ENVIRONMENTAL
GRANTMAKING
FOUNDATIONS

ENVIRONMENTAL GRANTMAKING FOUNDATIONS

1995
DIRECTORY

Environmental Data Research Institute
1655 Elmwood Avenue, Suite 225 • Rochester, NY 14620-3426

Allen D. Krusenstjerna: Production Coordinator

Edith C. Stein: Senior Editor

Terry Thurley: Associate Editor

Dora Hanninen: Assistant Editor

Peter Beckary: Production Assistant
Jonathan P. Brimfield: Production Assistant
Corinne Szymko: Production Assistant
Andrew D. Hopkins: Production Assistant

Carl Herrgesell: Information Systems Consultant

Environmental Grantmaking Foundations

© copyright 1995 by **Environmental Data Resources, Inc.**, all rights reserved. No part of this book may be used or reproduced in any manner whatsoever without written permission from the publisher.

The publisher makes every effort to accurately represent information made available to it by foundation personnel and by public sources, but is not responsible for and disclaims any liability for information inaccurate or incomplete at its source, for changes that result from the passage of time, or for the validity of the interpretation presented here.

Printed in the United States of America

3nd Edition 1995

ISBN 0–9631943–2–1

Environmental Data Research Institute is a nonprofit nonadvocacy organization that compiles, analyzes, and disseminates information on environmental funding. For further information write or call:

Environmental Data Research Institute • 1655 Elmwood Avenue, Suite 225 • Rochester, NY 14620–3426
800–724–1857 (Directory Sales)   716–473–3090 (Telephone)   716–473–0968 (Facsimile)
E–mail edri@eznet.net

Acknowledgments

The Environmental Data Research Institute wishes to express its gratitude to the individuals and grantmakers that helped fund *Environmental Grantmaking Foundations 1995*.

Anonymous

Porter W. Anderson, Jr.

Mary Reynolds Babcock Foundation, Inc.

The Blumenthal Foundation

The Bullitt Foundation

The Cabot Family Charitable Trust

The Clayton Fund, Inc.

Esprit Foundation

Flintridge Foundation

The Gap Foundation

General Service Foundation

The German Marshall Fund of the United States

Richard & Rhoda Goldman Fund

Great Lakes Protection Fund

The Luke B. Hancock Foundation

Teresa & H. John Heinz III Charitable Fund

The James Irvine Foundation

The Henry M. Jackson Foundation

The Robert S. and Grayce B. Kerr Foundation, Inc.

Kongsgaard-Goldman Foundation

Laurel Foundation

Joyce Mertz-Gilmore Foundation

Meyer Memorial Trust

The Curtis and Edith Munson Foundation, Inc.

The National Environmental Education & Training Foundation

National Geographic Society Education Foundation

New England Biolabs Foundation

Jessie Smith Noyes Foundation, Inc.

Philip Morris Companies, Inc.

Surdna Foundation, Inc.

The Trull Foundation

WMX Environmental Grants Program

Weeden Foundation

Margaret Cullinan Wray Charitable Lead Annuity Trust

We extend a special thanks to Stephen Toben of The William and Flora Hewlett Foundation, Jenny Russell of the Island Foundation, Inc., and Joshua Reichert of The Pew Charitable Trusts for their fundraising help with the 1995 edition.

We also wish to thank all the staff personnel who reviewed copy and patiently fielded our questions.

Finally, we gratefully acknowledge the generous grants from The Andrew W. Mellon Foundation and The Pew Charitable Trusts which allowed us to print and market *Environmental Grantmaking Foundations 1993*, but which were not noted in that edition.

Contents

Acknowledgments v

Contents vii

About The Directory xiii

How to Use The Directory xv

Profiles 3
   ARCO Foundation 3
   AT&T Foundation 4
   A Territory Resource 5
   The Abelard Foundation West 6
   The Abell Foundation 8
   Abell-Hanger Foundation 9
   The Achelis Foundation 10
   The Acorn Foundation 10
   The Ahmanson Foundation 11
   Airport Business Center Foundation ... 13
   Alaska Conservation Foundation 13
   The George I. Alden Trust 14
   Winifred & Harry B. Allen Foundation . 15
   The Jenifer Altman Foundation 16
   American Conservation Association, Inc. 17
   American Express Philanthropic Program 18
   American Foundation Corporation 19
   Americana Foundation, Inc. 20
   Ameritech Foundation 20
   Elmer L. & Eleanor J. Andersen Foundation ... 21
   Angelina Fund, Inc. 22
   Apple Computer, Inc. 23
   The Arca Foundation 23
   Arcadia Foundation 24
   Evenor Armington Fund 25
   The Vincent Astor Foundation 26
   Atherton Family Foundation 27
   Atkinson Foundation 28
   Atlantic Foundation 29
   The Austin Memorial Foundation 29
   Azadoutioun Foundation 30
   Mary Reynolds Babcock Foundation, Inc. 30
   The Bailey Wildlife Foundation 32
   The Cameron Baird Foundation 32
   Clayton Baker Trust 33
   The George F. Baker Trust 34
   Baltimore Gas and Electric Foundation, Inc. ... 35
   BankAmerica Foundation 36
   The Barra Foundation, Inc. 37
   The Theodore H. Barth Foundation, Inc. 38
   The Bauman Foundation 38
   Bay Area Community Foundation 39
   The Bay Foundation 40
   The Howard Bayne Fund 41

   L. L. Bean, Inc. 41
   S. D. Bechtel, Jr. Foundation 42
   The Beinecke Foundation, Inc. 43
   The Beirne Carter Foundation 44
   Beldon Fund 44
   David Winton Bell Foundation 45
   James Ford Bell Foundation 46
   The Ben & Jerry's Foundation 47
   Beneficia Foundation 49
   Benton Foundation 49
   Benua Foundation, Inc. 50
   The Bersted Foundation 50
   The Betterment Fund 51
   The Frank Stanley Beveridge Foundation, Inc. ... 52
   The William Bingham Foundation 53
   Bishop Pine Fund 54
   Blandin Foundation 55
   The Blumenthal Foundation 55
   The Bodman Foundation 56
   The Boeing Company 57
   Boettcher Foundation 58
   Mary Owen Borden Memorial Foundation . 59
   The Bothin Foundation 59
   Botwinick-Wolfensohn Foundation, Inc. . 60
   Helen Brach Foundation 61
   The Lynde and Harry Bradley
     Foundation, Inc. 62
   Otto Bremer Foundation 63
   Alexander H. Bright Charitable Trust . 64
   Alex. Brown & Sons Charitable
     Foundation, Inc. 64
   H. Barksdale Brown Charitable Trust .. 65
   Ruth H. Brown Foundation 66
   W. L. Lyons Brown Foundation 66
   The Robert Brownlee Foundation 67
   Kathleen Price and Joseph M. Bryan
     Family Foundation, Inc. 68
   The Buchanan Family Foundation 69
   Jesse Margaret Wilson Budlong
     Foundation for Animal Aid 69
   The Bullitt Foundation 70
   The Bunbury Company, Inc. 71
   The Bush Foundation 72
   The Butler Foundation 73
   J. E. & Z. B. Butler Foundation, Inc. 74
   Patrick and Aimee Butler Family
     Foundation 74
   The Bydale Foundation 75
   C. S. Fund 76
   The Cabot Family Charitable Trust 77
   The Morris and Gwendolyn
     Cafritz Foundation 77
   The Louis Calder Foundation 78
   California Community Foundation 79
   James & Abigail Campbell Foundation .. 80

© 1995 Environmental Data Resources, Inc.

Ward M. & Mariam C. Canaday Educational and Charitable Trust	81
The Cape Branch Foundation	82
The Cargill Foundation	82
Caribou Fund	83
Carolyn Foundation	84
The Carpenter Foundation	85
Mary Flagler Cary Charitable Trust	86
Centerior Energy Foundation	87
The Champlin Foundations	87
Changing Horizons Charitable Trust	88
Cheeryble Foundation	89
Ben B. Cheney Foundation	89
Chesapeake Bay Trust	90
Chesapeake Corporation Foundation	91
The Chevron Companies	92
The Chicago Community Trust	93
Chrysler Corporation Fund	94
Church & Dwight Co., Inc.	95
Liz Claiborne & Art Ortenberg Foundation	95
Claneil Foundation, Inc.	96
Clark Charitable Trust	97
The Clark Foundation	98
Robert Sterling Clark Foundation, Inc.	98
The Cleveland Foundation	99
The Clowes Fund, Inc.	100
Olive B. Cole Foundation	101
The Collins Foundation	102
Columbia Foundation	102
The Columbus Foundation	104
The Community Foundation of Greater New Haven	105
The Community Foundation of Santa Clara County	106
The Community Foundation of Sarasota County, Inc.	107
The Community Foundation Serving Coastal South Carolina	108
Community Foundation of Western North Carolina, Inc.	109
Compton Foundation, Inc.	110
The Conservation and Research Foundation	111
Conservation, Food & Health Foundation, Inc.	112
Cooke Foundation, Limited	113
Adolph Coors Foundation	114
S. H. Cowell Foundation	115
The Cowles Charitable Trust	116
Cox Foundation, Inc.	117
The James M. Cox, Jr. Foundation, Inc.	118
Jessie B. Cox Charitable Trust	119
The Cricket Foundation	120
The Mary A. Crocker Trust	120
Roy E. Crummer Foundation	121
Crystal Channel Foundation	122
Patrick and Anna M. Cudahy Fund	123
Charles E. Culpeper Foundation, Inc.	124
The Nathan Cummings Foundation	125
Damien Foundation	126
The Fred Harris Daniels Foundation, Inc.	126
Dart Foundation	127
The Arthur Vining Davis Foundations	128
Davis Conservation Foundation	128
Dayton Hudson Foundation	129
Deer Creek Foundation	130
The Nelson B. Delavan Foundation	131
The Aaron Diamond Foundation	132
Cleveland H. Dodge Foundation, Inc.	133
Geraldine R. Dodge Foundation, Inc.	133
Thelma Doelger Charitable Trust	135
Dolfinger-McMahon Foundation	135
Oliver S. and Jennie R. Donaldson Charitable Trust	136
Gaylord and Dorothy Donnelley Foundation	137
Donner Canadian Foundation	138
Douroucouli Foundation	139
The Herbert H. and Grace A. Dow Foundation	139
The Dragon Foundation, Inc.	140
The Max and Victoria Dreyfus Foundation, Inc.	140
The Elizabeth Ordway Dunn Foundation, Inc.	141
Jessie Ball duPont Religious, Charitable and Educational Fund	142
Eastman Kodak Company Charitable Trust	143
Echoing Green Foundation	144
Ederic Foundation, Inc.	145
The Educational Foundation of America	145
Arthur M. and Olga T. Eisig-Arthur M. and Kate E. Tode Foundation, Inc.	147
El Paso Community Foundation	147
El Pomar Foundation	148
The Emerald Foundation	149
The Thomas J. Emery Memorial	149
The Energy Foundation	150
The Charles Engelhard Foundation	151
English-Bonter-Mitchell Foundation	152
Environment Now Foundation	152
Environmental Education Foundation of Florida, Inc.	153
Environmental Endowment for New Jersey, Inc.	154
The Armand G. Erpf Fund, Inc.	155
The Ettinger Foundation, Inc.	156
Fair Play Foundation	157
Fanwood Foundation	157
The William Stamps Farish Fund	158
The Favrot Fund	158
Felburn Foundation	159
Samuel S. Fels Fund	160
The Hugh and Jane Ferguson Foundation	161
The Field Foundation of Illinois, Inc.	161
Jamee and Marshall Field Foundation	162
Fields Pond Foundation, Inc.	163
Fieldstead Charitable Trust	164
The 1525 Foundation	164
Leland Fikes Foundation, Inc.	165
Bert Fingerhut/Caroline Hicks Family Fund	165
FishAmerica Foundation	166
Flintridge Foundation	167
Ford Foundation	168
Ford Motor Company Fund	169
Walter and Josephine Ford Fund	170
Foundation for the Carolinas	171
Foundation for Deep Ecology	172
Foundation for Field Research	173

The Foundation for the National
  Capital Region 173
The Jacob and Annita France
  Foundation, Inc. 175
Mary D. and Walter F. Frear
  Eleemosynary Trust 176
The Freed Foundation, Inc. 177
Frelinghuysen Foundation 178
The Frost Foundation, Ltd. 178
Lloyd A. Fry Foundation 179
The Fund for New Jersey 180
The Fund for Preservation of Wildlife
  and Natural Areas 181
Fund of the Four Directions 181
Funding Exchange 182
The GAR Foundation 183
GE Fund 183
The Gap Foundation 184
Gates Foundation 185
The Barbara Gauntlett Foundation, Inc. .. 186
Gebbie Foundation, Inc. 187
The Fred Gellert Foundation 188
General Service Foundation 189
Georgia Power Foundation, Inc. 190
Georgia-Pacific Foundation 191
The Wallace Alexander Gerbode
  Foundation, Inc. 191
The German Marshall Fund of
  the United States 192
The Rollin M. Gerstacker Foundation 194
Bernard F. and Alva B. Gimbel
  Foundation, Inc. 194
Give to the Earth Foundation 195
Global Environmental Project Institute .. 196
Global Greengrants Fund 197
The Golden Rule Foundation, Inc. 197
The Goldman Environmental Foundation 198
Herman Goldman Foundation 199
Richard & Rhoda Goldman Fund 200
Good Samaritan, Inc. 201
Walter and Duncan Gordon
  Charitable Foundation 201
Great Lakes Protection Fund 202
Greater Piscataqua Community Foundation . 203
The Greenville Foundation 204
The William and Mary Greve
  Foundation, Inc. 205
The W. C. Griffith Foundation 206
The George Gund Foundation 207
HKH Foundation 208
Evelyn and Walter Haas, Jr. Fund 209
Walter and Elise Haas Fund 210
The Hahn Family Foundation 210
The Hall Family Foundation 211
The Ewing Halsell Foundation 212
The Hamer Foundation 213
James G. Hanes Memorial Fund 213
Harbor Lights Foundation 214
Harder Foundation 214
The Harding Educational and
  Charitable Foundation 215
Gladys and Roland Harriman Foundation ... 216

Mary W. Harriman Foundation 216
Hartford Foundation for Public Giving ... 217
The Hastings Trust 218
The Merrill G. & Emita E. Hastings
  Foundation 219
Hawaii Community Foundation 219
Hawaiian Electric Industries
  Charitable Foundation 220
Charles Hayden Foundation 221
The John Randolph Haynes and
  Dora Haynes Foundation 222
The Edward W. Hazen Foundation 223
The M. A. Healy Family Foundation, Inc. . 224
Howard Heinz Endowment 224
Vira I. Heinz Endowment 225
Heller Charitable & Educational Fund 226
The Clarence E. Heller Charitable Foundation 226
The William and Flora Hewlett Foundation 227
The Hitachi Foundation 228
The Hofmann Foundation 229
The Homeland Foundation 230
The Horn Foundation 231
Howfirma Foundation 232
Hudson-Webber Foundation 232
The Charles Evans Hughes Memorial
  Foundation, Inc. 233
The Roy A. Hunt Foundation 234
Hurdle Hill Foundation 234
The Hyams Foundation 235
The Hyde and Watson Foundation 236
IBM Corporation 237
Illilouette Fund 237
The Indian Point Foundation, Inc. 238
The Louise H. and David S. Ingalls
  Foundation, Inc. 238
The International Foundation, Inc. 239
Ireland Foundation 239
The James Irvine Foundation 240
Island Foundation, Inc. 241
Island Foundation 242
Ittleson Foundation, Inc. 243
The Richard Ivey Foundation 244
The Jackson Foundation 245
Jackson Hole Preserve, Inc. 246
The Henry M. Jackson Foundation 247
Martha Holden Jennings Foundation 248
The George Frederick Jewett Foundation .. 249
Helen K. and Arthur E. Johnson Foundation 250
The Howard Johnson Foundation 250
Walter S. Johnson Foundation 251
W. Alton Jones Foundation, Inc. 252
Joy Foundation for Ecological
  Education and Research 254
The Joyce Foundation 254
The J. M. Kaplan Fund, Inc. 255
W. K. Kellogg Foundation 256
Harris and Eliza Kempner Fund 258
The Henry P. Kendall Foundation 259
The Robert S. and Grayce B. Kerr
  Foundation, Inc. 259
The Helen & Milton Kimmelman Foundation . 260
Kinnoull Foundation 260

F. M. Kirby Foundation, Inc.	261
Caesar Kleberg Foundation for Wildlife Conservation	262
The Esther A. and Joseph Klingenstein Fund, Inc.	262
The Knapp Foundation, Inc.	263
The Seymour H. Knox Foundation, Inc.	264
Charles G. Koch Charitable Foundation	264
Kongsgaard-Goldman Foundation	265
The Kresge Foundation	266
The Lagemann Foundation	267
Laidlaw Foundation	267
Laird, Norton Foundation	269
Larsen Fund, Inc.	270
LaSalle Adams Fund	271
The Lauder Foundation, Inc.	271
Laurel Foundation	272
The Lazar Foundation	273
The Norman Lear Foundation	274
Levi Strauss Foundation	274
The Max and Anna Levinson Foundation	275
LifeWorks Foundation	277
Lilly Endowment, Inc.	277
Lintilhac Foundation	278
The Little Family Foundation	279
Longwood Foundation, Inc.	280
Richard Lounsbery Foundation, Inc.	280
Luster Family Foundation, Inc.	281
Lyndhurst Foundation	282
The John D. and Catherine T. MacArthur Foundation	283
James A. Macdonald Foundation	285
Magowan Family Foundation, Inc.	286
Maine Community Foundation, Inc.	286
Maki Foundation	287
Marbrook Foundation	288
Marin Community Foundation	289
MARPAT Foundation, Inc.	290
Mars Foundation	292
The Marshall Fund of Arizona	293
The Martin Foundation, Inc.	293
Massachusetts Environmental Trust	294
The McConnell Foundation	295
McCune Foundation	296
The Marshall L. & Perrine D. McCune Charitable Foundation	297
The Eugene McDermott Foundation	298
McDonnell Douglas Foundation	298
McGregor Fund	299
McInerny Foundation	300
The McIntosh Foundation	301
McKenzie River Gathering Foundation	302
McKesson Foundation, Inc.	303
The McKnight Foundation	304
McLean Contributionship	305
Giles W. and Elise G. Mead Foundation	306
Nelson Mead Fund	307
Meadows Foundation, Inc.	308
The Andrew W. Mellon Foundation	309
Richard King Mellon Foundation	310
Merck Family Fund	311
The John Merck Fund	313

Robert G. and Anne M. Merrick Foundation, Inc.	314
Joyce Mertz-Gilmore Foundation	314
Metropolitan Atlanta Community Foundation, Inc.	315
Metropolitan Life Foundation	316
Meyer Memorial Trust	317
Middlecott Foundation	318
Millbrook Tribute Garden, Inc.	319
The Milwaukee Foundation	319
The Minneapolis Foundation	320
Mobil Foundation, Inc.	321
Leo Model Foundation, Inc.	322
The Moody Foundation	323
J. P. Morgan Charitable Trust	323
The Moriah Fund, Inc.	325
Henry and Lucy Moses Fund, Inc.	326
Charles Stewart Mott Foundation	327
Ruth Mott Fund	329
The Mountaineers Foundation	331
The Curtis and Edith Munson Foundation, Inc.	332
M. J. Murdock Charitable Trust	333
John P. Murphy Foundation	334
Mustard Seed Foundation, Inc.	334
The National Environmental Education and Training Foundation, Inc.	335
National Fish and Wildlife Foundation	336
National Geographic Society Education Foundation	337
The Needmor Fund	338
New England Biolabs Foundation	339
New Hampshire Charitable Foundation	341
New Horizon Foundation	342
The New World Foundation	342
The New York Community Trust	343
New York Foundation	344
The New York Times Company Foundation, Inc.	345
The New-Land Foundation, Inc.	346
Edward John Noble Foundation, Inc.	346
The Samuel Roberts Noble Foundation, Inc.	347
Norcross Wildlife Foundation, Inc.	348
The Nord Family Foundation	349
Norman Foundation	350
Andrew Norman Foundation	351
Kenneth T. and Eileen L. Norris Foundation	351
Mary Moody Northen, Inc.	352
Northwest Area Foundation	353
Northwest Fund for the Environment	354
The Norton Foundation, Inc.	355
Jessie Smith Noyes Foundation, Inc.	356
Nicholas H. Noyes, Jr. Memorial Foundation	358
OCRI Foundation	358
Nathan M. Ohrbach Foundation, Inc.	359
The Ohrstrom Foundation	360
Spencer T. and Ann W. Olin Foundation	360
Onan Family Foundation	361
Orchard Foundation	362
Ottinger Foundation	362
Outdoor Industry Conservation Alliance	363
The Overbrook Foundation	364

The David and Lucile Packard Foundation	365
Patagonia, Inc.	366
Amelia Peabody Charitable Fund	367
Peninsula Community Foundation	368
The William Penn Foundation	369
James C. Penney Foundation	370
The Perkin Fund	371
Perkins Charitable Foundation	372
The Pew Charitable Trusts	372
Pew Scholars Program in Conservation and the Environment	374
The Pfizer Foundation, Inc.	375
The Philadelphia Foundation	377
The Philanthropic Group	377
Philip Morris Companies, Inc.	378
Phillips Petroleum Foundation, Inc.	379
Ellis L. Phillips Foundation	380
Howard Phipps Foundation	381
Pilot Trust	381
Pinewood Foundation	382
Henry B. Plant Memorial Fund, Inc.	382
The Polden-Puckham Charitable Foundation	383
The Powell Family Foundation	383
Lynn R. and Karl E. Prickett Fund	384
Prince Charitable Trusts	385
Pritzker Foundation	386
The Procter & Gamble Fund	386
The Prospect Hill Foundation	387
The Prudential Foundation	388
Public Welfare Foundation, Inc.	389
Recreational Equipment, Inc.	391
Philip D. Reed Foundation, Inc.	392
Z. Smith Reynolds Foundation, Inc.	392
The Rhode Island Community Foundation	394
Sid W. Richardson Foundation	395
Smith Richardson Foundation, Inc.	395
The Roberts Foundation	396
Rockefeller Brothers Fund, Inc.	397
Rockefeller Family Fund, Inc.	398
Rockefeller Financial Services, Philanthropy Department	400
The Rockefeller Foundation	400
The Winthrop Rockefeller Foundation	401
The Rockfall Foundation	403
Rockwell Fund, Inc.	403
Rockwood Fund, Inc.	404
Lee Romney Foundation, Inc.	405
Samuel and May Rudin Foundation, Inc.	406
Fran and Warren Rupp Foundation	406
Sacharuna Foundation	407
Sacramento Regional Foundation	407
San Diego Community Foundation	408
The San Francisco Foundation	410
The Sapelo Foundation	411
Sarkeys Foundation	412
Sarah Scaife Foundation Incorporated	413
The Scherman Foundation, Inc.	413
S. H. and Helen R. Scheuer Family Foundation, Inc.	414
Sarah I. Schieffelin Residuary Trust	415
The Schiff Foundation	415
Schultz Foundation, Inc.	416
The Schumann Fund for New Jersey, Inc.	417
The Florence and John Schumann Foundation	418
Ellen Browning Scripps Foundation	419
Sears-Swetland Foundation	419
Frances Seebe Trust	420
Sequoia Foundation	420
Seventh Generation Fund	421
Elmina B. Sewall Foundation	422
Ralph C. Sheldon Foundation, Inc.	423
Shell Oil Company Foundation	423
Thomas Sill Foundation	424
The Skaggs Foundation	425
The Kelvin and Eleanor Smith Foundation	426
Kelvin Smith 1980 Charitable Trust	426
Stanley Smith Horticultural Trust	427
Snee-Reinhardt Charitable Foundation	428
Solow Foundation	428
The Sonoma County Community Foundation	429
South Coast Foundation, Inc.	430
Southwestern Bell Foundation	430
Springhouse Foundation	431
Springs Foundation, Inc.	432
Sproul Foundation	432
Stackner Family Foundation, Inc.	433
Alfred T. Stanley Foundation	433
Anna B. Stearns Charitable Foundation, Inc.	434
The Stebbins Fund, Inc.	435
Steelcase Foundation	435
Stern Family Fund	436
Stoddard Charitable Trust	437
Stranahan Foundation	437
The Stratford Foundation	438
Margaret Dorrance Strawbridge Foundation of Pennsylvania II, Inc.	439
The Stroh Foundation	439
The Strong Foundation for Environmental Values	440
The Charles J. Strosacker Foundation	441
Stroud Foundation	442
The Morris Stulsaft Foundation	442
The Sudbury Foundation	443
The Sulzberger Foundation, Inc.	444
The Summerlee Foundation	445
The Summit Foundation	446
Surdna Foundation, Inc.	447
SURFREE	448
Edna Bailey Sussman Fund	448
The Switzer Foundation	449
Nelson Talbott Foundation	451
S. Mark Taper Foundation	451
The Telesis Foundation	452
Texaco Foundation	453
Thanksgiving Foundation	454
The Oakleigh L. Thorne Foundation	454
Threshold Foundation	455
The Tides Foundation	456
Times Mirror Magazines, Inc.	458
The Tinker Foundation Incorporated	459
Tortuga Foundation	460
Town Creek Foundation, Inc.	461
Toyota USA Foundation	462
The Travelers Foundation	463

© 1995 Environmental Data Resources, Inc.

Treacy Foundation, Inc.	464
Harry C. Trexler Trust	464
The Troy Foundation	465
True North Foundation	466
The Truland Foundation	467
The Trust For Mutual Understanding	467
Marcia Brady Tucker Foundation	468
Rose E. Tucker Charitable Trust	469
Alice Tweed Tuohy Foundation	470
Turner Foundation, Inc.	471
The USF&G Foundation, Inc.	472
USX Foundation, Inc.	473
Underhill Foundation	474
Union Camp Charitable Trust	475
Union Pacific Foundation	475
Unitarian Universalist Veatch Program at Shelter Rock	476
United States-Japan Foundation	477
Vancouver Foundation	478
R. T. Vanderbilt Trust	479
Vanguard Public Foundation	480
G. Unger Vetlesen Foundation	481
Victoria Foundation, Inc.	482
The Vidda Foundation	483
Vinmont Foundation, Inc.	484
Virginia Environmental Endowment	484
WMX Environmental Grants Program	486
Alex C. Walker Educational & Charitable Foundation	487
Wallace Genetic Foundation, Inc.	487
DeWitt Wallace-Reader's Digest Fund	488
Lila Wallace-Reader's Digest Fund	489
Bill & Edith Walter Foundation	490
C. A. Webster Foundation	490
Weeden Foundation	491
Welfare Foundation, Inc.	492
Henry E. and Consuelo S. Wenger Foundation, Inc.	492
Westinghouse Foundation	493
Weyerhaeuser Company Foundation	494
The William P. Wharton Trust	495
Whitecap Foundation	495
Joseph B. Whitehead Foundation	496
Wilburforce Foundation	497
G. N. Wilcox Trust	498
Robert W. Wilson Foundation	499
The Windham Foundation, Inc.	500
Mark and Catherine Winkler Foundation	500
The Winslow Foundation	501
The Winston-Salem Foundation, Inc.	501
The Dean Witter Foundation	502
Wodecroft Foundation	503
Robert W. Woodruff Foundation, Inc.	504
The Wortham Foundation, Inc.	505
Sidney & Phyllis Wragge Foundation	505
Margaret Cullinan Wray Charitable Lead Annuity Trust	506
Wrinkle in Time Foundation	507
The Wyomissing Foundation, Inc.	507

Appendixes

A. Grantmaker Types	513
B. Environmental Issues	515
C. Emphases and Limitations	519
D. Geographic Regions	521
E. Environmental Grantmakers Association	523
F. Application Deadlines	525
G. Grantmakers Added and Deleted	541
H. Grantmakers Alphabetical List	543

Indexes

Officers, Trustees, Directors, and Contacts	551
Grantmaker Location	597
United States	597
International	601
Recipient Location	603
United States	603
International	621
Activity Region	625
United States	625
International	635
Emphases	639
Limitations	673
Environmental Issues	701
Climate and Atmosphere	701
Biodiversity	701
Endangered Lands	704
Agriculture	707
Water	708
Oceans and Coasts	710
Energy	711
Solid Waste	712
Toxic Substances	712
Population	713
Development	715
Environmental Topics and Activities	717

About The Directory

Environmental Grantmaking Foundations 1995 was designed as a resource for the environmental community: grantmakers, grantseekers, and others who want to learn more about the field of environmental funding. The third edition of this unique publication provides in-depth information (including text, grants data, and analyses) on a broad cross-section of environmental grantmakers.

This third edition again represents an expanded field—featuring 183 more grantmaker profiles than the 1993 version, all in a single volume.

The 600 grantmakers profiled here have combined assets of more than $70 billion (excluding corporation assets). They collectively give more than $425 million in environmental grants each year. They are a somewhat heterogeneous group that consists mainly of independent grantmakers, but also includes more than a dozen U.S. community grantmakers, several U.S. company-sponsored grantmakers, and a few Canadian grantmakers. The directory includes some of the very largest U.S. grantmakers, and others that are quite small. Some have sizeable and well-established environmental programs; others have modest or nascent ones. Still others have no program as such but typically award a cluster of environmental grants each year. The directory includes several entities that are both environmental grantseekers and grantmakers. And it includes all 184 members of the Environmental Grantmakers Association.

The 600 grantmakers were selected from an environmental grants database at the Environmental Data Research Institute (EDRI), a nonprofit organization that studies environmental funding. EDRI now tracks environmental funding by some 2,200 grantmakers. Its database currently contains over 36,000 environmental grants awarded since 1988. We believe the group profiled here is fairly representative of the environmental grantmaking field, particularly as related to U.S. independent grantmakers. We expect to continue to increase the number of grantmakers profiled in each subsequent edition.

We gathered the data for each grantmaker profile from a number of sources. Most important were annual reports, guidelines, grants lists, IRS Forms 990, and other printed materials obtained directly from a grantmaker. After identifying a grantmaker of interest, we usually (but not always) drafted a profile and sent it to the grantmaker for review. For grantmakers listed in the first edition, we generally asked them to update last year's profile. In most (but not all cases) we received edits from a grantmaker and so were able to modify the profile to meet its needs. In most cases we generated the data analysis from the EDRI database, which represents our interpretation of the environmental grants awarded. The analyses thus generally reflect a consistent view of the environmental grants awarded by the 600 grantmakers, but a particular analysis may not exactly coincide with a grantmaker's view of its own awards.

We trust *Environmental Grantmaking Foundations 1995* will be useful to grantmakers and grantseekers alike. We look forward to your comments.

© 1995 Environmental Data Resources, Inc.

How to Use The Directory

Environmental Grantmaking Foundations 1995 contributes to the field of environmental grantmaking by providing accurate and detailed information on many of the most significant grantmakers.

The information in this directory has been compiled, verified, and systematically arranged. To approach it most efficiently, we suggest you read this section about the directory's format and content.

Elements of a Profile

Profiles are arranged alphabetically by grantmaker. Each entry may contain up to eleven items: contact information, history and philosophy, officers and directors, financial data, environmental awards, environmental issues funded, funding analysis, sample grants, application process, emphases, and limitations. We have reported information for each of these categories whenever it was available. Sometimes we could obtain only sketchy information, sometimes no information at all, and sometimes a grantmaker asked that we omit certain items. A few profiles contain slightly different information, usually at the grantmaker's request. The standard categories are:

Contact information. The heading for each entry includes the grantmaker's name, address, telephone number, facsimile number, e-mail address, employer identification number, grantmaker type (community, company-sponsored, independent, operating, or public), and the persons (and titles) to whom proposals or correspondence should be sent and from whom additional information may be requested. Appendix A presents a brief description of the grantmaker types. Members of the Environmental Grantmakers Association are identified here, as well as in Appendix E.

History and philosophy. This section gives a brief account of a grantmaker's history and philanthropic orientation, and typically contains details such as the date of founding, the original donor and business, categories of giving, and any special items of note.

Officers and directors. We list here, using the categories designated by the grantmaker, the individuals who set policy and priorities, review grant proposals, and make grants.

Financial data. This section briefly summarizes a grantmaker's financial picture for one recent fiscal year. *Assets* refers to total assets unless (net) is indicated. The assets figure is followed by a letter in parentheses denoting the way in which a grantmaker's investments are recorded in its financial statement (if available): (M)arket Value, (B)ook Value, (C)ost, (L)ower of cost or market value, or (U)nspecified. In some cases, particularly where a grantmaker is organized as a "pass-through" entity, *gifts received* may be listed instead of, or in addition to, assets. *Total grants authorized* is a dollar amount representing all new grants authorized for all categories of giving for the fiscal year of interest. In some cases the expression is *total grants disbursed,* a dollar amount representing grants actually given out during the fiscal year, regardless of when they were authorized. In cases where it was not clear whether the grants were authorized or disbursed, only *total grants* appears. Where numbers are rounded off or estimated, the notation (est.) is used.

Environmental awards. We offer data about issues and specific topics in two ways. *Program and interests* usually presents a grantmaker's own description of its environmental program and interests. *Recent grants* usually is our summary of environmental topics funded, based on a review of grants lists from one or more recent years.

Issues funded. This graphic presentation describes the broad environmental issues a grantmaker funds. The data are derived both from what a grantmaker says it funds and from what we believe its recent grantmaking activity shows. We list eleven environmental issues: climate and atmosphere (Cli), biodiversity (Bio), endangered lands (Lan), agriculture (Agr), water (Wat), oceans and coasts (Oce), energy (Ene), solid waste (Was), toxic substances (Tox), population (Pop), and development (Dev). Appendix B presents a detailed list of topics included under each of the eleven broad issue categories.

Each issue except population is listed only if a grantmaker has recently made, currently makes, or plans to make environmental grants that pertain to it. Population is listed if a grantmaker makes grants in the population field, whether or not those grants are considered related to its environmental giving. Population has been included in the **Issues funded** section because it is so intimately related to any consideration of environmental problems. However, grants for population are generally not included in the **Funding analysis** or **Sample grants** sections, because the Environmental Data Research Institute grants database currently does not include them, unless they specifically address the environment-population link.

Funding analysis. This section contains three tables for each grantmaker based on environmental grantmaking for a recent fiscal year. The first table summarizes the environmental grantmaking for the stated *fiscal year* (and in some cases, for two years) and lists: the *environmental grants authorized* (or *disbursed*), the *number* of awards, the dollar *range* of awards, and the *median* award. Finally, the *percent* of environmental grants is computed as a proportion of all grants made by a grantmaker in the fiscal year of interest. (Percent is computed either as environmental grants authorized/total grants authorized or environmental grants disbursed/total grants disbursed within the fiscal year.) It should be noted that different fiscal years may appear in **Financial data** and **Funding analysis**, but percent is always derived from data for one particular fiscal year.

The second table lists recipients of the top five environmental dollar amounts for that fiscal year. In cases where more than one recipient received the same dollar amount, more than five recipients may be listed. If the grantmaker gave less than five environmental grants, fewer recipients will appear. Here and in the **Sample grants** section, all grants are listed according to the recipient's current name and location; for the sake of consistency, in cases where a recipient has changed its name or moved, grants awarded in previous years will be listed under the most current name or location EDRI knows about. (An example of this is the Manomet Bird Observatory which recently changed its name to the Manomet Observatory for Conservation Science.)

The third table ranks the top (usually five) geographic regions targeted by a grantmaker's environmental grant activity. There are a total of 15 possible regions within the United States and 28 possible international regions. Appendix D lists the regions and the way we classify them. Again, more or less than five may appear.

Sample grants. This section usually lists some recent and representative environmental grants. For each grant we provide the recipient name, recipient location, grant amount, disbursement period (if other than one year), and a brief description if available. For multi-year grants, we usually show the total amount awarded even if the grant was authorized in a previous year.

Application process. This section describes how and when to initiate contact with a grantmaker, and provides details about what a grantee should include in written correspondence. It also includes a list of written materials available from a grantmaker. Although in many cases this section provides a list of required proposal elements, an applicant should never base a proposal solely on what is listed here; a grantmaker should always be contacted directly for detailed application procedures. In cases where we only know when the directors meet, we have noted this and included this date in lieu of the grant application date. Appendix F lists, in table format, application deadlines by month.

Emphases. This section highlights a grantmaker's funding preferences in four categories: *recipients*, *activities*, *types of support*, and *geography*. Appendix C lists examples of each category.

Limitations. This section highlights what a grantmaker generally will not support in the four categories: *recipients*, *activities*, *types of support*, and *geography*. Appendix C lists examples of each category.

Emphases and **Limitations** are not comprehensive. We compiled a list of those categories we thought most important and circulated it with a grantmaker's entry for review. Some (but not all) grantmakers responded. In other cases we used information gleaned elsewhere (e.g., IRS PF-990). Usually we include only those emphases and limitations mentioned in the written material obtained from a grantmaker.

Appendixes

Five appendixes provide expanded definitions for certain profile elements. Three provide various lists of grantmakers, and one provides new information about an index.

A. **Grantmaker Types.** Descriptions of the grantmaker types.

B. **Environmental Issues.** The 11 broad issues and a list of the sorts of topics each includes.

C. **Emphases and Limitations.** Examples of recipients, activities, types of funding, and geographic locations a grantmaker might prefer.

D. **Geographic Regions.** Our definitions of the 16 U.S. and 28 international geographic regions where a grantmaker might be located or grant activity might occur.

E. **Environmental Grantmakers Association.** A membership list as of October 1994. All EGA members are profiled in this volume.

F. **Application Deadlines.** A table listing each grantmaker by the month(s) in which its deadline(s), if any, occur(s).

G. **Grantmakers Added and Deleted.** A list of grantmakers that are new to the 1995 edition and those omitted from this edition that had appeared in the 1993 version.

H. **Grantmakers Alphabetical List.** An alphabetical list of grantmakers, last name first.

Indexes

Eight general indexes may help users identify the grantmakers most appropriate to their work.

Officers, Trustees, Directors, and Contacts: Lists personnel alphabetically along with the grantmaker(s) with which they are affiliated.

Grantmaker Location: Lists each grantmaker alphabetically by the state in which its main or official office is located. Non–U.S. grantmakers are listed at the end of this index.

Recipient Location: Lists grantmakers alphabetically by the states or countries in which its grant recipients are located. This index has two sections: U.S. recipients and international recipients. This index was generated for a grantmaker from a complete grants list for the most recent fiscal year contained in the EDRI database: usually 1993, sometimes 1992 or 1994.

Activity Region: Lists grantmakers alphabetically by the regions receiving the direct benefit of the grant monies. In many cases the activity location differs from the location of the recipient organization. Again, the index has two sections: 16 U.S. regions (usually comprised of multiple states) and 28 international regions (usually comprised of multiple countries). This index was generated for the same fiscal year as the grant recipient index.

Emphases: Lists 78 types of funding and the grantmakers that prefer to fund each type.

Limitations: Lists 78 types of funding and the grantmakers that prefer not to fund each type.

Environmental Issues: Lists grantmakers alphabetically under any of eleven broad environmental issues: climate and atmosphere, biodiversity, endangered lands, agriculture, water, oceans and coasts, energy, solid waste, toxic substances, population, and development. Appendix B describes the issues in more detail.

Environmental Topics and Activities: Lists 382 environmental topics and activities and the grantmakers that have funded each. These categories are not limited to specific environmental topics and activities such as composting, ecosystem restoration, pollution control, or sustainability, but also include such concepts as cultural diversity, conflict resolution, leadership, or volunteerism. This index was generated using the same grants data as the recipient location and activity region indexes.

Addendum

Not all grantmakers profiled in *Environmental Grantmaking Foundations 1995* are potential funders for all grantseekers. This book is a research document as well as a grantseekers' guide, and certain grantmakers only give to pre-selected recipients. In addition, users should not make this directory the *only* source they consult. Other valuable sources of information include The Foundation Center, The Taft Group, and the Environmental Grantmakers Association (EGA). All three publish directories and make information available through electronic databases. Finally and most importantly, there is no substitute for direct contact with a grantmaker.

Profiles

ARCO Foundation

515 South Flower Street
Los Angeles, California 90071
Tel: 213–486–3158
EIN: 953222292   Type: Company-sponsored
EGA member
Contact: Russell G. Sakaguchi, Program Officer

History and philosophy. Established in 1963, the ARCO Foundation attempts to stimulate and support the individual leadership and volunteerism efforts that enable nonprofit organizations to create positive social change. The Foundation chooses to "treat its philanthropic dollars as investments rather than as charitable gifts." Program areas are: Education, Community, Arts and Humanities, Environmental, and Public Information. Grants are awarded primarily to local nonprofits, located in communities where ARCO employees live and work.

Officers and directors. *Officers:* Lodwrick M. Cook, Chairman; Eugene R. Wilson, President; L. Marlene Bailey-Whiteside, Secretary; Martin C. Reccuite, Treasurer. *Directors:* Ronald J. Arnault, Mike R. Bowlin, Lodwrick M. Cook, Kenneth R. Dickerson, Stephen J. Giovanisci, James A. Middleton, James S. Morrison, Eugene R. Wilson, Robert E. Wycoff.

Financial data.* Data for fiscal year ended December 31, 1992. *Total grants disbursed:* $18,091,909.

*Includes employee matching grants totalling $6,669,881.

Environmental awards. *Program and interests:* "The ARCO Foundation invests in efforts to conserve and sustain the natural environment, supporting projects in which experts analyze and communicate the price both business and the community must pay for safeguarding that environment. Foundation investments also encourage organizations to develop and advocate responsible environmental positions and to balance the mandate for economic growth with the mandate to preserve and enhance environmental quality."

Priority is given to:

- Balanced environmental organizations that support rational land use and natural resource policies.
- Environmental education that:
  - Develops curriculum and programs in which the relationship between the economic cost and the public benefit of environmental decisions is articulated.
  - Increases the number of young people involved in community service to improve the environment.
- Land preservation initiatives that:
  - Preserve ecologically unique land for open space with public access.
  - Assist in the ecological restoration of unique locations that have been environmentally damaged.
- Conflict-resolution efforts that expedite mediation of sensitive environmental decisions.
- Conservation of wildlife and protection of endangered species.
- Recycling by community-based organizations as a means of reducing solid waste and creating jobs.
- Pollution prevention by identifying pollution-minimization opportunities and encouraging their adoption.

The Foundation is also interested in fostering the participation of minorities and inner-city residents in environmental programs.

Recent grants: 1992 grants included support for urban environment, land conservation (including deserts), river protection, wildlife conservation, marine issues, energy conservation, botanical gardens, various kinds of education, and youth and minority participation.

Issues.   Cli   Bio   Lan   Agr   Wat   Oce   Ene   Was   Tox   Pop   Dev
             •   •   •   •   •   •   •   •   •

Funding analysis.*

Fiscal year:	1991	1992
Env grants disb:	$1,120,166	$1,017,000
Number:	84	71
Range:	$1,000–$50,000	$1,000–$250,000
Median:	$10,000	$10,000
Pct $ disb (env/total):	9	9

Recipients (1992 highest):	Number:	Dollars:
Greater Los Angeles Zoo Association	1	250,000
American Enterprise Institute	1	50,000
Bird Treatment and Learning Center	1	45,000
Energy Source Education Council	2	27,000
Claremont University Center and Graduate School	1	25,000
National Park Foundation	1	25,000
Pacific Northwest Pollution Research Center	1	25,000
Resources for the Future	1	25,000
Southwest Museum of Science and Technology	1	25,000
Sustainable Conservation	1	25,000
TreePeople	1	25,000

Activity regions (1992 highest):	Number:	Dollars:
U.S. West	27	504,000
U.S. not specified	11	152,500
U.S. South Central	10	110,500
Alaska	8	110,000
U.S. Northwest	6	69,000

*Does not include employee matching gifts.

Sample grants (1992).

American Enterprise Institute. Washington, DC. $50,000. Study for alternative fuels.

Bird Treatment and Learning Center. Anchorage, AK. $45,000. Bird rescue education programs.

Claremont University Center and Graduate School. Claremont, CA. $25,000. Minority graduate fellowships in environmental policy.

Earth Science. Santa Monica, CA. $10,000. Startup of wood recycling furniture manufacturing plant.

© 1995 Environmental Data Resources, Inc.

A

Energy Source Education Council. Lakewood, CA. $20,000. Curricular materials on energy for Southern California schools.

Energy Source Education Council. Lakewood, CA. $7,000. Energy education programs in Louisiana and in Farmington, New Mexico.

Greater Los Angeles Zoo Association. Los Angeles, CA. $250,000. "Zoo Reach!" environmental education program for low-income children and families.

High Desert Museum. Bend, OR. $10,000. Exhibit program on Oregon's natural resources.

Korean Youth Center. Los Angeles, CA. $5,500. Community-based recycling project.

TreePeople. Beverly Hills, CA. $25,000. Neighborhood greening initiative and fruit tree distribution program.

Trout Unlimited. Vienna, VA. $5,000. "Embrace-a-Stream" program.

Wildlife on Wheels. Los Angeles, CA. $5,000. In school programs.

Application process. *Initial contact:* Brief proposal (5 pages) to include:
Cover letter.
1. Organization's mission.
2. Grant purpose.
3. Legal name of the organization.
4. Amount requested, and a list of any previous ARCO support.

Proposal.
1. Summary (1 page).
2. Organization's history and mission.
3. Needs statement.
4. Project description, goals, objectives, and plan.
5. Expected results and method of evaluation.

Attachments.
1. Financial information: most recent financial statement, organization budget, project budget including other possible sources of funding.
2. Most recent IRS Form 990.
3. List of board of directors and their affiliations.

Do not use binders or covers.
When to apply: Anytime.
Materials available: Annual report (includes "Application Procedures"), ARCO Foundation Priorities and Guidelines Investing for Results (brochure).

Emphases. *Recipients:* Educational institutions, museums, nonprofit organizations.
Activities: Conflict resolution, education, innovative programs, land acquisition, policy analysis/development, training, volunteerism.
Types of support: Education, general purposes.
Geography: Areas of ARCO operations; the West, Southwest, Rocky Mountain region, and Alaska.

Limitations. *Recipients:* Individuals, religious organizations.
Activities: Audiovisual materials, fundraising, lobbying, media projects, political activities, research.
Types of support: Annual campaigns, endowments, equipment, facilities, scholarships.
Geography: International programs.

AT&T Foundation

1301 Sixth Avenue, 31st Floor
New York, New York 10019
Tel: 212–841–4747 Fax: 212–841–4683
EIN: 133166495 Type: Company-sponsored
Contact: Laura M. Abbott, Secretary

History and philosophy. The AT&T Foundation is one of the world's largest endowed corporate foundations. Its core values include innovation, diversity, equal opportunity, human development, and cooperation and involvement. Program areas are: Arts and Culture, Education, Health and Human Services, and International. The company also operates the invitational AT&T University Equipment Donation Program, with computer equipment awards to selected schools. A local contributions program serves communities where AT&T is particularly active.

Officers and directors. *Officers:* Marilyn Laurie, Chairperson; Sarah Jepsen, Executive Director; Gary Doran, Vice President, Policy & Administration; Marilyn Reznick, Vice President, Education Programs; Suzanne Sato, Vice President, Arts & Culture Program; Milton Little, Vice President, Health & Human Services Program; Tim McClimon, Vice President, International Program & Director of Community Services; Laura M. Abbott, Secretary; Liz Jackson, Assistant Secretary; Robert E. Angelica, Treasurer. *Trustees:* Curtis A. Atis, Gerald J. Butters, W. Frank Cobbin, Jr., Melvin I. Cohen, Gary Doran, Mirian M. Graddick, John C. Guerra, Jr., Marilyn Laurie, Reynold Levy, Milton Little, Judith A. Maynes, Tim McClimon, Gail J. McGovern, Thomas H. Norris, Marilyn Reznick, Ray M. Robinson, Suzanne Sato, Yvonne M. Shephard, Lola A. Signom, Kent M. Takeda, Sara A. Tucker, Thomas C. Wajnert, Doreen S. Yochum.

Financial data. Data for fiscal year ended December 31, 1993. *Assets:* $128,925,000 (M). *Gifts received:* $249,500. *Total grants disbursed:* $37,100,000.

Environmental awards. *Program and interests:* AT&T provides environmental grants in two major categories:

- Grants to advance study in environmental engineering, particularly in the emerging field of industrial ecology, also called design for the environment, among college engineering students and scientists. Industrial ecology aims to eliminate or greatly reduce negative environmental effects at every step in a product's life, from its design to its manufacture.

- Grants to support community-based and national projects throughout the United States in the areas of clean air, clean water, and source reduction/recycling.

AT&T Corporation has received a number of awards for its environmental work. In 1993 the National Environmental Development Association (NEDA) Honor Roll Award (to the AT&T Contract Services Organization for its Recycling Program; the Clean Texas 2000 Award (to AT&T Microelectronics for recycling and cutting waste); Georgia Clean and Beautiful Award (for Innovator of the Year for the "Hub" recycling project in Atlanta); the Massachusetts/Columbus Quincentenial Award (to Aaron Frank of AT&T for the innovative development of n-butyl butyrate).

Issues. Cli Bio Lan Agr Wat Oce Ene Was Tox Pop Dev
• • • • • • •

Funding analysis.

Fiscal year:	1991	1993
Env grants auth:	$108,885	$751,500
Number:	4	23
Range:	$5,000–$47,185	$5,000–$75,000
Median:	$28,350	$30,000
Pct $ disb (env/total):	<1	<1

Recipients (1993 highest):	Number:	Dollars:
Environmental Compliance Support Association of California (ECoSA)	1	75,000
Massachusetts Institute of Technology	1	50,000
New York University	1	50,000
Princeton University	1	50,000
Spelman College	1	50,000
University of California	1	50,000
University of Michigan	1	50,000

Activity regions (1993 highest):	Number:	Dollars:
U.S. not specified	7	137,500
U.S. Great Lakes	4	134,000
U.S. West	2	125,000
New York/New Jersey	2	100,000
U.S. Southeast	2	80,000

Sample grants (1993).

Clean Dallas, Inc. Dallas, TX. $30,000. To support the Great Lakes Resources for the Future Program, a multi-year research, policy development, investment support, and communications project intended to catalyze widespread activity to increase the region's use of recycled and secondary materials.

Clean Sites. Alexandria, VA. $20,000. To support State Two of Clean Sites' Superfund Reauthorization Project.

E-Call. Boston, MA. $25,000. To support the start-up of E-Call's Ecology Hotline, which provides 24-hour access to accurate, timely, local information on recycling through voice-mail services.

Environmental Compliance Support Association of California (ECoSA). El Monte, CA. $75,000 (2 years). To support efforts to provide environmental regulation information to small minority-owned businesses in Greater Los Angeles. ECoSA will provide environmental regulation compliance seminars, workshops, consulting services, and information materials to merchants in Korean, Vietnamese, Japanese, Chinese, Spanish, and English.

The Georgia Conservancy. Atlanta, GA. $30,000. To support a series of 12 conservation seminars for small businesses in various Georgia cities. Each seminar will cover both general environmental issues and specific concerns of the seminar's audience.

INFORM. New York, NY. $25,000. To support INFORM's public education and technical assistance outreach programs, especially in the area of source reduction.

Massachusetts Institute of Technology. Cambridge, MA. $50,000. The AT&T Industrial Ecology Faculty Fellowship to MIT is one of six such grants totalling $300,000 for the first year and renewable for a second. Industrial Ecology seeks to eliminate or reduce environmental impacts at every stage of a product's life cycle, from design to manufacture, to use and disposal. The field, which deals with the integration of technology and environment in all economic activity, includes elements of engineering, physical science, economics, management, and law. The other recipients for 1993 were New York University, Princeton University, Spelman College, UCLA, and University of Michigan.

Application process. *Initial contact:* Telephone call or written request for application guidelines before submitting proposal.
When to apply: At any time, but the Foundation prefers to receive proposals by the end of January, April, July, and September.
Materials available: Biennial report, "Information for Grantseekers," "Guidelines."

Emphases. *Recipients:* Educational institutions, museums, nonprofit organizations.
Activities: Collaborative efforts, conferences, demonstration programs, direct services, education, exhibits, innovative programs, policy analysis/development, research (scholarly/scientific), seminars, symposia/colloquia, training, volunteerism.
Types of support: Annual campaigns, continuing support, emergency funding, fellowships, internships, lectureships, matching funds, multi-year grants, operating costs, pilot projects, program-related investments, scholarships, technical assistance.
Geography: National and international programs, cities with a major AT&T presence.

Limitations. *Recipients:* Individuals. Elementary and secondary schools (through direct funding), individual colleges and universities (general operations), local chapters of national organizations.
Activities: Lobbying, political activities.
Types of support: Advertising campaigns, endowments, facilities, scholarships (undergraduate).
The Foundation does not donate AT&T products or services.

A Territory Resource

603 Stewart Street, Suite 221
Seattle, Washington 98101
Tel: 206–624–4081 Fax: 206–382–2640
EIN: 911036971 Type: Public
EGA member
Contact: Carol T. Pencke, Executive Director
Alice Ito, Grants Program Coordinator
Stephen Hartnett, Office Manager

History and philosophy. Organized in 1978, A Territory Resource (ATR) is a nonprofit, public foundation that aims "to increase the funds available for social change activities in the Northwest and the Northern Rockies. ATR's goal is to be a resource for organizations attempting to establish a society that is politically and economically democratic, equitable, and environmentally sound. The five states within ATR's territory face common economic, political, and social problems. ATR encourages better communication in the region among groups facing similar problems so that common solutions can be developed and effective strategies shared."

A

Officers and directors. *Officers:* Suzanne Edison, Chair; Peter Titcomb, Treasurer. *Directors:* Beth Brunton, Suzanne Edison, Ellen Ferguson, Helen Gamble, Maxwell Milton, Diane Narasaki, Andrea Rabinowitz, Yolanda Russell-Alexander, Gary Sandusky, Gail Small, Hurdie Styles, Ebo Teichmann, Peter Titcomb.

Financial data. Data for fiscal year ended December 31, 1993. *Assets:* $573,000 (U). *Gifts received:* $544,778 (est). *Total grants disbursed:* $410,500.

Environmental awards. *Program and interests:* ATR funds in all areas of environmental work that empower local communities to control their own resources and management.
Recent grants: 1993 grants included support for sustainable forestry, water use, farmworker protection, toxic waste, and environmental justice.

Issues. Cli Bio Lan Agr Wat Oce Ene Was Tox Pop Dev
              •   •   •   •   •

Funding analysis.

Fiscal year:	1992	1993
Env grants auth:	$84,950	$48,300
Number:	18	12
Range:	$350–$10,000	$700–$8,000
Median:	$5,000	$5,000
Pct $ auth (env/total):	33	18

Recipients (1993 highest):	Number:	Dollars:
Idaho Citizen's Network Research & Education	1	8,000
Powder River Basin Resource Council	1	8,000
Palouse-Clearwater Environmental Institute	2	7,000
Convenio de Raices Mexicanas	1	6,000
Snake River Alliance Education Fund	1	6,000

Activity regions (1993):	Number:	Dollars:
U.S. Northwest	10	35,300
U.S. Mountain	2	13,000

Sample grants (1993).
Convenio de Raices Mexicanas. Phoenix, OR. $6,000. To partially support a bilingual, bicultural outreach worker for the Pesticide Outreach and Education Project in the Rogue Valley, educating farmworkers and orchard owners and assisting in documentation of pesticide use and abuse.
Idaho Citizen's Network Research & Education. Boise, ID. $8,000. For ongoing organizing, direct action, leadership development, coalition building, and other activities to accomplish health care reform, building support for statewide universal coverage; consensus building for groundwater clean-up and remediation; and assistance with cooperative small enterprise development.
Northern Plains Resource Council. Billings, MT. $5,000. For the Montana Waters Protection project, to prevent pollution of ground and surface water, bringing together family farmers and environmentalists to address policy development on agricultural pollution.
Palouse-Clearwater Environmental Institute. Moscow, ID. $6,000. To support the Volunteer Coordination and Organizational Development project of this multi-issue, community-based environmental research, education, and action group.
Powder River Basin Resource Council. Sheridan, WY. $8,000. For the Citizen Participation Project for Accountable Government, empowering community members through organizing, training, and education to ensure open, accessible, and accountable state and local governments, for citizen participation in resolving environmental and economic problems.
Rogue Institute for Ecology and Economy. Ashland, OR. $5,000. For the Applegate Partnership project, working with local residents, workers, and representatives of public agencies, industry, and other community groups, to develop and implement a model for managing forest lands.
Snake River Alliance Education Fund. Boise ID. $6,000. Funding for ongoing work to stop transportation and dumping of nuclear waste by the Department of Energy, including organizing, community education (production and distribution of the People's Guide to the Idaho National Engineering Laboratory), and coalition building.

Application process. *Initial contact:* Pre-application letter describing the proposed project. The Foundation may request a full proposal.
When to apply: Deadlines for pre-application letter are February 1 and August 1; deadlines for full proposal are March 1 and September 1.
Materials available: "General Funding Guidelines" (brochure), *ATR Report* (newsletter).

Emphases. *Recipients:* Nonprofit organizations.
Activities: Advocacy, citizen participation, collaborative efforts, publications.
Types of support: Annual campaigns, operating costs, pilot projects, seed money, technical assistance.
Geography: Idaho, Montana, Oregon, Washington, Wyoming.

Limitations. *Recipients:* Individuals, public agencies.
Activities: Conferences, direct services, land acquisition, litigation, publications, research.
Types of support: Equipment, emergency funding, endowments, facilities, fellowships, internships, loans, scholarships.

The Abelard Foundation West

c/o Common Counsel
2530 San Pablo Avenue, Suite B
Berkeley, California 94702-2013
Tel: 510-644-1904 Fax: 510-568-2359
EIN: 136064580 Type: Independent
EGA member
Contacts: Susan Beaudry, Executive Director
           Merle Bachman, Program Associate
           Ann Dowley, Grants Administrator

History and philosophy. Abelard is a small family foundation incorporated in 1958 and initially located in New York City. In 1978 Abelard opened an office on the West Coast where fewer foundation dollars are available. The Foundation's board of directors is committed to social change activities that expand and protect civil liberties and human rights; increase opportunities for the poor, the disenfranchised, and people of color; and enhance and expand community involvement in and control over economic and environmental decisions. The Foundation supports groups whose work reflects awareness of broader policy issues and their impact on other communities and the future.

Officers and directors. *Officers:* George B. Wells, II, President; Kristen Wells Buck, Frances W. Magee, Adele Neufeld, Joel Schreck, Susan Wells, Vice Presidents; Malcolm J. Edgerton, Jr., Secretary; Charles R. Schreck, Treasurer. *Directors:* Michael Bernhard, Nancy Bernhard, Sheryl Bernhard, Steven Bernhard, Kristen Wells Buck, Lewis H. Butler, Donald Collins, Susan Collins, Malcolm J. Edgerton, Jr., Andrew D. Heineman, David B. Magee, Frances W. Magee, Adele Neufeld, Peter Neufeld, Albert Schreck, Celeste G. Schreck, Charles R. Schreck, Christine Schreck, Daniel W. Schreck, Jean Schreck, Joel Schreck, Thomas A. Schreck, Albert B. Wells, II, George B. Wells, II, Laura Wells, Melissa R. Wells, Ruth D. Wells, Susan Wells.

Financial data. Data for fiscal year ended December 31, 1992. *Total grants authorized:* $185,000.

Environmental awards. *Program and interests:* Within the overall context of the Foundation's concern for social justice, Abelard West is particularly interested in supporting:

- Environmental justice.
- Community-based grassroots organizing on local and regional environmental issues.
- Preservation of indigenous agriculture.
- Sustainable development and agriculture.

The Foundation also gives occasional support for organizations addressing health consequences of environmental issues.
Recent grants: 1993 grants included support for rural and farmworker organizing, toxics education, environmental justice, and environmental health.

Issues. Cli Bio Lan Agr Wat Oce Ene Was Tox Pop Dev
                        •   •   •

Funding analysis.

Fiscal year:	1992	1993
Env grants auth:	$91,000	$49,000
Number:	10	4
Range:	$5,000–$16,000	$5,000–$18,000
Median:	$9,000	$8,000
Pct $ auth (env/total):	49	32

Recipients (1993):	Number:	Dollars:
La Organización de Trabajadores Agricolas	1	18,000
Concerned Citizens of South Central Los Angeles	1	16,000
Environmental Health Coalition	1	8,000
Denver Action for a Better Community	1	7,000

Activity regions (1993):	Number:	Dollars:
U.S. West	3	42,000
U.S. Mountain	1	7,000

Sample grants (1993).
Concerned Citizens of South Central Los Angeles. Los Angeles, CA. $16,000 (2 years). For CCSCLA's Environmental Awareness and Education program which emphasizes waste recycling as both an economic development strategy and a community environmental improvement strategy.
Denver Action for a Better Community. Denver, CO. $7,000. To address issues of environmental justice and community health access through direct action, community mobilization, and strong local leadership for a city lead abatement program in housing units.
Environmental Health Coalition. San Diego, CA. $8,000. For the Toxic-Free Neighborhoods project which develops ordinances and regulations that create buffer zones between industry and other land uses, encourages industry reduction in the use of chemicals, and organizes neighborhoods for thorough clean-up of hazardous facilities.
La Organización de Trabajadores Agricolas. Modesto, CA. $18,000 (2 years). To organize and empower agricultural workers to directly participate in the public policy decisions which affect their lives.

Application process. *Initial contact:* Short letter or full proposal to include:
1. Cover letter summarizing background and purposes of the applicant organization and how the funds will be used.
2. Project narrative explaining the problem or issue addressed, how the project will respond to or resolve that problem, and why the strategy will be effective.
3. Resumes of people who will do the work.
4. Project schedule.
5. Detailed budget for project, as well as for the sponsoring organization, if the project is part of a larger on-going effort.
6. Information on fundraising strategy, including the status of current requests and past sources of funding.
7. Documentation of the project's federal tax-exempt status.
8. List of board members and other references.

When to apply: Deadlines are January 15 and July 15. The board meets in April and October.
Materials available: "A Guide to Grantmaking" (brochure).

Emphases. *Recipients:* Nonprofit organizations.
Activities: Activism, advocacy, citizen participation, innovative programs, networking, political activities, policy analysis/development.
Types of support: General purposes, operating costs, seed money.
Geography: Hawaii, California, and states of the Pacific Northwest, the Rocky Mountains, and the Southwest for domestic projects only.

Limitations. *Recipients:* Educational institutions, individuals, public agencies.
Activities: Conferences (except when closely related to the initiation of new programs or organizations), direct services, education, research.
Types of support: Capital campaigns/expenses, facilities, scholarships.

© 1995 Environmental Data Resources, Inc.

A

The Abell Foundation
111 South Calvert Street, Suite 2300
Baltimore, Maryland 21202–6174
Tel: 410–547–1300 Fax: 410–539–6579
EIN: 526036106 Type: Independent
EGA member
Contact: Robert C. Embry, Jr., President

History and philosophy. The Abell Foundation was established in 1953 by Harry C. Black, chairman of the board of The A. S. Abell Company, publishers of the Baltimore Sunpapers. The resources of the Foundation were increased substantially from the sale of the company in 1986. Its mission is to ameliorate Maryland's societal problems and to enhance the quality of life for the citizens of Maryland. Program areas are: Education, Health and Human Services, Economic Development, Arts and Culture, and Conservation/Environment.

Officers and directors. *Officers:* Gary Black, Jr., Chairman; Robert C. Embry, Jr., President; Anna LaFarge Culman, Vice President; Esthel M. Summerfield, Secretary; Frances Murray Keenan, Treasurer. *Trustees:* Shepherdson Abell, Gary Black, Jr., W. George L. Bunting, Jr., Robert Garrett, William L. Jews, Sally J. Michel, Donald H. Patterson, Walter Sondheim, Jr.

Financial data. Data for fiscal year ended December 31, 1993. *Assets:* $171,457,771 (M). *Total grants authorized:* $5,557,645. *Total grants disbursed:* $7,995,300.

Environmental awards. *Program and interests:* The Conservation/Environment Program is designed to encourage greater public awareness, and to preserve ecologically significant and endangered habitats. Areas of special interest are:

- Conservation.
- Resource protection.
- Growth management.

The Foundation supports production of videos and reports, and the development of environmental curricula for school systems.

Issues. Cli Bio Lan Agr Wat Oce Ene Was Tox Pop Dev
•   •   •   •   •   •   •   •

Funding analysis.

Fiscal year:	1991	1993
Env grants auth:	$148,500	$417,775
Number:	6	11
Range:	$1,000–$60,000	$5,000–$160,000
Median:	$22,500	$24,150
Pct $ auth (env/total):	4	8

Recipients (1993 highest):	Number:	Dollars:
Johns Hopkins University, Environmental Forum	1	160,000
Chesapeake Bay Foundation	1	100,000
The Trust for Public Land	1	40,000
Save Our Streams	1	38,625
Greater Baltimore Committee Foundation	1	30,000

Activity region (1993):	Number:	Dollars:
U.S. Mid-Atlantic	11	417,775

Sample grants (1993).

Chesapeake Bay Foundation. Annapolis, MD. $100,000 (2 years). To develop and publish a middle school inter-disciplinary student service-based environmental education curriculum and teacher-training program.

Department of Planet Earth. Annapolis, MD. $5,000. For a study of five tributaries of the Chesapeake Bay in St. Mary's County to determine the water quality and degree of impact associated with watershed development.

Lower Shore Land Trust/Eastern Shore Land Conservancy. Queenstown, MD. $24,150. A challenge grant for start-up funding of the services of a land protection specialist and for related expenses in connection with the Nanticoke River Watershed Project.

Greater Baltimore Committee Foundation. Baltimore, MD. $30,000. For a feasibility study to develop an Ocean Thermal Energy Technology facility.

Irvine Natural Science Center. Stevenson, MD. $5,000. For expansion of the Natural Connections Project that recruits and trains high school student volunteers to teach elementary school students about neighborhood ecology.

Maryland Department of Natural Resources. Upper Marlboro, MD. <$5,000. Conservation/environment.

Pollution & Recycling Control Information Center. Baltimore, MD. <$5,000. Conservation/environment.

Save Our Streams. Glen Burnie, MD. $38,625. A challenge grant for general operating costs of the Baltimore City "Save Our Streams" initiative to clean up and monitor water quality in Gwynns Falls, Jones Falls, and Herring Run.

Application process. *Initial contact:* Telephone call or letter (1 page) describing applicant's mission and scope of activities, summary of the project, and amount requested. Full proposal, if invited, to include:

1. Completed application forms (from Foundation).
2. Copy of IRS tax-exempt status determination letter and foundation classification.
3. Most recent audited financial statement and copy of current operating budget.
4. Projected operating budget for each year in which funding is requested.
5. List of names and professional affiliations of current board.
6. Pertinent supporting materials.

When to apply: Deadlines are January 1, March 1, May 1, August 1, September 1, and November 1. The board meets in February, April, June, September, October, and December.

Materials available: Annual report (contains "Guidelines for Grantseekers"), "Policies and Guidelines," application form, *The Abell Report* (newsletter).

Emphases. *Recipients:* Aquariums, educational institutions, nonprofit organizations, research institutions, zoos.

Activities: Advocacy, audiovisual materials, citizen participation, conferences, demonstration programs, education, feasibility studies, innovative programs, land acquisition, networking, planning, volunteerism.

Types of support: Capital campaigns/expenses, endowments, equipment, facilities, leveraging funds, loans, matching funds,

pilot projects, program-related investments, seed money, single-year grants only.
Geography: Maryland, especially Baltimore.

Limitations. *Recipients:* Individuals.
Types of support: Continuing support, debt retirement, operating costs, multi-year grants (except in exceptional cases), scholarships.

Abell-Hanger Foundation
P.O. Box 430
Midland, Texas 79702
Tel: 915–684–6655   Fax: 915–684–4474
EIN: 756020781   Type: Independent
Contact: David L. Smith, Executive Director

History and philosophy. George Thomas Abell was a self-trained geologist who entered the petroleum business as an independent oil operator. Both Mr. Abell and his wife Gladys Hanger Abell were philanthropists helping a wide variety of organizations. In 1954 they created the Abell-Hanger Foundation to carry on their philanthropic endeavors. In Mr. Abell's words, "Business success provides the opportunity to do some of the things most of us dream about doing for our community and its various institutions, organizations, and agencies." The Foundation awards grants in the areas of Arts, Cultural, & Humanities; Education; Health; Human Services; Public/Society Benefit; and Religion.

Officers and directors. *Officers:* John F. Younger, President; James I. Trott, Vice President; Lester Van Pelt, Jr., Secretary/Treasurer; Robert M. Leibrock, Assistant Secretary. *Trustees:* Arlen L. Edgar, Jerome M. Fullinwider, Robert M. Leibrock, James I. Trott, Lester Van Pelt, Jr., John F. Younger. *Honorary Trustee:* Jno. P. Butler.

Financial data. Data for fiscal year ended June 30, 1993. *Assets:* $106,727,104 (M). *Total grants disbursed:* $5,079,276.

Environmental awards. *Recent grants:* 1993 grants included support for beautification, urban parks, and environmental education.
Issues. Cli Bio Lan Agr Wat Oce Ene Was Tox Pop Dev
           •   •

Funding analysis.

Fiscal year:	1993
Env grants disb:	$164,000
Number:	3
Range:	$5,000–$150,000
Median:	$9,000
Pct $ disb (env/total):	3

Recipients (1993):	*Number:*	*Dollars:*
City of Midland, Parks and Recreation Department	1	150,000
Keep Midland Beautiful	1	9,000
Prude Ranch Environmental Education, Inc.	1	5,000

Activity region (1993):	*Number:*	*Dollars:*
U.S. South Central	3	164,000

Sample grants (1993).
City of Midland, Parks and Recreation Department. Midland, TX. $150,000 (3 years). For public park renovation and development.
Keep Midland Beautiful. Midland, TX. $9,000. Unrestricted operating support.
Prude Ranch Environmental Education, Inc. Fort Davis, TX. $5,000. For an accredited environmental science workshop in environmental awareness for Midland/Odessa area teachers.

Application process. *Initial contact:* Telephone call or letter to request the "Pre-Proposal Questionnaire." Based on the completed questionnaire, the trustees may request a proposal (1 copy, unbound) to include:
1. Grant affidavit.
2. Institutional profile.
   - Summary income and expense data for previous, current, and next fiscal years.
   - Complete listing, in descending order of size, for each donation category for the previous and current fiscal years of all donations greater than 1 percent of the organization's operating budget.
3. Grant request summary.
   - Summary statement of request. Brief description of amount, purpose, and expenditure timing of funding need.
   - Statement of need. Identify need for the services or program(s).
   - Methodology statement. Specify techniques employed to meet these needs.
   - Evaluation of project statement. Identify procedure to determine program or project achievements.
   - Future funding needs. Identify any future operation, project, and capital funding needs from Abell-Hanger Foundation.
4. Detailed budget for current year.
5. Latest audited financial statement.
6. List of staff salaries, benefits, and length of employment.
7. IRS Form 990 Summarization, along with copies of the latest three years' Form 990.

Applicants must seek funding for the same proposal from various sources, as sole sponsorship of programs is rarely undertaken.
When to apply: Anytime.
Materials available: Annual report (includes "Grant Criteria and Procedures"), "Pre-Proposal Questionnaire."

Emphases. *Recipients:* Educational institutions, nonprofit organizations.
Types of support: Capital campaigns/expenses, challenge grants, endowments, general purposes, scholarships, seed money.
Geography: Texas only.

Limitations. *Recipients:* Individuals.
Types of support: Fellowships, loans, scholarships.

A

The Achelis Foundation
c/o Morris & McVeigh
767 Third Avenue
New York, New York 10017
Tel: 212–418–0588
EIN: 136022018   Type: Independent
Contact: Joseph S. Dolan, Executive Director and Secretary

History and philosophy. Elisabeth Achelis (1880–1974) established the Foundation in 1940. Grantmaking areas are: arts and civic affairs; education; health, medicine and rehabilitation; and social services, housing, and welfare.

Officers and directors. *Officers:* Guy G. Rutherfurd, President and Treasurer; John N. Irwin, III, First Vice President; Russell P. Pennoyer, Second Vice President; Joseph S. Dolan, Secretary. *Trustees:* Harry W. Albright, Jr., Mary B. Braga, Walter J. P. Curley, Jr., Anthony D. Duke, Peter Frelinghuysen, John N. Irwin, III, Leslie Lenkowsky, Ph.D., Marguerite S. Nichols, M.D., Russell P. Pennoyer, Mary S. Phipps, Guy G. Rutherfurd.

Financial data. Data for fiscal year ended December 31, 1993. *Assets:* $15,979,217 (M). *Total grants disbursed:* $914,852.

Environmental awards. *Program and interests:* The Foundation makes grants for ecology/environmental sciences through its health, medicine, and rehabilitation program.
Recent grants: 1993 grants included support for fisheries and public education.

Issues.   Cli   Bio   Lan   Agr   Wat   Oce   Ene   Was   Tox   Pop   Dev
                    •

Funding analysis.

Fiscal year:	1993
Env grants auth:	$30,000
Number:	3
Range:	$10,000–$10,000
Median:	$10,000
Pct $ disb (env/total):	3

Recipients (1993):	Number:	Dollars:
Central Park Conservancy	1	10,000
Friends of the Cold Spring Harbor Fish Hatchery	1	10,000
George Marshall Institute	1	10,000
Activity regions (1993):	Number:	Dollars:
New York/New Jersey	2	20,000
U.S. not specified	1	10,000

Sample grants (1993).
Central Park Conservancy. New York, NY. $10,000. For the Charles A. Dana Discovery Center's educational programs.
Friends of the Cold Spring Harbor Fish Hatchery. Cold Spring Harbor, NY. $10,000. A one-time grant for the current capital campaign, specifically for the Aquarium and Fairchild Exhibit Buildings.
George Marshall Institute. Washington, DC. $10,000. For the educational programs in science, technology, and public policy.

Application process. *Initial contact:* Letter (2 pages, 1 copy) and proposal (4–5 pages) to include:
1. Statement of organization's history and objectives.
2. List of board members and key personnel.
3. Current activities.
4. Description of project or purpose for fund request.
5. Budgets and audited financial statements for organization and project.
6. IRS tax-exempt status determination letter.

When to apply: Anytime. The board meets in May, September, and December.
Materials available: Annual report (includes "Grant Application Policies and Procedures").

Emphases. *Recipients:* Educational institutions.
Activities: Land acquisition, research, training.
Types of support: Annual campaigns, capital campaigns/expenses, continuing support, endowments, facilities, fellowships, general purposes, matching funds, multi-year grants, operating costs.
Geography: New York City metropolitan area.

Limitations. *Recipients:* Individuals.
Activities: Audiovisual materials, conferences, demonstration programs, publications.
Types of support: Loans, travel expenses.

The Acorn Foundation
c/o Common Counsel
2530 San Pablo Avenue, Suite B
Berkeley, California 94702-2013
Tel: 510–644–1904   Fax: 510–548–2358
EIN: 943025234   Type: Independent
EGA member
Contacts: Susan Beaudry, Executive Director
                Merle Bachman, Program Associate
                Ann Dowley, Grants Administrator

History and philosophy. A small family foundation founded in 1978, The Acorn Foundation has recently decided to focus on projects working for the restoration of a healthful global environment and a sustainable future. It supports the newer, smaller organizations based in the western United States, that are less likely to come to the attention of most donors and foundations that are working to: preserve and restore a natural habitat to support biological diversity; remedy air, water, and soil pollution from industrial, chemical, and nuclear sources; and limit new pollution from these and other sources; promote ecologically sound and appropriate technologies that ensure the preservation of our natural resources and improve the public health; and advocate environmental justice.

Officers and directors. *Officers:* Stephen C. Kimball, President; Anne Kimball, Secretary; Collier Kimball, William Kimball, Treasurers. *Directors:* Jeffrey Kimball, Julie C. Kimball, Stephen C. Kimball, Sergio Palleroni.

Financial data. Data for fiscal year ended December 31, 1992. *Assets:* $500,000 (U). *Total grants disbursed:* $37,000.

Environmental awards. *Program and interests:* The Acorn Foundation is particularly interested in:

- Community-based grassroots organizing on local environmental issues.
- Preservation of indigenous agriculture.
- Biodiversity.
- Sustainable development and agriculture.

Recent grants: 1993 grants included support for farmworker advocacy, community organizing, toxics issues, and environmental health.

Issues. Cli Bio• Lan• Agr• Wat Oce Ene Was• Tox Pop Dev

Funding analysis.

Fiscal year:	1992	1993
Env grants auth:	$30,000	$41,000
Number:	7	9
Range:	$2,500–$7,000	$3,000–$6,000
Median:	$4,000	$4,000
Pct $ auth (env/total):	81	100

Recipients (1993 highest):	Number:	Dollars:
Centro 16 de Septiembre	1	6,000
Rest the West	1	6,000
Bay Area Nuclear Waste Coalition	1	5,000
Fair Trade Campaign	1	5,000
Chickaloon Village Tribal Council	1	4,000
Citizen Alert	1	4,000
Labor/Community Strategy Center	1	4,000
West County Toxins Coalition	1	4,000

Activity regions (1993):	Number:	Dollars:
U.S. West	5	20,000
U.S. multiple regions	1	6,000
U.S. South Central	1	6,000
North America	1	5,000
Alaska	1	4,000

Sample grants (1993).

Bay Area Nuclear Waste Coalition. San Francisco, CA. $5,000. For a network of environmental, community, and native peoples' organizations working to prevent the construction of the nation's first shallow land burial dump for radioactive waste.

Centro 16 de Septiembre. Austin, TX. $6,000. For farmworker advocacy around living conditions and the establishment of self-sufficient organic farming.

Chickaloon Village Tribal Council. Palmer, AK. $4,000. For a grassroots outreach, education, and training effort assisting Alaskan Native communities in protecting their traditional lands from environmental contamination and resource exploitation.

Citizen Alert. Reno, NV. $4,000. For a statewide, citizens' organization working for greater public participation in Nevada's nuclear, military, and environmental decisions.

Fair Trade Campaign. San Francisco, CA. $5,000. For a national, grassroots effort among environmental, consumer, farm, labor, and community groups working to influence the outcome of the General Agreement of Tariffs and Trade (GATT) and the North American Free Trade Agreement (NAFTA).

Labor/Community Strategy Center. Los Angeles, CA. $4,000. To build a community base that holds public agencies and private corporations accountable for their environmental policies and practices.

Rest the West. Portland, OR. $6,000. For ecosystem protection by seeking limits to livestock grazing on federal lands in the Western United States.

Tucsonians for a Clean Environment. Tucson, AZ. $3,000. For organizing and education efforts to enforce accountable clean-up efforts of a nearby missile plant and for medical attention and compensation for victims of long-term pollution.

West County Toxins Coalition. Richmond, CA. $4,000. For organizing and advocacy by residents whose health and safety are jeopardized by the operations of petrochemical facilities in the area.

Application process. *Initial contact:* Full proposal to include:
1. A profile of the organization's purpose and structure.
2. A description of the project's history, goals, and timetable.
3. Budget and outline of fundraising strategy for the project.
4. Organization's annual income and expense statement for the previous fiscal year.
5. List of board members and resumes of key staff.
6. Copy of IRS tax-exempt status determination letter.

When to apply: Deadlines are April 1 and October 1, or at least twelve weeks prior to the semiannual board meetings held in January and July.

Materials available: "Application Procedures" (brochure).

Emphases. *Recipients:* Nonprofit organizations.
Activities: Activism, advocacy, citizen participation, collaborative efforts, networking, political activities, policy analysis/development.
Types of support: Continuing support, general purposes, operating costs.
Geography: Western United States primarily; some international grants.

Limitations. *Recipients:* Individuals, public agencies.
Activities: Audiovisual materials, media projects, research (medical/scholarly).
Types of support: Capital campaigns/expenses, facilities (construction).

The Ahmanson Foundation
9215 Wilshire Boulevard
Beverly Hills, California 90210
Tel: 310–278–0770
EIN: 956089998   Type: Independent
Contact: Leonard E. Walcott, Jr., Managing Director

History and philosophy. Financier Howard F. Ahmanson and his wife Dorothy incorporated the Foundation in 1952. "Currently the Foundation concentrates its funding on cultural projects support-

A

ing the arts, education at the collegiate and precollegiate levels, medicine and delivery of health care services, specialized library collections, programs related to homelessness and low-income populations, preservation of the environment, and a wide range of human service projects" in the greater Los Angeles community. Major program areas are: the Arts and Humanities, Education, Medicine and Health, and Human Services.

Officers and directors. *Officers:* Robert H. Ahmanson, President; Leonard E. Walcott, Jr., Vice President and Managing Director; William H. Ahmanson, Vice President; Karen A. Hoffman, Secretary and Senior Program Officer; Donald B. Stark, Treasurer; Frances Y. L. Chung, Assistant Secretary. *Trustees:* Howard F. Ahmanson, Jr., Robert H. Ahmanson, William H. Ahmanson, Daniel N. Belin, Lloyd E. Cotsen, Robert M. DeKruif, Robert F. Erburu, Franklin D. Murphy.

Financial data. Data for fiscal year ended October 31, 1993. *Assets:* $549,776,000 (M). *Total grants authorized:* $20,693,770.

Environmental awards. *Recent grants:* 1993 grants included support for river protection, land conservation, water reclamation, species protection, and public and teacher education.

Issues. Cli Bio Lan Agr Wat Oce Ene Was Tox Pop Dev
• • • • •

Funding analysis.

Fiscal year:	1991	1993
Env grants auth:	$759,000	$1,006,000
Number:	7	14
Range:	$14,000–$400,000	$5,000–$500,000
Median:	$25,000	$25,000
Pct $ auth (env/total):	4	5

Recipients (1993 highest):	Number:	Dollars:
The Nature Conservancy, California Field Office	1	500,000
University of California, Los Angeles	1	250,000
Omaha Zoological Society	1	50,000
Peregrine Fund	1	50,000
Conservation International Foundation	1	25,000
Earthwatch Expeditions, Inc.	1	25,000
Greater Los Angeles Zoo Association	1	25,000
University of California, Santa Cruz Foundation	1	25,000

Activity regions (1993):	Number:	Dollars:
U.S. West	12	931,000
U.S. Midwest	1	50,000
International*	1	25,000

*Multiple regions or not specified.

Sample grants (1993).
Conservation International Foundation. Washington, DC. $25,000. General support.
Earthwatch Expeditions, Inc. Santa Monica, CA. $25,000. Toward Los Angeles Unified School District teacher participation in Earthwatch Expeditions, 1993–94.
The Nature Conservancy, California Field Office. San Francisco, CA. $500,000. Toward the Santa Margarita River/Santa Ana Mountains Project.
University of California, Los Angeles. Los Angeles, CA. $250,000. Support toward the Water Reclamation Project.
University of California, Santa Cruz Foundation. Santa Cruz, CA. $25,000. Toward the Peregrine Falcon Restoration Monitoring Project of the Predatory Bird Research Group.

Application process. *Initial contact:* Written request for application guidelines. If appropriate, submit brief letter of inquiry to include:
1. Mission statement of applicant organization.
2. Brief description of organization background.
3. Needs statement.
4. Other potential sources of funding for the proposed project.

Foundation, if interested, will request full proposal to include:
1. Description of organization, its history, and current programs.
2. Needs statement.
3. Objectives of project or program.
4. Project timetable.
5. Overall cost.
6. Amount requested.

Supplementary data.
1. Detailed project budget.
2. Current annual operating budget for organization.
3. Most recent audited financial statement.
4. Copy of IRS tax-exempt status determination letter.
5. List of organization's governing board and officers.
6. Any other pertinent supplemental documents.

Requests for capital support are usually considered only after there is clear and assured evidence that the goal of the campaign will be achieved within a reasonable time period. Lead gifts are rarely granted.
When to apply: Anytime. The board meets quarterly.
Materials available: Annual report (includes "General Guidelines and Perspective of Interests," "Eligibility and Limitations," and "Suggested Procedures").

Emphases. *Recipients:* Educational institutions, museums, nonprofit organizations.
Activities: Conflict resolution, direct services, education, land acquisition, training, youth programs.
Types of support: Capital campaigns/expenses, computer hardware, emergency funding, endowments, equipment, facilities, projects, scholarships.
Geography: Southern California, especially Los Angeles County.

Limitations. *Recipients:* Individuals, religious organizations, research institutions.
Activities: Activism, advocacy, audiovisual materials, exhibits, feasibility studies, fundraising, litigation, lobbying, policy analysis/development, political activities, research, seminars, symposia/colloquia, workshops.
Types of support: Advertising campaigns, annual campaigns, continuing support, fellowships, indirect costs, internships, lectureships, loans, multi-year grants, operating costs, professorships, program-related investments, seed money, travel expenses.

Airport Business Center Foundation

303E Airport Business Center
Aspen, Colorado 81611
Tel: 303-925-7426
EIN: 841042661   Type: Independent
EGA member
Contact: John P. McBride, Trustee

History and philosophy. The Foundation was established in 1986. It makes grants in the areas of preservation of natural resources, research and educational programs on world overpopulation and family planning, amateur sports, and educational or medical services for distressed or underprivileged communities.

Officers and directors. *Trustees*: John P. McBride, John P. McBride, Jr., Katherine McBride, Laurie M. McBride, Lester P. Pedicord.

Financial data. Data for fiscal year ended December 31, 1992. *Assets:* $181,533 (M). *Gifts received:* $124,339. *Total grants disbursed:* $103,512.

Environmental awards. *Recent grants:* 1992 grants included support for land and wildlife preservation.

Issues.   Cli Bio Lan Agr Wat Oce Ene Was Tox Pop Dev
             •   •   •

Funding analysis.

Fiscal year:	1992
Env grants disb:	$14,825
Number:	10
Range:	$100–$5,000
Median:	$1,000
Pct $ disb (env/total):	14

Recipients (1992 highest):	*Number:*	*Dollars:*
Earthtrust	1	5,000
LightHawk	1	3,000
World Wildlife Fund	1	2,150
American Wildlife Foundation	1	2,000
American Wilderness Alliance	1	1,500

Activity regions (1992):	*Number:*	*Dollars:*
U.S. nonspecified	6	6,475
Hawaii	1	5,000
U.S. Mountain	3	3,350

Sample grants (1992).
American Wildlife Foundation. Washington, DC. $2,000.
American Wilderness Alliance. Englewood, CO. $1,500.
Colorado Bird Obervatory. Brighton, CO. $250.
Denver Audubon Society. Denver, CO. $100.
Ducks Unlimited, Inc. Long Grove, IL. $500.
Earthtrust. Kailua, HI. $5,000.
The Fund for Animals. New York, NY. $200.
LightHawk. Santa Fe, NM. $3,000.
Rainforest Action Network. San Francisco, CA. $125.
World Wildlife Fund. Washington, DC. $2,150.

Application process. *Initial contact:* The Foundation awards grants to pre-selected organizations only. No unsolicited applications accepted.

Emphases. *Recipients:* Pre-selected organizations only.
Geography: Aspen, Colorado, and Washington, D.C.

Alaska Conservation Foundation

750 West 2nd Avenue, Suite 104
Anchorage, Alaska 99501
Tel: 907-276-1917   Fax: 907-274-4145
EIN: 920061466   Type: Community
EGA member
Contact: Jim Stratton, Program and Finance Director

History and philosophy. The Alaska Conservation Foundation was founded in 1980. Its purpose is to protect Alaska's bioregional ecosystems through grants and technical and organizational assistance to the state's grassroots organizations and individuals. The Foundation acts to protect a pristine Alaska for all Americans, the state's diverse bioregions, human dignity, and Alaskans' right to a clean, healthy environment and a stable, sustainable economic future. It supports grassroots organizations and creative approaches to issues clarification and resolution. It works to foster trust and understanding among its grantees and their communities, and an active partnership among individuals, groups, and institutions working on conservation.

Officers and directors. *Officers:* Ken Leghorn, Chair; Matt Kirchhoff, David Rockefeller, Jr., Vice Chairs; Jan Konigsberg, Executive Director; Jim Stratton, Program and Finance Director; Cindy Adams, Secretary; Peg Tileston, Treasurer. *Honorary Chair:* Jimmy Carter. *Trustees:* Cindy Adams, Celia Hunter, Sally Kabisch, Matt Kirchhoff, Ken Leghorn, Caleb Pungowiyi, David Rockefeller, Jr., Eric Smith, Peg Tileston, Martha Vlasoff, William Wiener, Jr., Steve Williams.

Financial data. Data for fiscal year ended June 30, 1993. *Assets:* $916,218 (U). *Gifts received:* $1,705,145. *Total grants authorized:* $840,586.

Environmental awards. *Program and interests:* The Alaska Conservation Foundation supports the Alaskan conservation movement through grantmaking, technical and organizational assistance, and statewide coordination and planning. It offers its donors a variety of giving options including its unrestricted grantmaking fund and its donor-designated and field-of-interest funds. Current foci include circumpolar arctic environmental protection; southeast Alaska, the site of the Tongass ancient temperate rainforest; the offshore marine environment; and Prince William Sound.
Recent grants: Topics funded in 1992–93 included land conservation (wilderness, ancient forests, national forests), marine issues (fisheries, pollution), waste recycling, and toxic issues (oil spills, surface mining, air pollution, military waste). Activities included media programs and public education; citizen action, empowerment, and grassroots organizing; and environmental law.

A

Issues. Cli Bio Lan Agr Wat Oce Ene Was Tox Pop Dev
• • • • • • • • •

Funding analysis.

Fiscal year:	1991	1993
Env grants auth:	$367,479	$840,586
Number:	140	124
Range:	$50–$45,325	$75–$119,543
Median:	$2,000	$2,250
Pct $ auth (env/total):	100	100

Recipients (1993 highest):	Number:	Dollars:
Alaska Center for the Environment	8	151,568
Southeast Alaska Conservation Council	7	134,676
Natural Resources Defense Council	1	61,750
Alaska Rainforest Campaign Steering Committee	1	57,850
Alaska Environmental Assembly (AEA)	1	53,168

Activity region (1993):	Number:	Dollars:
Alaska	124	840,586

Sample grants (1993).
Alaska Center for the Environment. Anchorage, AK. $119,543. Grassroots organizing, public education, fax machines, and lobbying to protect private land in the western Gulf of Alaska (impacted by the Exxon Valdez oil spill), through purchase of timber and timber rights with oil spill settlement monies.
Alaska Center for the Environment. Anchorage, AK. $1,000. Printing of *Guide to Greener Living*.
Alaska Wildlife Alliance. Anchorage, AK. $3,000. Purchase of advertising time on Anchorage radio to promote the halt of state-sanctioned wolf control.
Lynn Canal Conservation, Inc. Haines, AK. $4,000. Support for local conservationists in the successful international campaign to halt the proposed Windy Craggy Mine, which would have been the world's largest copper mine, at the confluence of the Alsek and Tatshenshini rivers.
Natural Resources Defense Council. San Francisco, CA. $61,750. Legal expertise on national forest planning and Endangered Species Act; public education; media, and administrative lobbying in Washington, D.C.
Sierra Club, Alaska Chapter. Anchorage, AK. $18,350. Grassroots organizing in support of Rainforest Campaign goals, administrative lobbying, and public education to protect western Gulf of Alaska habitat with Exxon Valdez oil spill settlement monies.
Southeast Alaska Conservation Council. Juneau, AK. $114,026. To protect forest ecosystems in southeast Alaska through an improved Tongass Land Management Plan, analyze streams and rivers for possible Wild and Scenic River nomination, and to implement the Tongass Timber Reform Act.

Application process. *Initial contact:* For general support, send proposal summary (18 copies), signed by an officer and addressed to the chair of the board, to include:
1. Most recent financial statement.
2. Year-end financial statement.
3. Budget and fundraising plan.
4. Operating plan (see "Grantseeker's Guide").
5. Evaluation of previous year's operating plan.
6. List of staff, board, and officers.
7. Membership number.
8. Copy of IRS tax-exempt status determination letter.

For special project grants send full proposal (2–5 pages, 18 copies) to include:
1. Goals and objectives.
2. Problem statement.
3. Methods.
4. Timeline.
5. Expected results.
6. Evaluation.
7. Budget, including other sources of support.
8. Budget narrative.
9. Key personnel and qualifications.
10. If funding is not provided, how will this affect project implementation?

When to apply: Deadlines are in December or six weeks prior to the February board meeting for general support; in July or six weeks prior to the September board meeting for special projects.
Materials available: Annual report, "Grantseeker's Guide."

Emphases. *Recipients:* Individuals, nonprofit organizations.
Activities: Activism, advocacy, citizen participation, collaborative efforts, education, litigation, lobbying, policy analysis/development, publications, workshops.
Types of support: Advertising campaigns, continuing support, emergency funding, general purposes, internships, matching funds, membership campaigns, operating costs, projects, scholarships, travel expenses.
Geography: Alaska only.

Limitations. *Recipients:* Research institutions.
Activities: Land acquisition, political activities, research (scientific).
Types of support: Annual campaigns, capital campaigns/expenses, debt retirement, endowments, facilities, mortgage reduction, multi-year grants, program-related investments.

The George I. Alden Trust
370 Main Street, Suite 1250
Worcester, Massachusetts 01608
Tel: 508–798–8621 Fax: 508–791–1201
EIN: 046023784 Type: Independent
Contact: Francis H. Dewey, 3rd, Chairman

History and philosophy. The Trust was established in 1912 by George Alden (1843–1926), a nationally recognized inventor and educator. A professor for 28 years at Worcester Polytechnic Institute, Alden was an experienced and successful teacher who wanted to further the cause of education. The Trust continues to make education its primary focus; it favors institutions of higher education that combine academic excellence with administrative efficiency.

Officers and directors. *Officers:* Francis H. Dewey, 3rd, Chairman; Susan B. Woodbury, Vice Chairman; Warner S. Fletcher, Clerk; Harry B. Bayliss, Treasurer.

Financial data. Data for fiscal year ended December 31, 1992. *Assets:* $105,367,000 (M). *Total grants disbursed:* $3,567,000.

Environmental awards. *Recent grants:* 1992 grants included support for horticulture and an aquarium.

Issues. Cli Bio Lan Agr Wat Oce Ene Was Tox Pop Dev
              •   •

Funding analysis.

Fiscal year:	1991	1992
Env grants disb:	$50,000	$55,000
Number:	1	2
Range:	–	$5,000–$50,000
Median:	–	$27,500
Pct $ disb (env/total):	–	2

Recipients (1992):	Number:	Dollars:
Worcester County Horticultural Society	1	50,000
New England Aquarium	1	5,000

Activity region (1992):	Number:	Dollars:
U.S. Northeast	2	55,000

Sample grants (1992).
New England Aquarium. Boston, MA. $5,000. Operating support.
Worcester County Horticultural Society. Boylston, MA. $50,000 (multi-year grant). Capital campaign for new construction.

Application process. *Initial contact:* Full proposal (1 copy) in brief narrative form, signed by CEO of applicant institution, to include:
1. Purposes to be achieved.
2. Organization's qualifications to achieve the purpose.
3. How project's purpose integrates with existing activities.
4. Budget.
5. Copy of IRS tax-exempt status determination letter.
6. Most recent annual report, including audited financial statement.

When to apply: Anytime.
Materials available: Annual report (includes "Submission of Proposals").

Emphases. *Recipients:* Educational institutions.
Activities: Conferences, education, land acquisition, publications, research, seminars.
Types of support: Capital campaigns/expenses, emergency funding, endowments, equipment, facilities, internships, matching funds, professorships, scholarships, seed money.
Geography: Northeastern United States, particularly Worcester, Massachusetts.

Limitations. *Recipients:* Individuals.
Types of support: Loans.

Winifred & Harry B. Allen Foundation

c/o Allen Properties Company
83 Beach Road
Belvedere, California 94920-2363
Tel: 415-435-4525   Fax: 415-435-2439
EIN: 946100550   Type: Independent
Contact: Andrew E. Allen, Trustee

History and philosophy. The Winifred & Harry B. Allen Foundation was established in 1963. A sizeable portion of its funds go for environmental projects. Other interests include the arts, health, and human services.

Officers and directors. *Trustees:* Andrew E. Allen, David W. Allen, Howard B. Allen, Elizabeth Strauss.

Financial data. Data for fiscal year ended December 31, 1993. *Assets:* $1,385,728 (M). *Total grants disbursed:* $85,265.

Environmental awards. *Recent grants:* 1993 grants included support for land conservation (including state parks), wildlife preservation, horticulture, and coastal issues.

Issues. Cli Bio Lan Agr Wat Oce Ene Was Tox Pop Dev
              •   •   •   •   •   •

Funding analysis.

Fiscal year:	1993
Env grants disb:	$37,000
Number:	27
Range:	$200–$8,000
Median:	$1,000
Pct $ disb (env/total):	43

Recipients (1993 highest):	Number:	Dollars:
East Bay Sierra School	1	8,000
Audubon Canyon Ranch	1	5,000
San Francisco State University, Romberg Tiburon Center	1	4,000
Marin Conservation League	1	2,000
Point Reyes Bird Observatory	1	2,000
The Nature Conservancy, California Field Office	1	2,000

Activity regions (1993):	Number:	Dollars:
U.S. West	26	36,300
Alaska	1	700

Sample grants (1993).
Audubon Canyon Ranch. Stinson Beach, CA. $5,000. Permanent Endowment Fund.
Bay Institute of San Francisco. Sausalito, CA $1,500.
California State Parks Foundation. Kentfield, CA. $300.
East Bay Sierra School. El Cerrito, CA. $8,000.
Friends of the Sea Otter. Carmel, CA. $700. Support for the Alaska Project.
Golden Gate National Recreation Area. San Francisco, CA. $300.
Greenbelt Alliance. San Francisco, CA. $1,000.
Greenpeace. San Francisco, CA. $400.

© 1995 Environmental Data Resources, Inc.

A

Larkspur Parks & Recreation Department. Larkspur, CA. $500. Support for a community garden.
Local Earth Action Forum. Sonoma, CA. $1,000.
Marin Agricultural Land Trust (MALT). Point Reyes Station, CA. $600.
Marin Conservation League. San Rafael, CA. $2,000.
Marine Mammal Center. Sausalito, CA. $500.
National Audubon Society, Friends of the Richardson Bay Sanctuary. Tiburon, CA. $1,000.
The Nature Conservancy, California Field Office. San Francisco, CA. $2,000.
Pacific Horticulture Foundation. Berkeley, CA. $300.
Point Reyes Bird Observatory. Stinson Beach, CA. $2,000.
San Francisco Bay Bird Observatory. Alviso, CA. $1,000.
San Francisco State University, Romberg Tiburon Center for Environmental Studies. Tiburon, CA. $4,000.
Save the Redwoods League. San Francisco, CA. $500.
Save San Francisco Bay Association. Berkeley, CA. $300.
Sierra Club Foundation. San Francisco, CA. $400.
Sonoma Land Trust. Santa Rosa, CA. $1,000.
Strybling Arboretum Society of Golden Gate Park. San Francisco, CA. $200.
The Terwilliger Nature Education Center. Corte Madera, CA. $500.
The Trust for Public Land. San Francisco, CA. $1,000. National land preservation.

Application process. *Initial contact:* Letter stating organization's purpose, accompanied by proof of tax-exempt status.
When to apply: Anytime. The board meets June 15, September 15, December 15, and April 15. However, the Foundation's funds may be fully committed.

Emphases. *Recipients:* Nonprofit organizations.
Types of support: Endowments, facilities.
Geography: Primarily Marin County, California.

Limitations. *Recipients:* Individuals.

The Jenifer Altman Foundation

P.O. Box 1080
Bolinas, California 94924
Tel: 415–868–0821   Fax: 415–868–2230
EIN: 943146675   Type: Independent
EGA member
Contacts: Michael Lerner, President
            Beth Cleary, Program Associate
            Elise Miller, Program Associate

History and philosophy. Jenifer Altman was a Senior Research Associate of Commonweal, a health and environmental research institute in Bolinas, California. She originally came to the institute with a life-threatening cancer to participate in the Commonweal Cancer Help Program, but stayed on to work at the organization through the last two years of her life. Shortly before her death in 1991, Ms. Altman set up the Foundation to provide lasting support to Commonweal and other organizations pursuing similar goals.

The Foundation makes grants in the areas of environment, health care, and disadvantaged children. Special interests include parent advocacy for quality child care and research in complementary therapies for people with cancer. The Commonweal Sustainable Futures Project supports work on the environment and sustainable development. The Foundation awarded $800,000 to Commonweal in 1993.

Officers and directors. *Officers:* Celeste Bartos, Chair; Michael Lerner, President; Albert Wells, Treasurer. *Emeritus:* Philip R. Lee, M.D., Founding Chair. *Directors:* Peter O. Almond, Jonathan Altman, Jane Dustan, Philip R. Lee, M.D., Michael Lerner, Albert Wells. *Family Advisory Board:* Jonathan Altman, Kathleen Altman, Adam Bartos, Armand Bartos, Celeste Bartos, Erika Bilder, Peter Ungerleider.

Financial data. Data for fiscal year ended December 31, 1993. *Assets:* $14,000,000 (M) (est.). *Total grants disbursed:* $1,200,000.

Environmental awards. *Program and interests:* The Foundation is in the process of developing an environmental grantmaking program, through which it expects to award some $200,000 in grants in the $5,000–$10,000 range. In general, it prefers to award a number of small grants where they can make a significant difference. It tends not to contribute to general funds of major environmental organizations or to projects with large budgets.

Issues.   Cli   Bio   Lan   Agr   Wat   Oce   Ene   Was   Tox   Pop   Dev
                    •   •   •   •   •   •   •

Funding analysis.§

Fiscal year:	1993
Env grants auth:	$125,950
Number:	27
Range:	$550–$10,000
Median:	$5,000
Pct $ disb (env/total):	20

Recipients (1993 highest):	Number:	Dollars:
The Tides Foundation	6	25,550
African Wildlife Foundation	1	10,000
Balaton Group	1	10,000
Center for International Environmental Law	1	5,000
Center for Resource Economics/Island Press	1	5,000
Coalition for the Presidio Pacific Center	1	5,000
Earth Island Institute	1	5,000
Environmental Action Committee of West Marin	1	5,000
Institute for Agriculture and Trade Policy	1	5,000
Labor/Community Strategy Center	1	5,000
Oregon Trout	1	5,000
Philippine Institute for Alternative Futures	1	5,000
RARE Center for Tropical Conservation	1	5,000

The International Network of Resource Information Centers	1	5,000
The People-Centered Development Forum	1	5,000
The Whidbey Institute	1	5,000
United Nations Association of the United States (UN–USA)	1	5,000

Activity regions (1993 highest):	Number:	Dollars:
International*	11	44,850
U.S. not specified	4	18,600
U.S. West	3	15,000
Eastern and Southern Africa	1	10,000
Southeast Asia	2	10,000
U.S. Northwest	2	10,000

*Multiple regions or not specified.

§Based on a six-month period, July 1, 1992–December 31, 1993.

Sample grants (1993).

African Wildlife Foundation. Washington, DC. $10,000. For the International Gorilla Conservation Program. Balancing conservation with sustainable development geared to meet the needs of the local people is essential to the gorilla's survival.

Balaton Group. Hanover, NH. $10,000. Two grants to subsidize the travel of five Balaton members from Southern countries to attend two annual conferences at Lake Balaton, Hungary in 1993 and 1994.

Chinook Learning Community, The Whidbey Institute. Clintar, WA. $5,000. The Whidbey Institute works to promote greater understanding of the spiritual dimensions of the environmental crisis through education, research, publications, and special events for educators, policymakers, business leaders, environmental activists, clergy, and theological students.

Development Alternatives. New Delhi, India. $2,500. To support distribution of films on sustainable development to NGOs in India.

Institute for Agriculture and Trade Policy. Minneapolis, MN. $5,000. For the Citizen Dialogue on Forest Sustainability and North American Integration Project. The grant will fund an examination of the effects of NAFTA and GATT regulations on forest sustainability and North American integration.

RARE Center for Tropical Conservation. Philadelphia, PA. $5,000. To address environmental destruction in Ceduam, Mexico, associated with the recent introduction of modern agricultural practices. The grant supported educational programs including seminars to help communities organize themselves to solve environmental problems and courses in rural sustainable development.

Application process. *Initial contact:* Short letter (2 pages), briefly describing project, its budget, and amount requested. Supporting materials may be sent along. The Foundation vastly prefers letters to telephone inquiries. Facsimile transmission is acceptable. Note that external grants rarely exceed $5,000.
When to apply: Anytime.
Materials available: Annual report, "Jenifer Altman Fund Description," "Grant Application Form."

Emphases. *Recipients:* Educational institutions, nonprofit organizations, research institutions.

Activities: Activism, advocacy, audiovisual materials, capacity building, citizen participation, conferences, education.
Types of support: Pilot projects, program-related investments, seed money, travel expenses.
Geography: United States.

American Conservation Association, Inc.

1350 New York Avenue, NW, Suite 300
Washington, DC 20005
Tel: 202–624–9389
EIN: 131874023   Type: Operating
EGA member
Contact: Charles M. Clusen, Executive Director

History and philosophy. The American Conservation Association was founded in 1958 by Laurance S. Rockefeller. It typically receives a large annual contribution from the Jackson Hole Preserve, another environmental grantmaking entity supported by Rockefeller funds. Its grants address environmental and outdoor recreation issues.

Officers and directors. *Officers:* Laurance S. Rockefeller, President; George R. Lamb, Executive Vice President; Gene W. Setzer, Vice President; R. Scott Greathead, Secretary; Carmen Reyes, Treasurer. *Trustees:* John H. Adams, Frances G. Beinecke, Nash Castro, Charles M. Clusen, William G. Conway, Henry L. Diamond, Mrs. Lyndon B. Johnson, Fred I. Kent III, George R. Lamb, W. Barnabas McHenry, Patrick F. Noonan, Story Clark Resor, Laurance S. Rockefeller, David S. Sampson, Gene W. Setzer, Cathleen Douglas Stone, Russell E. Train, William H. Whyte, Jr., Conrad L. Wirth.

Financial data. Data for fiscal year ended December 31, 1992. *Assets:* $23,400 (M). *Gifts received:* $2,000,000. *Total grants disbursed:* $1,298,353.

Environmental awards. *Program and interests:* Grantmaking activities are directed toward information and action programs that increase public understanding of conservation issues and citizen participation in their resolution.
Recent grants: 1992 grants included support for land conservation, (public lands, open space, wilderness, forest protection), coastal issues, water quality, river protection, and wildlife.

Issues.   Cli   Bio   Lan   Agr   Wat   Oce   Ene   Was   Tox   Pop   Dev
             •   •   •   •   •   •   •

Funding analysis.

Fiscal year:	1991	1992
Env grants disb:	$1,846,000	$1,298,353
Number:	58	47
Range:	$3,000–$150,000	$5,000–$90,000
Median:	$25,000	$20,000
Pct $ disb (env/total):	100	100

Recipients (1992 highest):	Number:	Dollars:
Natural Resources Defense Council	1	90,000
Scenic America	1	90,000

Sierra Club Legal Defense Fund	2	90,000
The Wilderness Society	2	75,000
Cathedral Church of St. John the Divine	1	73,353

Activity regions (1992 highest):	Number:	Dollars:
U.S. not specified	15	453,353
New York/New Jersey	13	327,500
Alaska	7	285,000
U.S. Northeast	4	75,000
Latin America	2	60,000

Sample grants (1992).
The Adirondack Council, Inc. Elizabethtown, NY. $35,000. Campaign to Save the Adirondack Park.
Conservation Law Foundation. Boston, MA. $20,000.
Project for Public Spaces. New York, NY. $45,000.
Rails-to-Trails Conservancy. Washington, DC. $35,000. General budget and trail design manual project.
Sierra Club Legal Defense Fund. San Francisco, CA. $75,000. Protection of natural resources in Alaska.
Wyoming Outdoor Council. Lander, WY. $7,500. Protection of Wyoming wildlands and scenic conservation.

Application process. *Initial contact:* Short letter to include:
1. Description of project.
2. Estimated budget.
3. Possibilities of matching funds from other organizations.

When to apply: Deadline is May 1. The trustees meet in September or October.

Emphases. *Activities:* Citizen participation, conferences, publications, seminars, technical assistance.
Types of support: Continuing support, general purposes, loans, operating costs, projects.
Geography: United States.

Limitations. *Recipients:* Educational institutions (higher), individuals.
Types of support: Endowments, facilities, fellowships, scholarships.

American Express Philanthropic Program

American Express Tower
World Financial Center
New York, New York 10285–4845
Tel: 212–640–5661   Fax: 212–693–1033
EIN: 136123529   Type: Company-sponsored
EGA member
Contacts: Mary Beth Salerno, President (Domestic)
            Cornelia W. Higginson, Vice President (International)

History and philosophy. The American Express Philanthropic Program includes the American Express Foundation, American Express Minnesota Foundation, American Express Cultural Affairs, and corporate giving. All reflect the American Express family of companies, which now includes American Express Travel Related Services, IDS Financial Services, American Express Bank, and Lehman Brothers. Program areas include Education and Employment, Cultural Programs, and Community Service. Priority is given to projects supported by partnerships among public, private, and nonprofit sectors, and to efforts that involve American Express and its companies beyond grant support through employee participation in, and promotional support for, nonprofit organization activities.

Officers and directors. *Officers:* Mary Beth Salerno, President and Vice President; Cornelia W. Higginson, Vice President/Secretary; Susan Bloom, David A. Ruth, Vice Presidents. *Trustees:* Harvey Golub, Aldo Papone, James D. Robinson III, Mary Beth Salerno, Joan E. Spero.

Financial data. Data for fiscal year ended December 31, 1993. *Total grants disbursed:* $21,100,000.

Environmental awards. *Program and interests:* One focus of the Cultural Programs is to "Preserve historic and cultural assets, natural sites and parks, and encourage environmentally responsible tourism."
Recent grants: 1993 grants included support for urban environment, botanical gardens, parks, beautification, marine conservation, and outdoor education.

Issues.   Cli Bio Lan Agr Wat Oce Ene Was Tox Pop Dev
              •   •   •   •

Sample grants (1993).*
The Parks Council, Inc. New York, NY.
San Francisco Conservation Corps. San Francisco, CA.
The Student Conservation Association, Inc. Charlestown, NH.
Thompson Island Outward Bound Education Center. Boston, MA.
Brooklyn Botanic Garden. Brooklyn, NY.
Chesapeake Bay Foundation. Annapolis, MD.
Community Environmental Council. Santa Barbara, CA.
Institute of Marine Sciences. Santa Cruz, CA.
Keep Florida Beautiful. Tallahassee, FL.
Lincoln Park Zoological Society. Chicago, IL.
National Park Foundation. Washington, DC.
National Parks and Conservation Association. Washington, DC.
The New York Botanical Garden. Bronx, NY.
NYZS/The Wildlife Conservation Society. Bronx, NY.
The San Francisco Zoological Society. San Francisco, CA.
Twin Cities Tree Trust. St. Louis Park, MN.
Zoological Society of Florida. Miami, FL.

*Dollar amounts not available.

Application process. *Initial contact:* Letter (2–3 pages) to include:
Cover page.
1. Name and address of organization.
2. Contact person, title, and telephone and facsimile numbers.
3. Geographic area served by organization.
4. History of previous support from American Express-related entities.

Request details.
1. Funds requested.
2. Description of project, including objectives, target groups to be served, needs addressed, activities to be undertaken, expected outcomes, plans (if any) for utilizing volunteers, and project timetable.
3. Detailed project budget.

4. Plans for evaluating results.

Attachments.
1. Copy of IRS tax-exemption status determination letter.
2. Latest audited financial statement.
3. List of board of directors or governing body.
4. Current annual report (if not available, describe organization's overall mission and latest accomplishments).
5. Funding sources, including list of contributors.

When to apply: Anytime.
Materials available: "Philanthropy at American Express" (includes grants list), "Grant Guidelines."

Emphases. *Recipients:* Nonprofit organizations.
Activities: Collaborative efforts, education.
Types of support: Annual campaigns, emergency funding, general purposes, matching funds, projects, scholarships (employee-related), seed money.
Geography: Communities where American Express has a significant presence. Domestically, Arizona, California, Florida, Georgia, Illinois, Massachusetts, Michigan, Minnesota, New York metropolitan area, North Carolina, Ohio, Texas, Utah, and the District of Columbia. Internationally, Australia/New Zealand/South Pacific, Canada, Europe/Middle East/Africa; Japan/Pacific/Asia, and Latin America/Caribbean regions.

Limitations. *Recipients:* Individuals, religious organizations.
Activities: Fundraising, political activities, publications.
Types of support: Advertising campaigns, capital campaigns/expenses, endowments, scholarships (for individuals), travel expenses.

American Foundation Corporation

720 National City Bank Building
Cleveland, Ohio 44114
Tel: 216–241–6664 Fax: 216–241–6693
EIN: 237348126 Type: Independent
Contact: Maria G. Muth, Secretary/Treasurer

History and philosophy. Incorporated in 1974, the American Foundation Corporation succeeds a trust established in 1944 by members of the Corning and Murfey families and others. Grantmaking focuses on an arboretum, the arts and cultural programs, child welfare, education, conservation and environmental affairs, wildlife resources, religion, and scientific research.

Officers and directors. *Officers:* William W. Murfey, President; Nathan E. Corning, T. Dixon Long, Vice Presidents; Maria G. Muth, Secretary/Treasurer; Diane Saghy, Assistant Secretary/Treasurer. *Trustees:* Henry H. Corning, Nathan E. Corning, T. Dixon Long, Spencer L. Murfey, Jr., William W. Murfey.

Financial data. Data for fiscal year ended December 31, 1993. *Assets:* $25,648,050 (M). *Gifts received:* $3,064. *Total grants disbursed:* $857,718.

Environmental awards. *Recent grants:* 1993 grants included support for farmland preservation, river and forest protection, marine and coastal issues, habitats and wildlife, and an arboretum.

Issues. Cli Bio Lan Agr Wat Oce Ene Was Tox Pop Dev
• • • • • •

Funding analysis.

Fiscal year:	1991	1993
Env grants disb:	$384,096	$397,452
Number:	22	21
Range:	$100–$278,487	$100–$214,033
Median:	$1,000	$3,000
Pct $ disb (env/total):	30	45

Recipients (1993 highest):	Number:	Dollars:
The Holden Arboretum	3	300,417
Resource Renewal Institute	1	22,747
Point Reyes Bird Observatory	1	18,953
Santa Barbara Zoological Foundation	1	15,500
Bigelow Laboratory of Ocean Sciences	1	15,000

Activity regions (1993 highest):	Number:	Dollars:
U.S. Great Lakes	8	307,920
U.S. West	6	67,482
U.S. Northeast	3	16,450
U.S. Mountain	1	2,500
International*	1	2,000

*Multiple regions or not specified.

Sample grants (1993).
Bigelow Laboratory for Ocean Sciences. West Boothbay Harbor, ME. $15,000.
Camden Rockport Land Trust. Camden, ME. $1,000.
Cleveland Zoological Society. Cleveland, OH. $500.
Environmental Protection Information Center. Garberville, CA. $3,391.
Garden Center of Greater Cleveland. Cleveland, OH. $3,403.
Greater Yellowstone Coalition. Bozeman, MT. $2,500.
The Holden Arboretum. Mentor, OH. $300,417. Three grants, including support for the Horticulture Science Center and the Warren H. Corning Library.
Maine Coast Heritage Fund. Brunswick, MN. $450.
Marin Agricultural Land Trust. Point Reyes Station, CA. $1,891.
The Nature Conservancy, Ohio Field Office. Columbus, OH. $500.
Pacific Rivers Council. Eugene, OR. $1,000.
Point Reyes Bird Observatory. Stinson Beach, CA. $18,952.
Resource Renewal Institute. Sausalito, CA. $22,747.
Santa Barbara Zoological Foundation. Santa Barbara, CA. $15,500.
Trees for the Future. Silver Springs, MD. $100.
The Trust for Public Land. San Francisco, CA. $3,000.
Wilderness Inquiry. Minneapolis, MN. $100.
World Wildlife Fund. Washington, DC. $2,000.

Application process. *Initial contact:* The American Foundation awards grants to pre-selected organizations only. No unsolicited applications accepted.

Emphases. *Recipients:* Botanical gardens, educational institutions (private academies/colleges/universities/technical education), museums, pre-selected organizations only, zoos.

A

Activities: Youth programs.
Types of support: Annual campaigns, continuing support, general purposes.
Geography: Cleveland, Ohio; California.

Limitations. *Recipients:* Individuals.
Activities: Research.
Types of support: Capital campaigns/expenses, endowments, fellowships, loans, matching funds, projects, scholarships.

Americana Foundation, Inc.
Tollgate Farm
28115 Meadowbrook Road
Novi, Michigan 48377–1320
Tel: 810–347–3863 Fax: 810–347–3862
EIN: 382269431   Type: Independent
Contact: Thomas F. Ranger, Secretary/Treasurer

History and philosophy. The Americana Foundation was founded in 1956 by industrialist Adolph H. Meyer and his wife Ida. "Their success in industry and their interest in agriculture, horticulture, and related topics has inspired the trustees to continue to operate the Americana Foundation. The purpose of the Foundation is to support educational and advocacy programs that address preservation of Michigan's natural resources, conservation of American agriculture, and the American Heritage."

Officers and directors. *Officers:* Gary R. Rentrop, President; Marlene J. Fluharty, Executive Director; Thomas F. Ranger, Secretary/Treasurer. *Trustees:* Jack W. Barnes, Marlene J. Fluharty, Gordon E. Guyer, Barbara M. Livy, Ernest L. Morris, Thomas F. Ranger, Gary R. Rentrop, Jonathan M. Thomas.

Financial data. Data for fiscal years ended December 31, 1992 and 1993. *Assets (1992):* $5,362,136 (M). *Gifts received (1992):* $562,190. *Total grants disbursed (1993):* $130,500.

Environmental awards. *Recent grants:* 1993 grants included support for farmland preservation, land use planning, and habitat protection.

Issues. Cli Bio Lan Agr Wat Oce Ene Was Tox Pop Dev
            •   •   •

Funding analysis.

Fiscal year:	1990	1993
Env grants disb:	$55,000	$105,300
Number:	3	5
Range:	$10,000–$30,000	$10,000–$40,000
Median:	$15,000	$20,000
Pct $ disb (env/total):	11	81

Recipients (1993):	Number:	Dollars:
East Michigan Environmental Action Council	1	40,000
Little Traverse Conservancy	1	25,000
Michigan Environmental Council	1	20,000
Michigan Agricultural Stewardship Association	1	10,300
Capital Region Community Foundation	1	10,000

Activity region (1993):	Number:	Dollars:
U.S. Great Lakes	5	105,300

Sample grants (1993).
East Michigan Environmental Action Council. Birmingham, MI. $40,000. General purposes.
Little Traverse Conservancy. Harbor Springs, MI. $25,000.
Michigan Environmental Council. Grand Rapids, MI. $20,000.

Application process. *Initial contact:* Letter to include:
1. Brief description of basic needs and objectives of project.
2. Amount requested.
3. Brief history of organization making request.

Full proposal, if requested, to include:
1. Budget showing project costs and how funds will be used.
2. Names and affiliations of officers and board members.
3. Most recent audited financial report.
4. Current year's annual operating budget.
5. Other actual and potential sources of funding.
6. Copy of IRS tax-exempt status determination letter.

When to apply: Deadlines are February 28, May 31, August 31, and November 30. The board meets quarterly.
Materials available: Brochure (includes "How to Apply").

Emphases. *Recipients:* Museums, nonprofit organizations.
Activities: Activism, capacity building, citizen participation, collaborative efforts, symposia/colloquia, volunteerism.
Types of support: General purposes, matching funds, pilot projects, projects, technical assistance.
Geography: Primarily Michigan.

Limitations. *Recipients:* Individuals.
Activities: Fundraising, political activities.
Types of support: Scholarships.

Ameritech Foundation
30 South Wacker Drive, 34th Floor
Chicago, Illinois 60606
Tel: 312–750–5223
EIN: 363350561   Type: Company-sponsored
Contact: Michael E. Kuhlin, Director

History and philosophy. The Ameritech Foundation was established in 1984. The Ameritech Corporation is a parent company comprising Bell companies that serve Illinois, Indiana, Michigan, Ohio, and Wisconsin, and other information-related companies. With corporate headquarters in Chicago, the Foundation "will consider support for the city's major civic, educational, and cultural organizations which perform activities consistent with the Foundation's interests." It also joins with individual Ameritech companies to "support innovative local projects and programs which have national significance, stature, or implications." Current funding priorities are for grants "that advance the applications of technology in ways that improve education, economic development, and communications as it impacts the quality of life."

Officers and directors. *Officers:* William L. Weiss, Chairman; Richard H. Brown, President; Robert J. Kolbe, Vice President and CFO; Michael E. Kuhlin, Secretary; Arthur F. Naranjo, Treasurer; Ronald G. Pippin, Comptroller; Bruce B. Howat, Assistant Secretary. *Directors:* Ronald L. Blake, Richard H. Brown, Hanna Holborn Gray, Ph.D., James A. Henderson, Robert J. Kolbe, Michael E. Kuhlin, Martha L. Thornton, William L. Weiss, Jacqueline F. Woods.

Financial data. Data for fiscal year ended December 31, 1992. *Assets:* $64,684,653 (M). *Total grants disbursed:* $7,552,351.

Environmental awards. *Program and interests:* The Foundation makes environmental grants through its Civic and Community Program.
Recent grants: 1993 grants included support for hazardous waste cleanup and environmental education.

Issues. Cli Bio Lan Agr Wat Oce Ene Was Tox Pop Dev
                                                     •   •

Funding analysis.

Fiscal year:	1991	1992
Env grants disb:	$60,000	$60,000
Number:	2	2
Range:	$10,000–$50,000	$10,000–$50,000
Median:	$30,000	$30,000
Pct $ disb (env/total):	1	1

Recipients (1992):	Number:	Dollars:
Northeast-Midwest Institute	1	50,000
Clean Sites, Inc.	1	10,000

Activity region (1992):	Number:	Dollars:
U.S. Great Lakes	2	60,000

Sample grants (1993).*
Clean Sites, Inc. Alexandria, VA. Support to help clean up hazardous waste in the Midwest.
Great Lakes Museum of Science, Environment, and Technology. Cleveland, OH (3 years). Capital campaign.
*Dollar amounts not available.

Application process. *Initial contact:* Brief letter of inquiry to include:
1. Description of organization and its history and purpose.
2. Overview of project for which funding is requested.
3. Summary of program's budget.
4. Amount of support requested.
5. Geographic area served by organization or project.
6. Copy of IRS tax-exempt status determination letter.

In addition to the Ameritech Foundation, each Ameritech company has its own contributions program and priorities.
When to apply: Anytime.
Materials available: Annual report (includes "Application Procedures").

Emphases. *Recipients:* Educational institutions, nonprofit organizations, museums.
Activities: Conferences, education, policy analysis/development, research, seminars, projects, technical assistance, training.

Types of support: Advertising campaigns, annual campaigns, capital campaigns/expenses, fellowships, matching funds.
Geography: Illinois, Indiana, Michigan, Ohio, Wisconsin.

Limitations. *Recipients:* Individuals, religious organizations.
Activities: Fundraising, political activities.

Elmer L. & Eleanor J. Andersen Foundation

P.O. Box 130457
St. Paul, Minnesota 55113
Tel: 612–631–9102 Fax: 612–631–9102
EIN: 416032984 Type: Independent
Contact: Coral Berge, Program Associate

History and philosophy. The Foundation was established in 1957 "to enhance the quality of the civic, cultural, educational, environmental, and social aspect of life primarily in the metropolitan area of St. Paul and Minneapolis." Funding areas are: Arts & Humanities, Communications, Education, Environment, and Health & Human Services.

Officers and directors. *Officers:* Elmer L. Andersen, President; Eleanor J. Andersen, Vice President; Samuel H. Morgan, Secretary; Julian Andersen, Treasurer. *Directors:* Eleanor J. Andersen, Elmer L. Andersen, Emily Andersen, Julian Andersen, Tony Andersen, Barbara B. Miller.

Financial data. Data for fiscal year ended November 30, 1993. *Assets:* $4,136,626 (M). *Total grants disbursed:* $207,000.

Environmental awards. *Recent grants:* 1993 awards included support for wilderness, water, and species protection, urban forests, recreation, and environmental education.

Issues. Cli Bio Lan Agr Wat Oce Ene Was Tox Pop Dev
                •   •   •

Funding analysis.

Fiscal year:	1993
Env grants disb:	$77,750
Number:	17
Range:	$500–$55,000
Median:	$1,000
Pct $ disb (env/total):	38

Recipients (1993 highest):	Number:	Dollars:
Minnesota Landscape Arboretum Foundation	1	55,000
Minnesota Parks and Trails Council and Foundation	1	7,000
Friends-Parks & Trails, St. Paul/Ramsey Counties	1	2,000
National Outdoor Leadership School	1	2,000
Adams Elementary School	1	1,000
Boundary Waters Wilderness Foundation	1	1,000
Deep Portage Conservation Foundation	1	1,000

A

Eco Education	1	1,000
International Wolf Center	1	1,000
Izaak Walton League of America	1	1,000
Thomas Irvine Dodge Nature Center	1	1,000
Twin Cities Tree Trust	1	1,000
Washington County Land Trust	1	1,000
Wolf Ridge Environmental Learning Center	1	1,000

Activity region (1993):   *Number:*   *Dollars:*
U.S. Great Lakes   17   77,750

Sample grants (1993).
Boundary Waters Wilderness Foundation. Minneapolis, MN. $1,000.
Eco Education. St. Paul, MN. $1,000.
International Wolf Center. Brooklyn, MN. $1,000.
Izaak Walton League of America. Bloomington, MN. $1,000.
Minnesota Landscape Arboretum Foundation. Chanhassen, MN. $55,000. For the Andersen Horticultural Library.
Minnesota Parks & Trails Council and Foundation. St. Paul, MN. $7,000.
National Outdoor Leadership School. Lander, WY. $2,000.
Thomas Irvine Dodge Nature Center. West St. Paul, MN. $1,000.
Twin Cities Tree Trust. St. Louis Park, MN. $1,000.
Washington County Land Trust. Washington County, MN. $1,000.
Wolf Ridge Environmental Learning Center. Finland, MN. $1,000.

Application process. *Initial contact:* Full proposal to include:
1. Letter (1–2 pages).
   - Organization requesting funding.
   - Purpose for which funding is sought.
   - Constituency served and how it will benefit.
   - Amount requested.
2. Financial information.
   - Budget for upcoming year or project for requested funds.
   - Most current financial statement.
3. Lists.
   - Past major donors to organization.
   - Board members of organization.
4. Copy of IRS tax-exempt status determination letter.

When to apply: Deadlines are the first working day of February, May, August, and November. Board meetings are held in March, June, September, and December.
The Foundation is available by telephone Monday, Wednesday, and Friday from 8:30 to 11:30 A.M. All other days and times, you will reach a fax machine.
Materials available: "Annual Report & Proposal Guidelines."

Emphases. *Recipients:* Nonprofit organizations.
Activities: Publications
Types of support: Capital campaigns/expenses, operating costs, projects.
Geography: Minnesota, primarily the metropolitan area of St. Paul and Minneapolis.

Limitations. *Recipients:* Individuals.

Angelina Fund, Inc.
186 Sachems Head Road
Guilford, Connecticut 06437
EIN: 061244000   Type: Independent
EGA member

Application address:
100 East 85th Street
New York, New York 10028
Tel: 212–249–1023
Contact: Colin Greer, President

History and philosophy. The Fund was established in 1989 by Samuel G. Wiener, Jr. Its interests are in the areas of public policy, journalism, environment, and civil rights.

Officers and directors. *Officer:* Colin Greer, President. *Directors:* Richard Healy, Sara M. Wiener.

Financial data. Data for fiscal years ended December 31, 1991 and 1992. *Assets (1991):* $4,184,186 (M). *Total grants disbursed (1992):* $582,000.

Environmental awards. *Program and interests:* The Fund makes grants with an environmental component through its Media, Political Participation, and Special Grants programs.
Recent grants: 1992 grants included support for environmental justice, corporate responsibility, toxics issues and Right-To-Know, agricultural issues, and waste management.

Issues.   Cli   Bio   Lan   Agr   Wat   Oce   Ene   Was   Tox   Pop   Dev
                 •   •   •   •   •   •

Funding analysis.§

Fiscal year:	1992
Env grants disb:	$300,000
Number:	12
Range:	$20,000–$50,000
Median:	$25,000
Pct $ disb (env/total):	52

Recipients (1992 highest):	*Number:*	*Dollars:*
National Toxics Campaign Fund	1	50,000
DATACenter	1	25,000
Kentucky Coalition	1	25,000
Save Our Cumberland Mountains Resource Project	1	25,000
Southern Californian Ecumenical Council	1	25,000
The Focus Project	1	25,000
Western Organization of Resource Councils (WORC)	1	25,000

Activity regions (1992):	*Number:*	*Dollars:*
U.S. not specified	7	180,000
U.S. Southeast	2	50,000
U.S. Mountain	1	25,000
U.S. West	1	25,000
U.S. Northeast	1	20,000

§May overestimate environmental grant dollars because each grant also funds nonenvironmental concerns.

Sample grants (1992).
Cambridge Forum. Cambridge, MA. $20,000. Documentary Films/Pro-Media Social change Project. Pro-Media works with social justice organizations to gain mainstream media attention. Its issues include environmental justice, human rights, alternative economic policy, labor rights, education reform, and foreign policy. Through extensive contacts in the national and regional media, both print and mainstream, Pro-Media is able to promote coverage of specific stories and events.

DATACenter. Oakland, CA. $25,000. The library of the Data Center, which houses some 30 specialized collection, includes all major aspects of the U.S. political economy and its impact at home and abroad. The Center provides two monthly press monitors (one on Latin America and one on the corporate social and environmental record) to help subscribers keep abreast of developments in their fields. In addition, the Center runs the Right-to-Know project which is a response to recent government attempts to curb the flow of information from both public and private sectors.

National Toxics Campaign Fund. Allston, MA. $50,000. A special grant to support the Fund through a major restructuring, moving from a founder-led to a board-directed, multiracial organization, with a clear mission as a movement-building institution committed to functioning in a coherent, strategic, and democratic fashion.

OMB Watch. Washington, DC. $25,000. For the Focus Project, the 501(c)(3) arm of OMB Watch, which was founded in 1983 to monitor and counter the arbitrary authority of the Office of Management and Budget. Its regulatory monitoring reports and analyses are well regarded by the press and Congressional staffs, and its Action Alerts have proved an effective way to report to national and grassroots campaigns. The Project's work with grassroots groups was responsible for citizen participation in formulating fair IRS Anti-Lobbying Rules, and in safeguarding worker Right-to-Know regulations.

Public Media Center. San Francisco, CA. $20,000. This national resource organization specializes in public interest advertising campaigns and serves both large advocacy organizations and grassroots groups. PMC works with over 200 social justice organizations and its advertising campaigns on environmental issues, reproductive rights, and civil liberties and are considered models in the field.

Women's Peace Network/Riptide Communications, Inc. New York, NY. $20,000. This social issues public relations firm, founded in 1989, works primarily on the issues of racial justice, women's rights, peace, the environment, and human rights. In addition to the public relations services it provides, Riptide also trains its clients, thus building the progressive organizations it serves, and increasing their media capacity.

Application process. *Initial contact:* The Fund awards grants to pre-selected organizations only. No unsolicited applications accepted.

Emphases. *Recipients:* Pre-selected organizations only.

Apple Computer, Inc.
Community Affairs Department
20525 Mariani Avenue, MS 38J
Cupertino, California 95014
Tel: 408–974–2974   Fax: 408–974–5870
EIN: 942404110   Type: Company-sponsored
EGA member
Contact: Fred Silverman, Department Manager

History and philosophy. Since 1982, Apple Computer, Inc. has supported a wide range of nonprofit groups with grants of personal computers. In 1992 the company initiated a special program targeting environmental organizations. Its goal was to enable those active in a range of environmental areas to use Apple's technological tools to enhance their work. The grant program is only one of the ways Apple is addressing environmental issues. The company has also changed manufacturing processes, redesigned product packages, and implemented recycling programs.

Officers and directors. *Officers:* Fred Silverman, Department Manager; Beverly Long, Program Manager; Cristina Mendoza, Program Coordinator.

Financial data. Data for fiscal year ended September 30, 1993. *Total environmental grants disbursed:* $704,000 (est.)

Environmental awards. *Program and interests:* In 1993 Apple distributed computer equipment to groups working on environmental issues for more effective office administration and program management.

Application process. *Initial contact:* Telephone or write for "Guidelines for Fiscal Year 1994/95."
Materials available: Annual report, "Guidelines for Fiscal Year 1994/95."

Emphases. *Recipients:* Educational institutions (higher), nonprofit organizations.
Types of support: Computer hardware.
Geography: United States.

The Arca Foundation
1425 21st Street, N.W.
Washington, DC 20036
Tel: 202–822–9193   Fax: 202–785–1446
EIN: 132751798   Type: Independent
Contact: Janet Shenk, Executive Director

History and philosophy. The Arca Foundation was established in 1952 by Nancy Susan Reynolds, whose father founded R. J. Reynolds Tobacco Company. Her main philanthropic concern was population control. The Arca Foundation is dedicated to affecting public policy in the United States, by supporting groups who demonstrate an ability to expose the inequities of present-day policy, propose creative alternatives, and mobilize grassroots support for changing the status quo. It clusters its grantmaking around a specific set of issues, and supports a diverse set of organizations working toward common goals. It supports tax-exempt organizations engaged in activities of national significance that are likely to yield tangible public policy results.

The Foundation's priority areas include: (1) Campaign finance reform as part of an effort to reenergize and empower voters. (2) United States and Cuba relations, to create a climate more conducive to dialogue and democratization. (3) Human rights and democratic development in Central America. The Foundation also funds a number of policy-oriented social justice projects that reflect the diverse interests of its board.

Officers and directors. *Officers:* Smith W. Bagley, President; Ellsworth Culver, Vice President; Mary E. King, Secretary; Brian Topping, Treasurer. *Directors:* Elizabeth Frawley Bagley, Nancy R. Bagley, Nicole L. Bagley, Smith W. Bagley, Dick Clark, Ellsworth Culver, Mary E. King, Walter Russell Mead, Margery Tabankin, Brian Topping.

Financial data. Data for fiscal year ended December 31, 1993. *Assets:* $42,109,805 (M). *Total grants disbursed:* $1,605,608.

Environmental awards. *Recent grants:* 1993 awards included support for policy programs addressing industrial waste, production and regulation, trade policy (NAFTA), and sustainable development.

Issues. Cli Bio Lan Agr• Wat Oce Ene Was Tox• Pop• Dev•

Funding analysis.

Fiscal year:	1991	1993
Env grants disb:	$70,000	$50,000
Number:	2	3
Range:	$20,000–$50,000	$5,000–$25,000
Median:	$35,000	$20,000
Pct $ disb (env/total):	5	3

Recipients (1993):	Number:	Dollars:
Central America Working Group/National Council of Churches	1	25,000
Institute for Policy Studies	1	20,000
Institute for Development Research	1	5,000

Activity regions (1993):	Number:	Dollars:
Mexico and Central America	1	25,000
North America	1	20,000
International*	1	5,000

*Multiple regions or not specified.

Sample grants (1993).
Central America Working Group/National Council of Churches. Washington, DC. $25,000. To promote action by policymakers to defend human rights and reorient United States resources in support of pluralism, democratization, and sustainable development in Central America.
Institute for Development Research. Boston, MA. $5,000. To support exchange between NGOs in Central America and the Philippines on such issues as agrarian reform, peace negotiations, the environment, and foreign debt.

Institute for Policy Studies. Washington, DC. $20,000. To educate environmental, labor, consumer, religious, and farm constituencies about the North American Free Trade Agreement (NAFTA).

Application process. *Initial contact:* Full application (10 pages) written in a concise style to include:
1. Cover sheet. Brief summary (2 pages).
   - Organization's name and address.
   - Contact person(s) telephone and fax numbers.
   - Proposal summary (1 paragraph).
   - Total annual organizational budget and fiscal year.
   - Total project budget.
   - Amount being requested.
   - Amounts and dates of all previous Arca grants.
2. Narrative (10 pages).
3. Purpose of grant.
   - Description of project goals and objectives. State if new or ongoing part of sponsoring organization's activities.
   - Plans to accomplish goals and objectives with timetable.
   - List of names, qualifications or resumes, and job description of key staff responsible for the project.
   - Project budget, with anticipated income and expenditures.
4. Attachments.
   - IRS tax-exempt status determination letter.
   - Board of directors and their major organizational affiliation or occupation.
   - Organizational budget for the current fiscal year (1 page, line item).
   - List and amounts of other funding sources to which this proposal has been submitted and a list of all grants received during the most recent fiscal year.

When to apply: Deadlines are October 1 and April 1 for consideration at board meetings in December and June. Proposals sent by facsimile will not be considered.
Materials available: Annual report (includes "Application Procedures").

Emphases. *Recipients:* Educational institutions, nonprofit organizations.
Activities: Citizen participation, education, policy analysis/development, seminars.
Types of support: Emergency funding, travel expenses.
Geography: U.S.-based organizations only.

Limitations. *Recipients:* Individuals, public agencies.
Activities: Research (scholarly).
Types of support: Capital campaigns/expenses, endowments, fellowships, scholarships.

Arcadia Foundation
105 East Logan Street
Norristown, Pennsylvania 19401
Tel: 215-275-8460
EIN: 236399772   Type: Independent
Contact: Marilyn L. Steinbright, President

History and philosophy. The Foundation was established in 1964 by Edith C. and Marilyn L. Steinbright. It supports art, civic affairs, health and human services, and educational organizations working to improve the quality of life in Pennsylvania.

Officers and directors. *Officers:* Marilyn L. Steinbright, President; Tanya Hashorva, Vice President; David P. Sandler, Secretary; Harvey S. S. Miller, Treasurer. *Directors:* Tanya Hashorva, Edward L. Jones, Jr., Harvey S. S. Miller, David P. Sandler, Kathleen Shellington, Marilyn L. Steinbright.

Financial data. Data for fiscal year ended September 30, 1992. *Assets:* $37,788,255 (M). *Total grants disbursed:* $2,062,140.

Environmental awards. *Recent grants:* 1992 grants included support for watershed protection, water conservation, and wildlife protection.

Issues. Cli Bio Lan Agr Wat Oce Ene Was Tox Pop Dev
              •   •   •

Funding analysis.

Fiscal year:	1992
Env grants disb:	$85,500
Number:	9
Range:	$500–$25,000
Median:	$10,000
Pct $ disb (env/total):	4

Recipients (1992 highest):	Number:	Dollars:
Zoological Society of Philadelphia	1	25,000
Morris Arboretum of the University of Pennsylvania	1	15,000
Conservation International	1	10,000
Norristown Zoological Society	1	10,000
Wildlife Preservation Trust International	1	10,000

Activity regions (1992):	Number:	Dollars:
U.S. Mid-Atlantic	7	65,500
International*	2	20,000

*Multiple regions or not specified.

Sample grants (1992).
Clean Water Fund. Philadelphia, PA. $5,000.
Conservation International. Washington, DC. $10,000.
French and Pickering Creeks Conservation Trust. Pottstown, PA. $5,000.
Friends of the Delaware Canal. Point Pleasant, PA. $5,000.
Lower Merion–Narberth Watershed Association. Gladwyne, PA. $500.
Morris Arboretum of the University of Pennsylvania. Philadelphia, PA. $15,000.
Norristown Zoological Society. Norristown, PA. $10,000.
Wildlife Preservation Trust International. Philadelphia, PA. $10,000.
Zoological Society of Philadelphia. Philadelphia, PA. $25,000.

Application process. *Initial contact:* Proposal summary (1–2 pages) to include:
1. Brief history and purpose of organization.
2. How much money is requested.
3. How funds will be spent.

When to apply: Between July 1 and August 15. The board meets in September and November.

Emphases. *Recipients:* Nonprofit organizations.
Activities: Research.
Types of support: Annual campaigns, capital campaigns/expenses, continuing support, emergency funding, equipment, endowments, facilities, general purposes, operating costs, projects.
Geography: New proposals are limited to organizations located in Pennsylvania.

Limitations. *Recipients:* Individuals.
Activities: Conferences, demonstration programs, land acquisition, publications.
Types of support: Debt retirement, fellowships, loans.

Evenor Armington Fund

c/o Huntington Trust Company, N.A.
P.O. Box 1558
Columbus, Ohio 43216
Tel: 614–463–3707   Fax: 614–463–5223
EIN: 346525508   Type: Independent
Contact: David E. Armington, Advisor

History and philosophy. The Evenor Armington Fund was established in 1954 by Everett Armington and members of the family. It supports the arts, child welfare, education, the environment, medical research, population, and social justice issues.

Officers and directors. *Advisors:* David E. Armington, Paul Armington, Peter Armington. *Trustee:* Huntington Trust Company.

Financial data. Data for fiscal year ended June 30, 1993. *Assets:* $5,893,476 (M). *Total grants disbursed:* $286,000.

Environmental awards. *Recent grants:* 1993 grants included support for land conservation (including national parks) and river protection.

Issues. Cli Bio Lan Agr Wat Oce Ene Was Tox Pop Dev
              •   •   •   •

Funding analysis.

Fiscal year:	1991	1993
Env grants disb:	$62,300	$72,300
Number:	7	6
Range:	$3,700–$20,000	$4,000–$20,000
Median:	$8,000	$12,500
Pct $ disb (env/total):	21	26

Recipients (1993 highest):	Number:	Dollars:
The Trust for Public Land	1	20,000
Tin Mountain Conservation Center	1	18,300
American Rivers, Inc.	1	15,000
The Nature Conservancy, New Hampshire Field Office	1	10,000
Grand Teton Natural History Association	1	5,000

A

Activity regions (1993):	Number:	Dollars:
U.S. Northeast	2	28,300
U.S. Mid-Atlantic	1	20,000
U.S. not specified	1	15,000
U.S. Mountain	1	5,000
U.S. multiple regions	1	4,000

Sample grants (1993).
American Rivers, Inc. Washington, DC. $15,000.
Appalachian Trail Conference, Headquarters. Harpers Ferry, WV. $4,000.
Grand Teton Natural History Association. Moose, WY. $5,000.
The Nature Conservancy, New Hampshire Field Office. Concord, NH. $10,000. Peaked Mountain/Green Hills Project.
Tin Mountain Conservation Center. Jackson, NY. $18,300.
The Trust for Public Land. Cleveland, OH. $20,000.

Application process. *Initial contact:* The Foundation generally awards grants to pre-selected organizations. No unsolicited applications accepted.
When to apply: Deadline is November 15. The board meets during the summer.

Emphases. *Recipients:* Pre-selected organizations, generally.
Activities: Publications, research, projects.
Types of support: Annual campaigns/expenses, continuing support, emergency funding, operating costs.

Limitations. *Recipients:* Individuals.
Types of support: Debt retirement, general purposes.

The Vincent Astor Foundation
405 Park Avenue
New York, New York 10022–4456
Tel: 212–758–4110
EIN: 237167124   Type: Independent
Contact: Linda L. Gillies, Director

History and philosophy. Vincent Astor, descendant of John Jacob Astor, established the Foundation in 1948 "for the alleviation of human misery." After his death in 1959, the trustees determined that the Foundation should focus on the New York City metropolitan area. With few exceptions, the Foundation supports established nonprofit institutions and neighborhood programs that broaden the opportunities, enrich the lives, and sustain the vitality of New York City's population. Grants focus on the preservation and restoration of historic properties and literacy programs.

Officers and directors. *Officers:* Mrs. Vincent Astor, President; Anthony D. Marshall, Vice President; Peter P. McN. Gates, Secretary; Fergus Reid III, Treasurer; Linda L. Gillies, Director. *Trustees:* Mrs. Vincent Astor, Henry Christensen III, Thomas R. Coolidge, Henry N. Ess III, Peter P. McN. Gates, Linda L. Gillies, Anthony D. Marshall, Peter S. Paine, Richard S. Perkins, Howard Phipps, Jr., John Pierrepont, Fergus Reid III.

Financial data. Data for fiscal year ended December 31, 1993. *Assets:* $25,291,091. (M). *Total grants authorized:* $1,530,000.

Environmental awards. *Recent grants:* 1993 grants supported botanical and community gardens and urban beautification.

Issues.   Cli   Bio   Lan   Agr   Wat   Oce   Ene   Was   Tox   Pop   Dev
       •   •

Funding analysis.

Fiscal year:	1991	1993
Env grants auth:	$318,500	$50,300
Number:	11	10
Range:	$1,000–$250,000	$1,000–$25,000
Median:	$3,750	$1,650
Pct $ auth (env/total):	14	3

Recipients (1993 highest):	Number:	Dollars:
The New York Botanical Garden	2	26,650
Prospect Park Alliance	1	10,000
City Parks Foundation	1	5,000
The Parks Council, Inc.	1	3,000
NYZS/The Wildlife Conservation Society	1	1,650

Activity region (1993):	Number:	Dollars:
New York/New Jersey	10	50,300

Sample grants (1993).
City Parks Foundation. New York, NY. $5,000.
Council on the Environment of New York City. New York, NY. $1,000. General support.
Green Guerrillas. New York, NY. $1,000. Toward the Community Outreach Program.
The New York Botanical Garden. Bronx, NY. $25,000. Toward the Children's Education Program and Bronx Green-Up, a community garden project.
The Parks Council, Inc. New York, NY. $3,000. Toward "Forcing the Spring in Urban America," a colloquium held at the NYPL in April 1993.
Prospect Park Alliance. Brooklyn, NY. $10,000. Toward renovations at the Lefferts Homestead in Brooklyn's Prospect Park.
New York City Street Tree Consortium. New York, NY. $1,000.
West Side Community Garden. New York, NY. $1,000. General support.

Application process. *Initial contact:* Letter of inquiry to include:
1. Project description.
2. Description of sponsoring agency.
3. Budget.
4. Other potential sources of funds.

If the request falls within Foundation guidelines and appears to have a reasonable chance for funding, the Foundation will arrange a meeting and request more detailed information. All grant proposals to include:
1. Copy of most recently audited financial statement.
2. Copies of IRS tax-exempt status determination letter and proof that the organization is not a private foundation under Section 509(a).

When to apply: Anytime. The trustees consider grant applications in May, October, and December.
Materials available: Annual report (includes "Grant Policies").

Emphases. *Recipients:* Nonprofit organizations.
Activities: Education (literacy programs).
Types of support: Annual campaigns, capital campaigns/expenses, continuing support, endowments, equipment, facilities (renovation of historic properties), general purposes, operating costs, pilot projects, projects, seed money, single-year grants only, start-up costs.
Geography: New York City.

Limitations. *Recipients:* Individuals.
Activities: Activism, advocacy, audiovisual materials, capacity building, conferences, conflict resolution, direct services, exhibits, expeditions/tours, feasibility studies, fieldwork, fundraising, inventories, land acquisition, litigation, lobbying, networking, planning, policy analysis/development, political activities, publications, research, seminars, symposia/colloquia, technical assistance, training, volunteerism, workshops, youth programs.
Types of support: Advertising campaigns, annual campaigns/expenses, computer hardware, continuing support, debt retirement, emergency funding, facilities (construction), fellowships, indirect costs, internships, lectureships, leveraging funds, loans, membership campaigns, mortgage reduction, multi-year grants, professorships, program-related investments, scholarships, technical assistance, travel expenses.

Atherton Family Foundation

c/o Hawaii Community Foundation
222 Merchant Street, Second Floor
Honolulu, Hawaii 96813
Tel: 808–537–6333   Fax: 808–521–6286
EIN: 510175971   Type: Independent
Contact: Chris Sunada, Grants Manager

History and philosophy. The Atherton Family Foundation is the merged successor of two earlier family trusts: the Juliette M. Atherton Trust, established by the donor in 1915 in honor of her late husband Joseph Ballard Atherton; and the F. C. Atherton Trust, established by the philanthropist Frank C. Atherton in 1935. Organized as a nonprofit corporation in 1976, the Atherton Family Foundation is now one of the largest private resources in Hawaii devoted exclusively to charitable causes. Its six major program areas are: Education, Human Service, Health, Humanities & Religion, Culture & Art, and the Environment. Projects within the state of Hawaii receive preference.

Officers and directors. *Officers:* Robert R. Midkiff, President; Frank C. Atherton, James F. Morgan, Jr., John H. Rohlfing, Vice Presidents; Judith Dawson, Vice President and Secretary, Hawaiian Trust Company, Limited, Treasurer.

Financial data. Data for fiscal year ended December 31, 1992.
Assets: $32,970,362 (C). *Total grants authorized:* $2,080,425.

Environmental awards. *Program and interests:* The Foundation's special interests are species preservation and environmental education.
Recent grants: 1992 grants included support for land conservation, wildlife, energy conservation, recycling, and a botanical garden.

Issues.   Cli Bio Lan Agr Wat Oce Ene Was Tox Pop Dev
          •   •   •   •   •   •

Funding Analysis.

Fiscal year:	1992
Env grants auth:	$122,000
Number:	10
Range:	$2,000–$50,000
Median:	$5,000
Pct $ auth (env/total):	6

Recipients (1992 highest):	Number:	Dollars:
The Nature Conservancy, Hawaii Field Office	1	50,000
Bernice Pauahi Bishop Museum	1	30,000
Center for Plant Conservation	1	10,000
National Audubon Society, Hawaii State Office	1	10,000
Hawaii Nature Center	1	5,000
Natural Resources Defense Council	1	5,000

Activity region (1992):	Number:	Dollars:
Hawaii	10	122,000

Sample grants (1992).
Campaign Recycle Maui. Wailuku, HI. $3,000. Green waste source separation education for hotels.
Center for Plant Conservation. St. Louis, MO. $10,000. Plant conservation in Hawaii.
Kawai Nui Heritage Foundation. Hawaii. $2,000. "Na kia" i Pono "O Kawai Nui" program expansion.
National Audubon Society, Hawaii State Office. Honolulu, HI. $10,000. Second year support for Alien Species Alert Program.
Natural Resources Defense Council. Honolulu, HI. $5,000. Continued support for energy conservation project.
Outdoor Circle. Honolulu, HI. $4,000. Support for Anuenue Playground project.

Application process. *Initial contact:* Full proposal (1 copy) to include:
Proposal.
1. Description of organization, its history, mission and leadership.
2. Population to benefit by project and an estimate of the size or numbers.
3. The need for which project is responding (state source of statistics or opinions).
4. Project objectives, summary of activities to be funded.
5. Expense budget and revenue plan for project budget indicating categories of sources and amounts (2 copies).
6. Amount of funds requested, time funds will be needed, and anticipated source of funding when Foundation funding ceases.
7. Method used to determine effectiveness of funded project.
8. Information on organization's staff including those responsible for the project.

Executive summary (1–2 pages, 2 copies).
Attachments.
1. Copy of IRS tax-exempt status determination letter.
2. Organization's charter and bylaws.

A

3. Board of directors list, including occupations, positions, and a statement of board involvement and functions within the organization (2 copies).
4. Most recent budget or financial statement for the organization, preferably audited, showing the year's income and expenses, fund balances at year's end, and explanations for anything unusual reported in the statements.
5. Organization's current year operating budget.
6. Name and phone number of contact persons through whom the Foundation may arrange for an interview or site visit, or request further information.

Proposal should be signed by the presiding officer of the board and the organization's executive director to indicate that both the board and chief staff person have approved its submission (For proposals from units of government, signatures of the program or project director and the accountable department or division head are required.)

When to apply: Deadlines are February 1, April 1, June 1, August 1, October 1, and December 1 for board meetings in April, June, August, October, December, and February, respectively.

Materials available: Annual report (includes "Grant Application Procedures" and scholarship guidelines).

Emphases. *Recipients:* Individuals, nonprofit organizations, religious organizations.
Activities: Conferences, education, publications, research.
Types of support: Annual campaigns, continuing support, equipment, facilities, loans, matching funds, projects, scholarships, seed money.
Geography: Hawaii.

Limitations. *Activities:* Fundraising, lobbying, political activities.
Types of support: Operating costs.

Atkinson Foundation

1100 Grundy Lane, Suite 140
San Bruno, California 94066
Tel: 415-876-1359
EIN: 946075613   Type: Independent
Contact: Elizabeth H. Curtis, Administrator

History and philosophy. The Atkinson Foundation was established in 1939 by George H. Atkinson (1905–1978) and his wife Mildred (1904–1967). Co-founder of an international construction firm, Atkinson frequently travelled to developing countries. Firsthand experience of the problems faced by developing nations led the Atkinsons to a giving pattern "that serves human needs and contributes to the self-esteem and independence of individuals, families, and communities in the developing areas of the world." The Foundation also supports secondary and higher education through selected universities, community and minority colleges, the Methodist church, and social services in San Mateo County and the San Francisco Bay Area.

The Foundation's broad funding areas are: Community, International, Education, and Churches and Church Activities.

Officers and directors. *Officers:* Duane E. Atkinson, President; Ray N. Atkinson, Thomas J. Henderson, Vice Presidents; James C. Ingwersen, Secretary/Assistant Treasurer; John E. Herrell, Treasurer/Assistant Secretary. *Directors:* Duane E. Atkinson, Lavina M. Atkinson, Ray N. Atkinson, James R. Clark, Elizabeth H. Curtis, Thomas J. Henderson, John E. Herrell, James C. Ingwersen, Lawrence A. Wright.

Financial data. Data for fiscal year ended December 31, 1993. *Assets:* $12,466,509 (M). *Total grants disbursed:* $505,738.

Environmental awards. *Program and interests:* A major priority of the International program is "Technical assistance and training for the sustainable and ecologically sound development of local water and food resources, including reforestation."
Recent grants: 1993 grants included support for tropical forests, water resources, and agriculture in developing countries.

Issues. Cli Bio Lan Agr Wat Oce Ene Was Tox Pop Dev
               •   •   •   •   •   •

Funding analysis.

Fiscal year:	1991	1993
Env grants disb:	$21,000	$37,131
Number:	4	7
Range:	$5,000–$6,000	$4,631–$7,500
Median:	$5,000	$5,000
Pct $ disb (env/total):	12	7

Recipients (1993 highest):	Number:	Dollars:
The International Center	1	7,500
Ananda Marga Universal Relief Team	1	5,000
CODEL, Inc.	1	5,000
The Rainforest Foundation	1	5,000
The Resource Foundation	1	5,000
The Tides Foundation	1	5,000

Activity regions (1993):	Number:	Dollars:
Mexico and Central America	3	17,500
West Africa	2	9,631
Brazil	1	5,000
Eastern and Southern Africa	1	5,000

Sample grants (1993).
Africare. Washington, DC. $4,631. Water development project in Guinea-Bissau.
Ananda Marga Universal Relief Team. San Antonio, TX. $5,000. Pilot pond eco-system program in Ghana.
CODEL, Inc. New York, NY. $5,000. Water Project in Kenya.
The International Center. Washington, DC. $7,500. Support of Guatamalan Training Center providing resources for agroforestry, conservation, sustainable agriculture, solar box cookers, etc.
The Rainforest Foundation. New York, NY. $5,000. Xingu market project in Brazil.
The Resource Foundation. Larchmont, NY. $5,000. Water resource and sanitation development project in rural Honduras.
The Tides Foundation. Berkeley, CA. $5,000. Assistance to margin communities in the Los Tuxtlas rainforest in Mexico.

Application process. *Initial contact:* Telephone to determine if grant request is within the guidelines before submitting proposal.

Full proposal to include cover sheet (from Foundation) and:
1. Applicant's name, address, telephone number, names of applicant organization's president, executive director, and contact for the proposal.
2. Names, affiliations of applicant's directors and officers with evidence that the proposal has been approved by the applicant's governing body.
3. History and statement of organization's activities and goals.
4. Description of proposed program demonstrating need to be met, population to be served, and specific objectives; resources to be applied; description of staff and their qualifications; anticipated outcome; and method of evaluation.
5. Program budget showing projected income and expenses including current financial statement.
6. Sources of funding and anticipated sources of continuing support for project after termination of Foundation assistance.
7. Copy of IRS tax-exempt status determination letter, and evidence that the organization is not a private foundation.
8. Any supplementary information that may significantly strengthen the application.

When to apply: Anytime, but deadlines for the International program are March 31 and August 31.
Materials available: Annual report (includes "Application Guidelines & Procedures"), cover sheet.

Emphases. *Recipients:* Educational institutions, nonprofit organizations, religious institutions.
Activities: Collaborative efforts, education, innovative programs, technical assistance, training.
Types of support: Capital campaigns/expenses, facilities (construction), maintenance, seed money.
Geography: San Mateo County, California; U.S. organizations working in developing countries.

Limitations. *Recipients:* Individuals.
Activities: Conferences, fundraising, political activities, research (scholarly).
Types of support: Annual campaigns, loans, scholarships, travel expenses.
Geography: Organizations based outside the United States.

Atlantic Foundation
16 Farber Road
Princeton, New Jersey 08540
Tel: 609-799-8530 Fax: 609-799-7256
EIN: 226054882 Type: Independent
Contact: Louis R. Hewitt, Controller

History and philosophy. The Atlantic Foundation was established in 1963 by J. Seward Johnson, Sr., son of the founder of Johnson & Johnson pharmaceuticals. Johnson, a naval officer during World War I, was active in the development of Woods Hole Oceanographic Institution. In 1963, as part of his philanthropic activities, he established Harbor Branch Oceanographic Institution. The Atlantic Foundation gives one grant each year to Harbor Branch for marine research.

Officers and directors. *Officers:* J. Seward Johnson, Jr., Chairman, CEO, and Treasurer; Carl W. Shafer, President; C. Amos Bussmann, Vice President; Louis R. Hewitt, Controller and Secretary. *Directors:* C. Amos Bussmann, Michael H. Greenleaf, Garrett M. Heher, J. Seward Johnson, Jr., John S. Johnson III, Carl W. Schafer.

Financial data. Data for fiscal year ended December 31, 1991. *Assets:* $100,974,805 (M). *Total grants disbursed:* $3,481,063.

Environmental awards. *Program and interests:* The Foundation's annual grant supports programs in marine science, applied biology, sea pharmacy, and ocean engineering.

Issues. Cli Bio Lan Agr Wat Oce Ene Was Tox Pop Dev
                                        •

Funding analysis.

Fiscal year:	1991	1993
Env grants auth:	$3,257,763	$2,819,000
Number:	1	1
Range:	–	–
Median:	–	–
Pct $ auth (env/total):	92	79

Recipient (1993):	Number:	Dollars:
Harbor Branch Oceanographic Institution	1	2,819,000

Activity region (1993):	Number:	Dollars:
U.S. Southeast	1	2,819,000

Sample grant (1993).
Harbor Branch Oceanographic Institution. Fort Pierce, FL. $2,819,000. General support for the institution, which conducts research on marine and coastal resources.

Application process. *Initial contact:* The Foundation generally funds Harbor Branch Oceanographic Institution exclusively. No applications accepted.

Emphases. *Recipients:* Pre-selected organizations only.

The Austin Memorial Foundation
Aurora Commons Office Place, Suite 230
Aurora, Ohio 44202
Tel: 216-562-5155
EIN: 346528879 Type: Independent
Contact: Donald G. Austin, Jr., President

History and philosophy. Members of the Austin family incorporated the Foundation in 1961. Primary areas of interest are education, the environment, hospitals, and Protestant causes.

Officers and directors. *Officers:* Donald G. Austin, Jr., President; Winifred N. Austin, Margaret A. Grumhaus, Vice Presidents; Colette F. Mylott, Secretary; David A. Rodgers, Treasurer. *Trustees:* Donald G. Austin, Jr., James W. Austin, Richard C. Austin, Stewart G. Austin, Thomas G. Austin, Winifred N. Austin, Sarah R. Cole, Margaret A. Grumhaus, Ann R. Loeffler, David A. Rodgers.

B

Financial data. Data for fiscal year ended December 31, 1993. *Assets:* $7,720,879 (M). *Gifts received:* $16,375. *Total grants disbursed:* $290,804.

Environmental awards. *Recent grants:* 1993 grants included support for agricultural issues, land conservation, and wildlife.

Issues. Cli Bio Lan Agr Wat Oce Ene Was Tox Pop Dev
          •   •   •

Funding analysis.

Fiscal year:	1992
Env grants disb:	$93,500
Number:	6
Range:	$500–$51,500
Median:	$1,000
Pct $ disb (env/total):	38

Recipients (1992 highest):	Number:	Dollars:
The Land Institute	1	51,500
Center for Rural Affairs	1	38,500
New Hampshire Audubon Society	1	1,000
California Center for Wildlife	1	1,000
Marin Agricultural Land Trust (MALT)	1	1,000

Activity regions (1992):	Number:	Dollars:
U.S. Midwest	2	90,000
U.S. West	2	2,000
U.S. Northeast	2	1,500

Sample grants (1993).
California Center for Wildlife. San Rafael, CA. $1,000.
Center for Rural Affairs. Walthill, NE. $75,000.
Community Farm Alliance. Berea, KY. $10,000.
The Garden Conservancy. San Francisco, CA. $500.
The Land Institute. Salina, KS. $53,500.
Marin Agricultural Land Trust (MALT). Point Reyes Station, CA. $1,000.

Application process. *Initial contact:* The Foundation awards grants to pre-selected organizations only. No unsolicited applications accepted.

Emphases. *Recipients:* Pre-selected organizations only.

Limitations. *Recipients:* Individuals.

Azadoutioun Foundation
c/o Mugar Group, Inc.
Two Burlington Woods Drive
Burlington, Massachusetts 01803–4538
Tel: 617–229–2111   Fax: 617–270–9659
EIN: 042876245   Type: Independent
Contact: Janet M. Corpus, Director

History and philosophy. Carolyn G. Mugar established the Foundation in 1985. Its areas of interest are environment, social services, and international development.

Officers and directors. *Trustees:* Janet M. Corpus, Carolyn G. Mugar, Sidney Peck, Sharryn Ross.

Financial data. Data for fiscal year ended December 31, 1992. *Assets:* $2,529,559 (M). *Gifts received:* $80,000. *Total grants disbursed:* $400,000.

Environmental awards. *Recent grants:* 1992 grants included support for toxic substance control.

Issues. Cli Bio Lan Agr Wat Oce Ene Was Tox Pop Dev
                                                  •

Funding analysis.

Fiscal year:	1991	1992
Env grants auth:	$70,000	$97,000
Number:	1	3
Range:	–	$7,000–$65,000
Median:	–	$25,000
Pct $ auth (env/total):	61	

Recipients (1992):	Number:	Dollars:
Massachusetts Toxics Campaign	1	65,000
Center for Pollution Prevention, Inc.	1	25,000
Oklahoma Toxics Campaign	1	7,000

Activity regions (1992):	Number:	Dollars:
U.S. Northeast	1	65,000
U.S. not specified	1	25,000
U.S. South Central	1	7,000

Sample grants (1992).
Massachusetts Toxics Campaign. Brighton, MA. $65,000.
Oklahoma Toxics Campaign. Oklahoma City, OK. $7,000.

Application process. *Initial contact:* Full proposal. No standardized format.
When to apply: Anytime.

Emphases. *Types of support:* General purposes, projects.
Geography: Massachusetts.

Mary Reynolds Babcock Foundation, Inc.
102 Reynolda Village
Winston-Salem, North Carolina 27106–5123
Tel: 910–748–9222   Fax: 910–777–0095
EIN: 560690140   Type: Independent
EGA member
Contact: Gayle Williams Dorman, Executive Director

History and philosophy. The Foundation was created in 1953 with a $12 million bequest from Mary Reynolds Babcock, daughter of the founder of the R. J. Reynolds Tobacco Company. In keeping with its charter, the Foundation broadly seeks to promote the well-being and betterment of mankind. It favors programs that address emerging social needs as well as those that propose new approaches to old problems. Current grantmaking areas are: early childhood development, economic development, education, environment, government accountability, grassroots organizing, public policy, and other.

During 1994 the Foundation was engaged in a year-long reevaluation process, broadly "to analyze trends in urban and rural areas of the Southeast, to study more carefully the dynamics of social changes at the turn of this century, and to develop new sensibilities to human need and creative action in meeting that need." New guidelines will be available in January 1995.

Officers and directors. *Officers:* William R. Rogers, President; Barbara B. Millhouse, Vice President; Kenneth F. Mountcastle, Jr., Secretary; L. Richardson Preyer, Treasurer. *Directors:* Bruce M. Babcock, David L. Dodson, Barbara B. Millhouse, Katharine B. Mountcastle, Katharine R. Mountcastle, Kenneth F. Mountcastle, III, Laura L. Mountcastle, Mary Mountcastle, Wyndham Robertson, William R. Rogers, Zachary Smith.

Financial data. Data for fiscal year ended August 31, 1993. *Assets:* $65,937,226 (U). *Total grants authorized:* $3,525,993.

Environmental awards. *Program and interests:* Primary environmental interests are:

- Grassroots organization.
- Public policy development.
- Government accountability.

Recent grants: 1993 grants included support for growth management and land use planning, forest protection, coastal issues, water quality protection, hazardous waste reduction, and topics pertaining to environmental ethics. Activities funded included advocacy and citizen involvement.

Issues. Cli Bio Lan Agr Wat Oce Ene Was Tox Pop Dev
• • • • • • • • • •

Funding analysis.

Fiscal year:	1991	1993
Env grants auth:	$904,264	$783,100
Number:	30	31
Range:	$2,500–$61,310	$1,000–$150,000
Median:	$30,000	$25,000
Pct $ auth (env/total):	20	22

Recipients (1993 highest):	Number:	Dollars:
University of North Carolina, Environmental Resource Program	1	150,000
Government Accountability Project	1	40,000
The Agricultural Resources Center, Inc.	1	40,000
Coalition to Restore Coastal Louisiana	1	35,000
Food and Water, Inc.	1	35,000
INFORM	1	35,000
North Carolina Coastal Federation	1	35,000
Penn Community Services	1	35,000

Activity regions (1993):	Number:	Dollars:
U.S. Southeast	29	728,100
U.S. South Central	1	35,000
U.S. not specified	1	20,000

Sample grants (1993).
Association of Forest Service Employees for Environmental Ethics. Eugene, OR. $30,000. For Southeast Chapter organizing and monitoring teams.
Coalition to Restore Coastal Louisiana. Baton Rouge, LA. $35,000. For the Coastal Watch Program.
Kentucky Conservation Foundation. Frankfort, KY. $1,000. For the Sustainable Development Project.
Legal Environmental Assistance Foundation. Tallahassee, FL. $30,000. For the Justice and Empowerment Program.
Public Interest Projects. New York, NY. $20,000. On behalf of Public Employees for Environmental Responsibility (PEER).
University of North Carolina, Environmental Resource Program. Chapel Hill, NC. $150,000 (3 years). For the Environmental Resource Program's "Finding Common Ground: Toward a Sustainable North Carolina."
U.S. Catholic Conference, Appalachian Office for Justice and Peace. St. Paul, VA. $11,500. On behalf of the Coalition for Jobs and the Environment for sustainable development, waste reduction and quality, technical assistance, and training.

Application process. *Initial contact:* Telephone call, letter, or full proposal. As of mid-1994, criteria for application were:
1. Application form signed by organization's CEO or board chairman.
2. Proposal (5 pages maximum).
   - Program needs statement.
   - Objectives and purposes of program.
   - How needs and objectives will be met.
   - Organization's history and mission.
   - Staff qualifications.
   - Program's location and estimated duration.
   - Program's method and evaluation criteria.
3. Budget. Line-item (1 page) budget identifying projected expenses and income of program. If the total budget for the organization is different from the program budget, a summary (1 page) of the organization's budget, listing both expenses and revenues, should be included.
4. List of board of directors and their affiliations or occupations; racial and gender diversity of board members.
5. Copy of IRS tax-exempt status determination letter.

New guidelines will be available in January 1995 for application for the Spring 1995 grants cycle.

When to apply: Deadlines are March 1 and September 1. The board of directors meets in May and November.
Materials available: Annual report (contains "Application Information").

Emphases. *Recipients:* Nonprofit organizations.
Activities: Advocacy, capacity building, citizen participation, collaborative efforts, innovative programs, policy analysis/development, technical assistance.
Types of support: General purposes, leveraging funds, operating costs, pilot projects, program-related investments, projects, seed money, start-up costs.
Geography: Southeastern United States. International grants given on a very selective basis.

© 1995 Environmental Data Resources, Inc.

B

Limitations. *Recipients:* Individuals.
Types of support: Capital campaigns/expenses, computer hardware, equipment, facilities, fellowships, maintenance, professorships.
Geography: Individual community or county efforts unless there is potential for regional or statewide replication.

The Bailey Wildlife Foundation
10223 Bushveld Lane
Raleigh, North Carolina 27612
Tel: 919–848–7725
EIN: 546037402   Type: Independent
Contact: Harold W. Bailey, Jr., Treasurer and Trustee

History and philosophy. The Bailey Wildlife Foundation was established in 1987. It awards grants for research projects in the natural sciences and arts, with a focus on environment, conservation, and wildlife.

Officers and directors. *Trustees:* Gordon M. Bailey, Harold W. Bailey, Jr., Merritt P. Bailey, William H. Bailey.

Financial data. Data for fiscal year ended December 31, 1992. *Assets:* $2,667,258 (M). *Total grants disbursed:* $138,027.

Environmental awards. *Recent grants:* 1992 grants included support for species and wildlife preservation.

Issues.   Cli   Bio   Lan   Agr   Wat   Oce   Ene   Was   Tox   Pop   Dev
                      •

Funding analysis.

Fiscal year:	1990	1992
Env grants disb:	$56,185	$138,027
Number:	8	7
Range:	$3,000–$20,000	$3,000–$100,000
Median:	$3,000	$6,000
Pct $ disb (env/total):	90	100

Recipients (1992):	*Number:*	*Dollars:*
Southern Environmental Law Center	1	100,000
College of William and Mary	1	15,000
Smithsonian Institution, Conservation and Research Center	1	8,027
Carolina Raptor Center	1	6,000
NYZS/The Wildlife Conservation Society	1	3,000
Raptor Trust	1	3,000
Tufts University, School of Veterinary Medicine	1	3,000

Activity regions (1992):	*Number:*	*Dollars:*
U.S. Southeast	2	106,000
U.S. Mid-Atlantic	1	15,000
U.S. not specified	1	8,027
New York/New Jersey	2	6,000
U.S. Northeast	1	3,000

Sample grants (1992).
Carolina Raptor Center. Charlotte, NC. $6,000.
College of William and Mary. Williamsburg, VA. $15,000.
NYZS/The Wildlife Conservation Society. Bronx, NY. $3,000.
Raptor Trust. Livingston, NJ. $3,000.
Smithsonian Institution, Conservation and Research Center. Front Royal, VA. $8,027.
Southern Environmental Law Center. Charlottesville, VA. $100,000.
Tufts University, School of Veterinary Medicine. North Grafton, MA. $3,000.

Application process. *Initial contact:* Letter specifying the organization's purpose and intended use of the grant.
When to apply: Anytime.

Emphases. *Activities:* Research.

Limitations. *Recipients:* Individuals.

The Cameron Baird Foundation
120 Delaware Avenue, Sixth Floor
Buffalo, New York 14202
Tel: 716–845–6000
EIN: 166029481   Type: Independent
Contact: Brian D. Baird, Trustee

Application address:
Box 564
Hamburg, New York 14075

History and philosophy. Members of the Baird family established the Foundation in 1960. Grantmaking focuses on arts, civic affairs, and education. Special interests include music in Buffalo, the environment, and minority scholarships.

Officers and directors. *Trustees:* Brian D. Baird, Bridget B. Baird, Bruce C. Baird, Jane D. Baird, Bronwyn B. Clauson, Brenda B. Senturia.

Financial data. Data for fiscal year ended December 31, 1992. *Assets:* $18,744,518 (M). *Total grants disbursed:* $1,093,575.

Environmental awards. *Recent grants:* 1992 grants included support for land and wildlife conservation.

Issues.   Cli   Bio   Lan   Agr   Wat   Oce   Ene   Was   Tox   Pop   Dev
                      •   •   •

Funding analysis.

Fiscal year:	1991	1992
Env grants disb:	$72,000	$70,000
Number:	3	2
Range:	$2,000–$60,000	$10,000–$60,000
Median:	$10,000	$35,000
Pct $ disb (env/total):	8	6

Recipients (1992):	*Number:*	*Dollars:*
Sierra Club Foundation	1	60,000
World Wildlife Fund	1	10,000

Activity region (1992):   *Number:*   *Dollars:*
   U.S. not specified   2   70,000

Sample grants (1992).
Sierra Club Foundation. San Francisco, CA. $60,000. Conservation programs.
World Wildlife Fund. Washington, DC. $10,000. Conservation of natural resources.

Application process. *Initial contact:* Letter. Prospective applicants should note that Foundation favors pre-selected organizations.
When to apply: In the fall. The board meets annually.

Emphases. *Recipients:* Nonprofit organizations, pre-selected organizations.

Limitations. *Recipients:* Individuals, religious organizations.

Clayton Baker Trust
c/o John B. Powell, Jr.
250 West Pratt Street, 13th Floor
Baltimore, Maryland 21201
Tel: 410–539–5541   Fax: 410–659–1350
EIN: 526054237   Type: Independent
Contact: John B. Powell, Jr., Trustee

History and philosophy. Julia C. Baker established the Clayton Baker Trust in 1960. Most grants are awarded to organizations in the Baltimore area to help the disadvantaged and promote the welfare of children. Grants outside Baltimore generally focus on environmental protection, population control, arms control, and nuclear disarmament.

Officers and directors. *Trustees:* Julia C. Baker, William C. Baker, John B. Powell, Jr.

Financial data. Data for fiscal year ended December 31, 1992. *Assets:* $6,575,705 (M). *Total grants disbursed:* $266,500.

Environmental awards. *Recent grants:* 1992 grants included support for urban environment, wildlife, and marine issues.

Issues.   Cli   Bio   Lan   Agr   Wat   Oce   Ene   Was   Tox   Pop   Dev
              •   •   •   •   •   •   •   •

Funding analysis.

Fiscal year:	1992
Env grants disb:	$42,000
Number:	8
Range:	$2,000–$10,000
Median:	$5,000
Pct $ disb (env/total):	16

Recipients (1992 highest):	*Number:*	*Dollars:*
Chesapeake Bay Foundation	1	10,000
Fort Smallwood Marine Institute	1	10,000
Environmental Defense Fund	1	5,000
Johns Hopkins University, Institute for Policy Studies	1	5,000
The Wilderness Society	1	5,000

Activity regions (1992):	*Number:*	*Dollars:*
U.S. Mid-Atlantic	4	28,000
U.S. not specified	4	14,000

Sample grants (1992).
Chesapeake Bay Foundation. Annapolis, MD. $10,000.
Earth Action Network, Inc. Norwalk, CT. $2,000.
Earthwatch Expeditions, Inc. Watertown, MA. $2,000.
Environmental Defense Fund. New York, NY. $5,000.
Fort Smallwood Marine Institute. Fort Smallwood, MD. $10,000.
Johns Hopkins University, Institute for Policy Studies. Baltimore, MD. $5,000.
Maryland Public Interest Research. College Park, MD. $3,000.
The Wilderness Society. Washington, DC. $5,000.

Application process. *Initial contact:* Application to include:
Cover letter (2 pages).
1. Summary of program.
2. Need for program.
3. How the program seeks to meet that need.
4. Total funds required.
5. Amount requested.
Narrative (5 pages).
1. Organization.
   - History.
   - Purpose.
   - Current programs, activities, and accomplishments.
   - Plans for coming year.
   - Organization structure.
   - Board/staff responsibilities and volunteer involvement.
   - Affiliation with federated funds or public agencies.
2. Grant purpose.
   - Needs statement.
   - Population served and specific benefit.
   - Project goals and measurable objectives.
   - Program activities.
   - Timetable.
   - Other participating organizations (if any).
   - Names and qualifications of key project personnel.
   - Future funding sources; projected project budget.
3. Evaluation.
   - Expected results.
   - Criteria for success and methods for evaluation.
   - Means to use and/or disseminate project results.
Attachments.
1. Board of directors.
   - Names, occupations and/or community affiliations.
   - Board committee assignments.
   - Criteria for board selection.
2. Finances.
   - Organization's current annual operating budget.
   - Funding sources for organization, past major contributors.
   - Anticipated future funding sources.
   - Most recent annual financial statement (audited if available).
   - List of other foundations to which same proposal has been submitted.

3. Annual report (if available).
4. Current relevant newspaper or magazine articles or reviews about the organization's program, if available.
5. Copy of IRS tax-exempt status determination letter.

When to apply: Deadlines are April 5, August 5, & November 5.
Materials available: "Grant Application Format."

Emphases. *Recipients:* Nonprofit organizations.
Types of support: General purposes, operating costs, seed money, projects.
Geography: Greater Baltimore, Maryland.

Limitations. *Recipients:* Educational institutions (higher), research institutions.
Activities: Education, research.
Types of support: Continuing support, endowments, facilities, multi-year grants.

The George F. Baker Trust
767 Fifth Avenue, Suite 2850
New York, New York 10153
Tel: 212–755–1890
EIN: 136056818   Type: Independent
Contact: Rocio Suarez, Executive Director

History and philosophy. The Trust was created under the will of George F. Baker (1878–1937), former chairman of the First National Bank of New York. Primary program areas include: Education, Medical, Social Services, New York City Civic, Long Island Civic, Religion, International, and Miscellaneous.

Officers and directors. *Trustees:* Anthony K. Baker, George F. Baker III, Kane K. Baker.

Financial data. Data for fiscal year ended December 31, 1993.
Assets: $19,814,833 (C). *Total grants disbursed:* $2,653,750.

Environmental awards. *Recent grants:* 1993 grants included support for land conservation, marine issues, wildlife preservation, and environmental education.

Issues. Cli Bio• Lan• Agr Wat• Oce• Ene Was Tox Pop Dev

Funding analysis.

Fiscal year:	1993
Env grants auth:	$258,000
Number:	10
Range:	$3,000–$100,000
Median:	$17,500
Pct $ disb (env/total):	13

Recipients (1993 highest):	Number:	Dollars:
The Nature Conservancy, Headquarters	1	100,000
The Caribbean Marine Research Center–Perry Foundation	1	35,000
Sea Education Association	1	30,000
Quebec Labrador Foundation/ Atlantic Center for the Environment	1	25,000
Woods Hole Oceanographic Institution	1	25,000

Activity regions (1993):	Number:	Dollars:
U.S. South Central	2	110,000
U.S. Northeast	3	80,000
Caribbean and West Indies	1	35,000
New York/New Jersey	2	20,000
U.S. Southeast	2	13,000

Sample grants (1993).*
American Coastal Research & Education. West Palm Beach, FL. $10,000. General support of their efforts in the field of education and research of marine habitat.
The Caribbean Marine Research Center–Perry Foundation. Covington, VA. $35,000. For personnel, equipment, and travel involved in aquaculture research on the Nassau grouper which is the most important commercial finfish in the Bahamas and Caribbean.
The Nature Conservancy, Headquarters. Arlington, VA. $25,000. Toward the $100,000 grant for conservation costs of The Gray Ranch in New Mexico, a 500 square mile ranch that has for over 100 years kept intact the only remaining unfragmented series of natural communities in the southwest borderlands.
NYZS/The Wildlife Conservation Society. Bronx, NY. $100,000. Payment on the $1,000,000 grant voted in June 1991 which the Zoo wishes to apply to the Wildlife Crisis Campaign.
NYZS/The Wildlife Conservation Society. Bronx, NY. $10,000. For general support of the world's preeminent conservation organization.
North Shore Wildlife Sanctuary. Mill Neck, NY. $10,000. For operating expenses.
Quebec Labrador Foundation/Atlantic Center for the Environment. Ipswich, MA. $25,000. Matching grant.
Sea Education Association. Woods Hole, MA. $30,000. To support scholarships for the 1993 high school programs.
Woods Hole Oceanographic Institution. Woods Hole, MA. $25,000. For general support.
Zoological Society of the Palm Beaches–Dreher Park Zoo. West Palm Beach, FL. $20,000. Payment on the $100,000 grant voted in 1992 for educational environmental purposes and the possible acquisition of new specimens.
Zoological Society of the Palm Beaches–Dreher Park Zoo. West Palm Beach, FL. $3,000. For a fundraising event to support and maintain facility.

*Sample grants represent either new awards or disbursements on grants awarded in previous years.

Application process. *Initial contact:* Letter of inquiry describing the project. Proposal, signed by official of the organization, to include:
1. Amount requested and explanation of need.
2. Other sources of grants, how much, and by whom.

When to apply: Anytime. The board meets in June and November.
Materials available: Annual report (includes "General Policy in Regard to Applications").

Emphases. *Recipients:* Nonprofit organizations.
Types of support: General purposes, matching funds.
Geography: Primarily eastern United States with emphasis on New York City.

Limitations. *Recipients:* Individuals.
Types of support: Endowments, fellowships, loans, projects, scholarships.

Baltimore Gas and Electric Foundation, Inc.
Charles Center
P.O. Box 1475
1406B G&E Building
Baltimore, Maryland 21203–1475
Tel: 410–234–7481 Fax: 410–234–5004
EIN: 521452037 Type: Company-sponsored
Contact: Malinda B. Small, Chairman,
 Corporate Contributions Committee

History and philosophy. Baltimore Gas and Electric established the Foundation in 1986 to enhance the quality of life in the Baltimore area and central Maryland. Program areas are: Education; Matching Gifts; Health, Welfare, and Hospitals; Cultural; Civic and Other; Community Revitalization; and Environment. Special emphasis is placed on organizations whose services contribute to early childhood development. The Foundation looks for organizations that demonstrate community support as well as compliance with federal, state, and local laws and regulations.

Officers and directors. *Officers:* Christian H. Poindexter, Chairman and CEO; Edward A. Crooke, President; J. A. Tiernan, Vice President; C. W. Shivery, Vice President, CFO, and Secretary. *Directors:* H. Furlong Baldwin, Beverly B. Byron, J. Owen Cole, Dan A. Colussy, Edward A. Crooke, James R. Curtiss, Jerome W. Geckle, Freeman A. Hrabowski, III, Nancy Lampton, George V. McGowan, P. G. Miller, Christian H. Poindexter, G. L. Russell, C. W. Shivery, Michael Sullivan, J. A. Tiernan.

Financial data. Data for fiscal year ended December 31, 1993. *Assets:* $7,987,039 (M). *Total grants disbursed:* $4,700,000.

Environmental awards. *Program and interests:* The Foundation targets programs that seek solutions to environmental concerns, and programs that protect and preserve our natural resource. Education is of particular interest.
Recent grant: One grant in 1992 supported a zoo.

Issues. Cli Bio Lan Agr Wat Oce Ene Was Tox Pop Dev
          •

Funding analysis.

Fiscal year:	1992
Env grants disb:	$68,750
Number:	1
Range:	–
Median:	–
Pct $ disb (env/total):	3

Recipient (1992):	*Number:*	*Dollars:*
Baltimore Zoological Society	1	68,750

Activity region (1992):	*Number:*	*Dollars:*
U.S. Mid-Atlantic	1	68,750

Sample grant (1992).
Baltimore Zoological Society. Baltimore, MD. $68,750. Contribution to new Children's Zoo Building.

Application process. *Initial contact:* Proposal (2 copies) and cover letter. Full proposal to include:
Cover letter, on organization letterhead, signed by the executive director and/or board president. Include proposal summary and amount requested.
Narrative (5 pages maximum).
1. Agency information.
   - Brief summary of agency history, including mission, goals, and objectives.
   - Description of current programs, activities, and accomplishments.
   - Overall agency plans for the coming year.
   - Description of organizational structure, board/staff responsibilities, and level of volunteer involvement.
   - Agency affiliation with federated funds or public agencies.
2. Purpose of grant.
   - Statement of need/problem to be addressed; description of constituency served/target population; how they will benefit.
   - Description of project goals and measurable objectives.
   - Description of program/activities planned to accomplish these goals; is this a new or ongoing activity on the part of the sponsoring organization?
   - Timetable for implementation.
   - Other organizations, if any, participating in the project.
   - List of names and qualifications of key staff/volunteers responsible for project implementation.
   - Long-term sources/strategies for funding of this project.
   - Projected project budget.
3. Evaluation. Please discuss:
   - Expected results during the funding period.
   - How you define success and how it will be measured.
   - How project's results will be used and/or disseminated.

Attachments.
1. Board of directors.
   - Occupations and/or community affiliations; board committee assignments.
   - Criteria for board selection.
2. Finances.
   - Agency's current annual operating budget with summary of itemized expenses and revenues.
   - Funding sources for the organization with a listing of past major contributors with amounts and anticipated future funding sources.
   - Most recent annual financial statement (audited, if available).
3. Annual report.
4. Copy of IRS tax-exempt status determination letter.

When to apply: Anytime. The board meets six times a year.
Materials available: "BGE Corporate Contributions Program" (includes "Guidelines").

© 1995 Environmental Data Resources, Inc.

Emphases. *Recipients:* Nonprofit organizations.
Activities: Conferences, education, research, seminars.
Types of support: Annual campaigns, capital campaigns/expenses, general purposes, matching funds.
Geography: Baltimore and central Maryland (counties of Baltimore, Calvert, Harford, Carroll, Prince Georges, Anne Arundel, and Howard).

Limitations. *Recipients:* Individuals, religious organizations.
Activities: Fundraising, research (medical).

BankAmerica Foundation
Department 3246
P.O. Box 37000
San Francisco, California 94137
Tel: 415–953–3175
EIN: 941670382   Type: Company-sponsored
Contact: Caroline O. Boitano, President

History and philosophy. BankAmerica Foundation was established in 1968. It hopes "to improve the quality of life, to address the needs of education, and to create an atmosphere that will result in a stronger and richer community." Its recently adopted strategy is to collaborate with community-based nonprofit organizations working on: Community Development (particularly the creation and preservation of affordable housing); Economic Development (focusing on jobs in distressed communities); Education (focusing on continuing improvement of primary education and on increasing minorities' access to higher education and the opportunities it provides). The Foundation also continues to support previous interests: conservation and the environment, culture and the arts, and its Community Grants Program, which gives local branch managers the opportunity to direct Foundation resources into their communities.

Officers and directors. *Officers:* Donald A. Mullane, Chairman; Caroline O. Boitano, President and Executive Director; Joanne El-Gohary, James S. Wagele, Vice Presidents; Sandra Cohen, Secretary; Janet Nishioka, Treasurer. *Trustees:* Caroline O. Boitano, Kathleen J. Burke, Lewis S. Coleman, Raymond W. McKee, Donald A. Mullane, Thomas E. Peterson, Richard M. Rosenberg.

Financial data. Data for fiscal years ended December 31, 1991 and 1993. *Assets (1991):* $731,211 (M). *Gifts received (1991):* $7,172,022. *Total grants disbursed (1993):* $14,378,469.

Environmental awards. *Program and interests:* Each year some funding is allocated for a grassroots program to encourage direct involvement and volunteer activities inside the Bank of America as well as to support worthwhile environmental organizations at the local level.
Recent grants: 1993 grants included support for land and wildlife conservation, parks, fisheries, marine mammals, recycling, horticulture, public and youth education.

Issues. Cli • Bio • Lan • Agr • Wat • Oce • Ene • Was • Tox • Pop • Dev

---

Funding analysis.

Fiscal year:	1993
Env grants disb:	$487,787
Number:	63
Range:	$750–$100,000
Median:	$2,500
Pct $ disb (env/total):	3

Recipients (1993 highest):	Number:	Dollars:
California Institute of Technology	1	100,000
California Museum Foundation	1	50,000
Golden Gate National Recreation Area	1	50,000
Natural History Museum of Los Angeles County	1	25,000
Oregon Public Broadcasting Foundation	1	15,000
Oregon Trail Preservation Trust, Inc.	1	15,000
Peninsula Conservation Center	1	15,000

Activity regions (1993):	Number:	Dollars:
U.S. West	48	373,350
U.S. not specified	4	51,437
U.S. Northwest	8	48,000
U.S. South Central	3	15,000

Sample grants (1993).
Cabrillo Marine Aquarium. San Pedro, CA. $2,500. Support for the Educational Programs brochure.
Californians Against Waste Foundation. Sacramento, CA. $5,000. Support for a "Buy Recycled" campaign.
Golden Gate National Recreation Area. San Francisco, CA. $50,000 (2 years). For Presidio planning process.
Heal the Bay. Santa Monica, CA. $2,500.
Hulls Gulch Nature Preserve Trust. Boise, ID. $7,500. Establishment of a nature preserve and outdoor classroom.
The Lindsay Museum. Walnut Creek, CA. $10,000. Support for the permanent exhibit "Living with Nature."
Living Desert Reserve. Palm Desert, CA. $1,000.
Peninsula Conservation Center. Palo Alto, CA. $15,000. Support for the Environmental Business Cluster.
Texas State Aquarium Association. Corpus Christi, TX. $10,000. Support for Environmental Education Outreach program.

Application process. *Initial contact:* Letter to include:
1. Purpose for which grant is requested.
2. Information about organization including mailing address, name, and telephone number of contact.
3. Mission statement.
4. Copy of IRS tax-exempt status determination letter.
5. List of board of directors and affiliations.
6. Financial information for previous two years with audited statement if available.
7. Operating budget and project budget if applicable.
8. Population and geographic area served.
9. Amount requested.
10. List of sources and amounts of other funding obtained, pledged, or requested for this purpose.

When to apply: Anytime. Funding decisions are made quarterly.
Materials available: Annual report, "Guidelines."

Emphases. *Recipients:* Nonprofit organizations.
Activities: Collaborative efforts.
Types of support: Operating costs, projects.
Geography: Communities where the corporation has a significant presence except Washington State which is served by Seafirst Foundation.

Limitations. *Recipients:* Individuals, religious organizations.
Activities: Audiovisual materials, fundraising, political activities, publications, research.
Types of support: Advertising campaigns, endowments.

The Barra Foundation, Inc.
8200 Flourtown Avenue, Suite 12
Wyndmoor, Pennsylvania 19118
Tel: 215–236–1030
EIN: 236277885   Type: Independent
Contact: Robert L. McNeil, Jr., President

History and philosophy. Established in 1963 by Robert L. McNeil, Jr. the Foundation is dedicated to "advancing the frontiers of knowledge and its effective application to human needs." Interests include human services, education, arts and culture, and health. "The grants from the Foundation are used chiefly as the venture capital of philanthropy for the support of enterprises which require foresight and risk but are not likely to be supported by government, public, or private agencies."

Officers and directors. *Officers:* Robert L. McNeil, Jr., President and Treasurer; William T. Tredennick, Vice President; Frank R. Donahue, Jr., Secretary; H. R. Hutchinson, Assistant Treasurer. *Directors:* Frank R. Donahue, Jr., H. R. Hutchinson, Robert L. McNeil, Jr., William T. Tredennick.

Financial data. Data for fiscal year ended December 31, 1992. *Assets:* $28,270,081 (M). *Total grants disbursed:* $1,841,398.

Environmental awards. *Recent grants:* 1992 grants included support for land conservation, marine issues, environmental education, arboretums, parks, and a zoo.
Issues. Cli Bio Lan Agr Wat Oce Ene Was Tox Pop Dev

Funding analysis.

Fiscal year:	1992
Env grants disb:	$34,238
Number:	13
Range:	$1,000–$13,738
Median:	$1,000
Pct $ disb (env/total):	2

Recipients (1992):	Number:	Dollars:
Morris Arboretum of the University of Pennsylvania	2	16,238
Fairchild Tropical Garden	1	5,000
U.S., DOI, National Park Service	1	2,500
Zoological Society of Philadelphia	1	2,500
1000 Friends of Florida	1	1,000
Awbury Arboretum Association	1	1,000
Brandywine Conservancy, Inc.	1	1,000
Natural Lands Trust	1	1,000
New Jersey Academy for Aquatic Sciences	1	1,000
The Nature Conservancy, Florida Field Office	1	1,000
The Schuylkill Center for Environmental Education	1	1,000
World Wildlife Fund	1	1,000

Activity regions (1992):	Number:	Dollars:
U.S. Mid-Atlantic	8	25,238
U.S. Southeast	3	7,000
New York/New Jersey	1	1,000
U.S. not specified	1	1,000

Sample grants (1992).
Awbury Arboretum Association. Philadelphia, PA. $1,000.
Brandywine Conservancy, Inc. Chadds Ford, PA. $1,000.
Fairchild Tropical Garden. Miami, FL. $5,000.
Morris Arboretum of the University of Pennsylvania. Philadelphia, PA. $16,238.
Natural Lands Trust. Media, PA. $1,000.
The Nature Conservancy, Florida Field Office. Winter Park, FL. $1,000.
New Jersey Academy for Aquatic Sciences. Camden, NJ. $1,000.
1000 Friends of Florida. Tallahassee, FL. $1,000.
The Schuylkill Center for Environmental Education. Philadelphia, PA. $1,000.
U.S., DOI, National Park Service. Valley Forge, PA. $2,500.
World Wildlife Fund. Washington, DC. $1,000.
Zoological Society of Philadelphia. Philadelphia, PA. $2,500.

Application process. *Initial contact:* Brief letter (1–2 pages) to include:
1. The project's principal objectives and significance.
2. Methodology.
3. Qualifications of project personnel.
4. Estimated timetable.
5. Project budget and other anticipated sources of support.
6. Organization's history and goals.
7. List of officers and board of directors.
8. Copy of IRS tax-exempt status determination letter.

The Foundation may request a formal application.
When to apply: Anytime.
Materials available: "Statement of Policy/Application Guidelines and Procedures."

Emphases. *Recipients:* Nonprofit organizations.
Activities: Publications, research.
Types of support: Matching funds, pilot projects, projects.
Geography: Greater Philadelphia, Pennsylvania.

Limitations. *Recipients:* Individuals.
Types of support: Capital campaigns/expenses, continuing support, debt retirement, endowments, facilities, fellowships, loans, operating costs, scholarships.

B

The Theodore H. Barth Foundation, Inc.
1211 Avenue of the Americas, 17th Floor
New York, New York 10036
Tel: 212–704–6000
EIN: 136103401   Type: Independent
Contact: Irving P. Berelson, President

History and philosophy. Theodore H. Barth established the Foundation in 1953. Grants are made for education, health, and arts projects in the northeastern United States.

Officers and directors. *Officers:* Irving P. Berelson, President and Treasurer; Thelma D. Berelson, Secretary.

Financial data. Data for fiscal year ended December 31, 1992. *Assets:* $19,550,934 (M). *Total grants disbursed:* $910,300.

Environmental awards. *Recent grants:* 1992 grants included support for land conservation, horticulture, botanical gardens, and zoos in the New York metropolitan area.

Issues. Cli Bio Lan Agr Wat Oce Ene Was Tox Pop Dev
                •   •

Funding analysis.

Fiscal year:	1992
Env grants disb:	$52,500
Number:	6
Range:	$5,000–$15,000
Median:	$7,500
Pct $ disb (env/total):	6

Recipients (1992):	Number:	Dollars:
NYZS/The Wildlife Conservation Society	1	15,000
The New York Botanical Garden	1	12,500
Brooklyn Botanic Garden	1	10,000
Connecticut Audubon Society	1	5,000
Central Park Conservancy	1	5,000
The Horticultural Society of New York	1	5,000

Activity regions (1992):	Number:	Dollars:
New York/New Jersey	5	47,500
U.S. Northeast	1	5,000

Sample grants (1992).
Brooklyn Botanic Garden. Brooklyn, NY. $10,000.
Central Park Conservancy. New York, NY. $5,000.
The Horticulture Society of New York. New York, NY. $5,000.
The New York Botanical Garden. Bronx, NY. $12,500.
NYZS/The Wildlife Conservation Society. Bronx, NY. $15,000.

Application process. *Initial contact:* Proposal to include:
1. Brief description of problem to address.
2. Amount requested from the Foundation.
3. Statement of the project's main objectives.
4. Other planned sources of support.
5. Description of how you plan to address the problem (or, for research, project methodology).
6. Plans to evaluate or publish project results.
7. Expected results.
8. Plans to sustain the project after grant funds end.
9. Qualifications of personnel and grantholding institution.
10. Name and contact information.
11. Grant timetable.
12. Copy of IRS tax-exempt status determination letter.
13. Total estimated project budget.
14. Copy of most recent audited financial statement.

When to apply: Anytime.

Emphases. *Recipients:* Nonprofit organizations.
Geography: Northeastern United States.

Limitations. *Recipients:* Individuals.
Types of support: Capital campaigns/expenses.

The Bauman Foundation
2040 S Street, N.W.
Washington, DC 20009–1110
Tel: 202–328–2040   Fax: 202–328–2003
EIN: 133119290   Type: Independent
EGA member
Contact: Patricia Bauman, Co-Director

History and philosophy. The Bauman Foundation was established in 1987 through the estate of Lionel R. Bauman. A New York City lawyer, businessman, and philanthropist, Bauman supported education, the arts, social justice, and civil rights through his charitable and service activities. The Foundation's goal is to foster activities that encourage systematic social change. Program areas are: the Economy and the Environment, Citizen Access to Information, Civil Rights and Responsibilities, and Interdisciplinary Education.

The Foundation funds pre-selected organizations only. It will not review unsolicited proposals.

Officers and directors. *Officers:* Patricia Bauman, John L. Bryant, Jr., Co-Directors; Jessica B. Johnson, Program Officer. *Directors:* Patricia Bauman, John L. Bryant, Jr., C. Douglas Lewis.

Financial data. Data for fiscal year ended June 30, 1993. *Assets:* $25,068,710 (U). *Total grants authorized:* $1,495,043.

Environmental awards. *Program and interests:* Growing out of its interest in primary prevention of environmental problems, the Foundation supports work that focuses on the juncture of the economy and the environment. It favors projects that investigate issues such as jobs and the environment and the environmental consequences of international trade policies. The Foundation looks for innovation and experiments in practice, theory, and their interrelationships. It continues to support Right-to-Know as a crucial tool for social change. Specific target areas include:

- Primary prevention.
- Sustainable economic development.
- Right-to-Know.

Recent grants: In the last few years, the Foundation has funded a number of environmental topics: toxics use reduction has been a special focus. Activities of interest have included the promotion of enlightened trade policy, social justice, leadership development, and public information, especially Right-to-Know.

Issues. Cli Bio Lan Agr Wat Oce Ene Was Tox Pop Dev
                                                        •   •

Funding analysis.

Fiscal year:	1992	1993
Env grants auth:	$791,000	$917,000
Number:	39	40
Range:	$2,500–$55,000	$1,000–$75,000
Median:	$15,000	$20,000
Pct $ auth (env/total):	63	61

Recipients (1993 highest):	*Number:*	*Dollars:*
Institute for Agriculture and Trade Policy	1	75,000
Labor/Community Strategy Center	1	75,000
National Center for Economic Alternatives	1	75,000
Nuclear Times, Inc.	1	75,000
Public Health Institute	2	65,000

Activity regions (1993):	*Number:*	*Dollars:*
U.S. not specified	31	716,000
U.S. West	2	85,000
International	3	31,000
New York/New Jersey	1	25,000
North America	1	20,000
U.S. multiple regions	1	20,000
U.S. Northeast	1	20,000

Sample grants (1993).
Environmental Action Foundation. Takoma Park, MD. $20,000. General support for educational activities.
The Environmental Careers Organization, Inc. Boston, MA. $50,000. Renewal grant for the Technical Advisor Program for Toxics Use Reduction.
Environmental Grantmakers Association. New York, NY. $15,000. General support for *GREEN*, the newsletter of the Grantmakers Network on the Economy and the Environment.
National Religious Partnership for the Environment. New York, NY. $60,000. General support.
Public Citizen, Inc. Washington, DC. $20,000. General support.
World Wildlife Fund. Washington, DC. $20,000. Renewal grant to promote international right-to-know strategies for toxic chemicals.

Application process. *Initial contact:* The Foundation will not review unsolicited proposals.

Emphases. *Recipients:* Pre-selected organizations only.
Activities: Activism, advocacy, capacity building, citizen participation, collaborative efforts, innovative programs, networking, policy analysis/development, political activities, research, technical assistance.
Types of support: Continuing support, general purposes, pilot projects, technical assistance.
Geography: Programs with national impact.

Limitations. *Recipients:* Individuals.
Activities: Direct services, research (medical).
Geography: Local or state programs (unless there is a plan for their dissemination and use as models).

Bay Area Community Foundation
809 Saginaw Street
Bay City, Michigan 48708
Tel: 517–893–4438 Fax: 517–893–4448
EIN: 382418086 Type: Community
Contact: Bonnie Marsh, Executive Director

History and philosophy. The Bay Area Community Foundation was established in 1983 through a gift by the Kantzler Foundation. Its purpose is to receive donations and bequests, to hold and invest such gifts in trust, and to make grants from those trust funds to support charitable, cultural, artistic, civic, educational, and scientific organizations and programs in Bay County, Michigan.

Officers and directors. *Officers:* Kurt Rudolph, President; Ken Eshelman, Vice President; Richard Payne, Secretary; Peg Rowley, Treasurer. *Directors:* Gary Adelman, Dean Arbour, Bill Black, Bob Budzinski, Greg Demers, Dr. Ken Eshelman, Dr. Joe Gonzales, Michael Gray, Bill Herrera, Dr. Roger Hill, Lucy Horak, John Marra, David Murray, Richard Payne, Brenda Rowley, Peggy Rowley, Kurt Rudolph.

Financial data. Data for fiscal year ended December 31, 1993. *Assets:* $5,125,732 (M). *Gifts received:* 526,883. *Total grants disbursed:* $415,697.

Environmental awards. *Program and interests:* Three special interest endowment funds support beautification, environmental education, and parks. Ongoing projects include the Bay Hampton Railtrail and Riverwalk.
Recent grants: 1993 grants included support for beautification, recreation, and waste management.

Issues. Cli Bio Lan Agr Wat Oce Ene Was Tox Pop Dev
              •   •   •

Funding analysis.

Fiscal year:	1993
Env grants disb:	$26,910
Number:	6
Range:	$450–$13,247
Median:	$3,332
Pct $ disb (env/total):	6

Recipients (1993 highest):	*Number:*	*Dollars:*
City of Bay City	1	13,247
Kavanaugh Appraisal	1	6,000
Michigan State University	1	4,000
Pinconning Area Volunteers for Environment (PAVE)	1	2,663
University of Michigan	1	550

B

Activity region (1993):	Number:	Dollars:
U.S. Great Lakes	6	26,910

Sample grants (1993).
City of Bay City. Bay City, MI. $13,247. Railtrail construction.
Kavanaugh Appraisal. Bay City, MI. $6,000. Appraisal of property for future Railtrail.
Pinconning Area Volunteers for Environment (PAVE). Bay City, MI. $2,663. To install a hard surface pad for waste recycling.
Marquette Business District. Bay City, MI. $450. Tree planting.
Michigan State University. East Lansing, MI. $4,000. To design a muck remover machine for Bay City State Park.
University of Michigan. Ann Arbor, MI. $550. Archeological study of Tobico Marsh.

Application process. *Initial contact:* Complete proposal (5 copies) to include:
1. Brief description of the applicant organization: background, purpose, board of directors or trustees, officers, financial situation, including the most recent financial statement.
2. Copy of IRS tax-exempt status determination letter.
3. Comprehensive description of the project for which funding is requested, including a detailed budget for the project, a statement of other sources from which funding for the project is sought, and an explanation of the project's significance for the greater Bay City community.
4. Other information or documentation which seems pertinent.

When to apply: Deadlines are February 15, May 15, August 15, or November 15 for consideration at trustees meetings held quarterly in March, June, September, or December.
Materials available: Annual report, "Applying for a Grant: Policies & Procedures," grant application form.

Emphases. *Recipients:* Educational institutions, museums, nonprofit organizations, research institutions.
Activities: Education, fundraising, innovative programs, publications, research, seminars, workshops, youth programs.
Types of support: Equipment, facilities, matching funds, multi-year grants, pilot projects, scholarships.
Geography: Bay County, Michigan only.

Limitations. *Recipients:* Individuals.
Types of support: Annual campaigns, debt retirement, operating costs, travel expenses.

The Bay Foundation
17 West 94th Street, #1
New York, New York 10025
Tel: 212–663–1115
EIN: 135646283   Type: Independent
Contact: Robert W. Ashton, Executive Director

History and philosophy. "The Bay Foundation was established in 1950 with an endowment from Charles Ulrick Bay. Among Mr. Bay's enterprises were Bay Bandage Company, Bay Petroleum, the A. M. Kidder brokerage firm, Connecticut Railway and Lighting Company, and American Export Lines."

The Foundation currently supports children's services and education programs from pre-school through grade 12 with an emphasis on enhancement of science, math, and writing curricula; preservation of cultural and natural history collections and collections' care training in museums, zoos, libraries, and botanical gardens; advocacy and research programs for preserving biodiversity; and Native American cultural and economic development programs.

Officers and directors. *Officers:* Frederick U. Bay, Chairman; Synnova B. Hayes, President; Hans A. Ege, Vice President; Robert W. Ashton, Secretary; Daniel A. Demarest, Treasurer.
Directors: Robert W. Ashton, Frederick U. Bay, Christopher Bay-Hansen, Daniel A. Demarest, Hans A. Ege, Synnova B. Hayes.

Financial data. Data for fiscal year ended December 31, 1993.
Assets: $12,020,546 (M). *Total grants disbursed:* $473,866.

Environmental awards. *Program and interests:* Most environmental grants are awarded through the Biological Diversity/Science Grants program.
Recent grants: 1993 grants included support for marine conservation, wildlife preservation, and environmental education.

Issues. Cli Bio Lan Agr Wat Oce Ene Was Tox Pop Dev
            •   •   •   •   •

Funding analysis.§

Fiscal year:	1991	1993
Env grants disb:	$91,350	$101,500
Number:	8	10
Range:	$2,500–$60,000	$3,000–$25,000
Median:	$4,675	$9,000
Pct $ disb (env/total):	–	21

Recipients (1993 highest):	Number:	Dollars:
Center for Marine Conservation	1	25,000
The Resource Foundation	1	20,000
Cheetah Preservation Fund	1	12,000
American Museum of Natural History	1	10,000
University of Illinois	1	10,000

Activity regions (1993 highest):	Number:	Dollars:
U.S. not specified	1	25,000
New York/New Jersey	4	21,500
Andean Region and Southern Cone	1	20,000
Eastern and Southern Africa	1	12,000
U.S. Great Lakes	1	10,000

§Based on partial data.

Sample grants (1993).
American Museum of Natural History. New York, NY. $10,000. Support for new biodiversity and conservation center for the study of endangered species' ecosystems.
Center for Marine Conservation. Washington, DC. $25,000. Towards the establishment of the international Marine Conservation Network to promote marine conservation biology.
Cheetah Preservation Fund. Fort Collins, CO. $12,000. Continued support for Namibian cheetah preservation project.
Conservation International Foundation. Tucson, AZ. $8,000. Subsidy for flight services for animal and flora research in northern Mexico.

Enfield Elementary School. Ithaca, NY. $3,500. Support of the school's science and ecology program.
Hudson River Sloop Clearwater, Inc. Poughkepsie, NY. $3,000. Support of the Classrooms of the Waves environmental education program for elementary students.
The Resource Foundation. Larchmont, NY. $20,000. Support for an agro-ecology high school in Chile.
University of Illinois. Urbana, IL. $10,000. Continued support of integrative training in aquatic animal health and environmental toxicology.

Application process. *Initial contact:* Full proposal to include:
1. Description of the organization and the program.
2. Objectives, population served, and a budget or financial statements.
3. Anticipated sources of support.
4. Evidence of tax-exempt status.

When to apply: Deadlines are December 15, March 15, and September 1. The board meets in January, May, and October.
Materials available: Annual report (includes "Guidelines and Application Procedures"), "Guide to the Granting Process."

Emphases. *Recipients:* Educational institutions, nonprofit organizations.
Activities: Education, research.

Limitations. *Recipients:* Individuals, religious organizations.
Types of support: Facilities, multi-year grants.

The Howard Bayne Fund
c/o Simpson, Thacher & Bartlett
425 Lexington Avenue
New York, New York 10017–3909
Tel: 212–455–2734
EIN: 136100680   Type: Independent
Contact: Gurdon B. Wattles, President

History and philosophy. The Howard Bayne Fund was incorporated in 1960. Grantmaking focuses on conservation, culture, education, hospitals, medical research, and music.

Officers and directors. *Officers:* Gurdon B. Wattles, President; Daphne B. Shih, Vice President; Victoria B. Bjorklund, Secretary/Treasurer. *Directors:* Diana de Vegh, Pierre J. de Vegh, Daisy Paradis, Daphne B. Shih, Elizabeth C. Wattles, Gurdon B. Wattles, Elizabeth W. Wilkes.

Financial data. Data for fiscal year ended December 31, 1993. *Assets:* $11,162,764 (M). *Total grants disbursed:* $480,100.

Environmental awards. *Recent grants:* 1993 grants supported land conservation, species preservation, marine issues, a botanical garden, a zoo, and outdoor expeditions.

Issues. Cli Bio Lan Agr Wat Oce Ene Was Tox Pop Dev

Funding analysis.

Fiscal year:	1991	1993
Env grants disb:	$53,500	$56,000
Number:	16	13
Range:	$500–$10,000	$1,000–$10,000
Median:	$2,500	$5,000
Pct $ disb (env/total):	18	12

Recipients (1993 highest):	Number:	Dollars:
The Nature Conservancy, New Jersey Field Office	1	10,000
NYZS/The Wildlife Conservation Society	1	7,500
World Wildlife Fund	1	6,000
Brooklyn Botanic Garden	1	5,000
Duke University, Primate Center	1	5,000
Earthwatch	1	5,000
Sea Research Foundation, Inc.	1	5,000
Wildlife Preservation Trust International	1	5,000

Activity regions (1993):	Number:	Dollars:
New York/New Jersey	6	26,500
U.S. not specified	4	18,500
U.S. Northeast	2	6,000
U.S. Southeast	1	5,000

Sample grants (1993).
Brooklyn Botanic Garden. Brooklyn, NY. $5,000.
Duke University, Primate Center. Chapel Hill, NC. $5,000.
Earthwatch. Watertown, MA. $5,000.
The Nature Conservancy, New Jersey Field Office. Pottersville, NJ. $10,000.
NYZS/The Wildlife Conservation Society. Bronx, NY. $7,500.
Sea Research Foundation, Inc. Groton, CT. $5,000.
University of New Haven, Department of Environmental Studies. New Haven, CT. $1,000.
World Wildlife Fund. Washington, DC. $6,000.

Application process. *Initial contact:* The Fund awards grants to pre-selected organizations only. No applications accepted.

Emphases. *Recipients:* Pre-selected organizations only.
Geography: New York metropolitan area.

Limitations. *Recipients:* Individuals.

L. L. Bean, Inc.
Casco Street
Freeport, Maine 04033
Tel: 207–865–4761   Fax: 207–865–6738
Type: Company-sponsored
EGA member
Contacts: Janet Wyper, Senior Community Relations Specialist
            Jolene McGowan, Community Relations Associate
            Christopher Smith, Community Relations Assistant

History and philosophy. L. L. Bean, Inc. was founded in 1912 when Leon Leonwood Bean put his Maine Hunting Shoe on the market through mail order. From the beginning, Bean's marketing of practical, durable outdoor products at reasonable prices has been coupled with a stated appreciation for wild lands and the environment. Company operations stress environmental responsibility through recycling programs, energy efficiency, and product design and customer service that encourage reuse and rebuilding rather than replacement. The company also promotes environmental stewardship, through proceeds agreements that benefit organizations including the Maine Audubon Society and National Park Foundation, volunteer programs for employees, and grants.

L. L. Bean makes grants in the areas of Health and Human Services, Education, Culture and Art, and Conservation and Recreation. It tends to provide for, renew, and build upon its past relationships with conservation organizations. It has contributed over $1 million to conservation and environmental organizations in the last three years.

Financial data. Data for fiscal year ended February 28, 1993. *Sales:* $870,000,000 (U) (est.). *Total grants disbursed:* $930,000 (est.).

Environmental awards. *Program and interests:* Conservation and Recreation grants target stewardship of the outdoors through:

- Education.
- Membership support.
- Leadership training.
- Outdoor volunteerism.

Issues. Cli Bio Lan Agr Wat Oce Ene Was Tox Pop Dev

Funding analysis.§

Fiscal year:	1992	1993
Env grants disb:	$192,000	$263,000
Number	–	–
Range:	$1,000–$25,000	$1,000–$25,000
Median:	–	–
Pct $ disb (env/total):	28	30

§As reported by the Environmental Grantmakers Association.

Application process. *Initial contact:* Short letter.
When to apply: Anytime. Grants are approved in December.
Materials available: Information packet about the company.

Emphases. *Recipients:* Pre-selected organizations primarily.
Activities: Capacity building, citizen participation, collaborative efforts, feasibility studies, innovative programs, publications, training, volunteerism.
Types of support: Annual campaigns, capital campaigns/expenses, continuing support, endowments, facilities, general purposes, leveraging funds, multi-year grants.
Geography: Maine, regional, and national.

Limitations. *Recipients:* Aquariums, botanical gardens, individuals, museums, religious organizations, research institutions, zoos.
Activities: Activism, advocacy, audiovisual materials, litigation, lobbying, political activities, research, seminars, symposia/colloquia.

Types of support: Advertising campaigns, debt retirement, fellowships, internships, lectureships, loans, maintenance, mortgage reduction, professorships, travel expenses.
Geography: International.

S. D. Bechtel, Jr. Foundation

P.O. Box 193809
San Francisco, California 94119–3809
Tel: 415–768–4946   Fax: 415–768–3681
EIN: 946066138   Type: Independent
Contact: Theodore J. Van Bebber, Vice President and Treasurer

History and philosophy. The S. D. Bechtel, Jr. Foundation was incorporated in California in 1957. Grants are restricted to organizations pre-selected by the directors, and are usually cultural programs or educational institutions.

Officers and directors. *Officers:* S. D. Bechtel, Jr., President; Elizabeth H. Bechtel, Thomas G. Flynn, Vice Presidents; Theodore J. Van Bebber, Vice President and Treasurer. *Directors:* Theodore J. Van Bebber, Elizabeth H. Bechtel, S. D. Bechtel, Jr., Thomas G. Flynn.

Financial data. Data for fiscal year ended December 31, 1992. *Assets:* $23,606,301 (M). *Gifts received:* $792,152. *Total grants disbursed:* $1,395,767.

Environmental awards. *Recent grants:* 1992 grants included support for land conservation, wildlife, marine issues, horticulture, and recreation.

Issues. Cli Bio Lan Agr Wat Oce Ene Was Tox Pop Dev

Funding analysis.

Fiscal year:	1991	1992
Env grants disb:	$215,000	$111,000
Number:	29	15
Range:	$500–$50,000	$500–$35,000
Median:	$1,000	$2,000
Pct $ disb (env/total):	17	8

Recipients (1992 highest):	Number:	Dollars:
The Nature Conservancy, California Field Office	1	35,000
California Waterfowl Association	1	25,000
National Audubon Society, Western Region	1	25,000
Garden Club of America	1	5,000
Strybing Arboretum Society of Golden Gate Park	1	5,000
The Wildlife Conservation Fund of America	1	5,000

Activity regions (1992 highest):	Number:	Dollars:
U.S. West	9	100,500
U.S. not specified	1	5,000
U.S. Southeast	1	2,000

Alaska	1	1,000
New York/New Jersey	1	1,000
U.S. South Central	1	1,000

Sample grants (1992).
Audubon Canyon Ranch. Stinson Beach, CA. $1,000. Education and wildlife sanctuary.
China Poot Bay Society. Homer, AK. $1,000. Alaska coastal studies.
Monterey Bay Aquarium. Monterey, CA. $1,000. General operations.
The Nature Conservancy, California Field Office. San Francisco, CA. $35,000. California Riceland/Wetlands Use Project.
Strybing Arboretum Society of Golden Gate Park. San Francisco, CA. $5,000. Operating activities.
The Wildlife Conservation Fund of America. Columbus, OH. $5,000. Operating activities.

Application process. *Initial contact:* The Foundation awards grants to pre-selected organizations only. No unsolicited applications accepted.

Emphases. *Recipients:* Pre-selected organizations only.
Geography: San Francisco Bay Area, California.

Limitations. *Recipients:* Individuals.

The Beinecke Foundation, Inc.
c/o John R. Robinson
14–16 Elm Place
Rye, New York 10580
Tel: 203-861-7314   Fax: 203-861-7316
EIN: 136201175   Type: Independent
Contact: John R. Robinson, President

History and philosophy. The Foundation was established in 1966 with donations made by Sylvia B. Robinson. It funds a wide range of program areas including: arts, higher education, East Coast issues, population, historic preservation, and environment. It supports both unsolicited projects and projects developed in response to Foundation interests.

Officers and directors. *Officers:* John R. Robinson, President; Sylvia B. Robinson, Vice President; Theodore H. Ashford, Treasurer. *Directors:* Theodore H. Ashford, John R. Robinson, Sylvia B. Robinson.

Financial data. Data for fiscal year ended December 31, 1992. *Assets:* $48,726,030 (M). *Total grants disbursed:* $3,070,933.

Environmental awards. *Recent grants:* 1991 grants included support for land conservation, wildlife preservation, coastal issues, a botanical garden, and higher education.

Issues. Cli • Bio • Lan • Agr • Wat • Oce • Ene   Was   Tox • Pop   Dev

Funding analysis.

Fiscal year:	1990	1991
Env grants disb:	$490,325	$665,200
Number:	12	31
Range:	$500–$251,825	$190–$170,000
Median:	$1,000	$2,500
Pct $ disb (env/total):	25	27

Recipients (1991 highest):	Number:	Dollars:
Natural Resources Defense Council	3	200,190
Committee for the National Institute for the Environment	3	195,000
Open Space Institute, Inc.	2	195,000
Yale University, School of Forestry and Environmental Studies	3	25,310
The Nature Conservancy, Lower Hudson Chapter	1	15,000

Activity regions (1991):	Number:	Dollars:
U.S. not specified	16	608,390
New York/New Jersey	9	29,500
U.S. Northeast	4	26,310
North America	1	500
U.S. Mountain	1	500

Sample grants (1991).
Ducks Unlimited, Inc. Long Grove, IL. $500.
Long Island Soundkeeper Fund. Norwalk, CT. $1,000.
Natural Resources Defense Council. New York, NY. $100,000.
The New York Botanical Garden. Bronx, NY. $5,000.
Outward Bound USA. New York, NY. $2,500.
Scenic Hudson, Inc. Poughkeepsie, NY. $1,000.

Application process. *Initial contact:* Letter of inquiry (2 pages) to include:
1. Brief description of problem to be addressed.
2. Project objectives.
3. Expected outcome of project.
4. Qualifications of institution and project's principal personnel.
5. Grant timetable.
6. Total estimated project budget, other planned sources of support, and amount requested from Foundation.
7. Method of evaluation of the project's results and means of disseminating its findings.
8. Name of the primary contact person for follow-up.

Budgets and curricula vitae of key staff may be appended to the letter, as may any other relevant background information about the applicant's institution.
When to apply: Anytime.
Materials available: "Guidelines for Grant Applications," "Financial Statements and Supplementary Information" (includes recent grants.)

Emphases. *Recipients:* Botanical gardens, educational institutions, museums, nonprofit organizations, public agencies, research institutions, zoos.
Activities: Activism, advocacy, citizen participation, fieldwork, innovative programs, publications, seminars.
Types of support: Endowments, operating costs.

B

The Beirne Carter Foundation

P.O. Box 26903
Richmond, Virginia 23261
Tel: 804–788–2964   Fax: 804–788–2700
EIN: 541397827   Type: Independent
Contact: J. Samuel Gillespie, Jr., Ph.D., Advisor

History and philosophy. Established in 1986 by Beirne Carter, (d. 1984) former chairman and CEO of Carter Machinery Company. It was the hope of the founder that "primary emphasis would be placed upon helping citizens of all walks of life who live in all geographical areas of Virginia." The Foundation focuses its grantmaking on organizations interested in youth, cultural programs, history, health, ecology, and education impacting southwest Virginia.

Officers and directors. *Officers:* Mary Ross Carter Hutcheson, President; Mary Bryan Perkins, Vice President; Talfourd H. Kemper, Secretary/Treasurer; J. Samuel Gillespie, Jr., Ph.D., Advisor.

Financial data. Data for fiscal year ended December 31, 1993. *Assets:* $20,518,707 (M). *Total grants disbursed:* $866,335.

Environmental awards. *Program and interests:* The Foundation does not have a specific interest in environmental programs.
Recent grants: 1992 grants supported land conservation and a botanical garden.

Issues.   *Cli   Bio   Lan   Agr   Wat   Oce   Ene   Was   Tox   Pop   Dev*
                    •   •

Funding analysis.

Fiscal year:	1992
Env grants disb:	$250,000
Number:	3
Range:	$25,000–$150,000
Median:	$75,000
Pct $ disb (env/total):	31

Recipients (1992):	*Number:*	*Dollars:*
Corporation for Jefferson's Poplar Forest	1	150,000
The Nature Conservancy, Virginia Field Office	1	75,000
Lewis Ginter Botanical Gardens	1	25,000

Activity region (1992):	*Number:*	*Dollars:*
U.S. Mid-Atlantic	3	250,000

Sample grants (1992).
Corporation for Jefferson's Poplar Forest. Forest, VA. $150,000.
Lewis Ginter Botanical Gardens. Richmond, VA. $25,000.
The Nature Conservancy, Virginia Field Office. Charlottesville, VA. $75,000.

Application process. *Initial contact:* Proposal (4 copies), to include:
1. Brief description of the organization, its history, and purpose.
2. Description of the proposed project or activity, including purposes, benefits to be provided, and needs to be met.
3. Financial plan including cost, amount requested, amount raised to date, plans for procuring the remainder, other funding sources, and provision for contingencies and on-going support.
4. Background of person(s) conducting the proposed program.
5. Evaluation method and plans for sustaining the project after grant funds expire.
6. Letter from an official of the organization stating approval of the program.

Attachments (1 copy).
1. Names and affiliations of the organization's trustees, directors, advisors, and principal staff.
2. Copy of IRS tax-exempt status determination letter and evidence that the organization is not a private foundation.
3. Financial statements for the current and two prior years showing major sources of organization support and endowment, if any.

When to apply: Anytime. The board meets in March and September.
Materials available: "Application Guidelines."

Emphases. *Recipients:* Aquariums, botanical gardens, educational institutions, museums, nonprofit organizations, research institutions, zoos.
Activities: Education, land acquisition, youth programs.
Types of support: Capital campaigns/expenses, facilities, matching funds, pilot projects.
Geography: Primarily Virginia.

Limitations. *Recipients:* Individuals, religious organizations.
Types of support: Advertising campaigns, annual campaigns, continuing support, indirect costs, loans, operating costs.

Beldon Fund

2000 P Street N.W., Suite 410
Washington, DC 20036
Tel: 202–293–1928   Fax: 202–659–3897
EIN: 382786808   Type: Independent
EGA member
Contact: Diane Ives, Executive Director

History and philosophy. Established in 1982, the Beldon Fund awards all its grants for environmental purposes. The Fund's primary goal is to strengthen statewide multi-issue environmental organizations that educate and train their members and the public about significant issues that involve the grassroots.

Officers and directors. *Officers:* John R. Hunting, President; Diane Ives, Secretary/Treasurer; R. Malcolm Cumming, Sharon Miller, Assistant Secretaries.

Financial data. Data for fiscal year ended November 30, 1993. *Gifts received:* $885,992. *Total grants disbursed:* $649,000.

Environmental awards. *Program and interests:* The Fund's central concerns are to:

- Strengthen statewide multi-issue membership-based organizations through:
  - Membership development.
  - "Tech-ing up."
  - Skills training.
  - Coalition building.
- Strengthen activist national environmental organizations with:
  - Media projects.
  - Grassroots training.
  - Outreach "beyond the Beltway."

The Fund has limited involvement in selected national issues:
- Managing the solid waste crisis.
- Reducing toxic substance use.

The Fund does not award grants to preserve individual species.

Issues. Cli Bio Lan Agr Wat Oce Ene Was Tox Pop Dev
                            •   •   •

Funding analysis.

Fiscal year:	1991	1993
Env grants auth:	$979,500	$649,000
Number:	104	76
Range:	$1,500–$25,000	$1,000–$20,000
Median:	$10,000	$10,000
Pct $ auth (env/total):	100	100

Recipients (1993 highest):	Number:	Dollars:
Clean Water Fund	2	30,000
American Environment, Inc.	1	20,000
Environmental Action Foundation	1	20,000
Environmental Support Center	2	20,000
Arizona Toxics Information, Inc.	1	15,000
Illinois Environmental Council Education Fund	1	15,000

Activity regions (1993 highest):	Number:	Dollars:
U.S. not specified	19	185,000
U.S. Mountain	12	105,700
U.S. Southeast	10	86,500
U.S. Great Lakes	9	66,300
U.S. South Central	7	48,000

Sample grants (1993).
Border Ecology Project, Inc. Bisbee, AZ. $3,000. For work on border area environmental and occupational health problems.
Communications Consortium Media Center. Washington, DC. $5,000. Continued support for the Energy Efficiency Education Project, a national collaborative campaign on the critical importance of energy efficiency to the health of our economy, environment, and national security.
Environmental Federation of New England, Inc. Boston, MA. $10,000. Toward a unique multi-state model of a workplace giving program, serving environmental organizations throughout New England.
Heartwood, Inc. Morgantown, IN. $5,000. For the seventh annual Forest Reform Network PowWow to gain support for more effective forest protection programs.
Illinois Environmental Council Education Fund. Springfield, IL. $15,000. In support of Money Matters: Environmentalists Examine the State's Fiscal Choices project, demanding state fiscal accountability for needed environmental programs.
Louisiana Coalition. Baton Rouge, LA. $10,00. General support for its work to reform corporate tax breaks and to research the rapidly growing use of Enterprise Zones by Louisiana's petrochemical industry.
New Mexico Environmental Law Center. Santa Fe, NM. $10,000. For a self-sufficiency development campaign to increase support from non-foundation sources.
Silicon Valley Toxics Coalition. San Jose, CA. $7,500. General support for its organizing work to enable communities at risk from high-tech toxics pollution to respond effectively and create strategies for pollution prevention.
The Sonoran Institute. Tucson, AZ. $7,200. In support of its Greater Yellowstone Organizing Project, which will establish a nonprofit sustainable development organization in the Northern Rockies region.
Southern Utah Wilderness Alliance. Salt Lake City, UT. $12,500. To staff a development program which will provide an expanded membership base and increased organizational stability.

Application process. *Initial contact:* Telephone call or letter of inquiry.
When to apply: Anytime.
Materials available: Annual report (includes "Guidelines").

Emphases. *Recipients:* Nonprofit organizations.
Activities: Activism, advocacy, capacity building, citizen participation, collaborative efforts, conferences, fundraising, innovative programs, networking, political activities, technical assistance, training.
Types of support: General purposes, operating costs, projects, technical assistance.
Geography: State-level projects within the United States.

Limitations. *Recipients:* Aquariums, botanical gardens, educational institutions, individuals, museums, public agencies, religious organizations, research institutions, zoos.
Activities: Audiovisual materials, expeditions/tours, fieldwork, inventories, land acquisition, litigation, lobbying, research, seminars, symposia/colloquia, youth programs.
Types of support: Annual campaigns, capital campaigns/expenses, debt retirement, endowments, equipment, facilities, fellowships, internships, lectureships, loans, mortgage reduction, multi-year grants, professorships, program-related investments, scholarships.
Geography: International projects.

David Winton Bell Foundation

Carlson Center
601 Lakeshore Parkway, Suite 350
Minnetonka, Minnesota 55305
Tel: 612–540–4997   Fax: 612–540–4066
EIN: 416023104   Type: Independent
Contact: Diane B. Neimann

History and philosophy. The Foundation was established in 1956 by the family of Marine Corps flier David Winton Bell, lost over the Pacific in 1955. Son of Charles H. Bell, former

© 1995 Environmental Data Resources, Inc.

B

president of General Mills, Inc., David was a graduate of Brown University and an avid outdoorsman and sportsman. The Foundation's philanthropic focus reflects David's interests and concerns. Funding areas are the environment and social services.

Officers and Directors. *Trustees:* Charles H. Bell, Lucy W. Bell, John M. Hartwell, Lucy B. Hartwell.

Financial data. Data for fiscal year ended December 31, 1993. *Assets:* $1,533,086 (M). *Total grants disbursed:* $92,000.

Environmental awards. *Program and interests:* The Foundation funds programs addressing environmental preservation and education with an emphasis on Minnesota.
Recent grants: 1993 grants include support for wilderness, land, and waterfowl conservation.

Issues. Cli Bio Lan Agr Wat Oce Ene Was Tox Pop Dev

Funding analysis.

Fiscal year:	1993
Env grants disb:	$21,500
Number:	5
Range:	$1,500–$5,000
Median:	$5,000
Pct $ disb (env/total):	23

Recipients (1993):	Number:	Dollars:
Bell Museum	1	5,000
Delta Waterfowl Foundation	1	5,000
Minnesota Land Trust	1	5,000
The Nature Conservancy, Minnesota Field Office	1	5,000
Wilderness Inquiry	1	1,500

Activity region (1993):	Number:	Dollars:
U.S. Great Lakes	5	21,500

Sample grants (1993).
Bell Museum. Minneapolis, MN. $5,000. Wildlife Art Show.
Delta Waterfowl Foundation. Dearfield, IL. $5,000.
Minnesota Land Trust. Minneapolis, MN. $5,000.
The Nature Conservancy, Minnesota Field Office. Minneapolis, MN. $5,000.
Wilderness Inquiry. Minneapolis, MN. $1,500

Application process. *Initial contact:* Letter of inquiry and subsequently a proposal to include:
1. Completed Bell Foundation Cover Page.
2. Brief description of mission, history, background, and capabilities of the organization.
3. Purpose of project or program.
4. Statement of need.
5. Relevance to Foundation interests.
6. Implementation plans including work plan and timetable.
7. Collaboration. Partners and major sources of support.
8. Future funding.
9. Staff.
10. Evaluation plan.
11. How Bell Foundation funds will be used.

Attachments.
1. Copy of IRS tax-exempt status determination letter.
2. Copy of organization's budget for current fiscal year.
3. Copy of latest audit or financial statement.
4. List of board members and their affiliations.
5. Listing of current funders.

When to apply: Anytime. The trustees meet in February, June, and November.
Materials available: Guidelines, grants list.

Emphases. *Recipients:* Nonprofit organizations.
Geography: Minneapolis, Minnesota.

Limitations. *Recipients:* Individuals.
Activities: Fundraising, political activities.
Types of support: Membership campaigns.

James Ford Bell Foundation
Carlson Center
601 Lakeshore Parkway, Suite 350
Minnetonka, Minnesota 55305
Tel: 612–540–4997   Fax: 612–540–4066
Contact: Diane B. Neimann, Executive Director

History and philosophy. The Foundation was established in 1955 by James Ford Bell (1879–1961), a leading figure in the American flour milling industry who founded General Mills, Inc. in 1928. Bell was an inveterate outdoorsman, early conservationist, lifelong scientist, and leading philanthropist. He was instrumental in the building and development of the University of Minnesota's Museum of Natural History, subsequently re-named the James Ford Bell Museum of Natural History. He also founded the American Wildlife Foundation, now the Delta Waterfowl Foundation, set up to further the cause of waterfowl and wetlands. The Foundation generally funds projects with historical connections to the Bell family but also considers requests in the areas of the environment, the arts, social services, and education.

Officers and directors. *Officer:* Robert O. Mathson, Executive Secretary. *Trustees:* Ford W. Bell, Samuel H. Bell, Jr., David B. Hartwell.

Financial data. Data for fiscal year ended December 31, 1993. *Assets:* $15,259,102 (U). *Total grants disbursed:* $839,298.

Environmental awards. *Program and interests:* The program targets:

- Environmental preservation.
- Environmental education.
- Overpopulation and its environmental impact.

Recent grants: 1993 grants include support for wilderness and land conservation, forest preservation, biodiversity and species preservation (wolves, waterfowl, raptors), and environmental education.

Issues. Cli Bio Lan Agr Wat Oce Ene Was Tox Pop Dev

Funding analysis.

Fiscal year:	1993
Env grants auth:	$297,500
Number:	18
Range:	$500–$110,000
Median:	$8,750
Pct $ disb (env/total):	36

Recipients (1993 highest):	*Number:*	*Dollars:*
Delta Research Station	2	140,000
University of Minnesota, College of Natural Resources	1	36,000
Minnesota Land Trust	1	25,000
Special Projects Foundation	1	17,500
Delta Waterfowl Foundation	1	10,000
International Wolf Center	1	10,000
Minnesota Center for Environmental Advocacy	1	10,000
Minnesota Parks and Trails Council and Foundation	1	10,000
Northwoods Audubon Center	2	10,000

Activity regions (1993):	*Number:*	*Dollars:*
U.S. Great Lakes	14	254,500
Canada	1	30,000
U.S. Southeast	1	7,500
U.S. Mountain	1	5,000
U.S. not specified	1	500

Sample grants (1993).*

Concerts for the Environment, Inc. Minneapolis, MN. $25,000. Program-related investment; total commitment of $50,000 in support of concerts throughout the United States promoting environmental causes and education.

Delta Research Station. Winnipeg, Manitoba. $140,000. Support for waterfowl research and conservation in Manitoba, Canada.

Eco Education. St. Paul, MN. $2,000. General operating support for environmental education in Twin Cities schools.

International Wolf Center. Brooklyn, MN. $10,000. Capital grant for completion of construction of the Center in Ely.

Minnesota Department of Natural Resources. St. Paul, MN. $10,000. Second and final payment toward forest landscape project.

Minnesota Land Trust. Minneapolis, MN. $25,000. Seed money for organizational start-up.

Minnesota Parks & Trails Council and Foundation. St. Paul, MN. $10,000. For the land acquisition program.

Northwoods Audubon Center. Sandstone, MN. $5,500. Capital support for renovation and expansion of its residential environmental learning center.

Wilderness Inquiry. Minneapolis, MN. $1,500. General operating support for outdoor program for people of mixed abilities.

*Sample grants represent either new awards or disbursements on grants awarded in previous years.

Application process. *Initial contact:* Letter of inquiry and subsequently a proposal to include:
1. Completed James Ford Bell Foundation Cover Page.
2. Brief description of mission, history, background, and capabilities of organization.
3. Purpose of project or program.
4. Statement of need.
5. Relevance to Foundation.
6. Implementation: work plan, timeline.
7. Collaboration with others.
8. Future funding.
9. Staff capability.
10. Evaluation plan.
11. Use of Bell Foundation support.

Appendixes.
1. Copy of IRS tax-exempt status determination letter.
2. Copy of organization's budget for current fiscal year.
3. Copy of latest audit or financial statement.
4. Listing of board of directors and affiliations.
5. Listing of current funders.

When to apply: Deadlines are usually in December, April, and August or 45 working days before the first day of the month of a board meeting, held in February, June, and October.

Materials available: Guidelines, grants list.

Emphases. *Recipients:* Nonprofit organizations. *Geography:* Minnesota.

Limitations. *Recipients:* Individuals. *Activities:* Fundraising, political activities. *Types of support:* Fellowships, membership campaigns, scholarships.

The Ben & Jerry's Foundation

P.O. Box 299
Waterbury, Vermont 05676
Tel: 802–244–7105
EIN: 030300865   Type: Company-sponsored
EGA member
Contact: Rebecca Golden, Administrator

History and philosophy. Ben & Jerry's Homemade, Inc. established the Foundation in 1985 with a stock donation that now serves as its endowment. The Foundation's mission is "to support and contribute to progressive social change in the United States—efforts to change the underlying conditions that create social problems such as racism, sexism, poverty, and environmental destruction. We primarily fund small grassroots organizations, and are willing to take risks funding new projects and small organizations struggling to survive."

In 1994 the Foundation inaugurated a new grantmaking structure led by employees. Under the new program, significantly more grants will focus on Vermont—at least 35 percent of allocations—awarded through a decentralized decisionmaking process involving more employees. Grants to organizations outside Vermont will be awarded by a central board of representatives from company sites.

Grantmaking areas are: Children and Families; Disadvantaged Groups; and the Environment.

Officers and directors. *Officers:* Jerry Greenfield, President; Naomi Tannen, Secretary; Jeffrey Furman, Treasurer. *Employee Board:* Susan Bitterman, Ken Drew, Lisa Goodrich, Jesse Metcalf, Tom Noyes, Jean Stetter, John Turner, Michael Tutt.

B

Financial data. Data for fiscal year ended September 30, 1993. *Assets:* $1,000,000 (U) (est.). *Total grants disbursed:* $808,000.

Environmental awards. *Program and interests:* The Foundation targets three areas:

- Environmental justice.
- Grassroots efforts.
- Projects seeking to effect social change.

Recent grants: 1993 grants included support for education and advocacy on sustainable agriculture and food quality, hazardous waste and nuclear issues, environmental health, and environmental justice.

Issues. Cli Bio Lan Agr Wat Oce Ene Was Tox Pop Dev
          •   •   •   •   •   •   •   •   •   •

Funding analysis.

Fiscal year:	1990	1993
Env grants disb:	$48,700	$255,735
Number:	12	37
Range:	$700–$10,000	$500–$15,000
Median:	$3,750	$8,000
Pct $ disb (env/total):	15	32

Recipients (1993 highest):	Number:	Dollars:
Environmental Health Network	1	15,000
White Earth Land Recovery Project	1	15,000
California Rural Legal Assistance Foundation	1	10,000
CATA	1	10,000
Central Texas Health Project	1	10,000
Childhood Cancer Research Institute, Inc.	1	10,000
Citizens for a Clean Environment	1	10,000
Food Works	1	10,000
Gwich'in Steering Committee	1	10,000
Native Action	1	10,000
Save Our Cumberland Mountains	1	10,000
Student Environmental Action Coalition	1	10,000
Vermont Clean Water Project	1	10,000

Activity regions (1993 highest):	Number:	Dollars:
U.S. Northeast	14	74,485
U.S. Great Lakes	5	37,000
U.S. not specified	3	35,000
U.S. South Central	3	23,000
U.S. West	3	20,000

Sample grants (1993–94).

Chinese Progressive Association. San Francisco, CA. $7,000. The Chinatown Environmental Organizing Project will focus on neighborhood youth as a catalyst for organizing the community around environmental justice issues affecting Chinatown and other low-income communities of color.

Citizens for Safe Water Around Badger. Merrimac, WI. $8,000. To block location of a Superconductive Magnetic Energy Storage facility scheduled for the Badger Army Ammunition Plant. The group also fights for testing and cleanup of the community's soil and groundwater already polluted by BAAP.

Environmental Justice. Jackson, MS. $1,000. For a quarterly newsletter by this organization that provides a cohesive research, resource, and communication link for the numerous grassroots groups dealing with environmental racism in the state.

Georgia Elementary School. St. Albans, VT. $500. The Vermont Wild Kingdom project consists of fifth grade students generating fact sheets and other publications on the 44–state listed mammals of Vermont. The publications will be distributed to schools throughout the state as well as to the Fish & Wildlife Service for use in its educational outreach.

Northeast Sustainable Agricultural Working Group. Brooklyn, NY. $10,000. For the Leadership Congress, to form both traditional and non-traditional partnerships with leaders representing environmental, business, and consumer interests, to promote a more environmentally sound and economically just food and agriculture system.

Pineros y Campesinos Unidos del Noroeste. Woodburn, OR. $8,000. For this association of agricultural workers striving to improve working and living conditions especially in regard to pesticide poisoning. Their efforts include legal and medical networking, legislative campaigns, and farmworker education.

Southern Echo, Inc. Jackson, MS. $10,000. To empower African-American and poor communities in Mississippi through leadership training, development, and grassroots organizing so that they may become more active in the political process and stall further environmental degradation in their communities.

Wickford Middle School. North Kingstown, RI. $1,000. For the Environmental Classroom for Outdoor Studies project, to transform a wasteland of briar and bramble into a community garden that will provide produce for the local food pantry.

Application process. *Initial contact:* Telephone call, short letter, or post card requesting application form and guidelines. The Foundation generally invites 30 of some 350 potential applicants per quarter to submit a full proposal.

When to apply: Deadlines for complete proposals (invited applicants only) are January 1, April 1, July 1, and October 1.

Materials available: Annual report, application guidelines, quarterly grants lists.

Emphases. *Recipients:* Nonprofit organizations.

Activities: Activism, advocacy, capacity building, citizen participation, innovative programs, networking, political activities, volunteerism, youth programs.

Types of support: General purposes, matching funds, operating costs, projects, single-year grants only.

Geography: United States and its territories only. Emphasis on organizations based in Vermont.

Limitations. *Recipients:* Individuals, educational institutions, public agencies, religious organizations, research institutions.

Activities: Audiovisual materials, direct services, exhibits, expeditions/tours, fundraising, research, technical assistance.

Types of support: Computer hardware, continuing support, emergency funding, loans, multi-year grants, professorships, scholarships, technical assistance.

Geography: International.

Beneficia Foundation

165 Township Line Road
Jenkinton, Pennsylvania 19046-3593
Tel: 215-887-6700
EIN: 246015630   Type: Independent
EGA member
Contact: Carol Gairo, Secretary

History and philosophy. The Beneficia Foundation is a private foundation established in 1953 by Theodore Pitcairn. Directors of the Foundation are descendants of Theodore Pitcairn and their spouses. Beneficia's mission is to enhance the quality of life through conservation of the environment and promotion of the arts. Beneficia favors programs which are: innovative, catalytic, addressing unmet needs, and striving toward self-sustainability.

Officers and directors. *Officers:* Laren Pitcairn, President; J. Daniel Mitchell, Vice President; Feodor Pitcairn, Executive Secretary; Mark J. Pennink, Treasurer. *Directors:* Deana Duncan, Sharon Forsyth, J. Daniel Mitchell, Miriam Mitchell, Eshowe Pennick, Mark J. Pennick, Feodor Pitcairn, Jeremy Pitcairn, Kirstin Pitcairn, Laren Pitcairn, Mary Elenor Pitcairn, Heather Reynolds.

Financial data. Data for fiscal year ended April 30, 1993. *Assets:* $14,000,000 (M) (est.). *Total grants disbursed:* $783,024.

Environmental awards. *Program and Interests:* Priorities of the Environmental Committee are:

- Conservation of globally threatened terrestrial and marine ecosystems.
- Conservation of natural resources in the Delaware River watershed area.

Other interests include:

- Tropical biodiversity research, preservation, management.
- Endangered species.

Recent grants: 1993 grants included support for land conservation (wilderness, watersheds), wildlife protection, and air quality.

Issues. Cli • Bio • Lan • Agr Wat • Oce • Ene • Was Tox Pop Dev

Funding analysis.

Fiscal year:	1991	1993
Env grants disb:	$359,000	$463,707
Number:	12	16
Range:	$3,000–$139,500	$10,000–$112,995
Median:	$22,500	$20,000
Pct $ disb (env/total):	56	59

Recipients (1993 highest):	Number:	Dollars:
Pennypack Watershed Association	2	190,707
Center for Marine Conservation	1	30,000
Environmental Defense Fund	1	30,000
The Nature Conservancy, New Jersey Field Office	1	28,000
Zoological Society of Philadelphia	1	25,000

Activity regions (1993 highest):	Number:	Dollars:
U.S. Mid-Atlantic	7	293,707
U.S. not specified	2	50,000
Global	1	30,000
Andean Region and Southern Cone	1	20,000
New York/New Jersey	1	20,000
U.S. South Central	2	20,000
West Africa	1	20,000

Sample grants (1993).

Bat Conservation International. Austin, TX. $20,000. General support and building acquisition.
Center for Marine Conservation. Washington, DC. $30,000. Marine Biological Diversity Program.
Conservation International. Washington, DC. $10,000. Indonesia Program.
Delaware Valley Citizens Council for Clean Air. Philadelphia, PA. $20,000. General support.
Environmental Defense Fund. New York, NY. $30,000. Defense of the Endangered Species Act.
Natural Resources Defense Council. New York, NY. $20,000. Energy Efficiency Project with Chile.
Pennsylvania Environmental Council. Philadelphia, PA. $10,000. Building Better Communities Program.
The Wilderness Society. Washington, DC. $20,000. American Lifelands campaign.

Application process. *Initial contact:* Letter of inquiry addressed to the Environmental Committee.
When to apply: Deadline is January 15. The board generally meets in April.

Emphases. *Geography:* Philadelphia, Pennsylvania.

Limitations. *Recipients:* Individuals.

Benton Foundation

1634 Eye Street, N.W., 12th Floor
Washington, DC 20006
Tel: 202-638-5770   Fax: 202-638-5771
E-mail: benton@benton.org
EIN: 136075750   Type: Operating
EGA member
Contact: Larry Kirkman, Executive Director

History and philosophy. The Benton Foundation, established in 1980, builds on the belief of founder Senator William Benton that "communications media should be the backbone of informed participation in public life." The Foundation works with public interest groups "to demonstrate new forms of interaction and self-determination and to gain an effective voice for social change." Initiated and directed by Foundation staff, programs provide technical assistance and media resources to nonprofit public interest organizations; promote the importance of media to funders; and work to make media access and diversity subjects of widespread discussion and public decisionmaking.

Grantmaking programs are: Universal Service, Applications in Education and Health, The National Information Infrastructure

(NII) and Civic Networking, Educational and Outreach Efforts, Research, and Video and Print Materials.

Officers and directors. *Officers:* Charles Benton, Chairman and President; Richard M. Neustadt, Treasurer. *Directors:* Charles Benton, Craig H. Benton, Richard D. Mahoney, Michael Pertschuk, Dorothy S. Ridings, Henry M. Rivera, Carolyn Sachs.

Financial data. Data for fiscal year ended December 31, 1992. *Assets:* $13,000,000 (U) (est.). *Total grants disbursed:* $765,981.

Application process. *Initial contact:* Proposal by invitation only. Only proposals that directly complement Foundation operating projects and have been initiated by staff will be considered. No unsolicited applications accepted.

Emphases. *Recipients:* Pre-selected organizations only.
Activities: Audiovisual materials, conferences, education, publications.
Types of support: Technical assistance.

Benua Foundation, Inc.
c/o Eleanor L. Craig
1560 Fishinger Road
Columbus, Ohio 43221–2108
Tel: 614–442–5929   Fax: 614–442–1247
EIN: 316026443   Type: Independent
Contact: Eleanor L. Craig, Trustee/Director

History and philosophy. Incorporated in 1952 by A. R. Benua and Ebco Manufacturing Company, the Benua Foundation focuses its giving on pre-selected organizations working in conservation, culture, education, health, and social and youth services in Columbus, Ohio.

Officers and directors. *Trustees:* John M. Bowsher, Eleanor L. Craig, William L. Schmidt.

Financial data. Data for fiscal year ended December 31, 1993. *Assets:* $12,932,295 (M). *Total grants disbursed:* $477,000.

Environmental awards. *Recent grants:* 1993 grants included support for land conservation (botanical gardens, habitats, parks, nature preserves) forestry, wildlife, and a zoo.

Issues. Cli Bio Lan Agr Wat Oce Ene Was Tox Pop Dev
              •   •   •   •   •   •

Funding analysis.

Fiscal year:	1991	1993
Env grants disb:	$73,000	$43,000
Number:	14	9
Range:	$500–$25,000	$500–$15,000
Median:	$2,500	$2,500
Pct $ disb (env/total):	12	9

Recipients (1993 highest):	Number:	Dollars:
Ohio Department of Natural Resources	1	15,000
The Nature Conservancy, Ohio Field Office	2	12,000
Columbus Zoological Park Association	1	5,000
Ohio Forestry Association, Inc.	1	5,000
The Conservancy	1	2,500

Activity regions (1993):	Number:	Dollars:
U.S. Great Lakes	6	39,000
U.S. Southeast	1	2,500
Canada	1	1,000
U.S. not specified	1	500

Sample grants (1993).
Columbus Zoological Park Association. Powell, OH. $5,000.
The Conservancy. Naples, FL. $2,500.
Inniswood Botanical Garden and Nature Preserve. Westerville, OH. $2,000.
National Audubon Society. New York, NY. $500.
The Nature Conservancy, Ohio Field Office. Columbus, OH. $12,000.
Ohio Department of Natural Resources. Huron, OH. $15,000. To the Division of Natural Areas and Preserves for Old Woman Creek.
Ohio Forestry Association, Inc. Columbus, OH. $5,000.

Application process. *Initial contact:* The Foundation awards grants to pre-selected organizations only. No unsolicited applications accepted.

Emphases. *Recipients:* Pre-selected organizations only.
Geography: Primarily Columbus, Ohio.

Limitations. *Recipients:* Individuals.

The Bersted Foundation
c/o Bank of America
231 South LaSalle Street
Chicago, Illinois 60697
Tel: 312–828–1785
EIN: 366493609   Type: Independent
Contact: M. Catherine Ryan, Vice President, Bank of America

History and philosophy. Alfred Bersted (d. 1972), was former chairman of the board of McGraw Edison in Elgin, Illinois. The Foundation was established in 1973 in accord with Mr. Bersted's wishes. It continues his practice of charitable giving to organizations within the Illinois counties of DeKalb, DuPage, Kane, and McHenry. Its philosophy is shaped by "the spirit behind the creation of the Foundation, changing contemporary problems and the ability of the Foundation to contribute to their solution, and the availability of alternative sources of funding."

Officers and directors. *Trustee:* M. Catherine Ryan, Vice President, Bank of America.

Financial data. Data for fiscal year ended December 31, 1993. *Assets:* $6,300,00 (U) (est.). *Total grants disbursed:* $400,000.

Environmental awards. *Recent grants:* 1993 grants included support for land conservation and environmental education.

Issues. Cli Bio Lan Agr Wat Oce Ene Was Tox Pop Dev
              •   •

Funding analysis.

Fiscal year:	1993
Env grants disb:	$47,500
Number:	2
Range:	$2,500–$45,000
Median:	$23,750
Pct $ disb (env/total):	8

Recipients (1993):	*Number:*	*Dollars:*
Fox River Conservation Union of Nature Conservancy	1	45,000
DuPage Environmental Awareness Center	1	2,500

Activity region (1993):	*Number:*	*Dollars:*
U.S. Great Lakes	2	47,500

Sample grants (1993).
DuPage Environmental Awareness Center. Lisle, IL. $2,500.
Fox River Conservation Union of Nature Conservancy. Chicago, IL. $45,000.

Application process. *Initial contact:* Proposal (2 copies) to include:
Cover letter.
1. Brief summary of grant purpose.
2. Amount requested.
3. Name, address, and phone number of person submitting the request.

Proposal.
1. Organization name, address, and phone number.
2. Complete description of the program and explanation of why funds are needed.
3. Schedule for program implementation and names and qualifications of people responsible for the program.
4. Description of any programs in the same area, private or government-funded, that the program might duplicate.
5. Detailed program budget, information on other sources of funding available or being sought, and plans for permanent funding, if the program is to continue.
6. Description of evaluation methods and a statement showing how the grant was spent and that it was used only for the indicated purposes.

Attachments.
1. Copy of IRS tax-exempt status determination letter. If the letter does not state that the organization is "not a private foundation," a separate IRS letter on that ruling is required.
2. History of the organization, and description of additional programs operated by the organization, if any.
3. Names and affiliations of the organization's board of directors.
4. Certified financial statement (balance sheet and income statement) for the most current year.

When to apply: Deadlines are in February, May, August, and November for review in April, July, October, and January.

Materials available: Multi-year report 1973–1993 (includes "How to Apply for a Grant").

Emphases. *Recipients:* Nonprofit organizations, religious organizations.
Activities: Research (scientific).
Types of support: Facilities, general purposes, operating costs, technical assistance.
Geography: DeKalb, DuPage, Kane, and McHenry counties, Illinois.

Limitations. *Recipients:* Educational institutions, individuals.
Activities: Lobbying, political activities.
Types of support: Debt retirement, endowments.

The Betterment Fund
c/o Davidson, Dawson & Clark
330 Madison Avenue, Room 3500
New York, New York 10017
Tel: 212–557–7700   Fax: 212–286–8513
EGA member
Contact: Carolyn S. Wollen, Esq., Trustee

History and philosophy. The Betterment Fund was created by the will of William Bingham, 2nd in 1955. Mr. Bingham was a "philanthropist with an abiding interest in education and the improvement of health services in the state of Maine." The Fund's goal is to work for the betterment of the people of the state of Maine. It has expanded its areas of concern to include community service programs and environmental matters.

Officers and directors. *Trustees:* William M. Throop, Jr., William B. Winship, Carolyn S. Wollen, United States Trust Company of New York.

Financial data. Data for fiscal year ended December 31, 1993 and first six months of 1994. *Assets (1994):* $26,959,915 (M). *Total grants disbursed (1993):* $1,100,565.

Environmental awards. *Program and interests:* The Fund supports projects to promote thoughtful planning and preservation of Maine's natural resources. Specific interests include:

- Preservation of natural resources.
- Environmental education.
- Sustainable development policy.
- Public health.
- Environmental and economic development that is consistent with protecting natural resources.
- Land acquisition and preservation.

Recent grants: 1993 grants included support for natural resource inventories, wilderness and forest protection, rivers, coastal issues, air quality, and growth management.

Issues. Cli Bio Lan Agr Wat Oce Ene Was Tox Pop Dev
          •   •   •   •   •   •   •   •

B

Funding analysis.

Fiscal year:	1991	1993
Env grants auth:	$181,000	$181,100
Number:	8	8
Range:	$12,000–$60,000	$3,100–$72,000
Median:	$15,000	$20,000
Pct $ disb (env/total):	15	23

Recipients (1993 highest):	Number:	Dollars:
Rangeley Lakes Heritage Trust	1	72,000
College of the Atlantic	1	30,000
Hurricane Island Outward Bound School	1	25,000
Sierra Club Northern Forest Campaign	1	25,000
Friends of Casco Bay	1	15,000

Activity region (1993):	Number:	Dollars:
U.S. Northeast	8	181,100

Sample grants (1993).*
Appalachian Trail Conference, Headquarters. Harpers Ferry, WV. $5,000. Develop Trail Crew program.
College of the Atlantic. Bar Harbor, ME. $30,000. Support for ECO-ECO Priorities Project.
The Friends of Casco Bay. South Portland, ME. $15,000. To initiate the Baykeeper Program.
Hurricane Island Outward Bound School. Rockland, ME. $25,000. Teacher Development Project.
Mahoosuc Land Trust. Bethel, ME. $6,000.
Maine Audubon Society. Falmouth, ME. $15,000. To develop Environmental Centers.
Norway South Paris Heritage Trust. South Paris, ME. $3,100.
Rangeley Lakes Heritage Trust. Rangeley, ME. $72,000. Matching grant for acquisition of land for conservation.
Sierra Club Northern Forest Campaign. Saratoga Springs, NY. $25,000. Employment of Maine-based coordinator for the Northern Forest Campaign.

*Sample grants represent either new awards or disbursements on grants awarded from previous years.

Application process. *Initial contact:* Complete a grant application form and submit a summary (1 page) of the proposed budget for the project. More detail can be provided in a cover letter.
When to apply: Anytime. The trustees meet quarterly.
Materials available: Annual report, "Guidelines," application form.

Emphases. *Recipients:* Educational institutions.
Activities: Capacity building, collaborative efforts, demonstration programs, education, innovative programs, land acquisition, planning, policy analysis/development.
Types of support: Continuing support, general purposes, leveraging funds, matching funds, multi-year grants, operating costs, pilot projects, research (medical).
Geography: Maine only.

Limitations. *Recipients:* Individuals.
Activities: Audiovisual materials, political activities.
Types of support: Annual campaigns, endowments, facilities (construction), scholarships.

The Frank Stanley Beveridge Foundation, Inc.
301 N.E. 51st Street, Suite 1130
Boca Raton, Florida 33431-4929
Tel: 407-241-8388   Fax: 407-241-8332
EIN: 046032164   Type: Independent
Contact: Philip Caswell, President

History and philosophy. Frank Stanley Beveridge (1879–1956) was the founder of the Massachusetts company Stanhome, Inc. (formerly Stanley Home Products). He established The Foundation in 1947. The Foundation supports the arts, education, human welfare, medicine, and science; it also maintains a community park in Westfield, Massachusetts.

Officers and directors. *Officers:* Philip Caswell, President; David F. Woods, Clerk; Carole S. Lenhart, Treasurer. *Directors:* Sarah Caswell Bartelt, William R. Cass, John Beveridge Caswell, Philip Caswell, John G. Gallup, Carole S. Lenhart, Joseph Beveridge Palmer, Homer G. Perkins, Evelyn Beveridge Russell, Patsy Palmer Stecher, J. Thomas Touchton, David F. Woods.

Financial data. Data for fiscal year ended December 31, 1991. *Assets:* $42,161,192 (M). *Total grants disbursed:* $1,688,963.

Environmental awards. *Recent grants:* 1991 grants included support for land conservation (greenways, open lands, wetlands) and a zoo.

Issues.   Cli   Bio   Lan   Agr   Wat   Oce   Ene   Was   Tox   Pop   Dev
              •   •   •   •

Funding analysis.

Fiscal year:	1991
Env grants auth:	$835,395
Number:	8
Range:	$2,500–$665,000
Median:	$23,948
Pct $ disb (env/total):	43

Recipients (1991 highest):	Number:	Dollars:
The Stanley Park of Westfield, Inc.	1	665,000
Lowry Park Zoo Association	1	50,000
The Deerfield Land Trust	1	50,000
The Valley Land Fund, Inc.	1	25,000
Florida Audubon Society	1	22,895

Activity regions (1991):	Number:	Dollars:
U.S. Northeast	5	760,000
U.S. Southeast	2	72,895
U.S. not specified	1	2,500

Sample grants (1991).
The Deerfield Land Trust. Deerfield, MA. $50,000.
Florida Audubon Society. Maitland, FL. $22,895.
The Nature Conservancy, Headquarters. Arlington, VA. $2,500.
The Stanley Park of Westfield, Inc. Westfield, MA. $665,000.
The Valley Land Fund, Inc. Hadley, MA. $25,000. Capping grant to acquire and preserve 100 acres of sensitive wetlands.

Westfield River Watershed Association, Inc. Westfield, MA. $10,000. For the Greenway Plan to preserve the scenic and ecological characteristics of the Westfield River.

Application process. *Initial contact:* Letter or telephone call to request application form. Include proof of certification under Section 509(a) of the IRS Code. Applicants outside Hampden County, Massachusetts must be pre-selected by a director. If requested by the Foundation, submit formal proposal and accompanying documents.
1. Application.
   - Organization's purpose and history.
   - Objective of the proposed grant.
   - Timetable.
   - Total project budget; amount requested from Foundation.
   - List of special fundraising activities.
   - Name of person submitting the application.
2. IRS tax-exempt status determination letter.
3. IRS Form 990 for the two most recent years.
4. Most recent balance sheet and detailed income statement.
5. Verification that the grant request is submitted by someone authorized to represent the organization.
6. List of other funding sources for the proposed project.
7. List of board members' names and affiliations.
8. Name and qualifications of grant administrator.
9. Organizational chart.

When to apply: Deadlines are February 1 and August 1 for board meetings in April and October.
Materials available: Brochure, application guidelines.

Emphases. *Activities:* Technical assistance, projects.
Types of support: Capital campaigns/expenses, continuing support, equipment, facilities, matching funds, seed money.
Geography: Hampden and Hampshire counties, Massachusetts; Hillsborough and Palm Beach counties, Florida.

Limitations. *Recipients:* Individuals, public agencies.
Activities: Fundraising.
Types of support: Debt retirement, endowments, fellowships, loans, operating costs, scholarships, travel expenses.

The William Bingham Foundation
1250 Leader Building
Cleveland, Ohio 44114
Tel: 216-781-3275
EIN: 346513791   Type: Independent
EGA member
Contact: Laura C. Hitchcox, Director

History and philosophy. The William Bingham Foundation was established in 1955 by Elizabeth Bingham Blossom in memory of her brother, William Bingham, II, as a means of continuing the family's philanthropic tradition. Grants initially focused on cultural, educational, health, and welfare organizations in and around Cleveland, but broadened in 1977 to include less traditional programs and organizations in communities where the current trustees (all family members) now live. Grantmaking occurs in four areas: Arts and Culture, Education, Environmental Preservation, and Health and Human Services.

Officers and directors. *Officers:* Elizabeth B. Heffernan, President; Mary E. Gale, Vice President; Thomas F. Allen, Secretary; C. Bingham Blossom, Treasurer. *Trustees:* Thomas F. Allen, C. Bingham Blossom, C. Perry Blossom, Dudley S. Blossom, Laurel Blossom, Robin Dunn Blossom, Benjamin Gale, Mary E. Gale, Thomas H. Gale, Thomas V. Gale, Elizabeth B. Heffernan.

Financial data. Data for fiscal year ended December 31, 1993. *Assets:* $25,196,000 (C). *Gifts received:* $1,000. *Total grants disbursed:* $1,676,014.

Environmental awards. *Program and interests:* Since 1986 the Foundation has paid increasing attention to environmental issues, with some emphasis on climate change, global warming, and South Florida.
Recent grants: Overall, the two largest grants have gone to Natural Resources Defense Council to establish an environmental conflict negotiation fund to provide an institutional alternative to litigation in resolving differences among industry, government agencies, and environmentalists; and to Environmental Defense Fund to support research projects and policy development to halt ozone depletion and global climate change resulting from human activities.

Issues. Cli Bio Lan Agr Wat Oce Ene Was Tox Pop Dev
           •   •   •   •   •   •

Funding analysis.

Fiscal year:	1991	1993
Env grants auth:	$217,500	$455,000
Number:	13	8
Range:	$2,000–$50,000	$5,000–$250,000
Median:	$15,000	$25,000
Pct $ disb (env/total):	52	41

Recipients (1993 highest):	Number:	Dollars:
Yale University	1	250,000
Natural Resources Defense Council	1	50,000
The Climate Institute	1	50,000
Maine Wilderness Watershed Trust	1	25,000
National Public Radio	1	25,000
Pace Center for Environmental Legal Studies	1	25,000
The Wilderness Society	1	25,000

Activity regions (1993):	Number:	Dollars:
U.S. Northeast	2	275,000
U.S. not specified	3	80,000
International*	1	50,000
U.S. Southeast	2	50,000

*Multiple regions or not specified.

Sample grants (1993).*
Climate Institute. Washington, DC. $50,000. To continue efforts to educate the public and policymakers, in the United States and developing countries, on the implications of global climate change.
Environmental and Energy Study Institute. Washington, DC. $5,000. In general support of work to provide scientific and

---

© 1995 Environmental Data Resources, Inc.

B

policy information on environmental issues to members of Congress and their staff.

Environmental Defense Fund. New York, NY. $200,000. Final payment of a five-year, $1,000,000 grant for a program to identify and promote means to reduce climate change and the depletion of atmospheric ozone.

Maine Wilderness Watershed Trust. Portland ME. $25,000. To aid in efforts to protect the Pierce Pond Watershed in western Maine by acquisition of conservation easements.

National Public Radio. Washington, DC. $25,000. To expand in-depth coverage of environmental issues by hiring additional staff.

Natural Resources Defense Council. New York, NY. $50,000. For support of work addressing a wide range of environmental problems through legal action, conflict negotiation, public education, and policy development.

Pace University. White Plains, NY. $25,000. To aid its Center for Environmental Legal Studies in activities to promote the utility reforms necessary to encourage conservation in place of new electric generation in the state of Florida.

The Wilderness Society. Washington, DC. $25,000. To continue efforts to implement a comprehensive regional program of land and water management strategies needed to restore the Florida Everglades ecosystem.

Xerces Society. Portland, OR. $25,000. Second payment of a two-year $50,000 grant to help establish a captive breeding program for the endangered Homerus Swallowtail butterfly.

Yale University. New Haven, CT. $250,000. To help establish an endowment fund for Yale College's Studies in the Environment Program, a major course of study designed to introduce students to a broad range of economic, political, ethical, and scientific approaches to Environmental problem-solving.

*Sample grants represent either new awards or disbursements on grants awarded in previous years.

Application process. *Initial contact:* Brief letter (2 pages maximum) outlining:
1. Nature of project.
2. Budget requirements.
3. Contribution requested.

Please refrain from sending supporting materials. If the project coincides with the Foundation's interests, a full proposal will be requested.

When to apply: Anytime for a letter of intent. Deadlines for full proposals, submitted only at request of the Foundation, are March and August, or two months before semi-annual board meetings, usually held in May and October.

Materials available: Annual report (includes "Grantmaking Procedures").

Emphases. *Recipients:* Nonprofit organizations.
Geography: Eastern United States.

Limitations. *Recipients:* Individuals.
Geography: Organizations located outside the United States.

Bishop Pine Fund

P.O. Box 930
Inverness, California 94937–0930
Tel: 415–669–1184
EIN: 77000930   Type: Independent
Contact: William M. Eastman, Secretary

History and philosophy. The Bishop Pine Fund makes grants to pre-selected organizations in the San Francisco Bay Area.

Officers and directors. *Officers:* Barbara Booth Eastman, President; William M. Eastman, Secretary.

Financial data. Data for fiscal year ended June 30, 1993. *Assets:* $356,072 (M). *Total grants disbursed:* $27,750.

Environmental awards. *Recent grants:* 1993 grants included funds for land conservation, coastal issues, and river preservation.

Issues. Cli Bio Lan Agr Wat Oce Ene Was Tox Pop Dev
              •   •   •   •   •

Funding analysis.

Fiscal year:	1991	1993
Env grants disb:	$26,000	$24,500
Number:	18	16
Range:	$500–$4,750	$500–$5,000
Median:	$1,000	$1,000
Pct $ disb (env/total):	85	88

Recipients (1993 highest):	Number:	Dollars:
Greenbelt Alliance	1	5,000
Planning & Conservation League	1	5,000
Environmental Defense Fund	1	2,000
Natural Resources Defense Council	1	2,000
Audubon Canyon Ranch	1	1,000
Citizens for a Better Environment	1	1,000
Friends of the River Foundation	1	1,000
Marin Agricultural Land Trust	1	1,000
Marin Conservation League	1	1,000
Save San Francisco Bay Association	1	1,000
Save the Redwoods League	1	1,000
Sierra Club Foundation	1	1,000
The Nature Conservancy, California Field Office	1	1,000

Activity region (1993):	Number:	Dollars:
U.S. West	16	24,500

Sample grants (1993).
Audubon Canyon Ranch. Stinson Beach, CA. $1,000.
Environmental Defense Fund. Oakland, CA. $2,000.
Environmental Volunteers, Inc. Palo Alto, CA. $500.
Friends of the River Foundation. San Francisco, CA. $1,000.
Marin Agricultural Land Trust. Point Reyes, CA. $1,000.

Application process. *Initial contact:* The Foundation awards grants to pre-selected organizations only. No unsolicited applications accepted.

Emphases. *Recipients:* Pre-selected organizations only.
Geography: San Francisco Bay Area.

Blandin Foundation
100 North Pokegama Avenue
Grand Rapids, Minnesota 55744
Tel: 218–326–0523   Fax: 218–327–1949
EIN: 416038619   Type: Independent
Contact: Paul M. Olson, President

History and philosophy. The Blandin Foundation was founded in 1941 by Charles K. Blandin, newspaperman and owner of the Itasca Paper Company, "to promote the well-being of mankind as the board of trustees may from time-to-time determine." Today, the Foundation's stated mission is "to address the causes of problems and advance the viability of rural communities and the well-being of individuals throughout rural Minnesota." Central to the Foundation's philosophy is the belief that "building strong communities requires shared leadership, innovation, and commitment." Grants are awarded in seven areas: Health and Human Services, Education, Leadership, Arts and Humanities, Environment, Memberships, Economic and Community Development.

Officers and directors. *Officers:* Bruce W. Stender, Chair; James Hoolihan, Vice Chair; Paul M. Olson, President; Kathryn Jensen, Senior Vice President; Mary Jo Jess, Secretary; Vernae Hasbargen, Steve Shaler, Treasurers. *Trustees:* Ken Albrecht, Kathy Annette, Robert L. Bullard, Robert L. Comstock, Jr., Henry Doerr, Vernae Hasbargen, Peter A. Heegaard, James Hoolihan, Mary Jo Jess, Marcie McLaughlin, James R. Oppenheimer, Steve Shaler, Bruce W. Stender, Brian Vergin.

Financial data. Data for fiscal year ended December 31, 1993. *Assets:* $236,622,208 (C). *Total grants authorized:* $11,449,290.

Environmental awards. *Program and interests:* "For many years, the Blandin Foundation focused its attention in the Itasca County area on forestry-related issues. The Foundation's interest has been in the careful stewardship and management of this important environmental and economic resource."

The Trustees identified a specific focus area on the environment in 1990. In 1991 and 1992, environmental grants focused on forestry-related projects and on projects which improve and maintain the quality of Minnesota's freshwater resources. 1993 environmental grants focused on projects that provide an in-depth, experiential environmental education opportunity for young people outside the traditional classroom setting. 1994 grants will help to expand five environmental learning centers.

Issues.   Cli   Bio   Lan   Agr   Wat   Oce   Ene   Was   Tox   Pop   Dev
                  •   •   •   •

Funding analysis.

Fiscal year:	1991	1993
Env grants auth:	$1,489,550	$1,209,600
Number:	11	6
Range:	$18,000–$300,000	$5,000–$1,000,000
Median:	$100,000	$47,300
Pct $ auth (env/total):	19	11

Recipients (1993 highest):	Number:	Dollars:
St. Olaf College	1	1,000,000
St. Louis–Lake County Regional Railroad Authority	1	100,000
Lake Superior Center	1	84,600
City of Blackduck	1	10,000
The Minnesota Project	1	10,000

Activity region (1993):	Number:	Dollars:
U.S. Great Lakes	6	1,209,600

Sample grants (1993).
City of Blackduck. Blackduck, MN. $10,000. Development of Pine Tree Park as part of the Blandin Community Partnership Program.
Lake Superior Center. Duluth, MN. $84,600. To design an environmental education program.
St. Olaf College. Northfield, MN. $1,000,000 (5 years). Phase II of the Schoolside Nature Areas Project (SNAP) for rural Minnesota communities.
Voyageur Outward Bound School. Minnetonka, MN. $5,000. For the Red Road Pilot Project for Native Americans.

Application process. *Initial contact:* Telephone call or letter of inquiry to describe the request. A meeting with a staff member will be arranged if necessary.
When to apply: Deadlines are January 2, May 1, and September 1. The board of trustees meets three times a year, in April, August, and September.
Materials available: Annual report, "Information for Grant Applicants."

Emphases. *Recipients:* Nonprofit organizations.
Activities: Collaborative efforts, education.
Geography: Rural Minnesota.

Limitations. *Recipients:* Individuals.
Activities: Audiovisual materials (except for those on unique subjects of special interest to the region or state), camping programs, political activities, publications, and research (medical).
Types of support: Endowments, equipment, facilities, travel expenses.

The Blumenthal Foundation
P.O. Box 34689
Charlotte, North Carolina 28234
Tel: 704–377–6555   Fax: 800–421–9525
EIN: 560793667   Type: Independent
EGA member
Contact: Philip Blumenthal, Trustee

History and philosophy. The Blumenthal Foundation was established in 1953 by the late industrialist I. D. Blumenthal of Charlotte, North Carolina. It currently specializes in human services and Jewish causes, but plans to devote increasing resources to environmental concerns.

B

Officers and directors. *Trustees:* Alan Blumenthal, Anita Blumenthal, Herman Blumenthal, Philip Blumenthal, Samuel Blumenthal.

Financial data. Data for fiscal year ended April 30, 1993. *Assets:* $22,611,201 (M). *Total grants disbursed:* $1,057,773.

Environmental awards. *Program and interests:* The Foundation takes a special interest in environmental education.
Recent grants: 1992 grants included support for land conservation, outdoor education, and a zoo.

Issues. Cli Bio Lan Agr Wat Oce Ene Was Tox Pop Dev
           •   •   •

Funding analysis.

Fiscal year:	1991	1992
Env grants disb:	$137,145	$127,124
Number:	12	14
Range:	$45–$103,000	$55–$75,000
Median:	$1,000	$2,250
Pct $ disb (env/total):	14	13

Recipients (1992 highest):	Number:	Dollars:
Sierra Club Foundation	1	22,500
Botanical Garden Foundation, Inc.	1	12,169
The Nature Conservancy, North Carolina Field Office	1	5,000
Earth Coalition of Charlotte-Mecklenburg	1	2,500
Land Stewardship Council	1	2,500
Southern Environmental Law Center	1	2,500

Activity regions (1992):	Number:	Dollars:
U.S. Southeast	9	102,724
U.S. not specified	4	25,000

Sample grants (1993).
Botanical Garden Foundation, Inc. Chapel Hill, NC. $7,228.
Earth Coalition of Charlotte-Mecklenburg. Charlotte, NC. $2,500.
Environmental Defense Fund. Raleigh, NC. $3,000.
Land Stewardship Council. Pittsboro, NC. $2,500.
The Nature Conservancy, North Carolina Field Office. Carrboro, NC. $8,000.
North Carolina Outward Bound School. Morganton, NC. $1,000.
North Carolina Zoological Society. Asheboro, NC. $10,000.
Sierra Club Foundation. San Francisco, CA. $25,000.
Southern Environmental Law Center. Charlottesville, VA. $3,000.

Application process. *Initial contact:* Brief proposal in letter form (1 copy), signed by an authorized official of the petitioning organization. The first paragraph should state the specific amount and the purpose of the request, and the proposal should contain:
1. A concise description of project.
2. What project hopes to accomplish.
3. Total cost of project and duration.
4. Funds on hand or pledged and from what sources.
5. Other sources being approached for funding.
6. A plan for evaluation and how future funding will be obtained if the project is continuing.
7. Telephone number where a contact person may be reached during normal business hours.
8. Indication of to whom a check should be made payable.

Attachments.
1. Line-item budget for project for which funding is being requested, if applicable, and a budget for the organization's total operations including expected income and expenditures.
2. List of the governing board of petitioning organization.
3. Copy of the IRS tax-exempt status determination letter except in the case of governmental agencies and churches.

When to apply: Deadlines are 15 days before each quarterly board meeting, held in March, June, September, and December. Call for specific dates.
Materials available: "Procedures and Requirements for Submitting Grant Proposals."

Emphases. *Recipients:* Educational institutions, nonprofit organizations, zoos.
Activities: Activism, citizen participation, collaborative efforts, education, innovative programs, networking, volunteerism.
Types of support: Annual campaigns, capital campaigns/expenses, matching funds, operating costs, pilot projects, seed money.
Geography: North Carolina, particularly Charlotte.

Limitations. *Recipients:* Individuals.
Types of support: Loans, scholarships.

The Bodman Foundation
767 Third Avenue
New York, New York 10017–2023
Tel: 212–418–0500   Fax: 212–755–4476
EIN: 136022016   Type: Independent
Contact: Joe Dolan, Executive Director

History and philosophy. The Bodman Foundation was formed in 1945 by George M. Bodman (d. 1950) and his wife, Louise Clarke Bodman (d. 1955). Mr. Bodman was senior partner in the New York brokerage firm of Cyrus J. Lawrence and Sons. Designed to further the work of agencies and institutions that interested the Bodmans, the Foundation carries on its original mission to distribute funds in religious, educational, and charitable fields "for the moral, ethical, and physical well-being and progress of mankind."

Officers and directors. *Officers:* Guy G. Rutherfurd, President and Treasurer; John N. Irwin III, Russell P. Pennoyer, Vice Presidents; Joe Dolan, Secretary and Executive Director. *Trustees:* Harry W. Albright, Jr., Mary B. Braga, Walter J. P. Curley, Jr., Anthony D. Duke, Peter Frelinghuysen, John N. Irwin III, Leslie Lenkowsky, Ph.D., Marguerite S. Nichols, M.D., Russell P. Pennoyer, Mary S. Phipps, Guy G. Rutherfurd.

Financial data. Data for fiscal year ended December 31, 1993. *Assets:* $34,290,095 (C). *Total grants disbursed:* $1,875,000.

Environmental awards. *Recent grants:* 1993 grants included support for urban parks, a botanical garden, an aquarium, and environmental education.

Issues. *Cli* **Bio** **Lan** *Agr Wat Oce Ene Was Tox Pop Dev*

Funding analysis.

Fiscal year:	1991	1993
Env grants auth:	$15,000	$90,000
Number:	1	4
Range:	–	$15,000–$30,000
Median:	–	$22,500
Pct $ disb (env/total):	10	6

Recipients (1993):	Number:	Dollars:
National Audubon Society, Northeast Regional Office	1	30,000
Brooklyn Botanic Garden	1	25,000
Friends of the Cold Spring Harbor Fish Hatchery	1	20,000
Central Park Conservancy	1	15,000

Activity region (1993):	Number:	Dollars:
New York/New Jersey	4	90,000

Sample grants (1993).*
Brooklyn Botanic Garden. Brooklyn, NY. $25,000. For the Children's Garden.
Central Park Conservancy. New York, NY. $15,000. For the Charles A. Dana Discovery Center's educational programs.
Friends of the Cold Spring Harbor Fish Hatchery. Cold Spring Harbor, NY. $20,000. For capital campaign for the aquarium and Fairchild Exhibit Buildings.
National Audubon Society, Northeast Regional Office. Albany, NY. $30,000. For the Long Island Regional Effort.
The Nature Conservancy, Long Island Chapter. Cold Spring Harbor, NY. $25,000. Toward the cost of retaining a coordinator for the Peconic Bioreserve.

*Sample grants represent either new awards or disbursements on grants awarded in previous years.

Application process. *Initial contact:* Letter (2 pages) and full proposal (4–5 pages). Organizations with which the Foundation may not be familiar should include:
1. Statement of history and objectives.
2. Lists of board members and key personnel.
3. Scope of current activities.
4. Description of project or purpose for which funds are sought.
5. Financial data (including budgets and audited financial statements) for both the organization and the project.
6. Proof of IRS tax-exempt status.

When to apply: Anytime. The board of trustees meets in May, September, and December.
Materials available: Biennial report.

Emphases. *Geography:* New Jersey, specifically Monmouth County and Montclair.

Limitations. *Recipients:* Individuals.
Activities: Audiovisual materials, conferences, publications.
Types of support: Loans, travel expenses.

B

The Boeing Company
Office of Education, Affairs, and Contributions
P.O. Box 3707, Mail Stop 11–83
Seattle, Washington 98124–2207
Tel: 206–655–6679 Fax: 206–655–2000
EIN: 910425694   Type: Company-sponsored
Contact: Christine Jones, Manager, Corporate Contributions

History and philosophy. "The Boeing Company's contribution program is focused on four major categories: Education, Human Services, Arts and Culture, and Civic initiatives. The Company encourages proposals that involve collaboration between multiple organizations to address community needs."

Officers and directors. *Officers:* Frank Shrontz, Chairman and CEO; Philip M. Condit, President; B. Dan Pinick, Executive Vice President; Douglas P. Beighle, Deane D. Cruze, Boyd E. Given, A. D. Welliver, Senior Vice Presidents; Thomas M. Budinich, Jr., Arlington W. Carter, Lawrence W. Clarkson, F. G. Coffey, Theodore J. Collins, Dennis J. Crispin, Andre Gay, John F. Hayden, Larry G. McKean, Vice Presidents; David A. Jaeger, Vice President and Treasurer; Heather Howard, Corporate Secretary and Corporate Counsel. *Directors:* Robert A. Beck, Philip M. Condit, John B. Fery, Paul E. Gary, Harold J. Haynes, Stanley Hiller, Jr., George M. Keller, Donald E. Petersen, Charles M. Pigott, Rozanne L. Ridgway, Frank Shrontz, George P. Schultz, George H. Weyerhaeuser, T. A. Wilson.

Financial data. Data for fiscal year ended December 31, 1992. *Assets:* $18,147,000,000 (U) (est.). *Total grants disbursed:* $30,800,000 (est.).

Environmental awards. *Program and interests:* The Company's environmental grants are given primarily through Culture and Civic programs.
Recent grants: 1992 grants included support for land conservation, marine issues, energy conservation, environmental health, botanical gardens, and zoos.

Issues. *Cli* **Bio** **Lan** *Agr* Wat **Oce** **Ene** *Was* **Tox** *Pop Dev*

Sample grants (1992).*
Alliance to Save Energy. Washington, DC.
Camden Aquarium. Camden, NJ.
Environmental Health Center. Washington, DC.
The Nature Conservancy, Headquarters. Arlington, VA.
Northwest Renewable Resources Center. Seattle, WA.
The Wichita Botanical Gardens. Wichita, KS.
Woodland Park Zoological Society. Seattle, WA.

*Dollar amounts not available.

Application process. *Initial contact:* Proposal letter describing the applicant organization and the specific program for which support is sought. Letter to include:
1. History of service.
2. Statement of purpose and objectives.
3. Definition of project, with attention to:
   • Community need.
   • Goals project is designed to meet.

© 1995 Environmental Data Resources, Inc.

- Specific activities to meet these goals.
- Timeline.
- Plans for measurement and evaluation of results.
4. Itemized project budget.
5. List of project's committed financial supporters.
6. Plan for multi-year funding, if appropriate.

Attachments.
1. Copy of IRS tax-exempt status determination letter.
2. Copy of the most recent audited financial statements.
3. List of board of directors and officers with their affiliations.

When to apply: Anytime.
Materials available: Company annual report, Biennial "Report on Corporate Citizenship" (includes "Contribution Request Guidelines").

Emphases. *Recipients:* Nonprofit organizations.
Activities: Collaborative efforts, education.
Geography: Seattle, Washington; Portland, Oregon; Wichita, Kansas; Huntsville, Alabama; Philadelphia, Pennsylvania; Houston, Texas; and other areas of Company operations.

Limitations. *Recipients:* Individuals.
Activities: Political activities, research.
Types of support: Endowments, travel expenses.

Boettcher Foundation

600 17th Street, Suite 2210 South
Denver, Colorado 80202
Tel: 303-534-1937
EIN: 840404274   Type: Independent
Contact: William A. Douglas, Executive Director

History and philosophy. Claude K. Boettcher and his father, Charles Boettcher, incorporated the Boettcher Foundation in 1937 for "the well-being of mankind within the state of Colorado." The Foundation awards grants in the areas of: Education, Health and Hospitals, Cultural and Civic Organizations, and Community and Social Services. Giving is limited to Colorado.

Officers and directors. *Officers:* Claudia Boettcher Merthan, Chairman; Hover T. Lentz, Vice Chairman; William A. Douglas, President and Executive Director; Frederick K. Trask, III, Vice President and Assistant Secretary; John C. Mitchell, II, Secretary; George M. Wilfley, Treasurer; Edie R. Mattson, Assistant Treasurer. *Trustees:* Mrs. Charles Boettcher, II, E. Atwill Gilman, A. Barry Hirschfeld, Edward Lehman, Hover T. Lentz, Harry T. Lewis, Jr., Claudia Boettcher Merthan, John C. Mitchell, II, George M. Wilfley.

Financial data. Data for fiscal year ended December 31, 1993. *Assets:* $153,964,590 (M). *Total grants disbursed:* $7,109,106.

Environmental awards. *Recent grants:* 1993 grants included support for land conservation, beautification, parks, and a zoo.

Issues. Cli Bio Lan Agr Wat Oce Ene Was Tox Pop Dev
            •   •   •   •

Funding analysis.

Fiscal year:	1991	1993
Env grants auth:	$45,000	$1,081,000
Number:	4	7
Range:	$5,000–$25,000	$1,000–$650,000
Median:	$7,500	$50,000
Pct $ disb (env/total):	4	1

Recipients (1993 highest):	Number:	Dollars:
Denver Zoological Foundation	1	650,000
South Platte River Greenway Foundation, Inc.	1	200,000
The Nature Conservancy, Colorado Field Office	1	100,000
Colorado RiverFront Foundation	1	50,000
Pueblo Zoological Society	1	50,000

Activity region (1993):	Number:	Dollars:
U.S. Mountain	7	1,081,000

Sample grants (1993).*

Colorado RiverFront Foundation. Grand Junction, CO. $50,000. Toward completion (Phase II) of Blue Heron Trail.
Denver Zoological Foundation. Denver, CO. $650,000. Toward the Primate Panorama, Phase I.
The Nature Conservancy, Colorado Field Office. Boulder, CO. $100,000. Toward land acquisition and building at Aiken Canyon near Colorado Springs.
Pueblo Zoological Society. Pueblo, CO. $50,000. For capital improvements.
South Platte River Greenway Foundation, Inc. Denver, CO. $200,000. Toward renovation of Cherry Creek.

*Sample grants represent either new awards or disbursements on grants awarded in previous years.

Application process. *Initial contact:* Letter describing proposed project and its purpose. Formal application, if invited, to include:
1. Organization's name and address.
2. Copy of IRS tax-exempt status determination letter or a statement prepared by the organization's counsel.
3. Relationship, capacity, or title of person signing application.
4. List of officers and directors, together with the officers' occupations, positions, and places of employment.
5. Brief history of the organization, its principal programs, and accomplishments. (Especially important if the organization is new to the Foundation.) A separate document may be used.
6. Financial information, including the organization's latest annual report (preferably a certified audit or the most recent IRS Form 990) and a budget for the current year.
7. Concise and clear project description (supplemented by other material if needed) showing the need or problem and the proposed solution, its social or other significance, and its expected benefit for the citizens of Colorado. The trustees are especially interested in expected economic benefits.
8. Detailed budget for the project or program including the total amount to be raised, a list of expected funding sources, and the amount requested of the Foundation. If this is a pilot project, clearly indicate the expected and realistic sources of continued funding if the program is successful.
9. Qualifications of involved personnel.

10. An endorsement by the head of the institution, and copies of approval by regulatory agencies.
11. Program evaluation plan.
12. Description of amounts and kinds of contributed support received from foundations, corporations, and individuals, with detail. Information on last full fiscal year and current year-to-date, should be given for applicant organization and, if appropriate, for project for which funding is requested.

When to apply: Anytime.
Materials available: Annual report (includes "Guide to Applications for Grants").

Emphases. *Recipients:* Botanical gardens, museums, zoos.
Activities: Land acquisition, volunteerism.
Types of support: Capital campaigns/expenses, computer hardware, equipment, facilities.
Geography: Colorado only.

Limitations. *Recipients:* Individuals.
Activities: Research.
Types of support: Endowments.

Mary Owen Borden Memorial Foundation
160 Hodge Road
Princeton, New Jersey 08540
Tel: 609-924-3637
EIN: 136137137   Type: Independent
Contact: John Borden, Executive Director

History and philosophy. The Mary Owen Borden Memorial Foundation, established in 1934, makes grants in the areas of affordable housing, employment training and counseling, human services, conservation and environment, peace, substance abuse, education, and the arts. The Foundation's special focus is on economically disadvantaged youth at risk.

Officers and directors. *Officers:* Linda B. McKean, President; Lois Broder, Vice President; Mary L. Miles, Secretary; Joseph Lord, Treasurer; John Borden, Executive Director. *Trustees:* John Borden, Thomas A. Borden, Lois Broder, Gordon Litwin, Linda B. McKean, Mary L. Miles, Jerri Morrison, Dorothy Ransom.

Financial data. Data for fiscal year ended December 31, 1993. *Assets:* $10,050,000 (M). *Total grants disbursed:* $375,000.

Environmental awards. *Recent grants:* 1993 grants included support for open space, coastal issues, and waste management.

Issues. Cli Bio Lan Agr Wat Oce Ene Was Tox Pop Dev
              •   •   •   •   •

Funding analysis.

Fiscal year:	1991	1993
Env grants auth:	$7,500	$22,000
Number:	2	5
Range:	$2,500–$5,000	$3,000–$6,000
Median:	$3,750	$4,000
Pct $ auth (env/total):	2	6

Recipients (1993):	*Number:*	*Dollars:*
Delaware & Raritan Greenway, Inc.	1	6,000
The Trust for Public Land	1	5,000
American Littoral Society	1	4,000
Clean Water Fund	1	4,000
Poricy Park	1	3,000

Activity region (1993):	*Number:*	*Dollars:*
New York/New Jersey	5	22,000

Sample grants (1993).
American Littoral Society. Sandy Hook, NJ. $4,000. To help cover administrative expenses for this environmental organization working to preserve the New Jersey coastline through education campaigns and advocating responsible shoreline policies.
Clean Water Fund. New Brunswick NJ. $4,000. For educational efforts on their Reduce-Recycle First campaign and their environmentally sound alternatives to landfill disposals and incineration.
Delaware & Raritan Greenway, Inc. Princeton, NJ. $6,000. To fund the ongoing operations of this environmental organization which is supporting the preservation of an open space network linking regional parks and natural areas in central New Jersey.
Poricy Park. Middletown, NJ. $3,000. To cover some expenses for the teacher coordinator who will schedule teachers and volunteers for the hundreds of school children visiting the environmental center weekly.
The Trust for Public Land. Trenton, NJ. $5,000. To cover some of the purchase price for a new community park and nature retreat located in the west ward of Trenton.

Application process. *Initial contact:* Letter of inquiry describing applicant organization and proposed project. If the proposal meets Foundation guidelines, a questionnaire will be forwarded.
When to apply: Deadlines are January 1, April 1, and September 1. The board of trustees meets in January, May, and October.
Materials available: Annual report (includes "Guidelines").

Emphases. *Activities:* Advocacy, demonstration programs, education, land acquisition, technical assistance, youth programs.
Types of support: Annual campaigns, continuing support, general purposes, operating costs, pilot projects.
Geography: Mercer and Monmouth counties, New Jersey, only.

The Bothin Foundation
873 Sutter Street, Suite B
San Francisco, California 94109-6170
Tel: 415-771-4300   Fax: 415-771-4064
EIN: 941196182   Type: Independent
Contact: Lyman H. Casey, Executive Director

History and philosophy. Henry E. Bothin, his wife Ellen Chabot Bothin, and his daughter Genevieve Bothin de Limur established the Foundation (formerly the Bothin Helping Fund) in 1917. The broad purpose of the Foundation is to support public charities located in the five counties of San Francisco, Marin, Sonoma, San Mateo, and Santa Barbara. Interests are: youth, elderly, disabled, health care, minorities, community social services, and the environment. Grants for the arts are made only to groups serving youth or with youth participation.

Officers and directors. *Officers:* Genevieve Di San Faustino, President; Edmona Lyman Mansell, First Vice President; Benjamin J. Henley, Jr., Second Vice President; A. Michael Casey, Secretary; Lyman H. Casey, Treasurer. *Directors:* William W. Budge, A. Michael Casey, Lyman H. Casey, Genevieve Di San Faustino, William F. Geisler, Benjamin J. Henley, Jr., Stephanie C. MacColl, Edmona Lyman Mansell, Rhoda W. Schultz.

Financial data. Data for fiscal year ended December 31, 1993. *Assets:* $16,601,074 (U). *Total grants disbursed:* $899,849.

Environmental awards. *Recent grants:* 1993 grants included support for wilderness, urban forests, wildlife and fisheries protection, and youth education.

Issues. Cli Bio Lan Agr Wat Oce Ene Was Tox Pop Dev
         •   •   •   •   •

Funding analysis.

Fiscal year:	1993
Env grants auth:	$81,974
Number:	10
Range:	$2,200–$13,500
Median:	$8,137
Pct $ auth (env/total):	11

Recipients (1993 highest):	Number:	Dollars:
The Wilderness Society	1	13,500
Wildlife Associates	1	12,500
Pacific Crest Outward Bound School	1	12,000
Yosemite Institute	1	12,000
Camp Unalayee	1	9,200

Activity regions (1993):	Number:	Dollars:
U.S. West	9	68,474
U.S. not specified	1	13,500

Sample grants (1993).
California Center for Wildlife. San Rafael, CA. $2,200. Purchase telephone and voice mail system.
California Trout. San Francisco, CA. $7,074. Purchase computer equipment and copier.
Pacific Environmental Education Center. Mendocino, CA. $3,500.
The Wilderness Society. San Francisco, CA. $13,500. Purchase Novajet color inkjet plotter and computer equipment.
Yosemite Institute. Sausolito, CA. $12,000. Purchase walk-in refrigerator and convection oven.

Application process. *Initial contact:* Brief preliminary letter of request to include:
1. Purpose and history of the organization.
2. Project goals, objectives, and proposed budget.
3. Copy of IRS tax-exemption status determination letter.

Should additional information be desired, the Foundation will contact the applicant.

When to apply: Deadlines are in December, April, and August, ten weeks before distribution meetings held in February, June, and October.
Materials available: Biennial report (includes "Grant Making Guidelines" and "Application Procedure").

Emphases. *Types of support:* Capital campaigns/expenses, equipment, facilities.
Geography: California counties of San Francisco, Marin, Sonoma, San Mateo, and Santa Barbara.

Limitations. *Recipients:* Individuals.
Activities: Audiovisual materials, conferences, research (medical).
Types of support: Endowments, fellowships, loans, operating costs, scholarships.

Botwinick-Wolfensohn Foundation, Inc.
599 Lexington Avenue
New York, New York 10022
Tel: 212–909–8124
EIN: 136111833   Type: Independent
Contact: Jennifer Jacobson, Executive Director

History and philosophy. The Botwinick-Wolfensohn Foundation, Inc. was established in 1952. Funds are mainly committed to projects developed by the board of directors, but when funds are available, grants are given in the areas of: Jewish and Israeli interests, the homeless, music, education, social services, and medical research.

Officers and directors. *Officers:* James D. Wolfensohn, Chairman; Benjamin Botwinick, President; Edward Botwinick, Elaine Wolfensohn, Vice Presidents; Sara R. Wolfensohn, Treasurer.

Financial data. Data for fiscal year ended December 31, 1992. *Assets:* $3,531,535 (M). *Gifts received:* $1,005,000. *Total grants disbursed:* $1,599,262.

Environmental awards. *Recent grants:* 1992 grants included support for urban environment, parks, and outdoor education.

Issues. Cli Bio Lan Agr Wat Oce Ene Was Tox Pop Dev
         •   •

Funding analysis.

Fiscal year:	1992
Env grants disb:	$54,250
Number:	7
Range:	$1,000–$26,250
Median:	$4,000
Pct $ disb (env/total):	3

Recipients (1992 highest):	Number:	Dollars:
Central Park Conservancy	1	26,250
City Parks Foundation	1	15,000
Jackson Hole Land Trust	1	5,000
New York City Outward Bound Center	1	4,000
Environmental Defense Fund	1	2,000

Activity regions (1992):	Number:	Dollars:
New York/New Jersey	6	49,250
U.S. Mountain	1	5,000

Sample grant (1992).
Central Park Conservancy. New York, NY. $26,250.
City Parks Foundation. New York, NY. $15,000.
Environmental Defense Fund. New York, NY. $2,000.
Hurricane Island Outward Bound School. Rockland, ME. $4,000.
Jackson Hole Land Trust. Jackson, WY. $5,000.
New York Parks and Conservation Association. Albany, NY. $1,000.
The Preservation League of New York State. Albany, NY. $1,000.

Application process. *Initial contact:* Letter of intent including a description of organization, project, and financial requirements. *When to apply:* Anytime. The board meets annually.

Emphases. *Recipients:* Nonprofit organizations.
Types of support: Annual campaigns, capital campaigns/expenses, continuing support, facilities (construction), general purposes, projects, research, scholarships, seed money.
Geography: New York City.

Limitations. *Recipients:* Individuals.

Helen Brach Foundation
55 West Wacker Drive, Suite 701
Chicago, Illinois 60601
Tel: 312–372–4417
EIN: 237376427   Type: Independent
Contact: Raymond F. Simon, President

History and philosophy. Helen V. Brach was the wife of Frank Brach, a principal and owner of the E. J. Brach and Sons Candy Company of Chicago. Upon his retirement in 1966, Frank Brach sold the company. He died in 1970 and left the family fortune to his wife. Mrs. Brach created the Foundation in 1974 and disappeared in 1977. After she was declared legally deceased in 1984, as beneficiary, the Foundation received a bequest from the estate. Since 1985, the Foundation has awarded over $12.5 million in grants to organizations around the country.

The board has begun to develop particular areas of interest, which include "efforts to save wildlife, curtail the abuse of children and animals, provide funding for education at the secondary and college levels, and help those who serve the physically and mentally disabled, the poor, the blind, the homeless, the teenaged unwed mother, and the elderly." The Foundation generally makes smaller grants so as to serve a greater number of applicants.

Officers and directors. *Officers:* Charles M. Vorhees, Chairman; Raymond F. Simon, President; James J. O'Connor, Vice President; John J. Sheridan, Secretary/Treasurer. *Directors:* James J. O'Connor, John J. Sheridan, R. Matthew Simon, Raymond F. Simon, Charles A. Vorhees, Charles M. Vorhees.

Financial data. Data for fiscal year ended March 31, 1993. *Assets:* $69,509,958. *Total grants disbursed:* $2,455,994.

Environmental awards. *Recent grants:* 1993 grants included support for research and advocacy on wildlife, especially threatened or endangered species (elephants, primates, dolphins, cranes), and a zoo.

Issues.   Cli   Bio   Lan   Agr   Wat   Oce   Ene   Was   Tox   Pop   Dev
                      •

Funding analysis.

Fiscal year:	1991	1993
Env grants disb:	$102,000	$100,600
Number:	8	8
Range:	$5,000–$25,000	$600–$33,000
Median:	$10,000	$10,000
Pct $ disb (env/total):	5	4

Recipients (1993 highest):	Number:	Dollars:
Earth Action Network, Inc.	1	33,000
Brookfield Zoo	1	20,000
Earth News	1	12,000
Earth Island Institute	1	10,000
Environmental Investigation Agency	1	10,000
International Primate Protection League	1	10,000

Activity regions (1993):	Number:	Dollars:
U.S. not specified	3	53,000
U.S. Great Lakes	2	20,600
International*	2	15,000
U.S. West	1	12,000

*Multiple regions or not specified.

Sample grants (1993).
Brookfield Zoo. Brookfield, IL. $20,000. Support for animal health, conservation, and research on genetics and nutrition.
Earth Action Network, Inc. (E–The Environmental Magazine). Norwalk, CT. $33,000.
Earth Island Institute. San Francisco, CA. $10,000. In support of the Dolphin Project, and to prevent the use of driftnets.
Earth News. Agoura Hills, CA. $12,000.
Environmental Investigation Agency. Washington, DC. $10,000.
International Crane Foundation. Baraboo, WI. $5,000.
Lincoln Park Zoological Society. Chicago, IL. $600.

Application process. *Initial contact:* Application form (7 copies) accompanied by 1 copy of each of the following:
1. Cover letter summarizing the background and purposes of the organization and the proposed project or activity.
2. List of members of the organization's governing board.
3. Evidence of project approval from the organization's CEO or other authorized official.
4. Organization's most recent audited financial statement.
5. Copy of the IRS tax-exempt status determination letter.

When to apply: Deadline is December 31 for consideration in year ending March 31. The board meets quarterly.
Materials available: Annual report (includes "Grant Guidelines" and application form).

© 1995 Environmental Data Resources, Inc.

Emphases. *Recipients:* Museums, nonprofit organizations, zoos.
Activities: Advocacy, publications, research, projects.
Types of support: Annual campaigns, capital campaigns/expenses, equipment, facilities, general purposes, operating costs.

Limitations. *Recipients:* Individuals.
Activities: Political activities.
Types of support: Continuing support, multi-year grants.

The Lynde and Harry Bradley Foundation, Inc.
777 East Wisconsin Avenue, Suite 2285
Milwaukee, Wisconsin 53202
Tel: 414-291-9915 Fax: 414-291-9991
EIN: 396037928 Type: Independent
Contact: Michael S. Joyce, President

History and philosophy. The Lynde and Harry Bradley Foundation was established in 1985 with proceeds from the sale of the family business, the Allen-Bradley Company, an electronics firm acquired by Rockwell International Corporation.

The Foundation works "to commemorate Lynde and Harry Bradley by preserving and extending the principles and philosophy by which they lived and upon which they built the company." Among those principles are a belief in the power of ideas and the importance of political and economic freedom.

Current program areas are: Milwaukee Area Community Affairs, Independent Colleges and Universities of Wisconsin, Public Affairs, and Education.

Officers and directors. *Officers:* I. Andrew Rader, Chairman; Allen M. Taylor, Vice Chairman; Michael S. Joyce, President; Richard H. Lillie, M.D., Vice President; Hillel G. Fradkin, Vice President for Program; Wayne J. Roper, Secretary; Robert N. Berkopec, Treasurer/Assistant Secretary. *Directors:* Sarah D. Barder, Reed Coleman, Michael S. Joyce, Clayburn La Force, Richard H. Lillie, M.D., I. Andrew Rader, Wayne J. Roper, Frank Shakespeare, Allen M. Taylor, David V. Uihlein, Jr. *Honorary Director:* Urban T. Kuechle.

Financial data. Data for fiscal year ended December 31, 1993. *Assets:* $424,955,000 (M). *Total grants authorized:* $60,209,108. *Total grants disbursed:* $23,823,908.

Environmental awards. *Recent grants:* 1993 grants included support for land and wildlife conservation, coastal issues, and environmental education.

Issues. Cli Bio Lan Agr Wat Oce Ene Was Tox Pop Dev
             •   •   •   •

Funding analysis.

Fiscal year:	1990	1993
Env grants auth:	$1,521,400	$668,800
Number:	7	11
Range:	$11,900–$523,000	$2,000–$140,000
Median:	$100,000	$50,000
Pct $ auth (env/total):	8	1

Recipients (1993 highest):	Number:	Dollars:
Sand County Foundation, Inc.	2	200,000
Pamlico-Albemarle Study	1	140,000
Competitive Enterprise Institute (CEI)	1	100,000
George C. Marshall Institute	1	55,300
Harvard University, Center for Risk Analysis	1	50,000
The Nature Conservancy, Wisconsin Field Office	1	50,000

Activity regions (1993):	Number:	Dollars:
U.S. Great Lakes	6	278,500
U.S. not specified	2	155,300
U.S. Southeast	1	140,000
U.S. Northeast	1	50,000
International*	1	45,000

*Multiple regions or not specified.

Sample grants (1993).
Competitive Enterprise Institute (CEI). Milwaukee, WI. $100,000. To support a study of risk management.
Friends of Schlitz Audubon Center, Inc. Milwaukee, WI. $2,000. To support general operations.
George C. Marshall Institute. Washington, DC. $55,300. To support a study of environmental public policy issues.
Harvard University, Center for Risk Analysis. Cambridge, MA. $50,000. To support a project on risk management reform.
International Crane Foundation, Inc. Baraboo, WI. $45,000. To support an international training program.
The Nature Conservancy, Wisconsin Field Office. Madison, WI. $50,000. To support the Lulu Lake project.
Pamlico-Albemarle Study. Raleigh, NC. $140,000. To support Bradley Graduate and Post-Graduate Fellows in Environmental Policy.
Riveredge Nature Center, Inc. Newburg, WI. $20,000. To support general operations.
Sand County Foundation, Inc. Madison, WI. $200,000. To support general operations and program activities.
Wilderness Inquiry, Inc. Minneapolis, MN. $6,500. To support general program activities.

Application process. *Initial contact:* Brief letter of inquiry describing applicant organization, proposed project, and requesting guidelines and budget form. Detailed proposal, if requested, to include:
1. Objective of proposal, definition of problem being addressed, potential impact of proposal on the problem, population to benefit, and how will the population benefit.
2. Work plan and timeline for accomplishing objectives.
3. Period of time Foundation aid is required and desirable start and termination times for the support.
4. Sources of support after Foundation funding termination.
5. Discussion of whether project is new or ongoing, research performed to find similar projects, and their success or failure and why.
6. Description of evaluation plan.
7. Qualifications of individuals involved in project. (Include resumes for key personnel.)
8. Background of organization including list of board of directors/trustees.
9. Evidence of organization approval of project.

10. Most recent annual financial statement (audited if available).
11. List of other institutions participating in the project.
Guidelines and budget form.
When to apply: Deadlines are December 15, March 15, July 15, and September 15. The board of directors meets quarterly in February, May, September, and November.
Materials available: Annual report (includes "Application Procedure"), "Developing a Detailed Proposal," budget form.

Emphases. *Recipients:* Nonprofit organizations.
Activities: Conferences, education, media projects, policy analysis/development, publications, research, seminars.
Types of support: Annual campaigns, capital campaigns/expenses, continuing support, equipment, fellowships, internships, lectureships, matching funds, operating costs, professorships, scholarships.
Geography: Milwaukee and Wisconsin.

Limitations. *Recipients:* Individuals.
Types of support: Debt retirement, endowments.

Otto Bremer Foundation
445 Minnesota Street, Suite 2000
St. Paul, Minnesota 55101–2107
Tel: 612–228–8036   Fax: 612–227–2522
EIN: 416019050   Type: Independent
Contact: John Kostishack, Executive Director

History and philosophy. The Otto Bremer Foundation was established in 1944 "to enhance the quality of life in communities within the states of Minnesota, Wisconsin, and North Dakota with preference given to those communities currently served by the affiliates of Bremer Financial Corporation." Bremer, a German immigrant, was primarily a banker but also active in a broad range of political, financial, and corporate activities. Among other things, he was president of the Schmidt Brewing Company, treasurer of St. Paul, and counsel to Woodrow Wilson and Franklin D. Roosevelt.

Bremer's philanthropic interests in promoting citizenship and alleviating poverty continue to guide the Foundation today. Two areas of focus for its grantmaking activity are Racism and Rural Poverty. Other program areas are: Community Affairs, Education, Health, Human Services, and Religion.

Officers and directors. *Officers:* John Kostishack, Executive Director. *Trustees:* Charlotte S. Johnson, William H. Lipschultz, Robert J. Reardon.

Financial data. Data for fiscal years ended December 31, 1992 and 1993. *Assets (1992):* $95,805,165 (M). *Total grants disbursed (1993):* $5,624,367.

Environmental awards. *Recent grants:* 1993 awards included support for field research and environmental education.

Issues. Cli Bio Lan Agr Wat Oce Ene Was Tox Pop Dev
         •   •   •   •   •

Funding analysis.

Fiscal year:	1991	1992
Env grants auth:	$73,925	$113,150
Number:	8	12
Range:	$2,425–$24,000	$1,000–$20,000
Median:	$9,000	$10,000
Pct $ disb (env/total):	1	2

Recipients (1992 highest):	*Number:*	*Dollars:*
International Coalition for Land/Water Stewardship in the Red River Basin	1	20,000
Thomas Irvine Dodge Nature Center	1	15,900
The St. Paul Foundation	1	15,150
Clean Water Fund	1	10,000
Earthwatch Expeditions, Inc.	1	10,000
Mid-Min Rural Education and Resource Center	1	10,000
Neighbors United Resource Center	1	10,000

Activity regions (1992):	*Number:*	*Dollars:*
U.S. Great Lakes	10	108,650
U.S. Mountain	2	4,500

Sample grants (1993).
Earthwatch Expeditions, Inc. Watertown, MA. $10,000. To continue the fellowship program for teachers from rural Minnesota, North Dakota, and Wisconsin to engage in scientific field research.
Great Lakes Fish and Wildlife Commission. Odanah, WI. $1,925. To support the production and distribution of a videotape on consumption guidelines for mercury-contaminated fish.
Wilderness Inquiry. Minneapolis, MN. $5,000. To support participation of individuals with disabilities from rural communities in outdoor camping experiences and workshops.

Application process. *Initial contact:* Letter of inquiry or telephone call. Applicants are encouraged to contact Foundation staff for assistance in the development of a proposal. Proposals may be submitted through the local Bremer Bank affiliate or sent directly to the Foundation. Full proposal to include:
1. Organization's legal name, address, and telephone number; name and telephone number of contact person.
2. Description of organization including its goals, purposes, and a short history, if appropriate.
3. Description of project, what it is to achieve, and how this will be accomplished.
4. Specific amount requested.
5. Copy of IRS tax-exempt status determination letter.
6. Names and qualifications of key project staff.
7. Evidence of endorsement by the board of directors.
8. Complete project budget.
9. Audited financial statement.
10. Current operational budget.
11. Copy of most recent IRS Form 990.
12. Other funding sources.
13. Project's future plans.
14. Evaluation plans.
When to apply: Anytime. The trustees meet monthly.
Materials available: Annual report (includes "Proposal Guidelines").

© 1995 Environmental Data Resources, Inc.

Emphases. *Recipients:* Educational institutions, nonprofit organizations, public agencies.
Activities: Activism, advocacy, capacity building, citizen participation, conflict resolution, direct services, innovative programs, training, volunteerism.
Types of support: Facilities, general purposes, matching funds, multi-year grants, operating costs, program-related investments, seed money.
Geography: St. Paul, Minnesota; and Bremer-affiliated communities in Minnesota, North Dakota, and Wisconsin only.

Limitations. *Recipients:* Individuals, zoos.
Activities: Education (K–12), research.

Alexander H. Bright Charitable Trust

c/o Boston Safe Deposit & Trust Company
One Boston Place
Boston, Massachusetts 02108
Tel: 617–722–7337
EIN: 046013967   Type: Independent
Contact: Solange M. Bell, Trust Officer

History and philosophy. Established in 1952, the Trust makes grants in the areas of conservation and wildlife, education, social services, and youth.

Officers and directors. *Trustee:* Edward W. Weld.

Financial data. Data for fiscal year ended December 31, 1992. *Assets:* $2,001,573 (M). *Total grants disbursed:* $97,800.

Environmental awards. *Recent grants:* 1992 grants included support for land conservation, parks, species preservation, marine issues, and wildlife.

Issues. Cli Bio Lan Agr Wat Oce Ene Was Tox Pop Dev
              •   •   •   •   •   •   •

Funding analysis.

Fiscal year:	1992
Env grants disb:	$44,000
Number:	35
Range:	$500–$2,500
Median:	$1,250
Pct $ disb (env/total):	45

Recipients (1992 highest):	Number:	Dollars:
Natural Resources Defense Council	1	2,500
Conservation Law Foundation	1	2,000
Population-Environment Balance, Inc.	1	2,000
Sierra Club	1	2,000
Arnold Arboretum of Harvard University	1	1,500
Massachusetts Audubon Society	1	1,500
Bat Conservation International	1	1,500
Friends of the Earth/ Environmental Policy Institute	1	1,500
Greenpeace USA	1	1,500
Hurricane Island Outward Bound School	1	1,500
National Parks and Conservation Association	1	1,500
The Nature Conservancy, Headquarters	1	1,500
Trustees of Reservations	1	1,500
World Wildlife Fund	1	1,500

Activity regions (1992 highest):	Number:	Dollars:
U.S. not specified	13	18,000
U.S. Northeast	12	14,250
International*	4	5,000
U.S. South Central	1	1,500
Alaska	1	1,250

*Multiple regions or not specified.

Sample grants (1992).
The Adirondack Council, Inc. Elizabethtown, NY. $1,000.
Arnold Arboretum of Harvard University. Jamaica Plain, MA. $1,500.
Center for Marine Conservation. Washington, DC. $1,000.
Center for Plant Conservation. St. Louis, MO. $1,000.
Defenders of Wildlife. Washington, DC. $1,250.
Environmental Defense Fund. New York, NY. $1,000.
Grand Canyon Trust. Flagstaff, AZ. $1,000.
Massachusetts Audubon Society. Lincoln, MA. $1,500.
Natural Resources Defense Council. New York, NY. $2,500.
Trees for the Future. Silver Spring, MD. $1,000.
The Wilderness Society. Washington, DC. $1,250.

Application process. *Initial contact:* Letter to include:
1. Concise description of grant purpose.
2. Current year's operating budget.
3. Most recent audited financial statements.
4. List of current board members.
5. Resumes of all key staff people.
6. Copy of IRS tax-exempt status determination letter.

When to apply: Deadlines are February, May, August, and November for consideration at meetings in March, June, September, and December.

Limitations. *Recipients:* Individuals.

Alex. Brown & Sons Charitable Foundation, Inc.

c/o Alex. Brown and Sons, Inc.
135 East Baltimore Street
Baltimore, Maryland 21202
Tel: 410–727–1700
EIN: 526054236   Type: Company-sponsored
Contact: Walter W. Brewster, Secretary

History and philosophy. The Foundation was established in 1954 by Alex Brown and Sons, Inc. Areas of interest include culture, education, hospitals, social services, and conservation.

Officers and directors. *Officers:* Benjamin H. Griswold, IV, President; Truman T. Semans, Vice President; Walter W. Brewster, Secretary; Alvin B. Krongard, Treasurer.

Trustees: Walter W. Brewster, Benjamin H. Griswold, IV, F. Barton Harvey, Jr., Alvin B. Krongard, William F. Rienhoff, IV, Thomas Schweizer, Jr., Truman T. Semans, Mayo A. Shattuck, III.

Financial data. Data for fiscal year ended December 31, 1992. *Assets:* $8,438,125 (M). *Gifts received:* 2,384,353. *Total grants disbursed:* $909,542.

Environmental awards. *Recent grants:* 1992 grants include support for coastal and marine issues, river protection, an aquarium, a zoo, and outdoor education.

Issues. Cli Bio• Lan• Agr Wat• Oce• Ene Was Tox Pop Dev

Funding analysis.

Fiscal year:	1992
Env grants disb:	$57,083
Number:	9
Range:	$1,000–$22,500
Median:	$3,050
Pct $ disb (env/total):	6

Recipients (1992 highest):	Number:	Dollars:
Baltimore Zoological Society	1	22,500
Chesapeake Bay Foundation	1	13,533
National Aquarium in Baltimore	1	6,500
Garden Club of America	1	5,000
Irvine Natural Science Center	1	3,050

Activity regions (1992):	Number:	Dollars:
U.S. Mid-Atlantic	7	49,583
New York/New Jersey	2	7,500

Sample grants (1992).
Baltimore Harbor Endowment, Inc. Baltimore, MD. $1,000.
Baltimore Zoological Society. Baltimore, MD. $22,500.
Chesapeake Bay Foundation. Annapolis, MD. $13,533.
Fort Smallwood Marine Institute. Pasadena, MD. $2,000.
Garden Club of America. New York, NY. $5,000.
Garrison Forest School. Owings Mills, MD. $2,700.
Irvine Nature Science Center. Stevenson, MD. $3,050.
Maryland Save Our Streams. Glen Burnie, MD. $1,000.
Maryland Zoological Society. Baltimore, MD. $1,000.
National Aquarium in Baltimore. Baltimore, MD. $6,500.

Application process. *Initial contact:* Proposal.
When to apply: In the fall. The board meets in February, May, October, and December.

Emphases. *Recipients:* Aquariums, educational institutions, nonprofit organizations, zoos.
Types of support: Annual campaigns, capital campaigns/expenses, continuing support, endowments, facilities, general purposes, operating costs, scholarships.
Geography: Maryland.

Limitations. *Recipients:* Individuals, educational institutions (private), religious organizations (churches).

H. Barksdale Brown Charitable Trust

c/o Mercantile Safe Deposit & Trust Company
766 Old Hammonds Ferry Road
Linthicum, Maryland 21090
EIN: 526063083   Type: Independent
Contact: J. Michael Miller III, Vice President

Application address:
c/o Mercantile Safe Deposit & Trust Company
Two Hopkins Plaza
Baltimore, Maryland 21201
Tel: 410–237–5653

History and philosophy. The Trust was established in 1965. Its focus is arts and culture including theater, education, scientific research, and religious and social services.

Officers and directors. *Trustee:* Mercantile Safe Deposit & Trust Company.

Financial data. Data for fiscal year ended December 31, 1992. *Assets:* $1,004,927 (M). *Gifts received:* $35,000. *Total grants disbursed:* $100,000.

Environmental awards. *Recent grants:* 1992 grants included support for land conservation, and coastal and marine issues.

Issues. Cli Bio• Lan• Agr Wat Oce• Ene Was Tox Pop Dev

Funding analysis.

Fiscal year:	1992
Env grants disb:	$21,000
Number:	2
Range:	$1,000–$20,000
Median:	$10,500
Pct $ disb (env/total):	21

Recipients (1992):	Number:	Dollars:
The Nature Conservancy, Maryland Field Office	1	20,000
National Aquarium in Baltimore	1	1,000

Activity region (1992):	Number:	Dollars:
U.S. Mid-Atlantic	2	21,000

Sample grants (1992).
National Aquarium in Baltimore. Baltimore, MD. $1,000.
The Nature Conservancy, Maryland Field Office. Chevy Chase, MD. $20,000.

Application process. *Initial contact:* Proposal.
When to apply: Anytime.

Emphases. *Recipients:* Nonprofit organizations.
Activities: Education.
Geography: Baltimore Maryland.

Ruth H. Brown Foundation

420 North Spring
Aspen, Colorado 81611
Tel: 303-925-6071
EIN: 846023395   Type: Independent
Contact: Ruth Brown, Director

History and philosophy. The Ruth H. Brown Foundation was established in 1959. Until recently its giving was primarily for youth organizations, health services, and alcoholism treatment and research. Today the Foundation makes only environmental and population grants.

Officers and directors. *Officers:* Ruth Brown, President; David R. C. Brown, Vice President; Darcey B. Kelley, Secretary. *Director:* Ruth Brown.

Financial data. Data for fiscal years ended December 31, 1992 and 1993. *Assets (1992):* $1,563,798 (M). *Total grants disbursed (1993):* $93,000.

Environmental awards. *Program and interests:* Areas of interest include:

- Protection of critical land and wildlife resources.
- Public education programs in awareness of critical environmental issues facing the region.
- Energy conservation.

The Foundation also has "great interest in issues of access for regions that are not populated."
Recent grants: 1993 grants included support for wilderness protection, solar energy, and outdoor education.

Issues. Cli *Bio* *Lan* Agr Wat Oce *Ene* Was Tox *Pop* Dev

Funding analysis.

Fiscal year:	1992	1993
Env grants auth:	$76,000	$93,000
Number:	7	10
Range:	$4,000–$32,000	$2,000–$32,000
Median:	$6,000	$5,500
Pct $ auth (env/total):	95	100

Recipients (1993 highest):	Number:	Dollars:
Colorado Outward Bound School	1	32,000
Canyonlands Field Institute	1	15,000
Solar Technology Institute	1	10,000
Western Colorado Congress	1	10,000
The Nature Conservancy, Colorado Field Office	1	6,000

Activity region (1993):	Number:	Dollars:
U.S. Mountain	10	93,000

Sample grants (1993).
Canyonlands Field Institute. Moab, UT. $15,000.
Colorado Outward Bound School. Denver, CO. $32,000.
In Land We Trust. Creede, CO. $3,000. For the land trust.
The Nature Conservancy, Colorado Field Office. Boulder, CO. $6,000.
Solar Technology Institute. Carbondale, CO. $10,000.
Western Colorado Congress. Montrose, CO. $10,000.

Application process. *Initial contact:* Short letter of inquiry before submitting full proposal.
When to apply: Anytime.
Materials available: "Guidelines."

Emphases. *Recipients:* Nonprofit organizations, research institutions.
Activities: Education, fieldwork.
Types of support: Seed money.
Geography: Colorado and Western states.

Limitations. *Recipients:* Botanical gardens, museums, public agencies, religious organizations, zoos.
Types of support: Capital campaigns/expenses, endowments, operating costs.

W. L. Lyons Brown Foundation

c/o Louisville Community Foundation
Waterfront Plaza, Suite 1110
325 West Main Street
Louisville, Kentucky 40202
Tel: 502-585-4649
EIN: 610598511   Type: Independent
Contact: Eunice Blocker, Director

History and philosophy. The Foundation was established in 1962 by W. L. Lyons Brown and Sara S. Brown. It gives priority to organizations seeking to improve the quality of life in Kentucky. Interests include higher education, theater and the arts, and conservation.

Officers and directors. *Officers:* Ms. Ina B. Bond, President; Mrs. W. L. Lyons Brown, Secretary; Owsley Brown II, Treasurer. *Trustees:* Ms. Ina B. Bond, Martin S. Brown, Owsley Brown II, Mrs. W. L. Lyons Brown, W. L. Lyons Brown, Jr., Earl A. Dorsey, Adm. David L. McDonald, Benjamin H. Morris.

Financial data. Data for fiscal year ended December 31, 1993. *Assets:* $11,449,243 (M). *Total grants disbursed:* $535,896.

Environmental awards. *Recent grants:* 1993 grants included support for beautification, land and wildlife conservation, environmental education, and a zoo.

Issues. Cli *Bio* *Lan* Agr Wat Oce Ene Was Tox *Pop* Dev

Funding analysis.

Fiscal year:	1993
Env grants disb:	$110,833
Number:	9
Range:	$2,500–$33,333
Median:	$10,000
Pct $ disb (env/total):	21

Recipients (1993 highest):	Number:	Dollars:
Louisville Zoo Foundation, Inc.	1	33,333
University of Virginia, Department of Environmental Sciences	1	25,000
American Cave Conservation Association	1	10,000
Natural Resources Defense Council	1	10,000
The Student Conservation Association, Inc.	1	10,000
The Trust for Public Land	1	10,000

Activity regions (1993):	Number:	Dollars:
U.S. not specified	5	45,000
U.S. Southeast	2	35,833
U.S. Mid-Atlantic	1	25,000
International*	1	5,000

*Multiple regions or not specified.

Sample grants (1993).
American Cave Conservation Association. Horse Cave, KY. $10,000.

Louisville Zoo Foundation, Inc. Louisville, KY. $33,333.
University of Virginia, Department of Environmental Science. Charlottesville, VA. $25,000.
World Wildlife Fund. Washington, DC. $5,000.

Application process. *Initial contact:* Written proposal including "Contribution Request Form."
When to apply: Anytime. The board meets in October.
Materials available: Contribution Request Form.

Emphases. *Recipients:* Nonprofit organizations.
Geography: Metropolitan Louisville area and throughout Kentucky.

Limitations. *Recipients:* Individuals.

The Robert Brownlee Foundation
4125 Blackford Avenue, Suite 140
San Jose, California 95117-5330
Tel: 408-985-8596
EIN: 770131702   Type: Independent
Contact: Robert T. Borawski, President

History and philosophy. Robert Brownlee (1942–1991) was a naturalist and scientist. He created the Foundation in 1986 to support "community organizations that provide youngsters with hands-on and innovative methods of understanding the wonders of nature and the world." The Foundation preferentially funds science education programs for children grades K–12.

Officers and directors. *Officers:* Robert T. Borawski, President; Edith Eddy, Leonard Simon, Vice Presidents; Franklin Sunzeri, Secretary; Randall Blair, Treasurer. *Directors:* Randall Blair, Robert T. Borawski, Edith Eddy, Leonard Simon, Franklin Sunzeri.

Financial data. Data for fiscal year ended September 30, 1993. *Assets:* $2,263,174 (M). *Gifts received:* $324,000. *Total grants disbursed:* $162,248.

Environmental awards. *Recent grants:* 1993 grants included support for environmental educational experiences for California educators and children.

Issues.   Cli   Bio   Lan   Agr   Wat   Oce   Ene   Was   Tox   Pop   Dev
                    •   •   •

Funding analysis.

Fiscal year:	1991	1993
Env grants disb:	$71,000	$102,778
Number:	5	7
Range:	$6,000–$25,000	$1,000–$27,000
Median:	$10,000	$15,000
Pct $ disb (env/total):	66	63

Recipients (1993 highest):	Number:	Dollars:
Marine Science Institute	1	27,000
Hidden Villa Trust	1	20,000
Earthwatch Expeditions, Inc.	1	17,856
Environmental Volunteers, Inc.	1	15,000
Pacific Environmental Education Center	1	11,922

Activity region (1993):	Number:	Dollars:
U.S. West	7	102,778

Sample grants (1993).
Coyote Point Museum Association. San Mateo, CA. $10,000. For educational programs and training and general operations.
Earthwatch Expeditions, Inc. Los Angeles, CA. $17,856. Sponsors teachers to join an Earthwatch expedition.
Environmental Volunteers, Inc. Palo Alto, CA. $15,000. For educational programs and training and general operations.
Hidden Villa Trust. Los Altos, CA. $20,000. For educational programs and training.
Marine Science Institute. Redwood City, CA. $27,000. General operations.
Pacific Environmental Education Center. Mendocino, CA. $11,922. For educational programs and training.
The San Francisco Zoological Society. San Francisco, CA. $1,000. For educational programs and training.

Application process. *Initial contact:* Brief letter (2 pages) describing applicant organization, its purposes, amount requested, and proposed project. Include copies of organization's current annual budget and the IRS tax-exempt status determination letter.
When to apply: Deadlines are January 31 and July 31 for consideration at board meetings in March and September.
Materials available: Brochure.

Emphases. *Recipients:* Educational institutions, museums, nonprofit organizations.
Activities: Education, training.
Types of support: Capital campaigns/expenses, equipment, general purposes, projects.
Geography: San Francisco Bay Area and California.

Limitations. *Recipients:* Individuals.

Kathleen Price and Joseph M. Bryan Family Foundation, Inc.

One North Pointe, Suite 170
3101 North Elm Street
Greensboro, North Carolina 27408
Tel: 910–288–5455   Fax: 910–288–5458
EIN: 566046952   Type: Independent
EGA member
Contact: Robert K. Hampton, Executive Director

History and philosophy. The Kathleen Price and Joseph M. Bryan Family Foundation was established in 1955. Mrs. Bryan (1900–1984) was a daughter of Julian Price, president of Jefferson Standard Life Insurance Company. Joseph Bryan (b. 1896) was Senior Vice President of Jefferson Standard, Chairman of the Board of Pilot Life Insurance Company (now Jefferson-Pilot), and a pioneer of the broadcasting industry in the South. The Foundation's mission is to perpetuate the family's philanthropic involvement in "meaningful efforts" in North Carolina, including the arts, education, and community life.

The Foundation currently funds in the areas of: Public Interest, Education, Health, Human Service, Youth, and Arts and Culture.

Officers and directors. *Officers:* Joseph M. Bryan, Jr., President and Treasurer; S. Davis Phillips, Vice President; Robert K. Hampton, Secretary and Assistant Treasurer. *Trustees:* Joseph M. Bryan, Jr., David L. Dodson, Kathleen Bryan Edwards, Melanie Taylor Farland, Jane C. Kendall, S. Davis Phillips, John Guest Taylor. *Trustee Emeritus:* Joseph M. Bryan, Sr. *Members:* Joseph M. Bryan, Jr., Kathleen Bryan Edwards, Joel L. Fleishman, William C. Friday.

Financial data. Data for fiscal year ended December 31, 1993. *Assets:* $43,403,516 (M). *Total grants authorized:* $2,276,500.

Environmental awards. *Recent grants:* 1993 grants made within Education and Public Interest programs included support for land conservation, greenways, coastal issues, agricultural safety, toxics education, waste reduction, air quality, and energy-efficient transportation.

Issues.   Cli   Bio   Lan   Agr   Wat   Oce   Ene   Was   Tox   Pop   Dev
   •   •   •   •   •   •   •   •   •

Funding analysis.

Fiscal year:	1991	1993
Env grants auth:	$94,000	$148,500
Number:	6	15
Range:	$5,000–$40,000	$5,000–$15,000
Median:	$10,000	$10,000
Pct $ auth (env/total):	3	7

Recipients (1993 highest):	Number:	Dollars:
North Carolina Coastal Federation	1	15,000
Southern Environmental Law Center	1	15,000
The Conservation Fund	1	15,000
Mountain Area Gardeners in Communities (MAGIC)	1	11,000
Conservation Trust for North Carolina	1	10,000
Environmental Federation of North Carolina	1	10,000
Janus Farms Institute	1	10,000
North Carolina Coastal Land Trust	1	10,000
North Carolina Recycling Association	1	10,000
The Agricultural Resources Center, Inc.	1	10,000

Activity region (1993):	Number:	Dollars:
U.S. Southeast	15	148,500

Sample grants (1993).

The Agricultural Resources Center. Carrboro, NC. $10,000 challenge for the PESRed Project which promotes using alternatives to chemical pesticides through public education and technical assistance to other nonprofits.

Citizens for Waste Reduction and Recycling/Environmental Resource Center. Greensboro, NC. $7,500. To establish an environmental resource center in downtown Greensboro.

The Conservation Fund. Chapel Hill, NC. $15,000. Challenge toward support to plan, design, and implement a statewide network of greenways in North Carolina.

Conservation Trust for North Carolina. Raleigh, NC. $10,000. Challenge toward establishment of a statewide organization to help local and regional land trusts, communities, and public and private landowners protect property having scenic, cultural, and recreational value.

Environmental Federation of North Carolina. Durham, NC. $10,000. Challenge toward expansion of a workplace-giving campaign providing ongoing, operating support to a coalition of 20 environmental organizations in North Carolina.

The Nature Conservancy, North Carolina Field Office. Carrboro, NC. $7,500. To develop a preservation plan, including on-site mapping and aerial surveys, to protect 2,600 acres along the Black River whose banks contain the oldest living trees east of the Rocky Mountains.

Southern Environmental Law Center. Charlottesville, VA. $15,000. Toward initiation of the Western North Carolina Clean Air Project to improve air quality by working with environmental groups to develop and implement strategies to reduce air pollution.

Application process. *Initial contact:* Telephone call, personal visit, or full application to include:

1. Completed application form (in annual report).
2. Proposal (2 pages).
   - Description of need for project or program.
   - What it seeks to accomplish and when, where, and how.
   - Description of applicant organization.
   - Method and criteria for evaluation.
   - Other relevant information.
3. Line-item budget identifying projected expenses and income for project or program.
4. Current operating budget for organization.
5. Names and addresses of members of governing board.
6. Copy of most recent financial report for the organization, audited if available.
7. Copy of IRS tax-exempt status determination letter.
8. Additional materials if desired.

The Foundation does not consider grant requests for amounts under $5,000.

When to apply: Deadlines are March 1 and September 1. The trustees meet in May and November.

Materials available: Annual report (includes "Grantmaking Policies and Interests," "Application Information," and "Application Form").

Emphases. *Recipients:* Small nonprofit organizations.
Activities: Direct services.
Types of support: Endowments, equipment, facilities, matching funds, operating costs, program-related investments.
Geography: Greensboro and Guilford County; rural communities with financial need, and North Carolina.

Limitations. *Recipients:* Individuals.
Activities: Audiovisual materials, conferences, publications, research.
Types of support: Annual campaigns, travel expenses.

The Buchanan Family Foundation
222 East Wisconsin Avenue
Lake Forest, Illinois 60045
Tel: 708–234–0235
EIN: 366160998   Type: Independent
Contact: Huntington Eldridge, Jr., Treasurer

History and philosophy. DeWitt Wheeler Buchanan, Sr. and DeWitt Wheeler Buchanan, Jr. established the Foundation in 1967. The senior Buchanan was chairman of Old Ben Coal Company (which merged with Standard Oil of Ohio). The junior Buchanan was formerly president of Old Ben Coal Company and a director of Standard Oil Company of Ohio.

The Foundation funds in the areas of culture, environment, health, and higher education.

Officers and directors. *Officers:* Kenneth H. Buchanan, President; G. M. Walsh, Vice President and Secretary; Huntington Eldridge, Jr., Treasurer. *Directors:* Kenneth H. Buchanan, Kent Chandler, Huntington Eldridge, Huntington Eldridge, Jr., G. M. Walsh.

Financial data. Data for fiscal year ended December 31, 1992.
Assets: $40,559,297 (M). *Total grants disbursed:* $2,155,000.

Environmental awards. *Recent grants:* 1992 grants included support for land conservation, species preservation, and a zoo and an aquarium.

Issues.   Cli Bio Lan Agr Wat Oce Ene Was Tox Pop Dev
              •   •   •   •

Funding analysis.

Fiscal year:	1990	1992
Env grants disb:	$290,000	$345,000
Number:	11	12
Range:	$5,000–$100,000	$5,000–$100,000
Median:	$20,000	$22,500
Pct $ disb (env/total):	16	16

Recipients (1992 highest):	Number:	Dollars:
Chicago Horticultural Society	1	100,000
John G. Shedd Aquarium	1	50,000
Ducks Unlimited, Inc.	1	35,000
The Chicago Academy of Sciences	1	30,000
The Nature Conservancy, Illinois Field Office	1	30,000

Activity region (1992):	Number:	Dollars:
U.S. Great Lakes	12	345,000

Sample grants (1992).
The Chicago Academy of Science. Chicago, IL. $30,000.
Chicago Horticultural Society. Glencoe, IL. $100,000.
Chicago Zoological Society. Brookfield, IL. 20,000.
Ducks Unlimited, Inc. Northbrook, IL. $35,000.
International Crane Foundation. Baraboo, WI. $25,000.
Lake Forest Open Lands Association. Lake Forest, IL. $15,000.
Lincoln Park Zoological Society. Chicago, IL. $20,000.
The Morton Arboretum. Lisle, IL $10,000.
The Nature Conservancy, Illinois Field Office. Chicago, IL. $30,000.
Open Lands Project. Chicago, IL $5,000.
John G. Shedd Aquarium. Chicago, IL. $50,000.

Application process. *Initial contact:* Letter of inquiry. The Foundation generally funds pre-selected organizations and does not encourage unsolicited proposals.

Emphases. *Recipients:* Pre-selected organizations.
Geography: Chicago area.

Jessie Margaret Wilson Budlong Foundation for Animal Aid
c/o Hahn Gaintner & Associates
2198 East Camelback Road, Suite 205
Phoenix, Arizona 85016–4746
Tel: 602–381–0381
EIN: 860411447   Type: Independent
Contact: Frances W. Budlong, President

History and philosophy. The Jessie Margaret Wilson Budlong Foundation for Animal Aid supports animal welfare organizations with feeding, veterinary services, and maintaining Homes for Displaced Animals programs.

Officers and directors. *Officers:* Frances W. Budlong, President; Louise Frasher, Vice President; Richard Elliot, Secretary. *Directors:* Frances W. Budlong, Richard Elliot, Louise Frasher, Clara Howes, Frederick G. Lopes.

Financial data. Data for fiscal year ended December 31, 1991.
Assets: $90,095 (M). *Gifts received:* $80,000. *Total grants disbursed:* $27,755.

Environmental awards. *Program and interests:* The Foundation supports animal welfare through protection of animals and their habitats.

B

Issues. *Cli* **Bio** *Lan* **Agr** *Wat Oce Ene Was Tox Pop Dev*

Funding analysis.

Fiscal year:	1991
Env grants disb:	$5,200
Number:	16
Range:	$100–$500
Median:	$310
Pct $ disb (env/total):	19

Recipients (1991 highest):	Number:	Dollars:
Earth Island Institute	1	500
Greenpeace USA	2	500
National Audubon Society	1	500
National Parks and Conservation Association	1	500
National Wildlife Federation	2	500
Natural Resources Defense Council	1	500
World Wildlife Fund	1	500

Activity regions (1991):	Number:	Dollars:
U.S. not specified	13	4,400
International*	2	600
U.S. South Central	1	200

*Multiple regions or not specified.

Sample grants (1991).
American Rivers Inc. Washington, DC. $200.
Animal Protection Institute of America. Sacramento, CA. $500.
Center for Marine Conservation. Washington, DC. $100.
Environmental Defense Fund. New York, NY. $400.
Greenpeace USA. Washington, DC. $320.
Liberty Wildlife. Scottsdale, AZ. $100.
National Audubon Society. New York, NY. $500.
National Wildlife Federation. Washington, DC. $240.
Primarily Primates. San Antonio, TX. $200.
Sierra Club Legal Defense Fund. San Francisco, CA. $300.
The Wilderness Society. Washington, DC. $400.
World Wildlife Fund. Washington, DC. $500.

Application process. *Initial contact:* Letter stating purpose of grant. The Foundation's only limitation is that no more than $1,000 be spent annually on any given animal.
When to apply: Anytime.

The Bullitt Foundation

1212 Minor Avenue
Seattle, Washington 98101–2825
Tel: 206–343–0807   Fax: 206–343–0822
EIN: 916027795   Type: Independent
EGA member
Contact: Emory F. Bundy, Director

History and philosophy. The Bullitt Foundation was established in 1952 by Dorothy S. Bullitt, founder of King Broadcasting in Seattle. The Foundation has one primary goal: to protect and restore the natural physical environment of the Pacific Northwest. The Foundation prefers to fund projects that leverage resources, show possibilities for multiplier effects, address priority needs where government fails, and show discernible impact.

Officers and directors. *Officers:* Priscilla B. Collins, Chair; Denis A. Hayes, President; Katharine M. Bullitt, Vice President; David D. Buck, Secretary and Attorney; Stimson Bullitt, Treasurer; Emory F. Bundy, Director. *Trustees:* Pamela H. Brewster, Harriet S. Bullitt, Douglass A. Raff.

Financial data. Data for fiscal year ended December 31, 1993. *Assets:* $88,300,000 (C). *Total grants disbursed:* $4,198,941.

Environmental awards. *Program and interests:* The Foundation is committed to protect and restore the environment of the Northwest. Particular interests include:

- Puget Sound and the Strait of Georgia drainage basins.

  To reduce waste flow; restore streams, estuaries, and wetlands; and to regenerate a productive marine environment.

- The Columbia River Basin.

  To restore fish populations, assure sufficient water quantity, and markedly reduce the burden of pollutants.

- Open space.

  To acquire critical lands for their ecological value and recreational opportunities; manage growth to protect environmentally sensitive areas, agricultural lands, and forests; and preserve open space and separate communities.

- Northwest forests.

  To ensure careful management to maintain water quality, preserve biological diversity, and ensure the long-term health of northwestern forests and fisheries.

- Energy efficiency and transportation.

  To increase economic efficiency and environmental protection.

- Environmental justice.

  To promote robust, diverse, sustainable economies in urban and rural communities.

Issues. *Cli* **Bio** *Lan* **Agr** *Wat* **Oce** *Ene* **Was** *Tox* **Pop** *Dev*

Funding analysis.

Fiscal year:	1991	1993
Env grants auth:	$2,191,227	$4,189,441
Number:	60	152
Range:	$2,773–$250,000	$1,000–$150,000
Median:	$23,000	$20,000
Pct $ auth (env/total):	95	

Recipients (1993 highest):	Number:	Dollars:
Natural Resources Defense Council	1	150,000
People for Puget Sound	1	150,000
KCTS/9 Public Television	1	127,500
Washington Environmental Council	2	110,000
Alaska Conservation Foundation	1	100,000
Sierra Club Legal Defense Fund	1	100,000

Activity regions (1993):	Number:	Dollars:
U.S. Northwest	131	3,591,391
Canada	10	399,550
Alaska	4	129,000
U.S. Mountain	7	69,500

Sample grants (1993).
Alaska Conservation Foundation. Anchorage, AK. $100,000. Design and implementation of the Coastal Rainforest Campaign, an integrated forest conservation plan for southeast Alaska, the Cape Yakataga Coast, and Prince William Sound–Western Gulf.
Coast Range Association. Newport, OR. $25,000. To expand membership, strengthen the organization's ability to restore important coastal lands to a natural state, and promote sustainable timber and tourism practices.
Convenio de Raices Mexicanas. Phoenix, OR. $7,500. Pesticide awareness campaign for seasonal and migrant farmworkers in which community organizing, leadership development, and advocacy are used to address social and economic justice issues and effect institutional change.
Government Accountability Project. Seattle, WA. $35,000. To protect whistleblowers when they report violations of laws and safety standards regarding environmental hazards at Hanford, the world's largest repository of high-level nuclear wastes.
Idaho Conservation League. Boise, ID. $10,000. To support the project attorney at Wild Idaho Legal Project. Created in cooperation with Sierra Club Legal Defense Fund's northwest office and the Idaho Conservation League, the Project provides legal services to Idaho's conservation movement.
Mineral Policy Center. Washington, DC. $25,000. For the Northwest Circuit Rider project, which provides technical assistance to local, state, and regional groups working on mineral-related environmental concerns.
Prince William Sound Science Center. Cordova, AK. $13,000. Ecosystem monitoring program. Founded after the Exxon Valdez spill, the Center conducts scientific research on the Prince William Sound and Copper River regions' ecosystems and both educates and encourages local and regional participation in natural resource stewardship.
Thoreau Center. Portland, OR. $25,000. To improve public forest management. The Center provides research, consulting, and educational services to the environmental community.
University of Washington School of Law. Seattle, WA. $30,000. To found a Natural Resources/Environmental Law Center.
Wetlands Conservancy. Tualatin, OR. $35,000. To develop grassroots strategies for regional watershed protection involving public agencies, private landowners, and the business community. The Conservancy is a land trust that helps to acquire, restore, and manage Oregon wetlands and associated upland habitat.

Application process. *Initial contact:* Request "The Bullitt Foundation Grant Guidelines." Application procedures vary according to the size of the request.
When to apply: Deadlines are April 1, August 1, December 1.
Materials available: Annual report, "The Bullitt Foundation Grant Guidelines."

Emphases. *Recipients:* Educational institutions, nonprofit organizations. *Activities:* Advocacy, audiovisual materials, capacity building, citizen participation, collaborative efforts, education, fieldwork, innovative programs, land acquisition, litigation.
Types of support: Continuing support, emergency funding, general purposes, leveraging funds, loans, matching funds, operating costs, projects, single-year grants only, start-up costs.
Geography: The Pacific Northwest: Washington, Oregon, Idaho, western Montana, Alaska's coastal rainforests, and British Columbia.

Limitations. *Recipients:* Aquariums, individuals, museums, zoos. *Activities:* Conflict resolution, direct services, exhibits, expeditions/tours, feasibility studies, lobbying, political activities, research, seminars, technical assistance.
Types of support: Capital campaigns/expenses, computer hardware, debt retirement, facilities, fellowships, indirect costs, mortgage reduction, multi-year grants, professorships, scholarships.

The Bunbury Company, Inc.
169 Nassau Street
Princeton, New Jersey 08542
Tel: 609–683–1414 Fax: 609–683–0206
EIN: 136066172 Type: Independent
Contact: Barbara L. Ruppert, Assistant Secretary

History and philosophy. The Bunbury Company, Inc., is a private grantmaking foundation created in 1952 by Dean Mathey (1890–1972). Mr. Mathey was a longstanding trustee of Princeton University and the benefactor of many other educational and charitable institutions in New Jersey. Bunbury's grantmaking focus is on New Jersey organizations whose focus is handicapped or underprivileged youth, ecological and environmental concerns, the encouragement of arts, and education in its broadest sense.

Officers and directors. *Officers:* Samuel W. Lambert, III, President and CEO; Edward J. Toohey, Vice President; Charles C. Townsend, Jr., Secretary; James R. Cogan, Treasurer; Barbara L. Ruppert, Assistant Secretary; William McGuigan, Assistant Treasurer. *Directors:* Charles B. Atwater, James R. Cogan, Samuel W. Lambert, III, Stephan A. Morse, Robert M. Olmsted, Edward J. Toohey, Charles C. Townsend, Jr., William B. Wright, Edward J. Zuccaro.

Financial data. Data for fiscal year ended December 31, 1993. *Assets:* $14,146,266 (U). *Total grants disbursed:* $680,370.

Environmental awards. *Recent grants:* 1993 grants included support for land and water protection.

Issues. Cli Bio Lan Agr Wat Oce Ene Was Tox Pop Dev
• • • • •

Funding analysis.

Fiscal year:	1993
Env grants disb:	$17,500
Number:	5
Range:	$2,000–$5,000
Median:	$3,000
Pct $ disb (env/total):	3

Recipients (1993):	Number:	Dollars:
Delaware & Raritan Greenway, Inc.	1	5,000
Stony Brook–Millstone Watershed Association	1	5,000
The Nature Conservancy, New Jersey Field Office	1	3,000
New Jersey Conservation Foundation	1	2,500
Burlington Community Land Trust	1	2,000

Activity regions (1993):	Number:	Dollars:
New York/New Jersey	4	15,500
U.S. Northeast	1	2,000

Sample grants (1993).
Burlington Community Land Trust. Burlington, VT. $2,000.
Delaware & Raritan Greenway, Inc. Princeton, NJ. $5,000.
The Nature Conservancy, New Jersey Field Office. Pottersville, NJ. $3,000.
New Jersey Conservation Foundation. Morristown, NJ. $2,500.
Stony Brook–Millstone Watershed Association. Pennington, NJ. $5,000.

Application process. *Initial contact:* Information/Summary Sheet (from Foundation) and proposal to include:
1. Letter or memorandum describing the project to be funded.
2. Most recent balance sheet and income statement (preferably a certified public auditor's report).
3. Budget for the forthcoming year to fund the operation.
4. Copy of the IRS tax-exempt status determination letter that will classify the organization as a "public charity."

When to apply: Anytime. The board meets quarterly.
Materials available: Annual report, information summary sheet.

Emphases. *Recipients:* Educational institutions (higher/secondary), museums, nonprofit organizations.
Activities: Advocacy, audiovisual materials, collaborative efforts, direct services, education, exhibits, innovative programs, land acquisition, litigation, networking, planning, policy analysis/development, publications, workshops, youth programs.
Types of support: Annual campaigns, capital campaigns/expenses, computer hardware, continuing support, emergency funding, endowments, equipment, facilities, general purposes, maintenance, operating costs, pilot projects, projects, scholarships, seed money, start-up costs.
Geography: New Jersey only.

Limitations. *Recipients:* Individuals, pre-selected organizations only, public agencies, research institutions.
Activities: Conferences, research.
Types of support: Advertising campaigns, debt retirement, fellowships, loans, membership campaigns, mortgage reduction, technical assistance, travel expenses.

The Bush Foundation
E–900 First National Bank Building
332 Minnesota Street
St. Paul, Minnesota 55101
Tel: 612–227–0891   Fax: 612–297–6485
EIN: 416017815   Type: Independent
Contact: John W. Archabal, Senior Vice President

History and philosophy. The Bush Foundation was established in 1953 by Archibald Granville Bush and his wife, Edyth Bassler Bush. Bush worked at the 3M Company from 1909 to 1964, moving from assistant bookkeeper to chairman of the executive committee over the course of his career.

The Bush Foundation is predominantly a regional grantmaking foundation, with broad interests in education, human services, health, arts and humanities, and leadership development. Recent initiatives include: Education for Blacks, Native Americans, and Women; Rural Areas; Child Development; and Public Policy. Most recipients are located in Minnesota, North Dakota, South Dakota, or western Wisconsin.

Officers and directors. *Officers:* Thomas E. Holloran, Chairman; Frank B. Wilderson, Jr., First Vice Chairman; Anita M. Pampusch, Second Vice Chairman; Humphrey Doermann, President; John W. Archabal, Senior Vice President, Ellen Z. Green, Secretary; Richard D. McFarland, Treasurer. *Directors:* Sharon Sayles Belton, Merlin E. Dewing, Phyllis B. France, Ellen Z. Green, Thomas E. Holloran, Richard D. McFarland, John A. McHugh, Diana E. Murphy, Anita M. Pampusch, Kennon V. Rothchild, W. Richard West, Jr., Frank B. Wilderson, Jr., C. Angus Wurtele, Ann Wynia.

Financial data. Data for fiscal year ended November 30, 1993. *Assets:* $469,008,000. *Total grants disbursed:* $21,446,791.

Environmental awards. *Recent grants:* 1993 grants included support for wetlands and prairie protection, air quality, and recycling.

Issues.   Cli   Bio   Lan   Agr   Wat   Oce   Ene   Was   Tox   Pop   Dev
          •   •   •   •   •   •

Funding analysis.

Fiscal year:	1991	1993
Env grants auth:	$113,254	$500,411
Number:	3	7
Range:	$33,800–$45,000	$25,000–$102,820
Median:	$34,454	$75,000
Pct $ auth (env/total):	1	2

Recipients (1993 highest):	Number:	Dollars:
The Nature Conservancy, Headquarters	1	102,820
Prairie Island Tribal Council	1	101,831
Midwest Assistance Program, Inc.	1	95,760
Minnesota Food Association	1	75,000
Minnesota Audubon Society	1	60,000

Activity regions (1993):	Number:	Dollars:
U.S. Great Lakes	5	301,831
U.S. Mountain	2	198,580

Sample grants (1993).
Citizens for a Better Environment. Minneapolis, MN. $40,000. Continuing support for the Good Neighbor Project.
Midwest Assistance Program, Inc. New Prague, MN. $95,760. For a small community recycling assistance program in South Dakota.
Minnesota Center for Environmental Advocacy. St. Paul, MN. $25,000. For the Clean Air Project.
Minnesota Audubon Society. St. Paul, MN. $60,000. For the wetlands program at the Minnesota office.
The Nature Conservancy, Headquarters. Arlington, VA. $102,820. For the Northern Tallgrass Prairie Project of the Minnesota and Dakotas chapters.

Application process. *Initial contact:* Full proposal (2 copies) to include:
1. Organization information.
   - Organization's full name, address, and the name and position of the proposal contact person.
   - List of all involved officers and their qualifications.
   - Brief history and description of organization.
   - Organization's budget and most recent audited balance sheet.
   - Copy of IRS tax-exempt status determination letter, and a current declaration signed by an officer of organization that it has not received notice of any adverse action by the IRS with respect to its status or classification.
2. Project information.
   - Clear, concise project description, including needs statement and project goals.
   - Detailed project budget, including payment timeline and other sources of support.
   - Method of evaluation of the grant and the project.
   - Explanation of continuation of project past period of Foundation support.
   - Description of any similar work done by any other agencies, and the significance of this prior work to the current proposal.
   - Research proposals should be written so as to be understood by non-specialists, and also so that the specific work plan may be reviewed and understood by consultants in the specific discipline involved.

When to apply: Deadlines are January 1 (on odd-numbered years only), March 1, July 1, and November 1. The board meets quarterly.
Materials available: Annual report (includes "Grant Making Policies and Procedures").

Emphases. *Recipients:* Nonprofit organizations.
Geography: Minnesota, North Dakota, South Dakota.

Limitations. *Recipients:* Individuals.
Activities: Conferences, research (medical/scholarly), seminars.
Types of support: Continuing support, debt retirement, endowments, facilities (construction), general purposes, loans, operating costs, program-related investments.
Geography: Projects outside the United States.

B

The Butler Foundation
c/o Charter Trust Company
P.O. Box 1374
Concord, New Hampshire 03302
Tel: 603–224–1350   Fax: 603–224–1135
EIN: 222701588   Type: Independent
Contact: Clara W. Butler, Trustee

History and philosophy. The Butler Foundation, previously known as the Neslab Charitable Foundation, was established in 1985. Funding priorities include conservation, historic preservation, religion, youth, and women.

Officers and directors. *Trustees:* Bonnie B. Bunning, Barbara Y. Butler, Clara W. Butler, Marjorie W. Butler, Thomas Y. Butler, Henry Horner, Charter Trust Company.

Financial data. Data for fiscal year ended December 31, 1992. *Assets:* $2,604,108 (M). *Gifts received:* $14,260. *Total grants disbursed:* $66,000.

Environmental awards. *Recent grants:* 1992 grants included support for land conservation and river protection.

Issues.   Cli   Bio   Lan   Agr   Wat   Oce   Ene   Was   Tox   Pop   Dev
             •   •   •   •

Funding analysis.

Fiscal year:	1992
Env grants disb:	$58,000
Number:	5
Range:	$500–$50,000
Median:	$1,000
Pct $ disb (env/total):	88

Recipients (1992):	Number:	Dollars:
The Nature Conservancy, Headquarters	1	50,000
The Nature Conservancy, New Hampshire Field Office	1	6,000
Stewards of the Platte River	1	1,000
Friends of Odiorne Point	1	500
Plymouth State College, Environmental Science Department	1	500

Activity regions (1992):	Number:	Dollars:
U.S. not specified	1	50,000
U.S. Northeast	3	7,000
U.S. Midwest	1	1,000

Sample grants (1992).
Friends of Odiorne Point. Durham, NC. $500.
The Nature Conservancy, Headquarters. Arlington, VA. $50,000.
The Nature Conservancy, New Hampshire Field Office. Concord, NH. $6,000.
Stewards of the Platte River. Grand Island, NE. $1,000.

Application process. *Initial contact:* Letter.
When to apply: Anytime.

© 1995 Environmental Data Resources, Inc.

J. E. & Z. B. Butler Foundation, Inc.

c/o Schapiro Wisan & Krassner
122 East 42nd Street
New York, New York 10168-0005
Tel: 212-687-8440
EIN: 136082916   Type: Independent
Contact: Beatrice Doniger, President

History and philosophy. Established in 1958 by Jack E. and Zella B. Butler, the Foundation makes grants in the areas of Jewish welfare, health, social services, family services, cultural programs, and education.

Officers and directors. Beatrice Doniger, President; Bruce Doniger, Carole Parrish, Ruth Pearson, Vice Presidents; Joshua Morrison, Secretary; Leon Glaser, Treasurer. *Directors:* Beatrice Doniger, Bruce Doniger, Leon Glaser, Joshua Morrison, Carole Parrish, Ruth Pearson.

Financial data. Data for fiscal year ended December 31, 1992. *Assets:* $64,689,499 (M). *Gifts received:* $1,872,471. *Total grants disbursed:* $3,423,405.

Environmental awards. *Recent grants:* 1992 grants included support for air quality.

Issues. Cli Bio Lan Agr Wat Oce Ene Was Tox Pop Dev
                                •   •

Funding analysis.

Fiscal year:	1992
Env grants disb:	$150,000
Number:	2
Range:	$50,000–$100,000
Median:	$75,000
Pct $ disb (env/total):	4

Recipient (1992):	Number:	Dollars:
Natural Resources Defense Council	2	150,000

Activity region (1992):	Number:	Dollars:
U.S. not specified	2	150,000

Sample grants (1992).
Natural Resources Defense Council New York, NY. $100,000. Capital program.
Natural Resources Defense Council. New York, NY. $50,000. Clean air program.

Application process. *Initial contact:* The J. E. & Z. B. Butler Foundation, Inc. awards grants to pre-selected organizations only. No unsolicited applications accepted.

Emphases. *Recipients:* Pre-selected organizations only.
Geography: Primarily New York City.

Limitations. *Recipients:* Individuals.

Patrick and Aimee Butler Family Foundation

E-1420 First Bank Building
332 Minnesota Street
St. Paul, Minnesota 55101-1369
Tel: 612-222-2565
EIN: 416009902   Type: Independent
EGA member
Contact: Sandra K. Butler, Program Director

History and philosophy. Patrick and Aimee Mott Butler established the Foundation in 1951. Its mission is "to provide support for solid, progressive ideas in the areas of arts and culture, education, environment, social service, and social change." Program areas are: arts & culture, education, environment, philanthropy, and social services. Emphasis is placed on organizations that serve the St. Paul and Minneapolis area. A modest number of grants are made in Greater Minnesota and outside the state. Some international projects are funded but the sponsor must have headquarters in the United States and a longstanding relationship with the Foundation.

Officers and directors. *Officers:* Peter M. Butler, President; Patrick Butler, Jr., Vice President; Terence N. Doyle, Secretary; John K. Butler, Treasurer. *Trustees:* Cecelia M. Butler, Ellen M. Butler, Patricia M. Butler, Paul S. Butler, Sandra K. Butler, Suzanne A. LeFevour, Kate B. Peterson.

Financial data. Data for fiscal year ended December 31, 1993. *Assets:* $9,857,536 (M). *Gifts received:* $350,000. *Total grants disbursed:* $921,200.

Environmental awards. *Program and interests:* The Butler Family Foundation seeks to preserve and maintain natural resources for public use and enjoyment through Foundation initiated programs addressing one or more of its priority issues. Water quality of the Mississippi River in Minnesota, environmental education, land use and preservation, and sustainable agriculture are areas of particular interest to trustees.

Participation by the Foundation in environmental programs may range from annual support to multiple year collaboratives. Environmental proposals are by invitation only. This program area will be reviewed periodically by trustees.

Recent grants: 1994 grants included support for land conservation, water protection, sustainable agriculture, and outdoor education.

Issues. Cli Bio Lan Agr Wat Oce Ene Was Tox Pop Dev
                  •   •   •   •

Funding analysis.

Fiscal year:	1994
Env grants disb:	$80,300
Number:	7
Range:	$800–$40,000
Median:	$6,000
Pct $ disb (env/total):	9

Recipients (1994 highest):	Number:	Dollars:
Trustees of Reservations	1	40,000
Woods Hole Research Center	1	15,000
Technoserve	1	12,000

The Nature Conservancy, Minnesota Field Office	1	6,000
Freshwater Foundation	1	5,000

Activity regions (1994):	Number:	Dollars:
U.S. Northeast	1	40,000
Global	1	15,000
U.S. Great Lakes	4	13,300
Mexico and Central America	1	12,000

Sample grants (1994).
Freshwater Foundation. Wayzata, MN. $5,000.
The Minnesota Project. St. Paul, MN. $2,000.
Minnesota Parks and Trails Council and Foundation. St. Paul, MN. $3,000.
The Nature Conservancy, Minnesota Field Office. Minneapolis, MN. $6,000.
Technoserve. Norwalk, CT. $12,000.
Trustees of Reservations. Beverly, MA. $40,000.
Voyageur Outward Bound School. Minnetonka, MN. $1,500.
Woods Hole Research Center. Woods Hole, MA. $15,000.

Application process. *Initial contact:* Contact Foundation for a Letter of Intent Application. The trustees will request a full proposal if letter is approved.
When to apply: The 1995 deadline for letters is April 28. The trustees meet in June to review letters and in December to review full proposals.
Materials available: "Annual Report and Grant Guidelines," "Letter of Intent Application."

Emphases. *Recipients:* Nonprofit organizations.
Types of support: Annual campaigns, capital campaigns/expenses, continuing support, endowments, facilities, single-year grants only.
Geography: Minneapolis–St. Paul area, Minnesota.

Limitations. *Recipients:* Individuals.
Activities: Audiovisual materials, education (elementary/secondary), media projects, research (health/medical).
Types of support: Loans.

The Bydale Foundation
11 Martine Avenue
White Plains, New York 10606
Tel: 914–428–3232 Fax: 914–428–1660
EIN: 136195286 Type: Independent
Contact: Milton D. Solomon, Vice President

History and philosophy. The Bydale Foundation was incorporated in 1965. Interests include the arts and cultural programs, civil rights, education, the environment, health services, human rights, peace, public policy, and world affairs.

Officers and directors. *Officers:* Joan M. Warburg, President; Milton D. Solomon, Vice President and Secretary; Frank J. Kick, Treasurer. *Trustees:* Sarah W. Bliumis, Milton D. Solomon, James P. Warburg, Jr., Jennifer J. Warburg, Joan M. Warburg, Philip N. Warburg.

Financial data. Data for fiscal year ended December 31, 1993. *Assets:* $10,327,888 (M). *Total grants disbursed:* $400,750.

Environmental awards. *Recent grants:* 1993 grants included support for energy conservation, water quality, wildlife preservation, and toxics.

Issues. Cli Bio Lan Agr Wat Oce Ene Was Tox Pop Dev
            •   •   •   •   •

Funding analysis.§

Fiscal year:	1993
Env grants disb:	$37,500
Number:	4
Range:	$2,500–$20,000
Median:	$9,000
Pct $ disb (env/total):	9

Recipients (1993 highest):	Number:	Dollars:
Greenhouse Crisis Foundation	1	20,000
Clean Water Fund	1	5,000
The Israel Union for Environmental Defense	1	10,000
National Audubon Society	1	2,500

Activity regions (1993):	Number:	Dollars:
U.S. not specified	3	27,500
Middle East and Western Asia	1	10,000

§As reported by Foundation.

Sample grants (1993).
Clean Water Fund. Washington, DC. $5,000.
Greenhouse Crisis Foundation. Washington, DC. $20,000.
National Audubon Society. New York, NY. $2,500.

Application process. *Initial contact:* Letter briefly describing the proposal.
When to apply: Submit letter by November 1, preferably in July or August.

Emphases. *Activities:* Conferences, publications, research, seminars.
Types of support: Continuing support, matching funds, operating costs, seed money.

Limitations. *Recipients:* Individuals.
Activities: Demonstration programs.
Types of support: Annual campaigns, capital campaigns/expenses, debt retirement, emergency funding, endowments, fellowships, loans, scholarships.

C. S. Fund

469 Bohemian Highway
Freestone, California 95472
Tel: 707–874–2942   Fax: 707–874–1734
EIN: 953607882   Type: Independent
EGA member
Contacts: Martin Teitel, Executive Director
Roxanne Turnage, Deputy Director

History and philosophy. Established in 1981 by Maryanne Mott and Herman E. Warsh, the C. S. Fund seeks to address the global threats that endanger human survival. To do this it works "to expand our collective thinking beyond the habitual limits in order to discover and foster creative, imaginative, and effective strategies for survival." In addition to its grantmaking activities, the Fund operates a livestock breeding conservancy. The C. S. Fund administers its own grants and those of its sister fund, the Warsh-Mott Legacy. Both funds should be considered together (and applicants should apply only once), since they share a common grantmaking philosophy.

The Fund makes the majority of its grants in two categories: dissent and the environment. Within each of these broad categories the Fund has particular areas of interest. Over the next two years the Fund will be evaluating two other granting categories: peace and security, and children's health and the environment. During this period, the fund will be making a very limited number of grants in these areas.

Officers and directors. *Directors:* Maryanne Mott, Marise Meynet Stewart, Herman E. Warsh, Michael Warsh.

Financial data.* Data for fiscal years ended October 31, 1993 and 1994. *Assets (1993):* $473,372 (M). *Gifts received (1993):* $1,200,000. *Total grants disbursed (1994):* $696,500.

*C. S. Fund only.

Environmental awards. *Program and interests:* The Fund's environmental funding aims to encourage biological diversity and to eliminate toxins at their source. Its goals are:

- Conserving the rich diversity of food crop and livestock germplasm.
- Preventing the irreversible alteration of the earth's genetic legacy.
- Reducing or eliminating the production of toxic materials.
- Assessing the total burden of toxins on the biosphere and acting to reduce that burden.

Issues.   Cli   Bio   Lan   Agr   Wat   Oce   Ene   Was   Tox   Pop   Dev
                  •   •   •   •   •

Funding analysis.§

Fiscal year:	1991	1993
Env grants auth:	$247,600	$372,000
Number:	11	26
Range:	$10,000–$45,000	$2,000–$45,000
Median:	$20,000	$12,500
Pct $ disb (env/total):	49	50

Recipients (1993 highest):	Number:	Dollars:
Rural Advancement Fund International	1	45,000
Foundation on Economic Trends	2	40,000
Commission on Religion in Appalachia	1	25,000
Seed Savers Exchange, Inc.	1	25,000
Food & Water, Inc.	1	20,000
The Tides Foundation	1	20,000

Activity regions (1993 highest):	Number:	Dollars:
U.S. not specified	14	207,000
International*	4	85,000
U.S. West	4	40,000
North America	1	15,000
U.S. Northeast	1	15,000

*Multiple regions or not specified.

§C. S. Fund and Warsh-Mott Legacy dollar amounts are based on total award rather than one-year disbursement. This may be misleading because fewer multiple-year awards may be made in the future.

Sample grants (1993).*

California Academy of Sciences. San Francisco, Ca. $15,000. For Science in Action, a public education program on biological diversity.

Committee to Bridge the Gap. Los Angeles, CA. $10,000. To help prevent the opening of a low-level radioactive waste dump in Ward Valley, California.

Community Nutrition Institute. Washington, DC. $10,000. Toward the Environmental Policy and Trade Liberalization Project, which works to ensure that environmental impacts are given consideration in the negotiation and implementation of international trade agreements.

Council for Responsible Genetics. Boston, MA. $15,000. Support for public education and monitoring programs in the areas of human genetics, biological weapons, and commercial biotechnology products.

Earth Action. Fairbanks, AK. $15,000. Support the organization's efforts to coordinate citizen activism on environmental and peace issues around the world.

Native Seed/SEARCH. Tucson, AZ. $10,000. For renovation of an historic building to be used as a seed processing and office facility.

Pesticide Action Network (PAN), North American Regional Office. San Francisco, CA. $15,000. Support to educate the public about the dangers of toxic chemicals and the advantages of non-toxic alternatives.

Rural Advancement Fund International. Pittsboro, NC. $45,000. General support for the Foundation's educational programs on international public policy regarding genetic resource conservation.

Seed Savers Exchange, Inc. Decorah, IA. $25,000. General support for the organization's efforts to preserve endangered garden-seed varieties.

*Sample grants represent disbursements during fiscal year 1993.

Application process. *Initial contact:* Full proposal; proposals prepared for other funders are acceptable.

When to apply: The Fund has three granting cycles each year. 1995 deadlines will be April 17 for decision in July, August 15

for decision in November, and December 15 for decision in April 1996. No exceptions will be made for late proposals.
Materials available: Brochure (includes grants list and "Grant Application Procedures").

Emphases. *Recipients:* Educational institutions, nonprofit organizations.
Activities: Activism, advocacy, citizen participation, collaborative efforts, conferences, direct services, education, fieldwork, innovative programs, litigation, media projects, political activities, policy analysis/development, publications, research, seminars, technical assistance, workshops.
Types of support: Continuing support, general purposes, matching funds, operating costs, pilot projects.
Geography: Projects with national or international impact.

Limitations. *Recipients:* Individuals.
Activities: Audiovisual materials.
Types of support: Capital campaigns/expenses, debt retirement, emergency funding, endowments, fellowships, professorships, scholarships.
A 10 percent cap is placed on administrative expenses for grants made to universities.

The Cabot Family Charitable Trust
75 State Street
Boston, Massachusetts 02109
Tel: 617–342–6007   Fax: 617–342–6103
EIN: 046036446   Type: Independent
Contact: Ruth C. Sheer, Executive Director

History and philosophy. The Cabot Family Charitable Trust was established in 1942 by Godfrey L. Cabot, founder of the Cabot Corporation. It "extends support to a wide array of programs and organizations that pertain to the problems of overpopulation in the world, environmental issues of New England, and projects that represent volunteer efforts and educational interests of family members."

Officers and directors. *Trustees:* Jane C. Bradley, John G. L. Cabot, Louis W. Cabot. *Honorary Trustee:* Thomas D. Cabot.

Financial data. Data for fiscal year ended December 31, 1993.
Assets: $16,579,524 (U). *Total grants disbursed:* $623,930.

Environmental awards. *Recent grants:* 1993 grants included support for land conservation, coastal issues, agricultural education, outdoor education, and recreation.

Issues.   Cli   Bio   Lan   Agr   Wat   Oce   Ene   Was   Tox   Pop   Dev
              •   •   •   •   •   •   •

Funding analysis.

Fiscal year:	1991	1992
Env grants auth:	$212,500	$102,545
Number:	8	9
Range:	$1,000–$100,000	$5,000–$25,025
Median:	$17,000	$10,000
Pct $ disb (env/total):	20	15

Recipients (1993 highest):	Number:	Dollars:
Appalachian Mountain Club	1	25,040
Trustees of Reservations	1	25,040
Escuela Agricola Panamericana, Inc.	1	25,022
Earthwatch Expeditions, Inc.	1	20,051
Sea Education Association	1	15,031

Activity regions (1992):	Number:	Dollars:
U.S. Northeast	8	77,520
Latin America	1	25,025

Sample grants (1993).
Appalachian Mountain Club. Boston, MA. $25,040.
Earthwatch Expeditions, Inc. Watertown, MA. $20,051. General support.
Escuela Agricola Panamericana, Inc. Zamorano, Guatemala. $25,022. General endowment.
Sea Education Association. Woods Hole, MA. $15,031.
Trustees of Reservations. Beverly, MA. $25,040.

Application process. *Initial contact:* Proposal to include:
1. Statement about the proposed project (2 pages maximum).
   - Purpose of the project and its uniqueness.
   - Long-term goals and more specific short-term objectives.
   - Estimated time required for project completion.
   - Evaluation criteria.
2. Brief background information about organization, board of directors, qualifications of those leading the proposed effort.
3. Evidence of organization's tax-exempt status.
4. Total project cost, present and potential sources of funding, and amount requested from the Trust.
5. Latest audited financial statement (in cases where the organization's total budget exceeds $100,000).

When to apply: At least one month prior to the trustees' semiannual meetings in April and November.
Materials available: Annual report (includes "Application Procedures").

Emphases. *Activities:* Land acquisition, research (scholarly).
Types of support: Annual campaigns, capital campaigns/expenses, continuing support, endowments, facilities, general purposes, seed money.
Geography: New England.

Limitations. *Recipients:* Individuals, political organizations, fraternal organizations.
Activities: Fundraising, political activities.
Types of support: Advertising campaigns.

The Morris and Gwendolyn Cafritz Foundation
1825 K Street, N.W.
Washington, DC 20006
Tel: 202–223–3100   Fax: 202–296–7567
EIN: 526036989   Type: Independent
Contact: Anne Allen, Executive Director

History and philosophy. The Morris and Gwendolyn Cafritz Foundation was incorporated in 1948 with the purpose of serving Washington, D.C. where the Cafritz family lived. Morris Cafritz

(d. 1964) was a real estate developer. The Foundation currently funds nonprofit social, educational, and health organizations in the Greater Washington metropolitan area. The Foundation has a particular interest in low income, disadvantaged, and underserved sectors of the community. Program areas are: Arts and Humanities, Community Services, Education, Health, and Miscellaneous. It gives about 70 percent of its grants to small organizations.

Officers and directors. *Officers:* Calvin Cafritz, Chairman and President; Roger A. Clark, Secretary. *Directors:* Martin Atlas, Daniel J. Boorstin, J. Carter Brown, Warren E. Burger, Calvin Cafritz, William P. Rogers. *Advisory Board:* Roger A. Clark, Carolyn J. Deaver, Robert W. Duemling, Richard Hubbard Howland, Constance A. Morella, Julia S. Shepard, William Walton. *Emeritus:* S. Dillon Ripley, John Walker III.

Financial data. Data for fiscal year ended April 30, 1993. *Assets:* $169,080,009 (U). *Total grants authorized:* $8,616,973.

Environmental awards. *Recent grants:* 1993 grants made under the Community Services and Education programs included support for watershed protection, public lands restoration, urban gardens, and student and minority education and service.

Issues. Cli Bio Lan Agr Wat Oce Ene Was Tox Pop Dev

Funding analysis.

Fiscal year:	1992	1993
Env grants auth:	$327,320	$296,000
Number:	7	5
Range:	$3,200–$126,000	$20,000–$126,000
Median:	$35,500	$62,500
Pct $ auth (env/total):	4	3

Recipients (1993):	Number:	Dollars:
Chesapeake Bay Foundation	1	126,000
Anacostia Watershed Society	1	75,000
Echo Hill Outdoor School	1	50,000
Loudon Field Center	1	25,000
Friends of the U.S. National Arboretum	1	20,000

Activity region (1993):	Number:	Dollars:
U.S. Mid-Atlantic	5	296,000

Sample grants (1993).
Anacostia Watershed Society. College Park, MD. $75,000. General support.
Chesapeake Bay Foundation. Annapolis, MD. $126,000. Water Pollution and Wetlands Initiative.
Echo Hill Outdoor School. Worton, MD. $50,000. For an experiential educational program for students of District of Columbia public schools.
Friends of the U.S. National Arboretum. Washington, DC. $20,000. For the Youth Garden Project.
Loudon Field Center. Leesburg, VA. $25,000. To bring District of Columbia public school students to this outdoor education center during the 1992–93 school year.

Application process. *Initial contact:* Full proposal to include: Fact sheet (2 pages maximum).

1. Organization's name, address, telephone and facsimile numbers, contact person and title.
2. Brief organization description.
3. Annual organization budget, with listing of previous Cafritz Foundation support.

Project budget.
1. Other sources of funding.
2. The balance needed to complete the project.
3. The amount requested and the time period the grant will cover.

Purpose of the grant.
1. Explanatory narrative of less than 10 double-spaced, typewritten pages.
2. Needs statement including goals, method, and proposed benefits of project to its target community.

Accompanying documents.
1. Proof of IRS tax-exempt status.
2. Audited financial statement.
3. Other pertinent documents.

Proposals must be signed by the head of the applicant organization. Proposals signed by a division or department director must by countersigned by the head of the full institution or organization.

Detailed procedures for application are available from the Foundation upon request.

When to apply: Deadlines are March 1, July 1, and November 1. It takes at least six to nine months from deadline date to process a proposal for submission to the board.

Materials available: Annual report, guidelines.

Emphases. *Recipients:* Educational institutions, nonprofit organizations.
Activities: Citizen participation, collaborative efforts, education, training, volunteerism, youth programs.
Types of support: General purposes, internships, projects, scholarships.
Geography: Metropolitan Washington, D.C. area only.

Limitations. *Recipients:* Individuals.
Activities: Activism, litigation, lobbying, political activities.
Types of support: Endowments, facilities (construction), loans, mortgage reduction, program-related investments.

The Louis Calder Foundation

230 Park Avenue, Room 1530–1
New York, New York 10169
Tel: 212–687–1680
EIN: 136015562   Type: Independent
Contact: Barbara A. Sommer, Grant Program Manager

History and philosophy. The Foundation was established in 1951 by Louis Calder (1879–1963), past chairman of Perkins-Goodwin Co., a pulp and paper marketing and management firm. Louis Calder was instrumental in the development of the South's newsprint manufacturing industry, using indigenous southern pine. He was also a pioneer in the retail marketing of gasoline. Through the Kesbec Oil Company, he introduced drive-in, metered gasoline stations to the New York area during World

War I. A controlling interest in Kesbec was sold to Standard Oil in 1931.

The Foundation was set up to serve the people of New York City. Current priorities are health, welfare, and education. Of primary interest are programs to enhance the potential and increase the self-sufficiency of New York City's disadvantaged children and youth and their families. Additional grants support the performing arts, cultural education, and medical research.

Officers and directors. *Trustees:* Paul R. Brenner, Peter D. Calder, Chemical Bank.

Financial data. Data for fiscal year ended October 31, 1993. *Assets:* $102,254,810 (C). *Total grants disbursed:* $5,222,600.

Environmental awards. *Recent grants:* 1993 grants included support for educational programs at botanical gardens and a zoo.

Issues. Cli Bio Lan Agr Wat Oce Ene Was Tox Pop Dev
            •

Funding analysis.

Fiscal year:	1993
Env grants disb:	$95,000
Number:	4
Range:	$20,000–$25,000
Median:	$25,000
Pct $ disb (env/total):	2

Recipients (1993):	*Number:*	*Dollars:*
Brooklyn Botanic Garden	2	50,000
NYZS/The Wildlife Conservation Society	1	25,000
The New York Botanical Garden	1	20,000

Activity region (1993):	*Number:*	*Dollars:*
New York/New Jersey	4	95,000

Sample grants (1993).

Brooklyn Botanic Garden. Brooklyn, NY. $25,000. Support for Phase II of their Discovery Center Expansion Project, the development and construction of exhibit areas and to match the Hayden Challenge.

Brooklyn Botanic Garden. Brooklyn, NY. $25,000. Support of their science and environmental education programs for New York City school children.

The New York Botanical Garden. Bronx, NY. $20,000. Support of their Children's Education programming for New York City youth.

NYZS/The Wildlife Conservation Society. Bronx, NY. $25,000. Support of their Education Department's family program for Phipps Houses Residents.

Application process. *Initial contact:* Submit the New York Regional Association of Grantmakers Common Application Form accompanied by a concise statement of the purpose of the grant. If requested, provide:
1. Copy of IRS tax-exempt status determination letter.
2. Information on the organization's nature, history, and activities (in pamphlet form, if available).
3. Current list of the organization's members, trustees, directors, and/or officers.
4. Organization's current financial report or a summary thereof.
5. Detailed budget and prior income and expense statement for the project, program, or organization as applicable. The budget should list all sources and amounts of support.
6. List of other foundations currently contributing to the organization or project, the purpose, and amounts.

When to apply: Deadline March 31. Applications accepted only between November 1 and March 31.

Materials available: Annual report (includes "Guidelines" and "Grant Procedure").

Emphases. *Recipients:* Educational institutions, nonprofit organizations.
Types of support: Equipment, general purposes, operating costs, scholarships.
Geography: New York City.

Limitations. *Recipients:* Individuals, public agencies.
Types of support: Capital campaigns/expenses, continuing support, endowments, facilities, multi-year grants.

California Community Foundation
606 South Olive Street, Suite 2400
Los Angeles, California 90014–1526
Tel: 213–413–4042   Fax: 213–383–2046
EIN: 956013179   Type: Community
Contact: John Kim, Grants Coordinator

History and philosophy. Founded in 1915 by Joseph Sartori, a Los Angeles banker, the California Community Foundation is the second-oldest community foundation in the country and one of the largest. "Through [its] management of charitable trusts and bequests, [its] role as a convener and facilitator for important community initiatives, and, above all, through [its] grants for key community projects, [the Foundation helps] to meet basic human needs, celebrate cultural diversity, encourage cooperation among groups and communities, develop leadership, strengthen pluralism, and improve the quality of life and access to opportunity for all the residents of the [Greater Los Angeles] region." Whenever possible, it "will also favor the organization whose excellence in providing services is not yet recognized and supported adequately by other funding sources." Program areas are: arts and culture; children, youth and families; civic affairs and community development; community education; community health and medicine; environment and animal welfare; human services. The Foundation awards a large proportion of its grants through donor-advised funds.

Officers and directors. *Officers:* Stephen D. Gavin, Chair; Jack Shakely, President; Terri Jones, Vice President for Programs; Joe Lumarda, Vice President for Finance; Linda Shestock, Vice President for Finance/Administration; Debbie Andrade, Program Secretary. *Governors:* Caroline L. Ahmanson, Bruce C. Corwin, Susanne Fitger Donnelly, Stephen D. Gavin, Dr. Claudia H. Hampton, Nini Moore Horn, William G. Ouchi, David A. Peters, William F. Podlich, Bruce M. Ramer, Virgil Patrick Roberts, Ann Shaw, Jean French Smith, Danial L. Villanueva, Jr., Esther Wachtell, Ruth K. Watanabe, Peggy Fouke Wortz.

C

Financial data.* Data for fiscal year ended June 30, 1993. *Assets:* $126,703,562 (M). *Gifts received:* $16,891,468. *Total grants disbursed:* $8,435,951.

*Includes designated and donor-advised grants.

Environmental awards. *Program and interests:* Environmental grants are made to:
- Promote environmental appreciation and responsibility among all residents, but especially children and youth.
- Involve low-income and minority communities in considering alternatives for environmental protection and community development.
- Preserve opportunities for our urban population to enjoy and appreciate the natural world.
- Promote the welfare of birds and animals.

Grants are not made for programs that advocate a particular political position.
Recent grants: 1993 grants included support for land conservation, forests, wildlife, and education.

Issues. *Cli Bio Lan Agr Wat Oce Ene Was Tox Pop Dev*
          •   •

Funding analysis.§

Fiscal year:	1991*	1993
Env grants auth:	$956,666	$500,000
Number:	36	3
Range:	$100–$890,400	$25,000–$450,000
Median:	$500	$25,000
Pct $ disb (env/total):	8	11

*Based on disbursements.

Recipients (1993):	Number:	Dollars:
Greater Los Angeles Zoo Association	1	450,000
Mountains Education Association	1	25,000
Roar Foundation	1	25,000

Activity region (1993):	Number:	Dollars:
U.S. West	3	500,000

§Does not include designated or donor-advised grants.

Sample grants (1993).
Greater Los Angeles Zoo Association. Los Angeles, CA. $450,000. To create a program of animal education called Improving Animal Welfare, which will include an upgrading of an educational animal contact area.
Mountains Education Program. Calabasas, CA. $25,000. Support of an apprenticeship program that trains low-income young adults as naturalists.
Roar Foundation. Acton, CA. $25,000. General support for the Shambala Preserve, a haven for lions, tigers, and other exotic felines that have been abandoned or otherwise confiscated for improper captivity.

Application process. *Initial contact:* Contact Foundation for guidelines and application form.
The organization should be committed to any proposed program or project; the Foundation discourages speculative proposals. Application, signed by organization's CEO, chair, or president, to describe briefly:
1. Proposed project's purpose/goals and service population.
2. History and expertise of organization.
3. Specific needs or problems in the community that are trying to be solved.
4. What other agencies or services are addressing the same problem(s) and what methods are being used.
5. What is hoped to be accomplished and how will it solve or reduce the needs or problems of the project.
6. Project activities or steps to be taken.
7. Evaluation of progress and success of project.
8. If additional funds are needed, how will they be obtained.
9. Plans to continue beyond the period for which funds have been requested.
10. Additional information.

Attachments:
1. Organization budget.
2. List of board members.
3. IRS tax-exempt status determination letter.
4. Letters of Agreement from collaborating organization (if applicable).
5. Financial reports.
6. Most recent IRS 990 tax form.
7. Annual report.

When to apply: Deadlines for the Environmental program in 1995 are December 1, 1994 for May 1995 decision and December 1, 1995 for May 1996 decision.
Materials available: Annual report, application guidelines, application form, brochure, *Community Foundation Forum* (newsletter).

Emphases. *Recipients:* Nonprofit organizations.
Activities: Education, projects.
Types of support: Program-related investments, seed money, technical assistance.
Geography: Los Angeles, California (western edge of San Bernardino County, if criteria are met).

Limitations. *Recipients:* Individuals, religious organizations.
Activities: Conferences, fundraising, political activities.
Types of support: Annual campaigns, endowments, equipment, facilities, operating costs.

James & Abigail Campbell Foundation

1001 Kamokila Boulevard
Kapolei, Hawaii 96707
Tel: 808–674–6674   Fax: 808–674–3111
EIN: 990203078   Type: Independent
Contact: Theresia C. McMurdo, Assistant Secretary

History and philosophy. The Foundation, incorporated in 1980, is funded by family members and others in memory of James and Abigail Campbell. James Campbell transformed 41,000 acres of parched land into a thriving sugar plantation, Oahu Sugar Company, on the island of Oahu by drilling Hawaii's first artesian well. The well continues to provide the Leeward and Honolulu areas with water. The Campbell estate has holdings on three islands and assets valued at $2.05 billion.

The Foundation makes grants in five areas: youth, education, Hawaiian programs, environment, and recreation.

Officers and directors. *Officers:* Edward K. Kawananakoa, Chairman; James W. Growney, President; Thelma Hart, Dudley C. Pratt, Jr., Louise Stevenson, Vice Presidents; Stephen H. MacMillan, David H. McCoy, Assistant Vice Presidents; G. J. Liloa Willard, Secretary; Mary Philpotts McGrath, Treasurer; Theresia C. McMurdo, Assistant Secretary; Ronald M. Plumb, Assistant Treasurer. *Directors:* James W. Growney, Thelma Hart, Edward K. Kawananakoa, Mary Philpotts McGrath, Dudley C. Pratt, Jr., Louise Stevenson, G. J. Liloa Willard.

Financial data. Data for fiscal year ended December 31, 1993. *Assets:* $8,717,780 (M). *Gifts received:* $779,218. *Total grants disbursed:* $132,835.

Environmental awards. *Recent grants:* 1993 grants included support for land conservation, wetlands, parks, and gardens.

Issues. Cli Bio• Lan• Agr Wat Oce Ene Was Tox Pop Dev

Funding analysis.

Fiscal year:	1993
Env grants disb:	$47,335
Number:	4
Range:	$5,000–$17,335
Median:	$12,500
Pct $ disb (env/total):	36

Recipients (1993):	*Number:*	*Dollars:*
Lahaina Restoration Foundation	1	17,335
Hawaii Nature Center	1	15,000
The Nature Conservancy, Hawaii Field Office	1	10,000
Moanalua Gardens Foundation	1	5,000

Activity region (1993):	*Number:*	*Dollars:*
Hawaii	4	47,335

Sample grants (1993).
Hawaii Nature Center. Honolulu, HI. $15,000. Wetlands Field Education Program.
Lahaina Restoration Foundation. Lahaina, HI. $17,335. In trust for Campbell Park.
Moanalua Gardens Foundation. Honolulu, HI. $5,000. Education Materials Development Program.
The Nature Conservancy, Hawaii Field Office. Honolulu, HI. $10,000. Waianae Mountains Regional Conservation Partnership.

Application process. *Initial contact:* Letter (2–3 pages) to include:
1. Nature and purpose of the organization.
2. Program objectives, grant amount requested, and proposed use of funds.
3. Outline of methods to accomplish program objectives.
4. Population served and problems or needs addressed.
5. Duration that Foundation funds will be needed.
6. Other sources of funds currently being sought and future sources of funding.
7. Evaluation methods.

Appendixes.
1. Copy of IRS tax-exempt status determination letter.
2. Most current audited financial statement.
3. List of board of directors.
4. Proposed budget for the project.

When to apply: Deadlines are March 15, June 15, September 15, and December 15. The board meets at the end of April, July, October, and January.
Materials available: Annual report (includes "Grant Application Process").

Emphases. *Recipients:* Nonprofit organizations.
Activities: Education.
Types of support: Equipment, facilities (renovation), projects, scholarships, seed money.
Geography: Hawaii only, with emphasis on Ewa-Leeward, Kahuku, Maui, and the Big Island.

Limitations. *Recipients:* Individuals, religious organizations.
Activities: Political activities, research (technical).
Types of support: Endowments, loans.

Ward M. & Mariam C. Canaday Educational and Charitable Trust

c/o First National Bank of Boston
P.O. Box 1890, 01–04–06
Boston, Massachusetts 02105
Tel: 617–434–5669   Fax: 617–434–5785
EIN: 346523619   Type: Independent
EGA member
Contact: Sharon M. Driscoll, Executive Account Manager

History and philosophy. The Trust was established in 1945 in Ohio. Its primary interest is higher education with grantmaking to include colleges and universities.

Officers and directors. *Trustees:* Sharon M. Driscoll, George W. Ritter, Doreen C. Spitzer, Lyman Spitzer, Jr., First National Bank of Boston.

Environmental awards. *Program and interests:* Although an Environmental Grantmakers Association member as of 1994, the Trust had not yet awarded environmental grants.

Financial data. Data for fiscal year ended December 31, 1991. *Assets:* $6,854,316 (M). *Gifts received:* $754,656. *Total grants disbursed:* $1,284,120.

Application process. *Initial contact:* Proposal.
When to apply: Anytime.

Emphases. *Recipients:* Educational institutions.

© 1995 Environmental Data Resources, Inc.

The Cape Branch Foundation

c/o Danser, Balaam and Frank
5 Independence Way
Princeton, New Jersey 08540
Tel: 609–987–0300   Fax: 609–452–1024
EIN: 226054886   Type: Independent
Contact: Dorothy Frank, Partner

History and philosophy. The Cape Branch Foundation was established in 1964. It makes grants for secondary education, conservation, and museums in New Jersey. It also supports a university.

Officers and directors. *Trustees:* Gordon O. Danser, Frank J. Hoenemeyer, Gretchen W. Johnson. *Directors:* Gretchen W. Johnson, James L. Johnson.

Financial data. Data for fiscal year ended December 31, 1993. *Assets:* $12,121,298 (M). *Total grants disbursed:* $129,450.

Environmental awards. *Recent grants:* One 1993 grant supported watershed protection.

Issues.   Cli   Bio   Lan   Agr   Wat   Oce   Ene   Was   Tox   Pop   Dev
                                        •

Funding analysis.

Fiscal year:	1992	1993
Env grants disb:	$95,000	$10,000
Number:	3	1
Range:	$20,000–$50,000	—
Median:	$25,000	—
Pct $ disb (env/total):	34	8

Recipient (1993):	Number:	Dollars:
Upper Raritan Watershed Association	1	10,000

Activity region (1993):	Number:	Dollars:
New York/New Jersey	1	10,000

Sample grant (1993).
Upper Raritan Watershed Association. Gladstone, NJ. $10,000.

Application process. *Initial contact:* Letter outlining purpose and amount of request.
When to apply: Anytime.

Emphases. *Recipients:* Educational institutions, museums.
Activities: Education, land acquisition, research.
Types of support: General purposes, scholarships.
Geography: New Jersey.

Limitations. *Recipients:* Individuals.
Types of support: Fellowships, scholarships.

The Cargill Foundation

P.O. Box 5690
Minneapolis, Minnesota 55440
Tel: 612–742–6209   Fax: 612–742–7224
EIN: 416020221   Type: Company-sponsored
Contact: Audrey Tulberg, Senior Program Officer

History and philosophy. Cargill Incorporated is a privately held company with operations in 58 countries. Its numerous businesses deal with the buying, selling, processing, and storing of agricultural commodities such as grains and fertilizer. The Foundation was established in 1952. It supports "a broad range of programs that help achieve a better informed, healthier, more productive and prosperous citizenry. Special emphasis is placed on educational, social and community programs that assist individuals in becoming more self-reliant and on organizations that involve [Company] employees and their expertise." It makes grants in six program areas: Education, Civic/Community, Social Programs, Arts/Culture, Partnership Fund, and Health.

Officers and directors. *Officers:* William R. Pearce, President; Cargill MacMillan, Jr., John E. Pearson, Warren R. Staley, Vice Presidents; Thomas O. Moe, Secretary/Treasurer.

Financial data. Data for fiscal year ended December 31, 1993. *Assets:* $41,900,000 (M). *Gifts received:* $2,000,000. *Total grants disbursed:* $3,774,231.

Environmental awards. *Program and interests:* Grants are made to environmental projects through the Civic/Community Program. *Recent grants:* 1993 grants included support for wildlife protection, an arboretum, zoos, and outdoor education.

Issues.   Cli   Bio   Lan   Agr   Wat   Oce   Ene   Was   Tox   Pop   Dev
                  •   •   •

Funding analysis.

Fiscal year:	1992
Env grants disb:	$55,500
Number:	6
Range:	$500–$15,000
Median:	$10,000
Pct $ disb (env/total):	2

Recipients (1992 highest):	Number:	Dollars:
Minnesota Zoo Foundation	1	15,000
Voyageur Outward Bound School	1	15,000
The Nature Conservancy, Minnesota Field Office	1	12,500
Ducks Unlimited, Inc.	1	7,500
Project Environment Foundation	1	5,000

Activity region (1992):	Number:	Dollars:
U.S. Great Lakes	6	55,500

Sample grants (1993).
Minnesota Center for Environmental Advocacy. St. Paul, MN. $5,000.

Minnesota Landscape Arboretum. Chanhassen, MN. $25,000.
Minnesota Zoo. Apple Valley, MN. $25,000.
Voyageur Outward Bound School. Minnetonka, MN. $15,000.

Application process. *Initial contact:* Letter of inquiry to include:
1. Description of organization's history, mission, programs and services, and staffing support.
2. Description of the specific use of the funds requested, dollar amount, goals and objectives, and timetable.
3. Copy of IRS tax-exempt status determination letter.
4. Itemized annual budget and sources of financial support.
5. Most recent audited financial statement.
6. List of board of directors.

When to apply: Deadlines are three weeks before a meeting; the contributions committee usually meets every 6–8 weeks.
Materials available: Guidelines.

Emphases. *Recipients:* Nonprofit organizations.
Types of support: Capital campaigns/expenses, continuing support, general purposes, operating costs, projects.
Geography: Minneapolis–St. Paul metropolitan area; Minnesota; communities with Cargill operations.

Limitations. *Recipients:* Individuals, religious organizations.
Activities: Advocacy, audiovisual materials, conferences, fundraising, lobbying, political activities, publications, research, symposia/colloquia, workshops.
Types of support: Advertising campaigns, endowments, fellowships, loans, matching funds, multi-year grants, travel expenses.

Caribou Fund
3564 Pearl Street
Boulder, Colorado 80301
Tel: 303–786–8170   Fax: 303–786–8170
E-mail: greengrants@igc.apc.org
Type: Company-sponsored
EGA member
Contact: Chet Tchozewski, Executive Director

History and philosophy. Since 1991, the Caribou Fund "working in cooperation with the Rainforest Action Network, has provided limited assistance for grassroots activist organizations who are working to find innovative local solutions to the global environmental crisis." It assists "community-based grassroots environmental organizations in the Southern Hemisphere as well as exceptional programs in other regions where alternative sources of funding do not exist." The Fund is supported primarily by Nature's Own and Nature's Own Imagination, four science and natural history retail stores located in Colorado.

Officers and directors. *Officer:* Roy Young, President. *Director:* Chet Tchozewski.

Financial data. Data for fiscal year ended December 31, 1994.
Total grants disbursed: $100,000 (est.).

Environmental awards. Program and interests: Targets are development of:

- Infrastructure.
- Networking capability.
- Basic organizational requirements for community organizations in the Southern Hemisphere.

Recent grants: 1993 grants included support for tropical forest preservation, environmental education, and publications.

Issues.   Cli   Bio   Lan   Agr   Wat   Oce   Ene   Was   Tox   Pop   Dev

Funding analysis.

Fiscal year:	1993
Env grants auth:	$82,911
Number:	21
Range:	$600–$16,000
Median:	$2,000
Pct $ auth (env/total):	100

Recipients (1993 highest):	Number:	Dollars:
Rainforest Action Network	2	19,111
Boulder Area Communities Foundation	1	16,000
Asociación Ecologista Costarricense	1	5,000
Conference on the Socio-Ecological Problems of Central Siberia	1	5,000
Green November	1	5,000
Sarawak Campaign Committee	1	5,000

Activity regions (1993 highest):	Number:	Dollars:
Southeast Asia	4	25,000
Brazil	10	24,111
Russia	5	12,800
U.S. Mountain	1	16,000
Mexico and Central America	1	5,000

Sample grants (1993).
Agrias. Sao Paulo, Brazil. $1,000. To promote environmental education programs for public school teachers.
Friends of the Siberian Forests. Krasnoyarsk, Central Siberia, Russia. $1,200. General support for salary and operating costs.
Imagens da Terra. Sao Paulo, Brazil. $2,000. General support for photo documentation of environmentally unsound projects.
Rainforest Action Network. Sao Paulo, Brazil. $6,111. General support for communication among the worldwide network of grassroots rainforest groups.
Rainforest Action Network. Sao Paulo, Brazil. $13,000. For publication of the Southeast Asia Rainforests Resource Guide and Directory.
Sarawak Campaign Committee. Tokyo, Japan. $5,000. For organizing in Japan to help stop tropical deforestation and human rights abuses in Sarawak, Malaysia.
Wahana Lingkungan Hidup Indonesia (WALHI). Pejompongan, Indonesia. $2,000. General support for a national forum of Indonesians focused on sound management of natural resources.

Application process. *Initial contact:* Letter or telephone call.
When to apply: Anytime.
Materials available: Annual report.

C

Emphases. *Recipients:* Nonprofit organizations.
Activities: Activism, advocacy, citizen participation, conferences, education, publications.
Types of support: Continuing support, general purposes, operating costs, pilot projects, seed money.
Geography: Southern Hemisphere and Siberia.

Limitations. *Recipients:* Organizations in industrialized countries in the Northern Hemisphere.

Carolyn Foundation
4800 First Bank Place
Minneapolis, Minnesota 55402
Tel: 612–339–7101   Fax: 612–338–2084
EIN: 416044416   Type: Independent
Contact: Carol J. Fetzer, Executive Director and Secretary

History and philosophy. The Carolyn Foundation was established in 1964 by the will of Carolyn McKnight Christian, a daughter of Sumner T. McKnight, Minneapolis real estate entrepreneur, pioneer, and lumberman. The Foundation is predominately a regional general purpose foundation funding projects in the metropolitan areas of New Haven, Connecticut and Minneapolis–St. Paul, Minnesota. Areas of emphasis are education, the arts, programs addressing social problems, health, and the environment.

Officers and directors. *Officers:* Lucy C. Mitchell, Chair; Guido Calabresi, Vice Chair; Carol J. Fetzer, Secretary; Edwin L. Crosby, Treasurer. *Trustees:* Beatrice C. Booth, Guido Calabresi, Charles W. Case, Eugenie T. Copp, Edwin L. Crosby, Franklin M. Crosby III, G. Christian Crosby, Sumner McK. Crosby, Jr., Thomas M. Crosby, Jr., Carol J. Fetzer, Carolyn C. Graham, Lucy C. Mitchell. *Distribution Committee:* Susan W. Crosby, Chair; Eugenie T. Copp, Edwin L. Crosby, Carolyn C. Graham, Alexander L. Johnston, Jennifer Case Phelps.

Financial data. Data for fiscal year ended December 31, 1993. *Assets:* $26,320,938 (M). *Total grants disbursed:* $1,287,669.

Environmental awards. *Recent grants:* 1993 grants included support for land conservation, forest and watershed protection, coastal issues, species preservation, and energy.

Issues. Cli Bio Lan Agr Wat Oce Ene Was Tox Pop Dev

Funding analysis.

Fiscal year:	1991	1993
Env grants disb:	$169,000	$557,764
Number:	8	21
Range:	$7,000–$45,000	$3,000–$50,000
Median:	$20,000	$25,000
Pct $ disb (env/total):	16	43

Recipients (1993 highest):	Number:	Dollars:
American Wildlands	1	50,000
Connecticut Audubon Society	1	50,000
Rivers Alliance of Connecticut	1	50,000
South Central Connecticut Regional Water Authority	1	46,464
Minnesota Zoological Garden	1	45,000

Activity regions (1993):	Number:	Dollars:
U.S. Northeast	6	174,264
U.S. Great Lakes	6	153,500
U.S. not specified	5	110,000
U.S. Mountain	2	80,000
U.S. Northwest	2	40,000

Sample grants (1993).
American Wildlands. Lakewood, CO. $50,000.
Concerts for the Environment. Minneapolis, MN. $3,500.
Connecticut River Watershed Council. Easthampton, MA. $9,800
Garden Club of New Haven. New Haven, CT. $3,000.
Headwaters, Inc. Ashland, OR. $20,000.
International Crane Foundation. Baraboo, WI. $20,000.
Land Trust Alliance. Washington, DC. $15,000.
Minnesota Center for Environmental Advocacy. St. Paul, MN. $20,000.
Montana Land Reliance. Kalispell, MT. $30,000.
Save the Bay, Inc. Providence, RI. $15,000.
Western Ancient Forests Campaign. Washington, DC. $20,000.

Application process. *Initial contact:* Full proposal (1 copy) signed by an authorized official of the organization, to include:
Summary information.
1. Name and address and contact person.
2. Description of the applicant organization.
3. Demonstration of staff capability and list of board of directors.
4. IRS number and tax-exempt status determination letter, state registration certificate.
5. Dollar amount requested.
6. Detailed past and anticipated future sources of support.
Description of the project.
1. Overall purpose, specific goals, and objectives.
2. Assessment of need, client population, description of other programs operating parallel to or in cooperation with the proposed project.
3. Background, history of project, past record of project and staff.
4. Operational plan.
5. Future plans.
6. Licensing requirements, if any, and status of project with respect thereto.
7. Assessment and evaluation plans and methods—internal and external—during and following project completion.
When to apply: Deadlines for 1995 are January 31, decision made by mid-June and July 31, decision by mid-December.
Materials available: Annual report (includes "Guidelines" and "Grant Applications").

Emphases. *Recipients:* Educational institutions, museums, nonprofit organizations, zoos.
Activities: Conflict resolution, demonstration programs, education, innovative programs, land acquisition, litigation, volunteerism, workshops, youth programs.

Types of support: Capital campaigns/expenses, equipment, facilities, general purposes, maintenance, matching funds, operating costs, pilot projects, projects, seed money, single-year grants only, start-up costs, technical assistance.
Geography: Primarily the metropolitan areas of New Haven, Connecticut and Minneapolis–St. Paul, Minnesota.

Limitations. *Recipients:* Individuals, religious organizations.
Activities: Conferences, litigation, lobbying, seminars.
Types of support: Annual campaigns, debt retirement, multi-year grants, operating costs.
Geography: International.

The Carpenter Foundation
711 East Main Street, Suite 18
Medford, Oregon 97501
Tel: 503–772–5851
EIN: 930491360   Type: Independent
Contact: Jane H. Carpenter, President

History and philosophy. The Carpenter Foundation was established by Alfred S. V. Carpenter and Helen Bundy Carpenter in 1942. It was originally called the Jackson County Recreation Committee and provided recreational activities for servicemen at Camp White. The Committee was reorganized in 1958 to become a general purpose family foundation. It added associate trustees to the family-based board in 1972. Today the Foundation works with other agencies, organizations, and public entities to enhance opportunity, choice, enrichment, and a climate for change for those living in Oregon's Rogue Valley. Grants are made in the areas of human services, education, the arts, and certain public interest issues. Funding is limited to these topics and to the geographic area of Jackson and Josephine counties, Oregon.

Officers and directors. *Officers:* Jane H. Carpenter, President; Emily C. Mostue, Vice President; Karen C. Allan, Secretary; Dunbar Carpenter, Treasurer. *Directors:* Karen C. Allan, Patricia Blair, Dunbar Carpenter, Jane H. Carpenter, William E. Duhaime, William R. Moffat, A. Brian Mostue, Emily C. Mostue, Shirley Patton.

Financial data. Data for fiscal year ended June 30, 1993. *Assets:* $10,273,232 (B). *Total grants disbursed:* $483,096.

Environmental awards. *Program and interests:* Public interest grants, which include environmental grants, make up about 15 percent of Foundation funding.
Recent grants: 1993 grants included support for land conservation, watershed protection, and forest preservation.

Issues.   Cli   Bio   Lan   Agr   Wat   Oce   Ene   Was   Tox   Pop   Dev
                •   •   •   •

Funding analysis.

Fiscal year:	1991	1993
Env grants auth:	$45,800	$25,250
Number:	3	5
Range:	$8,800–$25,000	$1,250–$8,000
Median:	$12,000	$5,000
Pct $ disb (env/total):	9	5

Recipients (1993):	Number:	Dollars:
Rogue Institute for Ecology and Economy	1	8,000
Josephine Parks & Recreation Foundation	1	6,000
Headwaters, Inc.	1	5,000
Riverside West All Sports Park	1	5,000
Bear Creek Greenway Foundation	1	1,250

Activity region (1993):	Number:	Dollars:
U.S. Northwest	5	25,250

Sample grants (1993).
Bear Creek Greenway Foundation. Medford, OR. $1,250. To fund publication of the Bear Creek Greenway Activity Guide for use by teachers.
Headwaters, Inc. Ashland, OR. $5,000. Toward stream-flow monitoring in local watersheds by training volunteers.
Josephine Parks & Recreation Foundation. Grants Pass, OR. $6,000.
Riverside West All Sports Park. Grants Pass, OR. $5,000.
Rogue Institute for Ecology and Economy. Ashland, OR. $8,000. To encourage rural economic development using ecological forest management practices.

Application process. *Initial contact:* Full proposal to include:
Cover letter.
1. Summary of project scope.
2. Amount of request.
3. Name, address, and telephone number of a contact person.
Project description.
1. Description of project and the community need.
2. Budget for project and other possible funding sources.
3. Description of planning process, staffing, and schedule.
4. Result expected and proposed evaluation method.
Agency background.
1. Review of the organization: its purpose, services to the community, and staffing.
2. Budgets for both the organization's current year and the year for which the project is designed.
3. Current financial statement, audited if available.
4. List of the board of directors.
5. Board of directors' approval of project application.
6. Copy of the IRS tax-exempt status determination letter.
When to apply: Deadlines are generally about five weeks before the quarterly board meetings held in March, June, September, and December. Call for exact deadlines.
Materials available: Annual report (includes "Grant Application Guidelines").

Emphases. *Activities:* Capacity building, citizen participation, collaborative efforts, conflict resolution, demonstration programs, education, innovative programs, land acquisition, net-working.
Types of support: Leveraging funds, matching funds, pilot projects, program-related investments, seed money.
Geography: Jackson and Josephine counties, Oregon, only.

Limitations. *Recipients:* Individuals.

C

Mary Flagler Cary Charitable Trust
350 Fifth Avenue, Room 6622
New York, New York 10118
Tel: 212-563-6860 Fax: 212-695-6538
EIN: 136266964   Type: Independent
EGA member
Contact: Edward A. Ames, Trustee

History and philosophy. The Trust was established in January 1968 as a testamentary, charitable trust by the will of Mary Flagler Cary, daughter of Harry Harkness and Anne Lamont Flagler. Mrs. Cary's grandfather, Henry Morrison Flagler, was a founder and principal owner of the original Standard Oil Company. The Trust's primary purpose is to carry forward Mrs. Cary's interests in music and the environment. It has commitments undertaken relating to its history and origin. Each of these grants serves a public purpose, but none represents a general program of the Trust, and no additional, unrelated support is offered in these fields. These commitments are: the Institute of Ecosystem Studies, Inc. at the Mary Flagler Cary Arboretum; The New York Botanical Garden; and The Rockefeller University Field Research Center for Ecology and Ethology.

Officers and directors. *Trustees:* Edward A. Ames, William R. Grant, Phyllis J. Mills.

Financial data. Data for fiscal year ended June 30, 1993. *Assets:* $119,923,825 (M). *Total grants authorized:* $6,800,576.

Environmental awards. *Program and interests:* the Trust has two environmental programs:

- The Conservation Program supports efforts to protect coastal wetlands and estuaries as components of regional ecosystems from Virginia to Florida. Its first priority is to support selected programs (e.g., the Nanticoke River watershed in Delaware and Virginia; the Virginia Coast Reserve; the Albermarle and Pamlico Sounds, and the watersheds of four tributary rivers, in North Carolina; the ACE Base in South Carolina; and the Everglades watershed in Florida.) Grants go to organizations that provide credible, strategic information for conservation advocates, resource managers, and the general public. A portion of its budget goes to areas where support was provided prior to developing its protection of coastal resources program.

- The Urban Environment Program supports community initiatives and helps develop leadership to work on environmental problems within low-income New York City neighborhoods.

In addition, the scientific program of the Mary Flagler Cary Arboretum, the Institute of Ecosystem Studies, is of interest.

Issues. Cli Bio Lan Agr Wat Oce Ene Was Tox Pop Dev
             •   •   •   •   •

Funding analysis.

Fiscal year:	1991	1993
Env grants disb:	$3,907,031	$5,558,026
Number:	33	28
Range:	$3,000–$3,125,603	$5,000–$3,300,000
Median:	$20,000	$20,000
Pct $ disb (env/total):	74	82

Recipients (1993 highest):	Number:	Dollars:
The New York Botanical Garden	3	5,012,431
Southern Environmental Law Center	1	70,000
Center for Marine Conservation	1	45,000
Sierra Club Legal Defense Fund	1	40,000
Citizens Committee for New York City	1	32,500

Activity regions (1993 highest):	Number:	Dollars:
New York/New Jersey	11	5,154,026
U.S. Southeast	11	309,000
U.S. not specified	2	25,000
U.S. South Central	1	25,000
U.S. Northeast	1	18,000

Sample grants (1993).

Center for Marine Conservation. Washington, DC. $45,000. Toward the development and implementation of a management plan for the Florida Keys National Marine Sanctuary.

Citizens Committee for New York City. New York, NY. $32,500 (following $125,000 pre-payment made in prior fiscal year). For the Neighborhood Environmental Action Awards Program. Grants are awarded to neighborhood groups in low-income communities of New York City. About 20 grantees are selected by an independent panel, and awards of up to $5,000 support programs which deal with problems of air pollution, water quality, open space, lead poisoning and other toxic threats, noise, solid wastes and recycling, and energy issues. Technical assistance is provided by Citizen Committee staff.

Coast Alliance, Inc. Washington, DC. $15,000. Partial support of its public education project, primarily dealing with resource protection issues involving barrier islands and beaches on the Atlantic Coast.

Conservation Law Foundation. Boston, MA. $18,000. For the continuing effort to protect the Cape Cod National Seashore against off-road vehicles (ORVs). CLF's litigation and long-term advocacy before administrative forums have forced the National Park Service to enhance management plans, as required by law, to restrict the use of beach-destroying ORVs.

The New York Botanical Garden. Bronx, NY. $3,300,000. For the advancement of botanical science.

South Carolina Coastal Conservation League. Charleston, SC. $15,000. Support of the League's effort to increase public participation in long-term solutions to coastal environmental problems.

The Trust for Public Land. New York, NY. $14,095. (Prepayment of $55,000 made in prior fiscal year.) Support for TPL's Neighborhood Open Space Management Program. NOSM provides grants and technical assistance to community gardens in low-income neighborhoods of New York City to help strengthen organizational and leadership skills and increase local participation. One goal of the Program is to empower neighborhood groups to deal with more serious environmental issues in their communities.

Upward Fund, Inc. New York, NY. $20,000. Toward Upward's Environmental Education Program. Located in East Harlem, Upward provides afterschool and summer programs for community children. The Environment Education Program teaches children and their parents how to protect and improve their environment by conducting recycling and clean-up projects, gardening and plant care, and hydrant monitoring.

Application process. *Initial contact:* Letter to include:
1. A concise statement of program or project.
2. Amount of funding requested and how it fits within the overall budget of applicant.
3. Brief description of the nature and activities of applicant.
4. Applicant's legal name.
5. Current list of applicant's officers and directors or trustees.

If the Trust is interested, it will request additional information including:
1. Copy of IRS tax-exempt status determination letter and tax classification (determining that applicant is not a "private foundation") under Section 509(a).
2. Copy of applicant's most recent audited financial statement.
3. Official letter or request on the organization's letterhead, signed by its CEO on behalf of its governing body.

When to apply: Anytime. The trustees meet monthly.
Materials available: "Grants List and Financial Information," "Program Guidelines and General Information."

Emphases. *Recipients:* Nonprofit organizations.
Activities: Advocacy, citizen participation, collaborative efforts, litigation, planning, research (scientific).
Types of support: General purposes, multi-year grants, operating costs.
Geography: Eastern coastal states (Conservation Program); New York City (Urban Environment Program).

Limitations. *Recipients:* Educational institutions, individuals.
Types of support: Capital campaigns/expenses, endowments, professorships, scholarships.
Geography: International grants.

Centerior Energy Foundation
P.O. Box 94661
Cleveland, Ohio 44101–4661
Tel: 216–447–2574 Fax: 216–479–4826
EIN: 346514181   Type: Company-sponsored
Contact: Jacquita K. Hauserman, Chairperson,
Contributions Committee

History and philosophy. The Foundation was established in 1961 by the Cleveland Electric Illuminating Company, Centerior Energy Corporation. Grantmaking focuses on health, welfare, culture (including theater), education, and justice and human rights within the Centerior Corporation's service area in Ohio.

Officers and directors. *Officers:* Robert J. Farling, Chairman; Lyman C. Phillips, Vice Chairman; Jacquita K. Hauserman, President; Terrence G. Linnert, Vice President; E. Lyle Pepin, Secretary; Gary M. Hawkinson, Treasurer. *Directors:* Richard B. Anderson, Albert C. Bersticken, Leigh Carter, Wayne R. Embry, Robert J. Farling, Gary M. Hawkinson, George H. Kaull, Terrence G. Linnert, Frank E. Mosier, E. Lyle Pepin, Jans T. Percio, Lyman C. Phillips, Sister Mary Martha Reinhard, Robert A. Silwinski, Paul M. Smart, David W. Whitehead.

Financial data. Data for fiscal year ended December 31, 1992.
Assets: $17,741,094 (M). *Total grants disbursed:* $1,655,363.

Environmental awards. *Program and interests:* Special interests include:
- Energy conservation.
  Demand-side management programs designed to help customers use energy more efficiently.
- Solid waste.
  Technical and engineering support to local governments on waste management.
  Recycling programs.
- Forests.
  Green Up program donating trees for planting at elementary and secondary schools across Northern Ohio.
  Replacement of larger trees with smaller ones near power lines to reduce the chance of power outages.

Issues. Cli Bio Lan Agr Wat Oce Ene Was Tox Pop Dev
             •   •   •

Application process. *Initial contact:* Letter (1–2 pages) to include:
1. Amount requested.
2. Need for the grant.
3. Area served by applicant organization.
4. Brief history of organization.
5. Description of organization's contributions to the area.
6. Listing of organization's officers and trustees.
7. Current IRS verification—dated within one year of application date—showing nonprofit status.
8. Most current report from the Greater Cleveland Growth Association (for Cleveland area organizations only).

When to apply: Anytime. The Contributions Committee meets monthly.

Emphases. *Recipients:* Nonprofit organizations.
Types of support: Annual campaigns, capital campaigns/expenses, equipment, facilities, matching funds, operating costs, projects.
Geography: Northeastern and northwestern Ohio, especially the Cleveland and Toledo areas.

Limitations. *Recipients:* Individuals.
Activities: Research.
Types of support: Debt retirement, endowments, fellowships, loans, scholarships.

The Champlin Foundations
410 South Main Street
Providence, Rhode Island 02903
Tel: 401–421–3719
EIN: 516010168   Type: Independent
Contact: David A. King, Executive Director

History and philosophy. The Champlin Foundation Trust was established in Delaware in 1932 by George S. Champlin, Hope C. Neaves, and Florence C. Hamilton, who also founded the Second Champlin Foundation Trust in 1947. George S. Champlin

C

established The Third Champlin Foundation in 1975. Foundations grants have supported land conservation, environment, and a zoo; public schools, colleges and universities; libraries; social services, youth, and fitness; hospitals and health care; humane societies; arts and sciences; and historic preservation.

Officers and directors. *Officer:* David A. King, Executive Director. *Distribution Committee:* Francis C. Carter, John Gorham, Louis R. Hampton, Earl W. Harrington, Jr., Robert W. Kenyon, David A. King, Norma B. LaFreniere, John W. Linnell. *Trustee:* Bank of Delaware.

Financial data. Data for fiscal year ended December 31, 1993. *Assets:* $295,624,526 (M). *Total grants authorized:* $13,032,592.

Environmental awards. *Program and interests:* In 1993, 10 percent of the Foundations' awards were for open space, conservation, parks, and environment.
Recent grants: Most of the 1993 grant dollars went for acquisition of land bordering lakes, rivers, Narragansett Bay, or the Atlantic Ocean. A second major environmental focus was the Rhode Island Zoological Society at the Roger Williams Park Zoo.

Issues. Cli Bio Lan Agr Wat Oce Ene Was Tox Pop Dev
         •   •   •   •

Funding analysis.

Fiscal year:	1991	1993
Env grants auth:	$1,251,000	$1,317,000
Number:	3	5
Range:	$1,000–$1,000,000	$7,000–$1,000,000
Median:	$250,000	$85,000
Pct $ auth (env/total):	9	10

Recipients (1993):	Number:	Dollars:
The Nature Conservancy, Rhode Island Field Office	1	1,000,000
Rhode Island Zoological Society	1	200,000
Save the Bay, Inc.	1	85,000
The Mary Elizabeth Sharpe Street Tree Endowment	1	25,000
Norman Bird Sanctuary	1	7,000

Activity region (1993):	Number:	Dollars:
U.S. Northeast	5	1,317,000

Sample grants (1993).
The Nature Conservancy, Rhode Island Field Office. Providence, RI. $1,000,000. To be used in conjunction with the Rhode Island Department of Environmental Management for acquisition of land for open space and recreation.
Norman Bird Sanctuary. Middletown, RI. $7,000. For storage cases and equipment to house a bird collection.
Rhode Island Zoological Society. Providence, RI. $200,000. Toward the cost to construct an educational center.
Save the Bay, Inc. Providence, RI. $85,000. To construct an environmentally sound boat for patrolling Narragansett Bay.
The Mary Elizabeth Sharpe Street Tree Endowment. Providence, RI. $25,000. To increase the endowment to generate income for planting trees on the streets of Providence.

Application process. *Initial contact:* Letter (1 page) including:

1. Project description.
2. Intended purpose, cost, and amount requested.
3. Status of fundraising efforts and other sources of funding. Append documentation of tax-exempt status.

When to apply: Between April 1 and August 31. The distribution committee meets in November.
Materials available: Annual report, application guidelines.

Emphases. *Recipients:* Nonprofit organizations, zoos and aquariums.
Activities: Land acquisition.
Types of support: Capital campaigns/expenses, computer hardware, debt retirement, equipment, facilities, mortgage reduction.
Geography: Rhode Island.

Limitations. *Recipients:* Individuals.
Types of support: Annual campaigns, continuing support, loans, operating costs.

Changing Horizons Charitable Trust
2035 Twinbrook Road
Berwyn, Pennsylvania 19312
Tel: 215–296–5914
Type: Independent
EGA member
Contact: John A. Harris, Trustee

Officers and directors. *Trustee:* John A. Harris.

Financial data. Data for fiscal year ended December 31, 1992. *Total grants authorized:* $1,074,000.

Environmental awards. *Program and interests:* The Trust has had a longstanding interest in energy efficiency. It currently focuses on "the automobile and related media efforts."

Issues. Cli Bio Lan Agr Wat Oce Ene Was Tox Pop Dev
              •   •   •

Funding analysis.

Fiscal year:	1992
Env grants auth:	$1,047,900
Number:	34
Range:	$5,000–$215,000
Median:	$15,750
Pct $ auth (env/total):	—

Recipients (1992 highest):	Number:	Dollars:
Greenhouse Crisis Foundation	1	215,000
Communications Consortium	1	120,000
Advocacy Institute	1	90,000
Citizens Vote	1	60,000
Safe Energy Communication Council	1	50,000

Activity regions (1992):	Number:	Dollars:
U.S. not specified	30	963,900
U.S. Mid-Atlantic	2	52,500
New York/New Jersey	2	31,500

© 1995 Environmental Data Resources, Inc.

Sample grants (1992).
Advocacy Institute. Washington, DC. $90,000. Network for efficient, safe, and sustainable transportation.
American Horizons, Inc. Washington, DC. $5,000. For education efforts of the League of Conservation Voters.
Americans for the Environment. Washington, DC. $20,000. General support.
Clean Water Fund. Washington, DC. $45,000. To support efforts in Maryland to reduce automobile emissions and usage and general organizational expenses.
Greenhouse Crisis Foundation. Washington, DC. $215,000. For work on sustainable transportation ($100,000), Beyond Beef ($110,000), and a Green Wave Planning grant ($5,000).
Henry A. Wallace Institute of Alternative Agriculture. Greenbelt, MD. $7,900. General support.
Nuclear Information and Resource Service. Washington, DC. $25,000. General support.
Transportation Alternatives. New York, NY. $16,500. Win-win study on auto externality costs.

Application process. *Initial contact:* The Trust generally awards grants to pre-selected organizations. It does not solicit proposals.

Emphases. *Recipients:* Pre-selected organizations only.

Cheeryble Foundation
c/o Manny Flekman & Company
9171 Wilshire Boulevard, Suite 530
Beverly Hills, California 90210-5564
Tel: 301-274-5847
EIN: 954121906   Type: Independent
Contact: Zora Charles, President

History and philosophy. The Cheeryble Foundation was established in 1987 by Les and Zora Charles. Grantmaking interests include the arts, culture, literacy, and conservation.

Officers and directors. *Officers:* Zora Charles, President and Secretary; Les Charles, CFO. *Directors:* Les Charles, Zora Charles.

Financial data. Data for fiscal year ended December 31, 1993. *Assets:* $688,641 (M). *Gifts received:* $500,000. *Total grants disbursed:* $238,332.

Environmental awards. *Recent grants:* 1993 grants included support for forests, marine issues, wildlife, and zoos.

Issues. Cli Bio Lan Agr Wat Oce Ene Was Tox Pop Dev
              •   •   •   •   •

Funding analysis.

Fiscal year:	1991	1993
Env grants disb:	$48,145	$143,680
Number:	4	10
Range:	$300–$30,000	$100–$63,000
Median:	$8,923	$2,500
Pct $ disb (env/total):	40	60

Recipients (1993 highest):	Number:	Dollars:
World Wildlife Fund	1	63,000
TreePeople	1	30,000
American Oceans Campaign	1	25,000
Las Positas Park Foundation	1	17,910
Monterey Bay Aquarium	1	2,500
The Nature Conservancy, California Field Office	1	2,500

Activity regions (1993):	Number:	Dollars:
U.S. West	8	79,260
International	1	63,000
U.S. not specified	1	1,420

Sample grants (1993).
American Oceans Campaign. Santa Monica, CA. $25,000.
Greater Los Angeles Zoo Association. Los Angeles, CA. $1,000.
Greenpeace USA. Washington, DC. $1,420.
Las Positas Park Foundation. Santa Barbara, CA. $17,910.
Monterey Bay Aquarium. Monterey, CA. $2,500.
The Nature Conservancy, California Field Office. San Francisco, CA. $2,500.
Santa Barbara Zoological Society. Santa Barbara, CA. $100.
Sierra Club Foundation. San Francisco, CA. $250.
TreePeople. Beverly Hills, CA. $30,000.
World Wildlife Fund. Washington, DC. $63,000.

Application process. *Initial contact:* Proposal.
When to apply: Anytime.

Ben B. Cheney Foundation
First Interstate Plaza, Suite 1600
Tacoma, Washington 98402
Tel: 206-572-2442
EIN: 916053760   Type: Independent
Contact: William O. Rieke, M.D., Executive Director

History and philosophy. The Ben B. Cheney Foundation was established in 1955 by Ben B. Cheney and Marian Cheney Olrogg. Ben Cheney founded the Cheney Lumber Company. The Foundation began active grantmaking in 1975. Its mission is to address a wide range of needs in the communities where the Cheney Lumber Company operated. This includes Tacoma and Pierce County; southwestern Washington; southern Oregon; and the seven northernmost counties in California.

The Foundation prefers "projects which enable the development of new and innovative approaches to community problems, facilitate the improvement of services or programs, or that make an investment in equipment or facilities that will have a long-lasting impact on community needs." The Foundation has eight program areas: Charity, Civic, Culture, Education, Elderly, Health, Social Services, and Youth.

Officers and directors. *Officers:* Francis I. Cheney, President; Elgin E. Olrogg, Vice President; John F. Hansler, Secretary; Bradbury F. Cheney, Treasurer. *Directors:* Bradbury F. Cheney, R. Gene Grant, John F. Hansler, Elgin E. Olrogg.

Financial data. Data for fiscal year ended December 31, 1994. *Assets:* $65,000,000 (est.). *Total grants authorized:* $2,800,000 (est.).

Environmental awards. *Program and interests:* The Foundation does not consider itself an environmental grantmaker.
Recent grants: 1993 grants included support for preservation of natural areas, species preservation, and outdoor recreation.

Issues.   Cli   Bio   Lan   Agr   Wat   Oce   Ene   Was   Tox   Pop   Dev
                    •   •   •

Funding analysis.

Fiscal year:	1991	1993
Env grants auth:	$186,000	$117,500
Number:	9	8
Range:	$8,000–$50,000	$7,000–$25,000
Median:	$18,000	$12,500
Pct $ auth (env/total):	8	5

Recipients (1993 highest):	Number:	Dollars:
Foothills Rails-to-Trails Coalition	1	25,000
Mountain Circle	1	23,000
Jacksonville Woodlands Association	1	20,000
KCTS/9 Public Television	1	15,000
Mercy Medical Center	1	10,000
Point Defiance Zoo and Aquarium	1	10,000

Activity regions (1993):	Number:	Dollars:
U.S. Northwest	6	84,500
U.S. West	2	33,000

Sample grants (1993).
Columbia Pacific Resource Conservation & Development. Aberdeen, WA. $7,500. Support the Harbormill project.
Foothills Rails-to-Trails Coalition. Buckley, WA. $25,000. Complete the trail's model mile near Sumner.
Jacksonville Woodlands Association. Jacksonville, OR. $20,000. Purchase Beekman Woods to expand public park lands.
Mercy Medical Center. Mt. Shasta, CA. $10,000. Develop wheelchair-accessible nature trails at the hospital.
Mountain Circle. Greenville, CA. $23,000. Purchase a van for transporting foster children in the wilderness.
Wooden Boat Foundation. Port Townsend, WA. $7,000. Scholarships for the Summer Youth Sea Symposium.

Application process. *Initial contact:* Letter of inquiry (2 pages maximum), that outlines:
1. Organization history, mission, and scope of operations.
2. Proposal summary.
3. Specific amount requested from the Foundation and purpose for which it would be used.

The Foundation discourages applicants from submitting attachments with the initial query or unsolicited detailed proposals.
When to apply: Anytime. The board meets four times a year to review and approve grant requests.
Materials available: Annual report (includes "Application Process").

Emphases. *Recipients:* Nonprofit organizations.
Activities: Innovative programs.

Types of support: Equipment, facilities, general purposes, scholarships, seed money.
Geography: Tacoma and Pierce County, Washington; southwestern Washington; southern Oregon; the seven northernmost counties in California.

Limitations. *Recipients:* Individuals, public agencies, religious organizations.
Activities: Conferences, media projects, publications, research, seminars, travel (student).
Types of support: Endowments, loans, operating costs.

Chesapeake Bay Trust
60 West Street, Suite 200–A
Annapolis, Maryland 21401
Tel: 410–974–2941   Fax: 410–269–0387
EIN: 521454182
Contact: Thomas L. Burden, Executive Director

History and philosophy. "The Chesapeake Bay Trust is a nonprofit organization created by the Maryland General Assembly in 1985 to promote public awareness and participation in the restoration and protection of the Chesapeake Bay." With financial support from the private sector, the Trust offers grants for activities that contribute to protection and restoration of the Bay. Grants are limited to activities in the state of Maryland.

Officers and directors. *Officers:* Thomas L. Burden, Executive Director and Secretary. *Trustees:* Thomas H. Boggs, Jr., Honorable Torrey C. Brown, M.D., Leslie B. Disharoon, Honorable Arthur Dorman, Walter L. Dunkle, Frances H. Flanigan, Gary R. Fuhrman, Honorable Betty K. Gardner, James C. Johnson, Honorable Robert R. Neall, Honorable George W. Owings, III, Dr. Arnall Patz, Honorable Robert Perciasepe, Brice R. Phillips, JoAnn M. Roberts, Honorable Rosemary Roswell, Kathleen Cloyd Sher, Calman J. Zamoiski.

Financial data. Data for fiscal year ended June 30, 1993. *Assets:* $6,695,384 (M). *Gifts received:* $113,028. *Total grants disbursed:* $450,089.

Environmental awards. *Program and interests:* The Trust supports:

- Preservation of water quality and wildlife habitat.
- Restoration of aquatic and land resources.

It makes awards for direct conservation activities and also for the development of public awareness through publications, media programs, and training.
Recent grants: 1993 grants included support for watershed protection, coastal issues, ecosystem and habitat preservation, forest protection, sustainable agriculture, waste reduction, and classroom and public education.

Issues.   Cli   Bio   Lan   Agr   Wat   Oce   Ene   Was   Tox   Pop   Dev
                •   •   •   •   •   •   •   •   •

Funding analysis.

Fiscal year:	1991	1993
Env grants auth:	$778,115	$472,098
Number:	142	236
Range:	$135–$125,252	$53–$25,000
Median:	$1,000	$991
Pct $ disb (env/total):	100	100

Recipients (1993 highest):	*Number:*	*Dollars:*
Alliance for the Chesapeake Bay	3	31,460
Maryland Save Our Streams	2	23,939
Governor's Chesapeake Bay Communications Office	3	22,322
Maryland Citizens Planners Association	1	18,450
Audubon Naturalist Society of the Central Atlantic States	1	14,400

Activity region (1993):	*Number:*	*Dollars:*
U.S. Mid-Atlantic	236	472,098

Sample grants (1993).
Anne Arundel County Office of Planning and Zoning. Annapolis, MD. $2,900. To continue a citizens' water monitoring program.
Friends of Calvert Cliffs. Cove Point, MD. $5,000. For a boardwalk nature trail at Calvert State Park.
Harper's Choice Middle School. Columbia, MD. $600. Marsh grass planting and shoreline cleanup by seventh graders.
Havre de Grace High School. Havre de Grace, MD. $500. For a composting center, tree nursery, and stream testing equipment.
The Johns Hopkins University, Institute for Policy Studies. Baltimore, MD. $2,000. Educational program on the effect of air pollution on the Bay.
The Loading Dock, Inc. Baltimore, MD. $3,700. Paint recycling by commercial builders to nonprofit organizations and low-income homeowners.
Maryland Native Plant Society. Rockville, MD. $1,000. For materials describing the role of native plants in water conservation and pollution control.
The Park School. Brooklandville, MD. $375. For a sixth-grade organic gardening project to promote Bay conservation.
Partnership in Natural & Environmental Studies. Jessup, MD. $5,400. To develop an environmental study area on the grounds of Patuxent Valley Middle School.
Pickering Creek Environmental Center. Easton, MD. $14,350. Educational materials on sustainable agriculture for Eastern Shore schools.
Queen Anne's County Recreation and Parks. Centreville, MD. $1,000. Tree planting at Terrapin Beach Park.

Application process. *Initial contact:* Complete the grant application form available from the Trust. "For more comprehensive proposals" include:
1. A written description of project stating the need, its goals and objectives, and its significance to any other related activities. Appropriate details on location, drawings, etc., must be provided.
2. Name and description of requesting organization, along with names and qualifications of individuals working on project. The name, address, and telephone number of the project leader or coordinator of the activity.
3. Specific amount of grant requested.
4. Line-item budget, describing all estimated expenses, all sources and amounts of funding, and a proposed schedule of spending.
5. Schedule of project.
6. Description of plans and commitments for continuing support beyond the grant period (for activities of a long-term or ongoing nature).
7. Plan for evaluation of project success and effectiveness and a means to confirm completion of the activity.
8. Explanation of how proposed project might have a secondary, positive impact on other groups, inspiring them to undertake similar activities or serve as a model for others to design similar activities.

When to apply: Anytime. However, applications must be received not later than 60 days prior to the next quarterly meeting of the board of trustees. Call for submission deadlines.
Materials available: Annual report (includes "Criteria for Grants" and "Applying to the Trust"), grant application form.

Emphases. *Recipients:* Educational institutions, museums, nonprofit organizations, public agencies, research institutions, zoos.
Activities: Citizen participation, collaborative efforts, demonstration programs, education, publications, training, volunteerism, workshops, youth programs.
Types of support: Equipment, pilot projects, projects, seed money.
Geography: Chesapeake Bay region in Maryland, only.

Limitations. *Recipients:* Individuals.
Activities: Activism, advocacy, feasibility studies, fieldwork, fundraising, inventories, land acquisition, litigation, lobbying, research.
Types of support: Advertising campaigns, annual campaigns, capital campaigns/expenses, computer hardware, debt retirement, emergency funding, endowments, facilities, fellowships, general purposes, indirect costs, leveraging funds, loans, maintenance, membership campaigns, mortgage reduction, multi-year grants, operating costs, professorships, scholarships, travel expenses.

Chesapeake Corporation Foundation
1021 East Cary Street
P.O. Box 2350
Richmond, Virginia 23218–2350
Tel: 804–697–1000   Fax: 804–697–1199
EIN: 540605823   Type: Company-sponsored
Contact: Alvah H. Eubank, Jr., Secretary/Treasurer

History and philosophy. The Chesapeake Corporation Foundation was established in 1955. Chesapeake Corporation, the integrated paper and forest products company, is its sole donor and the Foundation's orientation is toward communities where Corporation employees live. Program areas are: Community Service, Culture, Education, and Health and Medicine.

C

Officers and directors. *Officer:* Alvah H. Eubank, Jr., Secretary/Treasurer. *Trustees:* O. D. Dennis, Jr., Thomas G. Harris, George P. Mueller, Sture G. Olsson, W. T. Robinson.

Financial data. Data for fiscal year ended December 31, 1992. *Assets:* $976,144 (M). *Gifts received:* $380,000. *Total grants disbursed:* $660,620.

Environmental awards. *Recent grants:* 1992 grants included support for education (higher and public), particularly pertaining to forests and coastal and marine issues.

Issues. Cli Bio• Lan• Agr Wat• Oce• Ene Was Tox Pop Dev

Funding analysis.

Fiscal year:	1991	1992
Env grants disb:	$91,000	$36,000
Number:	10	7
Range:	$3,000–$20,000	$1,000–$10,000
Median:	$6,000	$5,000
Pct $ disb (env/total):	14	5

Recipients (1992 highest):	Number:	Dollars:
Virginia Institute of Marine Science	2	15,000
Nature Science Center	1	6,000
North Carolina Forestry Foundation, Inc.	1	6,000
Chesapeake Bay Foundation	1	5,000
Virginia Forests Educational Fund	1	3,000

Activity regions (1992):	Number:	Dollars:
U.S. Mid-Atlantic	5	24,000
U.S. Southeast	2	12,000

Sample grants (1992).
Chesapeake Bay Foundation. Annapolis, MD. $5,000.
The Nature Conservancy, Virginia Field Office. Charlottesville, VA. $1,000.
North Carolina Forestry Foundation, Inc. Raleigh, NC. $6,000.
Virginia Forests Educational Fund. Richmond, VA. $3,000.
Virginia Institute of Marine Science. Gloucester Point, VA. $5,000.

Application process. *Initial contact:* Brief statement of the need for funds and grant purpose. If solicited, full proposal to include:
1. Concise statement of grant purpose and results sought.
2. Project budget, organization's budget and financial position.
3. Key project personnel and their qualifications.
4. List of members of the governing body.
5. Other sources to which the applicant has submitted or intends to submit proposals for funding, and amount(s) requested.
6. Copy of IRS tax-exempt status determination letter.
7. Statement from the applicant's governing body verifying that the proposal has been reviewed and approved for submission.

When to apply: The trustees meet in January, June, and October.
Materials available: Application guidelines.

Emphases. *Recipients:* Educational institutions, nonprofit organizations.
Activities: Education (elementary/secondary/higher).

Types of support: Capital campaigns/expenses, endowments, matching funds, program-related investments, scholarships.
Geography: Southeastern United States (areas of company operation).

Limitations. *Recipients:* Individuals.

The Chevron Companies

P.O. Box 7753
San Francisco, California 94120–7753
Tel: 415–894–6083 Fax: 415–894–5447
EIN: 940890210 Type: Company-sponsored
EGA member
Contact: David McMurry, Contributions Counsel

History and philosophy. Chevron is an integrated petroleum company involved in all aspects of the energy business: exploration, production, manufacturing, transportation, marketing, and research. Chevron has had a corporate giving program since 1939. Program areas include: Education, Health and Human Services, Civic Involvement, Arts, Environment, and International Relations.

Officers and directors. *Officers:* Kenneth T. Derr, Chairman and CEO; J. Dennis Bonney, James N. Sullivan, Vice Chairmen; Ray E. Galvin, David R. Hoyer, Richard H. Matzke, John E. Peppercorn, Corporate Vice Presidents; George K. Carter, William E. Crain, Lloyd E. Elkins, Roderick L. Hartung, Donald G. Henderson, Harvey D. Hinman, Ronald C. Kiskis, Martin R. Klitten, Jr., David J. O'Reilly, Vice Presidents; Malcolm J. McAuley, Corporate Secretary. *Directors:* Samuel H. Armacost, J. Dennis Bonney, William E. Crain, Kenneth T. Derr, Sam L. Ginn, Carla A. Hills, Charles M. Pigott, Condoleeza Rice, S. Bruce Smart, Jr., James N. Sullivan, George H. Weyerhaeuser, John A. Young.

Financial data. Data for fiscal year ended December 31, 1993. *Assets:* $34,736,000,000 (U) (est.). *Total grants disbursed:* $19,000,000.

Environmental awards. *Program and interests:* The premise of the environmental program is that human welfare depends on the wise management of the earth's natural resources. Funding interests include:

- Wildlife and habitat protection/restoration.
- Conservation.
- Risk assessment.
- Environmental education programs that present a balanced view of the issues.

Chevron in partnership with Times Mirror Magazines, Inc. co-sponsors a special Conservation Awards Program, which recognizes outstanding contributions by individuals and groups to the conservation of natural resources. Nominations are accepted each fall. Recent awards have been made for work in land and wetland habitat conservation, wildlife protection, and water resource protection.

Issues. Cli • Bio • Lan • Agr • Wat • Oce • Ene • Was • Tox • Pop • Dev •

Funding analysis.

Fiscal year:	1991	1992
Env grants disb:	$1,974,821	$1,673,526
Number:	127	114
Range:	$3,660–$104,645	$5,000–$107,769
Median:	$8,500	$8,550
Pct $ disb (env/total):	7	7

Recipients (1992 highest):	Number:	Dollars:
The San Francisco Zoological Society	1	105,000
Aquarium of the Americas	1	50,000
Media Institute–Environmental Reporting Forum	1	50,000
Yosemite Fund	1	35,000
Keystone Center	1	30,000

Activity regions (1992 highest):	Number:	Dollars:
U.S. not specified	27	637,073
U.S. West	37	468,350
U.S. South Central	9	106,000
International*	7	103,742
Canada	5	90,696

*Multiple regions or not specified.

Sample grants (1993).
Earthwatch Expeditions, Inc. Watertown, MA. $16,500.
Marine Mammal Center. Sausalito, CA. $10,000.
National Fish and Wildlife Foundation. Washington, DC. $27,500.
The Student Conservation Association, Inc. Arlington, VA. $5,000.
World Wildlife Fund. Washington, DC. $10,000
Yosemite Fund. San Francisco, CA. $35,000.

Application process. *Initial contact:* Concise letter (2 pages maximum) including:
Specific project request.
1. Brief description of activity or project.
2. Description of need and how project meets identified needs not being met by other community groups.
3. Timetable for project implementation.
4. Expected results: who will benefit and how.
5. Method of evaluating project effectiveness and communicating results to donors and similar organizations.
6. Project budget, including sources of financial support and amounts received, committed, or pending.
7. Plans for continued funding, if project will be ongoing.
General information.
1. Organization name, address, telephone number, and contact person.
2. Brief statement of organization's history, goals, and accomplishments.
3. Geographic area and number of people served by the organization.
4. Number of volunteers participating in the organization's activities.
5. Copy of IRS tax-exempt status determination letter and tax ID number.
6. Names and affiliations of the organization's governing board and brief background information on the executive director and key staff members.
7. Copy of the organization's most recent audited financial statement and current operating budget containing: amounts and percentages of income utilized for program, administration, fundraising, and general expenses; list of current sources of unrestricted and restricted funds (i.e., corporations, foundations, government, federated campaigns, individuals).
8. Copy of the organization's most recent IRS Form 990, including state supplement, if applicable.
When to apply: Anytime.
Community organizations should direct grant applications and requests for information to the Chevron Public Affairs Manager nearest their area of operation. To identify the appropriate contact, call 415–894–4193.
Materials available: Annual report, "Report of Contributions," "Grant Application Guidelines."

Emphases. *Recipients:* Nonprofit organizations.
Activities: Collaborative efforts, education, innovative programs, policy analysis/development, research (scientific), volunteerism.
Types of support: Annual campaigns, continuing support.
Geography: Projects near areas of company operations are preferred.

Limitations. *Recipients:* Individuals, public agencies, religious organizations.
Activities: Activism, audiovisual materials, conferences, fundraising, litigation, political activities.
Types of support: Advertising campaigns, capital campaigns/expenses, endowments, equipment, facilities, travel expenses.

The Chicago Community Trust
222 North LaSalle Street, Suite 1400
Chicago, Illinois 60601–1009
Tel: 312–372–3356   Fax: 312–580–7411
EIN: 362167000   Type: Community
EGA member
Contact: Janice Bennett, Senior Staff Associate

History and philosophy. One of some three hundred community foundations in the United States and Canada, The Chicago Community Trust, established in 1915, is the second oldest and the fourth largest. Albert W. Harris of Chicago's Harris Trust and Savings helped design The Trust using the model pioneered in Cleveland by Frederick Goff. The Trust receives its money from a wide range of individuals, families, and organizations. Funds are used "for such charitable purposes as will . . . best make for the mental, moral, intellectual, and physical improvement, assistance, and relief of the inhabitants of Cook County." The Trust gives grants in the broad areas of Health, Social Services, Arts and Humanities, Education, and Civic Affairs. It also has a number of special programs, each with unique guidelines.

Officers and directors. *Officers:* Edgar D. Jannotta, Chairman. *Executive Committee:* Judith S. Block, William M. Daley, Milton Davis, Margaret D. Hartigan, Edgar D. Jannotta, Margaret P. MacKimm, Richard M. Morrow, Virginia F. Ojeda, Cordell Reed, Shirley W. Ryan, Eugene A. Tracy, Ormand J. Wade.

Financial data. Data for fiscal year ended September 30, 1993. *Assets:* $291,524,501 (C). *Gifts received:* $4,429,522. *Total grants disbursed:* $34,428,947.

Environmental awards. *Program and interests:* The Trust usually makes environmental grants through its Civic Affairs program. Areas of interest include:

- Open space.
- Solid waste management.
- Water quality (Lake Michigan, groundwater).
- Ecosystem preservation/restoration.

Issues. Cli Bio Lan Agr Wat Oce Ene Was Tox Pop Dev
            •   •   •

Funding analysis.§

Fiscal year:	1991	1993
Env grants auth:	$820,288	$141,004
Number:	61	79
Range:	$250–$126,875	$400–$8,100
Median:	$5,000	$1,700
Pct $ auth (env/total):	3	1

Recipients (1993 highest):	Number:	Dollars:
Chicago/Cook County		
4–H Foundation	8	17,425
Chicago Horticultural Society	3	11,050
Field Museum of Natural History	1	7,365
Ducks Unlimited, Inc.	1	6,058
Izaak Walton League of America Endowment	1	6,058

Activity region (1993):	Number:	Dollars:
U.S. Great Lakes	79	141,004

§Does not include certain designated and matching grants.

Sample grants (1993).
Ducks Unlimited, Inc. Northbrook, IL. $6,058.
Izaak Walton League of America Endowment. Iowa City, IA. $6,058.
Urbs in Horto Fund/Tree Fund. Chicago, IL. $120,388 (multiple grants).

Application process. *Initial contact:* Telephone call or full proposal. Proposal to include:
1. Cover letter and brief background and purposes of request.
2. Written approval from CEO or other authorized individual.
3. Copy of IRS tax-exempt status determination letter.
4. List of members of the governing board.
5. Copy of most recent audited financial statement.
6. Current financial statement.
7. Current operating budget.

When to apply: Anytime.
Materials available: Annual report, *The Trust Quarterly* (quarterly report).

Emphases. *Recipients:* Charitable agencies or institutions that serve the inhabitants of Cook County, Illinois.
Geography: Cook County, Illinois; Lake Michigan.

Limitations. *Recipients:* Individuals, coalitions/networks, unless certain minimum conditions are satisfied.
Activities: Audio/visual/printed materials, conferences, exhibitions/tours, festivals, meetings.
Types of support: Certain requests to replace lost government funds, computer hardware without a feasibility study, debt retirement, endowments, equipment purchased by agencies engaged in program activities undertaken by a large number of similar agencies or institutes, facilities (construction), operating costs, scholarships.

Chrysler Corporation Fund

12000 Chrysler Drive
CIMS: 416–13–22
Highland Park, Michigan 48288–1919
Tel: 313-956-5194   Fax: 313-956-1462
EIN: 386087371   Type: Company-sponsored
Contact: Lynn A. Feldhouse, Manager

History and philosophy. The Chrysler Corporation Fund was established in 1953. It "was created to strengthen Chrysler's ability to support and enhance the well-being of the many communities in which the Company operates and to provide a means of support for selected national nonprofit organizations." Grants are awarded in four program areas: Education, Health and Human Services, Civic and Community, Culture and the Arts. Support for education is the Fund's highest priority. Each year almost half of all grants are designated for educational organizations and projects.

Officers and directors. *Officers:* A. C. Liebler, President; S. W. Bergeron, Vice President and Treasurer; L. A. Feldhouse, Secretary/Manager; C. A. Smith, Controller; J. A. Kozlowski, K. L. Trinh; Assistant Secretaries; T. J. Osborn, R. M. Sherwood, Assistant Treasurers. *Trustees:* S. W. Bergeron, F. J. Castaing, T. G. Denomme, M. M. Glusac, A. C. Liebler, W. J. O'Brien, III, E. T. Pappert, L. J. Piedra, L. C. Richie, G. C. Valade.

Financial data. Data for fiscal year ended December 31, 1993. *Assets:* $32,456,606 (M). *Gifts received:* $24,169,500. *Total grants disbursed:* $8,166,855.

Environmental awards. *Program and interests:* Most environmental grants are awarded through the Civic and Community program area. *Recent grants:* 1993 grants included support for beautification, wildlife protection, energy efficiency, and environmental careers.

Issues. Cli Bio Lan Agr Wat Oce Ene Was Tox Pop Dev
            •   •   •

Funding analysis.

Fiscal year:	1993
Env grants disb:	$33,000
Number:	9
Range:	$1,500–$10,000
Median:	$2,500
Pct $ disb (env/total):	<1

Recipients (1993 highest):	*Number:*	*Dollars:*
Racine Zoological Society	1	10,000
Keep America Beautiful	1	5,000
World Wildlife Fund	1	5,000
Alliance to Save Energy	1	2,500
Festival of Trees, Inc.	1	2,500
Indiana Environmental Institute, Inc.	1	2,500

Activity regions (1993):	*Number:*	*Dollars:*
U.S. Great Lakes	4	17,000
U.S. not specified	4	11,000
International*	1	5,000

*Multiple regions or not specified.

Sample grants (1993).
Alliance to Save Energy. Washington, DC. $2,500.
Detroit Zoological Society. Royal Oak, MI. $2,000.
The Environmental Careers Organization, Inc. Cleveland, OH. $2,000.
Environmental Law Institute. Washington, DC. $1,500.
Indiana Environmental Institute, Inc. Indianapolis, IN. $2,500.
Keep America Beautiful. New York, NY. $5,000.
World Wildlife Fund. Washington, DC. $5,000.

Application process. *Initial contact:* Letter to include:
1. Description of applicant organization: legal name, history, activities, goals, and objectives.
2. Summary of proposed project describing need, methods, population served, and proposed evaluation methods.
3. Annual budget for organization and proposed project, with amount requested.
4. Other sources and amounts of funding, actual and projected, from both public and private sources. List grants provided by other companies and foundations.
5. Explanation of the relationship, if any, to a United Way organization or government agency.
6. List of officers and board of directors.
7. Copy of IRS tax-exempt status determination letter.
8. Most recent audited financial report, audit statement (if available) and a copy of IRS Form 990.

Except in Michigan, organizations where Chrysler has major operations should forward the proposal to the Plant Manager of the local Chrysler facility. All other correspondence should be directed to the Fund Manager at the main address.
When to apply: Anytime.
Materials available: Manual report, "Chrysler Corporation Fund Guidelines."

Emphases. *Recipients:* Educational institutions.
Activities: Education, facilities (construction).

Types of support: Annual campaigns, continuing support, emergency funding, matching funds, operating costs, projects, scholarships.
Geography: Metropolitan Detroit, and Michigan; Alabama, Delaware, Illinois, Indiana, Missouri, New York, Ohio, Wisconsin; United States only.

Limitations. *Recipients:* Educational institutions (primary/secondary schools), individuals, religious organizations.
Activities: Conferences, political activities, research, seminars.
Types of support: Advertising campaigns, debt retirement, endowments, equipment, fellowships, loans, operating costs, travel expenses.

Church & Dwight Co., Inc.
469 North Harrison Street
Princeton, New Jersey 08543–4297
Tel: 609–683–5900   Fax: 609–497–7208
Type: Independent
EGA member
Contact: Bryan N. Thomlison, Director of Public Affairs

History and philosophy. This company manufactures Arm & Hammer Baking Soda. It is a member of the Environmental Grantmakers Association and anticipates developing a foundation in the future.

Liz Claiborne & Art Ortenberg Foundation
650 Fifth Avenue
New York, New York 10019
Tel: 212–333–2536   Fax: 212–956–3531
EIN: 133200329   Type: Independent
Contact: James Murtaugh, Program Manager

History and philosophy. "The Liz Claiborne and Art Ortenberg Foundation is a private body devoted to the conservation of nature and the amelioration of human distress. . . . It seeks to redress the breakdown in the processes linking nature and humanity. It concerns itself particularly with matters of species extinction, habitat destruction and fragmentation, resource depletion, and resource waste. It favors solutions which directly benefit local communities and serve as exemplars for saving species and wildlands. It recognizes the imperative to reconcile nature preservation with human needs and aspirations." While the Foundation "devotes a substantial portion of its funding to Third World countries," it also "supports conservation efforts in the United States, particularly Montana and those western states largely dependent upon extractive industries." Projects funded should be "designed with and supported by the local people most directly affected."

Officers and directors. *Trustees:* Liz Claiborne, Art Ortenberg.
Directors: David Quammen, David Western.

Financial data. Data for fiscal year ended January 31, 1994.
Assets: $37,327,203 (M). *Total grants disbursed:* $1,333,907.

C

Environmental awards. *Program and interests:* The board outlines two primary program interests:

- Mitigation of conflict between the land and resource use practices of rural communities and conservation of biological diversity.
- Implementation of field-based scientific, technical, and practical training programs in conservation biology for local people.

"The Foundation typically funds modest, carefully designed field activities in which local communities have a substantial *proprietary* interest."

Issues.   *Cli   Bio   Lan   Agr   Wat   Oce   Ene   Was   Tox   Pop   Dev*

Sample grants (1993).*

Missouri Botanical Garden. St. Louis, MO. $79,806. Botanical Training Program: botanical training and inventory of protected area system.

The Nature Conservancy, Montana Field Office. Helena, MT. $25,000. Madison River Land Protection: Reimbursement of landowner costs for conservation easements, first phase.

The Nature Conservancy, Montana Field Office. Helena, MT. $2,000. Hibbard Management Company Agricultural Study: Statewide study of tax and inheritance burden of agricultural properties.

Teton County Development Corporation. Choteau, MT. $3,450. Rangerider Program in Teton and Chotea counties: To coordinate and facilitate community access to state and federal development programs.

Teton Science Center. Kelly, WY. $27,500. ISLANDS Science Outreach Program in the Greater Yellowstone Ecosystem.

World Wildlife Fund. Washington, DC. $35,000. FIIT Agroecosystem Project in the Manchon region of southwestern Guatemala. Biological inventory and mapping preparatory to official consideration as a protected area.

Yale University. New Haven, CT. $61,040. Beza Mahafaly/School of Agronomy Project. Interdisciplinary research at Beza in collaboration with a community-based NGO.

*Sample grants represent either new awards or disbursements on grants awarded in previous years.

Application process. *Initial contact:* Letter of proposal to include:
1. Project objectives.
2. Anticipated duration and projected budget.
3. Evaluation criteria.
4. Information on local volunteer groups and other outside NGOs involved.

If funded, a semi-annual progress report will be required and Foundation trustees will schedule visits to the project site.
When to apply: Anytime.
Materials available: Brochure (includes application guidelines), Project Summary.

Emphases. *Recipients:* Botanical gardens, educational institutions.
Activities: Activism, citizen participation, education, fieldwork, planning, research, technical assistance, training, workshops.
Types of support: Scholarships, seed money.

Geography: Northern Rocky Mountains region; Third World countries.

Limitations. *Recipients:* Individuals.
Types of support: General purposes, operating costs.

Claneil Foundation, Inc.

630 West Germantown Pike, Suite 400
Plymouth Meeting, Pennsylvania 19462–1059
Tel: 610–828–6331   Fax: 610–828–6405
EIN: 236445450   Type: Independent
Contact: Dr. Henry A. Jordan, Executive Director

History and philosophy. The Claneil Foundation, Inc. was established in 1968 through donations by Henry S. McNeil. It supports innovative ideas from both public and private sectors, and, although loyal to proven efforts, is willing to assist start-up efforts. The Foundation concentrates its resources in four broad areas: the arts and humanities, education, the responsible stewardship of the natural and man-made environments, and health and human services.

Officers and directors. *Officers:* Lois F. McNeil, President; Barbara M. Jordan, Vice President; Henry A. Jordan, Secretary and Executive Director; Langhorne B. Smith, Treasurer. *Trustees:* Marjorie M. Findlay, Barbara M. Jordan, Henry A. Jordan, Lois F. McNeil, Robert D. McNeil, Langhorne B. Smith.

Financial data. Data for fiscal year ended December 31, 1993. *Assets:* $8,862,631 (M). *Total grants disbursed:* $380,900.

Environmental awards. *Recent grants:* 1993 grants included support for land conservation, watershed protection, beautification, horticulture, and publications.

Issues.   *Cli   Bio   Lan   Agr   Wat   Oce   Ene   Was   Tox   Pop   Dev*

Funding analysis.

Fiscal year:	1993
Env grants disb:	$51,750
Number:	12
Range:	$2,000–$8,000
Median:	$4,625
Pct $ disb (env/total):	14

Recipients (1993 highest):	Number:	Dollars:
Natural Lands Trust	1	8,000
Land Trust Alliance	1	6,000
Earth Action Network, Inc.	1	5,000
Pennsylvania Environmental Council	1	5,000
Schuylkill River Development Council	1	5,000
The Nature Conservancy, Pennsylvania Field Office	1	5,000

Activity regions (1993):	Number:	Dollars:
U.S. Mid-Atlantic	6	28,250
U.S. not specified	5	21,000
U.S. Northeast	1	2,500

Sample grants (1993).
Awbury Arboretum Association. Philadelphia, PA. $4,250.
Earth Action Network, Inc. Norwalk, CT. $5,000.
Land Trust Alliance. Washington, DC. $6,000.
Natural Lands Trust. Media, MD. $8,000.
The Nature Conservancy, Pennsylvania Field Office. Philadelphia, PA. $5,000.
The Nature Conservancy, Massachusetts Field Office. Boston, MA. $2,500.
Pennsylvania Environmental Council. Philadelphia, PA. $5,000.
Pennsylvania Horticultural Society. Philadelphia, PA. $2,000.
Scenic America. Washington, DC. $3,000.
Schuylkill River Development Council. Philadelphia, PA. $5,000.
Wissahickon Valley Watershed Association. Ambler, PA. $4,000.

Application process. *Initial contact:* Letter to include:
1. Description of organization and its goals.
2. Description of project including current status, objectives, and qualifications of personnel involved in the project.
3. Budget and timetable for project.
4. Other sources of funding; current and proposed.
5. Methods of evaluating the results of the program.

If the Foundation is interested, it will request:
1. Copy of latest IRS tax-exempt status determination letter.
2. Statement on the organization's letterhead that there has been no change in the purpose, character, or method of operations subsequent to the issuance of the IRS ruling.
3. Current operating budget for the organization.
4. Audited financial statements, if available.
5. An interim financial statement of income and expenses for the current fiscal period.
6. Names and affiliations of officers and directors or trustees.
7. Any printed materials.
8. If organization has been classified or applied for tax-exempt status, provide information to establish that the requested grant will not result in the loss of that status.

When to apply: Requests are accepted only between January 1 and March 31, and between July 1 and September 30. Grant decisions are made in April and October.
Materials available: Guidelines.

Emphases. *Recipients:* Educational institutions, museums, nonprofit organizations, research institutions.
Activities: Advocacy, capacity building, citizen participation, collaborative efforts, conferences, demonstration programs, education, feasibility studies, fieldwork, innovative programs, networking, publications, seminars, symposia/colloquia, training, volunteerism, workshops, youth programs.
Types of support: Annual campaigns, capital campaigns/expenses, computer hardware, continuing support, emergency funding, equipment, facilities (renovation), general purposes, internships, lectureships, pilot projects, projects, seed money, single-year grants only, technical assistance.
Geography: Southeastern Pennsylvania.

Limitations. *Recipients:* Aquariums, botanical gardens, individuals, public agencies, religious organizations, zoos.
Activities: Conflict resolution, expeditions/tours, inventories, land acquisition, litigation, lobbying, political activities.
Types of support: Advertising campaigns, debt retirement, fellowships, indirect costs, mortgage reduction, scholarships, travel expenses.

© 1995 Environmental Data Resources, Inc.

C

Clark Charitable Trust
P.O. Box 251
Lincoln, Massachusetts 01773
Tel: 617-259-8800
EIN: 046037650   Type: Independent
Contact: Timothy A. Taylor, Trustee

History and philosophy. Established in 1937, the Trust offers support for human welfare, environment, animal welfare, music, and higher education.

Officers and directors. *Trustees:* Russell T. Kopp, Timothy A. Taylor.

Financial data. Data for fiscal year ended December 31, 1992. *Assets:* $2,581,625 (M). *Total grants disbursed:* $78,000.

Environmental awards. *Recent grants:* 1992 grants included support for species preservation and outdoor recreation.

Issues.   Cli   Bio   Lan   Agr   Wat   Oce   Ene   Was   Tox   Pop   Dev
                •   •

Funding analysis.

Fiscal year:	1992
Env grants disb:	$18,000
Number:	4
Range:	$3,000–$5,000
Median:	$5,000
Pct $ disb (env/total):	23

Recipients (1992):	Number:	Dollars:
Appalachian Mountain Club	1	5,000
Massachusetts Audubon Society	1	5,000
World Wildlife Fund	1	5,000
Loon Preservation Committee	1	3,000

Activity regions (1992):	Number:	Dollars:
U.S. Northeast	2	10,000
U.S. not specified	1	5,000
New York/New Jersey	1	3,000

Sample grants (1992).
Appalachian Mountain Club. Boston, MA. $5,000.
Loon Preservation Committee. Meredith, NJ. $3,000.
Massachusetts Audubon Society. Lincoln, MA. $5,000.
World Wildlife Fund. Washington, DC. $5,000.

Application process. *Initial contact:* Letter describing the project's purpose and an audited financial statement.
When to apply: Anytime.
Materials available: Annual report and financial statement.

Emphases. *Activities:* Land acquisition.
Types of support: Annual campaigns, facilities (construction), capital campaigns/expenses, endowments, equipment, matching funds, operating costs, scholarships.

C

The Clark Foundation
30 Wall Street
New York, New York 10005
Tel: 212-269-1833   Fax: 212-747-0087
EIN: 135616528   Type: Independent
Contact: Joseph H. Cruickshank, Secretary

History and philosophy. The Clark Foundation was incorporated in 1931 by members of the family of Edward Clark, a Cooperstown lawyer and one of the founders of the Singer Company. In 1973 the Foundation merged with the Scriven Foundation, another Clark endowment. The Foundation supports community, educational, environmental, health, and youth organizations in the Cooperstown and New York City areas.

Officers and directors. *Officers:* Jane Forbes Clark, II, President; Edward W Stack, Vice President; Joseph H. Cruickshank, Secretary; Kevin S. Moore, Treasurer. *Directors:* Jane Forbes Clark, II, William M. Evarts, Jr., Gates Helms Hawn, Archie F. MacAllaster, Mrs. Edward B. McMenamin, Edward W. Stack, John Hoyt Stookey, A. Pennington Whitehead, Gov. Malcolm Wilson.

Financial data. Data for fiscal year ended June 30, 1993. *Assets:* $290,381,369 (M). *Gifts received:* $2,872,500. *Total grants disbursed:* $7,644,422.

Environmental awards. *Program and interests:* Most of the Foundation's grants are not environmental. *Recent grants:* 1993 grants included support for land conservation, wildlife, and outdoor education.

Issues. Cli Bio• Lan• Agr Wat Oce Ene Was Tox Pop• Dev

Funding analysis.

Fiscal year:	1991	1993
Env grants disb:	$278,184	$301,384
Number:	6	8
Range:	$15,000–$100,000	$6,384–$100,000
Median:	$39,092	$30,000
Pct $ disb (env/total):	5	4

Recipients (1993 highest):	Number:	Dollars:
The Wilderness Society	1	100,000
Outward Bound	2	56,384
Natural Resources Defense Council	1	50,000
National Fish and Wildlife Foundation	1	35,000
The Trust for Public Land	1	25,000

Activity regions (1993):	Number:	Dollars:
U.S. not specified	4	205,000
U.S. Northeast	2	56,384
New York/New Jersey	2	40,000

Sample grants (1993).
National Audubon Society. New York, NY. $20,000.
National Fish and Wildlife Foundation. Washington, DC. $35,000.
Natural Resources Defense Council. New York, NY. $50,000.
Otsego County Conservation Association. Cooperstown, NY. $15,000.
Outward Bound. Greenwich, CT. $50,000.
The Trust for Public Land. New York, NY. $25,000.
The Wilderness Society. Washington, DC. $100,000.

Application process. *Initial contact:* Letter of inquiry. If the Foundation is interested, a complete proposal will be requested. *When to apply:* Anytime. Board meetings are held in October and May.
Materials available: Foundation policy statement (includes "How to Apply" and "Proposal Check List").

Emphases. *Types of support:* Annual campaigns, capital campaigns/expenses, continuing support, emergency funding, equipment, facilities (construction), operating costs, pilot projects, scholarships, seed money.
Geography: New York. Scholarships limited to students in the Cooperstown, New York area.

Limitations. *Recipients:* Individuals.
Types of support: Endowments, research (non-medical).

Robert Sterling Clark Foundation, Inc.
112 East 64th Street, 6th Floor
New York, New York 10021
Tel: 212-308-0411   Fax: 212-755-2133
EIN: 131957792   Type: Independent
Contact: Margaret C. Ayers, Executive Director

History and philosophy. The Robert Sterling Clark Foundation was incorporated in 1952. The donor was Robert Sterling Clark, whose grandfather was one of the original partners in the Singer Sewing Machine Company.

The Foundation awards grants through three program areas: Ensuring Access to Family Planning Services, Improving the Performance of Public Institutions in New York, and Strengthening Cultural Institutions.

Officers and directors. *Officers:* Winthrop R. Munyan, President; Miner D. Crary, Jr., Secretary; Richardson Pratt, Jr., Treasurer. *Directors:* Miner D. Crary, Jr., Raymond D. Horton, Winthrop R. Munyan, Richardson Pratt, Jr., John N. Romans, Philip Svigals, Joanna D. Underwood.

Financial data. Data for fiscal year ended October 31, 1993. *Assets:* $76,455,090 (M). *Total grants disbursed:* $3,489,661.

Environmental awards. *Program and interests:* Environmental grants focus on "encouraging the implementation of solid waste management policies which will protect our environment in accordance with federal and state mandates." They are awarded through the program, "Improving the Performance of Public Institutions in New York."

Recent grants: 1993 grants included support for advocacy and public education to improve waste management and community planning and development.

Issues. Cli• Bio• Lan Agr Wat Oce Ene Was• Tox• Pop• Dev

Funding analysis.

Fiscal year:	1991	1993
Env grants auth:	$248,000	$330,000
Number:	5	7
Range:	$28,000–$60,000	$30,000–$60,000
Median:	$50,000	$50,000
Pct $ auth (env/total):	7	9

Recipients (1993 highest):	Number:	Dollars:
Environmental Defense Fund	1	60,000
INFORM	1	60,000
Natural Resources Defense Council	1	60,000
The New York Botanical Garden	1	50,000
Consumer Policy Institute	1	35,000
New York Environmental Institute	1	35,000

Activity region (1993):	Number:	Dollars:
New York/New Jersey	7	330,000

Sample grants (1993).

Environmental Defense Fund. New York, NY. $60,000. To develop and advocate for proposals to increase the efficiency and cost-effectiveness of New York City's waste prevention and recycling programs. EDF will collaborate with paper producers, large corporate users, and city officials to promote developing markets for recycled materials.

Natural Resources Defense Council. New York, NY. $60,000. New York Solid Waste Management Project. To work with city officials and community groups in resolving problems or disputes associated with the recycling provisions of the city's Solid Waste Plan; advocate for revised legislation; and develop business plans for two community-based recycling facilities.

The New York Botanical Garden. Bronx, NY. $50,000. For a telephone survey and focus groups of potential audiences; small scale test of various marketing strategies; and an analysis of how NYBG might market itself to the travel and tour industry.

New York Environmental Institute. New York, NY. $35,000. Public education and advocacy effort to ensure that Environmental Protection Act funds are used effectively to increase municipal recycling rates. Project staff will work with state officials to formulate energy and transport subsidy policies to attract manufacturers who use recycled materials to New York.

New York University Urban Research Center. New York, NY. $30,000. To identify industries that could process parts of New York's waste stream, provide the Department of Sanitation with data and analyses on them, suggest policies the city might use to attract the industries to the area, and determine how local companies and community development organizations might contribute to the effort.

Application process. *Initial contact:* Full proposal (not to exceed 15 pages) and accompanying materials.
Proposal.
1. Summary (1 page).
2. Description of project.
3. Project budget.
4. Expected results.
5. Plans for evaluation.
6. Plans for future support.
7. Background of those involved.

Accompanying materials.
1. Organization budget (previous, current, and projected years).
2. Most recent audited financial statement.
3. IRS tax-exempt status determination letter.
4. Name and occupations of trustees.
5. Examples of past accomplishments.

When to apply: Anytime. The board of directors meets in January, April, July, and October.
Materials available: Annual report (includes "Proposal Guidelines").

Emphases. *Recipients:* Educational institutions, nonprofit organizations, public agencies, research institutions.
Activities: Advocacy, education, litigation, policy analysis/development, political activities, publications.
Geography: New York City; New York State.

The Cleveland Foundation
1422 Euclid Avenue, Suite 1400
Cleveland, Ohio 44115–2001
Tel: 216–861–3810 Fax: 216–861–1729
EIN: 340714588 Type: Community
Contact: Susan N. Lajoie, Associate Director

History and philosophy. Founded in 1914 as the nation's first community trust, The Cleveland Foundation exists "to enhance the quality of life for all people of Greater Cleveland." The concept of a community foundation was originated by Cleveland banker Frederick Harris Goff, who sought a way for charitable bequests from many local donors to be managed for the long-term benefit of the community. The Foundation has a flexible grantmaking policy, attempting "to stimulate creative responses to changing needs. . . ." Its philanthropic philosophy is based on four imperatives: "Think strategically; focus on the most critical elements; seek and promote opportunities for collaboration; and, insist on results." Programs are: Civic Affairs, Cultural Affairs, Economic Development, Education, Health, Social Services, and Special Philanthropy.

Officers and directors. *Distribution Committee:* Alfred M. Rankin, Jr., Chairperson; Annie Lewis Garda, Vice Chairperson; Rev. Elmo A. Bean, James E. Bennett, James M. Delaney, Doris A. Evans, Russell R. Gifford, Jerry V. Jarrett, Adrienne Lash Jones, James V. Patton, Charles A. Ratner. *Trustees Committee:* David A. Daberko, Robert W. Gillespie, Richard L. Hargrove, Karen N. Horn, William J. Williams.

C

Financial data. Data for fiscal year ended December 31, 1993. *Assets:* $739,906,723 (M). *Gifts received:* $13,045,910. *Total grants authorized:* $33,183,780.

Environmental awards. *Program and interests:* With the exception of a few grants for zoos and similar institutions, the Foundation makes environmental awards through its Civic Affairs program.
Recent grants: 1993 grants included support for parks and open space, watershed protection, energy conservation, wildlife, toxics, and environmental education.

Issues. Cli Bio• Lan• Agr• Wat• Oce Ene• Was Tox• Pop• Dev

Funding analysis.§

Fiscal year:	1991	1993
Env grants auth:	$2,156,337	$462,929
Number:	23	16
Range:	$144–$1,700,000	$137–$75,000
Median:	$8,300	$21,489
Pct $ auth (env/total):	7	1

Recipients (1993 highest):	Number:	Dollars:
International Center for the Preservation of Wild Animals	1	75,000
Cuyahoga River Community Planning Organization	1	70,000
The Earth Day Coalition	2	67,000
City Hall of Cleveland	1	50,000
Lake Educational Assistance Foundation	1	40,000

Activity region (1993):	Number:	Dollars:
U.S. Great Lakes	16	462,929

§Includes designated grants.

Sample grants (1993).
The Center for Clean Air Policy. Washington, DC. $26,200. Training of local community groups in energy efficiency.
Cleveland Zoological Society. Cleaveland, OH. $137.
Cuyahoga River Community Planning Organization. Cleveland, OH. $70,000. (2 years). Staff support for the Cuyahoga River Remedial Action Plan.
The Earth Day Coalition. Cleveland, OH. $60,000 (2 years).
The Earth Day Coalition. Cleveland, OH. $7,000. Earthfest '94.
The Environmental Careers Organization, Inc. Boston, MA. $34,115 (15 months). Environmental careers presentations in Cleveland-area schools.
Environmental Health Watch. Cleveland, OH. $20,000. Public education on household hazardous wastes.
Hancock Parks Foundation. Beverly Hills, CA. $20,000. Professional design services for "Wild Encounters" display at Oakwood Nature Preserves.
International Center for the Preservation of Wild Animals. Columbus, OH. $75,000 (18 months). Wildlife conservation education program with the Cleveland Metroparks Zoo.
Lake Educational Assistance Foundation. Mentor, OH. $40,000 (2 years). Operating support.
Natural Resources Defense Council. New York, NY. $20,000. Water runoff project in Cleveland.
Roxboro Community Development Corporation. Cartersville, GA. $5,000. Community park and public space.
Shaker Lakes Regional Nature Center. Cleveland, OH. $5,000. Strategic plan.

Application process. *Initial contact:* Letter of inquiry describing nature of the project.
When to apply: Deadlines are March 31, June 30, September 15, and December 31. The distribution committee meets quarterly, in June, September, December, and March.
Materials available: Annual report, "Guidelines for Grant-seekers," *Keeping the Trust* (quarterly report).

Emphases. *Recipients:* Aquariums, museums, nonprofit organizations, public agencies, zoos.
Activities: Capacity building, direct services, education, planning, youth programs.
Types of support: Multi-year grants, seed money, start-up costs, technical assistance.
Geography: Greater Cleveland, Ohio.

Limitations. *Recipients:* Individuals.
Types of support: Advertising campaigns, annual campaigns, capital campaigns/expenses, computer hardware, continuing support, debt retirement, endowments, lectureships, maintenance, membership campaigns, mortgage reduction, operating costs, professorships, travel expenses.

The Clowes Fund, Inc.
250 East 38th Street
Indianapolis, Indiana 46205
Tel: 317–923–3264   Fax: 317–923–3265
EIN: 351079679   Type: Independent
Contact: Allen W. Clowes, President

History and philosophy. Edith W., George H. A., and Allen W. Clowes established the Clowes Foundation in 1952. The arts, civic services, educational institutions, health sciences and health services, marine science, and social services are areas of particular interest.

Officers and directors. *Officers:* Allen W. Clowes, President and Treasurer; Margaret J. Clowes, Vice President; Thomas M. Lofton, Secretary. *Directors:* Margaret C. Bowles, Alexander W. Clowes, Allen W. Clowes, Jonathan J. Clowes, Margaret J. Clowes, Thomas J. Clowes, Byron P. Hollett, Thomas M. Lofton, William H. Marshall.

Financial data. Data for fiscal year ended December 31, 1993. *Assets:* $42,556,679 (M). *Total grants disbursed:* $1,915,807.

Environmental awards. *Recent grants:* 1993 grants included support for a marine research institution, a zoo, and a wildlife sanctuary.

Issues. Cli Bio• Lan• Agr Wat Oce• Ene Was Tox Pop Dev

Funding analysis.

Fiscal year:	1993
Env grants disb:	$140,000
Number:	4
Range:	$10,000–$100,000
Median:	$15,000
Pct $ disb (env/total):	7

Recipients (1993):	*Number:*	*Dollars:*
Marine Biological Laboratory	1	100,000
Indianapolis Zoological Society	2	30,000
Salt Pond Area Bird Sanctuaries, Inc.	1	10,000

Activity regions (1993):	*Number:*	*Dollars:*
U.S. Northeast	2	110,000
U.S. Great Lakes	2	30,000

Sample grants (1993).
Indianapolis Zoological Society. Indianapolis, IN. $30,000.
Marine Biological Laboratory. Woods Hole, MA. $100,000. Education programs.
Salt Pond Area Bird Sanctuaries, Inc. Falmouth, MA. $10,000. For the Bourne Farm Fund.

Application process. *Initial contact:* Letter or proposal (2 copies) to include:
1. Description of organization.
2. Purpose of grant.
3. Amount requested.
4. Budget for proposal.
5. Financial statement.
6. Copy of IRS exempt-status determination letter.

When to apply: Deadline is January 31 for the board meeting held each spring.

Emphases. *Recipients:* Educational institutions, zoos.
Activities: Education.
Geography: Indianapolis, Indiana; Indiana; Boston, Massachusetts.

Limitations. *Recipients:* Individuals.
Activities: Conferences, publications, seminars.
Types of support: Loans.

Olive B. Cole Foundation
3242 Mallard Cove Lane
Fort Wayne, Indiana 46804
Tel: 219-436-2182
EIN: 356040491
Contact: John E. Hogan, Executive Vice President

History and philosophy. The Foundation was established in 1954 by Richard R. and Olive B. Cole with funds derived from stock in Flint and Walling, a water pump and conditioner manufacturer. Funding new organizations and maintaining old recipients are priorities of the Foundation. It makes grants primarily in education, civic and public affairs, and recreation in the Fort Wayne area.

Officers and directors. *Officers:* John N. Pichon, President; John E. Hogan, Executive Vice President; Maclyn T. Parker, Secretary; Gwen I. Tipton, Scholarship Administrator. *Directors:* Rev. Donald G. Fischer, Merrill B. Frick, John E. Hogan, Maclyn T. Parker, John N. Pichon, Victor B. Porter, John W. Riemke, Gwen I. Tipton.

Financial data. Data for fiscal year ended March 31, 1993. *Assets:* $21,614,181 (M). *Total grants disbursed:* $1,471,182.

Environmental awards. *Recent grants:* 1993 grants included support for land conservation, water resources, urban parks, and a zoo.

Issues. Cli Bio• Lan• Agr Wat• Oce Ene Was Tox Pop Dev

Funding analysis.

Fiscal year:	1993
Env grants disb:	$50,000
Number:	4
Range:	$5,000–$20,000
Median:	$12,500
Pct $ disb (env/total):	3

Recipients (1993):	*Number:*	*Dollars:*
Fort Wayne Children's Zoo	1	20,000
The Nature Conservancy, Indiana Field Office	1	20,000
LaGrange County Park Department	1	5,000
Town of Orland	1	5,000

Activity region (1993):	*Number:*	*Dollars:*
U.S. Great Lakes	4	50,000

Sample grants (1993).
Fort Wayne Children's Zoo. Fort Wayne, IN. $20,000. Indonesian tropical rainforest section.
LaGrange County Park Department. LaGrange, IN. $5,000. Commercial lawnmower.
The Nature Conservancy, Indiana Field Office. Indianapolis, IN. $20,000. Waters of Life campaign.
Town of Orland. Orland, IN. $5,000. Land acquisition for town park.

Application process. *Initial contact:* Letter of inquiry.
When to apply: Anytime. The board meets in February, May, August, and November.
Materials available: Application form.

Emphases. *Recipients:* Individuals (for scholarships), nonprofit organizations, public agencies.
Activities: Direct services, land acquisition.
Types of support: Capital campaigns/expenses, equipment, facilities, general purposes, loans, projects, scholarships.
Geography: Kendallville, Noble County, and northeastern Indiana. (Scholarships for graduates of secondary schools in Noble County, Indiana.)

Limitations. *Recipients:* Individuals, religious organizations.

C

The Collins Foundation

1618 Southwest First Avenue, Suite 305
Portland, Oregon 97201
Tel: 503-227-7171
Contact: William C. Pine, Executive Director

History and philosophy. The Foundation was established in 1947 by members of the E. S. Collins family. Its purpose is "to improve, enrich and give greater expression to the religious, educational, cultural and scientific endeavors in the state of Oregon and to assist in improving the quality of life in the state." The Foundation funds arts and humanities, science education, environment, medicine, religion, children and youth welfare, and general welfare.

Officers and directors. *Officers:* Maribeth W. Collins, President; Ralph Bollinger, Grace C. Goudy, Vice Presidents; Thomas B. Stoel, Secretary; Timothy R. Bishop, Treasurer; Rebecca Newhouse, Assistant Secretary; Barbara A. Johnson, Assistant Treasurer. *Trustees:* Ralph Bollinger, Maribeth W. Collins, Grace C. Goudy, Cherida C. Smith.

Financial data. Data for fiscal year ended December 31, 1993. *Assets:* $109,582,365 (M). *Total grants disbursed:* $5,065,125.

Environmental awards. *Recent grants:* 1993 awards included support for wilderness and forestry issues, river protection, and outdoor education.

Issues. Cli Bio• Lan• Agr Wat• Oce Ene Was• Tox Pop Dev•

Funding analysis.

Fiscal year:	1993
Env grants disb:	$260,500
Number:	12
Range:	$4,000–$75,000
Median:	$8,750
Pct $ disb (env/total):	5

Recipients (1993 highest):	Number:	Dollars:
1000 Friends of Oregon	1	75,000
High Desert Museum	1	75,000
Friends of the Rae Selling Berry Botanic Garden	1	25,000
World Forestry Center	1	25,000
Pacific Crest Outward Bound School	1	20,000

Activity region (1993):	Number:	Dollars:
U.S. Northwest	12	260,500

Sample grants (1993).

American Wilderness Foundation. Portland, OR. $5,000. Fifteen-passenger van.
Friends of the Columbia Gorge. Portland, OR. $4,000. Internship project.
Friends of Tryon Creek State Park. Portland, OR, $4,000. New field guide.
Home Gardening Project. Portland, OR. $7,500.
Josephine Parks & Recreation Foundation. Grants Pass, OR. $5,000. Merlin Community Center.
Pacific Crest Outward Bound School. Portland, OR. $20,000. Scholarship program.
Portland Youth Advocates, Inc. Portland, OR. $5,000. Youth Recycling Program.
World Forestry Center. Portland, OR. $25,000. Permanent exhibit of old growth forests.

Application process. *Initial contact:* Full application to include:
1. Narrative proposal describing applicant organization and the project for which funds are being sought including a description of the persons or groups to be served.
2. Detailed budget for proposed project, the amount of funds sought from the Foundation, and the date funds will be required.
3. Current financial statements.
4. Names and primary affiliations of applicant's current directors or trustees.
5. Copy of IRS tax-exempt status determination letter.
6. Statement on plans for future financing of the proposed project.
7. List of contributors to date and a list of other sources being approached for financial assistance for the project.

When to apply: Anytime.
Materials available: "Grant Applications Policies and Procedures."

Emphases. *Recipients:* Educational institutions (colleges/universities), nonprofit organizations, religious organizations.
Types of support: Equipment, facilities, internships, multi-year grants, scholarships.
Geography: Oregon only.

Limitations. *Recipients:* Individuals, educational institutions (elementary or secondary).
Activities: Fundraising.
Types of support: Annual campaigns, debt retirement, operating costs.

Columbia Foundation

One Lombard Street, Suite 305
San Francisco, California 94111
Tel: 415-986-5179   Fax: 415-986-4779
EIN: 941196186   Type: Independent
EGA member
Contact: Susan C. Silk, Executive Director

History and philosophy. The Columbia Foundation was established in 1940 by Madeleine H. Russell and her brother, the late William Haas. Its directors establish program priorities to meet needs as they arise. "The current focus is on projects that address issues critical to our times and that offer promise of significant impact in the areas of stopping the worldwide arms race, promoting international and cross-cultural understanding, protecting human rights, reversing the degradation of the environment, and enhancing urban life and culture."

Officers and directors. *Officers:* Madeleine H. Russell, President; Charles P. Russell, Vice President; Alice Russell-Shapiro, Secretary; Christine H. Russell, Treasurer. *Directors:* Christine H. Russell, Charles P. Russell, Madeleine H. Russell, Alice Russell-Shapiro.

Financial data. Data for fiscal year ended May 31, 1993. *Assets:* $44,669,117. *Total grants authorized:* $2,198,528. *Total grants disbursed:* $1,943,528.

Environmental awards. *Program and interests:* Current environmental interests are:

- Sustainable agriculture, especially reduction of the use of pesticides and fossil fuel-based fertilizers.
- Forest preservation.
- Urban environments.

Recent grants: 1993 grants included support for land use planning, forest protection, river and watershed preservation, sustainable agriculture, coastal issues, toxics control (including military pollution and pesticides), and sustainable development.

Issues. Cli Bio Lan Agr Wat Oce Ene Was Tox Pop Dev

Funding analysis.

Fiscal year:	1991	1993
Env grants auth:	$371,500	$648,150
Number:	18	26
Range:	$1,500–$50,000	$150–$75,000
Median:	$12,500	$15,000
Pct $ auth (env/total):	19	33

Recipients (1993 highest):	Number:	Dollars:
Natural Resources Defense Council	2	95,000
California Association of Family Farmers	1	75,000
Greenbelt Alliance	1	75,000
Ecology Action of the Midpeninsula	1	60,000
Mothers & Others for a Livable Planet	1	50,000

Activity regions (1993 highest):	Number:	Dollars:
U.S. West	14	373,000
U.S. not specified	8	165,150
Mexico and Central America	1	60,000
New York/New Jersey	1	20,000
International*	1	5,000

*Multiple regions or not specified.

Sample grants (1993).

Beginnings. Redway, CA. $50,000 (2 years). For the Institute for Sustainable Forestry's pilot project to test and demonstrate environmental logging techniques.

California Association of Family Farmers. Davis, CA. $75,000 (3 years). For the California Action Network to launch "Farmer to Farmer," a bulletin of practical information on sustainable agriculture for California farmers.

Center for the Study of Law and Politics. San Francisco, CA. $40,000 (2 years). For the Global Cities Project to define sustainability in the urban community, publish the best local policies that promote it, and build an agenda for a sustainable community in San Francisco.

Ecology Action of the Midpeninsula. Willits, CA. $60,000 (3 years). Public education and outreach on bio-intensive food-growing practices, and to develop a bio-intensive agriculture program in Mexico.

Greenbelt Alliance. San Francisco, CA. $75,000 (5 years). For the Greenbelt 2000 Campaign to protect the Bay Area's open space.

J. Walter Johnson Institute. Oakland, CA. $30,000 (2 years). For West Oakland Residents Turnout for Health (WORTH), a community-based program to reduce risks to residents from smoking, lead contamination, and other environmental hazards.

Pacific Energy and Resources Center. Sausalito, CA. $25,000 (2 years). For the Siberian Forest Protection Project to work with Siberian environmentalists and policymakers to develop and implement policies and legal strategies to protect Siberia's forests.

Save San Francisco Bay Association. San Francisco, CA. $50,000 (3 years). To develop a comprehensive plan for restoring and managing the Bay ecosystem and to develop a campaign to support the implementation of the plan.

Application process. *Initial contact:* Completed application cover sheet (see "Application Guidelines") and letter of inquiry (2 pages maximum). Letter to include:
1. Description of the organization.
2. Purpose for which funds are requested.
3. Amount requested.
4. Plan of action, including description of cooperating agencies, if any.
5. Intended results, including measurable objectives.

If requested, or if time before Foundation deadline is short, submit full application to include:
1. Proposal summary (2 pages) describing need for project, how project seeks to meet the need, amount requested.
2. Proposal (5 pages) stating:
   - Need for project.
   - Theoretical base or rationale for project's approach.
   - Specific project activities.
   - Significance of the project beyond its local need or focus.
   - Qualifications of organization and staff to implement project successfully.
   - Relationship of program to other similar programs and agencies.
   - Plans for the program's future, including dissemination of results.
3. Financial information.
   - Line-item budget identifying project income and expenses for years of project duration.
   - Statement of actual revenue and expenses for last two years for the organization as a whole and for the project (include an audited statement if available).
   - List of other contributions and sources of support for the project including any applications under current consideration.
4. Organizational information.
   - History of the organization including a description of current activities and an annual report, if available.

- List of the board of directors, including occupations and phone numbers of board members. Please indicate how and to what extent the board and staff represent the community served by the organization.
- Copy of the IRS letter of tax exemption.
- Copy of relevant articles or other publicity about the program or organization.
- Affirmative action statement regarding hiring standards.

The Foundation prefers that proposals be prepared double-sided on recycled paper (10 percent post-consumer waste). The Foundation does not accept proposals sent by facsimile machine. *When to apply:* Deadlines are February 1 and August 1. The board of directors holds semiannual meetings.
Materials available: Annual report (includes "Application Guidelines").

Emphases. *Recipients:* Nonprofit organizations.
Activities: Advocacy, demonstration programs, litigation, policy analysis/development.
Types of support: General purposes, multi-year grants, pilot projects, projects, seed money, start-up costs.
Geography: San Francisco Bay Area.

Limitations. *Recipients:* Individuals, public agencies.
Activities: Direct services, lobbying, political activities, research (medical).
Types of support: Emergency funding, fellowships, internships, lectureships, loans, program-related investments, scholarships.

The Columbus Foundation

1234 East Broad Street
Columbus, Ohio 43205
Tel: 614–251–4000   Fax: 614–251–4009
EIN: 131635260   Type: Community
Contact: Amy E. Eldridge, Grants Coordinator

History and philosophy. The Columbus Foundation was established in 1943. It now comprises more than 700 component funds organized in seven categories: unrestricted, field of interest, designated, organization endowment, donor advised, scholarship, and administrative. Gifts are made primarily to organizations in central Ohio in the fields of Arts and Humanities, Conservation, Education, Health, Social Services, Urban Affairs, and Advancing Philanthropy.

Officers and directors. *Officers:* John B. Gerlach, Chairman; Floradelle A. Pfahl, John F. Wolfe, Vice Chairmen. *Governing Committee:* Don M. Castro, III, John B. Gerlach, Charlotte P. Kessler, Floradelle A. Pfahl, Alex Shumate, Abigail Wexner, John F. Wolfe. *Trustees:* Bank One Ohio Trust Company, N.A., The Fifth Third Bank, The Huntington Trust Company, N.A., National City Bank, Columbus, Society National Bank.

Financial data. Data for fiscal year ended December 31, 1993. *Assets:* $258,722,775 (U). *Gifts received:* $30,781,784. *Total grants disbursed:* $18,979,374.

Environmental awards. *Program and interests:* The Foundation's Conservation Program has two priorities:

- Public education about the environment encouraging individual changes in behavior aimed at the prevention and alleviation of environmental problems.
- Acquisition of land for public parks, the protection of natural habitats, and land of historical and cultural significance.

Recent grants: 1993 grants included support for land conservation and wildlife protection.

Issues.   Cli   Bio   Lan   Agr   Wat   Oce   Ene   Was   Tox   Pop   Dev
          •   •   •   •

Funding analysis.§

Fiscal year:	1991	1993
Env grants disb:	$130,020	$129,490
Number:	30	35
Range:	$50–$42,000	$25–$23,000
Median:	$500	$1,000
Pct $ disb (env/total):	1	1

Recipients (1993 highest):	Number:	Dollars:
Columbus Zoological Park Association	9	52,150
Metro Parks	6	24,215
Heritage Rails-to-Trails Coalition	1	20,000
Ohio State University Development Fund	1	10,000
Rails-to-Trails Conservancy	2	5,025

Activity region (1993):	Number:	Dollars:
U.S. Great Lakes	35	129,490

§Includes designated, donor-advised, and unrestricted grants.

Sample grants (1993).
Columbus Zoological Park Association. Powell, OH. $52,150. Support of the capital campaign for the Columbus Zoo Aquarium and general support.
The Cousteau Society. Norfolk, VA. $100.
Environmental Defense Fund. New York, NY. $1,000.
Inniswood Garden Society. Columbus, OH. $1,000.
Little Traverse Conservancy. Harbor Springs, MI. $200.
Metro Parks. Columbus, OH. $24,215.
National Parks and Conservation Association. Washington, DC. $1,000.
Natural Resources Defense Council. Washington, DC. $900.
The Nature Conservancy, Ohio Field Office. Columbus, OH. $4,300.
Rails-to-Trails Conservancy. Washington, DC. $5,000. To assist central Ohio communities in developing rail-trail conversion projects.
Tip of the Mitt Watershed Council. Conway, MI. $5,000.
The Wilderness Society. Ann Arbor, MI. $1,000.
World Wildlife Fund. Washington, DC. $1,000.

Application process. *Initial contact:* Request "Information of Grant Applicants." Proposal (original and 3 copies) to include in this order:
1. Cover sheet (from Foundation).
2. History of the organization with an overview of current programs and activities.

3. Copy of IRS exempt-status determination letter.
4. Statement from organization's board authorizing the request and agreeing to carry out the project if funded.
5. Description of problem or need to be met.
6. Description of project including strategies, measurable objectives, and timetable.
7. Names and qualifications of persons carrying out the program.
8. Project budget and narrative, including income sources and expenditures; list of other funding requests, including those pending or approved.
9. Most recent audited financial statement and current operating budget.
10. Plan for continuing the project once Foundation funding ends.
11. Plan for evaluating the project.
12. Letters recommending project and supporting material.

When to apply: Refer to "Information for Grant Applicants."
Materials available: Annual report, "Information for Grant Applicants," *The Columbus Foundation Commentary* (newsletter).

Emphases. *Recipients:* Nonprofit organizations.
Activities: Land acquisition, publications, technical assistance.
Types of support: Capital campaigns/expenses, continuing support, facilities (renovation), seed money.
Geography: Central Ohio.

Limitations. *Recipients:* Individuals.
Activities: Conferences, research (scholarly).
Types of support: Debt retirement, endowments.

The Community Foundation of Greater New Haven
70 Audubon Street
New Haven, Connecticut 06510
Tel: 203-777-2386   Fax: 203-787-6584
EIN: 066032106   Type: Community
Contact: Alan E. Green, Executive Director

History and philosophy. Formerly the New Haven Foundation, the Community Foundation of Greater New Haven was established in 1928. Today its role is threefold: broad-based response to a range of community interests; strategic areas-of-emphasis that address important community needs as identified by the Foundation's board; and a transforming effect that involves the Foundation's ability to take a long-term approach to promoting fundamental social change. Program areas are: Health, Education, Community Vitalization (including arts, positive self esteem & cultural understanding, inter-group relations, economic development, environment, effective independent initiative, and spiritual well being), and Basic Human Needs. Two endowments also support environmental purposes: The Quinnipiac River Fund, and the Garden Club of New Haven.

Officers and directors. *Officers:* Richard G. Bell, Chair; Mary L. Pepe, Vice Chair. *Governing Board:* Richard G. Bell, Richard H. Bowerman, Carol A. Brown, Anne Tyler Calabresi, F. Patrick McFadden, John E. Padilla, Charles R. Twyman, Barbara C. Wareck.

Financial data. Data for fiscal year ended December 31, 1993. *Assets:* $113,320,856 (M). *Gifts received:* $3,913,538. *Total grants disbursed:* $4,787,250.

Environmental awards. *Program and interests:* Environmental grants are awarded through the Community Vitalization program. "Natural resources, open spaces, and historical structures enrich our communities and deserve to be used wisely. Grants have funded public education, preservation, conservation, and recreational activities."
Recent grants: 1993 grants included support for land conservation, marine issues and fisheries, parks, and environmental education.

Issues.   Cli Bio Lan Agr Wat Oce Ene Was Tox Pop Dev
              •   •   •   •   •

Funding analysis.§

Fiscal year:	1993
Env grants auth:	$130,901
Number:	20
Range:	$500–$30,000
Median:	$4,920
Pct $ auth (env/total):	3

Recipients (1993 highest):	Number:	Dollars:
Rainbow Recycling	1	30,000
Friends of the Ansonia Nature Center	1	20,000
New Haven Board of Park Commissioners, Park Department	1	11,466
University of New Haven, Department of Biology & Environment	1	10,450
National Marine Fisheries Service (NMFS)	2	9,890

Activity region (1993):	Number:	Dollars:
U.S. Northeast	20	130,901

§Includes designated and unrestricted grants.

Sample grants (1994).
Connecticut Department of Agriculture Aquaculture Division. Milford, CT. $7,000.
National Marine Fisheries Service (NMFS). Silver Spring, MD. $8,100.
New Haven County Soil & Water. New Haven, CT. $5,000.
Quinnipiac River Watershed Association. Meriden, CT. $5,000.
Sea Grant Marine Advisory Program. Milford, CT. $4,175.
Southern Connecticut State University. New Haven, CT. $4,826.
University of Connecticut, Department of Chemistry. Storrs, CT. $5,000.
University of New Haven, Department of Biology & Environment. New Haven, CT. $10,000.
University of New Haven, Institute of Analytical & Environmental Chemistry. New Haven, CT. $5,000.
Yale University, School of Forestry and Environmental Studies. New Haven, CT. $5,380.

Application process. *Initial contact:* Letter of intent (2 pages) to include:
1. Description of applicant and mission.
2. Description of proposed project. How does it differ from other such programs?
3. Importance of project and how the community will benefit.
4. Total projected cost of project, amount being requested, and potential for other funding. What is the plan for future funding?

Staff will follow up either with a request for additional information, or a recommendation on whether to proceed with a formal application.
When to apply: Anytime.
Materials available: Annual report (includes "Grantmaking Process").

Emphases. *Recipients:* Nonprofit organizations.
Activities: Capacity building, citizen participation, collaborative efforts, demonstration programs, feasibility studies, innovative programs, training, volunteerism, youth programs.
Types of support: Loans, matching funds, multi-year grants, pilot projects, projects, scholarships, seed money, start-up costs, technical assistance.
Geography: New Haven, Connecticut area: from the Long Island Sound to Wallingford, from Milford to Clinton, and within the Lower Naugatuck Valley.

Limitations. *Recipients:* Individuals.
Activities: Audiovisual materials, conferences, expeditions/tours, inventories, land acquisition, litigation, lobbying, publications, seminars.
Types of support: Annual campaigns, debt retirement, endowments, mortgage reduction, multi-year grants, professorships, program-related investments, travel expenses.
Geography: South Central Connecticut.

The Community Foundation of Santa Clara County

960 West Hedding, Suite 220
San Jose, California 95126-1215
Tel: 408-241-2666   Fax: 408-452-4636
EIN: 770066922   Type: Community
Contact: Winnie Chu, Associate Director

History and philosophy. The Community Foundation of Santa Clara County was established in 1954. Its mission is to nurture a greater sense of community, linking people together through a broad vision to achieve an integrated and united community. Its purpose is to strengthen and enrich the quality of life of individuals and their communities and to serve as a catalyst within the local community. It manages and invests a steadily-growing permanent endowment (as well as donor-advised funds) derived from contributions made by individuals, families, and organizations for the charitable benefit of the community. Grants are made in the categories of: arts and humanities, education, environment, community and social services, and health.

Officers and directors. *Officers:* Barbara Doyle Roupe, Chair; Kathie Priebe, Vice Chair; Bryan C. Polster, Treasurer. *Directors:* Frances C. Arrillaga, Phillip R. Boyce, Douglas C. Chance, Kenneth L. Coleman, Clarence J. Ferrari, Jr., Larry Jinks, Mary Katherine Kelley, Clayton J. Klein, Elaine Knoernschild, David W. Mitchell, Bryan C. Polster, Kathie Priebe, Barbara Doyle Roupe, Harry J. Saal, William F. Scandling, Sven-Erik Simonsen, Roger V. Smith, William E. Terry, John A. Wilson.

Financial data. Data for fiscal year ended June 30, 1993. *Assets:* $38,509,515 (M). *Gifts received:* $3,295,181. *Total grants disbursed:* $2,764,390.

Environmental awards. *Program and interests:* "The Foundation looks for programs that increase public understanding and awareness about environmental choices and consequences."

It emphasizes:

- Developing a environmentally literate public in order to manage our resources more effectively.
- Involving the public in the conservation of resources through projects such as trailbuilding, recycling programs, etc.

Recent grants: 1993 grants included support for land conservation and species preservation.

Issues.   Cli Bio Lan Agr Wat Oce Ene Was Tox Pop Dev
             •   •   •   •   •   •   •   •   •

Funding analysis.§

Fiscal year:	1993
Env grants disb:	$188,075
Number:	42
Range:	$50–$117,000
Median:	$975
Pct $ disb (auth/total):	7

Recipients (1993 highest):	Number:	Dollars:
Peninsula Conservation Center	1	117,000
San Jose Conservation Corps	1	11,550
Natural Resources Defense Council	1	10,300
Sempervirens Fund	1	6,800
Peninsula Open Space Trust	1	5,400

Activity regions (1993):	Number:	Dollars:
U.S. West	29	179,075
U.S. not specified	10	7,550
New York/New Jersey	1	1,000
Africa	1	250
Hawaii	1	200

§Includes designated, donor-advised, and unrestricted grants.

Sample grants (1993).
Audubon Society, California. Van Nuys, CA. $1,875.
Bay Area Ridge Trail Council San Francisco, CA. $3,750.
Big Sur Land Trust. Carmel, CA. $1,500.
California Waterfowl Association. Sacramento, CA. $1,000.
Californians Against Waste Foundation. Sacramento, CA. $1,150.
Defenders of Wildlife. Washington, DC. $200.
Environmental Defense Fund. New York, NY. $500.
Friends of the River Campaign. Sacramento, CA. $200.
Green Foothills Foundation. Palo Alto, CA. $1,600.
Greenbelt Alliance. San Francisco, CA. $1,100.
Greenpeace. San Francisco, CA. $1,100.

League to Save Lake Tahoe. South Lake Tahoe, CA. $500.
National Audubon Society. New York, NY. $400.
National Tropical Botanical Garden. Lawai, HI. $200.
National Wildlife Federation. Washington, DC. $600.
Peninsula Conservation Center. Palo Alto, CA. $117,000.
San Jose Conservation Corps. San Jose, CA. $11,550.

Application process. *Initial contact:* Contact a program officer and describe the project before submitting full proposal to include:
1. Proposal Summary Form (from Foundation).
2. Cover sheet (1 page).
   - Name, address, telephone and fax numbers.
   - Name and title of contact person.
   - Name and title of person responsible for project.
   - Organization's mission and goals.
   - Summary of proposal.
   - Total annual organization budget and fiscal year.
   - Total project budget.
   - Amount requested.
3. Narrative (2–5 pages).
   - Community issue(s)/problem(s) to be addressed.
   - Description of goals and measurable objectives and statement whether this is a new or ongoing project.
   - How community needs will be addressed; target populations; number of ethnic minorities served and how they will benefit; principal area(s) served.
   - Activities performed to accomplish goals.
   - How your services collaborate with community resources and how your project differs from other services offered.
   - Timetable.
   - Description of project staffing.
   - Budget including funding from other foundations or corporations to which this proposal has been submitted.
   - Funding strategies after Foundation support ends.
4. Attachments.
   - Annual operating budget for current year including revenue and expenses and most recent annual financial statement.
   - Copy of IRS tax-exempt status determination letter.
   - List of the board with occupations or affiliations.
   - Approval of submission by applicant's board.

When to apply: Deadlines are March and December. Call for exact dates. The board meets quarterly.
Materials available: Annual report, "Grant Guidelines and Application Procedures," brochures.

Emphases. *Recipients:* Botanical gardens, educational institutions, nonprofit organizations.
Activities: Citizen participation, innovative programs, land acquisition.
Types of support: Seed money, single-year grants only.
Geography: Santa Clara county, East Palo Alto, East Menlo Park, and Redwood City, California.

Limitations. *Recipients:* Individuals, educational institutions (for-profit schools), religious organizations.
Activities: Fundraising, political activities, research.
Types of support: Capital campaigns/expenses, debt retirement, endowments, equipment, facilities, operating costs, research.

C

The Community Foundation of Sarasota County, Inc.
1800 Second Street, Suite 740
P.O. Box 49587
Sarasota, Florida 34230–6587
Tel: 813–955–3000 Fax: 813–952–1951
EIN: 591956886 Type: Community
Contact: Stewart W. Stearns, Executive Director

History and philosophy. The Community Foundation of Sarasota County was established in 1987. Its role "is to provide a way for any individual or business to set up endowment funds for any charitable purpose; to use income from gifts to match the wishes of a donor with the needs of the community; to support all charitable areas; and to promote high professional standards in grantmaking, investment, and program development." Funding categories include: arts & culture, education (public and private), environment, health care, human services, and youth services.

Officers and directors. *Officers:* Carolyn A. Fitzpatrick, President; Jerome A. Jannopoulo, Vice President; Dr. Kay E. Glasser, Secretary; Ralph E. "Jack" Jaret, Treasurer. *Directors:* Dee Anderson, Kathy Baylis, John T. Berteau, Steven N. Dahlquist, John W. English, Carolyn A. Fitzpatrick, Letetia Flischel, Patrick L. Gallagher, Dr. Kay E. Glasser, Regina Hill-Faison, Wendy Hopkins, Jerome A. Jannopoulo, Ralph E. Jaret, Robert L. Kirce, Anthony Levering, Melville R. Levi, Gail Levin, Erik R. Lieberman, Isabel R. Lillie, Bill Little, Sandra Loevner, Rhoderick B. MacLeod, Thomas W. Moran, James M. Rothenburg, Tana Sandefur, Chuck Savidge, Edward J. Schmidt, Jr., J. Ronald Skipper, Barry F. Spivey, David A. Steves, Edwin D. Taylor, Mary G. Toundas, Judi Voigt.

Financial data. Data for fiscal year ended May 31, 1993. *Assets:* $2,346,166 (M). *Gifts received:* $480,050. *Total grants disbursed:* $217,215.

Environmental awards. *Recent grants:* 1993 grants included support for marine sciences and a nature center.

Issues. Cli Bio Lan Agr Wat Oce Ene Was Tox Pop Dev
              •   •   •

Funding analysis.§

Fiscal year:	1993
Env grants disb:	$13,550
Number:	3
Range:	$600–$8,000
Median:	$4,950
Pct $ disb (env/total):	6

Recipients (1993):	*Number:*	*Dollars:*
Mote Marine Laboratory	2	12,950
Wild Pine Nature Center	1	600

Activity region (1993):	*Number:*	*Dollars:*
U.S. Southeast	3	13,550

§Includes field-of-interest, donor-advised, restricted, and unrestricted grants.

C

Sample grants (1993).
Mote Marine Foundation. Sarasota, FL. $4,950. For general support.
Mote Marine Laboratory. Sarasota, FL. $8,000. To purchase laboratory equipment.
Wild Pine Nature Center. Sarasota, FL. $600. For start-up costs.

Application process. *Initial contact:* Contact the Foundation for grant guidelines and Grant Application Form. In reviewing proposals, the Foundation carefully considers:
1. Impact of request and the number of people who will benefit.
2. Imaginative or collaborative approach.
3. Extent of local volunteer involvement and support for project.
4. Commitment and composition of organization's board of directors.
5. Degree to which applicant works with or complements the services of other community organizations.
6. Organization's fiscal responsibility and management qualifications.
7. Possibility of use of its grant as seed money for matching funds from other sources.
8. Ability of program to obtain the necessary additional funding to implement project.
9. Ability of organization to provide ongoing funding after the term of the grant.
10. Potential visibility of project.

When to apply: Anytime.
Materials available: Grant Application Form, guidelines, "Information Guide."

Emphases. *Recipients:* Nonprofit organizations.
Activities: Innovative programs.
Types of support: Emergency funding, equipment, facilities, leveraging funds, pilot projects.
Geography: Sarasota County, Florida only.

Limitations. *Recipients:* Individuals, religious organizations.
Activities: Audiovisual materials, conferences, political activities, publications, research (scientific).
Types of support: Annual campaigns, debt retirement, endowments, operating costs, travel expenses.

The Community Foundation Serving Coastal South Carolina

456 King Street
Charleston, South Carolina 29403–6230
Tel: 803–723–3635; 803–723–2124   Fax: 803–577–3671
EIN: 237390313   Type: Community
Contact: Richard Hendry, Program Director

History and philosophy. The Foundation was established in 1974 and has grown to include a group of more than 100 separate funds, each established by a different donor for a distinct charitable purpose. The Foundation strives to build community, which means it chooses to help the community identify and articulate its fundamental principles upon which all can build. The methods of building include a kaleidoscope of traditions, beliefs, and talents. Discretionary funds offer funding to the community in five competitive programs: grants to "expansion artists"; grants to low/moderate-income neighborhood groups; mini-grants to public school teachers; scholarships for a college degree; and "open" grants to tri-county nonprofit groups.

The Foundation provides concentrated support in six program areas: arts, education, environment, health, human services, and neighborhood development.

Officers and directors. *Officers:* Thomas P. Anderson, President; Anita Zucker, Vice President; H. Louie Koester, III, Secretary; Susan P. Miller, Treasurer. *Directors:* William Ackerman, Scott Y. Barnes, Edward Bennett, Charlton deSaussure, Jr., Richard K. Gregory, Thomas D. Heneghan, Laura M. Hewitt, John Kinloch, Juanita W. LaRoche, Samuel F. Lyons, Joseph H. McGee, Bruce D. Murdy, Susan Pearlstine-Foster, Priscilla Robinson, Kenneth W. Shortridge, Jr., Sallie Sinkler, R. Dauer Stackpole, John D. Stewart, John L. Thompson.

Financial data. Data for fiscal year ended June 30, 1993. *Assets:* $6,710,482 (M). *Gifts received:* $962,042. *Total grants disbursed:* $616,164.

Environmental awards. *Recent grants:* 1993 grants included support for land conservation, urban forests, injured birds of prey, coastal issues, and youth education.

Issues. Cli Bio Lan Agr Wat Oce Ene Was Tox Pop Dev
              •   •   •

Funding analysis.

Fiscal year:	1993
Env grants disb:	$236,760
Number:	7
Range:	$500–$206,919
Median:	$4,000
Pct $ disb (env/total):	38

Recipients (1993 highest):	Number:	Dollars:
City of Charleston for Waterfront Park	1	206,919
Lowcountry ReLeaf	1	17,247
Waterfront Park Fund of TCF	1	6,594
The Nature Conservancy, South Carolina Field Office	1	4,000
South Carolina Wildlife Federation	1	1,000

Activity region (1993):	Number:	Dollars:
U.S. Southeast	7	236,760

Sample grants (1994).
American Friends of the Game Conservancy. Shreveport, LA. $7,500. General support.
Berkeley County Kids Who Care (About Our Environment). Berkeley County, SC. $3,223. General support and to open a grants program.
Charleston Raptor Center. Charleston, SC. $1,000.
Cherry Lakes Farm. Charleston, SC. $7,230. Thirty live oaks for East Bay Street.
Lowcountry Open Land Trust. Charleston, SC. $1,500.
Lowcountry ReLeaf. Charleston, SC. $15,455. General support and emergency funds.
South Carolina Coastal Conservation League. Charleston, SC. $2,000. General support.

Application process. *Initial contact:* Letter of intent (1 page) on agency's letterhead and signed by executive director or CEO to include:
1. Description of the organization, the community need, and the purpose of program.
2. Purpose of the organization, services provided, population receiving benefit, number of years in existence.
3. Brief nondiscrimination statement.
4. Program objectives, activities used to meet objectives, population to benefit, evaluation method.
5. Program's geographic area, type of program, and timeline.
6. Amount requested, total budget, and list of other requests.
7. Copy of IRS tax-exempt status determination letter.

Proposal (5 copies) if requested to include:
1. History of the agency, description of services, documentation of past program accomplishments, list of governing members, statement of current agency activities, qualifications to conduct the program.
2. Why program is needed, why it is different from existing programs, population to benefit (numbers included).
3. Goals and objectives of program.
4. How population is selected, activities, timeline including hours per week of provided services, method of evaluation.
5. List of staff involved in program, their responsibilities (with estimated hours), and qualifications (attach resumes).
6. Agency budget (income and expenses) for current year with audited financial statement and categorized program budget.

When to apply: Deadline for letter of intent is July 15 and September 15 for the requested proposal.
Materials available: Annual report, "How To Apply For a Grant," *What Gives?* (newsletter).

Emphases. *Recipients:* Nonprofit organizations.
Activities: Capacity building, citizen participation, collaborative efforts, demonstration programs, direct services, education, innovative programs, volunteerism, youth programs.
Types of support: General purposes, operating costs, pilot projects, seed money, single-year grants only, start-up costs.
Geography: Berkeley, Charleston, and Dorchester counties in South Carolina.

Limitations. *Recipients:* Individuals.
Activities: Lobbying.
Types of support: Endowments, fellowships, multi-year grants.

Community Foundation of Western North Carolina, Inc.

14 College Street
P.O. Box 1888
Asheville, North Carolina 28802
Tel: 704–254–4960
EIN: 561223384   Type: Community
Contact: Pat Smith, Executive Director

History and philosophy. The Foundation was established in 1978 to attend to the "current and future philanthropic needs as a whole" for the Greater Asheville area, one "whose beauty and healthful living conditions are complemented by its progressive spirit and social consciousness." It now serves 18 counties in Western North Carolina and maintains over 170 funds, each with a unique charitable purpose. Program areas include: Arts and Culture, Children and Youth, Community Development, Education, Environment, Health, Human Services, Religion, and Social Justice. The Foundation also awards scholarships.

Officers and directors. *Officers:* Mimi Cecil, Chairman; Philip G. Carson, Vice Chairman; Susan Kosma, Secretary; Raymond Spells, Jr., Treasurer. *Directors:* Garza Baldwin, Jr., Perry W. Bartsch, C. Robert Bell, Jr., Stephen D. Bitter, Elizabeth D. Bolton, Ellen Carr, Philip G. Carson, Mimi Cecil, Gran P. Childress, James McClure Clarke, Nancy L. Cole, Rebecca B. Cross, Sherri B. Free, Susan Kosma, Brian F. D. Lavelle, Doris Phillips Loomis, John W. Mason, Sue McClinton, Hugh E. McCollum, A. William McKee, Charles E. Nesbitt, Robert J. Robinson, John R. E. Ruhl, John Q. Schell, Lary A. Schulhof, M.D., Raymond Spells, Jr., Thomas L. Spradling.

Financial data. Data for fiscal year ended June 30, 1994. *Assets:* $13,549,571 (U). *Gifts received:* $1,086,165. *Total grants disbursed:* $4,248,588.

Environmental awards. *Program and interests:* With the underlying premise that "the mountains of western North Carolina are recognized as a significant international treasure, rich with endemic botanical and wildlife species," the Foundation works to deal with issues of "air and water pollution, land loss, and hazardous waste [that] pose a threat to the future of our environment."
Recent grants: The Foundation has identified education of young people as a particular goal, and recently supported four environmental education programs: the creation of a computer network for local teenagers, a new 4–H summer camp experience focusing on the interrelationship between people and nature, recycling programs on two college campuses, and a cooperative effort of six rural counties.

Issues.   Cli   Bio   Lan   Agr   Wat   Oce   Ene   Was   Tox   Pop   Dev
              •   •   •   •   •

Funding analysis.§

Fiscal year:	1993
Env grants auth:	$145,300
Number:	–
Range:	$2,500–$91,300
Median:	$5,000
Pct $ auth (env/total):	13

Recipients (1993 highest):	*Number:*	*Dollars:*
Long Branch Environmental Education Center	1	10,000
Black Swan Center	1	5,000
Clean Water Fund of North Carolina	1	5,000
Earth Dance Institute	1	5,000
Land-of-Sky Regional Council	1	5,000
Webster Enterprises	1	5,000

Activity region (1993):	*Number:*	*Dollars:*
U.S. Southeast	13	145,300

§Includes designated and donor-advised grants.

C

Sample grants (1994).
Clean Water Fund. Asheville, NC. $3,000. Organizational development consulting to benefit four regional environmental groups.
North Carolina Environmental Defense Fund. Raleigh, NC. $5,000. To develop and launch a citizen air quality monitoring project.
Southern Appalachian Highlands Conservancy. Asheville, NC. $7,500. To establish a regional land trust.
Southern Environmental Law Center. Chapel Hill, NC. $7,500. To support policy work on regional air quality.
Yancey County 4–H. Burnsville, NC. $1,500. For an environmental summer camp serving rural children.

Application process. *Initial contact:* Write or telephone the Foundation before submitting a proposal or application to obtain current guidelines, fund priorities, and requirements. Or visit the Foundation's Nonprofit Resource Center.
When to apply: Deadlines are August 15 and February 15.
Materials available: Annual report, *Quarterly* (newsletter).

Emphases. *Recipients:* Nonprofit organizations.
Activities: Education.
Types of support: Scholarships, seed money, technical assistance.
Geography: Western North Carolina counties of Avery, Buncombe, Burke, Cherokee, Clay, Graham, Haywood, Henderson, Jackson, Macon, Madison, McDowell, Mitchell, Polk, Rutherford, Swain, Transylvania, and Yancey.

Compton Foundation, Inc.
545 Middlefield Road, Suite 178
Menlo Park, California 94025
Tel: 415–328–0101   Fax: 415–328–0171
EIN: 237262706   Type: Independent
EGA member
Contact: Edith T. Eddy, Executive Director

History and philosophy. The Compton Foundation was established in 1973 as successor to the Compton Trust which Dorothy D. Compton and Randolph P. Compton had founded in 1946. The Comptons saw four world conditions threatening the fragile interdependence among nations: overpopulation, unequal distribution of resources, deterioration of the environment, and the chaotic status of human rights. The Foundation makes awards in the primary areas of Peace and World Order, Population, and Environment. Other concerns are Educational Opportunity, Community Welfare & Social Justice, and Culture & the Arts.

Officers and directors. *Officers:* James R. Compton, President; Ann C. Stephens, Vice President and Secretary; Michael P. Todaro, Treasurer. *Directors:* Randolph O. Compton, W. Danforth Compton, Lee Etta Powell, Kenneth W. Thompson, Laurie A. Wayburn.

Financial data. Data for fiscal year ended December 31, 1993.
Assets: $58,236,992 (M). *Total grants disbursed:* $3,909,159.

Environmental awards. *Program and interests:* The Foundation's main concern is to reverse the deterioration of the environment and the depletion of natural resources. Current foci are national and international programs for:

- Land, river, and watershed protection.

  For purposes of longterm habitat and ecosystem preservation and restoration, through means as securing water rights, purchasing land, providing technical assistance, and educating the public. Priorities are national projects and those likely to be taken over and managed by a long-term funding source.

- Graduate level training programs in environment and sustainable development for individuals from developing countries who are sponsored by cooperating institutions within their own countries. This is a Foundation-initiated program and thus is not open to unsolicited requests.

- Energy conservation including alternative energy sources and incentives for energy efficiency, both nationally and internationally.

- Promoting understanding of and solutions to the adverse environmental effects of population growth, especially in Mexico, Central America, and Sub-Saharan Africa. Priority will be given to projects which emphasize the impact of human behavior on the physical environment, and which encourage public awareness of and response to the interrelationship between population, consumption, and technology, both nationally and internationally.

Occasionally the Foundation will fund a local environmental project in the San Francisco Bay Area. In the Environment program as in all other areas, the Foundation has a special interest in providing support for minorities.

Issues. Cli Bio Lan Agr Wat Oce Ene Was Tox Pop Dev
• • • • • • • • • •

Funding analysis.

Fiscal year:	1992	1993
Env grants disb:	$845,420	$931,515
Number:	104	128
Range:	$100–$60,000	$100–$33,000
Median:	$2,500	$2,750
Pct $ disb (env/total):	23	24

Recipients (1993 highest):	Number:	Dollars:
Sierra Club Foundation	3	37,000
Ecotrust	2	35,500
Idaho Rivers United	2	35,000
Conservation International	1	33,000
Institute for Sustainable Forestry	1	30,000
Organization for Tropical Studies (OTS)	1	30,000
The Center for Development and Population Activities (CEDPA)	1	30,000

Activity regions (1993 highest):	Number:	Dollars:
U.S. West	50	259,155
U.S. Northwest	18	215,660
Mexico and Central America	4	113,000
U.S. not specified	31	87,400
International*	7	62,500

*Multiple regions or not specified.

Sample grants (1993).
American Wildlands. Bozeman, MT. $10,000. Tatshenshini campaign.
Bay Area Ridge Trail Council. San Francisco, CA. $10,000.
The Center for Development and Population Activities (CEDPA). Washington, DC. $30,000. Mexico Population/Environment Network.
Conservation International. Washington, DC. $33,000. Wetlands Program: Sonora, Mexico.
The Cousteau Society. Norfolk, VA. $900.
Environmental Enterprises Assistance Fund. Arlington, VA. $25,000. Environmental Enterprises of Central America.
Government Accountability Project. Seattle, WA. $10,000. Hanford Challenge Project.
Greenbelt Alliance. San Francisco, CA. $22,330. Multi-Media Analysis and Prevention.
International Crane Foundation. Baraboo, WI. $2,000.
International Rivers Network. Berkeley, CA. $20,000. Hidrovia, International Support Project.
Land and Water Fund of the Rockies. Boulder, CO. $25,000. Water and Toxics Program.
Learning Alliance. New York, NY. $10,000.
Oregon Natural Resources Council. Eugene, OR. $5,000. Forest Summit Account.
The Trust for Public Land. New York, NY. $20,000. Children's Gardening Program in New York City.
Washington Water Trails Association. Belleview, WA. $3,000. Cascadian Marina Trail.
Yosemite Restoration Trust. San Francisco, CA. $10,000.

Application process. *Initial contact:* Proposal (3–4 pages), after reviewing the Foundation's priorities and concerns. Proposal to include:
1. Brief description of applicant organization.
2. Project objective(s).
3. Means by which it will be accomplished and evaluated.
4. Qualifications of people involved.
5. Other sources of financial support.
6. Project budget.
7. Copy of IRS tax-exempt status determination letter.

When to apply: Deadlines are March 1 and October 1. The board of directors meets in May and December.
Materials available: Biennial report (includes "Application Procedures" and "Grantmaking Policies").

Emphases. *Recipients:* Nonprofit organizations.
Activities: Advocacy, capacity building, citizen participation, collaborative efforts, conflict resolution, direct services, education, land acquisition, networking, policy analysis/development, research (scholarly/scientific), training.
Types of support: Capital campaigns/expenses, continuing support, endowments, general purposes, multi-year grants, projects, technical assistance, travel expenses.
Geography: National projects in the United States and international projects.

Limitations. *Recipients:* Aquariums, botanical gardens, individuals, museums, religious organizations, zoos.
Activities: Audiovisual materials, conferences, exhibits, expeditions/tours, fundraising, inventories, lobbying, research (medical), seminars, single-year grants, symposia/colloquia, workshops, youth programs.

Types of support: Debt retirement, indirect costs, lectureships, loans, maintenance, mortgage reduction, multi-year grants, professorships, program-related investments, seed money, start-up costs.
Geography: Local projects are rarely funded, except for a few in the San Francisco Bay Area.

The Conservation and Research Foundation
Connecticut College
New London, Connecticut 06320
Tel: 203–447–1991
Type: Independent
Contact: Mary G. Wetzel, Secretary

History and philosophy. The Conservation and Research Foundation was established in 1953 to promote the conservation of the earth's natural resources, to encourage research in the biological sciences, and to deepen understanding of the intricate relationships between people and the environment that supports them. It implements this mission by giving direct grants to organizations to aid their conservation programs; initiating studies, supporting activities, and publishing information that might have a catalytic impact on the preservation of environmental quality; and by supporting biological research in neglected areas, especially those with environmental implications.

Officers and directors. *Officers:* Richard S. Goodwin, Sr., President; Mary G. Wetzel, Secretary; Richard H. Goodwin, Jr., Treasurer. *Directors:* Wallace D. Bowman, Winslow R. Briggs, Belton A. Copp, Richard H. Goodwin, Jr., Richard H. Goodwin, Sr., Hubert W. Vogelmann, Mary G. Wetzel, Alexander T. Wilson.

Financial data. Data for fiscal year ended December 31, 1993. *Assets:* $413,195 (M). *Gifts received:* $26,255. *Total grants authorized:* $42,675.

Environmental awards. *Program and interests:* The Foundation's major interests are in stabilizing the human population and preserving the world's natural ecosystems and biological diversity.

Issues. Cli Bio Lan Agr Wat Oce Ene Was Tox Pop Dev
　　　　　•　　•　　•　　　•　　　•　　　•　　•

Funding analysis.§

Fiscal year:	1992	1993
Env grants auth:	$62,471	$59,675
Number:	18	15
Range:	$150–$15,000	$500–$10,000
Median:	$3,471	$1,500
Pct $ auth (env/total):	100	100

Recipients (1993 highest):	Number:	Dollars:
Population Communications International	1	10,000
Carrying Capacity	1	4,000
Mary Lou Krause	1	3,000
Frances C. James	1	2,500
Lindwood H. Pendleton	1	2,500
Peter Siver	1	2,500

C

Activity regions (1993):	Number:	Dollars:
U.S. not specified	6	8,400
International*	3	5,500
Eastern and Southern Africa	1	3,000
Mexico and Central America	1	2,500
West Africa	1	1,500

*Multiple regions or not specified.

§Summary data table provided by Foundation. Recipients and Activity regions tables computed by EDRI based on partial data.

Sample grants (1993).
Lucy Braun Association for the Mixed Mesophytic Forest. Oxford, OH. $1,300. Start-up support.
Carrying Capacity. Washington, DC. $4,000. To support the information clearinghouse.
The Conservation Fund. Arlington, VA. $100. Organizational support.
Patrick Gonzales. Berkeley, CA. $1,500. Study of savanna ecology and human carrying capacity in the Senegal Sahel.
Grassroots Coalition for Environmental and Economic Justice, Inc. Clarksville, MD. $1,000. Organizational support.
International Society for Ecology and Culture. Berkeley, CA. $500. For "The Golden Harvest" television series.
Frances C. James. Tallahassee, FL. $2,500. To study long-term trends in populations of migratory land birds. Matched by Florida State University.
Population Communications International. New York, NY. $10,000. Organizational support.
The Rainbow Generation. Overland Park, KS. $1,000. Organizational support.

Application process. *Initial contact:* Exploratory letter outlining:
1. Nature of proposal.
2. Amount of funding required.
3. Reasons why project fits Foundation interests.

Full proposal (2 pages maximum, 9 copies) to include abstract and budget.
When to apply: Anytime.
Materials available: Five-year report, "Statement of Policies," "Report to Friends and Fellows."

Emphases. *Recipients:* Individuals, nonprofit organizations.
Activities: Citizen participation, collaborative efforts, fundraising, innovative programs, land acquisition, research (scientific), volunteerism.
Types of support: Continuing support, emergency funding, leveraging funds, matching funds, operating costs, pilot projects, projects, seed money, start-up costs.

Limitations. *Recipients:* Botanical gardens, museums, religious organizations, zoos.
Activities: Conflict resolution, exhibits, expeditions/tours, research (medical), seminars, technical assistance, training, youth programs.
Types of support: Annual campaigns, capital campaigns/expenses, endowments, fellowships, indirect costs, lectureships, maintenance, mortgage reduction, professorships, scholarships.

Conservation, Food & Health Foundation, Inc.
c/o Grants Management Associates
230 Congress Street, Third Floor
Boston, Massachusetts 02110
Tel: 617–426–7172   Fax: 617–426–5441
EIN: 222625024   Type: Independent
EGA member
Contact: Ann Fowler Wallace, Administrator

History and philosophy. The Conservation, Food & Health Foundation was established in 1985 to assist in the conservation of natural resources, the production and distribution of food, and the improvement and promotion of human health in the developing world. Through grants targeted toward specific problems, the Foundation works to build capacity within developing countries in its three areas of interest.

The Foundation's special interest is in projects leading to the transfer of responsibility to the citizens of developing countries for managing and solving their own problems and in self-help initiatives. Particular preference is given to projects in fields which tend to be underfunded.

Officers and directors. *Officer:* Philip M. Fearnside, President.

Financial data. Data for fiscal years ended December 31, 1992 and 1993. *Assets (1992):* $6,002,930 (M). *Total grants disbursed (1993):* $311,953.

Environmental awards. *Program and interests:* Conservation grants aim to assist in improving ecological and environmental conditions in the developing world. The Foundation is especially interested in field research and related research activities, training, and technical assistance efforts that:

- Help conserve viable ecosystems and protect biological diversity in developing countries.
- Educate Third World personnel in conservation and protection of resources.
- Train indigenous scientific personnel to work in conservation in the Third World.

Issues. Cli Bio Lan Agr Wat Oce Ene Was Tox Pop Dev
•   •   •   •   •   •   •

Funding analysis.

Fiscal year:	1991	1993
Env grants auth:	$322,894	$242,593
Number:	27	27
Range:	$2,880–$33,760	$250–$23,893
Median:	$10,000	$10,000
Pct $ disb (env/total):	72	85

Recipients (1993 highest):	Number:	Dollars:
Project Concern International	1	23,893
Rainforest Information Centre	1	15,890
Rainforest Alliance	1	15,000
Ashoka: Innovators for the Public	1	11,800
Coastal Resources Center, Inc.	1	11,700

Activity regions (1993 highest):	*Number:*	*Dollars:*
Brazil	6	57,600
Mexico and Central America	3	49,783
Southeast Asia	4	29,800
International*	2	18,250
Eastern and Southern Africa	2	16,170

*Multiple regions or not specified.

Sample grants (1993).
Arnold Arboretum of Harvard University. Cambridge, MA. $7,000. To provide partial support for a project to provide training in plant collecting and botanical inventory at the National Botanic Garden and National Herbarium in Indonesia.
Ashoka: Innovators for the Public. Arlington, VA. $11,800. To support Ashoka fellows Teresa Furtado and Pearl Nwashili working on projects in conservation and health in Brazil and Africa.
Coastal Resources Center, Inc. Boothbay Harbor, ME. $11,700. To provide training support for Sujitha Thomas, manager of an aquaculture program in Kerala, India to enable her to attend the Aquaculture Training Program at Auburn University, Alabama.
Foundation for International Environmental Law and Development. London, U.K. $10,000. To provide partial support for FIELD's efforts to ensure that the Global Environmental Facility provides financial assistance to small island and low-lying developing nations to help these countries adapt to the consequences of climate change, as called for in the 1992 Climate Change Convention.
Harvard University. Cambridge, MA. $10,000. To provide support for efforts to integrate Indonesian nationals into the research, training, and information dissemination activities of the Gunung Palung project, a tropical ecology research program in West Kalimantan, Indonesia.
Marine Biological Laboratory. Woods Hole, MA. $7,800. To support MBL's ecological internship and research program in the Amazon basin of Brazil.
Rainforest Alliance. New York, NY. $15,000. To provide partial support for a joint project with IMAZON to develop a Brazilian Amazon timber harvesting certification program.
Woods Hole Research Center. Woods Hole, MA. $10,000. To provide partial support for a collaborative project with the National Council of Rubber Tappers on forest management in Brazil.
Yale University. New Haven, CT. $5,520. To provide partial support for a research project in Malaysia developed by Dr. Kristina Vogt and Peter Palmiotto entitled: "The Influence of soil nutrients and moisture on species diversity."

Application process. *Initial contact:* Concept paper (3–4 pages) to include:
1. Brief background information on applicant organization and its purposes.
2. Outline of specific project to be supported including project goals, qualifications of personnel, and projected accomplishments.
3. Size, scope, and duration of project.
4. Itemized budget (1 page).
5. Indication of tax status.

See "Form for Concept Papers" for details.

The Foundation will review all concept papers and will invite a limited number of full proposals for review at the upcoming board meeting.
When to apply: Deadlines are January 1 and August 1 for review at the May/June and December meetings of the Foundation. Applicants who are invited to submit a full proposal will receive a minimum of two months to prepare the proposal. Applicants should submit no more than two concept papers to the Foundation in any calendar year.
Materials available: Annual report, "Guidelines—Policies: Information for Applicants," "List of Grants," "Form for Concept Papers."

Emphases. *Recipients:* Educational institutions, nonprofit organizations (especially smaller organizations working on underfunded topics), research institutions.
Activities: Advocacy, fieldwork, inventories, policy analysis/development, research (medical/scholarly), technical assistance, training.
Types of support: Matching funds, pilot projects, projects, seed money, single-year grants only, start-up costs.
Geography: Projects of benefit to Third World countries.

Limitations. *Recipients:* Individuals, public agencies, religious organizations.
Activities: Conflict resolution, fundraising, land acquisition, lobbying.
Types of support: Advertising campaigns, annual campaigns, capital campaigns/expenses, continuing support, debt retirement, emergency funding, endowments, general purposes, indirect costs, loans, membership campaigns, scholarships, technical assistance.

Cooke Foundation, Limited
222 Merchant Street, 2nd Floor
Honolulu, Hawaii 96813
Tel: 808–537–6333   Fax: 808–521–6286
EIN: 237120804   Type: Independent
Contact: Jane Smith, Chief Executive Officer

History and philosophy. In 1920 Anna Charlotte Rice Cooke established the charitable trust that later became the Cooke Foundation, Limited. The daughter of missionaries, Anna married Charles Montague Cooke in 1891. Over the years, they acquired substantial holdings through Charles' investments that ranged from sailing ships transporting sugar, molasses, and rice to Hawaiian Electric Company. Anna Cooke gave generously to the arts and founded the Honolulu Academy of Arts. The Foundation carries on Anna Cooke's tradition with its current program. Grantmaking areas (in order of priority) are: Arts and Culture, Human Services, Health, Science and the Environment, Education, and Humanities.

Officers and directors. *Officers:* Samuel A. Cooke, President; Dale S. Bachman, Anna D. Blackwell, Richard A. Cooke, Betty P. Dunford, Charles C. Spalding, Jr., Vice Presidents; Anna D. Blackwell, Secretary; Betty P. Dunford, Treasurer. *Trustees:* Dale S. Bachman, Anna D. Blackwell, Richard A. Cooke, Samuel A. Cooke, Betty P. Dunford, Charles C. Spalding, Jr.

© 1995 Environmental Data Resources, Inc.

C

Financial data. Data for fiscal year ended June 30, 1993. *Assets:* $12,572,174 (C). *Total grants authorized:* $665,518.

Environmental awards. *Program and interests:* From 1989 through 1993, the Foundation gave $205,500 (22 percent), $43,400 (10 percent), $455,000 (36 percent), $49,500 (6 percent), and $48,500 (7.3 percent), respectively, to environmental programs.
Recent grants: 1993 grants included support for a coastal water project, recycling education and materials development, and recovery from Hurricane Iniki.

Issues. Cli Bio Lan Agr Wat Oce Ene Was Tox Pop Dev
          •   •   •   •

Funding analysis.

Fiscal year:	1991	1993
Env grants auth:	$459,000	$78,500
Number:	8	10
Range:	$4,000–$400,000	$1,000–$25,000
Median:	$5,000	$5,000
Pct $ auth (env/total):	36	12

Recipients (1993 highest):	Number:	Dollars:
Amy B. H. Greenwell Ethnobotanical Garden	1	25,000
Center for Plant Conservation	1	15,000
National Tropical Botanical Garden	2	12,500
Natural Resources Defense Council	1	10,000
Campaign Recycle Maui	1	5,000
Moanalua Gardens Foundation	1	5,000

Activity region (1993):	Number:	Dollars:
Hawaii	10	78,500

Sample grants (1993).
Amy B. H. Greenwell Ethnobotanical Garden. Captain Cook, HI. $25,000. Capital improvements.
Campaign Recycle Maui. Wailuku, HI. $5,000. Support for program to educate hotels and condominiums about recycling.
Center for Plant Conservation. St. Louis, MO. $15,000. Operating support.
Moanalua Gardens Foundation. Honolulu, HI. $5,000. Support for educational materials development.
National Tropical Botanical Garden. Lawai, HI. $10,000. Support for damages to Lawai gardens due to Hurricane Iniki.
Natural Resources Defense Council. Honolulu, HI. $10,000. Support for coastal water project.

Application process. *Initial contact:* Telephone call or personal visit to discuss proposal. Full proposal to include:
1. Cover page (1 copy).
   - Organization name, address, phone number.
   - Nature of request.
   - Amount of request.
   - Contact person's name, phone number, and title.
   - Signatures of board president and executive director.
2. Executive summary: proposal abstract (1–2 pages, 2 copies).
3. Proposal (1 copy) in narrative form, as detailed as necessary to adequately describe the proposed program or project, and the purpose or mission of the organization. Describe in full:
   - Timetable.
   - Program objectives.
   - Plan of action.
   - Evaluation measures.
   - Population served.
   - The need or problem addressed.
4. Board and their occupations or affiliations (2 copies).
5. Operating budget for organization's current year and also for the project (2 copies).
6. Organization's financial statements for the period just completed, preferably audited (1 copy).
7. Copy of IRS tax-exempt status determination letter (1 copy).
8. Applicant's charter and bylaws (1 copy).

When to apply: Deadlines are July 1, November 1, and March 1 for board meetings in September, January, and May.
Materials available: Annual report (includes "Grantmaking Policies" and "Submitting a Proposal").

Emphases. *Recipients:* Botanical gardens, educational institutions, museums, nonprofit organizations.
Activities: Demonstration programs, direct services, education, innovative programs, policy analysis/development, youth programs.
Types of support: Capital campaigns/expenses, computer hardware, equipment, facilities, leveraging funds, matching funds, multi-year grants, pilot projects, projects, seed money, single-year grants, start-up costs, technical assistance.
Geography: Hawaii only.

Limitations. *Recipients:* Individuals, public agencies, religious organizations, research institutions, zoos.
Activities: Activism, conferences, expeditions/tours, land acquisition, litigation, lobbying, political activities, research, seminars, symposia/colloquia, workshops.
Types of support: Advertising campaigns, annual campaigns, continuing support, debt retirement, emergency funding, endowments, fellowships, general purposes, internships, lectureships, loans, membership campaigns, mortgage reduction, multi-year grants, operating costs, professorships, program-related investments, scholarships, travel expenses.

Adolph Coors Foundation
3773 Cherry Creek N. Drive, Suite 955
Denver, Colorado 80209
Tel: 303-388-1636   Fax: 303-388-1684
EIN: 510172279   Type: Independent
Contact: Linda S. Tafoya, Executive Director

History and philosophy. The Adolph Coors Foundation was established in 1975 by a bequest from the late Adolph Coors, Jr., whose father founded the Coors Brewing Company of Golden, Colorado. The Foundation has five primary areas of interest: Health, Education, Community & Human Services, Civic & Cultural, and Public Affairs.

Officers and directors. *Officers:* William K. Coors, President; Peter H. Coors, Vice President; Linda S. Tafoya, Secretary and Executive Director; Jeffrey H. Coors, Treasurer. *Trustees:* Ambassador Holland H. Coors, Jeffrey H. Coors, Joseph Coors, Peter H. Coors, William K. Coors, Robert G. Windsor.

Financial data. Data for fiscal year ended November 30, 1993. *Assets:* $146,924,928 (M). *Total grants disbursed:* $5,293,750.

Environmental awards. *Recent grants:* 1993 grants included support for recreation, outdoor education, and zoos.

Issues. Cli *Bio* *Lan* Agr Wat Oce Ene Was Tox Pop Dev

Funding analysis.

Fiscal year:	1993
Env grants disb:	$117,000
Number:	4
Range:	$10,000–$42,000
Median:	$32,500
Pct $ disb (env/total):	2

Recipients (1993):	*Number:*	*Dollars:*
Rocky Mountain National Park Associates	1	42,000
Colorado Outward Bound School	1	40,000
Pueblo Zoological Society	1	25,000
Doo Zoo Children's Museum	1	10,000

Activity region (1993):	*Number:*	*Dollars:*
U.S. Mountain	4	117,000

Sample grants (1993).

Colorado Outward Bound School. Denver, CO. $40,000. Underwrite the Instructor Development Program, an intensive training to prepare participants to meet the hiring qualifications for entry-level assistant instructors as a part of COBS' objective to achieve more diversity with people of color and women.

Doo Zoo Children's Museum. Grand Junction, CO. $10,000.

Pueblo Zoological Society. Pueblo, CO. $25,000. Capital construction; organization operates the Pueblo Zoo.

Rocky Mountain National Park Associates. Estes Park, CO. $42,000. Assist in making Sprague, Bear Lake, and the Colorado River Trail handicapped accessible.

Application process. *Initial contact:* Preliminary letter of request, including a general description of the program and pertinent financial information. Complete proposal to include:
1. Legal name and address of organization.
2. Contact person and telephone number.
3. Copy of IRS tax-exemption status determination letter.
4. Organization background: date established, brief history, mission statement.
5. Program information: unique aspects, relationships to similar programs.
6. Grant purpose, amount requested, project budget; substantiated need and anticipated results.
7. Other sources and amounts of funding.
8. Names and occupations of board of officers and directors.
9. Financial statement for most recent fiscal year (preferably audited).
10. Current and/or proposed income and expense budget.

When to apply: Deadlines are in February, May, August, and November for consideration at quarterly board meetings held in January, April, July, and October.

Materials available: Annual report (includes "Guidelines" and "Grant Application Procedures"), "Environmental Progress Report."

Emphases. *Recipients:* Nonprofit organizations.
Types of support: Facilities, general purposes, seed money, operating costs, projects.
Geography: Colorado.

Limitations. *Recipients:* Individuals, public agencies, religious organizations.
Activities: Media projects, research.
Types of support: Debt retirement, endowments.
Geography: Organizations or programs based outside the United States.

S. H. Cowell Foundation

120 Montgomery Street, Suite 2570
San Francisco, California 94104
Tel: 415–397–0285   Fax: 415–986–6786
EIN: 941392903   Type: Independent
EGA member
Contact: Max Thelan, Jr., Vice President

History and philosophy. The S. H. Cowell Foundation was formed in 1955 under the will of Samuel Henry Cowell (1861–1955), the last surviving child of California entrepreneur Henry Cowell (1819–1903). The elder Mr. Cowell began his career, with his brother John, in the drayage and storage business, and later owned the Henry Cowell Lime and Cement Company and lands extending from Canada to San Luis Obispo.

The Foundation's "focus is on the underlying causes of poverty and other social problems . . . and priorities include children, youth and families, early childhood education and housing for low income people . . . with concern about the negative impact of overpopulation on the environment and on the quality of life in California and around the world." "The Foundation prefers to award grants for one-time capital needs or for specific projects which are time-definite in nature and likely to become self-sufficient within the next few years." Program areas are: children, youth and families; education; housing; food and clothing distribution; disabled assistance; alcohol abuse prevention; population and environment; conventional arms control.

Officers and directors. *Officers:* J. D. Erickson, President; Max Thelan, Jr., Vice President; George A. Hopiak, Secretary/Treasurer. *Directors:* J. D. Erickson, George A. Hopiak, Dr. Mary S. Metz, Fredric C. Nelson, Max Thelan, Jr.

Financial data. Data for fiscal year ended December 31, 1993. *Assets:* $92,453,421 (M). *Total grants authorized:* $7,888,640.

Environmental awards. *Program and interests:* A priority is educating the public and government officials on the subject of degradation of the environment as a result of the patterns of consumption in developed countries. Other interests include:

- National environmental organizations with pollution policies or programs.

© 1995 Environmental Data Resources, Inc.

C

- Population organizations.
- Immigration organizations which seek to reduce the total amount of legal and illegal immigration.

Issues. Cli Bio Lan Agr Wat Oce Ene Was Tox **Pop Dev**

Funding analysis.

Fiscal year:	1992	1993
Env grants auth:	$481,000	$325,000
Number:	14	7
Range:	$10,000–$70,000	$25,000–$100,000
Median:	$40,000	$40,000
Pct $ auth (env/total):	6	4

Recipients (1993 highest):	Number:	Dollars:
Population Action International	1	100,000
Resource Renewal Institute	1	50,000
Union of Concerned Scientists	1	50,000
Natural Resources Defense Council	1	40,000
Parliamentarians for Global Action	1	30,000
Population-Environment Balance, Inc.	1	30,000

Activity regions (1993):	Number:	Dollars:
International*	5	245,000
U.S. not specified	2	80,000

*Multiple regions or not specified.

Sample grants (1993).
Natural Resources Defense Council. New York, NY. $40,000 (2 years). Support for Population, Consumption, and Environment Initiative.
Parliamentarians for Global Action. New York, NY. $30,000. General support for new Population and Development Project.
Population Action International. Washington, DC. $100,000 (2 years). Support for Population and Environment programs.
Population Communications International. New York, NY. $25,000. Support for the International Conference on Population and Development.
Resource Renewal Institute. Sausalito, CA. $50,000 (2 years). To educate, advocate, and consult for the implementation of a National Environmental Policy Plan (a Green Plan).
Union of Concerned Scientists. Cambridge, MA. $50,000. Global Resources Project.

Application process. *Initial contact:* Letter of inquiry, outlining the project and need for which support is requested and basic information about the applicant. If the Foundation requests a full proposal (1 copy), it should include:
1. Organization background: history, purpose, and goals.
2. Amount requested from the Foundation and detailed explanation of the use of funds.
3. Project scope, budget, and timetable.
4. List of other potential and actual sources of funding, along with amounts solicited or received. Notify the Foundation of grants received while application is pending.
5. Most recent copies of these tax-exemption documents:
   - IRS tax-exempt status determination letter and letter classifying the organization as not a private foundation.
   - Franchise Tax Board letter classifying the organization as exempt from California income tax.
   - Statement signed by a board member that the tax-exemption classifications have not been revoked or modified.

Address letters to Stephanie R. Wolf, Executive Director.
When to apply: Anytime. The board meets frequently.
Materials available: Annual report (includes "Grant Application Procedures").

Emphases. *Recipients:* Nonprofit organizations.
Types of support: Capital campaigns/expenses, equipment, facilities (renovation), matching funds, projects.
Geography: Northern California.

Limitations. *Recipients:* Individuals, public agencies, religious organizations.
Activities: Conferences, media projects, political activities, publications, research, seminars, symposia/colloquia, workshops.
Types of support: Annual campaigns, debt retirement, endowments, general purposes, operating costs, seed money.

The Cowles Charitable Trust
630 Fifth Avenue, Suite 1612
New York, New York 10111–0144
Tel: 212–765–6262
EIN: 136090295   Type: Independent
Contact: Martha Roby Stephens, Secretary

History and philosophy. The Cowles Charitable Trust was established in 1948 by Gardner Cowles, Jr. (1903–1985), founder of *LOOK* magazine. His company, Cowles Magazines and Broadcasting, Inc. (later renamed Cowles Communications, Inc.), owned newspapers, magazines, and radio and television stations. His father, Gardner Cowles, owned the *Des Moines Register* and *Tribune* newspapers and his brother, John Cowles, owned the *Minneapolis Star* and *Tribune* newspapers. The Des Moines newspapers were sold to the Gannett Company in 1985. The Minneapolis newspapers are owned by Cowles Media Company.

The Trust supports the arts, education, health, and environment.

Officers and directors. *Officers:* Gardner Cowles III, President; Martha Roby Stephens, Secretary; Mary Croft, Treasurer. *Trustees:* Charles Cowles, Gardner Cowles III, Jan Cowles, Lois Cowles Harrison, Kate Cowles Nichols, Virginia Cowles Schroth, Martha Roby Stephens.

Financial data. Data for fiscal year ended December 31, 1992. *Assets:* $17,022,877 (M). *Total grants disbursed:* $991,750.

Environmental awards. *Recent grants:* 1991 grants included support for land conservation, urban environment (parks and trees), marine issues, horticulture, a botanical garden, and a zoo. Most recipients were major national organizations.

Issues. Cli Bio• Lan• Agr Wat• Oce Ene• Was Tox Pop• Dev

Funding analysis.

Fiscal year:	1990	1991
Env grants disb:	$36,000	$41,000
Number:	9	10
Range:	$1,500–$10,000	$1,500–$10,000
Median:	$3,000	$4,000
Pct $ disb (env/total):	4	5

Recipients (1991 highest):	Number:	Dollars:
Horticultural Society of New York	1	10,000
City Parks Foundation	1	5,000
Environmental Defense Fund	1	5,000
NYZS/The Wildlife Conservation Society	1	5,000
Peconic Land Trust, Inc.	1	5,000

Activity regions (1991):	Number:	Dollars:
New York/New Jersey	7	30,500
U.S. not specified	3	10,500

Sample grants (1991).
Brooklyn Botanic Garden. Brooklyn, NY. $2,000.
Center for Marine Conservation. Washington, DC. $2,500.
City Parks Foundation. New York, NY. $5,000.
Environmental Defense Fund. New York, NY. $5,000.
Horticultural Society of New York. New York, NY. 10,000.
The Nature Conservancy, Headquarters. Arlington, VA. $3,000.
New York City Street Tree Consortium. New York, NY. $1,500.
NYZS/The Wildlife Conservation Society. Bronx, NY. $5,000.
The Parks Council, Inc. New York, NY. $2,000.
Peconic Land Trust, Inc. Southampton, NY. $5,000.

Application process. *Initial contact:* Letter and proposal packet. Letter, written on organization letterhead, to include:
1. Description of organization, including history and scope of current activities.
2. Statement describing need for project or activity, and project objectives: what it is intended to accomplish.
3. Brief description of activities to be included in project and the timetable for accomplishment.
4. Statement concerning overall cost of project, amount of funding requested and sources of additional support.

Proposal packet (7 copies).
1. Letter from organization's CEO (if letter of application has been written by someone else).
2. Project budget.
3. A list of organization's governing body and officers, showing business, professional, and community affiliations.

Attachments (1 copy).
1. Copy of IRS tax-exempt status determination letter.
2. Organization's most recent audited financial statement.

The Trust does not accept proposals sent by facsimile machine. *When to apply:* Deadlines are December 1, March 1, June 1, and September 1 for review in January, April, July, and October. *Materials available:* Annual report, "How to Apply for a Grant."

Emphases. *Recipients:* Nonprofit organizations.
Types of support: Annual campaigns, capital campaigns/expenses, continuing support, emergency funding, endowments, equipment, facilities, general purposes, matching funds, operating costs, pilot projects, professorships, seed money.
Geography: Florida, New York, and the East Coast.

Limitations. *Recipients:* Individuals, organizations that have applied within the last twelve months, organizations currently receiving multi-year grants until all payments have been made.
Types of support: Loans.

Cox Foundation, Inc.

c/o Choate, Hall & Stewart
Exchange Place
Boston, Massachusetts 02109-2841
Tel: 617-227-5020
EIN: 237068786   Type: Independent
Contact: Robert Perkins, Trust Administrator

History and philosophy. The Foundation was established in 1970 by William C. Cox, Jr.

Officers and directors. *Officers:* William C. Cox, Jr., President; David E. Place, Secretary; Martha W. Cox, Treasurer.

Financial data. Data for fiscal year ended January 31, 1992. *Assets:* $7,333,648 (M). *Gifts received:* $722,652. *Total grants disbursed:* $270,522.

Environmental awards. *Recent grants:* 1992 grants included support for land conservation, wildlife, and marine issues.

Issues. Cli Bio• Lan• Agr Wat• Oce Ene Was Tox Pop Dev

Funding analysis.

Fiscal year:	1992
Env grants disb:	$84,000
Number:	14
Range:	$1,000–$25,000
Median:	$3,750
Pct $ disb (env/total):	31

Recipients (1992 highest):	Number:	Dollars:
Nantucket Conservation Foundation	2	30,000
The Sconset Trust, Inc.	1	10,000
Marine Biological Laboratory	1	10,000
Woods Hole Oceanographic Institution	1	10,000
Conservation International	1	5,000
The Nature Conservancy, Headquarters	1	5,000

Activity regions (1992):	Number:	Dollars:
U.S. Northeast	7	63,500
U.S. not specified	3	9,500
International*	1	5,000
U.S. Southeast	2	3,500
U.S. Mid-Atlantic	1	2,500

*Multiple regions or not specified.

C

Sample grants (1992).
Brandywine Conservancy, Inc. Chadds Ford, PA. $2,500.
Conservation International. Washington, DC. $5,000.
International Game Fish Association. Fort Lauderdale, FL. $1,000.
Nantucket Conservation Foundation. Nantucket, MA. $5,000.
Nantucket Harbor Study Fund. Nantucket, MA. $1,000.
National Coalition for Marine Conservation. Savannah, GA. $2,500.
The Nature Conservancy, Headquarters. Arlington, VA. $5,000.
New England Aquarium. Boston, MA. $2,500.
North American Wildlife Foundation. Deerfield, IL. $2,000.
The Sconset Trust, Inc. Siasconset, MA. $10,000.
Woods Hole Oceanographic Institution. Woods Hole, MA. $10,000.

Application process. *Initial contact:* The Foundation awards grants to pre-selected organizations only. No unsolicited applications accepted.

Emphases. *Recipients:* Pre-selected organizations only.
Geography: Primarily Massachusetts and Florida.

Limitations. *Recipients:* Individuals

The James M. Cox, Jr. Foundation, Inc.
Fourth and Ludlow Street
Dayton, Ohio 45402
EIN: 237256190   Type: Independent

Application Address:
c/o Cox Enterprises, Inc.
P.O. Box 105720
Atlanta, Georgia 30348
Tel: 404-843-7912   Fax: 404-843-7926
Contact: Leigh Ann Korns, Administrative Assistant

History and philosophy. The Foundation was established in 1969. Funding priorities are conservation and the environment, education, health care, and cultural programs.

Officers and directors. *Officers:* James Cox Kennedy, President; Barbara Cox Anthony, Vice President; Andrew Merdek, Secretary; Carl R. Gross, Treasurer. *Trustees:* Barbara Cox Anthony, Carl R. Gross, James Cox Kennedy.

Financial data. Data for fiscal year ended December 31, 1992. *Assets:* $29,285,209 (M). *Total grants disbursed:* $1,330,833.

Environmental awards. *Recent grants:* 1992 grants supported land conservation, wildlife protection, and an arboretum.

Issues.   Cli   Bio   Lan   Agr   Wat   Oce   Ene   Was   Tox   Pop   Dev
                    •   •

Funding analysis.

Fiscal year:	1991	1992
Env grants disb:	$400,000	$425,000
Number:	5	5
Range:	$25,000–$250,000	$25,000–$250,000
Median:	$50,000	$50,000
Pct $ disb (env/total):	33	67

Recipients (1992):	Number:	Dollars:
The Nature Conservancy, Headquarters	1	250,000
Atlanta Outward Bound Center	1	50,000
Cox Arboretum Associates, Inc.	1	50,000
World Wildlife Fund	1	50,000
Ducks Unlimited, Inc.	1	25,000

Activity regions (1992):	Number:	Dollars:
U.S. not specified	2	275,000
U.S. Southeast	2	100,000
International*	1	50,000

*Multiple regions or not specified.

Sample grants (1992).
Atlanta Outward Bound Center. Decatur, GA. $50,000.
Cox Arboretum Associates, Inc. Dayton, OH. $50,000.
Ducks Unlimited, Inc. Long Grove, IL. $25,000.
The Nature Conservancy, Headquarters. Arlington, VA. $250,000.
World Wildlife Fund. Washington, DC. $50,000.

Application process. *Initial contact:* Written request to the trustees to include:
1. Outline of grant program or project, its needs, and goals.
2. Most recent annual report (if not available, send unaudited financial statements or the most recent tax return).
3. Interim financial reports.
4. Current budget.
5. Board of directors and officers, including top officers' salaries.
6. List of recent donors and amount contributed.
7. Copy of IRS tax-exempt status determination letter.

Applicants may send other materials as desired and relevant to the grant request. Send 4 copies of any materials submitted in booklet or bound format.
When to apply: Anytime. The board meets quarterly.

Emphases. *Recipients:* Botanical gardens, nonprofit organizations, public agencies, research institutions.
Activities: Direct services, innovative programs, land acquisition.
Types of support: Capital campaigns/expenses, facilities, general purposes, leveraging funds, multi-year grants.
Geography: Georgia and Ohio, and any locations of Cox Enterprises.

Limitations. *Recipients:* Educational institutions.

Jessie B. Cox Charitable Trust

c/o Grants Management Associates, Inc.
230 Congress Street, 3rd Floor
Boston, Massachusetts 02110
Tel: 617-426-7172   Fax: 617-426-5441
EIN: 046478024   Type: Independent
EGA member
Contacts: Ann Fowler Wallace, Administrator
Katherine McHugh, Administrator
Rachel Pohl, Administrator
Newell Flather, Advisor

History and philosophy. The Jessie B. Cox Charitable Trust was established in 1982 under the will of Jessie B. Cox. The Trust makes grants for projects which will address important societal issues in its fields of interest, and for which adequate funding from other sources cannot be obtained. The trustees also hope to increase significantly the ability of nonprofit organizations to carry out their stated missions in the fields of health, education, environment, and the development of philanthropy.

Officers and directors. *Trustees:* William C. Cox, Jr., Roy A. Hammer, Jane Cox MacElree, George T. Shaw.

Financial data. Data for fiscal years ended December 31, 1993. *Total grants disbursed:* $3,059,230.

Environmental awards. *Program and interests:* The Environment program protects the natural and urban environment, and conserves the natural resources of New England. Interests are:

- Natural resources and wildlife protection.
- Energy conservation.
- Conservation efforts with immediate public health benefit.
- Public awareness of critical environmental issues.

Issues. Cli Bio Lan Agr Wat Oce Ene Was Tox Pop Dev
              •   •   •   •   •   •

Funding analysis.

Fiscal year:	1991	1993
Env grants auth:	$639,590	$1,147,325
Number:	11	17
Range:	$25,000–$210,000	$325–$150,000
Median:	$45,000	$60,000
Pct $ disb (env/total):	39	33

Recipients (1993 highest):	Number:	Dollars:
Massachusetts Watershed Coalition	1	150,000
Elm Education Fund	1	120,000
Save the Bay, Inc.	1	120,000
Woods Hole Oceanographic Institution	1	120,000
Long Island Soundkeeper Fund	1	118,000

Activity regions (1993):	Number:	Dollars:
U.S. Northeast	14	1,067,000
U.S. Mid-Atlantic	1	50,000
U.S. not specified	2	30,325

Sample grants (1993).[*]

Boston GreenSpace Alliance. Boston, MA. $30,000. To support improvement of schoolyards and expansion of environmental education in the Boston public schools.

Boston Natural Areas Fund. Boston, MA. $34,000. Support of the Boston Urban Wilds Priority Action Project.

Center for Coastal Studies. Provincetown, MA. $15,000. Final support to develop new educational programs for the Center's Division of Conservation and Educational Programs.

Clean Water Fund. Boston, MA. $40,000. Support of the Heavy Metals Pollution Prevention Project, a project to prevent pollution and promote public health in New England.

Conservation Law Foundation. Boston, MA. $74,000. In support of a collaborative project of the Conservation Law Foundation, the Appalachian Mountain Club, and American Rivers to participate in hydropower relicensing proceedings in New England.

Gulf of Maine Aquarium. Portland, ME. $35,000. To support a mobile teaching laboratory using data from weather satellites to enhance science education through marine science applications.

Island Institute. Rockland, ME. $35,000. To support the Marine Resources Program to improve the health and economic wellbeing of Maine's wild and aquaculture fisheries.

Natural Resources Council of Maine. Augusta, ME. $40,000. Support of NRCM's air pollution initiative to reduce ground-level ozone and greenhouse gases in Maine.

Tellus Institute. Boston, MA. $50,000. To support a collaborative project of the Tellus Institute and the JSI Center for Environmental Health Studies to provide technical assistance to community groups concerned about the potential hazards of incinerators.

Vermont Natural Resources Council, Inc. Montpelier, VT. $100,000. Support of a collaborative project to create a network to promote water resource protection and improvement at local, regional, and state levels.

[*]Sample grants represent either new awards or disbursements on grants awarded in previous years.

Application process. *Initial contact:* Call to discuss project ideas or submit a concept paper (3–4 pages). Concept paper signed by executive director or board president to include:
1. Description of purposes of organization.
2. Outline of project to be supported.
3. Description of how proposed project will strengthen the ability of applicant organization to reach its goals.
4. Total amount desired.

Attach preliminary budget and IRS exempt-status determination letter.

When to apply: Deadlines are January 15, April 15, July 15, and October 15. The board of trustees meets in March, June, September, and December.

Materials available: Annual report, "Guidelines and Policies."

Emphases. *Recipients:* Nonprofit organizations.
Activities: Activism, advocacy, citizen participation, collaborative efforts, demonstration programs, education, planning, policy analysis/development.
Types of support: Multi-year grants, pilot projects, projects, seed money, start-up costs.
Geography: New England.

© 1995 Environmental Data Resources, Inc.

The Cricket Foundation

Exchange Place, Suite 2200
Boston, Massachusetts 02109–2881
Tel: 617–570–1130   Fax: 617–523–1231
EIN: 042655735   Type: Independent
Contact: George W. Butterworth III, Esq., Counsel

History and philosophy. The Cricket Foundation was established in 1978. It supports cultural and environmental organizations, primarily in New England.

Officers and directors. *Trustee:* A. Joshua Sherman.

Financial data. Data for fiscal year ended September 30, 1993. *Assets:* $2,150,000 (U). *Total grants authorized:* $83,000.

Environmental awards. *Recent grants:* 1993 grants included support for land conservation and coastal issues in New England.

Issues.   Cli   Bio   Lan   Agr   Wat   Oce   Ene   Was   Tox   Pop   Dev
                        •

Funding analysis.

Fiscal year:	1992	1993
Env grants auth:	$32,000	$30,500
Number:	8	5
Range:	$1,500–$7,000	$2,500–$10,000
Median:	$4,000	$5,000
Pct $ auth (env/total):	36	37

Recipients (1993):	Number:	Dollars:
Massachusetts Audubon Society	1	10,000
Appalachian Mountain Club	1	8,000
Laudholm Trust	1	5,000
The Environmental Careers Organization, Inc.	1	5,000
Charles River Watershed Association	1	2,500

Activity regions (1993):	Number:	Dollars:
U.S. Northeast	4	25,500
U.S. not specified	1	5,000

Sample grants (1993).
Appalachian Mountain Club. Boston, MA. $8,000. Climate research.
Charles River Watershed Association. Auburndale, MA. $2,500. General purposes.
The Environmental Careers Organization, Inc. Boston, MA. $5,000. General purposes.
Laudholm Trust. Wells, ME. $5,000. Volunteer coastal monitoring.
Massachusetts Audubon Society. Lincoln, MA. $10,000. Land protection.

Application process. *Initial contact:* Telephone inquiry to counsel at the number listed above. All proposals must include an IRS tax-exempt status determination letter.
When to apply: Deadlines are April 15 and October 15. Grants are awarded semiannually.

Emphases. *Recipients:* Nonprofit organizations.
Activities: Advocacy, land conservation, research.
Types of support: Operating costs, projects.
Geography: New England.

Limitations. *Recipients:* Individuals.
Types of support: Endowments, fellowships, scholarships.
Geography: Outside the United States.

The Mary A. Crocker Trust

233 Post Street, 2nd Floor
San Francisco, California 94108
Tel: 415–982–0138   Fax: 415–982–0141
EIN: 946051917   Type: Independent
EGA member
Contact: Barbaree Jernigan, Administrator

History and philosophy. Mary Crocker (1827–1889) was married to Charles Crocker, one of the "Big Four" who developed the Pacific Railroad. The Trust, established in 1889 by the four children of Mary Crocker, is the oldest family foundation west of the Mississippi. Five members of the Crocker family now serve as trustees. The Trust supports programs in Education, Environment, and Community Relations in the Bay Area.

Officers and directors. *Officers:* Tania Stepanian, Chairman; Lloyd Skjerdal, Treasurer. *Trustees:* Elizabeth Atcheson, Lucy Blake, Charles Crocker, Tania Stepanian, Fredrick Whitridge.

Financial data. Data for fiscal year ended December 31, 1993. *Assets:* $9,000,000 (M) (est.). *Total grants disbursed:* $49,070.

Environmental awards. *Program and interests:* The Trust seeks to fund education and advocacy projects that promote solutions to environmental problems and boost public awareness and participation. The Trust has a special interest in:

- Sustainable agriculture.
- Waste management and recycling.
- Water quality.
- Land use management.
- Population.

Recent grants: 1993 grants included support for coastal issues, forest preservation, river protection, and youth education.

Issues.   Cli   Bio   Lan   Agr   Wat   Oce   Ene   Was   Tox   Pop   Dev
                •   •   •   •   •   •   •

Funding analysis.

Fiscal year:	1992	1993
Env grants disb:	$137,500	$244,000
Number:	10	17
Range:	$2,500–$15,000	$5,000–$25,000
Median:	$10,000	$15,000
Pct $ disb (env/total):	25	47

Recipients (1993 highest):	Number:	Dollars:
Coastal Resources Center	1	25,000
Petaluma Wildlife & Natural Science Museum	1	25,000
Institute for Sustainable Forestry	1	20,000
Sierra Club Foundation	1	20,000
The Student Conservation Association, Inc.	1	20,000

Activity regions (1993):	Number:	Dollars:
U.S. West	15	223,000
U.S. not specified	2	21,000

Sample grants (1993).

Bay Area Ridge Trail Council. San Francisco, CA. $10,000. To help establish a comprehensive volunteer management program for the Council.

BayKeeper. San Francisco, CA. $15,000. Expansion support for legal and scientific programs—fish contamination study, water monitoring, agency reforms, and training.

California Communities Against Toxics. Rosamond, CA. $5,000. Support for this network of over 70 community groups and environmental organizations offering organizational leadership support to the grassroots toxics movement.

Californians Against Waste Foundation. Sacramento, CA. $15,000. For the education campaign designed to heighten awareness of California's need to develop recovered materials, industries, and jobs.

Earth Action Network, Inc. Westport, CT. For the California program of the Network, which offers "Alerts" to over 80 countries linking environmentalists worldwide with critical information on environmental issues.

Earthwatch Expeditions, Inc. Los Altos, CA. $5,000. For MESA (Math, Engineering, Science Achievement) scholarships for students to participate on scientific research expeditions in our national parks.

Environmental Defense Fund. New York, NY. $15,000. For the San Francisco Bay and Delta Protection program designed to improve water quality and management policies and standards.

Friends of the River Foundation. San Francisco, CA. $10,000. The Rivers Partners Program plans to bring environmental activists and organizations together to more effectively protect California rivers through education and leadership training.

Institute for Sustainable Forestry. Redway, CA. $20,000. Further funding for the Pacific Certified Ecological Forest Products Project—the certification, labeling, and marketing of ecologically harvested forest products.

Marine Science Institute. Redwood City, CA. $5,000. For environmental studies class to Bay Area school children.

The Pacific Forest Trust, Inc. Boonville, CA. $18,000. Private Lands–Public Trust program. Support for efforts in preservation and protection of forestland on private and public lands.

Petaluma Wildlife & Natural Science Museum. Petaluma, CA. $25,000. A technical assistance and general operating grant to support this unusual museum operated by Petaluma High School students.

Sierra Club Foundation. San Francisco, CA. $20,000. For the Western Water Policy Project, designed to implement the 1992 Central Valley Project Improvement Act and develop a model for water resource management in the West.

The Student Conservation Association, Inc. Charlestown, NH. $20,000. Matching grant for the Conservation Career Development Program of SCA. For recruitment, career training, and mentoring for minority youth in the Bay Area.

The Video Project. Oakland, CA. $16,000. To ensure the Ecological Film and Video Collection can be offered to schools and libraries at low cost.

Application process. *Initial contact:* Letter of inquiry. Formal proposal, if requested, to include:
1. Amount requested and the rationale.
2. Description of the innovative features of proposal.
3. Budgetary information, including the current budget of organization.
4. Other sources and amounts of support.
5. Contact persons.

When to apply: Deadlines for 1995 are January 31 and August 31. The trustees meet in April and November.

Materials available: Information packet, application guidelines, grants list.

Emphases. *Recipients:* Nonprofit organizations.
Activities: Advocacy, citizen participation, collaborative efforts, education, innovative programs, volunteerism.
Types of support: General purposes, matching funds, operating costs.
Geography: The Bay Area of Northern California only, including San Francisco, San Mateo, Santa Clara, Alameda, Contra Costa, Marin, Sonoma, Solano, and Napa counties.

Limitations. *Recipients:* Individuals.
Types of support: Annual campaigns, continuing support, debt retirement. Equipment, facilities, scholarships receive low priority.

Roy E. Crummer Foundation

130 Newport Center Drive, Suite 140
Newport Beach, California 92660
Tel: 714–644–4702
EIN: 886004422   Type: Independent
Contact: Jean Crummer Coburn, President

History and philosophy. The Roy E. Crummer Foundation was established in 1964. Primary fields of interest include: communications, media, higher education, social services, and wildlife.

Officers and directors. *Officers:* Jean Crummer Coburn, President; Milton Coburn, Vice President; Margarite Brown, Secretary/Treasurer. *Directors:* Margarite Brown, Jean Crummer Coburn, Milton Coburn, Ian Gow, Lee D. Strom.

C

Financial data. Data for fiscal year ended December 31, 1992. *Assets:* $6,961,839 (M). *Total grants disbursed:* $330,000.

Environmental awards. *Recent grants:* 1992 grants included support for coastal issues, wildlife, and public education.

Issues. Cli Bio Lan Agr Wat Oce Ene Was Tox Pop Dev
　　　　　　• 　 • 　　　 • 　　　 •

Funding analysis.

Fiscal year:	1992
Env grants disb:	$38,000
Number:	4
Range:	$1,000–$31,000
Median:	$3,000
Pct $ disb (env/total):	12

Recipients (1992):	Number:	Dollars:
Palm Springs Desert Museum	1	31,000
African Fund for Endangered Wildlife, Inc.	1	5,000
Defenders of Wildlife	1	1,000
Heal the Bay	1	1,000
Activity regions		
U.S. West	2	32,000
Africa	1	5,000
U.S. not specified	1	1,000

Sample grants (1992).
African Fund for Endangered Wildlife, Inc. Baltimore, MD. $5,000.
Defenders of Wildlife. Washington, DC. $1,000.
Heal the Bay. Santa Monica, CA. $1,000.
Palm Springs Desert Museum. Palm Springs, CA. $31,000.

Application process. *Initial contact:* The Foundation awards grants to pre-selected organizations only. No unsolicited applications accepted.

Emphases. *Recipients:* Pre-selected organizations only.

Crystal Channel Foundation
420 West Miner Street
West Chester, Pennsylvania 19382
Tel: 610–431–1642
EIN: 133384064　　Type: Independent
EGA member
Contact: Mary Radford, Executive Administrator

History and philosophy. The Crystal Channel Foundation was founded in 1986 by Christine Jurzykowski. It supports international grassroots organizations and projects where a small grant can serve as leverage. The Foundation is dedicated to funding fieldwork, conservation education, species preservation, and bridging spirituality and nature.

Officers and directors. *Officers:* Christine Jurzykowski, President; Mary Radford, Executive Administrator. *Directors:* James R. Jackson, Shirlee Stokes.

Financial data. Data for fiscal year ended December 31, 1994. *Assets:* $42,000 (M) (est.). *Total grants disbursed:* $16,750.

Environmental awards. *Program and interests:* The Foundation funds:

- Wildlife and species preservation, especially at the grassroots level.
- Fieldwork.
- Community outreach.
- Environmental education.
- Efforts to link spirituality and nature.

Recent grants: 1994 grants included support for reforestation, wildlife preservation, and education.

Issues. Cli Bio Lan Agr Wat Oce Ene Was Tox Pop Dev
　　　　　　• 　 • 　　　 • 　 • 　 • 　 •

Funding analysis.

Fiscal year:	1992	1994
Env grants auth:	$28,989	$18,250
Number:	18	15
Range:	$250–$10,000	$500–$3,500
Median:	$1,000	$1,000
Pct $ auth (env/total):	100	100

Recipients (1994 highest):	Number:	Dollars:
The Institute for Deep Ecology Education	1	3,500
Earth Action Network, Inc.	1	1,500
Ecoforestry Institute	1	1,500
Gladys Porter Zoo	1	1,500
Native Seeds/SEARCH	1	1,500

Activity regions (1994 highest):	Number:	Dollars:
U.S. not specified	4	7,000
U.S. South Central	3	3,500
U.S. West	2	2,250
International*	2	1,500
U.S. Northwest	1	1,500

*Multiple regions or not specified.

Sample grants (1994).
Aid to Artisans. Farmington, CT. $500. To support the Artisans and Ecology Program in Brazil.
Ecoforestry Institute. Portland, OR. $1,500. To help match a challenge grant to fund training of ecoforesters.
Eco Rap (Life on the Water). San Francisco, CA. $750. To help establish a multi-cultural Youth Corps to teach environmental education to at-risk children.
Earth Action Network, Inc. Norwalk, CT. $1,500. General support for one of the few remaining environmental magazines.
Endangered Species Project. San Francisco, CA. $1,000. To support a program to expose organized crime and illegal wildlife trade.
Friends of Conservation. Oak Brook, IL. $1,000. To support the Black Rhino Program.
Gladys Porter Zoo. Brownsville, TX. $1,500. For Kemp's Ridley Sea Turtle Program, to fund hands-on childrens' parties at nesting beaches and bi-lingual coloring books.

Grassroots Coalition for Environmental and Economic Justice. Clarksville, MD. $1,000. To support "Grassroots News" which is distributed to students and environmental church groups around the United States, Canada, and the United Kingdom.

The Institute for Deep Ecology Education. Boulder, CO. $3,500. For a scholarship program to allow environmental activists on low incomes to attend the 1994 IDEE Summer School in Applied Deep Ecology.

Native Seeds/SEARCH. Tucson, AZ. $1,500. General support.

SEARCH (Student Environmental Analysis Report Card to the Community and How to Improve It). Austin, TX. $1,000. To fund a program where all 420 students (half of whom are considered at-risk) participate in age-appropriate environmental activities and team students with adult mentors and senior citizens as well as professionals in specific environmental fields to study, create "Report Cards", and problem solve on four main areas of their community environment: waste, water, soil, and energy.

Trees for the Future. Silver Spring, MD. $500. To support the Tree Pals Project which will coordinate school reforestation programs around the world.

VCCF (Very Clever Conservation Folks). Glen Rose, TX. $1,000. To support a conference.

YES! Atlanta. Atlanta, GA. $1,000. To support the Green Schools Program, a follow-up program for YES! performances.

Cary Yeager, Fordham, University. Armonk, NY. $1,000. To support ongoing field research involving endangered species in Indonesia.

Application process. *Initial contact:* Brief proposal including "Summary Application Form."
When to apply: Deadlines are February 1 and August 1 for board meetings in March and September, respectively.
Materials available: "Guidelines," "Summary Application Form."

Emphases. *Recipients:* Educational institutions, nonprofit organizations, research institutions, zoos.
Activities: Advocacy, citizen participation, education, feasibility studies, fieldwork, innovative programs, research (scientific), training, volunteerism, youth programs.
Types of support: Annual campaigns, continuing support, general purposes, internships, leveraging funds, matching funds, pilot projects, seed money.

Limitations. *Activities:* Inventories, lobbying, research (scholarly).
Types of support: Debt retirement, facilities, mortgage reduction, professorships, program-related investments.

Patrick and Anna M. Cudahy Fund
P.O. Box 11978
Milwaukee, Wisconsin 53211–0978
Tel: 708–866–0760
EIN: 390991972   Type: Independent
Contact: Sister Judith Borchers, Executive Director

History and philosophy. Established in 1934 by Michael F. Cudahy in honor of his parents, the Patrick and Anna M. Cudahy Fund is a general purpose foundation which primarily supports social service, youth, and education. Some support is also given for local and national programs concerned with public interest and environmental issues, and for programs in Central America and southern Africa but only through U.S.-based organizations.

Officers and directors. *Officers:* Richard D. Cudahy, Chairman; Janet S. Cudahy, President; Sister Judith Borchers, OSB, Executive Director. *Directors:* James Bailey, Daniel Cudahy, Janet S. Cudahy, Richard D. Cudahy, Annette Stoddard Freeman, Dudley J. Godfrey, Jr., Jean Holtz, Philip Lerman, Wesley L. Scott.

Financial data. Data for fiscal year ended December 31, 1993. *Assets:* $19,517,931 (M). *Total grants disbursed:* $1,855,730.

Environmental awards. *Recent grants:* In 1993 grants included support for ecosystem preservation, wildlife, and education and training of women and teachers.

Issues. Cli Bio Lan Agr Wat Oce Ene Was Tox Pop Dev
          •   •   •

Funding analysis.

Fiscal year:	1991	1993
Env grants auth:	$60,900	$57,500
Number:	8	6
Range:	$2,400–$12,500	$5,000–$15,000
Median:	$8,000	$10,000
Pct $ disb (env/total):	4	3

Recipients (1993 highest):	Number:	Dollars:
Sierra Club Foundation	1	15,000
Coordination in Development, Inc.	1	10,000
Earthwatch Expeditions, Inc.	1	10,000
Northland College	1	10,000
The Wilderness Society	1	7,500

Activity regions (1993):	Number:	Dollars:
U.S. Great Lakes	2	25,000
U.S. not specified	3	22,500
New York/New Jersey	1	10,000

Sample grants (1993).

Coordination in Development, Inc. New York, NY. $10,000. Women's Literacy Environmental Training Program.

Earthwatch Expeditions, Inc. Watertown, MA. $10,000. Teacher Advancement Awards Program.

Environmental Defense Fund. New York, NY. $5,000. Wildlife Program.

Northland College. Ashland, WI. $10,000. Natural Resource Technology Program.

Sierra Club Foundation. San Francisco, CA. $15,000. Great Lakes Ecoregion Program.

The Wilderness Society. Washington, DC. $7,500. New Voices for the American West Campaign.

Application process. *Initial contact:* Telephone call or letter requesting application materials. Full proposal to include:
1. Completed form entitled "Summary of Requests" (sent by Foundation).
2. Brief description of applicant and outline of proposed project (5 pages maximum).

3. Financial summary for the applicant, preferably the most recent audited financial statement.
4. Projected income and expenses for current year, both for applicant and project.
5. List of other major donors for project.
6. List of applicant's current board of directors.
7. Copy of IRS tax-exempt status determination letter.

When to apply: Deadlines are in January, April, July, and October or at least six weeks before each quarterly board meeting held in March, June, September, and December. Call for specific dates.
Materials available: Grants list, "Guidelines," "Summary of Request Form."

Emphases. *Recipients:* Botanical gardens, educational institutions, museums, nonprofit organizations, public agencies.
Activities: Advocacy, citizen participation, collaborative efforts, direct services, education, fieldwork, innovative programs, networking, volunteerism.
Types of support: Annual campaigns, continuing support, equipment, general purposes, internships, matching funds, operating costs, scholarships, seed money.
Geography: Wisconsin; Chicago area.

Limitations. *Recipients:* Individuals.
Types of support: Endowments, loans.

Charles E. Culpeper Foundation, Inc.

Financial Centre
695 East Main Street, Suite 404
Stamford, Connecticut 06901–2138
Tel: 203–975–1240   Fax: 203–975–1847
EIN: 131956297   Type: Independent
Contact: Linda E. Jacobs, Vice President for Programs

History and philosophy. The Charles E. Culpeper Foundation is a private, nonprofit charitable foundation established under the will of the late Charles E. Culpeper, one of the pioneers in the bottling and marketing of Coca-Cola. In recent years, the Foundation has disbursed approximately $6 million a year to activities in health, education, arts and culture, and the administration of justice.

Officers and Directors. *Officers:* Francis J. McNamara, Jr., President; Philip M. Drake, Vice President and Secretary/Treasurer. *Trustees:* Colin G. Campbell, Philip M. Drake, Joseph F. Fahey, Jr., Ronald P. Lynch, Francis J. McNamara, Jr., John Morning, John C. Rose, M.D.

Financial data. Data for fiscal year ended December 31, 1993. *Assets:* $157,389,000 (M). *Total grants disbursed:* $5,972,000.

Environmental awards. *Program and interests:* "For many years the Foundation has played a large role in projects relating to conservation and the environment." Environmental studies is one of five principal areas within the Education program, where the Foundation mainly supports undergraduate education in the liberal arts and sciences at private colleges and universities.
Recent grants: In 1993 two grants supported environmental studies programs.

Funding analysis.§

Fiscal year:	1992	1993
Env grants auth:	$308,647	$250,000
Number:	3	2
Range:	$50,000–$158,647	$100,000–$150,000
Median:	$100,000	$125,000
Pct $ auth (env/total):	5	4

Recipients (1993):	Number:	Dollars:
Mount Holyoke College	1	150,000
The Environmental Careers Organization, Inc.	1	100,000

Activity regions (1993):	Number:	Dollars:
U.S. Northeast	1	150,000
U.S. not specified	1	100,000

§Does not include grants of less than $25,000.

Sample grants (1993).
The Environmental Careers Organization, Inc. Boston, MA. $100,000. Toward the formation of collective strategies to develop the role of college environmental studies programs in serving the goal of protecting the environment.
Mount Holyoke College. South Hadley, MA. $150,000. Toward a visiting professors program in environmental studies as a component of curriculum development.

Application process. *Initial contact:* Letter to include:
1. Amount requested and purpose.
2. Succinct description of project.
3. Budget.
4. Information on other funding received or anticipated.
5. Short history and background of applicant.
6. Copy of IRS tax-exempt status determination letter.

If interested, Foundation will send application and request for further information to include:
1. Name and telephone number of project contact.
2. Proposal summary (1 paragraph).
3. Statement of objectives and functions of proposed project.
4. Detailed budget by year.
5. List of other significant project/organizational support.
6. Timeline for project.
7. Qualifications of persons who will direct project.
8. History of the organization (1 page).
9. List of officers and/or trustees of organization.
10. Complete financial data on applicant organization.
11. Copy of IRS tax-exempt status determination letter.

When to apply: Anytime (except for the medical and medical humanities scholarship programs). The board meets quarterly.
Materials available: Annual report (includes "Program Guidelines," "Procedural Guidelines for Applications").

Emphases. *Activities:* Education.
Types of support: Projects.
Geography: United States only.

Limitations. *Recipients:* Individuals, organizations that merely distribute funds to beneficiaries of their own choosing.
Activities: Conferences and seminars are rarely funded.
Types of support: Loans, operating costs, travel expenses. Facilities and endowments are rarely funded.

The Nathan Cummings Foundation
1926 Broadway, Suite 600
New York, New York 10023
Tel: 212–787–7300   Fax: 212–787–7377
EIN: 237093201   Type: Independent
EGA member
Contact: Courtney Helgoe, Staff Associate

History and philosophy. The Nathan Cummings Foundation is a national grantmaking organization established in 1949 but operating as a staffed foundation only since 1990. Nathan Cummings (d. 1985) was the owner of Consolidated Foods (now Sara Lee) and a major investor in General Dynamics. Cummings left the bulk of his estate to the Foundation.

Grantmaking activity involves programs for the Arts, Environment, Health, and Jewish Life. Its primary focus is on programs within the United States.

Officers and directors. *Officers:* Ruth Cummings Sorensen, Chair; James K. Cummings, Vice Chair; Charles R. Halpern, President. *Trustees:* Diane M. Cummings, Herbert K. Cummings, James K. Cummings, Mark H. Cummings, Michael Cummings, Charles R. Halpern, Reynold Levy, Bevis Longstreth, Beatrice Cummings Mayer, Robert N. Mayer, Ruth Cummings Sorensen.

Financial data. Data for fiscal years ended December 31, 1992 and 1993. *Assets (1992):* $279,708,793 (M). *Total grants authorized (1993):* $10,500,000.

Environmental awards. *Program and interests:* Interests are:

- Energy-efficient transportation.
- Sustainable agriculture.
- Minorities and the environment.
- Describing and promoting a sustainable society.

Issues. Cli • Bio • Lan • Agr • Wat • Oce • Ene • Was   Tox • Pop • Dev •

Funding analysis.

Fiscal year:	1990	1992
Env grants auth:	$2,301,000	$2,899,000
Number:	62	64
Range:	$2,000–$200,000	$2,000–$300,000
Median:	$30,000	$35,000
Pct $ auth (env/total):	28	23

Recipients (1992 highest):	Number:	Dollars:
Cathedral Church of St. John the Divine	1	300,000
Natural Resources Defense Council	3	250,000
Environmental Defense Fund	1	200,000
Conservation Law Foundation	1	150,000
Business and Professional People for the Public Interest	1	100,000
Public Voice for Food and Health Policy	1	100,000

Activity regions (1992 highest):	Number:	Dollars:
U.S. not specified	32	1,564,500
U.S. West	7	395,000
U.S. Great Lakes	4	193,000
U.S. Northeast	3	159,000
Middle East and Western Asia	2	150,000

Sample grants (1992).

American Society for the Protection of Natural Resources in Israel. New York, NY. $45,000 (2 years). For general support of the Environmental Action Unit.

Business and Professional People for the Public Interest. Chicago, IL. $100,000. To help establish a five-organization partnership to advocate air quality and mass transit in northeastern Illinois.

Cathedral Church of St. John the Divine. New York, NY. $300,000 (3 years). For the continued organization and administration of the "National Religious Partnership for the Environment," an effort to educate and involve communities of faith in the work of environmental protection.

Center for Resource Economics. Washington, DC. $50,000. To pursue sustainable agriculture through public policy reform.

The Environmental Careers Organization, Inc. Boston, MA. $40,000. To place minority college and graduate students in nonprofit and environmental organizations.

Green Seal. Washington, DC. $20,000. Support for a program to identify, test, and certify consumer products that meet rigorous environmental standards.

Milkweed Editions. Minneapolis, MN. $30,000. For creation and publication of an anthology of essays and visual art on Native American responses to land issues.

Pesticide Action Network (PAN), North America Regional Center. San Francisco, CA. $35,000. For expanded bi-national efforts to promote sustainable pest management in Mexico.

Southwest Community Resources. Albuquerque, NM. $30,000. For continued development of a network of environmental activists concerned about environmental and economic justice.

Application process. *Initial contact:* Letter of inquiry (2–3 pages) to include:

1. Description of organization, including its activities, history, and tax-exempt status.
2. Name, address, and telephone number of a contact person.
3. Purposes and timeline for which funds are requested, including issues and problems the proposed project will address.
4. Names and qualifications of staff involved in project.
5. Budget information, including total budget of organization.
6. Total budget for project.
7. Total amount requested from the Foundation.
8. Other sources from which funding has been received or sought.

When to apply: Anytime.
Materials available: Annual report, "Grant Guidelines."

Emphases. *Recipients:* Educational institutions, nonprofit organizations, research institutions.
Activities: Advocacy, citizen participation, collaborative efforts, conferences, innovative programs, litigation, networking, planning, policy analysis/development, technical assistance, training, workshops.

Types of support: Equipment, general purposes, leveraging funds, matching funds, multi-year grants, operating costs, single-year grants, technical assistance, travel expenses.
Geography: National programs within the United States.

Limitations. *Recipients:* Individuals.
Activities: Land acquisition.
Types of support: Capital campaigns/expenses, endowments.

Damien Foundation
Russ Building
235 Montgomery Street, Suite 1120
San Francisco, California 94104
Tel: 415–421–7555   Fax: 415–421–0712
EIN: 133006359   Type: Independent
EGA member
Contact: Mark Rabine, Secretary

History and philosophy. Established in 1979 with donations from the Kristina Tara Fondaras Charitable Lead Trust, Damien's aim is "to empower those whose vision for humanity and the planet is democratic, fair, and environmentally sound." It "supports grassroots organizations and projects whose work reflects compassion, consciousness, and commitment. Generally, these are smaller organizations that rely on ingenuity, dedication, and imagination." A significant portion of Damien's grants are awarded for environmental purposes, often with an international focus. Other funding areas include health and social services. The Foundation favors projects that "evoke women's transformative potential," holistic approaches, and programs that "nurture the social, psychological, and spiritual dimensions of the individual."

Officers and directors. *Officers:* Tara Lamont, President; Mark Rabine, Secretary; Humberto Mafra, Executive Director and Treasurer. *Trustee:* Tara Lamont.

Financial data. Data for fiscal year ended December 31, 1993. *Assets:* $298,400 (U). *Gifts received:* $200,000. *Total grants disbursed:* $237,500.

Environmental awards. *Program and interests:* Damien's primary interest is in sustainable development in countries of the South, with an emphasis on the participation of women and grassroots approaches that involve the local population.
Recent grants: 1992 grants included support for sustainable development involving preservation of indigenous cultures, sustainable agriculture, spirituality, and ethical concerns.

Issues.   Cli   Bio   Lan   Agr   Wat   Oce   Ene   Was   Tox   Pop   Dev
                    •   •   •   •   •

Funding analysis.

Fiscal year:	1990	1992
Env grants disb:	$147,577	$193,300
Number:	5	20
Range:	$10,000–$50,000	$900–$40,000
Median:	$25,000	$6,515
Pct $ disb (env/total):	42	70

Recipients (1992 highest):	Number:	Dollars:
Rainforest Action Network	4	71,000
Fundacao Biodiversitas	1	20,000
Logistica e Assitencia Tecnica para ONG's	1	15,000
Fundacao Cicade da Paz	1	14,000
National Wildlife Federation	2	13,000

Activity regions (1992):	Number:	Dollars:
Brazil	8	131,000
International*	10	59,420
Europe	1	1,980
South America	1	900

*Multiple regions or not specified.

Sample grants (1992).
Ashoka: Innovators for the Public. Arlington, VA. $10,000. To support a woman fellow working in the Southern Hemisphere.
Environmental News Network. Berkeley, CA. $1,500. To enable participation at UNCED.
Fundacao Biodiversitas. Belo Horizante, Brazil. $20,000. To help cover salary and printing costs for one year for a grassroots environmental newspaper.
GAIA Foundation. London, U.K. $9,390. To promote exchange of information and ideas in the South to North Program.
Threshold Foundation. San Francisco, CA. $12,000. General support for international programs.
Women's Environmental Network. London, U.K. $7,030. General support for the International Program.

Application process. *Initial contact:* Short letter. The Foundation often awards grants to pre-selected organizations. It will, however, accept unsolicited applications.
Materials available: Brochure.

Emphases. *Recipients:* Nonprofit organizations, pre-selected organizations (often).
Activities: Citizen participation.
Types of support: General purposes, projects, seed money.
Geography: The South (developing countries), especially Brazil and India.

Limitations. *Recipients:* Botanical gardens, educational institutions, museums, public agencies, religious organizations, zoos.
Activities: Lobbying.

The Fred Harris Daniels Foundation, Inc.
c/o Mechanics Bank
Trust Tax Department
P.O. Box 15073
Worcester, Massachusetts 01615–0073
EIN: 046014333   Type: Independent
Contact: Bruce G. Daniels, President

History and philosophy. The Foundation was established in 1949 by Fred H. and Eleanor G. Daniels. Funding interests include science and technology, secondary and higher education, health, community funds, social services, child welfare, arts libraries, and Protestant programs.

Officers and directors. *Officers:* Bruce G. Daniels, President; William S. Nicholson, Secretary; William O. Pettit, Jr., Treasurer; John E. Arsenault, Assistant Secretary. *Directors:* Jonathan D. Blake, Bruce G. Daniels, Fred H. Daniels II, Janet B. Daniels, Eleanor D. Hodge, Amy Bronson Key, Sarah D. Morse, David A. Nicholson, William S. Nicholson, William O. Pettit, Jr., Meridith D. Wesbey.

Financial data. Data for fiscal year ended October 31, 1992. *Assets:* $9,217,637 (M). *Total grants disbursed:* $415,000.

Environmental awards. *Recent grants:* 1992 grants included support for conservation and marine biological research.

Issues. Cli Bio• Lan Agr Wat Oce• Ene Was Tox Pop Dev

Funding analysis.

Fiscal year:	1992
Env grants disb:	$57,500
Number:	5
Range:	$2,500–$25,000
Median:	$10,000
Pct $ disb (env/total):	14

Recipients (1992):	*Number:*	*Dollars:*
Worcester County Horticultural Society	1	25,000
Massachusetts Audubon Society, Environmental Affairs Office	1	10,000
Marine Biological Laboratory	1	10,000
Tower Hill Botanic Garden	1	10,000
Trustees of Reservations	1	2,500

Activity region (1992):	*Number:*	*Dollars:*
U.S. Northeast	5	57,500

Sample grants (1992).
Marine Biological Laboratory. Woods Hole, MA. $10,000.
Massachusetts Audubon Society, Environmental Affairs Office. Worcester, MA. $10,000.
Trustees of Reservations. Beverly, MA. $2,500.
Worcester County Horticultural Society. Boylston, MA. $25,000.

Application process. *Initial contact:* Letter stating amount and purpose for which grant is requested.
When to apply: Anytime. The board meets quarterly in March, June, September, and December.

Emphases: *Recipients:* Nonprofit organizations.
Activities: Land acquisition, research.
Types of support: Annual campaigns, capital campaigns/expenses, continuing support, emergency funding, endowments, equipment, facilities (construction), internships, matching funds, operating costs, professorships, projects, scholarships.
Geography: Primarily the Worcester, Massachusetts area.

Limitations. *Recipients:* Individuals.
Types of support: Debt retirement, loans, seed money.

Dart Foundation
500 Hogsback Road
Mason, Michigan 48854–9547
Tel: 517–676–3803 ext. 206   Fax: 517–676–6718
EIN: 382562664   Type: Independent
Contact: James Lammers, Vice President

History and philosophy. William A. Dart established the Foundation in 1984. All grants go for environmental purposes.

Officers and directors. *Officers:* William A. Dart, President; Claire T. Dart, James Lammers, Vice Presidents; Benjamin O. Schwendener, Jr., Secretary. *Directors:* Claire T. Dart, Kenneth B. Dart, Robert C. Dart, Thomas J. Dart, William A. Dart, James Lammers, Benjamin O. Schwendener, Jr.

Financial data. Data for fiscal year ended November 30, 1992. *Assets:* $13,810,475 (M). *Total grants disbursed:* $547,000.

Environmental awards. *Program and interests:* Waste management is a special focus.

Issues. Cli Bio Lan Agr Wat Oce Ene Was• Tox Pop Dev

Funding analysis.

Fiscal year:	1990	1992
Env grants disb:	$471,756	547,000
Number:	1	1
Range:	–	–
Median:	–	–
Pct $ disb (env/total):	100	100

Recipient (1992):	*Number:*	*Dollars:*
Solid Waste Management Foundation	1	547,000

Activity region (1992):	*Number:*	*Dollars:*
U.S. not specified	1	547,000

Sample grant (1992).
Solid Waste Management Foundation. Mason, MI. $547,000.

Application process. *Initial contact:* The Foundation awards grants to pre-selected organizations only. No unsolicited applications accepted. If invited, submit letter to include:
1. Description of the organization's structure, purpose, history, and program.
2. Summary of need for support and how it will be used.
3. Financial data such as an independent financial audit; budget; sources of income; breakdown of expenditures by program, administration, and fundraising; IRS tax-exempt status determination letter.

When to apply: Anytime. Grants are awarded a year in advance of start date.

Emphases. *Recipients:* Pre-selected organizations only.
Geography: Michigan.

Limitations. *Recipients:* Individuals.

D

The Arthur Vining Davis Foundations
645 Riverside Avenue, Suite 520
Jacksonville, Florida 32204–2901
Tel: 904–359–0670
EIN: 256018909   Type: Independent
Contact: Dr. Max King Morris, Executive Director

History and philosophy. Arthur Vining Davis was president and chairman of the board of the Aluminum Company of America (Alcoa), and a successful investor. His philanthropic activities emphasized higher education, religious activities, and medicine. The original Arthur Vining Davis Foundation (now known as Foundation No. 1) was organized in 1952; Foundations No. 2 and No. 3 were organized after Davis's death in 1952. The three now have similar boards. Together they fund organizations in the United States and its possessions in the areas of private higher education, health care, hospice, graduate theological education, secondary education, and public television.

Officers and directors. *Officer:* Nathanael V. Davis, Chairman. *Trustees:* Holbrook R. Davis, Joel P. Davis, J. H. Dow Davis, Maynard K. Davis, Nathanael V. Davis, Atwood Dunwody, Esq., The Reverend Davis Given, Mrs. Serena Davis Hall, Mrs. John L. Kee, Jr., William R. Wright. *Trustee Emeritus:* Carl H. Bruns. *Corporate Trustees:* The Mellon Bank N.A. (No. 1 and No. 2), Sun Bank/North Florida, N.A. (No. 3).

Financial data. Data for fiscal year ended December 31, 1993. *Assets:* $145,716,418 (M). *Total grants authorized:* $5,917,500. *Total grants disbursed:* $5,481,525.

Environmental awards. *Recent grants:* 1993 grants included support for marine issues and land conservation.

Issues.   Cli   Bio   Lan   Agr   Wat   Oce   Ene   Was   Tox   Pop   Dev
                        •   •

Funding analysis.

Fiscal year:	1991	1993
Env grants auth:	$100,000	$250,000
Number:	1	2
Range:	—	$100,000–$150,000
Median:	—	$125,000
Pct $ auth (env/total):	2	4

Recipients (1993):	*Number:*	*Dollars:*
Woods Hole Oceanographic Institution	1	150,000
The Nature Conservancy, Nantucket Island	1	100,000

Activity region (1993):	*Number:*	*Dollars:*
U.S. Northeast	2	250,000

Sample grants (1993).
The Nature Conservancy, Nantucket Island. Nantucket, MA. $100,000. To help fund the purchase of the Miacomet Moors on Nantucket Island.

Woods Hole Oceanographic Institution. Woods Hole, MA. $150,000. To help fund a graduate student summer fellowship program.

Application process. *Initial contact:* Letter describing applicant institution and proposed project, accompanied by an outline project budget.
All proposals must come from the applicant organization's president or primary executive. After initial review, more information may be requested.
When to apply: Anytime.
Materials available: Annual report (includes "Policies and Procedures").

Emphases. *Recipients:* Educational institutions, nonprofit organizations.
Activities: Direct services, education, research.

Limitations. *Recipients:* Individuals; educational institutions (public colleges, universities, other public entities except medical institutions).
Activities: Lobbying, political activities.
Types of support: Multi-year grants.
Geography: Institutions based outside the United States.

Davis Conservation Foundation
4 Fundy Road
Falmouth, Maine 04105
Tel: 207–781–5504
EIN: 222976811   Type: Independent
EGA member
Contact: Alden H. Sawyer, Jr., Executive Director

History and philosophy. Mr. and Mrs. H. Halsey Davis established the Davis Conservation Foundation in 1989 to support environmental protection and natural resource conservation. The Foundation's broad purpose is the wise utilization, protection, and enhancement of the physical environment and the natural life it hosts—including land-life, sea life, and mankind.

Officers and directors. *Officers:* H. Halsey Davis, Chairman; Alden H. Sawyer, Jr., Executive Director. *Trustees:* H. Halsey Davis, Phyllis C. Davis, Thomas S. Deans, Horace A. Hildreth, Jr., Alden H. Sawyer, Jr., Frederic A. Stott, Patricia B. Tozier.

Financial data. Data for fiscal year ended December 31, 1993. *Assets:* $6,615,200 (M). *Total grants disbursed:* $369,155.

Environmental awards. *Program and interests:* The Foundation gives exclusively for environmental/conservation purposes. Topics of particular interest include:

- Wildlife.
- Environmental protection.
- Outdoor recreation.

Of particular interest are research projects and those which strengthen volunteer activity in the New England area.

Recent grants: 1993 grants included support for land conservation (land use planning, greenways, forests, land preservation), marine issues (marine mammals, marine sanctuaries, coastal fisheries, shorebirds), water (watershed and river protection, water allocation, waste purification), wildlife conservation, organic farming, outdoor recreation, and environmental education.

Issues. Cli Bio Lan Agr Wat Oce Ene Was Tox Pop Dev
         •   •   •   •   •

Funding analysis.

Fiscal year:	1991	1993
Env grants auth:	$231,000	$369,155
Number:	33	45
Range:	$1,000–$15,000	$1,300–$25,000
Median:	$5,000	$7,500
Pct $ auth (env/total):	100	100

Recipients (1993 highest):	*Number:*	*Dollars:*
Appalachian Mountain Club	1	25,000
Arthur E. Howell Wildlife Conservation Center, Inc.	1	20,000
College of the Atlantic	1	20,000
Island Institute	1	15,000
Society for the Protection of New Hampshire Forests	1	15,000

Activity region (1993):	*Number:*	*Dollars:*
U.S. Northeast	45	369,155

Sample grants (1993).
American Rivers, Inc. Washington, DC. $10,000. New England Hydropower Relicensing Campaign.
Blue Hill Heritage Trust. Blue Hill, ME. $5,000. Acquisition of parcel of land on Blue Hill Mountain.
College of the Atlantic. Bar Harbor, ME. $20,000. ECO/ECO Environmental Priorities.
Conservation Law Foundation. Boston, MA. $10,000. Fisheries Management Project.
Friends of Acadia. Bar Harbor, ME. $3,500. Acadia Peregrine Management and Education Project.
Gulf of Maine Aquarium. Portland, ME. $10,000. Space Available: Learning from Satellites.
Island Institute. Rockland, ME. $15,000. Gulf of Maine Environmental Atlas.
Maine Conservation School. Bryant Pond, ME. $5,000. Sustaining the Maine Conservation School.
Portland Trails. Portland, ME. $5,000. Fore River Bridge.
Society for the Protection of New Hampshire Forests. Concord, NH. $15,000. Forests Forever.
The Sierra Club Foundation. San Francisco, CA. $10,000. Sierra Club Great Northern Forests Ecoregion Program.

Application process. *Initial contact:* Short letter. Full proposal to include:
1. Completed application form.
2. Proposal.
3. Current list of organization officers and board of directors.
4. Copy of IRS tax-exempt status determination letter.
5. Audit statement or current budget.
6. Other information necessary for a decision.

When to apply: Deadlines are April 15 and October 15. The trustees meet in May and November.
Materials available: Annual report, application form, guidelines.

Emphases. *Recipients:* Nonprofit organizations.
Activities: Research, volunteerism.
Geography: New England.

Limitations. *Recipients:* Individuals.
Types of support: Annual campaigns, debt retirement, fellowships, loans, multi-year grants, operating costs, scholarships, travel expenses.

Dayton Hudson Foundation
777 Nicollet Mall, Suite 1400
Minneapolis, Minnesota 55402-2055
Tel: 612-370-6608   Fax: 612-370-5542
EIN: 416017088   Type: Company-sponsored
Contact: Betsy Thomas, Administrator

History and philosophy. Since 1946, Dayton Hudson has invested 5 percent of its federally taxable income in the communities in which it operates as Target, Mervyn's, and the Dayton's, Hudson's, and Marshall Field's department stores. Eighty percent of its total giving is in two areas: social action and the arts. The balance is awarded for special community needs and opportunities in communities where stores operate. The company also supports the United Way through yearly contributions, matching funds, and by participating in the loaned executive program. The Foundation's grantmaking philosophy links its corporate, foundation, and divisional giving allowing it to achieve specific, long-lasting results. It pursues arts and social action giving opportunities in which it can provide significant leadership.

Officers and directors. *Officers:* Cynthia Mayeda, Chair; William E. Harder, Secretary; Stephen C. Kowalke, Treasurer; Michael J. Wahlig, Assistant Secretary. *Directors:* James T. Hale, Cynthia Mayeda, Robert J. Ulrich, Joseph C. Vesce, Stephen E. Watson, Edwin H. Wingate.

Financial data.* Data for fiscal year ended January 30, 1993. *Assets:* $21,924,000 (M). *Gifts received:* $3,097,824. *Total grants disbursed:* $9,917,850.

*As reported by Foundation.

Environmental awards. *Recent grants:* 1993 grants included support for urban forests, youth education, and a zoo.

Issues. Cli Bio Lan Agr Wat Oce Ene Was Tox Pop Dev
         •   •

Funding analysis.

Fiscal year:	1993
Env grants auth:	$20,000
Number:	2
Range:	$8,000–$12,000
Median:	$10,000
Pct $ disb (env/total):	4

D

Recipients (1993):	Number:	Dollars:
Voyageur Outward Bound School	1	12,000
Twin Cities Tree Trust	1	8,000

Activity region (1993):	Number:	Dollars:
U.S. Great Lakes	2	20,000

Sample grants (1993).*
Minnesota Zoological Garden. Apple Valley, MN. $250,000. Payment on a $1 million grant awarded in 1990 for construction of the outdoor amphitheater.
Twin Cities Tree Trust. St. Louis Park, MN. $8,000. General support for youth employment program.
Voyageur Outward Bound School. Minnetonka, MN. $12,000. For the Urban Education Initiative.

*Sample grants represent either new awards or disbursements on grants awarded in previous years.

Application process. *Initial contact:* Contact the Foundation for the "Grant Application Guidelines" to determine to which operating division to direct your proposal. Proposal to include:
1. Description of proposed program or project, the need, people to be served, and time period to be covered by the grant.
2. Explanation of results to be accomplished by the proposed program or project, and how the results will be evaluated.
3. Description of organization, its mission, and program objectives.
4. Names and qualifications of those who would manage the proposed program or project.
5. Copy of the IRS tax-exempt status determination letter.
6. List of organization's officers and directors.
7. Financial statement (audited, if available) for the most recent fiscal year.
8. Organization and program budgets for last year and the current year showing anticipated expenses and income sources.
9. Representative list of donors who contributed to your organization and/or program for the past 12 months, and amounts received.

When to apply: Anytime.
Materials available: Annual report, "Community Involvement," "Grant Application Guidelines," "Information for Applicants," grants list.

Emphases. *Recipients:* Nonprofit organizations, public agencies. *Activities:* Policy analysis/development, training, youth programs. *Types of support:* Annual campaigns, continuing support, general purposes, matching funds, operating costs. *Geography:* Twin Cities and areas of company operations: California, Michigan, Minnesota, Texas, and others.

Limitations. *Recipients:* Educational institutions, individuals, religious organizations.
Activities: Conferences, fundraising, land acquisition, research.
Types of support: Capital campaigns/expenses, emergency funding, endowments, fellowships, loans, professorships, scholarships, seed money, travel expenses.
Geography: International organizations or programs.

Deer Creek Foundation
720 Olive Street, Suite 1975
St. Louis, Missouri 63101
Tel: 314–241–3228
EIN: 436052774   Type: Independent
Contact: Mary Stake Hawker, Director

History and philosophy. Established in 1964, The Deer Creek Foundation is "a private philanthropy interested primarily in the advancement and preservation of the governance of society by rule of the majority, with protection of basic rights as provided by the Constitution and the Bill of Rights, and in education in its relation to this concept."

Officers and directors. *Trustees:* Lattie F. Coor, Pamela Ferguson, Aaron Fischer, M. Peter Fischer, Teresa M. Fischer, James C. Kautz, Philip B. Kurland.

Financial data. Data for fiscal year ended December 31, 1993. *Assets:* $9,500,000 (M) (est.). *Total grants authorized:* $689,608.

Environmental awards. *Program and interests:* The Foundation supports government accountability projects with respect to the environment among many other nonenvironmental issues.
Recent grants: 1993 grants included support for public education. In 1992 grants included support for government accountability projects pertaining to toxic substances and waste (including military waste), and natural resource conservation (including national forests). It should be noted that, although the Foundation supports reproductive choice "because choice is a privacy issue which comes within our concern for protecting constitutional rights," it does not fund projects working on any of the various aspects of population control.

Issues.   Cli   Bio   Lan   Agr   Wat   Oce   Ene   Was   Tox   Pop   Dev
              •   •   •   •   •   •

Funding analysis.

Fiscal year:	1991	1993
Env grants auth:	$147,500	$206,100
Number:	12	16
Range:	$5,000–$20,000	$2,500–$25,000
Median:	$12,500	$15,000
Pct $ auth (env/total):	27	30

Recipients (1993 highest):	Number:	Dollars:
Trees for the Planet	1	25,000
Government Accountability Project	1	20,000
Northwest Coalition for Alternatives to Pesticides	1	20,000
Citizens Environmental Coalition	1	15,000
Council on Economic Priorities	1	15,000
Environmental Health Network	1	15,000
Inland Empire Public Lands Council	1	15,000
Ohio River Valley Environmental Coalition, Inc.	1	15,000
The Tides Foundation, Military Toxics Project	1	15,000
Washington Environmental Council	1	15,000

Activity regions (1993 highest):	Number:	Dollars:
U.S. not specified	8	125,000
U.S. multiple regions	2	30,000
U.S. Northwest	3	21,500
New York/New Jersey	1	15,000
U.S. Northeast	1	7,500

Sample grants (1993).
Citizens Environmental Coalition. Albany, NY. $15,000. To support the efforts of a statewide coalition of groups and individuals seeking to hold the New York State government accountable to local citizens on toxic pollution problems.
Council on Economic Priorities. Washington, DC. $15,000. To support Corporate Environmental Data Clearinghouse efforts to educate the public about the impact individual corporations have upon the environment.
The Ecology Center. Missoula, MT. $7,100. For distribution of the documentary, "The Element of Doom," to educate the public about the environmental effects of, and governmental action with respect to, lead mining in the Big Spring area of the Missouri Ozarks.
Environmental Defense Institute. Troy, ID. $2,500. To monitor, educate, and litigate with respect to the Idaho National Engineering Laboratory's impact on human health.
Government Accountability Project. Washington, DC. $20,000. For whistleblower defense work with Public Employees for Environmental Ethics, a new organization of public employees seeking to promote integrity in federal environmental and resource agencies, and with the Association of Forest Service Employees for Environmental Ethics.
Northwest Coalition for Alternatives to Pesticides. Eugene, OR. $20,000. For a litigation and public education program aimed at requiring pesticide manufacturers to identify on product labels those "inert" ingredients which are toxic to humans.
Ohio River Valley Environmental Coalition. Proctorville, OH. $15,000. To insure citizen input into an EPA study of the Ohio–West Virginia–Kentucky Tri-State region's air, water soil, and toxic waste disposal practices, and hold environmental agencies accountable for implementing the study's recommendations and regulating polluters.
Trees for the Planet. Washington, DC. $25,000. To help launch a new organization which will monitor and educate the public about the performance of the U.S. Forest Service and Bureau of Land Management in protecting our nation's forests.
Washington Environmental Council. Seattle, WA. $15,000. To support the Council's Forest Resources Program which seeks to improve forest management practices in order to help preserve the forests of Washington State.
The Wilderness Society. Washington, DC. $5,000. For grants to small grassroots environmental organizations engaged in educating the public about the benefits of environmental regulation in response to claims of the "Wise Use" movement that such regulation stymies economic growth.

Application process. *Initial contact:* Proposal.
When to apply: Anytime.
Materials available: Brochure (includes "Guidelines" and "Grant Procedures").

Emphases. *Recipients:* Nonprofit organizations.
Types of support: Single-year grants only.

Geography: Programs of regional and national impact. Some preference for local grants in St. Louis, Missouri.

Limitations. *Types of support:* Endowments, equipment, facilities (construction), operating costs.

The Nelson B. Delavan Foundation
Chase Manhattan Bank, N.A.
Geneva Office
5 Seneca Street
Geneva, New York 14456
Tel: 315-781-0280
EIN: 166260274   Type: Independent
Contact: Gary Schultz, Trust Officer

History and philosophy. Elizabeth G. Delavan established the Foundation in 1983 in memory of her husband. During its first decade, the Foundation supported a variety of agencies and institutions pursuing social, historical, cultural and artistic, and environmental purposes, primarily in Seneca County, New York and New York State. Since Mrs. Delavan's death in 1993, the Foundation has redesigned its funding procedures and emphases to encompass a wider geographical focus.

Officers and directors. *Officers:* Nelson B. Delavan, Jr., Ann D. Harrop, Co-Chairpersons.

Financial data. Data for fiscal year ended March 31, 1992. *Assets:* $4,353,853 (M). *Total grants disbursed:* $229,200.

Environmental awards. *Program and interests:* African wildlife protection, biodiversity, and scientific research are of special interest to the Foundation.
Recent grants: 1992 grants included support for a nature center.

Issues.   Cli   Bio   Lan   Agr   Wat   Oce   Ene   Was   Tox   Pop   Dev
              •   •

Funding analysis.

Fiscal year:	1992
Env grants disb:	$19,700
Number:	3
Range:	$2,200–$10,000
Median:	$7,500
Pct $ disb (env/total):	9

Recipients (1992):	Number:	Dollars:
African Wildlife Foundation	1	10,000
Cayuga Nature Center, Inc.	1	7,500
African Wildlife News Service	1	2,200

Activity regions (1992):	Number:	Dollars:
Africa	2	12,200
New York/New Jersey	1	7,500

Sample grants (1992).
African Wildlife Foundation. Washington, DC. $10,000.
Cayuga Nature Center, Inc. Ithaca, NY. $7,500.process.

Application process. *Initial contact:* Proposal accompanied by copy of IRS tax-exempt status determination letter.
When to apply: Anytime.

Emphases. *Types of support:* Operating costs.

Limitations. *Recipients:* Individuals.

The Aaron Diamond Foundation
1270 Avenue of the Americas, Suite 2624
New York, New York 10020
Tel: 212–757–7680
EIN: 132678431   Type: Independent
Contact: Vincent McGee, Executive Director

History and philosophy. The Foundation was established in 1955 by Aaron and Irene Diamond as a vehicle for their personal giving. After Aaron Diamond's death, the Foundation was reorganized to distribute the fortune he had made in New York real estate. In 1987 the Foundation set a plan for a ten-year life: it will expend all income and principal and cease operation in 1996. Funding categories are: Medical Research, Minority Education, Culture (Arts, Human Rights, and Civil Liberties), and Other.

Officers and directors. *Officers:* Irene Diamond, President; Robert L. Bernstein, Vice President; Vincent McGee, Executive Director and Secretary; Peter Kimmelman, Treasurer. *Directors:* Robert L. Bernstein, Noreen M. Clark, Adrian W. DeWind, Irene Diamond, David N. Dinkins, Marian Wright Edelman, Alfred Gellhorn, Vartan Gregorian, Howard H. Hiatt, Peter Kimmelman. *Ex Officio:* Vincent McGee.

Financial data. Data for fiscal year ended December 31, 1992. *Assets:* $57,171,528 (M). *Total grants disbursed:* $21,966,509.

Environmental awards. *Recent grants:* 1992 grants included support for education for disadvantaged youth on urban environmental issues.

Issues.   Cli   Bio   Lan   Agr   Wat   Oce   Ene   Was   Tox   Pop   Dev
                    •   •

Funding analysis.

Fiscal year:	1991	1992
Env grants auth:	$335,000	$175,000
Number:	7	4
Range:	$10,000–$150,000	$20,000–$80,000
Median:	$40,000	$37,500
Pct $ disb (env/total):	1	1

Recipients (1992):	Number:	Dollars:
Brooklyn Center for the Urban Environment	1	80,000
NYZS/The Wildlife Conservation Society	1	50,000
New York City Outward Bound Center	1	25,000
The New York Botanical Garden	1	20,000

Activity region (1992):	Number:	Dollars:
New York/New Jersey	4	175,000

Sample grants (1993).*
Brooklyn Center for the Urban Environment. Brooklyn, NY. $30,000. For the tennis house, Prospect Park. Third and final payment of the $80,000 grant for educational programs, pursuant to the grant agreement letter of February 1992.
Clearpool, Inc. New York, NY. $40,000. Start-up funds for a new year-round alternative school with an environmental theme, pursuant to the grant agreement letter of February 1992.
NYZS/The Wildlife Conservation Society. Bronx, NY. $25,000. Final payment of $50,000 grant to the Society for the Expanding Horizons Teacher Training Project.

*Sample grants represent either new awards or disbursements on grants awarded in previous years.

Application process. *Initial contact:* Letter to include:
1. Short proposal (2 copies) giving history of the project and outlining goals to be achieved, methods, budget, and schedule for implementation.
2. Most recent audited annual financial statement.
3. List of board members and current grants.
4. Copy of IRS tax-exempt status determination letter.

When to apply: Anytime. The Foundation ceases activity in 1996. Proposals will not be accepted after April 30, 1995.
Materials available: Biennial report (includes "Application Guidelines").

Emphases. *Recipients:* Botanical gardens, nonprofit organizations, zoos.
Activities: Education, youth programs.
Types of support: Multi-year grants, projects.
Geography: New York City only.

Limitations. *Recipients:* Individuals.
Activities: Activism, advocacy, audiovisual materials, capacity building, citizen participation, collaborative efforts, conferences, conflict resolution, demonstration programs, direct services, exhibits, expeditions/tours, feasibility studies, fieldwork, fundraising, innovative programs, inventories, land acquisition, litigation, lobbying, networking, planning, policy analysis/development, political activities, publications, research, seminars, symposia/colloquia, technical assistance, training, volunteerism, workshops.
Types of support: Advertising campaigns, annual campaigns, capital campaigns/expenses, computer hardware, continuing support, debt retirement, emergency funding, endowments, equipment, facilities, fellowships, general purposes, indirect costs, internships, lectureships, leveraging funds, loans maintenance, matching funds, membership campaigns, mortgage reduction, operating costs, pilot projects, professorships, program-related investments, scholarships, seed money, single-year grants, start-up costs, technical assistance, travel expenses.

Cleveland H. Dodge Foundation, Inc.
670 West 247th Street
Bronx, New York 10471
Tel: 718–543–1220   Fax: 718–543–0737
EIN: 136015087   Type: Independent
Contact: Phyllis Criscuoli, Administrative Director

History and philosophy. Cleveland Hoadley Dodge was an official of the Phelps Dodge Corporation, a copper mining corporation founded in 1832 by his great-grandfather and grandfather that reaped a great fortune during World War I. Dodge set up the Foundation in 1917, consistent with his declaration that he would not "burn [his] pockets" with war profits.

The Foundation today makes three types of grants: (1) Annual grants to a few organizations in New York City and the Middle East that continue some of Mr. Dodge's original grant commitments; (2) Start-up funds and assistance for young organizations consistent with Mr. Dodge's interests; and (3) Matching grants to some institutions which have received donations from Mr. Dodge's descendants.

Officers and directors. *Officers:* Cleveland E. Dodge, Jr., President; Alfred H. Howell, Vice President; Gilbert Kerlin, Secretary; Phyllis Criscuoli, Treasurer. *Directors:* Cleveland E. Dodge, Jr., David S. Dodge, Robert Garrett, Alfred H. Howell, William D. Rueckert, Ingrid R. Warren, Mary Rea Weidlein. *Director Emeritus:* Margaret D. Garrett.

Financial data. Data for fiscal year ended December 31, 1992. *Assets:* $32,821,329 (M). *Total grants disbursed:* $1,693,925.

Environmental awards. *Recent grants:* 1992 grants included support for parks, zoos, botanical gardens, and educational programs in the New York metropolitan area.

Issues.   Cli Bio Lan Agr Wat Oce Ene Was Tox Pop Dev
                    •   •   •   •   •

Funding analysis.

Fiscal year:	1991	1992
Env grants disb:	$65,900	$180,600
Number:	16	19
Range:	$400–$15,000	$50–$100,000
Median:	$3,750	$2,000
Pct $ disb (env/total):	6	11

Recipients (1992 highest):	Number:	Dollars:
NYZS/The Wildlife Conservation Society	2	105,000
The New York Botanical Garden	3	31,500
Wave Hill, Inc.	1	12,000
Hurricane Island Outward Bound School	1	10,000
The Horticultural Society of New York	1	10,000

Activity regions (1992):	Number:	Dollars:
New York/New Jersey	12	167,000
U.S. Northeast	1	10,000
U.S. Mountain	2	2,000
U.S. not specified	2	1,500
U.S. Northwest	2	100

Sample grants (1992).
Adirondack Council. Elizabethtown, NY. $2,000. Matching grant.
The Horticulture Society of New York. New York, NY. $10,000. For Project Greenworks Program.
Hurricane Island Outward Bound School. Rockland, ME. $10,000. For its program for high school students.
The New York Botanical Garden. Bronx, NY. $25,000. For its Children's Educational Program.
NYZS/The Wildlife Conservation Society. Bronx, NY. $100,000 (2 years). For its Wildlife Crisis Campaign.
Wave Hill, Inc. Riverdale, NY. $12,000. For its Riverdale Park Project.

Application process. *Initial contact:* Brief letter, describing the proposed project and budget. If the Foundation finds the project within its guidelines, it will request a more detailed proposal. *When to apply:* Deadlines are January 15, April 15, and October 15. The board meets three times a year.
Materials available: Annual report, program policy statement.

Emphases. *Recipients:* Botanical gardens, nonprofit organizations, zoos.
Types of support: Endowments, equipment, facilities, matching funds.
Geography: New York metropolitan area; the Middle East (Greece, Lebanon).

Limitations. *Recipients:* Individuals.
Activities: Research (medical).
Types of support: Fellowships, general purposes, loans, scholarships.

Geraldine R. Dodge Foundation, Inc.
163 Madison Avenue
P.O. Box 1239
Morristown, New Jersey 07962–1239
Tel: 201–540–8442   Fax: 201–540–1211
EIN: 237406010   Type: Independent
EGA member
Contacts: Scott McVay, Executive Director
            Gary Tabor, Program Officer for Environmental Issues
            Alexandria Christy, Program Officer
            Ronald Thorpe, Program Officer

History and philosophy. The Geraldine R. Dodge Foundation was established in 1974 by the will of Geraldine Rockefeller Dodge, the daughter of William Rockefeller, a former president of Standard Oil Company.

The Foundation supports programs that promise to have an impact and to effect systemic change. Primary program areas are: Public Issues and the Environment, Pre-Collegiate Education, Arts, Welfare of Animals (including wildlife), and Local Issues.

D

Officers and directors. *Officers:* Robert H. B. Baldwin, Chairman; Robert LeBuhn, President; Scott McVay, Executive Director. *Trustees:* Robert H. B. Baldwin, Barbara Knowles Debs, Christopher J. Elliman, Henry U. Harder, John Lloyd Huck, Robert LeBuhn, Nancy D. Lindsay, Paul J. O'Donnell, James W. Stevens.

Financial data. Data for fiscal year ended December 31, 1993. *Assets:* $210,626,687 (M). *Total grants disbursed:* $11,198,622.

Environmental awards. *Program and interests:* Programs are nationally focused with particular interest in New Jersey and the northeast region of the United States. Special interests are:

- Ecosystem conservation.
- Pollution prevention and reduction.
- Biodiversity/species conservation.
- Energy conservation/alternative energy.
- Population issues/family planning.
- Enlightened environmental policy through education and communication.

The Foundation also supports efforts to establish enlightened environmental policy through education and communication.

Issues. Cli Bio Lan Agr Wat Oce Ene Was Tox Pop Dev
•   •   •   •   •   •   •   •   •   •   •

Funding analysis.

Fiscal year:	1992	1993
Env grants auth:	$2,942,786	$2,979,775
Number:	73	77
Range:	$6,000–$150,000	$6,000–$100,000
Median:	$27,500	$30,000
Pct $ auth (env/total):	31	30

Recipients (1993 highest):	Number:	Dollars:
American Museum of Natural History	1	100,000
Education Development Center	1	100,000
Environmental Defense Fund	1	100,000
National Public Radio	1	100,000
Natural Resources Defense Council	1	100,000
New Jersey Conservation Foundation	1	100,000
Second Nature	1	100,000
Worldwatch Institute	1	100,000
Yale University, School of Forestry and Environmental Studies	2	100,000

Activity regions (1993 highest):	Number:	Dollars:
New York/New Jersey	34	1,313,000
U.S. not specified	19	740,875
U.S. Northeast	9	426,500
International*	6	261,000
U.S. South Central	2	73,400

*Multiple regions or not specified.

Sample grants (1993).

Clean Ocean Action. Highlands, NJ. $40,000. To develop a management and disposal policy for the contaminated materials scraped off the bottom of New York Harbor each year and dumped in the ocean six miles off the coast of New Jersey.

Earth Promise. Glen Rose, TX. $23,400. To focus on the efforts in the captive breeding of the black rhinoceros, the most endangered large African mammal. Supporting a workshop to examine the practices and policies affecting the captive management of the black rhinoceros in the United States.

Global Learning, Inc. Union, NJ. $30,000. For the Sustainable Development Program, to design and disseminate an environmental component within New Jersey's required two years of U.S. history in high school. The lessons will link current environmental concerns to historical periods in order to foster critical thinking, informed decisionmaking, and responsible actions regarding environmental practices and policies.

Northern Rockies Conservation Cooperative. Jackson, WY. $20,000. To complete a one-year planning project to improve the conservation of four carnivores (wolves, grizzly bears, mountain lions, and wolverines) and at the same time chart a course for the ecological viability of the Greater Yellowstone Ecosystem, a bellwether for ecosystems of all national parks.

Project Urban Suburban Environments (USE). Long Branch, NJ. $30,000. For renewed support of the Newark/Jersey City Wilderness Coalition which provides outdoor learning to help disadvantaged youth, and for the continued development of a network of teachers and administrators whose wilderness training strengthens their capacity as educators.

Raptor Trust. Millington, NJ. $15,000. To provide continuing support for efforts to care for, rehabilitate, and reintroduce birds of prey into the wild. Over 17,000 wild birds have been helped since the trust opened, and of the 210 raptors treated for injuries in 1992, 118 were reintroduced to the wild.

Tri-State Bird Rescue and Research, Inc. Wilmington, DE. $16,500. To help Tri-State present five training workshops to assist 300 wildlife professionals and citizen volunteers in working together to provide a rapid informed response to wildlife contamination during oil spill crises and to write a workshop manual.

World Society for the Protection of Animals. Boston, MA. $15,000. To convene a workshop that will examine the conservation status of the American black bear, which is being threatened by a rapidly growing international market for its body parts and products.

Application process. *Initial contact:* Summary (1 page) followed by a full description (6 pages) to include:
1. Description of the proposed project and the need for it.
2. Qualifications and past accomplishments of the sponsoring organization.
3. How the project will proceed and who will carry it out.
4. Time frame and budget.
5. Benefits to be gained and for whom.
6. Plans for evaluating and funding the project in the future.

Attachments.
1. Recent financial statement (audited, if feasible).
2. Names and occupations of trustees.
3. Copy of IRS tax-exempt status determination letter.

The Foundation accepts the New York Area Common Application Form. Proposals should be submitted on letterhead of the

sponsoring organization. Two-sided copying when possible, no binders or plastic packaging, and no proposals sent by facsimile.
When to apply: Deadlines are December 15 for Pre-Collegiate Education, March 15 for The Arts, June 15 for Welfare of Animals and Local Issues, and September 15 for Public Issues and the Environment. The board of trustees meets quarterly.
Materials available: Annual report (includes "Guidelines for Applications.")

Emphases. *Recipients:* Educational institutions, nonprofit organizations, research institutions, zoos.
Activities: Conflict resolution, education, feasibility studies, innovative programs, planning, policy analysis/development, publications, workshops.
Types of support: Continuing support, matching funds, operating costs, pilot projects, seed money.
Geography: National, with particular emphasis on New Jersey and the northeastern United States.

Limitations. *Recipients:* Individuals, religious organizations.
Activities: Education (higher).
Types of support: Capital campaigns/expenses, debt retirement, endowments, equipment, indirect costs, scholarships.

Thelma Doelger Charitable Trust
950 John Daly Boulevard, Suite 300
Daly City, California 94015–3004
Tel: 415–755–2333
EIN: 946500318   Type: Independent
Contact: Edward M. King, Trustee

History and philosophy. The Thelma Doelger Charitable Trust was established in 1980. The Trust supports animal welfare, wildlife, zoos, and organizations to benefit human welfare.

Officers and directors. *Trustees:* Edward M. King, Chester W. Lebsack, D. Eugene Richard, Susan Doelger West.

Financial data. Data for fiscal year ended June 30, 1993. *Assets:* $18,587,761 (M). *Total grants disbursed:* $843,100.

Environmental awards. *Recent grants:* 1993 grants included support for wildlife (primates, marine mammals).

Issues. Cli Bio Lan Agr Wat Oce Ene Was Tox Pop Dev
                •   •

Funding analysis.

Fiscal year:	1991	1993
Env grants auth:	$1,113,446	$470,000
Number:	6	3
Range:	$10,000–$1,000,000	$20,000–$400,000
Median:	$21,723	$50,000
Pct $ disb (env/total):	55	56

Recipients (1993):	Number:	Dollars:
Primarily Primates	1	400,000
Coyote Point Museum Association	1	50,000
California Marine Mammal Center	1	20,000

Activity regions (1993):	Number:	Dollars:
U.S. South Central	1	400,000
U.S. West	2	70,000

Sample grants (1993).
California Marine Mammal Center. Sausalito, CA. $20,000.
Coyote Point Museum Association. San Mateo, CA. $50,000.
Primarily Primates. San Antonio, TX. $400,000.

Application process. *Initial contact:* Contact the Trust for a grant application form. Proposal to include:
1. IRS tax-exempt status determination letter.
2. Proposed budget for the year in which grant would be used.
3. Description of organization's activities.
4. List of organization's affiliations, if any.
5. List of organization's directors and their affiliations.
6. Description of how grant will be used.
7. Contact person's name and qualifications.

When to apply: Anytime.
Materials available: Application form.

Emphases. *Types of support:* General purposes.
Geography: San Francisco Bay Area.

Limitations. *Recipients:* Individuals.

Dolfinger-McMahon Foundation
c/o Duane, Morris & Heckscher
One Liberty Place
1650 Market Street
Philadelphia, Pennsylvania 19103–7396
Tel: 215–979–1768
EIN: 236232910   Type: Independent
Contact: Marlene Valcich, Executive Secretary

History and philosophy. The Dolfinger-McMahon Foundation is the financial legacy of Henry Dolfinger, manager of the Dolfinger Dairy, his daughter, Caroline D. McMahon and her daughter, Mary M. McMahon. It consists of two operating trusts that make grants in the Greater Philadelphia area for the initiation or support of: experimental or demonstrational projects, seed money projects, projects which can be accomplished by a single grant in a brief period of time, or an emergency grant. Program areas are: Arts & Culture, Education, Environment/Animals, Health, Human Services, and Public/Society Benefit.

Officers and directors. *Trustees:* Martin A. Heckscher, Roland Morris.

Financial data. Data for fiscal year ended September 30, 1993. *Assets:* $13,278,813 (M). *Total grants disbursed:* $505,000.

Environmental awards. *Recent grants:* 1993 grants included support for land conservation, urban parks and beautification, horticulture, recycling, and an arboretum.

Issues. Cli Bio Lan Agr Wat Oce Ene Was Tox Pop Dev
           •   •   •   •   •   •

D

Funding analysis.

Fiscal year:	1993
Env grants disb:	$42,000
Number:	8
Range:	$500–$16,000
Median:	$4,250
Pct $ disb (env/total):	8

Recipients (1993 highest):	*Number:*	*Dollars:*
Natural Lands Trust	1	16,000
Lucretia Mott Center	1	6,000
PhilaPride, Inc.	1	6,000
The Baldwin School	1	5,000
City Parks Association of Philadelphia	1	3,500

Activity region (1993):	*Number:*	*Dollars:*
U.S. Mid-Atlantic	8	42,000

Sample grants (1993).

Awbury Arboretum Association. Philadelphia, PA. $500. Unrestricted contribution to the general fund.

The Baldwin School. Bryn Mawr, PA. $5,000. To provide seed money for the development of an outdoor education program to foster confidence and leadership skills in young women.

City Parks Association of Philadelphia. Philadelphia, PA. $3,500. For the Regional Parks Clearinghouse and Cooperation Project, to expand and provide clearinghouse and technical assistance services to park, watershed, and land trust agencies, as well as organizations, coalitions, and projects.

Natural Lands Trust. Media, PA. $16,000. Toward development of the environmental education component of the new Community Land Stewardship programs around Philadelphia.

PhilaPride, Inc. Philadelphia, PA. $6,000. Toward a youth educational program offering information on litter prevention, recycling, waste reduction, and other environmental issues through assemblies, curricula, contest, and special events.

The Preservation Coalition of Greater Philadelphia. Philadelphia, PA. $2,500. Toward the October 1993 conference on environmental hazards in historic neighborhoods.

The Williamson Free School of Mechanical Trades. Philadelphia, PA. $2,500. To underwrite establishment of a required reference library for a new program in Horticulture, Landscaping, and Turf Management.

Application process. *Initial contact:* Proposal. The first six pages must include the following, one item per page, in this order:

1. Cover page.
   - Name and address of applicant.
   - Amount requested (and term, if more than one year).
   - Concise program description (one paragraph).
2. Statement (1 page) describing:
   - Need to be met.
   - Method by which program will be carried out.
   - Will program be completed at the end of the grant period, or will it then be self-supporting, or supported from other sources?
3. List of officers and board members.
4. Tax certification.
   - Copy of IRS tax-exempt status determination letter.
   - Copy of the IRS ruling stating the agency is not a private foundation.
5. Statement on whether support has been or is being requested from other foundations or sources and, if so, the source and amount of any commitments.
6. Itemized budget.

The applicant may supply additional information as appendixes. The trustees rarely award individual grants larger than $20,000.

When to apply: Deadlines are April 1 and October 1; the trustees meet in late spring and fall. Proposals for emergency funding are considered as needed.

Materials available: Annual "Report on Operations" (includes guidelines).

Emphases. *Recipients:* Nonprofit organizations.
Activities: Conferences, demonstration programs, innovative programs, publications, seminars.
Types of support: Debt retirement, emergency funding, matching funds, scholarships, seed money.
Geography: Greater Philadelphia, Pennsylvania.

Limitations. *Recipients:* Individuals.
Activities: Litigation, lobbying, research (medical/scientific).
Types of support: Advocacy, continuing support, endowments, equipment, facilities, operating costs, scholarships.

Oliver S. and Jennie R. Donaldson Charitable Trust

c/o U.S. Trust Co. of New York
114 West 47th Street
New York, New York 10036
Tel: 212–852–3683
EIN: 046229044   Type: Independent
Contact: Anne L. Smith-Ganey, U.S. Trust Co. of New York, Secretary

---

History and philosophy. The Oliver S. and Jennie R. Donaldson Charitable Trust was founded in 1969. Major interest areas are: cancer research and treatment, child welfare, education, health care, and wildlife preservation.

Officers and directors. *Officer:* Anne L. Smith-Ganey, Secretary. *Trustees:* Marjorie Atwood, Pamela Curtis, Elizabeth Lawrence, William E. Murray, John F. Sisk, U.S. Trust Company of New York.

Financial data. Data for fiscal year ended December 31, 1992. *Assets:* $19,000,000 (U) (unaudited). *Total grants disbursed:* $1,008,900.

Environmental awards. *Recent grants:* 1992 grants included support for habitat and wildlife conservation, and marine issues.

Issues.   Cli   Bio   Lan   Agr   Wat   Oce   Ene   Was   Tox   Pop   Dev
                    •   •   •

Funding analysis.

Fiscal year:	1991	1992
Env grants disb:	$158,500	$115,200
Number:	8	10
Range:	$3,500–$50,000	$3,000–$40,000
Median:	$8,000	$5,000
Pct $ disb (env/total):	11	11

Recipients (1992 highest):	Number:	Dollars:
Woods Hole Oceanographic Institution	2	45,000
National Audubon Society	1	30,000
Center for Respect of Life and Environment	1	10,200
Rainforest Alliance	1	10,000
The Student Conservation Association, Inc.	1	5,000

Activity regions (1992):	Number:	Dollars:
U.S. not specified	4	49,200
U.S. Northeast	3	48,000
Tropics	1	10,000
International*	2	8,000

*Multiple regions or not specified.

Sample grants (1992).
Center for Respect of Life and Environment. Washington, DC. $10,200.
National Audubon Society. New York, NY. $30,000.
The Nature Conservancy, Headquarters. Arlington, VA. $4,000.
Rainforest Alliance. New York, NY. $10,000.
The Student Conservation Association, Inc. Charlestown, MA. $5,000.
Woods Hole Oceanographic Institution. Woods Hole, MA. $5,000.
Woods Hole Oceanographic Institution. Woods Hole, MA. $40,000.
World Society for the Protection of Animals. Boston, MA. $4,000.
World Wildlife Fund. Washington, DC. $4,000.

Application process. *Initial contact:* Full proposal to include:
1. Letter (2–3 pages) outlining organization's purpose and needs.
2. Budget.
3. Audited statement.
4. Annual report.
5. Updated IRS tax-exempt status determination letter.

When to apply: Call for current deadlines. The trustees meet twice a year.

Emphases. *Recipients:* Pre-selected organizations (usually).
Types of support: General purposes.
Geography: U.S.-based organizations only.

Limitations. *Recipients:* Individuals.
Activities: Media projects, political activities.
Types of support: Direct services, equipment, fellowships, research, scholarships.

Gaylord and Dorothy Donnelley Foundation
350 East 22nd Street
Chicago, Illinois 60616–1428
Tel: 312–326–7255
EIN: 366108460   Type: Independent
Contact: Judith Stockdale, Executive Director

History and philosophy. The Gaylord and Dorothy Donnelle Foundation was founded in 1952 as the Gaylord Donnelley Foundation. Its name was changed in 1984. Following the death of Gaylord Donnelley in 1992, the board of directors has been reorganizing the Foundation to respond to new levels of funding opportunities. The new areas of interest are: conservation/ecology, education, cultural organizations/museums, and social welfare.

Officers and directors. *Officers:* Strachan Donnelley, Chairman; Jane Rishel, President and Treasurer; Dorothy Ranney Donnelley, Elliott R. Donnelley, Laura Donnelley-Morton, Vice Chairmen; Larry D. Berning, Secretary, Kathleen A. McShare, Assistant Secretary. *Directors:* Larry D. Berning, Robert T. Carter, Robert W. Carton, M.D., Dorothy Ranney Donnelley, Elliott R. Donnelley, Laura Donnelley-Morton, Strachan Donnelley, James B. Edwards, D.M.D., Joel L. Fleishman, Jane Rishel. *Life Director:* C. Bouton McDougal.

Financial data. Data for fiscal year ended December 31, 1993. *Assets:* $12,221,264 (M). *Gifts received:* $292,969. *Total grants disbursed:* $1,742,573.

Environmental awards. *Program and interests:* Conservation is one of the four areas of interest identified by the Foundation. *Recent grants:* 1993 grants included support for ecosystem and land conservation, and wildlife protection.

Issues. Cli Bio Lan Agr Wat Oce Ene Was Tox Pop Dev
              •   •   •   •   •

Funding analysis.

Fiscal year:	1992	1993
Env grants auth:	$171,500	$556,000
Number:	24	45
Range:	$1,000–$60,000	$1,000–$210,000
Median:	$4,000	$4,000
Pct $ disb (env/total):	23	32

Recipients (1993 highest):	Number:	Dollars:
Chicago Horticultural Society	1	210,000
Ducks Unlimited, Inc.	1	100,000
American Farmland Trust	1	27,500
Canal Corridor Association	1	25,000
Illinois Nature Preserves Commission	1	20,000

Activity regions (1993 highest):	Number:	Dollars:
U.S. Great Lakes	16	296,500
U.S. not specified	18	211,000
International*	5	29,000
U.S. Southeast	3	10,500
Africa	1	5,000

*Multiple regions or not specified.

© 1995 Environmental Data Resources, Inc.

D

Sample grants (1993).
American Farmland Trust. Washington, DC. $27,500.
Canal Corridor Association. Chicago, IL. $25,000.
Chicago Horticultural Society. Glencoe, IL. $210,000.
Ducks Unlimited, Inc. Memphis, TN. $100,000
Friends of the Parks. Chicago, IL. $2,000.
International Crane Foundation. Baraboo, WI. $10,000.
National Wildlife Federation. Washington, DC. $1,000.
Nitrogen Fixing Tree Association. Waimanalo, HI. $1,000.
Wildfowl Foundation. Washington, DC. $5,000.

Application process. *Initial contact:* Written request for guidelines, followed by proposal letter to include:
1. Summary (1 page) describing purpose of organization and purpose for which grant is requested.
2. List of directors.
3. Budget.
4. Financial statement and most recent audit report, if available.
5. Copy of IRS tax-exempt status determination letter.
6. Statement by representative of the organization that exemption letter is in full force and effect and that organization is a public charity with 501(c)(3) status.

When to apply: Anytime.
Materials available: Annual report, "Guidelines for Proposals/Application Procedure."

Emphases. *Recipients:* Nonprofit organizations.
Types of support: Continuing support, endowments, facilities (construction), general purposes.
Geography: Chicago, Illinois; South Carolina.

Limitations. *Recipients:* Individuals.
Activities: Conferences, fundraising.
Types of support: Loans, multi-year grants.

Donner Canadian Foundation

212 King Street West, Suite 402
Toronto, Ontario M5H 1K5
Canada
Tel: 416-593-5125
Type: Independent
EGA member
Contact: Mrs. Devon Gaffney Cross, President

History and philosophy. Like the William H. Donner Foundation, Donner Canadian Foundation was established by the American industrialist and philanthropist, William H. Donner, whose particular interest was medical research.

The current mission of the Donner Canadian Foundation is "to stimulate educated original debate on social and economic issues in Canada." Its grantmaking focuses largely on public policy issues and addresses topics surrounding the role of government in society. Specific interests include issues of public management, the appropriate role of government in the economy, and the responsibilities of citizenship. One concern is the role of the market and the economy and a host of related issues: regulatory reform, international trade, public finance, the environment, urban affairs, health care, educational reform, and social policy.

Officers and directors. *Governors:* Donald G. M. Coxe, Robert Donner, Jr., Timothy Donner, Constance Hunt, Geraldine Kenney-Wallace, Robert Donner Spencer, Curtin Winsor, Jr.

Financial data. Data for fiscal year ended December 31, 1993. *Assets:* $98,000,000 (U) (CDN) (est.). *Total grants disbursed:* $200,000 (est.).

Environmental awards. *Recent grants:* One grant in 1993 supported environmental policy in the Arctic.

Issues. Cli Bio Lan Agr Wat Oce Ene Was Tox Pop Dev
                 •   •   •   •   •

Funding analysis.

Fiscal year:	1991	1993
Env grants auth:	$355,000	$75,000
Number:	2	1
Range:	$175,000–$180,000	–
Median:	$177,500	–
Pct $ auth (env/total):	18	–

Recipients (1993):	Number:	Dollars:
Canadian Arctic Resource Committee	1	75,000

Activity region (1993):	Number:	Dollars:
Canada	1	75,000

Sample grant (1993).
Canadian Arctic Resource Committee. Ottawa, Ontario. $75,000 (3 years). For new directions group to bring business, government, and environmental leaders together.

Application process. *Initial contact:* Letter of inquiry (2–3 pages) to include:
1. Description of project and its objectives.
2. Explanation as to why project is needed, and how that need will be addressed.
3. Method for distributing results of project to a broad audience.
4. Approximate budget and work schedule.

All preliminary letters should be mailed, not faxed. The Foundation will ask for a full proposal, if interested.
When to apply: Anytime for letters of inquiry. Deadlines for full proposal are at least six weeks prior to a board meeting, held in January, May, and September.
Materials available: Brochure (includes "Funding Guide-Lines & Restrictions" and "Application Procedures.")

Emphases. *Recipients:* Charities registered under the Tax Act of Canada.
Activities: Collaborative efforts, innovative programs, multi-disciplinary projects, policy analysis/development, research.
Types of support: Multi-year grants, seed money.
Geography: Canada.

Limitations. *Recipients:* Individuals.
Activities: Audiovisual materials, conferences, fundraising, publications, seminars, workshops.
Types of support: Annual campaigns, capital campaigns/expenses, debt retirement, equipment, facilities, operating costs, scholarships, travel expenses.

Douroucouli Foundation

8332½ Melrose Avenue
Los Angeles, California 90069
Tel: 213–655–7010   Fax: 213–655–7016
EIN: 953880225   Type: Independent
Contact: Laura Lee Stearns, President

History and philosophy. The Douroucouli Foundation makes grants for environmental purposes.

Officers and directors. *Officer:* Laura Lee Stearns, President. *Directors:* Robert T. Higashi, Steven LeBlanc, Laura Lee Stearns.

Financial data. Data for fiscal year ended December 31, 1993. *Assets:* $4,691 (M). *Gifts received:* $23,500. *Total grants disbursed:* $23,000.

Environmental awards. *Recent grants:* 1993 grants included support for rainforest preservation.

Issues.   Cli   Bio   Lan   Agr   Wat   Oce   Ene   Was   Tox   Pop   Dev
                     •   •

Funding analysis.

Fiscal year:	1990	1993
Env grants disb:	$32,657	$10,000
Number:	8	2
Range:	$2,657–$6,500	$5,000–$5,000
Median:	$3,750	$5,000
Pct $ disb (env/total):	100	43

Recipients (1993):	Number:	Dollars:
Elizabeth A. Balko	1	5,000
Patricia Wright	1	5,000

Activity region (1993):	Number:	Dollars:
New York/New Jersey	2	10,000

Sample grants (1993).
Elizabeth A. Balko. Syracuse, NY. $5,000.
Patricia Wright. Sound Beach, NY. $5,000. Study of biodiversity in the rainforest.

Application process. *Initial contact:* Letter.
When to apply: Anytime.

Emphases. *Activities:* Research.

The Herbert H. and Grace A. Dow Foundation

1018 West Main Street
Midland, Michigan 48640–4292
Tel: 517–631–3699   Fax: 517–631–0675
EIN: 381437485   Type: Independent
Contact: Herbert H. Dow, President

History and philosophy. Mrs. Grace A. Dow created the Foundation in 1936 in memory of her husband, Dr. Herbert H. Dow, who founded Dow Chemical Company. The Foundation's giving program continues the donors' special interests in horticulture, culture, and community services (including the arts and programs for youth and the elderly), education, and local history in and around Midland, Michigan. Recent grants also support conservation and scientific research.

Officers and directors. *Officers:* Herbert H. Dow, President; Margaret A. Riecker, Vice President; Herbert D. Doan, Secretary; Michael L. Dow, Treasurer. *Trustees:* Julie C. Arbury, Ruth H. Buchanan, Herbert D. Doan, Herbert H. Dow, Michael L. Dow, Margaret A. Riecker.

Financial data. Data for fiscal years ended December 31, 1992 and 1993. *Assets (1993):* $277,056,678 (M). *Total grants disbursed (1992):* $9,770,900.

Environmental awards. *Program and interests:* The Foundation primarily supports the Dow Gardens, a botanical garden that displays cultures in landscape perspective.
Recent grants: One grant in 1993 supported a nature center.

Issues.   Cli   Bio   Lan   Agr   Wat   Oce   Ene   Was   Tox   Pop   Dev
                            •

Funding analysis.

Fiscal year:	1991	1992
Env grants disb:	$1,249,045	$210,000
Number:	5	3
Range:	$25,000–$1,101,045	$15,000–$120,000
Median:	$33,000	$75,000
Pct $ disb (env/total):	10	2

Recipients (1992):	Number:	Dollars:
City of Midland	1	120,000
Chippewa Nature Center	1	75,000
Midland Volunteers for Recycling	1	15,000

Activity region (1992):	Number:	Dollars:
U.S. Great Lakes	3	210,000

Sample grant (1993).
Chippewa Nature Center. Midland, MI. $75,000. Capital additions and renovation.

Application process. *Initial contact:* Letter outlining:
1. Nature and potential results of proposed project or program.
2. Institutions and personnel responsible for work.
3. Total project cost, including endowment operations, amount requested from the Foundation, and means and schedule for grant disbursements.
4. Provisions and procedures for continuing evaluation of proposed programs.

Attachments.
1. Copy of IRS tax-exempt status determination letter.
2. Current budget.
3. Names of management personnel; names and occupations of the organization's voluntary trustees or directors.

When to apply: Anytime. The board meets periodically during the year. Grant payments are usually made in late December.
Materials available: Annual report (includes "Application and Review Procedures"), application guidelines, program policy statement.

D

Emphases. *Recipients:* Botanical gardens, educational institutions, nonprofit organizations, religious organizations.
Activities: Education, research.
Types of support: Annual campaigns, endowments, equipment, facilities, general purposes, matching funds, operating costs, seed money.
Geography: Michigan only, especially Midland County.

Limitations. *Recipients:* Individuals.
Activities: Conferences, lobbying, political activities.
Types of support: Loans, scholarships, travel expenses.

The Dragon Foundation, Inc.
c/o Robert L. Clark
P.O. Box 16
Rockport, Maine 04856–0016
EIN: 010412143   Type: Independent
Contact: Robert L. Clark, Vice President

History and philosophy. The Foundation was created in 1985 by Robert L. and Mariana L. Clark. Funding interests include education, family planning, and environment.

Officers and directors. *Officers:* Mariana L. Clark, President; Robert L. Clark, Vice President; Peter Schmidt, Assistant Secretary. *Directors:* Mariana L. Clark, Paul E. Clark, Robert L. Clark, Peter Schmidt.

Financial data. Data for fiscal year ended November 30, 1992. *Assets:* $1,389,618 (M). *Total grants disbursed:* $137,000.

Environmental awards. *Recent grants:* 1992 grants included support for land conservation, coastal issues, and outdoor education.

Issues.   Cli   Bio   Lan   Agr   Wat   Oce   Ene   Was   Tox   Pop   Dev
                    •   •   •

Funding analysis.

Fiscal year:	1992
Env grants disb:	$124,000
Number:	4
Range:	$1,000–$120,000
Median:	$1,500
Pct $ disb (env/total):	91

Recipients (1992):	Number:	Dollars:
Outward Bound	1	120,000
The Nature Conservancy, Maine Chapter	2	2,500
Maine Audubon Society	1	1,500

Activity region (1992):	Number:	Dollars:
U.S. Northeast	4	124,000

Sample grants (1992).
Maine Audubon Society. Falmouth, ME. $1,500.
The Nature Conservancy, Maine Chapter. Brunswick, ME. $2,500 (2 grants).
Outward Bound. Greenwich, CT. $120,000.

Application process. *Initial contact:* Letter.

Limitations. *Recipients:* Individuals.

The Max and Victoria Dreyfus Foundation, Inc.
50 Main Street, Suite 1000
White Plains, New York 10022
Tel: 914–682–2008
EIN: 131687573   Type: Independent
Contact: Lucy Gioia, Administrative Assistant

History and philosophy. The Foundation was established in 1965 by Victoria Dreyfus (d. 1976), wife of music publisher Max Dreyfus. The Foundation makes grants primarily for health, education, culture, and social services, with an emphasis on the aged and handicapped.

Officers and directors. *Officers:* David J. Oppenheim, President; Nancy E. Oddo, Norman S. Portenoy, Mary P. Surrey, Vice Presidents; Winifred R. Portenoy, Secretary. *Directors:* Nancy E. Oddo, David J. Oppenheim, Norman S. Portenoy, Winifred R. Portenoy, Mary P. Surrey.

Financial data. Data for fiscal year ended December 31, 1992. *Assets:* $48,206,126 (M). *Total grants disbursed:* $1,558,300.

Environmental awards. *Recent grants:* 1992 grants included support for land conservation, urban forests, marine research, wildlife, and a zoo.

Issues.   Cli   Bio   Lan   Agr   Wat   Oce   Ene   Was   Tox   Pop   Dev
                    •   •   •

Funding analysis.

Fiscal year:	1991	1992
Env grants disb:	$67,000	$32,500
Number:	13	9
Range:	$1,000–$10,000	$1,000–$7,500
Median:	$5,000	$4,000
Pct $ disb (env/total):	4	2

Recipients (1992 highest):	Number:	Dollars:
National Park Foundation	1	7,500
Friends of the National Zoo	1	5,000
The Nature Conservancy, Headquarters	1	5,000
Vermont Land Trust	1	5,000
Concern, Inc.	1	4,000

Activity regions (1992):	Number:	Dollars:
U.S. not specified	3	14,500
U.S. Mid-Atlantic	3	10,000
U.S. Northeast	3	8,000

Sample grants (1992).
Environmental Investigation Agency. Washington, DC. $2,000.
Friends of the National Zoo. Washington, DC. $5,000.
Friends of Trees. Chatham, MA. $1,000.
L'Enfant Trust/Trees for the City. Washington, DC. $1,000.

Maine Sea, Inc. Lincoln, MA. $2,000.
The Nature Conservancy, Headquarters. Arlington, VA. $5,000.

Application process. *Initial contact:* Letter explaining grant purpose. Include a copy of the IRS tax-exempt status determination letter.
When to apply: Anytime.

Emphases. *Recipients:* Nonprofit organizations.
Activities: Research.

Limitations. *Recipients:* Individuals.
Geography: Outside the United States.

The Elizabeth Ordway Dunn Foundation, Inc.
c/o Grants Management Associates
12881 S.W. 63rd Court
Miami, Florida 33156
Tel: 305–665–0806
EIN: 592393843   Type: Independent
EGA member
Contact: Becky Roper Matkov, Associate

Alternate application address:
c/o Grants Management Associates
230 Congress Street, 3rd Floor
Boston, Massachusetts 02110
Tel: 617–426–7172
Contact: Ann Fowler Wallace, Associate

History and philosophy. The Elizabeth Ordway Dunn Foundation, Inc. was established in 1984 to assist nonprofit organizations to carry out their stated missions in fields of primary interest to the directors. The Foundation emphasizes "programs to protect important natural areas in the state, to preserve functioning natural ecosystems, to protect threatened plant and animal species, and to promote open space and recreational values." It also places "emphasis on funding diverse methods to promote environmental literacy and education among Florida's citizenry."

Officers and directors. *Officers:* Robert W. Jensen, President; Lynn F. Lummus, Vice President/Secretary; E. Rodman Titcomb, Jr., Vice President/Treasurer. *Directors:* Robert W. Jensen, Lynn F. Lummus, E. Rodman Titcomb, Jr.

Financial data. Data for fiscal year ended December 31, 1993. *Total grants authorized:* $609,450.

Environmental awards. *Program and interests:* Special interests include:

- Environmental education.
- Protection of coastal areas.
- Protection of fresh water resources.
- Land and wildlife preservation and protection.
- Environmental health.
- Energy conservation and development of renewable resources.
- Oceanography and the protection of marine life and natural resources.
- Comprehensive planning.

Issues. Cli Bio Lan Agr Wat Oce Ene Was Tox Pop Dev
          •   •   •   •   •   •   •   •

Funding analysis.

Fiscal year:	1992	1993
Env grants disb:	$618,500	$544,450
Number:	22	26
Range:	$5,000–$50,000	$5,000–$35,000
Median:	$30,000	$25,000
Pct $ disb (env/total):	100	89

Recipients (1993 highest):	Number:	Dollars:
1000 Friends of Florida	1	35,000
Pace University School of Law	1	35,000
Reef Relief, Inc.	1	35,000
American Planning Association	1	30,000
Environmental Law Institute	1	30,000
Tampa Baywatch, Inc.	1	30,000

Activity region (1993):	Number:	Dollars:
U.S. Southeast	26	544,450

Sample grants (1993).*
1000 Friends of Florida. Tallahassee, FL. $35,000. For the Apalachee Greenways prototype of the Florida Greenways Program to protect wildlife habitat and open space.
American Farmland Trust. Washington, DC. $10,000. For the Trust's work in south Florida on agricultural preservation which seeks to bridge the gap between agricultural and environmental communities.
Clean Water Fund. Annapolis, MD. $25,000. Continued support of start-up costs of the South Florida Organizing Project to expand grassroots citizen participation on behalf of the Florida Keys coral reef tract and the Everglades ecosystem.
Encounters in Excellence. Miami, FL. $12,000. For the production of "Mangrove Bay," an environmental lecture film on Florida Bay and the Biscayne National Park to be presented to students in Dade and Palm Beach counties.
Environmental Law Institute. Washington, DC. $30,000. To conduct a special judicial training course on environmental law in Florida for Florida trial and appellate judges.
Myakka Conservancy, Inc. Sarasota, FL. $10,000. Toward the start-up costs of a new land trust that will acquire conservation easements, land titles, and other legal rights to protect the Myakka River area in southwest Florida.
Planet Well, Inc. Tallahassee, FL. $15,000. Second year support of a statewide public education and organizing project to promote toxics use reduction in Florida.
Reef Relief, Inc. Key West, FL. $35,000. For the Coral Reef Awareness Campaign and its focus on the problems of water degradation in the Florida Keys.
Trout Lake Nature Center. Eustis, FL. $5,000. Toward instructor's expenses for the environmental interpretation program for school children at Trout Lake Nature Center.

*Sample grants represent either new awards or disbursements on grants awarded in previous years.

Application process. *Initial contact:* Telephone call or concept paper. Concept paper to describe the purposes of the organization, outline the specific project to be supported and the anticipated impact, describe how the proposed project will strengthen the ability of the applicant organization to reach its goals, and state the amount desired. A full proposal may be requested. Full proposal to include:
1. Cover letter (brief).
   - Summary of amount and purposes for request.
   - Definition of needs to be addressed.
   - Description of approach to be taken.
   - Indication of anticipated results to be achieved.
2. Concise case statement.
   - Description of project, activities to be undertaken, and benefits to be derived.
   - Project budget and complete fundraising plans for attaining self-sufficiency or for developing future funding sources.
   - Applicant's plan for conducting its own evaluation.
3. Attachments.
   - List of directors and principal project and agency staff.
   - Current and prior year's budgets.
   - Audited financial statements and the 990 return for the most recent two years with all attachments.
   - IRS tax-exempt status determination letter.

General correspondence, inquiries, and all concept papers should be directed to either of the Grants Management Associates offices. Proposals must be mailed in triplicate, one copy to each of the Grants Management Associates offices and one to:

The Elizabeth Ordway Dunn Foundation, Inc.
P.O. Box 016309
Miami, Florida 33101-6309

When to apply: Concept papers may be submitted at any time. Deadlines for full applications are March 15 and September 15. The directors meet in May and November.
Materials available: Annual report, "Guidelines—Policies."

Emphases. *Recipients:* Nonprofit organizations.
Activities: Advocacy, audiovisual materials, capacity building, citizen participation, collaborative efforts, education.
Types of support: Continuing support, seed money.
Geography: Florida.

Limitations. *Recipients:* Individuals.
Types of support: Capital campaigns/expenses, debt retirement, endowments, operating costs, scholarships.

Jessie Ball duPont Religious, Charitable and Educational Fund

225 Water Street, Suite 1200
Jacksonville, Florida 32202-5176
Tel: 904-353-0890 Fax: 904-353-3870
EIN: 596368632 Type: Independent
Contacts: Sherry P. Magill, Ph.D., Executive Director
Joan P. Bennett, Director of Administration

History and philosophy. When Jessie Ball duPont died in 1970, her will established the Jessie Ball duPont Religious, Charitable, and Educational Fund to carry on her philanthropic beliefs: "I believe that funds should be spent for the benefit of society—I have always believed it—don't call it charity; I think it is an obligation." Mrs. duPont, the widow of Alfred I. duPont, specified that the Fund make grants to the schools, colleges, churches, hospitals, charitable organizations and historic preservation efforts to which she had contributed from 1960 through 1964. Program grants are made in the areas of health and human services, education, religion, historic preservation, and culture. The Fund also has a cluster of special programs: Church Repair and Restoration, Small Liberal Arts Colleges, People-In-Need, Nonprofit Initiative, and Clergy Professional Development.

Officers and directors. *Officers:* The Rev. George C. Bedell, Ph.D., Chair; Mary K. Phillips, Vice Chair. *Directors:* The Rev. George C. Bedell, Ph.D., Jean W. Ludlow, Stephen A. Lynch III, Mary K. Phillips.

Financial data. Data for fiscal year ended October 31, 1993. *Assets:* $181,710,529 (M). *Total grants disbursed:* $6,896,953.

Environmental awards. *Recent grants:* 1993 grants included support for horticulture, water quality, and environmental education.

Issues. Cli Bio Lan Agr Wat Oce Ene Was Tox Pop Dev
             •   •

Funding analysis.

Fiscal year:	1992	1993
Env grants auth:	$41,632	$119,746
Number:	1	7
Range:	–	$5,000–$65,000
Median:	–	$5,000
Pct $ auth (env/total):	<1	2

Recipients (1993):	*Number:*	*Dollars:*
Randolph-Macon College	1	65,000
Saint Mary's Whitechapel	1	29,746
Garden Club of Jacksonville	2	10,000
National Audubon Society	2	10,000
Garden Club of Port St. Joe	1	5,000

Activity regions (1993):	*Number:*	*Dollars:*
U.S. Mid-Atlantic	2	94,746
New York/New Jersey	2	10,000
U.S. Southeast	2	10,000
U.S. not specified	1	5,000

Sample grants (1993).

Garden Club of Jacksonville. Jacksonville, FL. $5,000. To meet unexpected needs.

National Audubon Society. New York, NY. $5,000. Professional development, training, and consultation in nonprofit organizational management.

Randolph-Macon College. Ashland, VA. $65,000. For an environmental studies major.

Saint Mary's Whitechapel. Lively, VA. $29,746. For the SAIF Water project, ensuring the availability of safe, clean water to rural areas of Virginia.

Washington College. Chestertown, MD. $100,000. To support the creation of environmental internships.

Application process. *Initial contact:* "The Fund makes grants to a defined universe of eligible institutions. An institution is eligible if it received a contribution from Mrs. duPont during the period January 1, 1960 through December 31, 1964. Proof of eligibility is determined by the Fund from examination of Mrs. duPont's personal or tax records or by the applicant presenting written evidence of having received a contribution during the eligibility period."

Eligible institutions should begin by contacting program staff to discuss the proposed program and obtain application materials. Preliminary proposal (5 pages maximum) to include:
1. Description of need to be addressed.
2. Institution's unique ability to carry out the proposed program.
3. Specific program objectives.
4. Specific program activities.
5. Plans for program evaluation.
6. Program budget (1 page).

If invited by the Fund, final proposals must include an official application form and conform to the format specified in the guidelines.
When to apply: Anytime. The board of directors meets in March, May, July, September, and November.
Materials available: Annual report (includes "Guidelines for Applicants"), application form.

Emphases. *Recipients:* Pre-selected organizations only, educational institutions, museums, nonprofit organizations.
Activities: Collaborative efforts, conferences, education, feasibility studies, innovative programs, planning, policy analysis/development, technical assistance, training, volunteerism, workshops, youth programs.
Types of support: Computer hardware, continuing support, emergency funding, equipment, facilities (renovation), fellowships, general purposes, leveraging funds, multi-year grants, pilot projects, scholarships, seed money, start-up costs, technical assistance.
Geography: U.S. Southeast, especially Delaware, Florida, Maryland, North Carolina, South Carolina, Tennessee, Virginia.

Limitations. *Recipients:* Individuals.
Types of support: Endowments, facilities (construction).

Eastman Kodak Company Charitable Trust

343 State Street
Rochester, New York 14560–0316
Tel: 716–724–2434 Fax: 716–724–0665
EIN: 166015274 Type: Company-sponsored
Contact: Stanley C. Wright, Director of Corporate Contributions

---

History and philosophy. The Trust was established in 1953 by Eastman Kodak, the corporation which operates divisions in imaging, health sciences, and chemicals. The company's corporate giving program emphasizes investment and return: "contribut[ing] time, energy, and funding where we believe substantial gains can be made." "Most often, these investments are made in behalf of our employees, present and future, and the communities where they live and work." The Trust has three major program areas: Civic Community Revitalization and Culture, Education, and Health and Human Services.

Officers and directors. *Officer:* George Fisher, Chairman, President, and CEO. *Directors:* Richard S. Braddock, John F. Burlingame, Colby H. Chandler, Martha Layne Collins, Earnest W. Deavenport, Jr., Charles T. Duncan, Alice F. Emerson, Roberto C. Goizueta, Paul E. Gray, John J. Phelan, Jr., Wilbur J. Prezzano, Leo J. Thomas, Richard A. Zimmerman.

Financial data. Data for fiscal years ended December 31, 1992 and 1993. *Assets (1992):* $16,031,912 (M). *Gifts received (1992):* $10,000,000. *Total grants disbursed (1993):* $16,200,000.

Environmental awards. *Recent grants:* 1992 grants included support for environmental education, recreation, toxics and risk assessment, and energy.

Issues. Cli Bio Lan Agr Wat Oce Ene Was Tox Pop Dev
 •   •   •   •   •   •

Funding analysis.

Fiscal year:	1992
Env grants disb:	$583,750
Number:	12
Range:	$750–$500,000
Median:	$7,500
Pct $ disb (env/total):	6

Recipients (1992 highest):	*Number:*	*Dollars:*
World Wildlife Fund	1	500,000
Clean Sites, Inc.	1	20,000
Center for Environmental Information, Inc.	1	13,000
Institute for Evaluating Health Risks	1	10,000
Keep America Beautiful	1	10,000
World Resources Institute	1	10,000

Activity regions (1992 highest):	*Number:*	*Dollars:*
International*	2	510,000
U.S. not specified	5	50,000
New York/New Jersey	1	13,000
U.S. Great Lakes	1	5,000
North America	1	2,500
U.S. Southeast	1	2,500

*Multiple regions or not specified.

Sample grants (1992).
Appalachian Trail Conference. Harper's Ferry, VA. $750.
Center for Environmental Information, Inc. Rochester, NY. $13,000.
Center for the Great Lakes. Chicago, IL. $5,000.
Clean Kingsport. Kingsport, TN. $2,500.
Clean Sites, Inc. Alexandria, VA. $20,000.
Environmental & Energy Study Institute. Washington, DC. $5,000.
Institute for Evaluating Health Risks. Washington, DC. $10,000.
World Resources Institute. Washington, DC. $10,000.

E

Application process. *Initial contact:* Letter or full proposal including a summary of project activities, reason project is appropriate for Kodak, financial statement, and proof of tax-exempt status.
When to apply: Anytime.
Materials available: Annual report, corporate contributions report.

Emphases. *Types of support:* Continuing support, operating costs, scholarships.
Geography: Rochester, New York; Kingsport, Tennessee; Windsor, Colorado; Columbia, South Carolina; Longview, Texas, and other areas of company operations.

Limitations. *Recipients:* Individuals.
Types of support: Loans, matching funds.

Echoing Green Foundation

125 East 56th Street
New York, New York 10022
Tel: 212–756–4700   Fax: 212–319–4253
EIN: 133424419   Type: Independent
Contacts: Edwin C. Cohen, Chairman
          Dolly Saengswang, Program Director,
              Undergraduate Public Service Fellowships
          Rob Bowers, Program Director

History and philosophy. The Echoing Green Foundation (formerly General Atlantic Partners Foundation) was established in 1987. "Echoing Green applies techniques used by private sector venture capital firms to not-for-profit organizations: (1) We actively search for public service entrepreneurs rather than accepting proposals; (2) We fund start-up not-for-profit organizations and new innovative projects within existing not-for-profits; and (3) We work closely with many of the organizations we fund providing assistance in strategic planning, fundraising, marketing, operations, and personnel and board development." The Foundation funds projects in four major areas: the Arts, Education, the Environment, and Public Service. It also sponsors two Public Service Fellowship Programs, one for graduating college seniors and one for graduates of schools of business, law, forestry, and government, and for medical students. Central to all its programs is the goal "To invest in people with innovative ideas to effect positive change."

Officers and directors. *Officers:* Edwin C. Cohen, Chairman; Dolly Saengswang, Secretary; Stephen P. Reynolds, Treasurer; Stephen E. Hoey, Assistant Treasurer. *Directors:* Philip E. Aarons, Thomas A. Barron, Edwin C. Cohen, Stephen A. Denning, David C. Hodgson, Stephen E. Hoey, Stephen P. Reynolds.

Financial data. Data for fiscal year ended December 31, 1992. *Assets:* $630,723 (M). *Gifts received:* $2,000,000. *Total grants disbursed:* $1,194,472.

Environmental awards. *Recent grants:* 1991 grants included support for land conservation, species protection, and indigenous populations.

Issues. Cli Bio Lan Agr Wat Oce Ene Was Tox Pop Dev
            •   •   •   •

Funding analysis.

Fiscal year:	1990	1991
Env grants disb:	$187,125	$609,647
Number:	12	43
Range:	$125–$50,000	$20–$78,000
Median:	$10,000	$5,000
Pct $ disb (env/total):	15	30

Recipients (1991 highest):	Number:	Dollars:
The Wilderness Society	8	132,020
World Resources Institute	3	125,000
Ashoka: Innovators for the Public	5	106,000
Conservation International	4	67,076
Sierra Club Legal Defense Fund	1	50,000

Activity regions (1991 highest):	Number:	Dollars:
International*	17	345,377
U.S. not specified	20	243,670
U.S. Great Lakes	1	10,000
U.S. South Central	2	8,000
New York/New Jersey	2	2,100

*Multiple regions or not specified.

Sample grants (1991).
Adirondack Council. North Syracuse, NY. $2,100.
Ashoka: Innovators for the Public. Arlington, VA. $106,000.
CERES. Boston, MA. $500.
Charles River Foundation. Boston, MA. $500.
Conservation International. Washington, DC. $66,574.
Cultural Survival, Inc. Cambridge, MA. $67,500.
Friends of the Environment. Baton Rouge, LA. $5,000.
International Crane Foundation. Baraboo, WI. $10,000.
Louisiana Environmental Action Network. Baton Rouge, LA. $3,000.
National Parks and Conservation Association. Washington, DC. $3,500.
Natural Resources Defense Council. New York, NY. $40,000.
The Nature Conservancy, Headquarters. Arlington, VA. $14,250
The Wilderness Society. Washington, DC. $92,020.
World Resources Institute. Washington, DC. $75,000.
World Wildlife Fund. Washington, DC. $15,000.

Application process. *Initial contact:* The Foundation makes grants to pre-selected organizations only. No applications accepted.
Materials available: Fact sheet (includes mission and funding priorities).

Emphases. *Recipients:* Pre-selected individuals/organizations.
Activities: Advocacy, collaborative efforts, demonstration programs, direct services, education, innovative programs, technical assistance, training.
Types of support: Fellowships, multi-year grants, pilot projects, seed money, technical assistance.
Geography: United States (grants with national scope) or international.

Ederic Foundation, Inc.
P.O. Box 4420
Wilmington, Delaware 19807–0420
EIN: 516017927   Type: Independent
Contact: Harry S. Short, Secretary

History and philosophy. The Ederic Foundation was established in 1958. It makes grants in the areas of: community and youth activities, conservation, cultural activities, education, and hospitals and health services.

Officers and directors. *Officers:* John E. Riegel, President; Harry S. Short, Secretary/Treasurer. *Trustees:* Robert C. McCoy, John E. Riegel, Richard E. Riegel, Jr., Harry S. Short, Philip B. Weymouth, Jr.

Financial data. Data for fiscal year ended December 31, 1992. *Assets:* $4,693 (M). *Gifts received:* $453,392. *Total grants disbursed:* $455,850.

Environmental awards. *Recent grants:* 1992 grants included support for land conservation, forests, coastal issues, fishery and waterfowl protection, horticulture, outdoor education, and a zoo.

Issues. Cli Bio Lan Agr Wat Oce Ene Was Tox Pop Dev
              •   •   •   •   •   •

Funding analysis.

Fiscal year:	1992
Env grants disb:	$19,850
Number:	14
Range:	$100–$7,500
Median:	$500
Pct $ disb (env/total):	4

Recipients (1992 highest):	Number:	Dollars:
Garden Club of Wilmington	1	7,500
Wilmington Garden Center	1	5,000
Brandywine Conservancy, Inc.	1	3,000
Delaware Wild Lands	1	1,000
Chesapeake Bay Foundation	1	600

Activity regions (1992):	Number:	Dollars:
U.S. Mid-Atlantic	11	18,800
U.S. West	1	500
U.S. not specified	1	300
U.S. Northeast	1	250

Sample grants (1992).
Atlantic Salmon Federation. New York, NY. $250.
Brandywine Conservancy, Inc. Chadds Ford, PA. $3,000.
Chesapeake Bay Foundation. Annapolis, MD. $600.
Ducks Unlimited, Inc. Greenville, DE. $500.
Delaware Nature Education Center. Wilmington, DE. $500.
Delaware Wild Lands. Wilmington, DE. $1,000.
National Outdoor Leadership School. Lander, WY. $300.
Wilmington Garden Center. Wilmington, DE. $5,000.

Application process. *Initial contact:* Letter, specifying grant purpose and qualifications.

When to apply: Anytime.

Emphases. *Recipients:* Nonprofit organizations.
Geography: Wilmington, Delaware; Delaware.

Limitations. *Recipients:* Individuals.

The Educational Foundation of America
35 Church Lane
Westport, Connecticut 06880–3589
Tel: 203–226–6498   Fax: 203–227–0424
EIN: 136147947   Type: Independent
EGA member
Contact: Diane Allison, Executive Director

History and philosophy. Beginning his career as a professor at New York University, Richard Prentice Ettinger (d. 1971) authored a college textbook on finance, and then co-founded Prentice-Hall Publishing Company to publish textbooks. He had a lifelong interest in education, and in 1959 established The Educational Foundation of America. Partly as a result of his personal experience with cancer, Mr. Ettinger also developed an interest in medical and socio-medical problems, including disease prevention and patient care.

The Foundation (EFA) works to carry out Richard Ettinger's principles: (1) invest in people; (2) give "seed" money for innovative ventures; (3) focus grants sharply, so that goals are definable, progress discernible, and achievement measurable; (4) limit grants to the short-term; and (5) support organizations with competent financial management. Current program areas are: The Arts, Education, Environment, Native American, Population, and Other Interests.

Officers and directors. *Officer:* Barbara P. Ettinger, President. *Senior Directors:* Joan P. Andrews, Jerry Babicka, Lynn Babicka, David W. Ehrenfeld, Richard P. Ettinger, Jr., Sharon W. Ettinger, Wendy W. P. Ettinger, Elaine P. Hapgood, Edward E. Harrison, Heidi P. Landesman, John P. Powers, Rosalind C. Whitehead.

Financial data. Data for fiscal year ended December 31, 1993. *Assets:* $141,334,884 (M). *Total grants disbursed:* $5,719,828.

Environmental awards. *Program and interests:* EFA will make an effort to support smaller, more grassroots organizations and projects with sustainability, replicability, and the potential for long-term environmental impact. Areas of environmental interest include:

- Energy efficiency and conservation.
- Alternatives to nuclear energy.
- Sustainable agriculture and forest protection.
- Public land resource conservation.
- Opposition to anti-environmental organizations.

It should be noted that EFA's considerable Population program (1993 disbursements $942,150) "ultimately seeks to educate the public on the environmental impacts of overpopulation in order to raise awareness and help people make better choices regarding family size."

E

Issues. Cli Bio Lan Agr Wat Oce Ene Was Tox Pop Dev
• • • • • • • • • • •

Funding analysis.

Fiscal year:	1991	1993
Env grants auth:	$1,947,907	$2,188,271
Number:	43	44
Range:	$10,000–$175,000	$7,500–$200,000
Median:	$40,000	$40,000
Pct $ auth (env/total):	47	45

Recipients (1993 highest):	Number:	Dollars:
Conservation Law Foundation	1	200,000
University of Massachusetts, Environmental Science	1	150,943
Western Environmental Defenders	1	150,000
Safe Energy Communication Council	1	120,000
Mineral Policy Center	1	90,000

Activity regions (1993 highest):	Number:	Dollars:
U.S. not specified	15	743,000
U.S. Northeast	4	405,943
U.S. West	9	326,710
New York/New Jersey	4	180,000
North America	2	110,000

Sample grants (1993).

Altertec Incorporated. Mill Valley, CA. $9,210. Full Circle Solar, 1993—an innovative environmental education tool that features an integrated system of organic food, solar cooking, solar water heating, gray water recovery, worm composting, and information resources.

American Littoral Society. Highlands, NJ. $70,000. NJ/NY Harbor Baykeeper Project—to protect the Harbor Estuary from further degradation and to restore its biological integrity through an urban conservation corps and urban shoreline habitat restoration projects.

Center for Marine Conservation. Washington, DC. $50,000. Training Activists for Saving U.S. Fisheries—training for 250 activists in five regions to participate in the regional fishery management council decisionmaking process and to present their concerns as part of the national effort to reauthorize the Fisheries Conservation and Management Act.

Conservation Law Foundation. Boston, MA. $200,000. Energy Project—promotes energy conservation through collaboration with electric utilities throughout New England to design and implement large-scale efficiency programs.

Food and Water, Inc. Marshfield, VT. $60,000. Stop Pesticides Project—seeks to side-step the government's abdication of responsibility in the regulatory system and challenge the chemical industry's manufacturing of poisons for profit.

Institute of Agriculture and Trade Policy. Minneapolis, MN. $50,000. Citizens' Dialogue on the Environmental Impacts of Trade—a series of public forums to inform and enhance citizen participation in the process of international trade negotiations, especially the North American Free Trade Agreement.

Iowa Citizens for Community Improvement. Des Moines, IA. $70,000. Sustainable Agriculture Conservation Reserve Program—promotes sustainable farming practices in place of chemically intensive no-till farming through farmer-to-farmer educational activities and by mobilizing farmers to advocate institutional changes and policies.

Marin Conservation League. Fairfax, CA. $45,000. Save Cascade Ridge—funding to acquire 19 privately owned parcels of land for inclusion in the Elliot Preserve of the Marin County Open Space District.

Missouri Botanical Garden. St. Louis, MO. $60,000. The North American Lichen Project—completion of the photographic fieldwork for the first color guidebook to the lichens of the United States and Canada which will serve as a tool for environmental education, land management, and scientific research.

National Save the Family Farm Committee. Washington, DC. $40,000. Forging a Sustainable Agriculture System: Expanding the Grassroots—lays the groundwork for reforming farm policy toward sustainable agriculture, specifically targeting the 1995 Farm Bill.

Public Employees for Environmental Responsibility. Washington, DC. $40,000. An Environmental Expose of the Bureau of Land Management's Western Forest Management—documents the need to either remove forest management from the authority of the BLM or to institute changes which will ensure BLM's forest program is ecologically sustainable.

Rocky Mountain Institute. Snowmass, CO. $50,000. Energy Outreach Project—combines advanced technologies, creative use of market mechanisms, and varying ideological styles to foster the efficient and sustainable use of resources as a path to global security.

South Yuba River Citizens' League. Nevada City, CA. $7,500. Wild and Scenic River Study—delineates the value and reviews the alternative uses of the South Yuba River in order to form a campaign in Congress to gain protection for the river against impending dam threats.

The Tides Foundation, Global Action and Information Network. Santa Cruz, CA. $50,000. Comprehensive National Environmental Directory Project—creates a set of regional environmental organization directories to increase both effective citizen involvement in environmental activism and collaboration among organizations addressing environmental issues.

The Wilderness Society. Washington, DC. $50,000. New Voices for the American West—a mini-grants program ensures the preservation and proper management of America's public lands by supporting grassroots efforts to counter the "wise use" movement, which preaches that the protection of environmental quality and economic prosperity are mutually exclusive.

Application process. *Initial contact:* Letter of inquiry (2 pages), signed by an officer of the organization, to include:
Identification of the organization.
1. Mission.
2. Date of founding.
3. Location.
4. Region of focus.
5. Past and current projects.
6. Name(s) and brief description of founder(s).
7. Affiliation with other organizations.
8. Amount of its budget for the current year.
Description of the project for funding.
1. Purpose.
2. Intended results.
3. Duration.
4. Amount of its budget and amount requested.
5. Funding strategy.

Append a copy of IRS tax-exempt status determination letter. If approved, Foundation will request a full proposal.
When to apply: Anytime.
Materials available: Annual report (includes "Grant Application Procedures").

Emphases. *Recipients:* Educational institutions, museums, nonprofit organizations, public agencies, research institutions, zoos.
Activities: Activism, advocacy, conflict resolution, demonstration programs, innovative programs, litigation, planning, policy analysis/development, technical assistance, training.
Types of support: Pilot projects, seed money, technical assistance.
Geography: United States only.

Limitations. *Recipients:* Individuals.
Types of support: Annual campaigns, capital campaigns/expenses, debt retirement, endowments, facilities, mortgage reduction, operating costs.
Geography: International grants.

Arthur M. and Olga T. Eisig–Arthur M. and Kate E. Tode Foundation, Inc.

c/o Paul, Weiss, Rifkind, Wharton & Garrison
1285 Avenue of the Americas
New York, New York 10019–6064
Tel: 212–373–3000   Fax: 212–757–3990
EIN: 136161470   Type: Independent
Contact: John J. O'Neil, Esq., Assistant Secretary

History and philosophy. The Foundation was established in 1970 by the late Kate E. Tode. Grant priorities are conservation and the environment, higher education, and welfare of seamen.

Officers and directors. *Officers:* Howard A. Seitz, President; John J. O'Neil, Vice President and Assistant Secretary; Ralph J. Mills, Jr., Secretary/Treasurer. *Directors:* Ralph J. Mills, Jr., John J. O'Neil, Howard A. Seitz.

Financial data. Data for fiscal year ended December 31, 1992. *Assets:* $1,955,293 (M). *Gifts received:* $2,700,000. *Total grants disbursed:* $1,825,000.

Environmental awards. *Program and interests:* The Foundation does not have specific program areas, but conservation and the environment receive a substantial portion of grant funds.
Recent grants: 1992 grants included support for national parks, wildlife conservation, and marine issues.

Issues. Cli Bio Lan Agr Wat Oce Ene Was Tox Pop Dev
           •   •   •

Funding analysis.

Fiscal year:	1991	1992
Env grants disb:	$650,000	$1,275,000
Number:	6	4
Range:	$65,000–$130,000	$50,000–$1,000,000
Median:	$122,500	$112,500
Pct $ disb (env/total):	30	70

Recipients (1992):	Number:	Dollars:
Scripps Institution of Oceanography	1	1,000,000
National Audubon Society	1	125,000
National Parks and Conservation Association	1	100,000
National Wildlife Federation	1	50,000

Activity regions (1992):	Number:	Dollars:
U.S. West	1	1,000,000
U.S. not specified	3	275,000

Sample grants (1992).
National Audubon Society. New York, NY. $125,000.
National Parks & Conservation Association. Washington, DC. $100,000.
National Wildlife Federation. Washington, DC. $50,000.
Scripps Institution of Oceanography. La Jolla, CA. $1,000,000.

Application process. *Initial contact:* The Foundation awards grants to pre-selected organizations only. No unsolicited applications accepted.

Emphases. *Recipients:* Pre-selected organizations only.
Geography: Organizations generally based in New York City or Washington, D.C.

El Paso Community Foundation

1616 Texas Commerce Bank Building
El Paso, Texas 79901
Tel: 915–533–4020   Fax: 915–532–0716
EIN: 741839536   Type: Community
EGA member
Contact: Virginia Kemendo, Executive Vice President

History and philosophy. The El Paso Community Foundation was created in 1977. Its mission is to enrich the quality of life in the El Paso area. The Foundation has hundreds of component endowment funds. Some of these are for specific purposes; others are for general charitable purposes. It is the latter that generate a pool of income from which general grants can be made.

The Foundation's method involves developing a permanent endowment; assessing and responding to emerging and changing community needs; providing a vehicle for donors with varied interests; and serving as a resource and catalyst for charitable activities. Current funding areas include: Arts and Humanities, Civic Affairs/Public Benefit, Environment, Education, Health and Disabilities, and Human Services.

Officers and directors. *Officers:* Mary Carmen Saucedo, Chairman; Janice W. Windle, President; Virginia Kemendo, Executive Vice President; Carl E. Ryan, Secretary. *Trustees:* Joe Alcantar, Jr., Luis Chavez, Jackson V. Curlin, Jr., Mabel Fayant, Richard H. Feuille, Bette Hervey, Hector Holguin, Dr. Joe Kidd, Betty M. MacGuire, Carroll S. Maxon, Mary Lou Moreno, Guillermo Ochoa, Jim Paul, James R. Phillips.

Financial data. Data for fiscal year ended December 31, 1993. *Assets:* $37,891,718 (U). *Gifts received:* $6,665,105. *Total grants disbursed:* $2,145,980.

E

Environmental awards. *Recent grants:* During the past few years, environmental grants have focused on the preservation of drylands, water quality (including sewage treatment), and environmental health, as well as the provision of technical assistance to nonprofits working in the field of environment.

Issues. *Cli Bio Lan Agr Wat Oce Ene Was Tox Pop Dev*

Sample grants (1992–93).
Agua Limpia Project. El Paso, TX and Ciudad Juárez, Chihuahua, Mexico. $12,650. For coordination of a private initiative of United States corporations in partial funding of the first sewage treatment plant in Ciudad Juárez, Mexico.
Alert Citizens for Environmental Safety. El Paso, TX. $2,000. Seed money to set up a local office.
El Paso City County Health and Environmental District. El Paso, TX. $5,000. For an on-site sewage disposal project.
El Paso Zoological Society. El Paso, TX. $10,000. For Children's Village, an educational exhibit.
Westway Water District Technical Assistance Grant. El Paso, TX. $10,328. For construction accounting services for sewage lagoon project.

Application process. *Initial contact:* Letter of inquiry. Full proposal to include:
1. Project description with clear statement of purpose, expected results, work plan, financial plan, evaluation criteria and methods, and information on how project fits in with others in the same area (if any).
2. IRS tax-exempt status determination letter.
3. List of names, addresses, and ethnicity of board members.
4. Most recent financial audit or annual financial statement.
5. Any pertinent supporting materials.

When to apply: Anytime. Trustees consider proposals quarterly.
Materials available: Annual report, "Granting Guidelines and Procedures."

Emphases. *Activities:* Innovative programs.
Types of support: Leveraging funds, seed money.
Geography: El Paso, Texas area.

Limitations. *Recipients:* Individuals.
Activities: Expeditions/tours, fundraising, lobbying.
Types of support: Advertising campaigns, annual campaigns capital campaigns/expenses, continuing support, debt retirement, facilities, indirect costs, membership campaigns, mortgage reduction, travel expenses.

El Pomar Foundation
10 Lake Circle Drive
P.O. Box 158
Colorado Springs, Colorado 80906
Tel: 719-633-7733   Fax: 719-577-5702
EIN: 846002373   Type: Independent
Contact: David J. Palenchar, Vice President, Programs

History and philosophy. El Pomar Foundation was founded in 1937 by Spencer Penrose, a native of Philadelphia who made his fortune in the gold fields of Colorado and copper mines of Utah. Penrose was responsible for the construction of a number of Colorado landmarks including the Pikes Peak Highway, Cheyenne Mountain Zoo, and the Will Rogers Shrine of the Sun. His ultimate accomplishment was the construction in 1918 of the Broadmoor Hotel, a world-class resort in the foothills of Colorado Springs. Shortly before his death, Penrose established the El Pomar Foundation to help needy and worthwhile groups and institutions throughout Colorado. The Foundation currently makes grants in the areas of: Arts & Humanities; Civic & Community; Education; Health; Human Services; and Other.

Officers and directors. *Officers:* William J. Hybl, Chairman and CEO; R. Thayer Tutt, Jr., President and CIO; Robert J. Hilbert, Vice President, Administration; David J. Palenchar, Vice President, Programs; Dolores C. Fowler, Director, El Pomar Center. *Trustees:* Karl E. Eitel, Robert J. Hilbert, William J. Hybl, Kent O. Olin, R. Thayer Tutt, Jr.

Financial data. Data for fiscal year ended December 31, 1993. *Assets:* $301,666,371 (M). *Total grants authorized:* $18,845,808. *Total grants disbursed:* $9,977,658.

Environmental awards. *Recent grants:* 1993 grants included support for land conservation, parks, species protection, outdoor education, recreation, and zoos.

Issues. *Cli Bio Lan Agr Wat Oce Ene Was Tox Pop Dev*

Funding analysis.

Fiscal year:	1992	1993
Env grants disb:	$605,500	$1,073,000
Number:	10	11
Range:	$5,000–$250,000	$1,000–$450,000
Median:	$12,750	$25,000
Pct $ disb (env/total):	10	11

Recipients (1993 highest):	Number:	Dollars:
Cheyenne Mountain Zoo	1	450,000
Denver Zoological Foundation	1	300,000
The Nature Conservancy, Colorado Field Office	1	125,000
Pikes Peak Trail Coalition	1	85,000
South Platte River Greenway Foundation, Inc.	1	50,000

Activity region (1993):	Number:	Dollars:
U.S. Mountain	11	1,073,000

Sample grants (1993).
Cheyenne Mountain Zoological Park. Colorado Springs, CO. $450,00. General operating support.
Colorado Outward Bound School. Denver, CO. $23,000. For the Colorado Springs youth leadership program.
Denver Zoological Foundation. Denver, CO. $300,000. Primate Conservation Center.
The Nature Conservancy, Colorado Field Office. Boulder, CO. $125,000. Land acquisition in Aiken Canyon.
Pikes Peak Trail Coalition. Colorado Springs, CO. $85,000. For general support and Crestline Bridge project.

South Platte River Greenway Foundation, Inc. Denver, CO. $50,000. For "Punt the Creek" project.

Application process. *Initial contact:* Full proposal to include:
1. Name and address of applicant organization.
2. Brief history of organization, its mission, principal programs and accomplishments.
3. Statement of purpose for amount requested. Outline need for project, specific solutions to be reached, expected contributions to population served, and criteria for evaluation.
4. Organizational budget for current year, and a documented budget of project. Include total amount to be raised and a list of expected sources of funds. If request is for a program, indicate plans for funding after Foundation funding ceases.
5. Supplementary data (see annual report).

When to apply: Anytime.
Materials available: Annual report (includes "General Information" and "Application Guidelines").

Emphases. *Geography:* Colorado only.

Limitations. *Recipients:* Camps, seasonal facilities, conduit foundations, educational institutions (public elementary/secondary), public agencies.
Activities: Audiovisual materials, conferences, media projects, political activities, seminars.
Types of support: Debt retirement, endowments, travel expenses.

The Emerald Foundation
1010 Grand Avenue
Kansas City, Missouri 64106–2220
Tel: 816–842–3132
EIN: 431441085   Type: Independent
Contact: Vincent Rawson, Director

History and philosophy. The Foundation was founded by Ann Jennifer Dierks and Cynthia Grenfell. Its focus is wildlife conservation.

Officers and directors. *Directors:* Ann Jennifer Dierks, Cynthia Grenfell, Vincent Rawson.

Financial data. Data for fiscal year ended December 31, 1992. *Assets:* $502,558 (M). *Gifts received:* $20,000. *Total grants disbursed:* $25,000.

Environmental awards. *Recent grants:* 1992 grants included support for habitat and species conservation.

Issues. *Cli Bio Lan Agr Wat Oce Ene Was Tox Pop Dev*
          •   •

Funding analysis.

Fiscal year:	1992
Env grants disb:	$20,000
Number:	6
Range:	$3,000–$5,000
Median:	$3,000
Pct $ disb (env/total):	80

Recipients (1992):	Number:	Dollars:
The Nature Conservancy, Headquarters	1	5,000
Environmental Defense Fund	1	3,000
NYZS/The Wildlife Conservation Society	1	3,000
Technoserve	1	3,000
The Rainbow Generation	1	3,000
World Wildlife Fund	1	3,000

Activity regions (1992):	Number:	Dollars:
U.S. not specified	3	11,000
International*	2	6,000
New York/New Jersey	1	3,000

*Multiple regions or not specified.

Sample grants (1992).
Environmental Defense Fund. New York, NY. $3,000.
The Nature Conservancy, Headquarters. Arlington, VA. $5,000.
The Rainbow Generation. Overland Park, KS. $3,000.
Technoserve. Norwalk, CT. $3,000.
World Wildlife Fund. Washington, DC. $3,000.

Application process. *Initial contact:* The Foundation makes grants to pre-selected organizations only. No unsolicited applications accepted.

Emphases. *Recipients:* Pre-selected organizations only.

The Thomas J. Emery Memorial
c/o Frost & Jacobs
2500 PNC Center
Cincinnati, Ohio 45202
Tel: 513–621–6800
EIN: 310536711 Type: Independent
Contact: Henry W. Hobson, Jr., President

History and philosophy. Mary Muhlenberg Emery established the Memorial in 1925. Current grantmaking supports the arts, civic affairs, education, and health and social services in the Cincinnati area.

Officers and directors. *Officers:* Henry W. Hobson, President; Walter L. Lingle, Jr., Vice President; Frank T. Hamilton, Secretary; Lee A. Carter, Treasurer. *Trustees:* Lee A. Carter, Frank T. Hamilton, Henry W. Hobson, John T. Lawrence, Walter L. Lingle, Jr.

Financial data. Data for fiscal year ended December 31, 1993. *Assets:* $20,703,206 (M). *Total grants disbursed:* $1,078,124.

Environmental awards. *Recent grants:* 1993 grants included support for urban gardens and outdoor education.

Issues. *Cli Bio Lan Agr Wat Oce Ene Was Tox Pop Dev*
          •   •

E

Funding analysis.

Fiscal year:	1993
Env grants disb:	$20,000
Number:	2
Range:	$10,000–$10,000
Median:	$10,000
Pct $ disb (env/total):	2

Recipients (1993):	Number:	Dollars:
Civic Garden Center of Greater Cincinnati	1	10,000
Joy Outdoor Education Center	1	10,000

Activity region (1993):	Number:	Dollars:
U.S. Great Lakes	2	20,000

Sample grants (1993).
Civic Garden Center of Greater Cincinnati. Cincinnati, OH. $10,000.
Joy Outdoor Education Center. Clarksville, OH. $10,000.

Application process. *Initial contact:* Letter.
When to apply: Anytime.

Emphases. *Geography:* Cincinnati, Ohio.

The Energy Foundation
75 Federal Street
San Francisco, California 94107
Tel: 415–546–7400   Fax: 415–546–1794
EIN: 943126848   Type: Independent
EGA member
Contacts: Hal Harvey, Executive Director
    Rachel Finson, Program Officer
    Eric B. Heitz, Program Officer
    Ann Krumboltz, Program Officer

History and philosophy. The Energy Foundation was established in January 1991 with $20 million from the John D. and Catharine T. MacArthur Foundation, The Pew Charitable Trusts, and The Rockefeller Foundation. (The Foundation had previously been the Energy Project of The Trust for Public Land.) The Foundation's mission is "to assist in the transition to a sustainable energy future based on the efficient use of energy and the development of renewable energy supplies." It functions primarily as a grantmaker, but can also convene workshops, commission papers, and take other direct initiatives.

Officers and directors. *Officers:* Hal Harvey, Executive Director. *Directors:* Judith Espinosa, John Fox, Hal Harvey, Denis Hayes, Maya Lin, Mary Lou Munts, Meg Power, Kenneth Prewitt, Victor Rabinowitch, Fred Salvucci, Maxine Savitz, Robert Solow.

Financial data. Data for fiscal year ended December 31, 1993. *Assets:* $19,804,684 (M). *Gifts received:* $16,005,000 (est.). *Total grants authorized:* $4,407,903.

Environmental awards. *Program and interests:* The Energy Foundation supports research and analysis, advocacy for promising strategies, and implementation and replication of successful models in five major sectors:

- Utility reform.
- Buildings.
- Transportation.
- Renewable energy.
- Integrated issues.

The Foundation's geographic focus is the United States, with special emphasis on regional initiatives.

Recent grants: 1993 grants included support for utility reform, buildings, transportation, and renewable energy.

Issues.   Cli   Bio   Lan   Agr   Wat   Oce   Ene   Was   Tox   Pop   Dev
            •   •   •   •

Funding analysis.

Fiscal year:	1992*	1993
Env grants auth:	$6,079,985	$3,872,903
Number:	55	55
Range:	$5,000–$300,000	$2,822–$300,000
Median:	$50,000	$40,000
Pct $ auth (env/total):	100	100

*As reported by Foundation.

Recipients (1993 highest):	Number:	Dollars:
Environmental Defense Fund of Texas	2	500,000
Environmental Law and Policy Center of the Midwest	2	450,000
Northwest Conservation Act Coalition	2	350,000
1000 Friends of Oregon	2	237,000
Center for Neighborhood Technology	1	150,000
Land and Water Fund of the Rockies	1	150,000
Texas Citizens' Fund	2	150,000

Activity regions (1993 highest):	Number:	Dollars:
U.S. South Central	5	685,000
U.S. not specified	16	676,117
U.S. Northwest	5	600,000
U.S. Great Lakes	5	590,000
U.S. West	6	406,000

Sample grants (1993).
American Planning Association. Tallahassee, FL. $90,000. To bring together a "Coalition for an Energy-Efficient Florida."
Campaign for a Prosperous Georgia. Atlanta, GA. $35,000. To promote large-scale utility energy efficiency programs.
Center for Clean Air Policy. Washington, DC. $50,000. To promote increased utility investment in energy efficiency programs.
Citizens Energy Coalition Education Fund, Inc. Indianapolis, IN. $50,000. To promote efficiency as an alternative to new power

plant construction, and as a least-cost Clean Air Act compliance strategy.
Demand-Side Management Training Institute. Bala Cynwyd, PA. $30,000. To do market research to devise the best training program.
Energy Conservation Association. Denver, CO. $35,000. To promote demand-side management and low-income energy assistance programs.
Environmental Action Foundation. Takoma Park, MD. $14,000. To assess opportunities to promote efficiency.
Environmental Defense Fund of Texas. Austin, TX. $300,000. To reform Texas utility regulatory process with the goal of institutionalizing energy efficiency.
Environmental Law and Policy Center of the Midwest. Chicago, IL. $300,000. To launch a policy and technical-support center for a multi-state energy efficiency effort in the Midwest.
Kearns & West, Inc. San Francisco, CA. $15,000. To conduct a market research study with electric and gas utilities to determine the level of support and acceptable costs for Lawrence Berkeley Livermore's DEEP project.
National Association of State Utility Consumer Advocates. Washington, DC. $21,295. To investigate the opportunities for a grant from United States Department of Energy to conduct policy research on electricity issues.
Northwest Conservation Act Coalition. Seattle, WA. $50,000. To expand its promotion of regulations that make efficiency profitable in the Pacific Northwest.
Regulatory Assistance Project. Gardiner, ME. $39,886. To assist legislators in understanding the value of electric utility development of energy conservation and renewable resources.

Application process. *Initial contact:* Brief letter of inquiry to allow the Foundation to determine whether the project falls within its guidelines. Describe the project, its purpose, and the amount requested. If the applicant is confident the proposed project fits within the guidelines, the letter of inquiry is not necessary. Instead, send full proposal to include:
Cover sheet (included in annual report).
Proposal.
 1. Organization's history, mission and goals.
 2. Statement of need or problem.
 3. Background and purpose of project.
 4. Strategy.
 5. Target audience.
 6. Methods.
 7. Intended results.
 8. Timeline.
 9. Evaluation procedures.
 10. Project budget including other sources of actual and potential funding and plans to secure additional funding.
Supporting documents.
 1. Organization budget.
 2. Most recent audited financial statement.
 3. IRS tax-exempt status determination letter.
 4. Current annual report.
 5. Current list of board of trustees and officers.
 6. Resumes of key personnel involved in the project.
When to apply: Anytime. The board of directors meets three times a year, in March, June, and November.
Materials available: Annual report (includes "How to Apply for a Grant," "Proposal Cover Sheet," "Programs and Guidelines"), *Energy: From Crisis to Solution* (report).

Emphases. *Recipients:* Nonprofit organizations.
Activities: Advocacy, policy analysis/development, research.
Types of support: General purposes, pilot projects.
Geography: United States only.

Limitations. *Recipients:* Individuals.
Activities: Demonstration programs, fundraising, land acquisition, research (scientific technology).
Types of support: Annual campaigns, capital campaigns/expenses, debt retirement, endowments, equipment, facilities.
Geography: International projects.

The Charles Engelhard Foundation
645 Fifth Avenue
New York, New York 10022
Tel: 212–935–2430   Fax: 212–935–2434
EIN: 226063032   Type: Independent
Contact: Joan D. Ricci, Secretary

History and philosophy. The Foundation was established in 1940 with funds donated by Charles Engelhard, Jane Engelhard, and Engelhard Hanovia, Inc., the corporate successor to a metals refining business. Grants are awarded through five program areas: Education, Medical, Religion, Wildlife, and Other.

Officers and directors. *Officers:* Jane B. Englehard, President; Elaine Catterall, Joan D. Ricci, Secretaries; Edward G. Beimfohr, Treasurer. *Trustees:* Edward G. Beimfohr, Sophie Englehard Craighead, Anne E. de la Renta, Jane B. Englehard, Sally E. Pingree, Charlene B. Englehard Troy.

Financial data. Data for fiscal year ended December 31, 1992. *Assets:* $90,311,617 (M). *Total grants disbursed:* $5,760,256.

Environmental awards. *Recent grants:* 1992 grants included support for land conservation, parks, forests, watersheds, coastal issues, and native species protection.

Issues.   Cli Bio Lan Agr Wat Oce Ene Was Tox Pop Dev
                •   •   •   •   •

Funding analysis.

Fiscal year:	1991	1992
Env grants disb:	$1,004,450	$1,128,700
Number:	44	39
Range:	$250–$225,000	$1,000–$205,000
Median:	$9,000	$10,000
Pct $ disb (env/total):	15	21

Recipients (1992 highest):	*Number:*	*Dollars:*
Craighead Wildlife-Wildlands Institute	1	205,000
Conservation International	1	200,000
The Nature Conservancy, Headquarters	1	110,000
National Wildflower Research Center	1	100,000
Natural Resources Defense Council	1	82,500

© 1995 Environmental Data Resources, Inc.

E

Activity regions (1992 highest):	Number:	Dollars:
U.S. not specified	10	383,500
U.S. Mountain	3	226,000
International*	2	210,000
Africa	1	65,000
U.S. Northeast	5	62,000

*Multiple regions or not specified.

Sample grants (1992).
African Wildlife Foundation. Washington, DC. $65,000.
Americans for the Environment. Washington, DC. $10,000.
Concord Land Conservation Trust. Concord, MA. $7,000.
Conservation International. Washington, DC. $200,000.
Craighead Wildlife-Wildlands Institute. Missoula, MT. $205,000.
Great Bear Foundation. Missoula, MT. $1,000.
National Wildflower Research Center. Austin, TX. $100,000.
Owl Research Institute, Inc. Missoula, MT. $5,000.
Raptor Trust. Millington, NJ. $25,000.

Application process. *Initial contact:* The Foundation awards grants to pre-selected organizations only. No unsolicited applications accepted.
Materials available: Application guidelines.

Emphases. *Recipients:* Pre-selected organizations only.
Types of support: Continuing support, general purposes, operating costs.

Limitations. *Recipients:* Individuals.
Types of support: Facilities.

English-Bonter-Mitchell Foundation
c/o Fort Wayne National Bank
900 Fort Wayne National Bank Building
Fort Wayne, Indiana 46802
Tel: 219–426–0555
EIN: 356247168
Contact: Marlene Buesching, Trust Officer

History and philosophy. The English-Bonter-Mitchell Foundation was established in 1972, with donations from Mary Tower English, Louise Bonter, and others. The Foundation awards grants for: the arts, community development, cultural programs, churches and religious organizations, health, higher education, hospitals, and social services.

Officers and directors. *Member:* Mary E. Mitchell. *Trustee:* Fort Wayne National Bank

Financial data. Data for fiscal year ended December 31, 1993. *Assets:* $75,335,015 (M). *Total grants disbursed:* $2,568,900.

Environmental awards. *Recent grants:* 1993 grants included support for land conservation, parks, and a zoo.

Issues. Cli Bio Lan Agr Wat Oce Ene Was Tox Pop Dev
              •   •

Funding analysis.

Fiscal year:	1993
Env grants disb:	$147,000
Number:	5
Range:	$12,000–$50,000
Median:	$25,000
Pct $ disb (env/total):	6

Recipients (1993):	Number:	Dollars:
The Nature Conservancy, Indiana Field Office	1	50,000
Fort Wayne Children's Zoo	1	35,000
Fort Wayne Park Foundation	1	25,000
Headwaters Park Commission	1	25,000
Acres, Inc.	1	12,000

Activity region (1993):	Number:	Dollars:
U.S. Great Lakes	5	147,000

Sample grants (1993).
Acres, Inc. Huntertown, IN. $12,000.
Fort Wayne Children's Zoo. Fort Wayne, IN. $35,000.
Fort Wayne Park Foundation. Fort Wayne, IN. $25,000.
Headwaters Park Commission. Fort Wayne, IN. $25,000.
The Nature Conservancy, Indiana Field Office. Indianapolis, IN. $50,000.

Application process. *Initial contact:* The Foundation awards grants to pre-selected organizations only. No unsolicited applications accepted.

Emphases. *Recipients:* Pre-selected organizations only.
Geography: Fort Wayne, Indiana.

Limitations. *Recipients:* Individuals.

Environment Now Foundation
24955 Pacific Coast Highway, Suite C–201
Malibu, California 90265
Tel: 310–456–8775
EIN: 954247242   Type: Independent
EGA member
Contact: Rick Luskin, Executive Director

History and philosophy. Environment Now Foundation was established in 1988 by Frank G. and Luanne Wells. The Foundation makes grants to pre-selected organizations for environmental and other purposes. Its preferred role is as participant/partner rather than as sole grantmaker on a project.

Officers and directors. *Officers:* Paul C. Heeschen, President; Luanne Wells, Vice President; Shari Kimoto, Secretary.

Financial data. Data for fiscal year ended December 31, 1992. *Assets:* $15,424,934 (M). *Gifts received:* $4,130,000. *Total grants disbursed:* $572,075.

Environmental awards. *Program and interests:* Areas of interest include:

- Ancient forests.
- Forest ecosystems.
- Deserts.
- Water pollution.
- Rivers.

In addition to making grants, the Foundation supports direct charitable activities.

Recent grants: 1992 grants included support for climate issues, land conservation, park restoration, species preservation, coastal issues, and consumer education. Direct charitable activities included conferences, films, and publications.

Issues. *Cli Bio Lan Agr Wat Oce Ene Was Tox Pop Dev*
• • • • • • •

Funding analysis.

Fiscal year:	1990	1992
Env grants disb:	$118,500	$285,500
Number:	4	12
Range:	$1,000–$100,000	$1,000–$135,000
Median:	$8,750	$7,500
Pct $ disb (env/total):	100	50

Recipients (1992 highest):	*Number:*	*Dollars:*
Green Seal	1	135,000
Peregrine Fund	1	50,000
Yosemite Restoration Trust	1	50,000
Environmental Defense Fund	1	15,000
Environmental Media Association	1	10,000
Heal the Bay	1	10,000

Activity regions (1992):	*Number:*	*Dollars:*
U.S. not specified	4	153,500
U.S. West	6	77,000
U.S. Northwest	1	50,000
New York/New Jersey	1	5,000

Sample grants (1992).
Earth Island Institute. San Francisco, CA. $2,000.
Environmental Media Association. Los Angeles, CA. $10,000.
Green Seal. Washington, DC. $135,000.
Heal the Bay. Santa Monica, CA. $10,000.
Mountains Restoration Trust. Malibu, CA. $1,000.
Peregrine Fund. Santa Cruz, CA. $50,000.

Application process. *Initial contact:* The Foundation makes grants to pre-selected organizations only. No unsolicited applications accepted.

Emphases: *Recipients:* Pre-selected organizations only.

Environmental Education Foundation of Florida, Inc.

Suite 1501
The Capitol
Tallahassee, Florida 32399–0001
Tel: 904–488–5551   Fax: 904–488–5551
EIN: 592989880   Type: Independent
Contacts: Dr. Stan Kmet, Executive Director
            Mary Tanner, Staff Director

History and philosophy. In 1989 the Florida Legislature enacted the Florida Environmental Education Act to promote protection and restoration of Florida's environment through environmental education. The Environmental Education Foundation of Florida, Inc. was authorized by this legislation. The Foundation is a private, nonprofit corporation established to raise funds, promote, develop, and implement environmental education activities throughout the state. The program is administered by the Governor's Office of Planning and Budgeting, Environmental Policy/Community and Economic Development Unit. As a 501(c)(3) organization, the Foundation both seeks contributions and makes grants.

The Foundation is run by a non-partisan group of business people, civic leaders, educators, and environmental advocates who share a common desire: a "Sustainable Florida." A primary goal of the Foundation is to garner broad-based financial resources that can be sustained over the long term, in support of a comprehensive program of environmental education. While the Foundation itself does not actually carry out the projects that make up this program, it selects applicants, distributes funds, and monitors implementation by the grantees to ensure accountability in terms of quality performance and products.

Officers and directors. *Officers:* David Batt, President; Leah Schad, First Vice President; Lynda Long, Second Vice President; Andy Rackley, Secretary; Doug Shelby, Treasurer. *Directors:* David Batt, Pat Bergmann, Dr. Anthony J. Catanesee, Gordon Gaster, Pat Harden, Irene Hooper, Tom Hopkins, Reid Hughes, Ed Kolodzieski, Mary Kumpe, Jay Landers, Shirley Little, Charles Littlejohn, Lynda Long, Governor Buddy MacKay, Andy Rackley, Frank Reid, Leah Schad, Deedee Sharpe, Doug Shelby, Dr. Bernard Sliger, Elizabeth "Jonnie" Swann, James Welsh, Otis Wragg.

Financial data. Data for fiscal year ended June 30, 1991. *Assets:* $113,000 (U). *Total grants authorized:* $1,133,326.

Environmental awards. *Program and interests:* During 1994 the Foundation had four programs for which it invites proposals:

- Outreach programs.

    To educate our residents and visitors concerning the relationship between protecting and restoring the quality of Florida's environmental resources while at the same time growing a strong economy.

    Includes development of introductory materials, curricula, and consumer information.

E

- Leadership development.

    To help develop the future leadership that will be needed to bring groups together in a spirit of cooperation and compromise to surmount the many obstacles standing in the way of a "Sustainable Florida."

    Includes leadership forums to directly promote the positive, constructive interaction between business, environmental, and governmental leaders in the implementation of a "Sustainable Florida."

- Recognition programs.

    To encourage the development of environmental education programs that emphasize the link between the environment and economy.

    Includes the underwriting of high quality events which recognize organizations and individuals associated with exemplary environmental education programs that place an emphasis on the link between economic and environmental concerns.

- Innovation challenge grants.

    To encourage the transfer of innovative "Sustainable Florida" ideas that have significant potential for replication elsewhere in Florida.

    Includes limited grants to projects that do not necessarily conform to one of the other program categories, but do utilize innovation and creativity in supporting the principles of "Sustainable Florida" as well as the Foundation's strategic plan goals. Such proposals must have built-in evaluation mechanisms for documenting the effectiveness of the idea and the potential for replication throughout the state.

Issues.　Cli　Bio　Lan　Agr　Wat　Oce　Ene　Was　Tox　Pop　Dev
　　　　　　 •　　　　　　　•　　•　　　　　　　　　　•

Funding analysis.

Fiscal year:	1991	1992
Env grants auth:	$1,133,326	$132,120
Number:	36	14
Range:	$3,617–$118,594	$500–$30,000
Median:	$22,828	$6,315
Pct $ auth (env/total):	100	100

Recipients (1992 highest):	Number:	Dollars:
Lee County School District	1	30,000
Florida Audubon Society	1	23,513
Museum of Science and Industry	1	15,121
Manatee County School District	1	14,807
Hardee County School District	1	10,000

Activity region (1992):	Number:	Dollars:
U.S. Southeast	14	132,120

Sample grants (1994).

Broward County School Board. Broward County, FL. $5,000. For the Ely High School Science Magnet Program to study the fresh water and salt water ecology of south Florida by exploring how used oil from automobiles and boat engines is disposed.

Florida Council for Economic Education–The Environment and Economics. FL. $5,500. To develop a model curriculum to teach middle grade students how Florida's economy is inextricably linked to the health of the state's environment.

Volusia County School District. Volusia County, FL. $2,359. A hands-on environmental learning program for the handicapped to challenge students to offer an approach to handicap education that is enjoyable, enlightening, and rewarding. The program focuses on environmental problems, life sciences, and our role in protecting our unique ecosystems.

Application process. *Initial contact:* Apply directly to the Foundation's Projects and Programs Committee; or respond to a Request for Proposals (RFP) issued by the Foundation. Full proposal to include:
1. Cover page.
2. Table of contents.
3. Proposal summary (2 pages).
4. Evidence of financial stability and tax-exempt status.
5. Description of how the effectiveness of the project will be measured and monitored.
6. Description of tasks and schedules.
7. Summary of principal personnel/staffing qualifications.
8. Budget.
9. Other.

When to apply: Anytime.
Materials available: "Environmental Education Grant Guidelines" (brochure), "1993–94 Program Guide," *Environmental Education in Florida: A Joint Annual Report* (report).

Emphases. *Recipients:* Educational institutions, nonprofit organizations, public agencies.
Activities: Audiovisual materials, citizen participation, conferences, demonstration programs, education, exhibitions/tours, symposia/colloquia.
Types of support: Direct funding for environmental education products.
Geography: Florida only.

Limitations. *Types of support:* Equipment, facilities (construction), travel expenses.

Environmental Endowment for New Jersey, Inc.

Pennington Office Park
114 Titus Mill Road, Suite 204
Pennington, New Jersey 08534-4305
Tel: 609-737-9698　　Fax: 609-737-8622
EIN: 223107878　　Type: Independent
Contact: Richard J. Sullivan, President

History and philosophy. "The Environmental Endowment for New Jersey, Inc. was established in April, 1991 to receive and administer a $900,000 settlement of a Federal District Court case brought under the Federal Water Pollution Control Act by the New Jersey Public Interest Research Group (NJPIRG), et. al. In 1993, a settlement in a NJPIRG clean water citizen suit resulted in an additional $2 million court award to the Endowment." Another such case in 1994 involving Burlington County produced an additional $2.2 million for the Endowment.

Officers and directors. *Officers:* Richard J. Sullivan, President; Kenneth Ward, Vice President; Joan E. Burkholtz, Secretary; Thomas J. Gilmore, Treasurer. *Trustees:* Thomas J. Gilmore, Nancy K. Hedinger, Jane Nogaki, Ronald Sprague, Richard J. Sullivan, Kenneth Ward, Cindy Zipf, New Jersey First, Inc.

Financial data.* Data for fiscal year ended April 30, 1994. *Assets:* $5,200,000 (M) (est.). *Total grants disbursed:* $67,688.

*As reported by Endowment.

Environmental awards. *Program and interests:* The Endowment supports local, regional, or statewide projects that will have direct benefit in or near the tidally-related New York/New Jersey harbor complex. Projects may include research, litigation, or public education to promote the conservation, preservation, and improvement of the environment including air, land, and water. *Recent grants:* 1994 grants included support for coastal issues, watershed protection, waste management, and environmental education.

Issues. Cli• Bio• Lan• Agr Wat• Oce• Ene Was• Tox• Pop Dev

Funding analysis.

Fiscal year:	1994
Env grants auth:	$67,688
Number:	9
Range:	$2,988–$14,900
Median:	$7,500
Pct $ auth (env/total):	100

Recipients (1994 highest):	Number:	Dollars:
American Littoral Society	1	14,900
Keyport Partnership, Inc.	1	9,000
Bergen Save the Watershed Action Network	1	8,300
Clean Water Fund	1	7,500
Great Swamp Watershed Advisory Association	1	7,500

Activity region (1994):	Number:	Dollars:
New York/New Jersey	9	67,688

Sample grants (1994).
American Littoral Society. Sandy Hook-Highlands, NJ. $14,900. To support implementation of a Baykeeper legal strategy aimed at correcting past and current abuse of the Harbor and to protect it from further misuse.
Bergen Save the Watershed Action Network. Westwood, NJ. $8,300. Restoration of the Upper Hackensack River Watershed by deterring non-point pollution, decreasing erosion, and reestablishing wildlife populations.
Clean Water Fund. New Brunswick, NJ. $7,500. Pesticide Use Reduction–Watershed Protection project. CWF hopes to make significant progress in the NY/NJ estuary and watershed to reduce non-point pollution, specifically pesticide runoff.
Environmental Education Fund. Trenton, NJ. $6,000. An education effort to empower students to participate in New Jersey's environmental decision-making process.
Great Swamp Watershed Advisory Association. New Vernon, NJ. $7,500. Publication and promotion of the Open Space Master Plan.

Ironbound Community Corporation. Newark, NJ. $5,000. A project to promote the cleanup of dioxin and other pollutants in the Passaic River, and the tidally-related NY/NJ Harbor Complex.
Keyport Partnership, Inc. Keyport, NJ. $9,000. An environmental improvement project in Chingarora Creek.
Monmouth County Friends of Clearwater, Inc. Red Bank, NJ. $6,500. To establish an environmental education program and traveling festival to educate and empower young people in inner-city and suburban communities to understand more fully the interplay of the elements of land, water, and air in the NY/NJ Harbor Complex area.
New Jersey Concerned Citizens. Linden, NJ. $2,988. A pilot program combining indoor and outdoor classrooms, experiences, and experiments, into a full participation Wetlands Life Experience course. This will produce a curriculum guide, supplementary course books and a NY/NJ Harbor Estuary and Wetlands video.

Application process. *Initial contact:* Brief project description (2 pages, 7 copies). The Endowment may request an expanded proposal.
When to apply: Deadline for brief project description is March 1.
Materials available: "Report and Grant Guidelines."

Emphases. *Recipients:* Nonprofit organizations.
Activities: Education, litigation, research.
Geography: New Jersey; New York/New Jersey Harbor area, Delaware River Basin.

Limitations. *Recipients:* Individuals.
Types of support: Endowments, operating costs.

The Armand G. Erpf Fund, Inc.

c/o Peat Marwick
599 Lexington Avenue, 16th Floor
New York, New York 10022–6030
Tel: 212–872–7725   Fax: 212–872–7600
EIN: 136085594   Type: Independent
Contact: Gina Caimi, Secretary

Application address:
820 Fifth Avenue
New York, New York 10021

History and philosophy. Established by Armand G. Erpf in 1951, the Fund makes awards in the areas of environment and conservation, education, and culture.

Officers and directors. *Officers:* Sue Erpf Van de Bovenkamp, President; Douglass Campbell, Vice President; Gina Caimi, Secretary; Carl L. Kempner, Treasurer. *Trustees:* Gina Caimi, Douglas Campbell, Armand Bartholomew Erpf, Cornelia Aurelia Erpf, Henry B. Hyde, Carl L. Kempner, Roger Stone, Sue Erpf Van de Bovenkamp.

Financial data. Data for fiscal year ended November 30, 1991. *Assets:* $6,803,572 (M). *Gifts received:* $137,386. *Total grants disbursed:* $353,452.

E

Environmental awards. *Recent grants:* 1991 awards included support for land conservation, wildlife preservation, a botanical garden, and a zoo.

Issues. Cli Bio Lan Agr Wat Oce Ene Was Tox Pop Dev
• • • •

Funding analysis.

Fiscal year:	1990	1991
Env grants disb:	$154,715	$178,359
Number:	17	17
Range:	$20–$69,000	$60–$75,000
Median:	$500	$500
Pct $ disb (env/total):	43	51

Recipients (1991 highest):	Number:	Dollars:
NYZS/The Wildlife Conservation Society	1	75,000
World Wildlife Fund	1	69,667
Catskill Center for Conservation and Development	1	21,477
Catskill Forest Association	1	5,000
African Wildlife Foundation	1	2,000

Activity regions (1991):	Number:	Dollars:
New York/New Jersey	8	103,192
International*	3	71,167
Africa	1	2,000
U.S. Northeast	2	1,500
U.S. not specified	3	500

*Multiple regions or not specified.

Sample grants (1991).
African Wildlife Foundation. Washington, DC. $2,000.
Council on the Environment of New York City. New York, NY. $1,000.
Hudson River Sloop Clearwater, Inc. Poughkeepsie, NY. $75.
Museum of Comparative Zoology. Cambridge, MA. $500.
Natural Resources Defense Council. New York, NY. $60.
The Nature Conservancy, Headquarters. Arlington, VA. $100.
NYZS/The Wildlife Conservation Society. New York, NY. $75,000.
World Wildlife Fund. Washington, DC. $69,667.

Application process. *Initial contact:* Full proposal (1 copy).
When to apply: Anytime. The board meets quarterly.

Limitations. *Recipients:* Individuals.
Types of support: Endowments.

The Ettinger Foundation, Inc.
665 Fifth Avenue, No. 200
New York, New York 10022–5305
Tel: 212–688–5151
EIN: 066038938   Type: Independent
Contact: Richard P. Ettinger, Jr., Director

History and philosophy. The Ettinger Foundation was established in 1949 by members of the Ettinger family. Richard P. Ettinger, Sr. had been a founder of the Prentice-Hall publishing company. The Foundation supports projects in the arts, community service, education (secondary and higher), the environment, health, population, and youth.

Officers and directors. *Trustees:* Lynn P. Babicka, Richard P. Ettinger, Jr., Sharon W. Ettinger, Elaine P. Hapgood, Rocco Landesman, John P. Powers.

Financial data. Data for fiscal year ended December 31, 1992. *Assets:* $14,647,791 (M). *Total grants disbursed:* $599,420.

Environmental awards. *Recent grants:* 1992 grants included support for rainforest protection, wildlife, marine issues, protection of Antarctica, and Native American issues.

Issues. Cli Bio Lan Agr Wat Oce Ene Was Tox Pop Dev
• • • • • • •

Funding analysis.

Fiscal year:	1990	1992
Env grants disb:	$117,750	$56,500
Number:	23	13
Range:	$500–$10,000	$1,000–$10,000
Median:	$5,000	$2,500
Pct $ disb (env/total):	19	9

Recipients (1992 highest):	Number:	Dollars:
Native Americans for a Clean Environment	1	10,000
PIRG Toxics Action Research and Education Project	1	10,000
Malachite School and Small Farm	1	8,000
Food and Water, Inc.	1	6,500
Rainforest Action Network	1	5,000

Activity regions (1992):	Number:	Dollars:
U.S. West	4	20,000
U.S. not specified	4	19,500
U.S. Mountain	3	13,000
International*	2	4,000

*Multiple regions or not specified.

Sample grants (1992).
Antarctica Project. Washington, DC. $5,000.
Conservation International. Washington, DC. $3,000.
Marine Forests. Balboa Island, CA. $5,000.
Native Americans for a Clean Environment. Tahlequah, OK. $10,000.
Rainforest Action Network. San Francisco, CA. $5,000.
Sierra Club Legal Defense Fund. San Francisco, CA. $2,000.
World Wildlife Fund. Washington, DC. $500.

Application process. *Initial contact:* Letter outlining program objectives, proposed budget, and tax-exempt status.
When to apply: Anytime. The board meets in February, May, August, and November.

Emphases. *Recipients:* Nonprofit organizations.
Types of support: Scholarships.

Limitations. *Recipients:* Individuals (except for scholarships to relatives of Prentice-Hall employees).
Types of support: Endowments, facilities (construction), general purposes, loans.

Fair Play Foundation
350 Delaware Trust Building
Wilmington, Delaware 19801
Tel: 302-658-6771   Fax: 302-658-1192
EIN: 516017779   Type: Independent
Contact: Blaine T. Phillips, President

History and philosophy. Established in 1983, the Foundation awards grants to various civic, cultural, educational, and historical organizations, mainly in Middle Atlantic states and the Southeast.

Officers and directors. *Officers:* Blaine T. Phillips, President; James F. Burnett, Vice President; L. E. Grimes, Treasurer. *Trustees:* George P. Bissell, James F. Burnett, George P. Edmonds, L. E. Grimes, Blaine T. Phillips, D. P. Ross, Jr.

Financial data. Data for fiscal year ended December 31, 1992. *Assets:* $8,073,349 (M). *Total grants disbursed:* $492,722.

Environmental awards. 1991 grants included support for land conservation, habitat and wildlife preservation, watershed protection, and coastal issues.

Issues.   Cli   Bio   Lan   Agr   Wat   Oce   Ene   Was   Tox   Pop   Dev
               •   •   •   •

Funding analysis.

Fiscal year:	1991
Env grants disb:	$212,000
Number:	8
Range:	$5,000–$100,000
Median:	$15,000
Pct $ disb (env/total):	33

Recipients (1991 highest):	Number:	Dollars:
Chesapeake Bay Foundation	1	100,000
The Garden Club of Washington	1	25,000
African Wildlife Foundation	1	22,000
Brandywine Conservancy, Inc.	1	15,000
Conservation International	1	15,000
Delaware Nature Society	1	15,000
Delaware Wild Lands	1	15,000

Activity regions (1991):	Number:	Dollars:
U.S. Mid-Atlantic	6	175,000
Eastern and Southern Africa	1	22,000
International*	1	15,000

*Multiple regions or not specified.

Sample grants (1991).
Brandywine Conservancy, Inc. Chadds Ford, PA. $15,000. For the water project.
Chesapeake Bay Foundation. Annapolis, MD. $100,000. For Port Isabel, Fox Island.
Conservation International. Washington, DC. $15,000. For debt swap and the Tague Program.
Delaware Nature Society. Hockessin, DE. $15,000. To refurbish the new building.
Waterfowl Festival. Easton, MD. $5,000. To establish waterfowl habitat.

Application process. *Initial contact:* Submit a letter explaining the need for the proposed grant.
When to apply: Anytime.

Emphases. *Activities:* Land acquisition.
Types of support: Equipment, facilities (renovation).

Fanwood Foundation
c/o King, King & Goldsack
450 Somerset Street
P.O. Box 1106
Plainfield, New Jersey 07061-1106
Tel: 908-756-7804   Fax: 908-756-2184
EIN: 136051922   Type: Independent
Contact: Victor R. King, Esq., Trustee

History and philosophy. The Fanwood Foundation had its beginnings in a trust established by Dorothy W. Stevens in 1940. Grantmaking interests include community development, culture, education, environment, health, public policy, religion, women, and youth.

Officers and directors. *Trustees:* Victor R. King, Robert T. Stevens, Jr., Whitney Stevens.

Financial data. Data for fiscal year ended December 31, 1991. *Assets:* $11,537,453 (M). *Total grants disbursed:* $1,081,921.

Environmental awards. *Recent grants:* 1993 grants included support for land conservation, wildlife preservation, and marine issues.

Issues.   Cli   Bio   Lan   Agr   Wat   Oce   Ene   Was   Tox   Pop   Dev
               •   •   •   •

Funding analysis.

Fiscal year:	1991	1993
Env grants disb:	$221,600	$177,100
Number:	44	56
Range:	$500–$65,000	$250–$12,600
Median:	$2,000	$2,000
Pct $ disb (env/total):	20	–

Recipients (1993 highest):	Number:	Dollars:
The Nature Conservancy, International	4	24,600
The Nature Conservancy, Montana Field Office	1	10,000
Conservation International	1	7,000
Wildlife Conservation International	3	7,000
Greater Yellowstone Coalition	1	6,000
World Wildlife Fund	1	6,000

F

Activity regions (1993 highest):	Number:	Dollars:
International*	12	50,600
U.S. Mountain	18	49,500
U.S. not specified	12	33,000
New York/New Jersey	4	9,500
U.S. Northwest	2	4,000

*Multiple regions or not specified.

Sample grants (1993).
Montana Ecosystem Defense Council. Bozeman, MT. $250.
Montana Wilderness Association. Henena, MT. $1,000.
NYZS/The Wildlife Conservation Society. Bronx, NY. $5,000.
Predator Project. Bozeman, MT. $1,250.
Scenic America. Washington, DC. $1,000.

Application process. *Initial contact:* Brief statement of purpose, amount requested, and proof of IRS tax-exempt status.
When to apply: Anytime.

Emphases. *Types of support:* Annual campaigns, endowments, operating costs.

Limitations. *Recipients:* Individuals.

The William Stamps Farish Fund
10000 Memorial Drive, Suite 920
Houston, Texas 77024
Tel: 713–686–7373   Fax: 713–655–9124
EIN: 746043019   Type: Independent
Contact: Caroline P. Rotan, Secretary

History and philosophy. The William Stamps Farish Fund was established in 1951 by William Farish, one of the organizers of Humble Oil Company. Subsequent contributions have added to its assets. Education, medical research, and social services are the Fund's primary interests.

Officers and directors. *Officers:* William S. Farish, President; Martha F. Gerry, James O. Winston, Jr., Vice Presidents; Caroline P. Rotan, Secretary; Terry W. Ward, Treasurer. *Trustees:* Myrtle Camp, Cornelia Corbett, William S. Farish, Martha F. Gerry, Dan R. Japhet, James O. Winston.

Financial data. Data for fiscal year ended June 30, 1992. *Assets:* $94,157,203 (M). *Total grants disbursed:* $4,383,617.

Environmental awards. *Recent grants:* 1992 grants included support for land conservation and species preservation.

Issues. Cli Bio Lan Agr Wat Oce Ene Was Tox Pop Dev
              •   •   •

Funding analysis.

Fiscal year:	1991	1992
Env grants disb:	$116,200	$61,350
Number:	7	8
Range:	$1,200–$75,000	$1,200–$10,150
Median:	$10,000	$10,000
Pct $ disb (env/total):	3	1

Recipients (1992 highest):	Number:	Dollars:
Trees for Houston	1	10,150
Houston Audubon Society	1	10,000
Friends of Bellaire Parks	1	10,000
Houston Arboretum and Botanical Society	1	10,000
The New York Botanical Garden	1	10,000

Activity regions (1992):	Number:	Dollars:
U.S. South Central	5	45,150
New York/New Jersey	1	10,000
U.S. Southeast	2	6,200

Sample grants (1992).
Armand Bayou Nature Center. Houston, TX. $5,000. Educational and recreational programs.
Bluegrass Tomorrow, Inc. Lexington, KY. $5,000. Achieve regional solutions to problems related to land use in Fayette, Scott, Bourbon, Woodward, Clark, Madison, and Jessamine counties, Kentucky.
Friends of Bellaire Parks. Bellaire, TX. $10,000. Summer programs.
Houston Audubon Society. Houston, TX. $10,000. Fourth grade nature program.
Tall Timbers Research Stations. Tallahassee, FL. $1,200. Land and fire management programs.

Application process. *Initial contact:* Full proposal to include:
1. Organization history and detailed financial statement.
2. Description of proposed project and the need for it.
3. Amount requested, budget, and explanation of use of funds.
4. List of other potential funding sources.
5. Copy of IRS tax-exempt status determination letter.

When to apply: Anytime. The board meets annually.
Materials available: Annual report, application guidelines.

Emphases. *Geography:* Texas.

Limitations. *Recipients:* Individuals.
Types of support: Annual campaigns, debt retirement, endowments, loans, operating costs.

The Favrot Fund
1770 St. James, Suite 510
Houston, Texas 77056
Tel: 713–622–1442
EIN: 746045648   Type: Independent
Contact: Julie M. Richardson, Secretary

History and philosophy. Lawrence H. Favrot, Johanna A. Favrot, and George B. Strong were the principal donors for the Fund, which was established in 1952. The Fund supports programs in the arts and culture, community service, conservation and the environment, education, health, and social services.

Officers and directors. *Officers:* Mrs. Johanna A. Favrot, President; Mr. Lenoir Moody Josey, Vice President. *Directors:* Mrs. Celestine Favrot Arndt, Dr. Laurence DeKanter Favrot, Mr. Leo Mortimer Favrot, Mrs. Marcia Favrot, Mrs. Romelia Favrot, Mr. Lenoir Moody Josey, Dr. Jeanette Favrot Peterson.

Financial data. Data for fiscal year ending December 31, 1993. *Assets:** $12,427,580 (M). *Total grants disbursed:* $650,580.

*As of May 31, 1993.

Environmental awards. *Recent grants:* Grants in 1992 included support for land conservation, habitat and wildlife preservation, and education.

Issues. Cli • Bio • Lan • Agr Wat • Oce Ene • Was Tox Pop • Dev

Funding analysis.

Fiscal year:	1990	1992
Env grants disb:	$130,000	$155,000
Number:	5	11
Range:	$5,000–$50,000	$1,000–$45,000
Median:	$20,000	$7,000
Pct $ disb (env/total):	30	28

Recipients (1992 highest):	Number:	Dollars:
Natural Resources Defense Council	3	55,000
World Wildlife Fund	1	40,000
Houston Museum of Natural Science	1	20,000
Center for the Arts	1	15,000
Manomet Observatory for Conservation Science	1	10,000

Activity regions (1992 highest):	Number:	Dollars:
U.S. multiple regions	3	55,000
Indian Subcontinent and Indian Ocean Islands	1	40,000
U.S. South Central	1	20,000
U.S. West	1	15,000
New York/New Jersey	3	13,000

Sample grants (1992).

The Gorilla Foundation. Woodside, CA. $2,000. Toward current programs, to acquire a new gorilla, and to establish a gorilla preserve in Hawaii.

Hudson Highlands Land Trust. Garrison, NY. $7,000. Providing funds for a map that will spearhead an effort to create a master plan for the local planning board to preserve the local character of the land trust for future generations.

Natural Resources Defense Council. New York, NY. $45,000. Support of environmental laws in the United States. Monies for a recycling program in New York City and promoting clear air in the Los Angeles region.

Open Space Institute, Inc. New York, NY. $1,000. To establish land trusts on the east bank of the Hudson River and protect other public lands including the Highlands.

World Wildlife Fund. Washington, DC. $40,000. The fourth year of scholarship funds for Tshewang Wangchuk at the University of Maryland through the Bhutanese Scholarship Program of the National Women's Association of Bhutan.

Application process. *Initial contact:* Letter.
When to apply: Anytime. Board meets in September or October.

Emphases. *Types of support:* Equipment, facilities (construction), general purposes, operating costs.
Geography: California, New York, Texas, and Washington, D.C.

Felburn Foundation

c/o Robert Philipson & Co.
8601 Georgia Avenue, No. 1001
Silver Spring, Maryland 20910-3440
Tel: 301-608-3900
EIN: 510234331   Type: Independent
Contact: James F. Bergman, Advisor

History and philosophy. The Felburn Foundation was established in 1978 by J. Phil Felburn and The Aetna Freight Lines, Inc. Areas of interest are libraries and wildlife.

Officers and directors. *Officers:* J. Phil Felburn, President and Treasurer; Charles Freeman, Vice President; Don H. Norman, Secretary. *Directors:* J. Phil Felburn, Charles Freeman, Don H. Norman, Elmyra F. Schiller.

Financial data. Data for fiscal year ended December 31, 1992. *Assets:* $3,612,115 (M). *Gifts received:* $100,020. *Total grants disbursed:* $168,285.

Environmental awards. *Recent grants:* 1992 grants included support for nature study libraries and wildlife protection.

Issues. Cli • Bio • Lan Agr Wat Oce Ene Was Tox Pop Dev

Funding analysis.

Fiscal year:	1992
Env grants disb:	$165,423
Number:	4
Range:	$55–$98,024
Median:	$33,672
Pct $ disb (env/total):	98

Recipients (1992):	Number:	Dollars:
Bronson Nature Study Library	1	98,024
Bellview Nature Study Library	1	66,344
Southern Appalachian Highlands Conservancy	1	1,000
North Carolina Wildlife Federation	1	55

Activity region (1992):	Number:	Dollars:
U.S. Southeast	4	165,423

Sample grants (1992).
Bellview Nature Study Library. Ocala, FL. $66,344.
Bronson Nature Study Library. Bronson, FL. $98,024.
North Carolina Wildlife Federation. Raleigh, NC. $55.
Southern Appalachian Highland Conservancy. John City, TN. $1,000.

Application process. *Initial contact:* The Foundation awards grants to pre-selected organizations only. No unsolicited applications accepted.

Emphases. *Recipients:* Pre-selected organizations only.

Limitations. *Recipients:* Individuals.

Samuel S. Fels Fund
1616 Walnut Street, Suite 800
Philadelphia, Pennsylvania 19103
Tel: 215–731–9455
EIN: 231365325   Type: Independent
Contact: Helen Cunningham, Executive Director

History and philosophy. Samuel S. Fels (1860–1950) was president of Fels & Company soap manufacturers. A Philadelphia philanthropist and civic leader, Mr. Fels founded the Fund in 1935 to promote causes that "tend to improve human daily life and to bring to the average person greater health, happiness, and a fuller understanding of the meaning and purposes of life." It "seeks to support projects which prevent, lessen, or resolve contemporary social problems, or which seek to provide permanent improvements in the provision of services for the improvement of daily life. The Fund prefers to make grants on a modest scale that will have maximum impact upon institutions and service patterns in the Philadelphia area." Program areas are: Arts, Community Projects, Education, Health, and Winnet Internships in Community Service.

Officers and directors. *Officers:* David Melnicoff, President; Raymond K. Denworth, Jr., Sandra Featherman, Vice Presidents; Helen Cunningham, Secretary; David H. Wice, Treasurer. *Directors:* Iso Briselli, Daniel Burke, Ida K. Chen, Helen Cunningham, Raymond K. Denworth, Jr., Sandra Featherman, David Melnicoff, David H. Wice.

Financial data. Data for fiscal year ended December 31, 1993. *Assets:* $38,032,779 (M). *Total grants authorized:* $1,273,090.

Environmental awards. *Recent grants:* 1993 grants included support for an arboretum, energy conservation, urban environment, and environmental justice.

Issues. Cli Bio Lan Agr Wat Oce Ene Was Tox Pop Dev
          •   •   •   •   •

Funding analysis.

Fiscal year:	1993
Env grants auth:	$61,500
Number:	7
Range:	$2,500–$18,000
Median:	$6,000
Pct $ auth (env/total):	5

Recipients (1993):	Number:	Dollars:
Pennsylvania Environmental Council	1	18,000
Clean Air Council	1	15,000
Energy Coordinating Agency of Philadelphia	1	10,000
Awbury Arboretum Association	2	8,500
Board of Rabbis of Greater Philadelphia	1	5,000
Clean Water Fund	1	5,000

Activity regions (1993):	Number:	Dollars:
U.S. Mid-Atlantic	6	56,500
U.S. not specified	1	5,000

Sample grants (1993).
Awbury Arboretum Association. Philadelphia, PA. $6,000. Establish database of trees and shrubs.
Board of Rabbis of Greater Philadelphia. Philadelphia, PA. $5,000. Research on reduction of energy costs.
Clean Air Council. Philadelphia, PA. $15,000. Public education.
Clean Water Fund. Philadelphia, PA. $5,000. Environmental Justice Organizing Project.
Energy Coordinating Agency of Philadelphia. Philadelphia, PA. $10,000. Weatherization project.
Pennsylvania Environmental Council. Philadelphia, PA. $18,000. Philadelphia Green Agenda Project.

Application process. *Initial contact:* Proposal (1 copy, unbound) to include:
1. Proposal Cover Sheet (supplied by the Fund).
2. Narrative (5 pages).
   - Agency information. Brief summary of history; mission; current programs, activities, and accomplishments, with highlights of the past year; people involved and specific events; plans for the coming year.
   - Project request. How the project fits into the organization's mission; project goals and objectives; events and activities planned; key staff and volunteers; timetable; population served; interaction with other organizations (if relevant).
   - Evaluation. Methods during the funding period; expected results of the project; criteria for success; anticipated consequences of *not* conducting the project.
3. Attachments.
   - Board of directors. Addresses, occupations; minority, low-income, consumer, and/or neighborhood representatives.
   - Current agency annual operating budget.
   - Project budget.
   - Funding sources. For the organization: past major contributors with amounts; recent applications with results; anticipated future sources. For the project: applications for funds and their status.
   - Recent annual financial statement (audited, if available).
   - Personnel. Attach resumes of top staff for the organization and for key personnel/volunteers for the project.
   - Annual report (if available).
   - A few current relevant newspaper/magazine articles or reviews about the organization's programs (if available).
   - Copy of IRS tax-exempt status determination letter.

Applicants may be asked to submit additional materials. One proposal accepted per year. A written report is required from all grant recipients in order to be considered for subsequent grants.

When to apply: Anytime (except for Arts applications, which have deadlines of January 15 and June 15). The board meets regularly.
Materials available: Annual report, "Guidelines for Applicants," "Proposal Cover Sheet."

Emphases. *Recipients:* Nonprofit organizations.
Activities: Activism, advocacy, capacity building, citizen participation, collaborative efforts, conflict resolution, fieldwork, innovative programs, planning, political activities.
Types of support: Projects, start-up costs.
Geography: Philadelphia, Pennsylvania.

Limitations. *Recipients:* Individuals, public agencies, research institutions.
Activities: Education (private), litigation, publications, research (scholarly), training.
Types of support: Capital campaigns/expenses, debt retirement, emergency funding, endowments, equipment, facilities (construction), fellowships, scholarships, travel expenses.

The Hugh and Jane Ferguson Foundation
Two Union Square, #4512
601 Union Street
Seattle, Washington 98101
Tel: 206-633-0827   Fax: 206-628-3201
EIN: 911357603   Type: Independent
EGA member
Contact: Therese Ogle, Program Manager

History and philosophy. The Foundation was founded in 1987 and "is dedicated to the preservation and restoration of nature, including wildlife and their required habitats. It also supports the institutions that present nature to the public: museums, libraries, aquariums, zoos, and public media."

Officers and directors. *Officers:* Hugh S. Ferguson, President; Jane Avery Ferguson, Vice President; Ellen Lee Ferguson, Secretary.

Financial data. Data for fiscal year ended September 30, 1992. *Assets:* $886,244 (M). *Total grants disbursed:* $47,063.

Issues.   Cli   Bio   Lan   Agr   Wat   Oce   Ene   Was   Tox   Pop   Dev
                •   •

Sample grants (1988–93).
Friends of the Earth, Northwest. Seattle, WA. $4,500. Toward the Elwha River restoration project, for dam removal and fisheries restoration.
Long Live the Kings. Woodinville, WA. $3,500. To protect and restore productive wild salmon runs through innovative hatchery programs.
Montana Wilderness Association. Helena, MT. $1,500. To help create and protect federally designated wilderness areas in Montana.

Application process. *Initial contact:* Letter of inquiry. If requested, proposal to include:
1. Description of project.
2. History of organization.
3. List of involved staff and board members with resumes.
4. Evaluation method.
5. Project and/or organization budget.
6. Copy of IRS tax-exempt status determination letter.

When to apply: Deadlines are February 15 and August 15.

Emphases. *Recipients:* Aquariums, museums, nonprofit organizations, zoos.
Geography: Pacific Northwest and Alaska.

Limitations. *Recipients:* Individuals.
Types of support: Scholarships.

The Field Foundation of Illinois, Inc.
135 South LaSalle Street
Chicago, Illinois 60603
Tel: 312-263-3211   Fax: 312-263-3273
EIN: 366059408   Type: Independent
Contact: Joyce M. Alexander, Executive Assistant

History and philosophy. The Foundation was established in 1960 by Marshall Field, IV, whose family was active in newspapers and retailing in Chicago. It makes grants to institutions and agencies that operate in the fields of health, education, community welfare, culture, conservation, and urban and community affairs and that primarily serve the people of the Chicago metropolitan area. Special program areas: are Primary and Secondary Education and The Environment.

Officers and directors. *Officers:* Arthur F. Quern, Chairman; Handy L. Lindsey, Jr., Executive Director and Treasurer; Gary H. Kline, Secretary. *Directors:* Milton Davis, Marshall Field, V, Hanna H. Gray, Philip Wayne Hummer, George A. Ranney, Jr., Arthur E. Rasmussen.

Financial data. Data for fiscal year ended April 30, 1992. *Assets:* $32,953,467 (M). *Total grants disbursed:* $1,117,681.

Environmental awards. *Program and interests:* The Environment is the Foundation's newest area of grantmaking, approved in 1992. This program supports:

- Innovative initiatives in environmental protection and conservation at the neighborhood level in Chicago metropolitan communities lacking the resources to develop and implement this type of project.
- Efforts designed to educate and involve residents from Chicago's various social, racial and economic groups in the analysis and development of sound public policy on environmental protection and ecological conservation.
- Efforts which potentially serve as models for other communities.

Recent grants: 1992 grants supported ecosystem preservation (prairie and savanna), open lands, river protection, urban environment, parks, and a zoo.

F

Issues. Cli Bio Lan Agr Wat Oce Ene Was Tox Pop Dev
         •   •   •   •

Funding Analysis.

Fiscal year:	1992
Env grants auth:	$50,000
Number:	3
Range:	$5,000–$30,000
Median:	$15,000
Pct $ disb (env/total):	3

Recipients (1992):	Number:	Dollars:
Open Lands Project	1	30,000
Friends of the Chicago River	1	15,000
People for Community Recovery	1	5,000

Activity region (1992):	Number:	Dollars:
U.S. Great Lakes	3	50,000

Sample grants (1992).*

Friends of the Chicago River. Chicago, IL. $7,500. Payment on a $15,000 matching grant to establish a new full-time public policy and planning position.

The Nature Conservancy, Illinois Field Office. Chicago, IL. $10,000. Payment on a $30,000 grant for "Preserve the Preserves," a large-scale restoration of prairie and savannah (and their wildlife) in the Cook County Forest Preserves.

Open Lands Project. Chicago, IL. $7,500. Payment for a $30,000 grant for the America's Historic Tree and Project Tree Learning Program.

People for Community Recovery. Chicago, IL. $10,000. General operating expenses for this young, grassroots organization working to improve the environmental quality of low-income neighborhoods on Chicago's southeast side.

*Sample grants represent either new awards or disbursements on grants awarded in previous years.

Application process. *Initial contact:* Brief, concise proposal to include:
1. Detailed description of amount requested.
2. Duration of funding period.
3. Anticipated outcomes.
4. Implementation plans.
5. Personnel and their qualifications.
6. Evaluation plans.
7. Total project cost and funding sources and, if applicable, how project will be financed after the grant period.

Appendixes.
1. Cover letter summarizing why financial assistance is requested and the amount sought.
2. Brief history and background of applicant.
3. Budget for applicant's current year and most recent audited financial statement.
4. List of board of directors and their affiliations.
5. Copy of IRS tax-exempt status determination letter and a letter establishing its status as a publicly supported organization.

When to apply: Anytime. The board meets three times a year.
Materials available: Annual report (includes "Grant Application Procedures").

Emphases. *Activities:* Innovative programs, volunteerism.
Geography: Chicago metropolitan area.

Limitations. *Recipients:* Conduit agencies, educational institutions (private elementary/secondary), individuals, United Way member agencies.
Activities: Conferences, fundraising, political activities, publications.
Types of support: Advertising campaigns, endowments, equipment (video).

Jamee and Marshall Field Foundation
333 West Wacker Drive
Chicago, Illinois 60606
Tel: 312–917–1828   Fax: 312–917–1822
EIN: 363184245   Type: Independent
Contact: Iris J. Krieg, Executive Director

History and philosophy. The Jamee and Marshall Field Foundation was established in 1982 by the family of Marshall Field, V as a major means of realizing the Field family's commitment to philanthropy. Foundation program areas are: Conservation/Environment and Cultural Institutions.

Officers and directors. *Officers:* Marshall Field, V, President; Jamee J. Field, Vice President; Edwin H. Watkins, Secretary/Treasurer.

Financial data. Data for fiscal years ended September 30, 1993. *Assets:* $4,616,713 (M). *Total grants disbursed:* $233,550.

Environmental awards. *Program and interests:* The Foundation gives to organizations that bring together environmental and conservation concerns such as:

- Preservation of unique natural areas.
- Wildlife protection.
- Pollution abatement.

Most recipient organizations are national or international in scope.
Recent grants: 1993 grants included support for land conservation, coastal issues, and wildlife preservation.

Issues. Cli Bio Lan Agr Wat Oce Ene Was Tox Pop Dev
         •   •   •   •   •

Funding analysis.

Fiscal year:	1993
Env grants disb:	$29,800
Number:	16
Range:	$300–$4,000
Median:	$1,750
Pct $ disb (env/total):	13

Recipients (1993 highest):	Number:	Dollars:
Council on Economic Priorities	1	4,000
Restoration of Atlantic Salmon in America	1	4,000

The Student Conservation Association, Inc.	1	3,000
Chicago Academy of Science	1	2,500
National Audubon Society	1	2,500
American Littoral Society	1	2,000
Arlington Heights Park District/ Northgate Civic Association	1	2,000
Delta Waterfowl Foundation	1	2,000

Activity regions (1993):	Number:	Dollars:
U.S. not specified	9	19,000
U.S. Great Lakes	2	6,000
U.S. Northeast	2	4,300
U.S. Southeast	2	3,000
U.S. Mountain	1	500

Sample grants (1993).
American Littoral Society. Key Biscayne, FL. $2,000. Coral Reef Center.
Conservation Fund. Arlington, VA. $1,000.
Council on Economic Priorities. New York, NY. $4,000.
Montana Land Reliance. Helena, MT. $500.
National Fish and Wildlife Foundation. Washington, DC. $1,000.
Restoration of Atlantic Salmon in America. Dublin, NH. $4,000.
The Student Conservation Association, Inc. Arlington, VA. $3,000.
Wetlands Research, Inc. Chicago, IL. $1,500.

Application process. *Initial contact:* Full proposal to include:
1. Brief description of organization.
2. Current-year budget.
3. List of board of directors.
4. Copy of IRS tax-exempt status determination letter.
5. Copy of most recent audit.

When to apply: Deadlines are April 15, August 15, and December 15. The board of directors meets in February, June, and October.
Materials available: Letter outlining "Guidelines," "Limitations," and "Application Procedures."

Emphases. *Recipients:* Nonprofit organizations.
Activities: Advocacy, demonstration programs.
Types of support: Annual campaigns, continuing support, general purposes, operating costs, pilot projects, seed money.
Geography: Organizations in the Metropolitan Chicago area. However, for Conservation/Environment, recipient organizations may be located elsewhere if their activities are national or international in scope.

Limitations. *Recipients:* Individuals; United Way member agencies.
Activities: Audiovisual materials, conferences, fundraising, political activities, publications, research (medical/scholarly).
Types of support: Advertising campaigns, fellowships, scholarships.

F

Fields Pond Foundation, Inc.
77 Rumford Avenue, Suite 3C
P.O. Box 667
Waltham, Massachusetts 02254–06677
Tel: 617–899–9990   Fax: 617–899–2819
EIN: 043196041   Type: Independent
EGA member
Contact: Brian Rehrig, Vice President

History and philosophy. Established in 1993, the Fields Pond Foundation's mission is "to provide financial assistance to nature and land conservation organizations which are community-based, which address specific environmental challenges, and which serve to elevate environmental awareness by involving local inhabitants in conservation issues." The Foundation disbursed its initial grants in 1994.

Financial data.* Data as of November 21, 1994. *Assets:* $900,000 (U) (est.). *Total grants disbursed:* $10,100.

*As reported by Foundation.

Environmental awards. *Program and interests:* "The directors have experienced the positive impact that grassroots conservation efforts can achieve, and intend to nurture such efforts by making grants under the following priorities:

- Assistance in establishment of endowments, particularly as a method of funding specific ongoing programs.
- Specific project grants for land acquisition and conservation, enhancement of public access to conservation lands, rivers, coastlines and other natural resources, and related education programs and publications."

Recent grants: 1994 grants included support for land conservation, wildlife and habitats, coastal issues, and recreation.

Issues.   Cli Bio Lan Agr Wat Oce Ene Was Tox Pop Dev
              •   •   •

Sample grants (1994).
Boothbay Region Land Trust. East Boothbay, ME. $2,000. To establish a Trail Endowment Fund.
Damariscotta River Association. Damariscotta, ME. $1,100. To fund initial phase of bird species survey in connection with potential acquisition of Little Thrumcap Island.
The Nature Conservancy, Maine Chapter. Brunswick, ME. $5,000. Addition to Stewardship Endowment Fund.
Weston Forest & Trail Association. Weston, MA. $2,000. Addition to endowment fund for trail building and maintenance.

Application process. *Initial contact:* Proposal outline (1 page). Full proposal (4 pages, 2 copies), if requested, to include:
1. History of the organization, its mission and major accomplishments, its geographic scope, and populations served.
2. List of board and staff and qualifications of personnel involved in the project.
3. Current and projected budgets, current financial statement, and annual report, and a copy of the IRS Form 990.

5. Description of purpose, goals, objectives, and benefits to environment, organization, local residents, and population.
6. Proof proposal is consistent with Foundation's objectives.
7. Evidence that the funds will be used to address a need that would otherwise remain unmet.
8. Project budget, other sources of funding, and plan for ongoing funding.

Applicants are encouraged to contact the Foundation informally before proceeding to prepare a formal application.
When to apply: Anytime.
Materials available: "Application Guidelines."

Emphases. *Recipients:* Nonprofit organizations.
Activities: Education, land acquisition, publications.
Types of support: Capital campaigns/expenses, endowments, loans, matching funds, operating costs, projects, seed money.

Limitations. *Recipients:* Individuals, religious organizations.
Activities: Research.
Types of support: Debt retirement, general purposes, travel expenses.

Fieldstead Charitable Trust
P.O. Box 18613
Irvine, California 92713–8613
Tel: 718–474–0242
EIN: 330127363   Type: Independent
EGA member
Contact: Victor Porlier

History and philosophy. The Trust was established in 1985 by Roberta G. and Howard F. Ahmanson, Jr. The Trust is a member of the Environmental Grantmakers Association. No information about grantmaking is available.

Officers and directors. *Officers:* Howard F. Ahmanson, Jr. President; Roberta G. Ahmanson, Secretary.

Financial data. Data for fiscal year ended December 31, 1990. *Assets:* $138,239 (M). *Gifts received:* $136,600. *Total grants disbursed:* $191,088.

Application process. *Initial contact:* The Trust awards grants to pre-selected organization only. No unsolicited applications accepted.

Emphases. *Recipients:* Pre-selected organizations only.

The 1525 Foundation
1525 National City Bank Building
Cleveland, Ohio 44114
Tel: 216–696–4200   Fax: 216–696–7303
EIN: 341089206   Type: Independent
Contact: Phillip A. Ranney, Secretary/Treasurer

History and philosophy. Established in 1971, the Foundation makes grants primarily in the areas of higher education and the environment, or to Cuyahoga County organizations supported by the founder in his lifetime. The trustees look to fund organizations promoting self-help.

Officers and directors. *Officers:* Hubert G. Schneider, President; Thelma G. Smith, Vice President; Phillip A. Ranney, Secretary/Treasurer. *Trustees:* Elmer G. Beamer, William B. LaPlace, Phillip A. Ranney, Hubert G. Schneider, Thelma G. Smith.

Financial data. Data for fiscal year ended December 31, 1993. *Assets:* $8,449,955 (M). *Total grants disbursed:* $3,092,100.

Environmental awards. *Recent grants:* 1992 and 1993 grants included support for land planning, parks, watershed preservation, an arboretum, and recycling in the Cleveland area.

Issues. Cli Bio Lan Agr Wat Oce Ene Was Tox Pop Dev

Funding analysis.

Fiscal year:	1992
Env grants disb:	$340,800
Number:	4
Range:	$5,500–$300,000
Median:	$17,650
Pct $ disb (env/total):	13

Recipients (1992):	Number:	Dollars:
National Park Service	1	300,000
Cuyahoga Valley Preservation and Scenic Railway Association	1	25,000
Cleveland Recycling Center in St. Clair Superior	1	10,300
Cuyahoga River Community Planning Organization	1	5,500

Activity region (1992):	Number:	Dollars:
U.S. Great Lakes	4	340,800

Sample grants (1992–93).
Cleveland Recycling Center in St. Clair Superior. Cleveland, OH. $10,300.
Cuyahoga River Community Planning Organization. Cleveland, OH. $5,500.
Cuyahoga Valley Preservation and Scenic Railway Association. Peninsula, OH. $25,000.
The Holden Arboretum. Mentor, OH. $5,000.
National Park Service. Cleveland, OH. $300,000.

Application process. *Initial contact:* Short proposal to include:
1. Brief description of organization.
2. Purpose of grant request.
3. Applicable financial data.
4. Other contributors to project.
5. A copy of IRS tax-exempt status determination letter classifying the organization as not a private foundation under section 509(A).

When to apply: Anytime. The trustees meet often and will notify applicants within one month of application.
Materials available: "The 1525 Foundation."

Emphases. *Recipients:* Nonprofit organizations.
Types of support: Capital campaigns/expenses, endowments, equipment, general purposes, matching funds, seed money
Geography: Primarily northeastern Ohio.

Limitations. *Recipients:* Individuals.

Leland Fikes Foundation, Inc.
3050 Lincoln Plaza
500 North Akard
Dallas, Texas 75201
Tel: 214-754-0144   Fax: 214-855-1245
EIN: 756035984   Type: Independent
Contact: Nancy Solana, Vice President

History and philosophy. Leland Fikes, a Texas oil producer and philanthropist, created the Leland Fikes Foundation, Inc. in 1952. The Foundation works to better the quality of life in the Dallas area through its programs in Arts and Culture; Education; History, Heritage, and the Environment; Human Services; Medical; Population; Public Enlightenment; and Other Purposes.

Officers and directors. *Officer:* Lee Fikes, President. *Trustees:* Amy L. Fikes, Catherine W. Fikes, Lee Fikes.

Financial data. Data for fiscal year ended December 31, 1992. *Assets:* $50,460,000 (M) (est.). *Total grants disbursed:* $3,090,202.

Environmental awards. *Recent grants:* 1992 grants included support for habitat and species preservation, and public education.

Issues. Cli Bio Lan Agr Wat Oce Ene Was Tox Pop Dev
            •   •   •   •

Funding analysis.

Fiscal year:	1991	1992
Env grants disb:	$388,600	$113,500
Number:	7	5
Range:	$1,000–$177,000	$1,000–$60,000
Median:	$25,000	$1,500
Pct $ disb (env/total):	10	4

Recipients (1992 highest):	Number:	Dollars:
Species Survival Commission	1	60,000
La Ruta Maya Conservation Foundation	1	50,000
Dallas Zoological Society	1	1,500
Environmental Data Research Institute	1	1,000
Heard Natural Science Museum and Wildlife Sanctuary	1	1,000

Activity regions (1991 highest):	Number:	Dollars:
U.S. Great Lakes	1	60,000
U.S. Mid-Atlantic	1	50,000
U.S. South Central	2	2,500
U.S. Not specified	1	1,000

Sample grants (1992).
La Ruta Maya Conservation Foundation. Great Falls, VA. $50,000. General support to build an ecological park.
Species Survival Commission. Brookfield, IL. $60,000. To study declining amphibian population.

Application process. *Initial contact:* Concise but complete written proposal including:
1. Cover letter on organization letterhead, signed by CEO of the governing body. Briefly describe program or project to be funded, amount requested, and date funds are needed.
2. Copy of IRS tax-exempt status determination letter.
3. Names and affiliations of organization's board of directors or trustees.
4. Organization's budget for current year and previous year.
5. Budget for proposed program or project.
6. Information about principal staff or volunteers working on the proposed project.
7. Name and telephone number of contact person.
8. List of other sources that will fund or are considering funding the program or project.
9. Sources of future funds for program, project, or organization.
10. Program or project evaluation criteria and methods.

After reviewing the written proposal, trustees may request a meeting or additional written material.
When to apply: Anytime. The board meets bimonthly.
Materials available: Application guidelines.

Emphases. *Activities:* Land acquisition, research, projects.
Types of support: Annual campaigns, capital campaigns/expenses, continuing support, emergency funding, endowments, equipment, facilities, general purposes, matching funds, operating costs, professorships, scholarships, seed money.
Geography: Dallas, Texas.

Limitations. *Recipients:* Individuals.
Types of support: Loans.

Bert Fingerhut/Caroline Hicks Family Fund
1520 Silver King Drive
Aspen, Colorado 81611
Tel: 303-920-1934   Fax: 303-925-1820
Type: Independent
EGA member
Contact: Bert Fingerhut

History and philosophy. The Fund is primarily interested in public lands and wilderness preservation in the Colorado Plateau.

Financial data.* Data for fiscal year ended December 31, 1992. *Total grants disbursed:* $81,750.

*Does not include grants of less than $10,000.

Environmental awards. *Program and interests:* The Fund targets efforts to preserve:

- Public lands.
- Wilderness.

F

Issues. Cli Bio Lan Agr Wat Oce Ene Was Tox Pop Dev
                        •

Application process. *Initial contact:* Short letter.
When to apply: Anytime.

Emphases. *Geography:* Colorado Plateau.

Limitations. *Types of support:* Capital campaigns/expenses, endowments.

FishAmerica Foundation
1033 North Fairfax Street, Suite 200
Alexandria, Virginia 22314
Tel: 703–519–9691   Fax: 703–519–1872
EIN: 363219015
Contact: Andrew Loftus, Managing Director

History and philosophy. FishAmerica Foundation was created in 1983 for concern for the North America's waterways and fisheries. Established by the Zebco Corporation, the Foundation receives support from the sportfishing industry. Its goals: "To combat the continuing threats to our water quality; to stem shrinking fish populations; to improve the opportunity for sportfishing success; to supplement stagnating and/or declining federal and state monies for water and fisheries agencies; to go beyond current private efforts which are limited either geographically or programmatically; to provide funding for concerned groups to invest in projects in their local area; to encourage people to get involved in their local areas."

Officers and directors. *Officers:* Jim Hubbard, President; Don Sturdevant, Vice President. *Directors:* Howard Bach, Tom Bedell, John M. Charvat, Kim Erickson, Tony Estes, Tim Findlay, Edward J. Hochreiter, Gene Howard, Jim Hubbard, David Jones, Robert Keir, Al Lindner, Robert T. McNaney, Don Sturdevant, Dr. Howard Tanner, Jim Woodruff.

Financial data. Data for fiscal year ended December 31, 1992. *Gifts received:* $201,825. *Total grants disbursed:* $228,818.

Environmental awards. *Program and interests:* The Foundation favors projects that:

- Enhance fish populations and fisheries.
- Conserve and enhance waterways and water quality.

Recent grants: Grants in 1992 and 1993 included support for habitat construction and fishery enhancement.

Issues. Cli Bio Lan Agr Wat Oce Ene Was Tox Pop Dev
                •   •   •

Funding analysis.

Fiscal year:	1991	1992
Env grants auth:	$187,999	$228,818
Number:	33	34
Range:	$2,000–$10,000	$400–$10,000
Median:	$5,500	$7,500
Pct $ disb (env/total):	100	

Recipients (1992 highest):	Number:	Dollars:
Iowa Department of Natural Resources	2	15,000
State of Wisconsin, Department of Natural Resources	2	14,000
Benzie Fishery Coalition	1	10,000
City of Camdenton	1	10,000
Fairmont Lakes Foundation	1	10,000
Izaak Walton League of America	1	10,000
South Dakota Department of Game, Fish and Parks	1	10,000

Activity regions (1992 highest):	Number:	Dollars:
U.S. Great Lakes	11	78,445
U.S. Midwest	4	31,500
New York/New Jersey	4	24,335
U.S. Mountain	4	21,500
U.S. Mid-Atlantic	3	15,100

Sample grants (1992–93).
Benzie Fishery Coalition. Beulah, MI. $10,000. For continuation of a steelhead rearing program.
Cross Lake Association of Pine County. Pine City, MN. $4,800. For continuation of their walleye rearing program.
Down East Research, Conservation, and Development. Cherryfield, ME. $10,000. Support for the construction of an Atlantic salmon hatchery.
Inland Empire Fly Fishing Club/Spokane Fly Fishers. Spokane, WA. $400. Support for a wild rainbow and brook trout stream improvement project on Greers Ferry Lake.
Sullivan Trail Resource Conservation and Development Committee. Bath, NY. $8,035. For material for a stream bank stabilization project on Cohocton River.
Walleyes Unlimited of Washington. Des Moines, WA. $8,710. For equipment to aid in the continuation of a walleye spawning project in the Columbia River Basin.
Wisconsin Department of Natural Resources. Fitchburg, WI. $6,000. For materials for a trout stream habitat improvement project on Black Earth Creek.

Application process. *Initial contact:* Full proposal to include:
1. Complete budget for project, itemized by cost for equipment (purchase or rental), materials, and services. Indicate portion to which FAF grant monies will be applied.
2. Information about other possible sources of funding support.
3. Brief letter (on organization letterhead if available) containing: legal name; evidence of need for project or activity and benefits expected; history of any previous requests for support from the FishAmerica Foundation; description of purpose for which grant is sought, and specific details on how objectives are to be obtained.
4. If not a government agency, copy of IRS tax-exempt status determination letter.
5. Letter of approval from appropriate governmental agency(s) concerning the proposed project.

When to apply: Anytime.
Materials available: Annual report, brochure, information packet (includes "Criteria for Funding Grants" and application form); *Forum* (newsletter).

Emphases. *Recipients:* Nonprofit organizations, public agencies.
Activities: Citizen participation, collaborative efforts, fieldwork, innovative programs.
Types of support: Equipment, single-year grants only.
Geography: United States and Canada only.

Limitations. *Recipients:* Individuals.
Activities: Activism, advocacy, audiovisual materials, conferences, conflict resolution, exhibits, expeditions/tours, feasibility studies, fundraising, land acquisition, litigation, lobbying, net-working, planning, political activities, policy analysis/
development, research, seminars, symposia/colloquia, training, workshops.
Types of support: Advertising campaigns, annual campaigns, capital campaigns/expenses, debt retirement, endowments, fellowships, in-direct costs, internships, lectureships, loans, membership campaigns, mortgage reduction, multi-year grants, professorships, scholarships, travel expenses.

Flintridge Foundation

433 North Fair Oaks Avenue, Suite 200
Pasadena, California 91103
Tel: 818-449-6667   Fax: 818-585-0011
EIN: 953926331   Type: Independent
EGA member
Contact: Kelly Russell, Program Officer

History and philosophy. Founded in 1985, the Flintridge Foundation is the legacy of Francis and Louisa Moseley, who wanted to encourage people to seek new solutions to the complex problems of our rapidly changing society. Francis Moseley was a prolific inventor who worked on aerial navigation, electro-mechanical measuring instruments, and control mechanisms. He founded two manufacturing companies in California in graphic recording and machine tool control systems. Louisa Moseley was an artist whose paintings and sculptures were often exhibited in Southern California.

"The Flintridge Foundation intends to award grants that will help us understand our universe and preserve our biological and cultural heritage. It seeks energetic nonprofit organizations committed to similar goals and whose work reveals imagination, dedication, and clear focus on the problems they address." It currently awards grants in the areas of conservation and fine arts.

Officers and directors. *Officers:* Alexander Moseley, President; Ann Morris, Vice President; David Moseley, Secretary; Michael Addison, Treasurer. *Directors:* Michael Addison, Susan Addison, Armando Gonzalez, Judith Johnson, Ann Morris, Alexander Moseley, David Moseley, Jacqueline Moseley, Sarah Moseley.

Financial data. Data for fiscal year ended December 31, 1993.
Assets: $20,823,000 (C). *Total grants disbursed:* $772,618.

Environmental awards. *Program and interests:* The Flintridge Foundation is strongly committed to the preservation and restoration of native ecosystems. Conservation efforts include land acquisition, preservation of biodiversity, and science-based ecosystem restoration projects.

The Foundation's focus for 1994-96 is on preserving and restoring native ecosystems in the Pacific Northwest, primarily Oregon and Washington. Efforts of particular interest are:

- Preserving rivers, forests, and wetlands.
- Acquiring and protecting critical ecosystem components.
- Sustaining natural resources.

Recent grants: 1993 grants included support for ecosystem protection including land and habitat conservation, watershed preservation (in-stream issues, water use management, fisheries restoration), and forest issues.

Issues.   Cli   Bio   Lan   Agr   Wat   Oce   Ene   Was   Tox   Pop   Dev
               •   •   •   •

Funding analysis.

Fiscal year:	1991	1993
Env grants auth:	$97,950	$126,000
Number:	3	12
Range:	$27,950–$40,000	$1,000–$30,000
Median:	$30,000	$5,000
Pct $ disb (env/total):	30	44

Recipients (1993 highest):	Number:	Dollars:
Washington Environmental Council	1	30,000
Nature Center Associates of Los Angeles County	1	20,000
Pacific Rivers Council	1	20,000
Oregon Environmental Council	1	15,000
WaterWatch of Oregon	2	15,000

Activity regions (1993):	Number:	Dollars:
U.S. Northwest	9	100,000
U.S. West	2	25,000
U.S. not specified	1	1,000

Sample grants (1993).*

Ecotrust. Portland, OR. $50,000 (2 years). For the Clayoquot Sound Ecosystem Program.

Forest Conservation Council. Portland, OR. $10,000. For general operating expenses for the Portland office: State & Private Forestry Program.

Friends of the Earth, Northwest Office. Seattle, WA. $45,000 (2 years). For the Elway River Restoration Project.

Headwaters Community Association. Ashland, OR. $30,000. For Watershed Monitoring and Conservation Program; salary support for program aide.

Inland Empire Public Lands Council. Spokane, WA. $23,000 (2 years). For the Forest Watch Program.

Oregon Environmental Council. Portland, OR. $15,000. For the Water Conservation Project.

Oregon Trout. Portland, OR. $50,500 (2 years). Salary support for resource conservation associate.

Pacific Rivers Council. Eugene, OR. $45,000. For the Pacific Northwest Watershed Restoration Initiative and for the Pacific Northwest Salmonid Prioritization and Ecosystem Recovery Project.

WaterWatch of Oregon. Portland, OR. $30,000. For the Streamflow Restoration Program, Grants Pass Irrigation Project, and general operating expenses.

© 1995 Environmental Data Resources, Inc.

F

Wild Olympic Salmon. Chimacum, WA. $5,000. For general operating expenses.

*Sample grants represent either new awards or disbursements on grants awarded in previous years.

Application process. *Initial contact:* Call or write to request guidelines.
When to apply: Anytime.
Materials available: Annual report (includes "Grantmaking Procedures" and "Application Procedures").

Emphases. *Recipients:* Nonprofit organizations.
Activities: Capacity building, citizen participation, collaborative efforts, education, fieldwork, land acquisition, policy analysis/development, training, workshops.
Types of support: Continuing support, operating costs, projects.
Geography: Oregon, Washington.

Limitations. *Recipients:* Individuals.
Activities: Audiovisual materials, litigation, lobbying, media projects, political activities.
Types of support: Advertising campaigns, capital campaigns/expenses, debt retirement, endowments, facilities, funding for more than three years, loans, mortgage reduction, program-related investments.

Ford Foundation
320 East 43rd Street
New York, New York 10017
Tel: 212-573-4814   Fax: 212-490-7168
EIN: 131684331   Type: Independent
EGA member
Contacts: Janet Maughan, Program Officer
             E. Walter Coward, Director,
                Rural Poverty and Resources Program
             Frances Korten, Program Officer,
                Water and Forest Resources
             Anthony Romero, Environmental Justice

History and philosophy. Henry Ford, founder of the Ford Motor Company, created the Foundation in 1936 with his son Edsel. Until 1950 Foundation grants went largely to Michigan charitable institutions. Between 1943 and 1973 the Foundation became a major national and international donor under the direction of Henry Ford II. It no longer has ties to either the Ford family or Ford Motor Company.

The Foundation seeks to identify and contribute to the solution of problems of national or international importance. It works mainly by granting funds to institutions and organizations for experimental, demonstration, and developmental efforts that promise significant advances in a wide variety of fields. Major program areas are: Urban Poverty, Rural Poverty and Resources, Rights and Social Justice, Governance and Public Policy, Education and Culture, International Affairs, Reproductive Health and Population, and Media Projects.

Officers and directors. *Officers:* Henry B. Schacht, Chairman; Franklin A. Thomas, President; Susan V. Berresford, Vice President, Program Division; Linda B. Strumpf, Vice President and CIO; Barron M. Tenny, Vice President, Secretary, and General Counsel. *Directors:* Frances D. Fergusson, Kathryn S. Fuller, Robert D. Haas, Sir Christopher Hogg, Vernon E. Jordan, Jr., David T. Kearns, Wilma P. Mankiller, Luis G. Nogales, General Olusegun Obasanjo, Barbara Scott Preiskel, Dorothy S. Ridings, Monkombu S. Swaminathan, Ratan N. Tata, Thomas H. Wyman.

Financial data. Data for fiscal year ended September 30, 1993. *Assets:* $6,938,849,000 (M). *Total grants authorized:* $285,780,000.

Environmental awards. *Program and interests:* The Foundation does not have an environmental program as such, but rather a resource management program. It makes most of its environmental awards within the Rural Poverty and Resources Program, set up in the early 1950s to improve the welfare and opportunities of the rural poor. Initially targeting developing countries, the Program has included the United States since 1982. The general thrust of the Program is to address the relationship between resource management and the welfare of disadvantaged peoples.

Two premises underlie the Foundation's environment and development grantmaking: (1) the proposition that strengthening the economy and conserving the environment are interdependent goals; (2) the growing recognition that public bureaucracies managing natural resources such as forests and water must become more accountable to a broad constituency.

Within the United States, specific environmental foci include:

- Water.

    Water rights and equitable allocation.

- Forest resources.

    Enhanced income and employment potential through sustainable forestry in areas of persistent poverty (particularly northern New Mexico, Appalachia, the Deep South, and the U.S.-Mexico border region).

- Sustainable development in rural communities.

Overseas, interests include:

- Sustainable agriculture.

    Enhancement of agricultural productivity and more equitable and sustainable practices.

- Social forestry.

    Innovative programs that involve rural communities and forestry agencies in joint projects to improve management of public forest lands while creating economic opportunities for poor rural households.

- Sustainable development.

    Programs designed to find ways to reconcile environmental concerns with economic activities.

Other interests:

- Helping organizations shift their focus from environmental protection alone.

- Social justice.

Issues. *Cli Bio Lan Agr Wat Oce Ene Was Tox Pop Dev*
              •   •   •   •   •   •   •   •   •   •   •

Funding analysis.

Fiscal year:	1992	1993
Env grants auth:	$12,400,328	$14,084,477
Number:	114	110
Range:	$3,700–$600,000	$5,000–$775,000
Median:	$66,375	$100,000
Pct $ auth (env/total):	5	5

Recipients (1993 highest):	Number:	Dollars:
International Irrigation Management Institute	2	980,700
New Hampshire Charitable Fund	2	800,000
Latin American Scholarship Program of American Universities	1	740,000
Environmental Defense Fund	2	550,000
Western Governors' Association	2	500,000

Activity regions (1993 highest):	Number:	Dollars:
Indian Subcontinent and Indian Ocean Islands	26	2,593,220
Mexico and Central America	7	1,443,000
U.S. not specified	5	1,080,012
Eastern and Southern Africa	7	1,058,446
International*	5	975,000

*Multiple regions or not specified.

Sample grants (1993).
Agency for Integrated Development–Bangladesh. Dhaka, Bangladesh. $75,000. To support a project providing alternative employment in exchange for protection and conservation of the Sundarban Forest.
Environmental and Energy Study Institute. Washington, DC. $200,000. Support to improve federal policies and programs in western water conservation and management.
Institute for Policy Studies. Washington, DC. $50,000. Exchange with environment and development groups working on the U.S.-Mexico border.
National Wildlife Federation. Washington, DC. $250,000. Support for research and policy analysis on international trade and the environment.
New Hampshire Charitable Fund. Concord, NH. $25,000. To promote dialogue and communication on environment vs. economy conflicts in rural New England.
Pacific Rivers Council. Eugene, OR. $100,000. Support for its initiative to restore rural communities and watershed in the Pacific Northwest.
Pratt Institute, Center for Community and Environmental Development. Brooklyn, NY. $135,000. For exchange of community development practitioners in Chile and the United States.

Application process. *Initial contact:* Brief letter of inquiry. Full proposal, if invited, to include:
1. Objectives.
2. The proposed program for pursuing objectives.
3. Qualifications of persons engaged in the work.
4. Detailed budget.
5. Present means of support and status of applications to other funding sources.
6. Legal and tax status.

Grants to individuals are mainly limited to research, training, and other activities related to the Foundation's program interests. The Foundation does not award grants for programs for which substantial support from government or other sources is readily available.
When to apply: Anytime. Applications are considered throughout the year.
Materials available: Annual report (includes "Application Guidelines"), "Current Interests of the Ford Foundation" (booklet), *Report* (quarterly).

Emphases. *Recipients:* Individuals, nonprofit organizations.
Types of support: Program-related investments.
Geography: United States; developing countries.

Limitations. *Types of support:* Endowments, operating costs.

Ford Motor Company Fund
The American Road
P.O. Box 1899
Dearborn, Michigan 48121–1899
Tel: 313–845–8711   Fax: 313–323–2683
EIN: 381459376   Type: Company-sponsored
Contact: Leo J. Brennan, Jr., Executive Director

History and philosophy. Incorporated in 1949, the Ford Motor Company Fund is supported primarily by contributions from the Ford Motor Company. Grant activity is concentrated in communities of interest to the Company. Within these communities, a major portion of funding supports cultural organizations, economic education, educational institutions, social welfare, urban affairs, the United Way, and youth programs. In 1991, education received about half of all grant dollars through direct grants to educational institutions, matching funds for employees' contributions to colleges and universities, and student loans for children of employees. The Fund has six program areas: Arts and Humanities, Civic Activities and Public Policy, Education, Health and Welfare, U.S./International Relations, and Other.

Officers and directors. *Officers:* Harold A. Poling, President; Frank V. J. Darin, Vice President; John M. Rintamaki, Assistant Secretary; Dennis A. Tosh, Assistant Treasurer. *Trustees:* Alfred B. Ford, Allan D. Gilmour, Sheila F. Hamp, John W. Martin, Jr., David N. McCammon, Peter J. Pestillo, David W. Scott, Stanley A. Seneker, Alexander J. Trotman.

Financial data. Data for fiscal year ended December 31, 1993. *Assets:* $8,954,670 (M). *Gifts received:* $32,096. *Total grants disbursed:* $16,804,535.

Environmental awards. *Recent grants:* 1993 grants included support for beautification, parks, botanical gardens and zoos, wildlife conservation, energy research and education, Superfund cleanup, marine issues, and environmental expeditions.

Issues.   Cli   Bio   Lan   Agr   Wat   Oce   Ene   Was   Tox   Pop   Dev
             •   •   •   •   •   •   •

F

Funding analysis.

Fiscal year:	1991	1992
Env grants disb:	$324,875	$307,025
Number:	31	29
Range:	$200–$64,000	$500–$60,000
Median:	$2,500	$5,000
Pct $ disb (env/total):	2	2

Recipients (1992 highest):	Number:	Dollars:
Clean Sites, Inc.	1	60,000
Environmental Law Institute	2	40,000
National Park Foundation	1	31,725
Chicago Childrens Museum	1	25,000
Resources for the Future	1	25,000
The Environmental Careers Organization, Inc.	1	25,000

Activity regions (1992):	Number:	Dollars:
U.S. not specified	14	229,725
U.S. Great Lakes	8	47,050
International*	4	23,500
U.S. Southeast	2	6,000
U.S. Midwest	1	750

*Multiple regions or not specified.

Sample grants (1993).
Clean Sites, Inc. Alexandria, VA. $60,000.
Detroit Zoological Society. Royal Oak, MI. $2,500.
Environmental Education Foundation of Florida, Inc. Tallahassee, FL. $500.
Garden Center of Greater Cleveland. Cleveland, OH. $400.
Keep America Beautiful, Inc. New York, NY. $2,500
Keep America Beautiful, Inc. Farmington, MI. $500.
The Nature Conservancy, Michigan Field Office. East Lansing, MI. $10,000.
Resources for the Future. Washington, DC. $25,000.
Seven Ponds Endowment Fund. Dryden, MI. $1,000.
Toledo Zoological Society. Toledo, OH. $1,500.
World Wildlife Fund. Washington, DC. $10,000.

Application process. *Initial contact:* There is no application form except for the Ford Matching Gift Program to Advance Education and the Ford Fund Student Loan Program. For all other requests, submit a brief narrative. If the Fund is interested, it will request further information.
When to apply: Anytime. The board meets in April and October.
Materials available: Annual report, application guidelines, informational brochure.

Emphases. *Recipients:* Aquariums, educational institutions, museums, nonprofit organizations, zoos.
Activities: Conferences, education, exhibits, volunteerism.
Types of support: Annual campaigns, capital campaigns/expenses, facilities, lectureships, matching gifts (colleges only), scholarships (relatives of employees only).
Geography: Detroit, Michigan.

Limitations. *Recipients:* Individuals.
Types of support: Scholarships.

Walter and Josephine Ford Fund

100 Renaissance Center, 34th Floor
Detroit, Michigan 48243
Tel: 313-259-7777   Fax: 313-393-7579
EIN: 38606634   Type: Independent
Contact: Pierre V. Heftler, Secretary

History and philosophy. Walter B. Ford II and Josephine F. Ford established the Fund in 1951. Josephine F. Ford is the granddaughter of Henry Ford and daughter of Eleanor and Edsel Ford. Walter B. Ford II came from an unrelated Ford family, one of Detroit bankers. Funding areas are: arts, churches and religious organizations; community chests and other related organizations; hospitals and medical research; schools and educational; and miscellaneous.

Officers and directors. *Officers:* Josephine F. Ford, President; Pierre V. Heftler, Secretary; Richard M. Cundiff, Treasurer; George A. Straitor, Assistant Treasurer. *Trustees:* Josephine F. Ford, Pierre V. Heftler.

Financial data. Data for fiscal year ended December 31, 1993. *Assets:* $6,899,864 (M). *Gifts received:* $125,139. *Total grants disbursed:* $999,011.

Environmental awards. *Recent grants:* 1993 grants included support for forests, wildlife conservation, coastal issues, urban environment, and a zoo.

Issues.   Cli   Bio•   Lan•   Agr   Wat•   Oce•   Ene   Was   Tox   Pop•   Dev•

Funding analysis.

Fiscal year:	1991	1993
Env grants disb:	$57,650	$187,000
Number:	11	10
Range:	$50–$50,000	$500–$80,500
Median:	$500	$3,500
Pct $ disb (env/total):	10	19

Recipients (1993 highest):	Number:	Dollars:
Friends of Acadia	1	80,500
Maine Coast Heritage Trust	1	50,000
Tall Timbers Research Stations	1	38,000
The Greening of Detroit	1	7,000
Friends of the Everglades	1	5,000

Activity regions (1993):	Number:	Dollars:
U.S. Northeast	5	135,500
U.S. Southeast	2	43,000
U.S. Great Lakes	3	8,500

Sample grants (1993).
Detroit Zoological Society. Royal Oak, MI. $1,000.
Friends of Acadia. Bar Harbor, ME. $80,500.
Friends of the Everglades. Coconut Grove, FL. $5,000.
The Greening of Detroit. Detroit, MI. $7,000.
Island Institute. Rockland, ME. $1,000.
Maine Coast Heritage Trust. Brunswick, ME. $50,000.
Maine Seal. Lincoln, MA. $2,000.

Natural Resources Council of Maine. Augusta, ME. $2,000.
Tall Timbers Research Stations. Tallahassee, FL. $38,000.
The Wildlife Conservation Fund of America. Columbus, OH. $500.

Application process. *Initial contact:* Brief letter of intent accompanied by financial statement and copy of IRS tax-exempt status determination letter.
When to apply: Anytime.

Emphases. *Recipients:* Pre-selected organizations (usually).
Geography: Detroit, Michigan; New York, Maine.

Limitations. *Recipients:* Individuals.

Foundation for the Carolinas

1043 East Morehead Street, Suite 100
Charlotte, North Carolina 28204
Tel: 704–376–9541   Fax: 704–376–1243
EIN: 566047886   Type: Community
Contact: William L. Spencer, President

Application address:
P.O. Box 34769
Charlotte, North Carolina 28234–4769

History and philosophy. Established in 1958, Foundation for the Carolinas' mission is to better the communities it serves in the Central Piedmont area of the Carolinas. To accomplish this, it advocates philanthropy; assists donors, individuals, groups, and businesses in setting up funds; provides stewardship; builds permanent charitable resources; and makes grants to a wide range of community projects and interests. The Foundation aspires to be "the focal point for building and prudently managing permanent charitable capital in the communities it serves; a provider of quality philanthropic services to donors of all means; an ethical and representative organization; a catalyst for addressing community needs through creative grantmaking and other services that support philanthropy."

The Foundation has eight program areas: Education, Human Services, Religion, Health & Medical Research, Arts, Environment & Historical Preservation, Youth, and Senior Programs.

Officers and directors. *Officers:* Robin L. Hinson, Chairman; James R. Nisbet, First Vice Chairman; Edwin L. Jones, Jr., Vice Chairman; William L. Spencer, President; Marilyn M. Bradbury, Vice President/Assistant Secretary; James W. Thompson, Secretary; A. Zachary Smith III, Treasurer; Lawrence M. Kimbrough, Assistant Secretary. *Executive Committee:* Gordon Berg, Marilyn M. Bradbury, Larry J. Dagenhart, Charles T. Davidson, Thomas P. Dillon, Frank E. Emory Jr., Deborah S. Harris, Robin L. Hinson, F. Kenneth Iverson, Edwin L. Jones Jr., Lawrence M. Kimbrough, James R. Nisbet, A. Zachary Smith III, William L. Spencer, James W. Thompson.

Financial data. Data for fiscal year ended December 31, 1993. *Assets:* $74,575,499 (M). *Gifts received:* $12,324,737. *Total grants authorized:* $7,922,575.

Environmental awards. *Recent grants:* 1993 awards included support for land conservation and wildlife protection in North and South Carolina.

Issues.   Cli   Bio   Lan   Agr   Wat   Oce   Ene   Was   Tox   Pop   Dev
              •   •   •   •

Funding analysis.§

Fiscal year:	1991	1993
Env grants auth:	$96,600	$89,579
Number:	24	4
Range:	$2,500–$30,000	$5,000–$71,000
Median:	$6,000	$6,790
Pct $ auth (env/total):	–	1

Recipients (1993):	Number:	Dollars:
Sierra Club Foundation	1	71,000
Wing Haven Foundation	1	8,250
Southern Appalachian Highlands Conservancy	1	5,329
Clean Water Fund of North Carolina, Inc.	1	5,000

Activity region (1993):	Number:	Dollars:
U.S. Southeast	4	89,579

§Includes designated donor-advised, field-of-interest, and unrestricted grants.

Sample grants (1993).
Clean Water Fund of North Carolina, Inc. Asheville, NC. $5,000.
Sierra Club Foundation. San Francisco, CA. $71,000.
Southern Appalachian Highlands Conservancy. Asheville, NC. $5,329.
Wing Haven Foundation. Charlotte, NC. $8,250.

Application process. *Initial contact:* Proposal completed and signed by the applicant organization's board chairman or CEO. Attachments.
1. Cover letter (2 pages).
   • Project objectives and background.
   • Demonstrated need for project.
   • Specific plans and timetable for project.
   • Organization's current and long-term funding plans.
   • Qualifications of organization and project personnel.
2. Overall budget for organization; project budget. Show both sources of income and expenditures.
3. List of current board of directors.
4. Copy of IRS tax-exempt status determination letter.
5. One copy of applicant's most recent audit.

Priority is given to seed grants for both new and established organizations. In general, volunteer leadership and/or grassroots participation in program development are required. Foundation grants rarely exceed $5,000.
When to apply: Deadlines are February 1, June 1, and October 1. The board meets quarterly; the distribution committee, monthly.
Materials available: Annual report (includes "Special Project Grant Guidelines").

Emphases. *Recipients:* Nonprofit organizations.
Activities: Citizen participation, volunteerism.

Types of support: Matching funds, scholarships, seed money, single-year grants only.
Geography: North Carolina and South Carolina only, particularly the Central Piedmont area.

Limitations. *Recipients:* Individuals.
Activities: Conferences, media projects, publications.
Types of support: Capital campaigns/expenses, debt retirement, endowments, equipment, facilities, operating costs, publications, travel expenses.

Foundation for Deep Ecology
950 Lombard Street
San Francisco, California 94133
Tel: 415-771-1102   Fax: 415-771-1121
EIN: 943106115   Type: Independent
EGA member
Contact: Ms. Quincey Imhoff, Executive Director

History and philosophy. Deep ecology is a philosophy that rejects the notion of the world as a resource for human use, emphasizing instead the importance of natural systems and the capacities of the planet for self-renewal.

The Foundation for Deep Ecology is a new foundation, established to address the belief that "life on Earth has entered its most precarious phase in history," wherein there are threats to virtually all species of plants and animals as well as to the health and continued viability of the biosphere. The Foundation focuses on several issues which it regards as the root causes of this situation: the assumption of human superiority, overpopulation, the prevailing growth ethic of Western society, the worship of technology, the loss of appreciation for the natural world, domination of the technocratic-industrial world, concentration of power in an industrial elite, and the suppression of alternate views. It intends to fund programs that further articulate these root causes, that take action to reverse present trends, and that purchase threatened lands for permanent protection.

Officers and directors. *Directors:* Doug Tompkins, President; Debbie Sembler, Secretary/Treasurer.

Financial data. Data for fiscal year ended November 30, 1993.
Assets: $40,259,005 (M). *Total grants disbursed:* $2,164,996.

Environmental awards. *Program and interests:* The Foundation's program continues to develop. Areas of interest are:

- Forests and habitats.

    Campaigns to explore the ethics of economic growth, exploitation of resources and market-based economic systems. Activism to stop resource destruction.

- Traditional native communities.

    Support for efforts to maintain and disseminate their culture and philosophy.

- Education about the international spread of the Western technological ethic. Criticism and the development of alternative philosophical and practical frameworks.

- Expression of deep ecological principles.

    Support for writers, thinkers, grassroots activists, and those who provide a model for others to follow.

- International trade.

    Exploring the implications of free trade and its effects on the environment.

Issues.   Cli Bio Lan Agr Wat Oce Ene Was Tox Pop Dev
               •   •   •   •   •   •   •   •   •   •

Funding analysis.

Fiscal year:	1991	1992
Env grants disb:	$1,687,422	$3,109,891
Number:	66	199
Range:	$757–$100,000	$350–$100,000
Median:	–	$10,000
Pct $ disb (env/total):	100	100

Recipients (1992 highest):	Number:	Dollars:
Public Media Center	5	279,500
Foundation on Economic Trends	2	200,000
Consumers Association of Penang	3	165,000
Earth Island Institute	4	130,000
Greenhouse Crisis Foundation	2	115,000

Activity regions (1992 highest):	Number:	Dollars:
U.S. not specified	37	778,000
U.S. West	46	739,850
Andean Region and Southern Cone	13	247,000
U.S. Northwest	13	205,200
International*	11	165,500

*Multiple regions or not specified.

Sample grants (1992).
CEPAUR. Santiago, Chile. $28,000. Environmental awareness.
Earth Island Institute. San Francisco, CA. $100,000.
Earth Trust Foundation. Malibu, CA. $34,000.
Elmwood Institute. Berkeley, CA. $50,000.
International Society for Ecology. Berkeley, CA. $50,000.
The Land Institute. Salina, KS. $30,000.
LightHawk. Sante Fe, NM. $40,000.
Manitou Manitoba Foundation. Pine Falls, Manitoba. $20,000.
    Funding assistance for the Mother Earth Spiritual Camp.
Rainforest Action Network. San Francisco, CA. $50,000.
Rogue Institute for Ecology and Economy. Portland, OR. $75,000.
    For the ecoforestry institute.
Save America's Forests, Inc. Washington, DC. $20,000.
Western Ancient Forest Campaign. Portland, OR. $20,000.

Application process. *Initial contact:* Proposal to include:
1. Cover sheet (supplied by Foundation).
2. Copy of IRS tax-exempt status determination letter or equivalent.
3. Executive summary (1 page).
4. Organizational budget and projects budget.

The Foundation requests that you "Do not tailor the descriptions of programs but simply articulate what you are doing, why, and what you hope to achieve; also provide biographies of principals. Any form of application is acceptable including letters, tapes, proposals, and copies of previously written proposals to other foundations. Brevity is valued."

When to apply: Anytime.
Materials available: Foundation statement, cover sheet.

Emphases. *Recipients:* Individuals, nonprofit organizations.
Activities: Activism, advocacy, collaborative efforts, demonstration programs, innovative programs, litigation.
Types of support: Advertising campaigns, continuing support, general purposes, matching funds, membership campaigns, multi-year grants, pilot projects, projects.

Limitations. *Recipients:* Aquariums, botanical gardens, museums, religious organizations, research institutions, zoos.
Activities: Audiovisual materials, lobbying, research.
Types of support: Capital campaigns/expenses, debt retirement, emergency funding, mortgage reduction, scholarships.

Foundation for Field Research

P.O. Box 910078
San Diego, California 92191–0078
Tel: 619–687–3584   Fax: 619–452–6708
Contact: Thomas J. Banks, Director

History and philosophy. The Foundation for Field Research is a nonprofit organization founded in 1982 "to develop and select field research projects that can be assisted by non-specialist volunteers. The Foundation's goal is to unite researchers' needs with public support, and to strengthen mutual understanding through cooperative expeditions."

Officers and directors. *Officers:* Ramon Perez-Gil, President; Alexander Peal, Secretary/Treasurer. *Directors:* Thomas J. Banks, Andrew Bierzynski, Alexander Peal, Ramon Perez-Gil, Elvira Gonzalez de la Vega.

Financial data. Data for fiscal year ended December 31, 1990. *Assets:* $53,000 (U). *Gifts received:* $700,000 (est.) *Total grants disbursed:* $495,000.

Environmental awards. *Program and interests:* The Foundation's focus is on:

- Wildlife conservation.
- Habitat conservation.
- Archaeological salvage/conservation of selected sites.

Current projects are limited to the West Indies.

Issues.   Cli   Bio   Lan   Agr   Wat   Oce   Ene   Was   Tox   Pop   Dev

Funding analysis.§

Fiscal year:	1990
Env grants disb:	$495,000
Number:	–
Range:	$2,500–$15,000
Median:	–
Pct $ disb (env/total):	100

§As reported by Foundation.

Sample grant (1993).
Solar Ovens For Granada. Granada, W.I. Expeditions staffed by volunteers to help build solar ovens and teach Grenadians how to use them as an alternative to charcoal, in an effort to save the island's tropical vegetation.

Application process. *Initial contact:* Full proposal (4 copies) to include:

1. Title page, submission date, researcher's addresses, work telephone, facsimile, and home telephone.
2. Description and map of research area and/or site.
3. Background and significance of research.
4. Research objectives.
5. Specific plans for use of volunteers.
6. Curriculum vitae of applicant.
7. Itemized budget listing expendable supplies and estimated travel costs for principal investigator from home to site and return. Do not include logistical costs.
8. Past permit or letter indicating how permit is to be obtained and list of requirements to obtain permit.
9. List of three references (name, address, and telephone) competent to evaluate the project.

Appendixes.

1. Portrait photograph of researcher smiling.
2. Assorted photographs (black and white or sharp focus color) of people working on your project or a similar project.
3. Background reading: photocopies of two or three articles that will help the volunteer understand the project or get a feel for the type of research you are doing.

When to apply: Deadlines are country-specific; proposals are accepted at any time. In general, projects must be proposed fourteen months before fieldwork begins.
Materials available: "Grant Guidelines," *Explorer News* (newsletter).

Emphases. *Activities:* Expeditions/tours, fieldwork, research (scientific), volunteerism.
Types of support: Continuing support, fellowships, multi-year grants, operating costs, pilot projects, scholarships.
Geography: West Indies only.

Limitations. *Activities:* Seminars, symposia/colloquia.
Types of support: Endowments, lectureships, professorships, program-related investments.

The Foundation for the National Capital Region

1002 Wisconsin Avenue, N.W.
Washington, DC 20007
Tel: 202–338–8993   Fax: 202–337–6754
EIN: 237343119   Type: Community
Contact: Sylvana R. Straw, Program Officer

History and philosophy. The Foundation was established in 1973. The mission of the Foundation for the National Capital Region is to build philanthropic capital dedicated to improving the region's quality of life; to strengthen the region's nonprofit organizations and to improve their financial stability; and to fund projects offering new solutions to community needs.

Operating principles are: building financial, human and organizational resources; bridging groups, people and communities; enabling and facilitating others; encouraging models of inclusion and participation; and responding to changing community needs.

Program areas are: Arts, Culture, and Humanities; Conservation and Animal Welfare; Education; Family Literacy; Health; Human Services; Public/Society Benefit; and Other.

Officers and directors. *Officers:* R. Robert Linowes, Chair; Victoria P. Sant, Vice Chair; John D. Hawke, Jr., Secretary; William Harris, Treasurer; Thomas A. Troyer, General Counsel. *Trustees:* Stewart W. Bainum, John J. Barry, Diane Bernstein, Katharine Graham, Michele V. Hagans, Shirley Robinson Hall, John T. Hazel, Jr., Gov. Linwood Holton, Lawrence A. Hough, Ann D. Jordan, M. Charito Kruvant, Joan Maxwell, Ann McLaughlin, A. G. Newmyer, III, Elijah B. Rogers, Joshua I. Smith, Kenneth R. Thorton, Ladislaus von Hoffmann.

Financial data.* Data for fiscal year ended March 31, 1994. *Assets:* $38,000,000 (M) (est.). *Total grants disbursed:* $5,440,000 (est.).

*As reported by Foundation.

Environmental awards. *Program and interests:* The Foundation makes environmental grants in three ways:

- Conservation and Animal Welfare grants support organizations and projects of national and international scope.

In addition, there are two named funds designated for environmental purposes.

- The Bethesda Ever Green Project Fund "awards grants to involve and coordinate the citizens of Bethesda, Maryland, in the development of ecological enhancement projects within their community."
- The Environmentor's Fund "provides for the operations of the Environmentor's Project, which motivates high school students to develop community service projects that will benefit the environment."

Recent grants: 1993 grants included support for energy efficiency and wildlife preservation.

Issues. Cli • Bio • Lan Agr • Wat Oce • Ene Was • Tox Pop Dev

Funding analysis.

Fiscal year:	1993
Env grants disb:	$330,200
Number:	23
Range:	$500–$251,100
Median:	$1,100
Pct $ disb (env/total):	9

Recipients (1993 highest):	Number:	Dollars:
World Wildlife Fund	1	251,100
World Resources Institute	1	15,000
The Aspen Institute	1	11,750
Environmental and Energy Study Institute	1	10,000
INFORM	1	10,000
Piedmont Environmental Council	1	10,000

Activity regions (1993):	Number:	Dollars:
International*	6	270,400
U.S. not specified	9	42,350
U.S. Mid-Atlantic	6	15,850
Africa	1	1,100
U.S. Northeast	1	500

*Multiple regions or not specified.

Sample grants (1993).
African Wildlife Foundation. Washington, DC. $1,100.
Conservation International. Washington, DC. $1,000.
Environmental and Energy Study Institute. Washington, DC. $10,000.
Friends of the National Arboretum. Washington, DC. $2,000.
Garden Resources of Washington. Washington, DC. $500.
INFORM. New York, NY. $10,000.
National Audubon Society Productions. Washington, DC. $2,000.
Piedmont Environmental Council. Warrenton, VA. $10,000.
Prince George's County Parks and Recreation Foundation. Bowie, MD. $1,250.
Rocky Mountain Institute. Snowmass, CO. $1,000.
Squam Lakes Association. Holderness, NH. $500.
Wildlife Preservation Trust International. Philadelphia, PA. $1,100.
World Wildlife Fund. Washington, DC. $250,100.

Application process. *Initial contact:* Brief letter of intent. Full proposal, if requested, to include:
Washington Regional Association of Grantmakers' Common Grant Application.
Cover sheet (2 pages) to include, in this order:
1. Name and address of organization.
2. Contact person.
3. Phone and fax numbers.
4. One paragraph summary of organization's purpose and activities.
5. One paragraph proposal summary.
6. Relationship of proposal to organization's mission statement.
7. Total annual organizational budget and fiscal year.
8. Total project budget.
9. Dollar amount requested.
10. Previous support from this funder.
11. Grant period.

Narrative (10 double-spaced pages).
1. Organization information.
    - Brief summary of organization's history.
    - Brief statement of organization's mission and goals.
    - Description of current programs, activities, and accomplishments.
    - Overview of organizational structure, including board, staff, and volunteer involvement.
2. Purpose of the grant.
    - Statement of need/problems to be addressed; description of target population and how they will benefit.
    - Description of measurable project goals and objectives and statement as to whether this is a new or ongoing part of sponsoring organization.
    - Plans to accomplish goals and objectives.
    - Timetable for implementation, if applicable.
    - Other organizations participating in project and their roles.

- List of names, qualifications (or resume), and job description of key staff and/or volunteers responsible for the project.
- Long-term strategies for funding of this project at end of grant period.
- Project budget; use project budget format that follows.
3. Evaluation.
    - Plans for evaluation including how success will be defined and measured.
    - How evaluation results will be used and/or disseminated and, if appropriate, replicated.

Attachments.
1. Copy of IRS tax-exempt status determination letter. If not available, an explanation of application status.
2. Board of directors.
    - Description of board responsibilities.
    - List of board members with occupations, places of employment, and related community affiliations.
    - Criteria for board selection.
3. Finances.
    - Organization's previous and current annual operating budget, including expenses and revenue; indicate which sources of revenue have been received.
    - Most recent annual financial statement (audited, if available).
    - List and amounts requested of other foundations.
    - Agency affiliation with federated funds or public agencies.
4. Letters of support (4 maximum).
5. Annual report, if available.
6. Current relevant articles or reviews about the organization's program, if available.

Project Budget Format.
1. Organizational fiscal year.
2. Time period this budget covers.
3. Expenses.
    - Salaries (specify number of full-time equivalents).
    - Payroll taxes.
    - Fringe benefits.
    - Consultants and professional fees.
    - Travel.
    - Equipment.
    - Supplies.
    - Printing and copying.
    - Telephone and fax.
    - Postage and delivery.
    - Rent.
    - Utilities.
    - Maintenance.
    - Evaluation.
    - Other (specify).
    - Total expenses.
4. Revenue.
    - Grants and contracts.
    - Earned income.
    - Membership income.
    - In-kind support.
    - Other (specify).
    - Total revenue.

When to apply: Deadlines for letter of intent are in January and July; for full proposal (if requested) in March and September for review at board meetings held in May and November. Contact Foundation for exact dates.
Materials available: Annual report, application guidelines.

Emphases. *Recipients:* Nonprofit organizations.
Activities: Capacity building, collaborative efforts, fundraising, training, volunteerism.
Types of support: Capital campaigns/expenses, continuing support, emergency funding, general purposes, loans, projects, seed money, technical assistance.
Geography: Washington, D.C. and environs only, with National Capital area the priority.

Limitations. *Recipients:* Individuals.
Types of support: Annual campaigns, endowments, equipment, facilities (renovation), fellowships, land acquisition, matching funds, operating costs, scholarships.

The Jacob and Annita France Foundation, Inc.
The Exchange
1122 Kenilworth Drive, Suite 118
Baltimore, Maryland 21204
Tel: 410–832–5700   Fax: 410–832–5704
EIN: 520794585   Type: Independent
Contact: Frederick W. Lafferty, Executive Director

History and philosophy. The Jacob and Annita France Foundation, Inc., was created in 1959 by Jacob France, a prominent Baltimore lawyer and banker. Most of its grants are awarded through four program areas: Civic and Cultural Activities, Education, Historic Preservation and Conservation, and Health and Social Services.

Officers and directors. *Officers:* Anne M. Pinkard, President; Walter D. Pinkard, Jr., Vice President and Treasurer; Robert M. Pinkard, Secretary; Donna Silbersack, Assistant Secretary. *Directors:* Redmond C. S. Finney, Robert J. Merrick III, Anne M. Pinkard, Robert M. Pinkard, Walter G. Pinkard, Jr., Vernon T. Pittinger.

Financial data. Data for fiscal year ended May 31, 1993. *Assets:* $69,105,325 (M). *Total grants disbursed:* $3,160,474.

Environmental awards. *Recent grants:* 1993 grants included support for coastal issues.

Issues.   Cli   Bio   Lan   Agr   Wat   Oce   Ene   Was   Tox   Pop   Dev
                                              •

Funding analysis.

Fiscal year:	1991	1993
Env grants disb:	$168,500	$561,714
Number:	3	5
Range:	$30,000–$77,500	$800–$385,664
Median:	$61,000	$28,000
Pct $ disb (env/total):	7	18

© 1995 Environmental Data Resources, Inc.

F

Recipients (1993):	Number:	Dollars:
Echo Hill Outdoor School	2	505,414
Chesapeake Bay Foundation	1	28,000
Alliance for the Chesapeake Bay	1	27,500
Irvine Natural Science Center	1	800

Activity region (1993):	Number:	Dollars:
U.S. Mid-Atlantic	5	561,714

Sample grants (1993).
Alliance for the Chesapeake Bay. Baltimore, MD. $27,500.
Chesapeake Bay Foundation. Annapolis, MD. $28,000.
Echo Hill Outdoor School. Worton, MD. $385,664. Bay Project.
Irvine Natural Science Center. Stevenson, MD. $800.

Application process. *Initial contact:* Proposal and cover letter. Proposal to include:
1. Project description.
2. Brief description of applicant organization, including history, function, and goals.
3. Amount of funding requested and time period.
4. Budget for proposed project.
5. Number of employees on organization's staff; names and brief description of professional backgrounds of organization's key staff members.
6. List of board of directors.
7. Brief description of major funding sources for proposed project, e.g., other foundations approached, funding already received, etc.
8. Copy of organization's latest audit.
9. Brief statement regarding criteria and methods for project evaluation.
10. Copy of IRS tax-exempt status determination letter.

If request is within Foundation's guidelines and interests and funds are available, an interview may follow.
When to apply: Anytime.
Materials available: "Guidelines for Applying for a Grant."

Emphases. *Recipients:* Nonprofit organizations.
Geography: Maryland.

Mary D. and Walter F. Frear Eleemosynary Trust

c/o Hawaiian Trust Company, Ltd.
P.O. Box 3170
Honolulu, Hawaii 96802
Tel: 808–538–4945   Fax: 808–538–4944
EIN: 996002270   Type: Independent
Contact: Lois C. Loomis, Vice President,
Hawaiian Trust Company, Ltd.

History and philosophy. Walter Francis Frear, the only person to serve as both governor and chief justice of Hawaii, founded the Trust in 1936. The present distribution committee supports projects in the fields of health and social welfare. Its particular interest is in preventive programs and those that encourage youth to be self-reliant and industrious, and to have civic and community interest. The committee also continues to support programs that interested Walter Frear's wife, Mary: education through scholarships, family planning, and cultural programs in art, drama, music, and beauty in nature.

Officers and directors. *Trustee:* Hawaiian Trust Company, Ltd. *Distribution Committee:* Sharon McPhee, Chairman; Howard Hamamoto, Thomas J. Macdonald.

Financial data. Data for fiscal year ended December 31, 1993. *Assets:* $12,955,022 (M). *Total grants disbursed:* $512,413.

Environmental awards. *Recent grants:* 1993 grants included support for plant conservation, marine wildlife protection, energy conservation, recycling, and public education.

Issues.   Cli   Bio   Lan   Agr   Wat   Oce   Ene   Was   Tox   Pop   Dev
                        •   •   •   •   •

Funding analysis.

Fiscal year:	1991	1992
Env grants disb:	$27,500	$27,000
Number:	6	7
Range:	$2,000–$7,500	$2,000–$7,500
Median:	$5,000	$3,000
Pct $ disb (env/total):	4	5

Recipients (1992 highest):	Number:	Dollars:
Natural Resources Defense Council	1	7,500
Waimea Arboretum Foundation	1	6,000
Hawaii Nature Center	1	3,500
Hawaii Tropical Botanical Garden	1	3,000
Campaign Recycle Maui	1	2,500
Earthtrust	1	2,500

Activity region (1992):	Number:	Dollars:
Hawaii	7	27,000

Sample grants (1993).
Earthtrust. Kailua, HI. $2,500. Education program on Hawaii's endangered marine wildlife.
Hawaii Nature Center. Honolulu, HI. $3,500. Tree house.
National Tropical Botanical Garden. Lawai, HI. $1,000. Hurricane recovery.
Natural Resources Defense Council. Honolulu, HI. $5,000. Internship program.

Application process. *Initial contact:* Letter (2–3 pages, 4 copies), signed by presiding officer of the board of directors, to include:
1. Brief description of applicant organization and its purposes.
2. Concise summary of proposed activity including a statement of need or problem, description of how activity is to be carried out, indication of population to be served, and a plan for evaluating its effectiveness.
3. Total project cost, amount requested from the Trust, other funding sources, and plans for future support.
4. Statement as to qualifications of personnel responsible for carrying out project.
5. Statement as to active participation of board members.
6. Name and telephone number of appropriate contact person.

Attachments.
1. Budget for both project and organization, showing projected income and expenditures.
2. List of governing board members and their professional or business affiliations.
3. Letters (3 or 4) endorsing the activity.

Appendixes (1 copy).
1. IRS tax-exempt status determination letter and a letter advising that the organization has public foundation status under 509(a).
2. Organization's charter and bylaws.
3. Organization's most recent annual report and audited financial statements.

When to apply: Deadlines are January 15, April 15, July 15, and October 15. Organizations seeking funds for tuition aid or scholarship programs should submit proposals by January 15, and proposals for a major capital campaign should be submitted by October 15. The distribution committee meets quarterly.

Materials available: Annual report (includes "Grant Application Procedure").

Emphases. *Recipients:* Educational institutions.
Activities: Education, innovative programs, training.
Types of support: Capital campaigns/expenses, computer hardware, equipment, facilities.
Geography: Hawaii only.

Limitations. *Recipients:* Individuals.
Types of support: Debt retirement, endowments, "reserve purposes," travel expenses.

The Freed Foundation, Inc.
3050 K Street, N.W., Suite 335
Washington, DC 20007
Tel: 202–337–5487
EIN: 526047591   Type: Independent
Contact: Lorraine Barnhart, Executive Director

History and philosophy. The Freed Foundation was established in 1954. Its "mission is to address a number of compelling causes with impact and efficiency. We believe that to create workable solutions that make sense economically, we must make grants to organizations that have innovative leaders and programs. To promote the health and welfare of our society, these leaders must, in turn, engage in creative partnerships with others." Current grants focus on environmental protection, mental health, and public education programs addressing AIDS, nutrition, and substance abuse.

Officers and directors. *Officers:* Elizabeth Ann Freed, President/Treasurer; Lloyd J. Derrickson, Secretary. *Directors:* Lloyd J. Derrickson, Elizabeth Ann Freed, Joan F. Kahn, Sherwood Monahan.

Financial data. Data for fiscal year ended May 31, 1993. *Assets:* $18,100,068 (M). *Gifts received:* $18,100,068. *Total grants disbursed:* $397,900.

Environmental awards. *Recent grants:* 1993 grants included support for land conservation, species protection, and coastal issues.

Issues. Cli • Bio • Lan Agr • Wat • Oce Ene Was Tox • Pop Dev

Funding analysis.

Fiscal year:	1993
Env grants disb:	$35,000
Number:	4
Range:	$5,000–$15,000
Median:	$7,500
Pct $ disb (env/total):	9

Recipients (1993):	*Number:*	*Dollars:*
New Jersey Conservation Foundation	1	15,000
Poricy Park	1	10,000
American Littoral Society	1	5,000
Pinelands Preservation Alliance, Inc.	1	5,000

Activity region (1993):	*Number:*	*Dollars:*
New York/New Jersey	4	35,000

Sample grants (1993).
American Littoral Society. Highlands, NJ. $5,000. New Jersey Coastline Project.
New Jersey Conservation Foundation. Morristown, NJ. $15,000. Songbird education project.
Pinelands Preservation Alliance, Inc. Browns Mills, NJ. $5,000. General support.
Poricy Park. Middletown, NJ. $10,000. Freshwater Marsh Education Project.

Application process. *Initial contact:* Letter to include:
1. Description of applicant organization.
2. Need to be met.

Attachments.
1. Budget.
2. Proof of tax-exempt status.
3. Audited financial statement.

When to apply: Anytime, but proposals received after April 1 will not be funded within Foundation's current fiscal year. The board meets in February, May, August, and November.
Materials available: Annual report (includes "Application Procedures"), Application Form.

Emphases. *Recipients:* Nonprofit organizations.
Activities: Land acquisition, publications.
Types of support: Annual campaigns, continuing support, equipment, general purposes, matching funds, operating costs.
Geography: Washington, D.C. metropolitan area; New Jersey only.

Limitations. *Recipients:* Individuals.
Activities: Conferences, research.
Types of support: Endowments, scholarships.

Frelinghuysen Foundation

P.O. Box 726
Far Hills, New Jersey 07931–0726
Tel: 908–439–3499
EIN: 221723755   Type: Independent
Contact: Peter Frelinghuysen, President

History and philosophy. The Frelinghuysen Foundation was incorporated in 1950 by members of the Frelinghuysen family. Cultural programs, education, and hospitals are its primary funding interests.

Officers and directors. Peter Frelinghuysen, President; George L. K. Frelinghuysen, Vice President and Treasurer.

Financial data. Data for fiscal year ended December 31, 1993. *Assets:* $1,997,705 (M). *Total grants disbursed:* $226,139.

Environmental awards. *Recent grants:* 1993 grants included support for land conservation, parks, botanical gardens, species preservation, and public education.

Issues. Cli Bio Lan Agr Wat Oce Ene Was Tox Pop Dev
                 •   •

Funding analysis.

Fiscal year:	1993
Env grants disb:	$17,000
Number:	5
Range:	$1,000–$5,000
Median:	$5,000
Pct $ disb (env/total):	8

Recipients (1993):	*Number:*	*Dollars:*
Arizona–Sonora Desert Museum	1	5,000
Berkshire Garden Center	1	5,000
The New York Botanical Garden	1	5,000
Brandywine Conservancy, Inc.	1	1,000
Raptor Trust	1	1,000

Activity regions (1993):	*Number:*	*Dollars:*
New York/New Jersey	2	6,000
U.S. Northeast	1	5,000
U.S. West	1	5,000
U.S. Mid-Atlantic	1	1,000

Sample grants (1993).
The Arizona–Sonora Desert Museum. Tucson, AZ. $5,000.
Berkshire Garden Center. Stockbridge, MA. $5,000.
Brandywine Conservancy, Inc. Chadds Ford, PA. $1,000.
The New York Botanical Garden. Bronx, NY. $5,000.
Raptor Trust. Millington, NJ. $1,000.

Application process. *Initial contact:* Letter to include statement of purpose and amount requested.
When to apply: Anytime.

Emphases. *Recipients:* Botanical gardens, educational institutions, museums, nonprofit organizations.
Types of support: Capital campaigns/expenses, endowments, equipment, fellowships, general purposes, matching funds.

Geography: New Jersey and New York.

Limitations. *Recipients:* Individuals.

The Frost Foundation, Ltd.

314 McKenzie Street
Santa Fe, New Mexico 87501
Tel: 505–986–0208   Fax: 505–986–0430
EIN: 720520342   Type: Independent
Contact: Theodore Kauss, Executive Director

History and philosophy. Created in 1959, the Foundation was named in honor of Edwin Ambrose Frost and Virginia Chappelle Frost. Its mission: "To assist exemplary programs which can generate positive change beyond traditional boundaries, to encourage creative projects which recognize emerging needs, and to fund innovative programs which address current problems." From 1992 to 1994 the Foundation's focus is on Social Service and Humanitarian Needs, the Environment, and Education.

Officers and directors. *Officers:* Mary Amelia Whited-Howell, President; Mitchell R. Woddard, Secretary/Treasurer. *President Emeritus:* Edwin F. Whited. *Directors:* Ann Gerber, John A. LeVan, John W. Loftus, Taylor F. Moore, Lee Wheless, Edwin F. Whited, Mary Amelia Whited-Howell.

Financial data. Data for fiscal year ended December 31, 1992. *Assets:* $25,313,936 (M). *Total grants disbursed:* $1,293,417.

Environmental awards. *Program and interests:* The Foundation "recommends consideration of programs in research, education, and action to conserve and protect the environment for the well-being and safety of plants, animals, and human beings."

Issues. Cli Bio Lan Agr Wat Oce Ene Was Tox Pop Dev
                 •   •   •

Funding analysis.

Fiscal year:	1991	1992
Env grants disb:	$21,500	$21,000
Number:	3	2
Range:	$1,500–$15,000	$1,000–$20,000
Median:	$5,000	$10,500
Pct $ disb (env/total):	2	2

Recipients (1992):	*Number:*	*Dollars:*
Denver Zoological Foundation	1	20,000
South Suburban Parks and Recreation	1	1,000

Activity regions (1992):	*Number:*	*Dollars:*
U.S. Mountain	1	20,000
U.S. South Central	1	1,000

Sample grants (1991–92).
Concerned Citizens for Nuclear Safety. Santa Fe, NM. $1,500.
Land and Water Fund of the Rockies. Boulder, CO. $7,500. To help match a challenge grant to expand their efforts to develop the leadership support of their initial donors in Colorado.

Western Network. Santa Fe, NM. $15,000. To apply mediation and other consensus-based processes to the problems of dealing with hazardous and toxic materials.

Application process. *Initial contact:* Summary letter (1 page) to include:
At top of page.
1. Name of organization, address, telephone number, project director or executive director of applicant organization.
2. Title of specific project for which you are requesting funds.
3. Total cost of project and the amount requested from the Foundation.

Body of summary.
4. Age of organization.
5. Description of need or problem to be addressed.
6. Description of program and its goals and/or objectives.
7. Procedures used for planning and implementing program.
8. Estimated time for start-up and/or duration of program.
9. Qualified personnel to staff program.
10. Other proposed sources of funds.
11. Plans for cooperation with other organizations, if any.
12. Signature of your CEO.

If the Foundation is interested, it will request a full proposal. The Foundation does not accept summaries or proposals sent by facsimile machine.
When to apply: Deadlines are December 1 and June 1. The directors meet in March and September.
Materials available: Annual report, "Guidelines for Grant-Making Activity 1992–1994."

Emphases. *Recipients:* Educational institutions, individuals, museums, nonprofit organizations, research institutions, zoos.
Activities: Activism, education, innovative programs, land acquisition, research, training, volunteerism, youth programs.
Types of support: Emergency funding, equipment, pilot projects, seed money, start-up costs.
Geography: United States.

Limitations. *Recipients:* Individuals.
Activities: Advocacy, land acquisition, litigation, lobbying, political activities.
Types of support: Capital campaigns/expenses, debt retirement, endowments, facilities, leveraging funds, loans, mortgage reduction, operating costs, scholarships.
Geography: International.

Lloyd A. Fry Foundation

135 South LaSalle Street, Suite 1910
Chicago, Illinois 60603
Tel: 312–580–0310
EIN: 366108775   Type: Independent
Contact: Ben Rothblatt, Executive Director

History and philosophy. The Foundation was established in 1959 by Lloyd Fry, founder of the world's largest producer of asphalt roofing products. The Foundation received a significant testamentary bequest upon Mr. Fry's death in 1981. Grantmaking targets the Chicago metropolitan area in the four fields of education, arts, social service, and health. In each area, the Foundation seeks to channel its resources to the most disadvantaged members of the community, especially to children and youth.

Officers and directors. *Officers:* Edmund A. Stephan, Chairman; Roger E. Anderson, Vice Chairman; Howard M. McCue, Vice President and Secretary; M. James Termondt, President and Treasurer. *Directors:* Roger E. Anderson, Lloyd A. Fry, III, Howard M. McCue, Edmund A. Stephan, M. James Termondt.

Financial data. Data for fiscal year ended June 30, 1993. *Assets:* $93,718,829 (M). *Total grants disbursed:* $4,381,550.

Environmental awards. *Program and interests:* The Foundation makes environmental awards through two programs: Arts and Culture, and Civic Affairs and Social Service.
Recent grants: 1993 grants included support for open land conservation, horticulture, wildlife protection, and environmental education in the schools.

Issues.   Cli   Bio   Lan   Agr   Wat   Oce   Ene   Was   Tox   Pop   Dev
 •   •

Funding analysis.

Fiscal year:	1991	1993
Env grants auth:	$80,000	$73,000
Number:	5	8
Range:	$5,000–$35,000	$1,000–$25,000
Median:	$10,000	$7,500
Pct $ disb (env/total):	2	2

Recipients (1993 highest):	*Number:*	*Dollars:*
The Chicago Academy of Sciences	1	25,000
Chicago Horticultural Society	1	15,000
The Nature Conservancy, Illinois Field Office	1	15,000
Open Lands Project	1	10,000
World Wildlife Fund	1	5,000

Activity regions (1993):	*Number:*	*Dollars:*
U.S. Great Lakes	7	68,000
International*	1	5,000

*Multiple regions or not specified.

Sample grants (1993).
The Chicago Academy of Sciences. Chicago, IL. $25,000. For the Science Teaching Network and the Environmental Issues Forum.
Chicago Horticultural Society. Glencoe, IL. $15,000. For the Collaborative Outreach Education Program in Chicago public schools.
The Nature Conservancy, Illinois Field Office. Chicago, IL. $15,000. For a conservation program for inner-city school children.
Open Lands Project. Chicago, IL. $10,000. For a project to assist two communities on the west and south sides to convert vacant lots into neighborhood parks.
Save the Prairie Society. Westchester, IL. $1,000. Unrestricted.
Wild Life Theater. Chicago, IL. $1,000. Unrestricted.
Willowbrook Wildlife Foundation. Glen Ellyn, IL. $35,000. Unrestricted.
World Wildlife Fund. Washington, DC. $5,000. Unrestricted.

Application process. *Initial contact:* Letter of inquiry including a brief statement about the proposed project and a project budget. Full proposal to contain:
1. Brief history of organization, including a general statement of its primary functions and goals.
2. Brief summary of proposal, including a statement of need to be addressed, indication of how the project will ameliorate the need, a project budget, and a plan for evaluation.
3. Copy of organization's most recent audited financial report and approved operating budget. In addition, a statement of current and recent sources of support should be provided.
4. List of board members and professional staff.
5. Copy of IRS tax-exempt status determination letter.

When to apply: Anytime. The board meets in February, May, August, and November.
Materials available: Annual report (includes "Grant Application Guidelines and Procedures").

Emphases. *Recipients:* Nonprofit organizations.
Types of support: Projects, seed money.
Geography: Chicago metropolitan area.

Limitations. *Recipients:* Individuals, public agencies.
Activities: Fundraising.
Types of support: Capital campaigns/expenses, operating costs.

The Fund for New Jersey
Kilmer Square
65 Church Street, Suite 200
New Brunswick, New Jersey 08901
Tel: 908–220–8656   Fax: 908–220–8654
EIN: 221895028   Type: Independent
EGA member
Contact: Mark M. Murphy, Executive Director

History and philosophy. In December 1969 the family of the late Mr. and Mrs. Charles F. Wallace of Westfield, New Jersey, created what is known today as The Fund for New Jersey. The Fund makes grants to a broad range of organizations whose efforts have implications for future public policies in New Jersey. Grants are made in the areas of: Environment and Land Use, Social and Economic Opportunity, and Public Affairs.

Officers and directors. *Officers:* Joseph C. Cornwall, Chairman and Treasurer; Richard J. Sullivan, President; Hon. John J. Gibbons, Vice President; Mark M. Murphy, Secretary; Carol Head, Assistant Treasurer. *Trustees:* Candace McKee Ashmun, Ann L. Auerbach, William O. Baker, John W. Cornwall, Joseph C. Cornwall, Hon. Dickinson R. Debevoise, Hon. John J. Gibbons, Gustav Heningburg, Leonard Lieberman, Gordon A. MacInnes, Clement A. Price, Mary S. Strong, Richard J. Sullivan, Jane W. Thorne.

Financial data. Data for fiscal year ended December 31, 1993. *Assets:* $31,451,097 (M). *Total grants authorized:* $1,426,725.

Environmental awards. *Program and interests:* The Fund supports public policy to promote stewardship of land, air, and water for the benefit of all New Jersey residents.

Recent grants: 1993 grants included support for land use planning, watershed and wetlands protections, coastal issues, organic farming, solid waste reduction and recycling, and green product promotion.

Issues. Cli Bio Lan Agr Wat Oce Ene Was Tox Pop Dev
             •   •   •   •   •   •   •   •

Funding analysis.

Fiscal year:	1991	1993
Env grants auth:	$225,000	$474,500
Number:	12	14
Range:	$5,000–$40,000	$2,500–$110,000
Median:	$20,000	$25,000
Pct $ auth (env/total):	25	32

Recipients (1993 highest):	Number:	Dollars:
Association of New Jersey Environmental Commissions	1	110,000
Middlesex-Somerset-Mercer Regional Council, Inc.	1	54,000
Institute for Local Self-Reliance	1	50,000
North Camden Land Trust, Inc.	1	50,000
Regional Plan Association	1	35,000

Activity regions (1993):	Number:	Dollars:
New York/New Jersey	13	449,500
U.S. Mid-Atlantic	1	25,000

Sample grants (1993).
Association of New Jersey Environmental Commissions. Mendham, NJ. $110,000. To work with municipalities to devise future growth plans with the goal of protecting open space and revitalizing urban centers.
Clean Ocean Action. Seabright, NJ. $20,000. To secure the scientific analysis of dredged material and the technical advice on alternative disposal options.
Clean Water Fund. New Brunswick, NJ. $20,000. To support promotion of non-toxic pest control alternatives to the use of toxic chemical pesticides.
Great Swamp Watershed Advisory Association. New Vernon, NJ. $20,000. To support an open space master plan to protect the Great Swamp Watershed ecosystem.
Institute for Local Self-Reliance. Washington, DC. $50,000. Support to attract scrap-based industry to Patterson, New Jersey.
The Nature Conservancy, New Jersey Field Office. Pottersville, NJ. $25,000. To support the Delaware Bay Ecosystem Planning Project to develop a long-range strategic plan to protect the Delaware Bay ecosystem.
Northeast Organic Farming Association of New Jersey. Pennington, NJ. $30,000. To assist farmers to adopt organic methods of agriculture and develop markets for organic produce.

Application process. *Initial contact:* Telephone call or proposal cover sheet.
Cover sheet (1 page).
1. Organization and contact person: telephone number, street address, city, state, zip code.
2. Summary of request: description of proposed activity (1–2 sentences) and what it is expected to accomplish.
3. Amount requested.

© 1995 Environmental Data Resources, Inc.

4. Problem or need addressed by proposed activity.

Appendixes.
1. Copy of IRS tax-exempt status determination letter.
2. Names and affiliations of the board of directors of applicant organization, where appropriate.
3. Budget showing projected sources of income and anticipated expenditures.

When to apply: Anytime. The board of trustees meets quarterly.
Materials available: Annual report (includes "Information for Prospective Applicants").

Emphases. *Activities:* Citizen participation, conflict resolution, education, litigation, policy analysis/development, research.
Geography: New Jersey only.

Limitations. *Recipients:* Educational institutions, individuals.
Activities: Land acquisition.
Types of support: Capital campaigns/expenses, equipment, facilities, mortgage reduction, scholarships.

The Fund for Preservation of Wildlife and Natural Areas

c/o The Boston Foundation
One Boston Place, 24th Floor
Boston, Massachusetts 02108
Tel: 617–723–7415 Fax: 617–589–3616
Contact: Marshall Schell, Vice President for Development

History and philosophy. The Fund for Preservation of Wildlife and Natural Areas, established in 1962 by Boston Safe Deposit and Trust Company, is a public and charitable foundation dedicated to the preservation and protection of the natural heritage of land and wildlife. As of 1994 it is formally affiliated with The Boston Foundation.

"The Committee has decided to suspend discretionary grantmaking during 1994 while engaging in a year-long study to review objectives, to understand the changing needs of environmental organizations, and to assess how the Fund's grant program can complement the work of other grantmakers.

"We expect to complete this process in the spring of 1995, and plan to mail new guidelines with a request for proposals next summer."

Officers and directors. *Officer:* Martha A. Reardon, Chair.
Committee members: Gordon Abbott, Susanna Colloredo, Elizabeth McAfoose, Wilhelm M. Merck, Martha A. Reardon, John L. Thorndike, H. Wiley Vaughan.

Financial data.* Data for fiscal year ended August 31, 1991.
Assets: $4,593,201 (M). *Gifts received:* $300,270. *Total grants disbursed:* $623,102.

*Disbursements include special interest ($570,652) and discretionary ($52,450) grants.

Environmental awards. *Program and interests:* The Fund is reviewing its grantmaking objectives.

Issues. *Cli Bio Lan Agr Wat Oce Ene Was Tox Pop Dev*
          •   •

Sample grants (1990).*
Appalachian Mountain Club. Boston, MA. $5,000. To produce an educational brochure about the importance of preserving the West Parish Meadow.
Audubon Society of New Hampshire. Concord, NH. $4,000. For the Sanctuary Interpretation Project.
Boston Natural Areas Fund. Boston, MA. $5,000. To protect, preserve, and improve Boston's urban wilds.
Green Mountain Club. Montpelier, VT. $5,000. To preserve and protect land along the Long Trail in northern Vermont.
Nashua River Watershed Association. Fitchburg, MA. $1,950. To update and reprint the Greenway Brochure, an educational guide promoting waterway conservation and protection.
New England Wild Flower Society. Framingham, MA. $2,500. To produce a slide tape presentation to help launch the Plant Conservation Strategy for New England.
Whale and Dolphin Conservation Society. Lincoln, MA. $1,000. For research on the right whale.

*Sample grants include discretionary grants only.

Application process. *Initial contact:* Contact the Fund for new guidelines in the spring of 1995.
When to apply: Not before spring 1995.

Fund of the Four Directions

8 West 40th Street, 10th Floor
New York, New York 10018
Tel: 212–768–1430 Fax: 212–768–1471
Type: Independent
EGA member
Contact: Gary D. Schwartz, Director

History and philosophy. The Fund focuses on efforts toward "organizing and the empowering of disenfranchised peoples." It prefers to support relatively small organizations (budgets under $1 million), and in all program areas it "endeavor[s] to support work which strengthens multi-racial and multi-ethnic ties." Major areas for giving are: Environment and Environmental Justice, Social Justice, and Native Americans. Two additional areas of interest are: Central American Initiatives and Reproductive Rights.

Officers and directors. *Officer:* Ann R. Roberts, President and Founder. *Director:* Gary D. Schwartz.

Financial data. Data for fiscal year ended December 31, 1993.
Total grants: $1,160,378.

Environmental awards. *Program and interests:* Areas of interest include:

- Grassroots organizing.
- Toxics.
- Water quality.
- Safe energy.

F

Issues. Cli Bio Lan Agr Wat Oce Ene Was Tox Pop Dev
• • • • • • • •

Funding analysis.

Fiscal year:	1992
Env grants disb:	$355,000
Number:	42
Range:	$2,000–$20,000
Median:	$10,000
Pct $ disb (env/total):	29

Recipients (1992 highest):	Number:	Dollars:
National Toxics Campaign Fund	2	30,000
Citizen Alert	3	25,000
National Coalition Against the Misuse of Pesticides	3	25,000
Learning Alliance	2	15,000
White Earth Land Recovery Project	2	15,000

Activity regions (1992 highest):	Number:	Dollars:
U.S. not specified	16	147,500
U.S. West	6	50,000
U.S. Mountain	6	45,000
U.S. Great Lakes	4	27,500
Alaska	2	20,000

Sample grants (1992).

Alaska Conservation Foundation. Anchorage, AK. $10,000. General support.
American Rivers, Inc. Washington, DC. $7,500. General support.
Citizen Alert. Reno, NV. $25,000. General support, organizational development, and resource concepts land survey study.
Communications Consortium Media Center. Washington, DC. $10,000. General support.
Greater Yellowstone Coalition. Bozeman, MT. $10,000. General support.
Illinois Stewardship Alliance. Herrin, IL. $7,500. General support.
Ladakh Solar Project. Ladakh, India. $10,000. General support.
National Toxics Campaign Fund. Boston, MA. $30,000. General support and challenge grant met.
Nuclear Information and Resource Service. Washington, DC. $10,000. General support.
Public Citizen Foundation, Inc. Washington, DC. $5,000. Critical Mass Energy Project.
Southwest Research and Information Center. Albuquerque, NM. $10,000. General support.
Youth for Environmental Sanity. Santa Cruz, CA. $10,000. General support.

Application process. *Initial contact:* Brief letter of inquiry summarizing the proposed program and the organization (3 pages maximum). If the Fund is interested, it will request a full proposal to include:
1. Project/organization summary sheet.
2. Program description and organizational summary (15 pages maximum), including information on board and staff.
3. Line-item budget for organization and project (if applicable), including individual staff salaries.
4. List of past and current funders (large individual donors and foundations).
5. Copy of IRS tax-exempt status determination letter.

The Fund will not consider proposals received in plastic covers or binders and encourages the use of recycled paper when it is available and affordable in applicant's area.

When to apply: Deadlines for 1995 are January 13, March 31, and July 31.

Emphases. *Recipients:* Small nonprofit organizations.

Funding Exchange

666 Broadway, #500
New York, New York 10012
Tel: 212–529–5300   Fax: 212–982–9272
Type: Independent
EGA member
Contact: Cecilia Rodriguez, Executive Director

History and philosophy. The Funding Exchange includes both activist-advised and donor-advised funds and makes grants in the areas of: Lesbian and Gay Rights, Culture and Media, Native Americans, Community Organizing, Peace and Disarmament, Mental Health, Anti-racism, Environment, Government Accountability/Civil Liberties, Health Care, and International Human Rights.

Financial data. Data for fiscal year ended June 30, 1992. *Total grants disbursed:* $3,133,135.

Environmental awards. *Recent grants:* 1992 included support for land conservation, toxic and waste management, environmental justice, and wildlife.

Issues. Cli Bio Lan Agr Wat Oce Ene Was Tox Pop Dev
• • • • • • • •

Funding analysis.*

Fiscal year:	1992
Env grants disb:	$305,950
Number:	40
Range:	$500 $100,000
Median:	$3,000
Pct $ disb (env/total):	10

Recipients (1992 highest):	Number:	Dollars:
Woodlands Mountain Institute	1	100,000
Natural Resources Defense Council	1	50,000
Massachusetts Toxics Campaign	1	25,000
Native Americans for a Clean Environment	3	19,000
Indigenous Environmental Network	2	16,500

Activity regions (1992 highest):	Number:	Dollars:
U.S. not specified	15	108,500
U.S. Mid-Atlantic	1	100,000
U.S. Northeast	3	41,000
U.S. South Central	4	12,450
Puerto Rico	2	10,500

*Includes grants from donor-advised funds.

Sample grants (1992).*
Advocate for Wilderness the Wilderness Society. Washington, DC. $1,000.
Citizens for Environmental Justice. Savannah, GA. $7,000.
Environment and Democracy Campaign. New York, NY. $5,000.
Environmental Health Network. Harvey, LA. $1,000.
Indigenous Environmental Network. Tonawanda, NY. $16,500.
Massachusetts Toxics Campaign. Boston, MA. $25,000.
Native Americans for a Clean Environment. Ann Arbor, MI. $19,000.
Natural Resources Defense Council. New York, NY. $50,000.
Sacred Earth Coalition. Portland, OR. $4,500.
Woodlands Mountain Institute. Franklin, WV. $100,000.

*Sample grants include grants from donor-advised funds.

Application process. *Initial contact:* Letter of inquiry.
When to apply: Anytime.

The GAR Foundation
50 South Main Street
P.O. Box 1500
Akron, Ohio 44309
Tel: 216-376-5300
EIN: 346577710   Type: Independent
Contact: Hugh Colopy, Trustee

History and philosophy. The founder and CEO of a national trucking company established the GAR Foundation in 1967. Grantmaking continues to reflect its founders' interests in art, music, and education primarily in Akron and Summit County, secondarily in northeastern Ohio.

Officers and directors. *Trustees:* Robert W. Briggs, Hugh Colopy, National City Bank, Akron. *Distribution Committee:* Richard A. Chenoweth, Joseph Clapp, George C. Roush, G. James Roush, Thomas W. Roush, John L. Tormey, Ms. S. R. Werner, Douglas A. Wilson.

Financial data. Data for fiscal year ended December 31, 1993. *Assets:* $183,394,199 (M). *Total grants disbursed:* $9,164,317.

Environmental awards. *Recent grants:* 1993 grants included support for urban environment (beautification, litter control), parks, and an arboretum.

Issues. Cli Bio Lan Agr Wat Oce Ene Was Tox Pop Dev
                  •   •

Funding analysis.

Fiscal year:	1992	1993
Env grants disb:	$115,000	$217,700
Number:	2	6
Range:	$15,000–$100,000	$5,500–$100,000
Median:	$57,500	$27,500
Pct $ disb (env/total):	2	2

Recipients (1993 highest):	*Number:*	*Dollars:*
Akron Zoological Park	1	100,000
Cascades Locks Park Association	1	42,200
The Holden Arboretum	1	30,000
International Center for the Preservation of Wild Animals	1	25,000
Keep Akron Beautiful	1	15,000

Activity region (1993):	*Number:*	*Dollars:*
U.S. Great Lakes	6	217,700

Sample grants (1993).
Cascade Locks Park Association. Akron, OH. $42,200. To develop a conceptual plan for creating a park along Locks 10–16 of the Ohio and Erie Canal.
Cuyahoga River Community Planning Organization. Cleveland, OH. $5,500. To assist in producing and airing a series of ten 3–5 minute video vignettes for broadcast on public television.
The Holden Arboretum. Mentor, OH. $30,000. For endowment.
Keep Akron Beautiful. Akron, OH. $15,000. For the Litter Law Enforcement, the Clean Team, and Education Specialist Program.

Application process. *Initial contact:* Contact the Foundation for application form and guidelines.
When to apply: Deadlines are February 1, May 1, August 1, and November 1. The distribution committee generally meets the second Thursday of February, May, August, and November.
Materials available: Guidelines, application form.

Emphases. *Recipients:* Botanical gardens, museums, nonprofit organizations.
Activities: Collaborative efforts, education, innovative programs, land acquisition, research (scientific).
Types of support: Endowments, matching funds, seed money, single-year grants only.
Geography: Primarily Akron and Summit County, secondarily northeastern Ohio.

Limitations. *Recipients:* Individuals.
Activities: Research (medical).
Types of support: Multi-year grants.

GE Fund
3135 Easton Turnpike
Fairfield, Connecticut 06431
Tel: 203-373-3216   Fax: 203-373-3029
EIN: 146015766   Type: Company-sponsored
EGA member
Contact: Clifford V. Smith, Jr., President

History and philosophy. GE Fund comprises two entities: the GE Foundation, which awards grants only to organizations within the United States and its possessions; and the General Electric Foundation, Inc., which also awards grants internationally. The central goal of all Fund grantmaking is to make our communities better places to live and work. Programs are: Higher Education, Pre-College Education, Arts & Culture, International, Public Policy, Matching Gifts and United Way.

© 1995 Environmental Data Resources, Inc.

G

Officers and directors. *Officers:* Dennis D. Dammerman, Chairperson; Clifford V. Smith, Jr., President; Phyllis S. McGrath, Secretary; Michael J. Cosgrove, Jr., Treasurer; Jane L. Polin, Comptroller. *Trustees:* William J. Conaty, Dennis D. Dammerman, Frank P. Doyle, Benjamin W. Heineman, Jr., Joyce Hergenhan, Jack O. Peiffer, Lloyd G. Trotter.

Financial data. Data for fiscal years ended December 31, 1992 and 1993. *Assets (1992):* $12,331,000 (M). *Gifts received (1992):* $35,900,000. *Total grants disbursed (1993):* $24,363,883.

Environmental awards. *Program and interests:* Public Policy grants may have an environmental component. These grants target three key issues:

- Increasing scientific understanding of the environment.
- Expanding global trade.
- Strengthening the world economy through targeted research on employment, financial, and legal policy concerns.

Recent grants: 1993 grants included support for policy research pertaining to international trade issues and risk assessment.

Issues. Cli Bio Lan Agr Wat Oce Ene Was Tox Pop Dev
•   •   •   •

Funding analysis.§

Fiscal year:	1991	1993
Env grants disb:	$337,065	$172,500
Number:	23	11
Range:	$2,835–$58,983	$5,000–$40,000
Median:	$10,000	$10,000
Pct $ disb (env/total):	1	1

Recipients (1993 highest):	Number:	Dollars:
Housatonic Valley Association	1	40,000
Management Institute for Environment and Business	1	30,000
Resources for the Future	1	25,000
World Environment Center, Inc.	1	25,000
Environmental Law Institute	1	12,500

Activity regions (1993):	Number:	Dollars:
U.S. not specified	5	82,500
U.S. Northeast	4	55,000
New York/New Jersey	2	35,000

§Does not include $7,904,614 in matching gifts.

Sample grants (1993).
The Alliance to Save Energy. Washington, DC. $10,000.
Center for Ecological Technology Inc. Pittsfield, MA. $5,000.
Defenders of Wildlife. Washington, DC. $5,000.
Environmental Law Institute. Boston, MA. $12,500.
Presque Isle Audubon Society. Presque Isle, ME. $5,000.
Resources for the Future. Washington, DC. $25,000.

Application process. *Initial contact:* Proposals are generally submitted by invitation. Potential grantees may wish to submit a brief concept paper (1 copy) to assess Fund interest. The Fund favors concise proposals with minimum supporting documentation and materials. Proposal to include:
1. Executive summary.
2. Brief description of applicant organization and evidence of its tax-exempt status.
3. Program purpose and need; qualifications of key personnel.
4. Budget; sources of funding; work schedule; timetable.
5. Evaluation criteria; plans for publicity.

When to apply: Anytime. The board meets quarterly.
Materials available: Annual report, "Program and Guidelines" (brochure).

Emphases. *Recipients:* Educational institutions, nonprofit organizations, research institutions.
Activities: Education, policy analysis/development, publications, research, projects, training.
Types of support: Annual campaigns, continuing support, fellowships, general purposes, matching funds, multi-year grants, pilot projects, seed money.
Geography: Locations of company operations; national and international programs.

Limitations. *Recipients:* Individuals.
Types of support: Capital campaigns/expenses, endowments, equipment, loans, scholarships.

The Gap Foundation

One Harrison Street
San Francisco, California 94105
Tel: 415–291–2757   Fax: 415–495–2922
EIN: 942474426   Type: Company-sponsored
EGA member
Contact: Molly White, Director

History and philosophy. The Gap Foundation was created in 1977 by Donald G. Fisher, chairman and founder of The Gap clothing manufacturing company. Its goal is to improve the quality of public and private life in the communities where most Gap employees live. With primary interests in children and youth, the arts, and the environment, the Foundation awards grants in four major program areas: Arts and Culture, Education, Health and Human Services, and Environment. It also has a program to match employee contributions. It makes both cash and non-cash (gift certificate and merchandise) awards.

Officers and directors. *Officer:* Donald G. Fisher, Chairman and CEO. *Directors:* John P. Carver, Donald G. Fisher, Doris F. Fisher, Robert J. Fisher, Molly White.

Financial data. Data for fiscal year ended June 30, 1993. *Assets:* $1,345,711 (M). *Gifts received:* $1,975,000. *Total grants disbursed:* $1,676,666.

Environmental awards. *Program and interests:* Increasingly sensitive to environmental issues, the Foundation created an environmental program at the end of 1989. Topics include:

- Water quality in the San Francisco Bay-Delta region.
- Toxics.
- Sustainably managed resources, particularly cotton.

The Foundation emphasizes citizen advocacy and leadership development, and encourages grassroots participation.

Issues. Cli • Bio • Lan • Agr • Wat • Oce Ene • Was • Tox Pop • Dev •

Funding analysis.

Fiscal year:	1991	1993
Env grants auth:	$197,000	$334,275
Number:	24	32
Range:	$3,000–$13,000	$1,150–$30,000
Median:	$10,000	$10,000
Pct $ disb (env/total):	10	17

Recipients (1993 highest):	Number:	Dollars:
Presidio Pacific Center	1	30,000
KCET Community Television of Southern California	1	20,000
Materials for the Future Foundation	1	20,000
Natural Resources Defense Council	2	20,000
Sierra Club Legal Defense Fund	1	20,000

Activity regions (1993):	Number:	Dollars:
U.S. West	29	321,775
New York/New Jersey	1	5,000
U.S. not specified	1	5,000
U.S. Mid-Atlantic	1	2,500

Sample grants (1993).

Bay Area Ridge Trail Council. San Francisco, CA. $10,000. To create a recreational open space trail around San Francisco Bay.

BayKeeper. San Francisco, CA. $15,000. To support volunteer and staff monitoring of San Francisco Bay for water quality enforcement.

California Ancient Forest Alliance. San Francisco, CA. $10,000. Campaign to permanently protect remaining ancient forest stands in California.

Citizens for a Better Environment. San Francisco, CA. $15,000. Continuing support for Clean Bays and Coastal Waters Program targeting Bay clean-up.

Coyote Point Wildlife Habitat Center. San Mateo, CA. $5,000. Production of PSA to promote museum's environmental programs.

Greenbelt Alliance. San Francisco, CA. $10,000. To protect the San Francisco Greenbelt and enhance area livability.

Materials for the Future Foundation. Oakland, CA. $20,000. Multi-funder initiative to link economic development strategies and low income communities with the recycling industry.

Pesticide Action Network (PAN), North America Regional Office. San Francisco, CA. $15,000. Coalition of citizens organizations promoting pesticide use reduction.

The Trust for Hidden Villa, Inc. Los Altos Hills, CA. $5,000. To help provide access for economically disadvantaged and minority children to Hidden Villa's environmental program.

The Wilderness Society. Washington, DC. $20,000. Support of New Voices of the American West project to assess and publicize economic realities of and alternatives to the timber industry in the Sierra Nevada range, via media training and assistance to community-based volunteers.

Application process. *Initial contact:* Letter of inquiry (1–2 pages).
When to apply: Deadlines are the first day of the month preceding a board meeting. Call for dates of quarterly board meetings.
Materials available: Annual report (includes "Application Procedures").

Emphases. *Recipients:* Nonprofit organizations.
Types of support: Capital campaigns/expenses, general purposes, matching funds, operating costs.
Geography: Organizations located in northern California, especially San Mateo and San Francisco counties. Limited activity in Ventura, California; Erlanger, Kentucky; Baltimore, Maryland; and New York City.

Limitations. *Recipients:* Individuals.
Activities: Fundraising, lobbying, media projects, political activities, publications.
Types of support: Endowments.

Gates Foundation

3200 Cherry Creek South Drive, Suite 630
Denver, Colorado 80209-3247
Tel: 303-722-1881   Fax: 303-698-9031
EIN: 840474837   Type: Independent
Contact: Thomas C. Stokes, Executive Director

History and philosophy. The Gates Foundation was incorporated in 1946 by Charles C. Gates, Sr. and members of the Gates family. Charles Gates, Sr. founded the Gates Corporation, originally the Colorado Tire and Leather Company, which now makes non-tire rubber products and rechargeable batteries.

The Foundation's mission is to "aid, assist, encourage, help initiate, or carry on activities which will promote the health, welfare, and broad education of mankind whether by means of research, grants, publications, its own agencies and activities, or through cooperation with agencies and institutions already in existence, or by any other means which, from time to time, shall seem appropriate to the Foundation." Program areas are: Education, Humanities-Cultural Affairs-Historic Preservation, Youth Services, Human Services, Health, Parks-Conservation-Recreation, Public Policy Examination.

Officers and directors. *Officers:* Charles C. Gates, President; Diane Gates Wallach, Vice President; Thomas C. Stokes, Secretary; T. J. Gibson, Treasurer. *Trustees:* George B. Beardsley, Charles G. Cannon, F. Charles Froelicher, Charles C. Gates, William W. Grant III, Diane Gates Wallach, Mike Wilfley.

Financial data. Data for fiscal year ended December 31, 1993. *Assets:* $122,641,453 (M). *Total grants disbursed:* $5,416,034.

Environmental awards. *Program and interests:* The Foundation awards most of its environmental grants through its Parks-Conservation-Recreation program. It maintains an active interest in trail systems within urban and mountain parks and U.S. national forests.

G

Recent grants: 1993 grants included support for outdoor education and recreation, a botanical garden, and a local zoo.

Issues. Cli Bio Lan Agr Wat Oce Ene Was Tox Pop Dev
            •   •

Funding analysis:

Fiscal year:	1991	1993
Env grants auth:	$970,100	$1,794,285
Number:	9	6
Range:	$7,300–$500,000	$18,000–$1,600,000
Median:	$25,000	$43,143
Pct $ disb (env/total):	18	19

Recipients (1993 highest):	Number:	Dollars:
Denver Botanic Gardens	1	1,600,000
Breckenridge Outdoor Education Center	1	60,000
Volunteers for Outdoor Colorado	1	45,000
Colorado Outward Bound School	1	41,285
Doo Zoo Children's Museum	1	30,000

Activity region (1993):	Number:	Dollars:
U.S. Mountain	6	1,794,285

Sample grants (1993).
Breckenridge Outdoor Education Center. Breckenridge, CO. $60,000. Toward the construction of a new lodging facility.
Colorado Outward Bound School. Denver, CO. $41,285. To support the Leadership Scholarship Program.
Colorado School of Mines. Golden, CO. $50,000. To aid CSM in helping scientists and engineers develop the earth's natural resources without doing damage to the earth.
Colorado Trail Foundation. Golden, CO. $5,000. Final portion to establish an office and information coordinating center.
Denver Botanic Gardens. Denver, CO. $800,000. First portion toward the construction of the Garden Pavilion Building.
Doo Zoo Children's Museum. Grand Junction, CO. $30,000. Toward the renovation of the Doo Zoo building and construction of new exhibits.
The Student Conservation Association Inc. Charlestown, NH. $18,000. To support 10 Colorado students to work on Colorado's mountain trails.
Volunteers for Outdoor Colorado. Denver, CO. $20,000. First portion to support rehabilitation of trails and other natural areas around the state.

Application process. *Initial contact:* Telephone call requesting application guidelines pamphlet followed by a cover letter (1 page) and summary proposal. Proposal (2 pages) to include:
1. Organization's name, mission or purpose, and a brief history.
2. Description of applicant organization as it now stands.
3. Issue to be addressed, constituency served, target population, and how will they benefit.
4. Goals and objectives.
5. Activities planned to accomplish goals and is this project new to sponsoring organization.
6. Timetable for implementation.
7. Other contributing organizations.
8. Source of funding at end of grant period.
9. Expected results during funding period.
10. Method of defining and measuring success.
11. How project will be used or disseminated.
12. Board of director's occupations, community affiliations, and their antidiscrimination statement.
13. Names and qualifications of key staff.
14. Fiscal year-end financial statements, audited if available.
15. Current agency budget.
16. Annual report, if available.
17. Project budget.
18. Copy of IRS tax-exempt status determination letter.
19. List of major contributors.
20. List of volunteer involvement and in-kind contributions.

When to apply: Deadlines are January 15, April 1, July 15, and October 1. The trustees meet on or about April 1, June 15, October 1, and December 15.
Materials available: Annual report (includes "Common Grant Application," "Information for Grant Applicants," and "Information for Preparation of Proposals").

Emphases. *Recipients:* Botanical gardens, museums, nonprofit organizations, zoos.
Activities: Exhibits, land acquisition, volunteerism, workshops.
Types of support: Capital campaigns/expenses, endowments, equipment, facilities, multi-year grants.
Geography: Colorado only (unless initiated by trustees).

Limitations. *Recipients:* Individuals.
Activities: Conferences, fundraising, litigation.
Types of support: Annual campaigns, debt retirement, loans, operating costs, scholarships.

The Barbara Gauntlett Foundation, Inc.
c/o Gauntlett Group
5900 Hollis Street
Emeryville, California 94608
Tel: 510–658–9013   Fax: 510–658–3834
EIN: 115238046   Type: Independent
Contact: Jane Knecht

History and philosophy. The Foundation was established in 1986. Its focus is the environment.

Officers and directors. *Officers:* Suzanne Gauntlett, President; Charles C. Goodfellow III, Treasurer; Christopher C. Angell, Assistant Secretary. *Directors:* Christopher C. Angell, Suzanne Gauntlett, Charles C. Goodfellow III, Jerome Manning, Neal Myerberg.

Financial data. Data for fiscal year ended December 31, 1991. *Assets:* $18,664,092 (M). *Gifts received:* $3,548,739. *Total grants disbursed:* $1,258,720.

Environmental awards. *Recent grants:* One grant in 1991 supported rainforest preservation and marine mammals.

Issues. Cli Bio Lan Agr Wat Oce Ene Was Tox Pop Dev
            •   •   •

Funding analysis.

Fiscal year:	1991
Env grants disb:	$1,258,720
Number:	1
Range:	–
Median:	–
Pct $ disb (env/total):	100

Recipient (1991):	*Number:*	*Dollars:*
Earthtrust	1	1,258,720

Activity region (1991):	*Number:*	*Dollars:*
Hawaii	1	1,258,720

Sample grant (1991).
Earthtrust. Kailua, HI. $1,258,720. For preservation of rainforests and dolphins.

Application process. *Initial contact:* Letter.
When to apply: Anytime.

Emphases. *Recipients:* Nonprofit organizations.

Limitations. *Recipients:* Individuals.
Types of support: Annual campaigns, general purposes.

Gebbie Foundation, Inc.
Hotel Jamestown Building, Room 308
P.O. Box 1277
Jamestown, New York 14702–1277
Tel: 716–487–1062   Fax: 716–488–0387
EIN: 166050287   Type: Independent
Contact: John D. Hamilton, President

History and philosophy. Miss Marion Gebbie and Mrs. Geraldine Gebbie Bellinger established the Foundation in 1963 in memory of their parents, Frank and Harriet Louise Hubbell Gebbie. Along with Gail Borden, Frank Gebbie was one of the developers of condensed milk. He later founded the Mohawk Condensed Milk Company. "The Foundation's mission is to implement the intent of the funding benefactors and to focus on children, education, the arts, culture activities, family welfare, health care, and medical research to alleviate human suffering." Program areas are: Arts, Culture, Humanities; Education; Environment, Animals; Human Services; Public Society Benefit; and Religion. Focus is on the Jamestown, New York region.

Officers and directors. *Officers:* John D. Hamilton, President; Dr. Myron B. Franks, Vice President; William I. Parker, Secretary; Charles T. Hall, Treasurer; Dianne Eisenhardt, Assistant Secretary and Assistant Treasurer. *Directors:* Dr. Myron B. Franks, Charles T. Hall, John D. Hamilton, Rhoe B. Henderson III, Dr. Lillian Ney, Bertram Parker, Geraldine Parker, William I. Parker, Paul W. Sandberg.

Financial data. Data for fiscal year ended September 30, 1993. *Assets:* $51,754,659 (C). *Total grants disbursed:* $6,860,521.

Environmental awards. *Recent grants:* 1993 grants included support for lake protection, the local chapter of a national organization, and a natural history museum.

Issues.   Cli   Bio   Lan   Agr   Wat   Oce   Ene   Was   Tox   Pop   Dev
                                    •

Funding analysis.

Fiscal year:	1992	1993
Env grants disb:	443,000	$3,267,365
Number:	4	5
Range:	$18,000–$200,000	$19,500–$3,000,000
Median:	$112,000	$100,000
Pct $ disb (env/total):	—	48

Recipients (1993):	*Number:*	*Dollars:*
Roger Tory Peterson Institute of Natural History	1	3,000,000
Jamestown Audubon Society	2	144,500
Chautauqua Lake Association	1	100,000
Chautauqua Watershed Conservancy, Inc.	1	22,865

Activity region (1993):	*Number:*	*Dollars:*
New York/New Jersey	5	3,267,365

Sample grants (1993).
Chautauqua Lake Association. Lakewood, NY. $100,000 (3 years). General operating expenses.
Chautauqua Watershed Conservancy, Inc. Lakewood, NY. $22,865.
Jamestown Audubon Society. Jamestown, NY. $125,000 (4 years). Capital campaign.
Jamestown Audubon Society. Jamestown, NY. $19,500. Matching grant toward youth nature education.
Roger Tory Peterson Institute of Natural History. Jamestown, NY. $3,000,000. Matching grant toward construction of a building.

Application process. *Initial contact:* Letter of inquiry outlining need for funding and amount requested. If the request falls within the Foundation's areas of preferred interest or warrants consideration as a special project, further information will be solicited including formal application (12 copies) and 1 copy each of:
1. IRS tax-exempt status determination letter.
2. Most recent audited financial statements.
3. Most recent IRS Form 990.
4. Current/proposed budget for organization and/or program.

When to apply: Deadlines are January 1, May 1, September 1.
Materials available: Annual report (includes "Policy and Guidelines" and "Application Procedures").

Emphases. *Recipients:* Educational institutions, museums, nonprofit organizations.
Activities: Demonstration programs, direct services, education, innovative programs, training, youth programs.
Types of support: Annual campaigns, capital campaigns/expenses, computer hardware, continuing support, equipment, facilities, general purposes, matching funds, multi-year grants, operating costs, pilot projects, seed money, start-up costs.
Geography: Jamestown and Chautauqua County, New York.

G

Limitations. *Recipients:* Individuals, religious organizations, zoos.
Activities: Litigation, lobbying.
Types of support: Endowments.

The Fred Gellert Foundation
One Embarcadero Center, Suite 2480
San Francisco, California 94111
Tel: 415–433–6174   Fax: 415–433–7952
EIN: 946062859   Type: Independent
EGA member
Contacts: Fred Gellert, Jr., Chairman (for all requests and communications except telephone inquiries regarding environmental funding).
Jacqueline Young, Charitable Contributions Consultant (for telephone inquiries regarding environmental funding at 415–668–1119).

History and philosophy. The Foundation was created in 1958 by Fred Gellert, a San Francisco Bay Area real estate developer and builder. In accord with Mr. Gellert's interests, the Foundation supports programs for: environment, health care, disabled, social services, community services, education, arts, youth and senior services in the Bay Area.

Officers and directors. *Officers:* Fred Gellert, Jr., Chairman; John D. Howard; Secretary/Treasurer. *Directors:* Fred Gellert, Jr., Annette E. Gellert, John D. Howard, Marche H. Yoshioka.

Financial data. Data for fiscal year ended November 30, 1993. *Assets:* $11,078,718 (M). *Total grants disbursed:* $781,635.

Environmental awards. *Program and interests:* "The Directors have allocated one quarter of their annual grants for local and national groups organized to find solutions for a healthy planet. Interests are environmental organizations working to balance human numbers with earth's resources and organizations forming coalitions to make environmental planning a national priority."
Recent grants: 1993 grants included support for growth management, water issues, recycling, population/environment, and education efforts to develop a Green Plan in the United States.

Issues. Cli • Bio • Lan • Agr • Wat • Oce • Ene • Was • Tox • Pop • Dev •

Funding analysis.

Fiscal year:	1991	1993
Env grants auth:	$27,000	$245,000
Number:	6	34
Range:	$1,000–$15,000	$500–$75,000
Median:	$2,500	$5,000
Pct $ auth (env/total):	7	31

Recipients (1993 highest):	Number:	Dollars:
KCTS/9 Public Television	1	75,000
Resource Renewal Institute	3	40,000
Marine Science Institute	1	12,000
Materials for the Future Foundation	1	10,000
Population Action International	1	10,000

Activity regions (1993 highest):	Number:	Dollars:
U.S. West	17	85,000
U.S. Northwest	2	80,000
U.S. not specified	9	49,500
International*	4	25,000
Tropics	1	3,000

*Multiple regions or not specified.

Sample grants (1993).
Central California Coast Biosphere Reserve. San Francisco, CA. $5,000. For a three-day symposium bringing together resource managers, scientists, planners, policymakers, teachers, and conservationists to identify at-risk natural resources and find mechanisms of overall management for preserving biological diversity in the Coast.
EarthSave Foundation. Santa Cruz, CA. $3,000. For "Healthy People Healthy Planet" program. To duplicate around the country what is being done in the Santa Cruz school lunch program, teaching children and adults to make ecologically sound, healthy food choices.
Environmental Data Research Institute. Rochester, NY. $500. Toward production costs of the 1993 edition of *Environmental Grantmaking Foundations* directory.
LightHawk. Santa Fe, NM. $2,000. To carry out flights for Congresspeople on committees which oversee national forests and for new Congresspersons to show effects of unchecked logging.
Natural Resources Defense Council. San Francisco, CA. $6,000. For Oil Spill Prevention program in California, to follow through on the implementation phase of the 1990 state and federal oil spill laws ($3,000); for the Sierra Nevada Forestry Project, for staff support to insure that the interim policy of selective logging is adopted by the Forest Service ($3,000).
Point Reyes Bird Observatory. Stimson Beach, CA. $2,500. To support their collaborative work studying bird populations in North and South America and assessing key habitat features to provide objective information and policy direction on environmental issues.
Population Action International. Washington, DC. $10,000. To use international media to raise awareness, to assist family-planning colleagues by distributing information to 3,500 key leaders, to network and collaborate, to work with NGOs and governments towards UN 1994 Cairo conferences.
Rainforest Action Network. San Francisco, CA. $3,000. For the Tropical Timber Campaign aimed at changing consumer behavior and public policy in the United States regarding the use of tropical woods coming from unsustainable sources, particularly for production of information, action packets, and local research.
Sierra Club Foundation. San Francisco, CA. $6,000. To support the research, writing, publication, and distribution of the "Population Report" used to inform and mobilize members around the population issue.
World Affairs Council. San Francisco, CA. $3,000. To defray speaker expenses and for student scholarships for the Asilomar conference "The Environment and Population."
Youth for Environmental Sanity. Santa Cruz, CA. $2,000. To support the 1993–94 YES! Tour which travels the United States, giving school assemblies and workshops to educate and empower youth to make positive changes in the environment.

Zero Population Growth. Washington, DC. $6,000. To support coalition work with the Population Issues Forum, the Population and development Conference Task Force, Ad Hoc Policy Coalitions.

Application process. *Initial contact:* Proposal (3 copies), to include:
1. Letter or summary (1–3 pages) describing the organization's mission, goals, important accomplishments, and the amount and purpose of the funds requested. A list of any coalitions and an explanation of how cooperation impacts the problem-solving should also be included, if relevant.
2. Organization's current budget, including staffing and all operational costs, and the most recent financial statement.
3. List of funding sources for the past three years and a list of other foundations or organizations to whom you have submitted or will be submitting the current proposal.
4. Copy of IRS tax-exempt status determination letter.

When to apply: Deadlines are March 1 and September 1 to be eligible for funding in April and November, respectively.
Materials available: Annual financial statement, "Application Guidelines."

Emphases. *Recipients:* Nonprofit organizations.
Activities: Advocacy, audiovisual materials (films), collaborative efforts, education, networking, planning, policy analysis/development, volunteerism, youth programs.
Types of support: Projects, seed money.
Geography: San Francisco Bay Area; United States only.

Limitations. *Recipients:* Aquariums, botanical gardens, individuals, zoos.
Activities: Conferences, expeditions/tours, feasibility studies, fieldwork, fundraising, inventories, land acquisition, publications, seminars, technical assistance, training.
Types of support: Advertising campaigns, annual campaigns, capital campaigns/expenses, computer hardware, continuing support, debt retirement, emergency funding, endowments, equipment, facilities, indirect costs, lectureships, leveraging funds, loans, maintenance, matching funds, membership campaigns, mortgage reduction, technical assistance, travel expenses.

General Service Foundation

411 East Main Street, Suite 205
Aspen, Colorado 81611
Tel: 303-920-6834   Fax: 303-920-4578
EIN: 366018535   Type: Independent
EGA member
Contact: Robert W. Musser, President

History and philosophy. General Service Foundation is a private foundation endowed by Clifton R. Musser (1869–1956) and his wife, Margaret Kulp Musser (1875–1967). In an effort to address some of the world's basic long-term problems, the Foundation focuses on three areas: International Peace, Reproductive Health and Rights, and Resources.

Officers and directors. *Officers:* Robert W. Musser, President; Mary L. Estrin, Vice President; Marcie J. Musser, Vice President/Treasurer; Elizabeth W. Musser, Secretary. *Directors:* Mary L. Estrin, Robert L. Estrin, Margaret M. Halby, Gary S. Hartshorn, Patricia A. King, Heidi Lloyd, Elizabeth W. Musser, Marcie J. Musser, Robert W. Musser, James P. Shannon. *Honorary Director:* Marion M. Lloyd.

Financial data. Data for fiscal year ended December 31, 1993. *Assets:* $38,601,865 (M). *Total grants authorized:* $1,855,912. *Total grants disbursed:* $1,928,412.

Environmental awards. *Program and interests:* The Resources program has two priorities:

- Western Water.

    Improving the use, management, and quality of water in the United States, particularly west of the Mississippi River.

- International Resources.

    Promoting the conservation and sustainable utilization of natural resources in Latin America and the Caribbean, including tropical forests, wildlife, and fisheries.

Preference is given to field projects that have local community involvement and leadership as a central theme and that test community-led initiatives to integrate sustainable utilization with conservation.

Consideration will also be given to natural resource management training and leadership development programs for individuals from Latin America and the Caribbean.

Recent grants: 1993 grants included support for water (rights and use, river preservation and restoration) in the United States; and for the conservation and sustainable use of natural resources, including tropical forests, wildlife, and fisheries in Latin America and the Caribbean.

Issues.   Cli   Bio   Lan   Agr   Wat   Oce   Ene   Was   Tox   Pop   Dev
              •   •   •   •   •   •   •   •

Funding analysis.

Fiscal year:	1991	1993
Env grants auth:	$671,378	$987,792
Number:	25	39
Range:	$1,378–$150,000	$1,000–$80,000
Median:	$18,500	$25,000
Pct $ auth (env/total):	41	34

Recipients (1993 highest):	Number:	Dollars:
Native American Rights Fund	1	80,000
Woods Hole Research Center	1	65,000
American Rivers, Inc.	1	50,000
International Institute of Rural Reconstruction	1	45,000
Organization for Tropical Studies (OTS)	1	44,500

Activity regions (1993 highest):	Number:	Dollars:
Mexico and Central America	10	240,292
U.S. West	5	190,000
U.S. South Central	4	100,000
Latin America	4	84,500
U.S. Mountain	6	82,000

G

Sample grants (1993).
American Rivers, Inc. Seattle, WA. $50,000 (2 years). To support the Western Water Program, an effort to protect and restore western rivers and watersheds.
Denver Audubon Society. Denver, CO. $10,000. To support the West Mexico Connection Project, whose goal is to preserve important habitat within the Sierra de Manantlan Biosphere Reserve for western species of neotropical migratory birds.
International Voluntary Services, Inc. Washington, DC. $35,000. To support their program designed to reverse the destruction of tropical rainforests in Ecuador, and to revive and introduce sustainable means of producing food and income for the Shuar Indians.
Organization for Tropical Studies (OTS). Durham, NC. $44,500. For the Latin American Education Program, which offers training for Latin American students, professionals, and policymakers in tropical ecology, agroecology, and natural resource policy issues.
Woods Hole Research Center. Woods Hole, MA. $65,000 (2 years). To support a project designed to strengthen local communities' and institutions' capacity to manage and protect intact tropical forests in the Western Brazilian Amazon.
World Neighbors. Oklahoma City, OK. $35,000. For support of low-input agricultural and agroforestry projects in Honduras, Bolivia, and Mexico aimed at increasing food production while reversing environmental degradation.

Application process. *Initial contact:* Letter of inquiry describing the project. If project meets the Foundation's guidelines, an application form will be sent to be completed with a formal proposal. *When to apply:* Deadlines are February 1 and September 1. The board of directors meets semiannually, in the spring and fall. *Materials available:* Annual report (includes "Guidelines" and "Application Procedures").

Emphases. *Recipients:* Nonprofit organizations.
Activities: Advocacy, citizen participation, demonstration programs, fieldwork, innovative programs, litigation, training.
Types of support: Emergency funding, general purposes, operating costs, projects.
Geography: Western Water Program: West of the Mississippi; International Resources: Latin America, Mexico and the Caribbean.

Limitations. *Recipients:* Individuals.
Activities: Lobbying, publications.
Types of support: Annual campaigns, capital campaigns/expenses, continuing support, debt retirement, endowments, equipment, facilities, loans, matching funds, scholarships.
Geography: Non-U.S. organizations (usually).

Georgia Power Foundation, Inc.
20th Floor, 333 Piedmont Avenue, N.E.
Atlanta, Georgia 30308-3374
Tel: 404-526-6784   Fax: 404-526-2945
EIN: 581709417   Type: Company-sponsored
Contact: Judy M. Anderson, Executive Director

History and philosophy. Georgia Power Foundation, Inc. was established in 1986 to focus and extend its efforts under the utility company's motto: "A citizen wherever we serve." The Foundation "hopes to ensure not only the health and prosperity of these communities but also the happiness and success of its business, customers, and employees." Funding areas are: Civic & Community, Arts & Culture, Education, and Health & Human Services.

Officers and directors. *Officers:* Warren Y. Jobe, President; Judy M. Anderson, Secretary, Treasurer, and Executive Director. *Directors:* Judy M. Anderson, Robert L. Boyer, Wayne T. Dahlke, James K. Davis, Dwight H. Evans, Robert H. Haudein, Gene R. Hodges, Warren Y. Jobe, Brian D. Spickard.

Financial data. Data for fiscal year ended December 31, 1992. *Assets:* $56,216,697 (U). *Total grants disbursed:* $2,921,660.

Environmental awards. *Recent grants:* 1991 grants included support for land conservation, forests, wildlife, and a botanical garden.

Issues. Cli Bio Lan Agr Wat Oce Ene Was Tox Pop Dev
              •   •

Funding analysis.

Fiscal year:	1991
Env grants auth:	$289,000
Number:	16
Range:	$500–$100,000
Median:	$10,000
Pct $ disb (env/total):	7

Recipients (1991 highest):	Number:	Dollars:
Georgia Wildlife Federation	1	100,000
The Nature Conservancy, Georgia Field Office	1	55,000
Georgia Department of Natural Resources	2	25,000
The Atlanta Botanical Garden, Inc.	1	25,000
Friends of Zoo Atlanta	2	18,000

Activity regions (1991):	Number:	Dollars:
U.S. Southeast	14	283,500
International*	1	5,000
U.S. not specified	1	500

*Multiple regions or not specified.

Sample grants (1991).
The Atlanta Botanical Garden, Inc. Atlanta, GA. $25,000. Capital.
Friends of Zoo Atlanta. Atlanta, GA. $3,000. Operating expenses.
Georgia Conservancy. Atlanta, GA. $10,000. Operating expenses.
Georgia Department of Natural Resources. Atlanta, GA. $5,000. Operating expenses for the Nongame Wildlife Fund.
Georgia Wildlife Federation. Conyers, GA. $100,000. Capital.
Greater Atlanta Conservation Corps, Inc. Atlanta, GA. $3,500. Operating expenses.
International Society of Arboriculture Memorial Research Trust. Urbana, IL. $5,000. Operating expenses.

Application process. *Initial contact:* Letter to include:
1. Organization description including list of officers or board members.
2. Grant purpose.
3. Other sources of support and amounts assured or anticipated for the proposed project.
4. Evidence of current tax-exempt status.
5. Copy of most recent IRS Form 990 (including Schedule A).

When to apply: Anytime. Grant requests are considered bimonthly.
Materials available: Corporate report, brochure (includes "Application Procedures").

Emphases. *Recipients:* Botanical gardens, educational institutions, nonprofit organizations, public agencies, research institutions, zoos.
Activities: Conferences, research, seminars, volunteerism.
Types of support: Annual campaigns, capital campaigns/expenses, continuing support, debt retirement, emergency funding, endowments, facilities, general purposes, operating costs, professorships, scholarships, seed money, technical assistance.
Geography: Atlanta, Georgia; Georgia.

Georgia-Pacific Foundation

133 Peachtree Street, N.E.
P.O. Box 105605
Atlanta, Georgia 30303–5605
Tel: 404–521–4000
EIN: 936023726   Type: Company-sponsored
Contact: Joan E. Leininger, Director of Community Programs

History and philosophy. The Foundation acts as charitable donor on behalf of the forest products corporation. Interests include conservation and wildlife, historic preservation, medical education and research, and race relations. Major program areas are: arts and culture, civic and community services, education, and health and human services. Grantmaking is limited to areas where Georgia-Pacific has a plant or distribution center.

Officers and directors. *Officers:* Harold L. Airington, Chairman; Wayne I. Tamblyn, President and Treasurer; Ronald P. Hogan, Executive Vice President; Diane Durgin, Secretary; Cornelia B. Brewer, Assistant Secretary. *Trustees:* Harold L. Airington, Cornelia B. Brewer, Diane Durgin, Ronald P. Hogan, T. Marshall Hohn, Jr., Wayne I. Tamblyn, James C. Van Meter, Beth C. Zoffman.

Financial data. Data for fiscal year ended December 31, 1992. *Assets:* $701,341 (M). *Gifts received:* $759,081. *Total grants disbursed:* $2,106,607.

Environmental awards. *Recent grants:* 1991 grants included support for a beautification, land conservation, forest-related activities, outdoor education, a botanical garden, and a zoo.

Issues.   Cli   Bio   Lan   Agr   Wat   Oce   Ene   Was   Tox   Pop   Dev
                     •   •

Funding analysis.

Fiscal year:	1991
Env grants disb:	$82,500
Number:	12
Range:	$1,000–$25,000
Median:	$3,750
Pct $ disb (env/total):	4

Recipients (1991 highest):	Number:	Dollars:
The Atlanta Botanical Garden, Inc.	2	27,000
North Carolina Outward Bound School	1	15,000
Trees Atlanta, Inc.	1	12,000
Maine Tree Foundation	1	10,000
World Forestry Center	1	6,000

Activity regions (1991):	Number:	Dollars:
U.S. Southeast	8	64,500
U.S. Northeast	1	10,000
U.S. not specified	3	8,000

Sample grants (1991).
The Atlanta Botanical Garden, Inc. Atlanta, GA. $25,000.
Forest History Society. Durham, NC. $1,000.
North Carolina Outward Bound School. Morganton, NC. $15,000
Southern Forest World. Waycross, GA. $1,000.
World Forestry Center. Portland, OR. $6,000.

Application process. *Initial contact:* Proposal. There are no specific requirements.
When to apply: Anytime.
Materials available: Corporate report.

Emphases. *Recipients:* Nonprofit organizations.
Activities: Conferences, seminars, projects.
Types of support: Annual campaigns, capital campaigns/expenses, continuing support, debt retirement, emergency funding, endowments, equipment, facilities, general purposes, matching funds, operating costs, professorships, scholarships, seed money, technical assistance.
Geography: Georgia and locations where Georgia-Pacific has a significant presence.

The Wallace Alexander Gerbode Foundation, Inc.

470 Columbus Avenue, Suite 209
San Francisco, California 94133
Tel: 415–391–0911
EIN: 946065226   Type: Independent
EGA member
Contact: Thomas C. Layton, Executive Director

History and philosophy. The Foundation was established in 1953 by members of the Gerbode family. The Foundation funds innovative, positive programs and projects that affect residents of the California counties of Alameda, Contra Costa, Marin, San Francisco, and San Mateo and the state of Hawaii. Program areas are: Arts and Humanities, Community Affairs, Education, and the Environment.

Officers and directors. *Officers:* Maryanna G. Stockholm, Chairman and President; Frank A. Gerbode, M.D., Vice Chairman and Vice President; Joan Richardson, Secretary; Charles M. Stockholm, Treasurer; Thomas C. Layton, Assistant Secretary and Executive Director. *Directors:* Frank A. Gerbode, M.D., Thomas C. Layton, Joan Richardson, Charles M. Stockholm, Maryanna G. Stockholm.

Financial data. Data for fiscal year ended December 31, 1992. *Assets:* $42,890,672 (M). *Total grants disbursed:* $1,581,082.

Environmental awards. *Program and interests:* Topics of interest include:

- Toxics.
- Open space preservation.
- Coastal development issues.
- Marine issues.
- Energy policy.
- Ethnic diversity in environmental organizations.

The Foundation is also interested in population.

Recent grants: 1992 grants included support for conservation in the San Francisco Bay-Delta region, and in Hawaii for marine and coastal issues, solid waste, and toxics.

Issues. Cli Bio Lan Agr Wat Oce Ene Was Tox Pop Dev
• • •   • • •   • •

Funding analysis.

Fiscal year:	1991	1992
Env grants auth:	$308,000	$330,180
Number:	17	20
Range:	$5,000–$50,000	$500–$50,000
Median:	$15,000	$12,000
Pct $ auth (env/total):	25	16

Recipients (1992 highest):	Number:	Dollars:
Earth Island Institute	1	50,000
Greenbelt Alliance	1	45,000
Latino Issues Forum	1	30,000
Natural Resources Defense Council	1	30,000
Earthtrust	2	25,500

Activity regions (1992):	Number:	Dollars:
U.S. West	13	245,500
Hawaii	7	84,680

Sample grants (1992).

California Toxics Action. San Francisco, CA. $25,000. Support of its campaign to protect San Francisco Bay.
Center for Natural Lands Management. Sacramento, CA. $15,000. Organizational development.
Committee for Water Policy Consensus. Concord, CA. $5,000. Support of the Bay-Delta Hearings Coordination and Public Education Project.
Earthtrust. Kailua, HI. $25,000. To develop a long-term mechanism for the funding of dolphin and marine protection programs through the establishment of an independent "Flipper Foundation" and the Flipper Seal of Approval Program.
The Environmental Careers Organization, Inc. San Francisco, CA. $5,000. Support of its Minority Environmental Career Conference.
Friends of the River Foundation. San Francisco, CA. $3,500. Support of its long-range planning process.
Greenbelt Alliance. San Francisco, CA. $45,000 (3 years). Support of its Bay Area Ridge Trail Council Project.
Latino Issues Forum. San Francisco, CA. $30,000 (2 years). For the organizational development of its EDGE Program, an alliance of ethnic and environmental organizations.
The Trust for Public Land. San Francisco, CA. $20,000. Support of its efforts to develop and market a taxable, credit-enhanced debt instrument that TPL would use to finance multi-year real estate transactions with state and local governments.
Yosemite Institute. San Francisco, CA. $12,000. Organizational development.

Application process. *Initial contact:* Letter of inquiry to include:
1. Description of project.
2. Proposed budget.
3. Copy of IRS tax-exempt status determination letter.

Initial contact should not include materials to be returned. No applications or unsolicited materials accepted via facsimile.
When to apply: Anytime. The directors meet four times a year.
Materials available: Annual report.

Emphases. *Recipients:* Nonprofit organizations.
Activities: Advocacy, citizen participation, collaborative efforts, policy analysis/development.
Types of support: Program-related investments.
Geography: California counties of Alameda, Contra Costa, Marin, San Francisco, and San Mateo; Hawaii.

Limitations. *Recipients:* Individuals.
Activities: Direct services, fundraising, publications.
Types of support: Capital campaigns/expenses, debt retirement, equipment, facilities (construction), fellowships, general purposes, operating costs, scholarships, travel expenses.

The German Marshall Fund of the United States

11 Dupont Circle, N.W., Suite 750
Washington, DC 20036
Tel: 202-745-3950   Fax: 202-265-1662
EIN: 520954751   Type: Independent
EGA member
Contacts: Marianne L. Ginsburg, Program Officer
             Jessica Dax, Program Associate
             Irmgard Hunt, U.S. Project Director, Environmental Partnership for Central Europe

---

History and philosophy. The German Marshall Fund of the United States is an independent American organization created in 1972 by a gift from the Federal Republic of Germany as a memorial to the Marshall Plan. The Fund supports and carries out activities that: (1) promote a more informed understanding of Europe in the United States, and of the United States in Europe; (2) improve communication between these two industrial centers; and (3) strengthen public policy institutions addressing common problems. Since 1989 the Fund has supported programs in Western Europe, The Czech Republic and The Slovak Republic, Poland, and Hungary. The Fund currently has four substantive program areas: Exploring Changing U.S.-European Economic Roles, Supporting Reform in Central and Eastern Europe, Building U.S.-European Environmental Partnerships, and Fostering U.S.-European Cooperation after the Cold War.

Officers and directors. *Officer:* Franklin D. Raines, Chair. *Trustees:* Harry G. Barnes, Jr., Charles H. Dallara, Jessica Einhorn, Sandra Feldman, Guido Goldman, Geri M. Joseph, Frank E. Loy, Ray Marshall, Elizabeth Midgley, Steven Muller, Neal R. Peirce, William K. Reilly, Lois D. Rice, Richard C. Steadman, Fritz Stern, Victoria J. Tschinkel, J. Robinson West, William M. Woessner, Suzanne H. Woolsey, Robert B. Zoellick.

Financial data. Data for fiscal year ended May 31, 1993. *Assets:* $101,172,135 (U). *Total grants disbursed:* $8,548,155.

Environmental awards. *Program and interests:* Environmental grants are made through two programs: Supporting Reform in Central and Eastern Europe, and Building U.S.-European Environmental Partnerships.

- Supporting Reform.

    This program makes grants directly and indirectly through the Environmental Partnership for Central Europe, a Fund project supported by a consortium of foundations. Both encourage environmental reform and public participation.

    - Direct grants support projects with a national and region-wide outreach, and local pilot projects if these are not eligible under The Environmental Partnership.
    - The Environmental Partnership program focuses principally on local efforts and works through local representatives in the four countries of Central Europe (Poland, The Czech Republic, The Slovak Republic, and Hungary).

    The Supporting Reform program focuses on nongovernmental organizations (NGOs), specifically to:

    - Build NGO capacity to address environmental problems, implement projects, and determine the applicability of Western and other environmental models.
    - Transfer environmental management tools to environmental professionals in government and NGOs.
    - Further consensus building at national and local levels among NGOs, industry, and government.
    - Improve media coverage of environmental issues.

- Building Partnerships.

    With the recognition that global solutions are needed to deal with some of the most critical environmental problems, this program works with professionals and policymakers in government, business, and NGOs in two areas:

    - Integrated management policies in transportation, energy efficiency, and other fields essential to reduce greenhouse gas emissions.
    - Use of economic tools, such as taxes, fees, and pricing mechanisms to further environmental policies.

    The Building Partnerships program with an annual budget of $595,000 will support short-term trans-Atlantic fellowships and study tours for U.S. and European practitioners; workshops and conferences to bring together government, business, and NGOs; and NGO efforts to encourage governments and international organizations to adopt more effective environmental policies.

Issues. Cli • Bio • Lan Agr • Wat • Oce Ene • Was Tox • Pop Dev •

Funding analysis.

Fiscal year:	1992	1993
Env grants auth:	$898,661	$1,030,300
Number:	36	38
Range:	$615–$150,000	$1,200–$150,000
Median:	$30,000	$10,000
Pct $ disb (env/total):	13	12

Recipients (1993 highest):	Number:	Dollars:
German Marshall Fund, Administered Fellowships	4	383,900
Conservation Law Foundation	1	75,000
International Council for Local Environmental Issues	1	70,000
Environmental Health Center	1	55,000
Living on Earth	1	50,000
World Resources Institute	1	50,000

Activity region (1993):	Number:	Dollars:
International*	38	1,030,300

*All grants are U.S.-Europe.

Sample grants (1993).

Climate Network-Europe. Brussels, Belgium. $45,000 (2 years). To provide core support for CN-E's service office function.

International Council for Local Environmental Issues. Freiburg, Germany. $70,000. For start-up costs to expand linkages with North American initiatives and national climate campaigns and to develop training workshops.

Journaisten Aktion Umwelt. Germany. $15,000. For Central and Eastern European environmental journalists to participate in the 1993 International Communications Congress: "Perspectives of Environmental Communication: Environmental Consciousness in the Mass Media."

Living on Earth. Cambridge, MA. $50,000. To expand European coverage on the National Public Radio weekly half-hour environmental radio news magazine, *Living on Earth.*

World Resources Institute. Washington, DC. $50,000. To organize a workshop for U.S. and European NGOs, research institutes, policymakers, and business sector working on energy pricing that addresses global warming and to produce and coordinate policy analysis to educate constituencies.

Application process. *Initial contact:* Brief proposal to include:
1. Purpose and importance of project.
2. Link to U.S.-European relations.
3. Project budget.
4. Other potential funding sources.
5. Qualifications of the applicant (curriculum vitae or resume for individuals; descriptive brochures or annual reports for institutions, if available).
6. Plans for dissemination or follow-up.

When to apply: Anytime. Requests for grants of $25,000 or more should be submitted at least six weeks before a meeting of the board of trustees. These meetings take place in mid-October, mid-February, and late May.
Materials available: "Who We Are and How We Work" (brochure, contains application guidelines); *TransAtlantic Perspectives* (newsletter/journal published three times a year containing grants lists and financial statements). Special applications are required for research fellowships.

Emphases. *Recipients:* Nonprofit organizations, public agencies.
Activities: Advocacy, capacity building, citizen participation, collaborative efforts, conferences, conflict resolution, networking, planning, policy analysis/development, training, workshops.
Types of support: Fellowships, internships, leveraging funds, pilot projects, seed money, travel expenses.
Geography: Western Europe, United States, The Czech Republic, The Slovak Republic, Poland, Hungary.

Limitations. *Recipients:* Botanical gardens, museums, zoos.
Activities: Direct services, exhibits, inventories, land acquisition, litigation, lobbying, research.
Types of support: Advertising campaigns, annual campaigns, capital campaigns/expenses, debt retirement, loans, maintenance, membership campaigns, mortgage reduction, professorships, program-related investments.

The Rollin M. Gerstacker Foundation

P.O. Box 1945
Midland, Michigan 48641–1945
Tel: 517–631–6097   Fax: 517–832–8842
EIN: 386060276   Type: Independent
Contact: E. Ned Brandt, Vice President

History and philosophy. The Rollin M. Gerstacker Foundation was founded by Mrs. Eda U. Gerstacker in 1957 in memory of her husband. Its purpose is to continue to support charities of all kinds supported by the Gerstackers during their lifetimes. Most of these are located in Michigan and Ohio. Funding interests are: affordable housing for elderly persons in the Midland area; the Midland Hospital Association, research institutions, colleges and universities; youth work; and general community support. Recent grants have enhanced the quality of living in and around Midland through the downtown Streetscape project and the opening of the Pere Marquette Rail Trail.

Officers and directors. *Officers:* Gail E. Allen, President; E. Ned Brandt, Vice President and Secretary; Carl A. Gerstacker, Vice President and Treasurer; Gilbert A. Currie, Lisa J. Gerstacker, Julius Grosberg, Assistant Treasurers. *Trustees:* Frank Gerace, Esther S. Gerstacker, Paul F. Oreffice, Alan W. Ott, Jean Popoff, William D. Schuette.

Financial data. Data for fiscal year ended December 31, 1993.
Assets: $20,326,393 (M). *Total grants disbursed:* $3,743,127.

Environmental awards. *Recent grants:* 1993 grants included continuing support for wildlife recovery and a nature center.

Issues.   Cli   Bio   Lan   Agr   Wat   Oce   Ene   Was   Tox   Pop   Dev
                    •   •

Funding analysis.

Fiscal year:	1991	1993
Env grants disb:	$18,000	$32,000
Number:	2	3
Range:	$1,000–$17,000	$2,000–$20,000
Median:	$9,000	$10,000
Pct $ disb (env/total):	1	1

Recipients (1993)	*Number:*	*Dollars:*
Chippewa Nature Center	1	20,000
Midland Soil/Water Conservation District	1	10,000
Wildlife Recovery Association	1	2,000

Activity region (1993):	*Number:*	*Dollars:*
U.S. Great Lakes	3	32,000

Sample grants (1993).
Chippewa Nature Center. Midland, MI. $20,000.
Midland Soil/Water Conservation District. Midland, MI. $10,000.
Wildlife Recovery Association. Midland, MI. $2,000.

Application process. *Initial contact:* Brief letter describing proposed project.
When to apply: Deadlines are in May and November or at least one month before the trustees' meetings in June and December.
Materials available: Annual report.

Emphases. *Recipients:* Pre-selected organizations.
Geography: Midland, Michigan.

Limitations. *Recipients:* Individuals.
Types of support: Scholarships.

Bernard F. and Alva B. Gimbel Foundation, Inc.

c/o Bregman & Company
600 Summer Street, 3rd Floor
Stamford, Connecticut 06901–1403
Tel: 203–325–4155   Fax: 203–324–5454
EIN: 136090843   Type: Independent
Contact: Hope G. Solinger, Secretary/Treasurer

History and philosophy. The Foundation was established in 1943. It makes grants to pre-selected organizations in the fields of: arts (visual, performing, and literary), education, the environment, and human services for youth and the disadvantaged.

Officers and directors. *Officers:* Carol G. Lebworth, President; Hope G. Solinger, Secretary/Treasurer. *Directors:* Glenn H. Greenberg, Carol G. Lebworth, Hope G. Solinger, Lynn Stern.

Financial data. Data for fiscal year ended December 31, 1992.
Assets: $6,923,879 (M). *Total grants disbursed:* $425,000.

Environmental awards. *Recent grants:* 1992 grants included support for biodiversity and land conservation issues.

Issues. Cli Bio Lan Agr Wat Oce Ene Was Tox Pop Dev
         •   •   •

Funding analysis.

Fiscal year:	1991	1992
Env grants disb:	$56,000	$50,800
Number:	4	3
Range:	$1,000–$25,000	$800–$25,000
Median:	$15,000	$25,000
Pct $ disb (env/total):	15	12

Recipients (1992):	Number:	Dollars:
Environmental Defense Fund	1	25,000
Natural Resources Defense Council	1	25,000
The Nature Conservancy, Connecticut Chapter	1	800

Activity regions (1992):	Number:	Dollars:
U.S. not specified	2	50,000
U.S. Northeast	1	800

Sample grants (1992).

Environmental Defense Fund. New York, NY. $25,000.
Natural Resources Defense Council. New York, NY. $25,000.
The Nature Conservancy, Connecticut Chapter. Middletown, CT. $800.

Application process. *Initial contact:* The Foundation awards grants to pre-selected organizations only. No unsolicited applications accepted.

Emphases. *Recipients:* Pre-selected organizations only.
Types of support: Continuing support.
Geography: New York, Connecticut.

Limitations. *Types of support:* Fellowships, loans, matching funds, scholarships.

Give to the Earth Foundation

c/o Aveda Corporation
4000 Pheasant Ridge Drive
Blaine, Minnesota 55434
Tel: 612–783–4000 ext. 4220   Fax: 612–783–4110
800–933–6288
EIN: 411720153   Type: Independent
Contact: Ellen Liberatori, Executive Director

History and philosophy. The Foundation was established in 1991 by Aveda founder Horst Rechelbacher "to support activities that protect and sustain the planet." Give to the Earth is focused on environmental programs, especially "on funding grassroots, activist organizations making a direct, identifiable, and positive impact on the environment." The Foundation supports organizations with minimal administrative overhead.

Financial data. Data for fiscal year ended December 31, 1993. *Assets:* $190,257 (M). *Gifts received:* $198,008. *Total grants disbursed:* $137,705.

Environmental awards. *Program and interests:* The Foundation will consider grant requests that:

- Protect the integrity of the Earth's natural systems.
- Promote a sustainable society and work to eliminate the use of petrochemicals.
- Preserve biological diversity and conserve natural resources.
- Minimize pollution and contamination within the community.
- Improve the quality of human life.
- Communicate environmental information that assists in changing attitudes and facilitates practices compatible with a sustainable society.
- Respond to world emergency needs.

Recent grants: 1994 grants included support for toxics reduction and urban issues (transportation, community gardens, air quality).

Issues. Cli Bio Lan Agr Wat Oce Ene Was Tox Pop Dev
         •   •   •   •   •   •   •

Funding analysis.

Fiscal year:	1992
Env grants auth:	$86,500
Number:	12
Range:	$1,000–$17,000
Median:	$2,500
Pct $ disb (env/total):	52

Recipients (1992 highest):	Number:	Dollars:
Clean Water Action	1	17,000
International Alliance for Sustainable Agriculture	1	17,000
National Toxics Campaign Fund	1	17,000
Siskiyou Regional Education Project	1	17,000
White Earth Land Recovery Project	1	8,000

Activity regions (1992 highest):	Number:	Dollars:
U.S. not specified	3	36,000
International*	3	19,000
U.S. multiple regions	1	17,000
U.S. Great Lakes	1	8,000
Tropics	1	3,000

*Multiple regions or not specified.

Sample grants (1994).

Common Ground. Santa Fe, NM. $1,100. Organic community garden project that utilizes the talents of disadvantaged youth in the Twin Cities area. The grant provides matching funds to purchase *Seeds of Change* and a tiller to prepare three community sites.

Ohio Valley Environmental Coalition. Cleveland, OH. $5,000. To improve health and living standards of communities in Kentucky, Louisiana, and Ohio by minimizing toxic air emissions from local corporations. For a Citizen/Volunteer Monitoring and Action program that helps to enforce EPA regulations and to create a public forum, debate, and strategic planning for an environmental course that blends the interests of industry and the community.

G

The Rainbow Generation. Kansas City, KS. $2,000. Youth service and community action through the Stream Team Project, Local Weatherization Project for low-income residents, Christmas Tree Recycling Project, and Tree-Planting Project.

Sensible Transportation Options for People. Tigard, OR. $3,000. For public education and organizing to promote sensible and alternative transportation programs and sustainable city planning strat-egies in Washington County, Oregon.

Application process. *Initial contact:* Letter or telephone call. Proposal to include:
1. Organization's name, address, contact person, telephone number, and date of application.
2. Brief description and history of organization.
3. Purpose, need, and time period the grant will cover.
4. Description of results to be accomplished by project.
5. Amount of request.
6. Method for evaluating program.
7. List of funding proposed and received for project.
8. Evidence of IRS tax-exempt status.
9. Project and organization budget.
10. Audited financial information.

All funded projects must yield identifiable results. Environmental education programs must be action-oriented; the Foundation does not provide funding for those that focus on curriculum. The Foundation does not support organizations "that have developed excessive bureaucracy and administrative overhead," or individual projects involving the use of pesticides and/or herbicides.
When to apply: Anytime. The board meets bimonthly in January, March, May, July, September, and November.
Materials available: Foundation summary, application guidelines, grant recipient list, newsletter.

Emphases. *Recipients:* Pre-selected organizations (generally), nonprofit organizations.
Activities: Activism, advocacy, citizen participation, collaborative efforts, demonstration programs, direct services, innovative programs, training, volunteerism, youth programs.
Types of support: Continuing support, general purposes, leveraging funds, matching funds, pilot projects, projects.
Geography: Mainly Minnesota and the United States. Some international grants.

Limitations. *Activities:* Audiovisual materials, fundraising, land acquisition, lobbying.
Types of support: Operating costs.

Global Environmental Project Institute
P.O. Box 1111
Ketchum, Idaho 83340
Tel: 208–726–3025 Fax: 208–726–4068
EIN: 820421067 Type: Independent
EGA member
Contacts: J. Christopher Hormel, President
  Michelle Richer, Proposal Coordinator

History and philosophy. The Global Environmental Project Institute is a private foundation. Its central focus is public education about environmental issues.

Officers and directors. *Officers:* J. Christopher Hormel, President; Angela H. Ocone, Vice President; LuAnne Finch Hormel, Secretary/Treasurer. *Directors:* J. Christopher Hormel, LuAnne Finch Hormel, Thomas Hormel, Rampa Hormel.

Financial data. Data for fiscal year ended December 31, 1993. *Total grants:* $587,077.

Environmental awards. *Program and interests:* The Institute wishes to fund "anything that helps change people's attitudes about the planet: deep ecology, new economic theories, etc." Special interests are:

- Global environmental issues.
- Environmental education.
- Environmental citizenship.
- Grassroots organizations.
- Citizen action.

Recent grants: 1993 grants included support for forest and river protection and environmental education.

Issues. Cli Bio Lan Agr Wat Oce Ene Was Tox Pop Dev
  • • • • •

Funding analysis.

Fiscal year:	1992
Env grants disb:	$35,549
Number:	1
Range:	$35,549–$35,549
Median:	$35,549
Pct $ disb (env/total):	100

Recipient (1992):	*Number:*	*Dollars:*
Environmental Resource Center	1	35,549

Activity region (1992):	*Number:*	*Dollars:*
U.S. Northwest	1	35,549

Sample grants (1993).
E2: Environment & Education. Pacific Palisades, CA. $214,999.
East African Environmental Network. Niarobi, Kenya. $32,000.
Environmental Resource Center. Ketchum, ID. $83,300.
Global Action and Information Network. Santa Cruz, CA. $134,581.
Idaho Rivers United. Boise, ID. $5,000.
Save America's Forests, Inc. Washington, DC. $10,000.

Application process. *Initial contact:* Brief letter of inquiry.
When to a apply: Anytime.

Emphases. *Recipients:* Nonprofit organizations.
Activities: Activism, advocacy, citizen participation, conflict resolution, demonstration programs, education, innovative programs, lobbying, networking (international only), political activities.
Types of support: Matching funds, pilot projects, projects, single-year grants only, start-up costs, travel expenses.
Geography: Idaho; national United States; international.

Limitations. *Recipients:* Botanical gardens, educational institutions, individuals, museums, public agencies, research institutions, zoos.
Activities: Audiovisual materials, exhibits, expeditions/tours, inventories, land acquisition, litigation, research, seminars, symposia/colloquia.
Types of support: Advertising campaigns, debt retirement, emergency funding, facilities, fellowships, lectureships, loans, mortgage reduction, multi-year grants, professorships.
Geography: Local or regional organizations outside of Idaho.

Global Greengrants Fund
3564 Pearl Street
Boulder, Colorado 80301
Tel: 303-786-8170   Fax: 303-786-8170
E-mail: greengrants@igc.apc.org
Type: Community
Contact: Chet Tchozewshi, Director

History and philosophy. The Global Greengrants Fund was established in 1993 by the Damien Foundation and the Caribou Fund as a donor collaborative at The Tides Foundation. It is a community-based environmental grantmaker whose mission "is to make small grants to strengthen the international grassroots environmental movement in developing regions of the world with rich biodiversity of global importance." Most grants are made to pre-selected organizations on the basis of recommendations from an informal network of grassroots activists working with international, national, and regional networks of grassroots organizations.

Target areas are the Southern Hemisphere and other regions where alternative sources of funding do not exist.

Officers and directors. *Personnel:* Wendy Emrich, Humberto Mafra, Chet Tchozewshi, Roy Young.

Financial data. *Total grants disbursed as of December 1994:* $125,000 (est.).

Environmental awards. *Program and interests:* The Fund's premise is that "to prevent ecological collapse, it is necessary to build the capacity of the grassroots environmental movement by ensuring long-term organizational stability."
Recent grants: 1993 and 1994 grants included support for forest preservation, environmental education, and publications.

Issues. Cli   Bio   Lan   Agr   Wat   Oce   Ene   Was   Tox   Pop   Dev
                       •

Sample grants (1994).
Acao Democrática Feminina Gaucha Amigos de Terra. Porto Allegre, Brazil. $1,500.
Earth Island Institute. San Francisco, CA. $2,000.
Earth Trust Foundation. Malibu, CA. $5,000.
Pacific Environment and Resources Center. Sausalito, CA. $4,000.
Rainforest Action Network. Sao Paulo, Brazil. $2,000.
Sarawak Campaign Committee. Tokyo, Japan. $5,000.

Application process. *Initial contact:* Proposal (3 pages) to include:
1. Name, address, phone number, and title of contact person.
2. Timeline.
3. Amount requested.
4. Name, address, and phone and fax numbers of organization.
5. Telex, cable, and electronic mail address (if any).
6. Previous and current year's budget and sources of income.
7. Copy of IRS tax-exempt status determination letter.
8. Organization's bank name, contact, phone number, and account number.
9. Organization's history, goals, method of achieving goals, and population to benefit from project.
10. Description of past, current, and proposed activities and how these will enable organization to meet its long-term goals.

When to apply: Most grants are made to pre-selected organizations. No unsolicited applications accepted.
Materials available: Grant recommendation procedures, grant guidelines, grants list.

Emphases. *Recipients:* Nonprofit organizations, pre-selected organizations.
Activities: Activism, advocacy, citizen participation, conferences, education, publications.
Types of support: Continuing support, general purposes, operating costs, pilot projects, seed money.
Geography: Currently Latin America, Southeast Asia, and Siberia, but there are no firm geographic limitations.

Limitations. *Recipients:* Individuals.

The Golden Rule Foundation, Inc.
P.O. Box 825
Bowling Green Station
New York, New York 10274-0825
EIN: 599207701   Type: Independent
EGA member
Contact: John K. Evans, President

History and philosophy. The Golden Rule Foundation was established in 1982 by Jack Evans (d. 1991), who left most of his oil fortune to the Foundation. The Foundation's three main areas of interest reflect the founder's social concerns: (1) to correct the imbalance between energy supply and energy consumption, a concern over the long range effects which the development of necessary resources will have on the world for future generations; (2) to protect and preserve the environment; (3) to foster traditional American values of self-improvement and self-reliance by improving the management and entrepreneurial skills of young people engaged in business.

Officers and directors. John K. Evans, President; Sian Evans, Vice President; Gilbert Hsaio, Secretary/Treasurer.

Financial data. Data for fiscal year ended October 31, 1991. *Assets:* $515,065 (M). *Total grants disbursed:* $31,025.

G

Environmental awards. *Program and interests:* Two of the Foundation's three foci are environmental:

- Energy supply and conservation.
- Environmental protection and conservation.

Issues. *Cli Bio Lan Agr Wat Oce Ene Was Tox Pop Dev*
• •

Sample grants (1990).
International Energy Program–SAIS. Washington, DC. $1,000.
The Jefferson Energy Foundation. Washington, DC. $500.
Rocky Mountain Institute. Snowmass, CO. $1,000.

Application process. *Initial contact:* Preliminary letter (1,000 words maximum) to include:
1. Description of proposal, contact person, and fax number.
2. Objective of proposal.
3. Criteria and mechanisms for evaluating success of proposal.
4. Amount requested, time span involved, brief outline of budget and total project cost.

Letter should serve as an introduction to your proposal, not as actual detailed proposal. Append summary resumes of people involved (3 pages maximum).
When to apply: Anytime. Distribution takes place in October.
Materials available: Brochure (includes "Funding Criteria" and "Preliminary Procedures").

Emphases. *Activities:* Projects closely linked to specific geographical areas and small communities.

Limitations. *Recipients:* Individuals, religious organizations.
Activities: Education, training.
Types of support: Capital campaigns/expenses, endowments, political activities.

The Goldman Environmental Foundation

One Lombard Street, Suite 303
San Francisco, California 94111
Tel: 415–788–9090   Fax: 415–788–7890
EIN: 943094857   Type: Independent
EGA member
Contacts: Duane Silverstein, Executive Director
            Helena Brykarz, Program Officer
            Diana Donlon, Program Officer

History and philosophy. The Global Environmental Foundation was established in 1989 by the Richard & Rhoda Goldman Fund. Its makes an annual award of The Goldman Environmental Prize to six environmental "heroes"—one in each of the six continental regions: North America, South/Central America, Europe, Asia, Africa, and Island Nations.

Officers and directors. *Prize Jury:* Anwar Fazal, Susan R. Gelman, Douglas E. Goldman, M.D., John D. Goldman, Rhoda H. Goldman, Richard N. Goldman, Joan Martin-Brown, Robert T. Stafford, Dr. Alvaro Umaña, Linda J. Wong.

Financial data. Data for fiscal year ended December 31, 1993.
Total grants disbursed: $360,000.

Environmental awards. *Program and interests:* The Goldman Environmental Prize is the world's largest grassroots environmental prize. The Prize may be awarded for any environmental issue.

Issues. *Cli Bio Lan Agr Wat Oce Ene Was Tox Pop Dev*
•   •   •   •   •   •   •   •

Funding analysis.

Fiscal year:	1992	1993
Env grants auth:	$360,000	$360,000
Number:	6	6
Range:	—	—
Median:	$60,000	$60,000
Pct $ auth (env/total):	100	100

Recipients (1993):	Number:	Dollars:
Margaret Jacobsohn & Garth Owen-Smith	1	60,000
Juan Mayr	1	60,000
Dai Qing	1	60,000
John Sinclair	1	60,000
JoAnn Tall	1	60,000
Sviatoslav Zabelin	1	60,000

Activity regions (1993):	Number:	Dollars:
Africa	1	60,000
Australian Group	1	60,000
Far East	1	60,000
Northern South America	1	60,000
Russia	1	60,000
U.S. Mountain	1	60,000

Sample grants (1993).
Margaret Jacobsohn & Garth Owen-Smith. Africa. In a remote corner of Namibia, Margaret Jacobsohn and Garth Owen-Smith have started a successful natural resource management program linking wildlife conservation to sustainable rural development. This approach, "Community-Based Conservation Development," is a model for communities throughout Africa.
Juan Mayr. South/Central America. Colombia, one of the most biologically diverse countries on the planet, is home to the Sierra Nevada de Santa Marta. Despite dangerous working conditions, Juan Mayr has led an effective crusade for the Sierra Nevada's protection and has succeeded in getting disparate groups to come together for its preservation.
Dai Qing. Asia. Dai Qing, a journalist, has been outspoken in her opposition to China's Three Gorges Dam scheduled for the Yangtze River. At great personal risk, she published a collection of essays by Chinese intellectuals critical of what would be the world's largest hydroelectric dam.
John Sinclair. Island Nations. For 20 years, John Sinclair has fought to protect Fraser Island, the world's largest sand island, located off the coast of Queensland, Australia. Against strong local opposition, he succeeded in stopping sand mining on the island and logging of its unique rainforest. In 1992, Fraser Island was designated a World Heritage Site.
JoAnn Tall. North America. Inspired by the Native American tradition of respect for the land, JoAnn Tall, a Lakota woman, helped stop nuclear weapons testing in the Black Hills and prevented a hazardous waste dump from being located in Pine Ridge and the neighboring Rosebud Reservation. In 1989, Tall co-founded the Native Resource Coalition.

© 1995 Environmental Data Resources, Inc.

Sviatoslav Zabelin. Europe. In 1988, Russia's Sviatoslav Zabelin co-founded the Socio-Ecological Union, a coalition of 250 environmental organizations working throughout the republics of the former Soviet Union. Using a computer network, Zabelin has been able to help build the infrastructure necessary to combat the region's growing environmental problems.

Application process. *Initial contact:* Nominations are accepted from two sources only: a network of 19 internationally known environmental organizations and a confidential panel of environmental experts from 30 nations that includes citizen activists and prominent policymakers.
When to apply: Nominations are accepted from May 1 through September 1.
Materials available: Annual report, brochure.

Emphases. *Recipients:* Private citizens and grassroots groups; government employees are eligible only for work carried on outside the scope of their official responsibilities.
Activities: Citizen participation, education.
Geography: Africa, Asia, Europe, Island Nations, South/Central America, North America.

Herman Goldman Foundation

61 Broadway, 18th Floor
New York, New York 10006
Tel: 212–797–9090
EIN: 136066039   Type: Independent
Contact: Richard K. Baron, Executive Director

History and philosophy. The Herman Goldman Foundation was founded in 1942 by New York City attorney Herman Goldman (1880–1968). Originally organized as a charitable trust and reconstituted in 1943 as the Herman Goldman Foundation, Inc., the Foundation was renamed in 1972.

The Foundation's broad purpose is to enhance the quality of life in: Health, Education, Social Justice, and the Arts. "With few exceptions, grantmaking is confined to the New York metropolitan area."

Officers and directors. *Officers:* Stanley M. Klein, President; David A. Brauner, Vice President; Elias Rosenzweig, Secretary/Treasurer. *Directors:* Jules M. Baron, Raymond S. Baron, Paul Bauman, David A. Brauner, Robert N. Davies, Emanuel Goldstein, Michael L. Goldstein, Stanley M. Klein, Seymour H. Kligler, Elias Rosenzweig, Gail Schneider, Norman H. Sparber.

Financial data. Data for fiscal year ended February 28, 1993.
Assets: $19,572,823. *Total grants disbursed:* $2,910,424.

Environmental awards. *Recent grants:* 1993 grants included support for urban beautification; horticulture; and youth, citizen, and teacher education.

Issues.   Cli   Bio   Lan   Agr   Wat   Oce   Ene   Was   Tox   Pop   Dev
             •

Funding analysis.

Fiscal year:	1992	1993
Env grants auth:	$20,000	$30,000
Number:	2	3
Range:	$10,000–$10,000	$10,000–$10,000
Median:	$10,000	$10,000
Pct $ auth (env/total):	1	1

Recipients (1993):	Number:	Dollars:
Brooklyn Botanic Garden	1	10,000
Horticultural Society of New York	1	10,000
New York State Bar Association	1	10,000

Activity region (1993):	Number:	Dollars:
New York/New Jersey	3	30,000

Sample grants (1993).
Brooklyn Botanic Garden. Brooklyn, NY. $10,000. The Children's Garden has been teaching youngsters to grow and love plants for 79 years. The largest children's gardening program in the nation and the oldest continuously operating one in the world, it has positively affected the lives of some 15,000 children since it was established in 1914.
Horticultural Society of New York. New York, NY. $10,000. The Society's new program, The Harlem Project, is a hands-on environmental and beautification program designed to help the residents of north central Harlem better their neighborhood, strengthen their self-esteem, and elevate the quality of life for themselves and their children. The program's broad focus represents a significant step forward in The Society's community service work.
New York State Bar Association. New York, NY. $10,000. To develop a teacher's guide for *Shaping the Environment*. The guide would provide additional materials, activities, and instructional strategies with which the teacher could augment the use of, rewards from, and student response to, the text. It would also enable the teachers and students to become more comfortable with the complex issues in question.

Application process. *Initial contact:* Full proposal to include:
1. Amount requested.
2. Thorough description of existing activities, those intended, and their expected impact.
3. Other funding in hand, as well as anticipated.
4. Prospects for the project's continuation and support envisioned at the expiration of the requested grant.
5. Budget, if possible.
6. Copy of IRS tax-exempt status determination letter.

When to apply: Anytime.
Materials available: Annual report (includes "Information for Grant Applicants").

Emphases. *Recipients:* Nonprofit organizations.
Geography: New York metropolitan area.

Limitations. *Recipients:* Individuals.
Types of support: Debt retirement, emergency funding.

G

Richard & Rhoda Goldman Fund

One Lombard Street, Suite 303
San Francisco, California 94111
Tel: 415–788–1090   Fax: 415–788–7890
EIN: 946064502   Type: Independent
Contact: Duane Silverstein, Executive Director

History and philosophy. The Richard & Rhoda Goldman Fund, a private foundation established in 1951, reflects the founders' commitment to support charitable organizations that enhance the quality of life, primarily in the San Francisco Bay Area. The Fund supports programs the fields of: health, children and the elderly, civic affairs, cultural arts, population, and the environment.

Officers and directors. *Officers:* Richard N. Goldman, President; Rhoda H. Goldman, Secretary/Treasurer; Duane Silverstein, Executive Director. *Directors:* Michael C. Gelman, Susan R. Gelman, Douglas E. Goldman, John D. Goldman, Lisa M. Goldman, Marcia L. Goldman, Richard N. Goldman, Rhoda H. Goldman, Susan S. Goldman.

Financial data. Data for fiscal year ended October 31, 1993. *Assets:* $132,483,919 (M). *Total grants disbursed:* $5,451,933.

Environmental awards. *Program and interests:* The scope of the environment program is consistent with the Fund's primary focus on the San Francisco Bay Area.
Recent grants: 1993 grants included support for land and watershed protection, sustainable forestry, coastal and marine issues, recycling, environmental health, transportation, and education.

Issues. Cli Bio Lan Agr Wat Oce Ene Was Tox Pop Dev
           •   •   •   •   •   •   •   •   •   •   •

Funding analysis.

Fiscal year:	1991	1993
Env grants auth:	$192,500	$1,071,500
Number:	15	56
Range:	$1,000–$50,000	$1,000–$150,000
Median:	$10,000	$10,000
Pct $ disb (env/total):	24	29

Recipients (1993 highest):	Number:	Dollars:
International Rivers Network	1	150,000
Natural Resources Defense Council	1	150,000
American Friends of the Israel Union for Environmental Defense	1	70,000
National Geographic Society	1	50,000
Three Circles Center	1	40,000
Trees Foundation	1	40,000

Activity regions (1993 highest):	Number:	Dollars:
U.S. West	35	573,500
International*	6	201,000
U.S. not specified	10	163,000
Middle East and Western Asia	2	73,000
North America	1	30,000
U.S. Northwest	1	30,000

*Multiple regions or not specified.

Sample grants (1993).*
Council on Economic Priorities. New York, NY. $10,000. For corporate environmental data clearinghouse.
Earth Island Institute. San Francisco, CA. $30,000. For Sea Turtle Restoration Project and general support.
Environmental Defense Fund. Oakland, CA. $15,000. San Francisco Bay and Delta Program.
J. Walter Johnson Institute. Oakland, CA. $10,000. Project W.O.R.T.H., reducing the risk factors of diseases associated with environmental hazards.
National Audubon Society. Tiburon, CA. $5,000. Audubon Adventures program in Bay Area schools.
Pesticide Action Network (PAN), North America Regional Center. San Francisco, CA. $30,000. Information and Publications Program to promote safe alternatives to chemical pesticides.
Sierra Club Foundation. San Francisco, CA. $50,000. Final payment for the Ethnic Diversity Initiative.
Stanford University. Palo Alto, CA. $400,000. Second of five payments for the Environmental Studies Honors Program.
The Tides Foundation. Sacramento, CA. $10,000. WorldWise's program on multilateral development bank reform and California Communities Against Toxics.
The Wilderness Society. San Francisco, CA. $10,000. Campaign to protect the California desert.

*Sample grants represent either new awards or disbursements on grants awarded in previous years.

Application process. *Initial contact:* Letter of inquiry (2 pages) to include:
1. Executive summary (1 paragraph) describing project, its total budget, amount requested, and a short descriptive project title.
2. Primary contact person's name, title, address, and telephone number.
3. Project description: its necessity, objectives, significance, and plans for implementation.
4. Itemized project budget.
5. Other sources, or potential sources, of additional funding.
6. Organization's total annual budget.
7. Copy of IRS tax-exempt status determination letter.

If the project meets the Fund's guidelines and interests, a full proposal will be requested.
When to apply: Anytime.
Materials available: Annual report (includes "Application Guidelines").

Emphases. *Recipients:* Nonprofit organizations.
Activities: Activism, advocacy, citizen participation, education, innovative programs, land acquisition, litigation, policy analysis/development.
Types of support: Advertising campaigns, continuing support, multi-year grants, operating costs, pilot projects, seed money.
Geography: San Francisco Bay Area.

Limitations. *Recipients:* Individuals.
Activities: Conferences, fundraising, lobbying, research, symposia/colloquia.
Types of support: Debt retirement, endowments, operating costs, scholarships, travel expenses.

Good Samaritan, Inc.

600 Center Mill Road
Wilmington, Delaware 19807
Tel: 302-654-7558
EIN: 516000401   Type: Independent
Contact: Edmund N. Carpenter, II, Secretary/Treasurer

History and philosophy. Established in 1938 by Elias Ahuja, the foundation supports the study and treatment of dyslexia, higher education, medicine, projects relating to Spain, improvement of the administration of justice, and environmental protection.

Officers and directors. *Officers:* Reverend H. W. Sherrill, President; Elizabeth Lee DuPont, Vice President; Edmund N. Carpenter, II, Secretary/Treasurer.

Financial data. Data for fiscal year ended December 31, 1993. *Assets:* $3,254,244 (M). *Total grants disbursed:* $556,260.

Environmental awards. *Recent grants:* Grants in 1992 and 1993 included support of a focused effort to establish a national network of linked open spaces.

Issues.   Cli   Bio   Lan   Agr   Wat   Oce   Ene   Was   Tox   Pop   Dev
                            •

Funding analysis.

Fiscal year:	1990	1992
Env grants disb:	$300,000	$100,000
Number:	2	1
Range:	$50,000–$250,000	–
Median:	$150,000	–
Pct $ disb (env/total):	30	13

Recipients (1992):	Number:	Dollars:
The Conservation Fund	1	100,000

Activity region (1992):	Number:	Dollars:
U.S. not specified	1	100,000

Sample grant (1993).
The Conservation Fund. Arlington, VA. $100,000. In support of its "American Greenways Program," an effort to establish a national network of linked open spaces across America.

Application process. *Initial contact:* Written description of applicant organization's general activities and the specific purpose of and need for proposed project. Full application to include:
1. Organization's complete legal name and address.
2. Determination letters from the IRS indicating tax-exempt status; that the organization is not a private foundation; and, for private schools and colleges only, that the institution meets IRS non-discriminatory policy guidelines.
3. Most recent annual report and certified financial statements.
4. Detailed project budget, accompanied by a brief description (2 pages or less) of project purpose, rationale, and objectives.
5. For publicly supported charities qualifying under the provisions of IRS Code Sections 170(b), (1)(A)(vi), or 509(a)(2), a statement that foundation compliance with the grant request will not adversely affect its exemption status.
6. A short (1 paragraph) executive summary of the gist of the proposal including rationale, results to be achieved, and the amount of money requested.

When to apply: Deadlines are in early May and mid-October or at least four weeks before board meetings held approximately on the first Thursday in June and the third Thursday in November. The Foundation requests that no applications be sent to arrive within the four week period.
Materials available: "Guidelines for Grants and Suggested Procedure for Grant Application."

Emphases. *Recipients:* Nonprofit organizations.
Activities: Innovative programs.
Types of support: Seed money.

Limitations. *Recipients:* Individuals.

Walter and Duncan Gordon Charitable Foundation

11 Church Street, Suite 307
Toronto, Ontario M5E 1W1
Canada
Tel: 416-601-4776   Fax: 416-601-1689
Type: Independent
EGA member
Contact: Christine Lee, Executive Director

History and philosophy. The Gordon Foundation was established in 1965 by brothers Walter and Duncan Gordon and Mrs. Elizabeth Gordon. It has three grantmaking themes: Canadian Policy Development to Promote Common Security, Community Development in Canada North of 60° Latitude, and Improving Canadian Secondary Education through a Model Program in the Province of Manitoba.

Officers and directors. *Directors:* Dr. John R. Evans, Jane Glassco, Elizabeth Gordon, John Gordon, Kyra Montagu, Dr. Peter Nicholson.

Financial data. Data for fiscal year ended December 31, 1993. *Assets:* $34,721,115 (M) (CDN). *Total grants and program support disbursed:* $1,933,436.

Environmental awards. *Program and interests:* Primary interests are:

- Water management, particularly cross-border issues for Canada/United States.
- James Bay II hydroelectric project: implications for North America.
- Arctic wildlife nature reserve and the Administration's energy policy: implications for the caribou and the native people who rely on them.

Other interests are:

- Arctic circumpolar security.
- Sustainable community development in Canada north of 60° latitude.

G

Issues. Cli Bio Lan Agr Wat Oce Ene Was Tox Pop Dev
• • • • • •

Funding analysis.

Fiscal year:	1992	1993
Env grants disb:	184,800	$112,312
Number:	9	6
Range:	$2,000–$100,000	$3,000–$75,000
Median:	$5,000	$5,689
Pct $ disb (env/total):	12	6

Recipients (1993):	Number:	Dollars:
Municipality of Sanikiluaq–TEKMS	1	75,000
Porcupine Caribou Management Board	3	27,812
Yukon Conservation Society	2	9,500

Activity region (1993):	Number:	Dollars:
Canada	6	112,312

Sample grants (1993).
Municipality of Sanikiluaq–TEKMS. Sanikiluaq, Northwest Territories. $75,000. To support the traditional Ecological Knowledge and Management Systems Study of the Hudson Bay Program.
Porcupine Caribou Management Board. Whitehorse, Yukon. $9,000. The program is designed to encourage native students to pursue a career in wildlife management.
Yukon Conservation Society. Whitehorse, Yukon. $5,000. In support of a bursary fund to assist northern participants in their forum on northern protected areas.

Application process. *Initial contact:* Letter to include:
1. Brief description of applicant organization with the curriculum vitae of the person in charge of the project.
2. Description of proposed project with a detailed budget.
3. Explanation of how project will contribute to achievement of Foundation's specific program area and goals.
4. Steps to be taken to raise public awareness and support, disseminate the project's results, and influence policy and decisionmakers.
5. Suggested criteria for evaluation of the results of the project.
6. Copy of the Department of National Revenue's charitable gift number form.

When to apply: Anytime.
Publications available: "Priorities of the Foundation" brochure (includes "Funding Guidelines and Application Procedures").

Emphases. *Recipients:* Educational institutions, nonprofit organizations, public agencies, research institutions. All must be Canadian registered charitable organizations.
Activities: Activism, audiovisual materials, capacity building, citizen participation, collaborative efforts, conferences, conflict resolution, demonstration programs, education, fieldwork, networking, planning, policy analysis/development, publications, research, technical assistance, training, volunteerism, workshops, youth programs.

Types of support: Leveraging funds, matching funds, multi-year grants, pilot projects, program-related investments, seed money, technical assistance.
Geography: Canadian organizations providing services north of 60° latitude only.

Limitations. *Types of support:* Annual campaigns, capital campaigns/expenses, endowments, facilities, scholarships.

Great Lakes Protection Fund
35 East Wacker Drive, Suite 1880
Chicago, Illinois 60601
Tel: 312–201–0660   Fax: 312–201–0683
EIN: 363670734   Type: Public
EGA member
Contact: John Sherman, Program Director

History and philosophy. The Great Lakes Protection Fund, the nation's first multi-state environmental endowment, was formed in October 1989 by the governors of the eight Great Lakes states (Illinois, Indiana, Michigan, Minnesota, New York, Ohio, Pennsylvania, and Wisconsin). The Articles of Incorporation established a joint fund to be used as a permanent endowment, with its income disbursed through grants designed to improve water quality in the Great Lakes. The Fund is designed to maintain $100 million in contributions from the eight states. Each state's contribution is based on its pro-rated water use from the Great Lakes and ranges from $1.5 million (Minnesota and Pennsylvania) to $25 million (Michigan).

Officers and directors. *Officers:* Jeffrey L. Busch, Chairman; Sister Pat Lupo, Vice Chairman; H. Martin Jessen, Secretary/Treasurer. *Directors:* Jack Anderson, Jeffrey L. Busch, Ph.D., The Honorable Anthony S. Earl, H. Martin Jessen, Craig Kennedy, Sister Pat Lupo, W. Duncan MacMillan, Patrick Osborne, James B. Park, Jeffrey M. Reutter, Dennis L. Schornack, Ronald J. Scrudato, Ph.D., Maureen H. Smyth, David J. Sterret, Henry G. Williams.

Financial data. Data for fiscal year ended December 31, 1993. *Assets:* $84,554,815 (M). *Total grants authorized:* $1,798,000. *State share returns:* $1,593,050.

Environmental award. *Program and interests:* The Fund supports projects that promote regional action to enhance the health of the Great Lakes ecosystem. It has four funding priorities:

- Prevent toxic pollution.
- Support effective cleanup approaches in priority areas of concern.
- Support natural resource stewardship.
- Clarify effects of toxic pollution on humans and wildlife.

Issues. Cli Bio Lan Agr Wat Oce Ene Was Tox Pop Dev
• • • • •

Funding analysis.

Fiscal year:	1991	1993
Env grants auth:	$3,829,000	$1,798,000
Number:	30	15
Range:	$9,500–$450,000	$32,000–$350,000
Median:	$94,750	$100,000
Pct $ auth (env/total):	100	100

Recipients (1993 highest):	Number:	Dollars:
The Great Lakes Commission	1	350,000
Environmental Defense Fund	1	220,000
Ohio State University, School of Natural Resources	1	175,000
The Wetlands Initiative	1	166,000
Ohio State University	1	159,000

Activity regions (1993):	Number:	Dollars:
U.S. Great Lakes	14	1,448,000
International*	1	350,000

*U.S. Great Lakes and Canada.

Sample grants (1993).

Carnegie Mellon University, Center for Economic Development. Pittsburgh, PA. $73,000. To identify incentives for pollution prevention among supplier firms.

Council of Great Lakes Industries. Detroit, MI. $107,000 (3 years). To promote and evaluate use of "Total Quality Environmental Management."

The Great Lakes Commission. Anne Arbor, MI. $350,000 (2 years). To collaborate with the World Wildlife Fund and the University of Guelph, Ontario, on a profile of U.S. and Canadian agricultural practices.

Hazardous Waste Research and Information Center. Champaign, IL. $32,000 (9 months). To create a catalog of pollution prevention information resources.

National Environmental Law Center. Boston, MA. $90,000 (16 months). To promote compatibility of chemical accident and pollution prevention policies.

The Wetlands Initiative. Chicago, IL. $166,000 (18 months). To identify water quality improvements from wetland restorations.

Wisconsin Rural Development Center, Inc. Black Earth, WI. $100,000 (2 years). To test intensive rotational grazing to cut pollution and soil erosion.

Application process. *Initial contact:* Preproposal (2 pages maximum, 6 copies), to include:

1. Goals statement. Give specific reasons why the proposed work is consistent with the goals of the Fund.
2. Problem statement. Describe the issue that the project will resolve or address and its relevance to the Great Lakes.
3. Proposed work. Outline what will be done, how, and under what timetable.
4. Budget. Estimate the proposed budget by categories: salaries and benefits, equipment and supplies, travel, consultants, other. (The Fund generally will not consider fund overhead rates greater than 15 percent, excluding travel.)
5. List of key personnel, their experience and qualifications. Attach resume (2 pages) of principal investigator.
6. Regional collaboration. Provide a statement about any planned collaborations.
7. List of other funding sources, committed and potential.

A completed Applicant Information Sheet must be attached to the front of the preproposal. Full proposals will be invited from selected applicants. The Fund will not accept applications submitted via facsimile machine.

When to apply: There are typically several deadlines each year. 1995 pre-proposal deadlines are January 4 and June 30.

Materials available: Annual report (includes "Application Process"), "Priorities and Guidelines for Funding" (brochure), "Call for Preproposals" (application process for preproposals).

Emphases. *Recipients:* Educational institutions, nonprofit organizations, research institutions.

Activities: Capacity building, citizen participation, collaborative efforts, conflict resolution, demonstration programs, planning, policy analysis/development.

Types of support: Matching funds, multi-year grants, pilot projects, projects, travel expenses.

Geography: Great Lakes region only (Illinois, Indiana, Michigan, Minnesota, New York, Ohio, Pennsylvania, and Wisconsin in the United States; Ontario and Quebec in Canada).

Limitations. *Recipients:* Aquariums, botanical gardens, museums, religious organizations, zoos.

Activities: Exhibits, expeditions/tours, litigation, lobbying, seminars, symposia/colloquia. (Programs or projects that duplicate or replace existing state/regional/federal efforts.)

Types of support: Advertising campaigns, annual campaigns, capital campaigns/expenses, debt retirement, emergency funding, endowments, facilities, fellowships, general purposes, lectureships, loans, maintenance, membership campaigns, mortgage reduction, professorships, scholarships.

Greater Piscataqua Community Foundation

446 Market Street
Portsmouth, New Hampshire 03801
Tel: 603–430–9182   Fax: 603–431–6268
EIN: 026005625   Type: Community
Contact: Angela P. Matthews, Executive Director

History and philosophy. Established in 1983 as The Greater Portsmouth Community Foundation, the Greater Piscataqua Community Foundation is a regional division of the New Hampshire Charitable Foundation. The Foundation's assets are provided by contributions from many donors interested in the welfare and future of the seacoast region. As a regional division, the Foundation is supported in large part by program and administrative staff of the New Hampshire Charitable Foundation. Areas of giving include: Arts & Humanities, Education, Environment, Health, and Social and Community Services.

Officers and directors. *Officers:* Wilfred L. Sanders, Jr., Chair; Irving Gutin, Vice Chair. *Executive Committee:* H. Alfred Casassa, Patience Chamberlin, Irja Cilluffo, Geoffrey Clark, Charles A. DeGrandpre, Irving Gutin, Anna Grace Holloway, Elaine S. Krasker, James A. Labrie, Ala H. Reid, Richard W. Ridgway, Wilfred L. Sanders, Jr., John W. G. Tuthill. *Ex officio:* Nathan Greenberg, J. Bonnie Newman, Joseph G. Sawtelle.

G

Financial data. Data for fiscal year ended December 31, 1993. *Assets:* $13,500,000 (U) (est.). *Gifts received:* $352,000. *Total grants authorized:* $430,000.

Environmental awards. *Program and interests:* Environment is an area that donors may choose to support. The newly created GPCF Environmental Advisory Committee will work to build environmental endowment funds to support future environmental initiatives.
Recent grants: 1993 grants included support for land conservation, coastal issues, wildlife protection, and public school education.

Issues. Cli Bio Lan Agr Wat Oce Ene Was Tox Pop Dev
            •   •   •   •

Funding analysis.§

Fiscal year:	1992	1993
Env grants auth:	$1,733	$23,561
Number:	3	9
Range:	$233–$1,250	$200–$10,109
Median:	$250	$1,932
Pct $ auth:	<1	5

Recipients (1993 highest):	Number:	Dollars:
Friends of Odiorne Point	1	10,109
The Student Conservation Association, Inc.	1	5,000
Society for the Protection of New Hampshire Forests	2	3,219
University of New Hampshire, Cooperative Extension	1	2,000
New Hampshire Audubon Society	1	1,932

Activity region (1993):	Number:	Dollars:
U.S. Northeast	9	23,561

§Includes designated, field-of-interest, and unrestricted grants.

Sample grants (1993).
Collaboration of Community Foundations for the Gulf of Maine. Boston, MA. $2,500. To support the activities of the collaboration
Kittery Conservation Commission. Kittery, ME. $542. To support the development of a middle school curriculum on the study of estuaries.
Society for the Protection of New Hampshire Forests. Concord, NH. $2,500. To support two land protection workshops offered to the public.

Application process. *Initial contact:* Proposal (5–8 pages) to include:
Narrative.
1. Organization description, including history, mission, milestones, current programs, and services.
2. Needs assessment.
3. Planning, including how this project will be different from similar programs, if any.
4. Project description, goals, and objectives.
5. How project will be evaluated.
6. If the activity is intended to be ongoing, plans for continuation past the grant period.
7. Other support secured for the project.
Attachments.
1. Completed Application Cover Sheet.
2. Itemized project budget.
3. Last available audit or financial statement.
4. Current operating budget.
5. Current list of board members.
6. IRS tax-exempt status determination letter.

When to apply: Deadlines are April 1 and October 1 for board meetings in June and December, respectively.
Materials available: Annual report, "Program Priorities," application package (includes "Application Cover Sheet").

Emphases. *Recipients:* Nonprofit organizations.
Activities: Collaborative efforts, direct services, education, innovative programs, training, youth programs.
Types of support: Emergency funding, endowments, facilities, leveraging funds, matching funds, membership campaigns, pilot projects, projects, start-up costs.
Geography: The communities of Portsmouth, New Castle, Newington, Rye, Greenland, the Hamptons, Seabrook, Kensington, Kingston, East Kingston, Exeter, Newfields, Brentwood, Newton, Newmarket, and Stratham in New Hampshire; and Kittery, York, York Harbor, Eliot, and the Berwicks in Maine.

Limitations. *Recipients:* Individuals.
Activities: Land acquisition, litigation, lobbying, research (scholarly).
Types of support: Capital campaigns/expenses, continuing support, debt retirement, maintenance, mortgage reduction, operating costs, program-related investments, travel expenses.

The Greenville Foundation

283 Second Street East, Suite A
Sonoma, California 95476
Tel: 707–938–9377   Fax: 707–939–9311
EIN: 956043258   Type: Independent
EGA member
Contacts: Anne Fitzgerald, Administrator
Virginia Hubbell, Administrator

History and philosophy. The Greenville Foundation was established as a trust in 1949 by William Miles. It "seeks to encourage and fund unique, innovative, or other nonprofit programs designed to address problems facing the local and global human community. In most cases, the Foundation attempts to emphasize proposals aimed at those parts of the community least able, for whatever reason, to act on their own behalf. It generally limits funding to projects west of the Rockies." Current interests are: Education; Environment; Human and Social Issues; and International Development, Peace and Justice.

Officers and directors. *Officer:* Richard A. Crew, Chairman. *Trustees:* Donald W. Crew, Richard A. Crew, Brian Fish, L. M. Fish, Patricia Miles.

Financial data. Data for fiscal year ended December 31, 1993. *Assets:* $12,500,000 (M) (est.). *Total grants disbursed:* $535,000.

Environmental awards. *Program and interests:* Current interests are sustainable resource education, technology, and management. Special foci are:

- Alternative energy.
- Programs which comprehensively address the interrelationship of ecosystems and community economics.

Recent grants: 1993 grants included support for habitat restoration, watershed restoration, aerial surveillance, and education and training.

Issues. Cli• Bio• Lan• Agr• Wat• Oce• Ene• Was• Tox Pop Dev•

Funding analysis.

Fiscal year:	1993
Env grants auth:	$129,800
Number:	14
Range:	$4,800–$20,000
Median:	$7,500
Pct $ auth (env/total):	22

Recipients (1993 highest):	*Number:*	*Dollars:*
Pacific Rivers Council	1	20,000
Earthtrust New York	1	15,000
The International Center	1	15,000
The Nature Conservancy	1	15,000
American Friends Service Committee	1	10,000
Natural Resources Defense Council	1	10,000
The Wilderness Society	1	10,000

Activity regions (1993):	*Number:*	*Dollars:*
U.S. West	5	45,000
U.S. not specified	3	30,000
U.S. Northwest	2	25,000
Mexico and Central America	2	20,000
U.S. Mountain	2	9,800

Sample grants (1993).

American Oceans Campaign, Northwest Office. Seattle, WA. $5,000. To encourage cooperative and comprehensive efforts among the Tulalip tribes and rural landowners to restore and protect watersheds critical to tribal fishing resources.

Earthtrust. New York, NY. $15,000. To establish a network to monitor compliance with the recent U.N. ban on drift net fishing.

The International Center. Washington, DC. $15,000. Support for natural resource and community development programs in Guatemala.

Natural Resources Defense Council. Los Angeles, CA. $10,000. Educational efforts in support of local environmental groups participating in California's Natural Community Conservation Planning process. Aimed at proactive, cooperative approaches to ecosystem protection and development.

The Nature Conservancy. Los Angeles, CA. $15,000. For a project to hire at-risk inner-city youth to restore a desert oasis.

Pacific Rivers Council. Eugene, OR. $20,000. Support for cooperative approaches to economic and natural resource problems in the Pacific Northwest.

The Tides Foundation, Environmental Working Group. Washington, DC. $15,000. To support sustainable living strategies via training in nutrition, health, and gardening for women in Chimalpas, Mexico.

Application process. *Initial contact:* Brief narrative proposal (8 pages maximum, 3 copies) accompanied by:
1. Executive summary (1 page maximum).
2. Project budget.
3. Organization's current budget (income and expenses).
4. Financial statements for most recent complete fiscal year.
5. List of board of directors.
6. Annual report or other description of the organization's activities.
7. Copy of IRS tax-exempt status determination letter.

If you have previously received funding from the Foundation, include a report on the status and outcomes of the previously funded project.

When to apply: Deadlines are July 1 and December 1 for board meetings in mid-November and mid-March, respectively.

Materials available: "Funding Interests, Guidelines, & Selected Grants" brochure.

Emphases. *Recipients:* Educational institutions, nonprofit organizations.

Activities: Activism, advocacy, capacity building, citizen participation, collaborative efforts, conferences, education, innovative programs, political activities, technical assistance.

Types of support: General purposes, internships, matching funds, pilot projects, projects, seed money, technical assistance.

Geography: Projects located west of the U.S. Rockies are given priority. Projects of national impact; projects of international impact only through well-established U.S.-based or affiliated nonprofit organizations.

Limitations. *Recipients:* Individuals.
Types of support: Operating costs, capital campaigns/expenses.

The William and Mary Greve Foundation, Inc.

630 Fifth Avenue, Suite 1750
New York, New York 10111
Tel: 212–307–7850   Fax: 212–262–8340
EIN: 136020724   Type: Independent
Contact: Ellen A. Minucci, Executive Administrator

History and philosophy. The Foundation was established in 1964 with trust funds designated by Mrs. Mary Greve to be turned over to the Foundation upon her death. The Foundation currently focuses on three areas: Arts (performing and visual), Basic Education (pre-collegiate), and East-West Relations (particularly public education about the Former Soviet Union).

Officers and directors. *Officers:* John W. Kiser III, Chairman; Anthony C. M. Kiser, President; John J. Tommaney, Secretary. *Directors:* Anthony C. M. Kiser, John W. Kiser III, James W. Sykes, Jr., John J. Tommaney.

Financial data. Data for fiscal year ended December 31, 1992. *Assets:* $25,946,263 (M). *Total grants disbursed:* $1,175,538.

G

Environmental awards. *Recent grants:* 1992 grants included support for land conservation, farmland preservation, arboreta, and zoos.

Issues. Cli Bio Lan Agr Wat Oce Ene Was Tox Pop Dev
• • • •

Funding analysis.

Fiscal year:	1991	1992
Env grants disb:	$172,000	$61,290
Number:	8	7
Range:	$5,000–$50,000	$5,000–$25,000
Median:	$18,500	$5,000
Pct $ disb (env/total):	14	5

Recipients (1992):	Number:	Dollars:
Rhode Island Zoological Society	1	25,000
American Farmland Trust	1	11,290
Friends of the U.S. National Arboretum	1	5,000
INFORM	1	5,000
Montana Land Reliance	1	5,000
NYZS/The Wildlife Conservation Society	1	5,000
Piedmont Environmental Council	1	5,000

Activity regions (1992):	Number:	Dollars:
U.S. Northeast	1	25,000
U.S. not specified	2	16,290
U.S. Mid-Atlantic	2	10,000
New York/New Jersey	1	5,000
U.S. Mountain	1	5,000

Sample grants (1992).
American Farmland Trust. Washington, DC. $11,290.
Friends of the U.S. National Arboretum. Washington, DC. $5,000.
INFORM. New York, NY. $5,000.
Montana Land Reliance. Helena, MT. $5,000.
NYZS/The Wildlife Conservation Society. Bronx, NY. $5,000.
Piedmont Environmental Council. Warrenton, VA. $5,000.
Rhode Island Zoological Society. Providence, RI. $25,000.

Application process. *Initial contact:* Brief letter outlining:
1. Project purpose.
2. Project budget; detail use of grant funds.
3. Amount requested.
4. Organization's qualifications to undertake the project.
5. Copy of IRS tax-exempt status determination letter.

When to apply: Anytime.
Materials available: "Statement of Policy."

Emphases. *Types of support:* Continuing support, endowments, general purposes, matching funds, seed money.

Limitations. *Recipients:* Individuals.
Types of support: Fellowships, scholarships.

The W. C. Griffith Foundation

c/o National City Bank
P.O. Box 5031
Indianapolis, Indiana 46255
Tel: 317-267-7290   Fax: 317-267-7281
EIN: 356007742   Type: Independent
Contact: Mike Miner, Trust Officer

History and philosophy. The Foundation was established as a trust in 1959 by William C. and Ruth Perry Griffith. Areas of grantmaking interest include the visual and performing arts, education, the environment, health, human services, medical research, and religious organizations.

Officers and directors. *Advisors:* Ruthelen Griffith Burns, Charles P. Griffith, Jr., Walter S. Griffith, William C. Griffith III, Wendy Griffith Kortepeter. *Trustee:* National City Bank, Indiana.

Financial data. Data for fiscal year ended November 30, 1993.
Assets: $8,485,786 (M). *Total grants disbursed:* $400,000.

Environmental awards. *Recent grants:* 1993 grants included support for land conservation, water protection, urban environment, and a zoo.

Issues. Cli Bio Lan Agr Wat Oce Ene Was Tox Pop Dev
• • •

Funding analysis.

Fiscal year:	1993
Env grants disb:	$45,000
Number:	6
Range:	$1,000–$25,000
Median:	$4,000
Pct $ disb (env/total):	11

Recipients (1993):	Number:	Dollars:
Indianapolis Zoological Society	1	25,000
Indianapolis Parks Foundation	1	10,000
Lake Maxin Kuckee Environmental Fund, Inc.	1	5,000
The Nature Conservancy, Indiana Field Office	1	3,000
Hoosier Environmental Council	1	1,000
Indianapolis Clean City Committee	1	1,000

Activity region (1993):	Number:	Dollars:
U.S. Great Lakes	6	45,000

Sample grants (1993).
Hoosier Environmental Council. Indianapolis, IN. $1,000.
Indianapolis Clean City Committee. Indianapolis, IN. $1,000.
Indianapolis Parks Foundation. Indianapolis, IN. $10,000.
Indianapolis Zoological Society. Indianapolis, IN. $25,000.
Lake Maxin Kuckee Environmental Fund, Inc. Culver, IN. $5,000.
The Nature Conservancy, Indiana Field Office. Indianapolis, IN. $3,000.

Application process. *Initial contact:* Letter describing purpose of grant.
When to apply: Anytime. Board meets in June and November.

Emphases. *Recipients:* Educational institutions, museums, nonprofit organizations, religious organizations.
Types of support: Capital campaigns/expenses, continuing support, facilities (construction).
Geography: Indianapolis, Indiana.

Limitations. *Recipients:* Individuals.
Types of support: Fellowships, scholarships.

The George Gund Foundation
1845 Guildhall Building
45 Prospect Avenue West
Cleveland, Ohio 44115
Tel: 216–241–3114   Fax: 216–241–6560
EIN: 346519769   Type: Independent
EGA member
Contacts: Jon M. Jensen, Program Officer
David Bergholz, Executive Director

History and philosophy. The George Gund Foundation was established in 1952 as a private, nonprofit institution devoted to human well-being and social progress. George Gund (1888–1966), a businessman and philanthropist, had a lifelong interest in education and the institutions he attended.

The Foundation's mission is to enhance the quality of life; to solve community problems; to improve living conditions, particularly for the poor and underprivileged; and to provide opportunities for all people to live instructive lives in a peaceful world. Program areas are: Education, Economic and Community Revitalization, Human Services, Environment, Arts, and Civic Affairs.

Officers and directors. *Officers:* Geoffrey Gund, President and Treasurer; Llura N. Gund, Vice President; Ann L. Gund, Secretary. *Trustees:* Kathleen L. Barber, Ann L. Gund, Geoffrey Gund, George Gund III, Llura A. Gund.

Financial data. Data for fiscal year ended December 31, 1993.
Assets: $400,151,804 (M). *Total grants authorized:* $21,344,036.
Total grants disbursed: $25,060,897.

Environmental awards. *Program and interests:* The Foundation's grantmaking priorities are region-specific for Cleveland, Ohio, and the Great Lakes.

- Cleveland.
  Protection of ecosystems and natural features including rivers and watersheds, parks, and open space. Efforts to develop a broader ecological perspective for the region and encourage citizen awareness and advocacy.

- Ohio.
  State-wide issues and state-wide organizations promoting improved public policy or providing coordination and support for local environmental groups. Local projects outside Greater Cleveland will not be considered.

- Great Lakes basin.
  Region-wide protection of biological resources.
  Strengthening the infrastructure of the environmental community.

The Foundation has a special interest in programs that develop leadership and management capacity in nonprofit environmental organizations. Priority is given to programs which train and link networks of organizations.

Environmental grants may also be awarded through the Foundation's program in Education, and the Urban Design, Planning, & Amenities component of the Economic and Community Revitalization program.

Issues. Cli Bio Lan Agr Wat Oce Ene Was Tox Pop Dev
              •   •   •   •   •   •   •   •

Funding analysis.

Fiscal year:	1991	1993
Env grants auth:	$2,386,531	$2,661,191
Number:	67	63
Range:	$1,500–$477,146	$500–$160,000
Median:	$25,000	$30,000
Pct $ auth (env/total):	14	13

Recipients (1993 highest):	Number:	Dollars:
Case Western Reserve University	1	160,000
National Healthy Air License Exchange	2	157,500
Environmental Law and Policy Center of the Midwest	1	150,000
John Carroll University	1	115,420
Garden Center of Greater Cleveland	1	100,771

Activity regions (1993):	Number:	Dollars:
U.S. Great Lakes	57	2,370,191
U.S. not specified	5	241,000
Alaska	1	50,000

Sample grants (1993).

Alliance for Choice in Giving. Washington, DC. $4,000. Training program for environmental workplace fundraising federations.

American Rivers, Inc. Washington, DC. $30,000. Intervention in hydropower dam relicensing in the Great Lakes region.

City of Cleveland. Cleveland, OH. $40,000. Lead Hazard Abatement Project.

Coast Alliance. Washington, DC. $25,000. Technical assistance on coastal preservation to environmental groups.

Environmental Law and Policy Center of the Midwest. Chicago, IL. $150,000 (2 years). Start-up support for work on energy efficiency and transportation.

In Defense of Endangered Species. Columbus, OH. $5,000. State Coalition for Renewal of Endangered Species Act.

National Wildlife Federation. Washington, DC. $90,000 (2 years). Virtual Elimination of Great Lakes Toxics project.

The Ohio Environmental Council. Columbus, OH. $6,000.

Ohio State University, Research Foundation. Columbus, OH. $60,000 (2 years). Development and distribution of teaching materials on Great Lakes pollution issues.

H

Application process. *Initial contact:* Full proposal to include:
1. Summary abstract of proposal (1 page). Description of project and amount of funds requested.
2. Organizational background. History, mission, types of programs offered, constituencies served.
3. Project description. Justification of need, specific goals and objectives, activities to meet goals and objectives, project timeline, qualifications of personnel, methods of evaluation.
4. Project budget. Expenses, including details about how Foundation funds will be used, and anticipated income, including information about other foundations approached for funding.
5. Organizational budget. Current year budget and proposed budget for project year(s) showing income and expenses, along with most recent audited financial statement.
6. Supporting documents. Current board of trustees, letters of support, printed material such as an annual report or brochure, IRS tax-exempt status determination letter.

When to apply: Deadlines are January 15, March 30, June 30, and September 30. The board of trustees meets in March, June, September, and December.
Materials available: Annual report (includes "Grant Application Procedures"), "Guidelines for Grant Applicants."

Emphases. *Recipients:* Botanical gardens, educational institutions, museums, nonprofit organizations, public agencies, research institutions, zoos.
Activities: Activism, advocacy, capacity building, citizen participation, collaborative efforts, conferences, education, feasibility studies, inventories, networking, policy analysis/development, publications, seminars, symposia/colloquia, technical assistance, training, workshops.
Types of support: Continuing support, general purposes, internships, matching funds, multi-year grants, operating costs, projects, start-up costs, technical assistance, travel expenses.
Geography: Cleveland region; Ohio (statewide); Great Lakes; United States (sometimes).

Limitations. *Recipients:* Individuals.
Activities: Audiovisual materials, conflict resolution, direct services, exhibits, expeditions/tours, fundraising, land acquisition, litigation, lobbying, research (medical/scholarly), volunteerism, youth programs.
Types of support: Advertising campaigns, annual campaigns, capital campaigns/expenses, debt retirement, emergency funding, endowments, facilities, loans, maintenance, mortgage reduction, professorships, program-related investments.
Geography: Local grants outside of Cleveland; statewide issues outside of Ohio.

HKH Foundation
521 Fifth Avenue, Suite 1612
New York, New York 10175–1699
Tel: 518–352–7391
EIN: 136784950   Type: Independent
EGA member
Contact: Harriet Barlow, Advisor

History and philosophy. The Harold K. Hochschild (HKH) Foundation was founded in 1980. Primary areas of interest are: Reversing the Arms Race, Environmental Protection, and Civil Liberties. The Adirondack Historical Society also receives a substantial portion of Foundation funding. The Foundation does not respond to individual requests for funding. Instead, staff members consult with activists and researchers to formulate strategic plans for promoting work in areas of interest by funding a new project, supporting an existing project, or fostering cooperation between organizations.

Officers and directors. *Trustees:* Herman Von Hatzfelt, Adam Hochschild, Joseph Mische, Frederick A. Terry, Jr., Robert R. Worth.

Financial data. Data for fiscal year ended December 31, 1992. *Assets:* $40,392,513 (M). *Total grants disbursed:* $1,596,000.

Environmental awards. *Program and interests:* Environmental interests are:

- Environmental protection.
- Forest management.
- Renewable resources.
- Toxics.
- Trade.

Recent grants: 1992 grants included support for land conservation (public lands, rainforests), agricultural policy reform, toxics education, and citizen and grassroots organizing.

Issues. Cli Bio Lan Agr Wat Oce Ene Was Tox Pop Dev
              •   •   •   •   •

Funding analysis.

Fiscal year:	1991	1992*
Env grants disb:	$160,000	$350,000
Number:	9	–
Range:	$5,000–$35,000	$10,000–$30,000
Median:	$20,000	$20,000
Pct $ disb (env/total):	11	20

*As reported to the Environmental Grantmakers Association.

Recipients (1991 highest):	Number:	Dollars:
National Campaign Against Toxic Hazards	1	35,000
Institute for Local Self-Reliance	1	25,000
Rainforest Action Network	1	25,000
Earth Island Institute	1	20,000
Friends of the Earth	1	20,000
Nuclear Safety Campaign	1	20,000

Activity regions (1991):	Number:	Dollars:
U.S. not specified	7	125,000
New York/New Jersey	1	10,000
Tropics	1	25,000

Sample grants (1992).
Adirondack Council. Elizabethtown, NY. $5,000.
Environmental Research Foundation. Annapolis, MD. $25,000.
Institute for Energy and Environmental Research. Takoma Park, MD. $10,000.
National Audubon Society. New York, NY. $10,000.

National Resources Defense Council. New York, NY. $25,000.
National Toxics Campaign Fund. Boston, MA. $25,000.
Pesticide Action Network (PAN), North American Regional Center. San Francisco, CA. $15,000.
Residents Committee to Protect the Adirondacks. North Creek, NY. $5,000.
Western Ancient Forests Campaign. Portland, OR. $25,000.
Western States Center. Portland, OR. $35,000.

Application process. *Initial contact:* The Foundation does not review proposals on a competitive basis. However, "interested parties can submit a brief letter of inquiry."

Limitations. *Recipients:* Individuals.
Activities: Audiovisual materials, media projects, research.
Types of support: Capital expenses/expenses, endowments.

Evelyn and Walter Haas, Jr. Fund
One Lombard Street, Suite 305
San Francisco, California 94111
Tel: 415–398–3744   Fax: 415–986–4779
EIN: 946068932   Type: Independent
Contacts: Ira S. Hirschfield, President
Roberta Archer, Grants Coordinator

History and philosophy. The Evelyn and Walter Haas, Jr. Fund is a private foundation established in 1953 by the Haas family. Program concentrations include strengthening children, youth, families, and the elderly; strengthening neighborhoods and communities; reducing hunger and homelessness; encouraging volunteer service and philanthropy; and trustee-initiated grants. The Fund supports prevention and early intervention strategies; self-help and self-sufficiency; build on the strengths of individuals, families, and communities; and equality of opportunity.

Officers and directors. *Officers:* Walter A. Haas, Jr., Chairman; Evelyn D. Haas, Vice Chairman; Ira S. Hirshfield, President; Walter J. Haas, Secretary/Treasurer. *Trustees:* Elizabeth H. Eisenhardt, Evelyn D. Haas, Robert D. Haas, Walter A. Haas, Jr., Walter J. Haas, Ira S. Hirshfield.

Financial data. Data for fiscal year ended December 31, 1993. *Assets:* $219,970,295 (M). *Total grants disbursed:* $5,489,658.

Environmental awards. *Recent grants:* 1993 grants included support for parks, environmental career development for minorities, and youth programs.

Issues.   Cli   Bio   Lan   Agr   Wat   Oce   Ene   Was   Tox   Pop   Dev
                           •

Funding analysis.§

Fiscal year:	1993
Env grants auth:	$220,000
Number:	3
Range:	$50,000–$110,000
Median:	$60,000
Pct $ disb (env/total):	1

Recipients (1993):	Number:	Dollars:
Golden Gate National Recreation Area	1	110,000
San Francisco Conservation Corps	1	60,000
The Student Conservation Association, Inc.	1	50,000

Activity region (1993):	Number:	Dollars:
U.S. West	3	220,000

§Does not include grants less than $5,000.

Sample grants (1993).
Golden Gate National Recreation Area. San Francisco, CA. $110,000. Supports the planning and design phase of the Association's Crissy Field Project, which concentrates on shoreline restoration and recreational activities as part of efforts to preserve the park's natural and cultural resources.
San Francisco Conservation Corps. San Francisco, CA. $60,000 (2 years). Adds a Support Service Coordinator to the Corps, which works to improve the work skills, leadership potential, and academic abilities of at-risk youth.
The Student Conservation Association, Inc. Charlestown, NH. $50,000 (2 years). Supports the Oakland/San Francisco Conservation Career Development Program, which works with the National Park Service to identify promising minority high school students and guide them into conservation careers.

Application process. *Initial contact:* Letter of inquiry (3 pages) to include:
1. Brief statement of organization's purpose and goals.
2. If applicable, a description of project, need, and target population.
3. Information about capability of leadership implementing proposed project.
4. Anticipated short and long-term outcomes and plans for measuring achievements.
5. Grant amount needed.
6. Total agency budget and project budget (if different).
7. Other funding sources for agency and/or project.

If applicant knows a trustee, indicate the association in a letter of inquiry. If interested, the Fund will request a full proposal.
When to apply: The trustees meet three times a year; dates vary.
Materials available: Annual report (includes "Application Procedure"), "Guidelines and Application Procedures."

Emphases. *Recipients:* Educational institutions, museums, nonprofit organizations.
Activities: Capacity building, citizen participation, collaborative efforts, direct services, fundraising, planning, policy analysis/development, technical assistance, volunteerism, youth programs.
Types of support: Annual campaigns, general purposes, matching funds, multi-year grants, projects, start-up costs, technical assistance.
Geography: San Francisco and Alameda counties, California.

Limitations. *Recipients:* Individuals.
Activities: Audiovisual materials, conferences, fundraising, publications, research.
Types of support: Annual campaigns, capital campaigns/expenses, debt retirement, emergency funding, endowments, equipment, scholarships.

H

Walter and Elise Haas Fund
One Lombard Street, Suite 305
San Francisco, California 94111
Tel: 415–398–4474   Fax: 415–986–4779
EIN: 946068564   Type: Independent
Contact: Nancy M. Young, Program Officer

History and philosophy. "The Fund was established in 1952 by Walter and Elise Haas to provide support for charitable and cultural purposes consistent with traditions and values which they held in regard." Values of interest are: quality, ethics, compassion, pluralism, participation, leadership, and individual initiative.

The Fund makes grants in the areas of: Arts, Humanities, Education, Human Services, Health Care, Public Affairs, and Environment. Its primary focus is the San Francisco Bay Area.

Officers and directors. *Officers:* Rhoda H. Goldman, President; Peter E. Haas, Walter A. Haas, Jr., Vice Presidents; Bruce R. Sievers, Secretary/Treasurer. *Trustees:* Douglas E. Goldman, Rhoda H. Goldman, Peter E. Haas, Peter E. Haas, Jr., Walter A. Haas, Jr., Walter J. Haas.

Financial data. Data for fiscal year ended December 31, 1993. *Assets:* $150,768,302 (M). *Total grants authorized:* $6,286,168. *Total grants disbursed:* $11,242,873.

Environmental awards. *Program and interests:* Environmental grants may be made through Human Services, Public Affairs, and Environment programs.
Recent grants: 1993 grants included support for land conservation (land management, state parks, forest protection), coastal issues, wildlife, urban issues (forests, parks, ecology), and youth education.

Issues. Cli Bio Lan Agr Wat Oce Ene Was Tox Pop Dev
             •   •   •   •   •   •   •

Funding analysis.

Fiscal year:	1991	1993
Env grants auth:	$115,500	$124,000
Number:	12	14
Range:	$1,000–$30,000	$1,000–$25,000
Median:	$4,000	$4,000
Pct $ disb (env/total):	2	1

Recipients (1993 highest):	Number:	Dollars:
American Rivers, Inc.	1	25,000
Bay Area Ridge Trail Council	1	20,000
Greenbelt Alliance	1	20,000
California Trout	1	15,000
The Video Project	1	15,000

Activity region (1993):	Number:	Dollars:
U.S. West	14	124,000

Sample grants (1993).
Bay Area Ridge Trail Council. San Francisco, CA. $20,000. Creation of a 400-mile ridgeline trail surrounding the San Francisco Bay.
California Marine Mammal Center. Sausalito, CA. $3,000. General operating support.
Environmental Action Committee of West Marin. Point Reyes Station, CA. $3,000. Operating support and bridge challenge grant.
Greenbelt Alliance. San Francisco, CA. $20,000. Greenbelt Fieldwork Program.
Planet Drum Foundation. San Francisco, CA. $3,000. Green City Project.
Save the Redwoods League. San Francisco, CA. $1,000. General operating support.

Application process. *Initial contact:* Full proposal using Fund-supplied "Grant Request Cover Sheet" and including:
1. Organization's name and brief description.
2. Contact person's name, title, and address.
3. Project title or type (10 words maximum).
4. Brief description of project purpose.
5. Financial information. Amount requested, project budget, annual budget of sponsoring organization, and amount raised to date. Attach list of other sources from which funding is being sought and/or is committed to date for this project.

When to apply: Anytime.
Materials available: Annual report (includes "Application Process").

Emphases. *Recipients:* Educational institutions, nonprofit organizations.
Activities: Advocacy, education, land acquisition.
Types of support: General purposes, single-year grants only.
Geography: San Francisco and Alameda counties.

Limitations. *Recipients:* Individuals.
Activities: Audiovisual materials, lobbying.

The Hahn Family Foundation
1800 One M & T Plaza
Buffalo, New York 14203
Tel: 716–885–4931
EIN: 166128499   Type: Independent
Contact: Anne D. Hahn, Trustee

History and philosophy. Established in 1965 by Charles Hahn, the Foundation makes ecology its central focus and Buffalo and Erie County its geographic area of interest. Support is also given to organizations concerned with energy, agriculture, conservation, environment, and hunger.

Officers and directors. *Trustees:* Anne D. Hahn, Anne H. Hahn-Baker, Charles D. Hahn, Charles J. Hahn, Eric S. Hahn.

Financial data. Data for fiscal year ended December 31, 1992. *Assets:* $2,739,101 (M). *Gifts received:* $5,000. *Total grants disbursed:* $77,425.

Environmental awards. *Program and interests:* The special concerns of the Foundation are:

- Renewable energy sources.

- Wastes: radioactive, toxic, other.
- Farmland and sustainable organic farming.
- Environmental concerns of Buffalo and Erie County.

Recent grants: 1992 grants included support for renewable energy, sustainable agriculture, and environmental education.

Issues. Cli Bio Lan Agr Wat Oce Ene Was Tox Pop Dev
         •   •   •   •   •   •   •

Funding analysis.

Fiscal year:	1992
Env grants disb:	$23,675
Number:	15
Range:	$100–$10,000
Median:	$1,000
Pct $ disb (env/total):	31

Recipients (1992 highest):	Number:	Dollars:
State University College at Buffalo	1	10,000
Park School of Buffalo	1	5,000
Union of Concerned Scientists	1	1,100
Boys and Girls Club of Erie County	1	1,000
Camp Fire Council of Buffalo and Erie Counties	1	1,000
Gow School	1	1,000
National Organic Farmers' Association of New York, Inc.	1	1,000
The Wilderness Society	1	1,000

Activity regions (1992):	Number:	Dollars:
New York/New Jersey	8	10,925
U.S. Great Lakes	1	10,000
U.S. not specified	5	2,650
International*	1	100

*Multiple regions or not specified.

Sample grants (1992).
American Farmland Trust. Washington, DC. $200. General support.
Boys and Girls Clubs of Erie County. Buffalo, NY. $1,000. Environmental camperships.
Camp Fire Council of Buffalo and Erie Counties. Buffalo, NY. $1,000. Environmental camperships.
Citizens Environmental Coalition. Albany, NY. $925. To send youngsters to environmental conference at United Nations.
National Organic Farmers' Association of New York, Inc. Ithaca, NY. $1,000. Education on sustainable agriculture.
Park School of Buffalo. Buffalo, NY. $5,000. Ecology station.
The Wilderness Society. Washington, DC. $1,000. General support.

Application process. *Initial contact:* Letter or proposal including summary (1 page) and copy of IRS tax-exempt status determination letter.
When to apply: Anytime.
Materials available: Application guidelines.

Emphases. *Recipients:* Nonprofit organizations.
Activities: Education.

Types of support: General purposes, matching funds, projects, seed money.
Geography: Buffalo and Erie Counties, New York.

Limitations. *Recipients:* Individuals.
Types of support: Operating costs.

The Hall Family Foundation
Hallmark Cards, Inc.
P.O. Box 419580, Mail Drop 323
Kansas City, Missouri 64141–6580
Tel: 816–274–8516   Fax: 816–274–8547
EIN: 446006291   Type: Independent
EGA member
Contact: John W. Laney, Vice President

History and philosophy. The Hall Family Foundation was established in 1943 by Joyce C. Hall (b. 1891), former president and chairman of Hallmark Cards, Inc., his wife Elizabeth Ann Hall, and his brother, Rollie B. Hall.

The Foundation's mission is to enhance the quality of human life by supporting "programs that enrich the community, help people, and promote excellence." It seeks to act as a catalyst for interactive programs and for those that promise permanent solutions in the Kansas City community. The Foundation focuses on five areas: The Needs of Young People, The Arts, The Needs of Older Persons, Economic Development, and Civic Issues.

Officers and directors. *Officers:* Donald J. Hall, Chairman; William A. Hall, President; John W. Laney, Vice President. *Directors:* Donald J. Hall, Paul H. Henson, Irvine O. Hockaday, Jr., David H. Hughes, Robert A. Kipp, John P. Mascotte, Margaret Hall Pence, Morton I. Sosland.

Financial data. Data for fiscal year ended December 31, 1993. *Assets:* $430,300,000 (M). *Grants disbursed:* $17,800,000.

Environmental awards. *Program and interests:* The Foundation expects to have an environmental program in place by late 1995.
Recent grants: 1992–93 grants included support for outdoor education and community gardens.

Issues. Cli Bio Lan Agr Wat Oce Ene Was Tox Pop Dev
         •   •

Funding analysis.

Fiscal year:	1991	1993
Env grants auth:	$38,780	$212,000
Number:	2	2
Range:	$13,780–$25,000	$7,500–$204,500
Median:	$19,390	$106,000
Pct $ disb (env/total):	<1	1

Recipients (1993):	Number:	Dollars:
Wildwood Outdoor Education Center	1	204,500
Kansas City Community Gardens	1	7,500

© 1995 Environmental Data Resources, Inc.

H

Activity region (1993):   *Number:*   *Dollars:*
   U.S. Midwest   2   212,000

Sample grants (1992–93).*
Friends of the Zoo. Kansas City, MO. $5,000,000 (4 years). Capital grant for zoo reconstruction.
Kansas City Community Gardens. Kansas City, MO. $7,500. Self-help gardening for public housing residents.
Kansas State University, School of Architecture and Design. Project to study improvement of grounds maintenance in low-income, single-family homes.
Wildwood Outdoor Education Center. La Cygne, KS. $204,500. New programming and capital support.

*Sample grants represent either new awards or disbursements on grants awarded in previous years.

Application process. *Initial contact:* Letter of inquiry.
When to apply: Anytime.
Materials available: Annual report, "Guidelines and Procedures for Grant Applicants."

Emphases. *Recipients:* Botanical gardens, educational institutions, museums, nonprofit organizations, zoos.
Activities: Collaborative efforts.
Types of support: Facilities, fellowships, internships, leveraging funds, multi-year grants, pilot projects, program-related investments.
Geography: Kansas City area only.

Limitations. *Recipients:* Individuals.
Activities: Conferences, political activities, research (medical/scholarly).
Types of support: Advertising campaigns, debt retirement, endowments, travel expenses.

The Ewing Halsell Foundation

711 Navarro, Suite 537
San Antonio, Texas 78205
Tel: 210–223–2640   Fax: 210–271–9089
EIN: 746063016   Type: Independent
Contact: Robert Washington, Grants Coordinator

History and philosophy. The Ewing Halsell Foundation was established in 1957 with donations by Ewing Halsell, a cattle rancher with interests in Texas, Oklahoma, and Kansas, and his sister-in-law Grace Fortner Rider. The Foundation's mission is to help improve the quality of life for all Texans. Arts, education, and social services are its priorities.

Officers and directors. *Officer:* Gilbert M. Denman, Jr., Chairman. *Trustees:* Helen Campbell, Jean Deacy, Gilbert M. Denman, Jr., Leroy G. Denman, Hugh A. Fitzsimmons.

Financial data. Data for fiscal year ended June 30, 1992. Assets: $45,427,841 (M). Total grants disbursed: $1,999,759.

Environmental awards. *Recent grants:* 1992 grants supported species preservation and a botanical center.

Issues.   Cli   **Bio**   **Lan**   Agr   Wat   Oce   Ene   Was   Tox   **Pop**   Dev

Funding analysis.

Fiscal year:	1991
Env grants disb:	$307,500
Number:	3
Range:	$82,500–$125,000
Median:	$100,000
Pct $ disb (env/total):	18

Recipients (1991):   *Number:*   *Dollars:*
   San Antonio Botanical
     Center Society   2   207,500
   Bat Conservation International   1   100,000

Activity region (1991):   *Number:*   *Dollars:*
   U.S. South Central   3   307,500

Sample grants (1992).
Bat Conservation International. Austin, TX. $75,000. Toward acquiring undivided interest in Bracken Cave.
Texas Nature Conservancy. San Antonio, TX. $15,000. For a land ownership inventory program for hill country.

Application process. *Initial contact:* Proposal to include:
1. Brief history and purpose of applicant organization.
2. Description of the proposed project, use of funds, and anticipated results.
3. Statement of financial need and other sources of funds (if any) to be used for the project.
4. Copy of IRS tax-exempt status determination letter and verification that the organization is not a private foundation.
5. Information clearly indicating that any contribution made by the Halsell Foundation will be considered a "qualifying distribution" as defined in the IRS Code Section 4942(G) and not considered a "taxable expenditure" as in IRS Code Section 4945(d).

Applications should be signed or approved in writing by the CEO of the applicant organization. Applicants may be requested to provide additional information. The Foundation encourages matching funding and may initiate challenge grants.
When to apply: Anytime. The trustees meet quarterly.
Materials available: Annual report (includes application guidelines).

Emphases. *Types of support:* Matching funds.
Geography: Texas only, primarily San Antonio.

Limitations. *Recipients:* Individuals.
Activities: Conferences.
Types of support: Continuing support, debt retirement, emergency funding, endowments, fellowships, general purposes, loans, scholarships.

The Hamer Foundation

2470 Fox Hill Road
State College, Pennsylvania 16803
Tel: 814–355–8004   Fax: 814–335–2714
EIN: 251610780   Type: Independent
Contact: Diane M. Kerly, Trustee

History and philosophy. The Hamer Foundation was established in 1989. Its primary focus is to support organizations that benefit the citizens of Centre County, Pennsylvania.

Officers and directors. *Trustees:* Donald W. Hamer, Diane M. Kerly, Edward Matosziuk.

Financial data. Data for fiscal year ended December 31, 1993. *Assets:* $831,860 (M). *Gifts received:* $320,000. *Total grants disbursed:* $147,775.

Environmental awards. *Recent grants:* 1993 grants supported land conservation, water resources, wildlife, and horticulture.

Issues.   Cli   Bio   Lan   Agr   Wat   Oce   Ene   Was   Tox   Pop   Dev
              •   •   •

Funding analysis.

Fiscal year:	1991	1993
Env grants disb:	$36,500	$28,000
Number:	8	7
Range:	$500–$10,000	$1,000–$8,000
Median:	$5,000	$2,500
Pct $ disb (env/total):	34	20

Recipients (1993):	*Number:*	*Dollars:*
Clearwater Conservancy	2	9,000
The Nature Conservancy, Headquarters	1	7,500
National Fish and Wildlife Foundation	1	7,000
Western Pennsylvania Conservancy	1	2,500
British Virgin Islands Botanical Society	1	1,000
Ogletop Open Space and Park Fund	1	1,000

Activity regions (1993):	*Number:*	*Dollars:*
U.S. Mid-Atlantic	4	18,500
U.S. not specified	1	7,500
Caribbean and West Indies Islands	1	1,000
U.S. Great Lakes	1	1,000

Sample grants (1993).
British Virgin Islands Botanical Society. Roadtown, Tortola, British Virgin Islands. $1,000. Operating fund.
Clearwater Conservancy. State College, PA. $8,000. Creek study.
Ogletop Open Space and Park Fund. Byron, IL. $1,000. Operating fund.
Western Pennsylvania Conservancy. Pittsburgh, PA. $2,500. Operating fund.

Application process. *Initial contact:* The Foundation has no specific application requirements.
When to apply: Anytime.

Emphases. *Recipients:* Botanical gardens, educational institutions, museums, nonprofit organizations.
Activities: Education, land acquisition.
Types of support: Annual campaigns, capital campaigns/expenses, continuing support, endowments, general purposes, matching funds, multi-year grants, projects, scholarships.
Geography: Centre County, Pennsylvania.

Limitations. *Recipients:* Individuals.

James G. Hanes Memorial Fund

NationsBank Trust Division
NationsBank Plaza, NC1002–09–01
Charlotte, North Carolina 28255
Tel: 704–386–7581   Fax: 704–386–1729
EIN: 566036987   Type: Independent
Contact: Katherine Hardin, Vice President and Trust Officer

History and philosophy. The James G. Hanes Memorial Fund and Foundation were established from trusts founded in 1957 and 1972 by James G. Hanes and his wife, Mary Ruffin Hanes. Mr. Hanes was the former president and chairman of the board of Hanes Hosiery Corporation. Although the Fund and Foundation are separate entities, for grantmaking purposes the two are combined and share a distribution committee. Funding areas include: conservation, local and regional health/education projects, cultural institutions/projects, social services organizations, and community-based programs.

Officers and directors. *Officer:* Eldridge C. Hanes, Chairman. *Directors:* Edward C. Crawford, Gordon Hanes, James G. Hanes, III, Douglas R. Lewis, Drewry Hanes Nostitz, Frank F. Willingham. *Trustees:* NCNB National Bank of North Carolina, Wachovia Bank and Trust.

Financial data. Data for fiscal year ended October 31, 1991. *Assets:* $1,503,257 (M). *Gifts received:* $180,307. *Total grants disbursed:* $497,200.

Environmental awards. *Recent grant:* One grant in 1990 supported a regional zoo.

Issues.   Cli   Bio   Lan   Agr   Wat   Oce   Ene   Was   Tox   Pop   Dev
                    •

Funding analysis.

Fiscal year:	1990
Env grants auth:	$116,700
Number:	1
Range:	–
Median:	–
Pct $ auth (env/total):	23

H

Recipient (1990):	*Number:*	*Dollars:*
North Carolina Zoological Society	1	116,700

Activity region (1990):	*Number:*	*Dollars:*
U.S. Southeast	1	116,700

Sample grant (1990).
North Carolina Zoological Society. Asheboro, NC. $116,700.

Application process. *Initial contact:* Request guidelines and application form.
When to apply: Deadlines are December 15, March 15, June 15, and September 15. The board meets quarterly, at the end of January, April, July, and October.
Materials available: Brochure, information sheet (includes "Grant Application Form").

Emphases. *Recipients:* Nonprofit organizations.
Activities: Land acquisition, publications, research.
Types of support: General purposes, matching funds, seed money.
Geography: North Carolina; southeastern states. Applications from outside this geographic area will also be considered.

Limitations. *Recipients:* Individuals.
Types of support: Operating costs.

Harbor Lights Foundation
Goldman Sachs & Co.
85 Broad Street, Tax Department
New York, New York 10004-2408
Tel: 212-902-6897
EIN: 133052490   Type: Independent
Contact: Robin Perri-Gurniak, Vice President

History and philosophy. The Foundation was established in 1980 by J. Fred Weintz, Jr. It has no specified grantmaking programs and makes grants to pre-selected organizations only.

Officers and directors. *Trustees:* H. Fred Krimendahl II, Elisabeth B. Weintz, J. Fred Weintz, Jr.

Financial data. Data for fiscal year ended April 30, 1993. *Assets:* $1,963,325 (M). *Gifts received:* $100,625. *Total grants disbursed:* $71,375.

Environmental awards. *Recent grants:* 1993 grants included support for land conservation and wildlife protection.

Issues. Cli Bio Lan Agr Wat Oce Ene Was Tox Pop Dev
              •   •   •

Funding analysis.

Fiscal year:	1993
Env grants disb:	$11,550
Number:	9
Range:	$75-$10,000
Median:	$100
Pct $ disb (env/total):	16

Recipients (1993 highest):	*Number:*	*Dollars:*
Sierra Club Foundation	1	10,000
Sierra Club Legal Defense Fund	1	500
World Wildlife Fund	1	500
Wild Foundation	1	150
Environmental Defense Fund	1	100

Activity regions (1993):	*Number:*	*Dollars:*
U.S. not specified	6	10,825
International	2	575
U.S. Mountain	1	150

Sample grants (1993).
Cultural Survival. Cambridge, MA. $75.
Environmental Defense Fund. New York, NY. $100.
LightHawk. Santa Fe, NM. $75.
National Audubon Society. New York, NY. $75.
Rails-to-Trails Conservancy. Washington, DC. $75.
Sierra Club Foundation. San Francisco, CA. $10,000.
Sierra Club Legal Defense Fund. San Francisco, CA. $500.
Wild Foundation. Fort Collins, CO. $150.

Application process. *Initial contact:* The Foundation makes grants to pre-selected organizations only. No unsolicited applications accepted.

Emphases. *Recipients:* Pre-selected organizations only.

Harder Foundation
Main Office:
401 Broadway
Tacoma, Washington 98402
Tel: 206-593-2121   Fax: 206-593-2122
EIN: 386048242   Type: Independent
EGA member
Contacts: Del Langbauer, President
           Judy Loomis-Grover, Office Manager

Florida Office:
5051 Castello Drive, Suite 29
Naples, Florida 33940
Tel: 813-649-0565   Fax: 813-649-0565
Contact: Nathan B. Driggers, Vice President

History and philosophy. The Harder Foundation was established in 1955 by Delmar S. Harder. Its mission is to promote environmental quality and ecosystem preservation in the United States. It has a special interest in the preservation of biodiversity through habitat protection. The Foundation looks to support campaigns and specific projects that will result in concrete and identifiable gains in environmental quality or natural resource protection.

Officers and directors. *Officers:* Del Langbauer, President; Nathan B. Driggers, Vice President, Investments; Robert L. Langbauer, Vice President; Jay A. Herbst, Secretary; William H. Langbauer, Treasurer. *Trustees:* Nathan B. Driggers, Jay A. Herbst, Del Langbauer, Eldon N. Langbauer, Lucille H. Langbauer, Robert L. Langbauer, William H. Langbauer.

Financial data. Data for fiscal year ended December 31, 1993. *Assets:* $18,643,312 (U). *Total grants authorized:* $555,889.

Environmental awards. *Program and interests:* Except for certain prior commitments, all Harder Foundation grants are made for environmental purposes. Broad interests are:

- Preservation, acquisition, and restoration of natural areas.
- Preservation and restoration of biological species in their natural habitat, and maintenance of biodiversity.
- Endowment support of selected environmental groups.

Particular funding interests are:

- Wilderness preservation.
- Species and habitat preservation.
- Air, water, and soil protection.
- Natural resource conservation.
- Population.
- Ecosystem restoration.

The Foundation makes grants for projects and general support.

Project grants are made that will protect and preserve the greatest areas of environmentally valuable lands, or that will result in clear and explicit improvements in environmental quality for the greatest number of citizens at the least possible cost.

General support grants are made to organizations for basic operating expenses or special projects.

Occasionally a Foundation-initiated endowment grant ($100,000 to $250,000) will be made to a national, regional, or local organization with a very successful record of Harder Foundation-sponsored project grants. Then, no further grants of any kind will be made to such a grantee for at least five years. No applications for endowment grants will be accepted. All grants are expected to produce clear, concrete results.

Issues. Cli Bio Lan Agr Wat Oce Ene Was Tox Pop Dev
• • • • • • • •

Funding analysis.

Fiscal year:	1991	1993
Env grants auth:	$413,095	$540,889
Number:	31	46
Range:	$500–$102,000	$1,000–$102,000
Median:	$7,000	$9,500
Pct $ auth (env/total):	91	97

Recipients (1993 highest):	Number:	Dollars:
Sierra Club Foundation	2	114,000
Northern Plains Resource Council	2	39,000
Florida Wildlife Federation	1	31,200
The Conservancy	1	23,000
Idaho Rivers United	1	22,000

Activity regions (1993 highest):	Number:	Dollars:
U.S. Northwest	16	259,399
U.S. Mountain	11	110,500
U.S. not specified	10	71,500
U.S. Southeast	2	54,200
U.S. Great Lakes	5	26,290

Sample grants (1993).
American Farmland Trust. Washington, DC. $5,000.
Citizens for Alternatives to Chemical Contamination. Farwell, MI. $2,000.
Florida Wildlife Federation. Melbourne, FL. $31,200.
Greater Yellowstone Coalition. Bozeman, MT. $10,000.
Michigan Natural Areas Council. Ann Arbor, MI. $1,000.
New Mexico Environmental Law Center. Santa Fe, NM. $15,000.
Northern Plains Resource Council. Billings, MT. $32,000.
Oregon Environmental Council. Portland, OR. $11,000.
Southern Utah Wilderness Alliance. Cedar City, UT. $7,500.
Tip of the Mitt Watershed Council. Conway, MI. $11,290.

Application process. *Initial contact:* Application guidelines for project and general support grants differ. Write to the main office for "Grant Proposal Guidelines."
When to apply: Between March 1 and August 15 at the main office; between January 1 and August 15 at the Florida office. Proposals received after September may be considered for the following calendar year.
Materials available: Annual report, "Grant Proposal Guidelines."

Emphases. *Recipients:* Nonprofit organizations.
Activities: Activism, advocacy, land acquisition, litigation.
Types of support: General purposes, matching funds, membership campaigns.
Geography: Projects of regional, state, or local scope in the states of Washington, Oregon, Idaho, Montana, Wyoming, Colorado, Utah, Nevada, New Mexico, Arizona, Alaska, Florida, Louisiana, and the Great Lakes States: Michigan, Wisconsin, Illinois, Indiana, Minnesota, Ohio, Pennsylvania, and New York only.

Limitations. *Recipients:* Individuals, museums, public agencies.
Activities: Education, research.
Types of support: Facilities, professorships, scholarships.
Geography: No grants to proposed new grantees in the State of Michigan will be made in 1994 or 1995.

The Harding Educational and Charitable Foundation

c/o Chase Manhattan Bank, N.A.
1211 Sixth Avenue, 34th Floor
New York, New York 10036
Tel: 212–789–5332
EIN: 136083440   Type: Independent
Contact: Joseph Rotella, Trust Officer

History and philosophy. The Foundation was established in 1945 by Henry J. Harding, Martha Harding, and Robert L. Harding. Grant priorities are conservation, higher education, and Protestant causes.

Officers and directors. *Trustees:* Arthur R. Douglass, Robert L. Harding, Jr., Faith Harding Mori, Timothy L. Thompson, The Chase Manhattan Bank, N.A.

Financial data. Data for fiscal year ended December 31, 1992. *Assets:* $4,184,642 (M). *Gifts received:* $60,000. *Total grants disbursed:* $208,000.

H

Environmental awards. *Recent grants:* 1992 grants included support for native and urban forests and wildlife.

Issues. Cli Bio• Lan• Agr Wat Oce Ene Was Tox Pop Dev

Funding analysis.

Fiscal year:	1992
Env grants disb:	$65,000
Number:	6
Range:	$5,000–$15,000
Median:	$10,000
Pct $ disb (env/total):	31

Recipients (1992 highest):	*Number:*	*Dollars:*
Defenders of Wildlife	1	15,000
The Nature Conservancy, Headquarters	1	15,000
National Wildlife Federation	1	10,000
Save the Redwoods League	1	10,000
The Wilderness Society	1	10,000

Activity regions (1992):	*Number:*	*Dollars:*
U.S. not specified	4	50,000
U.S. West	1	10,000
New York/New Jersey	1	5,000

Sample grants (1992).
Defenders of Wildlife. Washington, DC. $15,000.
National Wildlife Federation. Washington, DC. $10,000.
The Nature Conservancy, Headquarters. Arlington, VA. $15,000.
Save the Redwoods League. San Francisco, CA. $10,000.
The Wilderness Society. Washington, DC. $10,000.

Application process. *Initial contact:* Letter indicating grant purpose. Include resume of personnel and their qualifications. *When to apply:* Anytime.

Emphases. *Recipients:* Pre-selected organizations, generally. *Activities:* Education (medical), research (medical). *Geography:* Primarily New York.

Gladys and Roland Harriman Foundation
63 Wall Street, 23rd Floor
New York, New York 10005
Tel: 212–493–8182
EIN: 510193915 Type: Independent
Contact: William F. Hibberd, Secretary

History and philosophy. The Foundation was established in 1966 by Gladys and Roland Harriman. Funding interests focus on education, health and medical research, public affairs (including the environment), and the arts.

Officers and directors. *Officers:* William Rich, III, Vice President; William F. Hibberd, Secretary; William J. Corcoran, Treasurer. *Directors:* William J. Corcoran, Thomas F. Dixon, Terrence M. Farley, Elbridge T. Gerry, Jr., William F. Hibberd, Edward H. Northrop, William Rich, III.

Financial data. Data for fiscal year ended December 31, 1992. *Assets:* $94,115,419 (M). *Gifts received:* $1,200,000. *Total grants disbursed:* $4,434,899.

Environmental awards. *Recent grants:* 1992 grants included support for land conservation, parks, wildlife, and environmental education.

Issues. Cli Bio• Lan• Agr Wat Oce Ene Was Tox Pop Dev

Funding analysis.

Fiscal year:	1992
Env grants disb:	$52,000
Number:	5
Range:	$1,000–$20,000
Median:	$10,000
Pct $ disb (env/total):	1

Recipients (1992):	*Number:*	*Dollars:*
Environmental Learning Center	1	20,000
The Student Conservation Association, Inc.	1	11,000
NYZS/The Wildlife Conservation Society	1	10,000
Palisades Interstate Park Commission	1	10,000
Scenic Hudson, Inc.	1	1,000

Activity regions (1992):	*Number:*	*Dollars:*
New York/New Jersey	3	21,000
U.S. Southeast	1	20,000
U.S. not specified	1	11,000

Sample grants (1992).
Environmental Learning Center. Vero Beach, FL. $20,000.
NYZS/The Wildlife Conservation Society. Bronx, NY. $10,000.
Palisades Interstate Park Commission. Bear Mountain, NY. $10,000.
Scenic Hudson, Inc. Poughkeepsie, NY. $1,000.
The Student Conservation Association, Inc. Charlestown, NH. $11,000.

Application process. *Initial contact:* Full proposal including history of applicant organization and details of its program. *When to apply:* Anytime. The board meets in April and October.

Emphases. *Recipients:* Nonprofit organizations. *Activities:* Education.

Mary W. Harriman Foundation
63 Wall Street, 23rd Floor
New York, New York 10005
Tel: 212–493–8182
EIN: 237356000 Type: Independent
Contact: William F. Hibberd, Secretary

History and philosophy. The Mary W. Harriman Foundation was established in 1925 by Mary W. Harriman, wife of Union

Pacific Railroad magnate and financier Edward Henry Harriman. Fields of interest include the arts, civic and public affairs, education, health, and social services.

Officers and directors. *Officers:* Kathleen H. Mortimer, President; William Rich, III, Vice President; William F. Hibberd, Secretary; William J. Corcoran, Treasurer. *Directors:* Mary A. Fisk, Elbridge T. Gerry, Sr., Pamela C. Harriman, Kathleen H. Mortimer, Edward H. Northrup.

Financial data. Data for fiscal year ended December 31, 1992. *Assets:* $20,719,594 (M). *Total grants disbursed:* $961,500.

Environmental awards. *Recent grants:* 1992 grants included support for wildlife, horticulture, and coastal and marine issues.

Issues. Cli Bio Lan Agr Wat Oce Ene Was Tox Pop Dev

Funding analysis.

Fiscal year:	1992
Env grants disb:	$82,500
Number:	10
Range:	$1,000–$30,000
Median:	$5,000
Pct $ disb (env/total):	9

Recipients (1992 highest):	*Number:*	*Dollars:*
World Wildlife Fund	1	30,000
Palisades Interstate Park Commission	1	15,000
Scenic Hudson, Inc.	1	13,000
Natural Resources Defense Council	1	5,000
NYZS/The Wildlife Conservation Society	1	5,000
The Horticultural Society of New York	1	5,000
The Nature Conservancy, Headquarters	1	5,000

Activity regions (1992):	*Number:*	*Dollars:*
New York/New Jersey	4	38,000
International*	1	30,000
U.S. not specified	3	11,000
U.S. Mid-Atlantic	1	2,500
U.S. Northwest	1	1,000

*Multiple regions or not specified.

Sample grants (1992).
Chesapeake Bay Foundation. Annapolis, MD. $2,500.
The Horticultural Society of New York. New York, NY. $5,000.
Idaho Conservation League. Boise, ID. $1,000.
National Wildflower Research Center. Austin, TX. $1,000.
Natural Resources Defense Council. New York, NY. $5,000.
The Nature Conservancy, Headquarters. Arlington, VA. $5,000.
NYZS/The Wildlife Conservation Society. Bronx, NY. $5,000.
Scenic Hudson, Inc. Poughkeepsie, NY. $13,000.
World Wildlife Fund. Washington, DC. $30,000.

Application process. Initial contact: Proposal to include history of applicant organization and details of its programs. *When to apply:* Anytime.

Emphases. *Activities:* General purposes, projects, research. *Geography:* New York metropolitan area.

Limitations. *Recipients:* Individuals.

Hartford Foundation for Public Giving
85 Gillett Street
Hartford, Connecticut 06105
Tel: 203–548–1888   Fax: 203–524–8346
EIN: 060699252   Type: Community
Contact: Michael Bangser, Executive Director

History and philosophy. The Hartford Foundation for Public Giving is a community foundation established in 1925 to serve the people of the capital region in and around Hartford, Connecticut. It makes grants in the categories of Arts and Culture, Education, Health, Housing, Neighborhood Development and Training, Social Services, and Other.

Officers and directors. *Officers:* James F. English, Jr., Chair; Sue Ann Shay, s.n.d., Vice Chair; Brewster B. Perkins, Treasurer. *Distribution Committee:* Paul Copes, James A. Crowley, James F. English Jr., Jon O. Newman, Brewster B. Perkins, Nancy Rankin, Rosaida Morales Rosario, Sue Ann Shay, s.n.d., Wilson Wilde.

Financial data. Data for fiscal year ended September 30, 1993. *Assets:* $251,455,365 (M). *Gifts received:* $10,645,875. *Total grants authorized:* $10,483,019.

Environmental awards. *Recent grants:* 1993 grants included support for parks and environmental health.

Issues. Cli Bio Lan Agr Wat Oce Ene Was Tox Pop Dev

Funding analysis.

Fiscal year:	1991	1993
Env grants auth:	$43,744	$354,083
Number:	2	5
Range:	$21,872–$21,872	$2,000–$321,425
Median:	$21,872	$12,829
Pct $ auth (env/total):	<1	3

Recipients (1993):	*Number:*	*Dollars:*
Saint Francis Hospital and Medical Center	1	321,425
Connecticut Department of Environmental Protection	1	12,829
Connecticut Forest and Park Association, Inc.	1	12,829
Friends of Keney Park	1	5,000
E.A.R.T.H. Camp	1	2,000

© 1995 Environmental Data Resources, Inc.

H

Activity region (1993):	Number:	Dollars:
U.S. Northeast	5	354,083

Sample grants (1993).
Connecticut Department of Environmental Protection. Hartford, CT. $12,829. From the Genevieve H. Goodwin Fund.
Connecticut Forest and Park Association, Inc. $12,829. For scholarship for the Genevieve H. Goodwin Fund.
Saint Francis Hospital and Medical Center. Hartford, CT. $321,425. For Greater Hartford Lead Treatment Center.

Application process. *Initial contact:* Telephone call or proposal using Application Packet. Full proposal to include:
1. Applicant's line-item budget for the most recently completed fiscal year and current fiscal year, including sources of income to meet estimated expenses.
2. Brief description (5 pages maximum) of the project for which you are seeking funding and including:
   - Reasons the project is needed, e.g., demographic information and number of people to be served.
   - Project goals, measurable objectives, plan, and timeline.
   - Relation of the proposal to your present operation.
   - Full names and qualifications of key personnel who will direct the project.
   - Name, home address, and business affiliation of each member of the board of directors.
   - Your provision (if any) for an independent, professional evaluation of project.
   - Project budget and explanation of sources of funds (if needed) to carry on the program after requested HFPG funds are spent; inclusion of a budget narrative is desirable.
   - Other organizations in the Hartford area which now furnish the type of service for which you are requesting funds, and the extent to which projected services would duplicate other services now available.
3. Latest financial audit and any other reports or documents you feel strengthen your application.
4. One copy of Project Workplan (supplied by the Foundation).

New applicants only:
1. Copy of IRS tax-exempt status determination letter and proof that organization is not a private foundation.
2. Explain any affiliations with a sectarian or religious group.
3. Report on charitable services rendered in your most recent fiscal year, including classification and age groups of persons served, types of services provided, and the number who benefitted from each service.

When to apply: Each subject area has its own deadline. Call for information.
Materials available: Annual report, "Application Packet."

Emphases. *Recipients:* Nonprofit organizations.
Activities: Demonstration programs, education, innovative programs, land acquisition.
Types of support: Capital campaigns/expenses, equipment, facilities, multi-year grants, seed money.
Geography: Grants given only in Hartford, Connecticut and the 29 towns comprising the capital region.

Limitations. *Recipients:* Individuals, public agencies.
Activities: Advocacy, conferences, lobbying, research.
Types of support: Debt retirement, endowments, loans.
Geography: National or international programs.

The Hastings Trust
544 Settlers Landing Road
Hampton, Virginia 23669
Tel: 804–722–2801
EIN: 546040247   Type: Independent
Contact: Robert C. Hastings, Trustee

History and philosophy. The Trust was established in 1964 by Charles E. and Mary C. Hastings. Grants are given for education, environment, and wildlife conservation.

Officers and directors. *Trustees:* John A. Hastings, Robert C. Hastings, Carol H. Saunders.

Financial data. Data for fiscal year ended December 31, 1992. *Assets:* $1,894,080 (M). *Total grants disbursed:* $113,235.

Environmental awards. *Recent grants:* 1992 grants included support for wildlife and species preservation.

Issues.   Cli   Bio   Lan   Agr   Wat   Oce   Ene   Was   Tox   Pop   Dev
              •   •

Funding analysis.

Fiscal year:	1992
Env grants disb:	$18,100
Number:	8
Range:	$500–$6,500
Median:	$1,050
Pct $ disb (env/total):	16

Recipients (1992 highest):	Number:	Dollars:
Ducks Unlimited, Inc.	1	6,500
American Chestnut Foundation	1	5,000
The Nature Conservancy, International Program	1	2,000
National Wild Turkey Federation, Inc.	1	1,100
The Nature Conservancy, California Field Office	1	1,000
The Wildlife Conservation Fund of America	1	1,000
Waterfowl Limited (USA)	1	1,000

Activity regions (1992):	Number:	Dollars:
U.S. not specified	4	13,500
International*	1	2,000
U.S. Southeast	2	1,600
U.S. West	1	1,000

*Multiple regions or not specified.

Sample grants (1992).
Dolphin Research Center. Marathon Shores, FL. $500.
Ducks Unlimited, Inc. Long Grove, IL. $6,500.
The Nature Conservancy, International Program. Arlington, VA. $2,000.
National Wild Turkey Federation, Inc. Edgefield, SC. $1,100.
Wildlife Conservation Fund of America. Columbus, OH. $1,000.
Waterfowl Limited, (USA). Edgefield, SC. $1,000.

Application process. *Initial contact:* Proposal.
When to apply: Anytime.

Emphases. *Geography:* Virginia.

Limitations. *Recipients:* Individuals

The Merrill G. & Emita E. Hastings Foundation
c/o Ernst & Young
787 7th Avenue, 20th Floor
New York, New York 10019
Tel: 212-773-1738
EIN: 136203465   Type: Independent
Contact: John Ablamsky, CPA

History and philosophy. The Foundation was established in 1966 by Emita E. Hastings. Grants are made for religious, educational, cultural, and youth activities.

Officers and directors. *Trustees:* Elizabeth H. Peterfreund, Janice Peterfreund, Joshua Peterfreund, Lisa Peterfreund.

Financial data. Data for fiscal year ended February 29, 1992. *Assets:* $2,960,460 (M). *Total grants disbursed:* $132,180.

Environmental awards. *Recent grants:* 1992 grants included support for beautification, land conservation, parks, forests, river protection, energy, population-environment, and wildlife.

Issues. Cli Bio Lan Agr Wat Oce Ene Was Tox Pop Dev
         •   •   •   •   •   •

Funding analysis.

Fiscal year:	1992
Env grants disb:	$54,400
Number:	20
Range:	$250-$12,000
Median:	$3,000
Pct $ disb (env/total):	41

Recipients (1992 highest):	Number:	Dollars:
America the Beautiful Fund	1	12,000
Wildlife Preservation Trust International	1	5,500
American Chestnut Foundation	1	3,000
American Farmland Trust	1	3,000
American Forestry Association	1	3,000
American Rivers, Inc.	1	3,000
Defenders of Wildlife	1	3,000
Grand Canyon Trust	1	3,000
Northern Rockies Conservation Cooperative	1	3,000
Rivers Unlimited	1	3,000
Scenic America	1	3,000

Activity regions (1992 highest):	Number:	Dollars:
U.S. not specified	11	38,500
International*	3	7,100
U.S. Mountain	2	6,000
U.S. Midwest	1	1,000
U.S. Southeast	1	1,000

*Multiple regions or not specified.

Sample grants (1992).
America The Beautiful Fund. Washington, DC. $12,000.
American Farmland Trust. Washington, DC. $3,000.
American Forestry Association. Washington, DC. $3,000.
American Rivers, Inc. Washington, DC. $3,000.
Grand Canyon Trust. Washington, DC. $3,000.
The International Institute for Energy Conservation. Washington, DC. $1,000.
The Land Institute. Salina, KS. $1,000.
Natural Resources Defense Council. New York, NY. $1,000.
NYZS/The Wildlife Conservation Society. Bronx, NY. $550.
Population-Environment Balance, Inc. Washington, DC. $600.
Rails-to-Trails Conservancy. Washington, DC. $2,500.
Renew America. Washington, DC. $2,000.
Scenic America. Washington, DC. $3,000.
Southern Environmental Law Center. Charlottesville, NC. $1,000.

Application process. *Initial contact:* Brief letter with outline of proposed budget.
When to apply: Anytime.
Materials available: Annual report.

Emphases. *Recipients:* Educational institutions, religious organizations.
Geography: Primarily the Metropolitan New York area.

Limitations. *Recipients:* Individuals.
Types of support: Endowments.

Hawaii Community Foundation
222 Merchant Street, 2nd Floor
Honolulu, Hawaii 96813
Tel: 808-537-6333   Fax: 808-521-6286
EIN: 990261283   Type: Community
Contact: Janet Smith, Grants Manager

History and philosophy. Established in 1916, the Hawaii Community Foundation ranks among the oldest community foundations in the country and is now the thirteenth largest. As of May 1992, it comprised 125 funds including three recently-established ones reserved for scientific study of Mamala Bay, support of the Honolulu Zoo and Hawaiian Humane Society, and general environmental purposes.

The Foundation's mission is to act as "a catalyst for the establishment of endowments to benefit the community now and in the future, and to provide leadership and resources to address changing community needs, challenges, and opportunities." Projects must demonstrate leadership that represents the community served and offer a program or project that responds to an identified opportunity or problem in the state of Hawaii. Discretionary grants are made in the fields of: Education; Health; Human Services; Arts, Culture, and Humanities; Housing; Environment and Species Protection; Community Development; and Other.

© 1995 Environmental Data Resources, Inc.

H

Officers and directors. *Officers:* Diane J. Plotts, Chair; Fujio Matsuda, Henry F. Rice, Vice Chairs; Jane Renfro Smith, President and CEO; Douglas Philpotts, Secretary; Charles R. Wichman, Treasurer. *Board of Governors:* Amy Agbayani, Evelyn J. Black, Zadoc Brown, Jr., Edwin L. Carter, Philip H. Ching, Samuel A. Cooke, Nora I. Cooper, Walter A. Dods, Jr., Julia Frohlich, James F. Gary, David Iha, Lawrence M. Johnson, Barbara L. Kalipi, Elia A. Long, Thomas J. Macdonald, Roderick McPhee, Robert R. Midkiff, Russell K. Okata, Wesley T. Park, David W. Pratt, H. M. Richards, Jr., Manuel R. Sylvester, John K. Tsui, Margaret S. Ushijima, James C. Wo.

Financial data. Data for fiscal year ended December 31, 1993. *Assets:* $179,028,889 (C). *Gifts received:* $64,993,832. *Total grants disbursed:* $17,933,857. *Discretionary grants disbursed:* $3,410,124.

Environmental awards. *Recent grants:* 1993 grants included support for species protection and renewable energy.

Issues. *Cli Bio Lan Agr Wat Oce Ene Was Tox Pop Dev*

Funding analysis.§

Fiscal year:	1993
Env grants disb:	$2,057,384
Number:	15
Range:	$265–$2,011,124
Median:	$500
Pct $ disb (env/total):	11

Recipients (1993 highest):	Number:	Dollars:
Mamala Bay Study Commission	1	2,011,124
National Tropical Botanical Garden	3	17,700
Moanalua Gardens Foundation	1	15,000
Center for Plant Conservation	1	5,000
Kauai Community College	1	5,000

Activity region (1993):	Number:	Dollars:
Hawaii	15	2,057,384

§Includes designated, discretionary, and donor-advised grants.

Sample grants (1993).*

Center for Plant Conservation. St. Louis, MO. $5,000. Matching funds for a grant to endow the National Collection of Endangered Plants.

Kauai Community College. Lihue, HI. $5,000. Design, build, test, and race a solar-powered vehicle.

Moanalua Gardens Foundation. Honolulu, HI. $15,000. For the third year of support for the Education Materials Development Project.

National Tropical Botanical Garden. Lawai, HI. $12,000. Recovery of the gardens following Hurricane Iniki.

*Discretionary grants only.

Application process. *Initial contact:* Telephone for guidelines. If appropriate, submit a written proposal.
When to apply: Anytime. The board meets monthly except in April and September.
Materials available: Annual report (includes "Information for Grantseekers").

Emphases. *Recipients:* Individuals, nonprofit organizations.
Activities: Conferences, education, research, seminars.
Types of support: Equipment, facilities (renovation), general purposes, operating costs, scholarships, seed money, technical assistance.
Geography: Hawaii only.

Limitations. *Types of support:* Annual campaigns, loans.

Hawaiian Electric Industries Charitable Foundation

P.O. Box 730
Honolulu, Hawaii 96808-0730
Tel: 808-532-5867   Fax: 808-532-5869
EIN: 990230697   Type: Company-sponsored
EGA member
Contact: Scott Shirai, Director, Community Relations

History and philosophy. The Foundation was established in 1984. It makes grants in the areas of: Education, Social Welfare, Environment, Youth Services, Culture and the Arts, and Health and Rehabilitation for programs in Hawaii. Particular consideration is given to organizations or programs that operate in communities where the company has a significant presence.

Officers and directors. *Officers:* Robert F. Clarke, President; Edward J. Blackburn, Harwood D. Williamson, Vice Presidents; Betty Ann M. Splinter, Secretary; Curtis Y. Harada, Treasurer. *Directors:* Edward J. Blackburn, Robert F. Clarke, Ben F. Kaito, Victor H. Li, Jeffrey N. Watanabe, Harwood D. Williamson.

Financial data. Data for fiscal year ended December 31, 1993. *Assets:* $3,162,000 (U). *Total grants disbursed:* $600,000.

Environmental awards. *Program and interests:* The Foundation developed an environmental grants program in 1992. Interests are:

- Local issues.
- Environmental education.
- Community outreach.

Recent grants: 1993 grants (awarded through the education program) included support for land conservation, indigenous species, and recycling in Hawaii.

Issues. *Cli Bio Lan Agr Wat Oce Ene Was Tox Pop Dev*

Funding analysis.

Fiscal year:	1991	1993
Env grants disb:	$57,440	$48,000
Number:	8	5
Range:	$500–$15,000	$2,365–$15,000
Median:	$5,400	$10,000
Pct $ disb (env/total):	6	8

Recipients (1993):	Number:	Dollars:
Hawaii Nature Center	1	15,000
National Audubon Society, Hawaii State Office	1	14,635

The Nature Conservancy, Hawaii Field Office	1	10,000
Recycling Association of Hawaii	2	8,365

Activity region (1993):	Number:	Dollars:
Hawaii	5	48,000

Sample grants (1993).
Hawaii Nature Center. Honolulu, HI. $15,000.
National Audubon Society, Hawaii State Office. Honolulu, HI. $14,635.
The Nature Conservancy, Hawaii Field Office. Honolulu, HI. $10,000.

Application process. *Initial contact:* Short letter. Full proposal to include:
1. Nature, scope, and purpose of organization.
2. Organization's mission statement.
3. Project objective. Include: needs statement; administration plan; how project will improve business, social, or surrounding environment in which the company operates; population served; and plans for project or program evaluation.
4. Amount requested from HEICF and reason why HEICF was asked for support.
5. Organization and project budgets, including sources of revenue, other funding requests outstanding, contributions already received, and donors, including support from officers and board members.
6. Copy of latest management audit, cost-effectiveness study, or lacking either, an explanation of methods employed to determine organization's cost-effectiveness.
7. Breakdown of monies spent on major program.
8. List of organization's board of directors and HEI employees involved with organization.
9. Copy of IRS tax-exempt status determination letter.
10. CEO's compensation and benefits.
11. Number of paid staff members and volunteers.
12. Names of affiliated organizations.
13. Outline of plans for acknowledging HEI's contribution.

When to apply: Anytime. The board meets twice a year, usually in February and August.
Materials available: Annual report, "HEICF Guidelines."

Emphases. *Recipients:* Botanical gardens, educational institutions, museums, nonprofit organizations, zoos.
Activities: Activism, advocacy, audiovisual materials, citizen participation, collaborative efforts, conflict resolution, demonstration programs, direct services, education, innovative programs, land acquisition, volunteerism, youth programs.
Types of support: Capital campaigns/expenses, equipment, facilities, maintenance, matching funds, multi-year grants, pilot projects, projects, scholarships, seed money.
Geography: Hawaii only.

Limitations. *Recipients:* Individuals, public agencies, religious organizations, research institutions.
Activities: Exhibits, expeditions/tours, feasibility studies, fieldwork, fundraising, inventories, litigation, lobbying, political activities, research, seminars, symposia/colloquia, workshops.
Types of support: Advertising campaigns, debt retirement, lectureships, leveraging funds, loans, membership campaigns, mortgage reduction, operating costs, travel expenses.

H

Charles Hayden Foundation
One Bankers Trust Plaza
130 Liberty Street
New York, New York 10006–1196
Tel: 212-938-0790   Fax:
EIN: 135562237   Type: Independent
Contact: William T. Wachenfeld, President

Additional application address:
c/o Grants Management Associates
230 Congress Street, Third Floor
Boston, Massachusetts 02110–2109

History and philosophy. Charles Hayden, founder of the Boston brokerage firm of Hayden, Stone and Company, established the Foundation in 1937 with a bequest of $45.9 million. Mr. Hayden was the primary benefactor of New York's Hayden Planetarium at the American Museum of Natural History.

The Foundation "assists those organizations concerned with the mental, moral, and physical development of youth in the New York and Boston metropolitan areas. Focus is on institutions and programs serving school-aged youth at risk of not reaching their full potential due to social and economic conditions." Program areas are: Youth Development, Education, and Miscellaneous.

Officers and directors. *Officers:* William T. Wachenfeld, President; Gilda G. Wray, Vice President; Kenneth D. Merin, Secretary; John C. Esty, Jr., Treasurer; Maureen T. Fletcher, Assistant Secretary; Raymond J. Rush, Assistant Treasurer. *Trustees:* Howard F. Cerny, John C. Esty, Jr., Malcolm MacKay, Kenneth D. Merin, William T. Wachenfeld, Gilda G. Wray

Financial data. Data for fiscal year ended September 30, 1993. *Assets:* $201,688,000 (M). *Total grants authorized:* $6,772,000. *Total grants disbursed:* $6,715,000.

Environmental awards. *Program and interests:* Environmental grants are awarded through the Education program area.
Recent grants: 1993 awards included support for energy conservation, urban parks and gardens, zoos, and youth education.

Issues.   Cli   Bio   Lan   Agr   Wat   Oce   Ene   Was   Tox   Pop   Dev
                •

Funding analysis.

Fiscal year:	1993
Env grants auth:	$494,000
Number:	6
Range:	$10,000–$276,000
Median:	$22,500
Pct $ auth (env/total):	8

Recipients (1993 highest):	Number:	Dollars:
The New York Botanical Garden	1	276,000
Central Park Conservancy	1	150,000
Council on the Environment of New York City	1	25,000
The Parks Council, Inc.	1	20,000
Girl Scout Council of Bergen County	1	13,000

H

Activity region (1993):   *Number:*   *Dollars:*
New York/New Jersey   6   494,000

Sample grants (1993).
Central Park Conservancy. New York, NY. $150,000 (3 years). For a Central Park Outward Bound program.
Council on the Environment of New York City. New York, NY. $25,000. To support a High School of Environmental Studies in New York City.
Girl Scout Council of Bergen County. Paramus, NJ. $13,000. To install electricity at their new environmental center at Camp Glen Spey.
New York Botanical Garden. Bronx, NY. $276,000. To support creation of a new Children's Adventure Garden and Children's Adventure Trails.
The Trust for Public Land. New York, NY. $10,000. To expand their Children's Gardening Program to public elementary schools in the Bronx.

Application process. *Initial contact:* Proposal. The New York Area Common Application Form is acceptable. Proposal to include:
1. Concise description of proposed project and its goals.
2. Number and ages of youth to be served.
3. Total cost of project, based on professional estimates.
4. If the request is for partial funding of the total project cost, outline plans for raising the balance of those costs.
5. Sources, if needed, for additional operating funds once a capital project is completed.
6. Copy of the most recent audited financial report, and an operating budget, including a breakdown of revenue sources and amounts, for the current and previous fiscal years.
7. Copy of IRS tax-exempt status determination letter.
8. Project's expected outcomes and the criteria the applicant prefers the Foundation use in evaluating the completed project.
9. Other printed material concerning the activities and history of the institution.

Boston applicants should send one copy to each address listed above.
When to apply: Anytime. The board meets monthly.
Materials available: Annual report (includes "Grant Application Guidelines").

Emphases. *Recipients:* Nonprofit organizations, public agencies. *Activities:* Collaborative efforts, education, exhibits, innovative programs. *Types of support:* Capital campaigns/expenses, equipment, facilities, matching funds, seed money, technical assistance. *Geography:* New York and Boston metropolitan areas.

Limitations. *Recipients:* Educational institutions (higher), individuals, religious organizations. *Activities:* Conferences, fundraising, publications, research (medical). *Types of support:* Annual campaigns, continuing support, debt retirement, emergency funding, endowments, fellowships, general purposes, loans, operating costs.

The John Randolph Haynes and Dora Haynes Foundation

888 West Sixth Street, Suite 1150
Los Angeles, California 90017-2737
Tel: 213-623-9151   Fax: 213-623-3951
EIN: 951644020   Type: Independent
Contact: F. Haynes Lindley, Jr., President

History and philosophy. The physician Dr. John Randolph Haynes and his wife Dora Haynes established the Foundation in 1926 to fund study and research in the social sciences. Grantmaking reflects the donors' interests in "study and research in political science, economics, public policy, history, social psychology, and sociology, favoring projects with specific application to the Los Angeles area. By dissemination of the results of the research, and by other means, the Foundation seeks to improve public awareness and understanding of current issues."

The Foundation provides undergraduate scholarships, graduate fellowships, and faculty research fellowships in the social sciences to select colleges and universities in the Los Angeles area.

Officers and directors. *Officers:* F. Haynes Lindley, Jr., President; Robert R. Dockson, First Vice President; Jack K. Horton, Second Vice President; Jane G. Pisano, Chair, Grants Committee. *Trustees:* Robert R. Dockson, Philip M. Hawley, Jack K. Horton, F. Haynes Lindley, Jr., Chauncey J. Medberry, III, Donn B. Miller, Jane G. Pisano, Gilbert T. Ray. *Trustee Emeritus:* R. Stanton Avery.

Financial data. Data for fiscal year ended August 31, 1993. *Assets:* $42,614,151 (M). *Total grants disbursed:* $2,095,842.

Environmental awards. *Recent grants:* 1993 grants included support for research on energy efficiency through better transportation, pricing mechanisms, and land use planning.

Issues.   Cli   Bio   Lan   Agr   Wat   Oce   Ene   Was   Tox   Pop   Dev
                          •   •

Funding analysis.

Fiscal year:	1991	1993
Env grants disb:	$113,000	$150,022
Number:	1	3
Range:	–	$10,785–$114,237
Median:	–	$25,000
Pct $ disb (env/total):	6	7

Recipients (1993):	*Number:*	*Dollars:*
Environmental Defense Fund	1	114,237
Reason Foundation	1	25,000
University of California, University Extension Public Policy Program	1	10,785

Activity region (1993):	*Number:*	*Dollars:*
U.S. West	3	150,022

Sample grants (1993).
Reason Foundation. Santa Monica, CA. $25,000. "Implementing Congestion Pricing in Greater Los Angeles: Taking the Next Step."
University of California, University Extension Public Policy Program. Los Angeles, CA. $10,785. For a study, "Land Use Planning and Intergovernmental Relations in the Highway 101 Corridor and Santa Monica Mountains."

Application process. *Initial contact:* Complete proposal (20 copies of project description items) to include:
1. Statement of project purpose.
2. Problems addressed; project methods.
3. Names and qualifications of key personnel.
4. Timetable.
5. Detailed project budget.
6. Cover letter on organization's letterhead.
7. Copies of tax exemption letters from the IRS and California Franchise Tax Board.

The Foundation does not award funds for institutional overhead; applications should not include such costs.
When to apply: Several weeks before one of the board's quarterly meetings, call for exact dates.
Materials available: "Programs and Purposes" (includes "Requests for Grants").

Emphases. *Recipients:* Educational institutions, nonprofit organizations, research institutions.
Activities: Planning, policy analysis/development, research (scholarly).
Types of support: Fellowships, projects (research), scholarships.
Geography: Greater Los Angeles, California.

Limitations. *Recipients:* Aquariums, botanical gardens, individuals, zoos.
Activities: Activism, advocacy, audiovisual materials, capacity building, demonstration programs, direct services, expeditions/tours, feasibility studies, fundraising, innovative programs, inventories, land acquisition, litigation, lobbying, media projects, networking, technical assistance, training, workshops, volunteerism.
Types of support: Advertising campaigns, annual campaigns, capital campaigns/expenses, computer hardware, continuing support, debt retirement, emergency funding, endowments, equipment, facilities, general purposes, indirect costs, leveraging funds, loans, maintenance, matching funds, membership campaigns, mortgage reduction, operating costs, pilot projects, professorships, program-related investments, seed money, technical assistance, travel expenses.

The Edward W. Hazen Foundation
60 Madison Avenue, Room 1110
New York, New York 10010–1600
Tel: 212-889-3034
EIN: 060646671   Type: Independent
Contact: Barbara A. Taveras, Executive Director

History and philosophy. Edward W. Hazen, an executive with the Curtis Publishing Company of Philadelphia who also served as Connecticut assemblyman, church deacon, and state senator, established the Foundation in 1925. The Foundation "seeks to assist young people, particularly minorities and those disadvantaged by poverty, to achieve their full potential as individuals and as active participants in a democratic society." Its objectives are: parent organizing and training initiatives, and proposals which focus on youth organizing around concrete social issues, or issues of concern to youth. Current grantmaking programs are Public Education and Youth Development.

Officers and directors. *Officers*: Mary L. Bundy, Chair; Arlene Adler, Vice Chair; Carol Anastasio, Secretary; Lewis M. Feldstein, Treasurer. *Trustees*: Arlene Adler, Carol Anastasio, Mary L. Bundy, Earl Durham, Lewis M. Feldstein, Barbara R. Hatton, Arturo Vargas.

Financial data. Data for fiscal year ended December 31, 1993. *Assets:* $15,262,112 (M). *Total grants disbursed:* $334,288.

Environmental awards. *Recent grants:* 1993 grants included support for marine issues, youth education, and environmental justice.

Issues.   Cli   Bio   Lan   Agr   Wat   Oce   Ene   Was   Tox   Pop   Dev
                      •   •   •

Funding analysis.

Fiscal year:	1993
Env grants auth:	$43,000
Number:	4
Range:	$1,000–$25,000
Median:	$8,500
Pct $ auth (env/total):	13

Recipients (1993):	*Number:*	*Dollars:*
Southern Organizing Committee for Economic and Social Justice	1	25,000
Save Our Cumberland Mountains	1	15,000
Schooner, Inc.	1	2,000
Kids Against Pollution	1	1,000

Activity regions (1993):	*Number:*	*Dollars:*
U.S. Southeast	2	40,000
U.S. Northeast	1	2,000
New York/New Jersey	1	1,000

Sample grants (1993).
Kids Against Pollution. Closter, NJ. $1,000. For Cape Ann Kids Against Pollution, which educates and empowers young people ages 8–13 about environmental issues.
Save Our Cumberland Mountains. Lake City, TN. $15,000. For the Youth Leadership project focusing on environmental and community issues.
Schooner, Inc. New Haven, CT. $2,000. For the Science Under Sail project, which seeks to introduce children to marine biology and to develop an appreciation for the ecology, history, and culture of New Haven Harbor and Long Island Sound.
Southern Organizing Committee for Economic and Social Justice. Atlanta, GA. $25,000. To help consolidate the Youth Task Force and strengthen its ability to reach out and organize young people across the South around environmental justice issues.

Application process. *Initial contact:* Letter of inquiry (2 pages) stating project goals, objectives, approach, target population, duration, and total project cost. Do not send additional materials unless requested by Foundation staff. If interested, the Foundation will send an application and guidelines.
When to apply: Deadlines are January 15 and July 15 for review at the trustees' spring and fall meetings.
Materials available: Annual report, "Guidelines for Grantseekers and Grants List," grant application.

Emphases. *Recipients:* Educational institutions, religious organizations.
Activities: Advocacy, education, litigation, policy analysis/development, research, technical assistance.
Types of support: General purposes, matching funds, pilot projects, seed money.
Geography: States having high concentrations of minority and poor youth: Arizona, California, Florida, Georgia, Illinois, Kentucky, Louisiana, Michigan, Montana, New Mexico, New Jersey, New York, North Carolina, North Dakota, Oklahoma, South Carolina, South Dakota, Texas, Washington, and the District of Columbia.

Limitations. *Recipients:* Individuals.
Types of support: Capital campaigns/expenses, debt retirement, endowments, fellowships, scholarships.

The M. A. Healy Family Foundation, Inc.
c/o Covington & Burling
P.O. Box 7566
1201 Pennsylvania Avenue, N.W.
Washington, DC 20044–0756
Tel: 202–662–6000   Fax: 202–662–5490
EIN: 521313820   Type: Independent
Contact: Doris D. Blazek-White, Director

History and philosophy. The Foundation was established in 1984 by Martha Ann Dumke Healy. Interests include civic affairs, education, museums, and environment.

Officers and directors. *Officers:* Martha Ann Dumke Healy, President; Nancy Healy Schwanfelder, Vice President and Secretary; Edmund Healy, Vice President and Treasurer. *Directors:* Doris D. Blazek-White, Edmund Healy, Martha Ann Dumke Healy, Nancy Healy Schwanfelder.

Financial data. Data for fiscal year ended May 31, 1993. *Assets:* $4,942,167 (M). *Gifts received:* $450,039. *Total grants disbursed:* $173,500.

Environmental awards. *Recent grants:* 1993 grants included support for recycling and forests in New Mexico.

Issues.   Cli   Bio   Lan   Agr   Wat   Oce   Ene   Was   Tox   Pop   Dev
                        •   •

Funding analysis.

Fiscal year:	1993
Env grants disb:	$15,000
Number:	2
Range:	$5,000–$10,000
Median:	$7,500
Pct $ disb (env/total):	9

Recipients (1993):	Number:	Dollars:
Roadrunners Recyclers	1	10,000
Forest Guardians	1	5,000

Activity region (1993):	Number:	Dollars:
U.S. South Central	2	15,000

Sample grants (1993).
Forest Guardians. Santa Fe, NM. $5,000.
Roadrunners Recyclers. El Prado, NM. $10,000.

Application process. *Initial contact:* The Foundation awards grants to pre-selected organizations only. No unsolicited applications accepted.

Emphases. *Recipients:* Pre-selected organizations only.
Geography: Washington, D.C., Bethesda, Maryland, and New Mexico.

Limitations. *Recipients:* Individuals.

Howard Heinz Endowment
30 CNG Tower
625 Liberty Avenue
Pittsburgh, Pennsylvania 15222
Tel: 412–281–5777   Fax: 412–281–5788
EIN: 251064784   Type: Independent
EGA member
Contacts: Frank Tugwell, Executive Director
                   Andrew McElwaine, Program Officer

History and philosophy. The Endowment was established by the will of Howard Heinz in 1941 and added to by Elizabeth Rust Heinz, widow of Howard Heinz, in 1952. It gives to organizations within the Commonwealth of Pennsylvania for issues including the encouragement of art and prevention of cruelty to children and animals.

Program areas are: The Arts and Humanities, Human Services, Health, Urban Affairs, and Education.

Officers and directors. *Officers:* Teresa F. Heinz, Chairman; Jack E. Kime, Associate Director/Chief Financial and Administrative Officer; Frank Tugwell, Executive Director. *Trustees:* Drue Maher Heinz, H. John Heinz IV, Maria Teresa Heinz, Teresa F. Heinz, Jack E. Kime, Howard M. Love, Joseph W. Oliver, William H. Rea, William W. Scranton, Frank Tugwell, Mellon Bank, N. A.

Financial data. Data for fiscal year ended December 31, 1992. *Assets:* $679,392,746 (M). *Total grants disbursed:* $22,047,718.

Environmental awards. *Program and interests:* The Endowment plans to pay "greater attention to environmental issues in the urban environment.... In future years, health and environmental assessments will be basic criteria for the Urban Affairs grants program."

Application process. *Initial contact:* Letter signed by head of the organization or the president of the board and proposal (3–5 pages) to include:
1. Need for program.
2. Objectives of program.
3. Description of target population.
4. Plan of action.
5. Staff and organizational qualifications.
6. Other organizations involved in similar programs and how the proposed project is similar or different.
7. Line-item budget with revenues and expenses.
8. Amount of funding requested.
9. Method of evaluation.
10. Budget including income sources and member contributions.
11. Organization's most recent certified audit.
12. Copy of IRS tax-exempt status determination letter.
13. List of organization's board of directors.

When to apply: Deadlines are mid-February for consideration in the spring and mid-September for December's agenda.
Materials available: Annual report (includes "Application Guidelines"), application form.

Emphases. *Recipients:* Educational institutions, nonprofit organizations, religious organizations.
Activities: Research.
Types of support: Capital campaigns/expenses, emergency funding, endowments, equipment, facilities, matching funds, program-related investments, projects, seed money.
Geography: Commonwealth of Pennsylvania.

Limitations. *Recipients:* Individuals.

Vira I. Heinz Endowment
30 CNG Tower
625 Liberty Avenue
Pittsburgh, Pennsylvania 15222
Tel: 412-281-5777   Fax: 412-281-5788
EIN: 256235878   Type: Independent
EGA member
Contacts: Frank Tugwell, Executive Director

History and philosophy. The Vira I. Heinz Endowment was established in 1986 upon her death. It supports human services, arts and humanities, economic development, education, health, nutrition, and religion in western Pennsylvania.

Officers and directors. *Officers:* James Mellon Walton, Chairman; Jack E. Kime, Associate Director/CFO and Chief Administrative Officer; Frank Tugwell, Executive Director.
Trustees: Jack E. Kime, William H. Rea, Helen P. Rush, John T. Ryan, Jr., Frank Tugwell, James Mellon Walton, S. Donald Wiley, Mellon Bank, N.A.

Financial data. Data for fiscal year ended December 31, 1992. *Assets:* $340,924,039 (M). *Total grants disbursed:* $13,500,448.

Environmental awards. *Program and interests:* The Endowment's Civic & Public Affairs Program has an interest in environmental affairs.
Recent grants: 1993 grants included support for urban environment.

Issues.   Cli   Bio   Lan   Agr   Wat   Oce   Ene   Was   Tox   Pop   Dev
                                                •

Sample grants (1993).
Council on Foundations. Washington, DC. $5,392. General support.
Environmental Defense Fund. New York, NY. $103,129. To cover anticipated expenses to help design the Center for Environmental Science and Economics.
Friends of the Riverfront. Pittsburgh, PA. $72,500. To plan and develop the Three Rivers Heritage Trail.
Regional Resources. Pittsburgh, PA. $50,000. To pursue several urban design and landscape projects in Pittsburgh.

Application process. *Initial contact:* Letter signed by head of the organization or the president of the board and proposal (3–5 pages) to include:
1. Need for program.
2. Objectives of program.
3. Description of target population.
4. Plan of action.
5. Staff and organizational qualifications for carrying out program.
6. Other organizations involved in similar programs and how proposed project is similar or different.
7. Line-item budget with revenues and expenses.
8. Amount of funding requested.
9. Method of evaluation.
10. Organization's budget including projected income sources and average annual contributions per member.
11. Organization's most recent certified audit.
12. Copy of IRS tax-exempt status determination letter.
13. List of organization's board of directors.

When to apply: Deadlines are in January and August, 60 days before board meetings, held in March and October.
Materials available: Annual report (includes "Application Guidelines"), application form.

Emphases. *Recipients:* Educational institutions, nonprofit organizations, religious organizations.
Activities: Education.
Types of support: Seed money.
Geography: Western Pennsylvania.

H

Heller Charitable & Educational Fund

P.O. Box 336
Kentfield, California 94914
Tel: 415-434-3160   Fax: 415-434-3807
EIN: 946066671   Type: Independent
Contact: Ruth B. Heller, Corresponding Secretary

History and philosophy. The Heller Charitable & Educational Fund was established in 1955. Its objectives are "to promote prison reform, especially programs to develop alternatives to incarceration; to support programs of research, litigation, or other means of arresting despoliation of the natural environment; to help preserve open space lands for agriculture, wilderness, and recreation through purchase and other means; and to support the acquisition of books, periodicals, and other educational materials for libraries."

Officers and directors. *Officers:* Rolf Lygren, President; Peter Mandell, Vice President; Anne E. Heller, Secretary; F. J. Tone IV, Treasurer; Ruth B. Heller, Corresponding Secretary. *Trustees:* Anne E. Heller, Katherine Heller, Miranda Heller, Ruth B. Heller, Rolf Lygren, Peter Mandell, F. J. Tone IV.

Financial data. Data for fiscal year ended December 31, 1993. *Assets:* $1,670,000 (M). *Total grants disbursed:* $73,000.

Environmental awards. *Program and interests:* Environmental grants have two foci:

- Supporting programs of research, litigation, or other means of arresting despoliation of the natural environment.
- Preserving open space lands for agriculture, wilderness, and recreation through purchase and other means.

Recent grants: Grants in 1993 included support for land conservation (greenbelts, public lands, national park restoration), coastal issues, river protection, sustainable and organic agriculture, and minority opportunities.

Issues. Cli Bio Lan Agr Wat Oce Ene Was Tox Pop Dev
          •   •   •   •   •

Funding analysis.

Fiscal year:	1992	1993
Env grants auth:	$34,500	$53,000
Number:	8	7
Range:	$1,000–$7,500	$3,000–$15,000
Median:	$5,000	$7,500
Pct $ auth (env/total):	78	73

Recipients (1993 highest):	Number:	Dollars:
The Trust for Public Land	1	15,000
Sierra Club Legal Defense Fund	1	7,500
Stanislaus River Council	1	7,500
The Pacific Forest Trust, Inc.	1	7,500
University of California, Santa Cruz	1	7,500

Activity region (1993):	Number:	Dollars:
U.S. West	7	53,000

Sample grants (1993).
Greenbelt Alliance. San Francisco, CA. $5,000. Greenbelt 2000 Campaign.
The Pacific Forest Trust, Inc. Boonville, CA. $7,500. Conservation in Northern California.
Stanislaus River Council. San Francisco, CA. $7,500. Preservation of the Stanislaus River.
The Trust for Public Land. San Francisco, CA. $15,000. To create parks in underserved areas of Los Angeles.
University of California, Santa Cruz. Santa Cruz, CA. $7,500. For the Lifelab Organic Farming Education program for 4th-, 5th- and 6th-grade students.

Application process. *Initial contact:* Full proposal (original and 6 copies) to include:
1. Text summary (3 pages maximum).
2. Budget.
3. Copy of IRS tax-exempt status determination letter.

A modest amount of supplementary material may be appended.
When to apply: Deadline is January 15, 1995 for spring distribution. Call for later deadlines.
Materials available: Information sheet.

Emphases. *Activities:* Innovative programs, land acquisition.
Types of support: Pilot projects, seed money.
Geography: California.

Limitations. *Recipients:* Individuals, religious organizations.
Activities: Fundraising.
Types of support: Capital campaigns/expenses, debt retirement, loans, mortgage reduction, technical assistance.

The Clarence E. Heller Charitable Foundation

One Lombard Street, Suite 305
San Francisco, California 94111-1130
Tel: 415-989-9839   Fax: 415-989-1909
EIN: 942814266   Type: Independent
EGA member
Contact: Bruce A. Hirsch, Executive Director

History and philosophy. The Clarence E. Heller Charitable Foundation was established in 1990. It makes grants in the areas of: Environment and Health, Sustainable Management of Natural Resources, Music, and Education for Economically Disadvantaged Children.

Officers and directors. *Officers:* Alfred E. Heller, President; Elizabeth H. Mandell, Vice President; Miranda Heller, Secretary/Treasurer. *Directors:* Anne Heller Anderson, Peter Harckham, Katherine Heller, Peter Mandell.

Financial data. Data for fiscal year ended December 31, 1993. *Assets:* $28,480,210 (M). *Total grants authorized:* $848,524.

Environmental awards. *Program and interests:* The Foundation has two program areas that address environmental topics:

- Environment and Health.

  To support programs in research, education, and policy development designed to identify, reduce, and prevent serious risk to human health from toxic substances and other environmental hazards.

- Sustainable Management of Natural Resources.

  To assist programs that demonstrate how natural resources can be managed on a sustainable and ecologically sound basis, consistent with amenable standards of living.

Recent grants: 1993 grants included support for alternative agriculture and organic farming, toxics issues (radioactive waste, industrial waste, pesticides), and sustainable development.

Issues. Cli Bio Lan Agr Wat Oce Ene Was Tox Pop Dev
                    •   •   •   •   •

Funding analysis.

Fiscal year:	1991	1993
Env grants auth:	$228,000	$238,800
Number:	10	9
Range:	$15,000–$30,000	$10,000–$90,000
Median:	$25,000	$20,000
Pct $ auth (env/total):	54	36

Recipients (1993 highest):	Number:	Dollars:
Natural Resources Defense Council	1	90,000
Henry A. Wallace Institute for Alternative Agriculture	1	25,000
Physicians for Social Responsibility	1	25,000
The Land Institute	1	20,000
The Nature Conservancy, California Field Office	1	20,000

Activity regions (1993):	Number:	Dollars:
U.S. West	6	168,800
U.S. not specified	2	50,000
U.S. Midwest	1	20,000

Sample grants (1993).

Committee to Bridge the Gap. Los Angeles, CA. $15,000. To support the Ward Valley Project to monitor plans to establish a radioactive waste facility near Needles, California.

The Land Institute. Salina, KS. $20,000. For the Sunshine Farm Project, to develop a 150-acre farm which uses renewable energy resources.

Natural Resources Defense Council. San Francisco, CA. $90,000 (3 years). To develop a plan for sustainable timber management in the eight national forests of the Sierra Nevada.

Organic Farming Research Foundation. Santa Cruz, CA. $15,000. For a survey of the needs of organic farmers and for general support of the Foundation's research program.

Physicians for Social Responsibility. Washington, DC. $25,000. For a program in professional and public education on the medical consequences of environmental degradation.

Henry A. Wallace Institute for Alternative Agriculture. Greenbelt, MD. $25,000. For the Alternative Agriculture Policy Studies Program, an initiative to develop policy reforms to encourage sustainable farming.

Application process. *Initial contact:* Short letter of inquiry to include:
1. Project purpose.
2. Background of sponsoring organization.
3. Project budget.
4. Amount requested.

Full proposal, if requested, to include:
1. Background and history of organization, with particular emphasis on relevant work leading to current project.
2. Statement of issue, problem, or need to be addressed by project, including appropriate evidence or documentation necessary for describing problem.
3. Project description, including objective or outcomes to be achieved, and methods and activities for accomplishing the objectives. Timeline for project should be attached. This section should also include qualifications of individuals with primary responsibility for project and demonstrate knowledge of organizations doing similar work in the field.
4. Description of steps organization will take to measure project's success, with particular emphasis on specific criteria to be used in evaluating project.
5. Total project and annual organization budgets; other sources of support, including amounts of current commitments and proposed funding sources. Also include a statement of plans for funding beyond the period of Foundation support.
6. Prior year's financial statement; list of board of directors; IRS tax-exempt status determination letter.

When to apply: The board of directors meets quarterly. Call for deadlines for each funding cycle.

Materials available: Annual report (includes "Guidelines for Applicants").

Emphases. *Recipients:* Educational institutions, nonprofit organizations, research institutions.

Activities: Demonstration programs, fieldwork, policy analysis/development, research.

Types of support: Leveraging funds, operating costs, pilot projects, seed money.

Geography: California.

Limitations. *Recipients:* Individuals.

Types of support: Capital campaigns/expenses, computer hardware, debt retirement, mortgage reduction.

The William and Flora Hewlett Foundation

525 Middlefield Road, Suite 200
Menlo Park, California 94025–3495
Tel: 415-329-1070   Fax: 415-329-9342
EIN: 941655673   Type: Independent
EGA member
Contact: Stephen Toben, Program Officer

History and philosophy. The Hewlett Foundation was established in 1966 by the Palo Alto industrialist William R. Hewlett,

H

his late wife Flora Lamson Hewlett, and their eldest son, Walter B. Hewlett. The Foundation's broad purpose is to promote the well-being of mankind by supporting charitable, religious, scientific, literary, and/or educational activities. Specific program areas are: Children, Youth, and Families; Conflict Resolution; Education; Environment; Performing Arts; Population; Regional Grants (San Francisco Bay Area); and Special Projects.

Officers and directors. *Officers:* William R. Hewlett, Chairman; Walter B. Hewlett, Vice Chairman; David P. Gardner, President; Marianne Pallotti, Vice President and Corporate Secretary; William F. Nichols, Treasurer. *Directors:* Robert F. Erburu, James C. Gaither, David P. Gardner, Eleanor H. Gimon, Walter B. Hewlett, William R. Hewlett, Roger W. Heyns, Mary H. Jaffe, Herant Katchadourian, M.D., Walter E. Massey, Arjay Miller, Loret M. Ruppe.

Financial data. Data for fiscal year ended December 31, 1993. *Assets:* $841,253,000 (U). *Total grants authorized:* $34,337,000.

Environmental awards. *Program and interests:* "In 1994 the Environment program adopted a new geographical focus. Grants are now awarded to organizations working on issues that affect western North America – west of the 100th meridian. The program supports organizations that produce nonpartisan, policy-oriented studies; disseminate information on western environmental issues to decisionmakers and the general public; demonstrate, document, or study how environmental decision-making processes can be improved; integrate rural community development and environmental protection through research, economic development and demonstration projects; and, in exceptional cases, acquire or preserve ecologically significant land."

Issues. Cli Bio Lan Agr Wat Oce Ene Was Tox Pop Dev
• • • • • • • • • • •

Funding analysis.

Fiscal year:	1992	1993
Env grants auth:	$2,810,000	$2,595,000
Number:	24	19
Range:	$20,000–$300,000	$50,000–$250,000
Median:	$100,000	$250,000
Pct $ auth (env/total):	10	8

Recipients (1993 highest):	Number:	Dollars:
Yale University	1	250,000
Duke University	1	250,000
Cornell University	1	250,000
Rocky Mountain Institute	1	250,000
Woods Hole Research Center	1	150,000
Greenbelt Alliance	1	150,000

Activity regions (1993):	Number:	Dollars:
U.S. West	9	1,010,000
U.S. Mid-Atlantic	5	585,000
U.S. Northeast	2	400,000
U.S. not specified	2	350,000
New York/New Jersey	1	250,000

Sample grants (1993).
American Farmland Trust. Washington, DC. $50,000. For general support.
American Forests. Washington, DC. $125,000 (3 years). For general support of the Forest Policy Center.
Center for Neighborhood Technology. Chicago, IL. $100,000 (2 years). For general support and for the Alliance for Sustainable Materials Economy.
Ecotrust. Portland, OR. $100,000 (2 years). For general support.
Greenbelt Alliance. San Francisco, CA. $150,000 (3 years). For general support to improve regional decisionmaking.
Management Institute for Environment and Business. Washington, DC. $150,000 (3 years). For the Environmental Partnerships Initiative.
Pacific Rivers Council. Eugene, OR. $100,000 (3 years). For general support.

Application process. *Initial contact:* Letter of inquiry, to the president, including a statement of needs and enough information for staff to determine whether the proposal falls within the Foundation's interests or warrants consideration as a special project.
When to apply: Anytime.
Materials available: Annual report, "Program Guidelines" (contains "Advice to Applicants").

Emphases. *Recipients:* Nonprofit organizations.
Activities: Capacity building, collaborative efforts, conflict resolution, planning, policy analysis/development, publications.
Types of support: Continuing support, general purposes, multi-year grants, operating costs.
Geography: Western North America, west of the 100th meridian.

Limitations. *Recipients:* Aquariums, individuals, museums, zoos.
Activities: Activism, advocacy, audiovisual materials, conferences, education, exhibits, expeditions/tours, litigation, lobbying, political activities, seminars, symposia/colloquia, workshops.
Types of support: Advertising campaigns, capital campaigns/expenses, endowments, internships, lectureships, professorships, program-related investments, scholarships.
Geography: Organizations located outside of the United States.

The Hitachi Foundation
1509 22nd Street, N.W.
Washington, DC 20037–1073
Tel: 202–457–0588 Fax: 202–296–1098
EIN: 521429292 Type: Company-sponsored
Contact: Lauri Regelbrugge, Director of Programs

History and philosophy. An endowment of $20 million established the Hitachi Foundation in 1985. In its first six years, the Foundation supported arts and museums, community development and technology, education, and international policy. Restructuring and new priorities in the early 1990s led to the three current program areas: Community Development, Education, and Global Citizenship. The Foundation's philosophy is to support "multidisciplinary, cross-ethnic, and collaborative organizational approaches that capitalize on individual organizational strengths while integrating services and programs within the context of a regional, national, and global perspective."

Officers and directors. *Officers:* Elliot Lee Richardson, Chairman; Delwin A. Roy, President; Soji Teramura, Secretary; Masayuki Yamada, Treasurer. *Directors:* Clara R. Apodaca, Patricia Albjerg Graham, Joseph E. Kasputys, Katsushige Mita, Percy A. Pierre, Elliot Lee Richardson, Delwin A. Roy.

Financial data. Data for fiscal year ended March 31, 1993. *Assets:* $27,286,961 (M). *Gifts received:* $1,204,860. *Total grants authorized:* $1,910,299. *Total grants disbursed:* $1,714,871.

Environmental awards. *Program and interests:* The Global Citizenship program focuses on the "roles and responsibilities that must be adopted by global corporations and organizations, governments, public and private institutions, communities, and individuals." Among other things, it seeks to "promote an understanding of the complex nature of global communication, rapidly changing technology, and environmental degradation."
Recent grants: Grants in 1992–93 included support for environmental cost accounting, marine issues, and high school education.

Issues. Cli Bio• Lan Agr Wat• Oce Ene Was Tox Pop Dev

Funding analysis.

Fiscal year:	1993
Env grants disb:	$67,825
Number:	9
Range:	$250–$25,000
Median:	$3,000
Pct $ disb (env/total):	4

Recipients (1993 highest):	*Number:*	*Dollars:*
World Resources Institute	2	50,000
The Environmentors Project	2	8,000
Council on Ocean Law	1	5,000
City of Daly City, Recreation and Parks	1	2,500
Hidden Villa Trust	1	1,050

Activity regions (1993):	*Number:*	*Dollars:*
International	2	50,000
U.S. not specified	3	13,000
U.S. West	4	4,825

Sample grants (1992–93).
Council on Ocean Law. Washington, DC. $5,000. For the United Nations' 1992 Conference on the Environment and Development and participation in a conference in Nova Scotia on the management of straddling stocks and high seas fisheries.
The Environmentors Project. Washington, DC. $5,000. For a summer intern to coordinate aspects of a demonstration project that matches high school students conducting environmental science projects with mentors from the environmental or scientific communities.
World Resources Institute. Washington, DC. $100,000. To support dissemination and outreach activities of the Environmental Cost Accounting project, which has developed a business accounting framework currently being tested and refined in specific companies. Funds will support the publication and dissemination of project findings, and outreach activities within the public and private sectors to promote adoption and use of the framework.

Application process. *Initial contact:* Global Citizenship Program grants are awarded to pre-selected organizations only. No unsolicited applications accepted. In the Community Development and Education programs, the Foundation considers funding requests in two stages: preliminary proposals and full proposals. Preliminary proposal to include:
1. Completed Grant Application Cover Sheet.
2. Preliminary proposal (5 pages maximum).
   - Statement of project need and specific purpose, and population to benefit.
   - Summary of proposed project activities and anticipated project outcomes.
   - Description of how project seeks to improve on present practice and/or contribute to the knowledge base in the field.
   - Description of why project is important to your community.
   - Brief description of applicant organization, its mission, objectives, activities, and scope.
3. Copy of IRS tax-exempt status determination letter.

No facsimile proposals will be accepted; no supplemental materials will be accepted with proposals at the preliminary stage. *When to apply:* Deadlines for preliminary proposals are February 1 and October 1.
Materials available: Annual Report (includes "Guidelines and Priorities" and "Grant Application Cover Sheet").

Emphases. *Types of support:* Multi-year grants, program-related investments.

Limitations. *Recipients:* Individuals.
Activities: Conferences, equipment, fundraising, political activities, publications, research (medical), seminars.
Types of support: Endowments, facilities, fellowships, scholarships.

The Hofmann Foundation

P.O. Box 907
Concord, California 94522
Tel: 510–682–4830
EIN: 946108897   Type: Company-sponsored
Contact: Lori Hoffman, Executive Director

History and philosophy. The Hofmann Foundation (previously the K. H. Hofmann Foundation) was established in 1963 with donations from the Alta Mortgage Company, Hofmann Company, New Discovery, Inc., and Kenneth H. Hofmann. Funding priorities are: environment, education, culture, and human welfare.

Officers and directors. *Officers:* Kenneth H. Hofmann, President; Lisa Hofmann-Sechres, Vice President; Albert T. Shaw, Secretary; Lori Hofmann, Treasurer.

Financial data. Data for fiscal year ended July 31, 1992. *Assets:* $16,005,105 (M). *Gifts received:* $1,262,902. *Total grants disbursed:* $2,888,708.

H

Environmental awards. *Program and interests:* The Environment program focuses on:

- Habitat acquisition, preservation, and conservation (wetlands in particular).
- Public education about the need for land conservation, tempered by a wish to preserve opportunities for sport and recreation.

Issues. *Cli Bio Lan Agr Wat Oce Ene Was Tox Pop Dev*
            •   •

Funding analysis.

Fiscal year:	1991	1992
Env grants disb:	$558,550	$108,960
Number:	6	6
Range:	$200–$500,000	$500–$98,050
Median:	$1,025	$1,530
Pct $ disb (env/total):	10	4

Recipients (1992 highest):	Number:	Dollars:
National Fish and Wildlife Foundation	1	98,050
Mzuri Wildlife Foundation	1	6,750
California Waterfowl Association	1	1,550
National Audubon Society	1	1,510
Ducks Unlimited, Inc.	1	600

Activity regions (1992):	Number:	Dollars:
U.S. not specified	2	99,560
U.S. West	4	9,400

Sample grants (1992).
California Waterfowl Association. Sacramento, CA. $1,550.
Ducks Unlimited, Inc. Long Grove, IL. $600.
National Audubon Society. New York, NY. $1,510.
National Fish and Wildlife Foundation. Washington, DC. $98,050.
Yosemite Fund. San Francisco, CA $500.

Application process. *Initial contact:* Letter of inquiry (3 pages maximum) describing the planned use of funds.
When to apply: Anytime. The board meets quarterly.
Materials available: Annual report (includes application guidelines).

Emphases. *Activities:* Research, projects.
Types of support: Emergency funding, endowments, facilities (construction), matching funds, scholarships.
Geography: Northern California, particularly the San Francisco Bay Area. Some funding for national organizations.

Limitations. *Types of support:* Debt retirement, general purposes, operating costs.

The Homeland Foundation

412 North Pacific Coast Highway, Suite 345
Laguna Beach, California 92651-1381
Tel: 714-494-0365   Fax: 714-494-8392
EIN: 330200133   Type: Independent
EGA member
Contact: H. M. Bedolfe, Environmental Program Director

History and philosophy. The Homeland Foundation was established in 1986. Grant priorities include conservation of species and habitat, the environment, and welfare of women.

Officers and directors. *Officers:* John E. Earhart, President; Anne Earhart, Secretary; Oliver Crary, Treasurer. *Directors:* Oliver Crary, Anne Earhart, John E. Earhart.

Financial data. Data for fiscal year ended December 31, 1992. *Assets:* $17,749,665 (M). *Gifts received:* $2,997,268. *Total grants disbursed:* $2,171,944.

Environmental awards. *Program and interests:* The environment program concentrates on preservation of species and habitat.
Recent grants: 1992 grants included support for organizations primarily in the far western United States, Pacific region, and New World Tropics. Topics included land conservation, parks, forests, plant and animal species preservation, river protection, and coastal and marine issues.

Issues. *Cli Bio Lan Agr Wat Oce Ene Was Tox Pop Dev*
            •   •   •   •   •   •   •   •

Funding analysis.

Fiscal year:	1990	1992
Env grants disb:	$661,730	$1,115,822
Number:	51	61
Range:	$1,000–$100,000	$1,000–$250,000
Median:	$5,000	$5,547
Pct $ disb (env/total):	41	51

Recipients (1992 highest):	Number:	Dollars:
The Nature Conservancy, California Field Office	1	250,000
Environmental Defense Fund	1	200,000
Center for Marine Conservation	1	55,000
Natural Resources Defense Council	1	50,000
Woods Hole Research Center	1	50,000

Activity regions (1992 highest):	Number:	Dollars:
U.S. not specified	20	511,629
U.S. West	21	348,296
U.S. Northeast	3	85,000
International*	3	71,000
Tropics	4	31,000

*Multiple regions or not specified.

Sample grants (1992).
American Cetacean Society. San Pedro, CA. $25,000.
American Rivers, Inc. Washington, DC. $5,000.
Consultative Group on Biodiversity. New York, NY. $5,000.
Dian Fossey Gorilla Fund. Englewood, CO. $10,000.
Friends of the Sea Lion. Laguna Beach, CA. $3,000.
Grand Canyon Trust. Washington, DC. $10,000.
International Primate Protection League. Summerville, SC. $20,000.
Manomet Observatory for Conservation Science. Manomet, MA. $25,000.
Marine Forests. Balboa Island, CA. $5,000.
Mono Lake Foundation. Bishop, CA. $5,000.
Mountain Lion Preservation Foundation. Sacramento, CA. $10,000.
National Wildflower Research Center. Austin, TX. $2,000.
The New York Botanical Garden. Bronx, NY. $14,850.
Rainforest Alliance. New York, NY. $5,000.
Tropical Forest Foundation. Alexandrea, VA. $5,000.
The Wilderness Society. Washington, DC. $30,000.
The Wolf Fund. Moose, WY. $5,000.

Application process. *Initial contact:* Short letter along with copy of IRS tax-exempt status determination letter.
When to apply: Application deadlines are March 1, June 1, September 1, and December 1. The board meets quarterly. Proposals are considered the quarter after they are received, i.e., proposals received by March 1 are considered at the June meeting.

Emphases. *Recipients:* Nonprofit organizations.
Activities: Capacity building, education, land acquisition, litigation, research (scientific).
Types of support: General purposes, multi-year grants, operating costs, pilot projects, seed money.
Geography: Far western United States; the Pacific region; and New World Tropics only.

Limitations. *Recipients:* Individuals, public agencies.
Activities: Audiovisual materials, conferences, conflict resolution, exhibits, expeditions/tours, feasibility studies, fundraising, inventories, lobbying, media projects, networking, political activities, publications, research (medical/scholarly), seminars, symposia/colloquia, workshops, volunteerism.
Types of support: Advertising campaigns, annual campaigns, capital campaigns/expenses, debt retirement, emergency funding, endowments, facilities, indirect costs, lectureships, loans, maintenance, mortgage reduction, professorships, program-related investments, travel expenses.

The Horn Foundation

335 North Maple Drive, Suite 135
Beverly Hills, California 90210-3867
Tel: 310-285-2330
EIN: 954247470   Type: Independent
Contact: Alan F. Horn, President

History and philosophy. Established in 1989 by Alan F. Horn. The Foundation funds pre-selected organizations working on issues including environment, health services, population, women's issues, and youth.

Officers and directors. *Officer:* Alan F. Horn, President.

Financial data. Data for fiscal year ended December 31, 1992. *Assets:* $3,553 (M). *Gifts received:* $275,000. *Total grants disbursed:* $328,407.

Environmental awards. *Program and interests:* "Because of our environmental concern and involvement, the biggest contributions made in the past have been to environmental organizations. These donations are made through personal knowledge of the beneficiaries or through the requests of friends and/or business associates. *Recent grants:* 1992 grants included support for land conservation, forests, coastal issues, and air quality.

Issues.   Cli   Bio   Lan   Agr   Wat   Oce   Ene   Was   Tox   Pop   Dev
               •   •   •   •   •   •

Funding analysis.

Fiscal year:	1991	1992
Env grants disb:	$162,400	$142,000
Number:	19	12
Range:	$100–$28,000	$1,000–$50,000
Median:	$1,000	$5,000
Pct $ disb (env/total):	52	43

Recipients (1992 highest):	Number:	Dollars:
Natural Resources Defense Council	1	50,000
Coalition for Clean Air	1	25,000
Heal the Bay	1	25,000
TreePeople	2	25,000
The Nature Conservancy, Headquarters	1	5,000
The Nature Conservancy, Montana Field Office	1	5,000

Activity regions (1992):	Number:	Dollars:
U.S. West	6	77,000
U.S. not specified	2	55,000
U.S. Mountain	2	8,000
Tropics	2	2,000

Sample grants (1992).
Coalition for Clean Air. Venice, CA. $25,000.
Montana Land Reliance. Helena, MT. $3,000.
The Nature Conservancy, Montana Field Office. Helena, MT. $5,000.
Natural Resources Defense Council. New York, NY. $50,000.
The Rainforest Foundation. New York, NY. $1,000.
TreePeople. Beverly Hills, CA. $5,000.

Application process. *Initial contact:* The Foundation awards grants to pre-selected organizations only. No unsolicited applications accepted.

Emphases. *Recipients:* Pre-selected organizations only.

H

Howfirma Foundation
14 Central Street
Woodstock, Vermont 05091
Tel: 802-457-1370
EIN: 222495072   Type: Independent
Contact: Gary R. Brown, Esq., Trustee

History and philosophy. The Foundation was established in about 1983. It makes grants to organizations in the Woodstock, Vermont area involved with child welfare, social services, health, conservation, history, historic preservation, and peace.

Officers and directors. *Trustees*: Gary R. Brown, Esq., Frank H. Teagle, Jr.

Financial data. Data for fiscal year ended December 31, 1992. *Assets*: $27,237 (M). *Total grants disbursed*: $156,887.

Environmental awards. *Recent grants*: 1992 grants included support for land conservation, parks, forests, watershed protection, wildlife and fisheries, energy conservation, toxics education, and recreation.

Issues.   Cli   Bio   Lan   Agr   Wat   Oce   Ene   Was   Tox   Pop   Dev
           •   •   •   •   •   •   •   •

Funding analysis.

Fiscal year:	1992
Env grants disb:	$13,600
Number:	39
Range:	$50–$2,500
Median:	$150
Pct $ disb (env/total):	9

Recipients (1992 highest):	Number:	Dollars:
Heifer Project International	2	3,000
The Nature Conservancy, Headquarters	1	2,000
New Society Educational Foundation	1	1,000
Sierra Club Foundation, Vermont Group	1	1,000
Vermont Land Trust	1	1,000

Activity regions (1992):	Number:	Dollars:
U.S. Northeast	22	6,400
U.S. not specified	13	3,900
International*	4	3,300

*Multiple regions or not specified.

Sample grants (1992).
American Forestry Association. Washington, DC. $50.
Connecticut River Watershed Council. Easthampton, MA. $250.
Environmental Defense Fund. New York, NY. $150.
Farm and Wilderness Camp Fund. Plymouth, VT. $500.
Green Mountain Club. Montpelier, VT. $200.
National Audubon Society. New York, NY. $50.
National Parks and Conservation Association. Washington, DC. $100.
Natural Resources Defense Council. New York, NY. $600.
The Nature Conservancy, Vermont Field Office. Montpelier, VT. $2,000.
Restoration of Atlantic Salmon in America. Dublin, NH. $100.
Rural Education Action Project. Montpelier, VT. $100.
Scenic Hudson, Inc. Poughkeepsie, NY. $100.
Sierra Club Foundation/Vermont Group. Montpelier, VT. $1,000.
Trees for the Future. Silver Springs, MD. $50.
Vermont Institute for Natural Science. Woodstock, VT. $500.
Vermont Land Trust. Montpelier, VT. $1,000.
Vermont Toxics Education Project. Barre, VT. $100.

Application process. *Initial contact:* Request application form. Proposal to include:
1. Name, address, telephone number of applicant.
2. Letter describing organization's purpose and activities.
3. Copy of IRS tax-exempt status determination letter.
4. Detailed budget.
5. Proposal description.
6. Grant amount desired.

Individuals must include:
1. List of educational institutions attended.
2. Copy of latest transcript.
3. Statement of personal finances (sworn to under oath before a notary public).
4. Statement of personal educational goals.

When to apply: Anytime.
Materials available: Application form.

Emphases. *Recipients:* Nonprofit organizations.
Geography: Woodstock, Vermont and its surrounding area.

Hudson-Webber Foundation
333 West Fort Street, Suite 1310
Detroit, Michigan 48226-3134
Tel: 313-963-7777
EIN: 386052131   Type: Independent
Contact: Gilbert Hudson, President

History and philosophy. The Hudson-Webber Foundation was established in 1943 with contributions from the J. L. Hudson Company, a major merchandiser in the Detroit area, and from Richard, Joseph, and Oscar Webber. "The basic purpose of the Foundation is to improve the vitality and quality of life of the metropolitan Detroit community... with a particular interest in the revitalization of the urban core because this area is a focus for community activity and pride and is of critical importance to the vitality of the entire metropolitan community."

At present the Foundation has five program missions: Development of Detroit Medical Center; Economic Development, with an emphasis on creating jobs; Detroit Physical Revitalization; Arts; and Crime Abatement.

Officers and directors. *Officers:* Joseph L. Hudson, Jr., Chairman; Gilbert Hudson, President and CEO; Hudson Holland, Jr., Secretary; Frank M. Hennessey, Treasurer. *Trustees:* Lawrence P. Doss, Alfred R. Glancy III, Frank M. Hennessey, Hudson Holland, Jr., Gilbert Hudson, Joseph L. Hudson, Jr., Joseph L. Hudson IV, John E. Lobbia, Philip J. Meathe, Theodore H. Mecke, Jr., Mrs. Alan E. Schwartz.

Financial data. Data for fiscal year ended December 31, 1993. *Assets:* $104,143,854 (M). *Total grants disbursed:* $2,889,823.

Environmental awards. *Recent grants:* 1993 grants included support for urban environment and a zoo.

Issues. Cli Bio Lan Agr Wat Oce Ene Was Tox Pop Dev
                                              •   •

Funding analysis.

Fiscal year:	1993
Env grants disb:	$21,000
Number:	2
Range:	$6,000–$15,000
Median:	$10,500
Pct $ disb (env/total):	1

Recipients (1993):	Number:	Dollars:
The Greening of Detroit	1	15,000
Detroit Zoological Society	1	6,000

Activity region (1993):	Number:	Dollars:
U.S. Great Lakes	2	21,000

Sample grants (1993).
Detroit Zoological Society. Royal Oak, MI. $6,000. General program support.
The Greening of Detroit. Detroit, MI. $15,000. General program support.

Application process. *Initial contact:* Brief letter, signed by a senior officer of the applicant organization, to include:
1. Brief description of organization seeking support.
2. Brief description of program in need of funding, its importance, and its goals.
3. Detailed income and expense budget for proposed program.
4. Information about other potential sources of funding.
5. Amount requested, purpose for funds, and timeline.
6. Copy of IRS tax-exempt status determination letter.

When to apply: Deadlines are April 15, August 15, and December 15 for review at board meetings in July, December, and April.
Materials available: Annual report (includes "Grantmaking Policies").

Emphases. *Recipients:* Public agencies.
Activities: Capacity building, innovative programs.
Types of support: Annual campaigns, continuing support, equipment, facilities, operating costs, seed money.
Geography: Detroit, Michigan; limited funding within the larger tri-county area of Macomb, Oakland, and Wayne counties in southeastern Michigan.

Limitations. *Recipients:* Individuals.
Activities: Conferences, exhibits, fundraising.
Types of support: Debt retirement, emergency funding, endowments, fellowships, loans, scholarships.

The Charles Evans Hughes Memorial Foundation, Inc.

Foundation Service
130 E. 59th Street, 15th Floor
New York, New York 10022
Tel: 212-836-1358
EIN: 136159445   Type: Independent
Contact: Lauren Katzowitz, Secretary

History and philosophy. The Charles Evans Hughes Memorial Foundation was established in 1962. Areas of interest are: legal education; organizations combatting prejudice; environmental protection, including population aspects and AIDS prevention; and the arts.

Officers and directors. *Officers:* Theodore H. Waddell, President; William G. Kirkland, Vice President and Treasurer; Lauren Katzowitz, Secretary/Assistant Treasurer; Suzanne T. Reardon, Assistant Secretary. *Directors:* Anthony C. Howkins, Marjory Hughes Johnson, William G. Kirkland, Karen A. G. Loud, Betty J. Stebman, Theodore H. Waddell.

Financial data. Data for fiscal year ended July 31, 1993. *Assets:* $13,173,604 (M). *Total grants disbursed:* $510,000.

Environmental awards. *Program and interests:* The Foundation does not consider itself an environmental grantmaker. It typically funds a few pre-selected conservation organizations each year.

Issues. Cli Bio Lan Agr Wat Oce Ene Was Tox Pop Dev
                                •   •   •   •

Funding analysis.

Fiscal year:	1992	1993
Env grants disb:	$105,000	$120,000
Number:	3	3
Range:	$15,000–$65,000	$20,000–$65,000
Median:	$25,000	$35,000
Pct $ disb (env/total):	24	23

Recipients (1993):	Number:	Dollars:
Natural Resources Defense Council	1	65,000
The Nature Conservancy, Headquarters	1	35,000
Center for Marine Conservation	1	20,000

Activity region (1992):	Number:	Dollars:
U.S. not specified	3	120,000

Sample grants (1993).
Center for Marine Conservation. Washington, DC. $20,000.
Natural Resources Defense Council. New York, NY. $65,000.
The Nature Conservancy, Headquarters. Arlington, VA. $35,000.

Application process. *Initial contact:* Letter (1 page).
When to apply: Deadline is August. The board meets in October.

H

Emphases. *Recipients:* Past recipients.
Geography: United States only.

Limitations. *Recipients:* Individuals.

The Roy A. Hunt Foundation
One Bigelow Square, Suite 630
Pittsburgh, Pennsylvania 15219–3030
Tel: 412–281–8734   Fax: 412–281–9463
EIN: 256105162   Type: Independent
Contact: Cynthia Lucas, Secretary

History and philosophy. The Roy A. Hunt Foundation was established in 1966 with a bequest from Roy Hunt, former president and chairman of the executive committee of Alcoa. It supports institutions that were of interest to Mr. Hunt and his wife as well as those of interest to the current trustees. The Hunt family also founded the Hunt Institute for Botanical Documentation at Carnegie-Mellon University in 1961, and the Hunt Foundation in 1952. Funding preferences include the arts, community service, education, and the sciences.

Officers and directors. *Officer:* Torrence M. Hunt, Jr., President. *Trustees:* Susan Hunt Hollingsworth, Andrew McQ. Hunt, Christopher M. Hunt, Daniel K. Hunt, Helen McM. Hunt, John B. Hunt, Marion Hunt-Badiner, Richard McM. Hunt, Roy A. Hunt, III, Torrence M. Hunt, Torrence M. Hunt, Jr., William E. Hunt, Rachel Hunt Knowles.

Financial data. Data for fiscal year ended May 31, 1993.*
Assets: $30,423,510 (M) (est). *Total grants disbursed:* $950,641.

*Considered by Foundation to be fiscal year 1992.

Environmental awards. *Recent grants:* 1993 awards included support for land conservation, watershed protection, and biodiversity.

Issues.   Cli   Bio   Lan   Agr   Wat   Oce   Ene   Was   Tox   Pop   Dev
              •   •   •   •   •

Funding analysis.

Fiscal year:	1992	1993
Env grants disb:	$57,000	$57,000
Number:	15	15
Range:	$1,000–$10,000	$1,000–$10,000
Median:	$3,000	$3,000
Pct $ disb (env/total):	9	6

Recipients (1993 highest):	Number:	Dollars:
The Nature Conservancy, Headquarters	1	10,000
Allegheny Conference on Community Development	1	7,000
Massachusetts Audubon Society	1	6,000
Garden Club of Oakmont	1	5,000
Global Action Plan for the Earth	1	5,000

Activity regions (1993 highest):	Number:	Dollars:
U.S. not specified	7	19,500
U.S. Mid-Atlantic	2	12,000
International*	1	10,000
U.S. Northeast	2	8,000
U.S. multiple regions	1	3,000

*Multiple regions or not specified.

Sample grants (1993).
Allegheny Conference on Community Development. Pittsburgh, PA. $7,000.
Garden Club of Oakmont. Oakmont, PA. $5,000.
Global Action Plan for the Earth. West Hurley, NY. $5,000.
Massachusetts Audubon Society. Lincoln, MA. $6,000.
The Nature Conservancy, Headquarters. Arlington, VA. $10,000.

Application process. *Initial contact:* Letter.
When to apply: Deadlines are April 15 and October 15.

Emphases. *Recipients:* Educational institutions, museums, non-profit organizations, zoos.
Activities: Education.
Types of support: Annual campaigns, capital campaigns/expenses, general purposes, multi-year grants, operating costs.

Hurdle Hill Foundation
c/o Woodstock Service Corporation
18 Tremont Street
Boston, Massachusetts 02108
Tel: 617–227–0600
EIN: 046012782   Type: Independent
Contact: Richard D. Phippen, Trustee

History and philosophy. Edith M. Adams and members of the Phippen family established the Hurdle Hill Foundation in 1960. Funding priorities include conservation and the environment, cultural programs, education, and health services.

Officers and directors. *Trustees:* Nelson J. Darling, Jr., Peter D. Phippen, Richard D. Phippen, Susanne LaCroix Phippen, William LaCroix Phippen.

Financial data. Data for fiscal year ended December 31, 1992.
Assets: $288,309 (M). *Gifts received:* $174,312. *Total grants disbursed:* $185,150.

Environmental awards. *Recent grants:* 1992 grants included support for land conservation, marine issues, wildlife, and outdoor education.

Issues.   Cli   Bio   Lan   Agr   Wat   Oce   Ene   Was   Tox   Pop   Dev
                    •   •   •   •   •

Funding analysis.

Fiscal year:	1992
Env grants disb:	$78,150
Number:	15
Range:	$100–$16,000
Median:	$4,000
Pct $ disb (env/total):	42

Recipients (1992 highest):	Number:	Dollars:
The Nature Conservancy, Headquarters	2	16,200
Trustees of Reservations	1	16,000
Essex County Green Belt Association	1	13,800
Center for Plant Conservation	1	10,000
Woods Hole Oceanographic Institution	1	5,000

Activity regions (1992):	Number:	Dollars:
U.S. Northeast	6	40,600
U.S. not specified	6	27,200
U.S. Midwest	1	10,000
International*	1	250
U.S. Mountain	1	100

*Multiple regions or not specified.

Sample grants (1992).
Colorado Outward Bound School. Denver, CO. $100.
Essex County Greenbelt Association. Essex, MA. $13,800.
Greenpeace USA. Washington, DC. $3,250.
Massachusetts Audubon Society. Lincoln, MA. $4,000.
Massachusetts Forestry Association. Belchertown, MA. $500.
Natural Resources Defense Council. New York, NY. $4,250.
Sierra Club Legal Defense Fund. San Francisco, CA. $3,000.
The Nature Conservancy, Headquarters. Arlington, VA. $10,000.
Trustees of Reservations. Beverly, MA. $16,000.
Woods Hole Oceanographic Society. Woods Hole, MA. $5,000.
World Wildlife Fund. Washington, DC. $250.

Application process. *Initial contact:* The Foundation awards grants to pre-selected organizations only. No unsolicited applications accepted.

Emphases. *Recipients:* Pre-selected organizations only.

The Hyams Foundation

One Boston Place, 32nd Floor
Boston, Massachusetts 02108
Tel: 617-720-2238   Fax: 617-720-2434
EIN: 042214849   Type: Independent
Contact: Elizabeth B. Smith, Executive Director

History and philosophy. Godfrey M. Hyams (1859–1927) was a metallurgist, engineer, and financier. He oversaw the growth of the Anaconda Mining Company, and planned and managed construction of the Virginia Railway which carried the coal east. He established The Godfrey Hyams Trust in 1921.

The Foundation's broad objectives are to "meet the needs of low-income and other underserved populations . . . address problems at the neighborhood level . . . and develop and maintain the capacity of local community-based organizations." Specific goals are to "promote understanding among people of different racial, ethnic, and economic backgrounds . . . [to] maintain open space for use by local residents and [to] promote clean and safe neighborhood environments." Most grants fund community development, health care, human and social services, and programs for the disadvantaged; some of them address environmental issues. The Boston area is the Foundation's geographic priority.

© 1995 Environmental Data Resources, Inc.

Officers and directors. *Officer:* John H. Clymer, Chairman. *Trustees:* Barbara E. Casey, John H. Clymer, James Jennings, Deborah Prothrow-Stith, Lewis H. Spence, Roslyn M. Watson.

Financial data. Data for fiscal year ended December 31, 1993. *Assets:* $75,568,010 (M). *Total grants authorized:* $3,245,561.

Environmental awards. *Recent grants:* 1993 grants included support for urban environment (including open space and gardens), coastal issues, and outdoor education.

Issues. Cli Bio Lan Agr Wat Oce Ene Was Tox Pop Dev
              •   •   •   •

Funding analysis.

Fiscal year:	1990	1993
Env grants auth:	$64,359	$50,000
Number:	6	4
Range:	$1,359–$20,000	$5,000–$20,000
Median:	$11,500	$12,500
Pct $ auth (env/total):	2	2

Recipients (1993):	Number:	Dollars:
Boston Urban Gardeners	1	20,000
Boston GreenSpace Alliance	1	15,000
Boston Natural Areas Fund	1	10,000
Thompson Island Outward Bound Education Center	1	5,000

Activity region (1993):	Number:	Dollars:
U.S. Northeast	4	50,000

Sample grants (1993).
Boston GreenSpace Alliance. Boston, MA. $15,000. Operating expenses.
Boston Natural Areas Fund. Boston, MA. $10,000. Operating expenses.
Boston Urban Gardeners. Boston, MA. $20,000. Operating expenses.
Thompson Island Outward Bound Education Center. Boston, MA. $5,000. Summer Project Island Discovery Program.

Application process. *Initial contact:* Letter of inquiry (1 page) outlining the proposed project and geographic area(s) and population(s) to be served or proposal (10 pages) to include:
1. Introduction.
   - Grant purpose, funding request, and anticipated results.
2. Grant request.
   - Organization's history, mission, and programs.
   - Objectives and activities and population served.
   - How the request addresses Foundation priorities.
   - Needs statement.
   - What makes project/organization unique.
   - Level of local involvement.
   - Organization's qualifications to carry out the project.
3. Staff and board of directors.
4. Financial information and status.
5. Evaluation criteria.
6. Appendixes.
   - Copy of IRS tax-exempt status determination letter and certification that the organization is "not a private foundation" under Section 509(a).

- Proof of incorporation in Massachusetts.
- Organization budget (board-approved) for the year in which funding is requested.
- Organization's year-to-date financial statement showing expenditures and sources of revenue.
- List of proposals pending with other funding sources for general operating expenses.
- Financial audit for previous fiscal year.
- Diversity Form (or Boston Foundation Diversity Form).
- Board of Directors Form (or United Way of Massachusetts Bay Form #7).

Organizations requesting a grant for a special or capital project must also submit:
- Board-approved special project or capital project budget, including projected income and expenses.
- Total amount and sources of funds received or committed to the project to date.
- List of proposals pending with other funding sources.

When to apply: Anytime. The trustees meet approximately every eight weeks from September through June.
Materials available: Annual report, "Statement of Principles and Funding Guidelines."

Emphases. *Recipients:* Nonprofit organizations.
Activities: Capacity building, youth programs.
Types of support: General purposes, operating costs.
Geography: Massachusetts only, especially Boston, Cambridge, Chelsea, Lynn, and Somerville. Focus is on low-income neighborhoods in these areas.

Limitations. *Recipients:* Botanical gardens, educational institutions, individuals, museums, public agencies, religious organizations, research institutions.
Activities: Audiovisual materials, conferences, conflict resolution, demonstration programs, education, exhibits, expeditions/tours, feasibility studies, fieldwork, fundraising, inventories, land acquisition, litigation, lobbying, networking, policy analysis/development, political activities, publications, research, seminars, symposia/colloquia, volunteerism, workshops.
Types of support: Advertising campaigns, annual campaigns, capital campaigns/expenses, computer hardware, debt retirement, emergency funding, endowments, fellowships, indirect costs, internships, lectureships, leveraging funds, loans, maintenance, matching funds, membership campaigns, mortgage reduction, multi-year grants, pilot projects, professorships, program-related investments, scholarships, seed money, travel expenses.

The Hyde and Watson Foundation

437 Southern Boulevard
Chatham Township, New Jersey 07928
Tel: 201-966-6024   Fax: 201-966-6404
EIN: 222425725   Type: Independent
Contact: Robert W. Parsons, Jr., President

History and philosophy. The Hyde and Watson Foundation was formed in 1983 through the consolidation of the Lillia Babbitt Hyde Foundation and the John Jay and Eliza Jane Watson Foundation. Lillia Babbitt (1856–1939) was the daughter of Benjamin Talbot Babbitt, a businessman and inventor who made his fortune in the chemical industry. She bequeathed her estate to the Foundation, which was established in 1924. John Jay Watson (1874–1939) was successful in the rubber and tire industries, and later in agricultural chemicals. His wife established a foundation in his name in 1939. The Hyde and Watson Foundation today makes grants in the areas of: health, education, religion, social services, arts, and humanities.

Officers and directors. *Officers:* John W. Holman, Jr., Chairman; Robert W. Parsons, Jr., President and Principal Officer; Hunter W. Corbin, Vice President; Roger B. Parsons, Vice President and Secretary; H. Corbin Day, Treasurer. *Directors:* Hunter W. Corbin, H. Corbin Day, William V. Engel, David Ferguson, John W. Holman, Jr., John G. MacKechnie, Robert W. Parsons, Jr., Roger B. Parsons, Kate B. Wood.

Financial data. Data for fiscal year ended December 31, 1993. *Assets:* $66,305,688 (M). *Total grants authorized:* $2,479,730.

Environmental awards. *Recent grants:* 1993 grants included support for capacity building of organizations working on land conservation, parks, and agriculture.

Issues.   Cli Bio Lan Agr Wat Oce Ene Was Tox Pop Dev
                   •   •   •   •

Funding analysis.

Fiscal year:	1991	1993
Env grants auth:	$74,980	$60,000
Number:	7	5
Range:	$2,480–$25,000	$5,000–$25,000
Median:	$7,500	$10,000
Pct $ auth (env/total):	3	2

Recipients (1993):	Number:	Dollars:
Reeves-Reed Arboretum	1	25,000
Natural Resources Defense Council	1	15,000
Pinelands Preservation Alliance, Inc.	1	10,000
Association of New Jersey Environmental Commissions	1	5,000
Great Swamp Watershed Advisory Association	1	5,000

Activity regions (1993):	Number:	Dollars:
New York/New Jersey	4	45,000
U.S. not specified	1	15,000

Sample grants (1993)

Association of New Jersey Environmental Commissions. Mendham, NJ. $5,000. Purchase of office and desktop publishing equipment.
Great Swamp Watershed Advisory Association. New Vernon, NJ. $5,000. Purchase of a computer system.
Natural Resources Defense Council. New York, NY. $15,000. Purchase equipment for Phases I and II of its information technology project.
Pinelands Preservation Alliance, Inc. Pemberton, NJ. $10,000. Purchase of computer equipment and software.
Reeves-Reed Arboretum. Summit, NJ. $25,000. Replacement and/or treatment of the siding on its main building.

Application process. *Initial contact:* Brief letter to include:
1. Description of the purpose and significance of the appeal and related operating programs.
2. Other support.
3. Board of directors.
4. Copy of IRS tax-exempt status determination letter.

When to apply: Deadlines are February 15 and September 15. The board of directors meets in the spring and fall.
Materials available: Annual report (includes "Grants Policy and Guidelines").

Emphases. *Recipients:* Educational institutions, museums, nonprofit organizations.
Types of support: Capital campaigns/expenses, computer hardware, equip-ment, facilities (construction/renovation).
Geography: New York City metropolitan area; Essex, Union, and Morris counties in New Jersey.

Limitations. *Recipients:* Individuals, public agencies.
Types of support: Endowments, operating costs.

IBM Corporation
Old Orchard Road
Armonk, New York 10504
Tel: 914–765–4266
Contact: Caleb Shutz, Program Manager

Regional office:
590 Madison Avenue, 39th Floor
New York, New York 10022
Tel: 212–745–4586 Fax: 212–745–4586
EGA member
Contacts: Robert N. Sellar
           Cynthia A. Pulliam

History and philosophy. IBM, the global technology company, has, from its earliest days, prided itself on its good citizenship in accord with the philosophy of founder, Thomas J. Watson, Sr.

IBM contributions are concentrated in six categories: Education, Environment, Health, Persons with Disabilities, Human Services, and Arts and Culture.

Financial data. Not available.

Environmental awards. *Program and interests:* In 1991, the company initiated an international, multi-year, multi-million dollar research program geared to promote the use of computer-based technology in studying and recommending solutions to such problems as groundwater pollution, depletion of the ozone layer, environmental education, environmental cost management systems, and waste minimization and disposal. Grants are made to ten universities and have been supplemented by the National Science Foundation (NSF), the Department of Energy (USDOE), the Environmental Protection Agency (USEPA), and The Fish and Wildlife Foundation.

Application process. *Initial contact:* Proposal to include:
1. Mission of applicant organization, amount requested, and purpose of contribution.
2. Current annual report, audited financial statement or Form 990, and IRS tax-exempt status determination letter.
3. Current budget with anticipated sources of income (state amount expected to be raised from business sources).
4. List of current contributions from business, including donor name and amount received.
5. List of officers and directors/trustees.
6. Method of evaluation.

When to apply: Anytime.
Materials available: Guidelines.

Emphases. *Recipients:* Educational institutions, nonprofit organizations.
Activities: Audiovisual materials, publications.
Types of support: Equipment, matching funds.
Geography: Locations where IBM has a presence.

Limitations. *Recipients:* Individuals, religious organizations.
Activities: Conferences, fundraising, political activities, symposia/colloquia.

Illilouette Fund
116 New Montgomery Street, Suite 800
San Francisco, California 94105
Tel: 415–543–2152 Fax: 415–543–6426
Type: Advisory service
EGA member
Contact: Kimery Wiltshire, Director

History and philosophy. Established in 1990, "the Fund advises individual donors on environmental giving and is not a foundation with pooled funds and published application procedures. While the Fund cannot accept unsolicited proposals, information from organizations is welcomed and appreciated."

Officers and directors. *Director:* Kimery Wiltshire.

Financial data. Not available.

Environmental awards. *Program and interests:* Interests depend on individual donors. Specific information is not available.

Application process. *Initial contact:* The Fund generally advises on grants to pre-selected organizations. Prospective applicants may initiate contact with a telephone call or short letter.
When to apply: Anytime.

Emphases. *Recipients:* Pre-selected organizations only.
Activities: Activism, advocacy, collaborative efforts, education, innovative programs, networking, planning, training.
Types of support: Continuing support, general purposes, leveraging funds, matching funds.
Geography: Western United States.

I

The Indian Point Foundation, Inc.
1095 Park Avenue, Room 11A
New York, New York 10128
Tel: 212–722–5752
EIN: 4728093000   Type: Independent
Contact: Clement C. Moore, President

History and philosophy. The Foundation was established in 1986 by members of the Moore family.

Officers and directors. *Officers:* Clement C. Moore, President; Elizabeth W. Moore, Secretary.

Financial data. Data for fiscal year ended June 30, 1993. *Assets:* $1,484,347 (M). *Total grants disbursed:* $53,508.

Environmental awards. *Recent grants:* 1993 grants included support for urban and national parks, river protection, marine issues, and outdoor education.

Issues.   Cli   Bio   Lan   Agr   Wat   Oce   Ene   Was   Tox   Pop   Dev
   •   •   •   •   •   •

Funding analysis.

Fiscal year:	1993
Env grants disb:	$13,890
Number:	6
Range:	$400–$5,750
Median:	$1,620
Pct $ disb (env/total):	26

Recipients (1993 highest):	Number:	Dollars:
Hurricane Island Outward Bound School	1	5,750
Quebec Labrador Foundation/ Atlantic Center for the Environment	1	3,500
Grand Canyon Trust	1	2,140
Central Park Conservancy	1	1,100
The New York Botanical Garden	1	1,000

Activity regions (1993):	Number:	Dollars:
U.S. Northeast	3	9,650
U.S. Mountain	1	2,140
New York/New Jersey	2	2,100

Sample grants (1993).
Central Park Conservancy. New York, NY. $1,100. General support.
Grand Canyon Trust. Washington, DC. $2,140. Computer support.
Hurricane Island Outward Bound School. Rockland, ME. $5,750. General support.
Mystic Marinelife Aquarium. Mystic, CT. $400. General support.
The New York Botanical Garden. Bronx, NY. $1,000. General support.
Quebec Labrador Foundation/Atlantic Center for the Environment. Ipswich, MA. $3,500. Connecticut River Project.

Application process. *Initial contact:* Telephone call to request guidelines and application form.
When to apply: Anytime.
Materials available: Guidelines and application form.

The Louise H. and David S. Ingalls Foundation, Inc.
301 Tower East
20600 Chagrin Boulevard
Shaker Heights, Ohio 44122
Tel: 216–921–6000   Fax: 216–921–7709
EIN: 346516550   Type: Independent
Contact: Jane W. Watson, Assistant Secretary

History and philosophy. The Foundation was established in 1953 for "improvement of the physical, educational, mental and moral condition of humanity throughout the world." Interests are: child development, cultural programming, disadvantaged persons, education at all levels, medical research, and public health.

Officers and directors. *Officers:* Louise I. Brown, President; Edith I. Vignos, Vice President; James H. Dempsey, Jr., Secretary; Willard W. Brown, Treasurer; Jane W. Watson, Assistant Secretary/Assistant Treasurer. *Trustees:* Louise I. Brown, Jane I. Davidson, Anne I. Lawrence, Edith I. Vignos.

Financial data. Data for fiscal year ended December 31, 1993. *Assets:* $16,483,870 (M). *Total grants disbursed:* $748,000.

Environmental awards. *Recent grants:* 1993 grants included support for land conservation and wildlife protection.

Issues.   Cli   Bio   Lan   Agr   Wat   Oce   Ene   Was   Tox   Pop   Dev
        •   •

Funding analysis.

Fiscal year:	1993
Env grants disb:	$51,000
Number:	4
Range:	$1,000–$40,000
Median:	$5,000
Pct $ disb (env/total):	7

Recipients (1993):	Number:	Dollars:
Jackson Laboratory	1	40,000
Lyme Land Conservation Trust, Inc.	1	5,000
Wildlife Management Institute, Inc.	1	5,000
National Audubon Society	1	1,000

Activity regions (1993):	Number:	Dollars:
U.S. Northeast	2	45,000
U.S. not specified	2	6,000

Sample grants (1993).
Jackson Laboratory. Bar Harbor, ME. $40,000.
Lyme Land Conservation Trust, Inc. Old Lyme, CT. $5,000. Capital.
National Audubon Society. New York, NY. $1,000.
Wildlife Management Institute, Inc. Washington, DC. $5,000.

Application process. *Initial contact:* Proposal (5 copies).
When to apply: Anytime.

Emphases. *Recipients:* Nonprofit organizations.
Activities: Research (medical/scholarly).
Types of support: Capital campaigns/expenses, endowments, facilities (construction), pilot projects.
Geography: Cleveland, Ohio.

Limitations. *Recipients:* Individuals.

The International Foundation, Inc.
c/o Carrico & Associates, P.A.
1700 Route 23 North, Suite 170
Wayne, New Jersey 07470
Tel: 201–633–6993   Fax: 201–633–7796
EIN: 131962255   Type: Independent
Contact: Edward A. Holmes, Grants Chairman

History and philosophy. Incorporated in 1948, the Foundation works to help people of the developing world in their endeavors to solve some of their problems, to attain a better standard of living, and to obtain a reasonable degree of self-sufficiency. Its five grantmaking areas are: agriculture (research and production); health (medical, nutrition, water); education (formal at all levels, research); social development (cultural, economic, community, entrepreneurial activity); and environment.

Officers and directors. *Officers:* Gary Dicovitsky, Chairman; Frank H. Madden, President; David S. Bate, Vice President; John D. Carrico, Secretary/Treasurer. *Directors:* David S. Bate, John D. Carrico, Duncan W. Clark, Gary Dicovitsky, J. Carter Hammel, Edward A. Holmes, Frank H. Madden, William M. McCormack.

Financial data. Data for fiscal year ended December 31, 1993.
Assets: $24,590,775 (M). *Total grants disbursed:* $1,103,200.

Environmental awards. *Recent grants:* 1991 grants included support for forest protection.

Issues. Cli Bio Lan Agr Wat Oce Ene Was Tox Pop Dev
                       •

Sample grants (1991).
Chol-Chol Foundation for Human Development. Washington, DC. $42,500. For animal husbandry and forestry in Chile.
International Union for Conservation of Nature and Natural Resources. Washington, DC. $30,000. For tropical forest management in Ecuador.

Application process. *Initial contact:* Letter requesting descriptive brochure. Proposal (2 copies and self-addressed envelope) to include:
1. IRS tax-exempt status determination letter.
2. Proposal description.
3. Amount of funds requested.
4. Background of organization.
5. Problem addressed by project.
6. Objectives of project.
7. Plan of operation/method of achieving objectives.
8. Beneficiaries of the project.
9. Methods of project evaluation and report.
10. Project budget.
11. Sources of other funding and date.

When to apply: From November to March. The board meets in January, April, July, and October.
Materials available: Brochure (includes "Proposals").

Emphases. *Recipients:* Nonprofit organizations.
Activities: Education, publications, research (scholarly), training.
Types of support: Emergency funding, equipment, facilities (construction), projects, seed money.
Geography: Projects based in the United States for work in Asia, the Caribbean, Latin America, the Middle East, the Philippines, the South Pacific, and Southern Africa.

Limitations. *Recipients:* Individuals.
Activities: Audiovisual materials, conferences.
Types of support: Endowments, fellowships, loans, matching funds, operating costs, scholarships.

Ireland Foundation
1422 Euclid Avenue, Suite 1030
Cleveland, Ohio 44115
Tel: 216–363–1033
EIN: 346525817   Type: Independent
Contact: Carole M. Nowak, Secretary

History and philosophy. The Foundation was established in 1951 by members of the Ireland family. Fields of interest include conservation and the environment, education (secondary and higher), hospitals, music, and nursing.

Officers and directors. *Officers:* Louise Ireland Humphrey, President; Kate Ireland, Vice President; Carole M. Nowak, Secretary; R. L. Ireland, III, Treasurer; Neil A. Brown, Assistant Treasurer. *Trustees:* Louise Ireland Humphrey, R. L. Ireland, III.

Financial data. Data for fiscal year ended December 31, 1993.
Assets: $9,538,654 (M). *Total grants disbursed:* $651,650.

Environmental awards. *Recent grants:* 1993 grants included support for forestry, coastal issues, wildlife, and education.

Issues. Cli Bio Lan Agr Wat Oce Ene Was Tox Pop Dev
                  •   •   •   •   •

Funding analysis.

Fiscal year:	1992
Env grants disb:	$544,250
Number:	14
Range:	$250–$505,000
Median:	$1,000
Pct $ disb (env/total):	47

Recipients (1992 highest):	Number:	Dollars:
Tall Timbers Research Stations	2	518,000
The Wildlife Conservation Fund of America	1	16,000

© 1995 Environmental Data Resources, Inc.

Gulf of Maine Foundation	2	2,500
National Outdoor Leadership School	1	1,500
Sea Education Association	1	1,500

Activity regions (1992):	Number:	Dollars:
U.S. Southeast	5	519,250
U.S. not specified	3	18,500
U.S. Northeast	4	5,000
New York/New Jersey	1	1,000
U.S. Great Lakes	1	500

Sample grants (1993).
Chicago Horticultural Society. Chicago, IL. $50.
Florida Audubon Society. Maitland, FL. $250.
Gulf of Maine Foundation. Orono, ME. $2,000.
Maine Coast Heritage Trust. Northeast Harbor, ME. $1,000.
National Audubon Society. Ithaca, NY. $200.
National Outdoor Leadership School. Lander, WY. $1,500.
The Nature Conservancy. Winter Park, FL. $1,500.
Sea Education Association. Mystic, CT. $1,500.

Application process. *Initial contact:* Proposal to include:
1. Current income and expense statement of operations.
2. Projected budget indicating use of grant funds.
3. Copy of IRS tax-exempt status determination letter.

When to apply: Anytime. The trustees meet annually on the first Tuesday in November.

Emphases. *Recipients:* Nonprofit organizations.
Activities: Education.
Types of support: General purposes.
Geography: Cleveland, Ohio.

Limitations. *Recipients:* Individuals.

The James Irvine Foundation
One Market Plaza
Spear Tower, Suite 1715
San Francisco, California 94105
Tel: 415–777–2244 Fax: 415–777–0869
EIN: 941236937 Type: Independent
EGA member
Contact: Constance Walker, Program Officer

Cultural Arts and Youth Grants:
777 South Figueroa Street, Suite 740
Los Angeles, California 90017
Tel: 213–236–0552 Fax: 213–236–0537

History and philosophy. The James Irvine Foundation was established in 1937 by James Irvine, a northern California miner, manufacturer, rancher, and farmer. The Foundation is dedicated to enhancing the social, economic, and physical quality of life throughout California and enriching the state's intellectual and cultural environment. Program areas are: Community Services, Cultural Arts, Health, Higher Education, and Youth.

Officers and directors. *Officers:* Myron Du Bain, Chairman; Roger W. Heyns, Vice Chairman; Dennis A. Collins, President; Larry R. Fies, Treasurer. *Directors:* Samuel H. Armacost, Angela G. Blackwell, Dennis A. Collins, Myron Du Bain, Larry R. Fies, Camilla C. Frost, James C. Gaither, Walter B. Gerken, Roger W. Heyns, Joan F. Lane, Donn B. Miller, Forrest N. Shumway, Kathryn L. Wheeler, Edward Zapanta, M.D.

Financial data. Data for fiscal year ended December 31, 1993.
Assets: $690,264,425 (M). *Total grants authorized:* $27,544,603.

Environmental awards. *Program and interests:* The Foundation does not have a specific environmental grantmaking program. However, it has been receptive to proposals that link environmental concerns with its interests in access to health care and in economic and human development.
Recent grants: 1993 grants included support for river and watershed protection, toxics and environmental health, recycling, sustainable development, and education.

Issues. Cli Bio Lan Agr Wat• Oce Ene• Was• Tox• Pop Dev•

Funding analysis.

Fiscal year:	1992	1993
Env grants auth:	$940,000	$790,350
Number:	7	8
Range:	$25,000–$400,000	$350–$200,000
Median:	$50,000	$100,000
Pct $ auth (env/total):	3	3

Recipients (1993 highest):	Number:	Dollars:
Environmental Defense Fund	1	200,000
The Tides Foundation	2	200,000
Earthwatch Expeditions, Inc.	1	115,000
Pacific Rivers Council	1	100,000
Urban Ecology	1	100,000

Activity regions (1993):	Number:	Dollars:
U.S. West	7	790,000
U.S. not specified	1	350

Sample grants (1993).
Californians Against Waste Foundation. Sacramento, CA. $75,000. To support the recycling and community economic development program.
Earthwatch Expeditions, Inc. Santa Monica, CA. $115,000. For Earthwatch's Inner City program to encourage and assist youth to consider environmental careers.
Environmental Defense Fund. New York, NY. $200,000. For support of "Cleaning Southern California's Air and Protecting its Economy," to improve transportation efficiency and equity.
Environmental Grantmakers Association. New York, NY. $350. For 1993 membership dues.
Pacific Rivers Council. Eugene, OR. $100,000. For start-up of a new California office and project focused on watershed protection and restoration, and sustainable community development in the north coast, Sierra, and other watershed regions of California.
The Tides Foundation. San Francisco, CA. $50,000. Staff support for the Defining Sustainable Communities Project.

The Tides Foundation. San Francisco, CA. $150,000. For the start-up of the California Center for Lead-Safe Housing.
Urban Ecology. Berkeley, CA. $100,000. Support of the Sustainable Bay Area Program.

Application process. *Initial contact:* Letter of inquiry. Full proposal (1 copy) to include:
1. Cover letter summarizing proposed project, need being addressed, total cost, amount requested from Foundation, and identity of applicant organization.
2. Proposal describing:
   - Organization's history and current programs.
   - Leadership.
   - Major funding sources.
   - The need being addressed.
   - Project strategy.
   - Staff requirements.
   - Timeline and evaluation criteria.
   - Project budget including current and anticipated revenue sources and amounts.
3. Letter signed by an officer of the board of directors stating the proposal is submitted with the board's support.
4. Copies of both IRS tax-exempt status determination letter and proof of private foundation status. A copy of 990 tax return will be requested at a later date.
5. Audited financial statements and management letters for the last three fiscal years. If revenues are under $500,000, statements signed by two board members are acceptable.
6. Current operating budget for organization.
7. Funding sources and amounts for most recent fiscal year.
8. Government sources and amounts for recent fiscal year.
9. Board of directors, titles, occupation, and address.

When to apply: Anytime. The board meets five times annually.
Materials available: Annual report, "Grantseekers Guide."

Emphases. *Recipients:* Nonprofit organizations.
Activities: Land acquisition, planning, policy analysis/development, volunteerism.
Types of support: General purposes, leveraging funds, multi-year grants, program-related investments.
Geography: California.

Limitations. *Recipients:* Organizations with substantial tax support, educational institutions (private elementary/secondary schools for activities primarily benefitting their own members).
Activities: Audiovisual materials, conferences, publications, research.
Types of support: Debt retirement, endowments, operating costs.

Island Foundation, Inc.
589 Mill Street
Marion, Massachusetts 02738-1418
Tel: 508-748-2809   Fax: 508-748-0991
EIN: 042670567   Type: Independent
EGA member
Contact: Jenny D. Russell, Executive Director

History and philosophy. William Van Alan Clark, Jr., his wife Mary H. Clark, and their seven offspring and spouses founded the Island Foundation in 1979 as a means of realizing the philanthropic interests of the family. The Foundation supports programs in Environment, Education, and Community. Its premise is that the condition of our lives and the condition of the environment are profoundly intertwined, and that "the preservation of habitats, our neighborhoods, and our families are all part of the same continuum of environmental grace and courtesy."

Officers and directors. *Officers:* Stephen Clark, President; JoAnn Watson, Vice President; Hannah T. C. Moore, Treasurer. *Directors:* Kim Clark, Stephen Clark, Mrs. Van Alan Clark, Hannah T. C. Moore, Michael Moore, Peter Nesbeda, Chris Tupper, JoAnn Watson.

Financial data. Data for fiscal year ended December 31, 1993. *Assets:* $24,000,000 (M). *Total grants disbursed:* $902,847.

Environmental awards. *Program and interests:* Since 1992, the Foundation has focused its environmental grantmaking on alternative wastewater treatment technologies. Somewhat new in the engineering and regulatory arenas, new technologies offer a tremendous opportunity to control the major source of pollution to coastal waters. The Foundation is interested in supporting:

- The acceptance and scientific understanding of those technologies based on natural systems which address nutrient-loading.
- Those programs which advocate for the implementation of appropriate and sustainable alternatives.

To a lesser extent, the Foundation is exploring the contributions and potential of environmental economics. This approach places high emphasis on sustainability, consumption, and documenting the real costs of environmental degradation.

The Foundation also maintains an interest in local coastal issues in New England and will respond in a moderate way to such requests.

Issues. Cli Bio Lan Agr Wat Oce Ene Was Tox Pop Dev
              •   •   •   •   •   •

Funding analysis.

Fiscal year:	1991	1993
Env grants auth:	$279,012	$273,916
Number:	17	21
Range:	$4,000–$45,000	$500–$50,000
Median:	$15,000	$5,000
Pct $ disb (env/total):	47	54

Recipients (1993 highest):	Number:	Dollars:
Coalition for the Advancement of Wastewater Treatment Alternatives	1	50,000
University of Maryland	1	50,000
Tufts University	2	31,000
Thompson Island Outward Bound Education Center	1	30,000
Massachusetts Bay Marine Studies Consortium	1	25,000
New England Aquarium	1	20,016

© 1995 Environmental Data Resources, Inc.

Activity regions (1993):	Number:	Dollars:
U.S. Northeast	13	132,466
U.S. not specified	4	57,000
U.S. Mid-Atlantic	1	50,000
International*	2	31,000
Indian Subcontinent and Indian Ocean Islands	1	3,450

*Multiple regions or not specified.

Sample grants (1993).*

Coalition for the Advancement of Wastewater Treatment Alternatives. Gloucester, MA. $50,000. Start-up support for a national network of information and expertise on alternative wastewater technologies. Fiscal agent: Action Energy, Inc.

Grantmakers Network on the Economy and the Environment (GREEN). Washington, DC. $5,000. Support for a two-day forum on environmental economics for public officials, practitioners, and researchers.

Maine Coast Heritage Trust. Brunswick, ME. $5,000. General operating support for land trust program concerned with protecting coastal Maine.

New England Aquarium. Boston, MA. $20,016. Research and conservation work concerning the right whale.

Save the Bay. Provincetown, RI. $15,000. Introduction of alternative wastewater technologies in Greenwich Bay.

Tufts University. Townsend, MD. $10,000. First installment of a five-year $50,000 commitment to support the appointment of Dr. Herman Daly to the faculty.

Woods Hole Oceanographic Institute. Woods Hole, MA. $210,000. Second installment of a three-year $662,000 grant to support denitrification research in the solar aquatic system used to treat wastewater.

*Sample grants represent either new awards or disbursements on grants awarded in previous years.

Application process. *Initial contact:* Brief letter or telephone call. The Foundation will review full proposals by invitation only.
When to apply: Anytime.
Materials available: "Annual Report and Application Procedures."

Emphases. *Recipients:* Nonprofit organizations, research institutions.
Activities: Advocacy, capacity building, citizen participation, education, networking, political activities, research (scientific), seminars, symposia/colloquia.
Types of support: Multi-year grants, operating costs, pilot projects, program-related investments, projects, start-up costs.
Geography: New England, priority in Maine, Massachusetts, and Rhode Island.

Limitations. *Recipients:* Religious organizations.
Activities: Lobbying.
Types of support: Capital campaigns/expenses.

Island Foundation

7500 East Arapahoe Road, Suite 305
Englewood, Colorado 80112
Tel: 303-773-1804   Fax: 303-773-1533
EIN: 840715001   Type: Operating
EGA member
Contact: Sally Ranney, Vice President

History and philosophy. The Foundation was incorporated in 1976 by Catherine M. Carrithers and R. Jelinek. It dedicates its energies and resources to conservation concerns and the relationship of human needs to agrarian development and the natural environment.

Island's grants are often aimed at helping organizations achieve self-sufficiency. Its most widely known achievement is the development of Island Press, the environmental publishing house.

Officers and directors. *Officers:* Ashley K. Carrithers, President; Sally Ranney, Vice President; Walter Sedgewick, Secretary/Treasurer.

Financial data. Data for fiscal year ended December 31, 1994. *Assets:* $750,000 (M). *Total grants disbursed:* $50,000.

Environmental awards. *Program and interests:* The Foundation is interested in organizational activities which:

- Address how humans can best interact with each other, other species, and the natural environment in a manner that supports the diversity and integrity of natural systems including, but not limited to, the use and care of soils, forestry practices, agricultural production of food and fiber, air and water quality, and the development and use of traditional and alternative sources of energy.

- Advance research relating to the understanding of, communications with, and relationships of humans with each other, other species, and the natural environment.

- Effectively serve human needs and habitat in the true spirit of responsible stewardship of the earth's resources for the purpose of a peaceful, sustainable future.

- Integrate research, education, and opportunity with creative, resourceful, and technically sound ideas that can be developed into successful, workable approaches and solutions to immediate as well as long-term human and natural resource problems.

Issues.   Cli   Bio   Lan   Agr   Wat   Oce   Ene   Was   Tox   Pop   Dev
              •   •   •   •

Sample grants (1976–93).

American Wilderness Alliance. Englewood, CO. $50,000. For seed capital for organization and membership development and educational work on selective river management and wilderness preservation issues.

Colorado Open Space Council. Denver, CO. $42,500. To provide funds for an Executive Director.

Four Corners Rediscover. Crestone, CO. $3,000. To support Native American youth and elder programs.

Friends of the Earth, Northwest. Seattle. WA. $10,000. For a new office in western Colorado and support of technical staff addressing oil shale development in the area.

Lincoln Institute of Land. Cambridge, MA. $5,000. For a conference regarding the concepts of private land conservation.

Montana Land Reliance. Helena, MT. $15,000. For a conference on the available techniques and tools for private land conservation.

Application process. *Initial contact:* The Foundation awards grants to pre-selected organizations only. No unsolicited applications accepted.

Emphases. *Recipients:* Pre-selected organizations only.
Activities: Conferences, publications, training.
Types of support: Seed money.
Geography: California and Colorado.

Ittleson Foundation, Inc.

645 Madison Avenue
New York, New York 10022
Tel: 212–838–5010   Fax: 212–751–2485
EIN: 510172757   Type: Independent
EGA member
Contact: Anthony C. Wood, Executive Director

History and philosophy. The Ittleson Foundation was established in 1932 by Henry Ittleson (d. 1948), founder of CIT Financial Corporation. Its original interests were health, welfare, public education for mental health, and intercultural relations. Today the Foundation's areas of particular interest are: mental health, AIDS, and the environment.

The Foundation "generally provides seed money for the start-up of innovative programs that will improve the social welfare of citizens of the United States. We look for pilot projects, test and demonstration projects, and applied research that would inform public policy, if successful. Such projects should be of national scope, or significance beyond the local area of implementation. Projects should result in a product or outcome of some consequence in the real world. The Foundation also supports dissemination projects."

Officers and directors. *Officers:* H. Anthony Ittleson, President; Pamela Syrmis, Vice President; Anthony C. Wood, Secretary and Executive Director; Lawrence O. Sneag, Treasurer. *Directors:* H. Anthony Ittleson, Marianne S. Ittleson, Lionel I. Pincus, Lawrence O. Sneag, Pamela Syrmis, Victor Syrmis, M.D., Anthony C. Wood.

Financial data. Data for fiscal year ended December 31, 1993. *Assets:* $18,319,759 (M). *Total grants disbursed:* $1,187,499.

Environmental awards. *Program and interests:* "As in other fields of activity, we seek pilot projects that will test new approaches to solving environmental problems, bring about changes through policy research, or add to our working knowledge through applied research. Examples might include pilot tests of innovative technology; analyses of regulations and laws; innovative coalitions and partnerships; and similar efforts.

"Because we are concerned about the future adequacy of human resources in this key field, the Foundation is interested in programs that provide new opportunities to recruit young people and new constituencies into the environmental field. Addressing the human resources issue could also mean undertaking broader kinds of public education for young people concerning the environment."

Recent grants: 1993 grants included support for land conservation, watershed protection, wildlife preservation, and environmental education.

Issues.   Cli   Bio   Lan   Agr   Wat   Oce   Ene   Was   Tox   Pop   Dev

Funding analysis.

Fiscal year:	1991	1993
Env grants auth:	$2,180,000	$220,000
Number:	8	6
Range:	$5,000–$2,000,000	$5,000–$75,000
Median:	$22,500	$27,500
Pct $ disb (env/total):	42	47

Recipients (1993 highest):	Number:	Dollars:
The Environmental Careers Organization, Inc.	1	75,000
Natural Resources Defense Council	1	60,000
Global Action Plan	1	30,000
World Resources Institute	1	25,000
World Wildlife Fund	1	25,000

Activity regions (1993):	Number:	Dollars:
U.S. Northeast	2	100,000
New York/New Jersey	2	90,000
U.S. not specified	2	30,000

Sample grants (1993).*

Brown University. Providence, RI. $400,000. Third payment of a five-year $2,000,000 grant for the environmental studies program.

The Environmental Careers Organization, Inc. Boston, MA. $75,000 (3 years). To support The New England Environmental Diversity Collaboration in its efforts to diversify the membership, agenda, staff, governing boards and operating cultures of a number of New England-based environmental organizations.

Friends of the Earth Foundation. Washington, DC. $5,000.

Global Action Plan. Woodstock, NY. $30,000. To support their Community Based Eco Team program as a pilot for mass replication. Ecoteams encourage and support people in living an environmentally sustainable lifestyle.

Independent Production Fund. New York, NY. $10,000. Final payment of a three-year $70,000 grant for the education outreach component for *Earth: A User's Guide,* an eight-part PBS series that will invite viewers to take practical steps to save the environment.

Natural Resources Defense Council. New York, NY. $60,000 (2 years). For the Watershed Initiative, NRDC's effort to protect New York City's watershed and water quality and to avoid costly mandatory water filtration by: advancing a pollution protection strategy for the watershed; building an informed public constituency in part by producing major new studies on the issue; developing a cooperative watershed partnership with upstate communities in the watershed; and securing additional time for strategies to work by obtaining a second filtration waiver for New York City.

World Resources Institute. Washington, DC. $25,000. To support the development and testing phase of DATASCOPE, a prototype interactive environmental educational software package to enable high school students to more deeply understand and analyze environmental issues.

World Wildlife Fund. Washington, DC. $25,000. To support WWF Marine Fisheries Conservation Program. WWF will investigate and work with regional fishing management council and consumers to effect better conservation and management of fisheries.

*Sample grants represent either new awards or disbursements on grants awarded in previous years.

Application process. *Initial contact:* Brief letter describing the organization and the work for which funds are sought, along with a budget and evidence of tax-exempt status. If the activity falls within the Foundation's current scope of interests, the applicant will be asked to supply additional information.
When to apply: Deadlines for the initial letter are April 1 and September 1. The board of directors meets twice each year, in the spring and fall.
Materials available: Annual report (includes "How to Apply").

Emphases. *Activities:* Demonstration programs, education, innovative programs, policy analysis/development, research (scholarly).
Types of support: Pilot projects, seed money.
Geography: Projects of national scope or impact.

Limitations. *Recipients:* Individuals.
Activities: Direct services (especially outside of New York City), research (medical).
Types of support: Endowments, facilities (construction), internships, scholarships.
Geography: International projects.

The Richard Ivey Foundation
618 Richmond Street
London, Ontario N6A 3G6
Canada
Tel: 519–673–1280   Fax: 519–672–4790
Type: Independent
EGA member
Contact: Marvi Ricker, Executive Director

History and philosophy. The Richard Ivey Foundation was founded in 1947 by the late Richard G. Ivey and his son Richard M. Ivey. Program areas are: Environmental Education, Biodiversity in Forest-Dominated Ecosystems, Health and Education, Social Development and the Environment, and Arts and Culture.

Officers and directors. *Officers:* Richard M. Ivey, President and Treasurer; Beryl M. Ivey, Vice President; Richard W. Ivey, Secretary; Yvonne Patrick-Maxwell, Assistant Secretary; Catherine I. Gauthier, Assistant Treasurer; Marvi Ricker, Executive Director; Marion D. Fraser, Director of Finance. *Directors:* Jennifer L. Ivey Bannock, Suzanne E. Ivey Cook, Beryl M. Ivey, Richard M. Ivey, Richard W. Ivey, Rosamond A. Ivey Thom.

Financial data. Data for fiscal year ended September 30, 1993. *Assets:* $40,861,247 (M) (CDN). *Total grants authorized:* $1,144,750.

Environmental awards. *Program and interests:* The Foundation has two primary interests covered in the Social Development and Environment program:

- Biodiversity in Forest-Dominated Ecosystems.

  To enhance public understanding of the importance of these ecosystems so that their destruction may be reversed. Support is provided primarily for projects that:

  - Educate and inform students and the public about forest-dominated ecosystems and the significance of biodiversity.
  - Add to the body of knowledge about biodiversity in forest-dominated ecosystems through research into biological, social, economic, legal, cultural, and ethical issues.
  - Through advocacy and/or conflict resolution, help to ensure that significant, threatened forest ecosystems and forest-dwelling species are preserved.

  The program's focus is on Ontario where 80 percent of the land is forested and about 170,000 people are employed in jobs directly or indirectly related to forests.

- Environmental Education.

  To support projects that:

  - Provide teachers with the academic and pedagogical knowledge needed to present environmental topics in their classrooms. These could include workshops and special courses for teachers, or secondments of qualified environmental educators to train or assist their colleagues within schools and/or boards of education.
  - Enable schools and/or boards of education to develop and/or implement environmental curricula. The Foundation is particularly interested in supporting a holistic approach, i.e., incorporating environmental topics in all school subjects, not isolating them in such courses as environmental science and environmental studies.
  - Assist faculties of education to train future primary and secondary school teachers to teach environmental topics. Again, the Foundation prefers to support projects aimed at incorporating environmental topics in all teaching subjects.

Issues.   Cli   Bio   Lan   Agr   Wat   Oce   Ene   Was   Tox   Pop   Dev
              •   •   •   •

Funding analysis.

Fiscal year:	1992	1993
Env grants auth:	$1,200,000	$972,750
Number:	17	16
Range:	$5,000–$373,000	$5,000–$300,000
Median:	$50,000	$44,000
Pct $ auth (env/total):	61	85

Recipients (1993 highest):	Number:	Dollars:
Federation of Ontario Naturalists	1	300,000
World Wildlife Fund Canada	1	185,350
Canadian Nature Federation	1	68,500
West Parry Sound Board of Education	1	56,000
Canadian Environmental Law Association	1	55,000
Lester B. Pearson College of the Pacific	1	55,000

Activity region (1993):	Number:	Dollars:
Canada	16	972,750

Sample grants (1993).

Canadian Foundation for Economic Education. Toronto, Ontario. $45,000. For the Environomics Project which will develop a model teaching kit for elementary and secondary school teachers, focusing on the link between the economy and the environment. The kit will contain material for up to 20 class periods of integrated instruction. A series of seminars will introduce educators to the kit and promote its effective use.

Federation of Ontario Naturalists. Toronto, Ontario. $300,000. The first year of a three-year research, community support and education project designed to accelerate government action to develop and implement land-use planning legislation and policies to conserve forest biodiversity, and it aims to build local capability in the monitoring and advocacy of such policies.

University of Guelph. Guelph, Ontario. $21,400. To support University of Guelph personnel who, with assistance from the Ministry of Natural Resources, will use two different sets of survey and economic methods to estimate non-market values associated with wilderness areas in Ontario.

West Parry Sound Board of Education. Parry Sound, Ontario. $56,000. The first year of a three-year effort to integrate environmental issues in its science programs, and eventually into all disciplines, using computer technology. The first year will be developing concepts and publishing a four-part newspaper series exploring issues of Biodiversity and old-growth in boreal forests as part of the Boreal Education Project.

World Wildlife Fund Canada. Toronto, Ontario. $185,350. To help complete a network of protected areas representing the full range of Canada's natural ecosystems, WWF is embarking on a project to identify and document gaps within Canada's protected areas network of ecologically significant lands. One part of the project is to examine current forest harvest levels, how they are set legally, and what changes are necessary to ensure sustainability. The project budget also includes funding to equip endangered spaces campaigners across the country to address forestry issues related to protected areas decisions in the respective regions and to assist WWF International in developing and applying performance measures for its global forest policy goals concerning temperate forests.

Application process. *Initial contact:* Short letter (2 pages maximum), outlining proposed project, budget and timeframe, and applicant organization's history, objectives, and activities.
When to apply: Anytime for Social Development and the Environment Program. Deadlines for the Biodiversity and Environmental Education programs are June 30 and December 31.

Materials available: Annual report, "Description of Grantmaking Programs and Application Guidelines." In addition, the Biodiversity and Environmental Education programs each have their own brochure entitled "Grantmaking Program Description and Application Guidelines."

Emphases. *Recipients:* Nonprofit organizations registered as charities with Revenue Canada.
Activities: Collaborative efforts, conferences,* demonstration programs, education, fieldwork, innovative programs, policy analysis/development, research (medical/scientific), symposia/colloquia,* training, workshops.*
Types of support: Computer hardware, equipment, leveraging funds, multi-year grants, pilot projects, seed money, start-up costs.
Geography: London and southwestern Ontario for the traditional giving program. For the two environmental programs, the Foundation will consider project proposals from organizations in Ontario. The only exception to this geographic restriction is proposals for projects that are national in scope and directly include the involvement of Ontario.

*Biodiversity and Environmental Education programs only.

Limitations. *Recipients:* Individuals, religious organizations.
Activities: Direct services, land acquisition.
Types of support: Annual campaigns, capital campaigns/expenses, debt retirement, endowments, facilities, operating costs, scholarships.

The Jackson Foundation

U.S. Bank of Oregon
P.O. Box 3168
Portland, Oregon 97208–0111
Tel: 503–275–6574   Fax: 503–275–3589
EIN: 936020752   Type: Independent
Contact: Robert H. Depew, Assistant Vice President, U.S. Bank of Oregon

History and philosophy. The Jackson Foundation was established in 1981 through the merger of several trusts set up in 1960 by Philip Ludwell Jackson and Maria C. Jackson. Under Maria Jackson's will, the Foundation supports efforts to promote the welfare of the public of the city of Portland and the state of Oregon. Current program areas are: Adult Care, Counseling, and Training; Arts and Humanities; Children and Youth Programs; Civic and Environmental; Domestic Violence; Education; Food, Fuel and Shelter; Medical; and Miscellaneous.

Officers and directors. *Trustee:* U.S. Bank of Oregon.
Directors: Milo E. Ormseth, Gordon M. Tretheway, U.S. Bank of Oregon.

Financial data. Data for fiscal years ended June 1992 and 1993. *Assets (1992):* $9,050,000 (M). *Total grants disbursed (1993):* $404,084.

Environmental awards. *Recent grants:* 1993 grants included support for land conservation, forest preservation, and a zoo.

Issues. Cli Bio Lan Agr Wat Oce Ene Was Tox Pop Dev
• • • •

Funding analysis.

Fiscal year:	1993
Env grants disb:	$30,500
Number:	8
Range:	$1,500–$7,500
Median:	$2,750
Pct $ disb (env/total):	8

Recipients (1993 highest):	Number:	Dollars:
Oregon Trail Foundation, Inc.	1	7,500
The Nature Conservancy, Oregon Field Office	1	6,000
Friends of Washington Park Zoo	1	5,000
Friends of Timberline	1	3,000
1000 Friends of Oregon	1	2,500
Friends of the Columbia Gorge	1	2,500
Pacific Crest Outward Bound School	1	2,500

Activity region (1993):	Number:	Dollars:
U.S. Northwest	8	30,500

Sample grants (1993).
Friends of the Columbia Gorge. Portland, OR. $2,500.
Friends of Washington Park Zoo. Portland, OR. $5,000.
The Nature Conservancy, Oregon Field Office. Portland, OR. $6,000.
1000 Friends of Oregon. Portland, OR. $2,500.
Oregon Trail Foundation, Inc. Baker City, OR. $7,500.
World Forestry Center. Portland, OR. $1,500.

Application process. *Initial contact:* Write for application form. *When to apply:* Deadlines are March 25, August 25, and November 25 for review at board meetings held in April, September, and December. *Materials available:* Annual report, "Required Information for Application," application form.

Emphases. *Geography:* Oregon only.

Limitations. *Recipients:* Individuals.

Jackson Hole Preserve, Inc.

30 Rockefeller Plaza, Room 5402
New York, New York 10112
Tel: 212-649-5669
EIN: 131813818   Type: Independent
Contact: George R. Lamb, President

History and philosophy. The Foundation was incorporated in 1940 by Laurance S. Rockefeller, Rockefeller Brothers Fund, and the late John D. Rockefeller, Jr., to support environmental affairs. "Grant-making activities are directed toward information and action programs that increase public understanding of conservation issues and citizen participation in their resolution." The Foundation is interested in wildlife and land conservation, as well as historic preservation in New York State.

Officers and directors. *Officers:* Laurance Spelman Rockefeller, Chairman; George R. Lamb, President; Gene W. Setzer, Vice President; Antonia M. Grumbach, Secretary; Ruth C. Haupert, Treasurer/Assistant Secretary; Carmen Reyes, Assistant Treasurer. *Trustees:* Nash Castro, Henry L. Diamond, William M. Dietel, Clayton W. Frye, Jr., Mrs. Lyndon B. Johnson, George R. Lamb, Franklin E. Parker, Howard Phipps, Jr., Laurance Rockefeller, Laurance Spelman Rockefeller, Gene W. Setzer, Fred Smith, Conrad L. Wirth.

Financial data. Data for fiscal year ended December 31, 1992. *Assets:* $31,871,036 (M). *Total grants disbursed:* $6,364,000.

Environmental awards. *Program and interests:* The primary focus of the Foundation is environment and wildlife conservation.

Issues. Cli Bio Lan Agr Wat Oce Ene Was Tox Pop Dev
• • •

Funding analysis.

Fiscal year:	1992
Env grants disb:	$3,329,000
Number:	13
Range:	$4,000–$2,000,000
Median:	$25,000
Pct $ disb (env/total):	52

Recipients (1992 highest):	Number:	Dollars:
American Conservation Association	1	2,000,000
Woodstock Foundation, Inc.	1	1,000,000
National Park Foundation	1	125,000
Jackson Hole Land Trust	1	65,000
Jackson Hole Alliance for Responsible Planning	1	35,000

Activity regions (1992):	Number:	Dollars:
U.S. not specified	3	2,140,000
U.S. Northeast	1	1,000,000
U.S. Mountain	5	140,000
U.S. Virgin Islands	2	29,000
Caribbean and West Indies Islands	1	10,000
U.S. West	1	10,000

Sample grants (1993).
American Conservation Association. New York, NY. $2,000,000.
American Wildlands. Englewood, CO. 10,000. Tatshenshini International Campaign.
Greater Yellowstone Coalition. Bozeman, MT. $20,000.
Jackson Hole Alliance for Responsible Planning. Jackson, WY. $30,000.
Jackson Hole Land Trust. Jackson, WY. $55,000.
Montana Land Reliance. Helena, MT. $5,000.
National Park Foundation. Washington, DC. $125,000.
National Wildlife Federation. Missoula, MT. $10,000. For the Wolf Recovery Project.
Woodstock Foundation, Inc. Woodstock, VT. $1,000,000. For land preservation and historic preservation.

Application process. *Initial contact:* Letter containing description of the project, estimated budget, possibility of matching funds from other organizations.
When to apply: Anytime. Preferably mid to late spring.

Emphases. *Activities:* Land acquisition, publications, technical assistance.
Types of support: Continuing support, general purposes, matching funds, technical assistance.
Geography: Jackson Hole, Wyoming; Hudson River Valley, New York; the eastern Caribbean.

Limitations. *Recipients:* Individuals.
Types of support: Endowments, facilities (construction), fellowships, loans, scholarships.

The Henry M. Jackson Foundation
1001 Fourth Avenue, Suite 3317
Seattle, Washington 98154–1101
Tel: 206–682–8565 Fax: 206–682–8961
EIN: 521313011   Type: Independent
EGA member
Contacts: Robin Pasquarella, Executive Director
           Lisa Napoli, Program Officer

History and philosophy. The Henry M. Jackson Foundation was established in 1983 at the time of the senator's death. Its purpose is to carry on Senator Jackson's commitments to education, public service, and the environment. To this end, it supports scholarship and research in the areas of: International Affairs, Human Rights, Public Service, and Environment & Natural Resources Management.

Officers and directors. *Officers:* Helen Hardin Jackson, Chairman; Stanley D. Golub, Vice Chairman; William J. Van Ness, Jr., President; Grenville Garside, Vice President; Joel Merkel, General Counsel; Julia P. Cancio, Secretary; Keith Grinstein, Treasurer; Donald D. Donohue, Executive Assistant to the Chairman.

Financial data. Data for fiscal year ended September 30, 1993. *Assets:* $15,453,202 (C). *Gifts received:* $104,835. *Total grants authorized:* $996,264.

Environmental awards. *Program and interests:* The Environment & Natural Resources Management Program initiates and supports programs that:

- Contribute to policy formulation.
- Train professionals for careers in environment and natural resource management.
- Enhance public awareness of national and international environmental issues.

The Foundation's current focus is on:

- Land use planning and growth management issues.

Priority is given to programs that have national significance or multi-state impact.

Issues. Cli Bio Lan Agr Wat Oce Ene Was Tox Pop Dev
              •   •   •   •   •

Funding analysis.

Fiscal year:	1992	1993
Env grants auth:	$280,950	$196,000
Number:	9	8
Range:	$6,000–$60,000	$1,000–$75,000
Median:	$24,950	$17,500
Pct $ auth (env/total):	13	20

Recipients (1993 highest):	Number:	Dollars:
American Planning Association	1	75,000
National Geographic Society	1	40,000
The Nature Conservancy, Washington Field Office	1	30,000
Rural Development Institute	1	20,000
The Trust for Public Land	1	15,000

Activity regions (1993):	Number:	Dollars:
U.S. not specified	4	131,000
U.S. Northwest	3	45,000
International*	1	20,000

*Multiple regions or not specified.

Sample grants (1993).

American Planning Association. Chicago, IL. $75,000. To support the "Growing Smart" program, helping state decisionmakers enhance and update the legal and institutional systems that authorize and empower towns, cities, counties, and regions to plan for and manage growth.

Central Washington University. Ellensburg, WA. $5,000. to support the Institute of Science and Society's program to enhance the quality of science education through workshops, special classes, and lectures for K–12 teachers and students.

National Geographic Society. Washington, DC. $40,000. To support the "Workshop on Water" program, providing intensive training for over 100 science and social studies teachers on issues of fresh water management.

Rural Development Institute. Seattle, WA. $20,000. To support agrarian reform and rural development efforts in Russia and China.

The Trust for Public Land. San Francisco, CA. $15,000. To support a year-long education and consulting program to help state, county, and municipal officers learn of innovative public financing strategies to acquire and manage new parks and other open spaces.

Application process. *Initial contact:* Brief letter of inquiry. Full proposal to include:
1. Cover letter. Briefly describe purpose of proposed program; give amount and use of funds requested, and contact person.
2. Proposal narrative (10 pages maximum).
   - Program goals and objectives.
   - Rationale and need for program.
   - Intended beneficiaries or participants.
   - Implementation strategy and timetable.
   - Detailed budget (including of other funding sources).
   - Experience and capability of organization administering the program (including identification of governing board and/or individuals responsible for program).

© 1995 Environmental Data Resources, Inc.

- Plans for program evaluation (list criteria for measuring project's success or failure).
3. Copy of organization's most recent financial statement and IRS tax-exempt status determination letter.

When to apply: Deadlines are December 15, March 15, June 15, and September 15. Grants are reviewed quarterly.
Materials available: Annual report (includes "Program Guidelines and Application Procedures"), *NewsLetter* (periodical).

Emphases. *Recipients:* Educational institutions, nonprofit organizations, public agencies, research institutions.
Activities: Demonstration programs, education, innovative programs, policy analysis/development, publications, research (scholarly/scientific), seminars, symposia/colloquia, technical assistance, training.
Types of support: Leveraging funds, matching funds, pilot projects, projects, scholarships, seed money, technical assistance.
Geography: Programs with U.S. national significance or having multi-state impact.

Limitations. *Recipients:* Individuals.
Activities: Lobbying, political activities.
Types of support: Capital campaigns/expenses, debt retirement, operating costs.

Martha Holden Jennings Foundation

710 Halle Building
1228 Euclid Avenue
Cleveland, Ohio 44115
Tel: 216-589-5700   Fax: 216-589-5730
EIN: 340934478   Type: Independent
Contact: Richard A. Boyd, Executive Director

History and philosophy. Martha Holden Jennings established the Foundation in 1959 "to foster the development of young people to the maximum possible extent through improving the quality of teaching in secular elementary and secondary schools." A resident of Cleveland, Jennings looked to improve programs and instruction in the Ohio Public School System. The Foundation focuses on public elementary and secondary education through: incentives and motivational training of teachers, students, and administrators; improved curricula, especially in the fields of science, math, written composition, and the fine arts; developing programs to help students with special needs; and increasing understanding and cooperation between public schools and the colleges and universities in the state of Ohio.

Officers and directors. *Officers:* Arthur S. Holden, Jr., Chairman; George B. Chapman, Jr., President; William F. Hauserman, Vice President; John H. Gherlein Secretary; Allen H. Ford, Treasurer. *Trustees:* George B. Chapman, Jr., Allen H. Ford, John H. Gherlein, Robert M. Ginn, William F. Hauserman, Arthur S. Holden, Jr., George B. Milbourne, William J. Williams.

Financial data. Data for fiscal year ended December 31, 1993. *Assets:* $64,683,774 (U). *Gifts received:* $3,800. *Total grants disbursed:* $2,701,854.

Environmental awards. *Recent grants:* Grants in 1993 included support for public and school-based education about biodiversity, and land conservation.

Issues. Cli Bio Lan Agr Wat Oce Ene Was Tox Pop Dev
              •   •

Funding analysis.

Fiscal year:	1991	1993
Env grants auth:	$50,550	$47,800
Number:	4	3
Range:	$5,000–$30,000	$5,300–$30,000
Median:	$7,775	$12,500
Pct $ disb (env/total):	2	2

Recipients (1993):	*Number:*	*Dollars:*
Cleveland Zoological Society	1	30,000
Cuyahoga Valley Preservation and Scenic Railway Association	1	12,500
Lake Parks Foundation, Concord Township	1	5,300

Activity region (1993):	*Number:*	*Dollars:*
U.S. Great Lakes	3	47,800

Sample grants (1993).
Cleveland Zoological Society. Cleveland, OH. $30,000. Fur, Feathers, and Scales: The Diversity of Life.
Cuyahoga Valley Preservation and Scenic Railway Association. Cleveland, OH. $12,500. School field trip program.

Application process. *Initial contact:* Proposal and application form (8 copies) to include:
1. Cover letter containing a list of all enclosures and signed by organization's CEO.
2. Project summary (1 page).
   - Amount requested.
   - Project purpose, needs, plan of action, and expected outcome.
   - Number of participants.
   - Sources of additional funding, if any.
3. Brief, detailed proposal.
4. Project budget listing use of Foundation funds, and amount and sources of any other funds.
5. "In the case of institutions that propose to provide services to schools, a letter indicating a need for the services and support for the project signed by the superintendent of schools."
6. Copy of IRS tax-exempt status determination letter.

When to apply: Anytime. Proposals should be received at the Foundation by the 20th of the month prior to that in which they are to be considered. The trustees meet ten times a year.
Materials available: Annual report (includes "Criteria for Grants").

Emphases. *Recipients:* Educational institutions, museums, nonprofit organizations, public agencies, zoos.
Activities: Direct services, education, exhibits, innovative programs, seminars, training, workshops.
Types of support: Continuing support, matching funds, pilot projects, seed money.
Geography: Ohio.

Limitations. *Recipients:* Individuals.
Activities: Activism, advocacy, capacity building, citizen participation, conflict resolution, feasibility studies, fundraising, inventories, land acquisition, litigation, lobbying, media projects, political activities, policy analysis/development.
Types of support: Advertising campaigns, annual campaigns, capital campaigns/expenses, computer hardware, debt retirement, endowments, facilities, fellowships, general purposes, loans, maintenance, membership campaigns, mortgage reduction, multi-year grants, professorships, program-related investments, scholarships, travel expenses.

The George Frederick Jewett Foundation
The Russ Building, Suite 612
235 Montgomery Street
San Francisco, California 94104
Tel: 415-421-1351
EIN: 046013832   Type: Independent
Contact: Theresa A. Mullen, Executive Director

History and philosophy. The Foundation was established in 1957 under the will of George Frederick Jewett (b. 1896), chairman of the Potlatch Corporation and a son of Margaret Weyerhaeuser. Grantmaking reflects the founding family's philanthropic interest in people and values. Interest areas are: Arts and Humanities; Conservation and Preservation; Education and Training; Education for Minority Groups; Medical Research, Services, and Training; Population; Public Affairs; Religion and Religious Training; Science; and Social Welfare. Grants are generally confined to eastern Washington and northern Idaho.

Officers and directors. *Officer:* George Frederick Jewett, Jr., Chairman. *Trustees:* Mary Jewett Gaiser, Margaret Jewett Greer, William Hershey Greer, Jr., George Frederick Jewett, Jr., Lucille McIntyre Jewett.

Financial data. Data for fiscal year ended December 31, 1992. *Assets:* $29,045,103 (M). *Total grants authorized:* $981,330.

Environmental awards. *Recent grants:* 1992 grants included support for land conservation, parks and recreation, and youth education.

Issues.   Cli   Bio   Lan   Agr   Wat   Oce   Ene   Was   Tox   Pop   Dev
          •   •   •   •   •

Funding analysis.

Fiscal year:	1991	1992
Env grants auth:	$62,000	$52,500
Number:	7	8
Range:	$1,000–$20,000	$500–$20,000
Median:	$5,000	$5,000
Pct $ auth (env/total):	7	5

Recipients (1992 highest):	Number:	Dollars:
Northern Lights Institute	1	20,000
Earthwatch Expeditions, Inc.	1	10,000
World Wildlife Fund	1	10,000
Forest History Society	1	5,000
The Student Conservation Association, Inc.	1	5,000

Activity regions (1992 highest):	Number:	Dollars:
U.S. Mountain	1	20,000
U.S. West	2	15,000
International*	1	10,000
U.S. Southeast	1	5,000
U.S. Northwest	1	1,000
U.S. not specified	1	1,000

*Multiple regions or not specified.

Sample grants (1992).
Forest History Society. Durham, NC. $5,000. General operating support.
Northern Lights Institute. Missoula, MT. $20,000. General support.
Spokane Park and Recreation Foundation. Spokane, WA. $1,000. Park developments and improvements.
The Student Conservation Association, Inc. Charleston, NH. $5,000. General operating support for the San Francisco/Golden Gate National Recreation Area program involving high school students in public service projects.
World Wildlife Fund. Washington, DC. $10,000. General support.

Application process. *Initial contact:* Full proposal to include:
Documentation.
1. Name and address of applicant organization.
2. Name(s) of chief administrative officer(s).
3. Official endorsement of proposal and agreement to assume full responsibility for fiscal management.
4. Statement of foundation status (private, non-private, or operating, if applicable).
5. Proof of tax-exempt status.
6. Statement that grant will compensate a government official.
7. Commitment to submit progress and financial reports.

Project information.
1. Brief description of project.
2. Plan of development.
3. Expected results.
4. Method of evaluation.
5. Key personnel (qualifications, role in project).
6. Itemized budget.
7. Timeline.
8. Information on funding requests to other grantmaking organizations and support received.

When to apply: Deadlines are February 15, May 15, August 15, and November 1.
Materials available: Annual report (includes "Policy and Guidelines"), "Outline of Policies, Guidelines and Application Procedures."

Emphases. *Recipients:* Nonprofit organizations.
Types of support: Endowments, operating costs, projects. (Fellowships, research, scholarships occasionally and at established universities only).
Geography: Pacific Northwest, especially eastern Washington and northern Idaho.

Limitations. *Recipients:* Individuals.
Activities: Political activities.

J

Helen K. and Arthur E. Johnson Foundation

1700 Broadway, Suite 2302
Denver, Colorado 80290
Tel: 303-861-4127   Fax: 303-861-0607
EIN: 846020702   Type: Independent
Contact: Stan Kamprath, Executive Director

History and philosophy. Established in 1948 as the Arthur E. Johnson Foundation, the Foundation assumed its present name in 1975. Grants support "a wide variety of organizations in an attempt to solve community problems and enrich the quality of life in Colorado." The Foundation has six program areas: Education, Community and Social Services, Youth, Civic and Cultural, Health, and Senior Citizens.

Officers and directors. *Officers:* Mrs. James R. Hartley, President; David R. Murphy, Vice President and Treasurer; Stan Kamprath, Vice President and Executive Director; Gerald R. Hillyard, Jr., Secretary; Betty J. Penner, Assistant Secretary. *Trustees:* Mrs. Lynn H. Campion, Thomas B. Campion, Jr., Mrs. James R. Hartley, Charles R. Hazelrigg, Gerald R. Hillyard, Jr., William H. Kistler, Roger D. Knight, Jr., Ronald L. Lehr, David R. Murphy, Stanley D. Neeleman.

Financial data. Data for fiscal year ended December 31, 1993. *Assets:* $76,514,696 (C). *Total grants authorized:* $3,256,731.

Environmental awards. *Program and interests:* Environmental grants are typically made through the Civic and Cultural, Community and Social Services, or Youth programs.
Recent grants: 1993 grants included support for youth education.

Issues.   Cli   Bio   Lan   Agr   Wat   Oce   Ene   Was   Tox   Pop   Dev
              •   •

Funding analysis.

Fiscal year:	1990	1992
Env grants auth:	$407,125	$325,000
Number:	4	3
Range:	$7,125–$250,000	$10,000–$300,000
Median:	$75,000	$15,000
Pct $ auth (env/total):	12	9

Recipients (1992):	Number:	Dollars:
Denver Zoological Foundation	1	300,000
Colorado Outward Bound School	1	15,000
Breckenridge Outdoor Education Center	1	10,000

Activity region (1992):	Number:	Dollars:
U.S. Mountain	3	325,000

Sample grants (1993).*
Colorado Outward Bound School. Denver, CO. Financial aid.
Sierra Club Defense Fund. Denver, CO. "Inner City Outings" program.

*Dollar amounts not available.

Application process. *Initial contact:* Preliminary proposal (2 pages) summarizing the grant request. If the Foundation is interested, it will request a full proposal. Alternatively, applicants may submit a full proposal to include:
1. Cover letter, describing the program and specifying the amount requested.
2. Narrative.
   - Organization's history, background, goals, and objectives.
   - Organization's programs and population served. If the grant request is for a specific project, campaign, or capital purchase, outline grant objectives.
   - Project's relevance to similar community programs.
   - Timetable.
3. List of current trustees or board of directors.
4. Board and Community Support Form (provided by the Foundation upon receipt of preliminary letter or full proposal).
5. Operating budget; project budget for the grant period.
6. Financial statements (preferably audited) for the last two fiscal years. Should include a balance sheet and statements of revenue and expenses.
7. List of other sources contacted for or providing funding.
8. Plan for long-term project funding.
9. Evaluation criteria.
10. IRS tax-exempt status determination letter.
11. Completed Tax Exempt Status Certification (provided by the Foundation upon receipt of preliminary or full proposal).

When to apply: Deadlines are January 1, April 1, July 1, and October 1. The board meets quarterly. (Reapplication is permitted only after a 12 month waiting period.)
Materials available: Annual report (includes "Application Guidelines").

Emphases. *Recipients:* Nonprofit organizations.
Types of support: Annual campaigns, capital campaigns/expenses, computer hardware, continuing support, equipment, facilities, general purposes, operating costs, pilot projects, scholarships, seed money, single-year grants only.
Geography: Colorado only.

Limitations. *Recipients:* Individuals.
Activities: Activism, advocacy, conferences, conflict resolution, exhibits, expeditions/tours, feasibility studies, litigation, lobbying, political activities, policy analysis/development, publications, seminars, symposia/colloquia.
Types of support: Advertising campaigns, debt retirement, emergency funding, endowments, fellowships, internships, lectureships, leveraging funds, loans, mortgage reduction, multi-year grants, program-related investments, travel expenses.

The Howard Johnson Foundation

c/o U.S. Trust Company
114 West 47th Street, Floor 9-H
New York, New York 10036
Tel: 212-852-3736
EIN: 046060965   Type: Independent
Contact: Edward Klein, Trustee

History and philosophy. The Foundation was established as a trust in 1961. It gives primarily for higher and secondary education and health and hospitals. It also supports museums, churches, religious welfare agencies, scientific programs, the environment, and animal welfare.

Officers and directors. *Officer:* Eugene J. Durgin, Secretary. *Trustees:* Marissa J. Brock, Eugene J. Durgin, Dorothy J. Henry, Howard Bates Johnson, Howard Brennan Johnson, Patricia B. Johnson, Joshua J. Weeks, William H. Weeks.

Financial data. Data for fiscal year ended December 31, 1992. *Assets:* $3,176,651 (M). *Total grants disbursed:* $211,500.

Environmental awards. *Recent grants:* 1992 grants included support for land conservation, parks, and wildlife.

Issues. Cli Bio• Lan• Agr Wat Oce• Ene Was Tox Pop• Dev

Funding analysis.

Fiscal year:	1992
Env grants disb:	$24,500
Number:	9
Range:	$1,000–$5,000
Median:	$2,500
Pct $ disb (env/total):	12

Recipients (1992 highest):	Number:	Dollars:
Connecticut Audubon Society	1	5,000
NYZS/The Wildlife Conservation Society	1	5,000
Central Park Conservancy	1	2,500
National Audubon Society	1	2,500
Natural Resources Defense Council	1	2,500
The Nature Conservancy, Headquarters	1	2,500
World Wildlife Fund	1	2,500

Activity regions (1992):	Number:	Dollars:
U.S. not specified	4	10,000
New York/New Jersey	2	7,500
U.S. Northeast	3	7,000

Sample grants (1992).
Central Park Conservancy. New York, NY. $2,500.
Connecticut Audubon Society. Fairfield, CT. $5,000.
National Audubon Society, Inc. New York, NY. $2,500.
Natural Resources Defense Council, Inc. New York, NY. $2,500.
The Nature Conservancy, Headquarters. Arlington, VA. $2,500.
New England Aquarium. Boston, MA. $1,000.
NYZS/The Wildlife Conservation Society. Bronx, NY. $5,000.
The Student Conservation Association, Inc. Charlestown, NH. $1,000.
World Wildlife Fund. Washington, DC. $2,500.

Application process. *Initial contact:* Letter outlining proposed project, accompanied by the organization's IRS tax-exempt determination letter.
When to apply: Anytime.
Materials available: Annual report.

Emphases. *Recipients:* Educational institutions, museums, religious organizations.
Geography: Connecticut, Massachusetts, New York.

Limitations. *Recipients:* Individuals.
Types of support: Scholarships.
Geography: United States.

Walter S. Johnson Foundation
525 Middlefield Road, Suite 110
Menlo Park, California 94025
Tel: 415–326–0485
EIN: 237003595   Type: Independent
Contact: Jean Parmelee, Executive Director

History and philosophy. The Foundation was established in 1968 by Walter S. Johnson, a California businessman who developed the American Forest Products Company and the Friden Calculating Machine Company. The Foundation carries on Mr. Johnson's philanthropic interests in education and the social services with a special emphasis on children.

Officers and directors. *Officers:* Gloria Eddie, President; Sandra Bruckner, First Vice President; Christopher Johnson, Second Vice President; Hathily Winston, Secretary; Scott Shackelton, Treasurer. *Trustees:* Sandra Bruckner, Gloria Eddie, Gloria Jeneal Eddie, Christopher Johnson, Mary Lanigar, Scott Shackelton, Hathily Winston.

Financial data. Data for fiscal year ended December 31, 1993. *Assets:* $61,101,875 (M). *Total grants authorized:* $2,635,854.

Environmental awards. The Foundation does not make awards for projects simply because they deal with environmental issues. However, some of the educational projects it funds happen to involve environmental subjects.
Recent grants: 1993 grants included support for public school education and recreation.

Issues. Cli Bio Lan• Agr Wat Oce Ene Was Tox Pop• Dev

Funding analysis.

Fiscal year:	1993
Env grants auth:	$80,109
Number:	1
Range:	—
Median:	—
Pct $ auth (env/total):	3

Recipient (1993):	Number:	Dollars:
Petaluma Wildlife and Natural Science Museum	1	80,109

Activity region (1993):	Number:	Dollars:
U.S. West	1	80,109

Sample grant (1993).
Petaluma Wildlife and Natural Science Museum. Petaluma, CA. $80,109. To launch the Science Education Project, developing high-quality supplemental science materials to prepare elementary students to make use of their visit to the museum.

Application process. *Initial contact:* Telephone call or brief letter of inquiry before full proposal. Proposal to contain:
1. Summary (1 page) describing project and request.
2. Narrative proposal.
   - Need for project.
   - Project plan including objectives to be achieved, activities, and how project outcomes will be evaluated.
   - Anticipated future funding needs and strategies to meet those needs when support ends.
3. Itemized budget for each year of requested support.
   - Total project cost and amount requested.
   - Resources contributed by applicant and other supporters.
4. Copy of audited financial statements for the past two years.
5. Copy of budget for current fiscal year and for first year of grant (if the two are different) with revenue sources itemized.
6. Optional attachments.
   - Purpose, background, and previous experience of applicant.
   - List of members of governing board.
   - Personnel involved in project and their qualifications.
   - Timeline for accomplishing goals of project.
   - Sample of project materials produced by staff.
   - Letters of support.

School districts must include a letter of endorsement from the superintendent.
When to apply: Anytime.
Materials available: Annual report.

Emphases. *Types of support:* Continuing support, general purposes, pilot projects, seed money, technical assistance.
Geography: California counties of Alameda, Contra Costa, San Francisco, San Mateo, and Santa Clara; Washoe County, Nevada.

Limitations. *Recipients:* Educational institutions (private), individuals.
Activities: Conferences, publications.
Types of support: Annual campaigns, capital campaigns/expenses, debt retirement, endowments, equipment, facilities (construction), fellowships, loans, matching funds, scholarships.

W. Alton Jones Foundation, Inc.

232 East High Street
Charlottesville, Virginia 22902–5178
Tel: 804–295–2134   Fax: 804–295–1648
EIN: 136034219   Type: Independent
EGA member
Contacts: J. P. Myers, Executive Director
Charles O. Moore, Sustainable Society Program Officer
Debra J. Callahan, Grassroots Program Director

History and philosophy. The W. Alton Jones Foundation was established in 1944 by "Pete" Jones (b. 1891), who had a distinguished career in the oil industry. The Foundation's mission is "to protect the Earth's life-support systems from environmental harm and to eliminate the possibility of nuclear war."

The Foundation makes grants in two areas: environmental protection through its Sustainable World Program, and nuclear warfare prevention through its Secure World Program. "The Foundation works principally through Foundation-defined initiatives addressing its priority issues. These initiatives usually take the form of coordinated grants to multiple institutions, each of which focuses on one or more components of an overall campaign defined by the Foundation's mission. Proposals for participation in these initiatives are invited by the Foundation."

Officers and directors. *Officers:* Patricia Jones Edgerton, President; Bradford W. Edgerton, Vice President; Diane Edgerton Miller, Secretary; Bernard F. Curry, Treasurer. *Trustees:* James S. Bennett, James R. Cameron, Bernard F. Curry, Bradford W. Edgerton, Patricia Jones Edgerton, William A. Edgerton, William A. McDonough, Scott McVay, Diane Edgerton Miller.

Financial data. Data for fiscal year ended December 31, 1993. *Assets:* $260,924,411 (M). *Total grants authorized:* $15,394,967. *Total grants disbursed:* $15,764,096.

Environmental awards. *Program and interests:* The Sustainable World Program makes grants in the areas of:

- Biodiversity. Focus is on preservation of six specific ecosystems and efforts to build a supportive international framework for the preservation of biological resources.

  The six ecosystems include three watersheds: the Amazon basin, the Pantanal and the Parana-Paraguay watershed, and the coastal wetlands of Louisiana; and three forest ecosystems: the Pacific Northwest of the United States and Canada, the Boreal forest of Siberia, and the tropical forests of Irian Jaya.

  Efforts to build a supportive international framework focus on global conventions such as the Convention on Biological Diversity signed at the Rio "Earth Summit" and entered into force in December 1993.

- Economics for a Sustainable Planet. Efforts to encourage the conduct of economic activity within realistic limits of the planet's physical and biotic environment. Focus areas are:
  - Externalities (estimating the true costs of economic activities, including environmental externalities, and to encourage their consideration).
  - Valuing Biodiversity (measuring the value and promote the understanding of biodiversity).
  - Grassroots.
  - Trade (ensuring that international trade supports environmental sustainability, with a focus on the Western Hemisphere.
  - Multilateral Development Bank Reform.

- Energy and Climate. Finding new ways to meet the gargantuan energy needs of human enterprise while not disrupting the planet's climate. Focus areas are:
  - Climate Treaties and Related Protocols.
  - Rural solar energy in developing countries.

- Urban energy policy in tropical Brazil and the former Soviet Union.
- Facilitating deployment of solar hydrogen fuel cells for transportation.
■ Systemic Contamination. Three target areas are:
  - Environmental factors that threaten children's health, specifically pesticides and related endocrine disrupters and air pollution.
  - Chemical contamination in Russia and the Newly Independent States.
  - Toxic contamination of aquifers in the United States.
■ Environmental Law/Media. Focus on activities that explicitly complement other parts of the Foundation's environmental funding.

Within the Sustainable World Program, special funds are set aside to support grassroots efforts on these issues by local organizations. Grants for this purpose are limited to $40,000. Activities funded must focus on local environmental protection, be undertaken by local organizations, and include volunteers.

Issues. Cli Bio Lan Agr Wat Oce Ene Was Tox Pop Dev
• • • • • • • • • •

Funding analysis.§

Fiscal year:	1992	1993
Env grants auth:	$9,386,930	$9,297,948
Number:	145	152
Range:	$5,000–$400,000	$6,000–$200,000
Median:	$40,000	$40,000
Pct $ auth (env/total):	67	60

Recipients (1993 highest):	Number:	Dollars:
Conservation International	2	230,600
Centro Mexicano de Derecho Ambiental	1	200,000
Stanford University, Center for Conservation Biology	1	200,000
The Carter Center, Inc.	1	200,000
The International Institute for Energy Conservation (IIEC)	1	200,000

Activity regions (1993 highest):	Number:	Dollars:
U.S. not specified	36	2,886,250
International*	15	970,600
U.S. Northwest	19	897,260
U.S. Southeast	10	405,000
Andean Region and Southern Cone	4	390,000

*Multiple regions or not specified.

§Includes a number of grants awarded within the Secure World Program that have an environmental health and/or toxic waste component.

Sample grants (1993).

Alliance to End Childhood Lead Poisoning. Washington, DC. $60,000. For policy analysis, implementation, and public education efforts to prevent childhood lead poisoning.

Asociación Peruana para la Conservación de la Naturaleza. Lima, Peru. $40,000. To promote sustainable development of Peruvian montane forest habitats in the western Amazon through public education, community outreach, and natural resource management efforts.

The Carter Center, Inc. Atlanta, GA. $200,000. To encourage the United States and multilateral banks to adopt sustainable economic policies, and to assist the Amazon Pact nation of Guyana to develop environmentally sustainable practices.

Center for Conservation Biology. Stanford, CA. $200,000. To continue policy research on ecological economics, Earth's carrying capacity, and environmental security and to disseminate this information to policymakers and the public.

Center for Independent Ecological Programs. Moscow, Russia. $40,000. For this branch of the Socio-Ecological Union to address environmental contamination issues in the Newly Independent States.

Climate Institute. Washington, DC. $100,000. To support efforts to implement the Framework Convention on Climate Change in the Asia-Pacific region.

Conservation International. Washington, DC. $200,000. For biological investigations in Amazonian Bolivia and for development of environmental policy in Suriname and in Guyana.

Endangered Species Coalition. Washington, DC. $50,000. For this project of the National Audubon Society for public education on preserving biodiversity and endangered species.

Environmental Defense Fund. New York, NY. $100,000. To coordinate a cooperative effort of organizations working to research and analyze policy issues related to the G-7 Economic Summits.

Environmental Strategies. Washington, DC. $125,000. To establish a new organization to improve national, regional, and local environmental protection efforts.

Greater Ecosystem Alliance. Bellingham, WA. $30,000. To protect ecosystems in the North Cascades and the Columbia Mountains in British Columbia, and in the U.S. Pacific Northwest.

International Institute for Energy Conservation (IIEC). Washington, DC. $200,000. To develop a statewide coalition to impact regional and state transportation planning toward energy conservation.

Louisiana State University. Baton Rouge, LA. $147,000. To implement a scientific panel assessing the causes of problems in Louisiana wetlands and addressing possible solutions.

National Audubon Society. New York, NY. $125,000. To monitor implementation of President Clinton's proposed forest plan for the Pacific Northwest.

National Coalition against the Misuse of Pesticides. Washington, DC. $50,000. For reform of pesticide regulations and to disseminate information on alternatives.

National Public Radio. Washington, DC. $150,000. For support of global environmental coverage, particularly in developing countries, by NPR's Science and Foreign Desks.

National Taxpayers Union Foundation. Washington, DC. $15,000. To examine the environmental and national security subsidies to agribusiness, the nuclear industry, and other industries whose activities pose a risk to surrounding populations.

Pacific Environmental and Resources Center. Sausalito, CA. $125,000. To promote sustainable forestry practices in Siberia.

Wetlands for the Americas. Manomet, MA. $21,000. This grant, for a project of the Manomet Observatory for Conservation Science, is to translate the report, "Hidrovia: An Initial

J

Application process. *Initial contact:* Letter of inquiry (2 pages maximum) describing project goals, summarizing methods, and specifying the amount of funding requested. If a proposal is invited, the Foundation will provide specifics to be included.

While most of the Foundation's grantmaking occurs through Foundation-initiated programs, unsolicited inquiries are considered. Proposals not directed toward the Foundation's stated priorities are unlikely to be funded.
When to apply: Anytime.
Materials available: Annual report (includes guidelines), "Guidelines and Application Procedures," *Review of Issues & Grants* (newsletter).

Emphases. *Recipients:* Nonprofit organizations.
Activities: Activism, advocacy, citizen participation, education, innovative programs, litigation, media projects, policy analysis/development, research (scientific), volunteerism.
Geography: Initiatives worldwide.

Limitations. *Recipients:* Individuals.
Activities: Conferences, international exchanges, research (basic).
Types of support: Annual campaigns, capital campaigns/expenses, emergency funding, endowments, facilities, general purposes, scholarships.

Joy Foundation for Ecological Education and Research
23 Sunrise Drive
P.O. Box 1104
Chincoteaque, Virginia 23336
Tel: 804-336-5688
EIN: 541575577   Type: Independent
EGA member
Contact: Joy Gilman, President

History and philosophy. The Foundation was established in 1991 by Joy Gilman Brown and Bertram Brown. It makes grants in the area of ecological education.

Officers and directors. *Officers:* Bertram Brown, Chairman; Rena Goehl, Vice Chairwomen; Joy Gilman Brown, President. *Directors:* Bertram Brown, Dale Brown, Joy Gilman Brown, Traci Brown, Wendy Brown, Kevin Browngoehl, Laurie Browngoehl, Rena Goehl, Art Spingarn.

Financial data. Data for fiscal years ended December 31, 1991 and 1993. *Assets (1991):* $26,431 (M). *Gifts received (1991):* $39,786. *Total grants disbursed (1993):* $15,600

Environmental awards. *Program and interests:* The Foundation has a special interest in linking local resources (parks, refuges, coastal reserves) to school systems.

Issues.   Cli   Bio   Lan   Agr   Wat   Oce   Ene   Was   Tox   Pop   Dev
                      •

Application process. *Initial contact:* Letter of inquiry.
When to apply: Anytime.

Emphases. *Recipients:* Educational institutions, nonprofit organizations.
Activities: Research.

The Joyce Foundation
135 South LaSalle Street, Suite 4010
Chicago, Illinois 60603-4886
Tel: 312-782-2464   Fax: 312-782-4160
EIN: 366079185   Type: Independent
EGA member
Contact: Margaret H. O'Dell, Program Officer

History and philosophy. The Joyce Foundation was established in 1948 by Beatrice Joyce Kean (d. 1972), heir to a lumber fortune. The Foundation targets the Midwest, making grants in the areas of: Conservation, Culture, Economic Development, Education, and Gun Violence. It also makes grants through three special funds: Special Opportunities, Special Projects, and the President's Discretionary Fund.

Officers and directors. *Officers:* John T. Anderson, Chairman; Deborah Leff, President; Joel D. Getzendanner, Linda K. Schelinski, Vice Presidents. *Directors:* John T. Anderson, Cushman B. Bissell, Jr., Lewis H. Butler, Charles U. Daly, Richard K. Donahue, Roger R. Fross, Carlton L. Guthrie, Marion T. Hall, Deborah Leff, Paula Wolff.

Financial data. Data for fiscal year ended December 31, 1993. *Assets:* $489,007,578 (M). *Total grants authorized:* $18,975,318.

Environmental awards. *Program and interests:* Natural resource conservation is a primary concern of the Foundation, which looks for ethical and economic solutions to problems of environmental protection. The Foundation funds projects in the Midwest pertaining to:

- Agricultural conservation.
- Soil conservation.
- Water quality and Great Lakes ecosystem management.
- Atmospheric pollution, particularly fossil fuel combustion.
- Biotechnology.

Preference is given to projects with a strong scientific base that build partnerships and use an integrated approach to environmental management.

Issues.   Cli   Bio   Lan   Agr   Wat   Oce   Ene   Was   Tox   Pop   Dev
              •   •   •   •   •   •   •   •   •   •

Funding analysis.

Fiscal year:	1991	1993
Env grants auth:	$4,643,363	$6,347,575
Number:	67	65
Range:	$407–$500,000	$2,940–$440,000
Median:	$50,000	$75,000
Pct $ auth (env/total):	32	33

Recipients (1993 highest):	Number:	Dollars:
Environmental Defense Fund	3	776,000
Environmental Law and Policy Center of the Midwest	2	480,000
Natural Resources Defense Council	3	474,445
Union of Concerned Scientists	1	440,000
Citizens for a Better Environment	2	300,000
Northeast-Midwest Institute	1	300,000
World Resources Institute	1	300,000

Activity regions (1993):	Number:	Dollars:
U.S. Great Lakes	41	3,679,935
U.S. not specified	16	2,054,655
U.S. Midwest	6	502,985
Canada	2	110,000

Sample grants (1993).
Center for Rural Affairs. Walthill, NE. $133,630 (2 years). To hire a policy analyst for the Washington, D.C. office of the Midwest Sustainable Agriculture Working Group.
Citizens for a Better Environment. Chicago, IL. $150,000. To promote new transportation approaches in southeast Wisconsin in partnership with the Sierra Club, New Transportation Alliance, and the Wisconsin Environmental Decade.
Conservation Law Foundation. Boston, MA. $75,493. To explore competitive approaches to the marketing of electric power and the implications of deregulation for efforts to promote energy conservation.
Ecology Center of Ann Arbor. Ann Arbor, MI. $64,800. For continued participation in the Auto Industry Pollution Prevention Project, a voluntary initiative between the auto industry and the state of Michigan to reduce the use and environmental impact of toxic chemicals.
Grand Calumet Task Force Corporation. Whiting, IN. $25,000. To promote pollution prevention in northwest Indiana.
Greenpeace USA. Washington, DC. $20,000. To explore the commercial potential of non-chemical dry cleaning.
Isaak Walton League of America. Arlington, VA. $25,000. For policy analysis and advocacy relating to controlling water pollution from agriculture.
National Academy of Sciences, National Research Council. Washington, DC. $20,000. To hold a Great Lakes roundtable on local priorities for addressing environmental degradation due to agriculture.
Northeast-Midwest Institute. Washington, DC. $300,000 (3 years). For work linking protection of the environment in the Great Lakes states to the economic well-being of the region.
Public Voice for Food & Health Policy. Washington, DC. $90,020. To continue the media campaign to inform the public about the benefits of sustainable agriculture.
Rails-to-Trails Conservancy. Washington, DC. $100,000. For work at the national and regional levels for new transportation priorities that de-emphasize building roads.
World Wildlife Fund. Washington, DC. $112,000 (2 years). To promote new ideas for preventing agricultural pollution in the Great Lakes region.

Application process. *Initial contact:* Short letter or full proposal to include:
1. Completed cover sheet (supplied by Foundation).
2. Description of organization, including a summary of its background, purpose, objectives, and experience in area for which funds are sought.
3. Information on project for which funding is requested, including organizational and project background, explanation of need including data or documentation, plans for implementation, means of assessing results, and plans for dissemination of project findings.
4. Itemized project budget with narrative and proposed funding sources, amount of funds requested from Joyce, their proposed use, and over what time period.
5. Names and qualifications of people involved in implementing the project.
6. Organizational expenses and income for previous, current, and coming fiscal year.
7. List of board members with their titles, outside affiliations, and telephone numbers.
8. IRS verification that the organization is not a private foundation. Copy of IRS tax-exempt status determination letter must accompany the proposal.
9. Audited financial statements (if available) or IRS Form 990 for most recently completed fiscal year.

When to apply: Inquiries are accepted throughout the year. Deadlines for 1995 are December 15, 1994, April 14, 1995, and August 15, 1995 for meetings in March, July, and November respectively.
Materials available: Annual report, "Program and Grant Proposal Guidelines," *Work in Progress* (newsletter).

Emphases. *Activities:* Advocacy, policy analysis/development.
Geography: Projects benefitting the Great Lake states: Minnesota, Wisconsin, Illinois, Indiana, Ohio, Michigan, and Iowa; or the Great Lakes region (United States and Canada).

Limitations. *Recipients:* Individuals.
Activities: Direct services, education.
Types of support: Capital campaigns/expenses, equipment, loans, scholarships.
Geography: International projects or organizations; activities outside the Midwest unless they relate to midwestern agriculture or air quality or to the Great Lakes ecosystem.

The J. M. Kaplan Fund, Inc.
30 Rockefeller Plaza, Suite 4250
New York, New York 10112
Tel: 212–767–0630   Fax: 212–767–0639
EIN: 136090286   Type: Independent
Contact: Henry Ng, Director

History and philosophy. Jacob Merrill Kaplan (1891–1987) established the Fund in 1945. In the 1950s the Fund's assets were greatly enhanced from the sale of the Welch Grape Juice Company, which Mr. Kaplan had long headed, to a grape-growers' cooperative. The Fund seeks to reinforce the tradition of progressive social policy in New York State. Principal program areas include: The Natural and Built Environment, Social Programs and Public Policy, Arts and Culture, and Education.

K

Officers and directors. *Trustees:* Betsy Davidson, G. Bradford Davidson, J. Matthew Davidson, Peter W. Davidson, Caio Fonseca, Elizabeth K. Fonseca, Isabel Fonseca, Quina Fonseca, Mary E. Kaplan, Richard D. Kaplan. *Honorary Trustee:* Alice M. Kaplan. *Trustee Emeritus:* Raymond S. Rubinow.

Financial data. Data for fiscal year ended November 30, 1993. *Assets:* $80,337,227 (M). *Total grants disbursed:* $3,014,500.

Environmental awards. *Program and interests:* The Natural and Built Environment comprises:

- Natural resources and environmental conservation.
- Land use and farmland protection.
- Environment and enterprise.
- Inner city greening.

All focus primarily on New York City and State.

Issues. Cli • Bio • Lan • Agr • Wat • Oce • Ene • Was Tox • Pop • Dev •

Funding analysis.

Fiscal year:	1992	1993*
Env grants auth:	$2,127,000	$1,104,000
Number:	49	31
Range:	$2,500–$200,000	$1,500–$140,000
Median:	$25,000	$25,000
Pct $ disb (env/total):	35	37

Recipients (1993 highest):	Number:	Dollars:
Land Trust Alliance	1	140,000
Preservation League of New York State	1	140,000
Natural Resources Defense Council	1	125,000
New York Planning Federation	1	125,000
Open Space Institute	1	120,000
Catskill Center for Conservation and Development	1	50,000
Hudson Riverkeeper Fund	1	50,000
American Farmland Trust	1	40,000

Activity region (1993):	Number:	Dollars:
New York/New Jersey	31	1,104,000

*As reported by Foundation.

Sample grants (1993).*

American Farmland Trust. New York, NY. $40,000. In support of their New York State office for farmland protection including educational programs for farmers on estate planning and conservation easements, assisting local land trusts with farmland protection, and promoting funding for a statewide farmland protection program.

Catskill Center for Conservation and Development, Inc. Arkville, NY. $50,000. For the Center to continue its watershed-related work in two areas: further development of upstate/downstate partnership strategy with NRDC, and their Farm Water Quality Incentive Program.

Hudson Riverkeeper Fund. New York, NY. $50,000. To continue review, oversight, and criticism of proposed regulations developed for watershed areas; and to continue their efforts to educate the public.

Land Trust Alliance. Washington, DC. $140,000. To administer the Rural New Land Trust Land Program which gives grants to provide critical support to land trusts and other land conservation organizations.

New York Planning Federation. New York, NY. $125,000. For the Rural New York Planning Grant Program which makes grants to aid the promotion of sound planning and zoning practices in small towns and rural communities; also $25,000 for general support.

Preservation League of New York State. Albany, NY. $140,000. For the Rural New York Historic Preservation Grant Program which makes grants to help preserve the architectural heritage of rural New York State; also, $40,000 for general support.

*Sample grants represent either new awards or disbursements on grants awarded in previous years.

Application process. *Initial contact:* Telephone for guidelines. Program is currently under review.
When to apply: Requests are accepted only between March 1 and October 15. Grant decisions are made on a rolling schedule.
Materials available: Annual report (includes "Information for Applicants"), "Application Checklist."

Emphases. *Recipients:* Nonprofit organizations.
Types of support: General purposes, program-related investments.
Geography: New York State.

Limitations. *Recipients:* Individuals.
Activities: Audiovisual materials, conferences, publications, research.
Types of support: Facilities, fellowships, operating costs, scholarships, travel expenses.

W. K. Kellogg Foundation

One East Michigan Avenue
Battle Creek, Michigan 49017
Tel: 616-968-1611   Fax: 616-968-0413
EIN: 381359264   Type: Independent
EGA member
Contact: Dr. Thomas Thorburn, Coordinator and Program Director for Food Systems, Rural Development, and Water Resources programs

---

History and philosophy. In 1906 W. K. Kellogg founded the Kellogg Company that pioneered the ready-to-eat breakfast cereal. When he established the Foundation in 1930, Kellogg said, "We will help people help themselves." This idea has remained central to the Foundation, which is not affiliated with the Kellogg Company except as a shareholder. The Foundation assists educational and service projects of potential national or international importance that emphasize the application of new knowledge in addressing significant human problems. Current major grant activity is limited to the fields of: Youth, Leadership, Philanthropy and Volunteerism, Community-Based Health Services, Higher Education, Food Systems, Rural Development, Groundwater Resources in the Great Lakes Area, and Economic Development in Michigan. The Foundation is conducting limited grantmaking in two fields: Families and Neighborhoods, and Human Resources for the Management of Information Systems.

Officers and directors. *Officers:* Russell G. Mawby, Chairman and CEO; Norman A. Brown, President and Chief Programming Officer; Helen Grace, Dan E. Moore, Valora Washington, Vice Presidents, Program; Laura A. Davis, Vice President, Corporate Affairs and Corporate Secretary; Karen R. Hollenbeck, Vice President, Administration and Assistant Corporate Secretary; William W. Fritz, Vice President, Finance and Treasurer; Katherine L. Saigeon, Assistant Vice President, Finance and Assistant Treasurer. *Trustees:* Shirley D. Bowser, Norman A. Brown, Chris T. Christ, William N. Hubbard, Jr., Dorothy A. Johnson, William La Mothe, Russell G. Mawby, Wenda Weekes Moore, Robert L. Raun, Howard F. Sims, Jonathan T. Walton.

Financial data.* Data for fiscal year ended August 31, 1993. *Assets:* $5,046,577,137 (M). *Total grants disbursed:* $277,448,031.

*Combined data for W. K. Kellogg Foundation and W. K. Kellogg Foundation Trust.

Environmental awards. *Program and interests:* The Foundation awards environmental grants under several sub-program areas, mainly Water Resources and Food Systems.

- Water Resources.

  Fostering cooperation between community projects and regional organizations to protect drinking water in Great Lakes states and provinces.

- Food Systems.

  Meeting the need for an adequate and nutritious diet while ensuring that food production systems are environmentally sensitive and sustainable. Here the Foundation's focus is on management practices designed to enhance productivity while protecting the environment and making farming economically viable for the farm family.

Issues. Cli Bio Lan Agr Wat Oce Ene Was Tox Pop Dev
        •   •   •   •   •   •   •

Funding analysis.§

Fiscal year:	1991*	1993**
Env grants disb:	$11,652,663	$8,890,908
Number:	43	41
Range:	$1,000–$3,200,000	$1,781–$3,000,000
Median:	$89,590	$88,875
Pct $ disb (env/total):	5	4

*Based on grants authorized.
**Based on grants disbursed.

Recipients (1993 highest):	Number:	Dollars:
Binder Park Zoological Society, Inc.	2	5,497,000
Eastern Michigan University	1	200,140
Alternative Energy Resources Organization	1	187,530
Michigan Technological University	1	175,930
Huron River Watershed Council	1	162,825

Activity regions (1993 highest):	Number:	Dollars:
U.S. Great Lakes	31	8,066,639
U.S. Midwest	3	313,725
U.S. not specified	3	304,119
U.S. Mid-Atlantic	2	120,875
U.S. Southeast	1	50,000

§Does not include a number of grants for alternative agriculture.

Sample grants (1993).*
Environmental Careers Organization. Cleveland, OH. $400,000. Improve groundwater protection in Great Lakes minority communities through a leadership development and placement program for college students and community education.
Michigan Department of Natural Resources. Lansing, MI. $95,530. Standardize the development of a groundwater database in Michigan through state-local partnerships of database users.
The Nature Conservancy, Ohio Field Office. Columbus, OH. $266,781. Empower the agricultural community of the Big Darby Watershed to implement economically and ecologically sound land use practices.
Northwest Michigan Resource Conservation and Development Council, Inc. Traverse City, MI. $101,700. Develop and implement a strategy for long-term success of the Grand Traverse Bay Watershed Initiative.
Practical Farmers of Iowa. Ames, IA. $729,076. Develop a model for communities to provide the support, guidance, and teamwork needed for the acceptance and use of sustainable farming systems.
Southern Illinois University. Edwardsville, IL. $501,219. Educate students, parents, and community members about groundwater quality issues through support of the Illinois Middle School Groundwater Project.
Tri-County Regional Planning Commission. Lansing, MI. $194,295. Protect drinking water quality by implementing a model for community cooperation and collaboration.

*Sample grants represent either new awards or disbursements on grants awarded in previous years.

Application process. *Initial contact:* Pre-proposal letter (1–2 pages) to include:
1. Description of basic problem and the plan for its solution.
2. Project objectives, operational procedures, and timeline.
4. Personnel and financial resources available and needed.

When to apply: Anytime.
Materials available: Annual report (includes "Application Procedure"), *International Journal* (semi-annual newsletter).

Emphases. *Recipients:* Nonprofit organizations, public agencies.
Activities: Capacity building, demonstration programs, direct services, education, innovative programs, networking, planning, training, volunteerism, youth programs.
Types of support: Equipment, multi-year grants, projects, technical assistance, travel expenses.
Geography: Michigan and the Great Lakes states and provinces. Groundwater programs must focus on the Great Lakes region. In general, the Foundation only supports programs in the United States, Latin America, the Caribbean, and southern Africa.

Limitations. *Recipients:* Individuals.
Activities: Activism.
Types of support: Advertising campaigns, annual campaigns, capital campaigns/expenses, indirect costs, loans.

© 1995 Environmental Data Resources, Inc.

K

Harris and Eliza Kempner Fund

P.O. Box 119
2201 Market Street, Suite 1200
Galveston, Texas 77553–0119
Tel: 409–762–1603 Fax: 409–762–5435
EIN: 746042458   Type: Independent
Contact: Elaine Perachio, Executive Director

History and philosophy. The Harris and Eliza Kempner Fund was established in 1946 to help fund Galveston charities during times of economic hardship. It was named to honor the progenitors of the Kempner family. Harris, a Jewish refugee from Poland acquired success in business enterprises ranging from wholesale merchandising to banking and investments in farm and timber lands. His wife Eliza played an active role in the social, cultural, and Jewish organizations of the community. Over the years the Fund has remained a family organization, now run by second- and third-generation family members.

Primary areas of concern—often with an emphasis on programs for youth—are: community development, cultural programming, health care, higher education, Jewish community organizations, social services, Third World development, and programs that preserve and enrich the environment, history, and beauty of the Galveston area. Family members and trustees also convene and contribute through three advisory committees on Education and Student Loans, Environment, and Global Issues.

Officers and directors. *Officers:* Lyda Ann Quinn Thomas, Chairman; Ann Oppenheimer Hamilton, Vice Chairman; Robert Lee Kempner Lynch, Secretary/Treasurer. *Emeritus:* Lenora Kempner Thompson, Chairman. *Trustees:* Arthur Malcolm Alpert, John Thornton Currie, Ann Oppenheimer Hamilton, Hetta Towler Kempner, Robert Lee Kempner Lynch, Barbara Weston Sasser, Lyda Ann Quinn Thomas, Edward Randall Thompson, Jr., Harris Kempner Weston

Financial data. Data for fiscal year ended December 31, 1993. *Assets:* $33,249,022 (C). *Total grants and matching gifts disbursed:* $1,334,212.

Environmental awards. *Recent grants:* 1993 grants included support for river protection, coastal issues, and environmental education.

Issues. Cli • Bio • Lan • Agr • Wat • Oce • Ene • Was • Tox • Pop • Dev

Funding analysis.

Fiscal year:	1993
Env grants disb:	$31,530
Number:	6
Range:	$2,000–$10,000
Median:	$4,765
Pct $ disb (env/total):	2

Recipients (1993):	*Number:*	*Dollars:*
Clean Galveston	1	10,000
Sierra Club Legal Defense Fund	1	8,000
Galveston Bay Foundation	1	5,000
City of Galveston	1	4,530
Association for Community Television/KUHT–Channel 8	1	2,000
Environmental Fund of Texas	1	2,000

Activity regions (1993):	*Number:*	*Dollars:*
U.S. South Central	5	23,530
U.S. not specified	1	8,000

Sample grants (1993).
Association for Community Television/KUHT–Channel 8. Houston, TX. $2,000. Underwriting for PBS documentary film, "River of Life—Rio Grande".
Clean Galveston. Galveston, TX. $10,000. Seawall cleanup in conjunction with beach renourishment.
Environmental Fund of Texas. Austin, TX. $2,000. Start-up funds.
Galveston Bay Foundation. Webster, TX. $5,000. Educational programs.
Sierra Club Legal Defense Fund. San Francisco, CA. $8,000. General operations.

Application process. *Initial contact:* Brief letter requesting application guidelines. Full proposal to include:
1. Brief letter, signed by the executive director and board chairman, stating need and amount requested.
2. Organization information.
   - Name and telephone number of contact person.
   - Names of present officers and board members.
   - Statement of purpose and brief history of organization.
   - List of previous Kempner Fund grants.
   - Financial statements (audited, if possible) and IRS Form 990 for most recent fiscal year.
   - Operating budget (revenue and expenses) for the year for which funds are sought.
   - Copy of IRS tax-exempt status determination letter.
   - Statement on organization letterhead that there has been no change in IRS status since issuance of ruling letter.
3. Project information (not required if for operating funds):
   - Objectives and potential benefits of project.
   - Proposed timetable.
   - Project budget (revenue and expenses).
   - Sources and amounts being solicited and/or received.
   - Plans to evaluate project progress and/or results.

When to apply: Deadlines are March 15, June 15, and October 15; December 1 is the deadline for national/international requests in the areas of education, environment, population control, and Third World development. The board meets in April, July, and December.
Materials available: Biennial report (includes "Application Guidelines").

Emphases. *Activities:* Conferences, publications, research, seminars.
Types of support: Annual campaigns, capital campaigns/expenses, continuing support, emergency funding, equipment, facilities, fellowships, general purposes, lectureships, loans, matching funds, operating costs, professorships, projects, scholarships, seed money.
Geography: Galveston, Texas.

Limitations. *Recipients:* Individuals.
Activities: Fundraising.

The Henry P. Kendall Foundation
176 Federal Street
Boston, Massachusetts 02110
Tel: 617-951-2525
EIN: 046029103   Type: Independent
EGA member
Contact: Theodore Smith, Executive Director

History and philosophy. The Foundation was established in 1957 through donations from the members of the Henry P. Kendall family. Primary interests are: conservation, environment, public policy, arms control, peace, and museums.

Officers and directors. *Officer:* John P. Kendall, President. *Trustees:* Henry W. Kendall, John P. Kendall, Anne W. Plimpton.

Financial data. Data for fiscal year ended December 31, 1992. *Assets:* $56,302,453 (M). *Total grants disbursed:* $1,405,697.

Environmental awards. *Program and interests:* The Foundation has a special interest in environmental protection and natural resource conservation.
Recent grants: 1992 grants included support for land conservation, wildlife, energy, and marine issues.

Issues. Cli • Bio • Lan Agr Wat • Oce • Ene Was Tox Pop • Dev

Funding analysis.

Fiscal year:	1992
Env grants disb:	$1,163,790
Number:	5
Range:	$15,000–$644,790
Median:	$100,000
Pct $ disb (env/total):	83

Recipients (1992):	Number:	Dollars:
Kendall Whaling Museum	1	644,790
Environmental Preservation Support Trust	1	354,000
Union of Concerned Scientists	1	100,000
National Wildlife Federation	1	50,000
High Country Foundation	1	15,000

Activity regions (1992):	Number:	Dollars:
U.S. Northeast	1	644,790
U.S. not specified	3	504,000
U.S. Mountain	1	15,000

Sample grants (1992).
Environmental Preservation Support Trust. Boston, MA. $354,000.
High Country Foundation. Paonia, CO. $15,000.
Kendall Whaling Museum. Sharon, MA. $644,790.
National Wildlife Federation. Washington, DC. $50,000.
Union of Concerned Scientists. Cambridge, MA. $100,000.

Application process. *Initial contact:* Proposal including budget, staff personnel, and IRS tax-exempt status determination letter.

When to apply: Deadlines are February 15, May 15, August 15, and November 15. The board meets in March, June, September, and December.

Emphases. *Recipients:* Educational institutions, museums, non-profit organizations, research institutions.
Activities: Conferences, publications, research, seminars.
Types of support: Continuing support, emergency funding, loans, operating costs, projects, seed money.
Geography: Massachusetts.

Limitations. *Recipients:* Individuals.
Types of support: Capital campaigns/expenses, endowments, fellowships, matching funds, scholarships.

The Robert S. and Grayce B. Kerr Foundation, Inc.
6301 North Western, Suite 220
Oklahoma City, Oklahoma 73118
Tel: 405-843-7064
EIN: 731256123   Type: Independent
EGA member
Contact: William G. Kerr, President

History and philosophy. The Foundation was established in 1986. It funds cultural activities, education, environmental projects, and human services, primarily in the state of Oklahoma.

Officers and directors. *Officers:* William G. Kerr, President and Chairman; Joffa Kerr, Sr., Vice President; Mara Kerr Burks, Secretary; James G. Anderson, Treasurer. *Trustees:* James G. Anderson, Mara Kerr Burks, Joffa Kerr, Sr., William G. Kerr.

Financial data. Data for fiscal year ended December 31, 1992. *Assets:* $27,036,372 (M). *Total grants disbursed:* $918,844.

Environmental awards. *Recent grants:* 1992 grants supported land conservation, plant conservation, and avian research.

Issues. Cli Bio • Lan • Agr Wat Oce Ene Was Tox Pop • Dev

Funding analysis.

Fiscal year:	1990	1992
Env grants disb:	$493,358	$451,416
Number:	4	14
Range:	$30,858–$375,000	$1,000–$125,000
Median:	$43,750	$11,250
Pct $ disb (env/total):	17	49

Recipients (1992 highest):	Number:	Dollars:
Wildlife of the American West Art Museum	5	253,916
The Nature Conservancy, Oklahoma Field Office	3	130,000
William Fremont Harn Gardens, Inc.	1	20,000
George Miksch Sutton Avian Research Center, Inc.	1	15,000
Teton Science School	1	15,000

K

Activity regions (1992):Number:Dollars:
U.S. Mountain 8 283,916
U.S. South Central 6 167,500

Sample grants (1992).
Jackson Hole Land Trust. Jackson, WY. $7,500.
National Wildflower Research Center. Austin, TX. $2,500.
The Nature Conservancy, Oklahoma Field Office. Tulsa, OK. $130,000.
Sutton Avian Research Center. Bartlesville, OK. $15,000.

Application process. *Initial contact:* The Foundation awards grants to pre-selected organizations only. No unsolicited applications accepted.

Emphases. *Recipients:* Pre-selected organizations only (museums, nonprofit organizations).
Types of support: Capital campaigns/expenses, continuing support, facilities, fellowships, general purposes, indirect costs, matching funds, multi-year grants.
Geography: Oklahoma.

Limitations. *Recipients:* Individuals.
Activities: Lobbying, research (medical/scientific).
Types of support: Annual campaigns, endowments, membership campaigns.

The Helen & Milton Kimmelman Foundation

445 Park Avenue, Suite 2100
New York, New York 10022
EIN: 133110688 Type: Independent
Contact: Helen Kimmel, Trustee

History and philosophy. The Foundation was established in 1982 by Milton Kimmelman. It makes grants to pre-selected organizations in the areas of Jewish concerns, arts, education, and medical research and education, and the environment.

Officers and directors. *Trustee:* Helen Kimmel.

Financial data. Data for fiscal year ended November 30, 1992. *Assets:* $18,734,537 (M). *Gifts received:* 2,417,090. *Total grants disbursed:* $1,377,940.

Environmental awards. *Recent grants:* 1992 grants included support for wilderness, wildlife, and wildfowl protection.

Issues. Cli Bio Lan Agr Wat Oce Ene Was Tox Pop Dev
• •   •

Funding analysis.

Fiscal year:	1992
Env grants disb:	$55,050
Number:	3
Range:	$50–$50,000
Median:	$5,000
Pct $ disb (env/total):	4

Recipients (1992): | Number: | Dollars:
The Wilderness Society | 1 | 50,000
NYZS/The Wildlife Conservation Society | 1 | 5,000
Southampton Wildfowl Association | 1 | 50

Activity regions (1992): | Number: | Dollars:
U.S. not specified | 1 | 50,000
New York/New Jersey | 2 | 5,050

Sample grants (1992).
NYZS/The Wildlife Conservation Society. Bronx, NY. $5,000.
Southampton Wildfowl Association. Quogue, NY. $50.
The Wilderness Society. Washington, DC. $50,000.

Application process. *Initial contact:* The Foundation awards grants to pre-selected organizations only. No unsolicited applications accepted.

Emphases. *Recipients:* Pre-selected organizations.
Types of support: General purposes, facilities, matching funds, program-related investments.

Limitations. *Recipients:* Individuals.

Kinnoull Foundation

Deloitte & Touche
c/o J. C. Vernon Miles
479 Pacific Street
Monterey, California 93940–2752
Tel: 408–372–7328 Fax: 408–372–5834
EIN: 946186982 Type: Independent
Contact: J. C. Vernor Miles, Chairman

History and philosophy. The Foundation was established in 1968. Its purpose is "to further the cause [of] prevention of cruelty to animals; and to support traditional teachings of the Catholic Church."

Officers and directors. *Officer:* J. C. Vernor Miles, Chairman. *Trustees:* J. C. Vernor Miles, Gloria Taviner, Paul Williams.

Financial data. Data for fiscal year ended June 30, 1993. *Assets:* $5,371,673 (M). *Total grants disbursed:* $356,500.

Environmental awards. *Recent grants:* 1993 grants included support for national and international efforts to protect wildlife.

Issues. Cli Bio Lan Agr Wat Oce Ene Was Tox Pop Dev
      •

Funding analysis.

Fiscal year:	1991	1993
Env grants disb:	$63,000	$33,500
Number:	3	4
Range:	$3,000–$40,000	$4,000–$15,000
Median:	$20,000	$7,250
Pct $ disb (env/total):	21	9

Recipients (1993):	Number:	Dollars:
Mauritius Wildlife Appeal Fund	1	15,000
NYZS/The Wildlife Conservation Society	2	14,500
Wildlife Preservation Trust International	1	4,000

Activity regions (1993):	Number:	Dollars:
Eastern and Southern Africa	1	15,000
International*	2	14,500
U.S. not specified	1	4,000

*Multiple regions or not specified.

Sample grants (1993).
Mauritius Wildlife Appeal Fund. Port-Louis, Mauritius. $15,000.
NYZS/The Wildlife Conservation Society. Bronx, NY. $10,000.
NYZS/The Wildlife Conservation Society. Bronx, NY. $4,500.
Wildlife Preservation Trust International. Philadelphia, PA. $4,000.

Application process. *Initial contact:* The Foundation awards grants to pre-selected organizations only. No unsolicited applications accepted.

Emphases. *Recipients:* Pre-selected organizations only.

Limitations. *Recipients:* Individuals.

F. M. Kirby Foundation, Inc.
17 DeHart Street
P.O. Box 151
Morristown, New Jersey 07963–0151
Tel: 201-538-4800
EIN: 516017929   Type: Independent
Contacts: F. M. Kirby, President
            Paul B. Mott, Jr., Executive Director

History and philosophy. The Foundation was established by Fred M. Kirby (1861–1940) in 1931. The Kirby family was associated with F. W. Woolworth Company, Allegheny Corporation, Investors Diversified Services, and Pittston Company. The Foundation's philosophy is "that a distinctive feature of American life dating back to colonial times is the remarkable richness and diversity of its voluntary, nonprofit sector. . . . People should be encouraged to solve their own problems exclusive of government aid and on the local level. Private philanthropy is there to help them."

The Foundation makes grants to a wide range of nonprofits in education, health and medicine, arts and the humanities, civic and public affairs, as well as religious, welfare, and youth organizations. Its grantees are generally located in geographic areas of interest to family members.

Officers and directors. *Officers:* F. M. Kirby, President; Walker D. Kirby, Vice President; Thomas J. Bianchini, Secretary/Treasurer. *Directors:* Alice Kirby Horton, F. M. Kirby; Fred M. Kirby III, Jefferson W. Kirby, S. Dillard Kirby, Walker D. Kirby.

Financial data. Data for fiscal year ended December 31, 1993. *Assets:* $268,353,392 (M). *Total grants disbursed:* $8,968,743.

Environmental awards. *Program and interests:* The Foundation's "support of environmental organizations is very limited." *Recent grants:* 1993 grants included support for land conservation, forestry, coastal issues, watershed protection, wildlife, fisheries, and urban environment.

Issues.   Cli   Bio   Lan   Agr   Wat   Oce   Ene   Was   Tox   Pop   Dev
              •   •   •   •   •

Funding analysis.

Fiscal year:	1992
Env grants disb:	$282,000
Number:	18
Range:	$1,500–$50,000
Median:	$12,500
Pct $ disb (env/total):	2

Recipients (1992 highest):	Number:	Dollars:
The Nature Conservancy, New Jersey Field Office	1	50,000
Lower James River Association	1	40,000
Morristown Clean Community	1	25,000
New Jersey Conservation Foundation	2	25,000
The Trust for Public Land	1	25,000

Activity regions (1992):	Number:	Dollars:
New York/New Jersey	10	180,000
U.S. Mid-Atlantic	3	70,000
U.S. not specified	3	25,500
U.S. Southeast	1	5,000
U.S. Great Lakes	1	1,500

Sample grants (1993).
Adirondack Nature Conservancy. Elizabethtown, NY. $10,000.
American Littoral Society. Highlands, NJ. $7,500.
Brandywine Conservancy, Inc. Chadds Ford, PA. $10,000. For the Brandywine River Museum and the Environmental Management Center.
Environmental Defense Fund. New York, NY. $25,000.
New Jersey Audubon Society. Franklin Lakes, NJ. $10,000.
The New York Botanical Garden. Bronx, NY. $15,000.
NYZS/The Wildlife Conservation Society. Bronx, NY. $15,000.
North Carolina Zoological Society. Asheboro, NC. $2,500.
Pinelands Preservation Alliance. Browns Mills, NJ. $20,000.

Application process. *Initial contact:* Full proposal to include:
1. Report on use of previous grants.
2. Report on current activities.
3. Amount requested.
4. Description of purpose for grant.
5. Type of support: general operations, specific project, capital needs, or endowment.
6. List of officers and directors.
7. Copy of current annual budget.
8. Copy of IRS tax-exempt status determination letter.

When to apply: Anytime. Proposals received after October 31 will be held for consideration the following year.
Materials available: "Solicitation Guidelines."

K

Emphases. *Recipients:* Botanical gardens, educational institutions, nonprofit organizations, religious organizations.
Activities: Education, research (medical).
Types of support: Annual campaigns, continuing support, equipment, facilities (renovation), general purposes, operating costs, seed money, projects.
Geography: New York, New Jersey, eastern Pennsylvania, North Carolina (Durham area).

Limitations. *Recipients:* Individuals, public agencies.
Activities: Fundraising.
Types of support: Loans.

Caesar Kleberg Foundation for Wildlife Conservation

711 Navarro, Suite 535
San Antonio, Texas 78205
Tel: 210–224–1011 Fax: 210–223–3657
EIN: 746038766 Type: Independent
Contact: Leroy G. Denman, Jr., Trustee

History and philosophy. The Caesar Kleberg Foundation for Wildlife Conservation began as a trust in 1951. Its donor, Caesar Kleberg, came from a prominent south Texas family that owned one of the world's largest oil and ranching operations. All contributions support wildlife conservation and studies.

Officers and directors. *Trustees:* Leroy G. Denman, Jr., Stephen J. Kleberg, Dr. Duane M. Leach.

Financial data. Data for fiscal year ended December 31, 1993. *Assets:* $18,684,014 (M). *Total grants disbursed:* $423,000.

Environmental awards. *Recent grants:* 1993 grants included support for wildlife conservation.

Issues. Cli Bio Lan Agr Wat Oce Ene Was Tox Pop Dev

Funding analysis.

Fiscal year:	1991	1992
Env grants disb:	$565,000	$545,000
Number:	3	5
Range:	$15,000–$450,000	$10,000–$450,000
Median:	$100,000	$25,000
Pct $ disb (env/total):	100	100

Recipients (1992):	Number:	Dollars:
Texas A&I University	1	450,000
Texas Technical University	1	50,000
University of Texas, Marine Science	1	25,000
State of Texas, Department of Agriculture	1	10,000
Texas Society of Biomedical Research	1	10,000

Activity region (1992):	Number:	Dollars:
U.S. South Central	5	545,000

Sample grants (1993).
C. K. W. Research Institute. Kingsville, TX. $213,000. Wildlife conservation.
National Audubon Society. New York, NY. $10,000. Wildlife conservation.
Texas A&M University. Kingsville, TX. $200,000. Wildlife conservation.

Application process. *Initial contact:* Letter of proposal, on organization letterhead, to include:
1. Nontechnical description of grant purpose.
2. Budget, indicating exact amount requested.

Append IRS tax-exempt status determination letter.
No grants will be made to organizations that discriminate.
When to apply: Anytime. The board meets at least twice a year.

Emphases. *Geography:* Southwest Texas.

Limitations. *Recipients:* Individuals.
Types of support: Endowments, facilities, fellowships, matching funds, loans, scholarships.

The Esther A. and Joseph Klingenstein Fund, Inc.

787 Seventh Avenue, 6th Floor
New York, New York 10019–6016
Tel: 212–492–6193 Fax: 212–492–7007
EIN: 136028788 Type: Independent
Contact: John Klingenstein, President

History and philosophy. The Fund was established in 1946 through the donations of Esther and Joseph Klingenstein, founding sponsors of the Mount Sinai School of Medicine. Joseph was chairman emeritus of the Mount Sinai Medical Center and senior partner of an investment banking firm. "During their lifetimes, their deep concern for individual human welfare was reflected in grants primarily to those institutions with which they were personally involved, mostly in the New York City area."

The Fund's two major areas of concern are neuroscience, especially research into epilepsy, and independent secondary education. Other interests include: animal research, communication and journalism, the environment, health, population and family planning, minority affairs, social and public policy, and separation of church and state.

Officers and directors. *Officers:* John Klingenstein, President and Treasurer; Frederick A. Klingenstein, Vice President and Secretary; Kenneth H. Fields, Assistant Treasurer. *Directors:* Kenneth H. Fields, Frederick A. Klingenstein, John Klingenstein, Patricia D. Klingenstein, Sharon L. Klingenstein.

Financial data. Data for fiscal year ended September 30, 1993. *Assets:* $83,129,152 (M). *Total grants disbursed:* $4,131,398.

Environmental awards. *Recent grants:* 1993 grants included support for rainforest protection and land conservation.

Issues. Cli Bio Lan Agr Wat Oce Ene Was Tox Pop Dev

Funding analysis.

Fiscal year:	1991	1993
Env grants disb:	$135,000	$85,000
Number:	3	4
Range:	$25,000–$60,000	$10,000–$30,000
Median:	$50,000	$22,500
Pct $ disb (env/total):	4	2

Recipients (1993):	Number:	Dollars:
Earthwatch Expeditions, Inc.	1	30,000
INFORM	1	30,000
Resources for the Future	1	15,000
Rainforest Alliance	1	10,000

Activity region (1993):	Number:	Dollars:
U.S. not specified	4	85,000

Sample grants (1993).
Earthwatch Expeditions, Inc. Watertown, MA. $30,000.
INFORM. New York, NY. $30,000.
Rainforest Alliance. New York, NY. $10,000.
Resources for the Future. Washington, DC. $15,000.

Application process. *Initial contact:* Proposal to include:
1. Brief description of organization.
2. Description of project, budget, and other sources of funding.
3. Organization's latest audited financial statement.
4. IRS tax-exempt status determination letter.

When to apply: Anytime. The board meets five/six times a year.
Materials available: Brochure.

Emphases. *Recipients:* Educational institutions, museums, non-profit organizations, research institutions.
Activities: Conferences, education, media projects, publications, research (medical), seminars.
Types of support: Continuing support, fellowships, general purposes, operating costs, pilot projects, seed money.
Geography: Primarily New York City area.

Limitations. *Recipients:* Individuals.
Types of support: Capital campaigns/expenses, endowments, facilities (construction).

The Knapp Foundation, Inc.
P.O. Box O
St. Michaels, Maryland 21663
Tel: 410–745–5660   Fax: 410–745–5713
EIN: 136001167   Type: Independent
Contact: Antoinette P. Vojvoda, President

History and philosophy. The Knapp Foundation, Inc. was founded in 1929 by the late Joseph P. Knapp. Through matching grants, it supports college and university libraries and efforts in wildlife conservation and preservation.

Officers and directors. *Officers:* Antoinette P. Vojvoda, President; Robert B. Vojvoda, Vice President; Ruth M. Capranica, Secretary. *Trustees:* Ruth M. Capranica, Margaret P. Newcomb, George L. Penny, Sylvia V. Penny, Antoinette P. Vojvoda, Robert B. Vojvoda.

Financial data. Data for fiscal year ended December 31, 1992. *Assets:* $20,917,548 (M). *Total grants disbursed:* $837,759.

Environmental awards. *Recent grants:* 1992 grants included support for habitat and wildlife conservation and environmental education, mainly along the Eastern Seaboard.

Issues.   Cli   Bio   Lan   Agr   Wat   Oce   Ene   Was   Tox   Pop   Dev
                    •   •   •   •

Funding analysis.

Fiscal year:	1991	1992
Env grants disb:	$305,625	$564,509
Number:	11	8
Range:	$1,500–$98,250	$3,000–$250,000
Median:	$10,000	$16,250
Pct $ disb (env/total):	70	67

Recipients (1992 highest):	Number:	Dollars:
Ducks Unlimited, Inc.	1	250,000
The Nature Conservancy, North Carolina Field Office	1	134,000
Wildfowl Trust of North America	1	127,009
Delaware Nature Society	1	22,500
Audubon Society, Massachusetts	1	10,000
National Aquarium in Baltimore	1	10,000

Activity regions (1992):	Number:	Dollars:
U.S. Southeast	2	384,000
U.S. Mid-Atlantic	4	167,509
U.S. Northeast	2	13,000

Sample grants (1992).*
Bigelow Laboratory for Ocean Sciences. West Boothbay Harbor, ME. $3,000. Computer equipment and software for Library and Retrieval Facility.
Calvert Marine Museum Society. Solomons, MD. $8,000. Purchase of habitat tank for Calvert Marine Museum.
Delaware Nature Society. Hockessin, DE. $11,250. First year of two-year commitment for purchase of audio-visual equipment.
Ducks Unlimited, Inc. Long Grove, IL. $250,000. Ace Basin conservation project for habitat protection in South Carolina.
Massachusetts Audubon Society. Lincoln, MA. $10,000. Second of two grants for land acquisition.
Monkey Island Education Project. Moyock, NC. $10,000. Second payment on two-year grant for environmental improvements for education center.
National Aquarium in Baltimore. Baltimore, MD. $10,000. Purchase of video equipment.
The Nature Conservancy, North Carolina Field Office. $134,000. Land acquisition, Resolution Trust Corporation tract, Nags Head Woods.
Wildfowl Trust of North America. Grasonville, MD. $127,009. For the Horsehead Sanctuary for maintenance of habitat for waterfowl and wildlife for educational purposes.

*Sample grants represent either new awards or disbursements on grants awarded in previous years.

K

Application process. *Initial contact:* Detailed letter to include project goals, project need, and other funding commitments to project or program (Foundation works on a matching grant basis). *When to apply:* Anytime. The board meets in December. The executive board meets quarterly when necessary.
Materials available: Application guidelines.

Emphases. *Recipients:* Educational institutions (colleges/universities), libraries, nonprofit organizations.
Activities: Audiovisual materials, conservation, education.
Types of support: Computer hardware, equipment (audiovisual), matching funds.
Geography: Primarily East Coast states.

Limitations. *Recipients:* Educational institutions (elementary/secondary), individuals.
Activities: Research.
Types of support: Facilities, operating costs.
Geography: Outside the United States.

The Seymour H. Knox Foundation, Inc.

3750 Marine Midland Center
Buffalo, New York 14203
Tel: 716–854–6811
EIN 160839066   Type: Independent
Contact: Northrup R. Knox, President

History and philosophy. The Foundation was established in 1945 by Seymour H. Knox, Marjorie K. C. Klopp, and Dorothy K. G. Rogers. Funding areas are: arts (academies, museums, and historical preservation); education (universities and private schools); health (hospitals); and civic affairs (environmental affairs, natural sciences, and community development).

Officers and directors. *Officers:* Seymour H. Knox III, Chairman; Northrup R. Knox, President and Treasurer; Hazard K. Campbell, Vice President and Secretary; James F. Wendel, Assistant Secretary/Assistant Treasurer. *Directors:* Benjamin E. Campbell, Northrup R. Knox, Northrup R. Knox, Jr., Seymour H. Knox III, Seymour H. Knox IV, Randolph A. Marks, Henry Z. Urban.

Financial data. Data for fiscal year ended December 31, 1992. *Assets:* $22,394,981 (M). *Total grants disbursed:* $961,600.

Environmental awards. *Recent grants:* 1992 grants included support for beautification, land conservation, wildlife, and fishery protection.

Issues.   Cli   Bio   Lan   Agr   Wat   Oce   Ene   Was   Tox   Pop   Dev
              •   •   •   •   •   •

Funding analysis.

Fiscal year:	1992
Env grants disb:	$95,200
Number:	17
Range:	$100–$75,000
Median:	$500
Pct $ disb (env/total):	10

Recipients (1992 highest):	Number:	Dollars:
Ducks Unlimited, Inc.	1	75,000
Genesee Valley Conservancy	1	11,500
Institute of Ecosystem Studies, New York Botanical Garden	1	2,500
Aiken County Open Land Trust, Inc.	1	1,000
Restigouche Atlantic Salmon Preservation Foundation	1	1,000

Activity regions (1992):	Number:	Dollars:
U.S. not specified	4	2,000
New York/New Jersey	8	91,200
U.S. Northeast	3	1,700
U.S. Southeast	2	300

Sample grants (1992).
Adirondack Museum. Blue Mountain Lake, NY. $100.
Aiken County Open Land Trust, Inc. Aiken County, NY. $1,000.
Atlantic Salmon Federation. New York, NY. $500.
Ducks Unlimited, Inc. Whitehall, NY. $75,000.
East Aurora Beautification. East Aurora, NY. $500.
Institute of Ecosystem Studies, New York Botanical Garden. Millbrook, NY $2,500.
National Audubon Society. New York, NY. $500.
World Wildlife Fund. Washington, DC. $500.

Application process. *Initial contact:* Letter of intent.
When to apply: Anytime.

Emphases. *Recipients:* Botanical gardens, educational institutions, museums, nonprofit organizations, religious organizations.
Types of support: General purposes.
Geography: Buffalo, New York area.

Limitations. *Recipients:* Individuals.

Charles G. Koch Charitable Foundation

1401 I Street, N.W., Suite 300
Washington, DC 20005
Tel: 202–842–4616
EIN: 480918408   Type: Independent
Contact: Lynn Taylor, Managing Director

History and philosophy. The Foundation was established in 1981 by Charles G. Koch and Fred C. Koch. Its "mission is to advance the well-being of mankind through the development and application of the principles of a free society. Recognizing that peace, prosperity, and human progress are only possible in a free society, the Foundation seeks opportunities to foster a deeper understanding of these principles and advance market-based solutions to society's most pressing problems." The Foundation supports public policy research and projects that support free enterprise and market-based solutions to social problems including crime, drug abuse, environment, and health care. It funds research institutions with doctorate-level candidates in disciplines such as economics, history, philosophy, political science, and organizational behavior.

Officers and directors. *Officers:* John Blundell, President; Elizabeth Koch, Vice President; Mary Ann Fox, Secretary; Vonda Holliman, Treasurer. *Directors:* Richard Fink, Charles G. Koch, Elizabeth Koch.

Financial data. Data for fiscal year ended December 31, 1992. *Assets:* $10,956,808 (U) (est.). *Total grants disbursed:* $1,507,221.

Environmental awards. *Recent grants:* 1990 grants included support for policy research on energy and other environmental issues.

Issues. Cli   Bio   Lan   Agr   Wat   Oce   Ene   Was   Tox   Pop   Dev
                                                    •

Funding analysis.

Fiscal year:	1990
Env grants disb:	$46,000
Number:	3
Range:	$1,000–$25,000
Median:	$20,000
Pct $ disb (env/total):	4

Recipient (1990):	Number:	Dollars:
Competitive Enterprise Institute	1	25,000
Political Economy Research Center	1	20,000
Institute for Energy Research	1	1,000

Activity region (1990):	Number:	Dollars:
U.S. not specified	3	46,000

Sample grants (1990).
Competitive Enterprise Institute. Washington, DC. $25,000. Environmental issues.
Institute for Energy Research. Houston, TX. $1,000.
Political Economy Research Center. Bozeman, MT. $20,000. Environmental issues.

Application process. *Initial contact:* Concise pre-proposal letter (3 pages maximum) describing proposed project and focusing on the Foundation's specific areas of interest. Please submit additional materials only if they are requested.
When to apply: Anytime.

Emphases. *Types of support:* General purposes, research, scholarships.

Limitations. *Recipients:* Individuals.

Kongsgaard-Goldman Foundation
1932 First Avenue, Suite 602
Seattle, Washington 98101
Tel: 206-448-1874   Fax: 206-448-1973
EIN: 943088217   Type: Independent
Contact: Martha Kongsgaard, Vice President

History and philosophy. The Kongsgaard-Goldman Foundation is a family foundation established in 1988 by Peter Goldman and Martha Kongsgaard. Grants focus on the environment, health, and social services, including grassroots organizing, Jewish welfare, and social change.

Officers and directors. *Officers:* Peter Goldman, President; Martha Kongsgaard, Vice President. *Directors:* Peter Goldman, Martha Kongsgaard.

Financial data. Data for fiscal years ended December 31, 1992 and 1993. *Assets (1992):* $329,900 (M). *Total grants disbursed (1993):* $519,933.

Environmental awards. *Recent grants:* 1993 grants included support for wildlife and habitat protection, recycling, toxics control, and land use.

Issues. Cli   Bio   Lan   Agr   Wat   Oce   Ene   Was   Tox   Pop   Dev
            •   •   •   •   •

Funding analysis.

Fiscal year:	1990	1992
Env grants disb:	$84,500	$83,500
Number:	12	14
Range:	$500–$15,000	$1,000–$15,000
Median:	$5,000	$5,000
Pct $ disb (env/total):	35	26

Recipients (1992 highest):	Number:	Dollars:
World Wildlife Fund	1	15,000
Washington Environmental Council	1	11,500
Greenpeace USA	1	10,000
Northwest Renewable Resources Center	1	8,500
Montana Environmental Information Center	1	8,000

Activity regions (1992 highest):	Number:	Dollars:
U.S. Northwest	6	33,000
U.S. not specified	3	17,000
International*	1	15,000
U.S. Mountain	1	8,000
Africa	1	5,000

*Multiple regions or not specified.

Sample grants (1992).
African Wildlife Foundation. Washington, DC. $5,000.
Alaska Wildlife Alliance. Anchorage, AK. $2,000.
Earth on the Air. Seattle, WA. $1,000.
Greenpeace USA. Washington, DC. $10,000.
Montana Environmental Information Center. Helena, MT. $8,000
Northwest Renewable Resources Center. Seattle, WA. $8,500.
Sierra Club. San Francisco, CA. $2,000.
Washington Citizens for Recycling Foundation. Seattle, WA. $5,000.
Washington Environmental Council. Seattle, WA. $11,500.
World Wildlife Fund. Washington, DC. $15,000.

Application process. *Initial contact:* Letter.
When to apply: Anytime. Contributions made in fall and winter.

K

Emphases. *Recipients:* Nonprofit organizations.
Activities: Advocacy, capacity building, citizen participation, conferences, conflict resolution, innovative programs, land acquisition, litigation, political activities.
Types of support: Continuing support, general purposes, multi-year grants, operating costs, seed money, technical assistance.
Geography: Primarily the Northwest.

The Kresge Foundation
3215 West Big Beaver Road
P.O. Box 3151
Troy, Michigan 48007-3151
Tel: 810-643-9630   Fax: 810-643-0588
EIN: 381359217   Type: Independent
Contact: Alfred H. Taylor, Jr., Chair

History and philosophy. Sebastian S. Kresge established the Foundation in 1924 on the twenty-fifth anniversary of his company, S. S. Kresge Company, known today as the Kmart Corporation. The Foundation directs its support toward the maintenance or expansion of charitable institutions in the area of "bricks and mortar." In 1988 the Trustees initiated an additional program, the Science Initiative, to upgrade and endow science laboratories through the purchase of instrumentation.

The Foundation makes grants in the categories of Arts and Humanities, Health and Long-Term Care, Higher Education, Science and Environment, Public Policy, and Social Services. Grants are awarded on a challenge basis—"approved in the midst of a fundraising effort, on the condition that the rest of the funds be raised by an agreed deadline."

Officers and directors. *Officers:* Alfred H. Taylor, Jr., Chair; John E. Marshall, III, President and CEO; Bruce A. Kresge, M.D., Vice President; Miguel A. Satut, Vice President and Secretary. *Trustees:* Jill K. Conway, Bruce A. Kresge, M.D., George D. Langdon, Jr., Robert C. Larson, John E. Marshall, III, David K. Page, Margaret T. Smith, Robert D. Storey, Alfred H. Taylor, Jr.

Financial data. Data for fiscal year ended December 31, 1993. *Assets:* $1,543,183,104 (M). *Total grants authorized:* $74,453,800. *Total grants disbursed:* $58,898,400.

Environmental awards. *Program and interests:* The Foundation does not have an environmental program as such. Within the last few years the Foundation has provided funds for buildings, equipment, and land acquisition for conservation organizations working on habitat and species protection.

Issues. Cli Bio Lan Agr Wat Oce Ene Was Tox Pop Dev
           •   •   •   •

Funding analysis.

Fiscal year:	1991	1993
Env grants auth:	$2,450,000	$5,223,000
Number:	7	12
Range:	$150,000–$750,000	$125,000–$850,000
Median:	$250,000	$484,000
Pct $ auth (env/total):	4	7

Recipients (1993 highest):	Number:	Dollars:
The Nature Conservancy, Oklahoma Field Office	1	850,000
Houston Museum of Natural Science	1	500,000
John Ball Zoological Society	1	500,000
Missouri Botanical Garden	1	500,000
Stanford University	1	500,000
Worcester County Horticultural Society	1	500,000

Activity regions (1993 highest):	Number:	Dollars:
U.S. South Central	3	1,750,000
U.S. Great Lakes	2	968,000
U.S. Northeast	2	700,000
U.S. Midwest	1	500,000
U.S. West	1	500,000

Sample grants (1992–93).*
John Ball Zoological Society. Grand Rapids, MI. $500,000. Expansion of facilities including Living Shores Immersion Habitat Aquarium.
Detroit Zoological Society. Detroit, MI. $468,000.
Ducks Unlimited, Inc. Memphis, TN. $750,000. Construction of International Center for Wetlands and Waterfowl Conservation.
Houston Museum of Natural Science. Houston, TX. $500,000. Renovation of exhibits and construction of Butterfly Center.
International Crane Foundation. Baraboo, WI. $150,000. For construction of International Guest House and Training Center.
The Lindsay Museum. Walnut Creek, CA. $250,000. Construction of replacement museum and wildlife rehabilitation center.
Massachusetts Audubon Society. Lincoln, MA. $200,000. Renovation of facilities at Wellfleet Bay Wildlife Sanctuary.
Missouri Botanical Garden. St. Louis, MO. $500,000. Renovation and expansion of facilities.
National Audubon Society. New York, NY. $750,000. Renovation of headquarters facility.
National Wildflower Research Center. Austin, TX. $400,000. Construction of Wildflower Center.
The Nature Conservancy, Maine Chapter. Brunswick, ME. $200,000. Purchase of the Waterboro Barrens.
The Nature Conservancy, Oklahoma Field Office. Tulsa, OK. $850,000. Purchase of Barnard Ranch.
The Nature Conservancy, Great Basin Field Office. Salt Lake City, UT. $430,000. Purchase of Mayberry property to preserve biological diversity.
New England Aquarium. Boston, MA. $200,000. Purchase and equipping of marine education vessel and construction of dock.
Sciencenter. Ithaca, NY. $100,000. Renovation of administrative areas and construction of outdoor science park and addition for exhibits.
Seed Savers Exchange, Inc. Dacorah, IA. $125,000. Construction of office and seed storage facility.
Stanford University. Stanford, CA. $500,000. Toward construction of the Green Earth Sciences Building.
Wilmington Garden Center. Wilmington, DE. $100,000. Purchase, renovation, and expansion of Garden Center.
Woodland Park Zoological Society. Seattle, WA. $400,000. Construction and renovation of Tropical Rain Forest Exhibit.

Worcester County Horticultural Society. Boylston, MA. $500,000. Construction of Education and Visitors' Center at Tower Hill Botanical Garden.

*Sample grants represent either new awards or disbursements on grants awarded in previous years.

Application process. *Initial contact:* Telephone call, or arrange to meet with Foundation staff before submitting a proposal. Proposal to include:
1. Cover letter, signed by the senior administrative official, briefly describing the grant request.
2. Fact sheet (form from "Policies and Application Procedures").
3. Organizational information.
   - Brief history.
   - Description of services provided and persons served.
   - Description of major affiliations, if any.
   - Description of policy for maintaining the present physical plant.
   - List of governing board.
4. Project information.
   - Description of the project and its expected impact on the organization.
   - Effect of the completed project on the organization's budget.
   - Status of architectural plans and basis for project cost estimates.
   - Small photograph or drawing of the project, if available.
5. Fundraising information.
   - Brief description of organization's previous fundraising track record, including annual giving appeals, endowment efforts, and earlier capital campaigns.
   - Complete fundraising plan for the project. Describe your strategy to date and indicate anticipated fundraising expected during the four or five months while the proposal is under consideration. Identify which constituencies are likely to respond to a Kresge challenge grant after its approval.
   - If the project is part of a larger campaign, outline the campaign goals and priorities. Indicate what gifts and grants have been designated for each. Also, indicate how unrestricted gifts have been or will be allocated to the proposed project.
6. Attachments.
   - Most recent audited financial statement.
   - Explanation of any long-term financing (bond sales, etc.).
   - Complete copy of the most recent accreditation and/or licensure report.
   - Copy of IRS tax-exempt status determination letter and proof the organization is not a private foundation.
   - Approvals: zoning approval, purchase agreements for real estate, etc. must be in hand before submission of an application.

When to apply: Anytime, with a limit of once per institution in a 12-month period.
Materials available: Annual report, "Policies and Application Procedures."

Emphases. *Recipients:* Aquariums, botanical gardens, educational institutions (higher), museums, nonprofit organizations, research institutions, zoos.
Activities: Land acquisition.

Types of support: Capital campaigns/expenses, equipment, facilities.

Limitations. *Recipients:* Educational institutions (community colleges, primary/secondary schools), individuals, religious organizations.
Activities: Research.
Types of support: Debt retirement, endowments, operating costs.

The Lagemann Foundation
c/o Diamond, Wohl, Fried & Leonard
1775 Broadway, Suite 419
New York, New York 10019
Tel: 212–687–3939
EIN: 136115306   Type: Independent
Contact: John H. Olding, Secretary

History and philosophy. The Lagemann Foundation was established in 1944. Funding interests include the environment, religious activities, social services, and youth centers.

Officers and directors. *Officers:* Peter J. Lagemann, President; John H. Olding, Secretary; Franklin E. Parker, Treasurer.

Financial data. Data for fiscal year ended December 31, 1992. *Assets:* $1,675,232 (M). *Total grants disbursed:* $178,000.

Environmental awards. *Recent grants:* 1991 grants included support for land conservation and recreation.

Issues.   Cli   Bio   Lan   Agr   Wat   Oce   Ene   Was   Tox   Pop   Dev
                        •

Sample grants (1991).
Appalachian Mountain Club. Gorham, NH. $10,000.
The Greenwich Land Trust, Inc. Greenwich, CT. $10,000.
Natural Resources Defense Council. New York, NY. $20,000.

Application process. *Initial contact:* Letter of inquiry.
When to apply: Anytime.

Emphases. *Recipients:* Nonprofit organizations.
Geography: New York and northeastern states.

Laidlaw Foundation
950 Yonge Street, Suite 700
Toronto, Ontario M4W 2J4
Canada
Tel: 416-964-3614   Fax: 416-975-1428
EGA member
Contacts: Mr. Nathan H. Gilbert, Executive Director
            Mr. Bruce Lourie, Programme Coordinator

History and philosophy. The Laidlaw Foundation was established in 1949 with an endowment by Robert A. Laidlaw to benefit charitable, educational, and cultural organizations in Ontario. Program areas are: Children at Risk (programs and

© 1995 Environmental Data Resources, Inc.

L

scholarships), Great Lakes Conservation, Law Fellowships, and Performing Arts. The board of directors make additional discretionary awards.

Officers and directors. *Officers:* Mrs. Lyn M. Apgar, President; Mr. Nathan H. Gilbert, Secretary. *Directors:* Mrs. Lyn M. Apgar, The Honorable David Crombie, Mr. Nathan H. Gilbert, Mr. Martin Hicks, The Honorable Dr. Lorna Marsden, Mr. Walter Ross, Mr. Jeffrey Smith, Mr. Robert D. Smith, Mr. George Thomson, Professor Joyce Zemans. *Advisors:* Ms. Helen Cooper, Professor George Francis, Mr. John Jackson, Ms. Julia Langer, Ms. Margaret Wanlin.

Financial data. Data for fiscal year ended December 31, 1993. *Assets:* $38,214,133 (C) (CDN). *Total grants authorized:* $1,925,694.

Environmental awards. *Program and interests:* The goal of the Great Lakes Conservation Programme is to preserve the natural heritage by supporting activities that balance the need for preservation with economic development. Broad interests are:

- Protecting the environment to ensure that human beings can meet their basic needs for clean air, fresh water, healthy food, and sanitation.
- Maintaining the ecological processes essential to human health and well-being including ecological succession, soil regeneration and protection, recycling of nutrients, and cleansing of air and water.
- Preserving biological diversity and ecological integrity.
- Restoring the sustainability of degraded terrestrial, aquatic, and atmospheric environments.
- Making decisions that will protect the interests of future generations.

Specific activities supported by the Programme include:

- Public involvement in policy and management issues for the Great Lakes.
- Applied research that is both innovative and has public policy relevance in the Great Lakes region.
- Effective cooperative ventures to protect ecologically important near-shore and coastal zone areas or critical wetlands.
- Environmental education/information projects that organize, analyze, and communicate scientific and other knowledge pertaining to Great Lakes issues to the public in a popular format or through special events.
- Demonstration projects for sound land-management measures to reduce non-point sources of pollution while enhancing soil conservation, cleaning up degraded areas, and showing how to live and work in a more environmentally sustainable manner.
- Professional development and training assistance to NGOs in management, fundraising, and communication skills, and in media, government, and public relations.
- Projects of national significance that fall outside the Great Lakes region, but where seed funding by the Foundation would act as a catalyst. Project must have some benefit, even if indirect, to the Great Lakes basin.
- Community-based sustainable society projects, such as recycling, pesticide-free lawns, organic food production, energy-saving measures, or water conservation.

Issues. Cli Bio Lan Agr Wat Oce Ene Was Tox Pop Dev

Funding analysis.

Fiscal year:	1992*	1993
Env grants auth:	$169,910	$246,538
Number:	14	19
Range:	$4,750–$25,000	$5,000–$30,000
Median:	$11,670	$10,000
Pct $ disb (env/total):	10	14

*As reported by Foundation.

Recipients (1993 highest):	*Number:*	*Dollars:*
World Wildlife Fund Canada	1	30,000
Canadian Environmental Law Association	2	25,000
Conservation Programme Development	1	21,237
Black Creek Project	1	20,000
University of Guelph, Centre for Land and Water Stewardship	1	20,000

Activity region (1993):	*Number:*	*Dollars:*
Canada	19	246,538

Sample grants (1993).*

Canadian Institute for Environmental Law and Policy. Toronto, Ontario. $15,000. For the Canadian Environmental Law Association to develop an environmental information service for environmental NGOs. Project focus is threefold: monthly publication and distribution of CELA Library Bulletin and Environmental Periodical contents; information delivering service; and market research into subscription feasibility.

Environment North. Thunder Bay, Ontario. $5,000 (18 months). To fund a newsletter for Lake Superior activists to assist in the efforts of making Lake Superior a test case for zero discharge of persistent toxic pollutants. The newsletter will help build a Lake Superior Alliance.

Grow T.O.Gether Community Gardens. Toronto, Ontario. $5,000. A coalition of groups and individuals seeking to advocate and support environmentally sound food production in metropolitan Toronto through community gardening. Includes support for a newsletter, community networking, and organizational development.

Hike Ontario. Toronto, Ontario. $5,000. For a trail-building project organized in tandem with the British Trust for Conservation Volunteers. Volunteers from Europe and the UK spent a two-week working vacation extending a hiking trail along the north shore of Lake Superior.

Nuclear Awareness Project. Toronto, Ontario. $12,500. To produce and disseminate the 1991/92 Nuclear Hazard Report and the Nuclear Hazards in Ontario Brochure Report. Both provide the environmental community, students, academics, decisionmakers, the media, and the general public with information on hazards associated with Ontario nuclear facilities, including accidents, radioactive emissions, and radioactive waste production in 1991 and 1992.

© 1995 Environmental Data Resources, Inc.

Trinity Theatre Toronto. Toronto, Ontario. $10,000. To develop a theatre program targeted at four key conferences around the lakes (including the IJC biennial meeting) over a one-year period, and as part of a larger focused program looking at health and social issues in areas of concern in the basin.

University of Guelph, Centre for Land and Water Stewardship. Guelph, Ontario. $20,000. For Watershed Regeneration: Principles and Practice. Dr. Stewart Hilts proposes to develop a strategy and guidelines for reforestation and revegetation in the Great Lakes basin. Such a plan could enhance the effectiveness of public participation in tree planting assistance programs as part of the ecosystem perspective for revegetation and reforestation.

*Sample grants represent either new awards or disbursements on grants awarded in previous years.

Application process. *Initial contact:* Telephone call, short letter, or proposal. Full proposal (10 copies) to include:
1. Cover sheet. Include:
   - Contact person responsible for administering the application.
   - Federal charitable registration number or that of a charitable trustee with an accompanying letter giving authorization.
2. Communication plan describing how the project's results will inform local communities, policymakers, and/or other NGOs.
3. Budgets and financial data.
   - Request for specific funding.
   - Project/programme budget (revenue and expenses).
   - Organization's current operating budget.
   - Organization's financial statement (audited, if available) for the most recent fiscal period.
4. For applicants new to the Foundation: Brief history of the organization and its purposes (an annual report outlining recent programme activities is acceptable).
5. Evaluation, progress, or final reports of projects previously supported by the Foundation (if not already submitted).
6. List of directors, and their community and professional affiliations.
7. Information on the status of applications submitted to other funding sources and on a long-range financial strategy for supporting the project.

When to apply: Deadlines are the first Mondays following January 1 and July 1.
Materials available: Biennial report, "Great Lakes Conservation Programme: Application Procedures and Guidelines."

Emphases. *Recipients:* Revenue Canada-approved institution including educational institutions, nonprofit organizations, research institutions.
Activities: Advocacy, citizen participation, collaborative efforts, conferences, demonstration programs, education, feasibility studies, fieldwork, innovative programs, lobbying, networking, planning, policy analysis/development, political activities, publications, research (scientific), symposia/colloquia, workshops, youth programs.
Types of support: Multi-year grants, pilot projects, projects, travel expenses.
Geography: Great Lakes ecosystem.

Limitations. *Activities:* Audiovisual materials, conferences, land acquisition, publications.

© 1995 Environmental Data Resources, Inc.

Types of support: Annual campaigns, capital campaigns/expenses, debt retirement, equipment, facilities, fellowships, operating costs, travel expenses.

Laird, Norton Foundation
801 Second Avenue, Suite 1600
Seattle, Washington 98104–1516
Tel: 206–464–3851   Fax: 206–464–5099
EIN: 916048373   Type: Independent
EGA member
Contact: Meg Shaw, Executive Director

History and philosophy. The Foundation was established in 1940 in Winona, Minnesota by descendants of William Harris Laird, Matthew George Norton, and James Laird Norton, founders of the Laird, Norton Company. Theirs was the first of several family-owned lumber companies working originally in the Midwest, later in the Pacific Northwest. The founders' descendants operate their plants and forests on a perpetual basis. Through the Foundation, they seek to support distinctive programs in conservation and forestry education.

Officers and directors. *Officers:* Marie K. Mentor, President; Anne M. Storm, Vice President; Patrick S. deFreitas, Secretary; Andreas W. Ueland, Treasurer; Sally J. Kelley, Assistant Treasurer. *Directors:* Margie B. Berger, Mary M. Cameron, James N. Clapp, II, Elizabeth L. Helmholz, Marie K. Mentor, Gail Nettleton, Rebecca S. Richardson, Anne M. Storm, Jeffrey W. Sullivan. *Honorary Director:* Norton Clapp.

Financial data. Data for fiscal year ended March 15, 1993. *Gifts received:* $665,420. *Total grants disbursed:* $609,070.

Environmental awards. *Program and interests:* Major interests are:
- Forestry education, including tree-growing projects.
- Conservation.

Special interests include rainforest protection and the sponsorship of distinguished visitor programs in forestry and global change at various universities.

Issues. Cli Bio Lan Agr Wat Oce Ene Was Tox Pop Dev
         •   •   •   •

Funding analysis.

Fiscal year:	1991	1992*
Environmental grants disb:	$109,020	$82,500
Number:	29	12
Range:	$100–$12,000	$2,000–$15,000
Median:	$2,000	$6,875
Pct $ disb (env/total)	35	20

*As reported by Foundation.

Recipients (1992 highest):	*Number:*	*Dollars:*
Pacific Energy and Resources Center	1	15,000
Ecotrust	1	15,000
Oregon Trout	1	9,000

L

Duke University	1	8,000
Earth Action Network, Inc.	1	7,000

Activity regions (1992):	Number:	Dollars:
U.S. not specified	7	32,500
U.S. Northwest	2	24,000
U.S. West	2	18,000
U.S. Southeast	1	8,000

Sample grants (1993).*

Appalachian Trail Conference. Harpers Ferry, WV. For the mid-Atlantic season trail crew program.

Ecotrust. Portland, OR. For the Clayoquot Biosphere Project promoting and protecting biodiversity.

The Environmental Careers Organization, Inc. Seattle, WA. To implement the Minority Opportunity Program designed to encourage cultural diversity in environmental careers.

Headwaters, Inc. Ashland, OR. For the Watershed Monitoring and Conservation Program by this organization whose focus is on watershed conservation, sustainable communities, and public forest management reform.

1000 Friends of Oregon. Portland, OR. For the staff forester's work on Goal 5 Primer, a document advising Oregon residents on local forestry issues.

Sound Experience. Poulsbo, WA. For a volunteer coordinator's salary for 1993 for this organization which owns and operates the schooner, Adventuress, which provides volunteer-based education programs on Puget Sound.

Washington Center for Environmental Internships. Washington, DC. To fund two internships for students from low-income families.

*Dollar amounts not available.

Application process. *Initial contact:* Letter (2 pages) outlining proposed project, its significance, overall budget requirements, and amount requested. Full proposal, if requested, to include:
1. Completed application form.
2. IRS tax-exempt status determination letter.
4. Organization's most recent annual report.
5. Plan for follow-up evaluation if proposal is funded.

When to apply: Deadlines are in January and September or 30 days before board meetings generally held in February and October.

Materials available: Annual report (contains "Application Procedure").

Emphases. *Recipients:* Educational institutions, nonprofit organizations, zoos.

Activities: Advocacy, audiovisual materials, citizen participation, conferences, education, exhibits, innovative programs, land acquisition, media projects, planning, publications, research, seminars, symposia/colloquia, training, workshops, volunteerism.

Types of support: Equipment, facilities, internships, program-related investments, single-year grants only, technical assistance, travel expenses.

Geography: United States.

Limitations. *Recipients:* Individuals.

Activities: Activism, fundraising, lobbying, political activities.

Types of support: Annual campaigns, debt retirement, loans, multi-year grants, scholarships.

Larsen Fund, Inc.
575 Madison Avenue, Suite 1006
New York, New York 10020
EIN: 136104430   Type: Independent

Application address:
2960 Post Road, Suite 100
Southport, Connecticut 06490
Tel: 203–255–5318
Contact: Patricia S. Palmer, Grants Administrator

History and philosophy. The Larsen Fund is a charitable foundation created in 1941 by the late Roy E. Larsen, a former president and vice chairman of Time, Inc. Currently most grants are made for education. Other significant funding areas are conservation; health services; and cultural, historical, or related organizations. Over the years Harvard University, The Nature Conservancy, the United Hospital Fund of New York, New York Public Library, and the Nantucket Conservation Foundation have received the largest grants.

Officers and directors. *Officers:* Robert R. Larsen, President; Christopher Larsen, Anne Larsen Simonson, Vice Presidents; Jonathan Z. Larsen, Secretary; David L. Johnson, Treasurer. *Members:* Christopher Larsen, Jonathan Z. Larsen, Robert R. Larsen, Anne Larsen Simonson.

Financial data. Data for fiscal year ended December 31, 1992. *Assets:* $8,433,831 (M). *Total grants disbursed:* $411,065.

Environmental awards. *Recent grants:* 1992 grants included support to national, state, and local organizations for land conservation and forest-related topics.

Issues.   Cli   Bio   Lan   Agr   Wat   Oce   Ene   Was   Tox   Pop   Dev
                    •   •   •   •   •   •

Funding analysis.

Fiscal year:	1991	1992
Env grants disb:	$47,900	$24,284
Number:	6	7
Range:	$500–$25,000	$500–$7,000
Median:	$4,850	$2,500
Pct $ disb (env/total):	13	6

Recipients (1992 highest):	Number:	Dollars:
Connecticut Audubon Society	1	7,000
Defenders of Wildlife	1	5,784
Environmental Learning Center	1	4,000
Earthwatch Expeditions, Inc.	1	2,500
The River Foundation	1	2,500

Activity regions (1992):	Number:	Dollars:
U.S. Northeast	2	9,500
U.S. not specified	1	5,784
U.S. Great Lakes	2	4,500
U.S. Mid-Atlantic	1	2,500
New York/New Jersey	1	2,000

Sample grants (1992).
Connecticut Audubon Society. Greenwich, CT. $7,000.

Council on the Environment of New York City. New York, NY. $2,000.
Defenders of Wildlife. Washington, DC. $5,784.
Earthwatch Expeditions, Inc. Watertown, MA. $2,500.
Environmental Learning Center. Isabella, MN. $4,000.
Minnesota Landscape Arboretum Foundation. Chanhassen, MN. $500.
The River Foundation. Roanoke, VA. $2,500.

Application process. *Initial contact:* Letter of request and short proposal to include:
1. History of project.
2. Outline of goals to be achieved.
3. Methods.
4. Budget.
5. Schedule for implementation.

Attachments.
1. Most recent annual financial statement.
2. List of board members and current grants.
3. Copy of IRS tax-exempt status determination letter.

When to apply: Six weeks before each semiannual board meeting, held in June and December. Call for exact deadlines.
Materials available: Annual report (includes "Application Guidelines and Grant Procedure").

Emphases. *Recipients:* Educational institutions, nonprofit organizations.
Activities: Direct services, education, exhibits, fieldwork, training, workshops.
Types of support: Computer hardware, continuing support, emergency funding, equipment, fellowships, internships, multi-year grants, professorships, scholarships.
Geography: New York City; Connecticut, Massachusetts, Minnesota.

Limitations. *Recipients:* Individuals.
Activities: Audiovisual materials.
Types of support: Loans.

LaSalle Adams Fund
c/o Sonnenschein, Nath and Carlin
8000 Sears Tower
Chicago, Illinois 60606
EIN: 366054247 Type: Independent
EGA member

Application address:
c/o EDRI
1655 Elmwood Avenue, Suite 225
Rochester, New York 14620
Tel: 716-473-3090 Fax: 716-473-0968
Contact: Edith C. Stein, M.D., Secretary

History and philosophy. The Fund was established by Sydney Stein, Jr., founder of the Chicago investment firm Stein Roe and Farnham. Originally set up for contributions by firm employees, the Fund became a family foundation in 1957. Stein had diverse interests including public administration and the out-of-doors. He was a generous philanthropist during his lifetime and left much of his estate to the Fund.

The current directors intend to carry on Fund giving in the spirit of its founder. For the next few years (1995–97), funds are essentially committed for the endowment of a chair of public management at the University of Chicago's Harris School and for ongoing contributions to The Brookings Institution. Future giving will support programs in the areas of environment, population, urban problems, public policy, and education.

Officers and directors. *Officers:* Rex J. Bates, Chairman and Treasurer; Edith C. Stein, M.D., Vice President and Secretary; Ferd Kramer, Vice President.

Financial data. Data for fiscal year ended December 31, 1994. *Total grants disbursed:* $600,000.

Environmental awards. *Program and interests:* The Fund will not be making environmental grants until at least 1996.

Issues. *Cli Bio Lan Agr Wat Oce Ene Was Tox Pop Dev*

Application process. *Initial contact:* At present the Fund makes grants to pre-selected organizations only. No unsolicited applications accepted.

Emphases. *Recipients:* Pre-selected organizations only.
Activities: Advocacy, education, research.

The Lauder Foundation, Inc.
767 Fifth Avenue
New York, New York 10153
Tel: 212-572-4426 Fax: 212-572-6745
EIN: 136153743 Type: Independent
EGA member
Contact: Barbara A. Capri, Administrator

History and philosophy. The Foundation was established in 1962 by members of the Lauder family, which founded the Estee Lauder cosmetics firm. It funds the arts, education, Jewish organizations, medical research, social services, and conservation.

Officers and directors. *Officers:* Estee Lauder, President; Ronald S. Lauder, Vice President; Leonard A. Lauder, Secretary/Treasurer. *Directors:* Estee Lauder, Leonard A. Lauder, Ronald S. Lauder.

Financial data. Data for fiscal year ended November 30, 1992. *Assets:* $7,511,879 (M). *Gifts received:* $410,000. *Total grants disbursed:* $728,605.

Environmental awards. *Recent grants:* 1991 grants included support for land conservation, parks, and urban issues.

Issues. *Cli Bio Lan Agr Wat Oce Ene Was Tox Pop Dev*

L

Funding analysis.

Fiscal year:	1991
Env grants disb:	$75,075
Number:	8
Range:	$1,000–$25,000
Median:	$6,038
Pct $ disb (env/total):	11

Recipients (1991):	Number:	Dollars:
Peconic Land Trust	2	50,000
Westchester Land Trust, Inc.	1	10,000
Central Park Conservancy	1	7,075
American Friends of the Game Conservancy	1	5,000
American Friends of the Council for a Beautiful Israel	1	1,000
Council on the Environment of New York City	1	1,000
Group for the South Fork	1	1,000

Activity regions (1991):	Number:	Dollars:
New York/New Jersey	6	69,075
U.S. not specified	1	5,000
Middle East and Western Asia	1	1,000

Sample grants (1991).

American Friends of the Council for a Beautiful Israel. New York, NY. $1,000.
American Friends of the Game Conservancy. Shreveport, LA. $5,000.
Central Park Conservancy. New York, NY. $7,075.
Peconic Land Trust, Inc. Southampton, NY. $50,000.
Westchester Land Trust, Inc. Bedford Hills, NY. $10,000.

Application process. *Initial contact:* Proposal describing applicant organization and project for which funds are sought. *When to apply:* Anytime.

Emphases. *Recipients:* Nonprofit organizations.
Types of support: Annual campaigns, continuing support, general purposes.
Geography: New York City area.

Limitations. *Recipients:* Individuals.

Laurel Foundation

Three Gateway Center, 6 North
Pittsburgh, Pennsylvania 15222
Tel: 412–765–2400 Fax: 412–765–2407
EIN: 256008073 Type: Independent
Contact: Donna M. Panazzi, Program Officer

History and philosophy. The Laurel Foundation was organized in 1951 giving grants in western Pennsylvania for "smaller, more innovative, perhaps riskier groups . . . whose causes and activities do not find so ready a response elsewhere." Program areas are: Arts and Culture, Education, Environment/Animals, Health, Human Services, International, and Public/Society Benefit.

Officers and directors. *Officers:* Cordelia S. May, Chairman; Roger F. Meyer, President; Mary Kraft, Vice President. *Trustees:* Mary Kraft, Cordelia S. May, Curtis S. Scaife, Thomas M. Schmidt.

Financial data. Data for fiscal year ended December 31, 1993. *Assets:* $23,279,370 (M). *Total grants disbursed:* $980,520.

Environmental awards. *Recent grants:* Grants in 1993 included support for land conservation, species and wildlife preservation, water quality, population-environment topics, and environmental careers.

Issues. Cli Bio• Lan• Agr• Wat• Oce Ene• Was• Tox Pop• Dev

Funding analysis.

Fiscal year:	1991	1993
Env grants auth:	$140,000	$213,000
Number:	6	12
Range:	$20,000–$25,000	$1,000–$50,000
Median:	$25,000	$12,500
Pct $ disb (env/total):	14	22

Recipients (1993 highest):	Number:	Dollars:
American Farmland Trust	1	50,000
The Carnegie	1	45,000
The Student Conservation Association, Inc.	1	30,000
The Conservation Fund	1	25,000
Alliance for a Paving Moratorium	1	15,000
Group for Recycling in Pennsylvania, Inc.	1	15,000

Activity regions (1993):	Number:	Dollars:
U.S. not specified	5	117,000
U.S. Mid-Atlantic	5	86,000
International*	1	5,000
U.S. Mountain	1	5,000

*Multiple regions or not specified.

Sample grants (1993).

Alliance for a Paving Moratorium. Fredericksburg, VA. $15,000. Support for land conservation.
American Chestnut Foundation. Bennington, VT. $10,000. Support for preservation of chestnut trees.
American Farmland Trust. Washington, DC. $50,000. Support for farmland preservation.
The Carnegie. Pittsburgh, PA. $45,000. Support for Powdermill Nature Reserve.
Rachel Carson Homestead Association. Pittsburgh, PA. $11,000.
The Conservation Fund. Arlington, VA. $25,000. Support the American Freshwater Initiative.
Environmental Data Research Institute. Rochester, NY. $2,000. Support for production costs of the *Environmental Grantmaking Foundations* directory.
Group for Recycling in Pennsylvania, Inc. Pittsburgh, PA. $15,000.
Population-Environment Balance, Inc. Washington, DC. $5,000.
The Student Conservation Association, Inc. Charlestown, NH. $30,000.

University of Colorado. Boulder, CO. $5,000. Support for production of: "The Forgotten Fundamentals of Energy Crisis" and "Arithmetic, Population, & Energy."

Application process. *Initial contact:* Letter to include:
Proposal summary.
1. Outline specific purpose and amount requested.
Narrative.
1. Organization information. Include a brief description (300 words maximum) of your organization and its mission, along with a brief summary (300 words maximum) of the project, or, if the request is for unrestricted funds, of the organization's goals for the period of the requested grant.
2. Funding request. Describe key staff involved, the timetable for implementation, and the constituency or target population to be served or addressed.
3. Evaluation. Discuss expected results and evaluation criteria.
Attachments.
1. Board of directors.
2. Finances. Current operating budget and annual financial statements for the past two years.
3. Sources of support. List major contributors with amounts, and summarize the balance of your contributions.
4. Personnel. List executive staff; give the total number of paid staff.
5. Annual report (if available).
6. Copy of IRS tax-exempt status determination letter.

When to apply: Deadlines are April 15 and October 15. The board of trustees meets in June and December. Early submission is encouraged, however, as proposals received after April 1 and October 1 necessarily receive less intensive review.
Materials available: Annual report (includes "Information for Applicants").

Emphases. *Recipients:* Botanical gardens, educational institutions, museums, nonprofit organizations, zoos.
Activities: Advocacy, conferences, direct services, education, exhibits, innovative programs, land acquisition, political activities, publications, research, training, volunteerism, workshops, youth programs.
Types of support: General purposes, operating costs, pilot projects, projects.
Geography: Western Pennsylvania.

Limitations. *Recipients:* Individuals.
Types of support: Annual campaigns, leveraging funds, loans.

The Lazar Foundation

510 S.W. Third Avenue, Suite 416
Portland, Oregon 97204
Tel: 503–225–0265   Fax: 503–225–9620
E-mail: LazFdn@aol.com
EIN: 136088182   Type: Independent
EGA member
Contact: William B. Lazar, Vice President

History and philosophy. The Lazar Foundation is a family foundation established in 1956 by Jack Lazar for general philanthropic purposes. It now makes grants in the area of Environment and Population as well as other topics. Unsolicited proposals are accepted only for the Environment and Population Program and only for projects within its geographic focus on the Pacific Northwest.

Officers and directors. *Officers:* Helen B. Lazar, President; William B. Lazar, Vice President and Secretary; Jeanne Morency, Treasurer. *Directors:* Helen B. Lazar, William B. Lazar, Jeanne Morency.

Financial data. Data for fiscal year ended December 31, 1993. *Assets:* $8,100,000 (M). *Total grants authorized:* $700,182.

Environmental awards. *Program and interests:* The Environment and Population program's major interests are:

- Building, sustaining grassroots organizations and coalitions.
- Bio-regional focus.
- Ecosystem level management of natural resources.

Recent grants: 1992 grants included support for ecosystem protection, forests, water issues (water quality, river protection), coastal issues, fisheries, and toxics (pesticides, mining wastes).

Issues. Cli Bio• Lan• Agr Wat• Oce• Ene Was• Tox• Pop Dev

Funding analysis.

Fiscal year:	1991	1993
Env grants auth:	$298,200	$336,882
Number:	38	39
Range:	$1,300–$30,000	$500–$20,000
Median:	$6,400	$7,500
Pct $ auth (env/total):	43	48

Recipients (1993 highest):	Number:	Dollars:
Oregon Trout	2	27,500
Southern Environmental Law Center	1	20,000
Oregon Natural Resources Council	1	18,782
Alaska Conservation Foundation	1	15,000
Cascade Holistic Economic Consultants	1	15,000
Western Environmental Law Clinic	1	15,000

Activity regions (1993 highest):	Number:	Dollars:
U.S. Northwest	21	173,082
U.S. Mid-Atlantic	5	45,500
U.S. Mountain	4	33,000
Canada	3	26,500
U.S. not specified	2	25,000

Sample grants (1993).
Alaska Conservation Association. Anchorage, AK. $15,000. For the small grants program and the ecosystem campaigns project.
Cascade Holistic Economic Consultants. Oak Grove, OR. $15,000. For computer equipment needed to study financial and ecological information on Forest Service's databases for all national forests.

L

Coast Range Association. Newport, OR. $7,000. For the Development/Capacity Building Campaign, to hire an Area Group organizer.

Flathead Lakers. Polson, MT. $5,000. Seed money for the program to build a citizen agenda for sustaining the Flathead Ecosystem.

Idaho Rivers United. Boise, ID. $12,000. For the Save our Wild Salmon campaign.

Montana Wilderness Association. Helena, MT. $10,000. For organizing work to develop grassroots support for wildlands protection in Montana.

Save Georgia Strait Alliance. Nanaimo, BC. $10,000. For efforts to protect water quality in Georgia Strait and Puget Sound.

Washington Environmental Council. Seattle, WA. $7,000. For the heap leach gold mining campaign.

Washington Toxics Coalition. Seattle, WA. $1,800. For the Information and Education Services Project.

Application process. *Initial contact:* Request guidelines by fax if possible and provide fax number. Full proposal to include:
1. Proposal summary.
2. Organization and project descriptions.
3. Organization and project budgets.
4. List of all staff with biographies for key staff.
5. List of board of directors with short biographies.
6. IRS tax-exempt status determination letter for applicant or fiscal agent (include agreement letter from fiscal agent).
7. List of secured and pending foundation funding.

When to apply: Anytime.
Materials available: Grants list, "Environmental Application Guidelines."

Emphases. *Recipients:* Nonprofit organizations.
Activities: Activism, advocacy, capacity building, citizen participation, collaborative efforts.
Types of support: Pilot projects, projects, seed money.
Geography: Oregon, Washington, Idaho, Montana, British Columbia, and Alaska only.

Limitations. *Recipients:* Botanical gardens, individuals, museums, public agencies, religious organizations, zoos.
Activities: Audiovisual materials, exhibits, expeditions/tours, land acquisition, publications.
Types of support: Capital campaigns/expenses, debt retirement, endowments, facilities, fellowships, loans, scholarships.

The Norman Lear Foundation
1999 Avenue of the Stars
Los Angeles, California 90067
Tel: 310–553–3636
EIN: 954036197   Type: Independent
Contact: Betsy Kenny, Secretary

History and philosophy. Established in 1986 by Norman Lear, the Foundation makes grants to pre-selected organizations in the fields of health, the arts, public policy, education, Jewish welfare, women, and conservation.

Officers and directors. *Officers:* Norman Lear, President; Lyn Lear, Vice President; Betsy Kenny, Secretary; Murray Neidorf, Treasurer. *Trustees:* Betsy Kenny, Lyn Lear, Norman Lear, Murray Neidorf.

Financial data. Data for fiscal year ended November 30, 1992. *Assets:* $711,779 (M). *Total grants disbursed:* $262,357.

Environmental awards. *Recent grants:* 1992 grants included support for coastal and marine issues, and media projects.

Issues. Cli Bio Lan Agr Wat Oce Ene Was Tox Pop Dev
              •   •   •

Funding analysis.

Fiscal year:	1992
Env grants disb:	$32,500
Number:	5
Range:	$500–$25,000
Median:	$1,000
Pct $ disb (env/total):	12

Recipients (1992):	*Number:*	*Dollars:*
Environmental Media Association	1	25,000
Heal the Bay	1	5,000
Isis Fund	1	1,000
Woods Hole Oceanographic Institution	1	1,000
The Colette Chuda Environmental Foundation	1	500

Activity regions (1992):	*Number:*	*Dollars:*
U.S. West	3	30,500
U.S. Northeast	2	2,000

Sample grants (1992).
Environmental Media Association. Los Angeles, CA. $25,000.
Heal the Bay. Santa Monica, CA. $5,000.
Woods Hole Oceanographic Institute. Woods Hole, MA. $1,000.

Application process. *Initial contact:* The Foundation awards grants to pre-selected organizations only. No unsolicited applications accepted.

Emphases. *Recipients:* Pre-selected organizations only.

Limitations. *Recipients:* Individuals.

Levi Strauss Foundation
1155 Battery Street
San Francisco, California 94111
Tel: 415–544–6579
EIN: 946064702   Type: Company-sponsored
Contact: Deborah Wallace, Executive Director

History and philosophy. The Levi Strauss Foundation was incorporated in 1941. It awards grants for projects both in the United States and abroad. Program areas are: Community Partnership (Economic Development, AIDS and Disease

Prevention, Social Justice); National, Community Involvement Teams; and Headquarters Fund. Its goal is to "contribute to the well-being of the communities in which it operates by: promoting volunteerism and community service among employees as individuals and as teams, through training, consulting, and recognition of effort; making cash and non-cash contributions including grants, donations of products, technical assistance, and advocacy to nonprofit organizations; and working with others to improve the well-being of society through, minority purchasing, education services for its employees, AIDS education, and other work."

The special Emphasis Program is designed to improve economic opportunities for the disadvantaged by economically empowering individuals in need and that affect the institutions and systems that surround them. This program operates on both the local and national level.

Officers and directors. *Officers:* Robert D. Haas, President; Robert H. Dunn, Executive Vice President; Judy Belk, Thomas W. Tusher, Vice Presidents. *Directors:* Ed Alvarez, Robert Friedman, Gordon T. Geballe, Rhoda H. Goldman, Peter E. Haas, Peter E. Haas, Jr., Peter A. Jacobi, Christine H. Russell, Donna Tewart.

Financial data. Data for fiscal year ended December 31, 1993. *Assets:* $56,900,000 (M). *Gifts received:* $14,113,000. *Total grants disbursed:* $8,354,104.

Environmental awards. *Program and interests:* Environmental grants are made by CITs (Community Involvement Teams) that identify projects of interest.
Recent grants: 1993 grants included support for urban forests, parks, and gardens; a zoo; and youth education.
Issues. Cli Bio Lan Agr Wat Oce Ene Was Tox Pop Dev
         •   •   •

Funding analysis.

Fiscal year:	1993
Env grants auth:	$52,100
Number:	10
Range:	$2,800–$10,000
Median:	$4,500
Pct $ auth (env/total):	

Recipients (1993 highest):	Number:	Dollars:
Earth Share	1	10,000
Hickman County Park & Recreation Authority	1	8,300
East Bay Conservation Corps	1	5,000
San Francisco League of Urban Gardeners	1	5,000
The San Francisco Zoological Society	1	5,000

Activity regions (1993):	Number:	Dollars:
U.S. West	9	43,800
U.S. Southeast	1	8,300

Sample grants (1993).
California State Parks Foundation. San Francisco, CA. $4,000. To distribute resource directories for San Francisco Bay Area.
Earth Share. San Francisco, CA. $10,000.
East Bay Conservation Corps. Oakland, CA. $5,000. To promote youth development through community service.
Hickman County Park & Recreation Authority. Centerville, TN. $8,300. To construct a family recreation park.
Planet Drum Foundation. San Francisco, CA. $2,800. To support gardening projects in the Tenderloin and Hunters Point districts of San Francisco.
San Francisco Friends of the Urban Forest. San Francisco, CA. $4,000. To support citizen-based tree planting efforts.
San Francisco League of Urban Gardeners. San Francisco, CA. $5,000. To create a children's learning area at the Garden for the Environment.
The San Francisco Zoological Society. San Francisco, CA. $5,000.
Sempervirens Fund. Mountain View, CA. $4,000. To support parklands restoration.
Tenderloin Neighborhood Development Corporation. San Francisco, CA. $4,000. To renovate a garden space in a low-income neighborhood.

Application process. *Initial contact:* The Levi Strauss Foundation does not conduct an environmental grants program which is open to application. Grants in this area are made by CITs (Community Involvement Teams) which identify projects of interest.
Materials available: "Social Investment Guidelines," listing of U.S. and International Contributions Staff, "Contributions Report and Funding Guidelines," "Grants."

Emphases. *Recipients:* Pre-selected organizations only.
Geography: Communities where Levi Strauss & Co. has plants or customer service centers: Arkansas, California, Florida, Georgia, Kentucky, Mississippi, Nevada, New Mexico, North Carolina, Tennessee, Texas, Virginia. International grants for Asia/Pacific (Australia, Hong Kong, Japan, New Zealand, Philippines), Brazil, Canada, European countries, Mexico.

Limitations. *Recipients:* Individuals, religious organizations.
Activities: Audiovisual materials, conferences, fundraising, political activities, research.

The Max and Anna Levinson Foundation
1411 Paseo de Peralta
Santa Fe, New Mexico 87501
Tel: 505–982–3662   Fax: 505–982–3665
EIN: 236282844   Type: Independent
EGA member
Contacts: Charlotte Talberth, Executive Director
            Kristine Schell, Executive Assistant

History and philosophy. The Levinson Foundation is a small national foundation incorporated in 1956. Its concern is the "development of a more humane and rewarding society, in which people have a greater ability and opportunity to determine directions for the future." Funding is allocated equally among three categories: The Environment, Social, and Jewish/Israel. Activities funded include public education, media, community organizing, policy and analysis, litigation, and citizen action.

L

Officers and directors. *Officers:* Carl A. Levinson, President; Carol Doroshow, Treasurer. *Directors:* Donald Bean, Carol Doroshow, Helen L. Doroshow, Anna B. Levinson, Doug Levinson, Edward Levinson, Ellen L. Levinson, Gordon R. Levinson, Julian A. Levinson, Lynda B. Levinson.

Financial data. Data for fiscal year ended September 30, 1992. *Assets:* $3,600,000 (U) (est.) *Total grants authorized:* $787,000.

Environmental awards. *Program and interests:* Environmental interests include:

- Preservation of ecosystems and biological diversity.
- Alternative energy and energy efficiency.
- Conservation of natural resources.
- Toxics and public health.
- Alternative agriculture.
- Public lands policy.
- Environmental restoration.
- Indigenous peoples and their environment.
- Low income and minority communities.

Issues. Cli Bio Lan Agr Wat Oce Ene Was Tox Pop Dev

Funding analysis.

Fiscal year:	1993
Env grants disb:	$213,000
Number:	30
Range:	$3,500–$10,000
Median:	$7,500
Pct $ disb (env/total):	31

Recipients (1993 highest):	Number:	Dollars:
Reef Relief, Inc.	1	10,000
Rocky Mountain Institute	1	10,000
The Wildlands Project	1	10,000
Center for International Environmental Law	1	8,500
Arizona Rainforest Alliance	1	8,000
Environmental Law Alliance Worldwide (E–LAW)	1	8,000
Forest Guardians	1	8,000
Institute for Agriculture and Trade Policy	1	8,000
Nuclear Free America	1	8,000
Round River Conservation Studies	1	8,000
Western Environmental Law Center, Inc.	1	8,000

Activity regions (1993 highest):	Number:	Dollars:
U.S. South Central	9	60,500
U.S. not specified	4	29,000
U.S. Mountain	3	20,500
Mexico and Central America	2	16,500
Middle East and Western Asia	2	15,000
U.S. Southeast	2	15,000

Sample grants (1993).
Arizona Rainforest Alliance. Tucson, AZ. $8,000. Sierra Madre Program. To address human rights and environmental protection in the Ejidos of the Sierra Madres, Mexico.
Environmental Law Alliance Worldwide (E–LAW). Eugene, OR. $8,000. To expand electronic access to legal and scientific information to advocates in Africa and Central America.
Forest Conservation Council. Santa Fe, NM. $7,500. Technical assistance to citizens' groups to create map-based inventories and forest conservation proposals in the Southwest.
Global Coral Reef Alliance. Chappaqua, NY. $5,000. Project development in Jamaica to preserve and protect the coral reef.
Rocky Mountain Institute. Snowmass, CO. $10,000. Public education about alternative-fuel cars.
Tonantzin Land Institute. Albuquerque, NM. $7,500. General support for organizing on land, water, youth, and cultural issues among traditional peoples of the Southwest.
The Wildlands Project. Tucson, AZ. $10,000. General support to create a Conservation Biology Proposal for North America.

Application process. *Initial contact:* Write for application form, guidelines, and grants list. If the project appears to coincide with Foundation interests, submit short proposal (2–6 pages) and attachments. Proposal to discuss:

1. What is the problem or opportunity you are seeking to address; scope, significance, impact, etc.?
2. Relevant to the above problem or opportunity, what specific changes are you seeking to bring about?
3. What are the activities you wish to carry out for which you are seeking funding?
4. Why do you believe your efforts, if successful, will achieve the desired changes?
5. What criteria would you use to evaluate the extent to which you have achieved your goals?

Attachments.

1. Completed application form.
2. Budget, including expenditures and income from current and anticipated sources.
3. Relevant information about the organization and its key individuals.
4. Copy of IRS tax-exempt status determination letter.

When to apply: Grants are currently awarded every eight months, but proposals may be submitted anytime. January 10, 1995 is the deadline to submit a proposal for consideration at the March 1995 meeting. Contact the Foundation for subsequent deadlines.
Materials available: Information sheet, grants list, application form.

Emphases. *Recipients:* Nonprofit organizations, research institutions.
Activities: Activism, advocacy, citizen participation, conferences, innovative programs, litigation, planning, policy analysis/development, political activities, publications, research, training, workshops.
Types of support: General purposes, leveraging funds, operating costs, pilot projects, projects, seed money, start-up costs.
Geography: Regional programs within United States; concerning North/South relations; national and international programs.

Limitations. *Recipients:* Botanical gardens, individuals, museums, public agencies, zoos.

Activities: Exhibits, expeditions/tours, land acquisition, lobbying.
Types of support: Advertising campaigns, capital campaigns/expenses, endowments, facilities, fellowships, lectureships, multi-year grants, professorships.
Geography: The Foundation generally does not fund local projects unless there is interest from a board member.

LifeWorks Foundation
P.O. Box 50276
Nashville, Tennessee 37205
Tel: 615–269–6663   Fax: 615–329–1302
EIN: 621428468   Type: Independent
EGA member
Contact: George N. Bullard, Director

History and philosophy. Established in 1967 as the George N. Bullard Foundation, the Foundation acquired its present name in 1990. LifeWorks supports local communities through community service and grassroots activism.

Officers and directors. *Director:* George N. Bullard.

Financial data. Data for fiscal years ended December 31, 1991 and 1993. *Assets (1991):* $5,928,023 (M). *Gifts received (1991):* $330,319. *Total grants disbursed (1993):* $289,987.

Environmental awards. *Program and interests:* LifeWorks funds grassroots organizations that recognize the connection between environmental and social justice issues. It carries out its founder's belief that environmental issues should be considered within the context of the entire community: they should not be used to further the goals of a particular interest group.

The Foundation is currently developing a retreat and sanctuary 65 miles east of Nashville.

Issues.   Cli   Bio   Lan   Agr   Wat   Oce   Ene   Was   Tox   Pop   Dev
       •   •   •   •

Funding analysis.

Fiscal year:	1991	1993
Env grants disb:	$49,500	$22,650
Number:	13	9
Range:	$500–$10,000	$150–$7,000
Median:	$3,000	$500
Pct $ disb (env/total):	15	8

Recipients (1993 highest):	*Number:*	*Dollars:*
B.U.R.N.T.	1	7,000
Tennessee Environmental Council	1	6,000
Recycle! Nashville	1	5,000
Good Works, Inc.	1	2,500
Dine C.A.R.E. (Citizens Against Ruining Our Environment)	1	500
L.E.A.P.S.	1	500
Waldens Puddle	1	500
Warner Park Nature Center	1	500

Activity regions (1993):	*Number:*	*Dollars:*
U.S. Southeast	4	11,650
U.S. not specified	4	10,500
U.S. West	1	500

Sample grants (1993).
B.U.R.N.T. Nashville, TN. $7,000.
Good Works, Inc. Nashville, TN. $2,500.
L.E.A.P.S. Nashville, TN. $500.
Recycle! Nashville. Nashville, TN. $5,000.
Tennessee Environmental Council. Nashville, TN. $6,000.
Warner Park Nature Center. Nashville, TN. $500.

Application process. *Initial contact:* The Foundation awards grants to pre-selected organizations only. No unsolicited applications accepted.

Emphases. *Recipients:* Pre-selected organizations only.
Activities: Activism, advocacy.
Types of support: General purposes.
Geography: Nashville, Tennessee area.

Lilly Endowment, Inc.
P.O. Box 88068
Indianapolis, Indiana 42608
Tel: 317–924–5471   Fax: 317–926–4431
EIN: 350868122   Type: Independent
Contact: Sue Ellen Walker, Program Administrator

History and philosophy. J. K. Lilly, Sr. and his sons J. K., Jr. and Eli Lilly created the Lilly Endowment in 1937 through gifts of stock in their pharmaceutical business. By 1990 the Endowment was the third largest U.S. private foundation. Its grant philosophy centers around "the power of partnerships that money can support." In recent years, it has shifted resources from capital projects toward human needs. Most of its funding goes for projects in Indianapolis and within Indiana, but geographic emphasis varies by program area.

The Endowment has three program areas: Education, Religion, and Community Development. It is also "interested in initiatives that benefit school-age youth and that promote leadership education for nonprofit boards of trustees." The Endowment "seeks to improve charitable giving and fundraising skills to help sustain nonprofit organizations." Economic education and public policy research also receive some funding.

Officers and directors. *Officers:* Thomas M. Lofton, Chairman and President; William C. Bonifield, Craig Dykstra, Charles A. Johnson, N. Clay Robbins, Vice Presidents; William M. Goodwin, Secretary/Treasurer. *Honorary Chairman:* Thomas H. Lake. *Directors:* Otis R. Bowen, William G. Enright, Earl B. Herr, Jr., Byron P. Hollett, Thomas H. Lake, Eli Lilly II, Thomas M. Lofton, Eugene F. Ratliff, Herman B. Wells.

Financial data. Data for fiscal year ended December 31, 1993. *Assets:* $2,520,098,381 (M). *Total grants disbursed:* $132,486,302.

Environmental awards. *Recent grants:* Grants in 1992 and 1993 funded urban environment, parks, and a zoo.

L

Issues. Cli Bio Lan• Agr Wat Oce Ene Was Tox Pop Dev

Funding analysis.

Fiscal year:	1991	1993
Env grants disb:	$3,760,000	$67,600
Number:	2	2
Range:	$10,000–$3,750,000	$17,600–$50,000
Median:	$1,880,000	$33,800
Pct $ disb (env/total):	3	<1

Recipient (1993):	Number:	Dollars:
Indianapolis Department of Parks and Recreation	2	67,600

Activity region (1993):	Number:	Dollars:
U.S. Great Lakes	2	67,600

Sample grants (1992–93).

Indianapolis Department of Parks and Recreation. Indianapolis, IN. $17,600. Development of a master plan for Tarkington Park.

James Bell Associates. Arlington, VA. $39,890. External review of the Center for Urban Policy and the Environment at Indiana University–Purdue University, Indianapolis.

Application process. *Initial contact:* Brief preliminary letter (2 pages maximum) describing:
1. Applicant organization.
2. Proposed project.
3. The amount required from the Endowment.

The Endowment may request a full proposal to include:
1. Copy of IRS tax-exempt status determination letter.
2. Description of background and qualifications to carry out proposed project.
3. Needs statement.
4. Project timetable
5. Evaluation criteria.
6. Proposed budget (listing additional sources of income).

When to apply: Preliminary requests are appropriate at any time. The executive committee meets in March, May, July, October, and December. The full board of directors meets in February, April, June, September, and November.
Materials available: Annual report (includes "Guidelines & Procedures"), "Grantmaking Portfolio."

Emphases. *Activities:* Conferences, research, seminars.
Types of support: Continuing support, fellowships, general purposes, matching funds, multi-year grants (2–3 years), operating costs, scholarships, seed money.
Geography: Indianapolis and Marion County, Indiana; Indiana.

Limitations. *Recipients:* Individuals, libraries (except in Marion County, Indiana).
Activities: Audiovisual materials, research (medical).
Types of support: Endowments, facilities (construction), loans, operating costs, professorships.

Lintilhac Foundation
100 Harbor Road
Shelbourne, Vermont 05482
Tel: 802–985–4106   Fax: 802–985–3725
EIN: 510176851   Type: Independent
Contact: Nancy R. Brink, Administrative Assistant

History and philosophy. Lintilhac is a family foundation, established in 1975 by Claire Lintilhac, once a travelling nurse in China, in order to create a nurse-midwifery program at the Medical Center Hospital of Vermont. Its objectives were restated in 1989 as follows: "To further natural science, teaching and research at qualified educational institutions, especially but not limited to the University of Vermont; to foster and maintain the midwifery program at the Medical Center Hospital of Vermont; to assist educational institutions and activities with an emphasis on such activities in Vermont; and to [assist] civic groups, associations, or communities, or to provide civic benefits and improvements within the state of Vermont." Most projects are identified by the directors, who work with organizations in north central Vermont to develop programs that meet community needs.

Officers and directors. *Officers:* Crea S. Lintilhac, President; Philip M. Lintilhac, Vice President and Secretary; Raeman P. Sopher, Treasurer. *Directors:* Crea S. Lintilhac, Philip M. Lintilhac, Raeman P. Sopher.

Financial data. Data for fiscal year ended December 31, 1993. *Assets:* $8,900,000 (M) (est.). *Total grants disbursed:* $420,436.

Environmental awards. *Program and interests:* The Foundation restricts its major grants to a few flagship projects, spreading the remainder of the funds over a number of smaller projects. Two special interests are Lake Champlain and Shelbourne Farms.
Recent grants: 1993 grants included support for land conservation, ecosystem monitoring, and environmental education (public schools, higher) in Vermont.

Issues. Cli• Bio• Lan• Agr• Wat• Oce Ene Was• Tox Pop Dev

Funding analysis.

Fiscal year:	1992	1993
Env grants auth:	$23,091	$118,100
Number:	7	8
Range:	$500–$16,591	$300–$100,000
Median:	$1,000	$1,000
Pct $ disb (env/total):	4	17

Recipients (1993 highest):	Number:	Dollars:
Shelburne Farms Resources, Inc.	2	105,000
University of Vermont, School of Natural Resources	1	9,800
The Nature Conservancy, Vermont Field Office	1	1,000
Vermont Institute of Natural Science	1	1,000
Vermont Natural Resources Council, Inc.	1	500
Vermont Youth Conservation Corps	1	500

Activity region (1993):	Number:	Dollars:
U.S. Northeast	8	118,100

Sample grants (1993).
George D. Aiken Resource Conservation and Development Area. Randolph, VT. $300. To support the Vermont Sludge Management Conference.
The Nature Conservancy, Vermont Field Office. Montpelier, VT. $1,000. General support.
Shelburne Farms Resources, Inc. Shelburne, VT. $5,000. For the Sustainable Agriculture Demonstration Project.
University of Vermont, School of Natural Resources. Burlington, VT. $9,800. Continuing support for the Lake Champlain Biological Monitoring Program which monitors and assesses the status of the Lake Champlain ecosystem.
Vermont Institute of Natural Science. Woodstock, VT. $1,000. For the ELF Program, a statewide environmental education program for elementary school students.
Vermont Natural Resource Council, Inc. Montpelier, VT. $500. General support.
Vermont Youth Conservation Corps. Waterbury, VT. $500. To support this statewide education, conservation, and service organization.

Application process. *Initial contact:* Full proposal.
When to apply: Anytime.
Materials available: Biennial report (includes "Guidelines").

Emphases. *Recipients:* Educational institutions (higher), nonprofit organizations.
Activities: Education, innovative programs, land acquisition, research, seminars, training, workshops.
Types of support: Annual campaigns, capital campaigns/expenses, endowments, equipment, facilities, fellowships, lectureships, matching funds, professorships, scholarships, seed money.
Geography: Projects in north central Vermont, including Chittenden, Lamoille, and Washington counties.

Limitations. *Recipients:* Individuals.
Types of support: Emergency funding.

The Little Family Foundation
33 Broad Street, 10th Floor
Boston, Massachusetts 02109
Tel: 617–723–6771 Fax: 617–723–7107
EIN: 056016740   Type: Independent
Contact: Arthur D. Little, Trustee

History and philosophy. The Foundation was established in 1946 by Royal Little, founder of Textron, Inc., the textile manufacturing company. The Foundation's primary interest is in education, but it also supports the arts and conservation organizations.

Officers and directors. *Trustees:* Augusta Willoughby Little Bishop, E. Janice Leeming, Arthur D. Little, Cameron R. Little, The Boston Company.

Financial data. Data for fiscal years ended December 31, 1992 and 1993. *Assets (1992):* $13,686,857 (M). *Total grants disbursed (1993):* $1,261,330.

Environmental awards. *Recent grants:* 1993 grants included support for wildlife conservation, raptors, and coastal and marine issues.

Issues.   Cli   Bio   Lan   Agr   Wat   Oce   Ene   Was   Tox   Pop   Dev
               •   •   •   •

Funding analysis.

Fiscal year:	1992
Env grants disb:	$131,250
Number:	10
Range:	$1,000–$50,000
Median:	$4,000
Pct $ disb (env/total):	10

Recipients (1992 highest):	Number:	Dollars:
Oregon Coast Aquarium	1	50,000
The Nature Conservancy, Rhode Island Field Office	1	40,000
Woodlands Park Zoo	1	17,500
Conservation International	1	10,000
Peregrine Fund	1	6,000

Activity regions (1992):	Number:	Dollars:
U.S. Northwest	4	75,500
U.S. Northeast	4	43,750
International*	2	12,000

*Multiple regions or not specified.

Sample grants (1993).
Conservation International. Washington, DC. $5,000.
Ecotrust. Portland, OR. $5,000.
NYZS/The Wildlife Conservation Society. Bronx, NY. $1,000.
Oregon Coast Aquarium. Newport, OR. $25,000.
Peregrine Fund. Boise, ID. $3,000.

Application process. *Initial contact:* Written request to include:
1. Reason for proposal.
2. Amount needed.
3. Plan for use of funds.
4. History and description of applicant organization.
5. Copy of IRS tax-exempt status determination letter.

When to apply: Anytime. The board meets quarterly.
Materials available: Application guidelines.

Emphases. *Recipients:* Educational institutions, museums, nonprofit organizations, zoos.
Activities: Education, exhibits, youth programs.
Types of support: Annual campaigns, continuing support.
Geography: New England, especially Massachusetts and Rhode Island; the Pacific Northwest, especially Washington and Oregon.

Limitations. *Recipients:* Individuals.
Activities: Land acquisition.
Types of support: Debt retirement, loans, seed money.

L

Longwood Foundation, Inc.
1004 Wilmington Trust Center
Wilmington, Delaware 19801
Tel: 302-654-2477   Fax: 302-654-2323
EIN: 510066734   Type: Independent
Contact: David D. Wakefield, Executive Secretary

History and philosophy. Pierre Samuel duPont established the Longwood Foundation in 1937. It is the major benefactor of Longwood Gardens, located on the donor's estate, one of the most extensive public gardens in the country. The Foundation supports efforts in conservation, education, hospitals, and social service agencies in the Greater Wilmington area.

Officers and directors. *Officers:* H. Rodney Sharp, III, President; Edward B. duPont, Vice President; Irene duPont May, Secretary; Henry H. Silliman, Jr., Treasurer. *Trustees:* Gerret van S. Copeland, David L. Craven, Edward B. duPont, Pierre S. duPont, IV, Irene duPont May, H. Rodney Sharp, III, Henry H. Silliman, Jr.

Financial data. Data for fiscal year ended September 30, 1993. *Assets:* $458,381,428 (M). *Total grants disbursed:* $15,749,985.

Environmental awards. *Recent grants:* 1993 grants included support for land conservation, water quality, coastal issues, and horticulture.

Issues. Cli Bio Lan Agr Wat Oce Ene Was Tox Pop Dev
           •   •   •   •

Funding analysis.

Fiscal year:	1992*	1993**
Env grants disb:	$1,086,100	$113,500
Number:	8	4
Range:	$2,500–$500,000	$2,500–$50,000
Median:	$76,800	$28,375
Pct $ disb (env/total):	5	1

*As reported by EDRI
**As reported by Foundation.

Recipients (1993):	Number:	Dollars:
Delaware Nature Society	1	50,000
Stroud Water Research Center	1	40,000
SHORE Foundation	1	21,000
National Junior Horticulture Foundation	1	2,500

Activity regions (1993):	Number:	Dollars:
U.S. Mid-Atlantic	3	111,000
U.S. not specified	1	2,500

Sample grants (1993).
Delaware Nature Society. Hockessin, DE. $50,000.
National Junior Achievement Horticulture Foundation. Fremont, MI. $2,500.
SHORE Foundation. North East, MD. $21,000.
Stroud Water Research Center. Avondale, PA. $40,000.

Application process. *Initial contact:* Letter (2 pages) describing grant purpose and need, pertinent financial statements, copy of IRS tax-exempt status determination letter.
When to apply: Deadlines are April 1 and October 1. The board meets in May and November.

Emphases. *Recipients:* Botanical gardens, libraries, museums.
Activities: Research.
Types of support: Capital campaigns/expenses, challenge grants, endowments, fellowships, general purposes.
Geography: Delaware and the Greater Wilmington area only.

Limitations. *Recipients:* Individuals.
Activities: Fundraising.

Richard Lounsbery Foundation, Inc.
159A East 61st Street
New York, New York 10021
Tel: 212-319-7033
EIN: 136081860   Type: Independent
Contact: Martha Norman, Principal Manager,
           Executive Director

History and philosophy. The Foundation was established in 1959 by the Richard Lounsbery Foundation Trust, Inc. It awards grants for: the arts, biomedical research, conservation and the environment, education (especially science and mathematics at the secondary and elementary levels), French cultural programs, human rights, and youth programs.

Officers and directors. *Officer:* Alan F. McHenry, President. *Directors:* Benjamin F. Bordon, William J. McGill, Alan F. McHenry, Dr. Frederick Seitz.

Financial data. Data for fiscal year ended December 31, 1992. *Assets:* $19,597,292 (M). *Gifts received:* $752,808. *Total grants disbursed:* $1,400,756.

Environmental awards. *Recent grants:* 1992 grants included support for parks, marine issues, outdoor expeditions, and botanical gardens.

Issues. Cli Bio Lan Agr Wat Oce Ene Was Tox Pop Dev
           •   •   •   •

Funding analysis.

Fiscal year:	1990	1992
Env grants disb:	$179,500	$43,700
Number:	15	7
Range:	$150–$30,000	$150–$25,000
Median:	$5,000	$2,500
Pct $ disb (env/total):	10	3

Recipients (1992 highest):	Number:	Dollars:
Earthwatch Expeditions, Inc.	1	25,000
Missouri Botanical Garden	1	10,000
The New York Botanical Garden	1	5,000

The Horticultural Society of New York	1	2,500
Central Park Conservancy	1	800

Activity regions (1992):	Number:	Dollars:
U.S. Northeast	2	25,250
U.S. Midwest	1	10,000
New York/New Jersey	4	8,450

Sample grants (1992).
Central Park Conservancy. New York, NY. $800.
Earthwatch Expeditions, Inc. Watertown, MA. $25,000.
Hudson River Sloop Clearwater, Inc. New York, NY. $2,000.
Missouri Botanical Garden. St. Louis, MO. $10,000.
The New York Botanical Garden. Bronx, NY. $5,000.
Woods Hole Oceanographic Institution. Woods Hole, MA. $250.

Application process. *Initial contact:* Proposal to include:
1. Statement of proposed need.
2. Description of project.
3. Amount of funds required.
4. Budget justifying the amount requested.

A copy of IRS tax-exempt status determination letter and other relevant exhibits should accompany the application.

When to apply: Deadlines are February 15, May 15, August 15, and November 15 for consideration at board meetings held in April, July, October, and January.

Emphases. *Recipients:* Pre-selected organizations.
Types of support: Fellowships, matching funds, seed money.

Limitations. *Recipients:* Individuals.
Activities: Conferences, seminars.
Types of support: Endowments, facilities, loans.

Luster Family Foundation, Inc.

6517 Dry Creek Road
Napa, California 94558
Tel: 707-944-8510
EIN: 954100318   Type: Independent
Contact: Elizabeth Luster, President

History and philosophy. The Foundation was established in 1987 by Elizabeth Luster. Its major areas of concern are animal welfare and conservation, child development, the environment, libraries, and medical research.

Officers and directors. *Officers:* Elizabeth Luster, President; Andrew Luster, Vice President and CFO; Amy Luster, Secretary. *Directors:* Shevy Healy, Amy Luster, Andrew Luster, Elizabeth Luster, Max Factor III.

Financial data. Data for fiscal year ended December 31, 1992. *Assets:* $6,691,304 (M). *Gifts received:* $417,785. *Total grants disbursed:* $73,804.

Environmental awards. *Program and interests:* Major foci are wildlife conservation and animal welfare. The Foundation also acquires and maintains properties used as wildlife refuge.
Recent grants: 1992 grants supported for wildlife conservation.

Issues. Cli Bio Lan Agr Wat Oce Ene Was Tox Pop Dev
          •   •   •   •

Funding analysis.

Fiscal year:	1990	1992
Env grants disb:	$47,000	$20,500
Number:	35	22
Range:	$500–$13,000	$500–$1,500
Median:	$1,000	$1,000
Pct $ disb (env/total):	27	28

Recipients (1992 highest):	Number:	Dollars:
African Wildlife Protection Trust	1	1,500
International Primate Protection League	1	1,500
Center for Marine Conservation	1	1,000
The Cousteau Society	1	1,000
Defenders of Wildlife	1	1,000
Forests Forever	1	1,000
Greenpeace USA	1	1,000
International Wildlife Coalition	1	1,000
Marine Mammal Center	1	1,000
Natural Resources Defense Council	1	1,000
NYZS/The Wildlife Conservation Society	1	1,000
Pacific Environmental Education Center	1	1,000
Primarily Primates	1	1,000
Sanctuary Forest	1	1,000
The Nature Conservancy, California Field Office	1	1,000
The Wilderness Society	1	1,000
World Resources Institute	1	1,000

Activity regions (1992):	Number:	Dollars:
U.S. West	12	9,500
U.S. not specified	4	4,000
Africa	1	1,500
U.S. Southeast	1	1,500
International*	1	1,000
New York/New Jersey	1	1,000
U.S. Northeast	1	1,000
U.S. South Central	1	1,000

*Multiple regions or not specified.

Sample grants (1992).
African Wildlife Protection Trust. Hanover, NH. $1,500.
California Nature Conservancy. Sausalito, CA. $1,000.
Center for Marine Conservation. San Francisco, CA. $1,000.
East Bay Conservation Corps. Oakland, CA. $500.
International Primate Protection League. Summerville, SC. $1,500.

L

The Wilderness Society. Washington, DC. $1,000.
World Resources Institute. Washington, DC. $1,000.

Application process. *Initial contact:* The Foundation awards grants to pre-selected organizations only. No unsolicited applications accepted.

Emphases. *Recipients:* Pre-selected organizations only.

Limitations. *Recipients:* Individuals.

Lyndhurst Foundation
Tallan Building, Suite 701
100 West Martin Luther King Boulevard
Chattanooga, Tennessee 37402–2561
Tel: 615–756–0767   Fax: 615–756–0770
EIN: 626044177   Type: Independent
EGA member
Contact: Benic M. Clark III, Associate

History and philosophy. The Lyndhurst Foundation had its beginnings in the establishment of the Memorial Welfare Foundation in 1938 by Thomas Carter Lupton, a pioneer in the Coca-Cola bottling business. For the first forty years, the Foundation divided its interests between charitable activities in Mr. Lupton's home town of Chattanooga and support for churches, colleges, and other charitable organizations located throughout the Southeast. Upon Mr. Lupton's death in 1977, the Foundation changed its name to Lyndhurst, a reference to the family home in Chattanooga, and revised its approach to philanthropy to emphasize regional initiatives in the fields of primary health care, the arts, and elementary and secondary education.

In the mid–1980s, the Foundation began to focus its attention almost exclusively on Chattanooga and its effort to revitalize its downtown and riverfront, enhance its arts and cultural life, and to improve its schools and natural environment.

In 1992, stimulated by the completion of a major phase in Chattanooga's redevelopment and a change in the Foundation board, Lyndhurst once again enlarged its focus. Although the Foundation continues to give special consideration to certain developments in Chattanooga, it now more actively considers initiatives in and requests from other areas of the South.

Officers and directors. *Officers:* Alice L. Montague, Chairman; Jack Murrah, President; Allen L. McCallie, Secretary; Charles B. Chitty, Treasurer. *Trustees:* Nelson Campbell, Robert Coles, Kate L. Crosland, George R. Fontaine, Jack Fontaine, Margaret L. Gerber, Alice L. Montague, Jack Murrah.

Financial data. Data for fiscal year ended December 31, 1993. *Assets:* $154,517,069 (M). *Total grants disbursed:* $7,948,821.

Environmental awards. *Program and interests:* Interests are:
- Growth management.
- Energy conservation.
- Forest and river protection.
- Biodiversity.
- Innovative urban projects.

All are pursued in the southeastern United States, with a special emphasis on the Southern Appalachian Highlands.

Issues. Cli Bio Lan Agr Wat Oce Ene Was Tox Pop Dev

Funding analysis.

Fiscal year:	1991	1993
Env grants disb:	$1,179,250	$858,000
Number:	25	26
Range:	$1,500–$625,000	$1,000–$100,000
Median:	$20,000	$30,000
Pct $ disb (env/total):	65	11

Recipients (1993 highest):	Number:	Dollars:
Southern Environmental Law Center	1	100,000
Tennessee Conservation League	1	64,000
Chattanooga Chamber Foundation	1	60,000
Alaska Conservation Foundation	1	50,000
American Chestnut Foundation	1	50,000
American Institute of Architects	1	50,000
North Carolina Environmental Defense Fund	1	50,000
Western North Carolina Tomorrow	1	50,000

Activity regions (1993):	Number:	Dollars:
U.S. Southeast	21	702,000
U.S. not specified	4	106,000
Alaska	1	50,000

Sample grants (1993).*

American Institute of Architects. Washington, DC. $50,000. To help further educate architects, engineers, builders, and related professionals about environmental design, the AIA's Center for the Environment has developed "Building Connections"–a program aimed at encouraging industry professionals to maintain environmental integrity and to use resources economically, responsibly, and intelligently. This grant provided partial support for the three-part series, which addresses the main themes of resource use, healthy buildings and materials, and urban ecology.

Cahaba River Society. Birmingham, AL. $25,000. Third year of support to the Society, founded in 1986 to protect this unique southern river through an active program in conservation, education, and recreation.

Georgia Citizens Fund. Decatur, GA. $25,000. Support for the Georgia Transportation Alliance, a project of the Fund, established to promote an alternative approach to transportation policy for Georgia and the region to counter the historical bias toward single occupancy automobiles and endless road construction.

Institute for Southern Studies. Durham, NC. $25,000. To enable the Institute to update and expand The Green Index: A State-by-State Guide to the Nation's Environmental Health."

Southern Environmental Law Center. Charlottesville, VA. $100,000. To assist SELC, a leading legal advocacy group for the protection of the natural resources and beauty of the Southeast, expand its services, and broaden its outreach and effectiveness.

Tennessee Environmental Council. Nashville, TN. $5,000. To enable the Council to engage in a long-range strategic planning process in its efforts to educate and advocate for the protection of public health and the environment in Tennessee.

Western North Carolina Alliance. Asheville, NC. $30,000. For this organization, which melds broad-based community organizing and education with sound ecological science to promote conservation and protection for the communities, forests, and waters of the North Carolina mountains. This grant is for expansion of WNCA's land-use planning project in the towns of Franklin and Highlands.

*Sample grants represent either new awards or disbursements on grants awarded in previous years.

Application process. *Initial contact:* Letter (3 pages maximum) describing the project and also including:
1. Description of sponsoring organization.
2. List of board of directors and staff.
3. Copy of organization's annual budget (both income and expenditure).
4. Estimated project budget with line items.
5. Copy of IRS tax-exempt status determination letter.

The staff requests interviews with some applicants.
When to apply: Deadlines are at the end of December, March, June, and September for consideration in February, May, August, and November, respectively. Contact Foundation for exact dates.
Materials available: Annual report, application guidelines.

Emphases. *Recipients:* Nonprofit organizations.
Types of support: General purposes, leveraging funds, matching funds, operating costs, pilot projects, seed money.
Geography: Southern Appalachian Highlands (environmental projects); six state area of the Southeast: Tennessee, Georgia, Alabama, North Carolina, South Carolina, Mississippi; Chattanooga, Tennessee.

Limitations. *Recipients:* Educational institutions, individuals (except for a limited number of awards at the initiative of the Foundation), religious organizations.
Activities: Research.
Types of support: Capital campaigns/expenses, debt retirement, endowments, equipment, mortgage reduction, scholarships, travel expenses.
Geography: Outside the Southeast.

The John D. and Catherine T. MacArthur Foundation

140 South Dearborn Street, Suite 1100
Chicago, Illinois 60603–5285
Tel: 312–726–8000   Fax: 312–917–0334
EIN: 237093598   Type: Independent
EGA member
Contacts: Dan M. Martin, Director, World Environment and Resources Program
Michael B. Jenkins, Associate Director

History and philosophy. The John D. and Catherine T. MacArthur Foundation was created in 1978 by John D. MacArthur (1897–1978) who owned an array of businesses—principally Bankers Life and Casualty Company—as well as property in Florida and New York.

"The Foundation has developed a limited number of programs in areas where it believes a focused philanthropic effort can make an important contribution." The Foundation seeks to be an active rather than a reactive force. Typically, it develops a philanthropic objective and then identifies the institutions and individuals that can best carry out program goals. In general, it aims "to encourage disparate disciplines to communicate and support people and organizations who are framing issues in a new way."

The Foundation currently has eight program areas: The Community Initiatives Program, The Education Program, The General Program (media projects and special initiatives), The Health Program, The MacArthur Fellows Program, The Program on Peace and International Cooperation, The Population Program, and The World Environment and Resources Program.

Officers and directors. *Officers:* Elizabeth J. McCormack, Chairman; Adele Simmons, President; Victor Rabinowitch, Senior Vice President; Lawrence L. Landry, Vice President and CFO; Woodward A. Wickham, Vice President for Public Affairs and Director of the General Program; Rebecca Reilly, Vice President for Chicago Affairs and Director, The Community Initiatives Program; Philip M. Grace, Treasurer; James T. Griffin, General Counsel and Assistant Secretary; David S. Chernoff, Associate General Counsel and Assistant Secretary. *Directors:* John E. Corbally, Robert E. Ewing, William H. Foege, James M. Furman, Murray Gell-Mann, Alan M. Hallene, Paul Harvey, John P. Holdren, Shirley Mount Hufstedler, Sara Lawrence Lightfoot, Margaret E. Mahoney, Elizabeth J. McCormack, George A. Ranney, Jr., Jonas Salk, M.D., Adele Simmons, Jerome B. Wiesner.

Financial data. Data for fiscal year ended December 31, 1993. *Assets:* $3,098,244,000 (M). *Total grants authorized:* $135,106,000. *Total grants disbursed:* $15,575,500.

Environmental awards. *Program and interests:* In 1988 the World Environment and Resources Program initiated a strategy to fund projects serving a limited number of geographic areas where biodiversity is maximal and danger of species extinction highest. Activities supported by the program include:

- Conservation science and policy studies including biological inventories, biogeography, and ecological research.

- Conservation action and education to foster the protection of biodiversity in the tropics.

- Conservation and sustainable economic development programs to promote sustainable management of natural resources combined with improving living standards in areas of high conservation value.

Because the conservation of biological diversity is the first objective of the World Environment Program, grants are frequently organized within specific biogeographic zones receiving high global priority ratings. A panel of consultants assists the Foundation in identifying these zones and in ranking them according to two criteria: the richness of species diversity and the threat of mass extinction within each area. The resulting rank order largely determines the sequence in which the Foundation organizes grantmaking initiatives in these "hotspots," the world's most urgent sites for conservation action.

M

Global Priority Areas:
1. Tropical Andes (eastern slopes from western Venezuela to central Bolivia, Pacific slopes in Colombia and northwestern Ecuador);
2. Atlantic Forest of Brazil;
3. Madagascar;
4. Philippine archipelago;
5. Malaysia (both insular and peninsular);
6. Eastern Himalayas (eastern Nepal to southwestern China, Western Ghats in India and Sinharaja Forest in Sri Lanka);
7. Indonesia;
8. New Caledonia and Melanesia;
9. Maya Forest (southern Mexico, northern Guatemala and Belize);
10. Western Ghats in India and Sinharaja Forest in Sri Lanka;
11. Eastern Arc Mountains of Tanzania;
12. Rift lakes of East Africa.

The Program will also consider supporting appropriate actions in areas of high diversity and less immediate endangerment, including: the Guiana Highlands of South America, New Guinea, and the Central African Forest.

Independent of the global priority list, the Program also conducts a continuing U.S. Tropical Initiative, begun in 1987 and supplemented annually. In this category, it supports actions described in the guidelines in or directly related to the tropical elements of the United States: Hawaii, Micronesia, the Florida Keys, Puerto Rico and the U.S. Virgin Islands. In 1988, before we began the "hotspots" approach, the Program also mounted a special initiative in the insular Caribbean.

Other categories in which the Program has been active include conservation science, sustainable development policy, environmental economics, and environmental law. These themes are elaborated on in the guidelines. Grants of this type can support actions with a broader geographic scope than the global priority areas. The Program also supports conservation media programs (publishing, exhibitions, films, and broadcasts) linked to the global priority initiatives.

Issues. Cli Bio Lan Agr Wat Oce Ene Was Tox Pop Dev

Funding analysis.§

Fiscal year:	1991	1993
Env grants auth:	$38,139,227	$36,547,235
Number:	199	171
Range:	$5,000–$10,000,000	$215–$13,500,000
Median:	$95,000	$100,000
Pct $ auth (env/total):	30	27

Recipients (1993 highest):	Number:	Dollars:
The Energy Foundation	1	13,500,000
Aspen Institute	1	1,200,000
World Wildlife Fund	6	890,000
Environmental Defense Fund	1	800,000
Non-Timber Forest Products Network	1	760,000

Activity regions (1993 highest):	Number:	Dollars:
U.S. not specified	13	15,234,500
Southeast Asia	28	3,666,000
International*	16	3,458,000
Andean Region and Southern Cone	16	3,331,000
Northern South America	7	1,940,000

*Multiple regions or not specified.

§Includes a number of environmental grants made outside of the World Environment and Resources Program.

Sample grants (1993).

Academy of Natural Sciences of Philadelphia. Philadelphia, PA. $210,000. To support the completion of research and development for an information service on commercially useful tropical tree species. The database will be marketed to architects, designers, builders, and other users of tropical hard woods.

Asian Wetland Bureau. Kuala Lumpur, Malaysia. $140,000 (3 years). In renewed support of wetland conservation programs including the formation of a global network for wetland conservation, public education programs, and small grants to support other institutions working on wetland biodiversity conservation in Malaysia and neighboring countries.

Association of Systematics Collections. Washington, DC. $180,000 (3 years). To support exchanges between Cuban and North American institutions of museum and herbarium collections and research materials.

Beijer International Institute of Ecological Economics. Stockholm, Sweden. $290,000 (2 years). To support the development of an interdisciplinary research program on the relationship of property rights to the performance of natural resource systems.

Chicago Collaborative Training Project. Chicago, IL. $435,000 (3 years) To support a new collaborative program among the Chicago Zoological Society, the Field Museum of Natural History, and the University of Illinois at Chicago that will offer advanced training in conservation biology for scientists and managers from tropical countries.

International Council of Scientific Unions. Paris, France. $190,000 (2 years). In support of the Scientific Committee for Problems of the Environment (SCOPE) program to assess the impact of species diversity on maintaining ecosystems.

Non-Timber Forest Products Network. Candela Peru, Lima, Peru; *Conservation International.* Washington, DC; *Fundacion de Capacitación e Investigación para el Desarrolo Socio-Ambiental.* Quito, Ecuador; *Fundación Inguedé para la Conservación del Trópico.* Bogota, Colombia. $760,000 (5 years). To support the establishment of a regional network developing economic alternatives to deforestation and bringing these activities to a commercial scale. National NGOs in Colombia, Ecuador, and Peru will focus on non-timber forest products, seeking to provide improved incomes to local populations while demonstrating the value of standing forests. Conservation International will provide the necessary technical assistance, facilitate access to international markets, and coordinate the exchange of information with group members.

Universidad Metropolitana. Rio Piedras, Puerto Rico. $225,000 (3 years). In renewed support of the teacher training and curriculum development programs of the University's Institute of Environmental Education.

Women's Environment and Development Organization. New York, NY. $300,000 (2 years). In support of policy and advocacy activities at the United Nations and for community organizing and education to raise awareness of gender and environment issues.

Application process. *Initial contact:* Letter of inquiry (2–3 pages) stating the problem, its relevance to the Program's interests, the proposed solution, funding requirements, and the applicant organization's identity and qualifications. The Foundation will request a formal proposal from applicants whose letters present a strong case for support from the Program. Do not submit a full proposal unless requested.
When to apply: Anytime. Deadline for letter of inquiry is at least four months before the board meeting. Call for specific dates.
Materials available: Annual report, "Programs and Policies," "Guidelines and Supplement to the Guidelines of the World Environment and Resource Program," *Update Memo: World Environmental and Resources Program* (newsletter).

Emphases. *Recipients:* Aquariums, botanical gardens, educational institutions, museums, nonprofit organizations, public agencies, research institutions, zoos.
Activities: Citizen participation, collaborative efforts, demonstration programs, education, policy analysis/development, research, technical assistance, training.
Types of support: Fellowships, leveraging funds, multi-year grants, operating costs, scholarships.
Geography: Areas of global priority for biodiversity as described in the guidelines. Current foci include: Indonesia, Papua New Guinea, Melanesia, southern Mexico, northern Guatemala and Belize, Atlantic Coastal Forest in Brazil, Philippines and Malaysia, Tropical Andes, Eastern Himalayas, Madagascar, Insular Caribbean, and U.S. Tropics.

Limitations. For limitations of the World Environment and Resources Program, refer to the guidelines. As a general policy, the Foundation does not fund:
Recipients: Individuals.
Activities: Conferences, political activities, lobbying, publications.
Types of support: Capital campaigns/expenses, endowments.

James A. Macdonald Foundation

One North Broadway
White Plains, New York 10601–2304
Tel: 914–428–9305
EIN: 136199690   Type: Independent
Contact: Walter J. Handelman, Vice President

History and philosophy. The James A. Macdonald Foundation was established in 1966 by Flora Macdonald Bonney. It supports Protestant giving, secondary education, community funds, hospitals, youth activities, and historic preservation.

Officers and directors. *Officers:* Alice H. Model, President; Walter J. Handelman, Vice President and Secretary; Alan L. Model, Treasurer. *Directors:* Walter J. Handelman, Alan L. Model, Alice H. Model.

Financial data. Data for fiscal year ended December 31, 1993.
Assets: $6,177,721 (M). *Total grants disbursed:* $382,800.

Environmental awards. *Recent grants:* 1993 grants included support for land conservation, parks, forests, watershed protection, wildlife, and beautification.

Issues. Cli **Bio** **Lan** **Agr** **Wat** Oce Ene Was Tox Pop Dev

Funding analysis.

Fiscal year:	1992
Env grants disb:	$12,750
Number:	18
Range:	$300–$1,300
Median:	$800
Pct $ disb (env/total):	3

Recipients (1992 highest):	Number:	Dollars:
The Nature Conservancy, Headquarters	1	1,300
The New York Botanical Garden	1	1,200
NYZS/The Wildlife Conservation Society	1	1,000
World Wildlife Fund	1	950
Mianus Gorge Preserve, Inc.	1	900
National Parks and Conservation Association	1	900
National Wildlife Federation	1	900

Activity regions (1992):	Number:	Dollars:
New York/New Jersey	13	8,500
U.S. not specified	4	3,900
U.S. West	1	350

Sample grants (1993).
American Farmland Trust. Washington, DC. $300.
Central Park Conservancy. New York, NY. $850.
Hudson River Sloop Clearwater. Poughkeepsie, NY. $350.
Mianus Gorge Preserve, Inc. Bedford, NY. $900.
National Parks and Conservation Association. Washington, DC. $900.
National Wildlife Federation. New York, NY. $900.
The Nature Conservancy, Headquarters. Arlington, VA. $1,800.
NYZS/The Wildlife Conservation Society. Bronx, NY. $1,000.
Peconic Land Trust, Inc. Southampton, NY. $300.
Save the Redwoods League. San Francisco, CA. $350.
White Plains Beautification Foundation. White Plains, NY. $500.
World Wildlife Fund. New York, NY. $950.

Application process. *Initial contact:* The Foundation awards grants to pre-selected organizations only. No unsolicited applications accepted.

Emphases. *Recipients:* Pre-selected organizations only.
Types of support: Annual campaigns, capital campaigns/expenses, computer hardware, continuing support, emergency funding, equipment, facilities, fellowships, general purposes, loans, operating costs, program-related investments, scholarships, seed money.
Geography: New York.

Limitations. *Recipients:* Individuals.
Activities: Lobbying, political activities.

Magowan Family Foundation, Inc.
c/o Merrill Lynch & Co.
100 Union Avenue
Cresskill, New Jersey 07626
EIN: 136085999   Type: Independent

Application address:
2100 Washington Street
San Francisco, California 94109
Tel: 415–563–5581   Fax: 415–563–0366
Contact: Mary Ann Chapin, Assistant Treasurer

History and philosophy. The Magowan Foundation was established in 1954. Grantmaking areas are: Educational, Medical, Religious, and Other.

Officers and directors. *Officers:* Peter A. Magowan, President; Doris M. Magowan, Mark E. Magowan, Merrill L. Magowan, Stephen C. Magowan, Vice Presidents; Charles M. Magowan, James Magowan, Kimberly Magowan, Robert A. Magowan, Jr., Thomas C. Magowan, Assistant Vice Presidents; Bernat Rosner, Secretary; Thomas J. Lombardi, Treasurer; Mary Ann Chapin, Rolando E. Fernandez, Assistant Treasurers. *Directors:* Mary Ann Chapin, Rolando E. Fernandez, Thomas J. Lombardi, Charles M. Magowan, Doris M. Magowan, James Magowan, Kimberly Magowan, Mark E. Magowan, Merrill L. Magowan, Peter A. Magowan, Robert A. Magowan, Jr., Stephen C. Magowan, Thomas C. Magowan, Bernat Rosner.

Financial data. Data for fiscal year ended October 31, 1993. *Assets:* $6,355,590 (M). *Gifts received:* $64,834. *Total grants disbursed:* $396,300.

Environmental awards. *Recent grants:* 1993 grants supported rainforest protection, coastal issues, wildlife, outdoor education, a botanical garden, and a zoo.

Issues.   Cli   Bio   Lan   Agr   Wat   Oce   Ene   Was   Tox   Pop   Dev
               •   •

Funding analysis.

Fiscal year:	1991	1993
Env grants disb:	$59,500	$52,183
Number:	13	13
Range:	$500–$17,500	$500–$13,683
Median:	$1,000	$2,000
Pct $ disb (env/total):	14	13

Recipients (1993 highest):	Number:	Dollars:
The San Francisco Zoological Society	1	13,683
National Tropical Botanical Garden	1	10,000
World Wildlife Fund	1	10,000
Environmental Defense Fund	1	7,500
Peconic Land Trust, Inc.	1	2,000
Rainforest Action Network	1	2,000
Southampton Garden Club	1	2,000

Activity regions (1993 highest):	Number:	Dollars:
U.S. West	2	14,183
International*	2	11,000
Hawaii	1	10,000
U.S. not specified	2	9,000
New York/New Jersey	3	5,000

*Multiple regions or not specified.

Sample grants (1993).
Environmental Defense Fund. New York, NY. $7,500.
The Garden Conservancy. Cold Spring Harbor, NY. $1,000.
Greenpeace USA. Washington, DC. $1,500.
Housatonic Audubon Society. Sharon, CT. $500.
National Tropical Botanical Garden. Lawai, HI. $10,000.
Peconic Land Trust, Inc. Southampton, NY. $2,000.
Rainforest Action Network. San Francisco, CA. $2,000.

Application process. *Initial contact:* Letter.
When to apply: Anytime.

Emphases. *Geography:* California, Florida, New York.

Limitations. *Recipients:* Individuals.

Maine Community Foundation, Inc.
210 Main Street
P.O. Box 148
Ellsworth, Maine 04605
Tel: 207–667–9735   Fax: 207–667–9738
EIN: 010391479   Type: Community
Contact: Elizabeth McKee, Program Officer

History and philosophy. "The Maine Community Foundation was created in 1983 to build a pool of individual charitable funds to serve the needs of Maine citizens. The Foundation is a nonprofit public charity that provides donors of all sizes and interests with a flexible, cost-effective vehicle for carrying out their charitable objectives in Maine." Its mission is to respond to human and community needs in Maine. Program areas are: Arts and Humanities, Education, Environment, Health, Historic Preservation, International Understanding, Nonprofit and Community Development, Scholarships, Scientific Research, and Social and Community Services.

Officers and directors. *Officers:* Rosalyne Bernstein, Chair; Marion Kane, President. *Directors:* Rosalyne Bernstein, Henry G. Brooks, Jr., Douglas H. Brown, Robert Carroll, Dorle K. Cartwright, Warren Cook, P. James Dowe, Jr., H. Allen Fernald, Christopher M. Harte, Horace A. Hildreth, Jr., Louis O. Hilton, Robert Kruger, Anita Leonard, P. Andrews Nixon, Paul E. Nordstrom, Elizabeth B. Noyce, Patricia Riley, Marilyn Rockefeller, Robert F. Rothschild, W. Tom Sawyer, Sidney St. F. Thaxter, Sally Vamvakias, Malcolm Warford, Richard J. Warren, Carol Wishcamper, Carolyn Wollen. *Ex officio:* Marion M. Kane.

Financial data. Data for fiscal year ended December 31, 1993. *Assets:* $12,982,187 (M). *Gifts received:* $3,590,211. *Total grants authorized:* $1,044,684.

Environmental awards. *Program and interests:* The Foundation supports programs that provide public education about critical environmental problems facing the state or that work toward long-term solutions to those problems.
Recent grants: 1993 grants included support for research and education on land conservation (greenways), coastal and marine issues, water quality, and organic gardening.

Issues. Cli Bio Lan Agr Wat Oce Ene Was Tox Pop Dev
           •   •   •   •   •   •

Funding analysis.§

Fiscal year:	1992	1993
Env grants auth:	$35,470	$20,297
Number:	21	24
Range:	$100–$15,000	$67–$2,500
Median:	$850	$1,000
Pct $ auth (env/total):	7	2

Recipients (1993 highest):	Number:	Dollars:
New Hampshire Charitable Fund	1	2,500
Quebec Labrador Foundation/ Atlantic Center for the Environment	1	2,500
Kittery Conservation Commission	2	1,250
Eliot Conservation Commission	1	1,082
Bremen Grade School	1	1,000
Friends of Evergreen	1	1,000
Friends of the Wilhelm Reich Museum	1	1,000
Georges River Tidewater Watch	1	1,000
Lubec Middle School	1	1,000
Mosman Memorial Park Association	1	1,000
MSAD #60/Berwick	1	1,000
Scarborough Coastal Pollution Committee	1	1,000
St. Croix International Waterway Commission	1	1,000

Activity region (1993):	Number:	Dollars:
U.S. Northeast	24	20,297

§Includes competitive grants only.

Sample grants (1993).
Beals Island Regional Shellfish Hatchery. Beals, ME. $114. For a water quality monitoring project.
Friends of Evergreen. Portland, ME. $1,000. To create a plan for the Evergreen Cemetery that links it with other greenways in Portland.
Maine Conservation School. Bryant Pond, ME. $2,500.
Maine Organic Farmers and Gardeners Association. Augusta, ME. $2,500. To develop gardens and teach gardening at 15 Head Start centers.
Quebec Labrador Foundation/Atlantic Center for the Environment. Ipswich, ME. $2,500. To fund a marine education program for young people in Eastport.

Application process. *Initial contact:* Telephone call or proposal. Full proposal to include:

1. Short cover letter signed by the executive director and/or president of the board containing:
   • Purpose of project and how it will be accomplished.
   • Relevant background information including evidence of need for proposed project.
   • Amount requested from MCF.
   • Amount raised or expected from other sources.
   • Explanation of how project is to be funded in the future (if applicable).
   • Criteria for measuring the results of the project.
   • Name and telephone number of project director.
2. Itemized income and expense budget for the project.
3. List of key personnel and a brief resume for each.
4. Copy of IRS tax-exempt status determination letter.
5. Completed Request for Information form available from the MCF office.

Foundation staff members will discuss project ideas by telephone or personal interview.
When to apply: Deadlines are January 15, April 1, July 15, and October 1. The board of directors meets quarterly.
Materials: Annual report (includes "Grantmaking Priorities"), Request for Information form.

Emphases. *Recipients:* Nonprofit organizations, public agencies.
Activities: Capacity building, citizen participation, collaborative efforts, conferences, conflict resolution, education, exhibits, innovative programs, policy analysis/development, workshops, youth programs.
Types of support: Emergency funding, matching funds, pilot projects, program-related investments, seed money, technical assistance.
Geography: Maine only.

Limitations. *Recipients:* Religious organizations.
Activities: Advocacy, expeditions/tours, fundraising, land acquisition, litigation, lobbying, research (medical).
Types of support: Advertising campaigns, annual campaigns, capital campaigns/expenses, computer hardware, continuing support, debt retirement, endowments, equipment, mortgage reduction.

Maki Foundation
421D Aspen Airport Business Center
Aspen, Colorado 81611-3551
Tel: 303-925-3272
EIN: 840836242   Type: Independent
EGA member
Contact: Patricia Humphry, Contact Person

History and philosophy. Established in 1981, the Foundation is concerned with environmental protection in the western United States. "Maki is the Lakota (Sioux) word for land, ground, earth, or the firmament upon which all living things are born and nourished and to which they return. The Lakota hold such a high regard for Earth that they call her mother or grandmother, and she is accorded honor, respect, and love. . . . Maki is viewed as the basic support for all things known to life, thus she should not be owned nor should she be injured for to do so is to diminish her nourishing powers upon which life depends."

Officers and directors. *Directors:* Ruth Adams, Ann Harvey, Constance Harvey.

Financial data. Data for fiscal year ended December 31, 1993. *Assets:* $1,616,077 (U). *Total grants authorized:* $81,000.

Environmental awards. *Program and interests:* The Foundation has four environmental priorities:

- Wilderness and wildlands protection.
- River and wetlands conservation.
- Biological diversity conservation.
- Public lands management.

Issues.   Cli   Bio   Lan   Agr   Wat   Oce   Ene   Was   Tox   Pop   Dev
                  •   •   •   •

Funding analysis.

Fiscal year:	1990	1992
Env grants auth:	$60,085	$71,000
Number:	21	23
Range:	$500–$5,000	$500–$5,000
Median:	$2,500	$3,000
Pct $ auth (env/total):	100	100

Recipients (1992 highest):	Number:	Dollars:
Colorado Environmental Coalition, Inc.	1	5,000
Teton Science School	1	5,000
The Teton Valley Land Trust	1	5,000
University of Colorado Foundation	1	5,000
Western Organization of Resource Councils (WORC)	1	5,000

Activity regions (1992 highest):	Number:	Dollars:
U.S. Mountain	15	46,500
U.S. not specified	3	7,500
U.S. multiple regions	1	5,000
U.S. Northwest	1	4,500
Alaska	1	4,000

Sample grants (1993).
American Wildlands. Bozeman, MT. $3,500. General support.
Colorado Environmental Coalition, Inc. Denver, CO. $5,000. To protect biological diversity on Colorado's national forests.
Four Corners School of Outdoor Education. Monticello, UT. $2,500.
Jackson Hole Alliance for Responsible Planning. Jackson, WY. $1,000. Summer/fall field trip program.
The Nature Conservancy, Colorado Field Office. Boulder, CO. $2,000. Biological inventory of the Roaring Fork River Basin.
The Northern Rockies Conservation Cooperative. Jackson, WY. $2,000. Environmental education.
Teton Science School. Kelly, WY. $5,000. For the I.S.L.A.N.D. Project.
The Teton Valley Land Trust. Driggs, ID. $5,000. Teton River and Wetlands Wildlife Project.
Western Colorado Congress. Montrose, CO. $5,000. Limiting oil and gas development on national forest lands in Colorado.

Application process. *Initial contact:* Letter of inquiry. Completed application form and project summary (1 page, 3 copies) must accompany full proposal. Full proposal to include:
1. Description of applicant organization, including name, number of years in operation, and mission.
2. Brief explanation of project or program for which funds are sought. Provide information about:
   - Grant purpose.
   - Project goals and objectives, including specific results to be achieved.
   - Plans for evaluation.
   - Project timetable.
   - Background of project director and staff.
3. Copy of organization's annual budget, including a detailed project budget. List all other sources of support for the project and amounts provided by each.
4. Organization's most recent financial statement, showing amounts and sources of current income.
5. List of organization's board of directors.
6. Copy of IRS tax-exempt status determination letter.

When to apply: Anytime for letters of inquiry. Deadline for full proposals is June 1 for consideration at board's annual mid-summer meeting.
Materials available: Application guidelines, application form.

Emphases. *Recipients:* Nonprofit organizations, public agencies. *Geography:* Colorado, New Mexico, Arizona, Nevada, Utah, Idaho, Montana, Wyoming, Washington, Alaska.

Limitations. *Activities:* Audiovisual materials, recycling programs, toxic waste cleanup, tree-planting projects.
Types of support: Acquisition/construction of community recreation, facilities (buildings), municipal parks, reservoirs, and similar projects; fellowships.

Marbrook Foundation
400 Baker Building
Minneapolis, Minnesota 55402
Tel: 612–332–2454   Fax: 612–342–2027
EIN: 416019899   Type: Independent
Contact: Conley Brooks, Jr., Executive Director

History and philosophy. Edward Brooks and Markell C. Brooks, longtime residents of Minnesota, created the Marbrook Foundation in 1948 to promote broad philanthropic objectives through grants and investments in the areas of physical and mental health, education, social welfare, visual and performing arts, conservation, and preservation. The Twin Cities have been the common denominator for most grants over the years; current grants are generally limited to the Twin Cities metropolitan area.

Officers and director. *Officer:* Conley Brooks, Jr., Executive Director. *Trustees:* John E. Andrus, III, Conley Brooks, Conley Brooks, Jr., Markell Brooks, William R. Humphrey, Jr.

Financial data. Data for fiscal year ended December 31, 1993. *Assets:* $6,482,045 (C). *Total grants disbursed:* $325,000.

Environmental awards. *Program and interests:* 1993 grants included support for land conservation and water issues in Minnesota.

Issues.   Cli   Bio   Lan   Agr   Wat   Oce   Ene   Was   Tox   Pop   Dev
                    •   •   •

Funding analysis.

Fiscal year:	1991	1993
Env grants disb:	$22,500	$29,000
Number:	4	5
Range:	$1,000–$10,000	$3,000–$10,000
Median:	$3,000	$4,500
Pct $ disb (env/total):	8	9

Recipients (1993):	Number:	Dollars:
The Nature Conservancy, Minnesota Field Office	1	10,000
Headwaters Fund	1	7,500
Concerts for the Environment Inc.	1	4,500
Minnesota Center for Environmental Advocacy	1	4,000
Freshwater Foundation	1	3,000

Activity region (1993):	Number:	Dollars:
U.S. Great Lakes	5	29,000

Sample grants (1993).
Concerts for the Environment, Inc. Minneapolis, MN. $4,500.
Freshwater Foundation. Navarre, MN. $3,000. Public water education program.
Headwaters Fund. Minneapolis, MN. $7,500.
Minnesota Center for Environmental Advocacy. St. Paul, MN. $4,000.
The Nature Conservancy, Minnesota Field Office. Minneapolis, MN. $10,000. For the Critical Areas Campaign.

Application process. *Initial contact:* Telephone call or full proposal to include:
1. Description of project objectives.
2. Specific details on how objectives are to be attained.
3. Budget, including information about other sources of support.
4. Proposed method of evaluation.
5. Description of the organization requesting support.
6. List of officers and board members.
7. Copy of IRS tax-exempt status determination letter and classification statement as a non-private foundation or a private operating foundation.

When to apply: Anytime. The trustees generally meet in May and November to review proposals.
Materials available: Annual report (includes "Application Procedures").

Emphases. *Recipients:* Nonprofit organizations.
Types of support: Operating costs.
Geography: Twin Cities metropolitan area of Minnesota.

Limitations. *Recipients:* Individuals
Activities: Advocacy, demonstration programs, lobbying, political activities, publications.
Types of support: Debt retirement, equipment, fellowships, scholarships.

© 1995 Environmental Data Resources, Inc.

Marin Community Foundation

17 East Sir Francis Drake Boulevard, Suite 200
Larkspur, California 94939
Tel: 415–461–3333   Fax: 415–461–3386
EIN: 943007979   Type: Community
EGA member
Contacts: Art Mills, Lead Program Officer, Environment
Sallyanne Wilson, Communications and Program Officer
Anne Cottrell, Program Assistant

History and philosophy. The Marin Community Foundation is a tax-exempt charity that administers private funds for public purposes. It was established in 1986 initially to serve the residents of Marin County through the Leonard and Beryl H. Buck Foundation (The Buck Trust). At the time of the original bequest, The Buck Trust was worth $15.4 million. Through the spectacular increase of a single stock (Belridge Oil), the value of the bequest increased to $534 million. In addition to the Trust, Marin County Foundation now also administers and oversees more than twenty other donor-advised funds, supporting organizations, and endowments. It also serves beneficiaries in the Greater San Francisco Bay Area and communities beyond Marin County.

The Foundation has six grantmaking programs: Human Needs, Education and Training, Community Development, Religion, Environment, and Arts. The Foundation encourages applications that unite and integrate two or more program areas.

Officers and directors. *Officers:* William Hamilton, Chair; Peter R. Arrigoni, Vice Chair. *Trustees:* Peter R. Arrigoni, William Hamilton, Grace A. Hughes, Rev. Douglas K. Huneke, Donald G. Linker, M.D., Shirley A. Thornton, Ed.D., David Werdegar, M.D.

Financial data.* Data for fiscal year ended June 30, 1993.
Assets: $497,670,000 (M). *Gifts received:* $6,910,000. *Total grants authorized:* $18,830,000.

*Assets do not include The Buck Trust, which supports the Foundation with assets of approximately $571 million as of June 1993.

Environmental awards. *Program and interests:* The purpose of the Environment program is to support the conservation of the natural environment in the community. The Foundation recognizes the regional context within which environmental resources exist, problems occur, and programs frequently operate. The Foundation will award grants based on the following goals:

- Environmental quality.

    To support efforts that sustain, enhance, or rehabilitate the quality of air, land, and water resources, and/or preserve habitats and species.

    Emphasis: Sustaining or rehabilitating biodiversity in watersheds, coastal regions, stream habitats, wetlands, and in the San Francisco Bay-Delta Estuary.

- Land conservation.

    To promote land conservation efforts that preserve agriculture, open space, and sensitive habitats.

    Emphasis: Preserving agricultural lands and open space.

M

- Environmental education.

To support environmental education that teaches a fundamental respect for the diversity of life and the interrelatedness of human life and the natural environment.

Emphasis: Encouraging comprehensive and integrative approaches to environment; education in elementary and secondary schools, community education, and coalition-building among environmental and other community leaders.

Recent grants: In 1993 the Foundation introduced "Food for Thought: Agricultural Classroom Activity for Growing Minds." Developed since 1991, this collaborative effort with the University of California Cooperative Extension and educators, ranchers, and environmentalists, seeks to educate children about Marin County's sources of food and fiber. Other grants in 1993 included support for land conservation, agricultural land preservation, open space, parks, watershed protection, and public education.

Issues. Cli Bio Lan Agr Wat Oce Ene Was Tox Pop Dev
              •   •   •   •   •

Funding analysis.§

Fiscal year:	1992	1993
Env grants auth:	$282,780	$2,641,300
Number:	5	9
Range:	$20,000–$75,000	$25,000–$2,000,000
Median:	$64,920	$50,000
Pct $ auth (env/total):	3	12

Recipients (1993 highest):	*Number:*	*Dollars:*
Beryl Buck Open Space Fund	1	2,000,000
Marin Agricultural Land Trust (MALT)	1	300,000
Marin Conservation League	1	80,000
Ecumenical Association for Housing	1	60,000
Earth Day Every Day Fund of MCF	1	50,000
Golden Gate National Park Association	1	50,000

Activity regions (1993):	*Number:*	*Dollars:*
U.S. West	8	2,601,300
Global	1	40,000

§Includes competitive grants only.

Sample grants (1993).*

Beryl Buck Open Space Fund. Larkspur, CA. $2,000,000. To reinvest in the open space fund so as to continue all the benefits originally anticipated at the fund's creation in 1988.

Environmental Action Committee of West Marin. Point Reyes Station, CA. $25,000. To produce a video in Spanish, with English subtitles, promoting environmental awareness in the West Marin Hispanic community.

Marin Agricultural Land Trust (MALT). Point Reyes Station, CA. $300,000. For continued general operating support.

Marin County Resource Conservation District. San Rafael, CA. $36,300. To complete a hydrodynamic analysis as part of development of an enhancement plan for the Estero de San Antonio/Stemple Creek Watershed.

Pacific Energy and Resources Center. Sausalito, CA. $40,000. To support the Global Environmental Education Program.

*Sample grants represent either new awards or disbursements on grants awarded in previous years.

Application process. *Initial contact:* Telephone call, followed by brief letter of intent (2–4 pages, 2 copies) to include:
1. Name and mission of organization.
2. Name, address, and phone number of contact person.
3. Description of project or program, including objective, expected outcomes, methods to be used to achieve them, and how achievements will be measured and evaluated.
4. Proposed starting date and duration of project or program.
5. Estimated total project or program cost, including amount requested from the Foundation and amounts requested of, or secured from, other funders.
6. Background information on organization, including year of incorporation and experience in the project or program area.

Attachments.
1. Copy of IRS tax-exempt status determination letter.
2. Names and affiliations of board of directors.
3. Equal employment policy statement.
4. Budget information:
   - Project budget executive summary.
   - Detailed project budget (see sample format).
   - Organization budget.
   - Funding sources.
   - Organization profile (use form from Foundation).

When to apply: Anytime.
Materials available: Annual report (includes "Application Information"), Newsletter.

Emphases. *Recipients:* Educational institutions, nonprofit organizations, public agencies.
Activities: Activism, advocacy, citizen participation, collaborative efforts, education, feasibility studies, policy analysis/development.
Types of support: Loans.
Geography: Projects benefitting Marin County, California and the surrounding area.

Limitations. *Recipients:* Individuals.
Activities: Excavation/protection of archeological sites; land acquisition; projects that should be funded by private, profit-making entities and government agencies; projects required by statute; research.
Types of support: Debt retirement, indirect costs, lectureships, mortgage reduction, professorships, scholarships, travel expenses.

MARPAT Foundation, Inc.

c/o Miller & Cheval
655 15th Street, N.W.
Washington, DC 20005
EIN: 521358159   Type: Independent
EGA member
Contact: Joan F. Koven, Secretary and Treasurer

History and philosophy. The MARPAT Foundation was established in 1985 by Marvin Breckinridge Patterson. It makes grants for peace through international understanding; education, libraries and museums; family planning and health care; scientific programs and research; and natural history and American human history and culture. Grants are generally made to organizations in the Washington, D.C. area.

Officers and directors. *Officers:* Marvin Breckinridge Patterson, President; Charles T. Akre, Vice President; Joan F. Koven, Secretary/Treasurer. *Directors:* Charles T. Akre, Isabella G. Breckinridge, Joan F. Koven, Marvin Breckinridge Patterson, Caroline T. Simmons, Samuel N. Stokes.

Financial data. Data for fiscal year ended December 31, 1993. *Assets:* $12,845,859 (M). *Total grants disbursed:* $915,823.

Environmental awards. *Program and interests:* The Foundation's interests are:

- Environmental education.
- Preservation.
- Conservation.
- Sustainable development.

Education on resource use is a particular thrust. In general the Foundation looks for an approach rather than specific species protection.

Recent grants: 1993 grants included support for land conservation, parks and forests, watershed protection, marine and coastal issues, water quality, wildlife and fisheries, and classroom education.

Issues. Cli Bio Lan Agr Wat Oce Ene Was Tox Pop Dev

Funding analysis.

Fiscal year:	1992	1993
Env grants disb:	$210,000	$251,000
Number:	12	18
Range:	$5,000–$50,000	$5,000–$28,000
Median:	$10,000	$12,500
Pct $ disb (env/total):	27	27

Recipients (1993 highest):	Number:	Dollars:
The Friends of Jefferson Patterson Park and Museum	1	28,000
Accokeek Foundation	1	25,000
Academy of Natural Sciences of Philadelphia	1	20,000
National Resources Council of Maine	1	20,000
Smithsonian Institution, National Museum of Natural History	1	18,000

Activity regions (1993):	Number:	Dollars:
U.S. Mid-Atlantic	8	128,000
U.S. not specified	6	68,000
U.S. Northeast	4	55,000

Sample grants (1993).

Academy of Natural Sciences of Philadelphia. Philadelphia, PA. $20,000. Toward building and equipping the new Estuarine Research Center to further the research and education program on the Chesapeake Bay and estuaries.

Accokeek Foundation. Accokeek, MD. $25,000. To preserve natural, historical, cultural resources of the Potomac River Basin, to foster public education programs to make people aware of the basin's diverse heritage, and to encourage land stewardship.

Audubon Naturalist Society. Chevy Chase, MD. $5,000. To help ANS and the Chesapeake Bay Trust carry out an 18-month phase of the Maryland-based Water Quality Monitoring program.

Chesapeake Wildlife Sanctuary. Bowie, MD. $10,000. For the Veterinary Graduate Intern who will learn as well as instruct other interns and volunteers during his/her one-year internship at the Sanctuary.

Earth Conservation Corps. Washington, DC. $10,000. To recruit at-risk young adults for a one-year program of conservation work and life skills training, to restore lower Beaverdam Creek, and remove man-made barriers reestablishing the historic herring migration.

Land Trust Alliance. Washington, DC. $10,000. For publication and distribution of a comprehensive guidebook for grassroots conservationists.

Laudholm Trust. Wells, ME. $15,000. To assist 17 schools in adopting Pathway to Change, a model educational program, and outreach program as a permanent part of each school's science curriculum.

Marine Environmental Research Institute (MERI). New York, NY. $10,000. To increase public awareness of current stresses affecting the marine environment, and to establish a model year-round community education program in Maine, replicable in other coastal communities.

Natural Resources Council of Maine. Augusta, ME. $20,000. To reduce dioxin to safe levels in Maine waters and to put programs in place to identify and reduce other harmful toxic substances there.

Scenic America. Washington, DC. $15,000. For research and report on how scenic byways can conserve valuable resources while stimulating economies by assisting activists and influencing policymakers to create scenic byways programs with strong conservation policies.

Application process. *Initial contact:* Short letter to request guidelines and summary sheet. Telephone calls are discouraged. Proposal (3 copies) to include:

1. Completed Summary Sheet (supplied by Foundation).
2. Description of project (2 pages maximum), need, how project will meet that need, and who will be served.
3. Project budget, indicating the use of MARPAT Foundation funds and other possible funding sources.
4. List of organization's officers and current board of directors or trustees.
5. Project staff and their qualifications.
6. Proof of IRS tax-exempt status.
7. Most recent annual report.
8. Most recent financial statement, audited if possible.
9. Report on any previous projects funded by MARPAT (2 pages maximum).

When to apply: Deadline is October 1 for consideration at the board's meeting in December.

Materials available: "Guidelines for Applicants," "Summary Sheet."

Emphases. *Recipients:* Educational institutions, museums, non-profit organizations, research institutions.
Activities: Demonstration programs, education, volunteerism.
Geography: Greater Washington, D.C. metropolitan area.

Limitations. *Recipients:* Individuals.
Activities: Expeditions/tours, research (medical).
Types of support: Endowments, loans, multi-year grants, scholarships.
Geography: International grants. No grants to organizations based outside the United States.

Mars Foundation
6885 Elm Street
McLean, Virginia 22101–3883
Tel: 703–821–4900   Fax: 703–448–9678
EIN: 546037592   Type: Independent
Contact: Robert C. Cargo, Secretary

History and philosophy. The Mars Foundation was established in 1958 with donations from Forrest E. Mars, Sr. Grantmaking interests are: Arts, Education (elementary, secondary, and higher), Medical, Historic Preservation, Wildlife Preservation/Environment, Animal Protection, Children and Young Adults, and Charitable Programs. Population issues are an additional interest.

Officers and directors. *Officers:* Jacqueline M. Vogel, President; Forrest E. Mars, Jr., John F. Mars, Vice Presidents; Robert C. Cargo, Secretary; Rita Langsam Davis, Assistant Secretary. *Directors:* Robert C. Cargo, Rita Langsam Davis, Forrest E. Mars, Jr., John F. Mars, William C. Turnbull, Jacqueline M. Vogel.

Financial data. Data for fiscal years ended December 31, 1992. *Assets:* $4,973,199 (M). *Gifts received:* $600,000. *Total grants disbursed:* $770,500.

Environmental awards. *Recent grants:* 1992 grants included support for land conservation (including wetlands), habitat and species preservation, coastal issues, and research on global warming.

Issues. Cli • Bio • Lan • Agr • Wat • Oce • Ene • Was • Tox • Pop • Dev

Funding analysis.

Fiscal year:	1991	1992
Env grants disb:	$71,000	$78,500
Number:	14	15
Range:	$1,000–$12,000	$1,000–$12,000
Median:	$5,000	$5,000
Pct $ disb (env/total):	9	10

Recipients (1992 highest):	Number:	Dollars:
The Nature Conservancy, Headquarters	1	12,000
Chesapeake Bay Foundation	1	10,000
World Wildlife Fund	1	10,000
African Wildlife Foundation	1	7,500
Shenandoah Valley Wildlife Treatment and Rehabilitation Center	1	6,000

Activity regions (1992):	Number:	Dollars:
U.S. Mid-Atlantic	5	29,000
International*	3	20,000
U.S. not specified	5	17,000
Africa	1	7,500
New York/New Jersey	1	5,000

*Multiple regions or not specified.

Sample grants (1992).
African Wildlife Foundation. Washington, DC. $7,500. Unrestricted gift to preserve African wildlife.
Chesapeake Bay Foundation. Annapolis, MD. $10,000. To help restore Chesapeake Bay.
Defenders of Wildlife. Washington, DC. $1,000. Unrestricted gift.
Ducks Unlimited, Inc. Long Grove, IL. $1,000. For the restoration, management, and preservation of wetland habitat for waterfowl and 350 other species dependent upon wetland habitats.
Environmental Defense Fund. New York, NY. $2,000. For research and implementation of solutions on global warming.
The Hastings Center. Briarcliff Manor, NY. $5,000. For ethics and environmental programs in biodiversity conservation and human and natural futures.
National Zoological Park. Washington, DC. $3,000. For the Reproduction Program of Noah's Center.
Ruffed Grouse Society. Coraopolis, PA. $5,000. For new ways to improve forest habitat for the grouse population.
Shenandoah Valley Wildlife Treatment and Rehabilitation Center. Weyers Cave, VA. $6,000. For treatment of sick, injured, and orphaned wild animals and educational programs for school children.
Trout Unlimited. Alexandria, VA. $5,000. For the cold water fishery for the Embrace-a-Stream program.
Wildlife Preservation Trust. Philadelphia, PA. $5,000. Unrestricted gift for species preservation.
World Resources Institute. Washington, DC. $5,000. Unrestricted gift for natural resource preservation.
World Wildlife Fund. Washington, DC. $10,000. For scientific research and conservation projects to save endangered wildlife.

Application process. *Initial contact:* Detailed letter of application, accompanied by a copy of IRS tax-exempt status determination letter. Application letter to include:
1. Organization background and purpose.
2. Project goals.
3. Description of project.
4. Amount of funding requested.

When to apply: Anytime. The board holds meetings in June and December.

Emphases. *Activities:* Research.
Types of support: Annual campaigns, continuing support, endowments, equipment, facilities, matching funds.

Limitations. *Recipients:* Individuals.
Types of support: Loans, scholarships.

The Marshall Fund of Arizona

4000 North Scottsdale Road, Suite 203
Scottsdale, Arizona 85251
Tel: 602–941–5249
EIN: 742470266   Type: Independent
Contact: Maxine B. Marshall, Vice President

History and philosophy. The Fund was established in 1987 by Maxine and Jonathan Marshall. Its philosophy of grantmaking rests on the belief "that a nonprofit charitable foundation has a serious responsibility to use its resources creatively in order to try to improve the quality of life in its community. . . . We look primarily for proposals which can have broad ramifications and a ripple effect. We also believe that a foundation should be willing to take chances by supporting groups which are not necessarily mainstream, and we are willing to take chances within the parameters of our guidelines." Grants are awarded in five areas: Cultural and Artistic Projects, Civil Liberties, Environmental Protection and Conservation, Human and Social Needs, and Promotion of World Peace and Understanding.

Officers and directors. *Officers:* Jonathan Marshall, President; Maxine B. Marshall, Vice President. *Directors:* Paul Eckstein, David R. Frazer, Gloria Heller, Jonathan Marshall, Laura Marshall, Maxine B. Marshall.

Financial data. Data for fiscal year ended December 31, 1993. *Assets:* $3,009,408 (M). *Total grants disbursed:* $131,110.

Environmental awards. *Recent grants:* 1992 and 1993 grants included support for habitat and species protection, forest protection, water conservation, and a botanical garden.

Issues.   Cli   Bio   Lan   Agr   Wat   Oce   Ene   Was   Tox   Pop   Dev
                    •   •   •   •   •

Funding analysis.

Fiscal year:	1992
Env grants auth:	$20,878
Number:	3
Range:	$3,378–$10,000
Median:	$7,500
Pct $ disb (env/total):	7

Recipients (1992):	Number:	Dollars:
Land and Water Fund of the Rockies	1	10,000
American Rivers, Inc.	1	7,500
The Wilderness Society	1	3,378

Activity regions (1992):	Number:	Dollars:
U.S. West	2	10,878
U.S. Mountain	1	10,000

**Sample grants (1992–93).*

American Rivers, Inc. Washington, DC. $7,500. Second-year funding for program to preserve and protect Arizona's rivers.
Desert Botanical Garden. Phoenix, AZ. $4,250. To support experiments in desert plant restoration on arid lands.
Land and Water Fund. Boulder, CO. $10,000. Adopt-a-Forest project.
Tucson Botanical Garden. Tucson, AZ. $2,800. Interpretive Tour Program "Discovering Plants."
The Wilderness Society. Santa Fe, NM. $3,378. Grand Canyon Management Plan.

*Sample grants represent either new awards or disbursements on grants awarded in previous years.

Application process. *Initial contact:* Letter (1–2 pages) to include:
1. Organization's description and purpose.
2. Project needs, purpose, and method.
3. Budget for grant and organization.
4. List of organization's board of directors.
5. Organization's tax-exempt ruling.

If proposal appears to meet the Fund's guidelines and interests, applicant will be asked to provide detailed information for formal board review.
When to apply: Deadlines are March 1, August 1, and November 1, for consideration at the spring, fall, and winter meetings.
Materials available: Annual report, brochure (includes "Applying for a Grant").

Emphases. *Recipients:* Botanical gardens, educational institutions, museums, nonprofit organizations.
Activities: Innovative programs.
Types of support: Matching funds, pilot projects, seed money.
Geography: Arizona only.

Limitations. *Recipients:* Individuals, public agencies.
Activities: Audiovisual materials, fundraising, publications, research (medical/scholarly).
Types of support: Annual campaigns, capital campaigns/expenses, debt retirement, endowments, facilities, operating costs.

The Martin Foundation, Inc.

500 Simpson Avenue
Elkhart, Indiana 46515–1167
Tel: 219–295–3343   Fax: 219–295–3488
EIN: 351070929   Type: Independent
EGA member
Contact: Geraldine F. Martin, President

History and philosophy. The Martin Foundation was established in 1953 by members of the Martin family. It funds "worthwhile local civic and community projects in Indiana and Illinois and has an interest in creative projects at the national and international level which attempt to address some of the world's challenging problems." Areas of interest are: Youth/Community and Social Service, Education, Civic Affairs/Public Interest, Culture, and Conservation/Environment.

Officers and directors. *Officers:* Geraldine F. Martin, President; Elizabeth Martin, Vice President and Secretary; Jennifer Martin, Treasurer. *Directors:* Casper Martin, Elizabeth Martin, Geraldine F. Martin, Jennifer Martin, Lee Martin, Rex Martin.

M

Financial data. Data for fiscal year ended June 30, 1994. *Assets:* $35,334,287 (M). *Total grants disbursed:* $1,389,340.

Environmental awards. *Program and interests:* Areas of interest include:

- Wildlife conservation and endangered species protection.
- Environmental education.
- Natural resource preservation.
- Energy and transportation.
- Recycling.

Recent grants: Grants in 1994 included endowment of the Lee & Geraldine Martin Professorship in Environmental Studies at the Massachusetts Institute of Technology, support for local nature programs, and land conservation in Third World countries.

Issues. Cli Bio• Lan• Agr Wat Oce Ene• Was• Tox Pop• Dev

Funding analysis.

Fiscal year:	1992	1993
Env grants auth:	$228,241	$3,046,725
Number:	15	14
Range:	$1,000–$90,000	$325–$3,000,000
Median:	$10,000	$2,950
Pct $ disb (env/total):	19	49

Recipients (1993 highest):	Number:	Dollars:
Massachusetts Institute of Technology	1	3,000,000
Antarctica Project	1	15,000
Hoosier Environmental Council	2	6,000
New England Wildlife Center, Inc.	1	5,000
Shirley Heinze Environmental Fund	1	5,000
Sierra Club Legal Defense Fund	1	5,000

Activity regions (1993 highest):	Number:	Dollars:
U.S. Northeast	2	3,005,000
U.S. Great Lakes	6	17,900
Antarctica	1	15,000
U.S. Mountain	3	7,000
Africa	1	1,500

Sample grants (1994).*

Chicago Recycling Coalition. Chicago, IL. $2,000. Support for the Chicago Compost Demonstration Site.

Forest Resource Center. Lanesboro, MN. $2,500. To develop an internship program for environmental educators at the Center which is dedicated to promoting the responsible use, renewal, and appreciation of our natural resources.

Global Greengrants Fund. Boulder, CO. $10,000. To this funders collaborative for environmental grantmakers who believe that giving small international grants to grassroots environmental groups is an effective grantmaking strategy to help save our endangered planet.

Goshen Park & Recreation Department. Goshen, IN. $4,000. To help with prairie restoration at Abshire Park.

Hoosier Environmental Council. Indianapolis, IN. $10,000. To help provide continued support of HEC's regional office in Michigan City, Indiana.

Massachusetts Institute of Technology. Cambridge, MA. $3,000,000. The second payment of $600,000 to endow the Lee & Geraldine Professorship in Environmental Studies & The Martin Fund to provide support for related activities.

*Sample grants represent either new awards or disbursements on grants awarded in previous years.

Application process. *Initial contact:* Full proposal to include:
1. Organization's legal name, address, telephone number, and name of contact person.
2. Copy of IRS tax-exempt status determination letter(s) confirming that the organization is tax-exempt and not a private foundation.
3. Brief history of the organization including goals, objectives, and activities.
4. Detailed statement describing the project or activities to which the requested grant monies would be directed.
5. Most recent annual report for the organization and an audited financial statement (if available) or IRS Form 990 for the most recently completed fiscal year.
6. List of other sources contacted for funds, along with results (or projected results).
7. Itemized budget for the organization and the specific project, showing both projected revenues and expenses for the current fiscal year.
8. List of the current board of directors.

When to apply: Anytime. The board meets four to six times each year.
Materials: Annual report (includes "Grant Application Guidelines."

Emphases. *Recipients:* Educational institutions, nonprofit organizations.
Activities: Education, innovative programs
Types of support: Matching funds, scholarships (funds only), start-up costs.
Geography: Indiana, Illinois, Massachusetts, Minnesota; national programs.

Limitations. *Recipients:* Individuals.
Activities: Litigation, lobbying.
Types of support: Endowments.

Massachusetts Environmental Trust
100 Cambridge Street, 20th Floor
Boston, Massachusetts 02202
Tel: 617–727–9800   Fax: 617–727–2754
EGA member
Contact: Robbin Peach, Executive Director

History and philosophy. The Trust was established in 1988 by the Massachusetts Legislature to receive settlement proceeds from the Commonwealth of Massachusetts and the Metropolitan District Commission for violations of the Clean Water Act in Boston Harbor. Its purpose is to "fund and coordinate projects to restore, protect, and improve the quality of Boston and Lynn

Harbors and Massachusetts, Buzzards, and Cape Cod bays; to increase public involvement of the bays and their resources and the effect of human activities upon them; and to encourage public involvement in activities which promote the harbors and bays as living resources and public treasures for present and future citizens of the Commonwealth of Massachusetts."

From 1988 to 1994, the Trust received proceeds from 13 environmental settlements, and a few private institutions. All money is redistributed to fund deserving environmental projects run by municipalities, nonprofits, schools, and scientists.

The Trust has three grant categories: general, focused, and restricted. (1) General; Depends on applicant proposals. (2) Focused; 1993 and 1994 priorities were source reduction, non-point source pollution, and citizen education on these issues. (3) Restricted; For settlements with conditions. Examples include $75,000 to educate photographic chemical users about handling and chemical waste disposal and $150,000 for pollution prevention curriculum for secondary schools in the Taunton River Watershed.

Officers and directors. *Officers:* Maynard Goldman, Chairman; Hannah T. C. Moore, Vice Chair; Trudy Coxe, Secretary. *Trustees:* Thomas M. Finneran, Charles H. W. Foster, Marion R. Fremont-Smith, Maynard Goldman, James S. Hoyte, John S. Llewellyn, Jr., Hannah T. C. Moore.

Financial data. Data for fiscal year ended June 30, 1994. *Assets:* $956,296 (U). *Total grants authorized:* $250,000 (est.). *Total grants disbursed:* $123,921.

Environmental awards. *Program and interests:* The interests of the Trust are:

- To restore, protect, and improve Massachusetts marine waters.
- To increase understanding of the bays, watersheds, and their resources.
- To engage the public in activities that promote the harbor, watersheds, and coastal zones.

Issues. Cli Bio Lan Agr Wat Oce Ene Was Tox Pop Dev

Sample grants (1988–93).
The Coalition for Buzzards Bay, Inc. Buzzards Bay, MA. $13,000. Support for the training and recruitment of a network of citizens to monitor the activities of the boards of local government whose decisions affect the future of Buzzards Bay.
Salem Sound 2000. Salem, MA. $5,000. For the Salem Partnership for a symposium and newsletters to promote community awareness and facilitate municipal and citizen management of the Salem Sound Estuary as a bioregion.
Thompson Island Outward Bound Education Center. Boston, MA. $200,000. Support to sponsor the Harbor Conservation Corps, enrolling about 200 youth.
University of Massachusetts. Boston, MA. $11,500. For Project Oceanology to introduce the study of the marine environment into five public schools, integrating classroom study with on-the-water research aboard Enviro Lab III.
Westport River Watershed Alliance (WRWA). Westport, MA. $10,000. To implement a model citizen water quality monitoring project in the Westport River.

Woods Hole Oceanographic Institution. Woods Hole. MA. $250,000. For a physical oceanographic survey of Massachusetts Bay.

Application process. *Initial contact:* Letter of inquiry. *When to apply:* Anytime.

Emphases. *Recipients:* Educational institutions, individuals (scientists), nonprofit organizations, public agencies. *Activities:* Education, research, symposia/colloquia, training. *Types of support:* General purposes. *Geography:* Massachusetts.

The McConnell Foundation
292 Hemsted Drive, Suite 100
P.O. Box 991870
Redding, California 96099–1870
Tel: 916–222–0696   Fax: 916–222–0695
EIN: 946102700   Type: Independent
Contact: Lee W. Salter, President and CEO

History and philosophy. The Foundation was established in 1964 by Carl R. and Leah F. McConnell. Its purpose is "to provide a professionally-managed source of funding for the promotion of innovative projects." The Foundation awards grants for the benefit of the northern California counties of Shasta and Siskiyou in the areas of: Arts and Culture, Community Enrichment, Designated Special Projects, Education, Environment, Health Care, Recreation, and Social Services.

Officers and directors. *Directors:* Doreeta Domke, John A. Mancasola, Leonard B. Nelson, William B. Nystrom, Lee W. Salter.

Financial data. Data for fiscal year ended December 31, 1993. *Assets:* $57,908,218 (M). *Total grants authorized:* $4,181,266.

Environmental awards. *Recent grants:* 1993 grants included support for an arboretum, wildlife preservation, and state and national parks and forests.

Issues. Cli Bio Lan Agr Wat Oce Ene Was Tox Pop Dev

Funding analysis.

Fiscal year:	1992	1993
Env grants auth:	$542,162	$1,853,957
Number:	10	7
Range:	$5,100–$195,000	$6,198–$1,395,579
Median:	$32,500	$47,594
Pct $ auth (env/total):	23	51

Recipients (1993 highest):	Number:	Dollars:
Shasta Natural Science Association	2	1,645,579
California Department of Fish and Game	1	119,156
Shasta and Siskiyou High Schools	1	47,594
USDA, Forest Service, Klamath National Forest	1	20,430

© 1995 Environmental Data Resources, Inc.

M

National Park Service,
Lava Beds National Monument　　　1　　　15,000

Activity region (1993):　　　*Number:*　　*Dollars:*
U.S. West　　　　　　　　　　7　　　1,853,957

Sample grants (1993).
Shasta Natural Science Association. Redding, CA. $250,000. Redding Arboretum by the River.
Shasta Wildlife Rescue and Rehabilitation, Inc. Anderson, CA. $6,198. Heating and cooling for the Wildlife Rescue Center.
USDA, Forest Service, Klamath National Forest. Yreka, CA. $20,430. Monitoring equipment.

Application process. *Initial contact:* Cover sheet (from Foundation) and letter of intent (3 pages, 1 copy) to include:
1. Signature of the executive director and board president (nongovernmental agencies).
2. Signature of the proposer and an authorized manager or school administrator (governmental and public school agencies).
3. Name of applicant organization, amount requested, and purpose of the grant.
4. History and description of organization.
5. Purpose of grant, why project is important to the community and how it would make a difference. (Include documentation of need.)
6. Goals and measurements of progress and success.
7. Description requirement of volunteers.
8. Projected budget, noting amount of proposed McConnell Foundation support and items affected.
9. Explanation of proposed expenditures and anticipated funds and/or in-kind from other sources.
10. Plans for continued support after one year of funding from Foundation.
11. Experience and expertise of key personnel.
12. Copy of Income and Expense Statement and Balance Sheet including disclosure of pension plans, deferred compensation plans, and the liability thereto.
13. Copy of IRS tax-exempt status determination letter.
14. List of current board of directors; (nongovernmental agencies); listing of governing board (governmental agencies).

If interested, Foundation will request full proposal.
When to apply: Deadlines are February 15 for letter of intent, May 31 for proposal.
Materials available: Annual report, application guidelines, policy statement.

Emphases. *Recipients:* Educational institutions, nonprofit organizations, public agencies.
Activities: Citizen participation, collaborative efforts, demonstration programs, direct services, education, exhibits, innovative programs, volunteerism.
Types of support: Equipment, matching funds, projects, scholarships, single-year grants only.
Geography: Shasta and Siskiyou counties, California only.

Limitations. *Recipients:* Individuals, religious organizations, research institutions.
Activities: Activism, advocacy, conferences, conflict resolution, expeditions/tours, feasibility studies, fieldwork, fundraising, inventories, land acquisition, litigation, lobbying, networking, planning, policy analysis/development, political activities, research, seminars, symposia/colloquia, technical assistance, training, workshops.
Types of support: Advertising campaigns, annual campaigns, capital campaigns/expenses, continuing support, debt retirement, emergency funding, endowments, facilities, fellowships, general purposes, indirect costs, internships, lectureships, loans, maintenance, membership campaigns, mortgage reduction, multi-year grants, pilot projects, professorships, program-related investments, seed money, start-up costs, travel expenses.

McCune Foundation
1104 Commonwealth Building
316 Fourth Avenue
Pittsburgh, Pennsylvania 15222
Tel: 412-644-8779
EIN: 256210269　　Type: Independent
Contact: Henry S. Beukema, Executive Director

History and philosophy. The Foundation was established in 1979 under the will of Charles L. McCune, former president of Union National Bank of Pittsburgh and director of several large corporations. The Foundation funds independent higher education, health, and social services in southwestern Pennsylvania, mainly in the Pittsburgh area.

Officers and directors. *Officers:* Henry S. Beukema, Executive Director; Martha J. Perry, Associate Executive Director. *Distribution Committee:* James McCune Edwards, Richard D. Edwards, John R. McCune, John R. McCune, Jr. *Trustee:* Integra Financial Corporation.

Financial data. Data for fiscal year ended November 30, 1993. *Assets:* $323,113,537 (M). *Total grants disbursed:* $13,616,950.

Environmental awards. *Recent grants:* One grant in 1993 supported trails.

Issues.　Cli　Bio　Lan　Agr　Wat　Oce　Ene　Was　Tox　Pop　Dev
　　　　　　　　　　　•

Funding analysis.

Fiscal year:	1993
Env grants disb:	$50,000
Number:	1
Range:	–
Median:	–
Pct $ disb (env/total):	<1

Recipient (1993):　　　　　　*Number:*　　*Dollars:*
Montour Trail Council　　　　　1　　　　50,000

Activity region (1993):　　　*Number:*　　*Dollars:*
U.S. Mid-Atlantic　　　　　　　1　　　　50,000

Sample grant (1993).
Montour Trail Council. Pittsburgh, PA. $50,000.

Application process. *Initial contact:* Brief letter to include:
1. Organizational background.
   - History.
   - Mission.
   - Types of programs offered.
   - Constituencies served.
2. Project description.
   - Justification of need.
   - Specific goals and objectives.
   - Activities planned to meet goals and objectives.
   - Project timeline.
   - Qualifications of key personnel.
   - Methods of evaluation.
3. Project budget.
   - Anticipated expenses, including details about how Foundation funds will be used.
   - Anticipated income, including information about other foundations approached for funding.
4. Organizational budget.
   - Current year budget and proposed budget for project year(s) showing both income and expenses.

When to apply: Anytime. The distribution committee meets in January and June.
Materials available: Annual report.

Emphases. *Types of support:* Endowments, facilities, projects.
Geography: Southwestern Pennsylvania.

Limitations. *Recipients:* Individuals.
Types of support: General purposes, operating costs.

The Marshall L. & Perrine D. McCune Charitable Foundation

123 East Marcy Street, Suite 201
Santa Fe, New Mexico 87501
Tel: 505-983-8300
EIN: 850375622   Type: Independent
Contact: S. J. Sanchez, Program Officer

History and philosophy. The Foundation was established in 1988 by Perrine Dixon McCune. Its mission is to memorialize the donors through grants that enrich the cultural life, health, education, environment, and spiritual life of the citizens of New Mexico. It favors programs that are foresighted, responsive, flexible and that help the people of New Mexico reach their human and spiritual potential.

Officers and directors. *Officer:* Sara McCune Losinger, Chairman. *Trustees:* James McCune Edwards, Sara McCune Losinger, John R. McCune VI, PNC Bank, N.A.

Financial data. Data for fiscal year ended December 31, 1992.
Assets: $79,977,723 (M). *Gifts received:* $77,625,427. *Total grants disbursed:* $821,680.

Environmental awards. *Recent grants:* 1992 grants included support for land conservation and air quality.

Issues.   Cli   Bio   Lan   Agr   Wat   Oce   Ene   Was   Tox   Pop   Dev
             •   •

Funding analysis.

Fiscal year:	1992
Env grants disb:	$25,000
Number:	4
Range:	$5,000–$10,000
Median:	$5,000
Pct $ disb (env/total):	3

Recipients (1992):	*Number:*	*Dollars:*
The Wilderness Society	1	10,000
LightHawk	1	5,000
The Nature Conservancy, New Mexico Field Office	1	5,000
NENIX	1	5,000

Activity region (1992):	*Number:*	*Dollars:*
U.S. South Central	4	25,000

Sample grants (1992).
LightHawk. Santa Fe, NM. $5,000.
The Nature Conservancy, New Mexico Field Office. Santa Fe, NM. $5,000.
NENIX. Santa Fe, NM. $5,000.
The Wilderness Society. Santa Fe, NM. $10,000.

Application process. *Initial contact:* Letter of inquiry (2 pages, 2 copies) to include:
1. Organization's name, address, telephone number, and contact name.
2. Description of project, intended result of project, amount requested.
3. Project duration.
4. Project budget.
5. Funding strategy.
6. Organizational budget for current year.
7. One sentence certifying tax-exempt status.

Full proposal, if requested (10 pages, 1 copy) to include:
1. Proposal Summary Report (use Foundation form).
2. Proposal summary including purpose, plan of execution, time frame, intended result, budget explanation.
3. History of organization.
   - Statement of current need or problem statement.
   - Statement of purpose and goals.
   - Description of programs, activities, and accomplishments, with highlights of past year.
   - Description of constituency and/or membership.
4. Description of how need to be addressed has been identified within a constituency.
5. How constituency will be involved in planning and implementation.
6. Funding request and plans for the coming year, including:
   - Line item budget for proposed program (revenues and expenses).
   - Fundraising objectives.
   - Future funding.
7. Program evaluation.
   - How organization will monitor and evaluate the project.
   - Evaluation should relate to the organization's objectives.

M

Attachments.
1. Resumes of top staff.
2. Board members, addresses, occupations, description of direct participation in programs.
3. Current annual operating budget.
4. Past major contributors and list of pending applications for the project and their status.
5. Most recent annual financial statement (audited if available).
6. Annual report.
7. Copy of IRS tax-exempt status determination letter.

When to apply: 1995 deadlines are January 4 for letters of inquiry and March 15 for proposals.
Materials available: "Applicant Information," grants list.

Emphases. *Recipients:* Nonprofit organizations.
Activities: Conferences, emergency funding, land acquisition, seminars.
Types of support: Annual campaigns, capital campaigns/expenses, continuing support, endowments, equipment, facilities, general purposes, matching funds, operating costs, projects, research, scholarships, seed money, technical assistance.
Geography: New Mexico, especially Santa Fe, and northern New Mexico.

Limitations. *Recipients:* Individuals.
Types of support: Debt retirement.

The Eugene McDermott Foundation

4701 Drexel Drive
Dallas, Texas 75205
Tel: 214–521–2924
EIN: 237237919   Type: Independent
Contact: Mrs. Eugene McDermott, President

History and philosophy. Eugene B. McDermott, a geophysicist and one of the founders of Texas Instruments, created the Foundation in 1972. The Foundation, which assimilated The McDermott Foundation in 1977, has supported the arts, cultural organizations, education, medical facilities, and scientific pursuits. Special interests include the Eugene McDermott Chair in Brain Sciences and Human Behavior at the Massachusetts Institute of Technology, the Dallas Museum of Fine Arts, and the Dallas Public Library. Grants are made primarily in the Southwest.

Officers and directors. *Officers:* Mrs. Eugene McDermott, President; Charles Cullum, Vice President; Mary McDermott Cook, Secretary/Treasurer; Patricia Brown, Assistant Secretary. *Trustees:* Mary McDermott Cook, Charles Cullum, Mrs. Eugene McDermott, C. J. Thomsen. *Agent:* Nations Bank of Texas, N. A.

Financial data. Data for fiscal year ended August 31, 1992. *Assets:* $43,983,737 (M). *Total grants disbursed:* $1,821,800.

Environmental awards. *Recent grants:* 1992 grants included support for plant conservation, a botanical garden, and a zoo.

Issues.   Cli   Bio   Lan   Agr   Wat   Oce   Ene   Was   Tox   Pop   Dev
                  •   •

Funding analysis.

Fiscal year:	1991	1992
Env grants disb:	$178,500	$132,500
Number:	6	$2,500–$100,000
Range:	$1,000–$100,000	4
Median:	$12,500	$15,000
Pct $ disb (env/total):	9	7

Recipients (1992):	Number:	Dollars:
Dallas Zoological Society	2	102,500
Dallas Arboretum and Botanical Society	1	20,000
Dallas Arboretum and Botanical Society Women's Council	1	10,000

Activity region (1992):	Number:	Dollars:
U.S. South Central	4	132,500

Sample grants (1992).
Dallas Arboretum and Botanical Society. Dallas, TX. $20,000. For house repair and restoration.
Dallas Arboretum and Botanical Society Women's Council. Dallas, TX. $10,000. For garden programs.
Dallas Zoological Society. Dallas, TX. $2,500. For operations.
Dallas Zoological Society. Dallas, TX. $100,000. For animal health care facility.

Application process. *Initial contact:* Letter of inquiry.
When to apply: Anytime. The board meets in April, July and November.

Emphases. *Activities:* Education.
Types of support: Equipment, facilities, operating costs.
Geography: Southwest.

Limitations. *Recipients:* Individuals.

McDonnell Douglas Foundation

P.O. Box 516
Mail Code 1001510
St. Louis, Missouri 63166
Tel: 314–234–0360   Fax: 314–232–7654
EIN: 431128093   Type: Company-sponsored
Contact: Antoinette M. Bailey, Vice President,
            Foundation Community Relations

History and philosophy. The Foundation was established in 1947 by the McDonnell Douglas Corporation. Funding areas in order of priority are: K–12 Education (Math and Science Focus); Minority Education and Development; Youth-at-Risk; Hunger/Homelessness; and Environment.

Officers and directors. *Officers:* John F. McDonnell, Chairman; Antoinette M. Bailey, President; Gerald A. Johnston, Vice President; D. R. Daniels, Secretary/Treasurer. *Directors:* Gerald A. Johnston, Mark Kuhlmann, James H. MacDonald, John F. McDonnell.

Financial data. Data for fiscal years ended December 31, 1992 and 1993. *Assets (1992):* $60,453,264 (M). *Total grants disbursed (1993):* $8,883,769.

Environmental awards. *Recent grants:* 1993 grants included support for wildlife protection, botanical gardens, and environmental education.

Issues. Cli Bio Lan Agr Wat Oce Ene Was Tox Pop Dev
• • • •

Fiscal year:	1992
Env grants disb:	$150,000
Number:	11
Range:	$2,500–$50,000
Median:	$5,000
Pct $ disb (env/total):	2

Recipients (1992 highest):	*Number:*	*Dollars:*
Missouri Botanical Garden	1	50,000
St. Louis Zoological Park	2	50,000
TreePeople	1	12,500
Earthways, Inc.	1	10,000
Arizona Clean and Beautiful, Inc.	1	5,000
Armand Bayou Nature Center	1	5,000
Los Angeles Beautiful	1	5,000
Orange County Marine Institute	1	5,000
The Nature Conservancy, Headquarters	1	5,000

Activity regions (1992):	*Number:*	*Dollars:*
U.S. Midwest	3	100,000
U.S. West	4	27,500
U.S. not specified	2	15,000
U.S. South Central	1	5,000
U.S. Mid-Atlantic	1	2,500

Sample grants (1993).*
Armand Bayou Nature Center. Houston, TX.
Huntsville Botanical Garden. Huntsville, AL.
Missouri Botanical Garden. St. Louis, MO.
National Audubon Society. New York, NY.
Pacific Crest Outward Bound School. San Francisco, CA.
Wildlife Habitat Enhancement Council. Silver Spring, MD.
World Wildlife Fund. Washington, DC.

*Dollar amounts not available.

Application process. *Initial contact:* Proposal to include:
1. Name, address, telephone number, contact person.
2. Statement of problem or need to be addressed.
3. Identification of geographic area or areas and number of people served.
4. Specific purpose for which funds are requested.
5. Specific dollar amount requested.
6. Annual organizational budget and detailed budget for any capital campaign or program to which the request relates.
7. Identification of sources of annual operating funds and of proposed sources and existing major contributors.
8. Explanation of how organization or program differs from others providing the same or similar services in the same geographic area.
9. Copy of IRS tax-exempt status determination letter.
10. Identification of board of directors and key staff members.
When to apply: Anytime. The board meets bimonthly.
Materials available: Annual report, "Funding Guidelines and Application Procedures."

Emphases. *Recipients:* Nonprofit organizations.
Types of support: Annual campaigns, capital campaigns/expenses, continuing support, facilities, general purposes, matching funds, projects, scholarships.
Geography: Areas where McDonnell Douglas has major concentrations of employees: Huntsville, Alabama; Mesa, Arizona; Huntington Beach and Long Beach, California; Titusville, Florida; Macon, Georgia; St. Louis, Missouri region; Houston, Texas; and Salt Lake City, Utah.

Limitations. *Recipients:* Individuals, religious organizations.
Activities: Fundraising, political activities.
Types of support: Loans.

McGregor Fund

333 West Fort Street, Suite 2090
Detroit, Michigan 48226-3115
Tel: 313-963-3495 Fax: 313-963-3512
EIN: 380808800 Type: Independent
Contact: Mrs. Sylvia L. McNarney, Director of Programs

History and philosophy. Tracy W. McGregor established the Fund in 1925 "to relieve the misfortunes and promote the well-being of mankind." Gifts from Mr. McGregor and his wife, Katherine Whitney McGregor, increased the fund to almost $10 million. Primary funding areas are: Education, Human Services, Health, Humanities, Public Benefit, and Other.

Officers and directors. *Officers:* Elliott H. Phillips, President; W. Warren Shelden, Vice President; Peter P. Thurber, Secretary; Robert M. Surdam, Treasurer; W. Calvin Patterson, III, Executive Director and Assistant Secretary. *Trustees:* Carlton M. Higbie, Jr., William T. McCormick, Jr., Eugene A. Miller, Elliott H. Phillips, W. Warren Shelden, Bruce W. Steinhauer, M.D., Peter W. Stroh, Robert M. Surdam, Peter P. Thurber.

Financial data. Data for fiscal year ended June 30, 1993. *Assets:* $98,373,480 (M). *Gifts received:* $1,000. *Total grants authorized:* $7,198,728. *Total grants disbursed:* $5,036,030.

Environmental awards. *Recent grants:* 1993 grants included support for urban environment and a zoo.

Issues. Cli Bio Lan Agr Wat Oce Ene Was Tox Pop Dev
• • •

Funding analysis.

Fiscal year:	1993
Env grants auth:	$125,000
Number:	2
Range:	$25,000–$100,000
Median:	$62,500
Pct $ auth (env/total):	2

M

Recipients (1993):	*Number:*	*Dollars:*
Detroit Zoological Society	1	100,000
The Greening of Detroit	1	25,000

Activity region (1993):	*Number:*	*Dollars:*
U.S. Great Lakes	2	125,000

Sample grants (1993).
Detroit Zoological Society. Royal Oak, MI. $100,000. Construction of an exhibit to house mandrills.
The Greening of Detroit. Detroit, MI. $25,000. Operations.

Application process. *Initial contact:* Contact Fund to request questionnaire. First-time applicants are encouraged to meet with staff to weigh potential trustee interest and to discuss the application process and materials. Proposal to include:
1. Completed questionnaire.
2. Cover letter stating purpose and amount of request.
3. IRS tax-exempt status determination letter; IRS Form 990.
4. Copy of current audited financial statements.
5. Detailed budget, including potential and committed revenues by source and expenditures.
6. Organization's operating budget, including potential and committed revenues by source and planned expenditures for the period covered by proposed project.
7. List of officers and directors and their affiliations.

When to apply: Anytime. The trustees meet four times a year.
Materials available: Annual report (includes "Application Procedures"), application form.

Emphases. *Recipients:* Educational institutions, museums, non-profit organizations, zoos.
Activities: Collaborative efforts, direct services, education, innovative programs, youth programs.
Types of support: Annual campaigns, capital campaigns/expenses, continuing support, endowments, equipment, facilities, general purposes, maintenance, matching funds, multi-year grants, operating costs, pilot projects, projects, seed money.
Geography: Detroit tri-county area (Wayne, Oakland, and Macomb); Michigan.

Limitations. *Recipients:* Individuals, research institutions.
Activities: Conferences, expeditions/tours, litigation, lobbying, research, seminars, symposia/colloquia, workshops.
Types of support: Advertising campaigns, computer hardware, debt retirement, emergency funding, lectureships, loans, membership campaigns, mortgage reduction, program-related investments, travel expenses (unrelated to a specific program).

McInerny Foundation

P.O. Box 3170
Honolulu, Hawaii 96802
Tel: 808–538–4944   Fax: 808–538–4647
EIN: 996002356   Type: Independent
Contact: Lois C. Loomis, Vice President,
    Hawaiian Trust Co., Ltd.

History and philosophy. The McInerny Foundation was created in 1937 by William, James, and Ella McInerny, descendants of Patrick Michael McInerny who arrived on the Hawaiian Islands from County Clare, Ireland in the mid-nineteenth century. The bulk of the founders' estates was left to the Foundation. "Use of this income was intended to be flexible, to cover changing conditions, and to best serve the charitable requirements of the people of the Hawaiian Islands." Current program areas are: Culture and Arts, Education, Environment, Health and Rehabilitation, Social Welfare, and Other.

Officers and directors. *Officers:* Thomas J. MacDonald, Chairman; Henry B. Clark, Jr., Vice Chairman. *Distribution Committee:* Mrs. Gerry Ching, Henry B. Clark, Jr., Thomas J. MacDonald. *Alternates:* Ms. Haunani Apoliona, Mark Fukunaga, Thurston Twigg-Smith.

Financial data. Data for fiscal year ended September 30, 1993. *Assets:* $39,939,619 (M). *Total grants disbursed:* $1,795,834.

Environmental awards. *Recent grants:* 1993 grants included support for preservation of Hawaii's indigenous marine and land-based species and environmental education.

Issues. Cli Bio Lan Agr Wat Oce Ene Was Tox Pop Dev
      •   •   •   •

Funding analysis.

Fiscal year:	1991	1993
Env grants auth:	$41,500	$43,862
Number:	6	7
Range:	$3,000–$10,000	$3,000–$10,000
Median:	$7,250	$7,250
Pct $ auth (env/total):	2	2

Recipients (1993 highest):	*Number:*	*Dollars:*
Hawaii Nature Center	1	10,000
Natural Resources Defense Council	1	7,500
National Tropical Botanical Garden	1	5,000
The Nature Conservancy, Hawaii Field Office	1	7,500

Activity region (1993):	*Number:*	*Dollars:*
Hawaii	7	43,862

Sample grants (1993).
Earthtrust. Kailua, HI. $3,000. Education program on Hawaii's endangered marine wildlife.
National Tropical Botanical Garden. Lawai, HI. $5,000. For hurricane recovery.
Natural Resources Defense Council. Honolulu, HI. $7,500. For Waianae Mountains conservation.

Application process. *Initial contact:* Full proposal (7 copies) to include:
1. Letter (3 pages) signed by presiding officer of the board of directors.
   - Summary of project, a description of how project is to be carried out, population served, and plan for evaluating project effectiveness.
   - Total project cost, amount requested, other sources of anticipated funding, and plans for continued support.
   - Qualifications of project personnel.
   - Contact person's name and telephone number.

2. Budget for both project and organization, showing projected income and expenditures.
3. List of governing board members and their professional or business affiliations.
4. Letters of endorsement (3–4).
5. Statement (1 page) explaining how project will benefit the lives of Hawaii's people and how those lives will be adversely affected if the activity is not carried out.

Attachments (1 copy each).
1. IRS tax-exempt status determination letter.
2. Organization's charter and bylaws.
3. Organization's financial statement for its last accounting period, preferably audited.
4. Other information pertinent to the request (optional).

When to apply: Anytime, except for capital funding requests (deadline is July 15 for consideration in September), and tuition aid/scholarships (deadline is January 15 for consideration in March).
Materials available: Questionnaires for requests for capital or scholarship funds are available from Foundation office.

Emphases. *Recipients:* Educational institutions, nonprofit organizations.
Activities: Education, innovative programs, training, volunteerism.
Types of support: Equipment, facilities, matching funds.
Geography: Hawaii only.

Limitations. *Recipients:* Individuals.
Types of support: Debt retirement, endowments.

The McIntosh Foundation

215 Fifth Street, Suite 300
West Palm Beach, Florida 33401
Tel: 407–832–8845 Fax: 407–832–3226
EIN: 136096459 Type: Independent
EGA member
Contact: Michael A. McIntosh, President

History and philosophy. The McIntosh Foundation was established in 1949 in New York by Josephine H. McIntosh, granddaughter of George Hamilton Hartford who founded the Great Atlantic and Pacific Tea Co. (A&P). Mrs. McIntosh made a bequest of $18.5 million to the Foundation in 1972. The Foundation funds in the areas of Environmental and Civil Rights Litigation, Education, and Social Services.

Officers and directors. *Officers:* Michael A. McIntosh, President; Peter H. McIntosh, Vice President and Treasurer; Winsome D. McIntosh, Vice President and Assistant Secretary; Joan H. McIntosh, Vice President and Assistant Treasurer; Frederick A. Terry, Jr., Secretary. *Directors:* Joan H. McIntosh, Michael A. McIntosh, Peter H. McIntosh, Winsome D. McIntosh, Frederick A. Terry, Jr.

Financial data. Data for fiscal years ended December 31, 1991 and 1992. *Assets (1991):* $28,329,898 (M). *Total grants disbursed (1992):* $1,600,000.

Environmental awards. *Program and interests:* The Foundation's main interest has been in the area of conservation and the environment. It funds organizations whose primary purpose is environmental. Particular foci are:

- Ancient forests.
- Toxics.

Recent grants: 1990 grants included support for land conservation and marine issues (including the protection of individual species).

Issues. Cli Bio Lan Agr Wat Oce Ene Was Tox Pop Dev
         •   •   •   •   •   •

Funding analysis.§

Fiscal year:	1991	1992
Env grants disb:	900,000	$900,000
Number:	–	–
Range:	$5,000–$150,000	$5,000–$150,000
Median:	20,000	$20,000
Pct $ disb (env/total):	–	–

Recipients (1990 highest):	Number:	Dollars:
Sierra Club Legal Defense Fund	1	90,500
Garden Club of America	1	45,000
Open Space Institute	3	38,000
Alaska Conservation Foundation	1	35,000
Southeast Alaska Conservation Council	1	20,000

Activity regions (1990):	Number:	Dollars:
U.S. not specified	6	167,500
Alaska	3	41,000
U.S. Southeast	6	36,500
U.S. Northwest	1	35,000
U.S. Mountain	1	5,000
U.S. West	1	5,000

§1991 and 1992 data as reported to the EGA.

Sample grants (1990).
Alaska Conservation Foundation. Anchorage, AK. $35,000.
Defenders of Wildlife. Washington, DC. $5,000.
Jackson Hole Land Trust. Jackson, WY. $5,000.
Save the Manatee. Maitland, FL. $1,000.

Application process. *Initial contact:* Letter of inquiry including description of proposed project, key staff, information about the applicant organization, and budget.
When to apply: Anytime.

Emphases. *Recipients:* Nonprofit organizations.

Limitations. *Recipients:* Individuals.
Activities: Conferences, research.
Types of support: Capital campaigns/expenses, equipment, endowments, facilities.

M

McKenzie River Gathering Foundation

454 Willamette
Eugene, Oregon 97401
Tel: 503–485–2790   Fax: 503–485–2790
EIN: 930691187   Type: Community
Contact: Linda Reymers, Co-Director

Portland office:
3558 S.E. Hawthorne
Portland, Oregon 97214
Tel: 503–223–0271
Contact: Brigette Sarabi, Co-Director

History and philosophy. Created in 1976, the McKenzie River Gathering Foundation (MRG) derives its name from a gathering of activists convened by founding donors Leslie Brockelbank and Charles Gray along the banks of the McKenzie River. From its inception MRG has been part of Oregon's "progressive" movement. It has also influenced funding for social change nationwide as a founding member of The Funding Exchange, a national group of 14 regionally-based social change foundations.

MRG supports groups that challenge social, economic, and political inequity and work towards a peaceful, just, and environmentally sound society. It focuses on groups with annual budgets below $100,000, unless the proposed project is so controversial that it is difficult to find funding through traditional sources. Interest areas include economic justice, environment, human rights, and peace and international solidarity. Specific topics, are secondary to MRG's other criteria: the applicant must be located in Oregon, with limited access to traditional funding.

Officers and directors. *Officers:* Tarso Ramos, President; Theresa Enrico, Vice President; Foncy Prescott, Treasurer. *Directors:* Peter Cervantes-Gautschi, Theresa Enrico, Jan Fenton, Cliff Jones, Scot Nakagawa, Cecil Prescod, Foncy Prescott, Tarso Ramos, Anne Sweet, Kelley Weigel, Marcy Westerline.

Financial data. Data for fiscal year ended June 30, 1993. *Assets:* $662,547 (U). *Gifts received:* $558,142. *Total grants disbursed:* $222,702.

Environmental awards. *Program and interests:* The environment program concentrates on issues that affect the people of Oregon such as forestry practices, water quality, pesticide use, mining, salmon habitat protection, and Native American sacred lands. Special interests are:

- Environmental protection.
- Sustainable forestry.
- Environmentalist coalition-building.

Recent grants: 1993 grants supported a wide range of topics including land conservation (wilderness, Native American lands); forests (ancient forests, sustainable forestry); water protection (watershed, river, and coastal waters); energy (renewable) and transportation policy; solid waste (incineration); toxics (mining, nuclear, and agricultural issues), all within Oregon.

Issues. Cli • Bio • Lan • Agr • Wat • Oce • Ene • Was • Tox • Pop • Dev •

Funding analysis.§

Fiscal year:	1992	1993
Env grants disb:	$23,150	$37,125
Number:	12	13
Range:	$750–$2,500	$1,700–$5,000
Median:	$2,200	$3,000
Pct $ disb (env/total):	7	12

Recipients (1993 highest):	Number:	Dollars:
Tygh of the Tlxni	1	5,000
Columbia River United	1	3,000
Concerned Friends of the Winema	1	3,000
Friends of the Greensprings	1	3,000
Kalmiopsis Audubon Society	1	3,000
Labor–Environmental Solidarity Network	1	3,000
Oregon Fair Trade Coalition	1	3,000
Rogue Institute for Ecology and Economy	1	3,000
Sacred Earth Coalition	1	3,000

Activity region (1993):	Number:	Dollars:
U.S. Northwest	13	37,125

§Does not include designated or donor-advised grants.

Sample grants (1993).

Citizens for Environmental Quality. Hermiston, OR. $1,925. To publish a newsletter to educate and organize opposition to a chemical weapons incinerator scheduled to be built at the Umatilla Army Depot.

Concerned Citizens for Responsible Mining. Ontario, OR. $2,000. To produce public education materials used to monitor the powerful mining industry and challenge cyanide heap leach gold mining.

Friends of the Greensprings. Ashland, OR. $3,000. General support for this group assisting grassroots involvement in resource management decisions, with a goal of producing sustainable forests and communities.

Oregon Shores Conservation Coalition. Depoe Bay, OR. $2,500. For a series of land-use activism training sessions for coastal residents concerned with countering the dramatically increased pressure for development of the coast.

Rogue Institute for Ecology and Economy. Ashland, OR. $3,000. General support for this coalition of timber union members, environmentalists, and community representatives promoting sustainable forest products enterprises that create living-wage jobs in rural communities.

Sacred Earth Coalition. Portland, OR. $3,000. General support for activities including those of the People of the Salmon Summit, and their continuing efforts to protect Native American treaty rights, sacred sites, and fishing rights.

Application process. *Initial contact:* Contact the Eugene office for application packet. Submit application form (16 copies) and IRS tax-exempt status determination letter (1 copy). Finalists will be interviewed and asked to make a presentation before the Grantmaking Committee. The maximum grant request is $3,000. *When to apply:* Deadlines in 1995 will be in mid-April and mid-October. Check with Foundation for precise dates. *Materials available:* Annual report, Application Packet (includes "Applying for a Grant," "Grant Application Form").

Emphases. *Recipients:* Nonprofit organizations.
Activities: Activism, advocacy, capacity building, citizen participation, collaborative efforts, conferences, fundraising, innovative programs, networking, planning, policy analysis/development, publications, technical assistance, training, volunteerism, workshops, youth programs.
Types of support: Annual campaigns, continuing support, equipment, general purposes, leveraging funds, matching funds, projects, seed money, single-year grants only, start-up costs, technical assistance, travel expenses.
Geography: Oregon-based groups working in Oregon.

Limitations. *Recipients:* Individuals.
Activities: Civil disobedience, lobbying.
Types of support: Scholarships.

McKesson Foundation, Inc.
One Post Street, 32nd Floor
San Francisco, California 94104
Tel: 415–983–8673   Fax: 415–983–7654
EIN: 596144455   Type: Company-sponsored
Contact: Marcia M. Argyris, President

History and philosophy. The McKesson Foundation was established in 1943. It supports organizations in the San Francisco Bay Area and other areas where the McKesson Company has a presence. Program areas are: youth and families, human services, higher education, culture and the arts, and the company's Community Action Fund.

Officers and directors. *Officers:* Marcia M. Argyris, President; John W. d'Alessio, Vice President and Treasurer; Dena G. Gardi, Secretary; Nancy A. Miller, Assistant Secretary; Alan Pearce, Assistant Treasurer. *Directors:* William A. Armstrong, Arthur Chong, James S. Cohune, John W. d'Alessio, Norma Garcia-Kennedy, Stanley A. Greenblatt, Marvin L. Krasnansky, David E. McDowell, Ivan D. Meyerson, Nancy A. Miller, Rhea Palmer, Cheryl L. Poinsette, Garret A. Scholz, Alan Seelenfreund, Gregory L. Tarr, Sonia Tom-Chew, Heidi Yodowitz.

Financial data.* Data for fiscal year ended March 31, 1993. *Assets:* $7,640,000 (M). *Total grants disbursed:* $2,011,000.

*Disbursements as reported by Foundation.

Environmental awards. *Recent grants:* 1993 grants included support for state and national parks and youth education.

Issues. Cli Bio Lan Agr Wat Oce Ene Was Tox Pop Dev
                    •

Funding analysis.

Fiscal year:	1993
Env grants disb:	$49,500
Number:	5
Range:	$2,500–$25,000
Median:	$5,000
Pct $ disb (env/total):	3

Recipients (1993):	Number:	Dollars:
National Park Foundation	1	25,000
Outward Bound USA	1	12,000
California State Parks Foundation	1	5,000
Golden Gate National Park Association	1	5,000
San Francisco Conservation Corps	1	2,500

Activity region (1993):	Number:	Dollars:
U.S. West	5	49,500

Sample grants (1993).
California State Parks Foundation. Kentfield, CA. $5,000.
Golden Gate National Park Association. San Francisco, CA. $5,000.
National Park Foundation. Washington, DC. $25,000.
Outward Bound USA. New York, NY. $12,000.
San Francisco Conservation Corps. San Francisco, CA. $2,500.

Application process. *Initial contact:* Full proposal to include:
1. Letter (2 pages).
   - Description of the organization.
   - Statement of purpose.
   - Request for a specific amount of money.
   - Explanation of how funds will be used.
2. List of board of directors.
3. Organizational budget for current operating year.
4. List of corporate, foundation, and other contributors and amounts for current year.
5. Copy of IRS tax-exempt status determination letter.

When to apply: Anytime. The trustees meet quarterly beginning in April.
Materials available: Annual report (includes "How to Apply for a Grant"), "Why We Do What We Do."

Emphases. *Recipients:* Nonprofit organizations.
Activities: Capacity building, citizen participation, collaborative efforts, direct services, education, innovative programs, volunteerism, youth programs.
Types of support: Operating costs, pilot projects, projects, single-year grants only.
Geography: San Francisco Bay Area.

Limitations. *Recipients:* Botanical gardens, individuals, public agencies, religious organizations, research institutions.
Activities: Activism, advocacy, audiovisual materials, conferences, exhibits, expeditions/tours, feasibility studies, fieldwork, fundraising, inventories, land acquisition, litigation, lobbying, political activities, publications, research, seminars, symposia/colloquia, technical assistance.
Types of support: Advertising campaigns, annual campaigns, capital campaigns/expenses, computer hardware, debt retirement, facilities, fellowships, indirect costs, internships, lectureships, leveraging funds, loans, maintenance, membership campaigns, mortgage reduction, multi-year grants, professorships, program-related investments, technical assistance, travel expenses.
Geography: International.

© 1995 Environmental Data Resources, Inc.

The McKnight Foundation

600 TCF Tower
121 South Eighth Street
Minneapolis, Minnesota 55402-2825
Tel: 612-333-4220   Fax: 612-332-3833
EIN: 410754835   Type: Independent
EGA member
Contact: Dan K. Ray, Program Officer

History and philosophy. The McKnight Foundation is a private grantmaking foundation established in 1953 by William L. and Maude L. McKnight. Mr. McKnight (d. 1978) was one of the early leaders of the 3M Company; however, the Foundation is independent of that corporation. The Foundation assumed its present structure in 1974 when a professional staff was hired. Since that time, its assets have grown from $8 million to more than $1 billion and grants have increased from $741,000 in 1974 to about $50 million in 1994.

The McKnight Foundation has a primary interest in assisting people who are poor or disadvantaged to enhance their capacity for productive living. The Foundation also seeks to strengthen community and community institutions, to enrich people's lives through the arts, to encourage preservation of the natural environment, and to advance scientific knowledge that can improve people's lives. The Foundation's primary geographic focus in its human services and arts grantmaking is the state of Minnesota.

The Foundation employs three strategies to pursue this mission: grantmaking that identifies and meets community needs in response to requests from nonprofit organizations; targeted initiatives developed by the Foundation to meet critical challenges; and support for research in selected fields. Current programs are: Human Services, Arts and Culture, Housing, Environment, International, and National Programs in Basic Research.

Officers and directors. *Officers:* Cynthia Binger Boynton, President; Michael O'Keefe, Executive Vice President; Marilyn Pidany, Vice President and Secretary; Carol Berde, Vice President; James M. Binger, Treasurer; Patricia S. Binger, Assistant Secretary/Assistant Treasurer. *Honorary Chair:* Virginia M. Binger. *Directors:* James H. Binger, James M. Binger, Patricia S. Binger, Virginia M. Binger, Cynthia Binger Boynton, Noa Boynton.

Financial data. Data for fiscal year ended December 31, 1993. *Assets:* $1,175,492,894 (M). *Total grants authorized:* $46,301,679. *Total grants disbursed:* $53,328,919.

Environmental awards. *Program and interests:* The Environment Program focuses on energy and the Mississippi basin.

- Energy Program.

    To ensure that Minnesota residents and institutions use energy as efficiently as possible, as part of a broader goal to encourage use of alternative energy sources throughout the nation.

    The program has two components:

    - Public policy.

        To promote state and local energy policies that encourage the fullest possible reliance on energy conservation and renewable energy in Minnesota.

    - Sustainable development.

        To engage Minnesota businesses in initiatives that encourage the development and marketing of energy-efficient products and services and improved renewable energy technologies.

- Mississippi River Program.

    To help maintain and, where necessary, restore a healthy and sustainable environment in the Mississippi River basin. Consistent with the Foundation's basic mission of assisting people who are poor or disadvantaged, the program places a priority on projects that provide new advantage to those whose ability to respond to environmental conditions along the Mississippi is now handicapped by prejudice, poverty, or lack of access or organization. The Foundation expects to commit about $10.4 million to this program between 1992 and 1996.

    The Mississippi River Program has three components:

    - Building networks.

        To create and strengthen networks of organizations—particularly citizen's groups—active in protecting the river and to examine the impacts of federal farm and navigation policies on the river's economy and environment.

    - Demonstration projects.

        Intensive efforts developed and overseen by the Foundation to address specific environmental issues. The Foundation has initiated two demonstration projects. One is on the Upper Mississippi River, from its headwaters in Minnesota to the Quad Cities of Illinois and Iowa. This project encourages state and federal agencies to reshape their services to better support the work of community-based river protection initiatives. The other is on the Lower Mississippi River between Baton Rouge and New Orleans, Louisiana.

    - General grants.

        To support projects that prevent toxic pollution, help farmers adopt less damaging practices, encourage less environmentally-harmful techniques to reduce flood damage, or address environmental issues of particular concern to poor people.

        Additional support for projects on tributaries of the Mississippi in Minnesota, along the Mississippi, its banks, and floodplain in all ten Mississippi River states.

Issues. Cli Bio Lan Agr Wat Oce Ene Was Tox Pop Dev
• • • • • • •

Funding analysis.

Fiscal year:	1991	1993
Env grants auth:	$81,650	$2,685,160
Number:	5	42
Range:	$7,200–$20,000	$2,280–$725,000
Median:	$18,000	$29,750
Pct $ auth (env/total):	<1	6

Recipients (1993 highest):

	Number:	Dollars:
Iowa Natural Heritage Foundation	2	740,000
Southern University, Baton Rouge, Center for Environmental		
Environmental Law and Policy Center of the Midwest	1	160,000
Friends of the Minnesota Valley	1	119,000
Coalition to Restore Coastal Louisiana	1	112,500

Activity regions (1993):

	Number:	Dollars:
U.S. Great Lakes	25	1,793,160
U.S. South Central	7	566,000
U.S. multiple regions*	7	221,000
U.S. Midwest	1	60,000
U.S. Southeast	2	45,000

*Mississippi River Basin.

Sample grants (1993).
American Rivers, Inc. Washington, DC. $10,000. Funds to advocate for improved protection of environmental resources following flooding of the Mississippi River.
Great Lakes Indian Fish & Wildlife Commission. Odanah, WI. $45,000. Funds to develop a wild rice restoration plan for the watersheds of the Rum and St. Croix rivers.
Institute for Conservation Leadership. Washington, DC. $28,000. Funds for a leadership training program for members of the Mississippi River Basin Alliance.
Louisiana Environmental Action Network. Baton Rouge, La. $93,000. Funds to strengthen the technical capacities of citizen groups working to reduce pollution and protect the Mississippi River.
Wetlands Research, Inc. Chicago, IL. $75,000. Funds to plan for the restoration of wetlands and floodplains at flood-damaged sites along the Mississippi River and in watersheds of the river's tributaries in Minnesota.

Application process. *Initial contact:* Request detailed guidelines for all program components from Foundation office. Potential applicants should review the guidelines, then send letter of inquiry (2–4 pages, 2 copies) before submitting a proposal. Letter to include:
1. Description of applicant organization.
2. Summary of proposed project or intended use of funds.
3. Brief explanation of how project will further the goals of the Foundation's programs.
4. Amount of support requested.

When to apply: Applications are considered quarterly. Deadlines vary for each program component. Deadlines for the Mississippi River Program are February 15, May 15, August 15, and November 15 for consideration in June, September, and December 1995 and March 1996. No facsimiles will be accepted.
Materials available: Annual report, "The Environment Program: The Mississippi River," "The Mississippi River Program Grantmaking Policies and Procedures," and "Energy Efficiency and Renewable Energy in Minnesota Guidelines."
Facsimiles will not be accepted.

Emphases. *Recipients:* Educational institutions, nonprofit organizations, public agencies.
Activities: Activism, advocacy, capacity building, citizen participation, collaborative efforts, conflict resolution, demonstration programs, direct services, innovative programs, networking, planning, policy analysis/development, technical assistance, training.
Types of support: Annual campaigns, capital campaigns/expenses, computer hardware, continuing support, general purposes, leveraging funds, matching funds, multi-year grants, operating costs, pilot projects, projects, seed money, start-up costs, technical assistance.
Geography: Minnesota (for the Energy Program); the ten Mississippi River corridor states (Louisiana, Mississippi, Tennessee, Arkansas, Kentucky, Missouri, Illinois, Iowa, Minnesota, Wisconsin) for the Mississippi River Program.

Limitations. *Recipients:* Botanical gardens, museums, religious organizations, research institutions, zoos.
Activities: Audiovisual materials, conferences, exhibits, expeditions/tours, inventories, land acquisition, litigation, lobbying, research, seminars, symposia/colloquia, youth programs.
Types of support: Advertising campaigns, debt retirement, emergency funding, endowments, equipment, facilities, fellowships, internships, lectureships, loans, maintenance, membership campaigns, mortgage reduction, professorships, program-related investments, scholarships, travel expenses.

McLean Contributionship
945 Haverford Road
Bryn Mawr, Pennsylvania 19010
Tel: 215–527–6330 Fax: 215–527–0338
EIN: 236396940 Type: Independent
Contact: John H. Buhsmer, President

History and philosophy. The McLean Contributionship was originally established in 1951 as the Bulletin Contributionship for charitable, educational, and scientific purposes. In 1980, when the association of the McLean family with the Philadelphia *Evening and Sunday Bulletin* ended, the philanthropy was renamed The McLean Contributionship. The Contributionship gives mainly to projects and programs in the Greater Philadelphia area where the McLean family has developed strong business and personal ties.

Funding areas are: environment; educational, medical, scientific, and cultural developments; health care; youth development; and responsible journalism.

Officers and directors. *Officers:* William L. McLean, III, Chairman; John H. Buhsmer, President and Secretary. *Trustees:* Jean G. Bodine, John H. Buhsmer, Joseph K. Gordon, William L. McLean, III, Carolyn M. Raymond. *Emeritus trustee:* R. Jean Brownlee. *Advisory trustees:* Leila G. Dyer, Sandra L. McLean.

Financial data. Data for fiscal year ended December 31, 1992. *Assets:* $23,514,546 (M). *Gifts received:* $27,127. *Total grants disbursed:* $1,097,500.

Environmental awards. *Program and interests:* The trustees prefer projects that "stimulate a better understanding of the physical environment [of the Greater Philadelphia area] and that work to preserve its best features."

M

Recent grants: 1992 grants included support for habitat protection and preservation (land acquisition, rivers, and bays/estuaries) and biodiversity (zoos and botanical gardens).

Issues. Cli Bio Lan Agr Wat Oce Ene Was Tox Pop Dev
          •   •   •   •

Funding analysis.

Fiscal year:	1991	1992
Env grants disb:	$171,000	$220,000
Number:	10	12
Range:	$1,000–$50,000	$1,000–$50,000
Median:	$15,000	$15,000
Pct $ disb (env/total):	17	20

Recipients (1992 highest):	Number:	Dollars:
The Nature Conservancy, Pennsylvania Field Office	1	50,000
The Schuylkill Center for Environmental Education	1	50,000
American Association of Botanical Gardens and Arboreta	1	25,000
Hawk Mountain Sanctuary Association	1	25,000
Academy of Natural Sciences of Philadelphia	1	20,000
Natural Lands Trust	1	20,000

Activity regions (1992):	Number:	Dollars:
U.S. Mid-Atlantic	10	209,000
South America	1	10,000
U.S. not specified	1	1,000

Sample grants (1992).
American Association of Botanical Gardens and Arboreta. Wayne, PA. $25,000. To help fund the development of the North America Plant Collections.
American Ornithologists' Union. Philadelphia, PA. $20,000. To support the National Fish and Wildlife Foundation.
The Nature Conservancy, Pennsylvania Field Office. Philadelphia, PA. $50,000. To help establish a Stewardship Endowment Fund.
Pennsylvania State University. DuBois, PA. $6,000. To support the Wildlife Technology Program.
Pennypack Watershed Association. Huntingdon Valley, PA. $8,000. To help repair Creek Road Bridge.
RARE Center for Tropical Conservation. Philadelphia, PA. $10,000. To support publication of *The Birds of South America.*
The Schuylkill Center for Environmental Education. Philadelphia, PA. $50,000. For the Teacher Research Center Project.
Zoological Society of Philadelphia. Philadelphia, PA. $2,500. For the 1992 Corporate Sponsors program.

Application process. *Initial contact:* Letter to include:
1. Description and justification of proposed project.
2. Budget.
3. Timetable.
4. Sources of other grants or alternative methods of financing.
5. Organization's financial statement.
6. Interim operating statements or budgets.
7. Evidence of tax-exempt status.

When to apply: Anytime.
Materials available: "Statement of History and Philosophy, Purposes, Procedures."

Emphases. *Recipients:* Nonprofit organizations.
Geography: The Greater Philadelphia area and other areas where the McLean family has developed ties.

Limitations. *Types of support:* Operating costs.

Giles W. and Elise G. Mead Foundation
P.O. Box 2218
Napa, California 94558
Tel: 707–257–6737   Fax: 707–226–2164
EIN: 956040921   Type: Independent
EGA member
Contact: Suzanne Easton, Executive Administrator

History and philosophy. The Giles W. and Elise G. Mead Foundation was established in 1961. Giles Mead was founder, chairman, and CFO of Union Carbide. His widow, Elise, was an astute business woman and a powerful force in Los Angeles County. The Foundation makes grants in the areas of: Education, Science, and the Environment.

Officers and directors. *Officers:* Giles W. Mead, Jr., President; Daniel E. McArthur, Vice President and Assistant Treasurer; Calder M. Mackay, Secretary/Treasurer. *Directors:* Stafford R. Grady, Katherine Cone Keck, Calder M. Mackay, Richard N. Mackay, Daniel E. McArthur, Giles W. Mead, Jr., Jane W. Mead, Parry W. Mead.

Financial data. Data for fiscal year ended October 31, 1993. *Assets:* $9,156,257 (U). *Total grants disbursed:* $453,263.

Environmental awards. *Program and interests:* The Environment Program's foci are:

- Forestry and fisheries development.
- Sustainable development.
- Public education.

The Foundation significantly increased its environmental funding in 1992. Its goal is to award about 50 percent of its grants for environmental purposes.
Recent grants: 1993 grants included support for land conservation, sustainable forestry, watershed protection, coastal issues, environmental ethics, and elementary education.

Issues. Cli Bio Lan Agr Wat Oce Ene Was Tox Pop Dev
          •   •   •   •   •

Funding analysis.

Fiscal year:	1991	1993
Env grants auth:	$57,500	$366,763
Number:	3	30
Range:	$7,500–$25,000	$1,000–$28,000
Median:	$25,000	$10,000
Pct $ disb (env/total):	12	81

Recipients (1993 highest):	Number:	Dollars:
Ecotrust	2	35,000
LightHawk	1	28,000
Center for Public Integrity	1	25,000
Grand Canyon Trust	1	25,000
Napa County Land Trust	1	25,000
Oregon Rivers Council	1	25,000
The Pacific Forest Trust, Inc.	1	25,000

Activity regions (1993 highest):	Number:	Dollars:
U.S. West	18	178,763
U.S. Northwest	5	65,000
U.S. not specified	2	35,000
Andean Region and Southern Cone	1	28,000
Canada	1	25,000
U.S. South Central	2	25,000

Sample grants (1993).

Andrea Torrice Productions. San Francisco, CA. $10,000. Grant to support production of video documentary, "Large Dams, False Promises," illustrating the environmental and social impacts of large dams around the world.

Association of Forest Service Employees. Eugene, OR. $10,000. To support public education project in efforts to reform U.S. Forest Service.

Bighorn Institute. Palm Desert, CA. $5,000. To help purchase research equipment in efforts to monitor and conserve bighorn sheep.

California Association of Resource Conservation Districts. Sacramento, CA. $3,500. To help create a supplemental "delivery network" as part of the Forest Stewardship Program.

Center for Public Integrity. Washington, DC. $25,000. For continued support of sustainable forestry initiatives in British Columbia and in support of Haisla Rediscovery Program, a cultural and environmental camp experience for native youth.

Forest Trust. Santa Fe, NM. $15,000. For forest-based rural development programs including organizing forest practitioners and promoting public policy initiatives.

Grand Canyon Trust. Flagstaff, AZ. $25,000. For the Navajo Nation Cultural Tourism Project, an effort to link resource conservation with economic development through tourism.

Greenbelt Alliance. San Francisco, CA. $15,000. For the North Bay Urban Growth Initiative. The Alliance works to promote land protection in the Bay Area through citizen action and land trust support.

Headwaters, Inc. Ashland, OR. $10,000. For watershed monitoring and conservation program in southern Oregon and northern California.

Institute for Sustainable Forestry. Redway, CA. $11,763. Matching grant for organizational development and printing costs of publication.

Klamath Forest Alliance. Etna, CA. $5,000. To enable additional staff time to follow up on Forest Summit activities by the Clinton administration.

KQED. San Francisco, CA. $5,000. For school demonstration project, using video shorts, "Green Means."

LightHawk. Santa Fe, NM. $28,000. For flight reconnaissance and monitoring of forest practices in Chile.

Plumas County Community Development Commission. Quincy, CA. $4,000. For sociological research on forest-dependent communities.

University of California, Davis. Davis, CA. $9,500. To support study by Dr. Peter B. Moyle, "Historical Abundance of Chinook Salmon in the Central Valley of California."

The Video Project. Oakland, CA. $10,000. To support the project, Teaching the Next Generation Campaign.

The Wilderness Society. San Francisco, CA. $10,000. To support participation of northern California groups in the North Coast Forest Watersheds and Fisheries Program.

Application process. *Initial contact:* Brief letter of inquiry describing the project. Complete proposal, if requested, to include:
1. Detailed project description (3–5 pages) with supporting documentation.
2. Project budget and time frame.
3. Other funding sources.
4. Copy of IRS tax-exempt status determination letter.
5. List of staff and directors associated with the project (including affiliation or expertise).
6. Current financial statement showing assets, liabilities, income and expenses, and an annual program report if available.

When to apply: Anytime.
Materials available: Biennial report (includes, "Application and Program Guidelines").

Emphases. *Recipients:* Nonprofit organizations.
Activities: Advocacy, audiovisual materials, collaborative efforts, conferences, education, land acquisition, media projects, policy analysis/development, research.
Types of support: Equipment, matching funds, seed money, technical assistance.
Geography: National programs, or those in the western United States.

Limitations. *Recipients:* Individuals.
Types of support: Operating costs.

Nelson Mead Fund
c/o Rend & Co.
1230 Kettering Tower
Dayton, Ohio 45423
Tel: 513-223-6414
EIN: 316064591   Type: Independent
Contact: Ruth C. Mead, Trustee

History and philosophy. The Fund was established in 1965 with contributions from the original founders and trustees. Interests include conservation, Protestant giving, health, culture, education, and civic affairs.

Officers and directors. *Trustee:* Ruth C. Mead.

Financial data. Data for fiscal year ended November 30, 1993. *Assets:* $5,670,559 (M). *Total grants disbursed:* $274,032.

Environmental awards. *Recent grants:* 1993 grants included support for land conservation, parks, marine issues, wildlife, arboreta, and horticulture.

M

Issues. Cli • Bio • Lan • Agr • Wat • Oce Ene Was • Tox Pop Dev •

Funding analysis.

Fiscal year:	1993
Env grants disb:	$52,990
Number:	33
Range:	$25–$10,150
Median:	$500
Pct $ disb (env/total):	19

Recipients (1993 highest):	Number:	Dollars:
World Wildlife Fund	1	10,150
1000 Friends of Florida	1	10,000
Cox Arboretum Associates, Inc.	2	7,000
The Nature Conservancy, Headquarters	2	6,700
Friends of Lincoln Park	1	5,000

Activity regions (1993 highest):	Number:	Dollars:
U.S. not specified	8	18,350
U.S. Great Lakes	11	16,115
U.S. Southeast	6	13,125
International*	1	2,200
New York/New Jersey	4	2,000

*Multiple regions or not specified.

Sample grants (1993).
The Billfish Foundation. Miami, FL. $500.
Cox Arboretum Associates, Inc. Dayton, OH. $2,000.
Defenders of Wildlife. Washington, DC. $500.
Friends of Aullwood, Inc. Dayton, OH. $2,000.
Friends of Lincoln Park. Chicago, IL. $5,000.
Hobe Sound Nature Center. Hobe Sound. FL. $500.
Jupiter Island Garden Club. Hobe Sound. FL. $25.
The Nature Conservancy, Headquarters. Arlington, VA. $6,500.
Reeves-Reed Arboretum. Summit, NJ. $250.
World Wildlife Fund. Washington, DC. $10,150.

Application process. *Initial contact:* The Fund awards grants to pre-selected organizations only. No unsolicited applications accepted.

Emphases. *Recipients:* Pre-selected organizations only.

Limitations. *Recipients:* Individuals.

Meadows Foundation, Inc.

Wilson Historic Block
3003 Swiss Avenue
Dallas, Texas 75204–6090
Tel: 214-826-9431   Fax: 214-827-7042
EIN: 756015322   Type: Independent
Contact: Bruce H. Esterline, Vice President for Grants

History and philosophy. The Meadows Foundation was established in 1948 by Algur Hurtle Meadows and his wife, Virginia Stuart Meadows. Algur Meadows was a lawyer and oil entrepreneur who founded the General American Oil Company of Texas. The Foundation's mission is to benefit the people of Texas. It seeks innovative ways to solve community problems. Grants are made in five areas of interest: Arts and Culture, Human Services, Health, Education, and Civic and Cultural Affairs.

Officers and directors. *Officers:* Curtis W. Meadows, Jr., President and CEO; Sally R. Lancaster, Executive Vice President; G. Thomas Rhodus, Vice President, Secretary, and Special Counsel; Robert E. Wise, Vice President and Treasurer; Robert E. Weiss, Vice President for Administration; Bruce H. Esterline, Vice President for Grants; Judy B. Culbertson, Linda P. Evans, Robert Al Meadows, Evy Kay Ritzen, Eloise Meadows Rouse, Vice Presidents; Anne P. Herrscher, Emily J. Jones, Assistant Vice Presidents; Nancy J. Nelson, Assistant Secretary; Ron Dugan, Assistant Treasurer. *Directors:* Evelyn Meadows Acton, John W. Broadfoot, Vela Meadows Broadfoot, J. W. Bullion, Eudine Meadows Cheney, Linda P. Evans, John A. Hammack, Sally R. Lancaster, Curtis W. Meadows, Jr., Robert Al Meadows, Harvey R. Mitchell, Evy Kay Ritzen, Eloise Meadows Rouse, Dorothy C. Wilson.

Financial data. Data for fiscal year ended December 31, 1993. *Assets:* $614,416,989 (M). *Total grants authorized:* $20,055,138. *Total grants disbursed:* $12,244,044.

Environmental awards. *Program and interests:* Topics of interest include environmental education and water issues.
Recent grants: 1993 grants included support for land conservation, beautification, and waste management.

Issues. Cli Bio • Lan • Agr • Wat • Oce Ene • Was Tox Pop Dev

Funding analysis.

Fiscal year:	1992	1993
Env grants disb:	$378,000	$930,281
Number:	3	10
Range:	$25,000–$300,000	$10,718–$213,633
Median:	$53,000	$73,238
Pct $ disb (env/total):	2	8

Recipients (1993 highest):	Number:	Dollars:
Texas State Aquarium Association	1	213,633
Ecology Action of Austin	1	206,000
Market Square Trust	1	105,000
City of Jasper	1	100,000
City of Elgin	1	83,275

Activity region (1993):	Number:	Dollars:
U.S. South Central	10	930,281

Sample grants (1993).
The Conservation Fund. Arlington, TX. $40,000. Toward expenses of a Texas office to facilitate land and resource conservation and historic preservation efforts.
Dallas Civic Garden Center. Dallas, TX. $63,200. Toward expansion of the Community Gardens Program that enables low-cost, shared gardens.
Dallas Parks Foundation. Dallas, TX. $48,455. Toward Cool Dallas, a tree planting project for low-income neighborhoods, to reduce residential utility costs.

Ecology Action of Austin. Austin, TX. $206,000. Toward purchase of a collection truck and containers for a rural, multi-county, solid-waste recycling program.

Texas State Aquarium Association. Corpus Christi, TX. $213,633. To construct a mobile aquarium, Ocean-On-Wheels, to travel to communities and schools.

Application process. *Initial contact:* Full proposal, unbound (1 copy), to include, in this order:
1. Brief history of organization's purpose and work.
2. Specific description of program or project proposed for funding.
3. Project income/expense budget.
4. Others asked to support this project, with amounts and responses to date.
5. Amount requested of the Meadows Foundation, with desired payment date.
6. Copy of IRS tax-exempt status determination letter.
7. Listing of trustees or directors, with information on profession, gender, and ethnicity.
8. Information on how many times a year the executive committee and board meet, and attendance figures.
9. Names and qualifications of principal staff.
10. Organization's current fiscal year-to-date financial statements and latest IRS Form 990 (for a young organization).

When to apply: Anytime.
Materials available: Annual report (includes "Grants Application Information").

Emphases. *Recipients:* Educational institutions, museums, non-profit organizations, public agencies, zoos.
Activities: Capacity building, citizen participation, demonstration programs, direct services, exhibits, innovative programs, land acquisition, youth programs.
Types of support: Capital campaigns/expenses, computer hardware, continuing support, equipment, facilities, multi-year grants.
Geography: Texas only.

Limitations. *Recipients:* Individuals.
Activities: Conferences, research (biomedical), symposia/colloquia.
Types of support: Annual campaigns.

The Andrew W. Mellon Foundation

140 East 62nd Street
New York, New York 10021
Tel: 212-838-8400   Fax: 212-223-2778
EIN: 131879954   Type: Independent
Contact: William Robertson IV, Program Officer,
   Conservation and Environment

History and philosophy. The Andrew W. Mellon Foundation was formed in 1969 by the consolidation of two foundations established by the children of Andrew W. Mellon: the Old Dominion Foundation (created in 1941 by Paul Mellon) and the Avalon Foundation (created in 1940 by Alisa Mellon Bruce). The Andrew W. Mellon Foundation's mission is to "aid and promote such religious, charitable, scientific, literary, and educational purposes as may be in the furtherance of the public welfare or tend to promote the well-doing or well-being of mankind." Within this broad charter the Foundation makes grants on a selective basis to institutions in higher education, in cultural affairs and the performing arts, in population, in certain areas of conservation and environment, and in public affairs."

Officers and directors. *Officers:* John C. Whitehead, Chairman; William G. Bowen, President; Harriet Zuckerman, Executive Vice President; T. Dennis Sullivan, Financial Vice President; Richard H. Ekman, Secretary; Eileen M. Scott, Treasurer/Assistant Secretary. *Trustees:* William G. Bowen, Charles E. Exley, Jr., Hanna Holborn Gray, Timothy Mellon, Frank H. T. Rhodes, Charles A. Ryskamp, John R. Stevenson, John C. Whitehead. *Honorary Trustee:* Paul Mellon.

Financial data. Data for fiscal year ended December 31, 1993. *Assets:* $2,305,385,000 (M). *Total grants disbursed:* $89,422,070.

Environmental awards. *Program and interests:* "The Foundation's program in Conservation and Environment has evolved from interests originally stated by the Avalon and Old Dominion Foundations as including the preservation of natural areas and the support of 'organizations concerned with increasing man's understanding of his natural environment, his relation to it, and the effects of his activities upon it.' Through the early 1970s, a substantial fraction of grants supported land acquisition. Between 1974 and 1979, the Foundation moved toward support of research in energy, natural resources, and the environment, including the oceans, and of important institutions working in these fields. It also supported the training of young scientists, engineers, resource managers, and potential policymakers.

"Our current program is devoted to basic research on how ecosystems work. It emphasizes the support of important institutions, innovative research, and the training of promising researchers. Our grants most often try to address several of these objectives simultaneously. Within the broad field of ecosystems research and training, we focus on botany and terrestrial ecosystems because of their key importance within larger systems and because other funding sources pay the least attention to them. We also invest in land preservation through The Trust for Public Land.

"In selecting both institutions and researchers, we look for independence, leadership in the field, vitality in questioning research and its results, and a commitment to objective research aimed at learning and understanding rather than at proving a point or supporting a position. As Hutchinson said in 1943, 'the point of view of the mind that delights in understanding nature rather than in attempting to reform her.' In reviewing training proposals, we look for programs that reach especially talented students and involve them with leading researchers and teachers."

A recent review committee recommended that the Foundation investigate two new areas for potential funding. "The first links scientific research to questions of public policy, particularly in the areas of governmental regulation. . . . The second . . . is the link between environmental concerns and population trends with a special emphasis on the Amazon basin."

"The Foundation does not make grants for work in such areas as energy, global warming, biodiversity, sustainable agriculture, pollution, or related policy."

M

Issues. Cli Bio Lan Agr Wat Oce Ene Was Tox Pop Dev
  •   •   •   •   •

Funding analysis.

Fiscal year:	1991	1993
Env grants auth:	$8,395,000	$11,734,000
Number:	23	40
Range:	$15,000–$1,200,000	$10,000–$1,500,000
Median:	$390,000	$172,500
Pct $ auth (env/total):	10	13

Recipients (1993 highest):	Number:	Dollars:
Carnegie Institution of Washington	1	1,500,000
Smithsonian Institution	1	900,000
The New York Botanical Garden	1	900,000
Center for Plant Conservation	1	750,000
Scripps Institution of Oceanography	1	720,000
University of Maryland, Coastal and Environmental Policy Program	1	720,000

Activity regions (1993 highest):	Number:	Dollars:
U.S. not specified	4	2,550,000
U.S. Northeast	9	2,234,000
New York/New Jersey	8	1,938,000
U.S. Mid-Atlantic	4	1,347,000
U.S. Midwest	2	1,100,000

Sample grants (1993).

Brooklyn Botanic Garden. Brooklyn, NY. $150,000. Toward costs of programs of plant conservation research.

Carnegie Institution of Washington. Washington, DC. $1,500,000. Matching endowment to support the research programs of its Department of Plant Biology.

Center for Plant Conservation. St. Louis, MO. $750,000. For general support.

Clemson University. Clemson, SC. $130,000. Toward costs of programs of ecological research and training.

Cornell University. Ithaca, NY. $188,000. Toward costs of a program of research on ecological processes.

Corporacion para el Desarrollo de Las Ciencias Vegetales en America Latina. Santiago, Chile. $300,000. For use toward continuing support of the Latin American Plant Sciences Network.

Environmental Data Research Institute. Rochester, NY. $50,000. Toward costs of producing and distributing the second edition of *Environmental Grantmaking Foundations* directory.

Harvard University. Cambridge, MA. $420,000. Toward costs of programs of ecological research and training.

Marine Biological Laboratory. Woods Hole, MA. $600,000. Toward costs of a program of ecological research.

United Negro College Fund, Inc. New York, NY. $100,000. Toward costs of programs for minority students in ecological research.

Yale University. New Haven, CT. $230,000. Toward costs of programs of research on components of ecosystems.

Application process. *Initial contact:* Letter of inquiry to include:
1. Need, nature, and the amount of the request and the justification for it.
2. Copy of IRS tax-exempt status determination letter.
3. Any supplementary exhibits an applicant may wish to submit.

When to apply: Anytime.
Materials available: Annual report.

Emphases. *Recipients:* Educational institutions, nonprofit organizations, research institutions.
Activities: Research (scientific).

Limitations. *Recipients:* Individuals, public agencies, zoos.
Activities: Activism, advocacy, audiovisual materials, capacity building, citizen participation, conferences, conflict resolution, direct services, exhibits, expeditions/tours, feasibility studies, fundraising, inventories, litigation, lobbying, media projects, political activities, policy analysis/development, research (medical), seminars, symposia/colloquia, technical assistance, workshops, volunteerism.
Types of support: Advertising campaigns, annual campaigns, capital campaigns/expenses, debt retirement, facilities, indirect costs, lectureships, loans, membership campaigns, mortgage reduction, program-related investments, technical assistance.

Richard King Mellon Foundation

P.O. Box 2930
Pittsburgh, Pennsylvania 15230–2930
Tel: 412–392–2800   Fax: 412–392–2837
EIN: 251127705   Type: Independent
Contact: George H. Taber, Vice President and Director

History and philosophy. The Richard King Mellon Foundation was established in 1947 by Richard King Mellon (1899–1970), president and chairman of the board of Mellon National Bank and Trust Company, and founder and president of T. Mellon and Sons. A dominant force in the renewal of Pittsburgh, R. K. Mellon was also a renowned sportsman and dedicated to the preservation of the national environment and its wildlife.

Since 1988 the Foundation has focused its grantmaking activities on two broad areas: the quality of life in Pittsburgh and southwestern Pennsylvania, and conservation of natural areas nationwide.

Officers and directors. *Officers:* Richard P. Mellon, Chairman; Seward Prosser Mellon, President and Chairman of the Executive Committee; George H. Taber, Vice President and Director; Michael Watson, Secretary; Arthur D. Miltenberger, Treasurer; Robert B. Burr, Jr., Assistant Treasurer; John J. Turcik, Controller. *Trustees:* Andrew W. Mathieson, Richard P. Mellon, Seward Prosser Mellon, Arthur M. Scully, Jr., George H. Taber, Mason Walsh, Jr.

Financial data. Data for fiscal year ended December 31, 1993. *Assets:* $1,057,577,335 (M). *Total grants authorized:* $51,369,980.

Environmental awards. *Program and interests:* The Foundation has two national conservation programs: The American Land Conservation Program and Conservation of Natural Areas. "At the forefront of the Foundation's activities is the American Land Conservation Program [initiated in 1988]. In December of 1993, the Foundation proudly published *Gifts to the Nation*, a report summarizing the first five years of this program. The report details our commitment to the conservation and preservation of Civil War battlefields, wildlife habitat, and scenic vistas throughout the United States."

The Conservation of Natural Areas Program targets:

- Land acquisition.
- Wetlands protection.
- Wildlife preservation.

Recent grants: Grants in 1993 included over $23 million for The American Land Conservation Program to secure public ownership and protection at ten sites around the nation. Under its Conservation of Natural Areas Program, the Foundation made grants in 1993 for topics including land and water conservation, farmland preservation, coastal issues, wildlife protection, and outdoor education.

Issues.   Cli Bio Lan Agr Wat Oce Ene Was Tox Pop Dev
              •   •   •   •   •   •   •   •

Funding analysis.

Fiscal year:	1991	1993
Env grants auth:	$33,244,053	$27,276,865
Number:	21	20
Range:	$5,000–$30,835,053	$50,000–$23,546,865
Median:	$50,000	$100,000
Pct $ auth (env/total):	74	53

Recipients (1993 highest):	*Number:*	*Dollars:*
Richard King Mellon Foundation, American Land Conservation Program	1	23,546,865
American Farmland Trust	1	750,000
The Ruffed Grouse Society	1	750,000
Chesapeake Bay Foundation	1	500,000
Zoological Society of Pittsburgh	1	300,000

Activity regions (1993):	*Number:*	*Dollars:*
U.S. not specified	6	24,621,865
U.S. Mid-Atlantic	9	2,085,000
U.S. Mountain	1	225,000
U.S. Northeast	3	225,000
U.S. Southeast	1	120,000

Sample grants (1993).

American Farmland Trust. Washington, DC. $750,000 (3 years). For ongoing farmland conservation activities.

American Wilderness Alliance. Englewood, CO. $225 (3 years). For its Corridors of Life project designed to help solve the problems of biodiversity protection in the Northern Rocky Mountain region.

Chesapeake Bay Foundation. Annapolis, MD. $500,000 (3 years). To support its programs in Pennsylvania designed to restore and protect the Susquehanna River and the Chesapeake Bay.

Maine Coast Heritage Trust. Brunswick, ME. $75,000. For support of a study for the creation of a Maine Island Greenway.

National Trust for Historic Preservation. Washington, DC. $75,000. Toward support of its American Resources Information Network designed to respond to groups which seek to eviscerate environmental protection and related land protection programs.

Resources for the Future. Washington, DC. $100,000. To assist in the development of a community risk profile for the city of Pittsburgh.

The Ruffed Grouse Society. Coraopolis, PA. $750,000 (5 years). To support its "Flight Plan" campaign designed to improve and expand habitat.

Scenic America. Washington, DC. $100,000 (2 years). For work on conserving the scenic character of Pennsylvania's highways while still encouraging economic development.

Application process. *Initial contact:* Full proposal and application form. Attachments to include:
1. Copy of IRS tax-exempt status determination letter.
2. Executive summary providing an overview of the organization, the proposed project, the problem it seeks to address, population served, and how it will be operated.
3. List of board of directors and name of chairman and/or president.
4. Background of organization, including history, purpose, and types of programs it provides.
5. Audited financial statements for the last two years.
6. Operating budget and timetable for proposed project.
7. Annual reports, brochures, catalogs, etc.
8. Other sources of funding and an explanation of how the project will be financed at the expiration of the proposed grant.
9. Method to be used to evaluate project success.

When to apply: Deadlines are April 1 and October 1. The board of trustees meets in June and December.

Materials available: Annual report (contains "Policy," application form, and "Checklist of Required Attachments").

Emphases. *Recipients:* Aquariums, educational institutions, museums, nonprofit organizations, public agencies, research institutions, zoos.

Activities: Conferences, education, land acquisition, research.

Types of support: Annual campaigns, capital campaigns/expenses, matching funds, operating costs, pilot projects, scholarships, seed money.

Geography: United States only.

Limitations. *Recipients:* Individuals.

Types of support: Fellowships, scholarships.

Merck Family Fund

6930 Carroll Avenue, Suite 500
Takoma Park, Maryland 20912
Tel: 301–270–2970 Fax: 301–270–2973
EIN: 226063382 Type: Independent
EGA member
Contact: Betsy Taylor, Executive Director

History and philosophy. George W. Merck created the Merck Family Fund in 1954. It "is dedicated to protecting the natural environment and addressing the root causes of problems faced by socially and economically disadvantaged people. Projects aimed at solutions to or the prevention of important problems through research or existing knowledge are favored over those which deal with consequences or react to needs." The Fund favors proposals that "emphasize self-help, sound management, and the ability to generate other support." "The Fund also favors proposals that address problems of national or regional significance but [it] recognizes that a solution may begin in a local project."

Officers and directors. *Officers:* Patience M. Chamberlin, President; Francis W. Hatch, III, Vice President; Anne Merck-Abeles, Secretary; Wilhelm M. Merck, Treasurer. *Trustees:* Anne Merck-Abeles, Patience M. Chamberlin, Francis W. Hatch, III, Albert W. Merck, Jr., Antony M. Merck, Josephine A. Merck, Wilhelm M. Merck, Serena Whitridge.

Financial data. Data for fiscal year ended December 31, 1993. *Assets:* $26,571,677 (M). *Total grants disbursed:* $1,280,500.

Environmental awards. *Program and interests:* In the environmental arena, the Fund targets two broad categories:

- Protecting and restoring vital eastern ecosystems.

  Of particular interest are efforts to preserve major tracts of private and public forests interconnected with critical rivers and woodlands, providing the necessary land and watersheds to preserve biodiversity and sustain local communities.

- Promoting economic practices that will assure a sustainable environment for future generations.

  Of interest are new initiatives that promote economic and consumer behavior which is ecologically sustainable for current and future generations.

Environmental grants are also made through the Fund's Human Needs program for:

- Community greening which includes urban gardens and open space.

Issues. Cli Bio Lan Agr Wat Oce Ene Was Tox Pop Dev

Funding analysis.

Fiscal year:	1991	1993
Env grants auth:	$340,000	$834,500
Number:	8	28
Range:	$5,000–$148,500	$10,000–$55,000
Median:	$26,000	$30,000
Pct $ auth (env/total):	37	65

Recipients (1993 highest):	Number:	Dollars:
The Tides Foundation	2	60,000
New York University	1	55,000
Appalachian Mountain Club	1	50,000
Enterprise Foundation	1	50,000
River Network	1	50,000
Southern Environmental Law Center	1	50,000

Activity regions (1993 highest):	Number:	Dollars:
U.S. Northeast	7	250,000
U.S. not specified	4	169,000
New York/New Jersey	7	155,000
U.S. Southeast	4	120,000
U.S. Mid-Atlantic	3	83,000

Sample grants (1993).
Government Accountability Project. Washington, DC. $35,000. Legal counsel and assistance to protect U.S. Forest Service whistleblowers in the southeastern United Sates and for efforts to reform management of national forests bordering the Chattooga River in the Southern Appalachian ecosystem.
International Society for Ecological Economics. Solomons, MD. $25,000. A post-conference "synthesis" workshop in conjunction with ISEE's third international conference on practical applications of ecological economics.
Natural Resources Council of Maine. Augusta, ME. $25,000. A two-day workshop on protecting Maine's biological diversity and for education and advocacy to protect Maine's north woods.
River Network. Portland, OR. $50,000 (2 years). Northeastern rivers project of the River Leadership program, with $9,000 earmarked to produce the handbook on riparian forest protection.
Tufts University. Medford, MA. $34,000. To develop a database and a series of publications summarizing the best analytic work on consumption and its impact on the environment and economy.
Green Guerillas. New York, NY. $25,000. To develop new community gardens and provide services to existing gardens, exclusively in low-income neighborhoods in New York City.

Application process. *Initial contact:* Brief letter describing the activities of the organization and the proposed grant, accompanied by a copy of the IRS tax-exempt status determination letter and an annual report (if available). If requested, complete proposal to include:
1. Statement of grant purpose and project's significance.
2. Explanation of problem and how proposed project will contribute effectively to its solution.
3. Specific objectives, including nature and size of population to benefit from project.
4. Plans to evaluate, use, and disseminate project results.
5. Qualifications of key project staff.
6. Timetable including proposed start date, schedule for completion, and any recurring regulatory approval.
7. Itemized project budget; justify and explain significant items.
8. Sources, amounts, and purposes of all internal and external support obtained, available, anticipated, or requested including name(s), address(es), and telephone number(s) of contact person(s).
9. Copy of IRS tax-exempt status determination letter, certification that organization is not a private foundation.

When to apply: Deadline for environmental proposal is March 16. The board meets three times a year: March, June, and November. Proposals should be in at least six weeks before the meeting. Preference will be given to proposals received early.
Materials available: Guidelines.

Emphases. *Recipients:* Nonprofit organizations.
Geography: Eastern ecosystem grants focus on the eastern United States.

Limitations. *Recipients:* Individuals, religious organizations.
Activities: Audiovisual materials, land acquisition, lobbying.
Types of support: Debt retirement, endowments, equipment, facilities, fellowships, loans, mortgage reduction, professorships, program-related investments, scholarships.

The John Merck Fund

11 Beacon Street, Suite 1230
Boston, Massachusetts 02108
Tel: 617-723-2932 Fax: 617-523-6029
EIN: 237082558 Type: Independent
EGA member
Contact: Ruth G. Hennig, Administrator

History and philosophy. The John Merck Fund was established in 1970 by the late Serena S. Merck. Until 1986 the Fund confined its grantmaking to research projects on developmental disabilities in children. It now makes grants in the categories of: Developmental Disabilities, Environment, Disarmament, Population Policy, and Human Rights.

Officers and directors. *Officers:* Francis W. Hatch, Chairman; Ruth G. Hennig, Secretary and Administrator. Huyler C. Held, Treasurer. *Trustees:* David Altshuler, Judith M. Buechner, Francis W. Hatch, Serena M. Hatch, Huyler C. Held, Arnold Hiatt, Robert M. Pennoyer, Serena Whitridge.

Financial data. Data for fiscal year ended December 31, 1993. *Assets:* $106,314,946 (M). *Total grants disbursed:* $5,408,296.

Environmental awards. *Program and interests:* The Fund makes selective grants to address global environmental threats relating to climate change, tropical deforestation, and loss of biological diversity. The exclusive focus is on projects that:

- Promote energy efficiency.
- Experiment with models of sustainable development that employ economic incentives for reducing forest destruction.

Additional selective grants are made for:

- Work to ensure that high standards of environmental protection are included in any agreements to encourage global trade.

In New England the Fund assists efforts to:

- Ensure sustainable management of the Great Northern Forest.
- Preserve and nurture the productive farmlands and forests of rural New England, primarily in Vermont.

Issues. Cli Bio Lan Agr Wat Oce Ene Was Tox Pop Dev
• • • • • • • • •

Funding analysis.

Fiscal year:	1991	1993
Env grants auth:	$1,717,700	$1,456,600
Number:	31	32
Range:	$5,000–$250,000	$600–$285,000
Median:	$35,000	$25,000
Pct $ auth (env/total):	31	27

Recipients (1993 highest):	Number:	Dollars:
Princeton University, Center for Energy and Environmental Studies	1	285,000
Conservation Law Foundation	1	150,000
Appalachian Mountain Club	1	135,000
American Farmland Trust	2	125,000
Woods Hole Research Center	1	70,000

Activity regions (1993 highest):	Number:	Dollars:
U.S. Northeast	10	390,000
U.S. not specified	6	346,600
International*	5	230,000
Europe	1	150,000
Southeast Asia	4	140,000

*Multiple regions or not specified.

Sample grants (1993).*

Academy of Natural Sciences. Washington, DC. $30,000. Final payment of two-year grant to support the Forest Resource Information System, an international database that will provide comprehensive information on characteristics of hundreds of underutilized common tree species available to architects, designers, and other users of commercial wood. This new, professional tool will reduce the pressure on overharvested species like teak and mahogany and encourage wood selections that protect biological diversity in forests.

American Farmland Trust. Washington, DC. $25,000. To acquire farmland of high scenic value adjacent to Shelburne Farms for demonstrations of state-of-the-art agricultural practices.

Conservation Law Foundation. Boston, MA. $150,000 (2 years). To collaborate with the Foundation for International Environmental Law and Development in promoting increased energy efficiency and demand-side management programs in the United Kingdom and the European Community.

Enersol Associates. Somerville, MA. $25,000. Continued support to provide technical training and small loans for installation and servicing of photovoltaic systems to electrify rural areas in Latin America and the Caribbean.

Harvard Institute for International Development. Cambridge, MA. $40,000. Continued support for field research conducted by an international network of scientists to develop sustainable management practices for Southeast Asian forests with high levels of biodiversity.

Manomet Observatory for Conservation Science. Manomet, MA. $60,000 (2 years). Continued support for a three-year study on the effects of industrial forest management on migratory birds in Maine's Northern Forest, and to develop management protocols for forests that maintain biodiversity without compromising economic value.

The Tides Foundation. San Francisco, CA. $50,000. To support the Fair Trade Campaign, which coordinates a national grassroots coalition of organizations concerned with the environmental impacts of international trade.

Vermont Milk Producers. Shoreham, VT. $151,400. Two program-related investments to enable a consortium of family-owned Vermont dairy farms to establish a market for premium milk products that rely on more sustainable farming practices and improved animal care.

Woods Hole Research Center. Woods Hole, MA. $70,000 (2 years). To provide general support for research and policy development in international forest management, global warming abatement, and marine conservation.

*Sample grants represent either new awards or disbursements on grants awarded in previous years.

© 1995 Environmental Data Resources, Inc.

M

Application process. *Initial contact:* The Fund generally funds pre-selected organizations. It discourages the submission of unsolicited applications. Instead, trustees request individuals to submit proposals for grants to support projects within their respective institutions. Candidates who are asked to apply should send a letter containing:
1. Concise statement describing the project or program.
2. Amount of funding requested and how it fits within the overall budget.
3. Summary of other major funding sources.
4. Brief description of the nature and activities of the sponsoring institution.
6. Sponsoring institution's legal name and a current list of officers and directors or trustees.

Appendixes.
1. Copy of IRS tax-exempt status determination letter and tax classification under Section 509(a).
2. Copy of the institution's most recent financial statement.

Materials available: Annual report (includes "Programs & Procedures").

Emphases. *Recipients:* Pre-selected organizations.
Activities: Advocacy, demonstration programs, litigation, pilot projects, policy analysis/development.
Types of support: Matching funds, operating costs, projects (selectively), seed money.
Geography: Rural New England, especially southern Vermont.

Limitations. *Recipients:* Individuals.
Activities: Political activities.
Types of support: Capital campaigns/expenses, endowments, facilities, operating funds, scholarships.

Robert G. and Anne M. Merrick Foundation, Inc.

The Exchange
1122 Kenilworth Drive, Suite 11B
Baltimore, Maryland 21204
Tel: 410–832–5700 Fax: 410–832–5704
EIN: 52–6072964 Type: Independent
Contact: Frederick W. Lafferty, Executive Director

History and philosophy. The Foundation was created by Robert G. Merrick in 1962. It makes grants within the state of Maryland in four program areas: Civic and Cultural Activities, Education, Historic Preservation and Conservation, and Health and Social Services.

Officers and directors. *Officers:* Anne M. Pinkard, President; Robert M. Pinkard, Vice President and Treasurer; Walter D. Pinkard, Jr, Secretary; Donna C. Silbersack, Assistant Secretary/Treasurer. *Directors:* Joseph S. Hall, Robert G. Merrick III, Vernon T. Pittinger, Donna C. Silbersack.

Financial data. Data for fiscal year ended May 31, 1993. *Assets:* $52,013,535 (M). *Gifts received:* $1,504. *Total grants disbursed:* $2,398,944.

Environmental awards. *Recent grants:* 1993 awards included support for coastal issues and outdoor education.

Issues. Cli Bio Lan Agr Wat Oce Ene Was Tox Pop Dev
           •   •   •   •   •

Funding analysis.

Fiscal year:	1993
Env grants disb:	$85,250
Number:	4
Range:	$20,000–$22,500
Median:	$21,375
Pct $ disb (env/total):	4

Recipients (1993):	Number:	Dollars:
Alliance for the Chesapeake Bay	1	22,500
Chesapeake Bay Foundation	1	22,500
Echo Hill Outdoor School	1	20,250
Irvine Natural Science Center	1	20,000

Activity region (1993):	Number:	Dollars:
U.S. Mid-Atlantic	4	85,250

Sample grants (1993).
Alliance for the Chesapeake Bay. Baltimore, MD. $22,500.
Chesapeake Bay Foundation. Anapolis, MD. $22,500.
Echo Hill Outdoor School. Worton, MD. $20,250.
Irvine Natural Science Center. Baltimore, MD. $20,000.

Application process. *Initial contact:* Cover letter and full proposal to include:
1. Description of project.
2. Description of applicant organization including history, function(s), goals.
3. Amount of funding requested and time period.
4. Copy of project budget.
5. Number of employees on organization staff.
6. Names of organization's key staff and brief description of professional backgrounds.
7. List of board of directors.
8. Description of major funding sources for proposed project.
9. Copy of organization's latest audit or details about income and expenses, assets and liabilities.
10. Evaluation plan.
11. Copy of IRS tax-exempt status determination letter.

When to apply: Anytime.

Emphases. *Recipients:* Nonprofit organizations.
Geography: Maryland.

Joyce Mertz-Gilmore Foundation

218 East 18th Street
New York, New York 10003
Tel: 212–475–1137
EIN: 132872722 Type: Independent
EGA member
Contacts: Robert Crane, Vice President, Program Officer
Stacey Cumberbatch, Program Officer

History and philosophy. The Mertz family of New York established the Mertz Foundation in 1956. Its name was changed in 1974 when Joyce Mertz Gilmore died and left a substantial bequest to the Foundation. Current program areas are: Human Rights, The Environment, World Security, New York City's Human and Built Environment, and the Arts in New York City.

Officers and directors. *Officers:* Larry E. Condon, President; Elizabeth B. Gilmore, Secretary; Charles Bloomstein, Treasurer; William B. O'Connor, Assistant Secretary; Golden Beckner, Jr., Assistant Treasurer. *Directors:* Charles Bloomstein, Harlan Cleveland, Larry E. Condon, Elizabeth B. Gilmore, Hal Harvey, Patricia Ramsay, Denise Nix Thompson, Franklin W. Wallin. *Trustee Emeritus:* C. Virgil Martin.

Financial data. Data for fiscal year ended December 31, 1993. *Assets:* $66,600,000 (M). *Total grants disbursed:* $10,864,431.

Environmental awards. *Program and interests:* "The Foundation's environmental program stresses support to organizations working to promote energy efficiency and the use of renewable energy sources. Grantmaking is focused on efforts to influence and change national energy policy and promote energy efficiency and the use of renewables through state and local utility regulation. In that context, the Foundation is interested in innovative projects linking energy efficiency and the use of renewable energy to economic development and job creation in low-income and underserved communities in the United States and in developing countries. The Foundation also supports a limited number of other environmental efforts focused on issues affecting the metropolitan region of New York State and City."

Issues. Cli Bio Lan Agr Wat Oce **Ene** Was Tox **Pop Dev**

Funding analysis.

Fiscal year:	1991	1993
Env grants disb:	$2,330,000	$2,870,500
Number:	46	73
Range:	$5,000–$450,000	$5,000–$270,000
Median:	$25,000	$25,000
Pct $ disb (env/total):	22	26

Recipients (1993 highest):	Number:	Dollars:
New York Community Trust	1	270,000
Conservation Law Foundation	3	228,000
Natural Resources Defense Council	2	155,000
Land and Water Fund of the Rockies	2	150,000
Environmental Defense Fund	1	125,000

Activity regions (1993 highest):	Number:	Dollars:
U.S. not specified	17	879,500
New York/New Jersey	28	753,000
International*	10	325,000
U.S. Northeast	3	228,000
U.S. Mountain	2	150,000

*Multiple regions or not specified.

Sample grants (1993).
Alliance for Affordable Energy. New Orleans, LA. $30,000. To support the state-of-the-art least-cost energy planning initiative begun in New Orleans by the Alliance, and to disseminate this initiative over a three-state area.

American Council For An Energy-Efficient Economy. Washington, DC. $125,000. For the Energy Efficiency and Economic Development Program which will demonstrate the employment and other economic development benefits associated with various energy efficiency policies.

Center for Neighborhood Technology. Chicago, IL. $125,000. To advocate for the adoption of an energy conservation plan for the all local government facilities and the reinvestment of energy savings in low-income communities to improve essential services and job opportunities.

Conservation Law Foundation. Boston, MA. $300,000. To promote energy efficiency and the use of renewables in New England.

Enersol Associates. Sommerville, MA. $65,000. To implement solar-based rural electrification in the Dominican Republic and Central America.

Environmental Enterprise Assistance Fund. Arlington, VA. $50,000. To promote the use of renewables and other environmentally sound technologies in developing countries. It invests in promising projects and provides technical assistance to entrepreneurs.

International Institute for Energy Conservation. Washington, DC. $100,000. Fosters sustainable development through energy efficiency by bringing energy conservation technologies and policies to institutions in developing countries.

New York Environmental Institute, Inc. Albany, NY. $20,000. This state-wide organization advocates for sound energy and environmental policies and strict enforcement of existing laws. Many environmental organizations which do not have a presence in the state capital rely on the Institute's voice there.

Application process. *Initial contact:* Letter of intent (2 pages maximum). If the Foundation is interested, it will request a full proposal and additional materials.
When to apply: Deadlines are January 31 for the spring meeting and July 31 for the fall meeting.
Materials available: Annual report (contains "How to Approach the Foundation").

Emphases. *Recipients:* Nonprofit organizations.
Activities: Advocacy, policy analysis/development.
Types of support: General purposes.

Limitations. *Recipients:* Individuals.
Activities: Audiovisual materials, conferences, expeditions/tours, publications, land acquisition, political activities, publications, seminars, symposia/colloquia.
Types of support: Annual campaigns, endowments, facilities, fellowships, loans, travel expenses.

Metropolitan Atlanta Community Foundation, Inc.
The Hurt Building, Suite 449
Atlanta, Georgia 30303
Tel: 404–688–5525   Fax: 404–688–3060
EIN: 581344646   Type: Community
Contact: Winsome Hawkins, Senior Program Officer

History and philosophy. Founded in 1951, the Metropolitan Atlanta Community Foundation works to improve the quality of life in the Greater Atlanta area. The Foundation provides grant support in six major program areas: Arts and Culture, Civic Affairs, Education, and Health, Social Services, and Community Development. The Foundation's recently established Nonprofit Resource Center encourages and facilitates management excellence.

Officers and directors. *Officer:* Cecil D. Conlee, President. *Directors:* Sam Allen, Spring Asher, Dr. James Brawner III, Cecil D. Conlee, The Hon. Clarence Cooper, Marie W. Dodd, Shirley C. Franklin, Bradley Hale, Roger I. Hallock, George H. Johnson, James R. Lientz, Jr., Clay Long, John McKinley, Ingrid Saunders-Jones, Don Speaks, Judith G. Taylor, Susan W. Wieland, Benjamin Neely Young.

Financial data. Data for fiscal year ended June 30, 1993. *Assets:* $120,412,891 (M). *Gifts received:* $18,588,756. *Total grants disbursed:* $19,545,629.

Environmental awards. *Recent grants:* 1993 grants included support for regional land conservation, wildlife, fisheries and coastal issues, urban parks, a botanical garden, a zoo, and outdoor education.

Issues. Cli Bio Lan Agr Wat Oce Ene Was Tox Pop Dev
• • • •

Funding analysis.§

Fiscal year:	1991	1993
Env grants auth:	$184,992	$46,501
Number:	16	15
Range:	$1,000–$50,000	$776–$15,000
Median:	$4,000	$2,500
Pct $ disb (env/total):	2	<1

Recipients (1993 highest):	*Number:*	*Dollars:*
Southeastern Environmental Law Center	1	15,000
The Atlanta Botanical Garden, Inc.	2	8,250
Edgewood Community Garden	1	5,050
Friends of Zoo Atlanta	1	3,275
Environmental Awareness Foundation	1	3,000

Activity regions (1993):	*Number:*	*Dollars:*
U.S. Southeast	12	43,501
U.S. Mid-Atlantic	1	1,000
U.S. Northeast	1	1,000
U.S. not specified	1	1,000

§Includes designated donor-advised, field-of-interest, and unrestricted grants.

Sample grants (1993).
Atlanta Salmon Federation. Atlanta, GA. $1,000.
The Cousteau Society. Norfolk, VA. $1,000.
Georgia Conservancy. Atlanta, GA. $2,500.
North American Wildlife Foundation. Deerfield, IL. $1,000.
Southern Environmental Law Center. Chapel Hill, NC. $15,000.
Friends of Zoo Atlanta. Atanta, GA. $3,275.

Application process. *Initial contact:* Telephone call to request "Grant Application Guidelines," "Grantsmanagement Policies: Unrestricted Grants," and application form. Proposal to include:
1. Grant application form.
2. Cover letter signed by the organization's president or chairman authorizing the grant request.
3. Detailed description of proposed project for which you seek funding (3 pages maximum).
4. Copy of IRS tax-exempt status determination letter.
5. List of organization's board of directors with their professional and/or civic affiliations.
6. Diversity table that indicates the total number of board and staff members by gender and race.
7. Listing of project staff with professional qualifications (if pertinent).
8. Financial information including current annual operating budget, previous year's actual budget, budget for proposed project, plans for securing ongoing support of project.

When to apply: 1994 and 1995 deadlines are March 15, July 15, and November 15. There are three grant review cycles: in May, September, and January.
Materials available: Annual report, "Grantsmanagement Policies: Unrestricted Grants," "Grant Application Guidelines," application form.

Emphases. *Recipients:* Botanical gardens, museums, nonprofit organizations, zoos.
Activities: Advocacy, capacity building, citizen participation, collaborative efforts, education.
Types of support: Capital campaigns/expenses, matching funds, single-year grants only.
Geography: Greater Metropolitan Atlanta, including the Georgia counties of Barrow, Bartow, Carroll, Cherokee, Clayton, Cobb, Coweta, DeKalb, Douglas, Fayette, Forsyth, Fulton, Gwinnett, Hall, Henry, Newton, Pickens, Paulding, Rockdale, Spalding, and Walton.

Limitations. *Recipients:* Individuals, public agencies.
Activities: Audiovisual materials, conferences, litigation, lobbying, political activities, research, symposia/colloquia.
Types of support: Computer hardware, continuing support, debt retirement, endowments, mortgage reduction, multi-year grants, scholarships.

Metropolitan Life Foundation
One Madison Avenue
New York, New York 10010–3690
Tel: 212–578–6272   Fax: 212–685–1435
EIN: 132878224   Type: Company-sponsored
Contact: Sibyl Jacobson, President and CEO

History and philosophy. Metropolitan Life Foundation was established in 1976 by MetLife, the health and life insurance company. Grantmaking philosophy encourages maximum benefit in the nonprofit sector by providing additional resources and by cost-effective measures including collaboration, volunteerism, and preventive health care. Program areas are: Civic Affairs, Culture, Education, Health, Public Broadcasting, Social Investment, and United Way.

Officers and directors. *Officers:* Robert J. Crimmins, Chairman; Sibyl Jacobson, President and CEO; Arthur G. Typermass, Treasurer. *Directors:* John J. Creedon, Robert J. Crimmins, William T. Friedewald, M.D., Sibyl Jacobson, John D. Moynahan, Jr., Catherine A. Rein, Vincent P. Reusing, Arthur G. Typermass.

Financial data. Data for fiscal year ended December 31, 1993. *Assets:* $99,516,568 (C). *Total grants disbursed:* $7,906,429.

Environmental awards. *Recent grants:* In 1993 environmental grants, awarded through the Culture and Civic Affairs programs, included support for land conservation, parks, coastal issues, botanical gardens, and zoos.

Issues. Cli Bio Lan Agr Wat Oce Ene Was Tox Pop Dev
             •   •   •   •

Funding analysis.

Fiscal year:	1993
Env grants auth:	$19,000
Number:	8
Range:	$1,000–$5,000
Median:	$1,500
Pct $ disb (env/total):	<1

Recipients (1993 highest):	*Number:*	*Dollars:*
Central Park Conservancy	1	5,000
The New York Botanical Garden	1	5,000
Brandywine Conservancy, Inc.	1	3,000
National Aquarium in Baltimore	1	1,500
Sedgwick County Zoological Society	1	1,500

Activity regions (1993):	*Number:*	*Dollars:*
New York/New Jersey	3	11,000
U.S. Mid-Atlantic	2	4,500
U.S. Midwest	1	1,500
U.S. Northeast	1	1,000
U.S. not specified	1	1,000

Sample grants (1993).
Central Park Conservancy. New York, NY. $5,000.
National Aquarium in Baltimore. Baltimore, MD. $1,500.
The Nature Conservancy, Headquarters. Arlington, VA. $1,000.
The New York Botanical Garden. Bronx, NY. $5,000.
Sedgwick County Zoological Society. Wichita, KS. $1,500.

Application process. *Initial contact:* Letter to include:
1. Brief description of the organization, including its legal name, history, activities, purpose, and governing board.
2. Grant purpose.
3. Amount requested, with a list of other sources of support.
4. Organization's most recent audited financial statement.
5. Copy of IRS tax-exempt status determination letter.
6. Copy of organization's most recent IRS Form 990.

When to apply: Anytime.
Materials available: Annual report (includes "How to Submit Requests for Contributions"), brochure, program policy statement.

Emphases. *Recipients:* Botanical gardens, nonprofit organizations, zoos.

Activities: Publications, research.
Types of support: Continuing support, general purposes, matching funds, operating costs, pilot projects, scholarships, seed money.
Geography: United States.

Limitations. *Recipients:* Educational institutions (public elementary/secondary), individuals, religious organizations.
Types of support: Advertising campaigns, capital campaigns/expenses, endowments.
Geography: International organizations.

Meyer Memorial Trust

1515 S.W. Fifth Avenue, Suite 500
Portland, Oregon 97201
Tel: 503-228-5512   Fax: 503-228-5840
EIN: 930806316   Type: Independent
Contact: Charles S. Rooks, Executive Director

History and philosophy. The Meyer Memorial Trust was created in 1982 with the residual of the Fred G. Meyer estate. Mr. Meyer (1886–1978) developed the Fred Meyer grocery chain of the Pacific Northwest. Throughout his life, Meyer displayed ingenuity, hard work, and a commitment to the communities where he built stores. In his will which established the Trust, he challenged the Trustees: "In all giving, give thought. With thoughtful giving, even small sums may accomplish great purposes."

The Trust currently groups its grants in three categories: Special Grants (Preserving the Future: Support for Children at Risk); General Purpose Grants (made in the fields of arts and humanities, education, health, social welfare, and other); and Small Grants ($500 to $8,000). General Purpose and Small Grants are limited to Oregon and that part of southwest Washington in the Portland metropolitan area. Proposals for the Children at Risk program are accepted from the five northwest states: Alaska, Idaho, Montana, Oregon, and Washington.

Officers and directors. *Officers:* Oran B. Robertson, Chairman; Charles S. Rooks, Executive Director; Wayne G. Pierson, Treasurer. *Trustees:* Travis Cross, Pauline Lawrence, Warne Nunn, Gerry Pratt, Oran B. Robertson.

Financial data. Data for fiscal year ended March 31, 1994. *Assets:* $304,249,724 (M). *Total grants authorized:* $10,164,979. *Total grants disbursed:* $15,498,935.

Environmental awards. *Recent grants:* 1993 grants included support for land conservation, river protection, recreation, and education for disadvantaged youth.

Issues. Cli Bio Lan Agr Wat Oce Ene Was Tox Pop Dev
             •   •   •

Funding analysis.

Fiscal year:	1992	1993
Env grants auth:	$1,322,900	$2,493,300
Number:	15	9
Range:	$4,500–$450,000	$2,300–$1,250,000
Median:	$25,000	$100,000
Pct $ auth (env/total):	7	15

M

Recipients (1993 highest):	Number:	Dollars:
High Desert Museum	1	1,250,000
Oregon State University	1	575,000
The Berry Botanic Garden	1	295,000
Pacific Rivers Council	1	150,000
Riverside West All Sports Park	1	100,000

Activity region (1993):	Number:	Dollars:
U.S. Northwest	9	2,493,300

Sample grants (1994).*

The Berry Botanic Garden. Portland, OR. $295,000. To renovate the facilities to provide more space for professional, horticultural, educational, and conservation programs.

Ecotrust. Portland, OR. $450,000. To support the Willapa Bay program, which assists local residents to protect the environment and promote sustainable economic development projects.

Oregon State University. Corvallis, OR. $575,000. To support construction of the Environmental Computing Center to house an advanced computer system and research team for the NASA Earth Observing System project.

*Sample grants represent either new awards or disbursements on grants awarded in previous years.

Application process. *Initial contact:* Full proposal (1 copy) to include:
1. Grant Application Cover Sheet (part of "Grant Applications Guidelines" booklet).
2. Narrative proposal describing applicant organization and proposed project.
3. Detailed proposal budget.
4. Description of financial condition of applicant organization.
5. Copy of IRS tax-exempt status determination letter.
6. List of names and primary affiliations of board of directors.

Review details of application procedure in the annual report and "Grant Application Guidelines" before preparing a proposal.
When to apply: Anytime for General Purpose Grants; deadlines for Small Grants ($500 to $8,000) are January 15, April 15, July 15, October 15; deadlines for Children at Risk are March 1 and September 1. Apply no more than one month before deadline.
Materials available: Annual report (includes "Grantmaking Policies and Procedures"), "Grant Application Guidelines," and individual program guidelines.

Emphases. *Recipients:* Botanical gardens, educational institutions, museums, nonprofit organizations, public agencies, research institutions, zoos.
Activities: Advocacy, citizen participation, demonstration programs, direct services, education, exhibits, innovative programs, training, youth programs.
Types of support: General purposes, matching funds, pilot projects, projects, seed money, start-up costs.
Geography: Oregon (General Purpose and Small Grants); five northwest states of Alaska, Idaho, Montana, Oregon, Washington (Children at Risk Grants).

Limitations. *Activities:* Litigation, lobbying.
Types of support: Indirect costs, scholarships.

Middlecott Foundation
c/o Saltonstall & Company
50 Congress Street, Suite 800
Boston, Massachusetts 02109-4007
Tel: 617-227-8660
EIN: 046155699   Type: Independent
Contact: William L. Saltonstall, Trustee

History and philosophy. The Foundation was established in 1967 by members of the Saltonstall family. It gives primarily to pre-selected organizations supporting education, arts and culture, health (including hospitals), and human services in the Boston area.

Officers and directors. *Trustees:* Robert A. Lawrence, George Lewis, William L. Saltonstall.

Financial data. Data for fiscal year ended December 31, 1992. *Assets:* $869,498 (M). *Gifts received:* $627,840. *Total grants disbursed:* $944,844.

Environmental awards. *Recent grants:* 1992 grants included support for land conservation, parks, greenbelts, forests, coastal issues, wildlife, and outdoor education.

Issues. Cli Bio Lan Agr Wat Oce Ene Was Tox Pop Dev
              •   •   •   •   •   •   •

Funding analysis.

Fiscal year:	1992
Env grants disb:	$29,600
Number:	35
Range:	$50–$5,000
Median:	$500
Pct $ disb (env/total):	3

Recipients (1992 highest):	Number:	Dollars:
Trustees of Reservations	6	6,500
Massachusetts Horticultural Society	2	5,050
Sherborn Rural Land Foundation	2	4,000
Massachusetts Audubon Society	4	3,000
New England Aquarium	3	3,000

Activity regions (1992):	Number:	Dollars:
U.S. Northeast	31	27,900
U.S. not specified	2	1,100
New York/New Jersey	2	600

Sample grants (1992).

Arnold Arboretum of Harvard University. Jamaica Plain, MA. $100. Park endowment.
Charles River Watershed Association. Auburndale, MA. $200.
Maine Coast Heritage Trust. Brunswick, ME. $350.
Massachusetts Audubon Society. Lincoln, MA. $3,000.
Massachusetts Horticulture Society. Boston, MA. $50.
New England Aquarium. Boston, MA. $3,000.
New England Forestry Foundation, Inc. Boston, MA. $100.
1000 Friends of Massachusetts. Lincoln Center, MA. $2,000.
Quebec Labrador Foundation/Atlantic Center for the Environment. Ipswich, MA. $500.

Sea Education Association. Woods Hole, MA. $1,600.
Thompson's Island Outward Bound Education Center. Boston, MA. $350.
Trustees of Reservations. Beverly, MA. $6,000.
Vinalhaven Land Trust. Vinalhaven, ME. $550.

Application process. *Initial contact:* The Foundation awards grants to pre-selected organizations only. No unsolicited applications accepted.

Emphases. *Recipients:* Pre-selected organizations only.

Limitations. *Recipients:* Individuals.

Millbrook Tribute Garden, Inc.
c/o D'Arcangelo & Co.
Franklin Avenue
Millbrook, New York 12545
Tel: 914-677-6823   Fax: 914-677-3526
EIN: 141340079   Type: Independent
Contact: George T. Whalen, Jr., Trustee

History and philosophy. Millbrook Tribute Garden, Inc. was incorporated in 1943. Its funding interests are secondary education, religion, child welfare, hospitals, and civic affairs. In addition to its grant programs, it maintains a playground and memorial park honoring war veterans.

Officers and directors. *Officers:* Oakleigh B. Thorne, President. *Trustees:* Felicitas S. Thorne, Oakleigh B. Thorne, Vincent N. Turtletes, George T. Whalen, Jr., Robert W. Whalen.

Financial data. Data for fiscal year ended September 30, 1993. *Assets:* $15,393,305 (M). *Total grants disbursed:* $889,000.

Environmental awards. *Recent grants:* 1993 grants included support for land and ecosystem conservation and wildlife protection.

Issues.   Cli   Bio   Lan   Agr   Wat   Oce   Ene   Was   Tox   Pop   Dev
                •   •   •

Funding analysis.

Fiscal year:	1991	1992
Env grants disb:	$167,500	$135,000
Number:	4	4
Range:	$7,500–$80,000	$5,000–$50,000
Median:	$40,000	$40,000
Pct $ disb (env/total):	16	15

Recipients (1992):	Number:	Dollars:
INFORM	1	50,000
Institute of Ecosystem Studies, New York Botanical Garden	1	50,000
Dutchess Land Conservancy, Inc.	1	30,000
Pet and Wildlife Preserve	1	5,000

Activity region (1992):	Number:	Dollars:
New York/New Jersey	4	135,000

Sample grants (1993).
Dutchess Land Conservancy, Inc. Bangall, NY. $30,000.
INFORM. New York, NY. $80,000.
Institute of Ecosystem Studies, New York Botanical Garden. Millbrook, NY. $50,000.
Pet and Wildlife Preserve. Amenia, NY. $5,000.

Application process. *Initial contact:* Proposal explaining the purpose for the grant request. Include a financial statement and a copy of the IRS tax-exempt status determination letter.
When to apply: Anytime.

Emphases. *Recipients:* Educational institutions, nonprofit organizations, public agencies.
Activities: Education.
Types of support: Annual campaigns, matching funds, scholarships.
Geography: Millbrook, New York area only.

Limitations. *Recipients:* Individuals.

The Milwaukee Foundation
1020 North Broadway
Milwaukee, Wisconsin 53202
Tel: 414-272-5805   Fax: 414-272-6235
EIN: 396036407   Type: Community
Contact: Douglas M. Jansson, Executive Director

History and philosophy. Founded in 1915, The Milwaukee Foundation works to promote the betterment of the Greater Milwaukee community and the enhancement of its citizens' quality of life. This is a community foundation and a vehicle through which individuals, companies, foundations, and charitable agencies may make gifts and bequests to Milwaukee-based organizations. The Foundation has five principal program areas: Education and Training, Health and Human Services, Arts and Culture, Conservation and Historic Preservation, and Community Development.

Officers and directors. *Officers:* Doris H. Chortek, Chair; Carl A. Weigell, Vice Chair; Douglas M. Jansson, Executive Director and Secretary. *Trustees:* Donald S. Buzard, Robert L. Hanley, Asher B. Nichols, Mark W. Sprenger, First Bank Milwaukee, Firstart Trust Company, Bank One Wisconsin Trust Company, N.A., Marshall and Ilsley Trust Company. *Directors:* Orren J. Bradley, Doris H. Chortek, William F. Fox, Harry F. Franke, John H. Hendee, Jr., Charles S. McNeer, Brenton H. Rupple, Polly H. Van Dyke, Carl A. Weigell, Walter H. White, Jr.

Financial data. Data for fiscal year ended December 31, 1993. *Assets:* $135,778,551 (M). *Gifts received:* $19,768,357. *Total grants authorized:* $5,632,421.

Environmental awards. *Program and interests:* The Foundation supports local efforts that promote more efficient use of natural resources, enhance the quality of the environment, and preserve the community's heritage.

M

Recent grants: 1993 grants included support for land conservation, wildlife protection, water quality, environmental health, and community education.

Issues. Cli Bio Lan Agr Wat Oce Ene Was Tox Pop Dev
          •   •   •   •   •   •

Funding analysis.§

Fiscal year:	1991	1993
Env grants auth:	$60,315	$102,615
Number:	13	16
Range:	$250–$18,000	$250–$18,000
Median:	$3,000	$4,118
Pct $ auth (env/total):	1	2

Recipients (1993 highest):	Number:	Dollars:
Friends of Schlitz Audubon Center	3	36,000
Milwaukee Bureau of Forestry	1	15,450
Friends of Riverside Nature Center	1	12,000
Sixteenth Street Community Health Center	1	10,000
Wisconsin Environmental Decade	1	10,000

Activity region (1993):	Number:	Dollars:
U.S. Great Lakes	16	102,615

§Includes competitive and noncompetitive grants.

Sample grants (1993).
Friends of Riverside Nature Center. Milwaukee, WI. $12,000. Environmental education program for families and residents of an elderly housing project implementing nature programs, walking tours, and environmental studies.
Friends of Schlitz Audubon Center. Bayside, WI. $15,000. Environmental education program using a Boston Whaler and Zodiac raft to transport students and teachers to study Lake Michigan, providing an outdoor laboratory.
Lake Michigan Federation. Chicago, IL. $15,000. Development of a Great Lakes Unique Habitats and Species pocket guide which will accompany public service announcements and a television special on the Great Lakes.
Wisconsin Environmental Decade. Milwaukee, WI. $10,000. Lead education project with the City Health Department to prevent lead exposure for children and adults in Milwaukee's low income neighborhoods.

Application process. *Initial contact:* Letter of intent to include:
1. Brief description of project.
2. Information about agency; its governance and financing.
3. Amount requested.
4. Total project budget.
5. Name, address, and telephone number of contact person.

Before submitting full proposal, request grant application and guidelines. A meeting with Foundation staff to discuss the proposal is encouraged. Proposal to include:
1. Application form (available from Foundation), completed and signed by the president or another officer of the organization's governing body.
2. Complete list of organization's officers and directors.
3. Organization's actual income and expense statement for past fiscal year, identifying principal sources of support.
4. Organization's projected income and expense budget for current year, identifying projected revenue sources.
5. Copies of IRS tax-exempt status determination letters.

When to apply: Submit proposal at least 10 weeks prior to a board meeting. Approximate dates are: January 1, April 1, July 1 (capital requests only), and October 1 for review in March, June, September, and December respectively.
Materials available: Annual report, "Instructions for Grant Applicants," application form, *The Community Trust* (newsletter). In addition, the Foundation holds Grantseeker Sessions at its offices.

Emphases. *Recipients:* Botanical gardens, educational institutions, museums, nonprofit organizations, public agencies, research institutions, zoos.
Activities: Advocacy, audiovisual materials, capacity building, collaborative efforts, conferences, demonstration programs, education, innovative programs, land acquisition, networking, planning, policy analysis/development, seminars, symposia/colloquia, technical assistance, training, volunteerism, workshops, youth programs.
Types of support: Equipment, facilities, leveraging funds, matching funds, pilot projects, projects, seed money, technical assistance.
Geography: The Greater Milwaukee area and the Wisconsin counties of Milwaukee, Waukesha, Ozaukee, and Washington.

Limitations. *Recipients:* Individuals.
Activities: Research (medical/scientific).
Types of support: Annual campaigns, capital campaigns/expenses, debt retirement, endowments, operating costs.

The Minneapolis Foundation

A200 Foshay Tower
821 Marquette Avenue
Minneapolis, Minnesota 55402
Tel: 612-339-7343   Fax: 612-672-3846
EIN: 416029402   Type: Community
Contact: Don Drake, Vice President for Programs

History and philosophy. The Minneapolis Foundation was established in 1915. Its mission is "to attract and mobilize community and philanthropic assets to promote equal access to resources needed for every individual, family, and community in Minnesota to reach full potential." In addition to making grants, the Foundation convenes meetings and seminars, and provides services to nonprofit organizations and the community at large. Grants are made in the areas of: Arts, Culture, Humanities; Education; Environment and Animal Welfare; Health; Human Services; International/Foreign Affairs; Public/Society Benefit; and Religion.

Officers and directors. *Officers:* Clinton A. Schroeder, Chair; Sue A. Bennett, Sandra L. Vargas, Vice Chairs; Rafael E. Ortega, Secretary; Susan S. Boren, Assistant Secretary; Conley Brooks, Jr., Treasurer. *Trustees:* Martha C. Atwater, Dr. Willarene P. Beasley, Sue A. Bennett, Susan S. Boren, Thomas H. Borman, William J. Brody, M. Elizabeth Craig, M.D., David P. Crosby, Edward N. Dayton, Barbara L. Forster, Anthony L. Genia,

Andrew C. Grossman, Peter A. Heegaard, Anne H. Hopkins, Curtis W. Johnson, Michele Keith, Ellen McInnis, Rafael E. Ortega, John E. Pearson, Matthew L. Ramadan, James R. Ryan, Robert H. Rydland, Richard W. Schoenke, Kathleen A. Speltz, Brenda St. Germaine, Lee Pao Xiong.

Financial data. Data for fiscal year ended March 31, 1994. *Assets:* $138,859,703 (M). *Gifts received:* $13,296,679. *Total grants disbursed:* $13,081,742.

Environmental awards. *Recent grants:* 1994 grants included support for land and farmland conservation, parks, an arboretum, and a zoo.

Issues. Cli Bio Lan Agr Wat Oce Ene Was Tox Pop Dev
• • • • •

Funding analysis.§

Fiscal year:	1992	1993
Env grants auth:	$511,579	$191,205
Number:	27	12
Range:	$100–$220,031	$500–$37,800
Median:	$2,700	$12,103
Pct $ auth (env/total):	10	3

Recipients (1993 highest):	Number:	Dollars:
Minnesota Landscape Arboretum Foundation	1	32,500
Population Communications International	1	30,000
The Nature Conservancy, Minnesota Field Office	1	28,400
National Audubon Society, Hunt Hill Audubon Sanctuary	1	20,500
Minnesota Zoo Foundation	1	12,805

Activity regions (1993):	Number:	Dollars:
U.S. Great Lakes	11	161,205
International*	1	30,000

*Multiple regions or not specified.
§Includes competitive and noncompetitive grants.

Sample grants (1994).*
Cedar Lake Park Preservation and Development Committee. MN. $20,000.
Land Stewardship Project. Marine on St. Croix, MN. $25,000. For the Metro Farm Program to provide advocacy for farmers in the metro area threatened by urban sprawl.
Minnesota Center for Environmental Advocacy. St. Paul, MN. $44,600.
Minnesota Landscape Arboretum Foundation. Chanhassen, MN. $45,050.
Minnesota Zoological Garden. MN. $850. For camperships for children who could not attend zoo camp without scholarship assistance.

*Includes Designated Beneficiary Funds, Field of Interest Funds, and Donor-Advised Funds.

Application process. *Initial contact:* Full proposal. Contact the Foundation for details.

When to apply: Deadlines for competitive (undesignated) funds for 1995 are January 10 and 15, March 1, and April 1.
Materials available: Annual report (includes "How to Apply for a Grant"), *Catalyst* (newsletter).

Emphases. *Recipients:* Nonprofit organizations.
Activities: Advocacy, collaborative efforts, innovative programs, policy analysis/development.
Types of support: Single-year grants only.
Geography: Greater Minneapolis–St. Paul area; Minnesota.

Limitations. *Recipients:* Individuals.
Activities: Conferences, fundraising, land acquisition, publications, research.
Types of support: Annual campaigns, debt retirement, endowments, facilities, matching funds, membership campaigns, scholarships.

Mobil Foundation, Inc.
3225 Gallows Road, Room 3D706
Fairfax, Virginia 22037
Tel: 703-846-3381   Fax: 703-846-3397
EIN: 136177075   Type: Company-sponsored
Contact: Richard G. Mund, Secretary

History and philosophy. Mobil Foundation, Inc., the philanthropic arm of Mobil Corporation, was established in 1965. It offers grants to charitable, federally tax-exempt civic, health, art and cultural organizations, hospitals, and educational institutions.

Officers and directors. *Officers:* Ellen Z. McCloy, President; Richard G. Mund, Secretary and Executive Director; Anthony L. Cavaliere, Treasurer. *Directors:* H. K. Acord, John M. Baitseil, Donald J. Bolger, G. Broadhead, Antony L. Cavaliere, Ellen Z. McCloy, Richard G. Mund, Harold B. Olson, Jr., Jerome F. Trautschold, Jr., John J. Wise.

Financial data. Data for fiscal years ended December 31, 1992 and 1993. *Assets (1992):* $7,610,494 (M). *Gifts received (1992):* $14,800,000. *Total grants disbursed (1993):* $8,942,958.

Environmental awards. *Program and interests:* The Foundation generally makes environmental awards through its Civic program. *Recent grants:* 1993 grants included support for land conservation, watershed protection, wildlife preservation, and recycling.

Issues. Cli Bio Lan Agr Wat Oce Ene Was Tox Pop Dev
• • • • • • •

Funding analysis.

Fiscal year:	1991	1993
Env grants auth:	$239,400	$163,300
Number:	25	26
Range:	$1,000–$55,000	$1,000–$20,000
Median:	$5,000	$5,000
Pct $ auth (env/total):	2	2

M

Recipients (1993 highest):	Number:	Dollars:
Woods Hole Oceanographic Institution	1	20,000
Nashua River Watershed Coalition	1	17,300
International Bird Rescue Research Center	1	15,000
Arizona Clean and Beautiful, Inc.	1	10,000
Bermuda Biological Station for Research, Inc.	1	10,000
Greater Caribbean Energy and Environment Foundation, Inc.	1	10,000
Wildlife Rehabilitation Center	1	10,000

Activity regions (1993 highest):	Number:	Dollars:
U.S. West	6	39,500
U.S. Mid-Atlantic	7	30,800
U.S. Northeast	2	30,000
Caribbean and West Indies Islands	2	20,000
U.S. not specified	4	18,000

Sample grants (1993).
Brandywine Conservancy, Inc. Chadds Ford, PA. $1,500.
Cabrilllo Marine Museum Volunteers. San Pedro, CA. $2,000.
California Living Museum. Bakersfield, CA. $3,500.
Environmental Law Institute. Washington, DC. $7,500.
The Jefferson Energy Foundation. Washington, DC. $2,500.
Nature Center of Charlestown. Devault, PA. $2,000.
Tri-State Bird Rescue and Research, Inc. Newark, DE. $5,000.

Application process. *Initial contact:* Full proposal to include:
1. Description of organization, its goals, and amount requested.
2. Specific purpose of funds and other sources of funding.
4. Budget and an audited financial statement.
5. Pertinent supporting data; an annual report, if available.
6. Copy of IRS tax-exempt status determination letter.
When to apply: Anytime.
Materials available: "Grant Guidelines," "Statement of Grants."

Emphases. *Recipients:* Educational institutions, nonprofit organizations, research institutions, zoos.
Activities: Education, research.
Types of support: General purposes, matching funds, scholarships.
Geography: Areas near company operations in California, Colorado, Illinois, Louisiana, New Jersey, and New York.

Limitations. *Recipients:* Individuals.
Activities: Fundraising, media projects, research (medical).
Types of support: Advertising campaigns, endowments, facilities (construction), loans, operating costs, professorships.

Leo Model Foundation, Inc.

310 South Juniper Street
Philadelphia, Pennsylvania 19107
Tel: 215-546-8058 Fax: 215-546-0664
EIN: 237084119 Type: Independent
Contact: Allen Model, President

History and philosophy. The Leo Model Foundation was established in 1970. Its program areas are: Culture, Education and Public Information, Environment, Health and Human Services, and Social and Economic Justice.

Officers and directors. *Officers:* Allen Model, President; Pamela Model, Peter H. Model, Vice Presidents; John A. Nevins, Secretary/Treasurer. *Directors:* Allen Model, Pamela Model, Peter H. Model, John A. Nevins, Marjorie Russell.

Financial data. Data for fiscal year ended December 31, 1993. *Assets:* $9,700,000 (M). *Total grants disbursed:* $1,509,775.

Environmental awards. *Recent grants:* 1993 grants included support for habitat conservation, watershed protection, and species preservation.

Issues. Cli Bio Lan Agr Wat Oce Ene Was Tox Pop Dev
 •   •   •   •   •

Funding analysis.

Fiscal year:	1991	1993
Env grants auth:	$157,940	$214,350
Number:	20	20
Range:	$100–$70,000	$100–$101,000
Median:	$2,500	$2,000
Pct $ auth (env/total):	12	14

Recipients (1993 highest):	Number:	Dollars:
The Nature Conservancy, Headquarters	1	101,000
NYZS/The Wildlife Conservation Society	2	49,500
RARE Center for Tropical Conservation	1	25,000
The Nature Conservancy, Pennsylvania Field Office	1	15,000
The New York Botanical Garden	1	4,000

Activity regions (1993):	Number:	Dollars:
U.S. not specified	6	106,250
New York/New Jersey	4	55,500
International*	5	32,000
U.S. Mid-Atlantic	5	20,600

*Multiple regions or not specified.

Sample grants (1993).
Academy of Natural Sciences of Philadelphia. Philadelphia, PA. $2,000.
American Museum of Natural History. New York, NY. $1,000.
Athenaeum of Philadelphia. Philadelphia, PA. $500.
Bat Conservation International. Austin, TX. $2,000.
Conservation International. Washington, DC. $2,000.
Environmental Data Research Institute. Rochester, NY. $250.
Environmental Defense Fund. New York, NY. $1,000.
Fresh Air Fund. New York, NY. $2,000.
The Nature Conservancy, Headquarters. Arlington, VA. $101,000.
The Nature Conservancy, Pennsylvania Field Office. Philadelphia, PA. $15,000.
NYZS/The Wildlife Conservation Society. Bronx, NY. $35,000.
RARE Center for Tropical Conservation. Philadelphia, PA. $25,000.

Application process. *Initial contact:* Full proposal to include:
1. Copy of IRS tax-exempt status determination letter.
2. Description of organization's purpose and programs.
3. Board list.
4. Staff list.
5. Financial statements.

When to apply: Anytime, but proposals received by July are most likely to be considered for funding in the calendar year.

Emphases. *Recipients:* Nonprofit organizations.

Limitations. *Recipients:* Individuals.

The Moody Foundation
2302 Post Office Street, Suite 704
Galveston, Texas 77550
Tel: 409–763–5333 Fax: 409–763–5564
EIN: 741403105 Type: Independent
Contact: Peter M. Moore, Grants Officer

History and philosophy. The Moody Foundation was created in 1942 for the perpetual benefit of present and future generations of Texans by William Lewis Moody, Jr. (1865–1954) and his wife, Libbie Shearn Moody (1869–1943). Financial interests of the Moody family included banks, newspapers, ranches, hotels, and the American National Insurance Company. The Foundation makes grants in the areas of: Community and Social Services, Health, Arts and Humanities, and Education.

Officers and directors. *Officers:* Frances Moody Newman, Chairman; Robert E. Baker, Executive Administrator. *Trustees:* Robert L. Moody, Ross R. Moody, Frances Moody Newman.

Financial data. Data for fiscal year ended December 31, 1993. *Assets:* $278,223,000 (C). *Total grants authorized:* $9,787,000.

Environmental awards. *Recent grants:* 1993 grants included support for rainforest education and for enhancement of the Moody Gardens. The Gardens emphasize environmental education and have a full K–12 curriculum on rainforest plants and animals.

Issues. Cli Bio Lan Agr Wat Oce Ene Was Tox Pop Dev
       •   •   •

Funding analysis.

Fiscal year:	1992	1993
Env grants auth:	$4,703,282	$1,920,490
Number:	2	3
Range:	$75,000–$4,628,282	$18,000–$1,834,490
Median:	$2,351,641	$68,000
Pct $ auth (env/total):	30	20

Recipients (1993):	Number:	Dollars:
Moody Gardens, Inc.	2	1,902,490
Houston Rainforest Action Group	1	18,000

Activity region (1993):	Number:	Dollars:
U.S. South Central	3	1,920,490

© 1995 Environmental Data Resources, Inc.

Sample grants (1993).
Houston Rainforest Action Group. Houston, TX. $18,000. Support of education staff visiting Galveston/Houston area schools, and for developing educational programs to increase awareness of the importance of rainforests in the earth's ecology.
Moody Gardens, Inc. Galveston, TX. $1,834,490. Operating expenses for fiscal year 1993, and for capital equipment and leasehold improvements.
Moody Gardens, Inc. Galveston, TX. $68,000. Additional allocation to fund an assessment of departmental policies and procedures, a review of the human resource effort, and an update on statutory compliance.

Application process. *Initial contact:* Letter of inquiry to include:
1. Nature of the request.
2. Amount requested.
3. Description of the applicant organization and its ability to carry out the proposed project.

When to apply: The board of trustees meets four times a year, but not on a regular quarterly basis. Deadlines are six weeks before each meeting. Call for precise dates.
Materials available: Annual report, "Guidelines."

Emphases. *Recipients:* Botanical gardens, educational institutions, nonprofit organizations, research institutions.
Activities: Education, exhibits, innovative programs, research.
Types of support: Continuing support, equipment, facilities, operating costs, pilot projects, seed money.
Geography: Texas only.

Limitations. *Recipients:* Individuals (except students covered by scholarship programs in Galveston County).

J. P. Morgan Charitable Trust
60 Wall Street, 46th Floor
New York, New York 10260
Tel: 212–648–9673 Fax: 212–648–5092
EIN: 136037931 Type: Company-sponsored
EGA member
Contact: Roberta A. Ruocco, Vice President

History and philosophy. The J. P. Morgan Charitable Trust was founded in 1961 "to make grants to worthy organizations for a variety of charitable purposes." Trust grants are funded by the New York financial corporation J. P. Morgan & Co.

The Trust favors comprehensive approaches to complex issues, "including those that look beyond service delivery to the policy and advocacy efforts crucial to bringing about constructive change." Central to the Trust's grantmaking philosophy is a belief that individuals and corporations must respond to important social issues, and that a long-term investment in human capital is an important means to that end. The Trust has six program areas: Arts, Education, Environment, Health and Related Services, International Affairs, and Urban Affairs. The Trust "rarely contributes to projects outside of New York City except in the fields of higher education and international affairs."

M

Officers and directors. *Advisory Committee:* Roberto G. Mendoza, Kurt F. Viermetz, Rodney B. Wagner, Douglas A. Warner III, Dennis Weatherstone. *Community Relations and Public Affairs Department:* Karen A. Erdos, Laura D. Roosevelt, Roberta A. Ruocco, Hildy J. Simmons, Gloria P. Turner.

Financial data. Data for fiscal years ended December 31, 1993. Assets: $34,041,410 (B). *Gifts received:* $15,000,000. *Total grants disbursed:* $14,026,579.

Environmental awards. *Program and interests:* "Morgan grants in the environmental area are to organizations that work to conserve and make wise use of natural resources. We support local environmental organizations addressing issues ranging from preservation of open space to recycling, and local and national organizations that conduct or promote scientific research, economic analysis, and advocacy for improved environmental quality. We also assist programs that educate policymakers, teachers, and the general public on current environmental issues."
Recent grants: 1993 grants supported land conservation (wilderness, rainforests, habitats); urban environment (parks, gardens, jobs, and recycling); and zoos and botanical gardens.

Issues. Cli Bio• Lan• Agr Wat Oce Ene• Was• Tox• Pop• Dev•

Funding analysis.§

Fiscal year:	1991	1993
Env grants auth:	$184,370	$364,946
Number:	—	—
Range:	$3,000–$20,000	$3,000–$30,000
Median:	$10,000	$15,000
Pct $ disb (env/total):	3	3

Recipients (1993 highest):	Number:	Dollars:
Brooklyn Botanic Garden	2	45,000
World Wildlife Fund	1	30,000
City Parks Foundation	1	20,000
INFORM	1	20,000
World Resources Institute	1	20,000

Activity regions (1993):	Number:	Dollars:
U.S. not specified*	4	181,946
New York/New Jersey	11	118,000
International*	3	65,000

*Multiple regions or not specified.

§Includes miscellaneous environmental contributions: $60,870 in 1991, $131,946 in 1993.

Sample grants (1993).*

Brooklyn Botanic Garden. Brooklyn, NY. $35,000. Includes first payment of $20,000 grant for Project Green Reach and $25,000 capital grant.
Center for the Biology of Natural Systems. Flushing, NY. $15,000. For the Community-Based Recycling Campaign in West Harlem.
City Parks Foundation. New York, NY. $10,000. First payment of $20,000 general support grant.
Conservation International. Washington, DC. $10,000. Final payment of a $20,000 general support grant.
New York City Audubon Society. New York, NY. $5,000. For start-up costs for the New York City office.
The Parks Council, Inc. New York, NY. $8,000. Includes $5,000 grant for the Urban Conservation Corps summer job program and $3,000 grant for "Forcing the Spring: Revitalizing Urban America Forum."
Rainforest Alliance. New York, NY. $7,500. First payment of a $15,000 general support grant.
World Resources Institute. Washington, DC. $10,000. First payment of a $20,000 grant for the Center for International Development and Environment.

*Sample grants represent disbursements during fiscal year 1993.

Application process. *Initial contact:* Completed grant application form (2 copies) and grant proposal (1 copy), accompanied by supporting materials. Include:

1. Organization's primary goals, need or problem that it works to address, and population it benefits.
2. Annual report (if available).
3. Brief history of organization (if not in the annual report).
4. Brief description of programs and accomplishments, emphasizing past year's achievements.
5. List of directors or trustees, with their affiliations.
6. List of senior staff members, number of paid full-time and part-time staff, and number of volunteers. Include a one-paragraph resume for each key staff member.
7. Most recent financial audit. If the audit for the most recent fiscal year is not complete, submit the most recent audited statement, along with the most recent year-end unaudited financial statement and the date of expected completion.
8. Current operating budget. Sources of projected income and a breakdown of actual income and expenses for the year to date should be aligned side-by-side on the same page.
9. Budget for the next fiscal year, if available.
10. List of foundation and corporate supporters and other sources of income, with amounts, for the most recent fiscal year and for the current fiscal year to date, aligned side by side on the same page.
11. Copy of IRS Form 990, including salary information and IRS tax-exempt status determination letter.
12. Outline of any plans for organization to enlarge its base of support from other potential funders.
13. If grant request is for a specific project, describe project including:
    - Statement of its primary purpose and the need or problem to address.
    - Population to serve and how this population will benefit from project.
    - Names and qualifications of project directors.
    - Anticipated project duration.
    - Current project budget.
    - When funds are needed.
14. If proposal is for capital support, provide a description of project including:
    - Total amount of funds required.
    - Amount raised to date.
    - Anticipated completion date of campaign.
15. Plans for project or program evaluation.
16. No more than three examples of recent articles about, or evaluations of applicant organization, if available.

When to apply: Anytime. The contributions committee meets frequently. Grants are awarded on a calendar-year basis. Apply by September 15 to receive a grant in the same calendar year.
Materials available: Annual report (includes "Information about the contributions program," "Supplementary information to be provided with a grant application," application form).

Emphases. *Recipients:* Botanical gardens, nonprofit organizations.
Activities: Advocacy, capacity building, collaborative efforts, direct services, education.
Types of support: Capital campaigns/expenses, general purposes.
Geography: New York City only.

Limitations. *Recipients:* Individuals.
Activities: Conferences, research (scholarly).
Types of support: Fellowships, loans, scholarships.

The Moriah Fund, Inc.

35 Wisconsin Circle, Suite 520
Chevy Chase, Maryland 20815
Tel: 301–951–3933   Fax: 301–951–3938
EIN: 311129589   Type: Independent
EGA member
Contact: Jack Vanderryn, Program Director for Environment

History and philosophy. Established in 1985, The Moriah Fund is a private foundation that makes grants in five geographic areas: Israel, Indiana, the United States, Eastern Europe, and the developing world. Each area has its own focus. In Israel the Fund supports efforts to promote pluralism and democracy, educational and economic opportunities for the disadvantaged, and relations among Israel's diverse communities, with some funding for higher education and research on desert agriculture. In Indiana The Fund supports basic human services, especially housing and family planning, strengthening of the Jewish community, and environmental protection. In the United States, Eastern Europe, and the developing world, it supports efforts to promote sustainable development, with an emphasis on reducing population growth and protecting the environment.

Officers and directors. *Officers:* Mary Ann Stein, President; Daniel Efroymson, Vice President and Secretary/Treasurer; Lori Efroymson, Vice President; Pat Cox, Assistant Secretary. *Directors:* Daniel Efroymson, Judith Lichtman, Mary Ann Stein.

Financial data. Data for fiscal year ended December 31, 1993. *Assets:* $190,023,859 (M) *Total grants authorized:* $10,856,045. *Total grants disbursed:* $8,901,045.

Environmental awards. *Program and interests:* The Fund makes most of its environmental grants in the United States and the developing world; some are restricted to the Indiana program. Revised environmental grantmaking guidelines were adopted in April 1994. Under these guidelines, the principal focus of the environmental program is on the conservation of biological diversity in the context of the sustainable management of ecosystems, with an emphasis on forests and wetlands.

Priority will be given to programs in the United States, Latin America, and the Caribbean that effectively combine several of the following program elements:

- Policy and economic research and analysis.

  Development of policies which encourage sustainable management of natural resources and ecosystems at the local, regional, or national level.

- On-the-ground projects and demonstrations.

  Giving priority to those that have broad regional or national implication and the possibility of replication in other settings.

- Enhancing the capacity of (NGOs).

  Providing support to grassroots, community-based, regional, national, or international NGOs for leadership development, strengthening management and technical capabilities and internal systems, and improving access to information.

- Assessment, evaluation, and dispersement of lessons learned.

  Efforts to better understand why initiatives failed or were successful, and dissemination of the lessons learned.

- Promoting joint efforts between local or regional actors.

  Projects or programs that combine the Moriah Fund's environmental program focus with one or more of the Fund's other program areas, which are:

  • Promoting reproductive health, stabilizing population growth, and strengthening the roles of women; and

  • Improving the quality of life of low-income families and children living in Indianapolis and the District of Columbia, under the Fund's poverty program grants.

Issues. Cli Bio Lan Agr Wat Oce Ene Was Tox Pop Dev
• • • • • • • • • • •

Funding analysis.

Fiscal year:	1992	1993
Env grants auth:	$1,647,000	$3,488,500
Number:	37	58
Range:	$2,000–$217,000	$2,000–$1,000,000
Median:	$40,000	$40,000
Pct $ disb (env/total):	22	31

Recipients (1993 highest):	Number:	Dollars:
The Nature Conservancy, Indiana Field Office	1	1,000,000
The Nature Conservancy, Headquarters	4	260,000
American Friends of Ben Gurion University	1	170,500
The Development Group for Alternative Policies	1	120,000
Citizens Action Coalition of Indiana, Inc.	1	110,000

Activity regions (1993 highest):	Number:	Dollars:
U.S. Great Lakes	10	1,410,000
U.S. not specified	20	685,500
Mexico and Central America	7	345,000
Middle East and Western Asia	2	225,500
Latin America	2	190,000

M

Sample grants (1993).*
American Horizons, Inc. Washington, DC. $30,000. To research campaign financing activities of the "wise use" movement.
Center for Marine Conservation. Washington, DC. $30,000. To support marine conservation in Samana Bay, Dominican Republic.
Center for International Environmental Law. Washington, DC. $42,500. To review the impact U.S. economic policies have on the conservation of biodiversity, stimulate coordination between organizations working on these issues, and identify gaps in research ($25,000); for the Biodiversity and Wildlife Law Program to provide legal analysis and consultation to protect biodiversity worldwide ($10,000); and to help build a public international environmental law movement in Chile ($7,500).
Clean Water Fund. Washington, DC. $40,000. To help create model strategies for environmentally and economically sustainable, community controlled development activities in the United States.
ECOLOGIA. Harford, PA. $35,000. For a small grants program for environmental organizations in the Baltic States to improve environmental conditions and support democracy and pluralism.
The Nature Conservancy, Headquarters. Arlington, VA. $220,000. For conservation of biodiversity projects: (a) Indigenous territories in large tropical landscapes—to develop a strategic plan to recommend ways in which TNC and its partners can cooperate with indigenous groups in Latin America to maximize biodiversity conservation efforts in large landscapes ($140,000); (b) To enhance TNC's remote sensing regional support center ($32,000); and (c) Eastern Caribbean Conservation—collaboration between TNC and the Island Resource Foundation to conserve biodiversity in Antigua and Montserrat ($48,000).
RARE Center for Tropical Conservation. Philadelphia, PA. $32,000. For a buffer zone management project to protect the bird population in the Monteverde Cloud Forest.
Solar Electric Light Fund. Washington, DC. $30,000. To bring a program of sustainable domestic solar electric power and light to a village in Nepal as a demonstration which could be widely replicated.
Synergos Institute. Syracuse, NY. $25,000. For its partnership effort with the campesinos in Mexico's Chimapalas rainforest.

*Sample grants represent either new awards or disbursements on grants awarded in previous years.

Application process. *Initial contact:* First-time applicants submit a letter of inquiry (2–3 pages) outlining history, purpose, and goals of organization; amount of funding requested; purpose and activities of project; and total budget of organization and project. If requested, full proposal to include:
Cover sheet summary.
1. Name, address, phone and fax numbers of organization.
2. Name and title of contact person.
3. Name of CEO.
4. Purpose of organization.
5. Organization budget for three years and dates of fiscal year.
6. Purpose, amount, and timeline for requested grant.
7. Total project budget for the past year (actual), current year (est.), and coming year (projected).
9. Other sources of income, committed and pending, for period in which Moriah support is requested.

Narrative (10 page maximum).
1. History, purpose, and goals of organization.
2. Description of organization's major programs and key accomplishments.
3. Plans and priorities for the year(s) for which funding is requested.
4. Qualifications of the organization for this work.
5. Methods of evaluation.
Project grant.
1. History of organization and a brief description of its major programs and key accomplishments.
2. Description of the activity for which funding is requested, and its
   - history
   - context within the organization
   - specific goals and measurable objectives
   - recent and anticipated accomplishments.
3. Project goals and plan of action with timeline.
4. Qualifications of organization for project.
5. Method of evalution.
6. Long-term project plans, including future financing.
Attachments.
1. Revenue and expense statements for past, current, and coming years for both organization and project.
2. List of organization's current major institutional funders with amounts.
3. Audit, if available.
4. Annual report, if available.
5. List of board of directors and their affiliations.
6. Copy of IRS tax-exempt status determination letter and proof of non-private status.
When to apply: Deadlines are March 15 and August 15.
Materials available: Annual report.

Emphases. *Recipients:* Nonprofit organizations.
Activities: Advocacy, capacity building, collaborative efforts, demonstration programs, fieldwork, innovative programs, networking, policy analysis/development, technical assistance, training.
Types of support: General purposes, leveraging funds, matching funds, multi-year grants, operating costs, pilot projects, program-related investments, projects, seed money, technical assistance.
Geography: Indiana.

Limitations. *Recipients:* Individuals.
Activities: Lobbying, political activities, research (medical).

Henry and Lucy Moses Fund, Inc.
c/o Moses & Singer
1301 Avenue of the Americas
New York, New York 10019–6016
Tel: 212–554–7800   Fax: 212–554–7700
EIN: 136092967   Type: Independent
Contact: Irving Sitnick, Secretary

History and philosophy. Attorney and banker Henry L. Moses and his wife Lucy G. Moses established the Fund in 1942. Mr.

Moses' broad philanthropic spirit and particular interest in hospitals were evident in his role as president and chairman of the board of Montefiore Hospital, and in the Fund's emphasis on health services. Today the Fund awards grants for: arts and culture, education, hospitals, social services, Jewish welfare and concerns, and environmental concerns.

Officers and directors. *Officers:* Henry Schneider, President; Joseph L. Fishman, Vice President; Alfred W. Bressler, Vice President and Treasurer; Irving Sitnick, Secretary. *Directors:* Alfred W. Bressler, Joseph L. Fishman, Henry Schneider, Irving Sitnick.

Financial data. Data for fiscal year ended December 31, 1993. *Assets:* $1,817,043 (M). *Total grants disbursed:* $1,771,770.

Environmental awards. *Recent grants:* 1993 grants included support for urban parks and open space, zoos, and botanical gardens.

Issues. Cli Bio Lan Agr Wat Oce Ene Was Tox Pop Dev
         •   •   •

Funding analysis.§

Fiscal year:	1992	1993
Env grants disb:	$178,500	$185,000
Number:	7	7
Range:	$1,000–$100,000	$2,500–$100,000
Median:	$10,000	$10,000
Pct $ disb (env/total):	8	10

Recipients (1993):	Number:	Dollars:
NYZS/The Wildlife Conservation Society	1	100,000
Central Park Conservancy	1	50,000
Brooklyn Botanic Garden	1	10,000
The New York Botanical Garden	1	10,000
Prospect Park Alliance	1	10,000
Environmental Defense Fund	1	2,500
The Parks Council, Inc.	1	2,500

Activity region (1993):	Number:	Dollars:
New York/New Jersey	7	185,000

§1993 analysis as reported by foundation.

Sample grants (1993).
Brooklyn Botanic Garden. Brooklyn, NY. $10,000.
Central Park Conservancy. New York, NY. $50,000.
Environmental Defense Fund. New York, NY. $2,500.
The New York Botanical Garden. Bronx, NY. $10,000.
NYZS/The Wildlife Conservation Society. Bronx, NY. $100,000.
The Parks Council, Inc. New York, NY. $2,500.
Prospect Park Alliance. Brooklyn, NY. $10,000.

Application process. *Initial contact:* Support generally limited to previous grant recipients. Prospective applicants may send a brief letter describing organization and project, along with a copy of the IRS tax-exempt status determination letter.
When to apply: Anytime. The board generally meets in February, May, August, and October.

Emphases. *Recipients:* Previous grant recipients.
Activities: Research.
Types of support: Annual campaigns, capital campaigns/expenses, continuing support, endowments, facilities, fellowships, general purposes, matching funds, operating costs, professorships, scholarships.
Geography: New York metropolitan area.

Limitations. *Recipients:* Individuals.
Types of support: Loans.

Charles Stewart Mott Foundation
1200 Mott Foundation Building
Flint, Michigan 48502–1851
Tel: 810–238–5651   Fax: 810–238–8152
EIN: 381211227   Type: Independent
EGA member
Contacts: Lois DeBacker, Program Officer
           Carlos Saavedra, Program Officer
           Edmund J. Miller, Associate Program Officer

History and philosophy. The Charles Stewart Mott Foundation, founded in Flint, Michigan in 1926, is a private foundation supporting programs throughout the United States and, on a limited basis, internationally. The Foundation's mission is to support efforts that promote a just, equitable, and sustainable society. It has four grantmaking programs: Environment, Poverty, Civil Society, and Flint Area.

Officers and directors. *Officers:* William S. White, Chairman, President, and CEO; William H. Piper, Vice Chairman; Richard K. Rappleye, Vice President and Secretary/Treasurer; Maureen H. Smyth, Vice President for Programs; Judy Y. Samelson, Vice President for Communications; Robert E. Swaney, Jr., Vice President and CIO. *Trustees:* Alonzo A. Crim, Katherine W. Fanning, Rushworth M. Kidder, Webb F. Martin, C. S. Harding Mott II, Maryanne Mott, William H. Piper, Willa B. Player, John W. Porter, William S. White.

Financial data. Data for fiscal year ended December 31, 1993. *Assets:* $1,273,305,723 (M). *Total grants authorized:* $49,031,475.

Environmental awards. *Program and interests:* The mission of the Environment program is to support efforts to achieve a healthy global environment capable of sustaining all forms of life. The program consists of four grantmaking areas:

- Reform of International Lending and Trade Policies.

    Promoting the transition to more sustainable forms of economic activity by reforming international lending and trade institutions. Emphases on reforming the multilateral development banks and the International Monetary Fund, particularly as they impact natural resource use in Latin America; and on influencing the General Agreement on Tariffs and Trade (GATT) and the North American Free Trade Agreement (NAFTA), especially through work in the United States, Canada, and Mexico.

- Prevention of Toxic Pollution.

  Improving and sustaining human and ecosystem health by reducing and, where possible, eliminating the use of toxic substances and their release into the environment. Emphases on pollution prevention in manufacturing and pesticide use reduction in agriculture in the United States; and on building a toxics movement in Latin America, particularly in Mexico.

- Protection of the Great Lakes Ecosystem.

  Restoring and protecting the health, diversity, and functioning of the Great Lakes ecosystem. Emphases on improving water quality, protecting natural areas, and improving environmental quality in urban areas bordering the lakes.

- Special Initiatives.

  Supporting efforts that address emerging environmental issues or offer unique opportunities to contribute to the resolution of environmental problems of national or global significance. Emphases on conservation of temperate rainforest ecosystems in Alaska and British Columbia, and advancement of public interest science.

In addition, within its Civil Society Program, the Foundation makes a limited number of grants to address environmental issues in Central Europe and the Independent (formerly Soviet) States.

Issues. Cli Bio Lan Agr Wat Oce Ene Was Tox Pop Dev

Funding analysis.

Fiscal year:	1992	1993*
Env grants auth:	$7,451,859	$7,436,378
Number:	107	69
Range:	$7,850–$375,000	$10,000–$300,000
Median:	$50,000	$57,000
Pct $ auth (env/total):	15	15

*As provided by Foundation. Data are said to be "annualized to account for multiple regions."

Recipients (1992 highest):	Number:	Dollars:
The Nature Conservancy, Headquarters	2	477,000
Natural Resources Defense Council	4	450,000
Friends of the Earth/ Environmental Policy Institute	2	350,000
Environmental Defense Fund	2	325,000
Center for Neighborhood Technology	1	225,000

Activity regions (1992 highest):	Number:	Dollars:
U.S. Great Lakes	20	1,937,932
U.S. not specified	20	1,820,000
Developing countries	9	648,650
U.S. Northeast	6	533,075
Eastern Europe	7	451,073

Sample grants (1993).

Bank Information Center. Washington, DC. $85,000. The Bank Information Center monitors and provides information on the policies and projects of the multilateral development banks to NGOs in donor and borrowing countries. Mott's support will expand the Center's capacity to assist NGOs in Latin America to become more involved in reform of multilateral development banks.

Center for Rural Affairs. Walthill, NE. $120,000 (2 years). For Policy Reform Efforts Aimed at Agricultural Pesticide Use Reduction. The next two years are a critical time for redirecting federal farm policy to support pesticide use reduction and sustainable agriculture more generally. The Clinton Administration is reorganizing the entire Department of Agriculture and, simultaneously, development is underway of the 1995 Farm Bill, which will guide U.S. farm policy for the rest of the decade. Through this project, CRA will promote policy reforms via a combination of grassroots organizing, administrative and legislative advocacy, outreach to farmers, policy option development, analysis of policy options put forth by others, coalition building, and work with the news media.

Citizens for a Better Environment. San Francisco, CA. $100,000. For the Campaign for Sustainable Manufacturing. The goal of this program is to move toward truly sustainable manufacturing in the San Francisco Bay Area and the Los Angeles basin. Targeting areas where pollution problems are most concentrated, CBE will work to advance pollution prevention strategies in the electronics and petrochemical sectors. Successful strategies will be shared with pollution prevention advocates in other states.

Community Nutrition Institute. Washington, DC. $50,000. For the Environmental Policy in Trade Liberalization Project. Two years ago, the OECD established a working group on trade and the environment to provide an opportunity for representatives of the major economic powers to work through the policy conflicts regarding trash and the environment in a nonbinding forum. The Community Nutrition Institute is the official representative of the environmental, health, and consumer communities on the U.S. delegation to those working group meetings. Through this project, the Institute will work to develop consensus positions among major U.S. environmental groups on trade-environment issues that will be addressed in the working group discussions, and then present those positions in that forum.

Grand Calumet Task Force Corporation. Whiting, IN. $60,000 (2 years). The "Calumet Region," which includes communities in northwest Indiana and southeast Chicago, is an area whose economic existence has long been dependent upon industrial production processes that create large amounts of toxic pollution. The Task Force will promote pollution prevention in that region by creating the Calumet Region Pollution Prevention Center. The Center will include an information library and meeting place for area environmental groups. Its staff will facilitate the establishment of the Calumet Region Pollution Prevention and Sustainable Communities Network, and prepare and distribute a Calumet Region Pollution Prevention Manual with information on industrial pollution sources in the region and possible options for reducing or preventing future pollution from those sources.

Industrial States Policy Center. Cleveland, OH. $60,000 (2 years). For the Great Lakes Water Quality Protection Project which will work to reduce inputs of toxic substances to the Great Lakes by documenting the contribution of Ohio sources to toxic pollution of the lakes, encouraging informed public comment on proposed water quality regulations, and working with officials of three northern Ohio communities to advance pollution prevention.

Keystone Center. Keystone, CO. $150,000 (2 years). For the Keystone Center and the Vermont School of Law to convene the National Commission on Superfund—a forum for developing practical recommendations to improve the federal Superfund program when it is reauthorized in 1994. The commission includes key organizations and constituencies whose views will influence Superfund reauthorization debates.

LightHawk. Santa Fe, NM. $180,000 (3 years). For the Ancient Temperate Rainforest Campaign. This grant will allow LightHawk, a public interest flying service, to undertake a major public awareness and action campaign to protect the remaining ancient forests in southeastern Alaska, British Columbia, and southern Chile. To achieve its objectives, LightHawk will use a combination of skills in flight, grassroots organizing, media communications, scientific research, and photo documentation.

Michigan Society of Planning Officials. Rochester, MI. $300,000 (15 months). For the Michigan Trend Future Report. This project will document key trends in patterns of land use in Michigan and assess the implications for Michigan's environmental and economic future, should those trends continue. A series of reports will be prepared, as well as summary publications intended for a general audience. An extensive computerized database will be developed and made accessible to Michigan citizens through an existing computer network. These trend future analyses will provide a common basis of information for decisionmakers in government and other organizations with an interest in improving land use policy.

Texas Center for Policy Studies. Austin, TX. $180,000 (3 years). For the Cross-Border Cooperation of Toxics Pollution Prevention and Control Project. Joint U.S.-Mexico efforts are essential to resolve common programs of toxic pollution along the border. Compared to their U.S. counterparts, NGOs in Mexico are generally weak and only have limited visibility. Given the nascent state of Mexican NGOs working on the U.S.-Mexico border, capacity building and access to information are two major needs to improve their ability to address the growing problems of toxic pollution in the region. This grant will allow the Center to: (1) promote networking and information dissemination; (2) provide technical assistance for research and policy development; and (3) provide seed grants for selected northern Mexico NGOs.

Urgewald. Sassenberg, Germany. $55,000. Reform of the Global Environmental Facility (GEF) and the Brazil Pilot Program. This project will further the international efforts to reform the policies of the multilateral development banks (MDBs) by focusing on two major World Bank-based initiatives—the Global Environmental Facility and the Brazil Pilot Program. Specifically, the project will target reform of German government policy because of that country's significant political and financial involvement in both efforts. Mott's grant will cover two half-time positions. Support will allow Mott to to target Europe in its efforts to reform the major MDBs.

Application process. *Initial contact:* Letter of inquiry or full proposal (letter of inquiry is preferred). Proposal to include:
1. Cover letter signed by person responsible for signing grant contracts on behalf of requesting organization.
2. Project description including goals, objectives, and projected timetable.
3. Needs statement.
4. Description of population served.
5. Documented line-item budget for proposed grant period, including list of other funding sources.
6. Starting and ending dates for project and, if project will continue, plans for post-grant funding.
7. Budget based on applicant's fiscal year (not required for major educational institutions or units of government).
8. Accomplishments to date and tax-exempt status letter.
9. Plans for project evaluation and dissemination.

When to apply: Anytime. Deadline for consideration in 1995 is August 31, 1995.

Materials available: Annual report (includes "How to Apply for a Grant"), "Philosophy, Programs, and Procedures: Environment," "Facts on Grants," and *Mott Exchange* (quarterly newsletter). Request materials by calling the Foundation's publications hotline at 810–766–1766.

Emphases. *Recipients:* Nonprofit organizations.
Activities: Advocacy, capacity building, citizen participation, collaborative efforts, demonstration programs, innovative programs, networking, policy analysis/development, technical assistance, training.
Types of support: General purposes, multi-year grants, projects.
Geography: Domestic United States; international (emphasis on Western Hemisphere).

Limitations. *Recipients:* Individuals.
Types of support: Loans, mortgage reduction.

Ruth Mott Fund

1726 Genesee Towers
Flint, Michigan 48502
Tel: 313–232–3180   Fax: 313–232–3272
EIN: 382284264   Type: Independent
EGA member
Contact: Deborah E. Tuck, Executive Director

History and philosophy. The Ruth Mott Fund was created in 1980 by Ruth Rawlings Mott. The Fund seeks to promote sensible health practices, sound nutrition, reduction of stress, a healthy environment, and artistic expression. "Because human health ultimately depends upon the well-being of the globe we all share, the Fund supports initiatives to protect the Earth's health. And because human beings have the power to destroy the entire web of life, it seeks opportunities to work for the prevention of war." Program areas are: Arts and Special Interests, Environment, Health Promotion, and National and International Security.

Officers and directors. *Officers:* Ruth R. Mott, Founder; Maryanne Mott, President; Leslie Dunbar, Chair; Joseph R. Robinson, Vice Chair and Treasurer; Susan Kleinpell, Secretary; Deborah E. Tuck, Executive Director. *Trustees:* Brooks Bollmen, III, Dudley Cocke, Leslie Dunbar, Jean E. Fairfax, Susan Kleinpell, Donna Metcalf, Maryanne Mott, Ruth R. Mott, Melissa Patterson, Joseph R. Robinson, Virginia M. Sullivan, Herman Warsh.

Financial data. Data for fiscal year ended November 30, 1993. *Assets:* $2,256,850 (M). *Gifts received:* $1,800,000. *Total grants disbursed:* $1,369,762.

© 1995 Environmental Data Resources, Inc.

M

Environmental awards. *Program and interests:* "The Fund seeks to foster public understanding and involvement in protecting our public resources. This includes the wealth of natural resources on public lands, the air we breathe, and the water we drink. The Fund is concerned particularly with the effect that private or public actions have on public resources.

"The Ruth Mott fund values organizations which are democratic and whose membership reflects the diversity of their community. While recognizing that organizations employ a range of strategies in regard to public resource issues, the Fund will give special attention to efforts to organize local citizens around issues of national significance. The Fund encourages efforts of local groups to work together and with regional or national organiza-tions on projects that promote public education, involvement, and advocacy."

Issues. Cli• Bio• Lan• Agr• Wat• Oce• Ene• Was Tox• Pop• Dev•

Funding analysis.

Fiscal year:	1991	1993
Env grants auth:	$419,500	$583,770
Number:	22	42
Range:	$2,500–$31,500	$100–$25,000
Median:	$20,000	$15,000
Pct $ auth (env/total):	24	33

Recipients (1993 highest):	Number:	Dollars:
Farm Labor Research Project, Inc.	1	25,000
Mineral Policy Center	1	25,000
Native Americans for a Clean Environment	1	25,000
Native Seeds/SEARCH	1	25,000
Western Ancient Forest Campaign	1	25,000

Activity regions (1993 highest):	Number:	Dollars:
U.S. not specified	8	130,500
U.S. Northwest	7	115,120
U.S. South Central	5	74,000
U.S. Southeast	3	60,000
U.S. Mountain	6	41,800

Sample grants (1993).

Alaska Conservation Foundation. Anchorage, AK. $20,000. Support for the Alaska Coastal Rainforest Campaign's work of research, education, and public advocacy on preserving Alaska's coastal rainforest ecosystem.

Inland Empire Public Lands Council. Spokane, WA. $20,000. For the Forest Watch Program to protect Washington's eastside forests from unsustainable cutting.

Institute for Agriculture and Trade Policy. Minneapolis, MN. $20,000. For organizing four Citizen Dialogues on the environmental impacts of NAFTA.

Mexicano/Chicano Chamber of Commerce. Silver City, NM. $7,000. Support for The San Vicente Community Education, Reclamation, and Monitoring Project.

Montana Wilderness Association. Helena, MT. $20,000. Support for the Montana Wilderness campaign.

Native Seeds/SEARCH. Tucson, AZ. $25,000. Support to expand the outreach and organizing programs by the traditional Native American Farmers Association.

Pacific Rivers Council. Eugene, OR. $15,000. Support for education and organizing efforts among timber workers and rural communities.

Pesticide Education Center. San Francisco, CA. $15,000. Support for the Farm Worker Education Project, to educate farm workers about the hazards and health effects of pesticide use.

Red Thunder, Inc. Dodson, MT. $10,000. Support for a project on mining and its impact on health, welfare, and culture of Native Americans.

Western Ancient Forest Campaign. Washington, DC. $25,000. Suppport for grassroots advocacy on the Northwest ancient forests.

Western North Carolina Alliance. Asheville, NC. $20,000. Support for the grassroots Forest Management Task Force and work in reforming U.S. Forest Service programs.

Application process. *Initial contact:* Letter of inquiry or full proposal. Proposal (2 copies) to include:

Summary page.
1. Name, address, and telephone number of organization.
2. Date of submission.
3. Contact person and title.
4. Title of project or other identification.
5. Total project budget amount.
6. Amount requested.
7. Period of time for which grant is requested.
8. Organization name as it appears on IRS exemption letter.
9. Brief description of project and purpose of funds, focusing on issues and problems and how they are to be addressed by this project.

Grant request (12 pages maximum).
1. What issues and problems are being addressed by the project or program and why are they important?
2. What is project plan and what are its measurable objectives?
3. How is the project expected to make a difference?
4. How will project results be evaluated?
5. What are your plans for continued funding (if applicable)?
6. How might this project benefit people beyond those immediately served by it?

Support material.
1. Project budget for grant period requested, including how much of budget has been raised.
2. Organization's operating budget for the grant period requested, including how much of the budget has been raised.
3. List showing funding organizations and amounts requested. Indicate which requests have already been submitted and which you plan to submit.
4. Financial statement of most recently completed fiscal year.
5. Summary of the organization's history and activities.
6. List of key personnel and resumes.
7. List of board members.
8. Description of racial/ethnic composition of board and staff.
9. Copy of IRS tax-exempt status determination letter.

Other supporting material (1 copy) can be included. Please do not include videotapes, cassettes, etc.

When to apply: Deadlines are November 1, March 1, and July 1. The trustees meet the first week of February, June, and October.

Materials available: Biennial report (includes "How to Apply for a Grant," "General Guidelines–All Program Areas").

Emphases. *Recipients:* Nonprofit organizations.
Activities: Advocacy, citizen participation, innovative programs, policy analysis/development.
Types of support: Continuing support, general purposes, operating costs, seed money.
Geography: United States.

Limitations. *Recipients:* Individuals.
Activities: Audiovisual materials, land acquisition.
Types of support: Annual campaigns, capital campaigns/expenses, debt retirement, emergency funding, endowments, equipment, facilities (renovation), fellowships, loans, scholarships.

The Mountaineers Foundation
c/o The Mountaineers
300 Third Avenue West
Seattle, Washington 98119
Tel: 206–284–6310
EIN: 237023350   Type: Public
Contact: Constance G. Pious, Chair, Grants Committee

History and philosophy. The Foundation was started in 1969 by members of The Mountaineers, an outdoors and conservation organization. Its objective is to study the mountains, forests, and streams; to gather into permanent form history and traditions; and to preserve the natural beauty of the Pacific Northwest. One of its special tasks is to preserve and protect over 180 acres of old growth forest called the Rhododendron Preserve.

Officers and directors. *Officers:* Constance G. Pious, Chair; James Dubuar, President.

Financial data. Data for fiscal year ended December 31, 1993. *Assets:* $407,872 (M). *Gifts received:* $98,968. *Total grants disbursed:* $17,141.

Environmental awards. *Recent grants:* 1993 grants included support for habitat and species preservation, education, and museums.

Issues. Cli Bio Lan Agr Wat Oce Ene Was Tox Pop Dev
         •   •   •   •

Funding analysis.

Fiscal year:	1993
Env grants disb:	$15,121
Number:	6
Range:	$1,000–$5,000
Median:	$2,288
Pct $ disb (env/total):	100

Recipients (1993):	Number:	Dollars:
The Nature Conservancy, Washington Field Office	1	5,000
Mountaineers Club	1	3,546
Washington State Capitol Museum	1	2,500
The Whale Museum	1	2,075
Sierra Club, Northwest Office	1	1,000
Washington Trails Association	1	1,000

Activity region (1993):	Number:	Dollars:
U.S. Northwest	6	15,121

Sample grants (1993).
Mountaineers Club. Seattle, WA. $3,546. To pay for development expenses for The Mountaineers' School Conservation/Education program consisting of 116 presentations in 38 schools to approximately 3,400 students.
The Nature Conservancy, Washington Field Office. Seattle, WA. $5,000. To help purchase 240 acres to protect shrub-steppe habitat on Barker Mountain in Douglas County, Washington for grouse. This property includes a key lek (mating dancing ground) of the Columbian sharp-tailed grouse.
Sierra Club, Northwest Office. Seattle, WA. $1,000. For a wilderness outing for ten inner-city youths to assist in training them to become "youth assistant-leaders," to pay for environmental education resource materials for use by outing leaders, and to plant trees and shrubs and make other landscape improvements in Martin Luther King Memorial Park.
Washington State Capital Museum. Olympia, WA. $2,500. To provide signs for the Cultural Botanical Garden surrounding the museum in Olympia.
Washington Trails Association. Seattle, WA. $1,000. To assist in publishing a guide book to barrier-free trails in the state of Washington.
The Whale Museum. Friday Harbor, WA. $2,075. To print whale descriptions, Puget Sound Pods, for public use to identify whales in Puget Sound.

Application process. *Initial contact:* Letter of inquiry (1 copy) briefly outlining proposed project. Proposal (7 copies) to include:
1. Completed Applicant Data Sheet.
2. Narrative (4 pages).
   - Organization's mission.
   - Description of project, why it's important, and how it addresses Foundation priorities.
   - List of personnel involved in project and their resumes.
   - Project schedule.
   - Project budget detailing how Foundation funds will be spent and funds of any other organization.
3. Copy of IRS tax-exempt status determination letter.
4. Evidence of support from other involved organizations.

Do not send elaborate brochures or other expensive materials.
When to apply: Deadlines are January 15, May 15, September 15, and November 15.
Materials available: "Guidelines For Grant Applications" and "What is the Mountaineers Foundation?" (flyer).

Emphases. *Recipients:* Educational institutions, individuals, museums, nonprofit organizations.
Activities: Audiovisual materials, conferences, education, publications, research, seminars.
Types of support: Capital campaigns/expenses, equipment, facilities (renovation), pilot projects, seed money.
Geography: Pacific Northwest.

Limitations. *Activities:* Fundraising, lobbying.
Types of support: Operating costs.

© 1995 Environmental Data Resources, Inc.

M

The Curtis and Edith Munson Foundation, Inc.
515 North State Street, Suite 2340
Chicago, Illinois 60610
Tel: 312-527-5545   Fax: 312-527-5544
EIN: 592235907   Type: Independent
EGA member
Contacts: C. Wolcott Henry III, President
            Angel Cunningham, Program Consultant

History and philosophy. Established in 1982 by Edith C. Munson, the Foundation's central focus is environmental issues in North America. It also supports interests of donor and board.

Officers and directors. *Officers:* Truman M. Hobbs, Chairman; C. Wolcott Henry III, President; Bruce S. Reid, Secretary; Michael C. Rausch, Treasurer. *Directors:* C. Wolcott Henry III, H. Alexander Henry, Truman M. Hobbs, Bruce S. Reid.

Financial data. Data for fiscal year ended December 31, 1994. *Assets:* $25,800,000 (M) *Total grants authorized:* $1,250,000.

Environmental awards. *Program and interests:* Interests include:
- Marine fisheries conservation and management.
- Southeast Florida issues.
- Environmental education.
- Management of NGOs.
- Population and the environment.

The Foundation also publishes a newsletter, *Conservation Digest*.

Issues.   Cli Bio Lan Agr Wat Oce Ene Was Tox Pop Dev
                   •   •   •   •   •   •   •   •   •

Funding analysis.

Fiscal year:	1990	1992
Env grants auth:	$630,000	$978,350
Number:	28	49
Range:	$5,000–$70,000	$3,350–$60,000
Median:	$20,000	$20,000
Pct $ disb (env/total):	65	89

Recipients (1992 highest):	Number:	Dollars:
World Wildlife Fund	2	85,000
National Fish and Wildlife Foundation	1	60,000
Lincoln Park Zoological Society	2	50,000
Center for Marine Conservation	1	40,000
National Coalition for Marine Conservation	1	32,500

Activity regions (1992 highest):	Number:	Dollars:
U.S. Southeast	20	325,000
U.S. not specified	6	205,000
Global	5	112,500
International*	6	155,000
U.S. Great Lakes	7	110,850

*Multiple regions or not specified.

Sample grants (1992).
Clean Water Fund. Coral Gables, FL. $15,000. Support to expand the diversity and inclusive popular base needed to produce effective and lasting policies that are protective of south Florida's water quality and quantity, and its unique and endangered natural resources areas.
Florida Conservation Association. Tallahassee, FL. $20,000. Continued support of the FCA fisheries conservation program, which includes the Ban the Nets Campaign.
Institute for Southern Studies. Durham, NC. $10,000. Support for a new *Green Index* which will profile activists using first-person testimony to dramatize the links between pollution and community health, and describe constructive steps taken to bring about change.
Management Institute for Environment and Business. Washington, DC. $30,000. Support for "The Pilot Program in Environment Management Education" to be added to the curriculum at the Kellogg School at Northwestern University.
National Coalition for Marine Conservation. Savannah, GA. $32,500. Support for three projects: (1) To compare marine fisheries issues with other environmental issues for which a broad constituency has been built, and explore how to begin building one for marine conservation; (2) To expand the brochure, "The Seas' Vanishing Bounty" to a poster; and (3) For NCM's Marine Fisheries Enhancement Project.
Natural Resources Defense Council. New York, NY. $20,000. To promote advocacy to improve the international regime governing fishing of species that migrate through or straddle the high seas or the Exclusive Economic Zones (EEZs) of other nations.
New England Aquarium. Boston, MA. $20,000. Salary support for a new conservation director who will oversee the Aquarium's conservation research and education efforts.
Open Lands Project. Chicago, IL. $12,500. For the environmental awareness and education portion of the Urban Greening Program.
Population Communications International. New York, NY. $30,000. For the Population/Environment Initiative and a media campaign.

Application process. *Initial contact:* No unsolicited grant proposals accepted. Telephone call and proposal summary (2 pages) to include:
1. Most recent annual report with audited financial statements.
2. List of major donors and those funding proposed project.
3. List of major program areas and budgets.
4. Two letters of reference on proposed project/program.
5. Copy of IRS tax-exempt status determination letter.

When to apply: Deadlines are June 1 and October 15. The directors review grants in July and November.
Materials available: "Guidelines," "Proposal Summary" (form), *Conservation Digest* (newsletter).

Emphases. *Recipients:* Pre-selected organizations only.
Types of support: Program-related investments, projects. Over 90 percent of grants are restricted.
Geography: North America, with emphasis on Florida, Illinois, and Alabama.

Limitations. *Recipients:* Individuals.
Types of support: Capital campaigns/expenses, endowments.

M. J. Murdock Charitable Trust

P.O. Box 1618
Vancouver, Washington 98668
Tel: 206-694-8415 or 503-285-4086
EIN: 237456468   Type: Independent
Contact: Ford A. Anderson, II, Executive Director

History and philosophy. The M. J. Murdock Charitable Trust was created in 1975 by the will of Melvin J. (Jack) Murdock (1917-1971), co-founder of Tektronix, Inc. In the spirit of Mr. Murdock, who sought "ways for humans to survive a little more constructively," the Trust funds programs that seek solutions to or the prevention of important problems; expand the knowledge of mankind; and promote social values and activities leading to happier, healthier, freer, and more productive lives. Projects or programs based on self-help and enterprise concepts are of particular interest. Program areas are: Education, Scientific and Medical Research, Health and Medicine, Community, Handicapped, Arts and Culture, and Public Affairs.

Officers and directors. *Trustees:* James B. Castles, Walter P. Dyke, Lynwood W. Swanson.

Financial data. Data for fiscal year ended December 31, 1992. *Assets:* $263,699,731 (M). *Total grants authorized:* $15,565,140.

Environmental awards. *Program and interests:* The Trust may make environmental grants through any of several funding categories. It has a particular interest in the free-market approach to environmental issues.
Recent grants: Grants in 1992 included support for ecosystem research, land conservation, and public education activities.

Issues.   Cli Bio Lan Agr Wat Oce Ene Was Tox Pop Dev
                   •   •   •   •   •   •

Funding analysis.

Fiscal year:	1991	1992
Env grants auth:	$2,766,800	$1,188,600
Number:	7	9
Range:	$12,000-$2,000,000	$15,000-$400,000
Median:	$175,000	$50,000
Pct $ auth (env/total):	20	8

Recipients (1992 highest):	Number:	Dollars:
Woodland Park Zoological Society	1	400,000
Prince William Sound Science Center	1	300,000
Oregon Coast Aquarium	1	220,500
Peregrine Fund	1	100,000
Montana Land Reliance	1	50,000

Activity regions (1992):	Number:	Dollars:
U.S. Northwest	7	838,600
Alaska	1	300,000
U.S. Mountain	1	50,000

Sample grants (1992).*
American Wilderness Foundation. Portland, OR. $4,000. Leadership training.
Columbia River Bicentennial Commission. Portland, OR. $46,400. Interactive computer-based exhibit.
Community Enterprises of Issaquah, Inc. Issaquah, WA. $15,000. Recycling equipment.
Friends of the Rae Selling Berry Botanic Garden. Portland, OR. $12,400. Public education.
Montana Tech Foundation. Butte, MT. $175,000. For the Environmental Engineering Program.
Oregon Coast Aquarium. Newport, OR. $220,500. Educational programs.
Oregon Graduate Institute of Science & Technology. Beaverton, OR. $2,000,000. New chemical and biological sciences/environmental science and engineering building.
Oregon Parks Foundation. Portland, OR. $40,000.
Prince William Sound Science Center. Cordova, AK. $300,000. Ecosystem conservation for the Greater Prince William Sound.
Washington Park Zoo Metropolitan Service District. Portland, OR. $16,700. Elementary teachers pilot science project.
Woodland Park Zoological Society. Seattle, WA. $400,000. New education center.

*Sample grants represent with new award on disbursements or grants awarded in previous years.

Application process. *Initial contact:* Telephone call to request information on application procedures. If proposal is research related, it requires the Research Application Form. The Trust defines three categories of proposal, each with its own application process:
1. Requests for less than $100,000. Complete and send 8 copies of the General Application Form, along with required attachments.
2. Requests for $100,000-$500,000. Develop a full proposal according to steps outlined by the Trust and submit with required attachments.
3. Requests of $500,000 or more. Complete and send 8 copies of the General Application Form. If the Trust is interested in the project, it will request submission of a full proposal or other appropriate information.

When to apply: Anytime. The board meets monthly.
Materials available: Annual report (contains "Grant Proposal Guidelines"), "General Application Packet."

Emphases. *Recipients:* Nonprofit organizations.
Activities: Research.
Types of support: Equipment, facilities (construction), projects, seed money.
Geography: Pacific Northwest states of Washington, Oregon, Idaho, Montana, and Alaska.

Limitations. *Recipients:* Conduit organizations, individuals.
Activities: Fundraising, lobbying, political activities.
Types of support: Annual campaigns, debt retirement, emergency funding, endowments, fellowships, general purposes, loans, matching funds, scholarships, operating costs.

M

John P. Murphy Foundation
Tower City Center
924 Terminal Tower
Cleveland, Ohio 44113–2203
Tel: 216–623–4770   Fax: 216–623–4773
EIN: 346528308
Contact: Herbert E. Strawbridge, President, Secretary, Treasurer

History and philosophy. The Foundation was established in 1960 by John P. Murphy, legal counsel to M. J. and O. P. Van Sweringen and director of many of their real estate and railroad corporations, and later president of The Higbee Company. The Foundation makes grants for: Community, Social Services, and Religion; Health; Education; and Arts and Culture.

Officers and directors. *Officers:* Herbert E. Strawbridge, President and Secretary/Treasurer; Claude M. Blair, Robert R. Broadbent, Marie S. Strawbridge, Robert G. Wright, Vice Presidents; Nancy W. McCann, Assistant Vice President; Allan J. Zambie, Assistant Secretary; *Directors:* Claude M. Blair, Robert R. Broadbent, Herbert E. Strawbridge, Marie S. Strawbridge, Robert G. Wright. *Honorary Director:* Frank E. Joseph, Sr.

Financial data. Data for fiscal year ended December 1993. *Assets:* $40,312,326 (M). *Total grants disbursed:* $1,955,175.

Environmental awards. *Recent grants:* 1993 grants included support for urban environment (trees, horticulture), and an aquarium.

Issues. Cli Bio Lan Agr Wat Oce Ene Was Tox Pop Dev

Funding analysis.

Fiscal year:	1993
Env grants disb:	$55,000
Number:	3
Range:	$5,000–$25,000
Median:	$25,000
Pct $ disb (env/total):	3

Recipients (1993):	Number:	Dollars:
Garden Center of Greater Cleveland	1	25,000
The CAQ Corporation	1	25,000
Cleanland, Ohio	1	5,000

Activity region (1993):	Number:	Dollars:
U.S. Great Lakes	3	55,000

Sample grants (1993).
Cleanland, Ohio. Cleveland, OH. $5,000. To purchase trees.
The CAQ Corporation. Cleveland, OH. $25,000. Membership drive for the Cleveland Aquarium.
Garden Center of Greater Cleveland. Cleveland, OH. $25,000. For office equipment.

Application process. *Initial contact:* Proposal (8 copies), signed by organization's president, to include:
1. Background of organization and its purpose.
2. Latest balance sheet with description of assets and liabilities.
3. Grant purpose and goal.
4. Total amount requested and total cost of project.
5. Manner in which you expect to raise the needed funds.

Attachments (1 copy).
1. Copies of tax-exempt certificates and letters.
2. Any other information you think will be helpful.

When to apply: Anytime. The trustees meet bi-monthly.
Materials available: Brochure (includes "Grant Application Requirements," application).

Emphases. *Recipients:* Aquariums, botanical gardens, educational institutions, museums, nonprofit organizations, zoos.
Activities: Education, exhibits, feasibility studies, innovative programs, land acquisition, publications, research (medical), volunteerism, workshops, youth programs.
Types of support: Annual campaigns, capital campaigns/expenses, computer hardware, continuing support, debt retirement, emergency funding, equipment, facilities, general purposes, indirect costs, internships, lectureships, leveraging funds, maintenance, matching funds, membership campaigns, mortgage reduction, multi-year grants, operating costs, pilot projects, professorships, program-related investments, projects, start-up costs, technical assistance, travel expenses.
Geography: Cuyahoga County and the adjacent counties in northeastern Ohio.

Limitations. *Recipients:* Individuals, public agencies, religious organizations.
Activities: Activism, advocacy.
Types of support: Advertising campaigns, endowments, fellowships, internships, lectureships, leveraging funds, loans, professorships, scholarships, start-up costs, travel expenses.

Mustard Seed Foundation, Inc.
c/o Edwards & Angell
2700 Hospital Trust Tower
Providence, Rhode Island 02903
Tel: 401–274–9200
EIN: 22-2714666   Type: Independent
Contact: Philip B. Barr, Jr., Secretary

History and philosophy. The Foundation was established in 1984 by the Russell family. It makes grants for higher education, environment, and Protestant causes.

Officers and directors. *Officers:* Rev. Thomas L. Crum, President; Philip B. Barr, Jr., Secretary; Benjamin G. Pastor, Treasurer. *Trustees:* Philip B. Barr, Jr., Rev. Thomas L. Crum, Benjamin G. Pastor, Carol L. Russell, Robert J. Russell.

Financial data. Data for fiscal year ended November 30, 1992. *Assets:* $167,425 (U). *Gifts received:* $157,835. *Total grants disbursed:* $116,711.

Environmental awards. *Recent grants:* 1992 grants included support for research expeditions.

Funding analysis.

Fiscal year:	1992
Env grants disb:	$45,360
Number:	2
Range:	$17,360–$28,000
Median:	$22,680
Pct $ disb (env/total):	39

Recipient (1992):	Number:	Dollars:
Earthwatch Expeditions, Inc.	2	45,360

Activity region (1992):	Number:	Dollars:
U.S. not specified	2	45,360

Sample grants (1992).
Earthwatch Expeditions, Inc. Watertown, MA. $28,000.
Earthwatch Expeditions, Inc. Watertown, MA. $17,360.

Application process. *Initial contact:* Letter indicating purpose, amount, and duration of program or product.
When to apply: Anytime.

Emphases. *Recipients:* Nonprofit organizations.

The National Environmental Education and Training Foundation, Inc.

915 15th Street, N.W., Suite 200
Washington, DC 20005
Tel: 202–628–8200   Fax: 202–628–8204
EIN: 541557043   Type: Independent
EGA member
Contact: Michelle Harvey, Program Director

History and philosophy. The Foundation was established by Congress in 1990 to foster environmental literacy through public/private partnerships and to increase support for environmental education. Grants are funded primarily through federal appropriations and require a cash match of at least one non-federal dollar for each Foundation dollar awarded.

It has three goals: to create an environmentally conscious and committed public, an environmentally literate workforce, and an environmentally advanced educational system; to promote environmental education partnerships among government, community, business, nonprofit, and academic organizations; and to increase funding for environmental education.

Officers and directors. *Program director:* Michelle Harvey.

Financial data. Data for fiscal year ended September 30, 1994. *Assets:* $1,197,812 (M). *Gifts received:* $26,460. *Total grants authorized:* $1,530,256.

Environmental awards. *Recent grants:* 1994 grants included support for land conservation, water resources, coastal and marine issues, toxics and environmental health, urban environment, and education on all levels.

Issues. Cli • Bio • Lan Agr • Wat • Oce Ene • Was Tox Pop Dev

Funding analysis.

Fiscal year:	1992
Env grants auth:	$532,050
Number:	14
Range:	$5,000–$85,000
Median:	$27,500
Pct $ auth (env/total):	100

Recipients (1992 highest):	Number:	Dollars:
City of Los Angeles	1	85,000
National Council for Geographic Education	1	80,000
Delaware Teachers Academy for Service Learning	1	70,000
Environmental Defense Fund	1	60,000
Global Tomorrow Coalition	1	60,000
Jane Goodall Institute	1	50,000

Activity regions (1992 highest):	Number:	Dollars:
U.S. not specified	5	230,000
U.S. West	4	147,500
U.S. Mid-Atlantic	1	70,000
New York/New Jersey	1	30,000
U.S. Northeast	1	25,000

Sample grants (1994).
Alliance for Community Education. Bowie, MD. $10,000. To train youth to start alternative lawn and garden care businesses, using concepts that reduce polluted run-off.
Citizens Committee for New York City. New York, NY. $75,000. To build and support environmental leadership among grassroots low-income and minority neighborhood leaders through an environmental training and education program.
Clean Air Council. Philadelphia, PA. $60,000. To provide low-income communities with environmental education and literacy programs focusing on health and the environment, with special emphasis on childrens' issues of lead poisoning and asthma.
Friends of Cabrillo Aquarium. San Pedro, CA. $24,000. To bring live marine specimens and a marine biology instructor to an additional 13,000 inner-city children in Los Angeles.
Management Institute for Environment and Business. Washington, DC. $50,000. To provide environmental management education and training for a consortium of 25 MBA programs.
National Technological University. Fort Collins, CO. $60,000. To develop and deliver two environmental training courses to be administered nationwide via satellite to engineers of small and medium-sized companies.
YMCA Earth Service Corps. Seattle, WA. $75,000. To combine environmental education with community service and leadership training for high school students.

Application process. *Initial contact:* Pre-proposal (1 page) to include a project summary with budget information itemized by project component.
When to apply: Deadlines are March 15 and August 15.
Materials available: "General Grant Guidelines."

Emphases. *Recipients:* Nonprofit organizations.
Activities: Conferences, education, publications, research, training, workshops.
Types of support: Advertising campaigns, matching funds.

Limitations. *Recipients:* Individuals.
Activities: Fellowships, political activities, research, scholarships.
Types of support: Capital campaigns/expenses, multi-year grants, operating costs.

National Fish and Wildlife Foundation

1120 Connecticut Avenue, N.W.
Bender Building, Suite 900
Washington, DC 20036
Tel: 202–857–0166   Fax: 202–857–0162
EIN: 521384139   Type: Independent
EGA member
Contact: Krishna K. Roy, Director,
         Development & Marketing

History and philosophy. The National Fish and Wildlife Foundation (NFWF) is a 501(c)(3) nonprofit organization dedicated to the conservation of natural resources—fish, wildlife, and plants. Among its goals are species habitat protection, environmental education, public policy development, natural resource management, habitat and ecosystem rehabilitation and restoration, and leadership training for conservation professionals. It meets these goals by forging partnerships between the public and private sectors and by supporting conservation activities that pinpoint and solve the root causes of environmental problems.

Headquartered in Washington, D.C., NFWF was established by Congress in 1984. NFWF invests in the best possible solutions to those problems by awarding challenge grants using its federally appropriated funds to match private sector funds. These combined resources fuel effective conservation projects; however, federal appropriations may not be used for NFWF's operating expenses. NFWF has awarded 962 grants that have leveraged $120 million for conservation projects. NFWF's work is local, regional, national, and international in scope. To date, project locations include the 50 states, Puerto Rico, and 17 countries.

Officers and directors. *Officers:* Magalen O. Bryant, Chairman; Amos S. Eno, Secretary. *Directors:* Kay K. Arnold, Magalen O. Bryant, Caroline Getty, Kenneth H. Hofmann, John L. Morris, Neil L. Oldridge, David B. Rockland, Ph.D., Lindsay Thomas. *Ex officio:* Mollie H. Beattie, Brig. Gen. Charles Y. Yeager. *Counsel:* Michael J. Brennan.

Financial data. Data for fiscal year ended September 30, 1993. *Assets:* $15,519,947 (M). *Revenues:* $19,370,164. *Total grants authorized:* $5,800,000. *Total grants disbursed:* $17,131,813.

Environmental awards. *Program and interests:* The Foundation awards the majority of its grants through six conservation programs:

- Wetland Conservation.

  The North American Waterfowl Management Plan and the North American Wetlands Partnership programs are cooperative undertakings by the United States, Canada, and Mexico to protect and restore wetland habitat both in public and private ownership. Thus far 223 projects totalling $48.1 million have been undertaken ($30.9 million were raised by NFWF and its partners to match $17.2 million in federal funds).

- Conservation Education and Leadership Training.

  Education programs are provided for the public and leadership training is provided for natural resource professionals, corporate leaders, and key policy and political decisionmakers in fish and wildlife stewardship and management policies. To date, 180 projects totalling $14.4 million have been undertaken ($10.9 million was raised by NFWF and its partners to match $3.5 million in federal funds).

- Fisheries Initiative.

  Addresses marine, estuarine, and inland fish resource and habitat depletion issues by funding projects that address high priority conservation challenges and improve federal and state policy, funding, and management practices. Thus far, 145 projects totalling $17.8 million have been undertaken ($12.3 million was raised by NFWF and its partners to match $5.5 million in federal funds).

- Neotropical Migratory Bird Conservation Program.

  Brings public and private partners together to conserve migratory songbirds. To date, 178 projects totalling $13.4 million have been undertaken ($8.7 million was raised by NFWF and its partners to match $4.7 million in federal funds).

- Fisheries and Wildlife Assessment.

  The Assessment functions as the policy arm of NFWF. This annual publication is made available to congressional representatives and staff, the executive branch, and conservation organizations. It provides the only nongovernmental, comprehensive, line-by-line budget analysis of the major federal agencies that have significant natural resource management and stewardship responsibilities. Over the years this study has become an influential guide for congressional appropriations to these agencies.

- Wildlife and Habitat Initiative.

  The initiative encompasses NFWF's broad interests in fish, wildlife, and plant conservation, including biodiversity preservation, threatened and endangered species recovery, and big game management. Thus far, 215 projects totalling $18.7 million have been undertaken ($14 million was raised by NFWF and its partners to match $4.7 million in federal funds).

Issues.   Cli   Bio   Lan   Agr   Wat   Oce   Ene   Was   Tox   Pop   Dev

Funding analysis.

Fiscal year:	1992	1993
Env grants auth:	$6,444,529	$18,803,768
Number:	168	190
Range:	$1,000–$500,000	$1,050–$1,172,000
Median:	$38,360	$45,000
Pct $ disb (env/total):	100	100

Recipients (1993 highest):	Number:	Dollars:
California Department of Fish and Game	1	1,172,000
Zoo Atlanta	1	1,000,000

National Fish and Wildlife Foundation	10	665,546
The Nature Conservancy, Hawaii Field Office	2	595,200
U.S. DOI, Fish and Wildlife Service, Region 2	2	585,000

Activity regions (1993 highest):	Number:	Dollars:
U.S. Southeast	16	3,103,300
U.S. not specified	31	2,682,044
U.S. West	14	2,486,760
U.S. South Central	14	1,935,120
Mexico and Central America	19	1,748,165

Sample grants (1993).
Idaho Fish and Wildlife Foundation. Boise, ID. $74,800. To purchase browse seed to restore more than 275,000 acres in Boise National Forest which were severely burned in 1992.
Manomet Observatory for Conservation Science. Manomet, MA. $8,300. To develop workshops that introduce science educators to issues affecting groundfish of the Gulf of Maine and their marine habitats in order to stimulate involvement of the New England education community in marine conservation.
Massachusetts Audubon Society. Lincoln, MA. $30,000. To protect 36 beach-nesting areas on the South Shore, Cape Cod, and the Islands of Massachusetts used by piping plovers and roseate, common, and arctic terns.
Montana Department of Fish, Wildlife and Parks. Kalispell, MT. $10,000. To support a bear-human conflict resolution position to implement a public education effort, with the goal of reducing bear-human interaction leading to conflicts.
North Carolina State University. Raleigh, NC. $350,000. To acquire a 242 acre upland and wetland tract to build a regional center for environmental education.
Wetlands for the Americas. Manomet, MA. $320,000. For workshops on how to manage private wetlands to benefit shorebirds and for establishment of demonstration sites.
World Wildlife Fund. Washington, DC. $60,000. To establish a North American network of fish and wildlife biologists working in the field of environmental contamination.
Zoo Atlanta. Atlanta, GA. $1,000,000. To construct a Discovery Center Complex where the U.S. Fish and Wildlife Service will have the opportunity to engage visitors in hands-on environmental education programs.

Application process. *Initial contact:* Obtain application from the Foundation. Full proposal (2 copies) to include:
1. Project description (use Foundation-supplied application form).
2. Project abstract (1 page) outlining project goals and benefits and organizations/individuals to be solicited to meet the challenge grant.
3. Agency/peer review (use form).
4. Project proposal outlining the need for the project, specific objectives, and purpose.
5. Project budget.
6. Additional information including list of board of directors, copy of IRS tax-exempt status determination letter, and additional descriptive materials.

When to apply: Deadlines are April 15 and August 15, 1995.

Materials available: Annual report, brochure on Foundation information on projects, articles on initiatives, *Partners in Flight* (quarterly newsletter), "NFWF Grant Procedures & Application."

Emphases. *Recipients:* Botanical gardens, educational institutions, individuals, museums, nonprofit organizations, public agencies, research institutions, zoos.
Activities: Audiovisual materials, capacity building, collaborative efforts, conferences, demonstration programs, education, fieldwork, innovative programs, land acquisition, litigation, publications, seminars, symposia/colloquia, training, workshops, youth programs.
Types of support: Equipment, general purposes, internships, leveraging funds, matching funds, operating costs, projects.
Geography: North and Central America.

Limitations. *Activities:* Advocacy, lobbying, political activities.
Types of support: Annual campaigns, capital campaigns/expenses, debt retirement, fellowships, indirect costs, loans, mortgage reduction, professorships.

National Geographic Society Education Foundation
1145 17th Street, N.W.
Washington, DC 20036-4468
Tel: 202-828-6672 Fax: 202-429-5709
EIN: 521544492 Type: Independent
EGA member
Contact: Missey Hyatt, Program Officer

History and philosophy. Established in 1988, the National Geographic Society Education Foundation was designed to provide a permanent and expanding source of financial support for geography education. Initial funding was provided by a gift of $20 million, with an additional $20 million pledged to match contributions through a challenge fund.

Grant categories are: the Geographic Alliance Network, Pre-Service Education, Teachers, and the Colorado, Mississippi, and Oklahoma Geography Education Fund. The Foundation expects to distribute approximately $3 million in 1995. The majority of these funds are earmarked for the Geographic Alliance Network.

Officers and directors. *Officers:* Gilbert M. Grosvenor, Chairman; Michela A. English, Vice Chairman; Terry Smith, Vice President and Executive Director; H. Gregory Platts, Treasurer; Richard T. Moreland, Assistant Treasurer. *Directors:* Gerald L. Baliles, Thomas E. Bolger, Martha E. Church, William Graves, James C. Kautz, Charles McGarry, Mac McGarry, Lloyd N. Morrisett, Patrick F. Noonan, B. Francis Saul, Robert C. Seamans, Jr., Robert B. Sims, Alex Trebek. *Advisors:* George Lucas, Floretta McKenzie.

Financial data. Data for fiscal year ended December 31, 1993. *Assets:* $54,000,000 (M) (est.). *Total grants authorized:* $3,000,000.

Environmental awards. *Program and interests:* All grants are related to geography. Special interests are teacher training, curriculum improvement, and public education. Consideration is given to programs for grades K-12 that relate geography to an enhanced understanding of our physical, cultural, and natural environments. Specific program elements include:

- Geographic Alliance Network.

  A 50-state network actively engaged in efforts to improve geography curriculum and classroom instruction. These Foundation-sponsored "Geographic Alliances" conduct curriculum conferences, summer institutes on regional geography, and in-service workshops for teachers.

- Pre-Service Education.

  Funds will be available for programs that enhance geography in the preparation of future teachers.

- Teacher Grants.

  Small awards, between $750 and $1,250, are awarded to teachers who have been trained at Society or Alliance-sponsored institutes.

- Restricted State Endowments.

  In 1989, the Society pledged up to $500,000 to create state-restricted endowments that would support geography education programs in individual states. Endowments have been established in Colorado, Mississippi, and Oklahoma.

Recent grants: All 1993 grants supported geographic education programs.

Issues. Cli Bio Lan Agr Wat• Oce Ene Was Tox Pop Dev

Funding analysis.

Fiscal year:	1991*	1993
Env grants auth:	$1,950,431	$85,644
Number:	–	9
Range:	$5,000–$50,000	$500–$34,840
Median:	$30,000	$3,653
Pct $ auth (env/total):	–	3

*As reported to the Environmental Grantmakers Association.

Recipients (1993 highest):	Number:	Dollars:
Alabama Geographic Alliance	1	34,840
The Geography Educator's Network of Indiana	1	20,400
Robert M. Ashley	1	14,750
Portland State University	1	4,813
Plymouth-Canton Community Schools	1	3,653

Activity regions (1993 highest):	Number:	Dollars:
U.S. Southeast	1	34,840
U.S. Great Lakes	1	20,400
U.S. not specified	3	16,438
U.S. Northeast	2	6,653
U.S. Northwest	1	4,813

Sample grants (1993).

Alabama Geographic Alliance. AL. $34,840. To support teachers who attended the Workshop on Water in the development of a "portable" workshop on "Geographic Approaches to Fresh Water Issues."

Environmental Data Research Institute. Rochester, NY. $500. Support for the publication of *Environmental Grantmaking Foundations 1993.*

Minot Public School District. Minot, ND. $2,500. To support a water festival, hosting a booth at the state's teacher convention, and developing a water unit.

Portland State University. Portland, OR. $4,813. Development of a teacher's guide on urban stream analysis.

Application process. *Initial contact:* Letter of inquiry.
When to apply: Anytime.
Materials available: "1994 Grant Information," Report of Programs, *Update* (quarterly newsletter).

Emphases. *Recipients:* Educational institutions, individuals.
Activities: Education, training, workshops.
Types of support: Program-related investments; technical assistance for Geographic Alliance groups to plan workshops and summer institutes, to discuss curriculum needs and objectives with school administrators, and to help raise funds for local programs.
Geography: United States and Canada.

Limitations. *Recipients:* Botanical gardens, museums, religious organizations, research institutions, zoos.
Activities: Activism, advocacy, audiovisual materials, capacity building, conflict resolution, feasibility studies, fundraising, inventories, land acquisition, litigation, lobbying, political activities, research.
Types of support: Advertising campaigns, annual campaigns, capital campaigns/expenses, computer hardware, continuing support, debt retirement, emergency funding, equipment, facilities, indirect costs, internships, leveraging funds, loans, maintenance, membership campaigns, mortgage reduction, professorships, scholarships, start-up costs, travel expenses.

The Needmor Fund

1730 15th Street
Boulder, Colorado 80302
Tel: 303-449-5801   Fax: 303-444-8055
EIN: 346504812   Type: Independent
Contact: Lynn Gisi, Coordinator

History and philosophy. The Needmor Fund was established in 1956 in Toledo, Ohio by members of the Stranahan family. Its interest is "to empower those individuals whose basic rights to justice and opportunity are systematically ignored or denied. We have identified community organizing as a highly effective process through which such people may learn to take control of their lives and change those conditions which adversely affect them." "Preference is given to organizations whose membership represents traditionally disenfranchised populations." "Funds are allocated from the Broad Common Pool, which accepts proposals from throughout the United States; and from the Toledo Common Pool, a fund dedicated to Toledo-based organizations."

The Fund is managed by a board of directors elected from three generations of the Stranahan family. The Fund's special interests are empowerment, grassroots involvement, and organizations that have difficulty finding funding from traditional sources. Areas of interest are: Civil and Human Rights, Economic Issues, Environment, Farm and Rural, Health, Housing, Indigenous Peoples, Multi-Issue, Women's Issues, and Workers' Rights.

Officers and Directors. *Directors:* Abbot Stranahan, Ann Stranahan, Mary C. Stranahan, Molly L. Stranahan, Sarah Stranahan, Stephen Stranahan.

Financial data.* Data for fiscal year ended December 31, 1992. *Assets:* $16,000,000 (U) (est.). *Total grants authorized:* $2,200,000.

*Grants include donor-advised: $1,200,000; common pool: $1,000,000.

Environmental awards. *Program and interests:* The Fund does not consider itself an environmental grantmaker as such. Rather than fund specific environmental issues or topics, its core interests are:

- Community organizing, primarily low income and minority communities.
- Grassroots organizations with limited access to foundation funds.

Issues. Cli Bio Lan Agr Wat Oce Ene Was Tox Pop Dev
•   •   •   •   •   •   •   •

Funding analysis.

Fiscal year:	1991	1992
Env grants auth:	$212,000	$257,000
Number:	11	14
Range:	$12,000–$26,000	$12,000–$20,000
Median:	$20,000	$20,000
Pct $ auth (env/total):	19	29

Recipients (1992 highest):	Number:	Dollars:
El Comité de Apoyo a los Trabajadores Agricolas	1	20,000
Dakota Rural Action	1	20,000
Kentucky Coalition	1	20,000
Klamath Forest Alliance	1	20,000
Leaders for Equality & Action in Dayton	1	20,000
San Jose Community Awareness Council	1	20,000
Save Our Cumberland Mountains	1	20,000
Western Colorado Congress	1	20,000

Activity regions (1992):	Number:	Dollars:
U.S. Mountain	5	87,000
U.S. West	3	55,000
U.S. Southeast	3	60,000
U.S. Great Lakes	1	20,000
U.S. Mid-Atlantic	1	20,000
U.S. Northwest	1	15,000

Sample grants (1993).

Alternative Energy Resources Organization. Helena, MT. $8,000. Farm Improvement Club Project, it creates local farmer groups cooperatively adapting more sustainable farming methods.

El Comité de Apoyo a los Trabajadores Agricolas. Glassboro, NJ. $20,000. Pennsylvania Leadership Development Project to assist migrant mushroom workers in developing leadership skills in their struggle for better living and working conditions.

Idaho Citizen's Network Research and Education. Boise, ID. $20,000. To build a statewide network through local organizing around issues such as health care, toxic waste clean-up, and civil rights for people with disabilities.

Native Action. Lame Deer, MT. $20,000. To promote natural resource protection, economic development, and youth leadership skills among the people of the Northern Cheyenne Reservation.

Naugatuck Valley Project, Inc. Waterbury, CT. $25,000. Institution-based organization addressing long term disinvestment and working for affordable housing, health care and a better environment.

Willamette Valley Law Project. Montrose, CO. $20,000. To promote the rights of primarily Mexican immigrant laborers in the fruit, vegetable, and reforestation agricultural industries.

Wisconsin Farmland Conservancy. Menomonie, WI. $15,000. Rural Wisconsin Communities' Organizing Project, organizes in rural communities around credit access, farm preservation, and the environment.

Application process. *Initial contact:* Telephone call or letter to request the Fund's Pre-Application Form. If the project is within the guidelines, a full proposal will be requested.

When to apply: There are two grantmaking cycles each year. Current deadlines for pre-proposal are May 1 and November 1, 1995. Deadlines for full proposal are July 10, 1995 and January 10, 1996. Contact Fund to confirm. The board meets in May and November.

Materials available: "The Needmor Fund Guidelines," "Needmor Fund Directory of Grantees," pre-application form, and proposal instructions.

Emphases. *Recipients:* Nonprofit organizations.
Activities: Activism, citizen participation, political activities.
Types of support: Continuing support, general purposes, leveraging funds, membership campaigns, multi-year grants (by invitation only), operating costs, seed money, technical assistance.

New England Biolabs Foundation

32 Tozer Road
Beverly, Massachusetts 01915
Tel: 508–927–2404   Fax: 508–921–1350
EIN: 042776213   Type: Independent
EGA member
Contacts: Martine Kellett, Executive Director
           Vickie Cataldo, Assistant to the Director

History and philosophy. New England Biolabs Foundation (NEBF) was established in 1982 by Donald G. Comb, molecular biologist and CEO of New England Biolabs, Inc. NEBF seeks to improve the quality of life in its community and around the world. The Foundation ordinarily limits its grants in the United States to the Greater Boston/North Shore area. And because even a small dollar amount can have a tremendous impact in certain parts of the world, the Foundation encourages proposals about developing countries with an emphasis on assisting local organizations in their endeavors. The Foundation prefers start-up projects with the understanding that, once they are established, funding from other sources will be sought. NEBF also initiates programs by contracting consultants for a specific undertaking. Funding areas are: Environment, Scientific Research (qualified), Education, the Arts, and Women's Issues in developing countries.

Officers and directors. *Trustees:* Donald G. Comb, Ph.D., Douglas I. Foy, Esq., Henry P. Paulus, Ph.D.

Financial data. Data for fiscal year ended November 30, 1993. *Assets:* $3,712,000 (M). *Total grants disbursed:* $120,000.

Environmental awards. *Program and interests:* The Foundation's interests have geographic specificity.

In developing countries they are:

- Marine conservation and research.
- Rainforest protection and management (except Central and South America).
- Biological diversity.
- Environmental education.

In the United States:

- Protection of wilderness in the Northeast.

Issues. Cli Bio Lan Agr Wat Oce Ene Was Tox Pop Dev
• • • • • • •

Funding analysis.

Fiscal year:	1991	1993
Env grants auth:	$70,393	$82,275
Number:	14	17
Range:	$1,000–$19,193	$1,000–$10,000
Median:	$4,500	$5,000
Pct $ disb (env/total):	44	69

Recipients (1993 highest):	Number:	Dollars:
Wau Ecology Institute	1	10,000
New Jersey Audubon Society	1	8,775
Missouri Botanical Garden	1	8,000
Kechuaymara	1	7,000
Maine Audubon Society	1	5,000
Boston Can and Project Place	1	5,000
Boston Recycling Coalition	1	5,000
Dudley Street Neighborhood Initiative	1	5,000
Earth Right Institute	1	5,000
Environmental Law Alliance Worldwide (E–LAW)	1	5,000
Underground Railway Theatre	1	5,000

Activity regions (1993 highest):	Number:	Dollars:
U.S. Northeast	8	32,000
Oceania	1	10,000
South America*	1	8,775
U.S. Midwest	1	8,000
Andean Region and Southern Cone	1	7,000

*Multiple regions or not specified.

Sample grants (1993).
AHEAD, Tanzania. Rockville, MD. For a solar powered water system for a rural health center in Shinyanga.
EarthRight Institute. White River Junction, VT. $5,000. To help communities in Vermont and New Hampshire with energy planning and conservation.
New Jersey Audubon Society. Franklin Lakes, NJ. $8,775. To promote ecotourism as a support for local economies and conservation efforts in South America.
Secdo Women Development Center. Ukwela, Sri Lanka. $6,740. For education and income generation for women working on plantations.

Application process. *Initial contact:* Letter of inquiry or telephone call. Full proposal (10 pages maximum), if requested, to include:
1. Brief history of the organization and its funding sources.
2. Summary (1 page).
3. Detailed project description, including goals, means for achieving those goals, a budget and timetable, and sources of support.

Appendixes:
1. Names and affiliations of board of directors.
2. Resumes of project principals.
3. Financial statements for the last two years or a current IRS Form 990.
4. Copy of IRS tax-exempt status determination letter.
5. Any literature or articles published, if available.

When to apply: Deadlines are March 1, September 1, and December 1 for review at trustees meeting held one month later.
Materials available: Brochure with guidelines, special grant application for individuals.

Emphases. *Recipients:* Nonprofit organizations.
Activities: Activism, advocacy, citizen participation, collaborative efforts, education, fieldwork, innovative programs, inventories, networking, research (scientific), training.
Types of support: Leveraging funds, matching funds, multi-year grants, pilot projects, seed money.
Geography: In the United States, Greater Boston and the North Shore of Massachusetts, New England (limited); in developing countries, Cameroon, Tanzania, Papua New Guinea, the Philippines, and Indonesia.

Limitations. *Recipients:* Educational institutions, museums, public agencies, zoos, species-specific programs.
Activities: Audiovisual materials, capacity development, conferences, direct services (needy/elderly/handicapped), expeditions/tours, fundraising, inventories, litigation, lobbying, media projects, political activities, policy analysis/development, research, seminars, symposia/colloquia, workshops.
Types of support: Advertising campaigns, annual campaigns, capital campaigns, computer hardware, debt retirement, endowments, facilities, fellowships, general purposes, indirect costs, internships, lectureships, membership campaigns, mortgage reduction, operating costs, professorships, scholarships, travel expenses.
Geography: Brazil, Costa Rica, former Eastern bloc countries and Former Soviet Union, South Africa, and the Middle East.

New Hampshire Charitable Foundation

37 Pleasant Street
Concord, New Hampshire 03301–4005
Tel: 603–225–6641   Fax: 603–225–1700
CompuServe: 74561,3407
EIN: 026005625   Type: Community
EGA member
Contacts: Thomas S. Deans, Vice President
Deborah Cowan, Associate Director

History and philosophy. New Hampshire Charitable Foundation is a statewide community foundation, established in 1962. It comprises 600 distinct component funds, each with its own donors, history, and purpose. These funds, which are pooled for investment purposes, represent a collection of the ideas and interests of individual donors who have united to increase the effectiveness and assure the future of their charitable giving.

Officers and directors. *Officers:* Martin L. Gross, Chair; Lewis M. Feldstein, President; Thomas S. Deans, Vice President.

Financial data.* Data for fiscal year ended December 31, 1993. *Assets:* $81,287,177 (M). *Gifts received:* 7,653,200. *Total grants and appropriations:* $4,569,346.

*Includes NHCF and Affiliated Trusts.

Environmental awards. *Program and interests:* The Foundation supports a variety of environmental issues. Particular interests include:

- Increasing general awareness of environmental values and public policy issues.
- Increasing sensitivity to the special qualities of the New Hampshire landscape and the design character of its communities, and demonstrating effective means to preserve those qualities in an era of rapid growth and development.

Other interests:

- Preserving the quality of New Hampshire's built environment.
- Environmental education.

Recent grants: 1993 grants included support for land use planning, land preservation (farmland, forests), river protection, sustainable agriculture, and public education.

Issues.   Cli   Bio   Lan   Agr   Wat   Oce   Ene   Was   Tox   Pop   Dev
  •   •   •   •   •   •   •   •   •

Funding analysis.§

Fiscal year:	1992	1993
Env grants disb:	$506,472	$268,083
Number:	69	75
Range:	$105–$200,000	$100–$50,000
Median:	$2,500	$1,500
Pct $ disb (env/total):	11	6

Recipients (1993 highest):	Number:	Dollars:
Tin Mountain Conservation Center	5	61,580
Lyme Foundation	1	23,613
The Student Conservation Association, Inc.	5	23,200
New Hampshire Farm Bureau Federation	1	21,887
Society for the Protection of New Hampshire Forests	7	21,044

Activity region (1993):	Number:	Dollars:
U.S. Northeast	75	268,083

§Includes advised, designated, and discretionary grants from all Affiliated Trusts except The Switzer Foundation and the Greater Piscatauga Community Foundation each of which has its own entry.

Sample grants (1993).

Audubon Society of New Hampshire. Concord, NH. $14,732. General support.

Beaver Brook Association. Hollis, NH. $4,000. For consulting services to develop a long-term fundraising plan.

Conservation Law Foundation. Boston, MA. $2,500. General support.

Conway Parks and Recreation Committee. Conway, NH. $1,000. To restore structure covering an active mineral spring on the Parks and Rec trail system.

Elaine Connors Center for Wildlife. Silver Lake, NH. $3,000. For the purchase of a vehicle to continue the Center's rehabilitation/education goals.

Natural Resources Defense Council. New York, NY. $2,750. General support.

Society for the Protection of New Hampshire Forests. Concord, NH. $1,500. General support.

Squam Lakes Association. Holderness, NH. $2,850. To support a sustainable economic study for five towns in the Squam Lakes watershed.

Student Conservation Association, Inc. Charlestown, NH. $1,200. To support the New Hampshire Conservation Corps.

Student Conservation Association, Inc. (New Hampshire Conservation Corps). Charlestown, NH. $7,000. To support the second-year program of Manchester Conservation Corps.

Application process. *Initial contact:* Telephone call or short letter. Full proposal to include:

Narrative.

1. Organization description. Briefly describe organization, its mission, current programs, and services. Include meaningful service statistics and a brief history highlighting significant milestones or achievements.
2. Needs assessment. Outline needs or the opportunity proposal addresses and how these were determined. Documentation may include in-house information and local or national data.
3. Planning. What other organizations are working on this problem and how will this program be different or better? Explain how organization will collaborate or work with others. Explain how proposed program is related to the organization's core mission and its growth and development. Why is it being undertaken at this time?
4. Project description, goals, and objectives. Describe what will be accomplished. Attach resumes of key people responsible.
5. Evaluation. Describe how the project will be evaluated and what information will be collected during the year to assess results. Criteria to include appropriate measurable outcomes.

© 1995 Environmental Data Resources, Inc.

6. Continuation. What resources will support the activity beyond the grant period?
7. Other support. What other support has already been secured?

Attachments.
1. Application cover sheet.
2. Project budget.
3. Financial statement.
4. Organization's current operating budget.
5. IRS tax-exempt status determination letter.
6. List of current board members.

When to apply: Deadlines are April 1, September 1, and December 1.
Materials available: Annual report, grants list, *Viewbook*.

Emphases. *Recipients:* Individuals, nonprofit organizations.
Types of support: Fellowships, loans, projects, scholarships.
Geography: New Hampshire only.

Limitations. *Types of support:* Capital campaigns/expenses, debt retirement, endowments, facilities, land acquisition, equipment. Support for operating costs of ongoing programs is rare.

New Horizon Foundation
820 A Street, Suite 345
Tacoma, Washington 98402
Tel: 206–627–1634
EIN: 911228957   Type: Independent
Contact: Frank D. Underwood, President

History and philosophy. The Foundation was established in 1983 by the Sequoia Foundation. It makes grants for social services, community development, education, arts and culture, and environment in the State of Washington.

Officers and directors. *Officers:* Frank D. Underwood, President and Treasurer; John F. Sherwood, Vice President. *Directors:* John F. Sherwood, Frank D. Underwood, Elvin J. Vandeberg.

Financial data. Data for fiscal year ended October 31, 1993. *Assets:* $52,473) (M). *Gifts received:* $1,355,000. *Total grants disbursed:* $1,185,567.

Environmental awards. *Recent grants:* One grant in 1993 supported single species preservation.

Issues.   Cli   Bio   Lan   Agr   Wat   Oce   Ene   Was   Tox   Pop   Dev
                    •   •

Funding analysis.

Fiscal year:	1993
Env grants disb:	$10,000
Number:	1
Range:	—
Median:	—
Pct $ disb (env/total):	1

Recipient (1993):	*Number:*	*Dollars:*
Wolf Haven	1	10,000

Activity region (1993):	*Number:*	*Dollars:*
U.S. Northwest	1	10,000

Sample grant (1993).
Wolf Haven. Tenino, WA. $10,000. Program support.

Application process. *Initial contact:* Summary letter (2 copies) requesting application guidelines.
When to apply: Anytime. The board meets bimonthly.
Materials available: Application guidelines.

Emphases. *Types of support:* Capital campaigns/expenses, matching funds, operating costs, projects.
Geography: South Puget Sound region of Washington, southwest Washington (except Clark County), and the Olympic Peninsula, with primary emphasis on Pierce County and secondary emphasis on Kitsap and Thurston counties.

Limitations. *Recipients:* Individuals.
Activities: Audiovisual materials, conferences, publications.
Types of support: Annual campaigns, debt retirement, endowments, travel expenses.

The New World Foundation
100 East 85th Street
New York, New York 10028
Tel: 212–249–1023
EIN: 131919791   Type: Independent
Contact: Colin Greer, President

History and philosophy. The New World Foundation grew out of the diversified philanthropic interests of its founder, Anita McCormick Blaine, daughter of Cyrus Hall McCormick who invented the reaper in 1831. His company was merged with Deering Harvester Company and other companies in the early 1900s to form International Harvester.

The Foundation seeks to foster connections between activists and policymakers, and decrease future levels of poverty, homelessness, and chronic unemployment. Five principal areas of interest are: Equal Rights and Opportunities, Public Education, Public Health, Community Initiatives, and Avoidance of War.

Officers and directors. *Officers:* David B. Harrison, Chairman; Colin Greer, President; Byllye Avery, Secretary. *Directors:* Byllye Avery, Anne Bartley, James P. Breeden, Adrian W. DeWind, Colin Greer, Herbert Chao Gunther, Sophia Bracey Harris, David B. Harrison, Donald Hazen, Sylvia I. Hill, Charles Hey Maestre, Peggy Kyoko Salka, Anthony Thigpenn.

Financial data. Data for fiscal year ended September 30, 1992. *Assets:* $21,624,965 (M). *Gifts received:* $175,571. *Total grants disbursed:* $1,461,500.

Environmental awards. *Program and interests:* The Foundation's public health program has a particular focus on community health protection, and with problems of occupational and environmental health and safety.
Recent grants: 1991 grants included support for land restoration, toxics issues, environmental justice, and public education.

Issues. Cli Bio• Lan• Agr• Wat Oce Ene Was Tox• Pop Dev

Funding analysis.

Fiscal year:	1991
Env grants auth:	$214,500
Number:	14
Range:	$500–$50,000
Median:	$12,500
Pct $ auth (env/total):	27

Recipients (1991 highest):	Number:	Dollars:
National Toxic Campaign Fund	1	50,000
Vermont Toxics Education Project	2	25,000
Louisiana Environmental Action Network	1	20,000
Silicon Valley Toxics Coalition	1	20,000
Comité de Apoyo a los Trabajadores Agricolas	1	15,000
Environmental Health Network	1	15,000
Farm Labor Research Project	1	15,000

Activity regions (1991 highest):	Number:	Dollars:
U.S. not specified	4	69,000
U.S. South Central	3	35,500
U.S. Great Lakes	2	25,000
U.S. Northeast	2	25,000
U.S. West	1	20,000

Sample grants (1992).
American Forum. Washington, DC. $10,000.
Center for Community Action. Lumberton, NC. $20,000.
Citizens Clearinghouse for Hazardous Wastes. Arlington, VA. $25,000.
Environmental Health Network. Harvey, LA. $5,000.
Highlander Research and Education Center. New Market, TN. $10,000.
Live Oak Fund. Austin, TX. $5,000.
Louisiana Environmental Action Network. Baton Rouge, LA. $25,000.
National Toxics Campaign Fund. Boston, MA. $75,000.
New England Citizen Action Resource Center. Hartford, CT. $22,500.
Save Our Cumberland Mountains. Jacksboro, TN. $10,000.
Vermont Toxics Education Project. Barre, VT. $25,000.

Application process. *Initial contact:* Letter or telephone call. Proposal to include:
1. Cover letter summarizing proposal and the amount requested.
2. Description of project.
3. Objectives, timetable for their achievement, and strategies and methods by which they will be attained.
4. Organization's budget for the fiscal year which funds are requested and a budget for the project being proposed.
5. Audited report for previous fiscal year if possible or a financial statement for the prior period.
6. Current sources of support and amount of income and a list of additional funds.
7. Copy of IRS tax-exempt status determination letter.

When to apply: Anytime.
Materials available: Biennial report (including "Guidelines For Grant Applications").

Emphases. *Recipients:* Nonprofit organizations, public agencies.
Activities: Activism, conferences.
Types of support: Loans, program-related investments, projects, seed money, technical assistance.
Geography: United States.

Limitations. *Recipients:* Educational institutions, individuals.
Activities: Audiovisual materials, fundraising, research.
Types of support: Capital campaigns/expenses, continuing support, debt retirement, endowments, fellowships, scholarships, matching funds.

The New York Community Trust

Two Park Avenue
New York, New York 10016
Tel: 212–686–0010   Fax: 212–532–8528
EIN: 133062214   Type: Community
EGA member
Contact: Anita Nager, Senior Program Officer

History and philosophy. Founded in 1924, The New York Community Trust serves the New York metropolitan area. The Trust acts as a permanent steward and administrator for the charitable assets of many individual donors. It makes grants in the areas of: Children, Youth, and Families; Community Development and the Environment; Education, Arts and the Humanities; and Health and People with Special Needs.

Officers and directors. *Officers:* Barbara Scott Preiskel, Chairman; Lorie A. Slutsky, President; Joyce M. Bove, Vice President. *Governing Body:* Arthur G. Altschul, Aida Alvarez, Bruce L. Ballard, M.D., William M. Evarts, Jr., Charlotte M. Fischman, Barry H. Garfinkel, Judah Gribetz, Alberto Ibarguen, Robert M. Kaufman, Lorie A. Slutsky, Carroll L. Wainwright, Jr., Lulu Wang.

Financial data. Data for fiscal year ended December 31, 1993. *Assets:* $988,874,697 (M). *Gifts received:* $33,830,825. *Total grants disbursed:* $61,669,270.

Environmental awards. *Program and interests:* Areas of interest include:

- Drinking water quality and supply.
- Solid waste.
- Air quality.
- Land planning.

For each of these issues the Trust promotes innovative public policy and public education. It also has a special focus on helping New Yorkers learn more about their environment through activities such as community action, citizen and student training, and coalition building.

© 1995 Environmental Data Resources, Inc.

Issues. Cli• Bio• Lan• Agr• Wat• Oce• Ene• Was• Tox Pop• Dev•

Funding analysis.§

Fiscal year:	1991	1993
Env grants disb:	$3,360,598	$1,861,141
Number:	16	41
Range:	$10,000–$1,469,599	$10,000–$215,547
Median:	$30,544	$30,450
Pct $ disb (env/total):	5	3

Recipients (1993 highest):	Number:	Dollars:
Environmental Defense Fund	1	215,547
Transportation Alternatives	1	180,000
Heifer Project International	1	125,500
Natural Resources Defense Council	1	106,569
Connecticut Fund for the Environment	1	80,000
Riverside Park Fund, Inc.	1	80,000

Activity regions (1993 highest):	Number:	Dollars:
New York/New Jersey	28	1,339,166
U.S. Northeast	6	225,200
International	2	155,950
U.S. not specified	3	80,825
U.S. Southeast	1	50,000

§Includes advised, designated, field-of-interest, and unrestricted grants over $10,000.

Sample grants (1993).
Catskill Center for Conservation and Development. Arkville, NY. $20,000. To build an upstate/downstate partnership for water quality protection.
Environmental Defense Fund. New York, NY. $215,547. To build an economically sustainable recycling infrastructure in New York City.
Natural Resources Defense Council. New York, NY. $106,569.
South Bronx 2000 Local Development Corporation. Bronx, NY. $32,000. To launch a wood pallet recycling business in the South Bronx.

Application process. *Initial contact:* Proposal on letterhead and signed by organization's CEO, to include:
Cover letter.
1. Proposal summary.
2. Amount requested.
3. Results expected.
Proposal.
1. Description of need to be addressed.
2. How need will be met.
3. What you hope to achieve.
4. Who will be served.
5. Why organization is the best to carry out the proposal.
6. Staff and their qualifications.
7. Budget for project and other sources of support.
8. Evaluation.
9. How program will be supported after the grant period.
10. Timetable.
Additional information.
1. Organizational background.
2. Board of directors.
3. Most recent audited financial statement.
4. Copy of current operating budget.
5. Evidence of tax-exempt status.
When to apply: Anytime.
Materials available: Annual report (includes "How to Apply for a Grant"), "Grant Guidelines" (booklet), *The New York Community Trust* (newsletter).

Emphases. *Recipients:* Nonprofit organizations.
Activities: Advocacy, innovative programs.
Geography: The five boroughs of New York City only.

Limitations. *Recipients:* Individuals.
Activities: Media projects (films).
Types of support: Capital campaigns/expenses, debt retirement, endowments.

New York Foundation
Empire State Building
350 Fifth Avenue, Room 2901
New York, New York 10118
Tel: 212–594–8009
EIN: 135626345   Type: Independent
Contact: Madeline Lee, Executive Director

History and philosophy. One of the oldest foundations, the New York Foundation was established in 1909 with a $1 million gift from Alfred M. Heinsheimer. This was soon supplemented by other personal gifts to be distributed "for altruistic purposes, charitable, benevolent, educational or otherwise." The Foundation originally gave nationally or regionally, but now focuses exclusively on New York City. Current emphases include empowerment of local community groups, participation of target populations in public debate on issues of pressing social concern, and projects that coordinate and improve communication among programs working on similar issues. Target populations are the disadvantaged, handicapped, minorities, youth, and the elderly.

Officers and directors. *Officers:* William M. Kelly, Chair; Stephen D. Heyman, Vice Chair; M. D. Taracido, Secretary; Malcolm Smith, Treasurer. *Trustees:* Susan Bellinger, R. Harcourt Dodds, Angelo Falcon, Margaret Fung, Madeline Einhorn Glick, Brian P. Mooney, Robert Pollack, Helen Rehr, Edgar Wachenheim, III, Arthur Zankel.

Financial data. Data for fiscal year ended December 31, 1993.
Assets: $58,083,000 (M). *Total grants authorized:* $2,780,000.

Environmental awards. *Program and interests:* The New York Foundation is concerned with environmental issues that affect the people of New York, such as parks and urban open space, toxic air pollution, radioactive waste storage, and community beautification.

Issues. Cli• Bio• Lan Agr• Wat Oce Ene Was• Tox• Pop Dev

Funding analysis.

Fiscal year:	1991	1992
Env grants auth:	$136,125	$90,400
Number:	4	3
Range:	$30,000–$40,000	$20,000–$35,400
Median:	$33,063	$35,000
Pct $ disb (env/total):	5	2

Recipients (1992):	Number:	Dollars:
Neighborhood Open Space Coalition	1	35,400
Radioactive Waste Campaign	1	35,000
The Trust for Public Land	1	20,000

Activity region (1992):	Number:	Dollars:
New York/New Jersey	3	90,400

Sample grant (1993).
The Student Environmental Action Coalition. New York, NY. $25,000. Support for this New York City network of students involved in environmental action.

Application process. *Initial contact:* Letter outlining project, budget needs, and amount requested. If a full proposal is requested, Foundation will send application guidelines and set up a personal meeting and site visit. The Foundation accepts New York Area Common Application Form.
When to apply: Deadlines are November 1, March 1, and July 1. The board of trustees meets in February, June, and October.
Materials available: Annual report (includes "Application Procedure").

Emphases. *Recipients:* Botanical gardens, educational institutions, nonprofit organizations, public agencies.
Activities: Activism, advocacy, citizen participation, collaborative efforts, conflict resolution, education, policy analysis/development, technical assistance, volunteerism, youth programs.
Types of support: General purposes, pilot projects, seed money.
Geography: New York City.

The New York Times Company Foundation, Inc.
299 West 43rd Street
New York, New York 10036–3959
Tel: 212–556–1091 Fax: 212–556–4450
EIN: 136066955 Type: Company-sponsored
Contact: Arthur Gelb, President

History and philosophy. The Foundation was established in 1955. Listed in order of grant dollars awarded in 1990, its five program areas are: Cultural Affairs, Education, Community Services, Journalism, and Environmental Concerns. A matching gift program adds $1.50 to each dollar employees, trustees, and retirees give to cultural, educational, and environmental organizations.

Officers and directors. *Officers:* Arthur Ochs Sulzberger, Chairman; Arthur Gelb, President; Lance R. Primis, Executive Vice President; David L. Gorham, Michael E. Ryan, Senior Vice Presidents; Solomon B. Watson IV, Vice President; Laura J. Corwin, Secretary; Richard Thomas, Treasurer; Martha Greenough, Assistant Treasurer. *Directors:* John F. Akers, Arthur Gelb, Richard L. Gelb, Louis V. Gerstner, Jr., Marian S. Heiskell, Hon. A. Leon Higginbotham, Jr., Ruth S. Holmberg, Robert A. Lawrence, Walter E. Mattson, George B. Munroe, The Honorable Charles H. Price II, George L. Shinn, Donald M. Stewart, Arthur Ochs Sulzberger, Judith P. Sulzberger, William O. Taylor, Cyrus R. Vance.

Financial data. Data for fiscal year ended December 31, 1993. *Assets:* $1,605,372 (C). *Gifts received:* $5,250,000. *Total grants disbursed:* $4,688,434.

Environmental awards. *Recent grants:* "Many of our major grants in 1993 focused on improving urban environment. . . . On a national scale, we gave support to organizations . . . concerned with the preservation of our nation's great natural heritage."

Issues. Cli • Bio • Lan Agr • Wat • Oce • Ene • Was Tox • Pop Dev

Funding analysis.§

Fiscal year:	1990	1993
Env grants disb:	$240,509	$393,921
Number:	105	122
Range:	$30–$25,000	$30–$40,000
Median:	$300	$285
Pct $ disb (env/total):	5	8

Recipients (1993 highest):	Number:	Dollars:
Central Park Conservancy	2	41,186
The New York Botanical Garden	2	35,269
The Parks Council, Inc.	1	35,000
Natural Resources Defense Council	2	30,446
New York City Outward Bound Center	1	25,000

Activity regions (1993 highest):	Number:	Dollars:
New York/New Jersey	56	290,390
U.S. not specified	22	70,358
U.S. Southeast	3	13,300
U.S. Northeast	29	9,986
Tropics	2	5,038

§Includes matching gifts.

Sample grants (1993).
Bellevue Center for New York City. New York, NY. $2,050. Transportation for children to the education series at NYZS/The Wildlife Conservation Society (the Bronx Zoo).
Central Park Conservancy. New York, NY. $40,000.
Council on the Environment of New York. New York, NY. $20,000. Education program.
Earthwatch Expeditions, Inc. Watertown, MA. $5,000. Environmental fellowship program.
Green Guerillas. New York, NY. $10,000. Newsletter for city gardeners and environmentalists.
INFORM. New York, NY. $7,000.
Mote Marine Laboratory. Sarasota, FL. $3,000.
New York City Outward Bound Center. New York, NY. $25,000.
The Parks Council, Inc. New York, NY. $35,000. Special grant to a coalition of 16 environmental groups.

N

The Trust for Public Land. New York, NY. $7,000.
We Care About New York. New York, NY. $5,00. Enlisting child volunteers to clean up neighborhoods.

Application process. *Initial contact:* Brief letter describing the purpose for requested, outlining amount of funds required, and other potential sources of funding. A copy of IRS tax-exempt status determination letter is required. The Foundation discourages organizations from investing excessive time and money in preparation of proposals and funding requests.
When to apply: Anytime. The board meets at least twice annually within the first and third quarters of the year.
Materials available: Annual report (includes "Grant Policies" and "Application Procedures").

Emphases. *Geography:* New York City; localities served by affiliates of The New York Times Company.

Limitations. *Recipients:* Individuals.

The New-Land Foundation, Inc.
1114 Avenue of the Americas, 46th Floor
New York, New York 10036-7798
Tel: 212-479-6162
EIN: 136086562   Type: Independent
Contact: Robert Wolf, President

History and philosophy. The New-Land Foundation was founded in 1941 by Joseph and Muriel Buttinger. It received contributions from Gladys Lack Unit Trust under the will of Muriel Buttinger and from the estate of M. Buttinger. The Foundation interests are: arts for children, civil rights/justice, leadership development, the environment (other than hazardous waste), population control, child development, peace, and arms control.

Officers and directors. *Officers:* Robert Wolf, President; Constance Harvey, Hal Harvey, Vice Presidents; Renee G. Schwartz, Secretary/Treasurer. *Directors:* Constance Harvey, Hal Harvey, Joan Harvey, Joseph Harvey, Anna Frank Loeb, Albert J. Solnit, Robert Wolf.

Financial data. Data for fiscal year ended December 31, 1992. *Assets:* $22,174,940 (M). *Gifts received:* $2,899,992. *Total grants disbursed:* $1,472,572.

Environmental awards. *Recent grants:* 1992 grants included support for land conservation, river preservation, wildlife protection, and energy conservation.

Issues. Cli Bio Lan Agr Wat Oce Ene Was Tox Pop Dev
              •   •   •   •   •   •   •

Funding analysis.

Fiscal year:	1991	1992
Env grants disb:	$400,500	$417,000
Number:	38	38
Range:	$2,500–$35,000	$1,000–$35,000
Median:	$5,000	$9,000
Pct $ disb (env/total):	22	28

Recipients (1992 highest):	Number:	Dollars:
Green Seal	1	35,000
American Wildlands	1	30,000
Alaska Conservation Foundation	1	25,000
American Rivers, Inc.	1	25,000
Land and Water Fund of the Rockies	1	25,000

Activity regions (1992 highest):	Number:	Dollars:
U.S. not specified	17	222,500
U.S. Mountain	11	103,000
Alaska	2	40,000
New York/New Jersey	4	23,500
U.S. Northwest	1	10,000

Sample grants (1992).
Alaska Conservation Foundation. Anchorage, AK. $25,000.
American Rivers, Inc. Seattle, WA. $25,000.
American Wilderness Alliance. Englewood, CO. $30,000.
Land and Water Fund of the Rockies. Boulder, CO. $25,000.
Rocky Mountain Institute. Snowmass, CO. $15,000.

Application process. *Initial contact:* Full proposal to include:
1. Application form and abstract of proposal (from Foundation).
2. Budget of organization/project and other sources of support.
3. List of board and executive staff members.
4. Copy of IRS tax-exempt status determination letter.
5. Annual report or current audited financial statement.

Letter (1 page) summarizing proposal to include:
1. Purpose, results, and method of evaluation.
2. Description of population to be served and its size.

When to apply: Deadlines are February 1 and August 1. The board of directors meets in the spring and fall.
Materials available: "Application Guidelines," application form, abstract of proposal.

Emphases. *Recipients:* Nonprofit organizations.
Activities: Education.
Types of support: General purposes, projects.

Limitations. *Recipients:* Educational institutions, individuals, religious organizations.
Activities: Audiovisual materials, conferences, publications.
Types of support: Capital campaigns/expenses, endowments, facilities (construction).

Edward John Noble Foundation, Inc.
32 East 57th Street
New York, New York 10022-2513
Tel: 212-759-4212   Fax: 212-888-4531
EIN: 061055586   Type: Independent
Contact: E. J. Noble Smith, Executive Director

History and philosophy. The Edward John Noble Foundation was established in 1940 by Edward John Noble (1882–1958), who founded the Life Saver Candy Company in 1913. Noble later was Undersecretary of Commerce and owner of the American Broadcasting Company (ABC). The Foundation concentrates its giving in New York City, but also has a particular interest in St.

Catherine's Island off the Georgia coast, and in Noble's home region of northern New York State. Program areas are: Arts, Conservation, Education, Health/Population, North Country, St. Catherine's Island Programs, and Miscellaneous.

Officers and directors. *Officers:* June Noble Larkin, Chairman and President; Frank Y. Larkin, Vice Chairman; E. J. Noble Smith, Treasurer. *Directors:* Howard Phipps, Jr., Frank P. Piskor, Bradford D. Smith, David S. Smith, Jeremy T. Smith, Carroll L. Wainwright, Jr.

Financial data. Data for fiscal year ended December 31, 1993. *Assets:* $112,352,773 (C). *Total grants authorized:* $3,791,089.

Environmental awards. *Program and interests:* Funds for conservation are devoted principally to several long-term programs on St. Catherine's Island, which include the breeding of endangered species, field research in biological and earth sciences, and archaeological studies. Concern about degradation of the environment has also motivated grants to selected national organizations that play leading roles in the protection of natural resources.

Issues. Cli Bio Lan Agr Wat Oce Ene Was Tox Pop Dev
          •   •   •   •   •   •

Funding analysis.

Fiscal year:	1990	1993
Env grants auth:	$1,693,980	$1,712,254
Number:	15	15
Range:	$5,000–$500,000	$10,000–$820,174
Median:	$40,000	$30,000
Pct $ auth (env/total):	37	45

Recipients (1993 highest):	Number:	Dollars:
St. Catherine's Island Foundation	1	820,174
NYZS/The Wildlife Conservation Society	1	477,000
Williams College, Center for Environmental Studies	1	75,000
Worldwatch Institute	1	75,000
South Bronx 2000 Local Development Corporation	1	60,000

Activity regions (1993 highest):	Number:	Dollars:
New York/New Jersey	3	1,322,174
U.S. not specified	5	145,000
International*	1	75,000
U.S. Northeast	1	75,000
U.S. Mountain	3	74,500

*Multiple regions or not specified.

Sample grants (1993).
Earthwatch Expeditions, Inc. Watertown, MA. $20,000. For Teacher Advancement Awards, specifically for ecological studies.
Environmental Defense Fund. New York, NY. $20,000. For the Toxic Chemicals Program.
Charles A. Lindberg Fund. Minneapolis, MN. $10,580. For a fellowship in environmental research.
National Audubon Society. New York, NY. $25,000. For the Audubon Adventures program for New York City school teachers.
South Bronx 2000 Local Development Corporation. Bronx, NY. $60,000. For their national recycled-product development center.
Teton Science School. Kelly, WY. $30,000 (3 years). For the ISLAND (Improving Scientific Literacy to Assure Natural Diversity) Project.
Williams College, Center for Environmental Studies. Williamstown, MA. $75,000 (3 years). For the Center for Environmental Studies.
Wyoming Outdoor Council. Lander, WY. $10,500. For the Conservation Biology Project for teachers and students.

Application process. *Initial contact:* Letter to include:
1. Brief description of organization's nature and purpose.
2. Concise statement of need for and objectives of project, including methods by which it will be carried out and its anticipated duration.
3. Qualifications of key personnel involved.
4. Program budget.
5. List of other sources of support assured and being sought.
6. Copy of IRS tax-exempt status determination letter.
7. Copy of organization's annual audit or financial statement.
8. List of officers and directors or trustees.

When to apply: Anytime.
Materials available: Annual report (includes "Applications for Grants").

Emphases. *Recipients:* Botanical gardens, educational institutions, museums, nonprofit organizations, public agencies, research institutions, zoos.
Activities: Education, fieldwork, innovative programs, planning, research, training, youth programs.
Types of support: Fellowships, general purposes, internships, multi-year grants, operating costs, pilot projects.
Geography: National projects. Areas of special interest are St. Catherine's Island, Georgia, and the New York counties of Jefferson and St. Lawrence.

Limitations. *Recipients:* Individuals.
Activities: Audiovisual materials, capacity building, conferences, expeditions/tours, inventories, land acquisition, litigation, lobbying.
Types of support: Debt retirement, equipment, facilities, loans.
Geography: Funding for international projects is rare.

The Samuel Roberts Noble Foundation, Inc.
P.O. Box 2180
2510 Highway 199 East
Ardmore, Oklahoma 73402
Tel: 405–223–5810 Fax: 405–221–7362
EIN: 730606209 Type: Independent
Contact: Michael A. Cawley, President

History and philosophy. The Foundation was established in 1945 by Lloyd Noble, who developed the Noble Drilling and Samedan Oil corporations. The Foundation was named for

Noble's father. The Foundation maintains its own operating programs in basic plant biology research, and agricultural research, consultation, and demonstration. It also makes grants for higher education, medical research and health care.

Officers and directors. *Officers:* Michael A. Cawley, President; Larry Pulliam, Sr. Vice President, CFO, and Treasurer; Elizabeth A. Aldridge, Secretary. *Trustees:* Elizabeth A. Aldridge, Ann Noble Brown, David R. Brown, Michael A. Cawley, Vivian N. Dubose, William R. Goddard, Shelley Mullins, Edward E. Noble, Mary Jane Noble, John F. Snodgrass.

Financial data. Data for fiscal year ended October 31, 1992. *Assets:* $410,121,659 (M). *Gifts received:* $3,565,350. *Total grants disbursed:* $4,995,499.

Environmental awards. *Program and interests:* The Foundation's plant biology and agricultural programs include:

- Plant research with the objective of genetic engineering of plants.
- Agricultural research, consultation, and demonstration along with wildlife management, for the benefit of rural and urban people.

Recent grants: 1992 grants included support for energy, horticulture, and agricultural research.

Issues. Cli Bio Lan Agr Wat Oce Ene Was Tox Pop Dev

Funding analysis.

Fiscal year:	1992
Env grants disb:	$97,000
Number:	5
Range:	$2,000–$50,000
Median:	$10,000
Pct $ disb (env/total):	2

Recipients (1992):	Number:	Dollars:
Center for Holistic Resource Management	1	50,000
William Fremont Harn Gardens, Inc.	1	30,000
Wildlife of the American West Art Museum	1	10,000
Timberline Trails, Inc.	1	5,000
Project Wildlife, Inc.	1	2,000

Activity regions (1992):	Number:	Dollars:
U.S. South Central	3	82,000
U.S. Mountain	2	15,000

Sample grants (1992).
Center for Holistic Resource Management. Albuquerque, NM. $50,000. Bartlett Energy and Security Studies program.
William Fremont Harn Gardens, Inc. Oklahoma City, OK. $30,000. General operating support.
Project Wildlife, Inc. Midwest City, OK. $2,000.
Timberline Trails, Inc. Almont, CO. $5,000.
Wildlife of the American West. Jackson, WY. $10,000.

Application process. *Initial contact:* Letter summarizing the project for which a grant is requested. If project is of interest to the trustees, a grant application will be forwarded.
When to apply: Deadlines are December 1, March 1, June 1, and September 1. The trustees meet in January, April, July, and October.
Materials available: Annual report, "Summary Granting Guidelines."

Emphases. *Activities:* Research.
Types of support: Capital campaigns/expenses, endowments, equipment, facilities, matching funds, scholarships, seed money.
Geography: Southwest, especially Oklahoma.

Limitations. *Recipients:* Individuals (except for scholarships for children of employees of Noble organizations).
Types of support: Loans.

Norcross Wildlife Foundation, Inc.

325 West 89th Street, #2
P.O. Box 0414
Planetarium Station
New York, New York 10024–0414
Tel: 212–362–4831   Fax: 212–362–4783
EIN: 132041622   Type: Independent
Contact: Richard S. Reagan, President

History and philosophy. The Foundation was established in 1964 by the late Arthur D. Norcross and June Norcross Webster. It gives mainly to environmental organizations.

Officers and directors. *Officers:* Richard S. Reagan, President and Treasurer; Ethel Stella, Executive Vice President; Fred C. Anderson, Secretary. *Directors:* Fred C. Anderson, Arthur Douglas, Edward Gallagher, Arthur D. Norcross, Jr., Richard S. Reagan, Anthony Schoendorf, Ethel Stella.

Financial data. Data for fiscal years ended December 31, 1992. *Assets:* $40,000,000 (M) (est.). *Total grants authorized:* $761,000.

Environmental awards. *Recent grants:* 1992 grants included support for land and habitat conservation, species protection, rivers, and coastal issues.

Issues. Cli Bio Lan Agr Wat Oce Ene Was Tox Pop Dev

Funding analysis.

Fiscal year:	1990	1992
Env grants auth:	$556,700	$529,874
Number:	33	70
Range:	$2,200–$65,000	$20–$50,000
Median:	$15,000	$6,000
Pct $ disb (env/total):	65	70

Recipients (1992 highest):	Number:	Dollars:
The Nature Conservancy, Maine Chapter	1	50,000
ANAI, Inc.	1	25,000

Recipients (1992 highest):	Number:	Dollars:
The Conservation Fund	1	25,000
National Audubon Society	1	16,000
The Billfish Foundation	1	15,000

Activity regions (1992 highest):	Number:	Dollars:
U.S. not specified	23	189,070
U.S. Northeast	16	136,954
New York/New Jersey	19	118,000
Mexico and Central America	1	25,000
U.S. Mid-Atlantic	4	17,250

Sample grants (1992).
ANAI, Inc. Puerto Limon, Costa Rica. $25,000.
Horticultural Society of New York. New York, NY. $5,000.
The Nature Conservancy, Maine Chapter. Topsham, ME. $50,000.
National Coalition for Marine Conservation. Boston, MA. $8,200.
Northern Alaska Environmental Center. Fairbanks, AK. $4,000.
Oregon Natural Resources Council. Eugene, OR. $8,000.
Reef Relief. Key West, FL. $5,000.
Riverwatch Network. Montpelier, VT. $9,000.
The Wilderness Society. Washington, DC. $5,400.
Wildlife Preservation Trust International. Philadelphia, PA. $8,000.

Application process. *Initial contact:* Letter (2 pages, 14 copies) describing organization's work and objectives, the request itself, and specific funding needs. Budget (1 page) is optional. Append IRS tax-exempt status determination letter (1 copy).
When to apply: Deadline is September 1 for consideration in late October. Additional deadline (by specific request only) is May 1 for consideration in early June.
Do not send annual reports, fancy brochures, abstracts, etc. Do not use binders. Use regular First Class mail only. Requests sent by Certified or Express Mail or Federal Express will be refused and returned automatically.
Materials available: "Current Grant-Request Guidelines."

Emphases. *Recipients:* Nonprofit organizations.
Activities: Education, land acquisition, media projects, publications.
Types of support: Equipment, projects.

Limitations. *Types of support:* Multi-year grants, operating costs.

The Nord Family Foundation
347 Midway Boulevard, Suite 312
Elyria, Ohio 44035
Tel: 216-324-2822; 216-233-8401   Fax: 216-324-6427
EIN: 341595929   Type: Independent
Contact: Laurie Mellchok, Assistant to President

History and philosophy. The Nord Family Foundation succeeded the Nordson Foundation, which was created as a trust by the late Walter G. Nord in 1952. In 1988 the Nordson Foundation was dissolved and two separate entities were established: The Nord Family Foundation and the Nordson Corporation Foundation. The Nord Family Foundation is now one of the ten largest private foundations in Ohio.

As founder of Nordson Corporation of Amherst, Ohio, Mr. Nord believed that business has a social responsibility to the community from which it draws its human resources. The mission of The Nord Family Foundation is "to enhance the ability and effectiveness with which individuals, organizations, and communities address problems as well as opportunities." It develops initiatives and supports programs "aimed at promoting the well-being of families, particularly those who are disadvantaged, and the area of the public service. Grants are also made to stimulate artistic creativity, protect and preserve the natural environment, and attack systemic causes of human adversity."

Current funding areas are: Civic Affairs, Health and Social Service, Education, Culture, and Miscellaneous.

Officers and directors. *Officers:* David W. Ignat, President; Henry J. Libicki, Vice President; William D. Ginn, Secretary; Virginia N. Barbato, Treasurer. *Trustees:* Virginia N. Barbato, William D. Ginn, David W. Ignat, Joseph N. Ignat, Marilyn Jenne, Henry J. Libicki, Emily McClintock, Cynthia W. Nord, Eric T. Nord, Jane B. Nord, Kathleen Nord-Petersen.

Financial data. Data for fiscal year ended October 31, 1992. *Assets:* $66,917,718 (M). *Total grants authorized:* $3,030,815.

Environmental awards. *Program and interests:* Environmental awards may be made through Education and Civic Affairs programs.
Recent grants: 1992 grants included support for river protection and public education.

Issues.   Cli   Bio   Lan   Agr   Wat   Oce   Ene   Was   Tox   Pop   Dev
                              •   •

Funding analysis.

Fiscal year:	1991	1992
Env grants auth:	$175,290	$51,196
Number:	8	3
Range:	$5,880–$71,000	$9,696–$25,000
Median:	$15,000	$16,500
Pct $ auth (env/total):	5	2

Recipients (1992):	Number:	Dollars:
Oberlin College	1	25,000
Lake Erie Nature and Science Center	1	16,500
Earth Action Network, Inc.	1	9,696

Activity region (1992):	Number:	Dollars:
U.S. Great Lakes	3	51,196

Sample grants (1992).
Earth Action Network, Inc. Norwalk, CT. $9,696. Support to provide one-year subscriptions of *E Magazine* for all Ohio libraries.
Lake Erie Nature and Science Center. Bay Village, OH. $16,500. Support for the Black River Corridor Collaborative Project.
Oberlin College. Oberlin, OH. $25,000. For Friends of the Black River and a project at Cascade Park in Elyria.

Application process. *Initial contact:* Proposal (1 copy) to include:
1. Cover letter from organization's executive director or board president.
2. Abstract of proposal (1 page).
3. Detailed description of proposed project.
   - Background information on problem to be addressed.
   - Statement of project goals and objectives.
   - Plan for evaluating project's results.
   - Project budget with anticipated income and expenditures.
4. Copy of IRS tax-exempt status determination letter.
5. List of current board members.
6. Copy of organization's most recent financial statement.

When to apply: Deadlines are April 1, August 1, and December 1. Decisions are made in June, October, and February.
Materials available: Annual report (includes "How to Make Application"), "Information for Grantseekers."

Emphases. *Recipients:* Nonprofit organizations.
Activities: Publications.
Types of support: Continuing support, general purposes, matching funds, multi-year grants, projects, seed money, technical assistance.
Geography: Lorain County, Ohio; with a lesser emphasis on Cuyahoga County, Ohio; Denver, Colorado; Columbia, South Carolina; and national organizations.

Limitations. *Recipients:* Individuals.
Activities: Fundraising, research.
Types of support: Capital campaigns/expenses, debt retirement, endowments, general purposes.

Norman Foundation
147 East 48th Street
New York, New York 10017
Tel: 212-230-9830   Fax: 212-230-9849
EIN: 131862694   Type: Independent
Contact: Mallika Dutt, Program Director

History and philosophy. The Foundation was established in 1935 by Aaron E. Norman and is now directed by members of the Norman family. "Since the late 1950s the Norman Foundation has concentrated on efforts to promote fairness and opportunity in this country, primarily by empowering the disempowered themselves to challenge the conditions and institutions that control major aspects of their lives. The Foundation has been focusing particularly on economic justice and environmental justice issues, while maintaining its broad commitment to basic issues of civil rights and individual liberties."

Officers and directors. *Officers:* Andrew E. Norman, Chairman; Frank A. Weil, President; Nancy N. Lassalle, Vice President; Lucinda W. Bunnen, Secretary. *Directors:* Lucinda W. Bunnen, Melissa Bunnen, Robert L. Bunnen, Jr., Alice Franklin, Andrew D. Franklin, Deborah Weil Harrington, Honor Lassalle, Nancy N. Lassalle, Philip E. Lassalle, Abigail Norman, Andrew E. Norman, Margaret Norman, Rebecca Norman, Sarah Norman, Belinda Bunnen Reusch, Diana Lassalle Turner, Amanda E. Weil, Frank A. Weil, Sandison E. Weil, William S. Weil.

Financial data. Data for fiscal year ended December 31, 1993.
Assets: $22,169,580 (M). *Total grants authorized:* $1,197,000.

Environmental awards. *Recent grants:* 1993 included support for environmental justice and health, water rights, waste management, and environmental education.

Issues. Cli Bio Lan Agr Wat Oce Ene Was Tox Pop Dev
                     •   •   •   •   •

Funding analysis.

Fiscal year:	1992	1993
Env grants auth:	$373,500	$330,500
Number:	14	24
Range:	$1,500–$25,000	$2,500–$25,000
Median:	$15,000	$15,000
Pct $ auth (env/total):	31	28

Recipients (1993 highest):	Number:	Dollars:
Environmental Community Action	1	25,000
Environmental Health Network	1	25,000
Blacks on the Serious Side	1	20,000
Community Farm Alliance	1	20,000
Sea Island Preservation Project	1	20,000
Southern Organizing Committee (SOC) Education Fund, Inc.	1	20,000

Activity regions (1993 highest):	Number:	Dollars:
U.S. Southeast	10	170,000
U.S. West	4	44,000
U.S. Mid-Atlantic	2	40,000
U.S. South Central	4	32,500
U.S. Mountain	2	25,000

Sample grants (1993).

Blacks on the Serious Side. Belle Glade, FL. $20,000. To improve electoral participation of African-Americans and confront economic and environmental issues through community organizing and education.

Center for Community Action, Inc. Lumberton, NC. $15,000. For the Low-Level Radioactive Waste Campaign to halt construction of a regional dump in North Carolina.

The Environmental and Economic Justice Project (EEJP). Los Angeles, CA. $15,000. To help build multi-racial organizations and alliances between local/regional environmental justice groups.

Environmental Health Network. Chesapeake, VA. $25,000. For the Health Registry Program and to support the provision of technical assistance to communities battling toxic waste.

Harvard University, Center for International Affairs. Cambridge, MA. $4,000. To support research that will analyze the impact environmental issues have on international policy making.

Occupational Safety and Health Law Center. Shepherdstown, WV. $15,000. For general support to provide technical assistance to groups organizing in the industries of coal mining and poultry.

The Rural Consortium. Enfield, NC. $15,000. To support a collaboration of Southern-based rural training centers that will focus on environmental education, land retention/development, and historic and cultural preservation and development.

Application process. *Initial contact:* Letter of inquiry to include:
1. Scope and significance of problem to be addressed.
2. Organization's proposed response and (if appropriate) how this strategy builds upon the organization's past work.
3. Specific, demonstrable effects the project would have if successful.
4. How the project promotes change on a national level and otherwise relates to the Foundation's guidelines.

If the project is deemed promising, a full proposal will be requested. Prospective grantees may use the New York Area Common Application Form and include:
1. A more detailed description of the proposed project as outlined in the initial letter.
2. Detailed organization and project budgets including a breakdown of current and prospective income from foundations and other sources.
3. Project staff background with ethnic and racial composition.
4. List of board members with ethnic and racial composition.
5. Letters of support as appropriate.
6. Copy of IRS tax-exempt status determination letter.

When to apply: Anytime.
Materials available: Annual report (contains "Application Process").

Emphases. *Recipients:* Educational institutions, nonprofit organizations.
Activities: Activism, advocacy, capacity building, citizen participation, collaborative efforts, conflict resolution, education, fundraising, innovative programs, land acquisition, litigation, networking, planning, policy analysis/development, political activities, publications, research, technical assistance, training, youth programs.
Types of support: Continuing support, emergency funding, general purposes, loans, matching funds, pilot projects, projects, seed money, start-up costs, technical assistance.
Geography: National and local programs in the United States.

Limitations. *Recipients:* Botanical gardens, individuals, museums, zoos.
Activities: Audiovisual materials, conferences, direct services, fundraising, media projects, research.
Types of support: Capital campaigns/expenses, scholarships.
Geography: International.

Andrew Norman Foundation
10960 Wilshire Boulevard, Suite 820
Los Angeles, California 90024
Tel: 310–478–1213   Fax: 310–478–1215
EIN: 953433781   Type: Independent
EGA member
Contact: Dan Olincy, Manager and Trustee

History and philosophy. The Andrew Norman Foundation was established in 1958. It gives grants in the areas of civil rights, medical research, education, and environment.

Officers and directors. *Officers:* Virginia Olincy, President; Bernice Kranson, Vice President; Dan Olincy, Secretary/Treasurer. *Trustees:* Bernice Kranson, Dan Olincy, Virginia Olincy.

Financial data. Data for fiscal year ended June 30, 1993. *Assets:* $3,514,915 (U). *Total grants authorized:* $59,400.

Environmental awards. *Recent grants:* 1993 grants included support for public education and environmental justice.

Issues.   Cli   Bio   Lan   Agr   Wat   Oce   Ene   Was   Tox   Pop   Dev
•

Funding analysis.

Fiscal year:	1992	1993
Env grants disb:	$40,000	$8,700
Number:	–	3
Range:	–	$200–$7,500
Median:	–	$1,000
Pct $ disb (env/total):	55	15

Recipients (1993):	Number:	Dollars:
Sierra Club Legal Defense Fund	1	7,500
Clean Air Now	1	1,000
Environmental Preservation Foundation	1	200

Activity region (1993):	Number:	Dollars:
U.S. West	3	8,700

Sample grants (1993).
Clean Air Now. Venice, CA. $1,000. Public education tour.
Environmental Preservation Foundation. San Francisco, CA. $200. General support.
Sierra Club Legal Defense Fund. San Francisco, CA, and *NAACP Legal Defense and Educational Fund, Inc.* Los Angeles, CA. $7,500. Joint environmental justice project.

Application process. *Initial contact:* The Foundation awards granted to pre-selected organizations only. No unsolicited applications accepted.

Emphases. *Recipients:* Pre-selected organizations only.
Types of support: Pilot projects, seed money.
Geography: California, primarily Los Angeles.

Limitations. *Recipients:* Individuals.
Types of support: Capital campaigns/expenses, endowments, fellowships, scholarships.

Kenneth T. and Eileen L. Norris Foundation
11 Golden Shore, Suite 450
Long Beach, California 90802
Tel: 310–435–8444   Fax: 310–436–0584
EIN: 956080374   Type: Independent
Contact: Ronald R. Barnes, Executive Director

History and philosophy. The Foundation was established in 1963 by Kenneth T. Norris and his wife Eileen. Mr. Norris, the founder and president of Norris Industries, wished to help support his company's surrounding community. The Foundation continues to support this community through grants for culture, education, health services, medical research, social services, and youth programs.

Officers and directors. *Officers:* Kenneth T. Norris, Jr., Chairman; Ronald R. Barnes, Executive Director. *Trustees:* Ronald R. Barnes, William G. Corey, M.D., George M. Gordon, Harlyne J. Norris, Kenneth T. Norris, Jr.

Financial data. Data for fiscal year ended November 30, 1992. *Assets:* $98,603,000 (M). *Total grants disbursed:* $3,519,822.

Environmental awards. *Recent grants:* 1992 grants included support for urban issues (parks, beautification), wildlife conservation, forests, and botanical gardens, mainly in California.

Issues. Cli Bio• Lan• Agr Wat Oce Ene Was Tox Pop Dev

Funding analysis.

Fiscal year:	1991	1992
Env grants disb:	$138,000	$66,000
Number:	6	4
Range:	$1,000–$50,000	$1,000–$50,000
Median:	$17,500	$7,500
Pct $ disb (env/total):	4	2

Recipients (1992):	Number:	Dollars:
Friends of Banning Park	1	50,000
National Wildlife Federation	1	10,000
Save the Redwoods League	1	5,000
Los Angeles Beautiful	1	1,000

Activity region (1992):	Number:	Dollars:
U.S. West	4	66,000

Sample grants (1992).
Friends of Banning Park. Wilmington, CA. $50,000.
Los Angeles Beautiful. Los Angeles, CA. $1,000.
National Wildlife Federation. Washington, DC. $10,000.
Save the Redwoods League. San Francisco, CA. $5,000.

Application process. *Initial contact:* Telephone call or brief letter of inquiry with a concise project outline.
When to apply: Anytime.
Materials available: Annual report.

Emphases. *Recipients:* Botanical gardens, educational institutions, museums, nonprofit organizations.
Activities: Education, publications, volunteerism.
Types of support: Annual campaigns, capital campaigns/expenses, continuing support, endowments, equipment, scholarships.
Geography: Los Angeles County, California.

Limitations. *Recipients:* Individuals.
Types of support: Loans.

Mary Moody Northen, Inc.
2628 Broadway
Galveston, Texas 77550
Tel: 409–765–9770
EIN: 751171741 Type: Independent
EGA member
Contact: Jeanette Moore, Administrative Director

Application address:
P.O. Box 1300
Galveston, Texas 77553

History and philosophy. The Foundation was established in 1964 by Mary Moody Northen. While most of its activities are geared towards the restoration of the historic Moody residence in Galveston and the preservation of the Foundation's properties at Mountain Lake, Virginia, the Foundation also supports civic affairs, community development, education, the environment, historic preservations, museums, and wildlife.

Officers and directors. *Officers:* Gilbert F. Orcutt, President and Treasurer; Edward L. Protz, Vice President and Secretary. *Directors:* Robert L. Moody, Gilbert F. Orcutt, Edward L. Protz.

Financial data. Data for fiscal years ended June 30, 1992 and 1993. *Assets (1992):* $52,052,067 (M). *Total grants disbursed (1993):* $798,275.

Environmental awards. *Program and interests:* The Foundation's primary interests are the arts and civic affairs.
Recent grants: 1993 grants included support for coastal issues and preservation of its Mountain Lake properties, which it maintains in the manner of a national or state park.

Issues. Cli Bio Lan Agr Wat• Oce Ene• Was Tox Pop Dev

Funding analysis.

Fiscal year:	1993
Env grants disb:	$30,000
Number:	2
Range:	$5,000–$25,000
Median:	$15,000
Pct $ disb (env/total):	4

Recipients (1993):	Number:	Dollars:
Wilderness Conservancy at Mountain Lake	1	25,000
Galveston Bay Foundation	1	5,000

Activity regions (1993):	Number:	Dollars:
U.S. Mid-Atlantic	1	25,000
U.S. South Central	1	5,000

Sample grants (1993).
Galveston Bay Foundation. Galveston, TX. $5,000. Save the Bay Program.
Wilderness Conservancy at Mountain Lake. Mountain Lake, VA. $25,000. Program development.

Application process. *Initial contact:* Brief letter of inquiry describing the project and its purpose. If deemed within its scope and budget, the Foundation will send formal application. Full proposal to include:
1. Name and address of tax-exempt organization.
2. Copy of IRS tax-exempt status determination letter.
3. Relationship, capacity, or title of person signing the application.
4. List of officers and directors.
5. Brief history including its principal program and accomplishments.
6. Recent annual report, preferably in the form of a certified audit, and budget for the current year.
7. Description of the project showing the need or problem and the proposed solution.
8. Detailed expense budget for the full term and for the period which assistance is requested. Provide amount to be raised, list of expected sources of funds, and amount requested. If this is a pilot project, include expected and realistic sources of continuing funding. State if the program is successful.
9. Qualifications of personnel involved.
10. Endorsements of the head of the institution and outside authorities, if indicated, and copies of approval of regulatory agencies.

Further information may be requested.
When to apply: Anytime.
Materials available: Application guidelines.

Emphases. *Recipients:* Educational institutions, research institutions.
Activities: Research
Types of support: Continuing support, general purposes, pilot projects, professorships.
Geography: Texas, Virginia.

Northwest Area Foundation
E–1201 First National Bank Building
332 Minnesota Street
St. Paul, Minnesota 55101–1373
Tel: 612–224–9635   Fax: 612–225–3881
EIN: 410719221   Type: Independent
Contact: Terry T. Saario, President

History and philosophy. Northwest Area Foundation was established in 1934 by Louis W. Hill, son of James J. Hill, pioneer builder of the Great Northern Railway. In setting up what was originally called the Lexington Foundation and later the Louis W. and Maud Hill Family Foundation, Louis Hill sought to create an institution that would "promote the public welfare." Today the Foundation is committed to the welfare of the eight-state area of Minnesota, Iowa, North Dakota, South Dakota, Montana, Idaho, Washington, and Oregon. The Foundation's mission is to contribute to the vitality of the region by promoting economic revitalization and improving the standard of living for the most vulnerable of its citizens.

"To accomplish its mission, the Foundation will focus, deepen, and enhance the public dialogue about important regional issues; seek innovative approaches to address these issues; and build the capacity to continue to address them effectively over the long term. Specific areas of interest are: alleviating rural and urban poverty and promoting economical development that is sustainable over the long term."

Officers and directors. *Officers:* Roger R. Conant, Chair; Marcia J. Bystrom, Vice Chair; Terry T. Saario, President, and Secretary, and Assistant Treasurer; Karl N. Stauber, Vice President and Assistant Secretary; Sandra T. Hokanson, Vice President; Worth Bruntjen, Treasurer. *Trustees:* Irving Clark, W. John Driscoll, Sheila Folliott, Louis W. Hill, Jr. *Directors:* Nina M. Archabal, W. E. Bye Barsness, Steven L. Belton, Worth Bruntjen, Marcia J. Bystrom, Roger R. Conant, W. John Driscoll, David F. Hickok, M.D., Richard S. Levitt, Hazel R. O'Leary, James R. Scott.

Financial data. Data for fiscal year ended February 29, 1993. *Assets:* $276,608,593 (M). *Total grants disbursed:* $11,462,373.

Environmental awards. *Program and interests:* The Foundation's sustainable development program focuses on planning for effective natural resource management and conservation, developing sustainable industries, and preserving ecosystems. In particular, its interest is in projects designed to resolve economic and environmental tensions around the use of the region's natural resource base:

- Water.

  Water management and use, rights, conservation, pollution, and allocation.

- Fisheries.

  Sustainability, resources, and aquaculture.

- Timber.

  Best-use practices, decisionmaking, and regulations.

- Agriculture.

  Sustainable agriculture and agricultural diversification.

- Citizen involvement.

  Capacity building, integrating scientific and citizen efforts.

- Waste management.

  Public education, recycling enterprises, networks, and public policy.

Recent grants: 1993 grants included support for sustainable agriculture, forestry, education, and policy development.

Issues. Cli Bio Lan Agr Wat Oce Ene Was Tox Pop Dev
              •   •   •   •   •

Funding analysis.

Fiscal year:	1991	1993
Env grants auth:	$2,004,807	$2,078,584
Number:	19	26
Range:	$7,774–$295,000	$10,000–$500,000
Median:	$76,010	$30,823
Pct $ auth (env/total):	15	42

Recipients (1993 highest):	Number:	Dollars:
North Dakota State University, Carrington Research Extension	1	500,000
People for Puget Sound	1	300,000

Eastern Plains Resource Conservation and Development	1	200,000
Prairiefire Rural Action	1	165,896
Oregon Trout	1	148,970

Activity regions (1993 highest):	Number:	Dollars:
U.S. Northwest	11	769,345
U.S. not specified	2	530,000
U.S. Mountain	3	254,248
U.S. multiple regions*	6	244,245
U.S. Midwest	3	205,896

*Grantmaking region as defined by Foundation.

Sample grants (1993).
Alternative Energy Resources Organization. Helena, MT. $64,740. Bridge grant. To ensure the continued involvement of the Alternative Energy Resources Organization in the Foundation's multi-state initiative examining the environmental, economic, and social implications of conventional and sustainable agriculture.
Center for Rural Affairs. Walthill, NE. $30,000. To conclude activities of the World Agriculture Project, which is providing information and analysis to agricultural organizations and policymakers within the Foundation's region concerning trade negotiations under the General Agreement on Trade and Tariffs (GATT) and the North American Free Trade Agreement (NAFTA).
Ecotrust. Portland, OR. $25,000. Multi-year Loan Fund Business Plan. To develop a business plan that will explore the economic viability of a multi-year loan fund supporting ecologically sustainable economic development in the Wallapa Bay region of southwest Washington.
Friends of the Columbia Gorge. Portland, OR. $20,000. To support citizen participation in implementing the permanent management plan for the Columbia River Gorge National Scenic Area by participating in the development of local and regional land-use ordinances.
Oregon State University, Department of Forest Science. Corvallis, OR. $28,000. For the Socioecological Approach to Resource Management Planning. To complete the planning and development of a new research tool for policymakers to use in determining some of the potential consequences of the difficult natural resource land management issues they are facing.
Pacific Rivers Council. Eugene, OR. $142,790. To develop a consensus plan for the recovery of Northwest salmon stocks, with consideration for cost, resource allocation, and economic impacts.

Application process. *Initial contact:* Letter of inquiry describing the applicant organization, the proposed project, and the project's finances. Full proposal, if requested, to include:
Cover Sheet (in "Guidelines for Grant Applicants").
Information about the applicant organization.
1. Name and address.
2. Name, title, address, and telephone number of project director.
3. Description of organization, including background, purpose, objectives, and experience in area for which funds are sought.
4. Names and affiliations of board of directors.
5. Statement of organization's financial status (preferably an audited balance sheet and income statement for the most recent fiscal year and a projected budget for current year).
6. Copy of IRS tax-exempt status determination letter.

Information about the project.
1. Explanation, with data or documentation, of need for project.
2. Comments on past or present attempts by the applicant and others to address the designated need.
3. Description of goals, objective, and specific outcomes the project is expected to achieve.
4. Activities or methods to reach goals and a timetable.
5. Date requested funds are needed.
6. Statement by director of organization that proposed project has the organization's full support.
7. Names and qualifications of people involved in implementing the project as well as percentage of time, on an annual basis, each person will devote to project activities.
8. Evaluation plan, including description of activities, timetable, and names of those responsible for conducting evaluation.
9. Plan for how project findings will be disseminated.

Information about the project's finances.
1. Itemized project budget showing how major expenses are estimated and how requested funds are to be spent. Sources, amounts, and use of funds other than those from Northwest Area Foundation should also be documented.
2. Explanation of how project will be financed after Foundation funds are expended.
3. Explanation of why organization cannot assume the costs of the project with its own resources.

When to apply: Anytime. The board meets bimonthly.
Materials available: Annual report (contains "Information for Applicants"), "Guidelines for Grant Applicants," *Northwest Report* (newsletter).

Emphases. *Recipients:* Nonprofit organizations.
Types of support: Program-related investments.
Geography: Minnesota, Iowa, North Dakota, South Dakota, Montana, Idaho, Washington, and Oregon.

Limitations. *Activities:* Conferences, lobbying, media projects, publications.
Types of support: Annual campaigns, capital campaigns/expenses, endowments, equipment, facilities, expansion or duplication of established programs, fellowships, operating costs, scholarships, travel expenses.

Northwest Fund for the Environment

4407 52nd Avenue, N.E.
Seattle, Washington 98105
Tel: 206-527-6350   Fax: 206-523-0567
EIN: 410719221   Type: Independent
Contacts: Marcy J. Golde, Vice President
Gayle Rothrock, Trustee
Walter Walkinshaw, Trustee

History and philosophy. The Northwest Fund was incorporated in 1934. Its purpose is to "undertake activities which will lead to the conservation, preservation, and wise use of the scenic, aesthetic, historic, wilderness, recreational, wildlife and other natural resources of the Pacific Northwest and the United States for the benefit of man and nature; to the protection of the ecology of the region and the nation; and to the creation of an environment which will enhance the quality of life."

Grants have historically been in the range of $1,500 – $10,000, with typically 10 to 14 grants made annually. In 1995 and thereafter, grants will be made in a broader financial range with a greater number of recipients under newly developed guidelines.

Officers and directors. *Officers:* Marcy J. Golde, Vice President; Walter Walkinshaw, Secretary/Treasurer. *Trustees:* Emory Bundy, Roger J. Contor, John DeYonge, Marcy J. Golde, James K. Penfield, Gayle Rothrock, Walter Walkinshaw.

Financial data. Data for fiscal year ended December 31, 1993. *Assets:* $45,000 (U). *Gifts received:* $43,600. *Total grants disbursed:* $60,000.

Environmental awards. *Program and interests:* Grants are made for projects that have the potential of major environmental benefit for Washington State.
Recent grants: 1993 and 1994 grants supported innovative wildlife habitat management, environmental volunteer and staff training, environmental litigation, toxic waste management and recycling legislation, and trails and recreation lands stewardship.

Issues. *Cli Bio Lan Agr Wat Oce Ene Was Tox Pop Dev*
•   •   •   •   •   •

Funding analysis.

Fiscal year:	1991
Env grants auth:	$74,923
Number:	14
Range:	$1,500–$10,000
Median:	$5,000
Pct $ auth (env/total):	100

Recipients (1991 highest):	*Number:*	*Dollars:*
Washington Environmental Council	2	17,500
Sierra Club Legal Defense Fund	2	12,500
Friends of the Columbia Gorge	1	10,000
Puget Sound Alliance	1	7,500
Northwest Rivers Council	1	5,500

Activity region (1991):	*Number:*	*Dollars:*
U.S. Northwest	14	74,923

Sample grants (1993–94).
Green Corps. Burlington, VT. $7,500. Support of training for college student grassroots organizers in the central Puget Sound area.
Hanford Education Action League. New Bedford, MA. $5,000. Continued support of work on public safety, health, and other problems related to the Hanford nuclear reservation.
Predator Project. Bozeman, MT. $5,000. Support for a road density and closure effectiveness inventory in the Wenatchee National Forest.
Sierra Club Legal Defense Fund. Seattle, WA. $10,000. Support for a water quality and civil rights campaign and test case on behalf of people of color and under-represented communities, to eliminate discrimination in the regulation of toxic water pollution.

Washington Toxics Coalition. Seattle, WA. $7,500. Information and education services project, to assist in meeting a matching challenge grant from an educational foundation.
Washington Trails Association. Seattle, WA. $5,000. Development of local trails advocacy and enhancement committees for Olympic, Okanogan, and Colville National Forests.
Washington Wildlife and Recreation Foundation. Seattle, WA. $5,000. Strengthen support for state land acquisition and stewardship program through a public education effort.

Application process. *Initial contact:* Letter of inquiry to include:
1. Brief proposal outline.
2. Amount requested.
3. Project needs.

When to apply: Deadlines are March 1 and September 1.

Emphases. *Recipients:* Nonprofit organizations.
Activities: Advocacy, citizen participation, collaborative efforts, demonstration programs, innovative programs, litigation, policy analysis/development, training (volunteers/staff).
Types of support: Leveraging funds, matching funds, operating costs.
Geography: Washington State only.

The Norton Foundation, Inc.
4350 Brownsboro Road, Suite 133
Louisville, Kentucky 40207–1667
Tel: 502–893–9549
EIN: 616024040   Type: Independent
Contact: Lucy Crawford, Executive Director

History and philosophy. Mrs. George W. Norton established the Foundation in 1958. It funds nonprofit organizations working in the areas of education, youth, social services, homeless, and the environment in the Metropolitan Louisville, Kentucky area.

Officers and directors. *Officers:* Jane Norton Dulaney, President; Robert W. Dulaney, Vice President; Lucy Crawford, Executive Director. *Directors:* Richard H. C. Clay, Jane Norton Dulaney, Robert W. Dulaney.

Financial data. Data for fiscal year ended December 31, 1993. *Assets:* $12,736,676 (M). *Total grants disbursed:* $597,805.

Environmental awards. *Recent grants:* 1993 grants included support for natural resources preservation and a zoo.

Issues. *Cli Bio Lan Agr Wat Oce Ene Was Tox Pop Dev*
•   •

Funding analysis.

Fiscal year:	1993
Env grants dsib:	$70,000
Number:	3
Range:	$20,000–$25,000
Median:	$25,000
Pct $ disb (env/total):	12

Recipients (1993):	Number:	Dollars:
Louisville Resource Conservation Council	1	25,000
Louisville Zoo Foundation, Inc.	1	25,000
Kentucky Resources Council	1	20,000

Activity region (1993):	Number:	Dollars:
U.S. Southeast	3	70,000

Sample grants (1993).
Kentucky Resources Council. Frankfort, KY. $20,000.
Louisville Resource Conservation Council. Louisville, KY. $25,000.
Louisville Zoo Foundation, Inc. Louisville, KY. $25,000.

Application process. *Initial contact:* Proposal to include:
1. Description (3 copies) of project to be funded.
2. Budget of all income and expenses.
3. Copy of IRS tax-exempt status determination letter.

When to apply: Anytime. The board meets quarterly.

Emphases. *Recipients:* Educational institutions, nonprofit organizations.
Types of support: Annual campaigns, capital campaigns/expenses, continuing support, endowments, general purposes, operating costs, projects, scholarships, seed money.
Geography: Metropolitan Louisville, Kentucky; Kentucky.

Limitations. *Recipients:* Individuals.

Jessie Smith Noyes Foundation, Inc.

16 East 34th Street
New York, New York 10016
Tel: 212–684–6577 Fax: 212–689–6549
E-mail: noyes@igc.org
EIN: 135600408 Type: Independent
EGA member
Contacts: Stephen Viederman, President
Environmental Justice
Victor De Luca, Program Officer,
Sustainable Agriculture
Jamie Fellner, Program Officer,
Groundwater and Toxics

History and philosophy. The Jessie Smith Noyes Foundation was established in 1947 by Charles F. Noyes as a memorial to his wife, Jessie Smith Noyes (b. 1885). Charles Noyes was known as the New York "Dean of Real Estate" and Jessie Smith Noyes was a champion of community needs, religious tolerance, and racial equality. In its early years the Foundation focused on minority education. The Foundation today has two goals: (1) preventing irreversible damage to the natural systems upon which all life depends; and (2) strengthening individuals and institutions committed to protecting natural systems and ensuring a sustainable society. Grants are primarily made in the interrelated areas of environment and population, favoring activities that also address the connections between environmental issues and issues of social justice.

Officers and directors. *Officers:* Nicholas Jacangelo, Chair; Dorothy E. Muma, Vice Chair; Edward B. Tasch, Treasurer. *Directors:* Dorothy Anderson, Catherine Bedell, Rosemary Bray, Donna Chavis, Donald S. Collat, Joan Gussow, Nicholas Jacangelo, Dorothy E. Muma, Edith N. Muma, David W. Orr, Chad Raphael, Elsa A. Rios, Edward B. Tasch, Stephen Viederman, Ann F. Wiener.

Financial data. Data for fiscal year ended December 31, 1993. *Assets:* $62,084,165 (M). *Total grants disbursed:* $3,599,555.

Environmental awards. *Program and interests:* The Foundation makes grants in three primary areas:

- Groundwater and Toxics in the United States, with particular emphasis on the Southeast, Southwest, and the Rocky Mountain West.

  Objective: To strengthen the ability of citizens to ensure for themselves and for future generations ample and uncontaminated groundwater resources.

  Priorities.
  - To strengthen the advocacy, outreach, and technical capabilities of organizations addressing groundwater protection.
  - To support efforts to improve public policies affecting groundwater protection, including initiatives to secure pollution prevention and waste reduction, and to strengthen their implementation.

- Sustainable Agriculture in the United States, with particular emphasis on the Southeast, Southwest, and the Rocky Mountain West.

  Objective: To strengthen the ability of citizens to promote a sustainable agricultural system that is environmentally sound, economically feasible, and socially just.

  Priorities.
  - To strengthen the advocacy, outreach, and technical capacity of organizations promoting sustainable agriculture, including the development of regional, national, and international collaborative efforts.
  - To improve the development and implementation of sustainable agriculture policies and programs at the state, regional, national, and international levels.
  - To demonstrate the agricultural and economical feasibility of sustainable agriculture; its social benefits; and its ability to strengthen rural communities.

- Population and Reproductive Rights in the United States.

  Objective: To ensure quality reproductive health care as a human right.

  Priorities.
  - To broaden the base and the agenda of the reproductive rights movement through the involvement of new constituencies.
  - To support legal and policy initiatives at the state and national level to safeguard reproductive freedom.
  - To ensure that reproductive health is included in health care policies and reform initiatives.

In addition, a few grants are made for activities that fall outside the programs described above, but which further the goals of the Foundation. Presently, two areas of special concern are:

- Environmental justice in the United States and Latin America.
- Strengthening the nonprofit sector in the United States.

Issues. Cli *Bio* *Lan* *Agr* Wat Oce *Ene* Was *Tox* *Pop* *Dev*

Funding analysis.

Fiscal year:	1992*	1993**
Env grants disb or auth:	$3,260,338	$1,754,125
Number:	162	79
Range:	$1,000–$40,000	$625–$80,000
Median:	$21,000	$20,000
Pct $ disb (env/total):	89	72

*As reported by Foundation based on grants disbursed. Included are $855,150 in 1992 for population and reproductive rights. Discretionary grants are not included.
**Based on grants authorized. Discretionary grants are not included.

Recipients (1993 highest):	*Number:*	*Dollars:*
The Global Fund for Women	1	80,000
Nucleo de Direitos Indigenas	1	62,000
Citizens Clearinghouse for Hazardous Wastes, Inc.	1	60,000
Center for Rural Affairs	1	50,000
Henry A. Wallace Institute for Alternative Agriculture	1	50,000
National Family Farm Coalition	1	50,000
The Focus Project	1	50,000

Activity regions (1993 highest):	*Number:*	*Dollars:*
U.S. not specified	27	613,625
U.S. Southeast	12	220,000
U.S. South Central	11	210,000
Brazil	3	129,000
U.S. West	5	110,000

Sample grants (1993).

Arkansas Land and Farm Development Corporation. Brinkley, AR. $20,000. For ALFDC's efforts to train and assist farmers in alternative crop production and low-input sustainable practices and to establish alternative marketing cooperatives. The ultimate purpose of the Corporation is to stop and reverse the causes and conditions leading to the loss of Black-owned land and the decline in the number of small farmers.

Committee on Women, Population, and the Environment. c/o Hampshire College. Amherst, MA. $15,000. The Committee is an informal network of women's health activists, environmentalists, community organizers, health practitioners, and scholars of diverse races, cultures, and countries of origin. This grant enables the Committee to provide alternative analyses, data documentation, and perspectives to improve policies and programs on population and environmental issues.

Eco-Justice Network Support Project. Washington, DC. $2,500. For information and resource material to environmental justice activists and organizations and for networking and communication among these groups.

Federation of Southern Cooperatives/Land Assistance Fund. Epes, AL. $25,000. The Federation was started in 1968 by African-American farmers and low-income people to organize and assist them in using their resources to form cooperatives and revitalize rural communities. This grant supports the Federation's efforts to provide technical assistance to and serve as an advocate on behalf of African-American and other low-income farmers in the Southeast.

The Focus Project. Washington, DC. $50,000 (2 years). General support for OMB Watch, founded in 1983 and operated by the Focus Project, to increase democratic participation in administrative governance and improve government accountability. OMB Watch began the Right-to-Know Computer Network to make government information more accessible to citizens. It contains information about toxic pollution from manufacturing facilities around the country and has more than 800 participants on its network.

Health and Development Policy Project. c/o The Tides Foundation. San Francisco, CA. $15,000. Seed money to this new Project which seeks to improve U.S. international policies on population, environment, and women's health. It will serve as a voice in Washington, D.C. for women's health and rights, and will alert women to political developments.

Midwest Sustainable Agriculture Working Group. Des Moines, IA. $25,000. SAWG was organized in 1988 as a coalition of more than 30 sustainable agriculture, environmental, food, religious, and rural development organizations. This grant supports the SAWG's efforts to develop and advocate for the adoption of policies and practices that advance sustainable agriculture in the region and nationally.

Rodale Institute. Emmaus, PA. $20,000. In 1988 the Rodale Institute developed farmer networks in three regions of the country thorough which 31 cooperating farms serve as bridges between conventional and low-input farming systems. This grant supports outreach and networking of coordinator and farmer cooperators of the Mid-South Farmers Network.

Southwest Research and Information Center. Albuquerque, NM. $25,000. To assist SRIC in providing technical assistance, training, and public education to grassroots groups in the region that are working on water pollution issues.

Texas Network for Environmental and Economic Justice. Austin, TX. $15,000. General support for the Network which seeks to provide a forum for examining and responding to the impact of environmental and economic development policies of communities of color in Texas and to permit leaders of communities of color from across the state to build alliances and provide support to one another.

Traditional Native American Farmers Association. c/o Native Seeds/SEARCH. Tucson, AZ. $15,000. Start-up funding for the Association, established in 1992 to bring together Native American farmers and gardeners in New Mexico and Arizona to ensure that the agricultural traditions of Native American people would be preserved and continued.

Henry A. Wallace Institute for Alternative Agriculture. Greenbelt, MD. $50,000 (2 years). The Henry A. Wallace Institute for Alternative Agriculture, founded in 1982, is both a convener and a catalyst linking farmers, agricultural scientists, and economists, federal and state policymakers, educators and extension agents, and agribusiness people. The Institute publishes the *American Journal of Alternative Agriculture* and two monthly newsletters, and convenes an annual symposium on major agricultural topics. This grant is for general support.

O

Application process. *Initial contact:* Letter of inquiry (2 pages) to include:
1. Brief statement of the issues to be addressed and organization's involvement.
2. Brief summary of activities for which support is requested, including an outline of objectives, and anticipated outcomes and implications.
3. Approximate start date and duration of proposed activities.
4. Total amount of funding needed, amount requested from the Foundation, and information about other sources of support, both assured and requested.

When to apply: Anytime. The board of directors meets three times a year.
Materials available: Annual report (includes "Applying for a Grant").

Emphases. *Recipients:* Nonprofit organizations.
Activities: Activism, advocacy, capacity building, citizen participation, collaborative efforts, innovative programs, networking, policy analysis/development, political activities.
Types of support: General purposes, pilot projects, program-related investments, projects, technical assistance.
Geography: United States. Especially South and Rocky Mountain West (groundwater and toxics); Southeast, Southcentral, Southwest, and Rocky Mountain West (sustainable agriculture); United States (population and reproductive rights).

Limitations. *Recipients:* Individuals.
Activities: Audiovisual materials, conferences, exhibits, expeditions/tours, fundraising, media projects, research, seminars, symposia/colloquia.
Types of support: Advertising campaigns, capital campaigns/expenses, debt retirement, endowments, fellowships, general purposes, lectureships, professorships, scholarships.

Nicholas H. Noyes, Jr. Memorial Foundation

7700B West 38th Street
Indianapolis, Indiana 46254
Tel: 317–293–1157
EIN: 351003699   Type: Independent
Contact: Evan L. Noyes, President

History and philosophy. The Foundation was established in 1951 by Nicholas H. and Marguerite Lilly Noyes. Its interests include secondary schools and private academies; united funds, housing, work centers, and day care; performing arts in Indianapolis; nursing and hospitals; zoos and conservation; and religion. Funding efforts focus on education, the arts, health, social services, and conservation.

Officers and directors. *Officers:* Evan L. Noyes, President; Robert H. Reynolds, Vice President; Frederic M. Ayres, Secretary; Kelly Glessner, Assistant Secretary; James M. Cornelius, Treasurer. *Directors:* Frederic M. Ayres, Nancy Ayres, Janet A. Carrington, James M. Cornelius, Diana C. Leslie, Evan L. Noyes, Nicholas S. Noyes, Robert H. Reynolds.

Financial data. Data for fiscal year ended December 31, 1993. *Assets:* $19,219,018 (M). *Total grants disbursed:* $1,050,000.

Environmental awards. *Recent grants:* 1993 grants included support for land conservation and a zoo.

Issues. Cli Bio Lan Agr Wat Oce Ene Was Tox Pop Dev
           •   •   •

Funding analysis.

Fiscal year:	1993
Env grants disb:	$55,000
Number:	2
Range:	$5,000–$50,000
Median:	$27,500
Pct $ disb (env/total):	5

Recipients (1993):	Number:	Dollars:
Indianapolis Zoological Society	1	50,000
The Nature Conservancy, Indiana Field Office	1	5,000

Activity region (1993):	Number:	Dollars:
U.S. Great Lakes	2	55,000

Sample grants (1993).
Indianapolis Zoological Society. Indianapolis, IN. $50,000. Operating fund.
The Nature Conservancy, Indiana Field Office. Indianapolis, IN. $5,000.

Application process. *Initial contact:* Letter describing the organization and the amount requested.
When to apply: Anytime. The board meets semiannually.

Emphases. *Recipients:* Nonprofit organizations.
Types of support: Endowments, matching funds, operating costs, scholarships.
Geography: Indiana.

Limitations. *Recipients:* Individuals.
Types of support: Facilities (construction), loans.

OCRI Foundation

P.O. Box 1705
Lake Oswego, Oregon 97035
Tel: 503–635–8010   Fax: 503–635–6544
EIN: 237120564   Type: Independent
Contact: Judith Anderson, Administrator

History and philosophy. Members of the Lamb family created the Foundation in 1971. Its primary interests are ecology, hunger, youth, and Christian religious organizations.

Officers and directors. *Officers:* Anita Lamb Bailey, Chairman; Paula L. Lamb, Vice Chairman; Helen Lamb, Secretary; F. Gilbert Lamb, Treasurer. *Directors:* Anita Lamb Bailey, Dorothy Lamb, F. Gilbert Lamb, Frank Lamb, Helen Lamb, Maryann Lamb, Paula L. Lamb, Peter Lamb, Walter Minnick.

Financial data. Data for fiscal year ended December 31, 1992. *Assets:* $4,387,228 (M). *Total grants disbursed:* $250,904.

Environmental awards. *Recent grants:* 1992 grants included support for wilderness, forest, and wildlife protection.

Issues. Cli Bio **Lan** **Agr** **Wat** Oce Ene Was Tox Pop Dev

Funding analysis.

Fiscal year:	1992
Env grants disb:	$56,754
Number:	12
Range:	$50–$25,204
Median:	$1,000
Pct $ disb (env/total):	23

Recipients (1992 highest):	Number:	Dollars:
High Desert Museum	1	25,204
Idaho Conservation League	1	11,000
Public Forestry Foundation	1	10,000
Headwaters Community Association	1	5,000
The Wilderness Society	1	2,000

Activity regions (1992):	Number:	Dollars:
U.S. Northwest	6	52,254
U.S. not specified	5	4,250
U.S. West	1	250

Sample grants (1992).
Association of Forest Service Employees for the Environment. Eugene, OR. $150.
Headwaters Community Association. Ashland, OR. $5,000.
High Desert Museum. Bend, OR. $25,204.
Home Gardening Project. Portland, OR. $1,000.
Idaho Conservation League. Boise, ID. $11,000.
National Audubon Society. New York, NY. $1,000.
The Nature Conservancy, Oregon Field Office. Portland, OR. $250.
Oregon Environmental Council. Portland, OR. $50.
Public Forestry Foundation. Eugene, OR. $10,000.
World Wildlife Fund. Washington, DC. $1,000.

Application process. *Initial contact:* Proposal to include:
1. Basic information about applicant organization.
2. Description of project, potential significance to community, anticipated costs, and sources of actual or potential support.
3. Financial statements.
4. Board of directors roster and relationship to the organization.
5. Copy of the IRS tax-exempt status determination letter.

When to apply: Anytime. The board meets in March, July, September, and December.
Materials available: Application guidelines, program policy statement.

Emphases. *Recipients:* Educational institutions, museums, non-profit organizations, religious organizations.
Types of support: Emergency funding, general purposes, matching funds, projects, seed money.
Geography: Oregon and northwestern states.

Limitations. *Recipients:* Individuals.

© 1995 Environmental Data Resources, Inc.

Nathan M. Ohrbach Foundation, Inc.

c/o Mitchell Rabbino
51 East 42nd Street, 17th Floor
New York, New York 10017
Tel: 212–682–8383
EIN: 136111585   Type: Independent
Contact: Caryl E. Ohrbach, President

History and philosophy. The Nathan M. Ohrbach Foundation was established in 1943. It makes grants in the areas of education, community development, medical research, cultural programs, youth, wildlife, and environment.

Officers and directors. *Officers:* Caryl E. Ohrbach, President; Lisa K. Ohrbach, Vice President; Suzan N. Ohrbach, Secretary; Barbara Kennedy Martin, Treasurer; Drummond M. Pike, Assistant Secretary/Treasurer. *Directors:* Barbara Kennedy Martin, Caryl E. Ohrbach, Lisa K. Ohrbach, Suzan N. Ohrbach, Mitchell W. Rabbino.

Financial data. Data for fiscal year ended April 30, 1993. *Assets:* $1,279,780 (M). *Total grants disbursed:* $67,000.

Environmental awards. *Recent grants:* 1993 grants included support for land conservation, wildlife preservation, and marine conservation.

Issues. Cli **Bio** **Lan** **Agr** **Wat** **Oce** **Ene** Was Tox Pop Dev

Funding analysis.

Fiscal year:	1993
Env grants disb:	$26,000
Number:	7
Range:	$2,500–$5,000
Median:	$3,000
Pct $ disb (env/total):	39

Recipients (1993 highest):	Number:	Dollars:
Life on the Water Theater	1	5,000
San Carlos Apache Tribe	1	5,000
The Wilderness Society	1	5,000
Earth Island Institute	1	3,000
Wolf Education & Research Center	1	3,000

Activity regions (1993):	Number:	Dollars:
U.S. West	5	18,000
U.S. not specified	1	5,000
U.S. Northwest	1	3,000

Sample grants (1993).
Dine CARE (Citizens Against Ruining Our Environment). Winslow, AZ. $2,500.
Earth Island Institute. San Francisco, CA. $3,000.
Life on the Water Theater. San Francisco, CA. $5,000.
Pesticide Education Center. San Francisco, CA. $2,500.
San Carlos Apache Tribe. San Carlos, AZ. $5,000.
The Wilderness Society. San Francisco, CA. $5,000.
Wolf Education & Research Center. Ketchum, ID. $3,000.

O

Application process. *Initial contact:* Letter to include:
1. Copy of IRS tax-exempt status determination letter.
2. Purpose of fund request.
3. Proposed use of funds.
4. Recent financial statements.

When to apply: Anytime. The board meets in April.

Emphases. *Recipients:* Educational institutions, nonprofit organizations, research institutions.
Activities: Innovative programs, research (medical).
Geography: Primarily New York and California.

Limitations. *Recipients:* Individuals.

The Ohrstrom Foundation

540 Madison Avenue
New York, New York 10022
Tel: 212–759–5380   Fax: 212–486–0935
EIN: 546039966   Type: Independent
Contact: George Ohrstrom, President

Alternate application address:
P.O. Box J
The Plains, Virginia
Tel: 703–253–5540
Contact: Colonel Dale Hogoboom, Administrator

History and philosophy. The Foundation was established in 1953 by members of the Ohrstrom family. It makes grants to pre-selected organizations in the areas of: education, civic affairs, conservation, education, health care and medical research, and museums.

Officers and directors. *Officers:* George Ohrstrom, President; Ricard R. Ohrstrom, Jr., Vice President; George L. Ohrstrom, Assistant Secretary; Palma Cifu, Treasurer; K. N. Levine, Assistant Secretary/Treasurer. *Trustees:* Magalen O. Bryant, Palma Cifu, George Ohrstrom, George L. Ohrstrom, Jr., Ricard R. Ohrstrom, Jr.

Financial data. Data for fiscal year ended May 31, 1992. *Assets:* $23,419,252 (M). *Total grants disbursed:* $910,260.

Environmental awards. *Recent grants:* 1992 grants included support for ecosystem preservation, river protection, wildlife, and education.

Issues. Cli Bio Lan Agr Wat Oce Ene Was Tox Pop Dev
         •   •   •   •   •   •

Funding analysis.

Fiscal year:	1991	1992
Env grants disb:	$361,000	$413,000
Number:	31	30
Range:	$500–$296,500	$500–$206,000
Median:	$1,000	$1,000
Pct $ disb (env/total):	44	45

Recipients (1992 highest):	Number:	Dollars:
Little River Foundation	2	330,000
Greater Yellowstone Coalition	1	25,000
River Foundation	1	10,000
National Fish and Wildlife Foundation	2	6,000
American Farmland Trust	1	5,000
Conservation Council of Virginia	1	5,000
Delta Environmental Land Trust Association	1	5,000

Activity regions (1992 highest):	Number:	Dollars:
U.S. not specified	8	341,000
U.S. Mid-Atlantic	9	26,500
U.S. Mountain	1	25,000
U.S. Southeast	3	11,000
International*	4	4,500

*Multiple regions or not specified.

Sample grants (1992).
African Wildlife Foundation. Washington, DC. $2,000.
American Farmland Trust. Washington, DC. $5,000.
Conservation Council of Virginia. Richmond, VA. $5,000.
Conservation International. Washington, DC. $1,500.
Friends of the National Zoo. Washington, DC. $2,500.
Izaak Walton League of America. Arlington, VA. $2,000.
Little River Foundation. Cincinnati, OH. $330,000.

Application process. *Initial contact:* The Foundation makes grants to pre-selected organizations only. No unsolicited applications accepted.

Emphases. *Recipients:* Pre-selected organizations only.
Activities: Land acquisition, research (medical).
Types of support: Annual campaigns, continuing support, emergency funding, endowments, equipment, facilities, matching funds, operating costs, seed money.
Geography: New York, Virginia.

Limitations. *Recipients:* Individuals.
Activities: Conferences, publications, research.
Types of support: Debt retirement, fellowships, loans, pilot projects, scholarships.

Spencer T. and Ann W. Olin Foundation

7701 Forsyth Boulevard, Suite 1040
St. Louis, Missouri 63105
Tel: 314–727–6202   Fax: 314–727–6157
EIN: 376044148   Type: Independent
Contact: Warren M. Shapleigh, President

History and philosophy. The Foundation was established in 1957 by Ann W. and Spencer T. Olin. The S. Truman Olin, Jr. Charitable Lead Trust and the Spencer T. Olin Charitable Lead Trust contribute to the Foundation. "Principal interests are in the fields of higher education, medical education and research, health services and facilities, and environmental conservation. Support is also given to community needs in the metropolitan St. Louis area, including cultural, civic, and welfare programs."

Officers and directors. *Officers:* Warren M. Shapleigh, President; Mary Olin Pritzlaff, Vice President; Eunice Olin Higgins, Secretary; J. Lester Willemetz, Treasurer; Marquita L. Kunce, Assistant Treasurer. *Trustees:* Eunice Olin Higgins, William W. Higgins, Rolla J. Mottaz, John C. Pritzlaff, Jr., Mary Olin Pritzlaff, Warren M. Shapleigh, Barbara Olin Taylor, F. Morgan Taylor, Jr., J. Lester Willemetz.

Financial data. Data for fiscal year ended December 31, 1992. *Assets:* $37,184,013 (M). *Gifts received:* $875,800. *Total grants disbursed:* $4,912,100.

Environmental awards. *Recent grants:* 1992 grants included support for species preservation and biodiversity issues.

Issues.   Cli   Bio   Lan   Agr   Wat   Oce   Ene   Was   Tox   Pop   Dev
                    •   •   •

Funding analysis.

Fiscal year:	1991	1992
Env grants disb:	$325,000	$382,500
Number:	2	3
Range:	$100,000–$225,000	$50,000–$232,500
Median:	$162,500	$100,000
Pct $ disb (env/total):	7	8

Recipients (1992):	Number:	Dollars:
The Nature Conservancy, Missouri Field Office	1	232,500
Missouri Botanical Garden	1	100,000
Desert Botanical Garden	1	50,000

Activity regions (1992):	Number:	Dollars:
U.S. Midwest	2	332,500
U.S. West	1	50,000

Sample grants (1992).
Desert Botanical Garden. Phoenix, AZ. $50,000.
Missouri Botanical Garden. St. Louis, MO. $100,000.
The Nature Conservancy, Missouri Field Office. St. Louis, MO. $232,500.

Application process. *Initial contact:* Brief letter to include:
1. Project description, including needs statement and timeline.
2. Budget including amount requested and other funding.
3. Most recent financial statement.
4. Copy of IRS tax-exempt status determination letter.

When to apply: The Foundation is currently fulfilling long-term commitments and not accepting new proposals.
Materials available: Annual report (includes "Interests and Guidelines" and "Application Procedures").

Emphases. *Activities:* Education (higher).
Types of support: General purposes, research.
Geography: St. Louis, Missouri.

Limitations. *Recipients:* Individuals, religious organizations.
Activities: Conferences, education (secondary), exhibits, seminars, workshops.

Types of support: Annual campaigns, debt retirement, endowments, facilities, fellowships, loans, matching funds, multi-year grants, operating costs, scholarships, travel expenses.

Onan Family Foundation
310 Interchange Plaza West
435 Ford Road, Suite 310
Minneapolis, Minnesota 55426
Tel: 612–544–4702   Fax: 612–544–4920
EIN: 416033631   Type: Independent
Contact: Susan J. Smith, Executive Director

History and philosophy. The Onan Family Foundation was established in 1942. For many years its major focus was on medical research. Its funding emphasis has since changed to meet the changing needs of the Twin Cities area. "David W. Onan, the founder, was a pioneer who held strong beliefs in free enterprise and personal generosity. He believed in defending the free market and fostering economic growth." To continue in David Onan's spirit, the Foundation emphasizes volunteerism and private support in the nonprofit community. Program areas are: Education, Social Welfare, Cultural and Civic Affairs, and Religion.

Officers and directors. *Officers:* David W. Onan, II, President and Treasurer; Bruce R. Smith, Secretary. *Trustees:* Judith O. Baragli, David W. Onan, II, David W. Onan, III, Bruce R. Smith.

Financial data. Data for fiscal year ended December 31, 1993. *Assets:* $5,861,065 (M). *Total grants disbursed:* $235,000.

Environmental awards. *Recent grants:* Two environmental grants in 1993 supported water resources and a local arboretum in Minnesota.

Issues.   Cli   Bio   Lan   Agr   Wat   Oce   Ene   Was   Tox   Pop   Dev
                    •   •

Funding analysis.

Fiscal year:	1992	1993
Env grants disb:	$12,500	$8,000
Number:	2	2
Range:	$2,500–$10,000	$3,000–$5,000
Median:	$6,250	$4,000
Pct $ disb (env/total):	6	3

Recipients (1993):	Number:	Dollars:
Freshwater Foundation	1	5,000
Minnesota Landscape Arboretum Foundation	1	3,000

Activity region (1993):	Number:	Dollars:
U.S. Great Lakes	2	8,000

Sample grants (1993).
Freshwater Foundation. Navarre, MN. $5,000.
Minnesota Landscape Arboretum Foundation. Chanhassen, MN. $3,000.

O

Application process. *Initial contact:* Full proposal to include:
1. Copy of tax-exempt status determination letter and 509(a)(1) classification.
2. Description of applicant organization, its history, objectives, and services.
3. Determination of quality, including how the applicant determines the needs for its services, and whether its activities meet that need.
4. Budget and current financial statement.
5. Current sources of all support, received and pending.

When to apply: The board of trustees meets twice a year in May and October. Requests should be sent well in advance.
Materials available: Annual report (includes "Grant Guidelines").

Emphases. *Recipients:* Nonprofit organizations.
Geography: Twin Cities metropolitan area.

Limitations. *Activities:* Advocacy, lobbying, political activities.
Types of support: Capital campaigns/expenses, endowments, travel expenses.

Orchard Foundation
P.O. Box 2587
South Portland, Maine 04116-2587
Tel: 207-799-0686   Fax: 207-799-0686
EIN: 046660214   Type: Company-sponsored
EGA member
Contact: Brigitte L. Kingsbury, Executive Director

History and philosophy. The Orchard Foundation was established in 1990 by Leigh Fibers, Inc. Program areas include: children's rights and welfare, the environment, family planning and reproductive rights.

Officers and directors. *Trustees:* M. Gordon Ehrlich, Carl P. Lehner, Peter Lehner, Philip Lehner.

Financial data. Data for fiscal year ended December 31, 1992. *Assets:* $1,477,855 (M). *Gifts received:* $850,625. *Total grants disbursed:* $393,95.

Environmental awards. *Program and interests:* The Foundation is interested in the preservation of aquatic systems, habitats, wildlife, and natural resources. It favors cooperative efforts among regional environmental groups.

Issues. *Cli Bio Lan Agr Wat Oce Ene Was Tox Pop Dev*

Application process. *Initial contact:* Letter of inquiry on letterhead signed by the executive director or board president and a proposal summary (1 page) to include:
1. Name and telephone number of project director.
2. Purpose of project, how it will be accomplished, proof of urgency of the project, and outcome expected.
3. Amount requested from the Foundation, budget of project, and amounts expected from other sources.

If requested, full proposal (4 pages, 4 copies) to include:
1. Problem statement.
2. Goals of project, plan of action, qualification of organization to fulfill plan, and a method of evaluation.
3. Preliminary income and expense budget for project (1 page).
4. Copy of IRS tax-exempt status determination letter.
5. List of organization officers and board of directors.
6. Audited financial statements and an annual report.

Send material, unbound, via first class mail.
When to apply: Deadline is August but mid-June is preferred.
Materials available: Application procedures and proposal guidelines.

Emphases. *Recipients:* Nonprofit organizations.
Types of support: Capital campaigns/expenses, operating costs, projects, seed money.
Geography: New York; New England. California and Florida if solicited by Foundation.

Limitations. *Recipients:* Individuals, religious organizations.
Types of support: Annual campaigns, endowments, fellowships, loans, scholarships, travel expenses.

Ottinger Foundation
265 North Pleasant Street, Suite 2
Amherst, Massachusetts 01002-1729
Tel: 413-256-0349   Fax: 413-256-3536
EIN: 136118423   Type: Independent
EGA member
Contact: Margaret E. Gage, Executive Director

History and philosophy. The Ottinger Foundation was established in 1945 by Lawrence Ottinger. It supports projects that promote environmental preservation, energy conservation, world peace, democratic participation, and economic justice. Projects with a strong component of citizen activism are preferred. The Foundation encourages submission of innovative proposals that address causes rather than symptoms of problems.

Officers and directors. *Officers:* Karen Heath, Chair; Louise L. Ottinger, President; Richard L. Ottinger, Vice President; William Zabel, Secretary/Treasurer. *Directors:* Karen Heath, David Hunter, Jennifer Ottinger, June Godfrey Ottinger, Lawrence Ottinger, LeaAnne Ottinger, Louise L. Ottinger, Randy Ottinger, Richard L. Ottinger, Ronald Ottinger, Sharon Kalemkiarian Ottinger, Peter Smith, Betsy Taylor, William Zabel.

Financial data. Data for fiscal years ended December 31, 1992 and 1993. *Assets (1992):* $3,387,394 (U). *Total grants authorized (1993):* $220,000.

Environmental awards. *Program and interests:* Areas of interest are:

- Energy.
- Military toxics.
- Coalition building and organizing.

Issues. *Cli Bio Lan Agr Wat Oce Ene Was Tox Pop Dev*

Funding analysis.

Fiscal year:	1991	1993
Env grants auth:	$52,500	$36,000
Number:	8	4
Range:	$2,500–$10,000	$1,000–$15,000
Median:	$6,250	$10,000
Pct $ auth (env/total):	29	16

Recipients (1993):	Number:	Dollars:
Legal Environmental Assistance Foundation	1	15,000
Environmental Health Coalition	1	10,000
Pace University School of Law	1	10,000
Kentucky Environmental Foundation, Inc.	1	1,000

Activity regions (1993):	Number:	Dollars:
U.S. Southeast	1	15,000
U.S. West	2	11,000
New York/New Jersey	1	10,000

Sample grants (1993).
Environmental Health Coalition. San Diego, CA. $10,000. To support the cleanup of military toxic waste sites in the San Diego area.
Kentucky Environmental Foundation, Inc. Berea, KY. $1,000. For the Chemical Weapons Working Group.
Legal Environmental Assistance foundation. Tallahassee, FL. $15,000. General support.
Pace University School of Law. White Plains, NY. $10,000. For the Pace Energy Project.

Application process. *Initial contact:* Full proposal (10 pages) to include:
1. Clear statement of need for support.
2. Project goals.
3. Action plan for achieving those goals. (Detailed notes on strategy and project implementation.)
4. Program evaluation.
5. IRS tax-exempt status determination letter.
6. Staff and organization's qualifications for carrying out the program.
7. List of other sources of financial support already committed.
8. Project and organizational line-item budget(s).
9. List of other organizations involved in similar programs and explanation of how the proposed project is different.

When to apply: Anytime. The board of directors meets twice a year.
Materials available: "Ottinger Foundation Guidelines," grants list.

Emphases. *Recipients:* Nonprofit organizations.
Activities: Activism, advocacy, citizen participation, collaborative efforts, political activities.
Types of support: Continuing support, leveraging funds, pilot projects.
Geography: United States, with an emphasis on national programs.

Limitations. *Recipients:* Educational institutions, individuals, museums, public agencies.

Activities: Audiovisual materials, conferences, media projects, publications, research (scholarly).
Types of support: Capital campaigns/expenses, endowments, facilities.
Geography: International projects, local programs.

Outdoor Industry Conservation Alliance

c/o Recreation Equipment, Inc. (REI)
P.O. Box 1938
Sumner, Washington 98390–0800
Tel: 707–961–0776
Type: Independent
EGA member
Contacts: Ron Nadeau, President
Kathleen Beamer, Grants Coordinator

History and philosophy. Founded in 1989, the Alliance is "made up of companies in the outdoor industry who want to do something to preserve the environment. Together, the money contributed by the Alliance members to individuals and organizations working to save our environment can make a difference."

Membership is open to "businesses based on self-propelled or muscle-powered outdoor activities, whose livelihood depends on conserving our outdoor environment, from all aspects of the outdoor industry." Each member-business makes a minimum annual donation of $10,000. The Alliance then seeks selected conservation groups that have developed programs to address important outdoor environmental issues. The Alliance will fund effective, special programs that might not happen without the Alliance's combined resources.

Financial data. Not available.

Environmental awards. *Program and interests:* Criteria for funding include:

- Grassroots.
- Volunteer based.
- Citizen action orientation.
- Muscle-powered.
- Lobbying for specific projects.
- Protection of endangered species habitats.
- Projects that begin and end.

Recent grants: Grants since 1989 have included support for land conservation, wilderness, mountains, forests, wild river protection, water use, coastal issues, and recreation.

Issues. Cli Bio Lan Agr Wat Oce Ene Was Tox Pop Dev

Sample grants (1989–92).
Appalachian Trail Conference. Harpers Ferry, WV. $55,000. For acquisition of lands adjacent to the trail.
Friends of the River Foundation. San Francisco, CA. $39,960. To protect recreational resources of the Colorado River in the Grand Canyon.

O

Friends of the Shawangunks. Accord, NY. $30,000. To protect lands in the Shawangunks Mountains.

Greater Yellowstone Coalition. Bozeman, MT. $20,000. To safeguard public recreational lands.

Ice Age Park and Trail Foundation. Sheboygan, WI. $38,800. For a new volunteer outreach program on this scenic Wisconsin trail.

Natural Resources Council of Maine. Augusta, ME. $18,572. To prevent the loss of recreational opportunities in the North Woods.

The Trust for Public Land. Seattle, WA. $15,000. For work to acquire the popular Peshastin Pinnacles climbing area in Washington.

The Utah Wilderness Coalition. Salt Lake City, UT. $40,000. To protect Boulder Mountain.

Western Ancient Forest Campaign. Washington, DC. $55,000. For lobbying efforts to protect remaining western U.S. ancient forests.

Application process. *Initial contact:* Prospective applicants must be recommended and formally endorsed by a member company. Endorsement to include name, address, telephone, and contact person. Direct endorsement to grant coordinator Kathleen Beamer at REI. She will then contact the recommended group and request a proposal. Unsolicited proposals will not be reviewed.
When to apply: Anytime.
Materials available: Brochures, *Works in Progress* (newsletter).

Emphases. *Recipients:* Nonprofit organizations.
Activities: Activism, advocacy, citizen participation, lobbying, projects, volunteerism.

Limitations. *Activities:* Education (traditional environmental projects such as the building of a nature center), media projects, research.

The Overbrook Foundation

521 Fifth Avenue, Room 1501
New York, New York 10175
Tel: 212–661–8710   Fax: 212–661–8664
EIN: 13608860   Type: Independent
Contact: Sheila McGoldrick, Corresponding Secretary

History and philosophy. The Overbrook Foundation was created in 1948 by Frank Altschul, chairman of the General American Investors Company. Grantmaking reflects the family's interests in arts and culture, child welfare, civil rights, community funds, conservation and environment, education, Jewish welfare, hospitals, international affairs, and social services. The Foundation prefers to award smaller grants, often for continuing support, in order to fund a larger number of organizations.

Officers and directors. *Officers:* Arthur G. Altshul, President and Treasurer; Edith A. Graham, Margaret A. Lang, Vice Presidents; Diana L. Altshul, Secretary. *Directors:* Arthur G. Altshul, Stephen F. Altshul, Edith A. Graham, Robert C. Graham, Jr., Frances A. Labaree, Margaret A. Lang.

Financial data. Data for fiscal year ended December 31, 1992. *Assets:* $76,113,154 (M). *Gifts received:* $537,700. *Total grants disbursed:* $3,167,357.

Environmental awards. *Recent grants:* 1992 grants included support for land conservation, rainforest preservation, watersheds, toxics issues, urban environment, a botanical garden, and a zoo.

Issues.   Cli   Bio   Lan   Agr   Wat   Oce   Ene   Was   Tox   Pop   Dev
                    •   •   •   •   •

Funding analysis.

Fiscal year:	1990	1992
Env grants disb:	$336,500	$353,000
Number:	23	21
Range:	$500–$50,000	$500–$55,000
Median:	$5,000	$5,000
Pct $ disb (env/total):	12	11

Recipients (1992 highest):	Number:	Dollars:
The New York Botanical Garden	1	55,000
Natural Resources Defense Council	1	54,250
Conservation International	1	50,000
Environmental Defense Fund	1	40,000
Stamford Museum and Nature Center	1	37,500

Activity regions (1992):	Number:	Dollars:
New York/New Jersey	10	225,000
International*	3	52,000
U.S. Northeast	2	38,500
U.S. not specified	5	35,000
Alaska	1	2,500

*Multiple regions or not specified.

Sample grants (1992).
Alaska Conservation Foundation. Anchorage, AK. $2,500.
Conservation International. Washington, DC. $50,000.
Council on the Environment of New York City. New York, NY. $2,000.
Earth Action Network, Inc. Norwalk, CT. $5,000.
Environmental Defense Fund. New York, NY. $40,000.
INFORM. New York, NY. $15,000.
National Toxics Campaign Fund. Boston, MA. $5,000.
Natural Resources Defense Council. New York NY. $54,250.
The Nature Conservancy, Connecticut Chapter. Middletown, CT. $1,000.
The New York Botanical Garden. Bronx, NY. $55,000.
NYZS/The Wildlife Conservation Society. Bronx, NY. $27,250.
The Trust for Public Land. New York, NY. $30,000.
Westchester Land Trust, Inc. Bedford Hills, NY. $10,000.

Application process. *Initial contact:* Letter describing the organization, its activities, and the proposed project, accompanied by a copy of IRS tax-exempt status determination letter.
When to apply: Anytime. The board usually meets in April and November.

Emphases. *Types of support:* General purposes.
Geography: Primarily Connecticut and New York.

Limitations. *Recipients:* Individuals.

The David and Lucile Packard Foundation

300 Second Street, Suite 200
Los Altos, California 94022
Tel: 415–948–7658   Fax: 415–948–5793
EIN: 942278431   Type: Independent
EGA member
Contact: Jeanne C. Sedgwick, Program Officer

History and philosophy. The Packard Foundation is a family foundation, established in 1964 by David Packard, one of the founders of the Hewlett-Packard Company, and his late wife, Lucile Salter Packard.

Current program areas are: Science (including Ocean Science, Fellowships for Science and Engineering, and science programs at historically black colleges and universities); Center for the Future of Children; Population; Conservation; Local Community; and Special Areas.

Officers and directors. *Officers:* David Packard, Chairman; Susan Packard Orr, President; Nancy Packard Burnett, David W. Packard, Julie E. Packard, Vice Presidents; Barbara Wright, Secretary; Edwin E. van Bronkhorst, Treasurer; Colburn S. Wilbur, Executive Director. *Trustees:* Edwin E. van Bronkhorst, Nancy Packard Burnett, Robin Chandler Duke, Robert J. Glaser, M.D., Dean O. Morton, Susan Packard Orr, David Packard, David W. Packard, Julie E. Packard, Frank H. Roberts.

Financial data. Data for fiscal year ended December 31, 1993. *Assets:* $1,271,780,000 (M). *Total grants disbursed:* $55,510,000.

Environmental awards. *Program and interests:* The Foundation concentrates its Conservation Program grants in five principal areas:

- Habitat protection.

  Focus is on wetlands protection, both in California and at the national policy level, and important coastal and marine habitats (including marine sanctuaries).

- Conservation of marine fisheries.
- Preservation of important open space.

  Focus is on providing support to the national land trust movement; start-up support for California land trusts; local (Bay Area to Monterey) growth management and greenbelt efforts; and limited funds for acquisition of important properties in habitats of interest.

- Initiatives combining the population and environment areas that have the potential for broad impacts.
- Wetlands and fisheries conservation and planning in Mexico.

In 1993 The Foundation awarded its largest single grant to the Monterey Bay Aquarium Research Institute (MBARI), founded in 1987 by David Packard. Part of the $20.6 million grant was for research on environmental issues, although the grant itself was not awarded within the Conservation Program.

Issues. Cli Bio Lan Agr Wat Oce Ene Was Tox Pop Dev
•   •   •   •   •   •   •   •   •   •   •

Funding analysis.

Fiscal year:	1991	1993
Env grants auth:	$9,545,400	$28,418,863
Number:	37	62
Range:	$6,000–$8,500,000	$720–$20,582,000
Median:	$20,000	$27,450
Pct $ auth (env/total):	29	43

Recipients (1993 highest):	Number:	Dollars:
Monterey Bay Aquarium Research Institute	1	20,582,000
Monterey Bay Aquarium	2	4,054,000
Stanford University	1	670,000
Michigan State University	1	500,000
Scripps Institution of Oceanography	1	500,000

Activity regions (1993 highest):	Number:	Dollars:
U.S. West	33	26,795,922
U.S. Great Lakes	1	500,000
U.S. not specified	11	396,000
Mexico and Central America	6	340,000
International*	2	95,000
U.S. Northwest	2	95,000

*Multiple regions or not specified.

Sample grants (1993).

American Fisheries Society. Bethesda, MD. $30,000. To support the Fisheries Action Network program activities.

Center for Marine Conservation. San Francisco, CA. $80,000 (2 years). To provide support for the project, "Creating a Model Sanctuary on the California Coast."

Centro Ecologico De Sonora. Mermosillo, Sonora, Mexico. $50,000. Support to develop management plans for three coastal and wetlands sites on the Sea of Cortez within the Sonora, Mexico system of proposed protected areas.

The Marine Resources Management Center, Inc. Gladstone, OR. $20,000. To support the West Coast F.I.S.H. Habitat Education Program.

The Nature Conservancy, California Field Office. San Francisco, CA. $20,000. To support the expanded Ricelands Project.

Point Reyes Bird Observatory. Stinson Beach, CA. $60,000 (2 years). For continued support of the Pacific Flyway Project, including its census of shorebird use of the flooded ricelands in the Central Valley.

Application process. *Initial contact:* Short letter of inquiry. If the project meets Foundation guidelines, a full proposal will be requested. Full proposal to include:

1. Cover letter. Brief descriptions of applicant organization and proposed program; amount of request; applicant organization's legal name, address, and telephone.
2. Background information. History and purpose of organization; people and groups organization serves.
3. Specific request. Description of proposed program and its objectives; evidence showing a need for the program and its value; geographic area to be served; an outline of phases of program from beginning to end; anticipated methods of evaluation.
4. Personnel. The agency personnel who will implement program and their qualifications; names and principal affiliations of directors, senior staff, and trustees.

5. Financial information. Detailed program budget showing other sources and amounts of funding; amount requested; financial statement from prior fiscal year, preferably audited; statement of sources of organization's funds, both public and private; and project budget.
6. Addenda. Copy of IRS tax-exempt status determination letter, documentation that proposal is supported by organization's board of directors, and any other supporting materials.

When to apply: Deadlines are March 15, June 15, September 15, and December 15. The trustees meet quarterly.

Materials available: Annual report (includes "Applying for a Grant," "What the Application Should Cover").

Emphases. *Recipients:* Nonprofit organizations.
Activities: Activism, advocacy, capacity building, citizen participation, collaborative efforts, conferences, conflict resolution, feasibility studies, fieldwork, innovative programs, inventories, land acquisition, planning, policy analysis/development, symposia/colloquia, technical assistance, training.
Types of support: Continuing support, general purposes, leveraging funds, loans, matching funds, multi-year grants, operating costs, pilot projects, program-related investments, technical assistance.
Geography: In the United States, projects on the national, state (California), and local levels. Local grants, to organizations that serve the people of San Mateo, Santa Clara, Santa Cruz, and Monterey counties. Occasionally staff-initiated grants are made for Hawaii. In Mexico, support for wetlands and fisheries only.

Limitations. *Recipients:* Individuals.
Activities: Education (public).
Geography: International projects (other than Mexico).

Patagonia, Inc.
259 West Santa Clara
Ventura, California 93001
Tel: 805–643–8616   Fax: 805–643–6384
EIN: 953526345   Type: Company-sponsored
EGA member
Contact: Libby Ellis, Environmental Grants Director

Application address:
Patagonia, Inc.
Grants Program
P.O. Box 150
Ventura, California 93002

History and philosophy. Patagonia, an outdoor-products manufacturer, commits 10 percent of its pre-tax profits or 1 percent of its sales, whichever is greater, to environmental causes. "Since 1984, our tithing program has distributed funds to over 350 different organizations. Rather than dilute the impact of our donations by spreading them thinly to a variety of causes, we have chosen to aim our dollars directly toward environmental issues. Patagonia products are designed for outdoor use and we feel a strong responsibility and commitment to keep the environment in its natural state for future generations. We are particularly interested in supporting environmental groups which operate at the most basic grassroots levels and which share our concern and sense of urgency about the state of the Earth."

Officers and directors. *Owner:* Yvon Chouinard.

Financial data. Data for fiscal year ended April 30, 1994. *Total grants disbursed:* $1,192,868.

Environmental awards. *Program and interests:* Patagonia makes grants and donates clothing to organizations working to support environmental issues. The Foundation's main priority is:

- Habitat protection.
  - Land acquisition, with special attention to endangered or protected species.
  - Habitat improvement.

Patagonia also has a strong interest in:

- Wild river preservation.
  - Efforts to block dam construction.

Other interests include issues that have an impact on habitat protection: toxic waste, acid rain, pesticide use, deforestation, ozone depletion, global warming, air and water pollution.

Issues. Cli Bio Lan Agr Wat Oce Ene Was Tox Pop Dev
• • • • • • • • • • •

Funding analysis.

Fiscal year:	1994
Env grants disb:	$1,072,411
Number:	240
Range:	$50–$72,000
Median:	$2,500
Pct $ disb (env/total):	90

Recipients (1994 highest):	*Number:*	*Dollars:*
Public Media Center	1	72,000
The Wildlands Project	1	30,000
Foundation for Deep Ecology	1	27,450
Mineral Policy Center	1	25,000
Alaska Conservation Foundation	1	20,000
Outdoor Industry Conservation Alliance	1	20,000

Activity regions (1994 highest):	*Number:*	*Dollars:*
U.S. not specified	24	211,150
U.S. Mountain	51	198,415
U.S. West	50	193,045
Canada	8	129,252
U.S. Northwest	27	118,934

Sample grants (1994).
Pesticide Action Network (PAN), North America Regional Office. San Francisco, CA. $5,000. To end the use of pesticides in agriculture and all other applications. PAN advocates and promotes the adoption of safe and sustainable pesticide use.
Preserve Appalachian Wilderness. Bondville, VT. $3,500. To protect and restore the eastern forests of America. Educating people to become active in preserving the ecosystems.
Snake River Alliance Education Fund. Boise, ID. $5,000. For support of work to end the disposal of spent nuclear fuel in Idaho. A watchdog political activist group which has launched a campaign in Idaho as well as the rest of the United States, to educate the public in preparation for spent fuel hearings.

White Earth Land Recovery Project. White Earth, MN. $5,000. To help recover Ojibwe land that has been taken from the Ojibwe people through unethical tax foreclosures, treaty abrogations and property theft. The White Earth Reservation consists of 837,000 acres of pine, rolling hills, prairie, hardwoods, marshlands and lakes. Only 8 percent of those acres are owned by the native peoples.

Wildlife Damage Review. Tucson, AZ. $5,000. To halt the destructive actions of Animal Damage Control (ADC). The ADC is responsible for the government-sponsored killing of wildlife on public lands. These killings threaten to destroy entire ecosystems by altering the predator-prey relationship.

Application process. *Initial contact:* Proposal (3 typewritten pages) that is short, personal, and to the point. Proposal to include:
1. Who you are.
2. What your mission is.
3. What you've accomplished.
4. How you're going to achieve your goals.
5. How Patagonia might fit into your overall financial scheme.
6. Copy of IRS tax-exempt status determination letter.

No telephone inquiries, please.
When to apply: January or August.
Materials available: "Grants Program."

Emphases. *Recipients:* Nonprofit organizations.
Activities: Activism, advocacy.
Types of support: Clothing donations.

Limitations. *Activities:* Media projects, research (scientific).

Amelia Peabody Charitable Fund
201 Devonshire Street
Boston, Massachusetts 02110-1401
Tel: 617-451-6178
EIN: 237364949   Type: Independent
EGA member
Contact: Jo Anne Borek, Executive Director

History and philosophy. The Amelia Peabody Charitable Fund was established in 1942. Its purpose is to assist local charitable and educational organizations, with an emphasis on hospitals, cultural programs, educational institutions, and environmental issues.

Officers and directors. *Trustees:* Jo Anne Borek, Richard A. Leahy, J. Elisabeth Rice, Harry F. Rice, Patricia E. Rice.

Financial data. Data for fiscal year ended December 31, 1992. *Assets:* $106,140,000 (U).* *Gifts received:* $9,776. *Total grants disbursed:* $4,686,264.

*As reported by the Fund.

Environmental awards. *Program and interests:* The Fund has no specific annual allocation for environmental grants. "Proposals are judged individually based on their merit without regard to whether they are necessarily environmental."

Recent grants: 1992 grants included support for land and water conservation, species preservation, freshwater quality, and marine topics.

Issues. Cli Bio Lan Agr Wat Oce Ene Was Tox Pop Dev
             •   •   •   •   •   •

Funding analysis.

Fiscal year:	1990	1992
Env grants disb:	$239,000	$130,300
Number:	11	9
Range:	$1,000–$100,000	$1,000–$50,000
Median:	$15,000	$5,000
Pct $ disb (env/total):	5	3

Recipients (1992 highest):	Number:	Dollars:
Natural Resources Council of Maine	1	50,000
Massachusetts Audubon Society	1	25,000
New England Aquarium	1	25,000
Laudholm Trust	1	15,000
Institute for Energy and Environmental Research	1	5,000
The Nature Conservancy, Headquarters	1	5,000

Activity regions (1992):	Number:	Dollars:
U.S. Northeast	6	119,300
U.S. not specified	2	10,000
International*	1	1,000

*Multiple regions or not specified.

Sample grants (1993).
Coalition for a Better Acre. Lowell, MA. $4,000.
Nashua River Watershed Coalition. Lunenburg, MA. $7,500.
New England Wild Flower Society. Framingham, MA. $75,000.

Application process. *Initial contact:* Proposal to include:
1. Nature of the nonprofit organization.
2. Outline of the project.
3. Financial statement for the past year.
4. Amount requested.
5. Other sources of funding.
6. Copy of the IRS tax-exempt status determination letter.

When to apply: Deadlines are April 1, July 1, and October 1. The trustees meet in May, August, and November. Reapply no more than every two years. If sending a video tape, provide a stamped return envelope.
Materials available: "Guidelines For Grantseekers."

Emphases. *Recipients:* Educational institutions, nonprofit organizations, research institutions.
Activities: Education, research (medical).
Types of support: Capital campaigns/expenses, endowments, equipment, facilities, matching funds, mortgage reduction, single-year grants.
Geography: New England, primarily the Greater Boston area.

Limitations. *Recipients:* Botanical gardens, individuals, public agencies, religious organizations.

© 1995 Environmental Data Resources, Inc.

Activities: Activism, advocacy, audiovisual materials, capacity building, citizen participation, collaborative efforts, conferences, conflict resolution, demonstration programs, direct services, exhibits, expeditions/tours, feasibility studies, fieldwork, fundraising, inventories, litigation, lobbying, planning, policy analysis/development, political activities, publications, seminars, symposia/colloquia, technical assistance, training.
Types of support: Advertising campaigns, annual campaigns, continuing support, general purposes, indirect costs, internships, lectureships, loans, membership campaigns, multi-year grants, operating costs, pilot projects, program-related investments, seed money, start-up costs, technical assistance, travel expenses.
Geography: Programs outside the United States.

Peninsula Community Foundation

1700 South El Camino Real, Suite 300
San Mateo, California 94402
Tel: 415–358–9369 Fax: 415–358–9817
EIN: 942746687   Type: Community
Contact: Jennifer A. Sims, Director of Programs

History and philosophy. The Peninsula Community Foundation was established in 1964 to serve San Mateo and northern Santa Clara counties—one of the most ethnically and economically diverse areas in the United States. The Foundation considers itself a "catalyst, convener, initiator, and grantor," dedicated to the quality of life on the San Francisco Peninsula. Its program areas are: Arts and Culture, Education, Civic/Public Benefit, Health, and Human Services. In addition to giving grants, the Foundation provides management assistance and funding information.

Officers and directors. *Officer:* Hon. Thomas M. Jenkins, Chair. *Directors:* Tom Bailard, Hugh C. Burroughs, T. Jack Foster, Jr., Albert J. Horn, Esq., Hon. Thomas M. Jenkins, Charles B. Johnson, Karen Olson, John P. Renshaw, Gordon Russell, William Wilson III, Rosemary Young.

Financial data. Data for fiscal year ended December 31, 1993. *Assets:* $62,000,000 (U) (est.). *Total grants disbursed:* $3,980,000.

Environmental awards. *Program and interests:* The Foundation funds few environmental programs. It only considers requests that address needs in the geographic area specified. Local environmental programs involving children have the highest priority.

Issues. Cli Bio• Lan• Agr Wat• Oce• Ene Was• Tox Pop• Dev

Funding analysis.§

Fiscal year:	1991	1992
Env grants auth:	$242,000	$39,940
Number:	28	6
Range:	$100–$100,900	$450–$17,000
Median:	$1,200	$3,495
Pct $ disb (env/total):	6	1

Recipients (1992):	Number:	Dollars:
Peninsula Open Space Trust	1	17,000
Environmental Volunteers, Inc.	1	15,000
Coyote Point Museum	2	6,990
East Palo Alto Historical and Agricultural Society	1	500
Menlo-Atherton High School	1	450

Activity region (1992):	Number:	Dollars:
U.S. West	6	39,940

§Analysis for 1991 includes designated, donor-advised, and unrestricted grants; for 1992 includes unrestricted grants only.

Sample grants (1992).
Environmental Volunteers, Inc. Palo Alto, CA. $15,000. Support for the "SHARE in Nature" program recruiting and training community volunteers who provide environmental education in the public schools.
Menlo-Atherton High School. Menlo Park, CA. $450. Support for an all-school performance by the Youth for Environmental Sanity (YES!) troupe.

Application process. *Initial contact:* Letter of inquiry (2 pages) to include answers to these questions:
1. Description of project and the needs to be met.
2. Description of population to be served.
3. Is project new, is it relative to the organizations goals.
4. What are expected outcomes what is the evaluation process?
5. Project cost and portion being requested from Foundation.
6. Compare to other agencies active in this area.
7. Will you be collaborating with other agencies?
8. What are the qualifications of the key personnel?

Append copy of IRS tax-exempt status determination letter.
When to apply: Anytime. The distribution committee meets quarterly, in February, May, August, and November.
Materials available: Annual report, "Program Guidelines and Application Procedures."

Emphases. *Recipients:* Nonprofit organizations, public agencies.
Activities: Education, innovative programs.
Types of support: Pilot projects, projects, single-year grants. (Multi-year grants will be considered depending on the goals of the project and the results.)
Geography: San Mateo and northern Santa Clara counties only.

Limitations. *Recipients:* Individuals, religious organizations, research institutions.
Activities: Activism, advocacy, conferences, conflict resolution, direct services, exhibits, expeditions/tours, feasibility studies, fieldwork, fundraising, inventories, land acquisition, litigation, lobbying, networking, planning, policy analysis/development, political activities, publications, research, seminars, symposia/colloquia, technical assistance, training, volunteerism, workshops.
Types of support: Advertising campaigns, annual campaigns, capital campaigns/expenses, computer hardware, continuing support, debt retirement, emergency funding, endowments, equipment, facilities, fellowships, general purposes, indirect costs, internships, lectureships, leveraging funds, loans, maintenance, matching funds, membership campaigns, mortgage reduction, multi-year grants, operating costs, professorships, program-related investments, scholarships, start-up costs, technical assistance, travel expenses.

The William Penn Foundation
1630 Locust Street
Philadelphia, Pennsylvania 19103–6305
Tel: 215–732–5114   Fax: 215–732–8780
EIN: 231503488   Type: Independent
EGA member
Contact: Kenneth S. Brecher, President

History and philosophy. The William Penn Foundation was established in 1945 by Otto Haas and his wife Phoebe. Haas (1872–1960) emigrated to Philadelphia in 1901, where he was a significant figure in the tanning industry. The mission of the Foundation is to improve the quality of life in the Delaware Valley. Program areas are: Human Development, Culture, Community Fabric, and Environment.

Officers and directors. *Officers:* Kenneth S. Brecher, President; Harry E. Cerino, Vice President for Programs; Eric R. Aird, Vice President for Finance and Treasurer. *Directors:* Kenneth S. Brecher, Ida K. Chen, Gloria Twine Chisum, Graham S. Finney, David W. Haas, Frederick R. Haas, Janet F. Haas, John O. Haas, Melinda A. Haas, Nancy B. Haas, William D. Haas, Phoebe A. Haddon, Barbara H. Hanrahan, Philip C. Herr, II, Stephanie W. Naidoff, Edmund B. Spaeth, Jr., Anita A. Summers.

Financial data.* Data for fiscal year ended December 31, 1993. *Assets:* $673,000,000 (M) (est.). *Total grants disbursed:* $35,770,176.

*Grants include matching gifts.

Environmental awards. *Program and interests:* In the tradition of William Penn, who helped ensure that parks and open space were an integral part of Philadelphia's design, the Foundation has long been active in preserving and improving the natural resources of the Philadelphia area. In 1986 the Board adopted Environment as one of its four major grantmaking categories. It also extended the geographic region of interest from the six-county Philadelphia metropolitan area to the much larger "natural support area" on which the city and its suburbs depend. At that time the Foundation's two goals were to improve the pattern of urban growth and development by preserving open space in the cities and by enhancing public parks, and to protect prime agricultural and other open land in the less developed parts of this region.

In 1989 The Foundation made the Delaware River the focus of almost half its environmental grantmaking over a five-year period. The new, cooperative effort to save the Delaware comprises:

- Land preservation.
- Creation of a greenway along the river and its tributaries.
- Development of an environmental ethic through education.
- Citizen participation in planning and monitoring activities affecting the river's health.

Other environmental priorities include:

- Urban environment in the six-county region.
- Open land preservation in southeastern Pennsylvania and southern New Jersey.

Recent grants: In addition to the above programs, the Foundation concluded a three-year initiative for the global environment in 1993. Grants "addressed international issues of importance for environmental protection, including population growth and energy consumption."

Issues.   Cli   Bio   Lan   Agr   Wat   Oce   Ene   Was   Tox   Pop   Dev
             •   •   •   •   •   •   •   •

Funding analysis.

Fiscal year:	1992*	1993**
Env grants auth or disb:	$1,336,006	$2,745,000
Number:	19	39
Range:	$2,300–$286,700	$3,500–$500,000
Median:	$50,000	$50,000
Pct $ disb (env/total):	–	8

*Based on grants authorized.
**Based on grants disbursed.

Recipients (1993 highest):	Number:	Dollars:
Pennsylvania Horticultural Society	2	545,000
Bucks County Conservancy	3	360,000
American Littoral Society	4	205,000
Lancaster Farmland Trust	2	180,000
New Jersey Conservation Foundation	2	173,739

Activity regions (1993):	Number:	Dollars:
U.S. Mid-Atlantic	28	2,080,962
New York/New Jersey	11	664,038

Sample grants (1993).*

American Littoral Society, Inc. Highlands, NJ. $200,000 (2 years). To continue a citizen water quality monitoring program on the Delaware River and its tributaries.

Bucks County Conservancy. Doylestown, PA. $330,000 (3 years). For a greenway project on the Delaware River.

Caribbean Natural Resources Institute. St. Croix, VI. $115,200. To involve more indigenous natural resource experts in the issues of the global environment and for its ongoing work in coral reef monitoring.

Delaware and Raritan Greenway, Inc. Princeton, NJ. $30,000. For a public education program on a freshwater tidal wetland.

Girl Scouts of Delaware County. Media, PA. $50,000 (2 years). For an environmental education program in five low-income school districts.

Lancaster Farmland Trust. Lancaster, PA. $150,000. Toward the agricultural easement acquisition fund.

New Jersey Conservation Foundation. Morristown, NJ. $206,000 (3 years). For a stream valleys/open land protection program in southern New Jersey.

Pennsylvania Environmental Council. Philadelphia, PA. $300,000 (3 years). To assist in creating environmental advisory councils throughout southeastern Pennsylvania.

WHYY, Inc. Philadelphia, PA. $245,000 (2 years). A declining grant for partial support to continue the environmental radio program *Earthtalk*.

World Resources Institute. Washington, DC. $170,000 (3 years). To develop support for alternatives to greenhouse gas-producing technologies.

*Sample grants represent either new awards or disbursements on grants awarded in previous years.

© 1995 Environmental Data Resources, Inc.

Application process. *Initial contact:* Full proposal to include:
Summary outline (1 page).
1. Agency name, address, telephone.
2. Names of contact, executive director.
3. Objective, target population, major activities, timetable.
4. Grant amount requested, and total project budget.
5. Other sources of support.
6. Agency's total income in the past fiscal year.

Information about the agency.
1. Brief historical sketch.
2. Statement of current goals and services.
3. Most recent annual report.

Complete description of proposed project.
1. Problem addressed, need for project, target population.
2. Activities to be carried out and timetable.
3. Staff required and their qualifications.
4. Clear statement of what will be accomplished.
5. Criteria for evaluation.

Complete financial information.
1. Detailed budget for income and expense of project.
2. Funds on hand or pledged and funds potentially available.
3. Plans for continuing support.

Attachments.
1. Copy of IRS tax-exempt status determination letter.
2. List of officers and directors of applicant organization.
3. Copy of most recent annual report and financial statement (audited if available).

When to apply: Anytime.
Materials available: Annual report, "Foundation Priorities and Grant Application Procedures" (brochure).

Emphases. *Recipients:* Botanical gardens, educational institutions, museums, nonprofit organizations, public agencies, zoos.
Activities: Citizen participation, direct services, education, land acquisition.
Types of support: Capital campaigns/expenses, equipment, facilities, multi-year grants, pilot projects, seed money.
Geography: Greater Philadelphia only, including southern Pennsylvania, northeastern Maryland, northern Delaware, and southern and western New Jersey (south of Delaware Water Gap).

Limitations. *Recipients:* Individuals, research institutions.
Activities: Conferences, expeditions/tours, lobbying, political activities, research, seminars, symposia/colloquia.
Types of support: Advertising campaigns, annual campaigns, debt retirement, endowments, fellowships, general purposes, internships, lectureships, loans, professorships, program-related investments, scholarships.

James C. Penney Foundation

1633 Broadway, 39th Floor
New York, New York 10019
Tel: 212–830–7490 Fax: 212–830–7509
EIN: 136114301 Type: Independent
EGA member
Contact: Anne Romasco, Managing Director

History and philosophy. "The James C. Penney Foundation is a small family foundation established in 1954 by J. C. Penney and Caroline A. Penney. The Foundation continues the philanthropic spirit of its founders and their vision of a society which honors the dignity of the individual and the belief that by working together people can make a difference in achieving basic human rights and a secure future."

The Foundation focuses on three main areas: Strengthening Youth and the Family, Community Economic Development, and Environment/Human Habitat.

Officers and directors. *Officers:* Carol P. Guyer, President; Mary Frances P. Wagley, Vice President and Treasurer; Andrew W. Bisset, Secretary. *Directors:* Andrew W. Bisset, Carol P. Guyer, Grant Guyer, Neal Keny-Guyer, Anne Paxton Wagley, James F. Wagley, Mary Frances P. Wagley.

Financial data. Data for fiscal year ended December 31, 1993. *Assets:* $15,728,464 (M). *Total grants authorized:* $815,000.

Environmental awards. *Program and interests:* The Foundation's priorities are:

- To build sustainable communities.

  Programs that simultaneously address environmental protection, economic development, and social and environmental justice. Areas of interest include coastal protection, recycling, sustainable agriculture, and transportation.

- To achieve safer workplace and community environments.

  Programs that address lead paint poisoning abatement and the reduction of toxic chemical use.

- To broaden the scope of environmental education.

  Outreach programs in economically disadvantaged communities that involve citizen groups and young people.

Issues. Cli Bio Lan Agr Wat Oce Ene Was Tox Pop Dev
 •   •   •   •   •   •   •   •   •

Funding analysis.

Fiscal year:	1992	1993
Env grants auth:	$160,000	$190,000
Number:	12	12
Range:	$10,000–$20,000	$10,000–$20,000
Median:	$10,000	$20,000
Pct $ auth (env/total):	31	23

Recipients (1993 highest):	Number:	Dollars:
Community Farm Alliance	1	20,000
Environmental Defense Fund	1	20,000
National Resources Council of Maine	1	20,000
Save the Bay, Inc.	1	20,000
Sea Island Preservation Project	1	20,000
Surface Transportation Policy Project	1	20,000
West Virginia-Citizen Research Group, Inc.	1	20,000

Activity regions (1993):	Number:	Dollars:
U.S. Northeast	3	50,000
U.S. not specified	3	50,000
U.S. Southeast	3	50,000
U.S. Mid-Atlantic	2	30,000
U.S. South Central	1	10,000

Sample grants (1993).

Appalachian Community Fund. Knoxville, TN. $10,000. For outreach to Japanese corporate leaders to increase their awareness of environmental and social justice issues and open up new sources of philanthropic giving in Central Appalachia.

Center for Policy Alternatives. Washington, DC. $10,000. To promote environmentally responsible economic development within the state and federal policy arenas.

Community Farm Alliance. Berea, KY. $20,000. For a training program that enables Southern farm leaders to become active participants in defining farm policy which will encourage sustainable agriculture and rural economic development.

Environmental Defense Fund. New York, NY. $20,000. For public education and public policy formulation for the development of lead paint poisoning prevention/abatement programs.

Hill Country Foundation. Austin, TX. $10,000. To protect Barton Springs, the Edwards Aquifer, and other highly sensitive areas in the Austin Hill Country from overdevelopment.

Natural Resources Council of Maine. Augusta, ME. $20,000. To promote reduction of toxic chemical use by Maine industries through education and advocacy at state and national levels.

Sea Island Preservation Project. St. Helena Island, SC. $20,000. To create alternatives to resort development that are environmentally sound and controlled by local residents. The project is sponsored by Penn Center, the South Carolina Coastal Conservation League, and the Neighborhood Legal Assistance Program.

Surface Transportation Policy Project. Washington, DC. $20,000. To prepare a handbook that outlines opportunities for citizens to participate effectively in the transportation decision-making process in order to make their communities more livable.

Application process. *Initial contact:* The Foundation does not review or consider any uninvited proposals.
When to apply: Anytime.
Materials available: 1993 Grants List and Guidelines.

Emphases. *Recipients:* Pre-selected organizations only.
Activities: Advocacy, capacity building, citizen participation, collaborative efforts, demonstration programs, education, feasibility studies, fieldwork, innovative programs, networking, planning, policy analysis/development, technical assistance, training, volunteerism, youth programs.
Types of support: Continuing support, general purposes, internships, leveraging funds, matching funds, pilot projects, seed money, technical assistance.
Geography: National with an emphasis on the Northeast, Central Appalachia, Texas, Oregon, and the Bay Area of California. State and local organizations are usually preferred, although national, regional, and intermediary organizations are considered when they work as advocates to reinforce the efforts of local groups.

Limitations. *Recipients:* Botanical gardens, individuals, museums, zoos.
Activities: Audiovisual materials, conflict resolution, expeditions/tours, inventories, land acquisition, litigation, research, seminars, symposia/colloquia.
Types of support: Annual campaigns, capital campaigns/expenses, computer hardware, debt retirement, emergency funding, equipment, facilities, lectureships, loans, maintenance, membership campaigns, mortgage reduction, professorships, travel expenses.
Geography: International.

P

The Perkin Fund
340 Country Club Road
New Canaan, Connecticut 06840
Tel: 203–966–1920
EIN: 136222498   Type: Independent
Contact: Gladys T. Perkin, Trustee

Application address:
c/o Morris & McVeigh
767 Third Avenue
New York, New York 10017

History and philosophy. The Perkin Fund was established in 1967 by Richard S. Perkin. Interest include higher education, medical research, medical sciences and physical sciences.

Officers and directors. *Trustees:* Dr. James G. Baker, Winifred P. Gray, Gladys T. Perkin, John T. Perkin, Mrs. Richard S. Perkin, Richard T. Perkin, Robert S. Perkin, Howard Phipps, Jr., Dr. Roderic M. Scott.

Financial data. Data for fiscal year ended December 31, 1992. *Assets:* $15,054,033 (M). *Total grants disbursed:* $521,000 (M).

Environmental awards. *Recent grants:* 1991 grants included support for marine issues and wildlife conservation.

Issues.   Cli   Bio   Lan   Agr   Wat   Oce   Ene   Was   Tox   Pop   Dev
                     •   •

Funding analysis.

Fiscal year:	1991
Env grants disb:	$55,000
Number:	2
Range:	$5,000–$50,000
Median:	$27,500
Pct $ disb (env/total):	9

Recipients (1991):	Number:	Dollars:
NYZS/The Wildlife Conservation Society	1	50,000
The Maritime Center	1	5,000

Activity region (1991):	Number:	Dollars:
New York/New Jersey	2	55,000

Sample grants (1991).
The Maritime Center. Mystic, CT. $5,000.
NYZS/The Wildlife Conservation Society. Bronx, NY. $50,000.

Application process. *Initial contact:* Letter to include description of program, dollar amount of grant requested, and copy of IRS tax-exempt status determination letter.
When to apply: Deadlines are March 15 and September 15.

Emphases. *Recipients:* Nonprofit organizations.
Activities: Research (medical).
Geography: United States.

Limitations. *Recipients:* Individuals.
Types of support: Scholarships.

P

Perkins Charitable Foundation

1030 Hanna Building
1422 Euclid Avenue
Cleveland, Ohio 44115
Tel: 216–621–0465
EIN: 346549753   Type: Independent
Contact: Marilyn Best, Secretary/Treasurer.

History and philosophy. The Foundation was established in 1950 by members of the Perkins family. Funding interests include education, health care, community, and conservation.

Officers and directors. *Officer:* Marilyn Best, Secretary/Treasurer. *Trustees:* George Oliva III, Leigh H. Perkins, Sallie Sullivan.

Financial data. Data for fiscal year ended December 31, 1993. *Assets:* $11,947,036 (M). *Total grants disbursed:* $547,400.

Environmental awards. *Recent grants:* 1993 grants included support for land conservation, river protection, and wildlife.

Issues.   Cli   Bio   Lan   Agr   Wat   Oce   Ene   Was   Tox   Pop   Dev
              •   •   •   •   •

Funding analysis.

Fiscal year:	1993
Env grants disb:	$139,000
Number:	7
Range:	$1,000–$69,000
Median:	$7,000
Pct $ disb (env/total):	25

Recipients (1993 highest):	Number:	Dollars:
The Nature Conservancy, Florida Field Office	1	69,000
The Nature Conservancy, Key West	1	30,000
Tall Timbers Research Stations	1	25,000
The Nature Conservancy, Wyoming Field Office	1	7,000
Forest Wildlife Foundation	1	4,000

Activity regions (1993):	Number:	Dollars:
U.S. Southeast	4	127,000
U.S. Mountain	1	7,000
U.S. Mid-Atlantic	1	4,000
U.S. not specified	1	1,000

Sample grants (1993).

American Rivers. Washington, DC. $1,000.

Florida Conservation Association. Tallahassee, FL. $3,000.

The Nature Conservancy, Florida Field Office. Winter Park, FL. $69,000.

The Nature Conservancy, Key West. Key West, FL. $30,000.

The Nature Conservancy, Wyoming Field Office. Lander, WY. $7,000.

Tall Timbers Research Stations. Tallahassee, FL. $25,000.

Application process. *Initial contact:* Proposal. *When to apply:* Anytime.

Emphases. *Recipients:* Nonprofit organizations, public agencies.

Limitations. *Recipients:* Individuals.

The Pew Charitable Trusts

One Commerce Square
2005 Market Street, Suite 1700
Philadelphia, Pennsylvania 19103–7017
Tel: 215–575–9050   Fax: 215–575–4939
EIN: 236299309   Type: Independent
EGA member
Contact: Joshua S. Reichert, Director, Environmental Division

History and philosophy. The Pew Charitable Trusts consists of seven individual trusts established between 1948 and 1979 by the four sons and daughters of Joseph N. Pew, founder of the Sun Oil Company. The first and largest of the seven trusts was created by the Pews in 1948 in memory of their parents, Joseph N. and Mary Anderson Pew; the other six trusts were created over the next 31 years. The Trusts currently make grants in the divisions of: Health and Human Services, Education, Culture and the Arts, Environment, Public Policy, and Religion.

Officers and directors. *Officers:* Thomas W. Langfitt, M.D., President; Rebecca W. Rimel, Executive Director; Michael Rubinger, Associate Executive Director. *Directors:* Susan W. Catherwood, Robert G. Dunlop, Thomas W. Langfitt, M.D., Robert E. McDonald, J. Howard Pew II, J. N. Pew III, Joseph N. Pew IV, M.D., R. Anderson Pew, William Richardson.

Financial data. Data for fiscal year ended December 31, 1993. *Assets:* $2,327,593,705 (M). *Total grants authorized:* $166,624,400.

Environmental awards. *Program and interests:* The Environment Program is designed to promote policies and practices that protect the environment and encourage the sustainable use of natural resources. The Program is particularly interested in "innovative ideas and creative solutions" to environmental problems. Its three primary foci are:

- Global Warming and Climate Change.

  Goal: To decrease emissions of carbon dioxide and other greenhouse gases that contribute to global warming.

  To increase energy efficiency and conservation in the United States by promoting efficiency improvements by gas and electric utilities.

  To eliminate the use of chlorofluorocarbons (CFCs) and related substances that contribute to the destruction of the global ozone layer.

  Requests will be considered for:

  - Developing and replicating successful models of least-cost planning by gas and electric utilities that include financial and other incentives for demand-reducing efficiency improvements.

- Increasing public awareness of the relationship between energy use and the environment, and encouraging energy-efficient consumer practices.
- Encouraging the rapid phase-out of ozone-depleting substances, the replacement of CFCs and related compounds with safe substitutes, as well as assisting developing countries in eliminating the use of ozone-depleting substances from their economies.

Note: Proposals in this category will be accepted only at the specific invitation of The Trusts.

- Environmental Pollution.

Goal: To reduce the production of toxic substances and other pollutants that may have adverse effects on the environment and public health.

To expand the development and widespread application of sustainable agricultural systems.

To reduce the toxicity and volume of the solid wastestream.

To promote changes in manufacturing processes that significantly reduce the production and emission of pollutants.

Requests will be considered for:

- Promoting economic and regulatory incentives that encourage innovative approaches to pollution prevention.
- Increasing consumer demand for products whose manufacture, use, and disposal do not pose adverse effects on public health and the natural environment, and developing better industrial planning procedures and evaluation methods needed to reduce environmental pollution.
- Developing and implementing policies and programs that encourage sustainable agricultural practices that conserve natural resources and reduce threats to public health stemming from the heavy use of chemical inputs.
- Promoting national, state, and municipal least-cost strategies to manage solid waste as well as policies that encourage the design and development of reusable/recyclable and nontoxic consumer products.
- Developing large-scale integrated recycling, processing, and manufacturing programs that can serve as models for waste management efforts throughout the country.

- Forest and Marine Conservation.

Goal: To halt the destruction and degradation of forests and marine ecosystems in North America.

To protect old-growth forest ecosystems.

To encourage the adoption of forest management practices that protect the diverse ecological values of public lands.

To raise public awareness about the rapid degradation of marine ecosystems so that marine conservation becomes a national priority.

To promote public policies that protect the biological integrity of marine ecosystems.

Requests will be considered for:

- Educating and mobilizing the general public to support preservation of forest and marine environments.
- Encouraging the adoption of policies that promote the sustainable management of marine ecosystems and public forest lands.
- Conducting applied research aimed at better informing policymakers and the general public regarding the economic, biological, and ecological values of forest and marine ecosystems and the extent to which they are being degraded by unsustainable harvesting, pollution, and other destructive practices.
- Establishing market mechanisms that encourage the purchase of products derived from ecologically sustainable forest and fishing practices.

Issues. Cli Bio Lan Agr Wat Oce Ene Was Tox Pop Dev

Funding analysis.

Fiscal year:	1992*	1993
Env grants auth:	$35,490,400	$28,876,400
Number:	94	110
Range:	$10,000–$12,000,000	$25,000–$3,000,000
Median:	$100,000	$100,000
Pct $ auth (env/total):	18	18

*As reported by The Trusts.

Recipients (1993 highest):	Number:	Dollars:
The Energy Foundation	2	6,000,000
The Tides Foundation	4	3,867,000
Pennsylvania Horticultural Society	1	2,560,000
National Religious Partnership for the Environment	1	1,200,000
Stanford University	1	750,000

Activity regions (1993 highest):	Number:	Dollars:
U.S. not specified	31	14,045,550
U.S. Mid-Atlantic	9	4,088,000
International*	17	3,151,000
U.S. West	5	1,100,000
U.S. Northwest	11	1,001,000

*Multiple regions or not specified.

Sample grants (1994).

American Oceans Campaign. Santa Monica, CA. $100,000. For the National Coastal Caucus. In support of a campaign to educate the public and policymakers on the need to strengthen the National Estuary Program by mobilizing the support of regional marine conservation organizations.

Environmental Defense Fund. New York, NY. $140,000 (18 months). In support of efforts to strengthen the provisions of the Montreal Protocol, ensure that it is effectively implemented, and research the potential impact of aircraft emissions on stratospheric ozone depletion.

Center for Resource Economics. Washington, DC. $300,000 (3 years). To develop and distribute publications on protection of North American forests and the marine environment, pollution prevention, and energy conservation and renewables.

Conservation Law Foundation. Boston, MA. $600,000 (2 years). To strengthen the energy program in New England and provide assistance to other regional projects.

Global Action Plan for the Earth. Woodstock, NY. $150,000. To support the development and delivery of a program educating children about how to live environmentally sustainable lives.

Greater Yellowstone Coalition. Bozeman, MT. $50,000. For the Forest Management and Reform Program. In support of the efforts by the Coalition to protect the forest ecosystems of the Northern Rockies.

The Humane Society of the United States. Washington, DC. $120,000 (2 years). For the Center for Respect of Life and Environment. In support of the project "Theological Education to Meet the Environmental Challenge," providing resource materials and technical assistance to seminaries and divinity schools to address population and environmental concerns.

Mothers & Others for a Livable Planet. New York, NY. $245,000 (2 years, partial matching grant). To support a consumer education effort to encourage more purchasing of foods that are produced in an environmentally sound manner.

National Wildlife Federation. Washington, DC. $240,000 (2 years). To increase public awareness and understanding of the links between population and the environment.

The Nature Conservancy, Headquarters. Arlington, VA. $175,000. For the second phase of a feasibility study to develop a network of "conservation lodges" in the United States.

Pesticide Action Network (PAN), North America Regional Center. San Francisco, CA. $70,000 (partial matching grant). For the National Pesticide Use Reduction project. To develop pesticide use reduction policies at the national and state level, and to disseminate this information through workshops, publications, and the media.

Regulatory Assistance Project. Gardiner, ME. $550,000 (2 years). To provide workshops and educational assistance to state public utility regulators and state legislators on integrated resource planning, energy conservation, and renewable resource policies.

Save the Bay, Inc. Providence, RI. $115,000 (2 years). To develop a national model for reducing water pollution by local communities using low-cost, low-technology pollution prevention techniques.

The Tides Foundation. San Francisco, CA. $650,000 (2 years, matching grant). For the Environmental Strategies, Inc. To establish a nonprofit organization to help coordinate the efforts of the environmental community to promote constructive environmental policies at the national level.

Application process. *Initial contact:* Letter of inquiry (5 pages maximum) to include:
1. Who: A description of organization and the nature of its work, as well as a brief history of organization's achievements, particularly as they relate to the problem or issue to be addressed.
2. What and how: A statement of problem or need and an explanation of how it will be addressed. A brief description of anticipated achievements or outcomes should also be included.
3. When: A description of timeframe of proposed activities.
4. How much: Estimated costs for project or activity and what is being requested from The Trusts.

When to apply: Anytime. Grants are awarded four times a year, in March, June, September, and December.
Materials available: Annual report, "Program Guidelines" (includes "Applying for a Grant").

Emphases. *Recipients:* Nonprofit organizations.
Activities: Activism, advocacy, collaborative efforts, demonstration programs, education (public), innovative programs, policy analysis/development.
Types of support: Leveraging funds, multi-year grants.
Geography: United States.

Limitations. *Recipients:* Individuals, public agencies.
Activities: Direct services (ongoing), museum or collections acquisitions, research (nonapplied).
Types of support: Capital campaigns/expenses, debt retirement, endowments, equipment, facilities (construction), scholarships/fellowships not initiated by The Trusts.

Pew Scholars Program in Conservation and the Environment

School of Natural Resources and Environment
University of Michigan
2042 Dana Building
430 East University
Ann Arbor, Michigan 48109–1115
Tel: 313–936–2556   Fax: 313–936–2195
EGA member
Contacts: James E. Crowfoot, Ph.D., Director
Stan Van Velsor, Assistant Director

History and philosophy. "The Pew Scholars Program in Conservation and the Environment was established in response to the critical need to identify and support a new generation of scholar-scientists who would apply their special knowledge and skills directly to finding solutions to pressing environmental problems." The Program was set up in 1988 by the board of directors of The Pew Charitable Trusts with an initial three-year commitment of $5.5 million. Under the program, ten outstanding scholars are selected annually, each to receive $150,000 fellowships over a three-year period. The first group of scholars was chosen in June 1990.

Officers and directors. *Advisory Committee:* James E. Crowfoot, Ph.D., Chair; Richard N. L. Andrews, Ph.D., Michael J. Bean, J.D., Herman E. Daly, Ph.D., Paul R. Ehrlich, Ph.D., Douglas I. Foy, J.D., Leslie S. Kaufman, Ph.D., Kenton R. Miller, Ph.D., Christine Padoch, Ph.D., Harold Salwasser, Ph.D., Kathryn A. Saterson, Ph.D., Stephen H. Schneider, Ph.D.

Financial data. Data for fiscal year ended June 30, 1993. *Gifts received:* $1,500,000. *Total fellowships authorized:* $1,500,000.

Environmental awards. *Program and interests:* The overall goals of the Program are:

- To identify and flexibly support individual leadership and initiative in the conservation of biological diversity.

- To stimulate the collection, analysis, and dissemination of information on biological diversity and natural resources, and to focus the application of this knowledge on urgent problems impeding the conservation of biological diversity.

- To encourage creative inter- and multidisciplinary approaches to the conservation of biological diversity.
- To encourage and inspire the next generation of conservation scholars by recognizing and rewarding outstanding individuals who are doing important work to conserve biological diversity.

Recent grants: 1993 scholars worked on the conservation of biology diversity by applying a range of disciplines including conservation biology, ecological economics, ecotoxicology, environmental law, land use planning, marine biology, ornithology, and rural sociology.

Issues. Cli Bio• Lan Agr• Wat Oce• Ene Was• Tox Pop• Dev•

Funding analysis.

Fiscal year:	1992	1993
Env grants auth:	$1,500,000	$1,500,000
Number:	10	10
Range:	—	—
Median:	$150,000	$150,000
Pct $ auth (env/total):	100	100

Recipients (1993):	Number:	Dollars:
Anil Gupta, Ph.D.	1	150,000
Bernard Nietschmann, Ph.D.	1	150,000
Madhav Gadgil, Ph.D.	1	150,000
Reed Noss, Ph.D.	1	150,000
Robert Costanza, Ph.D.	1	150,000
Robert Johannes, Ph.D.	1	150,000
Stuart Pimm, Ph.D.	1	150,000
Theodora Colborn, Ph.D.	1	150,000
Tomasz Zylicz, Ph.D.	1	150,000
Johanna Wald, J.D.	1	150,000

Activity regions (1993):	Number:	Dollars:
North America	3	450,000
U.S. not specified	2	300,000
Eastern Europe	1	150,000
Indian Subcontinent and Indian Ocean Islands	1	150,000
International*	1	150,000
Mexico and Central America	1	150,000
Southeast Asia	1	150,000

*Multiple regions or not specified.

Sample grants (1993).

Theodora Colborn, Ph.D., World Wildlife Fund. Washington, DC. $150,000 (3 years). Environmental health: toxic chemicals and the human/wildlife connection. Activity region–North America.

Robert Costanza, Ph.D., Maryland International Institute for Ecological Economics. Solomons, MD. $150,000 (3 years). Ecological economics: interface between ecological and economic systems. Activity region–North America.

Madhav Gadgil, Ph.D., India Institute of Science. Bangalore, India. $150,000 (3 years). Sustainable use of natural resources through bottom-up conservation planing. Activity region–India.

Anil Gupta, Ph.D., Indian Institute of Management. Gujarat, India. $150,000 (3 years). Analyzing indigenous knowledge: grassroots in innovation in resource conservation. Activity region–global.

Robert Johannes, Ph.D., Australian Commonwealth Scientific and Industrial Research Organization. Tasmania, Australia. $150,000 (3 years). Tropical marine conservation: integration of traditional knowledge into management strategies. Activity region–Pacific Islands and Southeast Asia.

Bernard Nietschmann, Ph.D., University of California, Berkeley. Berkeley, CA. $150,000 (3 years). Interdependence of biological and cultural diversity: contributions of indigenous people. Activity region–Caribbean Coast of Central America.

Reed Noss, Ph.D., The Wildlands Project. Corvallis, OR. $150,000 (3 years). Grassroots bioregional conservation: design of regional reserve networks. Activity region–North America.

Stuart Pimm, Ph.D., University of Tennessee. Knoxville, TN. $150,000 (3 years). Ecology of endangered species and ecosystems. Activity region–Hawaii and Guam.

Johanna Wald, J.D., Natural Resources Defense Council. New York, NY. $150,000 (3 years). Public land management: protection and restoration of public land ecosystems. Activity region–United States.

Tomasz Zylicz, Ph.D., Warsaw University. Warsaw, Poland. $150,000 (3 years). Ecological economics: modelling interactions of economic and ecological systems. Activity region–Eastern Europe.

Application process. *Initial contact:* Telephone call to discuss potential nominees. Application is by invitation only. The applicant pool consists of nominees from the Nominating Institutions (48 institutions representing academic centers, nonprofit environmental organizations, zoological and botanical gardens, and natural history museums) and the 12 Independent Nominators.

When to apply: Anytime. Nominations are generally due in November. Applications from nominated individuals are generally due in January. Call for exact deadlines.

Materials available: Annual report, "Application Guidelines."

Emphases. *Recipients:* Pre-selected individuals only.

Activities: Activism, advocacy, citizen participation, collaborative efforts, conflict resolution, education, fieldwork, innovative programs, litigation, networking, planning, policy analysis/development, publications, research, seminars, training, workshops.

Types of support: Fellowships.

The Pfizer Foundation, Inc.

235 East 42nd Street
New York, New York 10017
Tel: 212-573-3351
EIN: 136083839   Type: Company-sponsored
Contact: Kevin S. Keating, Treasurer

History and philosophy. The Pfizer Foundation, Inc. was established in 1953 by Pfizer, Inc., the global health care company. The broad objectives of the company's charitable contributions program are: to improve the quality of life in areas in which Pfizer facilities are located; to make grants to educational and research institutions, academic departments, and programs in which significant intellectual or scientific interests are involved; to support national institutions and organizations with programs that address issues of special interest to Pfizer; and to encourage community involvement through company programs. Program areas are: Education, Health Care, Civic Affairs, Culture, and International Affairs.

Officers and directors. *Officers:* Robert A. Wilson, President; Wyndham Anderson, Executive Vice President; Terence Gallagher, Secretary; Kevin S. Keating, Treasurer.

Financial data. Data for fiscal year ended December 31, 1992. *Assets:* $6,900,870 (M). *Gifts received:* $1,500,000. *Total grants disbursed:* $1,422,250.

Environmental awards. *Program and interests:* The Foundation's Civic Affairs program supports environmental/conservation efforts. The International Affairs program targets economic-based strategies for conserving natural resources.
Recent grants: 1992 grants included support for land conservation, parks, farmland preservation, biodiversity, a botanical garden, and environmental economics.

Issues. Cli Bio Lan Agr Wat Oce Ene Was Tox Pop Dev

Funding analysis.

Fiscal year:	1992
Env grants auth:	$141,500
Number:	17
Range:	$2,000–$50,000
Median:	$5,000
Pct $ auth (env/total):	10

Recipients (1992 highest):	*Number:*	*Dollars:*
The New York Botanical Garden	2	60,000
Central Park Conservancy	3	20,500
NYZS/The Wildlife Conservation Society	1	12,500
International Institute of Rural Reconstruction	1	8,500
Conservation International	1	5,000
Foundation for Research on Economics and the Environment	1	5,000
Marine Biological Laboratory	1	5,000
National Audubon Society	1	5,000
National Park Foundation	1	5,000
The Nature Conservancy, Headquarters	1	5,000

Activity regions (1992):	*Number:*	*Dollars:*
New York/New Jersey	8	98,000
U.S. not specified	6	25,000
International*	2	13,500
U.S. Northeast	1	5,000

*Multiple regions or not specified.

Sample grants (1992).
American Farmland Trust. Washington, DC. $2,500. General support.
Brooklyn Botanic Garden. Brooklyn, NY. $2,500. General support.
Central Park Conservancy. New York, NY. $15,000. Support for the Adopt-an-Acre Campaign.
Central Park Conservancy. New York, NY. $3,500. General support for program to maintain and improve Central Park.
Central Park Conservancy. New York, NY. $2,000. Support for You Gotta Have Park program.
The Conservation Fund. Arlington, VA. $2,500. General support.
Conservation International. Washington, DC. $5,000. Support for a program blending the biological science of ecosystem conservation with the social science of economics, to create new solutions for the deepening environmental crisis.
Council on the Environment of New York City. New York, NY. $2,500. General support.
Foundation for Research on Economics and the Environment. Seattle, WA. $5,000. General support.
National Audubon Society. New York, NY. $5,000. General support.
National Park Foundation. Washington, DC. $5,000. General support.
The Nature Conservancy, Headquarters. Arlington, VA. $5,000. General support to promote land conservation and preservation.
The New York Botanical Garden. Bronx, NY. $10,000. General support.
The New York Botanical Garden. Bronx, NY. $50,000. Support for the capital campaign.
NYZS/The Wildlife Conservation Society. Bronx, NY. 12,500. Support for the society's field veterinary program.

Application process. *Initial contact:* Proposal to include:
1. Description of program.
   - Rationale for program.
   - Projected budget.
   - Qualifications of program manager.
   - Methods of evaluation.
   - Timetable.
2. Other sources of funding.
3. How organization will acknowledge the Foundation's support.
4. Copy of the IRS tax-exempt status determination letter.
5. Most recent audited financial statements.
6. Names and affiliations of members of organization's board of directors or other governing body.
7. List of other contributors and grant amounts.

When to apply: Anytime.
Materials available: Annual report (includes "Guidelines").

Emphases. *Recipients:* Botanical gardens, museums, nonprofit organizations.
Activities: Conferences, education, fundraising, publications, research, seminars.
Types of support: Annual campaigns, capital campaigns/expenses, continuing support, emergency funding, endowments, equipment, facilities (construction), fellowships, internships, matching funds, operating costs, professorships, projects, research, scholarships, seed money, technical assistance.
Geography: Areas of company operations; New Jersey, New York City.

Limitations. *Recipients:* Individuals, religious organizations.
Activities: Land acquisition, political activities.
Types of support: Debt retirement, loans.

The Philadelphia Foundation
1234 Market Street, Suite 1900
Philadelphia, Pennsylvania 19107–3794
Tel: 215–563–6417 Fax: 215–563–6882
EIN: 231581832 Type: Community
Contact: Carrolle Fair Perry, Director

History and philosophy. Established in 1918, the Philadelphia Foundation is a consortium of 155 trust funds, active in the five counties of southwestern Pennsylvania. It makes grants "to support organizations working to change conditions that currently limit the access of low-income people to resources." Program areas are: Community, Culture, Education, Health, Housing & Economic Development, Social Service, and Children & Families. After awarding grants recommended by donors, the Foundation gives priority to organizations that benefit low-income communities, promote cultural pluralism and diversity, address the causes of social and economic inequities, facilitate development of new leaders, and have operating budgets under $1.5 million.

Officers and directors. *Officer:* Ernesta D. Ballard, Chair. *Board of Managers:* Ernesta D. Ballard, James F. Bodine, David W. Brenner, William C. Bullitt, Esq., Rev. Joan Salmon Campbell, Barbara D. Hauptfuhrer, Dona S. Kahn, Esq., Garry Maddox, M. Christine Murphy, Carmen Febo San Miguel, M.D., Leon C. Sunstein, Jr., Sheilah Vance-Lewis, Esq., Peter B. Vaughan, Ph.D.

Financial data. Data for fiscal year ended April 30, 1992. *Assets:* $76,227,347 (M). *Gifts received:* $2,881,579. *Total grants disbursed:* $5,107,051.

Environmental awards. *Program and interests:* The Foundation awards most of its environmental grants through the Community program.
Recent grants: 1992 grants included support for land and energy conservation, toxics, air quality, and urban environment.

Issues. Cli • Bio • Lan • Agr • Wat Oce Ene • Was Tox • Pop • Dev

Funding analysis.

Fiscal year:	1991	1992
Env grants disb:	$139,243	$157,412
Number:	14	14
Range:	$1,000–$38,437	$1,000–$25,000
Median:	$5,639	$10,000
Pct $ disb (env/total):	3	3

Recipients (1992 highest):	Number:	Dollars:
Clean Air Council	2	27,000
Friends of Farmworkers	1	25,000
Friends of Farmworkers for the Comité de Apoyo a los Trabajadore	1	21,000
Environmental Fund for Pennsylvania	1	15,000
Pennsylvania Environmental Council	1	12,000

Activity region (1992):	Number:	Dollars:
U.S. Mid-Atlantic	14	157,412

Sample grants (1992).
Delaware Valley Citizen's Council for Clean Air. Philadelphia, PA. $18,000.
Delaware Valley Toxics Coalition Educational Fund. Philadelphia, PA. $10,000.
Energy Coordinating Agency of Philadelphia. Philadelphia, PA. $11,370.
The Nature Conservancy, Pennsylvania Field Office. Philadelphia, PA. $1,000.
Neighborhood Gardens Association/A Philadelphia Trust. Philadelphia, PA. $9,000.
The Schuylkill Center for Environmental Education. Philadelphia, PA. $5,000.

Application process. *Initial contact:* Telephone call or letter requesting "Applicant Guidelines." If your organization is requesting more that $10,000 in multi-year funding or if you have not submitted a proposal in the past three years, you must submit a full application.
When to apply: Deadlines in 1995 are January 13 and July 28 for full proposals and June 30 for short proposals of previous applicants. The board meets twice a year.
Materials available: Annual report, (includes "Applying for a Grant"), "Applicant Guidelines."

Emphases. *Recipients:* Nonprofit organizations.
Activities: Education, innovative programs.
Types of support: Continuing support, emergency funding, general purposes, matching funds, operating costs, projects, seed money, technical assistance.
Geography: Bucks, Chester, Delaware, Montgomery, and Philadelphia counties in Pennsylvania.

Limitations. *Recipients:* Individuals, public agencies, religious organizations.
Activities: Advocacy, conferences, expeditions/tours, land acquisition, publications, research.
Types of support: Annual campaigns, capital campaigns/expenses, debt retirement, endowments, facilities, fellowships, loans, scholarships, travel expenses.
Geography: National and international organizations.

The Philanthropic Group
630 Fifth Avenue, Suite 2905
New York, New York 10111–0254
Tel: 212–332–1150 Fax: 212–332–1154
Type: Advisory service
EGA member
Contact: Barbara R. Greenberg, President

History and philosophy. The Philanthropic Group manages several foundations. One of these has been identified as an environmental grantmaker with an interest in environmental education for Newark, New Jersey youth and conservation projects in the Northeast. It makes grants to pre-selected organizations only. The Philanthropic Group has requested that this grantmaker be omitted from the Directory.

The Philanthropic Group is a member of the Environmental Grantmakers Association.

© 1995 Environmental Data Resources, Inc.

P

Philip Morris Companies, Inc.

Corporate Contributions
120 Park Avenue, 25th Floor
New York, New York 10017–5592
Tel: 212–880–3038 Fax: 212–907–5396
Type: Company-sponsored
EGA member
Contact: Joe Miloscia, Specialist, Corporate Contributions

History and philosophy. Philip Morris Companies together constitute the world's largest consumer packaged goods entity and the nation's largest food company. They consist of Kraft General Foods, Miller Brewing Company, Mission Viejo Company, Philip Morris International, and Philip Morris USA. Their focused giving program has three themes: the Arts, Educating the Future Work Force, and Hunger and Nutrition. In addition, general grants are made in the areas of: Education, Health and Human Services, Civic and Community, Culture and Humanities, and Conservation and Environment.

Officers and directors. *Director:* Mark L. Bodden, Manager of Corporate Contributions.

Financial data. Not available.

Environmental awards. *Program and interests:* The Conservation and Environment program focuses on future food sources and solid waste disposal. Objectives are to:

- Improve the quantity and quality of the world's food supply.
- Preserve and protect American farmlands.
- Promote awareness and stewardship of our nation's water resources.
- Improve waste management techniques in individual households, in our communities, and in commercial facilities.

Additional interests include:

- Minority involvement.
- Urban environmentalism.
- Partnerships among corporate, public, conservation, and academic communities in the development of public policies and environmental programs.
- Public education on environmental preservation and resource management.

Issues. Cli Bio Lan Agr Wat Oce Ene Was Tox Pop Dev

Funding analysis.§

Fiscal year:	1992
Env grants disb:	–
Number:	50
Range:	$1,000–$100,000
Median:	$20,000
Pct $ auth (env/total):	–

§As reported by the Environmental Grantmakers Association.

Sample grants (1993).*
American Farmland Trust. Washington, DC. To (1) establish innovative model test farms in the Chesapeake Bay watershed area. The grant allowed farmers to conduct on-farm research and demonstration projects to promote the development and use of alternative farming practices which are based on conservation and which will help to preserve the environment; and (2) promote Farming on the Edge, a comprehensive national study designed to collect data and affect public policy on the more than 58 percent of all U.S. agricultural production that comes from counties adjacent to metropolitan centers, so as to protect agricultural resources and sustain the farming industry in the critical areas around our growing cities.
Conservation Fund. Arlington, VA. Co-sponsor, National Geographic Society. For the 1993 Workshop on Water, a week-long water education workshop combining physical geography lectures and field sessions at Mammoth Lakes, California, with guided expeditions to several national lakes and parks. The workshop focused on water awareness and stewardship for 175 teachers and water officials from across the country. Workshop participants then undertook advocacy and taught lessons on freshwater in the fall.
The Izaak Walton League. Washington, DC. To produce a hands-on Stream Restoration Manual designed to help grassroots conservationists in reclaiming damaged waterways, bringing back ecosystems, and creating an amenity for communities.
Management Institute for Environment and Business. Arlington, VA. To comprehensively integrate environmental management education at leading business schools, and to establish at each school a center, institute, or some formalized degree program.

*Dollar amounts not available.

Application process. *Initial contact:* Brief proposal describing the purpose of the organization and specific activities. Also include:
1. Project description: needs statement, plan, evaluation method, and budget.
2. Current-year's operating budget, audited financial statement, or the most recent annual report.
3. List of other corporate and foundation support.
4. List of board of directors.
5. Copy of IRS tax-exempt status determination letter.

When to apply: Anytime.
Materials available: Informational brochure (includes "How to Apply for a General Grant").

Emphases. *Recipients:* Educational institutions, nonprofit organizations, research institutions.
Activities: Citizen participation, collaborative efforts, conferences, demonstration programs, education, innovative programs, policy analysis/development, research (scientific), symposia/colloquia.
Types of support: Continuing support, general purposes, multi-year grants, pilot projects.
Geography: Generally, areas where major company plants are located.

Limitations. *Recipients:* Botanical gardens, individuals, museums, public agencies, religious organizations, zoos.
Activities: Audiovisual materials, capacity building, expeditions/tours, fundraising, land acquisition, litigation, lobbying, political activities, publications, youth programs.

Types of support: Advertising campaigns, capital campaigns/expenses, computer hardware, debt retirement, emergency funding, endowments, loans, membership campaigns, mortgage reduction, professorships, scholarships.
Geography: International.

Phillips Petroleum Foundation, Inc.

16 C4 Phillips Building
Bartlesville, Oklahoma 74004
Tel: 918–661–9072
EIN: 237326611   Type: Company-sponsored
Contact: John C. West, Executive Manager

History and philosophy. The Foundation was established in 1973 by the Phillips Petroleum Company. Funding priorities are: Education, Environment, Civic, Youth, Health and Welfare, and Culture and the Arts.

Officers and directors. *Officers:* J. Bryan Whitworth, Stanley R. Mueller, Vice Presidents. *Trustees:* Dale J. Billam, W. F. Dausses, R. W. Holsapple, Stanley R. Mueller, J. Bryan Whitworth.

Financial data. Data for fiscal year ended December 31, 1993. *Assets:* $496,876 (U). *Gifts received:* $6,500,000. *Total grants disbursed:* $5,840,571.

Environmental awards. *Program and interests:* The Foundation favors:

- Grassroots efforts.
- Easily shared and replicated projects with high visibility and community involvement.
- Challenge grants.

Phillips sponsors the environmental sciences category of the International Science and Engineering Fair.
Recent grants: 1992 grants included support for land conservation, energy conservation, wildlife, fisheries, parks, a zoo, and outdoor education.

Issues.   Cli Bio Lan Agr Wat Oce Ene Was Tox Pop Dev
              •   •   •   •   •   •

Funding analysis.

Fiscal year:	1992
Env grants disb:	$131,100
Number:	18
Range:	$1,000–$50,000
Median:	$2,550
Pct $ disb (env/total):	2

Recipients (1992 highest):	*Number:*	*Dollars:*
The Nature Conservancy, Oklahoma Field Office	1	50,000
George Miksch Sutton Avian Research Center, Inc.	1	25,000
The Jefferson Energy Foundation	1	15,000
Foundation for Research on Economics and the Environment	1	10,000
American Fisheries Society, National Chapter	1	5,000
Izaak Walton League of America	1	5,000
The Student Conservation Association, Inc.	1	5,000

Activity regions (1992):	*Number:*	*Dollars:*
U.S. South Central	5	79,600
U.S. not specified	10	48,500
U.S. Mid-Atlantic	1	1,000
U.S. Midwest	1	1,000
U.S. Southeast	1	1,000

Sample grants (1992).
American Fisheries Society, National Chapter. Bethesda, MD. $5,000.
Appalachian Trail Conference, Headquarters. Harpers Ferry, WV. $1,000.
Foundation for Research on Economics and the Environment. Seattle, WA. $10,000.
Friends of Bellaire Parks. Bellaire, TX. $2,600.
The Jefferson Energy Foundation. Washington, DC. $15,000.
The Nature Conservancy, Oklahoma Field Office. Tulsa, OK. $50,000.
Oklahoma Wildlife Federation. Oklahoma City, OK. $1,000.
George Miksch Sutton Avian Research Center, Inc. Bartlesville, OK. $25,000.
Trout Unlimited. Vienna, VA. $1,000.
Tulsa Zoo Development. Tulsa, OK. $1,000.

Application process. *Initial contact:* Brief abstract of the proposal and:
1. Copy of IRS tax-exempt status determination letter.
2. Description of organization's aims and objectives, activities, and geographic scope, particularly as it relates to Phillips.
3. Names and affiliations of officers and board of directors or trustees, including relationships with Phillips Petroleum Company or its subsidiaries.
4. Number and total compensation of paid employees and number of volunteers.
5. Sources of all current income; list of other corporations, foundations, or agencies from which funding is requested.
6. Copy of most recent IRS Form 990.
7. List of organizations and foundations contributing to the organization during the previous 12 months.
8. Description of the project, the purpose of the sponsoring organization, how long the funds will be needed and:
   - What grant is expected to accomplish.
   - How program will be administered.
   - How program will be evaluated.
   - Budget.
   - Geographical scope.
   - Special funding costs.

When to apply: Anytime.
Materials available: "Contributions Policies and Guidelines," "Grant Application Guidelines."

Emphases. *Recipients:* Nonprofit organizations.
Activities: Conferences, demonstration programs, education, research.

P

Types of support: Annual campaigns, equipment, facilities, internships, land acquisition, matching funds, operating costs, professorships, scholarships, seed money, seminars.
Geography: Locations where the sponsoring company has a presence: Colorado, Oklahoma, Texas, and other states in the South and Southwest.

Limitations. *Recipients:* Individuals (except for scholarships for dependent children of employees), religious organizations.
Activities: Fundraising, political activities.
Types of support: Endowments, travel expenses.

Ellis L. Phillips Foundation
29 Commonwealth Avenue
Boston, Massachusetts 02116–2349
Tel: 617–424–7607
EIN: 135677691   Type: Independent
Contact: Janet Walsh, Executive Director

History and philosophy. The Foundation was founded in 1930 by Ellis L. Phillips, founder and president of the Long Island Lighting Company. The Foundation is today primarily interested in strategically significant modest project grants to certified 501(c)(3) institutions in New England. It supports work in: Informal and Women's Education, Advanced Training and Institutional Development in Music and the Visual Arts, Rural Human Services, Rural Historic Preservation, Biodiversity Conservation, and the Strengthening of Traditional Religion.

Officers and directors. *Officers:* Ellis L. Phillips, III, President; Ellis L. Phillips, Jr., Vice President; K. Noel Phillips Zimmermann, Secretary; George C. Thompson, Treasurer. *Directors:* David Lloyd Brown, Cornelia Grumman, David L. Grumman, George E. McCully, Walter C. Paine, Ellis L. Phillips, Jr., Ellis L. Phillips, III, George C. Thompson, Elise Phillips Watts, K. Noël Phillips Zimmermann. *Members:* David L. Grumman, Ellis L. Phillips, Jr., Ellis L. Phillips III.

Financial data. Data for fiscal year ended June 30, 1993. *Assets:* $5,293,151 (M). *Total grants authorized:* $165,450.

Environmental awards. *Program and interests:* The environmental program focuses on biodiversity conservation.

Issues.   Cli   Bio   Lan   Agr   Wat   Oce   Ene   Was   Tox   Pop   Dev
                    •   •

Funding analysis.

Fiscal year:	1992	1993
Env grants disb:	$19,000	$22,000
Number:	3	3
Range:	$5,000–$8,000	$6,000–$10,000
Median:	$6,000	$6,000
Pct $ disb (env/total):	7	13

Recipients (1993):	Number:	Dollars:
The Trust for Public Land	1	10,000
Appalachian Trail Conference, New England Regional Office	1	6,000
Social Science Institute	1	6,000

Activity region (1993):	Number:	Dollars:
U.S. Northeast	3	22,000

Sample grants (1993).*
Appalachian Trail Conference, New England Regional Office. Lyme, NH. $6,000. For Phase II of the Norwich-Hartford Greenway Project, to develop a 2,000 acre greenway and a 3.5 mile wildlife corridor.
Social Science Institute. Harborside, ME. $6,000. Second payment of a $12,000 grant in support of Eliot Coleman's research project involving sustainable soil fertility.
The Trust for Public Land. Boston, MA. $10,000. To fund an organizational development study to broaden the base of individual support and awareness of this land conservation organization.

*Sample grants represent either new awards or disbursements on grants awarded in previous years.

Application process. *Initial contact:* Concise letter (2–4 pages) to include descriptions of:
1. The organization, its history, and major accomplishments.
2. Problem to be solved, and its significance.
3. Solution proposed, its cost-effectiveness, and significance.
4. Specific project goals (quantified where possible).

Supporting documents.
1. Copy of IRS tax-exempt status determination letter.
2. Summary statement of the proposal (1 paragraph).
3. Project budget, indicating what proposed grant would cover.
4. Organization's budget for the current fiscal year.

Required of all proposals for grants of $5,000 or more, but optional for smaller proposals.
1. Most recent audited financial statements.
2. Board of directors, with institutional affiliations and titles.
3. List of all foundation grants received in the past two years, and of grant requests submitted or planned for proposed project.
4. Names, titles, and institutional affiliations of three independent references, with addresses and telephone numbers.

When to apply: Deadlines are January 1, April 1, and September 1. The board of directors meets in February, May, and October.
Materials available: Annual report (includes "Application Guidelines").

Emphases. *Recipients:* Nonprofit organizations.
Types of support: Capacity building, collaborative efforts, education, innovative programs, planning.
Geography: Northern New England and Greater Boston only.

Limitations. *Recipients:* Individuals, public agencies.
Activities: Litigation, lobbying.
Types of support: Loans.

Howard Phipps Foundation

c/o Bessemer Trust Company
100 Woodbridge Center Drive
Woodbridge, New Jersey 07095–0983
EIN: 226095226   Type: Independent

Application address:
Howard Phipps Foundation
c/o Bessemer Trust Company
630 Fifth Avenue
New York, New York 10111
Tel: 212–708–9242   Fax: 212–265–5826
Contact: Austin J. Power, Jr., Senior Vice President, Bessemer Trust Company

History and philosophy. Harriet Phipps established the Foundation in 1967. It awards grants for conservation, culture, and education.

Officers and directors. *Trustees:* Howard Phipps, Jr., Anne P. Sidamon-Eristoff, Bessemer Trust Company.

Financial data. Data for fiscal year ended June 30, 1992. *Assets:* $6,634,599 (M). *Gifts received:* $1,528,545. *Total grants disbursed:* $1,832,500.

Environmental awards. *Recent grants:* 1992 grants included support for land conservation, horticulture, wildlife preservation, and outdoor education.

Issues.   Cli Bio Lan Agr Wat Oce Ene Was Tox Pop Dev
                ●   ●   ●   ●

Funding analysis.

Fiscal year:	1991	1992
Env grants disb:	$685,000	$572,500
Number:	6	10
Range:	$10,000–$450,000	$2,500–$410,000
Median:	$50,000	$20,000
Pct $ disb (env/total):	41	31

Recipients (1992 highest):	Number:	Dollars:
NYZS/The Wildlife Conservation Society	2	425,000
World Wildlife Fund	1	50,000
Earthwatch Expeditions, Inc.	1	25,000
Environmental Defense Fund	1	25,000
Natural Resources Defense Council	1	25,000

Activity regions (1992):	Number:	Dollars:
New York/New Jersey	7	492,500
International*	1	50,000
U.S. Northeast	2	30,000

*Multiple regions or not specified.

Sample grants (1992).
Earthwatch Expeditions, Inc. Watertown, MA. $25,000.
Environmental Defense Fund. New York, NY. $25,000.
Manomet Observatory for Conservation Science. Manomet, MA. $5,000.
The New York Botanical Garden. Bronx, NY. $2,500.
Natural Resources Defense Council. New York, NY. $25,000.
NYZS/The Wildlife Conservation Society. Bronx, NY. $425,000.
Scenic Hudson, Inc. Poughkeepsie, NY. $5,000.
The Trust for Public Land. San Francisco, CA. $10,000.
World Wildlife Fund. Washington, DC. $50,000.

Application process. *Initial contact:* Letter of proposal. *When to apply:* Anytime.

Emphases. *Geography:* New York City.

Pilot Trust

c/o Norwest Bank of Boulder, N.A.
P.O. Box 299
Boulder, Colorado 80306–0299
Tel: 303–441–0309   Fax: 303–442–4614
EIN: 846030136   Type: Independent
Contact: Dwight V. Roberts, Trustee

History and philosophy. Roger Calvert established the Trust in 1960. Its grant monies support the Trust's own Cal-Wood Environmental Education Resource Center, a facility 22 miles northwest of Boulder, designed for those otherwise unable to access natural areas and outdoor experiences. Cal-Wood serves as a resource for various schools and universities as a retreat and a locus for environmental research.

Officers and directors. *Trustees:* Dan Calvert, Richard Meckley, Lawrence M. Wood, Norwest Bank of Boulder.

Financial data. Data for fiscal year ended December 31, 1993. *Assets:* $3,734,975 (M). *Total grants disbursed:* $177,962.

Environmental awards. *Program and interests:* The Trust is a funding trust for Cal-Wood Environmental Education Resource Center.

Funding analysis.

Fiscal year:	1991	1992
Env grants disb:	$174,620	$221,410
Number:	1	1
Range:	–	–
Median:	–	–
Pct $ disb (env/total):	100	100

Recipient (1992):	Number:	Dollars:
Cal-Wood Environmental Education Resource Center	1	221,410

Activity region (1992):	Number:	Dollars:
U.S. Mountain	1	221,410

Sample grant (1992).
Cal-Wood Environmental Education Resource Center. Boulder, CO. $221,410.

P

Application process. *Initial contact:* The Foundation awards grants to a pre-selected organization (Cal-Wood Environmental Education Resource Center) only.
When to apply: The board meets twice a year.

Emphases. *Recipients:* Pre-selected organization only.
Activities: Education, training.
Types of support: Continuing support.
Geography: Boulder County, Colorado.

Limitations. *Types of support:* Loans.

Pinewood Foundation
3 Manhattanville Road
Purchase, New York 10577–2110
Tel: 914–696–9000
EIN: 136101581   Type: Independent
Contact: Celeste G. Bartos, President

History and philosophy. Celeste G. Bartos established the Foundation (then the Celeste and Armand Bartos Foundation) in 1956. The Foundation makes grants to pre-selected organizations in the arts, cultural programs, education, and health. Conservation, the environment, and zoos and botanical gardens also receive a significant share of grant dollars.

Officers and directors. *Officers:* Celeste G. Bartos, President; Armand P. Bartos, Edgar Wachenheim, III, Vice Presidents; Peter C. Siegfried, Secretary; Irwin Markow, Treasurer; Joshua J. Eisenstein, Assistant Treasurer. *Directors:* Armand P. Bartos, Celeste G. Bartos, Joshua J. Eisenstein, Irwin Markow, Peter C. Siegfried, Edgar Wachenheim, III.

Financial data. Data for fiscal year ended September 30, 1993. *Assets:* $11,354,993 (M). *Total grants disbursed:* $2,420,572.

Environmental awards. *Recent grants:* 1993 grants included support for urban parks and gardens, and biodiversity (habitats, animals, and plants).

Issues.   Cli   Bio   Lan   Agr   Wat   Oce   Ene   Was   Tox   Pop   Dev
                •   •   •

Funding analysis.

Fiscal year:	1991	1993
Env grants disb:	$234,550	$191,300
Number:	11	6
Range:	$100–$195,000	$100–$175,000
Median:	$2,000	$3,000
Pct $ disb (env/total):	19	8

Recipients (1993 highest):	Number:	Dollars:
The New York Botanical Garden	1	175,000
Earth Island Institute	1	10,000
NYZS/The Wildlife Conservation Society	1	5,000
National Wildflower Research Center	1	1,000
The Nature Conservancy, Headquarters	1	200

Activity regions (1993):	Number:	Dollars:
New York/New Jersey	3	180,100
U.S. West	1	10,000
U.S. not specified	2	1,200

Sample grants (1993).
Earth Island Institute. La Honda, CA. $10,000.
National Wildflower Research Center. Austin, TX. $1,000.
The Nature Conservancy, Headquarters. Austin, TX. $200.
The New York Botanical Garden. Bronx, NY. $175,000.
NYZS/The Wildlife Conservation Society. Bronx, NY. $5,000.
The Parks Council, Inc. New York, NY. $3,000.

Application process. *Initial contact:* The Foundation awards grants to pre-selected organizations only. No unsolicited applications accepted.

Emphases. *Recipients:* Pre-selected organizations only.
Geography: New York City; Santa Fe, New Mexico.

Limitations. *Recipients:* Individuals.

Henry B. Plant Memorial Fund, Inc.
c/o U.S. Trust Company of New York
114 West 47th Street
New York, New York 10036–1532
Tel: 212–852–3719
EIN: 136077327   Type: Independent
Contact: Edward Sullivan

History and philosophy. The Foundation was established in 1947 by Amy P. Statter. Areas of interest include education, museums, and conservation.

Officers and directors. *Officers:* Mrs. J. Philip Lee, President; Mrs. David C. Oxman, Vice President.

Financial data. Data for fiscal year ended December 31, 1992. *Assets:* $6,796,094 (M). *Total grants disbursed:* $308,000.

Environmental awards. *Recent grants:* 1992 grants included support for urban parks, horticulture, marine issues, and outdoor education.

Issues.   Cli   Bio   Lan   Agr   Wat   Oce   Ene   Was   Tox   Pop   Dev
                •   •   •   •

Funding analysis.

Fiscal year:	1992
Env grants disb:	$40,000
Number:	14
Range:	$500–$10,000
Median:	$2,000
Pct $ disb (env/total):	13

Recipients (1992 highest):	Number:	Dollars:
Sea Education Association	1	10,000
Environmental Defense Fund	1	5,000
Quebec Labrador Foundation/ Atlantic Center for the Environment	1	5,000
Woods Hole Oceanographic Institution	1	5,000
Natural Resources Defense Council	1	4,000

Activity regions (1992):	Number:	Dollars:
U.S. Northeast	7	23,000
New York/New Jersey	4	12,000
U.S. not specified	3	5,000

Sample grants (1992).
Central Park Conservancy. New York, NY. $1,000.
Environmental Defense Fund. New York, NY. $5,000.
Greenwich Clean and Green. Greenwich, CT. $500.
Natural Resources Defense Fund. New York, NY. $4,000.
The Nature Center. Westport, CT. $1,000.
The New York Botanical Garden. Bronx, NY. $1,000.
Outward Bound. Greenwich, CT. $1,000.
Quebec Labrador Foundation/Atlantic Center for the Environment. Ipswich, MA. $5,000.
Sea Education Association. Woods Hole, MA. $10,000.
Sierra Club Foundation. San Francisco, CA. $2,000.
Woods Hole Oceanographic Institution. Woods Hole, MA. $5,000.

Application process. *Initial contact:* Letter describing activity of organization and purpose of grant.
When to apply: Anytime.

Emphases. *Recipients:* Nonprofit organizations.

Limitations. *Recipients:* Individuals.

The Polden-Puckham Charitable Foundation
41 Beauchamp Road, Bishopston
Bristol BS7 8LQ
United Kingdom
Tel: 011-0272-400324   Fax: 011-0272-400324
EGA member
Contact: M. Bevis Gillett, Secretary

History and philosophy. The Foundation was formed in 1990 by the merger of two family trusts, the A. B. and M. C. Charitable Foundation and the Puckham Charitable Trust. "The trustees are largely descendants of A. B. and M. C. Gillett, whilst the capital of the foundation comes from businesses with Quaker links." The Foundation supports work in the areas of peace, ecology and environment, and values and attitudes.

Officers and directors. *Trustees:* J. E. Barlow, R. R. Fruchter, A. N. Gillett, C. M. Gillett, D. B. Gillett, H. J. Gillett, J. Gordon.

Financial data. Data for 1991–92. *Assets:* 4,000,000£ (est.). *Total grants disbursed:* 223,000£ (est.).

Environmental awards. *Program and interests:* The Foundation's Ecology and Environment Program is involved in "work which demonstrates alternatives to current economic and social structures and thus tackles the underlying pressures and conditions which are tending to lead to global environmental catastrophe; particularly projects which promote sustainable lifestyles."

Issues. Cli Bio Lan Agr Wat Oce Ene Was Tox Pop Dev
                              •   •

Sample grants (1991–92).*
Friends of the Earth Trust. U.K.
Pesticides Trust. U.K.
Womens Environmental Network. London, U.K.

*Dollar amounts not available.

Application process. *Initial contact:* Proposal (2 pages) to include:
1. Description of project, goals, and methods to achieve goals.
2. Amount requested, names of current and potential funders, and expected sources after termination of PPCF funding.
3. Methods of monitoring, evaluating, and publicizing.
4. List and resumes of key personnel involved in organization.
5. Current audited financial documents, project budget, list of trustees, and two names not involved in organization.
6. Charity registration number or name and number of a charity which can accept funds on organization's behalf.

When to apply: Anytime. The trustees meet twice a year in late March/April and October.

Emphases. *Recipients:* Nonprofit organizations.

Limitations. *Recipients:* Individuals.
Activities: Research (scholarly).
Types of support: Capital campaigns/expenses, general purposes, travel expenses.

The Powell Family Foundation
10990 Roe Avenue
P.O. Box 7270
Overland Park, Kansas 66207-0563
Tel: 913-967-4321
EIN: 237023968   Type: Independent
Contact: Marjorie P. Allen, President

History and philosophy. The Foundation was established in 1969 by George E. Powell, Sr., former chairman of Yellow Freight System, Inc. Powell was a committed Christian Scientist who believed that assisting in the development of youth was the "most meaningful investment of time and finances" the Foundation could make. The Foundation continues to support the founder's interests in programs that benefit the residents of the Kansas City area. Funding areas are: Education, Community Support, and Youth Programs.

P

Officers and directors. *Officers:* George E. Powell, Jr., President; Marilyn P. Rinker, Vice President and Secretary; George E. Powell III, Treasurer. *Trustees:* Barbara P. Allen, George E. Powell, Jr., George E. Powell III, Nicholas K. Powell.

Financial data. Data for fiscal year ended December 31, 1993. *Assets:* $43,634,361 (M). *Total grants disbursed:* $2,265,998.

Environmental awards. *Program and interests:* The Foundation's central environmental effort is continuing support of Powell Gardens, a botanical garden and natural resource center dedicated to the promotion of horticulture and the appreciation of nature. *Recent grants:* 1993 grants included capital expenditures in anticipation of major building projects, horticulture, and community gardens.

Issues. Cli Bio• Lan• Agr Wat Oce Ene Was Tox Pop Dev

Funding analysis.

Fiscal year:	1993
Env grants disb:	$1,103,000
Number:	4
Range:	$8,000–1,050,000
Median:	$8,000
Pct $ disb (env/total):	49

Recipients (1993):	Number:	Dollars:
Powell Gardens, Inc.	1	1,050,000
Camping Connection	1	25,000
Wildwood Outdoor Education Center	1	20,000
Kansas City Community Gardens	1	8,000

Activity region (1993):	Number:	Dollars:
U.S. Midwest	4	1,103,000

Sample grants (1993).
Camping Connection. Kansas City, MO. $25,000. Camperships for at-risk youth.
Kansas City Community Gardens. Kansas City, MO. $8,000. Operating expenses for this organization that transforms vacant lots and backyard plots into productive vegetable and flower gardens mostly in the inner city.
Powell Gardens, Inc. Lonejack MO. $1,050,000. Operating expenses and pre-construction capital expenditures for this botanical garden and natural resource center which functions as a model of wise land use.
Wildwood Outdoor Education Center. LaCygne, KS. $20,000. Outdoor youth programs.

Application process. *Initial contact:* Proposal (3–5 pages) to include:
1. Description of project.
2. Proposed budget.
3. Objectives of program.
4. Other funders.
5. Board.
6. Most recent audited financial statement.
7. Copy of IRS tax-exempt status determination letter.

When to apply: Anytime. The trustees meet several times a year. Meetings are scheduled for the early spring and late fall.
Materials available: Biennial report, "Information for Applicants."

Emphases. *Recipients:* Botanical gardens, educational institutions, museums, nonprofit organizations.
Activities: Education, training, youth programs.
Types of support: Annual campaigns, continuing support, equipment, maintenance, operating costs, scholarships.
Geography: Kansas City area.

Limitations. *Recipients:* Individuals, public agencies, religious organizations, research institutions, zoos.
Activities: Activism, advocacy, audiovisual materials, conferences, conflict resolution, demonstration programs, exhibits, expeditions/tours, feasibility studies, fieldwork, fundraising, inventories, land acquisition, litigation, lobbying, political activities, publications, research, seminars, symposia/colloquia, technical assistance, volunteerism, workshops.
Types of support: Advertising campaigns, computer hardware, debt retirement, endowments, fellowships, indirect costs, internships, lectureships, leveraging funds, loans, membership campaigns, professorships, scholarships (to individuals).
Geography: International.

Lynn R. and Karl E. Prickett Fund

P.O. Box 20124
Greensboro, North Carolina 27420–0124
Tel: 919–274–5471 Fax: 919–272–8921
EIN: 566064788 Type: Independent
Contact: Dora Head, Account Administrator

History and philosophy. The Fund was established in 1964. It primarily supports civic affairs, social services, and education. The arts and health are also supported.

Officers and directors. *Trustees:* Charles S. Chapin, Chester F. Chapin, Samuel C. Chapin, C. W. Cheek, Lynn C. Gunzenhauser, Lisa V. Prochnow.

Financial data. Data for fiscal year ended June 30, 1992. *Assets:* $20,258,081 (M). *Total grants disbursed:* $882,415.

Environmental awards. *Recent grants:* 1992 grants included support for land and watershed preservation, wildlife conservation, marine issues, and outdoor education.

Issues. Cli Bio• Lan• Agr Wat• Oce• Ene Was• Tox Pop Dev

Funding analysis.

Fiscal year:	1991	1992
Env grants disb:	$217,000	$235,475
Number:	8	18
Range:	$5,000–$50,800	$1,000–$47,825
Median:	$24,200	$5,500
Pct $ disb (env/total):	27	27

Recipients (1992 highest):	Number:	Dollars:
Environmental Defense Fund	2	50,825
The Cousteau Society	1	47,825
Worldwatch Institute	1	47,825
Center for Marine Conservation	4	36,000
Natural Resources Defense Council	1	15,000

Activity regions (1992):	Number:	Dollars:
U.S. not specified	11	109,825
International*	4	108,650
U.S. Southeast	1	10,000
U.S. West	1	6,000
U.S. Northwest	1	1,000

*Multiple regions or not specified.

Sample grants (1992).
Center for Marine Conservation. Washington, DC. $36,000.
The Cousteau Society. Norfolk, VA. $47,825.
Environmental Defense Fund. New York, NY. $3,000.
The Gorilla Foundation. Woodside, CA. $5,000.
Natural Resources Defense Council. Washington, DC. $15,000.
North Carolina Outward Bound School. Morganton, NC. $10,000.
Worldwatch Institute. Washington, DC. $47,825.
World Wildlife Fund. Washington, DC. $10,000.

Application process. *Initial contact:* Proposal and copy of organization's IRS tax-exempt status determination letter. *When to apply:* Anytime.

Emphases. *Types of support:* General purposes.

Prince Charitable Trusts
10 South Wacker Drive, Suite 2575
Chicago, Illinois 60606
Tel: 312–454–9130 Fax: 312–454–9125
EIN: 362411865 Type: Independent
EGA member
Contact: Tracey Shafroth, Program Director

History and philosophy. The Prince Charitable Trusts were established in 1947 by Frederick Henry Prince. Their mission is to support a broad range of charitable institutions in Rhode Island, Chicago, Illinois, and Washington, D.C. The Trusts make grants in the areas of: Arts and Culture, Environment, Education, Social Services, and Health Care.

Officers and directors. *Trustees:* Frederick H. Prince, William Wood Prince.

Financial data. Data for fiscal year ended December 31, 1992. *Assets:* $100,000,000 (M) (est.). *Total grants authorized:* $4,635,550.

Environmental awards. *Program and interests:* Interests are education, advocacy, and citizen participation in relation to:

- Open space.
- Land use planning.
- Transportation.
- Recycling.

Recent grants: 1993 grants included support for land conservation, urban forests, botanic gardens, river protection, coastal issues, fisheries, transportation, and recycling.

Issues. Cli• Bio• Lan Agr• Wat• Oce• Ene• Was Tox Pop Dev

Funding analysis.

Fiscal year:	1991	1993
Env grants disb:	$597,000	$521,537
Number:	33	33
Range:	$5,000–$100,000	$400–$100,000
Median:	$12,500	$10,000
Pct $ disb (env/total):	13	–

Recipients (1993 highest):	Number:	Dollars:
Piedmont Environmental Council	2	125,000
Conservation Law Foundation	1	35,000
The Conservation Fund	2	30,000
Center for Neighborhood Technology	1	25,000
Environmental Law and Policy Center of the Midwest	1	25,000
Save the Bay, Inc.	1	25,000
Sierra Club Legal Defense Fund	1	25,000
Wetlands Research, Inc.	1	25,000

Activity regions (1993):	Number:	Dollars:
U.S. Mid-Atlantic	10	220,000
U.S. Great Lakes	7	127,000
U.S. Northeast	9	107,037
U.S. not specified	6	62,500
U.S. Midwest	1	5,000

Sample grants (1993).
Anacostia Watershed Society. College Park, MD. $10,000. Toward advocacy efforts for Children's Island.
Center for Marine Conservation. Washington, DC. $10,000. Toward the Fish for Future Program.
Center for Neighborhood Technology. Chicago, IL. $25,000. Toward support of the Material Reuse and Recycling Program.
Conservation Law Foundation. Boston, MA. $35,000. For their work on the issues of transportation and water in Rhode Island.
Earthwatch. Watertown, RI. $12,500. Toward five Education Awards for the middle schools on Aquidneck Island in Rhode Island.
Friends of Conservation. Oak Brook, IL. $20,000. General operating support.
Isaak Walton League of America. Arlington, VA. $15,000. Toward the Virginia Save Our Streams Program.
National Fund for the United States Botanic Garden. Washington, DC. $10,000. Capital campaign.
Open Lands Project. Chicago, IL. $15,000. Urban Greening Program.
Piedmont Environmental Council. Warrenton, VA. $100,00. Toward the Disney Take a Second Look Campaign.
Save the Bay, Inc. Providence, RI. $25,000. Toward the Baykeeper Program.

P

Application process. *Initial contact:* Letter of inquiry (2 pages). *When to apply:* Anytime. Call for annual meeting dates.

Emphases. *Recipients:* Nonprofit organizations.
Activities: Capacity building, citizen participation, collaborative efforts, education, land acquisition, litigation, policy analysis/development.
Types of support: Capital campaigns/expenses (limited), operating costs.
Geography: Chicago, Illinois; Rhode Island; organizations in Washington, D.C. that do not have a national focus.

Limitations. *Recipients:* Individuals.

Pritzker Foundation
200 West Madison Street, Suite 3800
Chicago, Illinois 60606
Tel: 312-621-4200
EIN: 366058062   Type: Independent
Contact: Simon Zunamon, Assistant Treasurer

History and philosophy. The Foundation was established in 1944 by members of the Pritzker family, owners of the Hyatt Corporation. The Foundation is run by the family and supports Jewish organizations, the arts, health, education, and social services in the Chicago metropolitan area.

Officers and directors. *Officers:* Robert A. Pritzker, Chairman and Vice President; Jay A. Pritzker, President; Nicholas J. Pritzker, Vice President and Secretary; Penny F. Pritzker, Vice President and Assistant Secretary; Thomas J. Pritzker, Vice President and Treasurer/Assistant Secretary; Daniel F. Pritzker, James N. Pritzker, John A. Pritzker, Vice Presidents; Glen Miller, Simon Zunamon, Assistant Treasurers. *Directors:* Daniel F. Pritzker, James N. Pritzker, Jay A. Pritzker, John A. Pritzker, Nicholas J. Pritzer, Penny F. Pritzker, Robert A. Pritzker, Thomas J. Pritzker.

Financial data. Data for fiscal year ended December 31, 1992. *Assets:* $58,680,020 (M). *Gifts received:* $1,659,063. *Total grants disbursed:* $2,299,597.

Environmental awards. *Recent grants:* 1992 grants included support for open lands, urban parks, an aquarium, and a zoo.

Issues.   Cli   Bio   Lan   Agr   Wat   Oce   Ene   Was   Tox   Pop   Dev
             •   •   •

Funding analysis.

Fiscal year:	1992
Env grants disb:	$301,200
Number:	5
Range:	$100–$200,000
Median:	$1,000
Pct $ disb (env/total):	13

Recipients (1992):	*Number:*	*Dollars:*
John G. Shedd Aquarium	1	200,000
Lincoln Park Zoological Society	2	100,100
Chicago Rainforest Action Group	1	1,000
Open Lands Project	1	100

Activity region (1992):	*Number:*	*Dollars:*
U.S. Great Lakes	5	301,200

Sample grants (1992).
Chicago Rainforest Action Group. Chicago, IL. $1,000.
Lincoln Park Zoological Society. Chicago, IL. $100,100.
Open Lands Project. Chicago, IL. $100.
John G. Shedd Aquarium. Chicago, IL. $200,000.

Application process. *Initial contact:* The Foundation awards grants to pre-selected organizations only. No unsolicited applications accepted.

Emphases. *Recipients:* Pre-selected organizations only.
Geography: Chicago metropolitan area.

Limitations. *Recipients:* Individuals.

The Procter & Gamble Fund
P.O. Box 599
Cincinnati, Ohio 45201
Tel: 513-945-8452   Fax: 513-945-8979
EIN: 316019594   Type: Company-sponsored
EGA member
Contact: Nathan H. Nattin, Program Manager

History and philosophy. The Procter & Gamble Fund was established in 1952. It focuses on organizations and institutions that (1) enhance societal conditions favorable to the company's future growth and prosperity; or (2) enhance the quality of life in communities with concentrations of company employees. Areas of giving are: Higher Education; Health and Social Service; and Civic, Cultural, and Environmental Organizations.

Officers and directors. *Officers:* R. L. Wehling, President; R. A. Bachhuber, E. G. Nelson, C. R. Otto, Vice Presidents; Robert R. Fitzpatrick, Jr., Vice President and Secretary; Raymond D. Mains, Treasurer; R. M. Neago, Assistant Secretary; Vicki F. Tylman, Assistant Treasurer. *Trustees:* R. A. Bachhuber, E. G. Nelson, C. R. Otto, R. L. Wehling.

Financial data. Data for fiscal year ended March 30, 1994. *Assets:* $26,000,000 (U) (est.). *Total grants authorized:* $19,000,000 (est).

Environmental awards. *Program and interests:* The Fund's environmental interests are:

- Solid waste.
- Air quality.
- Water quality.
- Land and wildlife.
- Wetlands.
- Coastal issues.

Recent grants: 1993 grants included support for land conservation, beautification, marine issues, air quality, and wildlife.

Issues. Cli Bio Lan Agr Wat Oce Ene Was Tox Pop Dev
· · · · · ·   ·

Funding analysis.

Fiscal year:	1991	1993
Env grants disb:	$505,000	$424,000
Number:	19	16
Range:	$1,000–$201,000	$1,000–$209,000
Median:	$10,000	$11,000
Pct $ disb (env/total):	3	2

Recipients (1993 highest):	Number:	Dollars:
Zoological Society of Cincinnati	1	209,000
Keep America Beautiful	1	68,000
Academy of Natural Sciences of Philadelphia	1	25,000
National Audubon Society	1	25,000
Memphis Zoo	1	20,000

Activity regions (1993):	Number:	Dollars:
U.S. Great Lakes	7	238,000
U.S. not specified	7	141,000
U.S. Mid-Atlantic	1	25,000
U.S. Southeast	1	20,000

Sample grants (1993).
Academy of Natural Sciences of Philadelphia. Philadelphia, PA. $25,000.
Air Pollution Control League of Greater Cincinnati. Cincinnati, OH. $2,000.
Civic Garden Center of Greater Cincinnati. Cincinnati, OH. $3,000.
Izaak Walton League of America. Arlington, VA. $10,000.
National Council for Environmental Balance. Louisville, KY. $3,000.
The Nature Conservancy, Headquarters. Arlington, VA. $15,000.
Zoological Society of Cincinnati. Cincinnati, OH. $209,000.

Application process. *Initial contact:* Short letter describing the organization and the request.
When to apply: Anytime.

Emphases. *Recipients:* Nonprofit organizations.
Types of support: Operating costs.
Geography: U.S., cities where Procter & Gamble has a significant presence only.

Limitations. *Recipients:* Individuals.
Activities: Publications, projects.
Types of support: Endowments.

The Prospect Hill Foundation
420 Lexington Avenue, Suite 3020
New York, New York 10170
Tel: 212–370–1144 Fax: 212–599–6282
EIN: 136075567 Type: Independent
EGA member
Contact: Constance Eiseman, Executive Director

History and philosophy. The Prospect Hill Foundation is a private foundation established in 1960 by William S. Beinecke, retired chairman of the Sperry and Hutchinson Company. In 1983, the Foundation merged with the Frederick W. Beinecke Fund, which had been established by the will of William Beinecke's father and later augmented by his mother, Carrie Sperry Beinecke.

The Foundation's program areas are: Environmental Conservation; Nuclear Weapons Control; Population (targeting Latin America); Social Services; and Arts, Cultural, and Educational Institutions selected by the directors.

Officers and directors. *Officers:* William S. Beinecke, President; Elizabeth G. Beinecke, Frederick W. Beinecke, John B. Beinecke, Vice Presidents; Constance Eiseman, Secretary and Executive Director; Robert J. Barletta, Treasurer. *Directors:* Elizabeth G. Beinecke, Frederick W. Beinecke, John B. Beinecke, William S. Beinecke, Frances Beinecke Elston, Sarah Beinecke Richardson.

Financial data.* Data for fiscal year ended June 30, 1994. *Assets:* $43,500,000 (U). *Total grants disbursed:* $2,210,093.

*Grants include $129,293 in matching funds.

Environmental awards. *Program and interests:* The Foundation's environmental grantmaking focuses on land and water protection, primarily in the northeastern United States. Proposals are encouraged from organizations exhibiting leadership that:

- Offer strategies and policies for the conservation of public and private lands.

- Strengthen policies and initiate means for improving water quality and protecting coastal areas.

The Foundation also makes a few grants each year for habitat and ecosystem preservation in Latin America. Related interests include family planning and nuclear weapons nonproliferation.

Issues. Cli Bio Lan Agr Wat Oce Ene Was Tox Pop Dev
· · · · ·   · · ·

Funding analysis.§

Fiscal year:	1992	1994
Env grants auth:	$352,500	$637,700
Number:	23	23
Range:	$2,500–$40,000	$2,500–$250,000
Median:	$15,000	$15,000
Pct $ auth (env/total):	44	34

Recipients (1994 highest):	Number:	Dollars:
NYZS/The Wildlife Conservation Society	1	250,000
Save the Bay, Inc.	1	90,000
Central Park Conservancy	1	25,000

National Audubon Society	1	25,000
American Littoral Society	1	20,000
City Parks Foundation	1	20,000
Manomet Observatory for Conservation Science	1	20,000
Natural Resources Defense Council	1	20,000
Prospect Park Alliance	1	20,000

Activity regions (1994 highest):	*Number:*	*Dollars:*
New York/New Jersey	15	448,200
U.S. Northeast	4	124,500
Mexico and Central America	1	20,000
U.S. not specified	1	20,000
U.S. Northwest	1	15,000

§Includes Cultural and Educational Institutions program grants.

Sample grants (1994).
Adirondack Land Trust. Keene Valley, NY. $15,000. General support.
American Littoral Society. Highlands, NY. $20,000. For the New York/New Jersey Harbor Baykeeper Project.
Bank Information Center. Washington, DC. $10,000. To monitor activities in the Caribbean and Latin America of the MLBs and to strengthen overseas NGOs working on reforms.
Central Park Conservancy. New York, NY. $25,000. Toward the salary of a zone gardener at Harlem Meer.
Clean Water Fund. Providence, RI. $7,500. For the Rhode Island War on Waste Campaign.
Ecotrust. Portland, OR. $15,000. Toward the costs of publishing a *Rain Forests of Home* Atlas.
Manomet Observatory for Conservation Sciences. Manomet, MA. $20,000 (2 years). To promote natural forest management of tropical forests in Belize.
National Audubon Society. New York, NY. $25,000. Toward Audubon Adventures Program in New York City and the Migratory Bird Conservation Program.
New York Environmental Institute. Albany, NY. $10,000. Toward the Communities of Place Project that promotes land use planning in New York State.
Save the Bay, Inc. Providence, RI. $90,000 (3 years). Toward protection of Narragansett Bay.
The Trust for Public Land. New York, NY. $10,000. For land preservation activities in New York State.
The Wilderness Society. Washington, DC. $15,000. For the 1994 Northern Forest Preservation Campaign.

Application process. *Initial contact:* Letter (3 pages maximum, 2 copies) to include:
1. Summary of applicant organization's history and goals.
2. Summary of project for which funding is sought.
3. Contribution of project to other work in the field and/or to organization's own development.
4. Organization's (current and proposed) budget and staff size.
5. Project budget.
6. Potential sources of project support.
7. List of organization's board of directors.

If the Foundation is interested, more detailed information will be requested including:
1. Line-item organizational and project income and expense budgets.
2. List of committed and prospective sources of support for project.
3. Timetable for project completion.
4. Qualifications of key personnel involved with project.
5. List of other organizations involved in similar projects with a description of how proposed program is different from or complements those efforts.
6. List of project's expected results and evaluation criteria.
7. Copy of IRS tax-exempt status determination letter.
8. Most recent audited financial statement.
9. Most recent IRS Form 990.

When to apply: Anytime. The directors meet five times annually.
Materials available: Annual report (includes "Application Requirements and Review Process").

Emphases. *Recipients:* Nonprofit organizations.
Activities: Land acquisition (in the Northeast), litigation, policy analysis/development.
Types of support: Multi-year grants, operating costs, pilot projects.
Geography: Northeastern United States; Latin America.

Limitations. *Recipients:* Individuals, public agencies, religious organizations.
Activities: Research (scholarly).

The Prudential Foundation
751 Broad Street, 15th Floor
Newark, New Jersey 07102–3777
Tel: 201–802–7354   Fax: 201–802–3345
EIN: 222175290   Type: Company-sponsored
Contact: Barbara L. Halaburda, Secretary

History and philosophy. The Prudential Insurance Company of America is the principal donor of The Prudential Foundation, which was incorporated in 1977. The Foundation's six primary grant categories are: Focus on Children (women, children and families; children's issues), Health and Human Services (including public policy), Education (precollegiate, minority teacher recruitment, conflict resolution), Urban & Community Development (neighborhood revitalization, employment and job-training opportunities), Business and Civic Affairs (public policy), Culture and the Arts (arts education and increased access), Social Investments (affordable housing, economic revital-ization), Volunteer Recognition, and Company Contributions.

Officers and directors. *Officers:* Dorothy K. Light, Chairman; Gabriella M. Coleman, President; Paul G. O'Leary, Vice President; Barbara L. Halaburda, Secretary; James J. Straine, Treasurer. *Trustees:* Lisle C. Carter, Jr., Carolyne K. Davis, James R. Gillen, Jon F. Hanson, Dorothy K. Light, Donald E. Procknow, Robert C. Winters, Edward D. Zinbarg.

Financial data. Data for fiscal year ended December 31, 1993. *Assets:* $131,705,000 (M). *Total grants disbursed:* $14,581,000.

Environmental awards. *Recent grants:* 1993 grants included support for environmental education.

Issues. *Cli Bio Lan Agr Wat Oce Ene Was Tox Pop Dev*
• • • •

Funding analysis.

Fiscal year:	1992
Env grants disb:	$94,000
Number:	11
Range:	$1,000–$50,000
Median:	$5,000
Pct $ disb (env/total):	1

Recipients (1992 highest):	*Number:*	*Dollars:*
The Trust for Public Land	1	50,000
New Jersey Conservation Foundation	1	10,000
The Student Conservation Association, Inc.	1	10,000
Heifer Project International	1	5,000
ISLES	1	5,000
North Camden Land Trust, Inc.	1	5,000

Activity regions (1992):	*Number:*	*Dollars:*
U.S. not specified	2	60,000
New York/New Jersey	4	22,500
U.S. Mid-Atlantic	3	5,500
International*	1	5,000
U.S. Great Lakes	1	1,000

*Multiple regions or not specified.

Sample grants (1993).
Pratt Institute, Center for Community and Environmental Development. Brooklyn, NY. $25,000. To produce and disseminate a television documentary on the community development corporation movement.
The Student Conservation Association, Inc. Charlestown, NH. $10,000. Newark Conservation Career Development Program.

Application process. *Initial contact:* Application form and concept paper (3 pages), optional. The Foundation may request additional information to include:
1. Copy of latest audited financial statement.
2. Copy of IRS tax-exempt status determination letter.
3. Complete itemized project budget.
4. List of funding sources and amounts.
5. Names and qualifications of staff involved in project.

When to apply: Anytime. The board meets in April, August, and December.
Materials available: Annual report, "Applying for a Grant" (includes The Prudential Foundation Grant Application).

Emphases. *Recipients:* Educational institutions, nonprofit organizations.
Activities: Conferences, innovative programs, seminars.
Types of support: Operating costs, equipment, matching funds, projects, seed money, technical assistance.
Geography: Newark, New Jersey; New Jersey; cities where Prudential has a significant presence.

Limitations. *Recipients:* Individuals, religious organizations.
Activities: Fundraising.
Types of support: Endowments, loans, scholarships.

Public Welfare Foundation, Inc.
2600 Virginia Avenue, N.W., Suite 505
Washington, DC 20037-1977
Tel: 202-965-1800   Fax: 202-625-1348
EIN: 540597601   Type: Independent
Contacts: Larry Kressley, Executive Director
Dana Alston, Program Officer
Jodi Williams, Grants Manager

History and philosophy. The Public Welfare Foundation was founded by Charles Edward Marsh in 1947. A newspaper executive, Marsh wanted the Foundation "to provide immediate and direct support to organizations serving those whose need was genuine and urgent, with a minimum of overhead and red tape."
Today the Public Welfare Foundation provides support "to organizations that provide direct services to low-income or otherwise seriously disadvantaged populations, where adequate financial support is otherwise unavailable." It has six priority areas: Population, Environment, Disadvantaged Youth, Disadvantaged Elderly, Criminal Justice, and Health.

Officers and directors. *Officers:* Donald T. Warner, Chairman; Larry Kressley, Executive Director; Thomas J. Scanlon, Vice President; Linda J. Campbell, Secretary/Assistant Treasurer; Veronica Keating, Treasurer. *Directors:* Peter B. Edelman, Antoinette M. Haskell, Robert H. Haskell, Veronica Keating, Robert R. Nathan, Myrtis H. Powell, Thomas J. Scanlon, Thomas W. Scoville, Jerome W. D. Stokes, C. Elizabeth Warner, Donald T. Warner. *Director Emeritus:* Claudia Haines Marsh.

Financial data. Data for fiscal year ended October 31, 1993. *Assets:* $277,308,139 (U). *Total grants authorized:* $17,193,500.

Environmental awards. *Program and interests:* "Environmental funding is primarily focused on advancing the grassroots movement, through direct support of either community-based groups or organizations that provide them with technical assistance. Other grants address the health effects of global warming and offer support for sustainable development." Particular concern are problems that pose an threat to disadvantaged communities.
Recent grants: In fiscal year 1993 the environmental initiative supported: (1) groups working to reduce existing and future threats to health and safety posed by toxic substances; (2) efforts to reduce the effects of unsustainable development prac-tices on Native, Chicano, and African American indigenous cul-ture; (3) assistance to state, regional, and national organizations that contribute to the efforts of the grassroots movement; (4) efforts to protect the global atmosphere; and (5) sound agricultural and development efforts in the United States and other countries.

Issues. *Cli Bio Lan Agr Wat Oce Ene Was Tox Pop Dev*
• • • • • • • • • • •

Funding analysis.

Fiscal year:	1992	1993
Env grants auth:	$3,326,100	$3,658,600
Number:	80	85
Range:	$10,000–$250,000	$10,000–$250,000
Median:	–	$30,000
Pct $ auth (env/total):	19	21

© 1995 Environmental Data Resources, Inc.

P

Recipients (1993 highest):	Number:	Dollars:
Friends of the Earth/Environmental Policy Institute	1	250,000
Natural Resources Defense Council	1	250,000
Environmental Defense Fund	1	200,000
Citizens Clearinghouse for Hazardous Wastes, Inc.	1	100,000
National Toxics Campaign Fund	1	100,000
Southern Environmental Law Center	1	100,000

Activity regions (1993 highest):	Number:	Dollars:
U.S. not specified	14	1,110,000
U.S. Southeast	15	561,000
U.S. West	11	380,000
International*	2	240,000
U.S. Northeast	8	235,000

*Multiple regions or not specified.

Sample grants (1993).
Calumet Project for Industrial Jobs, Inc. East Chicago, IN. $25,000. General support to establish a worker-based environmental monitoring system.
Chickaloon Village Traditional Council. Palmer, AK. $20,000. For the Chickaloon Village Environmental Protection Project, which focuses on current environmental threats to Native Alaskan communities.
Citizen's Clearinghouse for Hazardous Wastes, Inc. Falls Church, VA. $100,000. General support to grassroots groups protecting the environmental health and safety of their communities.
Comité de Apoyo a Los Trabajadores Agricolas. Glassboro, NJ. $25,000. For the Pesticide Project, working with farmworkers in Puerto Rico, New Jersey, and Pennsylvania to reduce the health hazards from exposure to agricultural chemicals.
Institute for Energy and Environmental Research. Takoma Park, MD. $50,000. General support to the organization and support for its Technical Assistance Project, which provides scientific and technical training on local and generic issues related to Energy Department nuclear weapons plants.
Labor Community Strategy Center. Los Angeles, CA. $50,000. For the Watchdog Environmental Organization to promote broad citizen involvement in developing an air-quality plan.
Louisiana Environmental Action Network. Baton Rouge, LA. $25,000. General support to provide technical support, education, organizing and networking assistance to grassroots organizations working on toxic contamination and environmental health issues in Louisiana.
Penn Center. St. Helena Island, SC. $30,000. For the Sea Island Preservation Project, working with island residents to resist immediate environmental threats creating long-term change and promoting environmentally sound strategies.
Western States Center. Portland, OR. $50,000. For the Wise Use Public Exposure Project, which opposes the activities of the Wise Use movement and builds support for environmentally sound and sustainable economic development alternatives.

Application process. *Initial contact:* Full proposal using Proposal Outline. A concisely written proposal is preferred, and must be written in English. Letters of inquiry are not encouraged. Proposal to include:
Cover Sheet (2 pages maximum).
1. Name and address of organization.
2. Contact person(s), telephone and facsimile numbers.
3. One paragraph summarizing organization's purpose and activities.
4. Relationship of proposal to organization's mission statement.
5. Total annual organizational budget for the fiscal year.
6. Dollar amount requested.
7. Previous support from this funder.
8. Period the grant will cover (beginning and end dates).

Narrative (10 double-spaced pages maximum).
1. Organizational information.
   - Brief organizational history.
   - Mission and goals.
   - Description of programs, activities, and accomplishments.
   - Overview of organizational structure, including board, staff, and volunteer involvement.
2. Purpose of grant.
   - Needs statement.
   - Description of target population and how it will benefit.
   - Project goals and objectives.
   - Timetable.
   - Other organizations participating in project.
   - List of names and qualifications of project's key staff.
   - Strategies for continuation of project after grant period.
   - Project budget, including expenses and revenue.
3. Evaluation.
   - Plans for evaluation, including how success will be defined and measured.
   - How evaluation results will be used and/or disseminated and, if appropriate, replicated.

Attachments.
1. Copy of IRS tax-exempt status determination letter, or, if unavailable, an explanation of application status.
2. Board of directors and description of responsibilities, occupations, and the criteria for selection.
3. Finances.
   - Previous and current annual operating budget, including expenses and revenue (see annual report for format).
   - Year-to-date figures if project or fiscal year has been in progress for more than one quarter (see annual report for format).
   - List of other foundations, corporations, and other funding sources to which the proposal has been submitted, and amounts requested.
   - Affiliation with federated funds or public agencies.
4. Letters of support (4 maximum).
5. Annual report, if available.
6. Relevant articles or reviews about the organization's program.

When to apply: Anytime.
Materials available: Annual report (includes "A Guide to Grant Requests"), "A Guide to Grant Requests."

Emphases. *Activities:* Activism, advocacy, citizen participation, collaborative efforts, innovative programs, networking, political activities, technical assistance.
Types of support: Projects, technical assistance.

Limitations. *Activities:* Conferences, exhibits, land acquisition, research.
Types of support: Capital campaigns/expenses, endowments, equipment, facilities, lectureships, loans, professorships.

Recreational Equipment, Inc.

P.O. Box 1938
Sumner, Washington 98390–0800
Tel: 206-395-5955   Fax: 206-395-4744
EIN: 910656890   Type: Company-sponsored
EGA member
Contacts: Kathleen Beamer, Vice President, Public Affairs
Marianne M. Jones, Grants Administrator
Judy Patrick, Public Affairs Secretary

History and philosophy. Recreational Equipment, Inc. (REI), the outdoor clothing and equipment manufacturer, began its corporate giving program in 1976. It supports grassroots efforts to protect public lands, rivers, and trails for muscle-powered outdoor recreation.

Officers and directors. *Officer:* Kathleen Beamer, Vice President.

Financial data. Data for fiscal year ended December 31, 1993. *Assets:* $181,668,000 (M). *Revenue:* $333,600,000. *Total grants authorized:* $550,645.

Environmental awards. *Program and interests:* REI's primary interest is in protection and enhancement of natural resources needed for muscle-powered outdoor sports, through:

- Preservation of wildlands/open space.
- Advocacy-oriented education of the public on specific conservation issues.
- Building the membership base of conservation organizations.
- Direct citizen action (lobbying) on specific public land and water recreation issues.
- Working to organize a trails constituency and to advocate for trails at the state and local levels.
- Helping trails happen that are: mixed ownership, used for commuting, rail-to-trail conversion projects, mixed or diverse use, used by road or mountain bicycles.

Issues. Cli • Bio • Lan • Agr Wat • Oce • Ene Was • Tox Pop Dev

Funding analysis.§

Fiscal year:	1992	1993
Env grants auth:	$262,188	$391,878
Number:	31	34
Range:	$250–$81,000	$1,000–$165,000
Median:	$2,000	$3,000
Pct $ auth (env/total):	100	100

Recipients (1993 highest):	Number:	Dollars:
The National Trails Coalition	1	165,000
American Rivers, Inc.	2	80,000
International Mountain Bicycling Association	1	23,000
The Trust for Public Land	1	19,500
Mineral Policy Center	1	18,000

Activity regions (1993 highest):	Number:	Dollars:
U.S. not specified	9	298,904
U.S. Northwest	9	43,790
U.S. Northeast	2	12,500
U.S. Mountain	3	6,500
U.S. West	2	5,500

§Includes cash contributions only.

Sample grants (1993).
American Rivers, Inc. Washington, DC. $5,000. To assist with the 25th Anniversary Conference of the Wild and Scenic Act.
American Rivers, Inc. Washington, DC. $75,000. For the coalition effort by eight organizations to protect the country's outstanding free-flowing rivers through the funding of national and state river protection work. The coalition members oversee a program making grants to grassroots river protection organizations all over the United States.
Ancient Forests Video Project. Seattle, WA. $5,000. To assist with a special broadcast on the economic value of the ancient forests of the Pacific Northwest.
Land Trust Alliance. Washington, DC. $2,500. To assist with the National Rally Scholarships project.
Mineral Policy Center. Washington, DC. $18,000. To assist with lobbying for the 1872 Mining Law Reform project.
The National Trails Coalition. (Managed by the Sierra Club. San Francisco, CA.) $165,000. A coalition effort to protect the nation's wilderness and trail system. The four coalition members oversee a grantsmaking program to grassroots organizations working on recreation trails and wild lands issues nationwide.
Washington Wilderness Coalition. Seattle, WA. $3,300. To assist with the Washington Wilderness Coalition's 1993 Membership Drive.

Application process. *Initial contact:* Short letter. Full application to include:
1. Application form.
2. Description of organization and project (4 pages).
3. Project budget.
4. Copy of IRS tax-exempt status determination letter.

All materials to be submitted to Judy Patrick, Public Affairs Secretary. Do not contact REI during the evaluation process.
When to apply: Anytime.
Materials available: Corporate annual report, "Proposal Guidelines," application form, grants list.

Emphases. *Recipients:* Nonprofit organizations.
Activities: Activism, advocacy, citizen participation, collaborative efforts, innovative programs, lobbying, networking, political activities, youth programs.
Types of support: Annual campaigns, emergency funding, leveraging funds, membership campaigns, pilot projects, projects, seed money, single-year grants only.
Geography: United States only.

Limitations. *Recipients:* Botanical gardens, educational institutions, individuals, museums, public agencies, religious organizations, research institutions, zoos.
Activities: Conferences, direct services, education, fundraising, research, training, workshops.

R

Types of support: Advertising campaigns, capital campaigns/expenses, computer hardware, continuing support, debt retirement, endowments, equipment, facilities, fellowships, general purposes, indirect costs, lectureships, loans, maintenance, mortgage reduction, multi-year grants, operating costs, professorships, program-related investments, scholarships.

Philip D. Reed Foundation, Inc.

570 Lexington Avenue, Room 923
New York, New York 10022
Tel: 212–836–3330
EIN: 136098916   Type: Independent
Contact: Patricia Anderson, Secretary

History and philosophy. The Foundation was established in 1955 by Philip D. Reed. It makes grants in the areas of: higher education, international studies, international affairs, public policy, energy, environment, conservation, and family planning.

Officers and directors. *Officers:* Philip D. Reed, Jr., Chairman and President; Harold A. Segall, Vice President and Treasurer; Patricia Anderson, Secretary. *Trustees:* Patricia Anderson, Philip D. Reed, Jr., Harold A. Segall, Kathryn R. Smith.

Financial data. Data for fiscal year ended June 30, 1993. *Assets:* $6,936,658 (M). *Gifts received:* $859,125. *Total grants disbursed:* $1,863,500.

Environmental awards. *Recent grants:* 1993 grants included support for land conservation, watershed protection, recycling, and environmental education.

Issues. Cli Bio Lan Agr Wat Oce Ene Was Tox Pop Dev

Funding analysis.

Fiscal year:	1993
Env grants disb:	$215,000
Number:	5
Range:	$5,000–$125,000
Median:	$20,000
Pct $ disb (env/total):	12

Recipients (1993):	Number:	Dollars:
Smithsonian Institution	1	125,000
The Nature Conservancy, New Jersey Field Office	1	50,000
Population Communications International	1	20,000
Environmental Defense Fund	1	15,000
Alternative Media Information Center	1	5,000

Activity regions (1993):	Number:	Dollars:
U.S. Mid-Atlantic	1	125,000
New York/New Jersey	3	70,000
International*	1	20,000

*Multiple regions or not specified.

Sample grants (1993).
Alternative Media Information Center. New York, NY. $5,000. To support the recycling educational program.
Environmental Defense Fund. New York, NY. $15,000. General support.
The Nature Conservancy, New Jersey Field Office. Pottersville, NJ. $50,000. Campaign for the Delaware.
Population Communications International. New York, NY. $20,000. Population/Environment initiative.
Smithsonian Institution. Washington, DC. $125,000. For the Environmental Research Educational Building.

Application process. *Initial contact:* Proposal.
When to apply: Anytime.

Limitations. *Recipients:* Individuals.

Z. Smith Reynolds Foundation, Inc.

101 Reynolda Village
Winston-Salem, North Carolina 27106–5199
Tel: 910-725-7541   Fax: 910-725-6069
EIN: 586038145   Type: Independent
EGA member
Contact: Joseph E. Kilpatrick, Assistant Director

History and philosophy. The Z. Smith Reynolds Foundation was established in 1936 in memory of Zachary Smith Reynolds (1911–1932). It makes grants to benefit the people of North Carolina.

Current areas of interest are: Precollegiate Education, Community Economic Development, Minority Issues, Women's Issues, Criminal Justice, and the Environment. In all its grants activity, the Foundation places a higher value on developing new programs than on sustaining well-established and well-funded ones.

Officers and directors. *Officers:* Mary Mountcastle, President; Zachary Smith, Vice President; Thomas W. Lambeth, Secretary; Joseph G. Gordon, Treasurer. *Trustees:* Smith W. Bagley, Josephine D. Clement, Daniel G. Clodfelter, Joseph G. Gordon, Hubert Humphrey, Katharine B. Mountcastle, Mary Mountcastle, Stephen L. Neal, Jane S. Patterson, Sherwood H. Smith, Jr., Zachary Smith, Lloyd P. Tate, Jr.

Financial data.* Data for fiscal year ended December 31, 1993. *Assets:* $259,496,464 (M). *Total grants authorized:* $9,461,100. *Total grants disbursed:* $9,073,566.

*Assets include contributions from the W. N. Reynolds Trust.

Environmental awards. *Program and interests:* The Foundation is interested in the full spectrum of environmental topics from water quality to public lands management and waste disposal. It supports several approaches to these topics, in particular:

- Advocacy.
- Public policy research.
- Public education.
- Citizen participation and empowerment.

- Environmental education.

All efforts are directed to the needs of North Carolina.

Issues. Cli • Bio • Lan • Agr • Wat • Oce • Ene • Was • Tox • Pop • Dev •

Funding analysis.

Fiscal year:	1992	1993
Env grants auth:	$940,000	$765,000
Number:	20	26
Range:	$3,000–$130,000	$15,000–$85,000
Median:	$32,500	$25,000
Pct $ auth (env/total):	9	8

Recipients (1993 highest):	Number:	Dollars:
North Carolina Coastal Federation	1	85,000
Western North Carolina Alliance	1	55,000
The Conservation Fund	1	50,000
North Carolina Outward Bound School	1	35,000
North Carolina Rural Communities Assistance Project (NC/RCAP)	1	35,000
North Carolina State University	1	35,000
Tyrrell County Community Development Corporation	1	35,000

Activity region (1993):*	Number:	Dollars:
North Carolina	26	765,000

*As reported by Foundation.

Sample grants (1993).

Agricultural Resources Center. Carrboro, NC. $30,000. Additional support for the Pesticide Education Project to reduce damage from pesticides by advocating better public policy, educating the public, assisting individuals, and promoting safer alternatives.

Albemarle Environmental Association. Hertford, NC. $25,000. To promote recycling and waste reduction.

Clean Water Fund of North Carolina. Asheville, NC. $30,000. Operational support to help grassroots groups and individuals fight environmental problems.

The Conservation Fund. Chapel Hill, NC. $50,000. To facilitate community-based development of the Albemarle-Pamlico Bioregional Greenway to create a prototype for development of a statewide greenway network to showcase natural, cultural, and historic resources to promote eco-tourism and environmental education as a sustainable economic development strategy for poor, rural counties.

Farm Plan Advocates, Inc. Charlotte, NC. $20,000. To help at-risk farmers restructure their debts and identify their options, prove farm viability, and shepherd the farm plan through the restructuring process with Farmer's Home Association (FmHA).

Fisheries Development Foundation of North Carolina. New Bern, NC. $25,000. To assist, encourage, enhance, and strengthen North Carolina's fishing industry through, research, technology and education to commercial fishermen/women so that they can change from the hunter/gatherer mode to the farmer mode of aquaculture production.

National Committee for the New River. Jefferson, NC. $25,000. To expand efforts to address the plight of the New River and develop a watershed organization to advocate for sound land use regulations and conservation-oriented development alternatives.

North Carolina Coastal Federation. Swansboro, NC. $85,000. For a comprehensive review of the impact and effectiveness of the North Carolina Coastal Area Management Act.

Pamlico–Tar River Foundation, Inc. Washington, NC. $20,000. To develop and implement a nutrient pollution abatement strategy and to facilitate public participation in establishing environmental policies and permit evaluations.

Sierra Club Foundation. San Francisco, CA. $15,000. Support for the North Carolina Alternative Transportation Project to establish a long-range vision for alternative transportation, including public transit, bicycle, and pedestrian circulation, overall quality of travel for all transportation modes, and land use action in the Boone and Blowing Rock communities.

Swain County. Bryson City, NC. $15,000. For a Water Quality Study to determine where man-made and/or natural pollution problems are occurring and then taking action to correct them.

Application process. *Initial contact:* Application including:
1. Completed application form (available from the Foundation).
2. Proposal (1 copy, unbound, limited to 3 single-spaced pages).
   - Concise description of project.
   - Total funds required for project.
   - Other funding sources.
   - Need for project.
   - Objectives and how they will be achieved.
   - Description of petitioning organization.
   - Method and criteria for evaluation of project.

   If this is not a new organization, include a separate report on previous accomplishments of the organization or project, people served, goals achieved, funding sources, etc.
3. Budget. Line-item budget (1 page), including both anticipated income and expenditures for the organization's current fiscal year. If funds requested are for a specific project (rather than for general support of your organization) also submit a line-item budget (1 page) for the specific project, including anticipated income and expenditures. State precisely how the funds requested from ZSRF will be spent.
4. Board of directors. A list of the members of the petitioning organization's governing board, with a brief explanation of how members are elected.
5. Tax-exempt status. Copy of IRS tax-exempt status determination letter and proof of status as publicly supported organization. Governmental units need not submit these documents.
6. Optional materials to supplement the application.

When to apply: Deadlines are February 1 and August 1. The board of trustees meets in May and November.

Materials available: Annual report (includes "Requirements and Procedures for Submitting Grant Proposals"), application form.

Emphases. *Recipients:* Nonprofit organizations, public agencies.
Activities: Advocacy, citizen participation, education, policy analysis/development.
Types of support: Operating costs, pilot projects.
Geography: North Carolina.

Limitations. *Recipients:* Individuals.
Types of support: Capital campaigns/expenses, endowments.

© 1995 Environmental Data Resources, Inc.

The Rhode Island Community Foundation

70 Elm Street
Providence, Rhode Island 02903
Tel: 401-274-4564   Fax: 401-331-8085
EIN: 050208270   Type: Community
Contact: Ronald V. Gallo, President

History and philosophy. The Rhode Island Foundation began in 1916 with a $10,000 endowment. By 1992, its assets had grown to more than $175 million. Over its 76 years the Foundation has distributed about $52 million to benefit the people of Rhode Island through diverse cultural and social programs. The Foundation has a four-part mission: to attract charitable funds, provide grants, exercise community leadership, and serve donors. It manages over 400 endowment funds and also gives grants in specified program areas: Arts, Culture, and Humanities; Education; Environment/Animals; Health; Human Services; Public/Society Benefit; and Other.

Officers and directors. *Officers:* Robert H. I. Goddard, Chairman; Melvin G. Alperin, Vice Chairman; Ronald V. Gallo, President; Carol Golden, Vice President for Development; Doris Stearn Donovan, Vice President for Program. *Directors:* Melvin G. Alperin, Paul J. Choquette, Jr., B. Jae Clanton, Ann F. Conner, Robert H. I. Goddard, William H. Heisler III, Edward L. Maggiacomo, Norman Estes McCulloch, Jr., Pablo Rodriguez M.D. *Trustees:* Citizen's Bank, Fleet National Bank, Rhode Island Hospital Trust National Bank, Van Liew Trust Company, Washington Trust Company.

Financial data. Data for fiscal year ended December 31, 1993. *Assets:* $197,142,952 (M). *Gifts received:* $4,000,000. *Total grants authorized:* $8,500,261.

Environmental awards. *Program and interests:* The Foundation is interested in inclusive education efforts to preserve and protect the state's natural resources. In addition, two Field-of-Interest funds support humane education and the well-being of animals.
Recent grants: 1993 grants included support for land conservation, watershed and river protection, coastal and marine issues, wildlife protection, and youth education.

Issues.   Cli   Bio   Lan   Agr   Wat   Oce   Ene   Was   Tox   Pop   Dev
              •   •   •   •   •

Funding analysis.§

Fiscal year:	1992	1993
Env grants auth:	$216,202	$346,731
Number:	26	23
Range:	$200–$36,707	$171–$118,342
Median:	$3,250	$5,270
Pct $ auth (env/total):	3	4

Recipients (1993 highest):	Number:	Dollars:
Audubon Society of Rhode Island	4	200,596
Save the Bay	1	45,000
Roger Williams Docent Council	1	21,540
Clean Water Fund	1	20,000
The Nature Conservancy, Rhode Island Field Office	1	10,000

Activity region (1993):	Number:	Dollars:
U.S. Northeast	23	346,731

§Includes advised, designated, and discretionary grants.

Sample grants (1993).*
Audubon Society of Rhode Island. Smithfield, RI. $118,342. Maintenance and supervision of two wildlife refuges.
Audubon Society of Rhode Island. Smithfield, RI. $25,000. Maintenance and supervision of Touisset Marsh Wildlife Refuge.
Audubon Society of Rhode Island. Smithfield, RI. $55,000. Maintenance and supervision of Fisherville Brook Wildlife Refuge.
Clean Water Fund. Providence, RI. $20,000. For general operating support.
The Nature Conservancy, Rhode Island Field Office. Providence, RI. $10,000. Third year operating support for species preservation efforts.
Roger Williams Docent Council. Bristol, RI. $21,540. To support pilot effort of youth urban environmental education and training program.
Save the Bay. Providence, RI. $45,000. To initiate a citizen monitoring program for Narragansett Bay.

*Sample grants represent either new awards or disbursements on grants awarded in previous years.

Application process. *Initial contact:* Letter of proposal; no application form required. Priority is given to the first 25 applications received before each board meeting.
When to apply: Anytime. The board meets in January, March, May, July, September, and November.
Materials available: Annual report, application guidelines, brochure, (program policy statement), *Foundation News* (newsletter).

Emphases. *Recipients:* Aquariums, educational institutions, museums, nonprofit organizations, zoos.
Activities: Advocacy, capacity building, citizen participation, collaborative efforts, direct services, education, exhibits, feasibility studies, innovative programs, land acquisition, planning, policy analysis/development, technical assistance, youth programs.
Types of support: Capital campaigns/expenses, computer hardware, continuing support, emergency funding, equipment, loans, matching funds, operating costs, pilot projects, program-related investments, projects, seed money, start-up costs, technical assistance.
Geography: Rhode Island only.

Limitations. *Recipients:* Individuals, public agencies, religious organizations, research institutions.
Activities: Litigation, lobbying, publications, research.
Types of support: Debt retirement, endowments, fellowships, internships, lectureships, leveraging funds, mortgage reduction, professorships, scholarships.

Sid W. Richardson Foundation

309 Main Street
Fort Worth, Texas 76102
Tel: 817-336-0494   Fax: 817-332-2176
EIN: 756015828   Type: Independent
Contact: Valleau Wilkie, Jr., Executive Vice President

History and philosophy. Sid W. Richardson (1891–1959), who made his fortune in oil, cattle, and land, established the Foundation in 1947 to support organizations serving the people of Texas. Mr. Richardson's interest in art of the American West is reflected in the Foundation's commitment to the Sid Richardson Collection of Western Art in Fort Worth. The Foundation has four program areas: Education, Human Services, Health, and the Arts.

Officers and directors. *Officers:* Perry R. Bass, President; Valleau Wilkie, Jr., Executive Vice President; Lee M. Bass, Nancy Lee Bass, Sid R. Bass, Vice Presidents; Jo Helen Rosacker, Secretary; M. E. Chappell, Treasurer. *Directors:* Lee M. Bass, Nancy Lee Bass, Perry R. Bass, Sid R. Bass, M. E. Chappell.

Financial data. Data for fiscal year ended December 31, 1993.
Assets: $254,042,318 (M). *Total grants disbursed:* $14,998,506.

Environmental awards. *Recent grants:* 1993 grants included support for botanical research, coastal issues, youth education, and zoos in the Fort Worth area.

Issues.   *Cli   Bio   Lan   Agr   Wat   Oce   Ene   Was   Tox   Pop   Dev*
                     •   •   •   •

Funding analysis.

Fiscal year:	1991	1993
Env grants auth:	$2,350,000	$452,500
Number:	4	3
Range:	$25,500–$2,200,000	$2,500–$440,000
Median:	$62,500	$10,000
Pct $ auth (env/total):	29	2

Recipients (1993):	Number:	Dollars:
Botanical Research Institute of Texas	1	440,000
Fort Worth Clean City, Inc.	1	10,000
Coastal Conservation Association	1	2,500

Activity region (1993):	Number:	Dollars:
U.S. South Central	3	452,500

Sample grants (1993).
Botanical Research Institute of Texas. Fort Worth, TX. $440,000. Support for the Sampling the Green World Symposium and the establishment of the Landscape Ecology Program.
Coastal Conservation Association. Houston, TX. $2,500. Sponsorship for one issue of *The Rising Tide.*
Fort Worth Clean City, Inc. Fort Worth, TX. $10,000. Support for the Youth Education Program.

Application process. *Initial contact:* Letter describing program or project. If the program falls within its guidelines, the Foundation will accept a formal proposal. Formal proposals must be submitted on the Foundation's grant application form. Applicants may also wish to submit a supplementary proposal in narrative form that describes the nature of the organization, its objectives, activities, and personnel; outline the need for and objectives of the proposed project; or add new information. If the grant is approved, the applicant will receive a Letter of Agreement outlining grant terms and conditions.
When to apply: Deadlines are March 1 and September 1. The board meets in the spring and fall.
Materials available: Annual report (includes "Guidelines for Grant Applications"), grant application form.

Emphases. *Recipients:* Educational institutions, museums, nonprofit organizations, public agencies, research institutions, zoos.
Activities: Collaborative efforts, conferences, education, feasibility studies, innovative programs, research (medical), workshops, youth programs.
Types of support: Endowments, equipment, facilities, general purposes, multi-year grants, operating costs, professorships, program-related investments.
Geography: Texas.

Limitations. *Recipients:* Individuals.

Smith Richardson Foundation, Inc.

60 Jesup Road
Westport, Connecticut 06880
Tel: 203-222-6222   Fax: 203-222-6282
EIN: 560611550   Type: Independent
EGA member
Contact: Peter L. Richardson, President

History and philosophy. The Foundation was established in 1935 by H. Smith Richardson and his wife Grace Jones Richardson. Mr. Richardson was president of Vick Chemical Company. The Foundation continues to reflect the Richardsons' philanthropic ideals. Since 1993 grantmaking has focused primarily on domestic and international public policy research. The domestic program supports "scholars whose research product is likely to have an impact on the broad policymaking community." Children and families is a special area of interest. The international program supports projects that attempt "to clarify international issues of direct concern to Americans, as demonstrated by our continued support of Harvard University's Olin Center's program, The Changing Security Environment and American National Interests."

Other program areas are: arts and humanities, civic affairs and community development, education, health care, and social welfare. The Foundation also maintains two special programs: Children and Families at Risk, and the Center for Creative Leadership in Greensboro, North Carolina.

Officers and directors. *Officers:* H. Smith Richardson, Jr., Chairman; Peter L. Richardson, President; Arvid R. Nelson, Secretary; Robert L. Coble, Treasurer; Diana B. Washburn, Assistant Secretary. *Trustees:* Robert H. DeMichele, Robert H. Mulreany, H. Smith Richardson, Jr., Peter L. Richardson, R. Randolph Richardson. *Governors:* Professor Donald Kagan,

General Edward C. Meyer, Honorable L. Richardson Preyer, Adele Richardson Ray, H. Smith Richardson, Jr., Heather S. Richardson, Lundsford Richardson, Jr., Peter L. Richardson, R. Randolph Richardson, Stuart S. Richardson, Professor Henry S. Rowen, E. William Stetson, III, Professor James Q. Wilson, Professor Edward F. Zigler.

Financial data. Data for fiscal year ended December 31, 1992. *Assets:* $322,031,655 (M). *Gifts received:* $2,546,847. *Total grants disbursed:* $11,791,823.

Environmental awards. *Recent grants:* 1992 public policy program area grants included several with an environmental component.

Issues. Cli Bio Lan Agr Wat Oce Ene Was Tox Pop Dev
•

Funding analysis.

Fiscal year:	1991	1992
Env grants disb:	$172,000	$205,900
Number:	3	3
Range:	$50,000–$67,000	$45,000–$98,000
Median:	$55,000	$62,900
Pct $ disb (env/total):	2	2

Recipients (1992):	Number:	Dollars:
Competitive Enterprise Institute (CEI)	1	98,000
Brandeis University	1	62,900
Political Economy Research Institute	1	45,000

Activity region (1992):	Number:	Dollars:
U.S. not specified	3	205,900

Sample grants (1992).*
Brandeis University. Waltham, MA. $62,900. Support for research and writing on the 1990 Clean Air Act.
Competitive Enterprise Institute (CEI). Washington, DC. $98,000. Support for an environmental studies program.
Political Economy Research Institute. McLean, VA. $45,000. Support for research and writing on environmental politics.

*Sample grants represent either new grants or disbursements on grants awarded in previous years.

Application process. *Initial contact:* Letter of inquiry to include:
1. Project description: need, purpose, and scope.
2. Organization description and credentials of key personnel.
3. Project budget and timeline.
4. Evidence that the project has not already been completed.
5. Description of population to benefit from project.
6. Copy of IRS tax-exempt status determination letter.

When to apply: Anytime. Grants are reviewed quarterly.
Materials available: Annual report.

Emphases. *Activities:* Nonprofit organizations, research.

Limitations. *Recipients:* Individuals.
Activities: Research (physical sciences).
Types of support: Debt retirement, facilities (construction).

The Roberts Foundation

873 Sutter Street, Suite B
San Francisco, California 94109
Tel: 415–771–4300   Fax: 415–771–4064
EIN: 942967074   Type: Independent
EGA member
Contacts: Lyman H. Casey, Executive Director
Jed Emerson, Program Director

History and philosophy. The Foundation was established in 1985 by George R. Roberts. Its primary interests are children, youth, and families; education; environmental issues; wildlife preservation; and animal welfare. Within the field of education, the Foundation is particularly interested in the learning disabled.

Officers and directors. *Officers:* Leanne B. Roberts, President and CEO; George R. Roberts, Vice President, Secretary, and CFO; Lyman H. Casey, Vice President and Assistant Secretary. *Directors:* Lyman H. Casey, George R. Roberts, Leanne B. Roberts.

Financial data. Data for fiscal year ended December 31, 1992. *Assets:* $9,961,365 (M). *Total grants disbursed:* $2,941,540.

Environmental awards. *Program and interests:* Current interests are:

- Sustainable development.
- Animal welfare issues.
- Habitat restoration.

Issues. Cli Bio Lan Agr Wat Oce Ene Was Tox Pop Dev
    •   •   •   •   •   •

Funding analysis.

Fiscal year:	1990	1992
Env grants auth:	$962,500	$278,200
Number:	13	8
Range:	$500–$500,000	$1,200–$62,000
Median:	$10,000	$47,500
Pct $ auth (env/total):	38	12

Recipients (1992 highest):	Number:	Dollars:
Marine Mammal Center	1	62,000
Environmental Defense Fund	1	50,000
Golden Gate National Recreation Area	1	50,000
Materials for the Future Foundation	1	50,000
Friends of the Garcia River	1	45,000

Activity regions (1992):	Number:	Dollars:
U.S. West	7	228,200
U.S. not specified	1	50,000

Sample grants (1991–92).
Carter House Natural Science Museum. Redding, CA. $17,640. Support for "Adopt-A-Stream" program.
Coyote Point Museum Association. San Mateo, CA. $10,000. Unrestricted grant.

Environmental Defense Fund. New York, NY. $50,000 (5 years). To endow an EDF environmental chair.

Institute for Sustainable Development. Montpelier, VT. $2,500. Unrestricted grant.

Petaluma Wildlife & Natural Science Museum. Petaluma, CA. $5,000. Toward construction of new museum exhibits.

Point Reyes Bird Observatory. Stinson Beach, CA. $20,000. Support for environmental studies on the Farallon Islands.

The San Francisco Zoological Society. San Francisco, CA. $25,000. Unrestricted grant.

The Trust for Hidden Villa, Inc. Los Altos Hills, CA. $10,000. Support for environmental education programs.

Application process. *Initial contact:* Preliminary letter to include:
1. Purpose and history of organization.
2. Goals and objectives of project.
3. Organization and project budgets.
4. Copy of IRS tax-exempt status determination letter.

When to apply: Deadlines are in November, March, and July. The board meets in February, June, and October (may vary to accommodate the board).

Materials available: Biennial report (includes "Grant Making Guidelines" and "Application Procedures").

Emphases. *Recipients:* Educational institutions, museums, non-profit organizations, zoos.

Activities: Citizen participation, demonstration programs, innovative programs, volunteerism.

Types of support: Projects.

Geography: Northern California only, especially the San Francisco Bay Area and the counties of Marin, Alameda, and Contra Costa.

Limitations. *Recipients:* Individuals, religious organizations.

Activities: Activism, fundraising, political activities, research (medical).

Types of support: Annual campaigns, endowments.

Rockefeller Brothers Fund, Inc.

1290 Avenue of the Americas, Suite 3450
New York, New York 10104–0233
Tel: 212–373–4200   Fax: 212–315–0996
TCN/Dialcom E-mail: 141:TCN300   Telex: 4900008630RBF
EIN: 131760106   Type: Independent
EGA member
Contact: Michael F. Northrop, Program Officer

History and philosophy. The Rockefeller Brothers Fund was founded in 1940 as a vehicle through which the children of John D. Rockefeller, Jr. could share advice and research on charitable activities and combine some of their philanthropic efforts.

In 1984 the trustees agreed to focus the Fund's grantmaking activities on the theme of global interdependence, specifically on resources and security. In addition, the Fund maintains an interest in the nonprofit sector, education, quality of life in New York City, and quality of education in South Africa.

Officers and directors. *Officers:* Abby M. O'Neill, Chairman; Steven C. Rockefeller, Vice Chairman; Colin G. Campbell, President; Russell A. Phillips, Jr., Executive Vice President; Benjamin R. Shute, Jr., Secretary/Treasurer. *Trustees:* Catharine O. Broderick, Colin G. Campbell, Jonathan F. Fanton, Neva R. Goodwin, Kenneth Lipper, William H. Luers, Jessica Tuchman Mathews, Abby M. O'Neill, Richard D. Parsons, David Rockefeller, Jr., Richard G. Rockefeller, Steven C. Rockefeller, S. Frederick Starr. *Advisory Trustee:* Mr. Russell E. Train.

Financial data. Data for fiscal year ended December 31, 1992. *Assets:* $342,426,742 (M). *Gifts received:* $1,192,607. *Total grants disbursed:* $11,059,856.

Environmental awards. *Program and interests:* The goal of the One World: Sustainable Resource Use program is "To encourage more efficient and renewable use of natural, human, and man-made resources, through an approach that blends social, economic, and ecological concerns." Strategies vary according to geographic target. They are:

- Globally. Refining and advocating the philosophy of sustainable resource use and furthering its implementation through support of international networks of organizations that are experimenting with practices which are less destructive to land, forest, air, water, and human resources.

- In the United States. Advancing progress on issues identified with a comprehensive sustainable growth agenda, including renewable agriculture, energy efficiency, municipal waste recycling, and water use efficiency; and assisting interest groups not generally concerned with environmental affairs to articulate their stakes in improved resource management.

- In East Central Europe and the Former Soviet Union. Supporting initiatives that improve local capacity to manage the environment, agriculture, and natural resources on a sustainable basis. Emphasis is given to education and training, policy formulation, institution building, and cooperating among local agencies and their foreign counterparts as well as to efforts linking environmental, economic, and business concerns.

- In East Asia. Strengthening the infrastructure of institutions needed to formulate policies that serve the region's twin goals of development and conservation, including public sector bureaucracies, universities, NGOs, and the media.

In addition, the Fund identifies global climate change as a special interest area. It seeks further discussion of coordinated international responses to the problem, while simultaneously focusing increased attention on promising practical solutions, particularly in the areas of reforestation, energy production, and consumption.

Finally, the Fund will support other compelling programs of special merit focusing effective action on the Fund's primary sustainable resource use objective.

Issues. Cli • Bio • Lan • Agr • Wat • Oce   Ene • Was • Tox • Pop • Dev •

Funding analysis.

Fiscal year:	1991	1992
Env grants auth:	$3,688,200	$3,343,840
Number:	34	25
Range:	$8,500–$375,000	$10,000–$1,000,000
Median:	$100,000	$75,000
Pct $ disb (env/total):	36	35

R

Recipients (1992 highest):	Number:	Dollars:
American Farmland Trust	1	1,000,000
Worldwatch Institute	1	525,000
Winrock International Institute for Agricultural Development	2	278,000
Center for Policy Alternatives	1	225,000
International Institute of Rural Reconstruction	1	210,000

Activity regions (1992 highest):	Number:	Dollars:
U.S. not specified	6	1,390,000
International*	3	599,340
Southeast Asia	5	465,000
Far East	5	458,000
Eastern Europe	5	421,500

*Multiple regions or not specified.

Sample grants (1992).*

American Council of Learned Societies. New York, NY. $100,000 (2 years). To support training, applied research, and conference travel for the Chinese and Mongolian participants in the Grassland Ecosystems of the Mongolian Steppe project of the Council's Committee on Scholarly Communication with China. The major goals of this joint project of the Mongolian, Chinese, and American academies of science are to study the impact of human incursion on the steppe ecosystem, to inform policymakers in China and Mongolia about the importance of grasslands management, and to address the larger question of how to balance the ecological health of the grasslands with the needs of a growing human population dependent on the land for livelihood.

Cathedral Church of St. John the Divine. New York, NY. $15,000. For a conference of senior American religious leaders and leading scientists, hosted by the Cathedral's Joint Appeal by Religion & Science for the environment. The con-ference was the culmination of an initial effort to facilitate collaboration among heads of religious faiths who seek to offer a scientifically informed, theological, and moral response to the deteriorating global environment.

Environmental Law Institute. Washington, DC. $120,000 (3 years). Continued support for the Institute's Environmental Program for Central and Eastern Europe, which advises governmental agencies and nongovernmental organizations in Poland, Hungary, and Czechoslovakia on the development of environmental protection laws and policies.

Institute for Environmental Policy. Prague, The Czech Republic. $150,000 (3 years). To launch the Institute for Environmental Policy, the first independent policy research institute established previously by Czechoslovakia to provide policy analysis regarding issues of sustainable development. Activities during its first year include an appraisal on the impact of the process of democratization on environmental policy formulation, and review of a blueprint for sustainable development in The Czech and The Slovak Republics.

Institute for Sustainable Communities. South Royalton, VT. $75,000. For a pilot project to encourage community-based sustainable development policymaking in Hungary. The project will introduce to selected communities in Hungary new methods for promoting cooperation between community leaders and local governments as they try to evaluate and balance the needs of economic development with the needs of environmental management. This will include training of public and private sector citizens in environmental analysis, democratic decisionmaking, and conflict resolution.

International Center for Research on Women. Washington, DC. $75,000. To support the Southeast Asian component of its project on women, development, and the environment. In collaboration with researchers in Southeast Asia, the ICRW will prepare case studies of efforts being made in developing countries to stem population growth and limit destruction of the environment while at the same time promoting economic development. Through these case studies, the project hopes to add a body of empirical data to the often subjective population-environment debate, and to distribute this information.

*Sample grants represent either new awards or disbursements on grants awarded in previous years.

Application process. *Initial contact:* Letter of inquiry (2–3 pages) including a description of the project or organization and its relationship to the Fund's program, information about principal staff, a synopsis of the budget, and the amount requested. Letters should be addressed to Benjamin R. Shute, Jr., Secretary. Full proposal, if requested, to include:

1. Description of purpose of project or organization.
2. Background and research that led to proposal.
3. Methods by which project is to be carried out.
4. Qualifications and experience of principal staff members.
5. Detailed, realistic budget.
6. List of board members or advisors.
7. Copy of IRS tax-exempt status determination letter.
8. Copy of recent financial statements, preferably audited.

When to apply: Anytime.
Materials available: Annual report (includes "How to Apply for a Grant"), *The Foundation Grants Index Quarterly*, *The Foundation Grants Index Annual*.

Emphases: *Recipients:* Nonprofit organizations.
Geography: East Asia, East Central Europe, (former) Soviet Union, United States.

Limitations. *Recipients:* Individuals (except for RBF fellowships and special grants for Ramon Magsaysay Awardees).
Activities: Land acquisition, research.
Types of support: Endowments, facilities.

Rockefeller Family Fund, Inc.

1290 Avenue of the Americas
New York, New York 10104
Tel: 212–373–4252   Fax: 212–315–0996
EIN: 136257658   Type: Independent (public charity status)
EGA member
Contact: Donald K. Ross, Director

History and philosophy. The Rockefeller Family Fund was established in 1967 by members of the Rockefeller family, principally the grandchildren of John D. Rockefeller, Jr. The Family Fund offers support for advocacy programs that are action-oriented and likely to yield tangible results. It makes grants in five program areas: Citizen Education and Participation, Economic Justice for Women, Environment, Institutional Responsiveness, and Self-Sufficiency.

Officers and directors. *Officers:* Richard G. Rockefeller, President; Anne Bartley, Clare P. Buden, Dana Chasin, Peter M. O'Neill, Wendy G. Rockefeller, Vice Presidents; Donald K. Ross, Director/Secretary; Leah D'Angelo, Treasurer. *Trustees:* Hope Aldrich, Nancy C. Anderson, Anne Bartley, Clare P. Buden, Dana Chasin, Laura Chasin, David W. Kaiser, Bruce Mazlish, Alida R. Messinger, Peter M. O'Neill, Mary Louise Pierson, Barbara Bellows Rockefeller, Diana N. Rockefeller, Lisenne Rockefeller, Richard G. Rockefeller, Steven C. Rockefeller, Wendy G. Rockefeller, Abby R. Simpson.

Financial data. Data for fiscal year ended December 31, 1993. *Assets:* $44,201,000 (M). *Total grants authorized:* $1,914,600.

Environmental awards. *Program and interests:* In 1992 and 1993 Environment was among the largest program areas. Budget priorities are, however, subject to change each year. The program emphasizes:

- Conservation of natural resources.
- Protection of health as affected by the environment.
- Cessation of pollution caused by the Departments of Energy and Defense.
- Domestic efforts to broaden the definition of national security and global stability to include environmental security.

Additional grants pertaining to environmental issues may be awarded under the Citizen Education and Participation and Institutional Responsiveness programs.

The Fund also provides hands-on assistance to environmental groups. It acts as administrator for the Environmental Grantmakers Association, and was instrumental in developing the Environmental Support Center, which provides technical assistance to state-based environmental groups.

Issues. Cli Bio Lan Agr Wat Oce Ene Was Tox Pop Dev

Funding analysis.

Fiscal year:	1991	1993
Env grants auth:	$810,000	$735,000
Number:	28	23
Range:	$15,000–$50,000	$2,000–$75,000
Median:	$25,000	$25,000
Pct $ disb (env/total):	48	41

Recipients (1993 highest):	Number:	Dollars:
Campaign for an Environmental Economy	1	75,000
Environmental Strategies	1	60,000
Government Accountability Project	1	60,000
Mineral Policy Center	1	60,000
Land and Water Fund of the Rockies	1	50,000
Western Ancient Forest Campaign	1	50,000

Activity regions (1993 highest):	Number:	Dollars:
U.S. not specified	13	452,000
U.S. Northwest	3	115,000
U.S. Mountain	1	50,000
U.S. Northeast	2	40,000
New York/New Jersey	1	25,000

Sample grants (1993).*

American Rivers, Inc. Washington, DC. $20,000. The second installment of a two-year grant totalling $50,000 for the National Hydropower Relicensing Campaign, which intends to use the upcoming relicensing of over 200 hydroelectric dams to press for greater energy efficiency and protection of river systems.

Association of Forest Service Employees for Environmental Ethics. Eugene, OR. $20,000. Support for an organizing campaign among Forest Service employees to influence resource management policies, and to protect the free speech rights of whistleblowers.

Campaign for an Environmental Economy. Washington, DC. $75,000. Support for an effort to raise awareness regarding federal subsidies that create disincentives for environmental preservation, such as subsidies for hardrock mining.

Coast Alliance. Washington, DC. $25,000. The second installment of a two-year grant totalling $50,000 for advocacy and public education to reverse destructive coastal development policies through reform of the federal flood insurance program, increased protection of coastal barriers, and strengthened state and federal coastal management policies.

Institute for Agriculture and Trade Policy. Minneapolis, MN. $20,000. Assistance to educate the environmental and farm communities about trade issues and to organize coalitions to develop and advance proposals to democratize the negotiating process.

Mothers & Others for a Livable Planet. New York, NY. $25,000. General support for this environmental organization geared towards families, and for work to promote an awareness of the dangers of pesticides in children's food through the Safe Food Program.

1000 Friends of Oregon. Portland, OR. $20,000. Support for a development campaign to increase membership of this advocacy organization which is building active support across Oregon on land use planning and growth management.

Pace Energy Center. New York, NY. $20,000. The second installment of a two-year grant totalling $45,000 for advocacy work on energy efficiency through intervention in state utility proceedings.

20/20 Vision Education Fund. Washington, DC. $20,000. General support for efforts to engage citizens in the public policy process, particularly on issues of environmental policy, by making grassroots activism accessible and convenient.

Western Ancient Forests Campaign. Washington, DC. $50,000. General support to help project the passion of grassroots activists to national decisionmakers as part of a multifaceted campaign to preserve the remaining ancient forests of the Pacific Northwest.

*Sample grants represent either new grants or disbursements on grants awarded in previous years.

Application process. *Initial contact:* Application to include:
1. Concisely written proposal.
   - Description of organization seeking funds.
   - Need for and objectives of the proposed program.
   - Strategy and plan of action.
   - Staff and organization's qualifications for carrying out the program.
   - Other organizations involved in similar programs and how the proposed project is similar or different.
   - Amount of funding requested.

- Line-item budget for the project.
- Method of evaluation.
2. Overall budget for the organization, including projected income and its sources.
3. Most recent certified audit, if available.
4. IRS tax-exempt status determination letter.

When to apply: Anytime.
Materials available: Annual report (includes "Application Procedures"), "Summary of Rockefeller Family Fund Program Areas and Guidelines."

Emphases. *Recipients:* Nonprofit organizations.
Activities: Activism, advocacy, capacity building, citizen participation, fundraising, litigation, lobbying, political activities.
Types of support: Annual campaigns, general purposes, matching funds, membership campaigns, multi-year grants.
Geography: United States only.

Limitations. *Recipients:* Individuals, museums.
Activities: Research (scholarly).
Types of support: Debt retirement, facilities.
Geography: International programs; projects pertaining to a single city, unless they may serve as a national model.

Rockefeller Financial Services, Philanthropy Department

30 Rockefeller Plaza, Room 5600
New York, New York 10112
Tel: 212–649–5600
Type: Advisory service
EGA member
Contacts: Marcia Townley, Philanthropic Advisor
Wade Greene, Philanthropic Advisor
Salvatore Laspada, Philanthropic Advisor
Charles Terry, Director

History and philosophy. The office provides philanthropic advice to members of the Rockefeller family and other individuals. Therefore, funding priorities and grants range vary widely from year to year.

Financial data. Not available.

Environmental awards. *Program and interests:* Funding patterns depend on the interest of individual donors. Priorities may range widely from year to year. Current interests are:

- Biodiversity.
- Energy.
- Conservation.
- Forests.
- Spirituality and the environment.
- Environmental justice.
- Population and the environment.

Issues. Cli Bio Lan Agr Wat Oce Ene Was Tox Pop Dev

Application process. *Initial contact:* Short letter.
When to apply: Anytime.

Emphases. *Recipients:* Educational institutions, nonprofit organizations.
Activities: Activism, advocacy, collaborative efforts, conflict resolution, direct services, education, policy analysis/development, youth programs.
Types of support: General purposes, operating costs, pilot projects, projects.

Limitations. *Recipients:* Individuals, public agencies.
Activities: Audiovisual materials, expeditions/tours, feasibility studies, fundraising, seminars.
Types of support: Debt retirement, lectureships, loans, mortgage reduction, professorships, program-related investments, travel expenses.
Geography: International.

The Rockefeller Foundation

420 Fifth Avenue
New York, New York 10018–2702
Tel: 212–869–8500 Fax: 212–764–3468 or 212–398–1858
EIN: 131659629 Type: Independent
EGA member
Contact: Dr. Al Binger, Director, Global Environment Program

History and philosophy. Endowed by John D. Rockefeller and chartered in 1893, The Rockefeller Foundation is one of the oldest private foundations in the United States and one of the few with strong international interests. The Foundation currently offers grants and fellowships in three principal areas: international science-based development (including agriculture, health, population, global environment, and special programming); the arts and humanities; and equal opportunity for U.S. minorities. The Foundation also has smaller programs in international security and in-school reform to improve public education for at-risk young people.

The Foundation focuses its efforts on selected programs with well-defined goals, but tries to adjust to new needs and opportunities as they arise. In addition to its grantmaking activities, The Foundation maintains the Bellagio Study and Conference Center in northern Italy which offers international conferences and residencies for artists and scholars.

Officers and directors. *Officers:* John R. Evans, Chair; Peter C. Goldmark, Jr., President; Kenneth Prewitt, Senior Vice President; Hugh B. Price, Vice President; Joyce L. Moock, Associate Vice President; Danielle Parris, Acting Vice President for Communications; Lynda Mullen, Secretary; David A. White, Treasurer; Webb Trammell, Assistant Treasurer. *Trustees:* Alan Alda, Ela R. Bhatt, Johnnetta B. Cole, David de Ferranti, Peggy Dulany, Frances FitzGerald, Daniel P. Garcia, Peter C. Goldmark, Jr., Ronald E. Goldsberry, Stephen Jay Gould, Linda Hill, Karen N. Horn, Alice Stone Ilchman, Richard H. Jenrette, Robert C. Maynard, Dr. Alvaro Umaña, Frank G. Wells.

Financial data.* Data for fiscal year ended December 31, 1993. *Assets:* $2,375,376,000 (U). *Total grants disbursed:* $109,923,248.

*As reported by Foundation.

Environmental awards. *Program and interests:* The Global Environment Program is an integral part of the Foundation's International Program to Support Science-Based Development, established in 1986. The premise of this program is that the well-being of people in developing nations can be advanced through the application of science and technology. Three broad areas of interest for grant and fellowship activity are:

- Supporting young environmental scientists, analysts, policy-makers, and community leaders who can be architects of future policy in development and the environment.

- Laying the groundwork for the multilateral bargains and accords that are necessary to address selected environmental issues.

- Advancing the development of alternative sources of energy and promoting energy efficiency.

In addition to the new Global Environment Program, related fields of interest are the agricultural, health, and population sciences organized under the International Program to Support Science-Based Development. The objective: "To help developing countries use, on their own terms, modern science and technology in ways that are environmentally sound to increase their people's access to food, health, reproductive choice, education, and life's other essentials."

Issues. Cli Bio Lan Agr Wat Oce Ene Was Tox Pop Dev
• • • • • • • • • •

Funding analysis.

Fiscal year:	1991	1993
Env grants disb:	$5,438,303	$16,683,490
Number:	82	129
Range:	$1,000–$775,000	$2,390–$2,400,000
Median:	$35,000	$50,000
Pct $ disb (env/total):	4	15

Recipients (1993 highest):	Number:	Dollars:
Rockefeller Foundation Administered Projects	13	4,714,600
The Energy Foundation	1	2,400,000
International Centre for Research in Agroforestry (ICRAF)	4	888,500
North Carolina State University	1	500,000
International Institute of Tropical Agriculture	1	423,000

Activity regions (1993 highest):	Number:	Dollars:
International*	29	4,618,100
Eastern and Southern Africa	22	2,831,250
U.S. not specified	2	2,525,000
Mexico and Central America	25	2,034,450
Brazil	8	1,348,330

*Multiple regions or not specified.

Sample grants (1993).
Africare. Washington, DC. $61,330. For a rural economic development project in Zimbabwe using photovoltaics.
Biomass Users Network. Washington, DC. $15,960. Toward the costs of a demonstration project using plant oil to replace diesel fuel for electricity generation in Brazil.
Council for Renewable Energy Education (CREE). Washington, DC. $48,000. For a study aimed at facilitating the inclusion of renewable energy projects in World Bank loans to Brazil.
Development and Environment Foundation. Moscow, Russia. $138,600. For support of the Leadership for Environment and Development (LEAD) national program in the Commonwealth of Independent States.
King Monghut's Institute of Technology Thonburi. Bankok, Thailand. $100,000. For a project recycling organic matter and reduce carbon dioxide emissions by composting cane trash.
Princeton University. Princeton, NJ. $200,000. For a study on renewable fuel utilization and improved technologies for conventional fuels, and to identify related model energy enterprises in the developing world.
World Resources Institute. Washington, DC. $10,000. To make possible the participation of three developing country scientists in a workshop on global environmental monitoring, co-sponsored by the California Institute of Technology, to be held in Pasadena, California June 1993.

Application process. *Initial contact:* Proposal to include:
1. Description of project, with plans and objectives.
2. Comprehensive plan for total funding of the project during and, where applicable, after the proposed grant period.
3. Listing of applicant's qualifications and accomplishments and, if applicable, a description of the institutional setting.

When to apply: Anytime.
Materials available: Annual report (includes "Information for Applicants").

Emphases. *Recipients:* Educational institutions, nonprofit organizations, public agencies. research institutions.
Activities: Demonstration programs, feasibility studies, policy analysis/development, training.
Types of support: Projects.
Geography: International, current focus on developing countries.

Limitations. *Recipients:* Botanical gardens, individuals (for personal aid), museums, religious organizations, zoos.
Activities: Lobbying.
Types of support: Endowments, general purposes (usually).

The Winthrop Rockefeller Foundation

308 East Eighth Street
Little Rock, Arkansas 72202-3999
Tel: 501-376-6854 Fax: 501-374-4797
EIN: 710285871 Type: Independent
Contact: Mahlon A. Martin, President

History and philosophy. The Foundation was established in 1956 as the Rockwin Fund by Winthrop Rockefeller (d. 1973), cattle rancher, businessman, and governor of Arkansas from 1966 to 1970. The Foundation was renamed in 1975. It is dedicated to the economic and social well-being of Arkansas. Its goals are to "encourage the development of Arkansas's ability to provide an equitable, quality education for all children; strengthen the capacity of local communities to break the cycle of poverty by supporting projects that promote local economic development; and nurture strong, broad-based grassroots leadership through the development of community-based organizations."

Officers and directors. *Officers:* Joe B. Hatcher, Chair; Winthrop Paul Rockefeller, Vice Chair; Mahlon A. Martin, President. *Directors:* Willard B. Gatewood, Jr., Ernest Green, Judith Berry Griffin, Joe B. Hatcher, Henry Jones, Olly Neal, Rae Rice Perry, Winthrop Paul Rockefeller, Jonathan Sher, Charles Thomas, Rachel Tompkins, Kathryn J. Waller.

Financial data. Data for fiscal year ended December 31, 1993. *Assets:* $79,323,260. (U) *Gifts received:* $690,000. *Total grants authorized:* $4,423,992.

Environmental awards. *Recent grants:* 1993 grants included support for sustainable agriculture and environmental education.

Issues. Cli Bio Lan Agr Wat Oce Ene Was Tox Pop Dev

Funding analysis.

Fiscal year:	1993
Env grants auth:	$202,190
Number:	14
Range:	$950–$56,910
Median:	$5,015
Pct $ auth (env/total):	5

Recipients (1993 highest):	Number:	Dollars:
Shirley Community Service and Development Corporation	1	56,910
Financing Ozarks Rural Growth and Economy	1	50,000
Arkansas Land and Farm Development Corporation	1	26,000
Ozark Foothills Resource Conservation & Development Project	1	25,000
Winrock International Institute for Agricultural Development	1	15,000

Activity regions (1993):	Number:	Dollars:
U.S. South Central	13	187,190
International*	1	15,000

*Multiple regions or not specified.

Sample grants (1993).
Arkansas Land and Farm Development Corporation. Brinkley, AR. $26,000. To support an analysis to determine the feasibility of a land-based development investment.
Arkansas Wildlife Federation. Little Rock, AR. $8,030. To update, publish, and distribute the Environmental Quality Index.
Berryville School District. Berryville, AR. $1,800. To increase student awareness of environmental issues and their role in solving environmental problems.
Financing Ozarks Rural Growth and Economy. Bass, AR. $50,000. To support efforts of a lending institution for financing development that creates sustainable economies and promotes ecologically sound and sustainable agricultural practices in the Ozark bio-region.
Heifer Project International. Little Rock, AR. $2,000. To support staff development activities.
Little Rock School District/Williams Magnet Elementary. Little Rock, AR. $950. To establish a mini-zoo used to teach science and to promote an appreciation for animals.
Ozark Foothills Resource Conservation & Development Project, Inc. Batesville, AR. $25,000. To develop a plan that meets the needs of the people and to address these needs.
Ozark Recycling Enterprise, Inc. Marshall, AR. $1,000. To support a rural recycling project.
Ozark Small Farm Viability Project. Mt. Judea, AR. $2,000. To support grassroots farmers in USDA agricultural programs and policy development.
Paris Public Schools. Paris, AR. $10,000. To help create an experimental farm to serve as an outdoor classroom.
Pulaski County. Little Rock, AR. $2,000. To support the Sweet Home community's public park project.
Shirley Community Service and Development Corporation. Shirley, AR. $56,910. To develop shiitake mushroom production as a sustainable industry using local resources.
Watson Chapel Schools. Pine Bluff, AR. $1,500. To develop students' appreciation and involvement in the protection of the environment.
Winrock International Institute for Agricultural Development. Morilton, AR. $15,000. To plan and conduct an international symposium held at Winrock International on Petit Jean Mountain.

Application process. *Initial contact:* Telephone call or letter requesting application guidelines. Proposal (2 copies) to include:
1. Legal name of organization.
2. Address, telephone number, and contact person.
3. List of current board and staff members.
4. Description of project (3–4 pages) including organization's activities, population served, problem to be addressed, goals and schedule, area and number of people served, description of similar projects, method of evaluation, and how project will be continued after grant ends.
5. Project budget and amount requested from the Foundation and other sources.
6. Funding received from other sources as a result of getting a Foundation grant.
7. Resume of the project coordinator.
8. Copy of IRS tax–exempt status determination letter.
9. Signatures of president and board chairperson.
10. Copy of recent audit, if available.
11. Answers to questions in "Guidelines for Grant Applicants."

When to apply: Deadlines are in early March and September or three months before board meetings held in June and December.
Materials available: Annual report (includes "Grant Applications"), "Guidelines for Grant Applicants."

Emphases. *Recipients:* Nonprofit organizations.
Activities: Advocacy, capacity building, citizen participation, planning, policy analysis/development.
Types of support:
Geography: Arkansas only.

Limitations. *Recipients:* Individuals.
Activities: Conferences, fundraising, research.
Types of support: Capital campaigns/expenses, continuing support, debt retirement, endowments, equipment, facilities, fellowships, general purposes, operating costs, scholarships, travel expenses.

The Rockfall Foundation
27 Washington Street
Middletown, Connecticut 06457
Tel: 203-347-0340
EIN: 066000700   Type: Independent
Contact: Virginia R. Rollefson, Executive Director

History and philosophy. Colonel Clarence S. Wadsworth established The Rockfall Foundation in 1935 to "establish and maintain parks, forest, and wild land for public use and enjoyment . . . ."

Over the years, Rockfall has preserved natural and historic resources for the people of Middlesex County, Connecticut, including Wadsworth Falls State Park and the deKoven House, an eighteenth-century Georgian brick mansion. Education on natural resource preservation and conservation is a priority. The Annual Rockfall Symposium convenes speakers around environmental issues of Middlesex County.

Officers and directors. *Officers:* Barbara S. Delaney, President; Leonard J. Mediavilla, Vice President; Frank J. Sutkowski, Secretary/Treasurer. *Directors:* Geoffrey L. Colegrove, Barbara S. Delaney, Jeanne C. Dilworth, C. James Gibbons, Joseph G. Lynch, Anthony S. Marino, Joan D. Mazzotta, Edward L. McMillan, Leonard J. Mediavilla, Sari A. Rosenbaum, Frank J. Sutkowski, J. Stanley Watson.

Financial data. Data for fiscal year ended June 30, 1993. *Assets:* $2,070,019 (M). *Gifts received:* $16,419. *Total grants authorized:* $4,700.

Environmental awards. *Program and interests:* The Foundation's Education and Environment Committee holds workshops on lake management and pollution problems and is developing a Map of Planned Open Space in Middlesex County. The recently published Middlesex Trails Map was a step in the completion of the county map.
Recent grants: 1993 grants included support for urban environment (forests, open space, greenbelts, land use planning); river protection; and landfill reclamation, landscaping, and education.

Issues. Cli Bio Lan Agr Wat Oce Ene Was Tox Pop Dev
         •   •   •   •   •

Funding analysis.

Fiscal year:	1993
Env grants auth:	$4,700
Number:	4
Range:	$700–$1,500
Median:	$1,250
Pct $ auth (env/total):	100

Recipients (1993):	*Number:*	*Dollars:*
The Nature Conservancy, Connecticut Chapter	1	1,500
Town of Portland	1	1,500
Essex Garden Club	1	1,000
Middletown Urban Forestry Commission	1	700

Activity region (1993):	*Number:*	*Dollars:*
U.S. Northeast	4	4,700

Sample grants (1993).
Essex Garden Club. Essex, CT. $1,000. To develop a master plan for "recycling" the Essex town landfill that includes how to navigate the regulatory requirements for a post-closure landfill site, community education concerning the role of waste in community culture, and history; development of educational and recreational aspects; and exploration of the potential for linkage with other open space to build a green corridor around Essex.
Middletown Urban Forestry Commission. Middletown, CT. $700. To establish the Notable Tree Program, teach volunteers to measure and record trees for entry and mapping to aid in local land use planning.
The Nature Conservancy, Connecticut Chapter. Middletown, CT. $1,500. To identify the most critical natural resources in the Tidelands of the Connecticut River; determine the current threats; design and implement solutions with an understanding of the economics of the landscape; and promote compatible human uses as models of how people can live with nature.
Town of Portland. Portland, CT. $1,500. To establish an urban park, the Portland Town Green, that would link major downtown public buildings, serve as a site for civic and cultural events, eliminate the hazardous traffic pattern, and re-use neglected space.

Application process. *Initial contact:* Write for application guidelines and application form.
When to apply: Deadline is January 15.
Materials available: Annual report, application form, application guidelines.

Emphases. *Recipients:* Nonprofit organizations.
Activities: Education, planning, publications, symposia, workshops.
Types of support: Matching funds.
Geography: Middlesex County, Connecticut only.

Rockwell Fund, Inc.
1360 Post Oak Boulevard, Suite 780
Houston, Texas 77056
Tel: 713-629-9022   Fax: 713-629-7702
EIN: 746040258   Type: Independent
Contact: Martha Vogt, Program Officer

History and philosophy. Members of the James M. Rockwell family, Rockwell Brothers & Company, and Rockwell Lumber Company donated the funds to establish the Rockwell Fund in 1931. The Fund incorporated in 1949 and absorbed Rockwell

R

Brothers Endowment, Inc. in 1981. Current funding priorities are: Arts/Humanity, Human Services, Civic, Education, Health, and Religion.

Officers and directors. *Officers:* R. Terry Bell, President; Helen N. Sterling, Vice President; Mary Jo Loyd, Secretary; Bennie Green, Treasurer. *Trustees:* R. Terry Bell, Bennie Green, Helen N. Sterling.

Financial data. Data for fiscal year ended December 31, 1993. *Assets:* $68,613,080 (M). *Total grants disbursed:* $2,932,800.

Environmental awards. *Recent grants:* 1993 grants included support for urban parks, plant research, coastal issues, and elementary and public education.

Issues. Cli Bio Lan Agr Wat Oce Ene Was Tox Pop Dev
•   •   •   •

Funding analysis.

Fiscal year:	1991	1993
Env grants disb:	$65,000	$125,000
Number:	5	7
Range:	$5,000–$20,000	$5,000–$50,000
Median:	$10,000	$10,000
Pct $ disb (env/total):	2	4

Recipients (1993 highest):	Number:	Dollars:
Texas Tech University Foundation	1	50,000
Houston Arboretum and Botanical Society	1	25,000
Zoo Friends of Houston	1	15,000
Armand Bayou Nature Center	1	10,000
Center for Marine Conservation	1	10,000
National Wildflower Research Center	1	10,000

Activity region (1993):	Number:	Dollars:
U.S. South Central	7	125,000

Sample grants (1993).
Armand Bayou Nature Center. Houston, TX. $10,000.
Center for Marine Conservation. Austin, TX. $10,000. Texas Coastal Clean-Up Program.
Houston Arboretum and Botanical Society. Houston, TX. $25,000. Capital campaign.
National Wildflower Research Center. Austin, TX. $10,000. Staff conferences and training.
The Park People. Houston, TX. $5,000. Publication of newsletter and bulletin.
Texas Tech University Foundation. Lubbock, TX. $50,000. Professorships in plant and soil science/merchandising, environmental design, and consumer economics.

Application process. *Initial contact:* Cover letter and proposal. Cover letter (3 pages), on organization's letterhead and signed by executive director or board chairman, stating specific need and amount requested. Proposal to include:
1. Name and telephone number of contact person.
2. Names of current officers and board members.
3. Statement of purpose and brief history of organization.
4. Financial statement of past fiscal year (audited if available).
5. Operating budget for year for which funds are sought.
6. Copy of IRS tax-exempt status determination letter.
7. Copy of most recent IRS 990 tax return.

Project/program information.
1. Specific description of proposed project/program.
2. Projected timetable for use of the grant sought.
3. Project/program budget (revenues and expenses).
4. Other sources of funding, amounts requested or received.

Do not bind proposal.
When to apply: Deadlines are in February, May, August, and November. The board meets in March, June, September, and December. Contact Fund for precise deadlines.
Materials available: Annual report, "Grant Policies and Procedures."

Emphases. *Recipients:* Educational institutions, nonprofit organizations, zoos.
Activities: Conferences, publications, research, training.
Types of support: Capital campaigns/expenses, endowments, facilities, operating costs, pilot projects, scholarships.
Geography: Houston, Texas; Texas only.

Limitations. *Recipients:* Individuals.
Activities: Fundraising.

Rockwood Fund, Inc.
P.O. Box 40368
Washington, DC 20016-0368
Tel: 202-363-3244
EIN: 521698396   Type: Independent
EGA member
Contact: Mary Weinmann, Secretary/Treasurer

History and philosophy. Mary Weinmann and Andre Carothers established the Fund in 1990. It makes grants in areas of environment and human rights, with interest in giving seed money.

Officers and directors. *Officers:* Andre Carothers, President; Robert O. Blake, Vice President; Mary Weinmann, Secretary/Treasurer. *Directors:* Robert O. Blake, Andre Carothers, Nicholas I. Morgan, Mary Weinmann.

Financial data. Data for fiscal year ended December 31, 1993. *Assets:* $912,452 (M). *Total grants disbursed:* $50,000.

Environmental awards. *Recent grants:* 1993 grants included support for land conservation, forestry, and education.

Issues. Cli Bio Lan Agr Wat Oce Ene Was Tox Pop Dev
•   •

Funding analysis.

Fiscal year:	1993
Env grants disb:	$36,000
Number:	11
Range:	$2,000–$5,000
Median:	$3,000
Pct $ disb (env/total):	72

Recipients (1993 highest):	Number:	Dollars:
Earth Trust Foundation	1	5,000
Mt. Graham Coalition	1	5,000
Piedmont Environmental Council	1	5,000
Southeast Asia Information Network	1	4,000
Biodiversity Legal Foundation	1	3,000
Ecomedia	1	3,000
Greater Ecosystem Alliance	1	3,000

Activity regions (1993 highest):	Number:	Dollars:
U.S. not specified	3	9,000
U.S. Mid-Atlantic	2	8,000
Mexico and Central America	1	5,000
U.S. Northwest	2	5,000
Southeast Asia	1	4,000

Sample grants (1993).
Biodiversity Legal Foundation. Boulder, CO. $3,000.
Blue Ridge Environmental Defense League. Glendale Springs, NC. $3,000.
Canopy Institute. Olympia, WA. $2,000. Information to researchers and students about the rainforest canopy.
Ecomedia. Washington, DC. $3,000. Environmental education.
Greater Ecosystem Alliance. Bellingham, WA. $3,000. Posters and videos to promote a Canadian–U.S. park.
Mt. Graham Coalition. Washington, DC. $5,000. To oppose the cultural and ecological threats posed by Mt. Graham Astronomy Laboratory.
Piedmont Environmental Council. Warrenton, VA. $5,000. To fight against Disney America.
Save America's Forests, Inc. Washington, DC. $2,000. Support for grassroots forest activists.
Southeast Asia Information Network. Berkeley, CA. $4,000. Information on human rights and environment abuses.
The Tides Foundation. San Francisco, CA. $2,000. Information on transnationals and the environment.

Application process. *Initial contact:* Request application form. *When to apply:* Deadline is October 15. *Materials available:* Application form.

Emphases. *Recipients:* Nonprofit organizations, research institutions.
Activities: Activism, advocacy, citizen participation, conferences, innovative programs, political activities, symposia/colloquia.
Types of support: Operating costs, projects, seed money, single-year grants only.

Limitations. *Recipients:* Educational institutions, individuals, museums, public agencies, religious organizations.
Activities: Demonstration programs, direct services, education, exhibits, expeditions/tours, feasibility studies, fundraising, inventories, land acquisition, research (medical/scholarly), technical assistance, youth programs.
Types of support: Advertising campaigns, capital campaigns/expenses, computer hardware, continuing support, debt retirement, endowments, facilities, fellowships, indirect costs, internships, lectureships, leveraging funds, loans, maintenance, matching funds, membership campaigns, mortgage reduction, multi-year grants, professorships, program-related investments, scholarships, technical assistance, travel expenses.

© 1995 Environmental Data Resources, Inc.

Lee Romney Foundation, Inc.
P.O. Box 495
Hartsdale, New York 10530
Tel: 914–693–4983
EIN: 133187997   Type: Independent
Contact: Mark A. Romney, President

History and philosophy. The Foundation makes grants to preselected organizations in support of environmental projects, social services, and family planning.

Officers and directors. *Officers:* Mark A. Romney, President; Stuart Kessler, Secretary; Charles Watson, Treasurer. *Directors:* Stanley M. Klein, Michael Romney, Sharon Rosenfeld Scott.

Financial data. Data for fiscal year ended November 30, 1992. *Assets:* $120,266 (M). *Gifts received:* $100,000. *Total grants disbursed:* $90,000.

Environmental awards. *Recent grants:* 1992 grants included support for wilderness, river protection, wildlife conservation, and coastal issues.

Issues.   Cli • Bio • Lan Agr • Wat • Oce Ene • Was Tox • Pop • Dev

Funding analysis.

Fiscal year:	1992
Env grants disb:	$50,000
Number:	15
Range:	$1,000–$5,000
Median:	$2,000
Pct $ disb (env/total):	56

Recipients (1992 highest):	Number:	Dollars:
African Wildlife Foundation	1	5,000
American Rivers, Inc.	1	5,000
Conservation International	1	5,000
Defenders of Wildlife	1	5,000
National Toxics Campaign Fund	1	5,000
NYZS/The Wildlife Conservation Society	1	5,000
Zoological Society of San Diego	1	5,000

Activity regions (1992 highest):	Number:	Dollars:
U.S. not specified	5	18,000
New York/New Jersey	2	7,000
Africa	1	5,000
International*	1	5,000
U.S. West	1	5,000

*Multiple regions or not specified.

Sample grants (1992).
African Wildlife Foundation. Washington, DC. $5,000.
Alliance for the Wild Rockies. Missoula, MT. $2,000.
American Rivers, Inc. Washington, DC. $5,000.
Chesapeake Bay Foundation. Annapolis, MD. $2,000.
Conservation International. Washington, DC. $5,000.
Defenders of Wildlife. Washington, DC. $5,000.
Environmental Concern. St. Michaels, MD. $5,000.

R

Sierra Club Legal Defense Fund. San Francisco, CA. $2,000.
Zoological Society of San Diego. San Diego, CA. $5,000.

Application process: *Initial contact:* The Foundation awards grants to pre-selected organizations only. No unsolicited applications accepted.

Emphases. *Recipients:* Pre-selected organizations only.

Samuel and May Rudin Foundation, Inc.
345 Park Avenue, 33rd Floor
New York, New York 10154
Tel: 212–407–2400   Fax: 212–407–2540
EIN: 132906946   Type: Independent
Contact: Donna Garber, Administrator

History and philosophy. The Foundation was established in 1976 by Samuel Rudin. It awards grants primarily for higher education, social services, religious welfare, hospitals, health associations, museums, performing arts groups, and other cultural programs.

Officers and directors. *Officers:* Lewis Rudin, Chairman; Jack Rudin, President; Eric Rudin, Vice President and Secretary/Treasurer; Madeleine Johnson, Katherine Rudin, William Rudin, Vice Presidents; Beth DeWoody, Executive Vice President. *Directors:* Beth DeWoody, Madeleine Johnson, Eric Rudin, Jack Rudin, Katherine Rudin, Lewis Rudin, William Rudin.

Financial data. Data for fiscal year ended June 30, 1993. *Assets:* $1,398,574 (M). *Gifts received:* $5,792,562. *Total grants disbursed:* $5,635,588.

Environmental awards. *Recent grants:* 1993 grants included support for parks, a botanical garden, and environmental education.

Issues.   Cli   Bio   Lan   Agr   Wat   Oce   Ene   Was   Tox   Pop   Dev
                    •   •   •

Funding analysis.

Fiscal year:	1991	1993
Env grants disb:	$162,750	$71,662
Number:	7	5
Range:	$3,500–$50,000	$3,150–$25,000
Median:	$15,000	$15,000
Pct $ disb (env/total):	2	2

Recipients (1993):	Number:	Dollars:
Central Park Conservancy	2	28,150
NYZS/The Wildlife Conservation Society	1	25,000
The New York Botanical Garden	1	15,000
The Rainforest Foundation	1	3,512

Activity region (1993):	Number:	Dollars:
New York/New Jersey	5	71,662

Sample grants (1993).
Central Park Conservancy. New York, NY. $28,150.
The New York Botanical Garden. Bronx, NY. $15,000. Children's educational programs.
NYZS/The Wildlife Conservation Society. Bronx, NY. $25,000. Educational program.
The Rainforest Foundation. New York, NY. $3,512.

Application process. *Initial contact:* Letter of request, accompanied by a brochure describing the organization's purpose and activities, and copy of IRS tax-exempt status determination letter. *When to apply:* Anytime.

Emphases: *Recipients:* Educational institutions, museums, nonprofit organizations, religious organizations.
Geography: New York City.

Fran and Warren Rupp Foundation
40 Sturges Avenue
Mansfield, Ohio 44902–1912
Tel: 419–522–2345
EIN: 341230690   Type: Independent
Contact: Timothy S. Smith, Secretary/Treasurer

History and philosophy. The Foundation was established in 1977 by Frances H. and Warren E. Rupp. Interests include the arts and theater, social services, conservation, environment, animal welfare.

Officers and directors. *Officers:* Frances R. Christian, Chairman; Donald E. Smith, President; Sheron A. Rupp, Suzanne R. Hartung, Vice Presidents; Timothy S. Smith, Secretary/Treasurer. *Trustees:* Frances R. Christian, Miles W. Christian, Suzanne R. Hartung, Sheron A. Rupp, Donald E. Smith.

Financial data. Data for fiscal year ended December 31, 1993. *Assets:* $14,044,365 (M). *Gifts received:* $194,766. *Total grants disbursed:* $241,500.

Environmental awards. *Recent grants:* 1993 grants included support for land conservation, wildlife protection, and toxics education.

Issues.   Cli   Bio   Lan   Agr   Wat   Oce   Ene   Was   Tox   Pop   Dev
                    •   •   •

Funding analysis.

Fiscal year:	1993
Env grants disb:	$60,000
Number:	4
Range:	$5,000–$25,000
Median:	$15,000
Pct $ disb (env/total):	25

Recipients (1993):	Number:	Dollars:
Mohican School In The Out-of-Doors, Inc.	1	25,000
The Nature Conservancy, Ohio Field Office	1	20,000

Environmental Defense Fund	1	10,000
The Wilds	1	5,000

Activity regions (1993):   *Number:*   *Dollars:*
U.S. Great Lakes	3	50,000
U.S. not specified	1	10,000

Sample grants (1993).
Environmental Defense Fund. New York, NY. $10,000. Health & Toxic Chemicals program.
Mohican School In The Out-of-Doors, Inc. Danville, OH. $25,000.
The Nature Conservancy, Ohio Field Office. Columbus, OH. $20,000. Kitty Todd Preserve.
The Wilds. Columbus, OH. $5,000. Rhino Management & Research Program.

Application process. *Initial contact:* Letter.
When to apply: Anytime. The board meets quarterly.
Materials available: Grant application form.

Emphases. *Recipients:* Nonprofit organizations.
Activities: Education, land acquisition.
Types of support: Endowments, leveraging funds, matching funds, projects.
Geography: Ohio.

Limitations. *Recipients:* Individuals, public agencies, religious organizations.
Activities: Conflict resolution, feasibility studies, fundraising, inventories, litigation, lobbying, political activities.
Types of support: Advertising campaigns, debt retirement, fellowships, internships, loans, membership campaigns, operating costs, professorships, program-related investments, travel expenses.
Geography: International.

Sacharuna Foundation
c/o Peregrine Financial Corporation
84 State Street
Boston, Massachusetts 02109–2202
Tel: 617–523–1031
EIN: 133264132   Type: Independent
EGA member
Contact: Paula Barta, Trustee

History and philosophy. The Sacharuna Foundation was established in 1985 with funds donated by Lavinia Currier and Jack Robinson. Conservation and the environment are its focus.

Officers and directors. *Trustees:* Paula Barta, Lavinia Currier, Nicholas Noon.

Financial data. Data for fiscal year ended December 31, 1992.
Assets: $10,491,067 (M). *Total grants disbursed:* $440,961.

Environmental awards. *Recent grants:* 1992 grants included support for land conservation, wilderness, forests, wildlife, environmental health, and spirituality.

Issues.   Cli   Bio   Lan   Agr   Wat   Oce   Ene   Was   Tox   Pop   Dev
        •   •   •

Funding analysis.
Fiscal year:	1990	1992
Env grants disb:	$172,500	$154,000
Number:	13	11
Range:	$1,000–$57,500	$1,000–$50,000
Median:	$5,000	$5,000
Pct $ disb (env/total):	91	35

Recipients (1992 highest):   *Number:*   *Dollars:*
The Conservation Fund	1	50,000
NYZS/The Wildlife Conservation Society	1	47,500
Southern Environmental Law Center	1	26,000
Earth Island Institute	1	10,000
Endangered Wildlife Trust	1	5,000
Valhalla Wilderness Society	1	5,000

Activity regions (1992 highest):   *Number:*   *Dollars:*
U.S. not specified	5	69,500
New York/New Jersey	1	47,500
U.S. Southeast	1	26,000
Canada	1	5,000
U.S. West	1	3,000

Sample grants (1992).
American Forestry Association. Washington, DC. $2,500.
The Conservation Fund. Arlington, VA. $50,000.
Earth Island Institute. San Rafael, CA. $10,000.
Klamath Forest Alliance. Etna, CA. $3,000.
NYZS/The Wildlife Conservation Society. Bronx, NY. $47,500.
Piedmont Environmental Council. Warrenton, VA. $2,000.
Southern Environmental Law Center. Charlottesville, VA. $26,000.
The Student Conservation Association, Inc. Charleston, NH. $2,000.
World Resources Institute. Washington, DC. $1,000.

Application process. *Initial contact:* The Foundation awards grants to pre-selected organizations only. No unsolicited applications accepted.

Emphases. *Recipients:* Pre-selected organizations only.
Types of support: General purposes.

Limitations. *Recipients:* Individuals.

Sacramento Regional Foundation
1610 Arden Way, Suite 298
Sacramento, California 95815–4028
Tel: 916–927–2241   Fax: 916–927–0110
EIN: 942891517   Type: Community
Contact: Lauren Wolkov, Executive Director

History and philosophy. Created in 1983, the Sacramento Regional Foundation (SRF) was designed to encourage "thoughtful giving to address community issues; building and managing a permanent endowment which can respond to changing needs as the community changes; [and] serving as a catalyst, a convener, and a partner with area citizens and organizations in order to foster cooperation and build a sense of community."

SRF supports "ideas that help individuals make informed decisions about themselves and others; ideas that encourage cooperation among organizations and groups; ideas that shed new light on the region's needs and aspirations, with emphasis on long-term solutions; ideas that promote ethnic harmony; and technical assistance to strengthen the professional, managerial, and fundraising skills of nonprofit organizations."

The Foundation comprises 130 funds. Among its donor-advised funds are several designated for environmental purposes. Grants from unrestricted funds are awarded in the areas of: Arts and Humanities; Conservation and Environment; Education; Health; Historic Preservation; Human Services; and Regional Affairs.

Officers and directors. *Officers:* Malcolm S. Weintraub, President; Frank Washington, Vice President; Sandra Yee, Secretary; Forrest A. Plant, Sr., Treasurer. *Directors:* Gerald F. Bays, Elfrena Foord, Marcy Friedman, Robert F. Gaines, Alice Gonzales, Muriel P. Johnson, Hon. Thomas J. MacBride, David K. Murphy, Melena Ose, Thomas J. O'Neil, Erwin Potts, C. John Tupper, M.D., Frank Washington, Sandra Yee.

Financial data. Data for fiscal year ended December 31, 1993. *Assets:* $8,300,000 (M). *Gifts received:* $1,353,962. *Total grants disbursed:* $1,104,000.

Environmental awards. *Recent grants:* 1992 grants from unrestricted funds included support for a nature center.

Issues.   Cli   Bio   Lan   Agr   Wat   Oce   Ene   Was   Tox   Pop   Dev
                    •   •

Funding analysis.§

Fiscal year:	1992
Env grants disb:	$4,539
Number:	9
Range:	$50–$2,500
Median:	$67
Pct $ disb (env/total):	1

Recipients (1992 highest):	Number:	Dollars:
Sacramento Zoological Society	2	2,550
Terwilliger Nature Education Center	1	1,000
Effie Yeaw Nature Center	1	500
The Nature Conservancy, California Field Office	1	255
California Waterfowl Association	1	67
National Audubon Society, Western Region	1	67

Activity region (1992):	Number:	Dollars:
U.S. West	9	4,539

§Includes discretionary, directed, and donor-advised grants.

Sample grants (1992).
California Waterfowl Association. Sacramento, CA. $67.
National Audubon Society, Western Region. Sacramento, CA. $67.
The Nature Conservancy, California Field Office. San Francisco, CA. $255.
Sacramento Zoological Society. Sacramento, CA. $2,550 (2 grants).
Terwilliger Nature Education Center. Corte Madera, CA. $1,000.
Effie Yeaw Nature Center. Sacramento, CA. $500.

Application process. *Initial contact:* Proposal (10 copies) to include:
1. Cover letter on organization letterhead, signed by a board officer.
2. Completed application form.
3. List of organization's governing body. Include professional or community affiliations, and indicate if they are paid for their services to the organization.
4. Financial statement (audited if available) for the most recent fiscal year.
5. Organization's budget for the current and preceding year.
6. Copy of IRS tax-exempt status determination letter.

When to apply: Deadline is in December. The board meets in March.
Materials available: Annual report (includes "Criteria for Grantseekers"), application form, *Update* (newsletter).

Emphases. *Recipients:* Nonprofit organizations.
Activities: Collaborative efforts, technical assistance.
Types of support: Leveraging funds.
Geography: Sacramento, Yolo, Placer, and El Dorado counties, California.

Limitations. *Recipients:* Individuals.
Types of support: Capital campaigns/expenses, debt retirement, facilities, mortgage reduction, multi-year grants, travel expenses.

San Diego Community Foundation
Wells Fargo Bank Building
101 West Broadway, Suite 1120
San Diego, California 92101
Tel: 619–239–8815   Fax: 619–239–1710
EIN: 952942582   Type: Community
Contact: Bob Kelly, President

History and philosophy. Established in 1975, the San Diego Community Foundation (SDCF) works to "fund programs that promote access, equity, diversity, and self-reliance and that reach key San Diego constituencies, especially children, youth, and families. Elders, persons with impaired abilities, racial and ethnic minorities, refugees and immigrants are also a primary focus."

Grantmaking priorities are demonstration projects that test practical approaches and models for community change; programs that significantly strengthen the capacity of existing institutions; programs that help coordinate community services; and programs that provide leverage for generating additional funds, resources, and community support. Program areas include: Arts and Culture, Civic Affairs and Community Planning, Conservation and

Civic Affairs and Community Planning, Conservation and Housing and Community Development, and Human Services.

Officers and directors. *Officers*: Ann Parode, Chairman; Susan A. Maddox, Vice Chairman; Bob Kelly, President and CEO; Frank Ault, Philip Blair, John Messner, Tom Robertson, Elsie Weston, Vice Presidents; Maria A. Vilar, Secretary. *Board of Governors:* Michel Anderson, Frank Ault, Philip Blair, Ron Blair, Hon. Federico Castro, Paul Ecke, Jr., Howard Goldfeder, Dr. Anita Harbert, Daniel Herde, Jerome Katzin, Hon. Judith Keep, Susan A. Maddox, Hon. Art Madrid, Robert McRann, John Messner, Sandra Fleet Mooers, Thomas Murphy, Ann Parode, Tom Robertson, Gail Stoorza-Gill, Albert Trepte, Maria A. Vilar, Barbara Walbridge, Mary Walshok, Elsie Weston, Su-Mei Yu.

Financial data. Data for fiscal year ended June 30, 1993. *Assets:* $81,593,138 (M). *Gifts received:* $8,509,284. *Total grants authorized:* $4,059,033.

Environmental awards. *Recent grants:* 1993 grants included support for beautification, land conservation, an arboretum, a park, a zoo, and environmental education.

Issues. Cli Bio Lan Agr Wat Oce Ene Was Tox Pop Dev

Funding analysis.§

Fiscal year:	1993
Env grants auth:	$137,715
Number:	18
Range:	$100–$48,700
Median:	$4,410
Pct $ disb (env/total):	3

Recipients (1993 highest):	Number:	Dollars:
Zoological Society of San Diego	10	110,370
San Diego Unified School District	2	17,962
Friends of the San Jacinto Mountains County Park	1	4,000
Carlsbad Arboretum Foundation, Inc.	1	2,565
City Beautiful–Poinsettia Fund	2	1,618

Activity region (1993):	Number:	Dollars:
U.S. West	18	137,715

§Includes advised, designated, field-of-interest, and unrestricted grants.

Sample grants (1993).
Carlsbad Arboretum Foundation, Inc. San Diego, CA. $2,565.
City Beautiful–Poinsettia Fund. San Diego, CA. $1,618.
The Environmental Trust. San Diego, CA. $1,100. Printing costs for land purchase.
Friends of the San Jacinto Mountains County Park. San Diego, CA. $4,000. Environmental education.
National Audubon Society. San Diego, CA. $100.
San Diego Unified School District. San Diego, CA. $17,962. For the Build Environment Education Program (BEEP).
Zoological Society of San Diego. San Diego, CA. $4,850. Heart of the Zoo Phase IIB.
Zoological Society of San Diego. San Diego, CA. $4,820. Support of construction of the Bonobo Exhibit.
Zoological Society of San Diego. San Diego, CA. $48,700. For the Center for the Reproduction of Endangered Species.
Zoological Society of San Diego. San Diego, CA. $52,000.

Application process. *Initial contact:* Letter of intent (2 pages), addressed to program director, to include:
1. Organization's mission.
2. Population to benefit from grant.
3. Description of program/project.
4. Results to be achieved.
5. Measurement strategy.
6. Project budget and plan for sustaining the project in the future.

Full proposal, if requested, to include:
1. Cover letter, signed by the agency's president and/or executive director, summarizing project and funding needs, and stating that the board of directors supports proposal.
2. Cover Sheet identifying project and key personnel.
3. Narrative proposal including organization's description, program description, statement of need, project objectives, methods or strategies to be used, project staffing and administration.
4. Methods to be used in evaluating project.
5. Funding sources.
6. Project future.
7. Project budget.
8. IRS tax-exempt status determination letter.
9. Most recent audited financial statements.
10. Board of directors and staff with race/ethnicity breakdown.

When to apply: Proposal deadlines are February 15, June 15, August 15, and December 15. Letters of intent should be submitted at least three weeks prior to the proposal deadline. The board of governors meet in March, May, September, and November.
Materials available: Annual report (includes "Grantmaking Guidelines"), "Discretionary Funding Guidelines," Appreciation packet.

Emphases. *Recipients:* Botanical gardens, educational institutions, museums, nonprofit organizations, public agencies, research institutions, zoos.
Activities: Capacity building, citizen participation, collaborative efforts, demonstration programs, education, feasibility studies, innovative programs, inventories, land acquisition, networking, planning, research, technical assistance, volunteerism, youth programs.
Types of support: Equipment, facilities, pilot projects, projects, seed money, single-year grants only, start-up costs, technical assistance.
Geography: San Diego County, California.

Limitations. *Recipients:* Individuals, religious organizations.
Activities: Conferences, exhibits, expeditions/tours, fundraising, litigation, lobbying, political activities, seminars, symposia/colloquia, workshops.
Types of support: Annual campaigns, capital campaigns/expenses, continuing support, debt retirement, endowments, general purposes, indirect costs, lectureships, maintenance, mortgage reduction, multi-year grants, operating costs, scholarships, travel expenses.

© 1995 Environmental Data Resources, Inc.

The San Francisco Foundation

685 Market Street, Suite 910
San Francisco, California 94105-9716
Tel: 415-495-3100   Fax: 415-442-0495
EIN: 941101547   Type: Community
EGA member
Contacts: Jane Rogers, Program Executive
Carol Campbell, Program Associate

History and philosophy. The San Francisco Foundation is a regional community foundation serving Alameda, Contra Costa, Marin, San Francisco, and San Mateo counties. Its purpose is to improve the quality of life, promote greater equality of opportunity, and assist those in need or at risk in the San Francisco Bay Area. The Foundation strives to protect and enhance the unique human and natural resources of the Bay Area, including "the beauty and quality of its land, air, and water—so that these resources may be enjoyed now and in the future." Its primary program areas are: Arts and Humanities, Community Health, Education, Environment, Urban Affairs, and Philanthropy. A significant portion of funds are donor-advised, and may be awarded to any program area.

Officers and directors. *Officer:* Mary Lee Widener, Chair. *Trustees:* Lucille S. Abrahamson, Peter E. Haas, Leonard E. Kingsley, Rolland C. Lowe, Stephanie C. MacColl, Ted J. Saenger, David J. Sanchez, Jr., Leslie Hume.

Financial data. Data for fiscal year ended June 30, 1993. *Assets:* $286,500,000 (M). *Gifts received:* $34,025,890. *Total grants disbursed:* $26,500,000.

Environmental awards. *Program and interests:* The purpose of the Environment program is to:

- Promote the highest possible quality natural and urban living environment for the culturally and ethnically diverse people of the Bay Area.
- Instill an enlightened environmental ethic in government, business, the independent sector, and the general public.

Priorities are:

- To protect and restore the ecosystem(s) of the Bay Area, including its land, water, air, and wildlife resources.
- To promote a livable, sustainable, and healthful urban environment for the 4 million Bay Area residents served by The San Francisco Foundation, with special emphasis on the needs of the disadvantaged.
- To promote multicultural participation and leadership in setting the Bay Area environmental action agenda and in programs and organizations working toward environmental betterment.
- To promote education for environmental literacy and to expand environmental career preparation and opportunities, especially for young people of color.
- To promote protection of the Bay Area greenbelt and provisions of park, open space, and outdoor recreation opportunities accessible to all Bay Area residents.

Special emphases are:

- Programs that improve environmental quality for those most in need.
- Work leading to the adoption and implementation of sound public policy related to the above program priorities.
- The ecological health and integrity of the San Francisco Bay-Delta ecosystem.

Issues. Cli • Bio • Lan • Agr • Wat • Oce • Ene • Was • Tox • Pop • Dev •

Funding analysis.§

Fiscal year:	1991	1993
Env grants auth:	$1,427,518	$1,214,512
Number:	80	77
Range:	$200–$165,000	$1,000–$109,600
Median:	$10,000	$10,000
Pct $ auth (env/total):	6	5

Recipients (1993 highest):	Number:	Dollars:
The San Francisco Zoological Society	1	109,600
Natural Resources Defense Council	3	78,600
Bay Institute of San Francisco	1	60,000
Living Desert Reserve	1	51,000
University of California, Botanical Garden	1	49,000

Activity regions (1993):	Number:	Dollars:
U.S. West	67	1,121,364
U.S. not specified	6	73,898
International*	2	13,750
U.S. Mountain	2	5,500

*Multiple regions or not specified.

§Includes donor-advised and program grants.

Sample grants (1993).

Alameda County Office of Education. Hayward, CA. $16,000. Family Ecology, an education program for K–6 students and their families.

Bay Area Ridge Trail Council. San Francisco, CA. $45,000 (2 years). Development of a comprehensive volunteer management plan for the Council's outreach program.

BayKeeper. San Francisco, CA. $25,000 (2 years). Enforcement of environmental protection for San Francisco Bay.

Committee for Water Policy Consensus. Concord, CA. $15,000. Coordination of Bay Area water resources activities affecting the San Francisco Bay-Delta.

East Palo Alto Agricultural and Historical Society. East Palo Alto, CA. $20,000. Activities to preserve the agricultural and community heritage of East Palo Alto.

Environmental Defense Fund. Oakland, CA. $30,000. Bay-Delta protection through water rights proceedings, negotiations, water management recommendations, and water marketing.

The Garden Project. San Francisco, CA. $25,000. Teaching former prisoners marketable skills in organic gardening.

The Nature Conservancy, California Field Office. San Francisco, CA. $25,000. Converting thousands of acres of fallow ricelands to managed wetlands and offstream winter storage.

People Organizing to Demand Environmental Rights. San Francisco, CA. $20,000. Education on lead poisoning.
Save San Francisco Bay Association. Oakland, CA. $20,000. Implementation of a restoration plan for San Francisco Bay.
The Student Conservation Association, Inc. Charleston, NH. $25,000. For the Conservation Career Development Program, for multicultural urban youth.
Tarlton Foundation. San Francisco, CA. $5,000 (6 months). Scholarships to Sea Camp, a summer marine science education program for disadvantaged youth.
University Oakland Metropolitan Forum. Berkeley, CA. $20,000 (6 months). Strategic planning and program development by the Ad Hoc Council on Replanting Needs (ACORN).

Application process. *Initial contact:* Letter of intent (3 pages maximum) outlining:
1. What is proposed project?
2. Why is project important?
3. Who is applicant?

When to apply: Anytime.
Materials available: Annual report (includes "How to Apply for a Grant"), *The Grant Application Process* (booklet). The Foundation also holds workshops on grant application.

Emphases. *Recipients:* Botanical gardens, educational institutions, museums, nonprofit organizations, public agencies, research institutions, zoos.
Activities: Activism, advocacy, capacity building, citizen participation, collaborative efforts, conflict resolution, demonstration programs, direct services, education, feasibility studies, fundraising, innovative programs, inventories, networking, planning, policy analysis/development, technical assistance, training, volunteerism, workshops, youth programs.
Types of support: General purposes, indirect costs, internships, leveraging funds, matching funds, multi-year grants, operating costs, pilot projects, program-related investments, projects, seed money, start-up costs, technical assistance.
Geography: Five Bay Area counties: San Francisco, Alameda, Contra Costa, Marin, and San Mateo only.

Limitations. *Recipients:* Individuals.
Activities: Audiovisual materials, conferences, expeditions/tours, land acquisition, litigation, lobbying, political activities, publications, research, seminars, symposia/colloquia.
Types of support: Advertising campaigns, annual campaigns, capital campaigns/expenses, computer hardware, continuing support, debt retirement, emergency funding, endowments, equipment, facilities, lectureships, maintenance, mortgage reduction, professorships.

The Sapelo Foundation
308 Mallory Street, Suite C
St. Simons Island, Georgia 31522
Tel: 912–638–6265 Fax: 912–634–6028
EIN: 580827472 Type: Independent
Contact: Alan McGregor, Executive Director

History and philosophy. The Foundation was established in 1949. It helps support a marine research laboratory on Sapelo Island through grants to the University of Georgia. It also gives grants in the areas of the environment, higher education, and social justice in the state of Georgia.

Officers and directors. Officers: Mr. Smith W. Bagley, President; Ms. Susan Lehman Carmichael, Vice President; Mr. William K. Broker, Secretary/Treasurer. *Honorary Chair:* Dr. Annemarie Reynolds. *Trustees:* Mr. Smith W. Bagley, Mr. William K. Broker, Ms. Susan Lehman Carmichael, Mr. Hubert Humphrey, Ms. Rosetta B. Johnson, Mrs. Katherine B. Mountcastle, Dr. Annemarie Reynolds.

Financial data. Data for fiscal year ended June 30, 1992. *Assets:* $18,352,025 (M). *Total grants disbursed:* $766,622.

Environmental awards. *Recent grants:* 1993 grants included support for sustainable development, racial justice, and solid and toxic waste issues along the Georgia coast.

Issues. Cli Bio Lan Agr Wat Oce Ene Was Tox Pop Dev
                             •   •   •   •

Funding analysis.

Fiscal year:	1991	1993
Env grants auth:	$312,000	$103,000
Number:	5	10
Range:	$2,000–$250,000	$5,000–$18,000
Median:	$10,000	$10,000
Pct $ auth (env/total):	47	24

Recipients (1993 highest):	Number:	Dollars:
St. Paul's Baptist Church	1	18,000
Corinth United Methodist Church, Environmental Fund	1	15,000
Campaign for a Prosperous Georgia	1	10,000
Environmental Community Action	1	10,000
McSap Development, Inc.	1	10,000
St. Paul's Missionary Baptist Church	1	10,000
University of Georgia Research Foundation	1	10,000
Ware County Community Coalition Board	1	10,000

Activity region (1993):	Number:	Dollars:
U.S. Southeast	10	103,000

Sample grants (1993).
Campaign for a Prosperous Georgia. Atlanta, GA. $10,000. For continued monitoring of the enforcement of Georgia's Solid Waste Act and for the education of the public concerning solid waste issues including waste reduction, recycling, and disposal technologies.
Environmental Community Action. Atlanta, GA. $10,000. To provide technical assistance, education, organizing assistance, and information to low income, minority, and rural communities in Georgia faced with environmental threats including irresponsible and unsafe hazardous and solid waste dumping, industrial pollution, and other environmental problems that threaten the health and development of these communities.

© 1995 Environmental Data Resources, Inc.

S

St. Paul's Missionary Baptist Church. Savannah, GA. $10,000. To educate the citizens of Savannah, particularly African Americans, about the severe environmental problems threatening their city and region and to organize citizens to advocate for cleanup of existing environmental hazards and to advocate pollution prevention policies. Also to conduct a regional education campaign about environmental hazards associated with the Savannah River Site nuclear fuel processing facility.

Sierra Club Foundation. Ty Ty, GA. $5,000. For the provision of technical assistance to rural communities working to create programs for the reduction and responsible management of solid and toxic waste, and for production of written materials promoting responsible waste management.

Application process. *Initial contact:* Proposal with project data. *When to apply:* Deadlines are March 15 and September 15 for review at the June and December board meetings, respectively. *Materials available:* Biennial report, application guidelines.

Emphases. *Recipients:* Nonprofit organizations, public agencies. *Activities:* Activism, advocacy, capacity building, citizen participation, collaborative efforts, education, fundraising, litigation, political activities, technical assistance, youth programs. *Types of support:* Continuing support, general purposes, leveraging funds, multi-year grants, operating costs, program-related investments, seed money, start-up costs, technical assistance, travel expenses. *Geography:* Georgia only.

Limitations. *Recipients:* Botanical gardens, individuals, museums, zoos. *Activities:* Exhibits, expeditions/tours, inventories, land acquisition, lobbying. *Types of support:* Debt retirement, emergency funding, endowments, facilities, fellowships, loans, mortgage reduction, professorships.

Sarkeys Foundation
116 South Peters, Suite 219
Norman, Oklahoma 73069-6066
Tel: 405-364-3703
EIN: 730736496   Type: Independent
Contact: Cheri D. Cartwright, Executive Director

History and philosophy. The Foundation was established in 1962 by S. J. Sarkeys. Main areas of interest are: Social Services, Arts and Cultural, Education, Health Care, and Medical Research.

Officers and directors. *Officers:* Richard A. Bell, President; Robert T. Rennie, Vice President; Robert S. Rizley, Secretary/Treasurer; Richard J. Hefler, Manager; Cheri D. Cartwright, Assistant Secretary/Treasurer and Executive Director. *Trustees:* Richard A. Bell, Molly Shi Boren, Joseph W. Morris, Robert T. Rennie, Robert S. Rizley, Dr. Paul F. Sharp, Preston A. Trimble, Terry W. West, Lee Anne Wilson.

Financial data. Data for fiscal year ended November 30, 1993. *Assets:* $62,202,647 (M). *Total grants disbursed:* $2,750,018.

Environmental awards. *Recent grants:* In 1993 the Foundation awarded a grant for a conservation study to identify and protect the biological systems in southeastern Oklahoma; assisted with the establishment of a biotechnology research laboratory; and made the final installment on an endowed university chair in environmental science.

Issues. Cli Bio Lan Agr Wat Oce Ene Was Tox Pop Dev
              •   •   •

Funding analysis.§

Fiscal year:	1991	1993
Env grants auth or disb:	$1,500,000*	$961,000
Number:	2	4
Range:	$500,000–$1,000,000	$5,000–$660,000
Median:	$750,000	$148,000
Pct $ disb (env/total):	8	35

*Based on grants authorized.

Recipients (1993):	Number:	Dollars:
University of Oklahoma, Energy Center	1	660,000
University of Tulsa	1	250,000
The Nature Conservancy, Oklahoma Field Office	1	46,000
William Fremont Harn Gardens, Inc.	1	5,000

Activity region (1993):	Number:	Dollars:
U.S. South Central	4	961,000

§Based on grants disbursed.

Sample grant (1993).
William Fremont Harn Gardens, Inc. Oklahoma City, OK. $5,000.
The Nature Conservancy, Oklahoma Field Office. Tulsa, OK. $46,000. Ouachita Mountain Conservation initiative.
University of Oklahoma, Energy Center. Norman, OK. $660,000.
University of Tulsa. Tulsa, OK. $250,000.

Application process. *Initial contact:* Letter or full proposal. Proposal (single-spaced, unbound, and printed on only one side of white 8½"x11" paper) to include:
1. Organization's legal name and address as stated on the IRS tax status letter.
2. Telephone number and name of contact person.
3. List of board and staff.
4. Project description (3–4 pages).
   - Brief description of organization's activities and people it serves.
   - Problem or need project will address and a description of how project will solve or alleviate problem.
   - Project outline containing a problem statement and project needs, goals, objectives, activities, and schedule.
   - Geographic area and number of people to be served by project.
   - Description of any similar programs and how organization will work cooperatively with them.
   - Description of project evaluation and how project will be continued at the end of grant period.
5. Project budget of other potantial or actual sources of funding.

6. Organization's budget, summarizing lists of funds and an indication of what percentage of the budget is spent on fundraising.
7. Copy of most recent audit or financial statement.
8. Copy of IRS tax-exempt status determination letter.

The Foundation does not accept proposals via facsimile machine.
When to apply: Deadlines are February 15 and August 15.
Materials available: Brochure (includes "Proposal Format").

Emphases. *Recipients:* Educational institutions, museums, nonprofit organizations, research institutions.
Activities: Collaborative efforts, education, innovative programs, research, youth programs.
Types of support: Capital campaigns/expenses, equipment, facilities, leveraging funds, matching funds, pilot projects, projects, scholarships.
Geography: Oklahoma.

Limitations. *Recipients:* Individuals, public agencies, religious organizations.
Activities: Activism, advocacy, conflict resolution, feasibility studies, litigation, lobbying, political activities.
Types of support: Annual campaigns, continuing support, debt retirement, loans, mortgage reduction, operating costs.

Sarah Scaife Foundation Incorporated
Three Mellon Bank Center
525 William Penn Place, Suite 3900
Pittsburgh, Pennsylvania 15219–1708
Tel: 412–392–2900
EIN: 251113452   Type: Independent
Contact: Richard M. Larry, President

History and philosophy. The Foundation was created in 1941 by Sarah Mellon Scaife, whose grandfather Judge Thomas Mellon founded the family's banking and investment fortune. Sarah Scaife died in 1965, leaving a large portion of her estate to the Foundation. In cooperation with other Scaife family charitable activities, the Foundation adopted an emphasis on public affairs related to selected domestic and international issues in the early 1970s. Program interests include economic growth, taxation, regulation, law and economics, public choice theory, educational reform, national and international security, arms control, defense capabilities, alliance systems, and support for graduate and postgraduate education and "think tanks."

Officers and directors. *Officers:* Richard M. Scaife, Chairman; Richard M. Larry, President; Barbara L. Slaney, Vice President and Assistant Secretary; Donald C. Sipp, Vice President, Investments and Treasurer; R. Daniel McMichael, Secretary.
Trustees: William J. Bennett, Anthony J. A. Bryan, T. Kenneth Cribb, Jr., Edwin J. Feulner, Jr., Richard M. Larry, Allan H. Meltzer, Richard M. Scaife, James M. Walton.

Financial data. Data for fiscal year ended December 31, 1992.
Assets: $212,232,889 (M). *Total grants disbursed:* $11,699,500.

Environmental awards. *Recent grants:* One grant in 1992 supported research on public choice theory related to climate issues.

Issues. Cli Bio Lan Agr Wat Oce Ene Was Tox Pop Dev
          •   •

Funding analysis.

Fiscal year:	1991	1992
Env grants auth:	$1,000,000	$100,000
Number:	7	1
Range:	$50,000–$500,000	–
Median:	$100,000	–
Pct $ auth (env/total):	7	1

Recipient (1992):	Number:	Dollars:
American Enterprise Institute	1	100,000

Activity region (1992):	Number:	Dollars:
U.S. not specified	1	100,000

Sample grant (1992).
American Enterprise Institute. Washington, DC. $100,000. For Dr. Robert Hahn of Carnegie Mellon University, who is examining the costs and benefits of stabilizing emissions of greenhouse gases and how to shape related policies.

Application process. *Initial contact:* Letter signed by organization's CEO or authorized representative, and approved by the organization's board of directors. The letter should provide a description of the purpose for the funds requested and a budget. Append:
1. Latest audited financial statements and annual report.
2. Current annual budget.
3. List of officers and directors and their major affiliations.
4. Copy of current IRS tax-exempt status determination letter.

Additional information may be requested.
When to apply: Anytime. The board meets in February, May, September, and November.
Materials available: Annual report (includes "Grant Application Procedures").

Emphases. *Recipients:* Educational institutions, nonprofit organizations.
Activities: Conferences, education, policy analysis/development, publications, research, seminars.
Types of support: Continuing support, fellowships, general purposes, matching funds, operating costs, projects, seed money.

Limitations. *Recipients:* Individuals, nationally organized fund-raising groups.
Types of support: Debt retirement, loans, scholarships.

The Scherman Foundation, Inc.
16 East 52nd Street, Suite 601
New York, New York 10022
Tel: 212–832–3086
EIN: 136098464   Type: Independent
Contact: Sandra Silverman, Executive Director

History and philosophy. The Scherman Foundation was incorporated in 1941 by Harry Scherman, founder of the Book-of-the-Month Club. Areas of interest are: the Arts, Conservation,

S

Disarmament and Peace, Family Planning, Human Rights and Liberties, and Social Welfare. The Foundation makes grants throughout the United States, but in the areas of Arts and Social Welfare emphasis is placed on organizations in New York City.

Officers and directors. *Officers:* Axel G. Rosin, Chairman; Karen R. Sollins, President; Katharine S. Rosin, Secretary; David F. Freeman, Treasurer; Sandra Silverman, Assistant Secretary and Executive Director. *Directors:* Hillary Brown, Helen Edey, Archibald R. Murray, Axel G. Rosin, Katharine S. Rosin, Anthony M. Schulte, Karen R. Sollins, Marcia Thompson.

Financial data. Data for fiscal year ended December 31, 1993. *Assets:* $72,052,977 (M). *Total grants disbursed:* $4,177,303.

Environmental awards. *Recent grants:* 1993 grants included support for land conservation, coastal issues, wildlife preservation, and urban environment.

Issues. Cli Bio Lan Agr Wat Oce Ene Was Tox Pop Dev

Funding analysis.

Fiscal year:	1991	1993
Env grants auth:	$380,000	$540,000
Number:	13	17
Range:	$10,000–$70,000	$5,000–$75,000
Median:	$25,000	$25,000
Pct $ auth (env/total):	10	13

Recipients (1993 highest):	Number:	Dollars:
Natural Resources Defense Council	1	75,000
The Parks Council, Inc.	2	60,000
Friends of the Earth/ Environmental Policy Institute	1	50,000
INFORM	1	50,000
Southern Environmental Law Center	1	40,000

Activity regions (1993):	Number:	Dollars:
New York/New Jersey	9	235,000
U.S. not specified	5	225,000
U.S. Southeast	2	55,000
Alaska	1	25,000

Sample grants (1993).
American Littoral Society. Highlands, NJ. $20,000 (2 years).
The Parks Council, Inc. New York, NY. $5,000. For the Committee to Preserve Brighton Beach and Manhattan Beach.
Legal Environmental Assistance Foundation. Tallahassee, FL. $15,000.
Prospect Park Alliance. New York, NY. $20,00 (2 years).
The Trust for Public Land. New York, NY. $25,000 (2 years). New York City Land Project.
The Wilderness Society. Washington, DC. $25,000 (2 years).

Application process. *Initial contact:* Letter outlining the purpose for which funds are sought. It is helpful to include:
1. Budget.
2. Names of the board of directors of organization.
3. Listing of key personnel.
4. Recent financial statement listing present sources of support.
5. Copy of IRS tax-exempt status determination letter.

When to apply: Anytime.
Materials available: Annual report (includes "Statement of Policy and Procedures").

Emphases. *Recipients:* Botanical gardens, museums, nonprofit organizations, zoos.
Activities: Advocacy, citizen participation, direct services, innovative programs, land acquisition, litigation, training, volunteerism, youth programs.
Types of support: Continuing support, emergency funding, general purposes, matching funds, multi-year grants, operating costs, program-related investments, seed money, technical assistance.
Geography: United States; New York City for Arts and Social Welfare programs.

Limitations. *Recipients:* Educational institutions, individuals, public agencies, religious organizations, research institutions
Activities: Audiovisual materials, conferences, education, exhibits, expeditions/tours, inventories, lobbying, networking, political activities, research, seminars, symposia/colloquia.
Types of support: Advertising campaigns, annual campaigns, capital campaigns/expenses, computer hardware, debt retirement, endowments, equipment, facilities, fellowships, lectureships, leveraging funds, membership campaigns, mortgage reduction, professorships, scholarships, travel expenses.

S. H. and Helen R. Scheuer Family Foundation, Inc.

c/o 61 Associates
350 Fifth Avenue, Suite 3410
New York, New York 10018
Tel: 212-947-9009
EIN: 136062661   Type: Independent
Contact: Linda Erlich, Executive Director

History and philosophy. The Scheuer Family Foundation was established in 1943 by S. H. Scheuer, an investor and philanthropist whose interests included housing for the elderly and Brandeis University. The Foundation primarily funds Jewish philanthropies, higher education, and arts and culture.

Officers and directors. *Officers:* Richard J. Scheuer, President; Amy Scheuer Cohen, Vice President; Harvey Brecher, Secretary; Harold Cohen, Treasurer; Eli S. Garber, Assistant Secretary/Treasurer. *Directors:* Harvey Brecher, Amy Scheuer Cohen, Harold Cohen, Eli S. Garber, Richard J. Scheuer.

Financial data. Data for fiscal year ended November 30, 1992. *Assets:* $25,370,836 (M). *Gifts received:* $4,924,653. *Total grants disbursed:* $6,410,762.

Environmental awards. *Recent grants:* 1992 grants included support for urban parks.

Issues. Cli Bio Lan Agr Wat Oce Ene Was Tox Pop Dev

Funding analysis.

Fiscal year:	1992
Env grants disb:	$12,500
Number:	2
Range:	$2,500–$10,000
Median:	$6,250
Pct $ disb (env/total):	<1

Recipients (1992):	Number:	Dollars:
Central Park Conservancy	1	10,000
Prospect Park Alliance	1	2,500

Activity region (1992):	Number:	Dollars:
New York/New Jersey	2	12,500

Sample grants (1992).
Central Park Conservancy. New York, NY. $10,000.
Prospect Park Alliance. Brooklyn, NY. $2,500.

Application process. *Initial contact:* Proposal and cover letter on letterhead including brief summary of proposal, amount requested, and results expected. Proposal to include:
1. Need to be addressed.
2. How need will be met.
3. Who will be served.
4. Expected outcome.
5. Why organization is appropriate for the job.
6. Staff and qualifications.
7. Organization's operating budget and sources of support.
8. Budget for proposed project and other sources of support.
9. Amount requested.
10. Evaluation plans.
11. Other sources of support.
12. Continuing support.
13. Timetable.
14. Contact person and telephone number.
15. Organizational background, board members, most recent audited financial statement, evidence of tax-exempt status.

When to apply: Anytime.
Materials available: "Information for Grant Application."

Emphases. *Types of support:* Capital campaigns/expenses, research, scholarships.
Geography: New York City and Israel.

Sarah I. Schieffelin Residuary Trust

c/o The Bank of New York
129 Avenue of the Americas, 29th Floor
New York, New York 10104
Tel: 212–495–1784
EIN: 136724459   Type: Independent
Contact: Herbert Rauser, Vice President

History and philosophy. The Sarah I. Schieffelin Residuary Trust was established in 1976 by Sarah I. Schieffelin. The Trust funds in the areas of conservation, wildlife, cultural programs, health, social services, and Protestant giving.

Officers and directors. *Trustees:* Thomas B. Fenlon, The Bank of New York.

Financial data. Data for fiscal year ended March 31, 1993. *Assets:* $8,036,239 (M). *Total grants disbursed:* $300,815.

Environmental awards. *Recent grants:* 1993 grants included support for land conservation, forests, and species protection.

Issues.   Cli   Bio   Lan   Agr   Wat   Oce   Ene   Was   Tox   Pop   Dev
 •   •

Funding analysis.

Fiscal year:	1993
Env grants disb:	$74,164
Number:	6
Range:	$1,000–$30,082
Median:	$5,500
Pct $ disb (env/total):	25

Recipients (1993 highest):	Number:	Dollars:
National Audubon Society	1	30,082
National Wildlife Federation	1	30,082
The Nature Conservancy, Headquarters	1	6,000
The Conservation Fund	1	5,000
Central Park Conservancy	1	2,000

Activity regions (1993):	Number:	Dollars:
U.S. not specified	4	71,164
New York/New Jersey	1	2,000
U.S. Mid-Atlantic	1	1,000

Sample grants (1993).
Central Park Conservancy. New York, NY. $2,000.
National Audubon Society. New York, NY. $30,082.
National Wildlife Federation. Washington, DC. $30,082.
The Nature Conservancy, Headquarters. Arlington, VA. $10,000.
Trees for the Future. Silver Springs, MD. $1,000.

Application process. *Initial contact:* The Trust awards grants to pre-selected organizations only. No unsolicited applications accepted. Potential applicants may send letter of inquiry.
When to apply: Deadline is March 31. The board meets May 31.

Emphases. *Recipients:* Pre-selected organizations.
Types of support: Continuing support.
Geography: New York City area.

The Schiff Foundation

485 Madison Avenue, 20th Floor
New York, New York 10022–5803
Tel: 212–751–3180
EIN: 136088221   Type: Independent
Contact: David T. Schiff, President

History and philosophy. This family foundation was established in 1946. Its primary areas of concern are: animal welfare, the arts, education, health services, social services, and youth.

Officers and directors. *Officers:* David T. Schiff, President; Sandra F. Davies, Secretary; Andrew N. Schiff, Treasurer. *Directors:* David T. Schiff, Peter G. Schiff.

Financial data. Data for fiscal year ended December 31, 1992. *Assets:* $11,524,935 (M). *Total grants disbursed:* $529,840.

Environmental awards. Recent grants: 1992 grants included support for land and wildlife conservation, urban environment, and outdoor education.

Issues. Cli Bio Lan Agr Wat Oce Ene Was Tox Pop Dev
 • •   •

Funding analysis.

Fiscal year:	1991	1992
Env grants disb:	$118,240	$182,340
Number:	11	17
Range:	$100–$100,000	$90–$150,000
Median:	$1,000	$1,000
Pct $ disb (env/total):	37	34

Recipients (1992 highest):	Number:	Dollars:
NYZS/The Wildlife Conservation Society	4	166,750
Outward Bound USA	1	5,000
Ducks Unlimited, Inc.	2	2,590
The Nature Conservancy, Headquarters	2	2,000
Environmental Defense Fund	1	1,000
National Wilderness Institute	1	1,000
The New York Botanical Garden	1	1,000
World Wildlife Fund	1	1,000

Activity regions (1992):	Number:	Dollars:
New York/New Jersey	10	175,250
U.S. not specified	7	7,090

Sample grants (1992).
Central Park Conservancy. New York, NY. $500.
Council on the Environment of New York City. New York, NY. $500.
Environmental Defense Fund. New York, NY. $1,000.
National Wilderness Institute. Alexandria, VA. $1,000.
NYZS/The Wildlife Conservation Society. Bronx, NY. $150,000.
Outward Bound USA. New York, NY. $5,000.
World Wildlife Fund. Washington, DC. $1,000.

Application process. *Initial contact:* The Foundation awards grants to pre-selected organizations only. No unsolicited applications accepted.

Emphases. *Recipients:* Pre-selected organizations only.
Types of support: Annual campaigns, capital campaigns/expenses, general purposes, pilot projects, professorships.

Limitations. *Recipients:* Individuals.

Schultz Foundation, Inc.
Schultz Building
P.O. Box 1200
Jacksonville, Florida 32201
Tel: 904–354–3603
EIN: 591055869   Type: Independent
Contact: Clifford G. Schultz, II, President

Application address:
50 North Laura Street, Suite 2725
Jacksonville, Florida 32202

History and philosophy. The Foundation was established in 1964 by members of the Schultz family. "The Schultz Foundation focuses on its home communities to do whatever it can to improve our world, our society, our lives." "The Foundation's range of giving is diverse, reflecting the various social concerns of its members. These concerns include: environment, the arts, children's needs, health care, education, and more." Giving focuses on Atlanta, Jacksonville, and the New York arts community.

Officers and directors. *Officers:* Clifford G. Schultz, II, President; John F. Reilly, Secretary/Treasurer. *Trustees:* Catherine Schultz Kelly, John F. Reilly, Clifford G. Schultz, II, Frederick H. Schultz, Jr., John R. Schultz, Nancy R. Schultz.

Financial data. Data for fiscal years ended December 31, 1991 and 1993. *Assets (1991):* $2,791,532 (M). *Total grants disbursed (1993):* $204,663.

Environmental awards. *Recent grants:* 1993 grants included support for land conservation, marine issues, wildlife protection, and environmental education.

Issues. Cli Bio Lan Agr Wat Oce Ene Was Tox Pop Dev
      •   •   •   •   •   •

Funding analysis.

Fiscal year:	1993
Env grants disb:	$21,675
Number:	24
Range:	$25–$3,500
Median:	$550
Pct $ disb (env/total):	11

Recipients (1993 highest):	Number:	Dollars:
The Nature Conservancy International	1	3,500
The Nature Conservancy, Florida Field Office	1	3,500
Green Seal	1	3,000
Greenpeace USA	1	1,500
The Wilderness Society	1	1,500

Activity regions (1993 highest):	Number:	Dollars:
U.S. not specified	9	8,650
U.S. Southeast	9	7,650

International*	1	3,500
U.S. West	1	1,000
U.S. Northwest	2	525

*Multiple regions or not specified.

Sample grants (1993).
BEAKS. Jacksonville, FL. $500.
Caribbean Conservation Corporation/Sea Turtle Coalition. Gainesville, FL. $250.
The Cousteau Society. Chesapeake, VA. $1,000.
Ducks Unlimited, Inc. Jacksonville, FL. $200.
Florida Defenders of the Environment. Gainesville, FL. $100.
Friends of the U.S. National Arboretum. Washington, DC. $100.
Greenpeace USA. Washington, DC. $1,500.
Mote Marine Laboratory. Sarasota, FL. $250.
The Nature Conservancy International. Arlington, VA. $3,500.
Rails-to-Trails Conservancy. Washington, DC. 200.
Sierra Club Legal Defense Fund. San Francisco, CA. $100.
The Wilderness Society. Washington, DC. $1,500.
Wildlife Rescue. Tampa, FA. $600.

Application process. *Initial contact:* Letter describing needs to be addressed and how funds are to be spent.
When to apply: Anytime.
Materials available: "Guidelines for Donation/Statement of Purpose."

Emphases. *Types of support:* General purposes.
Geography: Atlanta, Georgia; Jacksonville, Florida; and New York City (arts community).

The Schumann Fund for New Jersey, Inc.
33 Park Street
Montclair, New Jersey 07042
Tel: 201-509-9883   Fax: 201-783-7553
EIN: 521556076   Type: Independent
Contact: Julie Keenan, Executive Director

History and philosophy. The Schumann Fund for New Jersey was established in 1988 by its parent organization, the Florence and John Schumann Foundation. Its focus is "on organizations that address some of New Jersey's most formidable challenges." The Fund maintains a "strong interest in creative, innovative, and experimental programs involving community residents in their efforts to solve or alleviate problems." It has four program areas: Early Childhood, Environmental Protection, Essex County, and Public Policy.

Officers and directors. *Officers:* George R. Harris, Chairman; Leonard S. Coleman, Vice Chairman; Aubin Z. Ames, Secretary/Treasurer. *Trustees:* Aubin Z. Ames, Leonard S. Coleman, Christopher J. Daggett, Andrew C. Halvorsen, George R. Harris, Barbara H. Malcolm, Alan Rosenthal, Donald M. Wilson.

Financial data. Data for fiscal year ended December 31, 1993.
Assets: $27,915,430 (M). *Total grants disbursed:* $1,039,113.

Environmental awards. *Program and interests:* "We support the protection of natural resources, environmental quality, and wildlife. We believe that sound land use planning and balanced economic growth are essential to this goal."
Recent grants: 1993 grants included support for education and planning about land conservation and restoration, and river and riparian land preservation.

Issues. Cli Bio Lan Agr Wat Oce Ene Was Tox Pop Dev
              •   •   •   •

Funding analysis.

Fiscal year:	1991	1993
Env grants auth:	$168,000	$150,000
Number:	7	7
Range:	$15,000–$28,000	$20,000–$25,000
Median:	$25,000	$20,000
Pct $ disb (env/total):	19	20

Recipients (1993):	Number:	Dollars:
Association of New Jersey Environmental Commissions	1	25,000
The Trust for Public Land	1	25,000
Clean Water Fund	1	20,000
Greater Newark Conservancy	1	20,000
Isles, Inc.	1	20,000
New Jersey Audubon Society	1	20,000
Pinelands Preservation Alliance	1	20,000

Activity region (1993):	Number:	Dollars:
New York/New Jersey	7	150,000

Sample grants (1993).
Association of New Jersey Environmental Commissions. Mendham, NJ. $25,000. Support for efforts to establish regional coalitions of environmental commissions for natural resource protection and land use planning.
Clean Water Fund. New Brunswick NJ. $20,000. Support for CWF's work with the Camden City Garden Club to start a neighborhood composting/lead abatement project. Residents are being trained in establishing backyard composting and about the health threats posed by lead. Through greater use of compost bins, residents can reduce solid waste production. Soil from the bins will be transferred to vacant lots with high lead levels in a attempt to limit lead exposure to those walking through the neighborhood.
Isles, Inc. Trenton, NJ. $20,000. For efforts to create an Environmental Education Center in Trenton's largest public park.
New Jersey Audubon Society. Franklin Lakes, NJ. $20,000. To sponsor teacher education workshops on the use of "Bridges to the Natural World" for school districts and organizations in the state's urban areas.
Pinelands Preservation Alliance. Browns Mills, NJ. $20,000. Continuation of the Pinelands Education Program to schools and special interest groups throughout the state.
The Trust for Public Land. Morristown, NJ. $25,000. For open land and urban space preservation.

Application process. *Initial contact:* Proposal to include:
1. Organization objectives, activities, and leadership.
2. Project purpose, goals, and methods.

Accompanying documents.
1. Copy of latest financial statement.
2. Expense budget, specifically identifying all sources of income.
3. Project's time frame and future funding plans.
4. IRS documents confirming status as tax-exempt and not a private foundation.

When to apply: Deadlines are January 15, April 15, August 15, and October 15 for consideration at board meetings scheduled six weeks later.
Materials available: Annual report (includes "Program Guidelines").

Emphases. *Recipients:* Educational institutions, nonprofit organizations.
Activities: Advocacy, citizen participation, collaborative efforts, conferences, education, innovative programs, policy analysis/development, symposia/colloquia, training.
Types of support: General purposes, matching funds, multi-year grants, operating costs, seed money.
Geography: New Jersey only.

Limitations. *Recipients:* Botanical gardens, individuals, museums, religious organizations, zoos.
Types of support: Annual campaigns, capital campaigns/expenses, computer hardware, debt retirement, endowments, facilities, membership campaigns, mortgage reduction, scholarships.

The Florence and John Schumann Foundation

33 Park Street
Montclair, New Jersey 07042
Tel: 201–783–6660   Fax: 201–783–7553
EIN: 226044214   Type: Independent
EGA member
Contact: John Moyers, Program Officer

History and philosophy. The Florence and John Schumann Foundation was established in 1961 by Florence F. Schumann (d. 1991) and John J. Schumann, Jr. (d. 1964), who shared the "conviction that civilization is the result of the collaboration among caring men and women motivated by respect for all living things and a sense of personal responsibility."

In 1990 the trustees decided to focus their grantmaking on helping people renew the democratic process through cooperative acts of citizenship, particularly as they apply to governance and the environment.

Officers and directors. *Officers:* Robert F. Schumann, Chairman; Bill D. Moyers, President; W. Ford Schumann, Caroline Schumann Mark, Vice Presidents; Patricia A. McCarthy, Vice President, Administration; Howard D. Brundage, Vice President, Finance; David S. Bate, Secretary/Treasurer. *Trustees:* David S. Bate, Howard D. Brundage, Edwin D. Etherington, Caroline Schumann Mark, Bill D. Moyers, Robert F. Schumann, W. Ford Schumann, John C. Whitehead.

Financial data. Data for fiscal year ended December 31, 1993. *Assets:* $78,543,614 (U). *Total grants disbursed:* $7,001,600.

Environmental awards. *Program and interests:* The Foundation is primarily interested in national projects directly concerned with the renewing of democracy. To that end, it funds grassroots organizations and related support projects that bring citizens into the democratic conversation. Environmental justice and minority group organizing have been of particular interest.
Recent grants: 1993 grants included support for climate issues, land conservation (wilderness, wetlands, forests, public lands), toxics issues, and waste management. Activities funded included conferences, investigative reporting, media projects, public education, citizen monitoring, and grassroots organizing.

Issues. Cli Bio Lan Agr Wat Oce Ene Was Tox Pop Dev
 •   •   •   •   •   •   •   •   •   •

Funding analysis.

Fiscal year:	1991	1993
Env grants auth:	$2,454,500	$1,345,000
Number:	28	25
Range:	$5,000–$1,000,000	$5,000–$300,000
Median:	$32,500	$40,000
Pct $ auth (env/total):	36	19

Recipients (1993 highest):	Number:	Dollars:
Ozone Action	1	300,000
Environmental Research Foundation	1	100,000
The Wilderness Society	1	100,000
Citizens Clearinghouse for Hazardous Wastes, Inc.	1	80,000
Alaska Wilderness League	1	75,000
Kentucky Coalition	1	75,000

Activity regions (1993 highest):	Number:	Dollars:
U.S. not specified	9	655,000
U.S. Great Lakes	4	135,000
U.S. South Central	2	110,000
U.S. multiple regions	1	100,000
New York/New Jersey	4	90,000

Sample grants (1993).

Alaska Wilderness League. Washington, DC. $75,000. Support for the National Conference on Wildlife Law, January 1994.

The Calumet Project for Industrial Jobs, Inc. East Chicago, IN. $60,000 (2 years). For environmentally sustainable economic initiatives in low-income and disenfranchised communities in northwestern Indiana and eastern Illinois.

Clean Ocean Action, Inc. Highlands, NJ. $15,000. Support media campaign to prevent disposal of dioxin-contaminated sediments in the ocean.

Food and Water, Inc. Marshfield, VT. $40,000. For a grassroots campaign organizing consumers to demand pesticide-free foods.

Kentucky Coalition. Prestonburg, KY. $75,000 (3 years). For the Grassroots Environmental Project.

Ohio River Valley Environmental Coalition, Inc. Proctorville, OH. $20,000. For organizing, organization building, and leadership training activities.

Ozone Action. Marshall, NC. $300,000 (2 years). For work to address the issue of ozone depletion.
Public Policy and Education Fund of New York. Albany, NY. $45,000. Support the Slash Your Trash Campaign to reduce the amount of solid waste created in Broome County.
University of Maryland, College Park. College Park, MD. $50,000. To support efforts to train graduate students in ecological economics and public policy through the addition of Herman Daly to the faculty.
The Wilderness Society. Washington, DC. $100,000. For the New Voices for the American West Program.

Application process. *Initial contact:* Letter of inquiry. Proposal, if invited, to include:
1. Copy of organization's latest financial statement.
2. Budget which specifically identifies all sources of income.
3. Time frame and future funding plans.
4. Copy of IRS tax-exempt status determination letter and confirmation that the organization is not a private foundation.

When to apply: Deadlines are January 15, April 15 and August 15, six weeks prior to a meeting of the board of directors.
Materials available: Annual report (includes "Schumann Foundation Guidelines").

Emphases. *Recipients:* Nonprofit organizations.
Activities: Activism, advocacy, citizen participation.

Limitations. *Recipients:* Individuals.
Activities: Land acquisition.
Types of support: Annual campaigns, capital campaigns/expenses, debt retirement, endowments, equipment, loans.

Ellen Browning Scripps Foundation
Union Bank, Trust Department
P.O. Box 109
San Diego, California 92112–4103
Tel: 619–230–4709
EIN: 951644633   Type: Independent
Contact: E. Douglas Dawson, Vice President and
   Regional Manager, Union Bank

History and philosophy. The Ellen Browning Scripps Foundation was established in 1935 by the late Ellen Browning Scripps and the Late Robert Paine Scripps. Primary fields of interest include: the arts, child welfare, conservation, higher education, marine sciences, medical research, recreation, and youth.

Officers and directors. *Trustees:* Ellen Scripps Davis, Deborah M. Goddard, Edward S. Meanley, Paul K. Scripps.

Financial data. Data for fiscal year ended June 30, 1993. *Assets:* $16,082,315 (M). *Total grants disbursed:* $696,425.

Environmental awards. *Recent grants:* 1993 grants included support for marine issues and a zoo.

Issues.   Cli   Bio   Lan   Agr   Wat   Oce   Ene   Was   Tox   Pop   Dev
                    •   •   •   •

Funding analysis.

Fiscal year:	1993
Env grants disb:	$112,385
Number:	3
Range:	$1,000–$58,385
Median:	$53,000
Pct $ disb (env/total):	16

Recipients (1993):	Number:	Dollars:
Zoological Society of San Diego	2	111,385
San Diego Oceans Foundation	1	1,000

Activity region (1993):	Number:	Dollars:
U.S. West	3	112,385

Sample grants (1993).
San Diego Oceans Foundation. San Diego, CA. $1,000.
Zoological Society of San Diego. San Diego, CA. $58,385.
Zoological Society of San Diego. San Diego, CA. $53,000. For the San Pasqual Wild Animal Park.

Application process. *Initial contact:* The Foundation awards grants to pre-selected organizations only. No unsolicited applications accepted.

Emphases. *Recipients:* Pre-selected organizations only.
Geography: San Diego County, California.

Limitations. *Recipients:* Individuals.

Sears-Swetland Foundation
c/o Park Investment Company
907 Park Building
140 Public Square
Cleveland, Ohio 44114–2213
Tel: 216–241–6434
EIN: 346522143   Type: Independent
Contact: David W. Swetland, Trustee

History and philosophy. The Foundation was established in 1949 with contributions from members of the Sears and Swetland families. Areas of interest are: the arts, conservation and environment, youth development, education, health, and welfare.

Officers and directors. *Trustees:* Ruth Swetland Eppig, David Sears Swetland, David W. Swetland.

Financial data. Data for fiscal year ended December 31, 1993. *Assets:* $2,535,302 (M). *Gifts Received:* $7,387. *Total grants disbursed:* $109,225.

Environmental awards. *Recent grants:* 1993 grants included support for an arboretum, horticulture, and nature centers.

Issues.   Cli   Bio   Lan   Agr   Wat   Oce   Ene   Was   Tox   Pop   Dev
                    •   •   •   •

S

Funding analysis.

Fiscal year:	1993
Env grants disb:	$39,725
Number:	11
Range:	$500–$62,500
Median:	$1,000
Pct $ disb (env/total):	36

Recipients (1993 highest):	*Number:*	*Dollars:*
Rachel Carson Council, Inc.	2	15,000
Fairchild Tropical Garden	1	12,500
The Holden Arboretum	2	6,000
INFORM	1	2,500
Garden Center of Greater Cleveland	2	1,725

Activity regions (1993):	*Number:*	*Dollars:*
U.S. Great Lakes	10	27,225
U.S. Southeast	1	12,500

Sample grants (1993).
Cleanland, Ohio. Cleveland, OH. $500. General operating expenses.
Fairchild Tropical Garden. Miami, FL. $12,500. Capital campaign.
Garden Center of Greater Cleveland. Cleveland, OH. $1,000. General operating expenses.
Garden Center of Greater Cleveland. Cleveland, OH. $725. Transportable greenhouse.
The Holden Arboretum. Mentor, OH. $6,000 (2 grants). Annual fund, construction costs, Horticultural Science Center, and Lipp Horticultural Greenhouse.
INFORM. New York, NY. $2,500. For Ohio projects.
Rachel Carson Council, Inc. Chevy Chase, MD. $500. General operating expenses.
Shaker Lakes Regional Nature Center. Cleveland, OH. $1,000. General operating expenses.

Application process. *Initial contact:* Preliminary proposal to include:
1. Description and history of organization.
2. List of trustees.
3. Financial statement.
4. Description of need and/or project.
5. Methods and procedures to be used in project.
6. Personnel and financial resources available and/or needed.
7. Copy of IRS tax-exempt status determination letter.

When to apply: Anytime.
Materials available: "Grant Application Procedure."

Emphases. *Recipients:* Botanical gardens, educational institutions, museums, nonprofit organizations, research institutions, zoos.
Activities: Research.
Types of support: Annual campaigns, capital campaigns/expenses, continuing support, debt retirement, emergency funding, equipment, facilities (construction), general purposes, land acquisition, matching funds, operating costs, projects, seed money.
Geography: Cleveland, Ohio.

Limitations. *Recipients:* Individuals.
Types of support: Fellowships, loans, scholarships.

Frances Seebe Trust
c/o Wells Fargo Bank
525 Market Street, 17th Floor
San Francisco, California 94163
Tel: 415–396–0308
EIN: 956795278   Type: Independent
Contact: Charles K. Guttas, Trust Officer

History and philosophy. The Trust was established in 1983. It funds wildlife research, animal protection, and medical research.

Officers and directors. *Trustee:* Well Fargo Bank, N.A.

Financial data. Data for fiscal year ended January 31, 1993. *Assets:* $2,925,647 (M). *Total grants disbursed:* $177,506.

Environmental awards. *Recent grants:* 1993 grants included support for marine issues and wildlife protection.

Issues.   Cli   Bio   Lan   Agr   Wat   Oce   Ene   Was   Tox   Pop   Dev
         •   •

Funding analysis.

Fiscal year:	1993
Env grants disb:	$20,000
Number:	2
Range:	$5,000–$15,000
Median:	$10,000
Pct $ disb (env/total):	11

Recipients (1993):	*Number:*	*Dollars:*
Center for Marine Conservation	1	15,000
Palos Verdes Audubon Society	1	5,000

Activity region (1993):	*Number:*	*Dollars:*
U.S. West	2	20,000

Sample grants (1993).
Center for Marine Conservation. Washington, DC. $15,000.
Palos Verde Audubon Society. Palos Verde, CA. $5,000.

Application process. *Initial contact:* The Trust awards grants to pre-selected organizations only. No unsolicited applications accepted.

Emphases. *Recipients:* Pre-selected organizations only.

Sequoia Foundation
820 A Street, Suite 345
Tacoma, Washington 98402
Tel: 206–627–1634   Fax: 206–627–6249
EIN: 911178052   Type: Independent
EGA member
Contact: Frank D. Underwood, Executive Director

History and philosophy. The Sequoia Foundation was established in 1982 by C. Davis Weyerhaeuser of the lumber family.

Program areas are: conservation/environment, international conflict resolution, and social services where economic development is a program component. Current geographic areas of interest are: Mexico, Central America, and the Himalayan Mountain region.

Officers and directors. *Officers:* William Toycen Weyerhaeuser, President and Treasurer; Gail T. Weyerhaeuser, Vice President; Nicholas C. Spika, Secretary. *Directors:* James R. Hanson, Nicholas C. Spika, Annette Thayer Black Weyerhaeuser, Gail T. Weyerhaeuser, William Toycen Weyerhaeuser.

Financial data. Data for fiscal year ended August 31, 1993. *Assets:* $24,349,327 (M). *Gifts received:* $2,355,000. *Total grants disbursed:* $2,210,833.

Environmental awards. *Program and interests:* Interests include, but are not limited to:

- Maintenance of biodiversity.
- Habitat preservation.
- Conflict resolution between and among competing economic and environmental interests.

Both marine and terrestrial projects are of interest.

"Proposals should be directed to mediating the positions of divergent interests to develop creative solutions to environmental issues."

Issues. Cli Bio Lan Agr Wat Oce Ene Was Tox Pop Dev

Funding Analysis.

Fiscal year:	1993
Env grants disb:	$221,500
Number:	12
Range:	$3,000–$46,000
Median:	$17,500
Pct $ disb (env/total):	10

Recipients (1993 highest):	*Number:*	*Dollars:*
World Wildlife Fund	1	46,000
Center for Marine Conservation	1	25,000
Ecotrust	1	25,000
Environmental Defense Fund	1	25,000
New York Rainforest Alliance, Inc.	1	25,000

Activity regions (1993):	*Number:*	*Dollars:*
International*	4	88,500
U.S. not specified	4	68,000
U.S. Northwest	2	30,000
Tropics	1	25,000
U.S. Southeast	1	10,000

*Multiple regions or not specified.

Sample grants (1993).
Center for Marine Conservation. Washington, DC. $25,000. Program support.
Conflict Resolution, Research and Resource Institute. Tacoma, WA. $69,000. Operating budget and program support.
Conservation International. Washington, DC. $22,500. Operating budget and program support.
Consultative Group on Biodiversity. New York, NY. $3,000. Operating budget.
Enersol Associates, Inc. Sommerville, MA. $20,000. Operating budget.
Environmental Defense Fund. New York, NY. $25,000. Program support.
Forest History Society. Durham, NC. $10,000. Capital needs.
LightHawk. Santa Fe, NM. $15,000. Operating budget.
New York Rainforest Alliance, Inc. New York, NY. $25,000.
Northwest Trek Foundation Center. Eatonville, WA. $25,000. Capital needs.

Application process. *Initial contact:* Brief letter (2 copies) requesting application guidelines, to include:
1. Concise statement of proposed project including its objectives and significance.
2. Description of applicant organization.
3. Project budget.
4. Amount of money requested from the Foundation.
5. Copy or IRS tax-exempt status determination letter.

When to apply: Deadlines are March 15 and September 15 for consideration in May and November, respectively.
Materials available: Application guidelines.

Emphases. *Types of support:* Projects.
Geography: Mexico, Central America, the Himalayan Mountain region (Nepal and Bhutan); Northwest U.S. coastal area (Washington, Oregon, and Alaska).

Limitations. *Recipients:* Individuals.
Activities: Media projects, publications.
Types of support: Fellowships, scholarships.

Seventh Generation Fund
P.O. Box 4569
Arcata, California 95521
Tel: 707–829–7640   Fax: 707–829–7639
Type: Public
EGA member
Contact: Tia Oros, Program Coordinator

Application address:
Route 1, P.O. Box 308
Ponds Ford, Minnesota 56575
Contact: Winona Laduke, Environmental Program Director

History and philosophy. The Seventh Generation Fund is a national Native public foundation "dedicated to maintaining and promoting the uniqueness of Native people and nations." The Fund was established in 1977 and derives its name from the Great Law of the Haudenosaunne (six Nations Iroquois Confederacy) that requires chiefs to consider the impacts of their decisions on the seventh generation. The Fund supports activities that "protect land and natural resources; redevelop self-reliant economies; restore traditional ways of life; and support efforts by Native women to promote the well being of the family and the community." Funding areas include: Native American Community and Economic Renewal Initiatives, American Indian Religious Freedom, and Native American Environmental Initiatives.

S

Officers and directors. *Officers*: Dalee Sambo, Chair; Jeanette Armstrong, Vice Chair; John Mohawk, President. *Directors*: Jeanette Armstrong, Bob Antone, Larry Emerson, John Mohawk, Dalee Sambo, Reuben Snake, Jr.

Financial data. Data for fiscal year ended June 30, 1992. *Assets*: $778,577 (M). *Gifts received*: $758,817. *Total grants disbursed*: $481,064.

Environmental awards. *Program and interests*: "The Seventh Generation Fund believes that the spiritual relationship of Indigenous people with the natural environment derives from an ecologically centered consciousness and a unique world view. Within the wisdom of tribal legends, oral histories and prophecies lie the values for an ecologically enlightened social transformation that could reestablish a balance and renewed order in the world. The Fund's support of Native American Environmental Initiatives is critical to the ability of Native people to share traditional philosophies and facilitate new paradigm thinking."
Recent grants: 1992 grants included support for indigenous land conservation and toxic waste issues.

Issues. Cli • Bio • Lan • Agr • Wat Oce Ene • Was Tox • Pop Dev •

Funding analysis.§

Fiscal year:	1992
Env grants disb:	$73,394
Number:	18
Range:	$780–$14,459
Median:	$3,975
Pct $ disb (env/total):	15

Recipients (1992 highest):	Number:	Dollars:
The First People of Color Environmental Leadership Summit	1	14,459
Navajo Family Farms	1	5,711
Native Resource Coalition	1	5,500
The Columbia River Defense Project	1	5,000
Tonantzin Land Institute	1	5,000

Activity regions (1992 highest):	Number:	Dollars:
U.S. not specified	3	23,370
U.S. West	4	13,711
U.S. South Central	3	11,000
U.S. Great Lakes	3	6,160
U.S. Mountain	1	5,500

§Does not include training and technical assistance, or networking and advocacy grants.

Sample grants (1992).
Indigenous Environmental Network. Red Lake, MN. $450. For the Network and its participation in the Southwest Network for Environmental and Economic Justice and Knight writers conferences on indigenous peoples' environmental issues.
International Indian Treaty Council. San Francisco, CA. $2,000. For the International Human Rights Conference on protection of traditional lands, cultures and human rights.
Mother Earth Spiritual Camp. Pine Falls, Manitoba. $5,000. To provide assistance for the Mother Earth Spiritual Camp, community planning, exploration of appropriate energy technologies, and resource development strategies.
Native Resource Coalition. Porcupine, SD. $5,500. For protection of the natural and human resources of the Pine Ridge Indian Reservation.
Southwest Network for Environmental and Economic Justice. Albuquerque, NM. $2,000. Travel for six organizations and individuals to attend the Second Annual Gathering of the Southwest Network.
Tribal Concerns. Mescalero, NM. $500. To educate tribal members on the hazards of nuclear waste and to hold an informational meeting for concerned Mescalero tribal members.
White Earth Land Recovery Project. White Earth, MN. $2,000. To enroll two members in the Trust for Public Lands Training.

Application process. *Initial contact:* Telephone call.
When to apply: Anytime.
Materials available: Annual report, *Interim Report* (newsletter).

Emphases. *Recipients:* Native Americans only.
Activities: Capacity building.
Types of support: General purposes, operating costs, technical assistance, training.

Elmina B. Sewall Foundation

245 Commercial Street
Portland, Maine 04101-1117
EIN: 010387404   Type: Independent
Contact: Elmina B. Sewall, President

History and philosophy. The Elmina B. Sewall Foundation was established in 1983. It concentrates its giving in the areas of: animal welfare, social services, and youth.

Officers and directors. *Officers:* Elmina B. Sewall, President; Margaret Sewall Barbour, Vice President; Harold E. Woodsum, Jr., Secretary; William E. Curran, Treasurer; John S. Kaminski, Assistant Secretary. *Directors:* Margaret Sewall Barbour, William E. Curran, John S. Kaminski, Elmina B. Sewall, Harold E. Woodsum, Jr.

Financial data. Data for fiscal year ended September 30, 1991. *Assets:* $6,622,592 (M). *Gifts received:* $700,000. *Total grants disbursed:* $421,735.

Environmental awards. *Recent grants:* 1991 grants included support for land conservation, forest and river protection, coastal issues, wildlife, and outdoor education.

Issues. Cli Bio • Lan • Agr • Wat • Oce • Ene Was Tox Pop Dev

Funding analysis.

Fiscal year:	1990	1991
Env grants disb:	$113,000	$116,000
Number:	25	23
Range:	$500–$12,000	$1,000–$12,000
Median:	$3,500	$5,000
Pct $ disb (env/total):	29	28

Recipients (1991 highest):	Number:	Dollars:
NYZS/The Wildlife Conservation Society	1	12,000
World Wildlife Fund	1	12,000
The Nature Conservancy, Headquarters	1	10,000
Maine Coast Heritage Trust	1	7,500
Living Desert Reserve	1	6,000
The Wilderness Society	1	6,000

Activity regions (1991 highest):	Number:	Dollars:
U.S. not specified	8	37,500
U.S. Northeast	7	32,500
International*	2	17,000
New York/New Jersey	2	17,000
U.S. West	1	6,000

*Multiple regions or not specified.

Sample grants (1991).
African Wildlife Foundation. Washington, DC. $2,000.
American Farmland Trust. Washington, DC. $5,000.
American Rivers, Inc. Washington, DC. $5,000.
Defenders of Wildlife. Washington, DC. $3,000.
Laudholm Trust. Wells, ME. $3,000.
Living Desert Reserve. Palm Desert, CA. $6,000.
National Audubon Society. New York, NY. $5,000.
New England Forestry Foundation, Inc. Boston, MA. $4,000.
Primarily Primates. Wakefield, MA. $1,000.
Wildlife Preservation Trust International. Philadelphia, PA. $5,000.

Application process. *Initial contact:* The Foundation awards grants to pre-selected organizations only. No unsolicited applications accepted.

Emphases. *Recipients:* Pre-selected organizations only.
Geography: New England region.

Limitations. *Recipients:* Individuals.

Ralph C. Sheldon Foundation, Inc.
710 Hotel Jamestown Building
Jamestown, New York 14701
Tel: 716-664-9890
EIN: 166030502   Type: Independent
Contact: Paul B. Sullivan, Secretary

History and philosophy. The Foundation was established in 1948 by Julia S. Livengood and Isabell M. Sheldon. Interests include: youth programs, community development, com-munity funds, cultural programs, fine arts, performing arts, theater, hospitals, social services, environment, libraries, education.

Officers and directors. *Officers:* J. Elizabeth Sheldon, President; Robert G. Wright, Vice President; Paul B. Sullivan, Secretary/Assistant Treasurer; Miles L. Lasser, Treasurer/Assistant Secretary; Barclay O. Wellman, Assistant Secretary. *Directors:* Miles L. Lasser, J. Elizabeth Sheldon, Paul B. Sullivan, Barclay O. Wellman, Robert G. Wright.

Financial data. Data for fiscal year ended May 31, 1993. *Assets:* $5,808,403 (M). *Gifts received:* $1,139,305. *Total grants disbursed:* $1,302,763.

Environmental awards. *Recent grants:* 1993 grants included support for waste management and environmental education.

Issues.   Cli Bio Lan Agr Wat Oce Ene Was Tox Pop Dev
                                                      •

Funding analysis.

Fiscal year:	1991	1993
Env grants disb:	$75,000	$28,000
Number:	1	2
Range:	–	$2,000–$26,000
Median:	–	$14,000
Pct $ disb (env/total):	5	2

Recipients (1993):	Number:	Dollars:
Allegheny Highlands Council B.S.A.	1	26,000
Roger Tory Peterson Institute of Natural History	1	2,000

Activity region (1993):	Number:	Dollars:
New York/New Jersey	2	28,000

Sample grants (1993).
Allegheny Highlands Council B.S.A. Falconer, NY. $26,000. For waste disposal enhancement.
Roger Tory Peterson Institute of Natural History. Jamestown, NY. $2,000.

Application process. *Initial contact:* The Foundation usually makes grants to pre-selected organizations. Potential applicants may request application form.
When to apply: Anytime.
Materials available: Application form.

Emphases. *Recipients:* Nonprofit organizations, pre-selected organizations (usually).
Types of support: Annual campaigns, capital campaigns/expenses, emergency funding, equipment, facilities, general purposes.
Geography: Southern Chautauqua County, New York.

Limitations. *Recipients:* Individuals, religious organizations.

Shell Oil Company Foundation
Two Shell Plaza
P.O. Box 2099
Houston, Texas 77252
Tel: 713-241-3616   Fax: 713-241-3329
EIN: 136066583   Type: Company-sponsored
Contact: Jack N. Doherty, Senior Vice President

History and philosophy. Since the Foundation's inception in 1953, its basic mission remains unchanged: to help foster the general well-being of the society in which Shell Oil Company operates or has significant interests, offering the best possible

S

balance of contributions to education, community health and welfare, the arts, and other philanthropic activities. As nearly as possible, the Foundation focuses on specific needs identified by the publics it serves.

Officers and directors. *Officers:* J. P. Parrish, President; J. N. Doherty, B. W. Levan, P. G. Turberville, Vice Presidents; H. R. Hutchins, Secretary; M. S. Gerber, Treasurer; T. J. Howard, F. M. Rabbe, Assistant Secretaries; E. B. Kennair, Assistant Treasurer; J. M. Bishop, Assistant Secretary/Treasurer. *Directors:* B. E. Bernard, J. N. Doherty, M. H. Grasley, S. A. Lackey, B. W. Levan, J. M. Morgan, J. P. Parrish, L. L. Smith, S. C. Stryker, P. G. Turberville.

Financial data. Data for fiscal year ended December 31, 1993. *Assets:* $27,226,652 (M). *Total grants disbursed:* $13,270,082.

Environmental awards. *Program and interests:* "Environmental science has received attention since support was offered for research in water resources at Princeton University in 1964; it was included in seminars for precollege science teachers from 1956 through 1971; and its increasing importance has been recognized in Shell Graduate Grants and Shell Distinguished Chairs. Also, support is offered through a variety of programs related to the environment, i.e., nature centers, wildlife preservation, marine conservation, clean air, and the like". By the end of 1993, the Foundation had paid out $9,026,488 for such programs.
Recent grants: 1993 grants included support for environmental health, marine issues, energy policy, and urban beautification.

Issues. Cli • Bio • Lan • Agr Wat • Oce • Ene • Was Tox • Pop Dev

Funding analysis.

Fiscal year:	1991	1993
Env grants disb:	$648,250	$404,000
Number:	55	48
Range:	$500–$150,000	$1,000–$65,000
Median:	$5,000	$5,000
Pct $ disb (env/total):	4	3

Recipients (1993 highest):	Number:	Dollars:
University of Alabama	1	65,000
The Keystone Center	1	50,000
Louisiana Nature and Science Center	2	30,000
Center for Energy Policy Research	1	25,000
American Council on Science and Health	1	15,000
Friends of the Zoo	1	15,000
The Nature Conservancy, Headquarters	1	15,000
University of Colorado Foundation	1	15,000

Activity regions (1993 highest):	Number:	Dollars:
U.S. not specified	14	165,500
U.S. South Central	11	89,500
U.S. Southeast	3	73,000
U.S. West	10	25,500
U.S. Mountain	2	17,000

Sample grants (1993).
American Council on Science and Health. New York, NY. $15,000.
Foundation for Research on Economics and the Environment. Bozeman, MT. $10,000.
Marine Environmental Sciences Consortium. Dauphin Island, AL. $3,000.
M.I.T. Center of Energy Policy Research. Cambridge, MA. $25,000.
Princeton University. Princeton, NJ. $23,000.
University of Pittsburgh. Pittsburgh, PA. $10,000. Industrial health.

Application process. *Initial contact:* Letter to include:
1. Description of organization's structure, purpose, and history.
2. Project summary and budget.
3. Budget, including most recent audit, income and expenditure breakdown, corporate donors, and copy of IRS Form 990.
4. Copy of IRS tax-exempt status determination letter.

When to apply: Deadline is September 30 to be considered for the following year.
Materials available: "Pattern for Giving" (includes annual report for previous year and "Application Information").

Emphases. *Recipients:* Educational institutions, museums, nonprofit organizations, research institutions, zoos.
Activities: Citizen participation, collaborative efforts, education, exhibits, innovative programs, research (scientific), volunteerism, workshops, youth programs.
Types of support: Annual campaigns, capital campaigns/expenses, computer hardware, continuing support, equipment, facilities, fellowships, matching funds, multi-year grants, operating costs, pilot projects, professorships, projects, scholarships, start-up costs.
Geography: Areas of company operations.

Limitations. *Recipients:* Individuals.
Activities: Activism, advocacy, audiovisual materials, capacity building, conflict resolution, demonstration programs, direct services, expeditions/tours, feasibility studies, fieldwork, fundraising, inventories, land acquisition, litigation, lobbying, networking, political activities, publications.
Types of support: Advertising campaigns, debt retirement, endowments, indirect costs, leveraging funds, loans, maintenance, membership campaigns, mortgage reduction, seed money, travel expenses.

Thomas Sill Foundation

600–175 Hargrave Street
Winnipeg, Manitoba
Canada R0E 0K0
Tel: 204-947-3782   Fax: 204-947-3468
EGA member
Contact: Hugh Arklie, Executive Director

History and philosophy. The Foundation's purpose "is to provide encouragement and financial support to qualifying Manitoba organizations striving to improve the quality of life in the province." Its interests are the arts, education, environment, and social services.

Officers and directors. *Officers:* Norman Fiske, President; Robert Filuk, Vice President; Mr. E. Keith Urwin, Secretary; Mr. K. Milton McLean, Treasurer.

Financial data. *Total 1992 grants disbursed:* $1,077,000 (CDN) (est.).

Environmental awards. *Program and interests:* The Foundation's primary interests are:

- Protection of endangered ecosystems in the spirit of the United Nation's Brundtland Commission.
- Recycling.
- Environmental education.

Issues. Cli • Bio • Lan Agr Wat Oce Ene Was • Tox Pop • Dev

Funding analysis.§

Fiscal year:	1991	1992
Env grants auth:	$72,000	$26,000
Number:	–	–
Range:	$5,000–$25,000	$5,000–$25,000
Median:	$15,000	$14,000
Pct $ auth (env/total):	7	2

§As reported by the Environmental Grantmakers Association.

Sample grants (1990).
The Nature Conservancy, Canada. Toronto, ON. $8,754. Towards the purchase of an 80–acre remnant of tall grass prairie located near Vita.
Recycling Council of Manitoba. Winnipeg, MB. $15,250. Start-up operating grant.
Zoological Society of Manitoba. Winnipeg, MB. $105,000. Construction.

Application process. *Initial contact:* Telephone call. Proposal to include:
1. Application form.
2. Financial statements.
3. Organizations and project budget.
4. Annual report.

When to apply: Anytime. The board of governors meet monthly.
Materials available: Annual report, application form.

Emphases. *Recipients:* Registered Canadian Charities only.
Activities: Conferences, research, seminars.
Types of support: Capital campaigns/expenses, equipment, facilities, matching funds, pilot projects, seed money.
Geography: Province of Manitoba, Canada.

Limitations. *Recipients:* Individuals.
Types of support: Debt retirement, emergency funding, endowments, operating costs, program-related investments.

S

The Skaggs Foundation
P.O. Box 20510
Juneau, Alaska 99802
Tel: 907–463–4843   Fax: 907–463–4889
EIN: 946068822   Type: Independent
Contact: Samuel D. Skaggs, President

History and philosophy. The Skaggs Foundation is a small family foundation established in California in 1962 by M. B. Skaggs. In 1986 the Foundation's principal office was moved to Juneau, Alaska. The Foundation focuses on marine conservation, environmental education, and assistance to children with disabilities. Ninety percent of its funding goes to projects in Alaska, but it will also consider grants for California and the Pacific Northwest.

Officers and directors. *Officers:* Samuel D. Skaggs, President; Beverly R. Skaggs, Vice President; John C. Ricksen, Secretary. *Directors:* John C. Ricksen, Beverly R. Skaggs, Samuel D. Skaggs.

Financial data. Data for fiscal year ended December 31, 1993. *Assets:* $1,466,950 (M). *Total grants disbursed:* $71,000.

Environmental awards. *Program and interests:* Marine conservation and environmental education are two of the Foundation's primary areas of interest.
Recent grants: 1993 grants included support for land conservation, water quality, marine issues, outdoor recreation, and public education.

Issues. Cli Bio • Lan • Agr Wat • Oce • Ene Was Tox Pop Dev

Funding analysis.

Fiscal year:	1991	1993
Env grants disb:	$55,024	$67,000
Number:	10	11
Range:	$2,500–$10,574	$3,000–$10,000
Median:	$5,000	$5,000
Pct $ disb (env/total):	85	94

Recipients (1993 highest):	Number:	Dollars:
Homer Society of Natural History	1	10,000
Southeast Alaska Guidance Association	1	10,000
The Nature Conservancy, Alaska Field Office	1	10,000
Alaska Discovery Foundation	1	8,000
Ecotrust	1	5,000
Lynn Canal Conservation, Inc.	1	5,000
Musk Ox Development Corporation	1	5,000
Prince William Sound Science Center	1	5,000

Activity regions (1993):	Number:	Dollars:
Alaska	9	59,000
U.S. Northwest	1	5,000
U.S. West	1	3,000

S

Sample grants (1993).
Alaska Discovery Foundation. Juneau, AK. $8,000. For nature studies program.
Alaska Maritime Heritage Foundation. Juneau, AK. $3,000.
Environmental Traveling Companions. San Francisco, CA. $3,000. Program for physically challenged.
Homer Society of Natural History. Homer, AK. $10,000. Support of a marine education program and land acquisitions.
Lynn Canal Conservation, Inc. Haines, AK. $5,000. Monitoring water quality and public education.
Musk Ox Development Corporation. Palmer, AK. $5,000.
The Nature Conservancy, Alaska Field Office. Anchorage, AK. $10,000.
Prince William Sound Science Center. Cordova, AK. $5,000. For science education to outlying communities.
Southeast Alaska Guidance Association. Juneau, AK. $10,000. Development of a fitness trail.

Application process. *Initial contact:* Letter of inquiry (2 pages) to include:
1. Description of project.
2. Project budget.
3. Copy of IRS tax-exempt status determination letter.

The Foundation may not respond to all unsolicited grant requests. For further information, call the Foundation.
When to apply: Deadlines are May 1 and October 1.
Materials available: Annual report, guidelines.

Emphases. *Recipients:* Nonprofit organizations.
Activities: Activism, advocacy, citizen participation, collaborative efforts, demonstration programs, direct services, education, innovative programs, publications, volunteerism.
Types of support: Continuing support, facilities, general purposes, leveraging funds, matching funds, multi-year grants, operating costs, program-related investments, seed money.
Geography: Alaska, the Pacific Northwest.

Limitations. *Recipients:* Individuals.

The Kelvin and Eleanor Smith Foundation
1100 National City Bank Building
Cleveland, Ohio 44114
Tel: 216–566–5500
EIN: 346555349   Type: Independent
Contact: John L. Dampeer, Chairman

History and philosophy. The Kelvin and Eleanor Smith Foundation was established in 1955 by Kelvin Smith. "The foundation's principal interests are in the fields of non-sectarian education, the free enterprise system, the performing and visual arts, health care, and other activities of the type supported by the United Way Services of Cleveland."

Officers and directors. *Officers:* John L. Dampeer, Chairman and Treasurer; Lucia S. Nash, Cara S. Stirn, Vice Presidents; Ellen S. Mavec, Secretary; Andrew L. Fabens, III, Assistant Secretary. *Trustees:* M. Roger Clapp, John L. Dampeer, Michael D. Eppig, M.D., Ellen S. Mavec, Lucia S. Nash, Lincoln Reavis, Cara S. Stirn.

Financial data. Data for fiscal year ended October 31, 1993. *Assets:* $61,124,490 (M). *Total grants disbursed:* $2,671,100.

Environmental awards. *Recent grants:* 1993 grants included support for watershed preservation and an arboretum.

Issues. Cli Bio Lan Agr Wat Oce Ene Was Tox Pop Dev
              •   •

Funding analysis.

Fiscal year:	1993
Env grants disb:	$48,000
Number:	3
Range:	$4,500–$33,500
Median:	$10,000
Pct $ disb (env/total):	2

Recipients (1993):	Number:	Dollars:
The Holden Arboretum	2	38,000
Cuyahoga Valley Preservation and Scenic Railway Association	1	10,000

Activity region (1993):	Number:	Dollars:
U.S. Great Lakes	3	48,000

Sample grants (1993).
Cuyahoga Valley Preservation and Scenic Railway Association. Peninsula, OH. $10,000. General purposes.
The Holden Arboretum. Mentor, OH. $33,500. Horticulture Science Center.
The Holden Arboretum. Mentor, OH. $4,500.

Application process. *Initial contact:* Proposal to include:
1. Description of applicant organization and its tax status.
2. Nature of project.
3. Budget requirements.
4. Amount and scope of requested grant.

When to apply: Anytime. The board usually meets in May and October.

Emphases. *Activities:* Education.
Types of support: Annual campaigns, continuing support, equipment, operating costs, projects, seed money.
Geography: Cleveland, Ohio.

Limitations. *Recipients:* Individuals.
Types of support: Endowments, fellowships, loans, scholarships.

Kelvin Smith 1980 Charitable Trust
1100 National City Bank Building
Cleveland, Ohio 44114
Tel: 216–566–5500
EIN: 346789395   Type: Independent
Contact: John L. Dampeer, Trustee

History and philosophy. Kelvin Smith established the Trust in 1980. Aquariums and other marine life activities are its primary funding interests.

Officers and directors. *Trustees:* John L. Dampeer, Howard F. Stirn.

Financial data. Data for fiscal year ended May 31, 1994. *Assets:* $3,362,262 (M). *Total grants disbursed:* $175,000.

Environmental awards. *Recent grants:* A single grant in 1993 supported marine research.

Issues. *Cli   Bio   Lan   Agr   Wat   Oce   Ene   Was   Tox   Pop   Dev*
                                       •

Funding analysis.

Fiscal year:	1993
Env grants auth:	$160,000
Number:	1
Range:	—
Median:	—
Pct $ disb (env/total):	100

Recipient (1993):	Number:	Dollars:
Sea Research Foundation	1	160,000

Activity region (1993):	Number:	Dollars:
U.S. not specified	1	160,000

Sample grant (1993).
Sea Research Foundation. Cleveland, OH. $160,000. For operating support.

Application process. *Initial contact:* Proposal.
When to apply: Anytime.

Emphases. *Recipients:* Aquariums, nonprofit organizations.
Types of support: Operating costs, projects.
Geography: Cleveland, Ohio.

Limitations. *Recipients:* Individuals.
Types of support: Endowments, fellowships, loans, scholarships.

Stanley Smith Horticultural Trust
P.O. Box 12247
Berkeley, California 94701
Tel: 510–642–2089   Fax: 510–643–6264
EIN: 946209165   Type: Independent
Contact: Dr. Robert Ornduff, Grant Director

History and philosophy. The Trust was established in 1970 by May Smith. Its focus is horticultural research and education.

Officers and directors. *Trustees:* John P. Collins, Jr., J. R. Gibbs, N. D. Matheny, May Smith, Sir George Taylor.

Financial data. Data for fiscal year ended December 31, 1992. *Assets:* $9,202,887 (M). *Total grants disbursed:* $360,509.

Environmental awards. *Recent grants:* 1992 grants included support for horticulture and education at botanical gardens, for publishing projects, and membership surveys.

Issues. *Cli   Bio   Lan   Agr   Wat   Oce   Ene   Was   Tox   Pop   Dev*
        •   •   •

Funding analysis.

Fiscal year:	1991	1992
Env grants disb:	$249,400	$320,509
Number:	13	17
Range:	$1,500–$75,000	$4,109–$50,000
Median:	$15,000	$15,000
Pct $ disb (env/total):	100	100

Recipients (1992 highest):	Number:	Dollars:
University of California, Jepson Herbarium	1	50,000
Bernice Pauahi Bishop Museum	1	36,000
Tucson Botanical Garden	1	30,600
American Rhododendron Society, Vancouver Chapter	1	30,000
Organization for Tropical Studies (OTS)	1	26,800

Activity regions (1992 highest):	Number:	Dollars:
U.S. West	5	100,709
U.S. not specified	2	41,500
Hawaii	1	36,000
Canada	1	30,000
U.S. Midwest	2	29,000

Sample grants (1992).
American Association of Botanical Gardens and Arboreta. Swarthmore, PA. $17,500. For member and non-member surveys.
Amy B. H. Greenwell Ethnobotanical Garden. Captain Cook, HI. $36,000. Matching funds.
Historic Bartram's Garden. Philadelphia, PA. $10,000. For signage.
Powell Gardens. Kingsville, MO. $10,000. Toward construction of a rock and waterfall garden.

Application process. *Initial contact:* Proposal to include:
1. Description of organization and project.
2. Description of recipient population; size, and nature.
3. Budget for project and timetable for completion.
4. Audited financial statements.
5. Copy of IRS tax-exempt status determination letter.
6. Copy of current IRS 990 form.
7. Description of organization's sources of support and income.
8. List of sources of support being requested and confirmed sources.

When to apply: Deadline is September 15.
Materials available: "Guidelines for Grant Applicants."

Emphases. *Recipients:* Botanical gardens, educational institutions (horticultural/botanical studies), nonprofit organizations, research institutions, zoos.
Activities: Audiovisual materials, collaborative efforts, demonstration programs, education, exhibits, planning, publications, research (scientific), symposia/colloquia, training.
Types of support: Capital campaigns/expenses, equipment, facilities, internships, maintenance, matching funds, operating costs, pilot projects, seed money, single-year grants.
Geography: Primarily North and South America.

S

Limitations. *Recipients:* Individuals.
Activities: Litigation, lobbying, political activities.
Types of support: Continuing support, endowments, indirect costs, multi-year grants, professorships.
Geography: United Kingdom.

Snee-Reinhardt Charitable Foundation

2101 One Mellon Bank Center
500 Grant Street
Pittsburgh, Pennsylvania 15219
Tel: 412–471–2944   Fax: 412–471–3390
EIN: 256292908   Type: Independent
Contact: Joan E. Szymanski, Administrative Assistant

History and philosophy. The Foundation was established in 1987 by Katherine E. Snee. It makes grants in the areas of: Human Services, Hospital/Medical, Miscellaneous, Environment, Arts and Culture, and Education.

Officers and directors. *Officer:* Paul A. Heasley, Chair. *Directors:* Virginia M. Davis, Karen L. Heasley, Paul A. Heasley, Timothy Heasley, James W. Ummer, Richard T. Vail.

Financial data. Data for fiscal year ended December 31, 1992.
Assets: $5,419,269 (M). *Total grants disbursed:* $257,965.

Environmental awards. *Program and interests:* Consistent with the Foundation's belief that thoughtful and direct actions are needed to protect the environment, it supports:

- Natural resource conservation.
- Beautification.
- Environmental education
- Horticultural/botanical programs.
- Pollution control.

Recent grants: 1992 grants included support for land conservation and environmental education.

Issues.   Cli   Bio   Lan   Agr   Wat   Oce   Ene   Was   Tox   Pop   Dev

Funding analysis.

Fiscal year:	1992
Env grants disb:	$23,000
Number:	3
Range:	$3,000–$10,000
Median:	$10,000
Pct $ disb (env/total):	9

Recipients (1992):	Number:	Dollars:
Armstrong County Conservancy	1	10,000
Zoological Society of Pittsburgh	1	10,000
The Student Conservation Association, Inc.	1	3,000

Activity region (1992):	Number:	Dollars:
U.S. Mid-Atlantic	3	23,000

Sample grants (1992).
Armstrong County Conservancy. Kittanning, PA. $10,000.
The Student Conservation Association, Inc. Charlestown, NH. $3,000.
Zoological Society of Pittsburgh. Pittsburgh, PA. $10,000.

Application process. *Initial contact:* Letter summarizing the specific project and amount requested in the first paragraph. Also include:

1. Complete description of project.
2. Purpose and objective of project.
3. Procedures for implementation.
4. Itemized budget for project including income and expenses.
5. List of corporate and foundation donors.
6. Professionally prepared financial statement.
7. Copy of IRS tax-exempt status determination letter.
8. Organization's EIN.

When to apply: Deadlines vary, call for details.
Materials available: Report, "Grant Application Guidelines."

Emphases. *Recipients:* Nonprofit organizations.
Activities: Capacity building.
Geography: Southwestern Pennsylvania, northern West Virginia, northern Maryland; Pennsylvania; United States.

Limitations. *Recipients:* Individuals, religious organizations.
Activities: Political activities.
Types of support: Capital campaigns/expenses, endowments, operating costs, professorships.

Solow Foundation

Nine West 57th Street
New York, New York 10019–2601
Tel: 212–725–0024
EIN: 132950685   Type: Independent
Contact: Sheldon H. Solow, President

History and philosophy. The Foundation was established in 1978 by Sheldon H. Solow. It makes grants for education, libraries, museums, arts and culture, architecture, and Jewish causes.

Officers and directors. *Officers:* Sheldon H. Solow, President; Rosalie S. Wolff, Vice President; Leonard Lazarus, Secretary; Steven M. Chermiak, Treasurer. *Directors:* Steven M. Chermiak, Leonard Lazarus, Sheldon H. Solow, Rosalie S. Wolff.

Financial data. Data for fiscal year ended October 31, 1992.
Assets: $7,962,408 (M). *Total grants disbursed:* $382,785.

Environmental awards. *Recent grants:* 1992 grants included support for urban parks and wildlife conservation.

Issues.   Cli   Bio   Lan   Agr   Wat   Oce   Ene   Was   Tox   Pop   Dev

Funding analysis.

Fiscal year:	1992
Env grants disb:	$50,760
Number:	2
Range:	$500–$50,260
Median:	$25,380
Pct $ disb (env/total):	13

Recipients (1992):	*Number:*	*Dollars:*
Central Park Conservancy	1	50,260
NYZS/The Wildlife Conservation Society	1	500

Activity region (1992):	*Number:*	*Dollars:*
New York/New Jersey	2	50,760

Sample grants (1992).
Central Park Conservancy. New York, NY. $50,260.
NYZS/The Wildlife Conservation Society. Bronx, NY. $500.

Application process. *Initial contact:* Letter.
When to apply: Anytime.

The Sonoma County Community Foundation
Fountaingrove Center
3550 Round Barn Boulevard, Suite 212
Santa Rosa, California 95403
Tel: 707–579–4073   Fax: 707–579–4801
EIN: 680003212   Type: Community
Contact: Joan L. Stover, Program Officer

History and philosophy. The Sonoma County Community Foundation is a public charity established in 1983 as a philanthropic vehicle for individuals, families, organizations, corporations, or private foundations and trusts. The Foundation makes grants to a broad array of community organizations to meet diverse community needs. Its priorities include programs that (1) alleviate root causes or develop long-term solutions; (2) assist those residents whose needs are not met by existing services; (3) encourage more efficient use of community resources and promote coordination, cooperation, and sharing among organizations as well as the elimination of duplicated services; and (4) stimulate broad participation and reach a broader segment of the community.

Four main areas of interest are: arts and humanities, education, environment, and health and human services.

Officers and directors. *Officers:* John R. O'Brien, President; Lee Chandler, Vice President; Dee Richardson, Secretary; Peggy J. Bair, Treasurer. *Directors:* Ruben Arminana, Peggy J. Bair, John T. Blount, F. James Brock, Jr., Lee Chandler, Reverend James E. Coffee, Harry Friedman, Peggy J. Furth, Barbara Detrich Gallagher, Lucy Kishaba, Claire Lampson, Dan Libarle, Mark Matthews, John R. O'Brien, Peter Piasecki, Rhoann Ponseti, Dee Richardson, Irwin S. Rothenbeg, Jack Taylor, Kirk Veale. *Ex officio:* Harrison Comstock, John Moskowitz, Jean Schulz, John Shanahan.

Financial data. Data for fiscal year ended December 31, 1993. *Assets:* $5,000,000 (U) (est.). *Total grants disbursed:* $450,000.

Environmental awards. *Program and interests:* One of the member foundations, the Charles M. Schulz Foundation, awards grants up to $1,500 in the areas of youth and environment.
Recent grants: 1993 grants included support for tree care, horticulture, and environmental training.

Issues. Cli Bio Lan Agr Wat Oce Ene Was Tox Pop Dev
           •

Funding analysis.§

Fiscal year:	1993
Env grants disb:	$11,025
Number:	4
Range:	$1,075–$3,750
Median:	$3,100
Pct $ disb (env/total):	2

Recipients (1993):	*Number:*	*Dollars:*
Sonoma State University EarthLab	1	3,750
Circuit Rider Productions, Inc	1	3,200
Sonoma County ReLeaf	1	3,000
Operation Green Plant	1	1,075

Activity region (1993):	*Number:*	*Dollars:*
U.S. West	4	11,025

§Includes discretionary, donor-advised, and donor-designated grants.

Sample grants (1993).
Circuit Rider Productions, Inc. Windsor, CA. $3,200. To train high-risk, low-income adults enrolled in the Green Professions Training Program.
Operation Green Plant. Santa Rosa. CA. $1,075. To increase distribution and supplies.
Sonoma County ReLeaf. Santa Rosa, CA. $3,000 (12 weeks). For a tree care program.
Sonoma State University EarthLab. Rohnert Park, CA. $3,750. For a volunteer coordinator.

Application process. *Initial contact:* Request the Foundation's Grant Application Form and/or the Charles M. Schulz Mini-Grant Application Form.
When to apply: Deadlines for general grants are in February and August for May and November decisions. The deadline for Charles M. Schulz Mini-Grants is June for an August decision.
Materials available: Annual report, "Information For Organization Grant Applicants," brochures.

Emphases. *Recipients:* Museums, nonprofit organizations.
Activities: Collaborative efforts, conflict resolution, direct services, education, exhibits, innovative programs, volunteerism, youth programs.
Types of support: Matching funds, pilot projects, projects, seed money, single-year grants only, start-up costs.
Geography: Sonoma County, California; California only.

S

Limitations. *Recipients:* Individuals, religious organizations.
Activities: Advocacy, feasibility studies, fundraising, inventories, land acquisition, litigation, lobbying, political activities.
Types of support: Annual campaigns, capital campaigns, debt retirement, emergency funding, facilities, fellowships, general purposes, loans, mortgage reduction, multi-year grants, operating costs.

South Coast Foundation, Inc.
1563 Solano Avenue, Suite 354
Berkeley, California 94707
Tel: 510–527–2111
EIN: 770177830   Type: Independent
Contact: Kathleen M. Cook, President

History and philosophy. The Foundation was established in 1988 by Howard F. Cook as partial successor to Cook Brothers Educational Fund. It makes grants to South African nongovernment organ-izations to provide training services to community-based organizations in the areas of managerial and administrative skills, project and financial management, organizational development, and negotiating and advocacy skills.

Officers and directors. Kathleen M. Cook, President; Jason Hebel, Vice President; Frank Cook, Secretary/Treasurer.

Financial data. Data for fiscal year ended December 31, 1992. *Assets:* $2,348,595. (M) *Total grants disbursed:* $135,625.

Environmental awards. *Program and interests:* The Foundation's interests include environmental projects in South Africa.
Recent grants: 1992 grants included support for river protection, toxics, marine issues, and wildlife conservation.

Issues.   Cli   Bio   Lan   Agr   Wat   Oce   Ene   Was   Tox   Pop   Dev
                     •   •   •   •   •

Funding analysis.

Fiscal year:	1992
Env grants disb:	$33,000
Number:	5
Range:	$5,000–$10,000
Median:	$6,000
Pct $ disb (env/total):	24

Recipients (1992):	*Number:*	*Dollars:*
Earth Island Institute	1	10,000
The Tides Foundation, International Rivers Network	1	7,000
National Toxics Campaign Fund	1	6,000
African Water Network	1	5,000
Santa Barbara Wildlife Care Network	1	5,000

Activity regions (1992):	*Number:*	*Dollars:*
Eastern and Southern Africa	3	18,000
U.S. not specified	1	10,000
U.S. West	1	5,000

Sample grants (1992).
African Water Network. Nairobi, Kenya. $5,000. General support.
Earth Island Institute. San Francisco, CA. $10,000. Dolphin Project.
National Toxics Campaign Fund. Boston, MA. $6,000. South African Information and Technical Exchange Program.
Santa Barbara Wildlife Care Network. Santa Barbara, CA. $5,000. General support.
The Tides Foundation, International Rivers Network. San Francisco, CA. $7,000.

Application process. *Initial contact:* The South Coast Foundation awards grants to pre-selected organizations only. No unsolicited applications accepted.

Emphases. *Recipients:* Pre-selected organizations only.
Activities: Training.
Types of support: Continuing support, operating costs, projects.
Geography: South Africa.

Limitations. *Recipients:* Individuals.

Southwestern Bell Foundation
175 East Houston Street, Suite 200
San Antonio, Texas 78205
Tel: 201–351–2208   Fax: 210–351–2205
EIN: 431353948   Type: Company-sponsored
Contact: Charles O. DeRiemer, Executive Director

History and philosophy. The Foundation was established in 1984 by the Southwestern Bell Corporation to act as a "catalyst for change" in the communities in which it operates. Its two major objectives are: (1) to encourage innovative programs promoting volunteerism which provide services directly to those in need; and (2) to help find solutions for problems identified as areas of concern nationally and in communities where Southwestern Bell Corporation has a presence. The Foundation's programs are: Education, Community and Civic Needs, Health and Welfare, and the Arts. As of 1990 the Foundation added a special focus on public education and economic development.

Officers and directors. *Officers:* Gerald Blatherwick, Chairman; Larry J. Alexander, President; Harold E. Rainbolt, Vice President and Secretary; Roger W. Wohlert, Vice President and Treasurer. *Directors:* James R. Adams, Larry J. Alexander, Gerald Blatherwick, Royce S. Caldwell, James D. Ellis, Charles E. Foster, Robert G. Pope, Harold E. Rainbolt, Roger W. Wohlert.

Financial data. Data for fiscal year ended December 31, 1992. *Assets:* $39,011,627 (M). *Gifts received:* $14,000,000. *Total grants disbursed:* $13,809,593.

Environmental awards. *Recent grants:* 1992 grants included support for land conservation, species protection, beautification, botanical gardens, and zoos.

Issues.   Cli   Bio   Lan   Agr   Wat   Oce   Ene   Was   Tox   Pop   Dev
                     •   •

Funding analysis.

Fiscal year:	1990	1992
Env grants disb:	$636,500	$43,500
Number:	7	16
Range:	$10,000–$300,000	$500–$9,000
Median:	$35,000	$1,750
Pct $ disb (env/total):	4	<1

Recipients (1992 highest):	Number:	Dollars:
Oklahoma City Zoological Society/Zoological Trust	1	9,000
Raptor Rehabilitation	1	8,000
A More Beautiful Muskogee, Inc.	1	5,000
The Nature Conservancy, Oklahoma Field Office	1	5,000
Fort Worth Clean City, Inc.	2	3,500

Activity regions (1992):	Number:	Dollars:
U.S. South Central	14	33,000
U.S. Midwest	2	10,500

Sample grants (1992).
A More Beautiful Muskogee, Inc. Muskogee, OK. $5,000.
Abilene Zoological Society. Abilene, TX. $500.
Cameron Park Zoological. Waco, TX. $500.
Dallas Arboretum and Botanical Society. Dallas, TX. $3,000.
Dallas Zoological Society. Dallas, TX. $3,000.
Fort Worth Clean City, Inc. Fort Worth, TX. $3,500.
Keep Austin Beautiful, Inc. Austin, TX. $1,000.
Keep El Paso Beautiful. El Paso, TX. $500.
National Wildflower Research Center. Austin, TX. $500.
The Nature Conservancy, Oklahoma Field Office. Tulsa, OK. $5,000.
Oklahoma City Zoological Society/Zoological Trust. Oklahoma City, OK. $9,000.
Raptor Rehabilitation. Eureka, MO. $8,000.
San Antonio Zoo. San Antonio, TX. $1,000.
South Texas Zoological Society. Victoria, TX. $500.

Application process. *Initial contact:* Letter to include:
1. Copy of IRS tax-exempt status determination letter.
2. Description of organization's history and accomplishments.
3. Objectives, problem being addressed, project budget, and amount requested from Foundation.
4. How project's goals coincide with Foundation priorities.
5. Timetable and description of expected results.
6. Fundraising details including sources, amounts, and commitments.
7. Plans for continuation after Foundation support ceases.
8. Annual report or organization's budget showing all income sources and objectives.
9. List of board members and accrediting agencies, when appropriate.

When to apply: Anytime, but organizations are asked not to submit a proposal more than once a year.
Materials available: Annual report (includes "Grant Application Guidelines"), "Contribution Guidelines".

Emphases. *Recipients:* Nonprofit organizations.
Activities: Citizen participation, conferences, education, research, seminars, technical assistance, volunteerism.
Types of support: Lectureships, matching funds, pilot projects, seed money, technical assistance.
Geography: Arkansas, Kansas, Missouri, Oklahoma, Texas, and locations where Southwestern Bell has a presence.

Limitations. *Recipients:* Individuals, religious organizations.
Activities: Fundraising, political activities.
Types of support: Advertising campaigns, capital campaigns/expenses, continuing support, operating costs.

Springhouse Foundation

1505 Bridgeway, Suite 201
Sausalito, California 94965
Tel: 415–331–4400
EIN: 042947276   Type: Independent
Contact: Tracy Barbutes, Administrator

History and philosophy. The Springhouse Foundation is a small family foundation created in 1986 to "support worthwhile causes." Primary areas of interest are the arts, the elderly, the environment, the needy, and youth.

Officers and directors. *Trustees*: Bruce Katz, Roger Katz.

Financial data. Data for fiscal year ended November 30, 1992. *Assets:* $2,257,581 (M). *Gifts received:* 200,000. *Total grants disbursed:* $83,775.

Environmental awards. *Recent grants:* 1992 grants included support for forest protection and environmental education.

Issues.   Cli   Bio   Lan   Agr   Wat   Oce   Ene   Was   Tox   Pop   Dev
             •   •

Funding analysis.

Fiscal year:	1992
Env grants disb:	$27,000
Number:	5
Range:	$2,500–$12,000
Median:	$5,000
Pct $ disb (env/total):	83

Recipients (1992):	Number:	Dollars:
Forest Island Project	1	12,000
Farm and Wilderness Camp	1	5,000
Resource Renewal Institute	1	5,000
LightHawk	1	2,500
The Student Conservation Association, Inc.	1	2,500

Activity region (1992):	Number:	Dollars:
U.S. West	5	27,000

Sample grants (1992).
Forest Island Project. Berkeley, CA. $12,000.
LightHawk. Santa Fe, NM. $2,500.
Resource Renewal Institute. Sausalito, CA. $5,000.
The Student Conservation Association, Inc. Charlestown, NH. $2,500.

Application process. *Initial contact:* Postcard or brief letter describing applicant organization and its goals. If interested, Foundation will request:
1. Letter, signed by an officer, setting forth in detail project to be funded and amount requested.
2. IRS tax-exempt status determination letter, and signed statement that tax-exempt status has not changed.
3. Latest annual report.
4. Detailed budget and timeline for project.

When to apply: August through October, with grants awarded by November 15. Telephone calls are discouraged.
Materials available: "Eligibility Requirements and Guidelines."

Emphases. *Geography:* West Coast.

Limitations. *Activities:* Conferences, media projects, seminars.
Types of support: Endowments, general purposes, loans.

Springs Foundation, Inc.
104 East Springs Street
P.O. Box 460
Lancaster, South Carolina 29721
Tel: 803–286–2197 Fax: 803–286–3295
EIN: 570426344 Type: Independent
Contact: Charles A. Bundy, President

History and philosophy. Colonel Elliott White Springs (1896–1959), World War I pilot, author, and leader in the textile industry, founded the Foundation in 1942 with five areas of interest: Community Service, Recreation, Education, Health Care, and Religion, as well as a geographic restriction to Lancaster County, Chester, and Fort Mill, South Carolina. Frances Ley Springs (1900–1966), whose special interest was in health care and education, provided strong leadership for the Foundation following her husband's death. In 1992, the Trustees voted to add a special focus on early childhood education and support of an affordable housing development to the basic five areas of interest.

Officers and directors. *Officers:* Anne Springs Close, Chairman; Charles A. Bundy, President; H. W. Close, Jr., Vice President; James H. Hodges, Secretary/Treasurer. *Directors:* Crandall C. Bowles, James Bradley, Charles A. Bundy, Anne Springs Close, Derick S. Close, Elliott S. Close, H. W. Close, Jr., Katherine Anne Close, Leroy S. Close, Pat Close, Frances C. Hart, James H. Hodges, R. C. Hubbard, William G. Taylor.

Financial data. Data for fiscal year ended December 31, 1993. *Assets:* $20,731,341 (C). *Gifts received:* $850. *Total grants disbursed:* $1,466,468.

Environmental awards. *Recent grants:* 1993 grants included support for parks and environmental education.

Issues. *Cli Bio Lan Agr Wat Oce Ene Was Tox Pop Dev*
 •

Funding analysis.

Fiscal year:	1993
Env grants auth:	$30,300
Number:	2
Range:	$15,000–$15,300
Median:	$15,150
Pct $ auth (env/total):	2

Recipients (1993):	*Number:*	*Dollars:*
Environmental Education Center	1	15,300
Town of Kershaw	1	15,000

Activity region (1993):	*Number:*	*Dollars:*
U.S. Southeast	2	30,300

Sample grants (1993).
Environmental Education Center. Lake Wylie, SC. $15,300.
Town of Kershaw. Kershaw, SC. $15,000. Property for downtown park.

Application process. *Initial contact:* Letter (1 page) to include a statement of need and sponsoring organization. Additional information will be requested if needed.
When to apply: Anytime. Board meetings held in April and November.
Materials available: Annual report, "Guidelines For Grant Making."

Emphases. *Recipients:* Educational institutions, museums, non-profit organizations.
Activities: Education, land acquisition, training, youth programs.
Types of support: Annual campaigns, capital campaigns/expenses, computer hardware, continuing support, emergency funding, endowments, equipment, facilities, internships, loans (student), matching funds, multi-year grants, pilot projects, projects, scholarships, seed money, single-year grants, start-up costs.
Geography: Lancaster County and Fort Mill and Chester townships; South Carolina, only.

Limitations. *Recipients:* Individuals, research institutions.
Activities: Activism, advocacy, conferences, conflict resolution, demonstration programs, exhibits, expeditions/tours, feasibility studies, fieldwork, litigation, lobbying, policy analysis/development, political activities, publications, seminars, technical assistance, volunteerism, workshops.
Types of support: Advertising campaigns, indirect costs, lectureships, membership campaigns, professorships, program-related investments, technical assistance, travel expenses.

Sproul Foundation
1760 Bristol Road, Box 160
Warrington, Pennsylvania 18976–2700
Tel: 215–343–9000
EIN: 222725129 Type: Independent
Contact: David Finkelstone, Trustee

History and philosophy. The Foundation makes grants to pre-selected organizations in Pennsylvania in the fields of conservation, religion, and education.

Officers and directors. *Trustees:* David Finkelstone, Stephen B. Harris, T. Jefferies Rosengarten.

Financial data. Data for fiscal year ended October 31, 1992. *Assets:* $336,408 (M). *Total grants disbursed:* $56,500.

Environmental awards. *Recent grants:* 1992 grants supported land conservation, farmland preservation, and coastal issues.

Issues. Cli Bio Lan• Agr• Wat• Oce• Ene Was Tox Pop Dev

Funding analysis.

Fiscal year:	1992
Env grants disb:	$44,500
Number:	3
Range:	$5,000–$21,500
Median:	$18,000
Pct $ disb (env/total):	79

Recipients (1992):	*Number:*	*Dollars:*
Brandywine Conservancy, Inc.	1	21,500
Lancaster Farmland Trust	1	18,000
Chesapeake Bay Foundation	1	5,000

Activity region (1992):	*Number:*	*Dollars:*
U.S. Mid-Atlantic	3	44,500

Sample grants (1992).
Brandywine Conservancy, Inc. Chadds Ford, PA. $21,500.
Chesapeake Bay Foundation. Annapolis, MD. $5,000.
Lancaster Farmland Trust. Lancaster, PA. $18,000.

Application process. *Initial contact:* The Foundation awards grants to pre-selected organizations only.

Emphases. *Recipients:* Pre-selected organizations only.

Stackner Family Foundation, Inc.

c/o Patrick W. Cotter
411 East Wisconsin Avenue, #2500
Milwaukee, Wisconsin 53202
Tel: 414–277–5000
EIN: 396097597   Type: Independent
Contact: Patrick W. Cotter, Executive Director

History and philosophy. The Foundation was established in 1966 by John S. and Irene M. Stackner. It makes grants in the areas of: education, social services, medical research and health services, drug and alcohol abuse, historic preservation, and environmental conservation.

Officers and directors. *Officers:* Patricia S. Treiber, President; John A. Treiber, Vice President; Patrick W. Cotter, Secretary; David L. MacGregor, Treasurer. *Directors:* Patrick W. Cotter, David L. MacGregor, John A. Treiber, Patricia S. Treiber.

Financial data. Data for fiscal year ended August 31, 1993. *Assets:* $11,828,233 (M). *Total grants disbursed:* $618,300.

Environmental awards. *Recent grants:* 1993 grants included support for outdoor education and a zoo.

Issues. Cli• Bio Lan Agr Wat Oce Ene Was Tox Pop Dev

Funding analysis.

Fiscal year:	1993
Env grants disb:	$3,500
Number:	2
Range:	$1,000–$2,500
Median:	$1,750
Pct $ disb (env/total):	1

Recipients (1993):	*Number:*	*Dollars:*
Zoological Society of Milwaukee	1	2,500
Schlitz Audubon Center	1	1,000

Activity region (1993):	*Number:*	*Dollars:*
U.S. Great Lakes	2	3,500

Sample grants (1993).
Schlitz Audubon Center. Brown Deer, WI. $1,000. Annual fund drive.
Zoological Society of Milwaukee County. Milwaukee, WI. $2,500. Platypus Society membership.

Application process. *Initial contact:* Letter describing proposed program or project accompanied by:
1. Budget information.
2. IRS tax-exempt status determination letter.
3. Brochures or other descriptive material.

When to apply: Deadlines are March 15, June 15, September 15, and December 15. The board meets in January, April, July, and October.

Emphases. *Types of support:* Annual campaigns, capital campaigns/expenses, continuing support, equipment, facilities, matching funds, projects, research, seed money.
Geography: Greater Milwaukee area.

Limitations. *Recipients:* Individuals.
Types of support: Debt retirement, fellowships, loans, scholarships.

Alfred T. Stanley Foundation

c/o Daniel Jacobs
P.O. Box 1320
Bronx, New York 10471
EIN: 136133796   Type: Independent

Application address:
90 Bryant Avenue
White Plains, New York 10605
Tel: 914–683–5507
Contact: Daniel Jacobs

History and philosophy. Established in 1983, the Foundation makes grants in the areas of environment, welfare, Catholic welfare, medical research, health, social services, mainly in the New York City area.

Officers and directors. *Officers:* John Crane, President; Alfred T. Stanley, Vice President; Louise Pitkin, 2nd Vice President; Theodore Storey, Secretary; Beulah Stanley, Treasurer.
Directors: John Crane, Louise Pitkin, Alfred T. Stanley, Beulah Stanley.

Financial data. Data for fiscal year ended December 31, 1992. *Assets:* $1,243,715 (M). *Total grants disbursed:* $84,000.

Environmental awards. *Recent grants:* 1992 grants included support for parks, wildlife, and a nature center.

Issues. *Cli Bio Lan Agr Wat Oce Ene Was Tox Pop Dev*
         •   •   •

Funding analysis.

Fiscal year:	1992
Env grants disb:	$20,900
Number:	10
Range:	$500–$9,300
Median:	$1,000
Pct $ disb (env/total):	25

Recipients (1992 highest):	Number:	Dollars:
Environmental Defense Fund	1	9,300
Natural Resources Defense Council	1	3,000
Central Park Conservancy	1	2,600
Greenpeace USA	1	2,000
NYZS/The Wildlife Conservation Society	2	1,500

Activity regions (1992):	Number:	Dollars:
New York/New Jersey	8	17,900
U.S. not specified	2	3,000

Sample grants (1992).
Central Park Conservatory. New York, NY. $2,600.
Environmental Defense Fund. New York, NY. $9,300.
Flat Rock Brook Nature Association. Englewood, NJ. $500.
Greenpeace USA. Washington, DC. $2,000.
Natural Resources Defense Council. New York, NY. $3,000.
NYZS/The Wildlife Conservation Society. Bronx, NY. $500.
The Parks Council, Inc. New York, NY. $500.
Sierra Club Foundation. San Francisco, CA. $500.

Application process. *Initial contact:* Proposal from pre-selected organizations.
When to apply: Deadline is October 15.

Emphases. *Recipients:* Pre-selected organizations.

Anna B. Stearns Charitable Foundation, Inc.
c/o Grants Management Associates, Inc.
230 Congress Street
Boston, Massachusetts 02110
Tel: 617-426-7172
EIN: 046144732   Type: Independent
Contacts: Laura Henze, Administrator
          Suzanne Sack, Administrative Assistant

Alternate application address:
c/o Deborah Cowan, Associate Director
New Hampshire Charitable Foundation
37 Pleasant Street, P.O. Box 1335
Concord, New Hampshire 03302-1335

History and philosophy. Anna B. Stearns established the Foundation in 1966. It supports projects and organizations that "strengthen the education, independence, and/or socioeconomic status of women, children and youth; and protect and preserve the natural environment."

Officers and directors. *Officers:* Christine G. Franklin, President; Katherine L. Babson, Jr., Clerk and Treasurer.
Trustees: Katherine L. Babson, Jr., Christine G. Franklin, Gwendolyn Harper, Deborah C. Jackson, Leonard W. Johnson.

Financial data. Data for fiscal years ended December 31, 1992 and 1993. *Assets (1992):* $8,951,261 (M). *Total grants disbursed (1993):* $252,500.

Environmental awards. *Program and interests:* Environmental interests include land conservation, education, and programs for youth.
Recent grants: Grants in 1992 and 1993 included support for urban environment and open space.

Issues. *Cli Bio Lan Agr Wat Oce Ene Was Tox Pop Dev*
              •   •

Funding analysis.

Fiscal year:	1993
Env grants auth:	$10,000
Number:	1
Range:	—
Median:	—
Pct $ auth (env/total):	4

Recipient (1993):	Number:	Dollars:
Boston GreenSpace Alliance	1	10,000

Activity region (1993):	Number:	Dollars:
U.S. Northeast	1	10,000

Sample grants (1992–93).
Boston GreenSpace Alliance. Boston, MA. $10,000. Schoolyard improvement project.
Boston Natural Areas Fund. Boston, MA. $5,500. Planning grant to acquire land for parkland protection.

Application process. *Initial contact:* Cover letter summarizing the request, accompanying proposal to include:

1. Short narrative description of organization's history, mission, accomplishments, populations served; programs or services it provides; and qualifications to undertake the program for which funds are sought.
2. Description of specific purpose for which grant is sought and its relevance to Foundation's goals.
3. Timetable of activities and objectives to be met.
4. Clear statement of applicant's expectations with respect to the results of the grant, and how results will be measured.

Attachments.
1. Copy of the organization's most recent audited financial statement, IRS Form 990, and current annual budget.
2. Names and positions of board members and key staff, with information on how they reflect the diversity of the community served.
3. Information on the number, and racial and gender composition of program participants.
4. Budget for proposed project, including other sources of support already committed and requests pending.
5. Copy of IRS tax-exempt status determination letter and proof that the organization is not private.

Personal interviews are not always possible, but applicants are welcome to telephone Foundation staff.
Organizations serving Northern New Hampshire should contact Deborah Cowan at New Hampshire Charitable Foundation (see above).
When to apply: 1995 deadlines are May 1 and November 1 for review at trustees' winter and summer meetings.
Materials available: Guidelines.

Emphases. *Recipients:* Nonprofit organizations.
Activities: Education.
Types of support: General purposes, multi-year grants, projects, technical assistance.
Geography: Greater Boston area and Northern New Hampshire.

Limitations. *Types of support:* Capital campaigns/expenses, endowments.

The Stebbins Fund, Inc.
c/o Seymour Schneedman & Associates
400 Park Avenue, 2nd Floor
New York, New York 10022
Tel: 212-421-5380
EIN: 116021709   Type: Independent
Contact: Gary Castle, Accountant

History and philosophy. The Foundation was established in 1947 by members of the Stebbins family. Art, education, historic preservation, and museums are its main funding interests.

Officers and directors. *Officers:* James F. Stebbins, President; Theodore E. Stebbins, Vice President; Jane S. Sykes, Vice President and Treasurer; Meredith M. Brown, Secretary; Michael W. Galligan, Assistant Secretary/Treasurer. *Directors:* Victoria Stebbins Greenleaf, J. Wright Rumbough, Jr., Edwin E. F. Stebbins, James F. Stebbins, Michael Morgan Stebbins, Theodore E. Stebbins, Jr., Jane S. Sykes.

Financial data. Data for fiscal year ended December 31, 1992.
Assets: $2,153,430 (M). *Total grants disbursed:* $100,950.

Environmental awards. *Recent grants:* 1992 grants included support for land conservation, wildlife, horticulture, and recreation.

Issues.   Cli   Bio   Lan   Agr   Wat   Oce   Ene   Was   Tox   Pop   Dev
             •   •

Sample grants (1992).
Adirondack Trail Improvement Society. Keene Valley, NY. $1,000.
Association for the Protection of the Adirondacks. Schenectady, NY. $4,000.
INFORM. New York, NY. $1,000.
The Nature Conservancy, Long Island Chapter. Cold Spring Harbor, NY. $7,500.
North County Garden Club. Locust Valley, NY. $1,000.
Old Westbury Gardens. Westbury, NY. $1,000.
Theodore Roosevelt Sanctuary. Oyster Bay, NY. $500.

Application process. *Initial contact:* The Foundation generally makes grants to pre-selected organizations. "Unsolicited grant applications are not, as a general rule, entertained."
When to apply: Anytime. The board meets in June.

Emphases. *Recipients:* Nonprofit organizations.
Types of support: Annual campaigns, capital campaigns/expenses.
Geography: Northeastern United States.

Limitations. *Recipients:* Individuals.
Types of support: Endowments, loans.

Steelcase Foundation
Location CH.5C
P.O. Box 1967
Grand Rapids, Michigan 49501-1967
Tel: 616-246-4695   Fax: 616-246-4041
EIN: 386050470   Type: Company-sponsored
Contact: Kate Pew Wolters, Executive Director

History and philosophy. The Foundation was established in 1951 by Steelcase, the office furniture corporation, "to improve the health, education, recreational, and environmental opportunities for all Steelcase communities." Grants are made "to organizations, projects, and programs in the areas of human service, health, education, community/economic development, arts and culture, and the environment." Particular emphasis is given to the disadvantaged, disabled, the young, and the elderly.

Officers and directors. *Officer:* Robert C. Pew, Chairman. *Trustees:* David D. Hunting, Jr., Roger L. Martin, Frank H. Merlotti, Jerry K. Myers, Robert C. Pew, Peter M. Wege, Old Kent Bank and Trust Company.

Financial data. Data for fiscal year ended November 30, 1993.
Assets: $67,771,774 (M). *Gifts received:* $1,845,420. *Total grants disbursed:* $3,405,574.

Environmental awards. *Recent grants:* 1993 grants included support for ecosystem protection, water quality, horticulture, recreation, and public education.

Issues. Cli Bio Lan Agr Wat Oce Ene Was Tox Pop Dev
           •   •   •

Funding analysis.

Fiscal year:	1991	1993
Env grants disb:	$135,000	$1,148,800
Number:	3	6
Range:	$10,000–$100,000	$10,000–$500,000
Median:	$25,000	$61,900
Pct $ disb (env/total):	4	31

Recipients (1993 highest):	Number:	Dollars:
John Ball Zoological Society	1	500,000
West Michigan Horticultural Society, Inc.	1	500,000
The Nature Conservancy, Michigan Field Office	1	100,000
Natural Areas Conservancy of Western Michigan	1	23,800
Northview Education Foundation	1	10,000

Activity region (1993):	Number:	Dollars:
U.S. Great Lakes	6	1,148,800

Sample grants (1993).
John Ball Zoological Society. Grand Rapids, MI. $500,000. Funding for Phase II and III Zoo construction and renovation.
Grand Rapids Public Schools. Grand Rapids, MI. $15,000. Expansion of stream monitoring program through the "Environmental Educators Advisory Council" of KISD.
Natural Areas Conservancy of Western Michigan. Grand Rapids, MI. $23,800. Start-up funding for professional office and staff.
The Nature Conservancy, Michigan Field Office. East Lansing, MI. $100,000. Funding for "Great Lakes, Great Places" campaign for ecosystem protection.
Northview Education Foundation. Grand Rapids, MI. $10,000. Funding for the Northview Nature Trail and Outdoor Educational Center.
West Michigan Horticultural Society, Inc. Grand Rapids, MI. $500,000. Funding to develop the "Michigan Botanic Garden."

Application process. *Initial contact:* Letter, on organization letterhead and signed by CEO, requesting application materials and including:
1. Brief description of organization.
2. Description of project, amount requested, and expected results.
3. Copy of IRS tax-exempt status determination letter.

Applications for additional grants submitted within 12 months of your last grant will not be considered.
When to apply: Quarterly deadlines prior to each trustees' meeting. Exact dates will be sent with application materials.
Materials available: Annual report, "Guidelines."

Emphases. *Activities:* Education.
Types of support: Capital campaigns/expenses, facilities (construction), general purposes, pilot projects, scholarships, seed money.

Geography: Areas of company operations: Asheville, North Carolina; Athens, Alabama; Grand Rapids, Michigan; Orange County, California; Toronto, Ontario.

Limitations. *Recipients:* Individuals, religious organizations.
Activities: Conferences, seminars, symposia/colloquia.
Types of support: Endowments.

Stern Family Fund
256 North Pleasant Street
Amherst, Massachusetts 01002
Tel: 413–256–0349 Fax: 413–256–3536
EIN: 526037658 Type: Independent
EGA member
Contact: Margaret E. Gage, Executive Director

History and philosophy. Established in 1959 by Philip M. Stern, "the Stern Family Fund supports organizations working for systemic structural changes aimed at empowering the powerless, alleviating injustice, increasing government and corporate accountability, and strengthening the workings of American democracy."

Areas of special interest include campaign finance reform; election law reforms aimed at simplifying and encouraging voter participation; alleviating special problems faced by women, particularly women of color; fostering governmental accountability, open government, and the efforts of whistleblowers; providing technical assistance to progressive nonprofit groups to enable them to perform more effectively; and promoting corporate accountability and socially responsible corporate behavior.

Officers and directors. *Officers:* Philip M. Stern, President and Treasurer; Anne Plaster, Secretary. *Directors:* Anne Plaster, Walt Slocombe, Philip M. Stern.

Financial data. Data for fiscal year ended June 30, 1993. *Assets:* $409,668 (M). *Gifts received:* $14,098. *Total grants disbursed:* $414,095.

Environmental awards. *Program and interests:* The Fund's special interests are:

- Grassroots activism.
- Advocacy.

Recent grants: 1993 grants included support for advocacy on nuclear issues.

Issues. Cli Bio Lan Agr Wat Oce Ene Was Tox Pop Dev
                                             •   •

Funding analysis.

Fiscal year:	1991	1993
Env grants disb:	$55,000	$16,000
Number:	9	3
Range:	$1,000–$25,000	$1,000–$10,000
Median:	$2,500	$5,000
Pct $ disb (env/total):	10	4

Recipients (1993):	Number:	Dollars:
Nuclear Information and Resource Service	1	10,000
Institute for Conservation Leadership	1	5,000
Garden Resources of Washington	1	1,000

Activity regions (1993):	Number:	Dollars:
U.S. not specified	2	15,000
U.S. Mid-Atlantic	1	1,000

Sample grants (1993).
Garden Resources of Washington. Washington, DC. $1,000. General support.
Institute for Conservation Leadership. Washington, DC. $5,000. Scholarships to environmental activists who couldn't otherwise afford training to enhance their organizational skills.
Nuclear Information and Resource Center. Washington, DC. $10,000. General support.

Application process. *Initial contact:* Full proposal and short cover letter. Proposal to include:
1. Statement of the need for support, project goals, and an action plan for goal achievement. Preference is given to proposals which detail strategy and project implementation rather than those which focus primarily on the need for support. Include methods for evaluation.
2. Copy of IRS tax-exempt status determination letter.
3. Staff and organizational qualifications.
4. Other sources of financial support.
5. Project and organizational line item budget(s).
6. List of other organizations involved in similar programs and how the proposed project is different.
7. Hopes and/or expectations of achievement from the project, stated in terms as well quantified as possible.

When to apply: Anytime. The Fund meets approximately six times a year.
Materials available: Guidelines.

Emphases. *Recipients:* Nonprofit organizations.
Activities: Advocacy, citizen participation.
Geography: U.S. organizations only.

Limitations. *Recipients:* Organizations that traditionally enjoy popular support such as hospitals, museums, universities, or other grantmaking institutions.
Activities: Conferences, media projects, research.
Types of support: Capital campaigns/expenses, endowments, facilities, projects with budgets over $500,000.

Stoddard Charitable Trust

370 Main Street, 12th Floor
Worcester, Massachusetts 01608
Tel: 508–798–8621   Fax: 508–791–1201
EIN: 046023791   Type: Independent
Contact: Warner S. Fletcher, Chairman

History and philosophy. The Trust was established in 1939 by Harry G. Stoddard (d. 1969), chairman of the Wyman Gordon Company and the *Worcester Telegram and Gazette*. The Trust supports education, historic preservation, the arts, social services, community affairs, and the environment.

Officers and directors. *Officers:* Warner S. Fletcher, Chairman; Helen E. Stoddard, Vice Chairman; Valerie S. Loring, Secretary; Judith S. King, Treasurer. *Trustees:* Allen W. Fletcher, Warner S. Fletcher, Judith S. King, Valerie S. Loring, Helen E. Stoddard.

Financial data. Data for fiscal year ended December 31, 1992. *Assets:* $38,508,916 (M). *Total grants disbursed:* $2,493,700.

Environmental awards. *Recent grants:* Grants in 1992 included support for land conservation and horticulture in Massachusetts.

Issues.   Cli   Bio   Lan   Agr   Wat   Oce   Ene   Was   Tox   Pop   Dev
              •   •   •

Funding analysis.

Fiscal year:	1992
Env grants disb:	$176,000
Number:	5
Range:	$1,000–$90,000
Median:	$5,000
Pct $ disb (env/total):	7

Recipients (1992):	Number:	Dollars:
Worcester County Horticultural Society	1	90,000
Trustees of Reservations	1	75,000
Massachusetts Audubon Society	1	5,000
Sudbury Valley Trustees, Inc.	1	5,000
Metacomet Land Trust	1	1,000

Activity region (1992):	Number:	Dollars:
U.S. Northeast	5	176,000

Sample grants (1992).
Massachusetts Audubon Society. Lincoln, MA. $5,000.
Sudbury Valley Trustees, Inc. Sudbury, MA. $5,000.
Trustees of Reservations. Beverly, MA. $75,000.
Worcester County Horticulture Society. Worcester, MA. $90,000.

Application process. *Initial contact:* Letter.
When to apply: Anytime between January and November.

Emphases: *Geography:* Worcester, Massachusetts primarily.

Limitations. *Recipients:* Individuals.

Stranahan Foundation

4149 Holland Sylvania Road
Toledo, Ohio 43623
Tel: 419–882–6575
EIN: 346504818 Type: Independent
Contact: Charles G. Yeager, Trustee

History and philosophy. Robert A. Stranahan, former president and chairman of the Champion Spark Plug Company, established

S

the family trust with his brother Frank and other donors in 1944. The majority of grants fund community, education, and social service programs in Ohio.

Officers and directors. *Trustees:* Diana K. Foster, Gerald W. Miller, Frances Parry, Duane Stranahan, Sr., Duane Stranahan, Jr., Mark Stranahan, Mescal Stranahan, Robert A. Stranahan, Jr., Charles G. Yeager.

Financial data. Data for fiscal year ended December 31, 1993. *Assets:* $60,760,187 (M). *Total grants disbursed:* $2,693,238.

Environmental awards. *Recent grants:* In 1993 a single grant was awarded for wildlife preservation.

Issues. Cli Bio Lan Agr Wat Oce Ene Was Tox Pop Dev
•

Funding analysis.

Fiscal year:	1992
Env grants disb:	$75,000
Number:	1
Range:	–
Median:	–
Pct $ disb (env/total):	2

Recipient (1992):	Number:	Dollars:
International Center for the Preservation of Wild Animals	1	75,000

Activity region (1992):	Number:	Dollars:
International*	1	75,000

*Multiple regions or not specified.

Sample grant (1993).
International Center for the Preservation of Wild Animals. Columbus, OH. $25,000.

Application process. *Initial contact:* Letter to include:
1. Concise description of project or program to be funded.
2. Project or program budget.
Attachments.
1. Most recent audited financial statements and annual report.
2. Current annual budget.
3. List of officers and directors and their major affiliations.
4. Brief organization history.
5. Copy of IRS tax-exempt status determination letter.
When to apply: Deadline is October 1.

Emphases. *Recipients:* Nonprofit organizations.
Activities: Land acquisition.
Types of support: Annual campaigns, continuing support, equipment, facilities, general purposes.
Geography: Toledo, Ohio.

Limitations. *Recipients:* Individuals.

The Stratford Foundation

53 State Street, 17th Floor
Boston, Massachusetts 02109–2809
Tel: 617–248–7300   Fax: 617–248–7100
EIN: 222524023   Type: Independent
Contact: Peter A. Wilson, Executive Director

History and philosophy. The Foundation was established in 1983 through a donation of $80 million in Digital Equipment Corporation stock by Kenneth H. Olsen, founder and president of Digital. The Foundation makes grants primarily to organizations associated with Mr. Olsen. Areas of interest include: the arts and humanities, civic causes, conservation, education, health care, religious organizations, and social services.

Officers and directors. *Trustees:* Eeva-Liisa Aulikki Olsen, Kenneth H. Olsen, Ava-Liisa Memmen, Richard J. Testa.

Financial data. Data for fiscal year ended December 31, 1992. *Assets:* $52,385,208 (M). *Total grants disbursed:* $5,660,985.

Environmental awards. *Recent grants:* 1992 grants included support for land and habitat protection, and wildlife and plant conservation.

Issues. Cli Bio Lan Agr Wat Oce Ene Was Tox Pop Dev
•   •

Funding analysis.

Fiscal year:	1991	1992
Env grants disb:	$462,727	$350,269
Number:	7	7
Range:	$2,543–$267,250	$2,389–$237,138
Median:	$50,328	$20,288
Pct $ disb (env/total):	8	6

Recipients (1992 highest):	Number:	Dollars:
Arizona–Sonora Desert Museum	1	237,138
Massachusetts Audubon Society	2	46,850
Appalachian Mountain Club	1	33,841
The Nature Conservancy, Headquarters	1	19,906
Massachusetts Horticultural Society	1	10,144

Activity regions (1992):	Number:	Dollars:
U.S. West	1	237,138
U.S. Northeast	5	93,225
U.S. not specified	1	19,906

Sample grants (1992).
Appalachian Mountain Club. Boston, MA. $33,841.
Arizona–Sonora Desert Museum. Tucson, AZ. $237,138.
Lakes Region Conservation Trust. Meredith, NH. $2,389.
Massachusetts Audubon Society. Lincoln, MA. $46,850.
Massachusetts Horticultural Society. Boston, MA. $10,144.
The Nature Conservancy, Headquarters. Arlington, VA. $19,906.

Application process. *Initial contact:* Request application form. Required information includes description of background, services and needs of the organization, as well as a summary (2 pages) of project for which the grant is requested.
When to apply: Anytime.
Materials available: Application form.

Emphases. *Recipients:* Nonprofit organizations.
Activities: Education, research.
Types of support: General purposes.

Limitations. *Recipients:* Individuals.
Activities: Political activities.

Margaret Dorrance Strawbridge Foundation of Pennsylvania II, Inc.
125 Strafford Avenue, Suite 108
Wayne, Pennsylvania 19087–3367
Tel: 215–688–9261
EIN: 232371943   Type: Independent
Contact: Diana S. Norris, President

History and philosophy. Established in 1985, the Foundation gives grants in the areas of higher and secondary education, the environment, hospitals, and medical research.

Officers and directors. *Officer:* Diana S. Norris, President.

Financial data. Data for fiscal year ended December 31, 1992. *Assets:* $3,222,220 (M). *Gifts received:* $126,520. *Total grants disbursed:* $289,683.

Environmental awards. *Recent grants:* 1992 grants included support for land conservation, marine wildlife research and conservation, and horticulture.

Issues.   Cli Bio Lan Agr Wat Oce Ene Was Tox Pop Dev
                   •   •   •

Funding analysis.

Fiscal year:	1990	1992
Env grants disb:	$80,945	$74,400
Number:	15	14
Range:	$1,000–$26,000	$500–$26,200
Median:	$2,000	$2,000
Pct $ disb (env/total):	45	26

Recipients (1992 highest):	Number:	Dollars:
Brandywine Conservancy, Inc.	1	26,200
Pennsylvania Horticultural Society	1	15,000
Garden Club of America	1	10,000
Pine Jog Education Center	1	6,000
Delaware Center for Horticulture	1	5,000

Activity regions (1992):	Number:	Dollars:
U.S. Mid-Atlantic	3	46,200
U.S. not specified	5	14,700
U.S. Southeast	2	8,000
U.S. Northeast	3	4,500
Hawaii	1	1,000

Sample grants (1992).
American Horticultural Society. Mt. Vernon, VA. $1,200.
Brandywine Conservancy, Inc. Chadds Ford, PA. $26,200.
Delaware Center for Horticulture. Wilmington, DE. $5,000.
Dolphin Research Center. Washington, DC. $500.
Fairchild Tropical Garden. Miami, FL. $2,000.
Friends of Acadia. Bar Harbor, ME. $2,500.
Garden Club of America. New York, NY. $10,000.
Greenpeace USA. Washington, DC. $2,000.
Maine Audubon Society. Falmouth, ME. $1,000.
Maine Coast Heritage Trust. Brunswick, ME. $1,000.
National Audubon Society. New York, NY. $1,000.
National Tropical Botanical Garden. Lawai, HI. $1,000.
Pennsylvania Horticultural Society. Philadelphia, PA. $15,000.
Pine Jog Environmental Science Center. West Palm Beach, FL. $6,000.

Application process. *Initial contact:* Letter of inquiry. Solicitations for grants are not invited.
When to apply: Anytime.

Emphases. *Activities:* Research (medical).
Types of support: Annual campaigns, continuing support, operating costs.
Geography: Eastern United States, especially Florida and Pennsylvania.

Limitations. *Recipients:* Individuals.
Types of support: Capital campaigns/expenses, endowments, fellowships, loans, scholarships.

The Stroh Foundation
100 River Place, Suite 5000
Detroit, Michigan 48207
Tel: 313–446–5057   Fax: 313–446–2880
EIN: 386108732   Type: Company-sponsored
Contact: Gari M. Stroh, Jr., Secretary

History and philosophy. The Stroh Foundation was established by Stroh Brewery in 1965. It supports organizations that benefit the people of Detroit and Michigan where the company is located. "Its contributions are intended to reflect the highest standards for good citizenship and dedication to quality inherent in the Stroh management philosophies." Organizations that benefit from the Foundation's contributions have clear objectives and plans, active boards, and competent management; are beneficial to people in the Stroh communities; are respected by business and community groups; do not duplicate other services; use sound financial practices, minimal administration costs, financial information readily available, well-planned fundraising programs; and provide public recognition for The Stroh Companies.

The Foundation maintains programs in Education, Health Care and Research, Culture and the Arts, and Conservation and Ecology.

S

Officers and directors. *Officers:* John W. Stroh, III, President; Gari M. Stroh, Jr., Secretary; John W. Stroh, Jr., Treasurer. *Trustees:* C. Penfield Stroh, Gari M. Stroh, Jr., John W. Stroh, Jr., John W. Stroh, III, Peter W. Stroh.

Financial data. Data for fiscal year ended March 31, 1994. *Assets:* $5,171 (M). *Gifts received:* $300,000. *Total grants disbursed:* $148,275.

Environmental awards. *Recent grants:* 1994 grants included support for land conservation, biodiversity, marine issues, urban environment, and a zoo.

Issues.   Cli   Bio   Lan   Agr   Wat   Oce   Ene   Was   Tox   Pop   Dev
                •   •   •   •   •

Funding analysis.

Fiscal year:	1993
Env grants disb:	$48,334
Number:	14
Range:	$200–$15,000
Median:	$2,750
Pct $ disb (env/total):	16

Recipients (1993 highest):	*Number:*	*Dollars:*
Conservation International	1	15,000
The Nature Conservancy, Washington Field Office	3	7,500
Ecotrust	1	6,000
Aspen Center for Environmental Studies	1	4,334
Atlantic Salmon Federation	1	4,000
The Nature Conservancy, Headquarters	1	4,000

Activity regions (1993 highest):	*Number:*	*Dollars:*
International*	1	15,000
U.S. Northwest	4	13,500
U.S. Mountain	1	4,334
U.S. Northeast	1	4,000
U.S. not specified	1	4,000

*Multiple regions or not specified.

Sample grants (1994).
Aspen Center for Environmental Studies. Aspen, CO. $1,000.
Atlantic Salmon Federation. Calais, ME. $1,000.
Conservation International. Washington, DC. $7,400.
Detroit Zoological Society. Royal Oak, MI. $1,000.
The Nature Conservancy, Headquarters. Arlington, VA. $4,000.
The Nature Conservancy, Washington Field Office. Seattle, WA. $4,000.

Application process. *Initial contact:* Letter to include detailed budget, financial reports, and IRS tax-exempt status determination letter.
When to apply: Anytime.
Materials available: Annual report (including grants list), "Guidelines."

Emphases. *Recipients:* Nonprofit organizations.
Types of support: Matching funds.
Geography: Michigan, especially Detroit.

Limitations. *Recipients:* Individuals, religious organizations.
Activities: Fundraising, political activities.

The Strong Foundation for Environmental Values

116 New Montgomery Street, Suite 532
San Francisco, California 94105
Tel: 415–882–7928
EIN: 941167412   Type: Independent
Contact: Anne Bade, Executive Secretary

History and philosophy. Established in 1917 under another name, this grantmaker became The Strong Foundation for Environmental Values in 1982. Its mission is "to reflect a deep concern for our earthly environment and the people and animals that inhabit it." It makes grants primarily in California and the West.

Officers and directors. *Officers:* Thomas E. Bowman, President; Margaret Kelley, Vice President; Pat Bradley, Secretary; James T. Watters, Treasurer; Anne Bade, Executive Secretary. *Directors:* Thomas E. Bowman, Pat Bradley, Gerald Cullinane, Jean Farmer, Paul Grunland, John Hoffnagle, Margaret Kelley, Richard Millard, Tamra Peters, James T. Watters.

Financial data. Data for fiscal year ended August 31, 1993. *Assets:* $882,446 (C). *Total grants disbursed:* $62,000.

Environmental awards. *Program and interests:* The Foundation's primary interests are:

- Toxic waste.
- Land use.
- Water resources.

Recent grants: 1992 grants included support for conservation (land acquisition, farmland preservation, parks and public lands, open space, greenbelts, wilderness); forests (ancient forests, sustainable forestry); coastal issues; freshwater (watershed and river protection); species preservation and restoration; and toxics (environmental health, hazardous waste).

Issues.   Cli   Bio   Lan   Agr   Wat   Oce   Ene   Was   Tox   Pop   Dev
                •   •   •   •   •

Funding analysis.

Fiscal year:	1991	1992
Env grants disb:	$59,399	$62,500
Number:	40	39
Range:	$500–$4,500	$500–$5,000
Median:	$1,300	$1,300
Pct $ disb (env/total):	100	100

Recipients (1992 highest):	*Number:*	*Dollars:*
California Oak Foundation	1	5,000
Tuolumne River Preservation Trust	1	5,000
American Land Conservancy	1	4,400
South Yuba River Citizens League	1	3,000
BayKeeper	1	2,700

Activity regions (1992):	Number:	Dollars:
U.S. West	19	33,800
U.S. not specified	15	23,200
Alaska	2	4,000
U.S. Northwest	2	1,000
U.S. Great Lakes	1	500

Sample grants (1992).
American Land Conservancy. San Francisco, CA. $4,400.
American Friends Service Committee. San Francisco, CA. $800.
Center for Investigative Reporting. San Francisco, CA. $2,700.
Northern Alaska Environmental Center. Fairbanks, AK. $1,900.
Sacramento River Council. Redding, CA. $2,100.
Tuolumne River Preservation Trust. Oakland, CA. $5,000.

Application process. *Initial contact:* Full proposal (12 copies) to include:
1. Completed application form.
2. Project budget (income, expenses, and fundraising strategy).
3. Project statement (2 pages) including goals, objectives, timeline, and organizational qualifications.
4. State and federal tax exemption letters (1 copy).

No additional attachments will be accepted or considered.
When to apply: Deadlines are January 15, May 15, and September 15. Awards are made in March, July, and November.
Materials available: Application form, "Guidelines for Proposal Submission."

Emphases. *Recipients:* Nonprofit organizations.
Activities: Activism, advocacy, citizen participation, demonstration programs, education, feasibility studies, fieldwork, land acquisition, litigation, planning, political activities, policy analysis/development, publications, research, training.
Types of support: Equipment, general purposes, indirect costs, operating costs, pilot projects, single-year grants only.
Geography: Primarily Northern California and the Pacific Northwest.

Limitations. *Recipients:* Educational institutions, individuals, public agencies.
Activities: Conferences, lobbying.
Types of support: Endowments, fellowships, lectureships, multi-year grants, professorships.

The Charles J. Strosacker Foundation

P.O. Box 471
Midland, Michigan 48640-0471
Tel: 517-832-0066
EIN: 386062787   Type: Independent
Contact: Patricia E. McKelvey, Secretary

History and philosophy. Charles J. Strosacker (1882-1963), a pioneer of Dow Chemical Company, established the Foundation in 1957 to "assist and benefit political subdivisions of the state of Michigan, and religious, charitable, benevolent, scientific, or educational organizations." Major interests include education and youth programs. Midland County currently accounts for about 50 percent of grant dollars.

Officers and directors. *Officers:* Eugene C. Yehle, Chairman; Martha G. Arnold, President; Ralph A. Cole, Vice President; Charles J. Thrune, Assistant Vice President; Patricia E. McKelvey, Secretary; Lawrence E. Burks, Treasurer; Donna T. Morris, Assistant Secretary; John S. Ludington, Assistant Treasurer. *Trustees:* David J. Arnold, Martha G. Arnold, Lawrence E. Burks, Ralph A. Cole, John S. Ludington, Patricia E. McKelvey, Donna T. Morris, Charles J. Thrune, Eugene C. Yehle.

Financial data. Data for fiscal year ended December 31, 1993. *Assets:* $31,518,058 (M). *Total grants disbursed:* $1,003,090.

Environmental awards. *Recent grants:* 1993 grants included support for land and water conservation, recycling, and a nature center.

Issues.   Cli   Bio   Lan   Agr   Wat   Oce   Ene   Was   Tox   Pop   Dev
                    •   •   •

Funding analysis.

Fiscal year:	1993
Env grants auth:	$16,000
Number:	3
Range:	$2,000–$10,000
Median:	$4,000
Pct $ auth (env/total):	2

Recipients (1993):	Number:	Dollars:
Chippewa Nature Center	1	10,000
Midland Soil/Water Conservation District	1	4,000
Midland Volunteers for Recycling	1	2,000

Activity region (1993):	Number:	Dollars:
U.S. Great Lakes	3	16,000

Sample grants (1993).
Chippewa Nature Center. Midland, MI. $10,000.
Midland Soil/Water Conservation District. Midland, MI. $4,000.
Midland Volunteers for Recycling. Midland, MI. $2,000.

Application process. *Initial contact:* Letter to include:
1. Project purpose.
2. Major expenditures.
3. Major income sources.
4. Timing requirements.
5. Amount requested.

Attachments:
1. Copy of IRS tax-exempt status determination letter.
2. Organization's latest financial statements.

The trustees hold personal interviews with applicants only on Foundation initiative.
When to apply: Deadline is October of the year prior to that for which funding is desired.
Materials available: Annual report (includes "Application Guidelines").

Emphases. *Recipients:* Educational institutions, nonprofit organizations.

S

Types of support: Continuing support, equipment, facilities, fellowships, general purposes, operating costs, projects, seed money.
Geography: Primarily Midland County, Michigan.

Limitations. *Recipients:* Individuals.
Types of support: Loans, matching funds.

Stroud Foundation

c/o Mellon Bank, N.A.
P.O. Box 7236 AIM 193 0224
Philadelphia, Pennsylvania 19101–7236

Alternate address:
254 Stroud Lane
West Grove, Pennsylvania 19390
Tel: 215–869–9897
EIN: 236255701   Type: Independent
Contact: W. B. Dixon Stroud, Manager

History and philosophy. Joan M. Stroud established the Foundation in 1961.

Officers and directors. *Managers:* Mrs. Joan S. Blaine, T. Sam Means, Esq., W. B. Dixon Stroud, Truman Welling.

Financial data. Data for fiscal year ended December 31, 1992. *Assets:* $3,086,398 (M). *Gifts received:* $58,635. *Total grants disbursed:* $367,900.

Environmental awards. *Recent grants:* 1992 grants included support for land conservation and marine research.

Issues.   Cli   Bio   Lan   Agr   Wat   Oce   Ene   Was   Tox   Pop   Dev
                        •   •

Funding analysis.

Fiscal year:	1992
Env grants disb:	$70,000
Number:	2
Range:	$10,000–$60,000
Median:	$35,000
Pct $ disb (env/total):	19

Recipients (1992):	Number:	Dollars:
Marine Environmental Research Institute	1	60,000
Brandywine Conservancy, Inc.	1	10,000

Activity regions (1992):	Number:	Dollars:
New York/New Jersey	1	60,000
U.S. Mid-Atlantic	1	10,000

Sample grants (1992).
Brandywine Conservancy, Inc. Chadds Ford, PA. $10,000.
Marine Environmental Research Institute. New York, NY. $60,000.

Application process. *Initial contact:* The Foundation awards grants to pre-selected organizations only. No unsolicited applications accepted.

Emphases. *Recipients:* Pre-selected organizations only.

The Morris Stulsaft Foundation

100 Bush Street, Suite 825
San Francisco, California 94104
Tel: 415–986–7117
EIN: 946064379   Type: Independent
Contact: Joan Nelson Dills, Administrator

History and philosophy. The Morris Stulsaft Foundation was established in 1953 as a nonprofit public benefit corporation. It receives its support from the Morris Stulsaft Testamentary Trust, a tax-exempt charitable organization. The Foundation's purpose is to aid and assist needy and deserving children regardless of race, creed, or age. The Foundation supports projects in social services, education, health, arts, and recreation.

Officers and directors. *Officers:* J. Boatner Chamberlain, President; Adele Corvin, Vice President; Raymond Marks, Secretary/Treasurer. *Directors:* Roy L. Bouque, J. Boatner Chamberlain, Adele Corvin, Dorothy S. Corvin, Andrew C. Gaither, Edward A. Miller, Isadore Pivnick, Yori Wada.

Financial data. Data for fiscal year ended December 31, 1992. *Assets:* $139,074 (M). *Gifts received:* $1,067,006. *Total grants disbursed:* $906,580.

Environmental awards. *Recent grants:* 1992 grants included support for environmental education for the primary grades and for low-income youth.

Issues.   Cli   Bio   Lan   Agr   Wat   Oce   Ene   Was   Tox   Pop   Dev
                  •   •   •

Funding analysis.

Fiscal year:	1990	1992
Env grants disb:	$52,560	$30,000
Number:	8	6
Range:	$2,500–$20,000	$2,500–$10,000
Median:	$5,000	$5,000
Pct $ disb (env/total):	5	3

Recipients (1992):	Number:	Dollars:
East Bay Zoological Society	1	10,000
Marine Science Institute	1	5,000
San Jose Conservation Corps	1	5,000
The Trust for Hidden Villa, Inc.	1	5,000
Oakland Unified Schools	1	2,500
Strybing Arboretum & Botanical Gardens	1	2,500

Activity region (1992):	Number:	Dollars:
U.S. West	6	30,000

Sample grants (1992).
East Bay Zoological Society. Oakland, CA. $10,000. To support educational programs; conservation zoomobile, zoo camp, classrooms in school and at zoo.
Marine Science Institute. Redwood City, CA. $5,000. Toward the new building to house the Interpretive Center, a science lab for all ages.
Oakland Unified Schools. Oakland, CA. $2,500. Toward inner city fifth grade classes year-long environmental study and a week at Marin Headlands.
San Jose Conservation Corps. San Jose, CA. $5,000. To help corps members develop a work ethic and marketable skills while doing useful service.
Strybing Arboretum & Botanical Gardens. San Francisco, CA. $2,500. For Children and Gardens: Starting early for inner-city children from K–6th grades.
The Trust for Hidden Villa, Inc. Los Altos Hills, CA. $5,000. To purchase a work truck for farm chores and maintenance tasks.

Application process. *Initial contact:* Request application form. Completed application to include:
1. Detailed budget for project.
2. Current agency budget.
3. Most recent IRS Form 990 including all attached schedules.
4. List of officers, directors, and/or trustees, and occupations.
5. IRS tax-exempt status determination letter.
6. IRS letter classifying organization as 509(a).
7. Franchise Tax Board letter of 23701d exemption.
8. Articles of Incorporation and all amendments.

When to apply: Anytime, but not more than twice in any one year.
Materials available: Biennial report (includes "Grant Application Guidelines," "Grant Application Procedures"), application form.

Emphases. *Recipients:* Nonprofit organizations.
Types of support: Capital expenses, equipment, facilities, operating costs, projects, seed money.
Geography: Six counties in the San Francisco Bay Area: Alameda, Contra Costa, Marin, San Francisco, San Mateo, and Santa Clara.

Limitations. *Recipients:* Individuals, religious organizations.
Activities: Conferences, workshops.
Types of support: Annual campaigns, continuing support, debt retirement, emergency funding, endowments, multi-year grants.

The Sudbury Foundation
278 Old Sudbury Road
Sudbury, Massachusetts 01776
Tel: 508-443-0849   Fax: 508-443-0756
EIN: 046037026   Type: Operating
EGA member
Contact: Derry Tanner, Executive Director

History and philosophy. The Foundation was established in 1952 by Herbert J. and Esther M. Atkinson "to improve the quality of life in Sudbury, Massachusetts" where Mr. Atkinson's business, Sudbury Laboratory, was located. Foundation programs include a Student Aid Program of educational loans and scholarships for local college-bound youth and a Charitable Grants Program supporting nonprofit organizations in Sudbury and surrounding communities. In 1992 the trustees voted to establish a new program of environmental grantmaking not specifically tied to Sudbury.

Officers and directors. *Trustees:* Richard H. Davison, John E. Taft, John E. Arsenault for Mechanics Bank.

Financial data.* Data for fiscal year ended December 31, 1993. *Assets:* $19,025,276 (M). *Total grants disbursed:* $603,413.

*Grants includes scholarships.

Environmental awards. *Program and interests:* "With limited funds available to address complex and interrelated problems, many of global dimensions, the Foundation attempts to respond to those grantmaking opportunities where a modest investment of grant funds can help in a significant way to protect or restore the health and integrity of the environment.

"Applicants are typically based or active in New England, and working on issues of regional or national significance. Projects expected to have an impact beyond their local area of implementation are especially encouraged.

"The Foundation also supports environmental programs of direct benefit to the Sudbury area, including the conservation of ecologically significant parcels of land."

Recent grants: 1993 grants included support for coastal and marine issues, watershed protection, waste management, and environmental education.

Issues. Cli Bio Lan Agr Wat Oce Ene Was Tox Pop Dev
              •   •   •   •   •

Funding analysis.

Fiscal year:	1991	1993
Env grants auth:	$75,000	$100,360
Number:	2	11
Range:	$25,000–$50,000	$860–$20,000
Median:	$37,500	$7,500
Pct $ disb (env/total):	15	17

Recipients (1993 highest):	Number:	Dollars:
Appalachian Mountain Club	1	20,000
Center for Ecological Technology, Inc.	1	20,000
Audubon Society, Maine	1	10,000
Massachusetts Watershed Coalition	1	10,000
The Association for the Preservation of Cape Cod	1	10,000

Activity regions (1993):	Number:	Dollars:
U.S. Northeast	10	95,360
U.S. not specified	1	5,000

Sample grants (1993).
The Association for the Preservation of Cape Cod. Orleans, MA. $10,000. To help support the preparation and publication of a "State of the Cape" report and the convening of a follow-up conference to develop an environmental action agenda.

S

Center for Ecological Technology, Inc. Pittsfield, MA. $20,000 (2 years). For a model Rural Business Management Program which seeks to identify and overcome obstacles to waste reduction, recycling, and the use of secondary materials in the rural business community.

Cetacean Research Unit. Gloucester, MA. $5,000. For the Habitat Protection Project of targeted research and related advocacy to conserve New England's whales and their marine habitat.

Coolidge Center of Environmental Leadership. Cambridge, MA. $5,000. For an expanded Environmental Education Program, which will enable student and community audiences in Eastern Massachusetts to learn more about global environmental problems from a developing world perspective.

Massachusetts Watershed Coalition. Fitchburg, MA. $10,000. For the Massachusetts River and Stream Inventory Project, a statewide collaborative endeavor involving public agencies, watershed associations, and local communities in an effort to develop and use computer maps of riverine features to protect and restore the commonwealth's water resources.

Save the Harbor/Save the Bay. Boston, MA. $7,000. For the Bays Advocacy Project, which will give Save the Harbor/Save the Bay the organizational capacity to speak out more effectively for the protection of Boston Harbor and Massachusetts Bay while at the same time strengthening the agency's base of support.

Application process. *Initial contact:* Telephone call or brief concept paper followed by full proposal to include:
1. Applicant organization.
   - Organization's history, mission, and accomplishments.
   - Major programs and/or services, and numbers of people reached or served.
   - Location and geographic scope.
   - Management and finances, including numbers of staff and volunteers, board of directors, current operating budget showing both revenues and expenses, an audited financial statement (if available), and the most recent Form 990.
   - Copy of IRS tax-exempt status determination letter.
2. Proposed project.
   - Description of project or purpose for which funding is sought, including the rationale, general goals and specific objectives, methods to be used, time frame, and anticipated outcomes or benefits.
   - Evidence that applicant is an appropriate sponsor.
   - Discussion of how project is consistent with Foundation's interests and priorities.
   - Revenue and expense budget for the project, specifying other cash and in-kind support contemplated, requested, or committed (include the source and amount).
   - Evidence that alternate sources of project funding have been tapped or ruled out.
   - Plans for funding after Foundation support has ended.
   - Criteria and process for evaluating the project.
   - Report on results of any previous Sudbury Foundation grants.
3. Cover letter, signed by executive director or board president, and including overall cost of proposed project, amount of funding requested from the Foundation, and brief (1–2 paragraph) project summary.

When to apply: Call for deadlines and dates of grant review meetings.

Materials available: Biennial report (includes "Grant Guidelines" and "Application Procedures").

Emphases. *Recipients:* Nonprofit organizations.
Activities: Advocacy, capacity building, citizen participation, collaborative efforts, demonstration programs, education, innovative programs, planning, policy analysis/development, training.
Types of support: Capital campaigns/expanses, equipment, leveraging funds, loans, matching funds, multi-year grants, pilot projects, program-related investments, seed money, technical assistance.
Geography: Applicants are typically New England-based organizations working on environmental issues of regional or national significance.

Limitations. *Recipients:* Individuals, public agencies.
Activities: Research (medical).
Types of support: Advertising campaigns, annual campaigns, continuing support, debt retirement, fellowships, general purposes, lectureships, maintenance, operating costs, professorships, scholarships.

The Sulzberger Foundation, Inc.
229 West 43rd Street
New York, New York 10036
Tel: 212–556–1750   Fax: 212–556–3847
EIN: 136083166   Type: Independent
Contact: Marian S. Heiskell, President

History and philosophy. The Foundation was established in 1956 by members of the Sulzberger family, owners of *The New York Times*. Funding areas include: environmental organizations, zoos and botanical gardens, the arts, and education.

Officers and directors. *Officers:* Marian S. Heiskell, President; Arthur Ochs Sulzberger, Vice President and Secretary/Treasurer; Ruth S. Holmberg, Judith P. Sulzberger, Vice Presidents; Frederick T. Mason, Assistant Secretary/Treasurer. *Directors:* Marian S. Heiskell, Ruth S. Holmberg, Frederick T. Mason, Arthur Ochs Sulzberger, Judith P. Sulzberger.

Financial data. Data for fiscal year ended December 31, 1992. *Assets:* $21,521,964 (M). *Total grants disbursed:* $1,075,489.

Environmental awards. *Recent grants:* 1992 grants included support for urban environment, land conservation, river and fishery protection, zoos, and botanical gardens.

Issues.   Cli Bio Lan Agr Wat Oce Ene Was Tox Pop Dev
                    •   •   •   •   •

Funding analysis.

Fiscal year:	1991	1992
Env grants disb:	$244,688	$217,550
Number:	32	35
Range:	$100–$64,500	$100–$70,500
Median:	$1,000	$1,000
Pct $ disb (env/total):	24	20

Recipients (1992 highest):	Number:	Dollars:
Council on the Environment of New York City (CENYC)	1	70,500
The New York Botanical Garden	1	21,500
Tennessee River Gorge Trust	1	20,000
National Audubon Society	1	15,000
The Tennessee Aquarium	1	15,000

Activity regions (1992 highest):	Number:	Dollars:
New York/New Jersey	15	125,360
U.S. Southeast	6	47,000
U.S. not specified	5	16,850
U.S. Mid-Atlantic	1	13,500
International*	2	11,340

*Multiple regions or not specified.

Sample grants (1992).
Brooklyn Botanic Garden. Brooklyn, NY. $1,000.
Chattanooga Nature Center. Chattanooga, TN. $1,000.
Friends of the Sea Otter. Carmel, CA. $100.
International Atlantic Salmon Foundation. New York, NY. $2,100.
National Audubon Society. New York, NY. $15,000.
National Fish and Wildlife Foundation. Washington, DC. $250.
The New York Botanical Garden. Bronx, NY. $21,500.
New York Parks and Conservation Association. Albany, NY. $500.
NYZS/The Wildlife Conservation Society. Bronx, NY. $6,960.
Outboard. Morganton, NC. $5,000.
The Parks Council, Inc. New York, NY. $1,000.
Scenic Hudson, Inc. Poughkeepsie, NY. $250.
Tennessee River Gorge Trust. Chattanooga, TN. $20,000.

Application process. *Initial contact:* Telephone call or proposal letter.
When to apply: Anytime.

Emphases. *Activities:* Conferences, education, seminars.
Types of support: Annual campaigns, capital campaigns/expanses, continuing support, emergency funding, endowments, equipment, facilities, fellowships, general purposes, internships, lectureships, operating costs, pilot projects, professorships, program-related investments, scholarships, seed money, technical assistance.
Geography: New York; Chattanooga, Tennessee.

Limitations. *Recipients:* Individuals.
Types of support: Loans, matching funds.

The Summerlee Foundation

5956 Sherry Lane, Suite 1414
Dallas, Texas 75225
Tel: 214-363-9000   Fax: 214-363-1941
EIN: 758314010   Type: Independent
EGA member
Contact: Melanie A. Roberts, Program Director

History and philosophy. The Summerlee Foundation was established in 1988 by Dallas philanthropist Annie Lee Roberts. It makes for two purposes: (1) to alleviate fear, pain, and suffering of animals at the hands of humans and from natural disasters, and to promote animal protection and the prevention of cruelty to animals; and (2) to research, promote, preserve, and document all facets of Texas history.

Officers and directors. *Officers:* Judge David D. Jackson, Chairman and President; John W. Crain, Vice President; Melanie A. Roberts, Secretary. *Directors:* John W. Crain, Pat Davis, David D. Jackson, Melanie A. Roberts, Ron Tyler.

Financial data. Data for fiscal year ended June 30, 1993. *Assets:* $16,784,676 (M). *Gifts received:* $490,500. *Total grants authorized:* $462,907.

Environmental awards. *Program and interests:* The Foundation makes environmental grants within its Animals program. It takes special interest in projects through which the humane movement and the environmental movement can work together.

Issues.   Cli   Bio   Lan   Agr   Wat   Oce   Ene   Was   Tox   Pop   Dev
                     •   •

Funding analysis.

Fiscal year:	1992	1993
Env grants auth:	$119,950	$65,886
Number:	13	17
Range:	$3,250–$20,000	$1,000–$10,000
Median:	$10,000	$2,500
Pct $ auth (env/total):	22	15

Recipients (1993 highest):	Number:	Dollars:
The Association of Sanctuaries	1	10,000
Zoo Conservation Outreach Group	1	8,000
Defenders of Wildlife	1	7,500
Earth Island Institute	1	7,500
Fund for Animals	1	5,000

Activity regions (1993 highest):	Number:	Dollars:
U.S. not specified	2	17,500
U.S. South Central	5	16,260
International*	2	10,443
U.S. West	2	7,500
U.S. Mountain	3	7,183

*Multiple regions or not specified.

Sample grants (1993).
Defenders of Wildlife. Washington, DC. $7,500. Public education campaign to help protect endangered vaquita and totoaba.
Friends of Animals. Norwalk, CT. $2,500. Continued support for Ghana's anti-poaching program.
Forest Guardians. Santa Fe, NM. $2,500. Wildlife Protection Campaign.
Grounded Eagle Foundation. Condon, MT. $1,000. To help fund construction of a facility for rehabilitating eagles.
Mountain Lion Foundation. Sacramento, CA. $2,500. Anti-Poaching Campaign called "Crimes Against the Wild" to stop the slaughter of wildlife for illegal profit in California.
The Sierra Club, Lone Star Chapter. Austin, TX. $2,260. The Texas Mountain Lion Education Project.
Species Survival Commission. Brookfield, IL. $2,000. Support for the protection of Zimbabwean rhinos.

Application process. *Initial contact:* Full proposal signed by applicant organization's CEO, to include:
1. Description of organization.
   - Brief organizational history.
   - Statement of goals and purposes.
   - List of board of trustees and officers.
   - Most recent audited financial statement, if any.
2. Detailed project description.
   - Vitae of key personnel.
   - Project schedule.
   - Project budget.
   - Plan for project completion.
3. Copy of IRS tax-exempt status determination letter and copy of most recent IRS Form 990.

When to apply: Anytime. The board of directors meets bi-monthly.
Materials available: "Grant Application Information."

Emphases. *Recipients:* Educational institutions, museums, non-profit organizations.
Activities: Activism, advocacy, audiovisual materials, collaborative efforts, conferences, education, exhibits, fieldwork, fundraising, innovative programs, land acquisition, media projects, networking, publications, research (scholarly/scientific), seminars, technical assistance, training, workshops.
Types of support: Capital campaigns/expenses, computer hardware, emergency funding, equipment, facilities, lectureships, matching funds, membership campaigns, technical assistance.
Geography: Texas.

Limitations. *Recipients:* Individuals.
Types of support: Loans.

The Summit Foundation

1120 19th Street, N.W., Suite 550
Washington, DC 20036
Tel: 202–785–1724   Fax: 202–857–0025
EIN: 521743817   Type: Independent
EGA member
Contact: Victoria P. Sant, President

History and philosophy. "Established in 1991, The Summit Foundation encourages, supports, and funds innovative programs, projects, and organizations that have the potential to enhance global sustainability." The Foundation is currently concerned with population stabilization and environmental sustainability, and supports programs which encourage family planning and education in both developed and developing countries.

The Foundation gives preference to programs, projects, and organizations that are: innovative, catalytic, high-leverage, and replicable; express a global vision and impact; embody the principles and values of excellence and integrity; promote inclusion and partnership rather than division and confrontation; demonstrate strong leadership, management, and financial accountability; require initial seed money, yet have a clear potential to attract additional long-term support from other sources.

Officers and directors. *Officers:* Roger W. Sant, Chairman and Treasurer; Victoria P. Sant, President; Kristin W. Sant, Vice President; Alexis G. Sant, Secretary. *Directors:* Alexis G. Sant, Alison E. Sant, Kristin W. Sant, Michael J. Sant, Roger W. Sant, Shari L. Sant, Victoria P. Sant.

Financial data. *Total 1992 grants disbursed:* $348,500.

Environmental awards. *Program and interests:* Primary areas of environmental interest:

- Strengthening the use of market-based mechanisms to shift energy production to more environmentally benign systems.
- Demonstrating that economic success can best be achieved through investments in energy-efficient technologies.
- Encouraging a positive and supportive relationship between the industrial sector and organizations focused on environ-mental sustainability.
- Finding ways to compare and prioritize environmental risks.

Other interests:

- Programs in both the developed and developing world that enable individuals to control their own reproductive lives by providing universal access to safe, effective, voluntary family planning.
- Family planning activities in those countries where births are greater than one million per year, and where such activities are politically feasible.
- Initiatives that increase awareness among decisionmakers about the relationships of rapid population growth and environmental degradation.

Issues. Cli Bio Lan Agr Wat Oce Ene Was Tox Pop Dev
•   •   •   •   •   •   •   •

Sample grants.*
Aspen Institute. Washington, DC. For its program on public policy issues in energy and resources.
The Balaton Group. Hanover, NH. For an international association of scientists, teachers, and managers concerned with sustaining the long-term productivity of the world's resources and environment.
Environmental Defense Fund. Washington, DC. For studying methods of using marketable offsets to reduce global greenhouse gases.
Environmental and Energy Study Institute. Washington, DC. For its work to influence national policy on energy, groundwater protection, and global climate change.
Stanford University. Stanford, CA. To establish a program in Washington, D.C. designed to encourage undergraduates to study environmental problems and devote their professional lives to resolving them.
World Wildlife Fund. Washington, DC. To support innovative financing options to stimulate conservation.

*Year(s) of award and dollar amounts not available.

Application process. *Initial contact:* Telephone call or short letter of inquiry. Unsolicited proposals generally not accepted.
Materials available: Informational brochure.

Emphases. *Recipients:* Nonprofit organizations, pre-selected organizations.
Activities: Demonstration programs.
Types of support: Seed money.

Surdna Foundation, Inc.
1155 Avenue of the Americas, 16th Floor
New York, New York 10036
Tel: 212–730–0030   Fax: 212–391–4384
EIN: 136108163   Type: Independent
EGA member
Contacts: Edward Skloot, Executive Director
         Hooper Brooks, Program Officer for the Environment

History and philosophy. Surdna is a family foundation established in 1917 by John E. Andrus (d. 1934), whose businesses included gold, oil, timber, and real estate.

The Foundation maintains a longstanding interest in a children's home in Yonkers, New York and a retirement home in Hastings-on-Hudson, New York. About half of its annual distribution goes to these institutions. The other half of Surdna's distribution goes to two programs: Community Revitalization and the Environment.

Officers and directors. *Officers:* Peter B. Benedict, Chairman; Samuel S. Thorpe III, President; Lawrence S. C. Griffith, M.D., Vice President; John J. Lynagh, Secretary; Frederick F. Moon III, Treasurer. *Chairman Emeritus:* John E. Andrus III. *Directors:* John E. Andrus III, Julia A. Aubry, Peter B. Benedict, Christopher F. Davenport, Lawrence S. C. Griffith, Sandra T. Kaupe, Elizabeth Andrus Kelly, John J. Lynagh, Frederick F. Moon III, Edith D. Thorpe, Samuel S. Thorpe III.

Financial data. Data for fiscal year ended June 30, 1993. *Assets:* $354,728,991 (M). *Total grants authorized:* $11,175,618. *Program grants authorized:* $9,683,000.

Environmental awards. *Program and interests:* Surdna's goals are to prevent irreversible damage to the environment; support government, private, and voluntary actions that will produce a sustainable environment; and foster a population of environmentally informed, responsible, activist citizens.

Toward these ends the Foundation has selected three program themes for primary attention:

- Biological and Cultural Diversity.
  - Translating scientific concerns and findings into public policy.
  - Cataloging and demonstrating the value of biological and cultural diversity
  - Promoting public policies that ensure species preservation.
  - Creating programs that raise broad public awareness of these issues.
- Energy and Transportation.
  - Analyzing governmental policies and subsidies regarding the automobile and fostering alternative solutions to it.
  - Strengthening efforts to improve public policy and regulation in transportation and energy that produce locally sensitive solutions.
  - Supporting grassroots education and leadership.
  - Advancing consumer choice in the marketplace.
- Restoring the Environment in Urban and Suburban Areas.
  - Enhancing the participation of local communities through education, planning, and advocacy.
  - Encouraging governments and the private sector to promote responsible, cost-effective actions in transportation, open space planning, physical development, and energy use.
  - Supporting programs that foster open space, parkland creation, urban conservation, and livability.
  - Creating leadership programs that stimulate environmental awareness.
  - Communicating successful programs to other interested constituencies.

Issues. Cli Bio Lan Agr Wat Oce Ene Was Tox Pop Dev
            •   •   •   •   •   •   •   •

Funding analysis.

Fiscal year:	1992	1993
Env grants auth:	$4,553,000	$5,293,000
Number:	48	65
Range:	$15,000–$300,000	$20,000–$350,000
Median:	$72,500	$50,000
Pct $ auth (env/total):	27	47

Recipients (1993 highest):	Number:	Dollars:
National Religious Partnership for the Environment	1	350,000
NY/NJ/CT Transportation Campaign	1	350,000
Conservation Law Foundation	1	200,000
Transportation Legal Task Force	1	200,000
National Audubon Society	2	160,000
Rocky Mountain Institute	1	160,000
We Can	1	160,000

Activity regions (1993 highest):	Number:	Dollars:
U.S. not specified	23	2,240,000
New York/New Jersey	11	1,112,000
U.S. Northeast	11	688,000
U.S. Southeast	4	275,000
U.S. Northwest	6	263,000

Sample grants (1993).
Center for Neighborhood Technology. Chicago, IL. $100,000. For a leadership development, research, citizen action, and demonstration program to achieve transportation reform for the Chicago region which is both environmentally sound and socially equitable.
Center for Resource Economics. Washington, DC. $150,000. Continued support for a program to analyze the U.S. Environmental Protection Agency's annual budget and appropriations process and use the analysis to make the EPA more effective in protecting and improving environmental quality.
Endangered Species Coalition/National Audubon Society. Washington, DC. $60,000. To broaden grassroots support for endangered species protection and to reinforce the Endangered Species Act.

S

Environmental Defense Fund. New York, NY. $100,000. For a task force of six large corporate consumers of paper to use their purchasing power and assist the paper industry to make products that are better for the environment.

New England Wild Flower Society. Framingham, MA. $75,000 (2 years). To help implement the first systematic, comprehensive regional plant conservation program in the country.

1000 Friends of Oregon. Portland, OR. $48,000. To analyze how the national dissemination of a computerized planning process (LUTRAQ), which integrates land use, transportation, and air quality considerations, can be extended to other jurisdictions and be made self-supporting.

Pacific Forest Trust. Boonville, CA. $100,000 (2 years). Start-up grant for a group doing research, analysis, and education on how the private sector can use principles of sustainable forestry in its own economic interest.

Rocky Mountain Institute. Old Snowmass, CO. $160,000. Partial support for four components of RMI's program: to apply state-of-the-art technical knowledge to electric efficiency for low-income households; demonstrate a design approach yielding profitable, aesthetically pleasing and environmentally sound buildings; refine and build support for production of a supercar; and develop a book that integrates RMI's diverse environmental contributions.

World Wildlife Fund. Washington, DC. $50,000. To support involvement in the media and advocacy elements of a campaign by the Marine Fish Conservation Network to increase public awareness about, and press for sustainable management of, our nation's fisheries.

Yosemite Restoration Trust. San Francisco, CA. $40,000. To provide a third year of support for the Trust in its challenge to the concessions policies at Yosemite National Park.

Application process. *Initial contact:* Letter of inquiry (2–3 pages) to include:
1. Information about applicant organization's purposes and specific activities.
2. Brief description of program for which funds are being sought, including time period to be covered and principal outcome(s) expected.
3. Budget for proposed program and organization and amount requested from the Foundation.
4. Funding received to date for program, as well as sources from whom funding is being sought.
5. Most recent audited financial statements of organization and its operating subsidiaries, if any.
6. Names and qualifications of key personnel who will be responsible for program.
7. Copy of IRS tax-exempt status determination letter.

When to apply: Anytime. Grantmaking cycle is three times a year, in September, February, and May.
Materials available: Annual report (includes "Application Procedures").

Emphases. *Recipients:* Nonprofit organizations.
Activities: Advocacy, capacity building, collaborative efforts, fieldwork, innovative programs, planning, political activities, technical assistance.
Types of support: Continuing support, general purposes, leveraging funds, multi-year grants, pilot projects, seed money, technical assistance.
Geography: United States only, with a national focus.

Limitations. *Recipients:* Individuals.
Types of support: Capital campaigns/expenses, computer hardware, debt retirement, emergency funding, endowments, equipment, facilities, fellowships, lectureships, loans, membership campaigns, mortgage reduction, professorships, program-related investments, scholarships, travel expenses.

SURFREE
c/o Co-op America
1850 M Street, N.W., Suite 700
Washington, DC 20036
Tel: 202–872–5339   Fax: 202–331–8166
EIN: 237087207   Type: Independent
EGA member
Contact: Jeff Barber, Executive Director

History and philosophy. Surfree was established in 1970 in New York by Elizabeth Morse and John W. Morse and is a member of the Environmental Grantmakers Association.

Officers and directors. *Trustees:* Elizabeth Morse, John W. Morse.

Financial data. Data for fiscal year ended December 31, 1990. *Assets:* $630,234 (M). *Gifts received:* $1,465. *Total grants disbursed:* $26,507.

Application process. *Initial contact:* No applications are being accepted at this time.

Edna Bailey Sussman Fund
8072 Irish Mist Lane
Manlius, New York 13104–2500
Tel: 315–470–6599   Fax: 315–470–6779
EIN: 133187064   Type: Independent
EGA member
Contact: Robert H. Frey, Trustee

History and philosophy. In 1983 the will of Margaret Sussman established a trust with the net income to be distributed "to further the preservation of wildlife, the control of pollution, and the preservation of natural land and resources by funding internships . . . at institutions of higher learning in an area that significantly impacts upon the environment." Since 1985 the Fund has supported graduate students at pre-selected colleges and universities participating in internships in the environmental field.

Officers and directors. *Trustees:* Robert H. Frey, Edward S. Miller.

Financial data. Data for fiscal year ended April 30, 1993. *Assets:* $4,079,887 (M). *Total grants disbursed:* $207,013.

Environmental awards. *Program and interests:* The Fund has no stated preference for a particular environmental topic.

Recent grants: In the past the Fund has supported internships dealing with land use, water resources, wildlife and fisheries, waste management, environmental regulations and policy, and ecology.

Issues. Cli Bio Lan Agr Wat Oce Ene Was Tox Pop Dev
　　　　　　•　•　　•　•　　　•　•

Funding analysis.

Fiscal year:	1991*	1992**
Env grants disb:	$175,000	$197,828
Number:	62	9
Range:	$1,000–$4,000	$570–$40,037
Mean:	2,506	$21,300
Pct $ disb (env/total):	100	100

*Reflects number of students receiving awards.
**Reflects number of institutions receiving grants.

Recipients (1992 highest):	*Number:*	*Dollars:*
Duke University, School of Forestry	1	40,037
VPI & State University	1	36,500
SUNY, College of Environmental Science & Forestry	1	32,553
Cornell University	1	22,473
Colorado School of Mines	1	21,300

Activity regions (1992 highest):	*Number:*	*Dollars:*
New York/New Jersey	2	55,026
U.S. Southeast	1	40,037
U.S. Mountain	2	37,525
U.S. Mid-Atlantic	2	37,070
U.S. Great Lakes	1	20,170

Sample grants (1993).*

Colorado School of Mines. Golden, CO. $46,058.
Cornell University. Cornell, NY. $18,692.
Duke University, School of Forestry. Raleigh, NC. $21,648.
SUNY, College of Environmental Science & Forestry. Syracuse, NY. $37,035.
University of Colorado Foundation. Boulder, CO. $8,916.
University of Michigan. Ann Arbor, MI. $11,675.
Vanderbilt University, Center for Health Services. Nashville, TN. $4,360.
VPI and State University. Blacksburg, VA. $38,314.
Yale University, School of Forestry and Environmental Studies. New Haven, CT. $16,596.

*Each sample grant is similar to a recent Sussman fellowship.

Application process. *Initial contact:* Full proposal to be submitted through participating colleges and universities. At present these include: Colorado School of Mines, Cornell University, Duke University, Oregon State University, Pennsylvania State University School of Forest Resources, SUNY College of Environmental Science and Forestry, SUNY at Purchase, University of Michigan School of Natural Resources, Vanderbilt University, Virginia Polytechnic Institute and State University, Yale University School of Forestry and Environmental Studies. No new universities are being solicited at this time. Proposal (2 copies) to include:

1. Application cover page (from Fund).
2. Statement of applicant. Description of internship work and how it contributes to career goals (2–3 pages).
3. Letter from faculty sponsor. Addressed to the Fund indicating agreement with internship plan, credit hours assigned, and the suitability of the internship for overall plan of study.
4. Letter. On official stationery from immediate supervisor of the organization accepting you for the internship.
5. Budget. Start date, end date, number of weeks in all, and final amount requested. The Fund supports internships at $6.50/hr for a 35-hour work week. Contact Dr. Sanders on whether other items, such as travel and equipment, might be included and submit total.
6. ESF graduate transcript. Current course registration if not included.
7. Undergraduate transcript(s).
8. Resume or curriculum vitae.

When to apply: Deadlines are March 15 for work commencing in summer, June 15 for work commencing during fall semester, and October 15 for spring semester.

Materials available: Application cover page and application guidelines.

Emphases. *Recipients:* Graduate students enrolled at pre-selected colleges and universities.
Activities: Research.
Types of support: Internships.
Geography: United States.

Limitations. *Activities:* Lobbying.

The Switzer Foundation

c/o New Hampshire Charitable Foundation
37 Pleasant Street
Concord, New Hampshire 03301–4005
Tel: 603–225–6641   Fax: 603–225–4700
EGA member
Contact: Judith Burrows, Director of Student Aid Programs

Alternate application address:
The San Francisco Foundation
685 Market Street, Suite 910
San Francisco, California 94105–9716
Tel: 415–495–3100

History and philosophy. The Switzer Foundation was established in the mid-1980s by the Switzer family, founders of an Ohio chemical company that produced fluorescent chemicals and that later became Day-Glo Color Corporation. "In 1985 the newly formed Switzer Foundation focused its grantmaking activity on fellowships for graduate technical training of environmentalists, a need which became clear through the family background in the chemical industry. As the program expanded, the initial focus matured to include the identification and financial support of future environmental leaders and the encouragement of non-technical interdisciplinary environmentalists in their graduate training." The Fellowship Program gives one-year grants to scholars studying in California or New England. It is administered in California by The San Francisco Foundation and in New England by the New Hampshire Charitable Foundation (NHCF), a statewide community foundation.

S

The Foundation recently announced its new Environmental Leadership Grants program, designed to develop leadership and improve the effectiveness of environmental organizations in New England. Administered through the New Hampshire Charitable Foundation (NHCF), it has two components: NHCF grants to environmental organizations associated with Switzer Fellows, and small NHCF grants to individual Switzer Fellows. Both components of the Environmental Leadership Grants Program apply to individuals who have already received Switzer Fellowships for their graduate studies.

Officers and directors. *Trustees:* Lincoln Reavis, Ann Switzer Sander, Fred Switzer, Marge Switzer, Patricia Switzer, Paul Switzer, Robert Switzer.

Financial data. Data for fiscal year ended December 31, 1992. *Total grants authorized:* $385,000.

Environmental awards. *Program and interests:* The Foundation offers two programs:

- Switzer Fellowships.

  One-year, $10,000 scholarships for "highly qualified scholars planning graduate studies in California or New England directed toward the reduction or prevention of air, water, or soil pollution or the restoration of polluted resources."

- Environmental Leadership Grants to Organizations (New England only).

  "To facilitate the entry of Switzer Fellows into the public sector, and to give nonprofit organizations, educational institutions, and government agencies greater access to technical and scientific expertise." One-year grants of $3,000 to $15,000 are available for project support. Multi-year grants of up to $50,000 are available for major new project initiatives or to organizations proposing to add a Switzer Fellow to their permanent staff.

Issues. Cli • Bio • Lan • Agr • Wat • Oce • Ene • Was • Tox • Pop • Dev •

Funding analysis.

Fiscal year:	1991	1993
Env grants auth:	$362,845	$399,295
Number:	32	34
Range:	$10,000–$23,875	$7,956–$30,000
Median:	$10,000	$10,000
Pct $ auth (env/total):	100	100

Recipients (1993 highest):	Number:	Dollars:
Collaboration of Community Foundations/Greater Piscataqua Community Foundation	1	30,000
Massachusetts Audubon Society	1	25,000
Appalachian Mountain Club	1	23,000
Harvard University, School of Public Health	1	15,339
Massachusetts Division of Energy Resources	1	15,000

Activity regions (1993):	Number:	Dollars:
U.S. Northeast	19	249,295
U.S. West	15	150,000

Sample grants (1993).*

Appalachian Mountain Club. Boston, MA. $23,000. Switzer Fellow: Kathleen Fallon. Second year support for staff hydrologist within the AMC Research Department.

Harvard University, School of Public Health. Roxbury, MA. $15,339. Switzer fellow: Alison Taylor. To support research and remediation of contaminants in New Bedford Harbor. Management at the University of California at Berkeley.

Massachusetts Audubon Society. Lincoln, MA. $25,000. Switzer Fellow: Peter Vickery. Second year support for avian ecologist to implement an endangered bird conservation program.

The Nature Conservancy, New Hampshire Field Office. Concord, NH. $7,956. Switzer Fellow: Patrick McCarthy. Third year support to establish a preserve design and development program.

*Sample grants represent either new awards or disbursements on grants awarded in previous years.

Application process. *Initial contact:* Contact The San Francisco Foundation (for Fellowship applicants in California only) or the New Hampshire Charitable Foundation. Procedures differ for each program.

When to apply: See guidelines for individual programs.

Materials available: Switzer Foundation Environmental Fellowships (brochure), *Environmental Fellowship Program Directory* (annual publication), "Environmental Leadership Grants" (includes application guidelines).

Emphases. *Recipients: For Fellowships:* U.S. citizens who have completed at least one semester of environmental science at the graduate level. They may include scientists, engineers, or environmentalists who are policymakers, economists, writers, lawyers, or others.

For Leadership Grants: Nonprofit organizations, public agencies, and educational institutions for projects that will substantially involve a Switzer Foundation Fellow.

Activities: For Fellowships: Graduate studies.

For Leadership Grants: Demonstration programs, policy analysis/development, projects with potential for early application to critical New England environmental problems, technical assistance.

Types of support: For Fellowships: One-year fellowships for graduate studies.

For Leadership Grants: Project support, including salaries and benefits, consulting fees, travel expenses and materials.

Geography: For Fellowships: California or New England.
For Leadership Grants: New England.

Limitations. *Activities:* Projects not involving Switzer Fellows.
Types of support: Capital projects, equipment.

Nelson Talbott Foundation

1422 Euclid Avenue, Suite 1044
Cleveland, Ohio 44115
Tel: 216–696–8211   Fax: 216–696–8212
EIN: 316039441   Type: Independent
Contact: Nelson S. Talbott, Trustee

History and philosophy. This family foundation was established in 1947 by Nelson S. Talbott. Funding is given in the areas of: cultural programming, the environment, social services, and wildlife conservation.

Officers and directors. *Trustees:* Malvin Banks, Josephine L. Talbott, Nelson S. Talbott.

Financial data. Data for fiscal year ended September 30, 1993. *Assets:* $1,762,463 (M). *Total grants disbursed:* $25,726.

Environmental awards. *Recent grants:* 1993 grants included support for wilderness, national parks, wildlife conservation, species preservation, and environmental career development.

Issues. Cli Bio• Lan• Agr Wat• Oce Ene Was• Tox Pop• Dev•

Funding analysis.

Fiscal year:	1991	1993
Env grants disb:	$15,425	$9,811
Number:	25	27
Range:	$20–$5,000	$25–$5,000
Median:	$125	$100
Pct $ disb (env/total):	35	38

Recipients (1993 highest):	Number:	Dollars:
World Wildlife Fund	1	5,000
Cleveland Zoological Society	1	800
The Wilds	1	606
The Nature Conservancy, Ohio Field Office	2	550
Environmental Defense Fund	1	500
Environmental Law Institute	1	500

Activity regions (1993):	Number:	Dollars:
U.S. not specified	12	7,325
U.S. Great Lakes	10	2,331
Alaska	1	50
New York/New Jersey	1	30
U.S. Northeast	1	25
U.S. Northwest	1	25
U.S. South Central	1	25

Sample grants (1993).
Bat Conservation International. Austin, TX. $25.
Cleveland Zoological Society. Cleveland, OH. $800.
The Environmental Careers Organization, Inc. Boston, MA. $250.
Environmental Defense Fund. New York, NY. $500.
Environmental Law Institute. Washington, DC. $500.
Global Tomorrow Coalition. Washington, DC. $250.
Kirtlandia Society. Cleveland, OH. $25.
National Audubon Society. New York, NY. $150.
The Nature Conservancy, Ohio Field Office. Columbus, OH. $500.
Peregrine Fund, Inc. Boise, ID. $25.
Trout Unlimited, Inc. Vienna, VA. $100.
Trustees for Alaska. Anchorage, AK. $50.
The Wilds. Columbus, OH. $606.
World Wildlife Fund. Washington, DC. $5,000.

Application process. *Initial contact:* Letter of inquiry. *When to apply:* Anytime.

Emphases. *Geography:* Cleveland, Ohio.

Limitations. *Recipients:* Individuals.

S. Mark Taper Foundation

12011 San Vicente Boulevard, Suite 401
Los Angeles, California 90049
Tel: 310–476–5543   Fax: 213–471–4993
EIN: 954245076   Type: Independent
Contact: Janice Anne Lazarof, Director

History and philosophy. S. Mark Taper established the Foundation in 1989 to "support a better quality of life." Funding priorities include arts, the disadvantaged, education, environment, and family and housing issues.

Officers and directors. *Officers:* Janice Anne Lazarof, President; Cynthia Bolker, Vice President; Amelia Taper Stabler, Secretary; Deborah Taper Ringel, Treasurer/CFO. *Director:* Janice Anne Lazarof.

Financial data. Data for fiscal year ended December 31, 1993. *Assets:* $5,574,959 (M). *Gifts received:* $750,000. *Total grants disbursed:* $205,000.

Environmental awards. *Recent grants:* 1993 grants included support for environmental education.

Issues. Cli Bio Lan Agr Wat Oce Ene Was• Tox Pop Dev

Funding analysis.

Fiscal year:	1993
Env grants disb:	$6,000
Number:	2
Range:	$2,500–$3,500
Median:	$3,000
Pct $ disb (env/total):	3

Recipients (1993):	Number:	Dollars:
Earth Action Network, Inc.	1	3,500
Nursery Nature Walks	1	2,500

Activity regions (1993):	Number:	Dollars:
U.S. not specified	1	3,500
U.S. West	1	2,500

Sample grants (1993).
Earth Action Network, Inc. Norwalk, CT. $3,500.
Nursery Nature Walks. Santa Monica, CA. $2,500.

Application process. *Initial contact:* Letter of inquiry (3 pages) signed by an officer of the organization, to include:
Organizational background.
  1. Name of organization.
  2. Date of founding.
  3. Location.
  4. Region of focus.
  5. Name(s) and brief description of the founder(s).
  6. Affiliations with other organizations.
Proposed project.
  1. Specifically describe the project's purpose.
  2. Intended results.
  3. Duration.
  4. Amount of funds requested.
  5. Sources of funds already received.
  6. Estimate of total anticipated costs.
Documentation.
  1. IRS tax-exempt status determination letter.
  2. Most recent financial statement and current status of fundraising results.
When to apply: Anytime.
Materials available: "Grant Application Procedure," application form.

Emphases. *Recipients:* Nonprofit organizations.
Types of support: General purposes, projects, seed money.
Geography: Primarily California.

Limitations. *Recipients:* Individuals.

The Telesis Foundation
Pacific Telesis Center
130 Kearney Street, Room 3351
San Francisco, California 94108
Tel: 415–394–3769 Fax: 415–362–8605
EIN: 942950832 Type: Company-sponsored
Contact: Jere Jacobs, President

History and philosophy. Pacific Telesis Foundation was created in 1984 by the Pacific Telesis Group (PTG), a diversified telecommunications corporation with headquarters in San Francisco. Subsidiaries include Pacific Bell, Nevada Bell, and various companies that market telecommunications products and services in the United States and abroad.

In April 1994, Pacific Telesis Foundation was dissolved and replaced by two new foundations. The Telesis Foundation will continue with the PTG companies. Pacific Bell and Nevada Bell also manage their own separate contributions programs. The Telesis Foundation currently has three program areas: Arts and Culture, Community, and Education. Education is its primary focus.

Officers and directors. *Officers:* Phil Quigley, Chairman; Jere Jacobs, President.

Financial data. Data for fiscal year ended 1992. *Assets:* $68,750,000 (M). *Gifts received:* $1,041,135. *Total grants disbursed:* $7,987,570.

Environmental awards. *Recent grants:* 1993 grants included support for urban environment and a zoo.

Issues. Cli Bio Lan Agr Wat Oce Ene Was Tox Pop Dev
             •

Funding analysis.

Fiscal year:	1993
Env grants disb:	$55,000
Number:	2
Range:	$5,000–$50,000
Median:	$27,500
Pct $ disb (env/total):	1

Recipients (1993):	*Number:*	*Dollars:*
San Francisco Clean City Coalition	1	50,000
East Bay Zoological Society	1	5,000

Activity region (1993):	*Number:*	*Dollars:*
U.S. West	2	55,000

Sample grants (1993).
East Bay Zoological Society. Oakland, CA. $5,000. To support the Discovery Kit Educational Program at the Oakland Zoo.
San Francisco Clean City Coalition. San Francisco, CA. $50,000. To support 1993 activities and matching grants.

Application process. *Initial contact:* Brief letter of intent to include:
  1. Brief description of organization.
  2. Project description.
  3. Financial resources needed to complete the project.
Full proposal to include:
  1. Project description, including specific goals.
  2. Plan to evaluate project success.
  3. Description of how support would be recognized.
  4. Copy of IRS tax-exempt status determination letter.
  5. Copy of organization's most recent financial statement and most recent federal tax return (Form 990-PF).
  6. List of organization's board of directors, including their business, government, and educational affiliations.
  7. List of current funding sources and their funding levels.
When to apply: Anytime. The board meets quarterly.
Materials available: Annual report (includes "Application Procedures").

Emphases. *Recipients:* Nonprofit organizations.
Activities: Education.
Geography: California, Nevada.

Limitations. *Recipients:* Educational institutions (private K–12, public) individuals, religious organizations.
Activities: Research (medical).
Types of support: Capital campaigns/expenses, emergency funding, endowments, general purposes, loans, operating costs.

Texaco Foundation

2000 Westchester Avenue
White Plains, New York 10650
Tel: 914-253-4150 Fax: 914-253-4655
EIN: 237063751 Type: Company-sponsored
Contact: Maria Mike-Mayer, Secretary

History and philosophy. The Foundation was established in 1979. It operates under the belief that "a focal point of Texaco's commitment to good corporate citizenship is to enhance the quality of life wherever the company operates throughout the world." Interests include civic and public interests, health care, and social welfare, with "an intensified focus" on the arts, education, and the environment—areas designated as long-range priorities.

Officers and directors. *Officers:* J. Brademas, Chairman; Carl B. Davidson, President; Maria Mike-Mayer, Secretary; Robert W. Ulrich, Treasurer; George Eaton, Comptroller.

Financial data. Data for fiscal year ended December 31, 1993. *Assets:* $12,000,000 (U) (est.). *Total grants disbursed:* $11,831,399.

Environmental awards. *Program and interests:* The company has a "commitment to preserve and protect our natural resources through applied science, technology, and research," consistent with the "concept of sustainable growth; that is, the ability to balance natural, human, and material resources in ways that support the economic health of society while protecting the environment." Particular interests include:

- Scientific and scholarly research.
  - Global climate policy.
  - Air quality modeling.
  - Risk analysis.
  - Health and safety.
  - Tropical rainforest reforestation.
  - Soil bioremediation.

- Youth education.
  - Grants to inspire in young people an appreciation and respect for the environment. These grants range from providing opportunities for children to be exposed to natural and environmental sciences, to providing specialized training for their teachers.

Issues. Cli Bio Lan Agr Wat Oce Ene Was Tox Pop Dev
 •   •   •   •   •   •   •   •   •

Funding analysis.

Fiscal year:	1991	1993
Env grants auth:	$714,500	$828,000
Number:	38	41
Range:	$1,000–$250,000	$1,000–$150,000
Median:	$5,000	$7,500
Pct $ disb (env/total):	8	7

Recipients (1993 highest):	Number:	Dollars:
University of Notre Dame, Center for Bioengineering & Pollution Control	1	150,000
American Forests	1	100,000
The New York Botanical Garden	1	100,000
Marine Biological Laboratory	1	60,000
Harvard University, Center for Risk Analysis	1	50,000

Activity regions (1993 highest):	Number:	Dollars:
U.S. not specified	7	175,000
New York/New Jersey	7	150,000
U.S. Great Lakes	1	150,000
U.S. Northeast	3	111,000
U.S. West	11	98,500

Sample grants (1993).
Alliance to Save Energy. Washington, DC. $5,000.
American Forests. Washington, DC. $100,000. Urban tree research.
Americans for Energy Independence. Washington, DC. $5,000.
Cabrillo Marine Museum Volunteers, Inc. San Pedro, CA. $12,000.
Central Park Conservancy. New York, NY. $100,000.
Environmental Law Institute. Washington, DC. $5,000.
Friends of the Channel Islands National Park. Ventura, CA. $5,000.
Harvard University, Center for Risk Analysis. Cambridge, MA. $50,000.
Hudson River Museum. Yonkers, NY. $10,000.
International Bird Rescue and Research Center. Berkeley, CA. $10,000.
The Jefferson Energy Foundation. Washington, DC. $10,000.
Kern Environmental Education Program. Bakersfield, CA. $5,000.
Louisiana Nature and Science Center. New Orleans, LA. $25,000.
New York University. Tuxedo, NY. $20,000. Norton Nelson Institute for Environmental Medicine.

Application process. *Initial contact:* Full proposal to include:
1. Cover letter.
   - Brief project description, including objectives and timetable.
   - Specific reason(s) you consider the Foundation an appropriate donor.
   - Amount requested, prior history of funding or assistance from the Foundation, and why the organization considers Texaco Foundation an appropriate donor.
   - Description of how the organization will acknowledge the Foundation's support.
2. Project and organizational budget, listing additional sources of funding.
3. Size and composition of population served by the project.
4. Explanation of how the project is unique in its region.
5. Method of evaluation.
6. Organization's purpose and objectives.
7. List of names and primary professional affiliations of board of trustees.
8. Copy of IRS tax-exempt status determination letter.
9. Most recent audited financial statement.

10. Funding sources by category for your organization and, if available, a list of contributors and the size of gifts.
When to apply: Anytime.
Materials available: Annual report (includes "Application Procedure").

Emphases. *Activities:* Demonstration programs, research.
Types of support: Fellowships, matching funds, pilot projects, program-related investments, scholarships.
Geography: Areas of company operations.

Limitations. *Recipients:* Individuals, religious organizations.
Activities: Advocacy, lobbying, political activities, publications, seminars.
Types of support: Capital campaigns/expenses, endowments, loans, operating costs.

Thanksgiving Foundation

c/o Fiduciary Trust Company
Two World Trade Center
New York, New York 10048
Tel: 212–466–4100
EIN: 136861874   Type: Independent
Contact: Claudia Irving, Administrative Assistant

History and philosophy. Thomas M. Peters and Marion Post Peters created the Foundation in 1985. Program areas are: Animal Care & Protection, Birth & Population Control, Conservation & Reforestation, Education, Hospitals & Medical Research, Museums, Theatre & Fine Arts, Public Policy Research & Review, Religion & Churches, and Social Services.

Officers and directors. *Trustees:* Thomas Henry Stine, Mark C. Winmill, Fiduciary Trust Company International.

Financial data. Data for fiscal year ended July 31, 1992. *Assets:* $6,359,177 (M). *Total grants disbursed:* $288,030.

Environmental awards. *Recent grants:* 1992 grants included support for land conservation, watershed protection, marine issues, wildlife, and horticulture.

Issues. Cli Bio Lan Agr Wat Oce Ene Was Tox Pop Dev
              •   •   •   •   •   •

Funding analysis.

Fiscal year:	1992
Env grants disb:	$25,500
Number:	10
Range:	$1,000–$4,500
Median:	$2,000
Pct $ disb (env/total):	9

Recipients (1992 highest):	Number:	Dollars:
NYZS/The Wildlife Conservation Society	1	4,500
New Jersey Audubon Society	1	4,000
The Nature Conservancy, Headquarters	1	4,000
Mystic Marine Life Aquarium	1	3,000
National Wildlife Federation	1	2,000
Scenic Hudson, Inc.	1	2,000
Upper Raritan Watershed Association	1	2,000
Wildlife Preservation Trust International	1	2,000

Activity regions (1992):	Number:	Dollars:
New York/New Jersey	5	13,500
U.S. not specified	3	8,000
U.S. Northeast	1	3,000
U.S. Southeast	1	1,000

Sample grants (1992).
Christian Appalachian Project. Lancaster, KY. $1,000.
Garden Club of America. New York, NY. $1,000.
The Nature Conservancy, Headquarters. Arlington, VA. $4,000.
New Jersey Audubon Society. Franklin Lakes, NJ. $4,000.

Application process. *Initial contact:* The Foundation awards grants to pre-selected organizations only. No applications accepted.

Emphases. *Recipients:* Pre-selected organizations only.

Limitations. *Recipients:* Individuals.

The Oakleigh L. Thorne Foundation

1633 Broadway, 30th Floor
New York, New York 10019
Tel: 212–246–5070   Fax: 212–489–6101
EIN: 510243758   Type: Company-sponsored
Contact: Oakleigh B. Thorne, President

History and philosophy. The Foundation was established in 1959 with a donation by Commerce Clearing House, Inc. Grants support conservation, community funds, cultural programs, education, and health services.

Officers and directors. *Officers:* Oakleigh B. Thorne, Chairman, President, and Treasurer; Oakleigh Thorne, Vice President and Secretary; Theresa A. Milone, Vice President and Assistant Secretary; Joseph J. Finora, Assistant Secretary/Treasurer. *Directors:* Theresa A. Milone, Oakleigh B. Thorne, Oakleigh Thorne.

Financial data. Data for fiscal year ended December 31, 1992. *Assets:* $180,255 (M). *Gifts received:* $300,000. *Total grants disbursed:* $280,500.

Environmental awards. *Recent grants:* 1992 grants included support for farmland conservation, watershed protection, marine issues, wildlife, and environmental education.

Issues. Cli Bio Lan Agr Wat Oce Ene Was Tox Pop Dev
              •   •   •   •   •

Funding analysis.

Fiscal year:	1992
Env grants disb:	$25,000
Number:	13
Range:	$1,000–$5,000
Median:	$1,000
Pct $ disb (env/total):	9

Recipients (1992 highest):	Number:	Dollars:
Hudson River Film & Video	1	5,000
NYZS/The Wildlife Conservation Society	1	4,000
Quebec Labrador Foundation/ Atlantic Center for the Environment	1	4,000
The Nature Conservancy, Headquarters	1	2,000
World Wildlife Fund	1	2,000

Activity regions (1992):	Number:	Dollars:
New York/New Jersey	4	11,000
U.S. not specified	7	9,000
U.S. Northeast	1	4,000
U.S. Mountain	1	1,000

Sample grants (1992).
American Farmland Trust. Washington, DC. $1,000.
The Conservation Fund. Arlington, VA. $1,000.
Hudson Riverkeeper Fund. New York, NY. $1,000.
National Coalition for Marine Conservation. Boston, MA. $1,000.
NYZS/The Wildlife Conservation Society. Bronx, NY. $4,000.
The Student Conservation Association, Inc. Arlington, VA. $1,000.

Application process. *Initial contact:* Letter describing applicant institution and interests served.
When to apply: Anytime. The board meets quarterly.

Emphases. *Activities:* Land acquisition, projects, publications, research.
Types of support: Annual campaigns, capital campaigns/expenses, continuing support, debt retirement, emergency funding, equipment, facilities, general purposes, operating costs, seed money.

Limitations. *Recipients:* Individuals.
Types of support: Fellowships, loans, matching funds, scholarships.

Threshold Foundation
1388 Sutter Street, 10th Floor
San Francisco, California 94109
Tel: 415–771–4308   Fax: 415–771–0535
EIN: 133028214   Type: Independent
EGA member
Contact: Susan Muhlbach, Grants Administrator

History and philosophy. Established in 1982, "Threshold is a collection of more than three hundred individuals who together seek to discover the right relationship to our wealth in this time of human need and planetary peril. Through Threshold we pool a portion of our resources and make grants together."

Threshold raises funds on an annual basis. It works through five internally designated fund groups: Donor-Advised Fund, Pooled Fund, Network Fund, Conference and Education Fund, and Operating Fund. Threshold's grantmaking reflects its commitment to its members' areas of concern. These include: Arts and Media, International, Peace, Person, Planet, and Social Justice.

Officers and directors. *Officers:* Sandi Chamberlain, President; James K. Cummings, Secretary; Neal MacMillan, Treasurer. *Directors:* Andrew Beath, Joanie Bronfman, Ricki Gruhl, Christine Jurzykowski, Connie Packard, Howard Rower.

Financial data. Data for fiscal years ended December 31, 1991 and 1992. *Assets (1991):* $535,942 (M). *Gifts received (1991):* $1,528,181 *Total grants disbursed (1992):* $1,358,173.

Environmental awards. *Program and interests:* Threshold seeks projects that "deepen the understanding of inter-relatedness, and that offer strategic relief to the suffering of our planet and its inhabitants." Within the Planet focus area, specific topics of interest are:

- Overpopulation.
- Pollution of water, air, oceans.
- Global warming.
- Toxic and nuclear waste.
- Biodiversity.
- Forest preservation.
- Alternative agriculture.
- Creation of ecologically sustainable culture.

"The Foundation seeks projects which help us live lightly on the Earth, and which recognize and reflect the sacredness of Gaia—the Earth as a living organism. Programs should address these issues through transformational education, corporate responsibility and accountability, regional projects with national/ international impact, and other highly leveraged approaches."

Grants with an environmental component also may be given through the five areas of concern other than Planet.

Issues. Cli Bio Lan Agr Wat Oce Ene Was Tox Pop Dev
●   ●   ●   ●   ●   ●   ●   ●   ●   ●

Funding analysis.

Fiscal year:	1990	1991
Env grants auth:	$432,000	$558,370
Number:	43	46
Range:	$100–$30,000	$500–$5,000
Median:	$10,000	$12,220
Pct $ disb (env/total):	33	40

Recipients (1991 highest):	Number:	Dollars:
Heart of America Northwest	2	26,780
NEST Foundation	2	25,500
Resource Renewal Institute	1	25,000
Greyston Family Inn	1	24,000
Hanuman Foundation	1	23,000

T

Activity regions (1991 highest):	Number:	Dollars:
U.S. not specified	9	98,670
Mexico and Central America	5	67,850
U.S. Northwest	3	45,910
International*	3	41,660
U.S. West	3	30,850

*Multiple regions or not specified.

Sample grants (1991).
Antarctica Project. Washington, DC. $7,650. General support for the preservation of Antarctica.
Botanical Dimensions. Occidental, CA. $9,570. To collect and propagate medicinal and shamanic plants from the tropics around the world, and to gather and preserve their folklore and methods of use.
Commonweal. Bolinas, CA. $12,000. For the Green Gandhi Initiative. Green Gandhi tells the stories of women and men who resist the environmental degradation of their peoples and homelands. It will publicize stories of grassroots resistance to environmental destruction around the globe.
Earth Island Institute. San Francisco, CA. $14,350. For the Sea Turtle Restoration Project to protect and restore endangered sea turtle populations, and to shift economic dependency away from killing turtles.
Environmental Action Foundation. Takoma Park, MD. $12,440. For the Solid Waste Alternatives Project that works to reduce the solid waste stream and to conserve natural resources by informing activists, policymakers, politicians, and the media about the need for organic composting, recycling, and proper standards for labeling and packaging.
Headwaters Community Association. Ashland, OR. $19,130. To help develop an Ancient Forest Education program which will support action and broaden understanding of critical ancient forest issues in the Northwest.

Application process. *Initial contact:* Letter of inquiry (2 page) to include:
1. Description of organization.
2. Problem being addressed.
3. Strategy used to address the problem.
4. Organization's total operating budget.
5. Amount requested.
6. Description of use of funds.

Most proposals come to the Foundation through sponsorship by a Threshold member.
When to apply: Deadline for letters of inquiry is March 15. If requested, a full proposal is due by April 15.
Materials available: Annual report, "Guide to Grantseekers."

Emphases. *Recipients:* Nonprofit organizations.
Activities: Audiovisual materials, citizen participation, education, innovative programs, media projects.
Geography: Regional projects with national/international impact.

Limitations. *Types of support:* Capital campaigns/expenses, endowments.

The Tides Foundation
1388 Sutter Street
San Francisco, California 94109–5427
Tel: 415–771–4308   Fax: 415–771–0535
EIN: 510198509   Type: Independent
EGA member
Contacts: Drummond M. Pike, President
Jacqueline Schad, Director, Grantmaking Program
Clay Carter, Program Officer

History and philosophy. "The Tides Foundation was established in 1976 to promote creative nonprofit and philanthropic activity, particularly in the western United States. Since that time, the scope of The Foundation's work has widened beyond the western region to national and international dimensions."

"The Foundation seeks to link diverse individuals seeking social justice, creative new approaches to economic enterprise, and an enlightened stewardship of our natural environment. It supports efforts in five areas: Environment and Natural Resources; International Affairs; Economic Public Policy and Enterprise Development; Social Justice; and Community Affairs. In each of these areas, Tides encourages the participation of Asian, African-American, Latino, and Native American organizations."

Tides is a public charity with 501(c)(3) and 509(a)(1) designations, and as such seeks contributions to support its grantmaking activities. As a grantmaker, it administers over one hundred donor-advised funds and provides staff support to an additional five independent grantmaking organizations. All grants are made on the recommendation of donor-advised funds. Tides implements its purposes through three separate, yet inter-related, programs, each designed to offer, within an institutional framework, the greatest degree of flexibility for innovative nonprofit and philanthropic activity: The Grantmaking Program, The Projects Program, and The Management Program.

The Projects Program is viewed as an incubator, serving as a home for start-up projects and providing financial and administrative services for these new efforts. In fiscal year 1993 Tides had 180 projects supported by grants from foundations, other institutions, and individuals; project revenue was $10,313,700. In 1993 Environment and Natural Resource projects numbered 56 and included such entities as the Biotechnology Working Group, Green Media Team, Institute for Deep Ecology Education, and the Student Environmental Action Coalition (SEAC).

Officers and directors. *Officers:* Wade Rathke, Chair; Drummond M. Pike, President; Michael Kieschnick, Treasurer; Lynda Palevsky, Corporate Secretary. *Directors:* Richard Boone, Susan Lehman Carmichael, Michael Kieschnick, Andrea Kydd, Mary Mountcastle, Lynda Palevsky, Drummond M. Pike, Wade Rathke, Charles Savitt, Dagmar Thorpe.

Financial data. Data for fiscal year ended April 30, 1993. *Assets:* $34,437,200 (C). *Gifts received:* $16,087,000. *Total grants disbursed:* $6,321,300.

Environmental awards. *Program and interests:* Tides has sponsored a variety of efforts to explore and develop new concepts of environmental harmony. General concerns are:

- Natural resource conservation, policy alternatives and solutions.

- Global warming and the greenhouse effect.
- Sustainable development.
- Land use, preservation, and stewardship.
  - Wildlands and rainforests.
  - Land rights of indigenous peoples.
  - Public lands.
  - Sustainable agriculture.

Tides also maintains interests in:

- Water issues in the Colorado River Basin, particularly citizen groups working to ensure a more balanced use of this important resource. Groups working specifically on the challenges facing the Grand Canyon are of special interest.
- Environmental issues such as toxins, preservation of temperate forests and rainforests, and recycling.
- Social Justice groups organizing local constituencies and/or training young people as community leaders.
- Small scale economic development projects run by and for the benefit of low-income women and people of color.
- Organizations working to strengthen the spiritual and cultural traditions of indigenous peoples throughout the world.

Issues. Cli Bio Lan Agr Wat Oce Ene Was Tox Pop Dev
• • • • • • • • • • •

Funding analysis.§

Fiscal year:	1992	1993
Env grants auth:	$2,109,572	$1,236,555
Number:	61	80
Range:	$5,000–$484,887	$3,250–$70,000
Median:	$13,000	$10,000
Pct $ auth (env/total):	39	19

Recipients (1993 highest):	Number:	Dollars:
Living Earth	1	70,000
Global Action and Information Network	1	56,736
Global Action Plan	1	50,000
Widener University, School of Law	1	46,843
Earth Time Project	1	45,836

Activity regions (1993 highest):	Number:	Dollars:
International*	8	237,348
U.S. West	18	193,750
U.S. Mountain	11	166,500
U.S. not specified	9	143,751
U.S. South Central	5	77,250

*Multiple regions or not specified.

§Data for 1993 do not include grants less than $5,000.

Sample grants (1993).

Botanical Dimensions. Occidental, CA. $10,000. Hosaka Project.
Eastern Africa Environmental Network. Nairobi, Kenya. $10,000. General support.
Coolidge Center for Environmental Leadership. Cambridge, MA. $20,000. General support.
Eco-Rap Video Project. Berkeley, CA. $7,500. Post-production expenses.
Environmental Action Foundation. Takoma Park, MD. $5,000. MOBRO project.
Global Action and Information Network. Santa Cruz, CA. $56,736. General program support.
Grand Canyon Trust. Washington, DC. $13,000. General program support.
International Energy Initiative. New York, NY. $6,000. Research out of the Bangalore office.
International Society for Ecology and Culture. Berkeley, CA. $5,000. Ladakh project.
Living Earth. London, U.K. $70,000. General support.
Redwood Coast Watershed Alliance. Ukiah, CA. $6,250. General support.
Southwest Research and Information Center. Albuquerque, NM. $15,000. Four Corners Water and Cultural Project.
Western States Center. Portland, Oregon. $20,000. Wise Use Public Exposure Project.
White Earth Land Recovery Project. White Earth, MN. $10,000. Land acquisition.
The Wilderness Society. Washington, DC. $32,500. Work to preserve the ancient forests; general program support.

Application process. *Initial contact:* Proposal to include:
Summary (1 page).
1. Purpose of your agency.
2. Why you are requesting the grant.
3. What outcomes you hope to achieve.
4. How grant funds would be spent.

Narrative (5 pages maximum).
1. Background. Describe the work of your organization.
   - Brief description of its history and mission.
   - Need or problem that the organization works to address.
   - Current programs and accomplishments. Emphasize the achievements of the past year.
   - Population served, including geographic location, socio-economic status, race, ethnicity, gender, sexual orientation, age, physical ability, and language.
   - Number of paid staff (differentiate full-time and part-time) and volunteers.
   - Your organization's relationships with other organizations that work to meet the same needs or provide similar services. Explain how your organization differs from the others.
2. Funding request. Describe the program for which funding is sought.
   - Statement of its primary purpose and the need or problem you seek to address.
   - Population you plan to serve and how this population will benefit from the project.
   - Strategies used.
   - Names and qualifications of individuals who will direct the project.
   - Anticipated project length.
   - How the project contributes to the organization's overall mission.
3. List of foundations, corporations, and other sources that you are soliciting for funding and, to the best of your knowledge, the status of your proposal with each.
4. Evaluation.
   - Explain how you will measure the effectiveness of your activities.

- Describe your criteria for a successful program and the results you expect to have achieved by the end of the funding period.

Attachments.
Financial information.
1. Most recent annual financial statement, audited if available. The statement should reflect actual expenditures of funds received during your most recent fiscal year.
2. Operating budget for the current fiscal year.
3. List of foundation and corporate supporters and other sources of income, with amounts, for your current and most recent fiscal years.
4. If project funding is requested, provide a current budget for the project. List each staff line separately and include the percent of time spent on the project. Indicate specific uses of the requested grant, if possible.

Other supporting materials.
1. List of your board of directors, with their affiliations.
2. Copy of your most recent IRS letter indicating your agency's tax-exempt status or, if not available, an explanation.
3. One-paragraph resumes for key staff.
4. Most recent annual report, if available.
5. No more than three examples of recent articles about, or evaluations of, your organization, if available. You may also include your newsletter, brochure, or other literature.

When to apply: Anytime.
Materials available: Annual report (includes "How to Apply for a Grant from The Tides Foundation"), "Information for Grant Seekers," "Grant Proposal Format."

Emphases. *Recipients:* Nonprofit organizations.
Activities: Activism, advocacy, citizen participation, collaborative efforts, conflict resolution, innovative programs, networking, policy analysis/development, political activities, technical assistance, training, workshops, volunteerism, youth programs.
Types of support: Continuing support, general purposes, program-related investments, projects, single-year grants only, technical assistance.
Geography: National, international.

Limitations. *Types of support:* Capital campaigns/expenses, endowments, multi-year grants.

Times Mirror Magazines, Inc.
1705 DeSales Street, N.W., Suite 501
Washington, DC 20036
Tel: 202–467–4949   Fax: 202–467–4858
EIN: 132620517   Type: Company-sponsored
Contact: Consuelo A. Murtagh, Administrative Secretary, Partnership for Environmental Education

---

History and philosophy. Times Mirror Magazines, Inc. is the magazine subsidiary of the Times Mirror Company, a media and information company that publishes newspapers, books, and magazines, and owns cable and broadcast television stations. Times Mirror Magazines, Inc. publishes *Field & Stream, Golf Magazine, Home Mechanix, Outdoor Life, Popular Science, Salt Water Sportsman, Ski Magazine, Skiing, Skiing Trade News, Sporting Goods Dealer,* and *Yachting*.

In 1990 Times Mirror Magazines established the Partnership for Environmental Education "to ensure that tomorrow's leaders can make informed decisions on complex natural resource issues. A fundamental aspect of these solutions is the successful integration of economic development with environmental protection." Partnership grants are awarded by the Times Mirror Magazines Conservation Council, which consists of the company president, director of public relations, an executive director, and the twelve magazine editors. The Council funds a variety of projects, including college level research and studies, to reflect the variety of Times Mirror Magazines' publications. The average grant size is $3,300 and 2.5 percent of revenue is taken from ads in the various magazines with an environmental message.

Partnership funds derive primarily from environmentally conscious advertisements run in Times Mirror magazines and go for nonprofit environmental organizations, school programs for children under age 10, and for elementary, secondary, and higher education. Advertising revenue also supports the National Environmental Education and Training Foundation, college and university environmental studies scholarships, and other projects.

Officers and directors. *Officers:* Francis Pandolfi, President and CEO; Jim Kopper, Pat Campbell, Executive Vice Presidents; Michael Haugh, Scott Kabak, Senior Vice Presidents; George Bell, President, The Skiing Company; Nicholas Niles, President, The Sporting News Publishing Company. *Directors:* Dr. David B. Rockland and editors and staff from the magazines.

Financial data. Not available.

Environmental awards. *Program and interests:* Grants are made to education programs which focus on environmental issues, especially the successful integration of economic development and environmental protection. A project must be relevant to the subject matter of at least one of the Times Mirror magazines in order to qualify for funding.
Recent grants: 1993 grants included support for forest restoration, river protection, fisheries, wildlife conservation, and environmental education.

Issues.   Cli   Bio   Lan   Agr   Wat   Oce   Ene   Was   Tox   Pop   Dev
              •   •   •   •   •

Sample grants (1993).*
Billfish Foundation. Ft. Lauderdale, FL. Producing a video on how to release billfish.
Borough of North Plainfield. North Plainfield, NJ. For a local school to plant trees to stabilize a streambank.
Chesapeake Bay Foundation. Annapolis, MD. For the Careful Catch program to educate sport fishermen.
Dover School. East Dover, VT. To develop a school program to teach environmental awareness.
Harris Center for Conservation Education. Hancock, NH. To monitor an air quality project in several high schools.
Izaak Walton League of America. Arlington, VA. To distribute and produce "Save Our Streams" kits for children.
Jackson Hole Land Trust. Jackson, WY. To educate landowners about conservation easements.
Maryland Agricultural Education Foundation. Baltimore, MD. To train elementary school teachers in aquaculture and provide equipment.

National Anti-Poaching Foundation. Colorado Springs, CO. For the anti-poaching campaign, through a toll-free number and awareness stickers.

Sci-Tec Communications. Ridgefield, CT. To develop and prepare a booklet, "An Educator's Guide to Environmental Literacy."

Ski Windham. Windham, NH. Environmental fair for children and adults.

Tread Lightly! Ogden, UT. To teach responsible off-road vehicle use to high school students.

Trout Unlimited, Inc. Vienna, VA. To support the Lee Wulff scholar-ship for graduate students in fisheries management.

Wasatche-Cache National Forest. Salt Lake City, UT. To standardize a ski naturalist program with a roving Forest Service ranger.

*Dollar amounts not available.

Application process. *Initial contact:* Preliminary pre-proposal (1 page) is suggested. Full proposal to include:
1. Cover sheet.
2. Narrative (5 typed pages maximum, plus attachments) addressing the relevance of the request to the subject matter of one or more Times Mirror magazines and the specific accomplishment that will result from the donation.
3. Detailed budget.
4. Listing of other funding sources and amounts awarded.
5. Copy of operating budget and a most recent annual report.
6. Copy of IRS tax-exempt status determination letter.
7. Letters of reference (if possible), such as those from organizations or individuals familiar with your organization's project. Letters from participants in your projects are also of interest to the Council.
8. A description of the project's uniqueness and use as a model project.

Funding requests should not exceed $10,000.

When to apply: Deadlines are June 15 and December 15. Applications received after those dates will be held until the next cycle.

Materials available: Guidelines, Cover Sheet for Applications.

Emphases. *Activities:* Education.

Limitations. *Types of support:* Operating costs.

The Tinker Foundation Incorporated
55 East 59th Street
New York, New York 10022
Tel: 212-421-6858   Fax: 212-223-3326
EIN: 510175449   Type: Independent
EGA member
Contact: Renate Rennie, Executive Director

History and philosophy. The Tinker Foundation was established in 1959 by Edward Laroque Tinker (1881–1968). A writer and avid traveler, Dr. Tinker had a strong interest in people and cultures, particularly those of Latin America and Iberia. He believed that the future freedom and prosperity of the peoples of the Americas depended upon their mutual trust, friendship, and cooperation. The Foundation restricts its funding exclusively to activities with a geographic focus on Ibero-America, Portugal, Spain, and Antarctica. Projects deal primarily with issues of governance, economic policy, environmental policy, and the research, training, and public outreach initiatives associated with these areas.

Officers and directors. *Officers:* Martha Twitchell Muse, Chairman and President; Grayson Kirk, Vice President; Raymond L. Brittenham, Secretary; Gordon T. Wallis, Treasurer; Beatrice C. Treat, Assistant Treasurer; Renate Rennie, Executive Director. *Directors:* Raymond L. Brittenham, William R. Chaney, John N. Irwin III, Grayson Kirk, John A. Luke, Jr., Charles McC. Mathias, Jr., Martha Twitchell Muse, Renate Rennie, Susan L. Segal, Gordon T. Wallis.

Financial data. Data for fiscal year ended December 31, 1993. *Assets:* $60,423,517 (M). *Total grants authorized:* $1,646,700.

Environmental awards. *Program and interests:* The Foundation's particular interest is in policy issues.

Recent grants: 1993 grants included support for projects dealing with the development of environmental policy and law; trade and environment; the Antarctic Treaty System; forest and wetland management; air and water pollution within Latin America and on the U.S.-Mexican border; small industry environmental concerns; institutional development; training in environmental management and policy; and fisheries.

Issues. Cli Bio Lan Agr Wat Oce Ene Was Tox Pop Dev
         •   •   •   •   •   •   •

Funding analysis.

Fiscal year:	1991	1993
Env grants auth:	$845,500	$969,000
Number:	7	16
Range:	$12,500–$210,000	$15,000–$150,000
Median:	$150,000	$47,500
Pct $ auth (env/total):	33	59

Recipients (1993 highest):	Number:	Dollars:
Environmental Law Institute	1	150,000
Centro Ecologico de Sonora (CES)	1	139,000
Fundación Peruana para la Conservación de la Naturaleza	1	80,000
Center for Marine Conservation	1	75,000
Environmental Defense Fund	1	75,000
New York Rainforest Alliance, Inc.	1	75,000

Activity regions (1993 highest):	Number:	Dollars:
Andean Region and Southern Cone	5	240,000
U.S. not specified	1	150,000
Mexico and Central America	1	139,000
Brazil	1	75,000
Caribbean and West Indies	1	75,000
International*	1	75,000

*Multiple regions or not specified.

Sample grants (1993).

Center for Marine Conservation. Washington, DC. $75,000 (3 years). Community outreach efforts in Samana Bay, Dominican Republic (CMC is working cooperatively with Eco-Development of Samana Bay and Environs in the Dominican Republic).

Environmental Defense Fund. New York, NY. $75,000 (3 years). Project dealing with air pollution problems at the U.S.-Mexico border.

Fundación Peruana para la Conservación de la Naturaleza. Lima, Peru. $80,000 (2 years). Enhancing the current environmental knowledge among key policymakers in Peru.

The International Institute for Energy Conservation, Inc. Washington DC. $40,000. IIEC's energy efficiency and policy projects in Chile.

International Union for Conservation of Nature & Natural Resources–U.S. Washington, DC. $35,000. International Workshop on Antarctic Tourism.

Manomet Observatory for Conservation Science. Manomet, MA. $40,000. Supporting Wetlands for the Americas in its work on biodiversity conservation and policy developments in South America.

New York Rainforest Alliance, Inc. New York, NY. $75,000. Amazon Rivers Project for sustainable use of fishery resources in the Amazon Basin.

OCEANITES, Inc. Cooksville, MD. $15,000. Designing an Antarctic site inventory of significant resources for researchers, scientific organizations, national tourism bureaus, and national Antarctic programs.

Promoción de la Pequena Empresa Latinoamericana. Bogota, Colombia. $50,000. Addressing the environmental impact of small-scale Colombian tanneries and developing a framework for similar environmental assessments of small businesses.

Application process. *Initial contact:* Applicants are strongly urged to submit summary (2–3 pages) well in advance of deadline. Full proposal (2 copies), without binders and in the English language, to include:
1. Proposal cover sheet (supplied by Foundation).
2. Summary (1 page) describing objectives, target audience or beneficiaries, proposed methodology, and plan for dissemination of results.
3. Full proposal providing more detail on project's objectives and theoretical, practical, and/or policy-related significance (both as a discrete endeavor and within the broader field).
4. Plan of work describing the activities to be undertaken and indicating any factors which could serve to delay this plan, change the amount of time required to complete the project, or alter the proposed budgetary designations.
5. Anticipated results of the project.
6. Specific plan for the dissemination of those results (i.e., identification of the target audience and the means by which it will be reached).
7. Description of the plan to evaluate the short- and long-term impact of the project's results upon its completion.
8. Names and addresses of three individuals familiar with the proposed topic/field, but not directly involved in the project.
9. Qualifications of the project director and personnel, with curricula vitae attached.
10. Itemized budget for the costs of the entire project.
11. Itemized budget for those expenses for which Tinker Foundation funding is sought. (Please note that as a general rule the Foundation does not pay overhead or indirect costs. However, in those exceptional cases when it is considered absolutely necessary, a maximum of 10 percent of the project's direct costs may be included as overhead in the budget.)
12. Copy of IRS tax-exempt status determination letter.
13. Copy of the organization's latest federal/state Form 990.
14. Copy of the organization's latest financial statement.
15. Complete list of organization's staff and board of directors.
16. Brief narrative statement providing a historical overview of the institution.

When to apply: Deadlines are March 1 and October 1. The board of directors meets in June and December.

Materials available: Annual report, "Application Information: Institutional Grants."

Emphases. *Recipients:* Educational institutions, nonprofit organizations, research institutions.
Activities: Collaborative efforts, conferences, policy analysis/development, research, seminars, symposia/colloquia, training, workshops.
Types of support: Pilot projects, projects.
Geography: Latin America, Spain, Portugal, and Antarctica.

Limitations. *Recipients:* Individuals.
Activities: Lobbying, youth programs.

Tortuga Foundation
380 Riverside Drive, Suite 1D
New York, New York 10025
Tel: 212–315–0763
EIN: 510245279   Type: Independent
EGA member
Contact: Donald K. Ross, Secretary

History and philosophy. The Foundation was established in 1979. Its primary interests are the environment, family planning, health, and education.

Officers and directors. *Officers:* Millie L. Siceloff, President; Donald K. Ross, Secretary; William Breed, Treasurer; Christopher Angell, Assistant Secretary. *Trustees:* Patricia P. Livingston, Joan Tweedy.

Financial data. Data for fiscal years ended September 30, 1991 and 1993. *Assets (1991):* $5,425,475 (M). *Gifts received (1993):* $650,000. *Total grants disbursed (1993):* $650,000.

Environmental awards. *Recent grants:* 1993 grants included support for land conservation, forest and river protection, and toxic waste reduction. The Foundation also has an interest in population issues and awards several grants annually in the area of family planning.

Issues. Cli Bio Lan Agr Wat Oce Ene Was Tox Pop Dev
       •   •   •   •   •

Funding analysis.

Fiscal year:	1991	1993
Env grants disb:	$385,000	$480,000
Number:	15	19
Range:	$10,000–$50,000	$5,000–$50,000
Median:	$20,000	$25,000
Pct $ disb (env/total):	70	74

Recipients (1993 highest):	Number:	Dollars:
The Nature Conservancy, Headquarters	1	50,000
Mothers & Others for a Livable Planet	1	40,000
NYZS/The Wildlife Conservation Society	1	40,000
Public Employees for Environmental Responsibility, Inc.	1	35,000
Public Interest Projects, Inc.	1	35,000

Activity regions (1993):	Number:	Dollars:
U.S. not specified	12	330,000
New York/New Jersey	2	60,000
U.S. Northwest	3	50,000
U.S. Mountain	1	20,000
U.S. South Central	1	20,000

Sample grants (1993).
Environmental Research Foundation. Washington, DC. $15,000.
Environmental Support Center. Washington, DC. $30,000.
Mothers & Others for a Livable Planet. Ventura, CA. $40,000.
The Nature Conservancy, Headquarters. Arlington, VA. $50,000.
New York Environmental Institute. Albany, NY. $20,000.
NYZS/The Wildlife Conservation Society. Bronx, NY. $40,000.
Public Employees for Environmental Responsibility, Inc. New York, NY. $35,000.
Western Ancient Forest Campaign. Portland, OR. $25,000.

Application process. *Initial contact:* The Foundation awards grants to pre-selected organizations only. No unsolicited applications accepted.

Emphases. *Recipients:* Pre-selected organizations only, nonprofit organizations.
Activities: Advocacy, citizen participation, collaborative efforts, innovative program.
Types of support: General purposes.

Limitations. *Recipients:* Individuals.

Town Creek Foundation, Inc.
221 South Street
P.O. Box 159
Oxford, Maryland 21654
Tel: 410–226–5315
EIN: 521227030 Type: Independent
EGA member
Contact: Christine B. Shelton, Executive Director

History and philosophy. The Town Creek Foundation was established in 1981. It makes grants in the areas of environment, public radio and television, peace and justice, and improvement of life for disadvantaged persons in Talbot County, Maryland.

Officers and directors. *Officers:* Edmund A. Stanley, Jr., President; Jennifer Stanley, Vice President; Philip E. L. Dietz, Jr., Secretary/Treasurer. *Directors:* Philip E. L. Dietz, Jr., Edmund A. Stanley, Jr., Jennifer Stanley, Lisa A. Stanley, Betsy Taylor.

Financial data. Data for fiscal year ended December 31, 1993. *Assets:* $29,824,803 (M). *Total grants authorized:* $1,315,000.

Environmental awards. *Program and interests:* The Foundation's interests are:

- Preservation and enhancement of the human environment in the United States.

- Monitoring federal, state, and local officials and bodies responsible for enforcing environmental legislation.

Recent grants: 1993 grants supported a host of topics including protection of wilderness and forests, rivers, coastal lands, wildlife, and oceans; monitoring public lands; and waste reduction and toxic waste issues.

Issues. Cli Bio• Lan• Agr Wat• Oce• Ene• Was• Tox• Pop Dev

Funding analysis.

Fiscal year:	1991	1993
Env grants disb:	$801,000	$845,000
Number:	59	54
Range:	$5,000–$100,000	$5,000–$100,000
Median:	$10,000	$10,000
Pct $ disb (env/total):	69	64

Recipients (1993 highest):	Number:	Dollars:
The Wilderness Society	1	100,000
Chesapeake Bay Foundation	1	75,000
National Audubon Society	1	35,000
Natural Resources Defense Council	2	30,000
American Rivers, Inc.	1	25,000
Center for Marine Conservation	1	25,000

Activity regions (1993 highest):	Number:	Dollars:
U.S. not specified	34	565,000
U.S. Mid-Atlantic	4	100,000
U.S. Northwest	5	55,000
U.S. Mountain	5	45,000
U.S. Northeast	2	30,000

Sample grants (1993).
American Littoral Society. Philadelphia, PA. $10,000.
Center for Policy Alternatives. Washington, DC. $15,000.
Clean Water Fund. Washington, DC. $15,000.
Earth Action Network, Inc. Westport, CT. $10,000.
Environmental Law Institute. Washington, DC. $10,000.
Institute for Conservation Leadership. Washington, DC. $15,000.
Mineral Policy Center. Alexandria, VA. $15,000.
Pickering Creek Environmental Center. Easton, MD. $10,000.
Pinelands Preservation Alliance. Browns Mills, NJ. $10,000.
Scenic America. Washington, DC. $10,000.
Society of Environmental Journalists. Philadelphia, PA. $10,000.
Southern Environmental Law Center. Charlottesville, VA. $15,000.

Application process. *Initial contact:* Full proposal (10 pages maximum) to include:
1. Brief description (about 150 words) of organization, its goals and objectives.
2. Needs statement, including amount requested.

3. Project description, including goals, method and strategy, budget, and evaluation process.
4. Copy of organization's most recent financial statement, or a list of assets, total revenues, and expenses for the most recent fiscal year.

Additional information.
1. Copy of IRS tax-exempt status determination letter.
2. List of staff and organization's qualifications for carrying on work for which grant will be provided.
3. List of other sources of financial support, committed and potential, including sources to whom proposals have been sent in the last 12 months.

When to apply: Deadlines are January 15, May 15, and September 15 (or the next business day if deadline date falls on a weekend or holiday).
Materials available: "General Information and Grant Application Guidelines," grants list.

Emphases. *Recipients:* Nonprofit organizations.
Activities: Activism, advocacy, citizen participation, collaborative efforts, innovative programs, networking.
Types of support: Continuing support, general purposes, matching funds, operating costs, projects.
Geography: United States only. Emphasis on organizations working nationally, statewide, or over a large region.

Limitations. *Recipients:* Botanical gardens, educational institutions, individuals, museums, religious organizations, research institutions, zoos.
Activities: Conferences, exhibits, expeditions/tours, feasibility studies, fundraising, inventories, land acquisition, lobbying, policy analysis/development, publications, research, seminars, symposia/colloquia.
Types of support: Annual campaigns, capital campaigns/expenses, computer hardware, debt retirement, endowments, facilities, internships, lectureships, loans, mortgage reduction, professorships, program-related investments, scholarships.

Toyota USA Foundation
19001 South Western Avenue
Torrance, California 90509
Tel: 310–618–6766
EIN: 953255038   Type: Company-sponsored
Contact: Patricia Hull, Foundation Administrator

History and philosophy. Established in 1987, the Foundation is funded by a $20 million permanent endowment from Toyota Motor Sales, USA, Inc. "The Toyota USA Foundation is committed to enhancing America's academic environment, recognizing that a healthy, well-educated community creates a healthy and competitive business environment." Its grants are made primarily to educational programs with special emphasis in the area of pre-collegiate education. The Foundation is dedicated to improving the quality of K–12 education with a special interest in math, science, and environmental education. Secondary priority is given to the areas of: health & human services, arts & culture, and community & urban affairs.

Officers and directors. *Officers*: Shinji Sakai, President; Yale Gieszl, Executive Vice President. *Directors:* R. Chikuma, Tom Fujita, Yale Gieszl, John McGovern, Tom Nishiyana, James Olson, Shinji Sakai.

Financial data.* Data for fiscal year ended June 30, 1994. *Assets:* $20,000,000 (U). *Gifts received:* $1,000,000. *Total grants disbursed:* $1,001,517.

*As reported by Foundation.

Environmental awards. *Recent grants:* Grants in 1993 and 1994 included support for environmental education for minority and grade school students.

Issues.   Cli   Bio   Lan   Agr   Wat   Oce   Ene   Was   Tox   Pop   Dev
                                                   •

Funding analysis.

Fiscal year:	1993
Env grants auth:	$90,000
Number:	1
Range:	$90,000–$90,000
Median:	$90,000
Pct $ auth (env/total):	9

Recipient (1993):	Number:	Dollars:
University of California, Berkeley	1	90,000

Activity region (1993):	Number:	Dollars:
U.S. West	1	90,000

Sample grants (1993–94).
Clemson University. Clemson, SC. $60,000 (3 years). To support the teaching of "Kids About the Environment," a hands-on environmental education program for children in grade school.
University of California, Berkeley. Berkeley, CA. $90,000. For mathematics, engineering, and science achievement.

Application process. *Initial contact:* Letter of intent (1 page) summarizing the project. Use application form for full proposal if requested. Proposal to include:
1. Cover letter (1 page) stating purpose, amount requested, and timeline of project.
2. Organizational background.
    - History.
    - Major activities/purpose.
3. Project information.
    - Purpose of solicited funds.
    - Long-term goals.
    - Activities planned to reach goals.
    - Anticipated results.
    - Short-term measurable objectives.
    - Geographical area served.
    - Evaluation procedure.
4. Financial information.
    - Principal sources of funding.
    - Annual budget.
    - Administrative costs.
    - Amount to be raised by contributions.
5. Supporting documents.
    - Copy of IRS tax-exempt status determination letter.

- Audited financial statements for the past two years.
- Projected plan for 3–5 years.
- Full budget for one year.
- Copy of current 990 Form.
- List of board of directors.
- Annual report, clippings, brochures, etc.

When to apply: Anytime.
Materials available: Annual report (includes "Guidelines, Limitations and Funding Priorities"), Guidelines and Application Procedure, application form.

Emphases. *Recipients:* Educational institutions, nonprofit organizations.
Activities: Demonstration programs, education, training (teachers), youth programs.
Types of support: Multi-year grants, pilot projects, projects.
Geography: United States only.

Limitations. *Recipients:* Individuals, public agencies, religious organizations.
Activities: Advocacy, capacity building, conferences, expeditions/tours, feasibility studies, fundraising, inventories, land acquisition, litigation, lobbying, research, seminars, symposia/colloquia.
Types of support: Advertising campaigns, annual campaigns, capital campaigns/expenses, computer hardware, continuing support, debt retirement, emergency funding, endowments, facilities, fellowships, general purposes, indirect costs, internships, lectureships, loans, membership campaigns, mortgage reduction, operating costs, professorships, program-related investments, scholarships, travel expenses.

The Travelers Foundation
65 East 55th Street
New York, New York 10022
Tel: 212-891-8884 Fax: 212-891-8908
EIN: 136161154 Type: Company-sponsored
Contacts: Dee Topol, President
Patricia R. Byrne, Grants Manager

History and philosophy. Formerly Primerica Foundation, The Travelers Foundation adopted its present name in January 1994 when Primerica completed its acquisition of The Travelers Corporation, a diversified financial services company. Subsidiaries include Smith Barney, the New York investment banking and securities brokerage firm; The Travelers Insurance Companies, which provide life, health, and property/casualty insurance and are based in Hartford, Connecticut; and Commercial Credit Company, a nationwide consumer lending company with headquarters in Baltimore.

Grants are made in three categories: General Grants (awarded on behalf of the whole company), Local Contributions (identified and locally presented by each subsidiary company), and Volunteer Incentive Program grants (given to organizations recommended by Primerica employees who are directly involved as volunteers).

During 1993 Primerica Foundation grants and corporate contributions supported education, the arts and human services, and health and civic organizations.

Officers and directors. *Officers:* Sanford I. Weill, Chairman; Dee Topol, President; Robert I. Lipp, Vice President and Treasurer; Charles O. Prince III, Secretary. *Trustees:* James Dimon, Robert I. Lipp, Charles O. Prince III, Dee Topol, Sanford I. Weill.

Financial data.* Data for fiscal year ended December 31, 1993. *Assets:* $4,525,873 (U). *Total grants disbursed:* $5,001,794.

*As reported by Foundation.

Environmental awards. *Recent grants:* 1993 grants included support for a beautification, a botanical garden, urban environment, and wildlife.

Issues. Cli Bio Lan Agr Wat Oce Ene Was Tox Pop Dev
 •   •

Funding analysis.

Fiscal year:	1993
Env grants disb:	$42,750
Number:	13
Range:	$250–$15,500
Median:	$1,000
Pct $ disb (env/total):	1

Recipients (1993 highest):	Number:	Dollars:
City Parks Foundation	1	15,500
Brooklyn Botanic Garden	1	7,500
Council on the Environment of New York City	1	5,000
The Parks Council, Inc.	1	5,000
NYZS/The Wildlife Conservation Society	1	3,000

Activity regions (1993 highest):	Number:	Dollars:
New York/New Jersey	5	36,000
U.S. Mid-Atlantic	2	3,000
U.S. South Central	3	2,000
U.S. Northeast	1	1,000
U.S. West	1	500

Sample grants (1993).
Baltimore Zoological Society. Baltimore, MD. $2,250.
Baton Rouge Earth Day. Baton Rouge, LA. $500.
Brooklyn Botanic Garden. Brooklyn, NY. $7,500.
Chesapeake Wildlife Sanctuary. Bowie, MD. $750.
City Parks Foundation. New York, NY. $15,500.
Council on the Environment of New York City. New York, NY. $5,000.
Earth Circle Foundation. Santa Fe, NM. $500.
Friends of Keney Park. Hartford, CT. $1,000.
Living Desert Wildlife & Botanical Park. Palm Beach. CA. $500.
Operation City Beautiful. Evansville, IN. $250.
The Parks Council, Inc. New York, NY. $5,000.
NYZS/The Wildlife Conservation Society. Bronx, NY. $3,000.
Zoological Society of Houston. Houston, TX. $1,000.

Application process. *Initial contact:* Brief letter (3 pages) to include:
1. Program description and objectives.
2. Population served.

3. Need addressed.
4. Activities planned.
5. Timetable.
6. Budget.

Also provide:
1. General description of organization's nature and purpose; its address; and name, title, and telephone number of a contact.
2. Copy of the IRS tax-exempt status determination letter.
3. Current financial information on the organization, including the most recent audited financial statement, a list of recent contributors, and an annual report, if available.
4. A list of the members of the governing board and staff.

When to apply: Anytime.
Materials available: Annual report (includes "How to Apply for a Grant").

Emphases. *Recipients:* Nonprofit organizations.
Types of support: Operating costs, projects.
Geography: New York, Baltimore, Hartford, and Wilmington, Delaware metropolitan areas, and other areas of operations.

Limitations. *Recipients:* Individuals, religious organizations.
Activities: Fundraising, land acquisition, political activities, publications.
Types of support: Advertising campaigns, capital campaigns/expenses, continuing support, debt retirement, endowments, loans.

Treacy Foundation, Inc.
2963 East 75th Street
Tulsa, Oklahoma 74136
Tel: 918–492–1154
EIN: 731333867   Type: Independent
Contact: James B. Treacy, Chairman

History and philosophy. This Oklahoma family foundation makes grants for a wide range of causes including higher education, medical issues, Catholic charities, animal welfare, and conservation.

Officers and directors. *Officers:* James B. Treacy, Chairman; Francesca N. Treacy, Vice Chairman.

Financial data. Data for fiscal year ended December 31, 1992. *Assets:* $288,893 (M). *Total grants disbursed:* $20,925.

Environmental awards. *Recent grants:* 1992 grants included support for land conservation and wildlife protection.

Issues. Cli Bio Lan Agr Wat Oce Ene Was Tox Pop Dev
              •   •

Funding analysis.

Fiscal year:	1992
Env grants disb:	$8,900
Number:	6
Range:	$100–$6,500
Median:	$500
Pct $ disb (env/total):	43

Recipients (1992):	Number:	Dollars:
Tulsa Zoo Friends	1	6,500
The Nature Conservancy, Oklahoma Field Office	1	1,200
Greenpeace USA	1	500
NYZS/The Wildlife Conservation Society	1	500
Jane Goodall Institute for Wildlife Research Education	1	100
National Wildlife Federation	1	100

Activity regions (1992):	Number:	Dollars:
U.S. South Central	2	7,700
U.S. not specified	2	600
New York/New Jersey	1	500
U.S. West	1	100

Sample grants (1992).
Jane Goodall Institute for Wildlife Research Education. Tucson, AZ. $100.
Greenpeace USA. Washington, DC. $500.
The Nature Conservancy, Oklahoma Field Office. Tulsa, OK. $1,200.
National Wildlife Federation. Washington, DC. $100.
Tulsa Zoo Friends. Tulsa, OK. $6,500.
NYZS/The Wildlife Conservation Society. Bronx, NY. $500.

Application process. *Initial contact:* Proposal in any format.
When to apply: Anytime.

Harry C. Trexler Trust
33 South Seventh Street, Suite 205
Allentown, Pennsylvania 18101
Tel: 610–434–9645   Fax: 610–437–5721
EIN: 231162215   Type: Independent
Contact: Thomas H. Christman

History and philosophy. This charitable testamentary trust was established by the will of Harry C. Trexler (d. 1933), who owned one of the largest lumber companies in the East and one of the largest cement production companies in the world. During his lifetime, Trexler was involved with the growth and quality of life in the city of Allentown and the surrounding county of Lehigh. Under the terms of Trexler's will, one-half of the Trust's annual income is paid to charitable organizations in Allentown and Lehigh County; one-fourth goes to the Allentown parks system; and one-fourth is reinvested. The Trust currently makes grants in the areas of: culture, education, elderly, parks, social programs, and youth.

Officers and directors. *Trustees:* Dexter F. Baker, Philip I. Berman, Carl J. W. Hessinger, Kathryn Stephanoff, Richard K. White.

Financial data.* Data for fiscal year ended March 31, 1994. *Assets:* $48,907,026 (U). *Total grants disbursed:* $2,630,573.

*As reported by Trust.

Environmental awards. *Program and interests:* Most environmental grants support the Allentown park system.
Recent grants: 1994 grants included support for urban parks and wildlife preservation.

Issues. Cli Bio Lan Agr Wat Oce Ene Was Tox Pop Dev
          •   •

Funding analysis.

Fiscal year:	1993
Env grants disb:	$30,000
Number:	2
Range:	$10,000–$20,000
Median:	$15,000
Pct $ disb (env/total):	2

Recipients (1993):	*Number:*	*Dollars:*
Wildland Conservancy	1	20,000
Casa Guadalupe Center	1	10,000

Activity region (1993):	*Number:*	*Dollars:*
U.S. Mid-Atlantic	2	30,000

Sample grants (1994).
City of Allentown. Allentown, PA. $558,765. Toward park maintenance.
Trexler–Lehigh County Game Preserve. Lehigh County, PA. $43,750.
Wildland Conservancy. Emmaus, PA. $55,000. Construction costs of Bob Rodale Cycling and Fitness Park.
Wildland Conservancy. Emmaus, PA. $16,500. Jordan Creek Stream Corridor Conservation Project.
Wildlife Information Center. Allentown, PA. $2,500.

Application process. *Initial contact:* Contact by telephone before submitting proposal to include:
1. Articles of incorporation.
2. Current bylaws.
3. Board of directors.
4. Most recent audited financial statement.
5. Current operating budget.
6. IRS tax-exempt status determination letter.
7. Federal tax return.
8. Employer's First Quarterly Tax Form 941.
9. Client statistics.
   - Numbers served for each major category of services provided.
   - Fees charged, dues received, etc.
10. Purpose for funds.
11. Benefit to the community.
12. Amount of funds required to accomplish purpose.
13. Amount requested from the Trust.
14. Other sources from which funds are being requested and your relationship to them.
15. Analyses of receipts by county and client (if you serve clientele from counties other than Lehigh).

When to apply: Deadline is January 31.
Materials available: Annual report (includes "Grant Procedure").

Emphases. *Recipients:* Nonprofit organizations.
Activities: Education, fieldwork, youth programs.

Types of support: Capital campaigns/expenses, computer hardware, continuing support, equipment, facilities, operating costs.
Geography: Lehigh County, Pennsylvania.

The Troy Foundation
c/o Star Bank, Trust Department
910 West Main Street
Troy, Ohio 45373
Tel: 513-335-8351   Fax: 513-335-2458
EIN: 316018703   Type: Community
Contact: Richard J. Fraas, Secretary

History and philosophy. The Troy Foundation was created in 1924 with a bequest by A. G. Stouder, founder of the Hobart Corporation. The Foundation was patterned on The Cleveland Foundation, the first community trust in the Western Hemisphere. The purpose of the Foundation is to improve the quality of life for the community it serves. Within both unrestricted and restricted funds, target areas include: Education, Hospitals, Recreation, and Public Health.

Officers and directors. *Trustees Committee:* Michael E. Pfeffenberger, Chairperson; Rebekah Mohr Brown, Richard J. Fraas, Thomas B. Hamler, William H. Hobart, Jr., Robert R. Koverman, Stewart I. Lipp, Robert B. Meeker, Max A. Myers, Jerrold R. Stammen. *Distribution Committee:* R. Murray Dalton, Chairperson; Thomas E. Robinson, Vice Chairperson; Doris A. Blackmore, Helen N. Meeker, G. Joseph Reardon. *Trustee:* Star Bank, N.A.

Financial data. Data for fiscal year ended December 31, 1993. *Assets:* $16,643,365 (M). *Gifts received:* $1,652,209. *Total grants disbursed:* $888,594.

Environmental awards. *Recent grants:* 1993 grants included support for a nature center.

Issues. Cli Bio Lan Agr Wat Oce Ene Was Tox Pop Dev
          •   •

Funding analysis.§

Fiscal year:	1993
Env grants disb:	$108,915
Number:	5
Range:	$18–$87,147
Median:	$9,500
Pct $ disb (env/total):	12

Recipient (1993):	*Number:*	*Dollars:*
Brukner Nature Center	5	108,915

Activity region (1993):	*Number:*	*Dollars:*
U.S. Great Lakes	5	108,915

§Includes donor-advised grants.

Sample grants (1993).*
Brukner Nature Center. Troy, OH. $19,250. Environmental pilot program and maintenance and repair.

T

Brukner Nature Center. Troy, OH. $89,647. Administrative expenses.
Brukner Nature Center. Troy, OH. $18.

*Includes donor-advised grants.

Application process. *Initial contact:* Telephone or write the Foundation to determine eligibility. Full proposal to include:
1. Legal name and address of organization seeking grant.
2. Description of purpose of organization or activity, what it expects to accomplish, and how the program relates to the needs of the community.
3. Amount requested.
4. Detailed project budget indicating project sources and uses of funds.
5. Plans for future funding.
6. Parent organization's overall budget including income and expense.
7. Balance sheet and income statement from most recent fiscal year, preferably audited.
8. List of officers, directors, and staff.
9. Request authorization.
10. Copy of IRS tax-exempt status determination letter.
11. Background material on organization's history and operations.

When to apply: Anytime. The distribution committee meets six times a year.
Materials available: Annual report, "Information for Grant Applicants."

Emphases. *Recipients:* Educational institutions, nonprofit organizations.
Activities: Education, youth programs.
Types of support: Computer hardware, equipment.
Geography: Within the Troy, Ohio area.

Limitations. *Recipients:* Individuals, public agencies, religious organizations, research institutions, zoos.
Activities: Activism, advocacy, conferences, conflict resolution, expeditions/tours, fundraising, land acquisition, litigation, political activities, seminars, symposia/colloquia.
Types of support: Advertising campaigns, debt retirement, fellowships, internships, loans, membership campaigns, mortgage reduction, professorships, travel expenses.

True North Foundation
P.O. Box 271308
Fort Collins, Colorado 80527
Tel: 303–223–5285   Fax: 303–226–8646
EIN: 742421528   Type: Independent
EGA member
Contact: Kerry K. Hoffman, President

History and philosophy. True North Foundation, established in 1986, is "a private foundation that provides financial support for nonprofit organizations that work to improve our environment and our community." In addition to the environment, the Foundation supports social service and arts organizations, primarily those located in the San Francisco Area.

Officers and directors. *Officers:* Kerry K. Hoffman, President; K. F. Stephens, Vice President; S. O'Hara, Secretary. *Directors:* Kerry K. Hoffman, K. F. Stephens.

Financial data. Data for fiscal year ended December 31, 1993. *Assets:* $7,133,000 (M). *Total grants authorized:* $905,000.

Environmental awards. *Program and interests:* The Foundation allocates a large portion of its grant dollars for:
- Recycling and waste reduction.
- Clean air and water.
- Habitat and species protection.
- Energy conservation.

Issues. Cli Bio Lan Agr Wat Oce Ene Was Tox Pop Dev
         •   •   •   •   •   •   •   •   •

Funding analysis.

Fiscal year:	1991	1993
Env grants auth:	$224,000	$420,900
Number:	17	32
Range:	$2,500–$35,000	$700–$35,000
Median:	$10,000	$10,000
Pct $ auth (env/total):	35	47

Recipients (1993 highest):	Number:	Dollars:
Environmental Defense Fund	2	55,000
Natural Resources Defense Council	2	50,000
Pacific Rivers Council	2	28,200
Institute for Sustainable Forestry	1	25,000
Mineral Policy Center	1	25,000

Activity regions (1993):	Number:	Dollars:
U.S. West	18	187,700
U.S. Northwest	9	123,200
U.S. not specified	3	85,000
Alaska	1	15,000
U.S. Midwest	1	10,000

Sample grants (1993).
Alaska Conservation Foundation. Anchorage, AK. $15,000. General fund.
Cascade Holistic Economic Consultants. Portland, OR. $20,000. Forest Watch publication.
Citizens Fund of California. Sacramento, CA. $10,000. Food safety program.
Coastal Resources Center. San Francisco, CA. $10,000. Fisherman's Wharf Project.
Environmental Defense Fund. San Francisco, CA. $20,000. Bay-Delta.
Institute for Sustainable Forestry. Redway, CA. $25,000. Forestry certification program.
Mountain Lion Foundation. Sacramento, CA. $10,000. General fund.
Pacific Rivers Council. Eugene. OR. $15,000. Watershed restoration.
Yosemite Restoration Trust. San Francisco, CA. $5,000. General fund.

Application process. *Initial contact:* Brief letter (2 pages maximum) to include:
1. Name of organization, IRS status.
2. Contact person and title; address and telephone number.
3. Basic information about the organization (purpose, history, activities, etc.).
4. Description of grant proposal (project significance, timeline, cooperating agencies, etc.).
5. Budget, other sources of financial support, specific request of True North Foundation.
6. Descriptive brochure may be attached if related to this request.

When to apply: Anytime. The trustees meet bimonthly.
Materials available: Brochure.

Emphases. *Recipients:* Nonprofit organizations.
Geography: Regional grants in the San Francisco Bay Area. If the environment-related project has wide application or can be a model for other regions, the Foundation accepts requests from any part of the United States.

Limitations. *Recipients:* Individuals.
Activities: Lobbying, political activities.

The Truland Foundation
3330 Washington Boulevard, 7th Floor
Arlington, Virginia 22201
Tel: 703–516–2600   Fax: 703–522–1427
EIN: 546037172   Type: Independent
Contact: Ingred Moini, Trustee

History and philosophy. The Foundation was established in 1954 by Truland of Florida, Inc., and members of the Truland family. It makes grants in the areas of welfare, arts, higher education, and conservation.

Officers and directors. *Trustees:* Ingred Moini, Alice O. Truland, Robert W. Truland, Walter R. Truland.

Financial data. Data for fiscal year ended March 31, 1993.
Assets: $2,533,653 (M). *Total grants disbursed:* $117,177.

Environmental awards. *Recent grants:* 1993 grants included support for land conservation, marine issues, wildlife, and horticulture.
Issues. Cli • Bio • Lan • Agr • Wat • Oce Ene Was Tox Pop Dev

Funding analysis.

Fiscal year:	1993
Env grants disb:	$7,317
Number:	16
Range:	$22–$2,500
Median:	$250
Pct $ disb (env/total):	6

Recipients (1993 highest):	Number:	Dollars:
Caribbean Conservation Corporation	1	2,500
Royal Oak Foundation	1	1,060
The Conservation Fund	1	1,000
Wildlife Preservation Trust International	1	500
Brooklyn Botanic Garden	1	350
Virginia Wildlife Federation, Inc.	1	350

Activity regions (1993):	Number:	Dollars:
Caribbean and West Indies Islands	1	2,500
U.S. not specified	9	2,317
International*	2	1,500
U.S. Mid-Atlantic	3	650
New York/New Jersey	1	350

*Multiple regions or not specified.

Sample grants (1993).
American Horticultural Society. Alexandria, VA. $250.
Caribbean Conservation Corporation. Gainesville, FL. $2,500.
The Conservation Fund. Arlington, VA. $1,000.
Royal Oak Foundation. New York, NY. $1,060.
Virginia Wildlife Federation, Inc. Virginia Beach, VA. $350.
Wildlife Preservation Trust International. Philadelphia, PA. $500.
The Wildlife Society. Bethesda, MD. $300.

Application process. *Initial contact:* The Foundation awards grants to pre-selected organizations only. No unsolicited applications accepted.

Emphases. *Recipients:* Pre-selected organizations only.

The Trust For Mutual Understanding
30 Rockefeller Plaza, Room 5600
New York, New York 10112
Tel: 212–632–3405   Fax: 212–632–3409
EIN: 133212724   Type: Independent
EGA member
Contact: Richard S. Lanier, Director

History and philosophy. Established in 1984, "The Trust for Mutual Understanding is a private grantmaking organization which supports professional exchanges in the arts and in environmental conservation among the United States, the countries of the former Soviet Union, and Central Europe." Grants are awarded to American nonprofits for exchange activities conducted directly with institutions and individuals in the former Soviet Union and Central Europe. Activities eligible for Trust support are visual and performing arts programs, environmental ex-changes, workshops, conferences, seminars, and joint research projects.

Officers and directors. *Officer:* Richard S. Lanier, Director. *Trustees:* Richard S. Lanier, Elizabeth J. McCormack, Donal C. O'Brien, Jr. *Advisory Committee:* Ruth Adams, Wade Greene, William Luers, Isaac Shapiro.

Financial data. Data for fiscal year ended December 31, 1993.
Assets: $48,293,905 (U). *Total grants disbursed:* $1,960,035.

Environmental awards. *Program and interests:* Grants are made to American organizations for projects involving the exchange of environmental specialists among the United States, the Former Soviet Union, and Central and Eastern Europe. Priority is given to programs in which direct, professional interaction plays a major role and where a significant degree of collaboration exists.

Recent grants: 1993 grants included support for land use planning, forest and river protection, biodiversity, sustainable development, and protection of indigenous cultures. All grants are awarded to U.S. institutions working in the former Soviet Union or Central and Eastern Europe.

Issues. Cli Bio Lan Agr Wat Oce Ene Was Tox Pop Dev
         •   •   •   •   •

Funding analysis.

Fiscal year:	1992	1993
Env grants disb:	$303,132	$717,175
Number:	10	25
Range:	$2,052–$72,080	$4,500–$95,000
Median:	$26,500	$25,000
Pct $ disb (env/total):	15	37

Recipients (1993 highest):	Number:	Dollars:
Pacific Environment and Resources Center	1	95,000
Natural Resources Defense Council	1	75,000
Center for Post-Soviet Studies	1	50,000
German Marshall Fund of the United States	1	50,000
National Audubon Society	1	50,000

Activity regions (1993):	Number:	Dollars:
Russia	17	561,212
Eastern Europe	6	122,263
International*	2	33,700

*Multiple regions or not specified.

Sample grants (1993).

Center for Citizen Initiatives. San Francisco, CA. $7,500. To support filming in Russia of a documentary on Lake Baikal to be shown on public television as part of the NOVA series.

Center for Resource Management. Salt Lake City, UT. $20,000. To support an international working group of Russian and American environmental organizations involved in developing a model sustainable forestry project for Siberia.

Earth Island Institute. San Francisco, CA. $18,000. To enable Russian national park and nature reserve specialists to study methods of national park management in the United States in 1993 in a program developed by Baikal Watch.

National Fish and Wildlife Foundation. Washington, DC. $47,500. To provide renewed support for the international travel and related expenses of Russian environmental specialists participating in joint American-Russian research and exchange projects.

Physicians for Social Responsibility. Washington, DC. $25,000. To support the exchange in 1994 of physicians, scientists, and environmental health professionals from PSR chapters in the northwestern United States and from Chelyabinsk, Russia, in a program designed to promote improved safety and environmental conditions at nuclear plants in both countries.

Resources for the Future. Washington, DC. $15,000. To enable representatives from RFF to conduct collaborative research on environmental issues and concerns in the Ukraine.

River Watch Network. Montpelier, VT. $15,000. To enable representatives of the Goncol Foundation in Hungary to participate in a training program at River Watch focusing on organizational development, technical training, and strategic planning in spring 1993.

Tufts University. Boston, MA. $30,712. To support the international travel expenses of a project developed by the Program for the Study of Sustainable Change and Development at Tufts to incorporate environmental data and concerns into a new economics textbook for use in Russia.

University of California, Santa Cruz. Santa Cruz, CA. $35,000. To provide support to enable Russian and American scientists to participate in a project organized by the Predatory Bird Research Group at UCSC on the conservation of the habitat of the Altai falcon in Russia.

Application process. *Initial contact:* Short letter with brief project description. If the project qualifies for consideration by the Trust, more detailed information will be requested.
When to apply: At least six months before project date.
Materials available: "General Information" and "Application Procedures" (information sheet).

Emphases. *Recipients:* Educational institutions, museums, nonprofit organizations, research institutions.
Activities: Collaborative efforts, conferences, demonstration programs, direct services, exhibits, fieldwork, innovative programs, networking, planning, policy analysis/development, research (scholarly/scientific), seminars, symposia/colloquia, technical assistance, training, workshops.
Types of support: Fellowships, internships, leveraging funds, projects, technical assistance, travel expenses.
Geography: U.S. organizations working on projects involving the former Soviet Union and Central and Eastern Europe, only.

Limitations. *Recipients:* Individuals, public agencies, religious organizations.
Activities: Conflict resolution, education, expeditions/tours, land acquisition, lobbying, political activities, publications, volunteerism, youth programs.
Types of support: Advertising campaigns, annual campaigns, capital campaigns/expenses, computer hardware, continuing support, debt retirement, endowments, equipment, facilities, general purposes, loans, maintenance, membership campaigns, mortgage reduction, operating costs, program-related investments, scholarships.

Marcia Brady Tucker Foundation

11 South Washington Street
Easton, Maryland 21601
EIN: 136161561   Type: Independent
Contact: Luther Tucker, Jr., President

History and philosophy. The Foundation was established in 1941 by Marcia Brady Tucker. It makes grants in the areas of religion, welfare, medicine, education, culture, and environment.

Officers and directors. *Officers:* Elizabeth T. Sanders, Chairman; Luther Tucker, Jr., President; Naomi T. Stoehr, Secretary; Carll Tucker, Treasurer. *Directors:* Marcia T. Boogaard, Helen Sanders Gray, Elizabeth T. Sanders, Elizabeth Stoehr, Naomi T. Stoehr, Carll Tucker, Gay Tucker, Rev. Luther Tucker, Luther Tucker, Jr., Nicholas Tucker, Toinette Tucker.

Financial data.* Data for fiscal year ended December 31, 1993. Assets: $10,535,464 (M). *Total grants disbursed:* $502,776.

*As reported by Foundation.

Environmental awards. *Recent grants:* 1992 grants included support for parks, land conservation, forests, species preservation, and coastal issues.

Issues. Cli Bio Lan Agr Wat Oce Ene Was Tox Pop Dev
         •   •   •   •   •   •

Funding analysis.

Fiscal year:	1992
Env grants disb:	$65,580
Number:	9
Range:	$200–$24,800
Median:	$6,900
Pct $ disb (env/total):	12

Recipients (1992 highest):	Number:	Dollars:
Yale University, School of Forestry and Environmental Studies	1	24,800
National Fish and Wildlife Foundation	1	12,500
Westchester Land Trust, Inc.	1	10,500
Cincinnati Nature Center	1	8,000
Friends of Cincinnati Parks	1	6,900

Activity regions (1992):	Number:	Dollars:
U.S. Northeast	1	24,800
U.S. Great Lakes	3	15,500
U.S. not specified	2	13,780
New York/New Jersey	1	10,500
U.S. Mid-Atlantic	2	1,000

Sample grants (1992).
Center for Marine Conservation. Washington, DC. $1,280.
Cincinnati Nature Center. Cincinnati, OH. $8,000.
Friends of Cincinnati Parks. Cincinnati, OH. $6,900.
The Nature Conservancy, Maryland Chapter. Chevy Chase, MD. $800.
National Fish and Wildlife Foundation. Washington, DC. $12,500.
The Nature Conservancy, Ohio Chapter. Columbus, OH. $4,400.
Westchester Land Trust, Inc. Bedford Hills, NY. $10,500.
Yale University, School of Forestry and Environmental Studies. New Haven, CT. $24,800.

Application process. *Initial contact:* The Foundation awards grants to pre-selected organizations only. No unsolicited applications accepted.

Emphases. *Recipients:* Pre-selected organizations only.

Rose E. Tucker Charitable Trust

900 Southwest Fifth Avenue, Suite 2300
Portland, Oregon 97204
Tel: 503–224–3380   Fax: 503–220–2480
EIN: 936119091   Type: Independent
Contact: Thomas B. Stoel, Co-Trustee

History and philosophy. The Trust was established in 1976 through the will of Rose E. Tucker. Current priorities are: education, health and welfare, community development, social service, arts and culture, and human development, including the care and education of the underprivileged and the handicapped. Preference is given to projects within the state of Oregon, particularly within the Portland metropolitan area.

Officers and directors. *Trustees:* Milo E. Ormseth, Thomas B. Stoel, U.S. National Bank of Oregon.

Financial data. Data for fiscal year ended June 30, 1993. *Assets:* $17,239,680 (M). *Total grants disbursed:* $726,016.

Environmental awards. *Recent grants:* 1993 grants included support for land and watershed protection, land use planning, forests, and energy efficiency.

Issues. Cli Bio Lan Agr Wat Oce Ene Was Tox Pop Dev
         •   •   •   •   •   •

Funding analysis.

Fiscal year:	1991	1993
Env grants disb:	$83,000	$80,500
Number:	13	14
Range:	$2,500–$25,000	$1,500–$15,000
Median:	$3,500	$3,000
Pct $ disb (env/total):	11	11

Recipients (1993 highest):	Number:	Dollars:
1000 Friends of Oregon	1	15,000
Natural Resources Defense Council	1	15,000
The Nature Conservancy, Oregon Field Office	1	13,500
Audubon Society, Portland	1	10,000
Pacific Institute of Natural Sciences	1	5,000

Activity region (1993):	Number:	Dollars:
U.S. Northwest	14	80,500

Sample grants (1993).
Community Energy Project. Portland, OR. $2,500. Weatherization project.
Friends of Columbia River Gorge. Portland, OR. $2,500. Hearings on land use.
Natural Resources Defense Council. New York, NY. $15,000. Energy efficiency and conservation in the Pacific Northwest.
The Nature Conservancy, Oregon Field Office. Portland, OR. $13,500. Acquisition of protected areas.
1000 Friends of Oregon. Portland, OR. $15,000. Program and capacity building.

T

Pacific Rivers Council. Eugene, OR. $2,000. Plan to protect watersheds.
Public Forest Foundation. Eugene, OR. $2,000. Forest preservation program.
World Forestry Center. Portland, OR. $3,500. Timber exhibit.

Application process. *Initial contact:* Proposal including:
1. Copy of IRS tax-exempt status determination letter.
2. Basic organization background; brochure or other literature describing the applicant's purpose and activities, if available.
3. Budget or financial statement.
4. Project description.
   - Significance to the community.
   - Budget, listing other sources of income, present and future.
   - How the project will be funded in the future.
   - Project timeline, including date funds will be required.

When to apply: Anytime. The trustees meet at approximately two-month intervals to consider requests.
Materials available: Annual report, application guidelines, grants list, "Policies and Procedures."

Emphases. *Recipients:* Botanical gardens, museums, zoos.
Activities: Activism, capacity building, citizen participation, collaborative efforts, conferences, demonstration programs, direct services, education, exhibits, fieldwork, innovative programs, land acquisition, planning, policy analysis/development, publications, seminars, training, workshops, youth programs.
Types of support: Capital campaigns/expenses, equipment, facilities (construction), general purposes, multi-year grants, operating costs, pilot projects, scholarships.
Geography: Oregon, with an emphasis on Metropolitan Portland.

Limitations. *Recipients:* Individuals, religious organizations.
Activities: Advocacy, conflict resolution, expeditions/tours, litigation, lobbying, political activities, technical assistance.
Types of support: Debt retirement, fellowships, loans, program-related investments.

Alice Tweed Tuohy Foundation

P.O. Box 1328
Santa Barbara, California 93102
Tel: 805-962-6430   Fax: 805-962-6430
EIN: 956036471   Type: Independent
Contact: Harris W. Seed, President

History and philosophy. Alice Lyon Tweed Tuohy (1885–1973) was a teacher, art collector, and philanthropist. While married to mining industrialist and banker George Tweed, she was active in the civic life of Duluth, Minnesota, where she was a founder of the Tweed Museum of Art at the University of Minnesota. With her second husband Edward Tuohy, she moved to Santa Barbara where she set up the Foundation in 1956.

The Foundation continues to fund projects in Santa Barbara and at the University of Minnesota. It targets organizations that help young people by providing outstanding opportunities for performance, growth, and creativity. It also supports educational institutions, selected health care and medical organizations, and community projects.

Officers and directors. *Officers:* Harris W. Seed, President and CEO; Eleanor Van Cott, Executive Vice President and Secretary/Treasurer. *Directors:* Lorenzo Dall'Armi, Jr., Paul W. Hartloff, Jr., John R. Mackall, Harris W. Seed, Eleanor Van Cott.

Financial data. Data for fiscal year ended June 30, 1993. *Assets:* $11,040,753 (M). *Total grants disbursed:* $500,166.

Environmental awards. *Program and interests:* The Foundation does not consider environmental projects a primary interest. *Recent grants:* 1993 grants included support for a zoo.

Issues. Cli Bio Lan Agr Wat Oce Ene Was Tox Pop Dev
         •   •

Funding analysis.

Fiscal year:	1992	1993
Env grants auth:	$52,500	$17,910
Number:	3	2
Range:	$12,000–$25,000	$7,910–$10,000
Median:	$15,500	$8,955
Pct $ disb (env/total):	11	3

Recipients (1993):	Number:	Dollars:
Santa Barbara Zoological Foundation	1	10,000
Community Environmental Council	1	7,910

Activity region (1993):	Number:	Dollars:
U.S. West	2	17,910

Sample grants (1993).
Community Environmental Council. Santa Barbara, CA. $7,910.
Santa Barbara Zoological Foundation. Santa Barbara, CA. $10,000.

Application process. *Initial contact:* Full proposal (5 copies) to include:
1. Statement by the CEO that she/he has read the Tuohy Foundation's "General Guidelines" and "Application Procedures," the latest annual report, and the "Procedures and Policies Regarding Grant Requests," and that, to the best of her/his knowledge, the application complies.
2. Identity, prior history, and experience, if any, of the potential grantee and its management, including a list of the names and primary affiliations of governing board members.
3. Source of information regarding the Foundation.
4. Description in detail of the project for which funds are being solicited, including whether it is a multi-phase project, and how funds from the Foundation will be utilized.
5. Description of the amount currently expected to be spent on project, including an estimate of the total cost of all phases of the project (if it is multi-phased), and any amount presently available or obtainable, from other sources and the resources of the grantseeker.
6. Current budget of the potential grantee and any program for which funding is requested, and latest monthly comparison of operations to budget.
7. Grant or grant amounts requested, purposes, and reasons for selecting that amount. Untargeted requests for funding large projects will neither be considered nor acknowledged.
8. Each and every other person or organization to whom the same or similar request has been made and the amount of

pledge and/or gift received from each. This list should be certified as to correctness by a principal officer. Update will be required before actual award of grant.

9. Total amount of financial contributions made by members of the organization's board or equivalent body (including any advisory board), during each of the three years preceding the date of application to the Foundation. A statement identifying significant nonfinancial contributions by the board members may also be included. This list should be certified as to correctness by the CFO.

Attachments (1 copy).
1. Copies of IRS tax-exempt status determination letters and proof of the organization's status as a public organization.
2. A copy of the tax exemption letters from the applicant's state of incorporation or domicile.
3. Statement to the effect that the submitted tax exemption and private foundation rulings are current and no modifications have been made or are pending.
4. Statement that applicant has read the Expenditure Responsibility Grant Agreement, understands its terms, and willingly agrees to execute the same if and when grant is approved.
5. The last three annual accounting statements (preferably audited) and latest interim financial statements and reports.

Each proposal submitted should be able to stand by itself and not rely upon previously submitted material.

When to apply: Between July 1 and September 15. Requests received after September 15 may be deferred as long as one year or denied due to a lack of funds.

Materials available: Annual report (includes "General Guidelines" and "Application Procedures"), "Procedures and Policies Regarding Grant Requests."

Emphases. *Recipients:* Nonprofit organizations.
Activities: Citizen participation, collaborative efforts, innovative programs, technical assistance.
Types of support: General purposes, operating costs, pilot projects.
Geography: Santa Barbara area. The University of Minnesota at Duluth receives support for the visual arts and art education.

Limitations. *Recipients:* Individuals.
Activities: Conferences, feasibility studies, lobbying, political activities, publications, research, seminars.
Types of support: Capital campaigns/expenses, debt retirement, endowments, facilities, professorships.

Turner Foundation, Inc.
One CNN Center, Suite 425–South Tower
Atlanta, Georgia 30303
Tel: 404–681–9900 Fax: 404–681–0172
EIN: 581924590 Type: Independent
EGA member
Contact: Peter Bahouth, Program Director
Jan Memory, Assistant

History and philosophy. Turner Foundation, Inc. was founded in 1990 to support nonprofit organizations in their work to preserve the earth and its elements.

Officers and directors. *Officers:* R. E. Turner, President; Edward C. Harris, Executive Director. *Trustees:* Jane S. Fonda, Jennie Turner Garlington, Laura Turner Seydel, Beau Turner, Rhett Lee Turner, Robert Edward Turner IV.

Financial data. Data for fiscal years ended December 31, 1991 and 1993. *Assets:* (1991) $12,703,873 (M). *Total grants disbursed:* (1993) $2,575,000 (est.).

Environmental awards. *Program and interests:* The Foundation will support activities involved with:

- Water and toxics.

  To protect rivers, bays, wetlands, and oceans from contamination, degradation, and other abuses.

- Energy efficiency and renewables.

  To protect the atmosphere by promoting energy efficiency and renewable energy.

- Protection of forests and other habitat.

  To defend biodiversity by protecting natural habitats.

- Population issues.

  The development of a global population policy which addresses the relationships between population growth, access to reproductive health services, and global resources.

The Foundation will also support:

- Education about the need for preservation activities.
- Efforts to instill a sense of common responsibility for the fate of life on earth to citizens of all nations.

Issues. Cli Bio• Lan Agr• Wat• Oce• Ene• Was Tox Pop• Dev

Funding analysis.

Fiscal year:	1991
Env grants disb:	$581,500
Number:	10
Range:	$5,000–$250,000
Median:	$15,750
Pct $ disb (env/total):	99

Recipients (1991):	Number:	Dollars:
Better World Society	3	430,000
SatelLife	1	100,000
Greater Yellowstone Coalition	1	25,000
Worldwatch Institute	1	6,500
Environmental Defense Fund	1	5,000
Mission: Wolf	1	5,000
South Carolina Waterfowl Association	1	5,000
The Nature Conservancy, Montana Field Office	1	5,000

Activity regions (1991):	Number:	Dollars:
U.S. not specified	5	535,000
U.S. Mountain	3	35,000
International*	1	6,500
U.S. Southeast	1	5,000

*Multiple regions or not specified.

U

Sample grants (1992).
The Carter Center, Inc. Atlanta, GA. $200,000 (2 years).
Georgia Conservancy. Atlanta, GA. $10,000.
Greater Yellowstone Coalition. Bozeman, MT. $25,000.
Museum of the Rockies. Bozeman, MT. $50,000.
Native American Fish and Wildlife Society. Broomfield, CO. $50,000.
The Nature Conservancy, Montana Field Office. Helena, MT. $5,000.
Population Crisis Committee. Washington, DC. $65,000.
The Population Institute. Washington, DC. $50,000.
Smithsonian Institution. Washington, DC. $25,000.

Application process. *Initial contact:* Full proposal (2 pages) to include:
1. Proposal signed by executive or program director.
2. Legal name of organization.
3. Description of organization, its mission, and program.
4. Description of purpose of grant.
5. Amount requested.
6. List of board of directors.
7. Copy of IRS tax-exempt status determination letter.
8. Summary of the budget for project and organization.

Additional materials (5 pages maximum, 1 copy) are welcome. Send by regular mail only.
When to apply: Deadlines are April 1 and October 1. The board of trustees meets in July and December.
Materials available: Brochure.

Emphases. *Recipients:* Nonprofit organizations.
Activities: Activism, citizen participation, education.
Types of support: Multi-year grants.
Geography: Water and Toxics: Georgia, Florida, Montana, New Mexico, South Carolina; Energy: domestic and international; Forests and Other Habitats: Florida, Georgia, Montana, New Mexico, South Carolina, national programs and Russia. Population: domestic and international.

Limitations. *Activities:* Audiovisual materials, publications.
Types of support: Endowments, facilities, land acquisition, seed money.

The USF&G Foundation, Inc.
100 Light Street, 34th Floor
Baltimore, Maryland 21202
Tel: 410–547–3752   Fax: 410–547–3700
EIN: 521197155   Type: Company-sponsored
Contact: Sue Lovell, Corporate Foundation Administrator

History and philosophy. The Foundation was established in 1980 by the United States Fidelity and Guaranty Company. Grants are made in the areas of Education and Human and Community Services. In January 1995 two new focus areas will be selected.

Officers and directors. *Officers:* Norman P. Blake, Jr., Chairman, President, and CEO; Jack Hoffen, Jr., Secretary; Sue Lovell, Treasurer. *Employee Giving Council:* Mary-Lynn Antitomas, Fred Amy, Sr., John Barber, Julie Capocy, Vicki Coronel, Loretta Johnson, Mac Kennedy, Judy McClellan, Michael McNerney, Michael Norton, David C. Pease, Cecil M. Peer, Minnie Shorter, Dawn Purtell, Charlie Wancowicz, Frederick J. Wicker.

Financial data. Data for fiscal year ended December 31, 1993.
Assets: $13,212,490 (M). *Total grants disbursed:* $2,409,037.

Environmental awards. *Recent grants:* 1993 grants included support for land conservation, watershed protection, coastal issues, and outdoor education.

Issues. Cli Bio Lan Agr Wat Oce Ene Was Tox Pop Dev
                      •   •   •

Funding analysis.

Fiscal year:	1993
Env grants auth:	$37,400
Number:	3
Range:	$$6,500–$20,000
Median:	$10,900
Pct $ auth (env/total):	–

Recipients (1993):	Number:	Dollars:
The Wildfowl Trust of North America	1	20,000
Echo Hill Outdoor School	1	10,900
Chesapeake Watershed Reforestation Action Project (C–WRAP)	1	6,500

Activity region (1993 highest):	Number:	Dollars:
U.S. Mid-Atlantic	1	37,400

Sample grants (1993).
Chesapeake Watershed Reforestation Action Project (C–WRAP). Baltimore, MD. $6,500. Seton Keough High School and Cardinal Gibbons School students, through the C–WRAP program, are involved in an attempt to restore an urban watershed. The USF&G Foundation's grant provided computers to help the students identify problems and design solutions by analyzing physical and biological data.
Echo Hill Outdoor School. Worton, MD. $10,900. Environmental education targeted at elementary school age children is how Echo Hill hopes to promote a cleaner Chesapeake Bay. The *Chesapeake Baygull,* the school's newsletter, motivates teachers and students to learn about and improve the Chesapeake Bay. The USF&G Foundation's grant funded production of the newsletter.
The Wildfowl Trust of North America. Grasonville, MD. $20,000. The USF&G Foundation funded the Maryland Wetland Wise teacher outreach program. A curriculum on developing and conserving the wetlands was formed for regional and local schools, and the USF&G Foundation helped bring this environmental awareness course into the classroom.

Application process. *Initial contact:* Proposal and completed application form.
When to apply: Anytime.
Materials available: Annual report, "Policies and Guidelines" (includes application form).

Emphases. *Recipients:* Educational institutions, nonprofit organizations.
Activities: Advocacy, direct services, education, innovative programs, publications, training, youth programs.
Types of support: Matching funds, multi-year grants (2 years only), operating costs, projects, seed money.
Geography: United States.

Limitations. *Recipients:* Botanical gardens, individuals, research institutions.
Activities: Conferences, expeditions/tours, fundraising, inventories, land acquisition, litigation, lobbying, policy analysis/development, political activities, research.
Types of support: Advertising campaigns, capital campaigns/expenses, endowments, lectureships, loans, maintenance, multi-year grants, professorships, program-related investments, travel expenses.
Geography: International grants.

USX Foundation, Inc.
600 Grant Street, Room 2640
Pittsburgh, Pennsylvania 15219–4776
Tel: 412–433–5237
EIN: 136093185   Type: Company-sponsored
Contact: James L. Hamilton, III, General Manager

History and philosophy. USX Corporation (formerly United States Steel) created the Foundation in 1953. The Foundation was subsequently augmented by a merger with Marathon Oil Foundation, Inc. in 1989. USX Corporation and several of its subsidiaries remain the sole source of funds.

The Foundation "provides financial support in a planned and balanced manner to a variety of organizations and projects relating to charitable, health, educational, civic, cultural, and scientific endeavors." It has three grant programs: Education; Health and Human Services; and Public, Cultural, and Scientific Affairs.

Officers and directors. *Officers:* Charles A. Corry, Chairman; Robert M. Hernandez, CFO; Peter B. Mulloney, President; Gary A. Glynn, Vice President; Lewis B. Jones, Vice President and Comptroller; Dan D. Sandman, General Counsel and Secretary; Gretchen R. Haggerty, Vice President and Treasurer; M. Sharon Cassidy, John A. Hammerschmidt, David A. Lynch, Assistant Secretaries; John L. Richmond, Assistant Treasurer. *Trustees:* Victor G. Beghini, Charles A. Corry, Peter B. Mulloney, Dan D. Sandman, Thomas J. Usher, Louis A. Valli.

Financial data. Data for fiscal year ended November 30, 1993.
Assets: $928,591 (N). *Gifts received:* $500,208. *Total grants authorized:* $6,378,490.

Environmental awards. *Recent grants:* 1993 grants included support for beautification, land and wildlife conservation, avian research, and energy education.

Issues. Cli Bio Lan Agr Wat Oce Ene Was Tox Pop Dev
•   •   •   •   •   •   •   •

Funding analysis.

Fiscal year:	1992
Env grants disb:	$47,500
Number:	20
Range:	$1,000–$5,000
Median:	$2,000
Pct $ disb (env/total):	1

Recipients (1992 highest):	Number:	Dollars:
Indiana Environmental Institute, Inc.	1	5,000
International Bird Rescue Research Center	1	5,000
Izaak Walton League of America	1	5,000
National Energy Education Development Project (NEED)	1	5,000
University of Miami, Rosenstiel School of Marine and Atmospheric Science	1	5,000

Activity regions (1992 highest):	Number:	Dollars:
U.S. not specified	5	15,000
U.S. Great Lakes	4	9,000
U.S. Southeast	3	9,000
U.S. South Central	5	6,000
U.S. West	1	5,000

Sample grants (1993).
Canal Corridor Assocation. Chicago, IL. $7,500.
International Bird Rescue Research Center. Berkeley, CA. $5,000.
Keep America Beautiful. Stamford, CT. $20,000.
Louisiana State University Center for Energy Studies. Baton Rouge, LA. $60,000. Capital grant for endowment.
Western Pennsylvania Conservancy. Pittsburgh, PA. $2,500.
Zoological Society of Pittsburgh. Pittsburgh, PA. $20,000. Toward construction costs for the Education Complex.

Application process. *Initial contact:* Letter (2 pages) to include:
1. Description of organization and its mission.
2. Copy of IRS tax-exempt status determination letter.
3. Copy of organization's current budget and most recent audited financial report.
4. Full description of project and its goals.
5. Estimated project cost, amount requested, and explanation of need for funds in relation to total requirements of project and available resources.
6. Statement of sources of aid in hand and committed support.
7. Statement of sources of anticipated aid: prospective contributors, and amounts requested.
8. List of officers and directors.
9. Signature of authorized executive.
10. Signed statement of approval by CEO of parent organization if applicable.

When to apply: Deadlines: for Public, Cultural, and Scientific Affairs, January 15 for review in April; for Education, April 15 for review in June; for Health and Human Services, July 15 for review in October.
Materials available: Annual report (includes "Grant Application Guidelines").

© 1995 Environmental Data Resources, Inc.

Emphases. *Recipients:* Educational institutions, nonprofit organizations.
Types of support: Annual campaigns, capital campaigns/expenses, emergency funding, facilities, general purposes, operating costs, projects, scholarships.
Geography: United States only, primarily operating areas of USX Corporation.

Limitations. *Recipients:* Individuals, religious organizations (for religious purposes).
Activities: Audiovisual materials, conferences, publications, seminars, symposia/colloquia.
Types of support: Travel expenses.

Underhill Foundation

420 Lexington Avenue, Suite 3020
New York, New York 10170
Tel: 212-370-9388   Fax: 212-599-6282
EIN: 133096073   Type: Operating
Contact: Kim Elliman, Trustee

History and philosophy. The Foundation was established in 1987 by Gladys R. Underhill. Its mission is to conserve natural resources in the Americas and to provide educational and other assistance to the socially and economically disadvantaged. Substantially all funding goes to the direct operation of the Foundation's domestic and tropical conservation programs. A limited number of grants are made to other nonprofit organizations.

Officers and directors. *Officer:* Christopher J. Elliman, Program Director. *Directors:* Ann R. Elliman, Christopher J. Elliman, David D. Elliman.

Financial data. Data for fiscal year ended December 31, 1992.
Assets: $7,694,740 (M). *Gifts received:* $705,000. *Total grants disbursed:* $301,946.

Environmental awards. *Program and interests:* The Foundation's two programs each have their own foci:

The domestic program targets:

- Ancient forests in Alaska.
- Conservation education.
- Ranching and farming in the Rocky Mountains.
- Adirondack Park.
- Free-flowing rivers.

The tropical conservation program targets:

- Critical species and habitats
- Parks and other reserves
- Environmentally compatible economic development
- Indigenous environmental groups that oversee natural resources.

Recent grants: 1992 grants included support for wilderness and parks.

Issues. Cli Bio Lan Agr Wat Oce Ene Was Tox Pop Dev
           •   •   •

Funding analysis.

Fiscal year:	1992
Env grants disb:	$271,946
Number:	13
Range:	$5,000–$60,000
Median:	$15,000
Pct $ disb (env/total):	90

Recipients (1992 highest):	Number:	Dollars:
The Wilderness Society	1	60,000
Vermont Natural Resources Council, Inc.	1	41,346
The Adirondack Council, Inc.	1	30,000
Environmental Defense Fund	1	25,000
Yale University, School of Forestry and Environmental Studies	1	25,000

Activity regions (1992 highest):	Number:	Dollars:
New York/New Jersey	4	81,000
U.S. not specified	2	69,600
U.S. Northeast	2	66,346
U.S. West	3	30,000
Alaska	1	15,000

Sample grants (1992).
The Adirondack Council, Inc. Elizabethtown, NY. $30,000.
Central Park Conservancy. New York, NY. $5,500.
Environmental Defense Fund. New York, NY. $25,000.
Grand Canyon Trust. Flagstaff, AZ. $10,000.
The Parks Council, Inc. New York, NY. $20,500.
Sierra Club Legal Defense Fund. San Francisco, CA. $5,000.
The Trust for Public Land. San Francisco, CA. $15,000.
Trustees for Alaska. Anchorage, AK. $15,000.
Vermont Natural Resources Council, Inc. Montpelier, VT. $41,346.
Washington River Project. Washington, DC. $9,600.
The Wilderness Society. Washington, DC. $60,000.
Yale University, School of Forestry and Environmental Studies. New Haven, CT. $25,000.

Application process. *Initial contact:* The Foundation mainly awards grants to pre-selected organizations. Prospective applicants may send a letter (2 pages) that describes the applicant, and summarizes the goals of the project for which funding is sought. Include copy of IRS tax-exempt status determination letter.
When to apply: Anytime. The directors meet twice a year.
Materials available: Annual report (includes "Program and Grant Guidelines").

Emphases. *Recipients:* Nonprofit organizations.
Activities: Conferences, land acquisition, seminars.
Types of support: General purposes, scholarships.

Limitations. *Recipients:* Individuals.
Activities: Research (scholarly).

Union Camp Charitable Trust

c/o Union Camp Corporation
1600 Valley Road
Wayne, New Jersey 07470
Tel: 201-628-2248 Fax: 201-628-2848
EIN: 136034666 Type: Company-sponsored
Contact: Sydney N. Phin, Director, Human Resources

History and philosophy. The Trust was established in 1951 by the Union Camp Corporation. It makes grants for education, community funds, health, social services, youth and women, civic affairs, public interest, civil rights, law and justice, Jewish and Protestant causes, and culture.

Officers and directors. *Trustees:* R. W. Boekenheide, W. C. McClelland, J. M. Reed, Morgan Guaranty Trust Company of New York.

Financial data. Data for fiscal year ended December 31, 1992. *Assets:* $1,220,862 (M). *Gifts received:* $1,600,000. *Total grants disbursed:* $2,133,818.

Environmental awards. *Recent grants:* 1992 grants included support for land conservation, coastal issues, water quality, species preservation, and outdoor education.

Issues. Cli Bio Lan Agr Wat Oce Ene Was Tox Pop Dev
                    •   •   •   •   •

Funding analysis.

Fiscal year:	1992
Env grants disb:	$90,100
Number:	35
Range:	$50–$30,000
Median:	$500
Pct $ disb (env/total):	4

Recipients (1992 highest):	*Number:*	*Dollars:*
America's Clean Water Foundation	2	40,000
The Conservation Fund	2	11,000
National Audubon Society	2	10,200
Alliance for the Chesapeake Bay	1	4,000
Chesapeake Bay Foundation	1	4,000
College of William & Mary, Institute of Marine Sciences	1	4,000

Activity regions (1992 highest):	*Number:*	*Dollars:*
U.S. not specified	10	68,300
U.S. Mid-Atlantic	6	13,550
U.S. Southeast	13	5,400
New York/New Jersey	4	2,550
U.S. South Central	1	250

Sample grants (1992).
America's Clean Water Foundation. Washington, DC. $10,000.
Clean Coast, Inc. Savannah, GA. $500.
The Conservation Fund. Arlington, VA. $1,000.
Dolphin Project. Savannah, GA. $500.
Keep America Beautiful. Stamford, CT. $2,500.
Benton Mackaye Trail Association. Atlanta, GA. $300.
National Audubon Society. New York, NY. $10,000.
National Fish and Wildlife Foundation. Washington, DC. $1,000.
National Outdoor Leadership School. Lander, WY. $50.
North Carolina Forestry Foundation, Inc. Raleigh, NC. $50.
Outdoor Environmental Education Center. Sumter, SC. $500.
Rensselaer Polytechnic Institute, Department of Environmental Engineering. Troy, NY. $850.
Resources for the Future. Washington, DC. $2,500.

Application process. *Initial contact:* Proposal.
When to apply: January through August. The board meets in November.

Emphases. *Recipients:* Nonprofit organizations.
Activities: Research.
Types of support: Annual campaigns, capital campaigns/expenses, continuing support, emergency funding, endowments, equipment, facilities, fellowships, matching funds, operating costs, projects, scholarships, seed money.
Geography: Areas of company operations and national organizations in the eastern United States.

Limitations. *Recipients:* Individuals (employee scholarships only).
Types of support: Loans.

Union Pacific Foundation

Martin Tower
Eighth and Eaton Avenues
Bethlehem, Pennsylvania 18018
Tel: 215-861-3225
EIN: 136406825 Type: Company-sponsored
Contact: Judy L. Swantak, President

History and philosophy. Established in 1955, the Foundation administers the philanthropic program of Union Pacific Corporation and its operating companies—Union Pacific Railroad Company and Union Pacific Resources Company. Grants are awarded primarily to private institutions of higher education, and for health, social welfare and the arts in communities served by the Union Pacific Companies.

Officers and directors. *Officers:* Drew Lewis, Chairman; Judy L. Swantak, President; L. W. Matthews, III, Vice President, Finance; J. B. Gremillion, Jr., Vice President, Taxes; Gary M. Stuart, Treasurer; C. E. Billingsley, Controller; C. W. von Bernuth, General Counsel. *Directors:* W. L. Adams, R. P. Bauman, C. E. Billingsley, E. V. Conway, S. P. Eccles, E. T. Gerry, Jr., S. A. Goodsell, S. L. Groman, J. A. Hale, Jr., J. R. Hope, L. M. Jones, H. A. Kissinger, J. W. Leahy, Drew Lewis, C. B. Malone, L. W. Matthews, III, J. R. Mendenhall, J. R. Meyer, W. K. Peisley, T. A. Reynolds, Jr., J. D. Robinson, III, Robert W. Roth, Warren M. Shapleigh, Richard D. Simmons, M. B. Smith, Jr., G. M. Stuart, J. L. Swantak, C. W. von Bernuth, T. L. Whitaker, E. A. Willis.

Financial data. Data for fiscal year ended December 31, 1992. *Assets:* $1,835,000 (M). *Gifts received:* $7,200,000. *Total grants disbursed:* $7,162,670.

U

Environmental awards. *Recent grants:* 1992 grants included support for land conservation and public gardens.

Issues. Cli Bio• Lan• Agr Wat Oce Ene Was Tox Pop Dev

Sample grants (1992).
Idaho Botanical Gardens. Boise, ID. $3,000. To support renovation of heating plant into an Education/Visitors Center.
The Nature Conservancy, Louisiana Field Office. Baton Rouge, LA. $5,000.
Wilderness on Wheels. Lakewood, CO. $1,000.

Application process. *Initial contact:* Letter requesting the required application form.
When to apply: Deadline is August 15 for consideration during the next calendar year.
Materials available: "Application Guidelines."

Emphases. *Recipients:* Educational institutions, nonprofit organizations.
Activities: Education.
Types of support: Capital campaigns/expenses, continuing support, equipment, facilities, matching funds, program-related investments, projects, scholarships.
Geography: Primarily areas of company operations in the midwestern and western United States: Arizona, California, Colorado, Idaho, Illinois, Kansas, Louisiana, Missouri, Nebraska, Nevada, Oklahoma, Oregon, Texas, Utah, Washington, and Wyoming.

Limitations. *Recipients:* Individuals.
Activities: Fundraising, seminars.

Unitarian Universalist Veatch Program at Shelter Rock

48 Shelter Rock Road
Manhasset, New York 11030
Tel: 516-627-6576   Fax: 516-627-6596
Type: Independent
EGA member
Contact: Marjorie Fine, Executive Director

History and philosophy. The Veatch Program was established in 1959 with a gift by Mrs. Caroline Veatch to the North Shore Unitarian Universalist Society. The Program supports Unitarian Universalist organizations that foster the growth and development of the denomination and that increase the involvement of Unitarian Universalists in social action. It also supports non-denominational organizations that work in the spirit of Unitarian Universalism to strengthen the democratic process and promote justice, equity, and compassion in human relations.

The Program gives attention to projects that increase citizen participation in public policy and that promote changes in the way public and private institutions relate to disadvantaged sectors of the population. Program areas are: Denominational and Liberal Religion, Civil and Constitutional Rights, Social and Economic Justice, Environmental Protection, Global Democracy, and Training and Technical Assistance.

Officers and directors. *Officers:* Ida (Ollie) Cohen, Chair. Midge Jones, Vice Chair. *Governors:* Robert Adams, Ida (Ollie) Cohen, Midge Jones, Jean Judd, Ruth Reeves, Judith Rymer, Chester Thompson, Linda Welles. *Ex officio:* Nancy Van Dyke.

Financial data. Data for fiscal years ended June 30, 1993. *Total grants disbursed:* $9,300,000.

Environmental awards. *Program and interests:* The Environmental Protection Program "seeks to strengthen the rights and responsibilities of communities to care for the earth, air, and water that sustain them." It "funds organizations with a demonstrated ability to build bridges between environmental and economic concerns. . . ." "Because people of color have suffered the worst toxic exposure and received the least environmental attention, Veatch supports minority organizations. . . ." It also "looks for ways to push the margins of environmentalism to embrace other, overlooked environments: cities, workplaces, and rural communities; not simply wilderness."

The Program emphasizes activity as well as topic. Activities of interest include:

- Advocacy.
- Citizen participation.
- Community organizing.
- Minority involvement.
- Social and economic justice.

Topics of interest include:

- Grassroots toxics organizing.
- Military/nuclear production and waste.
- Genetic engineering/biotechnology.
- Sustainable agriculture/sustainable resource use.

Issues. Cli Bio• Lan• Agr• Wat• Oce Ene• Was• Tox• Pop Dev•

Funding analysis.

Fiscal year:	1992	1993
Env grants auth:	$1,809,000	$2,100,000
Number:	48	51
Range:	$15,000–$100,000	$10,000–$120,000
Median:	$30,000	$35,000
Pct $ auth (env/total):	20	23

Recipients (1993 highest):	Number:	Dollars:
Institute for Local Self-Reliance	1	120,000
Long Island Unitarian Universalist Fund	1	105,000
National Toxics Campaign Fund	1	100,000
Citizens Clearinghouse for Hazardous Wastes, Inc.	1	75,000
Military Production Network	1	75,000

Activity regions (1993 highest):	Number:	Dollars:
U.S. not specified	20	940,000

U.S. Southeast	5	190,000
U.S. Northeast	5	175,000
U.S. Great Lakes	5	170,000
New York/New Jersey	3	165,000

Sample grants (1993).

Campaign for Responsible Technology. San Jose, CA. $60,000 (2 years). To organize a "good neighbor" campaign in the electronics industry in the West and Southwest.

Citizens Coal Council. Washington, DC. $25,000. To support a coalition of citizen groups, individuals, and technical resource people working on coal mining and related water-protection issues.

Environmental Health Network. Chesapeake, VA. $60,000 (2 years). To give national expression to the public health consequences of toxic exposure.

Environment and Democracy Campaign. New Market, TN. $40,000. To enable U.S. environmental organizers and their international counterparts to share information and collaborate on strategies for environmental protection on the local, state, national, and international levels.

Indigenous Environmental Network. Red Lake, MN. $35,000. To strengthen a new network of grassroots Indian groups organized around environmental issues to protect the rights of Native peoples.

Long Island Unitarian Universalist Fund. Jericho, NY. $105,000. To foster social, economic, environmental, and political justice in Nassau and Suffolk counties on Long Island.

Sea Islands Preservation Project. St. Helena Island, SC. $40,000. To promote environmentally sound, community-controlled economic development on the Sea Islands while preserving the culture and land of the area's indigenous people.

Student Environmental Action Coalition. Chapel Hill, NC. $60,000. To support a national organization of students and student groups organizing around environmental issues.

Western Organization of Resource Councils. Billings, MT. $35,000. To strengthen and support grassroots organizing to counter the "Wise Use" movement in the Rocky Mountain and Great Plains regions.

White Earth Land Recovery Project. White Earth, MN. $25,000. To explore new options for the return of land to the Anishinaabeg people of northern Minnesota.

Wisconsin Farmland Conservancy. Menomonie, WI. $50,000 (2 years). To provide alternative financing and ownership options to preserve farmland for permanent sustainable production.

Application process. *Initial contact:* Written proposal, not telephone inquiry or request for personal meeting. Proposals prepared for other foundations are acceptable. Brief proposal (narrative 5–15 pages), to include:

1. Cover letter.
   - Name, address, and telephone number of the applicant.
   - Amount requested.
   - Period of time for which it is requested.
   - Description (1 paragraph) of proposed work.
2. Organizational background. History, purpose, accomplishments, decisionmaking structure, sources of financial support, membership, board and staff composition.
3. Background. Problem(s) to be addressed, universe of organizations working on the problem, how applicant fits within that universe, and why applicant is particularly well qualified to undertake the proposed activities.
4. Description of work to be undertaken. What will be done, methodology, time frame, and anticipated impact or results. If general support is sought, include outline of the work of the entire organization.
5. Budget. Organizational budget for current or upcoming year, including a list of projected income sources (including committed and solicited foundation grants), with amounts. If project support is sought, include project budget.
6. Financial information.
   - Actual income and expenses for the organization for the past two years, in a format comparable to the budget.
   - Copy of IRS tax-exempt status determination letter.
7. Supplemental information (optional). News articles, letters of support, annual reports. The submission of videotapes, audio tapes, or excessive amounts of paper is discouraged.

When to apply: Anytime. The board meets regularly throughout the year.

Materials available: Annual report (includes "Application Procedures").

Emphases. *Recipients:* Nonprofit organizations.
Activities: Citizen participation, policy analysis/development.
Geography: U.S.-based organizations with a focus of activity in the United States.

Limitations. *Recipients:* Individuals, public agencies.
Activities: Audiovisual materials, conferences, direct services, publications, research (scholarly/scientific).
Types of support: Annual campaigns, capital campaigns/expenses, endowments, loans.
Geography: International grants, non U.S.-based organizations.

United States-Japan Foundation

145 East 32nd Street
New York, New York 10016
Tel: 212–481–8753   Fax: 212–481–8762
EIN: 133054425   Type: Independent
Contact: Tom Foran, Senior Program Officer

History and philosophy. "The United States-Japan Foundation is a nonprofit, tax-exempt, philanthropic organization, incorporated in 1980 under the laws of the state of New York as a private grantmaking organization. Its principal mission "is to promote greater mutual knowledge between the United States and Japan and to contribute to a strengthened understanding of important public policy issues."

Grantmaking activities are focused in two main areas: Pre-college Education and Policy Studies. In Policy Studies, "the Foundation has established nongovernmental channels for on-going discussions between small groups of prominent experts representing academia, business, government, and the media who deal with some of the central issues facing the United States and Japan in today's changing international context. Policy study groups have been active in such fields as international finance, development assistance, multilateral crisis management, and regional security, environmental protection and energy, and science and technology. Groups have also focused on concerns in Latin America Asia, Central Europe, and the former Soviet Union."

Officers and directors. *Officers:* William D. Eberle, Chairman; Jiro Ushio, Vice Chairman; Stephen W. Bosworth, President; Ronald Aqua, Vice President; Takeaki Hori, Vice President and Director, Tokyo Office; Sander Lehrer, Secretary. *Trustees:* Thomas A. Bartlett, Stephen W. Bosworth, Robin Chandler Duke, William D. Eberle, William Frenzel, Shinji Fukukawa, Minoru Inouye, Robert McNamara, Moriyuki Motono, Isao Nakauchi, Henry Rosovsky, Yohei Sasakawa, Ryuzo Sejima, Ayako Sono, Phillips Talbot, Yoshio Terasawa, Jiro Ushio, John S. Wadsworth, Henry G. Walter, Jr. *Honorary Advisors:* Hon. Jimmy Carter; Hon. Gerald Ford; Rt. Hon. Takeo Fukada.

Financial data. Data for fiscal year ended December 31, 1993. *Assets:* $87,449,567 (M). *Total grants authorized:* $4,482,628.

Environmental awards. *Recent grants:* One grant in 1993 supported environmental justice.

Issues.   Cli   Bio   Lan   Agr   Wat   Oce   Ene   Was   Tox   Pop   Dev
                                                          •

Funding analysis.

Fiscal year:	1991	1993
Env grants auth:	$528,560	$164,538
Number:	3	1
Range:	$153,560–$200,000	—
Median:	$175,000	—
Pct $ auth (env/total):	12	4

Recipient (1993):	*Number:*	*Dollars:*
Atlantic Council of the United States	1	164,538

Activity region (1993):	*Number:*	*Dollars:*
International*	1	164,538

*United States-Japan.

Sample grants (1992–93).*
Atlantic Council of the United States. Washington, DC. $135,000. To support a U.S.-Japan consultative group on energy policies for the Newly Independent States of the Former Soviet Union (NIS).
Atlantic Council of the United States. Washington, DC. $164,538. to support second year of a U.S.-Japan consultative group on energy policies for the Newly Independent States of the Former Soviet Union (NIS).
Council of State Governments. Washington, DC. $153,560. To support the third year of exchanges between American state officials and their Japanese counterparts on the use of public-private partnerships to solve environmental problems.
Regional Plan Association. New York, NY. $157,250. To support the second year of an exchange of American and Japanese urban planners focusing on regional planning and land use issues.
World Resources Institute. Washington, DC. $50,000. To support joint U.S.-Japan research on the transfer of environmental protection technology between developed and Third World countries.

*Sample grants represent either new awards or disbursements on grants awarded in previous years.

Application process. *Initial contact:* Letter of inquiry (3 pages) to include:
1. Description of applicant organization.
2. Documentation of tax-exempt status.
3. Summary of proposed project.
4. Present sources of funds.
5. Amount of proposed grant.

When to apply: Anytime. The board of trustees meets in April and October.
Materials available: Annual report (includes "How to Apply for a Grant"), and *Forum* (newsletter).

Emphases. *Recipients:* Educational institutions, nonprofit organizations, research institutions.
Activities: Education (pre-college), policy analysis/development.
Types of support: Single-year grants only.
Geography: United States, Japan.

Limitations. *Recipients:* Individuals.
Activities: Conferences (research), education (undergraduate), exhibits, lobbying, political activities, publications, research (scholarly/scientific).
Types of support: Capital campaigns/expenses, debt retirement, endowments, equipment, facilities, loans, travel expenses.

Vancouver Foundation
505 Burrard Street
One Benthall Centre, Suite 230
Vancouver, British Columbia   V7X 1M3
Canada
Tel: 604–688–2204   Fax: 604–688–4170
Type: Community
EGA member
Contacts: Richard Mulcaster, President and CEO
                    John P. Binsted, Vice President

History and philosophy. The Foundation was founded in the early 1940s by W. J. VanDusen as a means of supporting charitable endeavors in British Columbia. The Foundation now administers more than 490 funds and makes grants with the income of their investments. Program areas are: Arts and Culture, Child and Family, Education, Environment, Health and Welfare, Youth, and Medical Services.

Officers and directors. *Officers:* Thomas G. Rust, Chairperson; Stanley Kwok, Vice Chairperson; Richard Mulcaster, President; John P. Binsted, Vice President. *Directors:* John Barnett, Bruce Buchanan, The Honorable Chief Justice William A. Esson, J. Haig deB. Farris, Peter H. Hebb, Christopher E. Hinkson, Stanley Kwok, Risa E. Levine, Maurice R. Mourton, Thomas G. Rust, Robert T. Stewart, Sandra Wilking. *Honorary Life Member:* W. Thomas Brown.

Financial data. Data for fiscal year ended December 31, 1993. *Assets:* $370,642,958 (U) (CDN). *Gifts received:* $18,252,510. *Total grants disbursed:* $22,090,918.

Environmental awards. *Program and interests:* The Environment Advisory Committee was established in 1991. It "strives to support projects based in British Columbia which are aimed at resolving environmental issues that effect the entire province, and which broaden the base of essential environmental knowledge. Grants are made to organizations which use representative and consensual processes in the development of strategies and supplementary research."

Changes in 1993 include: (1) a new focus on grants that are ecosystem-wide; and (2) a requirement that the constituencies affected by a grant be involved in its planning, management, and implementation. Activities targeted are:

- Research.
- Planning.
- Education.

Interest areas are:

- Land use planning.
- Urban open space.
- Critical habitat protection to preserve biodiversity.
- Expanding the pool of First Nations professionals in forest resource management and natural resource conservation.

Recent grants: 1993 grants included support for land conservation, (habitats, greenways, parks), biodiversity and species preservation, coastal issues, outdoor recreation and education.

Issues. Cli Bio Lan Agr Wat Oce Ene Was Tox Pop Dev
• • • •

Funding analysis.§

Fiscal year:	1991	1993
Env grants disb:	$583,340	$414,871
Number:	23	24
Range:	$750–$130,809	$712–$50,000
Median:	$15,000	$12,375
Pct $ disb (env/total):	3	2

Recipients (1993 highest):	*Number:*	*Dollars:*
Nature Trust of British Columbia	3	70,900
College of New Caledonia, Commission on Resources & the Environment	1	50,000
Spatsizi Association for Biological Research	1	38,550
Outward Bound Western Canada	2	38,306
Wildlife Rescue Association of British Columbia	2	32,298

Activity region (1993):	*Number:*	*Dollars:*
Canada	24	414,871

§Includes donor-advised and discretionary grants.

Sample grants (1993).*

British Columbia Conservation Foundation. Vancouver, British Columbia. $20,000. Study of coastal population of marbled murrelet.
College of New Caledonia, Commission on Resources & the Environment. Prince George, British Columbia. $50,000. Social profile and adjustment issues for Cariboo/Chilcotin Regional Land Use Strategy.
Nature Trust of British Columbia. Vancouver, British Columbia. $50,000. British Columbia Conservation Data Centre Program.
Northwest Wildlife Preservation Society. Vancouver, British Columbia. $10,000. Educational programs on wildlife and endangered species.
Outward Bound Western Canada. Vancouver, British Columbia. $30,600. Vista youth at risk.
Pacific Salmon Foundation. Vancouver, British Columbia. $20,570. Education projects.
Spatsizi Association for Biological Research. Smithers, British Columbia. $38,550. Studies on the Predator-Ungulate Ecosystem in the Spatsizi Wilderness Park Area.

*Includes donor-advised and discretionary grants.

Application process. *Initial contact:* Telephone or write to request funding guidelines and program area goals and objectives. Brief outline proposal (2–3 pages) to include:
1. Mandate of applicant organization.
2. Needs or specific problems project will address.
3. Proposed activities.
4. Proposed timeline.
5. Geographic scope of project.
6. Indication of community support.
7. Projected budget including other funding sources and amount requested from Vancouver Foundation.

If the proposal is deemed appropriate for the Foundation, a formal application form will be sent.
When to apply: Deadlines for completed proposals are in early January, April, and September.
Materials available: Annual report, "Application Process and Grants & Distribution," *Foundation Focus* (newsletter).

Emphases. *Recipients:* Nonprofit organizations registered under the Societies Act of British Columbia.
Activities: Policy analysis/development, research.
Types of support: Capital campaigns/expenses, pilot projects, program-related investments.
Geography: British Columbia.

Limitations. *Recipients:* Individuals.
Activities: Conferences, fundraising, land acquisition, seminars, symposia/colloquia, workshops.
Types of support: Debt retirement, equipment, operating costs, travel expenses.

R. T. Vanderbilt Trust
30 Winfield Street
Norwalk, Connecticut 06855
Tel: 203-853-1400
EIN: 066040981   Type: Independent
Contact: Hugh B. Vanderbilt, Sr., Chair

History and philosophy. The Trust was established in 1951. It's interests are education, conservation, hospitals, cultural programs, and historic preservation.

Officers and directors. *Officer:* Hugh B. Vanderbilt, Sr., Chairman. *Trustees:* Hugh B. Vanderbilt, Sr., Robert T. Vanderbilt.

V

Financial data. Data for fiscal year ended December 31, 1992. *Assets:* $7,917,554 (M). *Total grants disbursed:* $344,195.

Environmental awards. *Recent grants:* 1992 awards included support for land conservation and beautification, national parks, species preservation, coastal issues, and a zoo.

Issues. Cli Bio• Lan• Agr Wat Oce• Ene Was Tox Pop• Dev

Funding analysis.

Fiscal year:	1992
Env grants disb:	$24,000
Number:	10
Range:	$250–$10,000
Median:	$1,000
Pct $ disb (env/total):	7

Recipients (1992 highest):	Number:	Dollars:
NYZS/The Wildlife Conservation Society	1	10,000
National Audubon Society	1	5,000
America the Beautiful Fund	1	2,000
Suncoast Bird Sanctuary	1	1,750
Connecticut Audubon Society	1	1,000
Connecticut Forest and Park Association, Inc.	1	1,000
National Parks and Conservation Association	1	1,000
The Trust for Public Land	1	1,000
The Wilderness Society	1	1,000

Activity regions (1992):	Number:	Dollars:
New York/New Jersey	1	10,000
U.S. not specified	4	9,000
U.S. Northeast	2	2,000
U.S. Southeast	2	2,000
U.S. West	1	1,000

Sample grants (1992).
America the Beautiful Fund. Washington, DC. $2,000.
Connecticut Audubon Society. Fairfield, CT. $1,000.
Connecticut Forest and Park Association, Inc. Rockfall, CT. $1,000.
Mote Marine Laboratory. Sarasota, FL. $250.
National Audubon Society. New York, NY. $5,000.
National Parks and Conservation Association. Washington, DC. $1,000.
NYZS/The Wildlife Conservation Society. Bronx, NY. $10,000.
Suncoast Bird Sanctuary. Indian Shores, FL. $1,750.
The Trust for Public Land. San Francisco, CA. $1,000.
The Wilderness Society. Washington, DC. $1,000.

Application process. *Initial contact:* Full proposal along with appropriate printed matter and a copy of IRS tax-exempt status determination letter.
When to apply: November application preferred. The board meets in April, June, September, and December.

Emphases. *Recipients:* Nonprofit organizations.
Activities: Education.

Types of support: Endowments, facilities, operating costs, projects.
Geography: Connecticut and New York.

Limitations. *Recipients:* Individuals.

Vanguard Public Foundation
383 Rhode Island, Suite 301
San Francisco, California 94103
Tel: 415–487–2111   Fax: 415–487–2124
Type: Community
Contact: Linda Lucero, Grants Director

History and philosophy. The Foundation was founded in 1972 as a partnership of donors and community activists dedicated to the promotion of peace and social justice. Its major objective "is the empowerment of historically disenfranchised sectors of society through community organizing and advocacy." Through our General Fund and Donor-Advised Programs, "we promote the development of a grassroots, progressive, and democratic movement for social change, while facilitating the empowerment of both community activists and donors. We strive to forge an active and dynamic partnership of diverse communities, in order to realize the ideal of democratic and responsive philanthropy". Interests include civil rights, economic justice, workers' rights, women's rights, education, disability, health, housing, environment, cultural activism, indigenous peoples' rights, and international solidarity.

Officers and directors. *Officers:* Kimo Campbell, Nancy Feinstein, Co-Chairs; David Matchett, Treasurer. *Directors:* Janeen Antoine, Jane Baker, Kimo Campbell, Kitty Kelly Epstein, Nancy Feinstein, Paul Kivel, Linda Lucero, David Matchett, Rob McKay, Yvette Radford, Walter Riley, Peter Stern.

Financial data. Data for fiscal year ended June 30, 1993. *Assets:* $427,708 (M). *Gifts received:* $1,083,985. *Total grants authorized:* $644,973.

Environmental awards. *Recent grants:* 1993 grants included support for environmental health of low-income persons, farmworkers, and children.

Issues. Cli Bio• Lan• Agr• Wat• Oce Ene Was Tox• Pop Dev

Funding analysis.

Fiscal year:	1993
Env grants auth:	$21,750
Number:	9
Range:	$500–$6,000
Median:	$1,000
Pct $ auth (env/total):	3

Recipients (1993 highest):	Number:	Dollars:
Pesticide Education Center	1	6,000
California Communities at Risk	2	5,500
People Organizing to Demand Environmental Rights	1	5,000
American Farmland Trust	1	1,000

Marin Agricultural Land Trust (MALT)	1	1,000
The Trust for Public Land	1	1,000
Tri-Valley Citizens Against a Radioactive Environment (CARE)	1	1,000

Activity region (1993):	Number:	Dollars:
U.S. West	9	21,750

Sample grants (1993).
California Communities At Risk. San Francisco, CA. $5,000. To work with low-income communities of color that face a toxic risk, to organize opposition and build committees that can then take on other issues.
Klamath Forest Alliance. Forks of Salmon, CA. $5,000. For general support of this coalition of community-based rural organizations involved in resource management issues, protection and rehabilitation of ancient forests and key salmon rivers, assistance to Native American tribes and residents, political education and promotion of sustainable local economies based on conservation.
People Organizing to Demand Environmental Rights. San Francisco, CA. $5,000. To build community empowerment through leadership training and education, focusing on lead poisoning among children as a first organizing effort.
Pesticide Education Center. San Francisco, CA. $6,000. To research toxic chemicals and agricultural practices from a farmworker perspective. The Center has produced videos and training manuals in Spanish and English which demystify chemical technology.

Application process. *Initial contact:* Application form to include: Summary sheet.
1. Cover Sheet from Foundation.
2. Organizational Profile form from Foundation.
Narrative.
1. History and description.
2. Organizational structure.
3. Description of project.
4. Description of relationships with other groups working on similar issues.
5. Method of evaluation.
6. Affirmative action policies.
Attachments.
1. List of the governing body, one-paragraph biographies of key personnel.
2. Three contacts with phone numbers.
3. Project budget and amount requested.
4. Most recent income, expense statements, and balance sheet.
5. Copy of IRS tax-exempt status determination letter.
6. Support material.
When to apply: Deadlines are January 1, April 1, July 1, and October 1. The allocations committee meets quarterly.
Materials available: Annual report, brochure (includes "Application Instructions," Cover Sheet, and Organizational Profile form).

Emphases. *Recipients:* Nonprofit organizations.
Activities: Advocacy, citizen participation, publications.
Types of support: Emergency funding (political), projects.
Geography: Northern California (all counties north of Monterey).

Limitations. *Recipients:* Individuals.
Activities: Audiovisual materials, conferences, education, research.
Types of support: Capital campaigns/expenses, debt retirement, equipment, travel expenses.

G. Unger Vetlesen Foundation
One Rockefeller Plaza, Room 301
New York, New York 10020
Tel: 212–586–0700
EIN: 131982695   Type: Independent
Contact: George Rowe, Jr., President

History and philosophy. Established in 1955 by George Unger Vetlesen, the Foundation primarily supports oceanographic and geological research at scientific institutions. It also has an interest in cultural programs (emphasizing Norwegian-American relations), environment, libraries, and public policy.

Officers and directors. *Officers:* George Rowe, Jr., President; Harmon Duncombe, Vice President and Treasurer; Joseph T. C. Hart, Secretary. *Directors:* Harmon Duncombe, Joseph T. C. Hart, Eugene P. Grisanti, George Rowe, Jr., Henry G. Walter, Jr.

Financial data. Data for fiscal year ended December 31, 1992. *Assets:* $48,033,475 (M). *Total grants disbursed:* $2,413,818.

Environmental awards. *Program and interests:* The Foundation makes a biennial international science award for discoveries in the earth sciences. It also makes grants for biological, geophysical, and environmental research.
Recent grants: 1992 awards included support for fisheries and oceanographic research.

Issues. Cli Bio Lan Agr Wat Oce Ene Was Tox Pop Dev
           •   •   •

Funding analysis.

Fiscal year:	1992
Env grants disb:	$1,398,500
Number:	7
Range:	$10,000–$500,000
Median:	$163,500
Pct $ disb (env/total):	58

Recipients (1992 highest):	Number:	Dollars:
Scripps Institution of Oceanography	1	500,000
Woods Hole Oceanographic Institution	1	400,000
Marine Biological Laboratory	1	250,000
University of Washington, College of Fisheries Science	1	163,500
Resources for the Future	1	50,000

Activity regions (1992):	Number:	Dollars:
U.S. Northeast	3	660,000
U.S. West	1	500,000
U.S. Northwest	1	163,500
U.S. not specified	1	50,000
New York/New Jersey	1	25,000

Sample grants (1992).
Atlantic Salmon Federation. Calais, ME. $10,000.
Marine Biological Laboratory. Woods Hole, MA. $250,000.
NYZS/The Wildlife Conservation Society. Bronx, NY. $25,000.
Resources for the Future. Washington, DC. 50,000.
Scripps Institution of Oceanography. La Jolla, CA. $500,000.
University of Washington, College of Fisheries Science. Seattle, WA. $163,500.
Woods Hole Oceanographic Institution. Woods Hole, MA. $400,000.

Application process. *Initial contact:* Letter of intent.
When to apply: Anytime. The board meets in December.

Emphases. *Recipients:* Nonprofit organizations, research institutions.
Activities: Research.
Types of support: General purposes, projects.

Limitations. *Recipients:* Individuals.

Victoria Foundation, Inc.
40 South Fullerton Avenue
Montclair, New Jersey 07042
Tel: 201-783-4450 Fax: 201-783-6664
EIN: 221554541 Type: Independent
EGA member
Contact: Catherine M. McFarland, Secretary and Executive Officer

---

History and philosophy. The Victoria Foundation is a private foundation established in 1924 by Hendon Chubb. Over the past 25 years, the Foundation has focused on educational and socioeconomic challenges of the Greater Newark area and pressing environmental concerns throughout New Jersey. The Foundation's current program areas are: Education, Environment, Neighborhood Development and Urban Activities, and Youth and Families.

Officers and directors. *Officers:* Percy Chubb III, President; Margaret H. Parker, Vice President; Catherine M. McFarland, Secretary and Executive Officer; Kevin Shanley, Treasurer; Gordon A. Millspaugh, Jr., Assistant Treasurer. *Trustees:* Charles M. Chapin III, Corinne A. Chubb, Percy Chubb III, Sally Chubb, Mary Coggeshall, Robert Curvin, Gordon A. Millspaugh, Jr., Margaret H. Parker, Kevin Shanley, William Turnbull. *Emeritus:* S. Whitney Landon.

Financial data. Data for fiscal year ended December 31, 1993.
Assets: $144,916,085 (M) *Total grants disbursed:* $7,273,825.

Environmental awards. *Program and interests:* Objectives are the promotion of the sensible use of land, water, and energy throughout the state of New Jersey. The environmental program has four areas of focus:

- Promote protection and rehabilitation of the New Jersey coastline and the state's major waterways.
- Protect and conserve environmentally significant lands.
- Promote growth management in New Jersey, specifically implementation of the State Plan.
- Promote source reduction and appropriate waste management, including recycling of both solid and hazardous waste, and ameliorate the impact of toxic pollutants on residents.

1993 environmental grant composition: conservation of resources (47 percent); public education and advocacy (15 percent); research (4 percent); and education and leadership training (33 percent).

Issues. Cli Bio Lan Agr Wat Oce Ene Was Tox Pop Dev
             •   •   •   •   •   •   •   •   •

Funding analysis.

Fiscal year:	1992	1993
Env grants auth:	$989,400	$1,256,500
Number:	28	22
Range:	$4,000–$100,000	$1,000–$250,000
Median:	$30,000	$38,500
Pct $ disb (env/total):	14	16

Recipients (1993 highest):	Number:	Dollars:
The Nature Conservancy, Headquarters	1	250,000
The Trust for Public Land	1	250,000
New Jersey Conservation Foundation	1	80,000
American Littoral Society	1	62,000
INFORM	1	60,000

Activity region (1993):	Number:	Dollars:
New York/New Jersey	22	1,256,500

Sample grants (1993).
Clean Ocean Action. Sea Bright, NJ. $25,000. To build a strong, broad-based coalition dedicated to cleaning up and protecting the marine resources of the New York Bight through research, education, and citizen action.
Clean Water Fund. New Brunswick, NJ. $50,000. To support the lead demonstration project which is designed to test health risks and absorb financial costs associated with solid waste management and lead poisoning prevention and remediation.
Elliott Street School. Newark, NJ. $1,000. Toward the school's environmental beautification program.
Great Swamp Watershed Association. Madison, NJ. $42,000. To expand pilot watershed project that will link land use and wastewater allocation with watershed planning and the State Plan.
New Jersey Conservation Foundation. Morristown, NJ. $80,000. Renewed funding of the Greenways/Land Trusts Program and a planning grant to develop a reserves system for New Jersey.
Pinelands Preservation Alliance, Inc. Pemberton, NJ. $27,000. To act as the environmental voice in the legally mandated review of the Comprehensive Management Plan–the guiding land-use document of the Pinelands National Reserve.

Application process. *Initial contact:* Telephone call or short letter to request guidelines. Full proposal to include:
1. Cover sheet (1 page maximum).
   - Organization name, address, director, contact person, telephone and facsimile numbers.
   - Mission statement (1–2 sentences).
   - Services offered by organization.
   - Description of target population served.
   - Brief summary of request (1–2 sentences) stating proposed use of grant funds.
   - Amount requested.
2. Project summary (1 page).
3. Current operating budget itemizing expenses/revenue sources.
4. Project budget (1 page) itemizing projected expenses and sources of revenue.
5. Narrative (5 pages maximum).
   - Organization's purpose and needs statement.
   - Program goals and objectives.
   - Project plan, including timetable and the roles and responsibilities of program personnel.
   - Summary of program accomplishments of the last year.
6. Method of evaluation as related to program objectives.
7. Report of most recent Victoria grant.

Attachments.
1. Names and titles of people responsible for project.
2. List of board of directors.
3. Copies of organization's most recent annual report, financial statement and audit or IRS Form 990.
4. Copy of IRS tax-exempt status determination letter.

Submit only one copy of proposal. Do not use binders or staples. *When to apply:* Deadlines are February 1 and August 1. The board of trustees meets in June and November. *Materials available:* Annual report, "Grant Guidelines and Application Procedures."

Emphases. *Recipients:* Educational institutions, nonprofit organizations.
Activities: Capacity building, citizen participation, collaborative efforts, direct services, education, innovative programs, land acquisition, planning, training, youth programs.
Types of support: Continuing support, general purposes, leveraging funds, matching funds, operating costs, projects.
Geography: Newark only for Education, Neighborhood Development, Youth and Families; New Jersey for Environment.

Limitations. *Recipients:* Botanical gardens, individuals, (specific diseases, handicapped, aging).

The Vidda Foundation
c/o Carter, Carter & Rupp
10 East 40th Street, Suite 2103
New York, New York 10016
Tel: 212–696–4052
EIN: 132981105   Type: Independent
Contact: Gerald E. Rupp, Manager

History and philosophy. The Foundation was established in 1979 by Ursula Corning. Areas of interest include higher education, cultural programs, fine arts, museums, music, Catholic giving, Protestant giving, animal welfare, conservation, hospitals, social services, child welfare, and the aged.

Officers and directors. *Officer:* Gerald E. Rupp, Manager. *Trustees:* Ann F. Brewer, Ursula Corning, Thomas T. Fraser, Gerald E. Rupp, Christophe Velay.

Financial data. Data for fiscal year ended May 31, 1993. *Assets:* $1,647,910 (M). *Gifts received:* $900,000. *Total grants disbursed:* $970,276.

Environmental awards. *Recent grants:* 1993 grants included support for land conservation, urban parks, and environmental education.

Issues. Cli Bio Lan Agr Wat Oce Ene Was Tox Pop Dev
          •   •   •   •

Funding analysis.

Fiscal year:	1991	1993
Env grants disb:	$59,035	$77,500
Number:	6	5
Range:	$35–$25,000	$5,000–$25,000
Median:	$8,000	$15,000
Pct $ disb (env/total):	16	8

Recipients (1993):	Number:	Dollars:
The Student Conservation Association, Inc.	2	50,000
Central Park Conservancy	1	15,000
The Nature Conservancy, South Fork Shelter Island Chapter	1	7,500
Scenic Hudson, Inc.	1	5,000

Activity regions (1993):	Number:	Dollars:
U.S. not specified	2	50,000
New York/New Jersey	3	27,500

Sample grants (1993).
Central Park Conservancy. New York, NY. $15,000. Unrestricted operating grant.
The Nature Conservancy, South Fork Shelter Island Chapter. Sag Harbor, NY. $7,500. Unrestricted operating grant.
Scenic Hudson, Inc. Poughkeepsie, NY. $5,000.
The Student Conservation Association, Inc. Charleston, NH. $25,000. Publication of *Earth Work*.
The Student Conservation Association, Inc. Charleston, NH. $25,000. Michael Brewer scholarship fund.

Application process. *Initial contact:* Letter or full proposal (1 copy) along with copies of the organization's IRS tax-exempt status determination letter and financial statements.
When to apply: Anytime.

Emphases. *Recipients:* Educational institutions, museums, religious organizations.
Activities: Research.
Types of support: Endowments, facilities (construction), general purposes, operating costs, pilot projects.
Geography: New York.

Limitations. *Recipients:* Individuals.

V

Vinmont Foundation, Inc.
888 East 19th Street
Brooklyn, New York 11230
Tel: 718–338–5021
EIN: 131577203   Type: Independent
Contact: William R. Nye, President

History and philosophy. The Foundation was established in memory of Charles and Lily H. Weinberg in 1947. It makes grants in the areas of: civil rights and minorities' development; education and child welfare; criminal justice and services for offenders; urban and regional planning, and architectural preservation; performing and creative arts; population control; and environmental protection. Most of its funds go to the New York City area.

Officers and directors. *Officers:* William R. Nye, President; Carolyn S. Whittle, Vice President; Paul S. Byard, Secretary. *Directors:* Bruce Bozeman, Paul S. Byard, L. Franklyn Lowenstein, William R. Nye, Carolyn S. Whittle.

Financial data. Data for fiscal year ended December 31, 1993. *Assets:* $1,382,978 (M). *Total grants disbursed:* $166,500.

Environmental awards. *Recent grants:* 1993 grants included support for urban environment and wildlife preservation.

Issues. Cli Bio• Lan• Agr Wat• Oce Ene Was Tox Pop• Dev

Funding analysis.

Fiscal year:	1993
Env grants disb:	$11,000
Number:	7
Range:	$1,000–$3,000
Median:	$1,000
Pct $ disb (env/total):	7

Recipients (1993 highest):	Number:	Dollars:
Regional Plan Association	1	3,000
Environmental Defense Fund	1	2,000
Natural Resources Defense Council	1	2,000
Bronx River Restoration	1	1,000
City Parks Foundation	1	1,000
Council on the Environment of New York City (CENYC)	1	1,000
National Audubon Society	1	1,000

Activity region (1993):	Number:	Dollars:
New York/New Jersey	7	11,000

Sample grants (1993).
Bronx River Restoration. Bronx, NY. $1,000.
City Parks Foundation. New York, NY. $1,000.
Council on the Environment of New York City (CENYC). New York, NY. $1,000.
Environmental Defense Fund. New York, NY. $2,000.
National Audubon Society. New York, NY. $1,000.
Natural Resources Defense Council. New York, NY. $2,000.
Regional Plan Association. New York, NY. $3,000.

Application process. *Initial contact:* Proposal accompanied by a self-addressed stamped envelope.
When to apply: Anytime. The board meets quarterly.
Materials available: Program policy statement.

Emphases. *Recipients:* Nonprofit organizations.
Activities: Direct services, innovative programs.
Types of support: Annual campaigns, continuing support, general purposed, operating costs, pilot projects.
Geography: New York City area.

Limitations. *Recipients:* Individuals.

Virginia Environmental Endowment
Three James Center
1051 East Cary Street, Suite 1400
Richmond, Virginia 23206–0790
Tel: 804–644–5000
EIN: 541041973   Type: Independent
EGA member
Contact: Gerald P. McCarthy, Executive Director

Mailing address:
P.O. Box 790
Richmond, Virginia 23206–0790

History and philosophy. The Endowment was organized in 1977 as a nonprofit, independent corporation to improve the quality of Virginia's environment. The Endowment has been funded through a creative use of the judicial system: voluntary contributions from offending corporations. Donations have included $8 million from Allied Chemical Corporation (1977), $1 million from the FMC Corporation (1981), $193,600 from Bethlehem Steel (1990), and $200,000 from the Wheeling-Pittsburgh Steel Corporation (1991). During fiscal 1992, the Endowment received $25,000 settlements from both Hauni Richmond and IR International. The funds received from both settlements are to be used to provide information to Virginia businesses about opportunities for toxic substance use reduction.

The Endowment's purpose is to provide "venture capital" for projects that represent a commitment of public and private efforts to new ideas, and to promote public understanding of and participation in the decisions that affect environmental and natural resources on local, state, and regional levels.

Officers and directors. *Officers:* Virginia R. Holton, President; Dixon M. Butler, Senior Vice President; Jeannie P. Baliles, Vice President; Gerald P. McCarthy, Secretary; Byron L. Yost, Treasurer. *Directors:* Jeannie P. Baliles, Ross P. Bullard, Dixon M. Butler, Paul U. Elbling, Virginia R. Holton, Byron L. Yost.

Financial data. Data for fiscal year ended March 31, 1994. *Assets:* $17,822,241 (M). *Total grants authorized:* $772,588.

Environmental awards. *Program and interests:* The Endowment awards all its grants for environmental purposes. It has four major programs: the Virginia, the Virginia Mini-Grant, the Kanawha and Ohio River Valley, and the Martins Ferry–Ohio River.

Current priorities within the broad Virginia Program are environmental sustainability, water resources management, and environmental law and public policy. The Virginia Mini-Grant Program awards grants of $1,000 to $5,000 for community-based Virginia projects for river and stream protection, Chesapeake Bay restoration and protection, and environmental education. The Kanawha and Ohio River Valleys Program addresses water quality and the effects of water pollution on public health and the environment in Kentucky and West Virginia.

The Endowment also supports the Martins Ferry–Ohio River Program, which awards $33,000 in grants in one funding cycle each year to preserve, protect, and enhance the water quality, sediment quality, and aquatic life of the Ohio River in the Martins Ferry, Ohio region; and to fund Ohio River educational programs in public schools serving Martins Ferry, Ohio.

Issues. Cli Bio Lan Agr Wat Oce Ene Was Tox Pop Dev
• • • • • • • • • •

Funding analysis.

Fiscal year:	1992	1994
Env grants auth:	$887,989	$857,734
Number:	54	50
Range:	$338–$84,695	$525–$80,000
Median:	$10,000	$5,478
Pct $ auth (env/total):	100	100

Recipients (1994 highest):	Number:	Dollars:
Chesapeake Bay Foundation	4	131,500
Management Institute for Environment and Business	2	82,000
Old Dominion University	1	80,000
University of Virginia, Institute for Environmental Negotiations	1	80,000
West Virginia Rivers Coalition	1	50,000

Activity regions (1994):	Number:	Dollars:
U.S. Mid-Atlantic	48	823,209
U.S. Great Lakes	1	34,000
U.S. not specified	1	525

Sample grants (1994).

Appalshop, Inc. Whitesburg, KY. $6,000 (matched by $6,766). For a series of public forums and radio broadcasts on water issues in Dickenson County, Virginia by WMMT–FM radio.

Lord Fairfax Planning District Commission. Front Royal, VA. $3,750 (matched by $26,250). Partial support for the development of a River Corridor Management Plan for the South Fork of the Shenandoah River.

Management Institute for Environment and Business. Washington, DC. $42,000. Collaborative program between MEB and the University of Virginia's Darden School and the Institute for Environmental Negotiation to promote pollution prevention and toxics use reduction by Virginia's industries.

Maryland Save our Streams. Glen Burnie, MD. $10,000 (matched by $20,387). Partial support for a volunteer water quality training program in the Baltimore-area watershed of the Chesapeake Bay.

Old Dominion University. Norfolk, VA. $80,000 (matched by $320,000). To help establish the Virginia Coast Institute on the Eastern Shore to research and demonstrate sustainable community development.

University of Virginia, Institute for Environmental Negotiation. Charlottesville, VA. $80,000. General operating support for the Institute.

Application process. *Initial contact:* Full proposal (4 copies), signed by the organization's CEO or board chairman, to include:
1. Cover letter identifying the applicant, project title, grant request, matching funds, project schedule, and to which grants program the application is being submitted.
2. Project description (5 pages) clearly stating the need for the project, its goals and objectives and how they will be achieved, and its significance in relation to other work being done in the field.
3. Organization description, names and qualifications of key project personnel, list of members of governing board, and copy of IRS tax-exempt status determination letter, if applicable.
4. Line-item budget for proposed project, showing total project costs, all sources and amounts of matching funds (committed and anticipated), and proposed allocation of grant funds requested from VEE.
5. Project schedule.
6. Detailed plan for evaluating the project's results, including method and criteria.
7. Plans for continuing project activities and raising financial support beyond the grant period.

Additional descriptive materials may be submitted with the proposal at the applicant's discretion.

When to apply: Deadlines are January 15, May 15, and September 15 for the Virginia and Virginia Mini-Grant Programs. May 15 is the deadline for the Martins Ferry–Ohio River Program and the Kanawha and Ohio River Valley Program.

Materials available: Annual report, application materials for the Virginia Mini-Grant Program and the Martins Ferry–Ohio River Program.

Emphases. *Recipients:* Educational institutions, nonprofit organizations, public agencies.

Activities: Capacity building, citizen participation, collaborative efforts, conflict resolution, demonstration programs, education, feasibility studies, fieldwork, lobbying, networking, planning, policy analysis/development, volunteerism, youth programs.

Types of support: Continuing support, equipment, general purposes, leveraging funds, matching funds, multi-year grants, operating costs, pilot projects, program-related investments, seed money.

Geography: Grants currently awarded for programs only in Virginia, West Virginia, Kentucky, and Martins Ferry, Ohio.

Limitations. *Recipients:* Botanical gardens, individuals, religious organizations, zoos.

Activities: Activism, conferences, expeditions/tours, land acquisition, litigation, political activities, publications, research, seminars, symposia/colloquia.

Types of support: Annual campaigns, capital campaigns/expenses, debt retirement, emergency funding, endowments, facilities, indirect costs, maintenance, mortgage reduction, travel expenses.

WMX Environmental Grants Program

1155 Connecticut Avenue, N.W., Suite 800
Washington, DC 20036
Tel: 202–467–4480   Fax: 202–659–8752
Type: Company-sponsored
EGA member
Contacts: William Y. Brown, Vice President,
    Environmental Planning and Programs
    Leah Haygood, Manager Environmental Affairs
    Miren Cuenco, Executive Assistant,
    Environmental Planning and Programs

History and philosophy. The mission of WMX Technologies, Inc. is to be the acknowledged worldwide leader in providing comprehensive environmental services of the highest quality to industry, government, and consumers using state-of-the-art systems responsive to customer need, sound environmental policy, and the highest standards of corporate citizenship. In 1990 WMX established a detailed set of environmental principles, one of which directs that "[t]he company will encourage its employees to participate in and to support the world of environmental organizations, and . . . will provide support to environmental organizations for the advancement of environmental protection."

Officers and directors. *Officers:* Dean L. Buntrock, Chairman and CEO; Phillip B. Rooney, President and Chief Operating Officer; J. Steven Bergerson, James E. Koenig, Senior Vice Presidents; Joan Z. Bernstein, William Y. Brown, Herbert A. Getz, Thomas C. Hau, H. Vaughn Hooks, Ronald M. Jericho, Frank B. Moore, Susan C. Nustra, William J. Plunkett, Bruce D. Tobecksen, Donald A. Wallgren, Jane G. Witheridege, Thomas A. Witt, Linda R. Witte, Vice Presidents. *Directors:* H. Jesse Arnelle, Howard H. Baker, Jr., Dean L. Buntrock, Jerry E. Dempsey, Donald F. Flynn, Peter H. Huizenga, Peer Pedersen, James R. Peterson, Alexander B. Trowbridge.

Financial data. Data for fiscal years ended December 31, 1993. *Assets:* $16,264,476,000 (U). *Total grants and matching gifts disbursed:* $9,900,000 (est.).

Environmental awards. *Program and interests:* Current priorities for grantmaking include:

- Pollution prevention, including source reduction and energy conservation.
- Recycling of solid and hazardous waste.
- More effective regulation of industrial waste discharges.
- More effective regulation of sewage and other discharges.
- Projects to ensure proper management of waste by local authorities in developing nations, including restriction of the international export of waste.
- Conservation of biological diversity.
- Environmental internships.

Issues. *Cli* *Bio* *Lan* *Agr* *Wat* *Oce* *Ene* *Was* *Tox* *Pop* *Dev*
  •   •   •   •   •   •   •   •   •   •

Funding analysis.§

Fiscal year:	1992	1993
Env grants auth:	$754,000	$701,000
Number:	30	32
Range:	$10,000–$100,000	$10,000–$125,000
Median:	$22,500	$17,500

Pct $ disb (env/total):

Recipients (1993 highest):	Number:	Dollars:
National Audubon Society	1	125,000
World Wildlife Fund	1	40,000
National Wildlife Federation	1	59,000
Center for Marine Conservation	1	35,000
Keep America Beautiful, Inc.	1	31,000

Activity regions (1993 highest):	Number:	Dollars:
U.S. not specified	19	489,000
U.S. Great Lakes	4	67,000
International*	2	60,000
U.S. Northeast	2	35,000
U.S. Mountain	1	25,000

*Multiple regions or not specified.

§Does not includes grants of less than $10,000: 93 grants in 1993; 71 grants in 1992.

Sample grants (1993).
Center for Marine Conservation. Washington, DC. $35,000. To support CMC's wastewater management program.
Environmental Law Institute. Washington, DC. $20,000. To support ELI's international programs.
Friends of the Chicago River. Chicago, IL. $1,000. General support.
Isaak Walton League. Arlington, VA. $3,000. To support work on stream pollution monitoring.
National Audubon Society. New York, NY. $125,000. To prepare a report on the economic value of wetlands.
Wetlands Research, Inc. Chicago, IL. $5,000. To support wetlands restoration research.
World Resources Institute. Washington, DC. $20,000. To support a project on technologies for sustainable development.
World Wildlife Fund. Washington, DC. $40,000. To support biological diversity programs.

Application process. *Initial contact:* Short proposal to include:
1. Brief history of organization, including a general statement of its primary mission, purpose, and goals.
2. Brief summary of proposal (1–2 pages), including a statement of need to be addressed and explanation of how request meets grant program's guidelines.
3. Copy of organization's most recent audited financial statements and approved operating budget.
4. Project budget and plan for evaluating completed project.
5. List of other public and private contributors of support during the most recently completed fiscal year.
6. List of current trustees and board of directors and their affiliations.
7. Copy of IRS tax-exempt status determination letter.

When to apply: Anytime.
Materials available: Annual report, "Annual Environmental Report," "Annual Environmental Report Summary," "Annual Report of Corporate Contributions."

Emphases. *Recipients:* Nonprofit organizations.
Activities: Activism, advocacy, citizen participation, education, land acquisition, networking, policy analysis/development, publications, symposia/colloquia, workshops, youth programs.
Types of support: Internships, pilot projects, projects.

Limitations. *Recipients:* Individuals.

Alex C. Walker Educational & Charitable Foundation
c/o Pittsburgh National Bank, Trust Department 970
One Oliver Plaza, 28th Floor
Pittsburgh, Pennsylvania 15265–0970
Tel: 412–762–3866
EIN: 256109746   Type: Independent
Contact: Henry C. Flood, Jr., Vice President

History and philosophy. Established in 1967 by Alex C. Walker, the Foundation funds economic research and applied projects that subscribe to a conservative pro-market point-of-view.

Officers and directors. *Trustees:* Dr. Barrett C. Walker, T. Urling Walker, Pittsburgh National Bank.

Financial data. Data for fiscal year ended December 31, 1993. *Assets:* $5,181,721 (M). *Total grants disbursed:* $198,200.

Environmental awards. *Program and interests:* During the last several years the Foundation has made some environmental grants as an experiment, but considers them incidental to its main focus on economic research. Whether or not the Foundation will continue to fund environmental projects is uncertain.

Issues.   Cli   Bio   Lan   Agr   Wat   Oce   Ene   Was   Tox   Pop   Dev
                •   •

Funding analysis.

Fiscal year:	1993
Env grants disb:	$16,000
Number:	1
Range:	–
Median:	–
Pct $ disb (env/total):	8

Recipient (1993):	Number:	Dollars:
The Nature Conservancy, Latin America Division	1	16,000

Activity region (1993):	Number:	Dollars:
Latin America	1	16,000

Sample grant (1993).
The Nature Conservancy, Latin American Division. Arlington, VA. $16,000. Project grant.

Application process. *Initial contact:* Proposal.
When to apply: Anytime. The board meets quarterly.

Emphases. *Activities:* Research.

Limitations. *Recipients:* Individuals.
Types of support: Endowments, facilities.

Wallace Genetic Foundation, Inc.
4900 Massachusetts Avenue, N.W., Suite 220
Washington, DC 20016
Tel: 202–966–2932   Fax: 202–362–1510
EIN: 136162575   Type: Independent
EGA member
Contact: Polly Lawrence, Research Secretary

Sustainable Development Program:
1120 19th Street, N.W., Suite 550
Washington, DC 20036
Tel: 202–452–1530   Fax: 202–293–1795
E-mail: cfox@igc.org
Contact: Charlotte Fox, Program Officer

History and philosophy. The Foundation was established in 1959 by the late Henry A. Wallace, former Secretary of Agriculture. Grants are generally limited to organizations associated with personal interests of the Wallace family. Core interests include: agricultural research, population, environment, higher education, and health/cancer research.

Officers and directors. *Directors:* Jean W. Douglas, Henry B. Wallace, Robert B. Wallace.

Financial data. Data for fiscal year ended December 31, 1992. *Assets:* $95,929,158 (M). *Gifts received:* $417,000. *Total grants disbursed:* $2,680,722.

Environmental awards. *Program and interests:* Interests are:

- Agricultural research.
- Preservation of farmland.
- Ecology.
- Conservation.
- Sustainable development.

In its Sustainable Development Program, the Foundation seeks out and supports initiatives requiring private money that credibly promise to advance global progress towards and/or address major obstacles to an environmentally sustainable society. Obstacles include interrelated issues of population growth; nonsustainable corporate, government, and multi-lateral development bank policies; poverty; global climate change; pollution, waste and over-consumption; and threats to biodiversity and food production.

Issues.   Cli   Bio   Lan   Agr   Wat   Oce   Ene   Was   Tox   Pop   Dev
                •   •   •   •   •   •   •   •

Funding analysis.

Fiscal year:	1992
Env grants disb:	$945,864
Number:	30
Range:	$5,000–$105,595
Median:	$19,100
Pct $ disb (env/total):	35

W

Recipients (1992 highest):	Number:	Dollars:
Rocky Mountain Research Institute	1	105,595
Accokeek Foundation	1	100,000
Henry A. Wallace Institute for Alternative Agriculture	1	90,200
Natural Resources Defense Council	1	75,000
Drylands Institute	1	72,369

Activity regions (1992 highest):	Number:	Dollars:
U.S. not specified	11	392,200
U.S. Mid-Atlantic	2	115,000
U.S. West	3	107,369
U.S. Mountain	1	105,595
International*	2	57,500

*Multiple regions or not specified.

Sample grants (1992).
America the Beautiful Fund. Washington, DC. $20,000.
American Farmland Trust. Washington, DC. $50,000.
Environmental Defense Fund. New York, NY. $50,000.
Food and Water, Inc. New York, NY. $25,000.
Global Tomorrow Coalition. Washington, DC. $20,000.
International Council for Bird Preservation. Washington, DC. $50,000.
The Land Institute. Salina, KS. $25,000.
Land Stewardship Project. Marine on St. Croix, MN. $15,000.
National Audubon Society. New York, NY. $30,000.
National Fish and Wildlife Foundation. Tucson, AZ. $41,000.
Native Seeds/SEARCH. Tucson, AZ. $15,000.
Northwest Council of Alternatives to Pesticides. Eugene, OR. $15,000.
Resources Development Foundation. New York, NY. $15,000.
Union of Concerned Scientists. Cambridge, MA. $50,000.

Application process. *Initial contact:* Grants are usually made at the initiation of the directors.

Emphases. *Recipients:* Nonprofit organizations.
Activities: Education, research (medical).
Types of support: General purposes, projects.
Geography: National, international.

Limitations. *Recipients:* Individuals.
Types of support: Loans, operating costs, scholarships.

DeWitt Wallace–Reader's Digest Fund
261 Madison Avenue, 24th Floor
New York, New York 10016
Tel: 212–953–1201   Fax: 212–953–1279
EIN: 136183757   Type: Independent
Contact: Jane Quinn, President

History and philosophy. The Fund was created in 1965 by DeWitt Wallace. DeWitt and his wife Lila founded *Reader's Digest* with $5,000 in 1922. The "Digest" was the world's most widely read magazine by the time of Mr. Wallace's retirement in 1972.

The Fund focuses exclusively on education and youth services and has four program areas: improving elementary and secondary schools; encouraging school and community collaboration; strengthening organizations that serve youth; and increasing career, service, and education opportunities for youth.

Officers and directors. *Officers:* George V. Grune, Chairman; Jane Quinn, President; Jessica Chao, Vice President and Secretary; Rob D. Nagel, Treasurer and CFO. *Directors:* William G. Bowen, Theodore F. Brophy, M. Christine DeVita, George V. Grune, J. Edward Hall, Melvin R. Laird, Laurance S. Rockefeller, Walter V. Shipley.

Financial data. Data for fiscal year ended December 31, 1992. *Assets:* $1,133,580,423 (M). *Total grants disbursed:* $72,324,761.

Environmental awards. *Recent grants:* 1992 grants included support for youth in conservation and marine issues.

Issues.   Cli   Bio   Lan   Agr   Wat   Oce   Ene   Was   Tox   Pop   Dev
                    •   •   •

Funding analysis.

Fiscal year:	1992
Env grants auth:	$1,105,000
Number:	2
Range:	$300,000–$805,000
Median:	$552,500
Pct $ auth (env/total):	1

Recipients (1992):	Number:	Dollars:
National Association of Service and Conservation Corps	1	805,000
Miami Museum of Science, Inc.	1	300,000

Activity regions (1992):	Number:	Dollars:
U.S. not specified	1	805,000
U.S. Southeast	1	300,000

Sample grants (1992).
Miami Museum of Science, Inc. Miami, FL. $300,000 (3 years). To support a Miami Museum of Science program that enables minority students to use telecommunications and computers as tools for the investigation of the local marine environment.
National Association of Service and Conservation Corps. Washington, DC. $805,000 (3 years). To develop an ongoing program to train Corps staff and create a Technical Assistance Resource Center.

Application process. *Initial contact:* Letter (1–2 pages) to include:
1. Description of proposed project.
2. Description of organization.
3. Estimated total budget for project.
4. Portion of budget requiring funding.
When to apply: Anytime.
Materials available: Annual report (includes "Application Guidelines").

Emphases. *Recipients:* Educational institutions.
Activities: Citizen participation, education, policy analysis/development, training.

Types of support: Continuing support, fellowships, internships, operating costs, projects, scholarships, technical assistance.

Limitations. *Recipients:* Individuals, religious organizations, research institutions.
Activities: Research (medical/scholarly).
Types of support: Capital campaigns/expenses, endowments.

Lila Wallace–Reader's Digest Fund

261 Madison Avenue, 24th Floor
New York, New York 10016
Tel: 212-953-1248   Fax: 212-953-1017
EIN: 136086859   Type: Independent
Contact: Holly Sidford, Program Director

History and philosophy. Lila Acheson Wallace (1889–1984) was a graduate of the University of Oregon who worked during and after World War I to improve working conditions for women through a project run jointly by the YMCA and U.S. Department of Labor. In 1921, she married DeWitt Wallace, and a year later the two published the first issue of *Reader's Digest*. Nearly 75 years later, *Reader's Digest* is the world's most widely read magazine. Lila Wallace created the Fund in 1956 to support her belief that "the arts belong to and should be made accessible to people from diverse walks of life."

Today, to enhance the cultural life of communities and encourage people to make the arts and culture an active part of their everyday lives, the Fund supports the performing, visual, literary and folk arts. It also invests in programs for adult literacy and urban parks. Fund-initiated programs often incorporate community outreach, partnerships, and collaborations. It favors "comprehensive programs that can make substantial progress toward their goals in a period of three to five years." The Fund has nine program areas: Visual Arts, Theater, Dance, Music, Multidisciplinary, Literary Arts, Arts Education, Adult Literacy, and Urban Parks.

Officers and directors. *Officers:* George V. Grune, Chairman; M. Christine De Vita, President; Jessica Chao, Vice President and Secretary; Rob D. Nagel, Treasurer. *Directors:* William G. Bowen, Theodore F. Brophy, M. Christine DeVita, George V. Grune, J. Edward Hall, Melvin R. Laird, Laurance S. Rockefeller, Walter V. Shipley.

Financial data. Data for fiscal year ended December 31, 1993. *Assets:* $772,782,750 (M). *Total grants authorized:* $45,599,709.

Environmental awards. *Program and interests:* The Urban Parks program has an ongoing $7.9 million five-year plan to restore the natural forests of New York City parks. "Begun in 1990, this program also encourages community participation and promotes environmental education to raise residents' awareness, appreciation, and commitment to their parks." Components of the program include the Urban Forest and Education Program of the City Parks Foundation, restoration work at Wave Hill, The New York Botanical Garden's Forest Project, and other projects. The Fund does not award grants for conservation or other environmental purposes per se.

Recent grants: Grants in 1990 and 1991 included major support for New York City parks. In 1992, the Fund made a $300,000 grant to The Trust for Public Land to support a needs assessment and analysis of best practices for promoting urban open space for public use. In 1993 the Fund made a $300,000 grant to support the design of an initiative that will create parks in underserved communities in up to 12 mid-sized cities around the nation.

Issues.   Cli   Bio•   Lan•   Agr   Wat   Oce   Ene   Was   Tox   Pop   Dev

Funding analysis.

Fiscal year:	1991	1993
Env grants auth:	$50,000	$310,000
Number:	1	2
Range:	–	$10,000–$300,000
Median:	–	$155,000
Pct $ auth (env/total):	<1	1

Recipients (1993):	Number:	Dollars:
The Trust for Public Land	1	300,000
Jacksonville Zoological Society	1	10,000

Activity regions (1993):	Number:	Dollars:
U.S. not specified	1	300,000
U.S. Southeast	1	10,000

Sample grants (1993).*
City Parks Foundation, Inc. New York, NY. $1,274,990.
Jacksonville Zoological Society. Jacksonville, FL. $10,000. To upgrade teacher guides and other materials used in public schools.
The Trust for Public Land. San Francisco, CA. $300,000. Program design for a major multi-year initiative to create parks in underserved communities in eight to twelve mid-sized cities across the country. The Trust will work with the Fund to identify the cities and help each develop action plans to improve the number and quality of neighborhood parks.
Wave Hill, Inc. Bronx, NY. $110,000.

*Sample grants represent either new awards or disbursements on grants awarded in previous years.

Application process. *Initial contact:* Brief letter of inquiry (2–3 pages) describing the proposed project, the applicant organization, the project's estimated total budget, and the relationship between the project's goals and the Fund's mission. The Fund may then request additional information, including but not limited to:
1. A more complete proposal narrative.
2. Most recent audited financial statement.
3. Project budget.
4. Institutional operating budget for the current fiscal year.
5. Background information on the artists, key staff, and other professionals responsible for the project.
6. List of board of directors and their professional affiliations.
7. List of other funding sources, including pending requests.
8. Copy of IRS tax-exempt status determination letter.

Proposals are reviewed for their potential to advance the Fund's mission, the quality of the idea and qualifications of personnel involved, and the clarity of the project's goals and objectives. In addition, the organization's ability to complete the proposed project, measure its outcomes, and maintain its financial stability

will be considered. The Fund generally does not award grants of less than $50,000, or for long-term support of an organization.
When to apply: Anytime. The board meets four times a year.
Materials available: Annual report (includes "Application Guidelines").

Emphases. *Recipients:* Nonprofit organizations.
Types of support: Projects.
Geography: United States.

Limitations. *Recipients:* Individuals, public agencies.
Activities: Policy analysis/development, research (medical/scholarly).
Types of support: Annual campaigns, capital campaigns/expenses, endowments, facilities (construction).

Bill & Edith Walter Foundation
c/o Schottenstein, Zox & Dunn
41 South High Street
Huntington Center
Columbus, Ohio 43215
Tel: 614–462–2277   Fax: 614–464–1135
EIN: 311102570   Type: Independent
Contact: Frederick L. Fisher, Secretary/Treasurer

History and philosophy. Established in 1983, the Foundation awards grants for the performing arts, environment, nursing, and religious purposes in the Columbus area.

Officers and directors. *Officers:* James E. Lane, President, Frederick L. Fisher, Secretary/Treasurer. *Trustees:* Frederick L. Fisher, Betty B. Lane, James E. Lane.

Financial data. Data for fiscal year ended December 31, 1993.
Assets: $474,682 (M). *Total grants disbursed:* $88,400.

Environmental awards. *Recent grants:* The Foundation's largest grant in 1993 supported environmental projects at a local university.

Funding analysis.

Fiscal year:	1991	1993
Env grants disb:	$50,000	$54,400
Number:	1	1
Range:	–	–
Median:	–	–
Pct $ disb (env/total):	16	62

Recipient (1993):	Number:	Dollars:
The Ohio State University	1	54,400

Activity region (1993):	Number:	Dollars:
U.S. Great Lakes	1	54,400

Sample grant (1993).
The Ohio State University. Columbus, OH. $54,400.

Application process. *Initial contact:* The Foundation awards grants to pre-selected organizations only. No unsolicited applications accepted.

Emphases. *Recipients:* Pre-selected organizations only.
Geography: Central Ohio.

Limitations. *Recipients:* Individuals.

C. A. Webster Foundation
P.O. Box 126
Linden, California 95236
Tel: 209–887–3523
EIN: 946072116   Type: Independent
Contact: William H. Williams

History and philosophy. The Foundation's charitable interests involve higher education, animal welfare, social services, conservation, and religion in the Stockton, California area.

Officers and directors. *Directors:* Alberta Lewallen, Dorothy Lundblad, Marjorie Williams.

Financial data. Data for fiscal year ended December 31, 1992.
Assets: $1,341,156 (M). *Total grants disbursed:* $54,000.

Environmental awards. *Recent grants:* 1992 grants included support for farmland preservation, land conservation, coastal issues, and species protection.

Issues.   Cli   Bio•   Lan•   Agr•   Wat   Oce•   Ene   Was   Tox   Pop   Dev

Funding analysis.

Fiscal year:	1992
Env grants disb:	$13,500
Number:	6
Range:	$500–$5,000
Median:	$2,000
Pct $ disb (env/total):	25

Recipients (1992 highest):	Number:	Dollars:
Land Utility Trust	1	5,000
The Nature Conservancy, Headquarters	1	3,000
American Farmland Trust	1	2,000
Ducks Unlimited, Inc.	1	2,000
Audubon Canyon Ranch	1	1,000

Activity regions (1992):	Number:	Dollars:
U.S. not specified	5	12,500
U.S. West	1	1,000

Sample grants (1992).
American Farmland Trust. Washington, DC. $2,000.
Audubon Canyon Ranch. Stinson Beach, CA. $1,000.
Ducks Unlimited, Inc. Memphis, TN. $2,000.
The Nature Conservancy, Headquarters. Arlington, VA. $3,000.
National Wildflower Research Center. Austin, TX. $500.

Application process. *Initial contact:* Proposal to include:
1. Description of organization.
2. Purpose of grant.
3. List of officers and directors.
4. Copy of IRS tax-exempt status determination letter.

When to apply: Anytime.

Emphases. *Recipients:* Nonprofit organizations.
Geography: Stockton, California.

Weeden Foundation
747 Third Avenue, 34th Floor
New York, New York 10017
Tel: 212–888–1672   Fax: 212–888–1354
EIN: 946109313   Type: Independent
EGA member
Contacts: Alan N. Weeden, President
            James N. Sheldon, Executive Director

History and philosophy. The Weeden Foundation was established in 1963. The founder, Frank Weeden (d. 1984), was concerned about mankind's overuse and mindless destruction of the natural resource base and the population growth which helps fuel such abuse. He was particularly concerned about the consequences of increasing pressures on the biological diversity of the Earth through destruction of environmentally significant habitat. Almost all Foundation grants are awarded for either environmental purposes or population programs.

Officers and directors. *Officers:* Alan N. Weeden, President; William F. Weeden, M.D., Vice President; John D. Weeden, Secretary/Treasurer. *Directors:* Alan N. Weeden, Donald E. Weeden, John D. Weeden, William F. Weeden, M.D.

Financial data. Data for fiscal year ended June 30, 1993. *Assets:* $26,262,217. *Total grants disbursed:* $1,599,520.

Environmental awards. *Program and interests:* Interests include:
- Population and environment.
- Biodiversity.
- Ecosystem protection.
- Natural resource conservation.
- Rainforest and habitat protection.
- Wilderness.

Issues.   Cli   Bio   Lan   Agr   Wat   Oce   Ene   Was   Tox   Pop   Dev
              •   •   •   •   •   •   •   •   •   •

Funding analysis.§

Fiscal year:	1991	1993
Env grants auth:	$485,000	$990,000
Number:	22	79
Range:	$5,000–$100,000	$1,000–$125,000
Median:	$10,000	$10,000
Pct $ disb (env/total):	47	62

Recipients (1993 highest):	Number:	Dollars:
Center for Citizen Initiatives	1	125,000
Conservation International	2	75,000
NYZS/The Wildlife Conservation Society	1	50,000
The Nature Conservancy, California Field Office	1	50,000
Baikal Watch	1	25,000
Bird Life International	1	25,000
Center for Marine Conservation	1	25,000
Health and Habitat	1	25,000
National Fish and Wildlife Foundation	1	25,000
The Nature Conservancy, Hawaii Field Office	1	25,000

Activity regions (1993 highest):	Number:	Dollars:
U.S. not specified	18	183,000
International*	8	75,000
U.S. West	4	70,000
Andean Region and Southern Cone	6	68,000
Mexico and Central America	5	65,000

*Multiple regions or not specified.

§Does not include trustee-initiated grants.

Sample grants (1993).

Alaska Conservation Foundation. Anchorage, AK. $10,000. To promote ecosystem protection.

Baikal Watch. San Francisco, CA. $25,000. For fostering alternative economies in Siberia, and to help protect the Lake Baikal ecosystem.

Bird Life International. Cambridge, UK. $25,000. To help produce a land use management and development plan for the proposed Morne Diablotin National Park in Dominica.

Catholics for Free Choice. Washington, DC. $10,000. To help heighten awareness of reproductive health issues in Latin America.

Center for Immigration Studies. Washington, DC. $15,000. For a new book entitled: *How Many Americans: Immigration, Population and the Environment,* and for general support for their immigration education initiatives.

National Wildlife Federation. New York, NY. $5,000. For their forest protection and advocacy program.

Project Raft. Berkeley, CA. $5,000. To help facilitate the creation of a new coalition of international river activists in an effort to save six endangered rivers.

Southern Utah Wilderness Alliance. Cedar City, UT. $10,000. For their Wildlife Issues and Litigation Fund.

Wetlands for the Americas. Manomet, WA. $10,000.

Woods Hole Research Center. Woods Hole, MA. $25,000. For senior staff communication expenses that are not otherwise financed.

Application process. *Initial contact:* Clear, concise statement summarizing the proposed grant. The Foundation will contact the applicant if it is interested or needs more detailed information.
When to apply: Deadlines are generally in February, May, August, and November. The board of directors meets four times a year, in early March, June, September, and December. For proposals to be considered at a particular board meeting, they must be received three weeks before. Call for specific deadlines.

Materials available: Annual report (includes "Guidelines for Grant Applications").

Emphases. *Recipients:* Nonprofit organizations.
Activities: Advocacy, demonstration programs, innovative programs, land acquisition, litigation.

Limitations. *Recipients:* Individuals.
Activities: Audiovisual materials, conferences, exhibits, research (scientific).
Types of support: Equipment, facilities.

Welfare Foundation, Inc.
1004 Wilmington Trust Center
Wilmington, Delaware 19801
Tel: 302–654–2477
EIN: 516015916   Type: Independent
Contact: David D. Wakefield, Executive Secretary

History and philosophy. The Welfare Foundation was established in 1930 by Pierre Samuel du Pont to support plans for a public secondary school system. When that project was completed, the Foundation turned its support to the community at large.

Du Pont family members are the descendants of Pierre Samuel du Pont de Nemours, a Frenchman who emigrated to America in 1800. His son, Eleuthere Irenee, founded a gunpowder factory in 1801 which was the precursor to E. I. du Pont de Nemours & Company, a manufacturer of chemicals, plastics, fibers, and specialty products.

The Foundation supports social welfare organizations, civic associations, the arts, and educational institutions.

Officers and directors. *Officers:* Robert H. Bolling, Jr., President; J. Simpson Dean, Jr., Vice President; David D. Wakefield, Executive Secretary; W. Laird Stabler, Jr., Secretary; Robert C. Barlow, Assistant Secretary; Edward Bradford duPont, Treasurer; Stephen A. Martinenza, Assistant Treasurer. *Directors:* Robert H. Bolling, J. Simpson Dean, Jr., Edward Bradford du Pont, W. Laird Stabler, Jr., David D. Wakefield.

Financial data. Data for fiscal year ended December 31, 1992. *Assets:* $57,730,482. (M) *Total grants disbursed:* $2,472,100.

Environmental awards. *Recent grants:* 1992 grants included support for river preservation, coastal issues, and education.

Issues.   Cli   Bio   Lan   Agr   Wat   Oce   Ene   Was   Tox   Pop   Dev
              •   •   •   •

Funding analysis.

Fiscal year:	1992
Env grants disb:	$80,000
Number:	3
Range:	$10,000–$50,000
Median:	$20,000
Pct $ disb (env/total):	3

Recipients (1992):	*Number:*	*Dollars:*
Chesapeake Bay Foundation	1	50,000
Delaware Bay Marine Institute	1	20,000
Stroud Water Research Center	1	10,000

Activity region (1992):	*Number:*	*Dollars:*
U.S. Mid-Atlantic	3	80,000

Sample grants (1992).
Chesapeake Bay Foundation. Annapolis, MD. $50,000. Nanticoke River Project.
Delaware Bay Marine Institute. Delaware City, DE. $20,000. Computer Equipment.
Stroud Water Research Center. Avondale, PA. $10,000. Education Program.

Application process. *Initial contact:* Letter to include:
1. Reason for grant request.
2. Pertinent financial statements.
3. Copy of IRS tax-exempt status determination letter.

When to apply: Deadlines are April 1 and November 1.
Materials available: Annual report.

Emphases. *Recipients:* Educational institutions, museums, nonprofit organizations.
Types of support: Annual campaigns, capital campaigns/expenses, endowments, equipment, maintenance, matching funds, operating costs.
Geography: Delaware and the Greater Wilmington area.

Limitations. *Recipients:* Individuals.

Henry E. and Consuelo S. Wenger Foundation, Inc.
P.O. Box 43098
Detroit, Michigan 48243–0098
Tel: 313–567–1212   Fax: 313–567–1214
EIN: 386077419   Type: Independent
Contact: Henry Penn Wenger, President

History and philosophy. The Foundation was established in 1959. Primary areas of giving are: education, hospitals, cultural activities, environment, and conservation.

Officers and directors. *Officers:* Henry Penn Wenger, President; Diane Wenger, Vice President; Miles Jaffe, Secretary; William E. Slaughter, Jr., Treasurer. *Directors:* Miles Jaffe, William E. Slaughter, Jr., Diane Wenger, Henry Penn Wenger.

Financial data. Data for fiscal year ended December 31, 1993. *Assets:* $8,236,536 (M). *Total grants disbursed:* $758,900.

Environmental awards. *Recent grants:* 1993 grants included support for land and wildlife conservation.

Issues.   Cli   Bio   Lan   Agr   Wat   Oce   Ene   Was   Tox   Pop   Dev
                    •   •   •

Funding analysis.

Fiscal year:	1991	1992
Env grants disb:	$82,300	$37,100
Number:	13	9
Range:	$100–$50,000	$100–$12,500
Median:	$1,000	$2,500
Pct $ disb (env/total):	10	5

Recipients (1992 highest):	Number:	Dollars:
The Nature Conservancy, Illinois Field Office	1	12,500
NYZS/The Wildlife Conservation Society	3	10,000
Trout Unlimited, Inc.	1	10,000
Ducks Unlimited, Inc.	1	2,500
Little Traverse Conservancy	2	1,100

Activity regions (1992):	Number:	Dollars:
U.S. Great Lakes	4	14,600
U.S. not specified	2	12,500
New York/New Jersey	3	10,000

Sample grants (1993).
American Rivers, Inc. Washington, DC. $5,000.
Detroit Zoological Society. Royal Oak, MI. $1,000.
The Greenwich Land Trust, Inc. Greenwich, CT. $10,000.
Lake Forest Open Lands Association. Lake Forest, IL. $1,000.
Little Traverse Conservancy. Harbor Springs, MI. $1,100.
Montana Audubon Council. Helena, MT. $1,000.
Montana Land Reliance. Helena, MT. $50,000.
NYZS/The Wildlife Conservation Society. Bronx, NY. $10,000.
Williamstown Rural Lands Foundation. Williamstown, MA. $20,000.

Application process. *Initial contact:* The Foundation awards grants to pre-selected organizations only. No unsolicited applications accepted.

Emphases. *Recipients:* Pre-selected organizations only.

Limitations. *Recipients:* Individuals.

Westinghouse Foundation

c/o Westinghouse Electric Corporation
11 Stanwix Street
Pittsburgh, Pennsylvania 15222–1384
Tel: 412–642–6033   Fax: 412–642–4874
EIN: 251357168   Type: Company-sponsored
Contact: Cheryl L. Kubelick, Manager,
            Contributions and Community Affairs

History and philosophy. The Foundation serves as the funding program for the Westinghouse Electric Corporation. It was created in 1987 through a merger of Westinghouse's three previous funding programs: the Westinghouse Electric Fund, the Westinghouse Educational Foundation, and the Westinghouse International Educational Foundation. Program areas are: Education, Health and Welfare, Culture and the Arts, and Civic and Social.

Officers and directors. *Officers:* Frederick W. Hill, Chairman; G. Reynolds Clark, President; Cheryl L. Kubelick, Secretary; Eric H. Dussling, Treasurer. *Trustees:* Louis J. Briskman, Thomas P. Costello, Frederick W. Hill, Warren H. Hollinshead, Richard A. Linder, James Moore, John B. Yasinsky.

Financial data. Data for fiscal year ended December 31, 1992. *Assets:* $3,703,775 (M). *Gifts received:* $5,000,000. *Total grants disbursed:* $6,749,293.

Environmental awards. *Program and interests:* Environmental awards are made through Education, Health and Welfare, and Civic and Social programs.
Recent grants: 1992 grants included support for watershed and coastal protection, outdoor recreation, and education.

Issues. Cli Bio Lan Agr Wat Oce Ene Was Tox Pop Dev
              •   •   •   •

Funding analysis.

Fiscal year:	1991	1992
Env grants auth:	$74,704	$33,150
Number:	5	6
Range:	$5,000–$35,000	$1,690–$10,000
Median:	$9,704	$5,563
Pct $ disb (env/total):	1	<1

Recipients (1992 highest):	Number:	Dollars:
Earthwatch Expeditions, Inc.	1	10,000
Westmoreland Conservancy	1	7,835
The Nature Conservancy, Headquarters	1	6,125
Chesapeake Bay Foundation	1	5,000
Maryland Save Our Streams	1	2,500

Activity regions (1992):	Number:	Dollars:
U.S. Mid-Atlantic	4	17,025
U.S. not specified	2	16,125

Sample grants (1992).
Chesapeake Bay Foundation. Annapolis, MD. $5,000.
Mainstream, Inc. Bethesda, MD. $2,500.
Maryland Save Our Streams. Glen Burnie, MD. $2,500.

Application process. *Initial contact:* Full proposal to include:
1. Organization's mission statement.
2. Project summary.
   - Grant purpose and amount.
   - Project timetable.
   - Population served, and method of project evaluation.
3. Project budget.
4. List of trustees or board of directors, as well as the project head and his or her qualifications.
5. Proof of IRS tax-exempt status.

When to apply: Anytime.
Materials available: Annual report (includes "Guidelines," "Restrictions," and "Grant Application Process"), "Guidelines."

Emphases. *Recipients:* Botanical gardens, educational institutions, museums, nonprofit organizations, zoos.

Types of support: Matching funds, pilot projects, scholarships (employee-related).
Geography: Communities where company has significant presence.

Limitations. *Recipients:* Educational institutions (two-year and community colleges), individuals, public agencies, research institutions.
Activities: Activism, conferences, land acquisition, political activities, research.
Types of support: Advertising campaigns, debt retirement, emergency funding, endowments, equipment, facilities, fellowships, internships, lectureships, loans, mortgage reduction, professorships, scholarships, travel expenses.

Weyerhaeuser Company Foundation
CH 1F31
Tacoma, Washington 98477
Tel: 206-924-3159
EIN: 916024225   Type: Company-sponsored
Contact: Elizabeth A. Crossman, Vice President

History and philosophy. The Weyerhaeuser Company Foundation was created in 1948. It's two-fold mission is: (1) to improve the quality of life in communities where Weyerhaeuser has a major presence, and (2) to provide leadership that increases public understanding of issues where society's needs intersect with the interests of the forest products industry. The Foundation divides its grants between community giving and industry-related giving. Community grants focus on social services, education, civic improvements, emergency services, arts, and culture. Industry-related grants have an environmental thrust.

Officers and directors. *Officers:* Charles W. Bingham, Chairman; Mack L. Hogans, President; Elizabeth A. Crossman, Vice President; Karen L. Veitenhans, Secretary; David R. Edwards, Treasurer; Sandy D. McDade, Assistant Secretary; Linda L. Terrien, Assistant Treasurer. *Trustees:* Charles W. Bingham, William R. Corbin, John W. Creighton, Jr., Steven R. Hill, Mack L. Hogans, Norman E. Johnson, C. Stephen Lewis, W. Howarth Meadowcroft, Susan M. Mersereau, William C. Stivers, George H. Weyerhaeuser, Robert B. Wilson.

Financial data.* Data for fiscal year ended December 31, 1993. *Assets:* $14,356,779 (U). *Gifts received:* $4,887,276. *Total grants disbursed:* $5,532,517.

*Assets as reported by Foundation.

Environmental awards. *Program and interests:* Industry-related giving targets five priority areas:
- Forestry practices.
- Manufacturing's effects on air, land, and water.
- Free trade.
- Recycling.
- Diversity.

Recent grants: 1993 grants included support for land conservation, forest-related issues, wildlife protection, and environmental education.

Issues.   Cli Bio Lan Agr Wat Oce Ene Was Tox Pop Dev
              •   •   •   •   •   •

Funding analysis.

Fiscal year:	1993
Env grants auth:	$553,300
Number:	65
Range:	$1,000–$50,000
Median:	$5,000
Pct $ auth (env/total):	11

Recipients (1993 highest):	*Number:*	*Dollars:*
The Nature Conservancy, Washington Field Office	2	55,000
City of Washington	1	50,000
Resources for the Future	1	50,000
The Trust for Public Land	1	50,000
Woodland Park Zoological Society	1	25,000

Activity regions (1993 highest):	*Number:*	*Dollars:*
U.S. Northwest	32	289,500
U.S. not specified	10	97,000
U.S. Southeast	8	84,100
U.S. South Central	5	43,500
U.S. Great Lakes	7	31,200

Sample grants (1993).
American Forest Foundation. Washington, D.C. $5,000. To support the Arkansas Project Learning Tree program.
American Forestry Association. Washington, D.C. $5,000.
National Fish and Wildlife Foundation. Washington, D.C. $6,000. Supporting the Partners in Flight program for the conservation of neotropical migratory birds.
The Nature Conservancy, Mississippi Field Office. Jackson, MS. $1,000.
The Nature Conservancy, Virginia Field Office. Charlottsville, VA. $5,000.
The Nature Conservancy, Washington Field Office. Seattle, WA. $5,000.
North Carolina Forestry Foundation, Inc. Raleigh, NC. $2,100.
Oregon Women for Timber. La Grande, OR. $2,500. For the Trees are for People program.
Washington Environmental Council. Seattle, WA. $1,000. Toward purchase of computer equipment.
Wildlife Habitat Enhancement Council. Silver Spring, MD. $3,000.
Woodland Park Zoological Society. Seattle, WA. $25,000. Capital campaign.
World Forestry Center. Portland, OR. $12,500. Supporting a book project.

Application process. *Initial contact:* Telephone the Foundation to request application form.
When to apply: Anytime. Proposals are reviewed year-round but requests submitted in the fall may not be considered until the following year.

Materials available: Biennial report (includes "Grantmaking Guidelines" and application form).

Emphases. *Recipients:* Educational institutions, nonprofit organizations, research institutions.
Geography: U.S., Northwest (Washington, Oregon) and South (Arkansas, Alabama, Mississippi, North Carolina, Oklahoma).

Limitations. *Recipients:* Individuals, religious organizations.
Activities: Fundraising, political activities, research (medical).
Types of support: Debt retirement, endowments.

The William P. Wharton Trust
c/o Choate, Hall, & Stewart
53 State Street, Exchange Place, 35th Floor
Boston, Massachusetts 02109-2891
Tel: 617-227-5020   Fax: 617-227-7566
EIN: 046407797   Type: Independent
Contact: Mary A. Willert, Estate and Trust Administrator

History and philosophy. William P. Wharton (1880-1976) dedicated his life's work to the study and conservation of nature and forests. Over the years he served the conservation community as the executive director and president of the Massachusetts Forest and Park Association, director of the Massachusetts Audubon Society, chairman of the Town Forest Committee of Groton, and president of the National Parks Association. His particular interest was the scientific management and preservation of timber, especially the redwood forests of the West Coast. The Trust was established in 1976.

Officers and directors. *Trustees:* John M. Cornish, Thomas H. P. Whitney, Jr.

Financial data. Data for fiscal year ended September 30, 1993.
Assets: $1,942,655 (M). *Total grants disbursed:* $82,818.

Environmental awards. *Program and interests:* Grants are limited to projects that promote the conservation of renewable natural resources, including complete preservation of outstanding natural areas. Specific objectives include bird and forestry research and management, natural areas preservation (primarily in Massachusetts and New England), and management techniques designed to improve environmental quality and species diversity.
Recent grants: 1993 grants included support for land conservation, sustainable forestry, habitat protection, and species preservation.

Issues. Cli Bio Lan Agr Wat Oce Ene Was Tox Pop Dev
            •   •   •   •   •

Funding analysis.

Fiscal year:	1991	1993
Env grants disb:	$55,318	$82,818
Number:	17	21
Range:	$1,200–$5,000	$1,625–$5,000
Median:	$3,000	$4,450
Pct $ disb (env/total):	100	100

Recipients (1993 highest):	Number:	Dollars:
Friends of the Acton Arboretum	1	5,000
Merrimack River Watershed Council	1	5,000
Natural Resources Council of Maine	1	5,000
The Nature Conservancy, Rhode Island Field Office	1	5,000
The Student Conservation Association, Inc.	1	5,000
Tufts University, School of Veterinary Medicine	1	5,000
University of Vermont, Vermont Agricultural Experimental Station	1	5,000
Vermont Natural Resources Council, Inc.	1	5,000

Activity regions (1993):	Number:	Dollars:
U.S. Northeast	20	78,308
U.S. Mid-Atlantic	1	4,510

Sample grants (1993).
Beaver Brook Association. Hollis, NH. $5,000. To improve trail system and develop comprehensive plan for mailing.
DeCordova Museum and Sculpture Park. Lincoln, MA. $5,000. For the Sudbury River Project.
Dennis Conservation Department. Dennis, MA. $2,544. Wildlife management project at Crowe's Pasture.
Natural Resources Council of Maine. Augusta, ME. $5,000. Protection of Biological Diversity in Maine's North Woods: A Cooperative Approach.
Vermont Institute of Natural Science. Woodstock, VT. $5,000. Research related to "Bicknell's" grey-cheeked thrush.

Application process. *Initial contact:* Full proposal.
When to apply: Anytime, but deadlines are April 15 and October 15 for board meetings held in May and November.
Materials available: Brochure (includes "Grant Applications").

Emphases. *Recipients:* Nonprofit organizations.
Activities: Land acquisition, publications, research.
Types of support: Equipment, facilities, single-year grants.
Geography: Massachusetts, New England states.

Limitations. *Recipients:* Public agencies.

Whitecap Foundation
800 Wilshire Boulevard, Suite 1010
Los Angeles, California 90017
Tel: 213-624-5401   Fax: 213-624-0529
EIN: 954111120   Type: Independent
EGA member
Contact: Leslie A. Dorman, Executive Director

History and philosophy. The Foundation was established in 1986. It supports nonprofit organizations that focus on children and families, education, and wildlife conservation. Foundation funds support "safety net" programs that plug the holes where the

W

public sector has failed or has not yet found effective ways to address specific needs. These funds are not meant to replace government responsibility for social services, public education, or environmental protection.

Officers and directors. *Officers:* Elizabeth Duker, President; Brack Duker, Secretary and CFO. *Directors:* Brack Duker, Elizabeth Duker.

Financial data. Data for fiscal year ended November 30, 1992. *Assets:* $8,060,912 (M). *Gifts received:* $7,648,533. *Total grants disbursed:* $416,937.

Environmental awards. *Program and interests:* The Foundation supports a limited number of wildlife conservation projects, with particular emphasis on:

- Wetlands conservation.
- Restoration and maintenance of environmentally significant tracts of land, particularly in California's Central Valley.

Recent grants: 1992 grants included support for land and species conservation.

Issues. Cli Bio Lan Agr Wat Oce Ene Was Tox Pop Dev
              •   •

Funding analysis.

Fiscal year:	1992
Env grants disb:	$55,575
Number:	4
Range:	$8,575–$20,000
Median:	$13,500
Pct $ disb (env/total):	13

Recipients (1992):	Number:	Dollars:
The Nature Conservancy, California Field Office	1	20,000
National Audubon Society, Western Region	1	17,000
Ducks Unlimited, Inc.	1	10,000
National Audubon Society, Los Angeles Education Office	1	8,575

Activity region (1992):	Number:	Dollars:
U.S. West	4	55,575

Sample grants (1992).
Ducks Unlimited, Inc. Sacramento, CA. $10,000.
National Audubon Society, Los Angeles Education Office. Playa del Rey, CA. $8,575.
National Audubon Society, Western Region. Sacramento, CA. $17,000.
The Nature Conservancy, California Field Office. San Francisco, CA. $20,000.

Application process. *Initial contact:* Preliminary letter of introduction to include:
1. Purpose and program services of your organization.
2. Geographic area and population served.
3. Brief description of proposed project.
4. Copy of IRS tax-exempt status determination letter.

When to apply: Anytime.
Materials available: Brochure (includes "Application Procedures").

Emphases. *Recipients:* Nonprofit organizations.
Activities: Education.
Types of support: Continuing support, equipment, projects.
Geography: Los Angeles, California.

Limitations. *Recipients:* Individuals, religious organizations.
Activities: Fundraising, lobbying, political activities.
Types of support: Endowments, facilities, operating costs.

Joseph B. Whitehead Foundation
50 Hurt Plaza, Suite 1200
Atlanta, Georgia 30303
Tel: 404–522–6755   Fax: 404–522–7026
EIN: 586001954   Type: Independent
Contact: Charles H. McTier, President

History and philosophy. In 1900 Mr. Whitehead established what would become the Dixie Cocoa-Cola Bottling Company, serving the southeastern, southwestern, and midwestern United States. Mr. Whitehead was stricken with pneumonia and died at the age of 42 in 1906. The Joseph B. Whitehead Foundation was established in 1937 under the will of his son, Joseph B. Whitehead, Jr., who specified that the Foundation's giving should benefit the citizens of Atlanta, especially children.

The Foundation's grantmaking interests today include human services, particularly for children and youth; elementary and secondary education; health care; economic development and civic affairs; literacy and vocational training; art and cultural activities; and the environment.

Officers and directors. *Officers:* J. W. Jones, Chairman; James M. Sibley, Vice Chairman; Charles H. McTier, President; P. Russell Hardin, Vice President and Secretary; J. Lee Tribble, Treasurer. *Trustees:* Roberto C. Goizueta, J. W. Jones, James M. Sibley; J. Lee Tribble.

Financial data. Data for fiscal year ended December 31, 1993. *Assets:* $536,528,804 (M). *Total grants disbursed:* $24,258,500.

Environmental awards. *Recent grants:* 1993 grants included support for environmental education.

Issues. Cli Bio Lan Agr Wat Oce Ene Was Tox Pop Dev
              •   •

Funding analysis.

Fiscal year:	1993
Env grants disb:	$200,000
Number:	3
Range:	$50,000–$100,000
Median:	$50,000
Pct $ disb (env/total):	1

© 1995 Environmental Data Resources, Inc.

Recipients (1993):	Number:	Dollars:
The Path Foundation	1	100,000
Cochran Mill Nature Center & Arboretum	1	50,000
Visions United	1	50,000

Activity region (1993):	Number:	Dollars:
U.S. Southeast	3	200,000

Sample grants (1993).
Cochran Mill Nature Center & Arboretum. Atlanta, GA. $50,000. Construction of environmental education facility.
The Path Foundation. Atlanta, GA. $100,000.
Visions United. Atlanta, GA. $50,000. Environmental education.

Application process. *Initial contact:* Letter of inquiry followed by proposal in letter form to include:
1. Description of organization, its purposes, programs, staffing, and governing board.
2. Organization's latest financial statements including most recent audit report.
3. Description of proposed project and full justification for its funding.
4. Itemized project budget, including other sources of support in hand or anticipated.
5. Copy of IRS tax-exempt status determination letter.

When to apply: Deadlines are February 1 and September 1 for consideration in April and November, respectively.
Materials available: Brochure (includes "Application Procedures").

Emphases. *Recipients:* Botanical gardens, educational institutions, museums, nonprofit organizations, research institutions, zoos.
Activities: Demonstration programs, direct services, education, exhibits, land acquisition, policy analysis/development, youth programs.
Types of support: Capital campaigns/expenses, equipment, facilities, single-year grants.
Geography: Metropolitan Atlanta only.

Limitations. *Recipients:* Individuals.
Types of support: Operating costs.

Wilburforce Foundation

1200 Westlake Avenue North, Suite 414
Seattle, Washington 98109
Tel: 206-286-4554   Fax: 206-298-1320
EIN: 943137894   Type: Independent
EGA member
Contact: Rosanna W. Letwin, Chairperson

History and philosophy. Established in 1990, the Wilberforce Foundation is dedicated to support projects which protect the earth's natural habitats and environments, promote wildlife conservation, or reduce pressure on ecosystems through human population control. In general the Foundation prefers to fund projects most likely to have a favorable long-term impact. Except for population control projects, which may be regional, national, or international, the Foundation favors projects affecting regions in the western United States.

Officers and directors. *Officer:* Rosanna W. Letwin, Chairperson; James G. Letwin, President. *Directors:* Tim Greyhavens, William S. Holder, James G. Letwin, Rosanna W. Letwin.

Financial data. Data for fiscal year ended December 31, 1993. *Assets:* $4,400,000 (M) (est.). *Total grants disbursed:* $284,230.

Environmental awards. *Program and interests:* The Foundation provides support for projects that:

- Protect the earth's natural habitats and environments.
- Promote wildlife conservation.
- Reduce pressure on ecosystems through human population control.

Recent grants: 1993 grants included support for land conservation, land trusts, forests, water quality, wildlife, recycling, sustainable development, and population.

Issues.   Cli   Bio   Lan   Agr   Wat   Oce   Ene   Was   Tox   Pop   Dev
                    •   •   •   •   •   •   •

Funding analysis.

Fiscal year:	1991	1993
Env grants disb:	$27,700	$281,700
Number:	4	18
Range:	$50–$15,000	$500–$50,000
Median:	$6,325	$6,850
Pct $ disb (env/total):	100	99

Recipients (1993 highest):	Number:	Dollars:
The Nature Conservancy, Washington Field Office	1	50,000
The Trust for Public Land	1	50,000
Seattle–King County Land Conservancy	2	31,500
Hood Canal Land Trust	1	29,750
Carrying Capacity	1	25,000
World Wildlife Fund	1	25,000

Activity regions (1993):	Number:	Dollars:
U.S. Northwest	15	230,700
U.S. not specified	2	26,000
Alaska	1	25,000

Sample grants (1993).
Carrying Capacity Network. Washington, DC. $25,000. To research, write, and publish a book about the correlation between population increase and environmental degradation in the United States.
Greater Tacoma Community Foundation. Tacoma, WA. $500. For scholarships to pay for representatives of the Tacoma Land Conservancy to attend the 1993 National Land Trust Alliance Rally.
HOWL. Lynwood, WA. $6,000. For a student intern program (college and graduate level) at a wildlife rehabilitation clinic in Lynnwood, Washington.
Hood Canal Land Trust. Belfair, WA. $29,750. To provide a forum where Native American tribes, governmental agencies,

environmental advocates, affected communities, and other concerned parties can work to develop a plan for conserving and improving the resource base of the Hood Canal geographical area.

Land Trust Alliance. Washington, DC. $19,250. For general support of a new Northwest Land Trust Alliance.

Snohomish County Land Trust. Everett, WA. $21,000. For a Fee Steward program of land conservation in Snohomish County, Washington.

The Trust for Public Land. Seattle, WA. $50,000. For the Puget Sound Open Space Fund to be used for preserving critical open space in the Puget Sound area of Washington State.

Water Watch of Oregon. Portland, OR. $7,700. For board and staff development programs which will improve the effectiveness of the organization's oversight of water quality issues within the state of Oregon.

Application process. *Initial contact:* Request application packet from Foundation. Proposal (2 copies) to include:
1. Short letter (1–2 page) describing:
   - Proposed project and its total cost.
   - How Wilburforce and other funds will be used for the project.
   - The short- and long-term impacts of the project, if successful.
2. Copy of IRS tax-exempt status determination letter.
3. Completed copy of "About Your Organization."
4. Completed copy of "About Your Proposal."
5. Completed copy of "About Your project Budget."

When to apply: Anytime. The board meets every other month.
Materials available: "Initial Application Information."

Emphases. *Recipients:* Nonprofit organizations.
Activities: Collaborative efforts, demonstration programs, education, feasibility studies, fieldwork, fundraising, innovative programs, land acquisition, planning, training.
Types of support: Internships, leveraging funds, membership campaigns, multi-year grants, pilot projects, seed money, single-year grants, start-up costs.
Geography: Washington State.

Limitations. *Recipients:* Individuals, public agencies, religious organizations.
Activities: Expeditions/tours, lobbying.
Types of support: Continuing support, endowments, indirect costs, loans, professorships.

G. N. Wilcox Trust

c/o Hawaiian Trust Company, Ltd.
P.O. Box 3170
Honolulu, Hawaii 96802
Tel: 808-538-4944   Fax: 808-538-4647
EIN: 996002445   Type: Independent
Contact: Lois C. Loomis, Vice President
Hawaiian Trust Company, Ltd.

History and philosophy. George Norton Wilcox (1838–1933) was born to a missionary family in Hilo, Hawaii and educated at Punahou on Oahu and Sheffield Scientific School (Yale) in New Haven, Connecticut. A progressive sugar planter, Wilcox also worked to improve living conditions and develop the natural resources on Kauai. Wilcox's interests centered largely on religious and educational work. In 1916, he created a trust to build the Salvation Army Home for Boys. Before his death, he broadened the scope of the Trust which today has programs in Education, Social Welfare, Health, Culture & Arts, Youth Services, Religion, and Other (mostly environmental grants).

Officers and directors. *Officer:* Thomas J. MacDonald, Chairman. *Committee on Beneficiaries:* Thomas J. MacDonald, Gale F. Carswell, Aletha Kaohi. *Trustee:* Hawaiian Trust Co., Ltd.

Financial data. Data for fiscal year ended December 31, 1993. *Assets:* $15,775,600 (M). *Total grants disbursed:* $610,944.

Environmental awards. *Recent grants:* 1993 grants included support for land conservation, parks, forests, marine issues, and energy.

Issues.   Cli Bio Lan Agr Wat Oce Ene Was Tox Pop Dev
              •   •   •   •   •

Funding analysis.

Fiscal year:	1991	1993
Env grants disb:	$34,000	$17,000
Number:	8	5
Range:	$2,000–$5,000	$2,000–$5,000
Median:	$5,000	$4,000
Pct $ disb (env/total):	5	3

Recipients (1993):	Number:	Dollars:
Hui O Laka/Koke'e Natural History Museum	1	5,000
Natural Resources Defense Council	1	4,000
The Nature Conservancy, Hawaii Field Office	1	4,000
Earthtrust	1	2,000
Friends of He'eia State Park	1	2,000

Activity region (1993):	Number:	Dollars:
Hawaii	5	17,000

Sample grants (1993).

Earthtrust. Kailua, HI. $2,000. Educational program on Hawaii's endangered marine wildlife.

Friends of He'eia State Park. Honolulu, HI. $2,000. Environmental education program for children.

Hui O Laka/Koke'e Natural History Museum. Kauae, HI. $5,000. Support for the "Treasures of the Forest" exhibit.

Natural Resources Defense Council. Honolulu, HI. $4,000. Support of the energy conservation and planning project.

The Nature Conservancy, Hawaii Field Office. Honolulu, HI. $4,000. Support of the Waianae Mountains Regional Conservation Partnership.

Application process. *Initial contact:* Letter (2–3 pages, 5 copies), signed by the presiding officer of the board of directors and including:
1. Brief description of applicant organization and its purposes.

2. Concise summary of the proposed activity, including a statement of the need or problem, description of how the activity is to be carried out, indication of the population to be served, and a plan for evaluating its effectiveness.
3. Total project cost, amount requested from the Trust, other funding sources, and plans for future support of the project.
4. Statement regarding the qualifications of personnel responsible for carrying out the project.
5. Statement as to the active participation of board members.
6. Name and telephone number of the appropriate contact person.

Attachments (5 copies).
1. Budget for both the project and the applicant organization, showing projected income and expenditures.
2. List of the governing board members and their professional or business affiliations.
3. Three or four letters endorsing the activity.

Additional documents (1 copy).
1. IRS tax-exempt status determination letter and certification of public foundation status under 509(a).
2. Organization's charter and bylaws (not required if previously submitted).
3. Organization's most recent annual report and audited financial statements.

When to apply: Deadlines are January 15, April 15, July 15, and October 15. October 15 only is the deadline for capital campaign funding.
Materials available: Annual report (includes "Information for Applicants").

Emphases. *Recipients:* Educational institutions, nonprofit organizations.
Activities: Direct services, education.
Types of support: Capital campaigns/expenses, computer hardware, equip-ment, facilities, general purposes.
Geography: Hawaii only, especially Kauai.

Limitations. *Recipients:* Individuals, public agencies.
Types of support: Debt retirement, endowments.

Robert W. Wilson Foundation

145 Central Park West
New York, New York 10023
Tel: 212–799–3425
EIN: 116037280   Type: Independent
Contact: Robert W. Wilson, Trustee

History and philosophy. The Foundation was established in 1964. It makes grants in the areas of the arts and music, social services, historic preservation, population control, and conservation.

Officers and directors. *Trustees:* Richard Gilder, Jr., Robert W. Wilson.

Financial data. Data for fiscal year ended December 31, 1993.
Assets: $12,141,267 (M). *Total grants disbursed:* $1,630,050.

Environmental awards. *Recent grants:* 1992 grants included support for land conservation, water protection, a botanical garden, and a zoo.

Issues. Cli Bio Lan Agr Wat Oce Ene Was Tox Pop Dev
                    •   •   •   •   •

Funding analysis.

Fiscal year:	1992
Env grants disb:	$329,000
Number:	9
Range:	$1,000–$100,000
Median:	$25,000
Pct $ disb (env/total):	20

Recipients (1992 highest):	*Number:*	*Dollars:*
Environmental Defense Fund	2	125,000
The Nature Conservancy, Headquarters	2	125,000
Brooklyn Botanic Garden	1	45,000
NYZS/The Wildlife Conservation Society	1	23,000
The Adirondack Council, Inc.	1	5,000
The Trust for Public Land	1	5,000

Activity regions (1992):	*Number:*	*Dollars:*
U.S. not specified	4	250,000
New York/New Jersey	5	79,000

Sample grants (1992).
The Adirondack Council, Inc. Elizabethtown, NY. $5,000.
Brooklyn Botanic Garden. Brooklyn, NY. $45,000.
Environmental Defense Fund. New York, NY. $100,000.
Environmental Defense Fund. New York, NY. $25,000.
The Nature Conservancy, Headquarters. Arlington, VA. $100,000.
The Nature Conservancy, Headquarters. Arlington, VA. $25,000.
NYZS/The Wildlife Conservation Society. Bronx, NY. $23,000.
People for Westpride. New York, NY. $1,000.
The Trust for Public Land. New York, NY. $5,000.

Application process. *Initial contact:* The Foundation awards grants to pre-selected organizations only. No unsolicited applications accepted.

Emphases. *Recipients:* Pre-selected organizations only.
Activities: Land acquisition.
Types of support: Equipment, facilities, loans, matching funds.
Geography: Primarily New York City.

Limitations. *Recipients:* Individuals.
Activities: Research.
Types of support: Endowments, fellowships, scholarships.

W

The Windham Foundation, Inc.
P.O. Box 70
Grafton, Vermont 05146
Tel: 802–843–2211
EIN: 136142024 Type: Operating
Contact: Lora Graham, Grants Administrator

History and philosophy. Dean Mathey, a prominent investment banker with longstanding family ties to Grafton, established The Windham Foundation in 1963. Its purpose was threefold: "to restore buildings and economic vitality in the village of Grafton; to provide financial support for education and private charities; and to develop projects that will benefit the general welfare of Vermont and Vermonters." Today the Foundation owns about 2 percent of the land in Grafton, and owns and operates a number of local businesses including the Old Tavern, the Grafton Village Cheese Company, and Idyll Acres Farm. It supports projects that "assure the preservation of the rural nature of Vermont. . . . [including] sheep management, land conservation, forest management, and dairy operations," employing over 100 people in the area. The Foundation also promotes community dialogue at both state and local levels. It initiates and sponsors the Grafton Conference Project, a series of nonpartisan forums to discuss issues facing Vermonters. Locally, it holds regular meetings on issues including economic development, environmental protection, health care, education, and the arts. About 80 percent of Foundation giving takes the form of operational support for its various activities; only 20 percent is devoted to grants.

Officers and directors. *Officers:* James R. Cogan, Chairman; Stephan A. Morse, President and CEO; Samuel W. Lambert, III, Vice President; William B. Wright, Vice President and Treasurer; Charles B. Atwater, Secretary; Paula Sheehan, Assistant Secretary; Janet R. Moot, Assistant Treasurer. *Trustees:* Charles B. Atwater, James R. Cogan, Samuel W. Lambert, III, Stephan A. Morse, Robert M. Olmsted, Edward J. Toohey, Charles C. Townsend, Jr., William B. Wright, Edward R. Zuccaro.

Financial data. Data for fiscal year ended October 31, 1993. *Assets:* $37,367,259 (M). *Operational activities:* $1,170,026. *Total grants disbursed:* $178,309.

Environmental awards. *Program and interests:* Land conservation, land preservation, and forest management receive Foundation support through both operational moneys and grants.
Recent grants: 1993 grants included support for Vermont land acquisition, conservation, and preservation; outdoor activities and education; and parks.

Issues. Cli Bio Lan Agr Wat Oce Ene Was Tox Pop Dev
                      •

Funding analysis.

Fiscal year:	1993
Env grants disb:	$7,500
Number:	3
Range:	$2,000–$3,000
Median:	$2,500
Pct $ disb (env/total):	4

Recipients (1993):	*Number:*	*Dollars:*
Vermont Land Trust	1	3,000
Green Mountain Club, Inc.	1	2,500
Vermont Green Up, Inc.	1	2,000

Activity region (1993):	*Number:*	*Dollars:*
U.S. Northeast	3	7,500

Sample grants (1993).
Green Mountain Club, Inc. Brattleboro, VT. $2,500.
Vermont Green Up, Inc. Montpeliar, VT. $2,000.
Vermont Land Trust. Montpeliar, VT. $3,000.

Application process. *Initial contact:* Contact the Foundation for application guidelines.
When to apply: 1995 deadlines are March 17, June 16, and September 15. The board meets quarterly in January, April, July, and October.

Emphases. *Recipients:* Nonprofit organizations.
Types of support: Continuing support, facilities, matching funds, operating costs, projects, seed money.
Geography: Grafton and Windham County, Vermont; Vermont.

Limitations. *Recipients:* Individuals.
Types of support: Endowments, loans.

Mark and Catherine Winkler Foundation
4900 Seminary Road
Alexandria, Virginia 22311
Tel: 703–578–7768   Fax: 703–578–7899
EIN: 546054383   Type: Independent
Contact: Lynne S. Ball, Executive Director

History and philosophy. Mark and Catherine Winkler established the Foundation in 1964. Major areas of interest include: aid to single parents, environmental projects with an emphasis on global warming, medical research, and social welfare in northern Virginia. In addition, the Foundation has established endowment funds at several universities throughout the country for the purpose of tuition and/or child care assistance to single parents returning to college.

Officers and directors. *Officers:* Catherine W. Herman, Chairman; Margaret W. Hecht, Kathleen W. Wennesland, Presidents; Margaret W. Hecht, Vice President; Carolyn Winkler, Secretary; J. Dean Herman, Treasurer; Lynne S. Ball, Assistant Secretary. *Directors:* Margaret W. Hecht, Catherine W. Herman, J. Dean Herman, Carolyn Winkler.

Financial data. Data for fiscal year ended January 31, 1993. *Assets:* $2,084,579 (M) *Gifts received:* $625,000. *Total grants disbursed:* $758,386.

Environmental awards. *Program and interests:* The primary environmental interest is global warming.
Recent grants: 1993 grants also included support for land conservation and a botanical preserve.

Issues. Cli Bio Lan Agr Wat Oce Ene Was Tox Pop Dev
•   •   •   •

Funding analysis.

Fiscal year:	1991	1993
Env grants disb:	$254,000	$162,500
Number:	9	8
Range:	$1,000–$130,000	$500–$50,000
Median:	$20,000	$25,000
Pct $ disb (env/total):	31	21

Recipients (1993):	Number:	Dollars:
Winkler Botanical Preserve	3	110,000
Natural Resources Defense Council	2	26,000
INFORM	1	25,000
Advocates for Wilderness	1	1,000
The Conservation Fund	1	500

Activity regions (1993):	Number:	Dollars:
U.S. Mid-Atlantic	3	110,000
U.S. not specified	5	52,500

Sample grants (1993).
The Conservation Fund. Arlington, VA. $500.
INFORM. New York, NY. $25,000.
Natural Resources Defense Council. New York, NY. $1,000.
Winkler Botanical Preserve. Alexandria, VA. $80,000.

Application process. *Initial contact:* Letter or proposal to include:
1. Project's purpose and cost.
2. Evidence of need for project.
3. Amount of funding requested.
4. List of other sources of funding (including groups applicant has approached and/or intends to approach and their responses).
5. Background information on organization's general operations.
6. Background information on personnel responsible for organization.
7. Copy of IRS tax-exempt status determination letter.

When to apply: Anytime.

Emphases. *Recipients:* Educational institutions, nonprofit organizations.
Activities: Education, innovative programs, land acquisition, research.
Types of support: Annual campaigns, capital campaigns/expenses, emergency funding, endowments, general purposes, matching funds, multi-year grants, operating costs, professorships.
Geography: Global environmental issues with an emphasis on the Virginia area.

Limitations. *Recipients:* Individuals.
Activities: Media projects.

W

The Winslow Foundation

c/o Drinker Biddle & Reath
P.O. Box 627
Princeton, New Jersey 08542–0627
EIN: 222778703   Type: Independent
EGA member

Application address:
1425 21st Street, N.W.
Washington, DC 20036
Tel: 202–833–4714   Fax: 202–833–4716
Contact: Betty Ann Ottinger, Executive Director

History and philosophy. The Foundation was established in 1987 in New Jersey by Julia D. Winslow. Its giving is focused on women, environment, and ecology.

Officers and directors. *Trustees:* Teresa Heinz, Samuel W. Lambert III, Wren Winslow Wirth.

Financial data. Data for fiscal year ended December 31, 1992. *Assets:* $15,343,926 (M). *Gifts received:* $2,623,449. *Total grants disbursed:* $541,372.

Issues. Cli Bio Lan Agr Wat Oce Ene Was Tox Pop Dev
•   •   •   •

Sample grants (1992).
Council on Economic Priorities. New York, NY. $51,500. For environmental data clearinghouse.
University of Colorado Foundation, Natural Resources Law Center. Boulder, CO. $50,000. For Western Lands Program.
Heinz Family Foundation. Pittsburgh, PA. $38,492. To preserve the Amazon Basin.
University of California. Berkeley, CA. $37,900. For Berkeley-Stanford Carrying Capacities Project.

Application process. *Initial contact:* The Foundation awards grants to pre-selected organizations only. No unsolicited applications accepted.

Emphases. *Recipients:* Pre-selected organizations only.
Types of support: Continuing support.

Limitations. *Recipients:* Individuals.

The Winston-Salem Foundation, Inc.

310 West Fourth Street, Suite 229
Winston-Salem, North Carolina 27101–2889
Tel: 919–725–2382   Fax: 919–727–0581
EIN: 566037615   Type: Community
Contact: Donna Rader, Vice President of Grants and Programs

History and philosophy. Celebrating its 75th anniversary in 1994, The Winston-Salem Foundation has long been ranked among the nation's thirty largest community foundations. Colonel Francis Fries established the Foundation in 1919 with $1,000; today it consists of over 200 funds with assets of over $74 million. Yet, it maintains its original purpose of funding services to benefit the people of Forsyth County, North Carolina.

Grants are awarded from both discretionary and donor-advised funds in six program areas: Arts, Culture, and Religion; Education and Recreation; Health and Medical; Human Services; Public Interest; and Services for Youth and Older Adults. Only a few environmental grants have been made and those generally come from donor-advised rather than discretionary funds.

Officers and directors. *Foundation Committee:* A. Tab Williams, Jr., Chairman; Roberta Irvin, Vice Chairman; Willard W. Bass, Jr., Graham F. Bennett, Victor I. Flow, Jr., Robert C. Gulledge, Jr., Joseph F. Neely. *Directors:* Elizabeth Quick, President; Henry M. Carter, Jr., Secretary.

Financial data.* Data for fiscal year ended December 31 1993. *Assets:* $73,417,873 (M). *Gifts received:* $6,276,545. *Total grants disbursed:* $5,494,623.

*As reported by Foundation.

Environmental awards. *Program and interests:* Environmental grants have been awarded through Education and Recreation, Health and Medical, and Public Interest program areas. Several donor-advised funds target specific environmental purposes including energy conservation; scholarship aid for students majoring in water resource management; and outdoor activities, conservation, and environmental preservation. Discretionary grants for environmental purposes are rare.
Recent grants: 1992 grants included support for land conservation, forests, wildlife protection, and zoos and botanical gardens.

Issues. Cli Bio Lan Agr Wat Oce Ene Was Tox Pop Dev
• • • •

Funding analysis.§

Fiscal year:	1992
Env grants disb:	$55,561
Number:	25
Range:	$25–$12,698
Median:	$400
Pct $ disb (env/total):	1

Recipients (1992 highest):	Number:	Dollars:
The Nature Conservancy, North Carolina Field Office	1	12,698
Winston-Salem Parks and Recreation Department	1	10,000
Winston-Salem Journal Tree Fund	1	8,667
Sierra Club Foundation	1	6,100
Southern Environmental Law Center	1	5,000
The Atlanta Botanical Garden, Inc.	1	5,000

Activity regions (1992):	Number:	Dollars:
U.S. Southeast	14	43,934
U.S. not specified	9	10,977
U.S. Northeast	1	500
U.S. Great Lakes	1	150

§Includes donor-advised, designated, and discretionary grants.

Sample grants (1992).
Living Desert Wildlife & Botanical Park. Palm Beach, CA. $1,000.
Wildlife Waystation. Lakeview Terrace, CA. $300.
Winston-Salem Parks and Recreation Department. Winston-Salem, NC. $10,000. To provide funds for landscaping in Hanes Park.
Zoological Society of San Diego. San Diego, CA. $1,350.

Application process. *Initial contact:* Telephone call to set up an appointment with staff to introduce proposed project. Next, a letter (2 pages), signed by the chief officer of governing board, to include:
1. Background of the agency.
2. Concept and objectives of the project submitted.
3. Project methods.
4. Expected benefits.
5. Degree of project's priority to the requesting agency.
6. Grant amount requested.
7. Designated use of requested funds.

The applicant may also wish to supply a list of governing board members, supplementary budget materials, and other supporting data. If requested, the agency must supply a copy of its certification of IRS tax-exempt status.
When to apply: Deadlines are January 1, April 1, July 1, and October 1.
Materials available: Annual report (includes "How to Apply for Grants," and "The Grantmaking Policies").

Emphases. *Recipients:* Educational institutions, nonprofit organizations.
Activities: Capacity building, collaborative efforts, conflict resolution, demonstration programs, education, feasibility studies, innovative programs, planning, training.
Types of support: Capital campaigns/expenses, emergency funding, endowments, matching funds, pilot projects, scholarships, seed money.
Geography: Winston-Salem, Forsyth County, and the six contiguous North Carolina counties, only.

Limitations. *Recipients:* Individuals, research institutions.
Activities: Activism, advocacy, conferences, expeditions/tours, land acquisition, litigation, lobbying, policy analysis/development, political activities, research, seminars, symposia/colloquia.
Types of support: Annual campaigns, debt retirement, equipment, fellowships, indirect costs, lectureships, maintenance, professorships, program-related investments, travel expenses.

The Dean Witter Foundation

57 Post Street, Suite 510
San Francisco, California 94104
Tel: 415–981–2966 Fax: 415–981–5218
EIN: 946065150 Type: Independent
Contact: Lawrence I. Kramer, Jr., Administrative Director

History and philosophy. The Dean Witter Foundation is a grantmaking philanthropic foundation established in 1952. "During Dean Witter's lifetime his principal professional interest was in finance. He found recreation in hunting and fishing and in enjoyment of the outdoors. In business and as a fisherman Colonel Witter enjoyed pursuing the difficult task. He preferred the elusive trout to the easy fishing of a well-stocked pond. In this spirit the Foundation seeks to practice imaginative grant-making in the fields of finance and conservation."

Officers and directors. *Officers:* Dean Witter III, President; James R. Bancroft, Vice President; William D. Witter, Secretary/Treasurer; Frank H. Roberts, Assistant Secretary. *Trustees:* James R. Bancroft, Salvador O. Gutierrez, Stephen Nessier, Frank H. Roberts, Roland E. Tognazzini, Jr., Dean Witter III, William D. Witter.

Financial data. Data for fiscal year ended November 30, 1992. *Assets:* $10,489,535 (M). *Total grants disbursed:* $358,260.

Environmental awards. *Program and interests:* The Foundation occasionally makes small grants, usually on a matching basis, to support specific wildlife research and conservation projects, primarily in northern California.
Recent grants: 1992 grants included support for land conservation, coastal issues, habitat and species preservation, water management, waste and recycling, and public education.

Issues. Cli Bio Lan Agr Wat Oce Ene Was Tox Pop Dev
   •   •   •   •

Funding analysis.

Fiscal year:	1991	1992
Env grants auth:	$195,000	$158,860
Number:	18	10
Range:	$300–$50,000	$5,000–$50,000
Median:	$6,450	$10,000
Pct $ auth (env/total):	44	37

Recipients (1992 highest):	*Number:*	*Dollars:*
Natural Heritage Institute	1	50,000
California Trout	1	30,260
American Land Conservancy	1	20,000
Oakland Museum Foundation	1	12,000
California Academy of Sciences	1	10,000
Coastal Resources Center	1	10,000
Environmental Defense Fund	1	10,000

Activity region (1992):	*Number:*	*Dollars:*
U.S. West	10	158,860

Sample grants (1992).
American Land Conservancy. San Francisco, CA. $20,000. Towards purchasing Burdell Ranch (Marin) and returning it to wetlands.
Angel Island Association. Tiburon, CA. $5,000. To improve fundraising capability to provide volunteer support of educational and restoration services.
California Academy of Sciences. San Francisco, CA. $10,000. To support endangered species project.
California Trout. Sacramento, CA. $30,260. To support negotiations on Water Flow Control on the North Fork Feather River.
Coastal Resources Center. San Francisco, CA. $10,000. To establish a marine debris recycling and education program for San Francisco's Fisherman's Wharf.
Environmental Defense Fund. San Francisco, CA. $10,000. Development of negotiated water transfer agreements.
Marin County Resource Conservation District. Point Reyes Station, CA. $6,600.
Natural Heritage Institute. Sausalito, CA. $50,000. Toward development of a consensus plan for reforming California's water management system.
Oakland Museum Foundation. Oakland, CA. $12,000. Support of "To See the Sea" exhibit.

Application process. *Initial contact:* Brief letter to include:
1. Description of the program and its merits.
2. Estimated project budget.
3. Personnel.
4. Time required to carry out the proposal.
5. Copy of IRS tax-exempt status determination letter.
6. Explanation of any other sources of support such as volunteer workers and matching fund commitments.

If interested, Foundation will request a full proposal.
When to apply: Anytime.
Materials: Annual report (includes "How to Make a Proposal").

Emphases. *Recipients:* Educational institutions, museums, nonprofit organizations, research institutions, zoos.
Activities: Audiovisual materials, demonstration programs, education, fieldwork, innovative programs, planning, publications, research, technical assistance.
Types of support: Fellowships, general purposes, leveraging funds, matching funds, pilot projects.
Geography: Northern California, particularly the San Francisco Bay Area.

Limitations. *Recipients:* Individuals.
Types of support: Endowments.

Wodecroft Foundation
1900 Chemed Center
255 East Fifth Street
Cincinnati, Ohio 45202-3172
Tel: 513-977-8200
EIN: 316047601   Type: Independent
Contact: H. Truxton Emerson, Jr., Secretary/Treasurer

History and philosophy. The Foundation was established in 1958 with donations from Roger Drackett. Funding areas include health and human services, the arts, education, and conservation.

Officers and directors. *Officers:* Richard W. Barrett, Chairman; H. Truxton Emerson, Jr., Secretary/Treasurer. *Trustees:* Richard W. Barrett, Jeanne H. Drackett, H. Truxton Emerson, Jr.

Financial data. Data for fiscal year ended December 31, 1992. *Assets:* $8,475,470 (M). *Total grants disbursed:* $498,500.

Environmental awards. *Recent grants:* 1992 grants included support for land conservation, urban gardens, and a zoo.

W

Issues. *Cli Bio Lan Agr Wat Oce Ene Was Tox Pop Dev*
        •   •   •

Funding analysis.

Fiscal year:	1992
Env grants disb:	$41,500
Number:	5
Range:	$500–$35,000
Median:	$2,000
Pct $ disb (env/total):	8

Recipients (1992):	*Number:*	*Dollars:*
The Conservancy	2	35,500
Zoological Society of Cincinnati	1	3,000
Civic Garden Center of Greater Cincinnati	1	2,000
The Nature Conservancy, Ohio Field Office	1	1,000

Activity regions (1992):	*Number:*	*Dollars:*
U.S. Southeast	2	35,500
U.S. Great Lakes	3	6,000

Sample grants (1992).
Civic Garden Center of Greater Cincinnati. Cincinnati, OH. $2,000.
The Conservancy. Naples, FL. $35,500 (2 grants).
The Nature Conservancy, Ohio Field Office. Columbus, OH. $1,000.
Zoological Society of Cincinnati. Cincinnati, OH. $3,000.

Application process. *Initial contact:* Letter of intent.
When to apply: Anytime.

Emphases. *Recipients:* Nonprofit organizations.
Types of support: Annual campaigns, capital campaigns/expenses, equipment, facilities (construction).
Geography: Hilton County, Ohio and Collier County, Florida.

Limitations. *Recipients:* Individuals.

Robert W. Woodruff Foundation, Inc.

50 Hart Plaza, Suite 1200
Atlanta, Georgia 30303
Tel: 404–522–6755   Fax: 404–522–7026
EIN: 581695425   Type: Independent
Contact: Charles H. McTier, President

History and philosophy. The Foundation was established in 1937 by Robert W. Woodruff, president of the Coca-Cola Company, and an active philanthropist who left most of his estate to the Foundation. Funding areas are: Elementary, secondary, and higher education; Health care and education; Human services, particularly for children and youth; Economic development and civic affairs; Art and cultural activities; and Conservation of natural resources and environmental protection.

Officers and directors. *Officers:* J. W. Jones, Chairman; James M. Sibley, Vice Chairman; Charles H. McTier, President; P. Russell Hardin, Vice President and Secretary; J. Lee Tribble, Treasurer. *Trustees:* Ivan Allen, Jr., J. W. Jones, Wilton Looney, James M. Sibley, James Williams.

Financial data. Data for fiscal year ended December 31, 1993.
Assets: $1,562,461,708 (M). *Total grants disbursed:* $52,741,236.

Environmental awards. *Recent grants:* 1993 grants included support for environmental research.

Issues. *Cli Bio Lan Agr Wat Oce Ene Was Tox Pop Dev*
        •   •

Funding analysis.

Fiscal year:	1992	1993
Env grants disb:	$3,915,000	$10,272,343
Number:	2	1
Range:	$90,000–$3,825,000	–
Median:	$1,957,500	–
Pct $ disb (env/total):	7	19

Recipient (1993):	*Number:*	*Dollars:*
Ichauway, Inc.	1	10,272,343

Activity region (1993):	*Number:*	*Dollars:*
U.S. Southeast	1	10,272,343

Sample grant (1993).
Ichauway, Inc. Newton, GA. $10,272,343. For the Joseph W. Jones Ecological Research Center.

Application process. *Initial contact:* Letter of inquiry, followed by proposal to include:
1. Description of applicant organization, its purposes, programs, staffing, and governing board.
2. Copy of most recent financial statement including audit report.
3. Project description with full justification for its funding.
4. Itemized project budget with sources of support identified.
5. Copy of IRS tax-exempt status determination letter.

When to apply: February 1 and September 1 for consideration at the April and November board meetings.
Materials available: Application guidelines, informational brochure (includes "Application Procedures").

Emphases. *Recipients:* Botanical gardens, educational institutions, museums, nonprofit organizations, public agencies, research institutions, zoos.
Activities: Education, exhibits, inventories, land acquisition, policy analysis/development, publications, research (scientific).
Types of support: Capital campaigns/expenses, computer hardware, equipment, facilities, general purposes.
Geography: Georgia.

Limitations. *Recipients:* Individuals.
Activities: Lobbying.

The Wortham Foundation, Inc.

2727 Allen Parkway, Suite 2000
Houston, Texas 77019–2115
Tel: 713–526–8849
EIN: 741334356   Type: Independent
Contact: Barbara J. Snyder, Grants Administrator

History and philosophy. Gus S. Wortham and Lyndall F. Wortham established the Foundation in 1958. Mr. Wortham was a partner in John L. Wortham & Son, a forerunner of the American General Insurance Company now known as American General Corporation. The Worthams were active in civic, educational, and cultural affairs through organizations such as Rice University, the Houston Symphony Society, the Society for the Performing Arts, and the Houston Grand Opera Association.

For its first decade, the Foundation mainly supported cattle fertility research. Today it has more diverse interests, supporting the arts, civic and beautification projects, and community improvement in Houston.

Officers and directors. *Officers:* Allen H. Carruth, Chairman and President; H. Charles Boswell, Vice President and Treasurer; Fred C. Burns, Brady F. Carruth, E. A. Stupf III, R. W. Wortham III, Vice Presidents and Assistant Treasurers; William V. H. Clarke, Executive Secretary and Controller; Barbara J. Snyder, Secretary and Grants Administrator.

Financial data. Data for fiscal year ended September 30, 1993. *Assets:* $177,383,279 (M). *Total grants disbursed:* $8,015,400.

Environmental awards. *Program and interests:* Civic beautification is a stated interest: "The Foundation provides maintenance, repair, preservation, and rehabilitation services on an as needed basis for Houston City parks and Texas historic sites."
Recent grants: 1993 grants included support for urban lands (public parks, trees, beautification), a botanical garden, and a zoo.

Issues.   Cli   Bio   Lan   Agr   Wat   Oce   Ene   Was   Tox   Pop   Dev
                    •   •

Funding analysis.

Fiscal year:	1991	1993
Env grants disb:	$380,000	$478,300
Number:	10	8
Range:	$5,000–$100,000	$10,800–$200,000
Median:	$22,500	$37,500
Pct $ disb (env/total):	5	6

Recipients (1993 highest):	Number:	Dollars:
The Houston Parks Board	2	217,500
Houston Arboretum and Botanical Society	1	100,000
Houston Clean City Commission	1	50,000
The Park People	1	50,000
Armand Bayou Nature Center	1	25,000
Houston Beautification Foundation	1	25,000

Activity region (1993):	Number:	Dollars:
U.S. South Central	8	478,300

Sample grants (1993).
Armand Bayou Nature Center. La Porte, TX. $25,000. Park development.
Houston Arboretum and Botanical Society. Houston, TX. $100,000. Capital campaign.
Houston Clean City Commission. Houston, TX. $50,000. General operations.
Houston Zoological Society. Houston, TX. $10,800. General operations.
The Park People. Houston, TX. $50,000. Endowment.

Application process. *Initial contact:* Brief letter to request Grant Application Form. Complete form to include:
1. Organization name and address.
2. Administrator of proposed project.
3. Copy of IRS tax-exempt status determination letter.
4. Budget.
5. Copy of organization's IRS Form 990 or financial statement.
6. Brief statement of organization's activities.
7. List of board members and organization (or project) staff.
8. Amount requested and date needed.
9. Description of use of funds.
10. Description of population to benefit from the grant.

When to apply: Apply by the end of the first week of January, April, July, or October for consideration at trustees' meetings held in mid-February, May, August, or November.
Materials available: Annual report, Grant Application Form, informational brochure (includes application guidelines).

Emphases. *Recipients:* Botanical gardens, museums, nonprofit organizations, zoos.
Types of support: Annual campaigns, capital campaigns/expenses, endowments, matching funds, membership campaigns, operating costs.
Geography: Houston, Harris County, Texas.

Limitations. *Recipients:* Educational institutions, individuals, religious organizations, research institutions.
Types of support: Advertising campaigns, computer hardware, fellowships, internships, leveraging funds, loans, professorships, program-related investments, scholarships, travel expenses.

Sidney & Phyllis Wragge Foundation

46 Forest Street
Sherborn, Massachusetts 01770
Tel: 508–653–7852
EIN: 136271206   Type: Independent
Contact: Sara Wragge, President

History and philosophy. The Foundation was established by the late Phyllis Wragge. It makes grants in the areas of environment, wildlife welfare, social services, and health.

Officers and directors. *Officers*: Sara Wragge, President; Carla Wragge, Ellen Wragge, Vice Presidents.

Financial data. Data for fiscal year ended October 31, 1992. *Assets:* $538,128 (M). *Total grants disbursed:* $31,140.

W

Environmental awards. *Recent grants:* 1992 grants included support for land conservation, parks, and wildlife preservation.

Issues. Cli Bio• Lan• Agr Wat Oce Ene Was Tox Pop Dev

Funding analysis.

Fiscal year:	1992
Env grants disb:	$9,500
Number:	15
Range:	$250–$1,000
Median:	$500
Pct $ disb (env/total):	31

Recipients (1992 highest):	*Number:*	*Dollars:*
The Nature Conservancy, Headquarters	6	2,750
Conservation Law Foundation	2	1,500
Greater Yellowstone Coalition	1	1,000
Maudslay State Park Association	1	1,000
The Wilderness Society	1	1,000
Trustees of Reservations	1	1,000

Activity regions (1992):	*Number:*	*Dollars:*
U.S. not specified	10	5,000
U.S. Northeast	4	3,500
U.S. Mountain	1	1,000

Sample grants (1992).
Conservation Law Foundation. Boston, MA. $1,500.
Greater Yellowstone Coalition. Bozeman, MT. $1,000.
National Wildlife Federation. Washington, DC. $250.
The Nature Conservancy, Headquarters. Arlington, VA. $2,750.
Sierra Club Legal Defense Fund. San Francisco, CA. $500.
Trustees of Reservations. Beverly, MA. $1,000.
The Wilderness Society. Washington, DC. $1,000.
World Wildlife Fund. Washington, DC. $500.

Application process. *Initial contact:* The Foundation awards grants to pre-selected organizations only. No unsolicited applications accepted.

Emphases. *Recipients:* Pre-selected organizations only.

Margaret Cullinan Wray Charitable Lead Annuity Trust

c/o Board of Trustees
1724–A Sunset Boulevard
Houston, Texas 77005
Tel: 713–529–2229   Fax: 713–529–2353
EGA member
Contact: Claudia Blazek, Grants Coordinator

History and philosophy. The Trust was created in 1985 by the will of Margaret Cullinan Wray. Deeply involved in the community and environmental affairs of Houston, Mrs. Wray was a long-time board member of the Houston Museum of Natural Science and a lifetime member of the Audubon Society. The Wray Trust makes an effort to realize creative talents and protect natural resources. Gifts are made in the areas: of Arts, Education, and Environmental Conservation.

Officers and directors. *Trustees:* David Anderson Todd, Emily Leland Todd, Lucie Wray Todd.

Financial data. Data for fiscal year ended December 31, 1993. *Total grants authorized:* $370,354.

Environmental awards. *Program and interests:* The Wray Trust is interested in environmental protection and improvement, specifically:

- Air, water, and solid waste control.
- Resource conservation and reuse.
- Habitat and species protection.
- Aesthetic and recreational improvements.

Favored approaches include advocacy, education, litigation, and research.

Issues. Cli Bio• Lan• Agr• Wat• Oce• Ene• Was• Tox• Pop Dev

Funding analysis.

Fiscal year:	1992	1993
Env grants auth:	$289,885	$297,104
Number:	73	85
Range:	$500–$10,000	$500–$12,000
Median:	$3,000	$3,000
Pct $ auth (env/total):	78	80

Recipients (1993 highest):	*Number:*	*Dollars:*
Sierra Club Foundation	5	20,000
Houston Audubon Society	2	12,500
Environmental Defense Fund of Texas	1	12,000
National Audubon Society	1	10,000
Texas Committee on Natural Resources	1	9,750

Activity regions (1993):	*Number:*	*Dollars:*
U.S. South Central	78	262,604
International*	4	24,500
U.S. not specified	1	4,000
Asia	1	3,500
Mexico and Central America	1	2,500

*Texas and Mexico.

Sample grants (1993).
Bellaire Recycling Committee. Belaire, TX. $2,500. Study and advocacy of a volume-based garbage fee.
Center for Marine Conservation. Austin, TX. $4,000. Expert testimony on Gulf fishery regulation.
Coast Alliance. Washington, DC. $4,000. Work on flood insurance subsidies and coastal land use reform.
Houston Arboretum & Nature Center. Houston, TX. $4,500. Development of interactive and multi-media educational tools.
Katy Prairie Land Conservancy. Houston, TX. $2,500. Katy prairie ecotourism economic study.

League of Women Voters of Houston Education Fund. Houston. TX. $2,000. Clean Air Act discussion and advocacy work.
The Nature Conservancy, Texas Field Office. San Antonio, TX. $8,000. East Texas private forestlands initiative.
RARE Center for Tropical Conservation. Philadelphia, PA. $2,500. Guatemalan park design.
Texas A&M University, Kingsville. Kingsville, TX. $2,340. Atacosa River vegetation study.
Texas Parks and Wildlife Department. Austin, TX. $6,000. Butterfly project.

Application process. *Initial contact:* Proposal to include:
1. Project description (1 page) including means, ends, and cost.
2. Copy of IRS tax-exempt status determination letter.
3. Report on group's current financial status.
4. Contact name, telephone number, and address.

When to apply: Deadline is September 30 for annual gifts cycle at the end of December.
Materials available: Triennial grants report, "Grant Application Guidelines and Funding Cycle."

Emphases. *Recipients:* Botanical gardens, educational institutions, museums, nonprofit organizations, research institutions, zoos.
Activities: Activism, advocacy, citizen participation, collaborative efforts, conflict resolution, demonstration programs, education, fieldwork, innovative programs, land acquisition, litigation, planning, policy analysis/development, publications, research.
Types of support: Internships, pilot projects, projects, seed money, single-year grants only, start-up costs.
Geography: Texas only.

Limitations. *Recipients:* Individuals.
Activities: Lobbying, political activities.
Types of support: Capital campaigns/expenses, emergency funding, endowments.

Wrinkle in Time Foundation
P.O. Box 306
The Plains, Virginia 22171–0306
Tel: 703–253–5266   Fax: 703–253–5055
EIN: 222351518   Type: Independent
Contact: Andrea B. Currier, President

History and philosophy. The Foundation was established in 1980 by Andrea B. Currier. Its focus is "improving man's rural and urban environment."

Officers and directors. *Officer:* Andrea B. Currier, President, Chairman, Treasurer.

Financial data. Data for fiscal year ended December 31, 1992. *Assets:* $2,390,337. *Total grants disbursed:* $166,000.

Environmental awards. *Program and interests:* Stated interests are:

- Wildlife protection.
- Wilderness preservation.

- Environmental information gathering, preservation, and dissemination.
- Rural or urban environmental enhancement.
- Historic building, site, and antiquity preservation.
- Art and design that enhances the rural or urban environment.

Recent grants: 1992 grants included support for a regional organization dealing with land use issues.

Issues.   Cli   Bio   Lan   Agr   Wat   Oce   Ene   Was   Tox   Pop   Dev
              •   •

Funding analysis.

Fiscal year:	1990	1992
Env grants disb:	$25,000	$50,000
Number:	1	1
Range:	–	–
Median:	–	–
Pct $ disb (env/total):	71	30

Recipient (1992):	Number:	Dollars:
Piedmont Environmental Council	1	50,000

Activity region (1992):	Number:	Dollars:
U.S. Mid-Atlantic	1	50,000

Sample grant (1992).
Piedmont Environmental Council. Warrenton, VA. $50,000.

Application process. *Initial contact:* Letter.
When to apply: Anytime. The board meets in October.

Emphases. *Recipients:* Nonprofit organizations.
Types of support: Seed money, general purposes, projects.
Geography: Virginia.

The Wyomissing Foundation, Inc.
1015 Penn Avenue
Wyomissing, Pennsylvania 19610
Tel: 215–376–7496   Fax: 215–372–7626
EIN: 231980570   Type: Independent
Contact: Alfred G. Hemmerich, Secretary

History and philosophy. The Foundation was incorporated in 1929 by Ferdinand Thun. Primary concerns are: the arts and culture, education, environment, health care, and human services in Berks County, Pennsylvania.

Officers and directors. *Officers:* Paul R. Roedel, President; David L. Thun, Vice President; Alfred G. Hemmerich, Secretary; Fred D. Hafer, Treasurer. *Trustees:* Thomas A. Beaver, Fred D. Hafer, Sidney D. Kline, Jr., Timothy K. Lake, Marlin Miller, Jr., Paul R. Roedel, David L. Thun, Peter Thun. *Emeritus:* Ferdinand K. Thun, Louis R. Thun.

Financial data. Data for fiscal year ended December 31, 1993. *Assets:* $17,400,000 (M). *Total grants disbursed:* $612,000.

W

Environmental awards. *Recent grants:* 1993 grants included support for land conservation, wildlife (raptor) protection, and recycling.

Issues. Cli Bio Lan Agr Wat Oce Ene Was Tox Pop Dev
                •   •   •   •   •

Funding analysis.§

Fiscal year:	1992	1993
Env grants auth:	$72,500	$90,875
Number:	4	5
Range:	$2,500–$50,000	$5,000–$32,000
Median:	$10,000	$21,250
Pct $ disb (env/total):	16	15

Recipients (1993):	Number:	Dollars:
Hawk Mountain Sanctuary	1	32,000
Schuylkill River Greenway Association	1	23,000
Berks County Conservancy	1	21,250
Recycling Services, Inc.	1	7,500
Wildlands Trust Fund	1	5,125

Activity region (1992):	Number:	Dollars:
U.S. Mid-Atlantic	5	90,875

§As reported by Foundation.

Sample grants (1993).
Berks County Conservancy. Wyomissing, PA. $21,250. Open spaces program.
Hawk Mountain Sanctuary Association. Kempton, PA. $32,000.
Recycling Services, Inc. Pottstown, PA. $7,500.
Schuylkill River Greenway Association. Wyomissing, PA. $23,000.
Wildlands Trust Fund. Emmaus, PA. $5,125.

Application process. *Initial contact:* Letter (2 pages) to include:
1. Outline of need for the project and its intended scope.
2. Brief description of applicant organization.

When to apply: Deadlines are February 25, May 25, August 25, and October 25 for consideration at board meetings held in March, June, September, and November.
Materials available: Annual report, application guidelines, financial statement, program policy statement.

Emphases. *Recipients:* Educational institutions, museums, public agencies, zoos.
Activities: Capacity building, collaborative efforts, demonstration programs, direct services, education, feasibility studies, planning, policy analysis/development.
Types of support: Capital campaigns/expenses, continuing support, facilities (construction), general purposes, matching funds, operating costs, pilot projects, projects, seed money.
Geography: Berks County, Pennsylvania, and surrounding areas.

Limitations. *Recipients:* Individuals.
Activities: Conferences, publications.
Types of support: Debt retirement, endowments, fellowships, loans, scholarships.

Appendixes

A. Grantmaker Types

Independent foundation. A grantmaking fund or endowment classified as a private foundation by the IRS. An initial gift (and the interest thereupon accrued) from an individual or family accounts for most of the endowment. When an independent foundation is managed by family members, it may be called a "family foundation."

Community foundation. A publicly supported 501(c)(3) organization established to make grants to a specific community or region. An endowment may fund the community foundation, but grants are generally sought from many donors to enlarge the endowment.

Company-sponsored foundation. Classified as a private foundation, a company-sponsored foundation usually obtains its assets as contributions from a profit-making parent company or corporation. Although legally distinct from the company or corporation, the giving program usually reflects the parent entity's interests.

Operating foundation. An entity that makes grants to a few pre-selected organizations to carry out work designated by its charter or governing body. It is classified as a private foundation by the IRS.

Public foundation. A grantmaking fund whose endowment or annual contributions come from public sources such as the state or federal government.

Note: This directory includes a few entries for entities that act as advisors to grantmakers. We call them **Advisory services.** They are included because they are members of the Environmental Grantmakers Association, although they do not themselves make grants.

B. Environmental Issues

In most profiles an Issues Table summarizes the broad environmental issues a grantmaker funds. The data are derived both from what a grantmaker says it funds and from what we believe its recent grantmaking shows. For example:

Issues.   Cli   Bio   Lan   Agr   Wat   Oce   Ene   Was   Tox   Pop   Dev
        •   •   •   •

We generally assign one or more environmental issues to each grant. Issues are classified into eleven broad categories: Climate and Atmosphere (Cli), Biodiversity (Bio), Endangered Lands (Lan), Agriculture (Agr), Freshwater (Wat), Oceans and Coasts (Oce), Energy (Ene), Solid Waste (Was), Toxic Substances (Tox), Population (Pop), and Development (Dev).

Issue assignment is often an arduous (and sometimes arbitrary) task. Some grants have overlapping issues: grants for the San Francisco Bay-Delta, for example, may involve Freshwater, Oceans and Coasts, Endangered Lands, Biodiversity, and Agriculture. Other grants address no particular issue: grants awarded for broad environmental purposes such as "Environmental Conservation" or "Environmental Education" are examples. In *Environmental Grantmaking Foundations 1995*, grantmakers for which we know only such broad purposes have no Issues Table.

The eleven issues include but are not limited to the concepts listed here.

Climate and Atmosphere. The impact of modern industrial life on air quality, climate, and atmosphere.

Air pollution, indoor air quality
Atmospheric precipitation
Carbon dioxide emissions/levels/sources
Carbon monoxide emissions/levels/sources
Chlorofluorocarbons
Climate change

Clean Air Act
Global warming,
Greenhouse effect
Methane
Nitrogen oxides emissions/levels/sources
Ozone: atmospheric accumulation, stratospheric depletion

Biodiversity. The interaction between human settlement and development, species survival, and genetic variability.

Arboretums
Biological impoverishment
Biosphere reserves
Botanical gardens
CITES
Conservation biology
Conservation ethic
Ecosystems
Endangered species
Endangered Species Act
Exploitation
Extinction, extinction rate
Food web

Genetic diversity
Habitat fragmentation
Heirloom seedstocks
Intrinsic value
Island habitats
Migration
Refuges
Resource allocation, resource base
Species rights
Wildlife
Wildlife trade/poaching
Zoos/aquariums

Environmental Issues

Endangered Lands. Critical lands that perform an ecosystem service, represent a unique habitat, or have aesthetic value.

Acquisition	Lowlands
Beautification	Management
Conservation/preservation/protection	Mountain systems
Deserts/desertification	Parks
Forests	Riparian lands
Gardens	Sanctuaries
Grasslands, savannas	Tundra
Historic preservation	Uplands
Greenways	Wetlands
Land use planning	Wilderness

Agriculture. The impact of cultivation, crop production, and animal husbandry on soil, land, water, biodiversity, and human health.

Agroforestry	Land preservation
Alternative/organic agriculture	Low-input agriculture
Biotechnology	Low-till, no-till agriculture
Diversification	Monocropping
Drylands	Pest management
Energy efficiency	Pesticides; herbicides
External inputs	Polyculture
Farm Bill	Productivity
Farm size	Salinization
Federal policies	Seedstocks
Fertilizers	Soils
Food irradiation	Sustainable agriculture
Greenhouses	Trade policy
Hazardous chemicals	Traditional agriculture
Irrigation	Water depletion, pollution, quality, use

Water. All aspects of terrestrial freshwater in relation to environmental quality.

Allocation	Protection
Clean Water Act	Quality
Conservation	Resources
Diversion	Rights
Drinking water	Riverkeeper
Eutrophication	Rivers/streams
Groundwater	Sedimentation
Hydropower	Sewage
Instream issues	Use
Interbasin transfer	Watershed
Lakes	Wild and scenic rivers
Pollution	

Environmental Issues

Oceans and Coasts. Human impact on the biotic and abiotic components of the oceans and coastal areas of the earth.

Baykeeper	Islands
Coastal lands	Marine mammals
Development	Marine sanctuaries
Dumping	Oil
Entanglement	Sludge
Estuaries	Waste
Fisheries	Water diversion
International conventions	

Energy. The ways in which energy production, transportation, and use affect environmental quality.

Alternative sources	Incentives and markets
Biomass	Least-cost planning
Buildings	Mass transit
Clean Air Act	Nuclear power
Conservation	Renewable energy
Efficiency	Solar energy
Fossil fuel production/use	Surface Transportation Act
Fuel efficiency	Transportation
Geothermal power	Utilities
Hydropower	Wind power

Solid Waste. The generation and disposal of solid waste and its effects on the environment.

Disposal	Paper, glass, metals, fibers, plastics
Dumping	Recycling
Household/industrial/municipal waste	RCRA
Incineration	Source reduction
Landfills	Source separation
Markets	Waste-to-Energy

Toxic Substances. The production, use, and disposal of substances that can cause annoyance, irritation, illness, injury, or death to plants or animals.

Chemicals	International trade
Cleanup	Labeling
Consumer education	Radioactive wastes
Deep well injection	Right-to-Know
Departments of Defense/Energy	Risk management
Disposal	Source reduction
Hazardous materials	Superfund
Household chemicals	TSCA
Industrial chemicals	

© 1995 Environmental Data Resources, Inc.

Environmental Issues

Population. The human species, its distribution, and patterns of growth and consumption that affect the earth, its resources, and its ability to sustain other species.

- Abortion
- Age structure
- Birth rate
- Carrying capacity
- Consumption patterns
- Death rate
- Demographic transition
- Demographics
- Doubling time
- Exponential growth
- Family planning
- Fertility rate
- Food production
- Growth rate
- Income gap
- Infant mortality
- Life expectancy
- Overpopulation
- Population assistance/balance/density
- Population distribution/growth/pyramid
- Quality of life
- Reproductive rights
- Resource use
- Urbanization

Development. Economic growth and its effects on the environment through population increase, land settlement, agricultural and industrial modernization, and the use of energy, water, and the global commons such as oceans and atmosphere.

- Benefit-cost analysis
- The Commons
- Conservation banking
- Conservation economics
- Debt-for-nature
- Debt reduction
- Economic growth
- Economic self-sufficiency
- External costs
- GATT
- Industrialization
- International debt
- Less-developed nations
- More-developed nations
- Multilateral development banks
- NAFTA
- Sustainable development
- Trade policy
- UNCED

C. Emphases and Limitations

Recipients. Includes but is not limited to:

Aquariums
Botanical gardens
Educational institutions
Individuals
Museums
Nonprofit organizations

Pre-selected organizations
Public agencies
Religious organizations
Research institutions
Zoos

Activities. Includes but is not limited to:

Activism
Advocacy
Audiovisual materials
Capacity building
Citizen participation
Collaborative efforts
Conferences
Conflict resolution
Demonstration programs
Direct services
Education
Exhibits
Expeditions/tours
Feasibility studies
Fieldwork
Fundraising
Innovative programs
Inventories

Land acquisition
Litigation
Lobbying
Media projects
Networking
Planning
Political activities
Policy analysis/development
Publications
Research (medical/scholarly/scientific)
Seminars
Symposia/colloquia
Technical assistance (from the recipient)
Training
Workshops
Youth programs
Volunteerism

Types of support. Includes but is not limited to:

Advertising campaigns
Annual campaigns
Capital campaigns/expenses
Computer hardware
Continuing support
Debt retirement
Emergency funding
Endowments
Equipment
Facilities (construction/renovation)
Fellowships
General purposes
Indirect costs
Internships
Lectureships
Leveraging funds

Loans
Maintenance
Matching funds
Membership campaigns
Mortgage reduction
Multi-year projects
Operating costs
Pilot projects
Professorships
Program-related investments
Scholarships
Seed money
Single-year grants
Start-up costs
Technical assistance (for the recipient)
Travel expenses

Geography. Includes the geographic regional preferences or exclusions as stated by a grantmaker including location of recipient, activity, or scope of interest.

D. Geographic Regions

For analytic purposes, we classify grants according to the geographic location of their activity. We have defined 44 regions: 16 regions within the United States, and 28 international regions.

United States

The United States consists of 15 regions. Ten of these comprise the 48 contiguous states and are similar to the ten regions used by the Environmental Protection Agency (EPA); the other five regions correspond to the individual states of Alaska and Hawaii, the Commonwealth of Puerto Rico, and the territories of the U.S. Virgin Islands and Pacific Islands associated with the United States. The EPA classifies these with various mainland regions; we separate them to reflect their distinct geography and ecology. We added two extra categories: "U.S. multiple regions," and "U.S. not specified." Multiple regions denote a grant whose activity is carried out in more than one region. For example, a grant may target the Mississippi River basin, or for work in the southwestern United States. Grants with a national focus or that do not specify a particular geographic target within the United States are classified here as "U.S. not specified."

In this list, the first ten regions approximate the ten EPA regions; an asterisk (*) denotes cases where we have deleted a state or territory to create the five new regions. The first ten regions are:

U.S. Northeast (Connecticut, Maine, Massachusetts, New Hampshire, Rhode Island, Vermont)
U.S. New York/New Jersey*
U.S. Mid-Atlantic (Delaware, District of Columbia, Maryland, Pennsylvania, Virginia, West Virginia)
U.S. Southeast (Alabama, Florida, Georgia, Kentucky, Mississippi, North Carolina, South Carolina, Tennessee)
U.S. Great Lakes (Illinois, Indiana, Ohio, Michigan, Minnesota, Wisconsin)
U.S. South Central (Arkansas, Louisiana, Oklahoma, New Mexico, Texas)
U.S. Midwest (Iowa, Kansas, Missouri, Nebraska)
U.S. Mountain (Colorado, Montana, North Dakota, South Dakota, Utah, Wyoming)
U.S. West (Arizona, California, Nevada)*
U.S. Northwest (Idaho, Oregon, Washington)*

The five new regions are:

Alaska (EPA Region Northwest)
Hawaii (EPA Region West)
Puerto Rico (EPA Region New York/New Jersey)
U.S. Pacific Islands (EPA Region West)
U.S. Virgin Islands (EPA Region New York/New Jersey)

U.S. not specified

Geographic Regions

International Regions

International regions as defined in this directory are a somewhat heterogeneous group. They fall into three fairly well defined categories: (1) discrete geopolitical units (e.g., West Africa); (2) larger discrete geographic areas (e.g., Africa); and (3) areas defined by characteristics other than geography (e.g., Developing nations). Finally, we use the designation "international" for grants with an activity region that spans more than one of the international regions or areas or which is not regionally defined.

The 28 international regions are:

International not specified

Developing countries

Tropics

Africa

    Eastern and Southern Africa
    North Africa
    West Africa

Antarctica

Arctic

Asia

    Far East
    Indian Subcontinent and Indian Ocean Islands
    Middle East and Western Asia
    Russia and the Newly Independent States
    Southeast Asia

Australia/Oceania

Central Atlantic Islands

Eastern Europe

Western Europe and the United Kingdom

Latin America

    Caribbean and West Indies
    Mexico and Central America
    South America
        Andean Region and Southern Cone
        Brazil
        Northern South America

North America

    Canada

E. Environmental Grantmakers Association

ARCO Foundation
A Territory Resource
The Abelard Foundation West
The Abell Foundation
The Acorn Foundation
Airport Business Center Foundation
Alaska Conservation Foundation
The Jenifer Altman Foundation
American Conservation Association, Inc.
American Express Philanthropic Program
Angelina Fund, Inc.
Apple Computer, Inc.
Mary Reynolds Babcock Foundation, Inc.
The Bauman Foundation
L. L. Bean, Inc.
Beldon Fund
The Ben & Jerry's Foundation
Beneficia Foundation
Benton Foundation
The Betterment Fund
The William Bingham Foundation
The Blumenthal Foundation
Kathleen Price and Joseph M. Bryan Family Foundation, Inc.
The Bullitt Foundation
Patrick and Aimee Butler Family Foundation
C. S. Fund
Ward M. & Mariam C. Canaday Educational and Charitable Trust
Caribou Fund
Mary Flagler Cary Charitable Trust
Changing Horizons Charitable Trust
The Chevron Companies
The Chicago Community Trust
Church & Dwight Co., Inc.
Columbia Foundation
Compton Foundation, Inc.
Conservation, Food & Health Foundation, Inc.
S. H. Cowell Foundation
Jessie B. Cox Charitable Trust
The Mary A. Crocker Trust
Crystal Channel Foundation
The Nathan Cummings Foundation
Damien Foundation
Davis Conservation Foundation
Geraldine R. Dodge Foundation, Inc.
Donner Canadian Foundation
The Elizabeth Ordway Dunn Foundation, Inc.
The Educational Foundation of America
El Paso Community Foundation
The Energy Foundation
Environment Now Foundation
The Hugh and Jane Ferguson Foundation
Fields Pond Foundation, Inc.
Fieldstead Charitable Trust
Bert Fingerhut/Caroline Hicks Family Fund
Flintridge Foundation
Ford Foundation

Foundation for Deep Ecology
The Fund for New Jersey
Fund of the Four Directions
GE Fund
The Gap Foundation
The Fred Gellert Foundation
General Service Foundation
The Wallace Alexander Gerbode Foundation, Inc.
The German Marshall Fund of the United States
Global Environmental Project Institute
The Golden Rule Foundation, Inc.
The Goldman Environmental Foundation
Walter and Duncan Gordon Charitable Foundation
Great Lakes Protection Fund
The Greenville Foundation
The George Gund Foundation
HKH Foundation
The Hall Family Foundation
Harder Foundation
Hawaiian Electric Industries Charitable Foundation
Howard Heinz Endowment
Vira I. Heinz Endowment
The Clarence E. Heller Charitable Foundation
The William and Flora Hewlett Foundation
The Homeland Foundation
IBM Corporation
Illilouette Fund
The James Irvine Foundation
Island Foundation, Inc.
Island Foundation
Ittleson Foundation, Inc.
The Richard Ivey Foundation
The Henry M. Jackson Foundation
W. Alton Jones Foundation, Inc.
Joy Foundation for Ecological Education and Research
The Joyce Foundation
W. K. Kellogg Foundation
The Henry P. Kendall Foundation
The Robert S. and Grayce B. Kerr Foundation, Inc.
Laidlaw Foundation
Laird, Norton Foundation
LaSalle Adams Fund
The Lazar Foundation
The Max and Anna Levinson Foundation
LifeWorks Foundation
Lyndhurst Foundation
The John D. and Catherine T. MacArthur Foundation
Maki Foundation
Marin Community Foundation
MARPAT Foundation, Inc.
The Martin Foundation, Inc.
Massachusetts Environmental Trust
The McIntosh Foundation

The McKnight Foundation
Giles W. and Elise G. Mead Foundation
Merck Family Fund
The John Merck Fund
Joyce Mertz-Gilmore Foundation
J. P. Morgan Charitable Trust
The Moriah Fund, Inc.
Charles Stewart Mott Foundation
Ruth Mott Fund
The Curtis and Edith Munson Foundation, Inc.
The National Environmental Education and Training Foundation, Inc.
National Fish and Wildlife Foundation
National Geographic Society Education Foundation
New England Biolabs Foundation
New Hampshire Charitable Foundation
The New York Community Trust
Andrew Norman Foundation
Mary Moody Northen, Inc.
Jessie Smith Noyes Foundation, Inc.
Orchard Foundation
Ottinger Foundation
The David and Lucile Packard Foundation
Patagonia, Inc.
Amelia Peabody Charitable Fund
The William Penn Foundation
James C. Penney Foundation
The Pew Charitable Trusts
Pew Scholars Program in Conservation and the Environment
The Philanthropic Group
Philip Morris Companies, Inc.
The Polden-Puckham Charitable Foundation
Prince Charitable Trusts
The Procter & Gamble Fund
The Prospect Hill Foundation
Recreational Equipment, Inc.
Z. Smith Reynolds Foundation, Inc.
Smith Richardson Foundation, Inc.
The Roberts Foundation
Rockefeller Brothers Fund, Inc.
Rockefeller Family Fund, Inc.
Rockefeller Financial Services, Philanthropy Department
The Rockefeller Foundation
Rockwood Fund, Inc.
Sacharuna Foundation
The San Francisco Foundation
The Florence and John Schumann Foundation
Sequoia Foundation
Seventh Generation Fund
Thomas Sill Foundation
Stern Family Fund
The Sudbury Foundation
The Summerlee Foundation
The Summit Foundation
Surdna Foundation, Inc.
SURFREE

Environmental Grantmakers Association

Edna Bailey Sussman Fund
The Switzer Foundation
Threshold Foundation
The Tides Foundation
The Tinker Foundation Incorporated
Tortuga Foundation
Town Creek Foundation, Inc.
True North Foundation
The Trust For Mutual Understanding
Turner Foundation, Inc.
Unitarian Universalist Veatch Program
   at Shelter Rock
Vancouver Foundation
Victoria Foundation, Inc.
Virginia Environmental Endowment
WMX Environmental Grants Program
Wallace Genetic Foundation, Inc.
Weeden Foundation
Whitecap Foundation
Wilburforce Foundation
The Winslow Foundation
Margaret Cullinan Wray Charitable
   Lead Annuity Trust

F. Application Deadlines

Key:

* * = See individual entry for details.
* ♦ = No application deadline data available.
* ■ = Month(s) of deadline for application, pre-application, or letter of intent.
* ★ = Month(s) of board of directors meeting.
* / = Month(s) of preferred application.

Note: The "■" symbol in the X column indicates that applications may be submitted anytime. A grantmaker with no asterisk and a blank row is currently not accepting unsolicited proposals. If a deadline and a board meeting occur within the same month, only the deadline is shown.

We suggest this table be used only as a general guide: not as the sole source of deadline information. A prospective applicant should always consult an individual entry for complete deadline information.

Grantmaker	X	J	F	M	A	M	J	J	A	S	O	N	D
ARCO Foundation	■												
AT&T Foundation	■	/			/			/		/			
A Territory Resource	*		■	■					■	■			
The Abelard Foundation West			■		*		■			*			
The Abell Foundation			■	★	■	★	■	★		■	★	■	★
Abell-Hanger Foundation	■												
The Achelis Foundation	■					★				★			★
The Acorn Foundation			★			■		★			■		
The Ahmanson Foundation	■												
Airport Business Center Foundation													
Alaska Conservation Foundation			★					■		★			■
The George I. Alden Trust	■												
Winifred & Harry B. Allen Foundation	■				★		★			★			★
The Jenifer Altman Foundation	■												
American Conservation Association, Inc.						■				★			
American Express Philanthropic Program	■												
American Foundation Corporation													
Americana Foundation, Inc.			■			■			■			■	
Ameritech Foundation	■												
Elmer L. & Eleanor J. Andersen Foundation				■	★	■	★		■	★		■	★
Angelina Fund, Inc.													
Apple Computer, Inc.	*												
The Arca Foundation					■	★				■		★	
Arcadia Foundation	*							/	■	★		★	

Application Deadlines

Grantmaker	X	J	F	M	A	M	J	J	A	S	O	N	D
Evenor Armington Fund												■	
The Vincent Astor Foundation	■					★					★		★
Atherton Family Foundation			■		■		■		■		■		■
Atkinson Foundation				■					■				
Atlantic Foundation													
The Austin Memorial Foundation													
Azadoutioun Foundation	■												
Mary Reynolds Babcock Foundation, Inc.				■		★				■		★	
The Bailey Wildlife Foundation	■												
The Cameron Baird Foundation										/	/	/	
Clayton Baker Trust					■				■			■	
The George F. Baker Trust	■						★					★	
Baltimore Gas and Electric Foundation, Inc.	■												
BankAmerica Foundation	■												
The Barra Foundation, Inc.	■												
The Theodore H. Barth Foundation, Inc.	■												
The Bauman Foundation													
Bay Area Community Foundation			■	★		■	★		■	★		■	★
The Bay Foundation		★		■		★				■	★		■
The Howard Bayne Fund													
L. L. Bean, Inc.	■												★
S. D. Bechtel, Jr. Foundation													
The Beinecke Foundation, Inc.	■												
The Beirne Carter Foundation	■			★						★			
Beldon Fund	■												
David Winton Bell Foundation	■		★			★						★	
James Ford Bell Foundation			★		■		★		■		★		■
The Ben & Jerry's Foundation		■			■			■			■		
Beneficia Foundation			■		★								
Benton Foundation													
Benua Foundation, Inc.													
The Bersted Foundation		★	■		★	■		★	■		★	■	
The Betterment Fund	■												
The Frank Stanley Beveridge Foundation, Inc.			■		★				■		★		
The William Bingham Foundation	★			■		★			■		★		
Bishop Pine Fund													
Blandin Foundation		■			★	■			★	■			
The Blumenthal Foundation				■			■		■			■	
The Bodman Foundation	■					★				★			★

Application Deadlines

Grantmaker	X	J	F	M	A	M	J	J	A	S	O	N	D
The Boeing Company	■												
Boettcher Foundation	■												
Mary Owen Borden Memorial Foundation		■			■	★				■	★		
The Bothin Foundation			★		■		★			■	★		■
Botwinick-Wolfensohn Foundation, Inc.	■												
Helen Brach Foundation													■
The Lynde and Harry Bradley Foundation, Inc.			★	■		★		■		■		★	■
Otto Bremer Foundation	■	★	★	★	★	★	★	★	★	★	★	★	★
Alexander H. Bright Charitable Trust			■	★		■	★		■	★		■	★
Alex. Brown & Sons Charitable Foundation	★			★			★				★		★
H. Barksdale Brown Charitable Trust	■												
Ruth H. Brown Foundation	■												
W. L. Lyons Brown Foundation	■										★		
The Robert Brownlee Foundation		■			★			■		★			
Kathleen Price and Joseph M. Bryan Family Foundation, Inc.				■		★				■		★	
The Buchanan Family Foundation													
Jesse Margaret Wilson Budlong Foundation for Animal Aid	■												
The Bullitt Foundation					■				■				■
The Bunbury Company, Inc.	■												
The Bush Foundation		■		■			■					■	
The Butler Foundation	■												
J. E. and Z. B. Butler Foundation, Inc.													
Patrick and Aimee Butler Family Foundation					■		★						★
The Bydale Foundation							/	/				■	
C. S. Fund					■				■				■
The Cabot Family Charitable Trust	★			■	★						■	★	
The Morris and Gwendolyn Cafritz Foundation				■			■					■	
The Louis Calder Foundation	★	/	/	■								/	/
California Community Foundation	★					■							■
James & Abigail Campbell Foundation		★		■	★		■	★		■	★		■
Ward M. & Mariam C. Canaday Educational and Charitable Trust	■												
The Cape Branch Foundation	■												
The Cargill Foundation	★												
Caribou Fund	■												
Carolyn Foundation		■					★	■					★
The Carpenter Foundation	★				★		★			★			★
Mary Flagler Cary Charitable Trust	■	★	★	★	★	★	★	★	★	★	★	★	★
Centerior Energy Foundation	■	★	★	★	★	★	★	★	★	★	★	★	★
The Champlin Foundations					/	/	/	/	■			★	

© 1995 Environmental Data Resources, Inc.

Application Deadlines

Grantmaker	X	J	F	M	A	M	J	J	A	S	O	N	D
Changing Horizons Charitable Trust													
Cheeryble Foundation	■												
Ben B. Cheney Foundation	■												
Chesapeake Bay Trust													
Chesapeake Corporation Foundation		■				■					■		
The Chevron Companies	■												
The Chicago Community Trust	■												
Chrysler Corporation Fund	■												
Church & Dwight Co., Inc.													
Liz Claiborne & Art Ortenberg Foundation	■												
Claneil Foundation, Inc.		/	/	■	★		/	/		■	★		
Clark Charitable Trust	■												
The Clark Foundation	■				★						★		
Robert Sterling Clark Foundation, Inc.	■	★			★			★			★		
The Cleveland Foundation				■			■			■			■
The Clowes Fund, Inc.		■											
Olive B. Cole Foundation	■		★			★			★			★	
The Collins Foundation	■												
Columbia Foundation			■						■				
The Columbus Foundation	★												
The Community Foundation of Greater New Haven	■												
The Community Foundation of Santa Clara County	★			■									■
The Community Foundation of Sarasota County, Inc.	■												
The Community Foundation of Western North Carolina, Inc.			■						■				
The Community Foundation Serving Coastal South Carolina	★							■		■			
Compton Foundation, Inc.				■		★					■		★
The Conservation and Research Foundation	■												
Conservation, Food & Health Foundation, Inc.		■			★				■				★
Cooke Foundation, Limited		★		■		★	■			★		■	
Adolph Coors Foundation		★	■		★	■		★	■		★	■	
S. H. Cowell Foundation	■												
The Cowles Charitable Trust		★		■	★		■	★		■	★		■
Cox Foundation, Inc.													
The James M. Cox, Jr. Foundation, Inc.	■												
Jessie B. Cox Charitable Trust		■		★	■		★	■		★	■		★
The Cricket Foundation					■						■		
The Mary A. Crocker Trust			■		★				■			★	
Roy E. Crummer Foundation													
Crystal Channel Foundation			■	★					■	★			

Application Deadlines

Grantmaker	X	J	F	M	A	M	J	J	A	S	O	N	D
Patrick and Anna M. Cudahy Fund	*	■		★	■		★	■		★	■		★
Charles E. Culpeper Foundation, Inc.	■												
The Nathan Cummings Foundation	■												
Damien Foundation	*												
The Fred Harris Daniels Foundation, Inc.	■			★			★			★			★
Dart Foundation	■												
The Arthur Vining Davis Foundations	■												
Davis Conservation Foundation					■	★					■	★	
Dayton Hudson Foundation	■												
Deer Creek Foundation	■												
The Nelson B. Delavan Foundation	■												
The Aaron Diamond Foundation	*												
Cleveland H. Dodge Foundation, Inc.		■			■					■			
Geraldine R. Dodge Foundation, Inc.	*						■			■			
Thelma Doelger Charitable Trust	■												
Dolfinger-McMahon Foundation					■						■		
Oliver S. and Jennie R. Donaldson Charitable Trust	*												
Gaylord and Dorothy Donnelley Foundation	■												
Donner Canadian Foundation	*	★			★			★					
Douroucouli Foundation	■												
The Herbert H. and Grace A. Dow Foundation	■												
The Dragon Foundation, Inc.													
The Max and Victoria Dreyfus Foundation, Inc.	■												
The Elizabeth Ordway Dunn Foundation, Inc.				■		★				■		★	
Jessie Ball duPont Religious, Charitable and Educational Fund	■			★		★		★		★		★	
Eastman Kodak Company Charitable Trust	■												
Echoing Green Foundation													
Ederic Foundation, Inc.	■												
The Educational Foundation of America	■												
A. M. and O. T. Eisig-A. M. and K. E. Tode Foundation, Inc.													
El Paso Community Foundation	■												
El Pomar Foundation	■												
The Emerald Foundation													
The Thomas J. Emery Memorial	■												
The Energy Foundation	■			★			★					★	
The Charles Engelhard Foundation													
English-Bonter-Mitchell Foundation													
Environment Now Foundation													
Environmental Education Foundation of Florida, Inc.	■												

Application Deadlines

Grantmaker	X	J	F	M	A	M	J	J	A	S	O	N	D
Environmental Endowment for New Jersey, Inc.				■									
The Armand G. Erpf Fund, Inc.	■												
The Ettinger Foundation, Inc.	■		★			★			★			★	
Fair Play Foundation	■												
Fanwood Foundation	■												
The William Stamps Farish Fund	■												
The Favrot Fund	■												
Felburn Foundation													
Samuel S. Fels Fund	■												
The Hugh and Jane Ferguson Foundation			■						■				
The Field Foundation of Illinois, Inc.	■												
Jamee and Marshall Field Foundation			★		■		★		■		★		■
Fields Pond Foundation, Inc.	■												
Fieldstead Charitable Trust													
The 1525 Foundation	■												
Leland Fikes Foundation, Inc.	■												
Bert Fingerhut/Caroline Hicks Fund	■												
FishAmerica Foundation	■												
Flintridge Foundation	■												
Ford Foundation	■												
Ford Motor Company Fund	■				★						★		
Walter and Josephine Ford Fund	■												
Foundation for the Carolinas			■			■					■		
Foundation for Deep Ecology	■												
Foundation for Field Research	★												
The Foundation for the National Capital Region	★	■		■		★		■		■		★	
The Jacob and Annita France Foundation, Inc.	■												
Mary D. and Walter F. Frear Eleemosynary Trust	★	■			■			■			■		
The Freed Foundation, Inc.	★		★			★			★			★	
Frelinghuysen Foundation	■												
The Frost Foundation, Ltd.					★		■			★			■
Lloyd A. Fry Foundation	■		★			★			★			★	
The Fund for New Jersey	■												
The Fund for Preservation of Wildlife and Natural Areas	★												
Fund of the Four Directions			■		■			■					
Funding Exchange	■												
The GAR Foundation			■			■			■			■	
GE Fund	■												
The Gap Foundation	★												

Application Deadlines

Grantmaker	X	J	F	M	A	M	J	J	A	S	O	N	D
Gates Foundation		■			■		★	■			■		★
The Barbara Gauntlett Foundation, Inc.	■												
Gebbie Foundation, Inc.		■				■				■			
The Fred Gellert Foundation				■	★						■	★	
General Service Foundation			■							■			
Georgia Power Foundation, Inc.	■												
Georgia-Pacific Foundation	■												
The Wallace Alexander Gerbode Foundation, Inc.	■												
The German Marshall Fund of the United States	★		★		★						★		
The Rollin M. Gerstacker Foundation	★			■	★							■	★
Bernard F. and Alva B. Gimbel Foundation, Inc.													
Give to the Earth Foundation	■	★		★		★		★		★		★	
Global Environmental Project Institute	■												
Global Greengrants Fund													
The Golden Rule Foundation	■										★		
The Goldman Environmental Foundation	★					/	/	/	/	■			
Herman Goldman Foundation	■												
Richard & Rhoda Goldman Fund	■												
Good Samaritan, Inc.						■	★				■	★	
Walter and Duncan Gordon Charitable Foundation	■												
Great Lakes Protection Fund	★	■					■						
Greater Piscataqua Community Foundation					■		★				■		★
The Greenville Foundation				★		■						★	■
The William and Mary Greve Foundation, Inc.	■												
The W. C. Griffith Foundation	■					★						★	
The George Gund Foundation		■		■			■			■			★
HKH Foundation	★												
Evelyn and Walter Haas, Jr. Fund	★												
Walter and Elise Haas Fund	■												
The Hahn Family Foundation	■												
The Hall Family Foundation	■												
The Ewing Halsell Foundation	■												
The Hamer Foundation	■												
James G. Hanes Memorial Fund		★		■	★		■	★		■	★		■
Harbor Lights Foundation													
Harder Foundation	★			/	/	/	/	/	■				
The Harding Educational and Charitable Foundation	■												
Gladys and Roland Harriman Foundation	■				★						★		
Mary W. Harriman Foundation	■												

© 1995 Environmental Data Resources, Inc.

Application Deadlines

Grantmaker	X	J	F	M	A	M	J	J	A	S	O	N	D
Hartford Foundation for Public Giving	*												
The Hastings Trust	■												
The Merrill G. & Emita E. Hastings Foundation	■												
Hawaii Community Foundation	■	★	★	★		★	★	★	★		★	★	★
Hawaiian Electric Industries Charitable Foundation	■		★						★				
Charles Hayden Foundation	■	★	★	★	★	★	★	★	★		★	★	★
The John Randolph Haynes and Dora Haynes Foundation	*												
The Edward W. Hazen Foundation		■					■						
The M. A. Healy Family Foundation, Inc.													
Howard Heinz Endowment			■								■		
Vira I. Heinz Endowment		■		★					■		★		
Heller Charitable & Educational Fund	*	■											
The Clarence E. Heller Charitable Foundation	*												
The William and Flora Hewlett Foundation	■												
The Hitachi Foundation			■								■		
The Hofmann Foundation	■												
The Homeland Foundation				■			■			■			■
The Horn Foundation													
Howfirma Foundation	■												
Hudson-Webber Foundation					■		★	■					■
The Charles Evans Hughes Memorial Foundation, Inc.									■		★		
The Roy A. Hunt Foundation					■						■		
Hurdle Hill Foundation													
The Hyams Foundation	■												
The Hyde and Watson Foundation			■							■			
IBM Corporation	■												
Illilouette Fund													
The Indian Point Foundation, Inc.	■												
The Louise H. and David S. Ingalls Foundation, Inc.	■												
The International Foundation, Inc.		/	/	/	★		★			★		/	/
Ireland Foundation	■											★	
The James Irvine Foundation	■												
Island Foundation													
Island Foundation, Inc.	■												
Ittleson Foundation, Inc.					■					■			
The Richard Ivey Foundation	*						■						■
The Jackson Foundation				■	★				■	★		■	★
Jackson Hole Preserve, Inc.	■				/	/	/						
The Henry M. Jackson Foundation				■			■			■			■

Application Deadlines

Grantmaker	X	J	F	M	A	M	J	J	A	S	O	N	D
Martha Holden Jennings Foundation	■												
The George Frederick Jewett Foundation			■			■		■				■	
Helen K. and Arthur E. Johnson Foundation		■			■			■			■		
The Howard Johnson Foundation	■												
Walter S. Johnson Foundation	■												
W. Alton Jones Foundation, Inc.	■												
Joy Foundation for Ecological Education and Research	■												
The Joyce Foundation				★	■			★	■			★	■
The J. M. Kaplan Fund, Inc.				/	/	/	/	/	/	/	/		
W. K. Kellogg Foundation	■												
Harris and Eliza Kempner Fund				■	★		■	★			■		■
The Henry P. Kendall Foundation			■	★		■	★		■	★		■	★
The Robert S. and Grayce B. Kerr Foundation, Inc.													
The Helen & Milton Kimmelman Foundation													
Kinnoull Foundation													
F. M. Kirby Foundation, Inc.	■												
Caesar Kleberg Foundation for Wildlife Conservation	■												
The Esther A. and Joseph Klingenstein Fund, Inc.	■												
The Knapp Foundation, Inc.	■												★
The Seymour H. Knox Foundation, Inc.	■												
Charles G. Koch Charitable Foundation	■												
Kongsgaard-Goldman Foundation	■												
The Kresge Foundation	■												
The Lagemann Foundation	■												
Laidlaw Foundation		■						■					
Laird, Norton Foundation		■	★							■	★		
Larsen Fund, Inc.	★				■		★			■			★
LaSalle Adams Fund													
The Lauder Foundation, Inc.	■												
Laurel Foundation		/	/	/	■		★	/	/	/	■		★
The Lazar Foundation	■												
The Norman Lear Foundation													
Levi Strauss Foundation	★												
The Max and Anna Levinson Foundation	★	■		★									
LifeWorks Foundation													
Lilly Endowment, Inc.	■		★		★		★			★		★	
Lintilhac Foundation	■												
The Little Family Foundation	■												
Longwood Foundation, Inc.					■	★					■	★	

Application Deadlines

Grantmaker	X	J	F	M	A	M	J	J	A	S	O	N	D
Richard Lounsbery Foundation, Inc.			■			■			■			■	
Luster Family Foundation, Inc.													
Lyndhurst Foundation			★	■		★	■		★	■		★	■
The John D. and Catherine T. MacArthur Foundation	■												
James A. MacDonald Foundation													
Magowan Family Foundation, Inc.	■												
Maine Community Foundation, Inc.		■			■			■			■		
Maki Foundation	★						■						
Marbrook Foundation	■					★						★	
Marin Community Foundation	■												
MARPAT Foundation, Inc.											■		★
Mars Foundation	■						★						★
The Marshall Fund of Arizona				■					■			■	
The Martin Foundation, Inc.	■												
Massachusetts Environmental Trust	■												
The McConnell Foundation			■			■							
McCune Foundation	■	★					★						
Marshall L. & Perrine D. McCune Charitable Foundation		■		■									
The Eugene McDermott Foundation	■				★			★				★	
McDonnell Douglas Foundation	■												
McGregor Fund	■												
McInerny Foundation	★	■		★				■		★			
The McIntosh Foundation	■												
McKenzie River Gathering Foundation					■							■	
McKesson Foundation, Inc.	■												
The McKnight Foundation	★												
McLean Contributionship	■												
Giles W. and Elise G. Mead Foundation	■												
Nelson Mead Fund													
Meadows Foundation, Inc.	■												
The Andrew W. Mellon Foundation	■												
Richard King Mellon Foundation					■		★				■		★
Merck Family Fund	★			■			★					★	
The John Merck Fund													
Robert G. and Anne M. Merrick Foundation, Inc.	■												
Joyce Mertz-Gilmore Foundation		■						■					
Metropolitan Atlanta Community Foundation, Inc.		★		■		★		■		★		■	
Metropolitan Life Foundation	■												
Meyer Memorial Trust	★	■			■			■			■		

Application Deadlines

Grantmaker	X	J	F	M	A	M	J	J	A	S	O	N	D
Middlecott Foundation													
Millbrook Tribute Garden, Inc.	■												
The Milwaukee Foundation		■		★	■		★	■		★	■		★
The Minneapolis Foundation		■		■	■								
Mobil Foundation, Inc.	■												
Leo Model Foundation, Inc.	■												
The Moody Foundation	★												
J. P. Morgan Charitable Trust	■												
The Moriah Fund, Inc.	★			■					■				
Henry and Lucy Moses Fund, Inc.	■		★			★			★		★		
Charles Stewart Mott Foundation								■					
Ruth Mott Fund			★	■			★	■			★	■	
The Mountaineers Foundation		■				■				■		■	
The Curtis and Edith Munson Foundation, Inc.							■	★			■	★	
M. J. Murdock Charitable Trust	■	★	★	★	★	★	★	★	★	★	★	★	★
John P. Murphy Foundation	■												
Mustard Seed Foundation, Inc.	■												
The National Environmental Education & Training Foundation, Inc.				■					■				
National Fish and Wildlife Foundation					■				■				
National Geographic Society Education Foundation	■												
The Needmor Fund	★	■				■		■				■	
New England Biolabs Foundation		★		■	★					■	★		■
New Hampshire Charitable Foundation					■					■			■
New Horizon Foundation	■												
The New World Foundation	■												
The New York Community Trust	■												
New York Foundation			★	■			★	■			★	■	
The New York Times Company Foundation, Inc.	■												
The New-Land Foundation, Inc.			■						■				
Edward John Noble Foundation, Inc.	■												
The Samuel Roberts Noble Foundation, Inc.		★		■	★		■	★		■	★		■
Norcross Wildlife Foundation, Inc.	★			■	★					■	★		
The Nord Family Foundation			★		■		★		■		★		■
Norman Foundation	■												
Andrew Norman Foundation													
Kenneth T. and Eileen L. Norris Foundation	■												
Mary Moody Northen, Inc.	■												
Northwest Area Foundation	■												
Northwest Fund for the Environment				■						■			

Application Deadlines

Grantmaker	X	J	F	M	A	M	J	J	A	S	O	N	D
The Norton Foundation, Inc.	■												
Jessie Smith Noyes Foundation, Inc.	■												
Nicholas H. Noyes, Jr. Memorial Foundation	■												
OCRI Foundation	■			★				★		★			★
Nathan M. Ohrbach Foundation, Inc.	■				★								
The Ohrstrom Foundation													
Spencer T. and Ann W. Olin Foundation													
Onan Family Foundation	★			★								★	
Orchard Foundation	★								■				
Ottinger Foundation	■	/	/	/	/	/	/						
Outdoor Industry Conservation Alliance	■												
The Overbrook Foundation	■				★							★	
The David and Lucile Packard Foundation				■			■			■			■
Patagonia, Inc.		■							■				
Amelia Peabody Charitable Fund					■	★		■	★		■	★	
Peninsula Community Foundation	■		★			★			★			★	
The William Penn Foundation	■												
James C. Penney Foundation													
The Perkin Fund				■						■			
Perkins Charitable Foundation	■												
The Pew Charitable Trusts	■			★			★			★			★
Pew Scholars Program in Conservation and the Environment	★	■										■	
The Pfizer Foundation, Inc.	■												
The Philadelphia Foundation	★	■					■	■					
The Philanthropic Group													
Philip Morris Companies, Inc.	■												
Phillips Petroleum Foundation, Inc.	■												
Ellis L. Phillips Foundation			■	★		■	★				■	★	
Howard Phipps Foundation	■												
Pilot Trust													
Pinewood Foundation													
Henry B. Plant Memorial Fund, Inc.	■												
The Polden-Puckham Charitable Foundation	■			★							★		
The Powell Family Foundation	■												
Lynn R. and Karl E. Prickett Fund	■												
Prince Charitable Trusts	■												
Pritzker Foundation													
The Procter & Gamble Fund	■												
The Prospect Hill Foundation	■												

536 © 1995 Environmental Data Resources, Inc.

Application Deadlines

Grantmaker	X	J	F	M	A	M	J	J	A	S	O	N	D
The Prudential Foundation	■				★				★				★
Public Welfare Foundation, Inc.	■												
Recreational Equipment, Inc.	■												
Philip D. Reed Foundation, Inc.	■												
Z. Smith Reynolds Foundation, Inc.			■			★			■			★	
The Rhode Island Community Foundation	■	★		★		★		★		★		★	
Sid W. Richardson Foundation				■						■			
Smith Richardson Foundation, Inc.	■												
The Roberts Foundation			★	■			★	■			★	■	
Rockefeller Brothers Fund, Inc.	■												
Rockefeller Family Fund, Inc.	■												
Rockefeller Financial Services, Philanthropy Department	■												
The Rockefeller Foundation	■												
The Winthrop Rockefeller Foundation				■			★			■			★
The Rockfall Foundation			■										
Rockwell Fund, Inc.			■	★		■	★		■	★		■	★
Rockwood Fund, Inc.										■			
Lee Romney Foundation, Inc.													
Samuel and May Rudin Foundation, Inc.	■												
Fran and Warren Rupp Foundation	■												
Sacharuna Foundation													
Sacramento Regional Foundation					★								■
San Diego Community Foundation			■	★		★	■		■	★		★	■
The San Francisco Foundation	■												
The Sapelo Foundation				■			★			■			★
Sarkeys Foundation			■						■				
Sarah Scaife Foundation Incorporated	■		★			★				★		★	
The Scherman Foundation, Inc.	■												
S. H. and Helen R. Scheuer Family Foundation, Inc.	■												
Sarah I. Schieffelin Residuary Trust					■		★						
The Schiff Foundation													
Schultz Foundation, Inc.	■												
The Schumann Fund for New Jersey, Inc.			■		★	■		★		■		■	★
The Florence and John Schumann Foundation			■		★	■		★		■		★	
Ellen Browning Scripps Foundation													
Sears-Swetland Foundation	■												
Frances Seebe Trust													
Sequoia Foundation				■		★				■		★	
Seventh Generation Fund	■												

© 1995 Environmental Data Resources, Inc.

Application Deadlines

Grantmaker	X	J	F	M	A	M	J	J	A	S	O	N	D
Elmina B. Sewall Foundation													
Ralph C. Sheldon Foundation, Inc.	■												
Shell Oil Company Foundation										■			
Thomas Sill Foundation	■	★	★	★	★	★	★	★	★	★	★	★	★
The Skaggs Foundation						■					■		
The Kelvin and Eleanor Smith Foundation	■					★					★		
Kelvin Smith 1980 Charitable Trust	■												
Stanley Smith Horticultural Trust										■			
Snee-Reinhardt Charitable Foundation	★												
Solow Foundation	■												
The Sonoma County Community Foundation	★		■			★	■		■			★	
South Coast Foundation, Inc.													
Southwestern Bell Foundation	■												
Springhouse Foundation								/	/	/		★	
Springs Foundation, Inc.	■				★							★	
Sproul Foundation													
Stackner Family Foundation, Inc.		★		■	★		■	★		■	★		■
Alfred T. Stanley Foundation										■			
Anna B. Stearns Charitable Foundation, Inc.						■						■	
The Stebbins Fund, Inc.	■						★						
Steelcase Foundation	★												
Stern Family Fund	■												
Stoddard Charitable Trust		/	/	/	/	/	/	/	/	/	/		
Stranahan Foundation										■			
The Stratford Foundation	■												
Margaret Dorrance Strawbridge Foundation of Pennsylvania II, Inc.	■												
The Stroh Foundation	■												
The Strong Foundation for Environmental Values		■		★		■		★		■		★	
The Charles J. Strosacker Foundation											■		
Stroud Foundation													
The Morris Stulsaft Foundation	■												
The Sudbury Foundation	★												
The Sulzberger Foundation, Inc.	■												
The Summerlee Foundation	■												
The Summit Foundation													
Surdna Foundation, Inc.	■		★			★				★			
SURFREE													
Edna Bailey Sussman Fund				■			■				■		
The Switzer Foundation	★												

538

© 1995 Environmental Data Resources, Inc.

Application Deadlines

Grantmaker	X	J	F	M	A	M	J	J	A	S	O	N	D
Nelson Talbott Foundation	■												
S. Mark Taper Foundation	■												
The Telesis Foundation	■												
Texaco Foundation	■												
Thanksgiving Foundation													
The Oakleigh L. Thorne Foundation	■												
Threshold Foundation				■	■								
The Tides Foundation	■												
Times Mirror Magazines, Inc.							■						■
The Tinker Foundation Incorporated				■			★			■		★	
Tortuga Foundation													
Town Creek Foundation, Inc.		■			■					■			
Toyota USA Foundation	■												
The Travelers Foundation	■												
Treacy Foundation, Inc.	■												
Harry C. Trexler Trust		■											
The Troy Foundation	■												
True North Foundation	■												
The Truland Foundation													
The Trust For Mutual Understanding	★												
Marcia Brady Tucker Foundation													
Rose E. Tucker Charitable Trust	■												
Alice Tweed Tuohy Foundation							/	/	/				
Turner Foundation, Inc.				■			★			■			★
The USF&G Foundation, Inc.	■												
USX Foundation, Inc.		■			■		★	■		★			
Underhill Foundation	■												
Union Camp Charitable Trust		/	/	/	/	/	/	/	/			★	
Union Pacific Foundation								■					
Unitarian Universalist Veatch Program at Shelter Rock	■												
United States-Japan Foundation	■				★						★		
Vancouver Foundation		■		■						■			
R. T. Vanderbilt Trust					★		★			★		/	★
Vanguard Public Foundation		■			■			■		■			
G. Unger Vetlesen Foundation	■												★
Victoria Foundation, Inc.			■				★		■			★	
The Vidda Foundation	■												
Vinmont Foundation, Inc.	■												
Virginia Environmental Endowment		■				■				■			

© 1995 Environmental Data Resources, Inc.

Application Deadlines

Grantmaker	X	J	F	M	A	M	J	J	A	S	O	N	D
WMX Environmental Grants Program	■												
Alex C. Walker Educational & Charitable Foundation	■												
Wallace Genetic Foundation, Inc.	■												
DeWitt Wallace-Reader's Digest Fund	■												
Lila Wallace-Reader's Digest Fund	■												
Bill & Edith Walter Foundation													
C. A. Webster Foundation	■												
Weeden Foundation			■	★		■	★		■	★		■	★
Welfare Foundation, Inc.					■							■	
Henry E. and Consuelo S. Wenger Foundation, Inc.													
Westinghouse Foundation	■												
Weyerhaeuser Company Foundation	■												
William P. Wharton Trust					■	★					■	★	
Whitecap Foundation	■												
Joseph B. Whitehead Foundation			■		★					■		★	
Wilburforce Foundation	■												
G. N. Wilcox Trust		■			■			■			■		
Robert W. Wilson Foundation													
The Windham Foundation, Inc.		★		■	★		■	★		■	★		
Mark and Catherine Winkler Foundation	■												
The Winslow Foundation													
The Winston-Salem Foundation, Inc.		■			■			■			■		
The Dean Witter Foundation	■												
Wodecroft Foundation	■												
Robert W. Woodruff Foundation, Inc.			■		★					■		★	
The Wortham Foundation, Inc.			■	★		■	★		■	★		■	★
Sidney & Phyllis Wragge Foundation													
Margaret Cullinan Wray Charitable Lead Annuity Trust											■		★
Wrinkle in Time Foundation	■										★		
The Wyomissing Foundation, Inc.			■	★		■	★		■	★		■	★

G. Grantmakers Added and Deleted

Grantmakers added

Abell-Hanger Foundation
The Achelis Foundation
Airport Business Center Foundation
American Express Philanthropic Program
Elmer L. & Eleanor J. Andersen Foundation
Angelina Fund, Inc.
Arcadia Foundation
Atherton Family Foundation
Clayton Baker Trust
The George F. Baker Trust
Baltimore Gas and Electric Foundation, Inc.
BankAmerica Foundation
The Barra Foundation, Inc.
The Theodore H. Barth Foundation, Inc.
Bay Area Community Foundation
The Beirne Carter Foundation
David Winton Bell Foundation
James Ford Bell Foundation
Benton Foundation
The Bersted Foundation
The Boeing Company
The Bothin Foundation
Botwinick-Wolfensohn Foundation, Inc.
Alexander H. Bright Charitable Trust
Alex. Brown & Sons Charitable Foundation, Inc.
H. Barksdale Brown Charitable Trust
W. L. Lyons Brown Foundation
Jesse Margaret Wilson Budlong Foundation for Animal Aid
The Bunbury Company, Inc.
The Butler Foundation
J. E. & Z. B. Butler Foundation, Inc.
Patrick and Aimee Butler Family Foundation
The Louis Calder Foundation
James & Abigail Campbell Foundation
Ward M. & Mariam C. Canaday Educational and Charitable Trust
The Cargill Foundation
Caribou Fund
Centerior Energy Foundation
Chrysler Corporation Fund
Church & Dwight Co., Inc.
Liz Claiborne & Art Ortenberg Foundation
Claneil Foundation, Inc.
Clark Charitable Trust
Olive B. Cole Foundation
The Collins Foundation
The Community Foundation of Greater New Haven
The Community Foundation of Sarasota County, Inc.
The Community Foundation Serving Coastal South Carolina
Community Foundation of Western North Carolina, Inc.
Adolph Coors Foundation
Cox Foundation, Inc.

Roy E. Crummer Foundation
The Fred Harris Daniels Foundation, Inc.
Dayton Hudson Foundation
The Nelson B. Delavan Foundation
Dolfinger-McMahon Foundation
The Dragon Foundation, Inc.
Eastman Kodak Company Charitable Trust
Ederic Foundation, Inc.
The Emerald Foundation
The Thomas J. Emery Memorial
English-Bonter-Mitchell Foundation
Environmental Endowment for New Jersey, Inc.
Felburn Foundation
Samuel S. Fels Fund
The Hugh and Jane Ferguson Foundation
Fields Pond Foundation, Inc.
Fieldstead Charitable Trust
The 1525 Foundation
Bert Fingerhut/Caroline Hicks Family Fund
The Foundation for the National Capital Region
The Freed Foundation, Inc.
Frelinghuysen Foundation
Funding Exchange
The GAR Foundation
Global Greengrants Fund
The Golden Rule Foundation, Inc.
The W. C. Griffith Foundation
Evelyn and Walter Haas, Jr. Fund
The Hahn Family Foundation
Harbor Lights Foundation
The Harding Educational and Charitable Foundation
Gladys and Roland Harriman Foundation
Mary W. Harriman Foundation
The Hastings Trust
The Merrill G. & Emita E. Hastings Foundation
Hawaii Community Foundation
Charles Hayden Foundation
The Edward W. Hazen Foundation
The M. A. Healy Family Foundation, Inc.
Howard Heinz Endowment
Vira I. Heinz Endowment
The Hitachi Foundation
Howfirma Foundation
Hudson-Webber Foundation
Hurdle Hill Foundation
IBM Corporation
Illilouette Fund
The Indian Point Foundation, Inc.
The Louise H. and David S. Ingalls Foundation, Inc.
The International Foundation, Inc.
Ireland Foundation
Island Foundation
The Jackson Foundation
Jackson Hole Preserve, Inc.
The Howard Johnson Foundation

Joy Foundation for Ecological Education and Research
Harris and Eliza Kempner Fund
The Henry P. Kendall Foundation
The Helen & Milton Kimmelman Foundation
F. M. Kirby Foundation, Inc.
The Seymour H. Knox Foundation, Inc.
Charles G. Koch Charitable Foundation
The Lagemann Foundation
LaSalle Adams Fund
The Lauder Foundation, Inc.
The Norman Lear Foundation
Levi Strauss Foundation
The Little Family Foundation
James A. Macdonald Foundation
The Marshall Fund of Arizona
Massachusetts Environmental Trust
McCune Foundation
The Marshall L. & Perrine D. McCune Charitable Foundation
McDonnell Douglas Foundation
McGregor Fund
McKesson Foundation, Inc.
Nelson Mead Fund
Robert G. and Anne M. Merrick Foundation, Inc.
Metropolitan Life Foundation
Middlecott Foundation
The Mountaineers Foundation
John P. Murphy Foundation
Mustard Seed Foundation, Inc.
The National Environmental Education and Training Foundation, Inc.
New Horizon Foundation
The New World Foundation
The Samuel Roberts Noble Foundation, Inc.
Mary Moody Northen, Inc.
The Norton Foundation, Inc.
Nicholas H. Noyes, Jr. Memorial Foundation
OCRI Foundation
Nathan M. Ohrbach Foundation, Inc.
Orchard Foundation
Outdoor Industry Conservation Alliance
The Perkin Fund
Perkins Charitable Foundation
The Pfizer Foundation, Inc.
The Philanthropic Group
Phillips Petroleum Foundation, Inc.
Henry B. Plant Memorial Fund, Inc.
The Polden-Puckham Charitable Foundation
The Powell Family Foundation
Pritzker Foundation
The Prudential Foundation
Philip D. Reed Foundation, Inc.
The Winthrop Rockefeller Foundation
The Rockfall Foundation
Rockwood Fund, Inc.
Lee Romney Foundation, Inc.
Fran and Warren Rupp Foundation

© 1995 Environmental Data Resources, Inc.

Grantmakers Added and Deleted

Grantmakers added (cont.)

Sacramento Regional Foundation
San Diego Community Foundation
S. H. and Helen R. Scheuer Family Foundation, Inc.
Sarah I. Schieffelin Residuary Trust
Schultz Foundation, Inc.
Ellen Browning Scripps Foundation
Sears-Swetland Foundation
Frances Seebe Trust
Seventh Generation Fund
Thomas Sill Foundation
The Kelvin and Eleanor Smith Foundation
Kelvin Smith 1980 Charitable Trust
Snee-Reinhardt Charitable Foundation
Solow Foundation
The Sonoma County Community Foundation
South Coast Foundation, Inc.
Springhouse Foundation
Springs Foundation, Inc.
Sproul Foundation
Stackner Family Foundation, Inc.
Alfred T. Stanley Foundation
Anna B. Stearns Charitable Foundation, Inc.
The Stebbins Fund, Inc.
Stoddard Charitable Trust
Stranahan Foundation
The Stroh Foundation
The Charles J. Strosacker Foundation
Stroud Foundation
SURFREE
S. Mark Taper Foundation
The Telesis Foundation
Thanksgiving Foundation
The Oakleigh L. Thorne Foundation
Times Mirror Magazines, Inc.
Toyota USA Foundation
The Travelers Foundation
Treacy Foundation, Inc.
Harry C. Trexler Trust
The Troy Foundation
The Truland Foundation
Marcia Brady Tucker Foundation
The USF&G Foundation, Inc.
USX Foundation, Inc.
Underhill Foundation
Union Camp Charitable Trust
Union Pacific Foundation
R. T. Vanderbilt Trust
Vanguard Public Foundation
G. Unger Vetlesen Foundation
Vinmont Foundation, Inc.
Alex C. Walker Educational & Charitable Foundation
Wallace Genetic Foundation, Inc.
DeWitt Wallace-Reader's Digest Fund
C. A. Webster Foundation
Welfare Foundation, Inc.
Weyerhaeuser Company Foundation
Whitecap Foundation
Joseph B. Whitehead Foundation
Robert W. Wilson Foundation
The Windham Foundation, Inc.
The Winslow Foundation
The Winston-Salem Foundation, Inc.
Wodecroft Foundation
Sidney & Phyllis Wragge Foundation

Grantmakers deleted

Alpine Winter Foundation
The Baltimore Community Foundation, Inc.
George W. Barber, Jr. Foundation
Benwood Foundation, Inc.
Booth Ferris Foundation
Callaway Foundation, Inc.
Carnegie Corporation of New York
Amon G. Carter Foundation
The Catto Foundation
Chichester duPont Foundation, Inc.
Liz Claiborne Foundation
Close Foundation, Inc.
Communities Foundation of Texas, Inc.
Community Foundation of Greater Flint
The Charles A. Dana Foundation, Inc.
The Denver Foundation
The William H. Donner Foundation, Inc.
The Dunspaugh-Dalton Foundation, Inc.
The Durfee Foundation
Enron Foundation
Foellinger Foundation, Inc.
The Bradley L. Goldberg Charitable Trust
The Greater Cincinnati Foundation
Grotto Foundation, Inc.
Hoblitzelle Foundation
The Fletcher Jones Foundation
Mardag Foundation
Robert R. McCormick Tribune Foundation
The Ralph M. Parsons Foundation
The Payne Fund
Phipps Florida Foundation
Charles H. Revson Foundation, Inc.
Jacob G. Schmidlapp Trust No. 1
L. J. Skaggs & Mary C. Skaggs Foundation
Alfred P. Sloan Foundation
The Starr Foundation
The Steele-Reese Foundation
The Streisand Foundation
Martha P. and Joseph A. Thomas Foundation, Inc.
Vulcan Materials Company Foundation
The Walton Family Foundation
The Andy Warhol Foundation for the Visual Arts, Inc.

H. Grantmakers Alphabetical List

ARCO Foundation
AT&T Foundation
A Territory Resource
Abelard Foundation West, The
Abell Foundation, The
Abell-Hanger Foundation
Achelis Foundation, The
Acorn Foundation, The
Ahmanson Foundation, The
Airport Business Center Foundation
Alaska Conservation Foundation
Alden, George I. Trust, The
Allen, Winifred & Harry B. Foundation
Altman, Jenifer Foundation, The
American Conservation Association, Inc.
American Express Philanthropic Program
American Foundation Corporation
Americana Foundation, Inc.
Ameritech Foundation
Andersen, Elmer L. & Eleanor J. Foundation
Angelina Fund, Inc.
Apple Computer, Inc.
Arca Foundation, The
Arcadia Foundation
Armington, Evenor Fund
Astor, Vincent Foundation, The
Atherton Family Foundation
Atkinson Foundation
Atlantic Foundation
Austin Memorial Foundation, The
Azadoutioun Foundation
Babcock, Mary Reynolds Foundation, Inc.
Bailey Wildlife Foundation, The
Baird, Cameron Foundation, The
Baker, Clayton Trust
Baker, George F. Trust, The
Baltimore Gas and Electric Foundation, Inc.
BankAmerica Foundation
Barra Foundation, Inc., The
Barth, Theodore H. Foundation, Inc., The
Bauman Foundation, The
Bay Area Community Foundation
Bay Foundation, The
Bayne, Howard Fund, The
Bean, L.L., Inc.
Bechtel, S. D., Jr. Foundation
Beinecke Foundation, Inc., The
Beirne Carter Foundation, The
Beldon Fund
Bell, David Winton Foundation
Bell, James Ford Foundation
Ben & Jerry's Foundation, The
Beneficia Foundation
Benton Foundation
Benua Foundation, Inc.
Bersted Foundation, The
Betterment Fund, The
Beveridge, Frank Stanley Foundation, Inc., The

Bingham, William Foundation, The
Bishop Pine Fund
Blandin Foundation
Blumenthal Foundation, The
Bodman Foundation, The
Boeing Company, The
Boettcher Foundation
Borden, Mary Owen Memorial Foundation
Bothin Foundation, The
Botwinick-Wolfensohn Foundation, Inc.
Brach, Helen Foundation
Bradley, Lynde and Harry Foundation, Inc., The
Bremer, Otto Foundation
Bright, Alexander H. Charitable Trust
Brown, Alex. & Sons Charitable Foundation, Inc.
Brown, H. Barksdale Charitable Trust
Brown, Ruth H. Foundation
Brown, W. L. Lyons Foundation
Brownlee, Robert Foundation, The
Bryan, Kathleen Price and Joseph M. Family Foundation, Inc.
Buchanan Family Foundation, The
Budlong, Jesse Margaret Wilson Foundation for Animal Aid
Bullitt Foundation, The
Bunbury Company, Inc., The
Bush Foundation, The
Butler Foundation, The
Butler, J. E. & Z. B. Foundation, Inc.
Butler, Patrick and Aimee Family Foundation
Bydale Foundation, The
C. S. Fund
Cabot Family Charitable Trust, The
Cafritz, Morris and Gwendolyn Foundation, The
Calder, Louis Foundation, The
California Community Foundation
Campbell, James & Abigail Foundation
Canaday, Ward M. & Mariam C. Educational and Charitable Trust
Cape Branch Foundation, The
Cargill Foundation, The
Caribou Fund
Carolyn Foundation
Carpenter Foundation, The
Cary, Mary Flagler Charitable Trust
Centerior Energy Foundation
Champlin Foundations, The
Changing Horizons Charitable Trust
Cheeryble Foundation
Cheney, Ben B. Foundation
Chesapeake Bay Trust
Chesapeake Corporation Foundation
Chevron Companies, The
Chicago Community Trust, The
Chrysler Corporation Fund
Church & Dwight Co., Inc.

Claiborne, Liz and Art Ortenberg Foundation
Claneil Foundation, Inc.
Clark Charitable Trust
Clark Foundation, The
Clark, Robert Sterling Foundation, Inc.
Cleveland Foundation, The
Clowes Fund, Inc., The
Cole, Olive B. Foundation
Collins Foundation, The
Columbia Foundation
Columbus Foundation, The
Community Foundation of Greater New Haven, The
Community Foundation of Santa Clara County, The
Community Foundation of Sarasota County, Inc., The
Community Foundation Serving Coastal South Carolina, The
Community Foundation of Western North Carolina, Inc.
Compton Foundation, Inc.
Conservation and Research Foundation, The
Conservation, Food & Health Foundation, Inc.
Cooke Foundation, Limited
Coors, Adolph Foundation
Cowell, S. H. Foundation
Cowles Charitable Trust, The
Cox Foundation, Inc.
Cox, James M., Jr. Foundation, Inc., The
Cox, Jessie B. Charitable Trust
Cricket Foundation, The
Crocker, Mary A. Trust, The
Crummer, Roy E. Foundation
Crystal Channel Foundation
Cudahy, Patrick and Anna M. Fund
Culpeper, Charles E. Foundation, Inc.
Cummings, Nathan Foundation, The
Damien Foundation
Daniels, Fred Harris Foundation, Inc., The
Dart Foundation
Davis, Arthur Vining Foundations, The
Davis Conservation Foundation
Dayton Hudson Foundation
Deer Creek Foundation
Delavan, Nelson B. Foundation, The
Diamond, Aaron Foundation, The
Dodge, Cleveland H. Foundation, Inc.
Dodge, Geraldine R. Foundation, Inc.
Doelger, Thelma Charitable Trust
Dolfinger-McMahon Foundation
Donaldson, Oliver S. and Jennie R. Charitable Trust
Donnelley, Gaylord and Dorothy Foundation
Donner Canadian Foundation
Douroucouli Foundation
Dow, Herbert H. and Grace A. Foundation, The

© 1995 Environmental Data Resources, Inc.

Grantmakers Alphabetical List

Dragon Foundation, Inc., The
Dreyfus, Max and Victoria
  Foundation, Inc., The
Dunn, Elizabeth Ordway
  Foundation, Inc., The
DuPont, Jessie Ball Religious, Charitable
  and Educational Fund
Eastman Kodak Company Charitable Trust
Echoing Green Foundation
Ederic Foundation, Inc.
Educational Foundation of America, The
Eisig, Arthur M. and Olga T.-Arthur M.
  and Kate E. Tode Foundation, Inc.
El Paso Community Foundation
El Pomar Foundation
Emerald Foundation, The
Emery, Thomas J. Memorial, The
Energy Foundation, The
Engelhard, Charles Foundation, The
English-Bonter-Mitchell Foundation
Environment Now Foundation
Environmental Education Foundation
  of Florida, Inc.
Environmental Endowment for
  New Jersey, Inc.
Erpf, Armand G. Fund, Inc., The
Ettinger Foundation, Inc., The
Fair Play Foundation
Fanwood Foundation
Farish, William Stamps Fund, The
Favrot Fund, The
Felburn Foundation
Fels, Samuel S. Fund
Ferguson, Hugh and Jane Foundation, The
Field Foundation of Illinois, Inc., The
Field, Jamee and Marshall Foundation
Fields Pond Foundation, Inc.
Fieldstead Charitable Trust
1525 Foundation, The
Fikes, Leland Foundation, Inc.
Fingerhut, Bert/Caroline Hicks Family Fund
FishAmerica Foundation
Flintridge Foundation
Ford Foundation
Ford Motor Company Fund
Ford, Walter and Josephine Fund
Foundation for Carolinas
Foundation for Deep Ecology
Foundation for Field Research
Foundation for the National
  Capital Region, The
France, Jacob and Annita
  Foundation, Inc., The
Frear, Mary D. and Walter F.
  Eleemosynary Trust
Freed Foundation, Inc., The
Frelinghuysen Foundation
Frost Foundation, Ltd., The
Fry, Lloyd A. Foundation
Fund for New Jersey, The
Fund for Preservation of Wildlife
  and Natural Areas, The
Fund of the Four Directions
Funding Exchange
GAR Foundation, The
GE Fund
Gap Foundation, The

Gates Foundation
Gauntlett, Barbara Foundation, Inc., The
Gebbie Foundation, Inc.
Gellert, Fred Foundation, The
General Service Foundation
Georgia Power Foundation, Inc.
Georgia-Pacific Foundation
Gerbode, Wallace Alexander
  Foundation, Inc., The
German Marshall Fund of the
  United States, The
Gerstacker, Rollin M. Foundation, The
Gimbel, Bernard F. and Alva B.
  Foundation, Inc.
Give to the Earth Foundation
Global Environmental Project Institute
Global Greengrants Fund
Golden Rule Foundation, Inc., The
Goldman Environmental Foundation, The
Goldman, Herman Foundation
Goldman, Richard & Rhoda Fund
Good Samaritan, Inc.
Gordon, Walter and Duncan Charitable
  Foundation
Great Lakes Protection Fund
Greater Piscataqua Community Foundation
Greenville Foundation, The
Greve, William and Mary
  Foundation, Inc., The
Griffith, W. C. Foundation, The
Gund, George Foundation, The
HKH Foundation
Haas, Evelyn and Walter, Jr. Fund
Haas, Walter and Elise Fund
Hahn Family Foundation, The
Hall Family Foundation, The
Halsell, Ewing Foundation, The
Hamer Foundation, The
Hanes, James G. Memorial Fund
Harbor Lights Foundation
Harder Foundation
Harding Educational and Charitable
  Foundation, The
Harriman, Gladys and Roland Foundation
Harriman, Mary W. Foundation
Hartford Foundation for Public Giving
Hastings Trust, The
Hastings, Merrill G. & Emita E.
  Foundation, The
Hawaii Community Foundation
Hawaiian Electric Industries Charitable
  Foundation
Hayden, Charles Foundation
Haynes, John Randolph and Dora
  Foundation, The
Hazen, Edward W. Foundation, The
Healy, M. A. Family Foundation, Inc., The
Heinz, Howard Endowment
Heinz, Vira I. Endowment
Heller Charitable & Educational Fund
Heller, Clarence E. Charitable
  Foundation, The
Hewlett, William and Flora Foundation, The
Hitachi Foundation, The
Hofmann Foundation, The
Homeland Foundation, The
Horn Foundation, The

Howfirma Foundation
Hudson-Webber Foundation
Hughes, Charles Evans Memorial
  Foundation, Inc., The
Hunt, Roy A. Foundation, The
Hurdle Hill Foundation
Hyams Foundation, The
Hyde and Watson Foundation, The
IBM Corporation
Illilouette Fund
Indian Point Foundation, Inc., The
Ingalls, Louise H. and David S.
  Foundation, Inc., The
International Foundation, Inc., The
Ireland Foundation
Irvine, James Foundation, The
Island Foundation, Inc.
Island Foundation
Ittleson Foundation, Inc.
Ivey, Richard Foundation, The
Jackson Foundation, The
Jackson Hole Preserve, Inc.
Jackson, Henry M. Foundation, The
Jennings, Martha Holden Foundation
Jewett, George Frederick Foundation, The
Johnson, Helen K. and Arthur E. Foundation
Johnson, Howard Foundation, The
Johnson, Walter S. Foundation
Jones, W. Alton Foundation, Inc.
Joy Foundation for Ecological Education
  and Research
Joyce Foundation, The
Kaplan, J. M. Fund, Inc., The
Kellogg, W. K. Foundation
Kempner, Harris and Eliza Fund
Kendall, Henry P. Foundation, The
Kerr, Robert S. and Grayce B.
  Foundation, Inc., The
Kimmelman, Helen and Milton
  Foundation, The
Kinnoull Foundation
Kirby, F. M. Foundation, Inc.
Kleberg, Caesar Foundation for Wildlife
  Conservation
Klingenstein, Esther A. and Joseph
  Fund, Inc., The
Knapp Foundation, Inc., The
Knox, Seymour H. Foundation, Inc., The
Koch, Charles G. Charitable Foundation
Kongsgaard-Goldman Foundation
Kresge Foundation, The
Lagemann Foundation, The
Laidlaw Foundation
Laird, Norton Foundation
Larsen Fund, Inc.
LaSalle Adams Fund
Lauder Foundation, Inc., The
Laurel Foundation
Lazar Foundation, The
Lear, Norman Foundation, The
Levi Strauss Foundation
Levinson, Max and Anna Foundation, The
LifeWorks Foundation
Lilly Endowment, Inc.
Lintilhac Foundation
Little Family Foundation, The
Longwood Foundation, Inc.

Grantmakers Alphabetical List

Lounsbery, Richard Foundation, Inc.
Luster Family Foundation, Inc.
Lyndhurst Foundation
MacArthur, John D. and Catherine T. Foundation, The
Macdonald, James A. Foundation
Magowan Family Foundation, Inc.
Maine Community Foundation, Inc.
Maki Foundation
Marbrook Foundation
Marin Community Foundation
MARPAT Foundation, Inc.
Mars Foundation
Marshall Fund of Arizona, The
Martin Foundation, Inc., The
Massachusetts Environmental Trust
McConnell Foundation, The
McCune Foundation
McCune, Marshall L. & Perrine D. Charitable Foundation, The
McDermott, Eugene Foundation, The
McDonnell Douglas Foundation
McGregor Fund
McInerny Foundation
McIntosh Foundation, The
McKenzie River Gathering Foundation
McKesson Foundation, Inc.
McKnight Foundation, The
McLean Contributionship
Mead, Giles W. and Elise G. Foundation
Mead, Nelson Fund
Meadows Foundation, Inc.
Mellon, Andrew W. Foundation, The
Mellon, Richard King Foundation
Merck Family Fund
Merck, John Fund, The
Merrick, Robert G. and Anne M. Foundation, Inc.
Mertz-Gilmore, Joyce Foundation
Metropolitan Atlanta Community Foundation, Inc.
Metropolitan Life Foundation
Meyer Memorial Trust
Middlecott Foundation
Millbrook Tribute Garden, Inc.
Milwaukee Foundation, The
Minneapolis Foundation, The
Mobil Foundation, Inc.
Model, Leo Foundation, Inc.
Moody Foundation, The
Morgan, J.P. Charitable Trust
Moriah Fund, Inc., The
Moses, Henry and Lucy Fund, Inc.
Mott, Charles Stewart Foundation
Mott, Ruth Fund
Mountaineers Foundation, The
Munson, Curtis and Edith Foundation, Inc., The
Murdock, M. J. Charitable Trust
Murphy, John P. Foundation
Mustard Seed Foundation, Inc.
National Environmental Education and Training Foundation, Inc., The
National Fish and Wildlife Foundation
National Geographic Society Education Foundation
Needmor Fund, The

New England Biolabs Foundation
New Hampshire Charitable Foundation
New Horizon Foundation
New World Foundation, The
New York Community Trust, The
New York Foundation
New York Times Company Foundation, Inc., The
New-Land Foundation, Inc., The
Noble, Edward John Foundation, Inc.
Noble, Samuel Roberts Foundation, Inc., The
Norcross Wildlife Foundation, Inc.
Nord Family Foundation, The
Norman Foundation
Norman, Andrew Foundation
Norris, Kenneth T. and Eileen L. Foundation
Northen, Mary Moody, Inc.
Northwest Area Foundation
Northwest Fund for the Environment
Norton Foundation, Inc., The
Noyes, Jessie Smith Foundation, Inc.
Noyes, Nicholas H., Jr. Memorial Foundation
OCRI Foundation
Ohrbach, Nathan M. Foundation, Inc.
Ohrstrom Foundation, The
Olin, Spencer T. and Ann W. Foundation
Onan Family Foundation
Orchard Foundation
Ottinger Foundation
Outdoor Industry Conservation Alliance
Overbrook Foundation, The
Packard, David and Lucile Foundation, The
Patagonia, Inc.
Peabody, Amelia Charitable Fund
Peninsula Community Foundation
Penn, William Foundation, The
Penney, James C. Foundation
Perkin Fund, The
Perkins Charitable Foundation
Pew Charitable Trusts, The
Pew Scholars Program in Conservation and the Environment
Pfizer Foundation, Inc., The
Philadelphia Foundation, The
Philanthropic Group, The
Philip Morris Companies, Inc.
Phillips Petroleum Foundation, Inc.
Phillips, Ellis L. Foundation
Phipps, Howard Foundation
Pilot Trust
Pinewood Foundation
Plant, Henry B. Memorial Fund, Inc.
Polden-Puckham Charitable Foundation, The
Powell Family Foundation, The
Prickett, Lynn R. and Karl E. Fund
Prince Charitable Trusts
Pritzker Foundation
Procter & Gamble Fund, The
Prospect Hill Foundation, The
Prudential Foundation, The
Public Welfare Foundation, Inc.
Recreational Equipment, Inc.
Reed, Philip D. Foundation, Inc.
Reynolds, Z. Smith Foundation, Inc.
Rhode Island Community Foundation, The

Richardson, Sid W. Foundation
Richardson, Smith Foundation, Inc.
Roberts Foundation, The
Rockefeller Brothers Fund, Inc.
Rockefeller Family Fund, Inc.
Rockefeller Financial Services, Philanthropy Department
Rockefeller Foundation, The
Rockefeller, Winthrop Foundation, The
Rockfall Foundation, The
Rockwell Fund, Inc.
Rockwood Fund, Inc.
Romney, Lee Foundation, Inc.
Rudin, Samuel and May Foundation, Inc.
Rupp, Fran and Warren Foundation
Sacharuna Foundation
Sacramento Regional Foundation
San Diego Community Foundation
San Francisco Foundation, The
Sapelo Foundation, Inc.
Sarkeys Foundation
Scaife, Sarah Foundation Incorporated
Scherman Foundation, Inc., The
Scheuer, S. H. and Helen R. Family Foundation, Inc.
Schieffelin, Sarah I. Residuary Trust
Schiff Foundation, The
Schultz Foundation, Inc.
Schumann Fund for New Jersey, Inc., The
Schumann, Florence and John Foundation, The
Scripps, Ellen Browning Foundation
Sears-Swetland Foundation
Seebe, Frances Trust
Sequoia Foundation
Seventh Generation Fund
Sewall, Elmina B. Foundation
Sheldon, Ralph C. Foundation, Inc.
Shell Oil Company Foundation
Sill, Thomas Foundation
Skaggs Foundation, The
Smith, Kelvin and Eleanor Foundation, The
Smith, Kelvin 1980 Charitable Trust
Smith, Stanley Horticultural Trust
Snee-Reinhardt Charitable Foundation
Solow Foundation
Sonoma County Community Foundation, The
South Coast Foundation, Inc.
Southwestern Bell Foundation
Springhouse Foundation
Springs Foundation, Inc.
Sproul Foundation
Stackner Family Foundation, Inc.
Stanley, Alfred T. Foundation
Stearns, Anna B. Charitable Foundation, Inc.
Stebbins Fund, Inc., The
Steelcase Foundation
Stern Family Fund
Stoddard Charitable Trust
Stranahan Foundation
Stratford Foundation, The
Strawbridge, Margaret Dorrance Foundation of Pennsylvania II, Inc.
Stroh Foundation, The
Strong Foundation for Environmental Values, The

© 1995 Environmental Data Resources, Inc.

Grantmakers Alphabetical List

Strosacker, Charles J. Foundation, The
Stroud Foundation
Stulsaft, Morris Foundation, The
Sudbury Foundation, The
Sulzberger Foundation, Inc., The
Summerlee Foundation, The
Summit Foundation, The
Surdna Foundation, Inc.
SURFREE
Sussman, Edna Bailey Fund
Switzer Foundation, The
Talbott, Nelson Foundation
Taper, S. Mark Foundation
Telesis Foundation, The
Texaco Foundation
Thanksgiving Foundation
Thorne, Oakleigh L. Foundation, The
Threshold Foundation
Tides Foundation, The
Times Mirror Magazines, Inc.
Tinker Foundation Incorporated, The
Tortuga Foundation
Town Creek Foundation, Inc.
Toyota USA Foundation
Travelers Foundation, The
Treacy Foundation, Inc.
Trexler, Harry C. Trust
Troy Foundation, The
True North Foundation
Truland Foundation, The
Trust For Mutual Understanding, The
Tucker, Marcia Brady Foundation
Tucker, Rose E. Charitable Trust
Tuohy, Alice Tweed Foundation
Turner Foundation, Inc.
USF&G Foundation, Inc., The
USX Foundation, Inc.
Underhill Foundation
Union Camp Charitable Trust
Union Pacific Foundation
Unitarian Universalist Veatch Program
   at Shelter Rock
United States-Japan Foundation
Vancouver Foundation
Vanderbilt, R. T. Trust
Vanguard Public Foundation
Vetlesen, G. Unger Foundation
Victoria Foundation, Inc.
Vidda Foundation, The
Vinmont Foundation, Inc.
Virginia Environmental Endowment
WMX Environmental Grants Program
Walker, Alex C. Educational & Charitable
   Foundation
Wallace Genetic Foundation, Inc.
Wallace, DeWitt Reader's Digest Fund
Wallace, Lila Reader's Digest Fund
Walter, Bill & Edith Foundation
Webster, C. A. Foundation
Weeden Foundation
Welfare Foundation, Inc.
Wenger, Henry E. and Consuelo S.
   Foundation, Inc.
Westinghouse Foundation
Weyerhaeuser Company Foundation
Wharton, William P. Trust, The
Whitecap Foundation

Whitehead, Joseph B. Foundation
Wilburforce Foundation
Wilcox, G. N. Trust
Wilson, Robert W. Foundation
Windham Foundation, Inc., The
Winkler, Mark and Catherine Foundation
Winslow Foundation, The
Winston-Salem Foundation, Inc., The
Witter, Dean Foundation, The
Wodecroft Foundation
Woodruff, Robert W. Foundation, Inc.
Wortham Foundation, Inc., The
Wragge, Sidney & Phyllis Foundation
Wray, Margaret Cullinan Charitable
   Lead Annuity Trust
Wrinkle in Time Foundation
Wyomissing Foundation, Inc., The

Indexes

Officers, Trustees, Directors, and Contacts

A

Aarons, Philip E. Echoing Green Foundation
Abbott, Gordon. The Fund for Preservation of Wildlife and Natural Areas
Abbott, Laura M. AT&T Foundation
Abell, Shepherdson. The Abell Foundation
Ablamsky, John. The Merrill G. & Emita E. Hastings Foundation
Abrahamson, Lucille S. The San Francisco Foundation
Ackerman, William. The Community Foundation Serving Coastal South Carolina
Acord, H. K. Mobil Foundation, Inc.
Acton, Evelyn Meadows. Meadows Foundation, Inc.
Adams, Cindy. Alaska Conservation Foundation
Adams, James R. Southwestern Bell Foundation
Adams, John H. American Conservation Association, Inc.
Adams, Robert. Unitarian Universalist Veatch Program at Shelter Rock
Adams, Ruth. Maki Foundation, The Trust For Mutual Understanding
Adams, W. L. Union Pacific Foundation
Addison, Michael. Flintridge Foundation
Addison, Susan. Flintridge Foundation
Adelman, Gary. Bay Area Community Foundation
Adler, Arlene. The Edward W. Hazen Foundation
Agbayani, Amy. Hawaii Community Foundation
Ahmanson, Caroline L. California Community Foundation
Ahmanson, Howard F., Jr. The Ahmanson Foundation, Fieldstead Charitable Trust
Ahmanson, Robert H. The Ahmanson Foundation
Ahmanson, Roberta G. Fieldstead Charitable Trust
Ahmanson, William H. The Ahmanson Foundation
Aird, Eric R. The William Penn Foundation
Airington, Harold L. Georgia-Pacific Foundation
Akers, John F. The New York Times Company Foundation, Inc.
Akre, Charles T. MARPAT Foundation, Inc.
Albrecht, Ken. Blandin Foundation
Albright, Harry W., Jr. The Achelis Foundation, The Bodman Foundation
Alcantar, Joe, Jr. El Paso Community Foundation

Aldrich, Hope. Rockefeller Family Fund, Inc.
Aldridge, Elizabeth A. The Samuel Roberts Noble Foundation, Inc.
Alexander, Joyce M. The Field Foundation of Illinois, Inc.
Alexander, Larry J. Southwestern Bell Foundation
Allan, Karen C. The Carpenter Foundation
Allen, Andrew E. Winifred & Harry B. Allen Foundation
Allen, Anne. The Morris and Gwendolyn Cafritz Foundation
Allen, Barbara P. The Powell Family Foundation
Allen, David W. Winifred & Harry B. Allen Foundation
Allen, Gail E. The Rollin M. Gerstacker Foundation
Allen, Howard B. Winifred & Harry B. Allen Foundation
Allen, Ivan, Jr. Robert W. Woodruff Foundation, Inc.
Allen, Marjorie P. The Powell Family Foundation
Allen, Sam. Metropolitan Atlanta Community Foundation, Inc.
Allen, Thomas F. The William Bingham Foundation
Allison, Diane. The Educational Foundation of America
Almond, Peter O. The Jenifer Altman Foundation
Alperin, Melvin G. The Rhode Island Community Foundation
Alpert, Arthur Malcolm. Harris and Eliza Kempner Fund
Alston, Dana. Public Welfare Foundation, Inc.
Altman, Jonathan. The Jenifer Altman Foundation
Altman, Kathleen. The Jenifer Altman Foundation
Altschul, Arthur G. The New York Community Trust, The Overbrook Foundation
Altshul, Diana L. The Overbrook Foundation
Altshul, Stephen F. The Overbrook Foundation
Altshuler, David. The John Merck Fund
Alvarez, Aida. The New York Community Trust
Alvarez, Ed. Levi Strauss Foundation
Ames, Aubin Z. The Schumann Fund for New Jersey, Inc.
Ames, Edward A. Mary Flagler Cary Charitable Trust
Amy, Fred, Sr. The USF&G Foundation, Inc.

Anastasio, Carol. The Edward W. Hazen Foundation
Anderson, Anne Heller. The Clarence E. Heller Charitable Foundation
Andersen, Eleanor J. Elmer L. & Eleanor J. Andersen Foundation
Andersen, Elmer L. Elmer L. & Eleanor J. Andersen Foundation
Andersen, Emily. Elmer L. & Eleanor J. Andersen Foundation
Andersen, Julian. Elmer L. & Eleanor J. Andersen Foundation
Andersen, Tony. Elmer L. & Eleanor J. Andersen Foundation
Anderson, Dee. The Community Foundation of Sarasota County, Inc.
Anderson, Dorothy. Jessie Smith Noyes Foundation, Inc.
Anderson, Ford A., II. M. J. Murdock Charitable Trust
Anderson, Fred C. Norcross Wildlife Foundation, Inc.
Anderson, Jack. Great Lakes Protection Fund
Anderson, James G. The Robert S. and Grayce B. Kerr Foundation, Inc.
Anderson, John T. The Joyce Foundation
Anderson, Judith. OCRI Foundation
Anderson, Judy M. Georgia Power Foundation, Inc.
Anderson, Michel. San Diego Community Foundation
Anderson, Nancy C. Rockefeller Family Fund, Inc.
Anderson, Patricia. Philip D. Reed Foundation, Inc.
Anderson, Richard B. Centerior Energy Foundation
Anderson, Roger E. Lloyd A. Fry Foundation
Anderson, Thomas P. The Community Foundation Serving Coastal South Carolina
Anderson, Wyndham. The Pfizer Foundation, Inc.
Andrade, Debbie. California Community Foundation
Andrews, Joan P. The Educational Foundation of America
Andrews, Richard N. L. Pew Scholars Program in Conservation and the Environment
Andrus, John E., III. Marbrook Foundation, Surdna Foundation, Inc.
Angelica, Robert E. AT&T Foundation
Angell, Christopher. Tortuga Foundation
Angell, Christopher C. The Barbara Gauntlett Foundation, Inc.
Annette, Kathy. Blandin Foundation

© 1995 Environmental Data Resources, Inc.

Officers, Directors, Trustees, and Contacts

Anthony, Barbara Cox. The James M. Cox, Jr. Foundation, Inc.
Antitomas, Mary-Lynn. The USF&G Foundation, Inc.
Antoine, Janeen. Vanguard Public Foundation
Antone, Bob. Seventh Generation Fund
Apgar, Lyn M. Laidlaw Foundation
Apodaca, Clara R. The Hitachi Foundation
Apoliona, Ms. Haunani. McInerny Foundation
Aqua, Ronald. United States-Japan Foundation
Arbour, Dean. Bay Area Community Foundation
Arbury, Julie C. The Herbert H. and Grace A. Dow Foundation
Archabal, John W. The Bush Foundation
Archabal, Nina M. Northwest Area Foundation
Archer, Roberta. Evelyn and Walter Haas, Jr. Fund
Argyris, Marcia M. McKesson Foundation, Inc.
Arklie, Hugh. Thomas Sill Foundation
Armacost, Samuel H. The Chevron Companies, The James Irvine Foundation
Arminana, Ruben. The Sonoma County Community Foundation
Armington, David E. Evenor Armington Fund
Armington, Paul. Evenor Armington Fund
Armington, Peter. Evenor Armington Fund
Armstrong, Jeanette. Seventh Generation Fund
Armstrong, William A. McKesson Foundation, Inc.
Arnault, Ronald J. ARCO Foundation
Arndt, Mrs. Celestine Favrot. The Favrot Fund
Arnelle, H. Jesse. WMX Environmental Grants Program
Arnold, David J. The Charles J. Strosacker Foundation
Arnold, Kay K. National Fish and Wildlife Foundation
Arnold, Martha G. The Charles J. Strosacker Foundation
Arrigoni, Peter R. Marin Community Foundation
Arrillaga, Frances C. The Community Foundation of Santa Clara County
Arsenault, John E. The Fred Harris Daniels Foundation, Inc., The Sudbury Foundation
Asher, Spring. Metropolitan Atlanta Community Foundation, Inc.
Ashford, Theodore H. The Beinecke Foundation, Inc.
Ashmun, Candace McKee. The Fund for New Jersey
Ashton, Robert W. The Bay Foundaton
Astor del Valle, Janis. The Nathan Cummings Foundation

Astor, Mrs. Vincent. The Vincent Astor Foundation
Atcheson, Elizabeth. The Mary A. Crocker Trust
Atherton, Frank C. Atherton Family Foundation
Atis, Curtis A. AT&T Foundation
Atkinson, Duane E. Atkinson Foundation
Atkinson, Lavina M. Atkinson Foundation
Atkinson, Ray N. Atkinson Foundation
Atlas, Martin. The Morris and Gwendolyn Cafritz Foundation
Atwater, Charles B. The Bunbury Company, Inc, The Windham Foundation, Inc.
Atwater, Martha C. The Minneapolis Foundation
Atwood, Marjorie. Oliver S. and Jennie R. Donaldson Charitable Trust
Aubry, Julia A. Surdna Foundation, Inc.
Auerbach, Ann L. The Fund for New Jersey
Ault, Frank. San Diego Community Foundation
Austin, Donald G., Jr. The Austin Memorial Foundation
Austin, James W. The Austin Memorial Foundation
Austin, Maurice. The J. M. Kaplan Fund, Inc.
Austin, Richard C. The Austin Memorial Foundation
Austin, Stewart G. The Austin Memorial Foundation
Austin, Thomas G. The Austin Memorial Foundation
Austin, Winifred N. The Austin Memorial Foundation
Avery, Byllye. The New World Foundation
Avery, R. Stanton. The John Randolph Haynes and Dora Haynes Foundation
Ayers, Margaret C. Robert Sterling Clark Foundation, Inc.
Ayres, Frederic M. Nicholas H. Noyes, Jr. Memorial Foundation
Ayres, Nancy. Nicholas H. Noyes, Jr. Memorial Foundation

B

Babcock, Bruce M. Mary Reynolds Babcock Foundation, Inc.
Babicka, Jerry. The Educational Foundation of America
Babicka, Lynn. The Educational Foundation of America, The Ettinger Foundation, Inc.
Babson, Katherine L., Jr. Anna B. Stearns Charitable Foundation, Inc.
Bach, Howard. FishAmerica Foundation
Bachhuber, R. A. The Procter & Gamble Fund
Bachman, Dale S. Cooke Foundation, Limited

Bachman, Merle. The Abelard Foundation West, The Acorn Foundation
Bade, Anne. The Strong Foundation for Environmental Values
Bagley, Elizabeth Frawley. The Arca Foundation
Bagley, Nancy R. The Arca Foundation
Bagley, Nicole L. The Arca Foundation
Bagley, Smith W. The Arca Foundation, The Sapelo Foundation, Z. Smith Reynolds Foundation, Inc.
Bahouth, Peter. Turner Foundation, Inc.
Bailard, Tom. Peninsula Community Foundation
Bailey, Anita Lamb. OCRI Foundation
Bailey, Antoinette M. McDonnell Douglas Foundation
Bailey, Gordon M. The Bailey Wildlife Foundation
Bailey, Harold W., Jr. The Bailey Wildlife Foundation
Bailey, James. Patrick and Anna M. Cudahy Fund
Bailey, Merritt P. The Bailey Wildlife Foundation
Bailey, William H. The Bailey Wildlife Foundation
Bailey-Whiteside, L. Marlene. ARCO Foundation
Bainum, Stewart W. The Foundation for the National Capital Region
Bair, Peggy J. The Sonoma County Community Foundation
Baird, Brian D. The Cameron Baird Foundation
Baird, Bridget B. The Cameron Baird Foundation
Baird, Bruce C. The Cameron Baird Foundation
Baird, Jane D. The Cameron Baird Foundation
Baitseil, John M. Mobil Foundation, Inc.
Baker, Anthony K. The George F. Baker Trust
Baker, Dexter F. Harry C. Trexler Trust
Baker, George F., III. The George F. Baker Trust
Baker, Howard H., Jr. WMX Environmental Grants Program
Baker, James G. The Perkin Fund
Baker, Jane. Vanguard Public Foundation
Baker, Julia C. Clayton Baker Trust
Baker, Kane K. The George F. Baker Trust
Baker, Robert E. The Moody Foundation
Baker, William C. Clayton Baker Trust
Baker, William O. The Fund for New Jersey
Baldwin, Garza, Jr. Community Foundation of Western North Carolina, Inc.
Baldwin, H. Furlong. Baltimore Gas and Electric Foundation, Inc.
Baldwin, Robert H. B. Geraldine R. Dodge Foundation, Inc.
Baliles, Gerald L. National Geographic Society Education Foundation

Officers, Trustees, Directors, and Contacts

Baliles, Jeannie P. Virginia Environmental Endowment
Ball, Lynne S. Mark and Catherine Winkler Foundation
Ballard, Bruce L. The New York Community Trust
Ballard, Ernesta D. The Philadelphia Foundation
Bancroft, James R. The Dean Witter Foundation
Bangser, Michael. Hartford Foundation for Public Giving
Banks, Malvin. Nelson Talbott Foundation
Banks, Thomas J. Foundation for Field Research
Bannock, Jennifer L. Ivey. The Richard Ivey Foundation
Baragli, Judith O. Onan Family Foundation
Barbato, Virginia N. The Nord Family Foundation
Barber, Jeff. SURFREE
Barber, John. The USF&G Foundation, Inc.
Barber, Kathleen L. The George Gund Foundation
Barbour, Margaret Sewall. Elmina B. Sewall Foundation
Barbutes, Tracy. Springhouse Foundation
Barder, Sarah D. The Lynde and Harry Bradley Foundation, Inc.
Barletta, Robert J. The Prospect Hill Foundation
Barlow, Harriet. HKH Foundation
Barlow, J. E. The Polden-Puckham Charitable Foundation
Barlow, Robert C. Welfare Foundation, Inc.
Barnes, Harry G., Jr. The German Marshall Fund of the United States
Barnes, Jack W. Americana Foundation, Inc.
Barnes, Ronald R. Kenneth T. and Eileen L. Norris Foundation
Barnes, Scott Y. The Community Foundation Serving Coastal South Carolina
Barnett, John. Vancouver Foundation
Barnhart, Lorraine. The Freed Foundation, Inc.
Baron, Jules M. Herman Goldman Foundation
Baron, Raymond S. Herman Goldman Foundation
Baron, Richard K. Herman Goldman Foundation
Barr, Philip B., Jr. Mustard Seed Foundation, Inc.
Barrett, Richard W. Wodecroft Foundation
Barron, Thomas A. Echoing Green Foundation
Barry, John J. The Foundation for the National Capital Region
Barsness, W. E. Bye. Northwest Area Foundation
Barta, Paula. Sacharuna Foundation
Bartelt, Sarah Caswell. The Frank Stanley Beveridge Foundation, Inc.

Bartlett, Thomas A. United States-Japan Foundation
Bartley, Anne. The New World Foundation, Rockefeller Family Fund, Inc.
Bartos, Adam. The Jenifer Altman Foundation
Bartos, Armand P. The Jenifer Altman Foundation, Pinewood Foundation
Bartos, Celeste G. The Jenifer Altman Foundation, Pinewood Foundation
Bartsch, Perry W. Community Foundation of Western North Carolina, Inc.
Bass, Lee M. Sid W. Richardson Foundation
Bass, Nancy Lee. Sid W. Richardson Foundation
Bass, Perry R. Sid W. Richardson Foundation
Bass, Sid R. Sid W. Richardson Foundation
Bass, Willard W., Jr. The Winston-Salem Foundation, Inc.
Bate, David S. The International Foundation, Inc., The Florence and John Schumann Foundation
Bates, Rex J. LaSalle Adams Fund
Batt, David. Environmental Education Foundation of Florida, Inc.
Bauman, Patricia. The Bauman Foundation
Bauman, Paul. Herman Goldman Foundation
Bauman, R. P. Union Pacific Foundation
Bay, Frederick. The Bay Foundation
Bay-Hansen, Christopher. The Bay Foundation
Baylis, Kathy. The Community Foundation of Sarasota County, Inc.
Bayliss, Harry B. The George I. Alden Trust
Bays, Gerald F. Sacramento Regional Foundation
Beamer, Elmer G. The 1525 Foundation
Beamer, Kathleen. Outdoor Industry Conservation Alliance, Recreational Equipment, Inc.
Bean, Donald. The Max and Anna Levinson Foundation
Bean, The Reverend Elmo A. The Cleveland Foundation
Bean, Michael J. Pew Scholars Program in Conservation and the Environment
Beardsley, George B. Gates Foundation
Beasley, Willarene P. The Minneapolis Foundation
Beath, Andrew. Threshold Foundation
Beattie, Mollie H. National Fish and Wildlife Foundation
Beaudry, Susan. The Abelard Foundation West, The Acorn Foundation
Beaver, Thomas A. The Wyomissing Foundation, Inc.
Bechtel, Elizabeth H. S. D. Bechtel, Jr. Foundation
Bechtel, S. D., Jr. S. D. Bechtel, Jr. Foundation
Beck, Robert A. The Boeing Company
Beckner, Golden, Jr. Joyce Mertz-Gilmore Foundation

Bedell, Catherine. Jessie Smith Noyes Foundation, Inc.
Bedell, The Reverend George C. Jessie Ball duPont Religious, Charitable and Educational Fund
Bedell, Tom. FishAmerica Foundation
Bedolfe, H. M. The Homeland Foundation
Beghini, Victor G. USX Foundation, Inc.
Beighle, Douglas P. The Boeing Company
Beimfohr, Edward G. The Charles Engelhard Foundation
Beinecke, Elizabeth G. The Prospect Hill Foundation
Beinecke, Frances G. American Conservation Association, Inc.
Beinecke, Frederick W. The Prospect Hill Foundation
Beinecke, John B. The Prospect Hill Foundation
Beinecke, William S. The Prospect Hill Foundation
Belin, Daniel N. The Ahmanson Foundation
Belk, Judy. Levi Strauss Foundation
Bell, C. Robert, Jr. Community Foundation of Western North Carolina, Inc.
Bell, Ford W. James Ford Bell Foundation
Bell, George. Times Mirror Magazines, Inc.
Bell, Lucy W. David Winton Bell Foundation
Bell, R. Terry. Rockwell Fund, Inc.
Bell, Richard A. Sarkeys Foundation
Bell, Richard G. The Community Foundation of Greater New Haven
Bell, Samuel H., Jr. James Ford Bell Foundation
Bell, Solange M. Alexander H. Bright Charitable Trust
Bell, Charles H. David Winton Bell Foundation
Bellinger, Susan. New York Foundation
Belton, Sharon Sayles. The Bush Foundation
Belton, Steven L. Northwest Area Foundation
Benedict, Peter B. Surdna Foundation, Inc.
Bennett, Edward. The Community Foundation Serving Coastal South Carolina
Bennett, Graham F. The Winston-Salem Foundation, Inc.
Bennett, James E. The Cleveland Foundation
Bennett, James S. W. Alton Jones Foundation, Inc.
Bennett, Janice. The Chicago Community Trust
Bennett, Joan P. Jessie Ball duPont Religious, Charitable and Educational Fund
Bennett, Sue A. The Minneapolis Foundation
Bennett, William J. Sarah Scaife Foundation Incorporated
Benton, Charles. Benton Foundation
Benton, Craig H. Benton Foundation
Berde, Carol. The McKnight Foundation

© 1995 Environmental Data Resources, Inc.

Officers, Directors, Trustees, and Contacts

Berelson, Irving P. The Theodore H. Barth Foundation, Inc.
Berelson, Thelma D. The Theodore H. Barth Foundation, Inc.
Berg, Gordon. Foundation for the Carolinas
Berge, Coral. Elmer L. & Eleanor J. Andersen Foundation
Berger, Margie B. Laird, Norton Foundation
Bergeron, S. W. Chrysler Corporation Fund
Bergerson, J. Steven. WMX Environmental Grants Program
Bergholz, David. The George Gund Foundation
Bergman, James F. Felburn Foundation
Bergmann, Pat. Environmental Education Foundation of Florida, Inc.
Berkopec, Robert N. The Lynde and Harry Bradley Foundation, Inc.
Berman, Philip I. Harry C. Trexler Trust
Bernard, B. E. Shell Oil Company Foundation
Bernhard, Michael. The Abelard Foundation West
Bernhard, Nancy. The Abelard Foundation West
Bernhard, Sheryl. The Abelard Foundation West
Bernhard, Steven. The Abelard Foundation West
Berning, Larry D. Gaylord and Dorothy Donnelley Foundation
Bernstein, Diane. The Foundation for the National Capital Region
Bernstein, Joan Z. WMX Environmental Grants Program
Bernstein, Robert L. The Aaron Diamond Foundation
Bernstein, Rosalyne. Maine Community Foundation, Inc.
Berresford, Susan V. Ford Foundation
Bersticken, Albert C. Centerior Energy Foundation
Berteau, John T. The Community Foundation of Sarasota County, Inc.
Best, Marilyn. Perkins Charitable Foundation
Beukema, Henry S. McCune Foundation
Bianchini, Thomas J. F. M. Kirby Foundation, Inc.
Bierzynski, Andrew. Foundation for Field Research
Bilder, Erika. The Jenifer Altman Foundation
Billam, Dale J. Phillips Petroleum Foundation, Inc.
Billingsley, C. E. Union Pacific Foundation
Binger, Al. The Rockefeller Foundation
Binger, James H. The McKnight Foundation
Binger, James M. The McKnight Foundation
Binger, Patricia S. The McKnight Foundation
Binger, Virginia M. The McKnight Foundation

Bingham, Charles W. Weyerhaeuser Company Foundation
Binsted, John P. Vancouver Foundation
Bishop, Augusta Willoughby Little. The Little Family Foundation
Bishop, J. M. Shell Oil Company Foundation
Bishop, Timothy R. The Collins Foundation
Bissell, Cushman B., Jr. The Joyce Foundation
Bissell, George P. Fair Play Foundation
Bisset, Andrew W. James C. Penney Foundation
Bitter, Stephen D. Community Foundation of Western North Carolina, Inc.
Bitterman, Susan. The Ben & Jerry's Foundation
Bjorklund, Victoria B. The Howard Bayne Fund
Black, Bill. Bay Area Community Foundation
Black, Evelyn J. Hawaii Community Foundation
Black, Gary, Jr. The Abell Foundation
Blackburn, Edward J. Hawaiian Electric Industries Charitable Foundation
Blackmore, Doris A. The Troy Foundation
Blackwell, Angela G. The James Irvine Foundation
Blackwell, Anna D. Cooke Foundation, Limited
Blaine, Mrs. Joan S. Stroud Foundation
Blair, Claude M. John P. Murphy Foundation
Blair, Patricia. The Carpenter Foundation
Blair, Philip. San Diego Community Foundation
Blair, Randall. The Robert Brownlee Foundation
Blair, Ron. San Diego Community Foundation
Blake, Jonathan D. The Fred Harris Daniels Foundation, Inc.
Blake, Lucy. The Mary A. Crocker Trust
Blake, Norman P., Jr. The USF&G Foundation, Inc.
Blake, Robert O. Rockwood Fund, Inc.
Blake, Ronald L. Ameritech Foundation
Blatherwick, Gerald. Southwestern Bell Foundation
Blazek, Claudia. Margaret Cullinan Wray Charitable Lead Annuity Trust
Blazek-White, Doris D. The M. A. Healy Family Foundation, Inc.
Bliumis, Sarah W. The Bydale Foundation
Block, Judith S. The Chicago Community Trust
Blocker, Eunice. W. L. Lyons Brown Foundation
Bloom, Susan. American Express Philanthropic Program
Bloomstein, Charles. Joyce Mertz-Gilmore Foundation
Blossom, C. Bingham. The William Bingham Foundation

Blossom, C. Perry. The William Bingham Foundation
Blossom, Dudley S. The William Bingham Foundation
Blossom, Laurel. The William Bingham Foundation
Blossom, Robin Dunn. The William Bingham Foundation
Blount, John T. The Sonoma County Community Foundation
Blumenthal, Alan. The Blumenthal Foundation
Blumenthal, Anita. The Blumenthal Foundation
Blumenthal, Herman. The Blumenthal Foundation
Blumenthal, Philip. The Blumenthal Foundation
Blumenthal, Samuel. The Blumenthal Foundation
Blundell, John. Charles G. Koch Charitable Foundation
Bodden, Mark L. Philip Morris Companies, Inc.
Bodine, James F. The Philadelphia Foundation
Bodine, Jean G. McLean Contributionship
Boekenheide, R. W. Union Camp Charitable Trust
Boettcher, Mrs. Charles, II. Boettcher Foundation
Boggs, Thomas H., Jr. Chesapeake Bay Trust
Boitano, Caroline O. BankAmerica Foundation
Bolger, Donald J. Mobil Foundation, Inc.
Bolger, Thomas E. National Geographic Society Education Foundation
Bolker, Cynthia. S. Mark Taper Foundation
Bolling, Robert H. Welfare Foundation, Inc.
Bolling, Robert H., Jr. Welfare Foundation, Inc.
Bollinger, Ralph. The Collins Foundation
Bollmen, Brooks, III. Ruth Mott Fund
Bolton, Elizabeth D. Community Foundation of Western North Carolina, Inc.
Bond, Ms. Ina B. W. L. Lyons Brown Foundation
Bonifield, William C. Lilly Endowment, Inc.
Bonney, J. Dennis. The Chevron Companies
Boogaard, Marcia T. Marcia Brady Tucker Foundation
Boone, Richard. The Tides Foundation
Boorstin, Daniel J. The Morris and Gwendolyn Cafritz Foundation
Booth, Beatrice C. Carolyn Foundation
Borawski, Robert T. The Robert Brownlee Foundation
Borchers, Sister Judith. Patrick and Anna M. Cudahy Fund
Borden, John. Mary Owen Borden Memorial Foundation
Borden, Thomas A. Mary Owen Borden Memorial Foundation

Officers, Trustees, Directors, and Contacts

Bordon, Benjamin F. Richard Lounsbery Foundation, Inc.
Borek, Jo Anne. Amelia Peabody Charitable Fund
Boren, Molly Shi. Sarkeys Foundation
Boren, Susan S. The Minneapolis Foundation
Borman, Thomas H. The Minneapolis Foundation
Boswell, H. Charles. The Wortham Foundation, Inc.
Bosworth, Stephen W. United States-Japan Foundation
Botwinick, Benjamin. Botwinick-Wolfensohn Foundation, Inc.
Botwinick, Edward. Botwinick-Wolfensohn Foundation, Inc.
Bouque, Roy L. The Morris Stulsaft Foundation
Bove, Joyce M. The New York Community Trust
Bowen, Otis R. Lilly Endowment, Inc.
Bowen, William G. The Andrew W. Mellon Foundation, DeWitt Wallace-Reader's Digest Fund, Lila Wallace-Reader's Digest Fund,
Bowerman, Richard H. The Community Foundation of Greater New Haven
Bowers, Rob. Echoing Green Foundation
Bowles, Crandall C. Springs Foundation, Inc.
Bowles, Margaret C. The Clowes Fund, Inc.
Bowlin, Mike R. ARCO Foundation
Bowman, Thomas E. The Strong Foundation for Environmental Values
Bowman, Wallace D. The Conservation and Research Foundation
Bowser, Shirley D. W. K. Kellogg Foundation
Bowsher, John M. Benua Foundation, Inc.
Boyce, Phillip R. The Community Foundation of Santa Clara County
Boyd, Richard A. Martha Holden Jennings Foundation
Boyer, Robert L. Georgia Power Foundation, Inc.
Boynton, Cynthia Binger. The McKnight Foundation
Boynton, Noa. The McKnight Foundation
Bozeman, Bruce. Vinmont Foundation, Inc.
Bradbury, Marilyn M. Foundation for the Carolinas
Braddock, Richard S. Eastman Kodak Company Charitable Trust
Brademas, J. Texaco Foundation
Bradley, James. Springs Foundation, Inc.
Bradley, Jane C. The Cabot Family Charitable Trust
Bradley, Orren J. The Milwaukee Foundation
Bradley, Pat. The Strong Foundation for Environmental Values
Braga, Mary B. The Achelis Foundation, The Bodman Foundation

Brandt, E. Ned. The Rollin M. Gerstacker Foundation
Brauner, David A. Herman Goldman Foundation
Brawner, James, III. Metropolitan Atlanta Community Foundation, Inc.
Bray, Rosemary. Jessie Smith Noyes Foundation, Inc.
Brecher, Harvey. S. H. and Helen R. Scheuer Family Foundation, Inc.
Brecher, Kenneth S. The William Penn Foundation
Breckinridge, Isabella G. MARPAT Foundation, Inc.
Breed, William. Tortuga Foundation
Breeden, James P. The New World Foundation
Brennan, Leo J., Jr. Ford Motor Company Fund
Brennan, Michael J. National Fish and Wildlife Foundation
Brenner, David W. The Philadelphia Foundation
Brenner, Paul R. The Louis Calder Foundation
Bressler, Alfred W. Henry and Lucy Moses Fund, Inc.
Brewer, Ann F. The Vidda Foundation
Brewer, Cornelia B. Georgia-Pacific Foundation
Brewster, Pamela H. The Bullitt Foundation
Brewster, Walter W. Alex. Brown & Sons Charitable Foundation, Inc.
Briggs, Robert W. The GAR Foundation
Briggs, Winslow R. The Conservation and Research Foundation
Brink, Nancy R. Lintilhac Foundation
Briselli, Iso. Samuel S. Fels Fund
Briskman, Louis J. Westinghouse Foundation
Brittenham, Raymond L. The Tinker Foundation Incorporated
Broadbent, Robert R. John P. Murphy Foundation
Broadfoot, John W. Meadows Foundation, Inc.
Broadfoot, Vela Meadows. Meadows Foundation, Inc.
Broadhead, G. Mobil Foundation, Inc.
Brock, F. James, Jr. The Sonoma County Community Foundation
Brock, Marissa J. The Howard Johnson Foundation
Broder, Lois. Mary Owen Borden Memorial Foundation
Broderick, Catharine O. Rockefeller Brothers Fund, Inc.
Brody, William J. The Minneapolis Foundation
Broker, William K. The Sapelo Foundation
Bronfman, Joanie. Threshold Foundation
Brooks, Conley. Marbrook Foundation
Brooks, Conley, Jr. Marbrook Foundation, The Minneapolis Foundation

Brooks, Henry G., Jr. Maine Community Foundation, Inc.
Brooks, Hooper. Surdna Foundation, Inc.
Brooks, Markell. Marbrook Foundation
Brophy, Theodore F. DeWitt Wallace-Reader's Digest Fund Lila Wallace-Reader's Digest Fund
Brown, Ann Noble. The Samuel Roberts Noble Foundation, Inc.
Brown, Bertram. Joy Foundation for Ecological Education and Research
Brown, Carol A. The Community Foundation of Greater New Haven
Brown, Dale. Joy Foundation for Ecological Education and Research
Brown, David Lloyd. Ellis L. Phillips Foundation
Brown, David R. The Samuel Roberts Noble Foundation, Inc.
Brown, David R. C. Ruth H. Brown Foundation
Brown, Douglas H. Maine Community Foundation, Inc.
Brown, Gary R. Howfirma Foundation
Brown, Hillary. The Scherman Foundation, Inc.
Brown, J. Carter. The Morris and Gwendolyn Cafritz Foundation
Brown, Joy Gilman. Joy Foundation for Ecological Education and Research
Brown, Louise I. The Louise H. and David S. Ingalls Foundation, Inc.
Brown, Margarite. Roy E. Crummer Foundation
Brown, Martin S. W. L. Lyons Brown Foundation
Brown, Meredith M. The Stebbins Fund, Inc.
Brown, Neil. A. Ireland Foundation
Brown, Norman A. W. K. Kellogg Foundation
Brown, Owsley, II. W. L. Lyons Brown Foundation
Brown, Patricia. The Eugene McDermott Foundation
Brown, Rebekah Mohr. The Troy Foundation
Brown, Richard H. Ameritech Foundation
Brown, Ruth. Ruth H. Brown Foundation
Brown, The Honorable Torrey C. Chesapeake Bay Trust
Brown, Traci. Joy Foundation for Ecological Education and Research
Brown, W. L. Lyons, Jr. W. L. Lyons Brown Foundation
Brown, Mrs. W. L. Lyons. W. L. Lyons Brown Foundation
Brown, W. Thomas. Vancouver Foundation
Brown, Wendy. Joy Foundation for Ecological Education and Research
Brown, Willard W. The Louise H. and David S. Ingalls Foundation, Inc.
Brown, William Y. WMX Environmental Grants Program

Officers, Directors, Trustees, and Contacts

Brown, Zadoc, Jr. Hawaii Community Foundation
Browngoehl, Kevin. Joy Foundation for Ecological Education and Research
Browngoehl, Laurie. Joy Foundation for Ecological Education and Research
Brownlee, R. Jean. McLean Contributionship
Bruckner, Sandra. Walter S. Johnson Foundation
Brundage, Howard D. The Florence and John Schumann Foundation
Bruns, Carl H. The Arthur Vining Davis Foundations
Bruntjen, Worth. Northwest Area Foundation
Brunton, Beth. A Territory Resource
Bryan, Anthony J. A. Sarah Scaife Foundation Incorporated
Bryan, Joseph M., Jr. Kathleen Price and Joseph M. Bryan Family Foundation, Inc.
Bryan, Joseph M. Sr. Kathleen Price and Joseph M. Bryan Family Foundation, Inc.
Bryant, John L., Jr. The Bauman Foundation
Bryant, Magalen O. National Fish and Wildlife Foundation, The Ohrstrom Foundation
Brykarz, Helena. The Goldman Environmental Foundation
Buchanan, Bruce. Vancouver Foundation
Buchanan, Kenneth H. The Buchanan Family Foundation
Buchanan, Ruth H. The Herbert H. and Grace A. Dow Foundation
Buck, David D. The Bullitt Foundation
Buck, Kristen Wells. The Abelard Foundation West
Buden, Clare P. Rockefeller Family Fund, Inc.
Budge, William W. The Bothin Foundation
Budinich, Thomas M., Jr. The Boeing Company
Budlong, Frances W. Jesse Margaret Wilson Budlong Foundation for Animal Aid
Budzinski, Bob. Bay Area Community Foundation
Buechner, Judith M. The John Merck Fund
Buesching, Marlene. English-Bonter-Mitchell Foundation
Buhsmer, John H. McLean Contributionship
Bullard, George N. LifeWorks Foundation
Bullard, Robert L. Blandin Foundation
Bullard, Ross P. Virginia Environmental Endowment
Bullion, J. W. Meadows Foundation, Inc.
Bullitt, Harriet S. The Bullitt Foundation
Bullitt, Katharine M. The Bullitt Foundation
Bullitt, Stimson. The Bullitt Foundation
Bullitt, William C. The Philadelphia Foundation
Bundy, Charles A. Springs Foundation, Inc.

Bundy, Emory F. The Bullitt Foundation, Northwest Fund for the Environment
Bundy, Mary L. The Edward W. Hazen Foundation
Bunnen, Lucinda W. Norman Foundation
Bunnen, Melissa. Norman Foundation
Bunnen, Robert L., Jr. Norman Foundation
Bunning, Bonnie B. The Butler Foundation
Bunting, W. George L., Jr. The Abell Foundation
Buntrock, Dean L. WMX Environmental Grants Program
Burden, Thomas L. Chesapeake Bay Trust
Burger, Warren E. The Morris and Gwendolyn Cafritz Foundation
Burke, Daniel. Samuel S. Fels Fund
Burke, Kathleen J. BankAmerica Foundation
Burkholtz, Joan E. Environmental Endowment for New Jersey, Inc.
Burks, Lawrence E. The Charles J. Strosacker Foundation
Burks, Mara Kerr. The Robert S. and Grayce B. Kerr Foundation, Inc.
Burlingame, John F. Eastman Kodak Company Charitable Trust
Burnett, James F. Fair Play Foundation
Burnett, Nancy Packard. The David and Lucile Packard Foundation
Burns, Fred C. The Wortham Foundation, Inc.
Burr, Robert B., Jr. Richard King Mellon Foundation
Burns, Ruthelen Griffith. The W. C. Griffith Foundation
Burroughs, Hugh C. Peninsula Community Foundation
Burrows, Judith. The Switzer Foundation
Busch, Jeffrey L. Great Lakes Protection Fund
Bussmann, C. Amos. Atlantic Foundation
Butler, Barbara Y. The Butler Foundation
Butler, Cecelia M. Patrick and Aimee Butler Family Foundation
Butler, Clara W. The Butler Foundation
Butler, Dixon M. Virginia Environmental Endowment
Butler, Ellen M. Patrick and Aimee Butler Family Foundation
Butler, Jno. P. Abell-Hanger Foundation
Butler, John K. Patrick and Aimee Butler Family Foundation
Butler, Lewis H. The Abelard Foundation West, The Joyce Foundation
Butler, Marjorie W. The Butler Foundation
Butler, Patricia M. Patrick and Aimee Butler Family Foundation
Butler, Patrick, Jr. Patrick and Aimee Butler Family Foundation
Butler, Paul S. Patrick and Aimee Butler Family Foundation
Butler, Peter M. Patrick and Aimee Butler Family Foundation
Butler, Sandra K. Patrick and Aimee Butler Family Foundation

Butler, Thomas Y. The Butler Foundation
Butters, Gerald J. AT&T Foundation
Butterworth, George W., III. The Cricket Foundation
Buzard, Donald S. The Milwaukee Foundation
Byard, Paul S. Vinmont Foundation, Inc.
Byrne, Patricia R. The Travelers Foundation
Byron, Beverly B. Baltimore Gas and Electric Foundation, Inc.
Bystrom, Marcia J. Northwest Area Foundation

C

Cabot, John G. L. The Cabot Family Charitable Trust
Cabot, Louis W. The Cabot Family Charitable Trust
Cabot, Thomas D. The Cabot Family Charitable Trust
Cafritz, Calvin. The Morris and Gwendolyn Cafritz Foundation
Caimi, Ginna. The Armand G. Erpf Fund, Inc.
Calabresi, Anne Tyler. The Community Foundation of Greater New Haven
Calabresi, Guido. Carolyn Foundation
Calder, Peter D. The Louis Calder Foundation
Caldwell, Royce S. Southwestern Bell Foundation
Callahan, Debra J. W. Alton Jones Foundation, Inc.
Calvert, Dan. Pilot Trust
Cameron, James R. W. Alton Jones Foundation, Inc.
Cameron, Mary M. Laird, Norton Foundation
Camp, Myrtle. The William Stamps Farish Fund
Campbell, Benjamin E. The Seymour H. Knox Foundation, Inc.
Campbell, Carol. The San Francisco Foundation
Campbell, Colin G. Charles E. Culpeper Foundation, Inc., Rockefeller Brothers Fund, Inc.
Campbell, Douglas. The Armand G. Erpf Fund, Inc.
Campbell, Hazard K. The Seymour H. Knox Foundation, Inc.
Campbell, Helen. The Ewing Halsell Foundation
Campbell, The Reverend Joan Salmon. The Philadelphia Foundation
Campbell, Kimo. Vanguard Public Foundation
Campbell, Linda J. Public Welfare Foundation, Inc.
Campbell, Nelson. Lyndhurst Foundation
Campbell, Pat. Times Mirror Magazines, Inc.

Officers, Trustees, Directors, and Contacts

Campion, Mrs. Lynn H. Helen K. and Arthur E. Johnson Foundation
Campion, Thomas B., Jr. Helen K. and Arthur E. Johnson Foundation
Cancio, Julia P. The Henry M. Jackson Foundation
Cannon, Charles G. Gates Foundation
Capocy, Julie. The USF&G Foundation, Inc.
Capranica, Ruth M. The Knapp Foundation, Inc.
Capri, Barbara A. The Lauder Foundation, Inc.
Carmichael, Susan Lehman. The Sapelo Foundation, The Tides Foundation
Cargo, Robert C. Mars Foundation
Carothers, Andre. Rockwood Fund, Inc.
Carpenter, Dunbar. The Carpenter Foundation
Carpenter, Edmund N., II. Good Samaritan, Inc.
Carpenter, Jane H. The Carpenter Foundation
Carr, Ellen. Community Foundation of Western North Carolina, Inc.
Carrico, John D. The International Foundation, Inc.
Carrington, Janet A. Nicholas H. Noyes, Jr. Memorial Foundation
Carrithers, Ashley K. Island Foundation
Carroll, Robert. Maine Community Foundation, Inc.
Carruth, Allen H. The Wortham Foundation, Inc.
Carruth, Brady F. The Wortham Foundation, Inc.
Carson, Philip G. Community Foundation of Western North Carolina, Inc.
Carswell, Gale F. G. N. Wilcox Trust
Carter, Arlington W. The Boeing Company
Carter, Clay. The Tides Foundation
Carter, Edwin L. Hawaii Community Foundation
Carter, Francis C. The Champlin Foundations
Carter, George K. The Chevron Companies
Carter, Henry M., Jr. The Winston-Salem Foundation, Inc.
Carter, The Honorable Jimmy. Alaska Conservation Foundation, United States-Japan Foundation
Carter, Lee A. The Thomas J. Emery Memorial
Carter, Leigh. Centerior Energy Foundation
Carter, Lisle C., Jr. The Prudential Foundation
Carter, Robert T. Gaylord and Dorothy Donnelley Foundation
Carton, Robert W. Gaylord and Dorothy Donnelley Foundation
Cartwright, Cheri D. Sarkeys Foundation
Cartwright, Dorle K. Maine Community Foundation, Inc.
Carver, John P. The Gap Foundation
Casassa, H. Alfred. Greater Piscataqua Community Foundation

Case, Charles W. Carolyn Foundation
Casey, A. Michael. The Bothin Foundation
Casey, Barbara E. The Hyams Foundation
Casey, Lyman H. The Bothin Foundation, The Roberts Foundation
Cass, William R. The Frank Stanley Beveridge Foundation, Inc.
Cassidy, M. Sharon. USX Foundation, Inc.
Castaing, F. J. Chrysler Corporation Fund
Castle, Gary. The Stebbins Fund, Inc.
Castles, James B. M. J. Murdock Charitable Trust
Castro, Don M., III. The Columbus Foundation
Castro, The Honorable Federico. San Diego Community Foundation
Castro, Nash. American Conservation Association, Inc., Jackson Hole Preserve, Inc.
Caswell, John Beveridge. The Frank Stanley Beveridge Foundation, Inc.
Caswell, Philip. The Frank Stanley Beveridge Foundation, Inc.
Cataldo, Vickie. New England Biolabs Foundation
Catanesee, Anthony J. Environmental Education Foundation of Florida, Inc.
Catherwood, Susan W. The Pew Charitable Trusts
Catterall, Elaine. The Charles Engelhard Foundation
Cavaliere, Anthony L. Mobil Foundation, Inc.
Cawley, Michael A. The Samuel Roberts Noble Foundation, Inc.
Cecil, Mimi. Community Foundation of Western North Carolina, Inc.
Cerino, Harry E. The William Penn Foundation
Cerny, Howard F. Charles Hayden Foundation
Cervantes-Gautschi, Peter. McKenzie River Gathering Foundation
Chamberlain, J. Boatner. The Morris Stulsaft Foundation
Chamberlain, Sandi. Threshold Foundation
Chamberlin, Patience. Greater Piscataqua Community Foundation, Merck Family Fund
Chance, Douglas C. The Community Foundation of Santa Clara County
Chandler, Colby H. Eastman Kodak Company Charitable Trust
Chandler, Kent. The Buchanan Family Foundation
Chandler, Lee. The Sonoma County Community Foundation
Chaney, William R. The Tinker Foundation Incorporated
Chao, Jessica. DeWitt Wallace-Reader's Digest Fund, Lila Wallace-Reader's Digest Fund
Chapin, Charles M., III. Victoria Foundation, Inc.

Chapin, Charles S. Lynn R. and Karl E. Prickett Fund
Chapin, Chester F. Lynn R. and Karl E. Prickett Fund
Chapin, Mary Ann. Magowan Family Foundation, Inc.
Chapin, Samuel C. Lynn R. and Karl E. Prickett Fund
Chapman, George B., Jr. Martha Holden Jennings Foundation
Chappell, M. E. Sid W. Richardson Foundation
Charles, Les. Cheeryble Foundation
Charles, Zora. Cheeryble Foundation
Charvat, John M. FishAmerica Foundation
Chasin, Dana. Rockefeller Family Fund, Inc.
Chasin, Laura. Rockefeller Family Fund, Inc.
Chavez, Luis. El Paso Community Foundation
Chavis, Donna. Jessie Smith Noyes Foundation, Inc.
Cheek, C. W. Lynn R. and Karl E. Prickett Fund
Chen, Ida K. Samuel S. Fels Fund, The William Penn Foundation
Cheney, Bradbury F. Ben B. Cheney Foundation
Cheney, Eudine Meadows. Meadows Foundation, Inc.
Cheney, Francis I. Ben B. Cheney Foundation
Chenoweth, Richard A. The GAR Foundation
Chermiak, Steven M. Solow Foundation
Chernoff, David S. The John D. and Catherine T. MacArthur Foundation
Chikuma, R. Toyota USA Foundation
Childress, Gran P. Community Foundation of Western North Carolina, Inc.
Ching, Mrs. Gerry. McInerny Foundation
Chisum, Gloria Twine. The William Penn Foundation
Ching, Philip H. Hawaii Community Foundation
Chitty, Charles B. Lyndhurst Foundation
Chong, Arthur. McKesson Foundation, Inc.
Choquette, Paul J., Jr. The Rhode Island Community Foundation
Chortek, Doris H. The Milwaukee Foundation
Chouinard, Yvon. Patagonia, Inc.
Christ, Chris T. W. K. Kellogg Foundation
Christensen, Henry, III. The Vincent Astor Foundation
Christian, Frances R. Fran and Warren Rupp Foundation
Christian, Miles W. Fran and Warren Rupp Foundation
Christman, Thomas H. Harry C. Trexler Trust
Christy, Alexandria. Geraldine R. Dodge Foundation, Inc.
Chu, Winnie. The Community Foundation of Santa Clara County

Officers, Directors, Trustees, and Contacts

Chubb, Corinne A. Victoria Foundation, Inc.
Chubb, Percy, III. Victoria Foundation, Inc.
Chubb, Sally. Victoria Foundation, Inc.
Chung, Frances Y. L. The Ahmanson Foundation
Church, Martha E. National Geographic Society Education Foundation
Cifu, Palma. The Ohrstrom Foundation
Cilluffo, Irja. Greater Piscataqua Community Foundation
Claiborne, Liz. Liz Claiborne & Art Ortenberg Foundation
Clanton, B. Jae. The Rhode Island Community Foundation
Clapp, James N., II. Laird, Norton Foundation
Clapp, Joseph. The GAR Foundation
Clapp, M. Roger. The Kelvin and Eleanor Smith Foundation
Clapp, Norton. Laird, Norton Foundation
Clark, Benic M., III. Lyndhurst Foundation
Clark, Dick. The Arca Foundation
Clark, Duncan W. The International Foundation, Inc.
Clark, G. Reynolds. Westinghouse Foundation
Clark, Geoffrey. Greater Piscataqua Community Foundation
Clark, Henry B., Jr. McInerny Foundation
Clark, Irving. Northwest Area Foundation
Clark, James R. Atkinson Foundation
Clark, Jane Forbes, II. The Clark Foundation
Clark, Kim. Island Foundation, Inc.
Clark, Mariana L. The Dragon Foundation, Inc.
Clark, Noreen C. The Aaron Diamond Foundation
Clark, Paul E. The Dragon Foundation, Inc.
Clark, Robert L. The Dragon Foundation, Inc.
Clark, Roger A. The Morris and Gwendolyn Cafritz Foundation
Clark, Stephen. Island Foundation, Inc.
Clark, Mrs. Van Alan. Island Foundation, Inc.
Clarke, James McClure. Community Foundation of Western North Carolina, Inc.
Clarke, Robert F. Hawaiian Electric Industries Charitable Foundation
Clarke, William V. H. The Wortham Foundation, Inc.
Clarkson, Lawrence W. The Boeing Company
Clauson, Bronwyn B. The Cameron Baird Foundation
Clay, Richard H. C. The Norton Foundation, Inc.
Cleary, Beth. The Jenifer Altman Foundation
Clement, Josephine D. Z. Smith Reynolds Foundation, Inc.
Cleveland, Harlan. Joyce Mertz-Gilmore Foundation

Clodfelter, Daniel G. Z. Smith Reynolds Foundation, Inc.
Close, Anne Springs. Springs Foundation, Inc.
Close, Derick S. Springs Foundation, Inc.
Close, Elliott S. Springs Foundation, Inc.
Close, H. W., Jr. Springs Foundation, Inc.
Close, Katherine Anne. Springs Foundation, Inc.
Close, Leroy S. Springs Foundation, Inc.
Close, Pat. Springs Foundation, Inc.
Clowes, Alexander W. The Clowes Fund, Inc.
Clowes, Allen W. The Clowes Fund, Inc.
Clowes, Jonathan J. The Clowes Fund, Inc.
Clowes, Margaret J. The Clowes Fund, Inc.
Clowes, Thomas J. The Clowes Fund, Inc.
Clusen, Charles M. American Conservation Association, Inc.
Clymer, John H. The Hyams Foundation
Cobbin, W. Frank, Jr. AT&T Foundation
Coble, Robert L. Smith Richardson Foundation, Inc.
Coburn, Jean Crummer. Roy E. Crummer Foundation
Coburn, Milton. Roy E. Crummer Foundation
Cocke, Dudley. Ruth Mott Fund
Coffee, The Reverend James E. The Sonoma County Community Foundation
Coffey, F. G. The Boeing Company
Cogan, James R. The Bunbury Company, Inc., The Windham Foundation, Inc.
Coggeshall, Mary. Victoria Foundation, Inc.
Cohen, Amy Scheuer. S. H. and Helen R. Scheuer Family Foundation, Inc.
Cohen, Edwin C. Echoing Green Foundation
Cohen, Harold. S. H. and Helen R. Scheuer Family Foundation, Inc.
Cohen, Ida (Ollie). Unitarian Universalist Veatch Program at Shelter Rock
Cohen, Melvin I. AT&T Foundation
Cohen, Sandra. BankAmerica Foundation
Cohune, James S. McKesson Foundation, Inc.
Cole, J. Owen. Baltimore Gas and Electric Foundation, Inc.
Cole, Nancy L. Community Foundation of Western North Carolina, Inc.
Cole, Ralph A. The Charles J. Strosacker Foundation
Cole, Sarah R. The Austin Memorial Foundation
Colegrove, Geoffrey L. The Rockfall Foundation
Coleman, Gabriella M. The Prudential Foundation
Coleman, Kenneth L. The Community Foundation of Santa Clara County
Coleman, Leonard S. The Schumann Fund for New Jersey, Inc.
Coleman, Lewis S. BankAmerica Foundation

Coleman, Reed. The Lynde and Harry Bradley Foundation, Inc.
Coles, Robert. Lyndhurst Foundation
Collat, Donald S. Jessie Smith Noyes Foundation, Inc.
Collins, Dennis A. The James Irvine Foundation
Collins, Donald. The Abelard Foundation West
Collins, John P., Jr. Stanley Smith Horticultural Trust
Collins, Maribeth W. The Collins Foundation
Collins, Martha Layne. Eastman Kodak Company Charitable Trust
Collins, Priscilla B. The Bullitt Foundation
Collins, Susan. The Abelard Foundation West
Collins, Theodore J. The Boeing Company
Colloredo, Susanna. The Fund for Preservation of Wildlife and Natural Areas
Colopy, Hugh. The GAR Foundation
Colussy, Dan A. Baltimore Gas and Electric Foundation, Inc.
Comb, Donald G. New England Biolabs Foundation
Compton, James R. Compton Foundation, Inc.
Compton, Randolph O. Compton Foundation, Inc.
Compton, W. Danforth. Compton Foundation, Inc.
Comstock, Harrison. The Sonoma County Community Foundation
Comstock, Robert L., Jr. Blandin Foundation
Conant, Roger R. Northwest Area Foundation
Conaty, William J. GE Fund
Condit, Philip M. The Boeing Company
Condon, Larry E. Joyce Mertz-Gilmore Foundation
Conlee, Cecil D. Metropolitan Atlanta Community Foundation, Inc.
Conner, Ann F. The Rhode Island Community Foundation
Contor, Roger J. Northwest Fund for the Environment
Conway, E. V. Union Pacific Foundation
Conway, Jill K. The Kresge Foundation
Conway, William G. American Conservation Association, Inc.
Cook, Frank. South Coast Foundation, Inc.
Cook, Kathleen M. South Coast Foundation, Inc.
Cook, Lodwrick M. ARCO Foundation
Cook, Mary McDermott. The Eugene McDermott Foundation
Cook, Suzanne E. Ivey. The Richard Ivey Foundation
Cook, Warren. Maine Community Foundation, Inc.
Cooke, Richard A. Cooke Foundation, Limited

Officers, Trustees, Directors, and Contacts

Cooke, Samuel A. Cooke Foundation, Limited, Hawaii Community Foundation
Coolidge, Thomas R. The Vincent Astor Foundation
Cooper, The Honorable Clarence. Metropolitan Atlanta Community Foundation, Inc.
Cooper, Helen. Laidlaw Foundation
Cooper, Nora I. Hawaii Community Foundation
Coor, Lattie F. Deer Creek Foundation
Coors, Ambassador Holland H. Adolph Coors Foundation
Coors, Jeffrey H. Adolph Coors Foundation
Coors, Joseph. Adolph Coors Foundation
Coors, Peter H. Adolph Coors Foundation
Coors, William K. Adolph Coors Foundation
Copeland, Gerret van S. Longwood Foundation, Inc.
Copes, Paul. Hartford Foundation for Public Giving
Copp, Belton A. The Conservation and Research Foundation
Copp, Eugenie T. Carolyn Foundation
Corbally, John E. The John D. and Catherine T. MacArthur Foundation
Corbett, Cornelia. The William Stamps Farish Fund
Corbin, Hunter W. The Hyde and Watson Foundation
Corbin, William R. Weyerhaeuser Company Foundation
Corcoran, William J. Gladys and Roland Harriman Foundation, Mary W. Harriman Foundation
Corey, William G. Kenneth T. and Eileen L. Norris Foundation
Cornelius, James M. Nicholas H. Noyes, Jr. Memorial Foundation
Corning, Henry H. American Foundation Corporation
Corning, Nathan E. American Foundation Corporation
Corning, Ursula. The Vidda Foundation
Cornish, John M. The William P. Wharton Trust
Cornwall, John W. The Fund for New Jersey
Cornwall, Joseph C. The Fund for New Jersey
Coronel, Vicki. The USF&G Foundation, Inc.
Corpus, Janet M. Azadoutioun Foundation
Corry, Charles A. USX Foundation, Inc.
Corvin, Adele. The Morris Stulsaft Foundation
Corvin, Dorothy S. The Morris Stulsaft Foundation
Corwin, Bruce C. California Community Foundation
Corwin, Laura J. The New York Times Company Foundation, Inc.
Cosgrove, Michael J., Jr. GE Fund

Costello, Thomas P. Westinghouse Foundation
Cotsen, Lloyd E. The Ahmanson Foundation
Cott, Eleanor Van. Alice Tweed Tuohy Foundation
Cotter, Patrick W. Stackner Family Foundation, Inc.
Cottrell, Anne. Marin Community Foundation
Cowan, Deborah. New Hampshire Charitable Foundation
Coward, E. Walter. Ford Foundation
Cowles, Charles. The Cowles Charitable Trust
Cowles, Gardner, III. The Cowles Charitable Trust
Cowles, Jan. The Cowles Charitable Trust
Cox, Martha W. Cox Foundation, Inc.
Cox, Pat. The Moriah Fund, Inc.
Cox, William C., Jr. Jessie B. Cox Charitable Trust, Cox Foundation, Inc.
Coxe, Donald G. M. Donner Canadian Foundation
Coxe, Trudy. Massachusetts Environmental Trust
Craig, Eleanor L. Benua Foundation, Inc.
Craig, M. Elizabeth. The Minneapolis Foundation
Craighead, Sophie Englehard. The Charles Engelhard Foundation
Crain, John W. The Summerlee Foundation
Crain, William E. The Chevron Companies
Crane, John. Alfred T. Stanley Foundation
Crane, Robert. Joyce Mertz-Gilmore Foundation
Crary, Miner D., Jr. Robert Sterling Clark Foundation, Inc.
Crary, Oliver. The Homeland Foundation
Craven, David L. Longwood Foundation, Inc.
Crawford, Edward C. James G. Hanes Memorial Fund
Crawford, Lucy. The Norton Foundation, Inc.
Creedon, John J. Metropolitan Life Foundation
Creighton, John W., Jr. Weyerhaeuser Company Foundation
Crew, Donald W. The Greenville Foundation
Crew, Richard A. The Greenville Foundation
Cribb, T. Kenneth, Jr. Sarah Scaife Foundation Incorporated
Crim, Alonzo A. Charles Stewart Mott Foundation
Crimmins, Robert J. Metropolitan Life Foundation
Criscuoli, Phyllis. Cleveland H. Dodge Foundation, Inc.
Crispin, Dennis J. The Boeing Company
Crocker, Charles. The Mary A. Crocker Trust
Croft, Mary. The Cowles Charitable Trust

Crombie, The Honorable David. Laidlaw Foundation
Crooke, Edward A. Baltimore Gas and Electric Foundation, Inc.
Crosby, David P. The Minneapolis Foundation
Crosby, Edwin L. Carolyn Foundation
Crosby, Franklin M., III. Carolyn Foundation
Crosby, G. Christian. Carolyn Foundation
Crosby, Sumner McK., Jr. Carolyn Foundation
Crosby, Susan W. Carolyn Foundation
Crosby, Thomas M., Jr. Carolyn Foundation
Crosland, Kate L. Lyndhurst Foundation
Cross, Mrs. Devon Gaffney. Donner Canadian Foundation
Cross, Rebecca B. Community Foundation of Western North Carolina, Inc.
Cross, Travis. Meyer Memorial Trust
Crossman, Elizabeth A. Weyerhaeuser Company Foundation
Crowfoot, James E. Pew Scholars Program in Conservation and the Environment
Crowley, James A. Hartford Foundation for Public Giving
Cruickshank, Joseph H. The Clark Foundation
Crum, The Reverend Thomas L. Mustard Seed Foundation, Inc.
Cruze, Deane D. The Boeing Company
Cudahy, Daniel. Patrick and Anna M. Cudahy Fund
Cudahy, Janet S. Patrick and Anna M. Cudahy Fund
Cudahy, Richard D. Patrick and Anna M. Cudahy Fund
Cuenco, Miren. WMX Environmental Grants Program
Culbertson, Judy B. Meadows Foundation, Inc.
Cullinane, Gerald. The Strong Foundation for Environmental Values
Cullum, Charles. The Eugene McDermott Foundation
Culver, Ellsworth. The Arca Foundation
Cumberbatch, Stacey. Joyce Mertz-Gilmore Foundation
Cumming, R. Malcolm. Beldon Fund
Cummings, Diane M. The Nathan Cummings Foundation
Cummings, Herbert K. The Nathan Cummings Foundation
Cummings, James K. The Nathan Cummings Foundation, Threshold Foundation
Cummings, Mark H. The Nathan Cummings Foundation
Cummings, Michael. The Nathan Cummings Foundation
Cundiff, Richard M. Walter and Josephine Ford Fund
Cunningham, Angel. The Curtis and Edith Munson Foundation, Inc.

Officers, Directors, Trustees, and Contacts

Cunningham, Helen. Samuel S. Fels Fund
Curley, Walter J.P., Jr. The Achelis Foundation, The Bodman Foundation
Curlin, Jackson V., Jr. El Paso Community Foundation
Curran, William E. Elmina B. Sewall Foundation
Currie, Gilbert A. The Rollin M. Gerstacker Foundation
Currie, John Thornton. Harris and Eliza Kempner Fund
Currier, Andrea B. Wrinkle in Time Foundation
Currier, Lavinia. Sacharuna Foundation
Curry, Bernard F. W. Alton Jones Foundation, Inc.
Curtis, Elizabeth H. Atkinson Foundation
Curtis, Pamela. Oliver S. and Jennie R. Donaldson Charitable Trust
Curtiss, James R. Baltimore Gas and Electric Foundation, Inc.
Curvin, Robert. Victoria Foundation, Inc.

D

d'Alessio, John W. McKesson Foundation, Inc.
D'Angelo, Leah. Rockefeller Family Fund, Inc.
Daberko, David A. The Cleveland Foundation
Dagenhart, Larry J. Foundation for the Carolinas
Daggett, Christopher J. The Schumann Fund for New Jersey, Inc.
Dahlke, Wayne T. Georgia Power Foundation, Inc.
Dahlquist, Steven N. The Community Foundation of Sarasota County, Inc.
Daley, William M. The Chicago Community Trust
Dall'Armi, Lorenzo, Jr. Alice Tweed Tuohy Foundation
Dallara, Charles H. The German Marshall Fund of the United States
Dalton, R. Murray. The Troy Foundation
Daly, Charles U. The Joyce Foundation
Daly, Herman E. Pew Scholars Program in Conservation and the Environment
Dammerman, Dennis D. GE Fund
Dampeer, John L. Kelvin Smith 1980 Charitable Trust, The Kelvin and Eleanor Smith Foundation
Daniels, Bruce G. The Fred Harris Daniels Foundation, Inc.
Daniels, D. R. McDonnell Douglas Foundation
Daniels, Fred H., II. The Fred Harris Daniels Foundation, Inc.
Daniels, Janet B. The Fred Harris Daniels Foundation, Inc.
Danser, Gordon O. The Cape Branch Foundation

Darin, Frank V. J. Ford Motor Company Fund
Darling, Nelson J., Jr. Hurdle Hill Foundation
Dart, Claire T. Dart Foundation
Dart, Kenneth B. Dart Foundation
Dart, Robert C. Dart Foundation
Dart, Thomas J. Dart Foundation
Dart, William A. Dart Foundation
Dausses, W. F. Phillips Petroleum Foundation, Inc.
Davenport, Christopher F. Surdna Foundation, Inc.
Davidson, Betsy. The J. M. Kaplan Fund, Inc.
Davidson, Carl B. Texaco Foundation
Davidson, Charles T. Foundation for the Carolinas
Davidson, G. Bradford. The J. M. Kaplan Fund, Inc.
Davidson, J. Matthew. The J. M. Kaplan Fund, Inc.
Davidson, Jane I. The Louise H. and David S. Ingalls Foundation, Inc.
Davidson, Peter W. The J. M. Kaplan Fund, Inc.
Davies, Robert N. Herman Goldman Foundation
Davies, Sandra F. The Schiff Foundation
Davis, Carolyne K. The Prudential Foundation
Davis, Ellen Scripps. Ellen Browning Scripps Foundation
Davis, H. Halsey. Davis Conservation Foundation
Davis, Holbrook R. The Arthur Vining Davis Foundations
Davis, J. H. Dow. The Arthur Vining Davis Foundations
Davis, James K. Georgia Power Foundation, Inc.
Davis, Joel P. The Arthur Vining Davis Foundations
Davis, Laura A. W. K. Kellogg Foundation
Davis, Maynard K. The Arthur Vining Davis Foundations
Davis, Milton. The Chicago Community Trust, The Field Foundation of Illinois, Inc.
Davis, Nathanael V. The Arthur Vining Davis Foundations
Davis, Pat. The Summerlee Foundation
Davis, Phyllis C. Davis Conservation Foundation
Davis, Rita Langsam. Mars Foundation
Davis, Virginia M. Snee-Reinhardt Charitable Foundation
Davison, Richard H. The Sudbury Foundation
Dawson, E. Douglas. Ellen Browning Scripps Foundation
Dawson, Judith. Atherton Family Foundation
Dax, Jessica. The German Marshall Fund of the United States

Day, H. Corbin. The Hyde and Watson Foundation
Dayton, Edward N. The Minneapolis Foundation
Deacy, Jean. The Ewing Halsell Foundation
Dean, J. Simpson, Jr. Welfare Foundation, Inc.
Deans, Thomas S. Davis Conservation Foundation, New Hampshire Charitable Foundation
Deavenport, Earnest W., Jr. Eastman Kodak Company Charitable Trust
Deaver, Carolyn J. The Morris and Gwendolyn Cafritz Foundation
DeBacker, Lois. Charles Stewart Mott Foundation
Debevoise, The Honorable Dickinson R. The Fund for New Jersey
Debs, Barbara Knowles. Geraldine R. Dodge Foundation, Inc.
deFreitas, Patrick S. Laird, Norton Foundation
DeGrandpre, Charles A. Greater Piscataqua Community Foundation
DeKruif, Robert M. The Ahmanson Foundation
Delaney, Barbara S. The Rockfall Foundation
Delaney, James M. The Cleveland Foundation
de la Renta, Anne E. The Charles Engelhard Foundation
Delavan, Nelson B., Jr. The Nelson B. Delavan Foundation
de la Vega, Elvira Gonzalez. Foundation for Field Research
De Luca, Victor. Jessie Smith Noyes Foundation, Inc.
Demarest, Daniel A. The Bay Foundation
Demers, Greg. Bay Area Community Foundation
DeMichele, Robert H. Smith Richardson Foundation, Inc.
Dempsey, James H., Jr. The Louise H. and David S. Ingalls Foundation, Inc.
Dempsey, Jerry E. WMX Environmental Grants Program
Denman, Gilbert M., Jr. The Ewing Halsell Foundation
Denman, Leroy G. The Ewing Halsell Foundation
Denman, Leroy G., Jr. Caesar Kleberg Foundation for Wildlife Conservation
Denning, Stephen A. Echoing Green Foundation
Dennis, O. D., Jr. Chesapeake Corporation Foundation
Denomme, T. G. Chrysler Corporation Fund
Denworth, Raymond K., Jr. Samuel S. Fels Fund
Depew, Robert H. The Jackson Foundation
DeRiemer, Charles O. Southwestern Bell Foundation
Derr, Kenneth T. The Chevron Companies

Officers, Trustees, Directors, and Contacts

Derrickson, Lloyd J. The Freed Foundation, Inc.
deSaussure, Charlton, Jr. The Community Foundation Serving Coastal South Carolina
de Vegh, Diana. The Howard Bayne Fund
de Vegh, Pierre J. The Howard Bayne Fund
DeVita, M. Christine. DeWitt Wallace-Reader's Digest Fund, Lila Wallace-Reader's Digest Fund
Dewey, Francis H. The George I. Alden Trust
Dewey, Francis H., 3rd. The George I. Alden Trust
DeWind, Adrian W. The Aaron Diamond Foundation, The New World Foundation
Dewing, Merlin E. The Bush Foundation
DeWoody, Beth. Samuel and May Rudin Foundation, Inc.
DeYonge, John. Northwest Fund for the Environment
Diamond, Henry L. American Conservation Association, Inc., Jackson Hole Preserve, Inc.
Diamond, Irene. The Aaron Diamond Foundation
Dickerson, Kenneth R. ARCO Foundation
Dicovitsky, Gary. The International Foundation, Inc.
Dierks, Ann Jennifer. The Emerald Foundation
Dietel, William M. Jackson Hole Preserve, Inc.
Dietz, Philip E. L., Jr. Town Creek Foundation, Inc.
Dillon, Thomas P. Foundation for the Carolinas
Dills, Joan Nelson. The Morris Stulsaft Foundation
Dilworth, Jeanne C. The Rockfall Foundation
Dimon, James. The Travelers Foundation
Dinkins, David N. The Aaron Diamond Foundation
Di San Faustino, Genevieve. The Bothin Foundation
Disharoon, Leslie B. Chesapeake Bay Trust
Dixon, Thomas F. Gladys and Roland Harriman Foundation
Doan, Herbert D. The Herbert H. and Grace A. Dow Foundation
Dockson, Robert R. The John Randolph Haynes and Dora Haynes Foundation
Dodd, Marie W. Metropolitan Atlanta Community Foundation, Inc.
Dodds, R. Harcourt. New York Foundation
Dodge, Cleveland E., Jr. Cleveland H. Dodge Foundation, Inc.
Dodge, David S. Cleveland H. Dodge Foundation, Inc.
Dods, Walter A., Jr. Hawaii Community Foundation

Dodson, David L. Mary Reynolds Babcock Foundation, Inc., Kathleen Price and Joseph M. Bryan Family Foundation, Inc.
Doermann, Humphrey. The Bush Foundation
Doerr, Henry. Blandin Foundation
Doherty, Jack N. Shell Oil Company Foundation
Dolan, Joseph S. The Achelis Foundation, The Bodman Foundation
Domke, Doreeta. The McConnell Foundation
Donahue, Frank R., Jr. The Barra Foundation, Inc.
Donahue, Richard K. The Joyce Foundation
Doniger, Beatrice. J. E. & Z. B. Butler Foundation, Inc.
Doniger, Bruce. J. E. & Z. B. Butler Foundation, Inc.
Donlon, Diana. The Goldman Environmental Foundation
Donnelley, Dorothy Ranney. Gaylord and Dorothy Donnelley Foundation
Donnelley, Elliott R. Gaylord and Dorothy Donnelley Foundation
Donnelley, Strachan. Gaylord and Dorothy Donnelley Foundation
Donnelley-Morton, Laura. Gaylord and Dorothy Donnelley Foundation
Donnelly, Susanne Fitger. California Community Foundation
Donner, Robert, Jr. Donner Canadian Foundation
Donner, Timothy. Donner Canadian Foundation
Donohue, Donald D. The Henry M. Jackson Foundation
Donovan, Doris Stearn. The Rhode Island Community Foundation
Doran, Gary. AT&T Foundation
Dorman, The Honorable Arthur. Chesapeake Bay Trust
Dorman, Gayle Williams. Mary Reynolds Babcock Foundation, Inc.
Dorman, Leslie A. Whitecap Foundation
Doroshow, Carol. The Max and Anna Levinson Foundation
Doroshow, Helen L. The Max and Anna Levinson Foundation
Dorsey, Earl A. W. L. Lyons Brown Foundation
Doss, Lawrence P. Hudson-Webber Foundation
Douglas, Arthur. Norcross Wildlife Foundation, Inc.
Douglas, Jean W. Wallace Genetic Foundation, Inc.
Douglas, William A. Boettcher Foundation
Douglass, Arthur R. The Harding Educational and Charitable Foundation
Dow, Herbert H. The Herbert H. and Grace A. Dow Foundation
Dow, Michael L. The Herbert H. and Grace A. Dow Foundation

Dowe, P. James, Jr. Maine Community Foundation, Inc.
Dowley, Ann. The Abelard Foundation West, The Acorn Foundation
Doyle, Frank P. GE Fund
Doyle, Terence N. Patrick and Aimee Butler Family Foundation
Drackett, Jeanne H. Wodecroft Foundation
Drake, Don. The Minneapolis Foundation
Drake, Philip M. Charles E. Culpeper Foundation, Inc.
Drew, Ken. The Ben & Jerry's Foundation
Driggers, Nathan B. Harder Foundation
Driscoll, Sharon M. Ward M. & Mariam C. Canaday Educational and Charitable Trust
Driscoll, W. John. Northwest Area Foundation
Du Bain, Myron. The James Irvine Foundation
Dubose, Vivian N. The Samuel Roberts Noble Foundation, Inc.
Dubuar, James. The Mountaineers Foundation
Duemling, Robert W. The Morris and Gwendolyn Cafritz Foundation
Dugan, Ron. Meadows Foundation, Inc.
Duhaime, William E. The Carpenter Foundation
Duke, Anthony D. The Achelis Foundation, The Bodman Foundation
Duke, Robin Chandler. The David and Lucile Packard Foundation, United States-Japan Foundation
Duker, Brack. Whitecap Foundation
Duker, Elizabeth. Whitecap Foundation
Dulaney, Jane Norton. The Norton Foundation, Inc.
Dulaney, Robert W. The Norton Foundation, Inc.
Dunbar, Leslie. Ruth Mott Fund
Duncan, Charles T. Eastman Kodak Company Charitable Trust
Duncan, Deana. Beneficia Foundation
Duncombe, Harmon. G. Unger Vetlesen Foundation
Dunford, Betty P. Cooke Foundation, Limited
Dunkle, Walter L. Chesapeake Bay Trust
Dunlop, Robert G. The Pew Charitable Trusts
Dunn, Robert H. Levi Strauss Foundation
Dunwody, Atwood. The Arthur Vining Davis Foundations
duPont, Edward B. Longwood Foundation, Inc., Welfare Foundation, Inc.
DuPont, Elizabeth Lee. Good Samaritan, Inc.
duPont, Pierre S., IV. Longwood Foundation, Inc.
Durgin, Diane. Georgia-Pacific Foundation
Durgin, Eugene J. The Howard Johnson Foundation
Durham, Earl. The Edward W. Hazen Foundation

Officers, Directors, Trustees, and Contacts

Dussling, Eric H. Westinghouse Foundation
Dustan, Jane. The Jenifer Altman Foundation
Dutt, Mallika. Norman Foundation
Dyer, Leila G. McLean Contributionship
Dyke, Walter P. M. J. Murdock Charitable Trust
Dykstra, Craig. Lilly Endowment, Inc.

E

Earhart, Anne. The Homeland Foundation
Earhart, John E. The Homeland Foundation
Earl, The Honorable Anthony S. Great Lakes Protection Fund
Eastman, Barbara Booth. Bishop Pine Fund
Eastman, William M. Bishop Pine Fund
Easton, Suzanne. Giles W. and Elise G. Mead Foundation
Eaton, George. Texaco Foundation
Eberle, William D. United States-Japan Foundation
Eccles, S. P. Union Pacific Foundation
Ecke, Paul, Jr. San Diego Community Foundation
Eckstein, Paul. The Marshall Fund of Arizona
Eddie, Gloria. Walter S. Johnson Foundation
Eddie, Gloria Jeneal. Walter S. Johnson Foundation
Eddy, Edith T. The Robert Brownlee Foundation, Compton Foundation, Inc.
Edelman, Marian Wright. The Aaron Diamond Foundation
Edelman, Peter B. Public Welfare Foundation, Inc.
Edey, Helen. The Scherman Foundation, Inc.
Edgar, Arlen L. Abell-Hanger Foundation
Edgerton, Bradford W. W. Alton Jones Foundation, Inc.
Edgerton, Malcolm J., Jr. The Abelard Foundation West
Edgerton, Patricia Jones. W. Alton Jones Foundation, Inc.
Edgerton, William A. W. Alton Jones Foundation, Inc.
Edison, Suzanne. A Territory Resource
Edmonds, George P. Fair Play Foundation
Edwards, David R. Weyerhaeuser Company Foundation
Edwards, James B. Gaylord and Dorothy Donnelley Foundation
Edwards, James McCune. McCune Foundation, The Marshall L. & Perrine D. McCune Charitable Foundation
Edwards, Kathleen Bryan. Kathleen Price and Joseph M. Bryan Family Foundation, Inc.
Edwards, Richard D. McCune Foundation
Efroymson, Daniel. The Moriah Fund, Inc.
Efroymson, Lori. The Moriah Fund, Inc.
Ege, Hans A. The Bay Foundation

Ehrenfeld, David W. The Educational Foundation of America
Ehrlich, M. Gordon. Orchard Foundation
Ehrlich, Paul R. Pew Scholars Program in Conservation and the Environment
Einhorn, Jessica. The German Marshall Fund of the United States
Eiseman, Constance. The Prospect Hill Foundation
Eisenhardt, Dianne. Gebbie Foundation, Inc.
Eisenhardt, Elizabeth H. Evelyn and Walter Haas, Jr. Fund
Eisenstein, Joshua J. Pinewood Foundation
Eitel, Karl E. El Pomar Foundation
Ekman, Richard H. The Andrew W. Mellon Foundation
El-Gohary, Joanne. BankAmerica Foundation
Elbling, Paul U. Virginia Environmental Endowment
Eldridge, Amy E. The Columbus Foundation
Eldridge, Huntington. The Buchanan Family Foundation
Eldridge, Huntington, Jr. The Buchanan Family Foundation
Elkins, Lloyd E. The Chevron Companies
Elliman, Ann R. Underhill Foundation
Elliman, Christopher J. Geraldine R. Dodge Foundation, Inc., Underhill Foundation,
Elliman, David D. Underhill Foundation
Elliman, Kim. Underhill Foundation
Elliot, Richard. Jesse Margaret Wilson Budlong Foundation for Animal Aid
Ellis, James D. Southwestern Bell Foundation
Ellis, Libby. Patagonia, Inc.
Elston, Frances Beinecke. The Prospect Hill Foundation
Embry, Robert C., Jr. The Abell Foundation
Embry, Wayne R. Centerior Energy Foundation
Emerson, Alice F. Eastman Kodak Company Charitable Trust
Emerson, H. Truxton, Jr. Wodecroft Foundation
Emerson, Jed. The Roberts Foundation
Emerson, Larry. Seventh Generation Fund
Emory, Frank E., Jr. Foundation for the Carolinas
Emrich, Wendy. Global Greengrants Fund
Engel, William V. The Hyde and Watson Foundation
Englehard, Jane B. The Charles Engelhard Foundation
English, James F., Jr. Hartford Foundation for Public Giving
English, John W. The Community Foundation of Sarasota County, Inc.
English, Michela A. National Geographic Society Education Foundation
Eno, Amos S. National Fish and Wildlife Foundation

Enrico, Theresa. McKenzie River Gathering Foundation
Enright, William G. Lilly Endowment, Inc.
Eppig, Michael D. The Kelvin and Eleanor Smith Foundation
Eppig, Ruth Swetland. Sears-Swetland Foundation
Epstein, Kitty Kelly. Vanguard Public Foundation
Erburu, Robert F. The Ahmanson Foundation, The William and Flora Hewlett Foundation
Erdos, Karen A. J. P. Morgan Charitable Trust
Erickson, J. D. S. H. Cowell Foundation
Erickson, Kim. FishAmerica Foundation
Erlich, Linda. S. H. and Helen R. Scheuer Family Foundation, Inc.
Eshelman, Ken. Bay Area Community Foundation
Espinosa, Judith. The Energy Foundation
Ess, Henry N., III. The Vincent Astor Foundation
Esson, The Honorable Chief Justice William A. Vancouver Foundation
Esterline, Bruce H. Meadows Foundation, Inc.
Estes, Tony. FishAmerica Foundation
Estrin, Mary L. General Service Foundation
Estrin, Robert L. General Service Foundation
Esty, John C., Jr. Charles Hayden Foundation
Etherington, Edwin D. The Florence and John Schumann Foundation
Ettinger, Barbara P. The Educational Foundation of America
Ettinger, Richard P., Jr. The Educational Foundation of America, The Ettinger Foundation, Inc.
Ettinger, Sharon W. The Educational Foundation of America, The Ettinger Foundation, Inc.
Ettinger, Wendy W. P. The Educational Foundation of America
Eubank, Alvah H., Jr. Chesapeake Corporation Foundation
Evans, Doris A. The Cleveland Foundation
Evans, Dwight H. Georgia Power Foundation, Inc.
Evans, John R. Walter and Duncan Gordon Charitable Foundation
Evans, John K. The Golden Rule Foundation, Inc.
Evans, Linda P. Meadows Foundation, Inc.
Evans, Sian. The Golden Rule Foundation, Inc.
Evarts, William M., Jr. The Clark Foundation, The New York Community Trust
Ewing, Robert E. The John D. and Catherine T. MacArthur Foundation
Exley, Charles E., Jr. The Andrew W. Mellon Foundation

Officers, Trustees, Directors, and Contacts

F

Fabens, Andrew L., III. The Kelvin and Eleanor Smith Foundation
Factor, Max, III. Luster Family Foundation, Inc.
Fahey, Joseph F., Jr. Charles E. Culpeper Foundation, Inc.
Fairfax, Jean E. Ruth Mott Fund
Falcon, Angelo. New York Foundation
Fanning, Katherine W. Charles Stewart Mott Foundation
Fanton, Jonathan F. Rockefeller Brothers Fund, Inc.
Farish, William S. The William Stamps Farish Fund
Farley, Terrence M. Gladys and Roland Harriman Foundation
Farling, Robert J. Centerior Energy Foundation
Farmer, Jean. The Strong Foundation for Environmental Values
Farris, J. Haig deB. Vancouver Foundation
Favrot, Mrs. Johanna A. The Favrot Fund
Favrot, Laurence DeKanter. The Favrot Fund
Favrot, Leo Mortimer. The Favrot Fund
Favrot, Mrs. Marcia. The Favrot Fund
Favrot, Mrs. Romelia. The Favrot Fund
Fayant, Mabel. El Paso Community Foundation
Fazal, Anwar. The Goldman Environmental Foundation
Fearnside, Philip M. Conservation, Food & Health Foundation, Inc.
Featherman, Sandra. Samuel S. Fels Fund
Feinstein, Nancy. Vanguard Public Foundation
Felburn, J. Phil. Felburn Foundation
Feldhouse, Lynn A. Chrysler Corporation Fund
Feldman, Sandra. The German Marshall Fund of the United States
Feldstein, Lewis M. The Edward W. Hazen Foundation, New Hampshire Charitable Foundation
Fellner, Jamie. Jessie Smith Noyes Foundation, Inc.
Fenlon, Thomas B. Sarah I. Schieffelin Residuary Trust
Fenton, Jan. McKenzie River Gathering Foundation
Ferguson, David. The Hyde and Watson Foundation
Ferguson, Ellen Lee. The Hugh and Jane Ferguson Foundation, A Territory Resource
Ferguson, Hugh S. The Hugh and Jane Ferguson Foundation
Ferguson, Jane Avery. The Hugh and Jane Ferguson Foundation
Ferguson, Pamela. Deer Creek Foundation
Fergusson, Frances D. Ford Foundation

Fernald, H. Allen. Maine Community Foundation, Inc.
Fernandez, Rolando E. Magowan Family Foundation, Inc.
Ferrari, Clarence J., Jr. The Community Foundation of Santa Clara County
Fery, John B. The Boeing Company
Fetzer, Carol J. Carolyn Foundation
Feuille, Richard H. El Paso Community Foundation
Feulner, Edwin J., Jr. Sarah Scaife Foundation Incorporated
Field, Jamee J. Jamee and Marshall Field Foundation
Field, Marshall, V. The Field Foundation of Illinois, Inc.
Fields, Kenneth H. The Esther A. and Joseph Klingenstein Fund, Inc.
Fies, Larry R. The James Irvine Foundation
Fikes, Amy L. Leland Fikes Foundation, Inc.
Fikes, Catherine W. Leland Fikes Foundation, Inc.
Fikes, Lee. Leland Fikes Foundation, Inc.
Filuk, Robert. Thomas Sill Foundation
Findlay, Marjorie M. Claneil Foundation, Inc.
Findlay, Tim. FishAmerica Foundation
Fine, Marjorie. Unitarian Universalist Veatch Program at Shelter Rock
Fingerhut, Bert. Bert Fingerhut/Caroline Hicks Family Fund
Fink, Richard. Charles G. Koch Charitable Foundation
Finkelstone, David. Sproul Foundation
Finneran, Thomas M. Massachusetts Environmental Trust
Finney, Graham S. The William Penn Foundation
Finney, Redmond C. S. The Jacob and Annita France Foundation, Inc.
Finora, Joseph J. The Oakleigh L. Thorne Foundation
Finson, Rachel. The Energy Foundation
Fischer, Aaron. Deer Creek Foundation
Fischer, M. Peter. Deer Creek Foundation
Fischer, Teresa M. Deer Creek Foundation
Fischer, The Reverend Donald G. Olive B. Cole Foundation
Fischman, Charlotte M. The New York Community Trust
Fish, Brian. The Greenville Foundation
Fish, L. M. The Greenville Foundation
Fisher, Donald G. The Gap Foundation
Fisher, Doris F. The Gap Foundation
Fisher, Frederick L. Bill & Edith Walter Foundation
Fisher, George. Eastman Kodak Company Charitable Trust
Fisher, Robert J. The Gap Foundation
Fishman, Joseph L. Henry and Lucy Moses Fund, Inc.
Fisk, Mary A. Mary W. Harriman Foundation
Fiske, Norman. Thomas Sill Foundation

Fitzgerald, Anne. The Greenville Foundation
Fitzpatrick, Carolyn A. The Community Foundation of Sarasota County, Inc.
Fitzpatrick, Robert R., Jr. The Procter & Gamble Fund
Fitzsimmons, Hugh A. The Ewing Halsell Foundation
Flanigan, Frances H. Chesapeake Bay Trust
Flather, Newell. Jessie B. Cox Charitable Trust
Fleishman, Joel L. Kathleen Price and Joseph M. Bryan Family Foundation, Inc., Gaylord and Dorothy Donnelley Foundation
Fletcher, Allen W. Stoddard Charitable Trust
Fletcher, Maureen T. Charles Hayden Foundation
Fletcher, Warner S. The George I. Alden Trust, Stoddard Charitable Trust
Flischel, Letetia. The Community Foundation of Sarasota County, Inc.
Flood, Henry C., Jr. Alex C. Walker Educational & Charitable Foundation
Flow, Victor I., Jr. The Winston-Salem Foundation, Inc.
Fluharty, Marlene J. Americana Foundation, Inc.
Flynn, Donald F. WMX Environmental Grants Program
Flynn, Thomas G. S. D. Bechtel, Jr. Foundation
Foege, William H. The John D. and Catherine T. MacArthur Foundation
Folliott, Sheila. Northwest Area Foundation
Fonda, Jane S. Turner Foundation, Inc.
Fonseca, Bruno. The J. M. Kaplan Fund, Inc.
Fonseca, Caio. The J. M. Kaplan Fund, Inc.
Fonseca, Elizabeth K. The J. M. Kaplan Fund, Inc.
Fonseca, Isabel. The J. M. Kaplan Fund, Inc.
Fonseca, Quina. The J. M. Kaplan Fund, Inc.
Fontaine, George R. Lyndhurst Foundation
Fontaine, Jack. Lyndhurst Foundation
Foord, Elfrena. Sacramento Regional Foundation
Foran, Tom. United States-Japan Foundation
Ford, Alfred B. Ford Motor Company Fund
Ford, Allen H. Martha Holden Jennings Foundation
Ford, The Honorable Gerald. United States-Japan Foundation
Ford, Josephine F. Walter and Josephine Ford Fund
Forster, Barbara L. The Minneapolis Foundation
Forsyth, Sharon. Beneficia Foundation
Foster, Charles E. Southwestern Bell Foundation
Foster, Charles H. W. Massachusetts Environmental Trust
Foster, Diana K. Stranahan Foundation

Officers, Directors, Trustees, and Contacts

Foster, T. Jack, Jr. Peninsula Community Foundation
Fowler, Dolores C. El Pomar Foundation
Fox, Charlotte. Wallace Genetic Foundation, Inc.
Fox, John. The Energy Foundation
Fox, Mary Ann. Charles G. Koch Charitable Foundation
Fox, William F. The Milwaukee Foundation
Foy, Douglas I. New England Biolabs Foundation, Pew Scholars Program in Conservation and the Environment
Fraas, Richard J. The Troy Foundation
Fradkin, Hillel G. The Lynde and Harry Bradley Foundation, Inc.
France, Phyllis B. The Bush Foundation
Francis, George. Laidlaw Foundation
Frank, Dorothy. The Cape Branch Foundation
Franke, Harry F. The Milwaukee Foundation
Franklin, Alice. Norman Foundation
Franklin, Andrew D. Norman Foundation
Franklin, Christine G. Anna B. Stearns Charitable Foundation, Inc.
Franklin, Shirley C. Metropolitan Atlanta Community Foundation, Inc.
Franks, Myron B. Gebbie Foundation, Inc.
Fraser, Marion D. The Richard Ivey Foundation
Fraser, Thomas T. The Vidda Foundation
Frasher, Louise. Jesse Margaret Wilson Budlong Foundation for Animal Aid
Frazer, David R. The Marshall Fund of Arizona
Free, Sherri B. Community Foundation of Western North Carolina, Inc.
Freed, Elizabeth Ann. The Freed Foundation, Inc.
Freeman, Annette Stoddard. Patrick and Anna M. Cudahy Fund
Freeman, Charles. Felburn Foundation
Freeman, David F. The Scherman Foundation, Inc.
Frelinghuysen, George L. K. Frelinghuysen Foundation
Frelinghuysen, Peter. The Achelis Foundation, The Bodman Foundation, Frelinghuysen Foundation
Fremont-Smith, Marion R. Massachusetts Environmental Trust
Frenzel, William. United States-Japan Foundation
Frey, Robert H. Edna Bailey Sussman Fund
Frick, Merrill B. Olive B. Cole Foundation
Friday, William C. Kathleen Price and Joseph M. Bryan Family Foundation, Inc.
Friedewald, William T. Metropolitan Life Foundation
Friedman, Harry. The Sonoma County Community Foundation
Friedman, Marcy. Sacramento Regional Foundation
Friedman, Robert. Levi Strauss Foundation

Fritz, William W. W. K. Kellogg Foundation
Froelicher, F. Charles. Gates Foundation
Frohlich, Julia. Hawaii Community Foundation
Fross, Roger R. The Joyce Foundation
Frost, Camilla C. The James Irvine Foundation
Fruchter, R. R. The Polden-Puckham Charitable Foundation
Fry, Lloyd A., III. Lloyd A. Fry Foundation
Frye, Clayton W., Jr. Jackson Hole Preserve, Inc.
Fuhrman, Gary R. Chesapeake Bay Trust
Fujita, Tom. Toyota USA Foundation
Fukada, The Honorable Takeo. United States-Japan Foundation
Fukukawa, Shinji. United States-Japan Foundation
Fukunaga, Mark. McInerny Foundation
Fuller, Kathryn S. Ford Foundation
Fullinwider, Jerome M. Abell-Hanger Foundation
Fung, Margaret. New York Foundation
Furman, James M. The John D. and Catherine T. MacArthur Foundation
Furman, Jeffrey. The Ben & Jerry's Foundation
Furth, Peggy J. The Sonoma County Community Foundation

G

Gage, Margaret E. Ottinger Foundation, Stern Family Fund
Gaines, Robert F. Sacramento Regional Foundation
Gairo, Carol. Beneficia Foundation
Gaiser, Mary Jewett. The George Frederick Jewett Foundation
Gaither, Andrew C. The Morris Stulsaft Foundation
Gaither, James C. The William and Flora Hewlett Foundation, The James Irvine Foundation
Gale, Benjamin. The William Bingham Foundation
Gale, Mary E. The William Bingham Foundation
Gale, Thomas H. The William Bingham Foundation
Gale, Thomas V. The William Bingham Foundation
Gallagher, Barbara Detrich. The Sonoma County Community Foundation
Gallagher, Edward. Norcross Wildlife Foundation, Inc.
Gallagher, Patrick L. The Community Foundation of Sarasota County, Inc.
Gallagher, Terence. The Pfizer Foundation, Inc.
Galligan, Michael W. The Stebbins Fund, Inc.

Gallo, Ronald V. The Rhode Island Community Foundation
Gallup, John G. The Frank Stanley Beveridge Foundation, Inc.
Galvin, Ray E. The Chevron Companies
Gamble, Helen. A Territory Resource
Garber, Donna. Samuel and May Rudin Foundation, Inc.
Garber, Eli S. S. H. and Helen R. Scheuer Family Foundation, Inc.
Garcia-Kennedy, Norma. McKesson Foundation, Inc.
Garda, Annie Lewis. The Cleveland Foundation
Gardi, Dena G. McKesson Foundation, Inc.
Gardner, The Honorable Betty K. Chesapeake Bay Trust
Gardner, David P. The William and Flora Hewlett Foundation
Garfinkel, Barry H. The New York Community Trust
Garlington, Jennie Turner. Turner Foundation, Inc.
Garrett, Margaret D. Cleveland H. Dodge Foundation, Inc.
Garrett, Robert. The Abell Foundation, Cleveland H. Dodge Foundation, Inc.,
Garside, Grenville. The Henry M. Jackson Foundation
Gary, James F. Hawaii Community Foundation
Gary, Paul E. The Boeing Company
Gaster, Gordon. Environmental Education Foundation of Florida, Inc.
Gates, Charles C. Gates Foundation
Gates, Peter P. McN. The Vincent Astor Foundation
Gatewood, Willard B., Jr. The Winthrop Rockefeller Foundation
Gauntlett, Suzanne. The Barbara Gauntlett Foundation, Inc.
Gauthier, Catherine I. The Richard Ivey Foundation
Gavin, Stephen D. California Community Foundation
Gay, Andre. The Boeing Company
Geballe, Gordon T. Levi Strauss Foundation
Geckle, Jerome W. Baltimore Gas and Electric Foundation, Inc.
Geisler, William F. The Bothin Foundation
Gelb, Arthur. The New York Times Company Foundation, Inc.
Gelb, Richard L. The New York Times Company Foundation, Inc.
Gell-Mann, Murray. The John D. and Catherine T. MacArthur Foundation
Gellert, Annette E. The Fred Gellert Foundation
Gellert, Fred, Jr. The Fred Gellert Foundation
Gellhorn, Alfred. The Aaron Diamond Foundation

Officers, Trustees, Directors, and Contacts

Gelman, Michael C. Richard & Rhoda Goldman Fund
Gelman, Susan R. The Goldman Environmental Foundation, Richard & Rhoda Goldman Fund
Genia, Anthony L. The Minneapolis Foundation
Gerace, Frank. The Rollin M. Gerstacker Foundation
Gerber, Ann. The Frost Foundation, Ltd.
Gerber, M. S. Shell Oil Company Foundation
Gerber, Margaret L. Lyndhurst Foundation
Gerbode, Frank A. The Wallace Alexander Gerbode Foundation, Inc.
Gerken, Walter B. The James Irvine Foundation
Gerlach, John B. The Columbus Foundation
Gerry, Elbridge T., Jr. Gladys and Roland Harriman Foundation, Union Pacific Foundation
Gerry, Elbridge T., Sr. Mary W. Harriman Foundation
Gerry, Martha F. The William Stamps Farish Fund
Gerstacker, Carl A. The Rollin M. Gerstacker Foundation
Gerstacker, Esther S. The Rollin M. Gerstacker Foundation
Gerstacker, Lisa J. The Rollin M. Gerstacker Foundation
Gerstner, Louis V., Jr. The New York Times Company Foundation, Inc.
Getty, Caroline. National Fish and Wildlife Foundation
Getz, Herbert A. WMX Environmental Grants Program
Getzendanner, Joel D. The Joyce Foundation
Gherlein, John H. Martha Holden Jennings Foundation
Gibbons, C. James. The Rockfall Foundation
Gibbons, The Honorable John J. The Fund for New Jersey
Gibbs, J. R. Stanley Smith Horticultural Trust
Gibson, T. J. Gates Foundation
Gieszl, Yale. Toyota USA Foundation
Gifford, Russell R. The Cleveland Foundation
Gilbert, Nathan H. Laidlaw Foundation
Gilder, Richard, Jr. Robert W. Wilson Foundation
Gillen, James R. The Prudential Foundation
Gillespie, J. Samuel, Jr. The Beirne Carter Foundation
Gillespie, Robert W. The Cleveland Foundation
Gillett, A. N. The Polden-Puckham Charitable Foundation
Gillett, C. M. The Polden-Puckham Charitable Foundation
Gillett, D. B. The Polden-Puckham Charitable Foundation

Gillett, H. J. The Polden-Puckham Charitable Foundation
Gillett, M. Bevis. The Polden-Puckham Charitable Foundation
Gillies, Linda L. The Vincent Astor Foundation
Gilman, E. Atwill. Boettcher Foundation
Gilman, Joy. Joy Foundation for Ecological Education and Research
Gilmore, Elizabeth B. Joyce Mertz-GilmoreFoundation
Gilmore, Thomas J. Environmental Endowment for New Jersey, Inc.
Gilmour, Allan D. Ford Motor Company Fund
Gimon, Eleanor H. The William and Flora Hewlett Foundation
Ginn, Robert M. Martha Holden Jennings Foundation
Ginn, Sam L. The Chevron Companies
Ginn, William D. The Nord Family Foundation
Ginsburg, Marianne L. The German Marshall Fund of the United States
Gioia, Lucy. The Max and Victoria Dreyfus Foundation, Inc.
Giovanisci, Stephen J. ARCO Foundation
Gisi, Lynn. The Needmor Fund
Given, Boyd E. The Boeing Company
Given, The Reverend Davis. The Arthur Vining Davis Foundations
Glancy, Alfred R., III. Hudson-Webber Foundation
Glaser, Leon. J. E. & Z. B. Butler Foundation, Inc.
Glaser, Robert J. The David and Lucile Packard Foundation
Glassco, Jane. Walter and Duncan Gordon Charitable Foundation
Glasser, Kay E. The Community Foundation of Sarasota County, Inc.
Glessner, Kelly. Nicholas H. Noyes, Jr. Memorial Foundation
Glick, Madeleine Einhorn. New York Foundation
Glusac, M. M. Chrysler Corporation Fund
Glynn, Gary A. USX Foundation, Inc.
Goddard, Deborah M. Ellen Browning Scripps Foundation
Goddard, Robert H. I. The Rhode Island Community Foundation
Goddard, William R. The Samuel Roberts Noble Foundation, Inc.
Godfrey, Dudley J., Jr. Patrick and Anna M. Cudahy Fund
Goehl, Rena. Joy Foundation for Ecological Education and Research
Goizueta, Roberto C. Eastman Kodak Company Charitable Trust, Joseph B. Whitehead Foundation
Golde, Marcy J. Northwest Fund for the Environment
Golden, Carol. The Rhode Island Community Foundation

Golden, Rebecca. The Ben & Jerry's Foundation
Goldfeder, Howard. San Diego Community Foundation
Goldman, Douglas E. The Goldman Environmental Foundation, Richard & Rhoda Goldman Fund, Walter and Elise Haas Fund
Goldman, Guido. The German Marshall Fund of the United States
Goldman, John D. The Goldman Environmental Foundation, Richard & Rhoda Goldman Fund.
Goldman, Lisa M. Richard & Rhoda Goldman Fund
Goldman, Marcia L. Richard & Rhoda Goldman Fund
Goldman, Maynard. Massachusetts Environmental Trust
Goldman, Peter. Kongsgaard-Goldman Foundation
Goldman, Rhoda H. The Goldman Environmental Foundation, Richard & Rhoda Goldman Fund, Walter and Elise Haas Fund, Levi Strauss Foundation,
Goldman, Richard N. The Goldman Environmental Foundation, Richard & Rhoda Goldman Fund.
Goldman, Susan S. Richard & Rhoda Goldman Fund
Goldstein, Emanuel. Herman Goldman Foundation
Golub, Harvey. American Express Philanthropic Program
Golub, Stanley D. The Henry M. Jackson Foundation
Gonzales, Alice. Sacramento Regional Foundation
Gonzales, Joe. Bay Area Community Foundation
Gonzalez, Armando. Flintridge Foundation
Goodfellow, Charles C., III. The Barbara Gauntlett Foundation, Inc.
Goodrich, Lisa. The Ben & Jerry's Foundation
Goodsell, S. A. Union Pacific Foundation
Goodwin, Neva R. Rockefeller Brothers Fund, Inc.
Goodwin, Richard H., Jr. The Conservation and Research Foundation
Goodwin, Richard H., Sr. The Conservation and Research Foundation
Goodwin, Richard S., Sr. The Conservation and Research Foundation
Goodwin, William M. Lilly Endowment, Inc.
Gordon, Elizabeth. Walter and Duncan Gordon Charitable Foundation
Gordon, George M. Kenneth T. and Eileen L. Norris Foundation
Gordon, J. The Polden-Puckham Charitable Foundation
Gordon, John. Walter and Duncan Gordon Charitable Foundation

© 1995 Environmental Data Resources, Inc.

Officers, Directors, Trustees, and Contacts

Gordon, Joseph G. Z. Smith Reynolds Foundation, Inc.
Gordon, Joseph K. McLean Contributionship
Gorham, David L. The New York Times Company Foundation, Inc.
Gorham, John. The Champlin Foundations
Goudy, Grace C. The Collins Foundation
Gow, Ian. Roy E. Crummer Foundation
Grace, Helen. W. K. Kellogg Foundation
Grace, Philip M. The John D. and Catherine T. MacArthur Foundation
Graddick, Mirian M. AT&T Foundation
Grady, Stafford R. Giles W. and Elise G. Mead Foundation
Graham, Carolyn C. Carolyn Foundation
Graham, Edith A. The Overbrook Foundation
Graham, Katharine. The Foundation for the National Capital Region
Graham, Lora. The Windham Foundation, Inc.
Graham, Patricia Albjerg. The Hitachi Foundation
Graham, Robert C., Jr. The Overbrook Foundation
Grant, R. Gene. Ben B. Cheney Foundation
Grant, William R. Mary Flagler Cary Charitable Trust
Grant, William W., III. Gates Foundation
Grasley, M. H. Shell Oil Company Foundation
Graves, William. National Geographic Society Education Foundation
Gray, Hanna Holborn. Ameritech Foundation, The Field Foundation of Illinois, Inc., The Andrew W. Mellon Foundation
Gray, Helen Sanders. Marcia Brady Tucker Foundation
Gray, Michael. Bay Area Community Foundation
Gray, Paul E. Eastman Kodak Company Charitable Trust
Gray, Winifred P. The Perkin Fund
Greathead, R. Scott. American Conservation Association, Inc.
Green, Alan E. The Community Foundation of Greater New Haven
Green, Bennie. Rockwell Fund, Inc.
Green, Ellen Z. The Bush Foundation
Green, Ernest. The Winthrop Rockefeller Foundation
Greenberg, Barbara R. The Philanthropic Group
Greenberg, Glenn H. Bernard F. and Alva B. Gimbel Foundation, Inc.
Greenblatt, Stanley A. McKesson Foundation, Inc.
Greene, Wade. Rockefeller Financial Services, Philanthropy Department; The Trust For Mutual Understanding
Greenfield, Jerry. The Ben & Jerry's Foundation
Greenleaf, Michael H. Atlantic Foundation

Greenleaf, Victoria Stebbins. The Stebbins Fund, Inc.
Greenough, Martha. The New York Times Company Foundation, Inc.
Greer, Colin. The New World Foundation, Angelina Fund, Inc.
Greer, Margaret Jewett. The George Frederick Jewett Foundation
Greer, William Hershey, Jr. The George Frederick Jewett Foundation
Gregorian, Vartan. The Aaron Diamond Foundation
Gregory, Richard K. The Community Foundation Serving Coastal South Carolina
Gremillion, J. B., Jr. Union Pacific Foundation
Grenfell, Cynthia. The Emerald Foundation
Greyhavens, Tim. Wilburforce Foundation
Gribetz, Judah. The New York Community Trust
Griffin, James T. The John D. and Catherine T. MacArthur Foundation
Griffin, Judith Berry. The Winthrop Rockefeller Foundation
Griffith, Charles P., Jr. The W. C. Griffith Foundation
Griffith, Lawrence S. C. Surdna Foundation, Inc.
Griffith, Walter S. The W. C. Griffith Foundation
Griffith, William C., III. The W. C. Griffith Foundation
Grimes, L. E. Fair Play Foundation
Grinstein, Keith. The Henry M. Jackson Foundation
Grisanti, Eugene P. G. Unger Vetlesen Foundation
Griswold, Benjamin H., IV. Alex. Brown & Sons Charitable Foundation, Inc.
Groman, S. L. Union Pacific Foundation
Grosberg, Julius. The Rollin M. Gerstacker Foundation
Gross, Carl R. The James M. Cox, Jr. Foundation, Inc.
Gross, Martin L. New Hampshire Charitable Foundation
Grossman, Andrew C. The Minneapolis Foundation
Grosvenor, Gilbert M. National Geographic Society Education Foundation
Growney, James W. James & Abigail Campbell Foundation
Gruhl, Ricki. Threshold Foundation
Grumbach, Antonia M. Jackson Hole Preserve, Inc.
Grumhaus, Margaret A. The Austin Memorial Foundation
Grumman, Cornelia. Ellis L. Phillips Foundation
Grumman, David L. Ellis L. Phillips Foundation
Grune, George V. DeWitt Wallace-Reader's Digest Fund, Lila Wallace-Reader's Digest Fund

Grunland, Paul. The Strong Foundation for Environmental Values
Guerra, John C., Jr. AT&T Foundation
Gulledge, Robert C., Jr. The Winston-Salem Foundation, Inc.
Gund, Ann L. The George Gund Foundation
Gund, Geoffrey. The George Gund Foundation
Gund, George, III. The George Gund Foundation
Gund, Llura A. The George Gund Foundation
Gunther, Herbert Chao. The New World Foundation
Gunzenhauser, Lynn C. Lynn R. and Karl E. Prickett Fund
Gussow, Joan. Jessie Smith Noyes Foundation, Inc.
Guthrie, Carlton L. The Joyce Foundation
Gutierrez, Salvador O. The Dean Witter Foundation
Gutin, Irving. Greater Piscataqua Community Foundation
Guttas, Charles K. Frances Seebe Trust
Guyer, Carol P. James C. Penney Foundation
Guyer, Gordon E. Americana Foundation, Inc.

H

Haas, David W. The William Penn Foundation
Haas, Evelyn D. Evelyn and Walter Haas, Jr. Fund
Haas, Frederick R. The William Penn Foundation
Haas, Janet F. The William Penn Foundation
Haas, John O. The William Penn Foundation
Haas, Melinda A. The William Penn Foundation
Haas, Nancy B. The William Penn Foundation
Haas, Peter E. Walter and Elise Haas Fund The San Francisco Foundation, Levi Strauss Foundation
Haas, Peter E., Jr. Walter and Elise Haas Fund, Levi Strauss Foundation,
Haas, Robert D. Ford Foundation, Evelyn and Walter Haas, Jr. Fund, Levi Strauss Foundation
Haas, Walter A., Jr. Evelyn and Walter Haas, Jr. Fund, Walter and Elise Haas Fund
Haas, Walter J. Evelyn and Walter Haas, Jr. Fund, Walter and Elise Haas Fund
Haas, William D. The William Penn Foundation
Haddon, Phoebe A. The William Penn Foundation

Officers, Trustees, Directors, and Contacts

Hafer, Fred D. The Wyomissing Foundation, Inc.
Hagans, Michele V. The Foundation for the National Capital Region
Haggerty, Gretchen R. USX Foundation, Inc.
Hahn, Anne D. The Hahn Family Foundation
Hahn, Charles D. The Hahn Family Foundation
Hahn, Charles J. The Hahn Family Foundation
Hahn, Eric S. The Hahn Family Foundation
Hahn-Baker, Anne H. The Hahn Family Foundation
Halaburda, Barbara L. The Prudential Foundation
Halby, Margaret M. General Service Foundation
Hale, Bradley. Metropolitan Atlanta Community Foundation, Inc.
Hale, J. A., Jr. Union Pacific Foundation
Hale, James T. Dayton Hudson Foundation
Hall, Charles T. Gebbie Foundation, Inc.
Hall, Donald J. The Hall Family Foundation
Hall, J. Edward. DeWitt Wallace-Reader's Digest Fund, Lila Wallace-Reader's Digest Fund
Hall, Joseph S. Robert G. and Anne M. Merrick Foundation, Inc.
Hall, Marion T. The Joyce Foundation
Hall, Shirley Robinson. The Foundation for the National Capital Region
Hall, Mrs. Serena Davis. The Arthur Vining Davis Foundations
Hall, William A. The Hall Family Foundation
Hallene, Alan M. The John D. and Catherine T. MacArthur Foundation
Hallock, Roger I. Metropolitan Atlanta Community Foundation, Inc.
Halpern, Charles R. The Nathan Cummings Foundation
Halvorsen, Andrew C. The Schumann Fund for New Jersey, Inc.
Hamamoto, Howard. Mary D. and Walter F. Frear Eleemosynary Trust
Hamer, Donald W. The Hamer Foundation
Hamilton, Ann Oppenheimer. Harris and Eliza Kempner Fund
Hamilton, Frank T. The Thomas J. Emery Memorial
Hamilton, James L. USX Foundation, Inc.
Hamilton, John D. Gebbie Foundation, Inc.
Hamilton, William. Marin Community Foundation
Hamler, Thomas B. The Troy Foundation
Hammack, John A. Meadows Foundation, Inc.
Hammel, J. Carter. The International Foundation, Inc.
Hammer, Roy A. Jessie B. Cox Charitable Trust
Hammerschmidt, John A. USX Foundation, Inc.

Hamp, Sheila F. Ford Motor Company Fund
Hampton, Claudia H. California Community Foundation
Hampton, Louis R. The Champlin Foundations
Hampton, Robert K. Kathleen Price and Joseph M. Bryan Family Foundation, Inc.
Handelman, Walter J. James A. Macdonald Foundation
Hanes, Eldridge C. James G. Hanes Memorial Fund
Hanes, Gordon. James G. Hanes Memorial Fund
Hanes, James G., III. James G. Hanes Memorial Fund
Hanley, Robert L. The Milwaukee Foundation
Hanrahan, Barbara H. The William Penn Foundation
Hansler, John F. Ben B. Cheney Foundation
Hanson, James R. Sequoia Foundation
Hanson, Jon F. The Prudential Foundation
Hapgood, Elaine P. The Educational Foundation of America, The Ettinger Foundation, Inc.
Harada, Curtis Y. Hawaiian Electric Industries Charitable Foundation
Harbert, Anita. San Diego Community Foundation
Harckham, Peter. The Clarence E. Heller Charitable Foundation
Harden, Pat. Environmental Education Foundation of Florida, Inc.
Harder, Henry U. Geraldine R. Dodge Foundation, Inc.
Harder, William E. Dayton Hudson Foundation
Hardin, Katherine. James G. Hanes Memorial Fund
Hardin, P. Russell. Joseph B. Whitehead Foundation, Robert W. Woodruff Foundation, Inc.
Harding, Robert L., Jr. The Harding Educational and Charitable Foundation
Hargrove, Richard L. The Cleveland Foundation
Harper, Gwendolyn. Anna B. Stearns Charitable Foundation, Inc.
Harriman, Pamela C. Mary W. Harriman Foundation
Harrington, Deborah Weil. Norman Foundation
Harrington, Earl W., Jr. The Champlin Foundations
Harris, Deborah S. Foundation for the Carolinas
Harris, Edward C. Turner Foundation, Inc.
Harris, George R. The Schumann Fund for New Jersey, Inc.
Harris, John A. Changing Horizons Charitable Trust
Harris, Sophia Bracey. The New World Foundation

Harris, Stephen B. Sproul Foundation
Harris, Thomas G. Chesapeake Corporation Foundation
Harris, William. The Foundation for the National Capital Region
Harrison, David B. The New World Foundation
Harrison, Edward E. The Educational Foundation of America
Harrison, Lois Cowles. The Cowles Charitable Trust
Harrop, Ann D. The Nelson B. Delavan Foundation
Hart, Frances C. Springs Foundation, Inc.
Hart, Joseph T. C. G. Unger Vetlesen Foundation
Hart, Thelma. James & Abigail Campbell Foundation
Harte, Christopher M. Maine Community Foundation, Inc.
Hartigan, Margaret D. The Chicago Community Trust
Hartley, Mrs. James R. Helen K. and Arthur E. Johnson Foundation
Hartloff, Paul W., Jr. Alice Tweed Tuohy Foundation
Hartnett, Stephen. A Territory Resource
Hartshorn, Gary S. General Service Foundation
Hartung, Roderick L. The Chevron Companies
Hartung, Suzanne R. Fran and Warren Rupp Foundation
Hartwell, David B. James Ford Bell Foundation
Hartwell, John M. David Winton Bell Foundation
Hartwell, Lucy B. David Winton Bell Foundation
Harvey, Ann. Maki Foundation
Harvey, Constance. Maki Foundation, The New-Land Foundation, Inc.
Harvey, F. Barton, Jr. Alex. Brown & Sons Charitable Foundation, Inc.
Harvey, Hal. The Energy Foundation, Joyce Mertz-Gilmore Foundation, The New-Land Foundation, Inc.,
Harvey, Joan. The New-Land Foundation, Inc.
Harvey, Joseph. The New-Land Foundation, Inc.
Harvey, Michelle. The National Environmental Education and Training Foundation, Inc.
Harvey, Paul. The John D. and Catherine T. MacArthur Foundation
Hasbargen, Vernae. Blandin Foundation
Hashorva, Tanya. Arcadia Foundation
Haskell, Antoinette M. Public Welfare Foundation, Inc.
Haskell, Robert H. Public Welfare Foundation, Inc.
Hastings, John A. The Hastings Trust
Hastings, Robert C. The Hastings Trust
Hatch, Francis W. The John Merck Fund

© 1995 Environmental Data Resources, Inc.

Officers, Directors, Trustees, and Contacts

Hatch, Francis W., III. Merck Family Fund
Hatch, Serena M. The John Merck Fund
Hatcher, Joe B. The Winthrop Rockefeller Foundation
Hatton, Barbara R. The Edward W. Hazen Foundation
Hau, Thomas C. WMX Environmental Grants Program
Haudein, Robert H. Georgia Power Foundation, Inc.
Haugh, Michael. Times Mirror Magazines, Inc.
Haupert, Ruth C. Jackson Hole Preserve, Inc.
Hauptfuhrer, Barbara D. The Philadelphia Foundation
Hauserman, Jacquita K. Centerior Energy Foundation
Hauserman, William F. Martha Holden Jennings Foundation
Hawke, John D., Jr. The Foundation for the National Capital Region
Hawker, Mary Stake. Deer Creek Foundation
Hawkins, Winsome. Metropolitan Atlanta Community Foundation, Inc.
Hawkinson, Gary M. Centerior Energy Foundation
Hawley, Philip M. The John Randolph Haynes and Dora Haynes Foundation
Hawn, Gates Helms. The Clark Foundation
Hayden, John F. The Boeing Company
Hayes, Denis A. The Bullitt Foundation, The Energy Foundation
Hayes, Synnova B. The Bay Foundation
Haygood, Leah. WMX Environmental Grants Program
Haynes, Harold J. The Boeing Company
Hazel, John T., Jr. The Foundation for the National Capital Region
Hazelrigg, Charles R. Helen K. and Arthur E. Johnson Foundation
Hazen, Donald. The New World Foundation
Head, Carol. The Fund for New Jersey
Head, Dora. Lynn R. and Karl E. Prickett Fund
Healy, Edmund. The M. A. Healy Family Foundation, Inc.
Healy, Martha Ann Dumke. The M. A. Healy Family Foundation, Inc.
Healy, Richard. Angelina Fund, Inc.
Healy, Shevy. Luster Family Foundation, Inc.
Heasley, Karen L. Snee-Reinhardt Charitable Foundation
Heasley, Paul A. Snee-Reinhardt Charitable Foundation
Heasley, Timothy. Snee-Reinhardt Charitable Foundation
Heath, Karen. Ottinger Foundation
Hebb, Peter H. Vancouver Foundation
Hebel, Jason. South Coast Foundation, Inc.
Hecht, Margaret W. Mark and Catherine Winkler Foundation

Heckscher, Martin A. Dolfinger-McMahon Foundation
Hedinger, Nancy K. Environmental Endowment for New Jersey, Inc.
Heegaard, Peter A. Blandin Foundation, The Minneapolis Foundation
Heeschen, Paul C. Environment Now Foundation
Heffernan, Elizabeth B. The William Bingham Foundation
Hefler, Richard J. Sarkeys Foundation
Heftler, Pierre V. Walter and Josephine Ford Fund
Heher, Garrett M. Atlantic Foundation
Heineman, Andrew D. The Abelard Foundation West
Heineman, Benjamin W., Jr. GE Fund
Heinz, Drue Maher. Howard Heinz Endowment
Heinz, H. John, IV. Howard Heinz Endowment
Heinz, Maria Teresa. Howard Heinz Endowment
Heinz, Teresa. The Winslow Foundation
Heinz, Teresa F. Howard Heinz Endowment
Heiskell, Marian S. The New York Times Company Foundation, Inc., The Sulzberger Foundation, Inc.
Heisler, William H., III. The Rhode Island Community Foundation
Heitz, Eric B. The Energy Foundation
Held, Huyler C. The John Merck Fund
Helgoe, Courtney. The Nathan Cummings Foundation
Heller, Alfred E. The Clarence E. Heller Charitable Foundation
Heller, Anne E. Heller Charitable & Educational Fund
Heller, Gloria. The Marshall Fund of Arizona
Heller, Katherine. Heller Charitable & Educational Fund, The Clarence E. Heller Charitable Foundation
Heller, Miranda. Heller Charitable & Educational Fund, The Clarence E. Heller Charitable Foundation
Heller, Ruth B. Heller Charitable & Educational Fund
Helmholz, Elizabeth L. Laird, Norton Foundation
Hemmerich, Alfred G. The Wyomissing Foundation, Inc.
Hendee, John H., Jr. The Milwaukee Foundation
Henderson, Donald G. The Chevron Companies
Henderson, James A. Ameritech Foundation
Henderson, Rhoe B., III. Gebbie Foundation, Inc.
Henderson, Thomas J. Atkinson Foundation
Hendry, Richard. The Community Foundation Serving Coastal South Carolina

Heneghan, Thomas D. The Community Foundation Serving Coastal South Carolina
Heningburg, Gustav. The Fund for New Jersey
Henley, Benjamin J., Jr. The Bothin Foundation
Hennessey, Frank M. Hudson-Webber Foundation
Hennig, Ruth G. The John Merck Fund
Henry, C. Wolcott, III. The Curtis and Edith Munson Foundation, Inc.
Henry, Dorothy J. The Howard Johnson Foundation
Henry, H. Alexander. The Curtis and Edith Munson Foundation, Inc.
Henson, Paul H. The Hall Family Foundation
Henze, Laura. Anna B. Stearns Charitable Foundation, Inc.
Herbst, Jay A. Harder Foundation
Herde, Daniel. San Diego Community Foundation
Hergenhan, Joyce. GE Fund
Herman, Catherine W. Mark and Catherine Winkler Foundation
Herman, J. Dean. Mark and Catherine Winkler Foundation
Hernandez, Robert M. USX Foundation, Inc.
Herr, Earl B., Jr. Lilly Endowment, Inc.
Herr, Philip C., II. The William Penn Foundation
Herrell, John E. Atkinson Foundation
Herrera, Bill. Bay Area Community Foundation
Herrscher, Anne P. Meadows Foundation, Inc.
Hervey, Bette. El Paso Community Foundation
Hessinger, Carl J. W. Harry C. Trexler Trust
Hewitt, Laura M. The Community Foundation Serving Coastal South Carolina
Hewitt, Louis R. Atlantic Foundation
Hewlett, Walter B. The William and Flora Hewlett Foundation
Hewlett, William R. The William and Flora Hewlett Foundation
Heyman, Stephen D. New York Foundation
Heyns, Roger W. The William and Flora Hewlett Foundation, The James Irvine Foundation
Hiatt, Arnold. The John Merck Fund
Hiatt, Howard H. The Aaron Diamond Foundation
Hibberd, William F. Gladys and Roland Harriman Foundation, Mary W. Harriman Foundation
Hickok, David F. Northwest Area Foundation
Hicks, Martin. Laidlaw Foundation
Higashi, Robert T. Douroucouli Foundation

© 1995 Environmental Data Resources, Inc.

Officers, Trustees, Directors, and Contacts

Higbie, Carlton M., Jr. McGregor Fund
Higginbotham, The Honorable A. Leon, Jr. The New York Times Company Foundation, Inc.
Higgins, Eunice Olin. Spencer T. and Ann W. Olin Foundation
Higgins, William W. Spencer T. and Ann W. Olin Foundation
Higginson, Cornelia. American Express Philanthropic Program
Hilbert, Robert J. El Pomar Foundation
Hildreth, Horace A., Jr. Davis Conservation Foundation, Maine Community Foundation, Inc.
Hill, Frederick W. Westinghouse Foundation
Hill, Louis W., Jr. Northwest Area Foundation
Hill, Roger. Bay Area Community Foundation
Hill, Steven R. Weyerhaeuser Company Foundation
Hill, Sylvia I. The New World Foundation
Hill-Faison, Regina. The Community Foundation of Sarasota County, Inc.
Hiller, Stanley, Jr. The Boeing Company
Hills, Carla A. The Chevron Companies
Hillyard, Gerald R., Jr. Helen K. and Arthur E. Johnson Foundation
Hilton, Louis O. Maine Community Foundation, Inc.
Hinkson, Christopher E. Vancouver Foundation
Hinman, Harvey D. The Chevron Companies
Hinson, Robin L. Foundation for the Carolinas
Hirsch, Bruce A. The Clarence E. Heller Charitable Foundation
Hirschfeld, A. Barry. Boettcher Foundation
Hirschfield, Ira S. Evelyn and Walter Haas, Jr. Fund
Hitchcox, Laura C. The William Bingham Foundation
Hobart, William H., Jr. The Troy Foundation
Hobbs, Truman M. The Curtis and Edith Munson Foundation, Inc.
Hobson, Henry W. The Thomas J. Emery Memorial
Hochreiter, Edward J. FishAmerica Foundation
Hochschild, Adam. HKH Foundation
Hockaday, Irvine O., Jr. The Hall Family Foundation
Hodge, Eleanor D. The Fred Harris Daniels Foundation, Inc.
Hodges, Gene R. Georgia Power Foundation, Inc.
Hodges, James H. Springs Foundation, Inc.
Hodgson, David C. Echoing Green Foundation
Hoenemeyer, Frank J. The Cape Branch Foundation

Hoey, Stephen E. Echoing Green Foundation
Hoffen, Jack, Jr. The USF&G Foundation, Inc.
Hoffman, Karen A. The Ahmanson Foundation
Hoffman, Kerry K. True North Foundation
Hoffman, Lori. The Hofmann Foundation
Hoffnagle, John. The Strong Foundation for Environmental Values
Hofmann, Kenneth H. The Hofmann Foundation, National Fish and Wildlife Foundation
Hofmann-Sechres, Lisa. The Hofmann Foundation
Hogan, John E. Olive B. Cole Foundation
Hogan, Ronald P. Georgia-Pacific Foundation
Hogans, Mack L. Weyerhaeuser Company Foundation
Hogg, Sir Christopher. Ford Foundation
Hogoboom, Colonel Dale. The Ohrstrom Foundation
Hohn, T. Marshall, Jr. Georgia-Pacific Foundation
Hokanson, Sandra T. Northwest Area Foundation
Holden, Arthur S., Jr. Martha Holden Jennings Foundation
Holder, William S. Wilburforce Foundation
Holdren, John P. The John D. and Catherine T. MacArthur Foundation
Holguin, Hector. El Paso Community Foundation
Holland, Hudson, Jr. Hudson-Webber Foundation
Hollenbeck, Karen R. W. K. Kellogg Foundation
Hollett, Byron P. The Clowes Fund, Inc., Lilly Endowment, Inc.
Holliman, Vonda. Charles G. Koch Charitable Foundation
Hollinshead, Warren H. Westinghouse Foundation
Hollingsworth, Susan Hunt. The Roy A. Hunt Foundation
Holloran, Thomas E. The Bush Foundation
Holloway, Anna Grace. Greater Piscataqua Community Foundation
Holman, John W., Jr. The Hyde and Watson Foundation
Holmberg, Ruth S. The New York Times Company Foundation, Inc., The Sulzberger Foundation, Inc.
Holmes, Edward A. The International Foundation, Inc.
Holsapple, R. W. Phillips Petroleum Foundation, Inc.
Holton, Governor Linwood. The Foundation for the National Capital Region
Holton, Virginia R. Virginia Environmental Endowment
Holtz, Jean. Patrick and Anna M. Cudahy Fund

Hooks, H. Vaughn. WMX Environmental Grants Program
Hoolihan, James. Blandin Foundation
Hooper, Irene. Environmental Education Foundation of Florida, Inc.
Hope, J. R. Union Pacific Foundation
Hopiak, George A. S. H. Cowell Foundation
Hopkins, Anne H. The Minneapolis Foundation
Hopkins, Tom. Environmental Education Foundation of Florida, Inc.
Hopkins, Wendy. The Community Foundation of Sarasota County, Inc.
Horak, Lucy. Bay Area Community Foundation
Hori, Takeaki. United States-Japan Foundation
Hormel, J. Christopher. Global Environmental Project Institute
Hormel, LuAnne Finch. Global Environmental Project Institute
Hormel, Rampa. Global Environmental Project Institute
Hormel, Thomas. Global Environmental Project Institute
Horn, Alan F. The Horn Foundation
Horn, Albert J. Peninsula Community Foundation
Horn, Karen N. The Cleveland Foundation
Horn, Nini Moore. California Community Foundation
Horner, Henry. The Butler Foundation
Horton, Alice Kirby. F. M. Kirby Foundation, Inc.
Horton, Jack K. The John Randolph Haynes and Dora Haynes Foundation
Horton, Raymond D. Robert Sterling Clark Foundation, Inc.
Hough, Lawrence A. The Foundation for the National Capital Region
Howard, Gene. FishAmerica Foundation
Howard, Heather. The Boeing Company
Howard, John D. The Fred Gellert Foundation
Howard, T. J. Shell Oil Company Foundation
Howat, Bruce B. Ameritech Foundation
Howell, Alfred H. Cleveland H. Dodge Foundation, Inc.
Howes, Clara. Jesse Margaret Wilson Budlong Foundation for Animal Aid
Howkins, Anthony C. The Charles Evans Hughes Memorial Foundation, Inc.
Howland, Richard Hubbard. The Morris and Gwendolyn Cafritz Foundation
Hoyer, David R. The Chevron Companies
Hoyte, James S. Massachusetts Environmental Trust
Hrabowski, Freeman A., III. Baltimore Gas and Electric Foundation, Inc.
Hsaio, Gilbert. The Golden Rule Foundation, Inc.
Hubbard, Jim. FishAmerica Foundation

© 1995 Environmental Data Resources, Inc.

Officers, Directors, Trustees, and Contacts

Hubbard, R. C. Springs Foundation, Inc.
Hubbard, William N., Jr. W. K. Kellogg Foundation
Hubbell, Virginia. The Greenville Foundation
Huck, John Lloyd. Geraldine R. Dodge Foundation, Inc.
Hudson, Gilbert. Hudson-Webber Foundation
Hudson, Joseph L., Jr. Hudson-Webber Foundation
Hudson, Joseph L., IV. Hudson-Webber Foundation
Hufstedler, Shirley Mount. The John D. and Catherine T. MacArthur Foundation
Hughes, David H. The Hall Family Foundation
Hughes, Grace A. Marin Community Foundation
Hughes, Reid. Environmental Education Foundation of Florida, Inc.
Huizenga, Peter H. WMX Environmental Grants Program
Hull, Patricia. Toyota USA Foundation
Hume, Leslie. The San Francisco Foundation
Hummer, Philip Wayne. The Field Foundation of Illinois, Inc.
Humphrey, Hubert. Z. Smith Reynolds Foundation, Inc., The Sapelo Foundation
Humphrey, Louise Ireland. Ireland Foundation
Humphrey, William R., Jr. Marbrook Foundation
Humphry, Patricia. Maki Foundation
Huneke, The Reverend Douglas K. Marin Community Foundation
Hunt, Andrew McQ. The Roy A. Hunt Foundation
Hunt, Christopher M. The Roy A. Hunt Foundation
Hunt, Constance. Donner Canadian Foundation
Hunt, Daniel K. The Roy A. Hunt Foundation
Hunt, Helen McM. The Roy A. Hunt Foundation
Hunt, Irmgard. The German Marshall Fund of the United States
Hunt, John B. The Roy A. Hunt Foundation
Hunt, Richard McM. The Roy A. Hunt Foundation
Hunt, Roy A., III. The Roy A. Hunt Foundation
Hunt, Torrence M. The Roy A. Hunt Foundation
Hunt, Torrence M., Jr. The Roy A. Hunt Foundation
Hunt, William E. The Roy A. Hunt Foundation
Hunt-Badiner, Marion. The Roy A. Hunt Foundation
Hunter, Celia. Alaska Conservation Foundation
Hunter, David. Ottinger Foundation
Hunting, David D., Jr. Steelcase Foundation
Hunting, John R. Beldon Fund
Hutcheson, Mary Ross Carter. The Beirne Carter Foundation
Hutchins, H. R. Shell Oil Company Foundation
Hutchinson, H. R. The Barra Foundation, Inc.
Hyatt, Missey. National Geographic Society Education Foundation
Hybl, William J. El Pomar Foundation
Hyde, Henry B. The Armand G. Erpf Fund, Inc.

I

Ibarguen, Alberto. The New York Community Trust
Ignat, David W. The Nord Family Foundation
Ignat, Joseph N. The Nord Family Foundation
Iha, David. Hawaii Community Foundation
Imhoff, Ms. Quincey. Foundation for Deep Ecology
Ingwersen, James C. Atkinson Foundation
Inouye, Minoru. United States-Japan Foundation
Ireland, Kate. Ireland Foundation
Ireland, R. L., III. Ireland Foundation
Irvin, Roberta. The Winston-Salem Foundation, Inc.
Irving, Claudia. Thanksgiving Foundation
Irwin, John N., III. The Achelis Foundation, The Bodman Foundation, The Tinker Foundation Incorporated
Ito, Alice. A Territory Resource
Ittleson, H. Anthony. Ittleson Foundation, Inc.
Ittleson, Marianne S. Ittleson Foundation, Inc.
Iverson, F. Kenneth. Foundation for the Carolinas
Ives, Diane. Beldon Fund
Ivey, Beryl M. The Richard Ivey Foundation
Ivey, Richard M. The Richard Ivey Foundation
Ivey, Richard W. The Richard Ivey Foundation

J

Jacangelo, Nicholas. Jessie Smith Noyes Foundation, Inc.
Jackson, David D. The Summerlee Foundation
Jackson, Deborah C. Anna B. Stearns Charitable Foundation, Inc.
Jackson, Helen Hardin. The Henry M. Jackson Foundation
Jackson, James R. Crystal Channel Foundation
Jackson, John. Laidlaw Foundation
Jackson, Liz. AT&T Foundation
Jackson, The Honorable David D. The Summerlee Foundation
Jacobi, Peter A. Levi Strauss Foundation
Jacobs, Daniel. Alfred T. Stanley Foundation
Jacobs, Jere. The Telesis Foundation
Jacobs, Linda E. Charles E. Culpeper Foundation, Inc.
Jacobson, Jennifer. Botwinick-Wolfensohn Foundation, Inc.
Jacobson, Sibyl. Metropolitan Life Foundation
Jaeger, David A. The Boeing Company
Jaffe, Mary H. The William and Flora Hewlett Foundation
Jaffe, Miles. Henry E. and Consuelo S. Wenger Foundation, Inc.
Jannopoulo, Jerome A. The Community Foundation of Sarasota County, Inc.
Jannotta, Edgar D. The Chicago Community Trust
Jansson, Douglas M. The Milwaukee Foundation
Japhet, Dan R. The William Stamps Farish Fund
Jaret, Ralph E. "Jack". The Community Foundation of Sarasota County, Inc.
Jarrett, Jerry V. The Cleveland Foundation
Jenkins, Michael B. The John D. and Catherine T. MacArthur Foundation
Jenkins, The Honorable Thomas M. Peninsula Community Foundation
Jenne, Marilyn. The Nord Family Foundation
Jennings, James. The Hyams Foundation
Jensen, Jon M. The George Gund Foundation
Jensen, Robert W. The Elizabeth Ordway Dunn Foundation, Inc.
Jepsen, Sarah. AT&T Foundation
Jericho, Ronald M. WMX Environmental Grants Program
Jernigan, Barbaree. The Mary A. Crocker Trust
Jess, Mary Jo. Blandin Foundation
Jessen, H. Martin. Great Lakes Protection Fund
Jewett, George Frederick, Jr. The George Frederick Jewett Foundation
Jewett, Lucille McIntyre. The George Frederick Jewett Foundation
Jews, William L. The Abell Foundation
Jinks, Larry. The Community Foundation of Santa Clara County
Jobe, Warren Y. Georgia Power Foundation, Inc.
Johnson, Barbara A. The Collins Foundation
Johnson, Charles A. Lilly Endowment, Inc.
Johnson, Charles B. Peninsula Community Foundation
Johnson, Charlotte S. Otto Bremer Foundation

Officers, Trustees, Directors, and Contacts

Johnson, Christopher. Walter S. Johnson Foundation
Johnson, Curtis W. The Minneapolis Foundation
Johnson, David L. Larsen Fund, Inc.
Johnson, Dorothy A. W. K. Kellogg Foundation
Johnson, George H. Metropolitan Atlanta Community Foundation, Inc.
Johnson, Gretchen W. The Cape Branch Foundation
Johnson, Howard Bates. The Howard Johnson Foundation
Johnson, Howard Brennan. The Howard Johnson Foundation
Johnson, J. Seward, Jr. Atlantic Foundation
Johnson, James C. Chesapeake Bay Trust
Johnson, James L. The Cape Branch Foundation
Johnson, Jessica B. The Bauman Foundation
Johnson, John S., III. Atlantic Foundation
Johnson, Judith. Flintridge Foundation
Johnson, Lawrence M. Hawaii Community Foundation
Johnson, Leonard W. Anna B. Stearns Charitable Foundation, Inc.
Johnson, Loretta. The USF&G Foundation, Inc.
Johnson, Mrs. Lyndon B. American Conservation Association, Inc., Jackson Hole Preserve, Inc.
Johnson, Madeleine. Samuel and May Rudin Foundation, Inc.
Johnson, Marjory Hughes. The Charles Evans Hughes Memorial Foundation, Inc.
Johnson, Muriel P. Sacramento Regional Foundation
Johnson, Norman E. Weyerhaeuser Company Foundation
Johnson, Patricia B. The Howard Johnson Foundation
Johnson, Rosetta B. The Sapelo Foundation
Johnston, Alexander L. Carolyn Foundation
Johnston, Gerald A. McDonnell Douglas Foundation
Jones, Adrienne Lash. The Cleveland Foundation
Jones, Christine. The Boeing Company
Jones, Cliff. McKenzie River Gathering Foundation
Jones, David. FishAmerica Foundation
Jones, Edward L., Jr. Arcadia Foundation
Jones, Edwin L., Jr. Foundation for the Carolinas
Jones, Emily J. Meadows Foundation, Inc.
Jones, Henry. The Winthrop Rockefeller Foundation
Jones, J. W. Joseph B. Whitehead Foundation, Robert W. Woodruff Foundation, Inc.
Jones, L. M. Union Pacific Foundation
Jones, Lewis B. USX Foundation, Inc.

Jones, Marianne M. Recreational Equipment, Inc.
Jones, Midge. Unitarian Universalist Veatch Program at Shelter Rock
Jones, Terri. California Community Foundation
Jordan, Ann D. The Foundation for the National Capital Region
Jordan, Barbara M. Claneil Foundation, Inc.
Jordan, Henry A. Claneil Foundation, Inc.
Jordan, Vernon E., Jr. Ford Foundation
Joseph, Frank E., Sr. John P. Murphy Foundation
Joseph, Geri M. The German Marshall Fund of the United States
Josey, Lenoir Moody. The Favrot Fund
Joyce, Michael S. The Lynde and Harry Bradley Foundation, Inc.
Judd, Jean. Unitarian Universalist Veatch Program at Shelter Rock
Jurzykowski, Christine. Crystal Channel Foundation, Threshold Foundation

K

Kabak, Scott. Times Mirror Magazines, Inc.
Kabisch, Sally. Alaska Conservation Foundation
Kagan, Donald. Smith Richardson Foundation, Inc.
Kahn, Dona S. The Philadelphia Foundation
Kahn, Joan F. The Freed Foundation, Inc.
Kaiser, David W. Rockefeller Family Fund, Inc.
Kaito, Ben F. Hawaiian Electric Industries Charitable Foundation
Kalipi, Barbara L. Hawaii Community Foundation
Kaminski, John S. Elmina B. Sewall Foundation
Kamprath, Stan. Helen K. and Arthur E. Johnson Foundation
Kane, Marion. Maine Community Foundation, Inc.
Kaohi, Aletha. G. N. Wilcox Trust
Kaplan, Alice M. The J. M. Kaplan Fund, Inc.
Kaplan, Mary E. The J. M. Kaplan Fund, Inc.
Kaplan, Maurice C. The J. M. Kaplan Fund, Inc.
Kaplan, Richard D. The J. M. Kaplan Fund, Inc.
Kasputys, Joseph E. The Hitachi Foundation
Katchadourian, Herant. The William and Flora Hewlett Foundation
Katz, Bruce. Springhouse Foundation
Katzin, Jerome. San Diego Community Foundation
Katzowitz, Lauren. The Charles Evans Hughes Memorial Foundation, Inc.

Kaufman, Leslie S. Pew Scholars Program in Conservation and the Environment
Kaufman, Robert M. The New York Community Trust
Kaull, George H. Centerior Energy Foundation
Kaupe, Sandra T. Surdna Foundation, Inc.
Kauss, Theodore. The Frost Foundation, Ltd.,
Kautz, James C. Deer Creek Foundation, National Geographic Society Education Foundation
Kawananakoa, Edward K. James & Abigail Campbell Foundation
Kearns, David T. Ford Foundation
Keating, Kevin S. The Pfizer Foundation, Inc.
Keating, Veronica. Public Welfare Foundation, Inc.
Keck, Katherine Cone. Giles W. and Elise G. Mead Foundation
Kee, Mrs. John L., Jr. The Arthur Vining Davis Foundations
Keenan, Frances Murray. The Abell Foundation
Keenan, Julie. The Schumann Fund for New Jersey, Inc.
Keep, The Honorable Judith. San Diego Community Foundation
Keir, Robert. FishAmerica Foundation
Keith, Michele. The Minneapolis Foundation
Keller, George M. The Boeing Company
Kellett, Martine. New England Biolabs Foundation
Kelley, Darcey B. Ruth H. Brown Foundation
Kelley, Margaret. The Strong Foundation for Environmental Values
Kelley, Mary Katherine. The Community Foundation of Santa Clara County
Kelley, Sally J. Laird, Norton Foundation
Kelly, Bob. San Diego Community Foundation
Kelly, Catherine Schultz. Schultz Foundation, Inc.
Kelly, Elizabeth Andrus. Surdna Foundation, Inc.
Kelly, William M. New York Foundation
Kemendo, Virginia. El Paso Community Foundation
Kemper, Talfourd H. The Beirne Carter Foundation
Kempner, Carl L. The Armand G. Erpf Fund, Inc.
Kempner, Hetta Towler. Harris and Eliza Kempner Fund
Kendall, Henry W. The Henry P. Kendall Foundation
Kendall, Jane C. Kathleen Price and Joseph M. Bryan Family Foundation, Inc.
Kendall, John P. The Henry P. Kendall Foundation
Kennair, E. B. Shell Oil Company Foundation

© 1995 Environmental Data Resources, Inc.

Officers, Directors, Trustees, and Contacts

Kennedy, Craig. Great Lakes Protection Fund
Kennedy, James Cox. The James M. Cox, Jr. Foundation, Inc.
Kennedy, Mac. The USF&G Foundation, Inc.
Kenney-Wallace, Geraldine. Donner Canadian Foundation
Kenny, Betsy. The Norman Lear Foundation
Kent, Fred I., III. American Conservation Association, Inc.
Keny-Guyer, Neal. James C. Penney Foundation
Kenyon, Robert W. The Champlin Foundations
Kerlin, Gilbert. Cleveland H. Dodge Foundation, Inc.
Kerly, Diane M. The Hamer Foundation
Kerr, Joffa, Sr. The Robert S. and Grayce B. Kerr Foundation, Inc.
Kerr, William G. The Robert S. and Grayce B. Kerr Foundation, Inc.
Kessler, Charlotte P. The Columbus Foundation
Kessler, Stuart. Lee Romney Foundation, Inc.
Key, Amy Bronson. The Fred Harris Daniels Foundation, Inc.
Kick, Frank J. The Bydale Foundation
Kidd, Joe. El Paso Community Foundation
Kidder, Rushworth M. Charles Stewart Mott Foundation
Kieschnick, Michael. The Tides Foundation
Kilpatrick, Joseph E. Z. Smith Reynolds Foundation, Inc.
Kim, John. California Community Foundation
Kimball, Anne. The Acorn Foundation
Kimball, Collier. The Acorn Foundation
Kimball, Jeffrey. The Acorn Foundation
Kimball, Julie C. The Acorn Foundation
Kimball, Stephen C. The Acorn Foundation
Kimball, William. The Acorn Foundation
Kimbrough, Lawrence M. Foundation for the Carolinas
Kime, Jack E. Howard Heinz Endowment, Vira I. Heinz Endowment
Kimmel, Helen. The Helen & Milton Kimmelman Foundation
Kimmelman, Peter. The Aaron Diamond Foundation
Kimoto, Shari. Environment Now Foundation
King, David A. The Champlin Foundations
King, Edward M. Thelma Doelger Charitable Trust
King, Judith S. Stoddard Charitable Trust
King, Mary E. The Arca Foundation
King, Patricia A. General Service Foundation
King, Victor R. Fanwood Foundation
Kingsbury, Brigitte L. Orchard Foundation
Kingsley, Leonard E. The San Francisco Foundation

Kinloch, John. The Community Foundation Serving Coastal South Carolina
Kipp, Robert A. The Hall Family Foundation
Kirby, F. M. F. M. Kirby Foundation, Inc.
Kirby, Fred M., III. F. M. Kirby Foundation, Inc.
Kirby, Jefferson W. F. M. Kirby Foundation, Inc.
Kirby, S. Dillard. F. M. Kirby Foundation, Inc.
Kirby, Walker D. F. M. Kirby Foundation, Inc.
Kirce, Robert L. The Community Foundation of Sarasota County, Inc.
Kirchhoff, Matt. Alaska Conservation Foundation
Kirk, Grayson. The Tinker Foundation Incorporated
Kirkland, William G. The Charles Evans Hughes Memorial Foundation, Inc.
Kirkman, Larry. Benton Foundation
Kiser, Anthony C. M. The William and Mary Greve Foundation, Inc.
Kiser, John W., III. The William and Mary Greve Foundation, Inc.
Kishaba, Lucy. The Sonoma County Community Foundation
Kiskis, Ronald C. The Chevron Companies
Kissinger, H. A. Union Pacific Foundation
Kistler, William H. Helen K. and Arthur E. Johnson Foundation
Kivel, Paul. Vanguard Public Foundation
Kleberg, Stephen J. Caesar Kleberg Foundation for Wildlife Conservation
Klein, Clayton J. The Community Foundation of Santa Clara County
Klein, Edward. The Howard Johnson Foundation
Klein, Stanley M. Herman Goldman Foundation, Lee Romney Foundation, Inc.
Kleinpell, Susan. Ruth Mott Fund
Kligler, Seymour H. Herman Goldman Foundation
Kline, Gary H. The Field Foundation of Illinois, Inc.
Kline, Sidney D., Jr. The Wyomissing Foundation, Inc.
Klingenstein, Frederick A. The Esther A. and Joseph Klingenstein Fund, Inc.
Klingenstein, John. The Esther A. and Joseph Klingenstein Fund, Inc.
Klingenstein, Patricia D. The Esther A. and Joseph Klingenstein Fund, Inc.
Klingenstein, Sharon L. The Esther A. and Joseph Klingenstein Fund, Inc.
Klitten, Martin R., Jr. The Chevron Companies
Kmet, Stan. Environmental Education Foundation of Florida, Inc.
Knecht, Jane. The Barbara Gauntlett Foundation, Inc.
Knight, Roger D., Jr. Helen K. and Arthur E. Johnson Foundation

Knoernschild, Elaine. The Community Foundation of Santa Clara County
Knowles, Rachel Hunt. The Roy A. Hunt Foundation
Knox, Northrup R. The Seymour H. Knox Foundation, Inc.
Knox, Northrup R., Jr. The Seymour H. Knox Foundation, Inc.
Knox Seymour H., III. The Seymour H. Knox Foundation, Inc.
Knox, Seymour H., IV. The Seymour H. Knox Foundation, Inc.
Koch, Charles G. Charles G. Koch Charitable Foundation
Koch, Elizabeth. Charles G. Koch Charitable Foundation
Koenig, James E. WMX Environmental Grants Program
Koester, H. Louie, III. The Community Foundation Serving Coastal South Carolina
Kolbe, Robert J. Ameritech Foundation
Kolodzieski, Ed. Environmental Education Foundation of Florida, Inc.
Kongsgaard, Martha. Kongsgaard-Goldman Foundation
Konigsberg, Jan. Alaska Conservation Foundation
Kopp, Russell T. Clark Charitable Trust
Kopper, Jim. Times Mirror Magazines, Inc.
Korns, Leigh Ann. The James M. Cox, Jr. Foundation, Inc.
Korten, Frances. Ford Foundation
Kortepeter, Wendy Griffith. The W. C. Griffith Foundation
Kosma, Susan. Community Foundation of Western North Carolina, Inc.
Kostishack, John. Otto Bremer Foundation
Koven, Joan F. MARPAT Foundation, Inc.
Koverman, Robert R. The Troy Foundation
Kowalke, Stephen C. Dayton Hudson Foundation
Kozlowski, J. A. Chrysler Corporation Fund
Kraft, Mary. Laurel Foundation
Kramer, Ferd. LaSalle Adams Fund
Kramer, Lawrence I., Jr. The Dean Witter Foundation
Kranson, Bernice. Andrew Norman Foundation
Krasker, Elaine S. Greater Piscataqua Community Foundation
Krasnansky, Marvin L. McKesson Foundation, Inc.
Kresge, Bruce A. The Kresge Foundation
Kressley, Larry. Public Welfare Foundation, Inc.
Krieg, Iris J. Jamee and Marshall Field Foundation
Krimendahl, H. Fred, II. Harbor Lights Foundation
Krongard, Alvin B. Alex. Brown & Sons Charitable Foundation, Inc.
Kruger, Robert. Maine Community Foundation, Inc.

Officers, Trustees, Directors, and Contacts

Krumboltz, Ann. The Energy Foundation
Kruvant, M. Charito. The Foundation for the National Capital Region
Kubelick, Cheryl L. Westinghouse Foundation
Kuechle, Urban T. The Lynde and Harry Bradley Foundation, Inc.
Kuhlin, Michael E. Ameritech Foundation
Kuhlmann, Mark. McDonnell Douglas Foundation
Kumpe, Mary. Environmental Education Foundation of Florida, Inc.
Kunce, Marquita L. Spencer T. and Ann W. Olin Foundation
Kurland, Philip B. Deer Creek Foundation
Kwok, Stanley. Vancouver Foundation
Kydd, Andrea. The Tides Foundation

L

La Force, Clayburn. The Lynde and Harry Bradley Foundation, Inc.
La Mothe, William. W. K. Kellogg Foundation
Labaree, Frances A. The Overbrook Foundation
Labrie, James A. Greater Piscataqua Community Foundation
Lackey, S. A. Shell Oil Company Foundation
LaCroix Phippen, Susanne. Hurdle Hill Foundation
LaCroix Phippen, William. Hurdle Hill Foundation
Laduke, Winona. Seventh Generation Fund
LaFarge Culman, Anna. The Abell Foundation
Lafferty, Frederick W. The Jacob and Annita France Foundation, Inc., Robert G. and Anne M. Merrick Foundation, Inc.
LaFreniere, Norma B. The Champlin Foundations
Lagemann, Peter J. The Lagemann Foundation
Laird, Melvin R. DeWitt Wallace-Reader's Digest Fund, Lila Wallace-Reader's Digest Fund
Lajoie, Susan N. The Cleveland Foundation
Lake, Thomas H. Lilly Endowment, Inc.
Lake, Timothy K. The Wyomissing Foundation, Inc.
Lamb, Dorothy. OCRI Foundation
Lamb, F. Gilbert. OCRI Foundation
Lamb, Frank. OCRI Foundation
Lamb, George R. American Conservation Association, Inc., Jackson Hole Preserve, Inc.
Lamb, Helen. OCRI Foundation
Lamb, Maryann. OCRI Foundation
Lamb, Paula L. OCRI Foundation
Lamb, Peter. OCRI Foundation

Lambert, Samuel W., III. The Bunbury Company, Inc., The Windham Foundation, Inc., The Winslow Foundation,
Lambeth, Thomas W. Z. Smith Reynolds Foundation, Inc.
Lammers, James. Dart Foundation
Lamont, Tara. Damien Foundation
Lampson, Claire. The Sonoma County Community Foundation
Lampton, Nancy. Baltimore Gas and Electric Foundation, Inc.
Lancaster, Sally R. Meadows Foundation, Inc.
Landers, Jay. Environmental Education Foundation of Florida, Inc.
Landesman, Heidi P. The Educational Foundation of America
Landesman, Rocco. The Ettinger Foundation, Inc.
Landon, S. Whitney. Victoria Foundation, Inc.
Landry, Lawrence L. The John D. and Catherine T. MacArthur Foundation
Lane, Betty B. Bill & Edith Walter Foundation
Lane, James E. Bill & Edith Walter Foundation
Lane, Joan F. The James Irvine Foundation
Laney, John W. The Hall Family Foundation
Lang, Margaret A. The Overbrook Foundation
Langbauer, Del. Harder Foundation
Langbauer, Eldon N. Harder Foundation
Langbauer, Lucille H. Harder Foundation
Langbauer, Robert L. Harder Foundation
Langbauer, William H. Harder Foundation
Langdon, George D., Jr. The Kresge Foundation
Langer, Ms. Julia. Laidlaw Foundation
Langfitt, Thomas W. The Pew Charitable Trusts
Lanier, Richard S. The Trust For Mutual Understanding
Lanigar, Mary. Walter S. Johnson Foundation
LaPlace, William B. The 1525 Foundation
Larkin, Frank Y. Edward John Noble Foundation, Inc.
Larkin, June Noble. Edward John Noble Foundation, Inc.
LaRoche, Juanita W. The Community Foundation Serving Coastal South Carolina
Larry, Richard M. Sarah Scaife Foundation Incorporated
Larsen, Christopher. Larsen Fund, Inc.
Larsen, Jonathan Z. Larsen Fund, Inc.
Larsen, Robert R. Larsen Fund, Inc.
Larson, Robert C. The Kresge Foundation
Laspada, Salvatore. Rockefeller Financial Services, Philanthropy Department

Lassalle, Honor. Norman Foundation
Lassalle, Nancy N. Norman Foundation
Lassalle, Philip E. Norman Foundation
Lasser, Miles L. Ralph C. Sheldon Foundation, Inc.
Lauder, Estee. The Lauder Foundation, Inc.
Lauder, Leonard A. The Lauder Foundation, Inc.
Lauder, Ronald S. The Lauder Foundation, Inc.
Laurie, Marilyn. AT&T Foundation
Lavelle, Brian F. D. Community Foundation of Western North Carolina, Inc.
Lawrence, Anne I. The Louise H. and David S. Ingalls Foundation, Inc.
Lawrence, Elizabeth. Oliver S. and Jennie R. Donaldson Charitable Trust
Lawrence, John T. The Thomas J. Emery Memorial
Lawrence, Pauline. Meyer Memorial Trust
Lawrence, Polly. Wallace Genetic Foundation, Inc.
Lawrence, Robert A. Middlecott Foundation, The New York Times Company Foundation, Inc.
Layton, Thomas C. The Wallace Alexander Gerbode Foundation, Inc.
Lazar, Helen B. The Lazar Foundation
Lazar, William B. The Lazar Foundation
Lazarof, Janice Anne. S. Mark Taper Foundation
Lazarus, Leonard. Solow Foundation
Leach, Duane M. Caesar Kleberg Foundation for Wildlife Conservation
Leahy, J. W. Union Pacific Foundation
Leahy, Richard A. Amelia Peabody Charitable Fund
Lear, Lyn. The Norman Lear Foundation
Lear, Norman. The Norman Lear Foundation
LeBlanc, Steven. Douroucouli Foundation
Lebsack, Chester W. Thelma Doelger Charitable Trust
LeBuhn, Robert. Geraldine R. Dodge Foundation, Inc.
Lebworth, Carol G. Bernard F. and Alva B. Gimbel Foundation, Inc.
Lee, Christine. Walter and Duncan Gordon Charitable Foundation
Lee, Mrs. J. Philip. Henry B. Plant Memorial Fund, Inc.
Lee, Madeline. New York Foundation
Lee, Philip R. The Jenifer Altman Foundation
Leeming, E. Janice. The Little Family Foundation
LeFevour, Suzanne A. Patrick and Aimee Butler Family Foundation
Leff, Deborah. The Joyce Foundation
Leghorn, Ken. Alaska Conservation Foundation
Lehman, Edward. Boettcher Foundation
Lehner, Carl P. Orchard Foundation

Officers, Directors, Trustees, and Contacts

Lehner, Peter. Orchard Foundation
Lehner, Philip. Orchard Foundation
Lehr, Ronald L. Helen K. and Arthur E. Johnson Foundation
Lehrer, Sander. United States-Japan Foundation
Leibrock, Robert M. Abell-Hanger Foundation
Leininger, Joan E. Georgia-Pacific Foundation
Lenhart, Carole S. The Frank Stanley Beveridge Foundation, Inc.
Lenkowsky, Leslie. The Achelis Foundation, The Bodman Foundation
Lentz, Hover T. Boettcher Foundation
Leonard, Anita. Maine Community Foundation, Inc.
Lerman, Philip. Patrick and Anna M. Cudahy Fund
Lerner, Michael. The Jenifer Altman Foundation
Leslie, Diana C. Nicholas H. Noyes, Jr. Memorial Foundation
Letwin, James G. Wilburforce Foundation
Letwin, Rosanna W. Wilburforce Foundation
Levan, B. W. Shell Oil Company Foundation
LeVan, John A. The Frost Foundation, Ltd.
Levering, Anthony. The Community Foundation of Sarasota County, Inc.
Levi, Melville R. The Community Foundation of Sarasota County, Inc.
Levin, Gail. The Community Foundation of Sarasota County, Inc.
Levine, K. N. The Ohrstrom Foundation
Levine, Risa E. Vancouver Foundation
Levinson, Anna B. The Max and Anna Levinson Foundation
Levinson, Carl A. The Max and Anna Levinson Foundation
Levinson, Doug. The Max and Anna Levinson Foundation
Levinson, Edward. The Max and Anna Levinson Foundation
Levinson, Ellen L. The Max and Anna Levinson Foundation
Levinson, Gordon R. The Max and Anna Levinson Foundation
Levinson, Julian A. The Max and Anna Levinson Foundation
Levinson, Lynda B. The Max and Anna Levinson Foundation
Levitt, Richard S. Northwest Area Foundation
Levy, Reynold. AT&T Foundation, The Nathan Cummings Foundation
Lewallen, Alberta. C. A. Webster Foundation
Lewis, C. Douglas. The Bauman Foundation
Lewis, C. Stephen. Weyerhaeuser Company Foundation
Lewis, Douglas R. James G. Hanes Memorial Fund
Lewis, Drew. Union Pacific Foundation
Lewis, George. Middlecott Foundation
Lewis, Harry T., Jr. Boettcher Foundation
Li, Victor H. Hawaiian Electric Industries Charitable Foundation
Libarle, Dan. The Sonoma County Community Foundation
Liberatori, Ellen. Give to the Earth Foundation
Libicki, Henry J. The Nord Family Foundation
Lichtman, Judith. The Moriah Fund, Inc.
Lieberman, Erik R. The Community Foundation of Sarasota County, Inc.
Lieberman, Leonard. The Fund for New Jersey
Liebler, A. C. Chrysler Corporation Fund
Lientz, James R., Jr. Metropolitan Atlanta Community Foundation, Inc.
Light, Dorothy K. The Prudential Foundation
Lightfoot, Sara Lawrence. The John D. and Catherine T. MacArthur Foundation
Lillie, Isabel R. The Community Foundation of Sarasota County, Inc.
Lillie, Richard H. The Lynde and Harry Bradley Foundation, Inc.
Lilly, Eli, II. Lilly Endowment, Inc.
Lin, Maya. The Energy Foundation
Linder, Richard A. Westinghouse Foundation
Lindley, F. Haynes, Jr. The John Randolph Haynes and Dora Haynes Foundation
Lindner, Al. FishAmerica Foundation
Lindsay, Nancy D. Geraldine R. Dodge Foundation, Inc.
Lindsey, Handy L., Jr. The Field Foundation of Illinois, Inc.
Lingle, Walter L., Jr. The Thomas J. Emery Memorial
Linker, Donald G. Marin Community Foundation
Linnell, John W. The Champlin Foundations
Linnert, Terrence G. Centerior Energy Foundation
Linowes, R. Robert. The Foundation for the National Capital Region
Lintilhac, Crea S. Lintilhac Foundation
Lintilhac, Philip M. Lintilhac Foundation
Lipp, Robert I. The Travelers Foundation
Lipp, Stewart I. The Troy Foundation
Lipper, Kenneth. Rockefeller Brothers Fund, Inc.
Lipschultz, William H. Otto Bremer Foundation
Little, Arthur D. The Little Family Foundation
Little, Bill. The Community Foundation of Sarasota County, Inc.
Little, Cameron R. The Little Family Foundation
Little, Milton. AT&T Foundation
Little, Shirley. Environmental Education Foundation of Florida, Inc.
Littlejohn, Charles. Environmental Education Foundation of Florida, Inc.
Litwin, Gordon. Mary Owen Borden Memorial Foundation
Livingston, Patricia P. Tortuga Foundation
Livy, Barbara M. Americana Foundation, Inc.
Llewellyn, John S., Jr. Massachusetts Environmental Trust
Lloyd, Heidi. General Service Foundation
Lloyd, Marion M. General Service Foundation
Lobbia, John E. Hudson-Webber Foundation
Loeb, Anna Frank. The New-Land Foundation, Inc.
Loeffler, Ann R. The Austin Memorial Foundation
Loevner, Sandra. The Community Foundation of Sarasota County, Inc.
Lofton, Thomas M. Lilly Endowment, Inc., The Clowes Fund, Inc.
Loftus, Andrew. FishAmerica Foundation
Loftus, John W. The Frost Foundation, Ltd.
Lombardi, Thomas J. Magowan Family Foundation, Inc.
Long, Beverly. Apple Computer, Inc.
Long, Clay. Metropolitan Atlanta Community Foundation, Inc.
Long, Elia A. Hawaii Community Foundation
Long, Lynda. Environmental Education Foundation of Florida, Inc.
Long, T. Dixon. American Foundation Corporation
Longstreth, Bevis. The Nathan Cummings Foundation
Loomis, Doris Phillips. Community Foundation of Western North Carolina, Inc.
Loomis, Lois C. Mary D. and Walter F. Frear Eleemosynary Trust, McInerny Foundation, G. N. Wilcox Trust
Loomis-Grover, Judy. Harder Foundation
Looney, Wilton. Robert W. Woodruff Foundation, Inc.
Lopes, Frederick G. Jesse Margaret Wilson Budlong Foundation for Animal Aid
Lord, Joseph. Mary Owen Borden Memorial Foundation
Loring, Valerie S. Stoddard Charitable Trust
Losinger, Sara McCune. The Marshall L. & Perrine D. McCune Charitable Foundation
Lourie, Bruce. Laidlaw Foundation
Love, Howard M. Howard Heinz Endowment
Lovell, Sue. The USF&G Foundation, Inc.
Lowe, Rolland C. The San Francisco Foundation
Lowenstein, L. Franklyn. Vinmont Foundation, Inc.
Loy, Frank E. The German Marshall Fund of the United States
Loyd, Mary Jo. Rockwell Fund, Inc.

Officers, Trustees, Directors, and Contacts

Lucas, Cynthia. The Roy A. Hunt Foundation
Lucas, George. National Geographic Society Education Foundation
Lucero, Linda. Vanguard Public Foundation
Ludington, John S. The Charles J. Strosacker Foundation
Ludlow, Jean W. Jessie Ball duPont Religious, Charitable and Educational Fund
Luers, William H. Rockefeller Brothers Fund, Inc., The Trust For Mutual Understanding
Luke, John A., Jr. The Tinker Foundation Incorporated
Lumarda, Joe. California Community Foundation
Lummus, Lynn F. The Elizabeth Ordway Dunn Foundation, Inc.
Lundblad, Dorothy. C. A. Webster Foundation
Lupo, Sister Pat. Great Lakes Protection Fund
Luskin, Rick. Environment Now Foundation
Luster, Amy. Luster Family Foundation, Inc.
Luster, Andrew. Luster Family Foundation, Inc.
Luster, Elizabeth. Luster Family Foundation, Inc.
Lygren, Rolf. Heller Charitable & Educational Fund
Lynagh, John J. Surdna Foundation, Inc.
Lynch, David A. USX Foundation, Inc.
Lynch, Joseph G. The Rockfall Foundation
Lynch, Robert Lee Kempner. Harris and Eliza Kempner Fund
Lynch, Ronald P. Charles E. Culpeper Foundation, Inc.
Lynch, Stephen A., III. Jessie Ball duPont Religious, Charitable and Educational Fund
Lyons, Samuel F. The Community Foundation Serving Coastal South Carolina

M

MacAllaster, Archie F. The Clark Foundation
MacBride, The Honorable Thomas J. Sacramento Regional Foundation
MacColl, Stephanie C. The Bothin Foundation, The San Francisco Foundation
MacDonald, James H. McDonnell Douglas Foundation
Macdonald, Thomas J. Mary D. and Walter F. Frear Eleemosynary Trust, Hawaii Community Foundation, McInerny Foundation, G. N. Wilcox Trust
MacElree, Jane Cox. Jessie B. Cox Charitable Trust
MacGregor, David L. Stackner Family Foundation, Inc.

MacGuire, Betty M. El Paso Community Foundation
MacInnes, Gordon A. The Fund for New Jersey
Mackall, John R. Alice Tweed Tuohy Foundation
MacKay, Governor Buddy. Environmental Education Foundation of Florida, Inc.
Mackay, Calder M. Giles W. and Elise G. Mead Foundation
MacKay, Malcolm. Charles Hayden Foundation
Mackay, Richard N. Giles W. and Elise G. Mead Foundation
MacKechnie, John G. The Hyde and Watson Foundation
MacKimm, Margaret P. The Chicago Community Trust
MacLeod, Rhoderick B. The Community Foundation of Sarasota County, Inc.
MacMillan, Cargill, Jr. The Cargill Foundation
MacMillan, Neal. Threshold Foundation
MacMillan, Stephen H. James & Abigail Campbell Foundation
MacMillan, W. Duncan. Great Lakes Protection Fund
Madden, Frank H. The International Foundation, Inc.
Maddox, Garry. The Philadelphia Foundation
Maddox, Susan A. San Diego Community Foundation
Madrid, The Honorable Art. San Diego Community Foundation
Maestre, Charles Hey. The New World Foundation
Mafra, Humberto. Damien Foundation, Global Greengrants Fund
Magee, David B. The Abelard Foundation West
Magee, Frances W. The Abelard Foundation West
Maggiacomo, Edward L. The Rhode Island Community Foundation
Magill, Sherry P. Jessie Ball duPont Religious, Charitable and Educational Fund
Magowan, Charles M. Magowan Family Foundation, Inc.
Magowan, Doris M. Magowan Family Foundation, Inc.
Magowan, James. Magowan Family Foundation, Inc.
Magowan, Kimberly. Magowan Family Foundation, Inc.
Magowan, Mark E. Magowan Family Foundation, Inc.
Magowan, Merrill L. Magowan Family Foundation, Inc.
Magowan, Peter A. Magowan Family Foundation, Inc.
Magowan, Robert A., Jr. Magowan Family Foundation, Inc.

Magowan, Stephen C. Magowan Family Foundation, Inc.
Magowan, Thomas C. Magowan Family Foundation, Inc.
Mahoney, Margaret E. The John D. and Catherine T. MacArthur Foundation
Mahoney, Richard D. Benton Foundation
Mains, Raymond D. The Procter & Gamble Fund
Malcolm, Barbara H. The Schumann Fund for New Jersey, Inc.
Malone, C. B. Union Pacific Foundation
Mancasola, John A. The McConnell Foundation
Mandell, Elizabeth H. The Clarence E. Heller Charitable Foundation
Mandell, Peter. The Clarence E. Heller Charitable Foundation, Heller Charitable & Educational Fund
Mankiller, Wilma P. Ford Foundation
Manning, Jerome. The Barbara Gauntlett Foundation, Inc.
Mansell, Edmona Lyman. The Bothin Foundation
Marino, Anthony S. The Rockfall Foundation
Mark, Caroline Schumann. The Florence and John Schumann Foundation
Markow, Irwin. Pinewood Foundation
Marks, Randolph A. The Seymour H. Knox Foundation, Inc.
Marks, Raymond. The Morris Stulsaft Foundation
Marra, John. Bay Area Community Foundation
Mars, Forrest E., Jr. Mars Foundation
Mars, John F. Mars Foundation
Marsden, The Honorable Lorna. Laidlaw Foundation
Marsh, Bonnie. Bay Area Community Foundation
Marsh, Claudia Haines. Public Welfare Foundation, Inc.
Marshall, Anthony D. The Vincent Astor Foundation
Marshall, John E., III. The Kresge Foundation
Marshall, Jonathan. The Marshall Fund of Arizona
Marshall, Laura. The Marshall Fund of Arizona
Marshall, Maxine B. The Marshall Fund of Arizona
Marshall, Ray. The German Marshall Fund of the United States
Marshall, William H. The Clowes Fund, Inc.
Martin, Barbara Kennedy. Nathan M. Ohrbach Foundation, Inc.
Martin, C. Virgil. Joyce Mertz-Gilmore Foundation
Martin, Casper. The Martin Foundation, Inc.
Martin, Dan M. The John D. and Catherine T. MacArthur Foundation

© 1995 Environmental Data Resources, Inc.

Officers, Directors, Trustees, and Contacts

Martin, Elizabeth. The Martin Foundation, Inc.
Martin, Geraldine F. The Martin Foundation, Inc.
Martin, Jennifer. The Martin Foundation, Inc.
Martin, John W., Jr. Ford Motor Company Fund
Martin, Lee. The Martin Foundation, Inc.
Martin, Mahlon A. The Winthrop Rockefeller Foundation
Martin, Rex. The Martin Foundation, Inc.
Martin, Roger L. Steelcase Foundation
Martin, Webb F. Charles Stewart Mott Foundation
Martin-Brown, Joan. The Goldman Environmental Foundation
Martinenza, Stephen A. Welfare Foundation, Inc.
Mascotte, John P. The Hall Family Foundation
Mason, Frederick T. The Sulzberger Foundation, Inc.
Mason, John W. Community Foundation of Western North Carolina, Inc.
Massey, Walter E. The William and Flora Hewlett Foundation
Matchett, David. Vanguard Public Foundation
Matheny, N. D. Stanley Smith Horticultural Trust
Mathews, Jessica Tuchman. Rockefeller Brothers Fund, Inc.
Mathias, Charles McC., Jr. The Tinker Foundation Incorporated
Mathieson, Andrew W. Richard King Mellon Foundation
Mathson, Robert O. James Ford Bell Foundation
Matkov, Becky Roper. The Elizabeth Ordway Dunn Foundation, Inc.
Matosziuk, Edward. The Hamer Foundation
Matsuda, Fujio. Hawaii Community Foundation
Matthews, Angela P. Greater Piscataqua Community Foundation
Matthews, L. W., III. Union Pacific Foundation
Matthews, Mark. The Sonoma County Community Foundation
Mattson, Edie R. Boettcher Foundation
Mattson, Walter E. The New York Times Company Foundation, Inc.
Matzke, Richard H. The Chevron Companies
Maughan, Janet. Ford Foundation
Mavec, Ellen S. The Kelvin and Eleanor Smith Foundation
Mawby, Russell G. W. K. Kellogg Foundation
Maxon, Carroll S. El Paso Community Foundation
Maxwell, Joan. The Foundation for the National Capital Region
May, Cordelia S. Laurel Foundation

May, Irene duPont. Longwood Foundation, Inc.
Mayeda, Cynthia. Dayton Hudson Foundation
Mayer, Beatrice Cummings. The Nathan Cummings Foundation
Mayer, Robert N. The Nathan Cummings Foundation
Maynes, Judith A. AT&T Foundation
Mazlish, Bruce. Rockefeller Family Fund, Inc.
Mazzotta, Joan D. The Rockfall Foundation
McAfoose, Elizabeth. The Fund for Preservation of Wildlife and Natural Areas
McArthur, Daniel E. Giles W. and Elise G. Mead Foundation
McAuley, Malcolm J. The Chevron Companies
McBride, John P. Airport Business Center Foundation
McBride, John P., Jr. Airport Business Center Foundation
McBride, Katherine. Airport Business Center Foundation
McBride, Laurie M. Airport Business Center Foundation
McCallie, Allen L. Lyndhurst Foundation
McCammon, David N. Ford Motor Company Fund
McCann, Nancy W. John P. Murphy Foundation
McCarthy, Gerald P. Virginia Environmental Endowment
McCarthy, Patricia A. The Florence and John Schumann Foundation
McClellan, Judy. The USF&G Foundation, Inc.
McClelland, W. C. Union Camp Charitable Trust
McClimon, Tim. AT&T Foundation
McClintock, Emily. The Nord Family Foundation
McClinton, Sue. Community Foundation of Western North Carolina, Inc.
McCloy, Ellen Z. Mobil Foundation, Inc.
McCollum, Hugh E. Community Foundation of Western North Carolina, Inc.
McCormack, Elizabeth J. The John D. and Catherine T. MacArthur Foundation, The Trust For Mutual Understanding
McCormack, William M. The International Foundation, Inc.
McCormick, William T., Jr. McGregor Fund
McCoy, David H. James & Abigail Campbell Foundation
McCoy, Robert C. Ederic Foundation, Inc.
McCue, Howard M. Lloyd A. Fry Foundation
McCulloch, Norman Estes, Jr. The Rhode Island Community Foundation
McCully, George E. Ellis L. Phillips Foundation

McCune, John R. McCune Foundation
McCune, John R., Jr. McCune Foundation
McCune, John R., VI. The Marshall L. & Perrine D. McCune Charitable Foundation
McDade, Sandy D. Weyerhaeuser Company Foundation
McDonald, Admiral David L. W. L. Lyons Brown Foundation
McDermott, Mrs. Eugene. The Eugene McDermott Foundation
McDonald, Robert E. The Pew Charitable Trusts
McDonnell, John F. McDonnell Douglas Foundation
McDonough, William A. W. Alton Jones Foundation, Inc.
McDougal, C. Bouton. Gaylord and Dorothy Donnelley Foundation
McDowell, David E. McKesson Foundation, Inc.
McElwaine, Andrew. Howard Heinz Endowment
McFadden, F. Patrick. The Community Foundation of Greater New Haven
McFarland, Catherine M. Victoria Foundation, Inc.
McFarland, Richard D. The Bush Foundation
McGarry, Charles. National Geographic Society Education Foundation
McGarry, Mac. National Geographic Society Education Foundation
McGee, Joseph H. The Community Foundation Serving Coastal South Carolina
McGee, Vincent. The Aaron Diamond Foundation
McGill, William J. Richard Lounsbery Foundation, Inc.
McGoldrick, Sheila. The Overbrook Foundation
McGovern, Gail J. AT&T Foundation
McGovern, John. Toyota USA Foundation
McGowan, George V. Baltimore Gas and Electric Foundation, Inc.
McGowan, Jolene. L. L. Bean, Inc.
McGrath, Mary Philpotts. James & Abigail Campbell Foundation
McGrath, Phyllis S. GE Fund
McGregor, Alan. The Sapelo Foundation
McGuigan, William. The Bunbury Company, Inc.
McHenry, Alan F. Richard Lounsbery Foundation, Inc.
McHenry, W. Barnabas. American Conservation Association, Inc.
McHugh, John A. The Bush Foundation
McHugh, Katherine. Jessie B. Cox Charitable Trust
McInnis, Ellen. The Minneapolis Foundation
McIntosh, Joan H. The McIntosh Foundation
McIntosh, Michael A. The McIntosh Foundation

Officers, Trustees, Directors, and Contacts

McIntosh, Peter H. The McIntosh Foundation
McIntosh, Winsome D. The McIntosh Foundation
McKay, Rob. Vanguard Public Foundation
McKean, Larry G. The Boeing Company
McKean, Linda B. Mary Owen Borden Memorial Foundation
McKee, A. William. Community Foundation of Western North Carolina, Inc.
McKee, Elizabeth. Maine Community Foundation, Inc.
McKee, Raymond W. BankAmerica Foundation
McKelvey, Patricia E. The Charles J. Strosacker Foundation
McKenzie, Floretta. National Geographic Society Education Foundation
McKinley, John. Metropolitan Atlanta Community Foundation, Inc.
McLaughlin, Ann. The Foundation for the National Capital Region
McLaughlin, Marcie. Blandin Foundation
McLean, K. Milton. Thomas Sill Foundation
McLean, Sandra L. McLean Contributionship
McLean, William L., III. McLean Contributionship
McMenamin, Mrs. Edward B. The Clark Foundation
McMichael, R. Daniel. Sarah Scaife Foundation Incorporated
McMillan, Edward L. The Rockfall Foundation
McMurdo, Theresia C. James & Abigail Campbell Foundation
McMurry, David. The Chevron Companies
McNamara, Francis J., Jr. Charles E. Culpeper Foundation, Inc.
McNamara, Robert. United States-Japan Foundation
McNaney, Robert T. FishAmerica Foundation
McNarney, Mrs. Sylvia. McGregor Fund
McNeer, Charles S. The Milwaukee Foundation
McNeil, Lois F. Claneil Foundation, Inc.
McNeil, Robert D. Claneil Foundation, Inc.
McNeil, Robert L., Jr. The Barra Foundation, Inc.
McNerney, Michael. The USF&G Foundation, Inc.
McPhee, Roderick. Hawaii Community Foundation
McPhee, Sharon. Mary D. and Walter F. Frear Eleemosynary Trust
McRann, Robert. San Diego Community Foundation
McShare, Kathleen A. Gaylord and Dorothy Donnelley Foundation
McTier, Charles H. Joseph B. Whitehead Foundation, Robert W. Woodruff Foundation, Inc.

McVay, Scott. Geraldine R. Dodge Foundation, Inc., W. Alton Jones Foundation, Inc.
Mead, Giles W., Jr. Giles W. and Elise G. Mead Foundation
Mead, Jane W. Giles W. and Elise G. Mead Foundation
Mead, Parry W. Giles W. and Elise G. Mead Foundation
Mead, Ruth C. Nelson Mead Fund
Mead, Walter Russell. The Arca Foundation
Meadowcroft, W. Howarth. Weyerhaeuser Company Foundation
Meadows, Curtis W., Jr. Meadows Foundation, Inc.
Meadows, Robert Al. Meadows Foundation, Inc.
Meanley, Edward S. Ellen Browning Scripps Foundation
Means, T. Sam. Stroud Foundation
Meathe, Philip J. Hudson-Webber Foundation
Mecke, Theodore H., Jr. Hudson-Webber Foundation
Meckley, Richard. Pilot Trust
Medberry, Chauncey J., III. The John Randolph Haynes and Dora Haynes Foundation
Mediavilla, Leonard J. The Rockfall Foundation
Meeker, Helen N. The Troy Foundation
Meeker, Robert B. The Troy Foundation
Melchok, Laurie. The Nord Family Foundation
Mellon, Paul. The Andrew W. Mellon Foundation
Mellon, Richard P. Richard King Mellon Foundation
Mellon, Seward Prosser. Richard King Mellon Foundation
Mellon, Timothy. The Andrew W. Mellon Foundation
Melnicoff, David. Samuel S. Fels Fund
Meltzer, Allan H. Sarah Scaife Foundation Incorporated
Memmen, Ava-Liisa. The Stratford Foundation
Memory, Jan. Turner Foundation, Inc.
Mendenhall, J. R. Union Pacific Foundation
Mendoza, Cristina. Apple Computer, Inc.
Mendoza, Roberto G. J. P. Morgan Charitable Trust
Mentor, Marie K. Laird, Norton Foundation
Merck, Albert W., Jr. Merck Family Fund
Merck, Antony M. Merck Family Fund
Merck, Josephine A. Merck Family Fund
Merck, Wilhelm M. The Fund for Preservation of Wildlife and Natural Areas, Merck Family Fund
Merck-Abeles, Anne. Merck Family Fund
Merdek, Andrew. The James M. Cox, Jr. Foundation, Inc.
Merin, Kenneth D. Charles Hayden Foundation

Merkel, Joel. The Henry M. Jackson Foundation
Merlotti, Frank H. Steelcase Foundation
Merrick, Robert G., III. The Jacob and Annita France Foundation, Inc., Robert G. and Anne M. Merrick Foundation, Inc.
Mersereau, Susan M. Weyerhaeuser Company Foundation
Merthan, Claudia Boettcher. Boettcher Foundation
Messinger, Alida R. Rockefeller Family Fund, Inc.
Messner, John. San Diego Community Foundation
Metcalf, Donna. Ruth Mott Fund
Metcalf, Jesse. The Ben & Jerry's Foundation
Metz, Mary S. S. H. Cowell Foundation
Meyer, General Edward C. Smith Richardson Foundation, Inc.
Meyer, J. R. Union Pacific Foundation
Meyer, Roger F. Laurel Foundation
Meyerson, Ivan D. McKesson Foundation, Inc.
Michel, Sally J. The Abell Foundation
Middleton, James A. ARCO Foundation
Midgley, Elizabeth. The German Marshall Fund of the United States
Midkiff, Robert R. Atherton Family Foundation, Hawaii Community Foundation
Mike-Mayer, Maria. Texaco Foundation
Milbourne, George B. Martha Holden Jennings Foundation
Miles, J. C. Vernor. Kinnoull Foundation
Miles, Mary L. Mary Owen Borden Memorial Foundation
Miles, Patricia. The Greenville Foundation
Mill, Phyllis J. Mary Flagler Cary Charitable Trust
Millard, Richard. The Strong Foundation for Environmental Values
Miller, Arjay. The William and Flora Hewlett Foundation
Miller, Barbara B. Elmer L. & Eleanor J. Andersen Foundation
Miller, Diane Edgerton. W. Alton Jones Foundation, Inc.
Miller, Donn B. The James Irvine Foundation, The John Randolph Haynes and Dora Haynes Foundation
Miller, Edmund J. Charles Stewart Mott Foundation
Miller, Edward A. The Morris Stulsaft Foundation
Miller, Edward S. Edna Bailey Sussman Fund
Miller, Elise. The Jenifer Altman Foundation
Miller, Eugene A. McGregor Fund
Miller, Gerald W. Stranahan Foundation
Miller, Glen. Pritzker Foundation
Miller, Harvey S. S. Arcadia Foundation
Miller, J. Michael, III. H. Barksdale Brown Charitable Trust

© 1995 Environmental Data Resources, Inc.

577

Officers, Directors, Trustees, and Contacts

Miller, Kenton R. Pew Scholars Program in Conservation and the Environment
Miller, Marlin, Jr. The Wyomissing Foundation, Inc.
Miller, Nancy A. McKesson Foundation, Inc.
Miller, P. G. Baltimore Gas and Electric Foundation, Inc.
Miller, Sharon. Beldon Fund
Miller, Susan P. The Community Foundation Serving Coastal South Carolina
Millhouse, Barbara B. Mary Reynolds Babcock Foundation, Inc.
Mills, Art. Marin Community Foundation
Mills, Ralph J., Jr. Arthur M. and Olga T. Eisig-Arthur M. and Kate E. Tode Foundation, Inc.
Millspaugh, Gordon A., Jr. Victoria Foundation, Inc.
Milone, Theresa A. The Oakleigh L. Thorne Foundation
Miloscia, Joe. Philip Morris Companies, Inc.
Miltenberger, Arthur D. Richard King Mellon Foundation
Milton, Maxwell. A Territory Resource
Miner, Mike. The W. C. Griffith Foundation
Minnick, Walter. OCRI Foundation
Minucci, Ellen A. The William and Mary Greve Foundation, Inc.
Mische, Joseph. HKH Foundation
Mita, Katsushige. The Hitachi Foundation
Mitchell, David W. The Community Foundation of Santa Clara County
Mitchell, Harvey R. Meadows Foundation, Inc.
Mitchell, J. Daniel. Beneficia Foundation
Mitchell, John C., II. Boettcher Foundation
Mitchell, Lucy C. Carolyn Foundation
Mitchell, Mary E. English-Bonter-Mitchell Foundation
Mitchell, Miriam. Beneficia Foundation
Model, Alan L. James A. Macdonald Foundation
Model, Alice H. James A. Macdonald Foundation
Model, Allen. Leo Model Foundation, Inc.
Model, Pamela. Leo Model Foundation, Inc.
Model, Peter H. Leo Model Foundation, Inc.
Moe, Thomas O. The Cargill Foundation
Moffat, William R. The Carpenter Foundation
Mohawk, John. Seventh Generation Fund
Moini, Ingred. The Truland Foundation
Monahan, Sherwood. The Freed Foundation, Inc.
Montagu, Kyra. Walter and Duncan Gordon Charitable Foundation
Montague, Alice L. Lyndhurst Foundation
Moody, Robert L. The Moody Foundation, Mary Moody Northen, Inc.
Moody, Ross R. The Moody Foundation
Mooers, Sandra Fleet. San Diego Community Foundation

Moon, Frederick F., III. Surdna Foundation, Inc.
Mooney, Brian P. New York Foundation
Moore, Charles O. W. Alton Jones Foundation, Inc.
Moore, Clement C. The Indian Point Foundation, Inc.
Moore, Dan E. W. K. Kellogg Foundation
Moore, Elizabeth W. The Indian Point Foundation, Inc.
Moore, Frank B. WMX Environmental Grants Program
Moore, Hannah. Island Foundation, Inc., Massachusetts Environmental Trust
Moore, James. Westinghouse Foundation
Moore, Jeanette. Mary Moody Northen, Inc.
Moore, Kevin S. The Clark Foundation
Moore, Michael. Island Foundation, Inc.
Moore, Peter M. The Moody Foundation
Moore, Taylor F. The Frost Foundation, Ltd.
Moore, Wenda Weekes. W. K. Kellogg Foundation
Moot, Janet R. The Windham Foundation, Inc.
Moran, Thomas W. The Community Foundation of Sarasota County, Inc.
Moreland, Richard T. National Geographic Society Education Foundation
Morella, Constance A. The Morris and Gwendolyn Cafritz Foundation
Morency, Jeanne. The Lazar Foundation
Moreno, Mary Lou. El Paso Community Foundation
Morgan, J. M. Shell Oil Company Foundation
Morgan, James F., Jr. Atherton Family Foundation
Morgan, Nicholas I. Rockwood Fund, Inc.
Morgan, Samuel H. Elmer L. & Eleanor J. Andersen Foundation
Mori, Faith Harding. The Harding Educational and Charitable Foundation
Morning, John. Charles E. Culpeper Foundation, Inc.
Morris, Ann. Flintridge Foundation
Morris, Benjamin H. W. L. Lyons Brown Foundation
Morris, Donna T. The Charles J. Strosacker Foundation
Morris, Ernest L. Americana Foundation, Inc.
Morris, John L. National Fish and Wildlife Foundation
Morris, Joseph W. Sarkeys Foundation
Morris, Max King. The Arthur Vining Davis Foundations
Morris, Roland. Dolfinger-McMahon Foundation
Morrisett, Lloyd N. National Geographic Society Education Foundation
Morrison, James S. ARCO Foundation
Morrison, Jerri. Mary Owen Borden Memorial Foundation

Morrison, Joshua. J. E. & Z. B. Butler Foundation, Inc.
Morrow, Richard M. The Chicago Community Trust
Morse, Elizabeth. SURFREE
Morse, John W. SURFREE
Morse, Sarah D. The Fred Harris Daniels Foundation, Inc.
Morse, Stephan A. The Bunbury Company, Inc., The Windham Foundation, Inc.
Mortimer, Kathleen H. Mary W. Harriman Foundation
Morton, Dean O. The David and Lucile Packard Foundation
Moseley, Alexander. Flintridge Foundation
Moseley, David. Flintridge Foundation
Moseley, Jacqueline. Flintridge Foundation
Moseley, Sarah. Flintridge Foundation
Mosier, Frank E. Centerior Energy Foundation
Moskowitz, John. The Sonoma County Community Foundation
Mostue, A. Brian. The Carpenter Foundation
Mostue, Emily C. The Carpenter Foundation
Motono, Moriyuki. United States-Japan Foundation
Mott, C. S. Harding, II. Charles Stewart Mott Foundation
Mott, Maryanne. C. S. Fund, Charles Stewart Mott Foundation, Ruth Mott Fund
Mott, Paul B., Jr. F. M. Kirby Foundation, Inc.
Mott, Ruth R. Ruth Mott Fund
Mottaz, Rolla J. Spencer T. and Ann W. Olin Foundation
Mountcastle, Katharine B. Mary Reynolds Babcock Foundation, Inc., Z. Smith Reynolds Foundation, Inc., The Sapelo Foundation
Mountcastle, Katharine R. Mary Reynolds Babcock Foundation, Inc.
Mountcastle, Kenneth F., III. Mary Reynolds Babcock Foundation, Inc.
Mountcastle, Kenneth F., Jr. Mary Reynolds Babcock Foundation, Inc.
Mountcastle, Laura L. Mary Reynolds Babcock Foundation, Inc.
Mountcastle, Mary. Mary Reynolds Babcock Foundation, Inc., Z. Smith Reynolds Foundation, Inc. The Tides Foundation
Mourton, Maurice R. Vancouver Foundation
Moyers, Bill D. The Florence and John Schumann Foundation
Moyers, John. The Florence and John Schumann Foundation
Moynahan, John D., Jr. Metropolitan Life Foundation
Mueler, George P. Chesapeake Corporation Foundation

Officers, Trustees, Directors, and Contacts

Mueller, Stanley R. Phillips Petroleum Foundation, Inc.
Mugar, Carolyn G. Azadoutioun Foundation
Muhlbach, Susan. Threshold Foundation
Mulcaster, Richard. Vancouver Foundation
Mullane, Donald A. BankAmerica Foundation
Mullen, Theresa A. The George Frederick Jewett Foundation
Muller, Steven. The German Marshall Fund of the United States
Mullins, Shelley. The Samuel Roberts Noble Foundation, Inc.
Mulloney, Peter B. USX Foundation, Inc.
Mulreany, Robert H. Smith Richardson Foundation, Inc.
Muma, Dorothy E. Jessie Smith Noyes Foundation, Inc.
Muma, Edith N. Jessie Smith Noyes Foundation, Inc.
Mund, Richard G. Mobil Foundation, Inc.
Munroe, George B. The New York Times Company Foundation, Inc.
Munts, Mary Lou. The Energy Foundation
Munyan, Winthrop R. Robert Sterling Clark Foundation, Inc.
Murdy, Bruce D. The Community Foundation Serving Coastal South Carolina
Murfey, Spencer L., Jr. American Foundation Corporation
Murfey, William W. American Foundation Corporation
Murphy, David K. Sacramento Regional Foundation
Murphy, David R. Helen K. and Arthur E. Johnson Foundation
Murphy, Diana E. The Bush Foundation
Murphy, Franklin D. The Ahmanson Foundation
Murphy, M. Christine. The Philadelphia Foundation
Murphy, Mark M. The Fund for New Jersey
Murphy, Thomas. San Diego Community Foundation
Murrah, Jack. Lyndhurst Foundation
Murray, Archibald R. The Scherman Foundation, Inc.
Murray, David. Bay Area Community Foundation
Murray, William E. Oliver S. and Jennie R. Donaldson Charitable Trust
Murtagh, Consuelo A. Times Mirror Magazines, Inc.
Murtaugh, James. Liz Claiborne & Art Ortenberg Foundation
Muse, Martha Twitchell. The Tinker Foundation Incorporated
Musser, Elizabeth W. General Service Foundation
Musser, Marcie J. General Service Foundation

Musser, Robert W. General Service Foundation
Muth, Maria G. American Foundation Corporation
Myerberg, Neal. The Barbara Gauntlett Foundation, Inc.
Myers, J. P. W. Alton Jones Foundation, Inc.
Myers, Jerry K. Steelcase Foundation
Myers, Max A. The Troy Foundation
Mylott, Colette F. The Austin Memorial Foundation

N

Nadeau, Ron. Outdoor Industry Conservation Alliance
Nagel, Rob D. DeWitt Wallace-Reader's Digest Fund, Lila Wallace-Reader's Digest Fund
Nager, Anita. The New York Community Trust
Naidoff, Stephanie W. The William Penn Foundation
Nakagawa, Scot. McKenzie River Gathering Foundation
Nakauchi, Isao. United States-Japan Foundation
Napoli, Lisa. The Henry M. Jackson Foundation
Naranjo, Arthur F. Ameritech Foundation
Narasaki, Diane. A Territory Resource
Nash, Lucia S. The Kelvin and Eleanor Smith Foundation
Nathan, Robert R. Public Welfare Foundation, Inc.
Nattin, Nathan H. The Procter & Gamble Fund
Neago, R. M. The Procter & Gamble Fund
Neal, Olly. The Winthrop Rockefeller Foundation
Neal, Stephen L. Z. Smith Reynolds Foundation, Inc.
Neall, The Honorable Robert R.. Chesapeake Bay Trust
Neeleman, Stanley D. Helen K. and Arthur E. Johnson Foundation
Neely, Joseph F. The Winston-Salem Foundation, Inc.
Neidorf, Murray. The Norman Lear Foundation
Neimann, Diane B. James Ford Bell Foundation, David Winton Bell Foundation
Nelson, Arvid R. Smith Richardson Foundation, Inc.
Nelson, E. G. The Procter & Gamble Fund
Nelson, Fredric C. S. H. Cowell Foundation
Nelson, Leonard B. The McConnell Foundation
Nelson, Nancy J. Meadows Foundation, Inc.
Nesbeda, Peter. Island Foundation, Inc.
Nesbitt, Charles E. Community Foundation of Western North Carolina, Inc.

Nessier, Stephen. The Dean Witter Foundation
Nettleton, Gail. Laird, Norton Foundation
Neufeld, Adele. The Abelard Foundation West
Neufeld, Peter. The Abelard Foundation West
Neustadt, Richard M. Benton Foundation
Nevins, John A. Leo Model Foundation, Inc.
Newcomb, Margaret P. The Knapp Foundation, Inc.
Newhouse, Rebecca. The Collins Foundation
Newman, Frances Moody. The Moody Foundation
Newman, Jon O. Hartford Foundation for Public Giving
Newmyer, A. G., III. The Foundation for the National Capital Region
Ney, Lillian. Gebbie Foundation, Inc.
Ng, Henry. The J. M. Kaplan Fund, Inc.
Nichols, Asher B. The Milwaukee Foundation
Nichols, Kate Cowles. The Cowles Charitable Trust
Nichols, Marguerite S. The Achelis Foundation, The Bodman Foundation
Nichols, William F. The William and Flora Hewlett Foundation
Nicholson, David A. The Fred Harris Daniels Foundation, Inc.
Nicholson, Peter. Walter and Duncan Gordon Charitable Foundation
Nicholson, William S. The Fred Harris Daniels Foundation, Inc.
Niles, Nicholas. Times Mirror Magazines, Inc.
Nisbet, James R. Foundation for the Carolinas
Nishioka, Janet. BankAmerica Foundation
Nishiyana, Tom. Toyota USA Foundation
Nixon, P. Andrews. Maine Community Foundation, Inc.
Noble, Edward E. The Samuel Roberts Noble Foundation, Inc.
Noble, Mary Jane. The Samuel Roberts Noble Foundation, Inc.
Nogaki, Jane. Environmental Endowment for New Jersey, Inc.
Nogales, Luis G. Ford Foundation
Noon, Nicholas. Sacharuna Foundation
Noonan, Patrick F. American Conservation Association, Inc., National Geographic Society Education Foundation
Norcross, Arthur D., Jr. Norcross Wildlife Foundation, Inc.
Nord, Cynthia W. The Nord Family Foundation
Nord, Eric T. The Nord Family Foundation
Nord, Jane B. The Nord Family Foundation
Nord-Petersen, Kathleen. The Nord Family Foundation

© 1995 Environmental Data Resources, Inc.

Officers, Directors, Trustees, and Contacts

Nordstrom, Paul E. Maine Community Foundation, Inc.
Norman, Abigail. Norman Foundation
Norman, Andrew E. Norman Foundation
Norman, Don H. Felburn Foundation
Norman, Margaret. Norman Foundation
Norman, Martha. Richard Lounsbery Foundation, Inc.
Norman, Rebecca. Norman Foundation
Norman, Sarah. Norman Foundation
Norris, Diana S. Margaret Dorrance Strawbridge Foundation of Pennsylvania II, Inc.
Norris, Harlyne J. Kenneth T. and Eileen L. Norris Foundation
Norris, Kenneth T., Jr. Kenneth T. and Eileen L. Norris Foundation
Norris, Thomas H. AT&T Foundation
Northrop, Edward H. Gladys and Roland Harriman Foundation, Mary W. Harriman Foundation
Northrop, Michael F. Rockefeller Brothers Fund, Inc.
Norton, Michael. The USF&G Foundation, Inc.
Nostitz, Drewry Hanes. James G. Hanes Memorial Fund
Nowak, Carole M. Ireland Foundation
Noyce, Elizabeth B. Maine Community Foundation, Inc.
Noyes, Evan L. Nicholas H. Noyes, Jr. Memorial Foundation
Noyes, Nicholas S. Nicholas H. Noyes, Jr. Memorial Foundation
Noyes, Tom. The Ben & Jerry's Foundation
Nunn, Warne. Meyer Memorial Trust
Nustra, Susan C. WMX Environmental Grants Program
Nye, William R. Vinmont Foundation, Inc.
Nystrom, William B. The McConnell Foundation

O

O'Brien, John R. The Sonoma County Community Foundation
O'Brien, Jr, Donal C. The Trust For Mutual Understanding
O'Brien, W. J., III. Chrysler Corporation Fund
O'Connor, James J. Helen Brach Foundation
O'Connor, William B. Joyce Mertz-Gilmore Foundation
O'Dell, Margaret H. The Joyce Foundation
O'Donnell, Paul J. Geraldine R. Dodge Foundation, Inc.
O'Hara, S. True North Foundation
O'Keefe, Michael. The McKnight Foundation
O'Leary, Hazel R. Northwest Area Foundation
O'Leary, Paul G. The Prudential Foundation
O'Neil, John J. Arthur M. and Olga T. Eisig-Arthur M. and Kate E. Tode Foundation, Inc.
O'Neil, Thomas J. Sacramento Regional Foundation
O'Neill, Abby M. Rockefeller Brothers Fund, Inc.
O'Neill, Peter M. Rockefeller Family Fund, Inc.
O'Reilly, David J. The Chevron Companies
Obasanjo, General Olusegun. Ford Foundation
Ochoa, Guillermo. El Paso Community Foundation
Ocone, Angela H. Global Environmental Project Institute
Oddo, Nancy E. The Max and Victoria Dreyfus Foundation, Inc.
Ogle, Therese. The Hugh and Jane Ferguson Foundation
Ohrbach, Caryl E. Nathan M. Ohrbach Foundation, Inc.
Ohrbach, Lisa K. Nathan M. Ohrbach Foundation, Inc.
Ohrbach, Suzan N. Nathan M. Ohrbach Foundation, Inc.
Ohrstrom, George. The Ohrstrom Foundation
Ohrstrom, George L. The Ohrstrom Foundation
Ohrstrom, George L., Jr. The Ohrstrom Foundation
Ohrstrom, Ricard R., Jr. The Ohrstrom Foundation
Ojeda, Virginia F. The Chicago Community Trust
Okata, Russell K. Hawaii Community Foundation
Olding, John H. The Lagemann Foundation
Oldridge, Neil L. National Fish and Wildlife Foundation
Olin, Kent O. El Pomar Foundation
Olincy, Dan. Andrew Norman Foundation
Olincy, Virginia. Andrew Norman Foundation
Oliva, George, III. Perkins Charitable Foundation
Oliver, Joseph W. Howard Heinz Endowment
Olmsted, Robert M. The Bunbury Company, Inc., The Windham Foundation, Inc.
Olrogg, Elgin E. Ben B. Cheney Foundation
Olsen, Eeva-Liisa Aulikki. The Stratford Foundation
Olsen, Kenneth H. The Stratford Foundation
Olson, Harold B., Jr. Mobil Foundation, Inc.
Olson, James. Toyota USA Foundation
Olson, Karen. Peninsula Community Foundation
Olson, Paul M. Blandin Foundation
Olsson, Sture G. Chesapeake Corporation Foundation
Onan, David W., II. Onan Family Foundation
Onan, David W., III. Onan Family Foundation
Oppenheim, David J. The Max and Victoria Dreyfus Foundation, Inc.
Oppenheimer, James R. Blandin Foundation
Orcutt, Gilbert F. Mary Moody Northen, Inc.
Oreffice, Paul F. The Rollin M. Gerstacker Foundation
Ormseth, Milo E. Rose E. Tucker Charitable Trust, The Jackson Foundation
Ornduff, Robert. Stanley Smith Horticultural Trust
Oros, Tia. Seventh Generation Fund
Orr, David W. Jessie Smith Noyes Foundation, Inc.
Orr, Susan Packard. The David and Lucile Packard Foundation
Ortega, Rafael E. The Minneapolis Foundation
Ortenberg, Art. Liz Claiborne & Art Ortenberg Foundation
Osborn, T. J. Chrysler Corporation Fund
Osborne, Patrick. Great Lakes Protection Fund
Ose, Melena. Sacramento Regional Foundation
Ott, Alan W. The Rollin M. Gerstacker Foundation
Ottinger, Betty Ann. The Winslow Foundation
Ottinger, Jennifer. Ottinger Foundation
Ottinger, June Godfrey. Ottinger Foundation
Ottinger, Lawrence. Ottinger Foundation
Ottinger, LeaAnne. Ottinger Foundation
Ottinger, Louise L. Ottinger Foundation
Ottinger, Randy. Ottinger Foundation
Ottinger, Richard L. Ottinger Foundation
Ottinger, Ronald. Ottinger Foundation
Ottinger, Sharon Kalemkiarian. Ottinger Foundation
Otto, C. R. The Procter & Gamble Fund
Ouchi, William G. California Community Foundation
Owings, The Honorable George W., III. Chesapeake Bay Trust
Oxman, Mrs. David C. Henry B. Plant Memorial Fund, Inc.

P

Packard, Connie. Threshold Foundation
Packard, David. The David and Lucile Packard Foundation
Packard, David W. The David and Lucile Packard Foundation
Packard, Julie E. The David and Lucile Packard Foundation
Padilla, John E. The Community Foundation of Greater New Haven

Officers, Trustees, Directors, and Contacts

Padoch, Christine. Pew Scholars Program in Conservation and the Environment
Page, David K. The Kresge Foundation
Paine, Peter S. The Vincent Astor Foundation
Paine, Walter C. Ellis L. Phillips Foundation
Palenchar, David J. El Pomar Foundation
Palevsky, Lynda. The Tides Foundation
Palleroni, Sergio. The Acorn Foundation
Pallotti, Marianne. The William and Flora Hewlett Foundation
Palmer, Joseph Beveridge. The Frank Stanley Beveridge Foundation, Inc.
Palmer, Patricia S. Larsen Fund, Inc.
Palmer, Rhea. McKesson Foundation, Inc.
Pampusch, Anita M. The Bush Foundation
Panazzi, Donna M. Laurel Foundation
Pandolfi, Francis. Times Mirror Magazines, Inc.
Papone, Aldo. American Express Philanthropic Program
Pappert, E. T. Chrysler Corporation Fund
Paradis, Daisy. The Howard Bayne Fund
Park, James B. Great Lakes Protection Fund
Park, Wesley T. Hawaii Community Foundation
Parker, Bertram. Gebbie Foundation, Inc.
Parker, Franklin E. Jackson Hole Preserve, Inc., The Lagemann Foundation
Parker, Geraldine. Gebbie Foundation, Inc.
Parker, Maclyn T. Olive B. Cole Foundation
Parker, Margaret H. Victoria Foundation, Inc.
Parker, William I. Gebbie Foundation, Inc.
Parmelee, Jean. Walter S. Johnson Foundation
Parode, Ann. San Diego Community Foundation
Parrish, Carole. J. E. & Z. B. Butler Foundation, Inc.
Parrish, J. P. Shell Oil Company Foundation
Parry, Frances. Stranahan Foundation
Parsons, Richard D. Rockefeller Brothers Fund, Inc.
Parsons, Robert W., Jr. The Hyde and Watson Foundation
Parsons, Roger B. The Hyde and Watson Foundation
Pasquarella, Robin. The Henry M. Jackson Foundation
Pastor, Benjamin G. Mustard Seed Foundation, Inc.
Patrick, Judy. Recreational Equipment, Inc.
Patrick-Maxwell, Yvonne. The Richard Ivey Foundation
Patterson, Donald H. The Abell Foundation
Patterson, Jane S. Z. Smith Reynolds Foundation, Inc.
Patterson, Marvin Breckinridge. MARPAT Foundation, Inc.
Patterson, Melissa. Ruth Mott Fund
Patterson, W. Calvin, III. McGregor Fund
Patton, James V. The Cleveland Foundation
Patton, Shirley. The Carpenter Foundation
Patz, Arnall. Chesapeake Bay Trust
Paul, Jim. El Paso Community Foundation
Paulus, Henry P. New England Biolabs Foundation
Payne, Richard. Bay Area Community Foundation
Peach, Robbin. Massachusetts Environmental Trust
Peal, Alexander. Foundation for Field Research
Pearce, Alan. McKesson Foundation, Inc.
Pearce, William R. The Cargill Foundation
Pearlstine-Foster, Susan. The Community Foundation Serving Coastal South Carolina
Pearson, John E. The Cargill Foundation, The Minneapolis Foundation
Pearson, Ruth. J. E. & Z. B. Butler Foundation, Inc.
Pease, David C. The USF&G Foundation, Inc.
Peck, Sidney. Azadoutioun Foundation
Pedersen, Peer. WMX Environmental Grants Program
Pedicord, Lester P. Airport Business Center Foundation
Peer, Cecil M. The USF&G Foundation, Inc.
Peiffer, Jack O. GE Fund
Peirce, Neal R. The German Marshall Fund of the United States
Peisley, W. K. Union Pacific Foundation
Pelt, Lester Van, Jr. Abell-Hanger Foundation
Pence, Margaret Hall. The Hall Family Foundation
Pencke, Carol T. A Territory Resource
Penfield, James K. Northwest Fund for the Environment
Penner, Betty J. Helen K. and Arthur E. Johnson Foundation
Pennick, Eshowe. Beneficia Foundation
Pennick, Mark J. Beneficia Foundation
Pennoyer, Robert M. The John Merck Fund
Pennoyer, Russell P. The Achelis Foundation, The Bodman Foundation
Penny, George L. The Knapp Foundation, Inc.
Penny, Sylvia V. The Knapp Foundation, Inc.
Pepe, Mary L. The Community Foundation of Greater New Haven
Pepin, E. Lyle. Centerior Energy Foundation
Peppercorn, John E. The Chevron Companies
Perachio, Elaine. Harris and Eliza Kempner Fund
Perciasepe, The Honorable Robert. Chesapeake Bay Trust
Percio, Jans T. Centerior Energy Foundation
Perez-Gil, Ramon. Foundation for Field Research
Perkin, Gladys T. The Perkin Fund
Perkin, John T. The Perkin Fund
Perkin, Mrs. Richard S. The Perkin Fund
Perkin, Richard T. The Perkin Fund
Perkin, Robert S. The Perkin Fund
Perkins, Brewster B. Hartford Foundation for Public Giving
Perkins, Homer G. The Frank Stanley Beveridge Foundation, Inc.
Perkins, Leigh H. Perkins Charitable Foundation
Perkins, Mary Bryan. The Beirne Carter Foundation
Perkins, Richard S. The Vincent Astor Foundation
Perkins, Robert. Cox Foundation, Inc.
Perri-Gurniak, Robin. Harbor Lights Foundation
Perry, Carrolle Fair. The Philadelphia Foundation
Perry, Martha J. McCune Foundation
Perry, Rae Rice. The Winthrop Rockefeller Foundation
Pertschuk, Michael. Benton Foundation
Pestillo, Peter J. Ford Motor Company Fund
Peterfreund, Elizabeth H. The Merrill G. & Emita E. Hastings Foundation
Peterfreund, Janice. The Merrill G. & Emita E. Hastings Foundation
Peterfreund, Joshua. The Merrill G. & Emita E. Hastings Foundation
Peterfreund, Lisa. The Merrill G. & Emita E. Hastings Foundation
Peters, David A. California Community Foundation
Peters, Tamra. The Strong Foundation for Environmental Values
Petersen, Donald E. The Boeing Company
Peterson, James R. WMX Environmental Grants Program
Peterson, Jeanette Favrot. The Favrot Fund
Peterson, Kate B. Patrick and Aimee Butler Family Foundation
Peterson, Thomas E. BankAmerica Foundation
Pettit, William O., Jr. The Fred Harris Daniels Foundation, Inc.
Pew, J. Howard, II. The Pew Charitable Trusts
Pew, J. N., III. The Pew Charitable Trusts
Pew, Joseph N., IV. The Pew Charitable Trusts
Pew, R. Anderson. The Pew Charitable Trusts
Pew, Robert C. Steelcase Foundation
Pfahl, Floradelle A. The Columbus Foundation
Pfeffenberger, Michael E. The Troy Foundation
Phelan, John J., Jr. Eastman Kodak Company Charitable Trust
Phelps, Jennifer Case. Carolyn Foundation

Officers, Directors, Trustees, and Contacts

Phillips, Blaine T. Fair Play Foundation
Phillips, Brice R. Chesapeake Bay Trust
Phillips, Elliott H. McGregor Fund
Phillips, Ellis L., III. Ellis L. Phillips Foundation
Phillips, Ellis L., Jr. Ellis L. Phillips Foundation
Phillips, James R. El Paso Community Foundation
Phillips, Lyman C. Centerior Energy Foundation
Phillips, Mary K. Jessie Ball duPont Religious, Charitable and Educational Fund
Phillips, Russell A., Jr. Rockefeller Brothers Fund, Inc.
Phillips, S. Davis. Kathleen Price and Joseph M. Bryan Family Foundation, Inc.
Philpotts, Douglas. Hawaii Community Foundation
Phin, Sydney N. Union Camp Charitable Trust
Phippen, Peter D. Hurdle Hill Foundation
Phippen, Richard D. Hurdle Hill Foundation
Phipps, Howard, Jr. The Vincent Astor Foundation, Jackson Hole Preserve, Inc. Edward John Noble Foundation, Inc. Howard Phipps Foundation, The Perkin Fund
Phipps, Mary S. The Achelis Foundation, The Bodman Foundation
Piasecki, Peter. The Sonoma County Community Foundation
Pichon, John N. Olive B. Cole Foundation
Pidany, Marilyn. The McKnight Foundation
Piedra, L. J. Chrysler Corporation Fund
Pierre, Percy A. The Hitachi Foundation
Pierrepont, John. The Vincent Astor Foundation
Pierson, Mary Louise. Rockefeller Family Fund, Inc.
Pierson, Wayne G. Meyer Memorial Trust
Pigott, Charles M. The Chevron Companies
Pigott, Charles M. The Boeing Company
Pike, Drummond M. Nathan M. Ohrbach Foundation, Inc., The Tides Foundation
Pincus, Lionel I. Ittleson Foundation, Inc.
Pine, William C. The Collins Foundation
Pingree, Sally E. The Charles Engelhard Foundation
Pinick, B. Dan. The Boeing Company
Pinkard, Anne M. The Jacob and Annita France Foundation, Inc. Robert G. and Anne M. Merrick Foundation, Inc.
Pinkard, Robert M. The Jacob and Annita France Foundation, Inc., Robert G. and Anne M. Merrick Foundation, Inc.
Pinkard, Walter D., Jr. The Jacob and Annita France Foundation, Inc., Robert G. and Anne M. Merrick Foundation, Inc.
Pious, Constance G. The Mountaineers Foundation

Piper, William H. Charles Stewart Mott Foundation
Pippin, Ronald G. Ameritech Foundation
Pisano, Jane G. The John Randolph Haynes and Dora Haynes Foundation
Piskor, Frank P. Edward John Noble Foundation, Inc.
Pitcairn, Feodor. Beneficia Foundation
Pitcairn, Jeremy. Beneficia Foundation
Pitcairn, Kirstin. Beneficia Foundation
Pitcairn, Laren. Beneficia Foundation
Pitcairn, Mary Elenor. Beneficia Foundation
Pitkin, Louise. Alfred T. Stanley Foundation
Pittinger, Vernon T. The Jacob and Annita France Foundation, Inc., Robert G. and Anne M. Merrick Foundation, Inc.
Pivnick, Isadore. The Morris Stulsaft Foundation
Place, David E. Cox Foundation, Inc.
Plant, Forrest A., Sr. Sacramento Regional Foundation
Plaster, Anne. Stern Family Fund
Platts, H. Gregory. National Geographic Society Education Foundation
Player, Willa B. Charles Stewart Mott Foundation
Plimpton, Anne W. The Henry P. Kendall Foundation
Plotts, Diane J. Hawaii Community Foundation
Plumb, Ronald M. James & Abigail Campbell Foundation
Plunkett, William J. WMX Environmental Grants Program
Podlich, William F. California Community Foundation
Pohl, Rachel. Jessie B. Cox Charitable Trust
Poindexter, Christian H. Baltimore Gas and Electric Foundation, Inc.
Poinsette, Cheryl L. McKesson Foundation, Inc.
Polin, Jane L. GE Fund
Poling, Harold A. Ford Motor Company Fund
Pollack, Robert. New York Foundation
Polster, Bryan C. The Community Foundation of Santa Clara County
Ponseti, Rhoann. The Sonoma County Community Foundation
Pope, Robert G. Southwestern Bell Foundation
Popoff, Jean. The Rollin M. Gerstacker Foundation
Porlier, Victor. Fieldstead Charitable Trust
Portenoy, Norman S. The Max and Victoria Dreyfus Foundation, Inc.
Portenoy, Winifred R. The Max and Victoria Dreyfus Foundation, Inc.
Porter, John W. Charles Stewart Mott Foundation
Porter, Victor B. Olive B. Cole Foundation
Potts, Erwin. Sacramento Regional Foundation

Powell, George E., III. The Powell Family Foundation
Powell, George E., Jr. The Powell Family Foundation
Powell, John B., Jr. Clayton Baker Trust
Powell, Lee Etta. Compton Foundation, Inc.
Powell, Myrtis H. Public Welfare Foundation, Inc.
Powell, Nicholas K. The Powell Family Foundation
Power, Austin J., Jr. Howard Phipps Foundation
Power, Meg. The Energy Foundation
Powers, John P. The Educational Foundation of America, The Ettinger Foundation, Inc.
Pratt, David W. Hawaii Community Foundation
Pratt, Dudley C., Jr. James & Abigail Campbell Foundation
Pratt, Gerry. Meyer Memorial Trust
Pratt, Richardson, Jr. Robert Sterling Clark Foundation, Inc.
Preiskel, Barbara Scott. Ford Foundation, The New York Community Trust
Prescod, Cecil. McKenzie River Gathering Foundation
Prescott, Foncy. McKenzie River Gathering Foundation
Prewitt, Kenneth. The Energy Foundation
Preyer, The Honorable L. Richardson. Mary Reynolds Babcock Foundation, Inc. Smith Richardson Foundation, Inc.
Prezzano, Wilbur J. Eastman Kodak Company Charitable Trust
Price, The Honorable Charles H., II. The New York Times Company Foundation, Inc.
Price, Clement A. The Fund for New Jersey
Priebe, Kathie. The Community Foundation of Santa Clara County
Primis, Lance R. The New York Times Company Foundation, Inc.
Prince, Charles O., III. The Travelers Foundation
Prince, Frederick H. Prince Charitable Trusts
Prince, William Wood. Prince Charitable Trusts
Pritzker, Daniel F. Pritzker Foundation
Pritzker, James N. Pritzker Foundation
Pritzker, Jay A. Pritzker Foundation
Pritzker, John A. Pritzker Foundation
Pritzker, Nicholas J. Pritzker Foundation
Pritzker, Penny F. Pritzker Foundation
Pritzker, Robert A. Pritzker Foundation
Pritzker, Thomas J. Pritzker Foundation
Pritzlaff, John C., Jr. Spencer T. and Ann W. Olin Foundation
Pritzlaff, Mary Olin. Spencer T. and Ann W. Olin Foundation
Prochnow, Lisa V. Lynn R. and Karl E. Prickett Fund
Procknow, Donald E. The Prudential Foundation

Officers, Trustees, Directors, and Contacts

Prothrow-Stith, Deborah. The Hyams Foundation
Protz, Edward L. Mary Moody Northen, Inc.
Pulliam, Cynthia A. IBM Corporation
Pulliam, Larry. The Samuel Roberts Noble Foundation, Inc.
Pungowiyi, Caleb. Alaska Conservation Foundation
Purtell, Dawn. The USF&G Foundation, Inc.

Q

Quammen, David. Liz Claiborne & Art Ortenberg Foundation
Quern, Arthur F. The Field Foundation of Illinois, Inc.
Quick, Elizabeth. The Winston-Salem Foundation, Inc.
Quick, Sandy. The Community Foundation Serving Coastal South Carolina
Quigley, Phil. The Telesis Foundation
Quinn, Jane. DeWitt Wallace-Reader's Digest Fund

R

Rabbe, F. M. Shell Oil Company Foundation
Rabbino, Mitchell W. Nathan M. Ohrbach Foundation, Inc.
Rabine, Mark. Damien Foundation
Rabinowitch, Victor. The Energy Foundation, The John D. and Catherine T. MacArthur Foundation
Rabinowitz, Andrea. A Territory Resource
Rackley, Andy. Environmental Education Foundation of Florida, Inc.
Rader, Donna. The Winston-Salem Foundation, Inc.
Rader, I. Andrew. The Lynde and Harry Bradley Foundation, Inc.
Radford, Mary. Crystal Channel Foundation
Radford, Yvette. Vanguard Public Foundation
Raff, Douglass A. The Bullitt Foundation
Rainbolt, Harold E. Southwestern Bell Foundation
Raines, Franklin D. The German Marshall Fund of the United States
Ramadan, Matthew L. The Minneapolis Foundation
Ramer, Bruce M. California Community Foundation
Ramos, Tarso. McKenzie River Gathering Foundation
Ramsay, Patricia. Joyce Mertz-Gilmore Foundation
Ranger, Thomas F. Americana Foundation, Inc.
Rankin, Alfred M., Jr. The Cleveland Foundation
Rankin, Nancy. Hartford Foundation for Public Giving

Ranney, George A., Jr. The Field Foundation of Illinois, Inc., The John D. and Catherine T. MacArthur Foundation
Ranney, Phillip A. The 1525 Foundation
Ranney, Sally. Island Foundation
Ransom, Dorothy. Mary Owen Borden Memorial Foundation
Raphael, Chad. Jessie Smith Noyes Foundation, Inc.
Rappleye, Richard K. Charles Stewart Mott Foundation
Rasmussen, Arthur E. The Field Foundation of Illinois, Inc.
Rathke, Wade. The Tides Foundation
Ratliff, Eugene F. Lilly Endowment, Inc.
Ratner, Charles A. The Cleveland Foundation
Raun, Robert L. W. K. Kellogg Foundation
Rausch, Michael C. The Curtis and Edith Munson Foundation, Inc.
Rauser, Herbert. Sarah I. Schieffelin Residuary Trust
Rawson, Vincent. The Emerald Foundation
Ray, Adele Richardson. Smith Richardson Foundation, Inc.
Ray, Dan K. The McKnight Foundation
Ray, Gilbert T. The John Randolph Haynes and Dora Haynes Foundation
Rea, William H. Howard Heinz Endowment, Vira I. Heinz Endowment
Reagan, Richard S. Norcross Wildlife Foundation, Inc.
Reardon, G. Joseph. The Troy Foundation
Reardon, Martha A. The Fund for Preservation of Wildlife and Natural Areas
Reardon, Robert J. Otto Bremer Foundation
Reardon, Suzanne T. The Charles Evans Hughes Memorial Foundation, Inc.
Reavis, Lincoln. The Kelvin and Eleanor Smith Foundation, The Switzer Foundation
Reccuite, Martin C. ARCO Foundation
Reed, Cordell. The Chicago Community Trust
Reed, J. M. Union Camp Charitable Trust
Reed, Philip D., Jr. Philip D. Reed Foundation, Inc.
Reeves, Ruth. Unitarian Universalist Veatch Program at Shelter Rock
Regelbrugge, Lauri. The Hitachi Foundation
Rehr, Helen. New York Foundation
Rehrig, Brian. Fields Pond Foundation, Inc.
Reichert, Joshua S. The Pew Charitable Trusts
Reid, Ala H. Greater Piscataqua Community Foundation
Reid, Bruce S. The Curtis and Edith Munson Foundation, Inc.
Reid, Fergus, III. The Vincent Astor Foundation
Reid, Frank. Environmental Education Foundation of Florida, Inc.

Reilly, John F. Schultz Foundation, Inc.
Reilly, Rebecca. The John D. and Catherine T. MacArthur Foundation
Reilly, William K. The German Marshall Fund of the United States
Rein, Catherine A. Metropolitan Life Foundation
Reinhard, Sister Mary Martha. Centerior Energy Foundation
Rennie, Renate. The Tinker Foundation Incorporated
Rennie, Robert T. Sarkeys Foundation
Renshaw, John P. Peninsula Community Foundation
Rentrop, Gary R. Americana Foundation, Inc.
Resor, Story Clark. American Conservation Association, Inc.
Reusch, Belinda Bunnen. Norman Foundation
Reusing, Vincent P. Metropolitan Life Foundation
Reutter, Jeffrey M. Great Lakes Protection Fund
Reyes, Carmen. American Conservation Association, Inc., Jackson Hole Preserve, Inc.
Reymers, Linda. McKenzie River Gathering Foundation
Reynolds, Annemarie. The Sapelo Foundation
Reynolds, Heather. Beneficia Foundation
Reynolds, Robert H. Nicholas H. Noyes, Jr. Memorial Foundation
Reynolds, Stephen P. Echoing Green Foundation
Reynolds, T. A., Jr. Union Pacific Foundation
Reznick, Marilyn. AT&T Foundation
Rhodes, Frank H. T. The Andrew W. Mellon Foundation
Rhodus, G. Thomas. Meadows Foundation, Inc.
Ricci, Joan D. The Charles Engelhard Foundation
Rice, Condoleeza. The Chevron Companies
Rice, Harry F. Amelia Peabody Charitable Fund
Rice, Henry F. Hawaii Community Foundation
Rice, J. Elisabeth. Amelia Peabody Charitable Fund
Rice, Lois D. The German Marshall Fund of the United States
Rice, Patricia E. Amelia Peabody Charitable Fund
Rich, William, III. Gladys and Roland Harriman Foundation
Richard, D. Eugene. Thelma Doelger Charitable Trust
Richards, H. M., Jr. Hawaii Community Foundation
Richardson, Dee. The Sonoma County Community Foundation

© 1995 Environmental Data Resources, Inc.

Officers, Directors, Trustees, and Contacts

Richardson, Elliot Lee. The Hitachi Foundation
Richardson, H. Smith, Jr. Smith Richardson Foundation, Inc.
Richardson, Heather S. Smith Richardson Foundation, Inc.
Richardson, Joan. The Wallace Alexander Gerbode Foundation, Inc.
Richardson, Julie M. The Favrot Fund
Richardson, Lundsford, Jr. Smith Richardson Foundation, Inc.
Richardson, Peter L. Smith Richardson Foundation, Inc.
Richardson, R. Randolph. Smith Richardson Foundation, Inc.
Richardson, Rebecca S. Laird, Norton Foundation
Richardson, Sarah Beinecke. The Prospect Hill Foundation
Richardson, Stuart S. Smith Richardson Foundation, Inc.
Richardson, William. The Pew Charitable Trusts
Riche, Michelle. Global Environmental Project Institute
Richie, L. C. Chrysler Corporation Fund
Richmond, John L. USX Foundation, Inc.
Ricker, Marvi. The Richard Ivey Foundation
Ricksen, John C. The Skaggs Foundation
Ridgway, Richard W. Greater Piscataqua Community Foundation
Ridgway, Rozanne L. The Boeing Company
Ridings, Dorothy S. Benton Foundation, Ford Foundation
Riecker, Margaret A. The Herbert H. and Grace A. Dow Foundation
Riegel, John E. Ederic Foundation, Inc.
Riegel, Richard E., Jr. Ederic Foundation, Inc.
Rieke, William O. Ben B. Cheney Foundation
Riemke, John W. Olive B. Cole Foundation
Rienhoff, William F., IV. Alex. Brown & Sons Charitable Foundation, Inc.
Riley, Patricia. Maine Community Foundation, Inc.
Riley, Walter. Vanguard Public Foundation
Rimel, Rebecca W. The Pew Charitable Trusts
Ringel, Deborah Taper. S. Mark Taper Foundation
Rinker, Marilyn P. The Powell Family Foundation
Rintamaki, John M. Ford Motor Company Fund
Rios, Elsa A. Jessie Smith Noyes Foundation, Inc.
Ripley, S. Dillon. The Morris and Gwendolyn Cafritz Foundation
Rishel, Jane. Gaylord and Dorothy Donnelley Foundation
Ritter, George W. Ward M. & Mariam C. Canaday Educational and Charitable Trust
Ritzen, Evy Kay. Meadows Foundation, Inc.

Rivera, Henry M. Benton Foundation
Rizley, Robert S. Sarkeys Foundation
Robbins, N. Clay. Lilly Endowment, Inc.
Roberts, Ann R. Fund of the Four Directions
Roberts, Dwight V. Pilot Trust
Roberts, Frank. The David and Lucile Packard Foundation, The Dean Witter Foundation
Roberts, George R. The Roberts Foundation
Roberts, JoAnn M. Chesapeake Bay Trust
Roberts, Leanne B. The Roberts Foundation
Roberts, Melanie A. The Summerlee Foundation
Roberts, Virgil Patrick. California Community Foundation
Robertson, Oran B. Meyer Memorial Trust
Robertson, Tom. San Diego Community Foundation
Robertson, William, IV. The Andrew W. Mellon Foundation
Robertson, Wyndham. Mary Reynolds Babcock Foundation, Inc.
Robinson, James D., III. American Express Philanthropic Program, Union Pacific Foundation
Robinson, John R. The Beinecke Foundation, Inc.
Robinson, Joseph R. Ruth Mott Fund
Robinson, Priscilla. The Community Foundation Serving Coastal South Carolina
Robinson, Ray M. AT&T Foundation
Robinson, Robert J. Community Foundation of Western North Carolina, Inc.
Robinson, Sylvia B. The Beinecke Foundation, Inc.
Robinson, Thomas E. The Troy Foundation
Robinson, W. T. Chesapeake Corporation Foundation
Rockefeller, Barbara Bellows. Rockefeller Family Fund, Inc.
Rockefeller, David, Jr. Alaska Conservation Foundation, Rockefeller Brothers Fund, Inc.
Rockefeller, Diana N. Rockefeller Family Fund, Inc.
Rockefeller, Laurance. American Conservation Association, Inc., Jackson Hole Preserve, Inc., DeWitt Wallace-Reader's Digest Fund, Lila Wallace-Reader's Digest Fund
Rockefeller, Lisenne. Rockefeller Family Fund, Inc.
Rockefeller, Marilyn. Maine Community Foundation, Inc.
Rockefeller, Richard G. Rockefeller Brothers Fund, Inc., Rockefeller Family Fund, Inc.
Rockefeller, Steven C. Rockefeller Brothers Fund, Inc., Rockefeller Family Fund, Inc.
Rockefeller, Wendy G. Rockefeller Family Fund, Inc.

Rockefeller, Winthrop Paul. The Winthrop Rockefeller Foundation
Rockland, David B. National Fish and Wildlife Foundation, Times Mirror Magazines, Inc.
Rodgers, David A. The Austin Memorial Foundation
Rodriguez, Cecilia. Funding Exchange
Rodriguez, Pablo. The Rhode Island Community Foundation
Roedel, Paul R. The Wyomissing Foundation, Inc.
Rogers, Elijah B. The Foundation for the National Capital Region
Rogers, Jane. The San Francisco Foundation
Rogers, William P. The Morris and Gwendolyn Cafritz Foundation
Rogers, William R. Mary Reynolds Babcock Foundation, Inc.
Rohlfing, John H. Atherton Family Foundation
Rollefson, Virginia R. The Rockfall Foundation
Romans, John N. Robert Sterling Clark Foundation, Inc.
Romasco, Anne. James C. Penney Foundation
Romero, Anthony. Ford Foundation
Romney, Mark A. Lee Romney Foundation, Inc.
Romney, Michael. Lee Romney Foundation, Inc.
Rooks, Charles S. Meyer Memorial Trust
Rooney, Phillip B. WMX Environmental Grants Program
Roosevelt, Laura D. J. P. Morgan Charitable Trust
Roper, Wayne J. The Lynde and Harry Bradley Foundation, Inc.
Rosacker, Jo Helen. Sid W. Richardson Foundation
Rosario, Rosaida Morales. Hartford Foundation for Public Giving
Rose, John C. Charles E. Culpeper Foundation, Inc.
Rosenbaum, Sari A. The Rockfall Foundation
Rosenberg, Richard M. BankAmerica Foundation
Rosengarten, T. Jefferies. Sproul Foundation
Rosenthal, Alan. The Schumann Fund for New Jersey, Inc.
Rosenzweig, Elias. Herman Goldman Foundation
Rosin, Axel G. The Scherman Foundation, Inc.
Rosin, Katharine S. The Scherman Foundation, Inc.
Rosner, Bernat. Magowan Family Foundation, Inc.
Rosovsky, Henry. United States-Japan Foundation
Ross, D. P., Jr. Fair Play Foundation

Officers, Trustees, Directors, and Contacts

Ross, Donald K. Rockefeller Family Fund, Inc., Tortuga Foundation
Ross, Sharryn. Azadoutioun Foundation
Ross, Walter. Laidlaw Foundation
Roswell, The Honorable Rosemary. Chesapeake Bay Trust
Rotan, Caroline P. The William Stamps Farish Fund
Rotella, Joseph. The Harding Educational and Charitable Foundation
Roth, Robert W. Union Pacific Foundation
Rothblatt, Ben. Lloyd A. Fry Foundation
Rothchild, Kennon V. The Bush Foundation
Rothenbeg, Irwin S. The Sonoma County Community Foundation
Rothenburg, James M. The Community Foundation of Sarasota County, Inc.
Rothrock, Gayle. Northwest Fund for the Environment
Rothschild, Robert F. Maine Community Foundation, Inc.
Roupe, Barbara Doyle. The Community Foundation of Santa Clara County
Rouse, Eloise Meadows. Meadows Foundation, Inc.
Roush, G. James. The GAR Foundation
Roush, George C. The GAR Foundation
Roush, Thomas W. The GAR Foundation
Rowe, George, Jr. G. Unger Vetlesen Foundation
Rowen, Henry S. Smith Richardson Foundation, Inc.
Rower, Howard. Threshold Foundation
Rowley, Brenda. Bay Area Community Foundation
Rowley, Peggy. Bay Area Community Foundation
Roy, Delwin A. The Hitachi Foundation
Roy, Krishna K. National Fish and Wildlife Foundation
Rubinger, Michael. The Pew Charitable Trusts
Rubinow, Raymond S. The J. M. Kaplan Fund, Inc.
Rudin, Eric. Samuel and May Rudin Foundation, Inc.
Rudin, Jack. Samuel and May Rudin Foundation, Inc.
Rudin, Katherine. Samuel and May Rudin Foundation, Inc.
Rudin, Lewis. Samuel and May Rudin Foundation, Inc.
Rudin, William. Samuel and May Rudin Foundation, Inc.
Rudolph, Kurt. Bay Area Community Foundation
Rueckert, William D. Cleveland H. Dodge Foundation, Inc.
Ruhl, John R. E. Community Foundation of Western North Carolina, Inc.
Rumbough, J. Wright, Jr. The Stebbins Fund, Inc.
Ruocco, Roberta A. J. P. Morgan Charitable Trust

Rupert, Barbara L. The Bunbury Company, Inc.
Rupp, Gerald E. The Vidda Foundation
Rupp, Sheron A. Fran and Warren Rupp Foundation
Ruppe, Loret M. The William and Flora Hewlett Foundation
Ruppert, Barbara L. The Bunbury Company, Inc.
Rupple, Brenton H. The Milwaukee Foundation
Rush, Helen P. Vira I. Heinz Endowment
Rush, Raymond J. Charles Hayden Foundation
Russell, Carol L. Mustard Seed Foundation, Inc.
Russell, Charles P. Columbia Foundation
Russell, Christine H. Columbia Foundation, Levi Strauss Foundation
Russell, Evelyn Beveridge. The Frank Stanley Beveridge Foundation, Inc.
Russell, G. L. Baltimore Gas and Electric Foundation, Inc.
Russell, Gordon. Peninsula Community Foundation
Russell, Jenny D. Island Foundation, Inc.
Russell, Kelly. Flintridge Foundation
Russell, Madeleine H. Columbia Foundation
Russell, Marjorie. Leo Model Foundation, Inc.
Russell, Robert J. Mustard Seed Foundation, Inc.
Russell-Alexander, Yolanda. A Territory Resource
Russell-Shapiro, Alice. Columbia Foundation
Rust, Thomas G. Vancouver Foundation
Ruth, David A. American Express Philanthropic Program
Rutherfurd, Guy G. The Achelis Foundation, The Bodman Foundation
Ryan, Carl E. El Paso Community Foundation
Ryan, James R. The Minneapolis Foundation
Ryan, John T., Jr. Vira I. Heinz Endowment
Ryan, M. Catherine. The Bersted Foundation
Ryan, Michael E. The New York Times Company Foundation, Inc.
Ryan, Shirley W. The Chicago Community Trust
Rydland, Robert H. The Minneapolis Foundation
Rymer, Judith. Unitarian Universalist Veatch Program at Shelter Rock
Ryskamp, Charles A. The Andrew W. Mellon Foundation

S

Saal, Harry J. The Community Foundation of Santa Clara County

Saario, Terry T. Northwest Area Foundation
Saavedra, Carlos. Charles Stewart Mott Foundation
Sachs, Carolyn. Benton Foundation
Sack, Suzanne. Anna B. Stearns Charitable Foundation, Inc.
Saenger, Ted J. The San Francisco Foundation
Saengswang, Dolly. Echoing Green Foundation
Saghy, Diane. American Foundation Corporation
Saigeon, Katherine L. W. K. Kellogg Foundation
St. Germaine, Brenda. The Minneapolis Foundation
Sakaguchi, Russell G. ARCO Foundation
Sakai, Shinji. Toyota USA Foundation
Salerno, Mary Beth. American Express Philanthropic Program
Salk, Jonas. The John D. and Catherine T. MacArthur Foundation
Salka, Peggy Kyoko. The New World Foundation
Salter, Lee W. The McConnell Foundation
Saltonstall, William L. Middlecott Foundation
Salvucci, Fred. The Energy Foundation
Salwasser, Harold. Pew Scholars Program in Conservation and the Environment
Sambo, Dalee. Seventh Generation Fund
Samelson, Judy Y. Charles Stewart Mott Foundation
Sampson, David S. American Conservation Association, Inc.
San Miguel, Carmen Febo. The Philadelphia Foundation
Sanchez, David J., Jr. The San Francisco Foundation
Sanchez, S. J. The Marshall L. & Perrine D. McCune Charitable Foundation
Sandberg, Paul W. Gebbie Foundation, Inc.
Sandefur, Tana. The Community Foundation of Sarasota County, Inc.
Sander, Ann Switzer. The Switzer Foundation
Sanders, Elizabeth T. Marcia Brady Tucker Foundation
Sanders, Wilfred L., Jr. Greater Piscataqua Community Foundation
Sandler, David P. Arcadia Foundation
Sandman, Dan D. USX Foundation, Inc.
Sandusky, Gary. A Territory Resource
Sant, Alexis G. The Summit Foundation
Sant, Alison E. The Summit Foundation
Sant, Kristin W. The Summit Foundation
Sant, Michael J. The Summit Foundation
Sant, Roger W. The Summit Foundation
Sant, Shari L. The Summit Foundation
Sant, Victoria P. The Foundation for the National Capital Region, The Summit Foundation
Sarabi, Brigette. McKenzie River Gathering Foundation

Officers, Directors, Trustees, and Contacts

Sasakawa, Yohei. United States-Japan Foundation
Sasser, Barbara Weston. Harris and Eliza Kempner Fund
Saterson, Kathryn A. Pew Scholars Program in Conservation and the Environment
Sato, Suzanne. AT&T Foundation
Satut, Miguel A. The Kresge Foundation
Saucedo, Mary Carmen. El Paso Community Foundation
Saul, B. Francis. National Geographic Society Education Foundation
Saunders, Carol H. The Hastings Trust
Saunders-Jones, Ingrid. Metropolitan Atlanta Community Foundation, Inc.
Savidge, Chuck. The Community Foundation of Sarasota County, Inc.
Savitt, Charles. The Tides Foundation
Savitz, Maxine. The Energy Foundation
Sawyer, Alden H., Jr. Davis Conservation Foundation
Sawyer, W. Tom. Maine Community Foundation, Inc.
Scaife, Curtis S. Laurel Foundation
Scaife, Richard M. Sarah Scaife Foundation Incorporated
Scandling, William F. The Community Foundation of Santa Clara County
Scanlon, Thomas J. Public Welfare Foundation, Inc.
Schacht, Henry B. Ford Foundation
Schad, Jacqueline. The Tides Foundation
Schad, Leah. Environmental Education Foundation of Florida, Inc.
Schafer, Carl W. Atlantic Foundation
Schelinski, Linda K. The Joyce Foundation
Schell, John Q. Community Foundation of Western North Carolina, Inc.
Schell, Kristine. The Max and Anna Levinson Foundation
Schell, Marshall. The Fund for Preservation of Wildlife and Natural Areas
Scherman, John. Great Lakes Protection Fund
Scheuer, Richard J. S. H. and Helen R. Scheuer Family Foundation, Inc.
Schiff, Andrew N. The Schiff Foundation
Schiff, David T. The Schiff Foundation
Schiff, Peter G. The Schiff Foundation
Schiller, Elmyra F. Felburn Foundation
Schmidt, Edward J., Jr. The Community Foundation of Sarasota County, Inc.
Schmidt, Peter. The Dragon Foundation, Inc.
Schmidt, Thomas M. Laurel Foundation
Schmidt, William L. Benua Foundation, Inc.
Schneider, Gail. Herman Goldman Foundation
Schneider, Henry. Henry and Lucy Moses Fund, Inc.
Schneider, Hubert G. The 1525 Foundation
Schneider, Stephen H. Pew Scholars Program in Conservation and the Environment

Schoendorf, Anthony. Norcross Wildlife Foundation, Inc.
Schoenke, Richard W. The Minneapolis Foundation
Scholz, Garret A. McKesson Foundation, Inc.
Schornack, Dennis L. Great Lakes Protection Fund
Schreck, Albert. The Abelard Foundation West
Schreck, Celeste G. The Abelard Foundation West
Schreck, Charles R. The Abelard Foundation West
Schreck, Christine. The Abelard Foundation West
Schreck, Daniel W. The Abelard Foundation West
Schreck, Jean. The Abelard Foundation West
Schreck, Joel. The Abelard Foundation West
Schreck, Thomas A. The Abelard Foundation West
Schroeder, Clinton A. The Minneapolis Foundation
Schroth, Virginia Cowles. The Cowles Charitable Trust
Schuette, William D. The Rollin M. Gerstacker Foundation
Schulhof, Lary A. Community Foundation of Western North Carolina, Inc.
Schulte, Anthony M. The Scherman Foundation, Inc.
Schultz, Clifford G., II. Schultz Foundation, Inc.
Schultz, Frederick H., Jr. Schultz Foundation, Inc.
Schultz, Gary. The Nelson B. Delavan Foundation
Schultz, George P. The Boeing Company
Schultz, John R. Schultz Foundation, Inc.
Schultz, Nancy R. Schultz Foundation, Inc.
Schultz, Rhoda W. The Bothin Foundation
Schulz, Jean. The Sonoma County Community Foundation
Schumann, Robert F. The Florence and John Schumann Foundation
Schumann, W. Ford. The Florence and John Schumann Foundation
Schwanfelder, Nancy Healy. The M. A. Healy Family Foundation, Inc.
Schwartz, Mrs. Alan E. Hudson-Webber Foundation
Schwartz, Gary D. Fund of the Four Directions
Schwartz, Renee G. The New-Land Foundation, Inc.
Schweizer, Thomas, Jr. Alex. Brown & Sons Charitable Foundation, Inc.
Schwendener, Benjamin O., Jr. Dart Foundation
Scott, David W. Ford Motor Company Fund
Scott, Eileen M. The Andrew W. Mellon Foundation
Scott, James R. Northwest Area Foundation

Scott, Roderic M. The Perkin Fund
Scott, Sharon Rosenfeld. Lee Romney Foundation, Inc.
Scott, Wesley L. Patrick and Anna M. Cudahy Fund
Scoville, Thomas W. Public Welfare Foundation, Inc.
Scranton, William W. Howard Heinz Endowment
Scripps, Paul K. Ellen Browning Scripps Foundation
Scrudato, Ronald J. Great Lakes Protection Fund
Scully, Arthur M., Jr. Richard King Mellon Foundation
Seamans, Robert C., Jr. National Geographic Society Education Foundation
Sedgewick, Walter. Island Foundation
Sedgwick, Jeanne C. The David and Lucile Packard Foundation
Seed, Harris W. Alice Tweed Tuohy Foundation
Seelenfreund, Alan. McKesson Foundation, Inc.
Segal, Susan L. The Tinker Foundation Incorporated
Segall, Harold A. Philip D. Reed Foundation, Inc.
Seitz, Frederick. Richard Lounsbery Foundation, Inc.
Seitz, Howard A. Arthur M. and Olga T. Eisig-Arthur M. and Kate E. Tode Foundation, Inc.
Sejima, Ryuzo. United States-Japan Foundation
Sellar, Robert N. IBM Corporation
Semans, Truman T. Alex. Brown & Sons Charitable Foundation, Inc.
Sembler, Debbie. Foundation for Deep Ecology
Seneker, Stanley A. Ford Motor Company Fund
Senturia, Brenda B. The Cameron Baird Foundation
Setzer, Gene W. American Conservation Association, Inc., Jackson Hole Preserve, Inc.
Sewall, Elmina B. Elmina B. Sewall Foundation
Seydel, Laura Turner. Turner Foundation, Inc.
Shackelton, Scott. Walter S. Johnson Foundation
Shafer, Carl. Atlantic Foundation
Shafroth, Tracey. Prince Charitable Trusts
Shakely, Jack. California Community Foundation
Shakespeare, Frank. The Lynde and Harry Bradley Foundation, Inc.
Shaler, Steve. Blandin Foundation
Shanahan, John. The Sonoma County Community Foundation
Shanley, Kevin. Victoria Foundation, Inc.

Officers, Trustees, Directors, and Contacts

Shannon, James P. General Service Foundation
Shapiro, Isaac. The Trust For Mutual Understanding
Shapleigh, Warren M. Spencer T. and Ann W. Olin Foundation, Union Pacific Foundation
Sharp, H. Rodney, III. Longwood Foundation, Inc.
Sharp, Paul F. Sarkeys Foundation
Sharpe, Deedee. Environmental Education Foundation of Florida, Inc.
Shattuck, Mayo A., III. Alex. Brown & Sons Charitable Foundation, Inc.
Shaw, Albert T. The Hofmann Foundation
Shaw, Ann. California Community Foundation
Shaw, George T. Jessie B. Cox Charitable Trust
Shaw, Meg. Laird, Norton Foundation
Shay, Sue Ann. Hartford Foundation for Public Giving
Sheehan, Paula. The Windham Foundation, Inc.
Sheer, Ruth C. The Cabot Family Charitable Trust
Shelby, Doug. Environmental Education Foundation of Florida, Inc.
Shelden, W. Warren. McGregor Fund
Sheldon, J. Elizabeth. Ralph C. Sheldon Foundation, Inc.
Sheldon, James N. Weeden Foundation
Shellington, Kathleen. Arcadia Foundation
Shelton, Christine B. Town Creek Foundation, Inc.
Shenk, Janet. The Arca Foundation
Shepard, Julia S. The Morris and Gwendolyn Cafritz Foundation
Shephard, Yvonne M. AT&T Foundation
Sher, Jonathan. The Winthrop Rockefeller Foundation
Sher, Kathleen Cloyd. Chesapeake Bay Trust
Sheridan, John J. Helen Brach Foundation
Sherman, A. Joshua. The Cricket Foundation
Sherrill, The Reverend H. W. Good Samaritan, Inc.
Sherwood, John F. New Horizon Foundation
Sherwood, R. M. Chrysler Corporation Fund
Shestock, Linda. California Community Foundation
Shih, Daphne B. The Howard Bayne Fund
Shinn, George L. The New York Times Company Foundation, Inc.
Shipley, Walter V. DeWitt Wallace-Reader's Digest Fund, Lila Wallace-Reader's Digest Fund
Shirai, Scott. Hawaiian Electric Industries Charitable Foundation
Shivery, C. W. Baltimore Gas and Electric Foundation, Inc.
Short, Harry S. Ederic Foundation, Inc.

Shorter, Minnie. The USF&G Foundation, Inc.
Shortridge, Kenneth W., Jr. The Community Foundation Serving Coastal South Carolina
Shrontz, Frank. The Boeing Company
Shumate, Alex. The Columbus Foundation
Shumway, Forrest N. The James Irvine Foundation
Shute, Benjamin R., Jr. Rockefeller Brothers Fund, Inc.
Shutz, Caleb. IBM Corporation
Sibley, James M. Joseph B. Whitehead Foundation, Robert W. Woodruff Foundation, Inc.
Siceloff, Millie L. Tortuga Foundation
Sidamon-Eristoff, Anne P. Howard Phipps Foundation
Sidford, Holly. Lila Wallace-Reader's Digest Fund
Siegfried, Peter C. Pinewood Foundation
Sievers, Bruce R. Walter and Elise Haas Fund
Signom, Lola A. AT&T Foundation
Silbersack, Donna C. The Jacob and Annita France Foundation, Inc., Robert G. and Anne M. Merrick Foundation, Inc.
Silk, Susan C. Columbia Foundation
Silliman, Henry H., Jr. Longwood Foundation, Inc.
Silverman, Fred. Apple Computer, Inc.
Silverman, Sandra. The Scherman Foundation, Inc.
Silverstein, Duane. The Goldman Environmental Foundation, Richard & Rhoda Goldman Fund
Silwinski, Robert A. Centerior Energy Foundation
Simmons, Adele. The John D. and Catherine T. MacArthur Foundation
Simmons, Caroline T. MARPAT Foundation, Inc.
Simmons, Hildy J. J. P. Morgan Charitable Trust
Simmons, Richard D. Union Pacific Foundation
Simon, Leonard. The Robert Brownlee Foundation
Simon, R. Matthew. Helen Brach Foundation
Simon, Raymond F. Helen Brach Foundation
Simonsen, Sven-Erik. The Community Foundation of Santa Clara County
Simonson, Anne Larsen. Larsen Fund, Inc.
Simpson, Abby R. Rockefeller Family Fund, Inc.
Sims, Howard F. W. K. Kellogg Foundation
Sims, Jennifer A. Peninsula Community Foundation
Sims, Robert B. National Geographic Society Education Foundation
Sinkler, Sallie. The Community Foundation Serving Coastal South Carolina

Sipp, Donald C. Sarah Scaife Foundation Incorporated
Sisk, John F. Oliver S. and Jennie R. Donaldson Charitable Trust
Sitnick, Irving. Henry and Lucy Moses Fund, Inc.
Skaggs, Beverly R. The Skaggs Foundation
Skaggs, Samuel D. The Skaggs Foundation
Skipper, J. Ronald. The Community Foundation of Sarasota County, Inc.
Skjerdal, Lloyd. The Mary A. Crocker Trust
Skloot, Edward. Surdna Foundation, Inc.
Slaney, Barbara L. Sarah Scaife Foundation Incorporated
Slaughter, William E., Jr. Henry E. and Consuelo S. Wenger Foundation, Inc.
Sliger, Bernard. Environmental Education Foundation of Florida, Inc.
Slocombe, Walt. Stern Family Fund
Slutsky, Lorie A. The New York Community Trust
Small, Gail. A Territory Resource
Small, Malinda B. Baltimore Gas and Electric Foundation, Inc.
Smart, Paul M. Centerior Energy Foundation
Smart, S. Bruce, Jr. The Chevron Companies
Smith, A. Zachary, III. Foundation for the Carolinas
Smith, Bradford D. Edward John Noble Foundation, Inc.
Smith, Bruce R. Onan Family Foundation
Smith, C. A. Chrysler Corporation Fund
Smith, Cherida C. The Collins Foundation
Smith, Christopher. L. L. Bean, Inc.
Smith, Clifford V., Jr. GE Fund
Smith, David L. Abell-Hanger Foundation
Smith, David S. Edward John Noble Foundation, Inc.
Smith, Donald E. Fran and Warren Rupp Foundation
Smith, E. J. Noble. Edward John Noble Foundation, Inc.
Smith, Elizabeth B. The Hyams Foundation
Smith, Eric. Alaska Conservation Foundation
Smith, Fred. Jackson Hole Preserve, Inc.
Smith, Jane Renfro. Cooke Foundation, Limited, Hawaii Community Foundation
Smith, Janet. Hawaii Community Foundation
Smith, Jean French. California Community Foundation
Smith, Jeffrey. Laidlaw Foundation
Smith, Jeremy T. Edward John Noble Foundation, Inc.
Smith, Joshua I. The Foundation for the National Capital Region
Smith, Kathryn R. Philip D. Reed Foundation, Inc.
Smith, L. L. Shell Oil Company Foundation
Smith, Langhorne B. Claneil Foundation, Inc.
Smith, M. B., Jr. Union Pacific Foundation
Smith, Malcolm. New York Foundation

© 1995 Environmental Data Resources, Inc.

Officers, Directors, Trustees, and Contacts

Smith, Margaret T. The Kresge Foundation
Smith, May. Stanley Smith Horticultural Trust
Smith, Pat. Community Foundation of Western North Carolina, Inc.
Smith, Peter. Ottinger Foundation
Smith, Robert D. Laidlaw Foundation
Smith, Roger V. The Community Foundation of Santa Clara County
Smith, Sherwood H., Jr. Z. Smith Reynolds Foundation, Inc.
Smith, Susan J. Onan Family Foundation
Smith, Terry. National Geographic Society Education Foundation
Smith, Thelma G. The 1525 Foundation
Smith, Theodore. The Henry P. Kendall Foundation
Smith, Timothy S. Fran and Warren Rupp Foundation
Smith, Zachary. Mary Reynolds Babcock Foundation, Inc., Z. Smith Reynolds Foundation, Inc.
Smith-Ganey, Anne L. Oliver S. and Jennie R. Donaldson Charitable Trust
Smyth, Maureen H. Great Lakes Protection Fund, Charles Stewart Mott Foundation
Snake, Reuben, Jr. Seventh Generation Fund
Sneag, Lawrence O. Ittleson Foundation, Inc.
Snodgrass, John F. The Samuel Roberts Noble Foundation, Inc.
Snyder, Barbara J. The Wortham Foundation, Inc.
Solana, Nancy. Leland Fikes Foundation, Inc.
Solinger, Hope G. Bernard F. and Alva B. Gimbel Foundation, Inc.
Sollins, Karen R. The Scherman Foundation, Inc.
Solnit, Albert J. The New-Land Foundation, Inc.
Solomon, Milton D. The Bydale Foundation
Solow, Robert. The Energy Foundation
Solow, Sheldon H. Solow Foundation
Sommer, Barbara A. The Louis Calder Foundation
Sondheim, Walter, Jr. The Abell Foundation
Sono, Ayako. United States-Japan Foundation
Sopher, Raeman P. Lintilhac Foundation
Sorensen, Ruth Cummings. The Nathan Cummings Foundation
Sosland, Morton I. The Hall Family Foundation
Spaeth, Edmund B., Jr. The William Penn Foundation
Spalding, Charles C., Jr. Cooke Foundation, Limited
Sparber, Norman H. Herman Goldman Foundation
Speaks, Don. Metropolitan Atlanta Community Foundation, Inc.
Spells, Raymond, Jr. Community Foundation of Western North Carolina, Inc.
Speltz, Kathleen A. The Minneapolis Foundation
Spence, Lewis H. The Hyams Foundation
Spencer, Robert Donner. Donner Canadian Foundation
Spencer, William L. Foundation for the Carolinas
Spero, Joan E. American Express Philanthropic Program
Spickard, Brian D. Georgia Power Foundation, Inc.
Spika, Nicholas C. Sequoia Foundation
Spingarn, Art. Joy Foundation for Ecological Education and Research
Spitzer, Doreen C. Ward M. & Mariam C. Canaday Educational and Charitable Trust
Spitzer, Lyman, Jr. Ward M. & Mariam C. Canaday Educational and Charitable Trust
Spivey, Barry F. The Community Foundation of Sarasota County, Inc.
Splinter, Betty Ann M. Hawaiian Electric Industries Charitable Foundation
Spradling, Thomas L. Community Foundation of Western North Carolina, Inc.
Sprague, Ronald. Environmental Endowment for New Jersey, Inc.
Sprenger, Mark W. The Milwaukee Foundation
Stabler, Amelia Taper. S. Mark Taper Foundation
Stabler, W. Laird, Jr. Welfare Foundation, Inc.
Stack, Edward W. The Clark Foundation
Stackpole, R. Dauer. The Community Foundation Serving Coastal South Carolina
Stafford, Robert T. The Goldman Environmental Foundation
Staley, Warren R. The Cargill Foundation
Stammen, Jerrold R. The Troy Foundation
Stanley, Alfred T. Alfred T. Stanley Foundation
Stanley, Beulah. Alfred T. Stanley Foundation
Stanley, Edmund A., Jr. Town Creek Foundation, Inc.
Stanley, Jennifer. Town Creek Foundation, Inc.
Stanley, Lisa A. Town Creek Foundation, Inc.
Stark, Donald B. The Ahmanson Foundation
Starr, S. Frederick. Rockefeller Brothers Fund, Inc.
Stauber, Karl N. Northwest Area Foundation
Steadman, Richard C. The German Marshall Fund of the United States
Stearns, Laura Lee. Douroucouli Foundation
Stearns, Stewart W. The Community Foundation of Sarasota County, Inc.
Stebbins, Edwin E. F. The Stebbins Fund, Inc.
Stebbins, James F. The Stebbins Fund, Inc.
Stebbins, Michael Morgan. The Stebbins Fund, Inc.
Stebbins, Theodore E. The Stebbins Fund, Inc.
Stebbins, Theodore E., Jr. The Stebbins Fund, Inc.
Stebman, Betty J. The Charles Evans Hughes Memorial Foundation, Inc.
Stecher, Patsy Palmer. The Frank Stanley Beveridge Foundation, Inc.
Stein, Edith C. LaSalle Adams Fund
Stein, Mary Ann. The Moriah Fund, Inc.
Steinbright, Marilyn L. Arcadia Foundation
Steinhauer, Bruce W. McGregor Fund
Stella, Ethel. Norcross Wildlife Foundation, Inc.
Stender, Bruce W. Blandin Foundation
Stepanian, Tania. The Mary A. Crocker Trust
Stephan, Edmund A. Lloyd A. Fry Foundation
Stephanoff, Kathryn. Harry C. Trexler Trust
Stephens, Ann C. Compton Foundation, Inc.
Stephens, K. F. True North Foundation
Stephens, Martha Roby. The Cowles Charitable Trust
Sterling, Helen N. Rockwell Fund, Inc.
Stern, Fritz. The German Marshall Fund of the United States
Stern, Lynn. Bernard F. and Alva B. Gimbel Foundation, Inc.
Stern, Peter. Vanguard Public Foundation
Stern, Philip M. Stern Family Fund
Sterret, David J. Great Lakes Protection Fund
Stetson, E. William, III. Smith Richardson Foundation, Inc.
Stetter, Jean. The Ben & Jerry's Foundation
Stevens, James W. Geraldine R. Dodge Foundation, Inc.
Stevens, Robert T., Jr. Fanwood Foundation
Stevens, Whitney. Fanwood Foundation
Stevenson, John R. The Andrew W. Mellon Foundation
Stevenson, Louise. James & Abigail Campbell Foundation
Steves, David A. The Community Foundation of Sarasota County, Inc.
Stewart, Donald M. The New York Times Company Foundation, Inc.
Stewart, John D. The Community Foundation Serving Coastal South Carolina
Stewart, Marise Meynet. C. S. Fund
Stewart, Robert T. Vancouver Foundation
Stine, Thomas Henry. Thanksgiving Foundation
Stirn, Cara S. The Kelvin and Eleanor Smith Foundation
Stirn, Howard F. Kelvin Smith 1980 Charitable Trust

Officers, Trustees, Directors, and Contacts

Stivers, William C. Weyerhaeuser Company Foundation
Stockdale, Judith. Gaylord and Dorothy Donnelley Foundation
Stockholm, Charles M. The Wallace Alexander Gerbode Foundation, Inc.
Stockholm, Maryanna G. The Wallace Alexander Gerbode Foundation, Inc.
Stoddard, Helen E. Stoddard Charitable Trust
Stoehr, Elizabeth. Marcia Brady Tucker Foundation
Stoehr, Naomi T. Marcia Brady Tucker Foundation
Stoel, Thomas B. The Collins Foundation, Rose E. Tucker Charitable Trust
Stokes, Jerome W. D. Public Welfare Foundation, Inc.
Stokes, Samuel N. MARPAT Foundation, Inc.
Stokes, Shirlee. Crystal Channel Foundation
Stokes, Thomas C. Gates Foundation
Stone, Cathleen Douglas. American Conservation Association, Inc.
Stone, Roger. The Armand G. Erpf Fund, Inc.
Stookey, John Hoyt. The Clark Foundation
Stoorza-Gill, Gail. San Diego Community Foundation
Storey, Robert D. The Kresge Foundation
Storey, Theodore. Alfred T. Stanley Foundation
Storm, Anne M. Laird, Norton Foundation
Stott, Frederic A. Davis Conservation Foundation
Stover, Joan L. The Sonoma County Community Foundation
Straine, James J. The Prudential Foundation
Straitor, George A. Walter and Josephine Ford Fund
Stranahan, Abbot. The Needmor Fund
Stranahan, Ann. The Needmor Fund
Stranahan, Duane, Jr. Stranahan Foundation
Stranahan, Duane, Sr. Stranahan Foundation
Stranahan, Mark. Stranahan Foundation
Stranahan, Mary C. The Needmor Fund
Stranahan, Mescal. Stranahan Foundation
Stranahan, Molly L. The Needmor Fund
Stranahan, Robert A., Jr. Stranahan Foundation
Stranahan, Sarah. The Needmor Fund
Stranahan, Stephen. The Needmor Fund
Stratton, Jim. Alaska Conservation Foundation
Strauss, Elizabeth. Winifred & Harry B. Allen Foundation
Straw, Sylvana R. The Foundation for the National Capital Region
Strawbridge, Herbert E. John P. Murphy Foundation
Strawbridge, Marie S. John P. Murphy Foundation

Stroh, C. Penfield. The Stroh Foundation
Stroh, Gari M., Jr. The Stroh Foundation
Stroh, John W., Jr. The Stroh Foundation
Stroh, John W., III. The Stroh Foundation
Stroh, Peter W. McGregor Fund, The Stroh Foundation
Strom, Lee D. Roy E. Crummer Foundation
Strong, Mary S. The Fund for New Jersey
Stroud, W. B. Dixon. Stroud Foundation
Strumpf, Linda B. Ford Foundation
Stryker, S. C. Shell Oil Company Foundation
Stuart, Gary M. Union Pacific Foundation
Stupf, E. A., III. The Wortham Foundation, Inc.
Sturdevant, Don. FishAmerica Foundation
Styles, Hurdie. A Territory Resource
Suarez, Rocio. The George F. Baker Trust
Sullivan, Edward. Henry B. Plant Memorial Fund, Inc.
Sullivan, James N. The Chevron Companies
Sullivan, Jeffrey W. Laird, Norton Foundation
Sullivan, Michael. Baltimore Gas and Electric Foundation, Inc.
Sullivan, Paul B. Ralph C. Sheldon Foundation, Inc.
Sullivan, Richard J. Environmental Endowment for New Jersey, Inc., The Fund for New Jersey
Sullivan, Sallie. Perkins Charitable Foundation
Sullivan, T. Dennis. The Andrew W. Mellon Foundation
Sullivan, Virginia M. Ruth Mott Fund
Sulzberger, Arthur Ochs. The New York Times Company Foundation, Inc., The Sulzberger Foundation, Inc.
Sulzberger, Judith P. The New York Times Company Foundation, Inc., The Sulzberger Foundation, Inc.
Summerfield, Esthel M. The Abell Foundation
Summers, Anita A. The William Penn Foundation
Sunada, Chris. Atherton Family Foundation
Sunstein, Leon C., Jr. The Philadelphia Foundation
Sunzeri, Franklin. The Robert Brownlee Foundation
Surdam, Robert M. McGregor Fund
Surrey, Mary P. The Max and Victoria Dreyfus Foundation, Inc.
Sutkowski, Frank J. The Rockfall Foundation
Svigals, Philip. Robert Sterling Clark Foundation, Inc.
Swaminathan, Monkombu S. Ford Foundation
Swaney, Robert E., Jr. Charles Stewart Mott Foundation
Swann, Elizabeth. Environmental Education Foundation of Florida, Inc.
Swanson, Lynwood W. M. J. Murdock Charitable Trust

Swantak, Judy L. Union Pacific Foundation
Sweet, Anne. McKenzie River Gathering Foundation
Swetland, David Sears. Sears-Swetland Foundation
Swetland, David W. Sears-Swetland Foundation
Switzer, Fred. The Switzer Foundation
Switzer, Marge. The Switzer Foundation
Switzer, Patricia. The Switzer Foundation
Switzer, Paul. The Switzer Foundation
Switzer, Robert. The Switzer Foundation
Sykes, James W., Jr. The William and Mary Greve Foundation, Inc.
Sykes, Jane S. The Stebbins Fund, Inc.
Sylvester, Manuel R. Hawaii Community Foundation
Syrmis, Pamela. Ittleson Foundation, Inc.
Syrmis, Victor. Ittleson Foundation, Inc.
Szymanski, Joan E. Snee-Reinhardt Charitable Foundation

T

Tabankin, Margery. The Arca Foundation
Taber, George H. Richard King Mellon Foundation
Tabor, Gary. Geraldine R. Dodge Foundation, Inc.
Tafoya, Linda S. Adolph Coors Foundation
Taft, John E. The Sudbury Foundation
Takeda, Kent M. AT&T Foundation
Talberth, Charlotte. The Max and Anna Levinson Foundation
Talbot, Phillips. United States-Japan Foundation
Talbott, Josephine L. Nelson Talbott Foundation
Talbott, Nelson S. Nelson Talbott Foundation
Tamblyn, Wayne I. Georgia-Pacific Foundation
Tannen, Naomi. The Ben & Jerry's Foundation
Tanner, Derry. The Sudbury Foundation
Tanner, Howard. FishAmerica Foundation
Tanner, Mary. Environmental Education Foundation of Florida, Inc.
Taracido, M. D. New York Foundation
Tarr, Gregory L. McKesson Foundation, Inc.
Tasch, Edward B. Jessie Smith Noyes Foundation, Inc.
Tata, Ratan N. Ford Foundation
Tate, Lloyd P., Jr. Z. Smith Reynolds Foundation, Inc.
Taveras, Barbara A. The Edward W. Hazen Foundation
Taviner, Gloria. Kinnoull Foundation
Taylor Farland, Melanie. Kathleen Price and Joseph M. Bryan Family Foundation, Inc.
Taylor, Alfred H., Jr. The Kresge Foundation

Officers, Directors, Trustees, and Contacts

Taylor, Allen M. The Lynde and Harry Bradley Foundation, Inc.
Taylor, Barbara Olin. Spencer T. and Ann W. Olin Foundation
Taylor, Betsy. Merck Family Fund, Ottinger Foundation, Town Creek Foundation, Inc.
Taylor, Edwin D. The Community Foundation of Sarasota County, Inc.
Taylor, F. Morgan, Jr. Spencer T. and Ann W. Olin Foundation
Taylor, Jack. The Sonoma County Community Foundation
Taylor, John Guest. Kathleen Price and Joseph M. Bryan Family Foundation, Inc.
Taylor, Judith G. Metropolitan Atlanta Community Foundation, Inc.
Taylor, Lynn. Charles G. Koch Charitable Foundation
Taylor, Sir George. Stanley Smith Horticultural Trust
Taylor, Timothy A. Clark Charitable Trust
Taylor, William G. Springs Foundation, Inc.
Taylor, William O. The New York Times Company Foundation, Inc.
Tchozewshi, Chet. Caribou Fund, Global Greengrants Fund
Teagle, Frank H., Jr. Howfirma Foundation
Teichmann, Ebo. A Territory Resource
Teitel, Martin. C. S. Fund
Tenny, Barron M. Ford Foundation
Teramura, Soji. The Hitachi Foundation
Terasawa, Yoshio. United States-Japan Foundation
Termondt, M. James. Lloyd A. Fry Foundation
Terrien, Linda L. Weyerhaeuser Company Foundation
Terry, Charles. Rockefeller Financial Services, Philanthropy Department
Terry, Frederick A., Jr. HKH Foundation, The McIntosh Foundation
Terry, William E. The Community Foundation of Santa Clara County
Testa, Richard J. The Stratford Foundation
Tewart, Donna. Levi Strauss Foundation
Thaxter, Sidney St. F. Maine Community Foundation, Inc.
Thelan, Max, Jr. S. H. Cowell Foundation
Thigpenn, Anthony. The New World Foundation
Thom, Rosamond A. Ivey. The Richard Ivey Foundation
Thomas, Betsy. Dayton Hudson Foundation
Thomas, Charles. The Winthrop Rockefeller Foundation
Thomas, Franklin A. Ford Foundation
Thomas, Jonathan M. Americana Foundation, Inc.
Thomas, Leo J. Eastman Kodak Company Charitable Trust
Thomas, Lindsay. National Fish and Wildlife Foundation
Thomas, Lyda Ann Quinn. Harris and Eliza Kempner Fund

Thomas, Richard. The New York Times Company Foundation, Inc.
Thomlison, Bryan N. Church & Dwight Co., Inc.
Thompson, Chester. Unitarian Universalist Veatch Program at Shelter Rock
Thompson, Denise Nix. Joyce Mertz-Gilmore Foundation
Thompson, Edward Randall, Jr. Harris and Eliza Kempner Fund
Thompson, George C. Ellis L. Phillips Foundation
Thompson, James W. Foundation for the Carolinas
Thompson, John L. The Community Foundation Serving Coastal South Carolina
Thompson, Kenneth W. Compton Foundation, Inc.
Thompson, Lenora Kempner. Harris and Eliza Kempner Fund
Thompson, Marcia. The Scherman Foundation, Inc.
Thompson, Timothy L. The Harding Educational and Charitable Foundation
Thomsen, C. J. The Eugene McDermott Foundation
Thomson, George. Laidlaw Foundation
Thorburn, Thomas. W. K. Kellogg Foundation
Thorndike, John L. The Fund for Preservation of Wildlife and Natural Areas
Thorne, Felicitas S. Millbrook Tribute Garden, Inc.
Thorne, Jane W. The Fund for New Jersey
Thorne, Oakleigh. The Oakleigh L. Thorne Foundation
Thorne, Oakleigh B. The Oakleigh L. Thorne Foundation, Millbrook Tribute Garden, Inc.
Thornton, Martha L. Ameritech Foundation
Thornton, Shirley A. Marin Community Foundation
Thorpe, Dagmar. The Tides Foundation
Thorpe, Edith D. Surdna Foundation, Inc.
Thorpe, Ronald. Geraldine R. Dodge Foundation, Inc.
Thorpe, Samuel S., III. Surdna Foundation, Inc.
Thorton, Kenneth R. The Foundation for the National Capital Region
Throop, William M., Jr. The Betterment Fund
Thrune, Charles J. The Charles J. Strosacker Foundation
Thun, David L. The Wyomissing Foundation, Inc.
Thun, Ferdinand K. The Wyomissing Foundation, Inc.
Thun, Louis R. The Wyomissing Foundation, Inc.
Thun, Peter. The Wyomissing Foundation, Inc.

Thurber, Peter P. McGregor Fund
Tiernan, J. A. Baltimore Gas and Electric Foundation, Inc.
Tileston, Peg. Alaska Conservation Foundation
Tipton, Gwen I. Olive B. Cole Foundation
Titcomb, E. Rodman, Jr. The Elizabeth Ordway Dunn Foundation, Inc.
Titcomb, Peter. A Territory Resource
Tobecksen, Bruce D. WMX Environmental Grants Program
Toben, Stephen. The William and Flora Hewlett Foundation
Todaro, Michael P. Compton Foundation, Inc.
Todd, David Anderson. Margaret Cullinan Wray Charitable Lead Annuity Trust
Todd, Emily Leland. Margaret Cullinan Wray Charitable Lead Annuity Trust
Todd, Lucie Wray. Margaret Cullinan Wray Charitable Lead Annuity Trust
Tognazzini, Roland E., Jr. The Dean Witter Foundation
Tom-Chew, Sonia. McKesson Foundation, Inc.
Tommaney, John J. The William and Mary Greve Foundation, Inc.
Tompkins, Doug. Foundation for Deep Ecology
Tompkins, Rachel. The Winthrop Rockefeller Foundation
Tone, F. J., IV. Heller Charitable & Educational Fund
Toohey, Edward J. The Bunbury Company, Inc., The Windham Foundation, Inc.
Topol, Dee. The Travelers Foundation
Topping, Brian. The Arca Foundation
Tormey, John L. The GAR Foundation
Tosh, Dennis A. Ford Motor Company Fund
Touchton, J. Thomas. The Frank Stanley Beveridge Foundation, Inc.
Toundas, Mary G. The Community Foundation of Sarasota County, Inc.
Townley, Marcia. Rockefeller Financial Services, Philanthropy Department
Townsend, Charles C., Jr. The Bunbury Company, Inc., The Windham Foundation, Inc.
Tozier, Patricia B. Davis Conservation Foundation
Tracy, Eugene A. The Chicago Community Trust
Train, Russell E. American Conservation Association, Inc., Rockefeller Brothers Fund, Inc.
Trask, Frederick K., III. Boettcher Foundation
Trautschold, Jerome F., Jr. Mobil Foundation, Inc.
Treacy, Francesca N. Treacy Foundation, Inc.
Treacy, James B. Treacy Foundation, Inc.
Treat, Beatrice C. The Tinker Foundation Incorporated

Officers, Trustees, Directors, and Contacts

Trebek, Alex. National Geographic Society Education Foundation
Tredennick, William T. The Barra Foundation, Inc.
Treiber, John A. Stackner Family Foundation, Inc.
Treiber, Patricia S. Stackner Family Foundation, Inc.
Trepte, Albert. San Diego Community Foundation
Tretheway, Gordon M. The Jackson Foundation
Tribble, J. Lee. Joseph B. Whitehead Foundation, Robert W. Woodruff Foundation, Inc.
Trimble, Preston A. Sarkeys Foundation
Trinh, K. L. Chrysler Corporation Fund
Trotman, Alexander J. Ford Motor Company Fund
Trott, James I. Abell-Hanger Foundation
Trotter, Lloyd G. GE Fund
Trowbridge, Alexander B. WMX Environmental Grants Program
Troy, Charlene B Englehard. The Charles Engelhard Foundation
Troyer, Thomas A. The Foundation for the National Capital Region
Truland, Alice O. The Truland Foundation
Truland, Robert W. The Truland Foundation
Truland, Walter R. The Truland Foundation
Tschinkel, Victoria J. The German Marshall Fund of the United States
Tsui, John K. Hawaii Community Foundation
Tuck, Deborah E. Ruth Mott Fund
Tucker, Carll. Marcia Brady Tucker Foundation
Tucker, Gay. Marcia Brady Tucker Foundation
Tucker, Luther, Jr. Marcia Brady Tucker Foundation
Tucker, Nicholas. Marcia Brady Tucker Foundation
Tucker, Sara A. AT&T Foundation
Tucker, The Reverend Luther. Marcia Brady Tucker Foundation
Tucker, Toinette. Marcia Brady Tucker Foundation
Tugwell, Frank. Howard Heinz Endowment, Vira I. Heinz Endowment
Tulberg, Audrey. The Cargill Foundation
Tupper, C. John. Sacramento Regional Foundation
Tupper, Chris. Island Foundation, Inc.
Turberville, P. G. Shell Oil Company Foundation
Turcik, John J. Richard King Mellon Foundation
Turnage, Roxanne. C. S. Fund
Turnbull, William. Victoria Foundation, Inc.
Turner, Beau. Turner Foundation, Inc.
Turner, Diana Lassalle. Norman Foundation
Turner, Gloria P. J. P. Morgan Charitable Trust
Turner, John. The Ben & Jerry's Foundation
Turner, R. E. Turner Foundation, Inc.
Turner, Rhett Lee. Turner Foundation, Inc.
Turner, Robert Edward, IV. Turner Foundation, Inc.
Turtletes, Vincent N. Millbrook Tribute Garden, Inc.
Tusher, Thomas W. Levi Strauss Foundation
Tuthill, John W. G. Greater Piscataqua Community Foundation
Tutt, Michael. The Ben & Jerry's Foundation
Tutt, R. Thayer, Jr. El Pomar Foundation
Tweedy, Joan. Tortuga Foundation
Twigg-Smith, Thurston. McInerny Foundation
Twyman, Charles R. The Community Foundation of Greater New Haven
Tyler, Ron. The Summerlee Foundation
Tylman, Vicki F. The Procter & Gamble Fund
Typermass, Arthur G. Metropolitan Life Foundation

U

Ueland, Andreas W. Laird, Norton Foundation
Uihlein, David V., Jr. The Lynde and Harry Bradley Foundation, Inc.
Ulrich, Robert J. Dayton Hudson Foundation
Ulrich, Robert W. Texaco Foundation
Umana, Alvaro. The Goldman Environmental Foundation
Ummer, James W. Snee-Reinhardt Charitable Foundation
Underwood, Frank D. New Horizon Foundation, Sequoia Foundation
Underwood, Joanna D. Robert Sterling Clark Foundation, Inc.
Ungerleider, Peter. The Jenifer Altman Foundation
Urban, Henry Z. The Seymour H. Knox Foundation, Inc.
Urwin, E. Keith. Thomas Sill Foundation
Usher, Thomas J. USX Foundation, Inc.
Ushijima, Margaret S. Hawaii Community Foundation
Ushio, Jiro. United States-Japan Foundation

V

Vail, Richard T. Snee-Reinhardt Charitable Foundation
Valade, G. C. Chrysler Corporation Fund
Valcich, Marlene. Dolfinger-McMahon Foundation
Valli, Louis A. USX Foundation, Inc.
Vamvakias, Sally. Maine Community Foundation, Inc.
Van Bebber, Theodore J. S. D. Bechtel, Jr. Foundation
van Bronkhorst, Edwin E. The David and Lucile Packard Foundation
Van de Bovenkamp, Sue Erpf. The Armand G. Erpf Fund, Inc.
Van Dyke, Nancy. Unitarian Universalist Veatch Program at Shelter Rock
Van Dyke, Polly H. The Milwaukee Foundation
Van Meter, James C. Georgia-Pacific Foundation
Van Ness, William J., Jr. The Henry M. Jackson Foundation
Vance, Cyrus R. The New York Times Company Foundation, Inc.
Vance-Lewis, Sheilah. The Philadelphia Foundation
Vandeberg, Elvin J. New Horizon Foundation
Vanderbilt, Hugh B., Sr. R. T. Vanderbilt Trust
Vanderbilt, Robert T. R. T. Vanderbilt Trust
Vanderryn, Jack. The Moriah Fund, Inc.
Vargas, Arturo. The Edward W. Hazen Foundation
Vargas, Sandra L. The Minneapolis Foundation
Vaughan, H. Wiley. The Fund for Preservation of Wildlife and Natural Areas
Vaughan, Peter B. The Philadelphia Foundation
Veale, Kirk. The Sonoma County Community Foundation
Veitenhans, Karen L. Weyerhaeuser Company Foundation
Velay, Christophe. The Vidda Foundation
Velsor, Stan Van. Pew Scholars Program in Conservation and the Environment
Vergin, Brian. Blandin Foundation
Vesce, Joseph C. Dayton Hudson Foundation
Viederman, Stephen. Jessie Smith Noyes Foundation, Inc.
Viermetz, Kurt F. J. P. Morgan Charitable Trust
Vignos, Edith I. The Louise H. and David S. Ingalls Foundation, Inc.
Vilar, Maria A. San Diego Community Foundation
Villanueva, Danial L., Jr. California Community Foundation
Vlasoff, Martha. Alaska Conservation Foundation
Vogel, Jacqueline M. Mars Foundation
Vogelmann, Hubert W. The Conservation and Research Foundation
Vogt, Martha. Rockwell Fund, Inc.
Voigt, Judi. The Community Foundation of Sarasota County, Inc.

Officers, Directors, Trustees, and Contacts

Vojvoda, Antoinette P. The Knapp Foundation, Inc.
Vojvoda, Robert B. The Knapp Foundation, Inc.
von Bernuth, C. W. Union Pacific Foundation
Von Hatzfelt, Herman. HKH Foundation
von Hoffmann, Ladislaus. The Foundation for the National Capital Region
Vorhees, Charles A. Helen Brach Foundation
Vorhees, Charles M. Helen Brach Foundation

W

Wachenfeld, William T. Charles Hayden Foundation
Wachenheim, Edgar, III. New York Foundation, Pinewood Foundation
Wachtell, Esther. California Community Foundation
Wada, Yori. The Morris Stulsaft Foundation
Waddell, Theodore H. The Charles Evans Hughes Memorial Foundation, Inc.
Wade, Ormand J. The Chicago Community Trust
Wadsworth, John S. United States-Japan Foundation
Wagele, James S. BankAmerica Foundation
Wagley, Anne Paxton. James C. Penney Foundation
Wagley, James F. James C. Penney Foundation
Wagley, Mary Frances P. James C. Penney Foundation
Wagner, Rodney B. J. P. Morgan Charitable Trust
Wahlig, Michael J. Dayton Hudson Foundation
Wainwright, Carroll L., Jr. The New York Community Trust, Edward John Noble Foundation, Inc.
Wajnert, Thomas C. AT&T Foundation
Wakefield, David D. Longwood Foundation, Inc., Welfare Foundation, Inc.
Walbridge, Barbara. San Diego Community Foundation
Walcott, Leonard E., Jr. The Ahmanson Foundation
Walker, Barrett C. Alex C. Walker Educational & Charitable Foundation
Walker, Constance. The James Irvine Foundation
Walker, John, III. The Morris and Gwendolyn Cafritz Foundation
Walker, Sue Ellen. Lilly Endowment, Inc.
Walker, T. Urling. Alex C. Walker Educational & Charitable Foundation
Walkinshaw, Walter. Northwest Fund for the Environment

Wallace, Ann Fowler. Conservation, Food & Health Foundation, Inc., Jessie B. Cox Charitable Trust, The Elizabeth Ordway Dunn Foundation, Inc.
Wallace, Deborah. Levi Strauss Foundation
Wallace, Henry B. Wallace Genetic Foundation, Inc.
Wallace, Robert B. Wallace Genetic Foundation, Inc.
Wallach, Diane Gates. Gates Foundation
Waller, Kathryn J. The Winthrop Rockefeller Foundation
Wallgren, Donald A. WMX Environmental Grants Program
Wallin, Franklin W. Joyce Mertz-Gilmore Foundation
Wallis, Gordon T. The Tinker Foundation Incorporated
Walsh, G. M. The Buchanan Family Foundation
Walsh, Janet. Ellis L. Phillips Foundation
Walsh, Mason, Jr. Richard King Mellon Foundation
Walshok, Mary. San Diego Community Foundation
Walter, Henry G., Jr. United States-Japan Foundation, G. Unger Vetlesen Foundation
Walton, James M. Vira I. Heinz Endowment, Sarah Scaife Foundation Incorporated
Walton, Jonathan T. W. K. Kellogg Foundation
Walton, William. The Morris and Gwendolyn Cafritz Foundation
Wancowicz, Charlie. The USF&G Foundation, Inc.
Wang, Lulu. The New York Community Trust
Wanlin, Ms. Margaret. Laidlaw Foundation
Warburg, James P., Jr. The Bydale Foundation
Warburg, Jennifer J. The Bydale Foundation
Warburg, Joan M. The Bydale Foundation
Warburg, Philip N. The Bydale Foundation
Ward, Kenneth. Environmental Endowment for New Jersey, Inc.
Ward, Terry W. The William Stamps Farish Fund
Wareck, Barbara C. The Community Foundation of Greater New Haven
Warford, Malcolm. Maine Community Foundation, Inc.
Warner, C. Elizabeth. Public Welfare Foundation, Inc.
Warner, Donald T. Public Welfare Foundation, Inc.
Warner, Douglas A., III. J. P. Morgan Charitable Trust
Warren, Ingrid R. Cleveland H. Dodge Foundation, Inc.

Warren, Richard J. Maine Community Foundation, Inc.
Warsh, Herman. C. S. Fund, Ruth Mott Fund
Warsh, Michael. C. S. Fund
Washburn, Diana B. Smith Richardson Foundation, Inc.
Washington, Frank. Sacramento Regional Foundation
Washington, Robert. The Ewing Halsell Foundation
Washington, Valora. W. K. Kellogg Foundation
Watanabe, Jeffrey N. Hawaiian Electric Industries Charitable Foundation
Watanabe, Ruth K. California Community Foundation
Watkins, Edwin H. Jamee and Marshall Field Foundation
Watson, Charles. Lee Romney Foundation, Inc.
Watson, J. Stanley. The Rockfall Foundation
Watson, Jane W. The Louise H. and David S. Ingalls Foundation, Inc.
Watson, JoAnn. Island Foundation, Inc.
Watson, Michael. Richard King Mellon Foundation
Watson, Roslyn M. The Hyams Foundation
Watson, Solomon B., IV. The New York Times Company Foundation, Inc.
Watson, Stephen E. Dayton Hudson Foundation
Watters, James T. The Strong Foundation for Environmental Values
Wattles, Elizabeth C. The Howard Bayne Fund
Wattles, Gurdon B. The Howard Bayne Fund
Watts, Elise Phillips. Ellis L. Phillips Foundation
Wayburn, Laurie A. Compton Foundation, Inc.
Weatherstone, Dennis. J. P. Morgan Charitable Trust
Weeden, Alan N. Weeden Foundation
Weeden, Donald E. Weeden Foundation
Weeden, John D. Weeden Foundation
Weeden, William F. Weeden Foundation
Weeks, Joshua J. The Howard Johnson Foundation
Weeks, William H. The Howard Johnson Foundation
Wege, Peter M. Steelcase Foundation
Wehling, R. L. The Procter & Gamble Fund
Weidlein, Mary Rea. Cleveland H. Dodge Foundation, Inc.
Weigel, Kelley. McKenzie River Gathering Foundation
Weigell, Carl A. The Milwaukee Foundation
Weil, Amanda E. Norman Foundation
Weil, Frank A. Norman Foundation

Officers, Trustees, Directors, and Contacts

Weil, Sandison E. Norman Foundation
Weil, William S. Norman Foundation
Weill, Sanford I. The Travelers Foundation
Weinmann, Mary. Rockwood Fund, Inc.
Weintraub, Malcolm S. Sacramento Regional Foundation
Weintz, Elisabeth B. Harbor Lights Foundation
Weintz, J. Fred, Jr. Harbor Lights Foundation
Weiss, Robert E. Meadows Foundation, Inc.
Weiss, William L. Ameritech Foundation
Weld, Edward W. Alexander H. Bright Charitable Trust
Welles, Linda. Unitarian Universalist Veatch Program at Shelter Rock
Welling, Truman. Stroud Foundation
Welliver, A. D. The Boeing Company
Wellman, Barclay O. Ralph C. Sheldon Foundation, Inc.
Wells, Albert. The Jenifer Altman Foundation
Wells, Albert B., II. The Abelard Foundation West
Wells, George B., II. The Abelard Foundation West
Wells, Herman B. Lilly Endowment, Inc.
Wells, Laura. The Abelard Foundation West
Wells, Luanne. Environment Now Foundation
Wells, Melissa R. The Abelard Foundation West
Wells, Ruth D. The Abelard Foundation West
Wells, Susan. The Abelard Foundation West
Welsh, James. Environmental Education Foundation of Florida, Inc.
Wendel, James F. The Seymour H. Knox Foundation, Inc.
Wenger, Diane. Henry E. and Consuelo S. Wenger Foundation, Inc.
Wenger, Henry Penn. Henry E. and Consuelo S. Wenger Foundation, Inc.
Wennesland, Kathleen W. Mark and Catherine Winkler Foundation
Werdegar, David. Marin Community Foundation
Werner, Ms. S. R. The GAR Foundation
Wesbey, Meridith D. The Fred Harris Daniels Foundation, Inc.
West, J. Robinson. The German Marshall Fund of the United States
West, John C. Phillips Petroleum Foundation, Inc.
West, Susan Doelger. Thelma Doelger Charitable Trust
West, Terry W. Sarkeys Foundation
West, W. Richard, Jr. The Bush Foundation
Westerline, Marcy. McKenzie River Gathering Foundation
Western, David. Liz Claiborne & Art Ortenberg Foundation
Weston, Elsie. San Diego Community Foundation

Weston, Harris Kempner. Harris and Eliza Kempner Fund
Wetzel, Mary G. The Conservation and Research Foundation
Wexner, Abigail. The Columbus Foundation
Weyerhaeuser, Annette Thayer Black. Sequoia Foundation
Weyerhaeuser, Gail T. Sequoia Foundation
Weyerhaeuser, George H. The Boeing Company, The Chevron Companies, Weyerhaeuser Company Foundation
Weyerhaeuser, William Toycen. Sequoia Foundation
Weymouth, Philip B., Jr. Ederic Foundation, Inc.
Whalen, George T., Jr. Millbrook Tribute Garden, Inc.
Whalen, Robert W. Millbrook Tribute Garden, Inc.
Wheeler, Kathryn L. The James Irvine Foundation
Wheless, Lee. The Frost Foundation, Ltd.
Whitaker, T. L. Union Pacific Foundation
White, Molly. The Gap Foundation
White, Richard K. Harry C. Trexler Trust
White, Walter H., Jr. The Milwaukee Foundation
White, William S. Charles Stewart Mott Foundation
Whited, Edwin F. The Frost Foundation, Ltd.
Whited-Howell, Mary Amelia. The Frost Foundation, Ltd.
Whitehead, A. Pennington. The Clark Foundation
Whitehead, David W. Centerior Energy Foundation
Whitehead, John C. The Andrew W. Mellon Foundation, The Florence and John Schumann Foundation
Whitehead, Rosalind C. The Educational Foundation of America
Whitney, Thomas H. P., Jr. The William P. Wharton Trust
Whitridge, Fredrick. The Mary A. Crocker Trust
Whitridge, Serena. The John Merck Fund, Merck Family Fund
Whittle, Carolyn S. Vinmont Foundation, Inc.
Whitworth, J. Bryan. Phillips Petroleum Foundation, Inc.
Whyte, William H., Jr. American Conservation Association, Inc.
Wice, David H. Samuel S. Fels Fund
Wichman, Charles R. Hawaii Community Foundation
Wicker, Frederick J. The USF&G Foundation, Inc.
Wickham, Woodward A. The John D. and Catherine T. MacArthur Foundation
Widener, Mary Lee. The San Francisco Foundation
Wieland, Susan W. Metropolitan Atlanta Community Foundation, Inc.

Wiener, Ann F. Jessie Smith Noyes Foundation, Inc.
Wiener, Sara M. Angelina Fund, Inc.
Wiener, William, Jr. Alaska Conservation Foundation
Wiesner, Jerome B. The John D. and Catherine T. MacArthur Foundation
Wilbur, Colburn S. The David and Lucile Packard Foundation
Wilde, Wilson. Hartford Foundation for Public Giving
Wilderson, Frank B., Jr. The Bush Foundation
Wiley, S. Donald. Vira I. Heinz Endowment
Wilfley, George M. Boettcher Foundation
Wilfley, Mike. Gates Foundation
Wilke, Elizabeth W. The Howard Bayne Fund
Wilkie, Valleau, Jr. Sid W. Richardson Foundation
Wilkins, Sandra. Vancouver Foundation
Willard, G. J. Liloa. James & Abigail Campbell Foundation
Willemetz, J. Lester. Spencer T. and Ann W. Olin Foundation
Willert, Mary A. The William P. Wharton Trust
Williams, A. Tab, Jr. The Winston-Salem Foundation, Inc.
Williams, Henry G. Great Lakes Protection Fund
Williams, James. Robert W. Woodruff Foundation, Inc.
Williams, Jodi. Public Welfare Foundation, Inc.
Williams, Marjorie. C. A. Webster Foundation
Williams, Paul. Kinnoull Foundation
Williams, Steve. Alaska Conservation Foundation
Williams, William H. C. A. Webster Foundation
Williams, William J. The Cleveland Foundation, Martha Holden Jennings Foundation
Williamson, Harwood D. Hawaiian Electric Industries Charitable Foundation
Willingham, Frank F. James G. Hanes Memorial Fund
Willis, E. A. Union Pacific Foundation
Wilson, Alexander T. The Conservation and Research Foundation
Wilson, Donald M. The Schumann Fund for New Jersey, Inc.
Wilson, Dorothy C. Meadows Foundation, Inc.
Wilson, Douglas A. The GAR Foundation
Wilson, Eugene R. ARCO Foundation
Wilson, James Q. Smith Richardson Foundation, Inc.
Wilson, John A. The Community Foundation of Santa Clara County
Wilson, Lee Anne. Sarkeys Foundation
Wilson, Governor Malcolm. The Clark Foundation

© 1995 Environmental Data Resources, Inc.

Officers, Directors, Trustees, and Contacts

Wilson, Peter A. The Stratford Foundation
Wilson, Robert A. The Pfizer Foundation, Inc.
Wilson, Robert B. Weyerhaeuser Company Foundation
Wilson, Robert W. Robert W. Wilson Foundation
Wilson, Sallyanne. Marin Community Foundation
Wilson, T. A. The Boeing Company
Wilson, William, III. Peninsula Community Foundation
Wiltshire, Kimery. Illilouette Fund
Windle, Janice W. El Paso Community Foundation
Windsor, Robert G. Adolph Coors Foundation
Wingate, Edwin H. Dayton Hudson Foundation
Winkler, Carolyn. Mark and Catherine Winkler Foundation
Winmill, Mark C. Thanksgiving Foundation
Winship, William B. The Betterment Fund
Winsor, Curtin, Jr. Donner Canadian Foundation
Winston, Hathily. Walter S. Johnson Foundation
Winston, James O. The William Stamps Farish Fund
Winston, James O., Jr. The William Stamps Farish Fund
Winters, Robert C. The Prudential Foundation
Wirth, Conrad L. American Conservation Association, Inc., Jackson Hole Preserve, Inc.
Wirth, Wren Winslow. The Winslow Foundation
Wise, John J. Mobil Foundation, Inc.
Wise, Robert E. Meadows Foundation, Inc.
Wishcamper, Carol. Maine Community Foundation, Inc.
Witheridege, Jane G. WMX Environmental Grants Program
Witt, Thomas A. WMX Environmental Grants Program
Witte, Linda R. WMX Environmental Grants Program
Witter, Dean, III. The Dean Witter Foundation
Witter, William D. The Dean Witter Foundation
Wo, James C. Hawaii Community Foundation
Woddard, Mitchell R. The Frost Foundation, Ltd.
Woessner, William M. The German Marshall Fund of the United States
Wohlert, Roger W. Southwestern Bell Foundation
Wolf, Robert. The New-Land Foundation, Inc.
Wolfe, John F. The Columbus Foundation

Wolfensohn, Elaine. Botwinick-Wolfensohn Foundation, Inc.
Wolfensohn, James D. Botwinick-Wolfensohn Foundation, Inc.
Wolfensohn, Sara R. Botwinick-Wolfensohn Foundation, Inc.
Wolff, Paula. The Joyce Foundation
Wolff, Rosalie S. Solow Foundation
Wolkov, Lauren. Sacramento Regional Foundation
Wollen, Carolyn S. The Betterment Fund, Maine Community Foundation, Inc.
Wolters, Kate Pew. Steelcase Foundation
Wong, Linda J. The Goldman Environmental Foundation
Wood, Anthony C. Ittleson Foundation, Inc.
Wood, Kate B. The Hyde and Watson Foundation
Wood, Lawrence M. Pilot Trust
Woodburyn, Susan B. The George I. Alden Trust
Woodruff, Jim. FishAmerica Foundation
Woods, David F. The Frank Stanley Beveridge Foundation, Inc.
Woods, Jacqueline F. Ameritech Foundation
Woodsum, Harold E., Jr. Elmina B. Sewall Foundation
Woolsey, Suzanne H. The German Marshall Fund of the United States
Worth, Robert R. HKH Foundation
Wortham, R. W., III. The Wortham Foundation, Inc.
Wortz, Peggy Fouke. California Community Foundation
Wragg, Otis. Environmental Education Foundation of Florida, Inc.
Wragge, Carla. Sidney & Phyllis Wragge Foundation
Wragge, Ellen. Sidney & Phyllis Wragge Foundation
Wragge, Sara. Sidney & Phyllis Wragge Foundation
Wray, Gilda G. Charles Hayden Foundation
Wright, Barbara. The David and Lucile Packard Foundation
Wright, Lawrence A. Atkinson Foundation
Wright, Robert G. John P. Murphy Foundation, Ralph C. Sheldon Foundation, Inc.
Wright, Stanley C. Eastman Kodak Company Charitable Trust
Wright, William B. The Bunbury Company, Inc., The Windham Foundation, Inc.
Wright, William R. The Arthur Vining Davis Foundations
Wurtele, C. Angus. The Bush Foundation
Wycoff, Robert E. ARCO Foundation
Wyman, Thomas H. Ford Foundation
Wynia, Ann. The Bush Foundation
Wyper, Janet. L. L. Bean, Inc.

X

Xiong, Lee Pao. The Minneapolis Foundation

Y

Yamada, Masayuki. The Hitachi Foundation
Yasinsky, John B. Westinghouse Foundation
Yeager, Brigadier General Charles Y. National Fish and Wildlife Foundation
Yeager, Charles G. Stranahan Foundation
Yee, Sandra. Sacramento Regional Foundation
Yehle, Eugene C. The Charles J. Strosacker Foundation
Yochum, Doreen S. AT&T Foundation
Yodowitz, Heidi. McKesson Foundation, Inc.
Yoshioka, Marche H. The Fred Gellert Foundation
Yost, Byron L. Virginia Environmental Endowment
Young, Benjamin Neely. Metropolitan Atlanta Community Foundation, Inc.
Young, Jacqueline. The Fred Gellert Foundation
Young, John A. The Chevron Companies
Young, Nancy M. Walter and Elise Haas Fund
Young, Rosemary. Peninsula Community Foundation
Young, Roy. Caribou Fund, Global Greengrants Fund
Younger, John F. Abell-Hanger Foundation
Yu, Su-Mei. San Diego Community Foundation

Z

Zabel, William. Ottinger Foundation
Zambie, Allan J. John P. Murphy Foundation
Zamoiski, Calman J. Chesapeake Bay Trust
Zankel, Arthur. New York Foundation
Zapanta, Edward. The James Irvine Foundation
Zemans, Joyce. Laidlaw Foundation
Zigler, Edward F. Smith Richardson Foundation, Inc.
Zimmerman, Richard A. Eastman Kodak Company Charitable Trust
Zimmermann, K. Noël Phillips. Ellis L. Phillips Foundation
Zinbarg, Edward D. The Prudential Foundation
Zipf, Cindy. Environmental Endowment for New Jersey, Inc.
Zoellick, Robert B. The German Marshall Fund of the United States
Zoffman, Beth C. Georgia-Pacific Foundation

Officers, Trustees, Directors, and Contacts

Zuccaro, Edward J. The Bunbury Company, Inc.
Zuccaro, Edward R. The Windham Foundation, Inc.
Zucker, Anita. The Community Foundation Serving Coastal South Carolina
Zuckerman, Harriet. The Andrew W. Mellon Foundation
Zunamon, Simon. Pritzker Foundation

Grantmaker Location

United States

Alaska
Alaska Conservation Foundation
The Skaggs Foundation

Arkansas
The Winthrop Rockefeller Foundation

Arizona
Jesse Margaret Wilson Budlong
 Foundation for Animal Aid
The Marshall Fund of Arizona

California
ARCO Foundation
The Abelard Foundation West
The Acorn Foundation
The Ahmanson Foundation
Winifred & Harry B. Allen Foundation
The Jenifer Altman Foundation
Apple Computer, Inc.
Atkinson Foundation
BankAmerica Foundation
S. D. Bechtel, Jr. Foundation
Bishop Pine Fund
The Bothin Foundation
The Robert Brownlee Foundation
C. S. Fund
California Community Foundation
Cheeryble Foundation
The Chevron Companies
Columbia Foundation
The Community Foundation of
 Santa Clara County
Compton Foundation, Inc.
S. H. Cowell Foundation
The Mary A. Crocker Trust
Roy E. Crummer Foundation
Damien Foundation
Thelma Doelger Charitable Trust
Douroucouli Foundation
The Energy Foundation
Environment Now Foundation
Fieldstead Charitable Trust
Flintridge Foundation
Foundation for Deep Ecology
Foundation for Field Research
The Gap Foundation
The Barbara Gauntlett Foundation, Inc.
The Fred Gellert Foundation
The Wallace Alexander Gerbode
 Foundation, Inc.
The Goldman Environmental Foundation
Richard & Rhoda Goldman Fund
The Greenville Foundation
Evelyn and Walter Haas, Jr. Fund
Walter and Elise Haas Fund

The John Randolph Haynes and
 Dora Haynes Foundation
Heller Charitable & Educational Fund
The Clarence E. Heller Charitable
 Foundation
The William and Flora Hewlett
 Foundation
The Hofmann Foundation
The Homeland Foundation
The Horn Foundation
Illilouette Fund
The James Irvine Foundation
The George Frederick Jewett Foundation
Walter S. Johnson Foundation
Kinnoull Foundation
The Norman Lear Foundation
Levi Strauss Foundation
Luster Family Foundation, Inc.
Marin Community Foundation
The McConnell Foundation
McKesson Foundation, Inc.
Giles W. and Elise G. Mead Foundation
Andrew Norman Foundation
Kenneth T. and Eileen L. Norris
 Foundation
The David and Lucile Packard Foundation
Patagonia, Inc.
Peninsula Community Foundation
The Roberts Foundation
Sacramento Regional Foundation
San Diego Community Foundation
The San Francisco Foundation
Ellen Browning Scripps Foundation
Frances Seebe Trust
Seventh Generation Fund
Stanley Smith Horticultural Trust
The Sonoma County Community
 Foundation
South Coast Foundation, Inc.
Springhouse Foundation
The Strong Foundation for
 Environmental Values
The Morris Stulsaft Foundation
S. Mark Taper Foundation
The Telesis Foundation
Threshold Foundation
The Tides Foundation
Toyota USA Foundation
Alice Tweed Tuohy Foundation
Vanguard Public Foundation
C. A. Webster Foundation
Whitecap Foundation
The Dean Witter Foundation

Colorado
Airport Business Center Foundation
Boettcher Foundation

Ruth H. Brown Foundation
Caribou Fund
Adolph Coors Foundation
El Pomar Foundation
Bert Fingerhut/Caroline Hicks
 Family Fund
Gates Foundation
General Service Foundation
Global Greengrants Fund
Island Foundation
Helen K. and Arthur E. Johnson
 Foundation
Maki Foundation
The Needmor Fund
Pilot Trust
True North Foundation

Connecticut
Angelina Fund, Inc.
The Community Foundation of
 Greater New Haven
The Conservation and Research
 Foundation
Charles E. Culpeper Foundation, Inc.
The Educational Foundation of America
GE Fund
Bernard F. and Alva B. Gimbel
 Foundation, Inc.
Hartford Foundation for Public Giving
The Perkin Fund
Smith Richardson Foundation, Inc.
The Rockfall Foundation
R. T. Vanderbilt Trust

District of Columbia
American Conservation Association, Inc.
The Arca Foundation
The Bauman Foundation
Beldon Fund
Benton Foundation
The Morris and Gwendolyn Cafritz
 Foundation
The Foundation for the National
 Capital Region
The Freed Foundation, Inc.
The German Marshall Fund of
 the United States
The M. A. Healy Family Foundation, Inc.
The Hitachi Foundation
Charles G. Koch Charitable Foundation
MARPAT Foundation, Inc.
The National Environmental Education
 and Training Foundation, Inc.
National Fish and Wildlife Foundation
National Geographic Society Education
 Foundation
Public Welfare Foundation, Inc.

© 1995 Environmental Data Resources, Inc.

Grantmaker Location

District of Columbia (cont.)

Rockwood Fund, Inc.
The Summit Foundation
SURFREE
Times Mirror Magazines, Inc.
WMX Environmental Grants Program
Wallace Genetic Foundation, Inc.

Delaware

Ederic Foundation, Inc.
Fair Play Foundation
Good Samaritan, Inc.
Longwood Foundation, Inc.
Welfare Foundation, Inc.

Florida

The Frank Stanley Beveridge Foundation, Inc.
The Community Foundation of Sarasota County, Inc.
The Arthur Vining Davis Foundations
The Elizabeth Ordway Dunn Foundation, Inc.
Jessie Ball duPont Religious, Charitable and Educational Fund
Environmental Education Foundation of Florida, Inc.
The McIntosh Foundation
Schultz Foundation, Inc.

Georgia

Georgia Power Foundation, Inc.
Georgia-Pacific Foundation
Metropolitan Atlanta Community Foundation, Inc.
The Sapelo Foundation
Turner Foundation, Inc.
Joseph B. Whitehead Foundation
Robert W. Woodruff Foundation, Inc.

Hawaii

Atherton Family Foundation
James & Abigail Campbell Foundation
Cooke Foundation, Limited
Mary D. and Walter F. Frear Eleemosynary Trust
Hawaii Community Foundation
Hawaiian Electric Industries Charitable Foundation
McInerny Foundation
G. N. Wilcox Trust

Idaho

Global Environmental Project Institute

Illinois

Ameritech Foundation
The Bersted Foundation
Helen Brach Foundation
The Buchanan Family Foundation
The Chicago Community Trust
Gaylord and Dorothy Donnelley Foundation
The Field Foundation of Illinois, Inc.
Jamee and Marshall Field Foundation
Lloyd A. Fry Foundation
Great Lakes Protection Fund
The Joyce Foundation
LaSalle Adams Fund
The John D. and Catherine T. MacArthur Foundation
The Curtis and Edith Munson Foundation, Inc.
Prince Charitable Trusts
Pritzker Foundation

Indiana

The Clowes Fund, Inc.
Olive B. Cole Foundation
English-Bonter-Mitchell Foundation
The W. C. Griffith Foundation
Lilly Endowment, Inc.
The Martin Foundation, Inc.
Nicholas H. Noyes, Jr. Memorial Foundation

Kansas

The Powell Family Foundation

Kentucky

W. L. Lyons Brown Foundation
The Norton Foundation, Inc.

Massachusetts

The George I. Alden Trust
Azadoutioun Foundation
Alexander H. Bright Charitable Trust
The Cabot Family Charitable Trust
Ward M. & Mariam C. Canaday Educational and Charitable Trust
Clark Charitable Trust
Conservation, Food & Health Foundation, Inc.
Cox Foundation, Inc.
Jessie B. Cox Charitable Trust
The Cricket Foundation
The Fred Harris Daniels Foundation, Inc.
Fields Pond Foundation, Inc.
The Fund for Preservation of Wildlife and Natural Areas
Hurdle Hill Foundation
The Hyams Foundation
Island Foundation, Inc.
The Henry P. Kendall Foundation
The Little Family Foundation
Massachusetts Environmental Trust
The John Merck Fund
Middlecott Foundation
New England Biolabs Foundation
Ottinger Foundation
Amelia Peabody Charitable Fund
Ellis L. Phillips Foundation
Sacharuna Foundation
Anna B. Stearns Charitable Foundation, Inc.
Stern Family Fund
Stoddard Charitable Trust
The Stratford Foundation
The Sudbury Foundation
The William P. Wharton Trust
Sidney & Phyllis Wragge Foundation

Maryland

The Abell Foundation
Clayton Baker Trust
Baltimore Gas and Electric Foundation, Inc.
Alex. Brown & Sons Charitable Foundation, Inc.
H. Barksdale Brown Charitable Trust
Chesapeake Bay Trust
Felburn Foundation
The Jacob and Annita France Foundation, Inc.
The Knapp Foundation, Inc.
Merck Family Fund
Robert G. and Anne M. Merrick Foundation, Inc.
The Moriah Fund, Inc.
Town Creek Foundation, Inc.
Marcia Brady Tucker Foundation
The USF&G Foundation, Inc.

Maine

L. L. Bean, Inc.
Davis Conservation Foundation
The Dragon Foundation, Inc.
Maine Community Foundation, Inc.
Orchard Foundation
Elmina B. Sewall Foundation

Michigan

Americana Foundation, Inc.
Bay Area Community Foundation
Chrysler Corporation Fund
Dart Foundation
The Herbert H. and Grace A. Dow Foundation
Ford Motor Company Fund
Walter and Josephine Ford Fund
The Rollin M. Gerstacker Foundation
Hudson-Webber Foundation
W. K. Kellogg Foundation
The Kresge Foundation
McGregor Fund
Charles Stewart Mott Foundation
Ruth Mott Fund
Pew Scholars Program in Conservation and the Environment
Steelcase Foundation
The Stroh Foundation
The Charles J. Strosacker Foundation
Henry E. and Consuelo S. Wenger Foundation, Inc.

Grantmaker Location

Minnesota
Elmer L. & Eleanor J. Andersen Foundation
David Winton Bell Foundation
James Ford Bell Foundation
Blandin Foundation
Otto Bremer Foundation
The Bush Foundation
Patrick and Aimee Butler Family Foundation
The Cargill Foundation
Carolyn Foundation
Dayton Hudson Foundation
Give to the Earth Foundation
Marbrook Foundation
The McKnight Foundation
The Minneapolis Foundation
Northwest Area Foundation
Onan Family Foundation

Missouri
Deer Creek Foundation
The Emerald Foundation
The Hall Family Foundation
McDonnell Douglas Foundation
Spencer T. and Ann W. Olin Foundation

North Carolina
Mary Reynolds Babcock Foundation, Inc.
The Bailey Wildlife Foundation
The Blumenthal Foundation
Kathleen Price and Joseph M. Bryan Family Foundation, Inc.
Community Foundation of Western North Carolina, Inc.
Foundation for the Carolinas
James G. Hanes Memorial Fund
Lynn R. and Karl E. Prickett Fund
Z. Smith Reynolds Foundation, Inc.
The Winston-Salem Foundation, Inc.

New Hampshire
The Butler Foundation
Greater Piscataqua Community Foundation
New Hampshire Charitable Foundation
The Switzer Foundation

New Jersey
Atlantic Foundation
Mary Owen Borden Memorial Foundation
The Bunbury Company, Inc.
The Cape Branch Foundation
Church & Dwight Co., Inc.
Geraldine R. Dodge Foundation, Inc.
Environmental Endowment for New Jersey, Inc.
Fanwood Foundation
Frelinghuysen Foundation
The Fund for New Jersey
The Hyde and Watson Foundation
The International Foundation, Inc.

F. M. Kirby Foundation, Inc.
Magowan Family Foundation, Inc.
Howard Phipps Foundation
The Prudential Foundation
The Schumann Fund for New Jersey, Inc.
The Florence and John Schumann Foundation
Union Camp Charitable Trust
Victoria Foundation, Inc.
The Winslow Foundation

New Mexico
The Frost Foundation, Ltd.
The Max and Anna Levinson Foundation
The Marshall L. & Perrine D. McCune Charitable Foundation

New York
AT&T Foundation
The Achelis Foundation
American Express Philanthropic Program
The Vincent Astor Foundation
The Cameron Baird Foundation
The George F. Baker Trust
The Theodore H. Barth Foundation, Inc.
The Bay Foundation
The Howard Bayne Fund
The Beinecke Foundation, Inc.
The Betterment Fund
The Bodman Foundation
Botwinick-Wolfensohn Foundation, Inc.
J. E. & Z. B. Butler Foundation, Inc.
The Bydale Foundation
The Louis Calder Foundation
Mary Flagler Cary Charitable Trust
Liz Claiborne & Art Ortenberg Foundation
The Clark Foundation
Robert Sterling Clark Foundation, Inc.
The Cowles Charitable Trust
The Nathan Cummings Foundation
The Nelson B. Delavan Foundation
The Aaron Diamond Foundation
Cleveland H. Dodge Foundation, Inc.
Oliver S. and Jennie R. Donaldson Charitable Trust
The Max and Victoria Dreyfus Foundation, Inc.
Eastman Kodak Company Charitable Trust
Echoing Green Foundation
Arthur M. and Olga T. Eisig–Arthur M. and Kate E. Tode Foundation, Inc.
The Charles Engelhard Foundation
The Armand G. Erpf Fund, Inc.
The Ettinger Foundation, Inc.
Ford Foundation
Fund of the Four Directions
Funding Exchange
Gebbie Foundation, Inc.
The Golden Rule Foundation, Inc.
Herman Goldman Foundation
The William and Mary Greve Foundation, Inc.

HKH Foundation
The Hahn Family Foundation
Harbor Lights Foundation
The Harding Educational and Charitable Foundation
Gladys and Roland Harriman Foundation
Mary W. Harriman Foundation
The Merrill G. & Emita E. Hastings Foundation
Charles Hayden Foundation
The Edward W. Hazen Foundation
The Charles Evans Hughes Memorial Foundation, Inc.
IBM Corporation
The Indian Point Foundation, Inc.
Ittleson Foundation, Inc.
Jackson Hole Preserve, Inc.
The Howard Johnson Foundation
The J. M. Kaplan Fund, Inc.
The Helen & Milton Kimmelman Foundation
The Esther A. and Joseph Klingenstein Fund, Inc.
The Seymour H. Knox Foundation, Inc.
The Lagemann Foundation
Larsen Fund, Inc.
The Lauder Foundation, Inc.
Richard Lounsbery Foundation, Inc.
James A. Macdonald Foundation
The Andrew W. Mellon Foundation
Joyce Mertz-Gilmore Foundation
Metropolitan Life Foundation
Millbrook Tribute Garden, Inc.
J. P. Morgan Charitable Trust
Henry and Lucy Moses Fund, Inc.
The New World Foundation
The New York Community Trust
New York Foundation
The New York Times Company Foundation, Inc.
The New-Land Foundation, Inc.
Edward John Noble Foundation, Inc.
Norcross Wildlife Foundation, Inc.
Norman Foundation
Jessie Smith Noyes Foundation, Inc.
Nathan M. Ohrbach Foundation, Inc.
The Ohrstrom Foundation
The Overbrook Foundation
James C. Penney Foundation
The Pfizer Foundation, Inc.
The Philanthropic Group
Philip Morris Companies, Inc.
Pinewood Foundation
Henry B. Plant Memorial Fund, Inc.
The Prospect Hill Foundation
Philip D. Reed Foundation, Inc.
Rockefeller Brothers Fund, Inc.
Rockefeller Family Fund, Inc.
Rockefeller Financial Services, Philanthropy Department
The Rockefeller Foundation
Lee Romney Foundation, Inc.
Samuel and May Rudin Foundation, Inc.

Grantmaker Location

New York (cont.)

The Scherman Foundation, Inc.
S. H. and Helen R. Scheuer Family Foundation, Inc.
Sarah I. Schieffelin Residuary Trust
The Schiff Foundation
Ralph C. Sheldon Foundation, Inc.
Solow Foundation
Alfred T. Stanley Foundation
The Stebbins Fund, Inc.
The Sulzberger Foundation, Inc.
Surdna Foundation, Inc.
Edna Bailey Sussman Fund
Texaco Foundation
Thanksgiving Foundation
The Oakleigh L. Thorne Foundation
The Tinker Foundation Incorporated
Tortuga Foundation
The Travelers Foundation
The Trust For Mutual Understanding
Underhill Foundation
Unitarian Universalist Veatch Program at Shelter Rock
United States-Japan Foundation
G. Unger Vetlesen Foundation
The Vidda Foundation
Vinmont Foundation, Inc.
DeWitt Wallace-Reader's Digest Fund
Lila Wallace-Reader's Digest Fund
Weeden Foundation
Robert W. Wilson Foundation

Ohio

American Foundation Corporation
Evenor Armington Fund
The Austin Memorial Foundation
Benua Foundation, Inc.
The William Bingham Foundation
Centerior Energy Foundation
The Cleveland Foundation
The Columbus Foundation
The James M. Cox, Jr. Foundation, Inc.
The Thomas J. Emery Memorial
The 1525 Foundation
The GAR Foundation
The George Gund Foundation
The Louise H. and David S. Ingalls Foundation, Inc.
Ireland Foundation
Martha Holden Jennings Foundation
Nelson Mead Fund
John P. Murphy Foundation
The Nord Family Foundation
Perkins Charitable Foundation
The Procter & Gamble Fund
Fran and Warren Rupp Foundation
Sears-Swetland Foundation
The Kelvin and Eleanor Smith Foundation
Kelvin Smith 1980 Charitable Trust
Stranahan Foundation
Nelson Talbott Foundation
The Troy Foundation
Bill & Edith Walter Foundation
Wodecroft Foundation

Oklahoma

The Robert S. and Grayce B. Kerr Foundation, Inc.
The Samuel Roberts Noble Foundation, Inc.
Phillips Petroleum Foundation, Inc.
Sarkeys Foundation
Treacy Foundation, Inc.

Oregon

The Carpenter Foundation
The Collins Foundation
The Jackson Foundation
The Lazar Foundation
McKenzie River Gathering Foundation
Meyer Memorial Trust
OCRI Foundation
Rose E. Tucker Charitable Trust

Pennsylvania

Arcadia Foundation
The Barra Foundation, Inc.
Beneficia Foundation
Changing Horizons Charitable Trust
Claneil Foundation, Inc.
Crystal Channel Foundation
Dolfinger-McMahon Foundation
Samuel S. Fels Fund
The Hamer Foundation
Howard Heinz Endowment
Vira I. Heinz Endowment
The Roy A. Hunt Foundation
Laurel Foundation
McCune Foundation
McLean Contributionship
Richard King Mellon Foundation
Leo Model Foundation, Inc.
The William Penn Foundation
The Pew Charitable Trusts
The Philadelphia Foundation
Sarah Scaife Foundation Incorporated
Snee-Reinhardt Charitable Foundation
Sproul Foundation
Margaret Dorrance Strawbridge Foundation of Pennsylvania II, Inc.
Stroud Foundation
Harry C. Trexler Trust
USX Foundation, Inc.
Union Pacific Foundation
Alex C. Walker Educational & Charitable Foundation
Westinghouse Foundation
The Wyomissing Foundation, Inc.

Rhode Island

The Champlin Foundations
Mustard Seed Foundation, Inc.
The Rhode Island Community Foundation

South Carolina

The Community Foundation Serving Coastal South Carolina
Springs Foundation, Inc.

Tennessee

LifeWorks Foundation
Lyndhurst Foundation

Texas

Abell-Hanger Foundation
El Paso Community Foundation
The William Stamps Farish Fund
The Favrot Fund
Leland Fikes Foundation, Inc.
The Ewing Halsell Foundation
Harris and Eliza Kempner Fund
Caesar Kleberg Foundation for Wildlife Conservation
The Eugene McDermott Foundation
Meadows Foundation, Inc.
The Moody Foundation
Mary Moody Northen, Inc.
Sid W. Richardson Foundation
Rockwell Fund, Inc.
Shell Oil Company Foundation
Southwestern Bell Foundation
The Summerlee Foundation
The Wortham Foundation, Inc.
Margaret Cullinan Wray Charitable Lead Annuity Trust

Virginia

The Beirne Carter Foundation
Chesapeake Corporation Foundation
FishAmerica Foundation
The Hastings Trust
W. Alton Jones Foundation, Inc.
Joy Foundation for Ecological Education and Research
Mars Foundation
Mobil Foundation, Inc.
The Truland Foundation
Virginia Environmental Endowment
Mark and Catherine Winkler Foundation
Wrinkle in Time Foundation

Vermont

The Ben & Jerry's Foundation
Howfirma Foundation
Lintilhac Foundation
The Windham Foundation, Inc.

Washington

A Territory Resource
The Boeing Company
The Bullitt Foundation
Ben B. Cheney Foundation
The Hugh and Jane Ferguson Foundation
Harder Foundation
The Henry M. Jackson Foundation
Kongsgaard-Goldman Foundation
Laird, Norton Foundation
The Mountaineers Foundation
M. J. Murdock Charitable Trust
New Horizon Foundation
Northwest Fund for the Environment
Outdoor Industry Conservation Alliance

Grantmaker Location

Washington (cont.)

Recreational Equipment, Inc.
Sequoia Foundation
Weyerhaeuser Company Foundation
Wilburforce Foundation

Wisconsin

The Lynde and Harry Bradley
    Foundation, Inc.
Patrick and Anna M. Cudahy Fund
The Milwaukee Foundation
Stackner Family Foundation, Inc.

International

Canada

Donner Canadian Foundation
Walter and Duncan Gordon Charitable
    Foundation
The Richard Ivey Foundation
Laidlaw Foundation
Thomas Sill Foundation
Vancouver Foundation

United Kingdom

The Polden-Puckham Charitable
    Foundation

Recipient Location

United States

Alabama

The Nathan Cummings Foundation
W. Alton Jones Foundation, Inc.
Lyndhurst Foundation
McDonnell Douglas Foundation
Mobil Foundation, Inc.
National Geographic Society Education Foundation
Norman Foundation
Jessie Smith Noyes Foundation, Inc.
Patagonia, Inc.
Public Welfare Foundation, Inc.
The Rockefeller Foundation
Shell Oil Company Foundation
USX Foundation, Inc.
WMX Environmental Grants Program

Alaska

ARCO Foundation
The Acorn Foundation
Alaska Conservation Foundation
American Conservation Association, Inc.
S. D. Bechtel, Jr. Foundation
The Ben & Jerry's Foundation
Alexander H. Bright Charitable Trust
The Bullitt Foundation
C. S. Fund
The Nathan Cummings Foundation
The Energy Foundation
Foundation for Deep Ecology
Fund of the Four Directions
The George Gund Foundation
Harder Foundation
Kongsgaard-Goldman Foundation
The Lazar Foundation
Lyndhurst Foundation
The McIntosh Foundation
Charles Stewart Mott Foundation
Ruth Mott Fund
M. J. Murdock Charitable Trust
The New-Land Foundation, Inc.
Norcross Wildlife Foundation, Inc.
The Overbrook Foundation
Patagonia, Inc.
Public Welfare Foundation, Inc.
Recreational Equipment, Inc.
The Scherman Foundation, Inc.
Seventh Generation Fund
The Skaggs Foundation
The Strong Foundation for Environmental Values
Surdna Foundation, Inc.
Nelson Talbott Foundation
Town Creek Foundation, Inc.
True North Foundation
Underhill Foundation

Unitarian Universalist Veatch Program at Shelter Rock
Weeden Foundation

Arizona

ARCO Foundation
The Acorn Foundation
BankAmerica Foundation
The Bauman Foundation
The Bay Foundation
Beldon Fund
The Ben & Jerry's Foundation
Alexander H. Bright Charitable Trust
Jesse Margaret Wilson Budlong Foundation for Animal Aid
C. S. Fund
Liz Claiborne & Art Ortenberg Foundation
Compton Foundation, Inc.
Crystal Channel Foundation
Fanwood Foundation
Ford Foundation
Foundation for Deep Ecology
Frelinghuysen Foundation
General Service Foundation
W. Alton Jones Foundation, Inc.
The Max and Anna Levinson Foundation
The Marshall Fund of Arizona
McDonnell Douglas Foundation
Giles W. and Elise G. Mead Foundation
Joyce Mertz-Gilmore Foundation
Mobil Foundation, Inc.
Charles Stewart Mott Foundation
Ruth Mott Fund
National Fish and Wildlife Foundation
Jessie Smith Noyes Foundation, Inc.
Nathan M. Ohrbach Foundation, Inc.
Spencer T. and Ann W. Olin Foundation
Patagonia, Inc.
The Pew Charitable Trusts
Schultz Foundation, Inc.
Seventh Generation Fund
Stanley Smith Horticultural Trust
The Stratford Foundation
The Tides Foundation
Treacy Foundation, Inc.
Underhill Foundation
Wallace Genetic Foundation, Inc.
Margaret Cullinan Wray Charitable Lead Annuity Trust

Arkansas

Mary Reynolds Babcock Foundation, Inc.
Benton Foundation
FishAmerica Foundation
Ford Foundation
Howfirma Foundation

National Fish and Wildlife Foundation
Jessie Smith Noyes Foundation, Inc.
The Prudential Foundation
Rockefeller Brothers Fund, Inc.
The Winthrop Rockefeller Foundation
Weyerhaeuser Company Foundation

California

ARCO Foundation
AT&T Foundation
The Abelard Foundation West
The Acorn Foundation
The Ahmanson Foundation
Alaska Conservation Foundation
Winifred & Harry B. Allen Foundation
The Jenifer Altman Foundation
American Conservation Association, Inc.
American Express Philanthropic Program
American Foundation Corporation
Angelina Fund, Inc.
Atkinson Foundation
The Austin Memorial Foundation
The Cameron Baird Foundation
BankAmerica Foundation
The Bauman Foundation
S. D. Bechtel, Jr. Foundation
Beldon Fund
The Ben & Jerry's Foundation
Bishop Pine Fund
The Blumenthal Foundation
The Bothin Foundation
Helen Brach Foundation
Alexander H. Bright Charitable Trust
The Robert Brownlee Foundation
Jesse Margaret Wilson Budlong Foundation for Animal Aid
The Bullitt Foundation
C. S. Fund
California Community Foundation
Mary Flagler Cary Charitable Trust
Changing Horizons Charitable Trust
Cheeryble Foundation
Ben B. Cheney Foundation
The Chevron Companies
Columbia Foundation
The Community Foundation of Santa Clara County
Compton Foundation, Inc.
The Conservation and Research Foundation
Conservation, Food & Health Foundation, Inc.
S. H. Cowell Foundation
The Mary A. Crocker Trust
Roy E. Crummer Foundation
Crystal Channel Foundation
Patrick and Anna M. Cudahy Fund

Recipient Location

California (cont.)

The Nathan Cummings Foundation
Damien Foundation
Davis Conservation Foundation
Geraldine R. Dodge Foundation, Inc.
Thelma Doelger Charitable Trust
Gaylord and Dorothy Donnelley Foundation
Echoing Green Foundation
Ederic Foundation, Inc.
The Educational Foundation of America
Arthur M. and Olga T. Eisig-Arthur M. and Kate E. Tode Foundation, Inc.
The Energy Foundation
The Charles Engelhard Foundation
Environment Now Foundation
The Armand G. Erpf Fund, Inc.
The Ettinger Foundation, Inc.
Fanwood Foundation
The Favrot Fund
FishAmerica Foundation
Flintridge Foundation
Ford Foundation
Foundation for Deep Ecology
Fund of the Four Directions
Funding Exchange
The Gap Foundation
The Fred Gellert Foundation
General Service Foundation
The Wallace Alexander Gerbode Foundation, Inc.
The German Marshall Fund of the United States
Global Environmental Project Institute
Global Greengrants Fund
Richard & Rhoda Goldman Fund
The Greenville Foundation
The George Gund Foundation
HKH Foundation
Evelyn and Walter Haas, Jr. Fund
Walter and Elise Haas Fund
Harbor Lights Foundation
Harder Foundation
The Harding Educational and Charitable Foundation
The Hastings Trust
The John Randolph Haynes and Dora Haynes Foundation
Heller Charitable & Educational Fund
The Clarence E. Heller Charitable Foundation
The William and Flora Hewlett Foundation
The Hitachi Foundation
The Hofmann Foundation
The Homeland Foundation
The Horn Foundation
Howfirma Foundation
The Roy A. Hunt Foundation
Hurdle Hill Foundation
The James Irvine Foundation
Island Foundation, Inc.
Jackson Hole Preserve, Inc.
The Henry M. Jackson Foundation
The George Frederick Jewett Foundation
Walter S. Johnson Foundation
W. Alton Jones Foundation, Inc.

The Joyce Foundation
W. K. Kellogg Foundation
Harris and Eliza Kempner Fund
Kongsgaard-Goldman Foundation
The Kresge Foundation
The Lazar Foundation
The Norman Lear Foundation
Levi Strauss Foundation
The Max and Anna Levinson Foundation
Luster Family Foundation, Inc.
The John D. and Catherine T. MacArthur Foundation
James A. Macdonald Foundation
Magowan Family Foundation, Inc.
Marin Community Foundation
The Martin Foundation, Inc.
The McConnell Foundation
McDonnell Douglas Foundation
McKesson Foundation, Inc.
Giles W. and Elise G. Mead Foundation
The Andrew W. Mellon Foundation
Merck Family Fund
The John Merck Fund
Joyce Mertz-Gilmore Foundation
Middlecott Foundation
Mobil Foundation, Inc.
The Moriah Fund, Inc.
Charles Stewart Mott Foundation
Ruth Mott Fund
The National Environmental Education and Training Foundation, Inc.
National Fish and Wildlife Foundation
The New World Foundation
The New York Times Company Foundation, Inc.
The New-Land Foundation, Inc.
Norman Foundation
Andrew Norman Foundation
Kenneth T. and Eileen L. Norris Foundation
Jessie Smith Noyes Foundation, Inc.
Nathan M. Ohrbach Foundation, Inc.
The Ohrstrom Foundation
Orchard Foundation
Ottinger Foundation
Outdoor Industry Conservation Alliance
The Overbrook Foundation
The David and Lucile Packard Foundation
Patagonia, Inc.
Peninsula Community Foundation
The Pew Charitable Trusts
Pew Scholars Program in Conservation and the Environment
Howard Phipps Foundation
Pinewood Foundation
Henry B. Plant Memorial Fund, Inc.
Lynn R. and Karl E. Prickett Fund
Public Welfare Foundation, Inc.
Recreational Equipment, Inc.
The Roberts Foundation
Rockefeller Family Fund, Inc.
The Rockefeller Foundation
Rockwood Fund, Inc.
Lee Romney Foundation, Inc.
Sacharuna Foundation
Sacramento Regional Foundation

San Diego Community Foundation
The San Francisco Foundation
The Sapelo Foundation
The Scherman Foundation, Inc.
Schultz Foundation, Inc.
The Florence and John Schumann Foundation
Ellen Browning Scripps Foundation
Frances Seebe Trust
Elmina B. Sewall Foundation
Shell Oil Company Foundation
The Skaggs Foundation
Stanley Smith Horticultural Trust
The Sonoma County Community Foundation
South Coast Foundation, Inc.
Springhouse Foundation
Alfred T. Stanley Foundation
Steelcase Foundation
The Strong Foundation for Environmental Values
The Morris Stulsaft Foundation
The Sulzberger Foundation, Inc.
The Summerlee Foundation
The Summit Foundation
Surdna Foundation, Inc.
The Switzer Foundation
S. Mark Taper Foundation
The Telesis Foundation
Texaco Foundation
Threshold Foundation
The Tides Foundation
Tortuga Foundation
Town Creek Foundation, Inc.
Toyota USA Foundation
The Travelers Foundation
True North Foundation
The Trust For Mutual Understanding
Alice Tweed Tuohy Foundation
USX Foundation, Inc.
Underhill Foundation
Unitarian Universalist Veatch Program at Shelter Rock
R. T. Vanderbilt Trust
Vanguard Public Foundation
G. Unger Vetlesen Foundation
WMX Environmental Grants Program
Lila Wallace-Reader's Digest Fund
C. A. Webster Foundation
Weeden Foundation
Weyerhaeuser Company Foundation
Whitecap Foundation
The Winslow Foundation
The Dean Witter Foundation
Sidney & Phyllis Wragge Foundation
Margaret Cullinan Wray Charitable Lead Annuity Trust

Colorado

ARCO Foundation
The Abelard Foundation West
Airport Business Center Foundation
The Bay Foundation
Beldon Fund
The Ben & Jerry's Foundation

Recipient Location

Colorado (cont.)

Boettcher Foundation
Ruth H. Brown Foundation
Caribou Fund
Carolyn Foundation
Changing Horizons Charitable Trust
The Chevron Companies
Compton Foundation, Inc.
Adolph Coors Foundation
Crystal Channel Foundation
The Educational Foundation of America
El Pomar Foundation
The Energy Foundation
The Charles Engelhard Foundation
The Ettinger Foundation, Inc.
Ford Foundation
Foundation for Deep Ecology
The Foundation for the National Capital Region
The Frost Foundation, Ltd.
Gates Foundation
General Service Foundation
The Golden Rule Foundation, Inc.
Harbor Lights Foundation
Harder Foundation
The William and Flora Hewlett Foundation
The Homeland Foundation
Hurdle Hill Foundation
Island Foundation
Jackson Hole Preserve, Inc.
Helen K. and Arthur E. Johnson Foundation
W. Alton Jones Foundation, Inc.
The Joyce Foundation
The Henry P. Kendall Foundation
Laurel Foundation
The Lazar Foundation
The Max and Anna Levinson Foundation
The John D. and Catherine T. MacArthur Foundation
Maki Foundation
The Marshall Fund of Arizona
The Martin Foundation, Inc.
Richard King Mellon Foundation
The John Merck Fund
Joyce Mertz-Gilmore Foundation
The Moriah Fund, Inc.
Charles Stewart Mott Foundation
Ruth Mott Fund
The National Environmental Education and Training Foundation, Inc.
National Fish and Wildlife Foundation
The Needmor Fund
The New-Land Foundation, Inc.
The Samuel Roberts Noble Foundation, Inc.
Norman Foundation
The David and Lucile Packard Foundation
Patagonia, Inc.
The Pew Charitable Trusts
Pilot Trust
Public Welfare Foundation, Inc.
Recreational Equipment, Inc.
Rockefeller Family Fund, Inc.
Rockwood Fund, Inc.
The Schiff Foundation
Shell Oil Company Foundation

The Stroh Foundation
The Sulzberger Foundation, Inc.
The Summerlee Foundation
Surdna Foundation, Inc.
Edna Bailey Sussman Fund
Texaco Foundation
The Oakleigh L. Thorne Foundation
The Tides Foundation
Times Mirror Magazines, Inc.
True North Foundation
Turner Foundation, Inc.
USX Foundation, Inc.
Union Pacific Foundation
WMX Environmental Grants Program
Weeden Foundation
The Winslow Foundation

Connecticut

Angelina Fund, Inc.
Clayton Baker Trust
The Theodore H. Barth Foundation, Inc.
The Bauman Foundation
The Howard Bayne Fund
S. D. Bechtel, Jr. Foundation
The Beinecke Foundation, Inc.
Beldon Fund
The Ben & Jerry's Foundation
The William Bingham Foundation
Helen Brach Foundation
Patrick and Aimee Butler Family Foundation
Carolyn Foundation
Chrysler Corporation Fund
Liz Claiborne & Art Ortenberg Foundation
Claneil Foundation, Inc.
The Clark Foundation
The Community Foundation of Greater New Haven
Compton Foundation, Inc.
Conservation, Food & Health Foundation, Inc.
Jessie B. Cox Charitable Trust
Crystal Channel Foundation
The Nathan Cummings Foundation
Davis Conservation Foundation
Geraldine R. Dodge Foundation, Inc.
The Dragon Foundation, Inc.
Eastman Kodak Company Charitable Trust
The Emerald Foundation
GE Fund
Bernard F. and Alva B. Gimbel Foundation, Inc.
Richard & Rhoda Goldman Fund
Hartford Foundation for Public Giving
The Edward W. Hazen Foundation
The William and Flora Hewlett Foundation
The Indian Point Foundation, Inc.
The Louise H. and David S. Ingalls Foundation, Inc.
Ireland Foundation
The Howard Johnson Foundation
The Lagemann Foundation
Larsen Fund, Inc.
Magowan Family Foundation, Inc.
The Andrew W. Mellon Foundation

National Fish and Wildlife Foundation
The Needmor Fund
New England Biolabs Foundation
The New York Times Company Foundation, Inc.
The Nord Family Foundation
Orchard Foundation
The Overbrook Foundation
Patagonia, Inc.
The Perkin Fund
Henry B. Plant Memorial Fund, Inc.
The Procter & Gamble Fund
Public Welfare Foundation, Inc.
Recreational Equipment, Inc.
Rockefeller Brothers Fund, Inc.
The Rockfall Foundation
The Sulzberger Foundation, Inc.
The Summerlee Foundation
Surdna Foundation, Inc.
Edna Bailey Sussman Fund
The Switzer Foundation
S. Mark Taper Foundation
Texaco Foundation
Thanksgiving Foundation
Times Mirror Magazines, Inc.
Town Creek Foundation, Inc.
The Travelers Foundation
Marcia Brady Tucker Foundation
USX Foundation, Inc.
Underhill Foundation
Union Camp Charitable Trust
R. T. Vanderbilt Trust
WMX Environmental Grants Program
Weeden Foundation
Henry E. and Consuelo S. Wenger Foundation, Inc.
Margaret Cullinan Wray Charitable Lead Annuity Trust

Delaware

Chesapeake Bay Trust
The Chevron Companies
Geraldine R. Dodge Foundation, Inc.
Ederic Foundation, Inc.
Fair Play Foundation
The Knapp Foundation, Inc.
The Kresge Foundation
Longwood Foundation, Inc.
Mobil Foundation, Inc.
The William Penn Foundation
Margaret Dorrance Strawbridge Foundation of Pennsylvania II, Inc.
Texaco Foundation
The Tides Foundation
Welfare Foundation, Inc.

District of Columbia

ARCO Foundation
AT&T Foundation
The Achelis Foundation
The Ahmanson Foundation
Airport Business Center Foundation
Alaska Conservation Foundation
The Jenifer Altman Foundation

Recipient Location

District of Columbia (cont.)

American Conservation Association, Inc.
American Foundation Corporation
Angelina Fund, Inc.
The Arca Foundation
Arcadia Foundation
Evenor Armington Fund
Atkinson Foundation
Mary Reynolds Babcock Foundation, Inc.
The Cameron Baird Foundation
Clayton Baker Trust
BankAmerica Foundation
The Barra Foundation, Inc.
The Bauman Foundation
The Bay Foundation
The Howard Bayne Fund
Beldon Fund
Beneficia Foundation
The William Bingham Foundation
The Boeing Company
The Bothin Foundation
Helen Brach Foundation
The Lynde and Harry Bradley Foundation, Inc.
Alexander H. Bright Charitable Trust
W. L. Lyons Brown Foundation
Jesse Margaret Wilson Budlong Foundation for Animal Aid
The Bullitt Foundation
The Bydale Foundation
C. S. Fund
The Morris and Gwendolyn Cafritz Foundation
Carolyn Foundation
Mary Flagler Cary Charitable Trust
Changing Horizons Charitable Trust
Cheeryble Foundation
The Chevron Companies
Chrysler Corporation Fund
Liz Claiborne & Art Ortenberg Foundation
Claneil Foundation, Inc.
Clark Charitable Trust
The Clark Foundation
Columbia Foundation
Compton Foundation, Inc.
The Conservation and Research Foundation
Conservation, Food & Health Foundation, Inc.
S. H. Cowell Foundation
Cox Foundation, Inc.
The James M. Cox, Jr. Foundation, Inc.
Roy E. Crummer Foundation
Patrick and Anna M. Cudahy Fund
The Nathan Cummings Foundation
Damien Foundation
Davis Conservation Foundation
Deer Creek Foundation
The Nelson B. Delavan Foundation
Geraldine R. Dodge Foundation, Inc.
Gaylord and Dorothy Donnelley Foundation
The Max and Victoria Dreyfus Foundation, Inc.
The Elizabeth Ordway Dunn Foundation, Inc.
Eastman Kodak Company Charitable Trust

Echoing Green Foundation
The Educational Foundation of America
Arthur M. and Olga T. Eisig-Arthur M. and Kate E. Tode Foundation, Inc.
The Emerald Foundation
The Energy Foundation
The Charles Engelhard Foundation
Environment Now Foundation
The Armand G. Erpf Fund, Inc.
The Ettinger Foundation, Inc.
Fair Play Foundation
Fanwood Foundation
The Favrot Fund
Samuel S. Fels Fund
Jamee and Marshall Field Foundation
Ford Foundation
Ford Motor Company Fund
Foundation for Deep Ecology
The Foundation for the National Capital Region
Lloyd A. Fry Foundation
The Fund for New Jersey
Fund of the Four Directions
Funding Exchange
GE Fund
The Gap Foundation
The Fred Gellert Foundation
General Service Foundation
The German Marshall Fund of the United States
Global Environmental Project Institute
The Golden Rule Foundation, Inc.
Richard & Rhoda Goldman Fund
Great Lakes Protection Fund
The Greenville Foundation
The William and Mary Greve Foundation, Inc.
The George Gund Foundation
The Hahn Family Foundation
The Hamer Foundation
Harbor Lights Foundation
Harder Foundation
The Harding Educational and Charitable Foundation
Mary W. Harriman Foundation
The Merrill G. & Emita E. Hastings Foundation
Vira I. Heinz Endowment
The Clarence E. Heller Charitable Foundation
The William and Flora Hewlett Foundation
The Hitachi Foundation
The Hofmann Foundation
The Homeland Foundation
Howfirma Foundation
The Charles Evans Hughes Memorial Foundation, Inc.
The Roy A. Hunt Foundation
Hurdle Hill Foundation
The Indian Point Foundation, Inc.
The Louise H. and David S. Ingalls Foundation, Inc.
The International Foundation, Inc.
Ireland Foundation
Island Foundation, Inc.

Ittleson Foundation, Inc.
Jackson Hole Preserve, Inc.
The Henry M. Jackson Foundation
The George Frederick Jewett Foundation
The Howard Johnson Foundation
W. Alton Jones Foundation, Inc.
The Joyce Foundation
W. K. Kellogg Foundation
The Henry P. Kendall Foundation
The Helen & Milton Kimmelman Foundation
F. M. Kirby Foundation, Inc.
The Esther A. and Joseph Klingenstein Fund, Inc.
The Seymour H. Knox Foundation, Inc.
Charles G. Koch Charitable Foundation
Kongsgaard-Goldman Foundation
Laird, Norton Foundation
Larsen Fund, Inc.
Laurel Foundation
The Lazar Foundation
The Max and Anna Levinson Foundation
The Little Family Foundation
Luster Family Foundation, Inc.
Lyndhurst Foundation
The John D. and Catherine T. MacArthur Foundation
James A. Macdonald Foundation
Magowan Family Foundation, Inc.
MARPAT Foundation, Inc.
Mars Foundation
The Marshall Fund of Arizona
The Martin Foundation, Inc.
McDonnell Douglas Foundation
The McIntosh Foundation
McKesson Foundation, Inc.
The McKnight Foundation
Giles W. and Elise G. Mead Foundation
Nelson Mead Fund
The Andrew W. Mellon Foundation
Richard King Mellon Foundation
Merck Family Fund
The John Merck Fund
Joyce Mertz-Gilmore Foundation
The Milwaukee Foundation
Mobil Foundation, Inc.
Leo Model Foundation, Inc.
J. P. Morgan Charitable Trust
The Moriah Fund, Inc.
Charles Stewart Mott Foundation
Ruth Mott Fund
The Curtis and Edith Munson Foundation, Inc.
The National Environmental Education and Training Foundation, Inc.
National Fish and Wildlife Foundation
New Hampshire Charitable Foundation
The New York Times Company Foundation, Inc.
The New-Land Foundation, Inc.
Edward John Noble Foundation, Inc.
The Samuel Roberts Noble Foundation, Inc.
Norcross Wildlife Foundation, Inc.
Kenneth T. and Eileen L. Norris Foundation
Jessie Smith Noyes Foundation, Inc.

District of Columbia (cont.)

OCRI Foundation
The Ohrstrom Foundation
Outdoor Industry Conservation Alliance
The Overbrook Foundation
The David and Lucile Packard Foundation
Patagonia, Inc.
The William Penn Foundation
James C. Penney Foundation
Perkins Charitable Foundation
The Pew Charitable Trusts
Pew Scholars Program in Conservation and the Environment
The Pfizer Foundation, Inc.
Philip Morris Companies, Inc.
Phillips Petroleum Foundation, Inc.
Howard Phipps Foundation
Henry B. Plant Memorial Fund, Inc.
Lynn R. and Karl E. Prickett Fund
Prince Charitable Trusts
The Procter & Gamble Fund
The Prospect Hill Foundation
Public Welfare Foundation, Inc.
Recreational Equipment, Inc.
Philip D. Reed Foundation, Inc.
Smith Richardson Foundation, Inc.
Rockefeller Brothers Fund, Inc.
Rockefeller Family Fund, Inc.
The Rockefeller Foundation
Rockwood Fund, Inc.
Lee Romney Foundation, Inc.
Sacharuna Foundation
Sarah Scaife Foundation Incorporated
The Scherman Foundation, Inc.
Sarah I. Schieffelin Residuary Trust
The Schiff Foundation
Schultz Foundation, Inc.
The Florence and John Schumann Foundation
Sequoia Foundation
Seventh Generation Fund
Elmina B. Sewall Foundation
Shell Oil Company Foundation
Alfred T. Stanley Foundation
Stern Family Fund
Margaret Dorrance Strawbridge Foundation of Pennsylvania II, Inc.
The Stroh Foundation
The Sulzberger Foundation, Inc.
The Summerlee Foundation
The Summit Foundation
Surdna Foundation, Inc.
Nelson Talbott Foundation
Texaco Foundation
Thanksgiving Foundation
The Oakleigh L. Thorne Foundation
Threshold Foundation
The Tides Foundation
The Tinker Foundation Incorporated
Tortuga Foundation
Town Creek Foundation, Inc.
Treacy Foundation, Inc.
True North Foundation
The Truland Foundation
The Trust For Mutual Understanding

Marcia Brady Tucker Foundation
Turner Foundation, Inc.
USX Foundation, Inc.
Underhill Foundation
Union Camp Charitable Trust
Unitarian Universalist Veatch Program at Shelter Rock
United States-Japan Foundation
R. T. Vanderbilt Trust
G. Unger Vetlesen Foundation
Virginia Environmental Endowment
WMX Environmental Grants Program
Wallace Genetic Foundation, Inc.
DeWitt Wallace-Reader's Digest Fund
C. A. Webster Foundation
Weeden Foundation
Weyerhaeuser Company Foundation
Wilburforce Foundation
Sidney & Phyllis Wragge Foundation
Margaret Cullinan Wray Charitable Lead Annuity Trust

Florida

American Conservation Association, Inc.
American Express Philanthropic Program
Atlantic Foundation
Mary Reynolds Babcock Foundation, Inc.
The George F. Baker Trust
The Barra Foundation, Inc.
Beldon Fund
James Ford Bell Foundation
Benua Foundation, Inc.
The Frank Stanley Beveridge Foundation, Inc.
Mary Flagler Cary Charitable Trust
The Chevron Companies
Liz Claiborne & Art Ortenberg Foundation
The Community Foundation of Sarasota County, Inc.
The Conservation and Research Foundation
Conservation, Food & Health Foundation, Inc.
Cox Foundation, Inc.
The Elizabeth Ordway Dunn Foundation, Inc.
Jessie Ball duPont Religious, Charitable and Educational Fund
The Energy Foundation
The Charles Engelhard Foundation
Environmental Education Foundation of Florida, Inc.
The William Stamps Farish Fund
Felburn Foundation
Jamee and Marshall Field Foundation
FishAmerica Foundation
Walter and Josephine Ford Fund
The German Marshall Fund of the United States
Harder Foundation
Gladys and Roland Harriman Foundation
The Hastings Trust
Ireland Foundation
W. Alton Jones Foundation, Inc.
The Seymour H. Knox Foundation, Inc.
The Max and Anna Levinson Foundation

The John D. and Catherine T. MacArthur Foundation
The McIntosh Foundation
Nelson Mead Fund
Richard King Mellon Foundation
Joyce Mertz-Gilmore Foundation
Mobil Foundation, Inc.
Leo Model Foundation, Inc.
Charles Stewart Mott Foundation
The Curtis and Edith Munson Foundation, Inc.
National Fish and Wildlife Foundation
The Needmor Fund
The New York Times Company Foundation, Inc.
Norcross Wildlife Foundation, Inc.
Norman Foundation
Jessie Smith Noyes Foundation, Inc.
Orchard Foundation
Ottinger Foundation
Perkins Charitable Foundation
The Pew Charitable Trusts
Public Welfare Foundation, Inc.
The Rockefeller Foundation
The Scherman Foundation, Inc.
Schultz Foundation, Inc.
Sears-Swetland Foundation
Shell Oil Company Foundation
Margaret Dorrance Strawbridge Foundation of Pennsylvania II, Inc.
Surdna Foundation, Inc.
Texaco Foundation
The Tides Foundation
Times Mirror Magazines, Inc.
The Truland Foundation
USX Foundation, Inc.
Underhill Foundation
Union Camp Charitable Trust
R. T. Vanderbilt Trust
WMX Environmental Grants Program
DeWitt Wallace-Reader's Digest Fund
Lila Wallace-Reader's Digest Fund
Weeden Foundation
Wodecroft Foundation

Georgia

AT&T Foundation
Mary Reynolds Babcock Foundation, Inc.
S. D. Bechtel, Jr. Foundation
Beldon Fund
The Chevron Companies
Cox Foundation, Inc.
The Energy Foundation
Ford Foundation
Ford Motor Company Fund
Fund of the Four Directions
Funding Exchange
Georgia Power Foundation, Inc.
Georgia-Pacific Foundation
The Edward W. Hazen Foundation
W. Alton Jones Foundation, Inc.
Lyndhurst Foundation
Metropolitan Atlanta Community Foundation, Inc.
The Moriah Fund, Inc.

Recipient Location

Georgia (cont.)
Charles Stewart Mott Foundation
The Curtis and Edith Munson Foundation, Inc.
National Fish and Wildlife Foundation
Norman Foundation
Jessie Smith Noyes Foundation, Inc.
Rockefeller Family Fund, Inc.
The Sapelo Foundation
Schultz Foundation, Inc.
Turner Foundation, Inc.
Union Camp Charitable Trust
Unitarian Universalist Veatch Program at Shelter Rock
WMX Environmental Grants Program
Joseph B. Whitehead Foundation
Robert W. Woodruff Foundation, Inc.

Hawaii
Airport Business Center Foundation
Atherton Family Foundation
James & Abigail Campbell Foundation
The Chevron Companies
Compton Foundation, Inc.
Cooke Foundation, Limited
Geraldine R. Dodge Foundation, Inc.
Gaylord and Dorothy Donnelley Foundation
The Charles Engelhard Foundation
Foundation for Deep Ecology
Mary D. and Walter F. Frear Eleemosynary Trust
The Barbara Gauntlett Foundation, Inc.
General Service Foundation
The Wallace Alexander Gerbode Foundation, Inc.
Hawaii Community Foundation
Hawaiian Electric Industries Charitable Foundation
The Homeland Foundation
The John D. and Catherine T. MacArthur Foundation
Magowan Family Foundation, Inc.
McInerny Foundation
National Fish and Wildlife Foundation
The David and Lucile Packard Foundation
Patagonia, Inc.
The Rockefeller Foundation
Stanley Smith Horticultural Trust
Margaret Dorrance Strawbridge Foundation of Pennsylvania II, Inc.
The Tides Foundation
WMX Environmental Grants Program
Weeden Foundation
G. N. Wilcox Trust

Idaho
ARCO Foundation
A Territory Resource
The Ahmanson Foundation
BankAmerica Foundation
The Bullitt Foundation
Compton Foundation, Inc.
Deer Creek Foundation
The Educational Foundation of America
The Charles Engelhard Foundation
Environment Now Foundation
Fanwood Foundation
General Service Foundation
Global Environmental Project Institute
Harder Foundation
Mary W. Harriman Foundation
W. Alton Jones Foundation, Inc.
The Lazar Foundation
The Little Family Foundation
Maki Foundation
Charles Stewart Mott Foundation
Ruth Mott Fund
M. J. Murdock Charitable Trust
National Fish and Wildlife Foundation
The Needmor Fund
Jessie Smith Noyes Foundation, Inc.
OCRI Foundation
Nathan M. Ohrbach Foundation, Inc.
The Ohrstrom Foundation
Patagonia, Inc.
The Pew Charitable Trusts
Public Welfare Foundation, Inc.
Recreational Equipment, Inc.
Nelson Talbott Foundation
The Tides Foundation
Union Pacific Foundation
Unitarian Universalist Veatch Program at Shelter Rock
Weyerhaeuser Company Foundation

Illinois
ARCO Foundation
AT&T Foundation
Airport Business Center Foundation
American Express Philanthropic Program
The Bauman Foundation
The Bay Foundation
S. D. Bechtel, Jr. Foundation
The Beinecke Foundation, Inc.
Beldon Fund
The Ben & Jerry's Foundation
The Bersted Foundation
Helen Brach Foundation
The Buchanan Family Foundation
The Cargill Foundation
Changing Horizons Charitable Trust
The Chicago Community Trust
Cox Foundation, Inc.
Crystal Channel Foundation
The Nathan Cummings Foundation
Gaylord and Dorothy Donnelley Foundation
Eastman Kodak Company Charitable Trust
The Energy Foundation
The Field Foundation of Illinois, Inc.
Jamee and Marshall Field Foundation
Leland Fikes Foundation, Inc.
Ford Motor Company Fund
Foundation for Deep Ecology
Lloyd A. Fry Foundation
Fund of the Four Directions
Great Lakes Protection Fund
The George Gund Foundation
The Hamer Foundation
The William and Flora Hewlett Foundation
The Hofmann Foundation
Ireland Foundation
The Henry M. Jackson Foundation
The Joyce Foundation
W. K. Kellogg Foundation
The John D. and Catherine T. MacArthur Foundation
Mars Foundation
The Martin Foundation, Inc.
The McKnight Foundation
Nelson Mead Fund
Joyce Mertz-Gilmore Foundation
The Milwaukee Foundation
The Moriah Fund, Inc.
Charles Stewart Mott Foundation
Ruth Mott Fund
The Curtis and Edith Munson Foundation, Inc.
National Fish and Wildlife Foundation
Jessie Smith Noyes Foundation, Inc.
The Pew Charitable Trusts
Prince Charitable Trusts
Pritzker Foundation
Public Welfare Foundation, Inc.
The Summerlee Foundation
Surdna Foundation, Inc.
The Oakleigh L. Thorne Foundation
The Tides Foundation
USX Foundation, Inc.
Unitarian Universalist Veatch Program at Shelter Rock
WMX Environmental Grants Program
Henry E. and Consuelo S. Wenger Foundation, Inc.

Indiana
Beldon Fund
The Ben & Jerry's Foundation
Chrysler Corporation Fund
The Clowes Fund, Inc.
Olive B. Cole Foundation
The Energy Foundation
English-Bonter-Mitchell Foundation
Ford Motor Company Fund
The W. C. Griffith Foundation
The George Gund Foundation
The Joyce Foundation
Lilly Endowment, Inc.
The Martin Foundation, Inc.
The Moriah Fund, Inc.
Charles Stewart Mott Foundation
National Fish and Wildlife Foundation
Nicholas H. Noyes, Jr. Memorial Foundation
Public Welfare Foundation, Inc.
The Florence and John Schumann Foundation
Texaco Foundation
The Travelers Foundation
USX Foundation, Inc.
WMX Environmental Grants Program

Recipient Location

Iowa

C. S. Fund
The Educational Foundation of America
FishAmerica Foundation
Ford Foundation
W. Alton Jones Foundation, Inc.
The Joyce Foundation
W. K. Kellogg Foundation
The Kresge Foundation
The McKnight Foundation
Charles Stewart Mott Foundation
National Fish and Wildlife Foundation
Northwest Area Foundation
Jessie Smith Noyes Foundation, Inc.
Public Welfare Foundation, Inc.
True North Foundation

Kansas

The Austin Memorial Foundation
The Boeing Company
Compton Foundation, Inc.
The Conservation and Research Foundation
The Nathan Cummings Foundation
The Emerald Foundation
FishAmerica Foundation
Foundation for Deep Ecology
Give to the Earth Foundation
Richard & Rhoda Goldman Fund
The Hall Family Foundation
The Merrill G. & Emita E. Hastings Foundation
The Clarence E. Heller Charitable Foundation
The Roy A. Hunt Foundation
W. Alton Jones Foundation, Inc.
W. K. Kellogg Foundation
Metropolitan Life Foundation
Charles Stewart Mott Foundation
The New-Land Foundation, Inc.
The Pew Charitable Trusts
Phillips Petroleum Foundation, Inc.
The Powell Family Foundation
The Rockefeller Foundation
Wallace Genetic Foundation, Inc.

Kentucky

Angelina Fund, Inc.
The Austin Memorial Foundation
Mary Reynolds Babcock Foundation, Inc.
Beldon Fund
W. L. Lyons Brown Foundation
The Nathan Cummings Foundation
The William Stamps Farish Fund
The German Marshall Fund of the United States
W. Alton Jones Foundation, Inc.
W. K. Kellogg Foundation
Lyndhurst Foundation
Ruth Mott Fund
The New World Foundation
Norman Foundation
The Norton Foundation, Inc.
Jessie Smith Noyes Foundation, Inc.
Ottinger Foundation
James C. Penney Foundation
The Procter & Gamble Fund
Public Welfare Foundation, Inc.
The Florence and John Schumann Foundation
Thanksgiving Foundation
Unitarian Universalist Veatch Program at Shelter Rock
Virginia Environmental Endowment

Louisiana

Mary Reynolds Babcock Foundation, Inc.
S. D. Bechtel, Jr. Foundation
Beldon Fund
The Chevron Companies
Echoing Green Foundation
Funding Exchange
W. Alton Jones Foundation, Inc.
The Lauder Foundation, Inc.
The McKnight Foundation
Joyce Mertz-Gilmore Foundation
National Fish and Wildlife Foundation
The New World Foundation
Jessie Smith Noyes Foundation, Inc.
The Pew Charitable Trusts
Public Welfare Foundation, Inc.
The Florence and John Schumann Foundation
Shell Oil Company Foundation
Texaco Foundation
The Travelers Foundation
USX Foundation, Inc.
Union Pacific Foundation
Unitarian Universalist Veatch Program at Shelter Rock
WMX Environmental Grants Program

Maine

American Foundation Corporation
L. L. Bean, Inc.
Beldon Fund
The Ben & Jerry's Foundation
The Betterment Fund
The William Bingham Foundation
Botwinick-Wolfensohn Foundation, Inc.
Alexander H. Bright Charitable Trust
The Cabot Family Charitable Trust
Conservation, Food & Health Foundation, Inc.
Jessie B. Cox Charitable Trust
The Cricket Foundation
Davis Conservation Foundation
Cleveland H. Dodge Foundation, Inc.
Geraldine R. Dodge Foundation, Inc.
The Dragon Foundation, Inc.
The Energy Foundation
The Charles Engelhard Foundation
Jamee and Marshall Field Foundation
Fields Pond Foundation, Inc.
FishAmerica Foundation
Walter and Josephine Ford Fund
GE Fund
Greater Piscataqua Community Foundation
Howfirma Foundation
The Indian Point Foundation, Inc.
The Louise H. and David S. Ingalls Foundation, Inc.
Ireland Foundation
Island Foundation, Inc.
W. Alton Jones Foundation, Inc.
The Knapp Foundation, Inc.
The Seymour H. Knox Foundation, Inc.
The Kresge Foundation
Maine Community Foundation, Inc.
MARPAT Foundation, Inc.
Richard King Mellon Foundation
Merck Family Fund
The John Merck Fund
Middlecott Foundation
Charles Stewart Mott Foundation
National Fish and Wildlife Foundation
New England Biolabs Foundation
The New York Times Company Foundation, Inc.
Norcross Wildlife Foundation, Inc.
Orchard Foundation
Outdoor Industry Conservation Alliance
Patagonia, Inc.
Amelia Peabody Charitable Fund
James C. Penney Foundation
The Pew Charitable Trusts
Ellis L. Phillips Foundation
Public Welfare Foundation, Inc.
Recreational Equipment, Inc.
Rockefeller Family Fund, Inc.
Elmina B. Sewall Foundation
Margaret Dorrance Strawbridge Foundation of Pennsylvania II, Inc.
The Stroh Foundation
The Sudbury Foundation
Surdna Foundation, Inc.
Town Creek Foundation, Inc.
G. Unger Vetlesen Foundation
WMX Environmental Grants Program
Weeden Foundation
The William P. Wharton Trust

Maryland

ARCO Foundation
AT&T Foundation
The Abell Foundation
American Foundation Corporation
Clayton Baker Trust
Baltimore Gas and Electric Foundation, Inc.
The Bauman Foundation
Beldon Fund
Alexander H. Bright Charitable Trust
Alex. Brown & Sons Charitable Foundation, Inc.
H. Barksdale Brown Charitable Trust
The Bullitt Foundation
C. S. Fund
The Morris and Gwendolyn Cafritz Foundation
Mary Flagler Cary Charitable Trust
Changing Horizons Charitable Trust

Recipient Location

Maryland (cont.)

Chesapeake Bay Trust
Chesapeake Corporation Foundation
The Chevron Companies
Compton Foundation, Inc.
The Conservation and Research Foundation
Roy E. Crummer Foundation
Crystal Channel Foundation
The Nathan Cummings Foundation
Gaylord and Dorothy Donnelley Foundation
The Elizabeth Ordway Dunn
  Foundation, Inc.
Jessie Ball duPont Religious, Charitable
  and Educational Fund
Ederic Foundation, Inc.
The Educational Foundation of America
The Energy Foundation
The Charles Engelhard Foundation
Fair Play Foundation
Fanwood Foundation
The Foundation for the National
  Capital Region
The Jacob and Annita France
  Foundation, Inc.
Fund of the Four Directions
The Gap Foundation
HKH Foundation
Mary W. Harriman Foundation
The Clarence E. Heller Charitable
  Foundation
The Homeland Foundation
Howfirma Foundation
Island Foundation, Inc.
W. Alton Jones Foundation, Inc.
The Joyce Foundation
F. M. Kirby Foundation, Inc.
The Knapp Foundation, Inc.
The Kresge Foundation
The Lazar Foundation
The Max and Anna Levinson Foundation
The John D. and Catherine T. MacArthur
  Foundation
MARPAT Foundation, Inc.
Mars Foundation
McDonnell Douglas Foundation
The Andrew W. Mellon Foundation
Richard King Mellon Foundation
Merck Family Fund
Robert G. and Anne M. Merrick
  Foundation, Inc.
Metropolitan Life Foundation
The Moriah Fund, Inc.
Charles Stewart Mott Foundation
Ruth Mott Fund
The National Environmental Education
  and Training Foundation, Inc.
National Fish and Wildlife Foundation
New England Biolabs Foundation
The New York Times Company
  Foundation, Inc.
Jessie Smith Noyes Foundation, Inc.
The Ohrstrom Foundation
The Overbrook Foundation
The David and Lucile Packard Foundation
Amelia Peabody Charitable Fund

The William Penn Foundation
James C. Penney Foundation
The Pew Charitable Trusts
Pew Scholars Program in Conservation
  and the Environment
Phillips Petroleum Foundation, Inc.
Prince Charitable Trusts
Public Welfare Foundation, Inc.
Rockefeller Brothers Fund, Inc.
Rockefeller Family Fund, Inc.
Lee Romney Foundation, Inc.
Sarah I. Schieffelin Residuary Trust
The Florence and John Schumann
  Foundation
Sears-Swetland Foundation
Elmina B. Sewall Foundation
Shell Oil Company Foundation
Sproul Foundation
The Summerlee Foundation
Surdna Foundation, Inc.
Threshold Foundation
The Tides Foundation
Times Mirror Magazines, Inc.
The Tinker Foundation Incorporated
Town Creek Foundation, Inc.
The Travelers Foundation
The Truland Foundation
The Trust For Mutual Understanding
Marcia Brady Tucker Foundation
The USF&G Foundation, Inc.
Union Camp Charitable Trust
Unitarian Universalist Veatch Program
  at Shelter Rock
Virginia Environmental Endowment
WMX Environmental Grants Program
Wallace Genetic Foundation, Inc.
Welfare Foundation, Inc.
Westinghouse Foundation
Weyerhaeuser Company Foundation

Massachusetts

ARCO Foundation
AT&T Foundation
The Ahmanson Foundation
The George I. Alden Trust
American Conservation Association, Inc.
American Express Philanthropic Program
Angelina Fund, Inc.
The Arca Foundation
The Austin Memorial Foundation
Azadoutioun Foundation
The Bailey Wildlife Foundation
Clayton Baker Trust
The George F. Baker Trust
The Bauman Foundation
The Howard Bayne Fund
Beldon Fund
The Ben & Jerry's Foundation
The Frank Stanley Beveridge
  Foundation, Inc.
The Lynde and Harry Bradley
  Foundation, Inc.
Otto Bremer Foundation
Alexander H. Bright Charitable Trust
The Bullitt Foundation

Patrick and Aimee Butler Family
  Foundation
The Bydale Foundation
C. S. Fund
The Cabot Family Charitable Trust
Ward M. & Mariam C. Canaday
  Educational and Charitable Trust
Carolyn Foundation
Mary Flagler Cary Charitable Trust
The Chevron Companies
Chrysler Corporation Fund
Claneil Foundation, Inc.
Clark Charitable Trust
The Clowes Fund, Inc.
Compton Foundation, Inc.
Conservation, Food & Health
  Foundation, Inc.
S. H. Cowell Foundation
Cox Foundation, Inc.
Jessie B. Cox Charitable Trust
The Cricket Foundation
The Mary A. Crocker Trust
Patrick and Anna M. Cudahy Fund
Charles E. Culpeper Foundation, Inc.
The Nathan Cummings Foundation
The Fred Harris Daniels Foundation, Inc.
The Arthur Vining Davis Foundations
Davis Conservation Foundation
Deer Creek Foundation
Geraldine R. Dodge Foundation, Inc.
Oliver S. and Jennie R. Donaldson
  Charitable Trust
The Max and Victoria Dreyfus
  Foundation, Inc.
Echoing Green Foundation
The Educational Foundation of America
The Energy Foundation
The Charles Engelhard Foundation
The Armand G. Erpf Fund, Inc.
Fanwood Foundation
The Favrot Fund
Jamee and Marshall Field Foundation
Fields Pond Foundation, Inc.
Ford Foundation
Ford Motor Company Fund
Walter and Josephine Ford Fund
Foundation for Deep Ecology
The Foundation for the National
  Capital Region
Frelinghuysen Foundation
The Fund for Preservation of Wildlife
  and Natural Areas
Fund of the Four Directions
Funding Exchange
GE Fund
The Fred Gellert Foundation
General Service Foundation
The German Marshall Fund of
  the United States
Richard & Rhoda Goldman Fund
Great Lakes Protection Fund
Greater Piscataqua Community Foundation
The George Gund Foundation
HKH Foundation
The Hahn Family Foundation

Recipient Location

Massachusetts (cont.)
Harbor Lights Foundation
The William and Flora Hewlett Foundation
The Homeland Foundation
Howfirma Foundation
The Roy A. Hunt Foundation
Hurdle Hill Foundation
The Hyams Foundation
The Indian Point Foundation, Inc.
The James Irvine Foundation
Island Foundation, Inc.
Island Foundation
Ittleson Foundation, Inc.
The George Frederick Jewett Foundation
The Howard Johnson Foundation
W. Alton Jones Foundation, Inc.
The Joyce Foundation
W. K. Kellogg Foundation
The Henry P. Kendall Foundation
The Esther A. and Joseph Klingenstein Fund, Inc.
The Knapp Foundation, Inc.
The Seymour H. Knox Foundation, Inc.
The Kresge Foundation
Larsen Fund, Inc.
The Norman Lear Foundation
The Little Family Foundation
Richard Lounsbery Foundation, Inc.
Luster Family Foundation, Inc.
The John D. and Catherine T. MacArthur Foundation
Maine Community Foundation, Inc.
The Martin Foundation, Inc.
Massachusetts Environmental Trust
Nelson Mead Fund
The Andrew W. Mellon Foundation
Richard King Mellon Foundation
Merck Family Fund
The John Merck Fund
Joyce Mertz-Gilmore Foundation
Middlecott Foundation
Mobil Foundation, Inc.
J. P. Morgan Charitable Trust
The Moriah Fund, Inc.
Charles Stewart Mott Foundation
Ruth Mott Fund
The Curtis and Edith Munson Foundation, Inc.
Mustard Seed Foundation, Inc.
National Fish and Wildlife Foundation
National Geographic Society Education Foundation
New England Biolabs Foundation
New Hampshire Charitable Foundation
The New World Foundation
The New York Times Company Foundation, Inc.
The New-Land Foundation, Inc.
Edward John Noble Foundation, Inc.
Norcross Wildlife Foundation, Inc.
Norman Foundation
Northwest Fund for the Environment
Jessie Smith Noyes Foundation, Inc.
Orchard Foundation
The Overbrook Foundation

The David and Lucile Packard Foundation
Patagonia, Inc.
Amelia Peabody Charitable Fund
James C. Penney Foundation
The Pew Charitable Trusts
The Pfizer Foundation, Inc.
Ellis L. Phillips Foundation
Howard Phipps Foundation
Henry B. Plant Memorial Fund, Inc.
Lynn R. and Karl E. Prickett Fund
Prince Charitable Trusts
The Prospect Hill Foundation
Public Welfare Foundation, Inc.
Smith Richardson Foundation, Inc.
Rockefeller Brothers Fund, Inc.
Rockefeller Family Fund, Inc.
The Rockefeller Foundation
Lee Romney Foundation, Inc.
The Florence and John Schumann Foundation
Sequoia Foundation
Elmina B. Sewall Foundation
Shell Oil Company Foundation
South Coast Foundation, Inc.
Anna B. Stearns Charitable Foundation, Inc.
Stoddard Charitable Trust
The Stratford Foundation
The Sudbury Foundation
Surdna Foundation, Inc.
The Switzer Foundation
Nelson Talbott Foundation
Texaco Foundation
The Oakleigh L. Thorne Foundation
The Tides Foundation
The Tinker Foundation Incorporated
Tortuga Foundation
Town Creek Foundation, Inc.
The Trust For Mutual Understanding
Unitarian Universalist Veatch Program at Shelter Rock
G. Unger Vetlesen Foundation
WMX Environmental Grants Program
Wallace Genetic Foundation, Inc.
Weeden Foundation
Henry E. and Consuelo S. Wenger Foundation, Inc.
Westinghouse Foundation
The William P. Wharton Trust
Sidney & Phyllis Wragge Foundation

Michigan
AT&T Foundation
The Jenifer Altman Foundation
Americana Foundation, Inc.
Bay Area Community Foundation
Beldon Fund
Chrysler Corporation Fund
Dart Foundation
The Herbert H. and Grace A. Dow Foundation
FishAmerica Foundation
Ford Foundation
Ford Motor Company Fund
Walter and Josephine Ford Fund
Foundation for Deep Ecology

Funding Exchange
The Rollin M. Gerstacker Foundation
Great Lakes Protection Fund
Harder Foundation
Hudson-Webber Foundation
W. Alton Jones Foundation, Inc.
The Joyce Foundation
W. K. Kellogg Foundation
The Kresge Foundation
Longwood Foundation, Inc.
McGregor Fund
The Andrew W. Mellon Foundation
Charles Stewart Mott Foundation
Ruth Mott Fund
National Fish and Wildlife Foundation
The David and Lucile Packard Foundation
Patagonia, Inc.
Recreational Equipment, Inc.
Steelcase Foundation
The Stroh Foundation
The Charles J. Strosacker Foundation
Edna Bailey Sussman Fund
USX Foundation, Inc.
WMX Environmental Grants Program
Henry E. and Consuelo S. Wenger Foundation, Inc.
Weyerhaeuser Company Foundation

Minnesota
The Jenifer Altman Foundation
American Foundation Corporation
Elmer L. & Eleanor J. Andersen Foundation
The Bauman Foundation
Beldon Fund
David Winton Bell Foundation
James Ford Bell Foundation
The Ben & Jerry's Foundation
Blandin Foundation
The Lynde and Harry Bradley Foundation, Inc.
Otto Bremer Foundation
The Bush Foundation
Patrick and Aimee Butler Family Foundation
C. S. Fund
The Cargill Foundation
Carolyn Foundation
The Nathan Cummings Foundation
Dayton Hudson Foundation
Gaylord and Dorothy Donnelley Foundation
The Educational Foundation of America
The Energy Foundation
FishAmerica Foundation
Foundation for Deep Ecology
Fund of the Four Directions
Great Lakes Protection Fund
W. Alton Jones Foundation, Inc.
The Joyce Foundation
W. K. Kellogg Foundation
F. M. Kirby Foundation, Inc.
Larsen Fund, Inc.
The Max and Anna Levinson Foundation
The John D. and Catherine T. MacArthur Foundation
Marbrook Foundation

© 1995 Environmental Data Resources, Inc.

611

Recipient Location

Minnesota (cont.)

The Martin Foundation, Inc.
The McKnight Foundation
The John Merck Fund
Joyce Mertz-Gilmore Foundation
The Minneapolis Foundation
Charles Stewart Mott Foundation
Ruth Mott Fund
National Fish and Wildlife Foundation
Edward John Noble Foundation, Inc.
Norman Foundation
Northwest Area Foundation
Jessie Smith Noyes Foundation, Inc.
Onan Family Foundation
Patagonia, Inc.
The Pew Charitable Trusts
The Prudential Foundation
Public Welfare Foundation, Inc.
Rockefeller Family Fund, Inc.
Seventh Generation Fund
Surdna Foundation, Inc.
The Tides Foundation
Unitarian Universalist Veatch Program at Shelter Rock
Wallace Genetic Foundation, Inc.

Mississippi

Mary Reynolds Babcock Foundation, Inc.
The Ben & Jerry's Foundation
The Chevron Companies
The McKnight Foundation
National Fish and Wildlife Foundation
The Ohrstrom Foundation
Weyerhaeuser Company Foundation

Missouri

ARCO Foundation
Atherton Family Foundation
The Bay Foundation
Beldon Fund
Blandin Foundation
Alexander H. Bright Charitable Trust
Liz Claiborne & Art Ortenberg Foundation
The Elizabeth Ordway Dunn Foundation, Inc.
The Educational Foundation of America
FishAmerica Foundation
Ford Motor Company Fund
The Hall Family Foundation
Hurdle Hill Foundation
W. Alton Jones Foundation, Inc.
The Kresge Foundation
Richard Lounsbery Foundation, Inc.
The John D. and Catherine T. MacArthur Foundation
McDonnell Douglas Foundation
Nelson Mead Fund
The Andrew W. Mellon Foundation
Charles Stewart Mott Foundation
National Fish and Wildlife Foundation
New England Biolabs Foundation
Jessie Smith Noyes Foundation, Inc.
Spencer T. and Ann W. Olin Foundation
The David and Lucile Packard Foundation

Patagonia, Inc.
The Powell Family Foundation
Prince Charitable Trusts
Stanley Smith Horticultural Trust
Southwestern Bell Foundation
The Tides Foundation
Unitarian Universalist Veatch Program at Shelter Rock
Weeden Foundation

Montana

ARCO Foundation
A Territory Resource
The Abelard Foundation West
American Conservation Association, Inc.
American Foundation Corporation
Angelina Fund, Inc.
Beldon Fund
James Ford Bell Foundation
The Ben & Jerry's Foundation
The Bullitt Foundation
Carolyn Foundation
Liz Claiborne & Art Ortenberg Foundation
Compton Foundation, Inc.
The Nathan Cummings Foundation
Deer Creek Foundation
Gaylord and Dorothy Donnelley Foundation
The Educational Foundation of America
The Charles Engelhard Foundation
The Ettinger Foundation, Inc.
Fanwood Foundation
The Hugh and Jane Ferguson Foundation
Jamee and Marshall Field Foundation
FishAmerica Foundation
Ford Foundation
Foundation for Deep Ecology
Fund of the Four Directions
The Greenville Foundation
The William and Mary Greve Foundation, Inc.
Harder Foundation
The Merrill G. & Emita E. Hastings Foundation
The Horn Foundation
Island Foundation
Jackson Hole Preserve, Inc.
The George Frederick Jewett Foundation
W. K. Kellogg Foundation
Charles G. Koch Charitable Foundation
Kongsgaard-Goldman Foundation
The Lazar Foundation
The Max and Anna Levinson Foundation
Maki Foundation
The Martin Foundation, Inc.
Ruth Mott Fund
M. J. Murdock Charitable Trust
National Fish and Wildlife Foundation
The Needmor Fund
The New-Land Foundation, Inc.
Edward John Noble Foundation, Inc.
Norman Foundation
Northwest Area Foundation
Northwest Fund for the Environment
Jessie Smith Noyes Foundation, Inc.
The Ohrstrom Foundation

Outdoor Industry Conservation Alliance
Patagonia, Inc.
The Pew Charitable Trusts
Public Welfare Foundation, Inc.
Recreational Equipment, Inc.
Lee Romney Foundation, Inc.
Shell Oil Company Foundation
The Summerlee Foundation
The Tides Foundation
Town Creek Foundation, Inc.
Turner Foundation, Inc.
Unitarian Universalist Veatch Program at Shelter Rock
WMX Environmental Grants Program
Weeden Foundation
Henry E. and Consuelo S. Wenger Foundation, Inc.
Weyerhaeuser Company Foundation
Sidney & Phyllis Wragge Foundation

Nebraska

The Ahmanson Foundation
The Austin Memorial Foundation
The Butler Foundation
The Nathan Cummings Foundation
The Joyce Foundation
W. K. Kellogg Foundation
Charles Stewart Mott Foundation
Northwest Area Foundation
Jessie Smith Noyes Foundation, Inc.
Public Welfare Foundation, Inc.
The Tides Foundation
The Truland Foundation
Wallace Genetic Foundation, Inc.

Nevada

The Acorn Foundation
BankAmerica Foundation
C. S. Fund
The Educational Foundation of America
Fund of the Four Directions
Funding Exchange
W. Alton Jones Foundation, Inc.
The John Merck Fund
Ruth Mott Fund
The Needmor Fund
Norman Foundation
Jessie Smith Noyes Foundation, Inc.
Patagonia, Inc.
Public Welfare Foundation, Inc.

New Hampshire

ARCO Foundation
The Jenifer Altman Foundation
Evenor Armington Fund
The Austin Memorial Foundation
The Ben & Jerry's Foundation
Ruth H. Brown Foundation
W. L. Lyons Brown Foundation
The Butler Foundation
Changing Horizons Charitable Trust
The Chevron Companies
Compton Foundation, Inc.
The Mary A. Crocker Trust

Recipient Location

New Hampshire (cont.)

The Nathan Cummings Foundation
Davis Conservation Foundation
Geraldine R. Dodge Foundation, Inc.
Oliver S. and Jennie R. Donaldson
 Charitable Trust
Jamee and Marshall Field Foundation
Ford Foundation
The Foundation for the National
 Capital Region
The Fund for Preservation of Wildlife
 and Natural Areas
Fund of the Four Directions
The Gap Foundation
Gates Foundation
Greater Piscataqua Community Foundation
Gladys and Roland Harriman Foundation
The Homeland Foundation
Howfirma Foundation
The Roy A. Hunt Foundation
The George Frederick Jewett Foundation
The Howard Johnson Foundation
W. Alton Jones Foundation, Inc.
The Lagemann Foundation
Laurel Foundation
Luster Family Foundation, Inc.
Maine Community Foundation, Inc.
MARPAT Foundation, Inc.
Mars Foundation
The John Merck Fund
Charles Stewart Mott Foundation
National Fish and Wildlife Foundation
New Hampshire Charitable Foundation
The New World Foundation
The New York Times Company
 Foundation, Inc.
Orchard Foundation
Phillips Petroleum Foundation, Inc.
Ellis L. Phillips Foundation
The Prudential Foundation
Lee Romney Foundation, Inc.
Sacharuna Foundation
Schultz Foundation, Inc.
Elmina B. Sewall Foundation
Snee-Reinhardt Charitable Foundation
Springhouse Foundation
The Stratford Foundation
The Summit Foundation
The Switzer Foundation
The Oakleigh L. Thorne Foundation
The Vidda Foundation
The William P. Wharton Trust
Margaret Cullinan Wray Charitable
 Lead Annuity Trust

New Jersey

AT&T Foundation
The Bailey Wildlife Foundation
The Barra Foundation, Inc.
The Howard Bayne Fund
The Ben & Jerry's Foundation
Beneficia Foundation
The Boeing Company
Mary Owen Borden Memorial Foundation

The Bunbury Company, Inc.
The Cape Branch Foundation
The Chevron Companies
Clark Charitable Trust
Geraldine R. Dodge Foundation, Inc.
The Educational Foundation of America
The Charles Engelhard Foundation
Environmental Endowment for
 New Jersey, Inc.
Fanwood Foundation
FishAmerica Foundation
Foundation for Deep Ecology
The Freed Foundation, Inc.
Frelinghuysen Foundation
The Fund for New Jersey
Fund of the Four Directions
Charles Hayden Foundation
The Edward W. Hazen Foundation
The Hyde and Watson Foundation
W. Alton Jones Foundation, Inc.
F. M. Kirby Foundation, Inc.
Nelson Mead Fund
Merck Family Fund
The John Merck Fund
Middlecott Foundation
Ruth Mott Fund
National Fish and Wildlife Foundation
New England Biolabs Foundation
The New York Times Company
 Foundation, Inc.
The William Penn Foundation
The Pew Charitable Trusts
The Philadelphia Foundation
The Prospect Hill Foundation
The Prudential Foundation
Public Welfare Foundation, Inc.
Philip D. Reed Foundation, Inc.
Rockefeller Brothers Fund, Inc.
The Rockefeller Foundation
The Scherman Foundation, Inc.
The Schumann Fund for New Jersey, Inc.
The Florence and John Schumann
 Foundation
Stanley Smith Horticultural Trust
Alfred T. Stanley Foundation
Thanksgiving Foundation
The Tides Foundation
Times Mirror Magazines, Inc.
Town Creek Foundation, Inc.
Union Camp Charitable Trust
Unitarian Universalist Veatch Program
 at Shelter Rock
Victoria Foundation, Inc.

New Mexico

ARCO Foundation
Airport Business Center Foundation
Elmer L. & Eleanor J. Andersen Foundation
Beldon Fund
The Ben & Jerry's Foundation
Carolyn Foundation
The Nathan Cummings Foundation
Geraldine R. Dodge Foundation, Inc.
Fanwood Foundation
Ford Foundation

Foundation for Deep Ecology
The Frost Foundation, Ltd.
Fund of the Four Directions
Funding Exchange
The Gap Foundation
The Fred Gellert Foundation
General Service Foundation
Give to the Earth Foundation
The Greenville Foundation
Harbor Lights Foundation
Harder Foundation
The M. A. Healy Family Foundation, Inc.
The Homeland Foundation
W. Alton Jones Foundation, Inc.
The Max and Anna Levinson Foundation
The Marshall Fund of Arizona
The Marshall L. & Perrine D. McCune
 Charitable Foundation
Giles W. and Elise G. Mead Foundation
The Moriah Fund, Inc.
Charles Stewart Mott Foundation
Ruth Mott Fund
National Fish and Wildlife Foundation
The New-Land Foundation, Inc.
The Samuel Roberts Noble Foundation, Inc.
Norman Foundation
Jessie Smith Noyes Foundation, Inc.
Patagonia, Inc.
The Pew Charitable Trusts
Public Welfare Foundation, Inc.
Recreational Equipment, Inc.
The Florence and John Schumann
 Foundation
Sequoia Foundation
Seventh Generation Fund
Springhouse Foundation
The Summerlee Foundation
The Tides Foundation
Tortuga Foundation
Town Creek Foundation, Inc.
The Travelers Foundation
Unitarian Universalist Veatch Program
 at Shelter Rock
Margaret Cullinan Wray Charitable
 Lead Annuity Trust

New York

ARCO Foundation
AT&T Foundation
The Achelis Foundation
Airport Business Center Foundation
The Jenifer Altman Foundation
American Conservation Association, Inc.
American Express Philanthropic Program
Angelina Fund, Inc.
The Vincent Astor Foundation
Atkinson Foundation
Mary Reynolds Babcock Foundation, Inc.
The Bailey Wildlife Foundation
Clayton Baker Trust
The George F. Baker Trust
The Theodore H. Barth Foundation, Inc.
The Bauman Foundation
The Bay Foundation
The Howard Bayne Fund

Recipient Location

New York (cont.)

S. D. Bechtel, Jr. Foundation
The Beinecke Foundation, Inc.
Beldon Fund
James Ford Bell Foundation
The Ben & Jerry's Foundation
Beneficia Foundation
Benua Foundation, Inc.
The Betterment Fund
The William Bingham Foundation
The Bodman Foundation
Botwinick-Wolfensohn Foundation, Inc.
Alexander H. Bright Charitable Trust
Alex. Brown & Sons Charitable Foundation, Inc.
W. L. Lyons Brown Foundation
Jesse Margaret Wilson Budlong Foundation for Animal Aid
The Bullitt Foundation
J. E. & Z. B. Butler Foundation, Inc.
The Bydale Foundation
C. S. Fund
The Louis Calder Foundation
Carolyn Foundation
Mary Flagler Cary Charitable Trust
Changing Horizons Charitable Trust
The Chevron Companies
Liz Claiborne & Art Ortenberg Foundation
Claneil Foundation, Inc.
The Clark Foundation
Robert Sterling Clark Foundation, Inc.
Columbia Foundation
Compton Foundation, Inc.
Conservation, Food & Health Foundation, Inc.
S. H. Cowell Foundation
The Cowles Charitable Trust
Jessie B. Cox Charitable Trust
Crystal Channel Foundation
Patrick and Anna M. Cudahy Fund
The Nathan Cummings Foundation
Davis Conservation Foundation
Deer Creek Foundation
The Nelson B. Delavan Foundation
The Aaron Diamond Foundation
Cleveland H. Dodge Foundation, Inc.
Geraldine R. Dodge Foundation, Inc.
Oliver S. and Jennie R. Donaldson Charitable Trust
Gaylord and Dorothy Donnelley Foundation
Douroucouli Foundation
The Elizabeth Ordway Dunn Foundation, Inc.
Jessie Ball duPont Religious, Charitable and Educational Fund
Eastman Kodak Company Charitable Trust
Echoing Green Foundation
Ederic Foundation, Inc.
The Educational Foundation of America
Arthur M. and Olga T. Eisig-Arthur M. and Kate E. Tode Foundation, Inc.
The Emerald Foundation
The Energy Foundation
The Charles Engelhard Foundation
Environment Now Foundation

The Armand G. Erpf Fund, Inc.
The Ettinger Foundation, Inc.
Fanwood Foundation
The William Stamps Farish Fund
The Favrot Fund
Jamee and Marshall Field Foundation
FishAmerica Foundation
Flintridge Foundation
Ford Foundation
Ford Motor Company Fund
Foundation for Deep Ecology
The Foundation for the National Capital Region
Frelinghuysen Foundation
Fund of the Four Directions
Funding Exchange
GE Fund
The Gap Foundation
Gebbie Foundation, Inc.
The Fred Gellert Foundation
General Service Foundation
The German Marshall Fund of the United States
Bernard F. and Alva B. Gimbel Foundation, Inc.
Herman Goldman Foundation
Richard & Rhoda Goldman Fund
The Greenville Foundation
The William and Mary Greve Foundation, Inc.
The George Gund Foundation
HKH Foundation
The Hahn Family Foundation
Harbor Lights Foundation
Harder Foundation
Gladys and Roland Harriman Foundation
Mary W. Harriman Foundation
The Merrill G. & Emita E. Hastings Foundation
Charles Hayden Foundation
Vira I. Heinz Endowment
The William and Flora Hewlett Foundation
The Hofmann Foundation
The Homeland Foundation
The Horn Foundation
Howfirma Foundation
The Charles Evans Hughes Memorial Foundation, Inc.
The Roy A. Hunt Foundation
Hurdle Hill Foundation
The Hyde and Watson Foundation
The Indian Point Foundation, Inc.
The Louise H. and David S. Ingalls Foundation, Inc.
Ireland Foundation
The James Irvine Foundation
Island Foundation, Inc.
Ittleson Foundation, Inc.
Jackson Hole Preserve, Inc.
The Howard Johnson Foundation
W. Alton Jones Foundation, Inc.
The Joyce Foundation
The J. M. Kaplan Fund, Inc.
The Helen & Milton Kimmelman Foundation

Kinnoull Foundation
F. M. Kirby Foundation, Inc.
The Esther A. and Joseph Klingenstein Fund, Inc.
The Seymour H. Knox Foundation, Inc.
The Lagemann Foundation
Larsen Fund, Inc.
The Lauder Foundation, Inc.
Laurel Foundation
The Lazar Foundation
The Max and Anna Levinson Foundation
The Little Family Foundation
Richard Lounsbery Foundation, Inc.
Luster Family Foundation, Inc.
Lyndhurst Foundation
The John D. and Catherine T. MacArthur Foundation
James A. Macdonald Foundation
Magowan Family Foundation, Inc.
MARPAT Foundation, Inc.
Mars Foundation
The Martin Foundation, Inc.
McDonnell Douglas Foundation
McKesson Foundation, Inc.
Nelson Mead Fund
The Andrew W. Mellon Foundation
Richard King Mellon Foundation
Merck Family Fund
The John Merck Fund
Joyce Mertz-Gilmore Foundation
Metropolitan Life Foundation
Millbrook Tribute Garden, Inc.
The Minneapolis Foundation
Mobil Foundation, Inc.
Leo Model Foundation, Inc.
J. P. Morgan Charitable Trust
The Moriah Fund, Inc.
Henry and Lucy Moses Fund, Inc.
Charles Stewart Mott Foundation
Ruth Mott Fund
The Curtis and Edith Munson Foundation, Inc.
The National Environmental Education and Training Foundation, Inc.
National Fish and Wildlife Foundation
National Geographic Society Education Foundation
New Hampshire Charitable Foundation
The New York Community Trust
New York Foundation
The New York Times Company Foundation, Inc.
The New-Land Foundation, Inc.
Edward John Noble Foundation, Inc.
Norcross Wildlife Foundation, Inc.
Jessie Smith Noyes Foundation, Inc.
OCRI Foundation
The Ohrstrom Foundation
Orchard Foundation
Ottinger Foundation
Outdoor Industry Conservation Alliance
The Overbrook Foundation
The David and Lucile Packard Foundation
Patagonia, Inc.
James C. Penney Foundation

Recipient Location

New York (cont.)

The Perkin Fund
The Pew Charitable Trusts
The Pfizer Foundation, Inc.
Howard Phipps Foundation
Pinewood Foundation
Henry B. Plant Memorial Fund, Inc.
Lynn R. and Karl E. Prickett Fund
The Procter & Gamble Fund
The Prospect Hill Foundation
The Prudential Foundation
Public Welfare Foundation, Inc.
Recreational Equipment, Inc.
Philip D. Reed Foundation, Inc.
The Roberts Foundation
Rockefeller Brothers Fund, Inc.
Rockefeller Family Fund, Inc.
The Rockefeller Foundation
Lee Romney Foundation, Inc.
Samuel and May Rudin Foundation, Inc.
Fran and Warren Rupp Foundation
Sacharuna Foundation
The Scherman Foundation, Inc.
S. H. and Helen R. Scheuer Family
    Foundation, Inc.
Sarah I. Schieffelin Residuary Trust
The Schiff Foundation
The Florence and John Schumann
    Foundation
Sears-Swetland Foundation
Sequoia Foundation
Elmina B. Sewall Foundation
Ralph C. Sheldon Foundation, Inc.
Shell Oil Company Foundation
Stanley Smith Horticultural Trust
Solow Foundation
Alfred T. Stanley Foundation
The Stebbins Fund, Inc.
Margaret Dorrance Strawbridge Foundation
    of Pennsylvania II, Inc.
The Stroh Foundation
Stroud Foundation
The Sulzberger Foundation, Inc.
Surdna Foundation, Inc.
Edna Bailey Sussman Fund
Nelson Talbott Foundation
Texaco Foundation
Thanksgiving Foundation
The Oakleigh L. Thorne Foundation
The Tides Foundation
The Tinker Foundation Incorporated
Tortuga Foundation
Town Creek Foundation, Inc.
The Travelers Foundation
Treacy Foundation, Inc.
True North Foundation
The Truland Foundation
The Trust For Mutual Understanding
Marcia Brady Tucker Foundation
Rose E. Tucker Charitable Trust
Underhill Foundation
Union Camp Charitable Trust
Unitarian Universalist Veatch Program
    at Shelter Rock
United States-Japan Foundation

R. T. Vanderbilt Trust
G. Unger Vetlesen Foundation
The Vidda Foundation
Vinmont Foundation, Inc.
Virginia Environmental Endowment
WMX Environmental Grants Program
Wallace Genetic Foundation, Inc.
Lila Wallace-Reader's Digest Fund
Weeden Foundation
Henry E. and Consuelo S. Wenger
    Foundation, Inc.
Robert W. Wilson Foundation
Mark and Catherine Winkler Foundation
The Winslow Foundation
Margaret Cullinan Wray Charitable
    Lead Annuity Trust

North Carolina

Mary Reynolds Babcock Foundation, Inc.
The Bailey Wildlife Foundation
The Howard Bayne Fund
Beldon Fund
The Ben & Jerry's Foundation
The Blumenthal Foundation
The Lynde and Harry Bradley
    Foundation, Inc.
Kathleen Price and Joseph M. Bryan Family
    Foundation, Inc.
The Butler Foundation
C. S. Fund
Mary Flagler Cary Charitable Trust
Chesapeake Corporation Foundation
Community Foundation of
    Western North Carolina, Inc.
Compton Foundation, Inc.
Geraldine R. Dodge Foundation, Inc.
Gaylord and Dorothy Donnelley Foundation
Felburn Foundation
Ford Foundation
Foundation for the Carolinas
Funding Exchange
General Service Foundation
Georgia-Pacific Foundation
James G. Hanes Memorial Fund
The Merrill G. & Emita E. Hastings
    Foundation
The William and Flora Hewlett Foundation
The George Frederick Jewett Foundation
W. Alton Jones Foundation, Inc.
F. M. Kirby Foundation, Inc.
The Knapp Foundation, Inc.
Kongsgaard-Goldman Foundation
The Lazar Foundation
Lyndhurst Foundation
The McKnight Foundation
Merck Family Fund
Metropolitan Atlanta Community
    Foundation, Inc.
Charles Stewart Mott Foundation
Ruth Mott Fund
The Curtis and Edith Munson
    Foundation, Inc.
National Fish and Wildlife Foundation
The New York Times Company
    Foundation, Inc.

Norman Foundation
Jessie Smith Noyes Foundation, Inc.
Lynn R. and Karl E. Prickett Fund
Public Welfare Foundation, Inc.
Recreational Equipment, Inc.
Z. Smith Reynolds Foundation, Inc.
The Rockefeller Foundation
The Florence and John Schumann
    Foundation
Sequoia Foundation
Stanley Smith Horticultural Trust
The Sulzberger Foundation, Inc.
Edna Bailey Sussman Fund
The Tides Foundation
USX Foundation, Inc.
Union Camp Charitable Trust
Unitarian Universalist Veatch Program
    at Shelter Rock
Virginia Environmental Endowment
WMX Environmental Grants Program
Wallace Genetic Foundation, Inc.
Weeden Foundation
Weyerhaeuser Company Foundation
The Winston-Salem Foundation, Inc.

North Dakota

Otto Bremer Foundation
National Geographic Society Education
    Foundation
Northwest Area Foundation
Patagonia, Inc.

Ohio

American Foundation Corporation
Evenor Armington Fund
S. D. Bechtel, Jr. Foundation
Beldon Fund
Benua Foundation, Inc.
The Chevron Companies
The Cleveland Foundation
The Columbus Foundation
The Conservation and Research Foundation
The James M. Cox, Jr. Foundation, Inc.
Deer Creek Foundation
The Thomas J. Emery Memorial
Jamee and Marshall Field Foundation
The 1525 Foundation
FishAmerica Foundation
Ford Foundation
Ford Motor Company Fund
Walter and Josephine Ford Fund
Fund of the Four Directions
Funding Exchange
The GAR Foundation
Give to the Earth Foundation
Great Lakes Protection Fund
The George Gund Foundation
The Hastings Trust
The Roy A. Hunt Foundation
Ireland Foundation
Martha Holden Jennings Foundation
The Joyce Foundation
W. K. Kellogg Foundation
The Little Family Foundation

© 1995 Environmental Data Resources, Inc.

Recipient Location

Ohio (cont.)

The John D. and Catherine T. MacArthur Foundation
Nelson Mead Fund
Richard King Mellon Foundation
Charles Stewart Mott Foundation
John P. Murphy Foundation
National Fish and Wildlife Foundation
The Nord Family Foundation
The Procter & Gamble Fund
Public Welfare Foundation, Inc.
Fran and Warren Rupp Foundation
The Florence and John Schumann Foundation
Sears-Swetland Foundation
The Kelvin and Eleanor Smith Foundation
Kelvin Smith 1980 Charitable Trust
Stranahan Foundation
Nelson Talbott Foundation
The Troy Foundation
Marcia Brady Tucker Foundation
USX Foundation, Inc.
Virginia Environmental Endowment
Bill & Edith Walter Foundation
Wodecroft Foundation

Oklahoma

ARCO Foundation
Azadoutioun Foundation
Compton Foundation, Inc.
Conservation, Food & Health Foundation, Inc.
The Educational Foundation of America
The Ettinger Foundation, Inc.
Funding Exchange
General Service Foundation
The Robert S. and Grayce B. Kerr Foundation, Inc.
The Kresge Foundation
Ruth Mott Fund
National Fish and Wildlife Foundation
The New-Land Foundation, Inc.
The Samuel Roberts Noble Foundation, Inc.
Phillips Petroleum Foundation, Inc.
Public Welfare Foundation, Inc.
Sarkeys Foundation
Seventh Generation Fund
Shell Oil Company Foundation
Southwestern Bell Foundation
Treacy Foundation, Inc.
Weyerhaeuser Company Foundation

Oregon

ARCO Foundation
A Territory Resource
The Acorn Foundation
The Jenifer Altman Foundation
American Conservation Association, Inc.
American Foundation Corporation
Mary Reynolds Babcock Foundation, Inc.
BankAmerica Foundation
Beldon Fund
The Ben & Jerry's Foundation
The William Bingham Foundation
The Bullitt Foundation
C. S. Fund
The Morris and Gwendolyn Cafritz Foundation
Carolyn Foundation
The Carpenter Foundation
Ben B. Cheney Foundation
The Chevron Companies
The Collins Foundation
Compton Foundation, Inc.
Crystal Channel Foundation
The Nathan Cummings Foundation
Deer Creek Foundation
Cleveland H. Dodge Foundation, Inc.
Geraldine R. Dodge Foundation, Inc.
The Educational Foundation of America
The Energy Foundation
The Charles Engelhard Foundation
FishAmerica Foundation
Flintridge Foundation
Ford Foundation
Foundation for Deep Ecology
Fund of the Four Directions
Funding Exchange
The Fred Gellert Foundation
General Service Foundation
Georgia-Pacific Foundation
Give to the Earth Foundation
The Greenville Foundation
The George Gund Foundation
HKH Foundation
Harder Foundation
The William and Flora Hewlett Foundation
The Homeland Foundation
The James Irvine Foundation
The Jackson Foundation
W. Alton Jones Foundation, Inc.
Laird, Norton Foundation
The Lazar Foundation
The Max and Anna Levinson Foundation
The Little Family Foundation
McKenzie River Gathering Foundation
Giles W. and Elise G. Mead Foundation
Merck Family Fund
Meyer Memorial Trust
Charles Stewart Mott Foundation
Ruth Mott Fund
M. J. Murdock Charitable Trust
National Fish and Wildlife Foundation
National Geographic Society Education Foundation
New England Biolabs Foundation
The New-Land Foundation, Inc.
Northwest Area Foundation
Jessie Smith Noyes Foundation, Inc.
OCRI Foundation
The David and Lucile Packard Foundation
Patagonia, Inc.
The Pew Charitable Trusts
Pew Scholars Program in Conservation and the Environment
Lynn R. and Karl E. Prickett Fund
The Prospect Hill Foundation
Public Welfare Foundation, Inc.
Recreational Equipment, Inc.
Rockefeller Family Fund, Inc.
Schultz Foundation, Inc.
The Florence and John Schumann Foundation
Sequoia Foundation
Seventh Generation Fund
The Skaggs Foundation
The Stroh Foundation
The Strong Foundation for Environmental Values
Surdna Foundation, Inc.
Threshold Foundation
The Tides Foundation
Tortuga Foundation
Town Creek Foundation, Inc.
True North Foundation
Rose E. Tucker Charitable Trust
WMX Environmental Grants Program
Wallace Genetic Foundation, Inc.
Weeden Foundation
Weyerhaeuser Company Foundation
Wilburforce Foundation

Pennsylvania

AT&T Foundation
The Jenifer Altman Foundation
Arcadia Foundation
The Barra Foundation, Inc.
The Howard Bayne Fund
S. D. Bechtel, Jr. Foundation
Beldon Fund
Beneficia Foundation
Changing Horizons Charitable Trust
The Chevron Companies
Claneil Foundation, Inc.
Conservation, Food & Health Foundation, Inc.
Cox Foundation, Inc.
Jessie B. Cox Charitable Trust
The Nathan Cummings Foundation
Geraldine R. Dodge Foundation, Inc.
Dolfinger-McMahon Foundation
Gaylord and Dorothy Donnelley Foundation
Ederic Foundation, Inc.
The Educational Foundation of America
The Energy Foundation
The Charles Engelhard Foundation
Fair Play Foundation
Fanwood Foundation
Samuel S. Fels Fund
FishAmerica Foundation
Ford Foundation
The Foundation for the National Capital Region
Frelinghuysen Foundation
The German Marshall Fund of the United States
Great Lakes Protection Fund
The George Gund Foundation

Recipient Location

Pennsylvania (cont.)
The Hamer Foundation
The Merrill G. & Emita E. Hastings Foundation
Howard Heinz Endowment
Vira I. Heinz Endowment
The William and Flora Hewlett Foundation
The Homeland Foundation
The Roy A. Hunt Foundation
W. Alton Jones Foundation, Inc.
W. K. Kellogg Foundation
Kinnoull Foundation
F. M. Kirby Foundation, Inc.
The Seymour H. Knox Foundation, Inc.
Laurel Foundation
The Lazar Foundation
Longwood Foundation, Inc.
The John D. and Catherine T. MacArthur Foundation
MARPAT Foundation, Inc.
Mars Foundation
McCune Foundation
McLean Contributionship
Nelson Mead Fund
The Andrew W. Mellon Foundation
Richard King Mellon Foundation
Merck Family Fund
Metropolitan Life Foundation
Mobil Foundation, Inc.
Leo Model Foundation, Inc.
The Moriah Fund, Inc.
Charles Stewart Mott Foundation
Ruth Mott Fund
The National Environmental Education and Training Foundation, Inc.
National Fish and Wildlife Foundation
The New York Times Company Foundation, Inc.
Jessie Smith Noyes Foundation, Inc.
Patagonia, Inc.
The William Penn Foundation
Perkins Charitable Foundation
The Pew Charitable Trusts
The Philadelphia Foundation
The Procter & Gamble Fund
The Prudential Foundation
Public Welfare Foundation, Inc.
Recreational Equipment, Inc.
The Rockefeller Foundation
Elmina B. Sewall Foundation
Shell Oil Company Foundation
Stanley Smith Horticultural Trust
Snee-Reinhardt Charitable Foundation
Sproul Foundation
Margaret Dorrance Strawbridge Foundation of Pennsylvania II, Inc.
Stroud Foundation
Edna Bailey Sussman Fund
Thanksgiving Foundation
Town Creek Foundation, Inc.
Harry C. Trexler Trust
The Truland Foundation
USX Foundation, Inc.

WMX Environmental Grants Program
Weeden Foundation
Welfare Foundation, Inc.
Westinghouse Foundation
The William P. Wharton Trust
The Winslow Foundation
Margaret Cullinan Wray Charitable Lead Annuity Trust
The Wyomissing Foundation, Inc.

Rhode Island
The Ben & Jerry's Foundation
Carolyn Foundation
The Champlin Foundations
Jessie B. Cox Charitable Trust
Davis Conservation Foundation
The William and Mary Greve Foundation, Inc.
Island Foundation, Inc.
Ittleson Foundation, Inc.
The Little Family Foundation
Richard King Mellon Foundation
Metropolitan Life Foundation
The New York Times Company Foundation, Inc.
Orchard Foundation
James C. Penney Foundation
The Pew Charitable Trusts
Prince Charitable Trusts
The Prospect Hill Foundation
The Rhode Island Community Foundation
Surdna Foundation, Inc.
The Switzer Foundation
The William P. Wharton Trust

South Carolina
Mary Reynolds Babcock Foundation, Inc.
Beldon Fund
The Ben & Jerry's Foundation
Helen Brach Foundation
Alexander H. Bright Charitable Trust
Mary Flagler Cary Charitable Trust
The Community Foundation Serving Coastal South Carolina
Gaylord and Dorothy Donnelley Foundation
Fanwood Foundation
The Foundation for the National Capital Region
The Hastings Trust
The Homeland Foundation
W. Alton Jones Foundation, Inc.
The Seymour H. Knox Foundation, Inc.
Luster Family Foundation, Inc.
The Andrew W. Mellon Foundation
Merck Family Fund
The John Merck Fund
Metropolitan Atlanta Community Foundation, Inc.
Ruth Mott Fund
National Fish and Wildlife Foundation
Norman Foundation
James C. Penney Foundation
Phillips Petroleum Foundation, Inc.

Public Welfare Foundation, Inc.
Springs Foundation, Inc.
The Summerlee Foundation
Union Camp Charitable Trust
Unitarian Universalist Veatch Program at Shelter Rock
WMX Environmental Grants Program

South Dakota
Beldon Fund
FishAmerica Foundation
Seventh Generation Fund

Tennessee
Angelina Fund, Inc.
Beldon Fund
The Ben & Jerry's Foundation
The Buchanan Family Foundation
The Chevron Companies
Gaylord and Dorothy Donnelley Foundation
Eastman Kodak Company Charitable Trust
The Energy Foundation
Fanwood Foundation
Felburn Foundation
Foundation for Deep Ecology
The Foundation for the National Capital Region
Fund of the Four Directions
Funding Exchange
The Hastings Trust
The Edward W. Hazen Foundation
The Roy A. Hunt Foundation
W. Alton Jones Foundation, Inc.
The Knapp Foundation, Inc.
The Seymour H. Knox Foundation, Inc.
Levi Strauss Foundation
LifeWorks Foundation
Lyndhurst Foundation
Mars Foundation
The McKnight Foundation
Charles Stewart Mott Foundation
Ruth Mott Fund
National Fish and Wildlife Foundation
The New World Foundation
The New York Times Company Foundation, Inc.
Patagonia, Inc.
James C. Penney Foundation
Pew Scholars Program in Conservation and the Environment
Phillips Petroleum Foundation, Inc.
The Procter & Gamble Fund
Public Welfare Foundation, Inc.
The Rockefeller Foundation
The Schiff Foundation
The Sulzberger Foundation, Inc.
Nelson Talbott Foundation
Unitarian Universalist Veatch Program at Shelter Rock
WMX Environmental Grants Program
C. A. Webster Foundation
Henry E. and Consuelo S. Wenger Foundation, Inc.

© 1995 Environmental Data Resources, Inc.

Recipient Location

Texas

ARCO Foundation
AT&T Foundation
Abell-Hanger Foundation
The Acorn Foundation
American Conservation Association, Inc.
The George F. Baker Trust
BankAmerica Foundation
Beldon Fund
The Ben & Jerry's Foundation
Beneficia Foundation
Alexander H. Bright Charitable Trust
Jesse Margaret Wilson Budlong Foundation
    for Animal Aid
The Chevron Companies
Compton Foundation, Inc.
Crystal Channel Foundation
The Nathan Cummings Foundation
Geraldine R. Dodge Foundation, Inc.
Thelma Doelger Charitable Trust
The Educational Foundation of America
El Paso Community Foundation
The Energy Foundation
The Charles Engelhard Foundation
The William Stamps Farish Fund
The Favrot Fund
Ford Foundation
Foundation for Deep Ecology
The Ewing Halsell Foundation
Mary W. Harriman Foundation
The Homeland Foundation
Harris and Eliza Kempner Fund
The Robert S. and Grayce B. Kerr
    Foundation, Inc.
Caesar Kleberg Foundation for Wildlife
    Conservation
Charles G. Koch Charitable Foundation
The Kresge Foundation
Luster Family Foundation, Inc.
The Eugene McDermott Foundation
McDonnell Douglas Foundation
Meadows Foundation, Inc.
Joyce Mertz-Gilmore Foundation
Mobil Foundation, Inc.
Leo Model Foundation, Inc.
The Moody Foundation
Charles Stewart Mott Foundation
Ruth Mott Fund
National Fish and Wildlife Foundation
Mary Moody Northen, Inc.
Jessie Smith Noyes Foundation, Inc.
Patagonia, Inc.
James C. Penney Foundation
The Pew Charitable Trusts
Phillips Petroleum Foundation, Inc.
Pinewood Foundation
Sid W. Richardson Foundation
Rockwell Fund, Inc.
Elmina B. Sewall Foundation
Shell Oil Company Foundation
Southwestern Bell Foundation
The Summerlee Foundation
Nelson Talbott Foundation
Texaco Foundation

Town Creek Foundation, Inc.
The Travelers Foundation
USX Foundation, Inc.
Unitarian Universalist Veatch Program
    at Shelter Rock
WMX Environmental Grants Program
C. A. Webster Foundation
Weeden Foundation
The Wortham Foundation, Inc.
Margaret Cullinan Wray Charitable
    Lead Annuity Trust

Utah

Beldon Fund
Ruth H. Brown Foundation
The Chevron Companies
Fanwood Foundation
Foundation for Deep Ecology
Harder Foundation
The William and Flora Hewlett Foundation
W. Alton Jones Foundation, Inc.
The Kresge Foundation
National Fish and Wildlife Foundation
The New-Land Foundation, Inc.
Outdoor Industry Conservation Alliance
Patagonia, Inc.
Shell Oil Company Foundation
The Tides Foundation
Times Mirror Magazines, Inc.
Tortuga Foundation
Town Creek Foundation, Inc.
The Trust For Mutual Understanding
Weeden Foundation

Vermont

American Conservation Association, Inc.
Mary Reynolds Babcock Foundation, Inc.
The Ben & Jerry's Foundation
The Bunbury Company, Inc.
The Bydale Foundation
C. S. Fund
Changing Horizons Charitable Trust
Davis Conservation Foundation
The Max and Victoria Dreyfus
    Foundation, Inc.
The Educational Foundation of America
FishAmerica Foundation
The Fund for Preservation of Wildlife
    and Natural Areas
Fund of the Four Directions
Funding Exchange
General Service Foundation
The German Marshall Fund of
    the United States
The Merrill G. & Emita E. Hastings
    Foundation
Howfirma Foundation
Jackson Hole Preserve, Inc.
W. Alton Jones Foundation, Inc.
Laurel Foundation
Lintilhac Foundation
Lyndhurst Foundation
The Andrew W. Mellon Foundation

Merck Family Fund
The John Merck Fund
National Fish and Wildlife Foundation
New England Biolabs Foundation
New Hampshire Charitable Foundation
Norcross Wildlife Foundation, Inc.
Northwest Fund for the Environment
Jessie Smith Noyes Foundation, Inc.
Orchard Foundation
Patagonia, Inc.
Amelia Peabody Charitable Fund
The Pew Charitable Trusts
Public Welfare Foundation, Inc.
Recreational Equipment, Inc.
Rockefeller Brothers Fund, Inc.
The Florence and John Schumann
    Foundation
Stanley Smith Horticultural Trust
Springhouse Foundation
Surdna Foundation, Inc.
The Switzer Foundation
The Trust For Mutual Understanding
Underhill Foundation
Unitarian Universalist Veatch Program
    at Shelter Rock
Wallace Genetic Foundation, Inc.
The William P. Wharton Trust
The Windham Foundation, Inc.

Virginia

ARCO Foundation
AT&T Foundation
American Conservation Association, Inc.
Ameritech Foundation
Mary Reynolds Babcock Foundation, Inc.
The Bailey Wildlife Foundation
The George F. Baker Trust
The Bauman Foundation
The Beirne Carter Foundation
Beldon Fund
The Ben & Jerry's Foundation
The Frank Stanley Beveridge
    Foundation, Inc.
The Blumenthal Foundation
The Boeing Company
Alexander H. Bright Charitable Trust
W. L. Lyons Brown Foundation
Kathleen Price and Joseph M. Bryan Family
    Foundation, Inc.
The Bush Foundation
The Butler Foundation
Mary Flagler Cary Charitable Trust
Changing Horizons Charitable Trust
Chesapeake Corporation Foundation
The Chevron Companies
Liz Claiborne & Art Ortenberg Foundation
Compton Foundation, Inc.
The Conservation and Research Foundation
Conservation, Food & Health
    Foundation, Inc.
Cox Foundation, Inc.
The James M. Cox, Jr. Foundation, Inc.
The Nathan Cummings Foundation
Damien Foundation

Recipient Location

Virginia (cont.)

Deer Creek Foundation
Cleveland H. Dodge Foundation, Inc.
Oliver S. and Jennie R. Donaldson Charitable Trust
Gaylord and Dorothy Donnelley Foundation
The Max and Victoria Dreyfus Foundation, Inc.
Jessie Ball duPont Religious, Charitable and Educational Fund
Eastman Kodak Company Charitable Trust
Echoing Green Foundation
The Emerald Foundation
The Energy Foundation
The Charles Engelhard Foundation
Environment Now Foundation
The Armand G. Erpf Fund, Inc.
Fanwood Foundation
Jamee and Marshall Field Foundation
Leland Fikes Foundation, Inc.
FishAmerica Foundation
Ford Foundation
Ford Motor Company Fund
Foundation for Deep Ecology
The Foundation for the National Capital Region
The Jacob and Annita France Foundation, Inc.
General Service Foundation
The German Marshall Fund of the United States
Good Samaritan, Inc.
The William and Mary Greve Foundation, Inc.
The George Gund Foundation
The Hahn Family Foundation
The Hamer Foundation
The Harding Educational and Charitable Foundation
Mary W. Harriman Foundation
The Hastings Trust
The Merrill G. & Emita E. Hastings Foundation
The Homeland Foundation
The Horn Foundation
Howfirma Foundation
The Charles Evans Hughes Memorial Foundation, Inc.
The Roy A. Hunt Foundation
Hurdle Hill Foundation
Island Foundation, Inc.
Jackson Hole Preserve, Inc.
The Howard Johnson Foundation
W. Alton Jones Foundation, Inc.
The Joyce Foundation
W. K. Kellogg Foundation
F. M. Kirby Foundation, Inc.
The Seymour H. Knox Foundation, Inc.
Larsen Fund, Inc.
Laurel Foundation
The Lazar Foundation
Luster Family Foundation, Inc.
Lyndhurst Foundation
The John D. and Catherine T. MacArthur Foundation

James A. Macdonald Foundation
MARPAT Foundation, Inc.
Mars Foundation
McDonnell Douglas Foundation
Nelson Mead Fund
Meadows Foundation, Inc.
Richard King Mellon Foundation
Merck Family Fund
Joyce Mertz-Gilmore Foundation
Metropolitan Life Foundation
Middlecott Foundation
Mobil Foundation, Inc.
Leo Model Foundation, Inc.
J. P. Morgan Charitable Trust
The Moriah Fund, Inc.
Charles Stewart Mott Foundation
National Fish and Wildlife Foundation
The New World Foundation
The New York Times Company Foundation, Inc.
The New-Land Foundation, Inc.
Norman Foundation
Mary Moody Northen, Inc.
Jessie Smith Noyes Foundation, Inc.
OCRI Foundation
The Ohrstrom Foundation
The David and Lucile Packard Foundation
Patagonia, Inc.
Amelia Peabody Charitable Fund
The Pew Charitable Trusts
The Pfizer Foundation, Inc.
The Philadelphia Foundation
Philip Morris Companies, Inc.
Phillips Petroleum Foundation, Inc.
Pinewood Foundation
Lynn R. and Karl E. Prickett Fund
Prince Charitable Trusts
The Procter & Gamble Fund
Public Welfare Foundation, Inc.
Smith Richardson Foundation, Inc.
The Rockefeller Foundation
Rockwood Fund, Inc.
Sacharuna Foundation
The Scherman Foundation, Inc.
Sarah I. Schieffelin Residuary Trust
The Schiff Foundation
Schultz Foundation, Inc.
The Florence and John Schumann Foundation
Elmina B. Sewall Foundation
Shell Oil Company Foundation
Stanley Smith Horticultural Trust
The Stratford Foundation
Margaret Dorrance Strawbridge Foundation of Pennsylvania II, Inc.
The Stroh Foundation
The Sulzberger Foundation, Inc.
Surdna Foundation, Inc.
Edna Bailey Sussman Fund
Nelson Talbott Foundation
Texaco Foundation
Thanksgiving Foundation
The Oakleigh L. Thorne Foundation
The Tides Foundation
Times Mirror Magazines, Inc.

Tortuga Foundation
Town Creek Foundation, Inc.
The Truland Foundation
The Trust For Mutual Understanding
USX Foundation, Inc.
Union Camp Charitable Trust
Unitarian Universalist Veatch Program at Shelter Rock
Virginia Environmental Endowment
WMX Environmental Grants Program
Alex C. Walker Educational & Charitable Foundation
Wallace Genetic Foundation, Inc.
C. A. Webster Foundation
Henry E. and Consuelo S. Wenger Foundation, Inc.
Westinghouse Foundation
Weyerhaeuser Company Foundation
Robert W. Wilson Foundation
Mark and Catherine Winkler Foundation
Sidney & Phyllis Wragge Foundation
Wrinkle in Time Foundation

Washington

ARCO Foundation
A Territory Resource
Alaska Conservation Foundation
The Jenifer Altman Foundation
Beldon Fund
The Boeing Company
The Bullitt Foundation
Changing Horizons Charitable Trust
Ben B. Cheney Foundation
Compton Foundation, Inc.
The Nathan Cummings Foundation
Deer Creek Foundation
The Energy Foundation
Fanwood Foundation
The Hugh and Jane Ferguson Foundation
FishAmerica Foundation
Flintridge Foundation
Ford Foundation
Foundation for Deep Ecology
The Fred Gellert Foundation
General Service Foundation
Richard & Rhoda Goldman Fund
The Greenville Foundation
Harder Foundation
The Henry M. Jackson Foundation
The George Frederick Jewett Foundation
W. Alton Jones Foundation, Inc.
Kongsgaard-Goldman Foundation
Laird, Norton Foundation
The Lazar Foundation
The Little Family Foundation
Merck Family Fund
The John Merck Fund
Charles Stewart Mott Foundation
Ruth Mott Fund
The Mountaineers Foundation
M. J. Murdock Charitable Trust
The National Environmental Education and Training Foundation, Inc.
New Horizon Foundation
The New-Land Foundation, Inc.

© 1995 Environmental Data Resources, Inc.

619

Recipient Location

Washington (cont.)

Northwest Area Foundation
Northwest Fund for the Environment
Outdoor Industry Conservation Alliance
Patagonia, Inc.
The Pew Charitable Trusts
The Pfizer Foundation, Inc.
Phillips Petroleum Foundation, Inc.
Public Welfare Foundation, Inc.
Recreational Equipment, Inc.
Rockwood Fund, Inc.
Schultz Foundation, Inc.
Sequoia Foundation
Shell Oil Company Foundation
The Stroh Foundation
The Strong Foundation for Environmental Values
Texaco Foundation
The Tides Foundation
Town Creek Foundation, Inc.
True North Foundation
Unitarian Universalist Veatch Program at Shelter Rock
G. Unger Vetlesen Foundation
Weeden Foundation
Weyerhaeuser Company Foundation
Wilburforce Foundation

West Virginia

Evenor Armington Fund
The Betterment Fund
Chesapeake Bay Trust
The Chevron Companies
The Nathan Cummings Foundation
Davis Conservation Foundation
Eastman Kodak Company Charitable Trust
Fund of the Four Directions
Funding Exchange
The William and Flora Hewlett Foundation
Laird, Norton Foundation
Merck Family Fund
Ruth Mott Fund
Norman Foundation
Outdoor Industry Conservation Alliance
Patagonia, Inc.
James C. Penney Foundation
Phillips Petroleum Foundation, Inc.
Public Welfare Foundation, Inc.
Virginia Environmental Endowment

Wisconsin

Beldon Fund
The Ben & Jerry's Foundation
Helen Brach Foundation
The Lynde and Harry Bradley Foundation, Inc.
Otto Bremer Foundation
The Buchanan Family Foundation
Carolyn Foundation
The Chevron Companies
Liz Claiborne & Art Ortenberg Foundation
Compton Foundation, Inc.
Patrick and Anna M. Cudahy Fund
Geraldine R. Dodge Foundation, Inc.
Gaylord and Dorothy Donnelley Foundation
Echoing Green Foundation
FishAmerica Foundation
Ford Foundation
Ford Motor Company Fund
Foundation for Deep Ecology
Funding Exchange
Great Lakes Protection Fund
The John D. and Catherine T. MacArthur Foundation
The McKnight Foundation
The Andrew W. Mellon Foundation
The Milwaukee Foundation
The Minneapolis Foundation
Charles Stewart Mott Foundation
National Fish and Wildlife Foundation
The Needmor Fund
Edward John Noble Foundation, Inc.
Outdoor Industry Conservation Alliance
Patagonia, Inc.
The Pew Charitable Trusts
Recreational Equipment, Inc.
Lee Romney Foundation, Inc.
Seventh Generation Fund
Stackner Family Foundation, Inc.
The Trust For Mutual Understanding
Unitarian Universalist Veatch Program at Shelter Rock
WMX Environmental Grants Program
Weeden Foundation
Weyerhaeuser Company Foundation

Wyoming

A Territory Resource
American Conservation Association, Inc.
Elmer L. & Eleanor J. Andersen Foundation
Evenor Armington Fund
Beldon Fund
Botwinick-Wolfensohn Foundation, Inc.
The Chevron Companies
Liz Claiborne & Art Ortenberg Foundation
The Nathan Cummings Foundation
Cleveland H. Dodge Foundation, Inc.
Geraldine R. Dodge Foundation, Inc.
Ederic Foundation, Inc.
FishAmerica Foundation
Fund of the Four Directions
Harder Foundation
The Homeland Foundation
Ireland Foundation
Jackson Hole Preserve, Inc.
The Robert S. and Grayce B. Kerr Foundation, Inc.
Maki Foundation
The McIntosh Foundation
Nelson Mead Fund
National Fish and Wildlife Foundation
Edward John Noble Foundation, Inc.
The Samuel Roberts Noble Foundation, Inc.
Patagonia, Inc.
Perkins Charitable Foundation
Schultz Foundation, Inc.
Shell Oil Company Foundation
Town Creek Foundation, Inc.
Union Camp Charitable Trust

U.S. Commonwealth

Puerto Rico

The Ben & Jerry's Foundation
Funding Exchange
The John D. and Catherine T. MacArthur Foundation
Charles Stewart Mott Foundation
Public Welfare Foundation, Inc.
The Tides Foundation
Unitarian Universalist Veatch Program at Shelter Rock

U.S. Territory

Virgin Islands

The John D. and Catherine T. MacArthur Foundation

Recipient Location

International

Argentina
Ford Foundation
The Tinker Foundation Incorporated

Australia
Pew Scholars Program in Conservation and the Environment

Bangladesh
Ford Foundation
W. Alton Jones Foundation, Inc.

Belgium
The German Marshall Fund of the United States
W. Alton Jones Foundation, Inc.
The Rockefeller Foundation

Belize
W. Alton Jones Foundation, Inc.

Bermuda
ARCO Foundation
Mobil Foundation, Inc.

Bolivia
Conservation, Food & Health Foundation, Inc.
W. Alton Jones Foundation, Inc.
The John D. and Catherine T. MacArthur Foundation
New England Biolabs Foundation

Brazil
Caribou Fund
Damien Foundation
Ford Foundation
Global Greengrants Fund
W. Alton Jones Foundation, Inc.
The John D. and Catherine T. MacArthur Foundation
Charles Stewart Mott Foundation
Jessie Smith Noyes Foundation, Inc.
The Rockefeller Foundation

British Virgin Islands
The Hamer Foundation
Jackson Hole Preserve, Inc.

Burma
Caribou Fund

Canada
James Ford Bell Foundation
Benua Foundation, Inc.
The Bullitt Foundation
The Chevron Companies
Donner Canadian Foundation
Foundation for Deep Ecology
The German Marshall Fund of the United States
Walter and Duncan Gordon Charitable Foundation
The Richard Ivey Foundation
W. Alton Jones Foundation, Inc.
The Joyce Foundation
Laidlaw Foundation
The Lazar Foundation
The John D. and Catherine T. MacArthur Foundation
Charles Stewart Mott Foundation
National Fish and Wildlife Foundation
Patagonia, Inc.
Recreational Equipment, Inc.
The Rockefeller Foundation
Sacharuna Foundation
Thomas Sill Foundation
Stanley Smith Horticultural Trust
The Tides Foundation
Vancouver Foundation
Weeden Foundation

Chile
Ford Foundation
Foundation for Deep Ecology
The John D. and Catherine T. MacArthur Foundation
The Andrew W. Mellon Foundation
Patagonia, Inc.
The Rockefeller Foundation
The Tinker Foundation Incorporated
Weeden Foundation

China
Ford Foundation
The Rockefeller Foundation

Colombia
Ford Foundation
Funding Exchange
W. Alton Jones Foundation, Inc.
The John D. and Catherine T. MacArthur Foundation
Jessie Smith Noyes Foundation, Inc.
The Tinker Foundation Incorporated
Weeden Foundation

Costa Rica
Caribou Fund
Ford Foundation
National Fish and Wildlife Foundation
The Rockefeller Foundation
Weeden Foundation

Czech Republic
The German Marshall Fund of the United States
Charles Stewart Mott Foundation
Rockefeller Brothers Fund, Inc.

Dominican Republic
Ford Foundation
Public Welfare Foundation, Inc.

Ecuador
Conservation, Food & Health Foundation, Inc.
Foundation for Deep Ecology
W. Alton Jones Foundation, Inc.
The John D. and Catherine T. MacArthur Foundation
Charles Stewart Mott Foundation
Stanley Smith Horticultural Trust

Egypt
Ford Foundation

Estonia
The John D. and Catherine T. MacArthur Foundation

France
Foundation for Deep Ecology
The John D. and Catherine T. MacArthur Foundation
The Andrew W. Mellon Foundation
Patagonia, Inc.
The Rockefeller Foundation

French Antilles
New England Biolabs Foundation

Germany
The German Marshall Fund of the United States
W. Alton Jones Foundation, Inc.
Charles Stewart Mott Foundation
Patagonia, Inc.
The Rockefeller Foundation

Recipient Location

Guatemala
Ford Foundation

Honduras
The John D. and Catherine T. MacArthur Foundation

Hungary
Foundation for Deep Ecology
The German Marshall Fund of the United States
Charles Stewart Mott Foundation

India
The Jenifer Altman Foundation
Ford Foundation
Fund of the Four Directions
The John D. and Catherine T. MacArthur Foundation
Pew Scholars Program in Conservation and the Environment
Rockefeller Brothers Fund, Inc.
The Rockefeller Foundation

Indonesia
Ford Foundation
The John D. and Catherine T. MacArthur Foundation
The Rockefeller Foundation

Jamaica
The Rockefeller Foundation

Japan
Caribou Fund
Conservation, Food & Health Foundation, Inc.
Foundation for Deep Ecology
Global Greengrants Fund
W. Alton Jones Foundation, Inc.
Patagonia, Inc.
Rockefeller Brothers Fund, Inc.

Kenya
Ford Foundation
Global Environmental Project Institute
The Rockefeller Foundation
South Coast Foundation, Inc.
The Tides Foundation

Malawi
The Rockefeller Foundation

Malaysia
Foundation for Deep Ecology
The John D. and Catherine T. MacArthur Foundation

Mauritius
Kinnoull Foundation

Mexico
El Paso Community Foundation
Ford Foundation
W. Alton Jones Foundation, Inc.
The John D. and Catherine T. MacArthur Foundation
National Fish and Wildlife Foundation
The David and Lucile Packard Foundation
The Rockefeller Foundation
The Tinker Foundation Incorporated

Mozambique
The Rockefeller Foundation

Nepal
Ford Foundation

Netherlands
Ford Foundation
Foundation for Deep Ecology

New Zealand
Ford Foundation

Nigeria
The John D. and Catherine T. MacArthur Foundation
The Rockefeller Foundation

Norway
Foundation for Deep Ecology

Panama
Foundation for Deep Ecology

Papua New Guinea
New England Biolabs Foundation

Peru
The Homeland Foundation
W. Alton Jones Foundation, Inc.
The John D. and Catherine T. MacArthur Foundation
Jessie Smith Noyes Foundation, Inc.
The Tinker Foundation Incorporated

Philippines
The Jenifer Altman Foundation
Ford Foundation
The John D. and Catherine T. MacArthur Foundation
Rockefeller Brothers Fund, Inc.
The Rockefeller Foundation

Poland
Foundation for Deep Ecology
The John D. and Catherine T. MacArthur Foundation
Charles Stewart Mott Foundation
Pew Scholars Program in Conservation and the Environment

Russia
Caribou Fund
W. Alton Jones Foundation, Inc.
The John D. and Catherine T. MacArthur Foundation
The Rockefeller Foundation

Scotland
The Chevron Companies

Singapore
Conservation, Food & Health Foundation, Inc.

Slovak Republic
The German Marshall Fund of the United States
The John D. and Catherine T. MacArthur Foundation

South Africa
Ford Foundation

Spain
The Rockefeller Foundation

Sri Lanka
Ford Foundation
New England Biolabs Foundation

Sudan
Ford Foundation

Sweden
The John D. and Catherine T. MacArthur Foundation

Switzerland
Ford Foundation
W. Alton Jones Foundation, Inc.
Patagonia, Inc.

Thailand
Ford Foundation
The Ohrstrom Foundation
The Rockefeller Foundation

Uganda
The John D. and Catherine T. MacArthur Foundation
The Rockefeller Foundation

Ukraine
The John D. and Catherine T. MacArthur Foundation

United Kingdom
The Chevron Companies
Liz Claiborne & Art Ortenberg Foundation

United Kingdom (cont.)

Conservation, Food & Health
 Foundation, Inc.
Damien Foundation
Ford Foundation
Foundation for Deep Ecology
W. Alton Jones Foundation, Inc.
The John D. and Catherine T. MacArthur
 Foundation
The Polden-Puckham Charitable
 Foundation
The Tides Foundation
Weeden Foundation

Zambia

The Rockefeller Foundation

Zimbabwe

The Rockefeller Foundation

Activity Region

United States

Alaska

ARCO Foundation
The Acorn Foundation
Alaska Conservation Foundation
American Conservation Association, Inc.
S. D. Bechtel, Jr. Foundation
The Ben & Jerry's Foundation
The Bullitt Foundation
The Nathan Cummings Foundation
The Educational Foundation of America
The Energy Foundation
The Hugh and Jane Ferguson Foundation
Foundation for Deep Ecology
Fund of the Four Directions
Harder Foundation
Kongsgaard-Goldman Foundation
The Lazar Foundation
The McIntosh Foundation
Charles Stewart Mott Foundation
Ruth Mott Fund
M. J. Murdock Charitable Trust
National Fish and Wildlife Foundation
The New-Land Foundation, Inc.
Norcross Wildlife Foundation, Inc.
The Overbrook Foundation
Patagonia, Inc.
The Pew Charitable Trusts
Public Welfare Foundation, Inc.
Recreational Equipment, Inc.
The Florence and John Schumann Foundation
Seventh Generation Fund
The Skaggs Foundation
Surdna Foundation, Inc.
Town Creek Foundation, Inc.
True North Foundation
Underhill Foundation
Unitarian Universalist Veatch Program at Shelter Rock
Weeden Foundation

Great Lakes

AT&T Foundation
American Foundation Corporation
Americana Foundation, Inc.
Ameritech Foundation
Elmer L. & Eleanor J. Andersen Foundation
Evenor Armington Fund
Bay Area Community Foundation
The Bay Foundation
Beldon Fund
David Winton Bell Foundation
James Ford Bell Foundation
The Ben & Jerry's Foundation
Benua Foundation, Inc.
The Bersted Foundation
Blandin Foundation
Helen Brach Foundation
The Lynde and Harry Bradley Foundation, Inc.
Otto Bremer Foundation
The Buchanan Family Foundation
The Bush Foundation
Patrick and Aimee Butler Family Foundation
The Cargill Foundation
Carolyn Foundation
Centerior Energy Foundation
The Chevron Companies
The Chicago Community Trust
Chrysler Corporation Fund
The Cleveland Foundation
The Clowes Fund, Inc.
Olive B. Cole Foundation
The Columbus Foundation
Compton Foundation, Inc.
The James M. Cox, Jr. Foundation, Inc.
Patrick and Anna M. Cudahy Fund
The Nathan Cummings Foundation
Dart Foundation
Dayton Hudson Foundation
Gaylord and Dorothy Donnelley Foundation
The Herbert H. and Grace A. Dow Foundation
Eastman Kodak Company Charitable Trust
Echoing Green Foundation
The Thomas J. Emery Memorial
The Energy Foundation
English-Bonter-Mitchell Foundation
The Field Foundation of Illinois, Inc.
Jamee and Marshall Field Foundation
The 1525 Foundation
FishAmerica Foundation
Ford Foundation
Ford Motor Company Fund
Walter and Josephine Ford Fund
Foundation for Deep Ecology
Lloyd A. Fry Foundation
Fund of the Four Directions
Funding Exchange
The GAR Foundation
The Rollin M. Gerstacker Foundation
Great Lakes Protection Fund
The W. C. Griffith Foundation
The George Gund Foundation
Harder Foundation
Hudson-Webber Foundation
Ireland Foundation
Martha Holden Jennings Foundation
W. Alton Jones Foundation, Inc.
The Joyce Foundation
W. K. Kellogg Foundation
The Kresge Foundation
Laidlaw Foundation
Larsen Fund, Inc.
Lilly Endowment, Inc.
The John D. and Catherine T. MacArthur Foundation
Marbrook Foundation
The Martin Foundation, Inc.
McGregor Fund
The McKnight Foundation
Nelson Mead Fund
The Andrew W. Mellon Foundation
Joyce Mertz-Gilmore Foundation
The Milwaukee Foundation
The Minneapolis Foundation
Mobil Foundation, Inc.
The Moriah Fund, Inc.
Charles Stewart Mott Foundation
Ruth Mott Fund
The Curtis and Edith Munson Foundation, Inc.
John P. Murphy Foundation
National Fish and Wildlife Foundation
National Geographic Society Education Foundation
The New World Foundation
The Nord Family Foundation
Northwest Area Foundation
Nicholas H. Noyes, Jr. Memorial Foundation
Onan Family Foundation
Outdoor Industry Conservation Alliance
The David and Lucile Packard Foundation
Patagonia, Inc.
The Pew Charitable Trusts
Prince Charitable Trusts
Pritzker Foundation
The Procter & Gamble Fund
The Prudential Foundation
Public Welfare Foundation, Inc.
Recreational Equipment, Inc.
Lee Romney Foundation, Inc.
Fran and Warren Rupp Foundation
The Florence and John Schumann Foundation
Sears-Swetland Foundation
Seventh Generation Fund
The Kelvin and Eleanor Smith Foundation
Kelvin Smith 1980 Charitable Trust
Stackner Family Foundation, Inc.
Steelcase Foundation
Stranahan Foundation
The Stroh Foundation
The Charles J. Strosacker Foundation
Surdna Foundation, Inc.
Edna Bailey Sussman Fund
Nelson Talbott Foundation
Texaco Foundation
The Tides Foundation
The Travelers Foundation
The Troy Foundation

© 1995 Environmental Data Resources, Inc.

Activity Region

Great Lakes (cont.)

Marcia Brady Tucker Foundation
USX Foundation, Inc.
Union Pacific Foundation
Unitarian Universalist Veatch Program at Shelter Rock
WMX Environmental Grants Program
Wallace Genetic Foundation, Inc.
Bill & Edith Walter Foundation
Henry E. and Consuelo S. Wenger Foundation, Inc.
Wodecroft Foundation

Hawaii

The Abelard Foundation West
Atherton Family Foundation
James & Abigail Campbell Foundation
The Chevron Companies
Compton Foundation, Inc.
Cooke Foundation, Limited
The Charles Engelhard Foundation
Foundation for Deep Ecology
Mary D. and Walter F. Frear Eleemosynary Trust
The Wallace Alexander Gerbode Foundation, Inc.
Hawaii Community Foundation
Hawaiian Electric Industries Charitable Foundation
The Homeland Foundation
Magowan Family Foundation, Inc.
McInerny Foundation
National Fish and Wildlife Foundation
The David and Lucile Packard Foundation
Patagonia, Inc.
Stanley Smith Horticultural Trust
The Tides Foundation
WMX Environmental Grants Program
Weeden Foundation
G. N. Wilcox Trust

Mid-Atlantic

AT&T Foundation
The Abell Foundation
Arcadia Foundation
Evenor Armington Fund
The Bailey Wildlife Foundation
Clayton Baker Trust
Baltimore Gas and Electric Foundation, Inc.
The Barra Foundation, Inc.
The Beirne Carter Foundation
Beldon Fund
Beneficia Foundation
The Boeing Company
Alex. Brown & Sons Charitable Foundation, Inc.
H. Barksdale Brown Charitable Trust
The Morris and Gwendolyn Cafritz Foundation
Mary Flagler Cary Charitable Trust
Chesapeake Bay Trust
Chesapeake Corporation Foundation
The Chevron Companies
Chrysler Corporation Fund

Claneil Foundation, Inc.
S. H. Cowell Foundation
The Cowles Charitable Trust
The Nathan Cummings Foundation
Geraldine R. Dodge Foundation, Inc.
Dolfinger-McMahon Foundation
The Max and Victoria Dreyfus Foundation, Inc.
Jessie Ball duPont Religious, Charitable and Educational Fund
Ederic Foundation, Inc.
The Charles Engelhard Foundation
Fair Play Foundation
The Favrot Fund
Samuel S. Fels Fund
FishAmerica Foundation
Foundation for Deep Ecology
The Foundation for the National Capital Region
The Jacob and Annita France Foundation, Inc.
Fund of the Four Directions
Funding Exchange
The Gap Foundation
The William and Mary Greve Foundation, Inc.
The Hamer Foundation
Mary W. Harriman Foundation
Howard Heinz Endowment
Vira I. Heinz Endowment
The Roy A. Hunt Foundation
W. Alton Jones Foundation, Inc.
F. M. Kirby Foundation, Inc.
The Knapp Foundation, Inc.
The Kresge Foundation
Laurel Foundation
Longwood Foundation, Inc.
The John D. and Catherine T. MacArthur Foundation
MARPAT Foundation, Inc.
Mars Foundation
McCune Foundation
McLean Contributionship
The Andrew W. Mellon Foundation
Richard King Mellon Foundation
Merck Family Fund
Robert G. and Anne M. Merrick Foundation, Inc.
Metropolitan Life Foundation
Leo Model Foundation, Inc.
The Moriah Fund, Inc.
Charles Stewart Mott Foundation
Ruth Mott Fund
National Fish and Wildlife Foundation
The New York Times Company Foundation, Inc.
Norcross Wildlife Foundation, Inc.
Norman Foundation
Mary Moody Northen, Inc.
The Ohrstrom Foundation
Patagonia, Inc.
The William Penn Foundation
James C. Penney Foundation
The Pew Charitable Trusts
The Philadelphia Foundation

Prince Charitable Trusts
The Procter & Gamble Fund
The Prudential Foundation
Public Welfare Foundation, Inc.
Recreational Equipment, Inc.
Philip D. Reed Foundation, Inc.
Rockwood Fund, Inc.
Lee Romney Foundation, Inc.
Sacharuna Foundation
The Florence and John Schumann Foundation
Shell Oil Company Foundation
Stanley Smith Horticultural Trust
Snee-Reinhardt Charitable Foundation
Sproul Foundation
Stern Family Fund
Margaret Dorrance Strawbridge Foundation of Pennsylvania II, Inc.
Stroud Foundation
Surdna Foundation, Inc.
Edna Bailey Sussman Fund
Texaco Foundation
The Tides Foundation
Times Mirror Magazines, Inc.
Town Creek Foundation, Inc.
The Travelers Foundation
Harry C. Trexler Trust
The USF&G Foundation, Inc.
USX Foundation, Inc.
Union Camp Charitable Trust
Virginia Environmental Endowment
WMX Environmental Grants Program
Wallace Genetic Foundation, Inc.
Welfare Foundation, Inc.
Westinghouse Foundation
Mark and Catherine Winkler Foundation
Wrinkle in Time Foundation
The Wyomissing Foundation, Inc.

Midwest

The Austin Memorial Foundation
The Bay Foundation
Beldon Fund
The Boeing Company
Compton Foundation, Inc.
The Nathan Cummings Foundation
Deer Creek Foundation
The Educational Foundation of America
The Energy Foundation
FishAmerica Foundation
Ford Foundation
Ford Motor Company Fund
Foundation for Deep Ecology
General Service Foundation
The Hall Family Foundation
The Roy A. Hunt Foundation
W. Alton Jones Foundation, Inc.
The Joyce Foundation
W. K. Kellogg Foundation
The Kresge Foundation
McDonnell Douglas Foundation
The McKnight Foundation
Nelson Mead Fund
The Andrew W. Mellon Foundation
Metropolitan Life Foundation

Activity Region

Midwest (cont.)

Charles Stewart Mott Foundation
Ruth Mott Fund
National Fish and Wildlife Foundation
The New-Land Foundation, Inc.
Northwest Area Foundation
Spencer T. and Ann W. Olin Foundation
Patagonia, Inc.
The Pew Charitable Trusts
The Powell Family Foundation
Public Welfare Foundation, Inc.
Stanley Smith Horticultural Trust
Southwestern Bell Foundation
Surdna Foundation, Inc.
The Tides Foundation
Union Pacific Foundation
Unitarian Universalist Veatch Program
 at Shelter Rock
Wallace Genetic Foundation, Inc.

Mountain

ARCO Foundation
A Territory Resource
The Abelard Foundation West
Airport Business Center Foundation
American Conservation Association, Inc.
Angelina Fund, Inc.
Evenor Armington Fund
Beldon Fund
The Ben & Jerry's Foundation
Boettcher Foundation
Otto Bremer Foundation
Ruth H. Brown Foundation
The Bullitt Foundation
The Bush Foundation
The Chevron Companies
Liz Claiborne & Art Ortenberg Foundation
Compton Foundation, Inc.
Adolph Coors Foundation
The Nathan Cummings Foundation
Geraldine R. Dodge Foundation, Inc.
Eastman Kodak Company Charitable Trust
The Educational Foundation of America
El Pomar Foundation
The Energy Foundation
The Charles Engelhard Foundation
The Ettinger Foundation, Inc.
Fanwood Foundation
Jamee and Marshall Field Foundation
Bert Fingerhut/Caroline Hicks Family Fund
FishAmerica Foundation
Ford Foundation
Foundation for Deep Ecology
The Frost Foundation, Ltd.
Fund of the Four Directions
Gates Foundation
General Service Foundation
The Goldman Environmental Foundation
The Greenville Foundation
The William and Mary Greve
 Foundation, Inc.
Harbor Lights Foundation
Harder Foundation
The William and Flora Hewlett Foundation

The Homeland Foundation
The Horn Foundation
Illilouette Fund
The Indian Point Foundation, Inc.
Island Foundation
Jackson Hole Preserve, Inc.
The George Frederick Jewett Foundation
Helen K. and Arthur E. Johnson Foundation
W. Alton Jones Foundation, Inc.
The Robert S. and Grayce B. Kerr
 Foundation, Inc.
Kongsgaard-Goldman Foundation
The Kresge Foundation
The Lazar Foundation
The Max and Anna Levinson Foundation
Maki Foundation
The Martin Foundation, Inc.
Richard King Mellon Foundation
Joyce Mertz-Gilmore Foundation
Meyer Memorial Trust
Mobil Foundation, Inc.
Charles Stewart Mott Foundation
Ruth Mott Fund
M. J. Murdock Charitable Trust
National Fish and Wildlife Foundation
National Geographic Society Education
 Foundation
The New-Land Foundation, Inc.
Norman Foundation
Northwest Area Foundation
Jessie Smith Noyes Foundation, Inc.
The Ohrstrom Foundation
Outdoor Industry Conservation Alliance
The David and Lucile Packard Foundation
Patagonia, Inc.
Perkins Charitable Foundation
The Pew Charitable Trusts
Phillips Petroleum Foundation, Inc.
Pilot Trust
Public Welfare Foundation, Inc.
Recreational Equipment, Inc.
Rockefeller Family Fund, Inc.
Rockwood Fund, Inc.
Lee Romney Foundation, Inc.
Seventh Generation Fund
Shell Oil Company Foundation
The Summerlee Foundation
Edna Bailey Sussman Fund
Texaco Foundation
The Tides Foundation
Times Mirror Magazines, Inc.
Tortuga Foundation
Town Creek Foundation, Inc.
Turner Foundation, Inc.
USX Foundation, Inc.
Underhill Foundation
Union Pacific Foundation
Unitarian Universalist Veatch Program
 at Shelter Rock
Wallace Genetic Foundation, Inc.
Weeden Foundation
Henry E. and Consuelo S. Wenger
 Foundation, Inc.
The Winslow Foundation
Sidney & Phyllis Wragge Foundation

New York/New Jersey

AT&T Foundation
The Achelis Foundation
American Conservation Association, Inc.
The Vincent Astor Foundation
The Bailey Wildlife Foundation
The George F. Baker Trust
The Theodore H. Barth Foundation, Inc.
The Bauman Foundation
The Bay Foundation
The Howard Bayne Fund
The Beinecke Foundation, Inc.
Beldon Fund
The Ben & Jerry's Foundation
Beneficia Foundation
The Bodman Foundation
Mary Owen Borden Memorial Foundation
Botwinick-Wolfensohn Foundation, Inc.
Alexander H. Bright Charitable Trust
The Bunbury Company, Inc.
The Louis Calder Foundation
The Cape Branch Foundation
Mary Flagler Cary Charitable Trust
The Chevron Companies
Clark Charitable Trust
The Clark Foundation
Robert Sterling Clark Foundation, Inc.
Compton Foundation, Inc.
S. H. Cowell Foundation
The Cowles Charitable Trust
Deer Creek Foundation
The Nelson B. Delavan Foundation
The Aaron Diamond Foundation
Cleveland H. Dodge Foundation, Inc.
Geraldine R. Dodge Foundation, Inc.
Douroucouli Foundation
Echoing Green Foundation
The Educational Foundation of America
The Energy Foundation
The Charles Engelhard Foundation
Environmental Endowment for
 New Jersey, Inc.
The Armand G. Erpf Fund, Inc.
Fanwood Foundation
The William Stamps Farish Fund
The Favrot Fund
FishAmerica Foundation
Ford Foundation
Walter and Josephine Ford Fund
Foundation for Deep Ecology
The Freed Foundation, Inc.
Frelinghuysen Foundation
The Fund for New Jersey
Fund of the Four Directions
Funding Exchange
GE Fund
The Gap Foundation
Gebbie Foundation, Inc.
Herman Goldman Foundation
HKH Foundation
The Hahn Family Foundation
The Harding Educational and
 Charitable Foundation
Gladys and Roland Harriman Foundation
Mary W. Harriman Foundation

Activity Region

New York/New Jersey (cont.)

The Merrill G. & Emita E. Hastings Foundation
Charles Hayden Foundation
The Edward W. Hazen Foundation
The Hyde and Watson Foundation
The Indian Point Foundation, Inc.
Ittleson Foundation, Inc.
Jackson Hole Preserve, Inc.
The Howard Johnson Foundation
W. Alton Jones Foundation, Inc.
The J. M. Kaplan Fund, Inc.
The Helen & Milton Kimmelman Foundation
F. M. Kirby Foundation, Inc.
The Seymour H. Knox Foundation, Inc.
The Lagemann Foundation
Larsen Fund, Inc.
The Lauder Foundation, Inc.
Richard Lounsbery Foundation, Inc.
James A. Macdonald Foundation
Magowan Family Foundation, Inc.
Nelson Mead Fund
The Andrew W. Mellon Foundation
Merck Family Fund
Joyce Mertz-Gilmore Foundation
Metropolitan Life Foundation
Millbrook Tribute Garden, Inc.
Mobil Foundation, Inc.
Leo Model Foundation, Inc.
J. P. Morgan Charitable Trust
Henry and Lucy Moses Fund, Inc.
Charles Stewart Mott Foundation
Ruth Mott Fund
National Fish and Wildlife Foundation
The New York Community Trust
New York Foundation
The New York Times Company Foundation, Inc.
The New-Land Foundation, Inc.
Edward John Noble Foundation, Inc.
Norcross Wildlife Foundation, Inc.
Orchard Foundation
Ottinger Foundation
The Overbrook Foundation
The David and Lucile Packard Foundation
The William Penn Foundation
The Pew Charitable Trusts
The Pfizer Foundation, Inc.
Howard Phipps Foundation
Pinewood Foundation
Henry B. Plant Memorial Fund, Inc.
The Prospect Hill Foundation
The Prudential Foundation
Public Welfare Foundation, Inc.
Recreational Equipment, Inc.
Philip D. Reed Foundation, Inc.
Rockefeller Family Fund, Inc.
Lee Romney Foundation, Inc.
Samuel and May Rudin Foundation, Inc.
Sacharuna Foundation
The Scherman Foundation, Inc.
S. H. and Helen R. Scheuer Family Foundation, Inc.
Sarah I. Schieffelin Residuary Trust

The Schiff Foundation
The Schumann Fund for New Jersey, Inc.
The Florence and John Schumann Foundation
Ralph C. Sheldon Foundation, Inc.
Shell Oil Company Foundation
Stanley Smith Horticultural Trust
Solow Foundation
Alfred T. Stanley Foundation
The Stebbins Fund, Inc.
Stroud Foundation
The Sulzberger Foundation, Inc.
Surdna Foundation, Inc.
Edna Bailey Sussman Fund
Texaco Foundation
Thanksgiving Foundation
The Oakleigh L. Thorne Foundation
The Tides Foundation
Times Mirror Magazines, Inc.
Tortuga Foundation
Town Creek Foundation, Inc.
The Travelers Foundation
Marcia Brady Tucker Foundation
Underhill Foundation
Union Camp Charitable Trust
Unitarian Universalist Veatch Program at Shelter Rock
R. T. Vanderbilt Trust
Victoria Foundation, Inc.
The Vidda Foundation
Vinmont Foundation, Inc.
WMX Environmental Grants Program
Wallace Genetic Foundation, Inc.
Lila Wallace-Reader's Digest Fund
Weeden Foundation
Henry E. and Consuelo S. Wenger Foundation, Inc.
Robert W. Wilson Foundation

Northeast

AT&T Foundation
The George I. Alden Trust
American Conservation Association, Inc.
American Foundation Corporation
Angelina Fund, Inc.
Evenor Armington Fund
Azadoutioun Foundation
The Bailey Wildlife Foundation
The George F. Baker Trust
The Theodore H. Barth Foundation, Inc.
The Bauman Foundation
The Howard Bayne Fund
L. L. Bean, Inc.
The Beinecke Foundation, Inc.
Beldon Fund
The Ben & Jerry's Foundation
The Betterment Fund
The Frank Stanley Beveridge Foundation, Inc.
The William Bingham Foundation
Alexander H. Bright Charitable Trust
The Butler Foundation
C. S. Fund
The Cabot Family Charitable Trust
Carolyn Foundation

Mary Flagler Cary Charitable Trust
The Champlin Foundations
Clark Charitable Trust
The Clark Foundation
The Clowes Fund, Inc.
The Community Foundation of Greater New Haven
Cox Foundation, Inc.
Jessie B. Cox Charitable Trust
The Cricket Foundation
Charles E. Culpeper Foundation, Inc.
The Nathan Cummings Foundation
The Fred Harris Daniels Foundation, Inc.
The Arthur Vining Davis Foundations
Davis Conservation Foundation
Deer Creek Foundation
Cleveland H. Dodge Foundation, Inc.
Geraldine R. Dodge Foundation, Inc.
Oliver S. and Jennie R. Donaldson Charitable Trust
The Dragon Foundation, Inc.
The Max and Victoria Dreyfus Foundation, Inc.
Echoing Green Foundation
The Educational Foundation of America
The Energy Foundation
The Charles Engelhard Foundation
The Armand G. Erpf Fund, Inc.
Fanwood Foundation
Jamee and Marshall Field Foundation
Fields Pond Foundation, Inc.
FishAmerica Foundation
Ford Foundation
Walter and Josephine Ford Fund
The Foundation for the National Capital Region
The Fund for Preservation of Wildlife and Natural Areas
Funding Exchange
GE Fund
Bernard F. and Alva B. Gimbel Foundation, Inc.
Greater Piscataqua Community Foundation
Gladys and Roland Harriman Foundation
Hartford Foundation for Public Giving
The Edward W. Hazen Foundation
Howfirma Foundation
The Roy A. Hunt Foundation
Hurdle Hill Foundation
The Hyams Foundation
The Indian Point Foundation, Inc.
The Louise H. and David S. Ingalls Foundation, Inc.
Ireland Foundation
Island Foundation, Inc.
Ittleson Foundation, Inc.
Jackson Hole Preserve, Inc.
The Howard Johnson Foundation
W. Alton Jones Foundation, Inc.
The Henry P. Kendall Foundation
The Knapp Foundation, Inc.
The Kresge Foundation
The Lagemann Foundation
Larsen Fund, Inc.
Lintilhac Foundation

Activity Region

Northeast (cont.)

The Little Family Foundation
The John D. and Catherine T. MacArthur Foundation
Magowan Family Foundation, Inc.
Maine Community Foundation, Inc.
MARPAT Foundation, Inc.
The Martin Foundation, Inc.
Massachusetts Environmental Trust
The Andrew W. Mellon Foundation
Richard King Mellon Foundation
Merck Family Fund
The John Merck Fund
Joyce Mertz-Gilmore Foundation
Metropolitan Life Foundation
Middlecott Foundation
Charles Stewart Mott Foundation
Ruth Mott Fund
National Fish and Wildlife Foundation
National Geographic Society Education Foundation
New England Biolabs Foundation
New Hampshire Charitable Foundation
The New World Foundation
The New York Times Company Foundation, Inc.
Norcross Wildlife Foundation, Inc.
Orchard Foundation
The Overbrook Foundation
The David and Lucile Packard Foundation
Patagonia, Inc.
Amelia Peabody Charitable Fund
James C. Penney Foundation
The Perkin Fund
The Pew Charitable Trusts
Ellis L. Phillips Foundation
Howard Phipps Foundation
Henry B. Plant Memorial Fund, Inc.
Prince Charitable Trusts
The Prospect Hill Foundation
Public Welfare Foundation, Inc.
Recreational Equipment, Inc.
The Rhode Island Community Foundation
Rockefeller Family Fund, Inc.
The Rockfall Foundation
Lee Romney Foundation, Inc.
The Florence and John Schumann Foundation
Elmina B. Sewall Foundation
Stanley Smith Horticultural Trust
Anna B. Stearns Charitable Foundation, Inc.
Stoddard Charitable Trust
The Stratford Foundation
The Sudbury Foundation
Surdna Foundation, Inc.
Edna Bailey Sussman Fund
The Switzer Foundation
Texaco Foundation
The Oakleigh L. Thorne Foundation
The Tides Foundation
Times Mirror Magazines, Inc.
Town Creek Foundation, Inc.
The Travelers Foundation
Marcia Brady Tucker Foundation
Underhill Foundation

Unitarian Universalist Veatch Program at Shelter Rock
R. T. Vanderbilt Trust
G. Unger Vetlesen Foundation
Wallace Genetic Foundation, Inc.
Weeden Foundation
Henry E. and Consuelo S. Wenger Foundation, Inc.
The William P. Wharton Trust
The Windham Foundation, Inc.
Sidney & Phyllis Wragge Foundation

Northwest

ARCO Foundation
A Territory Resource
The Abelard Foundation West
The Jenifer Altman Foundation
American Conservation Association, Inc.
BankAmerica Foundation
Beldon Fund
The Ben & Jerry's Foundation
The Boeing Company
The Bullitt Foundation
C. S. Fund
The Carpenter Foundation
Ben B. Cheney Foundation
The Chevron Companies
The Collins Foundation
Compton Foundation, Inc.
Crystal Channel Foundation
Deer Creek Foundation
The Educational Foundation of America
The Energy Foundation
The Charles Engelhard Foundation
Fanwood Foundation
The Hugh and Jane Ferguson Foundation
FishAmerica Foundation
Flintridge Foundation
Ford Foundation
Foundation for Deep Ecology
Fund of the Four Directions
Funding Exchange
General Service Foundation
Georgia-Pacific Foundation
Global Environmental Project Institute
The Greenville Foundation
HKH Foundation
Harder Foundation
The William and Flora Hewlett Foundation
The Homeland Foundation
Illilouette Fund
The Jackson Foundation
The Henry M. Jackson Foundation
The George Frederick Jewett Foundation
W. Alton Jones Foundation, Inc.
Kongsgaard-Goldman Foundation
Laird, Norton Foundation
The Lazar Foundation
The Max and Anna Levinson Foundation
The Little Family Foundation
Maki Foundation
The McIntosh Foundation
McKenzie River Gathering Foundation
Giles W. and Elise G. Mead Foundation
Meyer Memorial Trust

Charles Stewart Mott Foundation
Ruth Mott Fund
The Mountaineers Foundation
M. J. Murdock Charitable Trust
National Fish and Wildlife Foundation
National Geographic Society Education Foundation
New Horizon Foundation
Norcross Wildlife Foundation, Inc.
Northwest Area Foundation
Northwest Fund for the Environment
OCRI Foundation
Nathan M. Ohrbach Foundation, Inc.
The Ohrstrom Foundation
Outdoor Industry Conservation Alliance
The David and Lucile Packard Foundation
Patagonia, Inc.
The Pew Charitable Trusts
Public Welfare Foundation, Inc.
Recreational Equipment, Inc.
Rockefeller Family Fund, Inc.
Rockwood Fund, Inc.
Sequoia Foundation
Seventh Generation Fund
Shell Oil Company Foundation
The Skaggs Foundation
Surdna Foundation, Inc.
Texaco Foundation
Threshold Foundation
The Tides Foundation
Tortuga Foundation
Town Creek Foundation, Inc.
True North Foundation
Rose E. Tucker Charitable Trust
Union Pacific Foundation
Unitarian Universalist Veatch Program at Shelter Rock
G. Unger Vetlesen Foundation
WMX Environmental Grants Program
Wallace Genetic Foundation, Inc.
Weeden Foundation
Weyerhaeuser Company Foundation
Wilburforce Foundation

South Central

ARCO Foundation
AT&T Foundation
The Abelard Foundation West
Abell-Hanger Foundation
The Acorn Foundation
American Foundation Corporation
Azadoutioun Foundation
The George F. Baker Trust
Beldon Fund
The Ben & Jerry's Foundation
Beneficia Foundation
The Boeing Company
The Chevron Companies
Compton Foundation, Inc.
Crystal Channel Foundation
The Nathan Cummings Foundation
Geraldine R. Dodge Foundation, Inc.
Thelma Doelger Charitable Trust
Echoing Green Foundation
The Educational Foundation of America

© 1995 Environmental Data Resources, Inc.

629

Activity Region

South Central (cont.)

El Paso Community Foundation
The Energy Foundation
The Charles Engelhard Foundation
The William Stamps Farish Fund
The Favrot Fund
Leland Fikes Foundation, Inc.
FishAmerica Foundation
Ford Foundation
Foundation for Deep Ecology
The Frost Foundation, Ltd.
Fund of the Four Directions
Funding Exchange
General Service Foundation
The Ewing Halsell Foundation
Harder Foundation
The M. A. Healy Family Foundation, Inc.
W. Alton Jones Foundation, Inc.
Harris and Eliza Kempner Fund
The Robert S. and Grayce B. Kerr Foundation, Inc.
Caesar Kleberg Foundation for Wildlife Conservation
The Kresge Foundation
The Max and Anna Levinson Foundation
The Marshall L. & Perrine D. McCune Charitable Foundation
The Eugene McDermott Foundation
McDonnell Douglas Foundation
The McKnight Foundation
Giles W. and Elise G. Mead Foundation
Meadows Foundation, Inc.
Joyce Mertz-Gilmore Foundation
Mobil Foundation, Inc.
The Moody Foundation
Charles Stewart Mott Foundation
Ruth Mott Fund
National Fish and Wildlife Foundation
The New World Foundation
The Samuel Roberts Noble Foundation, Inc.
Norman Foundation
Mary Moody Northen, Inc.
Jessie Smith Noyes Foundation, Inc.
Patagonia, Inc.
James C. Penney Foundation
The Pew Charitable Trusts
Phillips Petroleum Foundation, Inc.
Pinewood Foundation
Public Welfare Foundation, Inc.
Recreational Equipment, Inc.
Sid W. Richardson Foundation
The Winthrop Rockefeller Foundation
Rockwell Fund, Inc.
Sarkeys Foundation
The Florence and John Schumann Foundation
Seventh Generation Fund
Shell Oil Company Foundation
Southwestern Bell Foundation
The Summerlee Foundation
Texaco Foundation
The Tides Foundation
Tortuga Foundation
The Travelers Foundation
Treacy Foundation, Inc.

USX Foundation, Inc.
Union Camp Charitable Trust
Union Pacific Foundation
Unitarian Universalist Veatch Program at Shelter Rock
WMX Environmental Grants Program
Weeden Foundation
Weyerhaeuser Company Foundation
The Wortham Foundation, Inc.
Margaret Cullinan Wray Charitable Lead Annuity Trust

Southeast

AT&T Foundation
American Conservation Association, Inc.
Angelina Fund, Inc.
Atlantic Foundation
Mary Reynolds Babcock Foundation, Inc.
The Bailey Wildlife Foundation
The George F. Baker Trust
The Howard Bayne Fund
Beldon Fund
The Ben & Jerry's Foundation
The Frank Stanley Beveridge Foundation, Inc.
The William Bingham Foundation
The Blumenthal Foundation
The Boeing Company
The Lynde and Harry Bradley Foundation, Inc.
W. L. Lyons Brown Foundation
Kathleen Price and Joseph M. Bryan Family Foundation, Inc.
Mary Flagler Cary Charitable Trust
Chesapeake Corporation Foundation
The Chevron Companies
Chrysler Corporation Fund
The Community Foundation of Sarasota County, Inc.
The Community Foundation Serving Coastal South Carolina
Community Foundation of Western North Carolina, Inc.
Compton Foundation, Inc.
S. H. Cowell Foundation
The Cowles Charitable Trust
Cox Foundation, Inc.
The James M. Cox, Jr. Foundation, Inc.
The Nathan Cummings Foundation
Geraldine R. Dodge Foundation, Inc.
Gaylord and Dorothy Donnelley Foundation
The Elizabeth Ordway Dunn Foundation, Inc.
Jessie Ball duPont Religious, Charitable and Educational Fund
Eastman Kodak Company Charitable Trust
The Energy Foundation
The Charles Engelhard Foundation
Environmental Education Foundation of Florida, Inc.
Fanwood Foundation
The William Stamps Farish Fund
Felburn Foundation
Jamee and Marshall Field Foundation
FishAmerica Foundation

Ford Foundation
Ford Motor Company Fund
Foundation for the Carolinas
Foundation for Deep Ecology
Fund of the Four Directions
Funding Exchange
The Gap Foundation
Georgia Power Foundation, Inc.
Georgia-Pacific Foundation
James G. Hanes Memorial Fund
Harder Foundation
Gladys and Roland Harriman Foundation
The Hastings Trust
The Edward W. Hazen Foundation
W. Alton Jones Foundation, Inc.
F. M. Kirby Foundation, Inc.
The Knapp Foundation, Inc.
Laird, Norton Foundation
Levi Strauss Foundation
The Max and Anna Levinson Foundation
LifeWorks Foundation
Lyndhurst Foundation
The John D. and Catherine T. MacArthur Foundation
Magowan Family Foundation, Inc.
McDonnell Douglas Foundation
The McIntosh Foundation
The McKnight Foundation
Nelson Mead Fund
The Andrew W. Mellon Foundation
Richard King Mellon Foundation
Merck Family Fund
Joyce Mertz-Gilmore Foundation
Metropolitan Atlanta Community Foundation, Inc.
The Moriah Fund, Inc.
Charles Stewart Mott Foundation
Ruth Mott Fund
The Curtis and Edith Munson Foundation, Inc.
National Fish and Wildlife Foundation
National Geographic Society Education Foundation
The Needmor Fund
The New York Times Company Foundation, Inc.
Edward John Noble Foundation, Inc.
Norcross Wildlife Foundation, Inc.
Norman Foundation
The Norton Foundation, Inc.
Jessie Smith Noyes Foundation, Inc.
The Ohrstrom Foundation
Orchard Foundation
Ottinger Foundation
Outdoor Industry Conservation Alliance
Patagonia, Inc.
James C. Penney Foundation
Perkins Charitable Foundation
The Pew Charitable Trusts
Lynn R. and Karl E. Prickett Fund
The Procter & Gamble Fund
Public Welfare Foundation, Inc.
Recreational Equipment, Inc.
Z. Smith Reynolds Foundation, Inc.
Rockefeller Family Fund, Inc.

Activity Region

Southeast (cont.)

Sacharuna Foundation
The Sapelo Foundation
Schultz Foundation, Inc.
The Florence and John Schumann Foundation
Shell Oil Company Foundation
Stanley Smith Horticultural Trust
Springs Foundation, Inc.
Steelcase Foundation
Margaret Dorrance Strawbridge Foundation of Pennsylvania II, Inc.
The Sulzberger Foundation, Inc.
Surdna Foundation, Inc.
Edna Bailey Sussman Fund
Texaco Foundation
The Tides Foundation
Times Mirror Magazines, Inc.
Town Creek Foundation, Inc.
USX Foundation, Inc.
Union Camp Charitable Trust
Unitarian Universalist Veatch Program at Shelter Rock
WMX Environmental Grants Program
Wallace Genetic Foundation, Inc.
DeWitt Wallace-Reader's Digest Fund
Lila Wallace-Reader's Digest Fund
Weeden Foundation
Henry E. and Consuelo S. Wenger Foundation, Inc.
Weyerhaeuser Company Foundation
Joseph B. Whitehead Foundation
The Winston-Salem Foundation, Inc.
Wodecroft Foundation
Robert W. Woodruff Foundation, Inc.

West

ARCO Foundation
AT&T Foundation
The Abelard Foundation West
The Acorn Foundation
The Ahmanson Foundation
Winifred & Harry B. Allen Foundation
The Jenifer Altman Foundation
American Foundation Corporation
Angelina Fund, Inc.
The Austin Memorial Foundation
BankAmerica Foundation
The Bauman Foundation
S. D. Bechtel, Jr. Foundation
Beldon Fund
The Ben & Jerry's Foundation
Bishop Pine Fund
The Bothin Foundation
Helen Brach Foundation
The Robert Brownlee Foundation
C. S. Fund
California Community Foundation
Cheeryble Foundation
Ben B. Cheney Foundation
The Chevron Companies
Columbia Foundation
The Community Foundation of Santa Clara County

Compton Foundation, Inc.
The Mary A. Crocker Trust
Roy E. Crummer Foundation
Crystal Channel Foundation
The Nathan Cummings Foundation
Geraldine R. Dodge Foundation, Inc.
Thelma Doelger Charitable Trust
The Educational Foundation of America
Arthur M. and Olga T. Eisig-Arthur M. and Kate E. Tode Foundation, Inc.
The Energy Foundation
The Charles Engelhard Foundation
Environment Now Foundation
The Ettinger Foundation, Inc.
Fanwood Foundation
The Favrot Fund
FishAmerica Foundation
Flintridge Foundation
Ford Foundation
Foundation for Deep Ecology
Fund of the Four Directions
Funding Exchange
The Gap Foundation
The Fred Gellert Foundation
General Service Foundation
The Wallace Alexander Gerbode Foundation, Inc.
Richard & Rhoda Goldman Fund
The Greenville Foundation
Evelyn and Walter Haas, Jr. Fund
Walter and Elise Haas Fund
The Harding Educational and Charitable Foundation
The John Randolph Haynes and Dora Haynes Foundation
Heller Charitable & Educational Fund
The Clarence E. Heller Charitable Foundation
The William and Flora Hewlett Foundation
The Hofmann Foundation
The Homeland Foundation
The Horn Foundation
The Roy A. Hunt Foundation
Illilouette Fund
The James Irvine Foundation
Island Foundation
The George Frederick Jewett Foundation
Walter S. Johnson Foundation
W. Alton Jones Foundation, Inc.
The Kresge Foundation
Laird, Norton Foundation
The Norman Lear Foundation
Levi Strauss Foundation
The Max and Anna Levinson Foundation
Luster Family Foundation, Inc.
Magowan Family Foundation, Inc.
Marin Community Foundation
The Marshall Fund of Arizona
The McConnell Foundation
McDonnell Douglas Foundation
McKesson Foundation, Inc.
Giles W. and Elise G. Mead Foundation
The Andrew W. Mellon Foundation
Joyce Mertz-Gilmore Foundation
Mobil Foundation, Inc.

Charles Stewart Mott Foundation
Ruth Mott Fund
National Fish and Wildlife Foundation
The New York Times Company Foundation, Inc.
Norman Foundation
Andrew Norman Foundation
Kenneth T. and Eileen L. Norris Foundation
Jessie Smith Noyes Foundation, Inc.
OCRI Foundation
Nathan M. Ohrbach Foundation, Inc.
Orchard Foundation
Ottinger Foundation
Outdoor Industry Conservation Alliance
The David and Lucile Packard Foundation
Patagonia, Inc.
Peninsula Community Foundation
James C. Penney Foundation
The Pew Charitable Trusts
Lynn R. and Karl E. Prickett Fund
Public Welfare Foundation, Inc.
Recreational Equipment, Inc.
The Roberts Foundation
Rockefeller Family Fund, Inc.
Lee Romney Foundation, Inc.
Sacharuna Foundation
Sacramento Regional Foundation
San Diego Community Foundation
The San Francisco Foundation
Ellen Browning Scripps Foundation
Frances Seebe Trust
Seventh Generation Fund
Shell Oil Company Foundation
The Skaggs Foundation
Stanley Smith Horticultural Trust
The Sonoma County Community Foundation
South Coast Foundation, Inc.
Springhouse Foundation
Steelcase Foundation
The Stratford Foundation
The Strong Foundation for Environmental Values
The Morris Stulsaft Foundation
The Summerlee Foundation
Surdna Foundation, Inc.
The Switzer Foundation
S. Mark Taper Foundation
The Telesis Foundation
Texaco Foundation
Threshold Foundation
The Tides Foundation
Toyota USA Foundation
The Travelers Foundation
True North Foundation
Alice Tweed Tuohy Foundation
USX Foundation, Inc.
Underhill Foundation
Union Pacific Foundation
Unitarian Universalist Veatch Program at Shelter Rock
Vanguard Public Foundation
G. Unger Vetlesen Foundation
WMX Environmental Grants Program
Wallace Genetic Foundation, Inc.

© 1995 Environmental Data Resources, Inc.

Activity Region

West (cont.)

Lila Wallace-Reader's Digest Fund
C. A. Webster Foundation
Weeden Foundation
Whitecap Foundation
The Winslow Foundation
The Dean Witter Foundation

U.S. not specified

ARCO Foundation
AT&T Foundation
The Acorn Foundation
Airport Business Center Foundation
The Jenifer Altman Foundation
American Conservation Association, Inc.
American Express Philanthropic Program
Angelina Fund, Inc.
Apple Computer, Inc.
The Arca Foundation
Evenor Armington Fund
Azadoutioun Foundation
The Bailey Wildlife Foundation
The Cameron Baird Foundation
Clayton Baker Trust
BankAmerica Foundation
The Bauman Foundation
The Bay Foundation
The Howard Bayne Fund
L. L. Bean, Inc.
S. D. Bechtel, Jr. Foundation
The Beinecke Foundation, Inc.
Beldon Fund
James Ford Bell Foundation
The Ben & Jerry's Foundation
Beneficia Foundation
Benton Foundation
The William Bingham Foundation
Helen Brach Foundation
Alexander H. Bright Charitable Trust
Jesse Margaret Wilson Budlong Foundation for Animal Aid
The Butler Foundation
J. E. & Z. B. Butler Foundation, Inc.
The Bydale Foundation
C. S. Fund
Ward M. & Mariam C. Canaday Educational and Charitable Trust
Changing Horizons Charitable Trust
The Chevron Companies
Chrysler Corporation Fund
Clark Charitable Trust
The Clark Foundation
Compton Foundation, Inc.
The Conservation and Research Foundation
S. H. Cowell Foundation
Roy E. Crummer Foundation
Crystal Channel Foundation
Charles E. Culpeper Foundation, Inc.
The Nathan Cummings Foundation
Deer Creek Foundation
Cleveland H. Dodge Foundation, Inc.
Geraldine R. Dodge Foundation, Inc.
Oliver S. and Jennie R. Donaldson Charitable Trust

The Max and Victoria Dreyfus Foundation, Inc.
Echoing Green Foundation
The Educational Foundation of America
Arthur M. and Olga T. Eisig-Arthur M. and Kate E. Tode Foundation, Inc.
The Emerald Foundation
The Energy Foundation
The Charles Engelhard Foundation
Environment Now Foundation
The Armand G. Erpf Fund, Inc.
The Ettinger Foundation, Inc.
Fanwood Foundation
Jamee and Marshall Field Foundation
Ford Foundation
Ford Motor Company Fund
Foundation for Deep Ecology
The Foundation for the National Capital Region
Fund of the Four Directions
Funding Exchange
GE Fund
The Barbara Gauntlett Foundation, Inc.
The Fred Gellert Foundation
The German Marshall Fund of the United States
Bernard F. and Alva B. Gimbel Foundation, Inc.
Give to the Earth Foundation
Global Environmental Project Institute
The Golden Rule Foundation, Inc.
Good Samaritan, Inc.
The Greenville Foundation
The William and Mary Greve Foundation, Inc.
HKH Foundation
The Hamer Foundation
Harbor Lights Foundation
Harder Foundation
The Harding Educational and Charitable Foundation
Mary W. Harriman Foundation
The Hastings Trust
The Merrill G. & Emita E. Hastings Foundation
The Hitachi Foundation
The Hofmann Foundation
The Homeland Foundation
The Horn Foundation
The Charles Evans Hughes Memorial Foundation, Inc.
The Roy A. Hunt Foundation
Hurdle Hill Foundation
The Louise H. and David S. Ingalls Foundation, Inc.
Ireland Foundation
Island Foundation, Inc.
Ittleson Foundation, Inc.
The Henry M. Jackson Foundation
The Howard Johnson Foundation
W. Alton Jones Foundation, Inc.
Joy Foundation for Ecological Education and Research
The Helen & Milton Kimmelman Foundation

Kinnoull Foundation
The Esther A. and Joseph Klingenstein Fund, Inc.
Charles G. Koch Charitable Foundation
Kongsgaard-Goldman Foundation
The Kresge Foundation
Laird, Norton Foundation
Laurel Foundation
The Max and Anna Levinson Foundation
Richard Lounsbery Foundation, Inc.
Luster Family Foundation, Inc.
The John D. and Catherine T. MacArthur Foundation
Magowan Family Foundation, Inc.
MARPAT Foundation, Inc.
Mars Foundation
The Martin Foundation, Inc.
McDonnell Douglas Foundation
The McIntosh Foundation
Giles W. and Elise G. Mead Foundation
Nelson Mead Fund
The Andrew W. Mellon Foundation
Richard King Mellon Foundation
Merck Family Fund
The John Merck Fund
Joyce Mertz-Gilmore Foundation
Metropolitan Life Foundation
Mobil Foundation, Inc.
Leo Model Foundation, Inc.
The Moriah Fund, Inc.
Charles Stewart Mott Foundation
Ruth Mott Fund
The Curtis and Edith Munson Foundation, Inc.
Mustard Seed Foundation, Inc.
The National Environmental Education and Training Foundation, Inc.
National Fish and Wildlife Foundation
National Geographic Society Education Foundation
The Needmor Fund
The New World Foundation
The New York Times Company Foundation, Inc.
The New-Land Foundation, Inc.
Edward John Noble Foundation, Inc.
Norman Foundation
Jessie Smith Noyes Foundation, Inc.
OCRI Foundation
Nathan M. Ohrbach Foundation, Inc.
The Ohrstrom Foundation
Ottinger Foundation
Outdoor Industry Conservation Alliance
The Overbrook Foundation
The David and Lucile Packard Foundation
Patagonia, Inc.
James C. Penney Foundation
The Perkin Fund
Perkins Charitable Foundation
The Pew Charitable Trusts
Pew Scholars Program in Conservation and the Environment
The Pfizer Foundation, Inc.
Philip Morris Companies, Inc.
Phillips Petroleum Foundation, Inc.

Activity Region

U.S. not specified (cont.)

Howard Phipps Foundation
Henry B. Plant Memorial Fund, Inc.
Lynn R. and Karl E. Prickett Fund
Prince Charitable Trusts
The Procter & Gamble Fund
The Prospect Hill Foundation
The Prudential Foundation
Public Welfare Foundation, Inc.
Recreational Equipment, Inc.
Philip D. Reed Foundation, Inc.
Smith Richardson Foundation, Inc.
Rockefeller Brothers Fund, Inc.
Rockefeller Family Fund, Inc.
Rockefeller Financial Services, Philanthropy Department
Rockwood Fund, Inc.
Lee Romney Foundation, Inc.
Sacharuna Foundation
Sarah Scaife Foundation Incorporated
The Scherman Foundation, Inc.
The Schiff Foundation
Schultz Foundation, Inc.
The Florence and John Schumann Foundation
Seventh Generation Fund
Shell Oil Company Foundation
Stanley Smith Horticultural Trust
South Coast Foundation, Inc.
Alfred T. Stanley Foundation
Stern Family Fund
The Stratford Foundation
Margaret Dorrance Strawbridge Foundation of Pennsylvania II, Inc.
The Stroh Foundation
The Sulzberger Foundation, Inc.
The Summerlee Foundation
The Summit Foundation
Surdna Foundation, Inc.
Nelson Talbott Foundation
S. Mark Taper Foundation
Texaco Foundation
Thanksgiving Foundation
The Oakleigh L. Thorne Foundation
Threshold Foundation
The Tides Foundation
Times Mirror Magazines, Inc.
The Tinker Foundation Incorporated
Tortuga Foundation
Town Creek Foundation, Inc.
Treacy Foundation, Inc.
True North Foundation
The Truland Foundation
Marcia Brady Tucker Foundation
Turner Foundation, Inc.
USX Foundation, Inc.
Underhill Foundation
Union Camp Charitable Trust
Unitarian Universalist Veatch Program at Shelter Rock
R. T. Vanderbilt Trust
G. Unger Vetlesen Foundation
The Vidda Foundation
WMX Environmental Grants Program
Wallace Genetic Foundation, Inc.

DeWitt Wallace-Reader's Digest Fund
Lila Wallace-Reader's Digest Fund
C. A. Webster Foundation
Weeden Foundation
Henry E. and Consuelo S. Wenger Foundation, Inc.
Westinghouse Foundation
Weyerhaeuser Company Foundation
Robert W. Wilson Foundation
Mark and Catherine Winkler Foundation
The Winslow Foundation
Sidney & Phyllis Wragge Foundation
Margaret Cullinan Wray Charitable Lead Annuity Trust

U.S. Commonwealth

Puerto Rico

The Ben & Jerry's Foundation
Funding Exchange
The John D. and Catherine T. MacArthur Foundation
Charles Stewart Mott Foundation
Public Welfare Foundation, Inc.
The Tides Foundation
Unitarian Universalist Veatch Program at Shelter Rock

U.S. Territory

Virgin Islands

Jackson Hole Preserve, Inc.
The John D. and Catherine T. MacArthur Foundation

© 1995 Environmental Data Resources, Inc.

Activity Region

International

International not specified

The Acorn Foundation
The Jenifer Altman Foundation
American Foundation Corporation
The Arca Foundation
Atkinson Foundation
The George F. Baker Trust
The Bay Foundation
James Ford Bell Foundation
Beneficia Foundation
Benua Foundation, Inc.
The William Bingham Foundation
The Lynde and Harry Bradley
    Foundation, Inc.
The Bullitt Foundation
The Bydale Foundation
C. S. Fund
Caribou Fund
The Chevron Companies
Liz Claiborne & Art Ortenberg Foundation
Compton Foundation, Inc.
The Conservation and Research Foundation
Conservation, Food & Health
    Foundation, Inc.
Roy E. Crummer Foundation
Crystal Channel Foundation
The Nathan Cummings Foundation
Damien Foundation
The Nelson B. Delavan Foundation
Oliver S. and Jennie R. Donaldson
    Charitable Trustu
Donner Canadian Foundation
Douroucouli Foundation
The Emerald Foundation
The Energy Foundation
The Charles Engelhard Foundation
The Armand G. Erpf Fund, Inc.
The Ettinger Foundation, Inc.
Ford Foundation
Foundation for Deep Ecology
Foundation for Field Research
The Foundation for the National
    Capital Region
Fund of the Four Directions
Funding Exchange
GE Fund
The Fred Gellert Foundation
General Service Foundation
The German Marshall Fund of
    the United States
Give to the Earth Foundation
Global Environmental Project Institute
Global Greengrants Fund
The Goldman Environmental Foundation
Richard & Rhoda Goldman Fund

Walter and Duncan Gordon Charitable
    Foundation
Great Lakes Protection Fund
The Greenville Foundation
HKH Foundation
The Homeland Foundation
The Horn Foundation
The International Foundation, Inc.
The Richard Ivey Foundation
Jackson Hole Preserve, Inc.
The Henry M. Jackson Foundation
The George Frederick Jewett Foundation
W. Alton Jones Foundation, Inc.
The Joyce Foundation
W. K. Kellogg Foundation
Kinnoull Foundation
Laidlaw Foundation
The Lazar Foundation
The Max and Anna Levinson Foundation
The John D. and Catherine T. MacArthur
    Foundation
Magowan Family Foundation, Inc.
The Martin Foundation, Inc.
Giles W. and Elise G. Mead Foundation
The Andrew W. Mellon Foundation
The John Merck Fund
Joyce Mertz-Gilmore Foundation
The Moriah Fund, Inc.
Charles Stewart Mott Foundation
The Curtis and Edith Munson
    Foundation, Inc.
National Fish and Wildlife Foundation
The Needmor Fund
New England Biolabs Foundation
The New York Times Company
    Foundation, Inc.
Jessie Smith Noyes Foundation, Inc.
The Ohrstrom Foundation
The David and Lucile Packard Foundation
Patagonia, Inc.
The Pew Charitable Trusts
Pew Scholars Program in Conservation
    and the Environment
The Polden-Puckham Charitable Foundation
The Prospect Hill Foundation
Public Welfare Foundation, Inc.
Rockefeller Brothers Fund, Inc.
The Rockefeller Foundation
Rockwood Fund, Inc.
Lee Romney Foundation, Inc.
Sacharuna Foundation
Sequoia Foundation
Seventh Generation Fund
Shell Oil Company Foundation
Stanley Smith Horticultural Trust
South Coast Foundation, Inc.

Steelcase Foundation
The Summerlee Foundation
The Summit Foundation
Surdna Foundation, Inc.
Threshold Foundation
The Tides Foundation
The Tinker Foundation Incorporated
The Truland Foundation
The Trust For Mutual Understanding
United States-Japan Foundation
Vancouver Foundation
WMX Environemtnal Grants Program
Alex C. Walker Educational
    & Charitable Foundation
Wallace Genetic Foundation, Inc.
Weeden Foundation
The Winslow Foundation

Developing countries

The William Bingham Foundation
Caribou Fund
Liz Claiborne & Art Ortenberg Foundation
Compton Foundation, Inc.
Conservation, Food & Health
    Foundation, Inc.
Damien Foundation
Foundation for Deep Ecology
Ford Foundation
General Service Foundation
Global Greengrants Fund
The Homeland Foundation
The International Foundation, Inc.
W. Alton Jones Foundation, Inc.
The John D. and Catherine T. MacArthur
    Foundation
The Martin Foundation, Inc.
Joyce Mertz-Gilmore Foundation
Charles Stewart Mott Foundation
New England Biolabs Foundation
The New York Times Company
    Foundation, Inc.
The Pew Charitable Trusts
The Rockefeller Foundation
The Summit Foundation
The Tides Foundation
WMX Environmental Grants Program
Weeden Foundation

Tropics

Atkinson Foundation
Caribou Fund

Activity Region

Tropics (cont.)

Conservation, Food & Health
  Foundation, Inc.
Oliver S. and Jennie R. Donaldson
  Charitable Trust
Ford Foundation
Foundation for Deep Ecology
The Fred Gellert Foundation
General Service Foundation
Global Greengrants Fund
HKH Foundation
The Homeland Foundation
The Horn Foundation
The International Foundation, Inc.
W. Alton Jones Foundation, Inc.
The John D. and Catherine T. MacArthur
  Foundation
Magowan Family Foundation, Inc.
The John Merck Fund
The Moriah Fund, Inc.
Patagonia, Inc.
The Pew Charitable Trusts
Rockwood Fund, Inc.
Sequoia Foundation
Stanley Smith Horticultural Trust
The Tides Foundation
Weeden Foundation

Africa

Africa not specified

American Foundation Corporation
Compton Foundation, Inc.
Roy E. Crummer Foundation
The Nelson B. Delavan Foundation
The Charles Engelhard Foundation
The Armand G. Erpf Fund, Inc.
The Foundation for the National
  Capital Region
Give to the Earth Foundation
The Goldman Environmental Foundation
W. K. Kellogg Foundation
The Ohrstrom Foundation
The Rockefeller Foundation
Lee Romney Foundation, Inc.
South Coast Foundation, Inc.
The Tides Foundation

Eastern and Southern Africa

The Jenifer Altman Foundation
Atkinson Foundation
The Bay Foundation
The Conservation and Research Foundation
Conservation, Food & Health
  Foundation, Inc.
Ford Foundation
Global Environmental Project Institute
The International Foundation, Inc.
W. Alton Jones Foundation, Inc.
Kinnoull Foundation
The John D. and Catherine T. MacArthur
  Foundation

New England Biolabs Foundation
The Ohrstrom Foundation
Patagonia, Inc.
The Rockefeller Foundation
South Coast Foundation, Inc.
The Summerlee Foundation
The Tides Foundation
Weeden Foundation

North Africa

Ford Foundation

West Africa

Atkinson Foundation
Beneficia Foundation
The Conservation and Research Foundation
The John D. and Catherine T. MacArthur
  Foundation
New England Biolabs Foundation
Public Welfare Foundation, Inc.
The Summerlee Foundation

Antarctica

Patagonia, Inc.
Threshold Foundation
The Tinker Foundation Incorporated
Weeden Foundation

Asia

Asia not specified

The International Foundation, Inc.
W. Alton Jones Foundation, Inc.
The Moriah Fund, Inc.
The Rockefeller Foundation

Far East

American Foundation Corporation
Caribou Fund
Ford Foundation
Foundation for Deep Ecology
The Goldman Environmental Foundation
W. Alton Jones Foundation, Inc.
The John D. and Catherine T. MacArthur
  Foundation
Charles Stewart Mott Foundation
Patagonia, Inc.
Rockefeller Brothers Fund, Inc.
The Rockefeller Foundation
United States-Japan Foundation

Indian Subcontinent and Indian Ocean Islands

The Jenifer Altman Foundation
Conservation, Food & Health
  Foundation, Inc.
Ford Foundation
Foundation for Deep Ecology
Fund of the Four Directions
The John D. and Catherine T. MacArthur
  Foundation
The Moriah Fund, Inc.

The Ohrstrom Foundation
Patagonia, Inc.
Pew Scholars Program in Conservation
  and the Environment
Rockefeller Brothers Fund, Inc.
The Rockefeller Foundation
Sequoia Foundation
The Tides Foundation

Middle East and Western Asia

American Foundation Corporation
The Bydale Foundation
The Nathan Cummings Foundation
Richard & Rhoda Goldman Fund
The International Foundation, Inc.
W. Alton Jones Foundation, Inc.
The Max and Anna Levinson Foundation
The Moriah Fund, Inc.

Russia

Caribou Fund
Compton Foundation, Inc.
Ford Foundation
The Goldman Environmental Foundation
W. Alton Jones Foundation, Inc.
The John D. and Catherine T. MacArthur
  Foundation
Joyce Mertz-Gilmore Foundation
Charles Stewart Mott Foundation
New England Biolabs Foundation
Patagonia, Inc.
Rockefeller Brothers Fund, Inc.
The Rockefeller Foundation
The Trust For Mutual Understanding
Weeden Foundation

Southeast Asia

The Jenifer Altman Foundation
Beneficia Foundation
Caribou Fund
Conservation, Food & Health
  Foundation, Inc.
Crystal Channel Foundation
Ford Foundation
Foundation for Deep Ecology
The International Foundation, Inc.
The Max and Anna Levinson Foundation
The John D. and Catherine T. MacArthur
  Foundation
The John Merck Fund
New England Biolabs Foundation
The Ohrstrom Foundation
Pew Scholars Program in Conservation
  and the Environment
Rockefeller Brothers Fund, Inc.
The Rockefeller Foundation
Rockwood Fund, Inc.

Australian Group/Oceania

American Foundation Corporation
The Goldman Environmental Foundation
New England Biolabs Foundation

Activity Region

Europe

Eastern Europe

The Jenifer Altman Foundation
Foundation for Deep Ecology
The German Marshall Fund of
   the United States
W. Alton Jones Foundation, Inc.
The John D. and Catherine T. MacArthur
   Foundation
Joyce Mertz-Gilmore Foundation
The Moriah Fund, Inc.
Charles Stewart Mott Foundation
Pew Scholars Program in Conservation
   and the Environment
Rockefeller Brothers Fund, Inc.
The Trust For Mutual Understanding
Weeden Foundation

Western Europe

American Foundation Corporation
The Chevron Companies
Damien Foundation
Foundation for Deep Ecology
The German Marshall Fund of
   the United States
W. Alton Jones Foundation, Inc.
The John Merck Fund
Joyce Mertz-Gilmore Foundation
Charles Stewart Mott Foundation
Patagonia, Inc.
The Polden-Puckham Charitable Foundation
Rockefeller Brothers Fund, Inc.
The Rockefeller Foundation

Latin America

Latin America not specified

American Foundation Corporation
General Service Foundation
The International Foundation, Inc.
W. K. Kellogg Foundation
The John D. and Catherine T. MacArthur
   Foundation
The John Merck Fund
The Moriah Fund, Inc.
Charles Stewart Mott Foundation
Jessie Smith Noyes Foundation, Inc.
The Prospect Hill Foundation
The Rockefeller Foundation
The Tides Foundation
The Tinker Foundation Incorporated
Alex C. Walker Educational
   & Charitable Foundation
Wallace Genetic Foundation, Inc.
Weeden Foundation

Caribbean and West Indies

American Foundation Corporation
The George F. Baker Trust
Ford Foundation
Foundation for Field Research
General Service Foundation
The International Foundation, Inc.
Jackson Hole Preserve, Inc.
W. K. Kellogg Foundation
The Max and Anna Levinson Foundation
The John D. and Catherine T. MacArthur
   Foundation
The Moriah Fund, Inc.
National Fish and Wildlife Foundation
New England Biolabs Foundation
Public Welfare Foundation, Inc.
The Rockefeller Foundation
Shell Oil Company Foundation
The Tinker Foundation Incorporated
The Truland Foundation
Weeden Foundation

Mexico and Central America

The Jenifer Altman Foundation
The Arca Foundation
Atkinson Foundation
The Bay Foundation
Liz Claiborne & Art Ortenberg Foundation
Compton Foundation, Inc.
The Conservation and Research Foundation
Conservation, Food & Health
   Foundation, Inc.
The Nathan Cummings Foundation
The Armand G. Erpf Fund, Inc.
Ford Foundation
Foundation for Deep Ecology
General Service Foundation
The Greenville Foundation
W. Alton Jones Foundation, Inc.
The Max and Anna Levinson Foundation
The John D. and Catherine T. MacArthur
   Foundation
The Moriah Fund, Inc.
National Fish and Wildlife Foundation
New England Biolabs Foundation
Norcross Wildlife Foundation, Inc.
The David and Lucile Packard Foundation
Pew Scholars Program in Conservation
   and the Environment
The Prospect Hill Foundation
Public Welfare Foundation, Inc.
The Rockefeller Foundation
Rockwood Fund, Inc.
Sequoia Foundation
Threshold Foundation
The Tinker Foundation Incorporated
Weeden Foundation

South America not specified

Damien Foundation
W. Alton Jones Foundation, Inc.
The Moriah Fund, Inc.
New England Biolabs Foundation
Stanley Smith Horticultural Trust
The Tinker Foundation Incorporated

Andean Region and Southern Cone

The Bay Foundation
Beneficia Foundation
Compton Foundation, Inc.
Conservation, Food & Health
   Foundation, Inc.
Ford Foundation
Foundation for Deep Ecology
General Service Foundation
The Homeland Foundation
W. Alton Jones Foundation, Inc.
The John D. and Catherine T. MacArthur
   Foundation
Giles W. and Elise G. Mead Foundation
The Andrew W. Mellon Foundation
The Moriah Fund, Inc.
Charles Stewart Mott Foundation
New England Biolabs Foundation
Jessie Smith Noyes Foundation, Inc.
Patagonia, Inc.
The Rockefeller Foundation
Stanley Smith Horticultural Trust
The Tinker Foundation Incorporated
Weeden Foundation

Brazil

Atkinson Foundation
Caribou Fund
Conservation, Food & Health
   Foundation, Inc.
Crystal Channel Foundation
Damien Foundation
Ford Foundation
General Service Foundation
W. Alton Jones Foundation, Inc.
The John D. and Catherine T. MacArthur
   Foundation
The Andrew W. Mellon Foundation
The Moriah Fund, Inc.
Charles Stewart Mott Foundation
New England Biolabs Foundation
Jessie Smith Noyes Foundation, Inc.
The Rockefeller Foundation
The Tinker Foundation Incorporated
The Winslow Foundation

Northern South America

Conservation, Food & Health
   Foundation, Inc.
Ford Foundation
Funding Exchange
The Goldman Environmental Foundation
W. Alton Jones Foundation, Inc.
The John D. and Catherine T. MacArthur
   Foundation
The Andrew W. Mellon Foundation
Jessie Smith Noyes Foundation, Inc.
The Tinker Foundation Incorporated
Weeden Foundation
The Winslow Foundation

North America

North America not specified

The Acorn Foundation
The Jenifer Altman Foundation
The Arca Foundation

Activity Region

North America not specified (cont.)

C. S. Fund
The Charles Engelhard Foundation
Ford Foundation
Foundation for Deep Ecology
The German Marshall Fund of
  the United States
Richard & Rhoda Goldman Fund
W. Alton Jones Foundation, Inc.
The Max and Anna Levinson Foundation
The John D. and Catherine T. MacArthur
  Foundation
Charles Stewart Mott Foundation
The Curtis and Edith Munson
  Foundation, Inc.
National Fish and Wildlife Foundation
Patagonia, Inc.
The Pew Charitable Trusts
Pew Scholars Program in Conservation
  and the Environment
Stanley Smith Horticultural Trust

Canada

American Foundation Corporation
James Ford Bell Foundation
Benua Foundation, Inc.
The Bullitt Foundation
The Chevron Companies
Donner Canadian Foundation
Foundation for Deep Ecology
Give to the Earth Foundation
Walter and Duncan Gordon Charitable
  Foundation
Great Lakes Protection Fund
The Richard Ivey Foundation
W. Alton Jones Foundation, Inc.
The Joyce Foundation
Laidlaw Foundation
The Lazar Foundation
The John D. and Catherine T. MacArthur
  Foundation
Giles W. and Elise G. Mead Foundation
Charles Stewart Mott Foundation
National Fish and Wildlife Foundation
The Needmor Fund
Patagonia, Inc.
The Pew Charitable Trusts
Rockwood Fund, Inc.
Sacharuna Foundation
Seventh Generation Fund
Thomas Sill Foundation
Stanley Smith Horticultural Trust
Steelcase Foundation
The Tides Foundation
Vancouver Foundation
Weeden Foundation

Emphases

Activism

The Abelard Foundation West
The Acorn Foundation
Alaska Conservation Foundation
The Jenifer Altman Foundation
Americana Foundation, Inc.
The Bauman Foundation
The Beinecke Foundation, Inc.
Beldon Fund
The Ben & Jerry's Foundation
The Blumenthal Foundation
Otto Bremer Foundation
C. S. Fund
Caribou Fund
Liz Claiborne & Art Ortenberg Foundation
Jessie B. Cox Charitable Trust
The Educational Foundation of America
Samuel S. Fels Fund
Foundation for Deep Ecology
The Frost Foundation, Ltd.
Give to the Earth Foundation
Global Environmental Project Institute
Global Greengrants Fund
Richard & Rhoda Goldman Fund
Walter and Duncan Gordon Charitable Foundation
The Greenville Foundation
The George Gund Foundation
Harder Foundation
Hawaiian Electric Industries Charitable Foundation
Illilouette Fund
W. Alton Jones Foundation, Inc.
The Lazar Foundation
The Max and Anna Levinson Foundation
LifeWorks Foundation
Marin Community Foundation
McKenzie River Gathering Foundation
The McKnight Foundation
The Needmor Fund
New England Biolabs Foundation
The New World Foundation
New York Foundation
Norman Foundation
Jessie Smith Noyes Foundation, Inc.
Ottinger Foundation
Outdoor Industry Conservation Alliance
The David and Lucile Packard Foundation
Patagonia, Inc.
The Pew Charitable Trusts
Pew Scholars Program in Conservation and the Environment
Public Welfare Foundation, Inc.
Recreational Equipment, Inc.
Rockefeller Family Fund, Inc.
Rockefeller Financial Services, Philanthropy Department
Rockwood Fund, Inc.
The San Francisco Foundation
The Sapelo Foundation

The Florence and John Schumann Foundation
The Skaggs Foundation
The Strong Foundation for Environmental Values
The Summerlee Foundation
The Tides Foundation
Town Creek Foundation, Inc.
Rose E. Tucker Charitable Trust
Turner Foundation, Inc.
WMX Environmental Grants Program
Margaret Cullinan Wray Charitable Lead Annuity Trust

Advocacy

A Territory Resource
The Abelard Foundation West
The Abell Foundation
The Acorn Foundation
Alaska Conservation Foundation
The Jenifer Altman Foundation
Mary Reynolds Babcock Foundation, Inc.
The Bauman Foundation
The Beinecke Foundation, Inc.
Beldon Fund
The Ben & Jerry's Foundation
Mary Owen Borden Memorial Foundation
Helen Brach Foundation
Otto Bremer Foundation
The Bullitt Foundation
The Bunbury Company, Inc.
C. S. Fund
Caribou Fund
Mary Flagler Cary Charitable Trust
Claneil Foundation, Inc.
Robert Sterling Clark Foundation, Inc.
Columbia Foundation
Compton Foundation, Inc.
Conservation, Food & Health Foundation, Inc.
Jessie B. Cox Charitable Trust
The Cricket Foundation
The Mary A. Crocker Trust
Crystal Channel Foundation
Patrick and Anna M. Cudahy Fund
The Nathan Cummings Foundation
The Elizabeth Ordway Dunn Foundation, Inc.
Echoing Green Foundation
The Educational Foundation of America
The Energy Foundation
Samuel S. Fels Fund
Jamee and Marshall Field Foundation
Foundation for Deep Ecology
The Fred Gellert Foundation
General Service Foundation
The Wallace Alexander Gerbode Foundation, Inc.
The German Marshall Fund of the United States

Give to the Earth Foundation
Global Environmental Project Institute
Global Greengrants Fund
Richard & Rhoda Goldman Fund
The Greenville Foundation
The George Gund Foundation
Walter and Elise Haas Fund
Harder Foundation
Hawaiian Electric Industries Charitable Foundation
The Edward W. Hazen Foundation
Illilouette Fund
Island Foundation, Inc.
W. Alton Jones Foundation, Inc.
The Joyce Foundation
Kongsgaard-Goldman Foundation
Laidlaw Foundation
Laird, Norton Foundation
Laurel Foundation
The Lazar Foundation
The Max and Anna Levinson Foundation
LifeWorks Foundation
Marin Community Foundation
McKenzie River Gathering Foundation
The McKnight Foundation
Giles W. and Elise G. Mead Foundation
The John Merck Fund
Joyce Mertz-Gilmore Foundation
Metropolitan Atlanta Community Foundation, Inc.
Meyer Memorial Trust
The Milwaukee Foundation
The Minneapolis Foundation
J. P. Morgan Charitable Trust
Charles Stewart Mott Foundation
Ruth Mott Fund
New England Biolabs Foundation
The New York Community Trust
New York Foundation
Norman Foundation
Northwest Fund for the Environment
Jessie Smith Noyes Foundation, Inc.
Ottinger Foundation
Outdoor Industry Conservation Alliance
The David and Lucile Packard Foundation
Patagonia, Inc.
James C. Penney Foundation
The Pew Charitable Trusts
Pew Scholars Program in Conservation and the Environment
Public Welfare Foundation, Inc.
Recreational Equipment, Inc.
Z. Smith Reynolds Foundation, Inc.
The Rhode Island Community Foundation
Rockefeller Family Fund, Inc.
Rockefeller Financial Services, Philanthropy Department
The Winthrop Rockefeller Foundation
Rockwood Fund, Inc.
The San Francisco Foundation

© 1995 Environmental Data Resources, Inc.

639

Emphases

Advocacy (cont.)
The Sapelo Foundation
The Scherman Foundation, Inc.
The Schumann Fund for New Jersey, Inc.
The Florence and John Schumann Foundation
The Skaggs Foundation
Stern Family Fund
The Strong Foundation for Environmental Values
The Sudbury Foundation
The Summerlee Foundation
Surdna Foundation, Inc.
The Tides Foundation
Tortuga Foundation
Town Creek Foundation, Inc.
The USF&G Foundation, Inc.
Vanguard Public Foundation
WMX Environmental Grants Program
Weeden Foundation
Margaret Cullinan Wray Charitable Lead Annuity Trust

Annual campaigns
AT&T Foundation
A Territory Resource
The Achelis Foundation
American Express Philanthropic Program
American Foundation Corporation
Ameritech Foundation
Arcadia Foundation
Evenor Armington Fund
The Vincent Astor Foundation
Atherton Family Foundation
Baltimore Gas and Electric Foundation, Inc.
L. L. Bean, Inc.
The Blumenthal Foundation
Mary Owen Borden Memorial Foundation
Botwinick-Wolfensohn Foundation, Inc.
Helen Brach Foundation
The Lynde and Harry Bradley Foundation, Inc.
Alex. Brown & Sons Charitable Foundation, Inc.
The Bunbury Company, Inc.
Patrick and Aimee Butler Family Foundation
The Cabot Family Charitable Trust
Centerior Energy Foundation
The Chevron Companies
Chrysler Corporation Fund
Claneil Foundation, Inc.
Clark Charitable Trust
The Clark Foundation
The Cowles Charitable Trust
Crystal Channel Foundation
Patrick and Anna M. Cudahy Fund
The Fred Harris Daniels Foundation, Inc.
Dayton Hudson Foundation
The Herbert H. and Grace A. Dow Foundation
Fanwood Foundation
Jamee and Marshall Field Foundation
Leland Fikes Foundation, Inc.

Ford Motor Company Fund
The Freed Foundation, Inc.
GE Fund
Gebbie Foundation, Inc.
Georgia Power Foundation, Inc.
Georgia-Pacific Foundation
Evelyn and Walter Haas, Jr. Fund
The Hamer Foundation
Hudson-Webber Foundation
The Roy A. Hunt Foundation
Helen K. and Arthur E. Johnson Foundation
Harris and Eliza Kempner Fund
F. M. Kirby Foundation, Inc.
The Lauder Foundation, Inc.
Lintilhac Foundation
The Little Family Foundation
James A. Macdonald Foundation
Mars Foundation
The Marshall L. & Perrine D. McCune Charitable Foundation
McDonnell Douglas Foundation
McGregor Fund
McKenzie River Gathering Foundation
The McKnight Foundation
Richard King Mellon Foundation
Millbrook Tribute Garden, Inc.
Henry and Lucy Moses Fund, Inc.
John P. Murphy Foundation
Kenneth T. and Eileen L. Norris Foundation
The Norton Foundation, Inc.
The Ohrstrom Foundation
The Pfizer Foundation, Inc.
Phillips Petroleum Foundation, Inc.
The Powell Family Foundation
Recreational Equipment, Inc.
Rockefeller Family Fund, Inc.
The Schiff Foundation
Sears-Swetland Foundation
Ralph C. Sheldon Foundation, Inc.
Shell Oil Company Foundation
The Kelvin and Eleanor Smith Foundation
Springs Foundation, Inc.
Stackner Family Foundation, Inc.
The Stebbins Fund, Inc.
Stranahan Foundation
Margaret Dorrance Strawbridge Foundation of Pennsylvania II, Inc.
The Sulzberger Foundation, Inc.
The Oakleigh L. Thorne Foundation
USX Foundation, Inc.
Union Camp Charitable Trust
Vinmont Foundation, Inc.
Welfare Foundation, Inc.
Mark and Catherine Winkler Foundation
Wodecroft Foundation
The Wortham Foundation, Inc.

Aquariums
The Abell Foundation
The Beirne Carter Foundation
Alex. Brown & Sons Charitable Foundation, Inc.
Chesapeake Bay Trust
The Cleveland Foundation
Ford Motor Company Fund

The Kresge Foundation
The John D. and Catherine T. MacArthur Foundation
Richard King Mellon Foundation
Meyer Memorial Trust
John P. Murphy Foundation
The Rhode Island Community Foundation
Kelvin Smith 1980 Charitable Trust

Audiovisual materials
The Abell Foundation
The Jenifer Altman Foundation
Benton Foundation
The Bullitt Foundation
The Bunbury Company, Inc.
The Elizabeth Ordway Dunn Foundation, Inc.
Environmental Education Foundation of Florida, Inc.
The Fred Gellert Foundation
Walter and Duncan Gordon Charitable Foundation
Hawaiian Electric Industries Charitable Foundation
IBM Corporation
The Knapp Foundation, Inc.
Laird, Norton Foundation
Giles W. and Elise G. Mead Foundation
The Milwaukee Foundation
The Mountaineers Foundation
National Fish and Wildlife Foundation
Stanley Smith Horticultural Trust
The Summerlee Foundation
Threshold Foundation
The Dean Witter Foundation

Botanical gardens
American Foundation Corporation
The Beinecke Foundation, Inc.
The Beirne Carter Foundation
Boettcher Foundation
Liz Claiborne & Art Ortenberg Foundation
The Community Foundation of Santa Clara County
Cooke Foundation, Limited
The James M. Cox, Jr. Foundation, Inc.
Patrick and Anna M. Cudahy Fund
The Aaron Diamond Foundation
Cleveland H. Dodge Foundation, Inc.
The Herbert H. and Grace A. Dow Foundation
Frelinghuysen Foundation
The GAR Foundation
Gates Foundation
Georgia Power Foundation, Inc.
The George Gund Foundation
The Hall Family Foundation
The Hamer Foundation
Hawaiian Electric Industries Charitable Foundation
F. M. Kirby Foundation, Inc.
The Seymour H. Knox Foundation, Inc.
The Kresge Foundation
Laurel Foundation

Emphases

Botanical gardens (cont.)

Longwood Foundation, Inc.
The John D. and Catherine T. MacArthur Foundation
The Marshall Fund of Arizona
Metropolitan Atlanta Community Foundation, Inc.
Meyer Memorial Trust
The Milwaukee Foundation
The Moody Foundation
J. P. Morgan Charitable Trust
John P. Murphy Foundation
National Fish and Wildlife Foundation
New York Foundation
Edward John Noble Foundation, Inc.
Kenneth T. and Eileen L. Norris Foundation
The William Penn Foundation
The Pfizer Foundation, Inc.
The Powell Family Foundation
San Diego Community Foundation
The San Francisco Foundation
The Scherman Foundation, Inc.
Sears-Swetland Foundation
Stanley Smith Horticultural Trust
Rose E. Tucker Charitable Trust
Westinghouse Foundation
Joseph B. Whitehead Foundation
Robert W. Woodruff Foundation, Inc.
The Wortham Foundation, Inc.
Margaret Cullinan Wray Charitable Lead Annuity Trust

Capacity building

The Jenifer Altman Foundation
Americana Foundation, Inc.
Mary Reynolds Babcock Foundation, Inc.
The Bauman Foundation
L. L. Bean, Inc.
Beldon Fund
The Ben & Jerry's Foundation
The Betterment Fund
Otto Bremer Foundation
The Bullitt Foundation
The Carpenter Foundation
Claneil Foundation, Inc.
The Cleveland Foundation
The Community Foundation of Greater New Haven
The Community Foundation Serving Coastal South Carolina
Compton Foundation, Inc.
The Elizabeth Ordway Dunn Foundation, Inc.
Samuel S. Fels Fund
Flintridge Foundation
The Foundation for the National Capital Region
The German Marshall Fund of the United States
Walter and Duncan Gordon Charitable Foundation
Great Lakes Protection Fund
The Greenville Foundation
The George Gund Foundation

Evelyn and Walter Haas, Jr. Fund
The William and Flora Hewlett Foundation
The Homeland Foundation
Hudson-Webber Foundation
The Hyams Foundation
Island Foundation, Inc.
W. K. Kellogg Foundation
Kongsgaard-Goldman Foundation
The Lazar Foundation
Maine Community Foundation, Inc.
McKenzie River Gathering Foundation
McKesson Foundation, Inc.
The McKnight Foundation
Meadows Foundation, Inc.
Metropolitan Atlanta Community Foundation, Inc.
The Milwaukee Foundation
J. P. Morgan Charitable Trust
Charles Stewart Mott Foundation
National Fish and Wildlife Foundation
Norman Foundation
Jessie Smith Noyes Foundation, Inc.
The David and Lucile Packard Foundation
James C. Penney Foundation
Ellis L. Phillips Foundation
Prince Charitable Trusts
The Rhode Island Community Foundation
Rockefeller Family Fund, Inc.
The Winthrop Rockefeller Foundation
San Diego Community Foundation
The San Francisco Foundation
The Sapelo Foundation
Seventh Generation Fund
Snee-Reinhardt Charitable Foundation
The Sudbury Foundation
Surdna Foundation, Inc.
Rose E. Tucker Charitable Trust
Victoria Foundation, Inc.
Virginia Environmental Endowment
The Winston-Salem Foundation, Inc.
The Wyomissing Foundation, Inc.

Capital campaigns/expenses

The Abell Foundation
Abell-Hanger Foundation
The Achelis Foundation
The Ahmanson Foundation
The George I. Alden Trust
Ameritech Foundation
Elmer L. & Eleanor J. Andersen Foundation
Arcadia Foundation
The Vincent Astor Foundation
Atkinson Foundation
Baltimore Gas and Electric Foundation, Inc.
L. L. Bean, Inc.
The Beirne Carter Foundation
The Frank Stanley Beveridge Foundation, Inc.
The Blumenthal Foundation
Boettcher Foundation
The Bothin Foundation
Botwinick-Wolfensohn Foundation, Inc.
Helen Brach Foundation
The Lynde and Harry Bradley Foundation, Inc.

Alex. Brown & Sons Charitable Foundation, Inc.
The Robert Brownlee Foundation
The Bunbury Company, Inc.
Patrick and Aimee Butler Family Foundation
The Cabot Family Charitable Trust
The Cargill Foundation
Carolyn Foundation
Centerior Energy Foundation
The Champlin Foundations
Chesapeake Corporation Foundation
Claneil Foundation, Inc.
Clark Charitable Trust
The Clark Foundation
Olive B. Cole Foundation
The Columbus Foundation
Compton Foundation, Inc.
Cooke Foundation, Limited
S. H. Cowell Foundation
The Cowles Charitable Trust
The James M. Cox, Jr. Foundation, Inc.
The Fred Harris Daniels Foundation, Inc.
Fields Pond Foundation, Inc.
The 1525 Foundation
Leland Fikes Foundation, Inc.
Ford Motor Company Fund
The Foundation for the National Capital Region
Mary D. and Walter F. Frear Eleemosynary Trust
Frelinghuysen Foundation
The Gap Foundation
Gates Foundation
Gebbie Foundation, Inc.
Georgia Power Foundation, Inc.
Georgia-Pacific Foundation
The W. C. Griffith Foundation
The Hamer Foundation
Hartford Foundation for Public Giving
Hawaiian Electric Industries Charitable Foundation
Charles Hayden Foundation
Howard Heinz Endowment
The Roy A. Hunt Foundation
The Hyde and Watson Foundation
The Louise H. and David S. Ingalls Foundation, Inc.
The George Frederick Jewett Foundation
Helen K. and Arthur E. Johnson Foundation
Harris and Eliza Kempner Fund
The Robert S. and Grayce B. Kerr Foundation, Inc.
The Kresge Foundation
Lintilhac Foundation
Longwood Foundation, Inc.
James A. Macdonald Foundation
The Marshall L. & Perrine D. McCune Charitable Foundation
McDonnell Douglas Foundation
McGregor Fund
The McKnight Foundation
Meadows Foundation, Inc.
Richard King Mellon Foundation

© 1995 Environmental Data Resources, Inc.

641

Emphases

Capital campaigns/expenses (cont.)

Metropolitan Atlanta Community Foundation, Inc.
J. P. Morgan Charitable Trust
Henry and Lucy Moses Fund, Inc.
The Mountaineers Foundation
John P. Murphy Foundation
New Horizon Foundation
The Samuel Roberts Noble Foundation, Inc.
Kenneth T. and Eileen L. Norris Foundation
The Norton Foundation, Inc.
Orchard Foundation
Amelia Peabody Charitable Fund
The William Penn Foundation
The Pfizer Foundation, Inc.
Prince Charitable Trusts
The Rhode Island Community Foundation
Rockwell Fund, Inc.
Sarkeys Foundation
S. H. and Helen R. Scheuer Family Foundation, Inc.
The Schiff Foundation
Sears-Swetland Foundation
Ralph C. Sheldon Foundation, Inc.
Shell Oil Company Foundation
Thomas Sill Foundation
Stanley Smith Horticultural Trust
Springs Foundation, Inc.
Stackner Family Foundation, Inc.
The Stebbins Fund, Inc.
Steelcase Foundation
The Morris Stulsaft Foundation
The Sudbury Foundation
The Sulzberger Foundation, Inc.
The Summerlee Foundation
The Oakleigh L. Thorne Foundation
Harry C. Trexler Trust
Rose E. Tucker Charitable Trust
USX Foundation, Inc.
Union Camp Charitable Trust
Union Pacific Foundation
Vancouver Foundation
Welfare Foundation, Inc.
Joseph B. Whitehead Foundation
G. N. Wilcox Trust
Mark and Catherine Winkler Foundation
The Winston-Salem Foundation, Inc.
Wodecroft Foundation
Robert W. Woodruff Foundation, Inc.
The Wortham Foundation, Inc.
The Wyomissing Foundation, Inc.

Citizen participation

A Territory Resource
The Abelard Foundation West
The Abell Foundation
The Acorn Foundation
Alaska Conservation Foundation
The Jenifer Altman Foundation
American Conservation Association, Inc.
Americana Foundation, Inc.
The Arca Foundation
Mary Reynolds Babcock Foundation, Inc.
The Bauman Foundation

L. L. Bean, Inc.
The Beinecke Foundation, Inc.
Beldon Fund
The Ben & Jerry's Foundation
The Blumenthal Foundation
Otto Bremer Foundation
The Bullitt Foundation
C. S. Fund
The Morris and Gwendolyn Cafritz Foundation
Caribou Fund
The Carpenter Foundation
Mary Flagler Cary Charitable Trust
Chesapeake Bay Trust
Liz Claiborne & Art Ortenberg Foundation
Claneil Foundation, Inc.
The Community Foundation of Greater New Haven
The Community Foundation of Santa Clara County
The Community Foundation Serving Coastal South Carolina
Compton Foundation, Inc.
The Conservation and Research Foundation
Jessie B. Cox Charitable Trust
The Mary A. Crocker Trust
Crystal Channel Foundation
Patrick and Anna M. Cudahy Fund
The Nathan Cummings Foundation
Damien Foundation
The Elizabeth Ordway Dunn Foundation, Inc.
Environmental Education Foundation of Florida, Inc.
Samuel S. Fels Fund
FishAmerica Foundation
Flintridge Foundation
Foundation for the Carolinas
The Fund for New Jersey
General Service Foundation
The Wallace Alexander Gerbode Foundation, Inc.
The German Marshall Fund of the United States
Give to the Earth Foundation
Global Environmental Project Institute
Global Greengrants Fund
The Goldman Environmental Foundation
The Goldman Environmental Foundation
Richard & Rhoda Goldman Fund
Walter and Duncan Gordon Charitable Foundation
Great Lakes Protection Fund
The Greenville Foundation
The George Gund Foundation
Evelyn and Walter Haas, Jr. Fund
Hawaiian Electric Industries Charitable Foundation
Island Foundation, Inc.
W. Alton Jones Foundation, Inc.
Kongsgaard-Goldman Foundation
Laidlaw Foundation
Laird, Norton Foundation
The Lazar Foundation
The Max and Anna Levinson Foundation

The John D. and Catherine T. MacArthur Foundation
Maine Community Foundation, Inc.
Marin Community Foundation
The McConnell Foundation
McKenzie River Gathering Foundation
McKesson Foundation, Inc.
The McKnight Foundation
Meadows Foundation, Inc.
Metropolitan Atlanta Community Foundation, Inc.
Meyer Memorial Trust
Charles Stewart Mott Foundation
Ruth Mott Fund
The Needmor Fund
New England Biolabs Foundation
New York Foundation
Norman Foundation
Northwest Fund for the Environment
Jessie Smith Noyes Foundation, Inc.
Ottinger Foundation
Outdoor Industry Conservation Alliance
The David and Lucile Packard Foundation
The William Penn Foundation
James C. Penney Foundation
Pew Scholars Program in Conservation and the Environment
Philip Morris Companies, Inc.
Prince Charitable Trusts
Public Welfare Foundation, Inc.
Recreational Equipment, Inc.
Z. Smith Reynolds Foundation, Inc.
The Rhode Island Community Foundation
The Roberts Foundation
Rockefeller Family Fund, Inc.
The Winthrop Rockefeller Foundation
Rockwood Fund, Inc.
San Diego Community Foundation
The San Francisco Foundation
The Sapelo Foundation
The Scherman Foundation, Inc.
The Schumann Fund for New Jersey, Inc.
The Florence and John Schumann Foundation
Shell Oil Company Foundation
The Skaggs Foundation
Southwestern Bell Foundation
Stern Family Fund
The Strong Foundation for Environmental Values
The Sudbury Foundation
Threshold Foundation
The Tides Foundation
Tortuga Foundation
Town Creek Foundation, Inc.
Rose E. Tucker Charitable Trust
Alice Tweed Tuohy Foundation
Turner Foundation, Inc.
Unitarian Universalist Veatch Program at Shelter Rock
Vanguard Public Foundation
Victoria Foundation, Inc.
Virginia Environmental Endowment
WMX Environmental Grants Program
DeWitt Wallace-Reader's Digest Fund

Citizen participation (cont.)

Margaret Cullinan Wray Charitable Lead Annuity Trust

Collaborative efforts

AT&T Foundation
A Territory Resource
The Acorn Foundation
Alaska Conservation Foundation
American Express Philanthropic Program
Americana Foundation, Inc.
Atkinson Foundation
Mary Reynolds Babcock Foundation, Inc.
BankAmerica Foundation
The Bauman Foundation
L. L. Bean, Inc.
Beldon Fund
The Betterment Fund
Blandin Foundation
The Blumenthal Foundation
The Boeing Company
The Bullitt Foundation
The Bunbury Company, Inc.
C. S. Fund
The Morris and Gwendolyn Cafritz Foundation
The Carpenter Foundation
Mary Flagler Cary Charitable Trust
Chesapeake Bay Trust
The Chevron Companies
Claneil Foundation, Inc.
The Community Foundation of Greater New Haven
The Community Foundation Serving Coastal South Carolina
Compton Foundation, Inc.
The Conservation and Research Foundation
Jessie B. Cox Charitable Trust
The Mary A. Crocker Trust
Patrick and Anna M. Cudahy Fund
The Nathan Cummings Foundation
Donner Canadian Foundation
The Elizabeth Ordway Dunn Foundation, Inc.
Jessie Ball duPont Religious, Charitable and Educational Fund
Echoing Green Foundation
Samuel S. Fels Fund
FishAmerica Foundation
Flintridge Foundation
Foundation for Deep Ecology
The Foundation for the National Capital Region
The GAR Foundation
The Fred Gellert Foundation
The Wallace Alexander Gerbode Foundation, Inc.
The German Marshall Fund of the United States
Give to the Earth Foundation
Walter and Duncan Gordon Charitable Foundation
Great Lakes Protection Fund
Greater Piscataqua Community Foundation
The Greenville Foundation
The George Gund Foundation
Evelyn and Walter Haas, Jr. Fund
The Hall Family Foundation
Hawaiian Electric Industries Charitable Foundation
Charles Hayden Foundation
The William and Flora Hewlett Foundation
Illilouette Fund
The Richard Ivey Foundation
Laidlaw Foundation
The Lazar Foundation
The John D. and Catherine T. MacArthur Foundation
Maine Community Foundation, Inc.
Marin Community Foundation
The McConnell Foundation
McGregor Fund
McKenzie River Gathering Foundation
McKesson Foundation, Inc.
The McKnight Foundation
Giles W. and Elise G. Mead Foundation
Metropolitan Atlanta Community Foundation, Inc.
The Milwaukee Foundation
The Minneapolis Foundation
J. P. Morgan Charitable Trust
Charles Stewart Mott Foundation
National Fish and Wildlife Foundation
New England Biolabs Foundation
New York Foundation
Norman Foundation
Northwest Fund for the Environment
Jessie Smith Noyes Foundation, Inc.
Ottinger Foundation
The David and Lucile Packard Foundation
James C. Penney Foundation
The Pew Charitable Trusts
Pew Scholars Program in Conservation and the Environment
Philip Morris Companies, Inc.
Ellis L. Phillips Foundation
Prince Charitable Trusts
Public Welfare Foundation, Inc.
Recreational Equipment, Inc.
The Rhode Island Community Foundation
Sid W. Richardson Foundation
Rockefeller Financial Services, Philanthropy Department
Sacramento Regional Foundation
San Diego Community Foundation
The San Francisco Foundation
The Sapelo Foundation
Sarkeys Foundation
The Schumann Fund for New Jersey, Inc.
Shell Oil Company Foundation
The Skaggs Foundation
Stanley Smith Horticultural Trust
The Sonoma County Community Foundation
The Sudbury Foundation
The Summerlee Foundation
Surdna Foundation, Inc.
The Tides Foundation
The Tinker Foundation Incorporated
Tortuga Foundation
Town Creek Foundation, Inc.
The Trust For Mutual Understanding
Rose E. Tucker Charitable Trust
Alice Tweed Tuohy Foundation
Victoria Foundation, Inc.
Virginia Environmental Endowment
Wilburforce Foundation
The Winston-Salem Foundation, Inc.
Margaret Cullinan Wray Charitable Lead Annuity Trust
The Wyomissing Foundation, Inc.

Computer hardware

The Ahmanson Foundation
Apple Computer, Inc.
Boettcher Foundation
The Bunbury Company, Inc.
The Champlin Foundations
Claneil Foundation, Inc.
Cooke Foundation, Limited
Jessie Ball duPont Religious, Charitable and Educational Fund
Mary D. and Walter F. Frear Eleemosynary Trust
Gebbie Foundation, Inc.
The Hyde and Watson Foundation
The Richard Ivey Foundation
Helen K. and Arthur E. Johnson Foundation
The Knapp Foundation, Inc.
Larsen Fund, Inc.
James A. Macdonald Foundation
The McKnight Foundation
Meadows Foundation, Inc.
John P. Murphy Foundation
The Rhode Island Community Foundation
Shell Oil Company Foundation
Springs Foundation, Inc.
The Summerlee Foundation
Harry C. Trexler Trust
The Troy Foundation
G. N. Wilcox Trust
Robert W. Woodruff Foundation, Inc.

Conferences

AT&T Foundation
The Abell Foundation
The George I. Alden Trust
The Jenifer Altman Foundation
American Conservation Association, Inc.
Ameritech Foundation
Atherton Family Foundation
Baltimore Gas and Electric Foundation, Inc.
Beldon Fund
Benton Foundation
The Lynde and Harry Bradley Foundation, Inc.
The Bydale Foundation
C. S. Fund
Caribou Fund
Claneil Foundation, Inc.
The Nathan Cummings Foundation
Dolfinger-McMahon Foundation

Emphases

Conferences (cont.)

Jessie Ball duPont Religious, Charitable and Educational Fund
Environmental Education Foundation of Florida, Inc.
Ford Motor Company Fund
Georgia Power Foundation, Inc.
Georgia-Pacific Foundation
The German Marshall Fund of the United States
Global Greengrants Fund
Walter and Duncan Gordon Charitable Foundation
The Greenville Foundation
The George Gund Foundation
Hawaii Community Foundation
Island Foundation
The Richard Ivey Foundation
Harris and Eliza Kempner Fund
The Henry P. Kendall Foundation
The Esther A. and Joseph Klingenstein Fund, Inc.
Kongsgaard-Goldman Foundation
Laidlaw Foundation
Laird, Norton Foundation
Laurel Foundation
The Max and Anna Levinson Foundation
Lilly Endowment, Inc.
Maine Community Foundation, Inc.
The Marshall L. & Perrine D. McCune Charitable Foundation
McKenzie River Gathering Foundation
Giles W. and Elise G. Mead Foundation
Richard King Mellon Foundation
The Milwaukee Foundation
The Mountaineers Foundation
The National Environmental Education and Training Foundation, Inc.
National Fish and Wildlife Foundation
The New World Foundation
The David and Lucile Packard Foundation
The Pfizer Foundation, Inc.
Philip Morris Companies, Inc.
Phillips Petroleum Foundation, Inc.
The Prudential Foundation
Sid W. Richardson Foundation
Rockwell Fund, Inc.
Rockwood Fund, Inc.
Sarah Scaife Foundation Incorporated
The Schumann Fund for New Jersey, Inc.
Thomas Sill Foundation
Southwestern Bell Foundation
The Sulzberger Foundation, Inc.
The Summerlee Foundation
The Tinker Foundation Incorporated
The Trust For Mutual Understanding
Rose E. Tucker Charitable Trust
Underhill Foundation

Conflict resolution

ARCO Foundation
The Ahmanson Foundation
Otto Bremer Foundation
C. S. Fund
Carolyn Foundation
The Carpenter Foundation
Compton Foundation, Inc.
Geraldine R. Dodge Foundation, Inc.
The Educational Foundation of America
Samuel S. Fels Fund
The Fund for New Jersey
The German Marshall Fund of the United States
Global Environmental Project Institute
Walter and Duncan Gordon Charitable Foundation
Great Lakes Protection Fund
Hawaiian Electric Industries Charitable Foundation
The William and Flora Hewlett Foundation
Kongsgaard-Goldman Foundation
Maine Community Foundation, Inc.
The McKnight Foundation
New York Foundation
Norman Foundation
The David and Lucile Packard Foundation
Pew Scholars Program in Conservation and the Environment
Rockefeller Financial Services, Philanthropy Department
The San Francisco Foundation
The Sonoma County Community Foundation
The Tides Foundation
Virginia Environmental Endowment
The Winston-Salem Foundation, Inc.
Margaret Cullinan Wray Charitable Lead Annuity Trust

Continuing support

AT&T Foundation
The Achelis Foundation
The Acorn Foundation
Alaska Conservation Foundation
American Conservation Association, Inc.
American Foundation Corporation
Arcadia Foundation
Evenor Armington Fund
The Vincent Astor Foundation
Atherton Family Foundation
The Bauman Foundation
L. L. Bean, Inc.
The Betterment Fund
The Frank Stanley Beveridge Foundation, Inc.
Mary Owen Borden Memorial Foundation
Botwinick-Wolfensohn Foundation, Inc.
The Lynde and Harry Bradley Foundation, Inc.
Alex. Brown & Sons Charitable Foundation, Inc.
The Bullitt Foundation
The Bunbury Company, Inc.
Patrick and Aimee Butler Family Foundation
The Bydale Foundation C. S. Fund
The Cabot Family Charitable Trust
The Cargill Foundation
Caribou Fund
The Chevron Companies
Chrysler Corporation Fund
Claneil Foundation, Inc.
The Clark Foundation
The Columbus Foundation
Compton Foundation, Inc.
The Conservation and Research Foundation
The Cowles Charitable Trust
Crystal Channel Foundation
Patrick and Anna M. Cudahy Fund
The Fred Harris Daniels Foundation, Inc.
Dayton Hudson Foundation
Geraldine R. Dodge Foundation, Inc.
Gaylord and Dorothy Donnelley Foundation
The Elizabeth Ordway Dunn Foundation, Inc.
Jessie Ball duPont Religious, Charitable and Educational Fund
Eastman Kodak Company Charitable Trust
The Charles Engelhard Foundation
Jamee and Marshall Field Foundation
Leland Fikes Foundation, Inc.
Flintridge Foundation
Foundation for Deep Ecology
Foundation for Field Research
The Foundation for the National Capital Region
The Freed Foundation, Inc.
GE Fund
Gebbie Foundation, Inc.
Georgia Power Foundation, Inc.
Georgia-Pacific Foundation
Bernard F. and Alva B. Gimbel Foundation, Inc.
Give to the Earth Foundation
Global Greengrants Fund
Richard & Rhoda Goldman Fund
The William and Mary Greve Foundation, Inc.
The W. C. Griffith Foundation
The George Gund Foundation
The Hamer Foundation
The William and Flora Hewlett Foundation
Hudson-Webber Foundation
Illilouette Fund
Jackson Hole Preserve, Inc.
Martha Holden Jennings Foundation
Helen K. and Arthur E. Johnson Foundation
Walter S. Johnson Foundation
Harris and Eliza Kempner Fund
The Henry P. Kendall Foundation
The Robert S. and Grayce B. Kerr Foundation, Inc.
F. M. Kirby Foundation, Inc.
The Esther A. and Joseph Klingenstein Fund, Inc.
Kongsgaard-Goldman Foundation
Larsen Fund, Inc.
The Lauder Foundation, Inc.
Lilly Endowment, Inc.
The Little Family Foundation
James A. Macdonald Foundation
Mars Foundation
The Marshall L. & Perrine D. McCune Charitable Foundation

Emphases

Continuing support (cont.)

McDonnell Douglas Foundation
McGregor Fund
McKenzie River Gathering Foundation
The McKnight Foundation
Meadows Foundation, Inc.
Metropolitan Life Foundation
The Moody Foundation
Henry and Lucy Moses Fund, Inc.
Ruth Mott Fund
John P. Murphy Foundation
The Needmor Fund
The Nord Family Foundation
Norman Foundation
Kenneth T. and Eileen L. Norris Foundation
Mary Moody Northen, Inc.
The Norton Foundation, Inc.
The Ohrstrom Foundation
Ottinger Foundation
The David and Lucile Packard Foundation
James C. Penney Foundation
The Pfizer Foundation, Inc.
The Philadelphia Foundation
Philip Morris Companies, Inc.
Pilot Trust
The Powell Family Foundation
The Rhode Island Community Foundation
The Sapelo Foundation
Sarah Scaife Foundation Incorporated
The Scherman Foundation, Inc.
Sarah I. Schieffelin Residuary Trust
Sears-Swetland Foundation
Shell Oil Company Foundation
The Skaggs Foundation
The Kelvin and Eleanor Smith Foundation
South Coast Foundation, Inc.
Springs Foundation, Inc.
Stackner Family Foundation, Inc.
Stranahan Foundation
Margaret Dorrance Strawbridge Foundation of Pennsylvania II, Inc.
The Charles J. Strosacker Foundation
The Sulzberger Foundation, Inc.
Surdna Foundation, Inc.
The Oakleigh L. Thorne Foundation
The Tides Foundation
Town Creek Foundation, Inc.
Harry C. Trexler Trust
Union Camp Charitable Trust
Union Pacific Foundation
Victoria Foundation, Inc.
Vinmont Foundation, Inc.
Virginia Environmental Endowment
DeWitt Wallace-Reader's Digest Fund
Whitecap Foundation
The Windham Foundation, Inc.
The Winslow Foundation
The Wyomissing Foundation, Inc.

Debt retirement

The Champlin Foundations
Dolfinger-McMahon Foundation
Georgia Power Foundation, Inc.
Georgia-Pacific Foundation

John P. Murphy Foundation
Sears-Swetland Foundation
The Oakleigh L. Thorne Foundation

Demonstration programs

AT&T Foundation
The Abell Foundation
The Betterment Fund
Mary Owen Borden Memorial Foundation
Carolyn Foundation
The Carpenter Foundation
Chesapeake Bay Trust
Claneil Foundation, Inc.
Columbia Foundation
The Community Foundation of Greater New Haven
The Community Foundation Serving Coastal South Carolina
Cooke Foundation, Limited
Jessie B. Cox Charitable Trust
Dolfinger-McMahon Foundation
Echoing Green Foundation
The Educational Foundation of America
Environmental Education Foundation of Florida, Inc.
Jamee and Marshall Field Foundation
Foundation for Deep Ecology
Gebbie Foundation, Inc.
General Service Foundation
Give to the Earth Foundation
Global Environmental Project Institute
Walter and Duncan Gordon Charitable Foundation
Great Lakes Protection Fund
Hartford Foundation for Public Giving
Hawaiian Electric Industries Charitable Foundation
The Clarence E. Heller Charitable Foundation
Ittleson Foundation, Inc.
The Richard Ivey Foundation
The Henry M. Jackson Foundation
W. K. Kellogg Foundation
Laidlaw Foundation
The John D. and Catherine T. MacArthur Foundation
MARPAT Foundation, Inc.
The McConnell Foundation
The McKnight Foundation
Meadows Foundation, Inc.
The John Merck Fund
Meyer Memorial Trust
The Milwaukee Foundation
Charles Stewart Mott Foundation
National Fish and Wildlife Foundation
Northwest Fund for the Environment
James C. Penney Foundation
The Pew Charitable Trusts
Philip Morris Companies, Inc.
Phillips Petroleum Foundation, Inc.
The Roberts Foundation
The Rockefeller Foundation
San Diego Community Foundation
The San Francisco Foundation
The Skaggs Foundation

Stanley Smith Horticultural Trust
The Strong Foundation for Environmental Values
The Sudbury Foundation
The Switzer Foundation
Texaco Foundation
Toyota USA Foundation
The Trust For Mutual Understanding
Rose E. Tucker Charitable Trust
Virginia Environmental Endowment
Weeden Foundation
Joseph B. Whitehead Foundation
Wilburforce Foundation
The Winston-Salem Foundation, Inc.
The Dean Witter Foundation
Margaret Cullinan Wray Charitable Lead Annuity Trust
The Wyomissing Foundation, Inc.

Direct services

AT&T Foundation
The Ahmanson Foundation
Otto Bremer Foundation
Kathleen Price and Joseph M. Bryan Family Foundation, Inc.
The Bunbury Company, Inc.
C. S. Fund
The Cleveland Foundation
Olive B. Cole Foundation
The Community Foundation Serving Coastal South Carolina
Compton Foundation, Inc.
Cooke Foundation, Limited
The James M. Cox, Jr. Foundation, Inc.
Patrick and Anna M. Cudahy Fund
The Arthur Vining Davis Foundations
Echoing Green Foundation
Gebbie Foundation, Inc.
Give to the Earth Foundation
Greater Piscataqua Community Foundation
Evelyn and Walter Haas, Jr. Fund
Hawaiian Electric Industries Charitable Foundation
Martha Holden Jennings Foundation
W. K. Kellogg Foundation
Larsen Fund, Inc.
Laurel Foundation
The McConnell Foundation
McGregor Fund
McKesson Foundation, Inc.
The McKnight Foundation
Meadows Foundation, Inc.
Meyer Memorial Trust
J. P. Morgan Charitable Trust
The William Penn Foundation
The Rhode Island Community Foundation
Rockefeller Financial Services, Philanthropy Department
The San Francisco Foundation
The Scherman Foundation, Inc.
The Skaggs Foundation
The Sonoma County Community Foundation
The Trust For Mutual Understanding
Rose E. Tucker Charitable Trust

Emphases

Direct services (cont.)

The USF&G Foundation, Inc.
Victoria Foundation, Inc.
Vinmont Foundation, Inc.
Joseph B. Whitehead Foundation
G. N. Wilcox Trust
The Wyomissing Foundation, Inc.

Education

ARCO Foundation
AT&T Foundation
The Abell Foundation
The Ahmanson Foundation
Alaska Conservation Foundation
The George I. Alden Trust
The Jenifer Altman Foundation
American Express Philanthropic Program
Ameritech Foundation
The Arca Foundation
The Vincent Astor Foundation
Atherton Family Foundation
Atkinson Foundation
Baltimore Gas and Electric Foundation, Inc.
Bay Area Community Foundation
The Bay Foundation
The Beirne Carter Foundation
Benton Foundation
The Betterment Fund
Blandin Foundation
The Blumenthal Foundation
The Boeing Company
Mary Owen Borden Memorial Foundation
The Lynde and Harry Bradley Foundation, Inc.
H. Barksdale Brown Charitable Trust
Ruth H. Brown Foundation
The Robert Brownlee Foundation
The Bullitt Foundation
The Bunbury Company, Inc.
C. S. Fund
The Morris and Gwendolyn Cafritz Foundation
California Community Foundation
James & Abigail Campbell Foundation
The Cape Branch Foundation
Caribou Fund
Carolyn Foundation
The Carpenter Foundation
Chesapeake Bay Trust
Chesapeake Corporation Foundation
The Chevron Companies
Chrysler Corporation Fund
Liz Claiborne & Art Ortenberg Foundation
Claneil Foundation, Inc.
Robert Sterling Clark Foundation, Inc.
The Cleveland Foundation
The Clowes Fund, Inc.
The Community Foundation Serving Coastal South Carolina
Community Foundation of Western North Carolina, Inc.
Compton Foundation, Inc.
Cooke Foundation, Limited
Jessie B. Cox Charitable Trust

The Mary A. Crocker Trust
Crystal Channel Foundation
Patrick and Anna M. Cudahy Fund
Charles E. Culpeper Foundation, Inc.
The Arthur Vining Davis Foundations
The Aaron Diamond Foundation
Geraldine R. Dodge Foundation, Inc.
The Herbert H. and Grace A. Dow Foundation
The Elizabeth Ordway Dunn Foundation, Inc.
Jessie Ball duPont Religious, Charitable and Educational Fund
Echoing Green Foundation
Environmental Education Foundation of Florida, Inc.
Environmental Endowment for New Jersey, Inc.
Fields Pond Foundation, Inc.
Flintridge Foundation
Ford Motor Company Fund
Mary D. and Walter F. Frear Eleemosynary Trust
The Frost Foundation, Ltd.
The Fund for New Jersey
The GAR Foundation
GE Fund
Gebbie Foundation, Inc.
The Fred Gellert Foundation
Global Environmental Project Institute
Global Greengrants Fund
The Goldman Environmental Foundation
Richard & Rhoda Goldman Fund
Walter and Duncan Gordon Charitable Foundation
Greater Piscataqua Community Foundation
The Greenville Foundation
The George Gund Foundation
Walter and Elise Haas Fund
The Hahn Family Foundation
The Hamer Foundation
Gladys and Roland Harriman Foundation
Hartford Foundation for Public Giving
Hawaii Community Foundation
Hawaiian Electric Industries Charitable Foundation
Charles Hayden Foundation
The Edward W. Hazen Foundation
Vira I. Heinz Endowment
The Homeland Foundation
The Roy A. Hunt Foundation
Illilouette Fund
The International Foundation, Inc.
Ireland Foundation
Island Foundation, Inc.
Ittleson Foundation, Inc.
The Richard Ivey Foundation
The Henry M. Jackson Foundation
Martha Holden Jennings Foundation
W. Alton Jones Foundation, Inc.
The J. M. Kaplan Fund, Inc.
W. K. Kellogg Foundation
F. M. Kirby Foundation, Inc.
The Esther A. and Joseph Klingenstein Fund, Inc.

The Knapp Foundation, Inc.
Laidlaw Foundation
Laird, Norton Foundation
Larsen Fund, Inc.
LaSalle Adams Fund
Laurel Foundation
Lintilhac Foundation
The Little Family Foundation
The John D. and Catherine T. MacArthur Foundation
Maine Community Foundation, Inc.
Marin Community Foundation
MARPAT Foundation, Inc.
The Martin Foundation, Inc.
Massachusetts Environmental Trust
The McConnell Foundation
The Eugene McDermott Foundation
McGregor Fund
McInerny Foundation
McKesson Foundation, Inc.
Giles W. and Elise G. Mead Foundation
Richard King Mellon Foundation
Metropolitan Atlanta Community Foundation, Inc.
Meyer Memorial Trust
Millbrook Tribute Garden, Inc.
The Milwaukee Foundation
Mobil Foundation, Inc.
The Moody Foundation
J. P. Morgan Charitable Trust
The Mountaineers Foundation
John P. Murphy Foundation
The National Environmental Education and Training Foundation, Inc.
National Fish and Wildlife Foundation
National Geographic Society Education Foundation
New England Biolabs Foundation
New York Foundation
The New-Land Foundation, Inc.
Edward John Noble Foundation, Inc.
Norcross Wildlife Foundation, Inc.
Norman Foundation
Kenneth T. and Eileen L. Norris Foundation
Spencer T. and Ann W. Olin Foundation
Amelia Peabody Charitable Fund
Peninsula Community Foundation
The William Penn Foundation
James C. Penney Foundation
Pew Scholars Program in Conservation and the Environment
The Pfizer Foundation, Inc.
The Philadelphia Foundation
Philip Morris Companies, Inc.
Phillips Petroleum Foundation, Inc.
Ellis L. Phillips Foundation
Pilot Trust
The Powell Family Foundation
Prince Charitable Trusts
Z. Smith Reynolds Foundation, Inc.
The Rhode Island Community Foundation
Sid W. Richardson Foundation
Rockefeller Financial Services, Philanthropy Department
The Rockfall Foundation

Emphases

Education (cont.)

Fran and Warren Rupp Foundation
San Diego Community Foundation
The San Francisco Foundation
The Sapelo Foundation
Sarkeys Foundation
Sarah Scaife Foundation Incorporated
The Schumann Fund for New Jersey, Inc.
Shell Oil Company Foundation
The Skaggs Foundation
The Kelvin and Eleanor Smith Foundation
Stanley Smith Horticultural Trust
The Sonoma County Community Foundation
Southwestern Bell Foundation
Springs Foundation, Inc.
Anna B. Stearns Charitable Foundation, Inc.
Steelcase Foundation
The Stratford Foundation
The Strong Foundation for Environmental Values
The Sudbury Foundation
The Sulzberger Foundation, Inc.
The Summerlee Foundation
The Telesis Foundation
Threshold Foundation
Times Mirror Magazines, Inc.
Toyota USA Foundation
Harry C. Trexler Trust
The Troy Foundation
Rose E. Tucker Charitable Trust
Turner Foundation, Inc.
The USF&G Foundation, Inc.
Union Pacific Foundation
United States-Japan Foundation
R. T. Vanderbilt Trust
Victoria Foundation, Inc.
Virginia Environmental Endowment
WMX Environmental Grants Program
Wallace Genetic Foundation, Inc.
DeWitt Wallace-Reader's Digest Fund
Whitecap Foundation
Joseph B. Whitehead Foundation
Wilburforce Foundation
G. N. Wilcox Trust
Mark and Catherine Winkler Foundation
The Winston-Salem Foundation, Inc.
The Dean Witter Foundation
Robert W. Woodruff Foundation, Inc.
Margaret Cullinan Wray Charitable Lead Annuity Trust
The Wyomissing Foundation, Inc.

Educational institutions

ARCO Foundation
AT&T Foundation
The Abell Foundation
Abell-Hanger Foundation
The Achelis Foundation
The Ahmanson Foundation
The George I. Alden Trust
The Jenifer Altman Foundation
American Foundation Corporation
Ameritech Foundation

Apple Computer, Inc.
The Arca Foundation
Atkinson Foundation
Bay Area Community Foundation
The Bay Foundation
The Beinecke Foundation, Inc.
The Beirne Carter Foundation
The Betterment Fund
The Blumenthal Foundation
Otto Bremer Foundation
Alex. Brown & Sons Charitable Foundation, Inc.
The Robert Brownlee Foundation
The Bullitt Foundation
C. S. Fund
The Morris and Gwendolyn Cafritz Foundation
The Louis Calder Foundation
Ward M. & Mariam C. Canaday Educational and Charitable Trust
The Cape Branch Foundation
Carolyn Foundation
Chesapeake Bay Trust
Chesapeake Corporation Foundation
Chrysler Corporation Fund
Liz Claiborne & Art Ortenberg Foundation
Claneil Foundation, Inc.
Robert Sterling Clark Foundation, Inc.
The Clowes Fund, Inc.
The Collins Foundation
The Community Foundation of Santa Clara County
Conservation, Food & Health Foundation, Inc.
Cooke Foundation, Limited
Crystal Channel Foundation
Patrick and Anna M. Cudahy Fund
The Nathan Cummings Foundation
The Arthur Vining Davis Foundations
Geraldine R. Dodge Foundation, Inc.
The Herbert H. and Grace A. Dow Foundation
Jessie Ball duPont Religious, Charitable and Educational Fund
The Educational Foundation of America
Environmental Education Foundation of Florida, Inc.
Ford Motor Company Fund
Mary D. and Walter F. Frear Eleemosynary Trust
Frelinghuysen Foundation
The Frost Foundation, Ltd.
GE Fund
Gebbie Foundation, Inc.
Georgia Power Foundation, Inc.
Walter and Duncan Gordon Charitable Foundation
Great Lakes Protection Fund
The Greenville Foundation
The W. C. Griffith Foundation
The George Gund Foundation
Evelyn and Walter Haas, Jr. Fund
Walter and Elise Haas Fund
The Hall Family Foundation
The Hamer Foundation

The Merrill G. & Emita E. Hastings Foundation
Hawaiian Electric Industries Charitable Foundation
The John Randolph Haynes and Dora Haynes Foundation
The Edward W. Hazen Foundation
Howard Heinz Endowment
Vira I. Heinz Endowment
The Clarence E. Heller Charitable Foundation
The Roy A. Hunt Foundation
The Hyde and Watson Foundation
IBM Corporation
The Henry M. Jackson Foundation
Martha Holden Jennings Foundation
The Howard Johnson Foundation
Joy Foundation for Ecological Education and Research
The Henry P. Kendall Foundation
F. M. Kirby Foundation, Inc.
The Esther A. and Joseph Klingenstein Fund, Inc.
The Knapp Foundation, Inc.
The Seymour H. Knox Foundation, Inc.
The Kresge Foundation
Laird, Norton Foundation
Larsen Fund, Inc.
Laurel Foundation
Lintilhac Foundation
The Little Family Foundation
The John D. and Catherine T. MacArthur Foundation
Marin Community Foundation
MARPAT Foundation, Inc.
The Marshall Fund of Arizona
The Martin Foundation, Inc.
Massachusetts Environmental Trust
The McConnell Foundation
McGregor Fund
McInerny Foundation
The McKnight Foundation
Meadows Foundation, Inc.
The Andrew W. Mellon Foundation
Richard King Mellon Foundation
Meyer Memorial Trust
Millbrook Tribute Garden, Inc.
The Milwaukee Foundation
Mobil Foundation, Inc.
The Moody Foundation
The Mountaineers Foundation
John P. Murphy Foundation
National Fish and Wildlife Foundation
National Geographic Society Education Foundation
New York Foundation
Edward John Noble Foundation, Inc.
Norman Foundation
Kenneth T. and Eileen L. Norris Foundation
The Norton Foundation, Inc.
OCRI Foundation
Nathan M. Ohrbach Foundation, Inc.
Amelia Peabody Charitable Fund
The William Penn Foundation
Philip Morris Companies, Inc.

© 1995 Environmental Data Resources, Inc.

Emphases

Educational institutions (cont.)

The Powell Family Foundation
The Prudential Foundation
The Rhode Island Community Foundation
Sid W. Richardson Foundation
The Roberts Foundation
Rockefeller Financial Services, Philanthropy Department
The Rockefeller Foundation
Rockwell Fund, Inc.
Samuel and May Rudin Foundation, Inc.
San Diego Community Foundation
The San Francisco Foundation
Sarkeys Foundation
Sarah Scaife Foundation Incorporated
The Schumann Fund for New Jersey, Inc.
Sears-Swetland Foundation
Shell Oil Company Foundation
Stanley Smith Horticultural Trust
Springs Foundation, Inc.
The Charles J. Strosacker Foundation
The Summerlee Foundation
The Switzer Foundation
The Tinker Foundation Incorporated
Toyota USA Foundation
The Troy Foundation
The Trust For Mutual Understanding
The USF&G Foundation, Inc.
USX Foundation, Inc.
Union Pacific Foundation
United States-Japan Foundation
Victoria Foundation, Inc.
The Vidda Foundation
Virginia Environmental Endowment
DeWitt Wallace-Reader's Digest Fund
Welfare Foundation, Inc.
Westinghouse Foundation
Weyerhaeuser Company Foundation
Joseph B. Whitehead Foundation
G. N. Wilcox Trust
Mark and Catherine Winkler Foundation
The Winston-Salem Foundation, Inc.
The Dean Witter Foundation
Robert W. Woodruff Foundation, Inc.
Margaret Cullinan Wray Charitable Lead Annuity Trust
The Wyomissing Foundation, Inc.

Emergency funding

AT&T Foundation
The Ahmanson Foundation
Alaska Conservation Foundation
The George I. Alden Trust
American Express Philanthropic Program
The Arca Foundation
Arcadia Foundation
Evenor Armington Fund
The Bullitt Foundation
The Bunbury Company, Inc.
Chrysler Corporation Fund
Claneil Foundation, Inc.
The Clark Foundation
The Community Foundation of Sarasota County, Inc.
The Conservation and Research Foundation
The Cowles Charitable Trust
The Fred Harris Daniels Foundation, Inc.
Dolfinger-McMahon Foundation
Jessie Ball duPont Religious, Charitable and Educational Fund
Leland Fikes Foundation, Inc.
The Foundation for the National Capital Region
The Frost Foundation, Ltd.
General Service Foundation
Georgia Power Foundation, Inc.
Georgia-Pacific Foundation
Greater Piscataqua Community Foundation
Howard Heinz Endowment
The Hofmann Foundation
The International Foundation, Inc.
Harris and Eliza Kempner Fund
The Henry P. Kendall Foundation
Larsen Fund, Inc.
James A. Macdonald Foundation
Maine Community Foundation, Inc.
The Marshall L. & Perrine D. McCune Charitable Foundation
John P. Murphy Foundation
Norman Foundation
OCRI Foundation
The Ohrstrom Foundation
The Pfizer Foundation, Inc.
The Philadelphia Foundation
Recreational Equipment, Inc.
The Rhode Island Community Foundation
The Scherman Foundation, Inc.
Sears-Swetland Foundation
Ralph C. Sheldon Foundation, Inc.
Springs Foundation, Inc.
The Sulzberger Foundation, Inc.
The Summerlee Foundation
The Oakleigh L. Thorne Foundation
USX Foundation, Inc.
Union Camp Charitable Trust
Vanguard Public Foundation
Mark and Catherine Winkler Foundation
The Winston-Salem Foundation, Inc.

Endowments

The Abell Foundation
Abell-Hanger Foundation
The Achelis Foundation
The Ahmanson Foundation
The George I. Alden Trust
Winifred & Harry B. Allen Foundation
Arcadia Foundation
The Vincent Astor Foundation
L. L. Bean, Inc.
The Beinecke Foundation, Inc.
Alex. Brown & Sons Charitable Foundation, Inc.
Kathleen Price and Joseph M. Bryan Family Foundation, Inc.
The Bunbury Company, Inc.
Patrick and Aimee Butler Family Foundation
The Cabot Family Charitable Trust
Chesapeake Corporation Foundation
Clark Charitable Trust
Compton Foundation, Inc.
The Cowles Charitable Trust
The Fred Harris Daniels Foundation, Inc.
Cleveland H. Dodge Foundation, Inc.
Gaylord and Dorothy Donnelley Foundation
The Herbert H. and Grace A. Dow Foundation
Fanwood Foundation
Fields Pond Foundation, Inc.
The 1525 Foundation
Leland Fikes Foundation, Inc.
Frelinghuysen Foundation
The GAR Foundation
Gates Foundation
Georgia Power Foundation, Inc.
Georgia-Pacific Foundation
Greater Piscataqua Community Foundation
The William and Mary Greve Foundation, Inc.
The Hamer Foundation
Howard Heinz Endowment
The Hofmann Foundation
The Louise H. and David S. Ingalls Foundation, Inc.
The George Frederick Jewett Foundation
Lintilhac Foundation
Longwood Foundation, Inc.
Mars Foundation
McCune Foundation
The Marshall L. & Perrine D. McCune Charitable Foundation
McGregor Fund
Henry and Lucy Moses Fund, Inc.
The Samuel Roberts Noble Foundation, Inc.
Kenneth T. and Eileen L. Norris Foundation
The Norton Foundation, Inc.
Nicholas H. Noyes, Jr. Memorial Foundation
The Ohrstrom Foundation
Amelia Peabody Charitable Fund
The Pfizer Foundation, Inc.
Sid W. Richardson Foundation
Rockwell Fund, Inc.
Fran and Warren Rupp Foundation
The Sulzberger Foundation, Inc.
Union Camp Charitable Trust
R. T. Vanderbilt Trust
The Vidda Foundation
Welfare Foundation, Inc.
Mark and Catherine Winkler Foundation
The Winston-Salem Foundation, Inc.
The Wortham Foundation, Inc.

Equipment

The Abell Foundation
The Ahmanson Foundation
The George I. Alden Trust
Arcadia Foundation
The Vincent Astor Foundation
Atherton Family Foundation
Bay Area Community Foundation
The Frank Stanley Beveridge Foundation, Inc.
Boettcher Foundation

Emphases

Equipment (cont.)

The Bothin Foundation
Helen Brach Foundation
The Lynde and Harry Bradley Foundation, Inc.
The Robert Brownlee Foundation
Kathleen Price and Joseph M. Bryan Family Foundation, Inc.
The Bunbury Company, Inc.
The Louis Calder Foundation
James & Abigail Campbell Foundation
Carolyn Foundation
Centerior Energy Foundation
The Champlin Foundations
Ben B. Cheney Foundation
Chesapeake Bay Trust
Claneil Foundation, Inc.
Clark Charitable Trust
The Clark Foundation
Olive B. Cole Foundation
The Collins Foundation
The Community Foundation of Sarasota County, Inc.
Cooke Foundation, Limited
S. H. Cowell Foundation
The Cowles Charitable Trust
Patrick and Anna M. Cudahy Fund
The Nathan Cummings Foundation
The Fred Harris Daniels Foundation, Inc.
Cleveland H. Dodge Foundation, Inc.
The Herbert H. and Grace A. Dow Foundation
Jessie Ball duPont Religious, Charitable and Educational Fund
Fair Play Foundation
The Favrot Fund
The 1525 Foundation
Leland Fikes Foundation, Inc.
FishAmerica Foundation
Mary D. and Walter F. Frear Eleemosynary Trust
The Freed Foundation, Inc.
Frelinghuysen Foundation
The Frost Foundation, Ltd.
Gates Foundation
Gebbie Foundation, Inc.
Georgia-Pacific Foundation
Hartford Foundation for Public Giving
Hawaii Community Foundation
Hawaiian Electric Industries Charitable Foundation
Charles Hayden Foundation
Howard Heinz Endowment
Hudson-Webber Foundation
The Hyde and Watson Foundation
IBM Corporation
The International Foundation, Inc.
The Richard Ivey Foundation
Helen K. and Arthur E. Johnson Foundation
W. K. Kellogg Foundation
Harris and Eliza Kempner Fund
F. M. Kirby Foundation, Inc.
The Knapp Foundation, Inc.
The Kresge Foundation

Laird, Norton Foundation
Larsen Fund, Inc.
Lintilhac Foundation
James A. Macdonald Foundation
Mars Foundation
The McConnell Foundation
The Marshall L. & Perrine D. McCune Charitable Foundation
The Eugene McDermott Foundation
McGregor Fund
McInerny Foundation
McKenzie River Gathering Foundation
Giles W. and Elise G. Mead Foundation
Meadows Foundation, Inc.
The Milwaukee Foundation
The Moody Foundation
The Mountaineers Foundation
M. J. Murdock Charitable Trust
John P. Murphy Foundation
National Fish and Wildlife Foundation
The Samuel Roberts Noble Foundation, Inc.
Norcross Wildlife Foundation, Inc.
Kenneth T. and Eileen L. Norris Foundation
The Ohrstrom Foundation
Amelia Peabody Charitable Fund
The William Penn Foundation
The Pfizer Foundation, Inc.
Phillips Petroleum Foundation, Inc.
The Powell Family Foundation
The Prudential Foundation
The Rhode Island Community Foundation
Sid W. Richardson Foundation
San Diego Community Foundation
Sarkeys Foundation
Sears-Swetland Foundation
Ralph C. Sheldon Foundation, Inc.
Shell Oil Company Foundation
Thomas Sill Foundation
The Kelvin and Eleanor Smith Foundation
Stanley Smith Horticultural Trust
Springs Foundation, Inc.
Stackner Family Foundation, Inc.
Stranahan Foundation
The Strong Foundation for Environmental Values
The Charles J. Strosacker Foundation
The Morris Stulsaft Foundation
The Sudbury Foundation
The Sulzberger Foundation, Inc.
The Summerlee Foundation
The Oakleigh L. Thorne Foundation
Harry C. Trexler Trust
The Troy Foundation
Rose E. Tucker Charitable Trust
Union Camp Charitable Trust
Union Pacific Foundation
Virginia Environmental Endowment
Welfare Foundation, Inc.
The William P. Wharton Trust
Whitecap Foundation
Joseph B. Whitehead Foundation
G. N. Wilcox Trust
Robert W. Wilson Foundation
Wodecroft Foundation
Robert W. Woodruff Foundation, Inc.

Exhibits

AT&T Foundation
The Bunbury Company, Inc.
Environmental Education Foundation of Florida, Inc.
Ford Motor Company Fund
Gates Foundation
Charles Hayden Foundation
Martha Holden Jennings Foundation
Laird, Norton Foundation
Larsen Fund, Inc.
Laurel Foundation
The Little Family Foundation
Maine Community Foundation, Inc.
The McConnell Foundation
Meadows Foundation, Inc.
Meyer Memorial Trust
The Moody Foundation
John P. Murphy Foundation
The Rhode Island Community Foundation
Shell Oil Company Foundation
Stanley Smith Horticultural Trust
The Sonoma County Community Foundation
The Summerlee Foundation
The Trust For Mutual Understanding
Rose E. Tucker Charitable Trust
Joseph B. Whitehead Foundation
Robert W. Woodruff Foundation, Inc.

Facilities

The Abell Foundation
The Achelis Foundation
The Ahmanson Foundation
The George I. Alden Trust
Winifred & Harry B. Allen Foundation
Arcadia Foundation
The Vincent Astor Foundation
Atherton Family Foundation
Bay Area Community Foundation
L. L. Bean, Inc.
The Beirne Carter Foundation
The Bersted Foundation
The Frank Stanley Beveridge Foundation, Inc.
Boettcher Foundation
The Bothin Foundation
Helen Brach Foundation
Otto Bremer Foundation
Alex. Brown & Sons Charitable Foundation, Inc.
Kathleen Price and Joseph M. Bryan Family Foundation, Inc.
The Bunbury Company, Inc.
Patrick and Aimee Butler Family Foundation
The Cabot Family Charitable Trust
James & Abigail Campbell Foundation
Carolyn Foundation
Centerior Energy Foundation
The Champlin Foundations
Ben B. Cheney Foundation
Olive B. Cole Foundation
The Collins Foundation

Emphases

Facilities (cont.)

The Community Foundation of Sarasota County, Inc.
Cooke Foundation, Limited
Adolph Coors Foundation
The Cowles Charitable Trust
The James M. Cox, Jr. Foundation, Inc.
The Fred Harris Daniels Foundation, Inc.
Cleveland H. Dodge Foundation, Inc.
The Herbert H. and Grace A. Dow Foundation
Leland Fikes Foundation, Inc.
Ford Motor Company Fund
Mary D. and Walter F. Frear Eleemosynary Trust
Gates Foundation
Gebbie Foundation, Inc.
Georgia Power Foundation, Inc.
Georgia-Pacific Foundation
Greater Piscataqua Community Foundation
The Hall Family Foundation
Hartford Foundation for Public Giving
Hawaiian Electric Industries Charitable Foundation
Charles Hayden Foundation
Howard Heinz Endowment
Hudson-Webber Foundation
Helen K. and Arthur E. Johnson Foundation
Harris and Eliza Kempner Fund
The Robert S. and Grayce B. Kerr Foundation, Inc.
The Helen & Milton Kimmelman Foundation
The Kresge Foundation
Laird, Norton Foundation
Lintilhac Foundation
James A. Macdonald Foundation
Mars Foundation
The Marshall L. & Perrine D. McCune Charitable Foundation
The Eugene McDermott Foundation
McDonnell Douglas Foundation
McGregor Fund
McInerny Foundation
Meadows Foundation, Inc.
The Milwaukee Foundation
The Moody Foundation
Henry and Lucy Moses Fund, Inc.
John P. Murphy Foundation
The Samuel Roberts Noble Foundation, Inc.
The Ohrstrom Foundation
Amelia Peabody Charitable Fund
The William Penn Foundation
Phillips Petroleum Foundation, Inc.
Sid W. Richardson Foundation
Rockwell Fund, Inc.
San Diego Community Foundation
Sarkeys Foundation
Ralph C. Sheldon Foundation, Inc.
Shell Oil Company Foundation
Thomas Sill Foundation
The Skaggs Foundation
Stanley Smith Horticultural Trust
Springs Foundation, Inc.
Stackner Family Foundation, Inc.
Stranahan Foundation
The Charles J. Strosacker Foundation
The Morris Stulsaft Foundation
The Sulzberger Foundation, Inc.
The Summerlee Foundation
The Oakleigh L. Thorne Foundation
Harry C. Trexler Trust
USX Foundation, Inc.
Union Camp Charitable Trust
Union Pacific Foundation
R. T. Vanderbilt Trust
The William P. Wharton Trust
Joseph B. Whitehead Foundation
G. N. Wilcox Trust
Robert W. Wilson Foundation
The Windham Foundation, Inc.
Robert W. Woodruff Foundation, Inc.

Facilities (construction)

Atkinson Foundation
Botwinick-Wolfensohn Foundation, Inc.
Chrysler Corporation Fund
Clark Charitable Trust
The Clark Foundation
The Fred Harris Daniels Foundation, Inc.
Gaylord and Dorothy Donnelley Foundation
The Favrot Fund
The W. C. Griffith Foundation
Howard Heinz Endowment
The Hofmann Foundation
The Hyde and Watson Foundation
The Louise H. and David S. Ingalls Foundation, Inc.
The International Foundation, Inc.
McCune Foundation
M. J. Murdock Charitable Trust
The Pfizer Foundation, Inc.
Sears-Swetland Foundation
Steelcase Foundation
Rose E. Tucker Charitable Trust
The Vidda Foundation
Wodecroft Foundation
The Wyomissing Foundation, Inc.

Facilities (renovation)

The Vincent Astor Foundation
James & Abigail Campbell Foundation
Claneil Foundation, Inc.
The Columbus Foundation
S. H. Cowell Foundation
Jessie Ball duPont Religious, Charitable and Educational Fund
Fair Play Foundation
Hawaii Community Foundation
Howard Heinz Endowment
The Hyde and Watson Foundation
F. M. Kirby Foundation, Inc.
McCune Foundation
The Mountaineers Foundation

Feasibility studies

The Abell Foundation
L. L. Bean, Inc.
Claneil Foundation, Inc.
The Community Foundation of Greater New Haven
Crystal Channel Foundation
Geraldine R. Dodge Foundation, Inc.
Jessie Ball duPont Religious, Charitable and Educational Fund
The George Gund Foundation
Laidlaw Foundation
Marin Community Foundation
John P. Murphy Foundation
The David and Lucile Packard Foundation
James C. Penney Foundation
The Rhode Island Community Foundation
Sid W. Richardson Foundation
The Rockefeller Foundation
San Diego Community Foundation
The San Francisco Foundation
The Strong Foundation for Environmental Values
Virginia Environmental Endowment
Wilburforce Foundation
The Winston-Salem Foundation, Inc.
The Wyomissing Foundation, Inc.

Fellowships

AT&T Foundation
The Achelis Foundation
Ameritech Foundation
The Lynde and Harry Bradley Foundation, Inc.
Jessie Ball duPont Religious, Charitable and Educational Fund
Echoing Green Foundation
Foundation for Field Research
Frelinghuysen Foundation
GE Fund
The German Marshall Fund of the United States
The Hall Family Foundation
The John Randolph Haynes and Dora Haynes Foundation
Harris and Eliza Kempner Fund
The Robert S. and Grayce B. Kerr Foundation, Inc.
The Esther A. and Joseph Klingenstein Fund, Inc.
Larsen Fund, Inc.
Lilly Endowment, Inc.
Lintilhac Foundation
Longwood Foundation, Inc.
Richard Lounsbery Foundation
The John D. and Catherine T. MacArthur Foundation
James A. Macdonald Foundation
Henry and Lucy Moses Fund, Inc.
New Hampshire Charitable Foundation
Edward John Noble Foundation, Inc.
Pew Scholars Program in Conservation and the Environment
The Pfizer Foundation, Inc.
Sarah Scaife Foundation Incorporated
Shell Oil Company Foundation
The Charles J. Strosacker Foundation
The Sulzberger Foundation, Inc.
The Switzer Foundation

Emphases

Fellowships (cont.)
Texaco Foundation
The Trust For Mutual Understanding
Union Camp Charitable Trust
DeWitt Wallace-Reader's Digest Fund
The Dean Witter Foundation

Fieldwork
The Beinecke Foundation, Inc.
Ruth H. Brown Foundation
The Bullitt Foundation
C. S. Fund
Liz Claiborne & Art Ortenberg Foundation
Claneil Foundation, Inc.
Conservation, Food & Health
 Foundation, Inc.
Crystal Channel Foundation
Patrick and Anna M. Cudahy Fund
Samuel S. Fels Fund
FishAmerica Foundation
Flintridge Foundation
Foundation for Field Research
General Service Foundation
Walter and Duncan Gordon Charitable
 Foundation
The Clarence E. Heller Charitable
 Foundation
The Richard Ivey Foundation
Laidlaw Foundation
Larsen Fund, Inc.
National Fish and Wildlife Foundation
New England Biolabs Foundation
Edward John Noble Foundation, Inc.
The David and Lucile Packard Foundation
James C. Penney Foundation
Pew Scholars Program in Conservation
 and the Environment
The Strong Foundation for
 Environmental Values
The Summerlee Foundation
Surdna Foundation, Inc.
Harry C. Trexler Trust
The Trust For Mutual Understanding
Rose E. Tucker Charitable Trust
Virginia Environmental Endowment
Wilburforce Foundation
The Dean Witter Foundation
Margaret Cullinan Wray Charitable
 Lead Annuity Trust

Fundraising
Bay Area Community Foundation
Beldon Fund
The Conservation and Research Foundation
The Foundation for the National
 Capital Region
Evelyn and Walter Haas, Jr. Fund
McKenzie River Gathering Foundation
Norman Foundation
The Pfizer Foundation, Inc.
Rockefeller Family Fund, Inc.
The San Francisco Foundation
The Sapelo Foundation
The Summerlee Foundation

Wilburforce Foundation

General purposes
ARCO Foundation
The Abelard Foundation West
Abell-Hanger Foundation
The Achelis Foundation
The Acorn Foundation
Alaska Conservation Foundation
American Conservation Association, Inc.
American Express Philanthropic Program
American Foundation Corporation
Americana Foundation, Inc.
Arcadia Foundation
The Vincent Astor Foundation
Azadoutioun Foundation
Mary Reynolds Babcock Foundation, Inc.
Clayton Baker Trust
The George F. Baker Trust
Baltimore Gas and Electric Foundation, Inc.
The Bauman Foundation
L. L. Bean, Inc.
Beldon Fund
The Ben & Jerry's Foundation
The Bersted Foundation
The Betterment Fund
Mary Owen Borden Memorial Foundation
Botwinick-Wolfensohn Foundation, Inc.
Helen Brach Foundation
Otto Bremer Foundation
Alex. Brown & Sons Charitable
 Foundation, Inc.
The Robert Brownlee Foundation
The Bullitt Foundation
The Bunbury Company, Inc.
C. S. Fund
The Cabot Family Charitable Trust
The Morris and Gwendolyn Cafritz
 Foundation
The Louis Calder Foundation
The Cape Branch Foundation
The Cargill Foundation
Caribou Fund
Carolyn Foundation
Mary Flagler Cary Charitable Trust
Ben B. Cheney Foundation
Claneil Foundation, Inc.
Olive B. Cole Foundation
Columbia Foundation
The Community Foundation Serving
 Coastal South Carolina
Compton Foundation, Inc.
Adolph Coors Foundation
The Cowles Charitable Trust
The James M. Cox, Jr. Foundation, Inc.
The Mary A. Crocker Trust
Crystal Channel Foundation
Patrick and Anna M. Cudahy Fund
The Nathan Cummings Foundation
Damien Foundation
Dayton Hudson Foundation
Thelma Doelger Charitable Trust
Oliver S. and Jennie R. Donaldson
 Charitable Trust
Gaylord and Dorothy Donnelley Foundation

The Herbert H. and Grace A. Dow
 Foundation
Jessie Ball duPont Religious, Charitable
 and Educational Fund
The Energy Foundation
The Charles Engelhard Foundation
The Favrot Fund
Jamee and Marshall Field Foundation
The 1525 Foundation
Leland Fikes Foundation, Inc.
Foundation for Deep Ecology
The Foundation for the National
 Capital Region
The Freed Foundation, Inc.
Frelinghuysen Foundation
GE Fund
The Gap Foundation
Gebbie Foundation, Inc.
General Service Foundation
Georgia Power Foundation, Inc.
Georgia-Pacific Foundation
Give to the Earth Foundation
Global Greengrants Fund
The Greenville Foundation
The William and Mary Greve
 Foundation, Inc.
The George Gund Foundation
Evelyn and Walter Haas, Jr. Fund
Walter and Elise Haas Fund
The Hahn Family Foundation
The Hamer Foundation
James G. Hanes Memorial Fund
Harder Foundation
Mary W. Harriman Foundation
Hawaii Community Foundation
The Edward W. Hazen Foundation
The William and Flora Hewlett Foundation
The Homeland Foundation
The Roy A. Hunt Foundation
The Hyams Foundation
Illilouette Fund
Ireland Foundation
The James Irvine Foundation
Jackson Hole Preserve, Inc.
Helen K. and Arthur E. Johnson Foundation
Walter S. Johnson Foundation
The J. M. Kaplan Fund, Inc.
Harris and Eliza Kempner Fund
The Robert S. and Grayce B. Kerr
 Foundation, Inc.
The Helen & Milton Kimmelman
 Foundation
F. M. Kirby Foundation, Inc.
The Esther A. and Joseph Klingenstein
 Fund, Inc.
The Seymour H. Knox Foundation, Inc.
Charles G. Koch Charitable Foundation
Kongsgaard-Goldman Foundation
The Lauder Foundation, Inc.
Laurel Foundation
The Max and Anna Levinson Foundation
LifeWorks Foundation
Lilly Endowment, Inc.
Longwood Foundation, Inc.
Lyndhurst Foundation

© 1995 Environmental Data Resources, Inc.

Emphases

General purposes (cont.)

James A. Macdonald Foundation
Massachusetts Environmental Trust
The Marshall L. & Perrine D. McCune
  Charitable Foundation
McDonnell Douglas Foundation
McGregor Fund
McKenzie River Gathering Foundation
The McKnight Foundation
Joyce Mertz-Gilmore Foundation
Metropolitan Life Foundation
Meyer Memorial Trust
Mobil Foundation, Inc.
J. P. Morgan Charitable Trust
Henry and Lucy Moses Fund, Inc.
Charles Stewart Mott Foundation
Ruth Mott Fund
John P. Murphy Foundation
National Fish and Wildlife Foundation
The Needmor Fund
New York Foundation
The New-Land Foundation, Inc.
Edward John Noble Foundation, Inc.
The Nord Family Foundation
Norman Foundation
Mary Moody Northen, Inc.
The Norton Foundation, Inc.
Jessie Smith Noyes Foundation, Inc.
OCRI Foundation
Spencer T. and Ann W. Olin Foundation
The Overbrook Foundation
The David and Lucile Packard Foundation
James C. Penney Foundation
The Philadelphia Foundation
Philip Morris Companies, Inc.
Lynn R. and Karl E. Prickett Fund
Z. Smith Reynolds Foundation, Inc.
Sid W. Richardson Foundation
Rockefeller Family Fund, Inc.
Rockefeller Financial Services,
  Philanthropy Department
Sacharuna Foundation
The San Francisco Foundation
The Sapelo Foundation
Sarah Scaife Foundation Incorporated
The Scherman Foundation, Inc.
The Schiff Foundation
Schultz Foundation, Inc.
The Schumann Fund for New Jersey, Inc.
Sears-Swetland Foundation
Seventh Generation Fund
Ralph C. Sheldon Foundation, Inc.
The Skaggs Foundation
Anna B. Stearns Charitable Foundation, Inc.
Steelcase Foundation
Stranahan Foundation
The Stratford Foundation
The Strong Foundation for
  Environmental Values
The Charles J. Strosacker Foundation
The Sulzberger Foundation, Inc.
Surdna Foundation, Inc.
S. Mark Taper Foundation
The Oakleigh L. Thorne Foundation
The Tides Foundation

Tortuga Foundation
Town Creek Foundation, Inc.
Rose E. Tucker Charitable Trust
Alice Tweed Tuohy Foundation
USX Foundation, Inc.
Underhill Foundation
G. Unger Vetlesen Foundation
Victoria Foundation, Inc.
The Vidda Foundation
Vinmont Foundation, Inc.
Virginia Environmental Endowment
Alex C. Walker Educational
  & Charitable Foundation
Wallace Genetic Foundation, Inc.
G. N. Wilcox Trust
Mark and Catherine Winkler Foundation
The Dean Witter Foundation
Robert W. Woodruff Foundation, Inc.
Wrinkle in Time Foundation
The Wyomissing Foundation, Inc.

Indirect costs

The Robert S. and Grayce B. Kerr
  Foundation, Inc.
John P. Murphy Foundation
The San Francisco Foundation
The Strong Foundation for
  Environmental Values

Individuals

Alaska Conservation Foundation
Atherton Family Foundation
Olive B. Cole Foundation
The Conservation and Research Foundation
Ford Foundation
Foundation for Deep Ecology
The Frost Foundation, Ltd.
Hawaii Community Foundation
Massachusetts Environmental Trust
The Mountaineers Foundation
National Fish and Wildlife Foundation
National Geographic Society Education
  Foundation
New Hampshire Charitable Foundation

Innovative programs

ARCO Foundation
AT&T Foundation
The Abelard Foundation West
The Abell Foundation
Atkinson Foundation
Mary Reynolds Babcock Foundation, Inc.
The Bauman Foundation
Bay Area Community Foundation
L. L. Bean, Inc.
The Beinecke Foundation, Inc.
Beldon Fund
The Ben & Jerry's Foundation
The Betterment Fund
The Blumenthal Foundation
Otto Bremer Foundation
The Bullitt Foundation
The Bunbury Company, Inc.
C. S. Fund

Carolyn Foundation
The Carpenter Foundation
Ben B. Cheney Foundation
The Chevron Companies
Claneil Foundation, Inc.
The Community Foundation of
  Greater New Haven
The Community Foundation of
  Santa Clara County
The Community Foundation of
  Sarasota County, Inc.
The Community Foundation Serving
  Coastal South Carolina
The Conservation and Research Foundation
Cooke Foundation, Limited
The James M. Cox, Jr. Foundation, Inc.
The Mary A. Crocker Trust
Crystal Channel Foundation
Patrick and Anna M. Cudahy Fund
The Nathan Cummings Foundation
Geraldine R. Dodge Foundation, Inc.
Dolfinger-McMahon Foundation
Donner Canadian Foundation
Jessie Ball duPont Religious, Charitable
  and Educational Fund
Echoing Green Foundation
The Educational Foundation of America
El Paso Community Foundation
Samuel S. Fels Fund
The Field Foundation of Illinois, Inc.
FishAmerica Foundation
Foundation for Deep Ecology
Mary D. and Walter F. Frear
  Eleemosynary Trust
The Frost Foundation, Ltd.
The GAR Foundation
Gebbie Foundation, Inc.
General Service Foundation
Give to the Earth Foundation
Global Environmental Project Institute
Richard & Rhoda Goldman Fund
Good Samaritan, Inc.
Greater Piscataqua Community Foundation
The Greenville Foundation
Hartford Foundation for Public Giving
Hawaiian Electric Industries Charitable
  Foundation
Charles Hayden Foundation
Heller Charitable & Educational Fund
Hudson-Webber Foundation
Illilouette Fund
Ittleson Foundation, Inc.
The Richard Ivey Foundation
The Henry M. Jackson Foundation
Martha Holden Jennings Foundation
W. Alton Jones Foundation, Inc.
W. K. Kellogg Foundation
Kongsgaard-Goldman Foundation
Laidlaw Foundation
Laird, Norton Foundation
Laurel Foundation
The Max and Anna Levinson Foundation
Lintilhac Foundation
Maine Community Foundation, Inc.
The Marshall Fund of Arizona

Emphases

Innovative programs (cont.)

The Martin Foundation, Inc.
The McConnell Foundation
McGregor Fund
McInerny Foundation
McKenzie River Gathering Foundation
McKesson Foundation, Inc.
The McKnight Foundation
Meadows Foundation, Inc.
Meyer Memorial Trust
The Milwaukee Foundation
The Minneapolis Foundation
The Moody Foundation
Charles Stewart Mott Foundation
Ruth Mott Fund
John P. Murphy Foundation
National Fish and Wildlife Foundation
New England Biolabs Foundation
Edward John Noble Foundation, Inc.
Norman Foundation
Northwest Fund for the Environment
Jessie Smith Noyes Foundation, Inc.
Nathan M. Ohrbach Foundation, Inc.
The David and Lucile Packard Foundation
Peninsula Community Foundation
James C. Penney Foundation
The Pew Charitable Trusts
Pew Scholars Program in Conservation and the Environment
The Philadelphia Foundation
Philip Morris Companies, Inc.
Ellis L. Phillips Foundation
The Prudential Foundation
Public Welfare Foundation, Inc.
Recreational Equipment, Inc.
The Rhode Island Community Foundation
Sid W. Richardson Foundation
The Roberts Foundation
Rockwood Fund, Inc.
San Diego Community Foundation
The San Francisco Foundation
Sarkeys Foundation
The Scherman Foundation, Inc.
The Schumann Fund for New Jersey, Inc.
Shell Oil Company Foundation
The Skaggs Foundation
The Sonoma County Community Foundation
The Sudbury Foundation
The Summerlee Foundation
Surdna Foundation, Inc.
Threshold Foundation
The Tides Foundation
Tortuga Foundation
Town Creek Foundation, Inc.
The Trust For Mutual Understanding
Rose E. Tucker Charitable Trust
Alice Tweed Tuohy Foundation
The USF&G Foundation, Inc.
Victoria Foundation, Inc.
Vinmont Foundation, Inc.
Weeden Foundation
Wilburforce Foundation
Mark and Catherine Winkler Foundation
The Winston-Salem Foundation, Inc.

The Dean Witter Foundation
Margaret Cullinan Wray Charitable Lead Annuity Trust

Internships

AT&T Foundation
Alaska Conservation Foundation
The George I. Alden Trust
The Lynde and Harry Bradley Foundation, Inc.
The Morris and Gwendolyn Cafritz Foundation
Claneil Foundation, Inc.
The Collins Foundation
Crystal Channel Foundation
Patrick and Anna M. Cudahy Fund
The Fred Harris Daniels Foundation, Inc.
The German Marshall Fund of the United States
The Greenville Foundation
The George Gund Foundation
The Hall Family Foundation
Laird, Norton Foundation
Larsen Fund, Inc.
John P. Murphy Foundation
National Fish and Wildlife Foundation
Edward John Noble Foundation, Inc.
James C. Penney Foundation
The Pfizer Foundation, Inc.
Phillips Petroleum Foundation, Inc.
The San Francisco Foundation
Stanley Smith Horticultural Trust
Springs Foundation, Inc.
The Sulzberger Foundation, Inc.
Edna Bailey Sussman Fund
The Trust For Mutual Understanding
WMX Environmental Grants Program
DeWitt Wallace-Reader's Digest Fund
Wilburforce Foundation
Margaret Cullinan Wray Charitable Lead Annuity Trust

Inventories

Conservation, Food & Health Foundation, Inc.
The George Gund Foundation
New England Biolabs Foundation
The David and Lucile Packard Foundation
San Diego Community Foundation
The San Francisco Foundation
Robert W. Woodruff Foundation, Inc.

Land acquisition

ARCO Foundation
The Abell Foundation
The Achelis Foundation
The Ahmanson Foundation
The George I. Alden Trust
The Beirne Carter Foundation
The Betterment Fund
Boettcher Foundation
Mary Owen Borden Memorial Foundation
The Bullitt Foundation
The Bunbury Company, Inc.

The Cabot Family Charitable Trust
The Cape Branch Foundation
Carolyn Foundation
The Carpenter Foundation
The Champlin Foundations
Clark Charitable Trust
Olive B. Cole Foundation
The Columbus Foundation
The Community Foundation of Santa Clara County
Compton Foundation, Inc.
The Conservation and Research Foundation
The James M. Cox, Jr. Foundation, Inc.
The Cricket Foundation
The Fred Harris Daniels Foundation, Inc.
Fair Play Foundation
Fields Pond Foundation, Inc.
Leland Fikes Foundation, Inc.
Flintridge Foundation
The Freed Foundation, Inc.
The Frost Foundation, Ltd.
The GAR Foundation
Gates Foundation
Richard & Rhoda Goldman Fund
Walter and Elise Haas Fund
The Hamer Foundation
James G. Hanes Memorial Fund
Harder Foundation
Hartford Foundation for Public Giving
Hawaiian Electric Industries Charitable Foundation
Heller Charitable & Educational Fund
The Homeland Foundation
The James Irvine Foundation
Jackson Hole Preserve, Inc.
Kongsgaard-Goldman Foundation
The Kresge Foundation
Laird, Norton Foundation
Laurel Foundation
Lintilhac Foundation
The Marshall L. & Perrine D. McCune Charitable Foundation
Giles W. and Elise G. Mead Foundation
Meadows Foundation, Inc.
Richard King Mellon Foundation
The Milwaukee Foundation
John P. Murphy Foundation
National Fish and Wildlife Foundation
Norcross Wildlife Foundation, Inc.
Norman Foundation
The Ohrstrom Foundation
The David and Lucile Packard Foundation
The William Penn Foundation
Phillips Petroleum Foundation, Inc.
Prince Charitable Trusts
The Prospect Hill Foundation
The Rhode Island Community Foundation
Fran and Warren Rupp Foundation
San Diego Community Foundation
The Scherman Foundation, Inc.
Sears-Swetland Foundation
Springs Foundation, Inc.
Stranahan Foundation
The Strong Foundation for Environmental Values

© 1995 Environmental Data Resources, Inc.

653

Emphases

Land acquisition (cont.)

The Summerlee Foundation
The Oakleigh L. Thorne Foundation
Rose E. Tucker Charitable Trust
Underhill Foundation
Victoria Foundation, Inc.
WMX Environmental Grants Program
Weeden Foundation
The William P. Wharton Trust
Joseph B. Whitehead Foundation
Wilburforce Foundation
Robert W. Wilson Foundation
Mark and Catherine Winkler Foundation
Robert W. Woodruff Foundation, Inc.
Margaret Cullinan Wray Charitable
    Lead Annuity Trust

Lectureships

AT&T Foundation
The Lynde and Harry Bradley
    Foundation, Inc.
Claneil Foundation, Inc.
Ford Motor Company Fund
Harris and Eliza Kempner Fund
Lintilhac Foundation
John P. Murphy Foundation
Southwestern Bell Foundation
The Sulzberger Foundation, Inc.
The Summerlee Foundation

Leveraging funds

The Abell Foundation
Mary Reynolds Babcock Foundation, Inc.
L. L. Bean, Inc.
The Betterment Fund
The Bullitt Foundation
The Carpenter Foundation
The Community Foundation of
    Sarasota County, Inc.
The Conservation and Research Foundation
Cooke Foundation, Limited
The James M. Cox, Jr. Foundation, Inc.
Crystal Channel Foundation
The Nathan Cummings Foundation
Jessie Ball duPont Religious, Charitable
    and Educational Fund
El Paso Community Foundation
The German Marshall Fund of
    the United States
Give to the Earth Foundation
Walter and Duncan Gordon Charitable
    Foundation
Greater Piscataqua Community Foundation
The Hall Family Foundation
The Clarence E. Heller Charitable
    Foundation
Illilouette Fund
The James Irvine Foundation
The Richard Ivey Foundation
The Henry M. Jackson Foundation
The Max and Anna Levinson Foundation
Lyndhurst Foundation
The John D. and Catherine T. MacArthur
    Foundation

McKenzie River Gathering Foundation
The McKnight Foundation
The Milwaukee Foundation
John P. Murphy Foundation
National Fish and Wildlife Foundation
The Needmor Fund
New England Biolabs Foundation
Northwest Fund for the Environment
Ottinger Foundation
The David and Lucile Packard Foundation
James C. Penney Foundation
The Pew Charitable Trusts
Recreational Equipment, Inc.
Fran and Warren Rupp Foundation
Sacramento Regional Foundation
The San Francisco Foundation
The Sapelo Foundation
Sarkeys Foundation
The Skaggs Foundation
The Sudbury Foundation
Surdna Foundation, Inc.
The Trust For Mutual Understanding
Victoria Foundation, Inc.
Virginia Environmental Endowment
Wilburforce Foundation
The Dean Witter Foundation

Litigation

Alaska Conservation Foundation
The Bullitt Foundation
The Bunbury Company, Inc.
C. S. Fund
Carolyn Foundation
Mary Flagler Cary Charitable Trust
Robert Sterling Clark Foundation, Inc.
Columbia Foundation
The Nathan Cummings Foundation
The Educational Foundation of America
Environmental Endowment for
    New Jersey, Inc.
Foundation for Deep Ecology
The Fund for New Jersey
General Service Foundation
Richard & Rhoda Goldman Fund
Harder Foundation
The Edward W. Hazen Foundation
The Homeland Foundation
W. Alton Jones Foundation, Inc.
Kongsgaard-Goldman Foundation
The Max and Anna Levinson Foundation
The John Merck Fund
National Fish and Wildlife Foundation
Norman Foundation
Northwest Fund for the Environment
Pew Scholars Program in Conservation
    and the Environment
Prince Charitable Trusts
The Prospect Hill Foundation
Rockefeller Family Fund, Inc.
The Sapelo Foundation
The Scherman Foundation, Inc.
The Strong Foundation for
    Environmental Values
Weeden Foundation

Margaret Cullinan Wray Charitable
    Lead Annuity Trust

Loans

The Abell Foundation
American Conservation Association, Inc.
Atherton Family Foundation
The Bullitt Foundation
Olive B. Cole Foundation
The Community Foundation of
    Greater New Haven
Fields Pond Foundation, Inc.
The Foundation for the National
    Capital Region
Harris and Eliza Kempner Fund
The Henry P. Kendall Foundation
James A. Macdonald Foundation
Marin Community Foundation
New Hampshire Charitable Foundation
The New World Foundation
Norman Foundation
The David and Lucile Packard Foundation
The Rhode Island Community Foundation
Springs Foundation, Inc.
The Sudbury Foundation
Robert W. Wilson Foundation

Lobbying

Alaska Conservation Foundation
Global Environmental Project Institute
Laidlaw Foundation
Outdoor Industry Conservation Alliance
Recreational Equipment, Inc.
Rockefeller Family Fund, Inc.
Virginia Environmental Endowment

Matching funds

AT&T Foundation
The Abell Foundation
The Achelis Foundation
Alaska Conservation Foundation
The George I. Alden Trust
American Express Philanthropic Program
Americana Foundation, Inc.
Ameritech Foundation
Atherton Family Foundation
The George F. Baker Trust
Baltimore Gas and Electric Foundation, Inc.
The Barra Foundation, Inc.
Bay Area Community Foundation
The Beirne Carter Foundation
The Ben & Jerry's Foundation
The Betterment Fund
The Frank Stanley Beveridge
    Foundation, Inc.
The Blumenthal Foundation
The Lynde and Harry Bradley
    Foundation, Inc.
Otto Bremer Foundation
Kathleen Price and Joseph M. Bryan
    Family Foundation, Inc.
The Bullitt Foundation
The Bydale Foundation
C. S. Fund

Matching funds (cont.)

Carolyn Foundation
The Carpenter Foundation
Centerior Energy Foundation
Chesapeake Corporation Foundation
Chrysler Corporation Fund
Clark Charitable Trust
The Community Foundation of Greater New Haven
The Conservation and Research Foundation
Conservation, Food & Health Foundation, Inc.
Cooke Foundation, Limited
S. H. Cowell Foundation
The Cowles Charitable Trust
The Mary A. Crocker Trust
Crystal Channel Foundation
Patrick and Anna M. Cudahy Fund
The Nathan Cummings Foundation
The Fred Harris Daniels Foundation, Inc.
Dayton Hudson Foundation
Cleveland H. Dodge Foundation, Inc.
Geraldine R. Dodge Foundation, Inc.
Dolfinger-McMahon Foundation
The Herbert H. and Grace A. Dow Foundation
Fields Pond Foundation, Inc.
The 1525 Foundation
Leland Fikes Foundation, Inc.
Ford Motor Company Fund
Foundation for the Carolinas
Foundation for Deep Ecology
The Freed Foundation, Inc.
Frelinghuysen Foundation
The GAR Foundation
GE Fund
The Gap Foundation
Gebbie Foundation, Inc.
Georgia-Pacific Foundation
Give to the Earth Foundation
Global Environmental Project Institute
Walter and Duncan Gordon Charitable Foundation
Great Lakes Protection Fund
Greater Piscataqua Community Foundation
The Greenville Foundation
The William and Mary Greve Foundation, Inc.
The George Gund Foundation
Evelyn and Walter Haas, Jr. Fund
The Hahn Family Foundation
The Ewing Halsell Foundation
The Hamer Foundation
James G. Hanes Memorial Fund
Harder Foundation
Hawaiian Electric Industries Charitable Foundation
Charles Hayden Foundation
The Edward W. Hazen Foundation
Howard Heinz Endowment
The Hofmann Foundation
IBM Corporation
Ililouette Fund
Jackson Hole Preserve, Inc.
The Henry M. Jackson Foundation

Martha Holden Jennings Foundation
Harris and Eliza Kempner Fund
The Robert S. and Grayce B. Kerr Foundation, Inc.
The Helen & Milton Kimmelman Foundation
The Knapp Foundation, Inc.
Lilly Endowment, Inc.
Lintilhac Foundation
Richard Lounsbery Foundation, Inc.
Lyndhurst Foundation
Maine Community Foundation, Inc.
Mars Foundation
The Marshall Fund of Arizona
The Martin Foundation, Inc.
The McConnell Foundation
The Marshall L. & Perrine D. McCune Charitable Foundation
McDonnell Douglas Foundation
McGregor Fund
McInerny Foundation
McKenzie River Gathering Foundation
The McKnight Foundation
Giles W. and Elise G. Mead Foundation
Richard King Mellon Foundation
The John Merck Fund
Metropolitan Atlanta Community Foundation, Inc.
Metropolitan Life Foundation
Meyer Memorial Trust
Millbrook Tribute Garden, Inc.
The Milwaukee Foundation
Mobil Foundation, Inc.
Henry and Lucy Moses Fund, Inc.
John P. Murphy Foundation
The National Environmental Education and Training Foundation, Inc.
National Fish and Wildlife Foundation
New England Biolabs Foundation
New Horizon Foundation
The Samuel Roberts Noble Foundation, Inc.
The Nord Family Foundation
Norman Foundation
Northwest Fund for the Environment
Nicholas H. Noyes, Jr. Memorial Foundation
OCRI Foundation
The Ohrstrom Foundation
The David and Lucile Packard Foundation
Amelia Peabody Charitable Fund
James C. Penney Foundation
The Pfizer Foundation, Inc.
The Philadelphia Foundation
Phillips Petroleum Foundation, Inc.
The Prudential Foundation
The Rhode Island Community Foundation
Rockefeller Family Fund, Inc.
The Rockfall Foundation
Fran and Warren Rupp Foundation
The San Francisco Foundation
Sarkeys Foundation
Sarah Scaife Foundation Incorporated
The Scherman Foundation, Inc.
The Schumann Fund for New Jersey, Inc.
Sears-Swetland Foundation

Shell Oil Company Foundation
Thomas Sill Foundation
The Skaggs Foundation
Stanley Smith Horticultural Trust
The Sonoma County Community Foundation
Southwestern Bell Foundation
Springs Foundation, Inc.
Stackner Family Foundation, Inc.
The Stroh Foundation
The Sudbury Foundation
The Summerlee Foundation
Texaco Foundation
Town Creek Foundation, Inc.
The USF&G Foundation, Inc.
Union Camp Charitable Trust
Union Pacific Foundation
Victoria Foundation, Inc.
Virginia Environmental Endowment
Welfare Foundation, Inc.
Westinghouse Foundation
Robert W. Wilson Foundation
The Windham Foundation, Inc.
Mark and Catherine Winkler Foundation
The Winston-Salem Foundation, Inc.
The Dean Witter Foundation
The Wortham Foundation, Inc.
The Wyomissing Foundation, Inc.

Media projects

The Lynde and Harry Bradley Foundation, Inc.
C. S. Fund
W. Alton Jones Foundation, Inc.
The Esther A. and Joseph Klingenstein Fund, Inc.
Laird, Norton Foundation
Giles W. and Elise G. Mead Foundation
Norcross Wildlife Foundation, Inc.
The Summerlee Foundation
Threshold Foundation

Membership campaigns

Alaska Conservation Foundation
Foundation for Deep Ecology
Greater Piscataqua Community Foundation
Harder Foundation
John P. Murphy Foundation
The Needmor Fund
Recreational Equipment, Inc.
Rockefeller Family Fund, Inc.
The Summerlee Foundation
Wilburforce Foundation
The Wortham Foundation, Inc.

Multi-year grants

AT&T Foundation
The Achelis Foundation
Bay Area Community Foundation
L. L. Bean, Inc.
The Betterment Fund
Otto Bremer Foundation
C. S. Fund
Mary Flagler Cary Charitable Trust

Emphases

Multi-year grants (cont.)

The Cleveland Foundation
The Collins Foundation
Columbia Foundation
The Community Foundation of Greater New Haven
Compton Foundation, Inc.
Cooke Foundation, Limited
The James M. Cox, Jr. Foundation, Inc.
Jessie B. Cox Charitable Trust
The Nathan Cummings Foundation
The Aaron Diamond Foundation
Donner Canadian Foundation
Jessie Ball duPont Religious, Charitable and Educational Fund
Echoing Green Foundation
Foundation for Deep Ecology
Foundation for Field Research
GE Fund
Gates Foundation
Gebbie Foundation, Inc.
Richard & Rhoda Goldman Fund
Walter and Duncan Gordon Charitable Foundation
Great Lakes Protection Fund
The George Gund Foundation
Evelyn and Walter Haas, Jr. Fund
The Hall Family Foundation
The Hamer Foundation
Hartford Foundation for Public Giving
Hawaiian Electric Industries Charitable Foundation
The William and Flora Hewlett Foundation
The Hitachi Foundation
The Homeland Foundation
The Roy A. Hunt Foundation
The James Irvine Foundation
Island Foundation, Inc.
The Richard Ivey Foundation
W. K. Kellogg Foundation
The Robert S. and Grayce B. Kerr Foundation, Inc.
Kongsgaard-Goldman Foundation
Laidlaw Foundation
Larsen Fund, Inc.
Lilly Endowment, Inc.
The John D. and Catherine T. MacArthur Foundation
McGregor Fund
The McKnight Foundation
Meadows Foundation, Inc.
Charles Stewart Mott Foundation
John P. Murphy Foundation
The Needmor Fund
New England Biolabs Foundation
Edward John Noble Foundation, Inc.
The Nord Family Foundation
The David and Lucile Packard Foundation
The William Penn Foundation
The Pew Charitable Trusts
Philip Morris Companies, Inc.
The Prospect Hill Foundation
Sid W. Richardson Foundation
Rockefeller Family Fund, Inc.
The San Francisco Foundation

The Sapelo Foundation
The Scherman Foundation, Inc.
The Schumann Fund for New Jersey, Inc.
Shell Oil Company Foundation
The Skaggs Foundation
Springs Foundation, Inc.
Anna B. Stearns Charitable Foundation, Inc.
The Sudbury Foundation
Surdna Foundation, Inc.
Toyota USA Foundation
Rose E. Tucker Charitable Trust
Turner Foundation, Inc.
The USF&G Foundation, Inc.
Virginia Environmental Endowment
Wilburforce Foundation
Mark and Catherine Winkler Foundation

Museums

ARCO Foundation
AT&T Foundation
The Ahmanson Foundation
American Foundation Corporation
Americana Foundation, Inc.
Ameritech Foundation
Bay Area Community Foundation
The Beinecke Foundation, Inc.
The Beirne Carter Foundation
Boettcher Foundation
Helen Brach Foundation
The Robert Brownlee Foundation
The Bunbury Company, Inc.
The Cape Branch Foundation
Carolyn Foundation
Chesapeake Bay Trust
Claneil Foundation, Inc.
The Cleveland Foundation
Cooke Foundation, Limited
Patrick and Anna M. Cudahy Fund
Jessie Ball duPont Religious, Charitable and Educational Fund
The Educational Foundation of America
Ford Motor Company Fund
Frelinghuysen Foundation
The Frost Foundation, Ltd.
The GAR Foundation
Gates Foundation
Gebbie Foundation, Inc.
The W. C. Griffith Foundation
The George Gund Foundation
Evelyn and Walter Haas, Jr. Fund
The Hall Family Foundation
The Hamer Foundation
Hawaiian Electric Industries Charitable Foundation
The Roy A. Hunt Foundation
The Hyde and Watson Foundation
Martha Holden Jennings Foundation
The Howard Johnson Foundation
The Henry P. Kendall Foundation
The Robert S. and Grayce B. Kerr Foundation, Inc.
The Esther A. and Joseph Klingenstein Fund, Inc.
The Seymour H. Knox Foundation, Inc.
The Kresge Foundation

Laurel Foundation
The Little Family Foundation
Longwood Foundation, Inc.
The John D. and Catherine T. MacArthur Foundation
MARPAT Foundation, Inc.
The Marshall Fund of Arizona
McGregor Fund
Meadows Foundation, Inc.
Richard King Mellon Foundation
Metropolitan Atlanta Community Foundation, Inc.
Meyer Memorial Trust
The Milwaukee Foundation
The Mountaineers Foundation
John P. Murphy Foundation
National Fish and Wildlife Foundation
Edward John Noble Foundation, Inc.
Kenneth T. and Eileen L. Norris Foundation
OCRI Foundation
The William Penn Foundation
The Pfizer Foundation, Inc.
The Powell Family Foundation
The Rhode Island Community Foundation
Sid W. Richardson Foundation
The Roberts Foundation
Samuel and May Rudin Foundation, Inc.
San Diego Community Foundation
The San Francisco Foundation
Sarkeys Foundation
The Scherman Foundation, Inc.
Sears-Swetland Foundation
Shell Oil Company Foundation
The Sonoma County Community Foundation
Springs Foundation, Inc.
The Summerlee Foundation
The Trust For Mutual Understanding
Rose E. Tucker Charitable Trust
The Vidda Foundation
Welfare Foundation, Inc.
Westinghouse Foundation
Joseph B. Whitehead Foundation
The Dean Witter Foundation
Robert W. Woodruff Foundation, Inc.
The Wortham Foundation, Inc.
Margaret Cullinan Wray Charitable Lead Annuity Trust
The Wyomissing Foundation, Inc.

Networking

The Abelard Foundation West
The Abell Foundation
The Acorn Foundation
The Bauman Foundation
Beldon Fund
The Ben & Jerry's Foundation
The Blumenthal Foundation
The Bunbury Company, Inc.
The Carpenter Foundation
Claneil Foundation, Inc.
Compton Foundation, Inc.
Patrick and Anna M. Cudahy Fund
The Nathan Cummings Foundation
The Fred Gellert Foundation

Emphases

Networking (cont.)

The German Marshall Fund of the United States
Global Environmental Project Institute
Walter and Duncan Gordon Charitable Foundation
The George Gund Foundation
Illilouette Fund
Island Foundation, Inc.
W. K. Kellogg Foundation
Laidlaw Foundation
McKenzie River Gathering Foundation
The McKnight Foundation
The Milwaukee Foundation
Charles Stewart Mott Foundation
New England Biolabs Foundation
Norman Foundation
Jessie Smith Noyes Foundation, Inc.
James C. Penney Foundation
Pew Scholars Program in Conservation and the Environment
Public Welfare Foundation, Inc.
Recreational Equipment, Inc.
San Diego Community Foundation
The San Francisco Foundation
The Summerlee Foundation
The Tides Foundation
Town Creek Foundation, Inc.
The Trust For Mutual Understanding
Virginia Environmental Endowment
WMX Environmental Grants Program

Nonprofit organizations

ARCO Foundation
AT&T Foundation
A Territory Resource
The Abelard Foundation West
The Abell Foundation
Abell-Hanger Foundation
The Acorn Foundation
The Ahmanson Foundation
Alaska Conservation Foundation
Winifred & Harry B. Allen Foundation
The Jenifer Altman Foundation
American Express Philanthropic Program
Americana Foundation, Inc.
Ameritech Foundation
Elmer L. & Eleanor J. Andersen Foundation
Apple Computer, Inc.
The Arca Foundation
Arcadia Foundation
The Vincent Astor Foundation
Atherton Family Foundation
Atkinson Foundation
Mary Reynolds Babcock Foundation, Inc.
The Cameron Baird Foundation
Clayton Baker Trust
The George F. Baker Trust
Baltimore Gas and Electric Foundation, Inc.
BankAmerica Foundation
The Barra Foundation, Inc.
The Theodore H. Barth Foundation, Inc.
Bay Area Community Foundation
The Bay Foundation

The Beinecke Foundation, Inc.
The Beirne Carter Foundation
Beldon Fund
David Winton Bell Foundation
James Ford Bell Foundation
The Ben & Jerry's Foundation
The Bersted Foundation
The William Bingham Foundation
Blandin Foundation
The Blumenthal Foundation
The Boeing Company
Botwinick-Wolfensohn Foundation, Inc.
Helen Brach Foundation
The Lynde and Harry Bradley Foundation, Inc.
Otto Bremer Foundation
Alex. Brown & Sons Charitable Foundation, Inc.
H. Barksdale Brown Charitable Trust
Ruth H. Brown Foundation
W. L. Lyons Brown Foundation
The Robert Brownlee Foundation
Kathleen Price and Joseph M. Bryan Family Foundation, Inc.
The Bullitt Foundation
The Bunbury Company, Inc.
The Bush Foundation
Patrick and Aimee Butler Family Foundation
C. S. Fund
The Morris and Gwendolyn Cafritz Foundation
The Louis Calder Foundation
California Community Foundation
James & Abigail Campbell Foundation
The Cargill Foundation
Caribou Fund
Carolyn Foundation
Mary Flagler Cary Charitable Trust
Centerior Energy Foundation
The Champlin Foundations
Ben B. Cheney Foundation
Chesapeake Corporation Foundation
The Chevron Companies
Claneil Foundation, Inc.
Robert Sterling Clark Foundation, Inc.
The Cleveland Foundation
Olive B. Cole Foundation
The Collins Foundation
Columbia Foundation
The Columbus Foundation
The Community Foundation of Greater New Haven
The Community Foundation of Santa Clara County
The Community Foundation of Sarasota County, Inc.
The Community Foundation Serving Coastal South Carolina
Community Foundation of Western North Carolina, Inc.
Compton Foundation, Inc.
The Conservation and Research Foundation
Conservation, Food & Health Foundation, Inc.

Cooke Foundation, Limited
Adolph Coors Foundation
S. H. Cowell Foundation
The Cowles Charitable Trust
The James M. Cox, Jr. Foundation, Inc.
Jessie B. Cox Charitable Trust
The Cricket Foundation
The Mary A. Crocker Trust
Crystal Channel Foundation
Patrick and Anna M. Cudahy Fund
The Nathan Cummings Foundation
Damien Foundation
The Fred Harris Daniels Foundation, Inc.
The Arthur Vining Davis Foundations
Davis Conservation Foundation
Dayton Hudson Foundation
Deer Creek Foundation
The Aaron Diamond Foundation
Cleveland H. Dodge Foundation, Inc.
Geraldine R. Dodge Foundation, Inc.
Dolfinger-McMahon Foundation
Gaylord and Dorothy Donnelley Foundation
The Herbert H. and Grace A. Dow Foundation
The Max and Victoria Dreyfus Foundation, Inc.
The Elizabeth Ordway Dunn Foundation, Inc.
Jessie Ball duPont Religious, Charitable and Educational Fund
Ederic Foundation, Inc.
The Educational Foundation of America
The Energy Foundation
Environmental Education Foundation of Florida, Inc.
Environmental Endowment for New Jersey, Inc.
The Ettinger Foundation, Inc.
Samuel S. Fels Fund
The Hugh and Jane Ferguson Foundation
Jamee and Marshall Field Foundation
Fields Pond Foundation, Inc.
The 1525 Foundation
FishAmerica Foundation
Flintridge Foundation
Ford Foundation
Ford Motor Company Fund
Foundation for the Carolinas
Foundation for Deep Ecology
The Foundation for the National Capital Region
The Jacob and Annita France Foundation, Inc.
The Freed Foundation, Inc.
Frelinghuysen Foundation
The Frost Foundation, Ltd.
Lloyd A. Fry Foundation
Fund of the Four Directions
The GAR Foundation
GE Fund
The Gap Foundation
Gates Foundation
The Barbara Gauntlett Foundation, Inc.
Gebbie Foundation, Inc.
The Fred Gellert Foundation

© 1995 Environmental Data Resources, Inc.

Emphases

Nonprofit organizations (cont.)

General Service Foundation
Georgia Power Foundation, Inc.
Georgia-Pacific Foundation
The Wallace Alexander Gerbode Foundation, Inc.
The German Marshall Fund of the United States
Give to the Earth Foundation
Global Environmental Project Institute
Global Greengrants Fund
Herman Goldman Foundation
Richard & Rhoda Goldman Fund
Good Samaritan, Inc.
Walter and Duncan Gordon Charitable Foundation
Great Lakes Protection Fund
Greater Piscataqua Community Foundation
The Greenville Foundation
The W. C. Griffith Foundation
The George Gund Foundation
Evelyn and Walter Haas, Jr. Fund
Walter and Elise Haas Fund
The Hahn Family Foundation
The Hall Family Foundation
The Hamer Foundation
James G. Hanes Memorial Fund
Harder Foundation
Gladys and Roland Harriman Foundation
Hartford Foundation for Public Giving
Hawaii Community Foundation
Hawaiian Electric Industries Charitable Foundation
Charles Hayden Foundation
The John Randolph Haynes and Dora Haynes Foundation
Howard Heinz Endowment
Vira I. Heinz Endowment
The Clarence E. Heller Charitable Foundation
The William and Flora Hewlett Foundation
The Homeland Foundation
Howfirma Foundation
The Roy A. Hunt Foundation
The Hyams Foundation
The Hyde and Watson Foundation
IBM Corporation
The Louise H. and David S. Ingalls Foundation, Inc.
The International Foundation, Inc.
Ireland Foundation
The James Irvine Foundation
Island Foundation, Inc.
The Richard Ivey Foundation
The Henry M. Jackson Foundation
Martha Holden Jennings Foundation
The George Frederick Jewett Foundation
Helen K. and Arthur E. Johnson Foundation
W. Alton Jones Foundation, Inc.
Joy Foundation for Ecological Education and Research
The J. M. Kaplan Fund, Inc.
W. K. Kellogg Foundation
The Henry P. Kendall Foundation
The Robert S. and Grayce B. Kerr Foundation, Inc.
F. M. Kirby Foundation, Inc.
The Esther A. and Joseph Klingenstein Fund, Inc.
The Knapp Foundation, Inc.
The Seymour H. Knox Foundation, Inc.
Kongsgaard-Goldman Foundation
The Kresge Foundation
The Lagemann Foundation
Laidlaw Foundation
Laird, Norton Foundation
Larsen Fund, Inc.
The Lauder Foundation, Inc.
Laurel Foundation
The Lazar Foundation
The Max and Anna Levinson Foundation
Lintilhac Foundation
The Little Family Foundation
Lyndhurst Foundation
The John D. and Catherine T. MacArthur Foundation
Maine Community Foundation, Inc.
Maki Foundation
Marbrook Foundation
Marin Community Foundation
MARPAT Foundation, Inc.
The Marshall Fund of Arizona
The Martin Foundation, Inc.
Massachusetts Environmental Trust
The McConnell Foundation
The Marshall L. & Perrine D. McCune Charitable Foundation
McDonnell Douglas Foundation
McGregor Fund
McInerny Foundation
The McIntosh Foundation
McKenzie River Gathering Foundation
McKesson Foundation, Inc.
The McKnight Foundation
McLean Contributionship
Giles W. and Elise G. Mead Foundation
Meadows Foundation, Inc.
The Andrew W. Mellon Foundation
Richard King Mellon Foundation
Merck Family Fund
Robert G. and Anne M. Merrick Foundation, Inc.
Joyce Mertz-Gilmore Foundation
Metropolitan Atlanta Community Foundation, Inc.
Metropolitan Life Foundation
Meyer Memorial Trust
Millbrook Tribute Garden, Inc.
The Milwaukee Foundation
The Minneapolis Foundation
Mobil Foundation, Inc.
Leo Model Foundation, Inc.
The Moody Foundation
J. P. Morgan Charitable Trust
Charles Stewart Mott Foundation
Ruth Mott Fund
The Mountaineers Foundation
M. J. Murdock Charitable Trust
John P. Murphy Foundation
Mustard Seed Foundation, Inc.
The National Environmental Education and Training Foundation, Inc.
National Fish and Wildlife Foundation
The Needmor Fund
New England Biolabs Foundation
New Hampshire Charitable Foundation
The New World Foundation
The New York Community Trust
New York Foundation
The New-Land Foundation, Inc.
Edward John Noble Foundation, Inc.
Norcross Wildlife Foundation, Inc.
The Nord Family Foundation
Norman Foundation
Kenneth T. and Eileen L. Norris Foundation
Northwest Area Foundation
Northwest Fund for the Environment
The Norton Foundation, Inc.
Jessie Smith Noyes Foundation, Inc.
Nicholas H. Noyes, Jr. Memorial Foundation
OCRI Foundation
Nathan M. Ohrbach Foundation, Inc.
Onan Family Foundation
Orchard Foundation
Ottinger Foundation
The David and Lucile Packard Foundation
Patagonia, Inc.
Amelia Peabody Charitable Fund
Peninsula Community Foundation
The William Penn Foundation
The Perkin Fund
Perkins Charitable Foundation
The Pew Charitable Trusts
The Pfizer Foundation, Inc.
The Philadelphia Foundation
Philip Morris Companies, Inc.
Phillips Petroleum Foundation, Inc.
Ellis L. Phillips Foundation
Henry B. Plant Memorial Fund, Inc.
The Polden-Puckham Charitable Foundation
The Powell Family Foundation
Prince Charitable Trusts
The Procter & Gamble Fund
The Prospect Hill Foundation
The Prudential Foundation
Recreational Equipment, Inc.
Z. Smith Reynolds Foundation, Inc.
The Rhode Island Community Foundation
Sid W. Richardson Foundation
Smith Richardson Foundation, Inc.
The Roberts Foundation
Rockefeller Brothers Fund, Inc.
Rockefeller Family Fund, Inc.
Rockefeller Financial Services, Philanthropy Department
The Rockefeller Foundation
The Winthrop Rockefeller Foundation
The Rockfall Foundation
Rockwell Fund, Inc.
Rockwood Fund, Inc.
Samuel and May Rudin Foundation, Inc.
Fran and Warren Rupp Foundation
Sacramento Regional Foundation

Emphases

Nonprofit organizations (cont.)

San Diego Community Foundation
The San Francisco Foundation
The Sapelo Foundation
Sarkeys Foundation
Sarah Scaife Foundation Incorporated
The Scherman Foundation, Inc.
The Schumann Fund for New Jersey, Inc.
The Florence and John Schumann Foundation
Sears-Swetland Foundation
Ralph C. Sheldon Foundation, Inc.
Shell Oil Company Foundation
The Skaggs Foundation
Kelvin Smith 1980 Charitable Trust
Stanley Smith Horticultural Trust
Snee-Reinhardt Charitable Foundation
The Sonoma County Community Foundation
Southwestern Bell Foundation
Springs Foundation, Inc.
Anna B. Stearns Charitable Foundation, Inc.
The Stebbins Fund, Inc.
Stranahan Foundation
The Stratford Foundation
The Stroh Foundation
The Strong Foundation for Environmental Values
The Charles J. Strosacker Foundation
The Morris Stulsaft Foundation
The Sudbury Foundation
The Summerlee Foundation
The Summit Foundation
Surdna Foundation, Inc.
The Switzer Foundation
S. Mark Taper Foundation
The Telesis Foundation
Threshold Foundation
The Tides Foundation
The Tinker Foundation Incorporated
Tortuga Foundation
Town Creek Foundation, Inc.
Toyota USA Foundation
The Travelers Foundation
Harry C. Trexler Trust
The Troy Foundation
True North Foundation
The Trust For Mutual Understanding
Alice Tweed Tuohy Foundation
Turner Foundation, Inc.
The USF&G Foundation, Inc.
USX Foundation, Inc.
Underhill Foundation
Union Camp Charitable Trust
Union Pacific Foundation
Unitarian Universalist Veatch Program at Shelter Rock
United States-Japan Foundation
Vancouver Foundation
R. T. Vanderbilt Trust
Vanguard Public Foundation
G. Unger Vetlesen Foundation
Victoria Foundation, Inc.
Vinmont Foundation, Inc.
Virginia Environmental Endowment
WMX Environmental Grants Program
Wallace Genetic Foundation, Inc.
Lila Wallace-Reader's Digest Fund
C. A. Webster Foundation
Weeden Foundation
Welfare Foundation, Inc.
Westinghouse Foundation
Weyerhaeuser Company Foundation
The William P. Wharton Trust
Whitecap Foundation
Joseph B. Whitehead Foundation
Wilburforce Foundation
G. N. Wilcox Trust
The Windham Foundation, Inc.
Mark and Catherine Winkler Foundation
The Winston-Salem Foundation, Inc.
The Dean Witter Foundation
Wodecroft Foundation
Robert W. Woodruff Foundation, Inc.
The Wortham Foundation, Inc.
Margaret Cullinan Wray Charitable Lead Annuity Trust
Wrinkle in Time Foundation

Operating costs

AT&T Foundation
A Territory Resource
The Abelard Foundation West
The Achelis Foundation
The Acorn Foundation
Alaska Conservation Foundation
American Conservation Association, Inc.
Elmer L. & Eleanor J. Andersen Foundation
Arcadia Foundation
Evenor Armington Fund
The Vincent Astor Foundation
Mary Reynolds Babcock Foundation, Inc.
Clayton Baker Trust
BankAmerica Foundation
The Beinecke Foundation, Inc.
Beldon Fund
The Ben & Jerry's Foundation
The Bersted Foundation
The Betterment Fund
The Blumenthal Foundation
Mary Owen Borden Memorial Foundation
Helen Brach Foundation
The Lynde and Harry Bradley Foundation, Inc.
Otto Bremer Foundation
Alex. Brown & Sons Charitable Foundation, Inc.
Kathleen Price and Joseph M. Bryan Family Foundation, Inc.
The Bullitt Foundation
The Bunbury Company, Inc.
The Bydale Foundation
C. S. Fund
The Louis Calder Foundation
The Cargill Foundation
Caribou Fund
Carolyn Foundation
Mary Flagler Cary Charitable Trust
Centerior Energy Foundation
Chrysler Corporation Fund
Clark Charitable Trust
The Clark Foundation
The Community Foundation Serving Coastal South Carolina
The Conservation and Research Foundation
Adolph Coors Foundation
The Cowles Charitable Trust
The Cricket Foundation
The Mary A. Crocker Trust
Patrick and Anna M. Cudahy Fund
The Nathan Cummings Foundation
The Fred Harris Daniels Foundation, Inc.
Dayton Hudson Foundation
The Nelson B. Delavan Foundation
Geraldine R. Dodge Foundation, Inc.
The Herbert H. and Grace A. Dow Foundation
Eastman Kodak Company Charitable Trust
The Charles Engelhard Foundation
Fanwood Foundation
The Favrot Fund
Jamee and Marshall Field Foundation
Fields Pond Foundation, Inc.
Leland Fikes Foundation, Inc.
Flintridge Foundation
Foundation for Field Research
The Freed Foundation, Inc.
The Gap Foundation
Gebbie Foundation, Inc.
General Service Foundation
Georgia Power Foundation, Inc.
Georgia-Pacific Foundation
Global Greengrants Fund
Richard & Rhoda Goldman Fund
The George Gund Foundation
Hawaii Community Foundation
The Clarence E. Heller Charitable Foundation
The William and Flora Hewlett Foundation
The Homeland Foundation
Hudson-Webber Foundation
The Roy A. Hunt Foundation
The Hyams Foundation
Island Foundation, Inc.
The George Frederick Jewett Foundation
Helen K. and Arthur E. Johnson Foundation
Harris and Eliza Kempner Fund
The Henry P. Kendall Foundation
F. M. Kirby Foundation, Inc.
The Esther A. and Joseph Klingenstein Fund, Inc.
Kongsgaard-Goldman Foundation
Laurel Foundation
The Max and Anna Levinson Foundation
Lilly Endowment, Inc.
Lyndhurst Foundation
The John D. and Catherine T. MacArthur Foundation
James A. Macdonald Foundation
Marbrook Foundation
The Marshall L. & Perrine D. McCune Charitable Foundation
The Eugene McDermott Foundation
McGregor Fund
McKesson Foundation, Inc.

© 1995 Environmental Data Resources, Inc.

Emphases

Operating costs (cont.)

The McKnight Foundation
Richard King Mellon Foundation
The John Merck Fund
Metropolitan Life Foundation
The Moody Foundation
Henry and Lucy Moses Fund, Inc.
Ruth Mott Fund
John P. Murphy Foundation
National Fish and Wildlife Foundation
The Needmor Fund
New Horizon Foundation
Edward John Noble Foundation, Inc.
The Norton Foundation, Inc.
Nicholas H. Noyes, Jr. Memorial Foundation
The Ohrstrom Foundation
Orchard Foundation
The David and Lucile Packard Foundation
The Pfizer Foundation, Inc.
The Philadelphia Foundation
Phillips Petroleum Foundation, Inc.
The Powell Family Foundation
Prince Charitable Trusts
The Procter & Gamble Fund
The Prospect Hill Foundation
The Prudential Foundation
The Rhode Island Community Foundation
Sid W. Richardson Foundation
Rockefeller Financial Services, Philanthropy Department
Rockwell Fund, Inc.
Rockwood Fund, Inc.
The San Francisco Foundation
The Sapelo Foundation
Sarah Scaife Foundation Incorporated
The Scherman Foundation, Inc.
The Schumann Fund for New Jersey, Inc.
Sears-Swetland Foundation
Seventh Generation Fund
Shell Oil Company Foundation
The Skaggs Foundation
The Kelvin and Eleanor Smith Foundation
Kelvin Smith 1980 Charitable Trust
Stanley Smith Horticultural Trust
South Coast Foundation, Inc.
Margaret Dorrance Strawbridge Foundation of Pennsylvania II, Inc.
The Strong Foundation for Environmental Values
The Charles J. Strosacker Foundation
The Morris Stulsaft Foundation
The Sulzberger Foundation, Inc.
The Oakleigh L. Thorne Foundation
Town Creek Foundation, Inc.
The Travelers Foundation
Harry C. Trexler Trust
Rose E. Tucker Charitable Trust
Alice Tweed Tuohy Foundation
The USF&G Foundation, Inc.
USX Foundation, Inc.
Union Camp Charitable Trust
R. T. Vanderbilt Trust
Victoria Foundation, Inc.
The Vidda Foundation
Vinmont Foundation, Inc.
Virginia Environmental Endowment
DeWitt Wallace-Reader's Digest Fund
Welfare Foundation, Inc.
The Windham Foundation, Inc.
Mark and Catherine Winkler Foundation
The Wortham Foundation, Inc.
The Wyomissing Foundation, Inc.

Pilot projects

AT&T Foundation
A Territory Resource
The Abell Foundation
The Jenifer Altman Foundation
Americana Foundation, Inc.
The Vincent Astor Foundation
Mary Reynolds Babcock Foundation, Inc.
The Barra Foundation, Inc.
The Bauman Foundation
Bay Area Community Foundation
The Beirne Carter Foundation
The Betterment Fund
The Blumenthal Foundation
Mary Owen Borden Memorial Foundation
The Bunbury Company, Inc.
C. S. Fund
Caribou Fund
Carolyn Foundation
The Carpenter Foundation
Chesapeake Bay Trust
Claneil Foundation, Inc.
The Clark Foundation
Columbia Foundation
The Community Foundation of Greater New Haven
The Community Foundation of Sarasota County, Inc.
The Community Foundation Serving Coastal South Carolina
The Conservation and Research Foundation
Conservation, Food & Health Foundation, Inc.
Cooke Foundation, Limited
The Cowles Charitable Trust
Jessie B. Cox Charitable Trust
Crystal Channel Foundation
Geraldine R. Dodge Foundation, Inc.
Jessie Ball duPont Religious, Charitable and Educational Fund
Echoing Green Foundation
The Educational Foundation of America
The Energy Foundation
Jamee and Marshall Field Foundation
Foundation for Deep Ecology
Foundation for Field Research
The Frost Foundation, Ltd.
GE Fund
Gebbie Foundation, Inc.
The German Marshall Fund of the United States
Give to the Earth Foundation
Global Environmental Project Institute
Global Greengrants Fund
Richard & Rhoda Goldman Fund
Walter and Duncan Gordon Charitable Foundation
Great Lakes Protection Fund
Greater Piscataqua Community Foundation
The Greenville Foundation
The Hall Family Foundation
Hawaiian Electric Industries Charitable Foundation
The Edward W. Hazen Foundation
Heller Charitable & Educational Fund
The Clarence E. Heller Charitable Foundation
The Homeland Foundation
The Louise H. and David S. Ingalls Foundation, Inc.
Island Foundation, Inc.
Ittleson Foundation, Inc.
The Richard Ivey Foundation
The Henry M. Jackson Foundation
Martha Holden Jennings Foundation
Helen K. and Arthur E. Johnson Foundation
Walter S. Johnson Foundation
The Esther A. and Joseph Klingenstein Fund, Inc.
Laidlaw Foundation
Laurel Foundation
The Lazar Foundation
The Max and Anna Levinson Foundation
Lyndhurst Foundation
Maine Community Foundation, Inc.
The Marshall Fund of Arizona
McGregor Fund
McKesson Foundation, Inc.
The McKnight Foundation
Richard King Mellon Foundation
The John Merck Fund
Metropolitan Life Foundation
Meyer Memorial Trust
The Milwaukee Foundation
The Moody Foundation
The Mountaineers Foundation
John P. Murphy Foundation
New England Biolabs Foundation
New York Foundation
Edward John Noble Foundation, Inc.
Norman Foundation
Andrew Norman Foundation
Mary Moody Northen, Inc.
Jessie Smith Noyes Foundation, Inc.
Ottinger Foundation
The David and Lucile Packard Foundation
Peninsula Community Foundation
The William Penn Foundation
James C. Penney Foundation
Philip Morris Companies, Inc.
The Prospect Hill Foundation
Recreational Equipment, Inc.
Z. Smith Reynolds Foundation, Inc.
The Rhode Island Community Foundation
Rockefeller Financial Services, Philanthropy Department
Rockwell Fund, Inc.
San Diego Community Foundation

Emphases

Pilot projects (cont.)

The San Francisco Foundation
Sarkeys Foundation
The Schiff Foundation
Shell Oil Company Foundation
Thomas Sill Foundation
Stanley Smith Horticultural Trust
The Sonoma County Community
  Foundation
Southwestern Bell Foundation
Springs Foundation, Inc.
Steelcase Foundation
The Strong Foundation for
  Environmental Values
The Sudbury Foundation
The Sulzberger Foundation, Inc.
The Summit Foundation
Surdna Foundation, Inc.
Texaco Foundation
The Tinker Foundation Incorporated
Toyota USA Foundation
Rose E. Tucker Charitable Trust
Alice Tweed Tuohy Foundation
Vancouver Foundation
The Vidda Foundation
Vinmont Foundation, Inc.
Virginia Environmental Endowment
WMX Environmental Grants Program
Westinghouse Foundation
Wilburforce Foundation
The Winston-Salem Foundation, Inc.
The Dean Witter Foundation
Margaret Cullinan Wray Charitable
  Lead Annuity Trust
The Wyomissing Foundation, Inc.

Planning

The Abell Foundation
The Betterment Fund
The Bunbury Company, Inc.
Mary Flagler Cary Charitable Trust
Liz Claiborne & Art Ortenberg Foundation
The Cleveland Foundation
Jessie B. Cox Charitable Trust
The Nathan Cummings Foundation
Geraldine R. Dodge Foundation, Inc.
Jessie Ball duPont Religious, Charitable
  and Educational Fund
The Educational Foundation of America
Samuel S. Fels Fund
The Fred Gellert Foundation
The German Marshall Fund of
  the United States
Walter and Duncan Gordon Charitable
  Foundation
Great Lakes Protection Fund
Evelyn and Walter Haas, Jr. Fund
The John Randolph Haynes and
  Dora Haynes Foundation
The William and Flora Hewlett Foundation
Illilouette Fund
The James Irvine Foundation
The J. M. Kaplan Fund, Inc.
W. K. Kellogg Foundation

Laidlaw Foundation
Laird, Norton Foundation
The Max and Anna Levinson Foundation
McKenzie River Gathering Foundation
The McKnight Foundation
The Milwaukee Foundation
Edward John Noble Foundation, Inc.
Norman Foundation
The David and Lucile Packard Foundation
James C. Penney Foundation
Pew Scholars Program in Conservation
  and the Environment
Ellis L. Phillips Foundation
The Rhode Island Community Foundation
The Winthrop Rockefeller Foundation
The Rockfall Foundation
San Diego Community Foundation
The San Francisco Foundation
Stanley Smith Horticultural Trust
The Strong Foundation for
  Environmental Values
The Sudbury Foundation
Surdna Foundation, Inc.
The Trust For Mutual Understanding
Rose E. Tucker Charitable Trust
Victoria Foundation, Inc.
Virginia Environmental Endowment
Wilburforce Foundation
The Winston-Salem Foundation, Inc.
The Dean Witter Foundation
Margaret Cullinan Wray Charitable
  Lead Annuity Trust
The Wyomissing Foundation, Inc.

Policy analysis/development

ARCO Foundation
AT&T Foundation
The Abelard Foundation West
The Acorn Foundation
Alaska Conservation Foundation
Ameritech Foundation
The Arca Foundation
Mary Reynolds Babcock Foundation, Inc.
The Bauman Foundation
The Betterment Fund
The Lynde and Harry Bradley
  Foundation, Inc.
The Bunbury Company, Inc.
C. S. Fund
The Chevron Companies
Robert Sterling Clark Foundation, Inc.
Columbia Foundation
Compton Foundation, Inc.
Conservation, Food & Health
  Foundation, Inc.
Cooke Foundation, Limited
Jessie B. Cox Charitable Trust
The Nathan Cummings Foundation
Dayton Hudson Foundation
Geraldine R. Dodge Foundation, Inc.
Donner Canadian Foundation
Jessie Ball duPont Religious, Charitable
  and Educational Fund
The Educational Foundation of America
The Energy Foundation

Flintridge Foundation
The Fund for New Jersey
GE Fund
The Fred Gellert Foundation
The Wallace Alexander Gerbode
  Foundation, Inc.
The German Marshall Fund of
  the United States
Richard & Rhoda Goldman Fund
Walter and Duncan Gordon Charitable
  Foundation
Great Lakes Protection Fund
The George Gund Foundation
Evelyn and Walter Haas, Jr. Fund
The John Randolph Haynes and
  Dora Haynes Foundation
The Edward W. Hazen Foundation
The Clarence E. Heller Charitable
  Foundation
The William and Flora Hewlett Foundation
The James Irvine Foundation
Ittleson Foundation, Inc.
The Richard Ivey Foundation
The Henry M. Jackson Foundation
W. Alton Jones Foundation, Inc.
The Joyce Foundation
The J. M. Kaplan Fund, Inc.
Laidlaw Foundation
The Max and Anna Levinson Foundation
The John D. and Catherine T. MacArthur
  Foundation
Maine Community Foundation, Inc.
Marin Community Foundation
McKenzie River Gathering Foundation
The McKnight Foundation
Giles W. and Elise G. Mead Foundation
The John Merck Fund
Joyce Mertz-Gilmore Foundation
The Milwaukee Foundation
The Minneapolis Foundation
Charles Stewart Mott Foundation
Ruth Mott Fund
New York Foundation
Norman Foundation
Northwest Fund for the Environment
Jessie Smith Noyes Foundation, Inc.
The David and Lucile Packard Foundation
James C. Penney Foundation
The Pew Charitable Trusts
Pew Scholars Program in Conservation
  and the Environment
Philip Morris Companies, Inc.
Prince Charitable Trusts
The Prospect Hill Foundation
Z. Smith Reynolds Foundation, Inc.
The Rhode Island Community Foundation
Rockefeller Financial Services,
  Philanthropy Department
The Rockefeller Foundation
The Winthrop Rockefeller Foundation
The San Francisco Foundation
Sarah Scaife Foundation Incorporated
The Schumann Fund for New Jersey, Inc.
The Strong Foundation for
  Environmental Values

Emphases

Policy analysis/development (cont.)

The Sudbury Foundation
The Switzer Foundation
The Tides Foundation
The Tinker Foundation Incorporated
The Trust For Mutual Understanding
Rose E. Tucker Charitable Trust
Unitarian Universalist Veatch Program at Shelter Rock
United States-Japan Foundation
Vancouver Foundation
Virginia Environmental Endowment
WMX Environmental Grants Program
DeWitt Wallace-Reader's Digest Fund
Joseph B. Whitehead Foundation
Robert W. Woodruff Foundation, Inc.
Margaret Cullinan Wray Charitable Lead Annuity Trust
The Wyomissing Foundation, Inc.

Political activities

The Abelard Foundation West
The Acorn Foundation
The Bauman Foundation
Beldon Fund
The Ben & Jerry's Foundation
C. S. Fund
Robert Sterling Clark Foundation, Inc.
Samuel S. Fels Fund
Global Environmental Project Institute
The Greenville Foundation
Island Foundation, Inc.
Kongsgaard-Goldman Foundation
Laidlaw Foundation
Laurel Foundation
The Max and Anna Levinson Foundation
The Needmor Fund
Norman Foundation
Jessie Smith Noyes Foundation, Inc.
Ottinger Foundation
Public Welfare Foundation, Inc.
Recreational Equipment, Inc.
Rockefeller Family Fund, Inc.
Rockwood Fund, Inc.
The Sapelo Foundation
The Strong Foundation for Environmental Values
Surdna Foundation, Inc.
The Tides Foundation

Pre-selected organizations

Airport Business Center Foundation
American Foundation Corporation
Evenor Armington Fund
Atlantic Foundation
The Austin Memorial Foundation
The Cameron Baird Foundation
The Bauman Foundation
The Howard Bayne Fund
L. L. Bean, Inc.
S. D. Bechtel, Jr. Foundation
Benton Foundation
Benua Foundation, Inc.
Bishop Pine Fund

The Buchanan Family Foundation
J. E. & Z. B. Butler Foundation, Inc.
Changing Horizons Charitable Trust
Cox Foundation, Inc.
Roy E. Crummer Foundation
Dart Foundation
Oliver S. and Jennie R. Donaldson Charitable Trust
Jessie Ball duPont Religious, Charitable and Educational Fund
Echoing Green Foundation
Arthur M. and Olga T. Eisig-Arthur M. and Kate E. Tode Foundation, Inc.
The Emerald Foundation
The Charles Engelhard Foundation
English-Bonter-Mitchell Foundation
Environment Now Foundation
Felburn Foundation
Fieldstead Charitable Trust
Walter and Josephine Ford Fund
The Rollin M. Gerstacker Foundation
Bernard F. and Alva B. Gimbel Foundation, Inc.
Give to the Earth Foundation
Global Greengrants Fund
Harbor Lights Foundation
The Harding Educational and Charitable Foundation
The M. A. Healy Family Foundation, Inc.
The Horn Foundation
Hurdle Hill Foundation
Ililouette Fund
Island Foundation
The Robert S. and Grayce B. Kerr Foundation, Inc.
Kinnoull Foundation
LaSalle Adams Fund
The Norman Lear Foundation
Levi Strauss Foundation
LifeWorks Foundation
Richard Lounsbery Foundation, Inc.
Luster Family Foundation, Inc.
James A. Macdonald Foundation
Nelson Mead Fund
The John Merck Fund
Middlecott Foundation
The Curtis and Edith Munson Foundation, Inc.
Andrew Norman Foundation
The Ohrstrom Foundation
James C. Penney Foundation
Pew Scholars Program in Conservation and the Environment
Pilot Trust
Pinewood Foundation
Pritzker Foundation
Lee Romney Foundation, Inc.
Sacharuna Foundation
Sarah I. Schieffelin Residuary Trust
The Schiff Foundation
Ellen Browning Scripps Foundation
Frances Seebe Trust
Elmina B. Sewall Foundation
Ralph C. Sheldon Foundation, Inc.
South Coast Foundation, Inc.

Sproul Foundation
Alfred T. Stanley Foundation
Stroud Foundation
The Summit Foundation
Thanksgiving Foundation
Tortuga Foundation
The Truland Foundation
Marcia Brady Tucker Foundation
Bill & Edith Walter Foundation
Henry E. and Consuelo S. Wenger Foundation, Inc.
Robert W. Wilson Foundation
The Winslow Foundation
Sidney & Phyllis Wragge Foundation

Professorships

The George I. Alden Trust
The Lynde and Harry Bradley Foundation, Inc.
The Cowles Charitable Trust
The Fred Harris Daniels Foundation, Inc.
Leland Fikes Foundation, Inc.
Georgia Power Foundation, Inc.
Georgia-Pacific Foundation
Harris and Eliza Kempner Fund
Larsen Fund, Inc.
Lintilhac Foundation
Henry and Lucy Moses Fund, Inc.
John P. Murphy Foundation
Mary Moody Northen, Inc.
The Pfizer Foundation, Inc.
Phillips Petroleum Foundation, Inc.
Sid W. Richardson Foundation
The Schiff Foundation
Shell Oil Company Foundation
The Sulzberger Foundation, Inc.
Mark and Catherine Winkler Foundation

Program-related investments

AT&T Foundation
The Abell Foundation
The Jenifer Altman Foundation
Mary Reynolds Babcock Foundation, Inc.
Otto Bremer Foundation
Kathleen Price and Joseph M. Bryan Family Foundation, Inc.
California Community Foundation
The Carpenter Foundation
Chesapeake Corporation Foundation
Ford Foundation
The Wallace Alexander Gerbode Foundation, Inc.
Walter and Duncan Gordon Charitable Foundation
The Hall Family Foundation
Howard Heinz Endowment
The Hitachi Foundation
The James Irvine Foundation
Island Foundation, Inc.
The J. M. Kaplan Fund, Inc.
The Helen & Milton Kimmelman Foundation
Laird, Norton Foundation
James A. Macdonald Foundation

Emphases

Program-related investments (cont.)
Maine Community Foundation, Inc.
The Curtis and Edith Munson Foundation, Inc.
John P. Murphy Foundation
The New World Foundation
Northwest Area Foundation
Jessie Smith Noyes Foundation, Inc.
The David and Lucile Packard Foundation
The Rhode Island Community Foundation
Sid W. Richardson Foundation
The San Francisco Foundation
The Sapelo Foundation
The Scherman Foundation, Inc.
The Skaggs Foundation
The Sudbury Foundation
The Sulzberger Foundation, Inc.
Texaco Foundation
The Tides Foundation
Union Pacific Foundation
Vancouver Foundation
Virginia Environmental Endowment

Projects
The Ahmanson Foundation
Alaska Conservation Foundation
American Conservation Association, Inc.
American Express Philanthropic Program
Americana Foundation, Inc.
Ameritech Foundation
Elmer L. & Eleanor J. Andersen Foundation
Arcadia Foundation
Evenor Armington Fund
The Vincent Astor Foundation
Atherton Family Foundation
Azadoutioun Foundation
Mary Reynolds Babcock Foundation, Inc.
Clayton Baker Trust
BankAmerica Foundation
The Barra Foundation, Inc.
Beldon Fund
The Ben & Jerry's Foundation
The Frank Stanley Beveridge Foundation, Inc.
Botwinick-Wolfensohn Foundation, Inc.
Helen Brach Foundation
The Robert Brownlee Foundation
The Bullitt Foundation
The Bunbury Company, Inc.
The Morris and Gwendolyn Cafritz Foundation
California Community Foundation
James & Abigail Campbell Foundation
The Cargill Foundation
Carolyn Foundation
Centerior Energy Foundation
Chesapeake Bay Trust
Chrysler Corporation Fund
Claneil Foundation, Inc.
Olive B. Cole Foundation
Columbia Foundation
Compton Foundation, Inc.
The Conservation and Research Foundation

Conservation, Food & Health Foundation, Inc.
Cooke Foundation, Limited
Adolph Coors Foundation
S. H. Cowell Foundation
Jessie B. Cox Charitable Trust
The Cricket Foundation
Charles E. Culpeper Foundation, Inc.
Damien Foundation
The Fred Harris Daniels Foundation, Inc.
The Aaron Diamond Foundation
Samuel S. Fels Fund
Fields Pond Foundation, Inc.
Leland Fikes Foundation, Inc.
Flintridge Foundation
Foundation for Deep Ecology
The Foundation for the National Capital Region
Lloyd A. Fry Foundation
GE Fund
The Fred Gellert Foundation
General Service Foundation
Georgia-Pacific Foundation
Give to the Earth Foundation
Global Environmental Project Institute
The Golden Rule Foundation, Inc.
Great Lakes Protection Fund
Greater Piscataqua Community Foundation
The Greenville Foundation
The George Gund Foundation
Evelyn and Walter Haas, Jr. Fund
The Hahn Family Foundation
The Hamer Foundation
Mary W. Harriman Foundation
Hawaiian Electric Industries Charitable Foundation
The John Randolph Haynes and Dora Haynes Foundation
Howard Heinz Endowment
The Hofmann Foundation
The International Foundation, Inc.
Island Foundation, Inc.
The Henry M. Jackson Foundation
The George Frederick Jewett Foundation
W. K. Kellogg Foundation
Harris and Eliza Kempner Fund
The Henry P. Kendall Foundation
F. M. Kirby Foundation, Inc.
Laidlaw Foundation
Laurel Foundation
The Lazar Foundation
The Max and Anna Levinson Foundation
The McConnell Foundation
McCune Foundation
The Marshall L. & Perrine D. McCune Charitable Foundation
McDonnell Douglas Foundation
McGregor Fund
McKenzie River Gathering Foundation
McKesson Foundation, Inc.
The McKnight Foundation
The John Merck Fund
Meyer Memorial Trust
The Milwaukee Foundation

Charles Stewart Mott Foundation
The Curtis and Edith Munson Foundation, Inc.
M. J. Murdock Charitable Trust
John P. Murphy Foundation
National Fish and Wildlife Foundation
New Hampshire Charitable Foundation
New Horizon Foundation
The New World Foundation
The New-Land Foundation, Inc.
Norcross Wildlife Foundation, Inc.
The Nord Family Foundation
Norman Foundation
The Norton Foundation, Inc.
Jessie Smith Noyes Foundation, Inc.
OCRI Foundation
Orchard Foundation
Outdoor Industry Conservation Alliance
Peninsula Community Foundation
The Pfizer Foundation, Inc.
The Philadelphia Foundation
The Prudential Foundation
Public Welfare Foundation, Inc.
Recreational Equipment, Inc.
The Rhode Island Community Foundation
The Roberts Foundation
Rockefeller Financial Services, Philanthropy Department
The Rockefeller Foundation
Rockwood Fund, Inc.
Fran and Warren Rupp Foundation
San Diego Community Foundation
The San Francisco Foundation
Sarkeys Foundation
Sarah Scaife Foundation Incorporated
Sears-Swetland Foundation
Sequoia Foundation
Shell Oil Company Foundation
The Kelvin and Eleanor Smith Foundation
Kelvin Smith 1980 Charitable Trust
The Sonoma County Community Foundation
South Coast Foundation, Inc.
Springs Foundation, Inc.
Stackner Family Foundation, Inc.
Anna B. Stearns Charitable Foundation, Inc.
The Charles J. Strosacker Foundation
The Morris Stulsaft Foundation
The Switzer Foundation
S. Mark Taper Foundation
The Oakleigh L. Thorne Foundation
The Tides Foundation
The Tinker Foundation Incorporated
Town Creek Foundation, Inc.
Toyota USA Foundation
The Travelers Foundation
The Trust For Mutual Understanding
The USF&G Foundation, Inc.
USX Foundation, Inc.
Union Camp Charitable Trust
Union Pacific Foundation
R. T. Vanderbilt Trust
Vanguard Public Foundation
G. Unger Vetlesen Foundation

© 1995 Environmental Data Resources, Inc.

Emphases

Projects (cont.)

Victoria Foundation, Inc.
WMX Environmental Grants Program
Wallace Genetic Foundation, Inc.
DeWitt Wallace-Reader's Digest Fund
Lila Wallace-Reader's Digest Fund
Whitecap Foundation
The Windham Foundation, Inc.
Margaret Cullinan Wray Charitable
   Lead Annuity Trust
Wrinkle in Time Foundation
The Wyomissing Foundation, Inc.

Public agencies

The Beinecke Foundation, Inc.
Otto Bremer Foundation
Chesapeake Bay Trust
Robert Sterling Clark Foundation, Inc.
The Cleveland Foundation
Olive B. Cole Foundation
The James M. Cox, Jr. Foundation, Inc.
Patrick and Anna M. Cudahy Fund
Dayton Hudson Foundation
The Educational Foundation of America
Environmental Education Foundation
   of Florida, Inc.
FishAmerica Foundation
Georgia Power Foundation, Inc.
The German Marshall Fund of
   the United States
Walter and Duncan Gordon Charitable
   Foundation
The George Gund Foundation
Charles Hayden Foundation
Hudson-Webber Foundation
The Henry M. Jackson Foundation
Martha Holden Jennings Foundation
W. K. Kellogg Foundation
The John D. and Catherine T. MacArthur
   Foundation
Maine Community Foundation, Inc.
Maki Foundation
Marin Community Foundation
Massachusetts Environmental Trust
The McConnell Foundation
The McKnight Foundation
Meadows Foundation, Inc.
Richard King Mellon Foundation
Meyer Memorial Trust
Millbrook Tribute Garden, Inc.
The Milwaukee Foundation
National Fish and Wildlife Foundation
The New World Foundation
New York Foundation
Edward John Noble Foundation, Inc.
Peninsula Community Foundation
The William Penn Foundation
Perkins Charitable Foundation
Z. Smith Reynolds Foundation, Inc.
Sid W. Richardson Foundation
The Rockefeller Foundation
San Diego Community Foundation
The San Francisco Foundation
The Sapelo Foundation

The Switzer Foundation
Virginia Environmental Endowment
Robert W. Woodruff Foundation, Inc.
The Wyomissing Foundation, Inc.

Publications

A Territory Resource
Alaska Conservation Foundation
The George I. Alden Trust
American Conservation Association, Inc.
Elmer L. & Eleanor J. Andersen Foundation
Evenor Armington Fund
Atherton Family Foundation
The Barra Foundation, Inc.
Bay Area Community Foundation
L. L. Bean, Inc.
The Beinecke Foundation, Inc.
Benton Foundation
Helen Brach Foundation
The Lynde and Harry Bradley
   Foundation, Inc.
The Bunbury Company, Inc.
The Bydale Foundation
C. S. Fund
Caribou Fund
Chesapeake Bay Trust
Claneil Foundation, Inc.
Robert Sterling Clark Foundation, Inc.
The Columbus Foundation
Geraldine R. Dodge Foundation, Inc.
Dolfinger-McMahon Foundation
Fields Pond Foundation, Inc.
The Freed Foundation, Inc.
GE Fund
Global Greengrants Fund
Walter and Duncan Gordon Charitable
   Foundation
The George Gund Foundation
James G. Hanes Memorial Fund
The William and Flora Hewlett Foundation
IBM Corporation
The International Foundation, Inc.
Island Foundation
Jackson Hole Preserve, Inc.
The Henry M. Jackson Foundation
Harris and Eliza Kempner Fund
The Henry P. Kendall Foundation
The Esther A. and Joseph Klingenstein
   Fund, Inc.
Laidlaw Foundation
Laird, Norton Foundation
Laurel Foundation
The Max and Anna Levinson Foundation
McKenzie River Gathering Foundation
Metropolitan Life Foundation
The Mountaineers Foundation
John P. Murphy Foundation
The National Environmental Education
   and Training Foundation, Inc.
National Fish and Wildlife Foundation
Norcross Wildlife Foundation, Inc.
The Nord Family Foundation
Norman Foundation
Kenneth T. and Eileen L. Norris Foundation

Pew Scholars Program in Conservation
   and the Environment
The Pfizer Foundation, Inc.
The Rockfall Foundation
Rockwell Fund, Inc.
Sarah Scaife Foundation Incorporated
The Skaggs Foundation
Stanley Smith Horticultural Trust
The Strong Foundation for
   Environmental Values
The Summerlee Foundation
The Oakleigh L. Thorne Foundation
Rose E. Tucker Charitable Trust
The USF&G Foundation, Inc.
Vanguard Public Foundation
WMX Environmental Grants Program
The William P. Wharton Trust
The Dean Witter Foundation
Robert W. Woodruff Foundation, Inc.
Margaret Cullinan Wray Charitable
   Lead Annuity Trust

Religious organizations

Atherton Family Foundation
Atkinson Foundation
The Bersted Foundation
The Collins Foundation
The Herbert H. and Grace A. Dow
   Foundation
The W. C. Griffith Foundation
The Merrill G. & Emita E. Hastings
   Foundation
The Edward W. Hazen Foundation
Howard Heinz Endowment
Vira I. Heinz Endowment
The Howard Johnson Foundation
F. M. Kirby Foundation, Inc.
The Seymour H. Knox Foundation, Inc.
OCRI Foundation
Samuel and May Rudin Foundation, Inc.
The Vidda Foundation

Research

The Achelis Foundation
The George I. Alden Trust
Ameritech Foundation
Arcadia Foundation
Evenor Armington Fund
Atherton Family Foundation
The Bailey Wildlife Foundation
Baltimore Gas and Electric Foundation, Inc.
The Barra Foundation, Inc.
The Bauman Foundation
Bay Area Community Foundation
The Bay Foundation
Botwinick-Wolfensohn Foundation, Inc.
Helen Brach Foundation
The Lynde and Harry Bradley
   Foundation, Inc.
The Bydale Foundation
C. S. Fund
The Cape Branch Foundation
Liz Claiborne & Art Ortenberg Foundation
The Cricket Foundation

Emphases

Research (cont.)

The Fred Harris Daniels Foundation, Inc.
The Arthur Vining Davis Foundations
Davis Conservation Foundation
Donner Canadian Foundation
Douroucouli Foundation
The Herbert H. and Grace A. Dow Foundation
The Max and Victoria Dreyfus Foundation, Inc.
The Energy Foundation
Environmental Endowment for New Jersey, Inc.
Leland Fikes Foundation, Inc.
The Frost Foundation, Ltd.
The Fund for New Jersey
GE Fund
Georgia Power Foundation, Inc.
Walter and Duncan Gordon Charitable Foundation
James G. Hanes Memorial Fund
Mary W. Harriman Foundation
Hawaii Community Foundation
The Edward W. Hazen Foundation
Howard Heinz Endowment
The Clarence E. Heller Charitable Foundation
The Hofmann Foundation
Joy Foundation for Ecological Education and Research
Harris and Eliza Kempner Fund
The Henry P. Kendall Foundation
Caesar Kleberg Foundation for Wildlife Conservation
Charles G. Koch Charitable Foundation
Laird, Norton Foundation
LaSalle Adams Fund
Laurel Foundation
The Max and Anna Levinson Foundation
Lilly Endowment, Inc.
Lintilhac Foundation
Longwood Foundation, Inc.
The John D. and Catherine T. MacArthur Foundation
Mars Foundation
Massachusetts Environmental Trust
The Marshall L. & Perrine D. McCune Charitable Foundation
Giles W. and Elise G. Mead Foundation
Richard King Mellon Foundation
Metropolitan Life Foundation
Mobil Foundation, Inc.
The Moody Foundation
Henry and Lucy Moses Fund, Inc.
The Mountaineers Foundation
M. J. Murdock Charitable Trust
The National Environmental Education and Training Foundation, Inc.
Edward John Noble Foundation, Inc.
The Samuel Roberts Noble Foundation, Inc.
Norman Foundation
Mary Moody Northen, Inc.
Spencer T. and Ann W. Olin Foundation
Pew Scholars Program in Conservation and the Environment

The Pfizer Foundation, Inc.
Phillips Petroleum Foundation, Inc.
Smith Richardson Foundation, Inc.
Rockwell Fund, Inc.
San Diego Community Foundation
Sarkeys Foundation
Sarah Scaife Foundation Incorporated
S. H. and Helen R. Scheuer Family Foundation, Inc.
Sears-Swetland Foundation
Thomas Sill Foundation
Southwestern Bell Foundation
Stackner Family Foundation, Inc.
The Stratford Foundation
The Strong Foundation for Environmental Values
Edna Bailey Sussman Fund
Texaco Foundation
The Oakleigh L. Thorne Foundation
The Tinker Foundation Incorporated
Union Camp Charitable Trust
Vancouver Foundation
G. Unger Vetlesen Foundation
The Vidda Foundation
Alex C. Walker Educational & Charitable Foundation
The William P. Wharton Trust
Mark and Catherine Winkler Foundation
The Dean Witter Foundation
Margaret Cullinan Wray Charitable Lead Annuity Trust

Research (medical, scholarly, and/or scientific)

AT&T Foundation
The Bersted Foundation
The Betterment Fund
The Cabot Family Charitable Trust
Mary Flagler Cary Charitable Trust
The Chevron Companies
Compton Foundation, Inc.
The Conservation and Research Foundation
Conservation, Food & Health Foundation, Inc.
Crystal Channel Foundation
Foundation for Field Research
The GAR Foundation
The John Randolph Haynes and Dora Haynes Foundation
The Homeland Foundation
The Louise H. and David S. Ingalls Foundation, Inc.
The International Foundation, Inc.
Island Foundation, Inc.
Ittleson Foundation, Inc.
The Richard Ivey Foundation
The Henry M. Jackson Foundation
W. Alton Jones Foundation, Inc.
F. M. Kirby Foundation, Inc.
The Esther A. and Joseph Klingenstein Fund, Inc.
Laidlaw Foundation
The Andrew W. Mellon Foundation
John P. Murphy Foundation
New England Biolabs Foundation

Nathan M. Ohrbach Foundation, Inc.
Amelia Peabody Charitable Fund
The Perkin Fund
Philip Morris Companies, Inc.
Sid W. Richardson Foundation
Shell Oil Company Foundation
Stanley Smith Horticultural Trust
Margaret Dorrance Strawbridge Foundation of Pennsylvania II, Inc.
The Summerlee Foundation
The Trust For Mutual Understanding
Wallace Genetic Foundation, Inc.
Robert W. Woodruff Foundation, Inc.

Research institutions

The Abell Foundation
The Jenifer Altman Foundation
Bay Area Community Foundation
The Beinecke Foundation, Inc.
The Beirne Carter Foundation
Ruth H. Brown Foundation
Chesapeake Bay Trust
Claneil Foundation, Inc.
Robert Sterling Clark Foundation, Inc.
Conservation, Food & Health Foundation, Inc.
The James M. Cox, Jr. Foundation, Inc.
Crystal Channel Foundation
The Nathan Cummings Foundation
Geraldine R. Dodge Foundation, Inc.
The Educational Foundation of America
The Frost Foundation, Ltd.
GE Fund
Georgia Power Foundation, Inc.
Walter and Duncan Gordon Charitable Foundation
Great Lakes Protection Fund
The George Gund Foundation
The John Randolph Haynes and Dora Haynes Foundation
The Clarence E. Heller Charitable Foundation
Island Foundation, Inc.
The Henry M. Jackson Foundation
The Henry P. Kendall Foundation
The Esther A. and Joseph Klingenstein Fund, Inc.
The Kresge Foundation
Laidlaw Foundation
The Max and Anna Levinson Foundation
The John D. and Catherine T. MacArthur Foundation
MARPAT Foundation, Inc.
The Andrew W. Mellon Foundation
Richard King Mellon Foundation
Meyer Memorial Trust
The Milwaukee Foundation
Mobil Foundation, Inc.
The Moody Foundation
National Fish and Wildlife Foundation
Edward John Noble Foundation, Inc.
Mary Moody Northen, Inc.
Nathan M. Ohrbach Foundation, Inc.
Amelia Peabody Charitable Fund
Philip Morris Companies, Inc.

Emphases

Research institutions (cont.)

Sid W. Richardson Foundation
The Rockefeller Foundation
Rockwood Fund, Inc.
San Diego Community Foundation
The San Francisco Foundation
Sarkeys Foundation
Sears-Swetland Foundation
Shell Oil Company Foundation
Stanley Smith Horticultural Trust
The Tinker Foundation Incorporated
The Trust For Mutual Understanding
United States-Japan Foundation
G. Unger Vetlesen Foundation
Weyerhaeuser Company Foundation
Joseph B. Whitehead Foundation
The Dean Witter Foundation
Robert W. Woodruff Foundation, Inc.
Margaret Cullinan Wray Charitable Lead Annuity Trust

Scholarships

AT&T Foundation
Abell-Hanger Foundation
The Ahmanson Foundation
Alaska Conservation Foundation
The George I. Alden Trust
American Express Philanthropic Program
Atherton Family Foundation
Bay Area Community Foundation
Botwinick-Wolfensohn Foundation, Inc.
The Lynde and Harry Bradley Foundation, Inc.
Alex. Brown & Sons Charitable Foundation, Inc.
The Bunbury Company, Inc.
C. S. Fund
The Morris and Gwendolyn Cafritz Foundation
The Louis Calder Foundation
James & Abigail Campbell Foundation
The Cape Branch Foundation
Ben B. Cheney Foundation
Chesapeake Corporation Foundation
Chrysler Corporation Fund
Liz Claiborne & Art Ortenberg Foundation
Clark Charitable Trust
The Clark Foundation
Olive B. Cole Foundation
The Collins Foundation
The Community Foundation of Greater New Haven
Community Foundation of Western North Carolina, Inc.
Patrick and Anna M. Cudahy Fund
The Fred Harris Daniels Foundation, Inc.
Dolfinger-McMahon Foundation
Jessie Ball duPont Religious, Charitable and Educational Fund
Eastman Kodak Company Charitable Trust
The Ettinger Foundation, Inc.
Leland Fikes Foundation, Inc.
Ford Motor Company Fund
Foundation for Field Research

Foundation for the Carolinas
Georgia Power Foundation, Inc.
Georgia-Pacific Foundation
The Hamer Foundation
Hawaii Community Foundation
Hawaiian Electric Industries Charitable Foundation
The John Randolph Haynes and Dora Haynes Foundation
The Hofmann Foundation
The Henry M. Jackson Foundation
Helen K. and Arthur E. Johnson Foundation
Harris and Eliza Kempner Fund
Charles G. Koch Charitable Foundation
Larsen Fund, Inc.
Lilly Endowment, Inc.
Lintilhac Foundation
The John D. and Catherine T. MacArthur Foundation
James A. Macdonald Foundation
The Martin Foundation, Inc.
The McConnell Foundation
The Marshall L. & Perrine D. McCune Charitable Foundation
McDonnell Douglas Foundation
Richard King Mellon Foundation
Metropolitan Life Foundation
Millbrook Tribute Garden, Inc.
Mobil Foundation, Inc.
Henry and Lucy Moses Fund, Inc.
New Hampshire Charitable Foundation
The Samuel Roberts Noble Foundation, Inc.
Kenneth T. and Eileen L. Norris Foundation
The Norton Foundation, Inc.
Nicholas H. Noyes, Jr. Memorial Foundation
The Pfizer Foundation, Inc.
Phillips Petroleum Foundation, Inc.
The Powell Family Foundation
Rockwell Fund, Inc.
Sarkeys Foundation
S. H. and Helen R. Scheuer Family Foundation, Inc.
Shell Oil Company Foundation
Springs Foundation, Inc.
Steelcase Foundation
The Sulzberger Foundation, Inc.
Texaco Foundation
Rose E. Tucker Charitable Trust
USX Foundation, Inc.
Underhill Foundation
Union Camp Charitable Trust
Union Pacific Foundation
DeWitt Wallace-Reader's Digest Fund
Westinghouse Foundation
The Winston-Salem Foundation, Inc.

Seed money

A Territory Resource
The Abelard Foundation West
The Abell Foundation
Abell-Hanger Foundation
The George I. Alden Trust
The Jenifer Altman Foundation
American Express Philanthropic Program

The Vincent Astor Foundation
Atherton Family Foundation
Atkinson Foundation
Mary Reynolds Babcock Foundation, Inc.
Clayton Baker Trust
The Frank Stanley Beveridge Foundation, Inc.
The Blumenthal Foundation
Botwinick-Wolfensohn Foundation, Inc.
Otto Bremer Foundation
Ruth H. Brown Foundation
The Bunbury Company, Inc.
The Bydale Foundation
The Cabot Family Charitable Trust
California Community Foundation
James & Abigail Campbell Foundation
Caribou Fund
Carolyn Foundation
The Carpenter Foundation
Ben B. Cheney Foundation
Chesapeake Bay Trust
Liz Claiborne & Art Ortenberg Foundation
Claneil Foundation, Inc.
The Clark Foundation
The Cleveland Foundation
Columbia Foundation
The Columbus Foundation
The Community Foundation of Greater New Haven
The Community Foundation of Santa Clara County
The Community Foundation Serving Coastal South Carolina
Community Foundation of Western North Carolina, Inc.
The Conservation and Research Foundation
Conservation, Food & Health Foundation, Inc.
Cooke Foundation, Limited
Adolph Coors Foundation
The Cowles Charitable Trust
Jessie B. Cox Charitable Trust
Crystal Channel Foundation
Patrick and Anna M. Cudahy Fund
Damien Foundation
Geraldine R. Dodge Foundation, Inc.
Dolfinger-McMahon Foundation
Donner Canadian Foundation
The Herbert H. and Grace A. Dow Foundation
The Elizabeth Ordway Dunn Foundation, Inc.
Jessie Ball duPont Religious, Charitable and Educational Fund
Echoing Green Foundation
The Educational Foundation of America
El Paso Community Foundation
Jamee and Marshall Field Foundation
Fields Pond Foundation, Inc.
The 1525 Foundation
Leland Fikes Foundation, Inc.
Foundation for the Carolinas
The Foundation for the National Capital Region
The Frost Foundation, Ltd.

Emphases

Seed money (cont.)

Lloyd A. Fry Foundation
The GAR Foundation
GE Fund
Gebbie Foundation, Inc.
The Fred Gellert Foundation
Georgia Power Foundation, Inc.
Georgia-Pacific Foundation
The German Marshall Fund of the United States
Global Greengrants Fund
Richard & Rhoda Goldman Fund
Good Samaritan, Inc.
Walter and Duncan Gordon Charitable Foundation
The Greenville Foundation
The William and Mary Greve Foundation, Inc.
The Hahn Family Foundation
James G. Hanes Memorial Fund
Hartford Foundation for Public Giving
Hawaii Community Foundation
Hawaiian Electric Industries Charitable Foundation
Charles Hayden Foundation
The Edward W. Hazen Foundation
Howard Heinz Endowment
Vira I. Heinz Endowment
Heller Charitable & Educational Fund
The Clarence E. Heller Charitable Foundation
The Homeland Foundation
Hudson-Webber Foundation
The International Foundation, Inc.
Island Foundation
Ittleson Foundation, Inc.
The Richard Ivey Foundation
The Henry M. Jackson Foundation
Martha Holden Jennings Foundation
Helen K. and Arthur E. Johnson Foundation
Walter S. Johnson Foundation
Harris and Eliza Kempner Fund
The Henry P. Kendall Foundation
F. M. Kirby Foundation, Inc.
The Esther A. and Joseph Klingenstein Fund, Inc.
Kongsgaard-Goldman Foundation
The Lazar Foundation
The Max and Anna Levinson Foundation
Lilly Endowment, Inc.
Lintilhac Foundation
Richard Lounsbery Foundation, Inc.
Lyndhurst Foundation
James A. Macdonald Foundation
Maine Community Foundation, Inc.
The Marshall Fund of Arizona
The Marshall L. & Perrine D. McCune Charitable Foundation
McGregor Fund
McKenzie River Gathering Foundation
The McKnight Foundation
Giles W. and Elise G. Mead Foundation
Richard King Mellon Foundation
The John Merck Fund
Metropolitan Life Foundation

Meyer Memorial Trust
The Milwaukee Foundation
The Moody Foundation
Ruth Mott Fund
The Mountaineers Foundation
M. J. Murdock Charitable Trust
The Needmor Fund
New England Biolabs Foundation
The New World Foundation
New York Foundation
The Samuel Roberts Noble Foundation, Inc.
The Nord Family Foundation
Norman Foundation
Andrew Norman Foundation
The Norton Foundation, Inc.
OCRI Foundation
The Ohrstrom Foundation
Orchard Foundation
The William Penn Foundation
James C. Penney Foundation
The Pfizer Foundation, Inc.
The Philadelphia Foundation
Phillips Petroleum Foundation, Inc.
The Prudential Foundation
Recreational Equipment, Inc.
The Rhode Island Community Foundation
Rockwood Fund, Inc.
San Diego Community Foundation
The San Francisco Foundation
The Sapelo Foundation
Sarah Scaife Foundation Incorporated
The Scherman Foundation, Inc.
The Schumann Fund for New Jersey, Inc.
Sears-Swetland Foundation
Thomas Sill Foundation
The Skaggs Foundation
The Kelvin and Eleanor Smith Foundation
Stanley Smith Horticultural Trust
The Sonoma County Community Foundation
Southwestern Bell Foundation
Springs Foundation, Inc.
Stackner Family Foundation, Inc.
Steelcase Foundation
The Charles J. Strosacker Foundation
The Morris Stulsaft Foundation
The Sudbury Foundation
The Sulzberger Foundation, Inc.
The Summit Foundation
Surdna Foundation, Inc.
S. Mark Taper Foundation
The Oakleigh L. Thorne Foundation
The USF&G Foundation, Inc.
Union Camp Charitable Trust
Virginia Environmental Endowment
Wilburforce Foundation
The Windham Foundation, Inc.
The Winston-Salem Foundation, Inc.
Margaret Cullinan Wray Charitable Lead Annuity Trust
Wrinkle in Time Foundation
The Wyomissing Foundation, Inc.

Seminars

AT&T Foundation

The George I. Alden Trust
American Conservation Association, Inc.
Ameritech Foundation
The Arca Foundation
Baltimore Gas and Electric Foundation, Inc.
Bay Area Community Foundation
The Beinecke Foundation, Inc.
The Lynde and Harry Bradley Foundation, Inc.
The Bydale Foundation
C. S. Fund
Claneil Foundation, Inc.
Dolfinger-McMahon Foundation
Georgia Power Foundation, Inc.
Georgia-Pacific Foundation
The George Gund Foundation
Hawaii Community Foundation
Island Foundation, Inc.
The Henry M. Jackson Foundation
Martha Holden Jennings Foundation
Harris and Eliza Kempner Fund
The Henry P. Kendall Foundation
The Esther A. and Joseph Klingenstein Fund, Inc.
Laird, Norton Foundation
Lilly Endowment, Inc.
Lintilhac Foundation
The Marshall L. & Perrine D. McCune Charitable Foundation
The Milwaukee Foundation
The Mountaineers Foundation
National Fish and Wildlife Foundation
Pew Scholars Program in Conservation and the Environment
The Pfizer Foundation, Inc.
Phillips Petroleum Foundation, Inc.
The Prudential Foundation
Sarah Scaife Foundation Incorporated
Thomas Sill Foundation
Southwestern Bell Foundation
The Sulzberger Foundation, Inc.
The Summerlee Foundation
The Tinker Foundation Incorporated
The Trust For Mutual Understanding
Rose E. Tucker Charitable Trust
Underhill Foundation

Single-year grants only

The Abell Foundation
The Vincent Astor Foundation
The Ben & Jerry's Foundation
The Bullitt Foundation
Patrick and Aimee Butler Family Foundation
Carolyn Foundation
Claneil Foundation, Inc.
The Community Foundation of Santa Clara County
The Community Foundation Serving Coastal South Carolina
Conservation, Food & Health Foundation, Inc.
Cooke Foundation, Limited
The Nathan Cummings Foundation
Deer Creek Foundation

© 1995 Environmental Data Resources, Inc.

Emphases

Single-year grants only (cont.)

FishAmerica Foundation
Foundation for the Carolinas
The GAR Foundation
Global Environmental Project Institute
Walter and Elise Haas Fund
Helen K. and Arthur E. Johnson Foundation
Laird, Norton Foundation
The McConnell Foundation
McKenzie River Gathering Foundation
McKesson Foundation, Inc.
Metropolitan Atlanta Community Foundation, Inc.
The Minneapolis Foundation
Amelia Peabody Charitable Fund
Peninsula Community Foundation
Recreational Equipment, Inc.
Rockwood Fund, Inc.
San Diego Community Foundation
Stanley Smith Horticultural Trust
The Sonoma County Community Foundation
Springs Foundation, Inc.
The Strong Foundation for Environmental Values
The Tides Foundation
United States-Japan Foundation
The William P. Wharton Trust
Joseph B. Whitehead Foundation
Wilburforce Foundation
Margaret Cullinan Wray Charitable Lead Annuity Trust

Start-up costs

The Vincent Astor Foundation
Mary Reynolds Babcock Foundation, Inc.
The Bullitt Foundation
The Bunbury Company, Inc.
Carolyn Foundation
The Cleveland Foundation
Columbia Foundation
The Community Foundation of Greater New Haven
The Community Foundation Serving Coastal South Carolina
The Conservation and Research Foundation
Conservation, Food & Health Foundation, Inc.
Cooke Foundation, Limited
Jessie B. Cox Charitable Trust
Jessie Ball duPont Religious, Charitable and Educational Fund
Samuel S. Fels Fund
The Frost Foundation, Ltd.
Gebbie Foundation, Inc.
Global Environmental Project Institute
Greater Piscataqua Community Foundation
The George Gund Foundation
Evelyn and Walter Haas, Jr. Fund
Island Foundation, Inc.
The Richard Ivey Foundation
The Max and Anna Levinson Foundation
The Martin Foundation, Inc.
McKenzie River Gathering Foundation

The McKnight Foundation
Meyer Memorial Trust
John P. Murphy Foundation
Norman Foundation
The Rhode Island Community Foundation
San Diego Community Foundation
The San Francisco Foundation
The Sapelo Foundation
Shell Oil Company Foundation
The Sonoma County Community Foundation
Springs Foundation, Inc.
Wilburforce Foundation
Margaret Cullinan Wray Charitable Lead Annuity Trust

Symposia/colloquia

AT&T Foundation
Americana Foundation, Inc.
Claneil Foundation, Inc.
Environmental Education Foundation of Florida, Inc.
The George Gund Foundation
Island Foundation, Inc.
The Richard Ivey Foundation
The Henry M. Jackson Foundation
Laidlaw Foundation
Laird, Norton Foundation
Massachusetts Environmental Trust
The Milwaukee Foundation
National Fish and Wildlife Foundation
The David and Lucile Packard Foundation
Philip Morris Companies, Inc.
The Rockfall Foundation
Rockwood Fund, Inc.
The Schumann Fund for New Jersey, Inc.
Stanley Smith Horticultural Trust
The Tinker Foundation Incorporated
The Trust For Mutual Understanding
WMX Environmental Grants Program

Technical assistance

AT&T Foundation
A Territory Resource
American Conservation Association, Inc.
Americana Foundation, Inc.
Ameritech Foundation
Atkinson Foundation
Mary Reynolds Babcock Foundation, Inc.
The Bauman Foundation
The Bauman Foundation
Beldon Fund
Benton Foundation
The Bersted Foundation
The Frank Stanley Beveridge Foundation, Inc.
Mary Owen Borden Memorial Foundation
C. S. Fund
California Community Foundation
Carolyn Foundation
Liz Claiborne & Art Ortenberg Foundation
Claneil Foundation, Inc.
The Cleveland Foundation
The Columbus Foundation

The Community Foundation of Greater New Haven
Community Foundation of Western North Carolina, Inc.
Compton Foundation, Inc.
Conservation, Food & Health Foundation, Inc.
Cooke Foundation, Limited
The Nathan Cummings Foundation
Jessie Ball duPont Religious, Charitable and Educational Fund
Echoing Green Foundation
The Educational Foundation of America
The Foundation for the National Capital Region
Georgia Power Foundation, Inc.
Georgia-Pacific Foundation
Walter and Duncan Gordon Charitable Foundation
The Greenville Foundation
The George Gund Foundation
Evelyn and Walter Haas, Jr. Fund
Hawaii Community Foundation
Charles Hayden Foundation
The Edward W. Hazen Foundation
Jackson Hole Preserve, Inc.
The Henry M. Jackson Foundation
Walter S. Johnson Foundation
The J. M. Kaplan Fund, Inc.
W. K. Kellogg Foundation
Kongsgaard-Goldman Foundation
Laird, Norton Foundation
The John D. and Catherine T. MacArthur Foundation
Maine Community Foundation, Inc.
The Marshall L. & Perrine D. McCune Charitable Foundation
McKenzie River Gathering Foundation
The McKnight Foundation
Giles W. and Elise G. Mead Foundation
The Milwaukee Foundation
Charles Stewart Mott Foundation
John P. Murphy Foundation
The Needmor Fund
The New World Foundation
New York Foundation
The Nord Family Foundation
Norman Foundation
Jessie Smith Noyes Foundation, Inc.
The David and Lucile Packard Foundation
James C. Penney Foundation
The Pfizer Foundation, Inc.
The Philadelphia Foundation
The Prudential Foundation
Public Welfare Foundation, Inc.
The Rhode Island Community Foundation
Sacramento Regional Foundation
San Diego Community Foundation
The San Francisco Foundation
The Sapelo Foundation
The Scherman Foundation, Inc.
Seventh Generation Fund
Southwestern Bell Foundation
Anna B. Stearns Charitable Foundation, Inc.
The Sudbury Foundation

Emphases

Technical assistance (cont.)

The Sulzberger Foundation, Inc.
The Summerlee Foundation
Surdna Foundation, Inc.
The Switzer Foundation
The Tides Foundation
The Trust For Mutual Understanding
Alice Tweed Tuohy Foundation
DeWitt Wallace-Reader's Digest Fund
The Dean Witter Foundation

Training

ARCO Foundation
AT&T Foundation
The Achelis Foundation
The Ahmanson Foundation
Ameritech Foundation
Atkinson Foundation
L. L. Bean, Inc.
Beldon Fund
Otto Bremer Foundation
The Robert Brownlee Foundation
The Morris and Gwendolyn Cafritz Foundation
Chesapeake Bay Trust
Liz Claiborne & Art Ortenberg Foundation
Claneil Foundation, Inc.
The Community Foundation of Greater New Haven
Compton Foundation, Inc.
Conservation, Food & Health Foundation, Inc.
Crystal Channel Foundation
The Nathan Cummings Foundation
Dayton Hudson Foundation
Jessie Ball duPont Religious, Charitable and Educational Fund
Echoing Green Foundation
The Educational Foundation of America
Flintridge Foundation
The Foundation for the National Capital Region
Mary D. and Walter F. Frear Eleemosynary Trust
The Frost Foundation, Ltd.
GE Fund
Gebbie Foundation, Inc.
General Service Foundation
The German Marshall Fund of the United States
Give to the Earth Foundation
Walter and Duncan Gordon Charitable Foundation
Greater Piscataqua Community Foundation
The George Gund Foundation
Illilouette Fund
The International Foundation, Inc.
Island Foundation
The Richard Ivey Foundation
The Henry M. Jackson Foundation
Martha Holden Jennings Foundation
W. K. Kellogg Foundation
Laird, Norton Foundation
Larsen Fund, Inc.

Laurel Foundation
The Max and Anna Levinson Foundation
Lintilhac Foundation
The John D. and Catherine T. MacArthur Foundation
Massachusetts Environmental Trust
McInerny Foundation
McKenzie River Gathering Foundation
The McKnight Foundation
Meyer Memorial Trust
The Milwaukee Foundation
Charles Stewart Mott Foundation
The National Environmental Education and Training Foundation, Inc.
National Fish and Wildlife Foundation
National Geographic Society Education Foundation
New England Biolabs Foundation
Edward John Noble Foundation, Inc.
Norman Foundation
Northwest Fund for the Environment
The David and Lucile Packard Foundation
James C. Penney Foundation
Pew Scholars Program in Conservation and the Environment
Pilot Trust
The Powell Family Foundation
The Rockefeller Foundation
Rockwell Fund, Inc.
The San Francisco Foundation
The Scherman Foundation, Inc.
The Schumann Fund for New Jersey, Inc.
Seventh Generation Fund
Stanley Smith Horticultural Trust
South Coast Foundation, Inc.
Springs Foundation, Inc.
The Strong Foundation for Environmental Values
The Sudbury Foundation
The Summerlee Foundation
The Tides Foundation
The Tinker Foundation Incorporated
Toyota USA Foundation
The Trust For Mutual Understanding
Rose E. Tucker Charitable Trust
The USF&G Foundation, Inc.
Victoria Foundation, Inc.
DeWitt Wallace-Reader's Digest Fund
Wilburforce Foundation
The Winston-Salem Foundation, Inc.

Travel expenses

Alaska Conservation Foundation
The Jenifer Altman Foundation
The Arca Foundation
Compton Foundation, Inc.
The Nathan Cummings Foundation
The German Marshall Fund of the United States
Global Environmental Project Institute
Great Lakes Protection Fund
The George Gund Foundation
W. K. Kellogg Foundation
Laidlaw Foundation

Laird, Norton Foundation
McKenzie River Gathering Foundation
John P. Murphy Foundation
The Sapelo Foundation
The Switzer Foundation
The Trust For Mutual Understanding

Volunteerism

ARCO Foundation
AT&T Foundation
The Abell Foundation
Americana Foundation, Inc.
L. L. Bean, Inc.
The Ben & Jerry's Foundation
The Blumenthal Foundation
Boettcher Foundation
Otto Bremer Foundation
The Morris and Gwendolyn Cafritz Foundation
Carolyn Foundation
Chesapeake Bay Trust
The Chevron Companies
Claneil Foundation, Inc.
The Community Foundation of Greater New Haven
The Community Foundation Serving Coastal South Carolina
The Conservation and Research Foundation
The Mary A. Crocker Trust
Crystal Channel Foundation
Patrick and Anna M. Cudahy Fund
Davis Conservation Foundation
Jessie Ball duPont Religious, Charitable and Educational Fund
The Field Foundation of Illinois, Inc.
Ford Motor Company Fund
Foundation for Field Research
Foundation for the Carolinas
The Foundation for the National Capital Region
The Frost Foundation, Ltd.
Gates Foundation
The Fred Gellert Foundation
Georgia Power Foundation, Inc.
Give to the Earth Foundation
Walter and Duncan Gordon Charitable Foundation
Evelyn and Walter Haas, Jr. Fund
Hawaiian Electric Industries Charitable Foundation
The James Irvine Foundation
W. Alton Jones Foundation, Inc.
W. K. Kellogg Foundation
Laird, Norton Foundation
Laurel Foundation
MARPAT Foundation, Inc.
The McConnell Foundation
McInerny Foundation
McKenzie River Gathering Foundation
McKesson Foundation, Inc.
The Milwaukee Foundation
John P. Murphy Foundation
New York Foundation
Kenneth T. and Eileen L. Norris Foundation

Emphases

Volunteerism (cont.)

Outdoor Industry Conservation Alliance
James C. Penney Foundation
The Roberts Foundation
San Diego Community Foundation
The San Francisco Foundation
The Scherman Foundation, Inc.
Shell Oil Company Foundation
The Skaggs Foundation
The Sonoma County Community Foundation
Southwestern Bell Foundation
The Tides Foundation
Virginia Environmental Endowment

Workshops

Alaska Conservation Foundation
Bay Area Community Foundation
The Bunbury Company, Inc.
C. S. Fund
Carolyn Foundation
Chesapeake Bay Trust
Liz Claiborne & Art Ortenberg Foundation
Claneil Foundation, Inc.
The Nathan Cummings Foundation
Geraldine R. Dodge Foundation, Inc.
Jessie Ball duPont Religious, Charitable and Educational Fund
Flintridge Foundation
Gates Foundation
The German Marshall Fund of the United States
Walter and Duncan Gordon Charitable Foundation
The George Gund Foundation
The Richard Ivey Foundation
Martha Holden Jennings Foundation
Laidlaw Foundation
Laird, Norton Foundation
Larsen Fund, Inc.
Laurel Foundation
The Max and Anna Levinson Foundation
Lintilhac Foundation
Maine Community Foundation, Inc.
McKenzie River Gathering Foundation
The Milwaukee Foundation
John P. Murphy Foundation
The National Environmental Education and Training Foundation, Inc.
National Fish and Wildlife Foundation
National Geographic Society Education Foundation
Pew Scholars Program in Conservation and the Environment
Sid W. Richardson Foundation
The Rockfall Foundation
The San Francisco Foundation
Shell Oil Company Foundation
The Summerlee Foundation
The Tides Foundation
The Tinker Foundation Incorporated
The Trust For Mutual Understanding
Rose E. Tucker Charitable Trust
WMX Environmental Grants Program

Youth programs

The Ahmanson Foundation
American Foundation Corporation
Bay Area Community Foundation
The Beirne Carter Foundation
The Ben & Jerry's Foundation
Mary Owen Borden Memorial Foundation
The Bunbury Company, Inc.
The Morris and Gwendolyn Cafritz Foundation
Carolyn Foundation
Chesapeake Bay Trust
Claneil Foundation, Inc.
The Cleveland Foundation
The Community Foundation of Greater New Haven
The Community Foundation Serving Coastal South Carolina
Cooke Foundation, Limited
Crystal Channel Foundation
Dayton Hudson Foundation
The Aaron Diamond Foundation
Jessie Ball duPont Religious, Charitable and Educational Fund
The Frost Foundation, Ltd.
Gebbie Foundation, Inc.
The Fred Gellert Foundation
Give to the Earth Foundation
Walter and Duncan Gordon Charitable Foundation
Greater Piscataqua Community Foundation
Evelyn and Walter Haas, Jr. Fund
Hawaiian Electric Industries Charitable Foundation
The Hyams Foundation
W. K. Kellogg Foundation
Laidlaw Foundation
Laurel Foundation
The Little Family Foundation
Maine Community Foundation, Inc.
McGregor Fund
McKenzie River Gathering Foundation
McKesson Foundation, Inc.
Meadows Foundation, Inc.
Meyer Memorial Trust
The Milwaukee Foundation
John P. Murphy Foundation
National Fish and Wildlife Foundation
New York Foundation
Edward John Noble Foundation, Inc.
Norman Foundation
James C. Penney Foundation
The Powell Family Foundation
Recreational Equipment, Inc.
The Rhode Island Community Foundation
Sid W. Richardson Foundation
Rockefeller Financial Services, Philanthropy Department
San Diego Community Foundation
The San Francisco Foundation
The Sapelo Foundation
Sarkeys Foundation
The Scherman Foundation, Inc.
Shell Oil Company Foundation
The Sonoma County Community Foundation
Springs Foundation, Inc.
The Tides Foundation
Toyota USA Foundation
Harry C. Trexler Trust
The Troy Foundation
Rose E. Tucker Charitable Trust
The USF&G Foundation, Inc.
Victoria Foundation, Inc.
Virginia Environmental Endowment
WMX Environmental Grants Program
Joseph B. Whitehead Foundation

Zoos

The Abell Foundation
American Foundation Corporation
The Beinecke Foundation, Inc.
The Beirne Carter Foundation
The Blumenthal Foundation
Boettcher Foundation
Helen Brach Foundation
Carolyn Foundation
The Champlin Foundations
The Cleveland Foundation
The Clowes Fund, Inc.
Crystal Channel Foundation
The Aaron Diamond Foundation
Cleveland H. Dodge Foundation, Inc.
Geraldine R. Dodge Foundation, Inc.
The Educational Foundation of America
Ford Motor Company Fund
The Frost Foundation, Ltd.
Gates Foundation
Georgia Power Foundation, Inc.
The George Gund Foundation
The Hall Family Foundation
Hawaiian Electric Industries Charitable Foundation
The Roy A. Hunt Foundation
Martha Holden Jennings Foundation
The Kresge Foundation
Laird, Norton Foundation
Laurel Foundation
The Little Family Foundation
The John D. and Catherine T. MacArthur Foundation
McGregor Fund
Meadows Foundation, Inc.
Richard King Mellon Foundation
Metropolitan Atlanta Community Foundation, Inc.
Meyer Memorial Trust
The Milwaukee Foundation
Mobil Foundation, Inc.
John P. Murphy Foundation
National Fish and Wildlife Foundation
Edward John Noble Foundation, Inc.
The William Penn Foundation
The Rhode Island Community Foundation
Sid W. Richardson Foundation
The Roberts Foundation
Rockwell Fund, Inc.
San Diego Community Foundation

Zoos (cont.)

The San Francisco Foundation
The Scherman Foundation, Inc.
Sears-Swetland Foundation
Shell Oil Company Foundation
Kelvin Smith 1980 Charitable Trust
Stanley Smith Horticultural Trust
Rose E. Tucker Charitable Trust
Westinghouse Foundation
Joseph B. Whitehead Foundation
The Dean Witter Foundation
Robert W. Woodruff Foundation, Inc.
The Wortham Foundation, Inc.
Margaret Cullinan Wray Charitable
  Lead Annuity Trust
The Wyomissing Foundation, Inc.

Limitations

Activism

The Ahmanson Foundation
The Vincent Astor Foundation
L. L. Bean, Inc.
The Morris and Gwendolyn Cafritz Foundation
Chesapeake Bay Trust
The Chevron Companies
Cooke Foundation, Limited
The Aaron Diamond Foundation
FishAmerica Foundation
The John Randolph Haynes and Dora Haynes Foundation
The William and Flora Hewlett Foundation
Martha Holden Jennings Foundation
Helen K. and Arthur E. Johnson Foundation
W. K. Kellogg Foundation
Laird, Norton Foundation
The McConnell Foundation
McKesson Foundation, Inc.
The Andrew W. Mellon Foundation
John P. Murphy Foundation
National Geographic Society Education Foundation
Amelia Peabody Charitable Fund
Peninsula Community Foundation
The Powell Family Foundation
The Roberts Foundation
Sarkeys Foundation
Shell Oil Company Foundation
Springs Foundation, Inc.
The Troy Foundation
Virginia Environmental Endowment
Westinghouse Foundation
The Winston-Salem Foundation, Inc.

Advertising campaigns

AT&T Foundation
The Ahmanson Foundation
American Express Philanthropic Program
The Vincent Astor Foundation
BankAmerica Foundation
L. L. Bean, Inc.
The Beirne Carter Foundation
The Bunbury Company, Inc.
The Cabot Family Charitable Trust
The Cargill Foundation
Chesapeake Bay Trust
The Chevron Companies
Chrysler Corporation Fund
Claneil Foundation, Inc.
The Cleveland Foundation
Conservation, Food & Health Foundation, Inc.
Cooke Foundation, Limited
The Aaron Diamond Foundation
El Paso Community Foundation
The Field Foundation of Illinois, Inc.
Jamee and Marshall Field Foundation
FishAmerica Foundation

Flintridge Foundation
The Fred Gellert Foundation
The German Marshall Fund of the United States
Global Environmental Project Institute
Great Lakes Protection Fund
The George Gund Foundation
The Hall Family Foundation
Hawaiian Electric Industries Charitable Foundation
The John Randolph Haynes and Dora Haynes Foundation
The William and Flora Hewlett Foundation
The Homeland Foundation
The Hyams Foundation
Martha Holden Jennings Foundation
Helen K. and Arthur E. Johnson Foundation
W. K. Kellogg Foundation
The Max and Anna Levinson Foundation
Maine Community Foundation, Inc.
The McConnell Foundation
McGregor Fund
McKesson Foundation, Inc.
The McKnight Foundation
The Andrew W. Mellon Foundation
Metropolitan Life Foundation
Mobil Foundation, Inc.
John P. Murphy Foundation
National Geographic Society Education Foundation
New England Biolabs Foundation
Jessie Smith Noyes Foundation, Inc.
Amelia Peabody Charitable Fund
Peninsula Community Foundation
The William Penn Foundation
Philip Morris Companies, Inc.
The Powell Family Foundation
Recreational Equipment, Inc.
Rockwood Fund, Inc.
Fran and Warren Rupp Foundation
The San Francisco Foundation
The Scherman Foundation, Inc.
Shell Oil Company Foundation
Southwestern Bell Foundation
Springs Foundation, Inc.
The Sudbury Foundation
Toyota USA Foundation
The Travelers Foundation
The Troy Foundation
The Trust For Mutual Understanding
The USF&G Foundation, Inc.
Westinghouse Foundation
The Wortham Foundation, Inc.

Advocacy

The Ahmanson Foundation
The Vincent Astor Foundation
L. L. Bean, Inc.
The Cargill Foundation
Chesapeake Bay Trust

The Aaron Diamond Foundation
Dolfinger-McMahon Foundation
FishAmerica Foundation
The Frost Foundation, Ltd.
Hartford Foundation for Public Giving
The John Randolph Haynes and Dora Haynes Foundation
The William and Flora Hewlett Foundation
Martha Holden Jennings Foundation
Helen K. and Arthur E. Johnson Foundation
Maine Community Foundation, Inc.
Marbrook Foundation
The McConnell Foundation
McKesson Foundation, Inc.
The Andrew W. Mellon Foundation
John P. Murphy Foundation
National Fish and Wildlife Foundation
National Geographic Society Education Foundation
Onan Family Foundation
Amelia Peabody Charitable Fund
Peninsula Community Foundation
The Philadelphia Foundation
The Powell Family Foundation
Sarkeys Foundation
Shell Oil Company Foundation
The Sonoma County Community Foundation
Springs Foundation, Inc.
Texaco Foundation
Toyota USA Foundation
The Troy Foundation
Rose E. Tucker Charitable Trust
The Winston-Salem Foundation, Inc.

Annual campaigns

ARCO Foundation
The Ahmanson Foundation
Alaska Conservation Foundation
The Vincent Astor Foundation
Atkinson Foundation
Bay Area Community Foundation
The Beirne Carter Foundation
Beldon Fund
The Betterment Fund
Kathleen Price and Joseph M. Bryan Family Foundation, Inc.
The Bydale Foundation
California Community Foundation
Carolyn Foundation
The Champlin Foundations
Chesapeake Bay Trust
The Cleveland Foundation
The Collins Foundation
The Community Foundation of Greater New Haven
The Community Foundation of Sarasota County, Inc.
The Conservation and Research Foundation

© 1995 Environmental Data Resources, Inc.

673

Limitations

Annual campaigns (cont.)

Conservation, Food & Health
  Foundation, Inc.
Cooke Foundation, Limited
S. H. Cowell Foundation
The Mary A. Crocker Trust
Davis Conservation Foundation
The Aaron Diamond Foundation
Donner Canadian Foundation
The Educational Foundation of America
El Paso Community Foundation
The Energy Foundation
The William Stamps Farish Fund
FishAmerica Foundation
The Foundation for the National
  Capital Region
Gates Foundation
The Barbara Gauntlett Foundation, Inc.
The Fred Gellert Foundation
General Service Foundation
The German Marshall Fund of
  the United States
Walter and Duncan Gordon Charitable
  Foundation
Great Lakes Protection Fund
The George Gund Foundation
Evelyn and Walter Haas, Jr. Fund
Hawaii Community Foundation
Charles Hayden Foundation
The John Randolph Haynes and
  Dora Haynes Foundation
The Homeland Foundation
The Hyams Foundation
The Richard Ivey Foundation
Martha Holden Jennings Foundation
Walter S. Johnson Foundation
W. Alton Jones Foundation, Inc.
W. K. Kellogg Foundation
The Robert S. and Grayce B. Kerr
  Foundation, Inc.
Laidlaw Foundation
Laird, Norton Foundation
Laurel Foundation
Maine Community Foundation, Inc.
The Marshall Fund of Arizona
The McConnell Foundation
McKesson Foundation, Inc.
Meadows Foundation, Inc.
The Andrew W. Mellon Foundation
Joyce Mertz-Gilmore Foundation
The Milwaukee Foundation
The Minneapolis Foundation
Ruth Mott Fund
M. J. Murdock Charitable Trust
National Fish and Wildlife Foundation
National Geographic Society Education
  Foundation
New England Biolabs Foundation
New Horizon Foundation
Northwest Area Foundation
Spencer T. and Ann W. Olin Foundation
Orchard Foundation
Amelia Peabody Charitable Fund
Peninsula Community Foundation
The William Penn Foundation

James C. Penney Foundation
The Philadelphia Foundation
The Roberts Foundation
San Diego Community Foundation
The San Francisco Foundation
Sarkeys Foundation
The Scherman Foundation, Inc.
The Schumann Fund for New Jersey, Inc.
The Florence and John Schumann
  Foundation
The Sonoma County Community
  Foundation
The Morris Stulsaft Foundation
The Sudbury Foundation
Town Creek Foundation, Inc.
Toyota USA Foundation
The Trust For Mutual Understanding
Unitarian Universalist Veatch Program
  at Shelter Rock
Virginia Environmental Endowment
Lila Wallace-Reader's Digest Fund
The Winston-Salem Foundation, Inc.

Aquariums

L. L. Bean, Inc.
The Bullitt Foundation
Claneil Foundation, Inc.
Compton Foundation, Inc.
Damien Foundation
Foundation for Deep Ecology
The Fred Gellert Foundation
Great Lakes Protection Fund
The John Randolph Haynes and
  Dora Haynes Foundation
The William and Flora Hewlett Foundation

Audiovisual materials

ARCO Foundation
The Achelis Foundation
The Acorn Foundation
The Ahmanson Foundation
The Vincent Astor Foundation
BankAmerica Foundation
L. L. Bean, Inc.
Beldon Fund
The Ben & Jerry's Foundation
The Betterment Fund
Blandin Foundation
The Bodman Foundation
The Bothin Foundation
Kathleen Price and Joseph M. Bryan
  Family Foundation, Inc.
Patrick and Aimee Butler Family
  Foundation
C. S. Fund
The Cargill Foundation
The Chevron Companies
The Chicago Community Trust
The Community Foundation of
  Greater New Haven
The Community Foundation of
  Sarasota County, Inc.
Compton Foundation, Inc.
The Aaron Diamond Foundation

Donner Canadian Foundation
El Pomar Foundation
Jamee and Marshall Field Foundation
FishAmerica Foundation
Flintridge Foundation
Foundation for Deep Ecology
Give to the Earth Foundation
Global Environmental Project Institute
The George Gund Foundation
HKH Foundation
Evelyn and Walter Haas, Jr. Fund
Walter and Elise Haas Fund
The John Randolph Haynes and
  Dora Haynes Foundation
The William and Flora Hewlett Foundation
The Homeland Foundation
The Hyams Foundation
The International Foundation, Inc.
The James Irvine Foundation
The J. M. Kaplan Fund, Inc.
Laidlaw Foundation
Larsen Fund, Inc.
The Lazar Foundation
Levi Strauss Foundation
Lilly Endowment, Inc.
Maki Foundation
The Marshall Fund of Arizona
McKesson Foundation, Inc.
The McKnight Foundation
The Andrew W. Mellon Foundation
Merck Family Fund
Joyce Mertz-Gilmore Foundation
Metropolitan Atlanta Community
  Foundation, Inc.
Ruth Mott Fund
National Geographic Society Education
  Foundation
New England Biolabs Foundation
New Horizon Foundation
The New World Foundation
The New-Land Foundation, Inc.
Edward John Noble Foundation, Inc.
Norman Foundation
Jessie Smith Noyes Foundation, Inc.
Ottinger Foundation
Amelia Peabody Charitable Fund
James C. Penney Foundation
Philip Morris Companies, Inc.
The Powell Family Foundation
Rockefeller Financial Services,
  Philanthropy Department
The San Francisco Foundation
The Scherman Foundation, Inc.
Shell Oil Company Foundation
Turner Foundation, Inc.
USX Foundation, Inc.
Unitarian Universalist Veatch Program
  at Shelter Rock
Vanguard Public Foundation
Weeden Foundation

Botanical gardens

L. L. Bean, Inc.
Beldon Fund
Ruth H. Brown Foundation

Limitations

Botanical gardens (cont.)

Claneil Foundation, Inc.
Compton Foundation, Inc.
The Conservation and Research Foundation
Damien Foundation
Foundation for Deep Ecology
The Fred Gellert Foundation
The German Marshall Fund of
 the United States
Global Environmental Project Institute
Great Lakes Protection Fund
The John Randolph Haynes and
 Dora Haynes Foundation
The Hyams Foundation
The Lazar Foundation
The Max and Anna Levinson Foundation
McKesson Foundation, Inc.
The McKnight Foundation
National Geographic Society Education
 Foundation
Norman Foundation
Amelia Peabody Charitable Fund
James C. Penney Foundation
Philip Morris Companies, Inc.
Recreational Equipment, Inc.
The Rockefeller Foundation
The Sapelo Foundation
The Schumann Fund for New Jersey, Inc.
Town Creek Foundation, Inc.
The USF&G Foundation, Inc.
Victoria Foundation, Inc.
Virginia Environmental Endowment

Capacity building

The Vincent Astor Foundation
The Aaron Diamond Foundation
The John Randolph Haynes and
 Dora Haynes Foundation
Martha Holden Jennings Foundation
The Andrew W. Mellon Foundation
National Geographic Society Education
 Foundation
New England Biolabs Foundation
Edward John Noble Foundation, Inc.
Amelia Peabody Charitable Fund
Philip Morris Companies, Inc.
Shell Oil Company Foundation
Toyota USA Foundation

Capital campaigns/expenses

The Abelard Foundation West
The Acorn Foundation
Alaska Conservation Foundation
American Express Philanthropic Program
American Foundation Corporation
The Arca Foundation
Mary Reynolds Babcock Foundation, Inc.
The Barra Foundation, Inc.
The Theodore H. Barth Foundation, Inc.
Beldon Fund
Ruth H. Brown Foundation
The Bullitt Foundation
The Bydale Foundation
C. S. Fund

The Louis Calder Foundation
Mary Flagler Cary Charitable Trust
Chesapeake Bay Trust
The Chevron Companies
The Cleveland Foundation
The Community Foundation of
 Santa Clara County
The Conservation and Research Foundation
Conservation, Food & Health
 Foundation, Inc.
Jessie B. Cox Charitable Trust
The Nathan Cummings Foundation
Dayton Hudson Foundation
The Aaron Diamond Foundation
Geraldine R. Dodge Foundation, Inc.
Donner Canadian Foundation
The Elizabeth Ordway Dunn
 Foundation, Inc.
The Educational Foundation of America
El Paso Community Foundation
The Energy Foundation
Samuel S. Fels Fund
Bert Fingerhut/Caroline Hicks Family Fund
FishAmerica Foundation
Flintridge Foundation
Foundation for the Carolinas
Foundation for Deep Ecology
The Frost Foundation, Ltd.
Lloyd A. Fry Foundation
The Fund for New Jersey
GE Fund
The Fred Gellert Foundation
General Service Foundation
The Wallace Alexander Gerbode
 Foundation, Inc.
The German Marshall Fund of
 the United States
The Golden Rule Foundation, Inc.
Walter and Duncan Gordon Charitable
 Foundation
Great Lakes Protection Fund
Greater Piscataqua Community Foundation
The Greenville Foundation
The George Gund Foundation
HKH Foundation
Evelyn and Walter Haas, Jr. Fund
The John Randolph Haynes and
 Dora Haynes Foundation
The Edward W. Hazen Foundation
Vira I. Heinz Endowment
Heller Charitable & Educational Fund
The Clarence E. Heller Charitable
 Foundation
The William and Flora Hewlett Foundation
The Homeland Foundation
The Hyams Foundation
Island Foundation, Inc.
The Richard Ivey Foundation
The Henry M. Jackson Foundation
Martha Holden Jennings Foundation
Walter S. Johnson Foundation
W. Alton Jones Foundation, Inc.
The Joyce Foundation
W. K. Kellogg Foundation
The Henry P. Kendall Foundation

The Esther A. and Joseph Klingenstein
 Fund, Inc.
Laidlaw Foundation
The Lazar Foundation
The Max and Anna Levinson Foundation
Lyndhurst Foundation
The John D. and Catherine T. MacArthur
 Foundation
Maine Community Foundation, Inc.
The Marshall Fund of Arizona
The McConnell Foundation
The McIntosh Foundation
McKesson Foundation, Inc.
The Andrew W. Mellon Foundation
The John Merck Fund
Metropolitan Life Foundation
The Milwaukee Foundation
Ruth Mott Fund
The Curtis and Edith Munson
 Foundation, Inc.
The National Environmental Education
 and Training Foundation, Inc.
National Fish and Wildlife Foundation
National Geographic Society Education
 Foundation
New England Biolabs Foundation
New Hampshire Charitable Foundation
The New World Foundation
The New York Community Trust
The New-Land Foundation, Inc.
The Nord Family Foundation
Norman Foundation
Andrew Norman Foundation
Northwest Area Foundation
Jessie Smith Noyes Foundation, Inc.
Onan Family Foundation
Ottinger Foundation
Peninsula Community Foundation
James C. Penney Foundation
The Pew Charitable Trusts
The Philadelphia Foundation
Philip Morris Companies, Inc.
The Polden-Puckham Charitable Foundation
Public Welfare Foundation, Inc.
Recreational Equipment, Inc.
Z. Smith Reynolds Foundation, Inc.
The Winthrop Rockefeller Foundation
Rockwood Fund, Inc.
Sacramento Regional Foundation
San Diego Community Foundation
The San Francisco Foundation
The Scherman Foundation, Inc.
The Schumann Fund for New Jersey, Inc.
The Florence and John Schumann
 Foundation
Snee-Reinhardt Charitable Foundation
The Sonoma County Community
 Foundation
Southwestern Bell Foundation
Anna B. Stearns Charitable Foundation, Inc.
Stern Family Fund
Margaret Dorrance Strawbridge Foundation
 of Pennsylvania II, Inc.
Surdna Foundation, Inc.
The Switzer Foundation

Limitations

Capital campaigns/expenses (cont.)

The Telesis Foundation
Texaco Foundation
Threshold Foundation
The Tides Foundation
Town Creek Foundation, Inc.
Toyota USA Foundation
The Travelers Foundation
The Trust For Mutual Understanding
Alice Tweed Tuohy Foundation
The USF&G Foundation, Inc.
Unitarian Universalist Veatch Program at Shelter Rock
United States-Japan Foundation
Vanguard Public Foundation
Virginia Environmental Endowment
DeWitt Wallace-Reader's Digest Fund
Lila Wallace-Reader's Digest Fund
Margaret Cullinan Wray Charitable Lead Annuity Trust

Computer hardware

The Vincent Astor Foundation
Mary Reynolds Babcock Foundation, Inc.
The Ben & Jerry's Foundation
The Bullitt Foundation
Chesapeake Bay Trust
The Chicago Community Trust
The Cleveland Foundation
The Aaron Diamond Foundation
The Fred Gellert Foundation
The John Randolph Haynes and Dora Haynes Foundation
The Clarence E. Heller Charitable Foundation
The Hyams Foundation
Martha Holden Jennings Foundation
Maine Community Foundation, Inc.
McGregor Fund
McKesson Foundation, Inc.
Metropolitan Atlanta Community Foundation, Inc.
National Geographic Society Education Foundation
New England Biolabs Foundation
Peninsula Community Foundation
James C. Penney Foundation
Philip Morris Companies, Inc.
The Powell Family Foundation
Recreational Equipment, Inc.
Rockwood Fund, Inc.
The San Francisco Foundation
The Scherman Foundation, Inc.
The Schumann Fund for New Jersey, Inc.
Surdna Foundation, Inc.
Town Creek Foundation, Inc.
Toyota USA Foundation
The Trust For Mutual Understanding
The Wortham Foundation, Inc.

Conferences

A Territory Resource
The Abelard Foundation West
The Achelis Foundation
Arcadia Foundation
The Vincent Astor Foundation
Atkinson Foundation
The Bodman Foundation
The Bothin Foundation
Kathleen Price and Joseph M. Bryan Family Foundation, Inc.
The Bunbury Company, Inc.
The Bush Foundation
California Community Foundation
The Cargill Foundation
Carolyn Foundation
Ben B. Cheney Foundation
The Chevron Companies
The Chicago Community Trust
Chrysler Corporation Fund
The Clowes Fund, Inc.
The Columbus Foundation
The Community Foundation of Greater New Haven
The Community Foundation of Sarasota County, Inc.
Compton Foundation, Inc.
Cooke Foundation, Limited
S. H. Cowell Foundation
Charles E. Culpeper Foundation, Inc.
Dayton Hudson Foundation
The Aaron Diamond Foundation
Gaylord and Dorothy Donnelley Foundation
Donner Canadian Foundation
The Herbert H. and Grace A. Dow Foundation
El Pomar Foundation
The Field Foundation of Illinois, Inc.
Jamee and Marshall Field Foundation
FishAmerica Foundation
Foundation for the Carolinas
The Freed Foundation, Inc.
Gates Foundation
The Fred Gellert Foundation
Richard & Rhoda Goldman Fund
Evelyn and Walter Haas, Jr. Fund
The Hall Family Foundation
The Ewing Halsell Foundation
Hartford Foundation for Public Giving
Charles Hayden Foundation
The William and Flora Hewlett Foundation
The Hitachi Foundation
The Homeland Foundation
Hudson-Webber Foundation
The Hyams Foundation
IBM Corporation
The International Foundation, Inc.
The James Irvine Foundation
Helen K. and Arthur E. Johnson Foundation
Walter S. Johnson Foundation
W. Alton Jones Foundation, Inc.
The J. M. Kaplan Fund, Inc.
Laidlaw Foundation
Levi Strauss Foundation
Richard Lounsbery Foundation, Inc.
The John D. and Catherine T. MacArthur Foundation
The McConnell Foundation
McGregor Fund
The McIntosh Foundation
McKesson Foundation, Inc.
The McKnight Foundation
Meadows Foundation, Inc.
The Andrew W. Mellon Foundation
Joyce Mertz-Gilmore Foundation
Metropolitan Atlanta Community Foundation, Inc.
The Minneapolis Foundation
J. P. Morgan Charitable Trust
New England Biolabs Foundation
New Horizon Foundation
The New-Land Foundation, Inc.
Edward John Noble Foundation, Inc.
Norman Foundation
Northwest Area Foundation
Jessie Smith Noyes Foundation, Inc.
The Ohrstrom Foundation
Spencer T. and Ann W. Olin Foundation
Ottinger Foundation
Amelia Peabody Charitable Fund
Peninsula Community Foundation
The William Penn Foundation
The Philadelphia Foundation
The Powell Family Foundation
Public Welfare Foundation, Inc.
Recreational Equipment, Inc.
The Winthrop Rockefeller Foundation
San Diego Community Foundation
The San Francisco Foundation
The Scherman Foundation, Inc.
Springhouse Foundation
Springs Foundation, Inc.
Steelcase Foundation
Stern Family Fund
The Strong Foundation for Environmental Values
The Morris Stulsaft Foundation
Town Creek Foundation, Inc.
Toyota USA Foundation
The Troy Foundation
Alice Tweed Tuohy Foundation
The USF&G Foundation, Inc.
USX Foundation, Inc.
Unitarian Universalist Veatch Program at Shelter Rock
United States-Japan Foundation
Vancouver Foundation
Vanguard Public Foundation
Virginia Environmental Endowment
Weeden Foundation
Westinghouse Foundation
The Winston-Salem Foundation, Inc.
The Wyomissing Foundation, Inc.

Conflict resolution

The Vincent Astor Foundation
The Bullitt Foundation
Claneil Foundation, Inc.
The Conservation and Research Foundation
Conservation, Food & Health Foundation, Inc.
The Aaron Diamond Foundation
FishAmerica Foundation
The George Gund Foundation

Limitations

Conflict resolution (cont.)

The Homeland Foundation
The Hyams Foundation
Martha Holden Jennings Foundation
Helen K. and Arthur E. Johnson Foundation
The McConnell Foundation
The Andrew W. Mellon Foundation
National Geographic Society Education Foundation
Amelia Peabody Charitable Fund
Peninsula Community Foundation
James C. Penney Foundation
The Powell Family Foundation
Fran and Warren Rupp Foundation
Sarkeys Foundation
Shell Oil Company Foundation
Springs Foundation, Inc.
The Troy Foundation
The Trust For Mutual Understanding
Rose E. Tucker Charitable Trust

Continuing support

The Abell Foundation
The Ahmanson Foundation
The Vincent Astor Foundation
Clayton Baker Trust
The Barra Foundation, Inc.
The Beirne Carter Foundation
The Ben & Jerry's Foundation
Helen Brach Foundation
The Bush Foundation
The Louis Calder Foundation
The Champlin Foundations
The Cleveland Foundation
Conservation, Food & Health Foundation, Inc.
Cooke Foundation, Limited
The Mary A. Crocker Trust
The Aaron Diamond Foundation
Dolfinger-McMahon Foundation
El Paso Community Foundation
The Fred Gellert Foundation
General Service Foundation
Greater Piscataqua Community Foundation
The Ewing Halsell Foundation
Charles Hayden Foundation
The John Randolph Haynes and Dora Haynes Foundation
Maine Community Foundation, Inc.
The McConnell Foundation
Metropolitan Atlanta Community Foundation, Inc.
National Geographic Society Education Foundation
The New World Foundation
Amelia Peabody Charitable Fund
Peninsula Community Foundation
Recreational Equipment, Inc.
The Winthrop Rockefeller Foundation
Rockwood Fund, Inc.
San Diego Community Foundation
The San Francisco Foundation
Sarkeys Foundation
Stanley Smith Horticultural Trust

Southwestern Bell Foundation
The Morris Stulsaft Foundation
The Sudbury Foundation
Toyota USA Foundation
The Travelers Foundation
The Trust For Mutual Understanding
Wilburforce Foundation

Debt retirement

The Abell Foundation
Alaska Conservation Foundation
Arcadia Foundation
Evenor Armington Fund
The Vincent Astor Foundation
The Barra Foundation, Inc.
Bay Area Community Foundation
L. L. Bean, Inc.
Beldon Fund
The Bersted Foundation
The Frank Stanley Beveridge Foundation, Inc.
The Lynde and Harry Bradley Foundation, Inc.
The Bullitt Foundation
The Bunbury Company, Inc.
The Bush Foundation
The Bydale Foundation
C. S. Fund
Carolyn Foundation
Centerior Energy Foundation
Chesapeake Bay Trust
The Chicago Community Trust
Chrysler Corporation Fund
Claneil Foundation, Inc.
The Cleveland Foundation
The Collins Foundation
The Columbus Foundation
The Community Foundation of Greater New Haven
The Community Foundation of Santa Clara County
The Community Foundation of Sarasota County, Inc.
Compton Foundation, Inc.
Conservation, Food & Health Foundation, Inc.
Cooke Foundation, Limited
Adolph Coors Foundation
S. H. Cowell Foundation
Jessie B. Cox Charitable Trust
The Mary A. Crocker Trust
Crystal Channel Foundation
The Fred Harris Daniels Foundation, Inc.
Davis Conservation Foundation
The Aaron Diamond Foundation
Geraldine R. Dodge Foundation, Inc.
Donner Canadian Foundation
The Elizabeth Ordway Dunn Foundation, Inc.
The Educational Foundation of America
El Paso Community Foundation
El Pomar Foundation
The Energy Foundation
The William Stamps Farish Fund

Samuel S. Fels Fund
Fields Pond Foundation, Inc.
FishAmerica Foundation
Flintridge Foundation
Foundation for the Carolinas
Foundation for Deep Ecology
Mary D. and Walter F. Frear Eleemosynary Trust
The Frost Foundation, Ltd.
Gates Foundation
The Fred Gellert Foundation
General Service Foundation
The Wallace Alexander Gerbode Foundation, Inc.
The German Marshall Fund of the United States
Global Environmental Project Institute
Herman Goldman Foundation
Richard & Rhoda Goldman Fund
Great Lakes Protection Fund
Greater Piscataqua Community Foundation
The George Gund Foundation
Evelyn and Walter Haas, Jr. Fund
The Hall Family Foundation
The Ewing Halsell Foundation
Hartford Foundation for Public Giving
Hawaiian Electric Industries Charitable Foundation
Charles Hayden Foundation
The John Randolph Haynes and Dora Haynes Foundation
The Edward W. Hazen Foundation
Vira I. Heinz Endowment
Heller Charitable & Educational Fund
The Clarence E. Heller Charitable Foundation
The Hofmann Foundation
The Homeland Foundation
Hudson-Webber Foundation
The Hyams Foundation
The James Irvine Foundation
The Richard Ivey Foundation
The Henry M. Jackson Foundation
Martha Holden Jennings Foundation
Helen K. and Arthur E. Johnson Foundation
Walter S. Johnson Foundation
The Kresge Foundation
Laidlaw Foundation
Laird, Norton Foundation
The Lazar Foundation
The Little Family Foundation
Lyndhurst Foundation
Maine Community Foundation, Inc.
Marbrook Foundation
Marin Community Foundation
The Marshall Fund of Arizona
The McConnell Foundation
The Marshall L. & Perrine D. McCune Charitable Foundation
McGregor Fund
McInerny Foundation
McKesson Foundation, Inc.
The McKnight Foundation
The Andrew W. Mellon Foundation
Merck Family Fund

© 1995 Environmental Data Resources, Inc.

Limitations

Debt retirement (cont.)

Metropolitan Atlanta Community Foundation, Inc.
The Milwaukee Foundation
The Minneapolis Foundation
Ruth Mott Fund
M. J. Murdock Charitable Trust
National Fish and Wildlife Foundation
National Geographic Society Education Foundation
New England Biolabs Foundation
New Hampshire Charitable Foundation
New Horizon Foundation
The New World Foundation
The New York Community Trust
Edward John Noble Foundation, Inc.
The Nord Family Foundation
Jessie Smith Noyes Foundation, Inc.
The Ohrstrom Foundation
Spencer T. and Ann W. Olin Foundation
Peninsula Community Foundation
The William Penn Foundation
James C. Penney Foundation
The Pew Charitable Trusts
The Pfizer Foundation, Inc.
The Philadelphia Foundation
Philip Morris Companies, Inc.
The Powell Family Foundation
Recreational Equipment, Inc.
The Rhode Island Community Foundation
Smith Richardson Foundation, Inc.
Rockefeller Family Fund, Inc.
Rockefeller Financial Services, Philanthropy Department
The Winthrop Rockefeller Foundation
Rockwood Fund, Inc.
Fran and Warren Rupp Foundation
Sacramento Regional Foundation
San Diego Community Foundation
The San Francisco Foundation
The Sapelo Foundation
Sarkeys Foundation
Sarah Scaife Foundation Incorporated
The Scherman Foundation, Inc.
The Schumann Fund for New Jersey, Inc.
The Florence and John Schumann Foundation
Shell Oil Company Foundation
Thomas Sill Foundation
The Sonoma County Community Foundation
Stackner Family Foundation, Inc.
The Morris Stulsaft Foundation
The Sudbury Foundation
Surdna Foundation, Inc.
Town Creek Foundation, Inc.
Toyota USA Foundation
The Travelers Foundation
The Troy Foundation
The Trust For Mutual Understanding
Rose E. Tucker Charitable Trust
Alice Tweed Tuohy Foundation
United States-Japan Foundation
Vancouver Foundation
Vanguard Public Foundation
Virginia Environmental Endowment
Westinghouse Foundation
Weyerhaeuser Company Foundation
G. N. Wilcox Trust
The Winston-Salem Foundation, Inc.
The Wyomissing Foundation, Inc.

Demonstration programs

The Achelis Foundation
Arcadia Foundation
The Bydale Foundation
The Aaron Diamond Foundation
The Energy Foundation
The John Randolph Haynes and Dora Haynes Foundation
The Hyams Foundation
Marbrook Foundation
Amelia Peabody Charitable Fund
The Powell Family Foundation
Rockwood Fund, Inc.
Shell Oil Company Foundation
Springs Foundation, Inc.

Direct services

A Territory Resource
The Abelard Foundation West
The Vincent Astor Foundation
The Bauman Foundation
The Ben & Jerry's Foundation
The Bullitt Foundation
Columbia Foundation
The Aaron Diamond Foundation
Oliver S. and Jennie R. Donaldson Charitable Trust
The Wallace Alexander Gerbode Foundation, Inc.
The German Marshall Fund of the United States
The George Gund Foundation
The John Randolph Haynes and Dora Haynes Foundation
Ittleson Foundation, Inc.
The Richard Ivey Foundation
The Joyce Foundation
The Andrew W. Mellon Foundation
New England Biolabs Foundation
Norman Foundation
Amelia Peabody Charitable Fund
Peninsula Community Foundation
The Pew Charitable Trusts
Recreational Equipment, Inc.
Rockwood Fund, Inc.
Shell Oil Company Foundation
Unitarian Universalist Veatch Program at Shelter Rock

Education

The Abelard Foundation West
Clayton Baker Trust
Otto Bremer Foundation
Patrick and Aimee Butler Family Foundation
Geraldine R. Dodge Foundation, Inc.
Samuel S. Fels Fund
The Golden Rule Foundation, Inc.
Harder Foundation
The William and Flora Hewlett Foundation
The Hyams Foundation
The Joyce Foundation
Spencer T. and Ann W. Olin Foundation
Recreational Equipment, Inc.
Rockwood Fund, Inc.
The Scherman Foundation, Inc.
The Trust For Mutual Understanding
United States-Japan Foundation
Vanguard Public Foundation

Educational institutions

AT&T Foundation
The Abelard Foundation West
American Conservation Association, Inc.
Clayton Baker Trust
Beldon Fund
The Ben & Jerry's Foundation
The Bersted Foundation
Mary Flagler Cary Charitable Trust
Chrysler Corporation Fund
The Collins Foundation
The James M. Cox, Jr. Foundation, Inc.
Damien Foundation
Dayton Hudson Foundation
El Pomar Foundation
The Fund for New Jersey
Global Environmental Project Institute
Charles Hayden Foundation
The Hyams Foundation
The Knapp Foundation, Inc.
The Kresge Foundation
Lyndhurst Foundation
Metropolitan Life Foundation
New England Biolabs Foundation
The New World Foundation
The New-Land Foundation, Inc.
Ottinger Foundation
Recreational Equipment, Inc.
Rockwood Fund, Inc.
The Scherman Foundation, Inc.
The Strong Foundation for Environmental Values
The Telesis Foundation
Town Creek Foundation, Inc.
Westinghouse Foundation
The Wortham Foundation, Inc.

Emergency funding

A Territory Resource
The Vincent Astor Foundation
The Ben & Jerry's Foundation
The Bydale Foundation
C. S. Fund
Chesapeake Bay Trust
Columbia Foundation
Conservation, Food & Health Foundation, Inc.
Cooke Foundation, Limited
Jessie B. Cox Charitable Trust
Dayton Hudson Foundation
The Aaron Diamond Foundation

Limitations

Emergency funding (cont.)
Samuel S. Fels Fund
Foundation for Deep Ecology
The Fred Gellert Foundation
Global Environmental Project Institute
Herman Goldman Foundation
Great Lakes Protection Fund
The George Gund Foundation
Evelyn and Walter Haas, Jr. Fund
The Ewing Halsell Foundation
Charles Hayden Foundation
The John Randolph Haynes and
  Dora Haynes Foundation
The Homeland Foundation
Hudson-Webber Foundation
The Hyams Foundation
Helen K. and Arthur E. Johnson Foundation
W. Alton Jones Foundation, Inc.
Lintilhac Foundation
The McConnell Foundation
McGregor Fund
The McKnight Foundation
Ruth Mott Fund
M. J. Murdock Charitable Trust
National Geographic Society Education
  Foundation
Peninsula Community Foundation
James C. Penney Foundation
Philip Morris Companies, Inc.
The San Francisco Foundation
The Sapelo Foundation
Thomas Sill Foundation
The Sonoma County Community
  Foundation
The Morris Stulsaft Foundation
Surdna Foundation, Inc.
The Telesis Foundation
Toyota USA Foundation
Virginia Environmental Endowment
Westinghouse Foundation
Margaret Cullinan Wray Charitable
  Lead Annuity Trust

Endowments
ARCO Foundation
AT&T Foundation
A Territory Resource
Alaska Conservation Foundation
American Conservation Association, Inc.
American Express Philanthropic Program
American Foundation Corporation
The Arca Foundation
Clayton Baker Trust
The George F. Baker Trust
BankAmerica Foundation
The Barra Foundation, Inc.
Beldon Fund
The Bersted Foundation
The Betterment Fund
The Frank Stanley Beveridge
  Foundation, Inc.
Blandin Foundation
The Boeing Company
Boettcher Foundation

The Bothin Foundation
The Lynde and Harry Bradley
  Foundation, Inc.
Ruth H. Brown Foundation
The Bush Foundation
The Bydale Foundation
C. S. Fund
The Morris and Gwendolyn Cafritz
  Foundation
The Louis Calder Foundation
California Community Foundation
James & Abigail Campbell Foundation
The Cargill Foundation
Mary Flagler Cary Charitable Trust
Centerior Energy Foundation
Ben B. Cheney Foundation
Chesapeake Bay Trust
The Chevron Companies
The Chicago Community Trust
Chrysler Corporation Fund
The Clark Foundation
The Cleveland Foundation
The Columbus Foundation
The Community Foundation of
  Greater New Haven
The Community Foundation of
  Santa Clara County
The Community Foundation of
  Sarasota County, Inc.
The Community Foundation Serving
  Coastal South Carolina
The Conservation and Research Foundation
Conservation, Food & Health
  Foundation, Inc.
Cooke Foundation, Limited
Adolph Coors Foundation
S. H. Cowell Foundation
Jessie B. Cox Charitable Trust
The Cricket Foundation
Patrick and Anna M. Cudahy Fund
The Nathan Cummings Foundation
Dayton Hudson Foundation
Deer Creek Foundation
The Aaron Diamond Foundation
Geraldine R. Dodge Foundation, Inc.
Dolfinger-McMahon Foundation
The Elizabeth Ordway Dunn
  Foundation, Inc.
Jessie Ball duPont Religious, Charitable
  and Educational Fund
The Educational Foundation of America
El Pomar Foundation
The Energy Foundation
Environmental Endowment for
  New Jersey, Inc.
The Armand G. Erpf Fund, Inc.
The Ettinger Foundation, Inc.
The William Stamps Farish Fund
Samuel S. Fels Fund
The Field Foundation of Illinois, Inc.
Bert Fingerhut/Caroline Hicks Family Fund
FishAmerica Foundation
Flintridge Foundation
Ford Foundation

Foundation for the Carolinas
Foundation for Field Research
The Foundation for the National
  Capital Region
Mary D. and Walter F. Frear
  Eleemosynary Trust
The Freed Foundation, Inc.
The Frost Foundation, Ltd.
GE Fund
The Gap Foundation
Gebbie Foundation, Inc.
The Fred Gellert Foundation
General Service Foundation
The Golden Rule Foundation, Inc.
Richard & Rhoda Goldman Fund
Walter and Duncan Gordon Charitable
  Foundation
Great Lakes Protection Fund
The George Gund Foundation
HKH Foundation
Evelyn and Walter Haas, Jr. Fund
The Hall Family Foundation
The Ewing Halsell Foundation
Hartford Foundation for Public Giving
The Merrill G. & Emita E. Hastings
  Foundation
Charles Hayden Foundation
The John Randolph Haynes and
  Dora Haynes Foundation
The Edward W. Hazen Foundation
The William and Flora Hewlett Foundation
The Hitachi Foundation
The Homeland Foundation
Hudson-Webber Foundation
The Hyams Foundation
The Hyde and Watson Foundation
The International Foundation, Inc.
The James Irvine Foundation
Ittleson Foundation, Inc.
The Richard Ivey Foundation
Jackson Hole Preserve, Inc.
Martha Holden Jennings Foundation
Helen K. and Arthur E. Johnson Foundation
Walter S. Johnson Foundation
W. Alton Jones Foundation, Inc.
The Henry P. Kendall Foundation
The Robert S. and Grayce B. Kerr
  Foundation, Inc.
Caesar Kleberg Foundation for Wildlife
  Conservation
The Esther A. and Joseph Klingenstein
  Fund, Inc.
The Kresge Foundation
The Lazar Foundation
The Max and Anna Levinson Foundation
Lilly Endowment, Inc.
Richard Lounsbery Foundation, Inc.
Lyndhurst Foundation
The John D. and Catherine T. MacArthur
  Foundation
Maine Community Foundation, Inc.
MARPAT Foundation, Inc.
The Marshall Fund of Arizona
The Martin Foundation, Inc.
The McConnell Foundation

© 1995 Environmental Data Resources, Inc.

Limitations

Endowments (cont.)

McInerny Foundation
The McIntosh Foundation
The McKnight Foundation
Merck Family Fund
The John Merck Fund
Joyce Mertz-Gilmore Foundation
Metropolitan Atlanta Community Foundation, Inc.
Metropolitan Life Foundation
The Milwaukee Foundation
The Minneapolis Foundation
Mobil Foundation, Inc.
Ruth Mott Fund
The Curtis and Edith Munson Foundation, Inc.
M. J. Murdock Charitable Trust
John P. Murphy Foundation
New England Biolabs Foundation
New Hampshire Charitable Foundation
New Horizon Foundation
The New World Foundation
The New York Community Trust
The New-Land Foundation, Inc.
The Nord Family Foundation
Andrew Norman Foundation
Northwest Area Foundation
Jessie Smith Noyes Foundation, Inc.
Spencer T. and Ann W. Olin Foundation
Onan Family Foundation
Orchard Foundation
Ottinger Foundation
Peninsula Community Foundation
The William Penn Foundation
The Pew Charitable Trusts
The Philadelphia Foundation
Philip Morris Companies, Inc.
Phillips Petroleum Foundation, Inc.
The Powell Family Foundation
The Procter & Gamble Fund
The Prudential Foundation
Public Welfare Foundation, Inc.
Recreational Equipment, Inc.
Z. Smith Reynolds Foundation, Inc.
The Rhode Island Community Foundation
The Roberts Foundation
Rockefeller Brothers Fund, Inc.
The Rockefeller Foundation
The Winthrop Rockefeller Foundation
Rockwood Fund, Inc.
San Diego Community Foundation
The San Francisco Foundation
The Sapelo Foundation
The Scherman Foundation, Inc.
The Schumann Fund for New Jersey, Inc.
The Florence and John Schumann Foundation
Shell Oil Company Foundation
Thomas Sill Foundation
The Kelvin and Eleanor Smith Foundation
Kelvin Smith 1980 Charitable Trust
Stanley Smith Horticultural Trust
Snee-Reinhardt Charitable Foundation
Springhouse Foundation
Anna B. Stearns Charitable Foundation, Inc.
The Stebbins Fund, Inc.
Steelcase Foundation
Stern Family Fund
Margaret Dorrance Strawbridge Foundation of Pennsylvania II, Inc.
The Strong Foundation for Environmental Values
The Morris Stulsaft Foundation
Surdna Foundation, Inc.
The Telesis Foundation
Texaco Foundation
Threshold Foundation
The Tides Foundation
Town Creek Foundation, Inc.
Toyota USA Foundation
The Travelers Foundation
The Trust For Mutual Understanding
Alice Tweed Tuohy Foundation
Turner Foundation, Inc.
The USF&G Foundation, Inc.
Unitarian Universalist Veatch Program at Shelter Rock
United States-Japan Foundation
Virginia Environmental Endowment
Alex C. Walker Educational & Charitable Foundation
DeWitt Wallace-Reader's Digest Fund
Lila Wallace-Reader's Digest Fund
Westinghouse Foundation
Weyerhaeuser Company Foundation
Whitecap Foundation
Wilburforce Foundation
G. N. Wilcox Trust
Robert W. Wilson Foundation
The Windham Foundation, Inc.
The Dean Witter Foundation
Margaret Cullinan Wray Charitable Lead Annuity Trust
The Wyomissing Foundation, Inc.

Equipment

ARCO Foundation
A Territory Resource
Mary Reynolds Babcock Foundation, Inc.
Beldon Fund
Blandin Foundation
California Community Foundation
The Chevron Companies
The Chicago Community Trust
Chrysler Corporation Fund
The Community Foundation of Santa Clara County
The Mary A. Crocker Trust
Deer Creek Foundation
The Aaron Diamond Foundation
Geraldine R. Dodge Foundation, Inc.
Dolfinger-McMahon Foundation
Oliver S. and Jennie R. Donaldson Charitable Trust
Donner Canadian Foundation
The Energy Foundation
Environmental Education Foundation of Florida, Inc.
Samuel S. Fels Fund
Foundation for the Carolinas
The Foundation for the National Capital Region
The Fund for New Jersey
GE Fund
The Fred Gellert Foundation
General Service Foundation
The Wallace Alexander Gerbode Foundation, Inc.
Evelyn and Walter Haas, Jr. Fund
The John Randolph Haynes and Dora Haynes Foundation
The Hitachi Foundation
Walter S. Johnson Foundation
The Joyce Foundation
Laidlaw Foundation
Lyndhurst Foundation
Maine Community Foundation, Inc.
Marbrook Foundation
The McIntosh Foundation
The McKnight Foundation
Merck Family Fund
Ruth Mott Fund
National Geographic Society Education Foundation
New Hampshire Charitable Foundation
Edward John Noble Foundation, Inc.
Northwest Area Foundation
Peninsula Community Foundation
James C. Penney Foundation
The Pew Charitable Trusts
Public Welfare Foundation, Inc.
Recreational Equipment, Inc.
The Winthrop Rockefeller Foundation
The San Francisco Foundation
The Scherman Foundation, Inc.
The Florence and John Schumann Foundation
Surdna Foundation, Inc.
The Switzer Foundation
The Trust For Mutual Understanding
United States-Japan Foundation
Vancouver Foundation
Vanguard Public Foundation
Weeden Foundation
Westinghouse Foundation
The Winston-Salem Foundation, Inc.

Exhibits

The Ahmanson Foundation
The Vincent Astor Foundation
The Ben & Jerry's Foundation
The Bullitt Foundation
The Chicago Community Trust
Compton Foundation, Inc.
The Conservation and Research Foundation
The Aaron Diamond Foundation
FishAmerica Foundation
The German Marshall Fund of the United States
Global Environmental Project Institute
Great Lakes Protection Fund
The George Gund Foundation
Hawaiian Electric Industries Charitable Foundation
The William and Flora Hewlett Foundation

Limitations

Exhibits (cont.)

The Homeland Foundation
Hudson-Webber Foundation
The Hyams Foundation
Helen K. and Arthur E. Johnson Foundation
The Lazar Foundation
The Max and Anna Levinson Foundation
McKesson Foundation, Inc.
The McKnight Foundation
The Andrew W. Mellon Foundation
Jessie Smith Noyes Foundation, Inc.
Spencer T. and Ann W. Olin Foundation
Amelia Peabody Charitable Fund
Peninsula Community Foundation
The Powell Family Foundation
Public Welfare Foundation, Inc.
Rockwood Fund, Inc.
San Diego Community Foundation
The Sapelo Foundation
The Scherman Foundation, Inc.
Springs Foundation, Inc.
Town Creek Foundation, Inc.
United States-Japan Foundation
Weeden Foundation

Expeditions/tours

The Vincent Astor Foundation
Beldon Fund
The Ben & Jerry's Foundation
The Bullitt Foundation
Claneil Foundation, Inc.
The Community Foundation of Greater New Haven
Compton Foundation, Inc.
The Conservation and Research Foundation
Cooke Foundation, Limited
The Aaron Diamond Foundation
El Paso Community Foundation
FishAmerica Foundation
The Fred Gellert Foundation
Global Environmental Project Institute
Great Lakes Protection Fund
The George Gund Foundation
Hawaiian Electric Industries Charitable Foundation
The John Randolph Haynes and Dora Haynes Foundation
The William and Flora Hewlett Foundation
The Homeland Foundation
The Hyams Foundation
Helen K. and Arthur E. Johnson Foundation
The Lazar Foundation
The Max and Anna Levinson Foundation
Maine Community Foundation, Inc.
MARPAT Foundation, Inc.
The McConnell Foundation
McGregor Fund
McKesson Foundation, Inc.
The McKnight Foundation
The Andrew W. Mellon Foundation
Joyce Mertz-Gilmore Foundation
New England Biolabs Foundation
Edward John Noble Foundation, Inc.
Jessie Smith Noyes Foundation, Inc.

Amelia Peabody Charitable Fund
Peninsula Community Foundation
The William Penn Foundation
James C. Penney Foundation
The Philadelphia Foundation
Philip Morris Companies, Inc.
The Powell Family Foundation
Rockefeller Financial Services, Philanthropy Department
Rockwood Fund, Inc.
San Diego Community Foundation
The San Francisco Foundation
The Sapelo Foundation
The Scherman Foundation, Inc.
Shell Oil Company Foundation
Springs Foundation, Inc.
Town Creek Foundation, Inc.
Toyota USA Foundation
The Troy Foundation
The Trust For Mutual Understanding
Rose E. Tucker Charitable Trust
The USF&G Foundation, Inc.
Virginia Environmental Endowment
Wilburforce Foundation
The Winston-Salem Foundation, Inc.

Facilities

ARCO Foundation
AT&T Foundation
A Territory Resource
The Abelard Foundation West
Alaska Conservation Foundation
American Conservation Association, Inc.
Mary Reynolds Babcock Foundation, Inc.
Clayton Baker Trust
The Barra Foundation, Inc.
The Bay Foundation
Beldon Fund
Blandin Foundation
The Bullitt Foundation
The Louis Calder Foundation
California Community Foundation
Chesapeake Bay Trust
The Chevron Companies
The Community Foundation of Santa Clara County
Jessie B. Cox Charitable Trust
The Mary A. Crocker Trust
Crystal Channel Foundation
The Aaron Diamond Foundation
Dolfinger-McMahon Foundation
Donner Canadian Foundation
The Educational Foundation of America
El Paso Community Foundation
The Energy Foundation
The Charles Engelhard Foundation
Samuel S. Fels Fund
Flintridge Foundation
Foundation for the Carolinas
The Frost Foundation, Ltd.
The Fund for New Jersey
The Fred Gellert Foundation
General Service Foundation
Global Environmental Project Institute

Walter and Duncan Gordon Charitable Foundation
Great Lakes Protection Fund
The George Gund Foundation
Harder Foundation
The John Randolph Haynes and Dora Haynes Foundation
The Hitachi Foundation
The Homeland Foundation
The Richard Ivey Foundation
Martha Holden Jennings Foundation
W. Alton Jones Foundation, Inc.
The J. M. Kaplan Fund, Inc.
Caesar Kleberg Foundation for Wildlife Conservation
The Knapp Foundation, Inc.
Laidlaw Foundation
The Lazar Foundation
The Max and Anna Levinson Foundation
Richard Lounsbery Foundation, Inc.
Maki Foundation
The Marshall Fund of Arizona
The McConnell Foundation
The McIntosh Foundation
McKesson Foundation, Inc.
The McKnight Foundation
The Andrew W. Mellon Foundation
Merck Family Fund
The John Merck Fund
Joyce Mertz-Gilmore Foundation
The Minneapolis Foundation
National Geographic Society Education Foundation
New England Biolabs Foundation
New Hampshire Charitable Foundation
Edward John Noble Foundation, Inc.
Northwest Area Foundation
Spencer T. and Ann W. Olin Foundation
Ottinger Foundation
Peninsula Community Foundation
James C. Penney Foundation
The Philadelphia Foundation
Public Welfare Foundation, Inc.
Recreational Equipment, Inc.
Rockefeller Brothers Fund, Inc.
Rockefeller Family Fund, Inc.
The Winthrop Rockefeller Foundation
Rockwood Fund, Inc.
Sacramento Regional Foundation
The San Francisco Foundation
The Sapelo Foundation
The Scherman Foundation, Inc.
The Schumann Fund for New Jersey, Inc.
The Sonoma County Community Foundation
Stern Family Fund
Surdna Foundation, Inc.
Town Creek Foundation, Inc.
Toyota USA Foundation
The Trust For Mutual Understanding
Alice Tweed Tuohy Foundation
Turner Foundation, Inc.
United States-Japan Foundation
Virginia Environmental Endowment
Weeden Foundation

Limitations

Facilities (cont.)
Westinghouse Foundation
Alex C. Walker Educational & Charitable Foundation
Whitecap Foundation

Facilities (construction)
The Acorn Foundation
The Vincent Astor Foundation
The Betterment Fund
The Bush Foundation
The Morris and Gwendolyn Cafritz Foundation
The Chicago Community Trust
Deer Creek Foundation
Jessie Ball duPont Religious, Charitable and Educational Fund
Environmental Education Foundation of Florida, Inc.
The Ettinger Foundation, Inc.
The Wallace Alexander Gerbode Foundation, Inc.
Ittleson Foundation, Inc.
Jackson Hole Preserve, Inc.
Walter S. Johnson Foundation
The Esther A. and Joseph Klingenstein Fund, Inc.
Lilly Endowment, Inc.
Mobil Foundation, Inc.
The New-Land Foundation, Inc.
Nicholas H. Noyes, Jr. Memorial Foundation
The Pew Charitable Trusts
Smith Richardson Foundation, Inc.
Lila Wallace-Reader's Digest Fund

Facilities (renovation)
The Foundation for the National Capital Region
Ruth Mott Fund

Feasibility studies
The Ahmanson Foundation
The Vincent Astor Foundation
The Bullitt Foundation
Chesapeake Bay Trust
The Aaron Diamond Foundation
FishAmerica Foundation
The Fred Gellert Foundation
Hawaiian Electric Industries Charitable Foundation
The John Randolph Haynes and Dora Haynes Foundation
The Homeland Foundation
The Hyams Foundation
Martha Holden Jennings Foundation
Helen K. and Arthur E. Johnson Foundation
The McConnell Foundation
McKesson Foundation, Inc.
The Andrew W. Mellon Foundation
National Geographic Society Education Foundation
Amelia Peabody Charitable Fund

Peninsula Community Foundation
The Powell Family Foundation
Rockefeller Financial Services, Philanthropy Department
Rockwood Fund, Inc.
Fran and Warren Rupp Foundation
Sarkeys Foundation
Shell Oil Company Foundation
The Sonoma County Community Foundation
Springs Foundation, Inc.
Town Creek Foundation, Inc.
Toyota USA Foundation
Alice Tweed Tuohy Foundation

Fellowships
A Territory Resource
Abell-Hanger Foundation
The Ahmanson Foundation
American Conservation Association, Inc.
American Foundation Corporation
The Arca Foundation
Arcadia Foundation
The Vincent Astor Foundation
Mary Reynolds Babcock Foundation, Inc.
The George F. Baker Trust
The Barra Foundation, Inc.
L. L. Bean, Inc.
Beldon Fund
James Ford Bell Foundation
The Frank Stanley Beveridge Foundation, Inc.
The Bothin Foundation
The Bullitt Foundation
The Bunbury Company, Inc.
The Bydale Foundation
C. S. Fund
The Cape Branch Foundation
The Cargill Foundation
Centerior Energy Foundation
Chesapeake Bay Trust
Chrysler Corporation Fund
Claneil Foundation, Inc.
Columbia Foundation
The Community Foundation Serving Coastal South Carolina
The Conservation and Research Foundation
Cooke Foundation, Limited
The Cricket Foundation
Davis Conservation Foundation
Dayton Hudson Foundation
The Aaron Diamond Foundation
Cleveland H. Dodge Foundation, Inc.
Oliver S. and Jennie R. Donaldson Charitable Trust
Samuel S. Fels Fund
Jamee and Marshall Field Foundation
FishAmerica Foundation
The Foundation for the National Capital Region
The Wallace Alexander Gerbode Foundation, Inc.
Bernard F. and Alva B. Gimbel Foundation, Inc.
Global Environmental Project Institute

Great Lakes Protection Fund
The William and Mary Greve Foundation, Inc.
The W. C. Griffith Foundation
The Ewing Halsell Foundation
Charles Hayden Foundation
The Edward W. Hazen Foundation
The Hitachi Foundation
Hudson-Webber Foundation
The Hyams Foundation
The International Foundation, Inc.
Jackson Hole Preserve, Inc.
Martha Holden Jennings Foundation
Helen K. and Arthur E. Johnson Foundation
Walter S. Johnson Foundation
The J. M. Kaplan Fund, Inc.
The Henry P. Kendall Foundation
Caesar Kleberg Foundation for Wildlife Conservation
Laidlaw Foundation
The Lazar Foundation
The Max and Anna Levinson Foundation
Maki Foundation
Marbrook Foundation
The McConnell Foundation
McKesson Foundation, Inc.
The McKnight Foundation
Richard King Mellon Foundation
Merck Family Fund
Joyce Mertz-Gilmore Foundation
J. P. Morgan Charitable Trust
Ruth Mott Fund
M. J. Murdock Charitable Trust
John P. Murphy Foundation
The National Environmental Education and Training Foundation, Inc.
National Fish and Wildlife Foundation
New England Biolabs Foundation
The New World Foundation
Andrew Norman Foundation
Northwest Area Foundation
Jessie Smith Noyes Foundation, Inc.
The Ohrstrom Foundation
Spencer T. and Ann W. Olin Foundation
Orchard Foundation
Peninsula Community Foundation
The William Penn Foundation
The Philadelphia Foundation
The Powell Family Foundation
Recreational Equipment, Inc.
The Rhode Island Community Foundation
The Winthrop Rockefeller Foundation
Rockwood Fund, Inc.
Fran and Warren Rupp Foundation
The Sapelo Foundation
The Scherman Foundation, Inc.
Sears-Swetland Foundation
Sequoia Foundation
The Kelvin and Eleanor Smith Foundation
Kelvin Smith 1980 Charitable Trust
The Sonoma County Community Foundation
Stackner Family Foundation, Inc.
Margaret Dorrance Strawbridge Foundation of Pennsylvania II, Inc.

Limitations

Fellowships (cont.)

The Strong Foundation for Environmental Values
The Sudbury Foundation
Surdna Foundation, Inc.
The Oakleigh L. Thorne Foundation
Toyota USA Foundation
The Troy Foundation
Rose E. Tucker Charitable Trust
Westinghouse Foundation
Robert W. Wilson Foundation
The Winston-Salem Foundation, Inc.
The Wortham Foundation, Inc.
The Wyomissing Foundation, Inc.

Fieldwork

The Vincent Astor Foundation
Beldon Fund
Chesapeake Bay Trust
The Aaron Diamond Foundation
The Fred Gellert Foundation
Hawaiian Electric Industries Charitable Foundation
The Hyams Foundation
The McConnell Foundation
McKesson Foundation, Inc.
Amelia Peabody Charitable Fund
Peninsula Community Foundation
The Powell Family Foundation
Shell Oil Company Foundation
Springs Foundation, Inc.

Fundraising

ARCO Foundation
The Ahmanson Foundation
American Express Philanthropic Program
Americana Foundation, Inc.
Ameritech Foundation
The Vincent Astor Foundation
Atherton Family Foundation
Atkinson Foundation
Baltimore Gas and Electric Foundation, Inc.
BankAmerica Foundation
David Winton Bell Foundation
James Ford Bell Foundation
The Ben & Jerry's Foundation
The Frank Stanley Beveridge Foundation, Inc.
The Cabot Family Charitable Trust
California Community Foundation
The Cargill Foundation
Chesapeake Bay Trust
The Chevron Companies
The Collins Foundation
The Community Foundation of Santa Clara County
Compton Foundation, Inc.
Conservation, Food & Health Foundation, Inc.
Jessie B. Cox Charitable Trust
Dayton Hudson Foundation
The Aaron Diamond Foundation
Gaylord and Dorothy Donnelley Foundation
Donner Canadian Foundation

El Paso Community Foundation
The Energy Foundation
The Field Foundation of Illinois, Inc.
Jamee and Marshall Field Foundation
FishAmerica Foundation
Lloyd A. Fry Foundation
The Gap Foundation
Gates Foundation
The Fred Gellert Foundation
The Wallace Alexander Gerbode Foundation, Inc.
Give to the Earth Foundation
Richard & Rhoda Goldman Fund
The George Gund Foundation
Evelyn and Walter Haas, Jr. Fund
Hawaiian Electric Industries Charitable Foundation
Charles Hayden Foundation
The John Randolph Haynes and Dora Haynes Foundation
Vira I. Heinz Endowment
Heller Charitable & Educational Fund
The Hitachi Foundation
The Homeland Foundation
Hudson-Webber Foundation
The Hyams Foundation
IBM Corporation
Martha Holden Jennings Foundation
Harris and Eliza Kempner Fund
F. M. Kirby Foundation, Inc.
Laird, Norton Foundation
Levi Strauss Foundation
Longwood Foundation, Inc.
Maine Community Foundation, Inc.
The Marshall Fund of Arizona
The McConnell Foundation
McDonnell Douglas Foundation
McKesson Foundation, Inc.
The Andrew W. Mellon Foundation
The Minneapolis Foundation
Mobil Foundation, Inc.
The Mountaineers Foundation
M. J. Murdock Charitable Trust
National Geographic Society Education Foundation
New England Biolabs Foundation
The New World Foundation
The Nord Family Foundation
Norman Foundation
Jessie Smith Noyes Foundation, Inc.
Amelia Peabody Charitable Fund
Peninsula Community Foundation
Philip Morris Companies, Inc.
Phillips Petroleum Foundation, Inc.
The Powell Family Foundation
The Prudential Foundation
Recreational Equipment, Inc.
The Roberts Foundation
Rockefeller Financial Services, Philanthropy Department
The Winthrop Rockefeller Foundation
Rockwell Fund, Inc.
Rockwood Fund, Inc.
Fran and Warren Rupp Foundation
San Diego Community Foundation

The Sonoma County Community Foundation
Southwestern Bell Foundation
The Stroh Foundation
Town Creek Foundation, Inc.
Toyota USA Foundation
The Travelers Foundation
The Troy Foundation
The USF&G Foundation, Inc.
Union Pacific Foundation
Vancouver Foundation
Weyerhaeuser Company Foundation
Whitecap Foundation

General purposes

Evenor Armington Fund
The Bush Foundation
Chesapeake Bay Trust
Liz Claiborne & Art Ortenberg Foundation
Conservation, Food & Health Foundation, Inc.
Cooke Foundation, Limited
S. H. Cowell Foundation
The Aaron Diamond Foundation
Cleveland H. Dodge Foundation, Inc.
The Ettinger Foundation, Inc.
Fields Pond Foundation, Inc.
The Barbara Gauntlett Foundation, Inc.
The Wallace Alexander Gerbode Foundation, Inc.
Great Lakes Protection Fund
The Ewing Halsell Foundation
Charles Hayden Foundation
The John Randolph Haynes and Dora Haynes Foundation
The Hofmann Foundation
Martha Holden Jennings Foundation
W. Alton Jones Foundation, Inc.
The McConnell Foundation
McCune Foundation
The John Merck Fund
M. J. Murdock Charitable Trust
New England Biolabs Foundation
The Nord Family Foundation
Jessie Smith Noyes Foundation, Inc.
Amelia Peabody Charitable Fund
Peninsula Community Foundation
The William Penn Foundation
The Polden-Puckham Charitable Foundation
Recreational Equipment, Inc.
The Rockefeller Foundation
The Winthrop Rockefeller Foundation
San Diego Community Foundation
The Sonoma County Community Foundation
Springhouse Foundation
The Sudbury Foundation
The Telesis Foundation
Toyota USA Foundation
The Trust For Mutual Understanding

Indirect costs

The Ahmanson Foundation
The Vincent Astor Foundation

© 1995 Environmental Data Resources, Inc.

Limitations

Indirect costs (cont.)

The Beirne Carter Foundation
The Bullitt Foundation
Chesapeake Bay Trust
Claneil Foundation, Inc.
Compton Foundation, Inc.
The Conservation and Research Foundation
Conservation, Food & Health
  Foundation, Inc.
The Aaron Diamond Foundation
Geraldine R. Dodge Foundation, Inc.
El Paso Community Foundation
FishAmerica Foundation
The Fred Gellert Foundation
The John Randolph Haynes and
  Dora Haynes Foundation
The Homeland Foundation
The Hyams Foundation
W. K. Kellogg Foundation
Marin Community Foundation
The McConnell Foundation
McKesson Foundation, Inc.
The Andrew W. Mellon Foundation
Meyer Memorial Trust
National Fish and Wildlife Foundation
National Geographic Society Education
  Foundation
New England Biolabs Foundation
Amelia Peabody Charitable Fund
Peninsula Community Foundation
The Powell Family Foundation
Recreational Equipment, Inc.
Rockwood Fund, Inc.
San Diego Community Foundation
Shell Oil Company Foundation
Stanley Smith Horticultural Trust
Springs Foundation, Inc.
Toyota USA Foundation
Virginia Environmental Endowment
Wilburforce Foundation
The Winston-Salem Foundation, Inc.

Individuals

ARCO Foundation
AT&T Foundation
A Territory Resource
The Abelard Foundation West
The Abell Foundation
Abell-Hanger Foundation
The Achelis Foundation
The Acorn Foundation
The Ahmanson Foundation
The George I. Alden Trust
Winifred & Harry B. Allen Foundation
American Conservation Association, Inc.
American Express Philanthropic Program
American Foundation Corporation
Americana Foundation, Inc.
Ameritech Foundation
Elmer L. & Eleanor J. Andersen Foundation
The Arca Foundation
Arcadia Foundation
Evenor Armington Fund
The Vincent Astor Foundation

Atkinson Foundation
The Austin Memorial Foundation
Mary Reynolds Babcock Foundation, Inc.
The Bailey Wildlife Foundation
The Cameron Baird Foundation
The George F. Baker Trust
Baltimore Gas and Electric Foundation, Inc.
BankAmerica Foundation
The Barra Foundation, Inc.
The Theodore H. Barth Foundation, Inc.
The Bauman Foundation
Bay Area Community Foundation
The Bay Foundation
The Howard Bayne Fund
L. L. Bean, Inc.
S. D. Bechtel, Jr. Foundation
The Beirne Carter Foundation
Beldon Fund
David Winton Bell Foundation
James Ford Bell Foundation
The Ben & Jerry's Foundation
Beneficia Foundation
Benua Foundation, Inc.
The Bersted Foundation
The Betterment Fund
The Frank Stanley Beveridge
  Foundation, Inc.
The William Bingham Foundation
Blandin Foundation
The Blumenthal Foundation
The Bodman Foundation
The Boeing Company
Boettcher Foundation
The Bothin Foundation
Botwinick-Wolfensohn Foundation, Inc.
Helen Brach Foundation
The Lynde and Harry Bradley
  Foundation, Inc.
Otto Bremer Foundation
Alexander H. Bright Charitable Trust
Alex. Brown & Sons Charitable
  Foundation, Inc.
W. L. Lyons Brown Foundation
The Robert Brownlee Foundation
Kathleen Price and Joseph M. Bryan
  Family Foundation, Inc.
The Bullitt Foundation
The Bunbury Company, Inc.
The Bush Foundation
J. E. & Z. B. Butler Foundation, Inc.
Patrick and Aimee Butler Family
  Foundation
The Bydale Foundation
C. S. Fund
The Cabot Family Charitable Trust
The Morris and Gwendolyn Cafritz
  Foundation
The Louis Calder Foundation
California Community Foundation
James & Abigail Campbell Foundation
The Cape Branch Foundation
The Cargill Foundation
Carolyn Foundation
The Carpenter Foundation
Mary Flagler Cary Charitable Trust

Centerior Energy Foundation
The Champlin Foundations
Ben B. Cheney Foundation
Chesapeake Bay Trust
Chesapeake Corporation Foundation
The Chevron Companies
The Chicago Community Trust
Chrysler Corporation Fund
Liz Claiborne & Art Ortenberg Foundation
Claneil Foundation, Inc.
The Clark Foundation
The Cleveland Foundation
The Clowes Fund, Inc.
Olive B. Cole Foundation
The Collins Foundation
Columbia Foundation
The Columbus Foundation
The Community Foundation of
  Greater New Haven
The Community Foundation of
  Santa Clara County
The Community Foundation of
  Sarasota County, Inc.
The Community Foundation Serving
  Coastal South Carolina
Compton Foundation, Inc.
Conservation, Food & Health
  Foundation, Inc.
Cooke Foundation, Limited
Adolph Coors Foundation
S. H. Cowell Foundation
The Cowles Charitable Trust
Cox Foundation, Inc.
Jessie B. Cox Charitable Trust
The Cricket Foundation
The Mary A. Crocker Trust
Patrick and Anna M. Cudahy Fund
Charles E. Culpeper Foundation, Inc.
The Nathan Cummings Foundation
The Fred Harris Daniels Foundation, Inc.
Dart Foundation
The Arthur Vining Davis Foundations
Davis Conservation Foundation
Dayton Hudson Foundation
The Nelson B. Delavan Foundation
The Aaron Diamond Foundation
Cleveland H. Dodge Foundation, Inc.
Geraldine R. Dodge Foundation, Inc.
Thelma Doelger Charitable Trust
Dolfinger-McMahon Foundation
Oliver S. and Jennie R. Donaldson
  Charitable Trust
Gaylord and Dorothy Donnelley Foundation
Donner Canadian Foundation
The Herbert H. and Grace A. Dow
  Foundation
The Dragon Foundation, Inc.
The Max and Victoria Dreyfus
  Foundation, Inc.
The Elizabeth Ordway Dunn
  Foundation, Inc.
Jessie Ball duPont Religious, Charitable
  and Educational Fund
Eastman Kodak Company Charitable Trust
Ederic Foundation, Inc.

Limitations

Individuals (cont.)

The Educational Foundation of America
El Paso Community Foundation
The Energy Foundation
The Charles Engelhard Foundation
English-Bonter-Mitchell Foundation
Environmental Endowment for New Jersey, Inc.
The Armand G. Erpf Fund, Inc.
The Ettinger Foundation, Inc.
Fanwood Foundation
The William Stamps Farish Fund
Felburn Foundation
Samuel S. Fels Fund
The Hugh and Jane Ferguson Foundation
The Field Foundation of Illinois, Inc.
Jamee and Marshall Field Foundation
Fields Pond Foundation, Inc.
The 1525 Foundation
Leland Fikes Foundation, Inc.
FishAmerica Foundation
Flintridge Foundation
Ford Motor Company Fund
Walter and Josephine Ford Fund
Foundation for the Carolinas
The Foundation for the National Capital Region
Mary D. and Walter F. Frear Eleemosynary Trust
The Freed Foundation, Inc.
Frelinghuysen Foundation
The Frost Foundation, Ltd.
Lloyd A. Fry Foundation
The Fund for New Jersey
The GAR Foundation
GE Fund
The Gap Foundation
Gates Foundation
The Barbara Gauntlett Foundation, Inc.
Gebbie Foundation, Inc.
The Fred Gellert Foundation
General Service Foundation
The Wallace Alexander Gerbode Foundation, Inc.
The Rollin M. Gerstacker Foundation
Global Environmental Project Institute
Global Greengrants Fund
The Golden Rule Foundation, Inc.
Herman Goldman Foundation
Richard & Rhoda Goldman Fund
Good Samaritan, Inc.
Greater Piscataqua Community Foundation
The Greenville Foundation
The William and Mary Greve Foundation, Inc.
The W. C. Griffith Foundation
The George Gund Foundation
HKH Foundation
Evelyn and Walter Haas, Jr. Fund
Walter and Elise Haas Fund
The Hahn Family Foundation
The Hall Family Foundation
The Ewing Halsell Foundation
The Hamer Foundation

James G. Hanes Memorial Fund
Harder Foundation
The Harding Educational and Charitable Foundation
Gladys and Roland Harriman Foundation
Mary W. Harriman Foundation
Hartford Foundation for Public Giving
The Hastings Trust
The Merrill G. & Emita E. Hastings Foundation
Hawaiian Electric Industries Charitable Foundation
Charles Hayden Foundation
The John Randolph Haynes and Dora Haynes Foundation
The Edward W. Hazen Foundation
The M. A. Healy Family Foundation, Inc.
Howard Heinz Endowment
Vira I. Heinz Endowment
Heller Charitable & Educational Fund
The Clarence E. Heller Charitable Foundation
The William and Flora Hewlett Foundation
The Hitachi Foundation
The Homeland Foundation
Hudson-Webber Foundation
The Charles Evans Hughes Memorial Foundation, Inc.
The Hyams Foundation
The Hyde and Watson Foundation
IBM Corporation
Illilouette Fund
The International Foundation, Inc.
Ireland Foundation
Ittleson Foundation, Inc.
The Richard Ivey Foundation
The Jackson Foundation
Jackson Hole Preserve, Inc.
The Henry M. Jackson Foundation
Martha Holden Jennings Foundation
The George Frederick Jewett Foundation
Helen K. and Arthur E. Johnson Foundation
The Howard Johnson Foundation
Walter S. Johnson Foundation
W. Alton Jones Foundation, Inc.
The Joyce Foundation
The J. M. Kaplan Fund, Inc.
W. K. Kellogg Foundation
Harris and Eliza Kempner Fund
The Henry P. Kendall Foundation
The Robert S. and Grayce B. Kerr Foundation, Inc.
The Helen & Milton Kimmelman Foundation
Kinnoull Foundation
F. M. Kirby Foundation, Inc.
Caesar Kleberg Foundation for Wildlife Conservation
The Esther A. and Joseph Klingenstein Fund, Inc.
The Knapp Foundation, Inc.
The Seymour H. Knox Foundation, Inc.
Charles G. Koch Charitable Foundation
Kongsgaard-Goldman Foundation

The Kresge Foundation
Laird, Norton Foundation
Larsen Fund, Inc.
The Lauder Foundation, Inc.
Laurel Foundation
The Lazar Foundation
The Norman Lear Foundation
Levi Strauss Foundation
The Max and Anna Levinson Foundation
Lilly Endowment, Inc.
Lintilhac Foundation
The Little Family Foundation
Longwood Foundation, Inc.
Richard Lounsbery Foundation, Inc.
Luster Family Foundation, Inc.
Lyndhurst Foundation
James A. Macdonald Foundation
Magowan Family Foundation, Inc.
Marbrook Foundation
Marin Community Foundation
MARPAT Foundation, Inc.
Mars Foundation
The Marshall Fund of Arizona
The Martin Foundation, Inc.
The McConnell Foundation
McCune Foundation
The Marshall L. & Perrine D. McCune Charitable Foundation
The Eugene McDermott Foundation
McDonnell Douglas Foundation
McGregor Fund
McInerny Foundation
The McIntosh Foundation
McKenzie River Gathering Foundation
McKesson Foundation, Inc.
Giles W. and Elise G. Mead Foundation
Nelson Mead Fund
Meadows Foundation, Inc.
The Andrew W. Mellon Foundation
Richard King Mellon Foundation
Merck Family Fund
The John Merck Fund
Joyce Mertz-Gilmore Foundation
Metropolitan Atlanta Community Foundation, Inc.
Metropolitan Life Foundation
Middlecott Foundation
Millbrook Tribute Garden, Inc.
The Milwaukee Foundation
The Minneapolis Foundation
Mobil Foundation, Inc.
Leo Model Foundation, Inc.
The Moody Foundation
J. P. Morgan Charitable Trust
Henry and Lucy Moses Fund, Inc.
Charles Stewart Mott Foundation
Ruth Mott Fund
The Curtis and Edith Munson Foundation, Inc.
M. J. Murdock Charitable Trust
John P. Murphy Foundation
The National Environmental Education and Training Foundation, Inc.
New Horizon Foundation

© 1995 Environmental Data Resources, Inc.

Limitations

Individuals (cont.)

The New World Foundation
The New York Community Trust
The New York Times Company Foundation, Inc.
The New-Land Foundation, Inc.
Edward John Noble Foundation, Inc.
The Samuel Roberts Noble Foundation, Inc.
The Nord Family Foundation
Norman Foundation
Andrew Norman Foundation
Kenneth T. and Eileen L. Norris Foundation
The Norton Foundation, Inc.
Jessie Smith Noyes Foundation, Inc.
Nicholas H. Noyes, Jr. Memorial Foundation
OCRI Foundation
Nathan M. Ohrbach Foundation, Inc.
The Ohrstrom Foundation
Spencer T. and Ann W. Olin Foundation
Orchard Foundation
Ottinger Foundation
The Overbrook Foundation
The David and Lucile Packard Foundation
Amelia Peabody Charitable Fund
Peninsula Community Foundation
The William Penn Foundation
James C. Penney Foundation
The Perkin Fund
Perkins Charitable Foundation
The Pew Charitable Trusts
The Pfizer Foundation, Inc.
The Philadelphia Foundation
Philip Morris Companies, Inc.
Phillips Petroleum Foundation, Inc.
Ellis L. Phillips Foundation
Pinewood Foundation
Henry B. Plant Memorial Fund, Inc.
The Polden-Puckham Charitable Foundation
The Powell Family Foundation
Prince Charitable Trusts
Pritzker Foundation
The Procter & Gamble Fund
The Prospect Hill Foundation
The Prudential Foundation
Recreational Equipment, Inc.
Philip D. Reed Foundation, Inc.
Z. Smith Reynolds Foundation, Inc.
The Rhode Island Community Foundation
Sid W. Richardson Foundation
Smith Richardson Foundation, Inc.
The Roberts Foundation
Rockefeller Brothers Fund, Inc.
Rockefeller Family Fund, Inc.
Rockefeller Financial Services, Philanthropy Department
The Rockefeller Foundation
The Winthrop Rockefeller Foundation
Rockwell Fund, Inc.
Rockwood Fund, Inc.
Fran and Warren Rupp Foundation
Sacharuna Foundation
Sacramento Regional Foundation
San Diego Community Foundation
The San Francisco Foundation
The Sapelo Foundation
Sarkeys Foundation
Sarah Scaife Foundation Incorporated
The Scherman Foundation, Inc.
Sarah I. Schieffelin Residuary Trust
The Schiff Foundation
The Schumann Fund for New Jersey, Inc.
The Florence and John Schumann Foundation
Ellen Browning Scripps Foundation
Sears-Swetland Foundation
Sequoia Foundation
Elmina B. Sewall Foundation
Ralph C. Sheldon Foundation, Inc.
Shell Oil Company Foundation
Thomas Sill Foundation
The Skaggs Foundation
The Kelvin and Eleanor Smith Foundation
Kelvin Smith 1980 Charitable Trust
Stanley Smith Horticultural Trust
Snee-Reinhardt Charitable Foundation
The Sonoma County Community Foundation
South Coast Foundation, Inc.
Southwestern Bell Foundation
Springs Foundation, Inc.
Stackner Family Foundation, Inc.
The Stebbins Fund, Inc.
Steelcase Foundation
Stoddard Charitable Trust
Stranahan Foundation
The Stratford Foundation
Margaret Dorrance Strawbridge Foundation of Pennsylvania II, Inc.
The Stroh Foundation
The Strong Foundation for Environmental Values
The Charles J. Strosacker Foundation
The Morris Stulsaft Foundation
The Sudbury Foundation
The Sulzberger Foundation, Inc.
The Summerlee Foundation
Surdna Foundation, Inc.
Nelson Talbott Foundation
S. Mark Taper Foundation
The Telesis Foundation
Texaco Foundation
Thanksgiving Foundation
The Oakleigh L. Thorne Foundation
The Tinker Foundation Incorporated
Tortuga Foundation
Town Creek Foundation, Inc.
Toyota USA Foundation
The Travelers Foundation
The Troy Foundation
True North Foundation
The Trust For Mutual Understanding
Rose E. Tucker Charitable Trust
Alice Tweed Tuohy Foundation
The USF&G Foundation, Inc.
USX Foundation, Inc.
Underhill Foundation
Union Camp Charitable Trust
Union Pacific Foundation
Unitarian Universalist Veatch Program at Shelter Rock
United States-Japan Foundation
Vancouver Foundation
R. T. Vanderbilt Trust
Vanguard Public Foundation
G. Unger Vetlesen Foundation
Victoria Foundation, Inc.
The Vidda Foundation
Vinmont Foundation, Inc.
Virginia Environmental Endowment
WMX Environmental Grants Program
Alex C. Walker Educational & Charitable Foundation
Wallace Genetic Foundation, Inc.
DeWitt Wallace-Reader's Digest Fund
Lila Wallace-Reader's Digest Fund
Bill & Edith Walter Foundation
Weeden Foundation
Welfare Foundation, Inc.
Henry E. and Consuelo S. Wenger Foundation, Inc.
Westinghouse Foundation
Weyerhaeuser Company Foundation
Whitecap Foundation
Joseph B. Whitehead Foundation
Wilburforce Foundation
G. N. Wilcox Trust
Robert W. Wilson Foundation
The Windham Foundation, Inc.
Mark and Catherine Winkler Foundation
The Winslow Foundation
The Winston-Salem Foundation, Inc.
The Dean Witter Foundation
Wodecroft Foundation
Robert W. Woodruff Foundation, Inc.
The Wortham Foundation, Inc.
Margaret Cullinan Wray Charitable Lead Annuity Trust
The Wyomissing Foundation, Inc.

Internships

A Territory Resource
The Ahmanson Foundation
The Vincent Astor Foundation
L. L. Bean, Inc.
Beldon Fund
Columbia Foundation
Cooke Foundation, Limited
The Aaron Diamond Foundation
FishAmerica Foundation
The William and Flora Hewlett Foundation
The Hyams Foundation
Ittleson Foundation, Inc.
Helen K. and Arthur E. Johnson Foundation
The McConnell Foundation
McKesson Foundation, Inc.
The McKnight Foundation
John P. Murphy Foundation
National Geographic Society Education Foundation
New England Biolabs Foundation
Amelia Peabody Charitable Fund

Limitations

Internships (cont.)

Peninsula Community Foundation
The William Penn Foundation
The Powell Family Foundation
The Rhode Island Community Foundation
Rockwood Fund, Inc.
Fran and Warren Rupp Foundation
Town Creek Foundation, Inc.
Toyota USA Foundation
The Troy Foundation
Westinghouse Foundation
The Wortham Foundation, Inc.

Inventories

The Vincent Astor Foundation
Beldon Fund
Chesapeake Bay Trust
Claneil Foundation, Inc.
The Community Foundation of
  Greater New Haven
Compton Foundation, Inc.
Crystal Channel Foundation
The Aaron Diamond Foundation
The Fred Gellert Foundation
The German Marshall Fund of
  the United States
Global Environmental Project Institute
Hawaiian Electric Industries Charitable
  Foundation
The John Randolph Haynes and
  Dora Haynes Foundation
The Homeland Foundation
The Hyams Foundation
Martha Holden Jennings Foundation
The McConnell Foundation
McKesson Foundation, Inc.
The McKnight Foundation
The Andrew W. Mellon Foundation
National Geographic Society
  Education Foundation
New England Biolabs Foundation
Edward John Noble Foundation, Inc.
Amelia Peabody Charitable Fund
Peninsula Community Foundation
James C. Penney Foundation
The Powell Family Foundation
Rockwood Fund, Inc.
Fran and Warren Rupp Foundation
The Sapelo Foundation
The Scherman Foundation, Inc.
Shell Oil Company Foundation
The Sonoma County Community
  Foundation
Town Creek Foundation, Inc.
Toyota USA Foundation
The USF&G Foundation, Inc.

Land acquisition

A Territory Resource
Alaska Conservation Foundation
Arcadia Foundation
The Vincent Astor Foundation
Beldon Fund
Chesapeake Bay Trust

Claneil Foundation, Inc.
The Community Foundation of
  Greater New Haven
Conservation, Food & Health
  Foundation, Inc.
Cooke Foundation, Limited
Jessie B. Cox Charitable Trust
The Nathan Cummings Foundation
Dayton Hudson Foundation
The Aaron Diamond Foundation
The Energy Foundation
FishAmerica Foundation
The Foundation for the National
  Capital Region
The Frost Foundation, Ltd.
The Fund for New Jersey
The Fred Gellert Foundation
The German Marshall Fund of
  the United States
Give to the Earth Foundation
Global Environmental Project Institute
Greater Piscataqua Community Foundation
The George Gund Foundation
The John Randolph Haynes and
  Dora Haynes Foundation
The Hyams Foundation
The Richard Ivey Foundation
Martha Holden Jennings Foundation
Laidlaw Foundation
The Lazar Foundation
The Max and Anna Levinson Foundation
The Little Family Foundation
Maine Community Foundation, Inc.
Marin Community Foundation
The McConnell Foundation
McKesson Foundation, Inc.
The McKnight Foundation
Merck Family Fund
Joyce Mertz-Gilmore Foundation
The Minneapolis Foundation
Ruth Mott Fund
National Geographic Society Education
  Foundation
New Hampshire Charitable Foundation
Edward John Noble Foundation, Inc.
Peninsula Community Foundation
James C. Penney Foundation
The Pfizer Foundation, Inc.
The Philadelphia Foundation
Philip Morris Companies, Inc.
The Powell Family Foundation
Public Welfare Foundation, Inc.
Rockefeller Brothers Fund, Inc.
Rockwood Fund, Inc.
The San Francisco Foundation
The Sapelo Foundation
The Florence and John Schumann
  Foundation
Shell Oil Company Foundation
The Sonoma County Community
  Foundation
Town Creek Foundation, Inc.
Toyota USA Foundation
The Travelers Foundation
The Troy Foundation

The Trust For Mutual Understanding
Turner Foundation, Inc.
The USF&G Foundation, Inc.
Vancouver Foundation
Virginia Environmental Endowment
Westinghouse Foundation
The Winston-Salem Foundation, Inc.

Lectureships

The Ahmanson Foundation
The Vincent Astor Foundation
L. L. Bean, Inc.
Beldon Fund
The Cleveland Foundation
Columbia Foundation
Compton Foundation, Inc.
The Conservation and Research Foundation
Cooke Foundation, Limited
Jessie B. Cox Charitable Trust
The Aaron Diamond Foundation
FishAmerica Foundation
Foundation for Field Research
The Fred Gellert Foundation
Global Environmental Project Institute
Great Lakes Protection Fund
Hawaiian Electric Industries Charitable
  Foundation
The William and Flora Hewlett Foundation
The Homeland Foundation
The Hyams Foundation
Helen K. and Arthur E. Johnson Foundation
The Max and Anna Levinson Foundation
Marin Community Foundation
The McConnell Foundation
McGregor Fund
McKesson Foundation, Inc.
The McKnight Foundation
The Andrew W. Mellon Foundation
John P. Murphy Foundation
New England Biolabs Foundation
Jessie Smith Noyes Foundation, Inc.
Amelia Peabody Charitable Fund
Peninsula Community Foundation
The William Penn Foundation
James C. Penney Foundation
The Powell Family Foundation
Public Welfare Foundation, Inc.
Recreational Equipment, Inc.
The Rhode Island Community Foundation
Rockefeller Financial Services,
  Philanthropy Department
Rockwood Fund, Inc.
San Diego Community Foundation
The San Francisco Foundation
The Scherman Foundation, Inc.
Springs Foundation, Inc.
The Strong Foundation for
  Environmental Values
The Sudbury Foundation
Surdna Foundation, Inc.
Town Creek Foundation, Inc.
Toyota USA Foundation
The USF&G Foundation, Inc.
Westinghouse Foundation
The Winston-Salem Foundation, Inc.

Limitations

Leveraging funds

The Vincent Astor Foundation
Chesapeake Bay Trust
The Aaron Diamond Foundation
The Frost Foundation, Ltd.
The Fred Gellert Foundation
Hawaiian Electric Industries Charitable Foundation
The John Randolph Haynes and Dora Haynes Foundation
The Hyams Foundation
Helen K. and Arthur E. Johnson Foundation
Laurel Foundation
McKesson Foundation, Inc.
John P. Murphy Foundation
National Geographic Society Education Foundation
Peninsula Community Foundation
The Powell Family Foundation
The Rhode Island Community Foundation
Rockwood Fund, Inc.
The Scherman Foundation, Inc.
Shell Oil Company Foundation
The Wortham Foundation, Inc.

Litigation

A Territory Resource
The Ahmanson Foundation
The Vincent Astor Foundation
L. L. Bean, Inc.
Beldon Fund
The Morris and Gwendolyn Cafritz Foundation
Carolyn Foundation
Chesapeake Bay Trust
The Chevron Companies
Claneil Foundation, Inc.
The Community Foundation of Greater New Haven
Cooke Foundation, Limited
The Aaron Diamond Foundation
Dolfinger-McMahon Foundation
Samuel S. Fels Fund
FishAmerica Foundation
Flintridge Foundation
The Frost Foundation, Ltd.
Gates Foundation
Gebbie Foundation, Inc.
The German Marshall Fund of the United States
Global Environmental Project Institute
Great Lakes Protection Fund
Greater Piscataqua Community Foundation
The George Gund Foundation
Hawaiian Electric Industries Charitable Foundation
The John Randolph Haynes and Dora Haynes Foundation
The William and Flora Hewlett Foundation
The Hyams Foundation
Martha Holden Jennings Foundation
Helen K. and Arthur E. Johnson Foundation
Maine Community Foundation, Inc.
The Martin Foundation, Inc.

The McConnell Foundation
McGregor Fund
McKesson Foundation, Inc.
The McKnight Foundation
The Andrew W. Mellon Foundation
Metropolitan Atlanta Community Foundation, Inc.
Meyer Memorial Trust
National Geographic Society Education Foundation
New England Biolabs Foundation
Edward John Noble Foundation, Inc.
Amelia Peabody Charitable Fund
Peninsula Community Foundation
James C. Penney Foundation
Philip Morris Companies, Inc.
Ellis L. Phillips Foundation
The Powell Family Foundation
The Rhode Island Community Foundation
Fran and Warren Rupp Foundation
San Diego Community Foundation
The San Francisco Foundation
Sarkeys Foundation
Shell Oil Company Foundation
Stanley Smith Horticultural Trust
The Sonoma County Community Foundation
Springs Foundation, Inc.
Toyota USA Foundation
The Troy Foundation
Rose E. Tucker Charitable Trust
The USF&G Foundation, Inc.
Virginia Environmental Endowment
The Winston-Salem Foundation, Inc.

Loans

A Territory Resource
Abell-Hanger Foundation
The Achelis Foundation
The Ahmanson Foundation
The George I. Alden Trust
American Foundation Corporation
Arcadia Foundation
The Vincent Astor Foundation
Atkinson Foundation
The George F. Baker Trust
The Barra Foundation, Inc.
L. L. Bean, Inc.
The Beirne Carter Foundation
Beldon Fund
The Ben & Jerry's Foundation
The Frank Stanley Beveridge Foundation, Inc.
The Blumenthal Foundation
The Bodman Foundation
The Bothin Foundation
The Bunbury Company, Inc.
The Bush Foundation
Patrick and Aimee Butler Family Foundation
The Bydale Foundation
The Morris and Gwendolyn Cafritz Foundation
James & Abigail Campbell Foundation
The Cargill Foundation

Centerior Energy Foundation
The Champlin Foundations
Ben B. Cheney Foundation
Chesapeake Bay Trust
Chrysler Corporation Fund
The Clowes Fund, Inc.
Columbia Foundation
Compton Foundation, Inc.
Conservation, Food & Health Foundation, Inc.
Cooke Foundation, Limited
The Cowles Charitable Trust
Jessie B. Cox Charitable Trust
Patrick and Anna M. Cudahy Fund
Charles E. Culpeper Foundation, Inc.
The Fred Harris Daniels Foundation, Inc.
Davis Conservation Foundation
Dayton Hudson Foundation
The Aaron Diamond Foundation
Cleveland H. Dodge Foundation, Inc.
Gaylord and Dorothy Donnelley Foundation
The Herbert H. and Grace A. Dow Foundation
Eastman Kodak Company Charitable Trust
The Ettinger Foundation, Inc.
The William Stamps Farish Fund
Leland Fikes Foundation, Inc.
FishAmerica Foundation
Flintridge Foundation
The Frost Foundation, Ltd.
GE Fund
Gates Foundation
The Fred Gellert Foundation
General Service Foundation
The German Marshall Fund of the United States
Bernard F. and Alva B. Gimbel Foundation, Inc.
Global Environmental Project Institute
Great Lakes Protection Fund
The George Gund Foundation
The Ewing Halsell Foundation
Hartford Foundation for Public Giving
Hawaii Community Foundation
Hawaiian Electric Industries Charitable Foundation
Charles Hayden Foundation
The John Randolph Haynes and Dora Haynes Foundation
Vira I. Heinz Endowment
Heller Charitable & Educational Fund
The Homeland Foundation
Hudson-Webber Foundation
The Hyams Foundation
The International Foundation, Inc.
Jackson Hole Preserve, Inc.
Martha Holden Jennings Foundation
Helen K. and Arthur E. Johnson Foundation
Walter S. Johnson Foundation
The Joyce Foundation
W. K. Kellogg Foundation
F. M. Kirby Foundation, Inc.
Caesar Kleberg Foundation for Wildlife Conservation
Laird, Norton Foundation

© 1995 Environmental Data Resources, Inc.

Limitations

Loans (cont.)

Larsen Fund, Inc.
Laurel Foundation
The Lazar Foundation
Lilly Endowment, Inc.
The Little Family Foundation
Richard Lounsbery Foundation, Inc.
MARPAT Foundation, Inc.
Mars Foundation
The McConnell Foundation
McDonnell Douglas Foundation
McGregor Fund
McKesson Foundation, Inc.
The McKnight Foundation
The Andrew W. Mellon Foundation
Merck Family Fund
Joyce Mertz-Gilmore Foundation
Mobil Foundation, Inc.
J. P. Morgan Charitable Trust
Henry and Lucy Moses Fund, Inc.
Charles Stewart Mott Foundation
Ruth Mott Fund
M. J. Murdock Charitable Trust
John P. Murphy Foundation
National Fish and Wildlife Foundation
National Geographic Society Education Foundation
Edward John Noble Foundation, Inc.
The Samuel Roberts Noble Foundation, Inc.
Kenneth T. and Eileen L. Norris Foundation
Nicholas H. Noyes, Jr. Memorial Foundation
The Ohrstrom Foundation
Spencer T. and Ann W. Olin Foundation
Orchard Foundation
Amelia Peabody Charitable Fund
Peninsula Community Foundation
The William Penn Foundation
James C. Penney Foundation
The Pfizer Foundation, Inc.
The Philadelphia Foundation
Philip Morris Companies, Inc.
Ellis L. Phillips Foundation
Pilot Trust
The Powell Family Foundation
The Prudential Foundation
Public Welfare Foundation, Inc.
Recreational Equipment, Inc.
Rockefeller Financial Services, Philanthropy Department
Rockwood Fund, Inc.
Fran and Warren Rupp Foundation
The Sapelo Foundation
Sarkeys Foundation
Sarah Scaife Foundation Incorporated
The Florence and John Schumann Foundation
Sears-Swetland Foundation
Shell Oil Company Foundation
The Kelvin and Eleanor Smith Foundation
Kelvin Smith 1980 Charitable Trust
The Sonoma County Community Foundation
Springhouse Foundation
Stackner Family Foundation, Inc.

The Stebbins Fund, Inc.
Margaret Dorrance Strawbridge Foundation of Pennsylvania II, Inc.
The Charles J. Strosacker Foundation
The Sulzberger Foundation, Inc.
The Summerlee Foundation
Surdna Foundation, Inc.
The Telesis Foundation
Texaco Foundation
The Oakleigh L. Thorne Foundation
Town Creek Foundation, Inc.
Toyota USA Foundation
The Travelers Foundation
The Troy Foundation
The Trust For Mutual Understanding
Rose E. Tucker Charitable Trust
The USF&G Foundation, Inc.
Union Camp Charitable Trust
Unitarian Universalist Veatch Program at Shelter Rock
United States-Japan Foundation
Wallace Genetic Foundation, Inc.
Westinghouse Foundation
Wilburforce Foundation
The Windham Foundation, Inc.
The Wortham Foundation, Inc.
The Wyomissing Foundation, Inc.

Lobbying

ARCO Foundation
AT&T Foundation
The Ahmanson Foundation
The Vincent Astor Foundation
Atherton Family Foundation
L. L. Bean, Inc.
Beldon Fund
The Bersted Foundation
The Bullitt Foundation
The Morris and Gwendolyn Cafritz Foundation
The Cargill Foundation
Carolyn Foundation
Chesapeake Bay Trust
Claneil Foundation, Inc.
Columbia Foundation
The Community Foundation of Greater New Haven
The Community Foundation Serving Coastal South Carolina
Compton Foundation, Inc.
Conservation, Food & Health Foundation, Inc.
Cooke Foundation, Limited
Jessie B. Cox Charitable Trust
Crystal Channel Foundation
Damien Foundation
The Arthur Vining Davis Foundations
The Aaron Diamond Foundation
Dolfinger-McMahon Foundation
The Herbert H. and Grace A. Dow Foundation
El Paso Community Foundation
FishAmerica Foundation
Flintridge Foundation
Foundation for Deep Ecology

The Frost Foundation, Ltd.
The Gap Foundation
Gebbie Foundation, Inc.
General Service Foundation
The German Marshall Fund of the United States
Give to the Earth Foundation
Richard & Rhoda Goldman Fund
Great Lakes Protection Fund
Greater Piscataqua Community Foundation
The George Gund Foundation
Walter and Elise Haas Fund
Hartford Foundation for Public Giving
Hawaiian Electric Industries Charitable Foundation
The John Randolph Haynes and Dora Haynes Foundation
The William and Flora Hewlett Foundation
The Homeland Foundation
The Hyams Foundation
Island Foundation, Inc.
The Henry M. Jackson Foundation
Martha Holden Jennings Foundation
Helen K. and Arthur E. Johnson Foundation
The Robert S. and Grayce B. Kerr Foundation, Inc.
Laird, Norton Foundation
The Max and Anna Levinson Foundation
The John D. and Catherine T. MacArthur Foundation
James A. Macdonald Foundation
Maine Community Foundation, Inc.
Marbrook Foundation
The Martin Foundation, Inc.
The McConnell Foundation
McGregor Fund
McKenzie River Gathering Foundation
McKesson Foundation, Inc.
The McKnight Foundation
The Andrew W. Mellon Foundation
Merck Family Fund
Metropolitan Atlanta Community Foundation, Inc.
Meyer Memorial Trust
The Mountaineers Foundation
M. J. Murdock Charitable Trust
National Fish and Wildlife Foundation
National Geographic Society Education Foundation
New England Biolabs Foundation
Edward John Noble Foundation, Inc.
Northwest Area Foundation
Onan Family Foundation
Amelia Peabody Charitable Fund
Peninsula Community Foundation
The William Penn Foundation
Philip Morris Companies, Inc.
Ellis L. Phillips Foundation
The Powell Family Foundation
The Rhode Island Community Foundation
The Rockefeller Foundation
Fran and Warren Rupp Foundation
San Diego Community Foundation
The San Francisco Foundation
The Sapelo Foundation

© 1995 Environmental Data Resources, Inc.

Limitations

Lobbying (cont.)
Sarkeys Foundation
The Scherman Foundation, Inc.
Shell Oil Company Foundation
Stanley Smith Horticultural Trust
The Sonoma County Community
 Foundation
Springs Foundation, Inc.
The Strong Foundation for
 Environmental Values
Edna Bailey Sussman Fund
Texaco Foundation
The Tinker Foundation Incorporated
Town Creek Foundation, Inc.
Toyota USA Foundation
True North Foundation
The Trust For Mutual Understanding
Rose E. Tucker Charitable Trust
Alice Tweed Tuohy Foundation
The USF&G Foundation, Inc.
United States-Japan Foundation
Whitecap Foundation
Wilburforce Foundation
The Winston-Salem Foundation, Inc.
Robert W. Woodruff Foundation, Inc.
Margaret Cullinan Wray Charitable
 Lead Annuity Trust

Maintenance
Mary Reynolds Babcock Foundation, Inc.
L. L. Bean, Inc.
Chesapeake Bay Trust
The Cleveland Foundation
Compton Foundation, Inc.
The Conservation and Research Foundation
Jessie B. Cox Charitable Trust
The Fred Gellert Foundation
The German Marshall Fund of
 the United States
Great Lakes Protection Fund
Greater Piscataqua Community Foundation
The George Gund Foundation
The John Randolph Haynes and
 Dora Haynes Foundation
The Homeland Foundation
The Hyams Foundation
Martha Holden Jennings Foundation
The McConnell Foundation
McKesson Foundation, Inc.
The McKnight Foundation
National Geographic Society Education
 Foundation
Peninsula Community Foundation
James C. Penney Foundation
Recreational Equipment, Inc.
Rockwood Fund, Inc.
San Diego Community Foundation
The San Francisco Foundation
Shell Oil Company Foundation
The Sudbury Foundation
The Trust For Mutual Understanding
The USF&G Foundation, Inc.
Virginia Environmental Endowment
The Winston-Salem Foundation, Inc.

Matching funds
American Foundation Corporation
The Cargill Foundation
The Aaron Diamond Foundation
Eastman Kodak Company Charitable Trust
The Foundation for the National
 Capital Region
The Fred Gellert Foundation
General Service Foundation
Bernard F. and Alva B. Gimbel
 Foundation, Inc.
The John Randolph Haynes and
 Dora Haynes Foundation
The Hyams Foundation
The International Foundation, Inc.
Walter S. Johnson Foundation
The Henry P. Kendall Foundation
Caesar Kleberg Foundation for Wildlife
 Conservation
The Minneapolis Foundation
M. J. Murdock Charitable Trust
The New World Foundation
Spencer T. and Ann W. Olin Foundation
Peninsula Community Foundation
Rockwood Fund, Inc.
The Charles J. Strosacker Foundation
The Sulzberger Foundation, Inc.
The Oakleigh L. Thorne Foundation

Media projects
ARCO Foundation
The Acorn Foundation
Patrick and Aimee Butler Family
 Foundation
Ben B. Cheney Foundation
Adolph Coors Foundation
S. H. Cowell Foundation
Oliver S. and Jennie R. Donaldson
 Charitable Trust
El Pomar Foundation
Flintridge Foundation
Foundation for the Carolinas
The Gap Foundation
HKH Foundation
The John Randolph Haynes and
 Dora Haynes Foundation
The Homeland Foundation
Martha Holden Jennings Foundation
The Andrew W. Mellon Foundation
Mobil Foundation, Inc.
New England Biolabs Foundation
The New York Community Trust
Norman Foundation
Northwest Area Foundation
Jessie Smith Noyes Foundation, Inc.
Ottinger Foundation
Outdoor Industry Conservation Alliance
Patagonia, Inc.
Sequoia Foundation
Springhouse Foundation
Stern Family Fund
Mark and Catherine Winkler Foundation

Membership campaigns
The Vincent Astor Foundation
David Winton Bell Foundation
James Ford Bell Foundation
The Bunbury Company, Inc.
Chesapeake Bay Trust
The Cleveland Foundation
Conservation, Food & Health
 Foundation, Inc.
Cooke Foundation, Limited
Jessie B. Cox Charitable Trust
The Aaron Diamond Foundation
El Paso Community Foundation
FishAmerica Foundation
The Fred Gellert Foundation
The German Marshall Fund of
 the United States
Great Lakes Protection Fund
Hawaiian Electric Industries Charitable
 Foundation
The John Randolph Haynes and
 Dora Haynes Foundation
The Hyams Foundation
Martha Holden Jennings Foundation
The Robert S. and Grayce B. Kerr
 Foundation, Inc.
The McConnell Foundation
McGregor Fund
McKesson Foundation, Inc.
The McKnight Foundation
The Andrew W. Mellon Foundation
The Minneapolis Foundation
National Geographic Society Education
 Foundation
New England Biolabs Foundation
Amelia Peabody Charitable Fund
Peninsula Community Foundation
James C. Penney Foundation
Philip Morris Companies, Inc.
The Powell Family Foundation
Rockwood Fund, Inc.
Fran and Warren Rupp Foundation
The Scherman Foundation, Inc.
The Schumann Fund for New Jersey, Inc.
Shell Oil Company Foundation
Springs Foundation, Inc.
Surdna Foundation, Inc.
Toyota USA Foundation
The Troy Foundation
The Trust For Mutual Understanding

Mortgage reduction
Alaska Conservation Foundation
The Vincent Astor Foundation
L. L. Bean, Inc.
Beldon Fund
The Bullitt Foundation
The Bunbury Company, Inc.
The Morris and Gwendolyn Cafritz
 Foundation
Chesapeake Bay Trust
Claneil Foundation, Inc.
The Cleveland Foundation

Limitations

Mortgage reduction (cont.)

The Community Foundation of
   Greater New Haven
Compton Foundation, Inc.
The Conservation and Research Foundation
Cooke Foundation, Limited
Jessie B. Cox Charitable Trust
Crystal Channel Foundation
The Aaron Diamond Foundation
The Educational Foundation of America
El Paso Community Foundation
FishAmerica Foundation
Flintridge Foundation
Foundation for Deep Ecology
The Frost Foundation, Ltd.
The Fund for New Jersey
The Fred Gellert Foundation
The German Marshall Fund of
   the United States
Global Environmental Project Institute
Great Lakes Protection Fund
Greater Piscataqua Community Foundation
The George Gund Foundation
Hawaiian Electric Industries Charitable
   Foundation
The John Randolph Haynes and
   Dora Haynes Foundation
Vira I. Heinz Endowment
Heller Charitable & Educational Fund
The Clarence E. Heller Charitable
   Foundation
The Homeland Foundation
The Hyams Foundation
Martha Holden Jennings Foundation
Helen K. and Arthur E. Johnson Foundation
Lyndhurst Foundation
Maine Community Foundation, Inc.
Marin Community Foundation
The McConnell Foundation
McGregor Fund
McKesson Foundation, Inc.
The McKnight Foundation
The Andrew W. Mellon Foundation
Merck Family Fund
Metropolitan Atlanta Community
   Foundation, Inc.
Charles Stewart Mott Foundation
National Fish and Wildlife Foundation
National Geographic Society Education
   Foundation
New England Biolabs Foundation
Peninsula Community Foundation
James C. Penney Foundation
Philip Morris Companies, Inc.
Recreational Equipment, Inc.
The Rhode Island Community Foundation
Rockefeller Financial Services,
   Philanthropy Department
Rockwood Fund, Inc.
Sacramento Regional Foundation
San Diego Community Foundation
The San Francisco Foundation
The Sapelo Foundation
Sarkeys Foundation
The Scherman Foundation, Inc.

The Schumann Fund for New Jersey, Inc.
Shell Oil Company Foundation
The Sonoma County Community
   Foundation
Surdna Foundation, Inc.
Town Creek Foundation, Inc.
Toyota USA Foundation
The Troy Foundation
The Trust For Mutual Understanding
Virginia Environmental Endowment
Westinghouse Foundation

Multi-year grants

The Abell Foundation
The Ahmanson Foundation
Alaska Conservation Foundation
The Vincent Astor Foundation
Clayton Baker Trust
The Bay Foundation
Beldon Fund
The Ben & Jerry's Foundation
Helen Brach Foundation
The Bullitt Foundation
The Louis Calder Foundation
The Cargill Foundation
Carolyn Foundation
Chesapeake Bay Trust
The Community Foundation of
   Greater New Haven
The Community Foundation Serving
   Coastal South Carolina
Compton Foundation, Inc.
Cooke Foundation, Limited
The Arthur Vining Davis Foundations
Davis Conservation Foundation
Gaylord and Dorothy Donnelley Foundation
FishAmerica Foundation
Flintridge Foundation
The GAR Foundation
Global Environmental Project Institute
The Hyams Foundation
Martha Holden Jennings Foundation
Helen K. and Arthur E. Johnson Foundation
Laird, Norton Foundation
The Max and Anna Levinson Foundation
MARPAT Foundation, Inc.
The McConnell Foundation
McKesson Foundation, Inc.
Metropolitan Atlanta Community
   Foundation, Inc.
The National Environmental Education
   and Training Foundation, Inc.
Norcross Wildlife Foundation, Inc.
Spencer T. and Ann W. Olin Foundation
Amelia Peabody Charitable Fund
Peninsula Community Foundation
Recreational Equipment, Inc.
Rockwood Fund, Inc.
Sacramento Regional Foundation
San Diego Community Foundation
Stanley Smith Horticultural Trust
The Sonoma County Community
   Foundation
The Strong Foundation for
   Environmental Values

The Morris Stulsaft Foundation
The Tides Foundation
The USF&G Foundation, Inc.

Museums

L. L. Bean, Inc.
Beldon Fund
Ruth H. Brown Foundation
The Bullitt Foundation
Compton Foundation, Inc.
The Conservation and Research Foundation
Damien Foundation
Foundation for Deep Ecology
The German Marshall Fund of
   the United States
Global Environmental Project Institute
Great Lakes Protection Fund
Harder Foundation
The William and Flora Hewlett Foundation
The Hyams Foundation
The Lazar Foundation
The Max and Anna Levinson Foundation
The McKnight Foundation
National Geographic Society Education
   Foundation
New England Biolabs Foundation
Norman Foundation
Ottinger Foundation
James C. Penney Foundation
The Pew Charitable Trusts
Philip Morris Companies, Inc.
Recreational Equipment, Inc.
Rockefeller Family Fund, Inc.
The Rockefeller Foundation
Rockwood Fund, Inc.
The Sapelo Foundation
The Schumann Fund for New Jersey, Inc.
Stern Family Fund
Town Creek Foundation, Inc.

Networking

The Vincent Astor Foundation
The Chicago Community Trust
The Aaron Diamond Foundation
FishAmerica Foundation
The John Randolph Haynes and
   Dora Haynes Foundation
The Homeland Foundation
The Hyams Foundation
The McConnell Foundation
Peninsula Community Foundation
The Scherman Foundation, Inc.

Operating costs

The Abell Foundation
The Ahmanson Foundation
Atherton Family Foundation
The Barra Foundation, Inc.
Bay Area Community Foundation
The Beirne Carter Foundation
The Frank Stanley Beveridge
   Foundation, Inc.
The Bothin Foundation
Ruth H. Brown Foundation

© 1995 Environmental Data Resources, Inc.

Limitations

Operating costs (cont.)

The Bush Foundation
California Community Foundation
Carolyn Foundation
The Champlin Foundations
Ben B. Cheney Foundation
Chesapeake Bay Trust
The Chicago Community Trust
Chrysler Corporation Fund
Liz Claiborne & Art Ortenberg Foundation
The Cleveland Foundation
The Collins Foundation
The Community Foundation of Santa Clara County
The Community Foundation of Sarasota County, Inc.
Cooke Foundation, Limited
S. H. Cowell Foundation
Jessie B. Cox Charitable Trust
Charles E. Culpeper Foundation, Inc.
Davis Conservation Foundation
Deer Creek Foundation
The Aaron Diamond Foundation
Dolfinger-McMahon Foundation
Donner Canadian Foundation
The Elizabeth Ordway Dunn Foundation, Inc.
The Educational Foundation of America
Environmental Endowment for New Jersey, Inc.
The William Stamps Farish Fund
Ford Foundation
Foundation for the Carolinas
The Foundation for the National Capital Region
The Frost Foundation, Ltd.
Lloyd A. Fry Foundation
Gates Foundation
The Wallace Alexander Gerbode Foundation, Inc.
Give to the Earth Foundation
Richard & Rhoda Goldman Fund
Greater Piscataqua Community Foundation
The Greenville Foundation
The Hahn Family Foundation
James G. Hanes Memorial Fund
Hawaiian Electric Industries Charitable Foundation
Charles Hayden Foundation
The John Randolph Haynes and Dora Haynes Foundation
The Hofmann Foundation
The Hyde and Watson Foundation
The International Foundation, Inc.
The James Irvine Foundation
The Richard Ivey Foundation
The Henry M. Jackson Foundation
The J. M. Kaplan Fund, Inc.
The Knapp Foundation, Inc.
The Kresge Foundation
Laidlaw Foundation
Lilly Endowment, Inc.
The Marshall Fund of Arizona
McCune Foundation
McLean Contributionship
Giles W. and Elise G. Mead Foundation
The Milwaukee Foundation
Mobil Foundation, Inc.
The Mountaineers Foundation
M. J. Murdock Charitable Trust
The National Environmental Education and Training Foundation, Inc.
New England Biolabs Foundation
Norcross Wildlife Foundation, Inc.
Northwest Area Foundation
Spencer T. and Ann W. Olin Foundation
Amelia Peabody Charitable Fund
Peninsula Community Foundation
Recreational Equipment, Inc.
The Winthrop Rockefeller Foundation
Fran and Warren Rupp Foundation
San Diego Community Foundation
Sarkeys Foundation
Thomas Sill Foundation
Snee-Reinhardt Charitable Foundation
The Sonoma County Community Foundation
Southwestern Bell Foundation
The Sudbury Foundation
The Telesis Foundation
Texaco Foundation
Times Mirror Magazines, Inc.
Toyota USA Foundation
The Trust For Mutual Understanding
Vancouver Foundation
Wallace Genetic Foundation, Inc.
Whitecap Foundation
Joseph B. Whitehead Foundation

Policy analysis/development

The Ahmanson Foundation
The Vincent Astor Foundation
The Aaron Diamond Foundation
FishAmerica Foundation
The Hyams Foundation
Martha Holden Jennings Foundation
Helen K. and Arthur E. Johnson Foundation
The McConnell Foundation
The Andrew W. Mellon Foundation
New England Biolabs Foundation
Amelia Peabody Charitable Fund
Peninsula Community Foundation
Springs Foundation, Inc.
Town Creek Foundation, Inc.
The USF&G Foundation, Inc.
Lila Wallace-Reader's Digest Fund
The Winston-Salem Foundation, Inc.

Political activities

ARCO Foundation
AT&T Foundation
The Abelard Foundation West
The Ahmanson Foundation
Alaska Conservation Foundation
American Express Philanthropic Program
Americana Foundation, Inc.
Ameritech Foundation
The Vincent Astor Foundation
Atherton Family Foundation
Atkinson Foundation
BankAmerica Foundation
L. L. Bean, Inc.
David Winton Bell Foundation
James Ford Bell Foundation
The Bersted Foundation
The Betterment Fund
Blandin Foundation
The Boeing Company
Helen Brach Foundation
The Bullitt Foundation
The Cabot Family Charitable Trust
The Cabot Family Charitable Trust
The Morris and Gwendolyn Cafritz Foundation
California Community Foundation
James & Abigail Campbell Foundation
The Cargill Foundation
The Chevron Companies
Chrysler Corporation Fund
Claneil Foundation, Inc.
Columbia Foundation
The Community Foundation of Santa Clara County
The Community Foundation of Sarasota County, Inc.
Cooke Foundation, Limited
S. H. Cowell Foundation
The Arthur Vining Davis Foundations
The Aaron Diamond Foundation
Oliver S. and Jennie R. Donaldson Charitable Trust
The Herbert H. and Grace A. Dow Foundation
El Pomar Foundation
The Field Foundation of Illinois, Inc.
Jamee and Marshall Field Foundation
FishAmerica Foundation
Flintridge Foundation
The Frost Foundation, Ltd.
The Gap Foundation
The Golden Rule Foundation, Inc.
The Hall Family Foundation
Hawaiian Electric Industries Charitable Foundation
The William and Flora Hewlett Foundation
The Hitachi Foundation
The Homeland Foundation
The Hyams Foundation
IBM Corporation
The Henry M. Jackson Foundation
Martha Holden Jennings Foundation
The George Frederick Jewett Foundation
Helen K. and Arthur E. Johnson Foundation
Laird, Norton Foundation
Levi Strauss Foundation
James A. Macdonald Foundation
Marbrook Foundation
The McConnell Foundation
McDonnell Douglas Foundation
McKesson Foundation, Inc.
The Andrew W. Mellon Foundation
The John Merck Fund

Limitations

Political activities (cont.)

Joyce Mertz-Gilmore Foundation
Metropolitan Atlanta Community
 Foundation, Inc.
M. J. Murdock Charitable Trust
The National Environmental Education
 and Training Foundation, Inc.
National Fish and Wildlife Foundation
National Geographic Society Education
 Foundation
New England Biolabs Foundation
Onan Family Foundation
Amelia Peabody Charitable Fund
Peninsula Community Foundation
The William Penn Foundation
The Pfizer Foundation, Inc.
Philip Morris Companies, Inc.
Phillips Petroleum Foundation, Inc.
The Powell Family Foundation
The Roberts Foundation
Fran and Warren Rupp Foundation
San Diego Community Foundation
The San Francisco Foundation
Sarkeys Foundation
The Scherman Foundation, Inc.
Shell Oil Company Foundation
Stanley Smith Horticultural Trust
Snee-Reinhardt Charitable Foundation
The Sonoma County Community
 Foundation
Southwestern Bell Foundation
Springs Foundation, Inc.
The Stratford Foundation
The Stroh Foundation
Texaco Foundation
The Travelers Foundation
The Troy Foundation
True North Foundation
The Trust For Mutual Understanding
Rose E. Tucker Charitable Trust
Alice Tweed Tuohy Foundation
The USF&G Foundation, Inc.
United States-Japan Foundation
Virginia Environmental Endowment
Westinghouse Foundation
Weyerhaeuser Company Foundation
Whitecap Foundation
The Winston-Salem Foundation, Inc.
Margaret Cullinan Wray Charitable
 Lead Annuity Trust

Professorships

The Ahmanson Foundation
The Vincent Astor Foundation
Mary Reynolds Babcock Foundation, Inc.
L. L. Bean, Inc.
Beldon Fund
The Ben & Jerry's Foundation
The Bullitt Foundation
C. S. Fund
Mary Flagler Cary Charitable Trust
Chesapeake Bay Trust
The Cleveland Foundation

The Community Foundation of
 Greater New Haven
Compton Foundation, Inc.
The Conservation and Research Foundation
Cooke Foundation, Limited
Crystal Channel Foundation
Dayton Hudson Foundation
The Aaron Diamond Foundation
FishAmerica Foundation
Foundation for Field Research
The German Marshall Fund of
 the United States
Global Environmental Project Institute
Great Lakes Protection Fund
The George Gund Foundation
Harder Foundation
The John Randolph Haynes and
 Dora Haynes Foundation
The William and Flora Hewlett Foundation
The Homeland Foundation
The Hyams Foundation
Martha Holden Jennings Foundation
The Max and Anna Levinson Foundation
Lilly Endowment, Inc.
Marin Community Foundation
The McConnell Foundation
McKesson Foundation, Inc.
The McKnight Foundation
Merck Family Fund
Mobil Foundation, Inc.
John P. Murphy Foundation
National Fish and Wildlife Foundation
National Geographic Society Education
 Foundation
New England Biolabs Foundation
Jessie Smith Noyes Foundation, Inc.
Peninsula Community Foundation
The William Penn Foundation
James C. Penney Foundation
Philip Morris Companies, Inc.
The Powell Family Foundation
Public Welfare Foundation, Inc.
Recreational Equipment, Inc.
The Rhode Island Community Foundation
Rockefeller Financial Services,
 Philanthropy Department
Rockwood Fund, Inc.
Fran and Warren Rupp Foundation
The San Francisco Foundation
The Sapelo Foundation
The Scherman Foundation, Inc.
Stanley Smith Horticultural Trust
Snee-Reinhardt Charitable Foundation
Springs Foundation, Inc.
The Strong Foundation for
 Environmental Values
The Sudbury Foundation
Surdna Foundation, Inc.
Town Creek Foundation, Inc.
Toyota USA Foundation
The Troy Foundation
Alice Tweed Tuohy Foundation
The USF&G Foundation, Inc.
Westinghouse Foundation

Wilburforce Foundation
The Winston-Salem Foundation, Inc.
The Wortham Foundation, Inc.

Program-related investments

The Ahmanson Foundation
Alaska Conservation Foundation
The Vincent Astor Foundation
Beldon Fund
The Bush Foundation
The Morris and Gwendolyn Cafritz
 Foundation
Columbia Foundation
The Community Foundation of
 Greater New Haven
Compton Foundation, Inc.
Cooke Foundation, Limited
Jessie B. Cox Charitable Trust
Crystal Channel Foundation
The Aaron Diamond Foundation
Flintridge Foundation
Foundation for Field Research
The German Marshall Fund of
 the United States
Greater Piscataqua Community Foundation
The George Gund Foundation
The John Randolph Haynes and
 Dora Haynes Foundation
The William and Flora Hewlett Foundation
The Homeland Foundation
The Hyams Foundation
Martha Holden Jennings Foundation
Helen K. and Arthur E. Johnson Foundation
The McConnell Foundation
McGregor Fund
McKesson Foundation, Inc.
The McKnight Foundation
The Andrew W. Mellon Foundation
Merck Family Fund
Amelia Peabody Charitable Fund
Peninsula Community Foundation
The William Penn Foundation
Recreational Equipment, Inc.
Rockefeller Financial Services,
 Philanthropy Department
Rockwood Fund, Inc.
Fran and Warren Rupp Foundation
Thomas Sill Foundation
Springs Foundation, Inc.
Surdna Foundation, Inc.
Town Creek Foundation, Inc.
Toyota USA Foundation
The Trust For Mutual Understanding
Rose E. Tucker Charitable Trust
The USF&G Foundation, Inc.
The Winston-Salem Foundation, Inc.
The Wortham Foundation, Inc.

Public agencies

A Territory Resource
The Abelard Foundation West
The Acorn Foundation
The Arca Foundation

Limitations

Public agencies (cont.)

Beldon Fund
The Ben & Jerry's Foundation
The Frank Stanley Beveridge
 Foundation, Inc.
Ruth H. Brown Foundation
The Bunbury Company, Inc.
The Louis Calder Foundation
Ben B. Cheney Foundation
The Chevron Companies
Claneil Foundation, Inc.
Columbia Foundation
Conservation, Food & Health
 Foundation, Inc.
Cooke Foundation, Limited
Adolph Coors Foundation
S. H. Cowell Foundation
Jessie B. Cox Charitable Trust
Damien Foundation
El Pomar Foundation
Samuel S. Fels Fund
Lloyd A. Fry Foundation
Global Environmental Project Institute
Harder Foundation
Hartford Foundation for Public Giving
Hawaiian Electric Industries Charitable
 Foundation
The Homeland Foundation
The Hyams Foundation
The Hyde and Watson Foundation
F. M. Kirby Foundation, Inc.
The Lazar Foundation
The Max and Anna Levinson Foundation
The Marshall Fund of Arizona
McKesson Foundation, Inc.
The Andrew W. Mellon Foundation
Metropolitan Atlanta Community
 Foundation, Inc.
John P. Murphy Foundation
New England Biolabs Foundation
Ottinger Foundation
Amelia Peabody Charitable Fund
The Pew Charitable Trusts
The Philadelphia Foundation
Philip Morris Companies, Inc.
Ellis L. Phillips Foundation
The Powell Family Foundation
The Prospect Hill Foundation
Recreational Equipment, Inc.
The Rhode Island Community Foundation
Rockefeller Financial Services,
 Philanthropy Department
Rockwood Fund, Inc.
Fran and Warren Rupp Foundation
Sarkeys Foundation
The Scherman Foundation, Inc.
The Strong Foundation for
 Environmental Values
The Sudbury Foundation
Toyota USA Foundation
The Troy Foundation
The Trust For Mutual Understanding
Unitarian Universalist Veatch Program
 at Shelter Rock
Lila Wallace-Reader's Digest Fund

Westinghouse Foundation
The William P. Wharton Trust
Wilburforce Foundation
G. N. Wilcox Trust

Publications

A Territory Resource
The Achelis Foundation
American Express Philanthropic Program
Arcadia Foundation
The Vincent Astor Foundation
BankAmerica Foundation
Blandin Foundation
The Bodman Foundation
Kathleen Price and Joseph M. Bryan
 Family Foundation, Inc.
The Cargill Foundation
Ben B. Cheney Foundation
The Clowes Fund, Inc.
The Community Foundation of
 Greater New Haven
The Community Foundation of
 Sarasota County, Inc.
S. H. Cowell Foundation
Jessie B. Cox Charitable Trust
The Aaron Diamond Foundation
Donner Canadian Foundation
Samuel S. Fels Fund
The Field Foundation of Illinois, Inc.
Jamee and Marshall Field Foundation
Foundation for the Carolinas
The Gap Foundation
The Fred Gellert Foundation
General Service Foundation
The Wallace Alexander Gerbode
 Foundation, Inc.
Evelyn and Walter Haas, Jr. Fund
Charles Hayden Foundation
The Hitachi Foundation
The Homeland Foundation
The Hyams Foundation
The James Irvine Foundation
Helen K. and Arthur E. Johnson Foundation
Walter S. Johnson Foundation
The J. M. Kaplan Fund, Inc.
Laidlaw Foundation
The Lazar Foundation
The John D. and Catherine T. MacArthur
 Foundation
Marbrook Foundation
The Marshall Fund of Arizona
McKesson Foundation, Inc.
Joyce Mertz-Gilmore Foundation
The Minneapolis Foundation
New Horizon Foundation
The New-Land Foundation, Inc.
Northwest Area Foundation
The Ohrstrom Foundation
Ottinger Foundation
Amelia Peabody Charitable Fund
Peninsula Community Foundation
The Philadelphia Foundation
Philip Morris Companies, Inc.
The Powell Family Foundation
The Procter & Gamble Fund

The Rhode Island Community Foundation
The San Francisco Foundation
Sequoia Foundation
Shell Oil Company Foundation
Springs Foundation, Inc.
Texaco Foundation
Town Creek Foundation, Inc.
The Travelers Foundation
The Trust For Mutual Understanding
Alice Tweed Tuohy Foundation
Turner Foundation, Inc.
USX Foundation, Inc.
Unitarian Universalist Veatch Program
 at Shelter Rock
United States-Japan Foundation
Virginia Environmental Endowment
The Wyomissing Foundation, Inc.

Religious organizations

ARCO Foundation
The Ahmanson Foundation
American Express Philanthropic Program
Ameritech Foundation
The Cameron Baird Foundation
Baltimore Gas and Electric Foundation, Inc.
BankAmerica Foundation
The Bay Foundation
L. L. Bean, Inc.
The Beirne Carter Foundation
Beldon Fund
The Ben & Jerry's Foundation
Ruth H. Brown Foundation
California Community Foundation
James & Abigail Campbell Foundation
The Cargill Foundation
Carolyn Foundation
Ben B. Cheney Foundation
The Chevron Companies
Chrysler Corporation Fund
Claneil Foundation, Inc.
Olive B. Cole Foundation
The Community Foundation of
 Santa Clara County
The Community Foundation of
 Sarasota County, Inc.
Compton Foundation, Inc.
The Conservation and Research Foundation
Conservation, Food & Health
 Foundation, Inc.
Cooke Foundation, Limited
Adolph Coors Foundation
S. H. Cowell Foundation
Damien Foundation
Dayton Hudson Foundation
Geraldine R. Dodge Foundation, Inc.
Fields Pond Foundation, Inc.
Foundation for Deep Ecology
Gebbie Foundation, Inc.
The Golden Rule Foundation, Inc.
Great Lakes Protection Fund
Hawaiian Electric Industries Charitable
 Foundation
Charles Hayden Foundation
Vira I. Heinz Endowment
Heller Charitable & Educational Fund

Limitations

Religious organizations (cont.)

The Hyams Foundation
IBM Corporation
Island Foundation, Inc.
The Richard Ivey Foundation
The Kresge Foundation
The Lazar Foundation
Levi Strauss Foundation
Lyndhurst Foundation
The John D. and Catherine T. MacArthur Foundation
Maine Community Foundation, Inc.
The McConnell Foundation
McDonnell Douglas Foundation
McKesson Foundation, Inc.
The McKnight Foundation
Merck Family Fund
Metropolitan Life Foundation
John P. Murphy Foundation
National Geographic Society Education Foundation
The New-Land Foundation, Inc.
Spencer T. and Ann W. Olin Foundation
Orchard Foundation
Amelia Peabody Charitable Fund
Peninsula Community Foundation
The Pfizer Foundation, Inc.
The Philadelphia Foundation
Philip Morris Companies, Inc.
Phillips Petroleum Foundation, Inc.
The Powell Family Foundation
The Prospect Hill Foundation
The Prudential Foundation
Recreational Equipment, Inc.
The Rhode Island Community Foundation
The Roberts Foundation
The Rockefeller Foundation
Rockwood Fund, Inc.
Fran and Warren Rupp Foundation
San Diego Community Foundation
Sarkeys Foundation
The Scherman Foundation, Inc.
The Schumann Fund for New Jersey, Inc.
Ralph C. Sheldon Foundation, Inc.
Snee-Reinhardt Charitable Foundation
The Sonoma County Community Foundation
Southwestern Bell Foundation
Steelcase Foundation
The Stroh Foundation
The Morris Stulsaft Foundation
The Telesis Foundation
Texaco Foundation
Town Creek Foundation, Inc.
Toyota USA Foundation
The Travelers Foundation
The Troy Foundation
The Trust For Mutual Understanding
Rose E. Tucker Charitable Trust
USX Foundation, Inc.
Virginia Environmental Endowment
DeWitt Wallace-Reader's Digest Fund
Weyerhaeuser Company Foundation
Whitecap Foundation
Wilburforce Foundation

The Wortham Foundation, Inc.

Research

ARCO Foundation
A Territory Resource
The Abelard Foundation West
The Ahmanson Foundation
American Foundation Corporation
The Vincent Astor Foundation
Clayton Baker Trust
BankAmerica Foundation
L. L. Bean, Inc.
Beldon Fund
The Ben & Jerry's Foundation
The Boeing Company
Boettcher Foundation
Otto Bremer Foundation
Kathleen Price and Joseph M. Bryan Family Foundation, Inc.
The Bullitt Foundation
The Bunbury Company, Inc.
The Cargill Foundation
Centerior Energy Foundation
Chesapeake Bay Trust
Chrysler Corporation Fund
The Clark Foundation
The Community Foundation of Santa Clara County
Cooke Foundation, Limited
Adolph Coors Foundation
S. H. Cowell Foundation
Dayton Hudson Foundation
The Aaron Diamond Foundation
Oliver S. and Jennie R. Donaldson Charitable Trust
Samuel S. Fels Fund
Fields Pond Foundation, Inc.
FishAmerica Foundation
Foundation for Deep Ecology
The Freed Foundation, Inc.
The German Marshall Fund of the United States
Global Environmental Project Institute
Richard & Rhoda Goldman Fund
HKH Foundation
Evelyn and Walter Haas, Jr. Fund
Harder Foundation
Hartford Foundation for Public Giving
Hawaiian Electric Industries Charitable Foundation
The Hyams Foundation
The James Irvine Foundation
The J. M. Kaplan Fund, Inc.
The Knapp Foundation, Inc.
The Kresge Foundation
Levi Strauss Foundation
Lyndhurst Foundation
Marin Community Foundation
The McConnell Foundation
McGregor Fund
The McIntosh Foundation
McKesson Foundation, Inc.
The McKnight Foundation
Metropolitan Atlanta Community Foundation, Inc.

The Minneapolis Foundation
The National Environmental Education and Training Foundation, Inc.
National Geographic Society Education Foundation
New England Biolabs Foundation
The New World Foundation
The Nord Family Foundation
Norman Foundation
Jessie Smith Noyes Foundation, Inc.
The Ohrstrom Foundation
Outdoor Industry Conservation Alliance
Peninsula Community Foundation
The William Penn Foundation
James C. Penney Foundation
The Philadelphia Foundation
The Powell Family Foundation
Public Welfare Foundation, Inc.
Recreational Equipment, Inc.
The Rhode Island Community Foundation
Smith Richardson Foundation, Inc.
Rockefeller Brothers Fund, Inc.
The Winthrop Rockefeller Foundation
The San Francisco Foundation
The Scherman Foundation, Inc.
Stern Family Fund
Town Creek Foundation, Inc.
Toyota USA Foundation
Alice Tweed Tuohy Foundation
The USF&G Foundation, Inc.
Vanguard Public Foundation
Virginia Environmental Endowment
Westinghouse Foundation
Robert W. Wilson Foundation
The Winston-Salem Foundation, Inc.

Research (medical, scholarly, and/or scientific)

The Acorn Foundation
Alaska Conservation Foundation
The Arca Foundation
Atkinson Foundation
Baltimore Gas and Electric Foundation, Inc.
The Bauman Foundation
Blandin Foundation
The Bothin Foundation
The Bush Foundation
James & Abigail Campbell Foundation
Columbia Foundation
The Columbus Foundation
The Community Foundation of Sarasota County, Inc.
Compton Foundation, Inc.
The Conservation and Research Foundation
Crystal Channel Foundation
Cleveland H. Dodge Foundation, Inc.
Dolfinger-McMahon Foundation
The Energy Foundation
Jamee and Marshall Field Foundation
The GAR Foundation
Greater Piscataqua Community Foundation
The George Gund Foundation
The Hall Family Foundation
Charles Hayden Foundation
The Hitachi Foundation

Limitations

Research (medical, scholarly, and/or scientific) (cont.)

The Homeland Foundation
Ittleson Foundation, Inc.
The Robert S. and Grayce B. Kerr Foundation, Inc.
Lilly Endowment, Inc.
Maine Community Foundation, Inc.
MARPAT Foundation, Inc.
The Marshall Fund of Arizona
Meadows Foundation, Inc.
The Andrew W. Mellon Foundation
The Milwaukee Foundation
Mobil Foundation, Inc.
J. P. Morgan Charitable Trust
Ottinger Foundation
Patagonia, Inc.
The Polden-Puckham Charitable Foundation
The Prospect Hill Foundation
The Roberts Foundation
Rockefeller Family Fund, Inc.
Rockwood Fund, Inc.
The Sudbury Foundation
The Telesis Foundation
Underhill Foundation
Unitarian Universalist Veatch Program at Shelter Rock
United States-Japan Foundation
DeWitt Wallace-Reader's Digest Fund
Lila Wallace-Reader's Digest Fund
Weeden Foundation
Weyerhaeuser Company Foundation

Research institutions

The Ahmanson Foundation
Alaska Conservation Foundation
Clayton Baker Trust
L. L. Bean, Inc.
Beldon Fund
The Ben & Jerry's Foundation
The Bunbury Company, Inc.
Cooke Foundation, Limited
Samuel S. Fels Fund
Foundation for Deep Ecology
Global Environmental Project Institute
Hawaiian Electric Industries Charitable Foundation
The Hyams Foundation
The McConnell Foundation
McGregor Fund
McKesson Foundation, Inc.
The McKnight Foundation
National Geographic Society Education Foundation
Peninsula Community Foundation
The William Penn Foundation
The Powell Family Foundation
Recreational Equipment, Inc.
The Rhode Island Community Foundation
The Scherman Foundation, Inc.
Springs Foundation, Inc.
Town Creek Foundation, Inc.
The Troy Foundation
The USF&G Foundation, Inc.

DeWitt Wallace-Reader's Digest Fund
Westinghouse Foundation
The Winston-Salem Foundation, Inc.
The Wortham Foundation, Inc.

Scholarships

ARCO Foundation
AT&T Foundation
A Territory Resource
The Abelard Foundation West
The Abell Foundation
Abell-Hanger Foundation
American Conservation Association, Inc.
American Express Philanthropic Program
American Foundation Corporation
Americana Foundation, Inc.
The Arca Foundation
The Vincent Astor Foundation
Atkinson Foundation
The George F. Baker Trust
The Barra Foundation, Inc.
Beldon Fund
James Ford Bell Foundation
The Ben & Jerry's Foundation
The Betterment Fund
The Frank Stanley Beveridge Foundation, Inc.
The Blumenthal Foundation
The Bothin Foundation
The Bullitt Foundation
The Bydale Foundation
The Cape Branch Foundation
Mary Flagler Cary Charitable Trust
Centerior Energy Foundation
Chesapeake Bay Trust
The Chicago Community Trust
Claneil Foundation, Inc.
Columbia Foundation
The Conservation and Research Foundation
Conservation, Food & Health Foundation, Inc.
Cooke Foundation, Limited
Jessie B. Cox Charitable Trust
The Cricket Foundation
The Mary A. Crocker Trust
Davis Conservation Foundation
Dayton Hudson Foundation
The Aaron Diamond Foundation
Cleveland H. Dodge Foundation, Inc.
Geraldine R. Dodge Foundation, Inc.
Dolfinger-McMahon Foundation
Oliver S. and Jennie R. Donaldson Charitable Trust
Donner Canadian Foundation
The Herbert H. and Grace A. Dow Foundation
The Elizabeth Ordway Dunn Foundation, Inc.
Samuel S. Fels Fund
The Hugh and Jane Ferguson Foundation
Jamee and Marshall Field Foundation
FishAmerica Foundation
Ford Motor Company Fund
Foundation for Deep Ecology

The Foundation for the National Capital Region
The Freed Foundation, Inc.
The Frost Foundation, Ltd.
The Fund for New Jersey
GE Fund
Gates Foundation
General Service Foundation
The Wallace Alexander Gerbode Foundation, Inc.
The Rollin M. Gerstacker Foundation
Bernard F. and Alva B. Gimbel Foundation, Inc.
Richard & Rhoda Goldman Fund
Walter and Duncan Gordon Charitable Foundation
Great Lakes Protection Fund
The William and Mary Greve Foundation, Inc.
The W. C. Griffith Foundation
Evelyn and Walter Haas, Jr. Fund
The Ewing Halsell Foundation
Harder Foundation
The Edward W. Hazen Foundation
The William and Flora Hewlett Foundation
The Hitachi Foundation
Hudson-Webber Foundation
The Hyams Foundation
The International Foundation, Inc.
Ittleson Foundation, Inc.
The Richard Ivey Foundation
Jackson Hole Preserve, Inc.
Martha Holden Jennings Foundation
The Howard Johnson Foundation
Walter S. Johnson Foundation
W. Alton Jones Foundation, Inc.
The Joyce Foundation
The J. M. Kaplan Fund, Inc.
The Henry P. Kendall Foundation
Caesar Kleberg Foundation for Wildlife Conservation
Laird, Norton Foundation
The Lazar Foundation
Lyndhurst Foundation
Marbrook Foundation
Marin Community Foundation
MARPAT Foundation, Inc.
Mars Foundation
McKenzie River Gathering Foundation
The McKnight Foundation
Richard King Mellon Foundation
Merck Family Fund
The John Merck Fund
Metropolitan Atlanta Community Foundation, Inc.
Meyer Memorial Trust
The Minneapolis Foundation
J. P. Morgan Charitable Trust
Ruth Mott Fund
M. J. Murdock Charitable Trust
John P. Murphy Foundation
The National Environmental Education and Training Foundation, Inc.
National Geographic Society Education Foundation

Limitations

Scholarships (cont.)

New England Biolabs Foundation
The New World Foundation
Norman Foundation
Andrew Norman Foundation
Northwest Area Foundation
Jessie Smith Noyes Foundation, Inc.
The Ohrstrom Foundation
Spencer T. and Ann W. Olin Foundation
Orchard Foundation
Peninsula Community Foundation
The William Penn Foundation
The Perkin Fund
The Philadelphia Foundation
Philip Morris Companies, Inc.
The Powell Family Foundation
The Prudential Foundation
Recreational Equipment, Inc.
The Rhode Island Community Foundation
The Winthrop Rockefeller Foundation
Rockwood Fund, Inc.
San Diego Community Foundation
Sarah Scaife Foundation Incorporated
The Scherman Foundation, Inc.
The Schumann Fund for New Jersey, Inc.
Sears-Swetland Foundation
Sequoia Foundation
The Kelvin and Eleanor Smith Foundation
Kelvin Smith 1980 Charitable Trust
Stackner Family Foundation, Inc.
Margaret Dorrance Strawbridge Foundation of Pennsylvania II, Inc.
The Sudbury Foundation
Surdna Foundation, Inc.
The Oakleigh L. Thorne Foundation
Town Creek Foundation, Inc.
Toyota USA Foundation
The Trust For Mutual Understanding
Wallace Genetic Foundation, Inc.
Westinghouse Foundation
Robert W. Wilson Foundation
The Wortham Foundation, Inc.
The Wyomissing Foundation, Inc.

Seed money

The Ahmanson Foundation
Compton Foundation, Inc.
S. H. Cowell Foundation
The Fred Harris Daniels Foundation, Inc.
Dayton Hudson Foundation
The Aaron Diamond Foundation
The John Randolph Haynes and Dora Haynes Foundation
The Hyams Foundation
The Little Family Foundation
The McConnell Foundation
Amelia Peabody Charitable Fund
Shell Oil Company Foundation
Turner Foundation, Inc.

Seminars

The Ahmanson Foundation
The Vincent Astor Foundation
L. L. Bean, Inc.

Beldon Fund
The Bullitt Foundation
The Bush Foundation
Carolyn Foundation
Ben B. Cheney Foundation
Chrysler Corporation Fund
The Clowes Fund, Inc.
The Community Foundation of Greater New Haven
Compton Foundation, Inc.
The Conservation and Research Foundation
Cooke Foundation, Limited
S. H. Cowell Foundation
Charles E. Culpeper Foundation, Inc.
The Aaron Diamond Foundation
Donner Canadian Foundation
El Pomar Foundation
FishAmerica Foundation
Foundation for Field Research
The Fred Gellert Foundation
Global Environmental Project Institute
Great Lakes Protection Fund
Hawaiian Electric Industries Charitable Foundation
The William and Flora Hewlett Foundation
The Hitachi Foundation
The Homeland Foundation
The Hyams Foundation
Helen K. and Arthur E. Johnson Foundation
Richard Lounsbery Foundation, Inc.
The McConnell Foundation
McGregor Fund
McKesson Foundation, Inc.
The McKnight Foundation
The Andrew W. Mellon Foundation
Joyce Mertz-Gilmore Foundation
New England Biolabs Foundation
Jessie Smith Noyes Foundation, Inc.
Spencer T. and Ann W. Olin Foundation
Amelia Peabody Charitable Fund
Peninsula Community Foundation
The William Penn Foundation
James C. Penney Foundation
The Powell Family Foundation
Rockefeller Financial Services, Philanthropy Department
San Diego Community Foundation
The San Francisco Foundation
The Scherman Foundation, Inc.
Springhouse Foundation
Springs Foundation, Inc.
Steelcase Foundation
Texaco Foundation
Town Creek Foundation, Inc.
Toyota USA Foundation
The Troy Foundation
Alice Tweed Tuohy Foundation
USX Foundation, Inc.
Union Pacific Foundation
Vancouver Foundation
Virginia Environmental Endowment
The Winston-Salem Foundation, Inc.

Start-up costs

The Ahmanson Foundation

Compton Foundation, Inc.
The Aaron Diamond Foundation
The McConnell Foundation
John P. Murphy Foundation
National Geographic Society Education Foundation
Amelia Peabody Charitable Fund
Peninsula Community Foundation

Symposia/colloquia

The Ahmanson Foundation
The Vincent Astor Foundation
L. L. Bean, Inc.
Beldon Fund
The Cargill Foundation
Compton Foundation, Inc.
Cooke Foundation, Limited
S. H. Cowell Foundation
The Aaron Diamond Foundation
FishAmerica Foundation
Foundation for Field Research
Global Environmental Project Institute
Richard & Rhoda Goldman Fund
Great Lakes Protection Fund
Hawaiian Electric Industries Charitable Foundation
The William and Flora Hewlett Foundation
The Homeland Foundation
The Hyams Foundation
IBM Corporation
Helen K. and Arthur E. Johnson Foundation
The McConnell Foundation
McGregor Fund
McKesson Foundation, Inc.
The McKnight Foundation
Meadows Foundation, Inc.
The Andrew W. Mellon Foundation
Joyce Mertz-Gilmore Foundation
Metropolitan Atlanta Community Foundation, Inc.
New England Biolabs Foundation
Jessie Smith Noyes Foundation, Inc.
Amelia Peabody Charitable Fund
Peninsula Community Foundation
The William Penn Foundation
James C. Penney Foundation
The Powell Family Foundation
San Diego Community Foundation
The San Francisco Foundation
The Scherman Foundation, Inc.
Steelcase Foundation
Town Creek Foundation, Inc.
Toyota USA Foundation
The Troy Foundation
USX Foundation, Inc.
Vancouver Foundation
Virginia Environmental Endowment
The Winston-Salem Foundation, Inc.

Technical assistance

The Vincent Astor Foundation
The Ben & Jerry's Foundation
The Bullitt Foundation
The Bunbury Company, Inc.

Limitations

Technical assistance (cont.)
The Conservation and Research Foundation
Conservation, Food & Health Foundation, Inc.
The Aaron Diamond Foundation
The Fred Gellert Foundation
The John Randolph Haynes and Dora Haynes Foundation
Vira I. Heinz Endowment
Heller Charitable & Educational Fund
The McConnell Foundation
McKesson Foundation, Inc.
The Andrew W. Mellon Foundation
Amelia Peabody Charitable Fund
Peninsula Community Foundation
The Powell Family Foundation
Rockwood Fund, Inc.
Springs Foundation, Inc.
Rose E. Tucker Charitable Trust

Training
The Vincent Astor Foundation
The Conservation and Research Foundation
The Aaron Diamond Foundation
Samuel S. Fels Fund
FishAmerica Foundation
The Fred Gellert Foundation
The Golden Rule Foundation, Inc.
The John Randolph Haynes and Dora Haynes Foundation
The McConnell Foundation
Amelia Peabody Charitable Fund
Peninsula Community Foundation
Recreational Equipment, Inc.

Travel expenses
The Achelis Foundation
The Ahmanson Foundation
American Express Philanthropic Program
The Vincent Astor Foundation
Atkinson Foundation
Bay Area Community Foundation
L. L. Bean, Inc.
The Frank Stanley Beveridge Foundation, Inc.
Blandin Foundation
The Bodman Foundation
The Boeing Company
Kathleen Price and Joseph M. Bryan Family Foundation, Inc.
The Bunbury Company, Inc.
The Cargill Foundation
Ben B. Cheney Foundation
Chesapeake Bay Trust
The Chevron Companies
Chrysler Corporation Fund
Claneil Foundation, Inc.
The Cleveland Foundation
The Community Foundation of Greater New Haven
The Community Foundation of Sarasota County, Inc.
Cooke Foundation, Limited
Charles E. Culpeper Foundation, Inc.
Davis Conservation Foundation
Dayton Hudson Foundation
The Aaron Diamond Foundation
Donner Canadian Foundation
The Herbert H. and Grace A. Dow Foundation
El Paso Community Foundation
El Pomar Foundation
Environmental Education Foundation of Florida, Inc.
Samuel S. Fels Fund
Fields Pond Foundation, Inc.
FishAmerica Foundation
Foundation for the Carolinas
Mary D. and Walter F. Frear Eleemosynary Trust
The Fred Gellert Foundation
The Wallace Alexander Gerbode Foundation, Inc.
Richard & Rhoda Goldman Fund
Greater Piscataqua Community Foundation
The Hall Family Foundation
Hawaiian Electric Industries Charitable Foundation
The John Randolph Haynes and Dora Haynes Foundation
The Homeland Foundation
The Hyams Foundation
Martha Holden Jennings Foundation
Helen K. and Arthur E. Johnson Foundation
The J. M. Kaplan Fund, Inc.
Laidlaw Foundation
Lyndhurst Foundation
Marin Community Foundation
The McConnell Foundation
McGregor Fund
McKesson Foundation, Inc.
The McKnight Foundation
Joyce Mertz-Gilmore Foundation
John P. Murphy Foundation
National Geographic Society Education Foundation
New England Biolabs Foundation
New Horizon Foundation
Northwest Area Foundation
Spencer T. and Ann W. Olin Foundation
Onan Family Foundation
Orchard Foundation
Amelia Peabody Charitable Fund
Peninsula Community Foundation
James C. Penney Foundation
The Philadelphia Foundation
Phillips Petroleum Foundation, Inc.
The Polden-Puckham Charitable Foundation
Rockefeller Financial Services, Philanthropy Department
The Winthrop Rockefeller Foundation
Rockwood Fund, Inc.
Fran and Warren Rupp Foundation
Sacramento Regional Foundation
San Diego Community Foundation
The Scherman Foundation, Inc.
Shell Oil Company Foundation
Springs Foundation, Inc.
Surdna Foundation, Inc.
Toyota USA Foundation
The Troy Foundation
The USF&G Foundation, Inc.
USX Foundation, Inc.
United States-Japan Foundation
Vancouver Foundation
Vanguard Public Foundation
Virginia Environmental Endowment
Westinghouse Foundation
The Winston-Salem Foundation, Inc.
The Wortham Foundation, Inc.

Volunteerism
The Vincent Astor Foundation
The Aaron Diamond Foundation
The George Gund Foundation
The John Randolph Haynes and Dora Haynes Foundation
The Homeland Foundation
The Hyams Foundation
The Andrew W. Mellon Foundation
Peninsula Community Foundation
The Powell Family Foundation
Springs Foundation, Inc.
The Trust For Mutual Understanding

Workshops
The Ahmanson Foundation
The Vincent Astor Foundation
The Cargill Foundation
Compton Foundation, Inc.
Cooke Foundation, Limited
S. H. Cowell Foundation
The Aaron Diamond Foundation
Donner Canadian Foundation
FishAmerica Foundation
Hawaiian Electric Industries Charitable Foundation
The John Randolph Haynes and Dora Haynes Foundation
The William and Flora Hewlett Foundation
The Homeland Foundation
The Hyams Foundation
The McConnell Foundation
McGregor Fund
The Andrew W. Mellon Foundation
New England Biolabs Foundation
Spencer T. and Ann W. Olin Foundation
Peninsula Community Foundation
The Powell Family Foundation
Recreational Equipment, Inc.
San Diego Community Foundation
Springs Foundation, Inc.
The Morris Stulsaft Foundation
Vancouver Foundation

Youth programs
The Vincent Astor Foundation
Beldon Fund
Compton Foundation, Inc.
The Conservation and Research Foundation
The George Gund Foundation
The McKnight Foundation
Philip Morris Companies, Inc.

Youth programs (cont.)
Rockwood Fund, Inc.
The Tinker Foundation Incorporated
The Trust For Mutual Understanding

Zoos
L. L. Bean, Inc.
Beldon Fund
Otto Bremer Foundation
Ruth H. Brown Foundation
The Bullitt Foundation
Claneil Foundation, Inc.
Compton Foundation, Inc.
The Conservation and Research Foundation
Cooke Foundation, Limited
Damien Foundation
Foundation for Deep Ecology
Gebbie Foundation, Inc.
The Fred Gellert Foundation
The German Marshall Fund of
 the United States
Global Environmental Project Institute
Great Lakes Protection Fund
The John Randolph Haynes and
 Dora Haynes Foundation
The William and Flora Hewlett Foundation
The Lazar Foundation
The Max and Anna Levinson Foundation
The McKnight Foundation
The Andrew W. Mellon Foundation
National Geographic Society Education
 Foundation
New England Biolabs Foundation
Norman Foundation
James C. Penney Foundation
Philip Morris Companies, Inc.
The Powell Family Foundation
Recreational Equipment, Inc.
The Rockefeller Foundation
The Sapelo Foundation
The Schumann Fund for New Jersey, Inc.
Town Creek Foundation, Inc.
The Troy Foundation
Virginia Environmental Endowment

Environmental Issues

Climate and Atmosphere

ARCO Foundation
Alaska Conservation Foundation
BankAmerica Foundation
Beneficia Foundation
The Betterment Fund
The William Bingham Foundation
The Bush Foundation
J. E. & Z. B. Butler Foundation, Inc.
Patrick and Aimee Butler Family
  Foundation
The Bydale Foundation
Changing Horizons Charitable Trust
Chesapeake Bay Trust
The Chevron Companies
Robert Sterling Clark Foundation, Inc.
The Community Foundation of
  Santa Clara County
Conservation, Food & Health
  Foundation, Inc.
The Nathan Cummings Foundation
Deer Creek Foundation
Geraldine R. Dodge Foundation, Inc.
Eastman Kodak Company Charitable Trust
The Educational Foundation of America
The Energy Foundation
Environment Now Foundation
Environmental Endowment for
  New Jersey, Inc.
The Favrot Fund
Samuel S. Fels Fund
Ford Foundation
Foundation for Deep Ecology
The German Marshall Fund of
  the United States
Richard & Rhoda Goldman Fund
Great Lakes Protection Fund
The George Gund Foundation
HKH Foundation
The William and Flora Hewlett
  Foundation
The Horn Foundation
The James Irvine Foundation
W. Alton Jones Foundation, Inc.
The Joyce Foundation
The J. M. Kaplan Fund, Inc.
The Max and Anna Levinson Foundation
The John D. and Catherine T. MacArthur
  Foundation
Mars Foundation
The Marshall L. & Perrine D. McCune
  Charitable Foundation
The John Merck Fund
Joyce Mertz-Gilmore Foundation
Mobil Foundation, Inc.
Leo Model Foundation, Inc.
The Moriah Fund, Inc.
Charles Stewart Mott Foundation
Ruth Mott Fund
New Hampshire Charitable Foundation

New York Foundation
Andrew Norman Foundation
Patagonia, Inc.
Amelia Peabody Charitable Fund
The Pew Charitable Trusts
The Philadelphia Foundation
Pinewood Foundation
The Procter & Gamble Fund
Public Welfare Foundation, Inc.
Recreational Equipment, Inc.
Z. Smith Reynolds Foundation, Inc.
Smith Richardson Foundation, Inc.
Rockefeller Brothers Fund, Inc.
The Rockefeller Foundation
The San Francisco Foundation
Sarah Scaife Foundation Incorporated
The Florence and John Schumann
  Foundation
Shell Oil Company Foundation
The Summit Foundation
Surdna Foundation, Inc.
The Switzer Foundation
Texaco Foundation
Threshold Foundation
The Tides Foundation
Times Mirror Magazines, Inc.
True North Foundation
USX Foundation, Inc.
Weyerhaeuser Company Foundation
Mark and Catherine Winkler Foundation
Margaret Cullinan Wray Charitable
  Lead Annuity Trust

Biodiversity

ARCO Foundation
AT&T Foundation
The Abell Foundation
The Achelis Foundation
The Ahmanson Foundation
Airport Business Center Foundation
Alaska Conservation Foundation
The George I. Alden Trust
Winifred & Harry B. Allen Foundation
The Jenifer Altman Foundation
American Conservation Association, Inc.
American Express Philanthropic Program
American Foundation Corporation
Americana Foundation, Inc.
Elmer L. & Eleanor J. Andersen
  Foundation
Arcadia Foundation
Evenor Armington Fund
The Vincent Astor Foundation
Atherton Family Foundation
Atkinson Foundation
The Austin Memorial Foundation
Mary Reynolds Babcock Foundation, Inc.
The Bailey Wildlife Foundation
The Cameron Baird Foundation
The George F. Baker Trust

Baltimore Gas and Electric
  Foundation, Inc.
BankAmerica Foundation
The Barra Foundation, Inc.
The Theodore H. Barth Foundation, Inc.
Bay Area Community Foundation
The Bay Foundation
The Howard Bayne Fund
L. L. Bean, Inc.
S. D. Bechtel, Jr. Foundation
The Beinecke Foundation, Inc.
The Beirne Carter Foundation
David Winton Bell Foundation
James Ford Bell Foundation
The Ben & Jerry's Foundation
Beneficia Foundation
Benua Foundation, Inc.
The Betterment Fund
The Frank Stanley Beveridge
  Foundation, Inc.
The William Bingham Foundation
Bishop Pine Fund
Blandin Foundation
The Blumenthal Foundation
The Bodman Foundation
The Boeing Company
Boettcher Foundation
The Bothin Foundation
Botwinick-Wolfensohn Foundation, Inc.
Helen Brach Foundation
The Lynde and Harry Bradley
  Foundation, Inc.
Otto Bremer Foundation
Alexander H. Bright Charitable Trust
Alex. Brown & Sons Charitable
  Foundation, Inc.
H. Barksdale Brown Charitable Trust
Ruth H. Brown Foundation
W. L. Lyons Brown Foundation
The Robert Brownlee Foundation
Kathleen Price and Joseph M. Bryan
  Family Foundation, Inc.
The Buchanan Family Foundation
Jesse Margaret Wilson Budlong
  Foundation for Animal Aid
The Bullitt Foundation
The Bunbury Company, Inc.
The Bush Foundation
The Butler Foundation
Patrick and Aimee Butler Family
  Foundation
The Bydale Foundation
C. S. Fund
The Cabot Family Charitable Trust
The Morris and Gwendolyn Cafritz
  Foundation
The Louis Calder Foundation
California Community Foundation
James & Abigail Campbell Foundation
The Cargill Foundation

© 1995 Environmental Data Resources, Inc.

Environmental Issues

Biodiversity (cont.)

Caribou Fund
Carolyn Foundation
The Carpenter Foundation
Mary Flagler Cary Charitable Trust
Centerior Energy Foundation
The Champlin Foundations
Cheeryble Foundation
Ben B. Cheney Foundation
Chesapeake Bay Trust
Chesapeake Corporation Foundation
The Chevron Companies
The Chicago Community Trust
Chrysler Corporation Fund
Liz Claiborne & Art Ortenberg Foundation
Claneil Foundation, Inc.
Clark Charitable Trust
The Clark Foundation
Robert Sterling Clark Foundation, Inc.
The Cleveland Foundation
The Clowes Fund, Inc.
Olive B. Cole Foundation
The Collins Foundation
Columbia Foundation
The Columbus Foundation
The Community Foundation of Greater New Haven
The Community Foundation of Santa Clara County
The Community Foundation of Sarasota County, Inc.
The Community Foundation Serving Coastal South Carolina
Compton Foundation, Inc.
The Conservation and Research Foundation
Conservation, Food & Health Foundation, Inc.
Cooke Foundation, Limited
Adolph Coors Foundation
The Cowles Charitable Trust
Cox Foundation, Inc.
The James M. Cox, Jr. Foundation, Inc.
Jessie B. Cox Charitable Trust
The Mary A. Crocker Trust
Roy E. Crummer Foundation
Crystal Channel Foundation
Patrick and Anna M. Cudahy Fund
The Nathan Cummings Foundation
Damien Foundation
The Fred Harris Daniels Foundation, Inc.
Davis Conservation Foundation
Dayton Hudson Foundation
Deer Creek Foundation
The Nelson B. Delavan Foundation
The Aaron Diamond Foundation
Cleveland H. Dodge Foundation, Inc.
Geraldine R. Dodge Foundation, Inc.
Thelma Doelger Charitable Trust
Dolfinger-McMahon Foundation
Oliver S. and Jennie R. Donaldson Charitable Trust
Gaylord and Dorothy Donnelley Foundation
Douroucouli Foundation

The Dragon Foundation, Inc.
The Max and Victoria Dreyfus Foundation, Inc.
The Elizabeth Ordway Dunn Foundation, Inc.
Jessie Ball duPont Religious, Charitable and Educational Fund
Eastman Kodak Company Charitable Trust
Echoing Green Foundation
Ederic Foundation, Inc.
The Educational Foundation of America
Arthur M. and Olga T. Eisig–Arthur M. and Kate E. Tode Foundation, Inc.
El Paso Community Foundation
El Pomar Foundation
The Emerald Foundation
The Thomas J. Emery Memorial
The Charles Engelhard Foundation
English-Bonter-Mitchell Foundation
Environment Now Foundation
Environmental Education Foundation of Florida, Inc.
Environmental Endowment for New Jersey, Inc.
The Armand G. Erpf Fund, Inc.
The Ettinger Foundation, Inc.
Fair Play Foundation
Fanwood Foundation
The William Stamps Farish Fund
The Favrot Fund
Felburn Foundation
Samuel S. Fels Fund
The Hugh and Jane Ferguson Foundation
The Field Foundation of Illinois, Inc.
Jamee and Marshall Field Foundation
Fields Pond Foundation, Inc.
Leland Fikes Foundation, Inc.
FishAmerica Foundation
Flintridge Foundation
Ford Foundation
Ford Motor Company Fund
Walter and Josephine Ford Fund
Foundation for the Carolinas
Foundation for Deep Ecology
Foundation for Field Research
The Foundation for the National Capital Region
Mary D. and Walter F. Frear Eleemosynary Trust
The Freed Foundation, Inc.
Frelinghuysen Foundation
The Frost Foundation, Ltd.
Lloyd A. Fry Foundation
The Fund for Preservation of Wildlife and Natural Areas
Fund of the Four Directions
Funding Exchange
The GAR Foundation
GE Fund
The Gap Foundation
Gates Foundation
The Barbara Gauntlett Foundation, Inc.
The Fred Gellert Foundation
General Service Foundation
Georgia Power Foundation, Inc.

Georgia-Pacific Foundation
The Wallace Alexander Gerbode Foundation, Inc.
The Rollin M. Gerstacker Foundation
Bernard F. and Alva B. Gimbel Foundation, Inc.
Give to the Earth Foundation
Global Environmental Project Institute
Global Greengrants Fund
The Goldman Environmental Foundation
Herman Goldman Foundation
Richard & Rhoda Goldman Fund
Walter and Duncan Gordon Charitable Foundation
Great Lakes Protection Fund
Greater Piscataqua Community Foundation
The Greenville Foundation
The William and Mary Greve Foundation, Inc.
The W. C. Griffith Foundation
The George Gund Foundation
HKH Foundation
Walter and Elise Haas Fund
The Hahn Family Foundation
The Hall Family Foundation
The Ewing Halsell Foundation
The Hamer Foundation
James G. Hanes Memorial Fund
Harbor Lights Foundation
Harder Foundation
The Harding Educational and Charitable Foundation
Gladys and Roland Harriman Foundation
Mary W. Harriman Foundation
The Hastings Trust
The Merrill G. & Emita E. Hastings Foundation
Hawaii Community Foundation
Hawaiian Electric Industries Charitable Foundation
Charles Hayden Foundation
The M. A. Healy Family Foundation, Inc.
Heller Charitable & Educational Fund
The William and Flora Hewlett Foundation
The Hofmann Foundation
The Homeland Foundation
The Horn Foundation
Howfirma Foundation
Hudson-Webber Foundation
The Charles Evans Hughes Memorial Foundation, Inc.
The Roy A. Hunt Foundation
Hurdle Hill Foundation
The Hyams Foundation
The Hyde and Watson Foundation
The Indian Point Foundation, Inc.
The Louise H. and David S. Ingalls Foundation, Inc.
The International Foundation, Inc.
Ireland Foundation
Island Foundation, Inc.
Island Foundation
Ittleson Foundation, Inc.
The Richard Ivey Foundation

Environmental Issues

Biodiversity (cont.)
The Jackson Foundation
Jackson Hole Preserve, Inc.
Martha Holden Jennings Foundation
The George Frederick Jewett Foundation
Helen K. and Arthur E. Johnson Foundation
The Howard Johnson Foundation
Walter S. Johnson Foundation
W. Alton Jones Foundation, Inc.
The Joyce Foundation
The J. M. Kaplan Fund, Inc.
W. K. Kellogg Foundation
Harris and Eliza Kempner Fund
The Henry P. Kendall Foundation
The Robert S. and Grayce B. Kerr Foundation, Inc.
The Helen & Milton Kimmelman Foundation
Kinnoull Foundation
F. M. Kirby Foundation, Inc.
Caesar Kleberg Foundation for Wildlife Conservation
The Knapp Foundation, Inc.
The Seymour H. Knox Foundation, Inc.
Kongsgaard-Goldman Foundation
The Kresge Foundation
Laidlaw Foundation
Laird, Norton Foundation
Larsen Fund, Inc.
Laurel Foundation
The Lazar Foundation
Levi Strauss Foundation
The Max and Anna Levinson Foundation
LifeWorks Foundation
Lintilhac Foundation
The Little Family Foundation
Longwood Foundation, Inc.
Richard Lounsbery Foundation, Inc.
Luster Family Foundation, Inc.
Lyndhurst Foundation
The John D. and Catherine T. MacArthur Foundation
James A. Macdonald Foundation
Magowan Family Foundation, Inc.
Maine Community Foundation, Inc.
Maki Foundation
Marbrook Foundation
Marin Community Foundation
MARPAT Foundation, Inc.
Mars Foundation
The Marshall Fund of Arizona
The Martin Foundation, Inc.
The McConnell Foundation
The Eugene McDermott Foundation
McDonnell Douglas Foundation
McGregor Fund
McInerny Foundation
The McIntosh Foundation
McKenzie River Gathering Foundation
The McKnight Foundation
McLean Contributionship
Giles W. and Elise G. Mead Foundation
Nelson Mead Fund
Meadows Foundation, Inc.

The Andrew W. Mellon Foundation
Richard King Mellon Foundation
Merck Family Fund
The John Merck Fund
Robert G. and Anne M. Merrick Foundation, Inc.
Metropolitan Atlanta Community Foundation, Inc.
Metropolitan Life Foundation
Meyer Memorial Trust
Middlecott Foundation
Millbrook Tribute Garden, Inc.
The Milwaukee Foundation
The Minneapolis Foundation
Mobil Foundation, Inc.
Leo Model Foundation, Inc.
The Moody Foundation
J. P. Morgan Charitable Trust
The Moriah Fund, Inc.
Henry and Lucy Moses Fund, Inc.
Charles Stewart Mott Foundation
Ruth Mott Fund
The Mountaineers Foundation
The Curtis and Edith Munson Foundation, Inc.
M. J. Murdock Charitable Trust
John P. Murphy Foundation
The National Environmental Education and Training Foundation, Inc.
National Fish and Wildlife Foundation
The Needmor Fund
New England Biolabs Foundation
New Hampshire Charitable Foundation
New Horizon Foundation
The New York Community Trust
The New York Times Company Foundation, Inc.
The New-Land Foundation, Inc.
Edward John Noble Foundation, Inc.
The Samuel Roberts Noble Foundation, Inc.
Norcross Wildlife Foundation, Inc.
Kenneth T. and Eileen L. Norris Foundation
Northwest Area Foundation
Northwest Fund for the Environment
The Norton Foundation, Inc.
Nicholas H. Noyes, Jr. Memorial Foundation
OCRI Foundation
Nathan M. Ohrbach Foundation, Inc.
The Ohrstrom Foundation
Spencer T. and Ann W. Olin Foundation
Onan Family Foundation
Orchard Foundation
Outdoor Industry Conservation Alliance
The Overbrook Foundation
The David and Lucile Packard Foundation
Patagonia, Inc.
Amelia Peabody Charitable Fund
Peninsula Community Foundation
The William Penn Foundation
The Perkin Fund
Perkins Charitable Foundation
The Pew Charitable Trusts

Pew Scholars Program in Conservation and the Environment
The Pfizer Foundation, Inc.
The Philadelphia Foundation
Phillips Petroleum Foundation, Inc.
Ellis L. Phillips Foundation
Howard Phipps Foundation
Pinewood Foundation
Henry B. Plant Memorial Fund, Inc.
The Powell Family Foundation
Lynn R. and Karl E. Prickett Fund
Prince Charitable Trusts
Pritzker Foundation
The Procter & Gamble Fund
The Prospect Hill Foundation
The Prudential Foundation
Public Welfare Foundation, Inc.
Recreational Equipment, Inc.
Z. Smith Reynolds Foundation, Inc.
The Rhode Island Community Foundation
Sid W. Richardson Foundation
The Roberts Foundation
Rockefeller Brothers Fund, Inc.
Rockefeller Family Fund, Inc.
Rockefeller Financial Services, Philanthropy Department
The Rockefeller Foundation
The Winthrop Rockefeller Foundation
The Rockfall Foundation
Rockwell Fund, Inc.
Rockwood Fund, Inc.
Lee Romney Foundation, Inc.
Samuel and May Rudin Foundation, Inc.
Fran and Warren Rupp Foundation
Sacharuna Foundation
Sacramento Regional Foundation
San Diego Community Foundation
The San Francisco Foundation
Sarkeys Foundation
The Scherman Foundation, Inc.
Sarah I. Schieffelin Residuary Trust
The Schiff Foundation
Schultz Foundation, Inc.
The Florence and John Schumann Foundation
Ellen Browning Scripps Foundation
Sears-Swetland Foundation
Frances Seebe Trust
Sequoia Foundation
Seventh Generation Fund
Elmina B. Sewall Foundation
Shell Oil Company Foundation
Thomas Sill Foundation
The Skaggs Foundation
The Kelvin and Eleanor Smith Foundation
Stanley Smith Horticultural Trust
Snee-Reinhardt Charitable Foundation
Solow Foundation
The Sonoma County Community Foundation
South Coast Foundation, Inc.
Southwestern Bell Foundation
Springhouse Foundation
Sproul Foundation
Stackner Family Foundation, Inc.

© 1995 Environmental Data Resources, Inc.

Environmental Issues

Biodiversity (cont.)

Alfred T. Stanley Foundation
The Stebbins Fund, Inc.
Steelcase Foundation
Stern Family Fund
Stoddard Charitable Trust
Stranahan Foundation
The Stratford Foundation
Margaret Dorrance Strawbridge
 Foundation of Pennsylvania II, Inc.
The Stroh Foundation
The Strong Foundation for
 Environmental Values
The Charles J. Strosacker Foundation
The Morris Stulsaft Foundation
The Sudbury Foundation
The Sulzberger Foundation, Inc.
The Summerlee Foundation
The Summit Foundation
Surdna Foundation, Inc.
Edna Bailey Sussman Fund
The Switzer Foundation
Nelson Talbott Foundation
The Telesis Foundation
Texaco Foundation
Thanksgiving Foundation
The Oakleigh L. Thorne Foundation
Threshold Foundation
The Tides Foundation
Times Mirror Magazines, Inc.
The Tinker Foundation Incorporated
Tortuga Foundation
Town Creek Foundation, Inc.
The Travelers Foundation
Treacy Foundation, Inc.
Harry C. Trexler Trust
The Troy Foundation
True North Foundation
The Truland Foundation
The Trust For Mutual Understanding
Marcia Brady Tucker Foundation
Rose E. Tucker Charitable Trust
Alice Tweed Tuohy Foundation
Turner Foundation, Inc.
USX Foundation, Inc.
Underhill Foundation
Union Camp Charitable Trust
Union Pacific Foundation
Vancouver Foundation
R. T. Vanderbilt Trust
Vanguard Public Foundation
G. Unger Vetlesen Foundation
Victoria Foundation, Inc.
The Vidda Foundation
Vinmont Foundation, Inc.
Virginia Environmental Endowment
WMX Environmental Grants Program
Alex C. Walker Educational
 & Charitable Foundation
Wallace Genetic Foundation, Inc.
DeWitt Wallace-Reader's Digest Fund
Lila Wallace-Reader's Digest Fund
C. A. Webster Foundation
Weeden Foundation
Welfare Foundation, Inc.

Henry E. and Consuelo S. Wenger
 Foundation, Inc.
Westinghouse Foundation
Weyerhaeuser Company Foundation
The William P. Wharton Trust
Whitecap Foundation
Joseph B. Whitehead Foundation
Wilburforce Foundation
G. N. Wilcox Trust
Robert W. Wilson Foundation
Mark and Catherine Winkler Foundation
The Winslow Foundation
The Winston-Salem Foundation, Inc.
The Dean Witter Foundation
Wodecroft Foundation
Robert W. Woodruff Foundation, Inc.
The Wortham Foundation, Inc.
Sidney & Phyllis Wragge Foundation
Margaret Cullinan Wray Charitable
 Lead Annuity Trust
Wrinkle in Time Foundation
The Wyomissing Foundation, Inc.

Endangered Lands

ARCO Foundation
AT&T Foundation
A Territory Resource
The Abell Foundation
Abell-Hanger Foundation
The Acorn Foundation
The Ahmanson Foundation
Airport Business Center Foundation
Alaska Conservation Foundation
Winifred & Harry B. Allen Foundation
The Jenifer Altman Foundation
American Conservation Association, Inc.
American Express Philanthropic Program
American Foundation Corporation
Americana Foundation, Inc.
Elmer L. & Eleanor J. Andersen
 Foundation
Angelina Fund, Inc.
Arcadia Foundation
Evenor Armington Fund
The Vincent Astor Foundation
Atherton Family Foundation
Atkinson Foundation
The Austin Memorial Foundation
Mary Reynolds Babcock Foundation, Inc.
The Cameron Baird Foundation
Clayton Baker Trust
The George F. Baker Trust
BankAmerica Foundation
The Barra Foundation, Inc.
The Theodore H. Barth Foundation, Inc.
Bay Area Community Foundation
The Bay Foundation
The Howard Bayne Fund
L. L. Bean, Inc.
S. D. Bechtel, Jr. Foundation
The Beinecke Foundation, Inc.
The Beirne Carter Foundation
David Winton Bell Foundation
James Ford Bell Foundation
The Ben & Jerry's Foundation

Beneficia Foundation
Benua Foundation, Inc.
The Bersted Foundation
The Betterment Fund
The Frank Stanley Beveridge
 Foundation, Inc.
The William Bingham Foundation
Bishop Pine Fund
Blandin Foundation
The Blumenthal Foundation
The Bodman Foundation
The Boeing Company
Boettcher Foundation
Mary Owen Borden Memorial Foundation
The Bothin Foundation
Botwinick-Wolfensohn Foundation, Inc.
The Lynde and Harry Bradley
 Foundation, Inc.
Otto Bremer Foundation
Alexander H. Bright Charitable Trust
Alex. Brown & Sons Charitable
 Foundation, Inc.
H. Barksdale Brown Charitable Trust
Ruth H. Brown Foundation
W. L. Lyons Brown Foundation
The Robert Brownlee Foundation
Kathleen Price and Joseph M. Bryan
 Family Foundation, Inc.
The Buchanan Family Foundation
Jesse Margaret Wilson Budlong
 Foundation for Animal Aid
The Bullitt Foundation
The Bunbury Company, Inc.
The Bush Foundation
The Butler Foundation
Patrick and Aimee Butler Family
 Foundation
C. S. Fund
The Cabot Family Charitable Trust
The Morris and Gwendolyn Cafritz
 Foundation
California Community Foundation
James & Abigail Campbell Foundation
The Cargill Foundation
Caribou Fund
Carolyn Foundation
The Carpenter Foundation
Mary Flagler Cary Charitable Trust
The Champlin Foundations
Changing Horizons Charitable Trust
Cheeryble Foundation
Ben B. Cheney Foundation
Chesapeake Bay Trust
Chesapeake Corporation Foundation
The Chevron Companies
The Chicago Community Trust
Chrysler Corporation Fund
Liz Claiborne & Art Ortenberg Foundation
Claneil Foundation, Inc.
Clark Charitable Trust
The Clark Foundation
The Cleveland Foundation
The Clowes Fund, Inc.
Olive B. Cole Foundation
The Collins Foundation

Environmental Issues

Endangered Lands (cont.)

Columbia Foundation
The Columbus Foundation
The Community Foundation of Greater New Haven
The Community Foundation of Santa Clara County
The Community Foundation of Sarasota County, Inc.
The Community Foundation Serving Coastal South Carolina
Community Foundation of Western North Carolina, Inc.
Compton Foundation, Inc.
The Conservation and Research Foundation
Conservation, Food & Health Foundation, Inc.
Adolph Coors Foundation
The Cowles Charitable Trust
Cox Foundation, Inc.
The James M. Cox, Jr. Foundation, Inc.
Jessie B. Cox Charitable Trust
The Cricket Foundation
The Mary A. Crocker Trust
Roy E. Crummer Foundation
Crystal Channel Foundation
Patrick and Anna M. Cudahy Fund
The Nathan Cummings Foundation
Damien Foundation
The Arthur Vining Davis Foundations
Davis Conservation Foundation
Dayton Hudson Foundation
Deer Creek Foundation
The Nelson B. Delavan Foundation
Cleveland H. Dodge Foundation, Inc.
Geraldine R. Dodge Foundation, Inc.
Dolfinger-McMahon Foundation
Oliver S. and Jennie R. Donaldson Charitable Trust
Gaylord and Dorothy Donnelley Foundation
Donner Canadian Foundation
Douroucouli Foundation
The Herbert H. and Grace A. Dow Foundation
The Dragon Foundation, Inc.
The Max and Victoria Dreyfus Foundation, Inc.
The Elizabeth Ordway Dunn Foundation, Inc.
Eastman Kodak Company Charitable Trust
Echoing Green Foundation
Ederic Foundation, Inc.
The Educational Foundation of America
Arthur M. and Olga T. Eisig–Arthur M. and Kate E. Tode Foundation, Inc.
El Paso Community Foundation
El Pomar Foundation
The Emerald Foundation
The Energy Foundation
The Charles Engelhard Foundation
English-Bonter-Mitchell Foundation
Environment Now Foundation

Environmental Endowment for New Jersey, Inc.
The Armand G. Erpf Fund, Inc.
The Ettinger Foundation, Inc.
Fair Play Foundation
Fanwood Foundation
The William Stamps Farish Fund
The Favrot Fund
Felburn Foundation
Samuel S. Fels Fund
The Hugh and Jane Ferguson Foundation
The Field Foundation of Illinois, Inc.
Jamee and Marshall Field Foundation
Fields Pond Foundation, Inc.
The 1525 Foundation
Leland Fikes Foundation, Inc.
Bert Fingerhut/Caroline Hicks Family Fund
FishAmerica Foundation
Flintridge Foundation
Ford Foundation
Ford Motor Company Fund
Walter and Josephine Ford Fund
Foundation for the Carolinas
Foundation for Deep Ecology
Foundation for Field Research
The Foundation for the National Capital Region
The Freed Foundation, Inc.
Frelinghuysen Foundation
The Frost Foundation, Ltd.
Lloyd A. Fry Foundation
The Fund for New Jersey
The Fund for Preservation of Wildlife and Natural Areas
Fund of the Four Directions
Funding Exchange
The GAR Foundation
GE Fund
The Gap Foundation
Gates Foundation
The Barbara Gauntlett Foundation, Inc.
The Fred Gellert Foundation
General Service Foundation
Georgia Power Foundation, Inc.
Georgia-Pacific Foundation
The Wallace Alexander Gerbode Foundation, Inc.
The German Marshall Fund of the United States
The Rollin M. Gerstacker Foundation
Bernard F. and Alva B. Gimbel Foundation, Inc.
Give to the Earth Foundation
Global Environmental Project Institute
The Goldman Environmental Foundation
Richard & Rhoda Goldman Fund
Good Samaritan, Inc.
Walter and Duncan Gordon Charitable Foundation
Great Lakes Protection Fund
Greater Piscataqua Community Foundation
The Greenville Foundation
The William and Mary Greve Foundation, Inc.

The W. C. Griffith Foundation
The George Gund Foundation
HKH Foundation
Evelyn and Walter Haas, Jr. Fund
Walter and Elise Haas Fund
The Hahn Family Foundation
The Hall Family Foundation
The Ewing Halsell Foundation
The Hamer Foundation
Harbor Lights Foundation
Harder Foundation
The Harding Educational and Charitable Foundation
Gladys and Roland Harriman Foundation
Mary W. Harriman Foundation
Hartford Foundation for Public Giving
The Hastings Trust
The Merrill G. & Emita E. Hastings Foundation
Hawaii Community Foundation
Hawaiian Electric Industries Charitable Foundation
The John Randolph Haynes and Dora Haynes Foundation
The Edward W. Hazen Foundation
Vira I. Heinz Endowment
Heller Charitable & Educational Fund
The Clarence E. Heller Charitable Foundation
The William and Flora Hewlett Foundation
The Hitachi Foundation
The Hofmann Foundation
The Homeland Foundation
The Horn Foundation
Howfirma Foundation
The Charles Evans Hughes Memorial Foundation, Inc.
The Roy A. Hunt Foundation
Hurdle Hill Foundation
The Hyams Foundation
The Hyde and Watson Foundation
The Indian Point Foundation, Inc.
The Louise H. and David S. Ingalls Foundation, Inc.
Ireland Foundation
Island Foundation, Inc.
Island Foundation
Ittleson Foundation, Inc.
The Richard Ivey Foundation
The Jackson Foundation
Jackson Hole Preserve, Inc.
The Henry M. Jackson Foundation
Martha Holden Jennings Foundation
The George Frederick Jewett Foundation
The Howard Johnson Foundation
W. Alton Jones Foundation, Inc.
Joy Foundation for Ecological Education and Research
The Joyce Foundation
The J. M. Kaplan Fund, Inc.
W. K. Kellogg Foundation
Harris and Eliza Kempner Fund
The Henry P. Kendall Foundation

Environmental Issues

Endangered Lands (cont.)

The Robert S. and Grayce B. Kerr Foundation, Inc.
The Helen & Milton Kimmelman Foundation
F. M. Kirby Foundation, Inc.
The Esther A. and Joseph Klingenstein Fund, Inc.
The Knapp Foundation, Inc.
The Seymour H. Knox Foundation, Inc.
Kongsgaard-Goldman Foundation
The Kresge Foundation
The Lagemann Foundation
Laidlaw Foundation
Laird, Norton Foundation
Larsen Fund, Inc.
The Lauder Foundation, Inc.
Laurel Foundation
The Lazar Foundation
The Norman Lear Foundation
Levi Strauss Foundation
The Max and Anna Levinson Foundation
LifeWorks Foundation
Lilly Endowment, Inc.
Lintilhac Foundation
The Little Family Foundation
Longwood Foundation, Inc.
Richard Lounsbery Foundation, Inc.
Luster Family Foundation, Inc.
Lyndhurst Foundation
The John D. and Catherine T. MacArthur Foundation
James A. Macdonald Foundation
Magowan Family Foundation, Inc.
Maine Community Foundation, Inc.
Maki Foundation
Marbrook Foundation
Marin Community Foundation
MARPAT Foundation, Inc.
Mars Foundation
The Marshall Fund of Arizona
The Martin Foundation, Inc.
The McConnell Foundation
McCune Foundation
The Marshall L. & Perrine D. McCune Charitable Foundation
The Eugene McDermott Foundation
McDonnell Douglas Foundation
McGregor Fund
McInerny Foundation
The McIntosh Foundation
McKenzie River Gathering Foundation
McKesson Foundation, Inc.
The McKnight Foundation
McLean Contributionship
Giles W. and Elise G. Mead Foundation
Nelson Mead Fund
Meadows Foundation, Inc.
The Andrew W. Mellon Foundation
Richard King Mellon Foundation
Merck Family Fund
The John Merck Fund
Robert G. and Anne M. Merrick Foundation, Inc.

Metropolitan Atlanta Community Foundation, Inc.
Metropolitan Life Foundation
Meyer Memorial Trust
Middlecott Foundation
Millbrook Tribute Garden, Inc.
The Milwaukee Foundation
The Minneapolis Foundation
Mobil Foundation, Inc.
Leo Model Foundation, Inc.
The Moody Foundation
J. P. Morgan Charitable Trust
The Moriah Fund, Inc.
Henry and Lucy Moses Fund, Inc.
Charles Stewart Mott Foundation
Ruth Mott Fund
The Mountaineers Foundation
The Curtis and Edith Munson Foundation, Inc.
M. J. Murdock Charitable Trust
The National Environmental Education and Training Foundation, Inc.
National Fish and Wildlife Foundation
The Needmor Fund
New England Biolabs Foundation
New Hampshire Charitable Foundation
The New World Foundation
The New York Community Trust
New York Foundation
The New York Times Company Foundation, Inc.
The New-Land Foundation, Inc.
Edward John Noble Foundation, Inc.
The Samuel Roberts Noble Foundation, Inc.
Norcross Wildlife Foundation, Inc.
The Nord Family Foundation
Norman Foundation
Kenneth T. and Eileen L. Norris Foundation
Mary Moody Northen, Inc.
Northwest Area Foundation
Northwest Fund for the Environment
The Norton Foundation, Inc.
Jessie Smith Noyes Foundation, Inc.
Nicholas H. Noyes, Jr. Memorial Foundation
OCRI Foundation
Nathan M. Ohrbach Foundation, Inc.
The Ohrstrom Foundation
Spencer T. and Ann W. Olin Foundation
Outdoor Industry Conservation Alliance
The Overbrook Foundation
The David and Lucile Packard Foundation
Patagonia, Inc.
Amelia Peabody Charitable Fund
Peninsula Community Foundation
The William Penn Foundation
James C. Penney Foundation
Perkins Charitable Foundation
The Pew Charitable Trusts
Pew Scholars Program in Conservation and the Environment
The Pfizer Foundation, Inc.
The Philadelphia Foundation

Philip Morris Companies, Inc.
Phillips Petroleum Foundation, Inc.
Ellis L. Phillips Foundation
Howard Phipps Foundation
Pinewood Foundation
Henry B. Plant Memorial Fund, Inc.
The Powell Family Foundation
Lynn R. and Karl E. Prickett Fund
Prince Charitable Trusts
Pritzker Foundation
The Procter & Gamble Fund
The Prospect Hill Foundation
The Prudential Foundation
Public Welfare Foundation, Inc.
Recreational Equipment, Inc.
Philip D. Reed Foundation, Inc.
Z. Smith Reynolds Foundation, Inc.
The Rhode Island Community Foundation
Sid W. Richardson Foundation
The Roberts Foundation
Rockefeller Brothers Fund, Inc.
Rockefeller Family Fund, Inc.
Rockefeller Financial Services, Philanthropy Department
The Rockefeller Foundation
The Winthrop Rockefeller Foundation
The Rockfall Foundation
Rockwell Fund, Inc.
Rockwood Fund, Inc.
Lee Romney Foundation, Inc.
Samuel and May Rudin Foundation, Inc.
Fran and Warren Rupp Foundation
Sacharuna Foundation
Sacramento Regional Foundation
San Diego Community Foundation
The San Francisco Foundation
Sarkeys Foundation
The Scherman Foundation, Inc.
S. H. and Helen R. Scheuer Family Foundation, Inc.
Sarah I. Schieffelin Residuary Trust
The Schiff Foundation
Schultz Foundation, Inc.
The Schumann Fund for New Jersey, Inc.
The Florence and John Schumann Foundation
Sears-Swetland Foundation
Sequoia Foundation
Seventh Generation Fund
Elmina B. Sewall Foundation
Shell Oil Company Foundation
Thomas Sill Foundation
The Skaggs Foundation
The Kelvin and Eleanor Smith Foundation
Stanley Smith Horticultural Trust
Snee-Reinhardt Charitable Foundation
Solow Foundation
Southwestern Bell Foundation
Springhouse Foundation
Springs Foundation, Inc.
Sproul Foundation
Alfred T. Stanley Foundation
Anna B. Stearns Charitable Foundation, Inc.
The Stebbins Fund, Inc.

Environmental Issues

Endangered Lands (cont.)

Steelcase Foundation
Stoddard Charitable Trust
The Stratford Foundation
Margaret Dorrance Strawbridge
    Foundation of Pennsylvania II, Inc.
The Stroh Foundation
The Strong Foundation for
    Environmental Values
The Charles J. Strosacker Foundation
Stroud Foundation
The Morris Stulsaft Foundation
The Sudbury Foundation
The Sulzberger Foundation, Inc.
The Summerlee Foundation
The Summit Foundation
Surdna Foundation, Inc.
Edna Bailey Sussman Fund
The Switzer Foundation
Nelson Talbott Foundation
Texaco Foundation
Thanksgiving Foundation
The Oakleigh L. Thorne Foundation
Threshold Foundation
The Tides Foundation
Times Mirror Magazines, Inc.
The Tinker Foundation Incorporated
Tortuga Foundation
Town Creek Foundation, Inc.
The Travelers Foundation
Treacy Foundation, Inc.
Harry C. Trexler Trust
The Troy Foundation
True North Foundation
The Truland Foundation
The Trust For Mutual Understanding
Marcia Brady Tucker Foundation
Rose E. Tucker Charitable Trust
Turner Foundation, Inc.
The USF&G Foundation, Inc.
USX Foundation, Inc.
Underhill Foundation
Union Camp Charitable Trust
Union Pacific Foundation
Unitarian Universalist Veatch Program
    at Shelter Rock
Vancouver Foundation
R. T. Vanderbilt Trust
Vanguard Public Foundation
Victoria Foundation, Inc.
The Vidda Foundation
Vinmont Foundation, Inc.
Virginia Environmental Endowment
WMX Environmental Grants Program
Alex C. Walker Educational
    & Charitable Foundation
Wallace Genetic Foundation, Inc.
DeWitt Wallace-Reader's Digest Fund
Lila Wallace-Reader's Digest Fund
C. A. Webster Foundation
Weeden Foundation
Welfare Foundation, Inc.
Henry E. and Consuelo S. Wenger
    Foundation, Inc.
Westinghouse Foundation

Weyerhaeuser Company Foundation
The William P. Wharton Trust
Whitecap Foundation
Joseph B. Whitehead Foundation
Wilburforce Foundation
G. N. Wilcox Trust
Robert W. Wilson Foundation
The Windham Foundation, Inc.
Mark and Catherine Winkler Foundation
The Winslow Foundation
The Winston-Salem Foundation, Inc.
The Dean Witter Foundation
Wodecroft Foundation
Robert W. Woodruff Foundation, Inc.
The Wortham Foundation, Inc.
Sidney & Phyllis Wragge Foundation
Margaret Cullinan Wray Charitable
    Lead Annuity Trust
Wrinkle in Time Foundation
The Wyomissing Foundation, Inc.

Agriculture

A Territory Resource
The Abelard Foundation West
The Acorn Foundation
Alaska Conservation Foundation
Winifred & Harry B. Allen Foundation
The Jenifer Altman Foundation
American Conservation Association, Inc.
American Foundation Corporation
Americana Foundation, Inc.
Angelina Fund, Inc.
The Arca Foundation
Atkinson Foundation
The Austin Memorial Foundation
Mary Reynolds Babcock Foundation, Inc.
The Bay Foundation
The Ben & Jerry's Foundation
Bishop Pine Fund
Blandin Foundation
Otto Bremer Foundation
Alexander H. Bright Charitable Trust
Kathleen Price and Joseph M. Bryan
    Family Foundation, Inc.
The Bullitt Foundation
The Bush Foundation
Patrick and Aimee Butler Family
    Foundation
C. S. Fund
The Cabot Family Charitable Trust
Changing Horizons Charitable Trust
Chesapeake Bay Trust
The Chevron Companies
The Chicago Community Trust
The Cleveland Foundation
Columbia Foundation
Compton Foundation, Inc.
Conservation, Food & Health
    Foundation, Inc.
The Mary A. Crocker Trust
The Nathan Cummings Foundation
Damien Foundation
Geraldine R. Dodge Foundation, Inc.
Gaylord and Dorothy Donnelley
    Foundation

The Educational Foundation of America
El Paso Community Foundation
The Ettinger Foundation, Inc.
Ford Foundation
Ford Motor Company Fund
Foundation for Deep Ecology
The Fund for New Jersey
Fund of the Four Directions
The Gap Foundation
The Fred Gellert Foundation
General Service Foundation
Give to the Earth Foundation
Richard & Rhoda Goldman Fund
Great Lakes Protection Fund
The Greenville Foundation
The William and Mary Greve
    Foundation, Inc.
The Hahn Family Foundation
Harder Foundation
The Merrill G. & Emita E. Hastings
    Foundation
Heller Charitable & Educational Fund
The Clarence E. Heller Charitable
    Foundation
The William and Flora Hewlett
    Foundation
The Homeland Foundation
Howfirma Foundation
The Roy A. Hunt Foundation
Island Foundation
The Henry M. Jackson Foundation
W. Alton Jones Foundation, Inc.
The Joyce Foundation
The J. M. Kaplan Fund, Inc.
W. K. Kellogg Foundation
Kongsgaard-Goldman Foundation
Laidlaw Foundation
Laurel Foundation
Lintilhac Foundation
The John D. and Catherine T. MacArthur
    Foundation
James A. Macdonald Foundation
Marin Community Foundation
The McKnight Foundation
Richard King Mellon Foundation
The John Merck Fund
The Moriah Fund, Inc.
Charles Stewart Mott Foundation
Ruth Mott Fund
The Curtis and Edith Munson
    Foundation, Inc.
National Fish and Wildlife Foundation
The Needmor Fund
New England Biolabs Foundation
New Hampshire Charitable Foundation
The New World Foundation
The New York Community Trust
The New-Land Foundation, Inc.
The Samuel Roberts Noble
    Foundation, Inc.
Norman Foundation
Northwest Area Foundation
Jessie Smith Noyes Foundation, Inc.
Nathan M. Ohrbach Foundation, Inc.
The Ohrstrom Foundation

© 1995 Environmental Data Resources, Inc.

Environmental Issues

Agriculture (cont.)

The David and Lucile Packard Foundation
Patagonia, Inc.
The William Penn Foundation
James C. Penney Foundation
The Pew Charitable Trusts
The Pfizer Foundation, Inc.
The Philadelphia Foundation
Philip Morris Companies, Inc.
Phillips Petroleum Foundation, Inc.
The Polden-Puckham Charitable Foundation
The Procter & Gamble Fund
The Prudential Foundation
Public Welfare Foundation, Inc.
Z. Smith Reynolds Foundation, Inc.
Rockefeller Brothers Fund, Inc.
Rockefeller Family Fund, Inc.
The Rockefeller Foundation
The Winthrop Rockefeller Foundation
The San Francisco Foundation
The Sapelo Foundation
The Florence and John Schumann Foundation
Frances Seebe Trust
Seventh Generation Fund
Elmina B. Sewall Foundation
Sproul Foundation
The Strong Foundation for Environmental Values
The Switzer Foundation
The Oakleigh L. Thorne Foundation
Threshold Foundation
The Tides Foundation
Town Creek Foundation, Inc.
USX Foundation, Inc.
Unitarian Universalist Veatch Program at Shelter Rock
Vanguard Public Foundation
Virginia Environmental Endowment
Wallace Genetic Foundation, Inc.
C. A. Webster Foundation
Weeden Foundation
The William P. Wharton Trust
Margaret Cullinan Wray Charitable Lead Annuity Trust

Water

ARCO Foundation
AT&T Foundation
A Territory Resource
The Abell Foundation
The Ahmanson Foundation
Alaska Conservation Foundation
Winifred & Harry B. Allen Foundation
The Jenifer Altman Foundation
American Conservation Association, Inc.
American Express Philanthropic Program
American Foundation Corporation
Elmer L. & Eleanor J. Andersen Foundation
Angelina Fund, Inc.
Arcadia Foundation
Evenor Armington Fund

Atkinson Foundation
Mary Reynolds Babcock Foundation, Inc.
Clayton Baker Trust
BankAmerica Foundation
The Barra Foundation, Inc.
The Bay Foundation
The Beinecke Foundation, Inc.
Beldon Fund
The Ben & Jerry's Foundation
Beneficia Foundation
Benua Foundation, Inc.
The Bersted Foundation
The Betterment Fund
The Frank Stanley Beveridge Foundation, Inc.
The William Bingham Foundation
Bishop Pine Fund
Blandin Foundation
Boettcher Foundation
The Bothin Foundation
The Lynde and Harry Bradley Foundation, Inc.
Otto Bremer Foundation
Alex. Brown & Sons Charitable Foundation, Inc.
Kathleen Price and Joseph M. Bryan Family Foundation, Inc.
The Bullitt Foundation
The Bunbury Company, Inc.
The Butler Foundation
Patrick and Aimee Butler Family Foundation
The Bydale Foundation
The Morris and Gwendolyn Cafritz Foundation
The Cape Branch Foundation
Carolyn Foundation
The Carpenter Foundation
Mary Flagler Cary Charitable Trust
Chesapeake Bay Trust
The Chevron Companies
Claneil Foundation, Inc.
The Cleveland Foundation
Olive B. Cole Foundation
The Collins Foundation
Columbia Foundation
The Columbus Foundation
The Community Foundation of Greater New Haven
The Community Foundation of Santa Clara County
Community Foundation of Western North Carolina, Inc.
Compton Foundation, Inc.
The Conservation and Research Foundation
Conservation, Food & Health Foundation, Inc.
Cooke Foundation, Limited
Jessie B. Cox Charitable Trust
The Mary A. Crocker Trust
Crystal Channel Foundation
Patrick and Anna M. Cudahy Fund
The Nathan Cummings Foundation
Damien Foundation

Davis Conservation Foundation
Deer Creek Foundation
Cleveland H. Dodge Foundation, Inc.
Geraldine R. Dodge Foundation, Inc.
Dolfinger-McMahon Foundation
Gaylord and Dorothy Donnelley Foundation
Donner Canadian Foundation
The Elizabeth Ordway Dunn Foundation, Inc.
Jessie Ball duPont Religious, Charitable and Educational Fund
Echoing Green Foundation
Ederic Foundation, Inc.
The Educational Foundation of America
El Paso Community Foundation
El Pomar Foundation
The Charles Engelhard Foundation
Environment Now Foundation
Environmental Education Foundation of Florida, Inc.
Environmental Endowment for New Jersey, Inc.
The Armand G. Erpf Fund, Inc.
The Ettinger Foundation, Inc.
Fair Play Foundation
Fanwood Foundation
The Favrot Fund
The Field Foundation of Illinois, Inc.
Jamee and Marshall Field Foundation
The 1525 Foundation
FishAmerica Foundation
Flintridge Foundation
Ford Foundation
Ford Motor Company Fund
Walter and Josephine Ford Fund
Foundation for the Carolinas
Foundation for Deep Ecology
The Foundation for the National Capital Region
The Freed Foundation, Inc.
The Fund for New Jersey
Fund of the Four Directions
Funding Exchange
GE Fund
The Gap Foundation
Gebbie Foundation, Inc.
The Fred Gellert Foundation
General Service Foundation
The Wallace Alexander Gerbode Foundation, Inc.
The German Marshall Fund of the United States
Give to the Earth Foundation
Global Environmental Project Institute
The Goldman Environmental Foundation
Richard & Rhoda Goldman Fund
Walter and Duncan Gordon Charitable Foundation
Great Lakes Protection Fund
The Greenville Foundation
The W. C. Griffith Foundation
The George Gund Foundation
Walter and Elise Haas Fund
The Hahn Family Foundation

Environmental Issues

Water (cont.)

The Hamer Foundation
Harder Foundation
Mary W. Harriman Foundation
The Merrill G. & Emita E. Hastings Foundation
Heller Charitable & Educational Fund
The William and Flora Hewlett Foundation
The Homeland Foundation
Howfirma Foundation
The Roy A. Hunt Foundation
The Hyde and Watson Foundation
The Indian Point Foundation, Inc.
The James Irvine Foundation
Island Foundation, Inc.
Ittleson Foundation, Inc.
The Jackson Foundation
The Henry M. Jackson Foundation
W. Alton Jones Foundation, Inc.
The Joyce Foundation
The J. M. Kaplan Fund, Inc.
W. K. Kellogg Foundation
Harris and Eliza Kempner Fund
F. M. Kirby Foundation, Inc.
The Knapp Foundation, Inc.
The Seymour H. Knox Foundation, Inc.
Laidlaw Foundation
Laird, Norton Foundation
Larsen Fund, Inc.
Laurel Foundation
The Lazar Foundation
The Max and Anna Levinson Foundation
Lintilhac Foundation
Longwood Foundation, Inc.
Lyndhurst Foundation
The John D. and Catherine T. MacArthur Foundation
James A. Macdonald Foundation
Maine Community Foundation, Inc.
Maki Foundation
Marbrook Foundation
Marin Community Foundation
MARPAT Foundation, Inc.
Mars Foundation
The Marshall Fund of Arizona
Massachusetts Environmental Trust
McKenzie River Gathering Foundation
The McKnight Foundation
McLean Contributionship
Giles W. and Elise G. Mead Foundation
Nelson Mead Fund
Meadows Foundation, Inc.
Richard King Mellon Foundation
Merck Family Fund
The John Merck Fund
Robert G. and Anne M. Merrick Foundation, Inc.
Meyer Memorial Trust
Middlecott Foundation
The Milwaukee Foundation
The Minneapolis Foundation
Mobil Foundation, Inc.
Leo Model Foundation, Inc.

The Moriah Fund, Inc.
Charles Stewart Mott Foundation
Ruth Mott Fund
The Curtis and Edith Munson Foundation, Inc.
M. J. Murdock Charitable Trust
The National Environmental Education and Training Foundation, Inc.
National Fish and Wildlife Foundation
National Geographic Society Education Foundation
The Needmor Fund
New England Biolabs Foundation
New Hampshire Charitable Foundation
The New World Foundation
The New York Community Trust
The New York Times Company Foundation, Inc.
The New-Land Foundation, Inc.
Norcross Wildlife Foundation, Inc.
The Nord Family Foundation
Norman Foundation
Northwest Area Foundation
Northwest Fund for the Environment
Jessie Smith Noyes Foundation, Inc.
OCRI Foundation
Nathan M. Ohrbach Foundation, Inc.
The Ohrstrom Foundation
Onan Family Foundation
Orchard Foundation
Ottinger Foundation
Outdoor Industry Conservation Alliance
The Overbrook Foundation
The David and Lucile Packard Foundation
Patagonia, Inc.
Amelia Peabody Charitable Fund
Peninsula Community Foundation
The William Penn Foundation
James C. Penney Foundation
Perkins Charitable Foundation
The Pew Charitable Trusts
Philip Morris Companies, Inc.
Phillips Petroleum Foundation, Inc.
Howard Phipps Foundation
Lynn R. and Karl E. Prickett Fund
Prince Charitable Trusts
The Procter & Gamble Fund
The Prospect Hill Foundation
The Prudential Foundation
Public Welfare Foundation, Inc.
Recreational Equipment, Inc.
Philip D. Reed Foundation, Inc.
Z. Smith Reynolds Foundation, Inc.
The Rhode Island Community Foundation
The Roberts Foundation
Rockefeller Brothers Fund, Inc.
Rockefeller Family Fund, Inc.
The Rockefeller Foundation
Lee Romney Foundation, Inc.
The San Francisco Foundation
The Scherman Foundation, Inc.
Schultz Foundation, Inc.
The Schumann Fund for New Jersey, Inc.
The Florence and John Schumann Foundation

Sequoia Foundation
Seventh Generation Fund
Elmina B. Sewall Foundation
Shell Oil Company Foundation
The Skaggs Foundation
South Coast Foundation, Inc.
Sproul Foundation
Alfred T. Stanley Foundation
Steelcase Foundation
Margaret Dorrance Strawbridge Foundation of Pennsylvania II, Inc.
The Stroh Foundation
The Strong Foundation for Environmental Values
The Sudbury Foundation
The Sulzberger Foundation, Inc.
The Summit Foundation
Surdna Foundation, Inc.
Edna Bailey Sussman Fund
The Switzer Foundation
Nelson Talbott Foundation
Texaco Foundation
Thanksgiving Foundation
The Oakleigh L. Thorne Foundation
Threshold Foundation
The Tides Foundation
Times Mirror Magazines, Inc.
The Tinker Foundation Incorporated
Tortuga Foundation
Town Creek Foundation, Inc.
True North Foundation
The Truland Foundation
The Trust For Mutual Understanding
Marcia Brady Tucker Foundation
Rose E. Tucker Charitable Trust
Turner Foundation, Inc.
The USF&G Foundation, Inc.
Underhill Foundation
Union Camp Charitable Trust
Unitarian Universalist Veatch Program at Shelter Rock
Vancouver Foundation
Vanguard Public Foundation
G. Unger Vetlesen Foundation
Victoria Foundation, Inc.
The Vidda Foundation
Vinmont Foundation, Inc.
Virginia Environmental Endowment
WMX Environmental Grants Program
Wallace Genetic Foundation, Inc.
Weeden Foundation
Welfare Foundation, Inc.
Henry E. and Consuelo S. Wenger Foundation, Inc.
Westinghouse Foundation
Weyerhaeuser Company Foundation
The William P. Wharton Trust
Wilburforce Foundation
Robert W. Wilson Foundation
The Winslow Foundation
The Winston-Salem Foundation, Inc.
The Dean Witter Foundation
Margaret Cullinan Wray Charitable Lead Annuity Trust
The Wyomissing Foundation, Inc.

© 1995 Environmental Data Resources, Inc.

Environmental Issues

Oceans and Coasts

ARCO Foundation
The Abell Foundation
Alaska Conservation Foundation
The George I. Alden Trust
Winifred & Harry B. Allen Foundation
American Conservation Association, Inc.
American Express Philanthropic Program
American Foundation Corporation
Atherton Family Foundation
Atlantic Foundation
Mary Reynolds Babcock Foundation, Inc.
Clayton Baker Trust
The George F. Baker Trust
BankAmerica Foundation
The Bay Foundation
The Howard Bayne Fund
S. D. Bechtel, Jr. Foundation
The Beinecke Foundation, Inc.
The Ben & Jerry's Foundation
Beneficia Foundation
The Betterment Fund
Bishop Pine Fund
The Boeing Company
Mary Owen Borden Memorial Foundation
Alex. Brown & Sons Charitable Foundation, Inc.
H. Barksdale Brown Charitable Trust
The Robert Brownlee Foundation
Kathleen Price and Joseph M. Bryan Family Foundation, Inc.
The Buchanan Family Foundation
The Bullitt Foundation
The Cabot Family Charitable Trust
Carolyn Foundation
Mary Flagler Cary Charitable Trust
The Champlin Foundations
Cheeryble Foundation
Ben B. Cheney Foundation
Chesapeake Bay Trust
Chesapeake Corporation Foundation
The Chevron Companies
The Clowes Fund, Inc.
Columbia Foundation
The Columbus Foundation
The Community Foundation of Santa Clara County
The Community Foundation of Sarasota County, Inc.
The Community Foundation Serving Coastal South Carolina
Compton Foundation, Inc.
Conservation, Food & Health Foundation, Inc.
Cooke Foundation, Limited
The Cowles Charitable Trust
Cox Foundation, Inc.
Jessie B. Cox Charitable Trust
The Mary A. Crocker Trust
Roy E. Crummer Foundation
Crystal Channel Foundation
The Nathan Cummings Foundation
The Fred Harris Daniels Foundation, Inc.
The Arthur Vining Davis Foundations
Davis Conservation Foundation

Geraldine R. Dodge Foundation, Inc.
Thelma Doelger Charitable Trust
Oliver S. and Jennie R. Donaldson Charitable Trust
Gaylord and Dorothy Donnelley Foundation
Donner Canadian Foundation
The Elizabeth Ordway Dunn Foundation, Inc.
Ederic Foundation, Inc.
The Educational Foundation of America
Arthur M. and Olga T. Eisig–Arthur M. and Kate E. Tode Foundation, Inc.
The Energy Foundation
The Charles Engelhard Foundation
Environment Now Foundation
Environmental Education Foundation of Florida, Inc.
Environmental Endowment for New Jersey, Inc.
The Armand G. Erpf Fund, Inc.
The Ettinger Foundation, Inc.
Fair Play Foundation
Fanwood Foundation
Jamee and Marshall Field Foundation
Fields Pond Foundation, Inc.
Ford Foundation
Walter and Josephine Ford Fund
Foundation for Deep Ecology
Foundation for Field Research
The Jacob and Annita France Foundation, Inc.
Mary D. and Walter F. Frear Eleemosynary Trust
The Freed Foundation, Inc.
The Fund for New Jersey
The Gap Foundation
The Barbara Gauntlett Foundation, Inc.
The Fred Gellert Foundation
General Service Foundation
The Wallace Alexander Gerbode Foundation, Inc.
The Goldman Environmental Foundation
Richard & Rhoda Goldman Fund
Greater Piscataqua Community Foundation
The Greenville Foundation
Walter and Elise Haas Fund
Harder Foundation
Mary W. Harriman Foundation
Hawaii Community Foundation
The Edward W. Hazen Foundation
Heller Charitable & Educational Fund
The William and Flora Hewlett Foundation
The Hitachi Foundation
The Homeland Foundation
The Horn Foundation
The Charles Evans Hughes Memorial Foundation, Inc.
Hurdle Hill Foundation
The Hyams Foundation
The Indian Point Foundation, Inc.
Ireland Foundation
Island Foundation, Inc.
Ittleson Foundation, Inc.

The George Frederick Jewett Foundation
The Howard Johnson Foundation
W. Alton Jones Foundation, Inc.
The Joyce Foundation
Harris and Eliza Kempner Fund
The Henry P. Kendall Foundation
F. M. Kirby Foundation, Inc.
The Knapp Foundation, Inc.
The Seymour H. Knox Foundation, Inc.
The Kresge Foundation
Laird, Norton Foundation
The Lazar Foundation
The Norman Lear Foundation
The Max and Anna Levinson Foundation
The Little Family Foundation
Longwood Foundation, Inc.
Richard Lounsbery Foundation, Inc.
Luster Family Foundation, Inc.
The John D. and Catherine T. MacArthur Foundation
Maine Community Foundation, Inc.
MARPAT Foundation, Inc.
Mars Foundation
Massachusetts Environmental Trust
McDonnell Douglas Foundation
McInerny Foundation
The McIntosh Foundation
McKenzie River Gathering Foundation
Nelson Mead Fund
Meadows Foundation, Inc.
The Andrew W. Mellon Foundation
Richard King Mellon Foundation
The John Merck Fund
Robert G. and Anne M. Merrick Foundation, Inc.
Metropolitan Atlanta Community Foundation, Inc.
Metropolitan Life Foundation
Middlecott Foundation
Mobil Foundation, Inc.
The Moriah Fund, Inc.
Charles Stewart Mott Foundation
Ruth Mott Fund
The Mountaineers Foundation
The Curtis and Edith Munson Foundation, Inc.
M. J. Murdock Charitable Trust
John P. Murphy Foundation
The National Environmental Education and Training Foundation, Inc.
National Fish and Wildlife Foundation
New England Biolabs Foundation
The New York Community Trust
The New York Times Company Foundation, Inc.
Norcross Wildlife Foundation, Inc.
Mary Moody Northen, Inc.
Northwest Area Foundation
Northwest Fund for the Environment
Nathan M. Ohrbach Foundation, Inc.
The Ohrstrom Foundation
Orchard Foundation
The David and Lucile Packard Foundation
Patagonia, Inc.
Peninsula Community Foundation

Environmental Issues

Oceans and Coasts (cont.)

The William Penn Foundation
James C. Penney Foundation
The Perkin Fund
The Pew Charitable Trusts
Pew Scholars Program in Conservation
 and the Environment
The Pfizer Foundation, Inc.
Henry B. Plant Memorial Fund, Inc.
Lynn R. and Karl E. Prickett Fund
Prince Charitable Trusts
Pritzker Foundation
The Procter & Gamble Fund
The Prospect Hill Foundation
Public Welfare Foundation, Inc.
Recreational Equipment, Inc.
Z. Smith Reynolds Foundation, Inc.
The Rhode Island Community Foundation
Sid W. Richardson Foundation
The Roberts Foundation
The Rockfall Foundation
Rockwell Fund, Inc.
Lee Romney Foundation, Inc.
The San Francisco Foundation
The Scherman Foundation, Inc.
Schultz Foundation, Inc.
The Florence and John Schumann
 Foundation
Ellen Browning Scripps Foundation
Sequoia Foundation
Elmina B. Sewall Foundation
Shell Oil Company Foundation
The Skaggs Foundation
Kelvin Smith 1980 Charitable Trust
South Coast Foundation, Inc.
Sproul Foundation
The Stroh Foundation
The Strong Foundation for
 Environmental Values
Stroud Foundation
The Morris Stulsaft Foundation
The Sudbury Foundation
The Sulzberger Foundation, Inc.
Surdna Foundation, Inc.
Edna Bailey Sussman Fund
The Switzer Foundation
Texaco Foundation
Thanksgiving Foundation
The Oakleigh L. Thorne Foundation
Threshold Foundation
The Tides Foundation
Times Mirror Magazines, Inc.
The Tinker Foundation Incorporated
Town Creek Foundation, Inc.
True North Foundation
The Truland Foundation
Marcia Brady Tucker Foundation
The USF&G Foundation, Inc.
USX Foundation, Inc.
Union Camp Charitable Trust
Vancouver Foundation
R. T. Vanderbilt Trust
G. Unger Vetlesen Foundation
Victoria Foundation, Inc.
Virginia Environmental Endowment

WMX Environmental Grants Program
Wallace Genetic Foundation, Inc.
DeWitt Wallace-Reader's Digest Fund
C. A. Webster Foundation
Weeden Foundation
Welfare Foundation, Inc.
Westinghouse Foundation
G. N. Wilcox Trust
The Winston-Salem Foundation, Inc.
The Dean Witter Foundation
Margaret Cullinan Wray Charitable
 Lead Annuity Trust

Energy

ARCO Foundation
AT&T Foundation
A Territory Resource
The Abell Foundation
Alaska Conservation Foundation
Angelina Fund, Inc.
Atherton Family Foundation
Mary Reynolds Babcock Foundation, Inc.
BankAmerica Foundation
L. L. Bean, Inc.
The Ben & Jerry's Foundation
Beneficia Foundation
The William Bingham Foundation
The Boeing Company
Alexander H. Bright Charitable Trust
Ruth H. Brown Foundation
Kathleen Price and Joseph M. Bryan
 Family Foundation, Inc.
The Bullitt Foundation
C. S. Fund
Carolyn Foundation
Centerior Energy Foundation
Changing Horizons Charitable Trust
The Chevron Companies
Chrysler Corporation Fund
The Cleveland Foundation
Columbia Foundation
Community Foundation of
 Western North Carolina, Inc.
Compton Foundation, Inc.
The Conservation and Research
 Foundation
Jessie B. Cox Charitable Trust
Crystal Channel Foundation
The Nathan Cummings Foundation
Geraldine R. Dodge Foundation, Inc.
Donner Canadian Foundation
The Elizabeth Ordway Dunn
 Foundation, Inc.
Eastman Kodak Company Charitable Trust
The Educational Foundation of America
The Energy Foundation
The Favrot Fund
Samuel S. Fels Fund
Ford Foundation
Ford Motor Company Fund
The Foundation for the National
 Capital Region
Mary D. and Walter F. Frear
 Eleemosynary Trust
The Fund for New Jersey

Fund of the Four Directions
Funding Exchange
GE Fund
The Fred Gellert Foundation
The Wallace Alexander Gerbode
 Foundation, Inc.
The German Marshall Fund of
 the United States
The Golden Rule Foundation, Inc.
Richard & Rhoda Goldman Fund
Walter and Duncan Gordon Charitable
 Foundation
The Greenville Foundation
The George Gund Foundation
The Hahn Family Foundation
The Merrill G. & Emita E. Hastings
 Foundation
Hawaii Community Foundation
The John Randolph Haynes and
 Dora Haynes Foundation
The Clarence E. Heller Charitable
 Foundation
The William and Flora Hewlett
 Foundation
The Homeland Foundation
Howfirma Foundation
Hurdle Hill Foundation
The James Irvine Foundation
Island Foundation
W. Alton Jones Foundation, Inc.
The Joyce Foundation
The J. M. Kaplan Fund, Inc.
W. K. Kellogg Foundation
The Henry P. Kendall Foundation
Charles G. Koch Charitable Foundation
Laidlaw Foundation
Laurel Foundation
The Max and Anna Levinson Foundation
Lyndhurst Foundation
The John D. and Catherine T. MacArthur
 Foundation
The Martin Foundation, Inc.
The McKnight Foundation
Meadows Foundation, Inc.
The John Merck Fund
Joyce Mertz-Gilmore Foundation
Mobil Foundation, Inc.
The Moriah Fund, Inc.
Charles Stewart Mott Foundation
Ruth Mott Fund
The Curtis and Edith Munson
 Foundation, Inc.
The Needmor Fund
New England Biolabs Foundation
New Hampshire Charitable Foundation
The New York Community Trust
The New York Times Company
 Foundation, Inc.
The New-Land Foundation, Inc.
The Samuel Roberts Noble
 Foundation, Inc.
Ottinger Foundation
The David and Lucile Packard Foundation
Patagonia, Inc.
Amelia Peabody Charitable Fund

Environmental Issues

Energy (cont.)

James C. Penney Foundation
The Pew Charitable Trusts
The Philadelphia Foundation
Phillips Petroleum Foundation, Inc.
Prince Charitable Trusts
Public Welfare Foundation, Inc.
Z. Smith Reynolds Foundation, Inc.
Rockefeller Brothers Fund, Inc.
Rockefeller Family Fund, Inc.
Rockefeller Financial Services, Philanthropy Department
The Rockefeller Foundation
The San Francisco Foundation
Sarkeys Foundation
The Scherman Foundation, Inc.
Schultz Foundation, Inc.
Sequoia Foundation
Seventh Generation Fund
Shell Oil Company Foundation
The Summit Foundation
Surdna Foundation, Inc.
The Switzer Foundation
Texaco Foundation
The Tides Foundation
The Tinker Foundation Incorporated
Toyota USA Foundation
True North Foundation
The Trust For Mutual Understanding
Rose E. Tucker Charitable Trust
Turner Foundation, Inc.
USX Foundation, Inc.
Unitarian Universalist Veatch Program at Shelter Rock
United States-Japan Foundation
Virginia Environmental Endowment
WMX Environmental Grants Program
Weeden Foundation
G. N. Wilcox Trust
Sidney & Phyllis Wragge Foundation
Margaret Cullinan Wray Charitable Lead Annuity Trust

Solid Waste

ARCO Foundation
AT&T Foundation
The Abelard Foundation West
The Abell Foundation
Abell-Hanger Foundation
The Ahmanson Foundation
Alaska Conservation Foundation
The Jenifer Altman Foundation
Angelina Fund, Inc.
Atherton Family Foundation
Mary Reynolds Babcock Foundation, Inc.
BankAmerica Foundation
Bay Area Community Foundation
L. L. Bean, Inc.
Beldon Fund
The Ben & Jerry's Foundation
Mary Owen Borden Memorial Foundation
The Bothin Foundation
Otto Bremer Foundation

Kathleen Price and Joseph M. Bryan Family Foundation, Inc.
The Bullitt Foundation
The Bush Foundation
Centerior Energy Foundation
Chesapeake Bay Trust
Robert Sterling Clark Foundation, Inc.
The Collins Foundation
The Community Foundation of Greater New Haven
The Community Foundation of Santa Clara County
Community Foundation of Western North Carolina, Inc.
Compton Foundation, Inc.
Cooke Foundation, Limited
The Mary A. Crocker Trust
Crystal Channel Foundation
Dart Foundation
Davis Conservation Foundation
Geraldine R. Dodge Foundation, Inc.
Dolfinger-McMahon Foundation
The Herbert H. and Grace A. Dow Foundation
The Educational Foundation of America
El Paso Community Foundation
El Pomar Foundation
Environmental Endowment for New Jersey, Inc.
The Favrot Fund
The 1525 Foundation
Ford Foundation
Mary D. and Walter F. Frear Eleemosynary Trust
The Fund for New Jersey
The Gap Foundation
The Fred Gellert Foundation
Give to the Earth Foundation
Richard & Rhoda Goldman Fund
The Hahn Family Foundation
Hawaiian Electric Industries Charitable Foundation
The M. A. Healy Family Foundation, Inc.
The William and Flora Hewlett Foundation
Howfirma Foundation
The James Irvine Foundation
Island Foundation, Inc.
The Richard Ivey Foundation
W. Alton Jones Foundation, Inc.
The Joyce Foundation
Kongsgaard-Goldman Foundation
Laidlaw Foundation
Laurel Foundation
LifeWorks Foundation
Lyndhurst Foundation
The John D. and Catherine T. MacArthur Foundation
The Martin Foundation, Inc.
Meadows Foundation, Inc.
Mobil Foundation, Inc.
J. P. Morgan Charitable Trust
The Moriah Fund, Inc.
Charles Stewart Mott Foundation

The Curtis and Edith Munson Foundation, Inc.
M. J. Murdock Charitable Trust
The Needmor Fund
The New York Community Trust
New York Foundation
The New York Times Company Foundation, Inc.
Edward John Noble Foundation, Inc.
Norman Foundation
Northwest Fund for the Environment
Jessie Smith Noyes Foundation, Inc.
The David and Lucile Packard Foundation
Patagonia, Inc.
The William Penn Foundation
James C. Penney Foundation
The Pew Charitable Trusts
Philip Morris Companies, Inc.
Prince Charitable Trusts
The Procter & Gamble Fund
Public Welfare Foundation, Inc.
Philip D. Reed Foundation, Inc.
Z. Smith Reynolds Foundation, Inc.
Rockefeller Brothers Fund, Inc.
Rockefeller Family Fund, Inc.
The Rockefeller Foundation
The Winthrop Rockefeller Foundation
The Rockfall Foundation
The San Francisco Foundation
The Sapelo Foundation
The Florence and John Schumann Foundation
Ralph C. Sheldon Foundation, Inc.
Thomas Sill Foundation
Stanley Smith Horticultural Trust
The Charles J. Strosacker Foundation
The Sudbury Foundation
Surdna Foundation, Inc.
Edna Bailey Sussman Fund
The Switzer Foundation
The Telesis Foundation
Threshold Foundation
The Tides Foundation
Town Creek Foundation, Inc.
True North Foundation
Alice Tweed Tuohy Foundation
Unitarian Universalist Veatch Program at Shelter Rock
Victoria Foundation, Inc.
Virginia Environmental Endowment
WMX Environmental Grants Program
Weyerhaeuser Company Foundation
Wilburforce Foundation
Margaret Cullinan Wray Charitable Lead Annuity Trust
The Wyomissing Foundation, Inc.

Toxic Substances

ARCO Foundation
AT&T Foundation
A Territory Resource
The Abelard Foundation West
The Abell Foundation
The Acorn Foundation

Environmental Issues

Toxic Substances (cont.)

Alaska Conservation Foundation
The Jenifer Altman Foundation
American Conservation Association, Inc.
Ameritech Foundation
Angelina Fund, Inc.
The Arca Foundation
Azadoutioun Foundation
Mary Reynolds Babcock Foundation, Inc.
Clayton Baker Trust
The Bauman Foundation
Beldon Fund
The Ben & Jerry's Foundation
The Betterment Fund
The Boeing Company
The Lynde and Harry Bradley
  Foundation, Inc.
Kathleen Price and Joseph M. Bryan
  Family Foundation, Inc.
The Bullitt Foundation
The Bydale Foundation
C. S. Fund
The Morris and Gwendolyn Cafritz
  Foundation
Chesapeake Bay Trust
The Chevron Companies
Robert Sterling Clark Foundation, Inc.
The Cleveland Foundation
Columbia Foundation
Compton Foundation, Inc.
Conservation, Food & Health
  Foundation, Inc.
Jessie B. Cox Charitable Trust
The Mary A. Crocker Trust
The Nathan Cummings Foundation
Davis Conservation Foundation
Deer Creek Foundation
Geraldine R. Dodge Foundation, Inc.
Dolfinger-McMahon Foundation
The Elizabeth Ordway Dunn
  Foundation, Inc.
Eastman Kodak Company Charitable Trust
The Educational Foundation of America
The Energy Foundation
Environmental Endowment for
  New Jersey, Inc.
The Ettinger Foundation, Inc.
Ford Foundation
Ford Motor Company Fund
Foundation for Deep Ecology
The Foundation for the National
  Capital Region
The Frost Foundation, Ltd.
Fund of the Four Directions
Funding Exchange
The Gap Foundation
General Service Foundation
The Wallace Alexander Gerbode
  Foundation, Inc.
The German Marshall Fund of
  the United States
Give to the Earth Foundation
The Goldman Environmental Foundation
Richard & Rhoda Goldman Fund
Great Lakes Protection Fund

The William and Mary Greve
  Foundation, Inc.
The George Gund Foundation
HKH Foundation
The Hahn Family Foundation
Harder Foundation
Hartford Foundation for Public Giving
The Edward W. Hazen Foundation
Heller Charitable & Educational Fund
The Clarence E. Heller Charitable
  Foundation
The William and Flora Hewlett
  Foundation
The Homeland Foundation
Howfirma Foundation
The James Irvine Foundation
Island Foundation, Inc.
W. Alton Jones Foundation, Inc.
The Joyce Foundation
W. K. Kellogg Foundation
The Esther A. and Joseph Klingenstein
  Fund, Inc.
Kongsgaard-Goldman Foundation
Laidlaw Foundation
The Lazar Foundation
The Max and Anna Levinson Foundation
Lintilhac Foundation
Lyndhurst Foundation
The John D. and Catherine T. MacArthur
  Foundation
MARPAT Foundation, Inc.
The McIntosh Foundation
McKenzie River Gathering Foundation
The McKnight Foundation
Richard King Mellon Foundation
The John Merck Fund
Millbrook Tribute Garden, Inc.
The Milwaukee Foundation
J. P. Morgan Charitable Trust
The Moriah Fund, Inc.
Charles Stewart Mott Foundation
Ruth Mott Fund
The Curtis and Edith Munson
  Foundation, Inc.
The National Environmental Education
  and Training Foundation, Inc.
National Fish and Wildlife Foundation
The Needmor Fund
The New World Foundation
New York Foundation
Edward John Noble Foundation, Inc.
Norman Foundation
Northwest Fund for the Environment
Jessie Smith Noyes Foundation, Inc.
Nathan M. Ohrbach Foundation, Inc.
Ottinger Foundation
The Overbrook Foundation
Patagonia, Inc.
James C. Penney Foundation
The Pew Charitable Trusts
Pew Scholars Program in Conservation
  and the Environment
The Philadelphia Foundation
The Polden-Puckham Charitable
  Foundation

The Prospect Hill Foundation
Public Welfare Foundation, Inc.
Recreational Equipment, Inc.
Z. Smith Reynolds Foundation, Inc.
Rockefeller Brothers Fund, Inc.
Rockefeller Family Fund, Inc.
The Rockefeller Foundation
Lee Romney Foundation, Inc.
Fran and Warren Rupp Foundation
Sacharuna Foundation
The San Francisco Foundation
The Sapelo Foundation
The Scherman Foundation, Inc.
Schultz Foundation, Inc.
The Florence and John Schumann
  Foundation
Sears-Swetland Foundation
Seventh Generation Fund
Shell Oil Company Foundation
South Coast Foundation, Inc.
Stern Family Fund
The Strong Foundation for
  Environmental Values
The Summit Foundation
Edna Bailey Sussman Fund
The Switzer Foundation
Nelson Talbott Foundation
Texaco Foundation
Threshold Foundation
The Tides Foundation
Tortuga Foundation
Town Creek Foundation, Inc.
True North Foundation
The Trust For Mutual Understanding
USX Foundation, Inc.
Unitarian Universalist Veatch Program
  at Shelter Rock
Vanguard Public Foundation
Victoria Foundation, Inc.
Virginia Environmental Endowment
WMX Environmental Grants Program
Wallace Genetic Foundation, Inc.
Weeden Foundation
Mark and Catherine Winkler Foundation
Margaret Cullinan Wray Charitable
  Lead Annuity Trust

Population

Airport Business Center Foundation
Winifred & Harry B. Allen Foundation
American Foundation Corporation
The Arca Foundation
Evenor Armington Fund
Atkinson Foundation
Mary Reynolds Babcock Foundation, Inc.
The Cameron Baird Foundation
Clayton Baker Trust
The Beinecke Foundation, Inc.
James Ford Bell Foundation
Benua Foundation, Inc.
The Blumenthal Foundation
Mary Owen Borden Memorial Foundation
Alexander H. Bright Charitable Trust
Ruth H. Brown Foundation
W. L. Lyons Brown Foundation

© 1995 Environmental Data Resources, Inc.

Environmental Issues

Population (cont.)

The Buchanan Family Foundation
The Bunbury Company, Inc.
J. E. & Z. B. Butler Foundation, Inc.
The Bydale Foundation
The Cabot Family Charitable Trust
The Morris and Gwendolyn Cafritz Foundation
The Cargill Foundation
Carolyn Foundation
The Champlin Foundations
Cheeryble Foundation
Claneil Foundation, Inc.
The Clark Foundation
Robert Sterling Clark Foundation, Inc.
The Cleveland Foundation
The Clowes Fund, Inc.
The Community Foundation of Santa Clara County
Compton Foundation, Inc.
The Conservation and Research Foundation
Cooke Foundation, Limited
S. H. Cowell Foundation
The Cowles Charitable Trust
The Mary A. Crocker Trust
Roy E. Crummer Foundation
The Nathan Cummings Foundation
The Aaron Diamond Foundation
Cleveland H. Dodge Foundation, Inc.
Geraldine R. Dodge Foundation, Inc.
The Dragon Foundation, Inc.
The Max and Victoria Dreyfus Foundation, Inc.
Ederic Foundation, Inc.
The Educational Foundation of America
The Thomas J. Emery Memorial
The Ettinger Foundation, Inc.
Fanwood Foundation
The William Stamps Farish Fund
The Favrot Fund
Samuel S. Fels Fund
Leland Fikes Foundation, Inc.
Ford Foundation
Walter and Josephine Ford Fund
Foundation for the Carolinas
Foundation for Deep Ecology
Mary D. and Walter F. Frear Eleemosynary Trust
The Freed Foundation, Inc.
Fund of the Four Directions
Funding Exchange
The Fred Gellert Foundation
The Wallace Alexander Gerbode Foundation, Inc.
Bernard F. and Alva B. Gimbel Foundation, Inc.
Global Environmental Project Institute
Richard & Rhoda Goldman Fund
The George Gund Foundation
Walter and Elise Haas Fund
The Ewing Halsell Foundation
Harbor Lights Foundation
Harder Foundation
Mary W. Harriman Foundation

Hartford Foundation for Public Giving
The Merrill G. & Emita E. Hastings Foundation
Hawaii Community Foundation
The William and Flora Hewlett Foundation
The Horn Foundation
Howfirma Foundation
Hudson-Webber Foundation
The Charles Evans Hughes Memorial Foundation, Inc.
The Roy A. Hunt Foundation
Hurdle Hill Foundation
The Hyams Foundation
The Hyde and Watson Foundation
The Indian Point Foundation, Inc.
Ireland Foundation
The James Irvine Foundation
The George Frederick Jewett Foundation
Helen K. and Arthur E. Johnson Foundation
The Howard Johnson Foundation
Walter S. Johnson Foundation
The J. M. Kaplan Fund, Inc.
Harris and Eliza Kempner Fund
The Henry P. Kendall Foundation
The Robert S. and Grayce B. Kerr Foundation, Inc.
The Helen & Milton Kimmelman Foundation
F. M. Kirby Foundation, Inc.
The Esther A. and Joseph Klingenstein Fund, Inc.
The Seymour H. Knox Foundation, Inc.
The Kresge Foundation
Larsen Fund, Inc.
LaSalle Adams Fund
Laurel Foundation
The Lazar Foundation
The Norman Lear Foundation
Levi Strauss Foundation
The Little Family Foundation
Richard Lounsbery Foundation, Inc.
Luster Family Foundation, Inc.
The John D. and Catherine T. MacArthur Foundation
Marin Community Foundation
MARPAT Foundation, Inc.
Mars Foundation
The Marshall Fund of Arizona
The Martin Foundation, Inc.
McGregor Fund
Nelson Mead Fund
The Andrew W. Mellon Foundation
Merck Family Fund
The John Merck Fund
Joyce Mertz-Gilmore Foundation
Metropolitan Atlanta Community Foundation, Inc.
Middlecott Foundation
The Milwaukee Foundation
The Minneapolis Foundation
Leo Model Foundation, Inc.
The Moody Foundation
J. P. Morgan Charitable Trust

The Moriah Fund, Inc.
Henry and Lucy Moses Fund, Inc.
Charles Stewart Mott Foundation
The Curtis and Edith Munson Foundation, Inc.
New England Biolabs Foundation
New Hampshire Charitable Foundation
New Horizon Foundation
The New York Community Trust
The New York Times Company Foundation, Inc.
The New-Land Foundation, Inc.
Edward John Noble Foundation, Inc.
Jessie Smith Noyes Foundation, Inc.
Nicholas H. Noyes, Jr. Memorial Foundation
The Ohrstrom Foundation
Spencer T. and Ann W. Olin Foundation
Orchard Foundation
Ottinger Foundation
The Overbrook Foundation
The David and Lucile Packard Foundation
The William Penn Foundation
James C. Penney Foundation
Perkins Charitable Foundation
The Pew Charitable Trusts
The Philadelphia Foundation
Henry B. Plant Memorial Fund, Inc.
Lynn R. and Karl E. Prickett Fund
The Prospect Hill Foundation
Public Welfare Foundation, Inc.
Philip D. Reed Foundation, Inc.
Z. Smith Reynolds Foundation, Inc.
The Rhode Island Community Foundation
Sid W. Richardson Foundation
The Roberts Foundation
Rockefeller Brothers Fund, Inc.
Rockefeller Family Fund, Inc.
Rockefeller Financial Services, Philanthropy Department
The Rockefeller Foundation
Rockwell Fund, Inc.
Lee Romney Foundation, Inc.
Samuel and May Rudin Foundation, Inc.
San Diego Community Foundation
The San Francisco Foundation
Sarah Scaife Foundation Incorporated
The Scherman Foundation, Inc.
The Schiff Foundation
Elmina B. Sewall Foundation
Thomas Sill Foundation
Anna B. Stearns Charitable Foundation, Inc.
Stern Family Fund
Stoddard Charitable Trust
The Sulzberger Foundation, Inc.
The Summit Foundation
Nelson Talbott Foundation
S. Mark Taper Foundation
Thanksgiving Foundation
Threshold Foundation
The Tides Foundation
Tortuga Foundation
True North Foundation
Marcia Brady Tucker Foundation

Environmental Issues

Population (cont.)

Turner Foundation, Inc.
R. T. Vanderbilt Trust
Victoria Foundation, Inc.
Vinmont Foundation, Inc.
Wallace Genetic Foundation, Inc.
Weeden Foundation
Wilburforce Foundation
G. N. Wilcox Trust
Robert W. Wilson Foundation
The Winslow Foundation
Wodecroft Foundation
The Wyomissing Foundation, Inc.

Development

ARCO Foundation
The Abell Foundation
Alaska Conservation Foundation
The Jenifer Altman Foundation
American Conservation Association, Inc.
Ameritech Foundation
The Arca Foundation
Atkinson Foundation
Mary Reynolds Babcock Foundation, Inc.
The Bauman Foundation
The Ben & Jerry's Foundation
The Betterment Fund
Alexander H. Bright Charitable Trust
The Bullitt Foundation
Chesapeake Bay Trust
The Chevron Companies
The Collins Foundation
Columbia Foundation
The Community Foundation of Santa Clara County
Community Foundation of Western North Carolina, Inc.
Compton Foundation, Inc.
S. H. Cowell Foundation
The Nathan Cummings Foundation
Damien Foundation
Geraldine R. Dodge Foundation, Inc.
Donner Canadian Foundation
The Elizabeth Ordway Dunn Foundation, Inc.
The Educational Foundation of America
The Energy Foundation
Environment Now Foundation
Environmental Education Foundation of Florida, Inc.
Ford Foundation
Walter and Josephine Ford Fund
Foundation for Deep Ecology
The Fund for New Jersey
Fund of the Four Directions
Funding Exchange
The Gap Foundation
General Service Foundation
The German Marshall Fund of the United States
Give to the Earth Foundation
The Goldman Environmental Foundation
Richard & Rhoda Goldman Fund

Walter and Duncan Gordon Charitable Foundation
The Greenville Foundation
The George Gund Foundation
HKH Foundation
Walter and Elise Haas Fund
The Clarence E. Heller Charitable Foundation
The William and Flora Hewlett Foundation
Ireland Foundation
The James Irvine Foundation
Ittleson Foundation, Inc.
The Richard Ivey Foundation
Jackson Hole Preserve, Inc.
The Henry M. Jackson Foundation
W. Alton Jones Foundation, Inc.
The Joyce Foundation
The J. M. Kaplan Fund, Inc.
W. K. Kellogg Foundation
Laidlaw Foundation
Larsen Fund, Inc.
The Max and Anna Levinson Foundation
Lyndhurst Foundation
The John D. and Catherine T. MacArthur Foundation
The McIntosh Foundation
McKenzie River Gathering Foundation
The McKnight Foundation
Giles W. and Elise G. Mead Foundation
The Andrew W. Mellon Foundation
Richard King Mellon Foundation
Merck Family Fund
The John Merck Fund
Joyce Mertz-Gilmore Foundation
Middlecott Foundation
J. P. Morgan Charitable Trust
The Moriah Fund, Inc.
Charles Stewart Mott Foundation
Ruth Mott Fund
The Curtis and Edith Munson Foundation, Inc.
The Needmor Fund
New Hampshire Charitable Foundation
The New York Community Trust
Norcross Wildlife Foundation, Inc.
Northwest Area Foundation
Jessie Smith Noyes Foundation, Inc.
The David and Lucile Packard Foundation
Patagonia, Inc.
Peninsula Community Foundation
The William Penn Foundation
James C. Penney Foundation
The Pew Charitable Trusts
Pew Scholars Program in Conservation and the Environment
The Pfizer Foundation, Inc.
The Prospect Hill Foundation
Public Welfare Foundation, Inc.
Z. Smith Reynolds Foundation, Inc.
The Roberts Foundation
Rockefeller Brothers Fund, Inc.
Rockefeller Family Fund, Inc.
The Rockefeller Foundation

The Winthrop Rockefeller Foundation
The San Francisco Foundation
The Sapelo Foundation
Schultz Foundation, Inc.
The Schumann Fund for New Jersey, Inc.
The Florence and John Schumann Foundation
Seventh Generation Fund
The Summit Foundation
Surdna Foundation, Inc.
The Switzer Foundation
Threshold Foundation
The Tides Foundation
The Tinker Foundation Incorporated
The Trust For Mutual Understanding
Rose E. Tucker Charitable Trust
Turner Foundation, Inc.
Unitarian Universalist Veatch Program at Shelter Rock
Virginia Environmental Endowment
WMX Environmental Grants Program
Weeden Foundation
Wilburforce Foundation

© 1995 Environmental Data Resources, Inc.

Environmental Topics and Activities

Accountability

The Bullitt Foundation
Robert Sterling Clark Foundation, Inc.
Deer Creek Foundation
The Energy Foundation
The Fred Gellert Foundation
The William and Mary Greve Foundation, Inc.

Accountability: business

The Abelard Foundation West
The Acorn Foundation
Alaska Conservation Foundation
Angelina Fund, Inc.
Mary Reynolds Babcock Foundation, Inc.
The Bauman Foundation
Beldon Fund
The Bullitt Foundation
Chesapeake Bay Trust
Robert Sterling Clark Foundation, Inc.
Columbia Foundation
The Mary A. Crocker Trust
The Nathan Cummings Foundation
Deer Creek Foundation
Geraldine R. Dodge Foundation, Inc.
The Educational Foundation of America
Environment Now Foundation
The Fred Gellert Foundation
Great Lakes Protection Fund
The George Gund Foundation
W. Alton Jones Foundation, Inc.
The Joyce Foundation
Lyndhurst Foundation
The McKnight Foundation
Merck Family Fund
Joyce Mertz-Gilmore Foundation
The Curtis and Edith Munson Foundation, Inc.
The Needmor Fund
The New-Land Foundation, Inc.
Norman Foundation
Patagonia, Inc.
The Pew Charitable Trusts
Rockefeller Brothers Fund, Inc.
Schultz Foundation, Inc.
Surdna Foundation, Inc.
The Switzer Foundation
Threshold Foundation
The Tides Foundation
The Tinker Foundation Incorporated
Unitarian Universalist Veatch Program at Shelter Rock
WMX Environmental Grants Program
Wallace Genetic Foundation, Inc.
Weeden Foundation
The William P. Wharton Trust

Accountability: government

A Territory Resource
The Acorn Foundation
Alaska Conservation Foundation
Mary Reynolds Babcock Foundation, Inc.
The Bauman Foundation
Beldon Fund
The Bullitt Foundation
C. S. Fund
Columbia Foundation
Compton Foundation, Inc.
Deer Creek Foundation
The Educational Foundation of America
The Fred Gellert Foundation
General Service Foundation
The Lazar Foundation
The John D. and Catherine T. MacArthur Foundation
Giles W. and Elise G. Mead Foundation
Merck Family Fund
The Needmor Fund
Jessie Smith Noyes Foundation, Inc.
Patagonia, Inc.
Rockefeller Family Fund, Inc.
The Strong Foundation for Environmental Values
Threshold Foundation
Tortuga Foundation
Town Creek Foundation, Inc.
Unitarian Universalist Veatch Program at Shelter Rock
Wallace Genetic Foundation, Inc.
Margaret Cullinan Wray Charitable Lead Annuity Trust

Activism

California Community Foundation
Compton Foundation, Inc.
Norcross Wildlife Foundation, Inc.
Stern Family Fund
Vanguard Public Foundation

Advocacy

The Acorn Foundation
Alaska Conservation Foundation
The Jenifer Altman Foundation
The Bauman Foundation
Beldon Fund
James Ford Bell Foundation
The Ben & Jerry's Foundation
Mary Owen Borden Memorial Foundation
Helen Brach Foundation
The Bullitt Foundation
The Bush Foundation
California Community Foundation

Carolyn Foundation
Changing Horizons Charitable Trust
Robert Sterling Clark Foundation, Inc.
Compton Foundation, Inc.
Conservation, Food & Health Foundation, Inc.
S. H. Cowell Foundation
Jessie B. Cox Charitable Trust
The Nathan Cummings Foundation
Geraldine R. Dodge Foundation, Inc.
Echoing Green Foundation
The Educational Foundation of America
The Energy Foundation
Flintridge Foundation
Ford Foundation
The Gap Foundation
The Fred Gellert Foundation
General Service Foundation
The George Gund Foundation
The Richard Ivey Foundation
W. Alton Jones Foundation, Inc.
The Joyce Foundation
The J. M. Kaplan Fund, Inc.
Laidlaw Foundation
Lyndhurst Foundation
The John D. and Catherine T. MacArthur Foundation
Marbrook Foundation
McKenzie River Gathering Foundation
The McKnight Foundation
Merck Family Fund
The Minneapolis Foundation
Charles Stewart Mott Foundation
Ruth Mott Fund
The Curtis and Edith Munson Foundation, Inc.
The Needmor Fund
New Hampshire Charitable Foundation
Norman Foundation
Jessie Smith Noyes Foundation, Inc.
Patagonia, Inc.
James C. Penney Foundation
Prince Charitable Trusts
Public Welfare Foundation, Inc.
Recreational Equipment, Inc.
Z. Smith Reynolds Foundation, Inc.
Rockefeller Family Fund, Inc.
The San Francisco Foundation
The Sapelo Foundation
Seventh Generation Fund
Stern Family Fund
The Strong Foundation for Environmental Values
The Sudbury Foundation
Surdna Foundation, Inc.
The Tinker Foundation Incorporated

Environmental Topics and Activities

Advocacy (cont.)

The Trust For Mutual Understanding
Unitarian Universalist Veatch Program
　at Shelter Rock
Victoria Foundation, Inc.
Weeden Foundation
Margaret Cullinan Wray Charitable
　Lead Annuity Trust

Agricultural seedstocks

C. S. Fund
Crystal Channel Foundation
Foundation for Deep Ecology
The Kresge Foundation
Peninsula Community Foundation
Wallace Genetic Foundation, Inc.

Agriculture

Winifred & Harry B. Allen Foundation
American Foundation Corporation
Americana Foundation, Inc.
Angelina Fund, Inc.
The Arca Foundation
The Bauman Foundation
S. D. Bechtel, Jr. Foundation
Bishop Pine Fund
Kathleen Price and Joseph M. Bryan
　Family Foundation, Inc.
The Bullitt Foundation
The Cabot Family Charitable Trust
Changing Horizons Charitable Trust
Liz Claiborne & Art Ortenberg Foundation
The Community Foundation of
　Greater New Haven
Compton Foundation, Inc.
The Mary A. Crocker Trust
Damien Foundation
Geraldine R. Dodge Foundation, Inc.
Gaylord and Dorothy Donnelley Foundation
The Elizabeth Ordway Dunn
　Foundation, Inc.
The Educational Foundation of America
The Ettinger Foundation, Inc.
Ford Foundation
Ford Motor Company Fund
Foundation for Deep Ecology
The Fred Gellert Foundation
Great Lakes Protection Fund
HKH Foundation
Harder Foundation
The Clarence E. Heller Charitable
　Foundation
The William and Flora Hewlett Foundation
Howfirma Foundation
The Roy A. Hunt Foundation
Island Foundation
W. Alton Jones Foundation, Inc.
The Joyce Foundation
The J. M. Kaplan Fund, Inc.
W. K. Kellogg Foundation
The Lazar Foundation
The Max and Anna Levinson Foundation
The John D. and Catherine T. MacArthur
　Foundation

Marin Community Foundation
McKenzie River Gathering Foundation
Ruth Mott Fund
The Curtis and Edith Munson
　Foundation, Inc.
National Fish and Wildlife Foundation
The Needmor Fund
New Hampshire Charitable Foundation
Norcross Wildlife Foundation, Inc.
Northwest Area Foundation
Jessie Smith Noyes Foundation, Inc.
The David and Lucile Packard Foundation
The William Penn Foundation
The Pew Charitable Trusts
Public Welfare Foundation, Inc.
Z. Smith Reynolds Foundation, Inc.
The Rockefeller Foundation
The Winthrop Rockefeller Foundation
The San Francisco Foundation
Springhouse Foundation
The Strong Foundation for
　Environmental Values
The Morris Stulsaft Foundation
Threshold Foundation
Unitarian Universalist Veatch Program
　at Shelter Rock
Virginia Environmental Endowment
WMX Environmental Grants Program
Wallace Genetic Foundation, Inc.
Weeden Foundation
Weyerhaeuser Company Foundation

Agriculture: alternative/low input

The Acorn Foundation
The Ben & Jerry's Foundation
Kathleen Price and Joseph M. Bryan
　Family Foundation, Inc.
C. S. Fund
Changing Horizons Charitable Trust
Chesapeake Bay Trust
Columbia Foundation
Conservation, Food & Health
　Foundation, Inc.
The Nathan Cummings Foundation
Geraldine R. Dodge Foundation, Inc.
The Educational Foundation of America
Foundation for Deep Ecology
The Fund for New Jersey
The Gap Foundation
Give to the Earth Foundation
Heller Charitable & Educational Fund
The Clarence E. Heller Charitable
　Foundation
W. Alton Jones Foundation, Inc.
The Joyce Foundation
Kongsgaard-Goldman Foundation
The Max and Anna Levinson Foundation
Maine Community Foundation, Inc.
Merck Family Fund
The John Merck Fund
The Moriah Fund, Inc.
Charles Stewart Mott Foundation
National Fish and Wildlife Foundation
Jessie Smith Noyes Foundation, Inc.
Patagonia, Inc.

The Pew Charitable Trusts
Rockefeller Brothers Fund, Inc.
The Rockefeller Foundation
The San Francisco Foundation
The Strong Foundation for
　Environmental Values
Threshold Foundation
Wallace Genetic Foundation, Inc.

Agriculture: biointensive

C. S. Fund
Columbia Foundation
Compton Foundation, Inc.
Conservation, Food & Health
　Foundation, Inc.
Richard & Rhoda Goldman Fund
Threshold Foundation

Agriculture: family farms

A Territory Resource
Mary Reynolds Babcock Foundation, Inc.
The Ben & Jerry's Foundation
Otto Bremer Foundation
Changing Horizons Charitable Trust
Columbia Foundation
The Educational Foundation of America
Foundation for Deep Ecology
The J. M. Kaplan Fund, Inc.
W. K. Kellogg Foundation
The Needmor Fund
Northwest Area Foundation
Jessie Smith Noyes Foundation, Inc.
Patagonia, Inc.
Public Welfare Foundation, Inc.
Z. Smith Reynolds Foundation, Inc.
Rockefeller Brothers Fund, Inc.
Threshold Foundation
Unitarian Universalist Veatch Program
　at Shelter Rock

Agriculture: farm size

Mary Reynolds Babcock Foundation, Inc.
The Ben & Jerry's Foundation
Kathleen Price and Joseph M. Bryan
　Family Foundation, Inc.
The Ettinger Foundation, Inc.
General Service Foundation
Jessie Smith Noyes Foundation, Inc.
Public Welfare Foundation, Inc.
The Rockefeller Foundation
The Winthrop Rockefeller Foundation
The Sapelo Foundation
The Strong Foundation for
　Environmental Values
Threshold Foundation

Agriculture: hazardous chemicals

A Territory Resource
The Ben & Jerry's Foundation
General Service Foundation
Charles Stewart Mott Foundation
Patagonia, Inc.
The Pew Charitable Trusts

Environmental Topics and Activities

Agriculture: hazardous chemicals (cont.)

Public Welfare Foundation, Inc.
Vanguard Public Foundation

Agriculture: irrigation

Ford Foundation
Hawaii Community Foundation
Seventh Generation Fund
Weeden Foundation

Agriculture: land preservation

American Conservation Association, Inc.
American Foundation Corporation
Americana Foundation, Inc.
The Austin Memorial Foundation
Bishop Pine Fund
Alexander H. Bright Charitable Trust
Geraldine R. Dodge Foundation, Inc.
The William and Mary Greve Foundation, Inc.
The Hahn Family Foundation
The Merrill G. & Emita E. Hastings Foundation
Heller Charitable & Educational Fund
Howfirma Foundation
The J. M. Kaplan Fund, Inc.
Laurel Foundation
The Max and Anna Levinson Foundation
Lintilhac Foundation
James A. Macdonald Foundation
Marin Community Foundation
The McKnight Foundation
Richard King Mellon Foundation
The John Merck Fund
The Minneapolis Foundation
The Ohrstrom Foundation
The David and Lucile Packard Foundation
Patagonia, Inc.
The William Penn Foundation
The Pfizer Foundation, Inc.
Z. Smith Reynolds Foundation, Inc.
Rockefeller Brothers Fund, Inc.
Elmina B. Sewall Foundation
Sproul Foundation
The Strong Foundation for Environmental Values
The Oakleigh L. Thorne Foundation
USX Foundation, Inc.
Unitarian Universalist Veatch Program at Shelter Rock
Vanguard Public Foundation
Wallace Genetic Foundation, Inc.
C. A. Webster Foundation

Agriculture: livestock production/grazing

The Acorn Foundation
Mary Reynolds Babcock Foundation, Inc.
C. S. Fund
The Nathan Cummings Foundation
Foundation for Deep Ecology
Give to the Earth Foundation
Great Lakes Protection Fund
Hawaii Community Foundation
Howfirma Foundation
Laird, Norton Foundation
The Max and Anna Levinson Foundation
Ruth Mott Fund
National Fish and Wildlife Foundation
Norman Foundation
Northwest Area Foundation
Jessie Smith Noyes Foundation, Inc.
Patagonia, Inc.
The Prudential Foundation
Public Welfare Foundation, Inc.
The Winthrop Rockefeller Foundation
The Switzer Foundation
Threshold Foundation
Unitarian Universalist Veatch Program at Shelter Rock
Weeden Foundation

Agriculture: policy

The Abelard Foundation West
Mary Reynolds Babcock Foundation, Inc.
The Ben & Jerry's Foundation
The Educational Foundation of America
Ford Foundation
Give to the Earth Foundation
Great Lakes Protection Fund
The Henry M. Jackson Foundation
The J. M. Kaplan Fund, Inc.
Charles Stewart Mott Foundation
Jessie Smith Noyes Foundation, Inc.
James C. Penney Foundation
The Pew Charitable Trusts

Agriculture: sustainable

The Abelard Foundation West
The Acorn Foundation
The Jenifer Altman Foundation
Atkinson Foundation
Mary Reynolds Babcock Foundation, Inc.
The Bullitt Foundation
Patrick and Aimee Butler Family Foundation
C. S. Fund
Chesapeake Bay Trust
Columbia Foundation
Compton Foundation, Inc.
The Mary A. Crocker Trust
The Nathan Cummings Foundation
Damien Foundation
The Educational Foundation of America
Ford Foundation
General Service Foundation
Give to the Earth Foundation
Great Lakes Protection Fund
The Hahn Family Foundation
The Clarence E. Heller Charitable Foundation
W. Alton Jones Foundation, Inc.
The Joyce Foundation
The J. M. Kaplan Fund, Inc.
W. K. Kellogg Foundation
The Lazar Foundation
Lintilhac Foundation
The John D. and Catherine T. MacArthur Foundation
The John Merck Fund
The Moriah Fund, Inc.
Charles Stewart Mott Foundation
Ruth Mott Fund
The Needmor Fund
New England Biolabs Foundation
Northwest Area Foundation
Jessie Smith Noyes Foundation, Inc.
Patagonia, Inc.
James C. Penney Foundation
The Pew Charitable Trusts
Public Welfare Foundation, Inc.
Z. Smith Reynolds Foundation, Inc.
Rockefeller Brothers Fund, Inc.
The Rockefeller Foundation
The Winthrop Rockefeller Foundation
Seventh Generation Fund
Stanley Smith Horticultural Trust
The Strong Foundation for Environmental Values
The Switzer Foundation
Threshold Foundation
The Tides Foundation
Unitarian Universalist Veatch Program at Shelter Rock
Vanguard Public Foundation

Agroecosystems

The Bay Foundation
General Service Foundation
The John D. and Catherine T. MacArthur Foundation
The Rockefeller Foundation

Agroforestry

Atkinson Foundation
Ford Foundation
General Service Foundation
The Greenville Foundation
Laird, Norton Foundation
The Moriah Fund, Inc.
New England Biolabs Foundation
Jessie Smith Noyes Foundation, Inc.
The Rockefeller Foundation
Threshold Foundation

Air pollution: transportation

Changing Horizons Charitable Trust
The Energy Foundation
The Favrot Fund
The Max and Anna Levinson Foundation
The John Merck Fund
Threshold Foundation

Air quality/pollution

AT&T Foundation
The Acorn Foundation
Alaska Conservation Foundation
The Jenifer Altman Foundation
Beneficia Foundation
The Betterment Fund

Environmental Topics and Activities

Air quality/pollution (cont.)

Kathleen Price and Joseph M. Bryan Family Foundation, Inc.
The Bush Foundation
J. E. & Z. B. Butler Foundation, Inc.
Chesapeake Bay Trust
The Chevron Companies
Robert Sterling Clark Foundation, Inc.
The Cleveland Foundation
The Community Foundation of Santa Clara County
Jessie B. Cox Charitable Trust
The Nathan Cummings Foundation
Deer Creek Foundation
The Energy Foundation
Environmental Endowment for New Jersey, Inc.
The Favrot Fund
Samuel S. Fels Fund
Ford Foundation
The Fund for New Jersey
The German Marshall Fund of the United States
Give to the Earth Foundation
Richard & Rhoda Goldman Fund
The George Gund Foundation
Harder Foundation
The Clarence E. Heller Charitable Foundation
The Horn Foundation
The James Irvine Foundation
W. Alton Jones Foundation, Inc.
The Joyce Foundation
The J. M. Kaplan Fund, Inc.
Lyndhurst Foundation
Marin Community Foundation
Mobil Foundation, Inc.
The Moriah Fund, Inc.
Charles Stewart Mott Foundation
Ruth Mott Fund
The National Environmental Education and Training Foundation, Inc.
The New York Community Trust
New York Foundation
Andrew Norman Foundation
Patagonia, Inc.
The Pew Charitable Trusts
The Philadelphia Foundation
The Procter & Gamble Fund
Public Welfare Foundation, Inc.
Z. Smith Reynolds Foundation, Inc.
Rockefeller Brothers Fund, Inc.
The Rockefeller Foundation
The San Francisco Foundation
Shell Oil Company Foundation
Surdna Foundation, Inc.
The Switzer Foundation
Texaco Foundation
Threshold Foundation
Times Mirror Magazines, Inc.
The Tinker Foundation Incorporated
True North Foundation
Weyerhaeuser Company Foundation
Margaret Cullinan Wray Charitable Lead Annuity Trust

Arboretums

ARCO Foundation
Winifred & Harry B. Allen Foundation
American Foundation Corporation
Elmer L. & Eleanor J. Andersen Foundation
Arcadia Foundation
The Barra Foundation, Inc.
S. D. Bechtel, Jr. Foundation
Alexander H. Bright Charitable Trust
The Buchanan Family Foundation
The Morris and Gwendolyn Cafritz Foundation
The Cargill Foundation
Mary Flagler Cary Charitable Trust
The Chevron Companies
Claneil Foundation, Inc.
Conservation, Food & Health Foundation, Inc.
The James M. Cox, Jr. Foundation, Inc.
Dolfinger-McMahon Foundation
Fanwood Foundation
The William Stamps Farish Fund
Samuel S. Fels Fund
The Foundation for the National Capital Region
Mary D. and Walter F. Frear Eleemosynary Trust
The GAR Foundation
Georgia Power Foundation, Inc.
The William and Mary Greve Foundation, Inc.
The Homeland Foundation
The Hyde and Watson Foundation
W. K. Kellogg Foundation
Laird, Norton Foundation
Larsen Fund, Inc.
The John D. and Catherine T. MacArthur Foundation
The McConnell Foundation
The Eugene McDermott Foundation
McInerny Foundation
McLean Contributionship
Nelson Mead Fund
Middlecott Foundation
The Minneapolis Foundation
Mobil Foundation, Inc.
Ruth Mott Fund
The New York Community Trust
Onan Family Foundation
The Pew Charitable Trusts
The Philadelphia Foundation
Rockwell Fund, Inc.
San Diego Community Foundation
The San Francisco Foundation
Schultz Foundation, Inc.
Sears-Swetland Foundation
Shell Oil Company Foundation
The Kelvin and Eleanor Smith Foundation
Stanley Smith Horticultural Trust
The Truland Foundation
The William P. Wharton Trust
Joseph B. Whitehead Foundation
The Wortham Foundation, Inc.
Margaret Cullinan Wray Charitable Lead Annuity Trust

Atmosphere

Laird, Norton Foundation
Charles Stewart Mott Foundation
The Curtis and Edith Munson Foundation, Inc.
The David and Lucile Packard Foundation
Public Welfare Foundation, Inc.
Turner Foundation, Inc.
USX Foundation, Inc.

Beautification

ARCO Foundation
Abell-Hanger Foundation
The Ahmanson Foundation
American Conservation Association, Inc.
American Express Philanthropic Program
BankAmerica Foundation
Boettcher Foundation
W. L. Lyons Brown Foundation
The Chevron Companies
Chrysler Corporation Fund
Compton Foundation, Inc.
The Cowles Charitable Trust
Dolfinger-McMahon Foundation
The Max and Victoria Dreyfus Foundation, Inc.
Eastman Kodak Company Charitable Trust
Ford Motor Company Fund
The GAR Foundation
Georgia-Pacific Foundation
Herman Goldman Foundation
The Merrill G. & Emita E. Hastings Foundation
The J. M. Kaplan Fund, Inc.
The Seymour H. Knox Foundation, Inc.
Lyndhurst Foundation
James A. Macdonald Foundation
MARPAT Foundation, Inc.
McDonnell Douglas Foundation
Meadows Foundation, Inc.
The Minneapolis Foundation
Mobil Foundation, Inc.
New York Foundation
The New York Times Company Foundation, Inc.
Kenneth T. and Eileen L. Norris Foundation
Prince Charitable Trusts
The Procter & Gamble Fund
The Prudential Foundation
The Rhode Island Community Foundation
San Diego Community Foundation
Shell Oil Company Foundation
Snee-Reinhardt Charitable Foundation
Southwestern Bell Foundation
The Travelers Foundation
USX Foundation, Inc.
Union Camp Charitable Trust
R. T. Vanderbilt Trust
Victoria Foundation, Inc.
WMX Environmental Grants Program
Wallace Genetic Foundation, Inc.
The Wortham Foundation, Inc.

Environmental Topics and Activities

Billboards

The Mountaineers Foundation
Patagonia, Inc.
Margaret Cullinan Wray Charitable Lead Annuity Trust

Biodiversity

The Acorn Foundation
The Ahmanson Foundation
The Jenifer Altman Foundation
The Bay Foundation
James Ford Bell Foundation
Beneficia Foundation
The Bullitt Foundation
C. S. Fund
Mary Flagler Cary Charitable Trust
Liz Claiborne & Art Ortenberg Foundation
Compton Foundation, Inc.
The Conservation and Research Foundation
Conservation, Food & Health Foundation, Inc.
The Nathan Cummings Foundation
Geraldine R. Dodge Foundation, Inc.
Douroucouli Foundation
The Educational Foundation of America
Foundation for Deep Ecology
The Fred Gellert Foundation
Bernard F. and Alva B. Gimbel Foundation, Inc.
Give to the Earth Foundation
Harder Foundation
The Homeland Foundation
The Roy A. Hunt Foundation
The Richard Ivey Foundation
Martha Holden Jennings Foundation
W. Alton Jones Foundation, Inc.
The Kresge Foundation
Laidlaw Foundation
Laird, Norton Foundation
Laurel Foundation
The Lazar Foundation
Lyndhurst Foundation
The John D. and Catherine T. MacArthur Foundation
Maki Foundation
Mars Foundation
The Martin Foundation, Inc.
McLean Contributionship
Richard King Mellon Foundation
Merck Family Fund
The John Merck Fund
The Moriah Fund, Inc.
The Curtis and Edith Munson Foundation, Inc.
National Fish and Wildlife Foundation
New England Biolabs Foundation
Edward John Noble Foundation, Inc.
Northwest Fund for the Environment
The David and Lucile Packard Foundation
Patagonia, Inc.
The Pew Charitable Trusts
Pew Scholars Program in Conservation and the Environment
Rockefeller Family Fund, Inc.
Rockefeller Financial Services, Philanthropy Department
Rockwood Fund, Inc.
Sarkeys Foundation
Sequoia Foundation
Surdna Foundation, Inc.
Threshold Foundation
The Tinker Foundation Incorporated
Turner Foundation, Inc.
Vancouver Foundation
WMX Environmental Grants Program
Wallace Genetic Foundation, Inc.
Weeden Foundation
The William P. Wharton Trust

Biology

Clayton Baker Trust
The Howard Bayne Fund
The Robert Brownlee Foundation
The Chevron Companies
The Community Foundation of Greater New Haven
The Conservation and Research Foundation
Geraldine R. Dodge Foundation, Inc.
W. Alton Jones Foundation, Inc.
The Esther A. and Joseph Klingenstein Fund, Inc.
Larsen Fund, Inc.
Richard Lounsbery Foundation, Inc.
Giles W. and Elise G. Mead Foundation
National Fish and Wildlife Foundation
The New York Times Company Foundation, Inc.
Howard Phipps Foundation
The Rockefeller Foundation
The Switzer Foundation

Biosphere reserves

Geraldine R. Dodge Foundation, Inc.
Ford Foundation
General Service Foundation
Jackson Hole Preserve, Inc.
The John D. and Catherine T. MacArthur Foundation
The Curtis and Edith Munson Foundation, Inc.
National Fish and Wildlife Foundation
The David and Lucile Packard Foundation
The Rockefeller Foundation
The San Francisco Foundation

Biotechnology

C. S. Fund
Foundation for Deep Ecology
The Joyce Foundation
The John D. and Catherine T. MacArthur Foundation
Charles Stewart Mott Foundation
The Rockefeller Foundation
Sarkeys Foundation
Texaco Foundation
Unitarian Universalist Veatch Program at Shelter Rock

Birds

ARCO Foundation
Winifred & Harry B. Allen Foundation
American Foundation Corporation
The Beinecke Foundation, Inc.
Benua Foundation, Inc.
California Community Foundation
The Champlin Foundations
Chesapeake Bay Trust
The Chevron Companies
The Clowes Fund, Inc.
Compton Foundation, Inc.
The Conservation and Research Foundation
Jessie B. Cox Charitable Trust
Davis Conservation Foundation
Geraldine R. Dodge Foundation, Inc.
Gaylord and Dorothy Donnelley Foundation
Echoing Green Foundation
The Educational Foundation of America
The Charles Engelhard Foundation
The Freed Foundation, Inc.
The Fred Gellert Foundation
General Service Foundation
Richard & Rhoda Goldman Fund
The Hastings Trust
The Homeland Foundation
The Roy A. Hunt Foundation
Ireland Foundation
The Richard Ivey Foundation
W. Alton Jones Foundation, Inc.
The Helen & Milton Kimmelman Foundation
Longwood Foundation, Inc.
The John D. and Catherine T. MacArthur Foundation
Maki Foundation
Mars Foundation
The Martin Foundation, Inc.
McLean Contributionship
Nelson Mead Fund
Richard King Mellon Foundation
The John Merck Fund
Mobil Foundation, Inc.
Leo Model Foundation, Inc.
The Moriah Fund, Inc.
Charles Stewart Mott Foundation
The Mountaineers Foundation
The Curtis and Edith Munson Foundation, Inc.
National Fish and Wildlife Foundation
Norcross Wildlife Foundation, Inc.
The David and Lucile Packard Foundation
Patagonia, Inc.
Phillips Petroleum Foundation, Inc.
The Prospect Hill Foundation
The Rhode Island Community Foundation
Shell Oil Company Foundation
The Strong Foundation for Environmental Values
The Switzer Foundation
Nelson Talbott Foundation
Texaco Foundation
The Trust For Mutual Understanding
USX Foundation, Inc.

Environmental Topics and Activities

Birds (cont.)

Vancouver Foundation
R. T. Vanderbilt Trust
Virginia Environmental Endowment
WMX Environmental Grants Program
Wallace Genetic Foundation, Inc.
Weeden Foundation
Weyerhaeuser Company Foundation
The William P. Wharton Trust
Margaret Cullinan Wray Charitable
 Lead Annuity Trust

Birds: cranes

Helen Brach Foundation
The Lynde and Harry Bradley
 Foundation, Inc.
Geraldine R. Dodge Foundation, Inc.
Gaylord and Dorothy Donnelley Foundation
The Kresge Foundation
The John D. and Catherine T. MacArthur
 Foundation
The Milwaukee Foundation
Edward John Noble Foundation, Inc.
The Trust For Mutual Understanding
Weeden Foundation

Birds: raptors

ARCO Foundation
The Ahmanson Foundation
The Bailey Wildlife Foundation
BankAmerica Foundation
James Ford Bell Foundation
The Blumenthal Foundation
The Buchanan Family Foundation
Chesapeake Bay Trust
The Community Foundation Serving
 Coastal South Carolina
Davis Conservation Foundation
Geraldine R. Dodge Foundation, Inc.
The Charles Engelhard Foundation
Environment Now Foundation
Fanwood Foundation
Foundation for Deep Ecology
Frelinghuysen Foundation
The Robert S. and Grayce B. Kerr
 Foundation, Inc.
The Little Family Foundation
Maki Foundation
McLean Contributionship
M. J. Murdock Charitable Trust
National Fish and Wildlife Foundation
Norcross Wildlife Foundation, Inc.
Patagonia, Inc.
The William Penn Foundation
Shell Oil Company Foundation
Southwestern Bell Foundation
The Strong Foundation for
 Environmental Values
The Summerlee Foundation
Nelson Talbott Foundation
The Trust For Mutual Understanding
Weyerhaeuser Company Foundation
The Wyomissing Foundation, Inc.

Birds: shorebirds

Carolyn Foundation
Chesapeake Bay Trust
Compton Foundation, Inc.
Davis Conservation Foundation
Echoing Green Foundation
Flintridge Foundation
Ireland Foundation
National Fish and Wildlife Foundation
The David and Lucile Packard Foundation

Birds: waterfowl

BankAmerica Foundation
S. D. Bechtel, Jr. Foundation
The Beinecke Foundation, Inc.
David Winton Bell Foundation
James Ford Bell Foundation
The Buchanan Family Foundation
The Cargill Foundation
Chesapeake Bay Trust
The Chevron Companies
The Chicago Community Trust
Clark Charitable Trust
The Community Foundation of
 Santa Clara County
The James M. Cox, Jr. Foundation, Inc.
Davis Conservation Foundation
Geraldine R. Dodge Foundation, Inc.
Gaylord and Dorothy Donnelley Foundation
Ederic Foundation, Inc.
Fair Play Foundation
Fanwood Foundation
Jamee and Marshall Field Foundation
Flintridge Foundation
Ford Motor Company Fund
The Foundation for the National
 Capital Region
The Hastings Trust
The Clarence E. Heller Charitable
 Foundation
The Hofmann Foundation
The Roy A. Hunt Foundation
Island Foundation, Inc.
The Helen & Milton Kimmelman
 Foundation
The Knapp Foundation, Inc.
The Seymour H. Knox Foundation, Inc.
Mars Foundation
Nelson Mead Fund
National Fish and Wildlife Foundation
Phillips Petroleum Foundation, Inc.
The Rhode Island Community Foundation
The San Francisco Foundation
The Schiff Foundation
Schultz Foundation, Inc.
Nelson Talbott Foundation
Turner Foundation, Inc.
Union Camp Charitable Trust
Vancouver Foundation
WMX Environmental Grants Program
C. A. Webster Foundation
Henry E. and Consuelo S. Wenger
 Foundation, Inc.

The William P. Wharton Trust
Whitecap Foundation

Botany

California Community Foundation
Conservation, Food & Health
 Foundation, Inc.
Cooke Foundation, Limited
The Roy A. Hunt Foundation
The Andrew W. Mellon Foundation
Sid W. Richardson Foundation
The Rockefeller Foundation
Threshold Foundation
The Tides Foundation

Business community

The Abell Foundation
The Jenifer Altman Foundation
Angelina Fund, Inc.
BankAmerica Foundation
The Bullitt Foundation
Changing Horizons Charitable Trust
Chesapeake Bay Trust
The Chicago Community Trust
Robert Sterling Clark Foundation, Inc.
Community Foundation of
 Western North Carolina, Inc.
Geraldine R. Dodge Foundation, Inc.
Echoing Green Foundation
Environmental Education Foundation
 of Florida, Inc.
Foundation for Deep Ecology
The Fund for New Jersey
GE Fund
The Fred Gellert Foundation
The German Marshall Fund of
 the United States
Great Lakes Protection Fund
The William and Flora Hewlett Foundation
The Joyce Foundation
Lyndhurst Foundation
The McKnight Foundation
The Andrew W. Mellon Foundation
The Moriah Fund, Inc.
Charles Stewart Mott Foundation
The Curtis and Edith Munson
 Foundation, Inc.
National Fish and Wildlife Foundation
Northwest Area Foundation
Patagonia, Inc.
The Pew Charitable Trusts
Pew Scholars Program in Conservation
 and the Environment
Z. Smith Reynolds Foundation, Inc.
The San Francisco Foundation
The Sapelo Foundation
The Sudbury Foundation
Surdna Foundation, Inc.
The Switzer Foundation
Threshold Foundation
The Tinker Foundation Incorporated
WMX Environmental Grants Program
Weyerhaeuser Company Foundation

Environmental Topics and Activities

Butterflies

The William Bingham Foundation
Geraldine R. Dodge Foundation, Inc.
Environmental Education Foundation of Florida, Inc.
The Kresge Foundation
The John D. and Catherine T. MacArthur Foundation
National Fish and Wildlife Foundation
Virginia Environmental Endowment
WMX Environmental Grants Program
Margaret Cullinan Wray Charitable Lead Annuity Trust

Camps/camping

The Bothin Foundation
Otto Bremer Foundation
Chesapeake Bay Trust
Community Foundation of Western North Carolina, Inc.
Environmental Education Foundation of Florida, Inc.
Foundation for Deep Ecology
Greater Piscataqua Community Foundation
The Hahn Family Foundation
Hartford Foundation for Public Giving
Charles Hayden Foundation
Howfirma Foundation
Giles W. and Elise G. Mead Foundation
Meyer Memorial Trust
The Minneapolis Foundation
Patagonia, Inc.
Recreational Equipment, Inc.
The San Francisco Foundation
Springhouse Foundation
The Morris Stulsaft Foundation
Vancouver Foundation
Victoria Foundation, Inc.

Capacity building

Caribou Fund
The Cleveland Foundation
The Collins Foundation
Compton Foundation, Inc.
Ford Foundation
General Service Foundation
The German Marshall Fund of the United States
The Hyde and Watson Foundation
The J. M. Kaplan Fund, Inc.
The Lazar Foundation
The John D. and Catherine T. MacArthur Foundation
The Moriah Fund, Inc.
Charles Stewart Mott Foundation
Pew Scholars Program in Conservation and the Environment
Rose E. Tucker Charitable Trust

Carbon emissions/levels/sources

Changing Horizons Charitable Trust
The Energy Foundation
The German Marshall Fund of the United States
The George Gund Foundation
W. Alton Jones Foundation, Inc.
Laird, Norton Foundation
The John D. and Catherine T. MacArthur Foundation
The Pew Charitable Trusts
The Rockefeller Foundation

Careers: environmental

ARCO Foundation
Mary Reynolds Babcock Foundation, Inc.
The Bauman Foundation
W. L. Lyons Brown Foundation
Chrysler Corporation Fund
The Cleveland Foundation
The Cricket Foundation
The Mary A. Crocker Trust
Charles E. Culpeper Foundation, Inc.
The Nathan Cummings Foundation
Davis Conservation Foundation
Geraldine R. Dodge Foundation, Inc.
The Educational Foundation of America
Ford Motor Company Fund
The Gap Foundation
The Wallace Alexander Gerbode Foundation, Inc.
Walter and Duncan Gordon Charitable Foundation
The George Gund Foundation
Evelyn and Walter Haas, Jr. Fund
The William and Flora Hewlett Foundation
The James Irvine Foundation
Ittleson Foundation, Inc.
The Henry M. Jackson Foundation
The Joyce Foundation
W. K. Kellogg Foundation
Laird, Norton Foundation
Laurel Foundation
Charles Stewart Mott Foundation
The Curtis and Edith Munson Foundation, Inc.
National Fish and Wildlife Foundation
The David and Lucile Packard Foundation
Z. Smith Reynolds Foundation, Inc.
The San Francisco Foundation
The Schumann Fund for New Jersey, Inc.
The Sonoma County Community Foundation
Surdna Foundation, Inc.
Nelson Talbott Foundation
Town Creek Foundation, Inc.
Victoria Foundation, Inc.

Caves

W. L. Lyons Brown Foundation
The Ewing Halsell Foundation
Weeden Foundation

Center: outdoor education

Winifred & Harry B. Allen Foundation
Boettcher Foundation
Kathleen Price and Joseph M. Bryan Family Foundation, Inc.
The Morris and Gwendolyn Cafritz Foundation
Chesapeake Bay Trust
The Community Foundation of Sarasota County, Inc.
Dolfinger-McMahon Foundation
The Herbert H. and Grace A. Dow Foundation
The Thomas J. Emery Memorial
Environmental Education Foundation of Florida, Inc.
The Jacob and Annita France Foundation, Inc.
The Rollin M. Gerstacker Foundation
The Hall Family Foundation
Helen K. and Arthur E. Johnson Foundation
Maki Foundation
McDonnell Douglas Foundation
The Milwaukee Foundation
Patagonia, Inc.
Sacramento Regional Foundation
Sears-Swetland Foundation
Springs Foundation, Inc.
Steelcase Foundation
The Charles J. Strosacker Foundation
Texaco Foundation
The Troy Foundation
WMX Environmental Grants Program
Joseph B. Whitehead Foundation
The Wortham Foundation, Inc.
Margaret Cullinan Wray Charitable Lead Annuity Trust

Churches: environmental involvement

The Nathan Cummings Foundation
The Pew Charitable Trusts
Threshold Foundation

Citizen action

The Jenifer Altman Foundation
The Bauman Foundation
The Ben & Jerry's Foundation
Beneficia Foundation
C. S. Fund
Changing Horizons Charitable Trust
The Nathan Cummings Foundation
Deer Creek Foundation
Global Environmental Project Institute
Richard & Rhoda Goldman Fund
The Joyce Foundation
Levi Strauss Foundation
McKenzie River Gathering Foundation
Giles W. and Elise G. Mead Foundation
The John Merck Fund
The Needmor Fund
Outdoor Industry Conservation Alliance
Patagonia, Inc.
Public Welfare Foundation, Inc.
Z. Smith Reynolds Foundation, Inc.
Surdna Foundation, Inc.
Threshold Foundation

© 1995 Environmental Data Resources, Inc.

Environmental Topics and Activities

Citizen participation

A Territory Resource
The Acorn Foundation
Alaska Conservation Foundation
Angelina Fund, Inc.
Mary Reynolds Babcock Foundation, Inc.
Beldon Fund
The Ben & Jerry's Foundation
The Bullitt Foundation
Caribou Fund
Mary Flagler Cary Charitable Trust
Chesapeake Bay Trust
The Community Foundation of
    Santa Clara County
Jessie B. Cox Charitable Trust
Deer Creek Foundation
The Elizabeth Ordway Dunn
    Foundation, Inc.
The Educational Foundation of America
The Energy Foundation
Environmental Endowment for
    New Jersey, Inc.
Ford Foundation
Foundation for Deep Ecology
The Frost Foundation, Ltd.
Fund of the Four Directions
Laidlaw Foundation
Laird, Norton Foundation
The Lazar Foundation
MARPAT Foundation, Inc.
Massachusetts Environmental Trust
McKenzie River Gathering Foundation
The McKnight Foundation
The John Merck Fund
Charles Stewart Mott Foundation
The Needmor Fund
Northwest Area Foundation
Patagonia, Inc.
The William Penn Foundation
James C. Penney Foundation
The Pew Charitable Trusts
Public Welfare Foundation, Inc.
Recreational Equipment, Inc.
Z. Smith Reynolds Foundation, Inc.
The Rhode Island Community Foundation
Rockefeller Family Fund, Inc.
The Rockefeller Foundation
The Strong Foundation for
    Environmental Values
Surdna Foundation, Inc.
Threshold Foundation
The Tinker Foundation Incorporated
Unitarian Universalist Veatch Program
    at Shelter Rock
Vanguard Public Foundation
Victoria Foundation, Inc.
Virginia Environmental Endowment

Clean Air Act

The Nathan Cummings Foundation
The Energy Foundation
The Joyce Foundation

The Moriah Fund, Inc.
Charles Stewart Mott Foundation
New Hampshire Charitable Foundation
Smith Richardson Foundation, Inc.
Surdna Foundation, Inc.
Threshold Foundation
Margaret Cullinan Wray Charitable
    Lead Annuity Trust

Clean Water Act

Great Lakes Protection Fund
Charles Stewart Mott Foundation
WMX Environmental Grants Program

Clearinghouses

The Bauman Foundation
Kathleen Price and Joseph M. Bryan
    Family Foundation, Inc.
The Conservation and Research Foundation
The Nathan Cummings Foundation
Deer Creek Foundation
Dolfinger-McMahon Foundation
Richard & Rhoda Goldman Fund
The George Gund Foundation
Island Foundation, Inc.
W. Alton Jones Foundation, Inc.
Joyce Mertz-Gilmore Foundation
The Moriah Fund, Inc.
Charles Stewart Mott Foundation
Northwest Area Foundation
Rockefeller Brothers Fund, Inc.
The Strong Foundation for
    Environmental Values
Threshold Foundation
Town Creek Foundation, Inc.
Virginia Environmental Endowment
Weeden Foundation

Climate change

ARCO Foundation
The William Bingham Foundation
Patrick and Aimee Butler Family
    Foundation
Changing Horizons Charitable Trust
Conservation, Food & Health
    Foundation, Inc.
Ford Foundation
The German Marshall Fund of
    the United States
Give to the Earth Foundation
The Homeland Foundation
W. Alton Jones Foundation, Inc.
Laird, Norton Foundation
Charles Stewart Mott Foundation
Patagonia, Inc.
The Pew Charitable Trusts
Sarah Scaife Foundation Incorporated
The Florence and John Schumann
    Foundation
The Summit Foundation
Texaco Foundation
Wallace Genetic Foundation, Inc.

Coalitions/collaborations/consortia

A Territory Resource
Alaska Conservation Foundation
The Jenifer Altman Foundation
American Foundation Corporation
Angelina Fund, Inc.
Mary Reynolds Babcock Foundation, Inc.
BankAmerica Foundation
The Bauman Foundation
Beldon Fund
James Ford Bell Foundation
The Ben & Jerry's Foundation
Beneficia Foundation
The Blumenthal Foundation
Kathleen Price and Joseph M. Bryan
    Family Foundation, Inc.
The Bullitt Foundation
Carolyn Foundation
Changing Horizons Charitable Trust
Ben B. Cheney Foundation
Chesapeake Bay Trust
The Chevron Companies
Robert Sterling Clark Foundation, Inc.
Columbia Foundation
Community Foundation of
    Western North Carolina, Inc.
Compton Foundation, Inc.
The Conservation and Research Foundation
Conservation, Food & Health
    Foundation, Inc.
The Cowles Charitable Trust
Cox Foundation, Inc.
Jessie B. Cox Charitable Trust
Crystal Channel Foundation
The Nathan Cummings Foundation
Deer Creek Foundation
Geraldine R. Dodge Foundation, Inc.
Dolfinger-McMahon Foundation
The Elizabeth Ordway Dunn
    Foundation, Inc.
Echoing Green Foundation
The Educational Foundation of America
The Energy Foundation
Fanwood Foundation
Ford Foundation
Foundation for Deep Ecology
The Foundation for the National
    Capital Region
Lloyd A. Fry Foundation
Fund of the Four Directions
Funding Exchange
The Gap Foundation
The Fred Gellert Foundation
General Service Foundation
The German Marshall Fund of
    the United States
Global Greengrants Fund
The Goldman Environmental Foundation
Great Lakes Protection Fund
The George Gund Foundation
Harder Foundation
The Clarence E. Heller Charitable
    Foundation
The William and Flora Hewlett Foundation

Environmental Topics and Activities

Coalitions/collaborations/consortia (cont.)

The Hitachi Foundation
The Horn Foundation
The James Irvine Foundation
Island Foundation, Inc.
Ittleson Foundation, Inc.
The Richard Ivey Foundation
Jackson Hole Preserve, Inc.
W. Alton Jones Foundation, Inc.
The Joyce Foundation
The J. M. Kaplan Fund, Inc.
Laidlaw Foundation
Laird, Norton Foundation
The Max and Anna Levinson Foundation
Luster Family Foundation, Inc.
Lyndhurst Foundation
The John D. and Catherine T. MacArthur Foundation
Maine Community Foundation, Inc.
Maki Foundation
Marin Community Foundation
McKenzie River Gathering Foundation
The McKnight Foundation
Merck Family Fund
The John Merck Fund
Joyce Mertz-Gilmore Foundation
The Minneapolis Foundation
Mobil Foundation, Inc.
The Moriah Fund, Inc.
Charles Stewart Mott Foundation
Ruth Mott Fund
The Curtis and Edith Munson Foundation, Inc.
National Fish and Wildlife Foundation
The Needmor Fund
The New York Community Trust
New York Foundation
The New York Times Company Foundation, Inc.
The New-Land Foundation, Inc.
Norcross Wildlife Foundation, Inc.
The Nord Family Foundation
Norman Foundation
Jessie Smith Noyes Foundation, Inc.
The Ohrstrom Foundation
Ottinger Foundation
The David and Lucile Packard Foundation
Patagonia, Inc.
The Pew Charitable Trusts
Pew Scholars Program in Conservation and the Environment
The Philadelphia Foundation
Prince Charitable Trusts
Public Welfare Foundation, Inc.
Recreational Equipment, Inc.
Z. Smith Reynolds Foundation, Inc.
The Rhode Island Community Foundation
Rockefeller Brothers Fund, Inc.
Rockefeller Family Fund, Inc.
The Rockefeller Foundation
The San Francisco Foundation
The Schumann Fund for New Jersey, Inc.
The Florence and John Schumann Foundation
Seventh Generation Fund

Shell Oil Company Foundation
The Strong Foundation for Environmental Values
The Sudbury Foundation
Surdna Foundation, Inc.
The Switzer Foundation
Nelson Talbott Foundation
Texaco Foundation
The Oakleigh L. Thorne Foundation
Threshold Foundation
Town Creek Foundation, Inc.
True North Foundation
The Trust For Mutual Understanding
Union Camp Charitable Trust
Unitarian Universalist Veatch Program at Shelter Rock
Virginia Environmental Endowment
WMX Environmental Grants Program
Wallace Genetic Foundation, Inc.
Weeden Foundation
The William P. Wharton Trust
The Winston-Salem Foundation, Inc.
Sidney & Phyllis Wragge Foundation
Margaret Cullinan Wray Charitable Lead Annuity Trust

Coastal issues

ARCO Foundation
The Abell Foundation
Alaska Conservation Foundation
Winifred & Harry B. Allen Foundation
American Conservation Association, Inc.
American Foundation Corporation
Mary Reynolds Babcock Foundation, Inc.
Clayton Baker Trust
The George F. Baker Trust
BankAmerica Foundation
S. D. Bechtel, Jr. Foundation
The Beinecke Foundation, Inc.
Beldon Fund
The Ben & Jerry's Foundation
The Betterment Fund
Bishop Pine Fund
Mary Owen Borden Memorial Foundation
The Lynde and Harry Bradley Foundation, Inc.
Alex. Brown & Sons Charitable Foundation, Inc.
Kathleen Price and Joseph M. Bryan Family Foundation, Inc.
The Bullitt Foundation
The Morris and Gwendolyn Cafritz Foundation
Carolyn Foundation
Mary Flagler Cary Charitable Trust
The Champlin Foundations
Chesapeake Bay Trust
Chesapeake Corporation Foundation
The Chevron Companies
Columbia Foundation
The Community Foundation of Santa Clara County
The Community Foundation Serving Coastal South Carolina
Compton Foundation, Inc.

Cooke Foundation, Limited
Jessie B. Cox Charitable Trust
The Cricket Foundation
The Mary A. Crocker Trust
Roy E. Crummer Foundation
The Nathan Cummings Foundation
The Arthur Vining Davis Foundations
Davis Conservation Foundation
Geraldine R. Dodge Foundation, Inc.
Oliver S. and Jennie R. Donaldson Charitable Trust
Gaylord and Dorothy Donnelley Foundation
The Elizabeth Ordway Dunn Foundation, Inc.
Ederic Foundation, Inc.
The Educational Foundation of America
The Energy Foundation
The Charles Engelhard Foundation
Environment Now Foundation
Environmental Education Foundation of Florida, Inc.
Environmental Endowment for New Jersey, Inc.
Fair Play Foundation
Jamee and Marshall Field Foundation
Ford Foundation
Walter and Josephine Ford Fund
Foundation for Deep Ecology
The Jacob and Annita France Foundation, Inc.
The Freed Foundation, Inc.
The Fund for New Jersey
The Gap Foundation
The Fred Gellert Foundation
General Service Foundation
The Wallace Alexander Gerbode Foundation, Inc.
Give to the Earth Foundation
Richard & Rhoda Goldman Fund
Greater Piscataqua Community Foundation
The George Gund Foundation
Evelyn and Walter Haas, Jr. Fund
Walter and Elise Haas Fund
Mary W. Harriman Foundation
The Edward W. Hazen Foundation
Heller Charitable & Educational Fund
The Homeland Foundation
The Horn Foundation
Ireland Foundation
The James Irvine Foundation
Island Foundation, Inc.
W. Alton Jones Foundation, Inc.
Joy Foundation for Ecological Education and Research
The J. M. Kaplan Fund, Inc.
Harris and Eliza Kempner Fund
F. M. Kirby Foundation, Inc.
Laidlaw Foundation
Laird, Norton Foundation
The Lazar Foundation
The Norman Lear Foundation
Levi Strauss Foundation
The Max and Anna Levinson Foundation
The Little Family Foundation
Luster Family Foundation, Inc.

© 1995 Environmental Data Resources, Inc.

Environmental Topics and Activities

Coastal issues (cont.)

The John D. and Catherine T. MacArthur Foundation
Magowan Family Foundation, Inc.
Maine Community Foundation, Inc.
MARPAT Foundation, Inc.
Mars Foundation
Massachusetts Environmental Trust
McKenzie River Gathering Foundation
The McKnight Foundation
Giles W. and Elise G. Mead Foundation
The Andrew W. Mellon Foundation
Richard King Mellon Foundation
Merck Family Fund
Robert G. and Anne M. Merrick Foundation, Inc.
Metropolitan Life Foundation
Meyer Memorial Trust
Middlecott Foundation
The Moriah Fund, Inc.
Charles Stewart Mott Foundation
Ruth Mott Fund
The Curtis and Edith Munson Foundation, Inc.
M. J. Murdock Charitable Trust
The National Environmental Education and Training Foundation, Inc.
National Fish and Wildlife Foundation
New England Biolabs Foundation
The New York Community Trust
The New York Times Company Foundation, Inc.
Norcross Wildlife Foundation, Inc.
Mary Moody Northen, Inc.
Northwest Area Foundation
Northwest Fund for the Environment
The Ohrstrom Foundation
Outdoor Industry Conservation Alliance
The David and Lucile Packard Foundation
Patagonia, Inc.
Amelia Peabody Charitable Fund
Peninsula Community Foundation
The William Penn Foundation
James C. Penney Foundation
The Pew Charitable Trusts
Pew Scholars Program in Conservation and the Environment
Prince Charitable Trusts
The Prospect Hill Foundation
Public Welfare Foundation, Inc.
Z. Smith Reynolds Foundation, Inc.
The Rhode Island Community Foundation
Sid W. Richardson Foundation
Rockwell Fund, Inc.
Lee Romney Foundation, Inc.
The San Francisco Foundation
The Sapelo Foundation
The Scherman Foundation, Inc.
Elmina B. Sewall Foundation
Shell Oil Company Foundation
Sproul Foundation
Margaret Dorrance Strawbridge Foundation of Pennsylvania II, Inc.
The Stroh Foundation

The Strong Foundation for Environmental Values
The Morris Stulsaft Foundation
The Sudbury Foundation
Surdna Foundation, Inc.
The Switzer Foundation
Texaco Foundation
Threshold Foundation
The Tinker Foundation Incorporated
Town Creek Foundation, Inc.
True North Foundation
Marcia Brady Tucker Foundation
Turner Foundation, Inc.
Union Camp Charitable Trust
Vancouver Foundation
Victoria Foundation, Inc.
Virginia Environmental Endowment
WMX Environmental Grants Program
Wallace Genetic Foundation, Inc.
Welfare Foundation, Inc.
Westinghouse Foundation
Weyerhaeuser Company Foundation
Wilburforce Foundation
The Dean Witter Foundation
Margaret Cullinan Wray Charitable Lead Annuity Trust

Coastal lands

ARCO Foundation
Alaska Conservation Foundation
Winifred & Harry B. Allen Foundation
American Conservation Association, Inc.
American Foundation Corporation
Mary Reynolds Babcock Foundation, Inc.
Clayton Baker Trust
The George F. Baker Trust
BankAmerica Foundation
S. D. Bechtel, Jr. Foundation
The Beinecke Foundation, Inc.
The Ben & Jerry's Foundation
The Betterment Fund
Bishop Pine Fund
Mary Owen Borden Memorial Foundation
Alex. Brown & Sons Charitable Foundation, Inc.
Kathleen Price and Joseph M. Bryan Family Foundation, Inc.
The Bullitt Foundation
The Cabot Family Charitable Trust
The Morris and Gwendolyn Cafritz Foundation
Carolyn Foundation
Mary Flagler Cary Charitable Trust
The Champlin Foundations
Chesapeake Bay Trust
Chesapeake Corporation Foundation
The Chevron Companies
Columbia Foundation
The Community Foundation of Santa Clara County
The Community Foundation Serving Coastal South Carolina
Compton Foundation, Inc.
Jessie B. Cox Charitable Trust

The Mary A. Crocker Trust
Roy E. Crummer Foundation
The Arthur Vining Davis Foundations
Davis Conservation Foundation
Geraldine R. Dodge Foundation, Inc.
Oliver S. and Jennie R. Donaldson Charitable Trust
Gaylord and Dorothy Donnelley Foundation
The Elizabeth Ordway Dunn Foundation, Inc.
Ederic Foundation, Inc.
The Educational Foundation of America
The Energy Foundation
The Charles Engelhard Foundation
Environment Now Foundation
Environmental Endowment for New Jersey, Inc.
Fair Play Foundation
Jamee and Marshall Field Foundation
Walter and Josephine Ford Fund
Foundation for Deep Ecology
The Jacob and Annita France Foundation, Inc.
The Freed Foundation, Inc.
The Fund for New Jersey
The Gap Foundation
The Fred Gellert Foundation
General Service Foundation
The Wallace Alexander Gerbode Foundation, Inc.
Give to the Earth Foundation
The Goldman Environmental Foundation
Richard & Rhoda Goldman Fund
Great Lakes Protection Fund
The George Gund Foundation
Evelyn and Walter Haas, Jr. Fund
Walter and Elise Haas Fund
Mary W. Harriman Foundation
The Edward W. Hazen Foundation
Heller Charitable & Educational Fund
The Homeland Foundation
The Horn Foundation
Ireland Foundation
The James Irvine Foundation
Island Foundation, Inc.
W. Alton Jones Foundation, Inc.
Harris and Eliza Kempner Fund
F. M. Kirby Foundation, Inc.
Laird, Norton Foundation
The Lazar Foundation
The Norman Lear Foundation
Levi Strauss Foundation
The Max and Anna Levinson Foundation
The Little Family Foundation
Luster Family Foundation, Inc.
Lyndhurst Foundation
Maine Community Foundation, Inc.
MARPAT Foundation, Inc.
Mars Foundation
The Martin Foundation, Inc.
Massachusetts Environmental Trust
McKenzie River Gathering Foundation
The McKnight Foundation
Giles W. and Elise G. Mead Foundation

Environmental Topics and Activities

Coastal lands (cont.)
The Andrew W. Mellon Foundation
Richard King Mellon Foundation
Merck Family Fund
Robert G. and Anne M. Merrick Foundation, Inc.
Metropolitan Life Foundation
Middlecott Foundation
The Moriah Fund, Inc.
Ruth Mott Fund
The Curtis and Edith Munson Foundation, Inc.
National Fish and Wildlife Foundation
New England Biolabs Foundation
The New York Community Trust
The New York Times Company Foundation, Inc.
Norcross Wildlife Foundation, Inc.
Mary Moody Northen, Inc.
Northwest Area Foundation
Northwest Fund for the Environment
The Ohrstrom Foundation
The David and Lucile Packard Foundation
Patagonia, Inc.
Peninsula Community Foundation
The William Penn Foundation
James C. Penney Foundation
Perkins Charitable Foundation
The Pew Charitable Trusts
Pew Scholars Program in Conservation and the Environment
Prince Charitable Trusts
The Prospect Hill Foundation
Public Welfare Foundation, Inc.
Z. Smith Reynolds Foundation, Inc.
The Rhode Island Community Foundation
Sid W. Richardson Foundation
The Rockefeller Foundation
Rockwell Fund, Inc.
Lee Romney Foundation, Inc.
The San Francisco Foundation
The Scherman Foundation, Inc.
Elmina B. Sewall Foundation
Shell Oil Company Foundation
Sproul Foundation
Margaret Dorrance Strawbridge Foundation of Pennsylvania II, Inc.
The Stroh Foundation
The Strong Foundation for Environmental Values
The Sudbury Foundation
Texaco Foundation
Threshold Foundation
The Tides Foundation
The Tinker Foundation Incorporated
Town Creek Foundation, Inc.
True North Foundation
Marcia Brady Tucker Foundation
Union Camp Charitable Trust
Vancouver Foundation
Victoria Foundation, Inc.
Virginia Environmental Endowment
WMX Environmental Grants Program
Wallace Genetic Foundation, Inc.

Westinghouse Foundation
Wilburforce Foundation
Margaret Cullinan Wray Charitable Lead Annuity Trust

Communications
The Bullitt Foundation
Changing Horizons Charitable Trust
Ford Foundation
Fund of the Four Directions
The John D. and Catherine T. MacArthur Foundation
Merck Family Fund
The John Merck Fund
Charles Stewart Mott Foundation
The Rockefeller Foundation
Seventh Generation Fund
Surdna Foundation, Inc.
Threshold Foundation
Weyerhaeuser Company Foundation

Community development
Alaska Conservation Foundation
Atkinson Foundation
The Ben & Jerry's Foundation
Beneficia Foundation
The Bullitt Foundation
The Cleveland Foundation
Deer Creek Foundation
Geraldine R. Dodge Foundation, Inc.
Samuel S. Fels Fund
Ford Foundation
The Fred Gellert Foundation
General Service Foundation
The Greenville Foundation
The James Irvine Foundation
The Joyce Foundation
The J. M. Kaplan Fund, Inc.
The John D. and Catherine T. MacArthur Foundation
McKenzie River Gathering Foundation
Merck Family Fund
Jessie Smith Noyes Foundation, Inc.
Z. Smith Reynolds Foundation, Inc.
The Sapelo Foundation
Surdna Foundation, Inc.
Threshold Foundation
Vanguard Public Foundation
Virginia Environmental Endowment
Lila Wallace-Reader's Digest Fund

Community planning
Alaska Conservation Foundation
Robert Sterling Clark Foundation, Inc.
Ford Foundation
The George Gund Foundation
The Needmor Fund
Threshold Foundation

Community/local groups
A Territory Resource
The Abelard Foundation West
The Acorn Foundation

The Jenifer Altman Foundation
The Beinecke Foundation, Inc.
Beldon Fund
The Ben & Jerry's Foundation
Otto Bremer Foundation
Kathleen Price and Joseph M. Bryan Family Foundation, Inc.
The Bullitt Foundation
Chesapeake Bay Trust
Robert Sterling Clark Foundation, Inc.
The Cleveland Foundation
Jessie B. Cox Charitable Trust
The Mary A. Crocker Trust
Crystal Channel Foundation
Deer Creek Foundation
Dolfinger-McMahon Foundation
General Service Foundation
Great Lakes Protection Fund
HKH Foundation
The Richard Ivey Foundation
The Joyce Foundation
The J. M. Kaplan Fund, Inc.
Laidlaw Foundation
The John D. and Catherine T. MacArthur Foundation
The McKnight Foundation
The John Merck Fund
The Moriah Fund, Inc.
Charles Stewart Mott Foundation
National Fish and Wildlife Foundation
The Needmor Fund
Norcross Wildlife Foundation, Inc.
Northwest Area Foundation
Jessie Smith Noyes Foundation, Inc.
Patagonia, Inc.
James C. Penney Foundation
The Pew Charitable Trusts
Public Welfare Foundation, Inc.
Recreational Equipment, Inc.
Z. Smith Reynolds Foundation, Inc.
Rockefeller Brothers Fund, Inc.
The Sapelo Foundation
The Schumann Fund for New Jersey, Inc.
The Sudbury Foundation
Surdna Foundation, Inc.
Threshold Foundation
Unitarian Universalist Veatch Program at Shelter Rock

Composting
The Ben & Jerry's Foundation
Chesapeake Bay Trust
Robert Sterling Clark Foundation, Inc.
The Educational Foundation of America
Laird, Norton Foundation
Patagonia, Inc.
The William Penn Foundation
The Rockefeller Foundation
The Schumann Fund for New Jersey, Inc.
Stanley Smith Horticultural Trust
Threshold Foundation
Margaret Cullinan Wray Charitable Lead Annuity Trust

Environmental Topics and Activities

Conferences/colloquia/workshops, etc.

ARCO Foundation
The Abell Foundation
Abell-Hanger Foundation
Alaska Conservation Foundation
The Jenifer Altman Foundation
The Vincent Astor Foundation
Mary Reynolds Babcock Foundation, Inc.
The Bauman Foundation
Beldon Fund
The Blumenthal Foundation
Mary Owen Borden Memorial Foundation
Otto Bremer Foundation
Kathleen Price and Joseph M. Bryan Family Foundation, Inc.
The Bullitt Foundation
C. S. Fund
Ben B. Cheney Foundation
Chesapeake Bay Trust
The Chevron Companies
Robert Sterling Clark Foundation, Inc.
Columbia Foundation
Community Foundation of Western North Carolina, Inc.
Compton Foundation, Inc.
S. H. Cowell Foundation
Crystal Channel Foundation
The Nathan Cummings Foundation
Damien Foundation
Davis Conservation Foundation
Geraldine R. Dodge Foundation, Inc.
Dolfinger-McMahon Foundation
Eastman Kodak Company Charitable Trust
The Educational Foundation of America
The Energy Foundation
Environmental Education Foundation of Florida, Inc.
Flintridge Foundation
Ford Foundation
Foundation for Deep Ecology
Lloyd A. Fry Foundation
Fund of the Four Directions
The Gap Foundation
The Fred Gellert Foundation
General Service Foundation
The Wallace Alexander Gerbode Foundation, Inc.
The German Marshall Fund of the United States
Richard & Rhoda Goldman Fund
Great Lakes Protection Fund
Greater Piscataqua Community Foundation
The Greenville Foundation
The George Gund Foundation
The Hahn Family Foundation
The William and Flora Hewlett Foundation
The James Irvine Foundation
Island Foundation, Inc.
The Richard Ivey Foundation
The Henry M. Jackson Foundation
W. Alton Jones Foundation, Inc.
The Joyce Foundation
The J. M. Kaplan Fund, Inc.
Laidlaw Foundation
Laird, Norton Foundation
The Lazar Foundation
The Max and Anna Levinson Foundation
Lintilhac Foundation
Lyndhurst Foundation
The John D. and Catherine T. MacArthur Foundation
Maki Foundation
MARPAT Foundation, Inc.
McKenzie River Gathering Foundation
The McKnight Foundation
Giles W. and Elise G. Mead Foundation
The Andrew W. Mellon Foundation
Merck Family Fund
The John Merck Fund
Joyce Mertz-Gilmore Foundation
J. P. Morgan Charitable Trust
Charles Stewart Mott Foundation
The Curtis and Edith Munson Foundation, Inc.
National Fish and Wildlife Foundation
National Geographic Society Education Foundation
New Hampshire Charitable Foundation
The New York Times Company Foundation, Inc.
Norman Foundation
Northwest Area Foundation
Northwest Fund for the Environment
Jessie Smith Noyes Foundation, Inc.
The Ohrstrom Foundation
The David and Lucile Packard Foundation
Patagonia, Inc.
Peninsula Community Foundation
The Pew Charitable Trusts
Pew Scholars Program in Conservation and the Environment
Recreational Equipment, Inc.
Sid W. Richardson Foundation
Rockefeller Brothers Fund, Inc.
The Rockefeller Foundation
The Winthrop Rockefeller Foundation
Rockwell Fund, Inc.
The San Francisco Foundation
The Florence and John Schumann Foundation
Seventh Generation Fund
The Sudbury Foundation
Surdna Foundation, Inc.
Threshold Foundation
The Tides Foundation
The Tinker Foundation Incorporated
True North Foundation
The Trust For Mutual Understanding
Unitarian Universalist Veatch Program at Shelter Rock
Virginia Environmental Endowment
WMX Environmental Grants Program
Weeden Foundation
Weyerhaeuser Company Foundation
Wilburforce Foundation
Margaret Cullinan Wray Charitable Lead Annuity Trust

Conflict resolution/mediation

ARCO Foundation
The William Bingham Foundation
Liz Claiborne & Art Ortenberg Foundation
Compton Foundation, Inc.
Ford Foundation
The Frost Foundation, Ltd.
The Richard Ivey Foundation
The Max and Anna Levinson Foundation
The John D. and Catherine T. MacArthur Foundation
National Fish and Wildlife Foundation
Recreational Equipment, Inc.
Sequoia Foundation
Virginia Environmental Endowment

Conservation

The Ahmanson Foundation
Alaska Conservation Foundation
American Conservation Association, Inc.
Elmer L. & Eleanor J. Andersen Foundation
Arcadia Foundation
Evenor Armington Fund
Atkinson Foundation
Mary Reynolds Babcock Foundation, Inc.
The Cameron Baird Foundation
BankAmerica Foundation
The Bauman Foundation
Beldon Fund
Beneficia Foundation
Bishop Pine Fund
Ruth H. Brown Foundation
W. L. Lyons Brown Foundation
The Bullitt Foundation
The Bunbury Company, Inc.
C. S. Fund
California Community Foundation
The Cape Branch Foundation
Changing Horizons Charitable Trust
Chesapeake Bay Trust
The Chevron Companies
The Collins Foundation
The Columbus Foundation
The Community Foundation of Santa Clara County
Compton Foundation, Inc.
The Conservation and Research Foundation
Conservation, Food & Health Foundation, Inc.
Cooke Foundation, Limited
Cox Foundation, Inc.
The Mary A. Crocker Trust
Davis Conservation Foundation
Geraldine R. Dodge Foundation, Inc.
Oliver S. and Jennie R. Donaldson Charitable Trust
Gaylord and Dorothy Donnelley Foundation
Fair Play Foundation
Fanwood Foundation
Jamee and Marshall Field Foundation
Ford Foundation
Lloyd A. Fry Foundation
General Service Foundation

Environmental Topics and Activities

Conservation (cont.)

The German Marshall Fund of
 the United States
The Golden Rule Foundation, Inc.
Richard & Rhoda Goldman Fund
The Greenville Foundation
The George Gund Foundation
The Hahn Family Foundation
Harder Foundation
Gladys and Roland Harriman Foundation
The Merrill G. & Emita E. Hastings
 Foundation
Heller Charitable & Educational Fund
The Homeland Foundation
Howfirma Foundation
The Roy A. Hunt Foundation
Island Foundation, Inc.
The Howard Johnson Foundation
W. Alton Jones Foundation, Inc.
F. M. Kirby Foundation, Inc.
Laird, Norton Foundation
Laurel Foundation
The Lazar Foundation
The Little Family Foundation
The John D. and Catherine T. MacArthur
 Foundation
Maki Foundation
Marin Community Foundation
MARPAT Foundation, Inc.
Mars Foundation
The McIntosh Foundation
The McKnight Foundation
Giles W. and Elise G. Mead Foundation
Meyer Memorial Trust
The Moriah Fund, Inc.
The Curtis and Edith Munson
 Foundation, Inc.
National Fish and Wildlife Foundation
The New York Times Company
 Foundation, Inc.
The New-Land Foundation, Inc.
Edward John Noble Foundation, Inc.
Norcross Wildlife Foundation, Inc.
Northwest Fund for the Environment
The David and Lucile Packard Foundation
Peninsula Community Foundation
Perkins Charitable Foundation
The Pew Charitable Trusts
Phillips Petroleum Foundation, Inc.
Prince Charitable Trusts
The Prudential Foundation
Z. Smith Reynolds Foundation, Inc.
Rockefeller Financial Services,
 Philanthropy Department
Lee Romney Foundation, Inc.
Sacharuna Foundation
The San Francisco Foundation
Sarah I. Schieffelin Residuary Trust
Schultz Foundation, Inc.
Sequoia Foundation
Elmina B. Sewall Foundation
Snee-Reinhardt Charitable Foundation
Springhouse Foundation
Nelson Talbott Foundation
The Oakleigh L. Thorne Foundation

Town Creek Foundation, Inc.
The Trust For Mutual Understanding
Union Camp Charitable Trust
Vancouver Foundation
Victoria Foundation, Inc.
Virginia Environmental Endowment
WMX Environmental Grants Program
Wallace Genetic Foundation, Inc.
Weeden Foundation
The William P. Wharton Trust
Wilburforce Foundation
Margaret Cullinan Wray Charitable
 Lead Annuity Trust

Conservation biology

The Bay Foundation
Liz Claiborne & Art Ortenberg Foundation
Geraldine R. Dodge Foundation, Inc.
The Max and Anna Levinson Foundation
The John D. and Catherine T. MacArthur
 Foundation
Edward John Noble Foundation, Inc.
Patagonia, Inc.
The Switzer Foundation
Weeden Foundation

Conservation Corps

ARCO Foundation
The Chevron Companies
The Community Foundation of
 Santa Clara County
Compton Foundation, Inc.
The Educational Foundation of America
Georgia Power Foundation, Inc.
The German Marshall Fund of
 the United States
Evelyn and Walter Haas, Jr. Fund
Levi Strauss Foundation
Lintilhac Foundation
Luster Family Foundation, Inc.
MARPAT Foundation, Inc.
Massachusetts Environmental Trust
McKesson Foundation, Inc.
J. P. Morgan Charitable Trust
Charles Stewart Mott Foundation
National Fish and Wildlife Foundation
New Hampshire Charitable Foundation
Public Welfare Foundation, Inc.
The San Francisco Foundation
The Scherman Foundation, Inc.
The Morris Stulsaft Foundation
Victoria Foundation, Inc.
DeWitt Wallace-Reader's Digest Fund

Consumer education

Mary Reynolds Babcock Foundation, Inc.
Changing Horizons Charitable Trust
Chesapeake Bay Trust
Columbia Foundation
The Nathan Cummings Foundation
Deer Creek Foundation
Geraldine R. Dodge Foundation, Inc.
Environment Now Foundation
The George Gund Foundation

Joyce Mertz-Gilmore Foundation
The Needmor Fund
The New-Land Foundation, Inc.
The Pew Charitable Trusts
Schultz Foundation, Inc.
The Strong Foundation for
 Environmental Values
Surdna Foundation, Inc.
Threshold Foundation
The Tides Foundation

Coral reefs

The Beinecke Foundation, Inc.
Conservation, Food & Health
 Foundation, Inc.
The Elizabeth Ordway Dunn
 Foundation, Inc.
The Max and Anna Levinson Foundation
MARPAT Foundation, Inc.
McInerny Foundation
The Curtis and Edith Munson
 Foundation, Inc.
Norcross Wildlife Foundation, Inc.
The Pew Charitable Trusts
Pew Scholars Program in Conservation
 and the Environment

Cultural diversity

Mary Reynolds Babcock Foundation, Inc.
Crystal Channel Foundation
Geraldine R. Dodge Foundation, Inc.
Echoing Green Foundation
Richard & Rhoda Goldman Fund
Harbor Lights Foundation
Howfirma Foundation
Ittleson Foundation, Inc.
The Esther A. and Joseph Klingenstein
 Fund, Inc.
MARPAT Foundation, Inc.
Norman Foundation
Amelia Peabody Charitable Fund
Pew Scholars Program in Conservation
 and the Environment
The San Francisco Foundation
The Strong Foundation for
 Environmental Values
Surdna Foundation, Inc.
Threshold Foundation
Unitarian Universalist Veatch Program
 at Shelter Rock

Databases

ARCO Foundation
James Ford Bell Foundation
The Blumenthal Foundation
The Bullitt Foundation
Claneil Foundation, Inc.
Columbia Foundation
Conservation, Food & Health
 Foundation, Inc.
Jessie B. Cox Charitable Trust
Geraldine R. Dodge Foundation, Inc.
Samuel S. Fels Fund
Flintridge Foundation

© 1995 Environmental Data Resources, Inc.

Environmental Topics and Activities

Databases (cont.)

The Fred Gellert Foundation
General Service Foundation
Richard & Rhoda Goldman Fund
Great Lakes Protection Fund
The George Gund Foundation
Harder Foundation
The James Irvine Foundation
W. K. Kellogg Foundation
Laurel Foundation
The Lazar Foundation
Lyndhurst Foundation
The John D. and Catherine T. MacArthur
  Foundation
The Martin Foundation, Inc.
The Andrew W. Mellon Foundation
Merck Family Fund
The John Merck Fund
Leo Model Foundation, Inc.
The Moriah Fund, Inc.
Charles Stewart Mott Foundation
The Curtis and Edith Munson
  Foundation, Inc.
National Fish and Wildlife Foundation
National Geographic Society Education
  Foundation
Jessie Smith Noyes Foundation, Inc.
The David and Lucile Packard Foundation
Patagonia, Inc.
The Pew Charitable Trusts
The Summerlee Foundation
Threshold Foundation
Tortuga Foundation
Virginia Environmental Endowment
Weeden Foundation

Decisionmaking

Geraldine R. Dodge Foundation, Inc.
The Educational Foundation of America
The Energy Foundation
Great Lakes Protection Fund
The William and Flora Hewlett Foundation
The Henry M. Jackson Foundation
W. Alton Jones Foundation, Inc.
Laidlaw Foundation

Decisionmaking: participatory

The Acorn Foundation
The Educational Foundation of America
Environmental Endowment for
  New Jersey, Inc.
McKenzie River Gathering Foundation
The John Merck Fund
Jessie Smith Noyes Foundation, Inc.
Patagonia, Inc.
Rockefeller Brothers Fund, Inc.
Rockefeller Family Fund, Inc.
Seventh Generation Fund
Threshold Foundation

Deep ecology

Crystal Channel Foundation
The Nathan Cummings Foundation
Foundation for Deep Ecology
The German Marshall Fund of
  the United States
Global Environmental Project Institute
Patagonia, Inc.

Deserts

ARCO Foundation
The Ahmanson Foundation
BankAmerica Foundation
S. D. Bechtel, Jr. Foundation
California Community Foundation
The Chevron Companies
The Collins Foundation
Compton Foundation, Inc.
Roy E. Crummer Foundation
Environment Now Foundation
Frelinghuysen Foundation
Richard & Rhoda Goldman Fund
The Lazar Foundation
The Marshall Fund of Arizona
Mobil Foundation, Inc.
The Moriah Fund, Inc.
Spencer T. and Ann W. Olin Foundation
The San Francisco Foundation
Seventh Generation Fund
Elmina B. Sewall Foundation
The Stratford Foundation
The Travelers Foundation
True North Foundation
The Winston-Salem Foundation, Inc.

Developing countries

The Jenifer Altman Foundation
American Conservation Association, Inc.
The Arca Foundation
Atkinson Foundation
The Bay Foundation
Beneficia Foundation
The William Bingham Foundation
Patrick and Aimee Butler Family
  Foundation
Compton Foundation, Inc.
Conservation, Food & Health
  Foundation, Inc.
Crystal Channel Foundation
The Nathan Cummings Foundation
Damien Foundation
The Charles Engelhard Foundation
The Armand G. Erpf Fund, Inc.
Ford Foundation
Foundation for Deep Ecology
General Service Foundation
The William and Flora Hewlett Foundation
The Homeland Foundation
W. Alton Jones Foundation, Inc.
Laird, Norton Foundation
The John D. and Catherine T. MacArthur
  Foundation
The Martin Foundation, Inc.
Giles W. and Elise G. Mead Foundation
The Andrew W. Mellon Foundation
The John Merck Fund
Joyce Mertz-Gilmore Foundation

The Moriah Fund, Inc.
Charles Stewart Mott Foundation
National Fish and Wildlife Foundation
New England Biolabs Foundation
The New York Times Company
  Foundation, Inc.
Jessie Smith Noyes Foundation, Inc.
The Ohrstrom Foundation
Patagonia, Inc.
The Pew Charitable Trusts
Pew Scholars Program in Conservation
  and the Environment
The Prospect Hill Foundation
Public Welfare Foundation, Inc.
Rockefeller Brothers Fund, Inc.
The Rockefeller Foundation
Rockwood Fund, Inc.
Lee Romney Foundation, Inc.
The Summerlee Foundation
The Summit Foundation
The Switzer Foundation
Threshold Foundation
The Tides Foundation
The Tinker Foundation Incorporated
United States-Japan Foundation
WMX Environmental Grants Program
Weeden Foundation

Development: economic

The Ben & Jerry's Foundation
The Bullitt Foundation
The Carpenter Foundation
Mary Flagler Cary Charitable Trust
Chesapeake Bay Trust
Conservation, Food & Health
  Foundation, Inc.
Environmental Education Foundation
  of Florida, Inc.
Flintridge Foundation
The Gap Foundation
General Service Foundation
The James Irvine Foundation
The Henry M. Jackson Foundation
The John D. and Catherine T. MacArthur
  Foundation
MARPAT Foundation, Inc.
McKenzie River Gathering Foundation
Richard King Mellon Foundation
The Curtis and Edith Munson
  Foundation, Inc.
The Needmor Fund
James C. Penney Foundation
Public Welfare Foundation, Inc.
The Rockefeller Foundation
Seventh Generation Fund
Threshold Foundation
The Tinker Foundation Incorporated

Development: sustainable economic

ARCO Foundation
A Territory Resource
The Abelard Foundation West
The Acorn Foundation
The Jenifer Altman Foundation

Environmental Topics and Activities

Development: sustainable economic (cont.)

Ameritech Foundation
The Arca Foundation
Atkinson Foundation
Mary Reynolds Babcock Foundation, Inc.
The Bauman Foundation
Beldon Fund
The Betterment Fund
The Bullitt Foundation
Columbia Foundation
Compton Foundation, Inc.
The Nathan Cummings Foundation
Damien Foundation
Deer Creek Foundation
Geraldine R. Dodge Foundation, Inc.
The Educational Foundation of America
The Energy Foundation
Ford Foundation
Foundation for Deep Ecology
The Fund for New Jersey
General Service Foundation
Give to the Earth Foundation
The Goldman Environmental Foundation
Richard & Rhoda Goldman Fund
Walter and Duncan Gordon Charitable Foundation
The Clarence E. Heller Charitable Foundation
The William and Flora Hewlett Foundation
The James Irvine Foundation
The Richard Ivey Foundation
W. Alton Jones Foundation, Inc.
The Joyce Foundation
The J. M. Kaplan Fund, Inc.
Laird, Norton Foundation
Lyndhurst Foundation
The John D. and Catherine T. MacArthur Foundation
McKenzie River Gathering Foundation
The McKnight Foundation
Giles W. and Elise G. Mead Foundation
Richard King Mellon Foundation
The John Merck Fund
Joyce Mertz-Gilmore Foundation
The Moriah Fund, Inc.
Charles Stewart Mott Foundation
National Fish and Wildlife Foundation
New Hampshire Charitable Foundation
The New World Foundation
Norman Foundation
Northwest Area Foundation
Jessie Smith Noyes Foundation, Inc.
Patagonia, Inc.
James C. Penney Foundation
The Pew Charitable Trusts
Public Welfare Foundation, Inc.
Z. Smith Reynolds Foundation, Inc.
The Roberts Foundation
Rockefeller Brothers Fund, Inc.
The Rockefeller Foundation
The Winthrop Rockefeller Foundation
The Sapelo Foundation

The Florence and John Schumann Foundation
Seventh Generation Fund
Surdna Foundation, Inc.
The Switzer Foundation
Threshold Foundation
The Tides Foundation
The Tinker Foundation Incorporated
Underhill Foundation
Unitarian Universalist Veatch Program at Shelter Rock
Vanguard Public Foundation
Victoria Foundation, Inc.
Virginia Environmental Endowment
WMX Environmental Grants Program
Wallace Genetic Foundation, Inc.
Weeden Foundation
Wilburforce Foundation

Disabled persons

A Territory Resource
BankAmerica Foundation
James Ford Bell Foundation
Ben B. Cheney Foundation
The Chicago Community Trust
Community Foundation of Western North Carolina, Inc.
Adolph Coors Foundation
The Educational Foundation of America
Environmental Education Foundation of Florida, Inc.
The Fred Gellert Foundation
Richard & Rhoda Goldman Fund
National Fish and Wildlife Foundation
Patagonia, Inc.
The San Francisco Foundation
The Skaggs Foundation
The William P. Wharton Trust

Disadvantaged persons

ARCO Foundation
Beldon Fund
Otto Bremer Foundation
Ben B. Cheney Foundation
Crystal Channel Foundation
Geraldine R. Dodge Foundation, Inc.
The Educational Foundation of America
The Gap Foundation
MARPAT Foundation, Inc.
Meyer Memorial Trust
The Minneapolis Foundation
National Fish and Wildlife Foundation
New York Foundation
Patagonia, Inc.
James C. Penney Foundation
Public Welfare Foundation, Inc.
Z. Smith Reynolds Foundation, Inc.
The San Francisco Foundation
The Florence and John Schumann Foundation
Threshold Foundation
Weyerhaeuser Company Foundation

Drylands

Conservation, Food & Health Foundation, Inc.
El Paso Community Foundation
The Rockefeller Foundation

Earth Service Corps

The Bullitt Foundation
Victoria Foundation, Inc.
Weyerhaeuser Company Foundation

Ecology

A Territory Resource
The Abell Foundation
The Bauman Foundation
The Bay Foundation
Beldon Fund
Chesapeake Bay Trust
The Chevron Companies
The Community Foundation of Greater New Haven
Conservation, Food & Health Foundation, Inc.
Crystal Channel Foundation
The Nathan Cummings Foundation
The Educational Foundation of America
Ford Foundation
Foundation for Deep Ecology
Fund of the Four Directions
Funding Exchange
The Wallace Alexander Gerbode Foundation, Inc.
The Hahn Family Foundation
The Edward W. Hazen Foundation
The Homeland Foundation
W. Alton Jones Foundation, Inc.
Lyndhurst Foundation
The John D. and Catherine T. MacArthur Foundation
Maki Foundation
MARPAT Foundation, Inc.
McKenzie River Gathering Foundation
The Moody Foundation
Charles Stewart Mott Foundation
National Fish and Wildlife Foundation
Northwest Area Foundation
Patagonia, Inc.
The William Penn Foundation
Pew Scholars Program in Conservation and the Environment
Sid W. Richardson Foundation
Rockwood Fund, Inc.
Lee Romney Foundation, Inc.
The Strong Foundation for Environmental Values
The Oakleigh L. Thorne Foundation
The Tides Foundation
The Tinker Foundation Incorporated
Virginia Environmental Endowment
WMX Environmental Grants Program
Wallace Genetic Foundation, Inc.

Environmental Topics and Activities

Ecology: education

Chesapeake Bay Trust
Foundation for Deep Ecology
The Fred Gellert Foundation
Joy Foundation for Ecological
 Education and Research
Edward John Noble Foundation, Inc.
The San Francisco Foundation

Ecology: research

The Conservation and Research Foundation
The John D. and Catherine T. MacArthur
 Foundation
The Andrew W. Mellon Foundation
National Fish and Wildlife Foundation
Patagonia, Inc.
Edna Bailey Sussman Fund
Victoria Foundation, Inc.
The William P. Wharton Trust
Robert W. Woodruff Foundation, Inc.

Economic impact

Alaska Conservation Foundation
Angelina Fund, Inc.
Mary Reynolds Babcock Foundation, Inc.
C. S. Fund
The Energy Foundation
Ford Foundation
Great Lakes Protection Fund
W. Alton Jones Foundation, Inc.
Merck Family Fund
Northwest Area Foundation
The Pew Charitable Trusts
Public Welfare Foundation, Inc.
Rockefeller Brothers Fund, Inc.
Threshold Foundation
The Trust For Mutual Understanding
Unitarian Universalist Veatch Program
 at Shelter Rock
Weeden Foundation

Economic policy

The Bauman Foundation
The Bullitt Foundation
W. Alton Jones Foundation, Inc.
The John D. and Catherine T. MacArthur
 Foundation
The Moriah Fund, Inc.
The Strong Foundation for
 Environmental Values
The Tinker Foundation Incorporated
Weeden Foundation

Economic/social justice

The Abelard Foundation West
Angelina Fund, Inc.
The Ben & Jerry's Foundation
The Bullitt Foundation
C. S. Fund
The Conservation and Research Foundation
Crystal Channel Foundation
The Educational Foundation of America
The Energy Foundation
The Edward W. Hazen Foundation
The James Irvine Foundation
McKenzie River Gathering Foundation
The McKnight Foundation
The Moriah Fund, Inc.
The Needmor Fund
Norman Foundation
Jessie Smith Noyes Foundation, Inc.
James C. Penney Foundation
Public Welfare Foundation, Inc.
Z. Smith Reynolds Foundation, Inc.
The Sapelo Foundation
The Florence and John Schumann
 Foundation
Seventh Generation Fund
Threshold Foundation
The Tides Foundation
Unitarian Universalist Veatch Program
 at Shelter Rock
Vanguard Public Foundation

Economics

The Bauman Foundation
Beldon Fund
The Bullitt Foundation
The Conservation and Research Foundation
Jessie B. Cox Charitable Trust
The Nathan Cummings Foundation
Gaylord and Dorothy Donnelley Foundation
Echoing Green Foundation
Environmental Education Foundation
 of Florida, Inc.
Fanwood Foundation
Jamee and Marshall Field Foundation
Foundation for Deep Ecology
The German Marshall Fund of
 the United States
Island Foundation, Inc.
The Joyce Foundation
The John D. and Catherine T. MacArthur
 Foundation
McKenzie River Gathering Foundation
Giles W. and Elise G. Mead Foundation
Charles Stewart Mott Foundation
National Fish and Wildlife Foundation
The New-Land Foundation, Inc.
Norman Foundation
Jessie Smith Noyes Foundation, Inc.
The Pfizer Foundation, Inc.
Phillips Petroleum Foundation, Inc.
Recreational Equipment, Inc.
The Rockefeller Foundation
The Rockfall Foundation
Rockwell Fund, Inc.
The Sapelo Foundation
Shell Oil Company Foundation
The Tinker Foundation Incorporated
Town Creek Foundation, Inc.
The Trust For Mutual Understanding
Unitarian Universalist Veatch Program
 at Shelter Rock
Weyerhaeuser Company Foundation

Economics: ecological

The Bauman Foundation
The Hitachi Foundation
Island Foundation, Inc.
The Richard Ivey Foundation
W. Alton Jones Foundation, Inc.
Merck Family Fund
Jessie Smith Noyes Foundation, Inc.
Pew Scholars Program in Conservation
 and the Environment
The Florence and John Schumann
 Foundation
The Switzer Foundation
Threshold Foundation

Economics: tax policy

Angelina Fund, Inc.
Beldon Fund
The Nathan Cummings Foundation
The Energy Foundation
W. Alton Jones Foundation, Inc.
Merck Family Fund
Joyce Mertz-Gilmore Foundation
National Fish and Wildlife Foundation
Northwest Area Foundation
Public Welfare Foundation, Inc.
The Florence and John Schumann
 Foundation
Threshold Foundation

Ecosystems

ARCO Foundation
Atkinson Foundation
The Bay Foundation
The Bullitt Foundation
Chesapeake Bay Trust
Liz Claiborne & Art Ortenberg Foundation
The Clowes Fund, Inc.
Columbia Foundation
Compton Foundation, Inc.
The Conservation and Research Foundation
S. H. Cowell Foundation
Patrick and Anna M. Cudahy Fund
Geraldine R. Dodge Foundation, Inc.
Gaylord and Dorothy Donnelley Foundation
The Elizabeth Ordway Dunn
 Foundation, Inc.
The Educational Foundation of America
Environment Now Foundation
Great Lakes Protection Fund
The Greenville Foundation
Harder Foundation
The Richard Ivey Foundation
The Joyce Foundation
The Robert S. and Grayce B. Kerr
 Foundation, Inc.
The Seymour H. Knox Foundation, Inc.
Laidlaw Foundation
Laird, Norton Foundation
The Lazar Foundation
Lintilhac Foundation
The Andrew W. Mellon Foundation

Environmental Topics and Activities

Ecosystems

Charles Stewart Mott Foundation
Northwest Fund for the Environment
The David and Lucile Packard Foundation
Patagonia, Inc.
The Pew Charitable Trusts
The Rockefeller Foundation
Rockwood Fund, Inc.
The San Francisco Foundation
Thomas Sill Foundation
Surdna Foundation, Inc.
The Switzer Foundation
Threshold Foundation
Town Creek Foundation, Inc.
Vancouver Foundation
Virginia Environmental Endowment
Weeden Foundation
Wilburforce Foundation

Ecosystems: preservation

The Acorn Foundation
Alaska Conservation Foundation
Beldon Fund
Beneficia Foundation
The Bullitt Foundation
Mary Flagler Cary Charitable Trust
Chesapeake Bay Trust
Geraldine R. Dodge Foundation, Inc.
The Educational Foundation of America
Flintridge Foundation
Foundation for Deep Ecology
The Fund for New Jersey
The Gap Foundation
General Service Foundation
Give to the Earth Foundation
Richard & Rhoda Goldman Fund
The Greenville Foundation
The George Gund Foundation
The Henry M. Jackson Foundation
W. Alton Jones Foundation, Inc.
The Joyce Foundation
The Lazar Foundation
The Max and Anna Levinson Foundation
Lyndhurst Foundation
The John D. and Catherine T. MacArthur Foundation
Maki Foundation
MARPAT Foundation, Inc.
Merck Family Fund
Millbrook Tribute Garden, Inc.
The Moriah Fund, Inc.
Charles Stewart Mott Foundation
Ruth Mott Fund
The Curtis and Edith Munson Foundation, Inc.
M. J. Murdock Charitable Trust
National Fish and Wildlife Foundation
Patagonia, Inc.
The Pew Charitable Trusts
The Pfizer Foundation, Inc.
Public Welfare Foundation, Inc.
Rockefeller Brothers Fund, Inc.
The San Francisco Foundation

Seventh Generation Fund
Steelcase Foundation
Surdna Foundation, Inc.
The Switzer Foundation
The Tinker Foundation Incorporated
The Trust For Mutual Understanding
Weeden Foundation

Ecosystems: restoration

ARCO Foundation
The Ben & Jerry's Foundation
The William Bingham Foundation
The Bullitt Foundation
Mary Flagler Cary Charitable Trust
Chesapeake Bay Trust
The Chevron Companies
The Chicago Community Trust
Cooke Foundation, Limited
The Elizabeth Ordway Dunn Foundation, Inc.
Flintridge Foundation
The Fred Gellert Foundation
General Service Foundation
The Wallace Alexander Gerbode Foundation, Inc.
Richard & Rhoda Goldman Fund
Great Lakes Protection Fund
Harder Foundation
Hawaii Community Foundation
Richard King Mellon Foundation
The Curtis and Edith Munson Foundation, Inc.
National Fish and Wildlife Foundation
Northwest Fund for the Environment
Patagonia, Inc.
Pew Scholars Program in Conservation and the Environment
The Strong Foundation for Environmental Values
The Dean Witter Foundation

Education

ARCO Foundation
The Abell Foundation
Abell-Hanger Foundation
The Acorn Foundation
Alaska Conservation Foundation
The Jenifer Altman Foundation
American Express Philanthropic Program
The Arca Foundation
Atherton Family Foundation
The George F. Baker Trust
BankAmerica Foundation
The Barra Foundation, Inc.
The Bauman Foundation
L. L. Bean, Inc.
S. D. Bechtel, Jr. Foundation
Beldon Fund
The Ben & Jerry's Foundation
Benton Foundation
The Bersted Foundation
The Betterment Fund
The Blumenthal Foundation

The Bodman Foundation
Mary Owen Borden Memorial Foundation
Alexander H. Bright Charitable Trust
W. L. Lyons Brown Foundation
The Bullitt Foundation
Patrick and Aimee Butler Family Foundation
C. S. Fund
The Cabot Family Charitable Trust
The Morris and Gwendolyn Cafritz Foundation
The Louis Calder Foundation
California Community Foundation
James & Abigail Campbell Foundation
The Carpenter Foundation
The Champlin Foundations
Changing Horizons Charitable Trust
Chesapeake Bay Trust
The Chevron Companies
The Chicago Community Trust
The Clark Foundation
The Cleveland Foundation
The Collins Foundation
Compton Foundation, Inc.
Conservation, Food & Health Foundation, Inc.
Cooke Foundation, Limited
Adolph Coors Foundation
S. H. Cowell Foundation
The Mary A. Crocker Trust
Crystal Channel Foundation
The Nathan Cummings Foundation
Davis Conservation Foundation
Geraldine R. Dodge Foundation, Inc.
Gaylord and Dorothy Donnelley Foundation
The Elizabeth Ordway Dunn Foundation, Inc.
Eastman Kodak Company Charitable Trust
The Educational Foundation of America
El Pomar Foundation
The Energy Foundation
Environmental Education Foundation of Florida, Inc.
Environmental Endowment for New Jersey, Inc.
The Ettinger Foundation, Inc.
The William Stamps Farish Fund
The Field Foundation of Illinois, Inc.
Ford Foundation
Foundation for Deep Ecology
Mary D. and Walter F. Frear Eleemosynary Trust
The Freed Foundation, Inc.
Lloyd A. Fry Foundation
Funding Exchange
The GAR Foundation
The Gap Foundation
Gebbie Foundation, Inc.
The Fred Gellert Foundation
Give to the Earth Foundation
Global Environmental Project Institute
Global Greengrants Fund
Richard & Rhoda Goldman Fund
Great Lakes Protection Fund

© 1995 Environmental Data Resources, Inc.

Environmental Topics and Activities

Education (cont.)

Greater Piscataqua Community Foundation
The George Gund Foundation
HKH Foundation
The Hahn Family Foundation
Gladys and Roland Harriman Foundation
Hawaii Community Foundation
Howfirma Foundation
The Hyams Foundation
IBM Corporation
Ireland Foundation
The James Irvine Foundation
Island Foundation, Inc.
The Henry M. Jackson Foundation
W. Alton Jones Foundation, Inc.
The J. M. Kaplan Fund, Inc.
Harris and Eliza Kempner Fund
The Knapp Foundation, Inc.
The Kresge Foundation
Laidlaw Foundation
The Lazar Foundation
The Max and Anna Levinson Foundation
Lyndhurst Foundation
The John D. and Catherine T. MacArthur Foundation
Maine Community Foundation, Inc.
MARPAT Foundation, Inc.
McInerny Foundation
The McIntosh Foundation
The McKnight Foundation
The Andrew W. Mellon Foundation
Merck Family Fund
Meyer Memorial Trust
Middlecott Foundation
Charles Stewart Mott Foundation
Ruth Mott Fund
The Mountaineers Foundation
The Curtis and Edith Munson Foundation, Inc.
M. J. Murdock Charitable Trust
The National Environmental Education and Training Foundation, Inc.
National Fish and Wildlife Foundation
National Geographic Society Education Foundation
The Needmor Fund
New England Biolabs Foundation
New Hampshire Charitable Foundation
The New York Times Company Foundation, Inc.
Edward John Noble Foundation, Inc.
Norcross Wildlife Foundation, Inc.
Northwest Area Foundation
Northwest Fund for the Environment
Jessie Smith Noyes Foundation, Inc.
The David and Lucile Packard Foundation
Patagonia, Inc.
Peninsula Community Foundation
The William Penn Foundation
The Pew Charitable Trusts
The Prospect Hill Foundation
Public Welfare Foundation, Inc.
Philip D. Reed Foundation, Inc.
Z. Smith Reynolds Foundation, Inc.
The Rhode Island Community Foundation
The Roberts Foundation
Rockefeller Brothers Fund, Inc.
Rockefeller Family Fund, Inc.
Rockwood Fund, Inc.
Samuel and May Rudin Foundation, Inc.
San Diego Community Foundation
The San Francisco Foundation
The Sapelo Foundation
The Schiff Foundation
The Schumann Fund for New Jersey, Inc.
Ralph C. Sheldon Foundation, Inc.
Thomas Sill Foundation
Snee-Reinhardt Charitable Foundation
Springs Foundation, Inc.
The Morris Stulsaft Foundation
The Sudbury Foundation
The Summerlee Foundation
Surdna Foundation, Inc.
The Telesis Foundation
The Oakleigh L. Thorne Foundation
Threshold Foundation
Times Mirror Magazines, Inc.
True North Foundation
Underhill Foundation
Vancouver Foundation
Vanguard Public Foundation
Virginia Environmental Endowment
WMX Environmental Grants Program
Weeden Foundation
Welfare Foundation, Inc.
Weyerhaeuser Company Foundation
Joseph B. Whitehead Foundation
G. N. Wilcox Trust
The Dean Witter Foundation
Margaret Cullinan Wray Charitable Lead Annuity Trust

Education: agricultural

C. S. Fund
The Nathan Cummings Foundation
Threshold Foundation

Education: community

A Territory Resource
Beldon Fund
The Ben & Jerry's Foundation
The Bullitt Foundation
Laidlaw Foundation
Lyndhurst Foundation
MARPAT Foundation, Inc.
Merck Family Fund
Ruth Mott Fund
Norman Foundation
The Pew Charitable Trusts
The Rockfall Foundation
The Tinker Foundation Incorporated
Weeden Foundation

Education: curriculum development

ARCO Foundation
The Abell Foundation
The Bauman Foundation
The William Bingham Foundation
The Bullitt Foundation
The Butler Foundation
Mary Flagler Cary Charitable Trust
Chesapeake Bay Trust
Community Foundation of Western North Carolina, Inc.
Conservation, Food & Health Foundation, Inc.
The Mary A. Crocker Trust
Charles E. Culpeper Foundation, Inc.
The Nathan Cummings Foundation
The Aaron Diamond Foundation
Geraldine R. Dodge Foundation, Inc.
Dolfinger-McMahon Foundation
Gaylord and Dorothy Donnelley Foundation
Jessie Ball duPont Religious, Charitable and Educational Fund
Environmental Education Foundation of Florida, Inc.
Environmental Endowment for New Jersey, Inc.
The Favrot Fund
Ford Foundation
Great Lakes Protection Fund
Greater Piscataqua Community Foundation
The George Gund Foundation
Charles Hayden Foundation
The Clarence E. Heller Charitable Foundation
Island Foundation, Inc.
The Richard Ivey Foundation
The Henry M. Jackson Foundation
The John D. and Catherine T. MacArthur Foundation
MARPAT Foundation, Inc.
The Martin Foundation, Inc.
Merck Family Fund
The Moriah Fund, Inc.
The Curtis and Edith Munson Foundation, Inc.
National Fish and Wildlife Foundation
The David and Lucile Packard Foundation
Patagonia, Inc.
The Pew Charitable Trusts
Pew Scholars Program in Conservation and the Environment
Rockefeller Brothers Fund, Inc.
The Rockefeller Foundation
The Winthrop Rockefeller Foundation
Surdna Foundation, Inc.
Threshold Foundation
Toyota USA Foundation
Virginia Environmental Endowment
Weyerhaeuser Company Foundation
Margaret Cullinan Wray Charitable Lead Annuity Trust

Education: elementary

Atherton Family Foundation
The Bay Foundation
Chesapeake Bay Trust
The William Stamps Farish Fund
The Richard Ivey Foundation
Lintilhac Foundation
Maki Foundation
Massachusetts Environmental Trust

Environmental Topics and Activities

Education: elementary (cont.)

Giles W. and Elise G. Mead Foundation
M. J. Murdock Charitable Trust
New Hampshire Charitable Foundation
Peninsula Community Foundation
The Rhode Island Community Foundation
Rockwell Fund, Inc.
The San Francisco Foundation
The Morris Stulsaft Foundation
Toyota USA Foundation

Education: elementary/secondary

James Ford Bell Foundation
The Bullitt Foundation
Charles Hayden Foundation
Marin Community Foundation
Threshold Foundation

Education: government

The Educational Foundation of America
Give to the Earth Foundation
The Henry M. Jackson Foundation
The John Merck Fund
The Curtis and Edith Munson Foundation, Inc.
Threshold Foundation

Education: graduate/postdoctoral

ARCO Foundation
The Ben & Jerry's Foundation
The Lynde and Harry Bradley Foundation, Inc.
Conservation, Food & Health Foundation, Inc.
Geraldine R. Dodge Foundation, Inc.
Ford Foundation
The John D. and Catherine T. MacArthur Foundation
Charles Stewart Mott Foundation
Patagonia, Inc.
The Pew Charitable Trusts
The Rockefeller Foundation
The Florence and John Schumann Foundation
Edna Bailey Sussman Fund
The Switzer Foundation
Texaco Foundation
Times Mirror Magazines, Inc.

Education: higher

The Howard Bayne Fund
The Beinecke Foundation, Inc.
The William Bingham Foundation
W. L. Lyons Brown Foundation
Changing Horizons Charitable Trust
Chesapeake Corporation Foundation
The German Marshall Fund of the United States
Ittleson Foundation, Inc.
The Richard Ivey Foundation
Lilly Endowment, Inc.
The John D. and Catherine T. MacArthur Foundation

The Curtis and Edith Munson Foundation, Inc.
Edward John Noble Foundation, Inc.
Norcross Wildlife Foundation, Inc.
Sarkeys Foundation
Marcia Brady Tucker Foundation
USX Foundation, Inc.
Underhill Foundation
Union Camp Charitable Trust
Bill & Edith Walter Foundation

Education: low-income

The Nathan Cummings Foundation
The Milwaukee Foundation
Threshold Foundation

Education: minoritiy

The Morris and Gwendolyn Cafritz Foundation
Toyota USA Foundation

Education: professional

The Energy Foundation
The Clarence E. Heller Charitable Foundation

Education: public

The Achelis Foundation
The Ahmanson Foundation
Alaska Conservation Foundation
The Jenifer Altman Foundation
Ameritech Foundation
Elmer L. & Eleanor J. Andersen Foundation
Beldon Fund
The Ben & Jerry's Foundation
The William Bingham Foundation
Ruth H. Brown Foundation
Kathleen Price and Joseph M. Bryan Family Foundation, Inc.
The Bullitt Foundation
C. S. Fund
California Community Foundation
Mary Flagler Cary Charitable Trust
Changing Horizons Charitable Trust
Chesapeake Bay Trust
Chesapeake Corporation Foundation
Robert Sterling Clark Foundation, Inc.
The Cleveland Foundation
Columbia Foundation
The Columbus Foundation
The Community Foundation of Santa Clara County
Community Foundation of Western North Carolina, Inc.
Compton Foundation, Inc.
The Conservation and Research Foundation
Conservation, Food & Health Foundation, Inc.
Cooke Foundation, Limited
Roy E. Crummer Foundation
Damien Foundation
Davis Conservation Foundation
Deer Creek Foundation

Geraldine R. Dodge Foundation, Inc.
The Elizabeth Ordway Dunn Foundation, Inc.
The Educational Foundation of America
The Energy Foundation
Samuel S. Fels Fund
Flintridge Foundation
Foundation for Deep Ecology
Mary D. and Walter F. Frear Eleemosynary Trust
Fund of the Four Directions
The Fred Gellert Foundation
The Wallace Alexander Gerbode Foundation, Inc.
Give to the Earth Foundation
Herman Goldman Foundation
Richard & Rhoda Goldman Fund
The George Gund Foundation
The Clarence E. Heller Charitable Foundation
The Hofmann Foundation
Ittleson Foundation, Inc.
The Richard Ivey Foundation
The Henry M. Jackson Foundation
Martha Holden Jennings Foundation
W. Alton Jones Foundation, Inc.
The Joyce Foundation
The J. M. Kaplan Fund, Inc.
The Kresge Foundation
Laidlaw Foundation
Laird, Norton Foundation
The Max and Anna Levinson Foundation
Lyndhurst Foundation
The John D. and Catherine T. MacArthur Foundation
Marbrook Foundation
Marin Community Foundation
MARPAT Foundation, Inc.
The Martin Foundation, Inc.
Massachusetts Environmental Trust
McKenzie River Gathering Foundation
The McKnight Foundation
Giles W. and Elise G. Mead Foundation
Meadows Foundation, Inc.
Richard King Mellon Foundation
Merck Family Fund
The John Merck Fund
Joyce Mertz-Gilmore Foundation
The Moriah Fund, Inc.
Charles Stewart Mott Foundation
Ruth Mott Fund
The Mountaineers Foundation
The Curtis and Edith Munson Foundation, Inc.
National Fish and Wildlife Foundation
The Needmor Fund
New Hampshire Charitable Foundation
The New World Foundation
The New York Times Company Foundation, Inc.
Norcross Wildlife Foundation, Inc.
Andrew Norman Foundation
Northwest Area Foundation
Jessie Smith Noyes Foundation, Inc.
Patagonia, Inc.

Environmental Topics and Activities

Education: public (cont.)

The William Penn Foundation
James C. Penney Foundation
The Pew Charitable Trusts
Pew Scholars Program in Conservation
 and the Environment
The Pfizer Foundation, Inc.
Ellis L. Phillips Foundation
Public Welfare Foundation, Inc.
Recreational Equipment, Inc.
Z. Smith Reynolds Foundation, Inc.
Rockefeller Brothers Fund, Inc.
Rockefeller Family Fund, Inc.
The Rockefeller Foundation
The Winthrop Rockefeller Foundation
Rockwell Fund, Inc.
The San Francisco Foundation
The Sapelo Foundation
The Schumann Fund for New Jersey, Inc.
The Florence and John Schumann
 Foundation
Seventh Generation Fund
Steelcase Foundation
The Strong Foundation for
 Environmental Values
The Summerlee Foundation
Surdna Foundation, Inc.
The Switzer Foundation
S. Mark Taper Foundation
The Telesis Foundation
Threshold Foundation
The Tides Foundation
Times Mirror Magazines, Inc.
Harry C. Trexler Trust
True North Foundation
Union Pacific Foundation
Unitarian Universalist Veatch Program
 at Shelter Rock
Virginia Environmental Endowment
Weeden Foundation
Weyerhaeuser Company Foundation
The William P. Wharton Trust
Wilburforce Foundation
The Dean Witter Foundation
Margaret Cullinan Wray Charitable
 Lead Annuity Trust
Wrinkle in Time Foundation

Education: science

The Robert Brownlee Foundation
Kathleen Price and Joseph M. Bryan
 Family Foundation, Inc.
C. S. Fund
Mary Flagler Cary Charitable Trust
Jessie B. Cox Charitable Trust
The Nathan Cummings Foundation
The Favrot Fund
Lloyd A. Fry Foundation
The Fred Gellert Foundation
The Henry M. Jackson Foundation
The George Frederick Jewett Foundation
Walter S. Johnson Foundation
The John D. and Catherine T. MacArthur
 Foundation

Maki Foundation
MARPAT Foundation, Inc.
M. J. Murdock Charitable Trust
Edward John Noble Foundation, Inc.
The Pew Charitable Trusts
Pew Scholars Program in Conservation
 and the Environment
The Winthrop Rockefeller Foundation
The San Francisco Foundation
The Skaggs Foundation
Toyota USA Foundation

Education: secondary

Atherton Family Foundation
The George F. Baker Trust
The Bullitt Foundation
Cleveland H. Dodge Foundation, Inc.
The Foundation for the National
 Capital Region
Mary D. and Walter F. Frear
 Eleemosynary Trust
Great Lakes Protection Fund
The Hitachi Foundation
Ittleson Foundation, Inc.
National Fish and Wildlife Foundation
The David and Lucile Packard Foundation
Prince Charitable Trusts
Times Mirror Magazines, Inc.
Virginia Environmental Endowment

Education: teacher

ARCO Foundation
The Abell Foundation
Abell-Hanger Foundation
The Ahmanson Foundation
The Robert Brownlee Foundation
The Bullitt Foundation
The Cabot Family Charitable Trust
Caribou Fund
Chesapeake Bay Trust
Patrick and Anna M. Cudahy Fund
The Aaron Diamond Foundation
Geraldine R. Dodge Foundation, Inc.
The Educational Foundation of America
Environmental Education Foundation
 of Florida, Inc.
Herman Goldman Foundation
The Richard Ivey Foundation
The Henry M. Jackson Foundation
The John D. and Catherine T. MacArthur
 Foundation
McLean Contributionship
The Moody Foundation
J. P. Morgan Charitable Trust
National Fish and Wildlife Foundation
National Geographic Society Education
 Foundation
New England Biolabs Foundation
Edward John Noble Foundation, Inc.
The Schumann Fund for New Jersey, Inc.
Victoria Foundation, Inc.
Lila Wallace-Reader's Digest Fund
Weeden Foundation

Education: undergraduate

Charles E. Culpeper Foundation, Inc.
Jessie Ball duPont Religious, Charitable
 and Educational Fund
The Martin Foundation, Inc.
The Curtis and Edith Munson
 Foundation, Inc.
The Pew Charitable Trusts
Pew Scholars Program in Conservation
 and the Environment

Education: urban

ARCO Foundation
The Cabot Family Charitable Trust
Dayton Hudson Foundation
Lloyd A. Fry Foundation
The John D. and Catherine T. MacArthur
 Foundation
Edward John Noble Foundation, Inc.
Threshold Foundation

Education: youth

The Vincent Astor Foundation
Baltimore Gas and Electric Foundation, Inc.
BankAmerica Foundation
The Ben & Jerry's Foundation
The Bodman Foundation
Mary Owen Borden Memorial Foundation
The Bothin Foundation
The Robert Brownlee Foundation
The Cabot Family Charitable Trust
The Louis Calder Foundation
California Community Foundation
Mary Flagler Cary Charitable Trust
Ben B. Cheney Foundation
Chesapeake Bay Trust
Olive B. Cole Foundation
The Community Foundation Serving
 Coastal South Carolina
Community Foundation of
 Western North Carolina, Inc.
The Mary A. Crocker Trust
The Nathan Cummings Foundation
The Nelson B. Delavan Foundation
Geraldine R. Dodge Foundation, Inc.
Dolfinger-McMahon Foundation
The Elizabeth Ordway Dunn
 Foundation, Inc.
The Educational Foundation of America
Environmental Endowment for
 New Jersey, Inc.
Ford Motor Company Fund
Gates Foundation
The Fred Gellert Foundation
Herman Goldman Foundation
Walter and Elise Haas Fund
Charles Hayden Foundation
The Edward W. Hazen Foundation
Heller Charitable & Educational Fund
Martha Holden Jennings Foundation
The George Frederick Jewett Foundation
Helen K. and Arthur E. Johnson Foundation
W. Alton Jones Foundation, Inc.

Environmental Topics and Activities

Education: youth (cont.)

Laird, Norton Foundation
Levi Strauss Foundation
Maine Community Foundation, Inc.
Mars Foundation
McKesson Foundation, Inc.
Richard King Mellon Foundation
The Milwaukee Foundation
The Curtis and Edith Munson Foundation, Inc.
The New York Times Company Foundation, Inc.
Patagonia, Inc.
The Pew Charitable Trusts
Public Welfare Foundation, Inc.
Sid W. Richardson Foundation
The Winthrop Rockefeller Foundation
The San Francisco Foundation
The Morris Stulsaft Foundation
Threshold Foundation
The Tides Foundation
Vancouver Foundation
Victoria Foundation, Inc.
DeWitt Wallace-Reader's Digest Fund
Weeden Foundation
Westinghouse Foundation
Weyerhaeuser Company Foundation
G. N. Wilcox Trust

Employment

The Ben & Jerry's Foundation
The Carpenter Foundation
Compton Foundation, Inc.
Dayton Hudson Foundation
Ford Foundation
The German Marshall Fund of the United States
Northwest Area Foundation
Patagonia, Inc.
Public Welfare Foundation, Inc.
The Rockefeller Foundation
Weyerhaeuser Company Foundation

Endangered species: wild animal

ARCO Foundation
Alaska Conservation Foundation
The Jenifer Altman Foundation
The Bailey Wildlife Foundation
BankAmerica Foundation
The Bay Foundation
Beneficia Foundation
Helen Brach Foundation
The Lynde and Harry Bradley Foundation, Inc.
Alexander H. Bright Charitable Trust
The Buchanan Family Foundation
The Bullitt Foundation
The Chevron Companies
Compton Foundation, Inc.
Roy E. Crummer Foundation
Crystal Channel Foundation
The Nathan Cummings Foundation
Geraldine R. Dodge Foundation, Inc.
Echoing Green Foundation

The Educational Foundation of America
The Charles Engelhard Foundation
Environment Now Foundation
Fanwood Foundation
The Favrot Fund
Leland Fikes Foundation, Inc.
Foundation for Deep Ecology
Frelinghuysen Foundation
The Gap Foundation
Give to the Earth Foundation
Walter and Duncan Gordon Charitable Foundation
The George Gund Foundation
The Ewing Halsell Foundation
Harder Foundation
The Homeland Foundation
The Richard Ivey Foundation
Jackson Hole Preserve, Inc.
W. Alton Jones Foundation, Inc.
The J. M. Kaplan Fund, Inc.
W. K. Kellogg Foundation
The Robert S. and Grayce B. Kerr Foundation, Inc.
The Max and Anna Levinson Foundation
The John D. and Catherine T. MacArthur Foundation
Maki Foundation
Mars Foundation
The Martin Foundation, Inc.
McGregor Fund
McInerny Foundation
The McIntosh Foundation
The Milwaukee Foundation
Leo Model Foundation, Inc.
The Moriah Fund, Inc.
Charles Stewart Mott Foundation
The Curtis and Edith Munson Foundation, Inc.
M. J. Murdock Charitable Trust
National Fish and Wildlife Foundation
New Horizon Foundation
Edward John Noble Foundation, Inc.
Norcross Wildlife Foundation, Inc.
Outdoor Industry Conservation Alliance
The David and Lucile Packard Foundation
Patagonia, Inc.
The William Penn Foundation
The Pew Charitable Trusts
Lynn R. and Karl E. Prickett Fund
The Prospect Hill Foundation
San Diego Community Foundation
The San Francisco Foundation
Seventh Generation Fund
Elmina B. Sewall Foundation
Shell Oil Company Foundation
The Strong Foundation for Environmental Values
The Sulzberger Foundation, Inc.
The Summerlee Foundation
Surdna Foundation, Inc.
The Switzer Foundation
Nelson Talbott Foundation
Threshold Foundation
The Tides Foundation
True North Foundation

The Trust For Mutual Understanding
Turner Foundation, Inc.
Vancouver Foundation
WMX Environmental Grants Program
Weeden Foundation
The Dean Witter Foundation
Margaret Cullinan Wray Charitable Lead Annuity Trust

Endangered species: wild plant

ARCO Foundation
Alaska Conservation Foundation
The Bay Foundation
Alexander H. Bright Charitable Trust
The Bullitt Foundation
Roy E. Crummer Foundation
Crystal Channel Foundation
Geraldine R. Dodge Foundation, Inc.
The Elizabeth Ordway Dunn Foundation, Inc.
The Charles Engelhard Foundation
The Fund for Preservation of Wildlife and Natural Areas
The Gap Foundation
The George Gund Foundation
Mary W. Harriman Foundation
The Merrill G. & Emita E. Hastings Foundation
Hawaii Community Foundation
The Richard Ivey Foundation
W. Alton Jones Foundation, Inc.
The J. M. Kaplan Fund, Inc.
W. K. Kellogg Foundation
Lyndhurst Foundation
The John D. and Catherine T. MacArthur Foundation
Mars Foundation
McInerny Foundation
Charles Stewart Mott Foundation
The Curtis and Edith Munson Foundation, Inc.
National Fish and Wildlife Foundation
Edward John Noble Foundation, Inc.
Norcross Wildlife Foundation, Inc.
The David and Lucile Packard Foundation
Patagonia, Inc.
The Pew Charitable Trusts
Pew Scholars Program in Conservation and the Environment
The Prospect Hill Foundation
San Diego Community Foundation
The San Francisco Foundation
Seventh Generation Fund
Elmina B. Sewall Foundation
Stanley Smith Horticultural Trust
The Summerlee Foundation
Surdna Foundation, Inc.
Threshold Foundation
Vancouver Foundation
WMX Environmental Grants Program
C. A. Webster Foundation
Weeden Foundation
The Dean Witter Foundation
Margaret Cullinan Wray Charitable Lead Annuity Trust

Environmental Topics and Activities

Energy

ARCO Foundation
The Abell Foundation
Alaska Conservation Foundation
Angelina Fund, Inc.
BankAmerica Foundation
Beldon Fund
The Ben & Jerry's Foundation
The Bullitt Foundation
Changing Horizons Charitable Trust
The Chevron Companies
Robert Sterling Clark Foundation, Inc.
Compton Foundation, Inc.
Crystal Channel Foundation
Eastman Kodak Company Charitable Trust
The Energy Foundation
The Ettinger Foundation, Inc.
The Foundation for the National Capital Region
Fund of the Four Directions
Funding Exchange
The Wallace Alexander Gerbode Foundation, Inc.
Walter and Duncan Gordon Charitable Foundation
The George Gund Foundation
The Hahn Family Foundation
The Homeland Foundation
Hurdle Hill Foundation
Island Foundation
W. Alton Jones Foundation, Inc.
The Joyce Foundation
W. K. Kellogg Foundation
Charles G. Koch Charitable Foundation
Laurel Foundation
The John D. and Catherine T. MacArthur Foundation
Joyce Mertz-Gilmore Foundation
Mobil Foundation, Inc.
The Curtis and Edith Munson Foundation, Inc.
New Hampshire Charitable Foundation
The New-Land Foundation, Inc.
The Samuel Roberts Noble Foundation, Inc.
Ottinger Foundation
The David and Lucile Packard Foundation
Amelia Peabody Charitable Fund
The Pew Charitable Trusts
The Philadelphia Foundation
Phillips Petroleum Foundation, Inc.
Public Welfare Foundation, Inc.
Rockefeller Financial Services, Philanthropy Department
The Rockefeller Foundation
Sequoia Foundation
Shell Oil Company Foundation
The Summit Foundation
Surdna Foundation, Inc.
The Switzer Foundation
The Tides Foundation
USX Foundation, Inc.
Unitarian Universalist Veatch Program at Shelter Rock
United States-Japan Foundation
WMX Environmental Grants Program

G. N. Wilcox Trust
Margaret Cullinan Wray Charitable Lead Annuity Trust

Energy: alternative

ARCO Foundation
The Abell Foundation
Alaska Conservation Foundation
The Boeing Company
Changing Horizons Charitable Trust
Community Foundation of Western North Carolina, Inc.
The Elizabeth Ordway Dunn Foundation, Inc.
The Energy Foundation
Fund of the Four Directions
W. Alton Jones Foundation, Inc.
W. K. Kellogg Foundation
The Max and Anna Levinson Foundation
The McKnight Foundation
Joyce Mertz-Gilmore Foundation
Northwest Area Foundation
The Rockefeller Foundation
Seventh Generation Fund
Turner Foundation, Inc.

Energy: conservation

ARCO Foundation
Atherton Family Foundation
Beldon Fund
Beneficia Foundation
The William Bingham Foundation
Ruth H. Brown Foundation
Kathleen Price and Joseph M. Bryan Family Foundation, Inc.
The Bullitt Foundation
The Bydale Foundation
Centerior Energy Foundation
Changing Horizons Charitable Trust
The Chevron Companies
Chrysler Corporation Fund
The Cleveland Foundation
Compton Foundation, Inc.
Geraldine R. Dodge Foundation, Inc.
The Elizabeth Ordway Dunn Foundation, Inc.
The Educational Foundation of America
The Energy Foundation
Samuel S. Fels Fund
The Foundation for the National Capital Region
Mary D. and Walter F. Frear Eleemosynary Trust
GE Fund
The German Marshall Fund of the United States
Give to the Earth Foundation
The Golden Rule Foundation, Inc.
The George Gund Foundation
The Merrill G. & Emita E. Hastings Foundation
Howfirma Foundation
The Hyde and Watson Foundation
W. Alton Jones Foundation, Inc.

The Joyce Foundation
The J. M. Kaplan Fund, Inc.
The Max and Anna Levinson Foundation
Lyndhurst Foundation
The John D. and Catherine T. MacArthur Foundation
The McKnight Foundation
The John Merck Fund
Joyce Mertz-Gilmore Foundation
The Moriah Fund, Inc.
Charles Stewart Mott Foundation
The Needmor Fund
New England Biolabs Foundation
The New-Land Foundation, Inc.
The Pew Charitable Trusts
The Philadelphia Foundation
Prince Charitable Trusts
Rockefeller Brothers Fund, Inc.
Rockefeller Family Fund, Inc.
The Rockefeller Foundation
Surdna Foundation, Inc.
The Switzer Foundation
Texaco Foundation
Threshold Foundation
The Tinker Foundation Incorporated
True North Foundation
Rose E. Tucker Charitable Trust
Turner Foundation, Inc.
WMX Environmental Grants Program
The Winston-Salem Foundation, Inc.
Margaret Cullinan Wray Charitable Lead Annuity Trust

Energy: education

ARCO Foundation
Beldon Fund
Changing Horizons Charitable Trust
Compton Foundation, Inc.
The Educational Foundation of America
The Energy Foundation
Ford Motor Company Fund
The Rockefeller Foundation
Toyota USA Foundation
USX Foundation, Inc.

Energy: hydropower

The Bullitt Foundation
Carolyn Foundation
Jessie B. Cox Charitable Trust
Davis Conservation Foundation
Foundation for Deep Ecology
The Goldman Environmental Foundation
The George Gund Foundation
Charles Stewart Mott Foundation
National Fish and Wildlife Foundation
Patagonia, Inc.
The Pew Charitable Trusts
The Rockefeller Foundation
Surdna Foundation, Inc.
Weeden Foundation

Energy: petrochemical

The Acorn Foundation
Alaska Conservation Foundation

Environmental Topics and Activities

Energy: petrochemical (cont.)

The Jenifer Altman Foundation
Beldon Fund
Changing Horizons Charitable Trust
The Clarence E. Heller Charitable
  Foundation
The John D. and Catherine T. MacArthur
  Foundation
Charles Stewart Mott Foundation
Jessie Smith Noyes Foundation, Inc.
Patagonia, Inc.
Public Welfare Foundation, Inc.
The Florence and John Schumann
  Foundation
Seventh Generation Fund

Energy: photovoltaic/solar

The Bullitt Foundation
The Educational Foundation of America
The Energy Foundation
Fund of the Four Directions
Hawaii Community Foundation
W. Alton Jones Foundation, Inc.
The John Merck Fund
Joyce Mertz-Gilmore Foundation
The Moriah Fund, Inc.
Charles Stewart Mott Foundation
New England Biolabs Foundation
The Rockefeller Foundation
The Switzer Foundation
Margaret Cullinan Wray Charitable
  Lead Annuity Trust

Energy: solar box cookers

Atkinson Foundation
The Conservation and Research Foundation
The Educational Foundation of America
Foundation for Field Research

Energy: wind

The Energy Foundation

Environmental health

The Abelard Foundation West
The Acorn Foundation
The Bauman Foundation
Beldon Fund
The Ben & Jerry's Foundation
The Boeing Company
Otto Bremer Foundation
C. S. Fund
The Chevron Companies
The Cleveland Foundation
Columbia Foundation
Conservation, Food & Health
  Foundation, Inc.
Jessie B. Cox Charitable Trust
The Nathan Cummings Foundation
Deer Creek Foundation
The Elizabeth Ordway Dunn
  Foundation, Inc.
Eastman Kodak Company Charitable Trust
The Educational Foundation of America

El Paso Community Foundation
Foundation for Deep Ecology
Fund of the Four Directions
Funding Exchange
The German Marshall Fund of
  the United States
Richard & Rhoda Goldman Fund
Great Lakes Protection Fund
Hartford Foundation for Public Giving
Heller Charitable & Educational Fund
The Clarence E. Heller Charitable
  Foundation
The James Irvine Foundation
W. Alton Jones Foundation, Inc.
W. K. Kellogg Foundation
The Max and Anna Levinson Foundation
Lyndhurst Foundation
The John D. and Catherine T. MacArthur
  Foundation
Marin Community Foundation
The McKnight Foundation
The John Merck Fund
The Milwaukee Foundation
Charles Stewart Mott Foundation
Ruth Mott Fund
The Curtis and Edith Munson
  Foundation, Inc.
The National Environmental Education
  and Training Foundation, Inc.
The Needmor Fund
New England Biolabs Foundation
Norman Foundation
Jessie Smith Noyes Foundation, Inc.
Ottinger Foundation
The Pew Charitable Trusts
Pew Scholars Program in Conservation
  and the Environment
Public Welfare Foundation, Inc.
The Rockefeller Foundation
Fran and Warren Rupp Foundation
Sacharuna Foundation
The Sapelo Foundation
Shell Oil Company Foundation
The Strong Foundation for
  Environmental Values
Surdna Foundation, Inc.
The Switzer Foundation
Texaco Foundation
Threshold Foundation
The Tinker Foundation Incorporated
The Trust For Mutual Understanding
USX Foundation, Inc.
Unitarian Universalist Veatch Program
  at Shelter Rock
Vanguard Public Foundation
Victoria Foundation, Inc.
Virginia Environmental Endowment

Environmental history

The Jenifer Altman Foundation
C. S. Fund
California Community Foundation
The Chevron Companies
The Fred Gellert Foundation
The Edward W. Hazen Foundation

Environmental impact

Alaska Conservation Foundation
American Conservation Association, Inc.
Mary Reynolds Babcock Foundation, Inc.
Otto Bremer Foundation
The Bullitt Foundation
C. S. Fund
California Community Foundation
Chesapeake Bay Trust
Robert Sterling Clark Foundation, Inc.
Columbia Foundation
Jessie B. Cox Charitable Trust
The Nathan Cummings Foundation
Deer Creek Foundation
Geraldine R. Dodge Foundation, Inc.
The Educational Foundation of America
Flintridge Foundation
Ford Foundation
The German Marshall Fund of
  the United States
The Goldman Environmental Foundation
Richard & Rhoda Goldman Fund
The William and Mary Greve
  Foundation, Inc.
W. Alton Jones Foundation, Inc.
The Joyce Foundation
Laidlaw Foundation
The John D. and Catherine T. MacArthur
  Foundation
Giles W. and Elise G. Mead Foundation
Merck Family Fund
The John Merck Fund
Millbrook Tribute Garden, Inc.
J. P. Morgan Charitable Trust
The Moriah Fund, Inc.
Ruth Mott Fund
The Curtis and Edith Munson
  Foundation, Inc.
National Fish and Wildlife Foundation
Norcross Wildlife Foundation, Inc.
Northwest Area Foundation
The Overbrook Foundation
The David and Lucile Packard Foundation
Patagonia, Inc.
The Pew Charitable Trusts
Pew Scholars Program in Conservation
  and the Environment
Public Welfare Foundation, Inc.
Rockefeller Brothers Fund, Inc.
The Rockefeller Foundation
The Scherman Foundation, Inc.
Sears-Swetland Foundation
The Switzer Foundation
Nelson Talbott Foundation
Threshold Foundation
The Tinker Foundation Incorporated
The Trust For Mutual Understanding
Unitarian Universalist Veatch Program
  at Shelter Rock
Virginia Environmental Endowment
Weeden Foundation
The William P. Wharton Trust

© 1995 Environmental Data Resources, Inc.

Environmental Topics and Activities

Environmental justice

A Territory Resource
The Abelard Foundation West
The Acorn Foundation
The Jenifer Altman Foundation
Angelina Fund, Inc.
Mary Reynolds Babcock Foundation, Inc.
The Bauman Foundation
Beldon Fund
The Ben & Jerry's Foundation
The Bullitt Foundation
C. S. Fund
The Conservation and Research Foundation
Crystal Channel Foundation
The Nathan Cummings Foundation
Samuel S. Fels Fund
Ford Foundation
Fund of the Four Directions
Funding Exchange
Give to the Earth Foundation
The Edward W. Hazen Foundation
McKenzie River Gathering Foundation
The New York Community Trust
Norman Foundation
Andrew Norman Foundation
Jessie Smith Noyes Foundation, Inc.
James C. Penney Foundation
Public Welfare Foundation, Inc.
Rockefeller Financial Services,
 Philanthropy Department
The Sapelo Foundation
The Florence and John Schumann
 Foundation
Surdna Foundation, Inc.
Threshold Foundation
Unitarian Universalist Veatch Program
 at Shelter Rock
Vanguard Public Foundation
Margaret Cullinan Wray Charitable
 Lead Annuity Trust

Estuaries

The Bullitt Foundation
Mary Flagler Cary Charitable Trust
Chesapeake Bay Trust
Jessie B. Cox Charitable Trust
Geraldine R. Dodge Foundation, Inc.
The Elizabeth Ordway Dunn
 Foundation, Inc.
The Educational Foundation of America
Environmental Endowment for
 New Jersey, Inc.
The Gap Foundation
The Wallace Alexander Gerbode
 Foundation, Inc.
Marin Community Foundation
MARPAT Foundation, Inc.
McLean Contributionship
National Fish and Wildlife Foundation
The David and Lucile Packard Foundation
Patagonia, Inc.
The William Penn Foundation
The Pew Charitable Trusts
The San Francisco Foundation
The Tinker Foundation Incorporated
Victoria Foundation, Inc.
WMX Environmental Grants Program
Weyerhaeuser Company Foundation
The Dean Witter Foundation

Ethics: environmental

Mary Reynolds Babcock Foundation, Inc.
Compton Foundation, Inc.
The Nathan Cummings Foundation
Damien Foundation
Deer Creek Foundation
Foundation for Deep Ecology
The Homeland Foundation
Mars Foundation
Giles W. and Elise G. Mead Foundation
The New-Land Foundation, Inc.
OCRI Foundation
Patagonia, Inc.
The William Penn Foundation
The San Francisco Foundation
Threshold Foundation
Town Creek Foundation, Inc.
WMX Environmental Grants Program

Exchange programs

Compton Foundation, Inc.
Ford Foundation
Foundation for Deep Ecology
The John D. and Catherine T. MacArthur
 Foundation
Rockefeller Brothers Fund, Inc.
Seventh Generation Fund
South Coast Foundation, Inc.
The Trust For Mutual Understanding

Exhibits

ARCO Foundation
The Achelis Foundation
The Ahmanson Foundation
Alaska Conservation Foundation
BankAmerica Foundation
David Winton Bell Foundation
The Frank Stanley Beveridge
 Foundation, Inc.
The Bodman Foundation
The Louis Calder Foundation
Chesapeake Bay Trust
The Chevron Companies
The Cleveland Foundation
The Collins Foundation
Columbia Foundation
Adolph Coors Foundation
Geraldine R. Dodge Foundation, Inc.
The Favrot Fund
Leland Fikes Foundation, Inc.
Gates Foundation
The Fred Gellert Foundation
The George Gund Foundation
The Richard Ivey Foundation
W. Alton Jones Foundation, Inc.
The J. M. Kaplan Fund, Inc.
The Kresge Foundation
Laird, Norton Foundation
The John D. and Catherine T. MacArthur
 Foundation
McGregor Fund
Meadows Foundation, Inc.
Meyer Memorial Trust
M. J. Murdock Charitable Trust
National Fish and Wildlife Foundation
The New York Times Company
 Foundation, Inc.
The David and Lucile Packard Foundation
Patagonia, Inc.
The Pew Charitable Trusts
San Diego Community Foundation
Stanley Smith Horticultural Trust
The Tides Foundation
Rose E. Tucker Charitable Trust
WMX Environmental Grants Program
Weyerhaeuser Company Foundation
The William P. Wharton Trust
Wilburforce Foundation
G. N. Wilcox Trust
The Dean Witter Foundation

Expeditions

The Ahmanson Foundation
Clayton Baker Trust
The Howard Bayne Fund
Otto Bremer Foundation
The Robert Brownlee Foundation
The Chevron Companies
The Mary A. Crocker Trust
Ford Motor Company Fund
The Esther A. and Joseph Klingenstein
 Fund, Inc.
Larsen Fund, Inc.
Richard Lounsbery Foundation, Inc.
The McKnight Foundation
The Mountaineers Foundation
Mustard Seed Foundation, Inc.
The New York Times Company
 Foundation, Inc.
Howard Phipps Foundation
The Rhode Island Community Foundation
Threshold Foundation
WMX Environmental Grants Program
Westinghouse Foundation

Farmers/ranchers

A Territory Resource
The Abelard Foundation West
The Acorn Foundation
The Arca Foundation
Mary Reynolds Babcock Foundation, Inc.
The Ben & Jerry's Foundation
The Bullitt Foundation
C. S. Fund
Chesapeake Bay Trust
Columbia Foundation
The Mary A. Crocker Trust
The Nathan Cummings Foundation
Geraldine R. Dodge Foundation, Inc.
The Educational Foundation of America
Ford Foundation
Ford Motor Company Fund

Environmental Topics and Activities

Farmers/ranchers (cont.)

The Fund for New Jersey
Give to the Earth Foundation
Great Lakes Protection Fund
W. Alton Jones Foundation, Inc.
W. K. Kellogg Foundation
Laird, Norton Foundation
The Moriah Fund, Inc.
Charles Stewart Mott Foundation
Ruth Mott Fund
National Fish and Wildlife Foundation
The Needmor Fund
Norman Foundation
Northwest Area Foundation
Jessie Smith Noyes Foundation, Inc.
Patagonia, Inc.
Public Welfare Foundation, Inc.
Z. Smith Reynolds Foundation, Inc.
The Rockefeller Foundation
The Winthrop Rockefeller Foundation
The Strong Foundation for Environmental Values
Threshold Foundation
The Tides Foundation
Underhill Foundation
Unitarian Universalist Veatch Program at Shelter Rock
Vanguard Public Foundation

Farmworkers

A Territory Resource
The Needmor Fund
The Philadelphia Foundation
Public Welfare Foundation, Inc.
Rockefeller Family Fund, Inc.

Feasibility studies

The Abell Foundation
The Bullitt Foundation
Conservation, Food & Health Foundation, Inc.
The Energy Foundation
W. Alton Jones Foundation, Inc.
The Joyce Foundation
The John D. and Catherine T. MacArthur Foundation
Joyce Mertz-Gilmore Foundation
The Pew Charitable Trusts
The Rockefeller Foundation
The Winthrop Rockefeller Foundation
The San Francisco Foundation
Weeden Foundation
Margaret Cullinan Wray Charitable Lead Annuity Trust

Fellowships

ARCO Foundation
The George F. Baker Trust
The Lynde and Harry Bradley Foundation, Inc.
Otto Bremer Foundation
Mary Flagler Cary Charitable Trust

Conservation, Food & Health Foundation, Inc.
Damien Foundation
The Arthur Vining Davis Foundations
The Energy Foundation
Ford Foundation
General Service Foundation
The German Marshall Fund of the United States
The George Frederick Jewett Foundation
The Lazar Foundation
The Curtis and Edith Munson Foundation, Inc.
The New York Times Company Foundation, Inc.
The David and Lucile Packard Foundation
Samuel and May Rudin Foundation, Inc.
The Switzer Foundation
The Trust For Mutual Understanding
WMX Environmental Grants Program

Fisheries

The Achelis Foundation
The George F. Baker Trust
BankAmerica Foundation
The Bodman Foundation
The Bothin Foundation
Otto Bremer Foundation
The Bullitt Foundation
Chesapeake Bay Trust
The Community Foundation of Greater New Haven
Conservation, Food & Health Foundation, Inc.
Jessie B. Cox Charitable Trust
Davis Conservation Foundation
Ederic Foundation, Inc.
The Hugh and Jane Ferguson Foundation
Jamee and Marshall Field Foundation
FishAmerica Foundation
Flintridge Foundation
General Service Foundation
The Greenville Foundation
The Hitachi Foundation
Howfirma Foundation
F. M. Kirby Foundation, Inc.
The Seymour H. Knox Foundation, Inc.
Laird, Norton Foundation
Luster Family Foundation, Inc.
Maine Community Foundation, Inc.
Giles W. and Elise G. Mead Foundation
Metropolitan Atlanta Community Foundation, Inc.
The Curtis and Edith Munson Foundation, Inc.
National Fish and Wildlife Foundation
The New York Times Company Foundation, Inc.
Norcross Wildlife Foundation, Inc.
Northwest Area Foundation
The David and Lucile Packard Foundation
Patagonia, Inc.
Peninsula Community Foundation

The Pew Charitable Trusts
Prince Charitable Trusts
Z. Smith Reynolds Foundation, Inc.
The Stroh Foundation
The Sulzberger Foundation, Inc.
Surdna Foundation, Inc.
Edna Bailey Sussman Fund
Threshold Foundation
Times Mirror Magazines, Inc.
Town Creek Foundation, Inc.
Vanguard Public Foundation
G. Unger Vetlesen Foundation
WMX Environmental Grants Program
Weyerhaeuser Company Foundation
The Winston-Salem Foundation, Inc.
The Dean Witter Foundation

Fisheries: planning and regulation

ARCO Foundation
Alaska Conservation Foundation
The Bullitt Foundation
Chesapeake Bay Trust
The Chevron Companies
Compton Foundation, Inc.
Jessie B. Cox Charitable Trust
Davis Conservation Foundation
Geraldine R. Dodge Foundation, Inc.
The Educational Foundation of America
The Charles Engelhard Foundation
FishAmerica Foundation
The Gap Foundation
The Wallace Alexander Gerbode Foundation, Inc.
Howfirma Foundation
Ittleson Foundation, Inc.
W. Alton Jones Foundation, Inc.
Laidlaw Foundation
The Lazar Foundation
Maine Community Foundation, Inc.
Mars Foundation
Giles W. and Elise G. Mead Foundation
The Curtis and Edith Munson Foundation, Inc.
National Fish and Wildlife Foundation
The New York Times Company Foundation, Inc.
Norcross Wildlife Foundation, Inc.
Northwest Area Foundation
The David and Lucile Packard Foundation
Patagonia, Inc.
The Pew Charitable Trusts
Pew Scholars Program in Conservation and the Environment
Phillips Petroleum Foundation, Inc.
Shell Oil Company Foundation
Surdna Foundation, Inc.
The Tinker Foundation Incorporated
WMX Environmental Grants Program
Weeden Foundation
Henry E. and Consuelo S. Wenger Foundation, Inc.
Margaret Cullinan Wray Charitable Lead Annuity Trust

© 1995 Environmental Data Resources, Inc.

Environmental Topics and Activities

Fishing: sport

The Beinecke Foundation, Inc.
The Bullitt Foundation
Chesapeake Bay Trust
The Chevron Companies
The Mary A. Crocker Trust
Geraldine R. Dodge Foundation, Inc.
FishAmerica Foundation
Heller Charitable & Educational Fund
F. M. Kirby Foundation, Inc.
Laird, Norton Foundation
The Curtis and Edith Munson Foundation, Inc.
National Fish and Wildlife Foundation
The New York Times Company Foundation, Inc.
Norcross Wildlife Foundation, Inc.
The David and Lucile Packard Foundation
Phillips Petroleum Foundation, Inc.
The Prospect Hill Foundation
The Strong Foundation for Environmental Values
The Sulzberger Foundation, Inc.
Nelson Talbott Foundation
Times Mirror Magazines, Inc.
WMX Environmental Grants Program
Henry E. and Consuelo S. Wenger Foundation, Inc.
Weyerhaeuser Company Foundation
The Winston-Salem Foundation, Inc.

Food: industry

C. S. Fund
The Ettinger Foundation, Inc.
General Service Foundation
The J. M. Kaplan Fund, Inc.
Laidlaw Foundation
The Moriah Fund, Inc.
National Fish and Wildlife Foundation
Norman Foundation
Patagonia, Inc.
The Rockefeller Foundation
The Winthrop Rockefeller Foundation
Threshold Foundation

Food: safety

C. S. Fund
Beldon Fund
Changing Horizons Charitable Trust
Columbia Foundation
Rockefeller Family Fund, Inc.
The Florence and John Schumann Foundation
True North Foundation
Unitarian Universalist Veatch Program at Shelter Rock
Wallace Genetic Foundation, Inc.

Forestry

Alaska Conservation Foundation
The Beinecke Foundation, Inc.
Benua Foundation, Inc.
Blandin Foundation

The Bullitt Foundation
Chesapeake Bay Trust
Chesapeake Corporation Foundation
The Collins Foundation
Compton Foundation, Inc.
Geraldine R. Dodge Foundation, Inc.
Foundation for Deep Ecology
The Gap Foundation
The Fred Gellert Foundation
General Service Foundation
Georgia-Pacific Foundation
Walter and Elise Haas Fund
Harder Foundation
The Merrill G. & Emita E. Hastings Foundation
The Clarence E. Heller Charitable Foundation
The William and Flora Hewlett Foundation
Howfirma Foundation
Hurdle Hill Foundation
Island Foundation
The Richard Ivey Foundation
The Jackson Foundation
Jackson Hole Preserve, Inc.
Laird, Norton Foundation
The Max and Anna Levinson Foundation
The John D. and Catherine T. MacArthur Foundation
Maki Foundation
McKenzie River Gathering Foundation
Giles W. and Elise G. Mead Foundation
Merck Family Fund
The John Merck Fund
Middlecott Foundation
The Milwaukee Foundation
Ruth Mott Fund
National Fish and Wildlife Foundation
The Needmor Fund
New Hampshire Charitable Foundation
Northwest Area Foundation
OCRI Foundation
Patagonia, Inc.
Sacharuna Foundation
Elmina B. Sewall Foundation
Surdna Foundation, Inc.
Edna Bailey Sussman Fund
Threshold Foundation
True North Foundation
The Trust For Mutual Understanding
Rose E. Tucker Charitable Trust
Underhill Foundation
Union Camp Charitable Trust
WMX Environmental Grants Program
Weyerhaeuser Company Foundation
The William P. Wharton Trust
Margaret Cullinan Wray Charitable Lead Annuity Trust

Forests

Alaska Conservation Foundation
American Foundation Corporation
The Barra Foundation, Inc.
The Betterment Fund
Alexander H. Bright Charitable Trust
The Bullitt Foundation

Caribou Fund
Centerior Energy Foundation
The Champlin Foundations
Cheeryble Foundation
Chesapeake Bay Trust
Chesapeake Corporation Foundation
Chrysler Corporation Fund
Compton Foundation, Inc.
The Conservation and Research Foundation
Conservation, Food & Health Foundation, Inc.
Crystal Channel Foundation
Davis Conservation Foundation
Dayton Hudson Foundation
Geraldine R. Dodge Foundation, Inc.
Gaylord and Dorothy Donnelley Foundation
The Max and Victoria Dreyfus Foundation, Inc.
The Charles Engelhard Foundation
The Armand G. Erpf Fund, Inc.
Samuel S. Fels Fund
The Field Foundation of Illinois, Inc.
Bert Fingerhut/Caroline Hicks Family Fund
Ford Foundation
Foundation for Deep Ecology
The Freed Foundation, Inc.
General Service Foundation
Georgia Power Foundation, Inc.
Georgia-Pacific Foundation
Global Environmental Project Institute
Global Greengrants Fund
The Harding Educational and Charitable Foundation
Hartford Foundation for Public Giving
Heller Charitable & Educational Fund
The William and Flora Hewlett Foundation
The Homeland Foundation
The Horn Foundation
Howfirma Foundation
The Hyde and Watson Foundation
Ireland Foundation
The Richard Ivey Foundation
W. Alton Jones Foundation, Inc.
F. M. Kirby Foundation, Inc.
Laird, Norton Foundation
The Lazar Foundation
Luster Family Foundation, Inc.
The John D. and Catherine T. MacArthur Foundation
Mars Foundation
McDonnell Douglas Foundation
McInerny Foundation
Giles W. and Elise G. Mead Foundation
The Moriah Fund, Inc.
Ruth Mott Fund
National Fish and Wildlife Foundation
The Needmor Fund
New Hampshire Charitable Foundation
The New York Community Trust
The New York Times Company Foundation, Inc.
Norcross Wildlife Foundation, Inc.
Outdoor Industry Conservation Alliance
Patagonia, Inc.
James C. Penney Foundation

Environmental Topics and Activities

Forests (cont.)

The Pew Charitable Trusts
Recreational Equipment, Inc.
Rockefeller Brothers Fund, Inc.
Rockefeller Financial Services,
  Philanthropy Department
The Rockefeller Foundation
Sacharuna Foundation
The Florence and John Schumann
  Foundation
Springhouse Foundation
The Strong Foundation for
  Environmental Values
The Sulzberger Foundation, Inc.
Surdna Foundation, Inc.
The Tides Foundation
Times Mirror Magazines, Inc.
Tortuga Foundation
True North Foundation
The Truland Foundation
Rose E. Tucker Charitable Trust
Turner Foundation, Inc.
Union Camp Charitable Trust
R. T. Vanderbilt Trust
Weeden Foundation
Weyerhaeuser Company Foundation
The William P. Wharton Trust
G. N. Wilcox Trust
Margaret Cullinan Wray Charitable
  Lead Annuity Trust

Forests: ancient

Alaska Conservation Foundation
The Bullitt Foundation
Carolyn Foundation
Environment Now Foundation
Foundation for Deep Ecology
The Gap Foundation
Richard & Rhoda Goldman Fund
HKH Foundation
The Richard Ivey Foundation
W. Alton Jones Foundation, Inc.
The Lazar Foundation
MARPAT Foundation, Inc.
The McIntosh Foundation
McKenzie River Gathering Foundation
Giles W. and Elise G. Mead Foundation
Charles Stewart Mott Foundation
Ruth Mott Fund
Patagonia, Inc.
The Pew Charitable Trusts
Recreational Equipment, Inc.
Rockefeller Family Fund, Inc.
The Strong Foundation for
  Environmental Values
Surdna Foundation, Inc.
Threshold Foundation
The Tides Foundation
Tortuga Foundation
True North Foundation
Underhill Foundation
Vanguard Public Foundation
Weeden Foundation

Forests: deforestation

Alaska Conservation Foundation
The Ben & Jerry's Foundation
Beneficia Foundation
The Bullitt Foundation
The Nathan Cummings Foundation
The Energy Foundation
Flintridge Foundation
The Fred Gellert Foundation
The Goldman Environmental Foundation
The Richard Ivey Foundation
Laird, Norton Foundation
The Max and Anna Levinson Foundation
The John D. and Catherine T. MacArthur
  Foundation
McKenzie River Gathering Foundation
The Moriah Fund, Inc.
Ruth Mott Fund
Patagonia, Inc.
The Rockefeller Foundation
Seventh Generation Fund
The Switzer Foundation
Threshold Foundation
Virginia Environmental Endowment
WMX Environmental Grants Program
Weeden Foundation
Weyerhaeuser Company Foundation

Forests: history

Georgia-Pacific Foundation
The George Frederick Jewett Foundation
Sequoia Foundation
Weyerhaeuser Company Foundation

Forests: management

A Territory Resource
Alaska Conservation Foundation
Beldon Fund
The Bullitt Foundation
The Carpenter Foundation
Chesapeake Bay Trust
Conservation, Food & Health
  Foundation, Inc.
Jessie B. Cox Charitable Trust
Crystal Channel Foundation
Deer Creek Foundation
Geraldine R. Dodge Foundation, Inc.
The Educational Foundation of America
Ford Foundation
Foundation for Deep Ecology
General Service Foundation
HKH Foundation
Harder Foundation
The Clarence E. Heller Charitable
  Foundation
The Richard Ivey Foundation
Jackson Hole Preserve, Inc.
W. Alton Jones Foundation, Inc.
Laird, Norton Foundation
Maki Foundation
The Marshall Fund of Arizona
The Martin Foundation, Inc.
Giles W. and Elise G. Mead Foundation

Merck Family Fund
The John Merck Fund
The Moriah Fund, Inc.
Ruth Mott Fund
National Fish and Wildlife Foundation
The Needmor Fund
Patagonia, Inc.
The Prospect Hill Foundation
The Rockefeller Foundation
The Strong Foundation for
  Environmental Values
Threshold Foundation
The Tinker Foundation Incorporated
Weeden Foundation

Forests: national

Alaska Conservation Foundation
Beldon Fund
The Ben & Jerry's Foundation
The Bullitt Foundation
The Chevron Companies
Deer Creek Foundation
Geraldine R. Dodge Foundation, Inc.
The Fred Gellert Foundation
Give to the Earth Foundation
Richard & Rhoda Goldman Fund
The Greenville Foundation
The Clarence E. Heller Charitable
  Foundation
W. Alton Jones Foundation, Inc.
The Lazar Foundation
Lyndhurst Foundation
The John D. and Catherine T. MacArthur
  Foundation
Maki Foundation
MARPAT Foundation, Inc.
The Martin Foundation, Inc.
The McConnell Foundation
Merck Family Fund
Ruth Mott Fund
The Curtis and Edith Munson
  Foundation, Inc.
National Fish and Wildlife Foundation
Patagonia, Inc.
The Pew Charitable Trusts
Rockwood Fund, Inc.
Surdna Foundation, Inc.
Threshold Foundation
Weeden Foundation

Forests: non-timber products

Conservation, Food & Health
  Foundation, Inc.
The John D. and Catherine T. MacArthur
  Foundation
The John Merck Fund
The Rockefeller Foundation

Forests: protection

Alaska Conservation Foundation
Winifred & Harry B. Allen Foundation
American Conservation Association, Inc.
Mary Reynolds Babcock Foundation, Inc.

© 1995 Environmental Data Resources, Inc.

Environmental Topics and Activities

Forests: protection (cont.)

Beldon Fund
Bishop Pine Fund
Alexander H. Bright Charitable Trust
The Bullitt Foundation
California Community Foundation
Carolyn Foundation
Chesapeake Corporation Foundation
Columbia Foundation
The Community Foundation of Santa Clara County
Compton Foundation, Inc.
The Mary A. Crocker Trust
Davis Conservation Foundation
Deer Creek Foundation
Geraldine R. Dodge Foundation, Inc.
Ederic Foundation, Inc.
Fanwood Foundation
Flintridge Foundation
Ford Foundation
Foundation for Deep Ecology
Fund of the Four Directions
The Gap Foundation
The Fred Gellert Foundation
General Service Foundation
Richard & Rhoda Goldman Fund
Greater Piscataqua Community Foundation
The Greenville Foundation
Walter and Elise Haas Fund
Harbor Lights Foundation
The Harding Educational and Charitable Foundation
The M. A. Healy Family Foundation, Inc.
The Homeland Foundation
The Horn Foundation
Howfirma Foundation
The Richard Ivey Foundation
Jackson Hole Preserve, Inc.
W. Alton Jones Foundation, Inc.
Laurel Foundation
The Max and Anna Levinson Foundation
Luster Family Foundation, Inc.
Lyndhurst Foundation
The John D. and Catherine T. MacArthur Foundation
James A. Macdonald Foundation
McKenzie River Gathering Foundation
Richard King Mellon Foundation
Merck Family Fund
The John Merck Fund
The Moriah Fund, Inc.
Ruth Mott Fund
The Curtis and Edith Munson Foundation, Inc.
National Fish and Wildlife Foundation
The Needmor Fund
New England Biolabs Foundation
New Hampshire Charitable Foundation
The New York Times Company Foundation, Inc.
The New-Land Foundation, Inc.
Kenneth T. and Eileen L. Norris Foundation
Northwest Area Foundation
Patagonia, Inc.
Peninsula Community Foundation

The Pew Charitable Trusts
The Prospect Hill Foundation
Rockefeller Family Fund, Inc.
Rockwood Fund, Inc.
The San Francisco Foundation
Sarah I. Schieffelin Residuary Trust
The Schumann Fund for New Jersey, Inc.
Sequoia Foundation
The Sonoma County Community Foundation
Springhouse Foundation
The Strong Foundation for Environmental Values
Surdna Foundation, Inc.
The Switzer Foundation
Threshold Foundation
The Tides Foundation
Town Creek Foundation, Inc.
Weeden Foundation
Margaret Cullinan Wray Charitable Lead Annuity Trust

Forests: reforestation/afforestation

ARCO Foundation
Alaska Conservation Foundation
The Vincent Astor Foundation
Atkinson Foundation
BankAmerica Foundation
Bay Area Community Foundation
California Community Foundation
Chesapeake Bay Trust
The Community Foundation Serving Coastal South Carolina
The Cowles Charitable Trust
Crystal Channel Foundation
The Armand G. Erpf Fund, Inc.
Foundation for Deep Ecology
General Service Foundation
Give to the Earth Foundation
The George Gund Foundation
The Harding Educational and Charitable Foundation
Laidlaw Foundation
Laird, Norton Foundation
Levi Strauss Foundation
The John D. and Catherine T. MacArthur Foundation
The Mountaineers Foundation
National Fish and Wildlife Foundation
The Needmor Fund
New Hampshire Charitable Foundation
Patagonia, Inc.
The William Penn Foundation
Rockefeller Brothers Fund, Inc.
Threshold Foundation
WMX Environmental Grants Program
Weeden Foundation
Weyerhaeuser Company Foundation

Forests: sustainable yield

A Territory Resource
The Jenifer Altman Foundation
Beldon Fund
The Ben & Jerry's Foundation

The Bullitt Foundation
Compton Foundation, Inc.
The Mary A. Crocker Trust
Geraldine R. Dodge Foundation, Inc.
Foundation for Deep Ecology
Richard & Rhoda Goldman Fund
The Clarence E. Heller Charitable Foundation
The Richard Ivey Foundation
W. Alton Jones Foundation, Inc.
The John D. and Catherine T. MacArthur Foundation
McKenzie River Gathering Foundation
Giles W. and Elise G. Mead Foundation
Richard King Mellon Foundation
The John Merck Fund
The Moriah Fund, Inc.
Northwest Area Foundation
Northwest Fund for the Environment
Patagonia, Inc.
The Rockefeller Foundation
The Strong Foundation for Environmental Values
Surdna Foundation, Inc.
True North Foundation
The Trust For Mutual Understanding
Weeden Foundation
The William P. Wharton Trust

Forests: tropical

James & Abigail Campbell Foundation
Conservation, Food & Health Foundation, Inc.
Jessie B. Cox Charitable Trust
The Fred Gellert Foundation
General Service Foundation
The Homeland Foundation
Howfirma Foundation
The International Foundation, Inc.
W. Alton Jones Foundation, Inc.
Laird, Norton Foundation
The John D. and Catherine T. MacArthur Foundation
The John Merck Fund
The Moriah Fund, Inc.
The New York Times Company Foundation, Inc.
Patagonia, Inc.
The Prospect Hill Foundation
The Rockefeller Foundation
The Switzer Foundation
Texaco Foundation
Threshold Foundation

Forests: urban

American Express Philanthropic Program
Elmer L. & Eleanor J. Andersen Foundation
Bay Area Community Foundation
The Bothin Foundation
The Community Foundation Serving Coastal South Carolina
The Cowles Charitable Trust
Dayton Hudson Foundation

Environmental Topics and Activities

Forests: urban (cont.)

The Max and Victoria Dreyfus Foundation, Inc.
The William Stamps Farish Fund
The George Gund Foundation
Walter and Elise Haas Fund
The J. M. Kaplan Fund, Inc.
Harris and Eliza Kempner Fund
Levi Strauss Foundation
Lyndhurst Foundation
Meadows Foundation, Inc.
Joyce Mertz-Gilmore Foundation
John P. Murphy Foundation
National Fish and Wildlife Foundation
Norcross Wildlife Foundation, Inc.
Prince Charitable Trusts
The Rockfall Foundation
Texaco Foundation
The Winston-Salem Foundation, Inc.
The Wortham Foundation, Inc.

Gardens

S. D. Bechtel, Jr. Foundation
The Ben & Jerry's Foundation
Alex. Brown & Sons Charitable Foundation, Inc.
Kathleen Price and Joseph M. Bryan Family Foundation, Inc.
C. S. Fund
The Morris and Gwendolyn Cafritz Foundation
Carolyn Foundation
Chesapeake Bay Trust
The Chevron Companies
The Chicago Community Trust
The Collins Foundation
The Columbus Foundation
Geraldine R. Dodge Foundation, Inc.
Oliver S. and Jennie R. Donaldson Charitable Trust
Jessie Ball duPont Religious, Charitable and Educational Fund
Ederic Foundation, Inc.
El Pomar Foundation
The Thomas J. Emery Memorial
The Charles Engelhard Foundation
Environmental Education Foundation of Florida, Inc.
The Armand G. Erpf Fund, Inc.
Fair Play Foundation
The Foundation for the National Capital Region
Frelinghuysen Foundation
Greater Piscataqua Community Foundation
The George Gund Foundation
Charles Hayden Foundation
The Roy A. Hunt Foundation
Walter S. Johnson Foundation
The J. M. Kaplan Fund, Inc.
The Robert S. and Grayce B. Kerr Foundation, Inc.
Kongsgaard-Goldman Foundation
Laird, Norton Foundation
Longwood Foundation, Inc.

Magowan Family Foundation, Inc.
The McIntosh Foundation
Nelson Mead Fund
Meyer Memorial Trust
The Minneapolis Foundation
The Moody Foundation
New Hampshire Charitable Foundation
The Samuel Roberts Noble Foundation, Inc.
Norcross Wildlife Foundation, Inc.
OCRI Foundation
Patagonia, Inc.
Peninsula Community Foundation
The Pew Charitable Trusts
Prince Charitable Trusts
The Rockefeller Foundation
The San Francisco Foundation
Sarkeys Foundation
The Schiff Foundation
The Schumann Fund for New Jersey, Inc.
Sears-Swetland Foundation
Stanley Smith Horticultural Trust
The Stebbins Fund, Inc.
Stern Family Fund
Margaret Dorrance Strawbridge Foundation of Pennsylvania II, Inc.
Thanksgiving Foundation
Threshold Foundation
The Truland Foundation
Rose E. Tucker Charitable Trust
WMX Environmental Grants Program
The Winston-Salem Foundation, Inc.
Wodecroft Foundation

Gardens: botanical

ARCO Foundation
American Express Philanthropic Program
The Vincent Astor Foundation
Atherton Family Foundation
The Barra Foundation, Inc.
The Theodore H. Barth Foundation, Inc.
The Bay Foundation
The Howard Bayne Fund
The Beinecke Foundation, Inc.
The Beirne Carter Foundation
Beneficia Foundation
The Blumenthal Foundation
The Bodman Foundation
The Boeing Company
The Louis Calder Foundation
California Community Foundation
James & Abigail Campbell Foundation
Mary Flagler Cary Charitable Trust
Liz Claiborne & Art Ortenberg Foundation
Robert Sterling Clark Foundation, Inc.
The Collins Foundation
The Community Foundation of Santa Clara County
Cooke Foundation, Limited
The Cowles Charitable Trust
The Fred Harris Daniels Foundation, Inc.
The Aaron Diamond Foundation
Cleveland H. Dodge Foundation, Inc.
The Herbert H. and Grace A. Dow Foundation

The Elizabeth Ordway Dunn Foundation, Inc.
The Educational Foundation of America
The Charles Engelhard Foundation
The Armand G. Erpf Fund, Inc.
Fanwood Foundation
The William Stamps Farish Fund
Mary D. and Walter F. Frear Eleemosynary Trust
Frelinghuysen Foundation
Gates Foundation
Georgia Power Foundation, Inc.
Georgia-Pacific Foundation
Herman Goldman Foundation
The Ewing Halsell Foundation
The Hamer Foundation
Hawaii Community Foundation
Charles Hayden Foundation
The Homeland Foundation
The Indian Point Foundation, Inc.
W. Alton Jones Foundation, Inc.
The J. M. Kaplan Fund, Inc.
F. M. Kirby Foundation, Inc.
The Seymour H. Knox Foundation, Inc.
The Kresge Foundation
Laird, Norton Foundation
Richard Lounsbery Foundation, Inc.
The John D. and Catherine T. MacArthur Foundation
James A. Macdonald Foundation
Magowan Family Foundation, Inc.
The Marshall Fund of Arizona
The Eugene McDermott Foundation
McDonnell Douglas Foundation
McInerny Foundation
McLean Contributionship
The Andrew W. Mellon Foundation
Metropolitan Atlanta Community Foundation, Inc.
Metropolitan Life Foundation
Meyer Memorial Trust
Millbrook Tribute Garden, Inc.
The Milwaukee Foundation
Mobil Foundation, Inc.
Leo Model Foundation, Inc.
J. P. Morgan Charitable Trust
Henry and Lucy Moses Fund, Inc.
Charles Stewart Mott Foundation
The Mountaineers Foundation
National Fish and Wildlife Foundation
New England Biolabs Foundation
The New York Community Trust
The New York Times Company Foundation, Inc.
Norcross Wildlife Foundation, Inc.
Kenneth T. and Eileen L. Norris Foundation
Spencer T. and Ann W. Olin Foundation
The Overbrook Foundation
The Pfizer Foundation, Inc.
Howard Phipps Foundation
Pinewood Foundation
Henry B. Plant Memorial Fund, Inc.
Prince Charitable Trusts
The Rhode Island Community Foundation
The Rockefeller Foundation

© 1995 Environmental Data Resources, Inc.

Environmental Topics and Activities

Gardens: botanical (cont.)

Rockwell Fund, Inc.
Samuel and May Rudin Foundation, Inc.
The San Francisco Foundation
The Scherman Foundation, Inc.
The Schiff Foundation
Sears-Swetland Foundation
Shell Oil Company Foundation
Stanley Smith Horticultural Trust
Snee-Reinhardt Charitable Foundation
Southwestern Bell Foundation
Steelcase Foundation
Margaret Dorrance Strawbridge Foundation of Pennsylvania II, Inc.
The Morris Stulsaft Foundation
The Sulzberger Foundation, Inc.
Texaco Foundation
The Travelers Foundation
The Truland Foundation
WMX Environmental Grants Program
Weeden Foundation
Robert W. Wilson Foundation
Mark and Catherine Winkler Foundation
The Winston-Salem Foundation, Inc.
The Wortham Foundation, Inc.
Margaret Cullinan Wray Charitable Lead Annuity Trust

Gardens: public

Winifred & Harry B. Allen Foundation
The Vincent Astor Foundation
The Ben & Jerry's Foundation
The Cabot Family Charitable Trust
Laidlaw Foundation
Levi Strauss Foundation
Meadows Foundation, Inc.
Metropolitan Atlanta Community Foundation, Inc.
The William Penn Foundation
The Philadelphia Foundation
The Rhode Island Community Foundation
Union Pacific Foundation
Margaret Cullinan Wray Charitable Lead Annuity Trust

Gardens: urban

American Foundation Corporation
The Vincent Astor Foundation
The Morris and Gwendolyn Cafritz Foundation
Mary Flagler Cary Charitable Trust
Columbia Foundation
The Community Foundation of Greater New Haven
Compton Foundation, Inc.
The Cowles Charitable Trust
The Thomas J. Emery Memorial
Give to the Earth Foundation
The George Gund Foundation
The Hall Family Foundation
The Hyams Foundation
The J. M. Kaplan Fund, Inc.
Levi Strauss Foundation
Merck Family Fund

Metropolitan Life Foundation
Charles Stewart Mott Foundation
John P. Murphy Foundation
New England Biolabs Foundation
The New York Times Company Foundation, Inc.
The Pfizer Foundation, Inc.
The Procter & Gamble Fund
The Prospect Hill Foundation
Sears-Swetland Foundation
Wodecroft Foundation

Geographical information systems

The Bullitt Foundation
Compton Foundation, Inc.
The Greenville Foundation
National Fish and Wildlife Foundation
The David and Lucile Packard Foundation
The Pew Charitable Trusts

Global warming

BankAmerica Foundation
The William Bingham Foundation
Changing Horizons Charitable Trust
Conservation, Food & Health Foundation, Inc.
Foundation for Deep Ecology
The German Marshall Fund of the United States
Mars Foundation
The John Merck Fund
Charles Stewart Mott Foundation
The Curtis and Edith Munson Foundation, Inc.
The William Penn Foundation
Public Welfare Foundation, Inc.
Threshold Foundation
The Tides Foundation
Mark and Catherine Winkler Foundation

Grassroots/citizens organizations

The Acorn Foundation
Alaska Conservation Foundation
The Jenifer Altman Foundation
Angelina Fund, Inc.
Mary Reynolds Babcock Foundation, Inc.
Beldon Fund
The Ben & Jerry's Foundation
The Blumenthal Foundation
The Bullitt Foundation
Changing Horizons Charitable Trust
Liz Claiborne & Art Ortenberg Foundation
The Conservation and Research Foundation
The Mary A. Crocker Trust
Crystal Channel Foundation
The Nathan Cummings Foundation
Damien Foundation
Deer Creek Foundation
The Elizabeth Ordway Dunn Foundation, Inc.
The Educational Foundation of America
The Field Foundation of Illinois, Inc.
Fields Pond Foundation, Inc.
Foundation for Deep Ecology

Fund of the Four Directions
The Gap Foundation
The Fred Gellert Foundation
General Service Foundation
Give to the Earth Foundation
Global Environmental Project Institute
Global Greengrants Fund
The Goldman Environmental Foundation
Richard & Rhoda Goldman Fund
Great Lakes Protection Fund
The George Gund Foundation
HKH Foundation
Island Foundation, Inc.
W. Alton Jones Foundation, Inc.
The J. M. Kaplan Fund, Inc.
The Lazar Foundation
The Max and Anna Levinson Foundation
Lyndhurst Foundation
The John D. and Catherine T. MacArthur Foundation
MARPAT Foundation, Inc.
The Martin Foundation, Inc.
McKenzie River Gathering Foundation
The McKnight Foundation
The John Merck Fund
The Moriah Fund, Inc.
Charles Stewart Mott Foundation
The Curtis and Edith Munson Foundation, Inc.
National Fish and Wildlife Foundation
The Needmor Fund
Norcross Wildlife Foundation, Inc.
Jessie Smith Noyes Foundation, Inc.
Outdoor Industry Conservation Alliance
Patagonia, Inc.
Pew Scholars Program in Conservation and the Environment
The Pfizer Foundation, Inc.
The Prospect Hill Foundation
Public Welfare Foundation, Inc.
Recreational Equipment, Inc.
Z. Smith Reynolds Foundation, Inc.
The Winthrop Rockefeller Foundation
Rockwood Fund, Inc.
The Florence and John Schumann Foundation
Stern Family Fund
Surdna Foundation, Inc.
The Switzer Foundation
Threshold Foundation
Unitarian Universalist Veatch Program at Shelter Rock
Virginia Environmental Endowment
WMX Environmental Grants Program

Green products

Columbia Foundation
Compton Foundation, Inc.
The Mary A. Crocker Trust
The Nathan Cummings Foundation
Environment Now Foundation
The Fred Gellert Foundation
The Moriah Fund, Inc.
The New-Land Foundation, Inc.
Northwest Area Foundation

Environmental Topics and Activities

Green products (cont.)

The Pew Charitable Trusts
Schultz Foundation, Inc.
Surdna Foundation, Inc.
Threshold Foundation
The Tides Foundation

Greenways

ARCO Foundation
The Abell Foundation
Winifred & Harry B. Allen Foundation
BankAmerica Foundation
Beneficia Foundation
The Frank Stanley Beveridge Foundation, Inc.
Alex. Brown & Sons Charitable Foundation, Inc.
Kathleen Price and Joseph M. Bryan Family Foundation, Inc.
The Bunbury Company, Inc.
The Carpenter Foundation
Columbia Foundation
The Community Foundation of Santa Clara County
Compton Foundation, Inc.
Davis Conservation Foundation
Geraldine R. Dodge Foundation, Inc.
The Elizabeth Ordway Dunn Foundation, Inc.
El Pomar Foundation
The Fund for New Jersey
The Fund for Preservation of Wildlife and Natural Areas
The Gap Foundation
The Fred Gellert Foundation
The Wallace Alexander Gerbode Foundation, Inc.
Richard & Rhoda Goldman Fund
Good Samaritan, Inc.
Walter and Elise Haas Fund
Heller Charitable & Educational Fund
The William and Flora Hewlett Foundation
Howfirma Foundation
Hurdle Hill Foundation
The Hyams Foundation
Lyndhurst Foundation
The John D. and Catherine T. MacArthur Foundation
Maine Community Foundation, Inc.
MARPAT Foundation, Inc.
Giles W. and Elise G. Mead Foundation
Richard King Mellon Foundation
The Curtis and Edith Munson Foundation, Inc.
National Fish and Wildlife Foundation
New Hampshire Charitable Foundation
The David and Lucile Packard Foundation
Peninsula Community Foundation
The William Penn Foundation
Ellis L. Phillips Foundation
Z. Smith Reynolds Foundation, Inc.
The Rockfall Foundation
The San Francisco Foundation

The Strong Foundation for Environmental Values
Surdna Foundation, Inc.
Threshold Foundation
The Tides Foundation
True North Foundation
The Trust For Mutual Understanding
Vancouver Foundation
Victoria Foundation, Inc.
Virginia Environmental Endowment
Weeden Foundation
Weyerhaeuser Company Foundation
The William P. Wharton Trust
The Wyomissing Foundation, Inc.

Growth management

The Abell Foundation
Mary Reynolds Babcock Foundation, Inc.
The Betterment Fund
The Bullitt Foundation
The Fred Gellert Foundation
The Henry M. Jackson Foundation
The J. M. Kaplan Fund, Inc.
Lyndhurst Foundation
Richard King Mellon Foundation
The Curtis and Edith Munson Foundation, Inc.
New Hampshire Charitable Foundation
Northwest Area Foundation
The David and Lucile Packard Foundation
Rockefeller Family Fund, Inc.
Virginia Environmental Endowment
Weeden Foundation

Habitats

ARCO Foundation
Alaska Conservation Foundation
Americana Foundation, Inc.
The George F. Baker Trust
BankAmerica Foundation
S. D. Bechtel, Jr. Foundation
The Beinecke Foundation, Inc.
Benua Foundation, Inc.
The Frank Stanley Beveridge Foundation, Inc.
The Bothin Foundation
The Buchanan Family Foundation
The Bullitt Foundation
The Cargill Foundation
Mary Flagler Cary Charitable Trust
Chesapeake Bay Trust
The Chevron Companies
The Chicago Community Trust
Compton Foundation, Inc.
The James M. Cox, Jr. Foundation, Inc.
The Nathan Cummings Foundation
Geraldine R. Dodge Foundation, Inc.
Gaylord and Dorothy Donnelley Foundation
The Elizabeth Ordway Dunn Foundation, Inc.
Ederic Foundation, Inc.
The Educational Foundation of America
Fair Play Foundation

Fanwood Foundation
The Favrot Fund
FishAmerica Foundation
Flintridge Foundation
Ford Motor Company Fund
Foundation for Deep Ecology
Foundation for Field Research
The Gap Foundation
The Fred Gellert Foundation
General Service Foundation
The Wallace Alexander Gerbode Foundation, Inc.
Give to the Earth Foundation
The Greenville Foundation
Harder Foundation
The William and Flora Hewlett Foundation
The Hofmann Foundation
The Homeland Foundation
The Roy A. Hunt Foundation
The Richard Ivey Foundation
W. Alton Jones Foundation, Inc.
The J. M. Kaplan Fund, Inc.
The Knapp Foundation, Inc.
The Seymour H. Knox Foundation, Inc.
Kongsgaard-Goldman Foundation
The Kresge Foundation
Laidlaw Foundation
Lyndhurst Foundation
The John D. and Catherine T. MacArthur Foundation
Marin Community Foundation
Mars Foundation
McDonnell Douglas Foundation
The McKnight Foundation
McLean Contributionship
Richard King Mellon Foundation
The Mountaineers Foundation
The Curtis and Edith Munson Foundation, Inc.
National Fish and Wildlife Foundation
Norcross Wildlife Foundation, Inc.
Northwest Fund for the Environment
The Ohrstrom Foundation
Orchard Foundation
Outdoor Industry Conservation Alliance
The David and Lucile Packard Foundation
Patagonia, Inc.
Phillips Petroleum Foundation, Inc.
The Rhode Island Community Foundation
The Roberts Foundation
The San Francisco Foundation
The Schiff Foundation
Schultz Foundation, Inc.
Sequoia Foundation
Shell Oil Company Foundation
The Sudbury Foundation
Surdna Foundation, Inc.
The Switzer Foundation
Nelson Talbott Foundation
The Tinker Foundation Incorporated
True North Foundation
The Trust For Mutual Understanding
Turner Foundation, Inc.
Underhill Foundation

© 1995 Environmental Data Resources, Inc.

Environmental Topics and Activities

Habitats (cont.)

Union Camp Charitable Trust
Vancouver Foundation
Virginia Environmental Endowment
WMX Environmental Grants Program
C. A. Webster Foundation
Weeden Foundation
Henry E. and Consuelo S. Wenger Foundation, Inc.
Weyerhaeuser Company Foundation
The William P. Wharton Trust
Whitecap Foundation
Wilburforce Foundation
The Dean Witter Foundation
Margaret Cullinan Wray Charitable Lead Annuity Trust

Historic preservation

The Buchanan Family Foundation
The Educational Foundation of America
Jackson Hole Preserve, Inc.
The J. M. Kaplan Fund, Inc.
MARPAT Foundation, Inc.
McLean Contributionship
Meadows Foundation, Inc.
Norman Foundation
The San Francisco Foundation

Horticulture

Winifred & Harry B. Allen Foundation
American Foundation Corporation
Elmer L. & Eleanor J. Andersen Foundation
BankAmerica Foundation
The Theodore H. Barth Foundation, Inc.
Bay Area Community Foundation
S. D. Bechtel, Jr. Foundation
The Beinecke Foundation, Inc.
Alexander H. Bright Charitable Trust
The Buchanan Family Foundation
The Chicago Community Trust
Claneil Foundation, Inc.
The Cowles Charitable Trust
The Fred Harris Daniels Foundation, Inc.
Cleveland H. Dodge Foundation, Inc.
Dolfinger-McMahon Foundation
Gaylord and Dorothy Donnelley Foundation
Jessie Ball duPont Religious, Charitable and Educational Fund
Lloyd A. Fry Foundation
The GAR Foundation
Herman Goldman Foundation
Mary W. Harriman Foundation
Ireland Foundation
The J. M. Kaplan Fund, Inc.
The Kresge Foundation
Laird, Norton Foundation
Longwood Foundation, Inc.
Richard Lounsbery Foundation, Inc.
The John D. and Catherine T. MacArthur Foundation
Nelson Mead Fund
Meyer Memorial Trust
Middlecott Foundation

The New York Times Company Foundation, Inc.
Norcross Wildlife Foundation, Inc.
Amelia Peabody Charitable Fund
The William Penn Foundation
The Pew Charitable Trusts
The Pfizer Foundation, Inc.
The Procter & Gamble Fund
The Prospect Hill Foundation
The Prudential Foundation
Sears-Swetland Foundation
The Kelvin and Eleanor Smith Foundation
Stanley Smith Horticultural Trust
Snee-Reinhardt Charitable Foundation
Southwestern Bell Foundation
Steelcase Foundation
Stoddard Charitable Trust
The Stratford Foundation
Margaret Dorrance Strawbridge Foundation of Pennsylvania II, Inc.
The Sulzberger Foundation, Inc.
Threshold Foundation
The Truland Foundation
Rose E. Tucker Charitable Trust
Vancouver Foundation

Human rights

The Jenifer Altman Foundation
Angelina Fund, Inc.
The Arca Foundation
The Ben & Jerry's Foundation
The Nathan Cummings Foundation
The Max and Anna Levinson Foundation
Norman Foundation
Rockwood Fund, Inc.
Seventh Generation Fund
Threshold Foundation

Hunting

S. D. Bechtel, Jr. Foundation
The Beinecke Foundation, Inc.
The Curtis and Edith Munson Foundation, Inc.
Patagonia, Inc.
The Summerlee Foundation
Weyerhaeuser Company Foundation

Indigenous peoples

Alaska Conservation Foundation
American Conservation Association, Inc.
Angelina Fund, Inc.
Beldon Fund
The Bullitt Foundation
Damien Foundation
Geraldine R. Dodge Foundation, Inc.
Echoing Green Foundation
Ford Foundation
Foundation for Deep Ecology
Fund of the Four Directions
Funding Exchange
General Service Foundation
The Wallace Alexander Gerbode Foundation, Inc.

Give to the Earth Foundation
Walter and Duncan Gordon Charitable Foundation
Harbor Lights Foundation
Howfirma Foundation
The Esther A. and Joseph Klingenstein Fund, Inc.
Laidlaw Foundation
The Max and Anna Levinson Foundation
The John D. and Catherine T. MacArthur Foundation
The Moriah Fund, Inc.
Norman Foundation
Jessie Smith Noyes Foundation, Inc.
Patagonia, Inc.
Amelia Peabody Charitable Fund
The Pew Charitable Trusts
Public Welfare Foundation, Inc.
Rockefeller Brothers Fund, Inc.
The Rockefeller Foundation
Seventh Generation Fund
Threshold Foundation
The Tides Foundation
Underhill Foundation
Unitarian Universalist Veatch Program at Shelter Rock
Vancouver Foundation
Vanguard Public Foundation

Industry

A Territory Resource
The Abelard Foundation West
The Bauman Foundation
Beldon Fund
The Bullitt Foundation
Chesapeake Bay Trust
Robert Sterling Clark Foundation, Inc.
Columbia Foundation
Jessie B. Cox Charitable Trust
Geraldine R. Dodge Foundation, Inc.
The Educational Foundation of America
The Energy Foundation
Ford Foundation
The Fund for New Jersey
The Clarence E. Heller Charitable Foundation
W. Alton Jones Foundation, Inc.
The Joyce Foundation
Laird, Norton Foundation
The McKnight Foundation
Richard King Mellon Foundation
The John Merck Fund
The Moriah Fund, Inc.
Charles Stewart Mott Foundation
National Fish and Wildlife Foundation
Jessie Smith Noyes Foundation, Inc.
Patagonia, Inc.
James C. Penney Foundation
The Pew Charitable Trusts
Public Welfare Foundation, Inc.
The Winthrop Rockefeller Foundation
Surdna Foundation, Inc.
Threshold Foundation

Environmental Topics and Activities

Industry (cont.)

Unitarian Universalist Veatch Program
　at Shelter Rock
Virginia Environmental Endowment
Weyerhaeuser Company Foundation

Internships

Alaska Conservation Foundation
American Conservation Association, Inc.
Otto Bremer Foundation
Kathleen Price and Joseph M. Bryan
　Family Foundation, Inc.
Chrysler Corporation Fund
The Collins Foundation
Conservation, Food & Health
　Foundation, Inc.
The Nathan Cummings Foundation
Davis Conservation Foundation
Ford Foundation
Ford Motor Company Fund
Fund of the Four Directions
The German Marshall Fund of
　the United States
The George Gund Foundation
The Joyce Foundation
W. K. Kellogg Foundation
Laird, Norton Foundation
Maki Foundation
MARPAT Foundation, Inc.
Charles Stewart Mott Foundation
The Curtis and Edith Munson
　Foundation, Inc.
National Fish and Wildlife Foundation
Edward John Noble Foundation, Inc.
The Pew Charitable Trusts
Pew Scholars Program in Conservation
　and the Environment
The San Francisco Foundation
The Strong Foundation for
　Environmental Values
Edna Bailey Sussman Fund
Nelson Talbott Foundation
Town Creek Foundation, Inc.
The Trust For Mutual Understanding
Rose E. Tucker Charitable Trust
Victoria Foundation, Inc.
WMX Environmental Grants Program
Wilburforce Foundation
Margaret Cullinan Wray Charitable
　Lead Annuity Trust

Inventories

Liz Claiborne & Art Ortenberg Foundation
Conservation, Food & Health
　Foundation, Inc.
The Educational Foundation of America
The Fund for New Jersey
W. K. Kellogg Foundation
The Max and Anna Levinson Foundation
The John D. and Catherine T. MacArthur
　Foundation
Maki Foundation
National Fish and Wildlife Foundation
The Sudbury Foundation

The William P. Wharton Trust
Margaret Cullinan Wray Charitable
　Lead Annuity Trust

Islands

Atherton Family Foundation
Mary Reynolds Babcock Foundation, Inc.
Beldon Fund
The Bullitt Foundation
Mary Flagler Cary Charitable Trust
Chesapeake Bay Trust
The Conservation and Research Foundation
Conservation, Food & Health
　Foundation, Inc.
Cooke Foundation, Limited
The Arthur Vining Davis Foundations
Davis Conservation Foundation
Fair Play Foundation
Foundation for Deep Ecology
Foundation for Field Research
Mary D. and Walter F. Frear
　Eleemosynary Trust
The Wallace Alexander Gerbode
　Foundation, Inc.
The Goldman Environmental Foundation
Hawaii Community Foundation
The Hyams Foundation
The John D. and Catherine T. MacArthur
　Foundation
McInerny Foundation
Richard King Mellon Foundation
The Moriah Fund, Inc.
The Curtis and Edith Munson
　Foundation, Inc.
National Fish and Wildlife Foundation
New Hampshire Charitable Foundation
The New York Times Company
　Foundation, Inc.
Edward John Noble Foundation, Inc.
Norcross Wildlife Foundation, Inc.
Norman Foundation
Patagonia, Inc.
James C. Penney Foundation
Prince Charitable Trusts
Public Welfare Foundation, Inc.
The Rockefeller Foundation
Texaco Foundation
Threshold Foundation
Unitarian Universalist Veatch Program
　at Shelter Rock
The William P. Wharton Trust
Wilburforce Foundation

Islands: barrier

Beldon Fund
Mary Flagler Cary Charitable Trust

Job training

California Community Foundation
The Mary A. Crocker Trust
The Greenville Foundation
Laird, Norton Foundation
The John D. and Catherine T. MacArthur
　Foundation

McInerny Foundation
Merck Family Fund
The Moriah Fund, Inc.
The Needmor Fund
Threshold Foundation
Margaret Cullinan Wray Charitable
　Lead Annuity Trust

Journalism

The Bauman Foundation
The Bullitt Foundation
The Chevron Companies
Ford Foundation
Foundation for Deep Ecology
The Fred Gellert Foundation
The German Marshall Fund of
　the United States
The George Gund Foundation
Charles Stewart Mott Foundation
The Florence and John Schumann
　Foundation
The Strong Foundation for
　Environmental Values
Threshold Foundation
The Tides Foundation
The Tinker Foundation Incorporated
Town Creek Foundation, Inc.
Weyerhaeuser Company Foundation

Laboratory: testing/analysis

BankAmerica Foundation
The Ben & Jerry's Foundation
Chesapeake Bay Trust
Jessie B. Cox Charitable Trust
The Max and Anna Levinson Foundation
Meadows Foundation, Inc.
Charles Stewart Mott Foundation
National Fish and Wildlife Foundation
The New York Times Company
　Foundation, Inc.
Threshold Foundation
The William P. Wharton Trust

Lakes

Atkinson Foundation
The Ben & Jerry's Foundation
Blandin Foundation
The Bullitt Foundation
California Community Foundation
The Chicago Community Trust
Compton Foundation, Inc.
Adolph Coors Foundation
Patrick and Anna M. Cudahy Fund
Davis Conservation Foundation
Gaylord and Dorothy Donnelley Foundation
Eastman Kodak Company Charitable Trust
FishAmerica Foundation
The Foundation for the National
　Capital Region
Gebbie Foundation, Inc.
Great Lakes Protection Fund
The George Gund Foundation
The Hahn Family Foundation
The Homeland Foundation

Environmental Topics and Activities

Lakes (cont.)

W. Alton Jones Foundation, Inc.
The Joyce Foundation
W. K. Kellogg Foundation
Laidlaw Foundation
Lintilhac Foundation
The John D. and Catherine T. MacArthur Foundation
The McKnight Foundation
The Milwaukee Foundation
Charles Stewart Mott Foundation
Ruth Mott Fund
National Fish and Wildlife Foundation
New Hampshire Charitable Foundation
The New York Times Company Foundation, Inc.
The Pew Charitable Trusts
The Rockfall Foundation
Steelcase Foundation
The Trust For Mutual Understanding
Weeden Foundation
Weyerhaeuser Company Foundation

Lakes: preservation

The Lynde and Harry Bradley Foundation, Inc.
The Chevron Companies
The Community Foundation of Santa Clara County
Richard & Rhoda Goldman Fund
The John D. and Catherine T. MacArthur Foundation
The McKnight Foundation
Charles Stewart Mott Foundation
Norcross Wildlife Foundation, Inc.
The Strong Foundation for Environmental Values

Land acquisition

ARCO Foundation
Alaska Conservation Foundation
Winifred & Harry B. Allen Foundation
American Conservation Association, Inc.
American Foundation Corporation
Evenor Armington Fund
The Austin Memorial Foundation
The George F. Baker Trust
BankAmerica Foundation
The Barra Foundation, Inc.
The Howard Bayne Fund
The Beinecke Foundation, Inc.
The Beirne Carter Foundation
David Winton Bell Foundation
James Ford Bell Foundation
The Ben & Jerry's Foundation
Beneficia Foundation
Benua Foundation, Inc.
The Bersted Foundation
The Betterment Fund
The Frank Stanley Beveridge Foundation, Inc.
Bishop Pine Fund
The Blumenthal Foundation
Boettcher Foundation

Mary Owen Borden Memorial Foundation
Alexander H. Bright Charitable Trust
H. Barksdale Brown Charitable Trust
Ruth H. Brown Foundation
Kathleen Price and Joseph M. Bryan Family Foundation, Inc.
The Buchanan Family Foundation
The Bunbury Company, Inc.
The Bush Foundation
The Butler Foundation
California Community Foundation
James & Abigail Campbell Foundation
The Cargill Foundation
Carolyn Foundation
Mary Flagler Cary Charitable Trust
The Champlin Foundations
Cheeryble Foundation
Ben B. Cheney Foundation
Chesapeake Corporation Foundation
The Chevron Companies
Claneil Foundation, Inc.
Olive B. Cole Foundation
The Columbus Foundation
The Community Foundation of Santa Clara County
The Community Foundation Serving Coastal South Carolina
Compton Foundation, Inc.
The Conservation and Research Foundation
Conservation, Food & Health Foundation, Inc.
The Cowles Charitable Trust
Cox Foundation, Inc.
The James M. Cox, Jr. Foundation, Inc.
The Arthur Vining Davis Foundations
Davis Conservation Foundation
Cleveland H. Dodge Foundation, Inc.
Oliver S. and Jennie R. Donaldson Charitable Trust
Gaylord and Dorothy Donnelley Foundation
The Dragon Foundation, Inc.
The Max and Victoria Dreyfus Foundation, Inc.
Eastman Kodak Company Charitable Trust
Echoing Green Foundation
The Educational Foundation of America
El Pomar Foundation
The Emerald Foundation
The Charles Engelhard Foundation
English-Bonter-Mitchell Foundation
Environment Now Foundation
The Armand G. Erpf Fund, Inc.
Fanwood Foundation
Fields Pond Foundation, Inc.
Flintridge Foundation
Ford Motor Company Fund
The Foundation for the National Capital Region
The Fund for New Jersey
Fund of the Four Directions
Funding Exchange
Georgia Power Foundation, Inc.
Georgia-Pacific Foundation
Bernard F. and Alva B. Gimbel Foundation, Inc.

Richard & Rhoda Goldman Fund
The W. C. Griffith Foundation
The George Gund Foundation
The Hahn Family Foundation
The Ewing Halsell Foundation
The Hamer Foundation
The Harding Educational and Charitable Foundation
Mary W. Harriman Foundation
The Hastings Trust
The Merrill G. & Emita E. Hastings Foundation
Hawaii Community Foundation
Hawaiian Electric Industries Charitable Foundation
The Hofmann Foundation
The Homeland Foundation
The Horn Foundation
Howfirma Foundation
The Charles Evans Hughes Memorial Foundation, Inc.
Hurdle Hill Foundation
Ireland Foundation
The Jackson Foundation
Jackson Hole Preserve, Inc.
The Henry M. Jackson Foundation
The Howard Johnson Foundation
The J. M. Kaplan Fund, Inc.
W. K. Kellogg Foundation
The Robert S. and Grayce B. Kerr Foundation, Inc.
F. M. Kirby Foundation, Inc.
The Knapp Foundation, Inc.
The Seymour H. Knox Foundation, Inc.
The Kresge Foundation
Laird, Norton Foundation
Lintilhac Foundation
The Little Family Foundation
Longwood Foundation, Inc.
Lyndhurst Foundation
The John D. and Catherine T. MacArthur Foundation
James A. Macdonald Foundation
Maki Foundation
Marin Community Foundation
MARPAT Foundation, Inc.
Mars Foundation
McDonnell Douglas Foundation
McInerny Foundation
McLean Contributionship
Nelson Mead Fund
Richard King Mellon Foundation
The John Merck Fund
Metropolitan Life Foundation
Middlecott Foundation
The Milwaukee Foundation
The Minneapolis Foundation
Mobil Foundation, Inc.
Leo Model Foundation, Inc.
J. P. Morgan Charitable Trust
The Moriah Fund, Inc.
Charles Stewart Mott Foundation
The Mountaineers Foundation
The Curtis and Edith Munson Foundation, Inc.

Environmental Topics and Activities

Land acquisition (cont.)

National Fish and Wildlife Foundation
The Needmor Fund
New Hampshire Charitable Foundation
The New York Community Trust
The New York Times Company Foundation, Inc.
The New-Land Foundation, Inc.
Norcross Wildlife Foundation, Inc.
Norman Foundation
Northwest Fund for the Environment
Nicholas H. Noyes, Jr. Memorial Foundation
OCRI Foundation
The Ohrstrom Foundation
Spencer T. and Ann W. Olin Foundation
The Overbrook Foundation
The David and Lucile Packard Foundation
Patagonia, Inc.
Amelia Peabody Charitable Fund
Peninsula Community Foundation
The William Penn Foundation
Perkins Charitable Foundation
The Pfizer Foundation, Inc.
The Philadelphia Foundation
Phillips Petroleum Foundation, Inc.
Pinewood Foundation
Lynn R. and Karl E. Prickett Fund
The Procter & Gamble Fund
Recreational Equipment, Inc.
Philip D. Reed Foundation, Inc.
Z. Smith Reynolds Foundation, Inc.
The Rhode Island Community Foundation
The Winthrop Rockefeller Foundation
Fran and Warren Rupp Foundation
San Diego Community Foundation
The San Francisco Foundation
Sarah I. Schieffelin Residuary Trust
The Schiff Foundation
Schultz Foundation, Inc.
Seventh Generation Fund
Elmina B. Sewall Foundation
Shell Oil Company Foundation
The Skaggs Foundation
Southwestern Bell Foundation
Springs Foundation, Inc.
The Stebbins Fund, Inc.
The Stratford Foundation
The Stroh Foundation
The Strong Foundation for Environmental Values
The Sulzberger Foundation, Inc.
Nelson Talbott Foundation
Texaco Foundation
Thanksgiving Foundation
The Oakleigh L. Thorne Foundation
Threshold Foundation
The Tides Foundation
Tortuga Foundation
Treacy Foundation, Inc.
Rose E. Tucker Charitable Trust
Turner Foundation, Inc.
Union Camp Charitable Trust
Unitarian Universalist Veatch Program at Shelter Rock

Victoria Foundation, Inc.
The Vidda Foundation
WMX Environmental Grants Program
Alex C. Walker Educational & Charitable Foundation
C. A. Webster Foundation
Weeden Foundation
Henry E. and Consuelo S. Wenger Foundation, Inc.
Westinghouse Foundation
Weyerhaeuser Company Foundation
The William P. Wharton Trust
Whitecap Foundation
Wilburforce Foundation
G. N. Wilcox Trust
Robert W. Wilson Foundation
The Winston-Salem Foundation, Inc.
The Dean Witter Foundation
Wodecroft Foundation
Sidney & Phyllis Wragge Foundation
Margaret Cullinan Wray Charitable Lead Annuity Trust

Land conservation

ARCO Foundation
The Abell Foundation
The Acorn Foundation
The Ahmanson Foundation
Alaska Conservation Foundation
Winifred & Harry B. Allen Foundation
American Conservation Association, Inc.
American Foundation Corporation
Evenor Armington Fund
The Austin Memorial Foundation
The George F. Baker Trust
BankAmerica Foundation
The Barra Foundation, Inc.
The Howard Bayne Fund
S. D. Bechtel, Jr. Foundation
The Beinecke Foundation, Inc.
The Beirne Carter Foundation
David Winton Bell Foundation
James Ford Bell Foundation
The Ben & Jerry's Foundation
Beneficia Foundation
Benua Foundation, Inc.
The Bersted Foundation
The Betterment Fund
The Frank Stanley Beveridge Foundation, Inc.
Bishop Pine Fund
The Blumenthal Foundation
The Boeing Company
Boettcher Foundation
Mary Owen Borden Memorial Foundation
Otto Bremer Foundation
Alexander H. Bright Charitable Trust
H. Barksdale Brown Charitable Trust
Ruth H. Brown Foundation
W. L. Lyons Brown Foundation
Kathleen Price and Joseph M. Bryan Family Foundation, Inc.
The Buchanan Family Foundation
The Bullitt Foundation
The Bunbury Company, Inc.

The Bush Foundation
The Butler Foundation
Patrick and Aimee Butler Family Foundation
The Cabot Family Charitable Trust
California Community Foundation
James & Abigail Campbell Foundation
The Cargill Foundation
Carolyn Foundation
The Carpenter Foundation
Mary Flagler Cary Charitable Trust
The Champlin Foundations
Cheeryble Foundation
Chesapeake Corporation Foundation
The Chevron Companies
Liz Claiborne & Art Ortenberg Foundation
Claneil Foundation, Inc.
The Clark Foundation
Olive B. Cole Foundation
The Columbus Foundation
The Community Foundation of Santa Clara County
The Community Foundation Serving Coastal South Carolina
Compton Foundation, Inc.
The Conservation and Research Foundation
The Cowles Charitable Trust
Cox Foundation, Inc.
The James M. Cox, Jr. Foundation, Inc.
Jessie B. Cox Charitable Trust
The Cricket Foundation
The Mary A. Crocker Trust
Patrick and Anna M. Cudahy Fund
The Nathan Cummings Foundation
The Fred Harris Daniels Foundation, Inc.
The Arthur Vining Davis Foundations
Davis Conservation Foundation
Cleveland H. Dodge Foundation, Inc.
Geraldine R. Dodge Foundation, Inc.
Dolfinger-McMahon Foundation
Oliver S. and Jennie R. Donaldson Charitable Trust
Gaylord and Dorothy Donnelley Foundation
The Dragon Foundation, Inc.
The Max and Victoria Dreyfus Foundation, Inc.
Eastman Kodak Company Charitable Trust
Echoing Green Foundation
Ederic Foundation, Inc.
The Educational Foundation of America
El Pomar Foundation
The Emerald Foundation
The Charles Engelhard Foundation
English-Bonter-Mitchell Foundation
Environment Now Foundation
Environmental Endowment for New Jersey, Inc.
The Armand G. Erpf Fund, Inc.
Fanwood Foundation
The Favrot Fund
Jamee and Marshall Field Foundation
Fields Pond Foundation, Inc.
Flintridge Foundation
Ford Motor Company Fund
Foundation for Deep Ecology

© 1995 Environmental Data Resources, Inc.

Environmental Topics and Activities

Land conservation (cont.)

The Foundation for the National Capital Region
The Freed Foundation, Inc.
Frelinghuysen Foundation
Lloyd A. Fry Foundation
Fund of the Four Directions
Funding Exchange
The Gap Foundation
The Fred Gellert Foundation
General Service Foundation
Georgia Power Foundation, Inc.
Georgia-Pacific Foundation
The German Marshall Fund of the United States
Bernard F. and Alva B. Gimbel Foundation, Inc.
The Goldman Environmental Foundation
Richard & Rhoda Goldman Fund
Greater Piscataqua Community Foundation
The Greenville Foundation
The William and Mary Greve Foundation, Inc.
The W. C. Griffith Foundation
The George Gund Foundation
Walter and Elise Haas Fund
The Hahn Family Foundation
The Hamer Foundation
Harbor Lights Foundation
Harder Foundation
The Harding Educational and Charitable Foundation
Gladys and Roland Harriman Foundation
Mary W. Harriman Foundation
The Hastings Trust
The Merrill G. & Emita E. Hastings Foundation
Hawaii Community Foundation
Hawaiian Electric Industries Charitable Foundation
Heller Charitable & Educational Fund
The William and Flora Hewlett Foundation
The Homeland Foundation
The Horn Foundation
Howfirma Foundation
The Charles Evans Hughes Memorial Foundation, Inc.
The Roy A. Hunt Foundation
Hurdle Hill Foundation
The Hyams Foundation
The Hyde and Watson Foundation
The Indian Point Foundation, Inc.
The Louise H. and David S. Ingalls Foundation, Inc.
Ireland Foundation
Island Foundation, Inc.
Ittleson Foundation, Inc.
The Richard Ivey Foundation
The Jackson Foundation
Jackson Hole Preserve, Inc.
The Henry M. Jackson Foundation
The George Frederick Jewett Foundation
The Howard Johnson Foundation
W. Alton Jones Foundation, Inc.

The J. M. Kaplan Fund, Inc.
W. K. Kellogg Foundation
The Henry P. Kendall Foundation
The Robert S. and Grayce B. Kerr Foundation, Inc.
F. M. Kirby Foundation, Inc.
The Esther A. and Joseph Klingenstein Fund, Inc.
The Knapp Foundation, Inc.
The Seymour H. Knox Foundation, Inc.
The Kresge Foundation
Laird, Norton Foundation
Larsen Fund, Inc.
The Lauder Foundation, Inc.
Laurel Foundation
The Lazar Foundation
The Max and Anna Levinson Foundation
LifeWorks Foundation
Lintilhac Foundation
The Little Family Foundation
Longwood Foundation, Inc.
Lyndhurst Foundation
James A. Macdonald Foundation
Maki Foundation
Marbrook Foundation
Marin Community Foundation
MARPAT Foundation, Inc.
Mars Foundation
The Marshall Fund of Arizona
The Marshall L. & Perrine D. McCune Charitable Foundation
McDonnell Douglas Foundation
McInerny Foundation
The McIntosh Foundation
McLean Contributionship
Giles W. and Elise G. Mead Foundation
Nelson Mead Fund
Meadows Foundation, Inc.
Richard King Mellon Foundation
Metropolitan Atlanta Community Foundation, Inc.
Metropolitan Life Foundation
Middlecott Foundation
Millbrook Tribute Garden, Inc.
The Milwaukee Foundation
The Minneapolis Foundation
Mobil Foundation, Inc.
Leo Model Foundation, Inc.
J. P. Morgan Charitable Trust
The Moriah Fund, Inc.
Charles Stewart Mott Foundation
The Curtis and Edith Munson Foundation, Inc.
The National Environmental Education and Training Foundation, Inc.
National Fish and Wildlife Foundation
The Needmor Fund
New Hampshire Charitable Foundation
The New York Community Trust
The New York Times Company Foundation, Inc.
The New-Land Foundation, Inc.
Norcross Wildlife Foundation, Inc.
Norman Foundation

Mary Moody Northen, Inc.
Nicholas H. Noyes, Jr. Memorial Foundation
OCRI Foundation
The Ohrstrom Foundation
Spencer T. and Ann W. Olin Foundation
Outdoor Industry Conservation Alliance
The Overbrook Foundation
The David and Lucile Packard Foundation
Patagonia, Inc.
Amelia Peabody Charitable Fund
Peninsula Community Foundation
The William Penn Foundation
Perkins Charitable Foundation
The Pew Charitable Trusts
Pew Scholars Program in Conservation and the Environment
The Pfizer Foundation, Inc.
The Philadelphia Foundation
Phillips Petroleum Foundation, Inc.
Ellis L. Phillips Foundation
Pinewood Foundation
Lynn R. and Karl E. Prickett Fund
Prince Charitable Trusts
The Procter & Gamble Fund
The Prospect Hill Foundation
Public Welfare Foundation, Inc.
Recreational Equipment, Inc.
Philip D. Reed Foundation, Inc.
Z. Smith Reynolds Foundation, Inc.
The Rhode Island Community Foundation
Rockefeller Brothers Fund, Inc.
The Rockefeller Foundation
Lee Romney Foundation, Inc.
Fran and Warren Rupp Foundation
Sacharuna Foundation
The San Francisco Foundation
Sarkeys Foundation
The Scherman Foundation, Inc.
Sarah I. Schieffelin Residuary Trust
The Schiff Foundation
Schultz Foundation, Inc.
The Schumann Fund for New Jersey, Inc.
The Florence and John Schumann Foundation
Sequoia Foundation
Seventh Generation Fund
Elmina B. Sewall Foundation
Shell Oil Company Foundation
The Skaggs Foundation
The Kelvin and Eleanor Smith Foundation
Snee-Reinhardt Charitable Foundation
Southwestern Bell Foundation
Springhouse Foundation
Sproul Foundation
The Stebbins Fund, Inc.
The Stratford Foundation
Margaret Dorrance Strawbridge Foundation of Pennsylvania II, Inc.
The Stroh Foundation
The Strong Foundation for Environmental Values
The Charles J. Strosacker Foundation
Stroud Foundation

752

© 1995 Environmental Data Resources, Inc.

Environmental Topics and Activities

Land conservation (cont.)

The Sudbury Foundation
The Sulzberger Foundation, Inc.
Edna Bailey Sussman Fund
Nelson Talbott Foundation
Texaco Foundation
Thanksgiving Foundation
The Oakleigh L. Thorne Foundation
Threshold Foundation
The Tides Foundation
Times Mirror Magazines, Inc.
The Tinker Foundation Incorporated
Tortuga Foundation
Town Creek Foundation, Inc.
Treacy Foundation, Inc.
The Truland Foundation
Marcia Brady Tucker Foundation
Rose E. Tucker Charitable Trust
Turner Foundation, Inc.
Union Camp Charitable Trust
Union Pacific Foundation
Unitarian Universalist Veatch Program
 at Shelter Rock
Vancouver Foundation
Victoria Foundation, Inc.
The Vidda Foundation
Virginia Environmental Endowment
WMX Environmental Grants Program
Alex C. Walker Educational & Charitable
 Foundation
Wallace Genetic Foundation, Inc.
C. A. Webster Foundation
Weeden Foundation
Henry E. and Consuelo S. Wenger
 Foundation, Inc.
Westinghouse Foundation
Weyerhaeuser Company Foundation
The William P. Wharton Trust
Whitecap Foundation
Wilburforce Foundation
G. N. Wilcox Trust
Robert W. Wilson Foundation
The Winslow Foundation
The Winston-Salem Foundation, Inc.
The Dean Witter Foundation
Wodecroft Foundation
Sidney & Phyllis Wragge Foundation
Margaret Cullinan Wray Charitable
 Lead Annuity Trust
The Wyomissing Foundation, Inc.

Land development

Norman Foundation
The William Penn Foundation
The Pew Charitable Trusts
The Rockefeller Foundation

Land management

Alaska Conservation Foundation
The William Bingham Foundation
The Bullitt Foundation
Mary Flagler Cary Charitable Trust
Chesapeake Bay Trust
Compton Foundation, Inc.

Davis Conservation Foundation
Geraldine R. Dodge Foundation, Inc.
The Elizabeth Ordway Dunn
 Foundation, Inc.
The Educational Foundation of America
The William Stamps Farish Fund
Ford Foundation
The Wallace Alexander Gerbode
 Foundation, Inc.
Great Lakes Protection Fund
Walter and Elise Haas Fund
The Richard Ivey Foundation
W. Alton Jones Foundation, Inc.
The Max and Anna Levinson Foundation
The John D. and Catherine T. MacArthur
 Foundation
The Marshall Fund of Arizona
Merck Family Fund
The John Merck Fund
Charles Stewart Mott Foundation
National Fish and Wildlife Foundation
The Needmor Fund
New Hampshire Charitable Foundation
Northwest Area Foundation
Jessie Smith Noyes Foundation, Inc.
The David and Lucile Packard Foundation
Patagonia, Inc.
The William Penn Foundation
Pew Scholars Program in Conservation
 and the Environment
Z. Smith Reynolds Foundation, Inc.
The Rockefeller Foundation
Weyerhaeuser Company Foundation

Land reclamation/restoration

ARCO Foundation
Chesapeake Bay Trust
The Chevron Companies
Conservation, Food & Health
 Foundation, Inc.
Geraldine R. Dodge Foundation, Inc.
The Elizabeth Ordway Dunn
 Foundation, Inc.
Foundation for Deep Ecology
Evelyn and Walter Haas, Jr. Fund
Harder Foundation
Laird, Norton Foundation
Levi Strauss Foundation
Lyndhurst Foundation
Ruth Mott Fund
National Fish and Wildlife Foundation
Recreational Equipment, Inc.
The Schumann Fund for New Jersey, Inc.
True North Foundation
Whitecap Foundation

Land trusts

ARCO Foundation
Winifred & Harry B. Allen Foundation
American Conservation Association, Inc.
American Foundation Corporation
Elmer L. & Eleanor J. Andersen Foundation
The Austin Memorial Foundation
The Barra Foundation, Inc.

The Beinecke Foundation, Inc.
David Winton Bell Foundation
James Ford Bell Foundation
The Betterment Fund
The Frank Stanley Beveridge
 Foundation, Inc.
Bishop Pine Fund
Mary Owen Borden Memorial Foundation
Botwinick-Wolfensohn Foundation, Inc.
Alexander H. Bright Charitable Trust
Ruth H. Brown Foundation
W. L. Lyons Brown Foundation
Kathleen Price and Joseph M. Bryan
 Family Foundation, Inc.
The Bullitt Foundation
The Bunbury Company, Inc.
The Cabot Family Charitable Trust
Carolyn Foundation
Mary Flagler Cary Charitable Trust
Claneil Foundation, Inc.
The Community Foundation of
 Greater New Haven
The Community Foundation of
 Santa Clara County
The Community Foundation Serving
 Coastal South Carolina
Compton Foundation, Inc.
The Cowles Charitable Trust
The Mary A. Crocker Trust
Davis Conservation Foundation
Geraldine R. Dodge Foundation, Inc.
Dolfinger-McMahon Foundation
Gaylord and Dorothy Donnelley Foundation
The Max and Victoria Dreyfus
 Foundation, Inc.
The Elizabeth Ordway Dunn
 Foundation, Inc.
The Charles Engelhard Foundation
Fanwood Foundation
The Favrot Fund
The Fund for New Jersey
HKH Foundation
Harder Foundation
The Merrill G. & Emita E. Hastings
 Foundation
The William and Flora Hewlett Foundation
Howfirma Foundation
The Louise H. and David S. Ingalls
 Foundation, Inc.
Island Foundation, Inc.
Jackson Hole Preserve, Inc.
The J. M. Kaplan Fund, Inc.
The Robert S. and Grayce B. Kerr
 Foundation, Inc.
F. M. Kirby Foundation, Inc.
The Seymour H. Knox Foundation, Inc.
The Lagemann Foundation
Laidlaw Foundation
The Lauder Foundation, Inc.
Laurel Foundation
James A. Macdonald Foundation
Magowan Family Foundation, Inc.
Maki Foundation
Marin Community Foundation
MARPAT Foundation, Inc.

Environmental Topics and Activities

Land trusts (cont.)

The McIntosh Foundation
The McKnight Foundation
Giles W. and Elise G. Mead Foundation
Nelson Mead Fund
Merck Family Fund
Middlecott Foundation
National Fish and Wildlife Foundation
New Hampshire Charitable Foundation
The New York Community Trust
The New York Times Company Foundation, Inc.
Norcross Wildlife Foundation, Inc.
The Ohrstrom Foundation
The Overbrook Foundation
The David and Lucile Packard Foundation
The William Penn Foundation
The Prospect Hill Foundation
The Prudential Foundation
Recreational Equipment, Inc.
The Rhode Island Community Foundation
Sproul Foundation
Stoddard Charitable Trust
The Strong Foundation for Environmental Values
The Oakleigh L. Thorne Foundation
Threshold Foundation
The Tides Foundation
True North Foundation
Marcia Brady Tucker Foundation
Underhill Foundation
Victoria Foundation, Inc.
Wallace Genetic Foundation, Inc.
C. A. Webster Foundation
Henry E. and Consuelo S. Wenger Foundation, Inc.
Wilburforce Foundation
The Windham Foundation, Inc.

Land use planning

ARCO Foundation
The Abelard Foundation West
Americana Foundation, Inc.
Mary Reynolds Babcock Foundation, Inc.
The Beinecke Foundation, Inc.
The Bullitt Foundation
Patrick and Aimee Butler Family Foundation
The Cabot Family Charitable Trust
Chesapeake Bay Trust
Columbia Foundation
Compton Foundation, Inc.
Davis Conservation Foundation
Geraldine R. Dodge Foundation, Inc.
The Educational Foundation of America
The Energy Foundation
The William Stamps Farish Fund
The 1525 Foundation
Ford Foundation
The Fund for New Jersey
Great Lakes Protection Fund
The Greenville Foundation
The John Randolph Haynes and Dora Haynes Foundation

The Richard Ivey Foundation
Jackson Hole Preserve, Inc.
The Henry M. Jackson Foundation
W. Alton Jones Foundation, Inc.
The J. M. Kaplan Fund, Inc.
Kongsgaard-Goldman Foundation
Laidlaw Foundation
Laird, Norton Foundation
Lilly Endowment, Inc.
Lyndhurst Foundation
The John D. and Catherine T. MacArthur Foundation
MARPAT Foundation, Inc.
McKenzie River Gathering Foundation
Richard King Mellon Foundation
Merck Family Fund
Charles Stewart Mott Foundation
National Fish and Wildlife Foundation
The Needmor Fund
The New York Community Trust
Northwest Area Foundation
The David and Lucile Packard Foundation
Patagonia, Inc.
The Prospect Hill Foundation
Public Welfare Foundation, Inc.
Z. Smith Reynolds Foundation, Inc.
Rockefeller Family Fund, Inc.
The Rockefeller Foundation
The Rockfall Foundation
The San Francisco Foundation
The Schumann Fund for New Jersey, Inc.
Seventh Generation Fund
The Strong Foundation for Environmental Values
Surdna Foundation, Inc.
The Switzer Foundation
Threshold Foundation
The Tides Foundation
The Trust For Mutual Understanding
Rose E. Tucker Charitable Trust
United States-Japan Foundation
Vancouver Foundation
Victoria Foundation, Inc.
Vinmont Foundation, Inc.
Virginia Environmental Endowment
Weeden Foundation
The William P. Wharton Trust
Margaret Cullinan Wray Charitable Lead Annuity Trust

Landscaping

Chesapeake Bay Trust
Dolfinger-McMahon Foundation
The J. M. Kaplan Fund, Inc.
Larsen Fund, Inc.
Lyndhurst Foundation
Richard King Mellon Foundation
The Minneapolis Foundation
The Mountaineers Foundation
Onan Family Foundation
The William Penn Foundation
The Pew Charitable Trusts
Sid W. Richardson Foundation
The Rockfall Foundation

Stanley Smith Horticultural Trust
The Winston-Salem Foundation, Inc.

Law/regulation

AT&T Foundation
Alaska Conservation Foundation
The Jenifer Altman Foundation
American Conservation Association, Inc.
Mary Reynolds Babcock Foundation, Inc.
The Bailey Wildlife Foundation
Clayton Baker Trust
The Bauman Foundation
The Beinecke Foundation, Inc.
Beldon Fund
Beneficia Foundation
The William Bingham Foundation
The Blumenthal Foundation
Botwinick-Wolfensohn Foundation, Inc.
Alexander H. Bright Charitable Trust
W. L. Lyons Brown Foundation
Kathleen Price and Joseph M. Bryan Family Foundation, Inc.
Jesse Margaret Wilson Budlong Foundation for Animal Aid
The Bullitt Foundation
The Bush Foundation
The Bydale Foundation
California Community Foundation
Mary Flagler Cary Charitable Trust
Changing Horizons Charitable Trust
Chesapeake Bay Trust
Chrysler Corporation Fund
Robert Sterling Clark Foundation, Inc.
The Cleveland Foundation
Columbia Foundation
The Columbus Foundation
The Community Foundation of Santa Clara County
Compton Foundation, Inc.
Conservation, Food & Health Foundation, Inc.
The Cowles Charitable Trust
Jessie B. Cox Charitable Trust
The Mary A. Crocker Trust
Patrick and Anna M. Cudahy Fund
The Nathan Cummings Foundation
Davis Conservation Foundation
Deer Creek Foundation
Geraldine R. Dodge Foundation, Inc.
The Elizabeth Ordway Dunn Foundation, Inc.
Echoing Green Foundation
The Educational Foundation of America
The Emerald Foundation
The Energy Foundation
Environment Now Foundation
Environmental Endowment for New Jersey, Inc.
The Armand G. Erpf Fund, Inc.
The Ettinger Foundation, Inc.
Fanwood Foundation
The Favrot Fund
Flintridge Foundation
Ford Foundation

Environmental Topics and Activities

Law/regulation (cont.)

Ford Motor Company Fund
Walter and Josephine Ford Fund
Foundation for Deep Ecology
Funding Exchange
GE Fund
The Gap Foundation
General Service Foundation
The German Marshall Fund of the United States
Bernard F. and Alva B. Gimbel Foundation, Inc.
Richard & Rhoda Goldman Fund
Great Lakes Protection Fund
The Greenville Foundation
The George Gund Foundation
Harbor Lights Foundation
Harder Foundation
Mary W. Harriman Foundation
The Merrill G. & Emita E. Hastings Foundation
Heller Charitable & Educational Fund
The William and Flora Hewlett Foundation
The Hitachi Foundation
The Homeland Foundation
The Horn Foundation
Howfirma Foundation
The Charles Evans Hughes Memorial Foundation, Inc.
Hurdle Hill Foundation
The Richard Ivey Foundation
The Howard Johnson Foundation
W. Alton Jones Foundation, Inc.
The Joyce Foundation
The J. M. Kaplan Fund, Inc.
Harris and Eliza Kempner Fund
The Lagemann Foundation
Laidlaw Foundation
The Lazar Foundation
The Max and Anna Levinson Foundation
Lyndhurst Foundation
The John D. and Catherine T. MacArthur Foundation
Magowan Family Foundation, Inc.
Mars Foundation
The McIntosh Foundation
The McKnight Foundation
Giles W. and Elise G. Mead Foundation
Nelson Mead Fund
The Andrew W. Mellon Foundation
Richard King Mellon Foundation
Merck Family Fund
The John Merck Fund
Joyce Mertz-Gilmore Foundation
Metropolitan Atlanta Community Foundation, Inc.
Mobil Foundation, Inc.
Leo Model Foundation, Inc.
J. P. Morgan Charitable Trust
The Moriah Fund, Inc.
Henry and Lucy Moses Fund, Inc.
Charles Stewart Mott Foundation
Ruth Mott Fund
The Curtis and Edith Munson Foundation, Inc.

National Fish and Wildlife Foundation
New England Biolabs Foundation
New Hampshire Charitable Foundation
The New York Community Trust
The New York Times Company Foundation, Inc.
The New-Land Foundation, Inc.
Edward John Noble Foundation, Inc.
Norman Foundation
Northwest Fund for the Environment
Jessie Smith Noyes Foundation, Inc.
Ottinger Foundation
The Overbrook Foundation
The David and Lucile Packard Foundation
Patagonia, Inc.
The Pew Charitable Trusts
Phillips Petroleum Foundation, Inc.
Howard Phipps Foundation
Henry B. Plant Memorial Fund, Inc.
Lynn R. and Karl E. Prickett Fund
Prince Charitable Trusts
Public Welfare Foundation, Inc.
Recreational Equipment, Inc.
Z. Smith Reynolds Foundation, Inc.
The Rhode Island Community Foundation
The Roberts Foundation
Rockefeller Brothers Fund, Inc.
Lee Romney Foundation, Inc.
Sacharuna Foundation
The San Francisco Foundation
The Sapelo Foundation
The Scherman Foundation, Inc.
The Schiff Foundation
Schultz Foundation, Inc.
The Florence and John Schumann Foundation
Sequoia Foundation
Alfred T. Stanley Foundation
The Strong Foundation for Environmental Values
The Sulzberger Foundation, Inc.
Edna Bailey Sussman Fund
The Switzer Foundation
Nelson Talbott Foundation
Texaco Foundation
Threshold Foundation
The Tides Foundation
The Tinker Foundation Incorporated
Town Creek Foundation, Inc.
True North Foundation
The Trust For Mutual Understanding
Rose E. Tucker Charitable Trust
Turner Foundation, Inc.
USX Foundation, Inc.
Underhill Foundation
Unitarian Universalist Veatch Program at Shelter Rock
Vancouver Foundation
Vinmont Foundation, Inc.
WMX Environmental Grants Program
Wallace Genetic Foundation, Inc.
Weeden Foundation
Weyerhaeuser Company Foundation
G. N. Wilcox Trust
Robert W. Wilson Foundation

Mark and Catherine Winkler Foundation
The Winston-Salem Foundation, Inc.
The Dean Witter Foundation
Sidney & Phyllis Wragge Foundation
Margaret Cullinan Wray Charitable Lead Annuity Trust

Law/regulation: implementation/compliance

The Abelard Foundation West
Alaska Conservation Foundation
The Bauman Foundation
Beldon Fund
California Community Foundation
Robert Sterling Clark Foundation, Inc.
Jessie B. Cox Charitable Trust
The Mary A. Crocker Trust
Deer Creek Foundation
The Fred Gellert Foundation
General Service Foundation
W. Alton Jones Foundation, Inc.
The John D. and Catherine T. MacArthur Foundation
The McKnight Foundation
The Moody Foundation
The Moriah Fund, Inc.
Northwest Fund for the Environment
James C. Penney Foundation
The Pew Charitable Trusts
Public Welfare Foundation, Inc.
Surdna Foundation, Inc.
Weeden Foundation
The William P. Wharton Trust
Margaret Cullinan Wray Charitable Lead Annuity Trust

Leadership development

The Abelard Foundation West
Elmer L. & Eleanor J. Andersen Foundation
The Bauman Foundation
L. L. Bean, Inc.
The Mary A. Crocker Trust
Ederic Foundation, Inc.
El Pomar Foundation
Environmental Education Foundation of Florida, Inc.
Gates Foundation
General Service Foundation
The George Gund Foundation
The Edward W. Hazen Foundation
Walter S. Johnson Foundation
Merck Family Fund
The Curtis and Edith Munson Foundation, Inc.
National Fish and Wildlife Foundation
The Florence and John Schumann Foundation
Stern Family Fund
Surdna Foundation, Inc.
The Switzer Foundation
Threshold Foundation
Town Creek Foundation, Inc.
Union Camp Charitable Trust
WMX Environmental Grants Program

Environmental Topics and Activities

Least-cost approach

The Energy Foundation
Joyce Mertz-Gilmore Foundation
The Pew Charitable Trusts
Surdna Foundation, Inc.

Legislation

Beldon Fund
The Ben & Jerry's Foundation
The Chevron Companies
The Energy Foundation
Ford Foundation
The Richard Ivey Foundation
New Hampshire Charitable Foundation
Jessie Smith Noyes Foundation, Inc.
Patagonia, Inc.
Recreational Equipment, Inc.
Rockefeller Brothers Fund, Inc.
The Tinker Foundation Incorporated
WMX Environmental Grants Program
Weeden Foundation

Libraries

American Foundation Corporation
Elmer L. & Eleanor J. Andersen Foundation
Angelina Fund, Inc.
The Mary A. Crocker Trust
Dolfinger-McMahon Foundation
Felburn Foundation
The Knapp Foundation, Inc.
The Kresge Foundation
The John D. and Catherine T. MacArthur Foundation
The Andrew W. Mellon Foundation
Charles Stewart Mott Foundation
The Curtis and Edith Munson Foundation, Inc.
The Nord Family Foundation
The Rockefeller Foundation
Weyerhaeuser Company Foundation
Margaret Cullinan Wray Charitable Lead Annuity Trust

Litigation

Alaska Conservation Foundation
The Bullitt Foundation
Mary Flagler Cary Charitable Trust
Deer Creek Foundation
The Educational Foundation of America
Fund of the Four Directions
W. Alton Jones Foundation, Inc.
The Max and Anna Levinson Foundation
The John Merck Fund
Northwest Fund for the Environment
Patagonia, Inc.
Rockefeller Family Fund, Inc.
Surdna Foundation, Inc.
Threshold Foundation
Weeden Foundation
Margaret Cullinan Wray Charitable Lead Annuity Trust

Litter

ARCO Foundation
Abell-Hanger Foundation
BankAmerica Foundation
Dolfinger-McMahon Foundation
The GAR Foundation
WMX Environmental Grants Program

Low-income persons

ARCO Foundation
Angelina Fund, Inc.
Mary Reynolds Babcock Foundation, Inc.
The Bauman Foundation
Beldon Fund
The Ben & Jerry's Foundation
Kathleen Price and Joseph M. Bryan Family Foundation, Inc.
The Bullitt Foundation
California Community Foundation
Chesapeake Bay Trust
Columbia Foundation
Crystal Channel Foundation
The Nathan Cummings Foundation
Deer Creek Foundation
The Elizabeth Ordway Dunn Foundation, Inc.
The Energy Foundation
The Field Foundation of Illinois, Inc.
Ford Foundation
The Gap Foundation
Give to the Earth Foundation
The Joyce Foundation
The J. M. Kaplan Fund, Inc.
Laird, Norton Foundation
Levi Strauss Foundation
The Max and Anna Levinson Foundation
Marin Community Foundation
The McKnight Foundation
Meadows Foundation, Inc.
Merck Family Fund
Joyce Mertz-Gilmore Foundation
Meyer Memorial Trust
The Milwaukee Foundation
The Moriah Fund, Inc.
The National Environmental Education and Training Foundation, Inc.
National Fish and Wildlife Foundation
The Needmor Fund
New England Biolabs Foundation
Norman Foundation
Northwest Area Foundation
Jessie Smith Noyes Foundation, Inc.
Patagonia, Inc.
The William Penn Foundation
The Pew Charitable Trusts
Public Welfare Foundation, Inc.
Z. Smith Reynolds Foundation, Inc.
The Sapelo Foundation
The Florence and John Schumann Foundation
The Sonoma County Community Foundation
The Morris Stulsaft Foundation
Surdna Foundation, Inc.
The Tides Foundation
Unitarian Universalist Veatch Program at Shelter Rock
Vanguard Public Foundation
Virginia Environmental Endowment

Marine biology/sciences

ARCO Foundation
Atherton Family Foundation
The George F. Baker Trust
The Bay Foundation
The Howard Bayne Fund
California Community Foundation
Chesapeake Bay Trust
The Community Foundation of Sarasota County, Inc.
Conservation, Food & Health Foundation, Inc.
Cox Foundation, Inc.
The Fred Harris Daniels Foundation, Inc.
The Arthur Vining Davis Foundations
Oliver S. and Jennie R. Donaldson Charitable Trust
The Max and Victoria Dreyfus Foundation, Inc.
The Armand G. Erpf Fund, Inc.
The Edward W. Hazen Foundation
The William and Flora Hewlett Foundation
The Homeland Foundation
Hurdle Hill Foundation
The George Frederick Jewett Foundation
Richard Lounsbery Foundation, Inc.
Mobil Foundation, Inc.
Charles Stewart Mott Foundation
National Fish and Wildlife Foundation
Pew Scholars Program in Conservation and the Environment
The Pfizer Foundation, Inc.
Henry B. Plant Memorial Fund, Inc.
Kelvin Smith 1980 Charitable Trust
Texaco Foundation
R. T. Vanderbilt Trust
G. Unger Vetlesen Foundation
Virginia Environmental Endowment
Wallace Genetic Foundation, Inc.
Welfare Foundation, Inc.

Marine issues

ARCO Foundation
Alaska Conservation Foundation
American Express Philanthropic Program
Atlantic Foundation
Clayton Baker Trust
The George F. Baker Trust
BankAmerica Foundation
The Barra Foundation, Inc.
The Bay Foundation
S. D. Bechtel, Jr. Foundation
Beneficia Foundation
Alexander H. Bright Charitable Trust

Environmental Topics and Activities

Marine issues (cont.)

Alex. Brown & Sons Charitable Foundation, Inc.
The Robert Brownlee Foundation
Jesse Margaret Wilson Budlong Foundation for Animal Aid
The Bullitt Foundation
Patrick and Aimee Butler Family Foundation
The Cabot Family Charitable Trust
California Community Foundation
Cheeryble Foundation
Ben B. Cheney Foundation
Chesapeake Bay Trust
Chesapeake Corporation Foundation
The Chevron Companies
The Clowes Fund, Inc.
The Columbus Foundation
The Community Foundation of Sarasota County, Inc.
Compton Foundation, Inc.
Conservation, Food & Health Foundation, Inc.
The Cowles Charitable Trust
Cox Foundation, Inc.
Jessie B. Cox Charitable Trust
The Mary A. Crocker Trust
The Nathan Cummings Foundation
The Fred Harris Daniels Foundation, Inc.
The Arthur Vining Davis Foundations
Davis Conservation Foundation
Oliver S. and Jennie R. Donaldson Charitable Trust
The Elizabeth Ordway Dunn Foundation, Inc.
Arthur M. and Olga T. Eisig-Arthur M. and Kate E. Tode Foundation, Inc.
Environmental Education Foundation of Florida, Inc.
The Ettinger Foundation, Inc.
Fanwood Foundation
Jamee and Marshall Field Foundation
Ford Foundation
Ford Motor Company Fund
Foundation for Field Research
The Gap Foundation
The Fred Gellert Foundation
The Wallace Alexander Gerbode Foundation, Inc.
Greater Piscataqua Community Foundation
Walter and Elise Haas Fund
Hawaii Community Foundation
The Edward W. Hazen Foundation
The Homeland Foundation
The Charles Evans Hughes Memorial Foundation, Inc.
Hurdle Hill Foundation
The Indian Point Foundation, Inc.
Ireland Foundation
Island Foundation, Inc.
The Knapp Foundation, Inc.
The Kresge Foundation
The Norman Lear Foundation
Longwood Foundation, Inc.
Luster Family Foundation, Inc.

The John D. and Catherine T. MacArthur Foundation
Maine Community Foundation, Inc.
MARPAT Foundation, Inc.
Massachusetts Environmental Trust
McDonnell Douglas Foundation
McInerny Foundation
Nelson Mead Fund
The John Merck Fund
Metropolitan Atlanta Community Foundation, Inc.
Mobil Foundation, Inc.
The Moriah Fund, Inc.
Charles Stewart Mott Foundation
Ruth Mott Fund
The Curtis and Edith Munson Foundation, Inc.
National Fish and Wildlife Foundation
New England Biolabs Foundation
The New York Times Company Foundation, Inc.
Norcross Wildlife Foundation, Inc.
The Ohrstrom Foundation
Orchard Foundation
The David and Lucile Packard Foundation
Patagonia, Inc.
Amelia Peabody Charitable Fund
Peninsula Community Foundation
The Pew Charitable Trusts
Pew Scholars Program in Conservation and the Environment
Henry B. Plant Memorial Fund, Inc.
Lynn R. and Karl E. Prickett Fund
Prince Charitable Trusts
The Procter & Gamble Fund
Rockwell Fund, Inc.
The San Francisco Foundation
Schultz Foundation, Inc.
Ellen Browning Scripps Foundation
Frances Seebe Trust
Sequoia Foundation
Shell Oil Company Foundation
The Skaggs Foundation
Kelvin Smith 1980 Charitable Trust
South Coast Foundation, Inc.
Margaret Dorrance Strawbridge Foundation of Pennsylvania II, Inc.
The Stroh Foundation
The Strong Foundation for Environmental Values
Stroud Foundation
The Morris Stulsaft Foundation
The Sudbury Foundation
Texaco Foundation
Thanksgiving Foundation
The Oakleigh L. Thorne Foundation
Threshold Foundation
The Tides Foundation
The Tinker Foundation Incorporated
Town Creek Foundation, Inc.
The Truland Foundation
Marcia Brady Tucker Foundation
USX Foundation, Inc.
Union Camp Charitable Trust
Victoria Foundation, Inc.

Virginia Environmental Endowment
WMX Environmental Grants Program
DeWitt Wallace-Reader's Digest Fund
Weeden Foundation
Welfare Foundation, Inc.
Weyerhaeuser Company Foundation
G. N. Wilcox Trust
Robert W. Wilson Foundation
The Dean Witter Foundation
Margaret Cullinan Wray Charitable Lead Annuity Trust

Marine sanctuaries

The Bullitt Foundation
Mary Flagler Cary Charitable Trust
The Hitachi Foundation
The McIntosh Foundation
The National Environmental Education and Training Foundation, Inc.
New England Biolabs Foundation
The David and Lucile Packard Foundation
R. T. Vanderbilt Trust

Market approach

Atkinson Foundation
California Community Foundation
Robert Sterling Clark Foundation, Inc.
The Mary A. Crocker Trust
The Educational Foundation of America
The Energy Foundation
The Wallace Alexander Gerbode Foundation, Inc.
The Joyce Foundation
The J. M. Kaplan Fund, Inc.
Laidlaw Foundation
Lyndhurst Foundation
The John D. and Catherine T. MacArthur Foundation
The John Merck Fund
The Moriah Fund, Inc.
The Curtis and Edith Munson Foundation, Inc.
M. J. Murdock Charitable Trust
Northwest Area Foundation
Jessie Smith Noyes Foundation, Inc.
The David and Lucile Packard Foundation
The Pew Charitable Trusts
The Winthrop Rockefeller Foundation
Rockwell Fund, Inc.
The San Francisco Foundation
Surdna Foundation, Inc.
Threshold Foundation
The Tinker Foundation Incorporated

Media projects

Alaska Conservation Foundation
Beldon Fund
Benton Foundation
Otto Bremer Foundation
The Bullitt Foundation
C. S. Fund
California Community Foundation
Changing Horizons Charitable Trust
Ben B. Cheney Foundation

© 1995 Environmental Data Resources, Inc.

Environmental Topics and Activities

Media projects (cont.)

Columbia Foundation
Compton Foundation, Inc.
The Conservation and Research Foundation
The Cricket Foundation
The Mary A. Crocker Trust
Geraldine R. Dodge Foundation, Inc.
The Educational Foundation of America
Leland Fikes Foundation, Inc.
Foundation for Deep Ecology
Mary D. and Walter F. Frear
    Eleemosynary Trust
The Fund for New Jersey
The Fred Gellert Foundation
The Wallace Alexander Gerbode
    Foundation, Inc.
The German Marshall Fund of
    the United States
Richard & Rhoda Goldman Fund
The George Gund Foundation
Ittleson Foundation, Inc.
W. Alton Jones Foundation, Inc.
The J. M. Kaplan Fund, Inc.
Harris and Eliza Kempner Fund
The Knapp Foundation, Inc.
The Lazar Foundation
The Norman Lear Foundation
The John D. and Catherine T. MacArthur
    Foundation
McInerny Foundation
McKenzie River Gathering Foundation
Giles W. and Elise G. Mead Foundation
Merck Family Fund
The John Merck Fund
Charles Stewart Mott Foundation
The Curtis and Edith Munson
    Foundation, Inc.
National Fish and Wildlife Foundation
New Hampshire Charitable Foundation
Patagonia, Inc.
The William Penn Foundation
The Pew Charitable Trusts
Recreational Equipment, Inc.
Rockefeller Family Fund, Inc.
The Florence and John Schumann
    Foundation
The Strong Foundation for
    Environmental Values
The Oakleigh L. Thorne Foundation
Threshold Foundation
The Tides Foundation
The Trust For Mutual Understanding
Vanguard Public Foundation
Virginia Environmental Endowment
Weeden Foundation

Military issues

The Acorn Foundation
Beldon Fund
The Ben & Jerry's Foundation
Changing Horizons Charitable Trust
The Henry M. Jackson Foundation
Ruth Mott Fund
The Needmor Fund

Ottinger Foundation
Patagonia, Inc.
Public Welfare Foundation, Inc.
Rockefeller Family Fund, Inc.
Threshold Foundation

Mining

ARCO Foundation
Alaska Conservation Foundation
American Conservation Association, Inc.
Angelina Fund, Inc.
Beldon Fund
The Ben & Jerry's Foundation
The Bullitt Foundation
Deer Creek Foundation
The Educational Foundation of America
The Energy Foundation
Fanwood Foundation
Fund of the Four Directions
General Service Foundation
The Goldman Environmental Foundation
The Greenville Foundation
Harder Foundation
W. Alton Jones Foundation, Inc.
The Lazar Foundation
The Max and Anna Levinson Foundation
Maki Foundation
McKenzie River Gathering Foundation
Merck Family Fund
Ruth Mott Fund
The Needmor Fund
Norman Foundation
Patagonia, Inc.
The Pew Charitable Trusts
Recreational Equipment, Inc.
Rockefeller Family Fund, Inc.
The Florence and John Schumann
    Foundation
Seventh Generation Fund
Threshold Foundation
Tortuga Foundation
Town Creek Foundation, Inc.
True North Foundation
USX Foundation, Inc.
Weeden Foundation
Margaret Cullinan Wray Charitable
    Lead Annuity Trust

Minorities

ARCO Foundation
The Abelard Foundation West
Angelina Fund, Inc.
Mary Reynolds Babcock Foundation, Inc.
The Ben & Jerry's Foundation
The Bullitt Foundation
California Community Foundation
Mary Flagler Cary Charitable Trust
Columbia Foundation
Compton Foundation, Inc.
Adolph Coors Foundation
The Mary A. Crocker Trust
Crystal Channel Foundation
The Nathan Cummings Foundation
Geraldine R. Dodge Foundation, Inc.

Echoing Green Foundation
The Educational Foundation of America
El Paso Community Foundation
The Energy Foundation
Ford Foundation
Funding Exchange
The Gap Foundation
The Wallace Alexander Gerbode
    Foundation, Inc.
Give to the Earth Foundation
Evelyn and Walter Haas, Jr. Fund
Harbor Lights Foundation
The Joyce Foundation
W. K. Kellogg Foundation
The Esther A. and Joseph Klingenstein
    Fund, Inc.
Laird, Norton Foundation
The Max and Anna Levinson Foundation
Maki Foundation
Marin Community Foundation
The Andrew W. Mellon Foundation
The Minneapolis Foundation
Charles Stewart Mott Foundation
The Curtis and Edith Munson
    Foundation, Inc.
The National Environmental Education
    and Training Foundation, Inc.
National Fish and Wildlife Foundation
The Needmor Fund
New York Foundation
Norman Foundation
Jessie Smith Noyes Foundation, Inc.
The David and Lucile Packard Foundation
Amelia Peabody Charitable Fund
James C. Penney Foundation
The Pew Charitable Trusts
Pew Scholars Program in Conservation
    and the Environment
Public Welfare Foundation, Inc.
Z. Smith Reynolds Foundation, Inc.
Rockefeller Family Fund, Inc.
The San Francisco Foundation
The Sapelo Foundation
Seventh Generation Fund
Threshold Foundation
The Tides Foundation
USX Foundation, Inc.
Unitarian Universalist Veatch Program
    at Shelter Rock
Vanguard Public Foundation
Victoria Foundation, Inc.
Vinmont Foundation, Inc.
DeWitt Wallace-Reader's Digest Fund
Weyerhaeuser Company Foundation

Monitoring

ARCO Foundation
The Ahmanson Foundation
The Jenifer Altman Foundation
Mary Reynolds Babcock Foundation, Inc.
Beldon Fund
The Bullitt Foundation
C. S. Fund
Chesapeake Bay Trust
Jessie B. Cox Charitable Trust

Environmental Topics and Activities

Monitoring (cont.)

Deer Creek Foundation
The Educational Foundation of America
General Service Foundation
Richard & Rhoda Goldman Fund
The Greenville Foundation
The Clarence E. Heller Charitable Foundation
The Richard Ivey Foundation
W. Alton Jones Foundation, Inc.
The John D. and Catherine T. MacArthur Foundation
MARPAT Foundation, Inc.
Massachusetts Environmental Trust
McKenzie River Gathering Foundation
Giles W. and Elise G. Mead Foundation
Charles Stewart Mott Foundation
Ruth Mott Fund
National Fish and Wildlife Foundation
Patagonia, Inc.
The William Penn Foundation
Public Welfare Foundation, Inc.
The Rockefeller Foundation
The Florence and John Schumann Foundation
Threshold Foundation
Town Creek Foundation, Inc.
True North Foundation
The Trust For Mutual Understanding
Virginia Environmental Endowment
Weeden Foundation

Monitoring: pollution

The Ben & Jerry's Foundation
Jessie B. Cox Charitable Trust
Geraldine R. Dodge Foundation, Inc.
The Fred Gellert Foundation
The John D. and Catherine T. MacArthur Foundation
Maine Community Foundation, Inc.
The McKnight Foundation
The Curtis and Edith Munson Foundation, Inc.
National Fish and Wildlife Foundation
Steelcase Foundation

Mountainous areas

The Ahmanson Foundation
American Conservation Association, Inc.
American Foundation Corporation
Evenor Armington Fund
Beldon Fund
Alexander H. Bright Charitable Trust
Kathleen Price and Joseph M. Bryan Family Foundation, Inc.
The Bullitt Foundation
The Cabot Family Charitable Trust
California Community Foundation
James & Abigail Campbell Foundation
Changing Horizons Charitable Trust
The Chevron Companies
Clark Charitable Trust
Compton Foundation, Inc.
Adolph Coors Foundation

Jessie B. Cox Charitable Trust
The Cricket Foundation
Davis Conservation Foundation
Cleveland H. Dodge Foundation, Inc.
Geraldine R. Dodge Foundation, Inc.
Eastman Kodak Company Charitable Trust
Echoing Green Foundation
The Charles Engelhard Foundation
Environment Now Foundation
Fanwood Foundation
Felburn Foundation
Ford Foundation
Foundation for the Carolinas
Foundation for Deep Ecology
The Foundation for the National Capital Region
The Frost Foundation, Ltd.
The Fund for Preservation of Wildlife and Natural Areas
Fund of the Four Directions
The Goldman Environmental Foundation
HKH Foundation
Harder Foundation
The Merrill G. & Emita E. Hastings Foundation
The John Randolph Haynes and Dora Haynes Foundation
The Edward W. Hazen Foundation
The William and Flora Hewlett Foundation
Howfirma Foundation
The Roy A. Hunt Foundation
W. Alton Jones Foundation, Inc.
The J. M. Kaplan Fund, Inc.
The Seymour H. Knox Foundation, Inc.
The Lagemann Foundation
Laird, Norton Foundation
The Lazar Foundation
Lyndhurst Foundation
The John D. and Catherine T. MacArthur Foundation
Magowan Family Foundation, Inc.
Maki Foundation
McInerny Foundation
Giles W. and Elise G. Mead Foundation
Nelson Mead Fund
Richard King Mellon Foundation
Merck Family Fund
Joyce Mertz-Gilmore Foundation
The Moriah Fund, Inc.
Ruth Mott Fund
The Mountaineers Foundation
National Fish and Wildlife Foundation
New Hampshire Charitable Foundation
The New World Foundation
The New York Times Company Foundation, Inc.
The New-Land Foundation, Inc.
Norcross Wildlife Foundation, Inc.
Norman Foundation
Outdoor Industry Conservation Alliance
Patagonia, Inc.
Amelia Peabody Charitable Fund
The Pew Charitable Trusts
Phillips Petroleum Foundation, Inc.
The Prospect Hill Foundation

Recreational Equipment, Inc.
The Rhode Island Community Foundation
Rockefeller Brothers Fund, Inc.
Rockefeller Family Fund, Inc.
Lee Romney Foundation, Inc.
San Diego Community Foundation
Sarkeys Foundation
Seventh Generation Fund
The Stebbins Fund, Inc.
The Stratford Foundation
The Strong Foundation for Environmental Values
The Sudbury Foundation
The Sulzberger Foundation, Inc.
The Switzer Foundation
Thanksgiving Foundation
Threshold Foundation
The Tides Foundation
True North Foundation
USX Foundation, Inc.
Underhill Foundation
Unitarian Universalist Veatch Program at Shelter Rock
WMX Environmental Grants Program
Wallace Genetic Foundation, Inc.
Weeden Foundation
G. N. Wilcox Trust
Robert W. Wilson Foundation
The Windham Foundation, Inc.

Multilateral development banks

Richard & Rhoda Goldman Fund
W. Alton Jones Foundation, Inc.
Charles Stewart Mott Foundation
Ruth Mott Fund
The Prospect Hill Foundation
Public Welfare Foundation, Inc.
Threshold Foundation
Wallace Genetic Foundation, Inc.

Museums

ARCO Foundation
Ameritech Foundation
Atherton Family Foundation
BankAmerica Foundation
The Bay Foundation
S. D. Bechtel, Jr. Foundation
David Winton Bell Foundation
James Ford Bell Foundation
The Bothin Foundation
The Robert Brownlee Foundation
California Community Foundation
The Chevron Companies
The Chicago Community Trust
The Collins Foundation
Adolph Coors Foundation
Roy E. Crummer Foundation
The Nathan Cummings Foundation
Geraldine R. Dodge Foundation, Inc.
Thelma Doelger Charitable Trust
Oliver S. and Jennie R. Donaldson Charitable Trust
English-Bonter-Mitchell Foundation
Environment Now Foundation

© 1995 Environmental Data Resources, Inc.

Environmental Topics and Activities

Museums (cont.)

The Armand G. Erpf Fund, Inc.
Leland Fikes Foundation, Inc.
Ford Motor Company Fund
Frelinghuysen Foundation
The Gap Foundation
Gates Foundation
Richard & Rhoda Goldman Fund
The George Gund Foundation
The Richard Ivey Foundation
Walter S. Johnson Foundation
W. Alton Jones Foundation, Inc.
The Henry P. Kendall Foundation
The Robert S. and Grayce B. Kerr Foundation, Inc.
The Knapp Foundation, Inc.
The Seymour H. Knox Foundation, Inc.
Laurel Foundation
Luster Family Foundation, Inc.
The John D. and Catherine T. MacArthur Foundation
MARPAT Foundation, Inc.
Meyer Memorial Trust
Mobil Foundation, Inc.
The Mountaineers Foundation
National Fish and Wildlife Foundation
Norcross Wildlife Foundation, Inc.
OCRI Foundation
The Overbrook Foundation
Peninsula Community Foundation
The William Penn Foundation
The Pew Charitable Trusts
The Roberts Foundation
Shell Oil Company Foundation
Stanley Smith Horticultural Trust
The Stratford Foundation
Nelson Talbott Foundation
Texaco Foundation
The Tides Foundation
Town Creek Foundation, Inc.
Rose E. Tucker Charitable Trust
Virginia Environmental Endowment
DeWitt Wallace-Reader's Digest Fund
The William P. Wharton Trust
Wilburforce Foundation
The Dean Witter Foundation
Margaret Cullinan Wray Charitable Lead Annuity Trust

Museums: nature

ARCO Foundation
BankAmerica Foundation
The Mary A. Crocker Trust
Leland Fikes Foundation, Inc.
Gebbie Foundation, Inc.
The Fred Gellert Foundation
The Kresge Foundation
The John D. and Catherine T. MacArthur Foundation
Leo Model Foundation, Inc.
The David and Lucile Packard Foundation
The Strong Foundation for Environmental Values

Native Americans

ARCO Foundation
The Abelard Foundation West
The Acorn Foundation
Alaska Conservation Foundation
Beldon Fund
The Ben & Jerry's Foundation
Blandin Foundation
Otto Bremer Foundation
The Bullitt Foundation
The Bush Foundation
The Nathan Cummings Foundation
The Educational Foundation of America
The Ettinger Foundation, Inc.
Ford Foundation
Foundation for Deep Ecology
Fund of the Four Directions
Funding Exchange
General Service Foundation
Give to the Earth Foundation
The Goldman Environmental Foundation
Great Lakes Protection Fund
The Joyce Foundation
The Max and Anna Levinson Foundation
McKenzie River Gathering Foundation
Giles W. and Elise G. Mead Foundation
Charles Stewart Mott Foundation
Ruth Mott Fund
National Fish and Wildlife Foundation
The Needmor Fund
The New-Land Foundation, Inc.
Norman Foundation
Jessie Smith Noyes Foundation, Inc.
Patagonia, Inc.
Public Welfare Foundation, Inc.
Seventh Generation Fund
The Switzer Foundation
Threshold Foundation
The Tides Foundation
Unitarian Universalist Veatch Program at Shelter Rock
Vancouver Foundation
Wilburforce Foundation

Natural resources

ARCO Foundation
A Territory Resource
American Conservation Association, Inc.
Mary Reynolds Babcock Foundation, Inc.
The Cameron Baird Foundation
The Beinecke Foundation, Inc.
James Ford Bell Foundation
Beneficia Foundation
Benua Foundation, Inc.
The Blumenthal Foundation
Alexander H. Bright Charitable Trust
W. L. Lyons Brown Foundation
Jesse Margaret Wilson Budlong Foundation for Animal Aid
The Bullitt Foundation
California Community Foundation
The Cape Branch Foundation
Changing Horizons Charitable Trust
The Chevron Companies
Columbia Foundation
The Columbus Foundation
Compton Foundation, Inc.
The Conservation and Research Foundation
Jessie B. Cox Charitable Trust
Patrick and Anna M. Cudahy Fund
Geraldine R. Dodge Foundation, Inc.
Echoing Green Foundation
The Educational Foundation of America
The Armand G. Erpf Fund, Inc.
The Ettinger Foundation, Inc.
Ford Foundation
Walter and Josephine Ford Fund
Funding Exchange
The Fred Gellert Foundation
General Service Foundation
Georgia Power Foundation, Inc.
Bernard F. and Alva B. Gimbel Foundation, Inc.
Great Lakes Protection Fund
The Greenville Foundation
The George Gund Foundation
Mary W. Harriman Foundation
The Merrill G. & Emita E. Hastings Foundation
The Homeland Foundation
The Horn Foundation
Howfirma Foundation
The Charles Evans Hughes Memorial Foundation, Inc.
Hurdle Hill Foundation
The Richard Ivey Foundation
The Howard Johnson Foundation
W. Alton Jones Foundation, Inc.
The Lagemann Foundation
Laird, Norton Foundation
Lintilhac Foundation
Luster Family Foundation, Inc.
The John D. and Catherine T. MacArthur Foundation
Mars Foundation
McInerny Foundation
The McIntosh Foundation
The McKnight Foundation
The John Merck Fund
Joyce Mertz-Gilmore Foundation
The Curtis and Edith Munson Foundation, Inc.
National Fish and Wildlife Foundation
The Needmor Fund
The New York Times Company Foundation, Inc.
Edward John Noble Foundation, Inc.
Norcross Wildlife Foundation, Inc.
Northwest Area Foundation
Jessie Smith Noyes Foundation, Inc.
Orchard Foundation
The Overbrook Foundation
Patagonia, Inc.
Amelia Peabody Charitable Fund
The Pew Charitable Trusts
Howard Phipps Foundation
Lynn R. and Karl E. Prickett Fund

Environmental Topics and Activities

Natural resources (cont.)

Rockefeller Brothers Fund, Inc.
The Rockfall Foundation
The San Francisco Foundation
The Scherman Foundation, Inc.
The Schumann Fund for New Jersey, Inc.
Alfred T. Stanley Foundation
The Strong Foundation for
　Environmental Values
The Sudbury Foundation
Edna Bailey Sussman Fund
Texaco Foundation
The Tides Foundation
Tortuga Foundation
Town Creek Foundation, Inc.
Union Camp Charitable Trust
G. Unger Vetlesen Foundation
WMX Environmental Grants Program
Wallace Genetic Foundation, Inc.
Weeden Foundation
Weyerhaeuser Company Foundation
The William P. Wharton Trust
G. N. Wilcox Trust
Margaret Cullinan Wray Charitable
　Lead Annuity Trust

Natural resources: management

ARCO Foundation
AT&T Foundation
Beldon Fund
Bishop Pine Fund
The Bullitt Foundation
C. S. Fund
California Community Foundation
Mary Flagler Cary Charitable Trust
Ben B. Cheney Foundation
Chesapeake Bay Trust
The Chevron Companies
The Clark Foundation
The Community Foundation of
　Santa Clara County
Conservation, Food & Health
　Foundation, Inc.
The Energy Foundation
Ford Motor Company Fund
General Service Foundation
Give to the Earth Foundation
The Goldman Environmental Foundation
Great Lakes Protection Fund
W. Alton Jones Foundation, Inc.
The Joyce Foundation
The J. M. Kaplan Fund, Inc.
The Max and Anna Levinson Foundation
Lintilhac Foundation
Luster Family Foundation, Inc.
Lyndhurst Foundation
The John D. and Catherine T. MacArthur
　Foundation
McKenzie River Gathering Foundation
Giles W. and Elise G. Mead Foundation
Meadows Foundation, Inc.
The Moriah Fund, Inc.
National Fish and Wildlife Foundation

National Geographic Society Education
　Foundation
The New York Times Company
　Foundation, Inc.
Jessie Smith Noyes Foundation, Inc.
The David and Lucile Packard Foundation
Patagonia, Inc.
The Pew Charitable Trusts
Pew Scholars Program in Conservation
　and the Environment
Public Welfare Foundation, Inc.
Z. Smith Reynolds Foundation, Inc.
Rockefeller Brothers Fund, Inc.
Rockefeller Family Fund, Inc.
The Rockefeller Foundation
The Winthrop Rockefeller Foundation
The San Francisco Foundation
The Schumann Fund for New Jersey, Inc.
The Florence and John Schumann
　Foundation
Elmina B. Sewall Foundation
The Sulzberger Foundation, Inc.
Surdna Foundation, Inc.
The Switzer Foundation
Vancouver Foundation
Wallace Genetic Foundation, Inc.
The Dean Witter Foundation

Nature preserves

ARCO Foundation
The Ahmanson Foundation
BankAmerica Foundation
Benua Foundation, Inc.
The Bullitt Foundation
California Community Foundation
The Chevron Companies
The Cleveland Foundation
Davis Conservation Foundation
Geraldine R. Dodge Foundation, Inc.
Gaylord and Dorothy Donnelley Foundation
The Educational Foundation of America
The Favrot Fund
Ford Foundation
The Roy A. Hunt Foundation
The J. M. Kaplan Fund, Inc.
The Robert S. and Grayce B. Kerr
　Foundation, Inc.
Laurel Foundation
The John D. and Catherine T. MacArthur
　Foundation
James A. Macdonald Foundation
Millbrook Tribute Garden, Inc.
Mobil Foundation, Inc.
The Moriah Fund, Inc.
The Curtis and Edith Munson
　Foundation, Inc.
National Fish and Wildlife Foundation
The New York Community Trust
The New York Times Company
　Foundation, Inc.
Norcross Wildlife Foundation, Inc.
The David and Lucile Packard Foundation
Patagonia, Inc.
The Pew Charitable Trusts

Pew Scholars Program in Conservation
　and the Environment
Recreational Equipment, Inc.
The Rockefeller Foundation
Fran and Warren Rupp Foundation
Elmina B. Sewall Foundation
The Strong Foundation for
　Environmental Values
The Sulzberger Foundation, Inc.
The Switzer Foundation
The Trust For Mutual Understanding
Victoria Foundation, Inc.
WMX Environmental Grants Program
Weeden Foundation
Margaret Cullinan Wray Charitable
　Lead Annuity Trust

Neighborhoods

ARCO Foundation
The Abelard Foundation West
The Abell Foundation
The Ahmanson Foundation
Alaska Conservation Foundation
The Ben & Jerry's Foundation
The Bullitt Foundation
The Bush Foundation
Mary Flagler Cary Charitable Trust
Chesapeake Bay Trust
The Chicago Community Trust
The Nathan Cummings Foundation
Deer Creek Foundation
Geraldine R. Dodge Foundation, Inc.
Dolfinger-McMahon Foundation
The Field Foundation of Illinois, Inc.
Ford Foundation
Lloyd A. Fry Foundation
Give to the Earth Foundation
W. Alton Jones Foundation, Inc.
The Joyce Foundation
The J. M. Kaplan Fund, Inc.
Levi Strauss Foundation
Lyndhurst Foundation
The McKnight Foundation
Meadows Foundation, Inc.
Merck Family Fund
Joyce Mertz-Gilmore Foundation
Meyer Memorial Trust
The Milwaukee Foundation
The Minneapolis Foundation
The Moriah Fund, Inc.
Charles Stewart Mott Foundation
The Needmor Fund
New York Foundation
The New York Times Company
　Foundation, Inc.
The William Penn Foundation
The Pew Charitable Trusts
The Philadelphia Foundation
Public Welfare Foundation, Inc.
The Sapelo Foundation
The Florence and John Schumann
　Foundation
Surdna Foundation, Inc.

Environmental Topics and Activities

Neighborhoods (cont.)

The Tides Foundation
Unitarian Universalist Veatch Program at Shelter Rock
Lila Wallace-Reader's Digest Fund

Networks/networking

ARCO Foundation
A Territory Resource
The Acorn Foundation
Alaska Conservation Foundation
The Jenifer Altman Foundation
Angelina Fund, Inc.
BankAmerica Foundation
The Bauman Foundation
The Bay Foundation
Beldon Fund
The Ben & Jerry's Foundation
Mary Owen Borden Memorial Foundation
Helen Brach Foundation
Kathleen Price and Joseph M. Bryan Family Foundation, Inc.
The Bullitt Foundation
The Bydale Foundation
C. S. Fund
Caribou Fund
Columbia Foundation
Community Foundation of Western North Carolina, Inc.
Compton Foundation, Inc.
The Mary A. Crocker Trust
The Nathan Cummings Foundation
Damien Foundation
Davis Conservation Foundation
Geraldine R. Dodge Foundation, Inc.
Echoing Green Foundation
The Educational Foundation of America
The Energy Foundation
The Ettinger Foundation, Inc.
Ford Foundation
Foundation for Deep Ecology
Lloyd A. Fry Foundation
The Fund for New Jersey
Fund of the Four Directions
Funding Exchange
The Fred Gellert Foundation
General Service Foundation
The German Marshall Fund of the United States
Give to the Earth Foundation
Global Greengrants Fund
The Goldman Environmental Foundation
Richard & Rhoda Goldman Fund
Great Lakes Protection Fund
The George Gund Foundation
The Homeland Foundation
Howfirma Foundation
Island Foundation, Inc.
The Richard Ivey Foundation
W. Alton Jones Foundation, Inc.
The J. M. Kaplan Fund, Inc.
Laidlaw Foundation
Laird, Norton Foundation
The John D. and Catherine T. MacArthur Foundation
Magowan Family Foundation, Inc.
Maki Foundation
The McKnight Foundation
Giles W. and Elise G. Mead Foundation
The Andrew W. Mellon Foundation
Richard King Mellon Foundation
Merck Family Fund
The John Merck Fund
The Moriah Fund, Inc.
Charles Stewart Mott Foundation
Ruth Mott Fund
The Curtis and Edith Munson Foundation, Inc.
National Fish and Wildlife Foundation
New England Biolabs Foundation
The New York Times Company Foundation, Inc.
The New-Land Foundation, Inc.
Norcross Wildlife Foundation, Inc.
Norman Foundation
Northwest Area Foundation
Northwest Fund for the Environment
Jessie Smith Noyes Foundation, Inc.
The Overbrook Foundation
The David and Lucile Packard Foundation
Patagonia, Inc.
Amelia Peabody Charitable Fund
The Pew Charitable Trusts
Pew Scholars Program in Conservation and the Environment
Prince Charitable Trusts
Public Welfare Foundation, Inc.
Recreational Equipment, Inc.
Z. Smith Reynolds Foundation, Inc.
Rockefeller Brothers Fund, Inc.
The Rockefeller Foundation
The San Francisco Foundation
The Sapelo Foundation
Schultz Foundation, Inc.
Seventh Generation Fund
South Coast Foundation, Inc.
The Strong Foundation for Environmental Values
Surdna Foundation, Inc.
Threshold Foundation
The Tides Foundation
True North Foundation
Unitarian Universalist Veatch Program at Shelter Rock
Virginia Environmental Endowment
WMX Environmental Grants Program
Weeden Foundation
Margaret Cullinan Wray Charitable Lead Annuity Trust

Nitrogen fixation

Gaylord and Dorothy Donnelley Foundation
The Charles Engelhard Foundation
General Service Foundation
The Homeland Foundation
Laird, Norton Foundation

Nongovernmental organizations

The Jenifer Altman Foundation
The Arca Foundation
Conservation, Food & Health Foundation, Inc.
Damien Foundation
Ford Foundation
The Fred Gellert Foundation
General Service Foundation
The German Marshall Fund of the United States
W. Alton Jones Foundation, Inc.
Laidlaw Foundation
The John D. and Catherine T. MacArthur Foundation
The Moriah Fund, Inc.
Charles Stewart Mott Foundation
The Curtis and Edith Munson Foundation, Inc.
Jessie Smith Noyes Foundation, Inc.
The David and Lucile Packard Foundation
Pew Scholars Program in Conservation and the Environment
The Prospect Hill Foundation
Rockefeller Brothers Fund, Inc.
The Rockefeller Foundation
Threshold Foundation
The Tinker Foundation Incorporated
Weeden Foundation
Margaret Cullinan Wray Charitable Lead Annuity Trust
A Territory Resource
The Acorn Foundation
Angelina Fund, Inc.
Changing Horizons Charitable Trust
Compton Foundation, Inc.
Foundation for Deep Ecology
Fund of the Four Directions
Funding Exchange
W. Alton Jones Foundation, Inc.
Laidlaw Foundation
The Max and Anna Levinson Foundation
Ruth Mott Fund
The Needmor Fund
Public Welfare Foundation, Inc.
Seventh Generation Fund
Stern Family Fund
Threshold Foundation
Town Creek Foundation, Inc.
Margaret Cullinan Wray Charitable Lead Annuity Trust

Nuclear power

C. S. Fund
Changing Horizons Charitable Trust
Columbia Foundation
The Educational Foundation of America
The Max and Anna Levinson Foundation
The Sapelo Foundation
Threshold Foundation
The Trust For Mutual Understanding
Unitarian Universalist Veatch Program at Shelter Rock

Environmental Topics and Activities

Nuclear weapons

A Territory Resource
The Acorn Foundation
The Bullitt Foundation
C. S. Fund
Columbia Foundation
The Educational Foundation of America
The Fred Gellert Foundation
Richard & Rhoda Goldman Fund
W. Alton Jones Foundation, Inc.
The John D. and Catherine T. MacArthur Foundation
McKenzie River Gathering Foundation
The John Merck Fund
Ruth Mott Fund
Northwest Fund for the Environment
Public Welfare Foundation, Inc.
Rockefeller Family Fund, Inc.
Threshold Foundation
Unitarian Universalist Veatch Program at Shelter Rock

Nutrition

The Bauman Foundation
The Fred Gellert Foundation
Give to the Earth Foundation

Oceanography

ARCO Foundation
Atlantic Foundation
The George F. Baker Trust
California Community Foundation
Cox Foundation, Inc.
Jessie B. Cox Charitable Trust
The Arthur Vining Davis Foundations
Oliver S. and Jennie R. Donaldson Charitable Trust
Arthur M. and Olga T. Eisig-Arthur M. and Kate E. Tode Foundation, Inc.
The Armand G. Erpf Fund, Inc.
The Homeland Foundation
The Norman Lear Foundation
Richard Lounsbery Foundation, Inc.
The John D. and Catherine T. MacArthur Foundation
Massachusetts Environmental Trust
The Andrew W. Mellon Foundation
Mobil Foundation, Inc.
Charles Stewart Mott Foundation
Henry B. Plant Memorial Fund, Inc.
G. Unger Vetlesen Foundation
Wallace Genetic Foundation, Inc.

Oil spills

Alaska Conservation Foundation
Geraldine R. Dodge Foundation, Inc.
The Educational Foundation of America
Fund of the Four Directions
The Fred Gellert Foundation
Charles Stewart Mott Foundation
Patagonia, Inc.
The San Francisco Foundation

The Switzer Foundation
Victoria Foundation, Inc.

Open lands

American Conservation Association, Inc.
BankAmerica Foundation
The Beinecke Foundation, Inc.
Ruth H. Brown Foundation
The Buchanan Family Foundation
The Bullitt Foundation
Mary Flagler Cary Charitable Trust
The Champlin Foundations
The Chicago Community Trust
The Cleveland Foundation
Columbia Foundation
The Community Foundation of Santa Clara County
The Community Foundation Serving Coastal South Carolina
Compton Foundation, Inc.
Geraldine R. Dodge Foundation, Inc.
The Elizabeth Ordway Dunn Foundation, Inc.
The Educational Foundation of America
Environmental Endowment for New Jersey, Inc.
The Favrot Fund
The Field Foundation of Illinois, Inc.
Lloyd A. Fry Foundation
The Fund for New Jersey
The Fred Gellert Foundation
The Wallace Alexander Gerbode Foundation, Inc.
Richard & Rhoda Goldman Fund
Good Samaritan, Inc.
The Hamer Foundation
Heller Charitable & Educational Fund
The Hyams Foundation
The Henry M. Jackson Foundation
The J. M. Kaplan Fund, Inc.
The Seymour H. Knox Foundation, Inc.
Marin Community Foundation
The McIntosh Foundation
Joyce Mertz-Gilmore Foundation
Henry and Lucy Moses Fund, Inc.
The Curtis and Edith Munson Foundation, Inc.
National Fish and Wildlife Foundation
New Hampshire Charitable Foundation
The New York Community Trust
New York Foundation
The David and Lucile Packard Foundation
Patagonia, Inc.
Peninsula Community Foundation
The William Penn Foundation
Pritzker Foundation
Recreational Equipment, Inc.
Z. Smith Reynolds Foundation, Inc.
The Rockfall Foundation
The Schumann Fund for New Jersey, Inc.
The Strong Foundation for Environmental Values
Virginia Environmental Endowment

WMX Environmental Grants Program
Weyerhaeuser Company Foundation
The William P. Wharton Trust
Wilburforce Foundation
Margaret Cullinan Wray Charitable Lead Annuity Trust

Open lands: urban

American Conservation Association, Inc.
Mary Owen Borden Memorial Foundation
Kathleen Price and Joseph M. Bryan Family Foundation, Inc.
The Bullitt Foundation
Geraldine R. Dodge Foundation, Inc.
The J. M. Kaplan Fund, Inc.
Richard King Mellon Foundation
Merck Family Fund
The New York Times Company Foundation, Inc.
The Pew Charitable Trusts
Prince Charitable Trusts
Recreational Equipment, Inc.
Anna B. Stearns Charitable Foundation, Inc.
The Sulzberger Foundation, Inc.
Surdna Foundation, Inc.
Vancouver Foundation
Lila Wallace-Reader's Digest Fund

Open space: rural

The J. M. Kaplan Fund, Inc.
Henry E. and Consuelo S. Wenger Foundation, Inc.

Organizing

A Territory Resource
The Abelard Foundation West
The Acorn Foundation
Alaska Conservation Foundation
The Jenifer Altman Foundation
Mary Reynolds Babcock Foundation, Inc.
Beldon Fund
The Ben & Jerry's Foundation
The Bullitt Foundation
C. S. Fund
The Nathan Cummings Foundation
Deer Creek Foundation
The Elizabeth Ordway Dunn Foundation, Inc.
The Educational Foundation of America
Samuel S. Fels Fund
Foundation for Deep Ecology
The Fund for New Jersey
Fund of the Four Directions
Funding Exchange
The Gap Foundation
The Edward W. Hazen Foundation
W. Alton Jones Foundation, Inc.
The J. M. Kaplan Fund, Inc.
The Lazar Foundation
The Max and Anna Levinson Foundation
Lyndhurst Foundation
The John D. and Catherine T. MacArthur Foundation

Environmental Topics and Activities

Organizing (cont.)

Maki Foundation
McKenzie River Gathering Foundation
The McKnight Foundation
Giles W. and Elise G. Mead Foundation
Merck Family Fund
The Moriah Fund, Inc.
Charles Stewart Mott Foundation
Ruth Mott Fund
National Fish and Wildlife Foundation
The Needmor Fund
Norman Foundation
Northwest Area Foundation
Jessie Smith Noyes Foundation, Inc.
Patagonia, Inc.
Public Welfare Foundation, Inc.
Recreational Equipment, Inc.
Rockefeller Family Fund, Inc.
The Sapelo Foundation
The Florence and John Schumann Foundation
Seventh Generation Fund
Surdna Foundation, Inc.
Threshold Foundation
Unitarian Universalist Veatch Program at Shelter Rock
Victoria Foundation, Inc.

Outward Bound

The Ahmanson Foundation
American Express Philanthropic Program
The Beinecke Foundation, Inc.
The Betterment Fund
Blandin Foundation
The Blumenthal Foundation
Boettcher Foundation
The Bothin Foundation
Botwinick-Wolfensohn Foundation, Inc.
Alexander H. Bright Charitable Trust
Ruth H. Brown Foundation
Patrick and Aimee Butler Family Foundation
The Cabot Family Charitable Trust
California Community Foundation
The Cargill Foundation
The Clark Foundation
The Collins Foundation
Adolph Coors Foundation
Dayton Hudson Foundation
The Aaron Diamond Foundation
Cleveland H. Dodge Foundation, Inc.
The Dragon Foundation, Inc.
El Pomar Foundation
Fanwood Foundation
Gates Foundation
Georgia Power Foundation, Inc.
Georgia-Pacific Foundation
Richard & Rhoda Goldman Fund
Charles Hayden Foundation
Hurdle Hill Foundation
The Hyams Foundation
The Indian Point Foundation, Inc.
Island Foundation, Inc.
The Jackson Foundation

Helen K. and Arthur E. Johnson Foundation
MARPAT Foundation, Inc.
McDonnell Douglas Foundation
McKesson Foundation, Inc.
Nelson Mead Fund
Metropolitan Atlanta Community Foundation, Inc.
Middlecott Foundation
The Minneapolis Foundation
J. P. Morgan Charitable Trust
The New York Times Company Foundation, Inc.
Peninsula Community Foundation
Henry B. Plant Memorial Fund, Inc.
Lynn R. and Karl E. Prickett Fund
Z. Smith Reynolds Foundation, Inc.
The San Francisco Foundation
The Schiff Foundation
Elmina B. Sewall Foundation
The Sulzberger Foundation, Inc.
Vancouver Foundation
The Winston-Salem Foundation, Inc.

Ozone: stratospheric/depletion

The William Bingham Foundation
Changing Horizons Charitable Trust
Foundation for Deep Ecology
IBM Corporation
The Max and Anna Levinson Foundation
The Pew Charitable Trusts
Public Welfare Foundation, Inc.
Rockefeller Brothers Fund, Inc.
The Florence and John Schumann Foundation
Surdna Foundation, Inc.

Parks

Winifred & Harry B. Allen Foundation
American Express Philanthropic Program
The Barra Foundation, Inc.
The Ben & Jerry's Foundation
The Frank Stanley Beveridge Foundation, Inc.
Boettcher Foundation
Otto Bremer Foundation
The Bullitt Foundation
California Community Foundation
James & Abigail Campbell Foundation
The Champlin Foundations
Cheeryble Foundation
Ben B. Cheney Foundation
Chesapeake Bay Trust
The Chevron Companies
The Chicago Community Trust
The Collins Foundation
The Columbus Foundation
The Community Foundation of Greater New Haven
The Community Foundation Serving Coastal South Carolina
Compton Foundation, Inc.
The Cowles Charitable Trust
Davis Conservation Foundation
Cleveland H. Dodge Foundation, Inc.

Geraldine R. Dodge Foundation, Inc.
Gaylord and Dorothy Donnelley Foundation
El Pomar Foundation
The Charles Engelhard Foundation
English-Bonter-Mitchell Foundation
Fanwood Foundation
The William Stamps Farish Fund
Jamee and Marshall Field Foundation
Leland Fikes Foundation, Inc.
Ford Foundation
The Freed Foundation, Inc.
Frelinghuysen Foundation
Gates Foundation
The Fred Gellert Foundation
Georgia Power Foundation, Inc.
Richard & Rhoda Goldman Fund
The Greenville Foundation
Evelyn and Walter Haas, Jr. Fund
The Hamer Foundation
Harder Foundation
Gladys and Roland Harriman Foundation
Mary W. Harriman Foundation
Hartford Foundation for Public Giving
The Merrill G. & Emita E. Hastings Foundation
Charles Hayden Foundation
The Hitachi Foundation
The Homeland Foundation
Howfirma Foundation
The Hyde and Watson Foundation
The Henry M. Jackson Foundation
Martha Holden Jennings Foundation
The George Frederick Jewett Foundation
Joy Foundation for Ecological Education and Research
Laird, Norton Foundation
The Lauder Foundation, Inc.
Levi Strauss Foundation
Lilly Endowment, Inc.
The John D. and Catherine T. MacArthur Foundation
MARPAT Foundation, Inc.
The Martin Foundation, Inc.
Nelson Mead Fund
Meyer Memorial Trust
The Curtis and Edith Munson Foundation, Inc.
M. J. Murdock Charitable Trust
National Fish and Wildlife Foundation
New York Foundation
The New York Times Company Foundation, Inc.
The Nord Family Foundation
Kenneth T. and Eileen L. Norris Foundation
Patagonia, Inc.
The William Penn Foundation
Phillips Petroleum Foundation, Inc.
Prince Charitable Trusts
Recreational Equipment, Inc.
Z. Smith Reynolds Foundation, Inc.
Rockwell Fund, Inc.
Rockwood Fund, Inc.
San Diego Community Foundation
The San Francisco Foundation
Ellen Browning Scripps Foundation

Environmental Topics and Activities

Parks (cont.)

The Strong Foundation for Environmental Values
The Sulzberger Foundation, Inc.
Texaco Foundation
The Travelers Foundation
The Trust For Mutual Understanding
Underhill Foundation
Vancouver Foundation
Virginia Environmental Endowment
Lila Wallace-Reader's Digest Fund
Weyerhaeuser Company Foundation
G. N. Wilcox Trust
Margaret Cullinan Wray Charitable Lead Annuity Trust

Parks: local

Abell-Hanger Foundation
Mary Owen Borden Memorial Foundation
Otto Bremer Foundation
The Carpenter Foundation
The Cleveland Foundation
Olive B. Cole Foundation
The Cowles Charitable Trust
The Foundation for the National Capital Region
Lloyd A. Fry Foundation
The J. M. Kaplan Fund, Inc.
Maine Community Foundation, Inc.
The Winthrop Rockefeller Foundation
Weyerhaeuser Company Foundation

Parks: national

ARCO Foundation
Winifred & Harry B. Allen Foundation
American Conservation Association, Inc.
Evenor Armington Fund
BankAmerica Foundation
The Blumenthal Foundation
Alexander H. Bright Charitable Trust
Jesse Margaret Wilson Budlong Foundation for Animal Aid
California Community Foundation
The Chevron Companies
The Columbus Foundation
Conservation, Food & Health Foundation, Inc.
Adolph Coors Foundation
The Mary A. Crocker Trust
Geraldine R. Dodge Foundation, Inc.
Gaylord and Dorothy Donnelley Foundation
The Max and Victoria Dreyfus Foundation, Inc.
The Elizabeth Ordway Dunn Foundation, Inc.
Arthur M. and Olga T. Eisig-Arthur M. and Kate E. Tode Foundation, Inc.
Environment Now Foundation
Fanwood Foundation
The 1525 Foundation
Ford Foundation
Ford Motor Company Fund
Fund of the Four Directions
Richard & Rhoda Goldman Fund

Walter and Elise Haas Fund
Howfirma Foundation
Hurdle Hill Foundation
The Indian Point Foundation, Inc.
Jackson Hole Preserve, Inc.
The George Frederick Jewett Foundation
James A. Macdonald Foundation
Marin Community Foundation
MARPAT Foundation, Inc.
The Marshall Fund of Arizona
McKesson Foundation, Inc.
The John Merck Fund
The Curtis and Edith Munson Foundation, Inc.
National Fish and Wildlife Foundation
The New York Times Company Foundation, Inc.
The New-Land Foundation, Inc.
Edward John Noble Foundation, Inc.
Norcross Wildlife Foundation, Inc.
The Ohrstrom Foundation
Patagonia, Inc.
The Pfizer Foundation, Inc.
The Roberts Foundation
Margaret Dorrance Strawbridge Foundation of Pennsylvania II, Inc.
Surdna Foundation, Inc.
Nelson Talbott Foundation
Texaco Foundation
Town Creek Foundation, Inc.
The Trust For Mutual Understanding
Turner Foundation, Inc.
R. T. Vanderbilt Trust
Virginia Environmental Endowment
WMX Environmental Grants Program
Weeden Foundation
Wilburforce Foundation
Sidney & Phyllis Wragge Foundation
Margaret Cullinan Wray Charitable Lead Annuity Trust

Parks: state

Alaska Conservation Foundation
Winifred & Harry B. Allen Foundation
American Conservation Association, Inc.
Bay Area Community Foundation
James Ford Bell Foundation
Botwinick-Wolfensohn Foundation, Inc.
The Bullitt Foundation
Chesapeake Bay Trust
The Chevron Companies
The Collins Foundation
Columbia Foundation
Cleveland H. Dodge Foundation, Inc.
Geraldine R. Dodge Foundation, Inc.
Echoing Green Foundation
The Educational Foundation of America
Richard & Rhoda Goldman Fund
Greater Piscataqua Community Foundation
Walter and Elise Haas Fund
The J. M. Kaplan Fund, Inc.
Levi Strauss Foundation
The John D. and Catherine T. MacArthur Foundation
Maine Community Foundation, Inc.

McKesson Foundation, Inc.
Giles W. and Elise G. Mead Foundation
Merck Family Fund
Joyce Mertz-Gilmore Foundation
National Fish and Wildlife Foundation
Norcross Wildlife Foundation, Inc.
The David and Lucile Packard Foundation
Recreational Equipment, Inc.
The Sulzberger Foundation, Inc.
Rose E. Tucker Charitable Trust
Underhill Foundation
R. T. Vanderbilt Trust
WMX Environmental Grants Program
Weyerhaeuser Company Foundation

Parks: urban

The Achelis Foundation
Elmer L. & Eleanor J. Andersen Foundation
The Vincent Astor Foundation
BankAmerica Foundation
The Theodore H. Barth Foundation, Inc.
The Bay Foundation
Blandin Foundation
The Bodman Foundation
Mary Owen Borden Memorial Foundation
Botwinick-Wolfensohn Foundation, Inc.
Mary Flagler Cary Charitable Trust
The Columbus Foundation
The Community Foundation of Greater New Haven
The Cowles Charitable Trust
Cleveland H. Dodge Foundation, Inc.
Dolfinger-McMahon Foundation
The Herbert H. and Grace A. Dow Foundation
The Charles Engelhard Foundation
Fanwood Foundation
Lloyd A. Fry Foundation
The GAR Foundation
The W. C. Griffith Foundation
Charles Hayden Foundation
Heller Charitable & Educational Fund
The Hitachi Foundation
The Hofmann Foundation
The Indian Point Foundation, Inc.
The Howard Johnson Foundation
The J. M. Kaplan Fund, Inc.
Harris and Eliza Kempner Fund
Levi Strauss Foundation
Richard Lounsbery Foundation, Inc.
James A. Macdonald Foundation
Meadows Foundation, Inc.
Richard King Mellon Foundation
Joyce Mertz-Gilmore Foundation
Metropolitan Life Foundation
J. P. Morgan Charitable Trust
Henry and Lucy Moses Fund, Inc.
The New York Community Trust
The New York Times Company Foundation, Inc.
The New-Land Foundation, Inc.
Norcross Wildlife Foundation, Inc.
The Overbrook Foundation
The William Penn Foundation
The Pew Charitable Trusts

Environmental Topics and Activities

Parks: urban (cont.)

The Pfizer Foundation, Inc.
Pinewood Foundation
Henry B. Plant Memorial Fund, Inc.
The Prospect Hill Foundation
Recreational Equipment, Inc.
The Rockefeller Foundation
The Rockfall Foundation
Samuel and May Rudin Foundation, Inc.
The Scherman Foundation, Inc.
S. H. and Helen R. Scheuer Family Foundation, Inc.
Sarah I. Schieffelin Residuary Trust
The Schiff Foundation
The Schumann Fund for New Jersey, Inc.
Shell Oil Company Foundation
Solow Foundation
Springs Foundation, Inc.
Alfred T. Stanley Foundation
The Sulzberger Foundation, Inc.
Surdna Foundation, Inc.
Texaco Foundation
The Travelers Foundation
Harry C. Trexler Trust
Marcia Brady Tucker Foundation
Underhill Foundation
The Vidda Foundation
Vinmont Foundation, Inc.
WMX Environmental Grants Program
The Winston-Salem Foundation, Inc.
The Wortham Foundation, Inc.
Margaret Cullinan Wray Charitable Lead Annuity Trust

Performances

A Territory Resource
American Conservation Association, Inc.
Crystal Channel Foundation
Geraldine R. Dodge Foundation, Inc.
Foundation for Deep Ecology
Nathan M. Ohrbach Foundation, Inc.
Peninsula Community Foundation
Threshold Foundation
Weyerhaeuser Company Foundation

Pest management

The Nathan Cummings Foundation
The John D. and Catherine T. MacArthur Foundation
The Moriah Fund, Inc.
Z. Smith Reynolds Foundation, Inc.
The Rockefeller Foundation
Threshold Foundation

Pesticides/herbicides

A Territory Resource
Alaska Conservation Foundation
The Bauman Foundation
Compton Foundation, Inc.
The Fund for New Jersey
Fund of the Four Directions
Funding Exchange
The Gap Foundation
Great Lakes Protection Fund
HKH Foundation
Harder Foundation
The Homeland Foundation
W. Alton Jones Foundation, Inc.
Kongsgaard-Goldman Foundation
The Lazar Foundation
The John D. and Catherine T. MacArthur Foundation
Charles Stewart Mott Foundation
Ruth Mott Fund
National Fish and Wildlife Foundation
The Needmor Fund
Patagonia, Inc.
The Pew Charitable Trusts
Public Welfare Foundation, Inc.
The Rockefeller Foundation
The Florence and John Schumann Foundation
The Strong Foundation for Environmental Values
Threshold Foundation
Town Creek Foundation, Inc.
True North Foundation
Wallace Genetic Foundation, Inc.
Margaret Cullinan Wray Charitable Lead Annuity Trust

Pesticides: education

A Territory Resource
Mary Reynolds Babcock Foundation, Inc.
Beldon Fund
The Bullitt Foundation
Columbia Foundation
W. Alton Jones Foundation, Inc.
Charles Stewart Mott Foundation
Nathan M. Ohrbach Foundation, Inc.
Public Welfare Foundation, Inc.
Z. Smith Reynolds Foundation, Inc.
Rockefeller Family Fund, Inc.
The Strong Foundation for Environmental Values
Threshold Foundation

Pesticides: environmental hazards

The Ben & Jerry's Foundation
Columbia Foundation
The Educational Foundation of America
Environmental Endowment for New Jersey, Inc.
Richard & Rhoda Goldman Fund
W. Alton Jones Foundation, Inc.
Laidlaw Foundation
The Max and Anna Levinson Foundation
Threshold Foundation
True North Foundation

Pesticides: health hazards

The Ben & Jerry's Foundation
C. S. Fund
Deer Creek Foundation
W. Alton Jones Foundation, Inc.
Ruth Mott Fund
Jessie Smith Noyes Foundation, Inc.

Plants

California Community Foundation
Chesapeake Bay Trust
Columbia Foundation
The Columbus Foundation
Ederic Foundation, Inc.
The Charles Engelhard Foundation
Samuel S. Fels Fund
FishAmerica Foundation
Give to the Earth Foundation
The Homeland Foundation
The Joyce Foundation
The J. M. Kaplan Fund, Inc.
The Robert S. and Grayce B. Kerr Foundation, Inc.
The Kresge Foundation
Laird, Norton Foundation
The John D. and Catherine T. MacArthur Foundation
McLean Contributionship
The Andrew W. Mellon Foundation
The Curtis and Edith Munson Foundation, Inc.
National Fish and Wildlife Foundation
Norcross Wildlife Foundation, Inc.
Patagonia, Inc.
Rockwell Fund, Inc.
San Diego Community Foundation
Southwestern Bell Foundation
Threshold Foundation
C. A. Webster Foundation
The William P. Wharton Trust
Margaret Cullinan Wray Charitable Lead Annuity Trust

Plants: conservation

ARCO Foundation
American Conservation Association, Inc.
Atherton Family Foundation
Alexander H. Bright Charitable Trust
Chesapeake Bay Trust
The Elizabeth Ordway Dunn Foundation, Inc.
The Charles Engelhard Foundation
Mary D. and Walter F. Frear Eleemosynary Trust
Hawaii Community Foundation
Hurdle Hill Foundation
The Kresge Foundation
The John D. and Catherine T. MacArthur Foundation
Nelson Mead Fund
The Andrew W. Mellon Foundation
National Fish and Wildlife Foundation
The David and Lucile Packard Foundation
Pinewood Foundation
Prince Charitable Trusts
Rockwell Fund, Inc.
Stanley Smith Horticultural Trust
Surdna Foundation, Inc.
WMX Environmental Grants Program
Margaret Cullinan Wray Charitable Lead Annuity Trust

Environmental Topics and Activities

Plants: native

BankAmerica Foundation
Chesapeake Bay Trust
Flintridge Foundation
Hawaiian Electric Industries Charitable Foundation
The Homeland Foundation
The Robert S. and Grayce B. Kerr Foundation, Inc.
Patagonia, Inc.
Peninsula Community Foundation

Policy analysis/development

ARCO Foundation
A Territory Resource
Alaska Conservation Foundation
The Jenifer Altman Foundation
American Conservation Association, Inc.
Angelina Fund, Inc.
Mary Reynolds Babcock Foundation, Inc.
Clayton Baker Trust
The Bauman Foundation
Beldon Fund
The Ben & Jerry's Foundation
The William Bingham Foundation
The Lynde and Harry Bradley Foundation, Inc.
The Bullitt Foundation
Changing Horizons Charitable Trust
Robert Sterling Clark Foundation, Inc.
Columbia Foundation
Compton Foundation, Inc.
The Mary A. Crocker Trust
Geraldine R. Dodge Foundation, Inc.
Donner Canadian Foundation
The Educational Foundation of America
The Energy Foundation
Fanwood Foundation
Flintridge Foundation
Ford Foundation
GE Fund
The Fred Gellert Foundation
General Service Foundation
The Wallace Alexander Gerbode Foundation, Inc.
The German Marshall Fund of the United States
Give to the Earth Foundation
Great Lakes Protection Fund
The Clarence E. Heller Charitable Foundation
The Richard Ivey Foundation
Jackson Hole Preserve, Inc.
The Henry M. Jackson Foundation
W. Alton Jones Foundation, Inc.
The Joyce Foundation
The J. M. Kaplan Fund, Inc.
Charles G. Koch Charitable Foundation
The Max and Anna Levinson Foundation
Lilly Endowment, Inc.
Lyndhurst Foundation
The John D. and Catherine T. MacArthur Foundation

Marin Community Foundation
MARPAT Foundation, Inc.
Mars Foundation
The McKnight Foundation
The Andrew W. Mellon Foundation
The John Merck Fund
The Moody Foundation
The Moriah Fund, Inc.
Charles Stewart Mott Foundation
The Curtis and Edith Munson Foundation, Inc.
National Fish and Wildlife Foundation
The Needmor Fund
The New-Land Foundation, Inc.
Norman Foundation
Northwest Area Foundation
Jessie Smith Noyes Foundation, Inc.
The David and Lucile Packard Foundation
Patagonia, Inc.
James C. Penney Foundation
The Pew Charitable Trusts
Public Welfare Foundation, Inc.
Z. Smith Reynolds Foundation, Inc.
Rockefeller Brothers Fund, Inc.
Rockefeller Family Fund, Inc.
The Rockefeller Foundation
The Winthrop Rockefeller Foundation
The San Francisco Foundation
The Sapelo Foundation
Sarah Scaife Foundation Incorporated
The Florence and John Schumann Foundation
Shell Oil Company Foundation
The Strong Foundation for Environmental Values
The Summit Foundation
Surdna Foundation, Inc.
The Switzer Foundation
The Tinker Foundation Incorporated
Town Creek Foundation, Inc.
United States-Japan Foundation
Virginia Environmental Endowment
WMX Environmental Grants Program
Weeden Foundation
Weyerhaeuser Company Foundation
Margaret Cullinan Wray Charitable Lead Annuity Trust

Pollution

American Conservation Association, Inc.
Beldon Fund
Chesapeake Bay Trust
Robert Sterling Clark Foundation, Inc.
S. H. Cowell Foundation
Deer Creek Foundation
Richard & Rhoda Goldman Fund
The George Gund Foundation
The Edward W. Hazen Foundation
W. Alton Jones Foundation, Inc.
The Joyce Foundation
Laird, Norton Foundation
The McKnight Foundation
Millbrook Tribute Garden, Inc.
J. P. Morgan Charitable Trust

Charles Stewart Mott Foundation
The Curtis and Edith Munson Foundation, Inc.
The Overbrook Foundation
The Pew Charitable Trusts
Public Welfare Foundation, Inc.
Z. Smith Reynolds Foundation, Inc.
The Rockfall Foundation
The Sapelo Foundation
The Scherman Foundation, Inc.
The Florence and John Schumann Foundation
Sears-Swetland Foundation
Snee-Reinhardt Charitable Foundation
The Switzer Foundation
Nelson Talbott Foundation
Texaco Foundation
Unitarian Universalist Veatch Program at Shelter Rock
WMX Environmental Grants Program
Wallace Genetic Foundation, Inc.

Pollution: cleanup

ARCO Foundation
The Abell Foundation
The Acorn Foundation
Alaska Conservation Foundation
Mary Reynolds Babcock Foundation, Inc.
The Ben & Jerry's Foundation
Chesapeake Bay Trust
The Chevron Companies
Jamee and Marshall Field Foundation
Ford Motor Company Fund
The Gap Foundation
Island Foundation, Inc.
Harris and Eliza Kempner Fund
Longwood Foundation, Inc.
The McKnight Foundation
Charles Stewart Mott Foundation
John P. Murphy Foundation
National Fish and Wildlife Foundation
Norcross Wildlife Foundation, Inc.
Jessie Smith Noyes Foundation, Inc.
Ottinger Foundation
Patagonia, Inc.
Public Welfare Foundation, Inc.
Z. Smith Reynolds Foundation, Inc.
Rockwell Fund, Inc.
The Switzer Foundation
Unitarian Universalist Veatch Program at Shelter Rock
WMX Environmental Grants Program

Pollution: nonpoint source

Mary Flagler Cary Charitable Trust
Chesapeake Bay Trust
Environmental Endowment for New Jersey, Inc.
The Fund for New Jersey
Richard & Rhoda Goldman Fund
Great Lakes Protection Fund
Patagonia, Inc.
Threshold Foundation

© 1995 Environmental Data Resources, Inc.

Environmental Topics and Activities

Pollution: prevention

ARCO Foundation
A Territory Resource
The Abell Foundation
Alaska Conservation Foundation
The Jenifer Altman Foundation
Azadoutioun Foundation
The Bauman Foundation
Beldon Fund
The Ben & Jerry's Foundation
The Bullitt Foundation
The Nathan Cummings Foundation
Davis Conservation Foundation
Deer Creek Foundation
Geraldine R. Dodge Foundation, Inc.
Give to the Earth Foundation
Great Lakes Protection Fund
The George Gund Foundation
Ittleson Foundation, Inc.
W. Alton Jones Foundation, Inc.
The Joyce Foundation
Kongsgaard-Goldman Foundation
Lyndhurst Foundation
The McKnight Foundation
Charles Stewart Mott Foundation
Jessie Smith Noyes Foundation, Inc.
Patagonia, Inc.
The William Penn Foundation
The Pew Charitable Trusts
The Prospect Hill Foundation
Public Welfare Foundation, Inc.
Sid W. Richardson Foundation
The Sapelo Foundation
The Florence and John Schumann Foundation
The Switzer Foundation
Unitarian Universalist Veatch Program at Shelter Rock
Victoria Foundation, Inc.
Virginia Environmental Endowment
WMX Environmental Grants Program

Population

The Jenifer Altman Foundation
Alexander H. Bright Charitable Trust
California Community Foundation
Compton Foundation, Inc.
The Conservation and Research Foundation
S. H. Cowell Foundation
The Mary A. Crocker Trust
The Nathan Cummings Foundation
Davis Conservation Foundation
Geraldine R. Dodge Foundation, Inc.
Ford Foundation
Foundation for Deep Ecology
The Fred Gellert Foundation
The Wallace Alexander Gerbode Foundation, Inc.
Harder Foundation
The Horn Foundation
Laurel Foundation
The John D. and Catherine T. MacArthur Foundation
The Andrew W. Mellon Foundation
The Minneapolis Foundation
The Moriah Fund, Inc.
The Curtis and Edith Munson Foundation, Inc.
Jessie Smith Noyes Foundation, Inc.
The David and Lucile Packard Foundation
The Pew Charitable Trusts
Public Welfare Foundation, Inc.
Philip D. Reed Foundation, Inc.
Rockefeller Financial Services, Philanthropy Department
The Rockefeller Foundation
The Summit Foundation
Tortuga Foundation
Turner Foundation, Inc.
Vinmont Foundation, Inc.
Weeden Foundation
Wilburforce Foundation
The Winslow Foundation

Poverty

Ford Foundation
Laird, Norton Foundation
Joyce Mertz-Gilmore Foundation
The New York Times Company Foundation, Inc.
Northwest Area Foundation
Public Welfare Foundation, Inc.
Z. Smith Reynolds Foundation, Inc.
Rockefeller Brothers Fund, Inc.
The Rockefeller Foundation
Surdna Foundation, Inc.
Threshold Foundation
Wallace Genetic Foundation, Inc.

Prairies

ARCO Foundation
The Bush Foundation
Gaylord and Dorothy Donnelley Foundation
The Field Foundation of Illinois, Inc.
Lloyd A. Fry Foundation
The Robert S. and Grayce B. Kerr Foundation, Inc.
National Fish and Wildlife Foundation
Thomas Sill Foundation
Margaret Cullinan Wray Charitable Lead Annuity Trust

Problem solving

A Territory Resource
The Bauman Foundation
The Ben & Jerry's Foundation
The William Bingham Foundation
The Bullitt Foundation
Mary Flagler Cary Charitable Trust
The Energy Foundation
Ford Foundation
W. Alton Jones Foundation, Inc.
Mars Foundation
The Rockfall Foundation
Weeden Foundation

Program start-up/implementation

ARCO Foundation
The Abell Foundation
Atherton Family Foundation
The Bauman Foundation
The Bay Foundation
Beldon Fund
James Ford Bell Foundation
The William Bingham Foundation
Blandin Foundation
Kathleen Price and Joseph M. Bryan Family Foundation, Inc.
The Bullitt Foundation
C. S. Fund
Mary Flagler Cary Charitable Trust
Chesapeake Bay Trust
Robert Sterling Clark Foundation, Inc.
The Columbus Foundation
The Community Foundation of Sarasota County, Inc.
The Conservation and Research Foundation
S. H. Cowell Foundation
Jessie B. Cox Charitable Trust
The Mary A. Crocker Trust
Crystal Channel Foundation
The Nathan Cummings Foundation
Deer Creek Foundation
Geraldine R. Dodge Foundation, Inc.
The Elizabeth Ordway Dunn Foundation, Inc.
The Educational Foundation of America
The Energy Foundation
Environmental Education Foundation of Florida, Inc.
Environmental Endowment for New Jersey, Inc.
Ford Foundation
Mary D. and Walter F. Frear Eleemosynary Trust
The Fund for New Jersey
The Wallace Alexander Gerbode Foundation, Inc.
The German Marshall Fund of the United States
Richard & Rhoda Goldman Fund
Great Lakes Protection Fund
The George Gund Foundation
The James Irvine Foundation
Island Foundation, Inc.
W. Alton Jones Foundation, Inc.
The Joyce Foundation
The J. M. Kaplan Fund, Inc.
Harris and Eliza Kempner Fund
Laidlaw Foundation
The Lazar Foundation
Levi Strauss Foundation
The Max and Anna Levinson Foundation
Lyndhurst Foundation
The John D. and Catherine T. MacArthur Foundation
Richard King Mellon Foundation
J. P. Morgan Charitable Trust
The Moriah Fund, Inc.

Environmental Topics and Activities

Program start-up/implementation (cont.)
Charles Stewart Mott Foundation
The Curtis and Edith Munson
 Foundation, Inc.
National Fish and Wildlife Foundation
New England Biolabs Foundation
The Nord Family Foundation
Norman Foundation
Northwest Area Foundation
Jessie Smith Noyes Foundation, Inc.
The David and Lucile Packard Foundation
Patagonia, Inc.
The William Penn Foundation
James C. Penney Foundation
The Pew Charitable Trusts
Public Welfare Foundation, Inc.
Recreational Equipment, Inc.
Z. Smith Reynolds Foundation, Inc.
Rockefeller Brothers Fund, Inc.
Rockefeller Family Fund, Inc.
The Rockefeller Foundation
The Rockfall Foundation
The San Francisco Foundation
Sarkeys Foundation
The Schumann Fund for New Jersey, Inc.
Seventh Generation Fund
Thomas Sill Foundation
Steelcase Foundation
The Sudbury Foundation
Surdna Foundation, Inc.
The Switzer Foundation
Unitarian Universalist Veatch Program
 at Shelter Rock
Weeden Foundation
The William P. Wharton Trust

Programs: demonstration/pilot
ARCO Foundation
A Territory Resource
The Ahmanson Foundation
Atkinson Foundation
The Bauman Foundation
Beldon Fund
The Ben & Jerry's Foundation
Blandin Foundation
Otto Bremer Foundation
Kathleen Price and Joseph M. Bryan
 Family Foundation, Inc.
The Bullitt Foundation
Changing Horizons Charitable Trust
Ben B. Cheney Foundation
Chesapeake Bay Trust
Columbia Foundation
Compton Foundation, Inc.
Conservation, Food & Health
 Foundation, Inc.
The Mary A. Crocker Trust
The Nathan Cummings Foundation
Geraldine R. Dodge Foundation, Inc.
Dolfinger-McMahon Foundation
The Elizabeth Ordway Dunn
 Foundation, Inc.
The Energy Foundation

Environmental Education Foundation
 of Florida, Inc.
Environmental Endowment for
 New Jersey, Inc.
The Field Foundation of Illinois, Inc.
Ford Foundation
The Fund for New Jersey
General Service Foundation
The German Marshall Fund of
 the United States
The Goldman Environmental Foundation
Great Lakes Protection Fund
The William and Flora Hewlett Foundation
Island Foundation, Inc.
Ittleson Foundation, Inc.
The Richard Ivey Foundation
The Henry M. Jackson Foundation
W. Alton Jones Foundation, Inc.
The J. M. Kaplan Fund, Inc.
Laidlaw Foundation
The Max and Anna Levinson Foundation
Lintilhac Foundation
Lyndhurst Foundation
The John D. and Catherine T. MacArthur
 Foundation
MARPAT Foundation, Inc.
The Martin Foundation, Inc.
The McKnight Foundation
Giles W. and Elise G. Mead Foundation
The John Merck Fund
The Minneapolis Foundation
The Moriah Fund, Inc.
Charles Stewart Mott Foundation
The Curtis and Edith Munson
 Foundation, Inc.
M. J. Murdock Charitable Trust
National Fish and Wildlife Foundation
The Needmor Fund
Northwest Area Foundation
The David and Lucile Packard Foundation
The Pew Charitable Trusts
Pew Scholars Program in Conservation
 and the Environment
Z. Smith Reynolds Foundation, Inc.
Rockefeller Brothers Fund, Inc.
The Rockefeller Foundation
The Rockfall Foundation
The San Francisco Foundation
The Sapelo Foundation
Seventh Generation Fund
The Sudbury Foundation
Surdna Foundation, Inc.
The Switzer Foundation
Threshold Foundation
The Tinker Foundation Incorporated
The Trust For Mutual Understanding
Unitarian Universalist Veatch Program
 at Shelter Rock
Victoria Foundation, Inc.
Virginia Environmental Endowment
WMX Environmental Grants Program
Margaret Cullinan Wray Charitable
 Lead Annuity Trust

Programs: experimental/innovative
James Ford Bell Foundation
Geraldine R. Dodge Foundation, Inc.
The Energy Foundation
The J. M. Kaplan Fund, Inc.
The Curtis and Edith Munson
 Foundation, Inc.
The Pew Charitable Trusts
Threshold Foundation

Programs: international
The Ahmanson Foundation
Alaska Conservation Foundation
The Jenifer Altman Foundation
American Conservation Association, Inc.
Angelina Fund, Inc.
The Arca Foundation
Arcadia Foundation
Clayton Baker Trust
The Bauman Foundation
The Bay Foundation
The Howard Bayne Fund
The Lynde and Harry Bradley
 Foundation, Inc.
Alexander H. Bright Charitable Trust
Jesse Margaret Wilson Budlong Foundation
 for Animal Aid
The Bullitt Foundation
C. S. Fund
California Community Foundation
Changing Horizons Charitable Trust
The Chevron Companies
Columbia Foundation
Compton Foundation, Inc.
The Conservation and Research Foundation
Conservation, Food & Health
 Foundation, Inc.
S. H. Cowell Foundation
Cox Foundation, Inc.
The Mary A. Crocker Trust
Crystal Channel Foundation
The Nathan Cummings Foundation
Damien Foundation
Geraldine R. Dodge Foundation, Inc.
Gaylord and Dorothy Donnelley Foundation
Echoing Green Foundation
The Educational Foundation of America
The Energy Foundation
The Charles Engelhard Foundation
The Armand G. Erpf Fund, Inc.
The Ettinger Foundation, Inc.
Fanwood Foundation
The Favrot Fund
Ford Foundation
Foundation for Deep Ecology
Funding Exchange
The Fred Gellert Foundation
General Service Foundation
The German Marshall Fund of
 the United States
Give to the Earth Foundation
The Goldman Environmental Foundation
Richard & Rhoda Goldman Fund

© 1995 Environmental Data Resources, Inc.

769

Environmental Topics and Activities

Programs: international (cont.)

Great Lakes Protection Fund
The Greenville Foundation
Harbor Lights Foundation
The Merrill G. & Emita E. Hastings Foundation
Howfirma Foundation
The Roy A. Hunt Foundation
The Henry M. Jackson Foundation
W. Alton Jones Foundation, Inc.
The Esther A. and Joseph Klingenstein Fund, Inc.
Laidlaw Foundation
Laird, Norton Foundation
The Lazar Foundation
The Max and Anna Levinson Foundation
The John D. and Catherine T. MacArthur Foundation
Marin Community Foundation
Mars Foundation
Giles W. and Elise G. Mead Foundation
The Andrew W. Mellon Foundation
Merck Family Fund
The John Merck Fund
Joyce Mertz-Gilmore Foundation
The Minneapolis Foundation
J. P. Morgan Charitable Trust
The Moriah Fund, Inc.
Charles Stewart Mott Foundation
National Fish and Wildlife Foundation
The New York Times Company Foundation, Inc.
Norman Foundation
Northwest Area Foundation
Jessie Smith Noyes Foundation, Inc.
The Ohrstrom Foundation
The Overbrook Foundation
The David and Lucile Packard Foundation
Patagonia, Inc.
James C. Penney Foundation
The Pew Charitable Trusts
Pew Scholars Program in Conservation and the Environment
The Prudential Foundation
Public Welfare Foundation, Inc.
Philip D. Reed Foundation, Inc.
Rockefeller Brothers Fund, Inc.
The Rockefeller Foundation
The Winthrop Rockefeller Foundation
Rockwood Fund, Inc.
Lee Romney Foundation, Inc.
The San Francisco Foundation
Schultz Foundation, Inc.
Sequoia Foundation
Seventh Generation Fund
Shell Oil Company Foundation
The Sulzberger Foundation, Inc.
The Summerlee Foundation
Thanksgiving Foundation
Threshold Foundation
The Tides Foundation
The Tinker Foundation Incorporated
The Truland Foundation
The Trust For Mutual Understanding

Unitarian Universalist Veatch Program at Shelter Rock
United States-Japan Foundation
WMX Environmental Grants Program
Wallace Genetic Foundation, Inc.
Weeden Foundation
Margaret Cullinan Wray Charitable Lead Annuity Trust

Programs: outreach

ARCO Foundation
A Territory Resource
The Abell Foundation
The Vincent Astor Foundation
Mary Reynolds Babcock Foundation, Inc.
BankAmerica Foundation
S. D. Bechtel, Jr. Foundation
Beldon Fund
The Ben & Jerry's Foundation
Otto Bremer Foundation
The Bullitt Foundation
C. S. Fund
The Cabot Family Charitable Trust
California Community Foundation
Chesapeake Bay Trust
The Collins Foundation
Columbia Foundation
Davis Conservation Foundation
Geraldine R. Dodge Foundation, Inc.
The Educational Foundation of America
The Energy Foundation
Flintridge Foundation
Ford Foundation
Lloyd A. Fry Foundation
The Fred Gellert Foundation
Great Lakes Protection Fund
The George Gund Foundation
The Edward W. Hazen Foundation
W. Alton Jones Foundation, Inc.
The J. M. Kaplan Fund, Inc.
Laidlaw Foundation
Lyndhurst Foundation
The John D. and Catherine T. MacArthur Foundation
MARPAT Foundation, Inc.
The McKnight Foundation
Merck Family Fund
The John Merck Fund
Joyce Mertz-Gilmore Foundation
Charles Stewart Mott Foundation
Ruth Mott Fund
The Curtis and Edith Munson Foundation, Inc.
National Fish and Wildlife Foundation
Northwest Fund for the Environment
Jessie Smith Noyes Foundation, Inc.
Patagonia, Inc.
The William Penn Foundation
James C. Penney Foundation
The Pew Charitable Trusts
Public Welfare Foundation, Inc.
Recreational Equipment, Inc.
The San Francisco Foundation
The Florence and John Schumann Foundation

Surdna Foundation, Inc.
Threshold Foundation
The Tides Foundation
The Tinker Foundation Incorporated
True North Foundation
Rose E. Tucker Charitable Trust
Weeden Foundation
Margaret Cullinan Wray Charitable Lead Annuity Trust

Public health

Angelina Fund, Inc.
The Bauman Foundation
Beldon Fund
The Betterment Fund
The Bullitt Foundation
C. S. Fund
The Cleveland Foundation
Columbia Foundation
Conservation, Food & Health Foundation, Inc.
The Nathan Cummings Foundation
Deer Creek Foundation
Richard & Rhoda Goldman Fund
Great Lakes Protection Fund
W. Alton Jones Foundation, Inc.
The J. M. Kaplan Fund, Inc.
W. K. Kellogg Foundation
The Max and Anna Levinson Foundation
Lyndhurst Foundation
The John D. and Catherine T. MacArthur Foundation
The John Merck Fund
Charles Stewart Mott Foundation
Norman Foundation
Jessie Smith Noyes Foundation, Inc.
Patagonia, Inc.
Pew Scholars Program in Conservation and the Environment
Public Welfare Foundation, Inc.
Z. Smith Reynolds Foundation, Inc.
The Rockefeller Foundation
Seventh Generation Fund
Surdna Foundation, Inc.
The Switzer Foundation
Threshold Foundation
Unitarian Universalist Veatch Program at Shelter Rock
Virginia Environmental Endowment
Weeden Foundation

Public lands

Alaska Conservation Foundation
Winifred & Harry B. Allen Foundation
American Conservation Association, Inc.
American Foundation Corporation
Evenor Armington Fund
Beldon Fund
Bishop Pine Fund
Mary Owen Borden Memorial Foundation
Alex. Brown & Sons Charitable Foundation, Inc.
W. L. Lyons Brown Foundation

Environmental Topics and Activities

Public lands (cont.)

Kathleen Price and Joseph M. Bryan Family Foundation, Inc.
The Bullitt Foundation
The Morris and Gwendolyn Cafritz Foundation
Mary Flagler Cary Charitable Trust
The Chevron Companies
The Clark Foundation
The Community Foundation of Santa Clara County
Compton Foundation, Inc.
The Mary A. Crocker Trust
Davis Conservation Foundation
Deer Creek Foundation
The Elizabeth Ordway Dunn Foundation, Inc.
The Educational Foundation of America
The Favrot Fund
Bert Fingerhut/Caroline Hicks Family Fund
Flintridge Foundation
General Service Foundation
Georgia Power Foundation, Inc.
Georgia-Pacific Foundation
The Wallace Alexander Gerbode Foundation, Inc.
HKH Foundation
Harder Foundation
Charles Hayden Foundation
Heller Charitable & Educational Fund
The Henry M. Jackson Foundation
W. Alton Jones Foundation, Inc.
The J. M. Kaplan Fund, Inc.
F. M. Kirby Foundation, Inc.
The Max and Anna Levinson Foundation
The John D. and Catherine T. MacArthur Foundation
James A. Macdonald Foundation
Maki Foundation
MARPAT Foundation, Inc.
The Andrew W. Mellon Foundation
Richard King Mellon Foundation
Merck Family Fund
Middlecott Foundation
Ruth Mott Fund
National Fish and Wildlife Foundation
New Hampshire Charitable Foundation
New York Foundation
The New York Times Company Foundation, Inc.
The New-Land Foundation, Inc.
The Ohrstrom Foundation
The Overbrook Foundation
Patagonia, Inc.
The Pew Charitable Trusts
Pew Scholars Program in Conservation and the Environment
Ellis L. Phillips Foundation
Howard Phipps Foundation
The Prospect Hill Foundation
The Prudential Foundation
Rockefeller Family Fund, Inc.
The San Francisco Foundation
The Scherman Foundation, Inc.
The Schumann Fund for New Jersey, Inc.

The Florence and John Schumann Foundation
Seventh Generation Fund
The Strong Foundation for Environmental Values
The Sulzberger Foundation, Inc.
The Tides Foundation
Town Creek Foundation, Inc.
Underhill Foundation
R. T. Vanderbilt Trust
Vanguard Public Foundation
Victoria Foundation, Inc.
Lila Wallace-Reader's Digest Fund
Weeden Foundation
Weyerhaeuser Company Foundation
Wilburforce Foundation
Robert W. Wilson Foundation
Margaret Cullinan Wray Charitable Lead Annuity Trust

Public-private sector cooperation

National Fish and Wildlife Foundation
United States-Japan Foundation

Publications

ARCO Foundation
A Territory Resource
Alaska Conservation Foundation
The Jenifer Altman Foundation
American Conservation Association, Inc.
Mary Reynolds Babcock Foundation, Inc.
BankAmerica Foundation
The Bauman Foundation
Beldon Fund
James Ford Bell Foundation
The Ben & Jerry's Foundation
The Blumenthal Foundation
The Bullitt Foundation
C. S. Fund
The Carpenter Foundation
Changing Horizons Charitable Trust
Ben B. Cheney Foundation
Chesapeake Bay Trust
Claneil Foundation, Inc.
Robert Sterling Clark Foundation, Inc.
The Collins Foundation
Columbia Foundation
Compton Foundation, Inc.
The Conservation and Research Foundation
Conservation, Food & Health Foundation, Inc.
Jessie B. Cox Charitable Trust
Crystal Channel Foundation
The Nathan Cummings Foundation
Damien Foundation
Davis Conservation Foundation
Geraldine R. Dodge Foundation, Inc.
The Elizabeth Ordway Dunn Foundation, Inc.
The Educational Foundation of America
The Energy Foundation
Environmental Endowment for New Jersey, Inc.
The Ettinger Foundation, Inc.

The Favrot Fund
Flintridge Foundation
Ford Foundation
Foundation for Deep Ecology
Mary D. and Walter F. Frear Eleemosynary Trust
The Fred Gellert Foundation
General Service Foundation
The German Marshall Fund of the United States
Give to the Earth Foundation
Global Greengrants Fund
The Goldman Environmental Foundation
Herman Goldman Foundation
Richard & Rhoda Goldman Fund
Great Lakes Protection Fund
The George Gund Foundation
Harder Foundation
Island Foundation, Inc.
The Richard Ivey Foundation
The Henry M. Jackson Foundation
W. Alton Jones Foundation, Inc.
The Joyce Foundation
The J. M. Kaplan Fund, Inc.
Laidlaw Foundation
Laird, Norton Foundation
Laurel Foundation
The Max and Anna Levinson Foundation
Lyndhurst Foundation
The John D. and Catherine T. MacArthur Foundation
Maki Foundation
MARPAT Foundation, Inc.
McInerny Foundation
McKenzie River Gathering Foundation
The McKnight Foundation
McLean Contributionship
Giles W. and Elise G. Mead Foundation
The Andrew W. Mellon Foundation
Merck Family Fund
The John Merck Fund
Joyce Mertz-Gilmore Foundation
Leo Model Foundation, Inc.
The Moriah Fund, Inc.
Charles Stewart Mott Foundation
The Mountaineers Foundation
The Curtis and Edith Munson Foundation, Inc.
National Fish and Wildlife Foundation
National Geographic Society Education Foundation
New England Biolabs Foundation
New Hampshire Charitable Foundation
Edward John Noble Foundation, Inc.
The Nord Family Foundation
Northwest Area Foundation
Northwest Fund for the Environment
Jessie Smith Noyes Foundation, Inc.
The David and Lucile Packard Foundation
Patagonia, Inc.
James C. Penney Foundation
The Pew Charitable Trusts
The Prospect Hill Foundation
Recreational Equipment, Inc.
The Rhode Island Community Foundation

Environmental Topics and Activities

Publications (cont.)

Sid W. Richardson Foundation
Rockefeller Brothers Fund, Inc.
Rockefeller Family Fund, Inc.
The Rockefeller Foundation
The Winthrop Rockefeller Foundation
Rockwell Fund, Inc.
San Diego Community Foundation
The Sapelo Foundation
The Schumann Fund for New Jersey, Inc.
Seventh Generation Fund
The Sudbury Foundation
Surdna Foundation, Inc.
S. Mark Taper Foundation
Threshold Foundation
The Tinker Foundation Incorporated
True North Foundation
The Trust For Mutual Understanding
Rose E. Tucker Charitable Trust
The Vidda Foundation
Virginia Environmental Endowment
WMX Environmental Grants Program
Lila Wallace-Reader's Digest Fund
Weeden Foundation
Weyerhaeuser Company Foundation
The William P. Wharton Trust
Wilburforce Foundation
Margaret Cullinan Wray Charitable Lead Annuity Trust

Radiation: effects

The Bullitt Foundation
The Max and Anna Levinson Foundation
The John D. and Catherine T. MacArthur Foundation
Ruth Mott Fund
Unitarian Universalist Veatch Program at Shelter Rock

Radiation: food irradiation

C. S. Fund
Changing Horizons Charitable Trust
The Strong Foundation for Environmental Values
Threshold Foundation
Unitarian Universalist Veatch Program at Shelter Rock

Radioactive waste

The Acorn Foundation
Alaska Conservation Foundation
The Bullitt Foundation
Columbia Foundation
Funding Exchange
Richard & Rhoda Goldman Fund
The Hahn Family Foundation
The Clarence E. Heller Charitable Foundation
W. Alton Jones Foundation, Inc.
Laidlaw Foundation
Ruth Mott Fund
New York Foundation
Northwest Fund for the Environment
Public Welfare Foundation, Inc.
Seventh Generation Fund
Threshold Foundation
Unitarian Universalist Veatch Program at Shelter Rock
Vanguard Public Foundation

Radioactive waste: storage/disposal

A Territory Resource
The Acorn Foundation
The Bullitt Foundation
C. S. Fund
The Educational Foundation of America
Funding Exchange
W. Alton Jones Foundation, Inc.
The John Merck Fund
Ruth Mott Fund
Norman Foundation
Patagonia, Inc.
Public Welfare Foundation, Inc.
Seventh Generation Fund
Threshold Foundation
Unitarian Universalist Veatch Program at Shelter Rock

Rainforests

Alaska Conservation Foundation
Atkinson Foundation
The Bullitt Foundation
Caribou Fund
Olive B. Cole Foundation
Douroucouli Foundation
The Ettinger Foundation, Inc.
The Favrot Fund
Foundation for Deep Ecology
The Barbara Gauntlett Foundation, Inc.
The Fred Gellert Foundation
Give to the Earth Foundation
The Greenville Foundation
The Hitachi Foundation
The Homeland Foundation
The Kresge Foundation
Magowan Family Foundation, Inc.
The John Merck Fund
J. P. Morgan Charitable Trust
The Moriah Fund, Inc.
Charles Stewart Mott Foundation
Ruth Mott Fund
New England Biolabs Foundation
The New York Times Company Foundation, Inc.
The New-Land Foundation, Inc.
The Pew Charitable Trusts
Pritzker Foundation
The Prospect Hill Foundation
Rockwood Fund, Inc.
Sequoia Foundation
The Sulzberger Foundation, Inc.
Texaco Foundation
Threshold Foundation
The Tides Foundation
Weeden Foundation

Rainforests: education

The Bullitt Foundation
HKH Foundation
The Moody Foundation
Threshold Foundation

Rainforests: preservation

Alaska Conservation Foundation
The Bullitt Foundation
California Community Foundation
Conservation, Food & Health Foundation, Inc.
Damien Foundation
Oliver S. and Jennie R. Donaldson Charitable Trust
Foundation for Deep Ecology
General Service Foundation
HKH Foundation
The Homeland Foundation
The Horn Foundation
The Esther A. and Joseph Klingenstein Fund, Inc.
Maine Community Foundation, Inc.
The Overbrook Foundation
Patagonia, Inc.
Public Welfare Foundation, Inc.
Rockwood Fund, Inc.
Samuel and May Rudin Foundation, Inc.
Schultz Foundation, Inc.
Surdna Foundation, Inc.
Threshold Foundation

Ranch/rangelands/grasslands

Winifred & Harry B. Allen Foundation
The George F. Baker Trust
BankAmerica Foundation
Bishop Pine Fund
The Conservation and Research Foundation
The Kresge Foundation
The John D. and Catherine T. MacArthur Foundation
The Curtis and Edith Munson Foundation, Inc.
National Fish and Wildlife Foundation
Patagonia, Inc.
Rockefeller Brothers Fund, Inc.
C. A. Webster Foundation
The Dean Witter Foundation

Recreation

American Conservation Association, Inc.
Elmer L. & Eleanor J. Andersen Foundation
Atherton Family Foundation
BankAmerica Foundation
L. L. Bean, Inc.
Beldon Fund
The Ben & Jerry's Foundation
Beneficia Foundation
Blandin Foundation
Botwinick-Wolfensohn Foundation, Inc.
Otto Bremer Foundation
The Bullitt Foundation

Environmental Topics and Activities

Recreation (cont.)

C. S. Fund
The Cabot Family Charitable Trust
California Community Foundation
The Carpenter Foundation
The Champlin Foundations
Changing Horizons Charitable Trust
Ben B. Cheney Foundation
Chesapeake Bay Trust
The Chevron Companies
Clark Charitable Trust
The Collins Foundation
The Community Foundation of
  Greater New Haven
Adolph Coors Foundation
The Cricket Foundation
Davis Conservation Foundation
Eastman Kodak Company Charitable Trust
El Pomar Foundation
The William Stamps Farish Fund
The Foundation for the National
  Capital Region
The Gap Foundation
Gates Foundation
The Fred Gellert Foundation
Richard & Rhoda Goldman Fund
Evelyn and Walter Haas, Jr. Fund
The Hitachi Foundation
The Hofmann Foundation
Howfirma Foundation
The Jackson Foundation
Jackson Hole Preserve, Inc.
The George Frederick Jewett Foundation
The J. M. Kaplan Fund, Inc.
The Lagemann Foundation
Laird, Norton Foundation
Levi Strauss Foundation
Lilly Endowment, Inc.
Lyndhurst Foundation
Nelson Mead Fund
Meadows Foundation, Inc.
Meyer Memorial Trust
J. P. Morgan Charitable Trust
The Mountaineers Foundation
National Fish and Wildlife Foundation
The New York Times Company
  Foundation, Inc.
The New-Land Foundation, Inc.
Norcross Wildlife Foundation, Inc.
Northwest Area Foundation
Outdoor Industry Conservation Alliance
Patagonia, Inc.
The William Penn Foundation
Recreational Equipment, Inc.
Z. Smith Reynolds Foundation, Inc.
The Roberts Foundation
Rockefeller Family Fund, Inc.
The Rockfall Foundation
The San Francisco Foundation
The Skaggs Foundation
The Stebbins Fund, Inc.
Steelcase Foundation
The Stratford Foundation
The Strong Foundation for
  Environmental Values

The Sulzberger Foundation, Inc.
Threshold Foundation
Times Mirror Magazines, Inc.
Harry C. Trexler Trust
Union Camp Charitable Trust
Vancouver Foundation
Westinghouse Foundation
Weyerhaeuser Company Foundation
The Windham Foundation, Inc.
The Winston-Salem Foundation, Inc.
Margaret Cullinan Wray Charitable
  Lead Annuity Trust

Recycling

ARCO Foundation
AT&T Foundation
The Abelard Foundation West
The Abell Foundation
Abell-Hanger Foundation
The Ahmanson Foundation
Alaska Conservation Foundation
American Conservation Association, Inc.
Atherton Family Foundation
BankAmerica Foundation
Bay Area Community Foundation
The Ben & Jerry's Foundation
Mary Owen Borden Memorial Foundation
The Bothin Foundation
The Bullitt Foundation
The Bush Foundation
Centerior Energy Foundation
Chesapeake Bay Trust
Robert Sterling Clark Foundation, Inc.
The Collins Foundation
The Community Foundation of
  Greater New Haven
The Community Foundation of
  Santa Clara County
Community Foundation of
  Western North Carolina, Inc.
Cooke Foundation, Limited
The Mary A. Crocker Trust
Davis Conservation Foundation
Geraldine R. Dodge Foundation, Inc.
Dolfinger-McMahon Foundation
The Herbert H. and Grace A. Dow
  Foundation
El Pomar Foundation
The Favrot Fund
The 1525 Foundation
Mary D. and Walter F. Frear
  Eleemosynary Trust
The Fund for New Jersey
The Gap Foundation
The Fred Gellert Foundation
The William and Mary Greve
  Foundation, Inc.
Hawaiian Electric Industries Charitable
  Foundation
The M. A. Healy Family Foundation, Inc.
Howfirma Foundation
The James Irvine Foundation
Kongsgaard-Goldman Foundation
Laird, Norton Foundation
Laurel Foundation

LifeWorks Foundation
The John D. and Catherine T. MacArthur
  Foundation
The Martin Foundation, Inc.
Millbrook Tribute Garden, Inc.
Mobil Foundation, Inc.
J. P. Morgan Charitable Trust
The Moriah Fund, Inc.
Charles Stewart Mott Foundation
M. J. Murdock Charitable Trust
New England Biolabs Foundation
The New York Community Trust
The New York Times Company
  Foundation, Inc.
Edward John Noble Foundation, Inc.
The Overbrook Foundation
The David and Lucile Packard Foundation
Patagonia, Inc.
The William Penn Foundation
James C. Penney Foundation
The Pew Charitable Trusts
Prince Charitable Trusts
Public Welfare Foundation, Inc.
Philip D. Reed Foundation, Inc.
Z. Smith Reynolds Foundation, Inc.
Rockefeller Brothers Fund, Inc.
Rockefeller Family Fund, Inc.
The Rockefeller Foundation
The Winthrop Rockefeller Foundation
The Rockfall Foundation
The San Francisco Foundation
The Sapelo Foundation
The Scherman Foundation, Inc.
Sears-Swetland Foundation
Thomas Sill Foundation
The Charles J. Strosacker Foundation
The Sudbury Foundation
Surdna Foundation, Inc.
Nelson Talbott Foundation
Threshold Foundation
The Tides Foundation
True North Foundation
Virginia Environmental Endowment
WMX Environmental Grants Program
Weyerhaeuser Company Foundation
Wilburforce Foundation
The Dean Witter Foundation
Margaret Cullinan Wray Charitable
  Lead Annuity Trust
The Wyomissing Foundation, Inc.

Research

ARCO Foundation
A Territory Resource
The Ahmanson Foundation
The Jenifer Altman Foundation
Mary Reynolds Babcock Foundation, Inc.
The George F. Baker Trust
The Bauman Foundation
The Bay Foundation
S. D. Bechtel, Jr. Foundation
James Ford Bell Foundation
Beneficia Foundation
The Lynde and Harry Bradley
  Foundation, Inc.

Environmental Topics and Activities

Research (cont.)

The Bullitt Foundation
C. S. Fund
The Cabot Family Charitable Trust
Changing Horizons Charitable Trust
Chesapeake Bay Trust
The Chevron Companies
The Clowes Fund, Inc.
Columbia Foundation
The Conservation and Research Foundation
Conservation, Food & Health Foundation, Inc.
Jessie B. Cox Charitable Trust
The Nathan Cummings Foundation
Davis Conservation Foundation
Geraldine R. Dodge Foundation, Inc.
Gaylord and Dorothy Donnelley Foundation
Douroucouli Foundation
The Elizabeth Ordway Dunn Foundation, Inc.
The Educational Foundation of America
The Energy Foundation
The Ettinger Foundation, Inc.
Fanwood Foundation
Samuel S. Fels Fund
Jamee and Marshall Field Foundation
Ford Foundation
Walter and Josephine Ford Fund
Foundation for Deep Ecology
The GAR Foundation
The Fred Gellert Foundation
General Service Foundation
Georgia Power Foundation, Inc.
The German Marshall Fund of the United States
Give to the Earth Foundation
Great Lakes Protection Fund
The Hamer Foundation
The John Randolph Haynes and Dora Haynes Foundation
Heller Charitable & Educational Fund
The Clarence E. Heller Charitable Foundation
Island Foundation, Inc.
The Richard Ivey Foundation
W. Alton Jones Foundation, Inc.
The Joyce Foundation
The J. M. Kaplan Fund, Inc.
Laidlaw Foundation
Laird, Norton Foundation
The Max and Anna Levinson Foundation
Richard Lounsbery Foundation, Inc.
Luster Family Foundation, Inc.
The John D. and Catherine T. MacArthur Foundation
MARPAT Foundation, Inc.
The McKnight Foundation
Giles W. and Elise G. Mead Foundation
The Andrew W. Mellon Foundation
Richard King Mellon Foundation
The John Merck Fund
Joyce Mertz-Gilmore Foundation
Mobil Foundation, Inc.
The Moriah Fund, Inc.
Charles Stewart Mott Foundation

Ruth Mott Fund
The Curtis and Edith Munson Foundation, Inc.
National Fish and Wildlife Foundation
New Hampshire Charitable Foundation
The New York Times Company Foundation, Inc.
Edward John Noble Foundation, Inc.
Northwest Area Foundation
Jessie Smith Noyes Foundation, Inc.
The David and Lucile Packard Foundation
Patagonia, Inc.
Amelia Peabody Charitable Fund
The Pew Charitable Trusts
Pew Scholars Program in Conservation and the Environment
The Pfizer Foundation, Inc.
Phillips Petroleum Foundation, Inc.
Prince Charitable Trusts
Public Welfare Foundation, Inc.
Philip D. Reed Foundation, Inc.
Z. Smith Reynolds Foundation, Inc.
The Rhode Island Community Foundation
Sid W. Richardson Foundation
Smith Richardson Foundation, Inc.
Rockefeller Brothers Fund, Inc.
The Rockefeller Foundation
Rockwell Fund, Inc.
Fran and Warren Rupp Foundation
The Sapelo Foundation
Sarkeys Foundation
Sarah Scaife Foundation Incorporated
The Florence and John Schumann Foundation
Seventh Generation Fund
Shell Oil Company Foundation
Stanley Smith Horticultural Trust
The Sudbury Foundation
Surdna Foundation, Inc.
The Switzer Foundation
Nelson Talbott Foundation
Texaco Foundation
Threshold Foundation
The Tides Foundation
Town Creek Foundation, Inc.
Treacy Foundation, Inc.
The Trust For Mutual Understanding
Union Camp Charitable Trust
Unitarian Universalist Veatch Program at Shelter Rock
Vancouver Foundation
G. Unger Vetlesen Foundation
Virginia Environmental Endowment
Wallace Genetic Foundation, Inc.
Weeden Foundation
Weyerhaeuser Company Foundation
The William P. Wharton Trust
Wilburforce Foundation
Margaret Cullinan Wray Charitable Lead Annuity Trust

Research: field/fieldwork

ARCO Foundation
Atherton Family Foundation
BankAmerica Foundation
The Ben & Jerry's Foundation
Otto Bremer Foundation
The Bullitt Foundation
James & Abigail Campbell Foundation
Chesapeake Bay Trust
Crystal Channel Foundation
The Educational Foundation of America
Ford Foundation
Foundation for Field Research
Walter and Elise Haas Fund
Island Foundation, Inc.
The Richard Ivey Foundation
W. Alton Jones Foundation, Inc.
The John D. and Catherine T. MacArthur Foundation
The McConnell Foundation
The John Merck Fund
Charles Stewart Mott Foundation
National Fish and Wildlife Foundation
New England Biolabs Foundation
Norcross Wildlife Foundation, Inc.
Northwest Area Foundation
Patagonia, Inc.
Public Welfare Foundation, Inc.
The Rockefeller Foundation
Threshold Foundation
Victoria Foundation, Inc.
Virginia Environmental Endowment
The William P. Wharton Trust

Resources: management

The Bullitt Foundation
The Community Foundation of Santa Clara County
The Energy Foundation
Ford Foundation
The Fred Gellert Foundation
Laird, Norton Foundation
Norcross Wildlife Foundation, Inc.
Threshold Foundation
Margaret Cullinan Wray Charitable Lead Annuity Trust

Resources: renewable

The Boeing Company
The Bullitt Foundation
The Educational Foundation of America
The Energy Foundation
The Fred Gellert Foundation
HKH Foundation
The Clarence E. Heller Charitable Foundation
W. Alton Jones Foundation, Inc.
Kongsgaard-Goldman Foundation
The John D. and Catherine T. MacArthur Foundation
The McKnight Foundation
Joyce Mertz-Gilmore Foundation
The Moriah Fund, Inc.
Charles Stewart Mott Foundation
Patagonia, Inc.
The Pew Charitable Trusts
Public Welfare Foundation, Inc.
The Rockefeller Foundation

Environmental Topics and Activities

Resources: renewable (cont.)

Springhouse Foundation
The Switzer Foundation
The Tides Foundation
WMX Environmental Grants Program
Margaret Cullinan Wray Charitable
  Lead Annuity Trust

Right-to-Know

Angelina Fund, Inc.
The Bauman Foundation
Beldon Fund
Charles Stewart Mott Foundation
The Tides Foundation

Risk assessment/management

The Bauman Foundation
The Lynde and Harry Bradley
  Foundation, Inc.
The Bullitt Foundation
The Chevron Companies
Columbia Foundation
Eastman Kodak Company Charitable Trust
Fund of the Four Directions
GE Fund
Richard & Rhoda Goldman Fund
Great Lakes Protection Fund
Richard King Mellon Foundation
Charles Stewart Mott Foundation
The Summit Foundation
Texaco Foundation
Virginia Environmental Endowment

Rivers/streams

ARCO Foundation
Alaska Conservation Foundation
American Conservation Association, Inc.
American Foundation Corporation
Evenor Armington Fund
Mary Reynolds Babcock Foundation, Inc.
BankAmerica Foundation
The Ben & Jerry's Foundation
Benua Foundation, Inc.
Bishop Pine Fund
Boettcher Foundation
Jesse Margaret Wilson Budlong Foundation
  for Animal Aid
The Bullitt Foundation
Carolyn Foundation
Mary Flagler Cary Charitable Trust
Chesapeake Bay Trust
The Chicago Community Trust
Claneil Foundation, Inc.
The Collins Foundation
The Community Foundation of
  Greater New Haven
Compton Foundation, Inc.
Adolph Coors Foundation
Jessie B. Cox Charitable Trust
Davis Conservation Foundation
Geraldine R. Dodge Foundation, Inc.
Gaylord and Dorothy Donnelley Foundation

The Elizabeth Ordway Dunn
  Foundation, Inc.
The Educational Foundation of America
Environment Now Foundation
Environmental Endowment for
  New Jersey, Inc.
Fanwood Foundation
The Favrot Fund
The Hugh and Jane Ferguson Foundation
The Field Foundation of Illinois, Inc.
Fields Pond Foundation, Inc.
The 1525 Foundation
Ford Foundation
Ford Motor Company Fund
Foundation for Deep Ecology
GE Fund
The Fred Gellert Foundation
General Service Foundation
The Wallace Alexander Gerbode
  Foundation, Inc.
Global Environmental Project Institute
The Goldman Environmental Foundation
Richard & Rhoda Goldman Fund
The Greenville Foundation
The George Gund Foundation
The Hamer Foundation
Harder Foundation
Heller Charitable & Educational Fund
The William and Flora Hewlett Foundation
The Homeland Foundation
Howfirma Foundation
The Indian Point Foundation, Inc.
The James Irvine Foundation
Island Foundation, Inc.
Island Foundation
W. Alton Jones Foundation, Inc.
The Joyce Foundation
Laird, Norton Foundation
Larsen Fund, Inc.
The Lazar Foundation
Longwood Foundation, Inc.
The John D. and Catherine T. MacArthur
  Foundation
The Marshall Fund of Arizona
The McConnell Foundation
The McKnight Foundation
Merck Family Fund
The John Merck Fund
Joyce Mertz-Gilmore Foundation
Meyer Memorial Trust
The Moriah Fund, Inc.
Ruth Mott Fund
The Curtis and Edith Munson
  Foundation, Inc.
M. J. Murdock Charitable Trust
National Fish and Wildlife Foundation
National Geographic Society Education
  Foundation
The Needmor Fund
New Hampshire Charitable Foundation
The New York Times Company
  Foundation, Inc.
Norcross Wildlife Foundation, Inc.
The Nord Family Foundation

The Ohrstrom Foundation
Patagonia, Inc.
Amelia Peabody Charitable Fund
The William Penn Foundation
The Pew Charitable Trusts
Recreational Equipment, Inc.
Philip D. Reed Foundation, Inc.
Z. Smith Reynolds Foundation, Inc.
The Roberts Foundation
The Rockfall Foundation
The San Francisco Foundation
Elmina B. Sewall Foundation
South Coast Foundation, Inc.
Steelcase Foundation
The Strong Foundation for
  Environmental Values
The Sulzberger Foundation, Inc.
Surdna Foundation, Inc.
The Tides Foundation
Times Mirror Magazines, Inc.
The Tinker Foundation Incorporated
Tortuga Foundation
Harry C. Trexler Trust
True North Foundation
The Trust For Mutual Understanding
Rose E. Tucker Charitable Trust
Underhill Foundation
Vanguard Public Foundation
Victoria Foundation, Inc.
The Vidda Foundation
Vinmont Foundation, Inc.
Virginia Environmental Endowment
WMX Environmental Grants Program
Weeden Foundation
The William P. Wharton Trust
The Dean Witter Foundation
Margaret Cullinan Wray Charitable
  Lead Annuity Trust

Rivers/streams: instream issues

The Bullitt Foundation
General Service Foundation
The McKnight Foundation
Patagonia, Inc.
Recreational Equipment, Inc.

Rivers/streams: policy

The Bullitt Foundation
Chesapeake Bay Trust
The German Marshall Fund of
  the United States
The George Gund Foundation
Lyndhurst Foundation
Maki Foundation
The McKnight Foundation
Virginia Environmental Endowment

Rivers/streams: protection

ARCO Foundation
The Ahmanson Foundation
Alaska Conservation Foundation
The Jenifer Altman Foundation
American Conservation Association, Inc.

Environmental Topics and Activities

Rivers/streams: protection (cont.)

Arcadia Foundation
The Bay Foundation
The Beinecke Foundation, Inc.
Beldon Fund
The Ben & Jerry's Foundation
The Betterment Fund
The Frank Stanley Beveridge Foundation, Inc.
Alex. Brown & Sons Charitable Foundation, Inc.
The Bullitt Foundation
The Butler Foundation
Patrick and Aimee Butler Family Foundation
The Bydale Foundation
Chesapeake Bay Trust
The Chevron Companies
The Cleveland Foundation
Columbia Foundation
The Community Foundation of Santa Clara County
Compton Foundation, Inc.
The Mary A. Crocker Trust
The Nathan Cummings Foundation
Damien Foundation
Davis Conservation Foundation
Cleveland H. Dodge Foundation, Inc.
Geraldine R. Dodge Foundation, Inc.
The Elizabeth Ordway Dunn Foundation, Inc.
The Educational Foundation of America
El Pomar Foundation
Environmental Education Foundation of Florida, Inc.
The Armand G. Erpf Fund, Inc.
FishAmerica Foundation
Flintridge Foundation
Foundation for Deep Ecology
Fund of the Four Directions
General Service Foundation
Richard & Rhoda Goldman Fund
Walter and Elise Haas Fund
Gladys and Roland Harriman Foundation
Mary W. Harriman Foundation
The Merrill G. & Emita E. Hastings Foundation
Heller Charitable & Educational Fund
Howfirma Foundation
Jackson Hole Preserve, Inc.
W. Alton Jones Foundation, Inc.
The J. M. Kaplan Fund, Inc.
Harris and Eliza Kempner Fund
F. M. Kirby Foundation, Inc.
Laird, Norton Foundation
The Max and Anna Levinson Foundation
Richard Lounsbery Foundation, Inc.
Lyndhurst Foundation
James A. Macdonald Foundation
Maki Foundation
MARPAT Foundation, Inc.
McKenzie River Gathering Foundation
The McKnight Foundation
McLean Contributionship

Richard King Mellon Foundation
Joyce Mertz-Gilmore Foundation
The Moriah Fund, Inc.
Charles Stewart Mott Foundation
The Curtis and Edith Munson Foundation, Inc.
National Fish and Wildlife Foundation
The Needmor Fund
New Hampshire Charitable Foundation
The New York Community Trust
The New York Times Company Foundation, Inc.
The New-Land Foundation, Inc.
Norcross Wildlife Foundation, Inc.
Northwest Fund for the Environment
The Ohrstrom Foundation
Outdoor Industry Conservation Alliance
Patagonia, Inc.
Perkins Charitable Foundation
The Pew Charitable Trusts
Howard Phipps Foundation
Prince Charitable Trusts
The Prospect Hill Foundation
The Prudential Foundation
Recreational Equipment, Inc.
Z. Smith Reynolds Foundation, Inc.
Rockefeller Family Fund, Inc.
Lee Romney Foundation, Inc.
The Schumann Fund for New Jersey, Inc.
Seventh Generation Fund
The Strong Foundation for Environmental Values
The Sudbury Foundation
The Sulzberger Foundation, Inc.
Texaco Foundation
Thanksgiving Foundation
The Oakleigh L. Thorne Foundation
Threshold Foundation
Town Creek Foundation, Inc.
Union Camp Charitable Trust
Vinmont Foundation, Inc.
Virginia Environmental Endowment
WMX Environmental Grants Program
Weeden Foundation
Welfare Foundation, Inc.
Westinghouse Foundation
The Wyomissing Foundation, Inc.

Rivers/streams: riparian issues

Flintridge Foundation
The McKnight Foundation
Merck Family Fund
The Minneapolis Foundation
National Fish and Wildlife Foundation
The Schumann Fund for New Jersey, Inc.
Virginia Environmental Endowment

Rural development

The Carpenter Foundation
The Goldman Environmental Foundation
The Henry M. Jackson Foundation
The J. M. Kaplan Fund, Inc.
McKenzie River Gathering Foundation

Giles W. and Elise G. Mead Foundation
James C. Penney Foundation
Threshold Foundation

Rural issues

The Jenifer Altman Foundation
The Austin Memorial Foundation
Mary Reynolds Babcock Foundation, Inc.
The Bauman Foundation
Beldon Fund
The Ben & Jerry's Foundation
Blandin Foundation
Otto Bremer Foundation
Kathleen Price and Joseph M. Bryan Family Foundation, Inc.
The Bullitt Foundation
C. S. Fund
Changing Horizons Charitable Trust
Columbia Foundation
Community Foundation of Western North Carolina, Inc.
Compton Foundation, Inc.
The Nathan Cummings Foundation
Jessie Ball duPont Religious, Charitable and Educational Fund
The Educational Foundation of America
Ford Foundation
The J. M. Kaplan Fund, Inc.
W. K. Kellogg Foundation
Meadows Foundation, Inc.
Joyce Mertz-Gilmore Foundation
Meyer Memorial Trust
The Moriah Fund, Inc.
Charles Stewart Mott Foundation
Ruth Mott Fund
The Needmor Fund
New England Biolabs Foundation
Norman Foundation
Northwest Area Foundation
Jessie Smith Noyes Foundation, Inc.
Public Welfare Foundation, Inc.
Z. Smith Reynolds Foundation, Inc.
Rockefeller Brothers Fund, Inc.
The Rockefeller Foundation
The Winthrop Rockefeller Foundation
The Sapelo Foundation
The Strong Foundation for Environmental Values
The Sudbury Foundation
Surdna Foundation, Inc.
Unitarian Universalist Veatch Program at Shelter Rock
Vanguard Public Foundation
Wallace Genetic Foundation, Inc.
Wrinkle in Time Foundation

Sacred lands

The Acorn Foundation
The Jenifer Altman Foundation
The Ben & Jerry's Foundation
The Bullitt Foundation
Funding Exchange
The Wallace Alexander Gerbode Foundation, Inc.

Environmental Topics and Activities

Sacred lands (cont.)

McKenzie River Gathering Foundation
Patagonia, Inc.
Seventh Generation Fund
The Tides Foundation

Scholarships

The Ahmanson Foundation
The George F. Baker Trust
The Cabot Family Charitable Trust
California Community Foundation
Ben B. Cheney Foundation
The Collins Foundation
The Mary A. Crocker Trust
Crystal Channel Foundation
The Educational Foundation of America
Environmental Education Foundation of Florida, Inc.
The Favrot Fund
Ford Foundation
Foundation for Deep Ecology
Fund of the Four Directions
Gates Foundation
The Fred Gellert Foundation
Hartford Foundation for Public Giving
Ireland Foundation
The James Irvine Foundation
Helen K. and Arthur E. Johnson Foundation
Laird, Norton Foundation
Charles Stewart Mott Foundation
National Fish and Wildlife Foundation
Patagonia, Inc.
Recreational Equipment, Inc.
The San Francisco Foundation
Seventh Generation Fund
Stern Family Fund
USX Foundation, Inc.
The Vidda Foundation
Virginia Environmental Endowment
Weyerhaeuser Company Foundation
Wilburforce Foundation
Margaret Cullinan Wray Charitable Lead Annuity Trust

Schools: environmental

The Bay Foundation
The Bothin Foundation
Alexander H. Bright Charitable Trust
Davis Conservation Foundation
Ederic Foundation, Inc.
Environment Now Foundation
Foundation for Deep Ecology
The Jacob and Annita France Foundation, Inc.
The Gap Foundation
Charles Hayden Foundation
Hurdle Hill Foundation
Ireland Foundation
Helen K. and Arthur E. Johnson Foundation
Robert G. and Anne M. Merrick Foundation, Inc.
Metropolitan Atlanta Community Foundation, Inc.

The New York Times Company Foundation, Inc.
Patagonia, Inc.
Peninsula Community Foundation
Lynn R. and Karl E. Prickett Fund
Z. Smith Reynolds Foundation, Inc.
The San Francisco Foundation
Schultz Foundation, Inc.
Elmina B. Sewall Foundation
The Winston-Salem Foundation, Inc.

Sciences

The Bay Foundation
The Beinecke Foundation, Inc.
The Louis Calder Foundation
Chesapeake Bay Trust
The Aaron Diamond Foundation
Geraldine R. Dodge Foundation, Inc.
Oliver S. and Jennie R. Donaldson Charitable Trust
Gaylord and Dorothy Donnelley Foundation
Lloyd A. Fry Foundation
The Fred Gellert Foundation
Richard & Rhoda Goldman Fund
Greater Piscataqua Community Foundation
The Henry M. Jackson Foundation
The J. M. Kaplan Fund, Inc.
The Max and Anna Levinson Foundation
Maki Foundation
Mobil Foundation, Inc.
The Curtis and Edith Munson Foundation, Inc.
The David and Lucile Packard Foundation
Peninsula Community Foundation
Pew Scholars Program in Conservation and the Environment
Shell Oil Company Foundation
The Morris Stulsaft Foundation
The Switzer Foundation
Virginia Environmental Endowment
WMX Environmental Grants Program

Scientific assistance/support

The William Bingham Foundation
The Mary A. Crocker Trust
Deer Creek Foundation
The Fund for New Jersey
The Fred Gellert Foundation
W. Alton Jones Foundation, Inc.
The J. M. Kaplan Fund, Inc.
The Max and Anna Levinson Foundation
The John D. and Catherine T. MacArthur Foundation
McKenzie River Gathering Foundation
Charles Stewart Mott Foundation
New England Biolabs Foundation
The Pew Charitable Trusts
Public Welfare Foundation, Inc.
Weeden Foundation

Sewage/sludge

The Bullitt Foundation
El Paso Community Foundation

Environmental Endowment for New Jersey, Inc.
Lintilhac Foundation
Patagonia, Inc.
The Florence and John Schumann Foundation
Victoria Foundation, Inc.
WMX Environmental Grants Program

Soils

The Acorn Foundation
The Ben & Jerry's Foundation
Chesapeake Bay Trust
Conservation, Food & Health Foundation, Inc.
Crystal Channel Foundation
Deer Creek Foundation
Harder Foundation
Island Foundation
The John D. and Catherine T. MacArthur Foundation
The Andrew W. Mellon Foundation
Northwest Area Foundation
Patagonia, Inc.
The Rockefeller Foundation
Rockwell Fund, Inc.
The Switzer Foundation

Soils: conservation

Chesapeake Bay Trust
The Rollin M. Gerstacker Foundation
The Joyce Foundation
The John D. and Catherine T. MacArthur Foundation
New England Biolabs Foundation
Northwest Area Foundation
The Rockefeller Foundation
The Charles J. Strosacker Foundation

Soils: erosion

The Bullitt Foundation
Chesapeake Bay Trust
Environmental Endowment for New Jersey, Inc.
Great Lakes Protection Fund
The J. M. Kaplan Fund, Inc.
Laidlaw Foundation
Laird, Norton Foundation
Maine Community Foundation, Inc.
National Fish and Wildlife Foundation
Patagonia, Inc.
The Rockefeller Foundation
Threshold Foundation
Virginia Environmental Endowment

Solid waste

Beldon Fund
The Chicago Community Trust
Robert Sterling Clark Foundation, Inc.
Compton Foundation, Inc.
The Mary A. Crocker Trust
Crystal Channel Foundation
Dart Foundation

Environmental Topics and Activities

Solid waste (cont.)

Ford Foundation
Charles Stewart Mott Foundation
The Curtis and Edith Munson
  Foundation, Inc.
The New York Community Trust
Jessie Smith Noyes Foundation, Inc.
Patagonia, Inc.
Rockefeller Brothers Fund, Inc.
The Sapelo Foundation
The Florence and John Schumann
  Foundation
The Tides Foundation
Victoria Foundation, Inc.
WMX Environmental Grants Program
The Dean Witter Foundation
Margaret Cullinan Wray Charitable
  Lead Annuity Trust

Solid waste: disposal

The Bullitt Foundation
Jessie Smith Noyes Foundation, Inc.
Patagonia, Inc.
Public Welfare Foundation, Inc.
The Sapelo Foundation
The Florence and John Schumann
  Foundation
Weyerhaeuser Company Foundation

Solid waste: education

American Conservation Association, Inc.
Robert Sterling Clark Foundation, Inc.
The Mary A. Crocker Trust
The William and Mary Greve
  Foundation, Inc.
Millbrook Tribute Garden, Inc.
J. P. Morgan Charitable Trust
The Overbrook Foundation
The Scherman Foundation, Inc.
Sears-Swetland Foundation
Nelson Talbott Foundation

Solid waste: incineration

The Ben & Jerry's Foundation
Mary Owen Borden Memorial Foundation
Otto Bremer Foundation
McKenzie River Gathering Foundation

Solid waste: landfills

The Jenifer Altman Foundation
The Ben & Jerry's Foundation
Mary Owen Borden Memorial Foundation
The Bullitt Foundation
The Fund for New Jersey
The Rockfall Foundation
The Florence and John Schumann
  Foundation

Solid waste: ocean dumping

The Fund for New Jersey
The Florence and John Schumann
  Foundation
WMX Environmental Grants Program

Solid waste: source reduction

Mary Reynolds Babcock Foundation, Inc.
Beldon Fund
The Ben & Jerry's Foundation
The Bullitt Foundation
Chesapeake Bay Trust
Robert Sterling Clark Foundation, Inc.
Geraldine R. Dodge Foundation, Inc.
The Educational Foundation of America
The Fund for New Jersey
The Fred Gellert Foundation
Charles Stewart Mott Foundation
The Pew Charitable Trusts
Z. Smith Reynolds Foundation, Inc.
The Sapelo Foundation
The Florence and John Schumann
  Foundation
Threshold Foundation
WMX Environmental Grants Program

Spirituality: environmental/ecological

The Jenifer Altman Foundation
Crystal Channel Foundation
Damien Foundation
Foundation for Deep Ecology
Patagonia, Inc.
Rockefeller Financial Services,
  Philanthropy Department
Threshold Foundation
The Tides Foundation

Stewardship

L. L. Bean, Inc.
The Ben & Jerry's Foundation
Blandin Foundation
The Blumenthal Foundation
The Bullitt Foundation
Davis Conservation Foundation
Dolfinger-McMahon Foundation
The Fund for New Jersey
Fund of the Four Directions
The German Marshall Fund of
  the United States
Great Lakes Protection Fund
The George Gund Foundation
Island Foundation
MARPAT Foundation, Inc.
The McKnight Foundation
McLean Contributionship
Giles W. and Elise G. Mead Foundation
The Minneapolis Foundation
The Needmor Fund
New Hampshire Charitable Foundation
Northwest Area Foundation
The David and Lucile Packard Foundation
Patagonia, Inc.
The Pew Charitable Trusts
Recreational Equipment, Inc.
Surdna Foundation, Inc.
The Switzer Foundation
The Tides Foundation
Turner Foundation, Inc.
Vancouver Foundation

Virginia Environmental Endowment
Weyerhaeuser Company Foundation

Stewardship: land

Americana Foundation, Inc.
The Blumenthal Foundation
The Bullitt Foundation
Carolyn Foundation
Mary Flagler Cary Charitable Trust
The Educational Foundation of America
Foundation for Deep Ecology
The German Marshall Fund of
  the United States
The John D. and Catherine T. MacArthur
  Foundation
MARPAT Foundation, Inc.
Giles W. and Elise G. Mead Foundation
Charles Stewart Mott Foundation
M. J. Murdock Charitable Trust
National Fish and Wildlife Foundation
Northwest Area Foundation
Patagonia, Inc.
Wallace Genetic Foundation, Inc.
Weeden Foundation

Stewardship: water

The Bullitt Foundation
Patagonia, Inc.

Students

ARCO Foundation
A Territory Resource
The Abell Foundation
Alaska Conservation Foundation
The Jenifer Altman Foundation
Atherton Family Foundation
The Ben & Jerry's Foundation
Ruth H. Brown Foundation
W. L. Lyons Brown Foundation
Kathleen Price and Joseph M. Bryan
  Family Foundation, Inc.
The Bullitt Foundation
The Morris and Gwendolyn Cafritz
  Foundation
Chesapeake Bay Trust
The Chevron Companies
Columbia Foundation
The Columbus Foundation
Compton Foundation, Inc.
The Mary A. Crocker Trust
Crystal Channel Foundation
The Nathan Cummings Foundation
The Arthur Vining Davis Foundations
Davis Conservation Foundation
Cleveland H. Dodge Foundation, Inc.
Geraldine R. Dodge Foundation, Inc.
Oliver S. and Jennie R. Donaldson
  Charitable Trust
The Elizabeth Ordway Dunn
  Foundation, Inc.
The Educational Foundation of America
Environmental Education Foundation
  of Florida, Inc.

Environmental Topics and Activities

Students (cont.)

Environmental Endowment for New Jersey, Inc.
Jamee and Marshall Field Foundation
Mary D. and Walter F. Frear Eleemosynary Trust
Funding Exchange
The Gap Foundation
Gates Foundation
The Fred Gellert Foundation
General Service Foundation
Herman Goldman Foundation
Great Lakes Protection Fund
Greater Piscataqua Community Foundation
The Greenville Foundation
The George Gund Foundation
Evelyn and Walter Haas, Jr. Fund
Gladys and Roland Harriman Foundation
The Homeland Foundation
Howfirma Foundation
The Roy A. Hunt Foundation
Ittleson Foundation, Inc.
The Richard Ivey Foundation
The Henry M. Jackson Foundation
The George Frederick Jewett Foundation
The Howard Johnson Foundation
Walter S. Johnson Foundation
Laird, Norton Foundation
Laurel Foundation
The Lazar Foundation
The Max and Anna Levinson Foundation
The John D. and Catherine T. MacArthur Foundation
MARPAT Foundation, Inc.
Mars Foundation
McDonnell Douglas Foundation
McInerny Foundation
The Andrew W. Mellon Foundation
Charles Stewart Mott Foundation
The Mountaineers Foundation
The Curtis and Edith Munson Foundation, Inc.
National Fish and Wildlife Foundation
National Geographic Society Education Foundation
New Hampshire Charitable Foundation
Edward John Noble Foundation, Inc.
Norcross Wildlife Foundation, Inc.
Jessie Smith Noyes Foundation, Inc.
The Pew Charitable Trusts
Phillips Petroleum Foundation, Inc.
The Prudential Foundation
The Winthrop Rockefeller Foundation
Rockwood Fund, Inc.
Lee Romney Foundation, Inc.
Sacharuna Foundation
The San Francisco Foundation
Schultz Foundation, Inc.
The Florence and John Schumann Foundation
Elmina B. Sewall Foundation
Snee-Reinhardt Charitable Foundation
Springhouse Foundation
The Strong Foundation for Environmental Values
The Sudbury Foundation
Surdna Foundation, Inc.
Edna Bailey Sussman Fund
The Oakleigh L. Thorne Foundation
Threshold Foundation
Unitarian Universalist Veatch Program at Shelter Rock
Victoria Foundation, Inc.
The Vidda Foundation
Virginia Environmental Endowment
WMX Environmental Grants Program
DeWitt Wallace-Reader's Digest Fund
Weyerhaeuser Company Foundation
The William P. Wharton Trust
Wilburforce Foundation
Margaret Cullinan Wray Charitable Lead Annuity Trust

Superfund

A Territory Resource
The Bullitt Foundation
Charles Stewart Mott Foundation
Patagonia, Inc.
The Pew Charitable Trusts

Surveys

Beldon Fund
The Bullitt Foundation
Carolyn Foundation
The Columbus Foundation
The Energy Foundation
Fanwood Foundation
Foundation for Deep Ecology
Fund of the Four Directions
The Gap Foundation
The Fred Gellert Foundation
The Greenville Foundation
Harbor Lights Foundation
The Clarence E. Heller Charitable Foundation
The Homeland Foundation
The Richard Ivey Foundation
Richard Lounsbery Foundation, Inc.
National Fish and Wildlife Foundation
The New-Land Foundation, Inc.
Patagonia, Inc.
The San Francisco Foundation
Sequoia Foundation
Springhouse Foundation
The Strong Foundation for Environmental Values
The Summerlee Foundation
The Tides Foundation
The Tinker Foundation Incorporated
Town Creek Foundation, Inc.
Virginia Environmental Endowment
Margaret Cullinan Wray Charitable Lead Annuity Trust

Sustainability

A Territory Resource
Alaska Conservation Foundation
The Jenifer Altman Foundation
Mary Reynolds Babcock Foundation, Inc.
The Bauman Foundation
The Ben & Jerry's Foundation
The Bullitt Foundation
Changing Horizons Charitable Trust
Columbia Foundation
Community Foundation of Western North Carolina, Inc.
Conservation, Food & Health Foundation, Inc.
The Nathan Cummings Foundation
Geraldine R. Dodge Foundation, Inc.
The Educational Foundation of America
The Energy Foundation
Environmental Education Foundation of Florida, Inc.
Ford Foundation
Foundation for Deep Ecology
Fund of the Four Directions
The Gap Foundation
Give to the Earth Foundation
The George Gund Foundation
The William and Flora Hewlett Foundation
The James Irvine Foundation
Ittleson Foundation, Inc.
W. Alton Jones Foundation, Inc.
The Joyce Foundation
The Max and Anna Levinson Foundation
The John D. and Catherine T. MacArthur Foundation
MARPAT Foundation, Inc.
McKenzie River Gathering Foundation
Richard King Mellon Foundation
Merck Family Fund
The John Merck Fund
The Moriah Fund, Inc.
Charles Stewart Mott Foundation
The Curtis and Edith Munson Foundation, Inc.
Northwest Area Foundation
Jessie Smith Noyes Foundation, Inc.
The David and Lucile Packard Foundation
Patagonia, Inc.
James C. Penney Foundation
The Pew Charitable Trusts
Pew Scholars Program in Conservation and the Environment
Rockefeller Brothers Fund, Inc.
The Rockefeller Foundation
The San Francisco Foundation
Seventh Generation Fund
The Summit Foundation
Surdna Foundation, Inc.
Texaco Foundation
Threshold Foundation
The Tides Foundation
The Tinker Foundation Incorporated
The Trust For Mutual Understanding
Virginia Environmental Endowment
Weeden Foundation

Technical assistance/support

Alaska Conservation Foundation
Mary Reynolds Babcock Foundation, Inc.
Beldon Fund
The Ben & Jerry's Foundation

© 1995 Environmental Data Resources, Inc.

Environmental Topics and Activities

Technical assistance/support (cont.)

Kathleen Price and Joseph M. Bryan Family Foundation, Inc.
The Bullitt Foundation
Conservation, Food & Health Foundation, Inc.
Jessie B. Cox Charitable Trust
The Mary A. Crocker Trust
The Nathan Cummings Foundation
Deer Creek Foundation
The Aaron Diamond Foundation
Dolfinger-McMahon Foundation
The Elizabeth Ordway Dunn Foundation, Inc.
The Educational Foundation of America
The Energy Foundation
Ford Foundation
The Fund for New Jersey
General Service Foundation
The German Marshall Fund of the United States
Great Lakes Protection Fund
The Greenville Foundation
The George Gund Foundation
Hartford Foundation for Public Giving
W. Alton Jones Foundation, Inc.
The Joyce Foundation
The J. M. Kaplan Fund, Inc.
The Lazar Foundation
The Max and Anna Levinson Foundation
The John D. and Catherine T. MacArthur Foundation
The McKnight Foundation
Merck Family Fund
The John Merck Fund
The Moriah Fund, Inc.
Charles Stewart Mott Foundation
National Fish and Wildlife Foundation
The Needmor Fund
Norman Foundation
Jessie Smith Noyes Foundation, Inc.
Patagonia, Inc.
The Pew Charitable Trusts
Pew Scholars Program in Conservation and the Environment
Prince Charitable Trusts
Public Welfare Foundation, Inc.
Rockefeller Brothers Fund, Inc.
The Rockefeller Foundation
The Sapelo Foundation
The Schumann Fund for New Jersey, Inc.
The Florence and John Schumann Foundation
South Coast Foundation, Inc.
Surdna Foundation, Inc.
The Switzer Foundation
Threshold Foundation
The Tinker Foundation Incorporated
The Trust For Mutual Understanding
Unitarian Universalist Veatch Program at Shelter Rock
Victoria Foundation, Inc.
Virginia Environmental Endowment
DeWitt Wallace-Reader's Digest Fund

Technology

The Abell Foundation
Mary Reynolds Babcock Foundation, Inc.
Ruth H. Brown Foundation
Compton Foundation, Inc.
The Educational Foundation of America
Foundation for Deep Ecology
GE Fund
Great Lakes Protection Fund
The Hyde and Watson Foundation
IBM Corporation
Island Foundation, Inc.
W. Alton Jones Foundation, Inc.
The Joyce Foundation
The J. M. Kaplan Fund, Inc.
The John D. and Catherine T. MacArthur Foundation
McLean Contributionship
The Moriah Fund, Inc.
Charles Stewart Mott Foundation
The Curtis and Edith Munson Foundation, Inc.
Patagonia, Inc.
The Pew Charitable Trusts
The Rockefeller Foundation
The Winthrop Rockefeller Foundation
The Switzer Foundation
Threshold Foundation
The Tides Foundation
Unitarian Universalist Veatch Program at Shelter Rock
WMX Environmental Grants Program
Weyerhaeuser Company Foundation

Telecommunications projects

The Bullitt Foundation
Changing Horizons Charitable Trust
W. Alton Jones Foundation, Inc.
DeWitt Wallace-Reader's Digest Fund
Weeden Foundation

Tourism/travel: environmental

American Express Philanthropic Program
Kathleen Price and Joseph M. Bryan Family Foundation, Inc.
Environmental Education Foundation of Florida, Inc.
The J. M. Kaplan Fund, Inc.
The Kresge Foundation
The John D. and Catherine T. MacArthur Foundation
Maine Community Foundation, Inc.
MARPAT Foundation, Inc.
Giles W. and Elise G. Mead Foundation
National Fish and Wildlife Foundation
New England Biolabs Foundation
Andrew Norman Foundation
Northwest Area Foundation
Patagonia, Inc.
The Pew Charitable Trusts
Z. Smith Reynolds Foundation, Inc.
The Schumann Fund for New Jersey, Inc.
The Skaggs Foundation
The Tinker Foundation Incorporated
Margaret Cullinan Wray Charitable Lead Annuity Trust

Toxic/hazardous substances

Angelina Fund, Inc.
Azadoutioun Foundation
Clayton Baker Trust
The Bauman Foundation
Beldon Fund
The Ben & Jerry's Foundation
The Lynde and Harry Bradley Foundation, Inc.
Kathleen Price and Joseph M. Bryan Family Foundation, Inc.
The Bydale Foundation
C. S. Fund
Changing Horizons Charitable Trust
Compton Foundation, Inc.
The Nathan Cummings Foundation
Deer Creek Foundation
Eastman Kodak Company Charitable Trust
The Educational Foundation of America
The Ettinger Foundation, Inc.
Foundation for Deep Ecology
The Frost Foundation, Ltd.
Fund of the Four Directions
Funding Exchange
The Gap Foundation
The Fred Gellert Foundation
The Wallace Alexander Gerbode Foundation, Inc.
Give to the Earth Foundation
The Goldman Environmental Foundation
Richard & Rhoda Goldman Fund
Great Lakes Protection Fund
The George Gund Foundation
HKH Foundation
Harder Foundation
The Clarence E. Heller Charitable Foundation
The William and Flora Hewlett Foundation
Howfirma Foundation
W. Alton Jones Foundation, Inc.
The Joyce Foundation
W. K. Kellogg Foundation
The Lazar Foundation
The Max and Anna Levinson Foundation
The McIntosh Foundation
Charles Stewart Mott Foundation
The Needmor Fund
Edward John Noble Foundation, Inc.
Northwest Fund for the Environment
Jessie Smith Noyes Foundation, Inc.
The Overbrook Foundation
Patagonia, Inc.
Pew Scholars Program in Conservation and the Environment
The Philadelphia Foundation
Public Welfare Foundation, Inc.
Rockefeller Family Fund, Inc.
Lee Romney Foundation, Inc.
Fran and Warren Rupp Foundation

Environmental Topics and Activities

Toxic/hazardous substances (cont.)

The Florence and John Schumann
  Foundation
Sears-Swetland Foundation
South Coast Foundation, Inc.
The Strong Foundation for
  Environmental Values
The Switzer Foundation
Threshold Foundation
The Tides Foundation
True North Foundation
Turner Foundation, Inc.
Unitarian Universalist Veatch Program
  at Shelter Rock
Vanguard Public Foundation
WMX Environmental Grants Program

Toxic/hazardous substances: lead

The Abelard Foundation West
The Cleveland Foundation
Columbia Foundation
Deer Creek Foundation
The George Gund Foundation
Hartford Foundation for Public Giving
The William and Flora Hewlett Foundation
The James Irvine Foundation
W. Alton Jones Foundation, Inc.
Joyce Mertz-Gilmore Foundation
The Milwaukee Foundation
Norcross Wildlife Foundation, Inc.
James C. Penney Foundation
Public Welfare Foundation, Inc.
The San Francisco Foundation
The Schumann Fund for New Jersey, Inc.
The Switzer Foundation
Threshold Foundation
Victoria Foundation, Inc.
WMX Environmental Grants Program

Toxic/hazardous substances: military

C. S. Fund
Columbia Foundation
Deer Creek Foundation
Ottinger Foundation
Public Welfare Foundation, Inc.

Toxic/hazardous substances: source reduction

The Abelard Foundation West
The Bauman Foundation
Beldon Fund
C. S. Fund
Jessie B. Cox Charitable Trust
The Nathan Cummings Foundation
The Elizabeth Ordway Dunn
  Foundation, Inc.
The Joyce Foundation
Laidlaw Foundation
The Pew Charitable Trusts
Virginia Environmental Endowment

Toxic/hazardous waste

AT&T Foundation
The Abell Foundation
American Conservation Association, Inc.
Angelina Fund, Inc.
The Bauman Foundation
Beldon Fund
The Ben & Jerry's Foundation
The Bullitt Foundation
C. S. Fund
California Community Foundation
Robert Sterling Clark Foundation, Inc.
The Mary A. Crocker Trust
The Nathan Cummings Foundation
Davis Conservation Foundation
Deer Creek Foundation
Geraldine R. Dodge Foundation, Inc.
Funding Exchange
The Fred Gellert Foundation
The German Marshall Fund of
  the United States
The Goldman Environmental Foundation
Richard & Rhoda Goldman Fund
The William and Mary Greve
  Foundation, Inc.
The George Gund Foundation
Howfirma Foundation
Island Foundation, Inc.
W. Alton Jones Foundation, Inc.
The Joyce Foundation
W. K. Kellogg Foundation
Lyndhurst Foundation
Millbrook Tribute Garden, Inc.
J. P. Morgan Charitable Trust
Charles Stewart Mott Foundation
The Needmor Fund
The New World Foundation
Norman Foundation
Jessie Smith Noyes Foundation, Inc.
Ottinger Foundation
The Overbrook Foundation
Patagonia, Inc.
The Pew Charitable Trusts
The Prospect Hill Foundation
Public Welfare Foundation, Inc.
Rockefeller Family Fund, Inc.
The Sapelo Foundation
The Scherman Foundation, Inc.
The Florence and John Schumann
  Foundation
Sears-Swetland Foundation
Seventh Generation Fund
The Strong Foundation for
  Environmental Values
Nelson Talbott Foundation
Tortuga Foundation
Town Creek Foundation, Inc.
The Trust For Mutual Understanding
Unitarian Universalist Veatch Program
  at Shelter Rock
Vanguard Public Foundation
Victoria Foundation, Inc.

Toxic/hazardous waste: cleanup

A Territory Resource
The Abelard Foundation West
Alaska Conservation Foundation
Ameritech Foundation
The Bullitt Foundation
Deer Creek Foundation
Eastman Kodak Company Charitable Trust
Environmental Endowment for
  New Jersey, Inc.
Ford Motor Company Fund
The Gap Foundation
Great Lakes Protection Fund
The George Gund Foundation
The John Merck Fund
The Pew Charitable Trusts
Public Welfare Foundation, Inc.
Rockefeller Family Fund, Inc.
Threshold Foundation
WMX Environmental Grants Program

Toxic/hazardous waste: disposal

Angelina Fund, Inc.
The Ben & Jerry's Foundation
Deer Creek Foundation
Geraldine R. Dodge Foundation, Inc.
The Fund for New Jersey
Give to the Earth Foundation
W. Alton Jones Foundation, Inc.
McKenzie River Gathering Foundation
Jessie Smith Noyes Foundation, Inc.
Patagonia, Inc.
Seventh Generation Fund
The Strong Foundation for
  Environmental Values
Threshold Foundation

Toxic/hazardous waste: source reduction

The Jenifer Altman Foundation
Mary Reynolds Babcock Foundation, Inc.
The Bullitt Foundation
Geraldine R. Dodge Foundation, Inc.
The Elizabeth Ordway Dunn
  Foundation, Inc.
The Gap Foundation
Walter and Duncan Gordon Charitable
  Foundation
Great Lakes Protection Fund
HKH Foundation
W. Alton Jones Foundation, Inc.
The Joyce Foundation
MARPAT Foundation, Inc.
The McKnight Foundation
Charles Stewart Mott Foundation
New England Biolabs Foundation
Jessie Smith Noyes Foundation, Inc.
James C. Penney Foundation
Public Welfare Foundation, Inc.
The San Francisco Foundation
The Sapelo Foundation
Threshold Foundation

© 1995 Environmental Data Resources, Inc.

Environmental Topics and Activities

Toxic/hazardous waste: trade

Beldon Fund
Great Lakes Protection Fund
Threshold Foundation
WMX Environmental Grants Program

Toxicology

The Bay Foundation
Ford Motor Company Fund
Charles Stewart Mott Foundation

Trade policy

C. S. Fund
Donner Canadian Foundation
Ford Foundation
GE Fund
HKH Foundation
W. Alton Jones Foundation, Inc.
McKenzie River Gathering Foundation
The John Merck Fund
Charles Stewart Mott Foundation
The Pew Charitable Trusts
Weyerhaeuser Company Foundation

Trade policy: GATT

The Acorn Foundation
The Jenifer Altman Foundation
Foundation for Deep Ecology
Charles Stewart Mott Foundation
Northwest Area Foundation
Jessie Smith Noyes Foundation, Inc.
The Tinker Foundation Incorporated

Trade policy: NAFTA

The Acorn Foundation
The Jenifer Altman Foundation
The Arca Foundation
The Bauman Foundation
The Educational Foundation of America
Laidlaw Foundation
The Max and Anna Levinson Foundation
The John D. and Catherine T. MacArthur Foundation
McKenzie River Gathering Foundation
Charles Stewart Mott Foundation
Ruth Mott Fund
Northwest Area Foundation
Jessie Smith Noyes Foundation, Inc.
The Tinker Foundation Incorporated
Margaret Cullinan Wray Charitable Lead Annuity Trust

Trails

Elmer L. & Eleanor J. Andersen Foundation
Evenor Armington Fund
BankAmerica Foundation
Bay Area Community Foundation
James Ford Bell Foundation
The Ben & Jerry's Foundation
The Betterment Fund
Kathleen Price and Joseph M. Bryan Family Foundation, Inc.

The Bullitt Foundation
The Carpenter Foundation
Ben B. Cheney Foundation
Chesapeake Bay Trust
The Community Foundation of Santa Clara County
Community Foundation of Western North Carolina, Inc.
Compton Foundation, Inc.
The Mary A. Crocker Trust
Davis Conservation Foundation
Eastman Kodak Company Charitable Trust
El Pomar Foundation
Fields Pond Foundation, Inc.
The Gap Foundation
Walter and Elise Haas Fund
The Jackson Foundation
F. M. Kirby Foundation, Inc.
Laird, Norton Foundation
Maki Foundation
McCune Foundation
Meyer Memorial Trust
The Mountaineers Foundation
New Hampshire Charitable Foundation
The New York Times Company Foundation, Inc.
Norcross Wildlife Foundation, Inc.
Patagonia, Inc.
The William Penn Foundation
Phillips Petroleum Foundation, Inc.
Recreational Equipment, Inc.
The Skaggs Foundation
Springs Foundation, Inc.
The Stebbins Fund, Inc.
Steelcase Foundation
The Strong Foundation for Environmental Values
The Sudbury Foundation
The Tinker Foundation Incorporated
Union Camp Charitable Trust
Westinghouse Foundation
Weyerhaeuser Company Foundation
Margaret Cullinan Wray Charitable Lead Annuity Trust

Training

ARCO Foundation
A Territory Resource
Abell-Hanger Foundation
The Acorn Foundation
Alaska Conservation Foundation
Angelina Fund, Inc.
Mary Reynolds Babcock Foundation, Inc.
The Bauman Foundation
The Bay Foundation
Beldon Fund
The Ben & Jerry's Foundation
The Lynde and Harry Bradley Foundation, Inc.
Kathleen Price and Joseph M. Bryan Family Foundation, Inc.
The Bullitt Foundation
California Community Foundation

The Carpenter Foundation
Chesapeake Bay Trust
Liz Claiborne & Art Ortenberg Foundation
The Cleveland Foundation
Compton Foundation, Inc.
Conservation, Food & Health Foundation, Inc.
Adolph Coors Foundation
The Mary A. Crocker Trust
Crystal Channel Foundation
The Nathan Cummings Foundation
Deer Creek Foundation
The Aaron Diamond Foundation
Geraldine R. Dodge Foundation, Inc.
The Elizabeth Ordway Dunn Foundation, Inc.
The Educational Foundation of America
Ford Foundation
The Gap Foundation
General Service Foundation
The German Marshall Fund of the United States
Richard & Rhoda Goldman Fund
Great Lakes Protection Fund
The Greenville Foundation
The George Gund Foundation
The Richard Ivey Foundation
The Henry M. Jackson Foundation
W. Alton Jones Foundation, Inc.
The J. M. Kaplan Fund, Inc.
Laird, Norton Foundation
The Max and Anna Levinson Foundation
The John D. and Catherine T. MacArthur Foundation
MARPAT Foundation, Inc.
McInerny Foundation
McKenzie River Gathering Foundation
The McKnight Foundation
The Andrew W. Mellon Foundation
The John Merck Fund
J. P. Morgan Charitable Trust
The Moriah Fund, Inc.
Charles Stewart Mott Foundation
National Fish and Wildlife Foundation
Norman Foundation
Jessie Smith Noyes Foundation, Inc.
Patagonia, Inc.
Peninsula Community Foundation
James C. Penney Foundation
The Pew Charitable Trusts
Pew Scholars Program in Conservation and the Environment
The Pfizer Foundation, Inc.
Public Welfare Foundation, Inc.
Recreational Equipment, Inc.
Z. Smith Reynolds Foundation, Inc.
The Rhode Island Community Foundation
Rockefeller Brothers Fund, Inc.
Rockefeller Family Fund, Inc.
The Rockefeller Foundation
The Rockfall Foundation
Rockwell Fund, Inc.
The Schumann Fund for New Jersey, Inc.

Environmental Topics and Activities

Training (cont.)

The Florence and John Schumann Foundation
The Sonoma County Community Foundation
The Morris Stulsaft Foundation
Threshold Foundation
The Tinker Foundation Incorporated
True North Foundation
The Trust For Mutual Understanding
Unitarian Universalist Veatch Program at Shelter Rock
Vancouver Foundation
Vanguard Public Foundation
Victoria Foundation, Inc.
Virginia Environmental Endowment
DeWitt Wallace-Reader's Digest Fund
Weeden Foundation
The William P. Wharton Trust
Margaret Cullinan Wray Charitable Lead Annuity Trust

Transportation

AT&T Foundation
Alaska Conservation Foundation
Mary Reynolds Babcock Foundation, Inc.
The Bullitt Foundation
Changing Horizons Charitable Trust
Ben B. Cheney Foundation
Compton Foundation, Inc.
The Nathan Cummings Foundation
Geraldine R. Dodge Foundation, Inc.
The Elizabeth Ordway Dunn Foundation, Inc.
The Energy Foundation
The Fund for New Jersey
The Fred Gellert Foundation
The German Marshall Fund of the United States
Give to the Earth Foundation
Richard & Rhoda Goldman Fund
The George Gund Foundation
The John Randolph Haynes and Dora Haynes Foundation
W. Alton Jones Foundation, Inc.
The Joyce Foundation
Lyndhurst Foundation
The John D. and Catherine T. MacArthur Foundation
Joyce Mertz-Gilmore Foundation
New Hampshire Charitable Foundation
The New York Community Trust
The New York Times Company Foundation, Inc.
The New-Land Foundation, Inc.
Patagonia, Inc.
James C. Penney Foundation
Prince Charitable Trusts
Z. Smith Reynolds Foundation, Inc.
The Scherman Foundation, Inc.
Surdna Foundation, Inc.
The Switzer Foundation

Transportation: energy efficiency

A Territory Resource
Kathleen Price and Joseph M. Bryan Family Foundation, Inc.
The Bullitt Foundation
Changing Horizons Charitable Trust
The Nathan Cummings Foundation
Geraldine R. Dodge Foundation, Inc.
The Elizabeth Ordway Dunn Foundation, Inc.
The Energy Foundation
Hawaii Community Foundation
The John Randolph Haynes and Dora Haynes Foundation
The James Irvine Foundation
W. Alton Jones Foundation, Inc.
The Joyce Foundation
The Max and Anna Levinson Foundation
The Moriah Fund, Inc.
Charles Stewart Mott Foundation
Surdna Foundation, Inc.
The Switzer Foundation

Transportation: mass

Alaska Conservation Foundation
Kathleen Price and Joseph M. Bryan Family Foundation, Inc.
The Bullitt Foundation
The Chevron Companies
The Nathan Cummings Foundation
Geraldine R. Dodge Foundation, Inc.
The Energy Foundation
The Favrot Fund
Lyndhurst Foundation
The San Francisco Foundation
Surdna Foundation, Inc.
Threshold Foundation

Transportation: muscle-powered

BankAmerica Foundation
The Ben & Jerry's Foundation
Kathleen Price and Joseph M. Bryan Family Foundation, Inc.
The Bullitt Foundation
Compton Foundation, Inc.
Damien Foundation
The New York Times Company Foundation, Inc.
Outdoor Industry Conservation Alliance
Patagonia, Inc.
Recreational Equipment, Inc.
Z. Smith Reynolds Foundation, Inc.

Treaties

The Jenifer Altman Foundation
W. Alton Jones Foundation, Inc.
McKenzie River Gathering Foundation
The Pew Charitable Trusts
The Rockefeller Foundation
Seventh Generation Fund
The Tinker Foundation Incorporated

Tropical issues

Atherton Family Foundation
The Barra Foundation, Inc.
The Bay Foundation
Beneficia Foundation
Caribou Fund
The Chevron Companies
The Community Foundation of Santa Clara County
Conservation, Food & Health Foundation, Inc.
Cooke Foundation, Limited
Echoing Green Foundation
Ford Foundation
Foundation for Deep Ecology
Mary D. and Walter F. Frear Eleemosynary Trust
General Service Foundation
The Wallace Alexander Gerbode Foundation, Inc.
Hawaii Community Foundation
Hawaiian Electric Industries Charitable Foundation
Howfirma Foundation
The International Foundation, Inc.
W. Alton Jones Foundation, Inc.
The Esther A. and Joseph Klingenstein Fund, Inc.
The John D. and Catherine T. MacArthur Foundation
McInerny Foundation
McLean Contributionship
The Moriah Fund, Inc.
Patagonia, Inc.
Amelia Peabody Charitable Fund
Pew Scholars Program in Conservation and the Environment
Rockefeller Brothers Fund, Inc.
The Rockefeller Foundation
The San Francisco Foundation
Schultz Foundation, Inc.
Sears-Swetland Foundation
Shell Oil Company Foundation
Stanley Smith Horticultural Trust
Margaret Dorrance Strawbridge Foundation of Pennsylvania II, Inc.
Threshold Foundation
The Tides Foundation
The Truland Foundation
Weyerhaeuser Company Foundation

U.S. Congress

The William Bingham Foundation
The Educational Foundation of America
The Fred Gellert Foundation
The George Gund Foundation
The John D. and Catherine T. MacArthur Foundation
The John Merck Fund
Charles Stewart Mott Foundation
Patagonia, Inc.
Threshold Foundation
WMX Environmental Grants Program
Weeden Foundation

Environmental Topics and Activities

U.S. Department of Defense

Deer Creek Foundation
The Henry M. Jackson Foundation
W. Alton Jones Foundation, Inc.
Unitarian Universalist Veatch Program at Shelter Rock
WMX Environmental Grants Program

U.S. Environmental Protection Agency

Mary Reynolds Babcock Foundation, Inc.
Deer Creek Foundation
The German Marshall Fund of the United States
Give to the Earth Foundation
The Joyce Foundation
The Moriah Fund, Inc.
Surdna Foundation, Inc.

U.S. Fish and Wildlife Service

Alaska Conservation Foundation
The Ben & Jerry's Foundation
National Fish and Wildlife Foundation
WMX Environmental Grants Program

U.S. Forest Service

Mary Reynolds Babcock Foundation, Inc.
The Bullitt Foundation
Compton Foundation, Inc.
The Nathan Cummings Foundation
Deer Creek Foundation
Foundation for Deep Ecology
The Fred Gellert Foundation
The Homeland Foundation
Laird, Norton Foundation
The Lazar Foundation
The Max and Anna Levinson Foundation
The John D. and Catherine T. MacArthur Foundation
The McConnell Foundation
McKenzie River Gathering Foundation
Giles W. and Elise G. Mead Foundation
Merck Family Fund
Ruth Mott Fund
National Fish and Wildlife Foundation
The New-Land Foundation, Inc.
OCRI Foundation
Patagonia, Inc.
Recreational Equipment, Inc.
Rockefeller Family Fund, Inc.
Surdna Foundation, Inc.
Threshold Foundation
Tortuga Foundation
Town Creek Foundation, Inc.
Weeden Foundation

UNCED (U.N. Conference on Environment and Development)

Alaska Conservation Foundation
The Jenifer Altman Foundation
Damien Foundation
Ford Foundation
The William and Flora Hewlett Foundation

The John D. and Catherine T. MacArthur Foundation
The Andrew W. Mellon Foundation
Charles Stewart Mott Foundation
Threshold Foundation
The Tides Foundation

Uplands

Ford Foundation
W. Alton Jones Foundation, Inc.
The John D. and Catherine T. MacArthur Foundation
National Fish and Wildlife Foundation

Urban environment

ARCO Foundation
AT&T Foundation
The Abelard Foundation West
The Abell Foundation
The Vincent Astor Foundation
BankAmerica Foundation
The Bullitt Foundation
California Community Foundation
Mary Flagler Cary Charitable Trust
Robert Sterling Clark Foundation, Inc.
Columbia Foundation
The Community Foundation of Greater New Haven
The Community Foundation of Santa Clara County
The Cowles Charitable Trust
Jessie B. Cox Charitable Trust
The Nathan Cummings Foundation
Geraldine R. Dodge Foundation, Inc.
The Educational Foundation of America
The Armand G. Erpf Fund, Inc.
The Favrot Fund
Samuel S. Fels Fund
The Field Foundation of Illinois, Inc.
Ford Foundation
Ford Motor Company Fund
Walter and Josephine Ford Fund
Lloyd A. Fry Foundation
The Fund for New Jersey
The GAR Foundation
The Gap Foundation
The Wallace Alexander Gerbode Foundation, Inc.
The German Marshall Fund of the United States
Give to the Earth Foundation
Herman Goldman Foundation
Richard & Rhoda Goldman Fund
The W. C. Griffith Foundation
The George Gund Foundation
Walter and Elise Haas Fund
The Harding Educational and Charitable Foundation
Howard Heinz Endowment
Vira I. Heinz Endowment
The William and Flora Hewlett Foundation
Hudson-Webber Foundation
Ittleson Foundation, Inc.

The Richard Ivey Foundation
W. Alton Jones Foundation, Inc.
The J. M. Kaplan Fund, Inc.
F. M. Kirby Foundation, Inc.
Larsen Fund, Inc.
The Lauder Foundation, Inc.
Lyndhurst Foundation
The John D. and Catherine T. MacArthur Foundation
McGregor Fund
Giles W. and Elise G. Mead Foundation
Meadows Foundation, Inc.
Richard King Mellon Foundation
The John Merck Fund
Joyce Mertz-Gilmore Foundation
The Minneapolis Foundation
J. P. Morgan Charitable Trust
Charles Stewart Mott Foundation
The Curtis and Edith Munson Foundation, Inc.
The New York Community Trust
New York Foundation
The New York Times Company Foundation, Inc.
Norcross Wildlife Foundation, Inc.
Kenneth T. and Eileen L. Norris Foundation
Northwest Area Foundation
Jessie Smith Noyes Foundation, Inc.
The Overbrook Foundation
Patagonia, Inc.
The William Penn Foundation
The Pfizer Foundation, Inc.
Prince Charitable Trusts
The Procter & Gamble Fund
The Prospect Hill Foundation
The Prudential Foundation
The Rhode Island Community Foundation
The Rockfall Foundation
Rockwell Fund, Inc.
Rockwood Fund, Inc.
The San Francisco Foundation
The Scherman Foundation, Inc.
The Schiff Foundation
Shell Oil Company Foundation
Southwestern Bell Foundation
Springs Foundation, Inc.
The Stroh Foundation
The Strong Foundation for Environmental Values
The Sulzberger Foundation, Inc.
Surdna Foundation, Inc.
The Telesis Foundation
Threshold Foundation
The Travelers Foundation
Vinmont Foundation, Inc.
WMX Environmental Grants Program
Lila Wallace-Reader's Digest Fund
Robert W. Wilson Foundation
The Wortham Foundation, Inc.

Urban issues

ARCO Foundation
The Ahmanson Foundation
Beldon Fund

Environmental Topics and Activities

Urban issues (cont.)

The Cabot Family Charitable Trust
Carolyn Foundation
Columbia Foundation
Compton Foundation, Inc.
The Cowles Charitable Trust
The Educational Foundation of America
The Energy Foundation
Environmental Endowment for
   New Jersey, Inc.
Ford Foundation
The Fund for Preservation of Wildlife
   and Natural Areas
The Wallace Alexander Gerbode
   Foundation, Inc.
Give to the Earth Foundation
The John Randolph Haynes and
   Dora Haynes Foundation
Island Foundation, Inc.
The Henry M. Jackson Foundation
Joyce Mertz-Gilmore Foundation
The William Penn Foundation
Sears-Swetland Foundation
Threshold Foundation
Virginia Environmental Endowment
Wrinkle in Time Foundation

Volunteerism

ARCO Foundation
A Territory Resource
The Abell Foundation
Alaska Conservation Foundation
The Jenifer Altman Foundation
BankAmerica Foundation
Bay Area Community Foundation
L. L. Bean, Inc.
The Ben & Jerry's Foundation
Bishop Pine Fund
Mary Owen Borden Memorial Foundation
The Robert Brownlee Foundation
The Bullitt Foundation
The Carpenter Foundation
Chesapeake Bay Trust
The Chevron Companies
The Chicago Community Trust
The Cleveland Foundation
Compton Foundation, Inc.
Conservation, Food & Health
   Foundation, Inc.
The Mary A. Crocker Trust
Davis Conservation Foundation
Geraldine R. Dodge Foundation, Inc.
The Herbert H. and Grace A. Dow
   Foundation
Mary D. and Walter F. Frear
   Eleemosynary Trust
The Gap Foundation
Gates Foundation
The Fred Gellert Foundation
General Service Foundation
Richard & Rhoda Goldman Fund
Gladys and Roland Harriman Foundation
The Richard Ivey Foundation
The J. M. Kaplan Fund, Inc.

Laidlaw Foundation
Laird, Norton Foundation
MARPAT Foundation, Inc.
Mars Foundation
The McKnight Foundation
Richard King Mellon Foundation
Mobil Foundation, Inc.
National Fish and Wildlife Foundation
New Hampshire Charitable Foundation
The New York Times Company
   Foundation, Inc.
Norcross Wildlife Foundation, Inc.
Outdoor Industry Conservation Alliance
Patagonia, Inc.
Peninsula Community Foundation
The William Penn Foundation
Phillips Petroleum Foundation, Inc.
The Rhode Island Community Foundation
The Rockfall Foundation
Lee Romney Foundation, Inc.
The San Francisco Foundation
The Florence and John Schumann
   Foundation
Shell Oil Company Foundation
The Sonoma County Community
   Foundation
The Charles J. Strosacker Foundation
Texaco Foundation
The Oakleigh L. Thorne Foundation
Threshold Foundation
Rose E. Tucker Charitable Trust
Victoria Foundation, Inc.
Virginia Environmental Endowment
Weyerhaeuser Company Foundation
The William P. Wharton Trust
The Dean Witter Foundation
Margaret Cullinan Wray Charitable
   Lead Annuity Trust

Waste: disposal

The Richard Ivey Foundation
The McKnight Foundation
The Florence and John Schumann
   Foundation
Ralph C. Sheldon Foundation, Inc.
The Strong Foundation for
   Environmental Values
Threshold Foundation
Unitarian Universalist Veatch Program
   at Shelter Rock

Waste: management

Angelina Fund, Inc.
Beldon Fund
The Ben & Jerry's Foundation
Centerior Energy Foundation
The Community Foundation of
   Santa Clara County
Lintilhac Foundation
Mobil Foundation, Inc.
The Curtis and Edith Munson
   Foundation, Inc.
The Needmor Fund
Jessie Smith Noyes Foundation, Inc.

Patagonia, Inc.
The Sapelo Foundation
The Florence and John Schumann
   Foundation
The Sudbury Foundation
Victoria Foundation, Inc.
WMX Environmental Grants Program

Waste: reduction

ARCO Foundation
AT&T Foundation
Abell-Hanger Foundation
Mary Reynolds Babcock Foundation, Inc.
Beldon Fund
Kathleen Price and Joseph M. Bryan
   Family Foundation, Inc.
The Community Foundation of
   Santa Clara County
Community Foundation of
   Western North Carolina, Inc.
Dolfinger-McMahon Foundation
IBM Corporation
The Moriah Fund, Inc.
The Strong Foundation for
   Environmental Values
The Sudbury Foundation
Town Creek Foundation, Inc.
True North Foundation
Wallace Genetic Foundation, Inc.

Wastewater treatment

Mary Reynolds Babcock Foundation, Inc.
Chesapeake Bay Trust
The German Marshall Fund of
   the United States
Island Foundation, Inc.
The J. M. Kaplan Fund, Inc.
Charles Stewart Mott Foundation
Z. Smith Reynolds Foundation, Inc.
The Rhode Island Community Foundation
The Rockefeller Foundation
The Switzer Foundation
The Trust For Mutual Understanding
Victoria Foundation, Inc.
WMX Environmental Grants Program
Margaret Cullinan Wray Charitable
   Lead Annuity Trust

Water quality/pollution

ARCO Foundation
AT&T Foundation
The Abell Foundation
The Acorn Foundation
Alaska Conservation Foundation
American Conservation Association, Inc.
Mary Reynolds Babcock Foundation, Inc.
Beldon Fund
The Ben & Jerry's Foundation
Blandin Foundation
The Bullitt Foundation
Patrick and Aimee Butler Family
   Foundation
The Bydale Foundation
Carolyn Foundation

© 1995 Environmental Data Resources, Inc.

Environmental Topics and Activities

Water quality/pollution (cont.)

Changing Horizons Charitable Trust
Chesapeake Bay Trust
The Chicago Community Trust
Community Foundation of
 Western North Carolina, Inc.
Jessie B. Cox Charitable Trust
The Mary A. Crocker Trust
Crystal Channel Foundation
The Nathan Cummings Foundation
Davis Conservation Foundation
Deer Creek Foundation
The Elizabeth Ordway Dunn
 Foundation, Inc.
Jessie Ball duPont Religious, Charitable
 and Educational Fund
El Paso Community Foundation
The Energy Foundation
Environment Now Foundation
Environmental Endowment for
 New Jersey, Inc.
The Armand G. Erpf Fund, Inc.
Samuel S. Fels Fund
Ford Foundation
Foundation for the Carolinas
The Fund for New Jersey
Fund of the Four Directions
The Gap Foundation
The Fred Gellert Foundation
General Service Foundation
Give to the Earth Foundation
Richard & Rhoda Goldman Fund
Great Lakes Protection Fund
The W. C. Griffith Foundation
The George Gund Foundation
Harder Foundation
Ittleson Foundation, Inc.
W. Alton Jones Foundation, Inc.
The Joyce Foundation
The J. M. Kaplan Fund, Inc.
Laidlaw Foundation
The Lazar Foundation
Longwood Foundation, Inc.
Lyndhurst Foundation
Maine Community Foundation, Inc.
Marbrook Foundation
Marin Community Foundation
MARPAT Foundation, Inc.
The McKnight Foundation
Richard King Mellon Foundation
The Moriah Fund, Inc.
Charles Stewart Mott Foundation
Ruth Mott Fund
The Curtis and Edith Munson
 Foundation, Inc.
National Fish and Wildlife Foundation
National Geographic Society Education
 Foundation
The New-Land Foundation, Inc.
Northwest Area Foundation
Jessie Smith Noyes Foundation, Inc.
Patagonia, Inc.
Amelia Peabody Charitable Fund
The William Penn Foundation

The Pew Charitable Trusts
Prince Charitable Trusts
The Prospect Hill Foundation
The Prudential Foundation
Public Welfare Foundation, Inc.
Z. Smith Reynolds Foundation, Inc.
The Rhode Island Community Foundation
Rockefeller Brothers Fund, Inc.
The San Francisco Foundation
The Skaggs Foundation
Steelcase Foundation
The Strong Foundation for
 Environmental Values
The Switzer Foundation
Threshold Foundation
The Tides Foundation
Town Creek Foundation, Inc.
True North Foundation
Union Camp Charitable Trust
Virginia Environmental Endowment
WMX Environmental Grants Program
Welfare Foundation, Inc.
Weyerhaeuser Company Foundation
Wilburforce Foundation
Margaret Cullinan Wray Charitable
 Lead Annuity Trust

Water: allocation

The Jenifer Altman Foundation
Ford Foundation
Z. Smith Reynolds Foundation, Inc.
The Dean Witter Foundation

Water: conservation

American Conservation Association, Inc.
The Bullitt Foundation
California Community Foundation
Chesapeake Bay Trust
Robert Sterling Clark Foundation, Inc.
Olive B. Cole Foundation
Compton Foundation, Inc.
Flintridge Foundation
Ford Foundation
Funding Exchange
The Gap Foundation
The Rollin M. Gerstacker Foundation
The William and Mary Greve
 Foundation, Inc.
Harder Foundation
The Richard Ivey Foundation
The J. M. Kaplan Fund, Inc.
F. M. Kirby Foundation, Inc.
Laidlaw Foundation
The John D. and Catherine T. MacArthur
 Foundation
Maki Foundation
The Marshall Fund of Arizona
Millbrook Tribute Garden, Inc.
J. P. Morgan Charitable Trust
Charles Stewart Mott Foundation
National Fish and Wildlife Foundation
The New-Land Foundation, Inc.
Northwest Area Foundation

Onan Family Foundation
The Overbrook Foundation
The Scherman Foundation, Inc.
Seventh Generation Fund
The Charles J. Strosacker Foundation
Nelson Talbott Foundation
Threshold Foundation
Unitarian Universalist Veatch Program
 at Shelter Rock
WMX Environmental Grants Program

Water: drinking

The Ben & Jerry's Foundation
Changing Horizons Charitable Trust
Geraldine R. Dodge Foundation, Inc.
W. K. Kellogg Foundation
Lyndhurst Foundation
The John D. and Catherine T. MacArthur
 Foundation
The New York Community Trust
Jessie Smith Noyes Foundation, Inc.
The Strong Foundation for
 Environmental Values
Threshold Foundation

Water: ground

A Territory Resource
Angelina Fund, Inc.
The Ben & Jerry's Foundation
The Bullitt Foundation
The Chicago Community Trust
Jessie B. Cox Charitable Trust
Ford Foundation
General Service Foundation
IBM Corporation
W. K. Kellogg Foundation
Meadows Foundation, Inc.
Jessie Smith Noyes Foundation, Inc.
Patagonia, Inc.
Public Welfare Foundation, Inc.
The Summit Foundation
Threshold Foundation
Virginia Environmental Endowment
WMX Environmental Grants Program

Water: management

Beldon Fund
The William Bingham Foundation
The Bullitt Foundation
Jessie B. Cox Charitable Trust
The Mary A. Crocker Trust
Ford Foundation
General Service Foundation
The Richard Ivey Foundation
The Henry M. Jackson Foundation
The Lazar Foundation
New England Biolabs Foundation
Northwest Area Foundation
Outdoor Industry Conservation Alliance
The San Francisco Foundation
South Coast Foundation, Inc.
Edna Bailey Sussman Fund
The Switzer Foundation

Environmental Topics and Activities

Water: management (cont.)

Turner Foundation, Inc.
WMX Environmental Grants Program
Robert W. Wilson Foundation
The Winston-Salem Foundation, Inc.
The Dean Witter Foundation

Water: reclamation

The Ahmanson Foundation
Chesapeake Bay Trust
The Hugh and Jane Ferguson Foundation
Harris and Eliza Kempner Fund
Charles Stewart Mott Foundation
Patagonia, Inc.
Vinmont Foundation, Inc.

Water: rights

The Bullitt Foundation
Ford Foundation
General Service Foundation
The Max and Anna Levinson Foundation
National Fish and Wildlife Foundation
Norman Foundation
Northwest Area Foundation
The San Francisco Foundation
Seventh Generation Fund
Threshold Foundation

Water: use

A Territory Resource
Atkinson Foundation
The Mary A. Crocker Trust
FishAmerica Foundation
Ford Foundation
General Service Foundation
Northwest Area Foundation
Rockefeller Brothers Fund, Inc.

Watersheds: management

The Bullitt Foundation
Davis Conservation Foundation
Geraldine R. Dodge Foundation, Inc.
Richard & Rhoda Goldman Fund
Lyndhurst Foundation
Maki Foundation
Marin Community Foundation
The McKnight Foundation
The Tinker Foundation Incorporated
The Trust For Mutual Understanding
Weeden Foundation

Watersheds: preservation

The Abell Foundation
Arcadia Foundation
Beneficia Foundation
The Frank Stanley Beveridge
    Foundation, Inc.
The William Bingham Foundation
The Bullitt Foundation
The Morris and Gwendolyn Cafritz
    Foundation
The Cape Branch Foundation
Carolyn Foundation

The Carpenter Foundation
Mary Flagler Cary Charitable Trust
The Cleveland Foundation
Columbia Foundation
Compton Foundation, Inc.
Jessie B. Cox Charitable Trust
The Cricket Foundation
Geraldine R. Dodge Foundation, Inc.
Environmental Endowment for
    New Jersey, Inc.
The 1525 Foundation
Flintridge Foundation
The Fund for New Jersey
The Fund for Preservation of Wildlife
    and Natural Areas
Gebbie Foundation, Inc.
General Service Foundation
Richard & Rhoda Goldman Fund
Howfirma Foundation
The Roy A. Hunt Foundation
The Hyde and Watson Foundation
The James Irvine Foundation
Ittleson Foundation, Inc.
The J. M. Kaplan Fund, Inc.
W. K. Kellogg Foundation
F. M. Kirby Foundation, Inc.
Laird, Norton Foundation
The Lazar Foundation
The John D. and Catherine T. MacArthur
    Foundation
Marbrook Foundation
MARPAT Foundation, Inc.
Massachusetts Environmental Trust
McKenzie River Gathering Foundation
The McKnight Foundation
Giles W. and Elise G. Mead Foundation
Middlecott Foundation
Mobil Foundation, Inc.
Charles Stewart Mott Foundation
National Fish and Wildlife Foundation
The Overbrook Foundation
The David and Lucile Packard Foundation
Patagonia, Inc.
Amelia Peabody Charitable Fund
Z. Smith Reynolds Foundation, Inc.
The Kelvin and Eleanor Smith Foundation
The Strong Foundation for
    Environmental Values
The Sudbury Foundation
The Sulzberger Foundation, Inc.
Thanksgiving Foundation
The Oakleigh L. Thorne Foundation
The Tides Foundation
Rose E. Tucker Charitable Trust
Victoria Foundation, Inc.
Virginia Environmental Endowment
Weeden Foundation
Westinghouse Foundation

Watersheds: restoration

The Bullitt Foundation
Chesapeake Bay Trust
Environmental Endowment for
    New Jersey, Inc.
Flintridge Foundation

Ford Foundation
General Service Foundation
The Greenville Foundation
The James Irvine Foundation
Laidlaw Foundation
The Lazar Foundation
Giles W. and Elise G. Mead Foundation
Richard King Mellon Foundation
Meyer Memorial Trust
National Fish and Wildlife Foundation
Patagonia, Inc.
Surdna Foundation, Inc.
True North Foundation
The Dean Witter Foundation

Wetlands

ARCO Foundation
Alaska Conservation Foundation
BankAmerica Foundation
Bay Area Community Foundation
S. D. Bechtel, Jr. Foundation
The Beinecke Foundation, Inc.
Beldon Fund
The Frank Stanley Beveridge
    Foundation, Inc.
The Buchanan Family Foundation
The Bullitt Foundation
The Bush Foundation
The Morris and Gwendolyn Cafritz
    Foundation
James & Abigail Campbell Foundation
The Cargill Foundation
Mary Flagler Cary Charitable Trust
Chesapeake Bay Trust
The Chevron Companies
The Chicago Community Trust
Compton Foundation, Inc.
The James M. Cox, Jr. Foundation, Inc.
Geraldine R. Dodge Foundation, Inc.
Oliver S. and Jennie R. Donaldson
    Charitable Trust
Gaylord and Dorothy Donnelley Foundation
The Elizabeth Ordway Dunn
    Foundation, Inc.
Ederic Foundation, Inc.
Environmental Endowment for
    New Jersey, Inc.
Fanwood Foundation
The Favrot Fund
Jamee and Marshall Field Foundation
Flintridge Foundation
Ford Motor Company Fund
The Freed Foundation, Inc.
The Fund for New Jersey
Great Lakes Protection Fund
The George Gund Foundation
The Hastings Trust
The Clarence E. Heller Charitable
    Foundation
The Hofmann Foundation
The Roy A. Hunt Foundation
The Richard Ivey Foundation
W. Alton Jones Foundation, Inc.
The Joyce Foundation
The Knapp Foundation, Inc.

© 1995 Environmental Data Resources, Inc.

Environmental Topics and Activities

Wetlands (cont.)

The Seymour H. Knox Foundation, Inc.
Lyndhurst Foundation
The John D. and Catherine T. MacArthur Foundation
Maki Foundation
Marin Community Foundation
Mars Foundation
The Martin Foundation, Inc.
The McKnight Foundation
Richard King Mellon Foundation
The Moriah Fund, Inc.
Charles Stewart Mott Foundation
The Curtis and Edith Munson Foundation, Inc.
National Fish and Wildlife Foundation
Norcross Wildlife Foundation, Inc.
The David and Lucile Packard Foundation
Patagonia, Inc.
The William Penn Foundation
Phillips Petroleum Foundation, Inc.
Prince Charitable Trusts
The Rhode Island Community Foundation
The Rockefeller Foundation
The San Francisco Foundation
The Schiff Foundation
Schultz Foundation, Inc.
The Florence and John Schumann Foundation
The Strong Foundation for Environmental Values
The Switzer Foundation
Nelson Talbott Foundation
The Tides Foundation
The Tinker Foundation Incorporated
True North Foundation
The Trust For Mutual Understanding
Union Camp Charitable Trust
Virginia Environmental Endowment
WMX Environmental Grants Program
C. A. Webster Foundation
Weeden Foundation
Henry E. and Consuelo S. Wenger Foundation, Inc.
Weyerhaeuser Company Foundation
Whitecap Foundation
Wilburforce Foundation
The Dean Witter Foundation
Margaret Cullinan Wray Charitable Lead Annuity Trust

Whistle-blowers

Alaska Conservation Foundation
Mary Reynolds Babcock Foundation, Inc.
The Ben & Jerry's Foundation
The Bullitt Foundation
C. S. Fund
Compton Foundation, Inc.
Deer Creek Foundation
The Educational Foundation of America
The J. M. Kaplan Fund, Inc.
The Lazar Foundation
Giles W. and Elise G. Mead Foundation

Merck Family Fund
The John Merck Fund
Joyce Mertz-Gilmore Foundation
National Fish and Wildlife Foundation
Norman Foundation
Patagonia, Inc.
Public Welfare Foundation, Inc.
Recreational Equipment, Inc.
Rockefeller Family Fund, Inc.
Threshold Foundation
Tortuga Foundation
Town Creek Foundation, Inc.

Wilderness

ARCO Foundation
American Conservation Association, Inc.
American Foundation Corporation
Elmer L. & Eleanor J. Andersen Foundation
Clayton Baker Trust
The Beinecke Foundation, Inc.
Beldon Fund
David Winton Bell Foundation
James Ford Bell Foundation
The Ben & Jerry's Foundation
Beneficia Foundation
The Betterment Fund
The Bothin Foundation
The Lynde and Harry Bradley Foundation, Inc.
Alexander H. Bright Charitable Trust
Ruth H. Brown Foundation
Jesse Margaret Wilson Budlong Foundation for Animal Aid
The Bullitt Foundation
C. S. Fund
The Cabot Family Charitable Trust
Ben B. Cheney Foundation
The Chevron Companies
The Clark Foundation
The Collins Foundation
The Columbus Foundation
The Community Foundation of Santa Clara County
Compton Foundation, Inc.
Patrick and Anna M. Cudahy Fund
Geraldine R. Dodge Foundation, Inc.
Gaylord and Dorothy Donnelley Foundation
Echoing Green Foundation
The Educational Foundation of America
The Armand G. Erpf Fund, Inc.
Fanwood Foundation
The Hugh and Jane Ferguson Foundation
Bert Fingerhut/Caroline Hicks Family Fund
Ford Foundation
Foundation for Deep Ecology
Funding Exchange
Richard & Rhoda Goldman Fund
The Hahn Family Foundation
Harder Foundation
The Harding Educational and Charitable Foundation
The Hastings Trust
Heller Charitable & Educational Fund
The Homeland Foundation

Howfirma Foundation
Island Foundation
The Richard Ivey Foundation
The Helen & Milton Kimmelman Foundation
F. M. Kirby Foundation, Inc.
Laird, Norton Foundation
James A. Macdonald Foundation
Maki Foundation
MARPAT Foundation, Inc.
The Martin Foundation, Inc.
The Marshall L. & Perrine D. McCune Charitable Foundation
Giles W. and Elise G. Mead Foundation
Richard King Mellon Foundation
Merck Family Fund
Mobil Foundation, Inc.
Ruth Mott Fund
National Fish and Wildlife Foundation
The Needmor Fund
New England Biolabs Foundation
The New York Times Company Foundation, Inc.
The New-Land Foundation, Inc.
Norcross Wildlife Foundation, Inc.
Mary Moody Northen, Inc.
Northwest Fund for the Environment
OCRI Foundation
Nathan M. Ohrbach Foundation, Inc.
The Ohrstrom Foundation
Outdoor Industry Conservation Alliance
The Overbrook Foundation
The David and Lucile Packard Foundation
Patagonia, Inc.
The Pew Charitable Trusts
Pew Scholars Program in Conservation and the Environment
Lynn R. and Karl E. Prickett Fund
Recreational Equipment, Inc.
Z. Smith Reynolds Foundation, Inc.
The Roberts Foundation
Lee Romney Foundation, Inc.
Sacharuna Foundation
The San Francisco Foundation
The Scherman Foundation, Inc.
The Schiff Foundation
Schultz Foundation, Inc.
The Florence and John Schumann Foundation
Elmina B. Sewall Foundation
Springhouse Foundation
The Strong Foundation for Environmental Values
The Sulzberger Foundation, Inc.
Nelson Talbott Foundation
Threshold Foundation
The Tides Foundation
Tortuga Foundation
Town Creek Foundation, Inc.
The Truland Foundation
Underhill Foundation
Vancouver Foundation
R. T. Vanderbilt Trust
Weeden Foundation

Environmental Topics and Activities

Wilderness (cont.)

Mark and Catherine Winkler Foundation
The Winston-Salem Foundation, Inc.
Sidney & Phyllis Wragge Foundation
Margaret Cullinan Wray Charitable Lead Annuity Trust
Wrinkle in Time Foundation

Wildlife

ARCO Foundation
Alaska Conservation Foundation
American Express Philanthropic Program
The Austin Memorial Foundation
The Beinecke Foundation, Inc.
The Blumenthal Foundation
The Bothin Foundation
California Community Foundation
The Cargill Foundation
Chesapeake Bay Trust
The Chevron Companies
The Clark Foundation
The Columbus Foundation
The Mary A. Crocker Trust
Crystal Channel Foundation
Patrick and Anna M. Cudahy Fund
Davis Conservation Foundation
Gaylord and Dorothy Donnelley Foundation
The Max and Victoria Dreyfus Foundation, Inc.
The Elizabeth Ordway Dunn Foundation, Inc.
Fair Play Foundation
Fanwood Foundation
The Favrot Fund
Leland Fikes Foundation, Inc.
Foundation for Field Research
The Foundation for the National Capital Region
Lloyd A. Fry Foundation
The Gap Foundation
The Fred Gellert Foundation
Georgia Power Foundation, Inc.
Walter and Duncan Gordon Charitable Foundation
Great Lakes Protection Fund
Harbor Lights Foundation
Howfirma Foundation
Hurdle Hill Foundation
The J. M. Kaplan Fund, Inc.
The Robert S. and Grayce B. Kerr Foundation, Inc.
The Helen & Milton Kimmelman Foundation
The Kresge Foundation
Laidlaw Foundation
Laird, Norton Foundation
The John D. and Catherine T. MacArthur Foundation
McLean Contributionship
Metropolitan Atlanta Community Foundation, Inc.
Meyer Memorial Trust
The Milwaukee Foundation

The Moriah Fund, Inc.
Charles Stewart Mott Foundation
The Curtis and Edith Munson Foundation, Inc.
National Fish and Wildlife Foundation
The New York Times Company Foundation, Inc.
Norcross Wildlife Foundation, Inc.
Kenneth T. and Eileen L. Norris Foundation
The Ohrstrom Foundation
Orchard Foundation
Patagonia, Inc.
Phillips Petroleum Foundation, Inc.
The Rhode Island Community Foundation
The Roberts Foundation
The Winthrop Rockefeller Foundation
The Scherman Foundation, Inc.
Ellen Browning Scripps Foundation
Elmina B. Sewall Foundation
The Tides Foundation
Times Mirror Magazines, Inc.
Harry C. Trexler Trust
Union Camp Charitable Trust
Vancouver Foundation
WMX Environmental Grants Program
Weeden Foundation
The William P. Wharton Trust
Margaret Cullinan Wray Charitable Lead Annuity Trust
The Wyomissing Foundation, Inc.

Wildlife: conservation

ARCO Foundation
American Conservation Association, Inc.
American Foundation Corporation
Arcadia Foundation
The Bailey Wildlife Foundation
The Cameron Baird Foundation
The George F. Baker Trust
BankAmerica Foundation
The Barra Foundation, Inc.
The Theodore H. Barth Foundation, Inc.
The Bay Foundation
The Howard Bayne Fund
S. D. Bechtel, Jr. Foundation
James Ford Bell Foundation
Beneficia Foundation
The Blumenthal Foundation
The Bothin Foundation
Alexander H. Bright Charitable Trust
Ruth H. Brown Foundation
W. L. Lyons Brown Foundation
Jesse Margaret Wilson Budlong Foundation for Animal Aid
The Bullitt Foundation
The Bydale Foundation
California Community Foundation
Cheeryble Foundation
Ben B. Cheney Foundation
Chesapeake Bay Trust
The Chevron Companies
Chrysler Corporation Fund
Clark Charitable Trust

The Cleveland Foundation
The Columbus Foundation
The Community Foundation of Santa Clara County
The Community Foundation Serving Coastal South Carolina
Compton Foundation, Inc.
Cox Foundation, Inc.
The James M. Cox, Jr. Foundation, Inc.
Roy E. Crummer Foundation
Damien Foundation
Davis Conservation Foundation
The Nelson B. Delavan Foundation
The Aaron Diamond Foundation
Cleveland H. Dodge Foundation, Inc.
Geraldine R. Dodge Foundation, Inc.
Oliver S. and Jennie R. Donaldson Charitable Trust
Gaylord and Dorothy Donnelley Foundation
The Elizabeth Ordway Dunn Foundation, Inc.
Eastman Kodak Company Charitable Trust
Echoing Green Foundation
The Educational Foundation of America
Arthur M. and Olga T. Eisig-Arthur M. and Kate E. Tode Foundation, Inc.
The Emerald Foundation
The Charles Engelhard Foundation
Environmental Endowment for New Jersey, Inc.
The Armand G. Erpf Fund, Inc.
The Ettinger Foundation, Inc.
Fanwood Foundation
The Favrot Fund
Felburn Foundation
Jamee and Marshall Field Foundation
Flintridge Foundation
Ford Motor Company Fund
Walter and Josephine Ford Fund
The Foundation for the National Capital Region
GE Fund
The Barbara Gauntlett Foundation, Inc.
The Wallace Alexander Gerbode Foundation, Inc.
Give to the Earth Foundation
The Goldman Environmental Foundation
The William and Mary Greve Foundation, Inc.
The George Gund Foundation
The Hahn Family Foundation
Harbor Lights Foundation
Harder Foundation
The Harding Educational and Charitable Foundation
Gladys and Roland Harriman Foundation
Mary W. Harriman Foundation
The Hastings Trust
The Merrill G. & Emita E. Hastings Foundation
Heller Charitable & Educational Fund
The Hofmann Foundation
The Homeland Foundation
Howfirma Foundation

Environmental Topics and Activities

Wildlife: conservation (cont.)

The Roy A. Hunt Foundation
Hurdle Hill Foundation
Ireland Foundation
Ittleson Foundation, Inc.
The George Frederick Jewett Foundation
The Howard Johnson Foundation
The J. M. Kaplan Fund, Inc.
The Henry P. Kendall Foundation
The Helen & Milton Kimmelman Foundation
Kinnoull Foundation
F. M. Kirby Foundation, Inc.
Caesar Kleberg Foundation for Wildlife Conservation
The Knapp Foundation, Inc.
The Seymour H. Knox Foundation, Inc.
Kongsgaard-Goldman Foundation
Laird, Norton Foundation
Larsen Fund, Inc.
The Max and Anna Levinson Foundation
The Little Family Foundation
Luster Family Foundation, Inc.
The John D. and Catherine T. MacArthur Foundation
James A. Macdonald Foundation
Magowan Family Foundation, Inc.
Mars Foundation
McDonnell Douglas Foundation
The McIntosh Foundation
McLean Contributionship
Nelson Mead Fund
Richard King Mellon Foundation
Millbrook Tribute Garden, Inc.
Leo Model Foundation, Inc.
J. P. Morgan Charitable Trust
Henry and Lucy Moses Fund, Inc.
The Curtis and Edith Munson Foundation, Inc.
National Fish and Wildlife Foundation
New Hampshire Charitable Foundation
The New York Community Trust
The New York Times Company Foundation, Inc.
Norcross Wildlife Foundation, Inc.
Kenneth T. and Eileen L. Norris Foundation
OCRI Foundation
The Ohrstrom Foundation
The Overbrook Foundation
The David and Lucile Packard Foundation
Patagonia, Inc.
Perkins Charitable Foundation
The Pfizer Foundation, Inc.
Phillips Petroleum Foundation, Inc.
Ellis L. Phillips Foundation
Howard Phipps Foundation
Pinewood Foundation
Lynn R. and Karl E. Prickett Fund
The Prospect Hill Foundation
Z. Smith Reynolds Foundation, Inc.
The Rhode Island Community Foundation
Lee Romney Foundation, Inc.
Samuel and May Rudin Foundation, Inc.
Sacharuna Foundation
The San Francisco Foundation
Sarah I. Schieffelin Residuary Trust
The Schiff Foundation
Schultz Foundation, Inc.
The Florence and John Schumann Foundation
Sequoia Foundation
Seventh Generation Fund
Elmina B. Sewall Foundation
Shell Oil Company Foundation
Solow Foundation
South Coast Foundation, Inc.
Alfred T. Stanley Foundation
Stranahan Foundation
The Strong Foundation for Environmental Values
The Sulzberger Foundation, Inc.
The Summerlee Foundation
Surdna Foundation, Inc.
Edna Bailey Sussman Fund
The Switzer Foundation
Nelson Talbott Foundation
Thanksgiving Foundation
The Oakleigh L. Thorne Foundation
Threshold Foundation
Tortuga Foundation
Town Creek Foundation, Inc.
The Travelers Foundation
Treacy Foundation, Inc.
The Truland Foundation
Marcia Brady Tucker Foundation
USX Foundation, Inc.
Union Camp Charitable Trust
R. T. Vanderbilt Trust
G. Unger Vetlesen Foundation
WMX Environmental Grants Program
Wallace Genetic Foundation, Inc.
Weeden Foundation
Henry E. and Consuelo S. Wenger Foundation, Inc.
Weyerhaeuser Company Foundation
Wilburforce Foundation
Robert W. Wilson Foundation
The Winston-Salem Foundation, Inc.
Sidney & Phyllis Wragge Foundation
Wrinkle in Time Foundation

Wildlife: illegal trade

Crystal Channel Foundation
Ford Foundation

Wildlife: international programs

California Community Foundation
The Foundation for the National Capital Region

Wildlife: land mammals

The Bay Foundation
The Ben & Jerry's Foundation
Bishop Pine Fund
Alexander H. Bright Charitable Trust
The Robert Brownlee Foundation
The Chevron Companies
Compton Foundation, Inc.
Crystal Channel Foundation
The Nathan Cummings Foundation
Geraldine R. Dodge Foundation, Inc.
The Charles Engelhard Foundation
Fanwood Foundation
Leland Fikes Foundation, Inc.
Walter and Duncan Gordon Charitable Foundation
The Ewing Halsell Foundation
Harder Foundation
The Homeland Foundation
The Max and Anna Levinson Foundation
Giles W. and Elise G. Mead Foundation
Meyer Memorial Trust
Leo Model Foundation, Inc.
National Fish and Wildlife Foundation
Norcross Wildlife Foundation, Inc.
Patagonia, Inc.
Lynn R. and Karl E. Prickett Fund
Fran and Warren Rupp Foundation
The Sulzberger Foundation, Inc.
The Summerlee Foundation
Nelson Talbott Foundation
True North Foundation
Rose E. Tucker Charitable Trust
Turner Foundation, Inc.
Vancouver Foundation
Weyerhaeuser Company Foundation
Margaret Cullinan Wray Charitable Lead Annuity Trust

Wildlife: management

ARCO Foundation
Mary Flagler Cary Charitable Trust
Chesapeake Bay Trust
Davis Conservation Foundation
Gaylord and Dorothy Donnelley Foundation
The Louise H. and David S. Ingalls Foundation, Inc.
Laird, Norton Foundation
National Fish and Wildlife Foundation
Northwest Area Foundation

Wildlife: marine mammals

Winifred & Harry B. Allen Foundation
BankAmerica Foundation
The Ben & Jerry's Foundation
The Frank Stanley Beveridge Foundation, Inc.
Helen Brach Foundation
The Chevron Companies
The Community Foundation of Santa Clara County
Davis Conservation Foundation
Thelma Doelger Charitable Trust
Oliver S. and Jennie R. Donaldson Charitable Trust
Flintridge Foundation
Mary D. and Walter F. Frear Eleemosynary Trust
The Barbara Gauntlett Foundation, Inc.
The Wallace Alexander Gerbode Foundation, Inc.
The Greenville Foundation
Walter and Elise Haas Fund

Environmental Topics and Activities

Wildlife: marine mammals (cont.)

The Hastings Trust
The Homeland Foundation
Island Foundation, Inc.
The Richard Ivey Foundation
The Henry P. Kendall Foundation
Laird, Norton Foundation
Luster Family Foundation, Inc.
The McIntosh Foundation
The Mountaineers Foundation
The Curtis and Edith Munson Foundation, Inc.
National Fish and Wildlife Foundation
The David and Lucile Packard Foundation
Patagonia, Inc.
Peninsula Community Foundation
The Roberts Foundation
Schultz Foundation, Inc.
South Coast Foundation, Inc.
Stackner Family Foundation, Inc.
Margaret Dorrance Strawbridge Foundation of Pennsylvania II, Inc.
The Strong Foundation for Environmental Values
The Sudbury Foundation
The Sulzberger Foundation, Inc.
Thanksgiving Foundation
Threshold Foundation
Union Camp Charitable Trust
Weeden Foundation
G. N. Wilcox Trust
Margaret Cullinan Wray Charitable Lead Annuity Trust

Wildlife: marine turtles

ARCO Foundation
Compton Foundation, Inc.
Crystal Channel Foundation
Geraldine R. Dodge Foundation, Inc.
General Service Foundation
Richard & Rhoda Goldman Fund
Patagonia, Inc.
Schultz Foundation, Inc.
The Summerlee Foundation
Threshold Foundation
The Tides Foundation
Margaret Cullinan Wray Charitable Lead Annuity Trust

Wildlife: migration

Benua Foundation, Inc.
Compton Foundation, Inc.
The Conservation and Research Foundation
Jessie B. Cox Charitable Trust
Geraldine R. Dodge Foundation, Inc.
General Service Foundation
The Clarence E. Heller Charitable Foundation
The Richard Ivey Foundation
MARPAT Foundation, Inc.
McLean Contributionship
The John Merck Fund
National Fish and Wildlife Foundation

The Prospect Hill Foundation
Weeden Foundation
Weyerhaeuser Company Foundation

Wildlife: poaching

The McConnell Foundation
National Fish and Wildlife Foundation
Patagonia, Inc.
The Summerlee Foundation
Times Mirror Magazines, Inc.

Wildlife: primates

The Jenifer Altman Foundation
The Howard Bayne Fund
Boettcher Foundation
Helen Brach Foundation
Alexander H. Bright Charitable Trust
Jesse Margaret Wilson Budlong Foundation for Animal Aid
The Chevron Companies
Thelma Doelger Charitable Trust
El Pomar Foundation
Fanwood Foundation
The Favrot Fund
The Foundation for the National Capital Region
The Homeland Foundation
Luster Family Foundation, Inc.
McGregor Fund
Elmina B. Sewall Foundation
The Summerlee Foundation

Wildlife: rehabilitation

ARCO Foundation
The Ahmanson Foundation
BankAmerica Foundation
Jesse Margaret Wilson Budlong Foundation for Animal Aid
The Bullitt Foundation
California Community Foundation
The Chevron Companies
The Community Foundation Serving Coastal South Carolina
Compton Foundation, Inc.
Geraldine R. Dodge Foundation, Inc.
Foundation for Deep Ecology
General Service Foundation
The Rollin M. Gerstacker Foundation
Richard & Rhoda Goldman Fund
Mars Foundation
The Martin Foundation, Inc.
The McConnell Foundation
Nelson Mead Fund
Mobil Foundation, Inc.
Leo Model Foundation, Inc.
National Fish and Wildlife Foundation
Patagonia, Inc.
The William Penn Foundation
Southwestern Bell Foundation
The Summerlee Foundation
Wilburforce Foundation
Margaret Cullinan Wray Charitable Lead Annuity Trust

Wildlife: rescue

ARCO Foundation
BankAmerica Foundation
The Bullitt Foundation
The Chevron Companies
The Community Foundation of Santa Clara County
Geraldine R. Dodge Foundation, Inc.
Jackson Hole Preserve, Inc.
Longwood Foundation, Inc.
Luster Family Foundation, Inc.
The McConnell Foundation
Mobil Foundation, Inc.
Peninsula Community Foundation
Schultz Foundation, Inc.
Shell Oil Company Foundation
Texaco Foundation
Threshold Foundation
USX Foundation, Inc.
Vancouver Foundation
WMX Environmental Grants Program

Wildlife: sanctuary

Alaska Conservation Foundation
Winifred & Harry B. Allen Foundation
The George F. Baker Trust
BankAmerica Foundation
S. D. Bechtel, Jr. Foundation
The Ben & Jerry's Foundation
California Community Foundation
Mary Flagler Cary Charitable Trust
The Champlin Foundations
Chesapeake Bay Trust
The Chevron Companies
The Clowes Fund, Inc.
The Community Foundation of Santa Clara County
Davis Conservation Foundation
Geraldine R. Dodge Foundation, Inc.
Gaylord and Dorothy Donnelley Foundation
The Favrot Fund
Leland Fikes Foundation, Inc.
Flintridge Foundation
The Gap Foundation
The Fred Gellert Foundation
Greater Piscataqua Community Foundation
W. Alton Jones Foundation, Inc.
F. M. Kirby Foundation, Inc.
The Knapp Foundation, Inc.
Luster Family Foundation, Inc.
The John D. and Catherine T. MacArthur Foundation
MARPAT Foundation, Inc.
McLean Contributionship
National Fish and Wildlife Foundation
Norcross Wildlife Foundation, Inc.
The David and Lucile Packard Foundation
Patagonia, Inc.
The Pew Charitable Trusts
The Rhode Island Community Foundation
The San Francisco Foundation
The Florence and John Schumann Foundation

© 1995 Environmental Data Resources, Inc.

Environmental Topics and Activities

Wildlife: sanctuary (cont.)

Seventh Generation Fund
The Strong Foundation for
  Environmental Values
The Summerlee Foundation
Texaco Foundation
Threshold Foundation
Town Creek Foundation, Inc.
The Travelers Foundation
R. T. Vanderbilt Trust
WMX Environmental Grants Program
The William P. Wharton Trust
Margaret Cullinan Wray Charitable
  Lead Annuity Trust

Wildlife: wolves

Alaska Conservation Foundation
Elmer L. & Eleanor J. Andersen Foundation
James Ford Bell Foundation
Geraldine R. Dodge Foundation, Inc.
Fanwood Foundation
The Homeland Foundation
Jackson Hole Preserve, Inc.
National Fish and Wildlife Foundation
New Horizon Foundation
Nathan M. Ohrbach Foundation, Inc.
Patagonia, Inc.
Margaret Cullinan Wray Charitable
  Lead Annuity Trust

Women

The Abelard Foundation West
Angelina Fund, Inc.
The Bauman Foundation
The Ben & Jerry's Foundation
Kathleen Price and Joseph M. Bryan
  Family Foundation, Inc.
The Bullitt Foundation
Patrick and Anna M. Cudahy Fund
Damien Foundation
Dolfinger-McMahon Foundation
The Educational Foundation of America
The Favrot Fund
Leland Fikes Foundation, Inc.
Ford Foundation
Foundation for Deep Ecology
Island Foundation, Inc.
The John D. and Catherine T. MacArthur
  Foundation
The Moriah Fund, Inc.
Ruth Mott Fund
New England Biolabs Foundation
Jessie Smith Noyes Foundation, Inc.
Patagonia, Inc.
Peninsula Community Foundation
Public Welfare Foundation, Inc.
Rockefeller Brothers Fund, Inc.
The Rockefeller Foundation
Seventh Generation Fund
Threshold Foundation
The Tides Foundation
Unitarian Universalist Veatch Program
  at Shelter Rock

Vanguard Public Foundation
Victoria Foundation, Inc.
WMX Environmental Grants Program
Weyerhaeuser Company Foundation
Margaret Cullinan Wray Charitable
  Lead Annuity Trust

Work-place giving campaign

Beldon Fund
The George Gund Foundation
The Joyce Foundation
Jessie Smith Noyes Foundation, Inc.
Z. Smith Reynolds Foundation, Inc.
Rockefeller Family Fund, Inc.
Surdna Foundation, Inc.

World Bank

W. Alton Jones Foundation, Inc.
Laird, Norton Foundation
The Moriah Fund, Inc.
The Rockefeller Foundation

Youth

ARCO Foundation
The Abelard Foundation West
Abell-Hanger Foundation
American Conservation Association, Inc.
Atherton Family Foundation
BankAmerica Foundation
The Bodman Foundation
The Bothin Foundation
The Bullitt Foundation
The Cabot Family Charitable Trust
The Morris and Gwendolyn Cafritz
  Foundation
California Community Foundation
Ben B. Cheney Foundation
The Chicago Community Trust
The Collins Foundation
Compton Foundation, Inc.
Adolph Coors Foundation
The Mary A. Crocker Trust
Crystal Channel Foundation
The Nathan Cummings Foundation
Geraldine R. Dodge Foundation, Inc.
The Educational Foundation of America
El Pomar Foundation
English-Bonter-Mitchell Foundation
The William Stamps Farish Fund
Ford Motor Company Fund
Foundation for Deep Ecology
Fund of the Four Directions
The Gap Foundation
Gebbie Foundation, Inc.
Give to the Earth Foundation
Herman Goldman Foundation
Richard & Rhoda Goldman Fund
Greater Piscataqua Community Foundation
Evelyn and Walter Haas, Jr. Fund
The Hahn Family Foundation
The Edward W. Hazen Foundation
The James Irvine Foundation
Island Foundation, Inc.

Island Foundation
Ittleson Foundation, Inc.
Martha Holden Jennings Foundation
W. Alton Jones Foundation, Inc.
Laird, Norton Foundation
Levi Strauss Foundation
The Max and Anna Levinson Foundation
Longwood Foundation, Inc.
MARPAT Foundation, Inc.
McInerny Foundation
Giles W. and Elise G. Mead Foundation
Meyer Memorial Trust
The Milwaukee Foundation
The Minneapolis Foundation
The Moriah Fund, Inc.
The Mountaineers Foundation
The Curtis and Edith Munson
  Foundation, Inc.
The National Environmental Education
  and Training Foundation, Inc.
National Fish and Wildlife Foundation
The Needmor Fund
New Hampshire Charitable Foundation
New York Foundation
Jessie Smith Noyes Foundation, Inc.
Patagonia, Inc.
Peninsula Community Foundation
James C. Penney Foundation
The Pew Charitable Trusts
Public Welfare Foundation, Inc.
Z. Smith Reynolds Foundation, Inc.
The Rhode Island Community Foundation
Rockefeller Family Fund, Inc.
The San Francisco Foundation
The Sapelo Foundation
Sarkeys Foundation
The Schumann Fund for New Jersey, Inc.
Seventh Generation Fund
The Skaggs Foundation
Threshold Foundation
Vancouver Foundation
Virginia Environmental Endowment
WMX Environmental Grants Program
DeWitt Wallace-Reader's Digest Fund

Youth: urban

The Ahmanson Foundation
The Louis Calder Foundation
Community Foundation of
  Western North Carolina, Inc.
Crystal Channel Foundation
The Nelson B. Delavan Foundation
Environmental Endowment for
  New Jersey, Inc.
Lloyd A. Fry Foundation
The Fred Gellert Foundation
The James Irvine Foundation
National Fish and Wildlife Foundation
The New York Times Company
  Foundation, Inc.
Patagonia, Inc.
The San Francisco Foundation
The Morris Stulsaft Foundation

Environmental Topics and Activities

Youth: urban (cont.)

Threshold Foundation
Victoria Foundation, Inc.
WMX Environmental Grants Program

Zoos/aquariums

ARCO Foundation
The Achelis Foundation
The Ahmanson Foundation
The George I. Alden Trust
American Conservation Association, Inc.
American Express Philanthropic Program
American Foundation Corporation
Arcadia Foundation
The Vincent Astor Foundation
The Bailey Wildlife Foundation
The George F. Baker Trust
Baltimore Gas and Electric Foundation, Inc.
BankAmerica Foundation
The Barra Foundation, Inc.
The Theodore H. Barth Foundation, Inc.
The Bay Foundation
The Howard Bayne Fund
S. D. Bechtel, Jr. Foundation
The Beinecke Foundation, Inc.
The Ben & Jerry's Foundation
Beneficia Foundation
Benua Foundation, Inc.
The Frank Stanley Beveridge Foundation, Inc.
The Blumenthal Foundation
The Bodman Foundation
The Boeing Company
Boettcher Foundation
Helen Brach Foundation
Otto Bremer Foundation
Alexander H. Bright Charitable Trust
Alex. Brown & Sons Charitable Foundation, Inc.
H. Barksdale Brown Charitable Trust
W. L. Lyons Brown Foundation
The Robert Brownlee Foundation
The Buchanan Family Foundation
The Louis Calder Foundation
California Community Foundation
The Cargill Foundation
Carolyn Foundation
The Champlin Foundations
Cheeryble Foundation
Ben B. Cheney Foundation
Chesapeake Bay Trust
The Chevron Companies
Chrysler Corporation Fund
The Cleveland Foundation
The Clowes Fund, Inc.
Olive B. Cole Foundation
The Columbus Foundation
The Community Foundation of Santa Clara County
Compton Foundation, Inc.
Adolph Coors Foundation
The Cowles Charitable Trust
Cox Foundation, Inc.

Jessie B. Cox Charitable Trust
Crystal Channel Foundation
Davis Conservation Foundation
Dayton Hudson Foundation
The Aaron Diamond Foundation
Cleveland H. Dodge Foundation, Inc.
Geraldine R. Dodge Foundation, Inc.
Gaylord and Dorothy Donnelley Foundation
The Max and Victoria Dreyfus Foundation, Inc.
Ederic Foundation, Inc.
El Paso Community Foundation
El Pomar Foundation
The Emerald Foundation
The Charles Engelhard Foundation
The Armand G. Erpf Fund, Inc.
Fanwood Foundation
Leland Fikes Foundation, Inc.
Walter and Josephine Ford Fund
GE Fund
The Gap Foundation
Gates Foundation
Georgia Power Foundation, Inc.
Georgia-Pacific Foundation
Richard & Rhoda Goldman Fund
The Greenville Foundation
The William and Mary Greve Foundation, Inc.
The W. C. Griffith Foundation
James G. Hanes Memorial Fund
Gladys and Roland Harriman Foundation
Mary W. Harriman Foundation
The Merrill G. & Emita E. Hastings Foundation
Hawaii Community Foundation
The Horn Foundation
Hudson-Webber Foundation
The Indian Point Foundation, Inc.
Island Foundation, Inc.
The Jackson Foundation
Martha Holden Jennings Foundation
Helen K. and Arthur E. Johnson Foundation
The Howard Johnson Foundation
The Robert S. and Grayce B. Kerr Foundation, Inc.
The Helen & Milton Kimmelman Foundation
Kinnoull Foundation
F. M. Kirby Foundation, Inc.
The Knapp Foundation, Inc.
The Seymour H. Knox Foundation, Inc.
The Kresge Foundation
Levi Strauss Foundation
The Little Family Foundation
Longwood Foundation, Inc.
Luster Family Foundation, Inc.
The John D. and Catherine T. MacArthur Foundation
James A. Macdonald Foundation
Magowan Family Foundation, Inc.
Mars Foundation
The Eugene McDermott Foundation
McDonnell Douglas Foundation
McGregor Fund

The McIntosh Foundation
McLean Contributionship
Meadows Foundation, Inc.
Richard King Mellon Foundation
Metropolitan Atlanta Community Foundation, Inc.
Metropolitan Life Foundation
Meyer Memorial Trust
Middlecott Foundation
The Milwaukee Foundation
The Minneapolis Foundation
Mobil Foundation, Inc.
Leo Model Foundation, Inc.
Henry and Lucy Moses Fund, Inc.
The Curtis and Edith Munson Foundation, Inc.
M. J. Murdock Charitable Trust
John P. Murphy Foundation
The National Environmental Education and Training Foundation, Inc.
National Fish and Wildlife Foundation
The New York Community Trust
The New York Times Company Foundation, Inc.
Edward John Noble Foundation, Inc.
Norcross Wildlife Foundation, Inc.
The Norton Foundation, Inc.
Nicholas H. Noyes, Jr. Memorial Foundation
The Ohrstrom Foundation
The Overbrook Foundation
The David and Lucile Packard Foundation
Patagonia, Inc.
Amelia Peabody Charitable Fund
Peninsula Community Foundation
The Pew Charitable Trusts
The Pfizer Foundation, Inc.
Phillips Petroleum Foundation, Inc.
Howard Phipps Foundation
Pinewood Foundation
Pritzker Foundation
The Procter & Gamble Fund
The Prospect Hill Foundation
The Prudential Foundation
The Rhode Island Community Foundation
The Roberts Foundation
The Winthrop Rockefeller Foundation
Rockwell Fund, Inc.
Lee Romney Foundation, Inc.
Samuel and May Rudin Foundation, Inc.
Sacharuna Foundation
Sacramento Regional Foundation
San Diego Community Foundation
The San Francisco Foundation
The Schiff Foundation
Ellen Browning Scripps Foundation
Elmina B. Sewall Foundation
Thomas Sill Foundation
Solow Foundation
Southwestern Bell Foundation
Stackner Family Foundation, Inc.
Alfred T. Stanley Foundation
Steelcase Foundation
The Stroh Foundation

Environmental Topics and Activities

Zoos/aquariums (cont.)

The Morris Stulsaft Foundation
The Sulzberger Foundation, Inc.
The Summerlee Foundation
Nelson Talbott Foundation
The Telesis Foundation
Texaco Foundation
Thanksgiving Foundation
The Oakleigh L. Thorne Foundation
Tortuga Foundation
The Travelers Foundation
Treacy Foundation, Inc.
True North Foundation
Rose E. Tucker Charitable Trust
Alice Tweed Tuohy Foundation
USX Foundation, Inc.
R. T. Vanderbilt Trust
G. Unger Vetlesen Foundation
WMX Environmental Grants Program
Lila Wallace-Reader's Digest Fund
Henry E. and Consuelo S. Wenger Foundation, Inc.
Weyerhaeuser Company Foundation
Robert W. Wilson Foundation
The Winston-Salem Foundation, Inc.
Wodecroft Foundation
The Wortham Foundation, Inc.
Margaret Cullinan Wray Charitable Lead Annuity Trust